Modernism

Blackwell Anthologies

Editorial Advisers

Rosemary Ashton, University of London; Gillian Beer, University of Cambridge; Gordon Campbell, University of Leicester; Terry Castle, Stanford University; Margaret Ann Doody, Vanderbilt University; Richard Gray, University of Essex; Joseph Harris, Harvard University; Karen L. Kilcup, University of North Carolina, Greensboro; Jerome J. McGann, University of Virginia; David Norbrook, University of Oxford; Tom Paulin, University of Oxford; Michael Payne, Bucknell University; Elaine Showalter, Princeton University; John Sutherland, University of London; Jonathan Wordsworth, University of Oxford.

Blackwell Anthologies are a series of extensive and comprehensive volumes designed to address the numerous issues raised by recent debates regarding the literary canon, value, text, context, gender, genre, and period. While providing the reader with key canonical writings in their entirety, the series is also ambitious in its coverage of hitherto marginalized texts, and flexible in the overall variety of its approaches to periods and movements. Each volume has been thoroughly researched to meet the current needs of teachers and students.

Old and Middle English *c.* 890–*c.* 1400: An Anthology. Second edition
edited by Elaine Treharne

Medieval Drama: An Anthology
edited by Greg Walker

Chaucer to Spenser: An Anthology of English Writing 1375–1575
edited by Derek Pearsall

Renaissance Drama: An Anthology of Plays and Entertainments. Second edition
edited by Arthur F. Kinney

Renaissance Literature: An Anthology
edited by Michael Payne and John Hunter

Restoration Drama: An Anthology
edited by David Womersley

British Literature 1640–1789: An Anthology. Second edition
edited by Robert DeMaria, Jr

Romanticism: An Anthology. Third edition
edited by Duncan Wu

Children's Literature: An Anthology 1801–1902
edited by Peter Hunt

Victorian Women Poets: An Anthology
edited by Angela Leighton and Margaret Reynolds

The Victorians: An Anthology of Poetry and Poetics
edited by Valentine Cunningham

Modernism: An Anthology
edited by Lawrence Rainey

American Gothic: An Anthology 1787–1916
edited by Charles L. Crow

The Literatures of Colonial America: An Anthology
edited by Susan Castillo and Ivy T. Schweitzer

Nineteenth-Century American Women Writers: An Anthology
edited by Karen L. Kilcup

Nineteenth-Century American Women Poets: An Anthology
edited by Paula Bernat Bennett

Native American Women's Writing: An Anthology of Works *c.* 1800–1924
edited by Karen L. Kilcup

MODERNISM

AN ANTHOLOGY

EDITED BY LAWRENCE RAINEY

Blackwell
Publishing

BLACKWELL PUBLISHING
350 Main Street, Malden, MA 02148-5020, USA
9600 Garsington Road, Oxford OX4 2DQ, UK
550 Swanston Street, Carlton, Victoria 3053, Australia

First published 2005 by Blackwell Publishing Ltd

1   2005

Library of Congress Cataloging-in-Publication Data

Modernism : an anthology / edited by Lawrence Rainey.
p. cm.—(Blackwell anthologies)
Includes bibliographical references and index
ISBN-13: 978-0-631-20448-0 (hardback.: alk. paper)
ISBN-13: 978-0-631-20449-7 (pbk.: alk. paper)
ISBN-10: 0-631-20448-2 (hardback.: alk. paper)
ISBN-10: 0-631-20449-0 (pbk.: alk. paper)
1. English literature—20th century. 2. American literature—20th century.
3. Modernism (Literature)—English-speaking countries.
I. Rainey, Lawrence S. II. Title. III. Series.
PR1148.M63 2005
820.8'0112'0904—dc22
2004018067

A catalogue record for this title is available from the British Library.

Set in 9.5 on 11 pt Garamond 3
by SPI Publisher Services, Pondicherry, India
Printed and bound in the United Kingdom
by TJ International Ltd, Padstow, Cornwall

For further information on
Blackwell Publishing, visit our website:
www.blackwellpublishing.com

In Memory of Hugh Kenner (1913–2003),
Scholar and Critic of Literary Modernism

Contents

CONTINENTAL INTERLUDE II: DADA (1916–21) 461

Acknowledgments

The editor and publisher gratefully acknowledge the following for permission granted to reproduce the copyright material in this book:

Ezra Pound
"Canto LXXXI" first published in Ezra Pound, *The Pisan Cantos* (New York: New Directions, 1948); "From Canto CXV" first published in Ezra Pound, *Drafts and Fragments* (New York: New Directions, 1969), from *The Cantos of Ezra Pound* by Ezra Pound, copyright © 1934, 1937, 1940, 1948, 1956, 1959, 1962, 1963, 1966, and 1968 by Ezra Pound. Reprinted by permission of New Directions Publishing Corp.

Wyndham Lewis
"Enemy of the Stars," "Bestre," "The Death of the Ankou," "Manifesto," "Inferior Religions," "Foreword to *Tyros and Portraits*," and "The Children of the New Epoch" © Wyndham Lewis and the estate of the late Mrs G. A. Wyndham Lewis. Reprinted by kind permission of the Wyndham Lewis Memorial Trust (a registered charity).

James Joyce
Two short stories from *Dubliners*, two Episodes from *Ulysses*, and "Anna Livia Plurabelle" from *Finnegans Wake* reproduced with the permission of James Joyce's Estate. © Copyright, the Estate of James Joyce.

W. B. Yeats
"A Coat," "The Wild Swans at Coole," "In Memory of Major Robert Gregory," "Easter, 1916," and "The Second Coming"; the following poems from *The Tower* (London: Macmillan, 1928), "Sailing to Byzantium," "The Tower," "Meditations in Time of Civil War," "Nineteen Hundred and Nineteen," "The Wheel," "Youth and Age," "The New Faces," "A Prayer for my Son," "Two Songs from a Play," "Wisdom," "Leda and the Swan," "On a Picture of a Black Centaur by Edmund Dulac," "Among School Children," "Colonus' Praise," "The Hero, the Girl, and the Fool," "Owen Ahern and his Dancers," "A Man Young and Old," "The Three Monuments," "From 'Oedipus at Colonus,'" "The Gift of Harun Al-Rashid," and "All Souls' Night"; reprinted by permission of A. P. Watt Ltd., on behalf of Michael B. Yeats.

"Crazy Jane and the Bishop," "Byzantium," and "Coole and Ballylee, 1931" reprinted with the permission of Scribner, an imprint of Simon & Schuster Adult Publishing Group, from *The Collected Works of W. B. Yeats, Volume 1: The Poems Revised*, edited by Richard J. Finneran. Copyright © 1933 by The Macmillan Company; copyright renewed © 1961 by Bertha Georgie Yeats. Reprinted by permission of A. P. Watt Ltd., on behalf of Michael B. Yeats.

"Come Gather Round Me Parnellites," "The Statues," and "The Circus Animals' Desertion" reprinted with the permission of Scribner, an imprint of Simon & Schuster Adult Publishing Group, from *The Collected*

Works of W. B. Yeats, Volume 1: The Poems Revised, edited by Richard J. Finneran. Copyright © 1940 by Georgie Yeats; copyright renewed © 1968 by Bertha Georgie Yeats, Michael Butler Yeats and Anne Yeats. Reprinted by permission of A. P. Watt Ltd., on behalf of Michael B. Yeats.

At the Hawk's Well reprinted with the permission of Scribner, an imprint of Simon & Schuster Adult Publishing Group, from *The Collected Plays of W. B. Yeats, Revised Edition* by W. B. Yeats. Copyright © 1934, 1952, by Macmillan Publishing Company; copyright renewed © 1962 by Bertha Georgie Yeats and 1980 by Anne Yeats. Reprinted by permission of A. P. Watt Ltd., on behalf of Michael B. Yeats.

"Note on the First Performance of 'At the Hawk's Well'" reprinted by permission of A. P. Watt Ltd., on behalf of Michael B. Yeats.

"Introduction" to *Certain Noble Plays of Japan* reprinted with the permission of Scribner, an imprint of Simon & Schuster Adult Publishing Group, from *Essays and Introductions* by W. B. Yeats. Copyright © 1961 by Mrs W. B. Yeats. Reprinted by permission of A. P. Watt Ltd., on behalf of Michael B. Yeats.

"Rapallo" reprinted with the permission of Scribner, an imprint of Simon & Schuster Adult Publishing Group, from *The Collected Plays of W. B. Yeats, Revised Edition* by W. B. Yeats. Copyright © 1937, 1952 by W. B. Yeats; copyright renewed © 1965 by Bertha Georgie Yeats. Reprinted by permission of A. P. Watt Ltd., on behalf of Michael B. Yeats.

Gertrude Stein
Tender Buttons, "Tourty or Tourtebattre," "A Sweet Tail (Gypsies)," "A Description of the Fifteenth of November: A Portrait of T. S. Eliot," "Composition as Explanation," and "What Are Master-pieces and Why Are There So Few of Them," reprinted by permission of the Estate of Gertrude Stein, through its Literary Executor, Mr Stanford Gann, Jr, of Levin & Gann, PA.

Mina Loy
"Virgins Plus Curtains Minus Dots," "The Effectual Marriage," "Human Cylinders," "Joyce's Ulysses," "Brancusi's Golden Bird," "Lunar Baedeker," "Gertrude Stein," "Aphorisms on Futurism," "Psycho-Democracy," "Gertrude Stein," and "Modern Poetry," reprinted by permission of Carcanet Press Limited.

H.D.
"Orchard," "Oread," "Garden," "Sea Rose," "Night," "Eurydice," "Leda," "She Rebukes Hippolyta," "Demeter," "Helen," "Triplex," and "Magician," by H.D. (Hilda Doolittle), from *Collected Poems*, 1912–44, copyright © 1982 by The Estate of Hilda Doolittle. Reprinted by permission of New Directions Publishing Corp.

Hugo Ball
"Dada Fragments," reprinted by permission of Madame Betsy Jolas.

André Breton
"For Dada," "After Dada," and "The Mediums Enter," reprinted from *The Lost Footsteps (Les Pas perdus)* by André Breton, translated by Mark Polizzotti, by permission of the University of Nebraska Press. © Editions Gallimard 1924, 1969; translation ©1966 by Mark Polizzotti.

William Carlos Williams
Spring and All by William Carlos Williams, from *Collected Poems: 1909–1939, Volume I*, copyright © 1938 by New Directions Publishing Corp. Reprinted by permission of New Directions Publishing Corp and Carcanet Press Limited.

"A Note on the Recent Work of James Joyce," "The Work of Gertrude Stein," and "Marianne Moore" by Williams Carlos Williams, from *Imaginations*, copyright © 1970 by Florence H. Williams. Reprinted by permission of New Directions Publishing Corp.

"*A Draft of XXX Cantos* by Ezra Pound" by William Carlos Williams, from *Selected Essays of William Carlos Williams*, copyright © 1954 by William Carlos Williams. Reprinted by permission of New Directions Publishing Corp.

Ford Madox Ford
"Pink Flannel," "The Colonel's Shoes," "The Miracle," and "On Impressionism," reprinted by permission of David Higham Associates Limited.

Dorothy Richardson
"Sunday," "The Garden," "Sleigh Ride," "Nook on Parnassus," "The Reality of Feminism," "Women and the Future," "Women in the Arts," "Continuous Performance," and "Adventure for Readers," reprinted by permission of the Estate of Dorothy Richardson c/o Paterson Marsh Ltd.

Marianne Moore
"The Steeple-Jack," copyright 1951 © 1970 by Marianne Moore, © renewed 1979 by Lawrence E. Brinn and Louise Crain, Executors of the Estate of Marianne Moore, from *The Complete Poems of Marianne Moore* by Marianne Moore. Used by permission of Viking Penguin, a division of Penguin Group (USA) Inc.

"The Sacred Wood," copyright © 1921 by Marianne Moore; "Hymen," "A House-Party," "*A Draft of XXX Cantos*," and "Ideas of Order," copyright © 1936, copyright renewed © 1964 by Marianne Moore; "Well Moused, Lion (Wallace Stevens)," copyright © 1924, copyright renewed © 1952 by Marianne Moore; "A Poet of the Quattrocento," copyright © 1928, copyright renewed © 1956 by Marianne Moore, from *The Complete Prose of Marianne Moore* by Marianne Moore, edited by Patricia C. Willis, copyright © 1986 by Clive E. Driver, Literary Executor of the Estate of Marianne Moore. Used by permission of Viking Penguin, a division of Penguin Group (USA) Inc.

Rebecca West
"Indissoluble Matrimony" by Rebecca West (Copyright © Estate of Rebecca West 1914) first appeared in *Blast 1* in June 1914; "The 'Freewoman'" by Rebecca West (Copyright © Estate of Rebecca West 1926) first appeared in *Time and Tide* in July 1926; "High Fountain of Genius" by Rebecca West (Copyright © Estate of Rebecca West 1928) first appeared in the *New York Herald and Tribune* in October 1928; "What Is Mr. T. S. Eliot's Authority as a Critic?" by Rebecca West (Copyright © Estate of Rebecca West 1932) first appeared in the *Daily Telegraph* in September 1932. Reproduced by permission of PFD (www.pfd.co.uk) on behalf of the Estate of Rebecca West.

André Breton and Paul Eluard
"The Possessions, from the *Immaculate Conception*," translated by Jon Graham 1990 (London: Atlas Press). Reprinted by kind permission of Atlas Press (current edition of this title: *The Automatic Message*).

Nancy Cunard
"Wheels" and "The Carnivals of Peace" first appeared in Edith Sitwell, *Wheels: an Anthology of Verse* (Oxford: B. H. Blackwell, 1916); "Evenings" and "Voyages North" appeared in Nancy Cunard's first collection of poems titled *Outlaws* (London: Elkin Mathews, 1921); "Horns in the Valley" first published in Cunard's second collection of poems *Sublunary* (London: Hodder and Stoughton, 1923); "Simultaneous" first appeared in *Poems (Two) 1925* (London: Aquila Press, 1930); "'Black Man and White Ladyship'" was first published as an independent pamphlet in an unknown number of copies (Toloun: Imprimerie A. Bordato, 1931); "Harlem Reviewed" first appeared in *Negro* (London: Lawrence and Wishart, 1934); "The Exodus from Spain" was published in the *Manchester Guardian*, datelined 8 and 9 February, 1939. Copyright © Heirs of Nancy Cunard. Reprinted by kind permission of A. R. A. Hobson.

Mary Butts
"Speed the Plough," "Widdershins," "The House-party," "Green, " and "Friendship's Garland," reprinted by permission of the Mary Butts estate. Copyright © Mary Butts Estate.

Virginia Woolf
Between the Acts by Virginia Woolf, copyright 1941 by Harcourt Inc. and renewed 1969 by Leonard Woolf, reprinted by permission of Harcourt, Inc.

"Modern Fiction" from *The Common Reader* by Virginia Woolf, copyright 1925 by Harcourt Inc. and renewed 1953 by Leonard Woolf, reprinted by permission of the publisher.

"Mr Bennett and Mrs Brown" first published in the "Literary Review" section of the *New York Evening Post*, 17 November 1923.

"The Narrow Bridge of Art" from *Granite and Rainbows* by Virginia Woolf, copyright 1958 by Leonard Woolf and renewed 1986 by M. T. Parsons, Executor of Leonard Sidney Woolf, reprinted by permission of Harcourt Inc.

"The Leaning Tower" first published in a collection of essays by various authors edited by John Lehmann, *Folios of New Writing* (London: Hogarth Press, 1940).

All Virginia Woolf material reprinted by permission of The Society of Authors as the Literary Representative of the Estate of Virginia Woolf.

Elizabeth Bowen

"Foothold" first published in a collection of short stories by Elizabeth Bowen titled *Joining Charles, and Other Stories* (London: Constable, 1929). Reprinted by permission of Constable & Robinson Publishing Ltd.

"The Apple Tree" first appeared in *The Cat Jumps, and Other Stories* by Elizabeth Bowen (London: Victor Gollancz, 1934); "Attractive Modern Homes" first appeared in *Look at All Those Roses: Short Stories* by Elizabeth Bowen (London: Victor Gollancz, 1941); "Mysterious Kôr" first published in *Penguin New Writing* (January 1944), then collected in *The Demon Lover and Other Stories* (London: Jonathan Cape, 1945); "The Happy Autumn Fields" first published in *Cornhill*, no. 963 (November 1944), then collected in *The Demon Lover and Other Stories* (London: Jonathan Cape, 1945). Reproduced with permission of Curtis Brown Group Ltd., London, on behalf of the Estate of Elizabeth Bowen. Copyright © Elizabeth Bowen.

Eugene Jolas

"Revolution of the Word," "Notes on Reality," and "What is the Revolution of Language" reprinted with permission of Betsy Jolas.

Samuel Beckett

Texts for Nothing, "Dante . . . Bruno . Vico . . Joyce," "Three Dialogues," "Whoroscope," "Ennueg II," "Echo's Bones," "Ooftish," and "What is the Word" reprinted by permission of Calder Educational Trust Ltd, on behalf of The Samuel Beckett Estate.

Walter Benjamin

"Surrealism" from *Reflections: Essays, Aphorisms, Autobiographical Writings by Walter Benjamin*, English translation, copyright © 1978 by Harcourt Inc., reprinted by permission of the Publisher.

"The Work of Art in the Age of Mechanical Reproduction" from *Illuminations* by Walter Benjamin, copyright © 1955 by Suhrkamp Verlag, Frankfurt a.M. English translation by Harry Zohn copyright © 1968 and renewed 1996 by Harcourt Inc., reprinted by permission of Harcourt Inc.

Copyright © Walter Benjamin, alle Rechte beim Suhrkamp Verlag.

Theodor Adorno

"Looking Back on Surrealism" and "Trying to Understand *Endgame*" (originally titled "Ruckblickend auf den Surrealismus" and "Versuch das *Endspeil* zu verstehen") from *Noten zur Literatur* © Suhrkamp Verlag, Frankfurt am Main 1958 and 1961.

Every effort has been made to trace copyright holders and to obtain their permission for the use of copyright material. The publisher apologizes for any errors or omissions in the above list and would be grateful if notified of any corrections that should be incorporated in future reprints or editions of this book.

Introduction

The modernists were giants, monsters of nature who loomed so large that contemporaries could only gape at them in awe. Consider the case of Donald Hall, an American poet who was 23 in 1951, a recent graduate of Harvard who had served as editor of the university's celebrated literary magazine, the *Advocate*, just as T. S. Eliot had once done; his early poems were already drawing recognition, he had just won a fellowship to Oxford, and he was traveling to London, armed with an invitation to meet T. S. Eliot, the most honored poet of his age, the man who only three years before had received the Nobel Prize for literature, and the author of the century's greatest poem, *The Waste Land*. Eliot, notwithstanding his many distinctions, was still fulfilling his mundane duties as an editor at the firm of Faber and Faber, and Hall had been told that his meeting with the great man would take place at the publisher's offices at 24 Russell Square. Hall was terrified. His appointment was for 3:00 in the afternoon. He turned up an hour early, then decided to kill time by scrutinizing the neighboring buildings. Finally, at 3:00, he was duly escorted to Eliot's small office and greeted by the great man himself. He turned out to be as diffident and distant as report had portrayed him. Their conversation went poorly. "I was so convinced of the monumentality of this moment – 'I will be speaking of this, ages hence' – that I weighed every word as if my great-grandchildren were listening in," Hall later recalled, "and I feared to let them down by speaking idiomatically, or by seeing the humor in anything." Eliot commented briefly on some of Hall's poems, the hour passed swiftly, and by 4:00 it was time to leave. Hall leapt to his feet, sputtered ponderous thanks, and awaited Eliot's farewell:

> Then Eliot appeared to search for the right phrase with which to send me off. He looked me in the eyes, and set off into a slow, meandering sentence. "Let me see," said T. S. Eliot, "forty years ago I went from Harvard to Oxford. Now you are going from Harvard to Oxford. What advice can I give you?" He paused delicately, shrewdly, while I waited with greed for the words which I would repeat for the rest of my life, the advice from elder to younger, setting me on the road of emulation. When he had ticked off the comedian's exact milliseconds of pause, he said, "Have you any long underwear?"
>
> I told him that I had not, and paused to buy some on my dazzled walk back to the hotel. I suppose it was six months before I woke up enough to laugh.[1]

The reader who comes to modernism for the first time faces much the same dilemma as Hall did. Modernism is preceded by its reputation, or even by several reputations: it is endowed with authority so monumental that a reader is tempted to overlook the very experience of encountering modernist works; or it is attended with such opprobrium (the modernists were all fascists or anti-Semites, or if not that, "elitists") that one might wonder why anyone had bothered to read them at all. It is easy, too easy, to slight the grisly comedy or miss the mordant wit, to skim the surface of dazzling surprises, to neglect the sheer wildness and irredeemable opacity at the heart of modernist works.

Declaring modernism "finished" and "over" and "dead" has been a recurrent gesture in academic literary studies. We could epitomize it by inventing an imaginary professor (call him Professor X) who, let us say in

1956, would write an essay titled, "What Was Modernism?"[2] The *frisson* of the title would have been twofold: the term "modernism" was still a relatively new coinage, quite *au courant*, yet Professor X was already describing it with the past tense. Yet this daring gesture had at least a semblance of reason. To observant contemporaries of Professor X it was clear that modernism was receding into the past. Eliot was no longer writing works that startled and disturbed with the ferocious power of *The Waste Land*; instead he was attempting to write what is called "a well-made play," one that would conform to the standards of West End theaters in London – and this after the first English production of *Waiting for Godot* in 1955, a work which might have demolished the notion of the well-made play forever. Yet *Waiting for Godot* itself can remind us just how difficult it was to assign an ending to modernism. Beckett, after all, had served for years as amanuensis to James Joyce, whose influence in his early works is unmistakable. Worse still, his career would continue well into the 1980s. Would it never end?

Our imaginary Professor X was not entirely mistaken in adopting the past tense in his question about modernism. For by 1956 it was true that many of the first generation or even the first and second generations of modernists were in their grave. William Butler Yeats had died in 1939; Virginia Woolf and James Joyce had passed away in 1941; Gertrude Stein in 1946; Wallace Stevens only months before the appearance of Professor X's imaginary essay, in 1955. William Carlos Williams had already had the first of several strokes, while Wyndham Lewis was now blind. Lewis would die in 1957, Williams in 1963, and Eliot in 1965, leaving behind only Marianne Moore and Ezra Pound, who met one another for the third and last time in 1969, before they died in 1972. Samuel Beckett, who would live on till 1989, had already become "the last modernist."[3]

If dating modernism's ending has been difficult, defining the term's meaning has become something of an academic obsession. The task is all the more difficult because the term has been extended to cover disparate yet cognate fields, acquiring different chronologies and shadings of meaning as it moves from art history to architecture to music and intellectual history. Art historians, for example, agree in assigning a definite beginning to modernism. "Look there," they will say, pointing to a color reproduction of Manet's *Déjeuener sur l'herbe* (1863), or perhaps his *Olympia* (1865), or perhaps to the much later work, Picasso's *Demoiselles d'Avignon* (1907). "There is modernism, as plain as day." And music historians, however much they disagree about precursors and transitions, largely concur in citing Stravinsky's *Le Sacre de printemps* (1913) as the moment modernism appears in music. Architectural historians also disagree about precursors (the Crystal Palace in 1851?) and the steps that led to modernism's emergence; but while they are less inclined to name a specific building (Wright's Larkin Building of 1903? or his Robie House of 1906?) as marking an identifiable beginning, they agree in naming the grand figures of architectural modernism (Frank Lloyd Wright, Walter Gropius, Le Corbusier, Ludwig Mies van der Rohe), in specifying its basic principles (rationalism, functionalism, anti-ornamentalism, etc.), and even in tracing a broad, narrative arc in which the architectural idiom of daring pioneers slowly becomes the lingua franca of corporate office buildings and reigns supreme in the International Style of the 1950s. Such unanimity is much less prevalent in literary studies, for reasons we shall soon see.

One reason why the term "modernism" has undergone such a remarkable extension in the range of materials it can cover in English may be simply the result of historical-linguistic accident. In Italian, for example, the semantic potential of the cognate term *modernismo* had already been largely consumed by 1900, when it became current usage to designate a grouping of Catholic theologians and reformers who wanted the church to modernize. The same is true of the cognate terms in French (*le modernisme*) and German (*der Modernismus*), and even today "modernism" in either language is not used to demarcate an artistic and cultural phenomenon, but a theological one. (In both instead, one speaks of "the modern," or *le moderne, die Moderne*; and while some Italian academics have recently adopted the term *modernismo* in a manner analogous to that of Anglo-American usage, it has still not seeped into journalism or popular speech.) In the predominantly Protestant culture of the English-speaking world, instead, "modernism" was an invitingly empty term, a noun awaiting semantic content.

We should remember, too, that even the Anglophone adoption of "modernism" was relatively late and recent. Graham Hough, writing in 1960, wasn't sure what to call the phenomenon he was attempting to describe:

The years between 1910 and the Second World War saw a revolution in the literature of the English language as momentous as the Romantic one of a century before...[But it] has not yet acquired a name.[4]

And one year later, when Boris Ford edited *The Modern Age*, the last volume in the *Pelican Guide to English Literature*, the term "modernism" still made no appearance.[5] Only a decade further on, however, and the term was being freely used by Bernard Bergonzi in his essay on "The Advent of Modernism."[6] Somewhere between 1956, then, when Professor X had first pondered "What Was Modernism," and 1971, when Bernard Bergonzi felt that he could confidently trace "The Advent of Modernism," the term acquired a discernible currency among literary critics, shorthand to designate what Hough had called "a revolution in the literature of the English language," a change which took place during "the years between 1910 and the Second World War." From literary studies the term migrated into other disciplines of the humanities, the history of art, music, and architecture. "Modernism is a term now *frequently* used," Peter Faulkner could write in 1983, "in discussions of twentieth-century literature – indeed, of *all forms of twentieth-century art*" (italics mine).[7] Such was the vertiginous history of a word. But what did it mean? Or perhaps we should ask, what has it meant in various times and places?

If we return to Graham Hough for a moment, we can glimpse one answer, or maybe two answers, to that question: "The years between 1910 and the Second World War saw a revolution in the literature of the English language as momentous as the Romantic one of a century before..."[8] Hough, quite plainly, was alluding to a thesis about modernism which had gathered around the figure of T. S. Eliot. A deeply skeptical man who had always harbored reservations about the assumptions guiding Romantic culture and their lingering effects on the mindset of the twentieth century, in 1928 Eliot had announced a deep transformation of his life and thought: his express adherence to a programmatic aesthetics, his new-found affiliation with conservative politics, and his conversion to Christianity. He was, he now declared, a "classicist in literature, a royalist in politics, and anglo-Catholic in religion."[9] Those views, to which Eliot adhered for the rest of his life, could in turn be roughly squared with some of Ezra Pound's tenets. True, Pound's mature political views were considerably more extreme than Eliot's bland toryism (he was an early and ardent supporter of Mussolini), and he was a secularist who sometimes dreamed of an impossible return to some pre-Christian or mythological worldview. Yet he shared Eliot's distrust for Romantic culture and the Victorian heritage, and he intermittently issued declarations that might be considered "classicist." Moreover, their later divergences mattered less than their early collaboration in the years 1914–22. Yes, Hough regretted that the "revolution in the literature of the English language" had "not yet acquired a name," but he now proposed dubbing it not "modernism," but "Imagism," a name which had been adopted by Ezra Pound and a handful of other poets in 1912 to designate their programmatic ambitions. "Imagist ideas," wrote Hough, "are at the centre of the characteristic poetic procedures of our time."[10]

Though nobody would urge this thesis with such bluntness today, it summarized one early consensus about modernism. Its origins were somehow to be discerned in the early formulations of Ezra Pound, formulations whose premises had been deepened and extended by Eliot's work, ultimately bringing about a profound change in the literary and cultural climate of the age. This, in short, was one story that could be told about modernism, one which could also be broadened to accommodate Joyce, or at least one version of Joyce. After all, *Ulysses* had been published serially in the same reviews that sheltered Eliot and Pound. He too, despite the superficial unruliness of his work, might somehow be assimilated to a vague aesthetics of neoclassicism: the chaotic surface merely concealed the deep symbolic structures that shaped and informed his great work, structures that evinced a search for order every bit as profound as Pound's or Eliot's. London, then, was the critical setting for modernism, and the extraordinary decade that ran from 1912 to 1922, the *annus mirabilis*, culminating in the publication of *The Waste Land* (1922) and *Ulysses* (1922), was the critical period for debate and further investigation.

Another quite different account could also be given, however; one that was promulgated in its exemplary form in the pedagogy of that distinguished critic and teacher, Harry Levin. From the 1950s well into the 1970s, Levin taught an almost legendary, year-long course at Harvard on "Joyce, Proust, and Mann." Students were required to read all of *A la recherche*, all of *Ulysses*, and one or more novels by Thomas Mann, and it was even stipulated that they read either the French or the German author in the original. On many it left an indelible impression, and even today one can hear echoes of it in critical debates when these three names are unfurled like some triumvirate of High Modernism. "High Modernism" – and those capital letters are essential – was seen as both an extension of late Symbolism and an intransigent enactment of aesthetic aloofness. The Joyce which emerged from this view was lofty and patrician, utterly contemptuous of popular culture, and the *Ulysses* which came out of it was not the wild, unruly work which many have admired, but one in which every detail had been cunningly devised to accord with the dictates of a rigorous, coherent symbolic structure. Modernism, in this view, was a pan-European and cosmopolitan phenomenon, one promulgated by an international community effectively removed from the contingencies of time and place. Indeed, one key component of this account was the assertion that it was modernism's central achievement to have devised rigorous, difficult, yet coherent forms that were set over and against the chaotic contingencies of the present. And support for that view could be found among the modernists themselves. In a famous review of *Ulysses*, published in 1923, T. S. Eliot had argued that Joyce's use of Homeric myth had provided "a way of controlling, of ordering, of giving a shape and a significance to the immense panorama of futility and anarchy which is contemporary history" (see p. 167 this edition). Here was a view that could easily accommodate Yeats, for example, who became no longer an Irish poet mired in the tedious details of Irish politics, but an English-language counterpart to an aesthete such as Paul Valéry, one who shared with Joyce a concern with mythic or similar kinds of order. Here, in short, was another story one could tell about modernism, one in which its more unruly energies were seen as disciplined and controlled under the aegis of form, form dictated by mythic and symbolic structures located outside and against the historical horrors of the modern world.

Hough and Levin epitomize two of the recurrent stories or paradigms that have been invoked to account for modernism, one intensely focused on London and another resolutely breezing across the Continent in search of symbolic structure and intransigent aestheticism. For all their self-evident weaknesses, both identified points of debate which have continued into the present, albeit in much-altered terms. Though the kind of primacy which Hough assigned the London years of 1912 to 1922 is asserted by few scholars today, that place and time continue to exert an abiding fascination even now. Likewise, while few would accept the easy conflation of very different artists and traditions which Levin urged, the relationship between Anglo-American modernism and its Continental counterparts has remained a perennial subject of discussion, a topic which is also implicit in the shape and structure of this volume.

Another approach to modernism has been less interested in the stories or paradigms that we might use to account for modernism, more interested in modernism as an *-ism*, i.e. a body of doctrines (something on the order of stoicism or communism), a systematic or at least coherent collection of principles, ideas, or attitudes. Modernism, in this view, has identifiable contents, an ensemble of attitudes which either consciously or unconsciously were shared by the major modernists, or were embodied in their works. And these ideas – or so goes one important variant of this argument – had some significant relationship to the social and historical world in which they developed, even if that relationship was largely or wholly negative. Modernism, in short, is related to modernization, perhaps a product of it, perhaps a symptom of it, perhaps a reaction against it, or perhaps something that emerges in tandem with it. Stated so baldly and abstractly, such a view might seem to have little to commend it. But consider the prose of Marshall Berman:

> The maelstrom of modern life has been fed from many sources: great discoveries in the physical sciences, changing our images of the universe and our place in it; the industrialization of production, which transforms scientific knowledge into technology, creates new human environments and destroys old ones, speeds up the whole tempo of life, generates new forms of corporate power and class struggle; immense demographic upheavals, severing millions of people from their ancestral habitats, hurtling them halfway across the world into new lives; rapid and often cataclysmic urban growth; systems of mass communication, dynamic in their development, enveloping and binding together the most diverse people and societies; increasingly powerful national states, bureaucratically structured and operated, constantly striving to expand their powers; mass social movements of people, and peoples, challenging their political and economic rulers, striving to gain some control over their lives; finally, bearing and driving all these people and institutions along, an ever-expanding, drastically fluctuating capitalist world market. In the twentieth century, the social processes that bring this maelstrom into being and keep it in a state of perpetual becoming, have come to be called "modernization."

The visions and ideals nourished by these processes, Berman goes on, have "come to be loosely grouped together under the name of 'modernism'."[11] But many observers have found this definition of "modernism" much too vague, and even the definition of "modernization" which Berman offers, when stripped of its overheated prose, amounts to little more than a familiar catalogue often recited by sociologists of modernity: science, technology, industrialization, demographic changes, increasing urbanization, new mass communications technologies, growing state and corporate bureaucracies with attendant management systems. All can be readily found in the nineteenth century as well, and in themselves they hardly suffice to account for the precipitous rise of literary modernism, or contribute much to accounting for the dense specificity of modernist works.

Variants of arguments about modernism's contents or principles give importance to modernist attitudes towards history or the past, while others stress changing views of space and time. An extreme version of the latter has been argued by Stephen Kern in *The Culture of Time and Space, 1880–1918*. According to this account, sweeping changes in technology and culture "created distinctive new modes of thinking about and experiencing time and space," modes that can be readily discerned in artworks by the Italian Futurists or the French Cubists.[12] The problem with this argument is that the abstractions about space and time lack any organic connection with the works which Kern adduces; his readings of artworks remain wooden and unconvincing, strangely out of touch with contemporary art-historical writing, and almost willfully blind to aesthetic texture.

A very different kind of approach has focused not on the contents of modernism, not on the ideas or attitudes which it embodied or expressed, but on its procedures, the various devices, techniques, stratagems, and strategies by which modernist works achieve their effects. If modernism has a history, in such accounts, it is essentially a formal one, with one innovation paving the way or clearing the path for another. Multiple and unsteady points of view, stream of consciousness, illusionism with a self-consciousness of formal structure, collage, montage, juxtaposition, a display of raw medium (language, sound), a unified but lost order beneath apparent fragmentation – these are only a few of the techniques which have been repeatedly highlighted in these discussions. Such accounts, generally formalist in orientation, are often rather Whiggish in nature, with each new device or technique merely a prelude to still further innovation. In the most extreme formulations, the modernists even anticipate many of the concerns and devices which have been thought to characterize postmodern writing and art. Or in more comic variants, the term "postmodernist" is elevated to mean something like "very good" or "praiseworthy" and retroactively applied to individual modernists: Gertrude Stein or Ezra Pound, for example, are really "postmodernists" *avant la lettre*, and we should ignore their perverse propensity to associate with misogynists such as Picasso or that heir of late symbolism and proponent of neoclassicism, T. S. Eliot.[13]

The necessarily schematic account which I have just given suffices to indicate some of the major poles of thinking which have governed attempts to account for modernism. In recent years a new line of argumentation has attempted to draw a firm distinction between modernism and the historical avant-garde, one that allegedly pivots on their attitude toward popular culture. In this view, modernism is characterized above all by its suspicious, even hostile attitude towards the popular. "Mass culture has always been the hidden subtext of the modernist project," one in which popular culture is construed as a threat of encroaching formlessness, gendered as female, and held at bay by affirming and refortifying the boundaries between art and inauthentic mass culture. Here lies the dividing line between modernism and the avant-garde. "The avant garde," instead, "attempts to subvert art's autonomy, its artificial separation from life, and its institutionalization as 'high art'," and this impulse accounts for its "urge to validate other, formerly neglected or ostracized forms of cultural expression," chief among them popular culture. Modernism, in this view, becomes little more than a reactionary, even paranoid, fear of popular culture. Moreover, attached to this thesis about the avant-garde and modernism is a second claim: postmodernism, it is urged, seeks "to negotiate forms of high art with certain forms and genres of mass culture and the culture of everyday life," and therefore it is the legitimate heir of the historical avant-garde.[14] Indeed, "postmodernism itself can now be described as a search for a viable tradition apart from, say, the Proust–Joyce–Mann triad and outside the canon of classical modernism."[15]

Our old friends from Harry Levin's famous class have come back to haunt us – and with a vengeance. Yet many would quarrel with this curiously restricted definition of "classical modernism." After all, Thomas Mann's lifelong ambition was to develop a prose style that would approximate the style of Goethe's late masterpiece *Elective Affinities* (*Wahlverwandscaften*) (1809). But is this really an ambition that one would normally classify as modernist? Many would demur. Yes, Mann wrote a number of novels that take up themes and motifs found in modernism; but that does not make him a modernist, anymore than H. G. Wells becomes a modernist because of the modernist motifs discernible in his wonderful romp of a novel, *Tono-Bungay* (1908). Proust's position is notoriously complicated, and we can set him aside for now. But to have Joyce cited in the context of a thesis that modernism is hostile to popular culture is truly astonishing. For what book is more charged with the detritus of popular culture, each artifact treated respectfully or even lovingly, than *Ulysses*? And for some readers the central episodes of *Ulysses* are directly indebted to the structure of middle-brow forms such as British pantomime and music hall.[16]

An alternative approach, instead, has argued that it is futile to search for an ensemble of modernist ideas or attitudes (whether towards time, space, history, etc.) or to isolate a set of formal devices (collage, montage, stream-of-consciousness, juxtaposition, etc.), or even to correlate items from both categories and urge that together these embodied a vague yet potent ideology that challenged dominant cultural norms, assaulted the bourgeois concept of art, or anticipated the concerns of postmodernism. Such arguments are sustained only by confining one's attention to conceptual and formal values viewed in isolation from their social actualization. Viewed in institutional terms, the avant-garde was neither more nor less than a structural feature within the institutional configuration of modernism, the whole constituted by a specific array of marketing and publicity structures that were integrated in varying degrees with the larger economic apparatus of its time. Modernism itself, on this view, was more than just a series of texts, or a set of ideas that found expression in them, or a set of devices in which those were embodied. It was a social reality, a constellation of agents and practices that converged in the production, marketing, and publicization of an idiom, a shareable and serviceable language within the family of twentieth-century tongues. The institutional profile of that social constellation can be traced in the staging venues and social spaces where it operated – the salons and lecture halls, the little reviews and the deluxe or limited editions – the agoras in which the changing relations among authors and audiences were enacted, and in which the work, the "business" of modernism, got done. What drove that ensemble of institutions was a small elite of patron–investors: John Quinn, Harriet Shaw Weaver, Scofield Thayer, James Sibley Watson Jr., Otto Kahn, Peggy Guggenheim, the author Bryher – to name just a few. It was their money which funded the little reviews and purchased the limited or deluxe editions, both venues that were located in a profoundly ambiguous social space, simultaneously sequestered and semi-withdrawn from the larger institution of publishing, and instead situated within a submarket of collecting. What the patron–investors provided with their subsidies and endowments was an institutional space momentarily immune to the pressures of an expansive and expanding mass culture. Yet that same space was simultaneously being transformed by its proximity to the small (and hence malleable) submarket for rare books and deluxe editions, a submarket just then being "modernized," just then becoming aware of the potential value of works by authors still living, in part as a result of its interconnectedness with the world of collecting in the visual arts. Patronage was pervasive. Ezra Pound, James Joyce, T. S. Eliot, W. B. Yeats, Marianne Moore, the American poet H. D., Wyndham Lewis, Djuna Barnes – all of them received intermittent or sustained patronage in their careers. Only those who were already well-to-do or even wealthy, such as Virginia Woolf and Gertrude Stein, survived without it. Moreover, even those few who worked for a living, such as the insurance executive Wallace Stevens or the practicing doctor William Carlos Williams, were its beneficiaries insofar as the journals in which they published, such as the *Dial* (widely considered the preeminent review of Anglo-American literary modernism from 1920 to 1929), were sustained by patronage on a truly massive scale. How massive? The annual deficits for the *Dial* from 1920 through 1922 were, respectively, $100,000, $54,000, and $65,000, a cumulative deficit of $220,000 that was paid for by its two patrons at the rate of $4,000 per month from each. This was at a time when the annual salary of the private secretary to the editor of *Vanity Fair* was $1,400. A speculative reader may try to guess how much remuneration the same position receives today and accordingly scale up the size of the subsidy which kept the *Dial* afloat, translating it into current dollars. The result is staggering.

Modernism's interchanges with the emerging worlds of consumerism, fashion, and display were far more complicated, more ambiguous than often assumed. At times they brought modernism perilously close to being the kind of phenomenon that art critics deride with the scathing term "smart art." But they may also have been productive as well. The ambiguity of modernism's institutional status may itself account for much of its perennial uncertainty concerning the nature of representation in art, its insistent pressure on the means by which illusions and likenesses are made. Modernism's radical interrogation of the cultural repertoire, which permanently altered the relations of the arts with society at large, may owe much to its equivocal status as an institution that was half-withdrawn from, yet half-nestled within, the larger apparatus of cultural production.[17] Academic critics who postulate a schematic opposition between "the subversive, experimental energies of the avant-garde culture of the early part of the century" and the ways in which those were later "formulated, controlled, contained, marketed and cancelled" in the university or the museum, bear witness only to the poverty of historical imagination with which they address the past.[18]

But where does modernism stand today? What is its status among contemporary critics or intellectual historians, and is it still considered a compelling resource for the present? These questions are difficult to answer, in large part because every attempt to situate modernism within a narrative of cultural history inevitably brushes up against a problem at once historical and philosophical: what is the norm or background against which modernism is being assessed? Earlier critics who followed some of T. S. Eliot's hints, for example, typically set modernism against the background of Romanticism and either tacitly or explicitly characterized it as a form of neoclassicism. But Eliot's authority is no longer as monolithic as it was, and increasingly it is recognized that the neoclassical leanings of the later Eliot may be not only a poor guide to modernism, but also a poor guide to the earlier Eliot. Perhaps another approach to this issue might begin by taking up the question of narrative.

Whatever literary modernism was, it was impatient with or overtly hostile to received conventions of fiction. That hostility is often perceived as part of modernism's impulse to repudiate that Victorian literature (above all fiction), that had sold itself to a mass reading public – yet another instance of modernism's contempt for popular culture. But it may be more productive to take a more circuitous route and to situate the conventions of narrative in a broader perspective by turning back to Aristotle's *Poetics*, that seminal meditation on tragedy and epic, or fiction, which has exerted such influence over Western aesthetics. Aristotle, we recall, was bent on defending imaginative mimesis, or fictional resemblance, against the charges which Plato had earlier leveled against it, charges which had ultimately led Plato to exclude poets from his ideal Republic. For Aristotle, therefore, it was necessary to show that mimesis leads to forms of comprehension or understanding which have philosophical significance. To do so, he puts the experience of wonder at the heart of mimesis, for elsewhere Aristotle (following the lead of Plato) had placed wonder at the very origins of philosophy, a sign of humanity's primordial thirst for comprehension. The wonderful, therefore, becomes crucial to literary experience as well. Discussing those famous emotions, fear and pity, which tragedy must inspire, Aristotle writes toward the end of chapter 9:

> Such an effect is best produced when the events come on by surprise; and the effect is heightened *when*, at the same time, *they happen on account of one another*. The tragic wonder [*thaumaston*] will then be greater than if they happened of themselves, or by accident; for even coincidences are most wonderful when they have an air of design.[19]

Aristotle is saying that a fictional event can and should be surprising (or wonderful), but at the same time it must have an intelligible relationship with antecedent events, must entail sequential intelligibility. It may be surprising or shocking, for example, that Oedipus is blinded. But he must not be merely the victim of bad luck or the caprices of the gods; his fate must be a consequence of his earlier actions, must entail the kind of connectedness and relatedness which, if it is discerned by the audience, entails a form of comprehension that is analogous to, or of the same sort as, the comprehension which is achieved by philosophy.

Elsewhere, however, in a later part of the *Poetics* (ch. 24), Aristotle also expresses contradictory views about the wonderful or the marvelous:

> The element of the wonderful is required in tragedy. The irrational, on which the wonderful depends for its chief effects, has wider scope in epic poetry, because there the person is not seen [i.e., doesn't appear in the flesh onstage]. Thus, the pursuit of Hector [in Bk. 22 of the *Iliad*] would be ludicrous if placed upon the stage – the Greeks standing still and not joining in the pursuit, and Achilles waving them back. But in the epic poem this absurdity passes unnoticed. Now the wonderful is pleasing; a sign of this is the fact that everyone tells a story with some addition of his own, knowing that his hearers like it.... Accordingly, the poet should prefer probable impossibilities to improbable possibilities. The tragic plot must not be composed of irrational parts. Everything irrational should, if possible, be excluded; or, at all events, it should lie outside the action of the play.[20]

This is a curious passage. For while Aristotle plainly relates the wonderful to the irrational – "the irrational, on which the wonderful depends for its chief effects" – he also urges that every element of the irrational be excluded from tragic plots, a stipulation that would seem to entail excluding the wonderful as well, even though Aristotle elsewhere (ch. 9) makes wonder indispensable to the literary experience and assigns it kinship to pity and fear. One way to explain this contradiction would be to follow the suggestion of Aristotle's finest contemporary commentator, Stephen Halliwell, who urges that "there are degrees of wonder, which lies on the boundary between the explicable and the inexplicable, and so can slip into the latter (and hence become the irrational) or, properly used, may stimulate and challenge understanding."[21] In any event, wonder retains a troubled and potentially troubling status in Aristotelian aesthetics. But why should that matter in relation to modernism? To answer that we need a broad account of the place which Aristotle's aesthetics have come to occupy in modern cultural history.

The recovery of Aristotle during the Renaissance was one of the great achievements of the humanists. But it also dealt a virtual death-blow to the reputation of Dante, the greatest poet of the Middle Ages. For if there was ever a work in which there was an excess of the wonderful, a term explicitly related to the appearance of the divine in Aristotle's example from Book 22 of the *Iliad*, it is the *Divine Comedy*. The miraculous, a strong version of the wonderful, is pervasive in Dante's work. But Renaissance theorists of the epic, enthralled by Aristotle, would have none of it. So complete was the Renaissance demolition of Dante's masterpiece that from 1598 to 1703, a period of more than a century, only three editions of the *Divina Commedia* sufficed to satisfy demand in the whole of Western Christendom. Aristotle was the great theorist of realism, demanding that works have a high degree of spatiotemporal, logical, and causal connectedness; and it should also come as no surprise that Henry Fielding should have invoked the *Poetics* as his guiding light in the preface to *Joseph Andrews* (1742), that seminal work for the foundation of the English novel.

All which should give us a view of sufficient breadth to permit a sketch of modernism's place within a broader cultural history. For if we recognize that the wonderful, cognate with shocks and surprises, lies on the border of the inexplicable, we also begin to glimpse the discontinuous yet coherent outline of its family resemblance to terms which predominate in that most common yet legitimate complaint about modernism, its difficulty, its wild and irredeemable opacity, its resolute insistence on wonder so condensed that it turns into horror. Modernism, with all its machineries of extremism, was anything but eager to resolve the experience of wonder/horror into the ready comprehensibility of spatiotemporal and logical-causal connectedness. Quite the contrary. Its antinarratival aesthetics constituted an unprecedented rupture with a major strand, perhaps *the* major strand, of post-Renaissance aesthetics in the West.

To enquire about the cultural status of modernism today, then, may entail asking two further questions. One might be to ask what critics and intellectual historians posterior to the modernists have made of this recalcitrant, unruly heritage. There is no single answer, of course. Critics in the 1960s and 1970s still wrote in the shadow of Eliot's enormous reputation; modernism, it was held, was a reaction against Romanticism, and individual works by other authors were cajoled to conform to some vague standard of neoclassicism. Hugh Kenner, a ferociously intelligent and delightful contrarian, held out for an alternative view: the first half of the twentieth century was not the age of Eliot, but *The Pound Era*. But the advent of fiction and architecture that was labeled "postmodern" in the 1970s and 1980s made the question of defining modernism both less urgent and more urgent. Modernism was no longer the cutting edge in the arts; yet it was indispensable to understand it if one was to come to terms with contemporary developments. In this new climate, attempts to characterize modernism were often advanced with the idea of defending, justifying, or advocating the postmodern over and against modernism. The result was dispiriting, a travesty which eviscerated modernism of its wild opacity and reduced it to little more than a collection of the most reactionary political views which modernists such as Wyndham Lewis, T. S. Eliot, and Ezra Pound had adopted during the 1930s. Modernism was a closed, hermetic, elitist, misogynist, homophobic, moderately liberal or conservative (at best), reactionary (at second best), Fascist (at worst), and anti-Semitic (is there worse than worst?) movement which had cloaked its nefarious ideology under a spurius neoclassicism, a factitious formalism of the finished work of art. A sentence such as the immediately preceding became routine during the decade or so that ran from roughly 1985 to 1995. But since then, the climate has changed again. Postmodernism, which had been defined as anything from an arched eyebrow to a fundamental reordering of our perception of ourselves and our place in the world, is plainly waning in prestige. In literature, especially, it has been dismissed as little more than fiction and poetry for overeducated white males. The rise of ethnic fictions has been accompanied by a discernible revival of realism, sometimes labeled neorealism, while interest in postcolonialism has entailed a return to the kinds of systemic issues (globalization, diasporic or cosmopolitan communities) that have formed part of the modernism and modernity debates. Meanwhile, quietly and tenaciously, feminist critics have inexorably altered the scope of works included in the modernist canon: authors once deemed classic but then strangely forgotten (such as Gertrude Stein), authors swiftly hailed but just as swiftly forgotten (Djuna Barnes), and authors utterly forgotten but newly esteemed (Mary Butts), occupy a far more central place in the contemporary canon of modernism. Race, and the way it permeated modernist thinking about language and the arts, has also acquired a new centrality.[22]

Such changes might be easily dismissed as mere matters of academic fashion. But such a judgment would be premature. Of course the academy is prone to mercurial changes in fashion; but the same is true for journalism or even medicine. All these institutions form part of a complex civil society, and one dismisses such changes only at one's peril. Their internal debates inevitably filter out to form part of our common culture, however fractured and overloaded with information it may be.

There is a second, more urgent question embedded in the necessarily schematic account of how modernism has fared at the hands of critics since the 1960s, a question about the place which the future assumes in giving narrative shape and significance to events (or cultural events, such as modernism) which took place in the past. The philosopher Arthur Danto has usefully pointed out both the gaps and the possibilities created by shifting historical horizons. On the one hand, without a knowledge of events that are later to the one that we are describing, our historical account may be seriously inadequate and incomplete. On the other hand, we should be wary of "descriptions of events ... which make an essential reference to later events – events future to the time at which the description is given. In effect [such works] are trying to write the history of what happens *before* it has happened, and to give accounts of the past based upon accounts of the future."[23] But how can we thread our way between these conflicting imperatives?

Jürgen Habermas, in remarks directly indebted to Danto, has also emphasized the extent to which knowledge of the future is indispensable to enabling accounts of the past:

> Historical accounts make use of narrative statements. They are called narrative because they present events as elements of stories [*Geschichten*]. Stories have a beginning and an end; they are held together by an action. Historical events are reconstructed within the reference system of a story. They cannot be presented without relation to other, later events ... The sentence, "The thirty years war began in 1618," presupposes that at least those events have elapsed which are relevant for the history of the war up to the Peace of Westphalia, events that could not have been narrated by any observer at the outbreak of the war ... The predicates with which an event is narratively presented require the appearance of later events in the light of which the event in question appears as an historical event.[24]

Habermas, in effect, is reminding us how improbable is the imaginary scenario in which a German burgher of 1618 runs through his town shouting, "Oh my God! Today is the first day of the Thirty Years War!" There is nothing wrong with a historian narrating events from a perspective in time future to his subject-matter, of course, or knowing more about that subject than its contemporaries could have – e.g the length of a given war. "But such knowledge," Michael André Bernstein has warned, "should not delude the historian into thinking that the future was inevitable simply because it happened, nor should he use it to judge the way contemporaries, existing without such information, viewed their own circumstances and decided upon particular courses of action."[25]

This is pertinent to the question about the status of modernism because we are still so uncertain about which events will have to take place before we can give an adequate account of its significance. If postmodernism is now a spent force and neorealism is increasingly prevalent (it is certainly true at present that realism dominates all creative writing programs in the US), then perhaps a great age of literary experimentalism has simply drawn to a close, one inaugurated and sanctioned by modernism, one extended and finally depleted in postmodernism. But even that term, "experimentalism," puts too much emphasis on the purely formal dimensions of modernist writing and gives too little weight to the grim and grisly qualities of modernism, the tattered fabric of interruptions, gaps, and ruptures that make up modernist writing. Still, if nothing else, such an account reopens the question of modernism to a new generation of readers whose own experience of contemporary writing will inevitably be formed in ongoing dialogue with the contradictory heritage of modernism.

As for the modernists themselves, they could be disconcertingly cavalier about the transmission of their work to the future. Once again an example from T. S. Eliot springs to mind. Late in his life, in 1962, he was approached by a 17-year-old high school student about doing an interview. His claim on Eliot's attention was exceedingly slight: his parents had hosted dinners for Valerie Eliot, his second wife, before her marriage. But Eliot was never one to forget a kindness and he promptly agreed, even though the publication would only appear in a school magazine. Young Tim Jeal duly performed the interview, carefully gave the resultant text for approval to the illustrious interviewee, and finally sent it off to the printer. Proofs were subsequently checked by Jeal, his co-editor, and even a helpful teacher. Six weeks later, the moment at last came when the long-awaited publication arrived in the post. Jeal opened it eagerly, only to find to his horror that in every instance where the words "Waste Land" should have appeared, the word "Washstand" had been substituted. Horrified, Jeal telephoned Eliot and nervously explained that he had to come over right away, that something terrible had happened. When he arrived at Eliot's home, he hastily recounted the inexplicable disaster, then stood in terrified silence, awaiting the great man's castigation. A splutter broke from Eliot's lips, then another much louder and deeper, then a third so deep that it forced him to sit down. Eliot was laughing uncontrollably.

Eliot eventually calmed down and suggested to Jeal that he insert an erratum slip into the issues, which would more than suffice to rectify the error. As for himself, however, he wanted 12 copies of the journal – uncorrected and without the erratum slip, raw "Washstand." Later he wrote his final letter to young Jeal:

> When you have had as much experience of printers' errors as I have, you will not worry so much when you find a few. . . . I was delighted when I found *The Waste Land* turned into *The Washstand*. And there is another point worth mentioning. Some people (and a few libraries) now collect first editions of anything I write; and collectors are just as crazy as stamp collectors: if there is a misprint, that makes a first edition more valuable. In a few years time *The Washstand* text will be worth much more than *The Waste Land*.[26]

It might almost have been an allegory for critical understanding of modernism. The more carefully we scrutinize *The Waste Land*, the more we get *The Washstand*. But perhaps, if T. S. Eliot was right, that is no bad thing.

NOTES

1   Donald Hall, *Remembering Poets* (New York: Harper & Row, 1978), 91–2.
2   I am alluding to a famous essay by Harry Levin, "What Was Modernism?," first published in Stanley Burnshaw (ed.), *Varieties of Literary Experience* (New York: New York University Press, 1962), 307–29, and later collected in Harry Levin, *Refractions: Essays in Comparative Literature* (New York: Oxford University Press, 1966).
3   See Anthony Cronin, *Samuel Beckett: the Last Modernist* (London: HarperCollins, 1996).
4   Graham Hough, *Image and Experience: Studies in a Literary Revolution* (London: Duckworth, 1960), 4–5.
5   Boris Ford, *The Modern Age* (London: Penguin, 1961), vol. 7 in *The Pelican Guide to English Literature*.
6   Bernard Bergonzi, "The Advent of Modernism," in Bergonzi (ed.), *The Twentieth Century*, vol. 7 in *The Sphere History of Literature in the English Language* (London: Barrie and Jenkins, 1970).
7   Peter Faulkner, *Modernism* (London: Methuen, 1977), ix.
8   Hough, *Image and Experience*, 5.
9   T. S. Eliot, *For Lancelot Andrewes* (London: Faber and Gwyer, 1928), ix.
10   Hough, *Image and Experience*, 5.
11   Marshall Berman, *All That Is Solid Melts Into Air: The Experience of Modernity* (New York: Simon & Schuster, 1982), 16.
12   Stephen Kern, *The Culture of Time and Space, 1880–1918* (Cambridge, MA: Harvard University Press, 1983), 1.
13   The best examples of this kind of work are the many studies by Marjorie Perloff, which repeatedly turn on a distinction between a poetics derived from Symbolism (Eliot is the wicked examplar of this trend), and an anti-Symbolist poetics (Pound, Marinetti, Gertrude Stein, and various postmodern poets are the good exemplars of this trend): see *The Poetics of Indeterminacy: Rimbaud to Cage* (Princeton: Princeton University Press, 1981); *The Futurist Moment: Avant-Garde, Avant Guerre, and the Language of Rupture* (Chicago: University of Chicago Press, 1986); *Radical Aritifice: Writing Poetry in the Age of Media* (Chicago: University of Chicago Press, 1991); *Wittgenstein's Ladder: Poetic Language and the Strangeness of the Ordinary* (Chicago: University of Chicago Press, 1996).

14 Andreas Huyssen, *After the Great Divide: Modernism, Mass Culture, Postmodernism* (Bloomington: Indiana University Press, 1986), 47, 53, 61, 59.

15 Ibid., 169.

16 See Cheryl Herr, *Joyce's Anatomy of Culture* (Urbana, IL: University of Illinois, 1986).

17 See Lawrence Rainey, *Institutions of Modernism: Literary Elites and Public Culture* (New Haven: Yale University Press, 1998).

18 Steven Connor, *Postmodern Culture* (Oxford: Blackwell, 1989), 12, summarizing Charles Newman, *The Post-Modern Aura: the Act of Fiction in an Age of Inflation* (Evanston, IL: Northwestern University Press, 1985).

19 My translation; but see *The Poetics of Aristotle*, trans. Stephen Halliwell (Chapel Hill: University of North Carolina Press, 1987), 42.

20 My translation; but see *The Poetics of Aristotle*, 60.

21 Stephen Halliwell, *Aristotle's Poetics* (London: Duckworth, 1986), 75 n. 41.

22 See, for example, Michael North, *Dialectic of Modernism: Race, Language, and Twentieth Century Literature* (Oxford: Oxford University Press, 1994).

23 Arthur Danto, *Analytical Philosophy of History* (Cambridge: Cambridge University Press, 1965), 12.

24 Jürgen Habermas, "A Review of Gadamer's Truth and Method," in *Understanding and Social Inquiry*, eds. Fred R. Dallymayr and Thomas A. McCarthy (Notre Dame: University of Notre Dame Press, 1977), 346.

25 Michael André Bernstein, "Foregone Conclusions," *Modernism/Modernity* 1(1) (Jan. 1994): 64.

26 Tim Jeal, "Mr. Eliot and Me," *Daily Telegraph*, "Books," March 27, 2004, pp. 1–2.

A Note on the Selection, Texts, and Order of Presentation

This anthology contains selected works of 23 Anglo-American modernists, 12 women and 11 men. In addition it contains selected works of four movements or schools which interacted with Anglo-American modernism in various ways, either influencing it directly or offering commentary on it that has proved influential for subsequent critical discussion: Futurism, Dada, Surrealism, and the Frankfurt School. Large and very lengthy anthologies could be made for each of these movements, and what is presented here is necessarily more selective: fundamental texts that have repeatedly been at the center of critical debate about modernism's significance, or texts that enable a reader to acquire a basic sense of each movement's typical themes and scope. Modernism was a phenomenon at once stubbornly international and irreducibly local: even those writers who dogmatically urged that genuine art could be achieved only through a tenacious adherence to local particulars, such as William Carlos Williams, did so against the background of modernism's internationalism or cosmopolitanism, and did so too with an acute awareness of developments elsewhere.

There are some things this anthology is not designed to do. It cannot offer a survey of literary modernism's interactions with the contemporary visual arts or music, however rich those may have been. To do so would require yet another volume every bit as massive as this one, and perhaps larger still, since the volume would need to encompass not only the many primary materials (the many paintings, sculptures, artifacts, and musical scores), but the contemporary discourses that accompanied them, as well as the most influential critical descriptions or accounts that have become enshrined in subsequent discussion (e.g., Clement Greenberg). A multivolume anthology of modernism across the arts would be highly desirable, but it would also be a project much larger in scope than the present work.

A different yet related problem of scope concerns the novel. The case of Ford Madox Ford is instructive. To the overwhelming majority of readers Ford is known today as the author of two works, *The Good Soldier* and *Parade's End*, the latter comprising four books and running to nearly 1,000 pages in length. Neither could be easily accommodated in an anthology which must also encompass a good many other authors. Indeed, the same might be said of other novels and novelists. To try to represent entire novels with snippets of chapters or even entire chapters is a perilous and perhaps self-defeating enterprise. The amount of prefatory material required to explain the rationale behind the excerpt becomes overwhelming. Ford Madox Ford, in short, is poorly represented by the selection of his writing that is included here; but since his major novels are readily available in economical editions, one can at least hope that this selection of his writings can enhance and complement a reader's experience of those works.

Virginia Woolf ranks with James Joyce as one of modernism's major figures, and more space has been given over to these two authors than to any others. Woolf was first and foremost a novelist, or perhaps it might be better said that she was a writer who always thought through questions of form and style in terms that were ultimately derived from the novel. That is not to say that Woolf never wrote short stories, or that her short stories were uniformly poor. But it is the case that Woolf wrote relatively few of them, and that it was not a form that she turned to with any regularity, nor a form that consistently engaged her deepest imaginative resources. Under such circumstances, it is better to acknowledge the force of circumstances that cannot be altered, and on that basis to include an entire novel by Woolf, the form in which her imaginative world found its best and truest expression. *Between the Acts* may never be as popular as *To the Lighthouse* or *Mrs. Dalloway*; but it is nevertheless one of her best and most important works, and its dark meditations on the fate of culture in the midst of war and violence have a grimness that is especially compelling.

The cases of Ford Madox Ford and Virginia Woolf can serve to highlight the extent to which they differ from other novelists, writers for whom the short story was a more congenial form. Elizabeth Bowen, Djuna Barnes, Jean Rhys, Mary Butts, and Wyndham Lewis were all writers who were able to make good use of the short story, and although all of them also wrote major novels that are essential to an informed understanding of Anglo-American modernism, the selections of their short stories presented here can at least lay claim to offering a birds-eye view of the richly imagined worlds that are conjured in their longer works. The same claim could not, I think, have been made with respect to William Faulkner. His short stories were typically published in popular magazines such as the *Saturday Evening Post*, and were often written with the aim of earning a bit of money to tide him over while in the course of some larger project. To represent his achievement as a modernist by a selection of short stories would only be to misrepresent him, and on these grounds I have omitted his work from this collection.

A much larger omission concerns writers of the Harlem Renaissance. While it is self-evident that Langston Hughes, Zora Neale Hurston, and others took up modernist themes and concerns, or engaged in various ways with the formal experimentalism sometimes thought to typify modernism, any attempt to include them in an anthology containing Joyce, Eliot, Woolf, and Stein would inevitably smack of tokenism. Moreover, the present time is unusual in being able to boast a number of exceptionally good anthologies of the Harlem Renaissance, not least the *Portable Harlem Renaissance Reader*, edited by David Levering Lewis. I see no point in attempting to present an etiolated or shrunken version of that distinguished achievement, which runs to almost 800 pages. Likewise, it is certainly the case that Ralph Ellison's *Invisible Man* is the achievement of a distinctly modernist imagination; but to excerpt it is impossible, and to include excerpts from it alongside fuller representations of Woolf, Joyce, Stein, et al. would only, again, smack of tokenism.

Every anthologist must make hard choices. Other authors that could have been included in this volume – and indeed, at earlier points in time all of them were – are Roger Fry, Katherine Mansfield, Gilbert Seldes, Ernest Hemingway, Sylvia Townsend Warner, Nathanael West, Laura Riding Jackson, and Louis Zukovsky. Simple reasons of length combined with some of the already mentioned considerations to preclude them. On the plus side, however, this volume contains an impressive number of major works that have been presented whole:

Gertrude Stein, *Tender Buttons* (1914)
T. S. Eliot, *The Waste Land* (1922)
W. B. Yeats, *At the Hawk's Well* (1916) and *The Tower* (1928)
William Carlos Williams, *Spring and All* (1923)
Virginia Woolf, *Between the Acts* (1941)
Samuel Beckett, *Texts for Nothing* (1955) and *Endgame* (1957)

With the exception of the "Anna Livia Plurabelle" chapter of *Finnegans Wake*, all the works presented here are given in their entirety, and in the case of that exception the omission has been clearly signaled and the scope and nature of the omitted contents have been specified.

In preparing this collection, I have excluded materials such as diaries, letters, and private memoranda that were not originally in the public domain during the period from 1910 to 1940. While such materials can be gateways to important insights about modernism and its evolution, selecting one author's unpublished letters over another's is a delicate task; it invites the editor (and hence the reader) to favor one account over another, without a reader necessarily knowing what the alternatives are. Better, then, to decline that invitation.

In addition, I have given only limited attention to drama in making these selections – for two reasons, both pragmatic. The volume would have become far too long, and in practice American universities have tended to relegate drama to theater studies departments, a development that one may deplore, but one which made itself felt in the decision-making. My own hope is that a separate volume devoted to modernism and theater will follow this one.

The furious and widely publicized debates that have surrounded the text of *Ulysses* may prompt some readers to wonder about the version of any given text that is being presented here. The case of *Ulysses* is singular, but it can be useful for highlighting some problems common to many modernist texts. Perhaps the easiest way to illustrate those is through the case of Djuna Barnes and the short stories that she wrote during the decade that stretched from 1918 to 1928, stories that she collected in 1929 in *A Night among the Horses* (New York: Liveright). When Barnes was presented with the opportunity to revise them more than three decades later for her *Selected Works* (1962), she rewrote virtually every sentence. The result was to create something that her contemporaries, at least those of them who were still alive, would scarcely have recognized, and yet it is through the numerous reprintings of that later edition that Barnes's stories are known in libraries throughout the world. In the case of Barnes, I have restored all the readings of the 1929 edition. More generally I have followed the same policy with other authors, returning to the text presented in the first edition which the author oversaw, rather than (say) to the first publication in a journal or magazine, where "house style" would or could prevail over an author's intentions. In every case I have clearly indicated the text which has served as my authority in the first note that follows every title.

Finally, a word needs to be said about the order of these materials. The sequence of authors is broadly chronological, beginning with Ezra Pound and ending with Samuel Beckett. To begin with Pound is not to endorse a view which ascribes great importance to Imagism, as I myself have argued against that view elsewhere. It is to recognize, however, that Anglo-American literary modernism was unusual in the extent to which many of its principal protagonists interacted with one another through shared institutional structures during a brief yet crucial period from 1912 to 1922, roughly from the formation of Imagism to the publication of *Ulysses* (February 1922) and *The Waste Land* (October 1922). Such boundaries are, of course, arbitrary, slighting the extent to which Anglo-American modernism drew on cultural traditions extending much further back in time, minimizing developments in the decades that followed. But because that decade and the particular constellation of modernism which it nurtured have been so important to earlier criticism, and are likely to remain so in the years ahead, I have given them appropriate attention in the earlier selections.

Beyond that order, itself fairly minimal, I have aimed for an order that is broadly chronological and yet strives for productive juxtapositions that will help the student and general reader who encounters these materials for the first time to discern suggestive links among them. The four "Continental Interludes," which are devoted respectively to Futurism, Dada, Surrealism, and the Frankfurt School, can only be arranged in a chronological order. The first three movements in particular were, for contemporaries, associated with a specific period: the enormous uproar provoked by Futurism occurred before the outbreak of the First World War, just as Dada itself was very much a reaction against the Great War and an attempt to prolong that reaction into the period of the war's aftermath. Surrealism, though its intellectual roots are extraordinarily complex and rich, was at first a response to and a turn away from Dada, or at least that version of Dada that had prevailed in Paris during the early 1920s. And it was only in the later 1920s that the characteristic concerns and themes of the Frankfurt School first found voice. A chronological arrangement, in short, acknowledges the cumulative interaction and development of avant-garde motifs, themes, and devices; it is not, in other words, intended to imply that the Frankfurt School comes as a last, culminating, or definitive comment on modernism.

A similar caveat can be extended to the many essays included in this volume. Most of the modernists, though not all, were prodigious in their production of nonfiction prose. Over the course of his career T. S. Eliot published over 500 essays and reviews; Marianne Moore, more than 400; Ezra Pound, more than 1,500; and W. B. Yeats, at least 400. (Any selection of, say, four or five essays by these authors will inevitably entail distortions.) It is a commonplace that literary modernism is distinguished by this unprecedented production of critical and theoretical writings that were meant to articulate the historical, formal, or ideological grounds for the modernist experiment, that sought to create or shape an audience receptive to modernist artworks. Indeed, in the case of Futurism it can be plausibly argued that its manifestos *were* its principal artworks, effectively displacing or even replacing the paintings, poems, novels, buildings, and symphonies that were supposed to follow from them. Theory and practice, in short, had no straightforward or simple relationship to one another. It would be a mistake to assume that the essays explain or serve as reliable guides to the creative works. They, too, must be read with critical insight.

Continental Interlude I:
Futurism (1909–14)

Nothing did more to shape the concept of the "avant-garde" in twentieth-century culture than Futurism, the strange phenomenon – groping for words, cultural historians have typically labeled it a "movement" – that was unleashed by Filippo Tommaso Marinetti on February 20, 1909, when he published "The Founding and the Manifesto of Futurism" on the front page of the Parisian newspaper, *Le Figaro*. In subsequent decades Futurism became a paradigm for countless movements to come, some embodying the most vital currents among the twentieth-century arts (Vorticism, Dadaism, Surrealism, and the Internationale Situationiste). And already in the brief period that followed the first manifesto's publication, especially in the years from 1912 to 1914, Futurism became the focal point for a vast debate that stretched across Europe and the United States, spanned the spectrum of the arts, and encompassed the gamut of forums for critical discussion. In England alone during these years, more than 500 articles concerning Futurism were published, a number that also reflects Futurism's relentless expansion into nearly all the arts, including literature, music, the visual arts, architecture, drama, photography, film, dance, even fashion. Futurism had done something startling. It had revealed the power and potential of a novel type of intellectual formation: a small collectivity, buttressed by publicity and theatricality, that presented an array of cultural artifacts which were constructed in accordance with a coherent body of theoretical precepts, a set of axioms grounded not just in seemingly arbitrary aesthetic preferences, but in a systematic assessment of contemporary society. Futurism, in short, had irreversibly forged a fateful link between a theory of modernity and the project of the avant-garde. Still more, because Futurism would later be deeply involved with the genesis of Fascism, it would become the focal point for an immense and ongoing debate: in twentieth-century culture, Futurism has remained the litmus test for probing the relationship between art and power, aesthetics and politics.

F. T. Marinetti was born in 1876 in Alexandria, the son of a lawyer who specialized in commercial contracts and thrived in a city which was then a substantial center for trade. Marinetti was educated there at a French *collège*, a Jesuit institution, an experience which left him a predilection for writing in French which lasted into middle age. (A late as 1918 he would lapse into French in his diaries.) In 1894 Marinetti took up the study of law at the University of Pavia, followed by a transfer to the University of Genoa, where he received his degree in 1899. His family, meanwhile, had moved to Milan, the commercial center of Italy and a city which had a strong heritage of links with France.

In March 1898 he published his first poem, in French, "The Cup-Bearer" ("L'Échanson"), in the *Anthologie Revue*, a bilingual journal published in Milan. Marinetti soon became its "general secretary," a position that enabled him to take up correspondence with poets in Paris. The same year another poem by him won a French literary prize and he journeyed to Paris to receive the award and engage in literary networking. Marinetti's contributions to literary journals (all in French) multiplied at a prodigious rate. Three years later he published his first book, *The Conquest of the Stars* (*La Conquête des étoiles*), a long poem which recounts an apocalyptic war between the sea and the sky. The tempest, that great romantic topos, becomes a vast, lurid spectacle charged with elements of the macabre, and the demise of the stars dramatizes the withering of illusory ideals which the poet-narrator has long cherished. The poem was overtly allegorical, but its symbols reverberated beyond the bounds of its author's intentions. Consider only the sea, ostensibly the masculine element which defeats the feminine stars. Marinetti never tired of pointing out the link between the Italian word for sea, *mare*, and the beginning of his own name, *Mar*-inetti. But since the poem is written in French and is so explicitly fraught with issues of gender, who can fail to note that the French word for 'sea' (*mer*) rhymes with the French word for 'mother' (*mère*)? Albeit unconsciously, Marinetti was developing one of his characteristic rhetorical strategies, pushing the terms of a received polarity to such extremes that they would collapse back into their antitheses. Male and female were not the only terms that would be turned inside out; his best works would put insistent pressure on the deepest principles of individuation, the ways we draw elementary distinctions between self and world, figure and ground, objects and their contexts. His writings are often fraught with rhetoric of extraordinary violence and charged with elements of the grotesque and macabre – in short, the trappings of literary decadence, but trappings so strained, so overworked that they deliberately cross over into the comic, producing an uncanny effect that oscillates between elation and horror.

When a young composer joined the Futurist movement in 1910, Marinetti advised him how to achieve success:

In order to win over Paris and appear, in the eyes of all Europe, an absolute innovator, the most advanced of all, I urge you to get to work with all your heart, resolute on being bolder, crazier, more advanced, surprising, eccentric, incomprehensible, and grotesque than anybody else in music. I urge you to be a madman.

It was advice he never needed to give himself.

After launching Futurism with his manifesto in 1909, Marinetti gave a series of lectures in which he further explained his ideas, including one delivered in London in December 1910 (see pp. 6–9). The same year he was approached by a group of young painters in Milan who wished to join the "movement," which at this point consisted of himself alone. Marinetti decided to "launch" them on a colossal scale. They would have a show that would premiere in Paris, then tour the major capitals of Europe: first London, then Berlin, then other cities. When the exhibition opened in early 1912, accompanied by a flurry of manifestos, it provoked furious debate. The debate in Paris, inevitably, was duly noted by the press in London, where the second leg of the tour opened in March 1912 (see 000–000). Coming to London as it did, only 14 months after Roger Fry's first Post-Impressionist exhibition had sparked such enormous controversy, the exhibition prompted media furore. When Marinetti gave a lecture at Bechstein Hall (now Wigmore Hall), it was analyzed by a lead editorial or leader in the *Times*. Marinetti visited London for further exhibitions and lectures three more times over the next two years, concluding with a performance of Futurist music in the Coliseum in June 1914, at that time the largest music hall in London. By late 1913 his newest manifesto ("The Variety Theater," see pp. 34–8) was being published in English translation by the *Daily Mail*, then the newspaper with the largest circulation in the world.

Marinetti's manifestos of 1912 and 1913 increasingly turned to the question of Futurism's ramifications for literature, and these developments were dutifully followed by London literary journals. There can be little doubt that Imagism, often considered the very origin of Anglo-American literary modernism, arose in direct response to it.

The outbreak of the First World War in August 1914 effectively put an end to Futurism's influence in England. But its afterlife in Italy was quite another matter. From the moment that war broke out, Marinetti became a strident advocate of Italian intervention, and he was elated when Italy finally joined sides with France and Britain in 1915. He himself enrolled promptly, as did virtually all the Futurists. Many of their brightest talents (e.g., the painter Umberto Boccioni, the architect Antonio Sant'Elia) would be killed in the ensuing slaughter.

In 1917 Marinetti also had his first meeting with a dissident Socialist who had earlier broken with the Socialist party over the question of Italy's potential intervention in the war, Benito Mussolini. Mussolini, at this time, was an independent politician looking for a cause that would capture the political imagination of Italy in the aftermath of the war. In 1918, accompanied by Marinetti, he held the inaugural meeting of the Fascist Party in Milan, the city where he had lived for many years as editor of the Socialist newspaper *Avanti (Forward)*. Only four years later, propelled by years of paramilitary violence and the threat of a coup d'état, Mussolini would be named prime minister of Italy, in October 1922. Marinetti, paradoxically, had left the party already in 1920, angered by its refusal to adopt a sufficiently anticlerical position as part of its platform.

In the years that followed, from 1922 until the outbreak of the Second World War in 1939, Marinetti and the Futurists would occupy a strange, uneasy place within Fascist culture. They would be the recipients of a considerable amount of state patronage, with the Futurist style especially favored for projects in the visual arts and design which involved new technology, aviation, or other indices of modernity. At the same time, they were distrusted by many leaders within the Fascist regime, viewed as potential dissidents or even anarchists who had failed to make the transition from being outsiders to being members of a functioning government.

It should be noted here that Italian Fascism did not entail or otherwise advocate anti-Semitism. Indeed, Italian Jews joined the party in percentages which outstripped their relative weight within the population as a whole, and many occupied prominent places within the government and in local party chapters. But when Italy formally allied itself with Nazi Germany in 1936, anti-Semitism was quickly adopted as a prominent feature of government policy. Though Marinetti and others protested in private, and though Futurist journals were increasingly bereft of government support or even overtly repressed, the Futurists did not take a concerted public stance against the new government policies and for the most part acquiesced in their implementation.

Marinetti, it should also be noted, was a wealthy man who used his money to serve as a patron to the many artists and writers who joined his movement. After 1922, however, his wealth was seriously diminished, and Marinetti would allow the Futurist brand name (or the name of Marinetti's publishing firm) to be attached to the work of anyone who could afford to pay for a book's production costs.

Cultural historians remain sharply divided over the significance and the legacy of Futurism. Some underline the anarchist and utopian aspects of its early years, contrasting these sharply with the movement's later involvement with Fascism; others argue that Futurism was "proto-Fascist," an uncanny yet straightforward anticipation of the politics to come. Some view Futurist painting as work of dubious merit, and instead regard Futurism as a chapter in the history of the arts and their engagement with emerging mass media, an episode in the ongoing saga of public relations or the culture of celebrity. Whatever Futurism was, its impact during the period 1909–14 was indelible in the memory of contemporaries in Italy, France, England, Germany, and Russia.

The Founding and the Manifesto of Futurism (Feb. 1909)
F. T. Marinetti

We had stayed up[1] all night – my friends and I – beneath mosque lamps hanging from the ceiling. Their brass domes were filigreed, starred like our souls; just as they were illuminated, again like our souls, by the imprisoned brilliance of an electric heart. On the opulent oriental rugs, we had crushed our ancestral lethargy, arguing all the way to the final frontiers of logic and blackening reams of paper with delirious writings.

Our chests swelled with immense pride, for we alone were still awake and upright at that hour, like magnificent lighthouses or forward sentries facing an army of enemy stars, eyeing us from their encampments in the sky. Alone with the stokers who bustle in front of the boilers' hellish fires in massive ships; alone with the black specters who grope before the red-hot bellies of locomotives launched on insane journeys; alone with drunkards who feel their way against the city walls, with the beating of uncertain wings.

Suddenly we jumped at the tremendous noise of the large double-decker trams which jolted along outside, shimmering with multicolored lights, like villages on holiday which the flooding Po suddenly strikes and uproots, dragging them all the way to the sea, over waterfalls and through gorges.

Then the silence grew more gloomy. But as we were listening to the attenuated murmur of prayers muttered by the old canal and the bones of ailing palaces creaking above their beards of damp moss, suddenly we heard the famished automobiles roaring beneath the windows.

"Let's go!" I said. "Let's go, my friends! Let's leave! At last mythology and the mystical ideal have been superseded. We are about to witness the birth of the Centaur,[2] and soon we shall see the first Angels fly!... We have to shake the doors of life to test their hinges and bolts!... Let's leave! Look! There, on the earth, the earliest dawn! Nothing can match the splendor of the sun's red sword, skirmishing for the first time with our thousand-year-old shadows."

We drew close to the three snorting beasts, tenderly stroking their swollen breasts. I stretched out on my car like a corpse in its coffin, but revived at once under the steering wheel, a guillotine blade that menaced my stomach.

The furious sweep of madness drove us outside ourselves and through the streets, deep and precipitous as the beds of spring torrents. Here and there a sickly lamplight, behind the glass of a window, taught us to despise the errant mathematics of our transitory eyes.

I screamed: "The scent, the scent alone is enough for our beasts!"

And like young lions we ran after Death, its black hide stained with pale crosses, running across the vast livid sky, alive and throbbing.

And yet we did not have an ideal Beloved who raised her sublime form all the way to the clouds, nor a cruel Queen to whom we could offer our corpses, twisted in the shape of Byzantine rings! Nothing to make us wish to die except our desire to free ourselves from the burden of our own courage!

And so we raced on, hurling watchdogs back against the doorways; they were flattened and curled beneath our scorching tires like shirt collars beneath a pressing iron. Death, domesticated, was greeting me at every turn, gracefully holding out a paw, or sometimes stretching out on the

---

THE FOUNDING

First published on the front page of the Paris newspaper *Figaro* on February 20, 1909. Translation by Lawrence Rainey.

[1] *We stayed up* The verb translated here as "stayed up" can also mean "to watch over a dead man," as Catholics traditionally did, and so evoke a mythical motif of death and resurrection.

[2] *the birth of the Centaur* compare W. B. Yeats, "On a Picture of a Black Centaur by Edmund Dulac," p. 326. The centaur was a popular figure among late Symbolist poets and painters, uniting the animal and the human, the irrational and rational.

ground with a noise like that of grating jawbones, casting me velvety and tender looks from every puddle.

"Let's break out of wisdom, as if out of a horrible shell; and let's fling ourselves, like fruits swollen with pride, into the wind's vast and contorted mouth. Let's throw ourselves, like food, into the Unknown, not in desperation, but to fill up the deep wells of the Absurd."

Scarcely had I said these words, when I spun my car around as frantically as a dog trying to bite its own tail, and there, suddenly, were two bicyclists right in front of me, cutting me off, wobbling like two lines of reasoning, equally persuasive and yet contradictory. Their stupid argument was being discussed right in my path . . . What a bore! Damn! . . . I stopped short, and to my disgust rolled over into a ditch, with my wheels in the air. . . .

Oh! Maternal ditch, nearly full of muddy water! Fair factory drain! I gulped down your bracing slime, which reminded me of the sacred black breast of my Sudanese nurse.[3] . . . When I climbed out, a filthy and stinking rag, from underneath the capsized car, I felt my heart – deliciously – being slashed with the red-hot iron of joy!

A crowd of fishermen armed with hooks and naturalists stricken with gout formed a thronging circle around the prodigy. With patient and meticulous attention, they rigged up a derrick and enormous iron grapnels to fish out my car, stranded like a large shark. The car slowly emerged from the ditch, leaving behind in the depths its heavy chassis of good sense and its soft upholstery of comfort.

They thought it was dead, my beautiful shark, but one caress from me was enough to revive it, and there it was again, once more alive, running on its powerful fins.

And so, our faces covered with the good factory slime – a mix of metallic scum, useless sweat, heavenly soot – our arms bruised and bandaged, we have dictated our first intentions to all the *living* men of the earth:

The Manifesto of Futurism
1. We intend to sing to the love of danger, the habit of energy and fearlessness.
2. Courage, boldness, and rebelliousness will be the essential elements of our poetry.
3. Up to now literature has exalted contemplative stillness, ecstasy, and sleep. We intend to exalt movement and aggression, feverish insomnia, the racer's stride, the mortal leap, the slap and the punch.
4. We affirm that the beauty of the world has been enriched by a new form of beauty: the beauty of speed. A racing car with a hood that glistens with large pipes resembling a serpent with explosive breath . . . a roaring automobile that rides on grape-shot – that is more beautiful than the *Victory of Samothrace*.[4]
5. We intend to hymn man at the steering wheel, the ideal axis of which intersects the earth, itself hurled ahead in its own race along the path of its orbit.
6. Henceforth poets must do their utmost, with ardor, splendor, and generosity, to increase the enthusiastic fervor of the primordial elements.
7. There is no beauty that does not consist of struggle. No work that lacks an aggressive character can be considered a masterpiece. Poetry must be conceived as a violent assault launched against unknown forces to reduce them to submission under man.
8. We stand on the last promontory of the centuries! . . . Why should we look back over our shoulders, when we intend to breach the mysterious doors of the Impossible? Time and space died yesterday. We already live in the absolute, for we have already created velocity which is eternal and omnipresent.
9. We intend to glorify war – the only hygiene of the world – militarism, patriotism, the destructive gesture of emancipators, beautiful ideas worth dying for, and contempt for woman.

[3] *Sudanese nurse* On Marinetti's background in Africa, see the Introduction, p. 1.
[4] *Victory of Samothrace* is a Hellenistic statue that was found in 1863 by French archaeologists on the island of Samothrace, in the Aegean Sea off the coast of Thrace; from then until the 1980s it was placed opposite the entrance of the Louvre, where it greeted the museum's many visitors, and became a conventional figure of classical beauty.

10. We intend to destroy museums, libraries, academies of every sort, and to fight against moralism, feminism, and every utilitarian or opportunistic cowardice.

11. We shall sing the great masses shaken with work, pleasure, or rebellion: we shall sing the multicolored and polyphonic tidal waves of revolution in the modern metropolis; shall sing the vibrating nocturnal fervor of factories and shipyards burning under violent electrical moons; bloated railway stations that devour smoking serpents; factories hanging from the sky by the twisting threads of spiraling smoke; bridges like gigantic gymnasts who span rivers, flashing at the sun with the gleam of a knife; adventurous steamships that scent the horizon, locomotives with their swollen chest, pawing the tracks like massive steel horses bridled with pipes, and the oscillating flight of airplanes, whose propeller flaps at the wind like a flag and seems to applaud like a delirious crowd.

It is from Italy that we have flung this to the world, our manifesto of burning and overwhelming violence, with which we today establish "Futurism," for we intend to free this nation from its fetid cancer of professors, archaeologists, tour guides, and antiquarians.

For much too long Italy has been a flea market. We intend to liberate it from the countless museums that have covered it like so many cemeteries.

Museums: cemeteries! Identical, really, in the horrible promiscuity of so many bodies scarcely known to one another. Museums: public dormitories in which someone is put to sleep forever alongside others he hated or didn't know! Museums: absurd slaughterhouses for painters and sculptors who go on thrashing each other with blows of line and color along the disputed walls!

That once a year you might make a pilgrimage, much as one makes an annual visit to a graveyard . . . I'll grant you that. That once a year you can deposit a wreath of flowers in front of the *Mona Lisa*, I permit you that . . . But I cannot countenance the idea that our sorrows are daily shepherded on a tour through museums, or our weak courage, our pathological restlessness. Why would we wish to poison ourselves? Why wish to rot?

And what is there to see in an old painting besides the laborious distortion of the artist who tried to break through the insuperable barriers which blocked his desire to express fully his dream? . . . To admire an old painting is the same as pouring our sensibility into a funerary urn, instead of casting it forward into the distance in violent spurts of creation and action.

Do you wish to waste your best strength in this eternal and useless admiration of the past, an activity that will only leave you spent, diminished, crushed?

I declare, in all truth, that a daily visit to museums, libraries, and academies (cemeteries of futile efforts, Calvaries of crucified dreams, record books of broken assaults! . . .) is as dangerous for artists as a prolonged guardianship under the thumb of one's family is for certain young talents intoxicated with their own genius and ambitious aims. For the sickly, the ill, or the imprisoned – let them go and visit: the admirable past is perhaps a solace for their troubles, since the future is now closed to them. . . . But we intend to know nothing of it, nothing of the past – we strong and youthful *Futurists*!

And so, let the glad arsonists with charred fingers come! Here they are! Here they are! . . . Go ahead! Set fire to the shelves of the libraries! . . . Turn aside the course of the canals to flood the museums! . . . Oh, the joy of seeing all the glorious old canvasses floating adrift on the waters, shredded and discolored! . . . Grasp your pickaxes, axes, and hammers, and tear down, pitilessly tear down the venerable cities!

The oldest of us is thirty: so we have at least a decade left to fulfill our task. When we are forty, others who are younger and stronger will throw us into the wastebasket, like useless manuscripts. – We want it to happen!

They will come against us, our successors; they will come from far away, from every direction, dancing to the winged cadence of their first songs, extending predatory claws, sniffing doglike at the doors of the academies for the good smell of our decaying minds, long since promised to the libraries' catacombs.

But we won't be there.... They will find us, at last – one wintry night – in an open field, beneath a sad roof drummed by monotonous rain, crouched beside our trembling airplanes and in the act of warming our hands by the dirty little fire made by the books we are writing today, flaming beneath the flight of our imaginings.

Panting with contempt and anxiety, they will storm around us, and all of them, exasperated by our lofty daring, will attempt to kill us, driven by a hatred all the more implacable because their hearts will be intoxicated with love and admiration for us.

In their eyes, strong and healthy Injustice will radiantly burst. – Art, in fact, can be nothing if not violence, cruelty, and injustice.

The oldest of us is thirty: and yet already we have cast away treasures, thousands of treasures of force, love, boldness, cunning and raw will-power; have thrown them away impatiently, furiously, heedlessly, without hesitation, without rest, screaming for our lives. Look at us! We are still not weary! Our hearts feel no tiredness because they are fed with fire, hatred, and speed!... Are you astounded? Of course you are, because you can't even recall having ever been alive! Standing erect on the summit of the world, we fling, yet once more, our challenge to the stars!

You raise objections?... Stop! Stop! We know them... We've understood!... The refined and mendacious mind tells us that we are the summation and continuation of our ancestors – maybe! Suppose it so! But what difference does it make? We don't want to listen!... Woe to anyone who repeats those infamous words to us!

Lift up your heads!

Standing erect on the summit of the world, we fling, yet once more, our challenge to the stars.[5]

Futurist Speech to the English (Dec. 1910)
F. T. Marinetti

[...]

And there, with a few picturesque abridgments, you have some of our more interesting ideas and actions.

I don't know whether this lively account has been able to give you a sense of what Futurism really is.

In any case, you have already grasped one part of our philosophical, political, and artistic conception, its method of adopting the cruelest form of sincerity and the boldest kind of violence.

I couldn't imagine a better way of giving you an exact idea of what we are than to tell you what we think of you.

I will express myself with complete candor, carefully refraining from courting you in the style of cosmopolitan lecturers who crush their audiences with praise before cramming them full of banalities.

One of our young humorists has said that every good Futurist should be discourteous twenty times a day. So I will be discourteous with you, pluckily confessing to you all the ill that we think of the English, after having spoken much good of them. For as you well know, we love the indomitable and bellicose patriotism that sets you apart; we love the national pride that prompts

---

[5] The manifesto's ending with the word "stars" echoes Dante's practice of ending each of the three main parts of the *Divine Comedy* with the same word.

Marinetti spoke at the Lyceum Club for Women, in London, in late December of 1910. (The club was founded in the late 1890s, one of several established in reaction to the male-only clubs which had predominated till then.) It marked the first time that Marinetti spoke about Futurism outside of Italy; his lecture was doubtless given in French, as were his other lectures in England between 1912 and 14, and it was probably an impromptu performance

which drew on points already made in earlier manifestos. In early 1911 he published at least part of this lecture as "Discours futuristes aux Anglais" in *Le Futurisme* (Paris: E. Sansot), where it was followed by another essay titled "Ce déplorable Ruskin." In 1915, however, he oversaw a translation into Italian of *Le Futurisme*, which now acquired the title *Guerra sola igiene del mondo* (*War the only hygiene of the world*) (Milan: Edizioni di Poesia, 1915). In this new version, the first seven paragraphs from "Ce déplorable Ruskin" were added to the end of the "Futurist Speech to the English." This longer version of the speech is the one given here, with the 1915 additions plainly indicated. Translation by Lawrence Rainey.

your great muscularly courageous race; we love the generous and intelligent individualism that enables you to open your arms to individualists of every land, whether libertarians or anarchists.

But your broad love of liberty is not all we admire. What most sets you apart is that, amid so much pacifist nonsense and evangelical cowardice, you cherish an unbridled passion for struggle in all its forms, from boxing – simple, brutal, and rapid – to the monstrous roaring necks of the cannon on the decks of your dreadnoughts, crouched in their swivelling caves of steel, turning to scent the appetizing enemy squadrons in the distance.

You know perfectly well that there is nothing worse for a man's blood than the forgiveness of offenses; you know that prolonged peace, which has been fatal to the Latin races, is no less poisonous for the Anglo-Saxon races. . . . But I promised you discourtesies, and here they are:

To a degree you are the victims of your traditionalism and its medieval trappings, in which there persists a whiff of archives and a rattling of chains that hinder your precise and carefree forward march.

You will admit the oddness of this in a people of explorers and colonizers whose enormous ocean liners have obviously shrunk the world.

Most of all I reproach you for your maddening cult of aristocracy. No one admits to being a *bourgeois* in England: everyone despises his neighbor and calls *him* a bourgeois. You have an obsessive mania for being always *chic*. For love of the *chic* you renounce passionate action, violence of heart, exclamations, shouts, and even tears. The English want to be cold at any cost, everywhere, by the bedside of an adored person, in the face of death or at the prospect of happiness. For the love of *chic* you never discuss what you are doing, for one must always be light and airy in conversation. When the women leave after dinner, you chat a bit about politics, but not too much: it wouldn't be *chic*! . . .

Your writers have to be men of the world, for you can hardly imagine a novel whose action is set in high society. Try as you might to be modern, you still preserve an essentially medieval distinction between master and servant, grounded in an absurd adoration of wealth. It's one of your proverbs that a rich man never hangs in England. To that kind of thinking you add a no less absurd contempt for the poor. Their intellectual efforts, even their genius, strike you as useless; and yet you have a great love for intelligence and culture, and no other people devours books the way that you do.

Still, it remains only a way of passing one's leisure hours.

You lack consuming intellectual passions, a sharp and adventurous taste for ideas, an impulse toward the unknowns of the imagination, a passion for the future, a thirst for revolution. You are horribly custom-bound. Isn't it true that you firmly believe that the Puritans saved England, and that chastity is a nation's most important virtue?

Do you remember the dismal, ridiculous condemnation of Oscar Wilde, which Europe has never forgiven you for? Didn't all your newspapers cry out then that it was time to throw open every window, because the plague was over? . . .

Naturally, in such an atmosphere of habitual and hypocritical formality, your young women are skilled in the use of their naïve elegance to carry on the most audaciously lascivious games, to prepare themselves well for marriage: the intangible domain of the conjugal police.

As for your twenty-year-old young men, almost all of them are homosexuals for a time, which, after all, is absolutely respectable. This taste of theirs evolves through a kind of intensification of the *camaraderie* and friendship found in athletic sports in the years before they turn thirty, the time for work and good order, when they show their heels to Sodom in order to marry a young woman whose gown is shamelessly décolleté. Then they hasten to condemn the born invert severely, the counterfeit man, the half-woman who fails to conform.

Isn't it excessively formalistic of you to declare, as you do, that in order to know someone you must break bread with him, that is, have studied the way he eats? But how could you judge us, the Italians, from our way of eating when we always eat sloppily, our epigastric regions strangled by love or ambition?

To that one must add your obsessive desire to keep up appearances in all things, and a fussy mania for etiquette, masks, and folding screens of every sort, invented by prudishness and a conventional morality.

Yet I won't insist, but hasten on to speak about your greatest defect: a defect that you yourselves have bequeathed to Europe and that, in my opinion, is an obstacle to your marvelous practical instinct and your science of the rapid life.

I allude to your snobbery, whether it consists of a mad, exclusive cult of racial purity, in your aristocracy, or whether it creates a kind of religion out of fashion and transforms your illustrious tailors into so many high priests of lost religions.

I'm also referring to your dogmatic and imperious norms for good living and the Sacred Tables of *comme il faut*, in the light of which you neglect and abolish, with an astonishing light-heartedness, the fundamental worth of the individual, just as soon as he falls short of the supreme laws of snobbery.

All of this renders your existence singularly artificial, and makes you the most contradictory people on the planet; hence, all your intellectual maturity cannot save you from sometimes seeming a people in the process of formation.

You invented the love of hygiene, the adoration of muscles, a harsh taste for effort, all of which triumph in your beautiful sporting life.

But, unfortunately, you push your exaggerated cult of the body to the point of scorning ideas, and you care seriously only for physical pleasures. Platonic love is virtually absent among you – which is a good thing – but your love of succulent meals is excessive. And it's in the brutalizing religion of the table that you appease all your anxieties and all your worries! ...

From your sensuality you extract a formidable serenity in the face of moral suffering. Very well! ... Then you should stop giving so much importance to physical suffering!

You think yourselves very religious. It's pure illusion. You pay no attention to your inner lives, and your race lacks true mystical feeling! I congratulate you on this! But unfortunately you prefer to take refuge in Protestantism, *bonne-à-tout-faire* of your intelligence, which saves you the trouble of thinking freely, without fear and without hope, like a black banner among the shadows.

It's through intellectual laziness that you fall so often to your knees, and for love of a good conventional and puerile formalism.

No one loves the fleshly pleasures more than you, and yet you are the Europeans who pride themselves on their chastity! ...

You love and generously welcome every revolutionary, but that doesn't hinder you from solemnly defending the principles of order! You adore the fine swift machines that skim the earth, sea, and clouds, yet you carefully preserve every last debris from the past!

After all, is this a defect? You shouldn't treat all my remarks as reproofs. ... To contradict oneself is to live and you know how to contradict yourselves bravely.

But, besides, I know that you nurse a deep hatred for German clumsiness, and this is enough to absolve you completely.

[*Editor's note*: text from here on present only from 1915 edition onwards]

I have told you, in a synoptic way, what we think of England and the English.

Must I now hear the courteous reply that I already suspect is on your lips?

You surely want to stop my discourtesies by telling me how highly you think of Italy and the Italians. ... Well: no, I don't want to listen.

The compliments you are about to pay could only sadden me, because what you love in our dear peninsula is exactly the object of our hatreds. Indeed, you crisscross Italy only to meticulously sniff out the traces of our oppressive past, and you are happy, insanely happy, if you have the good fortune to carry home some miserable stone that has been trodden by our ancestors.

When, when will you disembarrass yourselves of the lymphatic ideology of that deplorable Ruskin, which I would like to cover with so much ridicule that you would never forget it?

With his morbid dream of primitive and rustic life, with his nostalgia for Homeric cheeses and legendary wool-winders, with his hatred for the machine, steam-power, and electricity, that maniac of antique simplicity is like a man who, after having reached full physical maturity, still wants to sleep in his cradle and feed himself at the breast of his decrepit old nurse in order to recover his thoughtless infancy.

Ruskin would certainly have applauded those passéist Venetians who wanted to rebuild the absurd bell-tower of San Marco,[1] as if a baby girl who has lost her grandmother were to be offered a little cloth and cardboard doll as a substitute.

Contempt for Woman (from Le Futurisme, 1911)
F. T. Marinetti

It is this hatred for the tyranny of love that we have expressed with the laconic phrase: "contempt for woman."[1]

We feel contempt for woman conceived as the reservoir of love, woman-poison, woman as a tragic bibelot, fragile woman, obsessing and fatal, whose voice, heavy with destiny, and whose dreamy tresses reach out and mingle with the foliage of forests bathed in moonlight.

We feel contempt for horrible and staid Love that encumbers the march of man and prevents him from transcending his own humanity, from redoubling himself, from going beyond himself and becoming what we call *multiplied man*.[2]

We feel contempt for horrible and staid Love, immense tether with which the sun chains the courageous earth in its orbit, which would doubtless rather leap at random, run every starry risk.

We are convinced that Love – sentimentality and lust – is the least natural thing in the world. There is nothing natural except coitus, whose purpose is the perpetuation of the species.

Love – romantic, voluptuary obsession – is nothing but an invention of the poets, who gave it to humanity. And it will be the poets who will take it away from humanity.

The great tragi-comic experience of love will be soon be ended, having yielded no profit and inflicted incalculable harm. There has always been conflict and never collaboration between the two sexes, who have proved themselves unequal to the grand task. That it is why we Futurists are officially withdrawing love today, as one withdraws a manuscript from a publisher who has shown himself incapable of printing it decently.

In this campaign for liberation, our best allies are the suffragettes, because the more rights and powers they win for woman, the more she will be impoverished of love, and by so much more will she cease to be a magnet for sentimental passion or an engine of lust.

Carnal life will be reduced to the conservation of the species, and that will be so much gain for the growing stature of man.

As for the supposed inferiority of woman, we think that if her body and spirit had, for many generations past, been subjected to the same physical and spiritual education as man, it would perhaps be legitimate to speak of the equality of the sexes.

It is obvious, nevertheless, that in her actual state of intellectual and erotic slavery, woman finds herself wholly inferior in respect to character and intelligence and can therefore be only a mediocre legislative instrument.

For just this reason we most enthusiastically defend the rights of the suffragettes, at the same time that we regret their infantile enthusiasm for the miserable, ridiculous right to vote.[3] For we are convinced that they will seize the right to vote with fervor, and thus involuntarily help us to

[1] *the absurd bell-tower of San Marco* the massive 324-foot tower, which dominates the center of Venice, collapsed in 1902; public sentiment dictated that it be rebuilt exactly as it was, rather than constructing a new one, and work was completed by 1912.

CONTEMPT FOR WOMEN

First published in *Le Futurisme* (Paris: E. Sansot, 1911). Translated by Lawrence Rainey.

[1] *"contempt for woman"* The phrase occurs for the first time in point number 9 of "The Founding and the Manifesto of Futurism"; see p. 4.

[2] *multiplied man* The concept of a "multiplied sensibility" that was being created by advancing modernity is first raised in "Fu-

turist Painting: Technical Manifesto," and elaborated in "Multiplied Man and the Reign of the Machine." For these, see Lawrence Rainey et al. (eds.), *Futurism: A Reader and Visual Repertoire* (New Haven: Yale University Press, 2005).

[3] *right to vote* By 1911 women had won the right to vote in national elections in New Zealand (1893), Australia (1902), and Finland (1906), with Norway soon to follow (1913). But in most Western countries enfranchisement took place after the First World War: Canada (1918), Germany, Austria, Poland, and Czechoslovakia (1919), the United States (1920), and Great Britain (1918 and 1928). In France and Italy, full enfranchisement occurred in 1945.

destroy that grand foolishness, made up of corruption and banality, to which Parliamentarianism is now reduced.

Parliamentarianism is exhausted almost everywhere. It accomplished a few good things: it created the illusory participation of the majority in government. I say *illusory* because it is clear that the people cannot be and never will be represented by spokesmen whom they do not know how to choose.

Consequently, the people have always remained estranged from government. On the other hand, it is precisely to Parliamentarianism that the people owe their real existence.

The pride of the masses has been inflated by the elective system. The stature of the individual has been heightened by the idea of representation. But this idea has completely undermined the value of intelligence by immeasurably exaggerating the worth of eloquence. This state of affairs worsens day by day. Which is why I welcome with pleasure the aggressive entrance of women beneath the garrulous cupolas. Where else could we find a more explosive dynamite of disorder and corruption?

Nearly all the European parliaments are mere noisy chicken coops, cow stalls, or sewers.

Their essential principles are: 1) financial corruption and shrewdness in graft, to win a seat in parliament; 2) empty eloquence, grandiose falsification of ideas, triumph of high-sounding phrases, tom-tom of Negroes and windmill gestures.

These gross elements of Parliamentarianism give an absolute power to the hordes of lawyers.

You know perfectly well that lawyers are alike in every country. They are beings deeply attached to everything mean and futile . . . minds that see only the small daily fact, who are wholly unable to handle the great general ideas, to imagine the collisions and fusions of races or the blazing flight of the ideal over individuals and peoples. They are argument-merchants, mental prostitutes, boutiques for subtle ideas and chiseled syllogisms.

It is because of Parliamentarianism that a whole nation is at the mercy of these fabricators of justice who, given the ductile iron of the law, can scarcely manage to build a workable mouse-trap.

Then let us hasten to give women the vote.

And this, furthermore, is the final and absolutely logical conclusion of the idea of democracy and universal suffrage as it was conceived by Jean-Jacques Rousseau and the other forebears of the French Revolution.

Let women, swift as lightning, hurry to make this great experiment in the total animalization of politics.

We who deeply despise politics are happy to abandon parliamentarianism to the spiteful claws of women; for it is precisely to them that the noble task of killing it for good has been reserved.

Oh! I'm not being in the least ironic; I'm speaking very seriously. Woman, as she has been shaped by our contemporary society, can only increase in splendor the principle of corruption which is intimately related to the principle of the vote.

Those who oppose the legitimate rights of the suffragettes do so for entirely personal reasons: they are tenaciously defending their own monopoly of harmful eloquence, which women won't hesitate to snatch away from them. Fundamentally, this bores us. We have very different mines to put under the ruins.

They tell us that a government composed of women or sustained by women would fatally drag us through the paths of pacifism and Tolstoyan cowardice into a definitive triumph of clericalism and moralistic hypocrisy . . .

Maybe! Probably! And I'm sorry! However, we will have the war of the sexes, inescapably prepared by the great agglomerations of the capital cities, by night life,[4] and the stabilizing of workers' salaries.

Maybe some misogynistic humorists are already dreaming of a Saint Bartholomew's Night for women.[5]

---

[4]   *night life* the word that Marinetti uses in both the French and Italian versions of this essay is "noctambulism." The social phenomenon that he is pointing to is indeed "night life," but Marinetti uses "noctambulism" to identify it with a pathological condition of personality multiplication, a process that was held to be a common denominator linking several similar conditions or ailments: hypnosis, somnambulism, hysteria, and shock.

[5]   *Saint Bartholomew's massacre* The slaughter of French Huguenots by Catholics in Paris on St. Bartholomew's Day, August 24, 1572, ordered by Charles IX at the instigation of his mother, Catherine de' Medici. The event has become a byword for a bloodbath.

I know, you think that I am amusing myself by offering you more or less fantastic paradoxes.

Nothing is as paradoxical or fantastic as reality, and I suspect there's little reason to believe in the logical probabilities of history.

The history of peoples runs at hazard, in any and every direction, like a flighty young woman who can't remember what her parents taught her except on New Year's Day, or only when abandoned by her lover.

But unfortunately she is still too wise and not disorderly enough, this young history of the world. So the sooner women mix into it, the better, because the men are putrescent with millenarian wisdom.

These aren't paradoxes, I assure you, but gropings into the night of the future.

You will admit, for example, that the victory of feminism and especially the influence of women on politics will end by destroying the principle of the family. It could easily be proved: but already you're bristling, terrified, and ready to oppose me with ingenious arguments because you do not want the family touched at all.

"Every right, every liberty should be given to women," you cry, "but the family must be preserved!"

Allow me to smile just a bit skeptically and say to you that if the family should disappear, we could try to do without it. "We," I was just saying, but obviously I am mistaken: it will be our children – the children whom we will not have – they will know very well how to do without the family.

And I should say, parenthetically, that we Futurists are such fighters that we won't have children, we who love the heroic instinct, we who sincerely want every masterpiece to be burned with the cadaver of its author, we who feel only repugnance at the idea of striving for immortality, for at bottom it's no more than the dream of minds vitiated by usury.

Beyond doubt, if modern woman dreams of winning her political rights, it is because without knowing it she is intimately sure of being, as a mother, as a wife, and as a lover, a closed circle, purely animal and absolutely devoid of usefulness.

You will certainly have watched the takeoff of a Blériot plane,[6] the moment when it's still held back by its mechanics, amid the mighty buffets of air from the propeller's first spins.

Ah well: before so intoxicating a spectacle, I confess, we male Futurists have felt ourselves abruptly detached from women, who have suddenly become too earthly or, better yet, have become a mere symbol of the earth that we ought to abandon.

We have even dreamed of one day being able to create a mechanical son,[7] the fruit of pure will, synthesis of all the laws that science is on the brink of discovering.

The Exhibitors to the Public (Feb. 1912)
Giacomo Balla, Umberto Boccioni, Carlo Carrà, Luigi Russolo, Gino Severini

We may declare, without boasting, that the first Exhibition of Italian Futurist Painting, recently held in Paris and now brought to London,[1] is the most important exhibition of Italian painting which has hitherto been offered to the judgment of Europe.

[6]   *a Blériot plane* Louis Blériot (1872–1936) was an inventor and aviator who finally got into the air with the Blériot VI, tested in July 1907. On July 25, 1909, piloting the Blériot XII, he crossed the English Channel, a distance of 38 kilometers, in a flight that lasted just under 37 minutes. The feat won him instant celebrity and a prize of £1,000 offered by the London *Daily Mail*.

[7]   *to create a mechanical son* Mafarka, the hero of Marinetti's novel *Mafarka the Futurist* (1909), gives birth to his mechanical son Gazourmah, who leaves his wife Coloubbi and abandons the earth for space.

The text was drafted by Umberto Boccioni in the first days of October 1911, then submitted to the other four Futurist painters (Giacomo Balla, Carlo Carrà, Luigi Russolo, and Gino Severini) for their ratification. It was published in French in February 1912, together with the exhibition catalogue for "Les Peintres Futuristes Italiens" (The Exhibition of Italian Futurist Painting); an English translation appeared a month later when the same exhibition went to London, and it is that translation from 1912 which is reproduced here, retaining its British spelling.

[1]   The Exhibition of Italian Futurist Painting was shown at the Gallerie Bernheim-Jeune in Paris from February 5 to 24, 1912, and at the Sackville Gallery in London from 1 to 20 March the same year.

For we are young and our art is violently revolutionary.

What we have attempted and accomplished, while attracting around us a large number of skillful imitators and as many plagiarists without talent, has placed us at the head of the European movement in painting by a road different from, yet, in a way, parallel with that followed by the Post-Impressionists, Synthetists and Cubists of France, led by their masters, Picasso, Braque, Derain, Metzinger, Le Fauconnier, Gleizes, Léger, Lhote, etc.[2]

While we admire the heroism of these painters of great worth, who have displayed a laudable contempt for artistic commercialism and a powerful hatred of academism, we feel ourselves and we declare our art to be absolutely opposed to their art.

They obstinately continue to paint objects motionless, frozen, and all the static aspects of Nature; they worship the traditionalism of Poussin, of Ingres, of Corot, ageing and petrifying their art with an obstinate attachment to the past, which to our eyes remains totally incomprehensible. We, on the contrary, with points of view pertaining essentially to the future, seek for a style of motion, a thing which has never been attempted before us.

Far from resting upon the examples of the Greeks and the Old Masters, we constantly extol individual intuition; our object is to determine completely new laws which may deliver painting from the wavering uncertainty in which it lingers.

Our desire, to give as far as possible to our pictures a solid construction, can never bear us back to any tradition whatsoever. Of that we are firmly convinced.

All the truths learnt in the schools or in the studios are abolished for us. Our hands are free enough and pure enough to start everything afresh.

It is indisputable that several of the aesthetic declarations of our French comrades display a sort of masked academism.

Is it not, indeed, a return to the Academy to declare that the subject, in painting, is of perfectly insignificant value?

We declare, on the contrary, that there can be no modern painting without the starting point of an absolutely modern sensation, and no one can contradict us when we state that *painting* and *sensation* are two inseparable words.

If our pictures are futurist, it is because they are the result of absolutely Futurist conceptions, ethical, aesthetic, political and social.

To paint from the posing model is an absurdity, and act of mental cowardice, even if the model be translated upon the picture in linear, spherical or cubic forms.

To lend an allegorical significance to an ordinary nude figure, deriving the meaning of the picture from the objects held by the model or from those which are arranged about him, is to our mind the evidence of a traditional and academic mentality.

This method, very similar to that employed by the Greeks, by Raphael, by Titian, by Veronese, must necessarily displease us.

---

[2]   Between 1909 and 1914, Braque and Picasso carried out their pioneering explorations of visual language as a small collective of two, collaborating in an intense dialogue. For a detailed history of their work, see William Rubin (ed.), *Picasso and Braque: Pioneering Cubism* (New York: Museum of Modern Art, 1999). The year 1911 saw the spread of Cubism into other circles. In the spring of that year, at the Salon des Indépendents, Albert Gleizes (1881–1953), together with Henri Le Fauconnier (1881–1946), whom he had met in 1909, and Jean Metzinger (1883–1956), whom he had met in 1910, exhibited with Robert Delaunay (1885–1941) and Fernand Léger (1881–1955) in a separate room, as self-styled "Cubists." The same five exhibited together again, this time joined by André Derain (1880–1954) and André Lhote (1885–1962), at the Salon d'Automne. Though Delaunay and Léger were independent and original artists who went on to produce important work of their own, the other five – Gleizes, Metzinger, Le Fauconnier, Derain, and Lhote – are generally considered mere imitators who contributed nothing new or essential to the Cubism of Picasso and Braque. In the autumn of 1911, at the time of the Salon D'Automne, Boccioni, Carrà, and Russolo went to Paris to get a first-hand view of Cubism, and through the offices of Luigi Severini, who resided in Paris, they were able to see the most recent of Braque and Picasso's works, as well as those of their imitators.

While we repudiate Impressionism, we emphatically condemn the present reaction which, in order to kill Impressionism, brings back painting to old academic forms.

It is only possible to react against Impressionism, by surpassing it.

Nothing is more absurd than to fight it by adopting the pictorial laws which preceded it.

The points of contact which the quest of style may have with the so-called *classic art* do not concern us.

Others will seek, and will, no doubt, discover, these analogies which in any case cannot be looked upon as a return to methods, conceptions and values transmitted by classical painting.

A few examples will illustrate our theory.

We see no difference between one of those nude figures commonly called *artistic* and an anatomical plate. There is, on the other hand, an enormous difference between one of these nude figures and our Futurist conception of the human body.

Perspective, such as it is understood by the majority of painters, has for us the very same value which they lend to an engineer's design.

The simultaneousness of states of mind in the work of art: that is the intoxicating aim of our art.[3]

Let us explain again by examples. In painting a person on a balcony, seen from inside the room, we do not limit the scene to what the square frame of the window renders visible; but we try to render the sum total of visual sensations which the person on the balcony has experienced; the sun-bathed throng in the street, the double row of houses which stretch to right and left, the beflowered balconies, etc.[4] This implies the simultaneousness of the ambient, and, therefore, the dislocation and dismemberment of objects, the scattering and fusion of details, freed from accepted logic, and independent from one another.

In order to make the spectator live in the center of the picture, as we express it in our manifesto,[5] the picture must be the synthesis of *what one remembers* and of *what one sees*.

You must render the invisible which stirs and lives beyond intervening obstacles, what we have on the right, on the left, and behind us, and not merely the small square of life artificially compressed, as it were, by the wings of a stage.

We have declared in our manifesto that what must be rendered is the *dynamic sensation*,[6] that is to say, the particular rhythm of each object, its inclination, its movement, or, to put it more exactly, its interior force.

It is usual to consider the human being in its different aspects of motion or stillness, of joyous excitement or grave melancholy.

What is overlooked is that all inanimate objects display, by their lines, calmness or frenzy, sadness or gaiety. These various tendencies lend to the lines of which they are formed a sense and character of weighty stability or of aerial lightness.

Every object reveals by its lines how it would resolve itself were it to follow the tendencies of its forces.

This decomposition is not governed by fixed laws but it varies according to the characteristic personality of the object and the emotions of the onlooker.

Furthermore, every object influences its neighbor, not by reflections of light (the foundation of *Impressionistic primitivism*), but by a real competition of lines and by real conflicts of planes, following the emotional law which governs the picture (the foundation of *futurist primitivism*).

---

[3] The concept of "simultaneousness," or "simultaneity" as it can also be translated, is introduced here for the first time.
[4] This account plainly corresponds to Boccioni's painting, *The Street Enters the House* (1911). But the larger question of how Futurist theory relates to Futurist practice is one that has been intensely debated.

[5] See "Futurist Painting: Technical Manifesto," in Lawrence Rainey et al. (eds.), *Futurism: A Reader and Visual Repertoire* (New Haven: Yale University Press, 2005).
[6] On the concept of dynamic sensation, see the text cited in n. 5.

With the desire to intensify the aesthetic emotions by blending, so to speak, the painted canvas with the soul of the spectator, we have declared that the latter "*must in future be placed in the center of the picture.*"[7]

He shall not be present at, but participate in the action. If we paint the phases of a riot, the crowd bustling with uplifted fists and the noisy onslaughts of cavalry are translated upon the canvas in sheaves of lines corresponding with all the conflicting forces following the general law of violence of the picture.

These *force-lines* must encircle and involve the spectator so that he will in a manner be forced to struggle himself with the persons in the picture.

All objects, in accordance with what the painter Boccioni happily terms *physical transcendentalism*, tend to the infinite by their *force-lines*, the continuity of which is measured by our intuition.

It is these *force-lines* that we must draw in order to lead back the work of art to true painting. We interpret nature by rendering these objects upon the canvas as the beginnings or the prolongations of the rhythms impressed upon our sensibility by these very objects.

After having, for instance, reproduced in a picture the right shoulder or the right ear of a figure, we deem it totally vain and useless to reproduce the left shoulder or the left ear. We do not draw sounds, but their vibrating intervals. We do not paint diseases, but their symptoms and their consequences.

We may further explain our idea by a comparison drawn from the evolution of music.

Not only have we radically abandoned the motive fully developed according to its determined and, therefore, artificial equilibrium, but we suddenly and purposely intersect each motive with one or more other motives of which we never give the full development but merely the initial, central, or final notes.

As you see, there is with us not merely variety, but chaos and clashing of rhythms, totally opposed to one another, which we nevertheless assemble into a new harmony.

We thus arrive at what we call the *painting of states of mind.*[8]

In the pictural description of the various states of mind of a leave-taking, perpendicular lines, undulating and as it were worn out, clinging here and there to silhouettes of empty bodies, may well express languidness and discouragement.

Confused and trepidating lines, either straight or curved, mingled with the outlined hurried gestures of people calling one another, will express a sensation of chaotic excitement.

On the other hand, horizontal lines, fleeting, rapid and jerky, brutally cutting into half lost profiles of faces or crumbling and rebounding fragments of landscape, will give the tumultuous feelings of the persons going away.

It is practically impossible to express in words the essential values of painting.

The public must also be convinced that in order to understand aesthetic sensations to which one is not accustomed, it is necessary to forget entirely one's intellectual culture, not in order to *assimilate* the work of art, but to *deliver one's self up* to it heart and soul.

We are beginning a new epoch of painting.

We are sure henceforward of realizing conceptions of the highest importance and the most unquestionable originality. Others will follow who, with equal daring and determination, will conquer those summits of which we can only catch a glimpse. That is why we have proclaimed ourselves to be the *primitives of a completely renovated sensitiveness.*[9]

---

[7] See Umberto Boccioni's paintings, *Riot at the Gallery* (1910) and *Charge of the Lancers* (1915), both in Rainey et al., *Futurism*, figs. 27, 39.

[8] *States of Mind* is also the title for two series, each of three paintings, that Boccioni did in 1911.

[9] This is the antepenultimate sentence from "Futurist Painting: Technical Manifesto"; see Rainey et al., *Futurism*. The 1912 translation into English adopted here is a more literal and less forceful rendering of it.

In several of the pictures which we are presenting to the public, vibration and motion endlessly multiply each object. We have thus justified our famous statement regarding the *"running horse which has not four legs, but twenty."*[10]

One may remark, also, in our pictures, spots, lines, zones of color which do not correspond to any reality, but which in accordance with a law of our interior mathematics, musically prepare and enhance the emotion of the spectator.

We thus create a sort of emotive ambience, seeking by intuition the sympathies and the links which exist between the exterior (concrete) scene and the interior (abstract) emotion. Those lines, those spots, those zones of color, apparently illogical and meaningless, are the mysterious keys to our pictures.

We shall no doubt be taxed with an excessive desire to define and express in tangible form the subtleties which unite our abstract interior with the concrete exterior.

Yet, could we leave an unfettered liberty of understanding to the public which always sees as it has been taught to see, through eyes warped by routine?

We go our way, destroying each day in ourselves and in our pictures the realistic forms and the obvious details which have served us to construct a bridge of understanding between ourselves and the public. In order that the crowd may enjoy our marvelous spiritual world, of which it is ignorant, we give it the material sensation of that world.

We thus reply to the coarse and simplistic curiosity which surrounds us by the brutally realistic aspects of our primitivism.

Conclusion: Our futurist painting embodies three new conceptions of painting:

1. That which solves the question of volumes in a picture, as opposed to the liquefaction of objections favored by the vision of the Impressionists.
2. That which leads us to translate objects according to the *force-lines* which distinguish them, and by which is obtained an absolutely new power of objective poetry.
3. That (the natural consequence of the other two) which would give the emotional ambience of a picture, the synthesis of the various abstract rhythms of every object, from which there springs a fount of pictural lyricism hitherto unknown.

Technical Manifesto of Futurist Literature (May 1912)
F. T. Marinetti

Sitting astride the fuel tank of an airplane, my stomach warmed by the aviator's head,[1] I felt the ridiculous inanity of the old syntax inherited from Homer. A raging need to liberate words, dragging them out from the prison of the Latin period. Like all imbeciles, this period, naturally, has a prudent head, a stomach, two legs, and two flat feet: but it will never have two wings. Just enough to walk, take a short run, and come up short, panting!

This is what the swirling propeller told me as I sped along at two hundred meters above the powerful smokestacks of Milan:

[10]   An inexact quotation from "Futurist Painting: Technical Manifesto"; see Rainey et al., *Futurism*.

The "Technical Manifesto of Futurist Literature" was published as an independent leaflet in May 1912, and appeared as part of a book when it was used as the preface to *The Futurist Poets* (Milan: Edizioni di Poesia, 1912), the first collective anthology of poetry which Marinetti edited. The volume sold more than 20,000 copies. Accounts of the manifesto figured in contemporary newspapers: *L'Intransigeant* (Paris), July 7, 1912; *Dernière Heure* (Paris), July 18; *Paris-Journal*, July 18; *Le Temps* (Paris), July 24. A German translation was also published in *Der Sturm*, no. 133 (Oct. 1912). This translation is by Lawrence Rainey.

[1]   Marinetti describes his one and only experience of flight prior to 1912, which took place at the first international air meet at Brescia in September 1909. Marinetti was given a brief ride with the Peruvian aviator Jean Bielovucic, who flew a Voisin biplane with a 50-horsepower ENV engine. The propellor was located not at the front of the plane, but immediately behind the wings. (The airplane, in other words, was what contemporaries called a "pusher.") Atop the lower wing, at its rear, sat the engine that drove the propellor, with its fuel tank in mid-wing. Marinetti, then, would have sat just in front of the fuel tank, while the pilot would have been located just in front of him. Because the airplane was a "pusher," pilot and passenger enjoyed an unimpeded view of the scene before and below them.

1. **It is imperative to destroy syntax and scatter one's nouns at random, just as they are born**.

2. **It is imperative to use verbs in the infinitive**, so that the verb can be elastically adapted to the noun and not be subordinated to the *I* of the writer who observes or imagines. Only the infinitive can give a sense of the continuity of life and the elasticity of the intuition that perceives it.

3. **Adjectives must be abolished**, so that the noun retains its essential color. The adjective, which by its nature tends to render shadings, is inconceivable within our dynamic vision, for it presupposes a pause, a meditation.

4. **Adverbs must be abolished**, old buckles strapping together two words. Adverbs give a sentence a tedious unity of tone.

5. **Every noun must have its double**, which is to say, every noun must be immediately followed by another noun, with no conjunction between them, to which it is related by analogy. Example: man–torpedo-boat, woman–bay, crowd–surf, piazza–funnel, door–faucet.

Just as aerial speed has multiplied our experience of the world, perception by analogy is becoming more natural for man. It is imperative to suppress words such as *like, as, so*, and *similar to*. Better yet, to merge the object directly into the image which it evokes, foreshortening the image to a single essential word.

6. **Abolish all punctuation**. With adjectives, adverbs, and conjunctions having been suppressed, naturally punctuation is also annihilated within the variable continuity of a *living* style that creates itself, without the absurd pauses of commas and periods. To accentuate certain movements and indicate their directions, mathematical signs will be used: $+ - \times := >$, along with musical notations.

7. Until now writers have been restricted to immediate analogies. For example, they have compared an animal to man or to another animal, which is more or less the same thing as taking a photograph. (They've compared, for example, a fox terrier to a tiny thoroughbred. A more advanced writer might compare that same trembling terrier to a telegraph. I, instead, compare it to gurgling water. In this there is **an ever greater gradation of analogies**, affinities ever deeper and more solid, however remote).

Analogy is nothing other than the deep love that binds together things that are remote, seemingly diverse or inimical. The life of matter can be embraced only by an orchestral style, at once polychromatic, polyphonic, and polymorphous, by means of the most extensive analogies.

In my *Battle of Tripoli*,[2] when I have compared a trench bristling with bayonets to an orchestra, or a machine-gun to a fatal women, I have intuitively introduced a large part of the universe into a brief episode of African combat.

Images are not flowers to be chosen and gathered with parsimony, as Voltaire said.[3] They constitute the very lifeblood of poetry. Poetry should be an uninterrupted flow of new images, without which it is merely anemia and green-sickness.

The vaster their affinities, the more images will retain their power to astound. One must – people say – spare the reader an excess of the marvelous.[4] Bah! We should worry instead about the fatal corrosion of time, which destroys not just the expressive value of a masterpiece, but its power to astound. Too often stimulated to enthusiasm, haven't our old ears perhaps already destroyed

---

[2]   Marinetti's book recounted his experiences (Oct–Nov. 1911) in the Italo-Turkish War between 1911 and 12, focusing on the siege of Tripoli, which Italian forces conquered swiftly on October 26, 1911, scarcely a month after war had begun. It appeared in Italy in both a French edition issued by Marinetti's own firm, *La Bataille de Tripoli* (Milan: Edizioni futuriste di Poesia, 1912), and in an Italian translation, *La Battaglia di Triopli* (Padua: Tipografia "Elzeviriana," 1912).

[3]   See François-Marie Aronet de Voltaire (1694–1778), *Dictionnaire Philosophique* (1764), s.v. "Fleuri," or "Flowered."

[4]   Aristotle's *Poetics* turned intelligible causation into the key notion that links together literary plot and the possibility of philosophical knowledge; doing so, he made the wonderful or the marvelous (*to thaumaston*) into a perennially ambiguous aesthetic value that lies on the boundary between the explicable and the inexplicable. Debate about the marvelous has been a recurrent feature of Italian literary culture because the rediscovery of Aristotelian aesthetics in the Renaissance meant that the greatest work of Italian literature, Dante's *Commedia*, stood condemned for having an excess of the marvelous and not conforming to Aristotelian demand for intelligible causation; and the same issue recurred in the later Renaissance debates about the poets Ariosto and Boiardo, and yet again in those concerning Tasso. Marinetti's bias, evident in all his writings, is for a poetics of the marvelous.

Beethoven and Wagner? It is imperative, then, to abolish whatever in language has become a stereotyped image, a faded metaphor, and that means nearly everything.

8. **There are no categories of images,** noble or gross or popular, eccentric or natural. The intuition that perceives them has no preferences or *partis pris*. Therefore the analogical style is the absolute master of all matter and its intense life.

9. To render the successive movements of an object, it is imperative to render the *chain of analogies* which it evokes, each condensed and concentrated into one essential word.

Here is an expressive example of a chain of analogies, though still masked and weighed down beneath traditional syntax:

> Ah yes! little machine gun, you are a fascinating woman, and sinister and divine, at the steering wheel of an invisible hundred-horse-power engine that roars with explosive impatience. Oh! surely you will soon leap into the circuit of death, to a shattering somersault or victory!... Do you wish me to compose madrigals full of grace and vivacity? At your pleasure, my dear... For me, you resemble a lawyer before the bar, whose tireless, eloquent tongue strikes to the heart of the surrounding listeners, who are deeply moved... You, at this moment, are like an omnipotent trephine that is boring deeply into the hard skull of the refractory night... And you are a rolling mill, an electric lathe, and what else? A great blowtorch that burns, chisels, and slowly melts the metallic tips of the final stars!... (*Battle of Tripoli*)[5]

In some cases it will be imperative to join images two by two, like those chained iron balls which can level a stand of trees in their flight.

To catch and gather whatever is most evanescent and ineffable in matter, it is imperative to shape **strict nets of images or analogies,** which will then be cast into the mysterious sea of phenomena. Except for the traditional festoons of its form, the following passage from my *Mafarka the Futurist* is an example of such a dense net of images:

> All the bitter-sweetness of bygone youth rose in his throat, as the cheerful shouts of children in the playground rise up to their old teachers, while they lean out over seaside balconies, watching boats skim across the sea...[6]

And here are three more nets of images:

> Around the well of Bumeliana, beneath the thick olive trees, three camels squatting comfortably in the sand gurgled with contentment, like rain pipes, mixing the *chack-chack* of their spitting with the steady thud of the steam pump that supplies water to the city. Shrieks and Futurist dissonances, in the deep orchestra of the trenches with their sensuous orifices and resonant cellars, amid the coming and going of bayonets, violin bows which the violet baton of twilight has inflamed with enthusiasm...
>
> The orchestra conductor-sunset, with a sweeping gesture, gathers in the scattered flutes of the birds in the trees, and the grieving harps of the insects, and the sound of crushed stones. Suddenly he stops the tympanums of the mess-kits and crashing rifles, so as to let the muted instruments sing out over the orchestra, all the golden stars, erect, arms akimbo, on the grand stage of the sky. And here comes the diva of the performance... A neckline plunging to her breasts, the desert displays her immense bosom in curvaceous liquefaction, aglow with rouge beneath the cascading jewels of the monstrous night. (*Battle of Tripoli*)[7]

10. As every kind of order is inevitably a product of the cautious and circumspect mind, it is imperative to orchestrate images, distributing them with a **maximum of disorder**.

11. **Destroy the "I" in literature:** that is, all psychology. The sort of man who has been damaged by libraries and museums, subjected to a logic and wisdom of fear, is absolutely of no interest anymore. We must abolish him in literature and replace him once and for all with matter, whose essence must be seized by strokes of intuition, something which physicists and chemists can never achieve.

5 Marinetti, *La battaglia di Tripoli* (Padua: Tipografia "Elzeviri-ana," 1912).

6 Marinetti, *Mafarka the Futurist: An African Novel*, trans. Carol

Diethe and Steve Cox (London: Middlesex University Press, 1999), ch. 10, "The Blacksmiths of Milmillah," p. 156.

7 From Marinetti, *La battaglia di Tripoli*.

To capture the breath, the sensibility, and the instincts of metals, stones, woods, and so on, through the medium of free objects and capricious motors. To substitute, for human psychology, now exhausted, **the lyrical obsession with matter.**

Be careful not to assign human sentiments to matter, but instead to divine its different governing impulses, its forces of compression, dilation, cohesion, disaggregation, its heaps of molecules massed together or its electrons whirling like turbines. There is no point in creating a drama of matter that has been humanized. It is the solidity of a steel plate which interests us as something in itself, with its incomprehensible and inhuman cohesion of molecules or electrons which can resist penetration by a howitzer. The heat of a piece of iron or wood leaves us more impassioned than the smile or tears of a woman.

We want literature to render the life of a motor, a new instinctive animal whose guiding principle we will recognize when we have come to know the instincts of the various forces that compose it.

Nothing, for a Futurist poet, is more interesting than the action of mechanical piano's keyboard.[8] Film offers us the dance of an object that disintegrates and recomposes itself without human intervention. It offers us the backward sweep of a diver whose feet fly out of the sea and bounce violently back on the springboard. Finally, it offers us the sight of a man driving at 200 kilometers per hour. All these represent the movements of matter which are beyond the laws of human intelligence, and hence of an essence which is more significant.

Three elements which literature has hitherto overlooked must now become prominent in it:

1. **Noise** (a manifestation of the dynamism of objects);
2. **Weight** (the capacity for flight in objects);
3. **Smell** (the capacity of objects to disperse themselves).

Take pains, for example, to render the landscape of odors that a dog perceives. Listen to engines and reproduce their speech.

Matter has always been contemplated by an *I* who is distanced, cold, too preoccupied with himself, full of pretensions to wisdom and human obsessions.

Man tends to befoul matter with his youthful joy or ageing sorrow – matter, which possesses an admirable continuity of impulse toward greater heat, greater movement, greater subdivision of itself. Matter is neither sad nor happy. Its essence is boldness, will, and absolute force. It wholly belongs to the divining poet who will know how to free himself of syntax which is traditional, burdensome, restrictive, and confined to the ground, armless and wingless because it is merely intelligent. Only the asyntactical poet with words set free will be able to penetrate the essence of matter and destroy the mute hostility that separates it from us.

The Latin period which has been used until now has been a pretentious gesture with which an overweening and myopic mind has tried to tame the multiform and mysterious life of matter. The Latin period has been stillborn.

Profound intuitions of life linked together one by one, word by word, according to their illogical surge – these will give us the general outlines for an **intuitive psychology of matter.** That is what was revealed to me from the heights of the airplane. Looking at objects from a new vantage point, no longer head on or from behind but straight down, foreshortened, I was able to break apart the old shackles of logic and the plumb lines of the old form of comprehension.

All of you, Futurist poets, who have loved and followed me until now, have been frenzied builders of images and bold explorers of analogies, just as I have. But the narrow nets of metaphor are, unfortunately, too weighted down by the plumb lines of logic. I urge you to make them lighter,

---

[8]   The player piano occupies a prominent role in many works of the period. In Joseph Conrad's novel *The Secret Agent* (1907), it epitomizes an empty mechanism that results in the futile anarchism of the characters who frequent *The Sirenus*, a lower class restaurant and beer hall; in the "Circe" episode of Joyce's *Ulysses* (1922), it becomes a vehicle for language or music in itself, freed from human authority or control.

so that your immensified gesture can hurl them farther, cast them out over a vaster expanse of ocean.

Together we will discover what I call **the wireless imagination**.[9] One day we will achieve an art that is still more essential, the day when we dare to suppress all the first terms of our analogies in order to render nothing other than an uninterrupted sequence of second terms. To achieve this, it will be necessary to forgo with being understood. It isn't necessary to be understood. We have already dispensed with that privilege anyway even when we have written fragments of a Futurist sensibility by means of traditional and intellective syntax.

Syntax has been a kind of abstract cipher which poets have used in order to inform the masses about the color, the musicality, the plasticity and architecture of the universe. It has been a sort of interpreter, a monotonous tour-guide. We must suppress this intermediary so that literature can directly enter into the universe and become one body with it.

My work sharply differs from anyone else's by virtue of its frightening power of analogy. Its inexhaustible wealth of images rivals the disorder of its illogical punctuation, and at the head of it all is the first Futurist manifesto, the synthesis of a hundred-horsepower engine racing at the most insane velocities over land.

Why should we still make use of four exasperated wheels that are boring, when we can break free of the ground once and for all? The liberation of words, unfolding wings of the imagination, the analogical synthesis of the earth embraced in a single view and gathered together whole in essential words.

They scream at us: "Your literature will not be beautiful! We'll no longer have a verbal symphony that is composed of harmonious rockings and tranquillizing cadences. "We understand that quite well! And how lucky! We, instead, make use of all the ugly sounds, the expressive screams of the violent life that surrounds us. **Let us boldly make "the ugly" in literature, and let us everywhere murder solemnity**. Go on! don't assume those grand priestly airs when listening to me. Every day we must spit upon the *Altar of Art*. We are entering the boundless domains of free intuition. After free verse, here at last are **words in freedom!**

There are no elements in this of either the absolute or the systematic. Genius has impetuous spurts and muddy torrents. Sometimes it requires analytical and explanatory languors. Nobody can renovate his own sensibility all at once. Dead cells are mixed together with live ones. Art is a need to destroy and disperse oneself, a great watering can of heroism that drowns the world. And don't forget: microbes are necessary for the health of the stomach and the intestines. Just so there is also a species of microbes that are necessary for the health of art – **art, which is a prolongation of the forest of our arteries**, prolongation which flows beyond the body and extends into the infinity of space and time.

Futurist Poets! I have taught you to hate libraries and museums, only in order to prepare you for the next step, **to hate intelligence**, reawakening in you divine intuition, the characteristic gift of the Latin races. By means of intuition we shall overcome the seeming irreducible divide which separates our human flesh from the metal of the motor.

After the reign of the animal, behold the beginning of the reign of the machine. Through growing familiarity and friendship with matter, which scientists can know only in its physical and chemical reactions, we are preparing the creation of the mechanical man with interchangeable parts. We will liberate man from the idea of death, and hence from death itself, the supreme definition of the logical mind.

---

[9]   The phrase "wireless imagination" translates the term *imaginazione senza fili*, which can be more literally translated as "imagination without strings," in which sense it refers to an imagination freed of the "plumb lines" or "strings" of logic, discussed in the preceding paragraph. But just as the word "wireless" – it was an abbreviation of "wireless telegraphy," the early term for radio – in British usage became the everyday term for radio, so in Italian *senza fili* (literally: without wires) also became a common name for radio. The term "wireless imagination" is more suggestive of these multiple connotations than either "imagination without strings" or "radio imagination," though nobody today uses "wireless" to mean a radio.

A Response to Objections (Aug. 1912)
F. T. Marinetti

I shall not reply to the jokes and countless ironic comments, but to the skeptical questions and important objections which have been directed by the European press against my "Technical Manifesto of Futurist Literature."

1. Those who have correctly understood what I meant by "hate for the intelligence" have wished to discern in that expression some influence from the philosophy of Bergson.[1] But evidently they are not aware that my first epic poem, "The Conquest of the Stars" (published in 1902), contained these three verses from Dante on the first page, serving as an epigraph:

> O insane labor of mortals,
> How defective are *syllogisms*
> Which *make men fold down their wings*.
>
> (*Paradiso*, Canto 11)[2]

Or this thought from Edgar Allan Poe, who describes:

> the poetic spirit – that faculty more sublime than any other, as we already know, – which, since truths of the greatest importance could not have been revealed to us except by means of that Analogy whose eloquence is irrefutable to the imagination, says nothing to weak and solitary reason. (Edgar Allan Poe, "The Colloquy of Monos and Una")[3]

Long before Bergson, these two creative geniuses coincided with my own temperament in distinctly affirming their hate for creeping, weak, and solitary intelligence, and according all powers to the intuitive and divining imagination.

2. When I speak of intuition and intelligence, I do not intend to speak of two domains that are distinct and wholly separate. Every creative mind has experienced how, during the labor of creation, the intuitive and intellectual dimensions have been fused together.

It is impossible, therefore, to specify exactly the point where unconscious inspiration leaves off and lucid will begins. Sometimes the latter suddenly generates inspiration, and sometimes instead it accompanies it. After several hours of unremitting and painful work, the creative spirit is suddenly freed from the weight of all obstacles and becomes, in some way, the prey of strange spontaneity of conception and execution. That hand that writes seems to separate from the body and freely leave far behind the brain, which, having itself in some way become detached from the

The text was first published as an independent manifesto in August 1912. An account and an extract from it appeared in the Parisian newspaper *L'Intransigeant*, August 20, 1912, followed by another extract with some ironic comments the next day. Another account of it appeared in *Paris-Journal*, August 20, 1912. A German translation was published in *Der Sturm*, no. 150–1 (March 1913), accompanied by a brief essay about it, "Futuristische Worttechnik" ("Futurist Language Techniques") by the great German writer Alexander Döblin. This translation into English is by Lawrence Rainey.

[1]   "hate for the intelligence" appears in the penultimate paragraph of the "Technical Manifesto of Futurist Literature"; see this edition, p. 19. The French philosopher Henri Bergson (1859–1941), in *Time and Free Will*, famously urged that our everyday notion that physical objects exist and occupy positions in the "empty homogeneous medium" of space had wrongly shaped our concept of time. Time is not, as we imagine it, an unbounded line composed of units or moments external to one another; nor is it a set of instants that can be specified in mathematical calculations. Such a view cannot account for the transition from one state to another. Instead it is a continuous flow or stream, pure duration or continuity of movement, *durée*, to which we can best gain access through the consciousness of our own inner mental life.

[2]   *epigraph* on Marinetti's first book, *La Conquête des Étoiles* (Paris: Editions de La Plume, 1902). The italics in the quotation from Dante are added by Marinetti.

[3]   Edgar Allan Poe wrote the "Colloquy of Monos and Una" in 1841 and it appeared for the first time in his collection of *Tales* (1845). It was translated into French by Charles Baudelaire under the title "Colloque entre Monos et Una," appearing first in the newspaper *Le Pays* (January 22, 23, 1855), then in the second of five volumes of translations which he made from Poe, *Nouvelles histoires extraordinaires par Edgar Poe* (1857). Baudelaire's translation of Poe is the text that Marinetti would have known. The story is a brief dialogue which takes place in the afterlife, with Monos explaining to Una his sensations and experience of death. Marinetti quotes from Monos's defense of "the poetic intellect" over and against utilitarian reason, which issues in "system" and "abstraction."

body and airborne, looks down from on high with terrible lucidity upon the unforeseen phrases emitted by the pen.

Does this domineering brain look passively on, or does it instead direct the leaps of fantasy that excite the hand? It is impossible to know. In such moments I have observed, from a physiological standpoint, little more than a great void in the stomach.

By *intuition*, I mean a state of mind almost entirely intuitive and unconscious. By *intelligence*, I mean a state of mind which is almost entirely intellective and a product of will.

3. The ideal kind of poetry which I dream of, which would be none other than the uninterrupted flow of the second terms of analogies, has nothing whatever to do with allegory. Allegory, in fact, is the succession of the second terms of several analogies that are all connected together *logically*. Sometimes, too, allegory can be the second term of an analogy which has been minutely developed and described.

On the contrary, I aspire to render the illogical succession, no longer explanatory but intuitive, of the second terms of many different analogies which are all disconnected and quite often opposed to one another.

4. All purebred stylists have easily been able to affirm that the adverb is not just a word that modifies a verb, adjective, or other adverb, but also a musical ligament that unites the different sounds of a sentence or period.

5. I believe it necessary to suppress the adjective and the adverb because they are simultaneously, and also on different occasions, many-colored festoons, draperies of subtle shading, pedestals, parapets and balustrades of the traditional period.

It is precisely through the deliberate use of the adjective and the adverb that writers give that melodious and monotonous rocking effect to the sentence, its moving and interrogative rise and its calming and gradual fall, like a wave on the beach. With an emotion that is always identical, the reader's spirit must momentarily hold its breath and tremble, beg to be calmed, until at last it can breathe freely again when the wave of words falls back, with a final punctuation of gravel and a last little echo.

The adjective and the adverb have a triple function, which is at once explanatory, decorative, and musical, by means of which they indicate the pace — light or heavy, slow or rapid — of the noun which is moving in the sentence. By turns, they are the noun's cudgel or its crutch. Their length and their weight govern the rhythm of a style which, necessarily, is always under guard, and they prevent it from reproducing the imagination's flight. For example: "A young and beautiful woman walks rapidly over the marble floor." The traditional mind hastens to explain that the woman is young and beautiful, even though the intuition always gives simply a beautiful movement. Later, the traditional mind announces that the woman is walking rapidly, and at last it adds that she is walking on a marble floor.

This purely explanatory procedure, imposed in advance of any arabesques, zigzags, or leaps of thought, no longer has any reason to exist. Whoever proceeds in just the opposite manner is almost certain not to deceive himself.

Further, it is undeniable that abolishing the adjective and the adverb will give back to the noun its value as something essential, total, and typical.

In addition, I have absolute faith in the feeling of horror that I experience when faced with a noun that strides forward yet is followed by its adjective, as if by some rag or puppy. Yes, sometimes the dog is held back on the leash of an elegant adverb. Sometimes the noun has an adjective in front and an adverb in back, like the two sign-boards of a sandwich man. But these too are unbearable spectacles.

6. For these reasons I have recourse to the abstract aridity of mathematical signs, which are used to render quantitative relations by epitomizing a longer explanation, without any fillers, and avoiding the dangerous mania for wasting time in all the crannies of the sentence, in the minute labors of the mosaic maker, the jeweler, or the shoeshine boy.

7.   Words freed from punctuation will irradiate one another, magnetic waves intersecting one another according to the ceaseless dynamism of thought. A shorter or longer blank space will tell the reader what are the pauses or the brief naps of intuition. Capital letters will tell the reader which nouns synthesize a dominant analogy.

8.   The destruction of the traditional period, the abolition of the adjective, the adverb, and punctuation, will necessarily bring about the collapse of that well-known type of harmonious style, with the result that the Futurist poet will finally use all the onomatopoeias, including the most cacophonous ones, which reproduce the countless noises of matter in motion.

All these elastic intuitions, with which I am supplementing my "Technical Manifesto of Futurist Literature," sprang to mind while I was creating my new Futurist work. Here is one of the more significant fragments from it:

Battle

Weight + Smell

Afternoon 3/4 flutes groans dog-days **boomboom** alarm Gargaresch bursting trembling march Tinkling/Ringing backpacks rifles hooves nails cannons manes wheels cartridge-boxes Jews pancakes bread-with-olive-oil sing-song shops whiffs cleaning eye-rheum stink cinnamon   mold flux and reflux pepper quarrel filth turbine orange-trees-in-blossom filigree poverty dice chess cards jasmine + ground-nutmeg + rose arabesque mosaic carcass stings tapping   machine guns = gravel + undertow + frogs Tinkling backpacks rifles cannons scrap-iron atmosphere = lead + lava + 300 stenches + 50 perfumes pavement mattress debris horse-dung carcasses flick-flack to crowded together camels donkeys **boom-boom** sewer Souk-of-the-silversmiths maze silk azure galabieh   purple oranges moucharabieh arches to dismount crossroads piazzetta teeming
    tannery shoeshine-boy gandouras burnous swarming to sift to sweat polychromia envelopment excrescences wounds fox-holes debris demolition phenol lime lice-swarm   Tinkling backpacks **tatatata** hooves nails cannons cartridge-boxes whippings uniform-cloth sheep-stench no-exit left-turn funnel right-turn crossroads chiaroscuro Turkish-bath fryings moss jonquils orange-blossoms nausea essence-of-rose trap ammonia claws excrements bits meat + 1000 flies dried-fruits carobs chick-peas pistachios nectarines banana-governments figs **boomboom**
    billy-goat couscous-moldy aromas saffron tar egg-soaked dog-drenched jasmine opopanax sandal carnation to ripen intensity boiling to ferment tuberose To rot to scatter rage to die dissolve pieces crumbs dust heroism   **Tatata** rifle-fire **pic pac pun pan pan** orange wool-fulvous machine-gun rattle leper-shelter sores forward   Meat-soaked dirty smoothness hetarae Tinkling backpacks rifles cartridge-boxes wheels gasoline tobacco incense anise village ruin burnt amber jasmine houses guttings abandonment terracotta-jar **boom-boom** violets shadow-zone wells donkey ass cadaver collapse sex exhibition   garlic bromines anise breeze fish fir-tree-new rosemary dashes palms sand cinnamon Sun gold scales even lead sky silk heat padding purple azure heat Sun = volcano + 3 − flags atmosphere precision corrida fury surgery lamps   Scalpel-rays sparkle sheets desert clinic × 20000 arms 20000 feet 10000 eyes gun-sights scintillation wait operation sands ship-ovens Italians Arabs 3000 meters battalions heats orders pistons sweat mouths ovens
        Lost forward-march oil **tatatata** ammonica > opopanax violets dung roses sands dazzle-of-mirrors everything to walk arithmetic footprints to obey irony enthusiasm
    Buzzing to sew dunes pillows zigzags to mend feet heap screeching sand pointlessness machine-guns = gavel + undertow + frogs
        Scouting parties: 200 meters loaded-to-the-brim forward-march Arteries swelling heat fermentation hair armpits drums tawniness blondness breaths + backpack 18 kilos fore-thought = sing-sing scrap-iron money-box softness: 3 shudders orders rocks anger enemy magnet

lightness glory   Heroism Scouting-parties: 100 meters machine-guns rifle-fire eruption violins bras **tim tum tak tak tim tum** machine-guns **tataratatarata**
        Scouting-parties: 20 meters battalions-ants cavalry-frogs streets-puddles general-islet sand-revolution howitzers-platforms clouds-gridirons rifles-martyrs shrapnel-halos multiplication addition division howitzer-subtraction grenade-erasure dripping draining landslide roadblock heap
        Scouting parties: 3 meters mix-up to-fro stuck unstuck wound fire uprooting yards heap deposits flames panic blinding smashing to enter to exit to run   Sugars Lives-rockets hearts-gluttonies bayonets-forks to bite to chop to stink to dance to leap anger dogs-explosion howitzers-gymnasts flashes-trapeze explosion rose joy stomachs-watering-cans heads-footballs scattering   Cannon 149-elephant limbs-cornacs issa-oh anger levy slowness heaviness center load infantry method monotony trainers distance grand-prize arc x light **pang-boom-boom** sprig infinite Sea = laces-emeralds-freshness-elasticity-abandonment-softness dread-nought-steel-concision-order Combat-flag   (fields skies-white-hot   blood)   = Italy force Italian-pride brothers wives mother insomnia newsboys-scream glory domination coffee war-stories   Towers cannons-virility-muzzles-erection range-finder ecstasy **boom-boom** 3 seconds **boomboom** waves smiles laughter chik chack plaff pluff   glooglooglooglooo play-hide-and-seek crystals virgins flesh jewels pearls iodine salts bromides skirts gas liqueurs bubbles 3 seconds boom-boom officer whiteness range-finder cross fire ring-ring megaphone height-4-thousand-meters left-face stop everybody halt troops-dismissed 7-degrees erection splendor pumping piercing immensity blue-woman deflowering doggedness hallways scream labyrinth mattresses sobs smashing down desert bed precision range-finder monoplane gallery applause monoplane = balcony-rose-wheel-drum buzzing-fly > defeat-Arab ox bloodiness slaughter wounds refuge oasis humidity fan coolness siesta stripes germination effort dilation-vegetal   I'll-be-more-green-tomorrow let's-stop-soaked save-this-drop-of-water   you-have-to-left-your-self-3-centimeters-to-overcome-20-grams-of-sand-and-3000-grams-of-shadows   milky-way-coco-nut-tree stars-coconuts milk to gush juice pleasure.

The Art of Noises: A Futurist Manifesto (Mar. 1913)
Luigi Russolo

Dear Balilla Pratella, great Futurist composer,

At the crowded Costanzi Theater in Rome, while I was listening to the orchestral performance of your overwhelming **Futurist music,**[1] together with my Futurist friends Marinetti, Boccioni, Carrà, Balla, Soffici, Papini, and Cavacchioli, there came to my mind the idea of a new art: the Art of Noises, a logical consequence of your marvelous innovations.

In older times life was completely silent. In the nineteenth century, with the invention of machines, Noise was born. Today, noise is triumphant and reigns supreme over the sensibility of men. For many centuries life went by in silence, or at most with muted sound. The loudest noises that interrupted this silence were neither intense, extended, nor varied. For if we set aside exceptional movements across the earth's surface, such as hurricanes, storms, avalanches, and waterfalls, nature is silent.

Amidst this scarcity of *noises*, the first *sounds* that men were able to extract from a hollow reed or a taut string were stupefying, something new and marvelous. Primitive peoples ascribed *sound* to the gods, deemed it sacred, and reserved it to the priests, who used it to enrich their rites with mystery. Thus was born the concept of sound as a thing itself, distinct from life and independent of it, and from that resulted music, a fantastic world superimposed on the real one, an inviolable and sacred world. It is easy to understand how such a concept of music must have inevitably hindered its progress in comparison with the other arts. The Greeks themselves, adopting a musical theory

ART OF NOISES
Firt published as an independent leaflet in March 1913. The translation given here is by Lawrence Rainey.

[1] The concert of Pratella's *Futurist Music* was given on March 9, 1913, at the Teatro Costanzi in Rome.

which was mathematically systematized by Pythagoras and which permitted only a few consonant intervals, limited the field of music considerably and rendered harmony, of which they remained ignorant, impossible.

The Middle Ages, with developments and modifications of the Greek tetrachord system,[2] with Gregorian chants and popular songs, enriched the art of music, but continued to consider sound only *in its unfolding in time*, a restricted concept that lasted for several centuries and can still be found in the extremely complicated polyphonies of Flemish contrapuntists. The *chord* did not exist; development of the different parts was not subordinated to the chord that these parts produced in their ensemble; and the conception of these parts was horizontal, not vertical. The desire, the search, and the taste for a simultaneous union of different sounds, i.e. for *the chord* (complex sound), arose only gradually, passing from perfect consonance with a few incidental dissonances to the complicated and persistent dissonances which characterize contemporary music.

At first the art of music sought and achieved purity, limpidity, and sweetness of sound; later it incorporated more diverse sounds, though it still took care to caress them with gentle harmonies. Today, growing ever more complicated, it is seeking those combinations of sounds that fall most dissonantly, strangely, and harshly on the ear. We are drawing ever closer to *noise-sound*.

This evolution of music is parallel to the multiplication of machines, which everywhere are collaborating with man. Not only amid the clamor of the metropolis, but also in the countryside, which until yesterday was normally silent, in our time the machine has created such a variety and such combinations of noises that pure sound, in its slightness and monotony, no longer arouses any feeling.

To excite and exalt our sensibilities, music has been developing toward extremely complex polyphony and the greatest possible variety of orchestral timbres, or colors, seeking out the most complex successions of dissonant chords, and preparing in a general way for the creation of **musical noise.** This evolution towards "noise-sound" was not possible before now. The ear of an eighteenth-century man could never have supported the dissonant intensity of certain chords produced by our orchestras (with three times as many performers as those of his day). Our ear instead takes pleasure in it, since it has already been trained by modern life, so teeming in different noises. Not, however, that it is fully satisfied: instead it demands an ever greater range of acoustical emotions.

Musical sound, on the other hand, is too limited in the qualitative variety of timbres. The most complicated orchestras are reduced to four or five classes of instruments, differing in timbre: instruments played with the bow, plucked instruments, brass winds, wood winds, and percussion instruments. So that modern music founders within this tiny circle as it vainly attempts to create new kinds of timbre.

We must break out of this restricted circle of pure sounds and conquer the infinite variety of noise-sounds.

Further, everyone will recognize that every sound carries with it a cluster of already familiar and stale associations which predispose the hearer to boredom, despite all the efforts of innovative musicians. We Futurists have all deeply loved and enjoyed the harmonies of the great masters. Beethoven and Wagner have stirred our hearts and nerves for many years. But now we are satiated with them, and **we derive far more pleasure from ideally combining the noises of trams, internal-combustion engines, carriages, and noisy crowds than from rehearing, for example, the "Eroica" or the "Pastorale."**[3]

We can hardly observe that enormous apparatus of forces represented by the modern orchestra without feeling the deepest disappointment at its petty acoustic achievements.

Is anything more ridiculous than the sight of twenty men furiously bent on redoubling the meowing of a violin? Naturally all this will make the musico-maniacs scream and perhaps disturb

---

[2] A tetrachord was a musical scale of four notes, bounded by the interval of a perfect fourth (an interval the size of two and one-half steps, such as from c to f). The descending tetrachord was the basic unit of analysis in Greek music, and scale systems were formed by joining successive tetrachords. Only the outer notes of each tetrachord were fixed, while the position of the inner pitches determined the genus of the tetrachord.

[3] *The Eroica* and *Pastorale* are popular names given to Beethoven's Symphonies No. 3 (1804) and No. 8 (1808).

the somnolent atmosphere of our concert-halls. But let us go together, as Futurists, into one of these hospitals for anaemic sounds. Listen to it: the first bar wafts to your ear the boredom of the already-heard and gives you a foretaste of the boredom to follow in the next. Let us savor, from one bar to the next, two or three species of pure boredom, forever waiting for the extraordinary sensation that never comes. Meanwhile, one is struck by that repugnant mixture which is created by emotional monotony and the cretinous religious excitement of the listeners, Bhuddhistically intoxicated by the thousandth repetition of their spurious and snobbish ecstasy. Away! Let's be gone, since it won't be long before we can't refrain our desire to create at least one new musical reality by generously handing out sonorous slaps, stamping with both feat on violins, pianos, contrabasses, and groaning organs. Away!

It's no good objecting that noise is simply loud and disagreeable to the ear. It seems to me pointless to enumerate all the graceful and delicate noises that afford pleasant acoustic sensations.

To be convinced of their astonishing variety one need only think of the rumbling of thunder, the whistling of the wind, the roaring of a waterfall, the gurgling of a brook, the rustling of leaves, the clatter of a horse trotting into the distance, the rattling jolt of a cart over cobblestones, or the deep, solemn, and white breath of a city at night, or all the noises made by wild and domestic animals, or all those that can be made by the mouth of man, apart from speech or song.

Let us wander through a great modern city with our ears more alert than our eyes and we shall find pleasure in distinguishing the rushing of water, gas, or air in metal pipes, the purring of motors that breathe and pulsate with indisputable animality, the throbbing of valves, the pounding of pistons, the screeching of mechanical saws, the jolting of trams on their tracks, the cracking of whips, the flapping of curtains and flags. We shall amuse ourselves by creating mental orchestrations of the crashing down of metal shop shutters, the slamming of doors, the bustle and shuffling of crowds, the varied racket of stations, railroads, iron foundries, spinning mills, printing works, electrical power stations, and subways.

Nor should the latest noises of modern warfare be forgotten. Recently the poet Marinetti, in a letter written from the Bulgarian trenches surrounding Adrianople, described for me the orchestration of a large battle, rendered in marvelous words-in-freedom:

every 5 seconds siege-cannons to disembowel space with a chord Bam-Booooomb mutiny of 500 in order to snap to break up to scatter to the infinite In the middle of those smashed Bam-Booomb range 50 square kilometers to bounce sweepings cuttings fists batteries in rapid fire Violence fierceness regularity this low weighty surging the strange madmen agitated taut from the battle Fury torment ears eyes nostrils open! straining! force! What pleasure to see to hear to smell everything taratatatata of the machine guns squealing breathless under bites slaps traack-traack lashes pic-pac-pum-boom oddities leaps height 200 meters of the rifle-fire Down down in the pit of the orchestra puddles to splash oxen buffalos goadings carts pliff plaff horses getting stuck flic flac zing zang riiiiinse playing neighing ayingayingaying . . . pawing pinging 3 Bulgarian battalions marching kroook-kraaaak (*lento double time*) Sciumi Maritza o Karvavena krooook-kraaak shout of officers to bang like brass plates pan over here paack over there chinck BOOOM chinck chack (*presto*) cha-cha-cha cha-chack up down there there around arms up attention on the head chack very nice! Blasts blasts blasts blasts blasts Blasts stage of the forts down there behind that smoke Shrkri Pasha communicates by telephone with 27 forts in Turkish in German hello! Ibrahim! Rudolph! hello! hello! actors roles echoes prompters stagehands comprised of smoke forests applause smell of hay mud dung I no longer feel my frozen feet odor of potassium nitrate smell of decay Tympanums flutes bass clarinets everywhere high low birds twittering beatitude shadows chirp-chirp-chirp breeze green flocks don-dan-don-din-bèèè Orchestra madmen to beat the orchestra musicians these badly beaten up to plaaaaay to plaaaaay Graaand clangings not to cancel to be precise reshaaaaaping them noises smaller minute-ute-ute wrecks of echoes in the theater size 300 square kilometers   Maritza Tungia Rivers spread out Rodopi Mountains straight up heights box-seats gallery 2000 shrapnel to saw the air to explode white kerchiefs ful of gold Boom-Boomb 2000 grenades straining to rip out with tearing shocks of dark hair ZANG-BOOM-ZANG-BOOM-

BOOOMB orchestra of the war noises to swell beneath a note of silence held in the high sky spherical balloon golden that surveys cannon-fire.[4]

We want to give pitches to these extraordinarily diverse sounds, regulating them harmonically and rhythmically. Giving pitches to noises doesn't mean depriving them of all the irregularity of tempo and intensity that characterize their movements and vibrations, but giving gradation or pitch to the strongest and predominant vibrations. Indeed, noise differs from sound only insofar as the vibrations that produce it are irregular and confused, both in tempo and intensity. **Every noise has a note, sometimes even a chord, that predominates in the ensemble of irregular vibrations.** Now, because of the predominating characteristic note, it is possible to "attune" it, or to assign a certain noise not just a single pitch but a variety of pitches, without losing its characteristic quality, by which I mean its timbre. Thus certain noises produced by rotary motion can offer an entire ascending or descending chromatic scale if the speed of the motion is increased or decreased.

Every manifestation of life is accompanied by noise. Noise is therefore familiar to our ears and has the power of immediately reminding us of life itself. But sound is alien to life, is always musical and a thing unto itself, an occasional and not an essential element, and it has become for our ears what a too familiar face is to our eyes. Noise, instead, comes to us in a confused and irregular way from the irregular confusion of life; it never reveals itself entirely to us and keeps innumerable surprises in reserve. We are convinced that by selecting, coordinating, and controlling noises we shall enrich mankind with a new and unexpected pleasure of the senses. Even though it is characteristic of noise to remind us brutally of life, **the art of noises must not be limited to an imitative reproduction**. It will achieve its greatest emotional power in acoustic pleasure in itself, which the artist's inspiration will evoke from combined noises.

These are the 6 **families of noises** in the Futurist orchestra, noises which we shall soon produce mechanically:

Rumbles	Whistles	Whispers	Screeches	Noises made	Voices of animals
Thundering	Hisses	Murmurs	Creaking	by percussion	and people;
Explosions	Snorts	Mutters	Rustles	on metals,	Shouts, Screams,
Crashes		Buzzes	Throbs	woods, skins,	Groans, Howls,
Splashes		Gurgles	Crackles	stones, terracotta	Wails, Laughs,
Booms			Scuffles		Wheezes, Sobs

In this we have included the most characteristic of the fundamental noises; the others are simply associations and combinations of these. **The rhythmic movements of a noise are infinite. There is always, as with a note, a predominant rhythm,** but around this there are many other secondary rhythms that can be perceived.

Conclusions

1. Futurist musicians must constantly enlarge and enrich the field of sound. This responds to a need in our sensibility. Indeed, we note that the most talented composers of today are tending to adopt the most complicated dissonances. As they move ever farther away from pure sound, they almost achieve *noise-sound*. This need and this tendency can be satisfied only *by adding and substituting noises for sounds*.
2. Futurist musicians must replace the limited variety of timbres offered by contemporary orchestral instruments with the infinite variety of the timbres of noises, reproduced by suitable mechanisms.

---

[4] This passage became the opening paragraphs in "Bombardment," chapter 10 in Marinetti's *Zang Tumb Tuuum* (Milan: Edizioni di Poesia, 1914), his free-word account of the siege that Italy conducted against the city of Adrianople, in Bulgaria, in October 1912. It was also Marinetti's most often recited piece at declamations and performances; in March 1914 he gave a recitation of it at the Doré Gallery in London, with the painter Christopher Nevinson making supporting noises on a large drum.

3. The sensibility of the musician, liberated from facile and traditional rhythm, must find the way to enhance and renew itself in noises, for every noise offers a union of the most diverse rhythms, aside from its predominant one.

4. Since every noise has a **general predominating tone** among its irregular vibrations, a sufficiently wide variety of tones, semitones, and quarter-tones will be easily attained in constructing the instruments that imitate it.

5. The practical difficulties facing the construction of these instruments are not serious. Once the mechanical principle for producing a certain noise has been found, its pitch can be varied applying the general laws of acoustics. If the instrument has a rotary movement, for example, its speed will be increased or decreased; if it doesn't have a rotary movement, the size or tension of the parts will be varied.

6. It will not be through a succession of noises imitating those of life, but through a fantastic combination of the varied timbres and rhythms that the new orchestra will achieve the newest and most complicated aural emotions. For that purpose every instrument will have to offer the possibility of varying its pitch, or will need a more or less extended range.

7. The variety of noises is infinite. If today when we have perhaps a thousand different machines, we can distinguish a thousand different noises, then tomorrow, as new machines multiply we shall be able to distinguish ten, twenty, or **thirty thousand different noises, not merely to be imitated, but to be combined as imagination dictates.**

8. We therefore invite young musicians of talent and audacity to listen continually and carefully to all noises in order to understand the various rhythms that go into their making, their principal tone, and their secondary ones. Then, by comparing their various timbres with those of sounds, they'll be persuaded how much more numerous are the former than the latter. This will not only give us an understanding of noises, but also a taste and a passion for them. Our multiplied sensibility, having already been conquered by the eyes of the Futurists, will at last have Futurist ears. In this way the motors and the machines of our industrial cities will one day be able to be consciously attuned, so that every factory will be made into an intoxicating orchestra of noises.

Dear Pratella, I submit these propositions to your Futurist genius and invite you to discuss them with me. I am not a musician, and therefore I don't have acoustical predilections or works that I have to defend. I am a Futurist painter who is using a much loved to art to project my determination to renew everything. Which is why, more daring than any professional musician could be, not worrying myself about my apparent incompetence and convinced that boldness possesses all rights and seizes all possibilities, I have been able to intuit the great renovation of music through the Art of noises.

Destruction of Syntax–Wireless Imagination–Words-in-Freedom (May 1913)
F. T. Marinetti

The Futurist sensibility

My "Technical Manifesto of Futurist Literature" (May 11, 1912), in which I first invented *synthetic and essential lyricism, wireless imagination*, and *words-in-freedom*, is concerned exclusively with poetic inspiration.[1]

DESTRUCTION

The text was first published as an independent leaflet in Italian in May 1913. It was read as a lecture by Marinetti in Paris at the Galérie La Boëtie on June 22, 1913. A French translation was published shortly thereafter, and is discussed in articles in the Parisian newspaper *Gil-Blas*, July 7, 1913, the *Magazine de la revue des Français*, July 10, 1913, and *Paris-Journal*, July 10, 1913. An English translation, by Arundel del Re, was published in what was then the leading journal of contemporary poetry in London, *Poetry and Drama* 1.3 (Sept. 1913): 266–76. It was prefaced by an account of Marinetti's activities written by Harold Monro, "Varia" (pp. 263–5), and followed by 30 pages of Futurist poetry in translation. The translation given here is by Lawrence Rainey.

[1]   For the "Technical Manifesto of Futurist Literature," see pp. 15–19. On the phrase "wireless imagination," see the "Technical Manifesto of Futurist Literature," note 9.

Philosophy, the exact sciences, politics, journalism, education, business, however much they may seek synthetic forms of expression, will still have to make use of syntax and punctuation. Indeed, I myself have to make use of them in order to advance the exposition of my concepts.

Futurism is based on the complete renewal of human sensibility which has been brought about as an effect of science's great discoveries. Those people who today make use of the telegraph, the telephone, the gramophone, the train, the bicycle, the motorcycle, the automobile, the ocean liner, the dirigible, the airplane, the cinema, the great newspaper (the synthesis of a day in the world's life) are not aware of the decisive influence that these various forms of communication, transportation, and information have on their psyches.

An ordinary man, spending a day's time in the train, can be transported from a small town, dead, with empty squares in which the sun, the dust, and the wind disport themselves in silence, to a great capital bristling with lights, movement, and street cries. By means of the newspaper, the inhabitant of a mountain village can tremble with anxiety every day, following the Chinese in revolt, the suffragettes of London or New York, Doctor Carrel, or the heroic dogsleds of the polar explorers.[2] The pusillanimous and sedentary inhabitant of any provincial town can allow himself the inebriation of danger by going to the movies and watching a great hunt in the Congo. He can admire Japanese athletes, Negro boxers, inexhaustible American eccentrics, the most elegant and Parisian women by spending a franc to go to the variety theater. Then, tucked up in his bourgeois bed, he can enjoy the distant and costly voice of a Caruso or a Burzio.[3]

Having becoming commonplace, such possibilities fail to arouse the curiosity of superficial minds which remain as incapable of grasping their deeper significance as *the Arabs who watched with indifference the first airplanes in the skies above Tripoli*. Yet to an acute observer these possibilities are so many modifiers of our sensibility, because they have caused the following significant phenomena:

1. Acceleration of life, which today has a rapid rhythm. Physical, intellectual, and emotional equilibrium on the cord of velocity stretched between contradictory magnetisms. Multiple and simultaneous awarenesses within the same individual.

2. Dread of whatever is old and already known. Love of the new, the unexpected.

3. Dread of quiet living, love of danger and an attitude of daily heroism.

4. Destruction of a sense of *the beyond* and an increased valorization of the individual who wants to *vivre sa vie*, to use the phrase of Condillac.[4]

5. Human desires and ambitions multiplying and going beyond all limits.

6. An exact knowledge of everything inaccessible and unrealizable in each person.

7. Semi-equality of man and woman, and less inequality in their social rights.

8. Contempt for love (sentimentalism or lechery) produced by greater freedom and erotic ease among women and by universal exaggeration of female luxury. Let me explain: today's women

[2]   Contemporary newspapers were filled with accounts of the Chinese Revolution (1911–12) and the ending of the Manchu dynasty in February 1912. Similarly, contemporaries were fascinated by accounts of suffragette violence in London, such as breaking shop windows with hammers. Dr. Alexis Carrel (1873–1944), a French surgeon, was in the news because he received the 1912 Nobel Prize for Medicine for developing a method of suturing blood vessels, work which he had achieved at the Rockefeller Institute for Medical Research in New York. Exploration of the South Pole was also much in the news. In 1908–9, Sir Ernest Henry Shackleton led a party to the Great Barrier, very close to the Pole. In January 1912 Scott and his party finally reached the Pole, only to discover that the Norwegian explorer Roald Amundsen had already been there a month

earlier. Scott's party, caught in a blizzard, died on their return journey.
[3]   Enrico Caruso (1873–1921) was a legendary Italian tenor and one of the first musicians to document his voice on gramophone recordings. Eugenia Burzio (1872–1922) was an Italian soprano. A violinist who turned to singing, she debuted in 1889 at Turin in *Cavalleria rusticana*. She made many appearances at *La Scala* in Milan, and during the years before the First World War was deemed one of the leading Italian sopranos. Her last appearance was in 1919.
[4]   Étienne Bonnot de Condillac (1715–80), French philosopher, is known chiefly as the leading advocate in France of the ideas of John Locke. The phrase that Marinetti cites could well have been said by almost anyone.

love luxury more than love. A visit to a great dressmaker's shop, escorted by a banker friend who is paunchy and gouty, but will pay the bill, has taken the place of some hot rendezvous with an adored young man. The element of mystery that was once found in love now resides in the selection of an amazing ensemble, latest model, preferably one which her friends don't yet have. Men no longer love a woman who is without *luxus*. The lover has lost all prestige, and Love has lost its absolute value. A complex question, one which I can only touch in passing.

9.   Modification of patriotism, which has today become the heroic idealizations of a people's commercial, industrial, and artistic solidarity.

10.   Modification of the conception of war, which has become the sanguinary and necessary test of the strength of a people.

11.   The passion, art, idealism of Business. New financial sensibility.

12.   Man multiplied by the machine.[5] New mechanical sense, a fusion of instinct with the output of a motor and forces conquered.

13.   The passion of art and idealism of Sport. Idea and love of "the record."

14.   The new tourist sensibility of ocean liners and grand hotels (annual synthesis of various races). Passion for the city. Negation of distances and solitary nostalgias. Derision for the "holy green silence" and the ineffable landscape.

15.   The earth shrunk by speed. New sense of the world. Let me explain: men have successively conquered a sense of the house, the neighborhood in which they live, the city, the region, the continent. Today man possesses a sense of the world; he has only a modest need to know what his forebears have done, but a burning need to know what his contemporaries are doing in every part of the globe. Whence the necessity, for the individual, of communicating with all the peoples of the earth. Whence the need to feel oneself at the center, to be judge and motor of the infinite both explored and unexplored. A gigantic increase in the sense of humanity and an urgent need to coordinate at every moment our relations with all humanity.

16.   Disgust for the curving line, the spiral, and the *tourniquet*. Love for the straight line and the tunnel. The habit of foreshortened views and visual syntheses created by the speed of trains and automobiles which look down over cities and country landscapes. Dread of slowness, minutiae, detailed analyses and explanations. Love of speed, abbreviation and synopsis. "Quick, tell me the whole story *in two words*."

17.   Love of depth and essence in every mental activity.

So these are some of the elements of a new Futurist sensibility which have generated our pictorial dynamism, our antigraceful music devoid of rhythmic regularity, our Art of noises and Futurist words-in-freedom.

Words-in-freedom

Casting aside all stupid definitions and confusing professorial verbalisms, I declare that *lyricism* is the rarely found *faculty* of *intoxicating oneself with life* and *with oneself*. The faculty of changing into wine the muddy waters of life that surround us and flow through us. The faculty of coloring the world with the unique colors of our changeable "I."

Now imagine that a friend of yours, gifted with this kind of lyrical faculty, should find himself in a zone of intense life (revolution, war, shipwreck, earthquake, etc.), and should come, immediately

[5]   See "Multiplied Man and the Reign of the Machine" in
Lawrence Rainey et al. (eds.), *Futurism: A Reader and Visual
Repertoire* (New Haven: Yale University Press, 2005).

afterwards, to recount his impressions. Do you know what your lyrical friend will do while he is still shocked? . . .

He will begin by brutally destroying the syntax of his speech. He will not waste time in constructing periodic sentences. He could care less about punctuation or finding the right adjective. He disdains subtleties and shadings, and in haste he will assault your nerves with visual, auditory, olfactory sensations, just as their insistent pressure in him demands. The rush of steam-emotion will burst the steampipe of the sentence, the valves of punctuation, and the regular clamp of the adjective. Fistfuls of basic words without a conventional order. Only preoccupation of the narrator, to render all the vibrations of his "I."

Moreover, if this same narrator gifted with lyricism has a mind stocked with general ideas, he will involuntarily link his sensations to the entire universe as he has known and intuited it. And in order to render the exact weight and proportion of the life he has experienced, he will hurl immense networks of analogies across the world. And thus will he render the analogical ground of life, telegraphically, which is to say with the same economical rapidity that the telegraph imposes on war correspondents and journalists for their synoptic accounts. This need for laconicism not only responds to the laws of velocity that regulate us today, but also the age-old relations that the public and the poet have had. For between the poet and the public, in fact, the same kind of relations exist as between two old friends. They can speak to each other with a half-word, a gesture, a wink. That is why the imagination of the poet must weave together distant things *without connecting wires*, by means of essential *words-in-freedom*.

Death of free verse

Free verse once had countless regions for existing, but it is now destined to be replaced by words-in-freedom.

The evolution of poetry and human sensibility have shown us the two irremediable defects of free verse.

1. Free verse fatally impels the poet toward facile effects of sonorousness, predictable mirror-games, monotonous cadences, absurd chiming, and inescapable echo-play, internal and external.

2. Free verse artificially channels the current of lyrical emotion between the banks of syntax and the weirs of grammar. The free intuitive inspiration that directly addresses the intuition of the ideal reader finds itself imprisoned, or redistributed into so many glasses of purified water for the alimentation of restless, fussy minds.

When I speak of destroying the canals of syntax, I am being neither peremptory nor systematic. In the words-in-freedom of my unchained lyricism, there will still be traces here and there of regular syntax and even of true, logical periods. This inequality in the conciseness and freedom is inevitable and natural. Since poetry, in reality, is nothing more than a superior form of life, more concentrated and intense than the one we lead everyday, – it too is composed of elements that are hyper-alive and moribund.

We need not, therefore, worry too much over the latter. But at all costs we must avoid rhetoric and commonplaces expressed telegraphically.

The wireless imagination

By wireless imagination, I mean the absolute freedom of images or analogies, expressed with disconnected words, and without the connecting syntactical wires and without punctuation.

Until now writers have been restricted to immediate analogies. For example, they have compared an animal to man or to another animal, which is more or less the same thing as taking a photograph. (They've compared, for example, a fox terrier to a tiny thoroughbred. A more advanced writer might compare that same trembling terrier to a telegraph. I, instead, compare it to gurgling water. In this there is an *ever greater gradation of analogies*, affinities ever deeper and more solid, however remote.) Analogy is nothing other than the deep love that binds together remote, seemingly diverse and hostile things. The life of matter can be embraced only by an orchestral style, at once polychromatic, polyphonic, and polymorphous, by means of the most extensive analogies. In my *Battle of Tripoli*, when I have compared a trench bristling with bayonets to an orchestra, or a machine-gun to a fatal women, I have intuitively introduced a large part of the universe into a brief episode of African combat. Images are not flowers to be chosen and gathered with parsimony, as Voltaire said. They constitute the very lifeblood of poetry. Poetry should be an uninterrupted flow of new images, without which it is merely anemia and green-sickness. The vaster their affinities, the more images will retain their power ("Technical Manifesto of Futurist Literature")

Wireless imagination and words-in-freedom will transport us into the essence of matter. With the discovery of new analogies between things remote and apparently contradictory, we shall value them ever more intimately. Instead of *humanizing* animals, vegetables, and minerals (a bygone system) we will be able to *animalize, vegetize, mineralize, electrify,* or *liquefy* our style, making it live the very life of matter. For example, to render the life of a blade of grass, we might say: "I will be greener tomorrow." But with words-in-freedom we might have: **Condensed Metaphors. –Telegraphic images. –Sums of vibrations. –Knots of thought. –Closed or open fans of movement. –Foreshortened analogies. –Color Balances. –The dimensions, weights, sizes and velocities of sensations. –The plunge of the essential word into the water of sensibility, without the concentric eddies produced by words. –Intuition's moments of repose. –Movements in two, three, four, five different rhythms. –Analytical explanatory telegraph poles that sustain the cable of intuitive wires.**

Death of the literary "I"
Matter and molecular life

My "Technical Manifesto" inveighed against the obsession with the "I"[6] that poets have described, sung, analyzed, and vomited forth until today. To rid ourselves of this obsessive "I," we must abandon the habit of humanizing nature, attributing human preoccupations and emotions to animals, plants, waters, stones, and clouds. Instead we should express the infinite smallness that surrounds us, the imperceptible, the invisible, the agitation of atoms, Brownian movements,[7] all the passionate hypothesis and all the dominions explored by high-powered microscopes. Let me explain: I want to introduce infinite molecular life into poetry not as a scientific document, but as an intuitive element. It should be mixed in with art works, with spectacles and dramas of what is infinitely grand, since the fusion of both constitutes the integral synthesis of life.

To help a bit the intuition of my ideal reader, I use *italics* for words-in-freedom that express infinite smallness and molecular life.

Semaphoric adjective
Adjective-lighthouse or atmosphere-adjective

Everywhere we tend to suppress a qualifying adjective, since it presupposes a halt in intuition, a too minute definition of the noun. That is not a categorical prohibition, but a tendency. What is necessary is to make use of the adjective as little as possible and to do so in a manner absolutely different from that which has prevailed until now. The adjective should be viewed as a railway signal or a semaphore of style, serving to regulate the impetus, the slowings and pauses of advancing analogies. As many as twenty of these semaphoric adjectives might be accumulated in this way.

What I call a semaphoric adjective, adjective-lighthouse, or atmosphere-adjective is an adjective separated from its noun and instead isolated in parentheses, which turns it into a sort of absolute noun, vaster and more powerful than a noun proper.

---

[6] See p. 19 in this edition, point 11 in the "Technical Manifesto."

[7] The Scottish scientist Robert Brown (1773–1858) published his discovery of Brownian movement, the natural continuous motion of minute particles in solution, in his pamphlet of 1828, *A Brief Account of Microscopical Observations*.

The semaphoric adjective or adjective-lighthouse, suspended above the ground in the glassy cage of parentheses, casts its whirling light into the distance all around.

The profile of this adjective crumbles, spreads abroad, illuminating, impregnating, and enveloping a whole zone of words-in-freedom. For example, I might place the following adjectives between parenthesis amid a group of words-in-freedom describing a voyage by sea: (calm blue methodical habitual). It would not be just the sea which is *calm blue methodical habitual*, but the ship, its machinery, the passengers, whatever I might be doing and my very mind.

The verb in the infinitive

Here, too, my pronouncements are not categorical. I maintain, however, that the verb in the infinitive is indispensable to a violent and dynamic lyricism, for the infinitive is round like a wheel, and like a wheel it is adaptable to all the railway-cars that make up the train of analogies, so constituting the very speed of style.

The verb in the infinitive denies by its very existence the classical period and prevents the style from slowing or sitting down at any specific point. While the **verb in the infinitive is round** and mobile as a wheel, the other moods and tenses of the verb are triangular, square, or oval.

Onomatopoeia and mathematical signs

When I said that it is "necessary to spit on the *Altar of Art*,"[8] I was inciting Futurists to liberate lyricism from the solemn atmosphere of compunction and incense that one usually calls Art with a capital A. Art with a capital A is a form of intellectual clericalism. That is why I incited Futurists to destroy and mock the garlands, palms, aureoles, exquisite frames, mantles and stoles, the whole historical wardrobe of romantic bric-a-brac that have comprised so much of all poetry until now. I urged instead a swift, brutal and immediate lyricism, one that would appear to all our predecessors as antipoetic, a telegraphic lyricism that would have nothing of the bookish about it, but as much as possible of the flavor of life. Whence the bold introduction of onomatopoeic harmonies to render all the sounds and noises of modern life, even the most cacophonous.

Onomatopoeia, which can help to vivify lyricism with raw and brutal elements of reality, has been used (from Aristophanes to Pascoli)[9] rather timidly used in poetry.(12) But we Futurists call for an audacious and ongoing use of onomatopoeia. It need not be systematic. For example, my "Adrianople Siege–Orchestra" and my "Battle Weight + Odor" required many onomatopoeic harmonies.[10] Always for the purpose of rendering a maximum quantity of vibrations and a deeper synthesis of life, we abolish all stylistic connectors, all the shiny buckles with which traditional poets have linked images to the period. Instead we employ very brief or anonymous mathematical and musical symbols, and between parentheses we place indications such as (fast) (faster) (slower) (two-beat time), to control the speed of the style. These parentheses can even cut into a word or an onomatopoeic harmony.

Typographical revolution

I have initiated a typographical revolution directed against the bestial, nauseating sort of book that contains passéist poetry or verse à la D'Annunzio[11] – handmade paper that imitates models of the seventeenth century, festooned with helmets, Minervas, Apollos, decorative capitals in red ink with loops and squiggles, vegetables, mythological ribbons from missals, epigraphs, and Roman

---

[8] In "The Technical Manifesto of Futurist Literature" (May 1912), p. 19 in this edition.

[9] Aristophanes (c. 450 to c. 385 BC) was the greatest poet of comedies in ancient Athens, an author who made liberal use of onomatopoeia in *The Frogs* and other plays. Giovanni Pascoli (1855–1912) was an Italian poet.

[10] "Adrianople Siege–Orchestra" was an independent poem which became the first half of chapter 10, "Bombardment," in

Marinetti's book *Zang Tumb Tuuum*. It is quoted in its entirety by Luigi Russolo in "the Art of Noises"; see pp. 25–26. "Battle Weight + Smell" is quoted in its entirety by Marinetti in "A Response to Objections," pp. 22–23.

[11] The Italian poet and novelist Gabriele D'Annunzio (1863–1938), a controversial Italian writer, did indeed have a love for fine book-making in the art-nouveau style.

numerals. The book must be the Futurist expression of Futurist thought. Not only that. My revolution is directed against the so-called typographical harmony of the page, which is contrary to the flux and reflux, the leaps and bursts of style that run through the page itself. For that reason we will use, in the very same page, *three or four different colors of ink*, and as many as 20 different typographical fonts if necessary. For example: *italics* for a series of swift or similar sensations, **boldface** for violent onomatopoeias, etc. The typographical revolution and the multicolored variety in the letters will mean that I can double the expressive force of words.

I oppose the decorative and precious aesthetic of Mallarmé and his search for the exotic word, the unique and irreplaceable, elegant, suggestive, exquisite adjective. I have no wish to suggest an idea of sensation by means of passéist graces and affectations: I want to seize them brutally and fling them in the reader's face.

I also oppose Mallarmé's static ideal.[12] The typographic revolution that I've proposed will enable me to imprint words (words already free, dynamic, torpedoing forward) every velocity of the stars, clouds, airplanes, trains, waves, explosives, drops of seafoam, molecules, and atoms.

And so I shall realize the fourth principle contained in my "First Manifesto of Futurism" (February 20, 1909) : "We affirm that the beauty of the world has been enriched by a new form of beauty: the beauty of speed."[13]

Multilineal lyricism

In addition, I have also devised *multilineal lyricism*, with which I am able to obtain that lyrical simultaneity which has obsessed Futurist painters, and by means of which I am convinced that we can achieve the most complex lyrical simultaneities.

On several parallel lines, a poet will launch several chains of colors, sounds, odors, noises, weights, densities, analogies. One line, for example, might be olfactory, another musical, another pictorial.

Let us imagine that one chain of sensations and pictorial analogies dominates several other chains of sensations and analogies: in that case it will be printed in a heavier typeface that the one used in the second or third lines (the one containing, for example, a chain of sensations and musical analogies; the other, a chain of sensations and olfactory analogies).

Given a page containing many groups of sensations and analogies, with each group composed of, say, three or four lines, then the first line of each group might be formed of pictorial sensations and analogies (printed in heavier typeface) and the same sort of chain would continue (always in heavier typeface) in the first line of each of the other groups.

The chain of musical sensations and analogies (second line), though less important than visual sensations and analogies (first line), yet more important than the olfactory sensations and analogies (third line), might be printed in a typeface lighter than that of the first line, but heavier than that of the third.

Free expressive orthography

The historical necessity of free expressive orthography is demonstrated by the successive revolutions that continuously freed the lyrical powers of the human race from shackles and rules.

1.   Poets, in fact, began by channeling their lyric intoxication in a series of equal breaths, with accents, echoes, assonances, or rhymes at pre-established intervals (**traditional metrics**), then varied these different breaths, measured by the lungs of preceding poets, with a certain freedom.

---

[12]   Stéphane Mallarmé's (1842–98) book *Un Cou de dés jamais n'abolira le hasard* (*A Throw of the Dice will Never Abolish Chance*) (1897) used special typographical features that might be thought to anticipate some of Marinetti's proposals here, a charge that he is attempting to forestall.
[13]   See "The Founding and the Manifesto of Futurism," p. 3.

2. Later, poets came to feel that differing moments of their lyrical intoxication required commensurate breath of various and unexpected lengths, with absolute freedom of accentuation. Thus they arrived at **free verse**, yet still preserved the syntactic order of words so that their lyrical intoxication could flow down to the listeners by the logical channel of syntax.

3. Today we no longer want lyrical intoxication to order words in syntactic order before launching them forth with the breaths that we have invented, and hence we have *words-in-freedom*. Further, our lyrical intoxication must be free to deform and reshape words, cutting them, lengthening them, reinforcing their centers or their extremities, increasing or diminishing the number of vowels and consonants. Thus we will have the *new orthography* which I call *free expressive*. This instinctive deformation of words corresponds to our natural tendency to use onomatopoeia. It matters little if a word, having been deformed, becomes ambiguous. For it will be wedded with onomatopoeic harmonies, synopses of noises, and these will enable us to swiftly reach an *onomatopoeic psychic* harmony, the sonorous but abstract expression of an emotion of pure thought. It may be objected that **words-in-freedom** or the wireless imagination require a special declamation, or else they will remain incomprehensible. Though I am not greatly worried about being understood by the masses, I will reply by noting that Futurist declaimers are rapidly increasing and further, that any greatly admired traditional poem has also required a special declamation in order to be fully savored.

The Variety Theater (Sept. 1913)
F. T. Marinetti

We have a deep distaste for the contemporary theater (verse, prose, and musical), because it oscillates stupidly between historical reconstruction (pastiche or plagiarism) and a photographic reproduction of everyday life; petty, slow, analytic, and diluted theater that is worthy, at best, of the age of the oil lamp.

FUTURISM EXALTS THE VARIETY THEATER because:

1. The Variety Theater, born as we are from electricity, is fortunate in having no traditions, no guiding lights, no dogmas, and in being nurtured with the swift pace of contemporary events.

2. The Variety Theater is absolutely practical, for it proposes to distract and amuse the public with comic effects, erotic stimulation, or imaginative astonishment.[1]

3. The authors, actors, and stage technicians of the Variety Theater have only one reason for existing and succeeding: incessantly to invent new means of astonishment. Whence the absolute impossibility of standing still or repeating oneself; whence the persistent competition of minds and muscles in order to break the various records of agility, speed, force, complication, and elegance.

4. The Variety Theater is unique today in making use of film, which enriches it with an incalculable number of visions and spectacles that couldn't otherwise be performed (battles, riots, horse races, automobile and airplane meets, travels, transatlantic steamers, the recesses of the city, of the countryside, of the oceans and the skies).

5. The Variety Theater, being a profitable shop-window for countless creative efforts, naturally generates what I call the *Futurist marvelous*, a product of modern machinism. Here are some of

The text was published as an independent leaflet in September 1913. It was published again in *Lacerba*, 1(19) (Oct. 1, 1913). A somewhat shortened version, with nine paragraphs lopped off, appeared in an anonymous English translation in the *Daily Mail* on Nov. 21, 1913, with the title of "The Meaning of the Music Hall." (The *Daily Mail* was then the largest mass-circulation newspaper in the world.) A different translation into English, this one by D. Nevile Lees, was published under the title "Futurism and the Theatre: A Futurist Manifesto by Marinetti,"

in *The Mask: A Quarterly Journal of the Art of the Theatre*, 6(3) (Jan. 1914): 188–93. The new translation also omitted several paragraphs. The translation given here is by Lawrence Rainey.

[1]   The phrase "imaginative astonishment" gives only a limited sense of the powerful state of shock that Marinetti characterizes with the expression *stupore immaginativo*, literally "imaginative stupor." Marinetti is transforming medical discussions of shock and trauma into the foundation for an aesthetics of shock.

the elements of this *marvelous*: 1. powerful caricatures; 2. abysses of the ridiculous; 3. improbable and delightful ironies; 4. comprehensive, definitive symbols; 5. cascades of uncontrollable humor; 6. deep analogies between the human, animal, vegetable, and mechanical worlds; 7. flashes of revelatory cynicism; 8. plots involving witticisms, puns, and conundrums that aerate the intelligence; 9. the entire gamut of laughter and smiles, to relax one's nerves; 10. the entire gamut of stupidity, imbecility, mindlessness, and absurdity, which imperceptibly push intelligence to the edge of insanity; 11. all the new productions of light, sound, noise, and language, with their mysterious and inexplicable extensions into the most unexplored regions of our sensibility; 12. a mass of current events dispatched within two minutes ("and now let's glance at the Balkans": King Nicholas, Enver-bey, Daneff, Venizelos, belly-slaps and fist-fights between Serbs and Bulgarians, a chorus number, and everything vanishes);[2] 13. satirical educational pantomimes; 14. caricatures of suffering and nostalgia, deeply impressed into the spectators' sensibility by means of gestures that exasperate with their spasmodic, hesitant, and weary slowness; weighty terms made ridiculous by comic gestures, bizarre disguises, mutilated words, smirks, pratfalls.

6. The Variety Theater in our time is the crucible in which the elements of a new emerging sensibility are seething. In it one can trace the ironic decomposition of all the outworn prototypes of the Beautiful, the Grand, the Solemn, the Religious, the Ferocious, the Seductive, and the Frightful, and the abstract elaboration of the new prototypes that will succeed them.

    The Variety Theater, therefore, is the synthesis of everything that humanity up till now has refined within its nervous system in order to amuse itself by laughing at material or moral suffering; and it is the seething fusion of all the laughter and all the smiles, all the guffaws, all the contortions, all the smirks of the humanity to come. The joy that will shake men in the next century, their poetry, their painting, their philosophy, the leaps of their architecture – all can be tasted in the Variety Theater of today.

7. Among the forms of contemporary spectacle, the Variety Theater is the most hygienic by virtue of the dynamism of its forms and colors (simultaneous movements of the jugglers, ballerinas, gymnasts, colorful riding masters, spiral cyclones of dancers spinning on the points of their feet). With its swift, overpowering dance rhythms, the Variety Theater forcibly drags the slowest souls out of their torpor and forces them to run and jump.

8. The Variety Theater is the only spectacle that makes use of audience collaboration. The audience is not static like a stupid voyeur, but joins noisily in the action, singing along with songs, accompanying the orchestra, communicating with the actors by speaking up at will or engaging in bizarre dialogues. The actors even bicker clownishly with the musicians.

    The Variety Theater uses the smoke of cigars and cigarettes to merge the atmosphere of the audience with that of the stage. And since the audience collaborates in this way with the actors' imaginations, the action develops simultaneously on the stage, in the boxes, and in the orchestra. And then it continues beyond the performance, among the battalions of fans and the sugared dandies at the stage door fighting over the starring lady; a double victory at the end; a chic dinner and bed.

---

[2] Throughout the period 1912–13, international diplomacy was preoccupied by the Balkan question. The Ottoman Empire or Turkey still controlled large amounts of territory across the Balkan peninsula, including what is now northern Greece (the area around Salonika), Macedonia, and Kosovo. But given Turkey's weakness, it was only a matter of time before the region's various peoples, incited by different powers, would rise in revolt. In October 1912, just at the moment when Turkey was concluding peace with Italy over the Italo-Turkish war (1911–12), the four countries of the Balkan League (Serbia, Montenegro, Greece, and Bulgaria) declared war against Turkey, sparking the First Balkan War. Bulgaria laid siege to Adrianople, a battle chronicled in Marinetti's *Zang Tumb Tuum*, while Greece took the city of Salonika. On December 3 an armistice was declared, and a peace conference called. But in January 1913, Enver Bey (also known as Enver Pasa, 1881–1922) led a coup d'état in Turkey, and the new government refused to accept the peace conditions. A settlement was finally reached in May 1913. But in June 1913, the Second Balkan War broke out, this time among the countries which had formerly been allies against Turkey. Greece and Serbia formed an alliance against Bulgaria, which they promptly defeated. Peace was signed in August 1913. King Nicholas I Petrovic (1860–1918) was the ruler of Bulgaria; Eleftherios Venizelos (1864–1936) was prime minister of Greece during the period 1910–15.

9. The Variety Theater is a school of sincerity for males because it exalts their rapacious instincts and snatches away from woman all the veils, all the phrases, all the sighs, all the romantic sobs that mask and deform her. Instead, it throws into relief all of woman's marvelous animal qualities, her power to grasp, seduce, betray, and resist.

10. The Variety Theater is a school of heroism in its stress on winning various records for difficulty and overcoming previous efforts, which gives the stage a strong and healthy atmosphere of danger. (For example, somersaults, looping the loop on bicycles, in cars, on horseback.)

11. The Variety Theater is a school of subtlety, complication, and cerebral synthesis because of its clowns, magicians, mind readers, brilliant calculators, character actors, imitators and parodists, its musical jugglers and eccentric Americans, its fantastic pregnancies that give birth to unexpected objects and mechanisms.

12. The Variety Theater is the only school that can give advice to adolescents and talented young people, because it briefly and incisively explains the most abstruse problems and complicated political events. Example: a year ago, at the Folies-Bergère, two dancers acted out the meandering discussions between Cambon and Kiderlen-Wächter on the question of Morocco and the Congo,[3] with a revealing symbolic dance that equaled at least three years of study in foreign policy. Facing the audience, their arms entwined, glued together, they kept making mutual territorial concessions, jumping back and forth, to the right and to the left, never separating, both of them keeping their sight fixed on their goal, which was to become ever more entangled. They gave an unrivaled rendering of diplomacy, of extreme courtesy, skillful vacillation, ferocity, diffidence, persistence, and pettiness.

   In addition, the Variety Theater luminously explains the laws that dominate life:

   a) the necessity of complications and differing rhythms;
   b) the inevitability of lies and contradictions (e.g. English *danseuses* with two faces: peaceful shepherd and terrible soldier);
   c) the omnipotence of a methodical will-power that modifies human powers [*forze*];
   d) syntheses of speed + transformations (example: Fregoli).[4]

13. The Variety Theater systematically disparages ideal love and its romantic obsessions by endlessly repeating the nostalgic languors of passion with the monotonous and automatic regularity of a daily job. It strangely mechanizes feelings; it disparages and hygienically tramples down the obsession with carnal possession; and it reduces lust to the natural function of coitus, stripping it of all mystery, depressing anxiety, anti-hygienic idealism.

   The Variety Theater, instead, communicates a sense of and a taste for facile, light, and ironic loves. Café-concert performances, given in the open air on the casino terraces, offer an amusing war between the spasmodic moonlight, tormented with endless desperation, and the electric light that sparkles violently over the false jewelry, the painted flesh, the colorful petticoats, the spangles, and the blood-red color of lipstick. Naturally it is the energetic electric light that triumphs, the moonlight that is defeated.

14. The Variety Theater is naturally anti-academic, primitive, and ingenuous, and hence more significant for the improvised character of its experiments and the simplicity of its means. (Example: the systematic tour of the stage that the *chanteuses* make, like caged animals, at the end of every refrain.)

---

[3] Jules Cambon (1845–1935) was a French diplomat and ambassador to Germany from 1907 to 1914, and in 1911 he negotiated with the German diplomat Alfred von Kiderlen-Wächter (1852–1912) over the Agadir crisis. In 1911 France had occupied the Moroccan cities of Rabat and Fès. Kiderlen demanded compensation for Germany and, to back up his demands, dispatched the German gunboat *Panther* to Agadir. Kiderlen refused conciliatory offers and demanded the whole of the French Congo in return for a free hand for France in Morocco. Cambon rejected that demand. In November, they finally agreed that Germany would receive two strips of territory from the French Congo and France would establish a protectorate over Morocco.

[4] Lepoldo Fregoli (1867–1936) was a comic actor who performed "transformations," rapidly changing from one character to another and often parodying recognizable types of people. His ensemble toured throughout the world.

15. The Variety Theater is destroying the Solemn, the Sacred, the Serious, the Sublime of Art with a capital *A*. It is helping along the Futurist destruction of immortal masterpieces by plagiarizing and parodying them, by making them seem commonplace in stripping them of their solemnity and presenting them as if they were just another turn or attraction. Hence we give our unconditional approval to the execution of *Parsifal* in 40 minutes, which is now in rehearsal in a great London music-hall.

16. The Variety Theater is destroying all our conceptions of perspective, proportion, time and space. (Example: a little doorway and gate that are 30 centimeters in height, isolated in the middle of the stage, which eccentric American comedians open and close with solemnity as they repeatedly enter and exit it, as though they couldn't do otherwise.)

17. The Variety Theater offers us all the records achieved until now: the greatest speed and the finest gymnastics and acrobatics of the Japanese, the greatest muscular frenzy of the Negroes, the highest examples of animal intelligence (trained horses, elephants, seals, dogs, birds), the finest melodic inspiration of the Gulf of Naples and the Russian steppes, the keenest Parisian wit, the greatest competitive force of different races (wrestling and boxing), the greatest anatomical monstrosity, the greatest female beauty.

18. While contemporary theater exalts the inner life, professorial meditation, the library, the museum, monotonous crises of conscience, stupid analyses of feelings – and in short, that filthy thing and filthy word *psychology*; the Variety theater exalts action, heroism, life in the open air, dexterity, the authority of instinct and intuition. To psychology it opposes what I call *body-madness* [*fisicofollia*].

19. Finally, the Variety Theater offers all nations that don't have a single great capital city (like Italy) a brilliant résumé of Paris, considered as the unique magnetic center of luxury and ultra-refined pleasure.

*Futurism wants to transform the Variety Theater into a theater
of astonishment, record-setting, and body-madness*

1.   Every trace of logic in Variety Theater performances must be destroyed, while their luxurious-ness must be grotesquely exaggerated, their contrasts multiplied, and on the stage their improbable and absurd dimensions must reign supreme. (Example: Require the *chanteuses* to dye their décolletage, their arms, and especially their hair, in all the colors hitherto neglected as means of seduction. Green hair, purple arms, blue décolletage, an orange chignon, etc. Interrupt a song and break into a revolutionary speech. Sprinkle over a romance some insults and profanity, etc.)

2.   Prevent any set of traditions from being established in the Variety Theater. Therefore fight to abolish the stupid Parisian *Revues*, as tedious as Greek tragedy with their *Compère* and *Commère* who play the part of the ancient chorus, and their parade of political personalities and events, punctuated by witticisms, which possess a tiresome logic and connectedness. The Variety Theater mustn't be a more or less humorous newspaper, as it is, unfortunately, today.

3.   Introduce surprise and the need to move among the spectators of the orchestra, the boxes, and the balcony. Some random suggestions: spread a strong glue on some of the seats, so that the male or female spectator will remain stuck to the seat and make everyone laugh (the damaged dinner jacket or toilette will be paid for at the door). –Sell the same ticket to ten people: resulting in traffic jams, bickering, and wrangling. –Give free tickets to men and women who are notoriously unbalanced, irritable, or eccentric and likely to provoke an uproar with obscene gestures, pinching women, or other freakishness. Sprinkle the seats with dusts that provoke itching, sneezing, etc.

4.   Systematically prostitute all of classical art on the stage, for example by performing all Greek, French, and Italian tragedies in a single evening, all highly condensed and mixed up. Put life

into the works of Beethoven, Wagner, Bach, Bellini, and Chopin by inserting Neapolitan songs into them. —Put on stage, side by side, Zacconi, Eleonora Duse, Felix Mayol, Sarah Bernhardt, and Fregoli.[5] —Perform a Beethoven symphony in reverse, starting from the last note —Condense all of Shakespeare into a single act. —Ditto for all the most venerated actors. —Have actors tied in sacks up to their necks recite Hugo's *Ernani*.[6] Soap the floorboards of the stage to cause amusing pratfalls at the most tragic moments.

5.   In every way encourage the *type* of the American eccentric, the effects of exciting grotesquerie which he achieves, the frightening dynamism, the crude jokes, the acts of enormous brutality, the trick weskits and trousers as deep as a ship's hold, out of which, along with a thousand different things, will come the great Futurist hilarity that must make the face of the world young again.

Because, and don't forget it, we Futurists are YOUNG ARTILLERYMEN ON A TOOT, as we proclaimed in our manifesto, "Let's murder the Moonlight," fire + fire + light against the moonlight and war every evening against the ageing firmaments great cities to blaze with electric signs   Immense face of a Negro (30 meters high + 150 meters high atop the building = 180 meters) golden eye to open to close to open to close height 3 meters SMOKE SMOKE MANOLI SMOKE MANOLI CIGARETTES   woman in blouse (50 meters high + 120 meters atop the house = 170 meters) bust to stretch to relax violet pink lilac blue   foam made up of electric lights in a champagne glass (30 meters high) to sparkle to evaporate within a shadowy mouth   electric signs to dim to die out beneath a dark tenacious hand to be reborn to continue to extend into night the effort of the day human courage + madness never to die to stop to fall asleep   electric signs = formation and dissolution of minerals and vegetables center of the earth   circulation of blood in the iron faces of the Futurist houses to pulse to turn purple (joy anger up up still more now stronger yet) the moment that pessimistic negative sentimental nostalgic shadows besiege the city   a brilliant reawakening of the streets that channel the smoky swarm of workers during the day   two horses (30 meters high) to role a golden ball with their hooves

MONA LISA PURGATIVE WATERS

cross cross of **trrr trrrrr** Elevated **trrrr trrrr** overhead **trombbooobooobooone** whiiiiiiiistles ambulance-sirens and fire trucks   transformation of the streets into splendid hallways to guide to push logical necessity the masses toward trepidation + laughter + uproar of Music-hall

FOLIE-BERGERE EMPIRE CREAM-ECLIPSE red red red

turquoise turquoise violet tubes of mercury   huge eel-letters of gold purple diamond Futurist defiance to the weepy nights   defeat of the stars warmth enthusiasm faith conviction will-power penetration of an electric sign in the house across the street **yellow slaps** for the gouty man dozing off in bibliophile slippers   3 mirrors watch him   the sign sinks into 3 red-gooooolden abysses to open to close to open to close depths of 3-thousand meters   horror   to leave to leave soon hat stick staircase taximeter pushings **zu zuoeu** here we are dazzle of the promenade   solemnity of the panther-cocottes in their tropics of light music   fat and warm smell of music hall gaiety = tireless ventilator of the world's Futurist brain.

---

[5]   Ernesto Zacconi (1857–1948) was an Italian actor notable for his performance in modern works such as Ibsen's *Ghosts*. In 1899 he starred opposite Eleonora Duse in D'Annunzio's play, *La Gioconda*, and again in 1901 in his *Città morta*. Eleonora Duse (1858–1924) was the most famous Italian actress of her time. In 1897 she played the lead role in D'Annunzio's *Il sogno di un mattino di primavera* (*The Dream of a Spring Morning*). Their notorious love affair and collaboration continued till 1904 and covered the period of her most celebrated performances. She retired from the stage in 1909. Félix Mayol (1872–1941) was a French singer who performed in café-concerto and music hall. He debuted in Paris in 1895 at the Concert Parisien, and was ranked

among the greatest performers of French song between 1895 and 1920. Sarah Bernhardt (1844–1923) was the most celebrated French actress of her time. She began her career at the Comédie Française in Paris, playing chiefly tragic roles. By 1899 she owned her own theater, the Théâtre Sarah Bernhardt, where she continued to perform a wide range of works. For Fregoli see p. 36 n. 4.

[6]   *Hernani* was a romantic historical drama by Victor Hugo first presented in 1830; it became the prototype of romantic drama, with audacious plot and setting, and a theatrical magnificence of verse.

Ezra Pound (1885–1972)

Ezra Pound was born in Hailey, Idaho, but moved with his family at the age of two to Wyncote, Pennsylvania, a Philadelphia suburb. He did his BA and an MA in Romance Philology at the University of Pennsylvania. Then, after a brief spell teaching in Indiana, he left for Europe. He arrived in London in 1908, and was soon frequenting the salons of Olivia Shakespeare, a close friend of Yeats, for Pound the greatest living poet. By 1913 he was serving as a reader and amanuensis for Yeats.

Pound has come to occupy an unusual place in the history of modernism. His energies as an impresario were indispensable to other writers such as Eliot and Joyce, and without his interventions they might never have had the careers they did. His generosity to them, and many others, is legendary. His gifts as an impresario were no less impressive. Much of the coherence of modernism as an institution derived from his canny capacity to bring together patrons, journals, and authors, creating and then exploiting institutional opportunities. He was Foreign Editor for the journal *Poetry* from 1912 to 1914, then a literary advisor to *The Egoist* from 1914 to 1917, then edited an independent section within *The Little Review* from 1917 to 1919, and then served as a foreign editor and seeker of talent for the *Dial* from 1920 to 1921. In these positions he was a tireless champion of Eliot and Joyce, and an early admirer of Marianne Moore. Unhappy and feeling unrecognized by literary London, he moved to Paris in early 1920, where he stayed until 1924, his residence punctuated by increasingly long travels in Italy. From now on his literary energies were directed entirely to his troubled masterpiece, *The Cantos*.

In late 1924 he moved to Rapallo, Italy. Already by then, and perhaps as early as 1923, he counted himself an admirer of Mussolini, a commitment which deepened in the years ahead. During the 1930s his admiration for Italian Fascism was wedded to an increasingly virulent anti-Semitism. During the Second World War he made a series of radio broadcasts sponsored by the Italian state, and for these he was indicted for treason. At the war's end he was briefly incarcerated in a prison camp for US army deserters and criminals located near Pisa, and there he wrote the *Pisan Cantos*, a part of his lifelong project which was published to acclaim and controversy in 1948. In 1945, meanwhile, Pound was flown to Washington DC for a trial, but was declared mentally unfit to stand trial before proceedings began. He was committed to St. Elizabeth's Hospital for the Insane, where he stayed until 1958, when he moved back to Italy, where he passed his last years in Venice. He continued to publish more parts of *The Cantos* during these years, but only the final volume, *Drafts and Fragments*, has found a warm reception from critics and readers.

His career and person continue to prompt debate. In earlier accounts of modernism, Imagism, which he created in 1912, was given a prominence which few would assign it today. Vorticism, begun in 1914 with Wyndham Lewis, continues to attract interest from a range of critics and commentators. But there is still much disagreement about the arc of his career. Many of his early poems seems slight and have worn poorly, though "Hugh Selwyn Mauberley" (1920) is undoubtedly a twentieth-century masterpiece. Because virtually all his energy after that was directed to *The Cantos*, and because some stretches of *The Cantos* (those written in the 1930s, for example) are undeniably tedious and wooden, while others are undeniably great, an assessment of his oeuvre is still highly contested.

The Seafarer (From the Anglo-Saxon) (1911)

> May I for my own self song's truth reckon,
> Journey's jargon, how I in harsh days
> Hardship endured oft.
> Bitter breast-cares have I abided,

THE SEAFARER

Pound's translation was first published in the *New Age* 10(5) (Nov. 30, 1922): 107.

  The *Seafarer* is a poem in Anglo-Saxon or Old English which is preserved in a single manuscript of the tenth century. Old English poetry typically had four stressed syllables, of which three were alliterations. Pound attempts to replicate that pattern in modern English. In accordance with many commentators of his period, who regarded the later lines of the poem as an interpolation, Pound omits some verses at the end.

5
Known on my keel many a care's hold,
And dire sea-surge, and there I oft spent
Narrow nightwatch nigh the ship's head
While she tossed close to cliffs. Coldly afflicted,
My feet were by frost benumbed.

10
Chill its chains are; chafing sighs
Hew my heart round and hunger begot
Mere-weary mood. Lest man know not
That he on dry land loveliest liveth,
List how I, care-wretched, on ice-cold sea,

15
Weathered the winter, wretched outcast
Deprived of my kinsmen;
Hung with hard ice-flakes, where hail-scur flew,
There I heard naught save the harsh sea
And ice-cold wave, at whiles the swan cries,

20
Did for my games the gannet's clamour,
Sea-fowls' loudness was for me laughter,
The mews' singing all my mead-drink.
Storms, on the stone-cliffs beaten, fell on the stern
In icy feathers; full oft the eagle screamed

25
With spray on his pinion.
                              Not any protector
May make merry man faring needy.
This he little believes, who aye in winsome life
Abides 'mid burghers some heavy business,

30
Wealthy and wine-flushed, how I weary oft
Must bide above brine.
Neareth nightshade, snoweth from north,
Frost froze the land, hail fell on earth then,
Corn of the coldest. Nathless there knocketh now

35
The heart's thought that I on high streams
The salt-wavy tumult traverse alone.
Moaneth alway my mind's lust
That I fare forth, that I afar hence
Seek out a foreign fastness.

40
For this there's no mood-lofty man over earth's midst,
Not though he be given his good, but will have in his youth greed;
Nor his deed to the daring, nor his king to the faithful
But shall have his sorrow for sea-fare
Whatever his lord will.

45
He hath not heart for harping, nor in ring-having
Nor winsomeness to wife, nor world's delight
Nor any whit else save the wave's slash,
Yet longing comes upon him to fare forth on the water.
Bosque taketh blossom, cometh beauty of berries,

50
Fields to fairness, land fares brisker,
All this admonisheth man eager of mood,
The heart turns to travel so that he then thinks
On flood-ways to be far departing.
Cuckoo calleth with gloomy crying,

55
He singeth summerward, bodeth sorrow,
The bitter heart's blood. Burgher knows not –
He the prosperous man – what some perform
Where wandering them widest draweth.
So that but now my heart burst from my breastlock,

60
My mood 'mid the mere-flood,
Over the whale's acre, would wander wide.
On earth's shelter cometh oft to me,

Eager and ready, the crying lone-flyer,
Whets for the whale-path the heart irresistibly,
O'er tracks of ocean; seeing that anyhow   65
My lord deems to me this dead life
On loan and on land, I believe not
That any earth-weal eternal standeth
Save there be somewhat calamitous
That, ere a man's tide go, turn it to twain.   70
Disease or oldness or sword-hate
Beats out the breath from doom-gripped body.
And for this, every earl whatever, for those speaking after –
Laud of the living, boasteth some last word,
That he will work ere he pass onward,   75
Frame on the fair earth 'gainst foes his malice,
Daring ado, . . .
So that all men shall honour him after
And his laud beyond them remain 'mid the English,
Aye, for ever, a lasting life's-blast,   80
Delight 'mid the doughty.
                            Days little durable,
And all arrogance of earthen riches,
There come now no kings nor Cæsars
Nor gold-giving lords like those gone.   85
Howe'er in mirth most magnified,
Whoe'er lived in life most lordliest,
Drear all this excellence, delights undurable!
Waneth the watch, but the world holdeth.
Tomb hideth trouble. The blade is layed low.   90
Earthly glory ageth and seareth.
No man at all going the earth's gait,
But age fares against him, his face paleth,
Grey-haired he groaneth, knows gone companions,
Lordly men, are to earth o'ergiven,   95
Nor may he then the flesh-cover, whose life ceaseth,
Nor eat the sweet nor feel the sorry,
Nor stir hand nor think in mid heart,
And though he strew the grave with gold,
His born brothers, their buried bodies   100
Be an unlikely treasure hoard.

Portrait d'une Femme (1912)

Your mind and you are our Sargasso Sea,
London has swept about you this score years
And bright ships left you this or that in fee:
Ideas, old gossip, oddments of all things,
Strange spars of knowledge and dimmed wares of price.   5
Great minds have sought you – lacking someone else.
You have been second always. Tragical?
No. You preferred it to the usual thing:
One dull man, dulling and uxorious,
One average mind – with one thought less, each year.   10

PORTRAIT D'UNE FEMME
The poem first appeared in Pound's 1912 collection of poems,
Ripostes (London: Swift, 1912), which was released in October.

Oh, you are patient, I have seen you sit
Hours, where something might have floated up.
And now you pay one. Yes, you richly pay.
You are a person of some interest, one comes to you
15   And takes strange gain away:
Trophies fished up; some curious suggestion;
Fact that leads nowhere; and a tale or two,
Pregnant with mandrakes, or with something else
That might prove useful and yet never proves,
20   That never fits a corner or shows use,
Or finds its hour upon the loom of days:
The tarnished, gaudy, wonderful old work;
Idols and ambergris and rare inlays,
These are your riches, your great store; and yet
25   For all this sea-hoard of deciduous things,
Strange woods half sodden, and new brighter stuff:
In the slow float of differing light and deep,
No! there is nothing! In the whole and all,
Nothing that's quite your own.
30   Yet this is you.

The Return (1912)

See, they return; ah, see the tentative
Movements, and the slow feet,
The trouble in the pace and the uncertain
Wavering!

5   See, they return, one, and by one,
With fear, as half-awakened;
As if the snow should hesitate
And murmur in the wind,
                  and half turn back;
10   These were the "Wing'd-with-Awe,"
                  Inviolable.

Gods of the wingèd shoe!
With them the silver hounds,
                  sniffing the trace of air!

15   Haie! Haie!
         These were the swift to harry;
These the keen-scented;
These were the souls of blood.

Slow on the leash,
20   pallid the leash-men!

THE RETURN
The poem was first published in the *English Review* 11(3) (June
1912), at that time edited by Ford Madox Ford (see pp. 553–77).

In a Station of the Metro (1913)

The apparition of these faces in the crowd;
Petals on a wet, black bough.

Salutation the Third (1914)

Let us deride the smugness of "The Times":
GUFFAW!
        So much the gagged reviewers,
It will pay them when the worms are wriggling in their vitals;
These were they who objected to newness,   5
HERE are their TOMB·STONES.
        They supported the gag and the ring:
A little black BOX contains them.
        SO shall you be also,
You slut-bellied obstructionist,   10
        You sworn foe to free speech and good letters,
You fungus, you continuous gangrene.

Come, let us on with the new deal,
        Let us be done with Jews and Jobbery,
Let us SPIT upon those who fawn on the JEWS for their money,   15
Let us out to the pastures.

PERHAPS I will die at thirty,
Perhaps you will have the pleasure of defiling my pauper's grave,
I wish you JOY, I proffer you ALL my assistance.
It has been your HABIT for long to do away with true poets,   20
You either drive them mad, or else you blink at their suicides,
Or else you condone their drugs, and talk of insanity and genius,
BUT I will not go mad to please you.
        I will not FLATTER you with an early death.
OH, NO! I will stick it out,   25
        I will feel your hates wriggling about my feet,
And I will laugh at you and mock you,
And I will offer you consolations in irony,
        O fools, detesters of Beauty.

I have seen many who go about with supplications,   30
        Afraid to say how they hate you.
HERE is the taste of my BOOT,
        CARESS it, lick off the BLACKING.

IN A STATION OF THE METRO
The poem was first published within a sequence of shorter poems collectively titled "Contemporania" in *Poetry* 2(1) (April 1913). The poem is often considered the epitome of Imagism, typically defined as a movement initiated by Pound, one which included writers such as H.D. (see pp. 441–60) and Richard Aldington and which emphasized verbal precision. See the essays in pp. 94–7 of this volume.

SALUTATION THE THIRD
The poem was published in the first issue of *Blast* (June 1914), an avant-garde journal edited by Wyndham Lewis. It was in *Blast* that Lewis and Pound announced the establishment of Vorticism; on that movement see "Vortex. Pound" (pp. 97–9) and Wyndham Lewis's "Manifesto" (pp. 201–6).

Meditatio (1914)

When I carefully consider the curious habits of dogs,
I am compelled to admit
That man is the superior animal.

When I consider the curious habits of man,
5   I confess, my friend, I am puzzled.

Song of the Bowmen of Shu (1915)

Here we are, picking the first fern-shoots
And saying: When shall we get back to our country?
Here we are because we have the Ken-in[1] for our foemen,
We have no comfort because of these Mongols.
5   We grub the soft fern-shoots,
When anyone says "Return," the others are full of sorrow.
Sorrowful minds, sorrow is strong, we are hungry and thirsty.
Our defence is not yet made sure, no one can let his friend return.
We grub the old fern-stalks.
10   We say: Will we be let to go back in October?
There is no ease in royal affairs, we have no comfort.
Our sorrow is bitter, but we would not return to our country.
What flower has come into blossom?
Whose chariot? The General's.
15   Horses, his horses even, are tired. They were strong.
We have no rest, three battles a month.
By heaven, his horses are tired.
The generals are on them, the soldiers are by them.
The horses are well trained, the generals have ivory arrows and quivers ornamented with fish-skin.
20   The enemy is swift, we must be careful.
When we set out, the willows were drooping with spring,
We come back in the snow,
We go slowly, we are hungry and thirsty,
Our mind is full of sorrow, who will know of our grief?

Bunno[2] (Shih-ching, 167)

MEDITATIO
See the note to the poem immediately preceding this one.

SONG OF THE BOWMEN OF SHU
The poem first appeared in Cathay (London: Elkin Mathews, 1915), a collection of Pound's translations largely from Chinese poetry; the translations were based on notes which had been made by the noted American Sinologist, Ernest Fenollosa (1853–1908). Pound had been introduced to Fenollosa's widow, Mary, who had invited him to look over some of her late husband's notes on Chinese poetry. Eventually, in late 1913, she turned over his papers to Pound, who became Fenollosa's literary executor, trying to make sense of the notes which Fenollosa had assembled under the guidance of professors in Japan. Pound worked on Fenollosa's papers throughout 1914 (the same year when he also collaborating with Wyndham Lewis on Blast). The poems appeared in April 1915, followed in September 1916 by Pound's translations of Japanese plays, again based on Fenollosa, Certain Noble Plays of Japan. For Pound the experience of working with Fenollosa's papers clarified some of his central aesthetic ideas (see his essay "The Chinese Written Character as a Medium for Poetry," pp. 99–112), while for Yeats it led to his discovery of the Noh theater as a model for a drama which could dispense with realism and address a small audience.
"Song of the Bowmen of Shu" is a version of MaoShih, II, which had been translated by the great Sinologist James Legge in 1871 in The Chinese Classic (vol. 4, part 2, pp. 258–61). "Shu" is the Japanese rendering of Legge's "Chow," the modern state of Si-chuan.
[1]   Ken-in Japanese rendering of the Chinese word Hsien-yun; Legge transliterates it as "Heen-yun" and says it means "wild tribes."
[2]   Bunno Japanese for the Chinese Wen-Wang, or "King Wen of the Chou dynasty," as one Sinologist has rendered it.

The River-Merchant's Wife: A Letter (1915)

While my hair was still cut straight across my forehead
  I played about the front gate, pulling flowers.
You came by on bamboo stilts, playing horse,
You walked about my seat, playing with blue plums.
And we went on living in the village of Chōkan: 5
Two small people, without dislike or suspicion.

At fourteen I married My Lord you.
I never laughed, being bashful.
Lowering my head, I looked at the wall.
Called to, a thousand times, I never looked back.   10

At fifteen I stopped scowling,
I desired my dust to be mingled with yours
Forever and forever and forever.[1]
Why should I climb the look out?

At sixteen you departed,   15
You went into far Ku-tō-en,[2] by the river of swirling eddies,
And you have been gone five months.
The monkeys make sorrowful noise overhead.

You dragged your feet when you went out.
By the gate now, the moss is grown, the different mosses,   20
Too deep to clear them away!
The leaves fall early this autumn, in wind.
The paired butterflies are already yellow with August
Over the grass in the West garden;
They hurt me. I grow older.   25
If you are coming down through the narrows of the river Kiang,[3]
Please let me know beforehand,
And I will come out to meet you
              As far as Chō-fū-Sa.[4]

                              By Rihaku (Li T'ai Po)

Poem by the Bridge at Ten-Shin (1915)

March has come to the bridge head,
Peach boughs and apricot boughs hang over a thousand gates,
At morning there are flowers to cut the heart,
And evening drives them on the eastward-flowing waters.
Petals are on the gone waters and on the going,   5
          And on the back-swirling eddies,

THE RIVER-MERCHANT'S WIFE
See introductory note to "Song of the Bowmen of Shu." The poem's title has been invented by Pound or Fenollosa; in Chinese the poem is the first of "Two Letters from Chang-kan," by the Chinese poet Li Po.
[1] *Forever ... forever* this line is not in the original poem, but has been added by Pound, drawing on Shakespeare's "To-morrow and to-morrow, and to-morrow" (*Macbeth* V.v.19).
[2] *Ku-tō-en* the Japanese rendering of the Chinese word *Yen-yu-tui*, an island in the river H'u-tang.

[3] *Kiang* the Japanese rendering of the Chinese *Ch'ut'ang*, the river alluded to in line 16.
[4] *Chō-fū-Sa* the Japanese rendering of the Chinese *Ch'ang-feng-sha*, a place several hundred miles upriver from Nanjing.

POEM BY THE BRIDGE
The poem was first published in *Cathay* (London: Elkin Mathews, 1915). Its original title is "Ku Feng no. 18 (After the Style of Ancient Poems," according to Wai-lim Yip, *Ezra Pound's Cathay* (Princeton: Princeton University Press, 1969), 196.

But to-day's men are not the men of the old days,
Though they hang in the same way over the bridge-rail.

10
The sea's colour moves at the dawn
And the princes still stand in rows, about the throne,
And the moon falls over the portals of Sei-jō-yō,[1]
And clings to the walls and the gate-top.
With head gear glittering against the cloud and sun,
The lords go forth from the court, and into far borders.
15
They ride upon dragon-like horses,
Upon horses with head-trappings of yellow metal,
And the streets make way for their passage.
                    Haughty their passing,
Haughty their steps as they go in to great banquets,
20
To high halls and curious food,
To the perfumed air and girls dancing,
To clear flutes and clear singing;
To the dance of the seventy couples;
To the mad chase through the gardens.
25
Night and day are given over to pleasure
And they think it will last a thousand autumns,
            Unwearying autumns.
For them the yellow dogs howl portents in vain,
And what are they compared to the lady Ryokushu,[2]
30
            That was cause of hate!
Who among them is a man like Han-rei[3]
            Who departed alone with his mistress,
With her hair unbound, and he his own skiffsman!
                    By Rihaku (Li T'ai Po)

The Jewel Stairs' Grievance (1915)

The jewelled steps are already quite white with dew,
It is so late that the dew soaks my gauze stockings,
And I let down the crystal curtain
And watch the moon through the clear autumn.
                    By Rihaku (Li T'ai Po)

NOTE.—Jewel stairs, therefore a palace. Grievance, therefore there is something to complain of. Gauze stockings, therefore a court lady, not a servant who complains. Clear autumn, therefore she has no excuse on account of weather. Also she has come early, for the dew has not merely whitened the stairs, but has soaked her stockings. The poem is especially prized because she utters no direct reproach.

The Coming of War: Actaeon (1915)

An image of Lethe,
and the fields

[1]   *Sei-jō-yō* the name of a palace.
[2]   *Ryokushu* Japanese from the Chinese *Lu-chu*, a courtesan who inspired much rivalry.
[3]   *Han-rei* Japanese from the Chinese *Fan-Li*, a hero who does not stay on at court once he has accomplished his mission.

THE JEWEL STAIRS' GRIEVANCE
The poem was first published in *Cathay* (London: Elkin Mathews, 1915).

THE COMING OF WAR
The poem first appeared in *Poetry* 5(6) (March 1915). Scholars are uncertain whether the poem is meant to refer to the First World War, and if so what attitude the poem takes toward the war. In the *Metamorphoses* (III, 143–252), Ovid recounts how Actaeon was punished for having seen Diana naked, changed into a stag, and then killed.

Full of faint light
  but golden,
Gray cliffs,   5
        and beneath them
A sea
Harsher than granite,
        unstill, never ceasing;
High forms   10
        with the movement of gods,
Perilous aspect;
        And one said:
"This is Actaeon."
        Actaeon of golden greaves![1]   15
Over fair meadows,
Over the cool face of that field,
Unstill, ever moving
Hosts of an ancient people,
The silent cortège.   20

Shop Girl (1915)

For a moment she rested against me
Like a swallow half blown to the wall,
And they talk of Swinburne's women,[1]
And the shepherdess meeting with Guido.[2]
And the harlots of Baudelaire.[3]   5

O Atthis (1916)

      Thy soul
Grown delicate with satieties,
Atthis.

            O Atthis,
I long for thy lips.   5

      I long for thy narrow breasts,
      Thou restless, ungathered.

[1] *golden greaves* an imitation of Homeric formula, such as "Hector of the flashing helm." Greaves is the piece of armor that protected the lower parts a man's legs, the shins.

SHOP GIRL
The poem first appeared in *Others* 1(5) (Nov. 1915), a journal published in New York.
[1] *Swinburne's women* in poems such as "Dolores," Algernon Swinburne (1837–1909) indulged in sensuous portraiture.
[2] *Guido* Guido Cavalcanti (1250–1300), an Italian poet of the generation immediately preceding Dante's, wrote a pastoral sonnet which begins: "In un boschetto trovai pastorella" ("In a little forest I found a shepherdess"). For the full text and an enface translation, see Lowry Nelson, ed. and trans., *The Poetry of Guido Cavalcanti* (New York: Garland, 1986), pp. 74–5.
[3] *Baudelaire* Pound may be alluding to "Confession," a poem by Charles Baudelaire (1821–1867), which begins:

  Un fois, une seule, aimable et douce femme,
    A mon bras votre bras poli

  S'appuya (sur le fond ténébreux de mon âme
    Ce souvenir n'est point pâli);

  Once, a woman sweet, friendly, and alone,
    Leaned her elegant arm against mine
  (Within the shadowy background of my soul
    This memory has never withered);

There are many poems in which Baudelaire takes up the subject of prostitutes; two of the most famous are "Muse venale" ("Venal Muse") and "A une passante" ("To a Girl Passing By").

O ATTHIS
The poem was first published in *Poetry* 8(6) (Sept. 1916). When it was collected in *Lustra* (London: Elkin Mathews, 1916), its title was changed to Ἰμέρω and it was placed immediately before "Shop Girl." The Greek word *imerrō* means "I long for," and Pound is alluding to a poem by Sappho (no. 86).

The Lake Isle (1916)

O God, O Venus, O Mercury, patron of thieves,
Give me in due time, I beseech you, a little
    tobacco-shop,
With the little bright boxes
    piled up neatly upon the shelves
5   And the loose fragrant cavendish
    and the shag,
And the bright Virginia
    loose under the bright glass cases,
And a pair of scales not too greasy,[1]
10   And the whores[2] dropping in for a word or two in
    passing,
For a flip word, and to tidy their hair a bit.

O God, O Venus, O Mercury, patron of thieves,
Lend me a little tobacco-shop,
    or install me in any profession
15   Save this damn'd profession of writing,
    where one needs one's brains all the time.

Hugh Selwyn Mauberley: Introduction

The poem was first published as an independent volume in a deluxe edition limited to 200 copies, *Hugh Selwyn Mauberley* (London: Ovid Press, 1920), which appeared in June. It was republished in a more public form 17 months later in Pound's *Poems 1918–1921* (New York: Boni and Liveright, 1921). The poem is often taken as marking a key moment in the transition from Pound's early work to his mature style of *The Cantos*.

The poem is divided into two parts. The first runs from the opening through "Envoi (1919)" (or Sections I–[VIII] in Pound's numbering), and concerns the literary contacts experienced by a persona named only E.P., one whose relationship to the "real Ezra Pound" has been the subject of much debate. The second, running from "Mauberley" through the final "Medallion," concerns Hugh Selwyn Mauberley, a fictitious minor poet and aesthete. Both explore the appeal and the limitations of aestheticism, epitomized by various poets of the 1890s. Throughout the poem makes use of quatrains which rhyme A–B–X–B, following a type of quatrain used by the French poet Théophile Gautier (1811–72) in his collection of poems *Émaux et Camées*. Eliot also used this form in seven poems which he wrote from mid-1917 to mid-1919 (for two examples, see pp. 118 and 120). For both poets it marked a turn away from free verse which, though controversial when it had first reappeared around 1912, now seemed an increasingly debased and formless medium.

Hugh Selwyn Mauberley (1920)
(Life and Contacts)

The sequence is so distinctly a farewell to London that the reader who chooses to regard this as an exclusively American edition may as well omit it and turn at once to page 61.[1]

"VOCAT ÆSTUS IN UMBRAM"[2]
Nemesianus, Ec. IV.

THE LAKE ISLE
The poem was first published in *Poetry* 8(6) (Sept. 1916). Its title alludes to W. B. Yeats's early poem, "The Lake Isle of Innisfree," which expresses an urge to escape from "the pavements gray" of modern city life.
1   *scales not too greasy* perhaps alluding to Yeats's poem "September 1913," which speaks of a shopkeeper fumbling "in a greasy till."
2   *whores* the word was altered to the French term *volailles* by Harriet Monroe when the poem was first published.

HUGH SELWYN MAUBERLEY
1   *farewell to London* Pound left London in January 1920, and after extensive travel, settled in Paris in April that year.
2   *"Vocat aestus in umbram"* Latin for "The summer invites us into the shade"; it comes from the Fourth Eclogue of Nemesianus, a third-century Latin poet.

E. P. Ode Pour L'Election de son Sepulchre[3]

I

For three years, out of key with his time,
He strove to resuscitate the dead art
Of poetry; to maintain "the sublime"
In the old sense. Wrong from the start —

No, hardly, but seeing he had been born   5
In a half savage country,[4] out of date;
Bent resolutely on wringing lilies from the acorn;
Capaneus;[5] trout for factitious bait;

Ἴδμεν γάρ τοι πάνθ', ὅσ' ἐνὶ Τροίη[6]
Caught in the unstopped ear;   10
Giving the rocks small lee-way
The chopped seas held him, therefore, that year.

His true Penelope was Flaubert,[7]
He fished by obstinate isles;
Observed the elegance of Circe's[8] hair   15
Rather than the mottoes on sun-dials.

Unaffected by "the march of events,"
He passed from men's memory in l'an trentuniesme
De son eage;[9] the case presents
No adjunct to the Muses' diadem.   20

II

The age demanded an image
Of its accelerated grimace,
Something for the modern stage,
Not, at any rate, an Attic grace;

Not, not certainly, the obscure reveries   25
Of the inward gaze;
Better mendacities
Than the classics in paraphrase!

The "age demanded" chiefly a mould in plaster,
Made with no loss of time,   30

---

[3] Ode pour L'Election de Son Sepulchre French for "Ode on the Choice of His Tomb," adapted from the title of a poem by the Renaissance writer Pierre de Ronsard (1524–85), "De l'Election de Son Sepulchre."

[4] Half savage country the United States.

[5] Capaneus One of the Seven against Thebes, who was struck down by Zeus on the city wall for his impiety. Dante portrays Capaneus (Inferno XIV, 49–72) as unrepentant in the afterworld.

[6] Ἴδμεν γάρ τοι πάνθ', ὅσ' ἐνὶ Τροίη From the Odyssey, XII, 189, where these words are sung by the Sirens; to resist their song, Odysseus fills the ears of his crew with wax, but has himself lashed to the mast with ears open so that he can hear it. Ancient Greek, meaning "For we know all the things that in

Troy ..." Pound goes on to rhyme the Greek word for Troy, pronounced "Troi-ee-ay" with "lee way," the first of many bilingual or international rhymes in the poem. Such rhymes were made famous by Byron (1788–1824), in Don Juan.

[7] Flaubert Gustave Flaubert (1821–80) is here a model of craftsmanship. Penelope was the wife of Odysseus, famous for her fidelity (20 years) to her husband while he was away at the Trojan Wars and voyaging home.

[8] Circe the sorceress with whom Odysseus spent a year, so delaying his return home.

[9] l'an trentuniesme / De son eage French for "the thirty-first year of his age," a translation of the famous first line of "The Testament" of Francois Villon (1431–c.1485).

A prose kinema,[10] not, not assuredly, alabaster
Or the "sculpture" of rhyme.

III

The tea-rose tea-gown,[11] etc.
Supplants the mousseline of Cos,[12]
35   The pianola "replaces"
Sappho's barbitos.[13]

Christ follows Dionysus,[14]
Phallic and ambrosial
Made way for macerations;
40   Caliban casts out Ariel.[15]

All things are a flowing,
Sage Heracleitus[16] says;
But a tawdry cheapness
Shall outlast our days.

45   Even the Christian beauty
Defects – after Samothrace;[17]
We see τὸ καλόν[18]
Decreed in the market place.

Faun's flesh is not to us,
50   Nor the saint's vision.
We have the press for wafer;
Franchise[19] for circumcision.

All men, in law, are equals.
Free of Pisistratus,[20]
55   We choose a knave or an eunuch
To rule over us.

O bright Apollo,
τίν' ἄνδρα, τίν' ἥρωα, τινα θεόν,[21]
What god, man, or hero
60   Shall I place a tin wreath upon!

[10]   *kinema* the Greek word for "movement," a term which gives rise to modern "cinema," the place where one sees "moving" or motion pictures.

[11]   *Tea-gown* a formal gown worn by women in the early 1900s, resembling a modern housecoat but more formal.

[12]   *Cos* a Greek island famous in antiquity for its muslin.

[13]   *Sappho's barbitos* "barbitos" is the ancient Greek word for a musical instrument of many strings, like the lyre, or the lyre itself. Sappho (sixth century BC) is here the model lyrical poet from antiquity.

[14]   *Dionysius* the Greek god of wine, associated with ecstatic and sensual celebrations, who is displaced by the "macerations" or excessive fastings of Christianity.

[15]   *Caliban . . Ariel* Caliban, a gross and monstrous earth-spirit who curses, and Ariel, a spirit of the air who makes music, are characters in Shakespeare's *Tempest*.

[16]   *Heraclitus* (c. 535–475 BC) was an ancient Greek philosopher whose famous pronouncement is translated here.

[17]   *after Samothrace* a Greek island whose religious cults had become extinct; even Christianity is now in danger of becoming equally extinct, or perhaps as fragmentary the *Victory of Samothrace* (see "The Founding and the Manifesto of Futurism," n. 4).

[18]   *to kalon* "the beautiful" in ancient Greek.

[19]   *Franchise* the right to vote, which was extended repeatedly to encompass more (male) citizens during the late nineteenth century; extending the franchise to women was the subject of intense debate in Britain throughout the period 1910–20. Many women were given the right to vote in 1920, which was extended to include all women in 1928.

[20]   *Pisistratus* (d. 527 BC) was a tyrant who ruled over Athens.

[21]   *tin andra, tin heroa, tina theon* Greek for "Which man, which hero, which God," a phrase from a poem by Pindar (*Olympian Odes*, II, 2). Pound achieves a bilingual pun with English "tin" played off against various forms of "which" (or "tin" and "tina") in ancient Greek.

IV

These fought in any case,
and some believing,
         pro domo,[22] in any case . . .

Some quick to arm,
some for adventure,   65
some from fear of weakness,
some from fear of censure,
some for love of slaughter, in imagination,
learning later . . .
some in fear, learning love of slaughter;   70

Died some, pro patria,
         non "dulce" non "et decor"[23] . . .
walked eye-deep in hell
believing in old men's lies, then unbelieving
came home, home to a lie,   75
home to many deceits,
home to old lies and new infamy;
usury age-old and age-thick
and liars in public places.

Daring as never before, wastage as never before.   80
Young blood and high blood,
fair cheeks, and fine bodies;

fortitude as never before

frankness as never before,
disillusions as never told in the old days,   85
hysterias, trench confessions,
laughter out of dead bellies.

V

There died a myriad,
And of the best, among them,
For an old bitch gone in the teeth,   90
For a botched civilization,

Charm, smiling at the good mouth,
Quick eyes gone under earth's lid,

For two gross of broken statues,
For a few thousand battered books.   95

---

[22] *Pro domo* Latin for "for the sake of home" and an adaptation of the phrase "pro patria," Latin for "for the sake of the fatherland," a phrase which is used in a poem by Horace quoted eight lines below this one (see next note).

[23] *Pro patria . . . "et decor"* Horace, *Odes* III, 2, 13, "Dulce et decorum est pro patria mori," or Latin for "It is sweet and honorable to die for the fatherland." Pounds adds the negative "non" to reverse Horace's sentiment.

Yeux Glauques[24]

Gladstone[25] was still respected,
When John Ruskin produced
"Kings' Treasuries"[26]; Swinburne
And Rossetti still abused.

5   Fœtid Buchanan[27] lifted up his voice
When that faun's head of hers[28]
Became a pastime for
Painters and adulterers.

    The Burne-Jones cartons
10   Have preserved her eyes;
Still, at the Tate, they teach
Cophetua to rhapsodize;

    Thin like brook-water,
With a vacant gaze.
15   The English Rubaiyat[29] was still-born
In those days.

    The thin, clear gaze, the same
Still darts out faun-like from the half-ruin'd face,
Questing and passive....
20   "Ah, poor Jenny's case"[30] ...

    Bewildered that a world
Shows no surprise
At her last maquero's[31]
Adulteries.

"Siena mi fe'; disfecemi Maremma"[32]

Among the pickled fœtuses and bottled bones,
Engaged in perfecting the catalogue,
I found the last scion of the
Senatorial families of Strasbourg, Monsieur Verog.[33]

[24] *Yeux Glauques* French for "sea-green eyes," an image in late nineteenth-century poetry; eyes recur through this passage.

[25] *Gladstone* William Ewart Gladstone (1809–98) was British prime minister 1868–74, 1880–5, 1886, 1892–4; he has a reputation as a self-righteous moralist.

[26] *"King's Treasuries"* the first chapter in John Ruskin's book *Sesame and Lilies* (1865), which denounces the contemporary culture for disdaining literature, art, science, natural beauty, and compassion.

[27] *Buchanan* Robert Buchanan (1841–1901) is remembered today only for having written a famous essay, "The Fleshly School of Poetry" (1871), which condemned the Pre-Raphaelite poets as immoral, chief among them Dante Gabriel Rossetti (1828–82) and Algernon Swinburne (1827–1909).

[28] *faun's head of hers* the head of Elizabeth Siddal, which inspired several paintings by Dante Gabriel Rossetti and one by Sir Edward Burne-Jones (1833–98), *Cophetua and the Beggar Maid* (Tate Gallery, London).

[29] *The Rubaiyat of Omar Khayyam*, a translation of Persian poetry by Edward Fitzgerald, was published in 1859, but disregarded until it was discovered by Rossetti a year later.

[30] *Poor Jenny's case* the poem "Jenny," by Rossetti, was singled out for attention in Robert Buchanan's attack against the Pre-Raphaelites. The poem is about a prostitute.

[31] *maquero* French for a pimp.

[32] *Siena ... Maremma* Italian for "Siena bore me; the Maremma undid me." The Maremma is a swampy area in southern Tuscany where Pia dei Tolomei, a character in Dante's *Purgatorio* (V, 133), was allegedly murdered by her husband. She represents souls who have found salvation at the last moment. Compare Eliot's adaption of this same line at the end of Part III of *The Waste Land*, ll. 293–4, in this edition p. 135.

[33] *Monsieur Verog* thought to be modeled on Victor Plarr (1863–1929), a lyric poet of the 1890s who became librarian to the Royal College of Surgeons in London and prepared a *Catalogue of Manuscripts in the Library of the Royal College of Surgeons of England*, finally completed in 1928. His poems were

For two hours he talked of Galliffet;[34]   5
Of Dowson;[35] of the Rhymers' Club;[36]
Told me how Johnson (Lionel)[37] died
By falling from a high stool in a pub . . .

But showed no trace of alcohol
At the autopsy, privately performed—   10
Tissue preserved—the pure mind
Arose toward Newman[38] as the whiskey warmed.

Dowson found harlots cheaper than hotels;
Headlam[39] for uplift; Image[40] impartially imbued
With raptures for Bacchus, Terpsichore and the Church.   15
So spoke the author of "The Dorian Mood,"[41]

M. Verog, out of step with the decade,
Detached from his contemporaries,
Neglected by the young,
Because of these reveries.   20

Brennbaum[42]

The sky-like limpid eyes,
The circular infant's face,
The stiffness from spats to collar
Never relaxing into grace;

The heavy memories of Horeb, Sinai and the forty years,[43]   5
Showed only when the daylight fell
Level across the face
Of Brennbaum "The Impeccable."

Mr. Nixon[44]

In the cream gilded cabin of his steam yacht
Mr. Nixon advised me kindly, to advance with fewer

collected in a volume titled *In the Dorian Mood* (London: John Lane; New York: George Richmond, 1896), which is mentioned below at line 135.
[34] *Galliffet* Gaston Alexandre Auguste de Gallifet (1830–1909) was a French general in the Franco-Prussian War.
[35] *Dowson* Ernest Dowson (1867–1900) was a lyrical poet of the 1890s.
[36] *the Rhymers' Club* an informal association of poets who from 1891 met at the Cheshire Cheese, a London restaurant; other members were Yeats and Ernest Dowson.
[37] *Johnson (Lionel)* Lionel Johnson was a prolific minor poet (1867–1902) who was a cousin of Dorothy Shakespeare, Pound's wife; Pound edited the *Poetical Works of Lionel Johnson* (London: Elkin Mathews) in 1915. The story that he died by falling from a stool in a pub was apocryphal.
[38] *Newman* John Henry Cardinal Newman (1801–90) was a convert to Catholicism, like Lionel Johnson and many writers of the 1890s.
[39] *Headlam* Rev. Stewart D. Headlam (1847–1924) was a friend of several writers of the 1890s.

[40] *Image* Selwyn Image (1849–1930) was a minor poet who wrote *New Poems* (1908); he drank excessively ("Bacchus"), wrote *The Art of Dancing* (London: Office of the "Church Reformer," 1891) ("Terpsichore" is the muse of dancing), and was interested in ecclesiastical matters ("the Church").
[41] *"The Dorian Mood"* See above, note 33.
[42] *Brennbaum* thought to be modeled on Max Beerbohm (1872–1956), a noted dandy, known as the "Incomparable Max," who left London for Italy in 1910.
[43] *Horeb, Sinai and the forty years* Horeb or Sinai was the mountain where Moses received the Tables of the Law, or the Ten Commandments; after the Exodus from Egypt, the Israelites spent 40 years in the wilderness before coming to the promised land. For some critics these words suggest that Brennbaum is ignoring the spiritual inheritance of Judaism; for others they are anti-Semitic.
[44] *Mr. Nixon* Thought to be modeled on Arnold Bennett (1867–1931), a highly successful English novelist who is also criticized by Virginia Woolf (see p. 901). To the modernists, he represented the established literary order: a writer in the realist tradition who actively courted popular success and large financial rewards.

Dangers of delay. "Consider
    "Carefully the reviewer.

5   "I was as poor as you are;
"When I began I got, of course,
"Advance on royalties, fifty at first," said Mr. Nixon,
"Follow me, and take a column,
"Even if you have to work free.

10   "Butter reviewers. From fifty to three hundred
"I rose in eighteen months;
"The hardest nut I had to crack
"Was Dr. Dundas.

15   "I never mentioned a man but with the view
"Of selling my own works.
"The tip's a good one, as for literature
"It gives no man a sinecure.

"And no one knows, at sight, a masterpiece.
"And give up verse, my boy,
20   "There's nothing in it."

.   .   .   .   .   .

Likewise a friend of Blougram's[45] once advised me:
Don't kick against the pricks,[46]
Accept opinion. The "Nineties" tried your game
And died, there's nothing in it.

X

Beneath the sagging roof
The stylist[47] has taken shelter,
Unpaid, uncelebrated,
At last from the world's welter

5   Nature receives him;
With a placid and uneducated mistress
He exercises his talents
And the soil meets his distress.

The haven from sophistications and contentions
10   Leaks through its thatch;
He offers succulent cooking;
The door has a creaking latch.

XI

"Conservatrix of Milésien"[48]
Habits of mind and feeling,

[45] *Blougram's* "Bishop Blougram" (1855) is a poem by Robert Browning (1812–99) in which a cynical priest offers a casuistic defense of himself.
[46] *Don't kick against the pricks* Christ tells Saul, later Saint Paul: "It is hard for thee to kick against the pricks" (Acts 9:5), i.e. make useless resistance against something that only hurts oneself.

[47] *stylist* sometimes thought to be modeled on Ford Madox Ford (1873–1939; see pp. 553–77), who in 1919 moved to a remote cottage in West Sussex. "The stylist," whether or not he is modeled on Ford, is in antithesis to Mr. Nixon.
[48] *"Conservatrix of Milésien"* an adaption of a phrase that appears in "Stratgemes," a short story by Remy de Gourmont

Possibly. But in Ealing[49]
With the most bank-clerkly of Englishmen?

No, "Milésian" is an exaggeration.   5
No instinct has survived in her
Older than those her grandmother
Told her would fit her station.

XII

"Daphne with her thighs in bark
Stretches toward me her leafy hands,"[50] –
Subjectively. In the stuffed-satin drawing-room
I await The Lady Valentine's commands,

Knowing my coat has never been   5
Of precisely the fashion
To stimulate, in her,
A durable passion;

Doubtful, somewhat, of the value
Of well-gowned approbation   10
Of literary effort,
But never of The Lady Valentine's vocation:

Poetry, her border of ideas,
The edge, uncertain, but a means of blending
With other strata   15
Where the lower and higher have ending;

A hook to catch the Lady Jane's attention,
A modulation toward the theatre,
Also, in the case of revolution,
A possible friend and comforter.   20

.   .   .   .

Conduct, on the other hand, the soul
"Which the highest cultures have nourished"[51]
To Fleet St. where
Dr. Johnson[52] flourished;

(1858–1915) which appears in his book, *Histoires Magiques* (1894), or *Magical Stories*. The phrase, in turn, owes its significance to the *Milesian Tales* by Aristides of Miletus (*c*. 100 BC), an ancient Greek collection of erotic, often obscene, short stories which have been lost, but were translated into Latin and sufficiently current that the expression *Milesiae fabulae* ("Milesian tales") became in Rome a generic title for erotic short stories. With this tradition in mind, Gourmont writes: "Some women, in the right situation, know how to bite. They should not be disdained, these preservers of Milesian traditions [ces conservatrices des traditions milesiennes] – but it can be a bit monotonous, and only rarely are they artists."

[49]   *Ealing* an eastern suburb of London, token of dull respectability.

[50]   *"Daphne ... hands"* Translated from Théophile Gautier (see introductory note to this poem) "Le Château du Souvenir" ("The Castle of Memory"):

Daphné, les hanches dans l'écorce
Étend toujours ses doigts touffus....

Lady Valentine possesses a copy of *Daphne and Apollo*, a famous statue by the Renaissance artist Benvenuto Cellini, which depicts a scene from Ovid's *Metamorphoses* (I.548–52), the foiled rape of Daphne by Apollo and her subsequent metamorphosis. Pound, in 1912 and 1913, gave a series of private lectures at the homes of wealthy socialites, one of whom was Lady Glenconner, sister-in-law of H. H. Asquith, at that time the prime minister.

[51]   *"Conduct ... nourished"* Pound is translating from the opening line of "Complainte des Pianos," a poem by Jules Laforgue (1860–87): "Menez l'âme que les Lettres ont bien nourrie" ("Guide the soul which Letters have well nourished").

[52]   *Dr. Johnson* Samuel Johnson (1709–84), the English author and essayist who is here the type of the eighteenth-century man of letters; Fleet Street was the center of London journalism until the 1970s.

25   Beside this thoroughfare
       The sale of half-hose has
       Long since superseded the cultivation
       Of Pierian roses.[53]

Envoi (1919)[54]

Go, dumb-born book,
Tell her that sang me once that song of Lawes:[55]
Hadst thou but song
As thou hast subjects known,
5   *Then were there cause in thee that should condone*
     Even my faults that heavy upon me lie,
     And build her glories their longevity.

     Tell her that sheds
     Such treasure in the air,
10   *Recking naught else but that her graces give*
     Life to the moment,
     I would bid them live
     As roses might, in magic amber laid,
     Red overwrought with orange and all made
15   *One substance and one colour*
     Braving time.

     Tell her that goes
     With song upon her lips
     But sings not out the song, nor knows
20   *The maker of it, some other mouth,*
     May be as fair as hers,
     Might, in new ages, gain her worshippers,
     When our two dusts with Waller's shall be laid,
     Siftings on siftings in oblivion,
25   *Till change hath broken down*
     All things save Beauty alone.

Mauberley (1920)

"Vacuos exercet in aera morsus."[56]

I

Turned from the "eau-forte
Par Jacquemart"[57]

[53] *Pierian roses* Pieria was a district near Mt. Olympus where the Muses were born. The line may also allude to Sappho, LXXI: "for you have no part in the roses that come from Pieria."
[54] *Envoi (1919)* this section is a pastiche of the song "Go, Lovely Rose," by Edmund Waller (1606–87), which begins:

    Go lovely Rose,
        Tell her that wastes her time and me,
        That now she knows
    When I resemble her to thee
        How sweet and fair she seems to be.

Whether this pastiche is spoken by "E.P." or the fictitious poet Mauberley is a subject of debate.
[55] *Lawes* Henry Lawes (1598–1687) was an English composer who set Waller's poem to music.
[56] *"Vacuos ... morsus"* Latin for "He bites the empty air," and quoted with a minor inaccuracy ("Vacuos" instead of "vanos") from Ovid, *Metamorphoses* (VII.786), where "he" is a dog named Laelaps that is trying to bite an elusive monster which is ravaging Thebes.
[57] *"eau-forte / Par Jacquemart"* an etching of the French poet Théophile Gautier (see introductory note to this poem) by

To the strait head
Of Messalina:[58]

"His true Penelope   5
Was Flaubert,"
And his tool
The engraver's.

Firmness,
Not the full smile,   10
His art, but an art
In profile;

Colourless
Pier Francesca,[59]
Pisanello[60] lacking the skill   15
To forge Achaia.

II

"Qu'est ce qu'ils savent de l'amour, et qu'est ce qu'ils peuvent en comprendre?
    S'ils ne comprennent pas la poésie, s'ils ne sentent pas la musique, qu'est ce qu'ils peuvent comprendre de
cette passion en comparaison avec laquelle la rose est grossière et le parfum des violettes un tonnerre?"

Caid Ali[61]

For three years, diabolus[62] in the scale,
He drank ambrosia,
All passes, ANANGKE[63] prevails,
Came end, at last, to that Arcadia.[64]

He had moved amid her phantasmagoria,   5
Amid her galaxies,
NUKTOS 'AGALMA[65]

.   .   .   .

Drifted . . . drifted precipitate,
Asking time to be rid of . . .
Of his bewilderment; to designate   10
His new found orchid. . . .

J. F. Jacquemart (1837–90) appears as the frontispiece for the 1881 edition of Gautier's *Émaux et Camées.*
[58] *Messalina* wife of the Roman emperor Claudius, noted for her licentiousness; the key contrast, however, is between Jacquemart's etching ("eau-forte") and a more classical portrait of Messalina.
[59] *Pier Francesca* Piero della Francesca (*c.* 1420–92), a Renaissance artist famous for his firm lines and pure forms; Piero also appears in the "Malatesta Cantos" by Pound (see p. 67n. 9).
[60] *Pisanello* Antonio Pisanello (1395–*c.*1455) is generally considered the greatest of the Renaissance medalists; he too figures in the "Malatesta Cantos," p. 78, Jacquemart, as an engraver, is like Pisanello, a medallist, but he cannot create art comparable to that of ancient Greece (Achaia).
[61] *Caid Ali* is a fictitious name and the French epigraph ascribed to him was actually written by Pound. It means:

"What do they know about love, and what can they understand of it? If they don't understand poetry, if they don't listen to music, what can they understand of this feeling, in comparison with which a rose is gross and the perfume of violets is thunderous?"
[62] *Diabolus* The diabolus – the term literally means "devil" in Latin – was the interval of the augmented fourth, one which gave medieval musicians great difficulty.
[63] *ANANGKE* Greek for "Necessity."
[64] *Arcadia* a land of idyllic peace and pastoral ease.
[65] *NUKTOS 'AGALMA* "the jewel of night" in Greek, from a poem by the Greek pastoral poet Bion (*c.* 100 BC), whose work survives in only 17 fragments. This phrase occurs in Fragment X.

To be certain . . . certain . . .
(Amid ærial flowers) . . . time for arrangements –
Drifted on
15   To the final estrangement;

Unable in the supervening blankness
To sift TO AGATHON[66] from the chaff
Until he found his sieve . . .
Ultimately, his seismograph:

20   – Given that is his "fundamental passion,"
This urge to convey the relation
Of eye-lid and cheek-bone
By verbal manifestation;

To present the series
25   Of curious heads in medallion –

He had passed, inconscient, full gaze,
The wide-banded irides
And botticellian sprays implied
In their diastasis;[67]

30   Which anæthesis,[68] noted a year late,
And weighed, revealed his great affect,
(Orchid), mandate
Of Eros, a retrospect.

                    .   .   .

Mouths biting empty air,
35   The still stone dogs,
Caught in metamorphosis, were
Left him as epilogues.

"The Age Demanded"

VIDE POEM II. PAGE 49

For this agility chance found
Him of all men, unfit
As the red-beaked steeds[69] of
The Cytheræan for a chain bit.

5   The glow of porcelain
Brought no reforming sense
To his perception
Of the social inconsequence.

Thus, if her colour
10   Came against his gaze,
Tempered as if
It were through a perfect glaze

---

[66]   TO AGATHON Greek for "the good."
[67]   diastasis separation.
[68]   anaesthesis inability to feel or perceive.

[69]   red-beaked steads doves which drew the carriage of Venus, the Cytherean (next line).

He made no immediate application
Of this to relation of the state
To the individual, the month was more temperate   15
Because this beauty had been.

      The coral isle, the lion-coloured sand
      Burst in upon the porcelain revery:
      Impetuous troubling
      Of his imagery.   20

Mildness, amid the neo-Nietzschean clatter,[70]
His sense of graduations,
Quite out of place amid
Resistance to current exacerbations,

Invitation, mere invitation to perceptivity   25
Gradually led him to the isolation
Which these presents place
Under a more tolerant, perhaps, examination.

By constant elimination
The manifest universe   30
Yielded an armour
Against utter consternation,

A Minoan[71] undulation,
Seen, we admit, amid ambrosial circumstances
Strengthened him against   35
The discouraging doctrine of chances,

And his desire for survival,
Faint in the most strenuous moods,
Became an Olympian *apathein*[72]
In the presence of selected perceptions.   40

A pale gold, in the aforesaid pattern,
The unexpected palms
Destroying, certainly, the artist's urge,
Left him delighted with the imaginary
Audition of the phantasmal sea-surge,[73]   45

Incapable of the least utterance or composition,
Emendation, conservation of the "better tradition,"
Refinement of medium, elimination of superfluities,
August attraction or concentration.

Nothing, in brief, but maudlin confession,   50
Irresponse to human aggression,
Amid the precipitation, down-float
Of insubstantial manna,
Lifting the faint susurrus[74]
Of his subjective hosannah.   55

---

[70] neo-Nietzschean clatter see *Nietzsche in England, 1890–1914: The Growth of a Reputation*, by David S. Thatcher (Toronto: University of Toronto Press, 1970).
[71] *Minoan* Minos was a legendary king of Crete, and the "Minoan" period ran from 2000 to 1500 BC in Crete; but the general sense here is that of "archaic."
[72] *apathein* imperviousness to feeling or suffering, indifference.
[73] *sea-surge* compare line 6 in Pound's translation of "The Seafarer," p. 40.
[74] *susurrus* whisper in Latin.

Ultimate affronts to
Human redundancies;

Non-esteem of self-styled "his betters"
Leading, as he well knew,
60   To his final
Exclusion from the world of letters.

IV

Scattered Moluccas[75]
Not knowing, day to day,
The first day's end, in the next noon;
The placid water
5   Unbroken by the Simoon;[76]

Thick foliage
Placid beneath warm suns,
Tawn fore-shores
Washed in the cobalt of oblivions;

10   Or through dawn-mist
The grey and rose
Of the juridical
Flamingoes;

A consciousness disjunct,
15   Being but this overblotted
Series
Of intermittences;

Coracle of Pacific voyages,
The unforecasted beach;
20   Then on an oar
Read this:

"I was
And I no more exist;
Here drifted
25   An hedonist."

Medallion[77]

Luini[78] in porcelain!
The grand piano
Utters a profane
Protest with her clear soprano.

---

[75] *Moluccas* spice-producing island in the Malaysian archipelago.
[76] *Simoon* hot, dry winds in the deserts of Arabia and North
Africa.

[77] *Medallion* it is widely agreed that this section reports a poem
written by the fictitious persona, Mauberley.
[78] *Luini* Bernardino Luini (c. 1475–1532), a Milanese painter
whose work is extremely mannered.

The sleek head emerges   5
From the gold-yellow frock
As Anadyomene[79] in the opening
Pages of Reinach.

Honey-red, closing the face-oval,
A basket-work of braids which seem as if they were   10
Spun in King Minos' hall
From metal, or intractable amber;

The face-oval beneath the glaze,
Bright in its suave bounding-line, as,
Beneath half-watt rays,   15
The eyes turn topaz.

From *The Cantos*: Introduction

Ezra Pound published drafts of the first three cantos in 1917, but he was continually revising these and adding more cantos until, by 1922, he had reached a total of eight. Then, from the middle of that year until the spring of 1923 he worked on the four "Malatesta Cantos" (see pp. 66–89), so called because they treat the life and doings of Sigismondo Malatesta (1417–68), the first time that Pound had worked on a block of cantos as a unit. Completing these enabled Pound to revise the earlier cantos, which he reduced to seven, then to write another five, and finally to publish *A Draft of XVI Cantos* (Paris: Three Mountains Press) in 1925. Three years later he issued *A Draft of the Cantos 17–27* (London: John Rodker, 1928), a block of cantos which concerned Renaissance rulers in Venice and Ferrara, Italy. Both these editions were deluxe editions limited to 90 and 94 copies.

Pound returned to Italian subject-matter once again, and in 1930 published *A Draft of XXX Cantos* (Paris: the Hours Press), this time in a limited edition of 200 copies, a volume reproduced three years later by Farrar Rinehart in the United States and Faber & Faber in Britain.

In the decade between 1930 and 1940, Pound issued new collections of cantos at a prodigious rate: *Eleven New Cantos* (1934), *The Fifth Decad of Cantos* (1937), and *Cantos LII–LXXI*. These treat early American presidents, such as Thomas Jefferson (31–3) and John Quincy Adams (34), medieval banking systems and Mussolini (42–51), Confucian ethics and Chinese history (52–61), and another early American president, John Adams (62–71). The rapid rate of production, coupled with Pound's numerous literary and political projects during this period, led to a perceptible waning of power, and many readers find this large block of cantos tedious and steadily coarsening in texture. Late during the Second World War Pound also wrote two cantos in Italian, exhorting Italians to fight against approaching American and British troops, though these were not included with editions of *The Cantos* until 1986.

Meanwhile, Pound wrote the Pisan Cantos in mid-1945 when, now 57 years old, he was confined in a small, outdoor cage in a prison for military criminals. In these hostile circumstances, Pound recorded a "dark night of the soul" which concludes with a vision of Aphrodite at the end. *The Pisan Cantos*, published in 1948, are sometimes racist and often defensive about Pound's adherence to Fascism, yet for many readers they have a compelling poetic power not seen in his work of the 1930s. While confined in St. Elizabeth's Hospital in Washington DC, Pound wrote two more books of cantos, *Section: Rock Drill* (1955) and *Thrones* (1959). His last volume of cantos appeared in 1969, *Drafts and Fragments of Cantos CX–CXVII*, a deeply moving mixture of intimate confession and fragmentary glimpses of visionary moments.

Canto I, except for the last nine lines, is a free translation of the beginning of Book XI of the *Odyssey*, which recounts Odysseus's descent to the underworld and his encounters with a series of ghosts. The incident acquires a paradigmatic status: the solitary individual, though firmly situated in the present, must confront a personal and cultural past which has been rendered weird and uncanny, simultaneously recognizable and yet alien, strange, distorted. The experience of Odysseus, in turn, becomes a paradigm for that of the reader: the incident of his descent to the underworld is immediately recognizable, yet the style and tone of the entire passage have turned it into something strange and

---

[79] *Anadyomene* i.e. Venus Anadyomene, or the image of Venus rising from the sea. Salomon Reinach (1858–1932), a French art historian, wrote *Apollo: Histoire générale des arts plastiques professée en 1902–1903 à l'École du Louvre* (Paris: Librairie Hachette, 1904), which was translated by Florence Simmonds into English as *Apollo: A General History of the Plastic Arts* (London: Heinemann, 1906). Figure 83 shows a "Head of Aphrodite" which Pound probably had in mind.

startling. This is not a translation that tries to achieve literal fidelity to its original. Nor is it a translation that seeks to convert ancient conventions (the unrhymed lines of 12 syllables that characterize Greek epic) into contemporary conventions (the iambic pentameter line, say, generally so typical of literary poetry in English). The Homeric line, instead, is converted into something almost bizarre: speech that partakes of the colloquial and discernibly modern ("And Anticlea came, whom I beat off, and then Tiresias Theban, / Holding his golden wand...") but is flavored with the stilted dignity of the archaic ("'Elpenor, how art thou come to this dark coast?'"). It is uneasy speech, in short, and it has been superimposed on the rhythm of Old English or Anglo-Saxon poetry, in which three stressed syllables out of four are marked by alliteration (line 4: "Bore sheep aboard her, and our bodies also"). Though this is ostensibly a translation of Homer into English, then, the identity of all the key terms is soon cast into doubt. Moreover, by the end of the canto, an unnamed narrator confesses that he (or is it she?) is translating not from Homer's Greek original, but from a Latin rendering of Homer which was published in 1538.

Canto I (1917/1925)

And then went down to the ship,
Set keel to breakers, forth on the godly sea, and
We set up mast and sail on that swart ship,
Bore sheep aboard her, and our bodies also
5   Heavy with weeping, and winds from sternward
Bore us out onward with bellying canvas,
Circe's[1] this craft, the trim-coifed goddess.
Then sat we amidships, wind jamming the tiller,
Thus with stretched sail, we went over sea till day's end.
10   Sun to his slumber, shadows o'er all the ocean,
Came we then to the bounds of deepest water,
To the Kimmerian lands,[2] and peopled cities
Covered with close-webbed mist, unpierced ever
With glitter of sun-rays
15   Nor with stars stretched, nor looking back from heaven
Swartest night stretched over wretched men there.
The ocean flowing backward, came we then to the place
Aforesaid by Circe.
Here did they rites, Perimedes and Eurylochus,[3]
20   And drawing sword from my hip
I dug the ell-square pitkin;[4]
Poured we libations unto each the dead,
First mead and then sweet wine, water mixed with white flour.
Then prayed I many a prayer to the sickly death's-heads;
25   As set in Ithaca, sterile bulls of the best
For sacrifice, heaping the pyre with goods,
A sheep to Tiresias only, black and a bell-sheep.[5]
Dark blood flowed in the fosse,[6]
Souls out of Erebus,[7] cadaverous dead, of brides
30   Of youths and of the old who had borne much;
Souls stained with recent tears, girls tender,
Men many, mauled with bronze lance heads,
Battle spoil, bearing yet dreory[8] arms,

---

[1]   *Circe's* Odysseus has left the island where he had spent a year with the goddess Circe. She has told him he must go to the mouth of the underworld to consult with the prophet Tiresias on how best to return to his home in Ithaca.

[2]   *Kimmerian lands* mythical places at the edge of the world.

[3]   *Perimedes and Eurylochus* two crew members.

[4]   *the ell-square pitkin* an ell is a measure of length equal to roughly a yard; a pitkin is a small pit.

[5]   *bell-sheep* the one that leads a flock. Tiresias has been given the gift of prophecy. Compare *The Waste Land*, Part III (p. 132 line 218 and note, in this edition).

[6]   *fosse* a trench or ditch.

[7]   *Erebus* another name for the underworld, or Hades.

[8]   *dreory* a modified version of *dreorig*, an Anglo-Saxon word meaning bloody.

These many crowded about me; with shouting,
Pallor upon me, cried to my men for more beasts;   35
Slaughtered the herds, sheep slain of bronze;
Poured ointment, cried to the gods,
To Pluto the strong, and praised Proserpine;[9]
Unsheathed the narrow sword,
I sat to keep off the impetuous impotent dead,   40
Till I should hear Tiresias.
But first Elpenor[10] came, our friend Elpenor,
Unburied, cast on the wide earth,
Limbs that we left in the house of Circe,
Unwept, unwrapped in sepulchre, since toils urged other.   45
Pitiful spirit. And I cried in hurried speech:
"Elpenor, how art thou come to this dark coast?
"Cam'st thou afoot, outstripping seamen?"
          And he in heavy speech:
"Ill fate and abundant wine. I slept in Circe's ingle.   50
"Going down the long ladder unguarded,
"I fell against the buttress,
"Shattered the nape-nerve, the soul sought Avernus.[11]
"But thou, O King, I bid remember me, unwept, unburied,
"Heap up mine arms, be tomb by sea-bord, and inscribed: 55
"A man of no fortune, and with a name to come.
"And set my oar up, that I swung mid fellows."

And Anticlea[12] came, whom I beat off, and then Tiresias Theban,
Holding his golden wand, knew me, and spoke first:
"A second time? why? man of ill star,   60
"Facing the sunless dead and this joyless region?
"Stand from the fosse, leave me my bloody bever[13]
"For soothsay."
          And I stepped back,
And he strong with the blood, said then: "Odysseus   65
"Shalt return through spiteful Neptune,[14] over dark seas,
"Lose all companions." And then Anticlea came.
Lie quiet Divus. I mean, that is Andreas Divus,[15]
In officina Wecheli, 1538, out of Homer.
And he sailed, by Sirens and thence outward and away   70
And unto Circe.
          Venerandam,[16]
In the Cretan's phrase,[17] with the golden crown, Aphrodite,
Cypri munimenta sortita est,[18] mirthful, orichalchi,[19] with golden

[9] *Pluto ... Proserpine* Pluto was the Roman lord of the under-world, Proserpina his wife.

[10] *Elpenor* a companion of Odysseus who had earlier fallen from the roof of Circe's house and, not having been discovered by his companions, had not received burial rites.

[11] *Avernus* a lake near Cumae and Naples, where there was a cave thought to lead to the underworld; the Trojan hero Aeneas descends there to Hades to learn the future. By extension, Avernus becomes Hades itself.

[12] *Anticlea* the mother of Odysseus, whom he cannot address until after he has spoken to Tiresias.

[13] *bever* a drink, as in the word *beverage*.

[14] *spiteful Neptune* the Roman god of the seas; Odysseus will be shipwrecked.

[15] *Andreas Divus* (fl. 1535) was a classical scholar who translated Homer's *Odyssey* into Latin; the speaker cites the 1538 edition published "in officina Wecheli," or "at the publishing house of Wechelus."

[16] *Venerandam* Latin for "to be reverenced"; the epithet is applied to Aphrodite in the sixth Homeric Hymn, a work also translated into Latin around 1535 and included in the same edition of 1538.

[17] *in the Cretan's phrase* a translation of the Homeric Hymns was made by Georgius Darton, from Crete, and included in the 1538 edition of the *Odyssey*.

[18] *Cypri ... est* Aphrodite "has been allotted the citadels of Cyprus," again from the sixth Homeric Hymn.

[19] *orichalchi* Latin for "of copper," alluding again to the Homeric Hymn in which votive gifts of copper and gold are made for Aphrodite.

Girdles and breast bands, thou with dark eyelids
Bearing the golden bough of Argicida.[20] So that:

The Malatesta Cantos, VIII to XI: Introduction

Ezra Pound first encountered the church of San Francesco in Rimini, Italy, in May of 1922, some five months after he had finished editing *The Waste Land* (see p. 123). To residents of Rimini the building is known simply as *il duomo* ("the cathedral"), but to art historians it is "the tempio malatestiano," or more simply, the "Tempio," a landmark building in architectural history because it was the first work of ecclesiastical architecture to incorporate a Roman triumphal arch into its design (see p. 66, fig. 2)

The "tempio malatestiano" (or "Malatestan temple") is so called after the man who sponsored its construction, Sigismondo Malatesta (1417–68), who succeeded his uncle Carlo as signore or lord of Rimini in 1432. Rimini and its adjacent territories (see figure 1) constituted a small state uneasily nestled between the five major powers of Italy: Milan and Venice in the north, Florence in central Italy, and Rome (or the papacy) and Naples in the south. Like other rulers of small city-states at this time, Sigismondo earned badly needed income by being a condottiere, one who received a *condotta* ("contract") to lead an army to war on behalf of a larger state. Sigismondo served all five of the major powers during his lifetime, but already by the late 1450s he was increasingly regarded with suspicion because he prosecuted his campaigns with insufficient vigor or was thought to engage in duplicitous dealings with opponents. In 1459 Sigismondo joined another condottiere, Giacomo Piccinino, in an imprudent attempt to unseat the Aragonese dynasty that ruled Naples and replace it with the Angevin dynasty of southern France. But to Milan, in the north, this scheme raised the specter of invasion from France, and Franceso Sforza (the ruler of Milan) reacted sharply. So did papal Rome: it too feared a French presence in the peninsula, and now saw an opportunity to reassert its claims over territories long lost to its control – the territories of Sigismondo himself. The papacy was assuming the contours of the modern state that would soon rule all of central Italy until 1860, and Sigismondo's state would become the first of many to disappear over the next century. In 1461 Sigismondo managed to survive a ferocious campaign, defeating the ecclesiastical army at the battle of Nidastore on July 2. The next season his luck ran out. On August 12, 1462, his troops were routed at the battle of Senigallia; and a few days later those of his ally Piccinino were annihilated at the battle of Troia. The next year, in 1463, Fano, a prominent town within Sigismondo's own territory, was besieged and captured. Sigismondo was ruined: all his territories outside the city of Rimini were seized. He tried to recoup his fortunes by serving Venice in a war in southern Greece (1464–6), but it availed him nothing. He died not long thereafter.

In 1447 Sigismondo began the reconstruction of a single chapel within the church of San Francesco. By 1450 his plans were growing much grander. Leon Battista Alberti (1404–72), one of the most important architects of the Renaissance, was commissioned to redesign the entire church. Since Alberti had to preserve the recently refurbished chapel, he designed the building as a shell that would be literally wrapped around the older building. The central doorway at the church's front would be a Roman triumphal arch, the sides a series of deeply niched arches, each of which would hold the funeral urn of a famous man. Soaring above the whole would be a grand cupola. The reality turned out quite different (see p. 66, figure 2). The front facade was only partially completed; much though not all of the building's right side was finished; and nothing of the cupola was ever constructed. By 1460 work had stopped, halted by a lack of funds. The interior had also been redesigned and it now housed a vast series of bas-reliefs with complicated allegorical and zodiacal references.

Pound returned to Paris in July 1922 and devoted his next five months to research about Sigismondo in the Bibliothèque Nationale. In early 1923 he returned to Italy for several months' research in Italian archives with stops in Rome, Florence, Bologna, Modena, Cesena, Rimini, the Republic of San Marino, Pennabilli, Fano, Pesaro, Urbino, again Rimini, Ravenna, Venice, and Milan. He returned to Paris where, after some 65 drafts and fragments, he completed the four Malatesta Cantos, which were published in July 1923 in *The Criterion* (edited by T. S. Eliot).

For some critics, the raw patches of prose documents set alongside passages of poetry make a text that bristles with vivid juxtapositions. For others, Pound's engagement with recalcitrant materials is too serious a breach of generic boundaries; the antiliterary nature of such materials is insuperable, and the historical detail overwhelming.

---

[20]   *Argicida* Latin for "slayer of Argives," or Greeks, and so referring to Aphrodite's championship of the Trojans against the Greeks; the word appears in the Latin translation of the first Homeric Hymn.

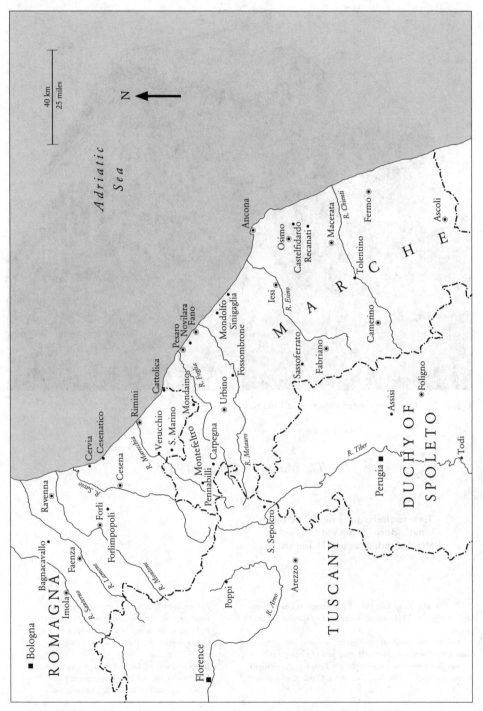

Figure 1: Fifteenth-century Rimini and its adjacent territories

Figure 2:   The church of San Francesco in Rimini, Italy

The Malatesta Cantos (1923)

VIII

These fragments you have shelved (shored).[1]
"Slut!" "Bitch!" Truth and Calliope[2]
Slanging each other sous les lauriers:[3]

---

[1]   Cf. *The Waste Land*, line 430: "These fragments I have shored against my ruins." This line is the first literary allusion to Eliot's poem.

[2]   *Calliope* the music of epic poetry, a figure for dignified narrative set over and against the messiness of history, truth.

[3]   *sous les lauriers* From a sonnet by the French poet Gérard de Nerval (1808–55), "Delfica," one of his *Chimères*, or *Chimeras* (1854):

> La connais-tu, Dafné, cette ancienne romance,
> Au pied du sycomore, ou sous les lauriers blancs,
> Sous l'olivers, le myrte, ou des saules tremblants,
> Cette chanson d'amour qui toujours recommence?

> Reconnais-tu le Temple au péristyle immense,
> Et les citrons amers où s'imprimaient tes dents,
> Et la grotte, fatale aux hôtes imprudents,
> Où du dragon vaincu dort l'antique semence?

> Ils reviendront, ces Dieux que tu pleures toujours!
> Le temps va ramener l'ordre des anciens jours;
> La terre a tressailli d'un souffle prophétique.

> Cependant la sibylle au visage latin
> Est endormie encor sous l'arc de Constantin
> —Et rien n'a dérangé le sévère portique.

That Alessandro[4] was negroid. And Malatesta Sigismund:

"*Frater tamquam et compater carissime*[5]:   5
        tergo[6]
    (...*hanni dc*
      ..*dicis*
      ... *entia*

Equivalent to: Giohanni of the Medici,[7] Florence)   10
Letter received, and in the matter of our Messire Gianozio
One from him also, sent on in form and with all due dispatch,
Having added your wishes and memoranda.
As to arranging peace between you and the King of Ragona,[8]
So far as I am concerned, it wd. give me the greatest possible pleasure,   15
At any rate nothing wd. give me more pleasure
      or be more acceptable to me,
And I shd. like to be party to it, as was promised me, either as participant or adherent.
As for my service money, perhaps you and your father wd. draw it
And send it on to me as quickly as possible.   20
And tell the *Maestro di pentore*[9]
That there can be no question of his painting the walls for the moment,
As the mortar is not yet dry
And it wd. be merely work chucked away
      (*buttato via*)[10]   25
But I want it to be quite clear, that until the chapels are ready
I will arrange for him to paint something else
So that both he and I shall get as much enjoyment as possible from it,
And in order that he may enter my service
And also because you write me that he needs cash,   30
I want to arrange with him to give him so much per year
And to assure him that he will get the sum agreed on.
You may say that I will deposit security for him wherever he likes.
And let me have a clear answer,
For I mean to give him good treatment   35
So that he may come to live the rest of his life in my lands –
Unless you put him off it –
And for this I mean to make due provision,
So that he can work as he likes,
Or waste his time as he likes   40

[4] *Alessandro* Alessandro de' Medici (1511–37), rumored to be the son of Pope Clement VII and a Moorish slave.

[5] *Frater tamquam / Et compater carissime* medieval Latin for "As dear to me as a brother and very dear companion," a courtly form of salutation in a letter.

[6] *tergo* scholarly Latin term meaning "On the verso or back of the leaf."

[7] *Giohanni of the Medici* Giovanni de' Medici (1421–63), the youngest son of Cosimo de' Medici, the head of the great family dynasty; fifteenth-century writing in Italian tolerated many variants in spelling, and the text is faithfully reproducing the orthography of the original letter, a document from April 7, 1449, which is preserved in the Archivio di stato (State Archive) in Florence, which Pound visited.

[8] *King of Ragona* Alfonso I of Aragon (1394–1458), king of Naples (1443–58). When the ruler of the duchy of Milan died in 1447, two major powers laid claim to it. Alfonso claimed it on the grounds that he had been named heir; Venice laid claim to it on still shakier grounds. The Milanese themselves declared the city a republic. Working as a condottiere for the Venetians,

Francesco Sforza (1401–66) besieged the city for three years, then entered and took the city for himself, declaring himself duke of Milan in 1450. Sforza was much aided by backing from Cosimo de' Medici, who wanted an independent Milan that could put a check to Venetian ambitions on the mainland. Sigismondo was ostensibly working for the Venetians, besieging Cremona and Sforza's troops defending the city.

[9] *the Maestro di pentore* it is uncertain who is being specified, but art historians have enjoyed the idea that it might be Piero della Francesca (1420?–92), the great quattrocento artist who painted a small fresco in one chapel in the Tempio malatestiano.

[10] *buttato via* the original Italian phrase which the poem has just translated as "chucked away." The original Italian is included because it corrects the work of the French historian Charles Yriarte (1832–98), whose study of Sigismondo Malatesta, *Un Condottiere au XVe siècle* (Paris: J. Rothschild, 1882) had also included a transcription of the same letter, but had incorrectly transcribed *gettato* instead of *buttato*; see Yriarte, p. 381.

(affatigandose per suo piacere o non
non gli manchera la provixione mai),[11]
never lacking provision.

SIGISMUNDUS PANDOLPHUS DE MALATESTIS,
In Campo Illus. Domini Venetorum die 7
aprilis 1449, contra Cremonam[12]
.... and because[13] the aforesaid most illustrious

45

Duke of Milan
Is content and wills that the aforesaid Lord Sigismundo
50   Go into the service of the most magnificent commune of the Florentines
For alliance defensive of the two states,
Therefore between the aforesaid Illustrious Sigismund
And the respectable man Agnolo della Stufa, ambassador, sindic and procurator
Appointed by the ten of the baily, etc., the half
55   Of these 50,000 florins, free of attainder,
For 1,400 cavalry and four hundred foot
To come into the terrene of the commune
or elsewhere in Tuscany,
As please the ten of the Baily,
60   And to be himself there with them in the service of the commune
With his horsemen and his footmen
(*gente di cauallo e da pie*), etc.
Aug. 5, 1452, *register of the Ten of the Baily.*

From the forked rocks of Penna and Billi, on Carpegna[14]
65   With the road leading under the cliff,
in the wind-shelter into Tuscany,
And the north road, toward the Marecchia
the mud-stretch full of cobbles.

Lyra:
70   "Ye spirits who of olde were in this land
Each under Love, and shaken,
Go with your lutes, awaken
The summer within her mind,[15]
Who hath not Helen for peer
75   Yseut nor Batsabe."[16]

---

[11]   *affatigandose ... la provixione mai* Italian for "working or not at his pleasure / provision for him will never be lacking."
[12]   *In campo ... Cremonam* medieval Latin for "In the camp of the Illustrious Lord of the Venetians on the seventh day of April 1449, campaigning against Cremona."
[13]   *and because* the poem quotes a contract drawn up between Sigismondo Malatesta and Agnolo della Stufa, who represents the commune of Florence. The contract is transcribed in Charles Yriarte, *Un Condottiere au XVᵉ siècle*, pp. 382–4. Lines 47–57 are from p. 382, lines 59–66 from p. 383.
[14]   *the forked rocks of Penna and Billi, on Carpegna* Pennabilli is a small town perched on forked rocks high on Monte Carpegna in the Appenines. From it rises the river Marecchia (line 67), creating a valley which flows down to Rimini and the Adriatic Sea. The Malatesta family originally stemmed from Pennabilli.
[15]   *Ye spirits who of olde ... within her mind* lines 70–3 are a translation from a poem (a *capitolo ternario*) ascribed to Sigismondo Malatesta by Charles Yriarte, *Un Condottiere au XVᵉ siècle*, pp. 389–92. Yriarte urged that the poem was written for Isotta da Rimini, that it was "the most characteristic of his [Sigismondo's] works" (139), and that it furnished "the key to the enigma" (218) of the allegorical bas-reliefs in the Tempio Malatestiano. His view was echoed in contemporary Baedeker guidebooks and

novels, and in the 1886 and 1911 editions of the *Encyclopaedia Britannica*. But in 1911, a scholar named Aldo Francesco Massèra (1860–1928) showed that the poem had been written by Simone Serdini, a Sienese poet who had enjoyed close relations with the court of Rimini. Serdini had died in 1419 or 1420, making it unlikely that his poem referred to Sigismondo (then three years old) or Isotta (then not yet born) or to the sculptures in the Tempio (then not yet sculpted). Yriarte had checked only one later manuscript which, in a fashion typical of the period, had mistakenly assigned a poem not to its author, but to the ruler to whom it was given or with whom it was associated. (Aldo Francesco Massàra, "I poeti isottei," *Giornale storico della letteratura italiana* 57 [1911]: 1–32.) Pound was unaware of Massèra's work and accepted Yriarte's claims.
[16]   *Who hath not ... nor Batsabe* is from a poem (a *serventese*) incorrectly ascribed to Sigismondo Malatesta by Charles Yriarte, *Un Condottiere au XVᵉ siècle*, p. 394; in 1911 it was established that the poem was by Carlo Valturi, a minor poet who labored at Sigismondo's court (see preceding note). The last two words ("nor Batsabe") are from a poem by Simone Serdini. Helen was the legendary figure whose abduction started the Trojan war, as recounted by Homer in the *Iliad*; Yseut is a variant spelling of Isotta or Isolda, of the famous medieval legend of Tristan and

With the interruption:

> *Magnifico, compater et carissime*
>
>> (Johanni di Cosimo)

Venice has taken me on again

>> At 7,000 a month, *fiorini di Camera*.   80

For 2,000 horse and four hundred footmen,

And it rains here by the gallon,

We have had to dig a new ditch.

In three or four days

I shall try to set up the bombards....[17]   85

Under the plumes, with the flakes and small wads of colour

Showering from the balconies,

With the sheets spread from windows,

>> with leaves and small branches pinned on them,

Arras hung from the railings; out of the dust,   90

With pheasant tails upright on their forelocks,

>> The small white horses, the

Twelve girls riding in order, green satin in pannier'd habits;

Under the baldachino, silver'd with heavy stitches,

Bianca Visconti, with Sforza,   95

The peasant's son and the duchess,

To Rimini, and to the wars southward,

Boats drawn on the sand, red-orange sails in the creek's mouth,

For two days' pleasure, mostly "*la pesca*," fishing,

Di cui in the which he, Francesco *godeva molto*.[18]   100

>> To the war southward

In which he, at that time, received an excellent hiding.

And the Greek emperor was in Florence[19]

Isolde; Batsabe is a medieval rendering of Bathsheba, the legendary queen who leads King David into sin in the Old Testament.

[17] *Magnifico compater ... bombards* the poem freely translates a letter, dated March 4, 1449, from Sigismondo Malatesta to Cosimo de' Medici (1389–1464), the banker and *de facto* ruler of Florence. It is transcribed in Yriarte, *Un Condottiere au XV*ᵉ *siècle*, pp. 384–5.

[18] *Under the plumes ... godeva molto* the poem adapts a passage in a work by Cesare Clementini, a Riminese historian who collated medieval and Renaissance chronicles to create his own history of the city, *Raccolto istorico della fondatione di Rimino, e dell' origine e vite de' Malatesti*, 2 vols. (Rimini: Simbeni, 1617), or in English, *Historical Collection of the Foundation of Rimini, and of the Origin and the Lives of the Malatestas*. Clementini, vol. 2, pp. 324–5 writes: "On the 23rd of May [1442], Count Francesco [Sforza] came into Rimini, bearing seven standards (the first from the Church, the second from Pope Eugenio, another from Venice, one from Florence, and the others kept enfolded), and with him was his wife Bianca, daughter of the Duke of Milan, accompanied by eight young women all dressed the same in green on eight little ponies, beneath a canopy [*baldacchino*] of silver brocade which was carried by the principal members of the Court and the City, the street being covered from the church of St. Julian to the Palazzo; and having rested two days with various recreations, in particular fishing [*la pesca*], which he much enjoyed [*di cui godeva molto*], he went on to La Marca, followed by his people, and two days later by Sigismondo Pandolfo." (My translation.)

[19] *And the Greek emperor...* John VIII Paleologus (ruled 1423–48) went to Ferrara in 1438 to participate in a council convened to discuss healing the schism between the eastern (Orthodox) and western (Catholic) churches. With him was Giorgios Gemistos Plethon (1355–1452), the leading thinker of the last age of Byzantium. When Ferrara was afflicted with the plague, the council moved to Florence where, it is sometimes argued, the presence of Gemistos Plethon sparked the neo-Platonism that would have such important literary and cultural ramifications. "The Temple at Delphos" or Delphi was the most sacred religious complex of ancient Greece, and "the war" around it was part of the larger war being fought between the growing Ottoman empire and the waning Byzantine empire, which would culminate in 1453 with the fall of Constantinople (modern Istanbul) to the Turks.

Poseidon was the ancient Greek god of earthquakes and the sea. In the allegorical reading of Poseidon which Gemistos Plethon offered, "Poseideon, the oldest of Zeus's sons, is an Idea, not just this or that idea, but the class of ideas which comprises all ideas in their unity" (quoted in Fritz Schultze, *Georgios Gemistos Plethon un seine reformatorischen Bestrebungen* [Jena: Maukes Verlag, 1874], p. 155 [my translation]). This was part of a more general allegorization of ancient divinities which Gemistos Plethon propounded, one that entailed the notion of a *concret Allgemeines*, German for a "concrete universal." As Schultze explains: "Because these gods are only ideas, or very universal concepts, so their genesis is only the logical development of a concept. For Plethon is completely a Platonic realist, in the medieval sense of that term. This universal is not an abstract universal, such as the nominalists understood it, but the concrete universal that contains all particulars within itself: it is not a mere extrapolation derived from all particulars, but the complete content of all particulars" (my translation; Schultze, *Georgios Gemistos Plethon*, p. 159).

(Ferrara having the pest)
105   And with him Gemisthus Plethon
             Talking of the war about the temple at Delphos,
             And of POSEIDON, *concret Allgemeine*,
             And telling of how Plato went to Dionysius of Syracuse
             Because he had observed that tyrants
110   Were most efficient in all that they set their hands to,
             But he was unable to persuade Dionysius
             To any amelioration.

             And in the gate at Ancona, between the foregate and the main-gates
             Sigismundo, ally, come through an enemy force,
115   To patch up some sort of treaty, passes one gate
             And they shut it before they open the next gate,
                          and he says:
             "Now you have me,
                          Caught like a hen in a coop."
120   And the captain of the watch says: "Yes Messire Sigismundo,
             But we want this town for ourselves."[20]

                    With the church against him,
             With the Medici bank for itself,
             With wattle Sforza against him,
125   Sforza Francesco, wattle-nose,
             Who married him (Sigismundo) his (Francesco's)
             Daughter in September,
             Who stole Pesaro in October
             (As Broglio says "*bestialmente*"),
130   Who stood with the Venetians in November,
             With the Milanese in December,
             Sold Milan in November, stole Milan in December
             Or something of that sort,
             Commanded the Milanese in the spring, the Venetians at mid-summer,
135   The Milanese in the autumn,
             And was Naples' ally in October,
                          He, Sigismundo, *templum aedificavit*
             In Romagna, teeming with cattle thieves,
                          with the game lost in mid-channel,
140   And never quite lost till '50, and never quite lost till the end, in Romagna,
             So that Galeaz sold Pesaro "to get pay for his cattle."[21]

The ancient Greek philosopher Plato (428–348 BC) went to visit Dionysius I, ruler of Syracuse, in Sicily, in 387 BC, and he went two more times to Syracuse during the reign of his successor, Dionysius II. He gives accounts of it in a document known as the *Seventh Letter*, in which he urges moderation and restraint and explains his role in the troubled relations between Dionysius II and a philosopher named Dion of Syracuse.

[20]   *And in the gate at Ancona ... for ourselves*. Source not identified.

[21]   *With the church ... for his cattle* this long sentence (126 words) presents a summary of Sigismondo's career, its clotted syntax a figure for the turbulent times that he lived through. Mention is made in passing of four events. In April 1442 the condottiere Francesco Sforza married his illegitimate daughter Polissena (1428–49) to Sigismondo (lines 126–7). Then, in late 1444, Galezzo Malatesta, the town's ruler and member of a collateral branch of the Malatesta family, sold the city of Pesaro to Alessandro Sforza (Francesco's brother) for 20,000 florins, in effect driving a wedge into the Malatestan territory and splitting it into two parts now connected only by sea (lines 128–9, 141). The event marked the end of the alliance between Sigismondo and Sforza which the wedding had sealed. And it elicited a comment from a contemporary observer, one Gaspare Broglio Taqrtaglia da Lavello (1407–93), or Broglio, a soldier of fortune and counselor who served at the court of Rimini from 1443 until Sigismondo's death in 1468. Broglio calls the sale of Pesaro a deed that was done *bestialmente* (line 129), "in a beastly fashion." These actions are all performed by others: by Francesco Sforza, by Galeazzo Malatesta, by Gaspare Broglio. Sigismondo performs only one action: *templum aedificavit* (line 137), Latin for "he built a temple," i.e the Tempio malatestiano. The Latin phrase comes from the *Commentarii* or *Commentaries* of Pope Pius II (1458–64), Enea Silvio Piccolimini (1405–64); see note to line 244.

And Poictiers, you know, Guillaume Poictiers,[22]
        had brought the song up out of Spain
With the singers and viels.[23] But here they wanted a setting
By Marecchia, where the water comes down over the cobbles   145
And Mastin had come to Verucchio,[24]
        and the sword, Paulo il Bello's,[25]
            caught in the arras
And, in Este's house, Parisina[26]
Paid   150
For this tribe paid always, and the house
Called also Atreides',[27]
And the wind is still for a little
And the dusk rolled
        to one side a little,   155
And he was twelve at the time, Sigismundo,
And no dues had been paid for three years,
And his elder brother gone pious;
And that year they fought in the streets,
And that year he got out to Cesena   160
        and brought back the levies,
And that year he crossed by night over the Foglia,[28]
        and ...

IX

One year[1] floods rose,
One year they fought in the snows,
One year hail fell, breaking the trees and walls.
Down here in the marsh[2] they trapped him
        in one year,   5
And he stood in the water up to his neck
        to keep the hounds off him,
And he floundered about in the marsh
        and came in after three days,
That was Astorre Manfredi of Faenza   10
        who worked the ambush, and set the dogs off to find him,

[22] *Guillaume Poictiers* Guillaume de Poitiers (1071–1126), Duke of Aquitaine, is widely considered the first troubadour, initiating a lyrical tradition that would have reverberations for the next two centuries, leading to the style of the early poems of Dante (1265–1321).

[23] *viels* medieval French for viols, more typically written *viells*.

[24] *Mastin ... Verucchio* Mastin, Italian "mastiff," nickname of Malatesta da Verucchio (1212–1312), treated as the founder of the Malatesta dynasty; before becoming lord of Rimini in 1293 he lived in the town of Verruchio.

[25] *Paolo il Bello* second son (c. 1247–c. 1283) of Malatesta da Verruchio, he is famous for appearing as a character in Dante's recounting of the story of Paolo and Francesca, *Inferno* V. Francesca, married to Paolo's brother Gianciotto, became Paolo's lover, and both were murdered by Gianciotto. The detail rehearsed by Pound, that Paolo's sword "caught in the arras," is one of countless novelistic embellishments furnished by medieval commentators on Dante.

[26] *in Este's house, Parisina* Parisina Malatesta, cousin to Sigismondo, married Niccolò d'Este in 1418, and in 1425 was executed by him for suspected adultery with his son by a previous marriage, Ugo. Both were beheaded.

[27] *Atreides* the house of Atreus, the family that includes Agamemnon, murdered by his wife Clytemnestra, who in turn is killed in revenge by her son Orestes; their stories are dramatized in the *Oresteia*, a trilogy by the Greek poet Aeschylus.

[28] *And that year ... over Foglia* in May 1431 there was a rebellion in Rimini led by Giovanni di Ramberto di Malatesta and instigated by Carlo Malatesta, ruler of nearby Pesaro; Sigismondo went to the neighboring town of Cesena and brought back troops to suppress it; his crossing over the Foglia formed part of the same series of events.

CANTO IX

[1] *One year* the style here evokes that of a contemporary or medieval chronicle.

[2] *Down here in the marsh ... under Mantua* in December 1446, when returning to Rimini from a campaign which he had been conducting for Filippo Maria Visconti, the duke of Milan, Sigismondo and a small party of retainers were ambushed by Astorre Manfredi, the ruler of Faenza, not far from Castello Rossi, a fortress in the town of Sasso Marconi (10 km south of Bologna). (Pound is mistaken about the location.)

In the marsh, down here under Mantua.
And he fought in Fano, in a street fight,
  and that was nearly the end of him;
15   And the Emperor came down and knighted us,[3]
And they had a wooden castle set up for fiesta,
And one year Bassinio went out into the courtyard
  Where the lists were, and the palisades
    had been set for the tourneys,
20   And he talked down the anti-Hellene,[4]
    And there was an heir male to the seignor,
    And Madame Genevra died.[5]
And he, Sigismundo, was Capitan for the Venetians.
And he had sold off small castles
25   and built the great Rocca[6] to his plan,
And he fought like ten devils at Monteluro[7]
    and got nothing but the victory
And old Sforza bitched us at Pesaro;[8]
    [sic], March the 16th:
30   "that Messire Alessandro Sforza
    is become lord of Pesaro
through the wangle of the Illus. Sgr. Mr. Fedricho d'Orbino,
Who worked the wangle with Galeaz
    through the wiggling of Messer Francesco
35   Who waggled it so that Galeaz should sell Pesaro
    to Alex and Fossembrone to Feddy;
and he hadn't the right to sell.
And this he did *bestialmente*; that is Sforza did *bestialmente*
as he had promised him, Sigismundo *per capitoli*
40   to see that he, Malatesta, should have Pesaro"
And this cut us off from our south half
   and finished our game, thus, in the beginning,
And he, Sigismundo, spoke his mind to Francesco
   and we drove them out of the Marches.

45   And the King o' Ragona,[9] Alphonse le roy d'Aragon,
    was the next nail in our coffin,

[3] *And the Emperor came down and knighted us* Sigismondo Malatesta and his brother Domenico Novello were knighted in September 1433 by Sigismund V (1368–1437), Holy Roman emperor (1433–7) of the house of Luxemburg. The knighting was a ceremonial gesture, a token of the emperor's gratitude for the solicitude with which he had been treated as a guest. The event was commemorated some 20 years later in a fresco by Piero della Francesca, housed in the Tempio malatestiano.

[4] *And one year Basinio ... the anti-Hellene* Basinio de Parma (1425–57) was a humanist active at the court of Sigismondo Malatesta from 1449 until his death; in 1455 he became embroiled in a dispute with two other humanists active in Rimini, Tommaso Seneca da Camerino and Poreclio Pandoni, over the utility of studying ancient Greek. Sigismondo, not without irony, was invoked as a judge of the quarrel, which ultimately produced three poems in Latin that are the principal record of these events.

[5] *And Madame Ginevra died* Ginevra d'Este, Sigismondo's first wife, died in the spring of 1437.

[6] *and built the great Rocca* construction of the Rocca or fortress-castle occupied Sigismondo from 1436–47; it still stands in the center of Rimini and has recently been restored, after having served for a century as a prison.

[7] *Monteluro* the battle took place on November 8, 1443, with Sigismondo acting as an ally of Sforza.

[8] *And old Sforza ... out of the Marches* (lines 28–44) see note to Canto ix, lines 133–55. Under the agreement detailed there, Pesaro was sold to Alessandro Sforza and Fossembrone to Frederico or Federico d'Urbino (1422–82), signore of Urbino (1444–72), who became Sigismondo's principal rival and ultimately defeated him. Federico's principal monument is the ducal palace at Urbino, one the purest and most harmonious expressions of Quattrocento aesthetic ideals. "Alex" and "Feddy" are colloquial renderings for Alessandro Sforza and Federico d'Urbino. The Marches, or *le Marche* in Italian, are the region to the south of Rimini (see figure 1).

[9] *And the King o' Ragona ... was worth afterward* (lines 45–53) this passage recounts a crucial moment in Sigismondo's political fortunes, one that transpired over the course of 1447. At the beginning of that year Italy as a whole was divided between two contending alliances: on the one side were the papacy, Milan, and Naples (headed by King Alfonso of Aragon); on the other were the two republics of Venice and Florence, with backing from the Angevin dynasty in southern France. In the spring and early summer, Sigismondo concluded a *condotta* with Alfonso, but in December he repudiated that agreement, signed on with

And all you can say is, anyhow, that he Sigismundo called a town council
And Valturio said "as well for a sheep as a lamb"
    And the change-over (*hæc traditio*)
As old bladder said "*rem eorum saluavit*"   50
      Saved the Florentine state; and that, maybe, was something,
And "Florence our natural ally" as they said in the meeting
    for whatever that was worth afterward.
And he began building the TEMPIO,
    and Polixena, his second wife, died.[10]   55
And the Venetians sent down an ambassador
    and said "speak humanely, but tell him
        it's no time for raising his pay."
And the Venetians[11] sent down an ambassador
    with three pages of secret instructions   60
To the effect: Did he think the campaign was a joy-ride?
And Old Wattle Wattle slipped into Milan
But he couldn't stand Sidg being so high with the Venetians
And he talked it over with Feddy; and Feddy said "Pesaro"
And old Foscari wrote "*Caro mio*,   65
"If we split with Francesco you can have it
"And we'll help you in every way possible."
      But Feddy offered it sooner.
And Sigismundo got up a few arches,

Florence, and then refused to repay Alfonso the sums which he had advanced for Sigismondo's service. It was a major decision, and to reach it he called a meeting of the town council to sound out alternatives. It was there that Roberto Valturio (1405–75) spoke against the views which had so far been advanced: "Against these views spoke up Valturio, in this case too much an intriguer and flatterer, alleging that Sigismondo would be just as disgraced with the king if he returned the money as he would be if he didn't, so that for now he might just as well make use of it (already partly spent), since the need for it was growing, and there was always plenty of time for restitution later: and certainly this pernicious advice was the ruin of his Lordship" (Clementini, *Raccolto istorico*, vol. 2, p. 355; see note 18 to Canto VIII). The poem's "as well for a sheep as a lamb" (line 48) is not a direct quotation, but a colloquial rendering of the spirit of Valturio's advice. The phrase "*hæc traditio . . . rem eorum saluavit*," medieval Latin for "this betrayal . . . saved their cause," is an adaption of a sentence by Pius II, contemptuously called "old bladder": "nec dubium quin ea Sigismundi proditio rem Florentinam salvaverit," or "There is no doubt that Sigismondo's betrayal saved the Florentine cause" (Enea Silvio Piccolomini, *I Commentarii*, ed. Luigi Totaro [Milan: Adelphi, 1984], vol. 1, p. 368).

[10] *Polixena . . . died* Polissena Sforza (1428–49), Sigismondo's second wife whom he married in 1442, died of the plague; it was later, in 1461 and thereafter, charged that Sigismondo had murdered her, an accusation debated down the centuries until the twentieth, when it has been accepted that the charge was without foundation.

[11] *And the Venetians . . . m'l'ha calata* (lines 56–68 and 95–101) these passages continue to recount the aftermath of Sigismondo's decision, taken in December 1447, to betray Alfonso and side with Florence. Setting out for Florentine territory in March 1448, in September he forced Alfonso to raise his siege at the city of Piombino, saving the Florentines. His success prompted more demand for his services, with Venice now in dire need of help to prevent Francesco Sforza from taking Milan. In Novem-

ber 1448 Sigismondo journeyed northwards to begin his long struggle against Sforza. It proved unsuccessful, and it was charged that Sigismondo was being less than assiduous in his conduct of the campaign ("Did he think the campaign was a joy-ride?"). In February 1450, a revolt within Milan itself meant that the city was open to be taken, and Sforza now seized control. Sigismondo, however, remained under orders to continue operations against him. It was now that Sforza devised a ruse to distract Sigismondo and gain time to consolidate his authority. At his initiative, Federico d'Urbino proposed to Sigismondo that he would help him conquer Pesaro (the city that in late 1444 had been purchased from a collateral member of the family and consigned to Alessandro Sforza), provided that Sigismondo returned some castles belonging to Federico. Sigismondo agreed, then requested permission from Venice to leave his post and pursue his plan. Venice gave him license to go and promised its aid ("you can have it and we'll help you in every way possible"). In May he set off for Rimini and his planned attack on Pesaro. But Sforza, fully aware of his plans through the agency of Federico, immediately sent troops from Milan to Pesaro. When Sigismondo finally arrived, ready to besiege the city, he found that none of Federico's promised troops had arrived, and that Sforza's had already arrived to reinforce the city's defenses. When he called on Federico to deliver the troops he had promised, Federico informed him that he would help defend the city, not attack it ("I am coming! . . . / . . . to help Alessandro.") Sigismondo, wild with indignation, had to suspend his attack and return to Rimini. When he realized how badly he'd been deceived, he said to his companion, Broglio: "*Misser Federico me l'ha pur calata!*" (line 101) ("Lord Federico has pulled a dirty trick on me."). These events, with the quotation from Broglio, are recounted in Luigi Tonini, *Storia di Rimini*, vol. 5, *Rimini nella signoria de' Malatesti* (Rimini: Tipografia Albertini, 1880), pp. 198–203, and Giovanni Soranzo, "Un fallito tentativo di Sigismondo Pandolfo Malatesta su Pesaro (giugno 1450)," *Le Marche*, 10 (1911): 221–34.

70 And stole that marble[12] in Classe, "stole" that is,
   Casus est talis:
   Foscari doge, to the prefect of Ravenna
   "Why, what, which, thunder, damnation ? ? ? ?"

   Casus est talis"
75   Filippo, commendatary of the *abbazia*
   Of Sant Apollinaire, Classe, Cardinal of Bologna
   That he did one night (*quadam nocte*) sell to the
   Illmo D° D° Sigismund Malatesta
   Lord of Arimnium, marble, porphyry, serpentine,
80 Whose men, Sigismundo's, came with more than an hundred
   two wheeled ox carts and deported, for the beautifying
   of the *tempio* where was Santa Maria in Trivio
   where the same are now on the walls. Four hundred
   ducats to be paid back to the *abbazia* by the said swindling
85 Cardinal or his heirs.
              grnnh! rrnnh, pthg.
   Wheels, *plaustra*, oxen under night-shield,
      And on the 13th of August: Aloysius Purtheo
   The next abbot to Sigismundo, receipt for 200 ducats
90 Corn-salve for the damage done in that scurry.

   And there was the row about the German-Bergundian female[13]
   And it was his messianic year, Poliorcetes,[14]
          but he was being a bit too POLUMETIS[15]
   And the Venetians wouldn't give him six months vacation.

95 And he went down to the old brick heap of Pesaro[16]
          and waited for Feddy
   And Feddy finally said "I am coming!!!!
                  ....to help Alessandro"
   And he said: "This time Mister Feddy has done it."
100 He said "Broglio, I'm the goat. This time

---

[12] *And stole that marble ... in that scurry* (lines 70–90) two passages interrupt the narrative of Sigismondo's failed attempt to seize Pesaro (see preceding note). This one, the first, concerns an allegation that Sigismondo stole marble and other precious stones from the church of San Apollinare in Classe, an important Byzantine church about five km south of Ravenna. The depredation took place in May 1449, and leading citizens from Ravenna promptly protested to the Venetian doge, Francesco Foscari, who ordered his agent in Ravenna to investigate ("Why ... damnation????"). In the end, it was agreed that Sigismondo would pay 200 gold coins for damages, and that the Abbot, Luigi dal Pozzo, would repay the 400 ducats he had received from Sigismondo to the abbey. The document acknowledging Sigismondo's payment is dated August 13, 1450. Pound cites isolated words (*quadam nocte*, or "on a certain night," l. 77 and *plaustra*, or "wagons" l. 87) from one sentence of the document, which reads: "In tantum ut predictus Illustrissimus dominus, quadam nocte ultra centum plaustra ad monasterium classense transmissa, ex decrustatis ecclesie parietibus oneraret; ac de illis postea ecclesiam sancti Francisci, quam Arimini aedificaverat, decoraret." Or in English: "Insofar as the aforesaid most illustrious lord, on a certain night over one hundred wagons having been sent to the monastery in Classe, loaded materials taken from the church's denuded walls, and with these decorated the church of Saint Francis, which he

had built in Rimini." Foscari's letter of May 15, 1449, is transcribed in Corrado Ricci, "Marmi ravennati erratici," *Ausonia* 4 (1909): 247–89, here 261; the quittance of August 13, 1450, is transcribed in Giovanni Benedetto Mittarelli (ed.), *Annales Camaldulenses ordinis Sancti Benedicti* (Venice: Jo. Baptisa Pasquali), 9 vols. (1755–73), vol. 7, p. 228.

[13] *the row about the German-Burgandian female* in June 1450 a woman returning from a Jubilee year pilgrimage to Rome was assaulted, robbed, and raped by a troop of soldiers in the area around Verona, where Sigismondo and his retainers were traveling on their way to Rimini and his subsequent misadventure in Pesaro. Sigismondo sent four of his soldiers to Venice, who were charged with being accomplices. But rumors that the culprit was Sigismondo persisted and found their way into charges leveled against Sigsmondo later in 1461.

[14] *Poliorcetes* "Taker of Cities," a learned epithet which humanist courtiers selected for medals commemorating Sigismondo's achievements; a celebrated medal of him executed by Pisanello (1395–1455), widely considered the greatest medallist of the age, contains the inscription: "Poliorcetes et semper invictus," or Latin for "Taker of cities and always undefeated."

[15] *POLUMETIS* "many-minded," in Greek, an epithet that Homer uses to describe Odysseus (*Odyssey* I, 1).

[16] See note 11.

Mr Feddy has done it (*m'l'a calata*)."
And he'd lost his job[17] with the Venetians,
And the stone didn't come in from Istria;
And we sent men to the silk war;
And Wattle never paid up on the nail   105
Though we signed on with Milan and Florence;
And he set up the bombards in muck down by Vada[18]
where nobody else could have set 'em
and he took the wood out of the bombs
and made 'em of two scoops of metal   110
And the jobs kept getting smaller and smaller,
Until he signed on with Siena;
and that time they grabbed his post-bag[19]
And what was it, anyhow?
Pitigliano, a man with a ten acre lot,   115
Two lumps of tufa,
and they'd taken his pasture land from him,
And Sidg had got back their horses,
and he had two big lumps of tufa
with six hundred pigs in the basements   120
And the poor devils were dying of cold.
And this is what they found in the post-bag:

Ex Arimino
die Decembris

"*Magnifice ac potens domine, mi singularissime*[20]   125
"I advise yr. Lordship how I have been with master Alwidge who has shown me the design of the
"nave that goes in the middle of the church and the design for the roof and . . ."[21]

"JHesus
"*Magnifico exso.* Signor Mio[22]
"Sence today I am recommanded that I hav to tel you my father's opinium that he has shode to   130
"Mr. Genare about the valts of the cherch . . . etc . . .
"Giovane of Master alwise P.S.I think it advisabl that I shud go to rome to talk to mister Albert[23]
"so as I can no what he thinks about it rite.
"Sagramoro has . . .
"*Illustre signor mio,*[24] Messire Battista,,, . . ."   135

---

[17] *And he'd lost his job* . . . after Sigismondo's failed attempt to take Pesaro in 1450, and Sforza's successful seizure of Milan, there was a change of climate in Italian politics, characterized by new efforts to establish peace throughout Italy. Sigismondo conducted desultory campaigns on behalf of Florence in 1452 and 1453. But in 1454, when the Peace of Lodi was proclaimed, which effectively promised an end to war among the major powers for the next 25 years, one could see signs of trouble coming for men dependent on war for their income. The next year, when the last of the major powers, Naples under Alfonso of Aragon, agreed to sign the peace of Lodi, it did so only with the proviso that Sigismondo Malatesta be excluded. His lands were now fair game for anyone.

[18] *And he set up . . . down by Vada* Sigismondo's campaign of 1453 was against a fort in Vada, on the southwest coast of Tuscany, a swampy and unhealthy area. Broglio chronicles the campaign in detail, and Pound took notes from Broglio's manuscript; see Broglio pp. 179–80.

[19] *signed with Siena . . . his post-bag* in November 1454 Sigismondo signed a condotta with Siena, which had been engaged in a local war with Aldobrandino Orsini, count of Pitiglano. Sigismondo besieged him at his castle in Sorano (the surrounding area

is famous for its tufa), but then treated secretly with him and arranged a truce. He was discharged by Siena and had to retreat quickly through Florentine territory back to Rimini, abandoning his baggage and correspondence; the latter was rediscovered in the nineteenth century, and transcriptions of some letters were included in Charles Yriarte, *Un Condottiere au XVᵉ siècle* (Paris: Rothschild, 1882).

[20] *Ex Arimino . . . singularissime* Latin for "From Rimini, day 22 of December / Magnificent and powerful lord, esteemed by me."

[21] The letter (lines 123–7) is from Matteo Nuti of Fano, the builder responsible for constructing the Tempio; the entire letter is found in Yriarte, *Un Condottiere au XVᵉ siècle*, pp. 421–2.

[22] The letter (lines 129–41), undated, is from a carpenter, Maestro Alvise; it begins with a Latin salutation, *Magnifico excelso,* or "to the mangificent and exalted," then shifts to Italian, "Signor Mio," or "my lord."

[23] *mister Albert* Leon Battista Alberti (1404–72), the architect who designed the Tempio malatestiano.

[24] *Illustre signor mio* "My illustrious lord," in Italian; this fragment does not lead on to a letter, but remains isolated.

"First: Ten slabs best red, seven by 15, by one third,
"Eight ditto, good red, 15 by three by one,
"Six of same, 15 by one by one,
"Eight columns 15 by three by one third
140   etc. . . . with carriage
                                      danars 151[25]
"MONSEIGNEUR:[26]
    "Madame Isotta has had me write today about Sr. Galeazzo's daughter. The man who said young
"pullets make thin soup, knew what he was talking about. We went to see the girl the other day, for
145 "all the good that did, and she denied the whole matter, and kept her end up without losing her
"temper. I think Madame Ixotta very nearly exhausted the matter. *Mi pare che avea decto hogni chossia.*[27]
"All the children are well. Where you are everyone is pleased and happy because of your taking the
"chateau here we are the reverse as you might say drifting without a rudder. Madame Lucrezia has
"probably, or should have, written to you, I suppose you have the letter by now. Everyone wants to
150 "be remembered to you.   "21 Dec,   D. de M."

" . . . *sagramoro* to put up the derricks. There is a supply of beams at . . . "[28]

"MAGNIFICENT LORD WITH DUE REVERENCE:[29]
    "Messire Malatesta is well and asks for you every day. He is so much pleased with his pony, It wd.
"take me a month to write you all the fun he gets out of that pony. I want to again remind you to
155 "write to Georgio Rambottom or to his boss to fix up that wall to the little garden that madame
"Isotta uses, for it is all flat on the ground now as I have already told him a lot of times, for all the
"good that does, so I am writing to your lordship in the matter I have done all that I can, for all
"the good that does as noboddy hear can do anything without you.
"your faithful   LUNARDA DA PALLA.
160   20 Dec. 1454."

" . . . gone over it with all the foremen and engineers. And about the silver for the small
"medal . . . "[30]

"*Magnifice ac poten* . . .

"   because the walls of . . . "[31]

165 "*Malatesta de Malatestis*[32] *ad Magnificum Dominum Patremque suum.*[33]
"Ex^{so} D^{no} et D^{no} sin D^{no} Sigismundum Pandolfi Filium

[25]   *First: Ten slabs ... danars 151* the document is a contract between Antonio de' Pasti (a sculptor) and Francesco Marangoni, representing Sigismondo, and Jacobo di Milano, resident in Verona, for marbles needed to make balustrades in the Tempio. The document is transcribed in Yriarte, *Un Condottiere au XVe siècle*, pp. 398–9.

[26]   *Monseigneur ... 21 Dec. D. de M.* (lines 142–50) written on behalf of Isotta degli Atti by "D. de M.," an otherwise unknown follower. The letter is reproduced in facsimile in Yriarte, *Un Condottiere au XVe siècle*, p. 158, while the letter is given in French translation on pp. 396–7. The opening salutation, "Monseigneur," is a careless mistake, since the facsimile plainly shows the word "Signore."

[27]   *Mi pare ... chossia* (Italian) "it seems to me that she said everything" or "nearly exhausted the matter."

[28]   *Sagramoro to ... beams at ...* from a letter to Sigismondo Malatesta, dated December 17, 1454, by Mateo de' Pasti (active 1441–67) and Pietro de' Genari; a transcription of the letter is given by Yriarte, *Un Condottiere au XVe siècle*, pp. 419–20.

[29]   *Magnificent Lord ... 20 Dec. 1454* (lines 152–60) Lundarda da Palla was a secretary and perhaps teacher of Sigismondo's children.

[30]   *"gone over it ... for the small medal ..."* this passage splices two phrases from a letter to Sigismondo Malatesta, dated December 17, 1454, by Mateo de' Pasti and Pietro de' Genari; a transcription of the letter is given by Yriarte, *Un Condottiere au XVe siècle*, pp. 419–20. The first phrase appears in line 4 of the letter, "e siamo stati con tutti li maestri e ingegneri," and the second five lines before its conclusion, "che mi dia argento per gettar la medaglia."

[31]   *Magnifice ac potens* another excerpt from the letter, dated December 22, 1454, by Matteo Nuti of Fano to Sigismondo; Nuti was the builder responsible for constructing the Tempio; the entire letter is found in Yriarte, *Un Condottiere au XVe siècle*, pp. 421–2.

[32]   *Malatesta de Malatestis ... his age* (lines 165–78) this letter is from Malatesta de Malatestis, the son of Sigismondo and Isotta degli Atti, a mistress who became his third wife in 1456; a transcription of it is given in Yriarte, *Un Condottiere au XVe siècle*, p. 445.

[33]   *Malatesta de Malatestis ... suum* Latin for "Malatesta of the Malatestas to the Magnificent Lord and his Father." These words are not in the original or in Yriarte, but are added by Pound, a sort of label describing the letter to follow, written by Sigismondo Malatesta's son.

"Malatestis Capitan General Magnificent and Exalted Lord and Father in especial my lord with
"due recommendation: your letter has been presented to me by Gentilino da Gradara and with
"it the bay pony (*ronzino baiectino*) the which you have sent me, and which appears in my eyes a fine
"caparison'd charger, upon which I intend to learn all there is to know about riding, in consider-   170
"ation of yr. paternal affection for which I thank your excellency thus briefly and pray you continue
"to hold me in this esteem notifying you by the bearer of this that we are all in good health, as I
"hope and desire your Ex^ct Lordship is also: with continued remembrance I remain
"   ‒ Your son and servant
"   MALATESTA DE MALATESTIS.   175
"   Given in Rimini, this the 22nd day of December
"   anno domini 1454"
"   (in the sixth year of his age)

"ILLUSTRIOUS PRINCE:
   "Unfitting as it is that I should offer counsels to Hannibal . . . "[34]   180

   "*Magnifice at potens domine, domine mi singularissime, humili recomendatione permissa* etc.[35] This to
"advise your M^gt Ld^shp how the second load of Veronese marble has finally got here, after being held
"up at Ferrara with no end of fuss and botheration, the whole of it having been there unloaded.
   "I learned how it happened, and it has cost a few florins to get back the said load which had been
"seized for the skipper's debt and defalcation; he having fled when the lighter was seized. But that   185
"Y^r M^gt Ld^shp may not lose the moneys paid out on his account I have had the lighter brought here
"and am holding it, against his arrival. If not we still have the lighter.
   "As soon as the Xmas fêtes are over I will have the stone floor laid in the sacresty, for which the
"stone is already cut. The wall of the building is finished and I shall now get the roof on.
   "We have not begun putting new stone into the martyr chapel; first because the heavy frosts wd.   190
"certainly spoil the job; secondly because the aliofants aren't yet here and one can't get the
"measurements for the cornice to the columns that are to rest on the aliofants.
   "They are doing the stairs to your room in the castle. . . . I have had Messire Antonio degli Atti's
"court paved and the stone benches put in it.
   "Ottavian is illuminating the bull. I mean the bull for the chapel. All the stone-cutters are   195
"waiting for spring weather to start work again.
   "The tomb is all done except part of the lid, and as soon as Messire Agostino gets back from
"Cesena I will see that he finishes it, ever recommending me to y^r M^gt Ld^shp
"   believe me y^r faithful
"   PETRUS GENARIIS."   200

That's what they found in the post-bag
And some more of it to the effect that
                          he "lived and ruled"

"et amava perdutamente Ixotta degli Atti"
e *"ne fu degna"*[36]   205

---

[34]   *Illustrious Prince . . . counsels to Hannibal* from a letter by the
humanist poet Servolo Trachulo, dated December 18, 1454, to
Sigismondo Malatesta; the letter, which is found in Yriarte, *Un
Condottiere au XVe siècle*, p. 444, is a sycophantic one that urges
Sigismondo to betray the Sienese and perhaps even conquer
them. Hannibal (247–182 BC) was a Carthaginian general
regarded as one of the world's greatest soldiers.

[35]   *Magnifice at potens . . . Petrus Genariis* (lines 181–200) a
letter by Pietro Genari, dated December 18, 1454, to Sigismondo Malatesta; it is transcribed in Yriarte, *Un Condottiere au
XVe siècle*, pp. 406–7.

[36]   *"et amava perdutamatmente Ixotta degli Atti" / e "ne fu degna"*
ultimately from Cardinal Jacopo Ammanati (1422–79), *Commentarii*, in Pius II, *Commentarii* (Frankfurt: in officina Aubriana,

1614), Book 5, p. 403, where he reports the death of Sigismondo:

> But in those days it happened that Sigismondo,
> who had returned to Italy from the Pelopon-
> nesian war on behalf of the Venetians exhausted
> by incessant ill health, departed from this life in
> Rimini, having entrusted custody of the city
> and its fortress to his wife Isotta, whom, earlier
> as a kept mistress, later as his wife, he had loved
> desperately [perdite amaverat].

Perdite amaverat was an expression which did not refer to depths
of romantic passion, but a humanist formula for describing love

> "constans in proposito
> "Placuit oculis principis
> "pulchra aspectu
> "populo grata"[37]   (Italiaeque decus)[38]

210   "and built a temple so full of pagan works"[39]
>   i.e. Sigismund
> and in the style "Past ruin'd Latium"[40]
> The filagree hiding the gothic,
>   with a touch of rhetoric in the whole
215   And the old sarcophagi,
>   such as lie, smothered in grass, by San Vitale.[41]

outside of marriage ("loved lostly" would be the most literal translation, signalling a loss of self-control). From Ammanati the passage was taken up by Gianmaria Mazzuchelli (1709–68), author of a biography of Isotta (*Notizie intorno ad Isotta da Rimino* [Brescia: Giambatista Bossini, 1759], p. 32), and from Mazzuchelli it was adopted by Gaetano Moroni in 1852 in a vast encyclopedia of Italian history (*Dizionario di erudizionestorico-ecclesiastica da S. Pietro ai nostri giorni*, vol. 57 [Venice: tip. Emiliana, 1852], p. 282, col. *a*). Thirty years later the passage was picked up from Moroni by the French journalist and art historian Yriarte (1832–98), in his study of Sigismondo Malatesa; he ascribed the quotation not to Jacopo Ammanati, but to Pius II, and he "improved" it by adding a new clause: "Pope Pius II has written: 'He loved Isotta desperately, and she was worthy of this love,'" or "Il a aimé éperdument Isotte et elle en était digne'" (Yriarte, *Un Condottiere au XVe siècle*, p. 155). Yet another 30 years later, Yriarte's nonquotation was adopted by the Italian journalist and novelist Antonio Beltramelli (1879–1930), in his work *Un tempio d'amore* (*A Temple of Love*) (Palermo: Remo Sandron, 1912): "Pius II, the historian who never spares a charge against Sigismondo, amò indeed who surpasses every limit, writes: 'Sigismondo loved Isotta desperately, and she was worthy of this love'" ("'Sigismondo perdutamente Isotta ed ella ne era degna'"). Beltramelli is the source of Pound's quotation, though Pound alters the verb tense (from *amò* to *amava*) and the spelling of Isotta's name (from *Isotta* to *Ixotta*).

[37]   *constans in proposito ... populo grata* Latin for "firm in her resolve / she pleased the eyes of the prince / lovely to behold / dear to the people." These phrases all come from the Chronicle of pseudo-Alessandro, a forgery composed around 1650 in order to create a history for spurious relics in a convent not far from Rimini. Though he had been warned of the chronicle's doubtful authenticity, Gianmaria Mazzuchelli, the author of a biography of Isotta (*Notizie intorno ad Isotta da Rimino* [Brescia: Giambatista Bossini, 1759], pp. 36–7), cited the passage that contained these phrases, and from his work it was next adopted by Yriarte (*Un Condottiere au XVe siècle*, [1882], p. 155 n. 1). From Yriarte, in turn, these phrases were adopted by Pound in 1922. The Chronicle of pseudo-Alessandro was identified and dismissed as worthless forgery in 1915 (see Giovanni Soranzo, "Due delitti attribuiti a Sigismondo Malatesta e una falsa cronachetta riminese," *Atti del Reale Istituto Veneto di scienze, lettere ed arti* 74 [1914] [Part 2]: 1881–1902).

[38]   *Italiaeque decus* Latin for "and the honor [*decus*] of Italy"; ultimately the phrase comes from Vergil, the *Aeneid* 11, 508, where a character named Turnus addresses the warrior-princess Camilla: "O decus Italiae virgo" ("O maiden, the honor of Italy").

The locution "Italiae decus" (classical Latin) or "Italie decus" (medieval Latin) appears in various testimonies of the Malatestan court, a humanist compliment comparing Isotta to the legendary Camilla. Pound chose the phrase specifically because it appeared on a medal that depicted Isotta and was allegedly made by Pisanello (Vittore Pisano) (1395–1455), the greatest of the Italian medallion makers. The medallion was attributed to Pisanello by Yriarte, *Un Condottiere au XVe siècle*, p. 150 n. 1. But, already dismissed as a forgery by Heiss in 1881, it was rejected by Armand in 1883, and rejected again by G. F. Hill in 1905. By 1917 it was considered "a well known forgery." (See Alfred Armand, *Les Médailleurs italiens*, vol. 1 [Paris: E. Plon, 1883], p. 13, note A; George Francis Hill, *Pisanello* [London: Duckworth, 1905]), p. 164; George Francis Hill, "The Medals of Matteo de' Pasti," *The Numismatic Chronicle*, ser. 4, vol. 17 (1917), pp. 298–312, here ["well known forgery"] p. 312; George Francis Hill, *Corpus of Italian Medals of the Renaissance Before Cellini* [London: British Museum, 1930] vol. 1, p. 10, n. 33.)

[39]   *"and built a temple so full of pagan works"* a translation of Pius II (Enea Silvio Piccolomini), *Commentarii*, ed. Luigi Tortaro (Milan: Adelphi, 1984; 1st ed. 1484), p. 366: "Aedificavit tamen nobile templum Arimini in honorem divi Fancisci; verum ita gentilibus operibus implevit ut non tam Christianorum quam Infidelium daemones adorantium templum esse videretur." Latin for: "Nevertheless he constructed in Rimini a noble temple in honor of Saint Francis, though he filled it with so many pagan [or gentile] works that it seemed less a temple for Christians than a temple for infidels worshipping demons."

[40]   *"past ruin'd Latium"* from Walter Savage Landor (1775–1864), untitled poem XVIII in his *Poems, Dialogues in Verse and Epigrams*, ed. Charles Crump, vol. 2 *Poems and Epigrams* (London: J. M. Dent, 1892), p. 97:

> Past ruin'd Ilion Helen lives,
>   Alcestis rises from the shades;
> Verse calls them forth; 'tis verse that gives
>   Immortal youth to mortal maids.
>
> Soon shall Oblvion's deepening veil
>   Hide all the peopled hills you see,
> The gay, the proud, while lovers hail
>   These many summers you and me.

[41]   *San Vitale* a Byzantine church in Ravenna which dates from the sixth century; the sarcophagi outside are shaped like those found in the arched niches of the Tempio malatestiano.

X

And the poor devils dying of cold,[1] outside Sorano,
And from the other side, from inside the château,
      Orsini, Count Pitigliano, on the 17th of November:
"Siggy, darlint, wd. you not stop making war on insensible
"objects, such as trees and domestic vines, that have no   5
"means to hit back . . . but if you will hire yourself out to
"a commune (Siena) which you ought rather to rule than
"serve . . ."[2]
         which with Trachulo's damn'd epistle!![3]
And what of it *any*how? a man with a ten acre lot,   10
Pitigliano !! . . . a lump of tufa,
      And S. had got back their horses
And the poor devils dying of cold . . .
(And there was another time, you know,
he signed on with the Fanesi,   15
         And just couldn't be bothered . . .)
And there were three men on a one-man job
      And Careggi wanting the baton[4]
And not getting it just now in any case,

And he, Sigismundo, refused an invitation to lunch   20
      In commemoration of Carmagnola
      (vide Venice, between the two columns
      where Carmagnola[5] was executed.)
      Et
      "anno messo a saccho el signor Sigismundo"   25
As Filippo Strozzi wrote to Zan, Lottieri, then in Naples,
      "I think they'll let him through at Campiglia"[6]
Archivio Storico, 4th series t,III. Florence e "La guerra dei Senesi col conte di Pitigliano."[7]

---

[1] *And the poor devils . . . just now in any case* (lines 1–19) the beginning of Canto X resumes the account of Sigismondo's campaign for Siena against Aldobrandino Orsini, count of Pitigliano, whom he besieged in the castle of Sorano during the winter of 1454–5, with brief interruption for a thematically related but chronologically disparate event, lines 20–3, Sigismondo's refusal of an invitation to Venice.

[2] *"Siggy, darlint . . . than serve . . . "* Pound splices together two passages, and also adds material of his own, from an essay by Luicano Banchi, "La Guerra de' Senesi col conte di Pitigliano" ("The War of the Sienese against the Count of Pitigliano"), *Archivio storico italiano*, ser. 4, vol. 3 (1879): 184–97. On p. 186 n. 2, Banchi quotes from a letter by Orsini, dated November 17, 1454, in which he asks Sigismondo to cease "far guerra ale cosse insensibili, le qualle non si possono defendere, come che de vigni e arbori domestici" (to stop "making war on insensibile objects that can't defend themselves, such as vines and domestic trees"). Elsewhere, in the text proper of the same page, Banchi presents a synopsis of Orsini's letter: "Orsini, who knew Sigismondo well, tried from the outset of the war to separate him from the Sienese, writing him that he was quite surprised to see him working in the pay of a community which it would be more fitting for him to rule." Pound converts Banchi's synopsis into a direct quotation and attaches it to the preceding genuine direct quotation, prefacing the whole with his own addition, "Siggy, darlint."

[3] *with Trachulo's damn'd epistle* the letter urges Sigismondo to betray the Sienese; see Canto IX, note 34.

[4] *three men . . . wanting the baton* the Venetians had sent troops to aid the Sienese, under the command of Pietro Brunoro and Carlo Careggi Gonzaga, while the troops of the Sienese were under the command of Giulio Cesare Varani. The entire force was under Sigismondo's supreme command.

[5] *Carmagnola* Francesco Bussone da Carmagnola (*c*. 1385–1432) was a condottiere who served Milan until 1425, then Venice. When, in 1432, it appeared that he was not conducting his campaign with sufficient vigor and was secretly negotiating for a state of his own, he was recalled to Venice, tried for treason, and executed between the columns on the Piazzetta, where the Doge's palace is. Sigismondo suspected that the Venetians were going to treat him similarly during his stalled campaign against Sforza in 1449–50.

[6] *Et "anno messo . . . at Campiglia"* the text is quoting from a letter in Italian by Filippo Strozi (1428–91), in Florence, to the Florentine ambassador Zanobi Lottieri in Naples, dated December 31, 1454, which is cited by Luciano Banchi, "La Guerra de' Senesi" (see note 2 above), p. 188 n. 3: "Da Siena ci è come anno messo a saccho el signor Sigismondo, et lui s'è fuggito sulli terreni nostri con poche genti. Ènne venuto verso Campiglia, et qui ha mandato per aver del passo per tornare a casa. Credo l'arà" Or: "From Siena it's reported how they've given the sack to Signor Sigismondo. He has come toward Campiglia, and has sent here requesting a 'pass' in order to return home. I think he'll have it."

[7] *Florence . . . di Pitigliano* see note 2 above.

And he found Carlo Gonzaga sitting like a mud-frog
30   in Orbetello[8]
And he said:
            "*Cara mio*, I can not receive you
It really is not the moment."
And Broglio says he ought to have tipped Gorro Lolli![9]
35   But he got back home here somehow,
And Piccinino was out of a job,[10]
And the old row with Naples[11] continued.
And what he said was all right in Mantua;
And Borso[12] had the pair of them up to Bel Fiore,
40   The pair of them, Sigismundo and Federico Urbino,

---

[8]   *Carlo Gonzaga ... in Orbetello* Carlo Gonzaga's troops retired from the Sienese campaign to Orbetello, a city on the west coast in the extreme south of Tuscany.

[9]   *Broglio says ... Gorro Lolli* Gaspare Broglio (1407–93) was an advisor and confidante to Sigismondo Malatesta; Gorro or Gregorio Lolli, a prominent lawyer in Siena, was a cousin and later secretary of Enea Silvio Piccolomini, later Pope Pius II (1458–64). This failure to give a tip is a feeble explanation for Pius II's later hostility toward Sigismondo.

[10] *And Piccinino was out of a job* Giacomo Piccinino (c. 1415–65) was a major condottiere; for him, as for Sigismondo and many lesser condottieri, the Peace of Lodi signed in 1454 by Venice, Milan, Florence, and the Papacy, and then ratified in 1455 by Naples, effectively meant discharge and destitution.

[11] *the old row with Naples* See Canto IX, note 9.

[12] *And Borso ... corata a te!* (lines 39–47) from Giovanni Soranzo, *Pio II e la politica italian nella lotta contro i Malatesti, 1457–1463* (or, *Pius II and Italian Politics in the Struggle against the Malatestas, 1456–1463* (Padua: Fratelli Drucker, 1911), p. 26: "Even in 1457, at the request of common friends, the two terrible adversaries decided to be reconciled and submitted their quarrel to the judgment of Borso d'Este, duke of Modena. In the d'Este villa at Belfiore on May 7 the two men met; there, in the presence of the duke and several common friends, they opened up their grievances and explained the causes of their resentment. At first the two maintained a calm and courteous conduct. But when Federico d'Urbino refused to withdraw a very serious charge that Sigismondo had secretly participated in a conspiracy to poison Alessandro Sforza, Sigismondo Malatesta could no longer contain himself: he launched into a furious invective and, faced with this stubborn opponent, saw no means of obtaining satisfaction other than setting his hand to his sword and advancing toward him screaming "By the body of God, I'll cut the guts out of your body!" [*io te caverò la budella del corpo!*] Federico di Montefeltro didn't hesitate, and imitating his taunter, he got up and said: "I'll cut your heart out of you" [*io te caverò la corata a te*]. (My translation)

The failure to reconcile Sigismondo and Federico d'Urbino in May 1457 proved the prelude to the turning point in Sigismondo's career. Five months later, in November, Federico and Jacomo Piccinino invaded Sigismondo's territory, now working together in the pay of Alfonso. Their aim was to compel Sigismondo to repay the money he had owed to Alfonso since 1447, when he had first signed a *condotta* with Alfonso and then had betrayed him, instead turning to Florence (see Canto IX, note 9). Alfonso would now be repaid, Federico would annex some Malatestan territories to his own, and Piccinino would acquire a state that would content him. But in the summer of 1458, just as the campaign against Sigismondo was beginning to progress, everything changed.

Alfonso of Aragon, King of Naples, died on June 27, 1458, and Pope Calixtus III on August 6. Piccinino halted his campaign against Sigismondo and instead seized several towns belonging to the Church, including the venerable city of Assisi. When Pius II was selected as the new pope, his first task was to force Piccinino out of Assisi, and to do so he struck a bargain with Alfonso's successor, Ferdinando I, still the ostensible paymaster of Piccinino. In return for papal recognition of Ferdinando's claim to the throne (Ferdinando was illegitimate), and papal help in pressing his dead father's old claim against Sigismondo, Ferdinando would compel Piccinino to abandon Assisi. To persuade Piccinino to leave, Ferdinando promised him that he would be able to keep some portion of the lands that, once again in conjunction with Federico d'Urbino, he would seize from the southernmost territories of Sigismondo. Piccinino finally left Assisi in late January, joined forces with Federico, and began a slow campaign against Sigismondo's territories in the March (the area south of Romagna) and Montefeltro. By August 1459, at a conference convened by the pope in Mantua, Sigismondo agreed to turn over a number of territories to papal commissioners, with these to serve as pledges for the debt to Ferdinando. But just when it seemed that the longstanding question of Sigismondo's debt was finally resolved, almost everything changed again.

In the summer of 1459, a rebellion against Ferdinando began among the major barons of the Neapolitan kingdom, headed by Giannantonio Orsini, the Prince of Taranto. Worse still, Jean d'Anjou now laid claim to the throne of Naples, and to advance his cause he poured in money and troops in aid of the barons. By the autumn it was clear that Ferdinando was vulnerable, and in January 1460 Piccinino threw his support behind the Angevins (supporters of Jean d'Anjou) and the rebel barons. Sigismondo, in exchange for Piccinino's return of some castles and towns he had taken, now agreed that Piccinino could pass through his lands in the course of his advance against Naples.

Six months later, on July 7, 1460, Ferdinando was badly defeated by the Angevins; and only days later Federico d'Urbino and Alessandra Sforza, jointly serving Ferdinando and the Church, were defeated by Piccinino. The final defeat of Ferdinando now seemed imminent, and in August Sigismondo threw in his lot with the Angevins and Piccinino. During the winter pause in combat, the Church began to marshal its finances and forces, including its spiritual weapons. Sigismondo was excommunicated on Christmas day, 1460, and in 1461 a series of consistories would judge him to be a heretic and excommunicate him again, culminating in a final excommunication and ceremony of effigy-burning in April 1462.

During the first year of the war, in 1461, Sigismondo managed to survive a ferocious campaign, defeating a superior ecclesiastical army at the battle of Nidastore on July 2. The next season

Or perhaps in the palace, Ferrara, Sigismund upstairs
And Urbino's gang in the basement,
And a regiment of guards in, to keep order,
For all the good that did:
"Te cavero la budella del corpo!"   45
El conte levatosi:
             "Io te cavero la corata a te!"

And that day[13] Cosimo smiled,
That is, the day they said:
            "Drusiana is to marry Count Giacomo ..."   50
(Piccinino) un sorriso malizioso.[14]
Drusiana, another of Franco Sforza's;
It would at least keep the row out of Tuscany.
And he fell out of a window, Count Giacomo,
Three days after his death, that was years later in Naples,   55
For trusting Ferdinando of Naples,
And old Wattle could do nothing about it.

                        Et:

INTEREA PRO GRADIBUS[15] BASILICAE S. PIETRI EX ARIDA MATERIA INGENS PYRA
EXTRUITUR IN CUJUS SUMMITATE IMAGO SIGISMUNDI COLLOCATUR, HOMINIS LINEA-   60
MENTA, ET VESTIMENTI MODUM ADEO PROPRIE REDDENS, UT VERA MAGIS PERSONA
QUAM IMAGO VIDERETUR; NE QUEM TAMEN IMAGO FALLERET, ET SCRIPTURA EX ORE
PRODIIT, QUAE DICERET: SIGISMUNDUS HIC EGO SUM MALATESTA, FILIUS PANDULPHI,
REX PRODITORUM, DEO ATQUE HOMINIBUS INFESTUS, SACRI CENSURA SENATUS IGNI
DAMNATUS;   65

---

his luck ran out. On August 13 his troops were routed at the battle of Senigallia, and less than a week later those of his ally Piccinino were annihilated at the battle of Troia. Sigismondo was finished. When peace terms were drafted, he lost everything except the city of Rimini.

[13] *And that day ... do nothing about it* (lines 48–57) Giacomo Piccinino had been betrothed to Drusiana Sforza, daughter of Francesco Sforza, since 1449; but it was not till 1458 that a plan to realize the marriage was first broached by Ferdinando I (1423–94), King of Naples (1458–94) who had succeeded his father Alfonso in 1458. Piccinino became a problem when he seized the city of Assisi from the papacy that year: it was a patent violation of the Peace of Lodi, and the major powers were to spend the next seven years trying to rid themselves of him. Ferdinando I, in proposing that Piccinino marry Sforza's daughter Drusiana, was hoping that her dowry might provide Piccinino with enough land to content him. But the plan was put off and not executed till late 1464, when Piccinino went to Milan, married her, and was showered with money and gifts. Sforza then persuaded Piccinino to honor his condotta with Ferdinando I and travel to Naples to see him. Piccinino arrived on June 23, 1465, was arrested on June 24, and was found dead on July 12. The story put about, that he fell out of a window, was not believed by contemporaries, and many believed that Sforza ("old Wattle") had cynically married his daughter to Piccinino only so that he would have faith in Sfroza's entreaties that he go to Naples. "Drusiana is to marry Count Giacomo ..." is not a direct quotation from a specific source.

[14] *un sorriso malizioso* (Italian) "a malicious smile," from Giovanni Soranzo, *Pio II e la politica italiana* (1911), pp. 73–4, n. 4. The phrase, in other words, is that of a modern historian, not that of a historical character in the poem.

[15] *Interea pro gradibus ... Yriarte, p. 288* (lines 59–126) having till now dwelled on events of 1455 (the aftermath of the Siena campaign), or 1457 (the failed reconciliation between Sigismondo and Federico di Montefelto) and 1458 (the idea that Piccinino marry Sforza's daughter Drusiana), the canto now leaps forward to events of May 1462, when three effigies of Sigismondo were publicly burnt in Rome, and he was formally excommunicated and declared a heretic. That event was the culmination of others. The first had been a public consistory on January 16, 1461, at which Andrea dei Benci, a lawyer for the treasury office of the Camera Apostolica, had read aloud a dramatic oration (thought by some to have been penned by Pius II himself), condemning Sigismondo for many crimes, an occasion which set in motion further proceedings. The second took place on October 14, 1461, when Nicolò da Cusa, charged with investigating the charges, reported his results. That led to the immediate publication of a papal bull, *Discipula veritatis*, which excommunicated Sigismondo. The third took place on April 27, 1462, a secret consistory comprising all the cardinals of the church, which decided on another public condemnation of Sigismondo and led to the ceremonial burning of his effigies a few days later in early May 1462. In effect, the text of this canto gives these events in a complex order: first (lines 59–70), it gives Pius II's account of the burning of the effigies in May, 1462; second (lines 71–106), it turns to the earlier oration by Andrea dei Benci (January 1461), quoting and paraphrasing extensively; third (lines 109–19), it turns to the proceeding conducted by Nicolò de Cusa (October 1461). Finally (lines 120–6), it gives a brief coda which comments, as if more comment were needed, on the preceding sections.

SCRIPTURAM

MULTI LEGERUNT, DEINDE ASTANTE POPULO IGNE IMMISSO, ET PYRA SIMULACRUM
REPENTE FLAGRAVIT.

Com, Pio II. Liv. VII p. 85.

Yriarte p. 288.

70

    So that in the end that pot-scraping little runt Andreas
        Benzi, da Siena[16]
    Got up to spout out the bunkum
    That that monstrous swollen, swelling

75

        Papa Pio Secundo
          Aeneas Silvius Piccolomini
            da Siena
    Had told him to spout, in their best bear's-greased latinity

    Stupro, caede, adulter,[17]

80

    homocidia, parricidia ac periurus,
    presbitericidia, audax, libidinosus,
    wives, jew-girls, nuns, necrophiliast, *fornicarium ac sicarium,*
    proditor, raptor, incestuosus, incendiarius, ac
    concubinarius,

85

    and that he rejected the whole symbol of the apostles,
    and that he said the monks ought not to own property
    and that he disbelieved in the temporal power,
    neither christian, jew, gentile
        nor any sect pagan, *nisi forsitan epicureae.*[18]

90

    And that he did[19] among other things
    Empty the fonts of the chiexa of holy water
    And fill up the same full with ink
    In order that he might in God's dishonour
    Stand before the doors of the said chiexa

95

    Making mock of the inky faithful, they
    Issuing thence by the doors in the pale light of the sunrise
    Which might be considered youthful levity
        but was really a profound indication;

    "Whence that his, Sigismundo's, foetor filled the earth

100

    And stank up through the air and stars to heaven
    Where, save they were immune from sufferings,
    It had made the emparadisèd spirits pewk"[20]
        from their jeweled terrace

---

[16] *So that ... uxoricido* (lines 71–106) Andrea dei Benci, or Benzi, was a lawyer in the treasury of the Camera Apostolica.

[17] *Stupro, caede ... concubinarius* (lines 79–84) Latin for: "Rape, slaughter, adultery, / homicide, patricide and perjuror, / priest-murderer, presumptuous, libidinous, / ... fornicator and assassin, / traitor, plunderer, incestuous, arsonist, and / keeper of concubines." The oration of Andrea dei Benci is printed in Giovanni Benedetto Mittarelli, *Bibliotheca codicum manuscriptorum Monasterii S. Michaelis Venetiarum prope Murianum* (Venice: ex typographia Fentiana, 1779), cols. 704–14.

[18] *nisi forsitan epicureae* in Latin, "except perhaps that of the epicureans" in Mittarelli, *Bibliotheca codicum manuscriptorum,* col. 713. The Epicureans, in the middle ages and Renaissance, were thought to be the ancient school of thought which was the most demonic or irreligious.

[19] *And that he did ... indication* (lines 90–6) translated loosely from Andrea dei Benci's oration, transcribed in Mittarelli, *Bibliotheca codicum manuscriptorum,* col. 712: Is quoque insolens

in magna sexta feria, quo tempore nemo homo Christianus est, qui conscientiam suam non inspeciat, et non corde mutato aliquo modo ad poenitentiam redeat, et bonis operibus Dei misericordiam imploret, perfidus Christianus, Saracenis, Turcisque nequior, et infidelior, Ecclesiam ingressus nocte, sacri roris vasa evacuata implevit atramento, ut ante lucem feminae, quae pro more illius diei templum ingredientes illo se conspergentes tamquam aqua benedicta, jam non homines sed daemonia viderentur. Juvinilia haec et levia, et ridicula dixerit aliquis; sed unde haec levitas, nisi in contemptum divinae domus, quae est Ecclesia.

[20] *"Whence that his ... spirits pewk"* freely translated again from the oration by Andrea dei Benci, in Mittarelli, *Bibliotheca codicum manuscriptorum,* col. 704: Nec facile putarim inveniri similem posse, cujus completa iniquitas est, cujus foetor non ecclesiam solum, et ipsum infecit terrarum orbem, sed in coelum usque sentitur, ipsis beatissimis spiritibus, nisi passiones essent incapaces, nauseam faceret.

"   *Lussurioso, incestuoso, perfide, sozzure ac crapulone*
assassino, ingordo, avaro, superbo, infedele   105
fattore di monete false, sodomitico, uxoricido,[21]

and the whole lump lot
given over to . . .

I mean after Pio had said, or at least Pio says that he
Said that this was elegant oratory *"Orationem*   110
Elegantissimam et ornatissimam
Audivimus venerabilis in Xti fratres ac dilectissimi
filii[22] . . . (stone in his bladder
                    . . . *testibus idoneis)*[23]
    The lump lot given over   115
To that kid-slapping fanatic il cardinale di San Pietro in Vincoli[24]
    To find him guilty, of the lump lot
As he duly did, calling rumour, and Messire Federico d'Urbino
And other equally unimpeachable witnesses.

So they burnt our brother in effigy   120
A rare magnificent effigy costing 8 florins 48 bol[25]
(i.e. for the pair, as the first one wasn't a good enough likeness)
And Borso said the time was ill suited
        to *tanta novità,*[26] such doings or innovations,

God's enemy and man's enemy, *stuprum, raptum*[27]   125
    I.N.R.I. Sigismund Imperator, Rex Proditorum.[28]

And old Pills[29] who tried to get him into a front rank action
In order to drive the rear guard at his buttocks

---

[21]   (lines 104–7) Italian for: "Lecherous incestuous man, foulness and glutton, / assassin, greedy, avaricious, haughty, unfaithful, / counterfeiter, sodomite, uxoricide." The Italian list is adapted from Giovanni Soranzo, *Pio II e la politica italiana nell lotta contro i Malatesti, 1457–1463* (Padua: Fratelli Drucker, 1922), p. 227, with only one error added to the Italian (*uxoricido* for *uxoricida*).

[22]   *Orationem ... filii* (lines 110–13) Latin for: "Brothers in venerable Christ and most beloved children, we have heard an elegant and highly ornamented speech." This is presumably said by Pius II immediately after the oration of dei Benci, but it appears nowhere in his *Commentarii.* See the bull, *Discipula veritatis,* in Pius, *Epistolae* (Milan: Zaroti, 1487), after Epistola VI (no pagination.)

[23]   *testibus idoneis* Latin for "by appropriate witnesses." The phrase occurs in a papal bull by Pius II, *Discipula veritatis* (*Disciple of the truth*), which is included in the 1487 edition of his *Epistolae,* Epistola VI, describing the report of Nicolò da Cusa on October 14, 1461: "retullit nobis in concistorio secreto crimina omnia et omnes excessus, super quibus Sigismundus fuisset delatus, aut testibus idoneis aut voce publica comprobari, quae vero maiora et atrociora essent ita vulgo et rumore plebium confirmari, ut manifesta et notoria iudicari possent; quibus cognitis certiores redditi sumus Sigismundum alium non esse quam fuerit per advocatum fisci descriptum." Or in English: "He recounted to us that all the crimes and all the excesses in which Sigismondo had indulged were proved either by appropriate witnesses or by public rumor, that in truth they were confirmed to be worse and more atrocious than vulgar or popular rumor supposed, that they were manifest and notorious; from

which facts being so well known, we have returned still more certain that Sigismondo is not different from the description that was given by the lawyer of the treasury [i.e. Andrea dei Benci]."

[24]   *il cardinale di San Pietro in Vincoli* Italian for "the cardinal of the church of Saint Peter in Chains," who was Nicolò da Cusa. Nicolò was charged with investigating the charges levied by dei Benci, and reported back on October 14, 1461 (see preceding note).

[25]   *costing 8 ... bol* The detail is derived from Yriarte, p. 287 n. 1.

[26]   *And Borso said ... tanta novita* Borso d'Este (1413–71), Duke of Ferrara (1450–71), wrote to his ambassador in Rome that the Pope, "se d'alcuno fosse laudata, non era ancora che non fosse da molti biasimata, perchè a questi tempi non pareva savio consiglio fare tanta novita" (the pope, "if he was praised by someone, it was not the case that he was not criticized by many, for in these times it did not seem to be a wise idea to perform such innovations"). Borso's remarks were reported in a letter from Ottone del Caretto in Rome to Francesco Sforza in Milan, January 25, 1461, and are reported by Giovani Soranzo, *Pio II e la politica italiana,* p. 231, which is Pound's source.

[27]   *stuprum, raptum* "rape, theft," in Latin; see note 17 above.

[28]   *I.N.R.I. ... Proditorum* Latin abbreviation for "Jesus of Nazareth, King of the Jews," said to have been posted on the cross at the crucifixion of Christ, and juxtaposed here with Latin for "Commander Sigismondo, King of Traitors."

[29]   *And old Pills ... living later* (lines 127–30) "Old Pills" is the text's sobriquet for Ugolini Pili, who served Pandolfo Malatesta (Sigismondo's father) as *condottiere,* councilor, and ambassador; he was named guardian of Pandolfo's three sons (including Sigis-

130
Old Pills listed among the murdered, although he
Came out of jail living later.

Et les angloys ne povans desraciner... venin de hayne.[30]
Had got back Gisors[31] from the Angevins,

And the Angevins were gunning after Naples
And we dragged in the Angevins,

135
And we dragged in Louis Eleventh,[32]
And the *tiers Calixte*[33] was dead, and Alfonso;
And against us we had "this Aeneas" and young Ferdinando
That we had smashed at Piombino[34] and driven out of the
Terrene of the Florentines;

140
And Piccinino, out of a job;
And he, Sidg, had had three chances of
Making it up with Alfonso, and an offer of
Marriage alliance;

And what he said was all right there in Mantua;[35]

145
But Pio, sometime or other, Pio lost his pustulous temper.
And they struck alum[36] at Tolfa, in the pope's land,
                To pay for their devilment.
And Francesco[37] said:
                I also have suffered.

150
When you take it, give me a slice.

        And they nearly jailed a chap for saying
The job was *mal hecho*;[38] and they caught poor old Pasti

mondo) upon his death. In his oration of early January 1461 Andrea dei Benci charged that he had been murdered by Sigismondo. Though it appears that he was jailed and his property confiscated in 1444 for some dealings with Pope Eugenio IV, he was still alive in 1469. Pound's information on him comes from Giovanni Soranzo, "Un'Invettiva della curia romana contro Sigismondo Pandolfo Malatesta [II]," *La Romagna* 8 (1911): 150–70, here 159–68.

[30]   *Et les angloys ... venin de hayne* medieval French for "And the English being unable to uproot ... the poison of hate." Source not identified.

[31]   *Gisors* site of a famous castle in Normandy that passed back and forth between English and French hands during the Hundred Years War; its relevance to the immediate context is obscure.

[32]   *Louis Eleventh* King of France, 1461–83; when he assumed the throne, Sigismondo sent the mayor of Rimini, Gregorio Bazolini, to France to offer condolences for the death of his father, present congratulations for his ascent to the throne, and sound out his intentions in connection with Italian politics. The king wrote to Sigismondo and explained his support for the Angevins against Ferdinando and the house of Aragon. See Soranzo, *Pio II e la politica italiana*, p. 268.

[33]   *tiers Calixte* Calixtus III (1378–1459), pope (1455–8), born Alfonso Borgia, founder of this infamous family; see note 12.

[34]   *smashed at Piombino* in 1448, when Sigismondo on behalf of the Florentines drove Alfonso and Ferdinando out of Piombino, a city in extreme southwestern Tuscany on the coast.

[35]   *there in Mantua* Pope Pius II convened an international conference in Mantua in 1459, aimed at resolving all local disputes within Italy and setting in motion longstanding plans

for a new crusade that would halt the advance of the Ottoman empire. Sigismondo met with him several times in efforts to resolve the question of his debt to the late Alfonso of Aragon, a debt inherited by his son Ferdinando I.

[36]   *And they struck alum* alum is a whitish, crystalline, mineral salt that was used in dying wool and tanning. It was discovered by Giovanni da Castro in 1462, or perhaps a bit earlier, in Tolfa, a small town about 30 km northeast of Civitavecchia, territory that at this time belonged to the Church. Until then alum had been imported at considerable expense from Asia Minor, then under the control of the Ottoman empire; the substantial revenues which were derived from this discovery accrued directly to the Church, and Pius II dedicated them all to the crusade against the Turks that he was bent on organizing. He recounts these events in his *Commentarii*, ed. Luigi Totaro (Milan: Adelphi, 1984), Book 7, 1450–9.

[37]   *Francesco* Francesco Sforza, Duke of Milan; here suggesting a secret arrangement of the sort he used on many occasions.

[38]   *mal hecho* Spanish for "badly done." From Giovanni Soranzo, *Pio II e la politica italiana*, p. 289, describing the burning of the effigy of Sigismondo Malatesta in early May 1462: "The ambassador of Mantua recounts a curious anecdote: a Florentine with a witty mind was among the crowd watching the event in Campo dei Fiori; all of a sudden he cried out loud: 'My God, that is badly done! [*Per Dio, èmal fatto!*].' The papal authorities immediately seized him and made ready to take him to prison. 'Why are you doing this?' said the Florentine. 'I'm not saying that the pope is doing something wicked; I'm only saying that the effigy of Sigismondo is so poor that it scarcely resembles him.' And to the laughter of the surrounding crowd he was set free."

In Venice,[39] and were like to pull all his teeth out;
   And they had a bow-shot at Borso
As he was going down the Grand Canal in his gondola,[40]   155
   (the nice kind with 26 barbs on it)
And they said: Novvy'll sell any man
   for the sake of Count Giacomo[41]
(Piccinino, the one that fell out of the window).

And they came[42] at us with their ecclesiastical legates   160
Until the eagle lit on his tent pole.
And he said: The Romans would have called that an augury
E grādment li antichi cavaler romanj
      davano fed a quisti annutii,[43]
All I want you to do is to follow the orders[44]   165
They've got a bigger army,
   but there are more men in this camp.[45]

XI

E grādment li antichi cavaler romanj
   davano fed a quisti annutii.[1]

[39] *Pasti in Venice* Matto de' Pasti (d. 1467 or 1468), originally from Verona, was an Italian medalist. In November, 1461 he was sent by Sigismondo to Mohammed II, head of the Ottoman empire, who had requested that he be allowed to have a portrait of himself made by de' Pasti. But while traveling to Constantinople, bearing a gift from Sigismondo (a copy of *De re militari* by the humanist Roberto Valturio), de' Pasti was detained by the Venetian authorities in the island of Candia, or Crete, and sent back to Venice. At first it was suspected that Sigismondo might be negotiating with Mohammed II about an invasion of Italy, and since Pope Pius II had only recently (1459) announced plans for a holy crusade, set to be launched in 1464, the incident was fraught with political repercussions that dissipated only when the mission's innocent nature was verified. "And were like to pull all his teeth out" is a fanciful extrapolation from the Venetians' liberal use of torture.

[40] *a bow-shot at Borso ... gondola* the source of this incident has not been identified.

[41] *Novvy'll sell any man for ... Giacomo* Malatesta Novella, or "Novvy," the ruler of Cesena and brother of Sigismondo Malatesta, served many times under Giacomo Piccinino and several times allowed Piccinino and his troops to winter in his territories during the period 1458–62 when Piccinino was intriguing with Federico d'Urbino and Ferdinando I to take territories away from Sigismondo.

[42] *And they came ... in this camp* (lines 160–7) this passage recounts the five-hour battle of Nidastore on July 2, 1461, when Sigismondo Malatesta, with 1,800 soldiers (1,300 cavalry and 500 infantry), defeated a much larger ecclesiastical force of 3,000, leading a surprise attack on the enemy camp. An eyewitness account of the battle is given by Gaspare Broglio (1407–93) in his *Cronaca universale*, an unpublished manuscript housed in the Biblioteca Gamabalunga in Rimini, Italy, where Pound consulted it in March 1923; Broglio's account of the battle was also transcribed and published in Carlo Tonini, *Rimini nella signoria de' Malatesti*, vol. 5 (Rimini: Albertini, 1880; ristampa Rimini: Bruno Ghigi, 1971), pp. 281–8.

[43] *E grādment ... quisti annutii* these words stem from a speech in Italian which Sigismondo gave to his men before the battle. In Italian, the text reads (with the words cited in the text in italics): "Or considerate se lla victoria è nostra – che iera sera un'aquila gientile se posò sull cima del nostro padiglione; *grandemente li antichi e valenti romani davano grandissima fede a questi annunti chiamati agurii*; per la quale part ne pigliamo gran conforto perchè essendo noi discessi della progienia e sanguinità dello illustrissimo Publio Scipone Affricano, nobile romano." In English translation: "Now consider whether the victory is ours – for yesterday evening a noble eagle landed on the top of our tent. *Greatly the ancient and valiant Romans placed great faith in these annunciations*, called auguries; therefore we take solace from this event, as our house descends from the progeny and blood-line of the famous Roman nobleman, Publius Scipio Africanus" (my translation). Pound's transcription differs from the Italian because he was not a palaeographer and had difficulty reading the script, known as *cancelleresca*, in which Broglio's manuscript was written, and because he did not check his transcription against that of Tonini, *Rimini nella signoria de' Malatesti*, vol. 5, p. 283.

[44] *All I want you to do is follow the orders* Broglio in Tonini, *Rimini nella signoria de' Malatesti*, vol. 5, p. 283: "Solo una cosa voglio da voi, che non vi partiate dalli disegni e ricordi dati, seguendo la vera ubbidientia." Or in English: "Only one thing I want from you, that you don't deviate from the plans and the orders that have been given, keeping true obedience."

[45] *They've got ... in this camp* Broglio in Tonini, *Rimini nella signoria de' Malatesti*, vol. 5, p. 283: "Ell' è vero che loro son più genti assai che noi semo; ma noi semo più homini." Or in English: "It's true that they are more numerous than we are; but we are more men."

[1] *E grādment ... annutii* see Canto X, note 43.

And he put us under the chiefs,[2]
    and the chiefs went back to their squadrons:

5   Bernardo Reggio, Nic Benzo, Giovan Nestorno,
Paulo Viterbo, Buardino of Brescia, Cetho Brandolino,
And Simone Malespina,
Petracco St Archangelo, Rioberto da Canossa,
And for the tenth Agniolo da Roma
10   and that gay bird Piero della Bella,
And to the eleventh Roberto,
And the papishes were three thousand on horses,
    dilly cavalli tre milia,[3]
And a thousand on foot,
15   And the Lord Sigismundo had but mille tre cento cavalli[4]
And hardly 500 fanti (and one spingard),[5]
And we beat the papishes and fought them back through the tents
And he came up to the dyke again
And fought through the dyke-gate
20   And it went on from dawn to sun-set
And we broke them and took their baggage
    and mille cinquecento cavalli
E li homini di Messire Sigismundo non furono che mille trecento[6]
And the Venetians sent in their compliments
25   And various and sundry sent in their compliments;
But we got it next August;[7]
And Roberto got beaten at Fano,[8]
And he went by ship to Tarentum,
I mean Sidg went to Tarentum[9]
30   And he found 'em, the anti-Aragons, busted and weeping into their beards.
And they, the papishes, came up to the walls.
And that nick-nosed s.o.b. Feddy Urbino
Said:
    "Par che è fuor di questo...Sigis...mundo."[10]
35   "They say he dodders about the streets
"And can put his hand to neither one thing nor the other,"
And he was in the sick wards, and on the high tower
And everywhere, keeping us at it.
And, thank god, they got the sickness outside
40   As we had the sickness inside,
And they had neither town nor castello
But dey got de mos' bloody rottenes' peace on us –

---

[2]   (lines 3–26) For the original account, see Broglio in Tonini, *Rimini nella signoria de' Malatesti*, vol. 5, pp. 281–8; the poem's account differs in a few places in rendering proper names, instances of Pound incorrectly transcribing them from the original manuscript in Rimini.

[3]   *dilly cavalli tre milia* Italian for: "Of men on horse, three thousand."

[4]   *mille tre cento cavalli* Italian for "One thousand three hundred cavalry."

[5]   *500 fanti (and one spingard)* Italian for "500 infantrymen," and one *spingarda*, or springald, a machine of war used in the fifteenth century for throwing stones; Broglio says that Sigismondo had several.

[6]   *mille cinqueceto...trecento* Italian for: "one thousand five hundred horses / And the men of Messire Sigismundo / were but one thousand three hundred."

[7]   *But we got it next August* Sigismondo's troops were routed at the battle of Senigallia on August 13, 1462.

[8]   *beaten at Fano* Roberto Malatesta (d. 1482), illegitimate son of Sigismondo, was defeated when the city fell on September 25, 1463.

[9]   *Sidg went to Tarentum* Sigismondo, together with Jacomo Piccinino and Jean d'Anjou, went to visit Gianantonio Orsini, the prince of Taranto, at his castle in Altamura on August 25, 1462.

[10]   *Par che e fuor di questo...Sigis...mundo* Federico d'Urbino, in a letter to Cicco Simonetta, dated October 21, 1463, wrote: "Et el Signore Sigismondo, per quanto intendo, *pare che sia fora de questo mondo* et va là e qua como balordo senza saper pigliare alcuno partito a cosa che luy habia ad fare" (my italics). Or in English: "And Signore Sigismondo, from what I hear, it seems that he is out of this world and goes here and there like a fool without knowing how to reach a decision about what he should do." The letter is transcribed in Giovanni Soranzo, *Pio II e la politica italiana*, pp. 509–10. In Italian, the word for "world" is *mondo*, which is also the last part of Sigismondo's name; Pound turns Federico's statement into a pun: "he is out of this Sigis-world."

Quali lochi sono questi:[11]

          Sogliano,

Torrano and La Serra, Sbrigara, San Martino,   45

Ciola, Pondo, Spinello, Cigna and Buchio,
Prataline, Monte Cogruzzo,
          and the villa at Rufiano
Right up to the door-yard
And anything else the Rev^{mo} Monsignore could remember.   50

And the water-rights on the Savio.
(And the salt heaps with the reed mats on them
          Gone long ago to the Venetians)
And when lame Novvy died, they got even Cesena.

And he wrote to young Piero:[12]   55
          Send me a couple of huntin' dogs,
They may take my mind off it.
And one day he was sitting in the chiexa,
On a bit of cornice, a bit of stone grooved for a cornice,
Too narrow to fit his big beam,   60
          hunched up and noting what was done wrong,
And an old woman came in and giggled to see him
          sitting there in the dark
She nearly fell over him,
          And he thought: 65
Old Zuliano[13] is finished,
If he's left anything we must see the kids get it,
Write that to Robert.
And Vanni must give that peasant a decent price for his horses,
Say that I will refund.   70

And the writs run in Fano,
          For the long room over the arches
Sub annulo piscatoris,
          Palatiam seu curiam OLIM *de Malatestis.*[14]
Gone, and Cesena, Zezena *d"e b"e colonne,*   75
And the big diamond pawned in Venice
And he gone out into Morea,
Where they sent him to do the Mo'ammeds,

---

[11] *Quali lochi ... Savio* (lines 43–51) "Which places are the following," in Italian; a list of the towns and territories that Sigismondo had to forfeit after his defeat. The list is part of a document titled "A Memoir of Things to be Included in the Peace Agreement between His Holiness the Pope and Signor Sigismondo Malatesta." The document is transcribed in Francesco Gaetano Battaglini, "Della vita e de' fatti di Sigismondo Pandolfo Malatesta Signor di Rimino, Commentario," in Basinii Parmensis poetae, *Opera praestantiora nunc primum edita et opportunis commentaries illustrata* (Rimin: ex typographia Albertiniana, 1794), vol. 2, pp. 653–60.

[12] *And he wrote to young Piero* Pierfrancesco de' Medici was uncle to Lorenzo il magnifico (1449–92); in 1458 he served as ambassador to the papal court in Rome, and in 1459 was elected one of the Priori in Florence. Sigismondo Malatesta wrote to Pierfrancesco on December 5, 1463: "You must have heard about the troubles and misfortunes I have borne in my war, and I am certain that for my continuing adversities you have felt that sadness which one friend feels for another. Now, in order to escape from my travails I have accepted everything that Fortune has brought me and made peace in the way that seemed best and pleased His Holiness of our Lord; and I remain in a state such as pleases God and I find my condition to be the opposite of that popular expression, that he who has few things has few thoughts; for I have very few things remaining and all too many thoughts. And to give scope to the bizarre and melancholy moods that strike me, I have decided to take up hunting and snaring birds for exercise, and being poorly supplied with dogs, in order to do such activities, would you please give me a couple of good harriers, for I know that you have them; or that, not having them, you will be able to get them from your many friendships. With these I can hunt away my troubles and sometimes give myself some pleasure; with confidence I request this of you because I am certain you would try to please me in much greater matters." The full text, in Italian, is given in Luigi Rossi, "Di un delitto di Sigismondo Malatesta," *Rivista di scienze storiche* 7 (1910), fasc. v–vi (maggio–giugno): pp. 262–382, here 382.

[13] *Old Zuliano* a fictional character named Giuliano, but with his name written to suggest the characteristic accent of Romagna. "Robert" would be Roberto Valturio and "Vanni" Giovanni, one of Sigismondo's sons.

[14] In the Malatestan houses (*case Malatestiane*) in Fano, above the sixteenth-century room called the *loggia del sansovino*, with six elegant columns that support airy arches, is an inscription in Latin which reads: "Under the seal of the Church, the palace or court formerly of the Malatestas."

With 5,000 against 25,000,
80   and he nearly died out in Sparta,
Morea, Lakadaemon,
                        and came back with no pep in him

And we sit here. I have sat here
                    For forty four thousand years,
85   And they trapped him down here in the marsh land,
                in '46 that was;
And the poor devils dying of cold, that was Rocca Sorano;
And he said in his young youth:
                        Vogliamo,
90   *che le donne*, we will that they, *le donne*, go ornate,
As be their pleasure, for the city's glory thereby.[15]

And Platina said afterward,[16]
                    when they jailed him
And the Accademia Romana, for singing to Zeus in the catacombs
95   Yes, I saw him when he was down here,
Ready to murder fatty Barbo, "Formosus,"
And they want to know what we talked about?
            "*de litteris et de armis, praestantibusque ingeniis,*
Both of ancient times and our own; books, arms,
100   And of men of unusual genius,
Both of ancient times and our own, in short the usual subjects
Of conversation between intelligent men."

And he with his luck gone out of him
64 lances in his company, and his pay 8,000 a *year,*
105   64 and no more, and he not to try to get any more
And all of it down on paper
sexaginta quatuor nec tentatur habere plures[17]
But leave to keep 'em in Rimini
                i.e. to watch the Venetians.

110   Damn pity[18] he didn't
                (i.e. get the knife into him)
Little fat squab "Formosus"
Barbo said "Call me Formosus"
But the conclave wouldn't have it
115   and they called him Paulo Secundo.

---

[15]   *Vogliamo ... glory thereby* in 1436, when he was 19 years old ("in his young youth"), Sigismondo Malatesta repealed the city of Rimini's laws against women wearing excessively ornate attire. In Italian, "We want women" to go ornate, or adorned.
[16]   *And Platina said afterward* Platina was the assumed Latin name of Bartolomeo Sacchi (1421–81), a humanist who worked in the papal chancery. He became a member of the Accademia Romana, a literary discussion group headed by Giulio Sanseverino, whose adopted name was Pomponio Leto. The group propagated an exaggerated devotion to Roman literature, names, and ceremonies. There were rumors that its members were plotting against Pope Paul II (1464–71), or Pietro Barbo (1417–71), and they were arrested in 1468. But only Leto was condemned for irreligion and pederasty, and even he was released. When Platina was questioned about conversations he had recently been having with Sigismondo, who was in Rome during this time to discuss revisions in the peace terms which had been imposed back in 1463, Platina replied: "De literis et de armis, de praestantibus ingeniis tum veterum tum nostrorum hominum," or "Of letters and of arms, of outstanding minds both of ancient times and our own." Ludwig Friedrich August von Pastor (1854–1928), *Geschichte der Päpste seit dem Ausgang des Mittelalters*, vol. 2 (Freiburg im Breisgau: Herer'sche Verlagshandlung, 1889), p. 384.
[17]   *64 lances ... habere plures* Battaglini, App. Doc. 69, 668–71.
[18]   *Damn pity ... "whom he could trust"* (lines 110–19) "El Papa, intrato in sospetione del prefato Signore, fece andare alla sua camera sette Cardinali delli suoi più confidati; e di poi mandò a dire al Signor mis Sigismondo che li era grato che sua Signoaria intrasse dentro." Or: "The Pope, having grown suspicious of Sigismondo, called seven of his most trusted Cardinals; then he sent someone to tell Sigismondo that he would be pleased for him to enter now." Broglio, in Tonini, *Rimini nella signoria de' Malatesti*, vol. 5, p. 313. The details about the horses at the gates are Pound's own, and Broglio never expresses the wish that Sigismondo had killed Pope Paul.

And he left three horses at one gate
        and three horses at the other,
And Fatty received him
        with a guard of seven cardinals whom he could trust.
And the castelan[19] of Montefiore wrote down,   120
"You'd better keep him out of the district,
"When he got back here from Sparta, the people
"Lit fires, and turned out yelling: 'PANDOLFO!!'"

In the gloom, the gold gathers the light against it.

And one day he said:[20] Henry, you can have it,   125
On condition, you can have it: for four months
You'll stand any reasonable joke that I play on you,
And you can joke back
        provided you don't get too ornrey.
And they put it all down in writing: 130
For a green cloak with silver brocade
Actum in Castro Sigismundo, presente Roberto de Valturibus
...sponte et ex certa scientia...to Enricho de Aquabello.[21]

Canto LXXXI (1948)

Zeus lies in Ceres' bosom[1]
Taishan[2] is attended of loves
        under Cythera,[3] before sunrise
and he said: "Hay aquí mucho catolicismo – (sounded catoli*th*ismo)
    y muy poco reliHion"[4]   5
and he said: "Yo creo que los reyes desaparecen"[5]

---

[19] *And the castelan...'PANDOLFO!'"* in 1466, when Sigismondo returned from his unsuccessful campaign against the Ottomans in Greece, his ship landed at the small coastal town of Montefore, formerly a Malatesta possession. The castellan wrote to his new overlords in Venice, warning them that Sigismondo was still very popular among the town's people.

[20] *And one day he...Enricho de Aquabello* (lines 125–34) in a legal document dated May 31, 1460, Sigismondo agreed to give Enrico Acquabello, a steward in Sigismondo's castle in Rimini, "a green cloak with silver brocade," provided that Enrico, for the next four months, stand or put up with any reasonable joke that Sigismondo might play on him, and with the proviso that Enrico could also play jokes on Sigismondo: "That Enrico himself, for the next four months, must be and will be held accountable for going to Aucumpaiandum [?] at the request of the Magnificent lord, and with an equitable spirit will bear all tricks and jokes that will be done by the Magnificent lord on the objects and person of Enrico, which must nevertheless be bearable, nor is he to quarrel or get annoyed or otherwise become indignant, the same Magnificent Lord also granting to Enrico full licence to joke and play tricks on the same Magnificent Lord and promising not to make any joke or trick against Enrico that would go against the gift, which nevertheless must also be bearable and will be received." Or in the original Latin: "Quod ipse Enricus debeat et teneatur per quatuor menses prossime futuros acedere cum prefato Mangnifico domino ad Aucumpaiandum (?) ad requisitionem ipsius Magnifici domini et equo animo suportare omnes nugas et omnia scripza fienda per ipsum Mafnificum dominum in rebus et persona ipsius Enrici que sint tamen suportabilia, nec ex ipsis altercari nec molestus esse nec indignationem aliquam sucipere ex epsis nugis et scripzis, Dans ipse Magnificus dominus dicto Enricho etiam plenam licteiam nugandi et scrizandi cump ipso Magnifico domino ac promictens non meloesta facere aliquam nugam sive scrizum fiendos contra ipsum Enricum contra donamtionem suam, que sint tamen suporatbili et recipienda." The entire document is found in Pound's source, Carlo Grigioni, "Un Cappricio di Sigismondo Malatesta" ("A Caprice of Sigismondo Malatesta"), *Arte e storia*, ser. 3, vol 10 (1908): 40–1.

[21] *Actum in...Aquabello* Latin for: "Executed in Castel Sigismono, witnessed by Roberto Valturio / of his free will and full knowledge...to Enricho de Aquabello." These are excerpts from the end (line 131) and the beginning (line 132) of the document.

Canto LXXX1 was first published as part of *The Pisan Cantos* (New York: New Directions, 1948; London: Faber & Faber, 1949).

[1] *Zeus...Ceres* in some accounts Zeus, the ruler of the ancient Greek Gods, is said to have married his sister Ceres, goddess of agriculture and fertility.

[2] *Taishan* a sacred mountain in China which is identified here with a cliff visible from the outdoor cage in the Disciplinary Training Center near Pisa where Pound was detained.

[3] *Cythera* an island sacred to Aphrodite, goddess of love, used as an epithet to describe her.

[4] *"Hay aquí...reliHion"* "There is much Catholicism here and very little religion," in Spanish. The speaker is Castilian, as evidenced by the way he pronounces the second "c" in *catolicismo* as *catolithismo*.

[5] *"Yo creo...desaprecen"* "I think that kings are disappearing," in Spanish

(Kings will, I think, disappear)
That was Padre José Elizondo[6]
      in 1906 and in 1917
10   or about 1917
          and Dolores said: "Come pan, niño," eat bread, me lad
Sargent[7] had painted her
          before he descended
(i.e. if he descended)
15   but in those days he did thumb sketches,
impressions of the Velázquez in the Museo del Prado
and books cost a peseta,
        brass candlesticks in proportion,
hot wind came from the marshes
20   and death-chill from the mountains.
And later Bowers[8] wrote: "but such hatred,
    I had never conceived such"
and the London reds wouldn't show up his friends
        (i.e. friends of Franco
25   working in London) and in Alcázar[9]
forty years gone, they said: "go back to the station to eat
you can sleep here for a peseta"
      goat bells tinkled all night
      and the hostess grinned: Eso es luto, *haw!*
30   mi marido es muerto[10]
        (it is mourning, my husband is dead)
when she gave me paper to write on
with a black border half an inch or more deep,
      say 5/8ths, of the locanda[11]
35   "We call *all* foreigners frenchies"
and the egg broke in Cabranez' pocket,
      thus making history.[12] Basil says
they beat drums for three days
till all the drumheads were busted
40   (simple village fiesta)
and as for his life in the Canaries . . .[13]
Possum[14] observed that the local portagoose folk dance
was danced by the same dancers in divers localities
      in political welcome . . .
45   the technique of demonstration
        Cole[15] studied that (not G.D.H., Horace)
"You will find" said old André Spire,[16]
that every man on that board (Crédit Agricole)[17]
has a brother-in-law
50   "You the one, I the few"
        said John Adams

[6] *Padre José Elizondo* a Catholic priest who helped Pound when he was researching Spanish manuscripts in the Escorial.

[7] *Sargent* John Singer Sargent (1856–1925), British painter much influenced by the Spanish painter Velasquez. Dolores is presumably a sitter for one of his works; his later paintings are mostly portraits of well-to-do sitters.

[8] *Bowers* Claude Gernade Bowers (1878–1958) was American ambassador to Spain during the Spanish Civil War (1936–9), won by the nationalists led by General Francisco Franco.

[9] *Alcázar* Alcazar de San Juan, a town in central Spain.

[10] *"Eso es . . . es muerto"* Translated in the next line.

[11] *locanda* Italian for inn or boarding house.

[12] *"We call . . . making history"*. Dr. Augustin Cabanès (1862–1928), author of some 60 volumes, chiefly concerning research into sexual behavior; the allusion remains obscure.

[13] *Basil says . . . Canaries* Basil Bunting (1900–85), British poet, recalled that in the Tyne Valley in England villagers beat drums night and day during the three days between the Crucifixion and the Resurrection, doing so till their hands bled.

[14] *Possum* nickname for T. S. Eliot (1888–1965), author *Old Possum's Book of Practical Cats* (London: Faber & Faber, 1939).

[15] *Cole* Horace de Vere Cole (1874–1935), a friend of the painter Augustus John, who organized a demonstration in support of Italy's entry into the First World War, as recounted in Canto LXXX; not G. D. H. Cole (1880–1959), an English economist and novelist.

[16] *André Spire* (1868–1966), French poet and advocate of Zionism.

[17] *Crédit Agricole* a bank specializing in lending to farmers.

speaking of fears in the abstract
    to his volatile friend Mr Jefferson.[18]
(To break the pentameter, that was the first heave)
or as Jo Bard[19] says: they never speak to each other,   55
if it is baker and concierge visibly
    it is La Rouchefoucauld and de Maintenon audibly.[20]
"Te cavero le budella"
        "La corata a te"[21]
In less than a geological epoch   60
    said Henry Mencken[22]
"Some cook, some do not cook
    some things cannot be altered"[23]
Ἴυγξ . . . ’ἐμὸν ποτί δῶμα τὸν ἄνδρα[24]
What counts is the cultural level,   65
    thank Benin[25] for this table ex packing box
    "doan yu tell no one I made it"
        from a mask fine as any in Frankfurt
"It'll get you offn th' groun"
        Light as the branch of Kuanon[26]   70
And at first disappointed with shoddy
the bare ram-shackle quais, but then saw the
high buggy wheels
    and was reconciled,
George Santayana[27] arriving in the port of Boston   75
and kept to the end of his life that faint *thethear*
of the Spaniard
    as a grace quasi imperceptible
as did Muss[28] the *v* for *u* of Romagna
and said the grief was a full act   80
    repeated for each new condoleress
working up to a climax.
and George Horace[29] said he wd/"get Beveridge" (Senator)
Beveridge wouldn't talk and he wouldn't write for the papers
but George got him by campin' in his hotel   85
and assailin' him at lunch breakfast an' dinner
    three articles
and my ole man went on hoein' corn
    while George was a-tellin' him,
come across a vacant lot   90
    where you'd occasionally see a wild rabbit

[18] *John Adams . . . Mr. Jefferson* John Adams (1756–1824), second president of the United States (1797–1801), told Thomas Jefferson (1743–1826), third president of the United States (1801–9) that he feared an aristocracy, whereas Jefferson feared monarchy.
[19] *Jo Bard* Joseph Bard (1882–1975), Hungarian-born British writer and friend of Pound.
[20] *"If it is . . . Maintenon audibly"* The Duc de Rochefoucauld (1747–1827) and Madame de Maintenon (1635–1727), the latter the second wife of Louis XIV of France, as exemplars of elegant prose style.
[21] *"Te cavero . . . corata a te"* see Canto X, note 12.
[22] *Henry Mencken* H. L. Mencken (1880–1956), American essayist and reformer, wrote Pound a letter, quoted in Pound's *Guide to Kulchur*, p. 182, in which he said: "I believe that all schemes of monetary reform collide inevitably with the nature of man in the mass. He can't be convinced in anything less than a geological epoch."
[23] *"Some cook . . . altered"* Dorothy Shakespeare Pound to Ezra Pound, stipulating that she not be requested to cook if they should marry.

[24] *Iugx . . . emon poti doma ton andra* ancient Greek for "Little wheel, [bring back] that man to my house." From the second Idyll of Theocritus, a dramatic monologue in which a girl uses a magic wheel to cast a spell on her unfaithful lover.
[25] *Benin* a district in Nigeria noted for its bronze masks which were collected by the German anthropologist Leo Frobenius (1873–1938) at the Institute for Cultural Morphology in Frankfurt. A black prisoner named Edwards has made a table as elegantly simple as one of the masks from Benin.
[26] *Kuanon* the Chinese goddess of mercy.
[27] *George Santayana* (1863–1952), American philosopher born in Spain, who also used the soft c or "th" sound of Castilian, which is described as the verb *cecear* in Spanish, pronounced *thethear*.
[28] *Muss* Benito Mussolini (1883–1945), Fascist dictator of Italy (1922–43), who made much of retaining the accent of his native province of Romagna.
[29] *George Horace* George Horace Lorimer (1868–1937), editor of the *Saturday Evening Post* for over 35 years, was trying to interview Albert Jeremiah Beveridge (1862–1927), the American senator and historian.

or mebbe only a loose one
AOI!
a leaf in the current
at my grates no Althea[30]

95 ___*libretto*___   Yet[31]

Ere the season died a-cold
Borne upon a zephyr's shoulder
I rose through the aureate sky

100
Lawes and Jenkyns guard thy rest
Dolmetsch ever be thy guest,[32]
Has he tempered the viol's wood
To enforce   both the grave   and the acute?
Has he curved us the bowl of the lute?

105
Lawes and Jenkyns guard thy rest
Dolmetsch ever be thy guest
Hast 'ou fashioned so airy a mood
To draw up leaf from the root?
Hast 'ou found   a cloud   so light

110
As seemed neither mist nor shade?

Then resolve me, tell me aright
If Waller sang or Dowland[33] played.

Your eyen two wol sleye me sodenly
I may the beauté of hem nat susteyne[34]

115
And for 180 years almost nothing.

Ed ascoltando al leggier mormorio[35]
there came new subtlety of eyes into my tent,
whether of spirit or hypostasis,[36]
but what the blindfold hides

120
or at carneval

nor any pair showed anger
Saw but the eyes and stance between the eyes,
colour, diastasis,[37]
careless or unaware it had not the

125
whole tent's room
nor was place for the full Εἰδὼς[38]
interpass, penetrate
casting but shade beyond the other lights
sky's clear

130
night's sea
green of the mountain pool
shone from the unmasked eyes in half-mask's space.
What thou lovest well remains,
the rest is dross

135
What thou lov'st well shall not be reft from thee

---

[30]   *no Althea* from the poem by Richard Lovelace (1618–57),
"To Althea, from Prison": When Love with unconfined wings /
Hovers within my Gates; / And my divine Althea brings / To
whisper at the grates..."

[31]   *libretto* a text to be sung to music.

[32]   *Lawes and Jenkins... Dolmetsch* Henry Lawes (1596–1662)
and John Jenkins (1592–1678) were English composers. Lawes
made a setting of Waller's poem, "Go, Lovely Rose," the source
of the "Envoi" in Pound's "Hugh Selwyn Mauberley" (see p. 56.
Arnold Dolmetsch (1858–1940) was a musicologist and builder
of modern reconstructions of old instruments who also advocated
reviving pre-Baroque music.

[33]   *Waller...Dowland* Edmund Waller (1606–87), English
poet, and John Dowland (1563–1626), English composer and
lutenist.

[34]   *Your eyen...nat susteyne* from Chaucer's "Merciless Beauté."

[35]   *Ed...mormorio* Italian for "And listening to the light
murmur." The passage is not a quotation; Pound had lived in
Italy for over 20 years.

[36]   *hypostasis* the substance of the godhead.

[37]   *diastasis* separation.

[38]   *Eidos* ancient Greek term for "knowing."

What thou lov'st well is thy true heritage
Whose world, or mine or theirs
                or is it of none?
First came the seen, then thus the palpable
      Elysium, though it were in the halls of hell,   140
What thou lovest well is thy true heritage
What thou lov'st well shall not be reft from thee

The ant's a centaur in his dragon world.
Pull down thy vanity,[39] it is not man
Made courage, or made order, or made grace,   145
      Pull down thy vanity, I say pull down.
Learn of the green world what can be thy place
In scaled invention or true artistry,
Pull down thy vanity,
                Paquin pull down!   150
The green casque has outdone your elegance.[40]

"Master thyself, then others shall thee beare"[41]
      Pull down thy vanity
Thou art a beaten dog beneath the hail,
A swollen magpie in a fitful sun,   155
Half black half white
Nor knowst'ou wing from tail
Pull down thy vanity
           How mean thy hates
Fostered in falsity,   160
           Pull down thy vanity,
Rathe[42] to destroy, niggard in charity,
Pull down thy vanity,
           I say pull down.

But to have done instead of not doing   165
           this is not vanity
To have, with decency, knocked
That a Blunt[43] should open
           To have gathered from the air a live tradition
or from a fine old eye the unconquered flame   170
This is not vanity.
           Here error is all in the not done,
all in the diffidence that faltered...

From Canto CXV (1969)

The scientists are in terror
      and the European mind stops
Wyndham Lewis[1] chose blindness

---

[39] *Pull down thy vanity* reminscent of Ecclesiastes I: "Saith the preacher, vanity of vanities, all is vanity."

[40] *Paquin...The green casque* Madame Paquin was a fashion designer who opened her house in Paris in 1896 and retired in 1920; Pound had ended the previous Canto with the words, "sunset grand couturier." "The green casque" is the shell of a green insect.

[41] *"Master thyself...beare"* a variation of Chaucer's "Ballade of Good Counsel": "Subdue thyself, and others thee shall hear."

[42] *Rathe* Middle English for "quick."

[43] *Blunt* Wilfred Scawen Blunt (1840–1922), English poet and political writer, who was given a testimonial dinner in 1914 organized by Yeats and Pound, which included an address that reads in part: "We who are little given to respect, / Respect you."

The fragment was first published in *Drafts and Fragments of Cantos CX-CXVII* (New York: New Directions, 1969).

[1] *Wyndham Lewis* (1884–1957) was afflicted after 1940 with the growth of a tumor in his brain which was pinching the optical nerves; Lewis chose not to have what at that time was a risky surgical procedure to remove it, and went blind.

rather than have his mind stop.

5   Night under wind mid garofani,[2]
          the petals are almost still
      Mozart, Linnaeus, Sulmona,[3]
      When one's friends hate each other
          how can there be peace in the world?

10   Their asperities diverted me in my green time.
      A blown husk that is finished
          but the light sings eternal
      a pale flare over marshes
          where the salt hay whispers to tide's change

15   Time, space,
          neither life nor death is the answer.
      And of man seeking good,
          doing evil.
      In meiner Heimat[4]

20   where the dead walked
            and the living were made of cardboard.

Imagisme* (1912)

Some curiosity has been aroused concerning *Imagisme*, and as I was unable to find anything definite about it in print, I sought out an *imagiste*, with intent to discover whether the group itself knew anything about the "movement." I gleaned these facts.

The *imagistes* admitted that they were contemporaries of the Post Impressionists and the Futurists;[1] but they had nothing in common with these schools. They had not published a manifesto. They were not a revolutionary school; their only endeavor was to write in accordance with the best tradition, as they found it in the best writers of all time, – in Sappho, Catullus, Villon.[2] They seemed to be absolutely intolerant of all poetry that was not written in such endeavor, ignorance of the best tradition forming no excuse. They had a few rules, drawn up for their own satisfaction only, and they had not published them. They were:

1. Direct treatment of the "thing," whether subjective or objective.

2. To use absolutely no word that did not contribute to the presentation.

3. As regarding rhythm: to compose in sequence of the musical phrase, not in sequence of a metronome.

By these standards they judged all poetry, and found most of it wanting. They held also a certain "Doctrine of the Image," which they had not committed to writing; they said that it did not concern the public, and would provoke useless discussion.

The devices whereby they persuaded approaching poetasters to attend their instruction were:

1. They showed him his own thought already splendidly expressed in some classic (and the school musters altogether a most formidable erudition).

2. They re-wrote his verses before his eyes, using about ten words to his fifty.

Even their opponents admit of them – ruefully – "At least they do keep bad poets from writing!"

---

[2]   *garofani* Italian for carnations.
[3]   *Mozart, Linnaeus, Sulmona* Wolfgang Amadeus Mozart (1756–91), Austrian composer; Karl von Linné (1707–78), or Linnaeus as his name was latinized for learned publications, was a Swedish botanist who founded the modern binomial method of designating plants and animals, an exemplar of keen observation; Sulmona, the birthplace of Ovid.
[4]   *In meiner Heimat* German for "In my homeland."

"Imagisme" was first published in *Poetry* 1(6) (March 1913), where it was ascribed to F. S. Flint. But it is now known that the essay was actually drafted by Pound and only touched up by Flint.

[1]   *The Post Impressionists and the Futurists* The Post-Impressionist Show opened in December 1910 in London and featured a wide range of recent and contemporary French artists who were largely unknown to the English public. The exhibition aroused enormous controversy, as did the first exhibition of the Italian Futurists, which opened on March 1, 1912.
[2]   *Sappho, Catullus, Villon* Sappho, Greek poet of the sixth century BC; Catullus (87–55 BC), Roman lyrical poet; François Villon (1431–c. 1463), French poet.

I found among them an earnestness that is amazing to one accustomed to the usual London air of poetic dilettantism. They consider that Art is all science, all religion, philosophy and metaphysic. It is true that *snobisme* may be urged against them; but it is at least *snobisme* in its most dynamic form, with a great deal of sound sense and energy behind it; and they are stricter with themselves than with any outsider.

F. S. Flint

*   Editor's Note [i.e. the editor of *Poetry*] – In response to many requests for information regarding *Imagism* and the *Imagistes*, we publish this note by Mr. Flint, supplementing it with further exemplification by Mr. Pound. It will be seen from these that *Imagism* is not necessarily associated with Hellenic subjects, or with *vers libre* as a prescribed form.

A Few Don'ts by an Imagiste (1912)

An "Image" is that which presents an intellectual and emotional complex in an instant of time. I use the term "complex" rather in the technical sense employed by the newer psychologists, such as Hart,[1] though we might not agree absolutely in our application.

It is the presentation of such a "complex" instantaneously which gives that sense of sudden liberation; that sense of freedom from time limits and space limits; that sense of sudden growth, which we experience in the presence of the greatest works of art.

It is better to present one Image in a lifetime than to produce voluminous works.

All this, however, some may consider open to debate. The immediate necessity is to tabulate A LIST OF DON'TS for those beginning to write verses. But I can not put all of them into Mosaic negative.

To begin with, consider the three rules recorded by Mr. Flint, not as dogma – never consider anything as dogma – but as the result of long contemplation, which, even if it is some one else's contemplation, may be worth consideration.

Pay no attention to the criticism of men who have never themselves written a notable work. Consider the discrepancies between the actual writing of the Greek poets and dramatists, and the theories of the Graeco-Roman grammarians, concocted to explain their metres.

Language

Use no superflous word, no adjective, which does not reveal something.

Don't use such an expression as "dim lands *of peace*." It dulls the image. It mixes an abstraction with the concrete. It comes from the writer's not realizing that the natural object is always the *adequate* symbol.

Go in fear of abstractions. Don't retell in mediocre verse what has already been done in good prose. Don't think any intelligent person is going to be deceived when you try to shirk all the difficulties of the unspeakably difficult art of good prose by chopping your composition into line lengths.

What the expert is tired of today the public will be tired of tomorrow.

Don't imagine that the art of poetry is any simpler than the art of music, or that you can please the expert before you have spent at least as much effort on the art of verse as the average piano teacher spends on the art of music.

Be influenced by as many great artists as you can, but have the decency either to acknowledge the debt outright, or to try to conceal it.

The essay first appeared in *Poetry* 1(6) (March 1913).

[1]   *Hart* Bernard Hart (b. 1879) was a distinguished Cambridge psychologist. He had published a contribution to *Subconscious Phenomena* (London: Rebman, 1911) and authored a popular primer *The Psychology of Insanity* (Cambridge: Cambridge Manuals of Science and Literature, 1912). He defined a complex as "a system of connected ideas, with a strong emotional tone, and a tendency to produce actions of a definite character." Pound's use of the term may have only a tenuous connection with Hart's.

Don't allow "influence" to mean merely that you mop up the particular decorative vocabulary of some one or two poets whom you happen to admire. A Turkish war correspondent was recently caught red-handed babbling in his dispatches of "dove-gray" hills, or else it was "pearl-pale," I can not remember.

Use either no ornament or good ornament.

Rhythm and rhyme

Let the candidate fill his mind with the finest cadences he can discover, preferably in a foreign language so that the meaning of the words may be less likely to divert his attention from the movement; e.g., Saxon charms, Hebridean Folk Songs, the verse of Dante, and the lyrics of Shakespeare — if he can dissociate the vocabulary from the cadence. Let him dissect the lyrics of Goethe coldly into their component sound values, syllables long and short, stressed and unstressed, into vowels and consonants.

It is not necessary that a poem should rely on its music, but if it does rely on its music that music must be such as will delight the expert.

Let the neophyte know assonance and alliteration, rhyme immediate and delayed, simple and polyphonic, as a musician would expect to know harmony and counterpoint and all the minutiae of his craft. No time is too great to give to these matters or to any one of them, even if the artist seldom have need of them.

Don't imagine that a thing will "go" in verse just because it's too dull to go in prose.

Don't be "viewy" — leave that to the writers of pretty little philosophic essays. Don't be descriptive; remember that the painter can describe a landscape much better than you can, and that he has to know a deal more about it.

When Shakespeare talks of the "Dawn in russet mantle clad"[2] he presents something which the painter does not present. There is in this line of his nothing that one can call description; he presents.

Consider the way of the scientists rather than the way of an advertising agent for a new soap.

The scientist does not expect to be acclaimed as a great scientist until he has *discovered* something. He begins by learning what has been discovered already. He goes from that point onward. He does not bank on being a charming fellow personally. He does not expect his friends to applaud the results of his freshman class work. Freshmen in poetry are unfortunately not confined to a definite and recognizable class room. They are "all over the shop." Is it any wonder "the public is indifferent to poetry?"

Don't chop your stuff into separate *iambs*. Don't make each line stop dead at the end, and then begin every next line with a heave. Let the beginning of the next line catch the rise of the rhythm wave, unless you want a definite longish pause.

In short, behave as a musician, a good musician, when dealing with that phase of your art which has exact parallels in music. The same laws govern, and you are bound by no others.

Naturally, your rhythmic structure should not destroy the shape of your words, or their natural sound, or their meaning. It is improbable that, at the start, you will be able to get a rhythm-structure strong enough to affect them very much, though you may fall a victim to all sorts of false stopping due to line ends and caesurae.

The musician can rely on pitch and the volume of the orchestra. You can not. The term harmony is misapplied to poetry; it refers to simultaneous sounds of different pitch. There is, however, in the best verse a sort of residue of sound which remains in the ear of the hearer and acts more or less as an organ-base. A rhyme must have in it some slight element of surprise if it is to give pleasure; it need not be bizarre or curious, but it must be well used if used at all.

Vide further Vildrac and Duhamel's notes on rhyme in *"Technique Poétique."*[3]

[2] *"Dawn in russet mantle clad"* Horatio to Hamlet, in *Hamlet*, Act I, Scene 1.
[3] *Vildrac and Duhamel* Charles Vildrac (1882–1971), the pen name of Charles Messager, and Georges Duhamel (1886–1966) were joint authors of *Notes sur la technique poétique* (Paris: [Chez les librairies et chez les auteurs], 1910), a short work that ran to 71 pages.

That part of your poetry which strikes upon the imaginative *eye* of the reader will lose nothing by translation into a foreign tongue; that which appeals to the ear can reach only those who take it in the original.

Consider the definiteness of Dante's presentation, as compared with Milton's rhetoric.[4] Read as much of Wordsworth as does not seem too unutterably dull.

If you want the gist of the matter go to Sappho, Catullus, Villon, Heine[5] when he is in the vein, Gautier[6] when he is not too frigid; or, if you have not the tongues, seek out the leisurely Chaucer. Good prose will do you no harm, and there is good discipline to be had by trying to write it.

Translation is likewise good training, if you find that your original matter "wobbles" when you try to rewrite it. The meaning of the poem to be translated can not "wobble."

If you are using a symmetrical form, don't put in what you want to say and then fill up the remaining vacuums with slush.

Don't mess up the perception of one sense by trying to define it in terms of another. This is usually only the result of being too lazy to find the exact word. To this clause there are possibly exceptions.

The first three simple proscriptions will throw out nine-tenths of all the bad poetry now accepted as standard and classic; and will prevent you from many a crime of production.

"...*Mais d'abord il faut etre un poete*," as MM. Duhamel and Vildrac have said at the end of their little book, "*Notes sur la Technique Poétique*"; but in an American one takes that at least for granted, otherwise why does one get born upon that august continent![7]

VORTEX.

POUND.

The vortex is the point of maximum energy,

It represents, in mechanics, the greatest efficiency.

We use the words "greatest efficiency" in the precise sense — as they would be used in a text book of MECHANICS.

You may think of man as that toward which perception moves. You may think of him as the TOY of circumstance, as the plastic substance RECEIVING impressions.

OR you may think of him as DIRECTING a certain fluid force against circumstance, as CONCEIVING instead of merely observing and reflecting.

THE PRIMARY PIGMENT.

The vorticist relies on this alone; on the primary pigment of his art, nothing else.

Every conception, every emotion presents itself to the vivid consciousness in some primary form.

It is the picture that means a hundred poems, the music that means a hundred pictures, the most highly energized statement, the statement that has not yet SPENT itself in expression, but which is the most capable of expressing.

---

[4] *Dante...Milton* Dante Alighieri (1265–1321), Italian poet; and John Milton (1608–72).

[5] *Sappho, Catullus, Villon, Heine* Sappho, Greek poet of the sixth century BC; Catullus (87–55 BC), Roman lyrical poet; François Villon (1431–*c*.1463) French poet; Heinrich Heine (1797–1856), German poet who absorbed both romantic and classical traditions.

[6] *Gautier* Théophile Gautier (1811–72), French poet.

[7] Vildrac and Duhamel, *Notes sur la techneque poètique*, p. 71. "Vortex. Pound." was first published in *Blast* 1 (July 1914).

THE TURBINE.

All experience rushes into this vortex. All the energized past, all the past that is living and worthy to live. All MOMENTUM, which is the past bearing upon us, RACE, RACE-MEMORY, instinct charging the PLACID,

NON-ENERGIZED FUTURE.

The DESIGN of the future in the grip of the human vortex. All the past that is vital, all the past that is capable of living into the future, is pregnant in the vortex, NOW.

Hedonism is the vacant place of a vortex, without force, deprived of past and of future, the vortex of a still spool or cone.

Futurism is the disgorging spray[1] of a vortex with no drive behind it, DISPERSAL.

EVERY CONCEPT, EVERY EMOTION PRESENTS ITSELF TO THE VIVID CONSCIOUS-NESS IN SOME PRIMARY FORM. IT BELONGS TO THE ART OF THIS FORM. IF SOUND, TO MUSIC; IF FORMED WORDS, TO LITERATURE; THE IMAGE, TO POETRY; FORM, TO DESIGN; COLOUR IN POSITION, TO PAINTING; FORM OR DESIGN IN THREE PLANES, TO SCULPTURE; MOVEMENT TO THE DANCE OR TO THE RHYTHM OF MUSIC OR OF VERSES.

Elaboration, expression of second intensities, of dispersedness belong to the secondary sort of artist. Dispersed arts HAD a vortex.

Impressionism, Futurism, which is only an accelerated sort of impressionism, DENY the vortex. They are the CORPSES of VORTICES. POPULAR BELIEFS, movements, etc., are the CORPSES OF VORTICES. Marinetti is a corpse.[2]

THE MAN.

The vorticist relies not upon similarity or analogy, not upon likeness or mimcry.

In painting he does not rely upon the likeness to a beloved grandmother or to a caressable mistress.

VORTICISM is art before it has spread itself into a state of flacidity, of elaboration, of secondary applications.

ANCESTRY.

"All arts approach the conditions of music." – Pater.[3]

"An Image is that which presents an intellectual and emotional complex in an instant of time." – Pound.[4]

"You are interested in a certain painting because it is an arrangement of lines and colours." – Whistler.[5]

Picasso, Kandinski,[6] father and mother, classicism and romanticism of the movement.

POETRY.

The vorticist will use only the primary media of his art.

The primary pigment of poetry is the IMAGE.

---

[1]   *Futurism is the disgorging spray...* see pp. 1–38.
[2]   F. T. Marinetti (1876–1944) was the founder and leader of Italian Futurism. See pp. 1–38.
[3]   "*All arts...* Walter Pater (1839–94), "The School of Giorgione" (*Fortnightly Review*, Oct. 1877), reprinted in his *The Renaissance: Studies in Art and Poetry (the 1893 Text)*, ed. Donald L. Hill (Berkeley: University of California Press, 1980), p. 106: "All art constantly aspires towards the condition of music."
[4]   "*An Image ...* see Pound, "A Few Don'ts," p. 95.

[5]   "*You are interested...* James McNeil Whistler (1834–1903) was a celebrated artist. This quotation is invented by Pound, though it accurately summarizes Whistler's views.
[6]   *Picasso, Kandinski* Pablo Picasso (1881–1973), Spanish artist who dominated twentieth-century painting; Wassily Kandinsky (1866–1944), Russian artist who pioneers new types of picture space.

The vorticist will not allow the primary expression of any concept or emotion to drag itself out into mimicry.

In painting Kandinski, Picasso.

In poetry this by, "H. D."

> Whirl up sea —
> Whirl your pointed pines,
> Splash your great pines
> On our rocks,
> Hurl your green over us,
> Cover us with your pools of fir.[7]

The Chinese Written Character as a Medium for Poetry (1918)
Ernest Fenollosa and Ezra Pound

[*This essay was practically finished by the late Ernest Fenollosa; I have done little more than remove a few repetitions and shape a few sentences.*

We have here not a bare philogical discussion but a study of the fundamentals of all esthetics. In his search through unknown art Fenollosa, coming upon unknown motives and principles unrecognized in the West, was already led into many modes of thought since fruitful in "new" western painting and poetry. He was a forerunner without being known as such.

He discerned principles of writing which he had scarcely time to put into practice. In Japan he restored, or greatly helped to restore, a respect for the native art. In America and Europe he cannot be looked upon as a mere searcher after exotics. His mind was constantly filled with parallels and comparisons between eastern and western art. To him the exotic was always a mean of fructification. He looked to an American renaissance. The vitality of his outlook can be judged from the fact that although this essay was written some time before his death in 1908 I have not had to change the allusions to western conditions. The later movements in art have corroborated his theories. – Ezra Pound.]

This twentieth century not only turns a new page in the book of the *world, but opens another and a startling chapter. Vistas of strange futures unfold for a man, of world-embracing cultures half weaned from Europe, of hitherto undreamed responsibilities for nations and races.*

The Chinese problem alone is so vast that no nation can afford to ignore it. We in America, especially, must face it across the Pacific, and master it or it will master us. And the only way to master it is to strive with patient sympathy to understand the best, the most hopeful and the most human elements in it.

It is unfortunate that England and America have so long ignored or mistaken the deeper problems of Oriental culture. We have misconceived the Chinese for a materialistic people, for a debased and wornout race. We have belittled the Japenese as a nation of copyists. We have stupidly assumed that Chinese history affords no glimpse of change in social evolution, no salient epoch of moral and spiritual crisis. We have denied the essential humanity of these peoples; and we have toyed with their ideals as if they were no better than comic songs in an "opera bouffé."

The duty that faces us is not to batter down their forts or to exploit their markets, but to study and to come to sympathize with their humanity and their generous aspirations. Their type of cultivation has been high. Their harvest of recorded experience doubles our own. The Chinese have been idealists, and experimenters in the making of great principles; their history opens a world of lofty aim and achievement, parallel to that of the ancient Mediterranean peoples. We need their best ideals to supplement our own – ideals enshrined in their art, in their literature and in the tragedies of their lives.

THE CHINESE WRITTEN CHARACTER
The essay was first published in four monthly installments in the
Little Review 6(5–8) (Sept.–Dec. 1919).

[7] For H. D. and her career, see pp. 441–60.

We have already seen proof of the vitality and practical value of oriental painting for ourselves and as a key to the eastern soul. It may be worth while to approach their literature, the intensest part of it, their poetry, even in an imperfect manner.

I feel that I should perhaps apologize[*] for presuming to follow that series of brilliant scholars, Davis, Legge, St. Denys and Giles,[1] who have treated the subject of Chinese poetry with a wealth of erudition to which I can proffer no claim. It is not as a professional linguist nor as a sinologue that I humbly put forward what I have to say. As an enthusiastic student of beauty in Oriental culture, having spent a large portion of my years in close relation with Orientals, I could not but breathe in something of the poetry incarnated in their lives.

I have been for the most part moved to my temerity by personal considerations. An unfortunate belief has spread both in England and in America that Chinese and Japanese poetry are hardly more than an amusement, trivial, childish, and not to be reckoned in the world's serious literary performance. I have heard well-known sinologues state that, save for the purpose of professional linguistic scholarship, these branches of poetry are fields too barren to repay the toil necessary for their cultivation.

Now my own impression has been so radically and diametrically opposed to such a conclusion, that a sheer enthusiasm of generosity has driven me to wish to share with other occidentals my newly discovered joy. Either I am pleasingly self-deceived in my positive delight, or else there must be some lack of æsthetic sympathy and of poetic feeling in the accepted methods of presenting the poetry of China. I submit my causes of joy.

Failure or success in presenting any alien poetry in English must depend largely upon poetic workmanship, in the chosen medium. It was perhaps too much to expect that aged scholars who had spent their youth in gladiatorial combats with the refractory Chinese characters should succeed also as poets. Even Greek verse might have fared equally ill had its purveyors been perforce content with provincial standards of English rhyming. Sinologues should remember that the purpose of poetical translation is the poetry, not the verbal definitions in dictionaries.

One modest merit I may, perhaps, claim for my work: it represents for the first time a Japanese school of study in Chinese culture. Hitherto Europeans have been somewhat at the mercy of contemporary Chinese scholarship. Several centuries ago China lost much of her creative self, and of her insight into the causes of her own life, but her original spirit still lives, grows, interprets, transferred to Japan in all its original freshness. The Japanese to-day represent a stage of culture roughly corresponding to that of China under the Sung dynasty. I have been fortunate in studying for many years as a private pupil under Professor Kainan Mori,[2] who is probably the greatest living authority on Chinese poetry. He has recently been called to a chair in the Imperial University of Tokio.

My subject is poetry, not language, yet the roots of poetry are in language. In the study of a language so alien in form to ours as is Chinese in its written character, it is necessary to inquire how those universal elements of form which constitute poetics can derive appropriate nutriment.

In what sense can verse, written in terms of visible hieroglyphics, be reckoned true poetry? It might seem that poetry, which like music is a *time art*, weaving its unities out of successive impressions of sound, could with difficulty assimilate a verbal medium consisting largely of semi-pictorial appeals to the eye.

Contrast, for example, Gray's line:

The curfew tolls the knell of parting day.[3]

with the Chinese line:

---

[*] [*The apology was unnecessary, but Professor Fenollosa saw fit to make it, and I therefore transcribe his words. – E. P.*]

[1] *Davis, Legge, St. Denys and Giles* John Francis Davis (1795–1890), James Legge (1850–1897), Hervey de Saint-Denys (1823–1892), and Herbert Giles (1845–1935), were all famous sinologists.

[2] *Professor Kainan Mori* (1863–1911) was a distinguished literary scholar and himself wrote poems in classical Chinese. He gave two years' intensive instruction to Ernest Fenollosa from 1899 to 1901.

[3] *Gray's line* Thomas Gray (1716–1771), "Elegy Written in a County Churchyard," line 1.

Moon   rays   like   pure   snow

Unless the sound of the latter be given, what have they in common? It is not enough to adduce that each contains a certain body of prosaic meaning; for the question is, how can the Chinese line imply, *as form*, the very element that distinguishes poetry from prose?

On second glance, it is seen that the Chinese words, though visible, occur in just as necessary an order as the phonetic symbols of Gray. All that poetic form requires is a regular and flexible sequence, as plastic as thought itself. The characters may be seen and read, silently by the eye, one after the other:

> Moon rays like pure snow.

Perhaps we do not always sufficiently consider that thought is successive, not through some accident or weakness of our subjective operations but because the operations of nature are successive. The transferences of force from agent to agent, which constitute natural phenomena, occupy time. Therefore, a reproduction of them in imagination requires the same temporal order.[*]

Suppose that we look out of a window and watch a man. Suddenly he turns his head and actively fixes his attention upon something. We look ourselves and see that his vision has been focussed upon a horse. We saw, first, the man before he acted; second, while he acted; third, the object toward which his action was directed. In speech we split up the rapid continuity of this action and of its picture into its three essential parts or joints in the right order, and say:

> Man sees horse.

It is clear that these three joints, or words, are only three phonetic symbols, which stand for the three terms of a natural process. But we could quite as easily denote these three stages of our thought by symbols equally arbitrary, *which had no basis in sound;* for example, by three Chinese characters:

If we all knew *what division* of this mental horse picture each of these signs stood for, we could communicate continuous thought to one another as easily by drawing them as by speaking words. We habitually employ the visible language of gesture in much this same manner.

But Chinese notation is something much more than arbitrary symbols. It is based upon a vivid shorthand picture of the operations of nature. In the algebraic figure and in the spoken word there is no natural connection between thing and sign: all depends upon sheer convention. But the Chinese method follows natural suggestion. First stands the man on his two legs. Second, his eye moves through space: a bold figure represented by running legs under an eye, a modified picture of an eye, a modified picture of running legs, but unforgettable once you have seen it. Third stands the horse on his four legs.

The thought-picture is not only called up by these signs as well as by words but far more vividly and concretely. Legs belong to all three characters: they are *alive*. The group holds something of the quality of a continuous moving picture.

[*] [*Style, that is to say, limpidity, as opposed to rhetoric. – E. P.*]

The untruth of a painting or a photograph is that, in spite of its concreteness, it drops the element of natural succession.

Contrast the Laocoon statue with Browning's lines:[4]

"I sprang to the saddle, and Jorris, and he

.   .   .   .   .   .

And into the midnight we galloped abreast."

One superiority of verbal poetry as an art rests in its getting back to the fundamental reality of *time*. Chinese poetry has the unique advantage of combining both elements. It speaks at once with the vividness of painting, and with the mobility of sounds. It is, in some sense, more objective than either, more dramatic. In reading Chinese we do not seem to be juggling mental counters, but to be watching *things* work out their own fate.

Leaving for a moment the form of the sentence, let us look more closely at this quality of vividness in the structure of detached Chinese words. The earlier forms of these characters were pictorial, and their hold upon the imagination is little shaken, even in later conventional modifications. It is not so well known, perhaps, that the great number of these ideographic roots carry in them a *verbal idea of action*. It might be thought that a picture is naturally the picture of a *thing*, and that therefore the root ideas of Chinese are what grammar calls nouns.

But examination shows that a large number of the primitive Chinese characters, even the so-called radicals, are shorthand pictures of actions or processes.

For example, the ideograph meaning "to speak" is a mouth with two words and a flame coming out of it. The sign meaning "to grow up with difficulty" is grass with a twisted root. But this concrete *verb* quality, both in nature and in the Chinese signs, becomes far more striking and poetic when we pass from such simple, original pictures to compounds. In this process of compounding, two things added together do not produce a third thing but suggest some fundamental relation between them. For example, the ideograph for a "messmate" is a man and a fire.

A true noun, an isolated thing, does not exist in nature. Things are only the terminal points, or rather the meeting points of actions, cross-sections cut through actions, snap-shots. Neither can a pure verb, an abstract motion, be possible in nature. The eye sees noun and verb as one: things in motion, motion in things, and so the Chinese conception tends to represent them.

The sun underlying the bursting forth of plants $=$ spring.

The sun tangled in the branches of the tree sign $=$ east.

"Rice-field" plus "struggle" $=$ male.

"Boat" plus "water" $=$ boat-water, a ripple.

Let us return to the form of the sentence and see what power it adds to the verbal units from which it builds. I wonder how many people have asked themselves why the sentence form exists at all, why it seems so universally necessary *in all languages?* Why *must* all possess it, and what is the normal type of it? If it be so universal it ought to correspond to some primary law of nature.

I fancy the professional grammarians have given but a lame response to this inquiry. Their definitions fall into two types: one, that a sentence expresses a "complete thought"; the other, that in it we bring about a union of subject and predicate.

The former has the advantage of trying for some natural objective standard, since it is evident that a thought can not be the test of its own completeness. But in nature there is *no* completeness. On the other hand, practical completeness may be expressed by a mere interjection, as "Hi! there!", or "Scat," or even by shaking one's fist. No sentence is needed to make one's meaning clear. On the other hand, no full sentence really completes a thought. The man who sees and the horse which is seen will not stand still. The man was planning a ride before he looked. The horse kicked when the man tried to catch him. The truth is that acts are successive, even continuous; one causes or passes

---

[4]   *Browning's lines* Robert Browning (1812–89), "How They Brought the Good News from Ghent to Aix," lines 1 and 6 of the first stanza. The correct reading of the first line is: "I sprang to the stirrup, and Joris, and he."

into another. And though we may string ever so many clauses into a single compound sentence, motion leaks everywhere, like electricity from an exposed wire. All processes in nature are inter-related; and thus there could be no complete sentence (according to this definition) save one which it would take all time to pronounce.

In the second definition of the sentence, as "uniting a subject and a predicate," the grammarian falls back on pure subjectivity. *We* do it all; it is a little private juggling between our right and left hands. The subject is that about which *I* am going to talk; the predicate is that which *I* am going to say about it. The sentence according to this definition is not an attribute of nature but an accident of man as a conversational animal.

If it were really so, then there could be no possible test of the truth of a sentence. Falsehood would be as specious as verity. Speech would carry no conviction.

Of course this view of the grammarians springs from the discredited, or rather the useless, logic of the middle ages. According to this logic, thought deals with abstractions, concepts drawn out of things by a sifting process. These logicians never inquired how the "qualities" which they pulled out of things came to be there. The truth of all their little checker-board juggling depended upon the natural order by which these powers or properties or qualities were folded in concrete things, yet they despised the "thing" as a mere "particular", or pawn. It was as if Botany should reason from the leafpatterns woven into our table-cloths. Valid scientific thought consists in following as closely as may be the actual and entangled lines of forces as they pulse through things. Thought deals with no bloodless concepts but watches *things move* under its microscope.

The sentence form was forced upon primitive men by nature itself. It was not we who made it; it was a reflection of the temporal order in causation. All truth has to be expressed in sentences because all truth is the *transference of power*. The type of sentence in nature is a flash of lightning. It passes between two terms, a cloud and the earth. No unit of natural process can be less than this. All natural processes are, in their units, as much as this. Light, heat, gravity, chemical affinity, human will have this in common, that they redistribute force. Their unit of process can be represented as:

term	transference	term
from	of	to
which	force	which

If we regard this transference as the conscious or unconscious act of an agent we can translate the diagram into:

agent	act	object

In this the act is the very substance of the fact denoted. The agent and the object are only limiting terms.

It seems to me that the normal and typical sentence in English as well as in Chinese expresses just this unit of natural process. It consists of three necessary words; the first denoting the agent or subject from which the act starts; the second embodying the very stroke of the act; the third pointing to the object, the receiver of the impact. Thus:

Farmer	pounds	rice.

The form of the Chinese transitive sentence, and of the English (omitting particles) exactly corresponds to this universal form of action in nature. This brings language close to *things*, and in its strong reliance upon verbs it erects all speech into a kind of dramatic poetry.

A different sentence order is frequent in inflected languages like Latin, German or Japanese. This is because they are inflected, i.e., they have little tags and word-endings, or labels to show which is the agent, the object, etc. In uninflected languages, like English and Chinese, there is nothing but the order of the words to distinguish their functions. And this order would be no sufficient indication, were it not the *natural order* – that is, the order of cause and effect.

It is true that there are, in language, intransitive and passive forms, sentences built out of the verb "to be," and finally negative forms. To grammarians and logicians these have seemed more primitive than the transitive, or at least exceptions to the transitive. I had long suspected that these apparently exceptional forms had grown from the transitive or worn away from it by alteration or modification. This view is confirmed by Chinese examples, wherein it is still possible to watch the transformation going on.

The intransitive form derives from the transitive by dropping a generalized, customary, reflexive or cognate object. "He runs (a race)." "The sky reddens (itself)." "We breathe (air)." Thus we get weak and incomplete sentences which suspend the picture and lead us to think of some verbs as denoting states rather than acts. Outside grammar the word "state" would hardly be recognized as scientific. Who can doubt that when we say, "The wall shines," we mean that it actively reflects light to our eye?

The beauty of Chinese verbs is that they are all transitive or intransitive at pleasure. There is no such thing as a naturally intransitive verb. The passive form is evidently a correlative sentence, which turns about and makes the object into a subject. That the object is not in itself passive, but contributes some positive force of its own to the action, is in harmony both with scientific law and with ordinary experience. The English passive voice with "is" seemed at first an obstacle to this hypothesis, but one suspected that the true form was a generalized transitive verb meaning something like "receive," which had degenerated into an auxiliary. It was a delight to find this the case in Chinese.

In nature there are no negations, no possible transfers of negative force. The presence of negative sentences in language would seem to corroborate the logicians' view that assertion is an arbitrary subjective act. We can assert a negation, though nature can not. But here again science comes to our aid against the logician: all apparently negative or disruptive movements bring into play other positive forces. It requires great effort to annihilate. Therefore we should suspect that, if we could follow back the history of all negative particles, we should find that they also are sprung from transitive verbs. It is too late to demonstrate such derivations in the Aryan languages, the clue has been lost, but in Chinese we can still watch positive verbal conceptions passing over into so-called negatives. Thus in Chinese the sign meaning "to be lost in the forest" relates to a state of non-existence. English "not" = the Sanskrit *na*, which may come from the root *na*, to be lost, to perish.

Lastly comes the infinitive which substitutes for a specific colored verb the universal copula "is," followed by a noun or an adjective. We do not say a tree "greens itself," but "the tree is green;" not that "monkeys bring forth live young," but that "the monkey is a mammal." This is an ultimate weakness of language. It has come from generalizing all intransitive words into one. As "live," "see," "walk," "breathe," are generalized into states by dropping their objects, so these weak verbs are in turn reduced to the abstractest state of all, namely, bare existence.

There is in reality no such verb as a pure copula, no such original conception, our very word *exist* means "to stand forth," to show oneself by a definite act. "Is" comes from the Aryan root *as*, to breathe. "Be" is from *bhu*, to grow.

In Chinese the chief verb for "is" not only means actively "to have," but shows by its derivation that it expresses something even more concrete, namely, "to snatch from the moon with the hand." Here the baldest symbol of prosaic analysis is transformed by magic into a splendid flash of concrete poetry.

I shall not have entered vainly into this long analysis of the sentence if I have succeeded in showing how poetical is the Chinese form and how close to nature. In translating Chinese, verse especially, we must hold as closely as possible to the concrete force of the original, eschewing adjectives, nouns and intransitive forms wherever we can, and seeking instead strong and individual verbs.

Lastly we notice that the likeness of form between Chinese and English sentences renders translation from one to the other exceptionally easy. The genius of the two is much the same. Frequently it is possible by omitting English particles to make a literal word-for-word translation which will be not only intelligible in English, but even the strongest and most poetical English. Here, however, one must follow closely what is said, not merely what is abstractly meant.

Let us go back from the Chinese sentence to the individual written word. How are such words to be classified? Are some of them nouns by nature, some verbs and some adjectives? Are there pronouns and prepositions and conjunctions in Chinese as in good Christian languages?

One is led to suspect from an analysis of the Aryan languages that such differences are not natural, and that they have been unfortunately invented by grammarians to confuse the simple poetic outlook on life. All nations have written their strongest and most vivid literature before they invented a grammar. Moreover, all Aryan etymology points back to roots which are the equivalents of simple Sanskrit verbs, such as we find tabulated at the back of our Skeat.[5] Nature herself has no grammar.[*]

Fancy picking up a man and telling him that he is a noun, a dead thing rather than a bundle of functions A "part of speech" is only *what it does*. Frequently our lines of cleavage fail, one part of speech acts for another. They *act for* one another because they were originally one and the same.

Few of us realize that in our own language these very differences once grew up in living articulation; that they still retain life. It is only when the difficulty of placing some odd term arises or when we are forced to translate into some very different language, that we attain for a moment the inner heat of thought, a heat which melts down the parts of speech to recast them at will.

One of the most interesting facts about the Chinese language is that in it we can see, not only the forms of sentences, but literally the parts of speech growing up, budding forth one from another. Like nature, the Chinese words are alive and plastic, because *thing* and *action* are not formally separated. The Chinese language naturally knows no grammar. It is only lately that foreigners, European and Japanese, have begun to torture this vital speech by forcing it to fit the bed of their definitions. We import into our reading of Chinese all the weakness of our own formalisms. This is especially sad in poetry, because the one necessity, even in our own poetry, is to keep words as flexible as possible, as full of the sap of nature.

Let us go further with our example. In English we call "to shine" a *verb in the infinitive*, because it gives the abstract meaning of the verb without conditions. If we want a corresponding adjective we take a different word, "bright." If we need a noun we say "luminosity," which is abstract, being derived from an adjective.[*] To get a tolerably concrete noun, we have to leave behind the verb and adjective roots, and light upon a thing arbitrarily cut off from its power of action, say "the sun" or "the moon." Of course there is nothing in nature so cut off, and therefore this nounizing is itself an abstraction. Even if we did have a common word underlying at once the verb "shine", the adjective "bright", and the noun "sun," we should probably call it an "infinitive of the infinitive." According to our ideas, it should be something extremely abstract, too intangible for use.

The Chinese have one word, *ming*, or *mei*. Its ideograph is the sign of the sun together with the sign of the moon. It serves as verb, noun, adjective. Thus you write literally, "the sun and moon of the cup" for "the cup's brightness." Placed as a verb, you write "the cup sun-and-moons," actually

---

[5]   Walter William Skeat (1835–1912) was born in London and educated at Christ's College, Cambridge. In 1878 he was elected Ellington and Bosworth Professor of Anglo-Saxon at Cambridge. His principal achievement in pure philology was his *Etymological Dictionary of the English Language*, 4 vols. (Oxford: Oxford University Press, 1879–82), which included tables of Sanskrit verbs in an appendix.

[*]   [Even Latin, (living Latin) had not the network they foist upon unfortunate school-children. These are borrowed sometimes from Greek grammarians, even as I have seen English grammars borrowing oblique cases from Latin grammars. Sometimes they sprang from the grammatizing or categorizing passion of pedants. Living Latin had only the feel of the cases. The ablative and dative eotion. – E. P.]

[*]   [A good writer would use "shine" (i. e., to shine), shining, and "the shine" or "sheen", possibly thinking of the German "shöne" and "Schönheit"; but this does not invalidate Prof. Fenollosa's next contention. – E. P.]

"cup sun-and-moon," or in a weakened thought, "is like sun," i.e., shines. "Sun-and-moon-cup" is naturally a bright cup. There is no possible confusion of the real meaning, though a stupid scholar may spend a week trying to decide what "part of speech" he should use in translating a very simple and direct thought from Chinese to English.

The fact is that almost every written Chinese word is properly just such an underlying word, and yet it is *not* abstract. It is not exclusive of parts of speech, but comprehensive; not something which is neither a noun, verb, or adjective, but something which is all of them at once and at all times. Usage may incline the full meaning now a little more to one side, now to another, according to the point of view, but through all cases the poet is free to deal with it richly and concretely, as does nature.

In the derivation of nouns from verbs, the Chinese language is forestalled by the Aryan. Almost all the Sanskrit roots, which seem to underlie European languages, are primitive verbs, which express characteristic actions of visible nature. The verb must be the primary fact of nature, since motion and change are all that we can recognize in her. In the primitive transitive sentence, such as "Farmer pounds rice," the agent and the object are nouns only in so far as they limit a unit of action. "Farmer" and "rice" are mere hard terms which define the extremes of the pounding. But in themselves, apart from this sentence-function, they are naturally verbs. The farmer is one who tills the ground, and the rice is a plant which grows in a special way. This is indicated in the Chinese characters. And this probably exemplifies the ordinary derivation of nouns from verbs. In all languages, Chinese included, a noun is originally "that which does something," that which performs the verbal action. Thus the moon comes from the root *ma*, and means "the measurer." The sun means that which begets.

The derivation of adjectives from the verb need hardly be exemplified. Even with us, to-day, we can still watch participles passing over into adjectives. In Japanese the adjective is frankly part of the inflection of the verb, a special mood, so that every verb is also an adjective. This brings us close to nature, because everywhere the quality is only a power of action regarded as having an abstract inherence. Green is only a certain rapidity of vibration, hardness a degree of tenseness in cohering. In Chinese the adjective always retains a substratum of verbal meaning. We should try to render this in translation, not be content with some bloodless adjectival abstraction plus "is."

Still more interesting are the Chinese "prepositions," they are often post-positions. Prepositions are so important, so pivotal in European speech only because we have weakly yielded up the force of our intransitive verbs. We have to add small supernumerary words to bring back the original power. We still say "I see a horse," but with the weak verb "look," we have to add the directive particle "at" before we can restore the natural transitiveness.[*]

Prepositions represent a few simple ways in which incomplete verbs complete themselves. Pointing toward nouns as a limit they bring force to bear upon them. That is to say, they are naturally verbs, of generalized or condensed use. In Aryan languages it is often difficult to trace the verbal origins of simple prepositions. Only in *"off"* do we see a fragment of the thought "to throw off." In Chinese the preposition is frankly a verb, specially used in a generalized sense. These verbs are often used in their specially verbal sense, and it greatly weakens an English translation if they are systematically rendered by colorless prepositions.

Thus in Chinese: By═to cause; to═to fall toward; in═to remain, to dwell; from═to follow; and so on.

Conjunctions are similarly derivative, they usually serve to mediate actions between verbs, and therefore they are necessarily themselves actions. Thus in Chinese: Because═to use; and═to be included under one; another form of "and"═to be parallel; or═to partake; if═to let one do, to permit. The same is true of a host of other particles, no longer traceable in the Aryan tongues.

---

[*] [*This is a bad example. We can say "I look a fool", "look", transitive, now means resemble. The main contention is however correct. We tend to abandon specific words like "resemble" and substitute, for them, vague verbs with prepositional directors, or riders. – E. P.*]

Pronouns appear a thorn in our evolution theory, since they have been taken as unanalyzable expressions of personality. In Chinese even they yield up their striking secrets of verbal metaphor. They are a constant source of weakness if colorlessly translated. Take, for example, the five forms of "I." There is the sign of a "spear in the hand"═a very emphatic I; five and a mouth═a weak and defensive I, holding off a crowd by speaking; to conceal═a selfish and private I; self (the cocoon sign) and a mouth═an egoistic I, one who takes pleasure in his own speaking; the self presented is used only when one is speaking to one's self.

I trust that this digression concerning parts of speech may have justified itself. It proves, first, the enormous interest of the Chinese language in throwing light upon our forgotten mental processes, and thus furnishes a new chapter in the philosophy of language. Secondly, it is indispensable for understanding the poetical raw material which the Chinese language affords. Poetry differs from prose in the concrete colors of its diction. It is not enough for it to furnish a meaning to philosophers. It must appeal to emotions with the charm of direct impression, flashing through regions where the intellect can only grope.* Poetry must render what is said, not what is merely meant. Abstract meaning gives little vividness, and fullness of imagination gives all. Chinese poetry demands that we abandon our narrow grammatical categories, that we follow the original text with a wealth of concrete verbs.

But this is only the beginning of the matter. So far we have exhibited the Chinese characters and the Chinese sentence chiefly as vivid shorthand pictures of actions and processes in nature. These embody true poetry as far as they go. Such actions are *seen*, but Chinese would be a poor language and Chinese poetry but a narrow art, could they not go on to represent also what is unseen. The best poetry deals not only with natural images but with lofty thoughts, spiritual suggestions and obscure relations. The greater part of natural truth is hidden in processes too minute for vision and in harmonies too large, in vibrations, cohesions and in affinities. The Chinese compass these also, and with great power and beauty.

You will ask, how could the Chinese have built up a great intellectual fabric from mere picture writing? To the ordinary western mind, which believes that thought is concerned with logical categories and which rather condemns the faculty of direct imagination, this feat seems quite impossible. Yet the Chinese language with its peculiar material has passed over from the seen to the unseen by exactly the same process which all ancient races employed. The process is metaphor, the use of material images to suggest immaterial relations.*

The whole delicate substance of speech is built upon substrata of metaphor. Abstract terms, pressed by etymology, reveal their ancient roots still embedded in direct action. But the primative metaphors do not spring from arbitrary subjective processes. They are possible only because they follow objective lines of relations in nature herself. Relations are more real and more important than the things which they relate. The forces which produce the branch-angles of an oak lay potent in the acorn. Similar lines of resistance, half curbing the out-pressing vitalities, govern the branching of rivers and of nations. Thus a nerve, a wire, a roadway, and a clearing-house are only varying channels which communication forces for itself. This is more than analogy, it is identity of structure. Nature furnishes her own clues. Had the world not been full of homologies, sympathies, and identities, thought would have been starved and language chained to the obvious. There would have been no bridge whereby to cross from the minor truth of the seen to the major truth of the unseen. Not more than a few hundred roots out of our large vocabularies could have dealt directly with physical processes. These we can fairly well identify in primitive Sanskrit. They are, almost without exception, vivid verbs. The wealth of European speech grew, following slowly the intricate maze of nature's suggestions and affinities. Metaphor was piled upon metaphor in quasigeological strata.

---

* [Cf. *principle of Primary apparition*, "Spirit of Romance". – E. P.]   * [Compare *Aristotle's Poetics*, – E. P.]

Metaphor, the revealer of nature, is the very substance of poetry. The known interprets the obscure, the universe is alive with myth. The beauty and freedom of the observed world furnish a model, and life is pregnant with art. It is a mistake to suppose, with some philosophers of aesthetics, that art and poetry aim to deal with the general and the abstract. This misconception has been foisted upon us by mediaeval logic. Art and poetry deal with the concrete of nature, not with rows of separate "particulars," for such rows do not exist. Poetry is finer than prose because it gives us more concrete truth in the same compass of words. Metaphor, its chief device, is at once the substance of nature and of language. Poetry only does consciously* what the primitive races did unconsciously. The chief work of literary men in dealing with language, and of poets especially, lies in feeling back along the ancient lines of advance.* He must do this so that he may keep his words enriched by all their subtle understones of meaning. The original metaphors stand as a kind of luminous background, giving color and vitality, forcing them closer to the concreteness of natural processes. Shakespeare everywhere teems with examples. For these reasons poetry was the earliest of the world arts; poetry, language and the care of myth grew up together.

I have alleged all this because it enables me to show clearly why I believe that the Chinese written language has not only absorbed the poetic substance of nature and built with it a second world of metaphor but has, through its very pictorial visibility, been able to retain its original creative poetry with far more vigor and vividness than any phonetic tongue. Let us first see how near it is to the heart of nature in its metaphors. We can watch it passing from the seen to the unseen, as we saw it passing from verb to pronoun. It retains the primitive sap, it is not cut and dried like a walking-stick. We have been told that these people are cold, practical, mechanical, literal, and without a trace of imaginative genius. That is nonsense.

Our ancestors built the accumulations of metaphor into structures of language and into systems of thought. Languages to-day are thin and cold because we think less and less into them. We are forced, for the sake of quickness and sharpness, to file down each word to its narrowest edge of meaning. Nature would seem to have become less like a paradise and more and more like a factory. We are content to accept the vulgar misuse of the moment. A late stage of decay is arrested and embalmed in the dictionary. Only scholars and poets feel painfully back along the thread of our etymologies and piece together our diction, as best they may, from forgotten fragments. This anemia of modern speech is only too well encouraged by the feeble cohesive force of our phonetic symbols. There is little or nothing in a phonetic word to exhibit the embryonic stages of its growth. It does not bear is metaphor on its face. We forget that personality once meant, not the soul, but the soul's mask. This is the sort of thing one can not possibly forget in using the Chinese symbols.

In this Chinese shows its advantage. Its etymology is constantly visible. It retains the creative impulse and process, visible and at work. After thousands of years the lines of metaphoric advance are still shown, and in many cases actually retained in the meaning. Thus a word, instead of growing gradually poorer and poorer as with us, becomes richer and still more rich from age to age, almost consciously luminous. Its uses in national philosophy and history, in biography and in poetry, throw about it a nimbus of meanings. These center about the graphic symbol. The memory can hold them and use them. The very soil of Chinese life seems entangled in the roots of its speech. The manifold illustrations which crowd its annals of personal experience, the lines of tendency which converge upon a tragic climax, moral character as the very core of the principle – all these are flashed at once on the mind as reinforcing values with an accumulation of meaning which a phonetic language can hardly hope to attain. Their ideographs are like blood-stained battle flags to an old campaigner. With us, the poet is the only one for whom the accumulated treasures of the race-words are real and active. Poetic language is always vibrant with fold on fold of overtones, and with natural affinities, but in Chinese the visibility of the metaphor tends to raise this quality to its intensest power.

---

*   [Vide also an article on "Vorticism"[6] in the Fortnightly Review for September, 1914. "The language of exploration", – E.P.]

*   [I would submit in all humility that this applies in the rendering of ancient texts. The poet in dealing with his own time, must also see to it that language does not petrify on his hands. He must prepare for new advances along the lines of true metaphor that is interpretive metaphor, or image, as diametrically opposed to untrue, or ornamental metaphor. – E. P.]

6   Ezra Pound, "Vorticism," Fortnightly Review 96 (N.S.), 573 (2 Sept. 1914): 461–471; reprinted in A. Walton Litz, ed., Ezra Pound's Poetry and Prose: Contributions to Periodicals, vol. 1 (New York: Garland, 1991), 275–85.

I have mentioned the tyranny of mediæval logic. According to this European logic thought is a kind of brickyard. It is baked into little hard units or concepts. These are piled in rows according to size and then labeled with words for future use. This use consists in picking out a few bricks, each by its convenient label, and sticking them together into a sort of wall called a sentence by the use either of white mortar for the positive copula "is," or black mortar for the negative copula "is not." In this way we produce such admirable propositions as "A ring-tailed baboon is not a constitutional assembly."

Let us consider a row of cherry trees. From each of these in turn we proceed to take an "abstract," as the phrase is, a certain common lump of qualities which we may express together by the name cherry or cherryness. Next we place in a second table several such characteristic concepts: cherry, rose, sunset, iron-rust, flamingo. From these we abstract some further common quality, dilutation or mediocrity, and label it "red" or "redness." It is evident that this process of abstraction may be carried on indefinitely and with all sorts of material. We may go on forever building pyramids of attenuated concept until we reach the apex "being."

But we have done enough to illustrate the characteristic process. At the base of the pyramid lie *things*, but stunned, as it were. They can never know themselves for things until they pass up and down among the layers of the pyramids. The way of passing up and down the pyramid may be exemplified as follows: We take a concept of lower attenuation, such as "cherry"; we see that it is contained under one higher, such as "redness." Then we are permitted to say in sentence form, "Cherryness is contained under redness," or for short, "(the) cherry is red." If, on the other hand, we do not find our chosen subject under a given predicate we use the black copula and say, for example, "(The) cherry is not liquid."

From this point we might go on to the theory of the syllogism, but we refrain. It is enough to note that the practised logician finds it convenient to store his mind with long lists of nouns and adjectives, for these are naturally the names of classes. Most text-books on language begin with such lists. The study of verbs is meager, for in such a system there is only one real working verb, to-wit, the quasi-verb "is." All other verbs can be transformed into participles and gerunds. For example, "to run" practically becomes a case of "running." Instead of thinking directly, "The man runs," our logician makes two subjective equations, namely: The individual in question is contained under the class "man"; and the class "man" is contained under the class of "running things."

The sheer loss and weakness of this method is apparent and flagrant. Even in its own sphere it can not think half of what to think. It has no way of bringing together any two concepts which do not happen to stand one under the other and in the same pyramid. It is impossible to represent change in this system or any kind of growth: This is probably, why the conception of evolution came so late in Europe. *It could not make way until it was prepared to destroy the inveterate logic of classification.*

Far worse than this, such logic can not deal with any kind of interaction or with any multiplicity of function. According to it, the function of my muscles is as isolated from the function of my nerves, as from an earthquake in the moon. For it the poor neglected things at the bases of the pyramids are only so many particulars or pawns.

Science fought till she got at the things. All her work has been done from the base of the pyramids, not from the apex. She has discovered how functions cohere in things. She expresses her results in grouped sentences which embody no nouns or adjectives but verbs of special character. The true formula for thought is: The cherry tree is all that it does. Its correlated verbs compose it. At bottom these verbs are transitive. Such verbs may be almost infinite in number.

In diction as in grammatical form science is utterly opposed to logic. Primitive men who created language agreed with science and not with logic. Logic has abused the language which they left to her mercy. Poetry agrees with science and not with logic.

The moment we use the copula, the moment we express subjective inclusions, poetry evaporates. The more concretely and vividly we express the interactions of things the better the poetry. We need in poetry thousands of active words, each doing its utmost to show forth the motive and vital forces. We can not exhibit the health of nature by mere summation, by the piling of sentences. Poetic thought works by suggestion, crowding maximum meaning into the single phrase pregnant, charged, and luminous from within.

In Chinese character each word accumulated this sort of energy in itself.

Should we pass formally to the study of Chinese poetry, we should warn ourselves against logicianized pitfalls. We should beware of modern narrow utilitarian meanings ascribed to the words in commercial dictionaries. We should try to preserve the metaphoric overtones. We should beware of English grammar, its hard parts of speech, and its lazy satisfaction with nouns and adjectives. We should seek and at least bear in mind the verbal undertone of each noun. We should avoid "is" and bring in a wealth of neglected English verbs. Most of the existing translations violate all of these rules.[*]

The development of the normal transitive sentence rests upon the fact that one action in nature promotes another; thus the agent and the object are secretly verbs. For example, our sentence, "Reading promotes writing," would be expressed in Chinese by three full verbs. Such a form is the equivalent of three expanded clauses and can be drawn out into adjectival, participial, infinitive, relative or conditional members. One of many possible examples is, "If one reads, it teaches him how to write." Another is, "One who reads becomes one who writes." But in the first condensed form a Chinese would write, "Read promote write." The dominance of the verb and its power to obliterate all other parts of speech give us the model of terse fine style.

I have seldom seen our rhetoricians dwell on the fact that the great strength of our language lies in the splendid array of transitive verbs, drawn both from Anglo-Saxon and from Latin sources. These give us the most individual characterizations of force. Their power lies in their recognition of nature as a vast storehouse of forces. We do not say in English that things seem, or appear, or eventuate, or even that they are; but that they *do*. Will is the foundation of our speech.[*] We catch the Demiurge in the act. I had to discover for myself why Shakespeare's English was so immeasurably superior to all others. I found that it was his persistent, natural, and magnificient use of hundreds of transitive verbs. Rarely will you find an "is" in his sentences. "Is" weakly lends itself to the uses of our rhythm, in the unaccented syllables; yet he sternly discards it. A study of Shakespeare's verbs should underlie all exercises in style.

We find in poetical Chinese a wealth of transitive verbs, in some way greater even than in the English of Shakespeare. This springs from their power of combining several pictorial elements in a single character. We have in English no verb for what two things, say the sun and moon, both do together. Prefixes and affixes merely direct and qualify. In Chinese the verb can be more minutely qualified. We find a hundred variants clustering about a single idea. Thus "to sail a boat for purposes of pleasure" would be an entirely different verb from "to sail for purposes of commerce." Dozens of Chinese verbs express various shades of grieving, yet in English translations they are usually reduced to one mediocrity. Many of them can be expressed only by periphrasis, but what right has the translator to neglect the overtones? There are subtle shadings. We should strain our resources in English.

It is true that the pictorial clue of many Chinese ideographs can not now be traced, and even Chinese lexicographers admit that combinations frequently contribute only a phonetic value. But I

---

[*] [These precautions should be broadly conceived. It is not so much their letter, as the underlying feeling of objectification, and activity that matters. – E. P.]

[*] [Compare Dante's definition of "rectitudo" as the direction of the will, probably taken from Aquinas. – E. P.]

find it incredible that any such minute subdivision of the idea could have ever existed alone as abstract sound without the concrete character. It contradicts the law of evolution. Complex ideas arise only gradually, as the power of holding them together arises. The paucity of Chinese sound could not so hold them. Neither is it conceivable that the whole list was made at once, as commercial codes of cipher are compiled. Therefore we must believe that the phonetic theory is in large part unsound. The metaphor once existed in many cases where we can not now trace it. Many of our own etymologies have been lost. It is futile to take the ignorance of the Han dynasty for omniscience.* It is not true, as Legge said, that the original picture characters could never have gone far in building up abstract thought.[7] This is a vital mistake. We have seen that our own languages have all sprung from a few hundred vivid phonetic verbs by figurative derivation. A fabric more vast could have been built up in Chinese by metaphorical composition. No attenuated idea exists which it might not have reached more vividly and more permanently than we could have been expected to reach with phonetic roots. Such a pictorial method, whether the Chinese exemplified it or not, would be the ideal language of the world.

Still, is it not enough to show that Chinese poetry gets back near to the processes of nature by means of its vivid figure, its wealth of such figure? If we attempt to follow it in English we must use words highly charged, words whose vital suggestion shall interplay as nature interplays. Sentences must be like the mingling of the fringes of feathered banners, or as the colors of many flowers blended into the single sheen of a meadow.

The poet can never see too much or feel too much. His metaphors are only ways of getting rid of the dead white plaster of the copula. He resolves its indifference into a thousand tints of verb. His figures flood things with jets of various light, like the sudden up-blaze of fountains. The prehistoric poets who created language discovered the whole harmonious framework of nature, they sang out her processes in their hymns. And this diffused poetry which they created Shakespeare has condensed into a more tangible substance. Thus in all poetry a word is like a sun, with its corona and chromosphere; words crowd upon words, and enwrap each other in their luminous envelopes until sentences become clear, continuous light-bands.

Now we are in condition to appreciate the full splendor of certain lines of Chinese verse. Poetry surpasses prose especially in that the poet selects for juxtaposition those words whose overtones blend into a delicate and lucid harmony. All arts follow the same law; refined harmony lies in the delicate balance of overtones. In music the whole possibility and theory of harmony is based on the overtones. In this sense poetry seems a more difficult art.

How shall we determine the metaphorical overtones of neighboring words? We can avoid flagrant breaches like mixed metaphor. We can find the concord or harmonizing at its intensest, as in Romeo's speech over the dead Juliet.

---

*   [Professor Fenollosa is well borne out by chance evidence. The vorticist sculptor Gaudier-Brzeska sat in my room a few months ago, before he went off to the war. He was able to read the Chinese radicals and many compound signs almost at pleasure. He is, of course, used to consider all life and nature in the terms of planes and of bounding lines. Nevertheless he had spent only a fortnight in the museum studying the Chinese characters. He was amazed at the stupidity of lexicographers who could not discern for all their learning the pictorial values which were to him perfectly obvious and apparent. Curiously enough, a few weeks later Edmond Dulac, who is of a totally different tradition, sat here, giving an impromptu panegyric on the elements of Chinese art, on the units of composition, drawn from the written characters. He did not use Professor Fenollosa's own words, he said "bamboo" instead of "rice". He said the essence of the bamboo is in a certain way it grows, they have this in their sign for bamboo, all designs of bamboo proceed from it. Then he went on rather to disparage vorticism, on the grounds that it could not hope to do for the Occident, in one life-time, what had required centuries of development in China – E. P.]

[7]   See note 6, p. 108.

Here also the Chinese ideography has its advantage, in even a simple line, for example, "The sun rises in the east."

Sun   rises   (in the)   East

The overtones vibrate against the eye. The wealth of composition in characters makes possible a choice of words in which a single dominant overtone colors every plane of meaning. That is perhaps the most conspicuous quality of Chinese poetry. Let us examine our line. The sun, the shining, on one side, on the other the sign of the east, which is the sun entangled in the branches of a tree. And in the middle sign, the verb "rise," we have further homology; the sun is above the horizon, but beyond that the single upright line is like the growing trunk-line of the tree sign. This is but a beginning, but it points a way to the method, and to the method of intelligent reading.

T. S. Eliot (1888–1965)

Introduction

T. S. Eliot was born in St. Louis, Missouri. His father was a successful businessman, his mother a thwarted intellectual. He attended private schools, then went to Harvard University, where he completed his BA in three years (1906–9), rather than the conventional four. He stayed on for another year to do an MA, then went to Europe for a year, spent chiefly in Paris, combined with a tour which took in Italy, Munich, and London. By now he had discovered the poetry of Jules Laforgue, a French author who exerted a strong influence over his early work, yet had also found a uniquely personal poetic voice (wistful and waspish, charged with longing and steeped in skepticism). He returned to Harvard to do a Ph.D. in philosophy, and won a fellowship which took him again to Europe in autumn 1914. With the outbreak of the First World War, he hastened to London, then to Oxford, where he was to write his Ph.D. thesis on F. H. Bradley, a British philosopher. In London he met Ezra Pound, who immediately recognized the power of Eliot's early poetry and encouraged him to write more. In Oxford he met Vivien Haigh-Wood, whom he married in 1915.

Eliot tried teaching and freelance writing for two years, then in 1917 took a position in Lloyds Bank, at that time one of the "Big Six" in British banking. He began a steady routine of working at the bank during the day, and writing at night and over the weekends. His poems, published in a series of little magazines, were soon attracting discerning attention. His first book, *Prufrock and Other Observations* (composed almost wholly of material written before 1911 or even earlier), was issued by the Egoist Press in an edition of 500 copies in 1917, secretly subsidized by Ezra Pound. His second book, *Poems*, was published by the Hogarth Press, a small publishing firm owned and managed by Virginia and Leonard Woolf. (The edition consisted of fewer than 250 copies.) His third, *Ara Vos Prec*, was issued in a limited edition of 250 copies in 1920, followed by an American edition issued by a more mainstream publisher, Alfred Knopf. In 1920 he also published his first book of criticism, *The Sacred Wood*, co-published by different firms in England and America. In 1921 he drafted *The Waste Land*, which he took with him to Paris in January 1922, and gave to Ezra Pound for criticism and counsel. Pound cut over 200 lines and helped to produce the poem as we have it today. The notes to the poem were completed late in July or early August 1922, necessitated by Eliot's wish to have material long enough to justify the poem's being published as an independent book. The poem was published without the notes in two journals late in October 1922, and with the notes as an independent book a month later. It was instantly hailed as a masterpiece, and overnight Eliot had become the foremost poet in the English language.

Eliot immediately began work on what would become *Sweeney Agonistes*, an experimental drama that he worked on intermittently over the next few years, a work that he could not bring to a satisfactory conclusion and one which he considered a failure. Meanwhile, his private life and his entire intellectual outlook were shifting profoundly. He left Lloyds Bank to become an editor at the publishing firm Faber and Gwyer, in 1925, where he stayed until his retirement. He also converted to Christianity and provocatively declared himself a "classicist in literature, a royalist in politics, and anglo-catholic in religion." Meanwhile, he continued to produce a series of important poems and provocative essays, the latter increasingly devoted to waspish meditations on the dwindling powers of literature and religion within modern culture. In 1939 he published *Old Possum's Book of Practical Cats*, a wonderfully whimsical book of poetry for children. During the late 1930s and the early years of the Second World War he wrote *The Four Quartets* (1943), a companion or rival to *The Waste Land*. In 1948 he received the Nobel Prize for Literature.

In 1933 Eliot had left his wife Vivien, a person beset by medical troubles, an array of dubious drugs and treatment regimes, and increasing psychological instability. She was committed by her brother to an asylum. Eliot married his second wife, Valerie, in 1956. After 1950 his interest was almost wholly centered on writing successful plays, and critics disagree sharply about the merits of these later works. Eliot had become a public figure of such stature that it is now difficult even to imagine. When he gave a lecture in 1956 at the University of Minnesota, the audience was so large (14,000) that it had to be given in a basketball stadium. When he died in 1965, there was a deep sense of public mourning over the passing of a figure who, however much one disagreed with him, had left an indelible impression on the literary culture of his age.

The Love Song of J. Alfred Prufrock (1915)

S'io credesse che mia risposta fosse
A persona che mai tornasse al mondo,
Questa fiamma staría senza più scosse.
Ma per ciò che giammai di questo fondo
Non tornò vivo alcun, s'i'odo il vero,
Senza tema d'infamia ti rispondo.[1]

Let us go then, you and I,
When the evening is spread out against the sky
Like a patient etherised upon a table;
Let us go, through certain half-deserted streets,
5   The muttering retreats
Of restless nights in one-night cheap hotels
And sawdust restaurants with oyster-shells:
Streets that follow like a tedious argument
Of insidious intent
10   To lead you to an overwhelming question ...
Oh, do not ask, "What is it?"
Let us go and make our visit.

In the room the women come and go
Talking of Michelangelo.

15   The yellow fog that rubs its back upon the window-panes,
The yellow smoke that rubs its muzzle on the window-panes
Licked its tongue into the corners of the evening,
Lingered upon the pools that stand in drains,
Let fall upon its back the soot that falls from chimneys,
20   Slipped by the terrace, made a sudden leap,
And seeing that it was a soft October night,
Curled once about the house, and fell asleep.

And indeed there will be time[2]
For the yellow smoke that slides along the street,
25   Rubbing its back upon the window-panes;
There will be time, there will be time
To prepare a face to meet the faces that you meet;
There will be time to murder and create,
And time for all the works and days[3] of hands
30   That lift and drop a question on your plate;
Time for you and time for me,
And time yet for a hundred indecisions,
And for a hundred visions and revisions,
Before the taking of a toast and tea.

The poem was first published in *Poetry* 6(3) (June 1915). It was composed in early 1911 when Eliot was in Paris, and completed later that year in July when he was in Munich.

[1] *Epigraph* "If I thought that my reply was made to someone who would return to the world, this flame [of my tongue] would no longer tremble. But since nobody has ever returned from these depths alive, if what I have heard is true, I'll answer you without fear of infamy." These words are spoken by Guido da Montefeltro (1212–98) in Dante's *Inferno*, XXVII, 61–6. Guido, with other deceitful counselors, is punished in a single prison of flame for the treacherous advice he gave to Pope Boniface.

[2] *there will be time* compare the poem "To His Coy Mistress," by Andrew Marvell (1621–78), which has the line "Had we but world enough and time."

[3] *works and days* echoing the title "Works and Days," a poem by the Greek writer Hesiod (fl. *c.* 750 BC), a poem which gives advice on living a life of honest work.

In the room the women come and go   35
Talking of Michelangelo.

    And indeed there will be time
To wonder, "Do I dare?" and, "Do I dare?"
Time to turn back and descend the stair,
With a bald spot in the middle of my hair –   40
[They will say: "How his hair is growing thin!"]
My morning coat, my collar mounting firmly to the chin,
My necktie rich and modest, but asserted by a simple pin –
[They will say: "But how his arms and legs are thin!"]
Do I dare   45
Disturb the universe?
In a minute there is time
For decisions and revisions which a minute will reverse.

    For I have known them all already, known them all: –
Have known the evenings, mornings, afternoons,   50
I have measured out my life with coffee spoons;
I know the voices dying with a dying fall[4]
Beneath the music from a farther room.
    So how should I presume?

    And I have known the eyes already, known them all –   55
The eyes that fix you in a formulated phrase,
And when I am formulated, sprawling on a pin,
When I am pinned and wriggling on the wall,
Then how should I begin
To spit out all the butt-ends of my days and ways?   60
    And how should I presume?

    And I have known the arms already, known them all –
Arms that are braceleted and white[5] and bare
[But in the lamplight, downed with light brown hair!]
Is it perfume from a dress   65
That makes me so digress?
Arms that lie along a table, or wrap about a shawl.
    And should I then presume?
    And how should I begin?

            .   .   .   .   .

Shall I say, I have gone at dusk through narrow streets   70
And watched the smoke that rises from the pipes
Of lonely men in shirt-sleeves, leaning out of windows? . . .

    I should have been a pair of ragged claws
Scuttling across the floors of silent seas.

            .   .   .   .   .

And the afternoon, the evening, sleeps so peacefully!   75
Smoothed by long fingers,
Asleep . . . tired . . . or it malingers,
Stretched on the floor, here beside you and me.
Should I, after tea and cakes and ices,
Have the strength to force the moment to its crisis?   80

---

[4]   *with a dying fall* "That strain again! It had a dying fall," says
Duke Orsino in Shakespeare's *Twelfth Night*, I.i, when he orders
an encore of a tune that suits his love-sick mood.

[5]   *braceleted and white* compare "The Relique" by John Donne
(1572–1631), which has the line: "A bracelet of bright hair
about the bone."

But though I have wept and fasted,[6] wept and prayed,
Though I have seen my head [grown slightly bald] brought in upon a platter,
I am no prophet[7] – and here's no great matter;
I have seen the moment of my greatness flicker,
85   And I have seen the eternal Footman hold my coat, and snicker,
And in short, I was afraid.

And would it have been worth it, after all,
After the cups, the marmalade, the tea,
Among the porcelain, among some talk of you and me,
90   Would it have been worth while,
To have bitten off the matter with a smile,
To have squeezed the universe into a ball[8]
To roll it toward some overwhelming question,
To say: "I am Lazarus,[9] come from the dead,
95   Come back to tell you all, I shall tell you all" –
If one, settling a pillow by her head,
   Should say: "That is not what I meant at all.
   That is not it, at all."

And would it have been worth it, after all,
100   Would it have been worth while,
After the sunsets and the dooryards and the sprinkled streets,
After the novels, after the teacups, after the skirts that trail along the floor –
And this, and so much more? –
It is impossible to say just what I mean!
105   But as if a magic lantern threw the nerves in patterns on a screen:
Would it have been worth while
If one, settling a pillow or throwing off a shawl,
And turning toward the window, should say:
   "That is not it at all,
110   That is not what I meant, at all."

. . . .

No! I am not Prince Hamlet,[10] nor was meant to be;
Am an attendant lord, one that will do
To swell a progress, start a scene or two,
Advise the prince; no doubt, an easy tool,
115   Deferential, glad to be of use,
Politic, cautious, and meticulous;
Full of high sentence,[11] but a bit obtuse;
At times, indeed, almost ridiculous –
Almost, at times, the Fool.[12]

---

[6] *wept and fasted* compare 2 Samuel 1:12: "they mourned, and wept and fasted."

[7] *my head . . . no prophet* John the Baptist, a prophet, rejected the love of Salome; in revenge Salome, when asked what she wanted as a reward for dancing before King Herod, asked for his head to be brought to her on a dish. The story is told in Mark 4:17–28 and Matthew 14:3–11.

[8] *universe into a ball* compare "Let us roll up all our strength and all / Our sweetness up into one ball," ll. 41–2 in "To His Coy Mistress," by Andrew Marvell; the speaker is beginning his final exhortation to seize the opportunity for love.

[9] *Lazarus* One Lazarus who appears in the Bible is the brother of Mary and Martha, a dead man whom Christ brings back to life (see John 11:1–44). Another Lazarus is a beggar juxtaposed with Dives, a rich man, in a parable (see Luke 16:19–31). Lazarus and Dives die at the same time, and while Lazarus goes to Heaven,

Dives goes to hell. Dives then wants to warn his brothers what hell is like, and asks God if Lazarus can be sent back to warn them. But God refuses: "If they hear not Moses and the prophets, neither will they be persuaded, though one rose from the dead."

[10] *Prince Hamlet* the hero of *Hamlet*, whose famous soliloquy ("To be or not to be") is echoed at the end of this line. Prufrock's soliloquy until now has had the kind of self-scrutiny and indecisiveness typified by Hamlet.

[11] *Full of high sentence* the phrase is used by Chaucer to characterize the conversation of the Clerk of Oxford in the General Prologue, 1. 306, to *The Canterbury Tales*; it means learned and full of noble sentiments. But many critics think that this line and the next two are meant to invoke the character Polonius, in *Hamlet*.

[12] *the Fool* a stock character in Elizabethan drama, a court entertainer whose seemingly nonsensical patter conceals wisdom.

I grow old . . . I grow old . . .   120
I shall wear the bottoms of my trousers rolled.[13]

Shall I part my hair behind? Do I dare to eat a peach?
I shall wear white flannel trousers, and walk upon the beach.
I have heard the mermaids singing, each to each.

I do not think that they will sing to me.   125

I have seen them riding seaward on the waves
Combing the white hair of the waves blown back
When the wind blows the water white and black.

We have lingered in the chambers of the sea
By sea-girls wreathed with seaweed red and brown   130
Till human voices wake us, and we drown.

La Figlia che piange (1916)

O quam te memorem virgo . . .[1]

Stand on the highest pavement of the stair –
Lean on a garden urn –
Weave, weave the sunlight in your hair –
Clasp your flowers to you with a pained surprise –
Fling them to the ground and turn   155
With a fugitive resentment in your eyes:
But weave, weave the sunlight in your hair.

So I would have had him leave,
So I would have had her stand and grieve,
So he would have left   140
As the soul leaves the body torn and bruised,
As the mind deserts the body it has used.
I should find
Some way incomparably light and deft,
Some way we both should understand,   145
Simple and faithless as a smile and shake of the hand.[2]

She turned away, but with the autumn weather
Compelled my imagination many days,
Many days and many hours:
Her hair over her arms and her arms full of flowers.
And I wonder how they should have been together!   150
I should have lost a gesture and a pose.

[13] *my trousers rolled* fastidiously arranged to prevent them getting wet.

LA FIGLIA

The poem was first published in *Poetry* 8(6) (September 1916); it was composed in the summer of 1911. Eliot later said that the title was that of a statue or stele in an Italian museum which a friend had recommended that he see, but which he had never actually found (Kristian Smidt, *Poetry and Belief in the Work of T. S. Eliot*, rev. ed. [London: Routledge, 1941], p. 41). The Italian phrase can be translated as "The Daughter Who Weeps," or, less accurately, as "The Girl Who Weeps."

[1] *O quam te memorem virgo* Latin for "Oh, how shall I address you, girl?" or "Oh, how shall I call you, maiden?" The phrase is spoken by Aeneas to Venus, his mother, though at this point she is disguised and he does not recognize her. He goes on: "For neither your appearance nor your voice are those of a mortal." See *Aeneid* I.327–8.
[2] *Simple and faithless as . . . hand* a free translation of a line by the poet Jules Laforgue, from "Petition": "Avec toutes, l'amour s'échange / Simple et sans foi comme un bonjour" ("With all women love is exchanged / Simply and as faithlessly as a 'good day'."

> Sometimes these cogitations still amaze
> The troubled midnight and the noon's repose.

Sweeney Among the Nightingales (1918)

ὤμοι, πέπληγμαι καιρίαν πληγὴν ἔσω.[1]

Apeneck Sweeney spreads his knees
Letting his arms hang down to laugh,
The zebra stripes along his jaw
Swelling to maculate[2] giraffe.

5   The circles of the stormy moon
Slide westward toward the River Plate,[3]
Death and the Raven[4] drift above
And Sweeney guards the hornèd gate.[5]

    Gloomy Orion and the Dog[6]
10   Are veiled; and hushed the shrunken seas;
The person in the Spanish cape
Tries to sit on Sweeney's knees

    Slips and pulls the table cloth
Overturns a coffee-cup,
15   Reorganized upon the floor
She yawns and draws a stocking up;

    The silent man in mocha brown
Sprawls at the window-sill and gapes;
The waiter brings in oranges
20   Bananas figs and hothouse grapes;

    The silent vertebrate in brown
Contracts and concentrates, withdraws;
Rachel née Rabinovitch
Tears at the grapes with murderous paws;

25   She and the lady in the cape
Are suspect, thought to be in league;
Therefore the man with heavy eyes
Declines the gambit, shows fatigue,

    Leaves the room and reappears
30   Outside the window, leaning in,
Branches of wistaria
Circumscribe a golden grin;

The poem was first published in *The Little Review* 5(5) (September 1918). Eliot has said that he thought of Sweeney, who appears in a number of poems, "as a man who in younger days was perhaps a pugilist, mildly successful; who then grew older and retired to keep a pub."
[1] *Epigraph* line 1343 of *Agamemnon* by the Greek dramatist Aeschylus (c. 512–c. 455 BC): "Ah, I am struck a deadly blow and deep within." The line is spoken offstage at the moment when Clytaemnestra murders him.
[2] *maculate* literally the word means marked or spotted; then, less literally, stained or soiled.

[3] *River Plate* the Rio de la Plata forms the border between Uruguay and Argentina in South America.
[4] *the Raven* the constellation Corvus.
[5] *the hornèd gate* in classical myth, the gate through which true dreams must pass on their way from Hades to the world of man (see *Aeneid* VI.892 ff., and *Odyssey* XIX.559 ff.).
[6] *Orion and the Dog* Orion, the hunter, is a constellation which includes the Dog Star (Sirius), one of the brightest in the night sky.

The host with someone indistinct
Converses at the door apart,
The nightingales[7] are singing near   35
The Convent of the Sacred Heart,[8]

And sang within the bloody wood[9]
When Agamemnon cried aloud,
And let their liquid siftings fall
To stain the stiff dishonoured shroud.   40

Sweeney Erect (1919)

And the trees about me,
Let them be dry and leafless; let the rocks
Groan with continual surges; and behind me
Make all a desolation. Look, look, wenches![1]

Paint me[2] a cavernous waste shore
    Cast in the unstilled Cyclades,[3]
Paint me the bold anfractuous[4] rocks
    Faced by the snarled and yelping seas.

Display me Aeolus[5] above   5
    Reviewing the insurgent gales
Which tangle Ariadne's[6] hair
    And swell with haste the perjured sails.[7]

Morning stirs the feet and hands
    (Nausicaa and Polypheme).[8]   10

[7] *nightingales* in Greek myth, Philomela was raped by Tereus, the husband of her sister Procne. To prevent her from revealing his crime, Tereus cut out her tongue; but Philomela depicted his crime on a piece of needlework and sent it to Procne. Philomela, in response, killed Tereus's son Itys and served his cooked flesh to him. When Tereus then attempted to kill the two sisters, Philomela was changed into a nightingale, Procne into a swallow. See Ovid's *Metamorphoses*, VI.424–674; see also *The Waste Land*, 97–103, 203–6.

[8] *Convent of the Sacred Heart* a convent of nuns who belong to the Roman Catholic Congregation of the Sisters of the Sacred Heart of Jesus and Mary.

[9] *bloody wood* Eliot has said that he had in mind the grove of the Furies at Colonus which is described as filled with singing nightingales by Sophocles (495–406 BC) in his play *Oedipus at Colonus*.

The poem was first published in *Arts and Letters* 2(3) (Summer 1919).

SWEENEY ERECT

[1] *Epigraph* from *The Maid's Tragedy* by Francis Beaumont (1584–1616) and John Fletcher (1579–1625). The speaker is Aspatia, the play's heroine, who has been betrayed by her lover Amintor. Aspatia is talking to her attendants, who are working on a tapestry which tells the story of Ariadne, a girl abandoned by Theseus in much the same way as Aspatia has been left. Aspatia criticizes the tapestry, suggesting that her own face would be a good model for that of Ariadne, then gives commands about how the landscape background should look.

[2] *Paint me . . . perjured sails* lines 1–8 imitate and amplify the directions that Aspatia gives to her attendants who are depicting the story of Ariadne and Theseus, who sailed away from her:

    Suppose I stand upon the sea-beach now,
    Mine arms thus, and mine hair blow with the wind . . .

[3] *Cyclades* islands in the Aegean Sea.
[4] *anfractuous* full of windings and turnings, circuitous.
[5] *Aeolus* Greek god of wind.
[6] *Ariadne*, in Greek myth, was the daughter of Minos, King of Crete. She falls in love with Theseus and helps him find his way out of the labyrinth where he has killed the Minotaur. They flee from Crete and are married, but he abandons her on the island of Naxos, where she hangs herself.
[7] *Perjured sails* Theseus had set out on his journey from Athens to Crete with black sails, because it was the custom to pay an annual tribute of young men and women who were sacrificed to the Minotaur. If he was successful in killing the monster, he was to return with white sails; but Theseus forgot to change them on his return journey and when his father, the king, saw the "perjured" black sails, he killed himself.
[8] *Nausicaa* the daughter of King Alicinous, Nausicaa is playing on the beach with friends one morning when she encounters Odysseus, who has been shipwrecked. Though naked, he covers himself with olive leaves and so charms Nausicaa that she takes him home to the palace of her father, where Odysseus is warmly welcomed. (See the *Odyssey* VI.) Polypheme or Polyphemus is one of the Cyclopses, one-eyed monsters who eat humans.

Gesture of orang-outang
    Rises from the sheets in steam.

This withered root of knots of hair
    Slitted below and gashed with eyes,
15   This oval O cropped out with teeth:
    The sickle motion from the thighs

Jackknifes upward at the knees
    Then straightens out from heel to hip
Pushing the framework of the bed
20   And clawing at the pillow slip.

Sweeney addressed full length to shave
    Broadbottomed, pink from nape to base,
Knows the female temperament
    And wipes the suds around his face.

25   (The lengthened shadow of a man
    Is history,[9] said Emerson
Who had not seen the silhouette
    Of Sweeney straddled in the sun.)

Tests the razor on his leg
30   Waiting until the shriek subsides.
The epileptic on the bed
    Curves backward, clutching at her sides.

The ladies of the corridor
    Find themselves involved, disgraced,
35   Call witness to their principles
    And deprecate the lack of taste

Observing that hysteria
    Might easily be misunderstood;
Mrs. Turner intimates
40   It does the house no sort of good.

But Doris, towelled from the bath,
    Enters padding on broad feet,
Bringing sal volatile
    And a glass of brandy neat.

Polyphemus captures Odysseus and his crew and imprisons them in his cave. But they manage to blind him, when he is sleeping, by dashing a huge spar of heated wood into his one eye. They then escape by hiding themselves in the thick wool on the underside of his sheep, whom he must let out to pasture. (See the *Odyssey* IX.)

[9] *The lengthened shadow . . . Is history* in his essay on "Self-Reliance," Emerson wrote that "an institution is the lengthened shadow of one man" and "all history resolves itself very easily into the biography of a few stout and earnest persons."

Gerontion (1920)

> *Thou hast nor youth nor age*
> *But as it were an after dinner sleep*
> *Dreaming of both.*[1]

Here I am, an old man in a dry month,
Being read to by a boy, waiting for rain.[2]
I was neither at the hot gates[3]
Nor fought in the warm rain
Nor knee deep in the salt marsh, heaving a cutlass,   5
Bitten by flies, fought.
My house is a decayed house,
And the jew[4] squats on the window sill, the owner,
Spawned in some estaminet[5] of Antwerp,
Blistered in Brussels, patched and peeled in London.   10
The goat coughs at night in the field overhead;
Rocks, moss, stonecrop, iron, merds.[6]
The woman keeps the kitchen, makes tea,
Sneezes at evening, poking the peevish gutter.[7]
                 I an old man,   15
A dull head among windy spaces.

Signs are taken for wonders. "We would see a sign!"[8]
The word within a word, unable to speak a word,
Swaddled with darkness.[9] In the juvescence of the year
Came Christ the tiger[10]   20

In depraved May, dogwood and chestnut, flowering judas,[11]
To be eaten, to be divided, to be drunk

The poem was first published in *Ara Vos Prec* (London: the Ovid Press, 1920), which was issued early in February that year; this was a deluxe edition limited to 264 copies. It was also included a few weeks later in *Poems* (New York: Alfred Knopf, 1920). "Geronion" is a transliteration of an ancient Greek word meaning "little old man."

[1]   *Epigraph* from Shakepeare's *Measure for Measure* III.i; spoken by the Duke to Claudio, who is about to be executed, offering the view that life is unreal.

[2]   *waiting for rain* an adaptation of lines that appear in a biography of Edward Fitzgerald, the poet who translated *The Rubaiyat of Omar Khayam*, by Arthur Christopher Benson (London: Macmillan, 1905), p. 142. Benson, summarizing a letter from Fitzgerald, describes the aging poet: "Here he sits, in a dry month, old and blind, being read to by a country boy, longing for rain."

[3]   *hot gates* a literal translation of the Greek place name Thermopylae, an important pass between northern and central Greece and the site of a famous battle between the Greeks and the Persians that took place in 480 BC. But plainly the recent experience of the Great War is also being invoked.

[4]   *the jew* whether this passage is anti-Semitic, and if so whose anti-Semitism it reflects, are questions that have been much debated. For an overview, see *Modernism/Modernity* 10(1) (January 2003): 1–70.

[5]   *estaminet* a small restaurant or café; the term entered English via soldiers returning from France and Belgium during the Great War.

[6]   *stonecrop . . . merds* stonecrop is a moss-like plant; merds is from French *merde*, meaning "shit" or "excrement."

[7]   *gutter* a spluttering fire.

[8]   *"We would see a sign!"* the cry of the Pharisees when they call on Christ to prove his divinity, in Matthew 12:38: "Then some of the scribes and Pharisees said unto him: 'Master, we would see a sign from thee'."

[9]   *The word . . . with darkness* Eliot's source for these lines is a Nativity Sermon preached before James I by Bishop Lancelot Andrewes (1555–1626) on Christmas Day, 1618. His text for the sermon is the cry of the Pharisees quoted in line 17. "Verbum infans [infant Word], the Word without a word; the eternal Word not able to speak a word: a wonder sure and . . . swaddled; and that a wonder too. He that takes the sea 'and rolls it about the swaddling bands of darkness,' to come thus into clouts [the baby's swaddling clothes], Himself!" Andrewes and Eliot are both using "word" in its original Greek sense of Logos, meaning the reason or principle informing all things, and Andrewes is marveling at the paradox that God, as Logos, should become a speechless child, unable to utter a word.

[10] *Christ the tiger* an allusion to Blake's poem "The Tiger," which makes this animal into a sign of God's aspect of power and wrath.

[11] *In depraved . . . judas* a condensed allusion to a passage in *The Education of Henry Adams* (Boston and New York: Houghton Mifflin, 1918), p. 400, where he speaks of settling in Washington: "The Potomac and its tributaries squandered beauty. . . . Here and there a Negro log cabin alone disturbed the dogwood and the judas-tree. . . . The tulip and the chestnut tree gave no sense of struggle against a stingy nature . . . The brooding heat of the profligate vegetation; the cool charm of the running

Among whispers; by Mr. Silvero
With caressing hands, at Limoges[12]
25   Who walked all night in the next room;

By Hakagawa, bowing among the Titians;[13]
By Madame de Tornquist, in the dark room
Shifting the candles; Fräulein von Kulp
Who turned in the hall, one hand on the door.
30   Vacant shuttles
Weave the wind.[14] I have no ghosts,
An old man in a draughty house
Under a windy knob.

After such knowledge, what forgiveness? Think now
35   History has many cunning passages, contrived corridors
And issues, deceives with whispering ambitions,
Guides us by vanities. Think now
She gives when our attention is distracted
And what she gives, gives with such supple confusions
40   That the giving famishes the craving. Gives too late
What's not believed in, or if still believed,
In memory only, reconsidered passion. Gives too soon
Into weak hands, what's thought can be dispensed with
Till the refusal propagates a fear. Think
45   Neither fear nor courage saves us. Unnatural vices
Are fathered by our heroism. Virtues
Are forced upon us by our impudent crimes.
These tears are shaken from the wrath-bearing tree.[15]

The tiger springs in the new year. Us he devours. Think at last
50   We have not reached conclusion, when I
Stiffen in a rented house. Think at last
I have not made this show purposelessly
And it is not by any concitation[16]
Of the backward devils.
55   I would meet you upon this honestly.
I that was near your heart was removed therefrom
To lose beauty in terror, terror in inquisition.
I have lost my passion: why should I need to keep it
Since what is kept must be adulterated?
60   I have lost my sight, smell, hearing, taste and touch:
How should I use them for your closer contact?

These with a thousand small deliberations
Protract the profit of their chilled delirium,
Excite the membrane, when the sense has cooled,

water, the terrific splendor of the June thundergust in the deep and solitary woods, were all sensual, animal, elemental. No European spring had shown him the same intermixture of delicate grace and passionate depravity that marked the Maryland May. He loved it too much as if it were Greek and half human."

[12] *Limoges* a French town, famous for its china.

[13] *the Titians* paintings by Titian (c. 1485–1576).

[14] *Vacant shuttles . . . wind* compare Job 7:6–7: "My days are swifter than a weaver's shuttle, and are spent without hope. O remember that my life is wind: mine eye shall see no more good."

[15] *wrath-bearing tree* perhaps the Tree of the Knowledge of Good and Evil in Genesis 1–2; "wrath-bearing" in the sense that man's violation of God's injunction not to eat of its fruit brings his wrath.

[16] *concitation* a neologism invented by Eliot from the Latin "concitatio," meaning stirring up, moving, exciting.

With pungent sauces, multiply variety   65
In a wilderness of mirrors. What will the spider do,
Suspend its operations, will the weevil
Delay? De Bailhache, Fresca, Mrs. Cammel, whirled
Beyond the circuit of the shuddering Bear[17]
In fractured atoms. Gull against the wind, in the windy straits   70
Of Belle Isle, or running on the Horn,[18]
White feathers in the snow, the Gulf claims,
And an old man driven by the Trades[19]
To a sleepy corner.

Tenants of the house,   75
Thoughts of a dry brain in a dry season.

The Waste Land: Introduction

The poem, without its notes, was published in England on October 16, 1922, in the first number of *The Criterion* (1 [1] [Oct. 1922]), a new journal edited by Eliot himself. Again without notes, it was published in the United States a few days later in *The Dial*, then the country's preeminent literary and cultural journal. A month later Eliot received the second annual Dial Award (the first had been granted to Sherwood Anderson), an award which was effectively the price that *The Dial* had chosen to pay to be the first journal in the US to publish the poem. Around December 1, 1922, the poem was published for a third time, now as an independent book issued by Boni and Liveright, a publishing house in New York. In this third version the poem came with the notes which have accompanied it ever since. The authority and status of the notes have been a subject of contentious debate, for reasons that will become clearer in a moment.

Eliot composed *The Waste Land* over the course of 1921. He began it in late January or February that year and completed a draft of it, about 220 lines longer than the published poem, in late December. His progress was relatively straightforward, in the sense that he composed the five parts of the poem in succession. But there were numerous turning points and digressions along the way. For example, in May of 1921 he appears to have added a new and very different beginning to Part I, one patently indebted to his recent reading of the manuscript version of episodes 14 ("Oxen of the Sun") and 15 ("Circe") of *Ulysses* (itself not published till February 1922). Likewise, the beginning to Part III, at this point, was very different from the published version presented here. It consisted of some 70 lines of satire depicting Fresca, a wealthy socialite. In early November, after composing the conclusion of Part III which we have today (11. 256–317), Eliot came to feel that there was too great a disparity between his new ending to Part III and the brittle satire of Fresca which was then the beginning to Part III. Sometime later in November or December, therefore, he added 17 more lines to Part III's beginning, an effort to achieve more connectedness between the part's beginning and its ending. Meanwhile, also during November and December, he composed Parts IV and V, with Part IV containing a lengthy story about the final voyage and shipwreck of a character named Phlebas. In early January 1922, he took the entire manuscript as it now stood to Ezra Pound in Paris for counsel and advice. Pound cut out the beginning to Part I, the passage so obviously indebted to Joyce; he also excised the entire depiction of Fresca which constituted the beginning to Part III; and he expunged the lengthy story of Phlebas's voyage and shipwreck that began Part IV. All total, he eliminated some 220 lines. As a result Eliot, while still in Paris, composed a new beginning to Part III, or lines 173–82, largely as we have them today.

By the end of January 1922, the poem proper was complete in the form we have it. As yet, however, there were no notes to it. Eliot did not begin working on them till much later, and even as late as July 1922, they had not been completed. It was only in August, some 8 months after

---

[17] *the shuddering Bear* the Great Bear, a northern constellation. The passage builds on a classical tradition that the sinners were punished by being sent into a whirling orbit that would take them into space.
[18] *Belle Isle... the Horn* Belle Isle and the Belle Isle straits are in the North Atlantic, off the eastern coast of Canada; Cape Horn is the southernmost tip of south America.

[19] *the Gulf... the Trades* the Gulf Stream in the Atlantic. A gull flying either to the north (Belle Isle) or the south (the Cape) will use "the Trades," or the Trade winds.

the poem was finished, that Eliot finished the notes. (Eliot's original notes, as opposed to my editorial footnotes, are printed here at the end of *The Waste Land*.) Moreover, the notes were produced in large part because Eliot was anxious that his poem be published as an independent book, and the text of the poem itself simply wasn't long enough to justify that, at least not by prevailing standards of the contemporary publishing industry. Ever since, the notes have been a subject of critical debate.

The reason why the notes have been so intensely debated is simple: they made reference to "the plan . . . of the poem," so suggesting that it had been composed and ordered by a purposeful design, perhaps obscure at first sight but ultimately discernible, a procedure very different from the more improvisational, more contingent process which, we know today, actually governed the poem's composition. Some critics, however, take Eliot's first note about "the plan . . . of the poem" at face value, and they urge that a proper understanding of the poem will begin with a contemporary book mentioned by Eliot, Jessie Weston's *From Ritual to Romance*.

That book contends that the Arthurian romances which recount a quest for the Holy Grail are underlain (or somehow informed) by pre-Christian fertility myths and rituals. In these romances, a Fisher king has been maimed or killed, and his country has therefore become a dry Waste Land; he can be regenerated and his land restored to fertility only when a knight (Perceval or Parsifal) perseveres through a series of ordeals to learn the answers to certain ritual questions about the Grail. The Fisher king, in short, is analogous to ancient vegetation gods (Adonis of Greece, Osiris of Egypt, etc.), whose deaths and rebirths were represented in ritual ceremonies intended to bring about the regeneration of plants after the sterile winter. The speaker of *The Waste Land*, then, is an identifiable character, a "quester," who is somehow performing actions analogous to those of Perceval or Parsifal, attempting to restore the land which has been wasted.

The text of this edition follows that found in Lawrence Rainey, *The Annotated Waste Land with Eliot's Contemporary Prose* (New Haven: Yale University Press, 2005).

The Waste Land (1922)

"Nam Sibyllam quidem Cumis ego ipse oculis meis vidi in ampulla pendere, et cum illi pueri dicerent: Σίβυλλα τί θέλεις; *respondebat illa:* ἀποθανεῖν θέλω."[1]

For Ezra Pound
il miglior fabbro[2]

I.   THE BURIAL OF THE DEAD[3]

April is the cruellest month, breeding
Lilacs out of the dead land, mixing
Memory and desire, stirring
Dull roots with spring rain.
5   Winter kept us warm, covering

---

[1]   *Epigraph* "For on one occasion I myself saw, with my own eyes, the Cumaean Sibyl hanging in a cage, and when some boys said to her, 'Sibyl, what do you want?' she replied, 'I want to die'." This account is given by Trimalchio, a character in the *Satyricon*, the satirical novel written by the Roman writer Petronius in the first century AD. Trimalchio, a wealthy vulgarian, is hosting a dinner which occupies the novel's middle section; he is vying with his guests in recounting tales of wonder, but merely muddles up commonplace stories of Hercules and Ulysses before turning to his account of the Cumaean Sibyl.

The Cumaean Sibyl (whose oracular cavern was rediscovered by archaeologists at the site of ancient Cumae near Naples in 1934) was a figure revered in antiquity. Her prophecies were delivered in Greek hexameter verses inscribed on palm-leaves and placed at the mouth of her cave. If no one came to collect them, they were scattered by the winds and never read. She figures prominently in Vergil's *Fourth Eclogue* and is described at length in Vergil's *Aeneid* VI.1–155. She also figures in Ovid's *Meta-*

morphoses XIV.101–53, the account to which Trimalchio alludes. Promised by Apollo that she could have one wish fulfilled, whatever it might be, she chose to live as many years as the grains of sand she could hold in her hand; but she forgot to choose eternal youth, and was condemned to grow ever older and more shriveled.

[2]   *il miglior fabbro* "the better craftsman" in Italian. Eliot dedicates the poem to Ezra Pound with the phrase that registers Dante's tribute to the Provençal poet Arnaut Daniel (fl. 1180–1200; see *Purgatorio* XXVI, line 117). The dedication first appeared in a presentation copy which Eliot gave Pound in January 1923; it was published for the first time in 1925 when *The Waste Land* was included in *Poems 1909–1925*.

[3]   *Title of Part I* "The Order for the Burial of the Dead" prescribes the words and actions of a burial service within the Church of England; the text appears in the *Book of Common Prayer*.

Earth in forgetful snow, feeding
A little life with dried tubers.
Summer surprised us, coming over the Starnbergersee
With a shower of rain; we stopped in colonnade,
And went on in sunlight, into the Hofgarten,   10
And drank coffee, and talked for an hour.
Bin gar keine Russin, stamm' aus Litauen, echt deutsch.[4]
And when we were children, staying at the archduke's,
My cousin's, he took me out on a sled,
And I was frightened. He said, Marie,   15
Marie,[5] hold on tight. And down we went.
In the mountains, there you feel free.
I read, much of the night, and go south in the winter.

What are the roots that clutch, what branches grow
Out of this stony rubbish? Son of man,   20
You cannot say, or guess, for you know only
A heap of broken images, where the sun beats,
And the dead tree gives no shelter, the cricket no relief,[6]
And the dry stone no sound of water. Only
There is shadow under this red rock,   25
(Come in under the shadow of this red rock),[7]
And I will show you something different from either
Your shadow at morning striding behind you
Or your shadow at evening rising to meet you;
I will show you fear in a handful of dust.   30

    Frisch weht der Wind
    Der Heimat zu,
    Mein Irisch Kind,
    Wo weilest du?[8]

"You gave me hyacinths first a year ago;   35
"They called me the hyacinth girl."
– Yet when we came back, late, from the Hyacinth Garden,
Your arms full, and your hair wet, I could not
Speak, and my eyes failed, I was neither
Living nor dead, and I knew nothing,   40

[4] *Starnbergersee... Hofgarten* the Starnbergersee is a lake 9 miles outside Munich, the Hofgarten (literally "court garden"), a park in the same city. One side of the park has a long arcade ("colonnade") which is flanked by a celebrated café. Eliot visited it in 1911.

Bin gar... echt deutsch "I am not a Russian, I come from Lithuania, a real German" (German).

[5] *Marie* Valerie Eliot, in her 1971 edition of *The Waste Land: A Facsimile*, has stated that Eliot "had met" the Countess Marie Larisch (1858–1940), a former intimate of the Hapsburg dynasty which ruled the Austro-Hungarian empire until 1818, and that "his description of the sledding... was taken verbatim from a conversation he had with" her (p. 126).

[6] *And the dead tree... no relief* Eliot's note cites Ecclesiastes 12:5, which describes the "evil days" that come when men are old and declining into darkness: "Also when they shall be afraid of that which is high, and fears shall be in the way, and the almond tree shall flourish, and the grasshopper shall be a burden, and desire shall fail: because man goeth to his long home, and the mourners go about in the streets."

[7] *Come in... this red rock* perhaps an echo of Isaiah 2:10: "Enter into the rock and hide thee in the dust, for fear of the Lord." Or it may also echo a more consoling prophecy in Isaiah 32:2: "And a man shall be as a hiding place from the wind, and a covert from the tempest; as rivers of water in a dry place, as the shadow of a great rock in a weary land."

[8] *Frisch weht... weilest du* as Eliot notes, his quotation is from the opera *Tristan and Isolde* (1865), by Richard Wagner (1813–83), I.i.5–8. "Fresh blows the wind / To the homeland / My Irish child, / Where are you tarrying?" (German). The scene opens on a ship transporting Isolde from Cornwall to Ireland, where she is to marry King Mark. She is accompanied by Tristan, Mark's nephew. From the ship's rigging, a sailor's voice resounds with a melancholy song about an Irish woman left behind, which includes the lines transcribed by Eliot. Later in the opera, Isolde decides to kill both Tristan and herself with poison; but her companion, Brangäne, substitutes a love potion for the poison, and the two fall hopelessly in love.

Looking into the heart of light, the silence.
Öd' und leer das Meer.[9]

Madame Sosotris,[10] famous clairvoyante,
Had a bad cold, nevertheless
45   Is known to be the wisest woman in Europe,
With a wicked pack of cards.[11] Here, said she,
Is your card, the drowned Phoenician Sailor,[12]
(Those are pearls that were his eyes. Look!)[13]
Here is Belladonna, the Lady of the Rocks,[14]
50   The lady of situations.
Here is the man with three staves, and here the Wheel,
And here is the one-eyed merchant,[15] and this card,
Which is blank, is something he carries on his back,
Which I am forbidden to see. I do not find
55   The Hanged Man. Fear death by water.
I see crowds of people, walking round in a ring.
Thank you. If you see dear Mrs. Equitone,
Tell her I bring the horoscope myself.
One must be so careful these days.

60   Unreal City,[16]
Under the brown fog of a winter dawn,
A crowd flowed over London Bridge, so many,

[9]   Öd' und leer das Meer "Desolate and empty the sea" (German). From Richard Wagner's opera, Tristan and Isolde, III.i.24. Tristan is lying grievously wounded outside Kareol, his castle in Brittany, tended by his companion Kurwenal. He will die unless Isolde can come and cure him with her magic arts. Tristan wakes from his delirium; he is clinging to life only so that he can find Isolde and take her with him into the realm of night. For a moment he thinks that he sees Isolde's ship approaching; but a shepherd who is watching with him pipes a sad tune: "Desolate and empty the sea."

[10]   Madame Sosotris the name indicates someone who equivocates, whose answer to every question is a variant of "so so." Not surprisingly, her friend is named Mrs. Equitone, a variant on the notion of equivocation. To learned readers her name may also recall the Greek work for "savior," soteros, which survives in the English word soteriological, of or having to do with the doctrine of salvation in Christian theology.

[11]   pack of cards the tarot cards consist of 22 cards, one unnumbered and the rest numbered through 21, which are added to a pack (British usage) or deck of 56 cards arranged in four suits (cups, wands, swords, and pentacles or pentangles). Jessie Weston suggested that these suits were repositories of primeval symbols of fertility corresponding to the four Grail talismans (grail-cup, lance, sword, dish) in her study From Ritual to Romance, pp. 77–9. Scholars have expended vast amounts of ink on establishing precise connections between the Tarot cards and Eliot's use of them, even though Eliot, in his notes to the poem, admitted that he had little familiarity with the Tarot and had "departed" from it "to suit my own convenience."

[12]   the drowned Phoenician Sailor there is no such card in the Tarot pack, but this looks forward to Part IV of The Waste Land.

[13]   Those are pearls...Look! from Shakespeare, The Tempest, I.ii.399. The play begins with a storm and shipwreck which bring young Prince Ferdinand and others to an unnamed island inhabited by Prospero, the former ruler of Naples

who has been deposed by his brother Antonio, and Alonso. The storm has been created at Prospero's behest by Ariel, a magical spirit of the island who serves him. When Ferdinand is lamenting his father's supposed death – he is mistaken, for his father is still alive – Ariel tries to comfort him with a song (396–405):

Full fathom five thy father lies;
    Of his bones are coral made;
Those are pearls that were his eyes;
    Nothing of him that doth fade
But doth suffer a sea change
Into something rich and strange.
Sea nymphs hourly ring his knell:
                    Burden. Ding-dong.
Hark! Now I hear them – ding-dong bell.

[14]   Here is Belladonna ... Rocks Belladonna is Italian for "beautiful woman." There is certainly no such card in the Tarot pack.

[15]   Here is the man ... the one-eyed merchant the first two cards, the man with three staves and the wheel, are genuine Tarot cards, but the one-eyed merchant is Eliot's invention.

[16]   Unreal City the City is the name for the financial district in London, located just beyond the north end of London Bridge. The area is home to the Royal Exchange, the Bank of England, and the head offices or headquarters of Britain's major commercial banks, including Lloyds Bank in Lombard Street, where Eliot worked from 1917 to 1925. The London Bridge that Eliot knew was built between 1825 and 1831 to a design by John Rennie (1761–1821); it was dismantled in 1967 and replaced with the current structure.

Eliot's note at this point invokes a poem by Charles Baudelaire (1821–67), "Les sept vieillards" (1859), which recounts a ghostly encounter in the street which sets the pattern for the incident that follows in this portion of The Waste Land.

I had not thought death had undone so many.[17]
Sighs,[18] short and infrequent, were exhaled,
And each man fixed his eyes before his feet.   65
Flowed up the hill and down King William Street,[19]
To where Saint Mary Woolnoth[20] kept the hours
With a dead sound on the final stroke of nine.
There I saw one I knew, and stopped him, crying: "Stetson!
"You who were with me in the ships at Mylae![21]   70
"That corpse you planted last year in your garden,
"Has it begun to sprout? Will it bloom this year?
"Or has the sudden frost disturbed its bed?
"Oh keep the Dog far hence hence, that's friend to men,
"Or with his nails he'll dig it up again![22]   75
"You! hypocrite lecteur! – mon semblable, – mon frère!"[23]

II.   A GAME OF CHESS[24]

The Chair she sat in, like a burnished throne,[25]
Glowed on the marble, where the glass

---

[17] *so many... so many* Eliot's note cites Dante, *Inferno* III.55–7:

> such a long stream
> of people, that I would not have thought
> that death had undone so many.

As soon as Dante passes through the gates of Hell, he hears first "sighs, lamentations, and loud wailings" (III.22), then "strange tongues, horrible languages, words of pain, tones of anger, voices loud and hoarse" (III.25–7). In the gloom he discerns "a long stream of people." He asks Vergil, his guide in the underworld, why these people are here, and Vergil explains that in life these did neither good nor evil, thinking only of themselves; like the Sybil in the epigraph to *The Waste Land*, they "have no hope of death, and so abject is their blind life that they are envious of every other lot" (III.46–8).

[18] *Sighs...* Eliot's note cites Dante, *Inferno* IV.25–7:

> Here, as far I could tell by listening,
> Was no lamentation more than sighs,
> Which kept the air forever trembling.

Dante has entered the first circle of Hell, or Limbo, and describes the sound that emanates from those who died without being baptized, and who therefore live with the torment of desiring to see God, but knowing that they never will.

[19] *King William Street* the thoroughfare which runs from the north end of London Bridge directly into the City, or financial district, of London.

[20] *St. Mary Woolnoth* the church, a neoclassical work designed by Nicholas Hawksmoor (1661–1736), who was a prominent architect in the early eighteenth century, was erected between 1716 and 1724. It is located at the intersection of King William Street and Lombard Street, directly opposite Eliot's office in Lloyds Bank. By his time the church had already become a relic, isolated and dwarfed by the larger office blocks of the City's banks, since people no longer resided within the City and the church had lost its parishioners.

[21] *Mylae* a city on the northern coast of Sicily, now called Milazzo, off the coast of which there occurred a naval battle between the Romans and the Carthaginians in 260 BC, the first engagement in the first of the Punic Wars. The Romans won, destroying some 50 ships, the first step in their battle for commercial domination of the Mediterranean.

[22] *Oh keep the Dog... again!* Eliot's note directs the reader to *The White Devil* (1612), a play by John Webster (c. 1580–c. 1635). It dramatizes numerous acts of political and sexual betrayal, among which Flamineo murders his own brother Marcello. Their mother, in Act V, scene 4, sings a demented dirge over Marcello's body; contemplating his future tomb, she says: "But keep the wolf far thence, that's foe to men."

[23] *hypocrite lecteur!... mon frère* Eliot's note cites "Au Lecteur" ("To the Reader," 1855), the first poem in *Les Fleurs du Mal* (*Flowers of Evil*, 1857), by Charles Baudelaire. Eliot quotes its last line in its entirety: "Hypocrite reader! – You! – My twin! – My brother!"

[24] *The Game of Chess* the title is indebted to the play by Thomas Middleton (1580–1627), *A Game at Chess* (1624), in which chess becomes an allegory of the diplomatic games between England and Spain. Middleton also authored *Women Beware Women* (date disputed, 1613–14 or 1619/1623), a play which Eliot cites in his note to line 137. In Act 2, scene 2, a game of chess is played between Livia, who is acting on behalf of the Duke of Florence, and the mother of Leantio, who is ostensibly watching over Leantio's young and beautiful wife. The game is a ruse to distract the mother, whose daughter-in-law is meanwhile being seduced by the Duke on the balcony above. The dialogue during the chess game ironically comments on the different mating moves being performed overhead by the Duke and the young wife.

[25] *The Chair she sat in... throne* Eliot cites Shakespeare's *Antony and Cleopatra*, II.ii.190. Enobarbus, a friend and follower of Marc Antony, describes Cleopatra as she was when floating on her ship down the Cydnus River to Antony (ll. 192–206):

> The barge she sat in, like a burnished throne,
> Burned on the water: the poop was beaten gold;
> Purple the sails, and so perfumèd that
> The winds were lovesick with them; the oars were silver,

80 Held up by standards wrought with fruited vines
From which a golden Cupidon peeped out
(Another hid his eyes behind his wing)
Doubled the flames of sevenbranched candelabra
Reflecting light upon the table as
85 The glitter of her jewels rose to meet it,
From satin cases poured in rich profusion;
In vials of ivory and coloured glass
Unstoppered, lurked her strange synthetic perfumes,
Unguent, powdered, or liquid – troubled, confused
90 And drowned the sense in odours; stirred by the air
That freshened from the window, these ascended
In fattening the prolonged candle-flames,
Flung their smoke into the laquearia,[26]
Stirring the pattern on the coffered ceiling.
Huge sea-wood fed with copper
95 Burned green and orange, framed by the coloured stone,
In which sad light a carvèd dolphin swam.
Above the antique mantel was displayed
As though a window gave upon the sylvan scene[27]
The change of Philomel,[28] by the barbarous king
100 So rudely forced; yet there the nightingale
Filled all the desert with inviolable voice
And still she cried, and still the world pursues,
"Jug Jug"[29] to dirty ears.
And other withered stumps of time
105 Were told upon the walls; staring forms
Leaned out, leaning, hushing the room enclosed.
Footsteps shuffled on the stair.
Under the firelight, under the brush, her hair
Spread out in fiery points
110 Glowed into words, then would be savagely still.

"My nerves are bad to-night. Yes, bad. Stay with me.
"Speak to me. Why do you never speak? Speak.
"What are you thinking of? What thinking? What?
"I never know what you are thinking. Think."

Which to the tune of flutes kept stroke, and made
The Water which they beat to follow faster,
As amorous of their strokes. For her own person,
It beggared all description: she did lie
In her pavilion, cloth-of-gold of tissue,
O'erpicturing that Venus where we see
The fancy outwork nature. On each side her
Stood pretty dimpled boys, like smiling Cupids,
With divers-colored fans, whose wind did seem
To glow the delicate cheeks which they did cool,
And what they undid did.

[26] *laquearia* a Latin term, in the plural, for a paneled or fretted ceiling. Eliot's note refers to Vergil, the *Aeneid* I.726–7. Aeneas and his crew have just arrived in Carthage after fleeing the ruins of Troy, destroyed by the Greeks at the end of the Trojan war; Dido, the queen of Carthage, has given them a royal welcome and gives them dinner in a banquet hall of great luxury. The gods have fated her to fall in love with Aeneas during this meal, which

will ensure that she provides him with aid and thus that he will go on to fulfill his destiny, the foundation of Rome; but to do this he will have to desert her, prompting her suicide. The story acquires irony from the reader's knowledge that Rome will eventually destroy Carthage.

Blazing torches hang down from the gilded ceiling,
And vanquish the night with their flames.

[27] *sylvan scene* Eliot's note refers us to Milton's *Paradise Lost* IV.140, a passage describing Satan as he approaches paradise (131–41) and sees "A Silvan Scene, a woody Theatre / Of stateliest view."
[28] *Philomel . . .* Eliot's note cites Ovid's *Metamorphoses*, VI.424–674. For a brief account of the myth, see "Sweeney Among the Nightingales," p. 119 n. 7 above.
[29] *Jug Jug* this was a conventional way of representing the nightingale's song in Elizabethan drama and poetry, and also a crude reference to sexual intercourse.

I think we are in rats' alley   115
Where the dead men lost their bones.

"What is that noise?"
                    The wind under the door.[30]
"What is that noise now? What is the wind doing?"
                    Nothing again nothing.   120
                        "Do
"You know nothing? Do you see nothing? Do you remember
"Nothing?"
                    I remember
                        Those are pearls that were his eyes.[31]   125
"Are you alive, or not? Is there nothing in your head?"
                    But
O O O O that Shakespeherian Rag –
It's so elegant
So intelligent[32]   130

"What shall I do now? What shall I do?"
"I shall rush out as I am, and walk the street
"With my hair down, so. What shall we do tomorrow?
"What shall we ever do?"
                    The hot water at ten.   135
And if it rains, a closed car at four.
And we shall play a game of chess,[33]
Pressing lidless eyes and waiting for a knock upon the door.

When Lil's husband got demobbed,[34] I said –
I didn't mince my words, I said to her myself,   140
HURRY UP PLEASE IT'S TIME[35]
Now Albert's coming back, make yourself a bit smart.
He'll want to know what you done with that money he gave you
To get yourself some teeth. He did, I was there.
You have them all out, Lil, and get a nice set,   145
He said, I swear, I can't bear to look at you.
And no more can't I, I said, and think of poor Albert,
He's been in the army four years, he wants a good time,
And if you don't give it him, there's others will, I said.
Oh is there, she said. Something o' that, I said.   150
Then I'll know who to thank, she said, and give me a straight look.
HURRY UP PLEASE IT'S TIME
If you don't like it you can get on with it, I said.
Others can pick and choose, if you can't.
But if Albert makes off, it won't be for lack of telling.   155
You ought to be ashamed, I said, to look so antique.
(And her only thirty-one.)
I can't help it, she said, pulling a long face,
It's them pills I took, to bring it off, she said.

[30]   *The wind under the door* Eliot's note directs the reader to the play by John Webster, *The Devil's Law Case*, III.ii.148. Contarino has been stabbed, and while undergoing treatment at the hands of two surgeons, is stabbed again by the villain Romelio, unbeknownst to the "surgeons" who have left the room. They return, thinking him dead, but he groans, and one surgeon asks the other, "Is the wind in that door still?"

[31]   *Those are pearls that were his eyes* see note 13 above.

[32]   *O O O O . . . So intelligent* the "Shakespearian Rag" was a popular song published in 1912 by Joseph W. Stern and Co.

and composed for performance at the Ziegfield Follies, with words by Gene Buck and Herman Ruby, music by David Stamper.

[33]   *chess* Eliot's note refers to the game of chess in Thomas Middleton's *Women Beware Women*; see the note to the title of Part II.

[34]   *demobbed* a popular contraction of "demobilized," or released from military service, a term first recorded in 1920.

[35]   *HURRY UP PLEASE IT'S TIME* a time-honored expression used by bartenders to announce the imminent closing of a pub, or public-house, in Britain.

160   (She's had five already,[36] and nearly died of young George.)
        The chemist[37] said it would be alright, but I've never been the same.
        You *are* a proper fool, I said.
        Well, if Albert won't leave you alone, there it is, I said,
        What you get married for if you don't want children?
165   HURRY UP PLEASE IT'S TIME
        Well, that Sunday Albert was home, they had a hot gammon,[38]
        And they asked me in to dinner, to get the beauty of it hot –
        HURRY UP PLEASE IT'S TIME
        HURRY UP PLEASE IT'S TIME
170   Goonight Bill. Goonight Lou. Goonight May. Goonight.
        Ta ta. Goonight. Goonight.
        Good night, ladies, good night, sweet ladies, good night, good night.[39]

III. THE FIRE SERMON[40]

        The river's tent is broken: the last fingers of leaf
        Clutch and sink into the wet bank. The wind
175   Crosses the brown land, unheard. The nymphs are departed.
        Sweet Thames, run softly, till I end my song.[41]
        The river bears no empty bottles, sandwich papers,
        Silk handkerchiefs, cardboard boxes, cigarette ends
        Or other testimony of summer nights. The nymphs are departed.
180   And their friends, the loitering heirs of city directors;
        Departed, have left no addresses.
        By the waters of Leman I sat down and wept . . . [42]
        Sweet Thames, run softly till I end my song,
        Sweet Thames, run softly, for I speak not loud or long.
185   But at my back in a cold blast I hear[43]
        The rattle of the bones, and chuckle spread from ear to ear.

        A rat crept softly through the vegetation
        Dragging its slimy belly on the bank
        While I was fishing in the dull canal
190   On a winter evening round behind the gashouse

---

[36] *She's had five already* The size of the British family had shrunk from an average of 5.5 members in the mid-Victorian era to 2.2 between 1924 and 1929. Systematic practice of birth control had started among the middle classes in the 1870s and had spread downwards before the First World War. After the war, popular interest in birth control surged; Marie Stopes's book, *Married Love: A New Contribution to the Solution of Sex Difficulties* (London: Fifield, 1918), sold 400,000 copies between 1918 and 1923.

[37] *chemist* or a pharmacist, in American usage.

[38] *gammon* smoked ham, in American usage.

[39] *Good night . . . good night* the last line of Part II quotes from Ophelia's mad scene, where she appears distracted by the news that Hamlet has murdered her father and her sense that he will repudiate his affection for her, *Hamlet* IV.v.72–3. Later Ophelia is drowned.

[40] *The Fire Sermon* the title is taken from a sermon by the great religious teacher Siddhartha Gautama (c. 563–483 BC), called by his followers the Buddha or the Enlightened One. The text was translated and edited by Henry Clarke Warren (1854–99), a Harvard University professor whose *Buddhism in Translations*

(Cambridge, MA: Harvard University Press, 1896) became a standard text (for the Fire Sermon, see pp. 151–2).

[41] *Sweet Thames . . . my song* Eliot's note cites the refrain to the "Prothalamion" (1596) by Edmund Spenser (1552–99), a poem which celebrated the ideal of marriage to commemorate the wedding of the two daughters of the Earl of Worcester.

[42] *By the waters of Leman . . .* Eliot is adapting the first verse of Psalm 137: "By the rivers of Babylon, there sat we down, yea, we wept, when we remembered Zion." The ancient Hebrews are lamenting their exile in Babylon and remembering the lost city of Jerusalem. Eliot has substituted for Babylon, the word "Leman," which is the French name for the Lake of Geneva, where he spent some six weeks, from November 22, 1921, to January 2, 1922, ostensibly resting his nerves and also writing Parts IV and V of *The Waste Land*. As Eliot was also aware, "leman" is an archaic term, used by Elizabethan and Jacobean poets to designate an illicit mistress.

[43] *But at my back . . .* an adaptation which virtually reverses the original sense of lines 21–2 of "To His Coy Mistress" by Andrew Marvell (1621–78): "But at my back I always hear / Time's wingèd chariot hurrying near."

Musing upon the king my brother's wreck
And on the king my father's death before him.[44]
White bodies naked on the low damp ground
And bones cast in a little low dry garret,
Rattled by the rat's foot only, year to year.   195
But at my back from time to time I hear[45]
The sound of horns and motors,[46] which shall bring
Sweeney to Mrs. Porter in the spring.[47]
O the moon[48] shone bright on Mrs. Porter
And on her daughter   200
They wash their feet in soda water[49]
Et O ces voix d'enfants, chantant dans la coupole![50]

Twit twit twit
Jug jug jug jug jug jug
So rudely forc'd.   205
Tereu[51]

Unreal City
Under the brown fog of a winter noon
Mr. Eugenides, the Smyrna merchant[52]
Unshaven, with a pocket full of currants   210

---

[44] *And on the king my father's death* Eliot's note directs the reader to *The Tempest*, I.ii.388–93; Ferdinand, musing by himself on the shore where he has been shipwrecked, hears a song by one of the spirits of the air and asks:

Where should this music be? I' th' air or th' earth?
It sounds no more; and sure it waits upon
Some god o' th' island. Sitting on a bank,
Weeping again the king my father's wrack
This music crept by me upon the waters,
Allaying both their fury and my passion
With its sweet air.

[45] *But at my back* ... see note 43.
[46] *The sound of horns and motors* Eliot's note directs the reader to a poem by John Day (1574–1640?), *The Parliament of Bees* (1641), a series of pastoral eclogues about "the doings, the births, the wars, the wooings" of bees. See "The Parliament of Bees," edited by Arthur Symons, in *Nero and Other Plays*, edited by Herbert P. Horne, Havelock Ellis, Arthur Symons, and A. Wilson Verity (London: T. Fisher Unwin; New York: Charles Scribner's Sons, 1904), p. 227.
[47] *Sweeney to Mrs. Porter* ... Sweeney figures in two earlier poems by Eliot, "Sweeney Erect" and "Sweeney Among the Nightingales" (see pp. 118–20).
[48] *O the moon* ... Eliot's note says that this ballad "was reported to me from Sydney, Australia." According to one scholar, who cites no evidence for his claim, this soldiers' ballad originally had the word "cunts" instead of feet. Contemporary reviewers, instead, cited an anonymous American ballad known as "Red Wing," with the refrain:

Now the moon shines bright on pretty Red Wing,
The breezes sighing, the night birds crying,
For afar 'neath his star her brave is sleeping,
While Red Wing's weeping her heart away.

[49] *soda water* bicarbonate of soda, or baking soda, used for cleaning.
[50] *Et O ces voix d'enfants* ... the last line of a sonnet by the French poet Paul Verlaine (1844–96), "Parsifal," first published in the *Revue Wagnérienne* (June 6, 1886). "And O these children's voices, singing in the cupola." Verlaine's poem refers to Richard Wagner's opera, *Parsifal* (1882), in which the innocent knight Parsifal overcomes first the temptations of the flower maidens in Klingsor's magic garden, then the temptations of the beautiful Kundry, who acts under a spell cast by Klingsor. Parsifal recovers the sacred Spear with which Christ's side had been pierced and returns to the Castle of Monsalvat, where the Knights of the Holy Grail are waiting, and Anfortas, the Fisher King, will be healed by a touch from the Spear. Before he heals Anfortas, Kundry (now free from Klingsor's spell) washes his feet (compare with Mrs. Porter and her daughter), and after Anfortas is healed, a choir of young boys sings.
[51] *Jug* ... *Tereu* see note 29.
[52] *Mr. Eugenides the Smyrna merchant* in both ancient Greek and Latin, *euge* means "well done" or "bravo!" In ancient Greek, *eugeneia* meant "high descent, nobility of birth," and *eugenes* "well-born." The word persists in the modern term "eugenics." Smyrna, modern day Izmir, is on the western coast of modern Turkey, or Asia Minor, and until 1914 was part of the Ottoman Empire, hosting a heterogenous population. It was divided into Turkish, Jewish, Armenian, Greek, and Frankish quarters. With the end of the First World War, obtaining Smyrna became a primary goal of Greece. In May 1919, a Greek occupation force, protected by allied warships, disembarked in the city. Meanwhile, the Ottoman empire was being swept away by the Turkish nationalist movement headed by Mustafa Kemal (Atatürk). In March 1921, after an international conference failed to resolve the problem of Asia Minor, the Greeks launched a major offensive and by the end of the summer were only 40 miles from Ankara. But in August Mustafa Kemal launched a counteroffensive which completely routed the Greeks. On September 8 the Greek army evacuated Smyrna; the next day the Turks entered it and massacred the city's Christian inhabitants, killing some 30,000. The conflict was not resolved until the Treaty of Lausanne was signed in July 1923, in which Greece ceded all territories in Asia Minor to the newly created Republic of Turkey. Greece and Smyrna, then, were much in the news throughout the period when Eliot was writing *The Waste Land*.

C.i.f. London: documents at sight,
Asked me in demotic[53] French
To luncheon at the Cannon Street Hotel[54]
Followed by a weekend at the Metropole.[55]

215   At the violet hour, when the eyes and back
Turn upward from the desk, when the human engine waits
Like a taxi throbbing waiting,
I Tiresias, though blind, throbbing between two lives,[56]
Old man with wrinkled female breasts, can see

220   At the violet hour, the evening hour that strives
Homeward, and brings the sailor home from sea,[57]
The typist[58] home at teatime, clears her breakfast, lights
Her stove, and lays out food in tins.
Out of the window perilously spread

225   Her drying combinations[59] touched by the sun's last rays,

[53] *demotic* as spoken by ordinary people, versus correct or learned speech.

[54] *Cannon Street Hotel* Cannon Street runs westward from King William Street (see notes 19 and 20). The Cannon Street Station was designed and built between 1863 and 1866; it became a terminus for suburban commuters and businessmen traveling to and from the Continent. Attached to it was the Cannon Street Hotel, designed by Edward Middleton Barry (1830–80) and opened in May 1867, demolished in 1963.

[55] *a weekend at the Metropole* the Metropole is a hotel in Brighton, a holiday resort on the southern coast of England. Designed by Alfred Waterhouse and opened in July 1890, it was the largest hotel in Britain outside London, and is still there.

[56] *I Tiresias ... two lives* a legendary blind seer from Thebes. One day, when he saw snakes coupling and struck them with his stick, he was instantly transformed into a woman; seven years later the same thing happened again and he was turned back into a man. Since he had experienced the body in both sexes, he was asked by Jove and Juno to settle a dispute concerning whether men or women had greater pleasure in making love. Tiresias took the side of Jove and answered that women had more pleasure. Juno, angered, blinded him. In compensation, Jove gave him the gift of prophecy and long life. The story is told in Ovid's *Metamorphoses*, III.316–38 (Eliot, in his notes, gives the original Latin for lines 320–38), given here in Rolfe Humphries' translation:

So, while these things were happening on earth
And Bacchus, Semele's son, was twice delivered,
Safe in his cradle, Jove, they say, was happy
And feeling pretty good (with wine) forgetting
Anxiety and care, and killing time
Joking with Juno. "I maintain," he told her,
"You females get more pleasure out of loving
Than we poor males do, ever." She denied it,
So they decided to refer the question
To wise Tiresias' judgment: he should know
What love was like, from either point of view.
Once he had come upon two serpents mating
In the green woods, and struck them from each other,
And thereupon, from man was turned to woman,
And was a woman seven years, and saw
The serpents once again, and once more struck them
Apart, remarking: "If there is such magic
In giving you blows, that man is turned to woman,
It may be that woman is turned to man. Worth trying."

And so he was a man again; as umpire,
He took the side of Jove. And Juno
Was a bad loser, and she said that umpires
Were nearly always blind, and made him so forever.
No god can over-rule another's action,
But the Almighty Father, out of pity,
In compensation, gave Tiresias power
To know the future, so there was some honor
Along with punishment.

Tiresias also figures prominently in Sophocles' play, *Oedipus Rex*, where he recognizes that the curse on Thebes has come about because Oedipus has unknowingly committed incest with his mother Jocasta and killed his father. Thebes has been turned into a waste land, its land and people infertile.

[57] *Homeward .. the sailor home from sea* Eliot's note refers to Fragment 149 by Sappho, a Greek poet of the seventh century BC:

Hesperus, you bring home all the bright dawn disperses,
bring home the sheep,
bring home the goat, bring the child home its mother.

[58] *The typist...* it is difficult today to appreciate just how radical Eliot was in making a typist a protagonist in a serious poem. Prior to *The Waste Land* typists had appeared almost exclusively in light verse, humorous or satirical in nature. Their increasing presence in offices after 1885 was registered instead in fiction, and often they were shown being tempted by unscrupulous bosses or fellow workers. Early novels about typists, from 1893 to 1908, were often melodramatic and lurid (see, for example, Clara Del Rio, *Confessions of a Type-Writer* [Chicago: Rio Publishing Co., 1893]), but these vanished after 1910. Instead, typists became a subject increasingly explored by writers working in the tradition of realism. American writers who did this were David Graham Phillips, *The Grain of Dust* (New York: D. Appleton, 1911); Sinclair Lewis, *The Job* (New York: Harcourt, Brace, 1917); and Winston Churchill, *The Dwelling Place of Light* (New York: Macmillan, 1917). In Great Britain authors who did this were Ivy Low, *The Questing Beast* (London, Secker, 1914), Arnold Bennett, *Lilian* (London: Cassell, 1922), and Rebecca West, *The Judge* (London: Hutchinson, 1922). In four of these novels the heroine engages in what would now be termed consensual premarital sex.

[59] *Her drying combinations* a "combination" was the popular term for a "combination-garment," so called because it combined

On the divan are piled (at night her bed)
Stockings, slippers, camisoles, and stays.
I Tiresias, old man with wrinkled dugs
Perceived the scene, and foretold the rest —
I too awaited the expected guest.   230
He, the young man carbuncular, arrives,
A small house agent's clerk, with one bold stare,
One of the low on whom assurance sits
As a silk hat on a Bradford millionaire.⁶⁰
The time is now propitious, as he guesses,   235
The meal is ended, she is bored and tired,
Endeavours to engage her in caresses
Which still are unreproved, if undesired.
Flushed and decided, he assaults at once;
Exploring hands encounter no defence;   240
His vanity requires no response,
And makes a welcome of indifference.
(And I Tiresias have foresuffered all
Enacted on this same divan or bed;
I who have sat by Thebes below the wall   245
And walked among the lowest of the dead.)⁶¹
Bestows one final patronising kiss,
And gropes his way, finding the stairs unlit ...

She turns and looks a moment in the glass,
Hardly aware of her departed lover;   250
Her brain allows one half-formed thought to pass:
"Well now that's done: and I'm glad it's over."
When lovely woman stoops to folly⁶² and
Paces about her room again, alone,
She smoothes her hair with automatic hand,   255
And puts a record on the gramophone.

"This music crept by me upon the waters"⁶³
And along the strand, up Queen Victoria Street.⁶⁴
O City City, I can sometimes hear
Beside a public bar in Lower Thames Street,⁶⁵   260
The pleasant whining of a mandoline
And a clatter and a chatter from within
Where fishmen lounge at noon: where the walls

---

a chemise with drawers or panties in a single undergarment. Combinations were introduced in the 1880s and vanished after the Second World War.

⁶⁰ *a Bradford millionaire* Bradford is located in the western part of Yorkshire, a county in the northeast of England; it has always been a woolen and textile center, and its mills prospered during the First World War by manufacturing serge, khaki uniforms, and blankets for the armed forces. After the war there were charges of wartime profiteering.

⁶¹ *And walked among ... the dead* see Homer, *Odyssey*, Book XI, which recounts Odysseus's journey to the underworld, where he consults Tiresias.

⁶² *When lovely woman* ... Eliot's note directs the reader to a novel by Oliver Goldsmith (1730?–74), *The Vicar of Wakefield* (1762), ch. 24. The chapter begins with the song of Livia, who has been seduced (it will later turn out that she has not been):

When Lovely woman stoops to folly,
And finds too late that men betray,

What charm can sooth her melancholy,
What art can wash her guilt away?

The only art her guilt to cover,
To hide her shame from every eye,
To give repentance to her lover,
And wring his bosom — is to die.

⁶³ *'This music ... upon the waters'* see note 44 above.

⁶⁴ *the Strand*, three-quarters of a mile long, connects the City (or financial district) with Westminster (the political district). The street contains many restaurants, theaters, pubs, and hotels. Queen Victoria Street runs from Bank Junction, the very heart of the City, southwest and then west to Blackfriars Bridge.

⁶⁵ *Lower Thames Street* runs westward from London Bridge along the north bank of the Thames; on it stands Billingsgate Market, the great London fish market, and the church of St. Magnus Martyr (see below). In Eliot's time the area was still lively with colorful fishmongers and local tradespeople.

Of Magnus Martyr[66] hold
265   Inexplicable splendour of Ionian white and gold.

The river sweats[67]
Oil and tar
The barges drift
With the turning tide
270   Red sails
Wide
To leeward, swing on the heavy spar.
The barges wash
Drifting logs
275   Down Greenwich reach
Past the Isle of Dogs.[68]
            Weialala leia
            Wallala leialala
Elizabeth and Leicester[69]
280   Beating oars
The stern was formed
A gilded shell
Red and gold
The brisk swell
285   Rippled both shores
Southwest wind
Carried down stream
The peal of bells
White towers

---

[66]   *Magnus Martyr* built between 1671 and 1676 by Sir Christopher Wren, one of the many which Wren built in the wake of the fire of London of 1666. Wren is best known as the architect of St. Paul's Cathedral. Eliot refers to the slender Ionic columns which grace the church's interior.

[67]   *The river sweats...* Eliot's note states that "the song of the (three) Thames-daughters begins here" and continues to line 306, and compares their song with that of the Rhine-daughters in Wagner's opera, *Götterdämmerung* (*The Twilight of the Gods*) (1876), the fourth and final part of *Der Ring der Nibelungen* (*The Ring Cycle*). The Rhine-daughters first appear in Wagner's *Das Rheingold* (1869), part I of the cycle. They are nymphs who guard a lump of gold in the river, and their ecstatic joy is expressed in their repeated cry, "Weialala leia wallala leialala." At the start of the opera Alberich, the leader of the Nibelung dwarfs, interrupts their play and wants them to satisfy his lust. But he is made to flounder in the waters as they mock him with these cries. Only he who overcomes the lusts of the flesh, they tell him, can hope to possess the Rhine gold. Alberich curses love and steals the gold. In *Götterdämmerung* the three Rhine-daughters reappear to sing of the Rhine gold they have lost. Even here their song is not mournful, but joyously praises the gold and looks foward to the hero who will return it to them. When Siegfried returns with the ring and refuses to give it to them, they prophesy his death. Siegfried is then murdered. His beloved Brünnhilde orders a vast funeral pyre to be built, which she lights and mounts. The flames destroy the hall and engulf all of Valhalla, destroying all the gods (whence the opera's title). The Rhine overflows its banks, and the Rhine-daughters take back their gold. The two-beat measure which typifies much of this passage is adapted from Wagner's nymphs, who adopt it whenever they sing.

[68]   *Greenwich reach...the Isle of Dogs* the Isle of Dogs is a peninsula created by a loop in the River Thames. Past the peninsular Isle of Dogs the Thames is called Greenwich Reach.

[69]   *Elizabeth and Leicester* Eliot's note refers the reader to James Anthony Froude (1818–94), *History of England from the Fall of Wolsey to the Death of Elizabeth*, 12 vols. (London: Longman, Green, 1856–70), vol. 7, *Reign of Elizabeth: Volume 1* (1863). Froude was Regius Professor of History at Oxford. His history draws heavily on the reports sent by Alvarez de Quadra (the Bishop of Aquila), the Spanish ambassador to Queen Elizabeth's court, to his master Philip II, King of Spain. Since Elizabeth was only 25 years old when she became queen in 1558, the question of whom she might marry loomed large. One perennial candidate was Lord Robert Dudley, Earl of heicester, whose fortunes she encouraged from the moment she became queen, naming him her Master of the Horse, a high-ranking position. But when Dudley's wife was found dead on September 8, 1560, it was widely speculated that he had had some hand in her death. He was banished from the court until a coroner's jury had found him innocent, then returned. Throughout the early months of 1561, de Quadra reported his growing conviction that Elizabeth would marry Dudley and that together they would return England to the Catholic faith. But when a papal nuncio applied to come to Elizabeth's court in June that year, the Council of State (headed by William Cecil, who opposed Robert Dudley) rejected his application, leaving de Quadra enraged. It was in this context that De Quadra wrote to Philip on June 30, a letter which Froude reports in translation, pp. 347–9. That the poem seems to link the historical Elizabeth with the legendary Cleopatra, or with Mrs. Porter, has troubled some critics. And unlike the Thames-daughters who appear in the following passages, Elizabeth did not become a victim of her lover (if Dudley was indeed her lover).

     Weialala leia   290
     Wallala leialala

    "Trams and dusty trees.
    Highbury bore me. Richmond and Kew
    Undid me.[70] By Richmond I raised my knees
    Supine on the floor of a narrow canoe."   295

    "My feet are at Moorgate,[71] and my heart
    Under my feet. After the event
    He wept. He promised 'a new start.'
    I made no comment. What should I resent?"

    "On Margate Sands.[72]   300
    I can connect
    Nothing with nothing.
    The broken fingernails of dirty hands.
    My people humble people who expect
    Nothing."   305
      la la

    To Carthage then I came[73]

    Burning burning burning burning[74]
    O Lord Thou pluckest me out
    O Lord Thou pluckest[75]   310

    burning

IV. DEATH BY WATER

    Phlebas the Phoenician,[76] a fortnight dead,
    Forgot the cry of gulls, and the deep sea swell

[70] *Highbury bore me. Richmond and Kew / Undid me* Eliot's note directs the reader to Dante, *Purgatorio* V.130–6. In canto V, Dante encounters three spirits who have died a violent death and repented only at the last moment. The last one says:

> "Remember me, who am La Pia:
> Sienna bore me; the Maremma undid me:
>   He knows of it who, first being engaged to me,
> Married me with his gem."

Medieval commenators agreed in idenifying her as the wife of Nello d'Inghiramo dei Pannocchieschi, a ruler in the Maremma, an area in southern Tuscany. She was murdered by him. But the historical details matter less than the mood evoked by her speech, one which Eliot captures perfectly and transposes in a modern key. Highbury was a drab, middle-class suburb in the north of London which had been developed in the late Victorian and Edwardian eras. Kew Gardens (officially, the Royal Botanic Gardens), is situated on the banks of the River Thames between Richmond and Kew in southwest London, a popular excursion site for city-dwellers.

[71] *Moorgate* was originally a gate within the London wall, built in 1415 and pulled down in 1761. The street that led to it, still called Moorgate, runs due north, starting from the southwest corner of the Bank of England.

[72] *Margate Sands* is the principal beach in Margate, a seaside resort in the county of Kent; it grew enormously with the growth of large-scale tourism in the later nineteenth century, and the majority of its tourists were tyically from the lower middle classes, shopkeepers and typists. Eliot stayed at the Albemarle Hotel, in Cliftonville, Margate, for three weeks in October 1921, the first part of a three-month leave from work to rest his nerves. Lines 259–311 were written while he was there.

[73] *To Carthage then I came* Eliot cites a passage from Book III of *The Confessions of Saint Augustine*, trans. Edward B. Pusey (London: Dent, 1907), pp. 31–2.

[74] *Burning burning burning burning* Eliot cites "The Fire Sermon" by the Buddha; for the text, see the note to the title of Part III.

[75] *O Lord Thou . . . pluckest* compare this passage from Book X of *The Confessions of Saint Augustine*, trans. Edward B. Pusey (London: Dent, 1907), pp. 237–8 "But the framers and followers of the outward beauties derive thence the rule of judging of them, but not of using them. And He is there, though they perceive Him not, that so they might not wander, but keep their strength for Thee, and not scatter it abroad upon pleasurable wearinesses. And I, though I speak and see this, entangle my steps with these beauties; but Thou pluckest me out, O Lord, Thou pluckest me out; because Thy loving-kindness is before my eyes."

[76] *Phlebas the Phoenician* this section is a close adaptation of the last seven lines of a poem in French by Eliot, "Dans le Restaurant" ("In the Restaurant"), written 1916–17. The name "Phlebas" may be derived from the Latin adjective *flebilis*, meaning "to be wept over, to be lamented."

And the profit and loss.

315   A current under sea
Picked his bones in whispers. As he rose and fell
He passed the stages of his age and youth
Entering the whirlpool.
                              Gentile or Jew

320   O you who turn the wheel and look to windward,
Consider Phlebas, who was once handsome and tall as you.

V.   WHAT THE THUNDER SAID[77]

After the torchlight[78] red on sweaty faces
After the frosty silence in the gardens
After the agony in stony places[79]

325   The shouting and the crying
Prison and palace and reverberation
Of thunder of spring over distant mountains
He who was living is now dead
We who were living are now dying

330   With a little patience

Here is no water but only rock
Rock and no water and the sandy road
The road winding above among the mountains
Which are mountains of rock without water

335   If there were water we should stop and drink
Amongst the rock we cannot stop or think
Sweat is dry and feet are in the sand
If there were only water amongst the rock
Dead mountain mouth of carious teeth that cannot spit

340   Here one can neither stand nor lie nor sit
There is not even silence in the mountains
But dry sterile thunder without rain
There is not even solitude in the mountains
But red sullen faces sneer and snarl

345   From doors of mudcracked houses
                              If there were water
And no rock
If there were rock
And also water
And water

350   A spring
A pool among the rock
If there were the sound of water only
Not the cicada
And dry grass singing

355   But sound of water over a rock

---

[77]   *What the Thunder Said* see note 88.

[78]   *torchlight* while the verse paragraph from lines 322 to 330 draws on images associated with the betrayal and arrest of Christ in the garden of Gethsemane, Eliot's lines are highly stylized and remote from Biblical particulars.

[79]   *After the agony in stony places* in the garden of Gethsemane, Jesus withdraws to pray, according to Luke 22:44: "And being in an agony he prayed more earnestly: and his sweat was as it were great drops of blood falling down on the ground." The phrase "stony places" is also Biblical. It occurs in Psalm 141:6: "When their judges are overthrown in stony places, they shall hear my words; for they are sweet." It occurs again in Matthew 3:5, in the parable of the sower whose seeds are cast in various places: "Some fell upon stony places, where they had not much earth: and forthwith they sprung up, because they had no deepness of earth." And it occurs a third time in Matthew 13:20, when the meaning of the parable is expounded: "But he that received the seed into stony places, the same is he that heareth the word, and anon with joy receiveth it."

Where the hermit-thrush sings in the pine trees
Drop drop drip drop drop drop drop[80]
But there is no water

Who is the third who walks always beside you?[81]
When I count,[82] there are only you and I together   360
But when I look ahead up the white road
There is always another one walking beside you
Gliding wrapt in a brown mantle, hooded
I do not know whether a man or a woman
– But who is that on the other side of you?   365
What is that sound high in the air
Murmur of maternal lamentation[83]
Who are those hooded hordes swarming
Over endless plains, stumbling in cracked earth
Ringed by the horizon only   370
What is the city over the mountains
Cracks and reforms and bursts in the violet air
Falling towers
Jerusalem Athens Alexandria
Vienna London   375
Unreal

A woman[84] drew her long black hair out tight
And fiddled whisper music on those strings

[80]   Eliot's factitious note directs the reader to a book by the Canadian author Frank M. Chapman (1864–1945), titled *Handbook of Birds of Eastern North America* (New York: D. Appleton, 1895). But the quotation that Eliot cites is actually taken by Chapman from the American naturalist Eugene Pintard Bicknell (1859–1925), *A Study of the Singing of Our Birds* (Boston: 1885).

[81]   *Who is the third...* Eliot's note at the beginning of Part V outlines "three themes" to appear in the first part of Part V, and refers to the story of the journey to Emmaus. The story is recounted in the Bible, Luke 24:13–32. It takes place immediately after the disciples of Jesus return to his grave on Easter Sunday and discover that his body is no longer there, leaving them bewildered "at that which was come to pass." Two disciples, on their way to Emmaus, discuss this mystery, and "Jesus himself drew near, and went with them. But their eyes were holden that they should not know him." Later, when they stop at a village, "their eyes were opened, and they knew him; and he vanished out of their sight."

[82]   *When I count* Eliot's note directs the reader to "the account of the one of the Antarctic expeditions (I forget which, but think one of Shackleton's)." Sir Ernest Shackleton (1874–1922) made three journeys to the Antarctic, each beset with problems. On his third attempt he tried to cross the entire Antarctic ice-cap on foot, a journey of 1,500 miles. The expedition set sail on the *Endurance* from the island of South Georgia in December 1914, but their ship became trapped in ice and was eventually crushed. To return they made an almost 2-year journey. Three years later Shackleton published his account of the trip, *South: The Story of Shackleton's Last Expedition, 1914–1917* (London: W. Heinemann, 1919), which includes the following passage (p. 209):

When I look back at those days I have no doubt that Providence guided us, not only across those snow-fields, but across the storm-white sea that separated Elephant Island from our landing-place on South Georgia. I know

that during that long and racking march of thirty-six hours over the unnamed mountains and glaciers of South Georgia it seemed to me often that we were four, not three. I said nothing to my companions on the point, but afterwards Worsely said to me, "Boss, I had a curious feeling on the march that there was another person with us." Crean confessed to the same idea. One feels "the dearth of human words, the roughness of mortal speech" in trying to describe things intangible, but a record of our journeys would be incomplete without a reference to a subject very near to our hearts.

[83]   *What is that sound...lamentation* Eliot's note directs the reader to a book by the German author Hermann Hesse (1872–1962), *Blick ins Chaos: drei Aufsätze (A Look into the Chaos)* (Berne: Verlag Seldwyla, 1920), from which Eliot quotes a passage in the original German, one that refers to the Russian Revolution and the collapse of the German and Austro-Hungarian empires: "Already half of Europe, and at the least half of Eastern Europe, is on the way toward chaos; it is drunkenly driving forward in a holy frenzy toward the abyss, drunkenly singing, as if singing hymns, the way Dmitri Karamazov sang. The offended bougeois laughs over these songs; the holy seer hears them with tears." (Dimitri Karamazov is a character in the novel *The Brothers Karamazov* by Feodor Doestoevsky [1821–81].) Eliot was so taken with this book that he urged his friend Sydney Schiff (1868–1948) to translate it into English. His translation, titled *In Sight of Chaos*, appeared a year later, under Schiff's *nom de plume*, Stephen Hudson (Zurich: Verlag Seldwyla, 1923).

[84]   *A woman...rain* (lines 377–94) Eliot's note at the beginning of Part V states that "The approach to the Chapel Perilous" is one of "three themes" employed in this part's opening section (322–94), and he tells the reader to "see Miss Weston's book."

And bats with baby faces in the violet light
380 Whistled, and beat their wings
And crawled head downward down a blackened wall
And upside down in air were towers
Tolling reminiscent bells, that kept the hours
And voices singing out of empty cisterns and exhausted wells.

385 In this decayed hole among the mountains
In the faint moonlight, the grass is singing
Over the tumbled graves, about the chapel
There is the empty chapel, only the wind's home,
It has no windows, and the door swings,
390 Dry bones can harm no one.
Only a cock stood on the rooftree
Co co rico co co rico[85]
In a flash of lightning. Then a damp gust
Bringing rain
395 Ganga[86] was sunken, and the limp leaves
Waited for rain, while the black clouds
Gathered far distant, over Himavant.[87]
The jungle crouched, humped in silence.
Then spoke the thunder[88]
400 DA
Datta: what have we given?
My friend, blood shaking my heart
The awful daring of a moment's surrender
Which an age of prudence can never retract
405 By this, and this only, we have existed
Which is not to be found in our obituaries
Or in memories draped by the beneficent spider[89]
Or under seals broken by the lean solicitor

Weston's *From Ritual to Romance* devotes a chapter (ch. 13, pp. 175–88) to "The Perilous Chapel," a motif which she summarizes in her opening paragraph: "Students of the Grail romances will remember that in many of the versions the hero – sometimes it is a heroine – meets with a strange and terrifying adventure in a mysterious Chapel, an adventure which, we are given to understand, is fraught with extreme peril to life. The details vary: sometimes there is a Dead Body laid on the altar; sometimes a Black Hand extinguishes the tapers; there are strange and threatening voices, and the general impression is that this is an adventure in which supernatural, and evil, forces are engaged."
[85] *Co co rico* in French and Italian, "cocorico" is the onomatopoetic word which represents the sound of a rooster, or "cock-a-doodle-do."
[86] *Ganga* variant of the Ganges, the sacred river of India.
[87] *Himavant* a Sanskrit adjective meaning "snowy," applied to one or more mountains in the Himalayas.
[88] *Then spoke the thunder* Eliot's note to line 401 directs the reader to "the fable of the meaning of the Thunder," recounted in the *Brihadaranyaka Upanishad* 5. The Upanishads are sacred texts written in Sanskrit, the earliest of which belong to the eighth and seventh centuries BC, a group which includes the *Brihadaranyaka Upanishad*. Their number exceeds 200, though Indian tradition put it at 108. The Indian philosopher Shankara, who flourished around 800 AD, commented on 11 Upanishads, including the *Brihadaranyaka Upanishad*, and these with two or

three others are considered the principal Upanishads. The German translation cited by Eliot, Paul Deussen's *Sechzig Upanishads des Veda* (Leipzig: F. A. Brockhaus, 1897) comprised 60 Upanishads. Eliot studied Sanskrit at Harvard between 1911 and 13. In the fable of the Thunder which he cites, the Lord of Creation, Prajapati, thunders three times, the sound being represented by the Sanskrit word "DA." He instructs the lesser gods to "Control" their unruly natures; men to "give" to others; and demons to sympathize. In one tradition of commentary, it was said that self-control was demanded of the gods because they were naturally unruly, charity of men because they were naturally greedy, and compassion of the demons because they were naturally cruel. But it was also suggested that there were no gods or demons other than men. Men who lack self-control, while endowed with other good qualities, are gods. Men who are particularly greedy are men. And those who are cruel are demons.
[89] Eliot's note directs the reader to John Webster's play, *The White Devil* V.vi.154–8. Flamineo, a villain who has prostituted his sister and murdered both his brother-in-law and his brother, discovers that his sister Vittoria has betrayed him:

O men
That lie upon your death-beds, and are haunted
With howling wives, ne'er trust them: they'll re-marry
Ere the worm pierce your winding-sheet, ere the spider
Make a thin curtain for your epigraphs

In our empty rooms
DA
Dayadhvam: I have heard the key[90]   410
Turn in the door once and turn once only
We think of the key, each in his prison
Thinking of the key, each confirms a prison
Only at nightfall, aethereal rumours
Revive for a moment a broken Coriolanus[91]   415
DA
Damyata: The boat responded
Gaily, to the hand expert with sail and oar
The sea was calm, your heart would have responded   420
Gaily, when invited, beating obedient
To controlling hands

I sat upon the shore
Fishing, with the arid plain behind me[92]
Shall I at least set my lands in order?[93]   425

London Bridge is falling down falling down falling down[94]
Poi s'ascose nel foco che gli affina[95]
Quando fiam ceu chelidon – O swallow swallow[96]

---

[90]   I have heard the key Eliot's note refers the reader to Dante's Inferno, XXXIII.46–7. In the previous canto Dante has come upon Ugolino dell Gherardesca, who is forever devouring the head of Archbishop Ruggieri of Pisa. Ugolino now explains that Ruggieri had locked up him and his four children in a tower, leaving them to starve. His four children had died first, and then Ugolino had eaten their corpses. Ugolino had "heard the key / Turn in the door once and turn once only" because the guards were leaving him and his children to starve. Eliot also quotes from Appearance and Reality: A Metaphysical Essay (London: Swan Sonnenschein, 1893), a book by the philosopher Francis Herbert Bradley (1846–1924). Eliot wrote his Ph.D. thesis on Bradley for Harvard University, begun in 1911 and completed in 1916 (though never formally submitted). His thesis, Knowledge and Experience in the Philosophy of F. H. Bradley, was published in 1964.

[91]   a broken Coriolanus the protagonist of Shakespeare's play Coriolanus (1607–8). Coriolanus is a Roman general who despises the fickle mob. Driven by pride and his desire to punish an ungrateful Roman populace, he joins the Volscian forces against Rome. Though victorious, he is persuaded by his mother, wife, and son to spare Rome from sacking. To punish this new treachery, the Volscians hack him to death.

[92]   Fishing...behind me Eliot's note refers the reader to chapter 9, "The Fisher King" (pp. 112–36), in Jessie Weston's From Ritual to Romance. Weston sums up her arguments concerning the Fisher King up to this point when she declares: "We have already seen that the personality of the King, the nature of the disability under which he is suffering, and the reflex effect exercised upon his folk and his land, correspond, in a most striking manner, to the intimate relation at one time held to exist between the ruler and his land; a relation mainly dependent upon the identification of the King with the Divine principle of Life and Fertility" (p. 114). She goes on to argue that the Fisher King's name in no way derived from early Christian use of the fish as a symbol, nor from any Celtic myth or legend. Instead, fish played "an important part in Mystery Cults, as being the 'holy' food" (129), partly because of "the belief...that all life comes from the water" (133), partly because "the Fish was

considered a potent factor in ensuring fruitfulness" among certain prehistoric peoples (135), a belief which had persisted and played a role in shaping the figure of the Fisher King.

[93]   Shall I... in order compare Isaiah 38:1: "Thus saieth the Lord, Set thine house in order: for thou shalt die, and not live."

[94]   London Bridge...falling down from a children's nursery rhyme.

[95]   Poi s'ascose...affina Italian for "Then he vanished into the fire which refines them." Eliot's note cites Dante, Purgatorio XXVI. 145–8:

"Now I beseech you, by that virtue
which conducts you to the summit of the steps [in Purgatory]
at times bethink yourself of my suffering."
Then he vanished into the fire which refines them.

Dante hears these words from the Provençal poet Arnaut Daniel, whom he meets in the seventh circle of Purgatory, reserved for the lustful.

[96]   Quando fiam... swallow Latin for "When shall I become like the swallow?" Eliot's note refers the reader to the anonymous Latin poem, the Pervigilium Veneris, or "The Vigil of Venus," now thought to have been written in the early fourth century, most likely by Tiberianus. But in Eliot's day the poem's date and authorship were uncertain. Eliot quotes from line 90, three lines before the poem ends, set within a passage which shifts from religious hymn to a deeply personal note:

The swans, with hoarse voice, are trumpeting over the pools;
The young wife of Tereus [Procne] sings under the poplar shade,
making you think her melodious mouth was moved by love,
and not a sister's [Philomela's] complaint of her barbarous husband.
She is singing, I am mute. When will my springtime come?
When shall I become like the swallow, that I cease being silent?
I have lost my Muse through being silent, and Phoebus does not regard me.

Le Prince d'Aquitaine à la tour abolie[97]

430   These fragments I have shored against my ruins
Why then Ile fit you. Hieronymo's mad againe.[98]
Datta. Dayadhvan. Damyata.

Shantih   shantih   shantih[99]

Notes

Not only the title, but the plan and a good deal of the incidental symbolism of the poem were suggested by Miss Jessie L. Weston's book on the Grail legend: *From Ritual to Romance* (Cambridge). Indeed, so deeply am I indebted, Miss Weston's book will elucidate the difficulties of the poem much better than my notes can do; and I recommend it (apart from the great interest of the book itself) to any who think such elucidation of the poem worth the trouble. To another work of anthropology I am indebted in general, one which has influenced our generation profoundly; I mean *The Golden Bough*; I have used especially the two volumes *Adonis, Attis, Osiris*. Anyone who is acquainted with these works will immediately recognise in the poem certain references to vegetation ceremonies.

I.   The Burial of the Dead

Line 20. Cf. Ezekiel II, i.

23. Cf. Ecclesiastes XII, v.

31. V. Tristan und Isolde, I, verses 5–8.

42. Id. III, verse 24.

46. I am not familiar with the exact constitution of the Tarot pack of cards, from which I have obviously departed to suit my own convenience. The Hanged Man, a member of the traditional pack, fits my purpose in two ways: because he is associated in my mind with the Hanged God of Frazer, and because I associate him with the hooded figure in the passage of the disciples in Part V. The Phoenician Sailor and the Merchant appear later; also the "crowds of people," and Death by Water is executed in Part IV. The Man with Three Staves (an authentic member of the Tarot pack) I associate, quite arbitrarily, with the Fisher King himself.

60. Cf. Baudelaire:

"Fourmillante cité, cité pleine de rêves,
"Où le spectre en plein jour raccroche le passant."

63. Cf. Inferno III, 55–7:

"Si lunga tratta
di gente, ch'io non avrei mai creduto
che morte tanta n'avesse disfatta."

---

[97] *Le Prince . . . tour abolie* French for "The Prince of Aquitaine, his tower in ruins." Eliot's note directs the reader to "El Desdichado" (1853), a celebrated but cryptic sonnet by the French poet Gérard de Nerval (1808–55), which begins: "Je suis le ténébreux, – la veuf, – l'inconsolé, / Le Prince d'Aquitane à la tour abolie" ("I am the man of gloom, – the widower, – the unconsoled, / The Prince of Aquitania, his tower in ruins.")

[98] *Why then . . . mad againe* Eliot's note refers to *The Spanish Tragedy* (1592) by Thomas Kyd (1557?–95), subtitled *Hieronymo is Mad Againe*. Hieronymo has been driven mad by the murder of his son. He is asked to write a court entertainment or play, and he

convinces the murderers to act in it. Crucially, he also convinces them to speak their parts in different languages, much as in the *The Waste Land*. See *The Spanish Tragedy*, IV.i.59–106.

[99] *Shantih Shantih Shantih* Eliot's note explains that the repetition of this word marks the ending of an Upanishad, and is a loose counterpart to the phrase, "The Peace which passeth understanding." That phrase, in turn, comes from Saint Paul's letter to the Philippians 4:7: "And the peace of God, which passeth all understanding, shall keep your hearts and minds through Christ Jesus."

64. Cf. Inferno IV, 25–7:

> "Quivi, secondo che per ascoltare,
> "non avea pianto, ma' che di sospiri,
> "che l'aura eterna facevan tremare."

68. A phenomenon which I have often noticed.

74. Cf. The Dirge in Webster's *White Devil*.

76. V. Baudelaire, Preface to *Fleurs du Mal*.

II.   A Game of Chess

77. Cf. *Antony and Cleopatra*, II, ii, l. 190.

92. Laquearia. V. *Aeneid*, I, 726:

> "dependent lychni laquearibus aureis
> incensi, et noctem flammis funalia vincunt."

98. Sylvan scene. V. Milton, *Paradise Lost*, IV, 140.

99. V. Ovid, *Metamorphoses*, VI, Philomela.

100. Cf. Part III l. 204.

115. Cf. Part III l. 195.

118. Cf. Webster: "Is the wind in that door still?"

126. Cf. Part I ll. 37, 48.

138. Cf. The game of chess in Middleton's *Women beware Women*.

III.   The Fire Sermon

176. Spenser, *Prothalamion*.

192. Cf. *The Tempest*, I, ii.

196. Cf. Marvell, *To His Coy Mistress*.

197. Cf. Day, *Parliament of Bees*:

> "When of the sudden, listening, you shall hear,
> "A noise of horns and hunting, which shall bring
> "Actaeon to Diana in the spring,
> "Where all shall see her naked skin..."

199. I do not know the origin of the ballad from which these lines are taken; it was reported to me from Sydney, Australia.

202. V. Verlaine, *Parsifal*.

210. The currants were quoted at a price "carriage and insurance free to London"; and the Bill of Lading etc. were to be handed to the buyer upon payment of the sight draft.

218. Tiresias, although a mere spectator and not indeed a "character," is yet the most important personage in the poem, uniting all the rest. Just as the one-eyed merchant, seller of currants, melts into the Phoenician Sailor, and the latter is not wholly distinct from Ferdinand Prince of Naples, so all the women are one woman, and the two sexes meet in Tiresias. What Tiresias *sees*, in fact, is the substance of the poem. The whole passage from Ovid is of great anthropological interest:

> ...Cum Iunone iocos et maior vestra profecto est
> Quam, quae contingit 'maribus', dixisse, 'voluptas.'
> Illa negat; placuit quae sit sententia docti
> Quaerere Tiresiae: venus huic erat utraque nota.

Nam duo magnorum viridi coeuntia silva
Corpora serpentum baculi violaverat ictu
Deque viro factus, mirabile, femina septem
Egerat autumnos; octavo rursus eosdem
Vidit et 'est vestrae si tanta potentia plagae,'
Dixit, 'ut auctoris sortem in contraria mutet,
Nunc quoque vos feriam!' percussis anguibus isdem
Forma prior rediit genetivaque venit imago.
Arbiter hic igitur sumptus de lite iocosa
Dicta Iovis firmat; gravius Saturnia iusto
Nec pro materia fertur doluisse suique
Iudicis aeterna damnavit lumina nocte,
At pater onmipotens (neque enim licet inrita cuiquam
Facta dei fecisse deo) pro lumine adempto
Scire futura dedit poenamque levavit honore.

221. This may not appear as exact as Sappho's lines, but I had in mind the "longshore" or "dory" fisherman, who returns at nightfall.

253. V. Goldsmith, the song in *The Vicar of Wakefield*.

257. V. *The Tempest*, as above.

264. The interior of St. Magnus Martyr is to my mind one of the finest among Wren's interiors. See *The Proposed Demolition of Nineteen City Churches* (P. S. King & Son Ltd.).

266. The song of the (three) Thames-daughters begins here. From line 292 to 306 inclusive they speak in turn. V. *Götterdämmerung*, III, i: the Rhine-daughters.

276. V. Froude, *Elizabeth*, vol. I, ch. iv, letter of De Quadra to Philip of Spain: "In the afternoon we were in a barge, watching the games on the river. (The queen) was alone with Lord Robert and myself on the poop, when they began to talk nonsense, and went so far that Lord Robert at last said, as I was on the spot there was no reason why they should not be married if the queen pleased."

293. Cf. *Purgatorio*, V. 133:

"Ricorditi di me, che son la Pia;
"Siena mi fe', disfecemi Maremma."

307. V. St. Augustine's *Confessions*: "to Carthage then I came, where a cauldron of unholy loves sang all about mine ears."

308. The complete text of the Buddha's Fire Sermon (which corresponds in importance to the Sermon on the Mount) from which these words are taken, will be found translated in the late Henry Clarke Warren's *Buddhism in Translation* (Harvard Oriental Series). Mr. Warren was one of the great pioneers of Buddhist studies in the occident.

312. From St. Augustine's *Confessions* again. The collocation of these two representatives of eastern and western asceticism, as the culmination of this part of the poem, is not an accident.

V. What the Thunder Said

In the first part of Part V three themes are employed: the journey to Emmaus, the approach to the Chapel Perilous (see Miss Weston's book) and the present decay of eastern Europe.

357. This is *Turdus aonalaschkae pallasii*, the hermit-thrush which I have heard in Quebec County. Chapman says (*Handbook of Birds of Eastern North America*) "it is most at home in secluded woodland and thickety retreats.... Its notes are not remarkable for variety or volume, but in purity and sweetness of tone and exquisite modulation they are unequaled." Its "water-dripping song" is justly celebrated.

360. The following lines were stimulated by the account of one of the Antarctic expeditions (I forget which, but I think one of Shackleton's): it was related that the party of explorers, at the extremity of their strength, had the constant delusion that there was *one more member* than could actually be counted.

366–76. Cf. Hermann Hesse, *Blick ins Chaos*: "Schon ist halb Europa, schon ist zumindest der halbe Osten Europas auf dem Wege zum Chaos, fährt betrunken im heiligen Wahn am Abgrund entlang and singt dazu, singt betrunken and hymnisch wie Dmitri Karamasoff sang. Ueber diese Lieder lacht der Bürger beleidigt, der Heilige and Seher hört sie mit Tränen."

401. "Datta, dayadhvam, damyata" (Give, sympathise, control). The fable of the Thunder is found in the *Brihadaranyaka–Upanishad*, 5, I. A translation is found in Deussen's *Sechzig Upanishads des Veda*, p. 489.

407. Cf. Webster, *The White Devil*, V. vi:

> " . . . they'll remarry
> Ere the worm pierce your winding-sheet, ere the spider
> Make a thin curtain for your epitaphs."

411. Cf. *Inferno*, XXXIII, 46:

> "ed io sentii chiavar l'uscio di sotto
> all'orribile torre."

Also F. H. Bradley, *Appearance and Reality*, p. 346.
"My external sensations are no less private to myself than are my thoughts or my feelings. In either case my experience falls within my own circle, a circle closed on the outside; and, with all its elements alike, every sphere is opaque to the others which surround it. . . . In brief, regarded as an existence which appears in a soul, the whole world for each is peculiar and private to that soul."

424. V. Weston: *From Ritual to Romance*; chapter on the Fisher King.

427. V. *Purgatorio*, XXVI, 148.

> " 'Ara vos prec, per aquella valor
> 'Que vos guida al som de l'escalina,
> 'Sovegna vos a temps de ma dolor.'
> Poi s'ascose nel foco che gli affina."

428. V. *Pervigilium Veneris*. Cf. Philomela in Parts II and III.

429. V. Gerard de Nerval, Sonnet *El Desdichado*.

431. V. Kyd's *Spanish Tragedy*.

433. Shantih. Repeated as here, a formal ending to an Upanishad. "The Peace which passeth understanding" is a feeble translation of the content of this word.

Sweeney Agonistes: Introduction

Sweeney Agonistes was first published in the October 1926 and the January 1927 issues of *The Criterion*, a journal edited by T. S. Eliot. In the first of these the opening prologue was titled "Fragment of a Prologue"; in the second, a brief scene was titled "Fragment of an Agon from *Wanna go Home, Baby?*" In December 1932, both parts appeared as a small book (31 numbered pages), with the title *Sweeney Agonistes: Fragments of an Aristophanic Melodrama* (London: Faber & Faber). In May 1933, there was a production of the work at Vassar College, which included a short final scene that was first printed in 1943 but never admitted by Eliot into his *Collected Poems* (first published in 1936) or his *Collected Poems and Plays* (1962).

The work was largely neglected by critics writing before 1980.

Eliot wrote the work in 1923 and 1924, a process contemporaneous with his work on "The Hollow Men." In 1926, the same year that he published the "Prologue" to *Sweeney Agonistes*, Eliot also wrote: "The next form of drama will have to be a verse drama but in new verse forms. Perhaps the conditions of modern life (think how large a part is now played in our sensory life by the internal combustion engine!) have altered our perception of rhythms. At any rate the recognized forms of speech-verse are not as efficient as they should be; probably a new form will be devised out of colloquial speech." (See T. S. Eliot,

"Introduction" to *Savonarola: A Dramatic Poem* by Charlotte Eliot [London: R. Cobden–Sanderson, 1926], xi.) To Hallie Flannagan, who presented the work at Vassar in 1933, Eliot wrote:

The action should be stylized as in the Noh drama – see Ezra Pound's book and Yeats' preface [pp. 362–70 this edn.] and notes to *The Hawk's Well* [pp. 360–2 this edn.]. Characters *ought* to wear masks; the ones wearing old masks ought to give the impression of being young persons (as actors) and vice versa. Diction should not have too much expression. I had intended the whole play to be accompanied by light drum taps to accentuate the beats (esp. the chorus, which ought to have a noise like a street drill). The characters should be in a shabby flat, seated at a refectory table, facing the audience; Sweeney in the middle with a chafing dish, scrambling eggs (See "you see this egg.") (See also F. M. Cornford, Origins of Attic Comedy, which is important to read before you do the play. I am talking about the *second* fragment of course; the other one is not much good. The second should end as follows . . .

Eliot then went on to give an ending to the work which is deeply inconsistent with the rest of *Sweeney Agonistes* and reflects Eliot's later religious concerns. It is not included here in deference to Eliot's own decision not to include it in any edition of his collected writings. Also not given here is a two-page synopsis of the work, evidently made around 1925, which was first printed in 1960.

Francis M. Cornford (1874–1943) was a classicist with strong anthropological interests and the author of *The Origin of Attic Comedy* (London: Edward Arnold, 1914). He described the Agon, one part of the primitive fertility ritual underlying the comedy of Aristophanes, thus: "The *Agon* is the beginning of the sacrifice in its primitive form – the conflict between the good and evil principles, Summer and Winter, Life and Death. The good spirit is slain, dismembered, cooked, and eaten in the communal feast, and yet brought back to life" (103–4).

Sweeney Agonistes[1] (1932)

Fragments of an Aristophanic Melodrama[2]

ORESTES: *You don't see them, you don't – but I see them: they are hunting me down, I must move on.*
–Choephoroi.[3]

Hence the soul cannot be possessed of the divine union, until it has divested itself of the love of created beings.
–St. John of the Cross.[4]

Fragment of a Prologue

DUSTY. DORIS.

DUSTY: How about Pereira?
DORIS: What about Pereira?
       I don't care.
DUSTY: You don't care!
       Who pays the rent?
DORIS: Yes he pays the rent
DUSTY: Well some men don't and some men do
       Some men don't and you know who
DORIS: You can have Pereira
DUSTY: What about Pereira?

[1]   Agonistes the title alludes to *Samson Agonistes* (1671) the last major work by John Milton (1608–74); "agonistes" literally means "in struggle."

[2]   *Aristophanic Melodrama* Aristophanes (*c.* 450–*c.* 385) was the greatest poet of comedies in ancient Athens. Melodrama is a word that first appears in 1809 and designates a stage play, with songs, of sensational incident and violent appeals to the emotions. The title signals Eliot's attempt to conjoin "high" and

"low" cultures, or even to see "high" and "low" as sharing the same preoccupations.

[3]   Aeschylus, *The Oresteia*, trans. Richard Lattimore (Chicago: University of Chicago Press, 1953), "The Libation Bearers" (or "Choephoroi"), lines 1161–2.

[4]   St. John of the Cross, *The Ascent of Mount Carmel*, bk. I, ch. 4, para. 1. The translation that Eliot was using has not been identified.

DORIS: He's no gentleman, Pereira:
    You can't trust him!
DUSTY: Well that's true.
    He's no gentleman if you can't trust him
    And *if* you can't trust him –
    Then you never know what he's going to do.
DORIS: No it wouldn't do to be too nice to Pereira.
DUSTY: Now Sam's a gentleman through and through.
DORIS: I like Sam
DUSTY: *I* like Sam
    Yes and Sam's a nice boy too.
    He's a funny fellow
DORIS: He *is* a funny fellow
    He's like a fellow once I knew.
    He could make you laugh.
DUSTY: Sam can make you laugh:
    Sam's all right
DORIS: But Pereira won't do.
    We can't have Pereira
DUSTY: Well what you going to do?
TELEPHONE: Ting a ling ling
         Ting a ling ling
DUSTY: That's Pereira
DORIS: Yes that's Pereira
DUSTY: Well what you going to do?
TELEPHONE: Ting a ling ling
         Ting a ling ling
DUSTY: That's Pereira
DORIS: Well can't you stop that horrible noise?
    Pick up the receiver
DUSTY: What'll I say!
DORIS: Say what you like: say I'm ill,
    Say I broke my leg on the stairs
    Say we've had a fire
DUSTY: Hello Hello are you there?
    Yes this is Miss Dorrance's *flat* –
    Oh Mr. Pereira is that you? how do you do!
    Oh I'm *so* sorry. I *am* so sorry
    But Doris came home with a terrible chill
    No, just a chill
    Oh I *think* it's only a chill
    Yes indeed I hope so too –
    Well I *hope* we shan't have to call a doctor
    Doris just hates having a doctor
    She says will you ring up on Monday
    She hopes to be all right on Monday
    I say do you mind if I ring off now
    She's got her feet in mustard and water
    I said I'm giving her mustard and water
    All right, Monday you'll phone through.
    Yes I'll tell her. Good bye. Goooood bye.
    I'm sure, that's very kind of *you*.
                Ah-h-h
DORIS: Now I'm going to cut the cards for to-night.
    Oh guess what the first is
DUSTY: First is. What is?
DORIS: The King of Clubs

DUSTY: That's Pereira
DORIS: It might be Sweeney
DUSTY: It's Pereira
DORIS: It might *just* as well be Sweeney
DUSTY: Well anyway it's very queer.
DORIS: Here's the four of diamonds, what's that mean?
DUSTY [*reading*]: "A small sum of money, or a present
                    Of wearing apparel, or a party."
                    That's queer too.
DORIS: Here's the three. What's that mean?
DUSTY: "News of an absent friend." – Pereira!
DORIS: The Queen of Hearts! – Mrs. Porter!
DUSTY: Or it might be you
DORIS: Or it might be you
    We're all hearts. You can't be sure.
    It just depends on what comes next.
    You've got to *think* when you read the cards,
    It's not a thing that anyone can do.
DUSTY: Yes I know you've a touch with the cards
    What comes next?
DORIS: What comes next. It's the six.
DUSTY: "A quarrel. An estrangement. Separation of friends."
DORIS: Here's the two of spades.
DUSTY: The *two* of *spades!*
    THAT'S THE COFFIN!!
DORIS: THAT'S THE COFFIN?
    Oh good heavens what'll I do?
    Just before a party too!
DUSTY: Well it needn't be yours, it may mean a friend.
DORIS: No it's mine. I'm sure it's mine.
    I dreamt of weddings all last night.
    Yes it's mine. I know it's mine.
    Oh good heavens what'll I do.
    Well I'm not going to draw any more,
    You cut for luck. You cut for luck.
    It might break the spell. You cut for luck.
DUSTY: The Knave of Spades.
DORIS: That'll be Snow
DUSTY: Or it might be Swarts
DORIS: Or it might be Snow
DUSTY: It's a funny thing how I draw court cards
DORIS: There's a lot in the way you pick them up
DUSTY: There's an awful lot in the way you feel
DORIS: Sometimes they'll tell you nothing at all
DUSTY: You've got to know what you want to ask them
DORIS: You've got to know what you want to know
DUSTY: It's no use asking them too much
DORIS: It's no use asking more than once
DUSTY: Sometimes they're no use at all.
DORIS: I'd like to know about that coffin.
DUSTY: Well I never! What did I tell you?
    Wasn't I saying I always draw court cards?
    The Knave of Hearts!
                    [*Whistle outside of the window.*]
                    Well I *never*
    What a co*in*cidence! Cards are queer!
                    [*Whistle again.*]

DORIS: Is that Sam?
DUSTY: Of course it's Sam!
DORIS: Of course, the Knave of Hearts *is* Sam!
DUSTY [*leaning out of the window*]: Hello Sam!
WAUCHOPE: Hello dear
    How many's up there?
DUSTY: Nobody's up here
    How many's down there?
WAUCHOPE: Four of us here.
    Wait till I put the car round the corner
    We'll be right up
DUSTY: All right, come up.
DUSTY [*to* DORIS]: Cards are queer.
DORIS: I'd like to know about that coffin.
    KNOCK KNOCK KNOCK
    KNOCK KNOCK KNOCK
    KNOCK
    KNOCK
    KNOCK

   DORIS. DUSTY. WAUCHOPE. HORSFALL. KLIPSTEIN. KRUMPACKER.

WAUCHOPE: Hello Doris! Hello Dusty! How do you do!
    How come? how come? will you permit me –
    I think you girls both know Captain Horsfall –
    We want you to meet two friends of ours,
    American gentlemen here on business.
    Meet Mr. Klipstein. Meet Mr. Krumpacker.
KLIPSTEIN: How do you do
KRUMPACKER: How do you do
KLIPSTEIN: I'm very pleased to make your acquaintance
KRUMPACKER: Extremely pleased to become acquainted
KLIPSTEIN: Sam – I should say Loot Sam Wauchope
KRUMPACKER: Of the Canadian Expeditionary Force –
KLIPSTEIN: The Loot has told us a lot about you.
KRUMPACKER: We were all in the war together
    Klip and me and the Cap and Sam.
KLIPSTEIN: Yes we did our bit, as you folks say,
    I'll tell the world we got the Hun on the run
KRUMPACKER: What about that poker game? eh what Sam?
    What about that poker game in Bordeaux?
    Yes Miss Dorrance you get Sam
    To tell about that poker game in Bordeaux.
DUSTY: Do you know London well, Mr. Krumpacker?
KLIPSTEIN: No we never been here before
KRUMPACKER: We hit this town last night for the first time
KLIPSTEIN: And I certainly hope it won't be the last time.
DORIS: You like London, Mr. Klipstein?
KRUMPACKER: Do we like London? do we like London!
    Do we like London!! Eh what Klip?
KLIPSTEIN: Say, Miss – er – uh – London's swell.
    We like London fine.
KRUMPACKER: Perfectly slick.
DUSTY: Why don't you come and live here then?
KLIPSTEIN: Well, no, Miss – er – you haven't quite got it
    (I'm afraid I didn't quite catch your name –

But I'm very pleased to meet you all the same) –
London's a little too gay for us
Yes I'll say a little too gay.
KRUMPACKER: Yes London's a little too gay for us
Don't think I mean anything *coarse* –
But I'm afraid we couldn't stand the pace.
What about it Klip?
KLIPSTEIN: You said it, Krum.
London's a slick place, London's a swell place,
London's a fine place to come on a visit –
KRUMPACKER: Specially when you got a real live Britisher
A guy like Sam to show you around.
Sam of course is at *home* in London,
And he's promised to show us around.

Fragment of an Agon

SWEENEY. WAUCHOPE. HORSFALL. KLIPSTEIN. KRUMPACKER. SWARTS. SNOW. DORIS. DUSTY.

SWEENEY: I'll carry you off
To a cannibal isle.
DORIS: You'll be the cannibal!
SWEENEY: You'll be the missionary!
You'll be my little seven stone missionary!
I'll gobble you up. I'll be the cannibal.
DORIS: You'll carry me off? To a cannibal isle?
SWEENEY: I'll be the cannibal.
DORIS: I'll be the missionary.
I'll convert you!
SWEENEY: I'll convert *you!*
Into a stew.
A nice little, white little, missionary stew.
DORIS: You wouldn't eat me!
SWEENEY: Yes I'd eat you!
In a nice little, white little, soft little, tender little,
Juicy little, right little, missionary stew.
You see this egg
You see this egg
Well that's life on a crocodile isle.
There's no telephones
There's no gramophones
There's no motor cars
No two-seaters, no six-seaters,
No Citroën, no Rolls-Royce.
Nothing to eat but the fruit as it grows.
Nothing to see but the palmtrees one way
And the sea the other way,
Nothing to hear but the sound of the surf.
Nothing at all but three things
DORIS: What things?
SWEENEY: Birth, and copulation, and death.
That's all, that's all, that's all, that's all,
Birth, and copulation, and death.
DORIS: I'd be bored.
SWEENEY: You'd be bored.
Birth, and copulation, and death.
DORIS: I'd be bored.
SWEENEY: You'd be bored.

Birth, and copulation, and death.
That's all the facts when you come to brass tacks:
Birth, and copulation, and death.
I've been born, and once is enough.
You dont remember, but I remember,
Once is enough.

SONG BY WAUCHOPE AND HORSFALL
SWARTS AS TAMBO. SNOW AS BONES[5]

Under the bamboo[6]
Bamboo bamboo
Under the bamboo tree
Two live as one
One live as two
Two live as three
Under the bam
Under the boo
Under the bamboo tree.

Where the breadfruit fall
And the penguin call
And the sound is the sound of the sea
Under the bam
Under the boo
Under the bamboo tree.

Where the Gauguin maids
In the banyan shades
Wear palmleaf drapery
Under the bam
Under the boo
Under the bamboo tree.

[5] *Swarts as Tambo. Snow as Bones* Tambo and Bones are stock names from minstrel theater; Tambo was the parodically dandified urban Negro and Bones the rustic. Snow[ball] is one of the possible names for the antic "Jim Crow" figure in minstrel shows from about 1830 on; Swarts is a variant of the German word *schwartz* and may suggest a neo-Yiddish allusion.

[6] *Under the bamboo* Eliot is adapting here a popular song, first published in 1902, with words by Robert Cole and music by J. Rosamond Johnson (1873–1954) and James Weldon Johnson (1871–1938), all three African-Americans. It became a big hit in a musical play called *Sally in the Alley* and sold over 400,000 copies in sheet music. Eliot first heard it in 1904 at the St. Louis World's Fair.

Under the Bamboo Tree (1902)
Down in the jungles lived a maid,
Of royal blood though dusky shade,
A marked impression once she made
Upon a Zulu from Matabooloo;
And ev'ry morning he would be
Down underneath the bamboo tree,
Awaiting there his love to see
And then to her he'd sing:

CHORUS 2 times
If you lak-a-me, lak I lak-a-you
And we lak-a-both the same,
I lak-a say, this very day,

I lak-a-change your name;
'Cause I love-a-you and love-a-you true
And if you-a love-a-me.
One live as two, two live as one
Under the bamboo tree.

And in this simple jungle way,
He wooed the maiden ev'ry day,
By singing what he had to say;
One day he seized her and gently squeezed her;
And then beneath the bamboo green,
He begged her to become his queen;
The dusky maiden blushed unseen
And joined him in his song.

(CHORUS 2 times)

This little story strange but true,
Is often told in Mataboo,
Of how this Zulu tried to woo
His jungle lady in tropics shady;
Although the scene was miles away,
Right here at home I dare to say,
You'll hear some Zulu ev'ry day,
Gush out this soft refrain:

(CHORUS 2 times)

> Tell me in what part of the wood
> Do you want to flirt with me?
> Under the breadfruit, banyan, palmleaf
> Or under the bamboo tree?
> Any old tree will do for me
> Any old wood is just as good
> Any old isle is just my style
> Any fresh egg
> Any fresh egg
> And the sound of the coral sea.

DORIS: I dont like eggs; I never liked eggs;
    And I dont like life on your crocodile isle.

SONG BY KLIPSTEIN AND KRUMPACKER
SNOW AND SWARTS AS BEFORE

> My little island girl
> My little island girl
> I'm going to stay with you
> And we wont worry what to do
> We wont have to catch any trains
> And we wont go home when it rains
> We'll gather hibiscus flowers
> For it wont be minutes but hours
> For it wont be hours but years

diminuendo
> And the morning
> And the evening
> And noontime
> And night
> Morning
> Evening
> Noontime
> Night

DORIS: That's not life, that's no life
    Why I'd just as soon be dead.
SWEENEY: That's what life is. Just is
DORIS: What is?
    What's that life is?
SWEENEY: Life is death.
    I knew a man once did a girl in –
DORIS: Oh Mr. Sweeney, please dont talk,
    I cut the cards before you came
    And I drew the coffin
SWARTS: You drew the coffin?
DORIS: I drew the COFFIN very last card.
    I dont care for such conversation
    A woman runs a terrible risk.
SNOW: Let Mr. Sweeney continue his story.
    I assure you, Sir, we are very interested.
SWEENEY: I knew a man once did a girl in
    Any man might do a girl in
    Any man has to, needs to, wants to
    Once in a lifetime, do a girl in.
    Well he kept her there in a bath
    With a gallon of lysol in a bath
SWARTS: These fellows always get pinched in the end.
SNOW: Excuse me, they dont all get pinched in the end.
    What about them bones on Epsom Heath?

> I seen that in the papers
> You seen it in the papers
> They *dont* all get pinched in the end.

DORIS: A woman runs a terrible risk.

SNOW: Let Mr. Sweeney continue his story.

SWEENEY: This one didn't get pinched in the end
> But that's another story too.
> This went on for a couple of months
> Nobody came
> And nobody went
> But he took in the milk and he paid the rent.

SWARTS: What did he do?
> All that time, what did he do?

SWEENEY: What did he do! what did he do?
> That dont apply.
> Talk to live men about what they do.
> He used to come and see me sometimes
> I'd give him a drink and cheer him up.

DORIS: Cheer him up?

DUSTY: Cheer him up?

SWEENEY: Well here again that dont apply
> But I've gotta use words when I talk to you.
> But here's what I was going to say.
> He didn't know if he was alive
>   and the girl was dead
> He didn't know if the girl was alive
>   and he was dead
> He didn't know if they both were alive
>   or both were dead
> If he was alive then the milkman wasn't
>   and the rent-collector wasn't
> And if they were alive then he was dead.
> There wasn't any joint
> There wasn't any joint
> For when you're alone
> When you're alone like he was alone
> You're either or neither
> I tell you again it dont apply
> Death or life or life or death
> Death is life and life is death
> I gotta use words when I talk to you
> But if you understand or if you dont
> That's nothing to me and nothing to you
> We all gotta do what we gotta do
> We're gona sit here and drink this booze
> We're gona sit here and have a tune
> We're gona stay and we're gona go
> And somebody's gotta pay the rent

DORIS: I know who

SWEENEY: But that's nothing to me and nothing to you.

FULL CHORUS: WAUCHOPE, HORSFALL, KLIPSTEIN, KRUMPACKER

> When you're alone in the middle of the night and you wake in a sweat and a hell of a fright
> When you're alone in the middle of the bed and you wake like someone hit you on the head
> You've had a cream of a nightmare dream and you've got the hoo-ha's coming to you.
> Hoo hoo hoo
> You dreamt you waked up at seven o'clock and it's foggy and it's damp and it's dawn and it's dark
> And you wait for a knock and the turning of a lock for you know the hangman's waiting for you.
> And perhaps you're alive

And perhaps you're dead
Hoo ha ha
Hoo ha ha
Hoo
Hoo
Hoo
KNOCK KNOCK KNOCK
KNOCK KNOCK KNOCK
KNOCK
KNOCK
KNOCK

Tradition and the Individual Talent (1919)

In English writing we seldom speak of tradition, though we occasionally apply its name in deploring its absence. We cannot refer to "the tradition" or to "a tradition"; at most, we employ the adjective in saying that the poetry of So-and-so is "traditional" or even "too traditional." Seldom, perhaps, does the word appear except in a phrase of censure. If otherwise, it is vaguely approbative, with the implication, as to the work approved, of some pleasing archaeological reconstruction. You can hardly make the word agreeable to English ears without this comfortable reference to the reassuring science of archaeology.

Certainly the word is not likely to appear in our appreciations of living or dead writers. Every nation, every race, has not only its own creative, but its own critical turn of mind; and is even more oblivious of the shortcomings and limitations of its critical habits than of those of its creative genius. We know, or think we know, from the enormous mass of critical writing that has appeared in the French language the critical method or habit of the French; we only conclude (we are such unconscious people) that the French are "more critical" than we, and sometimes even plume ourselves a little with the fact, as if the French were the less spontaneous. Perhaps they are; but we might remind ourselves that criticism is as inevitable as breathing, and that we should be none the worse for articulating what passes in our minds when we read a book and feel an emotion about it, for criticizing our own minds in their work of criticism. One of the facts that might come to light in this process is our tendency to insist, when we praise a poet, upon those aspects of his work in which he least resembles any one else. In these aspects or parts of his work we pretend to find what is individual, what is the peculiar essence of the man. We dwell with satisfaction upon the poet's difference from his predecessors, especially his immediate predecessors; we endeavour to find something that can be isolated in order to be enjoyed. Whereas if we approach a poet without this prejudice we shall often find that not only the best, but the most individual parts of his work may be those in which the dead poets, his ancestors, assert their immortality most vigorously. And I do not mean the impressionable period of adolescence, but the period of full maturity.

Yet if the only form of tradition, of handing down, consisted in following the ways of the immediate generation before us in a blind or timid adherence to its successes, "tradition" should positively be discouraged. We have seen many such simple currents soon lost in the sand; and novelty is better than repetition. Tradition is a matter of much wider significance. It cannot be inherited, and if you want it you must obtain it by great labour. It involves, in the first place, the historical sense, which we may call nearly indispensable to any one who would continue to be a poet beyond his twenty-fifth year; and the historical sense involves a perception, not only of the pastness of the past, but of its presence; the historical sense compels a man to write not merely with his own generation in his bones, but with a feeling that the whole of the literature of Europe from

The essay was first published in the *Egoist* 6(4) (Sept. 1919) and 6(5) (Nov. 1919). In 1932, when Eliot published the first edition of his *Selected Essays*, he made it the volume's first essay and, perhaps inadvertently, assigned it to 1917, so signaling that it constituted the gateway to his entire oeuvre. This edition follows the text of the *Selected Essays*.

Homer and within it the whole of the literature of his own country has a simultaneous existence and composes a simultaneous order. This historical sense, which is a sense of the timeless as well as of the temporal and of the timeless and of the temporal together, is what makes a writer traditional. And it is at the same time what makes a writer most acutely conscious of his place in time, of his own contemporaneity.

No poet, no artist of any art, has his complete meaning alone. His significance, his appreciation is the appreciation of his relation to the dead poets and artists. You cannot value him alone; you must set him, for contrast and comparison, among the dead. I mean this as a principle of aesthetic, not merely historical, criticism. The necessity that he shall conform, that he shall cohere, is not onesided; what happens when a new work of art is created is something that happens simultaneously to all the works of art which preceded it. The existing monuments form an ideal order among themselves, which is modified by the introduction of the new (the really new) work of art among them. The existing order is complete before the new work arrives; for order to persist after the supervention of novelty, the *whole* existing order must be, if ever so slightly, altered; and so the relations, proportions, values of each work of art toward the whole are readjusted; and this is conformity between the old and the new. Whoever has approved this idea of order, of the form of European, of English literature will not find it preposterous that the past should be altered by the present as much as the present is directed by the past. And the poet who is aware of this will be aware of great difficulties and responsibilities.

In a peculiar sense he will be aware also that he must inevitably be judged by the standards of the past. I say judged, not amputated, by them; not judged to be as good as, or worse or better than, the dead; and certainly not judged by the canons of dead critics. It is a judgment, a comparison, in which two things are measured by each other. To conform merely would be for the new work not really to conform at all; it would not be new, and would therefore not be a work of art. And we do not quite say that the new is more valuable because it fits in; but its fitting in is a test of its value – a test, it is true, which can only be slowly and cautiously applied, for we are none of us infallible judges of conformity. We say: it appears to conform, and is perhaps individual, or it appears individual, and many conform; but we are hardly likely to find that it is one and not the other.

To proceed to a more intelligible exposition of the relation of the poet to the past: he can neither take the past as a lump, an indiscriminate bolus, nor can he form himself wholly on one or two private admirations, nor can he form himself wholly upon one preferred period. The first course is inadmissible, the second is an important experience of youth, and the third is a pleasant and highly desirable supplement. The poet must be very conscious of the main current, which does not at all flow invariably through the most distinguished reputations. He must be quite aware of the obvious fact that art never improves, but that the material of art is never quite the same. He must be aware that the mind of Europe – the mind of his own country – a mind which he learns in time to be much more important than his own private mind – is a mind which changes, and that this change is a development which abandons nothing *en route*, which does not superannuate either Shakespeare, or Homer, or the rock drawing of the Magdalenian draughtsmen.[1] That this development, refinement perhaps, complication certainly, is not, from the point of view of the artist, any improvement. Perhaps not even an improvement from the point of view of the psychologist or not to the extent which we imagine; perhaps only in the end based upon a complication in economics and machinery. But the difference between the present and the past is that the conscious present is an awareness of the past in a way and to an extent which the past's awareness of itself cannot show.

Some one said: "The dead writers are remote from us because we *know* so much more than they did." Precisely, and they are that which we know.

---

[1] *Magdalenian draughtsman* caves near the village of Madeleine, in the province of Dordogne, were discovered by a French archaeologist Edouard Lartet (1801–71 and his English colleague Henry Christy (1810–65); they contained prehistoric carvings and drawings of animals such as reindeer and mammoths. "Madelein" is the French word for the Latin "Magdalene," and by 1885 "Magdalenian" was becoming current to describe late paleolithic culture (17,000–11,000 BC) represented by these remains. Eliot took a walking tour in southern France in August 1919 and may have visited the Grotte de Niaux, or Cave of Niaux (on the banks of the Vicdessos River), which houses extraordinary drawings of horses and bison.

I am alive to a usual objection to what is clearly part of my programme for the *métier* of poetry. The objection is that the doctrine requires a ridiculous amount of erudition (pedantry), a claim which can be rejected by appeal to the lives of poets in any pantheon. It will even be affirmed that much learning deadens or perverts poetic sensibility. While, however, we persist in believing that a poet ought to know as much as will not encroach upon his necessary receptivity and necessary laziness, it is not desirable to confine knowledge to whatever can be put into a useful shape for examinations, drawing-rooms, or the still more pretentious modes of publicity. Some can absorb knowledge, the more tardy must sweat for it. Shakespeare acquired more essential history from Plutarch[2] than most men could from the whole British Museum. What is to be insisted upon is that the poet must develop or procure the consciousness of the past and that he should continue to develop this consciousness throughout his career.

What happens is a continual surrender of himself as he is at the moment to something which is more valuable. The progress of an artist is a continual self-sacrifice, a continual extinction of personality.

There remains to define this process of depersonalization and its relation to the sense of tradition. It is in this depersonalization that art may be said to approach the condition of science. I, therefore, invite you to consider, as a suggestive analogy, the action which takes place when a bit of finely filiated platinum is introduced into a chamber containing oxygen and sulphur dioxide.

II

Honest criticism and sensitive appreciation and directed not upon the poet but upon the poetry. If we attend to the confused cries of the newspaper critics and the *susurrus* of popular repetition that follows, we shall hear the names of poets in great numbers; if we seek not Blue-book knowledge but the enjoyment of poetry, and ask for a poem, we shall seldom find it. I have tried to point out the importance of the relation of the poem to other poems by other authors, and suggested the conception of poetry as a living whole of all the poetry that has ever been written. The other aspect of this Impersonal theory of poetry is the relation of the poem to its author. And I hinted, by an analogy, that the mind of the mature poet differs from that of the immature one not precisely in any valuation of "personality," not being necessarily more interesting, or having "more to say," but rather by being a more finely perfected medium in which special, or very varied, feelings are at liberty to enter into new combinations.

The analogy was that of the catalyst. When the two gases previously mentioned are mixed in the presence of a filament of platinum, they form sulphurous acid. This combination takes place only if the platinum is present; nevertheless the newly formed acid contains no trace of platinum, and the platinum itself is apparently unaffected; has remained inert, neutral, and unchanged. The mind of the poet is the shred of platinum. It may partly or exclusively operate upon the experience of the man himself; but, the more perfect the artist, the more completely separate in him will be the man who suffers and the mind which creates; the more perfectly will the mind digest and transmute the passions which are its material.

The experience, you will notice, the elements which enter the presence of the transforming catalyst, are of two kinds: emotions and feelings. The effect of a work of art upon the person who enjoys it is an experience different in kind from any experience not of art. It may be formed out of one emotion, or may be a combination of several; and various feelings, inhering for the writer in particular words or phrases or images, may be added to compose the final result. Or great poetry may be made without the direct use of any emotion whatever: composed out of feelings solely.

---

[2]   *Shakespeare acquired more essential history* Plutarch (c. 50 AD–c. 120 AD) wrote the *Lives*, brief biographies of famous men from the ancient Greek and Roman worlds which were highly regarded and influential. But after 1800 his lack of historical perspective, unsophisticated moral attitudes, and naive reliance on the work of others undermined his reputation. Eliot's point is that even so untrustworthy a historian as Plutarch could be useful to a writer of genius such as Shakespeare in plays such as *Antony and Cleopatra* or *Julius Caesar*.

Canto XV of the *Inferno* (Brunetto Latini)[3] is a working up of the emotion evident in the situation; but the effect, though single as that of any work of art, is obtained by considerable complexity of detail. The last quatrain gives an image, a feeling attaching to an image, which "came," which did not develop simply out of what precedes, but which was probably in suspension in the poet's mind until the proper combination arrived for it to add itself to. The poet's mind is in fact a receptacle for seizing and storing up numberless feelings, phrases, images, which remain there until all the particles which can unite to form a new compound are present together.

If you compare several representative passages of the greatest poetry you see how great is the variety of types of combination, and also how completely any semi-ethical criterion of "sublimity" misses the mark. For it is not the "greatness," the intensity, of the emotions, the components, but the intensity of the artistic process, the pressure, so to speak, under which the fusion takes place, that counts. The episode of Paolo and Francesca[4] employs a definite emotion, but the intensity of the poetry is something quite different from whatever intensity in the supposed experience it may give the impression of. It is no more intense, furthermore, than Canto XXVI, the voyage of Ulysses, which has not the direct dependence upon an emotion. Great variety is possible in the process of transmutation of emotion: the murder of Agamemnon, or the agony of Othello, gives an artistic effect apparently closer to a possible original than the scenes from Dante. In the *Agamemnon*, the artistic emotion approximates to the emotion of an actual spectator; in *Othello* to the emotion of the protagonist himself. But the difference between art and the event is always absolute; the combination which is the murder of Agamemnon is probably as complex as that which is the voyage of Ulysses. In either case there has been a fusion of elements. The ode of Keats contains a number of feelings which have nothing particular to do with the nightingale, but which the nightingale, partly, perhaps, because of its attractive name, and partly because of its reputation, served to bring together.[5]

The point of view which I am struggling to attack is perhaps related to the metaphysical theory of the substantial unity of the soul: for my meaning is, that the poet has, not a "personality" to express, but a particular medium, which is only a medium and not a personality, in which impressions and experiences combine in peculiar and unexpected ways. Impressions and experiences which are important for the man may take no place in the poetry, and those which become important in the poetry may play quite a negligible part in the man, the personality.

I will quote a passage which is unfamiliar enough to be regarded with fresh attention in the light – or darkness – of these observations:

> And now methinks I could e'en chide myself
> For doating on her beauty, though her death
> Shall be revenged after no common action.
> Does the silkworm expend her yellow labours
> For thee? For thee does she undo herself?
> Are lordships sold to maintain ladyships
> For the poor benefit of a bewildering minute?
> Why does yon fellow falsify highways,
> And put his life between the judge's lips,
> To refine such a thing – keeps horse and men
> To beat their valours for her? . . . [6]

---

[3] *Canto XV of the* Inferno *(Brunetto Latini)* in Canto XV Dante encounters Brunetto Latini (*c.* 1220–94), an esteemed teacher and rhetorician whose example and influence had been felt by Dante when young. Their dramatic and poignant encounter has always been one of the most esteemed cantos of the *Inferno*. The last four lines come at the moment when Brunetto's naked form must return to the group of "sodomites" (Dante's term), condemned to run forever along the bank of a stream, with flames falling about them:

> Then he turned away, and he seemed like one of those
> Who run for the green cloth in the field

> At Verona [an annual foot-race]; and of those he seemed
> Like the one who wins, not one who loses.

[4] *the episode of Paolo and Francesca* see Dante's *Inferno*, V.
[5] *the* Agamemnon . . . *ode of Keats* the *Agamemnon* is a Greek tragedy by Aeschylus (*c.* 525–456 BC); the "Ode to a Nightingale" is by John Keats (1795–1821).
[6] *And now methinks . . . To beat their valours for her?* from *The Revenger's Tragedy* (1607), III.5, by Cyril Tourneur (*c.* 1580–1626). The revenger is speaking about the skull of a dead woman, his beloved.

In this passage (as is evident if it is taken in its context) there is a combination of positive and negative emotions: an intensely strong attraction toward beauty and an equally intense fascination by the ugliness which is contrasted with it and which destroys it. This balance of contrasted emotion is in the dramatic situation to which the speech is pertinent, but that situation alone is inadequate to it. This is, so to speak, the structural emotion, provided by the drama. But the whole effect, the dominant tone, is due to the fact that a number of floating feelings, having an affinity to this emotion by no means superficially evident, have combined with it to give us a new art emotion.

It is not in his personal emotions, the emotions provoked by particular events in his life, that the poet is in any way remarkable or interesting. His particular emotions may be simple, or crude, or flat. The emotion in his poetry will be a very complex thing, but not with the complexity of the emotions of people who have very complex or unusual emotions in life. One error, in fact, of eccentricity in poetry is to seek for new human emotions to express; and in this search for novelty in the wrong place it discovers the perverse. The business of the poet is not to find new emotions, but to use the ordinary ones and, in working them up into poetry, to express feelings which are not in actual emotions at all. And emotions which he has never experienced will serve his turn as well as those familiar to him. Consequently, we must believe that "emotion recollected in tranquillity"[7] is an inexact formula. For it is neither emotion, nor recollection, nor, without distortion of meaning, tranquillity. It is a concentration, and a new thing resulting from the concentration, of a very great number of experiences which to the practical and active person would not seem to be experiences at all; it is a concentration which does not happen consciously or of deliberation. These experiences are not "recollected," and they finally unite in an atmosphere which is "tranquil" only in that it is a passive attending upon the event. Of course this is not quite the whole story. There is a great deal, in the writing of poetry, which must be conscious and deliberate. In fact, the bad poet is usually unconscious where he ought to be conscious, and conscious where he ought to be unconscious. Both errors tend to make him "personal." Poetry is not a turning loose of emotion, but an escape from emotion; it is not the expression of personality, but an escape from personality. But, of course, only those who have personality and emotions know what it means to want to escape from these things.

III

ὁ δὲ νοῦς ἴσως Θειότερόν τι καὶ ἀπαθές ἐστιν.[8]

This essay proposes to halt at the frontier of metaphysics or mysticism, and confine itself to such practical conclusions as can be applied by the responsible person interested in poetry. To divert interest from the poet to the poetry is a laudable aim: for it would conduce to a juster estimation of actual poetry, good and bad. There are many people who appreciate the expression of sincere emotion in verse, and there is a smaller number of people who can appreciate technical excellence. But very few know when there is an expression of *significant* emotion, emotion which has its life in the poem and not in the history of the poet. The emotion of art is impersonal. And the poet cannot reach this impersonality without surrendering himself wholly to the work to be done. And he is not likely to know what is to be done unless he lives in what is not merely the present, but the present moment of the past, unless he is conscious, not of what is dead, but of what is already living.

The Lesson of Baudelaire (1921)

With regard to certain intellectual activities across the Channel, which at the moment appear to take the place of poetry in the life of Paris, some effort ought to be made to arrive at an intelligent

---

[7]   *emotion recollected in tranquillity* a famous definition of poetry given by William Wordsworth (1770–1850) in his "Preface" to the *Lyrical Ballads* (1798).

[8]   From Aristotle, *De Anima*, 1.4, 408b: "The mind is doubtless something more divine and unaffected" (Greek).

The essay was published in the first number of *The Tyro*, a journal edited by Wyndham Lewis, which was published on April 9, 1921.

point of view on this side. It is probable that this French performance is of value almost exclusively for the local audience; I do not here assert that it has any value at all, only that its pertinence, if it has any, is to a small public formidably well instructed in its own literary history, erudite and stuffed with tradition to the point of bursting. Undoubtedly the French man of letters is much better read in French literature than the English man of letters is in any literature; and the educated English poet of our day must be too conscious, by his singularity in that respect, of what he knows, to form a parallel to the Frenchman. If French culture is too uniform, monotonous,[1] English culture, when it is found, is too freakish and odd. Dadaism is a diagnosis of a disease of the French mind; whatever lesson we extract from it will not be directly applicable in London.[2]

Whatever value there may be in Dada depends upon the extent to which it is a moral criticism of French literature and French life. All first-rate poetry is occupied with morality: this is the lesson of Baudelaire.[3] More than any poet of his time, Baudelaire was aware of what most mattered: the problem of good and evil. What gives the French Seventeenth Century literature its solidity is the fact that it had its Morals, that it had a coherent point of view. Romanticism endeavoured to form another Morals – Rousseau, Byron, Goethe, Poe were moralists. But they have not sufficient coherence; not only was the foundation of Rousseau rotten, his structure was chaotic and inconsistent. Baudelaire, a deformed Dante (somewhat after the intelligent Barbey d'Aurevilly's phrase)[4] aimed, with more intellect *plus* intensity, and without much help from his predecessors, to arrive at a point of view toward good and evil.

English poetry, all the while, either evaded the responsibility, or assumed it with too little seriousness. The Englishman had too much fear, or too much respect, for morality to dream that possibly or necessarily he should be concerned with it, *vom Haus aus*, in poetry.[5] This it is that makes some of the most distinguished English poets so trifling. Is anyone seriously interested in Milton's view of good and evil? Tennyson decorated the morality he found in vogue; Browning really approached the problem, but with too little seriousness, with too much complacency; thus *The Ring and the Book* just misses greatness – as the revised version of *Hyperion* almost, or just, touches it.[6] As for the verse of the present time, the lack of curiosity in technical matters, of the academic poets of to-day (Georgian et caetera) is only an indication of their lack of curiosity in moral matters. On the other hand, the poets who consider themselves most opposed to

---

[1] [T. S. Eliot's note:] Not without qualification. M. Valéry is a mathematician; M. Benda is a mathematician and a musician. These, however, are men of exceptional intelligence. [Editor's note:] Paul Valéry (1871–1945) was a French poet of the twentieth century. Eliot wrote several essays on him in the years after *The Waste Land*. Julien Benda (1867–1956) was a French writer and philosopher, an anti-Romantic thinker who defended reason against the philosophical intuitionism of Henri Bergson. In 1919 he had published *Belphégor: essai sur l'esthétique de la société française dans la première moitié du XXᵉ siècle* (*Belphegor: An Essay on the Esthetics of French Society in the First Half of the Twentieth Century*), an attack on contemporary intellectual fashions.

[2] On Dada, see the Introductory note to "Continental Interlude II: Dada," pp. 461–2. Dada effectively moved to Paris in January 1920, when Tristan Tzara moved there. His arrival sparked a flurry of Dada events, performances, and manifesto-readings over the next months, but Eliot would not have known about these. His knowledge of Dada probably came from the *Nouvelle revue française*, a journal he subscribed to and read regularly. In April 1920 André Gide published an essay in the *Nouvelle revue française* in which he viewed Dada as an instance of "the mind . . . in ruins." Four months later, in August, André Breton replied to Gide's essay with "Pour Dada" ("For Dada," see pp. 489–93).) Breton's essay was accompanied by another in the same issue, "Reconnaissance à Dada," a sympathetic analysis of Dada by Jacques Rivière, editor of the *Nouvelle revue*. (The essay is reprinted in Jacques Rivière, *Nouvelles Études* [Paris: Gallimard,

1947], pp. 294–310). Eliot may also have derived knowledge of Dada from Fritz Vanderpyl, a Belgian poet and novelist who was art critic for the *Petit Parisien*.

[3] Charles Baudelaire (1821–67) was a French poet, translator, and literary and art critic. His reputation as a poet rests on *Les Fleurs du mal* (1857; *The Flowers of Evil*), the most influential poetry collection published in Europe in the nineteenth century, and on *Le Spleen de Paris* (1869), a collection of prose poems.

[4] *a deformed Dante . . . Barbey d'Aurevilly's phrase* "There is something of Dante in the author of *Flowers of Evil*, but it is a Dante of a fallen age, it is of a modern and atheist Dante, a Dante who has come after Voltaire, who lives in an age that has no Saint Thomas Aquinas," wrote Jules Barbey d'Aurevilly (1808–89) in his essay "Les Fleurs du Mal, par M. Charles Baudelaire" (1858). His essay has frequently been reprinted with editions of *Les Fleurs du mal* (see Charles Baudelaire, *Oeuvres complètes*, ed. Claude Pichois [Paris: Gallimard, Bibliothèque de la Pléiade, 1975], vol. 1, pp. 1191–6, here p. 1195).

[5] *vom Haus aus*, a German expression meaning "beginning with the house and going out from there," or more simply, "thoroughly."

[6] Milton (1608–74), Tennyson (1809–92), and Robert Browning (1812–89) were all English poets. *Hyperion* (1818–19) is an incomplete poem in three books by John Keats (1795–1821). It attempts to recount the legend of the overthrow of the Titans by the Olympian gods. Keats undertook a revised version of the poem later in 1819, now known as *The Fall of Hyperion*, but abandoned it after three months' work.

Georgianism, and who know a little French, are mostly such as could imagine the Last Judgment only as a lavish display of Bengal lights, Roman candles, catherine-wheels, and inflammable fire-balloons.[7] *Vous, hypocrite lecteur...*[8]

London Letter: May 1921

The Phoenix Society

In my last letter I mentioned an approaching performance by the Phoenix Society of Ben Jonson's *Volpone*; the performance proved to be the most important theatrical event of the year in London.[1] The play was superbly carried out; the performance gave evidence of Jonson's consummate skill stage technique, proceeding without a moment of tedium from end to end; it was well acted and both acted and received with great appreciation.

Almost the only opportunity for seeing a good play is that given by a few private societies, which by reason of their "private" character are allowed to give performances (for subscribers) on Sunday evenings. These are not commercial enterprises, but depend on the enthusiasm of a few patrons and the devotion of a few actors, most of whom have other engagements during the week. The Phoenix, which restricts itself to Elizabethan and Restoration drama, is an off-shoot of the Incorporated Stage Society, which produces modern and contemporary plays of the better sort – the better sort usually being translations.[2] At the beginning of its venture, last year, the Phoenix was obliged to suffer a good deal of abuse in the daily press, especially from the *Daily News* and the *Star*. These two journals are, to my mind, the least objectionable of the London newspapers in their political views, but their Manchester-School politics gives a strong aroma of the Ebenezer Temperance Association to their views on art.[3] The bloodiness of Elizabethan tragedy, and the practice of the Society in presenting the complete text of the plays, were the points of attack. The *Daily News* reviewed the performance of *The Duchess of Malfi* under the heading, "Funnier than Farce!" Mr. William Archer mumbled "this farrago of horrors...shambling and ill-composed...funereal affectation...I am far from calling *The Duchess of Malfi* garbage, but..."[4] Still droller was a certain Sir Leo Money:

[7] *Bengal lights* and other things listed here are all types of fireworks.

[8] "You, hypocrite reader..." The last two words are the beginning of the last line in "Au Lecteur" ("To the Reader"), Baudelaire's famous preface to *Les Fleurs du mal*. Eliot quotes the entire line in *The Waste Land*, l. 76, p. 127 this edition.

LONDON LETTER
The essay was first published in the *Dial*, vol. 70, no. 6 (June 1921), pp. 686–91. The "London Letter" was a regular feature that Eliot wrote for the *Dial* in1921–2, reporting on literary and cultural events in London.

[1] The Phoenix Society was founded by Montague Summers (1880–1948) in September 1919, dedicated to the revival of Jacobean and Restoration plays and to having them performed in their entirety. It gave two performances of Ben Jonson's *Volpone* on Sunday January 30 and on Tuesday February 1, 1921, at the Lyric Theatre, Hammersmith.

[2] Eliot was misled because the early Phoenix Society programs stated that their plays were produced "Under the Auspices of the Incorporated Stage Society." But the two societies had no real connection.

[3] The *Daily News* was founded in 1845 and its circulation in 1920 was 800,000 a day. It was a Liberal newspaper allied with the wing of the party that was loyal to Herbert Asquith, the former prime minister who had resigned in 1916. It opposed the policies of David Lloyd George, also a Liberal, but one who had succeeded Asquith as prime minister by forging a coalition with the Conservative party, so abandoning his party for the sake of achieving power. In 1918, at the end of the First World War, Lloyd George stood for election on the platform of preserving Coalition government. Though he won, the Liberal party was further weakened. Many, sensing that Lloyd George was destroying the Liberal party, began to shift allegiances to the young Labour party, and that is what the *Daily News* was doing in 1921: whence Eliot's comments about "Manchester-School politics." The *Star* was an evening paper launched in 1888. In 1912 both the *Star* and the *Daily News* were purchased by the Cadbury family, famous makers of chocolate in England, who retained them until 1960, when both disappeared. The United Grand Junction Ebenezer Temperance Association is a creation of Charles Dickens in *The Pickwick Papers*, ch. 33, which details a comical meeting of its Brick Lane Branch in the East End of London.

[4] *The Duchess of Malfi*, sponsored by the Phoenix Society, was performed at the Lyric Theatre, Hammersmith, on November 23 and 24, 1919. William Archer (1856–1924), was the most influential drama critic of the New Drama movement in the 1890s and a translator of Ibsen. His review of *The Duchess of Malfi* appeared in the *Star*, November 25 (Tuesday), 1919, p. 3, col. 5, under the headline: "PHOENIX SOCIETY. | "The Duchess of Malfy" [*sic*] in an | Elizabethan Setting." Another review of *The Duchess of Malfi*, this one by "K. A. N.," appeared in the

"I agree with Mr. Robert Lynd that 'there are perhaps a dozen Elizabethan plays apart from Shakespeare that are as great as his third-best work,' but I should not include *The Duchess of Malfi* in the dozen.... I did not see the Phoenix production, but I hope that some fumigation took place."[5] Sir Leo writes frequently about the Tariff, the income tax, and kindred topics. For my part I am more and more convinced that the Phoenix is wholly justified in its refusal to admit any expurgation whatever. The sense of relief, in hearing the indecencies of Elizabethan and Restoration drama, leaves one a better and a stronger man.

I do not suggest that Jonson is comparable to Shakespeare. But we do not know Shakespeare; we only know Sir J. Forbes-Robertson's Hamlet and Irving's Shylock, and so on.[6] The performance of *Volpone* had a significance for us which no contemporary performance of Shakespeare has had; it brought the great English drama to life as no contemporary performance of Shakespeare has done. Shakespeare (that is to say, such of his plays as are produced at all), strained through the nineteenth century, has been dwarfed to the dimensions of a part for Sir Johnston Forbes-Robertson, Sir Frank Benson, or other histrionic nonentities: Shakespeare is the avenue to knighthood.[7] But the continued popularity of Shakespeare perhaps has this meaning, that the appetite for poetic drama, and for a peculiarly English comedy or farce, has never disappeared; and that a native popular drama, if it existed, would be nearer to Shakespeare than to Ibsen or Chekhov. It is curious that the popular desire for Shakespeare, and for the operas of Gilbert and Sullivan, should be insatiable, although no attempt is ever made to create anything similar; and that on the other hand the crudest American laughter-and-tears plays, such as *Romance* or *Peg o' My Heart* should be constantly imported.[8] Curious, again, that with so much comic talent in England – more than any other country – no intelligent attempt has been made to use it to advantage in a good comic opera or revue.

Music-Hall and Revue

This is an age of transition between the music-hall and the revue. The music-hall is older, more popular, and is sanctified by the admiration of the Nineties.[9] It has flourished most vigorously in the North; many of its most famous stars are of Lancashire origin. (Marie Lloyd, if I am not mistaken, has a bit of a Manchester accent.) Lancashire wit is mordant, ferocious, and personal; the

---

Daily News, November 25 (Tuesday) 1919, p. 7, col. 7, under the headline: "AN ELIZABETHAN | MELODRAMA. | Wholesale Butchery in | "Duchess of Malfi." | FUNNIER THAN FARCE." For the text of both reviews see Lawrence Rainey (ed.), *The Annotated Waste Land with Eliot's Contemporary Prose* (New Haven: Yale University Press, 2005), pp. 226–9. Eliot himself also wrote a review of the performance; see " 'The Duchess of Malfi' at the Lyric; and Poetic Drama," *Art and Letters* 3(1) (Winter [1919]/1920): 36–9).

[5]   Sir Leo George Chiozza Money (1870–1944) was a statistician and politician. Born in Genoa, he moved to London when young and in 1903 adopted his additional surname. In 1906 he was elected a Member of Parliament and from 1910 to 1918 he sat for East Northants. He resigned from the Liberal party in 1918 and turned to journalism. His review of *The Duchess of Malfi* has not been identified. For Robert Wilson Lynd, whom he cites, see n. 20 to this essay.

[6]   Sir Johnston Forbes-Robertson (1853–1937) was a noted Shakespearian actor who played Hamlet many times both in London and New York. He was knighted in 1913. Sir Henry Irving (1838–1905) was the most famous actor of the late Victorian stage. He played Shylock in *The Merchant of Venice* for the first time in 1879 and became famous for it, repeating the role many times in the years ahead. He was the first actor to be knighted in 1895.

[7]   Sir Frank Benson (1858–1938) was a Shakespearian actor who

was knighted in 1916. He was noted for his performances of Hamlet, Coriolanus, Richard II, Lear, and Petruchio.

[8]   *Romance* was a play by Edward Brewster Sheldon (1886–1946), which opened in New York in 1913 and became a big hit. A young man who is planning to marry receives a cautionary tale from his bishop, based on the sad story of the bishop's own early romance. Its London production, starring Doris Keane, had over 1,000 performances. *Peg o' My Heart: A Comedy of Youth* was a romantic comedy by J. Hartly Manners (1870–1928). It opened on Broadway in 1912 and in London in 1914. It dramatizes the story of Peg, a poor, young Irish girl from New York who learns that she has inherited a fortune; she must leave for London, where she will be introduced into society by her aunt, and her life is about to be turned upside down (but in a good way, of course).

[9]   The poet and critic Arthur Symons (1865–1945) and the novelist and essayist Max Beerbohm (1872–1956) were only two of many writers of the 1890s who wrote about music hall. Symons's essay "A Spanish Music Hall" (1892) is reprinted in his *Cities and Sea-Coasts and Islands* (London: W. Collins, 1918), pp. 145–57. Beerbohm wrote several essays: "The Blight on Music Hall" (1899), "Demos' Mirror" (1900), "At the Music Hall" (1901), "The Older and Better Music Hall" (1903), and "Idolum Aularum" (1906), all collected in *Around Theatres*, 2 vols. (London: W. Heinemann, 1924).

Lancashire music-hall is excessively *intime*; success depends upon the relation established by a comedian of strong personality with an audience quick to respond with approval or contempt. The fierce talent of Nellie Wallace (who also has a Lancashire accent) holds the most boisterous music hall in complete subjection.[10] Little Tich and George Robey (though the latter has adapted himself in recent years to some inferior revues) belong to this type and generation.[11] The Lancashire comedian is at his best when unsupported and making a direct set, pitting himself, against a suitable audience; he is seen to best advantage at the smaller and more turbulent halls. As the smaller provincial or suburban hall disappears, supplanted by the more lucrative Cinema, this type of comedian disappears with it.

The music-hall comedian, however, can still be seen to perfection, whereas the revue comedian never is, because the revue is never good enough. Our best revue comedienne, Miss Ethel Levey, has seldom had the revue, and never the appreciation, that she deserves.[12] Her type is quite different from that of Marie Lloyd or Nellie Wallace. She is the most aloof and impersonal of personalities; indifferent, rather than contemptuous, towards the audience; her appearance and movement are of an extremely modern type of beauty. Hers is not broad farce, but a fascinating inhuman grotesquerie; she lays for herself rather than for the audience. Her art requires a setting which (in this country at least) it has never had. It is not a comedy of mirth.

An element of *bizarrerie* is present in most of the comedians whom we should designate as of the revue stage rather than the music-hall stage: in Lupino Lane, in Robert Hale and George Graves; a *bizarrerie* more mature, perhaps more cosmopolitan, than that of Little Tich.[13] But the revue itself is still lacking.

Caricature

Baudelaire, in his essay on "Le Rire" (*qui vaut bien celui de Bergson*), remarks of English caricature:

Pour trouver du comique féroce et très-féroce, il faut passer la Manche et visiter les royaumes brumeux du spleen... le signe distinctif de ce genre de comique était la violence.[14]

[10] Marie Lloyd (1870–1922) was born in Hoxton, then a working-class area just north of the City (or financial district) in the heart of London, far from Lancashire. Nellie Wallace (1870–1948) was born in Glasgow, Scotland (she did not have "a Lancashire accent"). She first appeared on the stage in 1888 in Birmingham as a clog dancer, then joined a singing group known as the Three Sisters Wallace. Success arrived when she became a solo turn, famous for her characterization of the frustrated spinster. In a strange, rapid account, she told of many romances that went wrong or never really got started.

[11] "Little Tich" was the stage name of Harry Relph (1867–1928), a minuscule man (barely four feet tall) who created an unforgettable stage character, wearing slap shoes almost as long as himself and doing his Big Boot Dance. George Robey (1869–1954), born George Edward Wade in London, was the son of an engineer. He left Cambridge University and took up life on the stage; his music hall character was a somewhat saucy country person with big black eyebrows and a red rose.

[12] Ethel Levey (1881–1955) was a Vaudeville singer and dancer who married (1899) and then divorced (1907) the American songwriter George M. Cohan. She continued with her own performing career which, in the early 1920s, in a stage act, featured her rendition of the Grizzly Bear Dance. From September 1 to October 23, 1920 she had the lead role in *Oh! Julie*, a musical comedy in three acts, in London.

[13] Lupino Lane (1892–1959) was an acrobatic music-hall performer and comedian. He starred in the Broadway show *Afgar* from 1920 to 1922, went on to make several films, and later become a stage and television comedian in England. Robert Hale (1876–1940) was a comic actor and music hall performer. His first success came in the musical comedy *Florodora* at the Lyric Theatre in 1898, which ran for 455 performances. Thereafter he alternated between musical comedy productions and runs at various music halls. George Graves (1876–1949) was a comic actor and music hall and pantomime performer. He first appeared on stage in 1896 and in 1903 he had his first London hit as General Marchmont in *The School Girl*. In 1907 he scored another success as Baron Popoff in the operetta *The Merry Widow* (*Die Lustige Witwe*, by Franz Lehár) at Daly's Theatre, his voice adapted to suggest the popping of champagne corks, with an exaggerated nose and peculiar wig. He became a regular at Daly's and played pantomime at Drury Lane at Christmas, with occasional forays into the music halls.

[14] The title of Baudelaire's famous essay is "De l'essence du rire, et généralement du comique dans les arts plastiques" ("On the Essence of Laughter, and more generally, on the Comic Element in the Plastic Arts") (1855/7). The ellipsis is Eliot's, and signals the omission of nine sentences from Baudelaire's original text. The sentences cited by Eliot can be translated: "To find something of ferocious and very-ferocious comedy, one has to cross the Channel and visit the foggy realms of spleen... the distinctive mark of this kind of comedy is its violence." In his sentence introducing the quotation from Baudelaire, Eliot notes in French that Baudelaire's essay "is much better than that of Bergson," referring to the French philosopher Henri Bergson (1859–1951), whose book *Le Rire*, or *Laughter*, was published in 1900.

Perhaps the best of the English caricaturists of journalism is H. M. Bateman. He has lately held a very interesting exhibition at the Leicester Galleries.[15] It is curious to remark that some of his drawings descend to the pure and insignificant funniness without seriousness which appeals to the readers of *Punch*; while others continue the best tradition from Rowlandson and Cruikshank.[16] They have some of the old English ferocity. Bateman is, I imagine, wholly unconscious of the two distinct strains in his work; Mr. Wyndham Lewis, in his exhibition now on show at the same gallery, is wholly conscious and deliberate in his attempt to restore this peculiarly English caricature and to unite it with serious work in paint. Mr. Lewis is the most English of English painters, a student of Hogarth and Rowlandson; his fantastic imagination produces something essentially different from anything across the Channel.[17] I have always thought his design at its greatest when it approached the border of satire and caricature; and his Tyros may be expected to breed a most interesting and energetic race.

The State of Criticism

The disappearance of the *Athenaeum* as an independent organ and its gradual suffocation under the ponderous mass of the *Nation* are greatly to be deplored. It leaves the *Times Literary Supplement* and the *London Mercury* as the only literary papers.[18] The former is a useful bibliographer; it fills, and always will fill, an important place of its own. This place it can only hold by maintaining the anonymity of its contribution; but this anonymity, and the large number of its contributors, prevents it from upholding any definite standard of criticism. Nevertheless it possesses more authority than the *Mercury*, which is homogeneous enough, but suffers from the mediocrity of the minds most consistently employed upon it. Mr. Murry, as editor of the *Athenaeum*, was genuinely studious to maintain a serious criticism. With his particular tastes, as well as his general statements, I find myself frequently at variance: the former seem to me often perverse or exaggerated, the latter tainted by some unintelligible Platonism. But there is no doubt that he had much higher standards and greater ambitions for literary journalism than any other editor in London. When he is not deceived by some aberration of enthusiasm or dislike, and when he is not deluded by philosophy, he is the only one of the accredited critics whom I can read at all. There is Mr. Clutton-Brock, whose attention is not focussed upon literature but upon a very mild type of philosophic humanitarian religion; he is like a very intelligent archdeacon.[19] There is Mr. Robert Lynd, who has successfully cultivated the typical vices of daily journalism and has risen to the top of his profession; and there is Mr. Squire, whose solemn trifling fascinates multitudes; and there are

[15] Henry Mayo Bateman (1887–1970) became a celebrated caricaturist. His cartoons appeared in variety of periodicals and he published many books. His exhibition at the Leicester Galleries took place from February 1 to 28, 1921, timed to coincide with his publication of a volume entitled *A Book of Drawings*, with a preface by G. K. Chesterton (London: Methuen, 1921), which contains the works shown in the exhibition.

[16] Thomas Rowlandson (1756–1827) is one of the most celebrated of all English illustrators. George Cruikshank (1792–1878) was a British illustrator, by some considered the best that Britain has produced. From 1805 to 1820 he was a maker of satirical prints and caricatures, many of them bawdy. But his career began to change as he became an illustrator for books, his best-known works being his illustrations for Dickens's early novels.

[17] Wyndham Lewis's exhibition, "Portraits and Tyros," ran from April 9 to 30, 1921, at the Leicester Galleries. The tyros were a race of imaginary, caricature creatures, and Lewis included five oils of them in the show. William Hogarth (1697–1764) is for many the best English painter and printmaker. His most famous sets of prints are: *A Harlot's Progress, A Rake's Progress, Marriage A La Mode, Beer Street and Gin Lane, The Four Times of Day*, and *Four Prints of an Election*.

[18] The *Athenaeum* was an established weekly periodical which had begun publication in 1830. It was read largely by academics and consisted mainly of book reviews. Under the ownership of the Labour politician Arthur Greenwood, it had fallen on hard times, and in 1919 it was bought by Arthur Rowntree, who hired John Middleton Murry (1889–1957) to be editor at a very princely salary of £800 per year; Murry offered Eliot the job of Assistant Editor at £500 per year, but he declined. Contributors were generously paid, and Murry was discerning in selecting a roster that included Virginia Woolf, T. S. Eliot, Clive Bell, Leonard Woolf, Bertrand Russell, Walter de la Mare, Julian Huxley, Kathryn Mansfield, E. M. Forster, and Lytton Strachey. Alas, it failed to attract many new subscribers and in early 1921 was sold to *The Nation*. The *London Mercury* was a literary journal created by J. C. Squire in 1920 and much disliked by Eliot and the Bloomsbury circle, who dismissed contributors to the journal as members of the "Squire-archy." The *Times Literary Supplement* was founded in 1902 and edited by Bruce Richmond. Its circulation was 24,000 at this time.

[19] Arthur Clutton-Brock (1868–1924) was a literary critic, reviewer, and author. He advocated a wooly version of Christian socialism and wrote more than 30 books.

several writers, like Mr. Edmund Gosse and Sir Sidney Colvin, whom I have never read and so cannot judge.[20]

I cannot find, after this muster, that there is any ground for the rumour current in the chatty paragraphs of the newsprint several months ago, that the younger generation has decided to revive criticism. There has been a brisk business in centenaries. Keats and Marvell have been celebrated in this way.[21] The former has been particularly fortunate. All the approved critics, each in a different paper, blew a blast of glory enough to lay Keats' ghost for twenty years. I have never read such unanimous rubbish, and yet Keats was a poet. Possibly, after the chatty columns of newsprint have ceased to cheer the "revival" of criticism, they will get a tip to lament its decay.[22] Yet the "revival" of criticism as a "form" is not the essential thing; if we are intelligent enough, and really interested in the arts, both criticism and "creation" will in some form flourish.

The True Church and the Nineteen Churches

While the poetry lovers have been subscribing to purchase for the nation the Keats house in Hampstead as a museum, the Church of England has apparently persisted in its design to sell for demolition nineteen religious edifices in the City of London.[22] Probably few American visitors, and certainly few natives, ever inspect these disconsolate fanes; but they give to the business quarter of London a beauty which its hideous banks and commercial houses have not quite defaced. Some are by Christopher Wren himself, others by his school; the least precious redeems some vulgar street, like the plain little church of All Hallows at the end of London Wall. Some, like St. Michael Paternoster Royal, are of great beauty.[23] As the prosperity of London has increased, the City churches have fallen into desuetude; for their destruction the lack of congregation is the ecclesiastical excuse, and the need of money the ecclesiastical reason. The fact that the erection of these churches was apparently paid for out of a public coal tax and their decoration probably by the parishioners, does not seem to invalidate the right of the True Church to bring them to the ground. To one who, like the present writer, passes his days in this City of London (*quand'io sentii chiavar l'uscio di sotto*)[24] the loss of these towers, to meet the eye down a grimy lane, and of these empty naves, to receive the solitary visitor at noon from the dust and tumult of Lombard Street, will be irreparable and unforgotten.

[20]   Robert Wilson Lynd (1879–1949), the son of a Presbyterian minister, was born in Belfast. He became a successful reviewer, critic, and author. From 1912 on he was literary editor at the *Daily News*, and from 1918 wrote a weekly feature for the *New Statesman* under the pseudonym "YY." Eliot reviewed his book, *Old and New Masters* (London: F. Unwin, 1919), somewhat harshly (see "Criticism in England," *Athenaeum* 4650 [June 13, 1919]: 456–7) and Lynd, in turn, reviewed *The Sacred Wood* very harshly. Edward Gosse (1849–1928) was the most influential critic of his day, and at this time was editor of *The Sunday Times*. Sir Sidney Colvin (1845–1927) was a prominent critic of art and literature who wrote more than 50 books.
[21]   Andrew Marvell (1621–78) was a poet known for a handful of exceptional lyric poems. The tercentenary of his birth in 1921 was marked by having the Bishop of Durham conduct a special service in Hull (Marvell's home town) in the presence of the Mayor, the Corporation, and various civic representatives. Later, Augustine Birrell (1850–1933), who had written a critical study of Marvell in 1905 (*Andrew Marvell* [London: Macmillan]), gave a speech about Marvell at a public meeting. For these events, see "Andrew Marvell: Character and Poetry," the *Times*, April 1 (Friday) 1921, p. 5, col. 3. The centenary of Keats's death was marked by the announcement of a public subscription to buy the house in Hampstead where he lived. (See "John Keats: Centenary of His Death," *The Times*, February 22, 1921, p. 13, col. 4.)
[22]   Eliot had mentioned "the revival of criticism" in a previous "London Letter," but his source for this phrase has not been identified.
[23]   The City of London is the name for the financial district. Christopher Wren (1632–1723) is often considered the greatest British architect, famous for designing St. Paul's in London. But in the aftermath of the Great Fire of 1666, Wren designed and built some 50 churches in the City. Many of these were destroyed in subsequent years, and the question of preserving those that remained was becoming urgent by the early twentieth century. The church of All Hallows on the Wall is located at 83 London Wall, a street that runs east–west and forms a northern boundary to the City. All Hallows, built between 1765 and 1767, was designed by George Dance the younger (1741–1825). It has a fine plaster ceiling with blue and gold decorations, and parts of the medieval London wall, which gave the street its name, can be seen in its churchyard. St. Michael Paternoster Royal is located on College Street, also in the City. The church was rebuilt by Christopher Wren between 1689 and 1694, with a tower dating from 1713, the last of Wren's City churches.
[24]   Eliot quotes from Dante, *Inferno* XXXIII.46, a passage which can be translated as "When I heard the door down below being nailed up." It is spoken by Ugolino di Guelfo di Gherardesca, as he recounts how he was locked up in a tower, together with his two sons and two nephews, whom he cannibalized before dying of starvation himself. The same passage is echoed in *The Waste Land*, lines 411–12. Lombard Street houses the home office or headquarters of Lloyds Bank, where Eliot worked from 1917 to 1925.

A small pamphlet issued for the London County Council: P. S. King & Son, 2–4 Gt. Smith Street, Westminster, S.W.1, 3s.6d.net) should be enough to persuade of what I have said.

London Letter: November 1922 (Marie Lloyd)

It requires some effort of analysis to understand why one person, among many who do a thing with accomplished skill, should be greater than the others; nor is it always easy to distinguish superiority from great popularity, when the two go together. I am thinking of Marie Lloyd,[1] who has died only a short time before the writing of this letter. Although I have always admired her genius I do not think that I always appreciated its uniqueness; I certainly did not realize that her death would strike me as the most important event which I have had to chronicle in these pages. Marie Lloyd was the greatest music-hall artist in England: she was also the most popular. And popularity in her case was not merely evidence of her accomplishment; it was something more than success. It is evidence of the extent to which she represented and expressed that part of the English nation which has perhaps the greatest vitality and interest.

Marie Lloyd's funeral became a ceremony which surprised even her warmest admirers:

"The scenes from an early hour yesterday, had been eloquent of the supreme place which Marie Lloyd held in the affection of the people. Wreaths had poured into the house in Woodstock Road from all parts of the country. There were hundreds of them from people whose names are almost household words on the variety stage, and from such people as 'a flower boy' in Piccadilly Circus: the taxi-drivers of Punter's Garage: and the Costermongers' Union of Farringdon Road. . . . Bombardier Wells sent a wreath. It was a white cushion, and across it in violets were the words 'At Rest: With deepest sympathy from Mrs and Billie Wells.' . . . Tributes were also sent by Hetty King, Clarice Mayne, Clara Mayne, Little Tich, Arthur Prince, George Mozart, Harry Weldon, Charles Austin, Gertie Gitana, the Brothers Egbert, Zetta Mare, Julia Neilson, and Fred Terry, Mr and Mrs Frank Curzon, Marie Loftus, many of the provincial music-halls, the Gulliver halls, and dressers from most of the theatres, and many of Miss Lloyd's old school chums. . . . A favourite song of Miss Lloyd's was recalled by a wreath fashioned like a bird's cage. The cage was open, but the old cock linnet had flown. . . . A large floral horseshoe, with whip, cap, and stirrups, was from 'Her Jockey Pals' – Donoghue, Archibald, and other men famous in the racing world. . . . There were other wreaths from the National Sporting Club, the Eccentric Club, the Ladies' Theatrical Guild, the Variety Artists' Federation, Albert and Mrs Whelan, Lorna and Toots Pound, Kate Carney, Nellie Wallace, the Ring at Blackfriars, Connie Ediss (who sent red roses), the Camberwell Palace (a white arch with two golden gates), Lew Lake, Major J. Arnold Wilson, and innumerable other people."[2]

Among all of that small number of music-hall performers, whose names are familiar to what is called the lower class, Marie Lloyd had far the strongest hold on popular affection. She is known to many audiences in America. I have never seen her perform in America, but I cannot imagine that she would be seen there at her best; she was only seen at her best under the stimulus of those audiences (in England, and especially in Cockney London), who had crowded to hear her for thirty

The essay was first published in the *Dial*, 73(6) (Dec. 1922). With revisions it was reprinted as "In Memoriam: Marie Lloyd" in the *Criterion* 1(2) (Jan. 1923), and then included under the title "Marie Lloyd" in Eliot's *Selected Essays* (1932) this latter being the text followed here:

[1] Marie Lloyd (1870–1922) was born in Hoxton, a working-class district in London just north of the City (or financial district). She was widely considered the greatest of all music-hall performers. When she died, nearly 100,000 people mourned her funeral cortege, and Max Beerbohm thought it the biggest funeral that London had witnessed since the death of Wellington. Noted for her risqué lyrics and double entrendres, Marie (who

pronounced her name to rhyme with "starry") collapsed on stage while performing at the Edmonton Empire on October 7, 1922, and died. Her funeral took place on October 12.

[2] Eliot is quoting from a contemporary newspaper account of Marie Lloyd's funeral: "MISS MARIE | LLOYD | Bareheaded Thousands At | To-day's Funeral | COSTERS' WREATH | Houses Filled With Beautiful | Flowers." It appeared in the *Star*, Oct. 12, 1922, p. 1, col. 5, an extensive report which carried over to p. 8, cols. 1–2. It was accompanied by a photo of the funeral cortege, p. 1, cols. 3–4. On the *Star*, see note 3 to "London Letter: May 1921, p. 158 this edition."

years. The attitude of these audiences was different, toward Marie Lloyd, from what it was toward any other of their favourites, and this difference represents the difference in her art. Marie Lloyd's audiences were invariably sympathetic, and it was through this sympathy that she controlled them. Among living music-hall artists none can so well control an audience as Nellie Wallace. I have seen Nellie Wallace interrupted by jeering or hostile comment from a boxful of East-Enders; I have seen her, hardly pausing in her act, make some quick retort that silenced her tormenters for the rest of the evening.[3] But I have never known Marie Lloyd to be confronted by this kind of hostility; in any case the feeling of the vast majority of the audience was so manifestly on her side, that no objector would have dared to lift his voice. And the difference is this: that whereas other comedians amuse their audiences as much and sometimes more than Marie Lloyd, no other comedian succeeded so well in giving expression to the life of that audience, in raising it to a kind of art. It was, I think, this capacity for expressing the soul of the people that made Marie Lloyd unique and that made her audiences, even when they joined in the chorus, not so much hilarious as happy.

It is true that in the details of acting Marie Lloyd was perhaps the most perfect, in her own line, of British actresses. There are – thank God – no cinema records of her; she never descended to this form of money-making; it is to be regretted, however, that there is no film of her to preserve for the recollection of her admirers the perfect expressiveness of her smallest gestures. But it is more in the thing that she made it, than in the accomplishment of her act, that she differed from other comedians. There was nothing about her of the grotesque; none of her comic appeal was due to exaggeration; it was all a matter of selection and concentration. The most remarkable of the survivors of the music-hall stage, to my mind, are Nellie Wallace and Little Tich;[4] but each of these is a kind of grotesque; their acts are an inconceivable orgy of parody of the human race. For this reason, the appreciation of these artists requires less knowledge of the environment. To appreciate for instance the last turn in which Marie Lloyd appeared, one ought to know already exactly what objects a middle-aged woman of the charwoman class would carry in her bag; exactly how she would go through her bag in search of something; and exactly the tone of voice in which she would enumerate the objects she found in it. This was only part of the acting in Marie Lloyd's last song, "I'm One of the Ruins That Cromwell Knocked Abaht a Bit."

Marie Lloyd was of London – in fact of Hoxton – and on the stage from her earliest years. It is pleasing to know that her first act was for a Hoxton audience, when at the age of ten she organized the Fairy Bell Minstrels for the Nile Street Mission of the Band of Hope; at which she sang and acted a song entitled "Throw Down the Bottle and Never Drink Again," which is said to have converted at least one member of the audience to the cause now enforced by law in America. It was similar audiences to her first audience that supported her to the last.

Marie Lloyd's art will I hope be discussed by more competent critics of the theatre than I. My own chief point is that I consider her superiority over other performers to be in a way a moral superiority:[5] it was her understanding of the people and sympathy for them, and the people's recognition of the fact that she embodied the virtues which they genuinely most respected in private life, that raised her to the position she occupied at her death. And her death is itself a significant moment in English history. I have called her the expressive figure of the lower classes. There has been no such expressive figure for any other class. The middle classes have no such idol: the middle classes are morally corrupt. That is to say, it is themselves and their own life which find no expression in such a person as Marie Lloyd; nor have they any independent virtues as a class which might give them as a conscious class any dignity. The middle classes, in England as elsewhere, under democracy, are morally dependent upon the aristocracy, and the aristocracy are morally in fear of the middle class which is gradually absorbing and destroying them. The lower classes still exist; but perhaps they will not exist for long. In the music-hall comedians they find the artistic expression and dignity of their own lives; and this is not found for any life in the most

[3]   See note 10 to Eliot's "London Letter: May 1921" (p. 160 this edition). The East End of London, at this time, was a poor district inhabited by working-class people.

[4]   See note 11 to Eliot's "London Letter: May 1921," p. 160.

[5]   Compare Eliot's comments on Baudelaire: "All first-rate poetry is occupied with morality: this is the lesson of Baudelaire" (p. 157 above).

elaborate and expensive revue. In England, at any rate, the revue expresses almost nothing. With the dwindling of the music-hall, by the encouragement of the cheap and rapid-breeding cinema, the lower classes will tend to drop into the same state of amorphous protoplasm as the bourgeoisie. The working-man who went to the music-hall and saw Marie Lloyd and joined in the chorus was himself performing part of the work of acting; he was engaged in that collaboration of the audience with the artist which is necessary in all art and most obviously in dramatic art. He will now go to the cinema, where his mind is lulled by continuous senseless music and continuous action too rapid for the brain to act upon, and he will receive, without giving, in that same listless apathy with which the middle and upper classes regard any entertainment of the nature of art. He will also have lost some of his interest in life. Perhaps this will be the only solution. In a most interesting essay in the recent volume of *Essays on the Depopulation of Melanesia* the great psychologist W. H. R. Rivers adduces evidence which has led him to believe that the natives of that unfortunate archipelago are dying out principally for the reason that the "Civilization" forced upon them has deprived them of all interest in life.[6] They are dying from pure boredom.

When every theatre has been replaced by 100 cinemas, when every musical instrument has been replaced by 100 gramaphones, when every horse has been replaced by 100 cheap motor cars, when electrical ingenuity has made it possible for every child to hear its bed-time stories through a wireless receiver attached to both ears, when applied science has done everything possible with the materials on this earth to make life as interesting as possible, it will not be surprising if the population of the entire civilized world rapidly follows the fate of the Melanesians. You will see that the death of Marie Lloyd has had a depressing effect, and that I am quite incapable of taking any interest in any literary events in England in the last two months, if any have taken place.

Ulysses, Order, and Myth (1923)

Mr. Joyce's book has been out long enough for no more general expression of praise, or expostulation with its detractors, to be necessary; and it has not been out long enough for any attempt at a complete measurement of its place and significance to be possible. All that one can usefully do at this time, and it is a great deal to do, for such a book, is to elucidate any aspect of the book – and the number of aspects is indefinite – which has not yet been fixed. I hold this book to be the most important expression which the present age has found; it is a book to which we are all indebted, and from which none of us can escape. These are postulates for anything that I have to say about it, and I have no wish to waste the reader's time by elaborating my eulogies; it has given me all the surprise, delight, and terror that I can require, and I will leave it at that.

Among all the criticisms I have seen of the book, I have seen nothing – unless we except, in its way, M. Valéry Larbaud's valuable paper which is rather an Introduction than a criticism – which seemed to me to appreciate the significance of the method employed – the parallel to the *Odyssey*, and the use of appropriate styles and symbols to each division. Yet one might expect this to be the first peculiarity to attract attention; but it has been treated as an amusing dodge, or scaffolding erected by the author for the purpose of disposing his realistic tale, of no interest in the completed structure. The criticism which Mr. Aldington[1] directed upon *Ulysses* several years ago seems to me to fail by this oversight – but, as Mr. Aldington wrote before the complete work had appeared, fails more honourably than the attempts of those who had the whole book before them. Mr. Aldington treated Mr. Joyce as a prophet of chaos; and wailed at the flood of Dadaism which his prescient eye saw bursting forth at the tap of the magician's rod. Of course, the influence which Mr. Joyce's book may have is from my point of view an irrelevance. A very great book may have a very bad influence indeed; and a mediocre book may be in the event most salutary. The next generation is responsible

[6] *Essays on the Depopulation of Melanesia*, by W. H. R. Rivers (1864–1922) was published by Cambridge University Press in 1922.

ULYSSES, ORDER, AND MYTH
The essay was first published in the *Dial* 75(5) (Nov. 1923), 21 months after the publication of *Ulysses*.
[1] Eliot is referring to Richard Aldington, "The Influence of Mr. James Joyce," *English Review* 32 (April 1921): 333–41.

for its own soul; a man of genius is responsible to his peers, not to a studio full of uneducated and undisciplined coxcombs. Still, Mr. Aldington's pathetic solicitude for the half-witted seems to me to carry certain implications about the nature of the book itself to which I cannot assent; and this is the important issue. He finds the book, if I understand him, to be an invitation to chaos, and an expression of feelings which are perverse, partial, and a distortion of reality. But unless I quote Mr. Aldington's words I am likely to falsify. "I say, moreover," he says, "that when Mr. Joyce, with his marvellous gifts, uses them to disgust us with mankind, he is doing something which is false and a libel on humanity." It is somewhat similar to the opinion of the urbane Thackeray upon Swift.[2] "As for the moral, I think it horrible, shameful, unmanly, blasphemous: and giant and great as this Dean is, "I say we should hoot him." (This, of the conclusion of the Voyage to the Houyhnhnms – which seems to me one of the greatest triumphs that the human soul has ever achieved. It is true that Thackeray later pays Swift one of the finest tributes that a man has ever given or received: "So great a man he seems to me that thinking of him is like thinking of an empire falling." And Mr. Aldington, in his time, is almost equally generous.)

Whether it is possible to libel humanity (in distinction to libel in the usual sense, which is libelling an individual or a group in contrast with the rest of humanity) is a question for philosophical societies to discuss; but of course if *Ulysses* were a "libel" it would simply be a forged document, a powerless fraud, which would never have extracted from Mr. Aldington a moment's attention. I do not wish to linger over this point: the interesting question is that begged by Mr. Aldington when he refers to Mr. Joyce's "great *undisciplined* talent."

I think that Mr. Aldington and I are more or less agreed as to what we want in principle, and agreed to call it classicism. It is because of this agreement that I have chosen Mr. Aldington to attack on the present issue. We are agreed as to what we want, but not as to how to get it, or as to what contemporary writing exhibits a tendency in that direction. We agree, I hope, that "classicism" is not an alternative to "romanticism," as of political parties, Conservative and Liberal, Republican and Democrat, on a "turn-the-rascals-out" platform. It is a goal toward which all good literature strives, so far as it is good, according to the possibilities of its place and time. One can be "classical," in a sense, by turning away from nine-tenths of the material which lies at hand and selecting only mummified stuff from a museum – like some contemporary writers, about whom one could say some nasty things in this connection, if it were worth while (Mr. Aldington is not one of them). Or one can be classical in tendency by doing the best one can with the material at hand. The confusion springs from the fact that the term is applied to literature and to the whole complex of interests and modes of behaviour and society of which literature is a part; and it has not the same bearing in both applications. It is much easier to be a classicist in literary criticism than in creative art – because in criticism you are responsible only for what you want, and in creation you are responsible for what you can do with material which you must simply accept. And in this material I include the emotions and feelings of the writer himself, which, for that writer, are simply material which he must accept – not virtues to be enlarged or vices to be diminished. The question, then, about Mr. Joyce, is: how much living material does he deal with, and how does he deal with it: deal with, not as a legislator or exhorter, but as an artist?

It is here that Mr. Joyce's parallel use of the *Odyssey* has a great importance. It has the importance of a scientific discovery. No one else has built a novel upon such a foundation before: it has never before been necessary. I am not begging the question in calling *Ulysses* a "novel"; and if you call it an epic it will not matter. If it is not a novel, that is simply because the novel is a form which will no longer serve; it is because the novel, instead of being a form, was simply the expression of an age which had not sufficiently lost all form to feel the need of something stricter. Mr. Joyce has written one novel – the *Portrait*; Mr. Wyndham Lewis has written one novel – *Tarr*.[3] I do not suppose that

[2]   Eliot's quotations are both from William Makepeace Thackeray, "Jonathan Swift," in Thackeray's *The English Humourists of the Eighteenth Century*, in *The Works of William Makepeace Thackeray* (London: Smith, Elder & Co.; Philadelphia: Lippincott & Co., 1876), vol. 10, pp. 381–415. His second quotation is the essay's penultimate sentence.

[3]   Wyndham Lewis published *Tarr* in 1917, with the Egoist Press; *Portrait of the Artist as a Young Man* appeared the same year with the same publisher.

either of them will ever write another "novel." The novel ended with Flaubert and with James. It is, I think, because Mr. Joyce and Mr. Lewis, being "in advance" of their time, felt a conscious or probably unconscious dissatisfaction with the form, that their novels are more formless than those of a dozen clever writers who are unaware of its obsolescence.

In using the myth, in manipulating a continuous parallel between contemporaneity and antiquity, Mr. Joyce is pursuing a method which others must pursue after him. They will not be imitators, any more than the scientist who uses the discoveries of an Einstein in pursuing his own, independent, further investigations. It is simply a way of controlling, of ordering, of giving a shape and a significance to the immense panorama of futility and anarchy which is contemporary history. It is a method already adumbrated by Mr. Yeats, and of the need for which I believe Mr. Yeats to have been the first contemporary to be conscious. It is a method for which the horoscope is auspicious. Psychology (such as it is, and whether our reaction to it be comic or serious), ethnology, and *The Golden Bough* have concurred to make possible what was impossible even a few years ago. Instead of narrative method, we may now use the mythical method. It is, I seriously believe, a step toward making the modern world possible for art, toward that order and form which Mr. Aldington so earnestly desires. And only those who have won their own discipline in secret and without aid, in a world which offers very little assistance to that end, can be of any use in furthering this advance.

Baudelaire (Introduction to Journaux intimes) (1930)

Anything like a just appreciation of Baudelaire has been slow to arrive in England, and still is defective or partial even in France. There are, I think, special reasons for the difficulty in estimating his worth and finding his place. For one thing, Baudelaire was in some ways far in advance of the point of view of his own time, and yet was very much of it, very largely partook of its limited merits, faults, and fashions. For another thing, he had a great part in forming a generation of poets after him; and in England he had what is in a way the misfortune to be first and extravagantly advertised by Swinburne, and taken up by the followers of Swinburne.[1] He was universal, and at the same time confined by a fashion which he himself did most to create. To dissociate the permanent from the temporary, to distinguish the man from his influence, and finally to detach him from the associations of those English poets who first admired him, is no small task. His comprehensiveness itself makes difficulty, for it tempts the partisan critic, even now, to adopt Baudelaire as the patron of his own beliefs.

It is the purpose of this essay to affirm the importance of Baudelaire's prose works, a purpose justified by the translation of one of those works which is indispensable for any student of his poetry. This is to see Baudelaire as something more than the author of the *Fleurs du mal*, and consequently to revise somewhat our estimate of that book. Baudelaire came into vogue at a time when "Art for Art's sake" was a dogma. The care which he took over his poems, and the fact that contrary to the fluency of his time, both in France and England, he restricted himself to this one volume, encouraged the opinion that Baudelaire was an artist exclusively for art's sake. The doctrine does not, of course, really apply to anybody; no one applied it less than Pater, who spent many years, not so much in illustrating it, as in expounding it as a *theory of life*, which is not the same thing at all. But it was a doctrine which did affect criticism, and appreciation, and which did obstruct a proper judgment of Baudelaire. He is in fact a greater man than was imagined, though perhaps not such a perfect poet.

The essay was first published as the "Introduction" to Charles Baudelaire, *Intimate Journals*, trans. Christopher Isherwood (London: Blackamore Press; New York: Random House, 1930), a limited edition in 700 copies, of which 400 were for sale in Britain, 250 in the US, and another 50 were copies autographed by Eliot. With some slight revisions and the omission of Part IV, the essay's concluding section, it was republished in Eliot's *Selected Essays* (London: Faber & Faber, 1930).

[1]   Algernon Swinburne (1837–1909), a British poet, wrote the first review of Baudelaire in English and imitated him in many poems. By 1930 Swinburne's lush style was viewed with some embarrassment. See his "Charles Baudelaire: Les Fleurs du Mal," *Spectator*, September 6, 1862: 998–1000; reprinted in Clyde K. Hyder (ed.), *Swinburne as Critic* (London and Boston: Routledge, 1972), pp. 27–36.

Baudelaire has, I believe, been called a fragmentary Dante,[2] for what that description is worth. It is true that many people who enjoy Dante enjoy Baudelaire, but the differences are as important as the similarities. Baudelaire's inferno is very different in quality and significance from that of Dante. Truer, I think, would be the description of Baudelaire as a later and more limited Goethe. As we begin to see him now, he represents his own age in somewhat the same way as that in which Goethe represents an earlier age. As a critic of the present generation, Mr. Peter Quennell, has recently said in his book, *Baudelaire and the Symbolists:*[3]

> He had enjoyed a *sense of his own age*, had recognized its pattern while the pattern was yet incomplete, and – because it is only our misapprehension of the present which prevents our looking into the immediate future, our ignorance of to-day and of its real as apart from its spurious tendencies and requirements – had anticipated many problems, both on the aesthetic and on the moral plane, in which the fate of modern poetry is still concerned.

Now the man who has this sense of his age is apt to be very hard to analyse. He is exposed to its follies as well as sensitive to its inventions; and in Baudelaire, as well as in Goethe, is some of the outmoded nonsense of his time. The parallel between the German poet who has always been the symbol of perfect "health" in every sense, as well as of universal curiosity, and the French poet who has been the symbol of morbidity in mind and concentrated interests in work, may see paradoxical. But after this lapse of time the difference between "health" and "morbidity" in the two men becomes more negligible; there is something artificial and even priggish about Goethe's healthiness, as there is about Baudelaire's unhealthiness; we have passed beyond both fashions, of health or malady, and they are both merely men with restless, critical, curious minds and the "sense of the age"; both men who understood and foresaw a great deal. Goethe, it is true, was interested in a great many subjects which Baudelaire left alone; but by Baudelaire's time it was no longer necessary for a man to embrace such varied interests in order to have the sense of the age; and in retrospect some of Goethe's studies seem to us (not altogether justly) to have been merely dilettante hobbies. The most of Baudelaire's prose writings (with the exception of the translations from Poe, which are of less interest to an English reader) are as important as the most of Goethe. They throw light on the *Fleurs du mal* certainly, but they also expand immensely our appreciation of their author.

It was once the mode to take Baudelaire's Satanism seriously, as it is now the tendency to present Baudelaire as a serious and Catholic Christian. Especially as a prelude to the *Journaux Intimes* this diversity of opinion needs some discussion. I think that the latter view – that Baudelaire is essentially Christian – is nearer the truth than the former, but it needs considerable reservation. When Baudelaire's Satanism is dissociated from its less creditable paraphernalia, it amounts to a dim intuition of a part, but a very important part, of Christianity. Satanism itself, so far as it is not merely an affectation, was an attempt to get into Christianity by the back door. Genuine blasphemy, genuine in spirit and not purely verbal, is the product of partial belief, and is as impossible to the complete atheist as to the perfect Christian. It is a way of affirming belief. This state of partial belief is manifest throughout the *Journaux Intimes*. What is significant about Baudelaire is his theological innocence. He is discovering Christianity for himself; he is not assuming it as a fashion or weighing social or political reasons, or any other accidents. He is beginning, in a way, at the beginning; and being a discoverer, is not altogether certain what he is exploring and to what it leads; he might almost be said to be making again, as one man, the effort of scores of generations. His Christianity is rudimentary or embryonic; at best, he has the excesses of a Tertullian (and even Tertullian is not considered wholly orthodox and well balanced). His business was not to practise Christianity, but – what was much more important for his time – to assert its *necessity*.

---

[2]   See Eliot, "The Lesson of Baudelaire," note 4, p. 157.   [3]   London: Chatto and Windus, 1929; p. 64.

Baudelaire's morbidity of temperament cannot, of course, be ignored: and no one who has looked at the work of Crépet[4] or the recent small biographical study of François Porché[5] can forget it. We should be misguided if we treated it as an unfortunate ailment which can be discounted or to attempt to detach the sound from the unsound in his work. Without the morbidity none of his work would be possible or significant; his weaknesses can be composed into a larger whole of strength, and this is implied in my assertion that neither the health of Goethe nor the malady of Baudelaire matters in itself: it is what both men made of their endowments that matters. To the eye of the world, and quite properly for all questions of private life, Baudelaire was thoroughly perverse and insufferable: a man with a talent for ingratitude and unsociability, intolerably irritable, and with a mulish determination to make the worst of everything; if he had money, to squander it; if he had friends, to alienate them; if he had any good fortune, to disdain it. He had the pride of the man who feels in himself great weakness and great strength. Having great genius, he had neither the patience nor the inclination, had he had the power, to overcome his weakness; on the contrary, he exploited it for theoretical purposes. The morality of such a course may be a matter for endless disputation; for Baudelaire, it was the way to liberate his mind and give us the legacy and lesson that he has left.

He was one of those who have great strength, but strength merely to *suffer*. He could not escape suffering and could not transcend it, so he *attracted* pain to himself. But what he could do, with that immense passive strength and sensibilities which no pain could impair, was to study his suffering. And in this limitation he is wholly unlike Dante, not even like any character in Dante's Hell. But, on the other hand, such suffering as Baudelaire's implies the possibility of a positive state of beatitude. Indeed, in his way of suffering is already a kind of presence of the supernatural and of the superhuman. He rejects always the purely natural and the purely human; in other words, he is neither "naturalist" nor "humanist." Either because he cannot adjust himself to the actual world he has to reject it in favour of Heaven and Hell, or because he has the perception of Heaven and Hell he rejects the present world: both ways of putting it are tenable. There is in his statements a good deal of romantic detritus; *ses ailes de géant l'empêchent de marcher*,[6] he says of the Poet and of the Albatross, but not convincingly; there is also truth about himself and about the world. His *ennui* may of course be explained, as everything can be explained, in psychological or pathological terms; but it is also, from the opposite point of view, a true form of *acedia*, arising from the unsuccessful struggle towards the spiritual life.

II

From the poems alone, I venture to think, we are not likely to grasp what seems to me the true sense and significance of Baudelaire's mind. Their excellence of form, their perfection of phrasing, and their superficial coherence, may give them the appearance of presenting a definite and final state of mind. In reality, they seem to me to have the external but not the internal form of classic art. One might even hazard the conjecture that the care for perfection of form, among some of the romantic poets of the nineteenth century, was an effort to support, or to conceal from view, an inner disorder. Now the true claim of Baudelaire is not that he found a superficial form but that he was searching for a form of life. In minor form he never indeed equalled Théophile Gautier, to whom he significantly dedicated the book: in the best of the slight verse of Gautier there is a satisfaction, a balance of inwardness and form, which we do not find in Baudelaire.[7] He had a greater technical ability than Gautier, and yet the content of feeling is constantly bursting the receptacle. His apparatus, by which I do not mean his command of words and rhythms, but his stock of imagery (and every poet's stock of imagery is circumscribed somewhere), is not wholly perdurable or

---

[4] Eugène Crépet (1827–92) edited a collection of Baudelaire's writings in 1887 which included a long biographical appendix. The appendix was revised, updated, and published as an independent book by his son, Jacques Crépet, in editions of 1906 and 1919, *Charles Baudelaire: étude biographique* (Paris: A. Messein).

[5] François Porché (1877–1944) wrote *La vie douloureuse de Charles Baudelaire* (Paris: Plon, 1926), which was translated by

John Mavin as *Charles Baudelaire* (London: Wishart; New York: Liveright, 1928).

[6] French for "his gigantic wings prevent him from walking," the last line of "The Albatross" ("L'Albatros"), a poem by Baudelaire.

[7] For Théophile Gautier, see "Hugh Selwyn Mauberley: Introduction," p. 48.

adequate. His prostitutes, mulattoes, Jewesses, serpents, cats, corpses form a machinery which has not worn very well; his Poet, or his Don Juan, has a romantic ancestry which is too clearly traceable. Compare with the costumery of Baudelaire the stock of imagery of the *Vita Nuova* or of Cavalcanti, and you find Baudelaire's does not everywhere wear as well as that of several centuries earlier; compare him with Dante or Shakespeare, for what such a comparison is worth, and he is found not only a much smaller poet, but one in whose work much more that is perishable has entered.

To say this is only to say that Baudelaire belongs to a definite place in time. Inevitably the offspring of romanticism, and by his nature the first counter-romantic in poetry, he could, like any one else, only work with the materials which were there. It must not be forgotten that a poet in a romantic age cannot be a "classical" poet except in tendency. If he is sincere, he must express with individual differences the general state of mind – not as a *duty*, but simply because he cannot help participating in it. For such poets, we may expect often to get much help from reading their prose works and even notes and diaries; help in deciphering the discrepancies between head and heart, means and end, material and ideals.

What preserves Baudelaire's poetry from the fate of most French poetry of the nineteenth century up to his time, and has made him, as M. Valéry has said in a recent introduction to *Fleurs du mal*, the one modern French poet to be widely read abroad, is not quite easy to conclude.[8] It is partly that technical mastery which can hardly be overpraised, and which has made his verse an inexhaustible study for later poets, not only in his own language. When we read

> *Maint joyau dort enseveli*
> *Dans les ténèbres et l'oubli,*
> *Bien loin des pioches et des sondes;*
> *Mainte fleur épanche à regret*
> *Son parfume doux comme un secret*
> *Dans les solitudes profondes,*[9]

we might for a moment think it a more lucid bit of Mallarmé; and so original is the arrangement of words that we might easily overlook its borrowing from Gray's "Elegy."[10] When we read

> *Valse mélancholique et langoureux vertige!*[11]

we are already in the Paris of Laforgue. Baudelaire gave to French poets as generously as he borrowed from English and American poets. The renovation of the versification of Racine has been mentioned often enough; quite genuine, but might be overemphasized, as it sometimes comes near to being a trick. But even without this, Baudelaire's variety and resourcefulness would still be immense.

Furthermore, besides the stock of images which he used that seems already second-hand, he gave new possibilities to poetry in a new stock of imagery of contemporary life.

> *...Au coeur d'un vieux faubourg, labyrinthe fangeux*
> *Où l'humanité grouille en ferments orageux,*
> *On voit un vieux chiffonier qui vient, hochant le tête*
> *Buttant, et se cognant aux murs comme un poète.*[12]

---

[8] See Charles Baudelaire, *Les fleurs du mal*, Texte de la 2. édition, publié avec une introduction de Paul Valéry (Paris: Payot, 1926). Paul Valery (1871–1945) was an influential French poet, much admired by Eliot.

[9] From "Le Guignol," or "Punch" (as in Punch and Judy), by Charles Baudelaire:

> Some jewel is sleeping buried
> In shadows and forgetfulness,
> Far away from drill and pickaxes;
> Some flower is regretfully pouring out,

> Its perfume as sweet as a secret
> In profound solitude

[10] "Elegy in a Country Churchyard," by Thomas Gray (1716–71).

[11] French, meaning "Mechanical waltz and langorous vertigo!" From a poem titled "Harmonie du soir," or "Evening Harmony," by Charles Baudelaire. On Jules Laforgue, see the introduction to the T. S. Eliot section, p. 113.

[12] French, from a poem Charles Baudelaire called "Le vin des chiffoniers" ("The Wine of the Ragpickers"):

This introduces something new, and something universal in modern life. (The last line quoted, which in ironic terseness anticipates Corbière, might be contrasted with the whole poem "Béné-diction" which begins the volume.[13]) It is not merely in the use of imagery of common life, not merely in the use of imagery of the sordid life of a great metropolis, but in the elevation of such imagery to the *first intensity* – presenting it as it is, and yet making it represent something much more than itself – that Baudelaire has created a mode of release and expression for other men.

This invention of language, at a moment when French poetry in particular was famishing for such invention, is enough to make of Baudelaire a great poet, a great landmark in poetry. Baudelaire is indeed the greatest exemplar in *modern* poetry in any language, for his verse and language is the nearest thing to a complete renovation that we have experienced. But his renovation of an attitude towards life is no less radical and no less important. In his verse, he is now less a model to be imitated or a source to be drained than a reminder of the duty, the consecrated task, of sincerity. From a fundamental sincerity he could not deviate. The superficies of sincerity (as I think has not always been remarked) is not always there. As I have suggested, many of his poems are insuffi-ciently removed from their romantic origins, from Byronic paternity and Satanic fraternity. The "Satanism" of the Black Mass was very much in the air; in exhibiting it Baudelaire is the voice of his time; but I would observe that in Baudelaire, as in no one else, it is redeemed by *meaning something else*. He uses the same paraphernalia, but cannot limit its symbolism even to all that of which he is conscious. Compare him with Huysmans in *A rebours*, *En route*, and *Là-bas*.[14] Huysmans, who is a first rate realist novelist of his time, only succeeds in making his diabolism interesting when he treats it externally, when he is merely describing a manifestation of his period (if such it was). His own interest in such matters is, like his interest in Christianity, a petty affair. Huysmans merely provides a document. Baudelaire would not even provide that, if he had been really absorbed in that ridiculous hocus-pocus. But actually Baudelaire is concerned, not with demons, black masses, and romantic blasphemy, but with the real problem of good and evil. It is hardly more than an accident of time that he uses the current imagery and vocabulary of blasphemy. In the nineteenth century, the age which (at its best) Goethe had prefigured, an age of bustle, programmes, platforms, scientific progress, humanitarianism, and sanguine revolutions which improved nothing, an age of progressive degradation, Baudelaire perceived that what really matters is Sin and Redemption. It is a proof of his honesty that he went as far as he could go and no further. To a mind observant of the post-Voltaire France (*Voltaire . . . prédicateur des concierges*[15]), a mind which saw the world of *Napoléon le petit* more lucidly than did that of Victor Hugo, a mind which at the same time had no affinity for the *Saint-Sulpicerie* of the day, the recognition of the reality of Sin is a New Life; and the possibility of damnation a relief in a world of electoral reform, plebiscites, sex reform and dress reform, that damnation itself is an immediate form of salvation – of salvation from the ennui of modern life, because it at last gives some significance to living. It is this, I believe, that Baudelaire is trying to express; and it is this which separates him from the modernist Protestantism of Byron and Shelley. It is apparently Sin in the Swinburnian sense, but really Sin in the permanent Christian sense, that occupies the mind of Baudelaire.

Yet, as I said, the sense of Evil implies the sense of good. Here too, as Baudelaire apparently confuses, and perhaps did confuse, Evil with its theatrical representations, Baudelaire is not always certain in his notion of the Good. The romantic idea of Love is never quite exorcised, but never quite surrendered to. In "Le Balcon,"[16] which M. Valéry considers, and I think rightly, one of

---

In the heart of an aging suburb, a muddy labyrinth
Where humanity teems in tempestuous discord,
One sees an old ragpicker who is coming, nodding his head,
Bumping against the wall like a poet.

[13]   Tristan Corbière (1845–75) was a French poet. "Benedic-tion" is the first poem (after the prefatory poem "To the Reader") in Baudelaire's work, *Les Fleurs du mal*.
[14]   Joris-Karl Huysmans (1848–1907) wrote *A rebours* (1884), or *Against the Grain*, a novel about an aesthete who cultivates a

spiritualism full of strange thrills; *Là-bas* (1891), a novel about diabolism and black magic; and *En route* (1895), a novel informed by Huysmans's deepening Christian mysticism.
[15]   French for "the preacher of the concierges," Baudelaire's scathing dismissal of Voltaire's atheism as itself a debased religion taken up only by concierges. See his *Journaux intimes*, "Mon coeur mis à nu," XVIII.
[16]   French for "The Balcony," by Baudelaire.

Baudelaire's most beautiful poems, there is all the romantic idea, but something more: the reaching out towards something which cannot be had *in*, but which may be had partly *through*, personal relations. Indeed, in much romantic poetry the sadness is due to the exploitation of the fact that no human relations are adequate to human desires, but also to the disbelief in any further object for human desires than that which fails to satisfy them. One of the unhappy necessities of human existence is that we have to "find things out for ourselves." If it were not so, the statement of Dante would have, at least for poets, have done once and for all. Baudelaire has all the romantic sorrow, but invents a new kind of romantic nostalgia, a derivative of his nostalgia being the *poésie des départs*, the *poésie des salles d'attente*.[17] In a beautiful paragraph of the present volume, he imagines the vessels lying in harbour as saying: *Quand partons-nous vers le bonheur?*[18] And his minor successor Laforgue exclaims: *Comme ils sont beaux, les trains manqués.*[19] The poetry of flight – which, in contemporary France, owes a great debt to the poems of the A. O. Barnabooth of Valery Larbaud[20] – is, in its origin in this paragraph of Baudelaire, a dim recognition of the direction of beatitude.

But in the adjustment of the natural to the spiritual, of the bestial to the human and the human to the supernatural, Baudelaire is a bungler compared with Dante; the best that can be said, and that is a very great deal, is that what he knew he found out for himself. In his book, the *Journaux intimes*, and especially in *Mon coeur mis à nu*, he has a great deal to say of the love of man and woman. One aphorism which has been especially noticed is the following: *la volupté unique et suprême de l'amour gît dans la certitude de faire le mal.*[21] This means, I think, that Baudelaire has perceived that what distinguishes the relations of man and woman from the copulation of beasts is the knowledge of Good and Evil (of *moral* Good and Evil, which are not natural Good and Bad or puritan Right and Wrong). Having an imperfect, vague romantic conception of Good, he was at least able to see that to conceive of the sexual act as evil is more dignified, less boring, than as the natural "life-giving," cheery automatism of the modern world. For Baudelaire, sexual operation is at least something not analogous to Kruschen Salts.

So far as we are human, what we do must be either evil or good; so far as we do evil or good, we are human; and it is better, in a paradoxical way, to do evil than to do nothing: at least, we exist. It is true to say that the glory of man is his capacity for salvation; it is also true to say that his glory is his capacity for damnation. The worst that can be said of most of our malefactors, from statesmen to thieves, is that they are not men enough to be damned. Baudelaire was man enough for damnation: whether he *is* damned is, of course, another question, and we are not prevented from praying for his repose. In all his humiliating traffic with other beings, he walked secure in this high vocation, that he was capable of a damnation denied to the politicians and the newspaper editors of Paris.

III

Baudelaire's notion of beatitude certainly tended to the wishy-washy; and even in one of the most beautiful of his poems, "L'Invitation au voyage," he hardly exceeds the *poésie des départs*. And because his vision is here so restricted, there is for him a gap between human love and divine love. His human love is definite and positive, his divine love vague and uncertain: hence his insistence upon the evil of love, hence his constant vituperations of the female. In this there is no need to pry for psychopathological causes, which would be irrelevant at best; for his attitude towards women is

---

[17]   French for "poetry of departures" and the "poetry of waiting rooms."

[18]   French for "When shall we set sail towards happiness?" from Baudelaire, *Journaux intimes*, "Fusées," VIII, or *Intimate Journals*, "Rockets", VIII; Eliot is mistaken in citing the "Mon coeur mis à nu" section of the *Intimate Journals*.

[19]   Eliot misremembers a line from Jules Laforgue, which reads: "Oh, qu'ils sont pittoresques les trains manqués." French for "Oh, how picturesque are trains that have been missed," or in Eliot's transformed version, "How beautiful are trains that have

been missed." The poem, untitled, is poem X or 10 in Jules Laforgue, *Derniers Vers* (*Last Poems*).

[20]   Valery Larbaud (1881–1957) wrote *Poêmes d'un riche amateur ou oeuvres françaises de M. Barnabooth* or *Poems of a Wealthy Amateur or the French Works of M. Barnabooth* in 1908. In 1910 he converted to Catholicism.

[21]   In French, "the unique and supreme pleasure of love lies in the certainty of committing evil." Charles Baudelaire, *Journeaux intimes*, "Fusées," III; or *Intimate Journals*, "Rockets," III.

consistent with the point of view which he had reached. Had he been a woman, he would, no doubt, have held the same views about men. He has arrived at the perception that a woman must be to some extent a symbol; he did not arrive at the point of harmonising his experience with his ideal needs. The complement, and the correction to the *Journaux Intimes*, so far as they deal with the relations of man and woman, is the *Vita Nuova*, and the *Divine Comedy*. But – and I cannot assert it too strongly – Baudelaire's view of life, such as it is, is objectively apprehensible, that is to say, his idiosyncrasies can partly explain his view of life, but they cannot explain it away. And this view of life is one which has grandeur and which exhibits heroism; it was an evangel to his time and to ours. *La vraie civilisation*, he wrote, *n'est pas dans le gaz, ni dans la vapeur, ni dans les table tournantes. Elle est dans la diminution des traces du péché originel.*[22] It is not quite clear exactly what *diminution* here implies, but the tendency of his thought is clear, and the message is still accepted by but few. More than half a century later T. E. Hulme left behind him a paragraph which Baudelaire would have approved:

> In the light of these absolute values, man himself is judged to be essentially limited and imperfect. He is endowed with Original Sin. While he can occasionally accomplish acts which partake of perfection, he can never himself *be* perfect. Certain secondary results in regard to ordinary human action in society follow from this. A man is essentially bad, he can only accomplish anything of value by discipline – ethical and political. Order is thus not merely negative, but creative and liberation. Institutions are necessary.[23]

IV

To translate successfully an imperfect series of notes and jottings like the *Journaux Intimes* is a more difficult task than the whole of Baudelaire's formal prose. There are repetitions (of thoughts which are probably all the more important to the author because of being repeated); there are short phrases and single words which seem to be memoranda for thoughts, unknown to us, to be developed later; and there are many references to Baudelaire's familiars and to personages of the day. There is the opportunity for vast annotation by some French student who can devote much time to the subject. Pending the appearance of a definitive text of this book in one or other of the two large French editions which are in process of publication, it would be absurd to make such an attempt in an English translation. The reader need not, however, be deterred. The most important passages are also the most comprehensible. We need not stop to guess at meanings in cryptogram, or to enquire the identity of all the persons mentioned. There is enough to be done in pondering the passages which are fully expressed. And the more we study it, the more coherence appears, the more sane and severe and clear-sighted we find a view of life which is, I believe, much more modern for us than are most philosophies between Baudelaire's time and our own.

---

[22] French for: "True civilization is not found in gas lighting, steam-power, or table-turning spiritualism. It is in the diminution of the marks of original sin." Charles Baudelaire, *Journaux intimes*, "Mon coeur mis à nu," XXXII; *Intimate Journals*, "My Heart Laid Naked," XXXIII.

[23] Eliot is quoting from T. E. Hulme (1883–1917), *Speculations* (London: Routledge, 1924), p. 47.

Wyndham Lewis (1882–1957)

Introduction

Born in Canada, Lewis moved to England with his family at age 6. His American father soon left the family, and Lewis's English mother started a laundering business in north London. Lewis was enrolled in the Slade School of Art at age 16. Though he received a prestigious scholarship, he proved a troublesome student. In a gesture of deliberate defiance he lit a cigarette just outside the office of the school's director. He was promptly seized, flung through the school's double doors, and told never to return.

For the next 10 years Lewis lived a bohemian life supported by his mother, much of it abroad in Madrid, Munich, and Paris. He published his first short story in 1908, and by 1910 he seemed more poised to become a writer than a painter. But in 1911 he contributed to his first group exhibition. His works were immediately noticed by contemporary critics. His taut draftsmanship was unmistakable, and already by 1912 he was producing works that drew on the latest idioms of modernism to create a distinctly personal style: strange automatons, their faces locked in rigid grimaces, stagger through disturbing fields of piercing arcs and angles.

It was a propitious moment. In 1910 Roger Fry had staged his famous Exhibition of Post-Impressionism, while in early 1912 the first Exhibition of Futurist Painting took London by storm, prompting unprecedented debate about contemporary art. Lewis admired the concerted polemical onslaught which the Futurists had mounted and resolved to be every bit as truculent in shaping a movement of his own. It was his good fortune to team up with Ezra Pound, whose canny sense of polemics and publicity served Lewis well. In 1914 they launched Vorticism with *Blast*, an avant-garde journal bristling with pugnacious manifestos and typography. In 1917 he published his novel *Tarr*, a minor classic that bristles with mannered allegories.

Lewis was becoming a celebrity. But he was also leading a double life. His first illegitimate child was born in 1911, his second in 1913. Both were entrusted to Lewis's aging mother, with Lewis promising what he could from his erratic earnings. In 1919 and 1920, he produced two more illegitimate children, duly sent off to a "Home for the Infants and Children of Gentlepeople," with Lewis undertaking to pay the bill. Chronically behind on his rent and beleaguered by creditors, Lewis fled from flat to flat, studio to studio. Even a successful show couldn't rectify his indigence. A major exhibition in 1921 yielded £616 in sales. But when the gallery commission and studio costs were deducted, Lewis was left with £54. Lewis's next major exhibition didn't occur until 1937.

During the early 1920s Lewis had turned to portraiture to make money. He also took up writing in earnest. His massive volumes of political-cultural criticism, *The Art of Being Ruled* and *Time and Western Man*, often lapse into tiresome jeremiads. His novel *The Childermass* offers flashes of brilliant writing and pages of dreary speechifying. *The Apes of God* is a mordant satire on wealthy bohemia, blemished by ugly undercurrents of anti-Semitism. Over and over Lewis asserted the modernist credo that art is infinitely superior to life. His career, instead, was an endless dramatization of life's revenge.

In 1930, after a 3-week jaunt to Berlin, Lewis cobbled together a biography of Hitler, the first in any language. Most reviewers damned its sloppy writing and poor research, a few praised its impressionistic vivacity. But by 1933, when the climate of opinion had irrevocably altered, passers-by would spit at shop windows displaying the book. Lewis's reputation was permanently damaged.

None of that deterred Lewis, who continued to write travel books, novels, and topical commentary, as well as some of the finest portraits of the twentieth century. In 1930 he married Gladys Anne Hoskins. In 1937 he published *Revenge for Love*, his most accessible novel and one that epitomizes all his recurrent themes. It brought no relief to his desperate financial straits. Desperate to change his luck, Lewis left for the United States and Canada in 1939. Things went no better, and commissions failed to materialize. By late 1941 he excused his delay in replying to one correspondent by explaining that he couldn't afford the postage stamp. The next year there was a 3-month period when Gladys couldn't leave their one-room flat because she lacked serviceable shoes. Despite these conditions, Lewis developed a curious fondness for Americanisms, which he carefully recorded in his diaries. "The American idiom is catching. The other day I caught myself saying golly, for instance." And he added: "I must be careful not to talk like that!" Yet when one correspondent asked Lewis about a new suit which he had acquired for a special occasion, Lewis proudly replied, "I think it will be a lulu."

When Lewis finally returned to England in 1945, the arrears on rent from his London flat and unpaid rates amounted to over £600. He also learned that he was going blind. For some years a tumor had been growing in his brain, slowly crushing his optical nerves. Lewis completed his last portrait in 1949, and two years later publicly announced his blindness when he resigned as art critic for the *Listener*. His last years were spent writing the novels

Monstre Gai and *Malign Festa*. In 1956, only 8 months before his death, he was taken to the Tate Gallery for the private viewing of a major retrospective exhibition. One observer noted tears in the blind man's eyes.

Enemy of the Stars (1914)

ADVERTISEMENT

THE SCENE:

SOME BLEAK CIRCUS, UNCOVERED, CAREFULLY-CHOSEN, VIVID NIGHT.
IT IS PACKED WITH POSTERITY, SILENT AND EXPECTANT.
POSTERITY IS SILENT, LIKE THE DEAD, AND MORE PATHETIC.

CHARACTERS:

TWO HEATHEN CLOWNS, GRAVE BOOTH ANIMALS, CYNICAL ATHLETES.

DRESS:

ENORMOUS YOUNGSTERS, BURSTING EVERYWHERE THROUGH HEAVY
TIGHT CLOTHES, LABOURED IN BY DULL EXPLOSIVE MUSCLES, full of fiery
dust and sinewy energetic air, not sap. BLACK CLOTH CUT SOMEWHERE, NOW-
ADAYS, ON THE UPPER BALTIC.

VERY WELL ACTED BY YOU AND ME.

ENEMY OF THE STARS

ONE IS IN IMMENSE COLLAPSE OF CHRONIC PHILOSOPHY. YET HE BULGES ALL
OVER, COMPLEX FRUIT, WITH SIMPLE FIRE OF LIFE. GREAT MASK, VENUSTIC AND
VERIDIC, TYPE OF FEMININE BEAUTY CALLED 'MANNISH'.

FIRST HE IS ALONE. A HUMAN BULL RUSHES INTO THE CIRCUS. THIS SUPER IS
NO MORE IMPORTANT THAN LOUNGING STAR OVERHEAD. HE IS NOT EVEN A
"STAR." HE RUSHES OFF, INTO THE EARTH.

CHARACTERS AND PROPERTIES BOTH EMERGE FROM GANGWAY INTO
GROUND AT ONE SIDE.

THEN AGAIN THE PROTAGONIST REMAINS NEGLECTED, AS THOUGH HIS TWO
FELLOW ACTORS HAD FORGOTTEN HIM, CAROUSING IN THEIR PROFESSIONAL
CAVERN.

SECOND CHARACTER, APPALLING "GAMIN," BLACK BOURGEOIS ASPIRATIONS
UNDERMINING BLATANT VIRTUOSITY OF SELF.

His criminal instinct of intemperate bilious heart, put at service of unknown Humanity, our King,
to express its violent royal aversion to Protagonist, statue-mirage of Liberty in the great desert.

Mask of discontent, anxious to explode, restrained by qualms of vanity, and professional coyness.
Eyes grown venturesome in native temperatures of Pole – indulgent and familiar, blessing with
white nights.

Type of characters taken from broad faces where Europe grows arctic, intense, human and
universal.

The work was first published in *Blast*, 1 (June 1914). The story which the play recounts is briefly this. Arghol, the main character, has previously been a student in Berlin. While there he had increasingly felt that his social relationships and studies were obscuring his true, original self with a layer of falsity. Alienating or repudiating his acquaintances, he has left Berlin and gone north to work in his uncle's yard as a wheelwright. This early part of the narrative is given in the middle of section V, an account of Arghol's dream. When the "play" begins, instead, Arghol has been working at his uncle's for some time, and we see the routine he goes through after finishing a day's work. His uncle kicks him to within an inch of his life, and supper-time is spent in talking to Hanp, the other worker in the yard. Arghol explains to Hanp why he has turned his back on life to work in the yard. They argue, but Arghol, suddenly realizing that his new way of life is also false in its way, asserts his authority and orders Hanp to leave. A fight ensues, which Arghol wins. He then falls asleep and dreams about what has happened and his own past. He begins snoring. Hanp takes up a knife and plunges it into Arghol, but Hanp, suddenly afflicted with despair, jumps off a bridge into a canal, where he drowns.

"Yet you and me: why not from the English metropolis?" – Listen: it is our honeymoon. We go abroad for the first scene of our drama. Such a strange thing as our coming together requires a strange place for initial stages of our intimate ceremonious acquaintance.

THERE ARE TWO SCENES

STAGE ARRANGEMENT:

RED OF STAINED COPPER PREDOMINANT COLOUR. OVERTURNED CASES AND OTHER IMPEDIMENTA HAVE BEEN COVERED, THROUGHOUT ARENA, WITH OLD SAIL-CANVAS.
HUT OF SECOND SCENE IS SUGGESTED BY CHARACTERS TAKING UP THEIR POSITION AT OPENING OF SHAFT LEADING DOWN INTO MIMES' QUARTERS.
A GUST, SUCH AS IS MET IN THE CORRIDORS OF THE TUBE, MAKES THEIR CLOTHES SHIVER OR FLAP, AND BLARES UP THEIR VOICES. MASKS FITTED WITH TRUMPETS OF ANTIQUE THEATRE, WITH EFFECT OF TWO CHILDREN BLOWING AT EACH OTHER WITH TIN TRUMPETS.
AUDIENCE LOOKS DOWN INTO SCENE, AS THOUGH IT WERE A HUT ROLLED HALF ON ITS BACK, DOOR UPWARDS, CHARACTERS GIDDILY MOUNTING IN ITS OPENING.

THE PLAY

ARGHOL

INVESTMENT OF RED UNIVERSE.
EACH FORCE ATTEMPTS TO SHAKE HIM.
CENTRAL AS STONE, POISED MAGNET OF SUBTLE, VAST, SELFISH THINGS.
HE LIES LIKE HUMAN STRATA OF INFERNAL BIOLOGIES. WALKS LIKE WARY SHIFTING OF BODIES IN DISTANT EQUIPOISE. SITS LIKE A GOD BUILT BY AN ARCHITECTURAL STREAM, FECUNDED BY MAD BLASTS OF SUNLIGHT.

———————

The first stars appear and Arghol comes out of the hut. This is his cue. The stars are his cast. He is rather late and snips into its place a vest button. A noise falls on the cream of Posterity, assembled in silent banks. One hears the gnats' song of the thirtieth centuries.

They strain to see him, a gladiator who has come to fight a ghost, Humanity – the great Sport of Future Mankind.

He is the prime athlete exponent of this sport in its palmy days. Posterity slowly sinks into the hypnotic trance of Art, and the Arena is transformed into the necessary scene.

THE RED WALLS OF THE UNIVERSE NOW SHUT THEM IN, WITH THIS CON-DEMNED PROTAGONIST.
THEY BREATHE IN CLOSE ATMOSPHERE OF TERROR AND NECESSITY TILL THE EXECUTION IS OVER, THE RED WALLS RECEDE, THE UNIVERSE SATISFIED.
THE BOX OFFICE RECEIPTS HAVE BEEN ENORMOUS.

———————

THE ACTION OPENS

THE YARD

The Earth has burst, a granite flower, and disclosed the scene.
A wheelwright's yard.
Full of dry, white volcanic light.
Full of emblems of one trade: stacks of pine, iron, wheels stranded.

Rough Eden of one soul, to whom another man, and not Eve, would be mated.

A canal at one side, the night pouring into it like blood from a butcher's pail.

Rouge mask in aluminum mirror, sunset's grimace through the night.

A leaden gob, slipped at zenith, first drop of violent night, spreads cataclysmically in harsh water of evening. Caustic Reckitt's stain.[1]

Three trees, above canal, sentimental, black and conventional in number, drive leaf flocks, with jeering cry.

Or they slightly bend their joints, impassible acrobats; step rapidly forward, faintly incline their heads.

Across the mud in pond of the canal their shadows are gawky toy crocodiles, sawed up and down by infant giant?

Gollywog[2] of arabian symmetry, several tons, Arghol[3] drags them in blank nervous hatred.

THE SUPER.

Arghol crosses yard to the banks of the canal: sits down.

"Arghol!"

"I am here."

His voice raucous and disfigured with a catarrh of lies in the fetid bankrupt atmosphere of life's swamp: clear and splendid among Truth's balsamic hills, shepherding his agile thoughts.

"Arghol!"

It was like a child's voice hunting its mother.

A note of primitive distress edged the thick bellow. The figure rushed without running. Arghol heeled over to the left. A boot battered his right hand ribs. These were the least damaged: it was their turn.

Upper lip shot down, half covering chin, his body reached methodically. At each blow, in muscular spasm, he made the pain pass out. Rolled and jumped, crouched and flung his grovelling Enceladus[4] weight against it, like swimmer with wave.

The boot, and heavy shadow above it, went. The self-centred and elemental shadow, with whistling noise peculiar to it, passed softly and sickly into a doorway's brown light.

The second attack, pain left by first shadow, lashing him, was worse. He lost consciousness.

THE NIGHT

His eyes woke first, shaken by rough moonbeams. A white, crude volume of brutal light blazed over him. Immense bleak electric advertisement of God, it crushed with wild emptiness of stress.

The ice field of the sky swept and crashed silently. Blowing wild organism into the hard splendid clouds, some will cast its glare, as well, over him.

The canal ran in one direction, his blood, weakly, in the opposite.

The stars shone madly in the archaic blank wilderness of the universe, machines of prey.

Mastodons, placid in electric atmosphere, white rivers of power. They stood in eternal black sunlight.

Tigers are beautiful imperfect brutes.

---

[1]   Probably Maurice B. Reckitt (1888–1980), who attended St. John's College, Oxford, and from 1912 to 1914 contributed essays to *The New Age*, which urged a combination of Christianity and Guild Socialism, a view sustained at more length in a book he wrote with C. E. Bechhofer, *The Meaning of National Guilds* (London: C. Palmer & Haywood, 1918).

[2]   A golliwog was a name invented for a black-faced, grotesquely dressed (male) doll with a shock of fuzzy hair. The term is first recorded in 1895.

[3]   Alan Munton has noted that the name is sometimes spelled as *Argol* in Lewis's typescript. According to the *OED*, argol is either the tartar deposited inside casks of fermented wines, and the source of cream of tartar; or dried cow dung which is used as fuel in Tartary.

[4]   In Greek mythology Enceladus was a Titan who was defeated in battle and buried under Mount Etna by Athena.

Throats iron eternities, drinking heavy radiance, limbs towers of blatant light, the stars poised, immensely distant, with their metal sides, pantheistic machines.

The farther, the more violent and vivid, Nature: weakness crushed out of creation! Hard weakness, a flea's size, pinched to death in a second, could it get so far.

He rose before this cliff of cadaverous beaming force, imprisoned in a messed socket of existence.

Will Energy some day reach Earth like violent civilization, smashing or hardening all? In his mind a chip of distant hardness, tugged at dully like a tooth, made him ache from top to toe.

But the violences of all things had left him so far intact.

HANP

I.

Hanp comes out of hut, coughing like a goat, rolling a cigarette. He goes to where Arghol is lying. He stirs him with his foot roughly.

Arghol strains and stretches elegantly, face over shoulder, like a woman.

"Come, you fool, and have supper." Hanp walks back to hut, leaving him.

Arghol lies, hands clasped round his knees. This new kick has put him into a childish lethargy. He gets to his feet soon, and walks to hut. He puts his hand on Hanp's shoulder, who has been watching him, and kisses him on the cheek.

Hanp shakes him off with fury and passes inside hut.

Bastard violence of his half-disciple, métis[5] of an apache[6] of the icy steppe, sleek citizen, and his own dumbfounding soul.

Fungi of sullen violent thoughts, investing primitive vegetation. Hot words drummed on his ear every evening: abuse: question. Groping hands strummed toppling Byzantine organ of his mind, producing monotonous black fugue.

Harsh bayadère-shepherdess[7] of Pamir, with her Chinese beauty: living on from month to month in utmost tent with wastrel, lean as mandrake root, red and precocious: with heavy black odour of vast Manchurian garden-deserts, and the disreputable muddy gold squandered by the unknown sun of the Amur.

His mind unlocked, free to this violent hand. It was his mind's one cold flirtation, then cold love. Excelling in beauty, marked out for Hindu fate of sovereign prostitution, but clear of the world, with furious vow not to return. The deep female strain succumbed to this ragged spirt of crude manhood, masculine with blunt wilfulness and hideous stupidity of the fecund horde of men, phallic wand-like cataract incessantly poured into God. This pip of icy spray struck him on the mouth. He tasted it with new pleasure, before spitting it out: acrid.

To be spat back among men. The young man foresaw the event.

They ate their supper at the door of the hut. An hour passed in wandering spacious silence.

"Was it bad tonight?" a fierce and railing question often repeated.

Arghol lay silent, his hands a thick shell fitting back of head, his face grey vegetable cave.

"Can't you kill him, in the name of God? A man has his hands, little else. Mote and speck, the universe illimitable!" Hanp gibed. "It is true he is a speck, but all men are. To you he is immense."

They sat, two grubby shadows, unvaccinated as yet by the moon's lymph, sickened by the immense vague infections of night.

---

[5]   French for a half-breed or mestizo.

[6]   Not a member of the Apathcaan Indians who live in New Mexico, but a ruffian of a type that infested Paris during the period 1900–14 and became the subject of journalistic lore; and more generally, any man of ruffian behavior. The term first appears in English in 1902 and is last recorded in 1933. "The leader of the band of roughs in Paris known as the 'Apaches'" (1902 *Westminster Gazette*, Oct. 22, 1902, 8/1; or "Those apaches with which Brussels is haunted," London *Times*, Feb. 9, 1909, 4/4).

[7]   Bayadère is French for a dancing-girl from India.

"That is absurd. I have explained to you. Here I get routine, the will of the universe manifested with directness and persistence. Figures of persecution are accidents or adventures for some. Prick the thin near heart, like a pea, and the bubble puffs out. That would not be of the faintest use in my case."

Two small black flames, wavering, as their tongues moved, drumming out thought, with low earth-draughts and hard sudden winds dropped like slapping birds from climaxes in the clouds.

No Morris-lens would have dragged them from the key of vastness. They must be severe midgets, brain specks of the vertiginous, seismic, vertebrate, slowly-living lines, of landscape.

"Self, sacred act of violence, is like murder on my face and hands. The stain won't come out. It is the one piece of property all communities have agreed it is illegal to possess. The sweetest-tempered person, once he discovers you are that sort of criminal, changes any opinion of you, and is on his guard. When mankind cannot overcome a personality, it has an immemorial way out of the difficulty. It becomes it. It imitates and assimilates that Ego until it is no longer one.... This is success.

"Between Personality and Mankind it is always a question of dog and cat; they are diametrically opposed species. Self is the ancient race, the rest are the new one. Self is the race that lost. But Mankind still suspects Egotistic plots, and hunts Pretenders.

"My uncle is very little of a relation. It would be foolish to kill him. He is an échantillon, acid advertisement slipped in letter-box: space's store-rooms dense with frivolous originals. I am used to him, as well."

Arghol's voice had no modulations of argument. Weak now, it handled words numbly, like tired compositor. His body was quite strong again and vivacious. Words acted on it as rain on a plant. It got a stormy neat brilliance in this soft shower. One flame balanced giddily erect, while other larger one swerved and sang with speech coldly before it.

They lay in a pool of bleak brown shadow, disturbed once by a rat's plunging head. It seemed to rattle along, yet slide on oiled planes. Arghol shifted his legs mechanically. It was a hutch with low loft where they slept.

Beyond the canal, brute-lands, shuttered with stoney clouds, lay in heavy angles of sand. They were squirted on by twenty ragged streams; legions of quails hopped parasitically in the miniature cliffs.

Arghol's uncle was a wheelwright on the edge of the town.

Two hundred miles to north the Arctic circle swept. Sinister tramps, its winds came wandering down the high road, fatigued and chill, doors shut against them.

"First of all; lily pollen of Ideal on red badge of your predatory category. Scrape this off and you lose your appetite. Obviously. – But I don't want in any case to eat Smith, because he is tough and distasteful to me. I am too vain to do harm, too superb ever to lift a finger when harmed.

"A man eats his mutton chop, forgetting it is his neighbour; drinks every evening blood of the Christs, and gossips of glory.

"Existence; loud feeble sunset, blaring like lumpish, savage clown, alive with rigid tinsel, before a misty door: announcing events, tricks and a thousand follies, to penniless herds, their eyes red with stupidity.

"To leave violently slow monotonous life is to take header into the boiling starry cold. (For with me some guilty fire of friction unspent in solitariness, will reach the stars.)

"Hell of those Heavens uncovered, whirling pit, every evening! You cling to any object, dig your nails in earth, not to drop into it."

The night plunged gleaming nervous arms down into the wood, to wrench it up by the roots. Restless and rhythmical, beyond the staring red rimmed doorway, giddy and expanding in drunken walls, its heavy drastic lights shifted.

Arghol could see only ponderous arabesques of red cloud, whose lines did not stop at door's frame, but pressed on into shadows within the hut, in tyrannous continuity. As a cloud drove eastward, out of this frame, its weight passed, with spiritual menace, into the hut. A thunderous atmosphere thickened above their heads.

Arghol, paler, tossed clumsily and swiftly from side to side, as though asleep.

He got nearer the door. The clouds had room to waste themselves. The land continued in dull form, one per cent. animal, these immense bird-amoebas. Nerves made the earth pulse up against his side and reverberate. He dragged hot palms along the ground, caressing its explosive harshness.

All merely exterior attack.

His face calm seismograph of eruptions in Heaven.

Head of black, eagerly carved, herculean Venus, of iron tribe, hyper-barbarous and ascetic. Lofty tents, sonorous with October rains, swarming from vast bright doll-like Asiatic lakes.

Faces following stars in blue rivers, till sea-struck, thundering engine of red water.

Pink idle brotherhood of little stars, passed over by rough cloud of sea.

Cataclysm of premature decadence.

Extermination of the resounding, sombre, summer tents in a decade, furious mass of images left: no human.

Immense production of barren muscular girl idols, wood verdigris, copper, dull paints, flowers.

Hundred idols to a man, and a race swamped in hurricane of art, falling on big narrow souls of its artists.

Head heavy and bird-like, weighted to strike, living on his body, ungainly red Atlantic wave.

"To have read all the books of the town, Arghol, and to come back here to take up this life again."

Coaxing: genuine stupefaction: reproach, a trap.

Arghol once more preceded him through his soul, unbenevolent. Doors opened on noisy blankness, coming through from calm, reeling noon-loudness beyond. Garrets waking like faces. A shout down a passage to show its depth, horizon as well. Voice coming back with suddenness of expert pugilistics.

Perpetual inspector of himself.

"I must live, like a tree, where I grow. An inch to left or right would be too much.

"In the town I felt unrighteous in escaping blows, home anger, destiny of here.

"Selfishness, flouting of destiny, to step so much as an inch out of the bull's eye of your birth. (When it is obviously a bull's eye!)

"A visionary tree, not migratory: visions from within.

"A man with headache lies in deliberate leaden inanimation. He isolates his body, floods it with phlegm, sucks numbness up to his brain.

"A soul wettest dough, doughiest lead: a bullet. To drop down Eternity like a plummet.

"Accumulate in myself, day after day, dense concentration of pig life. Nothing spent, stored rather in strong stagnation, till rid at last of evaporation and lightness characteristic of men. So burst Death's membrane through, slog beyond, not float in appalling distances.

"Energy has been fixed on me from nowhere – heavy and astonished: resigned. Or is it for remote sin! I will use it, anyway, as prisoner his bowl or sheet for escape: not as means of idle humiliation.

"One night Death left his card. I was not familiar with the name he chose: but the black edge was deep. I flung it back. A thousand awakenings of violence.

"Next day I had my knife up my sleeve as my uncle came at me, ready for what you recommend. But a superstition, habit, is there, curbing him mathematically: that of not killing me. I should know an ounce of effort more. – He loads my plate, even. He must have palpable reasons for my being alive."

A superb urchin watching some centre of angry commotion in the street, his companion kept his puffed slit eyes, generously cruel, fixed on him. God and Fate, constant protagonists, one equivalent to Police, his simple sensationalism was always focussed on. But God was really his champion. He longed to see God fall on Arghol, and wipe the earth with him. He egged God on: then egged on Arghol. His soft rigid face grinned with intensity of attention, propped contemplatively on hand.

Port-prowler, serf of the capital, serving its tongue and gait within the grasp and aroma of the white, matt, immense sea. Abstract instinct of sullen seafarer, dry-salted in slow acrid airs, aerian flood not stopped by shore, dying in dirty warmth of harbour-boulevards.

His soul like ocean-town: leant on by two skies. Lower opaque one washes it with noisy clouds: or lies giddily flush with street crevices, wedges of black air, flooding it with red emptiness of dead light.

It sends ships between its unchanging slight rock of houses periodically, slowly to spacious centre. Nineteen big ships, like nineteen nomad souls for its amphibious sluggish body, locked there.

II.

"What is destiny? Why yours to stay here, more than to live in the town or cross to America?"

"My dear Hanp, your geography is so up-to-date!

"Geography doesn't interest me. America is geography.

"I've explained to you what the town is like.

"Offences against the discipline of the universe are registered by a sort of conscience, prior to the kicks. Blows rain on me. Mine is not a popular post. It is my destiny right enough: an extremely unpleasant one."

"It is not the destiny of a man like you to live buried in this cursed hole."

"Our soul is wild, with primitiveness of its own. Its wilderness is anywhere – in a shop, sailing, reading psalms: its greatest good our destiny.

"Anything I possess is drunk up here on the world's brink, by big stars, and returned me in the shape of thought heavy as a meteorite. The stone of the stars will do for my seal and emblem. I practise with it, monotonous 'putting,' that I may hit Death when he comes."

"Your thought is buried in yourself."

"A thought weighs less in a million brains than in one. No one is conjuror enough to prevent spilling. Rather the bastard form infects the original. Famous men are those who have exchanged themselves against a thousand idiots. When you hear a famous man has died penniless and diseased, you say, 'Well served.' Part of life's arrangement is that the few best become these cheap scarecrows.

"The process and condition of life, without any exception, is a grotesque degradation, and *souillure*[8] of the original solitude of the soul. There is no help for it, since each gesture and word partakes of it, and the child has already covered himself with mire.

"Anything but yourself is dirt. Anybody that is. I do not feel clean enough to die, or to make it worth while killing myself."

A laugh, packed with hatred, not hoping to carry, snapped like a fiddle-cord.

"Sour grapes! That's what it's all about! And you let yourself be kicked to death here out of spite.

"Why do you talk to me, I should like to know? Answer me that?"

Disrespect or mocking is followed, in spiritualistic séances, with offended silence on part of the spooks. Such silence, not discernedly offended, now followed.

The pseudo-rustic Master, cavernously, hemicyclically real, but anomalous shamness on him in these circumstances, poudre de riz on face of knight's sleeping effigy, lay back indifferent, his feet lying, two heavy closed books, before the disciple.

Arghol was a large open book, full of truths and insults.

He opened his jaws wide once more in egotistic self castigation.

"The doctoring is often fouler than disease.

"Men have a loathsome deformity called Self: affliction got through indiscriminate rubbing against their fellows: social excrescence.

"Their being is regulated by exigencies of this affliction. Only one operation can cure it: the suicide's knife.

"Or an immense snuffling or taciturn parasite, become necessary to victim, like abortive poodle, all nerves, vice and dissatisfaction.

"I have smashed it against me, but it still writhes, turbulent mess.

---

[8]   French for a stain or spot.

"I have shrunk it in frosty climates, but it has filtered filth inward through me, dispersed till my deepest solitude is impure.

"Mire stirred up desperately, without success in subsequent hygiene."

This focussed disciple's physical repulsion: nausea of humility added. Perfect tyrannic contempt: but choking respect, curiosity; consciousness of defeat. These two extremes clashed furiously. The contempt claimed its security and triumph: the other sentiment baffled it. His hatred of Arghol for perpetually producing this second sentiment grew. This would have been faint without physical repulsion to fascinate him, make him murderous and sick.

He was strong and insolent with consciousness stuffed in him in anonymous form of vastness of Humanity: full of rage at gigantic insolence and superiority, combined with utter uncleanness and despicableness – all back to physical parallel – of his Master.

The more Arghol made him realize his congenital fatuity and cheapness, the more a contemptible matter appeared accumulated in the image of his Master, sunken mirror. The price of this sharp vision of mastery was contamination.

Too many things inhabited together in this spirit for cleanliness or health. Is one soul too narrow an abode for genius?

To have humanity inside you – to keep a doss-house! At least impossible to organize on such a scale.

People are right who would disperse these impure monopolies! Let everyone get his little bit, intellectual Balham rather than Bedlam!

III.

In sluggish but resolute progress towards the City and centre, on part of young man was to be found cause of Arghol's ascendancy in first place. Arghol had returned some months only from the great city of their world.

He showed Hanp picture postcards. He described the character of each scene. Then he had begun describing more closely. At length, systematically he lived again there for his questioner, exhausted the capital, put it completely in his hands. The young man had got there without going there. But instead of satisfying him, this developed a wild desire to start off at once. Then Arghol said: –

"Wait a moment."

He whispered something in his ear.

"Is that true?"

"Aye and more."

He supplemented his description with a whole life of comment and disillusion. – The young man felt now that he had left the city. His life was being lived for him. – But he forgot this and fought for his first city. Then he began taking a pleasure in destruction.

He had got under Arghol's touch.

But when he came to look squarely at his new possession, which he had exchanged for his city, he found it wild, incredibly sad, hateful stuff.

Somehow, however, the City had settled down in Arghol. He must seek it there, and rescue it from that tyrannic abode. He could not now start off without taking this unreal image city with him. He sat down to invest it, Arghol its walls.

IV.

Arghol had fallen. His Thébaide[9] had been his Waterloo.

He now sat up slowly.

"Why do I speak to you?

---

[9] Solitary retreat.

"It's not to you but myself. – I think it's a physical matter: simply to use one's mouth.

"My thoughts to walk abroad and not always be stuffed up in my head: ideas to banjo this resounding body.

"You seemed such a contemptible sort of fellow that there was some hope for you. Or to be clear, there was NOTHING to hope from your vile character.

"That is better than little painful somethings!

"I am amazed to find that you are like me.

"I talk to you for an hour and get more disgusted with myself.

"I find I wanted to make a naif yapping Poodle-parasite of you. – I shall always be a prostitute.

"I wanted to make you my self: you understand?

"Every man who wants to make another HIMSELF, is seeking a companion for his detached ailment of a self.

"You are an unclean little beast, crept gloomily out of my ego. You are the world, brother, with its family objections to me.

"Go back to our Mother and spit in her face for me!

"I wish to see you no more here! Leave at once. Here is money. Take train at once: Berlin is the place for your pestilential little carcass. Get out! Here! Go!"

Amazement had stretched the disciple's face back like a mouth, then slowly it contracted, the eyes growing smaller, chin more prominent, old and clenched like a fist.

Arghol's voice rang coldly in the hut, a bell beaten by words.

Only the words, not tune of bell, had grown harder. At last they beat virulently.

When he had finished, silence fell like guillotine between them, severing bonds.

The disciple spoke with his own voice, which he had not used for some weeks. It sounded fresh, brisk and strange to him, half live garish salt fish.

His mouth felt different.

"Is that all?"

Arghol was relieved at sound of Hanp's voice, no longer borrowed, and felt better disposed towards him. The strain of this mock life, or real life, rather, was tremendous on his underworld of energy and rebellious muscles. This cold outburst was not commensurate with it. It was twitch of loud bound nerve only.

"Bloody glib-tongued cow! You think you can treat me that way!"

Hanp sprang out of the ground, a handful of furious movements: flung himself on Arghol.

Once more the stars had come down.

Arghol used his fists.

To break vows and spoil continuity of instinctive behaviour, lose a prize that would only be a trophy tankard never drunk from, is always fine.

Arghol would have flung away his hoarding and scraping of thought as well now. But his calm, long instrument of thought, was too heavy. It weighed him down, resisted his swift anarchist effort, and made him giddy.

His fear of death, anti-manhood, words coming out of caverns of belief – synthesis, that is, of ideal life – appalled him with his own strength.

Strike his disciple as he had abused him. Suddenly give way. Incurable self taught you a heroism.

The young man brought his own disgust back to him. Full of disgust: therefore disgusting. He felt himself on him. What a cause of downfall!

V.

The great beer-coloured sky, at the fuss, leapt in fête of green gaiety.

Its immense lines bent like whalebones and sprang back with slight deaf thunder.

The sky, two clouds, their two furious shadows, fought.

The bleak misty hospital of the horizon grew pale with fluid of anger.

The trees were wiped out in a blow.

The hut became a new boat inebriated with electric milky human passion, poured in.

It shrank and struck them: struck, in its course, in a stirred up unmixed world, by tree, or house-side grown wave.

First they hit each other, both with blows about equal in force – on face and head.

Soul perched like aviator in basin of skull, more alert and smaller than on any other occasion. Mask stoic with energy: thought cleaned off slick – pure and clean with action. Bodies grown brain, black octopi.

Flushes on silk epiderm and fierce card-play of fists between: emptying of "hand" on soft flesh-table.

Arms of grey windmills, grinding anger on stone of the new heart.

Messages from one to another, dropped down anywhere when nobody is looking, reaching brain by telegraph: most desolating and alarming messages possible.

The attacker rushed in drunk with blows. They rolled, swift jagged rut, into one corner of shed: large insect scuttling roughly to hiding.

Stopped astonished.

Fisticuffs again: then rolled kicking air and each other, springs broken, torn from engine.

Hanp's punch wore itself out, soon, on herculean clouds, at mad rudder of boat on Arghol.

Then like a punch-ball, something vague and swift struck him on face, exhausted and white.

Arghol did not hit hard. Like something inanimate, only striking as rebound and as attacked.

He became soft, blunt paw of Nature, taken back to her bosom, mechanically; slowly and idly winning.

He became part of responsive landscape: his friend's active punch key of the commotion.

Hanp fell somewhere in the shadow: there lay.

Arghol stood rigid.

As the nervous geometry of the world in sight relaxed, and went on with its perpetual mystic invention, he threw himself down where he had been lying before.

A strong flood of thought passed up to his fatigued head, and at once dazed him. Not his body only, but being was out of training for action: puffed and exhilarated. Thoughts fell on it like punches.

His mind, baying mastiff, he flung off.

In steep struggle he rolled into sleep.

Two clear thoughts had intervened between fight and sleep.

Now a dream began valuing, with its tentative symbols, preceding events.

A black jacket and shirt hung on nails across window: a gas jet turned low to keep room warm, through the night, sallow chill illumination: dirty pillows, black and thin in middle, worn down by rough head, but congested at each end.

Bedclothes crawling over bed never-made, like stagnant waves and eddies to be crept beneath. – Picture above pillow of Rosa Bonheur horses[10] trampling up wall like well-fed toffyish insects. Books piled on table and chair, open at some page.

Two texts in Finnish. Pipes half smoked, collars: past days not effaced beneath perpetual tidiness, but scraps and souvenirs of their accidents lying in heaps.

His room in the city, nine feet by six, grave big enough for the six corpses that is each living man.

Appalling tabernacle of Self and Unbelief.

He was furious with this room, tore down jacket and shirt, and threw the window open.

The air made him giddy.

He began putting things straight.

[10] Rosa Bonheur (1806–56) was a French artist who painted
animals and landscapes with great attention to detail.

The third book, stalely open, which he took up to shut, was the *Einzige und Sein Eigentum*. Stirner.[11]

One of seven arrows in his martyr mind.

Poof! he flung it out of the window.

A few minutes, and there was a knock at his door. It was a young man he had known in the town, but now saw for the first time, seemingly. He had come to bring him the book, fallen into the roadway.

"I thought I told you to go!" he said.

The young man had changed into his present disciple.

Obliquely, though he appeared now to be addressing Stirner.

"I thought I told you to go!"

His visitor changed a third time.

A middle aged man, red cropped head and dark eyes, self-possessed, loose, free, student-sailor, fingering the book: coming to a decision. Stirner as he had imagined him.

"Get out, I say. Here is money."

Was the money for the book?

The man flung it at his head; its cover slapped him sharply.

"Glib tongued cow! Take that!"

A scrap ensued, physical experiences of recent fight recurring, ending in eviction of this visitor, and slamming of door.

"These books are all parasites. Poodles of the mind, Chows and King Charles; eternal prostitute.

"The mind, perverse and gorgeous.

"All this Art life, posterity and the rest, is wrong. Begin with these."

He tore up his books.

A pile by door ready to sweep out.

He left the room, and went round to Café to find his friends.

"All companions of parasite Self. No single one a brother.

"My dealings with these men is with their parasite composite selves, not with Them."

The night had come on suddenly. Stars like clear rain soaked chillily into him.

No one was in the street.

The sickly houses oozed sad human electricity.

He had wished to clean up, spiritually, his room, obliterate or turn into deliberate refuse, accumulations of Self.

Now a similar purging must be undertaken among his companions preparatory to leaving the city.

But he never reached the Café.

His dream changed; he was walking down the street in his native town, where he now was, and where he knew no one but his school-mates, workmen, clerks in export of hemp, grain and wood.

Ahead of him he saw one of the friends of his years of study in Capital.

He did not question how he had got there, but caught him up. Although brusquely pitched elsewhere, he went on with his plan.

"Sir, I wish to know you!"

Provisional smile on face of friend, puzzled.

"Hallo, Arghol, you seem upset."

"I wish to make your acquaintance."

"But, my dear Arghol, what's the matter with you?

"We already are very well acquainted."

---

[11]   Max Stirner (1806–56) was a German philosopher known for one book, *Der Einzige und sein Eigentum* (*The Individual and His Individuality*; 1844), an early and extreme statement of philosophic egoism. It immediately caused controversy, most notably a rebuttal from Marx and Engels in *The German Ideology*. But when John Henry Mackay (1864–1933) published a biographical and critical study of Stirner in 1898, *Max Stirner: Sen Leben und sein Werk* (*Max Stirner: His Life and Work*), it sparked new interest in him. In the next 10 years his major work was translated into Italian, Russian, and twice into French. The English version, *The Ego and His Own*, by Benjamin Tucker, appeared in 1908. It led Dora Marsden and Harriet Shaw Weaver to change the title of their dissident feminist journal from the *New Freewoman* to the *Egoist* in 1913.

"I am not Arghol."

"No?"

The good-natured smug certitude offended him.

This man would never see anyone but Arghol he knew. – Yet he on his side saw a man, directly beneath his friend, imprisoned, with intolerable need of recognition.

Arghol, that the baffling requirements of society had made, impudent parasite of his solitude, had foregathered too long with men, and bore his name too variously, to be superseded.

He was not sure, if they had been separated surgically, in which self life would have gone out and in which remained.

"This man has been masquerading as me."

He repudiated Arghol, nevertheless.

If eyes of his friends-up-till-then could not be opened, he would sweep them, along with Arghol, into rubbish heap.

Arghol was under a dishonouring pact with all of them.

He repudiated it and him.

"So I am Arghol."

"Of course. But if you don't want –."

"That is a lie. Your foolish grin proves you are lying. Good day."

Walking on, he knew his friend was himself. He had divested himself of something.

The other steps followed, timidly and deliberately: odious invitation.

The sound of the footsteps gradually sent him to sleep.

Next, a Café; he, alone, writing at table.

He became slowly aware of his friends seated at other end of room, watching him, as it had actually happened before his return to his uncle's house. There he was behaving as a complete stranger with a set of men he had been on good terms with two days before.

"He's gone mad. Leave him alone," they advised each other.

As an idiot, too, he had come home; dropped, idle and sullen, on his relative's shoulders.

VI.

Suddenly, through confused struggles and vague successions of scenes, a new state of mind asserted itself.

A riddle had been solved.

What could this be?

He was Arghol once more.

Was that a key to something? He was simply Arghol.

"I am Arghol."

He repeated his name – like sinister word invented to launch a new Soap, in gigantic advertisement – toilet-necessity, he, to scrub the soul.

He had ventured in his solitude and failed. Arghol he had imagined left in the city. – Suddenly he had discovered Arghol who had followed him, in Hanp. Always à deux!

———————————

Flung back to extremity of hut, Hanp lay for some time recovering. Then he thought. Chattel for rest of mankind, Arghol had brutalized him.

Both eyes were swollen pulp.

Shut in: thought for him hardly possible so cut off from visible world.

Sullen indignation at Arghol ACTING, he who had not the right to act. Violence in him was indecent: again question of taste.

How loathsome heavy body, so long quiet, flinging itself about: face strained with intimate expression of act of love.

Firm grip still on him; outrage.

"Pudeur,"[12] in races accustomed to restraint, is the most violent emotion, in all its developments. Devil ridicule, heroism of vice, ideal, god of taste. Why has it not been taken for root of great Northern tragedy?

Arghol's unwieldy sensitiveness, physical and mental, made him a monster in his own eyes, among other things. Such illusion, imparted with bullet-like directness to a companion, falling on suitable soil, produced similar conviction.

This humility of perverse asceticism opposed to vigorous animal glorification of self.

He gave men one image with one hand, and at same time a second, its antidote, with the other.

He watched results a little puzzled.

The conflict never ended.

Shyness and brutality, chief ingredients of their drama, fought side by side.

Hanp had been "ordered off," knocked about. Now he was going. Why? Because he had been sent off like a belonging.

Arghol had dragged him down: had preached a certain life, and now insolently set an example of the opposite.

Played with, debauched by a mind that could not leave passion in another alone.

Where should he go? Home. Good natured drunken mother, recriminating and savage at night.

Hanp had almost felt she had no right to be violent and resentful, being weak when sober. He caught a resemblance to present experiences in tipsy life stretching to babyhood.

He saw in her face a look of Arghol.

How disgusting she was, his own flesh. Ah! That was the sensation! Arghol, similarly disgusted through this family feeling, his own flesh: though he was not any relation.

Berlin and nearer city was full of Arghol. He was comfortable where he was.

Arghol had lived for him, worked: impaired his will. Even wheel-making had grown difficult, whereas Arghol acquitted himself of duties of trade quite easily.

WHOSE energy did he use?

Just now the blows had leapt in his muscles towards Arghol, but were sickened and did not seem hard. Would he never be able again to hit? Feel himself hard and distinct on somebody else?

That mass, muck, in the corner, that he hated: was it hoarded energy, stolen or grabbed, which he could only partially use, stagnating?

Arghol was brittle, repulsive and formidable through this sentiment.

Had this passivity been holy, with charm of a Saint's?

Arghol was glutted with others, in coma of energy.

He had just been feeding on him – Hanp!

He REFUSED to act, almost avowedly to infuriate: prurient contempt.

His physical strength was obnoxious: muscles affecting as flabby fat would in another.

Energetic through self-indulgence.

Thick sickly puddle of humanity, lying there by door.

Death, taciturn refrain of his being.

Preparation for Death.

Tip him over into cauldron in which he persistently gazed: see what happened!

This sleepy desire leapt on to young man's mind, after a hundred other thoughts – clown in the circus, springing on horse's back, when the elegant riders have hopped, with obsequious dignity down gangway.

VII.

Bluebottle, at first unnoticed, hurtling about, a snore rose quietly on the air.

Drawn out, clumsy, self-centred! It pressed inflexibly on Hanp's nerve of hatred, sending hysteria gyrating in top of diaphragm, flooding neck.

---

12   French for "shame."

It beckoned, filthy, ogling finger.

The first organ note abated. A second at once was set up: stronger, startling, full of loathsome unconsciousness.

It purred a little now, quick and labial. Then virile and strident again.

It rose and fell up centre of listener's body, and along swollen nerves, peachy, clotted tide, gurgling back in slimy shallows. Snoring of a malodorous, bloody, sink, emptying its water.

More acutely, it plunged into his soul with bestial regularity, intolerable besmirching.

Aching with disgust and fury, he lay dully, head against ground. At each fresh offence the veins puffed faintly in his temples.

All this sonority of the voice that subdued him sometimes: suddenly turned bestial in answer to his vision.

"How can I stand it! How can I stand it!"

His whole being was laid bare: battened on by this noise. His strength was drawn raspingly out of him. In a minute he would be a flabby yelling wreck.

Like a sleek shadow passing down his face, the rigour of his discomfort changed, sly volte-face of Nature.

Glee settled thickly on him.

The snore crowed with increased loudness, glad, seemingly, with him; laughing that he should have at last learnt to appreciate it. A rare proper world if you understand it!

He got up, held by this foul sound of sleep, in dream of action. Rapt beyond all reflection, he would, martyr, relieve the world of this sound.

Cut out this noise like a cancer.

He swayed and groaned a little, peeping through patches of tumified flesh, boozer collecting his senses; fumbled in pocket.

His knife was not there.

He stood still wiping blood off his face.

Then he stepped across shed to where fight had occurred.

The snore grew again: its sonorous recoveries had amazing and startling strength. Every time it rose he gasped, pressing back a clap of laughter.

With his eyes, it was like looking through goggles.

He peered round carefully, and found knife and two coppers where they had slipped out of his pocket a foot away from Arghol.

He opened the knife, and an ocean of movements poured into his body. He stretched and strained like a toy wound up.

He took deep breaths: his eyes almost closed. He opened one roughly with two fingers, the knife held stiffly at arm's length.

He could hardly help plunging it in himself, the nearest flesh to him.

He now saw Arghol clearly: knelt down beside him.

A long stout snore drove his hand back. But the next instant the hand rushed in, and the knife sliced heavily the impious meat. The blood burst out after the knife.

Arghol rose as though on a spring, his eyes glaring down on Hanp, and with an action of the head, as though he were about to sneeze. Hanp shrank back, on his haunches. He over-balanced, and fell on his back.

He scrambled up, and Arghol lay now in the position in which he had been sleeping.

There was something incredible in the dead figure, the blood sinking down, a moist shaft, into the ground. Hanp felt friendly towards it.

There was only flesh there, and all our flesh is the same. Something distant, terrible and eccentric, bathing in that milky snore, had been struck and banished from matter.

Hanp wiped his hands on a rag, and rubbed at his clothes for a few minutes, then went out of the hut.

The night was suddenly absurdly peaceful, trying richly to please him with gracious movements of trees, and gay processions of arctic clouds.

Relief of grateful universe.

A rapid despair settled down on Hanp, a galloping blackness of mood. He moved quickly to outstrip it, perhaps.

Near the gate of the yard he found an idle figure. It was his master. He ground his teeth almost in this man's face, with an aggressive and furious movement towards him. The face looked shy and pleased, but civil, like a mysterious domestic.

Hanp walked slowly along the canal to a low stone bridge.

His face was wet with tears, his heart beating weakly, a boat slowed down.

A sickly flood of moonlight beat miserably on him, cutting empty shadow he could hardly drag along.

He sprang from the bridge clumsily, too unhappy for instinctive science, and sank like lead, his heart a sagging weight of stagnant hatred.

Bestre (1922)

As I walked along the quay at Kermanac,[1] there was a pretty footfall in my rear. Turning my head, I found an athletic French woman, about forty years old, of the bourgeois class, looking at me.

The crocket-like[2] floral postiches on the ridges of her head-gear looked crisped down in a threatening way: her nodular pink veil was an apoplectic gristle round her stormy brow: steam came out of her lips upon the harsh white atmosphere. Her eyes were dark, and the contiguous colour of her cheeks of a redness quasi-venetian, with something like the feminine colouring of battle. This was surely a feline battle-mask, then; but in such a pacific and slumbrous spot I thought it an anomalous ornament.

My dented bidon[3] of a hat – cantankerous beard – Austrian boots, the soles like the rind of a thin melon slice, the uppers in stark calcinous segments; my cassock-like blue broad-cloth coat (why was I like this? – the habits of needy travel grew this composite shell), this uncouthness might have raised in her the question of defiance and offence. I glided swiftly along on my centipedal boots, dragging my eye upon the rough walls of the houses to my right like a listless cane. Low houses faced the small vasey[4] port. It was there I saw Bestre.

This is how I became aware of Bestre.

The detritus of some weeks' hurried experience was being dealt with in my mind, on this crystalline, extremely cold, walk, through Kermanac to Rot;[5] and was being established in orderly heaps. At work in my untidy hive, I was alone: the atmosphere of the workshop dammed me in. That I moved forward was no more strange than if a carpenter's shop or chemist's laboratory, installed in a boat, should move forward on the tide of a stream. Now, what seemed to happen was that, as I bent over my work, an odiously grinning face peered in at my window. The impression of an intrusion was so strong, that I did not even realise at first that it was I who was the intruder. That the window was not *my* window, and that the face was not peering in but *out*: that, in fact, it was I myself who was guilty of peering into somebody else's window: this was hidden from me in the first moment of consciousness about the odious brown person of Bestre. It is a wonder that the curse did not at once fall from me on this detestable inquisitive head. What I did do was to pull up

The story was published in three distinct versions in 1909, 1922, and 1927. This edition follows the 1922 version, which appeared in the *Tyro* 2 (1922).

The story was one of nine which Lewis first wrote between 1909 and 1917, all of them set in Brittany, a northwestern province of France which was noted for sustaining primitive, peasant, or premodern modes of life which had vanished elsewhere, life-forms that could also be explained by invoking the region's Celtic heritage – the famous megaliths and dolmens in Carnac, for example. The tale begins when the narrator observes a Fenchwoman immediately after she has witnessed a scene of sexual exhibitionism on the part of Bestre, the story's principal character and an innkeeper in the town where the narrator, an

artist, is staying. The rest of the story turns on the narrator's observations of Bestre, who in turn has made observing or looking at others into a form of minor art which enables him to impose a rudimentary order on the world about him.

[1] A fictional name, but one very close to *Kermanec*, the name of a real town near Finisterre, in Brittany, France.

[2] A crocket, in architecture, is a carved ornament which resembles foliage and is placed on the sloping edges of spires or pinnacles.

[3] French for a can or milk-churn.

[4] From the French word for mud, *vase*, hence "muddy."

[5] A fictional town.

in my automatic progress, and, instead of passing on, to continue to stare in at Bestre's kitchen window, and scowl at Bestre's sienna-coloured gourd of a head.

Bestre in his turn was nonplussed. He knew that someone was looking in at his kitchen window all right: he had expected someone to do so, someone who in fact had contracted the habit of doing that. But he had mistaken my steps for this other person's; and the appearance of my face was in a measure as disturbing to him, as his had been to me. My information on these points afterwards became complete. With a flexible imbrication reminiscent of a shutter-lipped ape, a bud of tongue still showing, he shot the latch of his upper lip down in front of the nether one, and depressed the interior extremities of his eyebrows sharply from their quizzing perch – only this monkey-on-a-stick mechanical pull – down the face's centre. At the same time, his arms still folded like bulky lizards, blue tattoo on brown ground, upon the escarpment of his vesicular[6] middle, not a hair or muscle moving, he made a quick, slight motion to me with one hand to get out of the picture without speaking – to efface myself. It was the gesture of a theatrical French sportsman. I was in the line of fire. I moved on: a couple of steps did it. That lady was twenty yards distant. But nowhere anything apparently related to Bestre's gestures. "Pension de Famille?"[7] What prices? – and how charmingly placed. I passed along the side of Bestre's house to the principal door. I concluded that this entrance was really disused, although more imposing. So emerging on the quay once more, and turning along the front of the house, I again discovered myself in contact with Bestre. He was facing towards me, and down the quay, still as before and the attitude so much a replica as to make it seem a plagiarism of his kitchen piece: only now his head was on one side, a verminous grin had dispersed the equally unpleasant entity of his shut mouth. The new facial arrangement and angle for the head imposed on what seemed his stock pose for the body, must mean: "Am I not rather smart? Not just a little bit smart? Don't you think? A little, you will concede? You did not expect that, did you? That was a nasty jar for you, was it not? Ha! my lapin,[8] that was unexpected, that is plain! Did you think you would find Bestre asleep? He is always awake! He watched you being born, and has watched you ever since. Don't be too sure that he did not play some part in planting the little seed from which you grew into such a big, fine (many withering exclamation marks) boy (or girl). He will be in at your finish too. But he is in no hurry about that. He is never in a hurry! He bides his time. Meanwhile he laughs at you. He finds you a little funny. That's right! Yes! I am still looking!"

His very large eyeballs, the small saffron ocellation[9] in their centre, the tiny spot through which light entered the obese wilderness of his body; his bronzed, bovine arms, swollen handles for a variety of indolent little ingenuities; his inflated digestive case, lent their combined expressiveness to say these things; with every tart and biting condiment that eye-fluid, flaunting of fatness (the well-filled!), the insult of the comic, implications of indecence, could provide. Every variety of bottom-tapping resounded from his dumb bulk. His tongue stuck out, his lips eructated with the incredible indecorum that appears to be the monopoly of liquids, his brown arms were for the moment genitals, snakes in one massive twist beneath his mamillary slabs, gently riding on a pancreatic swell, each hair on his oil-bearing skin contributing its message of porcine affront.

Taken fairly in the chest by this magnetic attack, I wavered. Turning the house corner it was like confronting a hard meaty gust. But I perceived that the central gyroduct[10] passed a few feet clear of me. Turning my back, arching it a little, perhaps, I was just in time to receive on the boko[11] a parting volley from the female figure of the obscure encounter, before she disappeared behind a rock which brought Kermanac to a close on this side of the port. She was evidently replying to Bestre. It was the rash grating philippic of a battered cat, limping into safety. At the moment that she vanished behind the boulder, Bestre must have vanished too, for a moment later the quay was empty. On reaching the door into which he had sunk, plump and slick as into a stage trap, there he was inside – this grease-bred old mammifer[12] – his tufted vertex charging about the plank ceiling –

---

[6] From *vesicle*, meaning a small bladder or cyst filled with fluid, such as a blister.

[7] French for a "family boarding-house."

[8] French for a "rabbit," or a "crafty creature."

[9] An eye-like spot or marking.

[10] A term invented by Lewis, combining the Greek word *gyros*, meaning a "circle" or "spiral," with the medical sense of a *duct* as a tube or canal that carries a bodily fluid.

[11] British slang for "nose."

[12] An animal which has mammary glands, a mammal.

generally ricochetting like a dripping sturgeon in a boat's bottom – arms warm brown, ju-jitsu of his guts, tan canvas shoes and trousers rippling in ribbed planes as he darted about – with a filthy snicker for the scuttling female, and a stark cock of the eye for an unknown figure miles to his right: he filled this short tunnel with clever parabolas and vortices, little neat stutterings of triumphs, goggle-eyed hypnotisms, in restropect, for his hearers.

"T'as vu? T'as vu? Je l'ai fiché c'es'qu'elle n'attendait pas! Ah, la rosse! Qu'elle aille raconter ça à son crapule de mari. Si, si, s'il vient ici, tu sais –!"[13]

His head nodded up and down in batches of blood-curdling affirmations; his hand, pudgy hieratic disk, tapped the air gently, then sawed tenderly up and down.

Bestre, on catching sight of me, hailed me as a witness. "Tiens! Ce monsieur peut vous le dire: il etait là. Il m'a vu là didans qui l'attendait!"[14]

I bore witness to the subtleties of his warlike ambush. I told his sister and two boarders that I had seldom been privy to such a rich encounter. They squinted at me, and at each other, dragging their eyes off with slow tosses of the head. I took rooms in this house, and was constantly entertained for a week.

Before attempting to discover the significance of Bestre's proceedings when I clattered into the silken zone of his hostilities, I settled down in his house; watched him idly, from both my windows – cleaning his gun in the back yard – rather shyly sucking up to a fisherman on the quay. I went into his kitchen and his shed and watched him. I realised as little as he did that I was patting and prodding a subject of these stories. There was no intention in these stoppages on my zigzag trek across Western France of taking a human species, as an entomologist would take a Distoma[15] or a Narbonne Lycosa,[16] to study. It was at the end of a few months' roaming in the country that I saw I had been a good deal in contact with a tribe, some more and some less generic. It seemed to me an amusing labour to gather some of these individuals in retrospect and group them under their function, to which all in some diverting way were attached. My stoppage at Kermanac, for example, was because Bestre was a little excitement. I had never seen brown flesh put to those uses. And the situation of his boarding-house would allow of unlimited pococurantism, idling and eating: the small cliffs of the scurfy little port, as well, its desertion and queer train of life, reaching a system of dreams I had considered effaced. But all the same I went laughing after Bestre, tapping him, setting traps for the game that he decidedly contained for my curiosity. So it was almost as though Fabre[17] could have established himself within the masonries of the bee, and lived on its honey, while investigating for the human species: or stretched himself on a bed of raphia and pebbles at the bottom of the Lycosa's pit, and lived on flies and locusts. I lay on Bestre's billowy beds, fished from his boat; he brought me birds and beasts that he had chased and killed. It was an idyllic life of the calmest adventure. We were the best of friends: he thought I slapped him because contact with his fat gladdened me; and to establish contact with the feminine vein in his brown-coated ducts and muscles. Also he was Bestre, and it must be nice to pat and buffet him as it would be to do that with a dreadful lion.

He offered himself, sometimes wincing coquettishly, occasionally rolling his eyes a little, as the lion might do to remind you of your fear, and heighten the luxurious privilege.

---

[13]   Bestre's very low and ungrammatical French means: "Did you see? Did you see? I gave her something that she wasn't expecting! Ah, the bitch! Let her go tell that to her bastard of a husband. Yes, yes, if he were to come here, you know –"

[14]   "Ah! This gentleman can tell you all about it; he was there. He saw me inside there, waiting for her!"

[15]   The name of a genus of trematode worms, which are parasitic worms or flukes that have two suckers (whence the name, *di*, Greek for two, and *stoma*, Greek for mouth) and infest the alimentary canals, livers, etc., of vertebrates.

[16]   The scientific name for the black-bellied tarantula, a species of spider; the female, after copulating, devours the male. See also the next note.

[17]   Jean Henri Fabre (1832–1915) was a celebrated French entomologist whose essays were frequently published in translation in pre-First World War issues of the *English Review*, the same journal in which Lewis published "Some Innkeepers and Bestre," the first version of "Bestre," in June 1909. Fabre's study of *Mason-Bees* was published in English in 1914 (New York: Dodd, Mead; London: Hodder and Stoughton), while his *Life of the Spider*, published in English a year earlier in 1913 (New York: Dodd, Mead), devoted four chapters (chs. 3–6) to the black-bellied tarantula, or Narbonne Lycosa, including one chapter on its burrow or "pit."

Bestre's boarding-house is only open from June to October: the winter months he passes in hunting and trapping. He is a stranger to Kermanac, a Boullonais,[18] and at constant feud with the natives. For some generations his family have been strangers where they lived; and he carries on his face the mark of an origin even more distant than Picardy. His great-grandfather came into France from the Peninsula, with the armies of Napoleon. Possibly his alertness, combativeness and timidity are the result of these exilings and difficult adjustments to new surroundings, working in his blood, and in his own history.

He is a large, tall man, corpulent and ox-like: you can see by his movements that the slow aggrandisement of his stomach has hardly been noticed by him. It is still compact with the rest of his body, and he is as nimble as a flea. It has been for him like the peculations of a minister, enriching himself under the nose of the Pasha: Bestre's kingly indifference can be accounted for by the many delights and benefits procured through this subtle misappropriation of the general resources of the body. Sunburnt, with large yellow-white moustache, little eyes protruding with the cute strenuosity already noticed, when he meets anyone for the first time his mouth stops open, a cigarette-end adhering to the lower lip. He will assume an expression of expectancy, and repressed amusement, like a man accustomed to nonplussing: the expression the company wears in those games of divination when they have made the choice of an object, and he whose task it is to guess its nature is called in, and commences the cross-examination. Bestre is jocose: he will beset you with mocking thoughts as the man is danced round in a game of blind man's buff. He may have regarded my taps as a myopic clutch at his illusive person. He gazes at a new acquaintance as though this poor man, without guessing it, were entering a world of astonishing things! A would-be boarder arrives and asks him if he has a room with two beds. Bestre fixes him steadily for twenty seconds with an amused yellow eye. Without uttering a word, he then leads the way to a neighbouring door, lets the visitor pass into the room, stands watching him with the expression of a conjurer who has just drawn a curtain aside and revealed to the stupefied audience a horse and cart, or a life-size portrait of Mr. H. G. Wells, where a moment ago there was nothing.

Suppose the following thing happened. A madman, who believes himself a hen, escapes from Charenton,[19] and gets, somehow or another, as far as Finisterre. He turns up at Kermanac, knocks at Bestre's door and asks him with a perfect stereotyped courtesy for a large, airy room, with a comfortable perch to roost on, and a little straw in the corner where he might sit. Bestre a few days before has been visited by the very idea of arranging such a room: all is ready. He conducts his demented client to it. Now his manner with his everyday client would be thoroughly appropriate under these circumstances. They are carefully suited to a very weak-minded and whimsical visitor indeed.

Bestre has another group of tricks, pertaining directly to the commerce of his hospitable trade. When a customer is confessing in the fullest way his paraesthesias,[20] allowing this new host an engaging glimpse of his nastiest propriums[21] and kinks, Bestre behaves, with unconscious logic, as though a secret of the most disreputable nature were being imparted to him. Were, in fact, the requirements of a vice being enumerated, he could not display more plainly the qualms caused by his role of accessory. He will lower his voice, whisper in the client's ear; before doing so glance over his shoulder apprehensively two or three times, and push his guest roughly into the darkest corner of the passage or kitchen. It is his perfect understanding – is he not the only man that does, at once, forestall your eager whim: there is something of the fortune-teller in him – that produces the air of mystery. For his information is not always of the nicest, is it? He must know more about you than I daresay you would like many people to know. And Bestre will in his turn mention certain little delicacies that he, Bestre, will see that you have, and that the other guests will not share with you. So there you are committed at the start to a subtle collusion. But Bestre means it. Everyone he sees for the first time he is thrilled about, until they have got used to him. He would give you anything

---

[18] A native of Boulogne.
[19] A suburb of Paris.
[20] A paraesthesia or paresthesia is an abnormal sensation of prickling, tingling, or itching of the skin.

[21] A proprium is an attribute essentially belonging to something, a distinctive characteristic; essential nature or selfhood.

while he is still strange to you. But you see the interest die down in his eyes, at the end of twenty-four hours, whether you have assimilated him or not. He only gives you about a day for your meal. He then assumes that you have finished him, and he feels chilled by your scheduled disillusion. A fresh face and an enemy he depends on for that "new" feeling – or what can we call this firework that he sends up for the stranger, that he enjoys so much himself – or this rare bottle he can only open when hospitality compels – his own blood?

I had arrived at the master-moment of one of Bestre's campaigns. These were long and bitter affairs. But they consisted almost entirely of dumb show. The few words that passed were generally misleading. A vast deal of talking went on in the different camps. But a dead and pulverising silence reigned on the field of battle, with few exceptions.

It was a matter of who could be most silent and move least: it was a stark stand-up fight between one personality and another, unaided by adventitious muscle or tongue. It was more like phases of a combat or courtship in the insect-world. The Eye was really Bestre's weapon: the ammunition with which he loaded it was drawn from all the most skunk-like provender, the most ugly mucins, fungoid glands, of his physique. Excrement as well as sputum would be shot from this luminous hole, with the same certainty in its unsavoury appulsion. Every resource of metonomy, bloody mind transfusion or irony were also his. What he selected as an arm in his duels, then, was the Eye. As he was always the offended party he considered that he had this choice. I traced the predilection for this weapon and method to a very fiery source – to the land of his ancestry – Spain. How had the knife dropped out of his outfit? Who can tell? But he retained the mirada[22] whole and entire enough to please anyone, all the more active for the absence of the dagger. I pretend that Bestre behaved as he did directly because his sweet forbears had to rely so much on the furious languishing and jolly conversational properties of their eyes to pull off life's business at all. The Spanish beauty imprisoned behind her casement can only roll her eyes at her lover in the street below. The result of these and similar Eastern restraints develops the eye almost out of recognition. Bestre in his kitchen, behind his casement, was unconsciously employing this gift from his half-African past. And it is not even the unsupported female side of Bestre. For the lover in the street as well must keep his eye in constant training to bear out the furibond jugular drops, the mettlesome stamping, of the guitar. And all the haughty chevaleresque habits of this bellicose race have substituted the eye for the mouth in a hundred ways. The Grandee's eye is terrible, and at his best is he not speechless with pride? Eyes, eyes: for defiance, for shrivelling subordinates, for courtesy, for love. A "Spanish" eye might be used as we say "Toledo blade." There, anyway, is my argument, I place on the one side Bestre's eye: on the other I isolate the Iberian eye. Bestre's grandfather, we know, was a Castilian. To show how he was beholden to this extraction, and again how the blood clung to him, Bestre was in no way grasping. It went so far that he was noticeably careless about money. This, in France, could not be accounted for in any other way.

Bestre's quarrels turned up as regularly as work for a good shoemaker. Antagonism after antagonism flushed forth: became more acute through several weeks: detonated in the dumb pyrotechnic I have described: then wore itself out with its very exhausting and exacting violence. At the passing of an enemy Bestre will pull up his blind with a snap. There he is, with his insult stewing lusciously in his yellow sweat. The eyes fix on the enemy, on his weakest spot, and do their work. He has the anatomical instinct of the hymenopter for his prey's most morbid spot; for an old wound; for a lurking vanity. He goes into the other's eye, seeks it, and strikes. On a physical blemish he turns a scornful and careless rain like a garden hose. If the deep vanity is on the wearer's back, or in his walk or gaze, he sluices it with an abundance you would not expect his small eyes to be capable of delivering. But the *mise-en-scène* for his successes is always the same.

Bestre is *discovered* somewhere, behind a blind, in a doorway, beside a rock, when least expected. He regards the material world as so many ambushes for his body.

Then the key principle of his strategy is provocation. The enemy must be exasperated to the point at which it is difficult for him to keep his hands off his aggressor. The desire to administer the blow is as painful as a blow received. That the blow should be taken back into the enemy's own

---

[22]   Spanish for a glance, or for a gaze, a steadfast look.

bosom, and that he should be stifled by his own oath – *that* Bestre regards as so many blows, and so much abuse, of *his*, Bestre's, although he has never so much as taken his hands out of his pockets, or opened his mouth.

His immediate neighbours on the quay afford him a constant war-food. I have seen him slipping out in the evening and depositing refuse in front of his neighbour's house. I have seen a woman screeching at him in pidgin French from a window of the débit[23] two doors off, while he pared his nails a yard from his own front door. This was to show his endurance. The subtle notoriety, too, of his person is dear to him. But local functionaries and fishermen are not his only fare. During summer, time hangs heavy with the visitor from Paris. When the first great ennui comes upon him, he wanders about desperately, and his eye in due course falls on Bestre. It depends how busy Bestre is at the moment. But often enough he will take on the visitor in his canine way. The visitor shivers, opens his eyes, bristles at the quizzing pursuit of Bestre's œillade:[24] the remainder of his holiday flies in a round of singular plots, passionate conversations and prodigious encounters with this born broiler.

Now a well-known painter and his family, who rented a house in the neighbourhood, were, it seemed, particularly responsive to Bestre. I could not, at the bottom of it, find any cause for his quarrel. The most insignificant pretext was absent. The pompous, peppery Paris salon artist, and this Boulogne-bred innkeeper inhabited the same village and grew larger and larger in each other's eyes at a certain moment, in this bare Breton wild. As Bestre swelled and swelled for the painter, he was seen to be the possessor of some insult incarnate that was an intolerable element in so lonely a place. War was inevitable. Bestre saw himself growing and growing, with the glee of battle in his heart, and the flicker of budding effront in his little eye. He did nothing to arrest this alarming aggrandisement. Pretexts could have been found. But they were dispensed with by mutual consent. This is how I reconstructed the obscure and early phases of that history. What is certain is that there had been much eye-play on the quay between Monsieur Riviere and Monsieur Bestre. And the scene that I had taken part in was the culmination of a rather humiliating phase in the annals of Bestre's campaigns.

The distinguished painter's wife had contracted the habit of passing Bestre's kitchen window of a morning when Mademoiselle Marie was alone there – gazing glassily in, but never looking at Mademoiselle Marie. This had such a depressing effect on Bestre's old sister, that it reduced her vitality considerably, and in the end brought on diarrhœa. Why did Bestre permit the war to be brought into his own camp with such impunity? The only reason that I could discover for this was that the attacks were of very irregular timing, and that he had been out fishing in one or two cases when it had occurred. But on the penultimate occasion Madame Riviere had practically finished off the last surviving female of Bestre's notable stock. As usual she had looked into the kitchen; but this time *at* Mademoiselle Marie, and in such a way as practically to curl her up on the floor. Bestre's sister had none of her brother's ferocity, and in every way departed considerably from his type, except in a mild and sentimental imitation of his colouring. The distinguished painter's wife on the other hand had a touch of Bestre about her. It was because Bestre did not have it all his own way, and recognized, probably with misgiving, the redoubtable and Bestre-like quality of his enemy, that he resorted to such extreme measures as I suspect him of employing to rout her on the ground she had chosen – his kitchen.

On that morning when I drifted into the picture what happened to induce such a disarray in the female? Bestre was lying in wait for her. What means did he employ during the second or two that she would take in passing his kitchen window, to bring her to her knees? In principle, as I have said, Bestre sacrificed the claims any individual portion of his anatomy might have to independent expressiveness to a tyrannical appropriation of all this varied battery of bestial significance by his eye. Had he any theory, however, that certain occasions warranted, or required, the auxiliary offices of units of the otherwise subordinated mass? Can the sex of his assailant give us a clue? I am convinced in my own mind that another agent was called in on this occasion. I am certain that he struck the death-blow with another engine than his eye. I believe that the most savage and

---

[23] French for a "small shop."

[24] French for "a glance, an ogle."

obnoxious means of affront were employed to cope with the distinguished painter's wife.

Monsieur Riviere, with his painting-pack and campstool, came along the quay shortly after-wards, going in the same direction as his wife. Bestre was at his door; and he came in later and let us know how he had behaved.

"I wasn't such a fool as to insult him, there were witnesses: let him do that. But if I come upon him in one of those lanes at the back there, you know——! I was standing at my door; he came along and looked at my house and scanned my windows" (this is equivalent in Bestre warfare to a bombardment). "As he passed I did not move. I thought to myself 'Hurry home, old fellow, and ask Madame what she has seen during her little walk!' I looked him in the white of the eyes: he thought I'd lower mine; he doesn't know me. And, after all, what is he, though he's got the Riband of the Legion of Honour? I don't carry *my* decorations on my coat! I have mine marked on my body. Yes, I fought in 1870; did I ever show you what I've got here? No; I'm going to show you." He had shown all this before, but my presence encouraged a repetition of former successes. So while he was speaking he jumped up, quickly undid his shirt, bared his chest and stomach, and pointed to something beneath his arm. Then, rapidly rolling up his sleeve, he pointed to a cicatrice rather like a vaccination mark, but larger. While showing his scars he slaps his body, with a sort of sneering rattle or chuckle between his words, his eyes protruding more than usual. His customary wooden expression is disintegrated: this compound of a constant foreboded reflection of the expression of astonishment your face will acquire when you learn of his wisdom, valour, or wit: the slightest shade of sneering triumph: and a touch of calm relish at your wonder. Or he seems teaching you by his staring grimace the amazement you should feel; and his grimace gathers force and blooms as the full sense of what you are witnessing, hearing, bursts upon you, while your gaping face conforms more and more to Bestre's prefiguring mask.

As to his battles, Bestre is profoundly unaware of what strange category he has got himself into. The principles of his strategy are possibly the possession of his libido, but most certainly not that of the bulky and surface citizen, Bestre. On the contrary, he considers himself on the verge of a death struggle at any moment when in the presence of one of his enemies.

Like all people who spend their lives talking about their deeds, he presents a very particular aspect in the moment of action. When discovered in the thick of one of his dumb battles, he has the air of a fine company promoter, cornered, trying to corrupt some sombre fact into shielding for an hour his unwieldy fiction, until some fresh wangle can retrieve it. Or he will display a great empirical expertness in reality, without being altogether at home in it.

Bestre in the moment of action feels as though he were already talking. His action has the exaggerated character of his speech, only oddly curbed by the exigencies of reality. In his moments of most violent action he retains something of his dumb-passivity. He never seems quite entering into reality, but observing it. He is looking at the reality with a professional eye, so to speak: with a professional liar's.

I have noticed that the more cramped and meagre his action has been, the more exuberant his account of the affair is afterwards. The more restrictions reality has put on him, the more unbridled is his gusto as historian of his deeds, immediately afterwards.

Then he has the common impulse to avenge that self that has been perishing under the famine and knout of a bad reality, by glorifying and surfeiting it on its return to the imagination.

The Death of the Ankou (1927)

'And Death once dead, there's no more dying then.'
                                          – William Shakespeare[1]

Ervoanik Plouillo – meaning the death-god of Ploumilliau;[2] I said over the words, and as I did so I saw the death-god. – I sat in a crowded inn at Vandevennec, in the *argoat*, not far from Rot,[3] at the Pardon,[4] deafened by the bitter screech of the drinkers, finishing a piece of cheese. As I avoided the maggots I read the history of the Ankou, that is the armorican[5] death-god. The guide-book to the antiquities of the district made plain, to the tourist, the ancient features of this belief. It recounted how the gaunt creature despatched from the country of death traversed at night the breton region. The peasant, late on the high-road and for the most part drunk, staggering home at midnight, felt around him suddenly the atmosphere of the shades, a strange cold penetrated his tissues, authentic portions of the *Néant* pushed in like icy wedges within the mild air of the fields and isolated him from Earth, while rapid hands seized his shoulders from behind, and thrust him into the ditch. Then, crouching with his face against the ground, his eyes shut fast, he heard the hurrying wheels of the cart. Death passed with his assistants. As the complaint of the receding wheels died out, he would cross himself many times, rise from the ditch, and proceed with a terrified haste to his destination.

There was a midnight mass at Ploumilliau, where the Ankou, which stood in a chapel, was said to leave his place, pass amongst the kneeling congregation, and tap on the shoulders those he proposed to take quite soon. These were memories. The statue no longer stood there, even. It had been removed some time before by the priests, because it was an object of too much interest to local magicians. They interfered with it, and at last one impatient hag, disgusted at its feebleness after it had neglected to assist her in a deadly matter she had on hand, introduced herself into the chapel one afternoon and, unobserved by the staff, painted it a pillar-box red. This she imagined would invigorate it and make it full of new mischief. When the priest's eyes in due course fell upon the red god, he decided that that would not do: he put it out of the way, where it could not be tampered with. So one of the last truly pagan images disappeared, wasting its curious efficacy in a loft, dusted occasionally by an ecclesiastical *bonne*.

Such was the story of the last authentic plastic Ankou. In ancient Brittany the people claimed to be descended from a redoubtable god of death. But long passed out of the influence of that barbarity, their early death-god, competing with gentler images, saw his altars fall one by one. In a semi-'parisian' parish, at last, the cult which had superseded him arrived in its turn at a universal decline, his ultimate representative was relegated to a loft to save it from the contemptu-ous devotions of a disappointed sorceress. Alas for Death! or rather for its descendants, thought I, a little romantically: that chill in the bone it brought was an ancient tonic: so long as it ran down the spine the breton soul was quick with memory. So, *alas!*

But I had been reading after that, and immediately prior to my encounter, about the peasant in the ditch, also the blinding of the god. It was supposed, I learnt, that formerly the Ankou had his eyesight. As he travelled along in his cart between the hedges, he would stare about him, and spot likely people to right and left. One evening, as his flat, black, breton peasants' hat came rapidly along the road, as he straddled attentively bolt-upright upon its jolting floor, a man and his master,

---

[1]   The last line of Sonnet 146.
[2]   A village situated on the northern coast of Brittany, on the English Channel. The church of Sant Millau in the village currently houses the statue of the Ankou, or death-god, a med-ieval wood carving of a skeleton holding a large scythe, in effect a Grim Reaper. *Ervoanik Plouillou* is the name of the statue in Breton, the Celtic language spoken by natives of Brittany.
[3]   Vandevennec is an imaginary name, while the Argoat is a real region in the extreme northwest of Brittany, comprising the towns of Canihuel, Kerpert, St-Conan et St-Gilles-Pligeaux.

Rot is another imaginary place name, though it means "belch" in French.
[4]   A church festival at which indulgence is granted, often the festival of the patron saint. Compare John Mounteny Jephson, *Narrative of a Walking Tour in Brittany* (London: A. W. Bennett, 1859): "To-day was the village 'Pardon,' and the whole popula-tion were assembled in the church to celebrate it."
[5]   Of or having to do with Brittany, a region also known as Armor.

in an adjoining field, noticed his approach. The man broke into song. His scandalized master attempted to stop him. But this bright bolshevik continued to sing an offensively carefree song under the nose of the supreme authority. The scandal did not pass unnoticed by the touchy destroyer. He shouted at him over the hedge, that for his insolence he had eight days to live, no more, which perhaps would teach him to sing etcetera! As it happened St. Peter was there. St. Peter's record leaves little question that a suppressed communist of an advanced type is concealed beneath the archangelical robes. It is a questionable policy to employ such a man as doorkeeper, and many popular airs in latin countries facetiously draw attention to the possibilities inherent in such a situation. In this case Peter was as scandalized at the behaviour of the Ankou as was the farmer at that of his farm-hand.

"Are you not ashamed, strange god, to condemn a man in that way, *at his work?*" he exclaimed. It was the *work* that did it, as far as Peter was concerned. Also it was his interference with work that brought his great misfortune on the Ankou. St. Peter, so the guide-book said, was as touchy as a captain of industry or a demagogue on that point. Though how could poor Death know that work, of all things, was sacred? Evidently he would have quite different ideas as to the attributes of divinity. But he had to pay immediately for his blunder. The revolutionary archangel struck him blind on the spot – struck Death blind; and, true to his character, that of one at all costs anxious for the applause of the *muchedumbre*,[6] he returned to the field, and told the astonished labourer, who was still singing – because in all probability he was a little soft in the head – that he had his personal guarantee of a very long and happy life, and that he, Peter, had punished Death with blindness. At this the labourer, I daresay, gave a hoarse laugh; and St. Peter probably made his way back to his victim well-satisfied in the reflection that he had won the favour of a vast mass of mortals.

In the accounts in the guide-book, it was the dating, however, connected with the tapping of owls, the crowing of hens, the significant evolutions of magpies, and especially the subsequent time-table involved in the lonely meetings with the plague-ridden death-cart, that seemed to me most effective. If the peasant were overtaken by the cart on the night-road towards the morning, he must die within the month. If the encounter is in the young night, he may have anything up to two years still to live. It was easy to imagine all the calculations indulged in by the distracted man after his evil meeting. I could hear his screaming voice (like those at the moment tearing at my ears as the groups of black-coated figures played some game of chance that maddened them) when he had crawled into the large, carved cupboard that served him for a bed, beside his wife, and how she would weigh this living, screaming, man, in the scales of time provided by superstition, and how the death damp would hang about him till his time had expired.

I was persuaded, finally, to go to Ploumilliau, and see the last statue of the blind Ankou. It was not many miles away. *Ervoanik Plouillo* – still to be seen for threepence: and while I was making plans for the necessary journey, my mind was powerfully haunted by that blind and hurrying apparition which had been so concrete there.

It was a long room where I sat, like a gallery: except during a Pardon it was not so popular. When I am reading something that interests me, the whole atmosphere is affected. If I look quickly up, I see things as though they were a part of a dream. They are all penetrated by the particular medium I have drawn out of my mind. What I had last read on this occasion, although my eyes at the moment were resting on the words *Ervoanik Plouillo*, was the account of how it affected the person's fate at what hour he met the Ankou. The din and smoke in the dark and crowded gallery was lighted by weak electricity, and a wet and lowering daylight beyond. Crowds of umbrellas moved past the door which opened on to the square. Whenever I grew attentive to my surroundings, the passionate movement of whirling and striking arms was visible at the tables where the play was in progress, or a furious black body would dash itself from one chair to another. The 'celtic screech' meantime growing harsher and harsher, sharpening itself on caustic snarling words, would soar to a paroxysm of energy. "Garce!"[7] was the most frequent sound. All the voices would clamour for a moment together. It was a shattering noise in this dusky tunnel. – I had stopped reading, as I have said, and I lifted my eyes. It was then that I saw the Ankou.

---

[6]   Spanish for "crowd."

[7]   French for "bitch" or "whore."

With revulsed and misty eyes almost in front of me, an imperious figure, apparently armed with a club, was forcing its way insolently forward towards the door, its head up, an eloquently moving mouth hung in the air, as it seemed, for its possessor. It forced rudely aside everything in its path. Two men who were standing and talking to a seated one flew apart, struck by the club, or the sceptre, of this king amongst afflictions. The progress of this embodied calamity was peculiarly straight. He did not deviate. He passed my table and I saw a small, highly coloured, face, with waxed moustaches. But the terrible perquisite of the blind was there in the staring, milky eyeballs: and an expression of acetic[8] ponderous importance weighted it so that, mean as it was in reality, this mask was highly impressive. Also, from its bitter immunity and unquestioned right-of-way, and from the habit of wandering through the outer jungle of physical objects, it had the look that some small boy's face might acquire, prone to imagine himself a steam-roller, or a sightless Juggernaut.

The blinded figure had burst into my daydream so unexpectedly and so pat, that I was taken aback by this sudden close-up of so trite a tragedy. Where he had come was compact with an emotional medium emitted by me. In reality it was a private scene, so that this overweening intruder might have been marching through my mind with his taut convulsive step, club in hand, rather than merely traversing the eating-room of a hotel, after a privileged visit to the kitchen. Certainly at that moment my mind was lying open so much, or was so much exteriorized, that almost literally, as far as I was concerned, it was inside, not out, that this image forced its way. Hence, perhaps, the strange effect.

The impression was so strong that I felt for the moment that I had met the death-god, a garbled version with waxed moustaches. It was noon. I said to myself that, as it was noon, that should give me twelve months more to live. I brushed aside the suggestion that day was not night, that I was not a breton peasant, and that the beggar was probably not Death. I tried to shudder. I had not shuddered. His attendant, a sad-faced child, rattled a lead mug under my nose. I put two sous in it. I had no doubt averted the omen, I reflected, with this bribe.

The weather improved in the afternoon. As I was walking about with a fisherman I knew, who had come in twenty miles for this Pardon, I saw the Ankou again, collecting pence. He was strolling now, making a leisurely harvest from the pockets of these religious crowds. His attitude was, however, peremptory. He called out hoarsely his requirements, and turned his empty eyes in the direction indicated by his acolyte, where he knew there was a group who had not paid. His clothes were smart, all in rich, black broadcloth and black velvet, with a ribboned hat. He entered into every door he found open, beating on it with his club-like stick. I did not notice any *Thank you!* pass his lips. He appeared to snort when he had received what was due to him, and to turn away, his legs beginning to march mechanically like a man mildly shell-shocked.

The fisherman and I both stood watching him. I laughed.

"Il ne se gêne pas!"[9] I said. "He does not *beg*. I don't call that a *beggar*."

"Indeed, you are right. — That is Ludo," I was told.

"Who is Ludo, then?" I asked.

"Ludo is the king of Rot!" my friend laughed. "The people round here spoil him, according to my idea. He's only a beggar. It's true he's blind. But he takes too much on himself."

He spat.

"He's not the only blind beggar in the world!"

"Indeed, he is not," I said.

"He drives off any other blind beggars that put their noses inside Rot. You see his stick? He uses it!"

We saw him led up to a party who had not noticed his approach. He stood for a moment shouting. From stupidity they did not respond at once. Turning violently away, he dragged his attendant after him.

"He must not be kept waiting!" I said.

"Ah, no. With Ludo you must be nimble!"

---

[8] Vinegary.   [9] "He is not ashamed in the least!"

The people he had left remained crestfallen and astonished.

"Where does he live?" I asked.

"Well, he lives, I have been told, in a cave, on the road to Kermarquer.[10] That's where he lives. Where he banks I can't tell you!"

Ludo approached us. He shouted in breton.

"What is he saying?"

"He is telling you to get ready; that he is coming!" said my friend. He pulled out a few sous from his pocket, and said: "Faut bien! Needs must!" and laughed a little sheepishly.

I emptied a handful of coppers into the mug.

"Ludo!" I exclaimed. "How are you? Are you well?"

He stood, his face in my direction, with, except for the eyes, his mask of an irritable Jack-in-office, with the waxed moustaches of a small pretentious official.

"Very well! And you?" came back with unexpected rapidity.

"Not bad, touching wood!" I said. "How is your wife?"

"Je suis garçon! I am a bachelor!" he replied at once.

"So you are better off, old chap!" I said. "Women serve no good purpose, for serious boys!"

"You are right," said Ludo. He then made a disgusting remark. We laughed. His face had not changed expression. Did he try, I wondered, to picture the stranger, discharging remarks from empty blackness, or had the voice outside become for him or had it always been what the picture is to us? If you had never seen any of the people you knew, but had only talked to them on the telephone – what under these circumstances would So-and-So be as a voice, I asked myself, instead of mainly a picture?

"How long have you been a beggar, Ludo?" I asked.

"Longtemps!" he replied. I had been too fresh for this important beggar. He got in motion and passed on, shouting in breton.

The fisherman laughed and spat.

"Quel type!"[11] he said. "When we were in Penang, no it was at Bankok, at the time of my service with the fleet, I saw just such another. He was a blind sailor, an Englishman. He had lost his sight in a shipwreck. – He would not beg from the black people."

"Why did he stop there?"

"He liked the heat. He was a *farceur*.[12] He was such another as this one."

Two days later I set out on foot for Kermarquer. I remembered as I was going out of the town that my friend had told me that Ludo's cave was there somewhere. I asked a woman working in a field where it was. She directed me.

I found him in a small, verdant enclosure, one end of it full of half-wild chickens, with a rocky bluff at one side, and a stream running in a bed of smooth boulders. A chimney stuck out of the rock, and a black string of smoke wound out of it. Ludo sat at the mouth of his cave. A large dog rushed barking towards me at my approach. I took up a stone and threatened it. His boy, who was cooking, called off the dog. He looked at me with intelligence.

"Good morning, Ludo!" I said. "I am an Englishman. I met you at the Pardon, do you remember? I have come to visit you, in passing. How are you? It's a fine day."

"Ah, it was you I met? I remember. You were with a fisherman from Kermanec?"

"The same."

"So you're an Englishman?"

"Yes."

"Tiens!"[13]

I did not think he looked well. My sensation of mock-superstition had passed. But although I was now familiar with Ludo, when I looked at his staring mask I still experienced a faint reflection of my first impression, when he was the death-god. That impression had been a strong one, and it was associated with superstition. So he was still a feeble death-god.

[10]   An imaginary toponym.
[11]   "What a character!"
[12]   A joker.
[13]   "Well, well!"

The bodies of a number of esculent[14] frogs lay on the ground, from which the back legs had been cut. These the boy was engaged in poaching.

"What is that you are doing them in?" I asked him.

"White wine," he said.

"Are they best that way?" I asked.

"Why, that is a good way to do them," said Ludo. "You don't eat frogs in England, do you?"

"No, that is repugnant to us."

I picked one up.

"You don't eat the bodies?"

"No, only the thighs," said the boy.

"Will you try one?" asked Ludo.

"I've just had my meal, thank you all the same."

I pulled out of my rucksack a flask of brandy.

"I have some eau-de-vie here," I said. "Will you have a glass?"

"I should be glad to," said Ludo.

I sat down, and in a few minutes his meal was ready. He disposed of the grenouilles[15] with relish, and drank my health in my brandy, and I drank his. The boy ate some fish that he had cooked for himself, a few yards away from us, giving small pieces to the dog.

After the meal Ludo sent the boy on some errand. The dog did not go with him. I offered Ludo a cigarette which he refused. We sat in silence for some minutes. As I looked at him I realized how the eyes mount guard over the face, as well as look out of it. The faces of the blind are hung there like a dead lantern. Blind people must feel on their skins our eyes upon them: but this sheet of flesh is rashly stuck up in what must appear far outside their control, an object in a foreign world of sight. So in consequence of this divorce, their faces have the appearance of things that have been abandoned by the mind. What is his face to a blind man? Probably nothing more than an organ, an exposed part of the stomach, that is a mouth.

Ludo's face, in any case, was *blind*; it looked the blindest part of his body, and perhaps the deadest, from which all the functions of a living face had gone. As a result of its irrelevant external situation, it carried on its own life with the outer world, and behaved with all the disinvolture of an internal organ, no longer serving to secrete thought any more than the foot. For after all to be lost *outside* is much the same as to be hidden in the dark *within*. – What served for a face for the blind, then? What did they have instead, that was expressive of emotion in the way that our faces are? I supposed that all the responsive machinery must be largely readjusted with them, and directed to some other part of the body. I noticed that Ludo's hands, all the movement of his limbs, were a surer indication of what he was thinking than was his face.

Still the face registered something. It was a health-chart perhaps. He looked very ill I thought, and by that I meant, of course, that his *face* did not look in good health. When I said, "You don't look well," his hands moved nervously on his club. His face responded by taking on a sicklier shade.

"I'm ill," he said.

"What is it?"

"I'm indisposed."

"Perhaps you've met the Ankou." I said this thoughtlessly, probably because I had intended to ask him if he had ever heard of the Ankou, or something like that. He did not say anything to this, but remained quite still, then stood up and shook himself and sat down again. He began rocking himself lightly from side to side.

"Who has been telling you about the Ankou, and all those tales?" he suddenly asked.

"Why, I was reading about it in a guide-book, as a matter of fact, the first time I saw you. You scared me for a moment. I thought you might be he."

He did not reply to this, nor did he say anything, but his face assumed the expression I had noticed on it when I first saw it, as he forced his way through the throngs at the inn.

"Do you think the weather will hold?" I asked.

---

[14] Edible.   [15] French for "frogs."

He made no reply. I did not look at him. With anybody with a face you necessarily feel that they can see you, even if their blank eyes prove the contrary. His fingers moved nervously on the handle of his stick. I felt that I had suddenly grown less popular. What had I done? I had mentioned an extinct god of death. Perhaps that was regarded as unlucky. I could not guess what had occurred to displease him.

"It was a good Pardon, was it not, the other day?" I said.

There was no reply. I was not sure whether he had not perhaps moods in which, owing to his affliction, he just entered into his shell, and declined to hold intercourse with the outside. I sat smoking for five minutes, I suppose, expecting that the boy might return. I coughed. He turned his head towards me.

"Vous êtes toujours là?"[16] he asked.

"Oui, toujours,"[17] I said. Another silence passed. He placed his hand on his side and groaned.

"Is there something hurting you?" I asked.

He got up and exclaimed:

"Merde!"[18]

Was that for me? I had the impression, as I glanced towards him to enquire, that his face expressed fear. Of what?

Still holding his side, shuddering and with an unsteady step, he went into his cave, the door of which he slammed. I got up. The dog growled as he lay before the door of the cave. I shouldered my rucksack. It was no longer a hospitable spot. I passed the midden on which the bodies of the grenouilles now lay, went down the stream, and so left. If I met the boy I would tell him his master was ill. But he was nowhere in sight, and I did not know which way he had gone.

I connected the change from cordiality to dislike on the part of Ludo with the mention of the Ankou. There seemed no other explanation. But why should that have affected him so much? Perhaps I had put myself in the position of the Ankou, even – unseen as I was, a foreigner and, so, ultimately dangerous – by mentioning the Ankou, with which he was evidently familiar. He may even have retreated into his cave, because he was afraid of me. Or the poor devil was simply ill. Perhaps the frogs had upset him: or maybe the boy had poisoned him. I walked away. I had gone a mile probably when I met the boy. He was carrying a covered basket.

"Ludo's ill. He went indoors," I said. "He seemed to be suffering."

"He's not very well to-day," said the boy. "Has he gone in?"

I gave him a few sous.

Later that summer the fisherman I had been with at the Pardon told me that Ludo was dead.

MANIFESTO (1914)

I.

1   Beyond Action and Reaction we would establish ourselves.

2   We start from opposite statements of a chosen world. Set up violent structure of adolescent clearness between two extremes.

3   We discharge ourselves on both sides.

4   We fight first on one side, then on the other, but always for the SAME cause, which is neither side or both sides and ours.

5   Mercenaries were always the best troops.

---

[16] "Are you still there."
[17] "Yes, still here."
[18] "Shit!"

6   We are Primitive Mercenarles in the Modern World.

7   Our *Cause* is NO-MAN'S.

8   We set Humour at Humour's throat. Stir up Civil War among peaceful apes.

9   We only want Humour if it has fought like Tragedy.

10   We only want Tragedy if it can clench its side-muscles like hands on it's belly, and bring to the surface a laugh like a bomb.

II.

1   We hear from America and the Continent all sorts of disagreeable things about England: "the unmusical, anti-artistic, unphilosophic country."

2   We quite agree.

3   Luxury, sport, the famous English "Humour," the thrilling ascendancy and idée fixe of Class, producing the most intense snobbery in the World; heavy stagnant pools of Saxon blood, incapable of anything but the song of a frog, in home-counties: – these phenomena give England a peculiar distinction in the wrong sense, among the nations.

4   This is why England produces such good artists from time to time.

5   This is also the reason why a movement towards art and imagination could burst up here, from this lump of compressed life, with more force than anywhere else.

6   To believe that it is necessary for or conducive to art, to "Improve" life, for instance – make architecture, dress, ornament, in "better taste," is absurd.[1]

7   The Art-instinct is permanently primitive.

8   In a chaos of imperfection, discord, etc., it finds the same stimulus as in Nature.

9   The artist of the modern movement is a savage (in no sense an "advanced," perfected, democratic, Futurist individual of Mr. Marinetti's limited imagination[2]): this enormous, jangling, journalistic, fairy desert of modern life serves him as Nature did more technically primitive man.

10   As the steppes and the rlgours of the Russian winter, when the peasant has to lie for weeks in his hut, produces that extraordinary acuity of feeling and intelligence we associate with the Slav; so England is just now the most favourable country for the appearance of a great art.

---

[1]   *To believe ... is absurd.* an attack on Roger Fry and the Omega Workshop which he had founded in 1913 with just this aim in mind.

[2]   *Mr. Marinetti's limited imagination* see the Introduction" to "Continental Interlude I: Futurism" and the related texts, pp. 1ff. above.

III.

1   We have made it quite clear that there is nothing Chauvinistic or picturesquely patriotic about our contentions.[3]

2   But there is violent boredom with that feeble Europeanism, abasement of the miserable "intellectual" before anything coming from Paris,[4] Cosmopolitan sentimentality, which prevails in so many quarters.

3   Just as we believe that an Art must be organic with its Time, So we insist that what is actual and vital for the South, is ineffectual and unactual in the North.[5]

4   Fairies have disappeared from Ireland (despite foolish attempts to revive them) and the bull-ring languishes in Spain.

5   But mysticism on the one hand, gladiatorial instincts, blood and asceticism on the other, will be always actual, and springs of Creation for these two peoples.

6   The English Character is based on the Sea.

7   The particular qualities and characteristics that the sea always engenders in men are those that are, among the many diagnostics of our race, the most fundamentally English.

8   That unexpected universality as well, found in the completest English artists, is due to this.

IV.

1   We assert that the art for these climates, then, must be a northern flower.

2   And we have implied what we believe should be the specific nature of the art destined to grow up in this country, and models of whose flue decorate the pages of this magazine.

3   It is not a question of the characterless material climate around us.
     Were that so the complication of the Jungle, dramatic Tropic growth, the vastness of American trees, would not be for us.

4   But our industries, and the Will that determined, face to face with its needs, the direction of the modern world, has reared up steel trees where the green ones were lacking; has exploded in useful growths, and found wilder intricacies than those of Nature.

---

[3]   *We have made it quite clear ... our contentions.* an attack on the patriotic claims of the Italian Futurists.
[4]   *anything coming from Paris* an attack on the art critic Roger Fry and hs praise of contemporary French painting, but also a criticism of Marinetti and the Italian Futurists, who had enjoyed considerable success in Paris before bringing their exhibition of paintings to London in March, 1912.
[5]   *inneffectual and unactual in the North* another attack on Italian Futurism ("the South").

V.

1 We bring clearly forward the following points, before further defining the character of this necessary native art.

2 At the freest and most vigorous period of ENGLAND'S history, her literature, then chief Art, was in many ways identical with that of France.

3 Chaucer was very much cousin of Villon as an artist.

4 Shakespeare and Montaigne formed one literature.

5 But Shakespeare reflected in his imagination a mysticism, madness and delicacy peculiar to the North, and brought equal quantities of Comic and Tragic together.

6 Humour is a phenomenon caused by sudden pouring of culture into Barbary.

7 It is intelligence electrified by flood of Naivety.

8 It is Chaos invading Concept and bursting it like nitrogen.

9 It is the Individual masquerading as Humanity like a child in clothes too big for him.

10 Tragic Humour is the birthright of the North.

11 Any great Northern Art will partake of this insidious and volcanic chaos.

12 No great ENGLISH Art need be ashamed to share some glory with France, to-morrow it may be with Germany, where the Elizabethans did before it.

13 But it will never be French, any more than Shakespeare was, the most catholic and subtle Englishman.

VI.

1 The Modern World is due almost entirely to Anglo-Saxon genius, – its appearance and its spirit.

2 Machinery, trains, steam-ships, all that distinguishes externally our time, came far more from here than anywhere else.

3 In dress, manners, mechanical inventions, LIFE, that is, ENGLAND, has influenced Europe in the same way that France has in Art.

4 But busy with this LIFE-EFFORT, she has been the last to become conscious of the Art that is an organism of this new Order and Will of Man.

5   Machinery is the greatest Earth-medium: incidentally it sweeps away the doctrines of a narrow and pedantic Realism at one stroke.

6   By mechanical inventiveness, too, just as English-men have spread themselves all over the Earth, they have brought all the hemispheres about them in their original island.

7   It cannot be said that the complication of the Jungle, dramatic tropic growths, the vastness of American trees, is not for us.

8   For, in the forms of machinery, Factories, new and vaster buildings, bridges and works, we have all that, naturally, around us.

VII.

1   Once this consciousness towards the new possibilities of expression in present life has come, however, it will be more the legitimate property of English-men than of any other people in Europe.

2   It should also, as it is by origin theirs, inspire them more forcibly and directly.

3   They are the inventors of this bareness and hardness, and should be the great enemies of Romance.

4   The Romance peoples will always be, at bottom, its defenders.

5   The Latins are at present, for instance, in their "discovery" of sport, their Futuristic gush over machines, aeroplanes, etc., the most romantic and sentimental "moderns" to be found.

6   It is only the second-rate people in France or Italy who are thorough revolutionaries.

7   In England, on the other hand, there is no vulgarity in revolt.

8   Or, rather, there is no revolt, it is the normal state.

9   So often rebels of the North and the South are diametrically opposed species.

10   The nearest thing in England to a great traditional French artist, is a great revolutionary English one.

Signatures for Manifesto[6]

R. Aldington

Arbuthnot

L. Atkinson

Gaudier Brzeska

J. Dismorr

C. Hamilton

E. Pound

W. Roberts

H. Sanders

E. Wadsworth

Wyndham Lewis

---

[6] Of the 11 people who signed the "Manifesto" of Vorticism, two were authors. Richard Aldington (1892–1962) was thought of at this time as an Imagist poet. He went on to become an esteemed novelist and critic. On the poet Ezra Pound, see p. 39. Malcolm Arbuthnot (1877–1967) was a British photographer, painter, and watercolorist who, after marrying someone wealthy in 1931, retired to the island of Jersey. Lawrence Atkinson (1873–1914) had a multiplicity of interests as a singer, poet, and painter. He participated briefly in the Rebel Art Centre, the chief institution of Vorticism, and exhibited in the first exhibition of Vorticism. From 1918 until his death Atkinson concentrated on severe, near-abstract carvings. Henri Gaudier-Brzeska (1891–1915) was a Polish sculptor who had migrated to London; for many critics he was, together with Jacob Epstein, the most talented sculptor at work in London before the First World War. He left many works, including a *Hieratic Head of Ezra Pound*. He was killed in the war in early 1915 and was commemorated by Ezra Pound in a brief book, *Gaudier-Brzeska: A Memoir* (London and New York: John Lane, 1916). Jessica Dismorr (1885–1939) studied fine arts at the Slade School in London, then studied with various painters in Paris during the period 1910–13. She became associated with the Vorticists, exhibited with them in 1915, and exhibited again with Wyndham Lewis in the *Group X* exhibition in 1920. She suffered from recurrent bouts of depression and died by her own hand just before the outbreak of the Second World War. Cuthbert Hamilton (1885–1959) was a British artist and sculptor who joined Roger Fry's Omega Workshops in 1913, then broke with it to join Wyndham Lewis and the Vorticists in 1914. After completing his wartime duties as a special constable, he exhibited again with Lewis in the *Group X* exhibition in 1920. Shortly thereafter he founded Yeoman Potteries, a firm which became his principal concern for the rest of his life. William Roberts (1895–1980) was a promising artist who had won a scholarship to the Slade School in London. Like Cuthbert Hamilton, he had joined Rober Fry's Omega Workshops in 1913, then broke with it to join Wyndham Lewis and the Vorticists in 1914. During the 1920s he took up a style of stripped-down portraiture, with stiff and stylized figures, and continued to work in this style throughout the 1970s. He was given a retrospective exhibition at the Tate Gallery in 1965 and then was elected to the Royal Academy a year later. Helen Saunders (1885–1963) studied at the Slade and the Central School of Arts and Crafts and was among the handful of women artists active in the Modernist avant-garde before the First World War. A regular exhibitor at Vorticist exhibitions, she was reluctant to exhibit her work after 1916 and there are no published sources to document her long career as an artist. Her later works included landscape, still-life, and portraits of friends. An exhibition of works from her entire life was held at the Ashmoleon Museum, Oxford University, in January to March 1996. Edward Wadsworth (1889–1949) was born in Cleckheaton, Yorkshire. He studied engineering, then turned to art in 1907, obtaining a scholarship to the Slade School from 1908 to 12. He joined Roger Fry's Omega Workshops, then seceded and joined Wyndham Lewis and the Vorticists. During the war he was charged with designing dazzle camouflage for ships. After the war, in 1920, he exhibited a series of woodcuts depicting facets of life in the coal-mining districts of Lancashire, *The Black Country* (London: Ovid Press, 1920), a series still much esteemed by collectors. During the rest of his career he alternated between realist and Cubistic modes of painting.

Inferior Religions (1917)

I

To introduce my puppets, and the Wild Body, the generic puppet of all, I must look back to a time when the antics and solemn gambols of these wild children filled me with triumph.

The fascinating imbecility of the creaking men-machines some little restaurant or fishing-boat works, is the subject of these studies. The boat's tackle and dirty little shell keep their limbs in a monotonous rhythm of activity. A man gets drunk with his boat as he would with a merry-go-round. Only it is the staid, everyday drunkeness of the normal real. We can all see the ascendance a "carrousel" has on men, driving them into a set narrow intoxication. The wheel at Carisbrooke[1] imposes a set of movements on the donkey inside it, in drawing water from the well, that it is easy to grasp. But in the case of a fishing-boat the variety is so great, the scheme so complex, that it passes as open and untrammeled life. This subtle and wider mechanism merges, for the spectator, in the general variety of Nature. Yet we have in most lives a spectacle as complete as a problem of Euclid.

Moran, Bestre and Brobdingnag[2] are essays in a new human mathematic. But they are each simple shapes, little monuments of logic. I should like to compile a book of forty of these propositions, one deriving from and depending on the other.

These intricately moving bobbins are all subject to a set of objects or one in particular. Brobdingnag is fascinated by one object for instance; one at once another vitality. He bangs up against it wildly at regular intervals, blackens it, contemplates it, moves round it and dreams. All such fascination is religious. Moran's damp napkins are the altar cloths of his rough illusion, Julie's bruises are the markings on an idol.

These studies of rather primitive people are studies in a savage worship and attraction. Moran rolls between his tables ten million times in a realistic rhythm that is as intense and superstitious as the figures of a war-dance. He worships his soup, his damp napkins, the lump of flesh that rolls everywhere with him called Madame Moran.

INFERIOR RELIGIONS

This essay was first published in the *Little Review* 4(5) (Sept. 1917). It was accompanied by an "Editor's Note" written by Ezra Pound:

> This essay was written as the introduction to a volume of short stories containing "Inn-Keepers and Bestre," "Unlucky for Pringle," and some others ... The book was in process of publication (the author had even been paid an advance on it) when war broke out. The last member of the publishing firm has been killed in France, and the firm disbanded. The essay is complete in itself and need not stand as an "introduction." It is perhaps the most important single document that Wyndham Lewis has written.

The essay draws heavily on, but also sharply revises, the theory of comedy developed by the French philosopher Henri Bergson in his book, *Le Rire: essai sur la signification du comique* (Paris: Félix Alcan, 1900), a work widely discussed throughout Europe and translated into English in 1911, by Cloudesley Brereton and Fred Rothwell, under the title *Laughter: An Essay on the Meaning of the Comic* (London: Macmillan & Co., 1911). Bergson's theory of comedy depends on his assumption that matter (the body), conceived as inert material or raw thing-ness that is active only through automatism, differs starkly from life (*élan*, or spirit), which possesses an irreducibly purposive dimension:

> The comic is that side of a person in which he resembles a thing; it is that aspect of human events which, by a special kind of rigidity, imitates a mechanism pure and simple, an automatism, a lifeless movement. It thus expresses an individual or collective imperfection which calls for immediate correction. Laughter is this very corrective. (Bergson, *Oeuvre Complètes*, 66–7)

The comic, in this view, is the result of life celebrating its distance from matter and the merely mechanical. But Lewis reverses the hierarchic polarity implicit in Bergson's thought: for him, the comic results from life recognizing its identity with the material and mechanical. The outcome is the grim and cruel form of humor that Lewis revels in, a celebration of what he calls "the wild body."

[1] Carisbrooke Castle, a medieval fortress on the Isle of Wight which once featured, in a courtyard, a donkey that drew water from a well.

[2] Moran is a fictional character in a story that Lewis wrote and subsequently lost, or one that he planned to write but never did. Bestre is a fictional character who appears in a story that Lewis wrote and published in three different versions (see pp. 189–95). Brobdingnag is a fictional character in a short story of the same name, published in *The New Age* of January 5, 1911. In 1927 the story was heavily revised, its name changed from "Brobdingnag" to "Brotcotnaz," and published in *The Wild Body* (London: Chatto and Windus, 1927). For the texts of both

All religion has the mechanism of the celestial bodies, has a dance. When we wish to renew our idols, or break up the rhythm of our naïvety, the effort postulates a respect which is the summit of devoutness.

II

I would present these puppets, then, as carefully selected specimens of religious fanaticism. With their attendant objects or fetishes they live and have a regular food for vitality. They are not creations but puppets. You can be as exterior to them, and live their life as little, as the showman grasping from beneath and working about a Polichinelle.[3] They are only shadows of energy, and not living beings. Their mechanism is a logical structure and they are nothing but that.

Sam Weller, Jingle, Malvolio, Bouvard and Pécuchet,[4] the "commissaire" in *Crime and Punishment*, do not live; they are congealed and frozen into logic, and an exuberant, hysterical truth. They transcend life and are complete cyphers, but they are monuments of dead imperfection. Their only reference is to themselves, and their only significance their egoism.

The great intuitive figures of creation live with the universal egoism of the Poet. They are not picturesque and over palpable. They are supple with this rare impersonality; not stiff with a common egotism. The "realists" of the Flaubert, Maupassant, and Tchekoff school are all satirists. "Realism", understood as applied to them, implies either photography or satire.

Satire, the great Heaven of Ideas, where you meet the Titans of red laughter, is just below Intuition, and Life charged with black Illusion.

III

When we say "types of humanity," we mean violent individualities, and nothing stereotyped. But Othello, Falstaff and Pecksniff attract, in our memory, a vivid following. All difference is energy, and a category of humanity a relatively small group, and not the myriads suggested by a generalisation.

A comic type is a failure of considerable energy, an imitation and standardising of self, suggesting the existence of a uniform humanity, – creating, that is, a little host as like as ninepins; instead of one synthetic and various Ego. It is the laziness of a successful personality. It is often part of our own organism become a fetish.

Sarah Gamp and Falstaff[5] are minute and rich religions. They are illusions hugged and lived in. They are like little dead Totems. Just as all Gods are a repose for humanity, the big religions an important refuge and rest, so these little grotesque idols are. One reason for this is that, for the spectator or participator, it is a world in a corner of the world, full of rest and security.

Moran, even, advances in life with his rows of bottles and napkins; Julie is Brobdingnag's Goddess, and figures for intercessions, if the occasion arises.

All these are forms of static and traditional art, then. There is a great deal of divine Olympian sleep in English Humour. The most gigantic spasm of laughter is sculptural, isolated and essentially simple.

IV

1   Laughter is the Wild Body's song of triumph.
2   Laughter is the climax in the tragedy of seeing, hearing and smelling self-consciously.
3   Laughter is the bark of delight of a gregarious animal at the proximity of its kind.
4   Laughter is an independent, tremendously important, and lurid emotion.

---

versions, see Bernard Lafourcade (ed.), *The Complete Wild Body* (Santa Barbara, CA: Black Sparrow, 1982), pp. 133–48, 291–8.

[3]   The French name for a Punch and Judy puppet.

[4]   Sam Weller and Jingle are comic characters in Charles Dickens's *Pickwick Papers* (1836); Malvolio is a comic character in Shakespeare's *Twelfth Night* (1602); Bouvard and Pécuchet are the comic heroes of Gustave Flaubert's novel of the same name (1880).

[5]   Fictional characters in Charles Dickens's novel *Martin Chuzzlewit* (1843–4) and Shakespeare's *Henry IV* (1598) and *The Merry Wives of Windsor* (1599).

5   Laughter is the representative of Tragedy, when Tragedy is away.
6   Laughter is the emotion of tragic delight.
7   Laughter is the female of Tragedy.
8   Laughter is the strong elastic fish, caught in Styx, springing and flapping about until it dies.
9   Laughter is the sudden handshake of mystic violence and the anarchist.
10 Laughter is the mind sneezing.
11 Laughter is the one obvious commotion that is not complex, or in expression dynamic.
12 Laughter does not progress. It is primitive, hard and unchangeable.

V

The chemistry of personality (subterranean in a sort of cemetery whose decompositions are our lives) puffs in frigid balls, soapy Snow-men, arctic Carnival-Masks, which we can photograph and fix.

Upwards from the surface of Existence a lurid and dramatic scum oozes and accumulates into the characters we see. The real and tenacious poisons, and sharp forces of vital vitality, do not socially transpire. Within five yards of another man's eyes, we are on a little crater, which, if it erupted, would split up as a cocoa-tin of nitrogen would. Some of these bombs are ill-made, or some erratic in their timing. But they are all potential little bombs.

Capriciously, however, the froth-forms of these darkly-contrived machines, twist and puff in the air, in our legitimate and liveried masquerade.

Were you the female of Moran (the first Innkeeper) and beneath the counterpane with him, you would be just below the surface of life, in touch with a nasty and tragic organism. The first indications of the proximity of the real soul would be apparent. You would be for hours beside a filmy crocodile, conscious of it like a bone in an Ex-Ray, and for minutes in the midst of a tragic wallowing. The soul lives in a cadaverous activity; its dramatic corruption thumps us like a racing engine in the body of a car. The finest humour is the great Play-Shapes blown up or given off by the tragic corpse of Life underneath the world of the Camera. This futile, grotesque and sometimes pretty spawn, is what in this book is Kodacked by the Imagination.

Any great humourist is an artist; Dickens as an example. It is just this character of uselessness and impersonality in Laughter, the fibre of anarchy in the comic habit of mind, that makes a man an artist in spite of himself when he begins living on his laughter. Laughter is the arch-luxury that is as simple as bread.

VI

In this objective Play-World, corresponding to our social consciousness as opposed to our solitude, no final issue is decided. You may blow away a Man-of-bubbles with a Burgundian gust of laughter, but that is not a personality, it is an apparition of no importance. Its awkwardness, or prettiness is accidental. But so much correspondence it has with its original that if the cadaveric travail beneath is vigorous and bitter, the mask and figurehead will be of a more original and intense grotesqueness. The opposing armies in Flanders stick up dummy men on poles for their enemies to pot at, in a spirit of fierce friendliness. It is only a dummy of this sort that is engaged in the sphere of laughter. But the real men are in the trenches underneath all the time, and are there on a more "decisive" affair. In our rather drab Revel there is certain category of spirit that is not quite anaemic, and yet not very funny. It consists of those who take, at the Clarkson's[6] situated at the opening of their lives, some conventional Pierrot costume, with a minimum of inverted vigour and the assurance of superior insignificance.

---

[6] "A London theatrical costumer," according to an "Editor's note" written by Ezra Pound.

The King of Play is not a phantom corresponding to the Sovereign force beneath the surface. The latter must always be accepted as the skeleton of the Feast. That soul or dominant corruption is so real that he cannot rise up and take part in man's festival as a Falstaff of unwieldy spume; if he comes at all it must be as he is, the skeleton or bogey of True Life, stuck over corruptions and vices. He may a certain "succès d' hystérie."

VII

A scornful optimism, with its confident onslaughts on our snobbism, will not make material existence a peer for our energy. The gladiator is not a perpetual monument of triumphant health. Napoleon was harried with Elbas. Moments of vision are blurred rapidly and the poet sinks into the rhetoric of the will.

But life is invisible and perfection is not in the waves or houses that the poet sees. Beauty is an icy douche of ease and happiness at something suggesting perfect conditions for an organism. A stormy landscape, and a Pigment consisting of a lake of hard, yet florid waves; delight in each brilliant scoop or ragged burst, was John Constable's[7] beauty. Leonardo's consisted in a red rain on the shadowed side of heads, and heads of massive female aesthetes. Uccello[8] accumulated pale parallels, and delighted in cold architectures of distinct colour. Korin[9] found in the symmetrical gushing of water, in waves like huge vegetable insects, traced and worked faintly, on a golden pâte, his business. Cézanne liked cumbrous, democratic slabs of life, slightly leaning, transfixed in vegetable intensity.

Beauty is an immense predilection, a perfect conviction of the desirability of a certain thing. To a man with long and consumptive fingers a sturdy hand may be heaven. Equilibrium and "perfection" may be a bore to the perfect. The most *universally* pleasing man is something probably a good way from "perfection." Henri Fabre was in every way a superior being to Bernard,[10] and he knew of elegant grubs which he would prefer to the painter's nymphs.

It is obvious, though, that we should live a little more in small communities.

---

[7] John Constable (1776–1837) was an English painter, one of the greatest British landscape artists.
[8] Paolo di Dono, known as Paolo Uccello (1397–1475), was a Florentine painter and mosaicist.
[9] Ogata Korin (1658–1716) was a Japanese artist whose famous landscapes are often set against a gold background.

[10] On Henri Fabre, the French entomologist, see p. 191, n. 17; Emile Bernard (1868–1941) was a French painter and writer who associated with Gauguin, Cézanne, and others, and who continued to paint well after 1900 in a style that had become conspcuously dated.

James Joyce (1882–1941)

James Joyce was born in Dublin, the son an improvident father who had drifted into politics and been rewarded for helping secure a Liberal victory in the general elections of 1880, granted the post of Collector of Rates or taxes for Dublin, one which earned the princely salary of £500 per year. The position was taken away from him in 1892 and he was given a pension of £132 per year. Joyce, in effect, grew up in two worlds: first, a middle-class one, from birth to age 12; then a world of sham gentility as his father's improvidence made it increasingly difficult for him to support his 10 children. The family moved from house to house, often leaving rents unpaid. He attended University College, a Catholic institution struggling for distinction. After graduating, he tried writing poems and short stories, went to Paris briefly to study medicine, then returned to Dublin. On June 10, 1904, he met Nora Barnacle, a young woman from Galway. Four months later, though still not married (their marriage would only take place much later, in 1931), the two left Ireland to move to the Continent. They had only enough money to travel to Paris, but Joyce stopped in London, borrowed more, and the couple made it to Trieste, at that time a part of the Austro-Hungarian Empire (though most of its inhabitants were Italian). There Joyce would reside for more than a decade. He became a teacher of English at the local Berlitz school and took up writing in earnest. He completed *Dubliners*, and by 1913 had begun to work on *Portrait of the Artist as a Young Man*. His life changed forever in late 1913 when he received a letter from Ezra Pound, who had been told about Joyce by William Butler Yeats, asking if he had any materials that Pound might see for any of several journals with which he was connected. Joyce sent him *Dubliners* and the first chapter of *Portrait*. "In Ezra Pound," as Joyce's great biographer Richard Ellmann wrote, "as eager to discover as Joyce was to be discovered, the writings of Joyce found their missionary."

Pound arranged for serial publication of *Portrait* in the *Egoist*, a monthly journal devoted to philosophical ideas about "egoism." The journal had some 200 subscribers and was supported by subsidies from Harriet Shaw Weaver, a prim Englishwoman who had a deep sense of her duty to contribute to bettering the world. Joyce now had an audience, however small, and he relished it. In 1917, *A Portrait of the Artist* was published by the Egoist Press, the book-publishing wing of Harriet's enterprise. By then Joyce was already at work on *Ulysses*, widely recognized as the greatest novel of the twentieth century, and was living in Zurich, where he had moved with his family after the outbreak of the Great War. Though he was paid for installments of *Ulysses*, the sums were too little to make ends meet, and in 1916 Harriet Shaw Weaver began to act as Joyce's patron, sending him small but essential sums on an increasingly regular basis. Joyce, as improvident as his father, never found the money to be enough, but he continued to work with extraordinary energy on *Ulysses*. He had decided that each chapter would be written in a different style, but it was with episode 7, "Aeolous," that this ambition became more pronounced. Joyce was clearly fascinated by the idea of having an audience (he probably didn't know just how small it was), and he was determined to dazzle. Each episode now became the occasion for a bravura performance, and Joyce became ever more determined to disturb, startle, and provoke. In 1919 the *Egoist* ceased publication, but *Ulysses* continued to enjoy serial publication in the *Little Review*, an American journal with which Pound had become involved. In 1920 he moved to Paris, largely at Pound's urging (Pound himself was moving there that spring), and he now contemplated the final episodes of his epic work. But because the *Little Review* was charged late that year with publishing obscenity when it had issued episode 13, or "Nausicaa," the prospects for book publication grew clouded, both in the United States and Britain. In April 1921, Sylvia Beach, an American who owned an English-language bookshop in Paris, offered to take on the novel, a limited and deluxe edition to be issued in 1,000 copies. Harriet Shaw Weaver, meanwhile, was still proceeding with her plans for a normal English edition. Beach dissuaded her from proceeding, since that edition would lessen demand for the deluxe one. Joyce, meanwhile worked frantically on the book's final episodes, simultaneously writing these while he revised all the earlier ones as they went through proof. He completed the last writing on October 30, 1921, though proofs for the later episodes kept coming in. Finally, on February 2, 1922, the first copies of *Ulysses* arrived in Paris. Within 18 weeks the edition was sold out, and by September 1922, copies which had originally sold at £3 3s. were selling in London and New York for as much as £40. The next year Beach did a second edition, and each year she did another until 1935, when a celebrated court ruling declared the book not indecent, and hence publishable in the US.

Weaver, meanwhile, settled £23,000 on Joyce, a sum that meant his annual income from it was £1,050 per year, a sizeable figure in those days. Joyce now turned his attention to *Finnegans Wake*, a project that would culminate with that work's publication in 1939. When he died in 1941, all of Weaver's money had disappeared. Joyce had consumed not just the income, but also the principal.

Araby[1] *(1914), from* Dubliners

North Richmond Street,[2] being blind,[3] was a quiet street except at the hour when the Christian Brothers' School[4] set the boys free. An uninhabited house of two storeys stood at the blind end, detached from its neighbours in a square ground. The other houses of the street, conscious of decent lives within them, gazed at one another with brown imperturbable faces.

The former tenant of our house, a priest, had died in the back drawing-room. Air, musty from having been long enclosed, hung in all the rooms, and the waste room behind the kitchen was littered with old useless papers. Among these I found a few paper-covered books, the pages of which were curled and damp: *The Abbot*, by Walter Scott,[5] *The Devout Communicant*[6] and *The Memoirs of Vidocq*.[7] I liked the last best because its leaves were yellow. The wild garden behind the house contained a central apple-tree and a few straggling bushes under one of which I found the late tenant's rusty bicycle-pump. He had been a very charitable priest; in his will he had left all his money to institutions and the furniture of his house to his sister.

When the short days of winter came dusk fell before we had well eaten our dinners. When we met in the street the houses had grown sombre. The space of sky above us was the colour of ever-changing violet and towards it the lamps of the street lifted their feeble lanterns. The cold air stung us and we played till our bodies glowed. Our shouts echoed in the silent street. The career of our play brought us through the dark muddy lanes behind the houses where we ran the gantlet[8] of the rough tribes from the cottages, to the back doors of the dark dripping gardens where odours arose from the ashpits, to the dark odorous stables where a coachman smoothed and combed the horse or shook music from the buckled harness. When we returned to the street light from the kitchen windows had filled the areas.[9] If my uncle was seen turning the corner we hid in the shadow until we had seen him safely housed. Or if Mangan's sister[10] came out on the doorstep to call her brother in to his tea we watched her from our shadow peer up and down the street. We waited to see whether she would remain or go in and, if she remained, we left our shadow and walked up to Mangan's steps resignedly. She was waiting for us, her figure defined by the light from the half-opened door. Her brother always teased her before he obeyed and I stood by the railings looking at her. Her dress swung as she moved her body and the soft rope of her hair tossed from side to side.

Every morning I lay on the floor in the front parlour watching her door. The blind was pulled down to within an inch of the sash so that I could not be seen. When she came out on the doorstep my heart leaped. I ran to the hall, seized my books and followed her. I kept her brown figure always in my eye and, when we came near the point at which our ways diverged, I quickened my pace and passed her. This happened morning after morning. I had never spoken to her, except for a few casual words, and yet her name was like a summons to all my foolish blood.

---

[1]   Araby is a poetic name for Arabia. The bazaar in this story took place between May 14 and 19, 1894, in aid of Jervis Street Hospital, and its theme song was "I'll sing these songs of Araby." The title may also allude to the Irish poet Thomas Moore (1772–1859) and his ballad, "Farewell – Farewell to Thee, Araby's Daughter."

[2]   A street on the north side of the city.

[3]   A dead-end or cul-de-sac.

[4]   A Roman Catholic school for boys, one of many of the same name which made strenuous efforts on behalf of the Irish poor. Joyce attended the one in North Richmond Street in 1893.

[5]   A novel (1820), one that deals with Mary Queen of Scots and the social crisis of the Protestant Reformation, by Sir Walter Scott (1771–1832).

[6]   Work of Catholic devotional literature by Pacificus Baker (1695–1774), an English Franciscan.

[7]   Memoirs by François-Eugène Vidocq (1775–1857), a sensationalist account of a criminal turned detective, translated into English by the Irishman William Maginn (1793–1842) in 1828 and reprinted countless times.

[8]   *gantlet* absolete spelling of *gauntlet*.

[9]   The sunken space at the front of Victorian buildings which was meant to provide light to the basements or cellars of houses.

[10]   Perhaps alluding to the Irish romantic poet James Clarence Mangan (1803–49) and his works of doomed love and biting despair.

Her image accompanied me even in places the most hostile to romance. On Saturday evenings when my aunt went marketing I had to go to carry some of the parcels. We walked through the flaring streets, jostled by drunken men and bargaining women, amid the curses of labourers, the shrill litanies of shop-boys who stood on guard by the barrels of pigs' cheeks, the nasal chanting of street-singers, who sang a *come-all-you*[11] about O'Donovan Rossa,[12] or a ballad about the troubles in our native land.[13] These noises converged in a single sensation of life for me: I imagined that I bore my chalice safely through a throng of foes. Her name sprang to my lips at moments in strange prayers and praises which I myself did not understand. My eyes were often full of tears (I could not tell why) and at times a flood from my heart seemed to pour itself out into my bosom. I thought little of the future. I did not know whether I would ever speak to her or not or, if I spoke to her, how I could tell her of my confused adoration. But my body was like a harp and her words and gestures were like fingers running upon the wires.

One evening I went into the back drawing-room in which the priest had died. It was a dark rainy evening and there was no sound in the house. Through one of the broken panes I heard the rain impinge upon the earth, the fine incessant needles of water playing in the sodden beds. Some distant lamp or lighted window gleamed below me. I was thankful that I could see so little. All my senses seemed to desire to veil themselves and, feeling that I was about to slip from them, I pressed the palms of my hands together until they trembled, murmuring: *O love! O love!* many times.

At last she spoke to me. When she addressed the first words to me I was so confused that I did not know what to answer. She asked me was I going to *Araby*. I forget whether I answered yes or no. It would be a splendid bazaar, she said; she would love to go.

— And why can't you? I asked.

While she spoke she turned a silver bracelet round and round her wrist. She could not go, she said, because there would be a retreat that week in her convent. Her brother and two other boys were fighting for their caps and I was alone at the railings. She held one of the spikes, bowing her head towards me. The light from the lamp opposite our door caught the white curve of her neck, lit up her hair that rested there and, falling, lit up the hand upon the railing. It fell over one side of her dress and caught the white border of a petticoat, just visible as she stood at ease.

— It's well for you, she said.

— If I go, I said, I will bring you something.

What innumerable follies laid waste my waking and sleeping thoughts after that evening! I wished to annihilate the tedious intervening days. I chafed against the work of school. At night in my bedroom and by day in the classroom her image came between me and the page I strove to read. The syllables of the word *Araby* were called to me through the silence in which my soul luxuriated and cast an Eastern enchantment over me. I asked for leave to go to the bazaar on Saturday night. My aunt was surprised and hoped it was not some Freemason affair.[14] I answered few questions in class. I watched my master's face pass from amiability to sternness; he hoped I was not beginning to idle. I could not call my wandering thoughts together. I had hardly any patience with the serious work of life which, now that it stood between me and my desire, seemed to me child's play, ugly monotonous child's play.

On Saturday morning I reminded my uncle that I wished to go to the bazaar in the evening. He was fussing at the hallstand, looking for the hat-brush, and answered me curtly:

— Yes, boy, I know.

---

[11] "Come all you gallant Irishmen and listen to my song" was a conventional beginning to many popular songs and ballads.

[12] Jeremiah O'Donovan (1831–95) was a Fenian revolutionary and Member of Parliament elected in 1869 while serving a life sentence for treason-felony. He was nicknamed Dynamite Rossa.

[13] Irish nationalism drew on a vast repertoire of self-pitying ballads which recounted Ireland's wrongs and the daring deeds of patriots.

[14] The Masons were thought to be influential in the professional life of Victorian Protestant Dublin. Roman Catholics suspected them of atheism, anti-Catholicism, and Protestant bigotry.

As he was in the hall I could not go into the front parlour and lie at the window. I left the house in bad humour and walked slowly towards the school. The air was pitilessly raw and already my heart misgave me.

When I came home to dinner my uncle had not yet been home. Still it was early. I sat staring at the clock for some time and, when its ticking began to irritate me, I left the room. I mounted the staircase and gained the upper part of the house. The high cold empty gloomy rooms liberated me and I went from room to room singing. From the front window I saw my companions playing below in the street. Their cries reached me weakened and indistinct and, leaning my forehead against the cool glass, I looked over at the dark house where she lived. I may have stood there for an hour, seeing nothing but the brown-clad figure cast by my imagination, touched discreetly by the lamplight at the curved neck, at the hand upon the railings and at the border below the dress.

When I came downstairs again I found Mrs Mercer sitting at the fire. She was an old garrulous woman, a pawnbroker's widow, who collected used stamps for some pious purpose.[15] I had to endure the gossip of the tea-table. The meal was prolonged beyond an hour and still my uncle did not come. Mrs Mercer stood up to go: she was sorry she couldn't wait any longer, but it was after eight o'clock and she did not like to be out late, as the night air was bad for her. When she had gone I began to walk up and down the room, clenching my fists. My aunt said:

— I'm afraid you may put off your bazaar for this night of Our Lord.[16]

At nine o'clock I heard my uncle's latchkey in the halldoor. I heard him talking to himself and heard the hallstand rocking when it had received the weight of his overcoat. I could interpret these signs. When he was midway through his dinner I asked him to give me the money to go to the bazaar. He had forgotten.

— The people are in bed and after their first sleep now, he said.

I did not smile. My aunt said to him energetically:

— Can't you give him the money and let him go? You've kept him late enough as it is.

My uncle said he was very sorry he had forgotten. He said he believed in the old saying: *All work and no play makes Jack a dull boy.* He asked me where I was going and, when I had told him a second time he asked me did I know *The Arab's Farewell to his Steed.*[17] When I left the kitchen he was about to recite the opening lines of the piece to my aunt.

I held a florin[18] tightly in my hand as I strode down Buckingham Street[19] towards the station. The sight of the streets thronged with buyers and glaring with gas recalled to me the purpose of my journey. I took my seat in a third-class carriage of a deserted train. After an intolerable delay the train moved out of the station slowly. It crept onward among ruinous houses and over the twinkling river. At Westland Row Station[20] a crowd of people pressed to the carriage doors; but the porters moved them back, saying that it was a special train for the bazaar. I remained alone in the bare carriage. In a few minutes the train drew up beside an improvised wooden platform. I passed out on to the road and saw by the lighted dial of a clock that it was ten minutes to ten. In front of me was a large building which displayed the magical name.

I could not find any sixpenny entrance and, fearing that the bazaar would be closed, I passed in quickly through a turnstile, handing a shilling to a weary-looking man. I found myself in a big hall girdled at half its height by a gallery. Nearly all the stalls were closed and the greater part of the hall was in darkness. I recognized a silence like that which pervades a church after a service. I walked into the centre of the bazaar timidly. A few people were gathered about the stalls which were still open. Before a curtain, over which the words *Café Chantant*[21] were written in coloured lamps, two men were counting money on a salver. I listened to the fall of the coins.

Remembering with difficulty why I had come I went over to one of the stalls and examined porcelain vases and flowered tea-sets. At the door of the stall a young lady was talking and laughing

---

[15]   Postage stamps were collected and sold to collectors, with the proceeds going to some church cause, typically foreign missions.

[16]   Pious and conventional reference to the present evening.

[17]   Poem by the Irish poet Caroline Norton (1808–77), one often recited for school prizes.

[18]   A silver coin worth 2 shillings when there were 20 shillings to the pound; for the boy in the story, a vast sum.

[19]   Street on the north side of the Liffey in central Dublin.

[20]   A railway station on the south side of the Liffey.

[21]   A Parisian institution which, being imported into Dublin, was meant to evoke romance and risqué temptation.

with two young gentlemen. I remarked their English accents and listened vaguely to their conversation.

— O, I never said such a thing!

— O, but you did!

— O, but I didn't!

— Didn't she say that?

— Yes. I heard her.

— O, there's a . . . fib!

Observing me the young lady came over and asked me did I wish to buy anything. The tone of her voice was not encouraging; she seemed to have spoken to me out of a sense of duty. I looked humbly at the great jars that stood like eastern guards at either side of the dark entrance to the stall and murmured:

— No, thank you.

The young lady changed the position of one of the vases and went back to the two young men. They began to talk of the same subject. Once or twice the young lady glanced at me over her shoulder.

I lingered before her stall, though I knew my stay was useless, to make my interest in her wares seem the more real. Then I turned away slowly and walked down the middle of the bazaar. I allowed the two pennies to fall against the sixpence in my pocket. I heard a voice call from one end of the gallery that the light was out. The upper part of the hall was now completely dark.

Gazing up into the darkness I saw myself as a creature driven and derided by vanity; and my eyes burned with anguish and anger.

A Little Cloud¹ (1914), from Dubliners

Eight years before he had seen his friend off at the North Wall² and wished him godspeed. Gallaher had got on. You could tell that at once by his travelled air, his well-cut tweed suit and fearless accent. Few fellows had talents like his and fewer still could remain unspoiled by such success. Gallaher's heart was in the right place and he had deserved to win. It was something to have a friend like that.

Little Chandler's thoughts ever since lunch-time had been of his meeting with Gallaher, of Gallaher's invitation and of the great city London where Gallaher lived. He was called Little Chandler because, though he was but slightly under the average stature, he gave one the idea of being a little man. His hands were white and small, his frame was fragile, his voice was quiet and his manners were refined. He took the greatest care of his fair silken hair and moustache and used perfume discreetly on his handkerchief. The half-moons of his nails were perfect and when he smiled you caught a glimpse of a row of childish white teeth.

As he sat at his desk in the King's Inns³ he thought what changes those eight years had brought. The friend whom he had known under a shabby and necessitous guise had become a brilliant figure on the London Press.⁴ He turned often from his tiresome writing to gaze out of the office window. The glow of a late autumn sunset covered the grass plots and walks. It cast a shower of kindly golden dust on the untidy nurses and decrepit old men who drowsed on the benches; it flickered upon all the moving figures – on the children who ran screaming along the gravel paths and on everyone who passed through the gardens. He watched the scene and thought of life; and (as always happened when he thought of life) he became sad. A gentle melancholy took possession of him. He felt how useless it was to struggle against fortune, this being the burden of wisdom which the ages had bequeathed to him.

---

¹ Possibly alluding to Elijah's prophesy that a drought, brought about as a punishment for worshiping the foreign god Baal, will be ended by rain from "a little cloud, like a man's hand" (see I Kings 18:44).

² Quay on the docks on the north side of the the Liffey, where a packet steamer to England departed.

³ Buildings in central Dublin that were occupied by the legal societies which called people to the bar and so enabled them to practice as barristers or lawyers in Irish courts. The complex included the Deeds Registry Office and similar entities, in any of which Little Chandler might have worked as a clerk.

⁴ As a journalist writing for English national newspapers.

He remembered the books of poetry upon his shelves at home. He had bought them in his bachelor days and many an evening, as he sat in the little room off the hall, he had been tempted to take one down from the bookshelf and read out something to his wife. But shyness had always held him back; and so the books had remained on their shelves. At times he repeated lines to himself and this consoled him.

When his hour had struck he stood up and took leave of his desk and of his fellow-clerks punctiliously. He emerged from under the feudal arch of the King's Inns, a neat modest figure, and walked swiftly down Henrietta Street.[5] The golden sunset was waning and the air had grown sharp. A horde of grimy children populated the street. They stood or ran in the roadway or crawled up the steps before the gaping doors or squatted like mice upon the thresholds. Little Chandler gave them no thought. He picked his way deftly through all that minute vermin-like life and under the shadow of the gaunt spectral mansions in which the old nobility of Dublin had roistered.[6] No memory of the past touched him, for his mind was full of a present joy.

He had never been in Corless's[7] but he knew the value of the name. He knew that people went there after the theatre to eat oysters and drink liqueurs; and he had heard that the waiters there spoke French and German. Walking swiftly by at night he had seen cabs drawn up before the door and richly dressed ladies, escorted by cavaliers, alight and enter quickly. They wore noisy dresses and many wraps. Their faces were powdered and they caught up their dresses, when they touched earth, like alarmed Atalantas.[8] He had always passed without turning his head to look. It was his habit to walk swiftly in the street even by day and whenever he found himself in the city late at night he hurried on his way apprehensively and excitedly. Sometimes, however, he courted the causes of his fear. He chose the darkest and narrowest streets and, as he walked boldly forward, the silence that was spread about his footsteps troubled him, the wandering silent figures troubled him; and at times a sound of low fugitive laughter made him tremble like a leaf.

He turned to the right towards Capel Street.[9] Ignatius Gallaher on the London Press! Who would have thought it possible eight years before? Still, now that he reviewed the past, Little Chandler could remember many signs of future greatness in his friend. People used to say that Ignatius Gallaher was wild. Of course, he did mix with a rakish set of fellows at that time, drank freely and borrowed money on all sides. In the end he had got mixed up in some shady affair, some money transaction: at least, that was one version of his flight. But nobody denied him talent. There was always a certain . . . something in Ignatius Gallaher that impressed you in spite of yourself. Even when he was out at elbows and at his wits' end for money he kept up a bold face. Little Chandler remembered (and the remembrance brought a slight flush of pride to his cheek) one of Ignatius Gallaher's sayings when he was in a tight corner:

— Half time,[10] now, boys, he used to say light-heartedly. Where's my considering cap?[11]

That was Ignatius Gallaher all out; and, damn it, you couldn't but admire him for it.

Little Chandler quickened his pace. For the first time in his life he felt himself superior to the people he passed. For the first time his soul revolted against the dull inelegance of Capel Street. There was no doubt about it: if you wanted to succeed you had to go away. You could do nothing in Dublin. As he crossed Grattan Bridge[12] he looked down the river towards the lower quays and pitied the poor stunted houses. They seemed to him a band of tramps, huddled together along the

---

5   Street in central Dublin that led to the rear of the King's Inns; at the time of the story, it was lined by tenements filled with poor people.
6   The slums of central Dublin were often Georgian mansions that had been divided and subdivided to create tenements; in the popular imagination, the aristocrats had led lives of Bacchanalian pleasure.
7   Well-known restaurant in central Dublin, its full name being the Burlington Hotel, Restaurant and Dining room, at one time owned by Thomas Corless.
8   In Greek mythology, Atalanta would marry only a man who could beat her in a race. If a candidate failed, she would spear him in the back. Eventually she married Hippomenes, who delayed

her by throwing three golden apples in her path, gifts to him from Aphrodite. But Hippomenes failed to thank Aphrodite and, when the couple impiously lay together in a holy place, she turned them into lions.
9   Street in central Dublin north of the river; it ends at Grattan Bridge over the Liffey.
10   The interval between two halves of a football or soccer match.
11   Silas Wegg, a wily character in the novel *Our Mutual Friend* (1864–5) by Charles Dickens (1812–70), uses this phrase when he is about to deceive someone.
12   Bridge over the Liffey which connects Capel Street on the north to Parliament Street on the south side.

river-banks, their old coats covered with dust and soot, stupefied by the panorama of sunset and waiting for the first chill of night to bid them arise, shake themselves and begone. He wondered whether he could write a poem to express his idea. Perhaps Gallaher might be able to get it into some London paper for him. Could he write something original? He was not sure what idea he wished to express but the thought that a poetic moment had touched him took life within him like an infant hope. He stepped onward bravely.

Every step brought him nearer to London,[13] farther from his own sober inartistic life. A light began to tremble on the horizon of his mind. He was not so old – thirty-two. His temperament might be said to be just at the point of maturity. There were so many different moods and impressions that he wished to express in verse. He felt them within him. He tried to weigh his soul to see if it was a poet's soul. Melancholy was the dominant note of his temperament, he thought, but it was a melancholy tempered by recurrences of faith and resignation and simple joy. If he could give expression to it in a book of poems perhaps men would listen. He would never be popular: he saw that. He could not sway the crowd but he might appeal to a little circle of kindred minds. The English critics, perhaps, would recognize him as one of the Celtic school by reason of the melancholy tone of his poems; besides that, he would put in allusions. He began to invent sentences and phrases from the notices which his book would get. *Mr Chandler has the gift of easy and graceful verse.... A wistful sadness pervades these poems ... The Celtic note.*[14] It was a pity his name was not more Irish-looking.[15] Perhaps it would be better to insert his mother's name before the surname: Thomas Malone[16] Chandler, or better still: T. Malone Chandler. He would speak to Gallaher about it.

He pursued his revery so ardently that he passed his street and had to turn back. As he came near Corless's his former agitation began to overmaster him and he halted before the door in indecision. Finally he opened the door and entered.

The light and noise of the bar held him at the doorway for a few moments. He looked about him, but his sight was confused by the shining of many red and green wine-glasses. The bar seemed to him to be full of people and he felt that the people were observing him curiously. He glanced quickly to right and left (frowning slightly to make his errand appear serious), but when his sight cleared a little he saw that nobody had turned to look at him: and there, sure enough, was Ignatius Gallaher leaning with his back against the counter and his feet planted far apart.

— Hallo, Tommy, old hero, here you are! What is it to be? What will you have? I'm taking whisky: better stuff than we get across the water.[17] Soda? Lithia?[18] No mineral? I'm the same. Spoils the flavour.... Here, *garçon*,[19] bring us two halves of malt whisky, like a good fellow.... Well, and how have you been pulling along since I saw you last? Dear God, how old we're getting! Do you see any signs of aging in me – eh, what? A little grey and thin on the top – what?

Ignatius Gallaher took off his hat and displayed a large closely cropped head. His face was heavy, pale and clean-shaven. His eyes, which were of bluish slate-colour, relieved his unhealthy pallor and shone out plainly above the vivid orange tie he wore. Between these rival features the lips appeared very long and shapeless and colourless. He bent his head and felt with two sympathetic fingers the thin hair at the crown. Little Chandler shook his head as a denial. Ignatius Gallaher put on his hat again.

— It pulls you down, he said, Press life. Always hurry and scurry, looking for copy and sometimes not finding it: and then, always to have something new in your stuff. Damn proofs

---

[13]   Chandler is walking south and east, or toward London, and also toward Gallaher, associated with London.

[14]   Matthew Arnold (1822–88), in his *Study of Celtic Literature*, poularized the idea that the Celt (or Irish) possessed "natural magic" and was incapable of submitting to "the despotism of fact." Many Irish writers satisfied this stereotype by supplying poetry on Irish mythology or other work suffused with melancholy. In 1904 A.E. (George Russell) was involved in publishing an anthology titled *A Celtic Christmas*, which Joyce disdained.

[15]   Chandler, which is the English term for a candlemaker or general dealer in groceries and small wares, is a name that has material and Anglo-saxon associations at odds with the "Celtic note" he wants to strike.

[16]   A very Irish name, as the Malones were distinguished Catholic landowners in the seventeenth century.

[17]   Britain.

[18]   A mineral water that had lithium salts and was often drunk with whisky.

[19]   French for "boy." Gallaher is flaunting Continental airs.

and printers, I say, for a few days. I'm deuced glad, I can tell you, to get back to the old country. Does a fellow good, a bit of a holiday. I feel a ton better since I landed again in dear dirty Dublin.[20] . . . Here you are, Tommy. Water? Say when.

Little Chandler allowed his whisky to be very much diluted.

— You don't know what's good for you, my boy, said Ignatius Gallaher. I drink mine neat.

— I drink very little as a rule, said Little Chandler modestly. An odd half-one or so when I meet any of the old crowd: that's all.

— Ah, well, said Ignatius Gallaher, cheerfully, here's to us and to old times and old acquaintance. They clinked glasses and drank the toast.

— I met some of the old gang to-day, said Ignatius Gallaher. O'Hara seems to be in a bad way. What's he doing?

— Nothing, said Little Chandler. He's gone to the dogs.

— But Hogan has a good sit,[21] hasn't he?

— Yes; he's in the Land Commission.[22]

— I met him one night in London and he seemed to be very flush.[23] . . . Poor O'Hara! Boose, I suppose?

— Other things, too, said Little Chandler shortly.

Ignatius Gallaher laughed.

— Tommy, he said, I see you haven't changed an atom. You're the very same serious person that used to lecture me on Sunday mornings when I had a sore head and a fur on my tongue. You'd want to knock about a bit in the world. Have you never been anywhere, even for a trip?

— I've been to the Isle of Man,[24] said Little Chandler.

Ignatius Gallaher laughed.

— The Isle of Man! he said. Go to London or Paris: Paris, for choice. That'd do you good.

— Have you seen Paris?

— I should think I have! I've knocked about there a little.

— And is it really so beautiful as they say? asked Little Chandler.

He sipped a little of his drink while Ignatius Gallaher finished his boldly.

— Beautiful? said Ignatius Gallaher, pausing on the word and on the flavour of his drink. It's not so beautiful, you know. Of course, it is beautiful. . . . But it's the life of Paris; that's the thing. Ah, there's no city like Paris for gaiety, movement, excitement. . . .

Little Chandler finished his whisky and, after some trouble, succeeded in catching the barman's eye. He ordered the same again.

— I've been to the Moulin Rouge,[25] Ignatius Gallaher continued when the barman had removed their glasses, and I've been to all the Bohemian cafés. Hot stuff! Not for a pious chap like you, Tommy.

Little Chandler said nothing until the barman returned with the two glasses: then he touched his friend's glass lightly and reciprocated the former toast. He was beginning to feel somewhat disillusioned. Gallaher's accent and way of expressing himself did not please him. There was something vulgar in his friend which he had not observed before. But perhaps it was only the result of living in London amid the bustle and competition of the Press. The old personal charm was still there under this new gaudy manner. And, after all, Gallaher had lived, he had seen the world. Little Chandler looked at his friend enviously.

— Everything in Paris is gay, said Ignatius Gallaher. They believe in enjoying life – and don't you think they're right? If you want to enjoy yourself properly you must go to Paris. And, mind you, they've a great feeling for the Irish there. When they heard I was from Ireland they were ready to eat me, man.

[20] A popular and affectionate phrase to refer to Dublin, first popularized by the Irish novelist Lady Sydney Morgan (*c.* 1783–1859).

[21] Or "a good situation."

[22] The Irish Land Commission Court was the British government agency charged with giving effect to land reform, a process whereby tenant farmers, aided by substantial government credits, were to buy land from large estates. A result of the land agitation of the 1880s, the Commission disbursed considerable sums of money.

[23] Slang for having money to spend.

[24] Island in the Irish sea betweeen Dublin and Liverpool.

[25] A highly publicized music hall in Paris and the embodiment of "gay Paree" in popular accounts.

Little Chandler took four or five sips from his glass.

— Tell me, he said, is it true that Paris is so . . . immoral as they say?

Ignatius Gallaher made a catholic gesture[26] with his right arm.

— Every place is immoral, he said. Of course you do find spicy bits in Paris. Go to one of the students' balls[27] for instance. That's lively, if you like, when the *cocottes* begin to let themselves loose. You know what they are, I suppose?

— I've heard of them, said Little Chandler.

Ignatius Gallaher drank off his whisky and shook his head.

— Ah, he said, you may say what you like. There's no woman like the Parisienne — for style, for go.

— Then it is an immoral city, said Little Chandler, with timid insistence — I mean, compared with London or Dublin?

— London! said Ignatius Gallaher. It's six of one and half-a-dozen of the other. You ask Hogan, my boy. I showed him a bit about London when he was over there. He'd open your eye. . . . I say, Tommy, don't make punch of that whisky: liquor up.

— No, really. . . .

— O, come on, another one won't do you any harm. What is it? The same again, I suppose?

— Well . . . all right.

— *François*, the same again. . . . Will you smoke, Tommy?

Ignatius Gallaher produced his cigar-case. The two friends lit their cigars and puffed at them in silence until their drinks were served.

— I'll tell you my opinion, said Ignatius Gallaher, emerging after some time from the clouds of smoke in which he had taken refuge, it's a rum world. Talk of immorality! I've heard of cases — what am I saying? — I've known them: cases of . . . immorality. . . .

Ignatius Gallaher puffed thoughtfully at his cigar and then, in a calm historian's tone, he proceeded to sketch for his friend some pictures of the corruption which was rife abroad. He summarised the vices of many capitals and seemed inclined to award the palm to Berlin. Some things he could not vouch for (his friends had told him), but of others he had had personal experience. He spared neither rank nor caste. He revealed many of the secrets of religious houses on the Continent[28] and described some of the practices which were fashionable in high society and ended by telling, with details, a story about an English duchess[29] — a story which he knew to be true. Little Chandler was astonished.

— Ah, well, said Ignatius Gallaher, here we are in old jog-along Dublin where nothing is known of such things.

— How dull you must find it, said Little Chandler, after all the other places you've seen!

— Well, said Ignatius Gallaher, it's a relaxation to come over here, you know. And, after all, it's the old country, as they say, isn't it? You can't help having a certain feeling for it. That's human nature. . . . But tell me something about yourself. Hogan told me you had . . . tasted the joys of connubial bliss. Two years ago, wasn't it?

Little Chandler blushed and smiled.

— Yes, he said. I was married last May twelve months.

— I hope it's not too late in the day to offer my best wishes, said Ignatius Gallaher. I didn't know your address or I'd have done so at the time.

He extended his hand, which Little Chandler took.

— Well, Tommy, he said, I wish you and yours every joy in life, old chap, and tons of money, and may you never die till I shoot you. And that's the wish of a sincere friend, an old friend. You know that?

[26] One that implies a comprehensive knowledge of the subject; perhpas also a "Catholic gesture," making the sign of the cross in the face of widespread sin.

[27] Dances in Parisian restaurants and cafés which were depicted as occasions for licentious behavior in popular novels and press accounts.

[28] Victorian pornography and gutter press newspapers combined salacious accounts of life in Catholic convents and monasteries with anti-Catholic bigotry.

[29] Popular novels of the period often portrayed English aristocrats as dissolute and licentious.

— I know that, said Little Chandler.

— Any youngsters? said Ignatius Gallaher.

Little Chandler blushed again.

— We have one child, he said.

— Son or daughter?

— A little boy.

Ignatius Gallaher slapped his friend sonorously on the back.

— Bravo, he said, I wouldn't doubt you, Tommy.

Little Chandler smiled, looked confusedly at his glass and bit his lower lip with three childishly white front teeth.

— I hope you'll spend an evening with us, he said, before you go back. My wife will be delighted to meet you. We can have a little music and —

— Thanks awfully, old chap, said Ignatius Gallaher, I'm sorry we didn't meet earlier. But I must leave to-morrow night.

— To-night, perhaps . . . ?

— I'm awfully sorry, old man. You see I'm over here with another fellow, clever young chap he is too, and we arranged to go to a little card-party. Only for that . . .

— O, in that case. . . .

— But who knows? said Ignatius Gallaher considerately. Next year I may take a little skip over here now that I've broken the ice. It's only a pleasure deferred.

— Very well, said Little Chandler, the next time you come we must have an evening together. That's agreed now, isn't it?

— Yes, that's agreed, said Ignatius Gallaher. Next year if I come, *parole d'honneur*.[30]

— And to clinch the bargain, said Little Chandler, we'll just have one more now.

Ignatius Gallaher took out a large gold watch and looked at it.

— Is it to be the last? he said. Because you know, I have an a.p.[31]

— O, yes, positively, said Little Chandler.

— Very well, then, said Ignatius Gallaher, let us have another one as a *deoc an doruis*[32] — that's good vernacular for a small whisky, I believe.

Little Chandler ordered the drinks. The blush which had risen to his face a few moments before was establishing itself. A trifle made him blush at any time: and now he felt warm and excited. Three small whiskies had gone to his head and Gallaher's strong cigar had confused his mind, for he was a delicate and abstinent person. The adventure of meeting Gallaher after eight years, of finding himself with Gallaher in Corless's surrounded by lights and noise, of listening to Gallaher's stories and of sharing for a brief space Gallaher's vagrant and triumphant life, upset the equipoise of his sensitive nature. He felt acutely the contrast between his own life and his friend's, and it seemed to him unjust. Gallaher was his inferior in birth and education. He was sure that he could do something better than his friend had ever done, or could ever do, something higher than mere tawdry journalism if he only got the chance. What was it that stood in his way? His unfortunate timidity! He wished to vindicate himself in some way, to assert his manhood. He saw behind Gallaher's refusal of his invitation. Gallaher was only patronizing him by his friendliness just as he was patronizing Ireland by his visit.

The barman brought their drinks. Little Chandler pushed one glass towards his friend and took up the other boldly.

— Who knows? he said, as they lifted their glasses. When you come next year I may have the pleasure of wishing long life and happiness to Mr and Mrs Ignatius Gallaher.

---

[30] "My word of honor," in French, with Gallaher affecting cosmopolitan sophistication.

[31] Slang meaning either an "appointment" or "author's proof," the final version of a text which is sent to an author for checking before a work goes into print.

[32] Irish for "a door-drink," a final round or one for the road.

Ignatius Gallaher in the act of drinking closed one eye expressively over the rim of his glass. When he had drunk he smacked his lips decisively, set down his glass and said:

— No blooming fear of that, my boy. I'm going to have my fling first and see a bit of life and the world before I put my head in the sack – if I ever do.

— Some day you will, said Little Chandler calmly.

Ignatius Gallaher turned his orange tie and slate-blue eyes full upon his friend.

— You think so? he said.

— You'll put your head in the sack, repeated Little Chandler stoutly, like everyone else if you can find the girl.

He had slightly emphasised his tone and he was aware that he had betrayed himself; but, though the colour had heightened in his cheek, he did not flinch from his friend's gaze. Ignatius Gallaher watched him for a few moments and then said:

— If ever it occurs, you may bet your bottom dollar there'll be no mooning and spooning about it. I mean to marry money. She'll have a good fat account at the bank or she won't do for me.

Little Chandler shook his head.

— Why, man alive, said Ignatius Gallaher, vehemently, do you know what it is? I've only to say the word and to-morrow I can have the woman and the cash. You don't believe it? Well, I know it. There are hundreds – what am I saying? – thousands of rich Germans and Jews, rotten with money, that'd only be too glad.... You wait a while, my boy. See if I don't play my cards properly. When I go about a thing I mean business, I tell you. You just wait.

He tossed his glass to his mouth, finished his drink and laughed loudly. Then he looked thoughtfully before him and said in a calmer tone:

— But I'm in no hurry. They can wait. I don't fancy tying myself up to one woman, you know.

He imitated with his mouth the act of tasting and made a wry face.

— Must get a bit stale, I should think, he said.

.   .   .   .

Little Chandler sat in the room off the hall, holding a child in his arms. To save money they kept no servant but Annie's young sister Monica came for an hour or so in the morning and an hour or so in the evening to help. But Monica had gone home long ago. It was a quarter to nine. Little Chandler had come home late for tea and, moreover, he had forgotten to bring Annie home the parcel of coffee from Bewley's.[33] Of course she was in a bad humour and gave him short answers. She said she would do without any tea but when it came near the time at which the shop at the corner closed she decided to go out herself for a quarter of a pound of tea and two pounds of sugar. She put the sleeping child deftly in his arms and said:

— Here. Don't waken him.

A little lamp with a white china shade stood upon the table and its light fell over a photograph which was enclosed in a frame of crumpled horn. It was Annie's photograph. Little Chandler looked at it, pausing at the thin tight lips. She wore the pale blue summer blouse which he had brought her home as a present one Saturday. It had cost him ten and elevenpence;[34] but what an agony of nervousness it had cost him! How he had suffered that day, waiting at the shop door until the shop was empty, standing at the counter and trying to appear at his ease while the girl piled ladies' blouses before him, paying at the desk and forgetting to take up the odd penny of his change, being called back by the cashier, and, finally, striving to hide his blushes as he left the shop by examining the parcel to see if it was securely tied. When he brought the blouse home Annie kissed him and said it was very pretty and stylish; but when she heard the price she threw the blouse on the table and said it was a regular swindle to charge ten and elevenpence for that. At first she wanted to take it back but when she tried it on she was delighted with it, especially with the make of the sleeves, and kissed him and said he was very good to think of her.

---

[33] Well-known chain of tea and coffee houses owned by a prominent Quaker family.

[34] Ten shillings and 11 pence, almost 11 shillings (there were 12 pence in the shilling), a considerable sum for someone earning a clerk's salary.

Hm!...

He looked coldly into the eyes of the photograph and they answered coldly. Certainly they were pretty and the face itself was pretty. But he found something mean in it. Why was it so unconscious and lady-like? The composure of the eyes irritated him. They repelled him and defied him: there was no passion in them, no rapture. He thought of what Gallaher had said about rich Jewesses. Those dark Oriental eyes, he thought, how full they are of passion, of voluptuous longing!... Why had he married the eyes in the photograph?

He caught himself up at the question and glanced nervously round the room. He found something mean in the pretty furniture which he had bought for his house on the hire system.[35] Annie had chosen it herself and it reminded him of her. It too was prim and pretty. A dull resentment against his life awoke within him. Could he not escape from his little house? Was it too late for him to try to live bravely like Gallaher? Could he go to London? There was the furniture still to be paid for. If he could only write a book and get it published, that might open the way for him.

A volume of Byron's poems[36] lay before him on the table. He opened it cautiously with his left hand lest he should waken the child and began to read the first poem in the book:

> *Hushed are the winds and still the evening gloom,*
> *Not e'en a Zephyr wanders through the grove,*
> *Whilst I return to view my Margaret's tomb*
> *And scatter flowers on the dust I love.*[37]

He paused. He felt the rhythm of the verse about him in the room. How melancholy it was! Could he, too, write like that, express the melancholy of his soul in verse? There were so many things he wanted to describe: his sensation of a few hours before on Grattan Bridge, for example. If he could get back again into that mood....

The child awoke and began to cry. He turned from the page and tried to hush it: but it would not be hushed. He began to rock it to and fro in his arms but its wailing cry grew keener. He rocked it faster while his eyes began to read the second stanza:

> *Within this narrow cell reclines her clay,*
> *That clay where once...*

It was useless. He couldn't read. He couldn't do anything. The wailing of the child pierced the drum of his ear. It was useless, useless! He was a prisoner for life. His arms trembled with anger and suddenly bending to the child's face he shouted:

— Stop!

The child stopped for an instant, had a spasm of fright and began to scream. He jumped up from his chair and walked hastily up and down the room with the child in his arms. It began to sob piteously, losing its breath for four or five seconds, and then bursting out anew. The thin walls of the room echoed the sound. He tried to soothe it but it sobbed more convulsively. He looked at the contracted and quivering face of the child and began to be alarmed. He counted seven sobs without a break between them and caught the child to his breast in fright. If it died!...

The door was burst open and a young woman ran in, panting.

— What is it? What is it? she cried.

The child, hearing its mother's voice, broke out into a paroxysm of sobbing.

— It's nothing, Annie... it's nothing.... He began to cry...

She flung her parcels on the floor and snatched the child from him.

— What have you done to him? she cried, glaring into his face.

---

[35] Purchase on credit with payments in installments and considerable interest.
[36] George Gordon, Lord Byron (1788–1824), became a byword for Romantic excess and heroic posing.

[37] First stanza of Byron's poem "On the Death of a Young Lady, Cousin of the Author, and Very Dear to Him" (1802), first published in *Hours of Idleness* (1807), a sentimental piece at odds with the more romantic myth of Byron.

Little Chandler sustained for one moment the gaze of her eyes and his heart closed together as he met the hatred in them. He began to stammer:

— It's nothing....He...he began to cry....I couldn't...I didn't do anything....What?

Giving no heed to him she began to walk up and down the room, clasping the child tightly in her arms and murmuring:

— My little man! My little mannie! Was 'ou frightened, love?...There now, love! There now!...Lambabaun![38] Mamma's little lamb of the world![39]...There now!

Little Chandler felt his cheeks suffused with shame and he stood back out of the lamplight. He listened while the paroxysm of the child's sobbing grew less and less; and tears of remorse started to his eyes.

Aeolus: Introduction

In survey after survey, writers and critics have named *Ulysses* the most important novel of the twentieth century. Preceded by its legendary stature, daunting in its formidable length, accompanied or encumbered by heaps of exegetical commentary, it can provoke a feeling of anxiety in a reader who approaches it for the first time. But such anxiety will, when one actually begins to read it, soon give way to other sensations, not least among them unalloyed pleasure at the uncanny inventiveness in Joyce's use of language. The virtuoso shifts in style from episode to episode are so pronounced that *Ulysses*, with some legitimacy, can be viewed not as a single book, but as a series of books which have been welded around a somewhat slender plot.

Indeed, ever since its first appearance it has always been viewed as at least two very different sorts of book. In one view famously articulated by Ezra Pound *Ulysses* was a work of hyperbolic realism, one that embodied a sustained and unstinting satire of middle-class life as epitomized in the novel's hero, Leopold Bloom. (See Pound's "Paris Letter," rpt. in Forrest Read [ed.], *Pound/Joyce* [New York: New Directions, 1967], pp. 194–200.) In another view famously articulated by T. S. Eliot (see pp. 165–7), it was not the book's realism which mattered, but "the parallel to the *Odyssey*, and the use of appropriate styles and symbols to each division." This had "the importance of a scientific discovery," Eliot urged, for it offered "a way of controlling, or ordering, of giving a shape and a significance to the immense panorama of futility and anarchy which is contemporary history." The difference between these views turned on their attitude toward what Eliot had called "the parallel to the *Odyssey*," or what Pound called "the correspondences," which is to say the emphasis which one should give to the novel's insinuation (already formulated in its title, *Ulysses*) that the fictional events that take place on June 16, 1904, in Dublin, somehow "correspond" or are "parallel" to events recounted in Homer's *Odyssey*. Pound was dismissive of that insinuation. "These correspondences are part of Joyce's mediaevalism and are chiefly his own

affair, a scaffold, a means of construction, justified by the result, and justifiable by it only." Eliot, in turn, was dismissive of those who dismissed it: "one might expect this to be the first peculiarity to attract attention; but it has been treated as an amusing dodge, or scaffolding erected by the author for the purpose of disposing his realistic tale, of no interest in the completed structure."

These contrasting views of *Ulysses*, which first appeared in the immediate wake of its publication in 1922, were still more sharply and more fully articulated in two important works of the 1930s. One was *James Joyce and the Making of Ulysses* (1934) by Frank Budgen, a painter who had been Joyce's closest friend in the years when he was writing *Ulysses* in Zurich, from 1915 to 1920. The other was *James Joyce's Ulysses* (1930), by Stuart Gilbert, a former civil servant who had retired early and moved to Paris, where he first met Joyce in 1927. Joyce himself intervened in the writing of both, offering suggestions and anecdotes. Yet their views of *Ulysses* were very different and their divergence largely replicated the difference between Pound and Eliot. Budgen drew heavily on his own unique experience, the special authority which accrued to him from his having read or listened to Joyce reading aloud successive episodes and passages of *Ulysses* while he was composing them in Zurich:

Joyce's first question when I had read a completed episode or when he had read out a passage of an uncompleted one was always: "How does Bloom strike you?" Technical considerations, problems of Homeric correspondence, the chemistry of the human body, were secondary matters.

Budgen, in other words, shared Ezra Pound's skepticism about the authority that should be assigned to "technical considerations, problems of Homeric correspondence, the chemistry of the human body." The novel's center of gravity was not there, he thought, but in the everyday reality of cups and saucers, chairs and tables. And above all it was to

---

[38]   Irish for "lamb-child," a term of affection.

[39]   John 1:29 describes Jesus as the "lamb of God."

be found in the character of Bloom, who was not merely a butt of satirical observation (here Budgen departed from Pound), but a bearer of central values and precepts, "a complete man, a good man," as Joyce had allegedly told Budgen in Zurich. Indeed, Budgen's tart dismissal of "problems of Homeric correspondence" was probably a direct shot at Stuart Gilbert's book, which, published only four years earlier, had been the first to contain a document that has since been named after Gilbert, the so-called "Gilbert schema," an elaborate table of Homeric correspondences which Joyce had worked out when he was finishing the novel in 1921. Needless to say, Gilbert's view of *Ulysses* differed sharply. Every detail of the novel contributed to make up a fictional world of extraordinary symbolic density, and the Homeric parallels or correspondences were the gateway to exploring that world. (Realism counted for little here.) Moreover, Gilbert also laid claim to a unique authority derived from Joyce: "the ideas, interpretations and explanations put forward in these pages are not capricious or speculative, but were endorsed by Joyce himself." Yet in practice the results were sometimes strained. Many pages of *Ulysses*, according to Gilbert, could be understood only through thorough familiarity with the knottier points of esoteric Buddhism. The novel's elaborate parallels with the Homeric world, too, could seem oddly pointless: does it really matter that Leopold Bloom waves a cigar at the same moment when Odysseus brandishes a spear in the *Odyssey*?

The battle between heavily "symbolic" readings of *Ulysses*, such as Gilbert's, and broadly "realist" readings, such as Budgen's, would be staged again and again during the half-century or so that followed the book's publication. But more recent readings have largely abandoned such sharp polarities, the result of several different but converging trends. One has been a growing recognition that Joyce, though in everyday life a man prone to making statements every bit as one-sided as either Budgen's or Gilbert's, possessed when writing a unique responsiveness to ambivalence and complexity. Bloom is indeed the warm, heroic figure idealized by Budgen, but at the same time he is often the object of the satirical glance celebrated by Pound. Individuals, within *Ulysses*, have a perceptible psychological and moral integrity; but they are also suffused with ideas, values, thoughts, and phrases not of their own making, some the result of new communications and transcription technologies, some dictated by the aleatory or uncanny meanderings of the subconscious. Another trend has been poststructuralist theory, which has helped readers become more responsive to the aleatory dimensions of language.

Still a third trend which has led critics to be skeptical about the dichotomies epitomized by Gilbert and Budgen has been our deepening knowledge about the protracted process of composition and revision that went into making *Ulysses*. Gilbert apparently assumed that the famous "schema" of correspondences which he published had been present from the beginning, a sort of guide or working plan which Joyce had elaborated at the very outset, then put into effect as he worked his way through each successive episode. In fact, however, the schema that Gilbert published had been devised very late, in 1921, as the book was drawing toward its conclusion; and unbeknownst to Gilbert there was even another schema, known as the Linati schema (after the Italian critic for whom Joyce prepared it), which Joyce had prepared a year earlier in 1920 and which differed in crucial details. When he first began writing, Joyce had only a vague sense of the final shape that *Ulysses* would assume when completed. And because it was published first in serial form, each episode acquired a certain autonomy and independence, offered an occasion for an experiment in a discrete mode of literary form and linguistic coherence. Joyce seized almost every opportunity and turned the book into a dazzling series of improvisations. It was only as the book entered its final stage of composition, which began after its serial publication had been suspended in late 1920 on charges of obscenity and the decision had been taken in early 1921 to proceed with publication as a book, that the question of his work's unity became a pressing concern. Indeed, the question became pressing precisely because hostile critics, during the course of its serial publication, had repeatedly damned it as formless, rambling, and chaotic (and obscene, of course). The schemata that Joyce devised were partly defensive attempts to forestall further instances of just this sort of sniping. The unique circumstances that surrounded the book's publication as a book also presented Joyce with an unusual opportunity. For now, throughout most of 1921, Joyce was writing the book's final episodes at the same time that he was correcting proofs for the book version of its earliest episodes. The proofs, in effect, became an occasion for inserting countless interwoven details that would suggest an overarching, architectonic unity. They also became an occasion for further exploring the range of the numerous styles he had established. As much as one-third of *Ulysses*, it has been estimated, was composed directly in the over-sized margins of the numerous sets of proofs that Joyce received. Even today one can only marvel at the prodigious quantity of inventive prose which Joyce distilled over the course of that extraordinary year.

Ulysses is divided into 18 episodes. There are several competing ways in which we can describe the structure that informs those episodes. But whichever description we choose will depend to some degree on a prior account of the relationship between *Ulysses* and the *Odyssey* of Homer. One crucial dimension of that relationship is already indicated by Joyce's title, *Ulysses*. For "Ulysses" is the Latin word which was used to render the Greek "Odysseus," the name of the hero in Homer's *Odyssey*. *Ulysses*, in other words, is not a straightforward or literal rendering of the *Odyssey*; it is a translation, an adaptation that involves reworking materials originally shaped within one set of cultural, historical, and linguistic horizons into another, very different set of horizons.

Homer's *Odyssey*, conventionally divided into 24 "books" or chapters, recounts the 10-year career of Odysseus from the fall of Troy to his return to his own small kingdom, the island of Ithaca. The work has three readily identifiable parts. The first (Books 1–4) concerns Telemachus, Odysseus's son, who leaves Ithaca and sails to mainland Greece to seek information about his father, absent for 20 years since he left home as part of the expedition to besiege Troy. Nothing has been heard of him since the fall of the city. Telemachus visits old companions of his father to see if he can learn more, visiting first Nestor, then Menelaeus. This part of the *Odyssey* is often termed a "Telemachiad," so called because it centers on Telemachus (in the same way that the *Aeneid* is named after its protagonist, Aeneas). The second part of the *Odyssey* (Books 5–14) concerns Odysseus; it traces his journey from the island of Ogygia to Scheria and thence to Ithaca, but it also recounts the whole series of earlier travels and adventures which had brought him to Ogygia. This second part is sometimes called the "wanderings" or the "adventures." The third part of the *Odyssey* (Books 15–24) recounts the meeting of Odysseus and Telemachus on Ithaca, and the execution of their plan to rid the kingdom of the suitors who, believing Odysseus dead, have been scheming to marry his wife Penelope and murder Telemachus. This part is often called the *nostos*, the ancient Greek word for "a return home."

Ulysses, broadly speaking, follows this tripartite structure. The first part consists of three episodes ("Telemachus," "Nestor," and "Proteus") that concern Stephen Dedalus, the character who is cast as the counterpart to Telemachus, Odysseus' son. The second consists of 12 episodes that focus on Leopold Bloom, the character who is the counterpart of Odysseus or Ulysses, and his peregrinations through the cityscape of Dublin. Though Bloom's and Stephen's journeys in the city intersect at three points (in episodes 6, 7, and 9), they do not actually address one another until the fourteenth episode ("Oxen of the Sun"). Yet even this long-delayed meeting occurs much earlier than the analogous encounter of Odysseus and Telemachus in the *Odyssey*, where it transpires only after both have returned to Ithaca. Bloom and Stephen, instead, are together in the final two episodes of what are supposed to be the wanderings of Odysseus, or Bloom, a conjuncture that would be manifestly impossible if *Ulysses* were following the *Odyssey* as strictly as might be supposed from accounts. The parallel to the *Odyssey*, in other words, is extremely flexible, and readers must learn to alter the expectations which they bring to bear on it from one episode to the next, or even within the same episode. The third part of *Ulysses* consists of three episodes, all set in Bloom's house at 7 Eccles Street, his miniature Ithaca. But Stephen is together with him for only two of those episodes, and the nature of their relationship when they finally part paths has been the subject of much debate. In the book's final episode, Bloom and Stephen vanish as protagonists of narrated action, appearing only in the drowsy thoughts of Molly Bloom, the character cast as the counterpart of Penelope.

Though the structure of *Ulysses* broadly follows that of the *Odyssey*, it also employs various substructures that are embedded within that vaster architecture, or even alternative structures that stand alongside it. One alternative structure, for example, is a bipartite scheme that divides the 18 episodes into two halves. The first half consists of episodes 1 through 9, followed by the interlude that makes up episode 10, which is not especially concerned with either Bloom or Stephen, and then followed by a second half consisting of episodes 11 through 18.

One substructure that is embedded within these two larger structures is readily identifiable in the first 6 episodes of the book. While the first 3 introduce Stephen Dedalus, the next 3 introduce Bloom through a series of conspicuous parallels. Episodes 1 and 4, for example, both take place at the same time of day, and both depict the situation of the protagonist at home. Stephen is in danger of being dispossessed of his home by Buck Mulligan, his housemate, while Bloom is in danger of being dispossessed of his wife Molly by Blazes Boylan, a popular singer who is scheduled to visit her later that day. In the second episode Stephen performs his duties as a teacher and broods on the theme of history and whether the power of the past can be escaped. In the corresponding fifth episode, Bloom perorms a number of domestic errands and resolutely tries to escape from the history of his relationship with Molly, whom he has sorely neglected. In the third episode we see Stephen in isolation as he walks along Sandymount Strand, bitterly meditating on his own identity and change. Stephen is estranged from his father, and the plans which he once had for his future, his ambitions to write successful books, have come to nothing. In the corresponding sixth episode, we see Bloom, though surrounded by a small group of fellow-citizens who are attending the funeral of Patrick Dignam with him, similarly isolated. His fellow citizens pointedly neglect him in their conversation or make clumsy allusions to his Jewishness, and Bloom himself broods on the death of both his father and his son Rudy, deaths which have devastated him. Both characters are isolated from their community (isolated in space, as it were), and both are cut off from the past and future they had experienced or hoped for (isolated in time, so to speak).

Episodes 1 through 6 also share a common formal repertoire. The narrative proceeds by oscillating between the voice of an omniscient narrator and that of the protagonist's "interior monologue," a term which the French writer and critic Valéry Larbaud first adopted in 1921 to describe the seemingly direct transcription of a character's thoughts. Sometimes the transition from one to the other is quite abrupt, as when Buck Mulligan hands Stephen a mirror, urging him to look at himself:

Stephen bent forward and peered at the mirror held out to him, cleft by a crooked crack. As he and others see me. Who chose this face for me? This dogsbody to rid of vermin. It asks me too.

At other times the transition is smoothed over by the use of what is called "free indirect style," the style that results when a third-person omniscient narrator adopts the perspective and the verbal mannerisms of a character. Here, for example, is a passage in which Stephen is recalling a dream of his mother, one that shifts from free indirect style (signaled by third-person pronouns such as "him") to the interior monologue (signaled by first-person terms such as "me" or "my"):

In a dream, silently, she had come to him, her wasted body within its loose graveclothes giving off an odour of wax and rosewood, her breath, bent over him with mute secret words, a faint odour of wetted ashes.

Her glazing eyes, staring out of death, to shake and bend my soul. On me alone. The ghostcandle to light her agony. Ghostly light on the tortured face. Her hoarse loud breath rattling in horror, while all prayed on their knees. Her eyes on me to strike me down.

To be sure, the contrast that I have been drawing between an omniscient third-person narrator and a first-person interior monologue is a bit too schematic. Even within the first 6 episodes, Joyce subtly alters the omniscient narrator's tone and level of diction to make it harmonize better with the principal characters and events that dominate each episode. (In the first one which introduces Stephen, for example, the omniscient narrator adopts a more learned and literary vocabulary; in the fourth, which introduces Bloom, the tone is plainer and more matter-of-fact.) The key point, however, is that these stylistic modulations plainly work to advance purposes of traditional storytelling: they complement the delineation of character, or they enhance the logical, causal, or thematic connections that are binding together actions and events.

Despite these modulations of style, the overall contrast between third-person omniscient narrator and first-person interior monologue remains dominant throughout the first 6 episodes of Ulysses, and it is used to achieve an extraordinary range of effects, from the poignant juxtaposition of lyricism and bitterness in "Proteus," the third episode, to the mixture of sharp-eyed observation and comic commentary of "Hades," the sixth episode. But the basic contrast between third-person omniscient narrator and first-person interior monologue also entails a certain limitation, one that is momentarily obscured by the range of moods and tones which are unfurled in the novel's opening episodes. However inadvertently, it establishes and reinforces a rather static opposition between objective world and subjective experience, a schematic binary that is too brittle to address the highly mediated character of modern experience, too rigid to probe the grids of interlocking systems (transportation, communication, economics) that constitute the modern metropolis.

Which makes what happens in the seventh episode of Ulysses, known as "Aeolus," all the more remarkable. For it is here that style undergoes a pronounced elaboration. It is as if Ulysses were no longer content with the range of effects that could be achieved through the juxtaposition of third-person omniscient narrator and first-person interior monologue; now it assimilates and incorporates the voice of a social force, the modern newspaper, through the use of 63 headlines that conspicuously punctuate the text. That is not all, however. For the 63 headlines are not themselves a fixed or stable element. Whereas the earlier ones have a bland and innocuous quality ("GENTLEMEN OF THE PRESS" or "HOW A GREAT DAILY ORGAN IS TURNED OUT") that might let them qualify as headlines to conceivable feature stories in a newspaper, the later ones grow increasingly wild and irreverent ("DIMINISHED DIGITS PROVE TOO TITILLATING FOR FRISKY FRUMPS. ANN WIMBLES, FLO WANGLES – YET CAN YOU BLAME THEM?"). Yes, one can argue that this last example parodies the tabloids' penchant for excessive alliteration (diminished digits, too titillating, frisky frumps), or urge that it obliquely comments on the parable which Stephen Dedalus has just told – though a great deal of strain is resting on the adverb *obliquely* in that claim. Moreover, the pronounced elaboration of style which is discernible in the headlines finds a counterpart in the prose of the omniscient third-person narrator. Consider only the account of workers loading barrels on a wagon:

Grossbooted draymen rolled barrels dullthudding out of Prince's stores and bumped them up on the brewery float. On the brewery float bumped dullthudding barrels rolled by grossbooted draymen of Prince's stores.

Whatever else one might say about this passage, it is hardly advancing the story, at least not in any conventional sense. If anything, it retards the story, doubling back and reversing the action with its chiastic word order. "But just what is its purpose then?" an impatient reader may ask. The answer to that question reaches to the heart of debate about the "Aeolus" episode.

Adopting an older view of Ulysses, one which saw it as a work of hyperbolic realism, we might argue that the passage about "grossbooted draymen" doubles back on itself in order to underscore the repetitive nature of the task being performed, and then relate this to other actions that transpire later in the episode (several characters repeat long passages from speeches, for example). In this view, the increasing prominence of stylistic techniques and strategies would still be strictly tethered to narrative function, to storytelling in some form. Adopting instead a poststructuralist view, we might emphasize, rather than paper over, the gap between technique and storytelling functionalism, noting how the style is now spotlighting language as a sequence of words and sentences that can be played with, moved about, substituted for one another, or reinserted elsewhere to create

The Linati Schema (1920)

Title	Hour	Color	Persons	Technic	Science, Art	Sense (Meaning)	Organ	Symbol
Aeolus	12–1	Red	Aeolus	Symbouleutike	Rhetoric	The Derision	Lungs	Machines,
Fame,			Sons	Dikanike		of Victory		Wind, Fame
Failed			Telemachus	Epideictic				Kite, Failed
Destinies,			Mentor	Tropes				Destinies,
Mutability			Ulysses					The press,
								Mutability

The Gilbert Schema (1921)

Title	Scene	Hour	Organ	Art	Colour	Symbol	Technic	Correspondences
Aeolus	The Newpaper	12 noon	Lungs	Rhetoric	Red	Editor	Enthymemic	Aeolus: Crawford; Incest; Journalism; Floating Island: Press

surprising effects. In this view, textness would now be taking precedence over storyness. Adopting yet a third view, we might claim that the chiastic doubling of the "grossbooted draymen" passage was a local variant of a comprehensive program of reversals, repetitions, and doublings deployed throughout the episode, a program that was part of Joyce's exploration of the new mass media (the headlines) and their power to duplicate or "double" the modern metropolis (an extended pun on Dublin, as it were, doublin'). If formulated in a way that addressed the flippant irrelevance so evident in the later headlines, this view might go on to mediate the competing claims of storyness and textness. Of course our account of these three approaches has been overly schematic, slighting the more nuanced positions that actually emerge from more extended analysis. But at least it has enabled us to survey the questions raised by the pronounced elaboration of style which becomes unmistakable in "Aeolus" and is only further accentuated in the succeeding episodes of *Ulysses*.

"Aeolus" corresponds to an incident in Book 10 of the *Odyssey*. Odysseus, traveling homeward after the Trojan war together with his men, comes to the island of Aeolia, ruled by Aeolus, whom Zeus has designated as a keeper or warden of all the winds. After entertaining Odysseus, who returns the favor by recounting stories of his adventures, Aeolus gives him a bag in which he has penned up all the winds that are unfavorable to his journey, which means that only the west wind, which will take him to Ithaca, will continue to blow. Odysseus sets sail and after 9 days finds himself drawing close to home. But exhausted by his journey, he falls asleep at the tiller. His crewmen, suspicious that the sack of Aeolus contains valuable treasure, decide to open it. The adverse winds are released, and Odysseus and his ships are blown all the way back to Aeolia. Odysseus asks for Aeolus's help a second time, but he refuses, urging that Odysseus is a man "detested by the blessed gods."

Mention was made earlier of the Linati and Gilbert Schemata, the tables of correspondences which Joyce elaborated and gave to interested critics and admirers. The two versions of table for the "Aeolus" episode are reproduced above.

If these seem somewhat less than helpful, that is in part because of the tension between Joyce's wish to write a novel and the claims of his Homeric parallel. By this point in the novel, Joyce needs to have some sort of encounter between Bloom and Stephen; but the parallel with the *Odyssey* makes this difficult, since Odysseus is alone or with his crew during his many adventures, not accompanied by Telemachus. The result is a difficult accommodation, if one insists on strict parallelism, or a productive tension if one is more flexible.

Most of the action in "Aeolus" takes place inside the rambling offices of the *Freeman's Journal* and the *Evening Telegraph*, morning and evening newspapers that were owned by a single firm. There circulations were 40,000 and 26,000, respectively, and their chief competitor was the *Irish Times*, with a circulation of about 45,000. Both were pro-home-rule newspapers. Their offices were at 4–8, Prince's Street North, the southern side of an east–west street that debouches into what was then Sackville Street, the principal north–south artery of Dublin. Most of the north side of Prince's Street North is consumed by the flank of the General Post Office, which in turn faces the central terminus for most of the tramways, electrified only a few years earlier in 1901. Here, in other words, is the nexus of modern communications (post office, newspaper) and transportation (electrified tramways) technologies.

Though most of the action transpires in rooms within the newspaper building, the episode frames that indoor setting with outdoor scenes that precede and follow it, and in both these scenes the reader's attention is directed to Nelson's pillar, the massive Doric column, built in 1809, which dominated the heart of Dublin and commemorated Lord Nelson's celebrated victory at the battle of Trafalgar. Significantly, another pillar of a different kind is also mentioned in one of three speeches that are recited during the main action within the newspaper offices, "the pillar of the cloud" which guided the Israelites during their wanderings in the desert on their journey to the Promised Land. The analogy implied by this textual juxtaposition, that the modern Irish are like the ancient Hebrews who were oppressed but then delivered from bondage and led to the promised land, is all but stated by Professor MacHugh when he discusses the Roman empire:

– What was their civilisation? Vast, I allow: but vile. *Cloacae*: sewers. The jews in the wilderness and on the mountaintop said: *It is meet to be here. Let us build an altar to Jehovah.* The Roman, like the Englishman who follows in his footsteps, brought to every new shore on which he set his foot (on our shore he never set it) only his cloacal obsession. He gazed about him in his toga and he said: *It is meet to be here. Let us construct a water-closet.*

Stephen Dedalus has not yet entered the room when MacHugh makes this comment, but he is present later when MacHugh recites the speech that refers to "the pillar of the cloud," a speech constructed around a sustained analogy between the modern Irish and the ancient Hebrews, and he is also present when MacHugh draws a second analogy, this one also pointing obliquely to Nelson's pillar via a reference to the battle of Trafalgar:

– The Greek! he said again. *Kyrios*. Shining word! ...*Kyrie*! The radiance of the intellect. I ought to profess Greek, the language of the mind. *Kyrie eleison*! The closetmaker and the cloacamaker will never be lords of our spirit. We are liege subjects of the catholic chivalry of Europe that foundered at Trafalgar and of the empire of the spirit, not an *imperium*, that went under with the Athenian fleets at Aegospotami. [Ellipsis mine.]

The second analogy, one that compares ancient Greeks to modern Irish and ancient Romans to modern Britons, pivots on the polarity of "spirit" and "matter," but also on the distinction between Catholic and Protestant. The true Irish are Catholic, akin to the French who were defeated at Trafalgar, akin also to that "empire of the spirit" made up of the ancient Greeks defeated at Aegospotami. Both have been subdued by coarse, sewer-building materialists, be they Romans or Britons. Yet these claims to the realm of "spirit" are severely undermined by pointed details in the episode. For the "spirits" that animate the conversationalists in the newspaper office are of a decidedly more material kind. Simon Dedalus, unemployed, leaves the office with Ned Lambert, on a day off work, to have a drink at nearby pub – though it is scarcely past noon. When the editor Miles Crawford makes an incoherent comment, Lambert whispers to J. J. O'Molloy: "Incipient jigs. Sad case." Crawford, in other words, is suffering from advancing alcoholism. Lambert's comment to O'Molloy is doubly ironic, for when O'Molloy first enters the newspaper office, Bloom thinks: "Cleverest fellow at the bar he used to be. Decline, poor chap. That hectic flush spells finis for a man." He, too, is suffering from alcoholism, and he has come to

the office to cadge a loan, which is not granted, from Miles Crawford. Lenehan, too, is an unemployed idler, cadging cigarettes and drinks as best he can. When O'Madden Burke suggests that the company retire for a drink, Lenehan seconds him and deftly turns the proposal into a fixed plan.

One of the most beguiling features of the "Aeolus" episode is its delicate choreographing of characters' movements. It begins with Bloom conversing with Red Murray, who works for the newspaper and helps Bloom find an old ad; then exchanging words with Joe Hynes, who happens to drop off a press notice of Paddy Dignam's funeral (which Bloom has attended the previous episode, "Hades"); then discussing with Joseph Nannetti the potential terms for an ad which Bloom can offer to Aleander Keyes. Keyes has already agreed to renew his ad for a month, but Nannetti wants Bloom to try for a three-month renewal. As Bloom stands in a gallery that connects the various parts of the building, he is undecided whether he should tram it to Keyes, return home first (and so perhaps prevent the tryst of his wife with Blazes Boylan), or simply telephone Keyes. He decides to telephone from the office of the newspaper editor, Miles Crawford, and so comes upon a group of three people (Professor MacHugh, Simon Dedalus, and Ned Lambert) who have gathered in the editor's outer office, where they are laughing over a speech which was recently delivered by Dowie Dawson. The group, momentarily swollen to four, is soon joined by a fifth person, the solicitor and alcoholic J. J. O'Molloy. When Crawford steps out of his inner office to join the group, Bloom seizes the opportunity and retreats into that office to telephone Keyes who, it so happens, is just around the corner in Dillon's auction rooms. Meanwhile, Simon Dedalus and Ned Lambert leave for a pub, momentarily reducing the group to three till Lenehan, who has been left behind by Miles Crawford in the inner office, steps out and joins the group in the outer office. The group now consists of four: Miles Crawford, Professor MacHugh, Lenehan, and J. J. O'Molloy. Bloom briefly passes through the outer office again as he leaves the newspaper building to go find Alexander Keyes. Shortly after he leaves, Stephen Dedalus arrives, accompanied by O'Madden Burke, and now delivers a letter about foot-and-mouth disease which Mr. Deasy, in the second episode, had asked him to convey to the newspaper. The group has now swollen to six. It is while Stephen is in the room that J. J. O'Molloy and Professor MacHugh each recite a passage from a celebrated speech of some years back. Both speeches make reference to Moses. O'Madden Burke now proposes that everyone retire to Mooney's, a nearby pub. Four of the group leave first – Stephen Dedalus, O'Madden Burke, Lenehan, and Professor MacHugh – while Miles Crawford stays behind to find his keys and J. J. O'Molloy lingers with him in order to ask for a loan. Once outside, Stephen begins to recount to Professor MacHugh a parable, one intended to respond to the speeches that have been recited by O'Molloy and MacHugh back in the office. Bloom, meanwhile, returns from Dillon's auction room and catches up with Miles Crawford and J. J. O'Molloy in the street, who are some distance behind the group of four. Keyes has offered to renew his advertisement for only two months, not the three which Bloom had hoped to attain, and he wants the newspaper to furnish "a little puff," a small feature article that would be advertising thinly disguised. When Bloom reports this to Crawford, the editor tartly tells Bloom that Keyes "can kiss my royal Irish arse." Bloom is now left behind by Crawford and O'Molloy, and the narrative briefly focuses on Crawford's polite refusal of O'Molloy's request for a loan. When these two swiftly catch up with the group of four, the narrative turns to Stephen's story, which he now completes, and which the others comment on.

Aeolus (1922), from Ulysses

IN THE HEART OF THE HIBERNIAN METROPOLIS

Before Nelson's pillar[1] trams slowed, shunted, changed trolley, started for Blackrock, Kingstown and Dalkey, Clonskea, Rathgar and Terenure, Palmerston park and upper Rathmines, Sandymount Green, Rathmines, Ringsend and Sandymount Tower, Harold's Cross. The hoarse Dublin United Tramway Company's timekeeper bawled them off:
— Rathgar and Terenure !   5
— Come on, Sandymount Green !
Right and left parallel clanging ringing a doubledecker and a singledeck moved from their railheads, swerved to the down line, glided parallel.
— Start, Palmerston park!

THE WEARER OF THE CROWN

Under the porch of the general post office[2] shoeblacks called and polished. Parked in North   10
Prince's street His Majesty's vermilion mailcars, bearing on their sides the royal initials, E. R.,[3] received loudly flung sacks of letters, postcards, lettercards, parcels, insured and paid, for local, provincial, British and overseas delivery.

GENTLEMEN OF THE PRESS

Grossbooted draymen rolled barrels dullthudding out of Prince's stores[4] and bumped them up on the brewery float. On the brewery float bumped dullthudding barrels rolled by grossbooted   15
draymen out of Prince's stores.
— There it is, Red Murray said. Alexander Keyes.
— Just cut it out, will you? Mr Bloom said, and I'll take it round to the *Telegraph* office.
The door of Ruttledge's office creaked again. Davy Stephens,[5] minute in a large capecoat, a small felt hat crowning his ringlets, passed out with a roll of papers under his cape, a king's courier.   20
Red Murray's long shears sliced out the advertisement from the newspaper in four clean strokes. Scissors and paste.

---

[1] Nelson's pillar, located in the very center of Dublin on Sackville Street (now O'Connell Street), served as the departure point for most of Dublin's trams. Electrification of the tramways began in 1896 and was completed in 1901. Nelson's pillar was erected to commemorate Lord Horatio Nelson, victorious naval commander at the Battle of Trafalgar; its foundation stone was laid in February 1808, and its construction finished the next year, three decades before the Nelson Monument in Trafalgar Square, London, was built. The Doric column was designed by the architect Francis Johnston (1760–1829), then Dublin architect of the Board of Works, and the surmounting statue of Nelson was by Thomas Kirk (1781–1845), a sculptor from Cork. It towered over the city center, 134 feet high. (It was blown up by Republicans in 1966 to commemorate the fiftieth anniversary of the Easter Rising; nobody was ever arrested in connection with this crime.)

[2] The General Post Office was built between 1815 and 1817, designed by Francis Johnston (see preceding note). Its neoclassical facade faces Sackville Street (now O'Connell Street), and it is situated just southwest of the site of Nelson's Pillar.

[3] Initials of *Edward Rex*, or Edward VII, King of England.

[4] A warehouse at 13, Prince's Street North, and so midway between the General Post Office and and the offices of *Freeman's Journal* and the *Evening Telegraph*.

[5] A vendor who kept a newstand at Kingstown (now Dun Laoghaire), the port which served the mailboat between Dublin and Liverpool. He became celebrated for his uninhibited wit, and for meeting leading politicians and public figures, including Edward VII (whence the epigraph "a king's courier"). For a contemporary postcard with a photograph of him, see David Pierce, *Jame Joyce's Ireland* (New Haven: Yale University Press, 1992), p. 106.

— I'll go through the printing works, Mr Bloom said, taking the cut square.

— Of course, if he wants a par, Red Murray said earnestly, a pen behind his ear, we can do him

25   one.

— Right, Mr Bloom said with a nod. I'll rub that in.

We.

WILLIAM BRAYDEN, ESQUIRE, OF OAKLANDS, SANDYMOUNT[6]

Red Murray touched Mr Bloom's arm with the shears and whispered:

— Brayden.

30   Mr Bloom turned and saw the liveried porter raise his lettered cap as a stately figure entered between the newsboards of the *Weekly Freeman and National Press* and the *Freeman's Journal and National Press*. Dullthudding Guinness's barrels. It passed statelily up the staircase steered by an umbrella, a solemn beardframed face. The broadcloth back ascended each step: back. All his brains are in the nape of his neck, Simon Dedalus says. Welts of flesh behind on him. Fat folds of neck, fat,

35   neck, fat, neck.

— Don't you think his face is like Our Saviour? Red Murray whispered.

The door of Ruttledge's office whispered: ee: cree. They always build one door opposite another for the wind to. Way in. Way out.

Our Saviour: beardframed oval face: talking in the dusk Mary, Martha.[7] Steered by an umbrella

40   sword to the footlights: Mario the tenor.[8]

— Or like Mario, Mr Bloom said.

— Yes, Red Murray agreed. But Mario was said to be the picture of Our Saviour.

Jesus Mario with rougy cheeks, doublet and spindle legs. Hand on his heart. In *Martha*.[9]

Co-ome thou lost one,
45   *Co-ome thou dear one*

THE CROZIER AND THE PEN

— His grace[10] phoned down twice this morning, Red Murray said gravely.

---

[6]   William Braydon (1865–1933) was editor of the *Freeman's journal* from 1892 to 1916. His house, named "Oaklands," was situated on the Serpentine Avenue in Sandymount, a Dublin suburb.

[7]   Mary and Martha are sisters of Lazarus and friends of Jesus who, in an incident recounted in Luke 10:38–42, host a meal for him. When Martha complains that Mary is not helping do chores, but sits listening to Jesus, Jesus answers that "Mary has chosen that good part, which shall not be taken away from her." Earlier in the day, in episode 5 of "Lotus-Eaters," Bloom has received a letter from a woman who signs as "Martha Clifford." Bloom is conducting an epistolary affair with her (he signs his letters "Henry Flower"), an attempt to displace his anxiety over the state of his marriage with his wife, Marion. As a consequence of the coincidence of names, Bloom thinks back to a painting of Mary and Martha throughout the day.

[8]   Giovanni Mario (1810–83), an Italian tenor whose original name was Giovanni Matteo, Cavaliere di Candia, sang in London from 1839 to 1871 at various theaters. Like Enrico Caruso or Luciano Pavarotti, he became a legendary figure, his image reproduced in postcards many years after his death.

[9]   *Martha, oder der Markt von Richmond* or *Martha, the Fair at Richmond* (1847), was a light opera by Friedrich von Flotow (1812–83). The noblewoman Lady Harriet Durham disguises herself as "Martha," a servant girl and, together with her maid Nancy, also disguised, escapes the stultifying life of the court by going to a country fair at Richmond. There they meet two well-to-do farmers, Lionel and Plunkett, who hire them as servants. Of course the women prove utterly incompetent at household chores, but the men fall in love with them anyway, Lionel with "Martha" and Plunkett with Nancy. The two women escape back to court, but one day when they are out riding their singing is immediately recognized by Lionel and Plunkett. They escape a second time, and Lionel loses his reason in grief over his lost love. But Nancy and Plunkett stage a repeat performance of the fair at Richmond, where Lionel again meets "Martha," recovers his reason, and at last marries her. The opera interests Bloom because of his clandestine correspondence with Martha Clifford, whose name may be as fictitious as that of the character in Flotow's opera. There are two arias from the opera that recur throughout *Ulysses*. One is called "Ach! so fromm, ach so traut" ("Oh so innocent, oh so faithful"), which has always been a favorite for tenors because of the sustained high note at the end; it was translated into English under the title "When First I Saw that Form Endearing," and into Italian as "M'appari" ("You Appeared to Me"); the latter is still a concert aria for Italian tenors. It is from the English version that Bloom recalls, in this episode, "Co-ome thou lost one, / Co-ome thou dear one!" The other aria that recurs in *Ulysses* is a musical setting of Thomas Moore's "The Last Rose of Summer."

[10]   It is not clear whether this is newspaper slang for Brayden, the publisher, or is really meant to refer to William J. Walsh (1841–1921), the Archbishop of Dublin. The former seems more likely.

They watched the knees, legs, boots vanish. Neck.

A telegram boy stepped in nimbly, threw an envelope on the counter and stepped off posthaste with a word.

— *Freeman* ! 50

Mr Bloom said slowly:

— Well, he is one of our saviours also.

A meek smile accompanied him as he lifted the counterflap, as he passed in through the sidedoor and along the warm dark stairs and passage, along the now reverberating boards. But will he save the circulation? Thumping, thumping. 55

He pushed in the glass swingdoor and entered, stepping over strewn packing paper. Through a lane of clanking drums he made his way towards Nannetti's[11] reading closet.

Hynes here too:[12] account of the funeral probably. Thumping thump.

WITH UNFEIGNED REGRET IT IS WE ANNOUNCE THE DISSOLUTION OF A MOST RESPECTED DUBLIN BURGESS

This morning the remains of the late Mr Patrick Dignam. Machines. Smash a man to atoms if they got him caught. Rule the world today. His machineries are pegging away too. Like these, got 60 out of hand: fermenting. Working away, tearing away. And that old grey rat tearing to get in.

HOW A GREAT DAILY ORGAN IS TURNED OUT

Mr Bloom halted behind the foreman's spare body, admiring a glossy crown.

Strange he never saw his real country. Ireland my country.[13] Member for College green. He boomed that workaday worker tack for all it was worth. It's the ads and side features sell a weekly not the stale news in the official gazette.[14] Queen Anne is dead.[15] Published by authority in the year one thousand and. Demesne situate in the townland of Rosenallis, barony of Tinnahinch.[16] To all whom 65 it may concern schedule pursuant to statute showing return of number of mules and jennets exported from Ballina. Nature notes. Cartoons. Phil Blake's weekly Pat and Bull story. Uncle Toby's page for tiny tots. Country bumpkin's queries. Dear Mr Editor, what is a good cure for flatulence? I'd like that part. Learn a lot teaching others. The personal note. M. A. P.[17] Mainly all pictures. Shapely bathers on golden strand. World's biggest balloon. Double marriage of sisters celebrated. Two 70 bridegrooms laughing heartily at each other.[18] Cuprani too, printer. More Irish than the Irish.

[11] Joseph Patrick Nannetti (1851–1915) was an Irish-Italian master printer and politician. He served as Member of Parliament for the College Division of Dublin (whence the reference, a bit further below, to "Member for College Green") and was also a member of the Dublin Corporation.

[12] Joe Hynes had earlier attended the funeral of Patrick Dignam, along with Bloom himself, recounted in "Hades," the episode preceding this one.

[13] The newspaper the *United Irishman* (founded by the nationalist Arthur Griffith in 1901) had made the question of who was to be considered Irish a topical question. Griffith argued that only Gaels were truly Irish; anyone else would not count. The question recurs when Bloom first enters the outer office of Miles Crawford, further below in this episode.

[14] The *Dublin Gazette*, printed by His Majesty's Stationer's office, reported legal notices and official news.

[15] A retort to someone who reports stale news, ostensibly an expression that arose when Joseph Addison (1672–1719) reported the death of Queen Anne in the *Spectator* long after it was well known to all.

[16] The name of a house in the parish of Rosenallis in what was then Queens County (now County Laois), some 12 miles southeast of Dublin; it was presented to Henry Grattan (1746–1820), an Irish statesman, by the Irish Parliament in 1797, a gift in recognition of his labors on behalf of the nation. Grattan had cam-

paigned successfully for increased legislative independence and Catholic emancipation; he had returned from retirement to oppose the Act of Union (1799–1800), then become a Member of Parliament after its passage.

[17] *Mainly About People* was a penny weekly edited by T. P. O'Connor (1848–1929), one of several newspapers and journals that he launched, all of which typified what contemporaries called "the New Journalism." Newspapers most representative of this trend were the *Pall Mall Gazette*, which was redesigned by W. T. Stead (1849–1912) in 1883; the *Star*, which was founded and edited by O'Connor in 1888; and the *Daily Mail*, which was launched in 1896 by Alfred Harmsworth (1865–1922; later Lord Northcliffe) and which had a circulation of more than one million a day by 1902, then the largest circulation in the world. The politics of these newspapers varied widely, from nonconformist reformism to deep conservatism, but they were united in adopting larger headlines, many illustrations, a style that was bright, personal, and lively, and a tendency to blur the distinction between news and entertainment. For some they represented a significant lowering of the standards of cultural debate; for others they marked an enlargement of public debate to include vast, new audiences.

[18] *To all whom ... heartily at each other* these phrases parody features that appeared in *The Weekly Freeman*, a weekly version of *The Freeman's Journal*. "Market News" listed sales of livestock,

The machines clanked in threefour time. Thump, thump, thump. Now if he got paralysed there and no one knew how to stop them they'd clank on and on the same, print it over and over and up and back. Monkeydoodle the whole thing. Want a cool head.

75   — Well, get it into the evening edition, councillor, Hynes said.

Soon be calling him my lord mayor. Long John[19] is backing him they say.

The foreman, without answering, scribbled press on a corner of the sheet and made a sign to a typesetter. He handed the sheet silently over the dirty glass screen.

— Right: thanks, Hynes said moving off.

80   Mr Bloom stood in his way.

— If you want to draw the cashier is just going to lunch, he said, pointing backward with his thumb.

— Did you? Hynes asked.

— Mm, Mr Bloom said. Look sharp and you'll catch him.

85   — Thanks, old man, Hynes said. I'll tap him too.

He hurried on eagerly towards the *Freeman's Journal*.

Three bob I lent him in Meagher's.[20] Three weeks. Third hint.

WE SEE THE CANVASSER AT WORK

Mr Bloom laid his cutting on Mr Nannetti's desk.

— Excuse me, councillor, he said. This ad, you see. Keyes, you remember.

90   Mr Nannetti considered the cutting awhile and nodded.

— He wants it in for July, Mr Bloom said.

The foreman moved his pencil towards it.

— But wait, Mr Bloom said. He wants it changed. Keyes, you see. He wants two keys at the top.

Hell of a racket they make. He doesn't hear it. Nannan. Iron nerves. Maybe he understands

95   what I.

The foreman turned round to hear patiently and, lifting an elbow, began to scratch slowly in the armpit of his alpaca jacket.

— Like that, Mr Bloom said, crossing his forefingers at the top.

Let him take that in first.

100   Mr Bloom, glancing sideways up from the cross he had made, saw the foreman's sallow face, think he has a touch of jaundice, and beyond the obedient reels feeding in huge webs of paper. Clank it. Clank it. Miles of it unreeled. What becomes of it after? O, wrap up meat, parcels: various uses, thousand and one things.

Slipping his words deftly into the pauses of the clanking he drew swiftly on the scarred

105   woodwork.

HOUSE OF KEY(E)S[21]

— Like that, see. Two crossed keys here.[22] A circle. Then here the name Alexander Keyes, tea, wine and spirit merchant. So on.

Better not teach him his own business.

---

sometimes reporting on places as unimportant as Balina, in County Mayo; "Nature Notes" carried advice on agriculture; still other pages indulged Irish stereoptyes, addressed children, or offered advice.

[19]   Nannetti became lord mayor of Dublin in 1906; Long John Fanning is a fictional subsheriff of Dublin, who is described in "Grace," a short story in Joyce's *Dubliners*.

[20]   A public house, or pub, in central Dublin. "Three bob" are three shillings.

[21]   Bloom assimilates the fictional grocer, Alexander Keyes, to the House of Keys, the lower house of the Parliament in the Isle

of Man. Since the island enjoyed a qualified home rule (Parliament acting in consort with a governor), it was a model for Irish aspirations to home rule.

[22]   The emblem of the House of Keys on the Isle of Man. But throughout the opening episodes of *Ulysses*, keys acquire a range of values. In "Telemachus" (episode 1), Stephen Dedalus relinquishes the key to the Martello tower which he has rented to Buck Mulligan, a sign of the power or authority which Mulligan is usurping. Bloom, in "Calypso" (episode 4), forgets his key in another pair of trousers; it becomes a sign of the sexual power which he has relinquished.

— You know yourself, councillor, just what he wants. Then round the top in leaded: the house of keys. You see? Do you think that's a good idea? 110

The foreman moved his scratching hand to his lower ribs and scratched there quietly.

— The idea, Mr Bloom said, is the house of keys. You know, councillor, the Manx parliament. Innuendo of home rule. Tourists, you know, from the isle of Man. Catches the eye, you see. Can you do that?

I could ask him perhaps about how to pronounce that *voglio*.[23] But then if he didn't know only 115
make it awkward for him. Better not.

— We can do that, the foreman said. Have you the design?

— I can get it, Mr Bloom said. It was in a Kilkenny[24] paper. He has a house there too. I'll just run out and ask him. Well, you can do that and just a little par calling attention. You know the usual. High class licensed premises. Longfelt want. So on. 120

The foreman thought for an instant.

— We can do that, he said. Let him give us a three months' renewal.

A typesetter brought him a limp galleypage. He began to check it silently. Mr Bloom stood by, hearing the loud throbs of cranks, watching the silent typesetters at their cases.

ORTHOGRAPHICAL

Want to be sure of his spelling. Proof fever. Martin Cunningham forgot to give us his spellingbee 125
conundrum this morning. It is amusing to view the unpar one ar alleled embarra two ars is it? double ess ment of a harassed pedlar while gauging au the symmetry of a peeled pear under a cemetery wall. Silly, isn't it? Cemetery put in of course on account of the symmetry.

I could have said when he clapped on his topper. Thank you. I ought to have said something about an old hat or something. No, I could have said. Looks as good as new now. See his phiz[25] then. 130

Sllt. The nethermost deck of the first machine jogged forward its flyboard[26] with sllt the first batch of quirefolded[27] papers. Sllt. Almost human the way it sllt to call attention. Doing its level best to speak. That door too sllt creaking, asking to be shut. Everything speaks in its own way. Sllt.

NOTED CHURCHMAN AN OCCASIONAL CONTRIBUTOR

The foreman handed back the galleypage suddenly, saying: 135
— Wait. Where's the archbishop's letter? It's to be repeated in the *Telegraph*. Where's what's his name?

He looked about him round his loud unanswering machines.

— Monks, sir? a voice asked from the castingbox.[28]

---

[23] In "Calypso" (episode 4 of *Ulysses*), Bloom's wife Molly tells him that she will be singing *La ci darem la mano* ("There we shall give each other our hands") in her upcoming concert in Belfast, together with Blazes Boylan. This part of the aria, a duet from Mozart's opera *Don Giovanni*, is sung by the character Zerlina (read: Molly) to the character Don Giovanni (read: Blazes Boylan) in response to his seductive proposal that they retreat alone to his secluded house, leaving behind her fiancé, Massetto (read: Bloom). Zerlina's reply is ambiguous: *Vorrei e non vorrei* ("I would like to and I wouldn't like to"). Bloom, as it so happens, is also looking for Molly's stocking while talking with her:

> He felt here and there. *Voglio e non vorrei.*
> Wonder if she pronounces that right: *voglio.*
> Not in the bed.

Bloom substitutes *voglio* ("I want") for *vorrei* ("I would like to") because subconsciously he knows that Molly (Zerlina) wants

Blazes Boylan (her Don). At the same time, his sequence of thoughts (*voglio*. Not in the bed.), though ostensbily tracing a change in the focus of his thoughts from the aria (*voglio*, or "I want") to the missing stocking ("Not in the bed."), inadvertently recognizes his own problem: he has not made love to Molly since the death of their son Rudy, 9 years earlier.

[24] A town some 70 miles southwest of Dublin.

[25] Physiognomy.

[26] The horizontal board on which an old-fashioned printing press would deposit the printed sheets.

[27] Four sheets folded in half to make a quire of 8 pages.

[28] A box, into which a body of typeset matter would be inserted; a plaster mold was then made of the type, which in turn was used to produce a metal plate, or stereo type, that would then be used for the actual process of printing.

140   — Ay. Where's Monks?
        — Monks!
        Mr Bloom took up his cutting. Time to get out.
        — Then I'll get the design, Mr Nannetti, he said, and you'll give it a good place I know.
        — Monks!
145   — Yes, sir.
        Three months' renewal. Want to get some wind off my chest first. Try it anyhow. Rub in August: good idea: horseshow month. Ballsbridge.[29] Tourists over for the show.

A DAYFATHER[30]

        He walked on through the caseroom, passing an old man, bowed, spectacled, aproned. Old Monks, the dayfather. Queer lot of stuff he must have put through his hands in his time: obituary
150   notices, pubs' ads, speeches, divorce suits, found drowned. Nearing the end of his tether now. Sober serious man with a bit in the savingsbank I'd say. Wife a good cook and washer. Daughter working the machine in the parlour. Plain Jane, no damn nonsense.

AND IT WAS THE FEAST OF THE PASSOVER[31]

        He stayed in his walk to watch a typesetter neatly distributing type. Reads it backwards first. Quickly he does it. Must require some practice that. mangiD. kcirtaP.[32] Poor papa with his
155   hagadah[33] book, reading backwards with his finger to me. Pessach.[34] Next year in Jerusalem.[35] Dear, O dear! All that long business about that brought us out of the land of Egypt and into the house of bondage *alleluia.*[36] *Shema Israel Adonai Elohenu.*[37] No, that's the other. Then the twelve brothers,[38] Jacob's sons. And then the lamb and the cat and the dog and the stick and the water and the butcher and then the angel of death kills the butcher and he kills the ox and the dog kills the
160   cat.[39] Sounds a bit silly till you come to look into it well. Justice it means but it's everybody eating everyone else. That's what life is after all. How quickly he does that job. Practice makes perfect. Seems to see with his fingers.
        Mr Bloom passed on out of the clanking noises through the gallery on to the landing. Now am I going to tram it out all the way and then catch him out perhaps. Better phone him up first.
165   Number? Same as Citron's house. Twentyeight. Twentyeight double four.

[29] Ballsbridge, a southeastern suburb of Dublin, was the site of an annual horse show held in August.

[30] *DAYFATHER* in the specialized world of printing, a "chapel" was the term used to designate either a printers' workshop (i.e., a printing office) or a meeting or association of the journeymen employed in a printing office, typically for promoting and enforcing order among themselves or for settling disputes concerning wages, etc. It was presided over by a "father" of the chapel who was annually elected; a "dayfather" was the father of the day staff, a "nightfather" of the night staff.

[31] From the Hebrew word *pesach*, meaning "to pass over"; Passover is a Jewish feast which commemorates God's "passing over" or sparing the homes of the Israelites on the evening when he killed all the firstborn children of the Egyptians to punish them for their wickedness (see Exodus 12:1–14). This is the first of many allusions connecting the Exodus story with that of modern Ireland.

[32] *mangiD. kcirtaP* Patrick Dignam, whose name Bloom is reading in reverse because that is how the characters appear to the eye when a compositor sets type, is a fictional character whose

funeral Bloom has attended in the preceding episode ("Hades") of *Ulysses.*

[33] The Hagadah is the prayerbook for the family observance of the Passover in Judaism.

[34] A variant spelling of the Hebrew word *pesach*, or Passover.

[35] The final phrase that climaxes the last prayer to God and concludes the ceremonies on the first night of Passover.

[36] Bloom mistakenly reverses an often cited phrase of the Old Testament: "the Lord brought us out from Egypt, from the house of bondage" (Exodus 13:14).

[37] "Alleluia" is the Latin and Greek rendering of the Hebrew Hallelujah, "Praise ye the Lord." "Shema Israel Adona Elohenu" is Hebrew for "hear, oh Israel, the Lord our God" (Deuteronomy 6:4).

[38] Bloom associates the 12 sons of Jacob (Genesis 35:22–7) with the 12 tribes of Israel.

[39] *And then lamb ... kills the cat* Bloom recalls an idiosyncratic version of a chant, the *Chad Gadya* ("One Kid"), which is recited on the second day of Passover. His interpretation of it is broadly correct.

ONLY ONCE MORE THAT SOAP

He went down the house staircase. Who the deuce scrawled all over these walls with matches? Looks as if they did it for a bet. Heavy greasy smell there always is in those works. Lukewarm glue in Thom's next door[40] when I was there.

He took out his handkerchief to dab his nose. Citronlemon? Ah, the soap I put there. Lose it out of that pocket. Putting back his handkerchief he took out the soap and stowed it away, buttoned, into the hip pocket of his trousers.   170

What perfume does your wife use?[41] I could go home still: tram: something I forgot. Just to see: before: dressing. No. Here. No.

A sudden screech of laughter came from the *Evening Telegraph* office. Know who that is. What's up? Pop in a minute to phone. Ned Lambert it is.   175

He entered softly.

ERIN, GREEN GEM OF THE SILVER SEA[42]

— The ghost walks,[43] professor MacHugh murmured softly, biscuitfully to the dusty windowpane.

Mr Dedalus, staring from the empty fireplace at Ned Lambert's quizzing face, asked of it sourly:

— Agonising Christ, wouldn't it give you a heartburn on your arse? Ned Lambert, seated on the table, read on: 180

— *Or again, note the meanderings of some purling rill as it babbles on its way, tho' quarrelling with the stony obstacles, to the tumbling waters of Neptune's blue domain, mid mossy banks, fanned by gentlest zephyrs, played on by the glorious sunlight or 'neath the shadows cast o'er its pensive bosom by the overarching leafage of the giants of the forest.* What about that, Simon? he asked over the fringe of his newspaper. How's that for high?   185

— Changing his drink, Mr Dedalus said.

Ned Lambert, laughing, struck the newspaper on his knees, repeating:

— *The pensive bosom and the overarsing leafage.* O boys! O, boys!

— And Xenophon looked upon Marathon, Mr Dedalus said, looking again on the fireplace and to the window, and Marathon looked on the sea.[44]   190

— That will do, professor MacHugh cried from the window. I don't want to hear any more of the stuff.

He ate off the crescent of water biscuit he had been nibbling and, hungered, made ready to nibble the biscuit in his other hand.

High falutin stuff. Bladderbags. Ned Lambert is taking a day off I see. Rather upsets a man's day a funeral does. He has influence they say. Old Chatterton,[45] the vice-chancellor is his granduncle or his greatgranduncle. Close on ninety they say. Subleader[46] for his death written this long time perhaps. Living to spite them. Might go first himself. Johnny, make room for your uncle. The right   195

---

[40] The publishing firm of Alexander Thom and Co., which printed a directory of Dublin.

[41] *What perfume does your wife use?* Bloom is recalling a phrase from a letter by "Martha Clifford," a woman with whom he is having a clandestine affair by correspondence. (Bloom receives her letter in "Lotus Eaters," episode 5 in *Ulysses*.) Her letter ends: "P.S. Do tell what kind of perfume does your wife use. I want to know."

[42] *ERIN, GREEN GEM OF THE SILVER SEA* compare "Cuisle Mo Chroidhe," by John Philpot Curran, which begins: "Dear Erin, how sweetly thy green bosom rises! An emerald set in the ring of the sea."

[43] Theatrical and journalistic slang for "salaries are being paid," and an allusion to *Hamlet* I.i.

[44] *And Xenophon . . . on the sea* from "The Isles of Greece," a lyric by Lord Byron (1788–1824) which is interpolated between stanzas 86 and 87 of *Don Juan* (1821): "The mountains look on Marathon / And Marathon looks on the sea." Xenophon (c. 434–c.354) was an ancient Greek historian. Marathon, on the northeast coast of Attica, some 20 miles outside Athens, was the site of a battle in 490 BC in which the Athenians defeated the invading Persians.

[45] Hedges Eyre Chatterton (1820–1910) was a solictor and vice-chancellor of Ireland, a judge who assisted or substituted for the chancellor.

[46] An account of a well-known person's life which is kept on file, then updated and added to the "leader," the first paragraph of an obituary notice.

honourable Hedges Eyre Chatterton. Daresay he writes him an odd shaky cheque or two on gale
200   days.[47] Windfall when he kicks out. Alleluia.

— Just another spasm, Ned Lambert said.

— What is it? Mr Bloom asked.

— A recently discovered fragment of Cicero's,[48] professor MacHugh answered with pomp of
tone. *Our lovely land.*

SHORT BUT TO THE POINT

205   — Whose land? Mr Bloom said simply.

— Most pertinent question, the professor said between his chews. With an accent on the whose.

— Dan Dawson's[49] land, Mr Dedalus said.

— Is it his speech last night? Mr Bloom asked.

Ned Lambert nodded.

210   — But listen to this, he said.

The doorknob hit Mr Bloom in the small of the back as the door was pushed in.

— Excuse me, J. J. O'Molloy said, entering.

Mr Bloom moved nimbly aside.

— I beg yours, he said.

215   — Good day, Jack.

— Come in. Come in.

— Good day.

— How are you, Dedalus?

— Well. And yourself?

220   J. J. O'Molloy shook his head.

SAD

Cleverest fellow at the junior bar he used to be. Decline poor chap. That hectic flush spells finis
for a man. Touch and go with him. What's in the wind, I wonder. Money worry.

— *Or again if we but climb the serried mountain peaks.*

— You're looking extra.

225   — Is the editor to be seen? J. J. O'Molloy asked, looking towards the inner door.

— Very much so, professor MacHugh said. To be seen and heard. He's in his sanctum with
Lenehan.[50]

J. J. O'Molloy strolled to the sloping desk and began to turn back the pink pages[51] of the file.

Practice dwindling. A mighthavebeen. Losing heart. Gambling. Debts of honour. Reaping the
230   whirlwind.[52] Used to get good retainers from D. and T. Fitzgerald.[53] Their wigs to show their grey
matter. Brains on their sleeve like the statue in Glasnevin.[54] Believe he does some literary work for
the *Express* with Gabriel Conroy.[55] Wellread fellow. Myles Crawford began on the *Independent*.[56]

---

[47]   Days when installment payments are due.

[48]   (106–43 BC) Roman orator and statesman, noted for his
achievements in rhetoric.

[49]   A successful baker who became a politician, twice lord
mayor of Dublin (1882, 1883), and in 1904 collector of rates
(taxes) for the Dublin Corporation. His speech is fictional.

[50]   A fictional character, an unemployed cadger whose doings
are recounted in "Two Gallants," a short story in Joyce's *Dubliners.*

[51]   The Last Pink Edition of the *Evening Telegraph* was printed
on light pink paper.

[52]   Hosea 8:7, "For they have sown the wind, and they shall reap
the whirlwind."

[53]   A legal firm in north central Dublin.

[54]   A Dublin cemetery which Bloom has visited earlier in the
day (in the "Hades" episode), where he noticed a statue that wore
a heart as a symbol of devotion.

[55]   The *Daily Express* (1851–1921) was a conservative newspaper; Gabriel Conroy is a fictional character in "The Dead,"
the last short story in Joyce's *Dubliners.*

[56]   the *Irish Daily Independent* was founded in 1891 by Charles
Parnell; it was bought out by William Martin Murphy in 1900,
renamed the *Irish Independent*, and given a different editorial
policy.

Funny the way those newspaper men veer about when they get wind of a new opening. Weathercocks. Hot and cold in the same breath. Wouldn't know which to believe. One story good till you hear the next. Go for one another baldheaded in the papers and then all blows over.   235
Hailfellow well met the next moment.

— Ah, listen to this for God' sake, Ned Lambert pleaded. *Or again if we but climb the serried mountain peaks . . .*

— Bombast! the professor broke in testily. Enough of the inflated windbag!

— *Peaks*, Ned Lambert went on, *towering high on high, to bathe our souls, as it were . . .*   240

— Bathe his lips, Mr Dedalus said. Blessed and eternal God! Yes? Is he taking anything for it.

— *As 'twere, in the peerless panorama of Ireland's portfolio, unmatched, despite their wellpraised prototypes in other vaunted prize regions, for very beauty, of bosky grove and undulating plain and luscious pastureland of vernal green, steeped in the transcendent translucent glow of our mild mysterious Irish twilight . . .*

— The moon, professor MacHugh said. He forgot Hamlet.[57]   245

HIS NATIVE DORIC[58]

— *That mantles the vista far and wide and wait till the glowing orb of the moon shines forth to irradiate her silver effulgence.*

— O! Mr Dedalus cried, giving vent to a hopeless groan, shite and onions! That'll do, Ned. Life is too short.

He took off his silk hat and, blowing out impatiently his bushy moustache, welshcombed[59] his   250
hair with raking fingers.

Ned Lambert tossed the newspaper aside, chuckling with delight. An instant after a hoarse bark of laughter burst over professor MacHugh's unshaven blackspectacled face.

— Doughy Daw! he cried.

WHAT WETHERUP SAID

All very fine to jeer at it now in cold print but it goes down like hot cake that stuff. He was in   255
the bakery line too wasn't he? Why they call him Doughy Daw. Feathered his nest well anyhow.
Daughter engaged to that chap in the inland revenue office with the motor. Hooked that nicely.
Entertainments open house. Big blow out. Wetherup always said that. Get a grip of them by the stomach.

The inner door was opened violently and a scarlet beaked face, crested by a comb of feathery hair,   260
thrust itself in. The bold blue eyes stared about them and the harsh voice asked:

— What is it?

— And here comes the sham squire[60] himself, professor MacHugh said grandly.

— Getououthat, you bloody old pedagogue! the editor said in recognition.

— Come, Ned. Mr Dedalus said, putting on his hat. I must get a drink after that.   265

— Drink! the editor cried. No drinks served before mass.

— Quite right too, Mr Dedalus said, going out. Come on, Ned.

Ned Lambert sidled down from the table. The editor's blue eyes roved towards Mr Bloom's face, shadowed by a smile.

— Will you join us, Myles? Ned Lambert asked.   270

---

[57] Dawson, having described Ireland by moonlight, should carry on his flourish to include dawn, as Horatio does in *Hamlet* I.i.166–7.

[58] The Doric dialect of ancient Greek was considered broad or rustic; by extension the term was applied to nonstandard dialects of English.

[59] to comb one's hair with the thumb and four fingers; the Welsh were popularly thought to be unkempt.

[60] Francis Higgens (1746–1802) was known as "the sham squire" because he married a respectable young woman by pretending to be a country gentleman when he was merely an attorney's clerk in Dublin.

MEMORABLE BATTLES RECALLED

— North Cork militia! the editor cried, striding to the mantelpiece. We won every time! North Cork and Spanish officers!

— Where was that, Myles? Ned Lambert asked with a reflective glance at his toecaps.

— In Ohio! the editor shouted.[61]

275   — So it was, begad, Ned Lambert agreed.

Passing out, he whispered to J. J. O'Molloy:

— Incipient jigs.[62] Sad case.

— Ohio! the editor crowed in high treble from his uplifted scarlet face. My Ohio!

— A perfect cretic![63] the professor said. Long, short and long.

O, HARP EOLIAN![64]

280   He took a reel of dental floss from his waistcoat pocket and, breaking off a piece, twanged it smartly between two and two of his resonant unwashed teeth.

— Bingbang, bangbang.

Mr Bloom, seeing the coast clear, made for the inner door.

— Just a moment, Mr Crawford, he said. I just want to phone about an ad. He went in.

285   — What about that leader[65] this evening? professor MacHugh asked, coming to the editor and laying a firm hand on his shoulder.

— That'll be all right, Myles Crawford said more calmly. Never you fret. Hello, Jack. That's all right.

— Good day, Myles, J. J. O'Molloy said, letting the pages he held slip limply back on the file. Is

290   that Canada swindle case[66] on today?

The telephone whirred inside.

— Twenty eight . . . No, twenty . . . Double four . . . Yes.

SPOT THE WINNER

Lenehan came out of the inner office with *Sport's* tissues.[67]

— Who wants a dead cert for the Gold cup?[68] he asked. Sceptre with O. Madden up.

295   He tossed the tissues on to the table.

Screams of newsboys barefoot in the hall rushed near and the door was flung open.

— Hush, Lenehan said. I hear feetstoops.

---

[61]   *North Cork militia ... In Ohio!* Crawford's claims are so incoherent that Ned Lambert, a few lines further, ascribes them to the effects of alcoholism.

[62]   Formed from *jig*, to hop or skip around, the term indicates the incoherent mental processes of advancing alcoholism.

[63]   In the metrics of ancient Greek and Latin, a poetic foot with three syllables: long, short, long.

[64]   An aeolian harp is a stringed instrument which is activated by the winds. The harp also is a symbol of Ireland, since Celtic bards reportedly used them.

[65]   In British usage, a "leader" is the leading editorial, which Crawford must write.

[66]   A case that was currently before the court which concerned a man known variously as Saphiro, Sparks, or James Wought, who was charged with swindling people by promising to secure passage to Canada for £1, when the going fare was £2.

[67]   Racing forms prepared by *Sport*, a weekly newspaper published by the same company that published *The Freeman* and the *Evening Telegraph*.

[68]   The Gold Cup was a horse race held on June 16, 1904, at Ascot Heath, a racetrack located 26 miles from London. The race, over a course of two miles and a half, began at 3:00 p.m., and was won by a dark horse with the delightful name Throwaway. The text of *Ulysses* gradually weaves a series of associative links which connect this horse to Bloom, who is himself a "throwaway," someone who will be cast off or rejected by his wife Molly during the course of the day, but someone who will also, if we insist on the parallel with the horse, prevail in the end. In earlier and later episodes, comic misunderstandings ensue as various Dubliners mistakenly assume that Bloom has inside information about the race, that he is predicting the race's outcome, or (later in the day) that he has earned a great deal of money by betting on Throwaway against steep odds. "With O. Madden up" means that "O. Madden," a wholly fictional character, is to be the jockey riding Sceptre.

Professor MacHugh strode across the room and seized the cringing urchin by the collar as the others scampered out of the hall and down the steps. The tissues rustled up in the draught, floated softly in the air blue scrawls and under the table came to earth. 300

— It wasn't me, sir. It was the big fellow shoved me, sir.

— Throw him out and shut the door, the editor said. There's a hurricane blowing.

Lenehan began to paw the tissues up from the floor, grunting as he stooped twice.

— Waiting for the racing special, sir, the newsboy said. It was Pat Farrell shoved me, sir.

He pointed to two faces peering in round the doorframe. 305

— Him, sir.

— Out of this with you, professor MacHugh said gruffly.

He hustled the boy out and banged the door to.

J. J. O'Molloy turned the files crackingly over, murmuring, seeking:

— Continued on page six, column four. 310

— Yes ... *Evening Telegraph* here, Mr Bloom phoned from the inner office. Is the boss ...? Yes, *Telegraph* ... To where? ... Aha! Which auction rooms? ... Aha! I see ... Right. I'll catch him.

A COLLISION ENSUES

The bell whirred again as he rang off. He came in quickly and bumped against Lenehan who was struggling up with the second tissue. 315

— *Pardon, monsieur*, Lenehan said, clutching him for an instant and making a grimace.

— My fault, Mr Bloom said, suffering his grip. Are you hurt? I'm in a hurry.

— Knee, Lenehan said.

He made a comic face and whined, rubbing his knee:

— The accumulation of the *anno Domini*.[69] 320

— Sorry, Mr Bloom said.

He went to the door and, holding it ajar, paused. J. J. O'Molloy slapped the heavy pages over. The noise of two shrill voices, a mouthorgan, echoed in the bare hallway from the newsboys squatted on the doorsteps:

> We are the boys of Wexford 325
> Who fought with heart and hand.[70]

EXIT BLOOM

— I'm just running round to Bachelor's walk, Mr Bloom said, about this ad of Keyes's. Want to fix it up. They tell me he's round there in Dillon's.

He looked indecisively for a moment at their faces. The editor who, leaning against the mantelshelf, had propped his head on his hand suddenly stretched forth an arm amply. 330

— Begone! he said. The world is before you.[71]

— Back in no time, Mr Bloom said, hurrying out.

J. J. O'Molloy took the tissues from Lenehan's hand and read them, blowing them apart gently, without comment.

— He'll get that advertisement, the professor said, staring through his blackrimmed spectacles 335 over the crossblind. Look at the young scamps after him.

— Show. Where? Lenehan cried, running to the window.

[69] Latin for "in the year of our Lord."
[70] *We are the boys ... hand* words from the chorus to the ballad "The Boys of Wexford" by R. Dwyer Joyce (1830–83). The boys of Wexford are patriots who, in the Irish Rebellion of 1798, defeat the English but then, in the song, collapse in alcoholic excesses.
[71] *The world is before you* a proverbial expression that ultimately derives from Milton's *Paradise Lost*, where it is used to describe the state of Adam and Eve when they must leave Paradise (Bk. 12, ll. 646–7):

> The World was all before them, where to choose
> Their place of rest, and Providence their guide.

A STREET CORTEGE

Both smiled over the crossblind at the file of capering newsboys in Mr Bloom's wake, the last zigzagging white on the breeze a mocking kite, a tail of white bowknots.

340 — Look at the young guttersnipe behind him hue and cry, Lenehan said, and you'll kick. O, my rib risible! Taking off his flat spaugs and the walk. Small nines. Steal upon larks.[72]

He began to mazurka in swift caricature cross the floor on sliding feet past the fireplace to J. J. O'Molloy who placed the tissues in his receiving hands.

— What's that? Myles Crawford said with a start. Where are the other two gone?

345 — Who? the professor said, turning. They're gone round to the Oval for a drink. Paddy Hooper is there with Jack Hall.[73] Came over last night.

— Come on then, Myles Crawford said. Where's my hat?

He walked jerkily into the office behind, parting the vent of his jacket, jingling his keys in his back pocket. They jingled then in the air and against the wood as he locked his desk 350 drawer.

— He's pretty well on, professor MacHugh said in a low voice.

— Seems to be, J. J. O'Molloy said, taking out a cigarette case in murmuring meditation, but it is not always as it seems. Who has the most matches?

THE CALUMET[74] OF PEACE

He offered a cigarette to the professor and took one himself. Lenehan promptly struck a match 355 for them and lit their cigarettes in turn. J.J. O'Molloy opened his case again and offered it.

— *Thanky vous*, Lenehan said, helping himself.

The editor came from the inner office, a straw hat awry on his brow. He declaimed in song, pointing sternly at professor MacHugh:

> 'Twas rank and fame that tempted thee,
360 > 'Twas empire charmed thy heart.[75]

The professor grinned, locking his long lips.

— Eh? You bloody old Roman empire? Myles Crawford said.

He took a cigarette from the open case. Lenehan, lighting it for him with quick grace, said:

— Silence for my brandnew riddle!

365 — *Imperium romanum*,[76] J. J. O'Molloy said gently. It sounds nobler than British or Brixton.[77] The word reminds one somehow of fat in the fire.

Myles Crawford blew his first puff violently towards the ceiling.

— That's it, he said. We are the fat. You and I are the fat in the fire. We haven't got the chance of a snowball in hell.

THE GRANDEUR THAT WAS ROME[78]

370 — Wait a moment, professor MacHugh said, raising two quiet claws. We mustn't be led away by words, by sounds of words. We think of Rome, imperial, imperious, imperative.

---

[72] *Taking off his spaugs … larks* "Taking off his spaugs," i.e., imitating the movements of Bloom's big, clumsy feet (spaugs); "small nines" means that the newsboys are "up to all the dodges and tricks"; and "Steal upon larks" means they are clever enough to creep up on something as difficult to surprise as a lark.
[73] The Oval was a pub in Abbey Street Middle, just south of the *Freeman* offices; Patrick Hooper and J. B. Hall were Dublin journalists.
[74] the long tobacco pipe smoked by native Americans on ceremonial occasions; here applied to the cigarette that J. J. O'Molloy offers to professor MacHugh.

[75] *'Twas rank and fame … charmed thy heart* the first two lines of an aria from Act III of *The Rose of Castile* (1857), by Anglo-Irish composer Michael Balfe (1808–70).
[76] Latin for "the Roman empire."
[77] A London suburb which, around 1900, was a byword for drab respectability.
[78] From the poem "To Helen" (1831, 1845) by Edgar Allan Poe (1809–49):

> On desperate seas long wont to roam,
> Thy hyacinth hair, thy classic face,

He extended elocutionary arms from frayed stained shirtcuffs, pausing:

— What was their civilisation? Vast, I allow: but vile. Cloacae:[79] sewers. The Jews in the wilderness and on the mountaintop said: *It is meet to be here. Let us build an altar to Jehovah.* The Roman, like the Englishman who follows in his footsteps, brought to every new shore on   375 which he set his foot (on our shore he never set it) only his cloacal obsession. He gazed about him in his toga and he said: *It is meet to be here. Let us construct a watercloset.*

— Which they accordingly did do, Lenehan said. Our old ancient ancestors, as we read in the first chapter of Guinness's,[80] were partial to the running stream.

— They were nature's gentlemen, J. J. O'Molloy murmured. But we have also Roman law.   380

— And Pontius Pilate is its prophet,[81] professor MacHugh responded.

— Do you know that story about chief baron Palles?[82] J. J. O'Molloy asked. It was at the royal university dinner. Everything was going swimmingly...

— First my riddle, Lenehan said. Are you ready?

Mr O'Madden Burke,[83] tall in copious grey of Donegal tweed, came in from the hallway. Stephen   385 Dedalus, behind him, uncovered as he entered.

— *Entrez, mes enfants!*[84] Lenehan cried.

— I escort a suppliant, Mr O'Madden Burke said melodiously. Youth led by Experience visits Notoriety.

— How do you do? the editor said, holding out a hand. Come in. Your governor[85] is just gone.   390

???

Lenehan said to all:

— Silence! What opera resembles a railway line? Reflect, ponder, excogitate, reply.

Stephen handed over the typed sheets, pointing to the title and signature.

— Who? the editor asked.

Bit torn off.   395

— Mr Garrett Deasy, Stephen said.

— That old pelters,[86] the editor said. Who tore it? Was he short taken?

> *On swift sail flaming*
> *From storm and south*
> *He comes, pale vampire,*
> *Mouth to my mouth.*[87]

Thy Naiad airs have brought me home
To the glory that was Greece,
And the grandeur that was Rome.

[79] Latin for sewers. Sewers, or drainage systems, were one of the great achievements of nineteenth-century urbanism. The London sewer system was designed and built by Joseph Bazalgette between 1856 and 1859; the Paris sewer system was designed and built by Eugène Belgrand and Georges Haussmann between 1856 and 1865. In Paris the sewers even became popular with tourists. Dublin, instead, did not begin work on a sewer system until 1896, and it was not completed till 1906. Predictably, the death rate from typhoid in Dublin was higher than that of any other city in the UK, except Belfast.

[80] Lenehan uses a commonplace pun in Dublin to conjoin the book of Genesis with the famous Dublin Brewery: as the Jews were inclined to build altars, so the Irish have been inclined to drink.

[81] *Pontius Pilate is its prophet* MacHugh's remark echoes the Moslem profession of faith: "There is no god but Allah, and Mohammed is his Prophet."

[82] Christopher Palles (1831–1920), an Irish barrister and Lord

Chief Baron of the Exchequer, or chief judge in the Exchequer court, which was a division of the High Court of Justice in Ireland.

[83] A fictional character who appears in "A Mother," a short story in Joyce's *Dubliners*.

[84] French for "Enter, my children!"

[85] Slang for "father."

[86] Archaic term for a tramp or paltry person.

[87] *On swift sail ... mouth* some critics think that Stephen's poem is a free adaption of the last stanza in "My Grief on the Sea," a poem translated fom the Irish by Douglas Hyde (1869–1949) in his *Love Songs of Connacht* (Dublin, 1893):

> And my love came behind me –
> He came from the South;
> His breast to my bosom,
> His mouth to my mouth.

The poem is written by Stephen in "Proteus" (episode 3), and to write it he tears off a piece of paper from a letter to the editor written by Mr. Deasy, headmaster at the school where Stephen teaches; Stephen is now delivering the letter to Miles Crawford. Whence Crawford's question, "Who tore it?"

— Good day, Stephen, the professor said, coming to peer over their shoulders. Foot and mouth? Are you turned . . . ?

400   Bullockbefriending bard.

SHINDY IN WELLKNOWN RESTAURANT

— Good day, sir, Stephen answered, blushing. The letter is not mine. Mr Garrett Deasy asked me to . . .

— O, I know him, Myles Crawford said, and knew his wife too. The bloodiest old tartar God ever made. By Jesus, she had the foot and mouth disease and no mistake! The night she threw the
405   soup in the waiter's face in the Star and Garter.[88] Oho!

A woman brought sin into the world. For Helen, the runaway wife of Menelaus, ten years the Greeks. O'Rourke, prince of Breffni.[89]

— Is he a widower? Stephen asked.

— Ay, a grass one,[90] Myles Crawford said, his eye running down the typescript. Emperor's horses.
410   Habsburg. An Irishman saved his life on the ramparts of Vienna. Don't you forget! Maximilian Karl O'Donnell, graf von Tirconnel in Ireland.[91] Sent his heir over to make the king an Austrian fieldmarshal now.[92] Going to be trouble there one day. Wild geese.[93] O yes, every time. Don't you forget that!

— The moot point is did he forget it, J. J. O'Molloy said quietly, turning a horseshoe
415   paperweight. Saving princes is a thank you job.

Professor MacHugh turned on him.

— And if not? he said.

— I'll tell you how it was, Myles Crawford began. A Hungarian it was one day . . .

LOST CAUSES
NOBLE MARQUESS MENTIONED

— We were always loyal to lost causes, the professor said. Success for us is the death of the
420   intellect and of the imagination. We were never loyal to the successful. We serve them. I teach the blatant Latin language. I speak the tongue of a race the acme of whose mentality is the maxim: time is money. Material domination. *Dominus!*[94] Lord! Where is the spirituality? Lord Jesus! Lord Salisbury.[95] A sofa in a westend club. But the Greek!

KYRIE ELEISON![96]

A smile of light brightened his darkrimmed eyes, lengthened his long lips.
425   — The Greek! he said again. *Kyrios!* Shining word! The vowels the Semite and the Saxon know not.[97] *Kyrie!* The radiance of the intellect. I ought to profess Greek, the language of the mind. *Kyrie*

---

[88]   A Dublin hotel with a restaurant.

[89]   *A woman . . . Breffni* Stephen alludes to three stories. The first is that of Eve, who "brought sin into the world," in the book of Genesis. The second is that of Helen, the wife of the Greek king Menelaus, who runs away with Paris, and so starts the 10 years' war between the Greeks and the Trojans, recounted in Homer's *Iliad*. The third is that of Devorgilla, wife of O'Rourke, the Prince of Breffni (or Briefny, in some spellings), who runs away with Dermod MacMurrough in 1152, setting off a chain of events which leads him to solicit aid from Henry II of England and sparks the first Anglo-Norman invasion of Ireland in 1169.

[90]   A grass widower was a man separated from his wife.

[91]   *An Irishman saved . . . in Ireland* Maximilian Karl Lamoral Graf O'Donnell von Tirconnell (b. 1812), the son of an Irish expatriate in Austria, saved the life of Emperor Francis Joseph in 1853 when he was attacked by a Hungarian tailor.

[92]   *Sent his heir . . . now* Archduke Francis Ferdinand, son and "heir" of Emperor Francis Ferdinand (see preceding note) gave

Edward VII the baton of an Austrian field marshal on June 9, 1904.

[93]   The term was used to denote Irish who had deliberately expatriated rather than live in an Ireland ruled by England, such as the Tirconnell just described.

[94]   Latin for Lord.

[95]   Robert Arthur Talbot Gascoigne-Cecil, third Marquess of Salisbury, was the Conservative party leader who opposed Gladstone and Home Rule for the Irish. He was prime minister in 1885–6, 1886–92, and 1895–1902. The West End is the better and fashionable part of London.

[96]   Greek for "Lord, have mercy" and the name of a litany that forms a regular part of the Mass. "Kyrios" is the Greek word for "lord."

[97]   *vowels the Semite and the Saxon know not* The Greek vowel upsilon has no direct equivalent in the Hebrew alphabet or the Roman alphabet used in English.

eleison! The closetmaker and the cloacamaker will never be lords of our spirit. We are liege subjects of the catholic chivalry of Europe that foundered at Trafalgar[98] and of the empire of the spirit, not an *imperium*, that went under with the Athenian fleets at Ægospotami.[99] Yes, yes. They went under. Pyrrhus,[100] misled by an oracle, made a last attempt to retrieve the fortunes of Greece. Loyal to a   430
lost cause.

He strode away from them towards the window.

— They went forth to battle, Mr O'Madden Burke said greyly, but they always fell.[101]

— Boohoo! Lenehan wept with a little noise. Owing to a brick received in the latter half of the *matinée*. Poor, poor, poor Pyrrhus!   435

He whispered then near Stephen's ear:

LENEHAN'S LIMERICK

—There's a ponderous pundit MacHugh
Who wears goggles of ebony hue.
As he mostly sees double
To wear them why trouble?   440
I can't see the Joe Miller.[102] Can you?

In mourning for Sallust,[103] Mulligan says. Whose mother is beastly dead.

Myles Crawford crammed the sheets into a sidepocket.

— That'll be all right, he said. I'll read the rest after. That'll be all right.

Lenehan extended his hands in protest.   445

— But my riddle! he said. What opera is like a railway line?

— Opera? Mr O'Madden Burke's sphinx face reriddled.

Lenehan announced gladly:

— *The Rose of Castile.*[104] See the wheeze? Rows of cast steel. Gee!

He poked Mr O'Madden Burke mildly in the spleen. Mr O'Madden Burke fell back with grace   450
on his umbrella, feigning a gasp.

— Help! he sighed. I feel a strong weakness.

Lenehan, rising to tiptoe, fanned his face rapidly with the rustling tissues.

The professor, returning by way of the files, swept his hand across Stephen's and Mr O'Madden Burke's loose ties.   455

— Paris, past and present, he said. You look like communards.[105]

[98] The naval battle of Trafalgar took place on October 21, 1805; Admiral Horatio Nelson defeated the combined fleets of France and Spain. A pillar commemorating the battle was erected in the center of Dublin in 1808–9, where it stood till 1966. See note 1 p.229.

[99] In 405 BC the Spartans defeated the Athenians at Aegospotami in Thrace, destroying their fleet and 3,000 men, and so winning the Peloponnesian War.

[100] Pyrrhus (319–272 BC) was king of Epirus, a region in the northwest of modern Greece and therefore a kingdom poised between Macedonia (in northeastern Greece, the territory that had been shaped into a powerful kingdom by Alexander the Great [356–323 BC], and the expanding republic of Rome. He led many military expeditions into both Italy and Greece, but it is anachronistic to say that he sought "to retrieve the fortunes of Greece." Chiefly he sought to advance his own. His last campaign was against Sparta in the Peloponnesus; it failed and he was killed in Argos by a "brick" or roof tile supposedly thrown at his head. Stephen thinks about him because he has earlier (in "Nestor," episode 2) been teaching ancient history to children at Mr. Deasy's school and trying to summarize Pyrrhus's career. The extent to which Pyrrhus was "misled by an oracle," as Professor MacHugh claims, is a subject of debate.

[101] *They went forth ... they always fell* the original title of "The Rose of Battle," a poem by William Butler Yeats in *The Rose* (1893), taken from Matthew Arnold's epigraph to the the *Study of Celtic Literature* (London, 1867).

[102] *the Joe Miller* a stale joke named after a comedian whose book of anecdotes was repeatedly revised and reissued in the nineteenth century, and so came to be synonymous with old chestnuts.

[103] Gaius Sallustius Crispus (86–34 BC), a Roman historian and supporter of Caesar. Stephen is evidently recalling a quip that the fictional character Buck Mulligan has made in the past about MacHugh, one underscoring the sentimental anachronism of mourning for Sallust, who was charged with extortion in public office and escaped only through Caesar's intervention.

[104] A light opera (1857) by Michael William Balfe (1808–70). Myles Crawford, earlier in this episode, has sung two lines from one of its arias to Professor MacHugh (see note 74 and text).

[105] Members of the left-wing Commune de Paris which, after after the defeat of Napoleon III by Germany in 1870–1, briefly seized control of Paris (March–May 1871), but was defeated after a bloody siege.

— Like fellows who had blown up the Bastille,[106] J. J. O'Molloy said in quiet mockery. Or was it you shot the lord lieutenant of Finland between you? You look as though you had done the deed. General Bobrikoff.[107]

460 — We were only thinking about it, Stephen said.

OMNIUM GATHERUM[108]

— All the talents, Myles Crawford said. Law, the classics . . .

— The turf, Lenehan put in.

— Literature, the press.

— If Bloom were here, the professor said. The gentle art of advertisement.

465 — And Madam Bloom, Mr O'Madden Burke added. The vocal muse. Dublin's prime favourite. Lenehan gave a loud cough.

— Ahem! he said very softly. O, for a fresh of breath air! I caught a cold in the park. The gate was open.

« YOU CAN DO IT! »

The editor laid a nervous hand on Stephen's shoulder.

— I want you to write something for me, he said. Something with a bite in it. You can do it. I see

470 it in your face. *In the lexicon of youth* . . .[109]

See it in your face. See it in your eye. Lazy idle little schemer.[110]

— Foot and mouth disease! the editor cried in scornful invective. Great nationalist meeting in Borris-in-Ossory.[111] All balls! Bulldosing the public! Give them something with a bite in it. Put us all into it, damn its soul. Father, Son and Holy Ghost and Jakes M' Carthy.[112]

475 — We can all supply mental pabulum, Mr O'Madden Burke said.

Stephen raised his eyes to the bold unheeding stare.

— He wants you for the pressgang, J. J. O'Molloy said.

THE GREAT GALLAHER[113]

— You can do it, Myles Crawford repeated, clenching his hand in emphasis. Wait a minute. We'll paralyse Europe as Ignatius Gallaher used to say when he was on the shaughraun, doing

480 billiardmarking in the Clarence.[114] Gallaher, that was a pressman for you. That was a pen. You know how he made his mark? I'll tell you. That was the smartest piece of journalism ever known. That was in eightyone, sixth of May, time of the invincibles, murder in the Phœnix park,[115] before you were born, I suppose. I'll show you.

---

[106] A fortress-prison in Paris that was stormed by a revolutionary mob on July 14, 1789, an event that marks the beginning of the French Revolution, and still celebrated as a national holiday in France.

[107] Nikolai Ivanovitch Bobrikoff (1857–1904), the Russian commander in chief (or lord lieutenant) of the military district of Finland, was assassinated on June 16, 1904, the day when *Ulysses* unfolds. The news will have just reached Dublin in the course of the morning.

[108] "A gathering of all" in dog Latin, i.e. a phrase formed by making an English word (gather) take on a specious Latin form (gatherum) and pairing it with a genuine Latin word (omnium).

[109] *In the lexicon of youth* from a play, *Richelieu, or the Conspiracy* (1837) by Edward Bulwer-Lytton (1803–73), III.i: "Fail – fail? In the lexicon of youth, which fate reserves / For a bright manhood, there is no such word / As 'fail'."

[110] *See it in your face . . . idle little schemer* Stephen is recalling his unjust punishment at the hands of Father Dolan, an incident recounted in ch. 1 of *A Portrait of the Artist as a Young Man*.

[111] *nationalist meeting in Borris-in-Ossory* the site, some 25 miles southwest of Dublin, of a meeting held by Daniel O'Connell (1775–1847), an Irish political leader who advocated repeal of the Act of Union which had united the parliaments of England and Ireland in 1800.

[112] A "jakes" is an outdoor toilet or privy.

[113] Ignatius Gallaher, a fictional journalist, appears in "A Little Cloud," one of the stories in Joyce's *Dubliners*; see pp. 215–23 above.

[114] *shaughran in the Clarence* the Gaelic word *seachrán*, i.e. wandering about, unemployed; the Clarence was a commercial hotel in central Dublin.

[115] On May 6, 1882 (Crawford's date is off by a year), a small splinter group of Fenians, known as the Invincibles, stabbed and killed two members of the government not far from the Viceregal Lodge in Phoenix Park.

He pushed past them to the files.

— Look at here, he said, turning. The *New York World* cabled for a special. Remember that time?   485
Professor MacHugh nodded.

— *New York World*, the editor said, excitedly pushing back his straw hat. Where it took place.
Tim Kelly, or Kavanagh I mean, Joe Brady and the rest of them. Where Skin-the-goat drove the
car.[116] Whole route, see?

— Skin-the-goat, Mr O'Madden Burke said. Fitzharris. He has that cabman's shelter, they say,   490
down there at Butt bridge.[117] Holohan told me. You know Holohan?

— Hop and carry one, is it? Myles Crawford said.

— And poor Gumley is down there too, so he told me, minding stones for the corporation.
A night watchman.

Stephen turned in surprise.   495

— Gumley? he said. You don't say so? A friend of my father's, is he?

— Never mind Gumley, Myles Crawford cried angrily. Let Gumley mind the stones, see they
don't run away. Look at here. What did Ignatius Gallaher do? I'll tell you. Inspiration of genius.
Cabled right away. Have you *Weekly Freeman* of 17 March? Right. Have you got that?

He flung back pages of the files and stuck his finger on a point.   500

— Take page four, advertisement for Bransome's coffee let us say. Have you got that? Right.
The telephone whirred.

A DISTANT VOICE

— I'll answer it, the professor said going.

— B is parkgate. Good.

His finger leaped and struck point after point, vibrating.   505

— T is viceregal lodge. C is where murder took place. K is Knockmaroon gate.[118]

The loose flesh of his neck shook like a cock's wattles. An illstarched dicky jutted up and with a
rude gesture he thrust it back into his waistcoat.

— Hello? *Evening Telegraph* here ... Hello? ... Who's there? ... Yes ... Yes ... Yes ...

— F to P is the route Skin-the-goat drove the car for an alibi. Inchicore, Roundtown, Windy   510
Arbour, Palmerston Park, Ranelagh.[119] F. A. B. P. Got that? X is Davy's publichouse[120] in upper
Leeson street.

The professor came to the inner door.

— Bloom is at the telephone, he said.

— Tell him go to hell, the editor said promptly. X is Burke's public house, see?   515

CLEVER, VERY

— Clever, Lenehan said. Very.

— Gave it to them on a hot plate, Myles Crawford said, the whole bloody history.

Nightmare from which you will never awake.[121]

— I saw it, the editor said proudly. I was present, Dick Adams, the besthearted bloody Corkman
the Lord ever put the breath of life in, and myself.   520

Lenehan bowed to a shape of air, announcing:

— Madam, I'm Adam. And Able was I ere I saw Elba.

---

[116] *Tim Kelly ... Skin-the-Goat* Joe Brady was the principal
assassin, Tim Kelly the second, while Kavanagh drove the get-
away cab. "Skin-the-Goat," or James Fitzharris, drove a decoy cab
from Phoenix Park to the center of Dublin. He reappears in
episode 16 ("Eumaeus"), minding a cabman's shelter.
[117] A real bridge over the Liffey, in 1904 the easternmost one
in Dublin.

[118] A gate at the western edge of Phoenix Park.
[119] Places in Dublin along the route which the murderers took.
[120] A pub at which the assassins stopped, located where the
text indicates.
[121] *Nightmare from which you will never awake* a definition of
history which Stephen proposes to himself earlier in the day, in
"Nestor," the second episode of *Ulysses*.

525 — History! Myles Crawford cried. The Old Woman of Prince's street[122] was there first. There was weeping and gnashing of teeth over that. Out of an advertisement. Gregor Grey made the design for it. That gave him the leg up. Then Paddy Hooper worked Tay Pay who took him on to the *Star*. Now he's got in with Blumenfeld.[123] That's press. That's talent. Pyatt![124] He was all their daddies.

— The father of scare journalism, Lenehan confirmed, and the brother-in-law of Chris Callinan.[125]

— Hello?... Are you there?... Yes, he's here still. Come across yourself.

530 — Where do you find a pressman like that now, eh? the editor cried.

He flung the pages down.

— Clamn dever, Lenehan said to Mr O'Madden Burke.

— Very smart, Mr O'Madden Burke said.

Professor MacHugh came from the inner office.

535 — Talking about the invincibles, he said, did you see that some hawkers were up before the recorder...

— O yes, J. J. O'Molloy said eagerly. Lady Dudley[126] was walking home through the park to see all the trees that were blown down by that cyclone last year[127] and thought she'd buy a view of Dublin. And it turned out to be a commemoration postcard of Joe Brady or Number One or Skin-

540 the-goat. Right outside the viceregal lodge, imagine!

— They're only in the hook and eye department, Myles Crawford said. Psha! Press and the bar! Where have you a man now at the bar like those fellows, like Whiteside, like Isaac Butt, like silvertongued O'Hagan?[128] Eh? Ah, bloody nonsense! Only in the halfpenny place![129]

His mouth continued to twitch unspeaking in nervous curls of disdain.

545 Would anyone wish that mouth for her kiss? How do you know? Why did you write it then?

RHYMES AND REASONS

Mouth, south. Is the mouth south someway? Or the south a mouth? Must be some. South, pout, out, shout, drouth. Rhymes: two men dressed the same, looking the same, two by two.

............*la tua pace*
..........*che parlar ti piace*
550 ....*mentreche il vento, come fa, si tace*.[130]

He saw them three by three, approaching girls, in green, in rose, in russet, entwining, *per l'aer perso* in mauve, in purple, *quella pacifica oriafiamma*, in gold of oriflamme, *di rimirar fè più ardenti*. But I old men, penitent, leadenfooted, underdarkneath the night: mouth south: tomb womb.[131]

— Speak up for yourself, Mr O'Madden Burke said.

[122] A nickname for the *Freeman's Journal*.

[123] *Tay Pay... Blumenfield* "Tay Pay" represents the Irish pronunciation of T. P., the well-known initials of Thomas Power O'Connor (1848–1929), who founded the *Star* in 1888 (see the annotation to M.A.P., note 17 above); Ralph Blumenfield was editor of the *Daily Express* in London, a newspaper launched in 1900 and associated with "the New Journalism" typified by T. P. O'Connor.

[124] Félix Pyat (1810–89), a French social revolutionary who went to London after 1871 and edited several revolutionary journals.

[125] *the father ... the brother-in-law* the real Pyat and the fictional Gallaher, respectively; Chris Callinan was a Dublin journalist.

[126] The wife of William Humble Ward, early of Dudley (1866–1932) and Lord Lieutenant of Ireland (1902–6). Contemporary newspapers in June 1904 did record a case of people hawking mementoes of the Phoenix Park murders, though they were taken to a police court, not the recorder's court.

[127] Severe gales from February 26 to 27, 1903, caused much damage in Dublin and uprooted trees in Phoenix Park.

[128] James Whiteside (1804–76), Isaac Butt (1813–79), and Thomas O'Hagan (1812–95) were Irish barristers and orators who supported Home Rule.

[129] *the halfpenny place* second rate.

[130] *la tua pace ... si tace* Stephen Dedalus recalls the line endings, or in the last instance the entire line, of a famous passage in Dante's *Inferno* 5.91–6. The three lines mean "your peace," "that speaking pleases you," and "While the wind is silent, as it is now." They are spoken by Paolo and Francesca to Dante, and they precede their recounting their famous story.

[131] *He saw them ... womb* as a whole, the passage echoes the Divine Pageant in Dante's *Purgatorio* 29. Interwoven with that are phrases from elsewhere in the *Divine Comedy*: *per l'aer perso*, "through the dark air," is from *Inferno* 5.89; *quella pacifica oriafiamma*, "that peaceful oriflamme" or "gold-flame," is from *Paradiso* 35.127; *di rimirar fé piè ardenti*, "it made them more eager to look again," is from *Paradiso* 31.142.

SUFFICIENT FOR THE DAY... [132]

J. J. O'Molloy, smiling palely, took up the gage.   555

— My dear Myles, he said, flinging his cigarette aside, you put a false construction on my words. I hold no brief, as at present advised, for the third profession *qua* profession but your Cork legs are running away with you. Why not bring in Henry Grattan and Flood and Demosthenes and Edmund Burke?[133] Ignatius Gallaher we all know and his Chapelizod boss, Harmsworth of the farthing press, and his American cousin of the Bowery gutter sheet[134] not to mention *Paddy Kelly's* 560 *Budget, Pue's Occurrences* and our watchful friend *The Skibereen Eagle*.[135] Why bring in a master of forensic eloquence like Whiteside? Sufficient for the day is the newspaper thereof.

LINKS WITH BYGONE DAYS OF YORE

— Grattan and Flood wrote for this very paper, the editor cried in his face. Irish volunteers. Where are you now? Established 1763. Dr Lucas. Who have you now like John Philpot Curran?[136] Psha!

— Well, J. J. O'Molloy said, Bushe K. C.,[137] for example.   565

— Bushe? the editor said. Well, yes. Bushe, yes. He has a strain of it in his blood. Kendal Bushe[138] or I mean Seymour Bushe.

— He would have been on the bench long ago, the professor said, only for . . . But no matter.

J. J. O'Molloy turned to Stephen and said quietly and slowly:

— One of the most polished periods I think I ever listened to in my life fell from the lips of 570 Seymour Bushe. It was in that case of fratricide, the Childs murder case.[139] Bushe defended him.

And in the porches of mine ear did pour.[140]

By the way how did he find that out?[141] He died in his sleep. Or the other story, beast with two backs?

— What was that? the professor asked.   575

[132] *SUFFICIENT FOR THE DAY* ... Jesus, in the Sermon on the Mount, urges "Take therefore no thought for the morrow: for the morrow shall take thought for the things of itself. Sufficient unto the day is the evil thereof" (Matthew 6:34)

[133] On Henry Grattan, see n. 16 above; Henry Flood (1732–91) was an Irish statesman and orator. Demosthenes (c. 384–322 BC) was an Athenian orator. Edmund Burke (1729–97) was an Anglo-Irish member of parliament, barrister, orator, and political philosopher.

[134] *his Chapelizod boss, Harmsworth ... gutter sheet* Alfred Harmsworth, later Baron Northcliffe (1865–1922), was born in Chapelizod, just outside Dublin. He became the classic example of the journalist who became a press tycoon, famous for launching the *Daily Mail* in 1896, which by 1902 had the largest circulation of any newspaper in the world. It featured concise writing, a tabloid format, attractive competitions, and advertisements, and was thought to embody the New Journalism, deplored by some for its vulgarity, applauded by others for attracting new readerships. His "American cousin" was Joseph Pulitzer (1847–1911), his friend and the editor of the *New York World*.

[135] *Paddy Kelly's Budget* (1832–4) was a Dublin newspaper that became a byword for vulgarity, while *Pue's Occurrences* (1700–50)

was the first daily newspaper in Dublin. The *Skibereen Eagle* was a small weekly newspaper which, when it announced "that the *Skibbereen Eagle* was keeping its eye on the Czar of Russia," became synonymous with provincial self-importance.

[136] Charles Lucas (1713–71) was an Irish physician and contributor to the *Freeman's Journal*. John Philpot Curran (1750–1817) was an Irish barrister, orator, and MP, a supporter of Catholic relief and an opponent of Union.

[137] Seymour Bushe (1853–1922), was an Irish Barrister and Crown Counsel for the county and city of Dublin (1901), before he became King's Counsel (KC) and moved to England in 1904.

[138] Charles Kendal Bushe (1767–1843) was an Irish jurist and orator, an ally of Grattan in opposing the Act of Union.

[139] Samuel Childs was acquitted of the murder of his brother Thomas in October 1899. The case is briefly discussed in the previous episode of *Ulysses*, "Hades," when Bloom and his fellow funeral-goers pass by the house where the murder occurred.

[140] The Ghost in *Hamlet* recounts his murder by Claudius, who poured poison into his ear (*Hamlet* I.v.63).

[141] How could the Ghost know how he died if he was asleep at the time. And how did he then learn about "the other story" that his wife Gertrude was committing adultery ("the beast with two backs," from *Othello*, I.i.117) before he died?

ITALIA, MAGISTRA ARTIUM[142]

— He spoke on the law of evidence, J. J. O'Molloy said, of Roman justice as contrasted with the earlier Mosaic code, the *lex talionis*.[143] And he cited the Moses of Michelangelo in the Vatican.[144]

— Ha.

— A few wellchosen words, Lenehan prefaced. Silence!

580 Pause. J. J. O'Molloy took out his cigarette case.

False lull. Something quite ordinary.

Messenger took out his matchbox thoughtfully and lit his cigar.

I have often thought since on looking back over that strange time that it was that small act, trivial in itself, that striking of that match, that determined the whole aftercourse of both our

585 lives.[145]

A POLISHED PERIOD

J. J. O'Molloy resumed, moulding his words:

— He said of it: *that stony effigy in frozen music,*[146] *horned and terrible, of the human form divine, that eternal symbol of wisdom and of prophecy which, if aught that the imagination or the hand of sculptor has wrought in marble of soultransfigured and of soultransfiguring deserves to live, deserves to live.*

590 His slim hand with a wave graced echo and fall.

— Fine! Myles Crawford said at once.

— The divine afflatus, Mr O'Madden Burke said.

— You like it? J. J. O'Molloy asked Stephen.

Stephen, his blood wooed by grace of language and gesture, blushed. He took a cigarette from

595 the case. J. J. O'Molloy offered his case to Myles Crawford. Lenehan lit their cigarettes as before and took his trophy, saying:

— Muchibus thankibus.

A MAN OF HIGH MORALE

— Professor Magennis was speaking to me about you, J. J. O'Molloy said to Stephen. What do you think really of that hermetic crowd, the opal hush poets : A. E. the master mystic? That

600 Blavatsky woman started it.[147] She was a nice old bag of tricks. A. E. has been telling some yankee interviewer that you came to him in the small hours of the morning to ask him about planes of consciousness. Magennis thinks you must have been pulling A. E.'s leg. He is a man of the very highest morale, Magennis.

Speaking about me. What did he say? What did he say? What did he say about me? Don't ask.

605 — No, thanks, professor MacHugh said, waving the cigarette case aside. Wait a moment. Let me say one thing. The finest display of oratory I ever heard was a speech made by John F. Taylor[148] at

[142]   Latin for "ITALY, TEACHER OF THE ARTS."

[143]   *Lex talionis* is Latin for "law of equal punishment," which is also a principle of Mosaic law, an eye for an eye, a tooth for a tooth (Exodus 21:23–5).

[144]   The statue (1513–16), part of the mausoleum of Julius II by Michelangelo (1475–1564), is in the church of San Pietro in Vincoli in Rome, not in the Vatican.

[145]   *I have often thought ... of both our lives* the style here suddenly adopts the tone of Dickens in *David Copperfield* (1849–50) and *Great Expectations* (1861).

[146]   The German philosospher Frederick von Schilling (1775–1854) defined architecture as "music in space, as it were a frozen music" (*Philosophy of Art*, trans. 1845).

[147]   *that hermetic crowd ... A.E. ... That Blavatsky woman* Theosophy was an eclectic blend of doctrines from Hinduism,

Buddhism, and Jewish and Christian sources. It was invented by Helen Petrovna Blavatsky (1831–91), who founded the Theosophical Society in 1875 and published *Isis Unveiled* in 1876. The movement adopted complicated systems of psychology and cosmology and advocated belief in the transmigration of souls and the universal brotherhood of man, regardless of race or creed. George Russell, known by his pen name A.E. (1867–1935), was her most active follower in Dublin, a member of a lodge of the Society which was opened in 1904. In 1909 it changed into an independent organization known as the Hermetic Society.

[148]   John F. Taylor (*c*. 1850–1902) was an Irish barrister, orator, and journalist who, on October 24, 1901, made the speech that Professor MacHugh recalls.

the college historical society. Mr Justice Fitzgibbon,[149] the present lord justice of appeal, had spoken and the paper under debate was an essay (new for those days), advocating the revival of the Irish tongue.

He turned towards Myles Crawford and said: 610

— You know Gerald Fitzgibbon. Then you can imagine the style of his discourse.

— He is sitting with Tim Healy,[150] J. J. O'Molloy said, rumour has it, on the Trinity college estates commission.

— He is sitting with a sweet thing in a child's frock, Myles Crawford said. Go on. Well?

— It was the speech, mark you, the professor said, of a finished orator, full of courteous 615 haughtiness and pouring in chastened diction, I will not say the vials of his wrath but pouring the proud man's contumely upon the new movement.[151] It was then a new movement. We were weak, therefore worthless.

He closed his long thin lips an instant but, eager to be on, raised an outspanned hand to his spectacles and, with trembling thumb and ringfinger touching lightly the black rims, steadied 620 them to a new focus.

IMPROMPTU

In ferial tone he addressed J. J. O'Molloy:

— Taylor had come there, you must know, from a sick bed. That he had prepared his speech I do not believe for there was not even one shorthandwriter in the hall. His dark lean face had a growth of shaggy beard round it. He wore a loose neckcloth and altogether he looked (though he was not) a 625 dying man.

His gaze turned at once but slowly from J. J. O'Molloy's towards Stephen's face and then bent at once to the ground, seeking. His unglazed linen collar appeared behind his bent head, soiled by his withering hair. Still seeking, he said:

— When Fitzgibbon's speech had ended John F. Taylor rose to reply. Briefly, as well as I can 630 bring them to mind, his words were these.

He raised his head firmly. His eyes bethought themselves once more. Witless shellfish swam in the gross lenses to and fro, seeking outlet.

He began:

— *Mr chairman, ladies and gentlemen: Great was my admiration in listening to the remarks* 635 *addressed to the youth of Ireland a moment since by my learned friend. It seemed to me that I had been transported into a country far away from this country, into an age remote from this age, that I stood in ancient Egypt and that I was listening to the speech of some highpriest of that land addressed to the youthful Moses.*

His listeners held their cigarettes poised to hear, their smokes ascending in frail stalks that 640 flowered with his speech. *And let our crooked smokes.*[152] Noble words coming. Look out. Could you try your hand at it yourself?

— *And it seemed to me that I heard the voice of that Egyptian highpriest raised in a tone of like haughtiness and like pride. I heard his words and their meaning was revealed to me.*

[149] Gerald Fitzgibbon (1837–1909) was a staunch Conservative, one opposed to Home Rule. As commissioner of national education, he was thought to be Anglicizing Ireland.

[150] Timothy Healy (1855–1931) was secretary to Charles Parnell, then led the move to oust him from leadership of the Irish Nationalist party. He was appointed to the Trinity College estates commission on June 9, 1904, which investigated how the university could comply with Irish land reform legislation yet retain its income from landholdings.

[151] *vials of his wrath ... proud man's contumely* "And I heard a great voice out of the temple saying to the seven angels, Go your ways, and pour out the vials of the wrath of God upon the earth" (Revelation 16:1). "The proud man's contumely" is from Hamlet's soliloquy in *Hamlet* III.i.70.

[152] *And let our crooked smokes* "Laud we the gods / And let our crooked smokes climb to their nostrils From our blest altars." Spoken by Cymbeline when peace and tranquillity have been restored at the end (*Cymbeline*, V.v.476–8).

FROM THE FATHERS[153]

645   It was revealed to me that those things are good which yet are corrupted which neither if they
were supremely good nor unless they were good could be corrupted.[154] Ah, curse you! That's saint
Augustine.

— *Why will you jews not accept our culture, our religion and our language? You are a tribe of nomad
herdsmen; we are a mighty people. You have no cities nor no wealth: our cities are hives of humanity and our*
650   *galleys, trireme and quadrireme, laden with all manner merchandise furrow the waters of the known globe. You
have but emerged from primitive conditions: we have a literature, a priesthood, an agelong history and a polity.*

Nile.

Child, man, effigy.

By the Nilebank the babemaries kneel, cradle of bulrushes: a man supple in combat: stone-
655   horned, stonebearded, heart of stone.

— *You pray to a local and obscure idol: our temples, majestic and mysterious, are the abodes of Isis and
Osiris, of Horus and Ammon Ra.*[155] *Yours serfdom, awe and humbleness: ours thunder and the seas. Israel is
weak and few are her children: Egypt is an host and terrible are her arms. Vagrants and daylabourers are you
called: the world trembles at our name.*

660   A dumb belch of hunger cleft his speech. He lifted his voice above it boldly:

— *But, ladies and gentlemen, had the youthful Moses listened to and accepted that view of life, had he
bowed his head and bowed his will and bowed his spirit before that arrogant admonition he would never have
brought the chosen people out of their house of bondage nor followed the pillar of the cloud by day. He would
never have spoken with the Eternal amid lightnings on Sinai's mountaintop nor ever have come down with the*
665   *light of inspiration shining in his countenance and bearing in his arms the tables of the law,*[156] *graven in the
language of the outlaw.*

He ceased and looked at them, enjoying silence.

OMINOUS — FOR HIM!

J. J. O'Molloy said not without regret:

— And yet he died without having entered the land of promise.[157]
670   — A-sudden-at-the-moment-though-from-lingering-illness-often-previously-expectorated-de-
mise, Lenehan said. And with a great future behind him.

The troop of bare feet was heard rushing along the hallway and pattering up the staircase.

— That is oratory, the professor said, uncontradicted.

Gone with the wind.[158] Hosts at Mullaghmast and Tara of the kings.[159] Miles of ears of porches. The
675   tribune's words howled and scattered to the four winds. A people sheltered within his voice. Dead
noise. Akasic records[160] of all that ever anywhere wherever was. Love and laud him: me no more.

---

[153]   The Church fathers are the early leaders and writers of the
Christian church, among whom is Augustine.

[154]   *It was revealed … could be corrupted* a passage from the
Confessions (397 AD) of St. Augustine (354–430), vii.12.

[155]   Egyptian gods. Isis and Osiris were the female and male
principles (sister and brother, wife and husband); Horus, their
son, avenged his father's death and was god of light. Ammon Ra
was the sun god and supreme divinity.

[156]   *the tables of the law* in Exodus 19 the Israelites come to
Mount Sinai and Moses communes with God for three days. In
the course of this experience he received the Ten Commandments
and other laws (Exodus 20–31). "And the tables were the work of
God, and the writing was the writing of God, graven upon the
tables" (Exodus 34:29).

[157]   *the land of promise* Moses went to "the mountain of Nebo, to
the top of Pisgah," where he is allowed to see the promised land,
but told that he will not be able to enter it.

[158]   *Gone with the wind* from the poem "Non Sum Qualis
Eram Bonae Sub Regno Cynarae" (1896), by Ernest
Dowson (1867–1900). The title is Latin for "I am not what
I once was under the spell of kind Cynara," a line from Horace,
Odes IV.i.3. It is used to describe how much the speaker has
forgotten.

[159]   The "hosts" are the people who came to "monster meetings" called by Daniel O'Connell, self-styled "tribune" of Ireland, in Rath of Mullaghmast on October 1, 1843, and at the
hill of Tara on August 13, 1843. The hill of Tara, 20 miles
northwest of Dublin, is associated with Irish kings of a golden-
age Ireland.

[160]   A theosophical term referring to Akasa, the eternal memory
of Nature which registers every thought, silent or expressed.

I have money.

— Gentlemen, Stephen said. As the next motion on the agenda paper may I suggest that the house do now adjourn?

— You take my breath away. It is not perchance a French compliment?[161] Mr O'Madden Burke 680
asked. 'Tis the hour, methinks, when the winejug, metaphorically speaking, is most grateful in Ye ancient hostelry.

— That it be and hereby is resolutely resolved. All who are in favour say ay, Lenehan announced. The contrary no. I declare it carried. To which particular boosing shed . . . ? My casting vote is: Mooney's![162] 685

He led the way, admonishing:

— We will sternly refuse to partake of strong waters, will we not? Yes, we will not. By no manner of means.

Mr O'Madden Burke, following close, said with an ally's lunge of his umbrella:

— Lay on, Macduff![163] 690

— Chip of the old block! the editor cried, slapping Stephen on the shoulder. Let us go. Where are those blasted keys?

He fumbled in his pocket, pulling out the crushed typesheets.

— Foot and mouth. I know. That'll be all right. That'll go in. Where are they? That's all right.

He thrust the sheets back and went into the inner office. 695

LET US HOPE

J. J. O'Molloy, about to follow him in, said quietly to Stephen:

— I hope you will live to see it published. Myles, one moment.

He went into the inner office, closing the door behind him.

— Come along, Stephen, the professor said. That is fine, isn't it? It has the prophetic vision. *Fuit Ilium!*[164] The sack of windy Troy. Kingdoms of this world. The masters of the Mediterranean are fellaheen[165] today. 700

The first newsboy came pattering down the stairs at their heels and rushed out into the street, yelling:

— Racing special!

Dublin. I have much, much to learn.

They turned to the left along Abbey street. 705

— I have a vision too, Stephen said.

— Yes? the professor said, skipping to get into step. Crawford will follow. Another newsboy shot past them, yelling as he ran:

— Racing special! 710

DEAR DIRTY DUBLIN[166]

Dubliners.

— Two Dublin vestals,[167] Stephen said, elderly and pious, have lived fifty and fiftythree years in Fumbally's lane.

— Where is that? the professor asked.

---

[161] *a French compliment* a compliment that is an empty gesture or promise.

[162] A pub at 1 Abbey Street Lower, near the street's intersection with Sackville (now O'Connell) Street.

[163] Macbeth's words to Macduff when he learns that Macduff will kill him (*Macbeth*, V.ii.33), but by this time a cliché for "Let the action begin."

[164] Latin for "Troy once was!" (from Vergil, *Aeneid*, 2.325).

[165] A peasant or laborer in Egypt and other Arab-speaking countries.

[166] An expression coined by Lady Sydney Morgan (1780–1859), which became a cliché.

[167] The six vestal virgins were priestesses of Vesta, Roman goddess of hearth and home, whose temple was the oldest in the city; they were dedicated to a life of chastity and charged with maintaining the temple's eternal flame.

715   — Off Blackpitts,[168] Stephen said.

Damp night reeking of hungry dough. Against the wall. Face glistening tallow under her fustian shawl. Frantic hearts. Akasic records. Quicker, darlint!

On now. Dare it. Let there be life.[169]

    — They want to see the views of Dublin from the top of Nelson's pillar. They save up three and

720 tenpence in a red tin letterbox moneybox. They shake out the threepenny bits and a sixpence and coax out the pennies with the blade of a knife. Two and three in silver and one and seven in coppers. They put on their bonnets and best clothes and take their umbrellas for fear it may come on to rain.

    — Wise virgins,[170] professor MacHugh said.

LIFE ON THE RAW

    — They buy one and fourpenceworth of brawn and four slices of panloaf[171] at the north city

725 dining rooms in Marlborough street from Miss Kate Collins, proprietress . . . [172] They purchase four and twenty ripe plums from a girl at the foot of Nelson's pillar to take off the thirst of the brawn. They give two threepenny bits to the gentleman at the turnstile and begin to waddle slowly up the winding staircase, grunting, encouraging each other, afraid of the dark, panting, one asking the other have you the brawn, praising God and the Blessed Virgin, threatening to come down, peeping

730 at the airslits. Glory be to God. They had no idea it was that high.

Their names are Anne Kearns and Florence MacCabe. Anne Kearns has the lumbago for which she rubs on Lourdes water[173] given her by a lady who got a bottleful from a passionist father.[174] Florence Mac Cabe takes a crubeen[175] and a bottle of double X[176] for supper every Saturday.

    — Antithesis, the professor said, nodding twice. Vestal virgins. I can see them. What's keeping

735 our friend?

He turned.

A bevy of scampering newsboys rushed down the steps, scampering in all directions, yelling, their white papers fluttering. Hard after them Myles Crawford appeared on the steps, his hat aureoling his scarlet face, talking with J. J. O'Molloy.

740   — Come along, the professor cried, waving his arm.

He set off again to walk by Stephen's side.

    — Yes, he said. I see them.

RETURN OF BLOOM

Mr Bloom, breathless, caught in a whirl of wild newsboys near the offices of the *Irish Catholic* and *Dublin Penny Journal*,[177] called:

745   — Mr Crawford! A moment!

    — *Telegraph*! Racing special!

---

[168] *Fumbally's lane . . . Off Blackpitts* both streets in the Liberties, in the southwest area of central Dublin, a notorious slum.

[169] *Let there be life* compare Genesis 1:3: "And God said, Let there be light; and there was light."

[170] In the New Testament, Jesus recounts the parable of the 10 virgins (Matthew 25:1–3). Five wise and five foolish virgins go to meet the bridegroom at a wedding. The wise virgins take both lamps and oil, the foolish only lamps. When the bridegroom arrives at midnight, the wise virgins are ready and go in with him to the marriage. The foolish virgins are left out. "Watch therefore, for ye know neither the day nor the hour wherein the Son of man cometh."

[171] *brawn . . . panloaf* brawn is a headcheese that is a jellied loaf of hogs' head. Panloaf is a small loaf of bread.

[172] *at the north . . . proprietress* the North City Dining Rooms were located at 11 Marlborough Street, a north–south street

parallel to and just east of Sackville Street, the principal artery of central Dublin and the site of Nelson's pillar.

[173] Lourdes, in southern France, is a major shrine for Catholic pilgrims. It was there the Virgin Mary reportedly appeared to 14-year-old Bernadette Soubirous (St. Bernadette) in 1858. A nearby spring furnishes waters diverted into basins in which ailing pilgrims bathe.

[174] *a passionist father* a member of the Catholic order "Barefooted Clerks of the Holy Cross and Passion of Our Lord," established in 1737 by St. Paul of the Cross (1697–1775).

[175] A pig's foot.

[176] The standard Dublin pub beer manufactured by Guinness, in contrast to "triple x," manufactured for export.

[177] Weekly newspapers with offices at 90 Abbey Street Middle, close to the intersection with Sackville Street.

— What is it? Myles Crawford said, falling back a pace.

A newsboy cried in Mr Bloom's face:

— Terrible tragedy in Rathmines! A child bit by a bellows!

INTERVIEW WITH THE EDITOR

— Just this ad, Mr Bloom said, pushing through towards the steps, puffing, and taking the   750
cutting from his pocket. I spoke with Mr Keyes just now. He'll give a renewal for two months, he
says. After he'll see. But he wants a par to call attention in the *Telegraph* too, the Saturday pink. And
he wants it if it's not too late I told councillor Nannetti from the *Kilkenny People*.[178] I can have access
to it in the national library. House of keys, don't you see? His name is Keyes. It's a play on the
name. But he practically promised he'd give the renewal. But he wants just a little puff. What will   755
I tell him, Mr Crawford?

K. M. A.

— Will you tell him he can kiss my arse? Myles Crawford said, throwing out his arm for
emphasis. Tell him that straight from the stable.

A bit nervy. Look out for squalls. All off for a drink. Arm in arm. Lenehan's yachting cap on the
cadge beyond. Usual blarney. Wonder is that young Dedalus the moving spirit. Has a good pair of   760
boots on him today. Last time I saw him he had his heels on view. Been walking in muck
somewhere. Careless chap. What was he doing in Irishtown?

— Well, Mr Bloom said, his eyes returning, if I can get the design I suppose it's worth a short
par. He'd give the ad I think. I'll tell him . . .

K. M. R. I. A.[179]

— He can kiss my royal Irish arse, Myles Crawford cried loudly over his shoulder. Any time he   765
likes, tell him.

While Mr Bloom stood weighing the point and about to smile he strode on jerkily.

RAISING THE WIND[180]

— *Nulla bona*,[181] Jack, he said, raising his hand to his chin. I'm up to here. I've been through the
hoop myself. I was looking for a fellow to back a bill for me no later than last week. Sorry, Jack. You
must take the will for the deed. With a heart and a half if I could raise the wind anyhow.   770

J. J. O'Molloy pulled a long face and walked on silently. They caught up on the others and
walked abreast.

— When they have eaten the brawn and the bread and wiped their twenty fingers in the paper
the bread was wrapped in, they go nearer to the railings.

— Something for you, the professor explained to Myles Crawford. Two old Dublin women on   775
the top of Nelson's pillar.

SOME COLUMN! – THAT'S WHAT WADDLER ONE SAID

— That's new, Myles Crawford said. That's copy. Out for the waxies' Dargle.[182] Two old trickies,
what?

---

[178] A weekly newspaper; Kilkenny is some 70 miles southwest
of Dublin.
[179] MRIA can also be an abbreviation for Member of the Royal
Irish Academy.
[180] *RAISING THE WIND* slang expression for obtaining necessary money.

[181] Latin for "no possessions," an expression used in law to say
that someone has nothing that can be sold or mortgaged to pay
debts.
[182] "Waxies" were candlemakers, and the Dargle was the name
for their annual trip to a homonymous site near Bray.

— But they are afraid the pillar will fall, Stephen went on. They see the roofs and argue about
780 where the different churches are: Rathmines' blue dome,[183] Adam and Eve's, saint Laurence
O'Toole's. But it makes them giddy to look so they pull up their skirts . . .

THOSE SLIGHTLY RAMBUNCTIOUS FEMALES

— Easy all, Myles Crawford said, no poetic licence. We're in the archdiocese here.
— And settle down on their striped petticoats, peering up at the statue of the onehandled
adulterer.[184]
785 — Onehandled adulterer! the professor cried. I like that. I see the idea. I see what you mean.

DAMES DONATE DUBLIN'S CITS SPEEDPILLS VELOCITOUS AEROLITHS, BELIEF[185]

— It gives them a crick in their necks, Stephen said, and they are too tired to look up or down or
to speak. They put the bag of plums between them and eat the plums out of it, one after another,
wiping off with their handkerchiefs the plumjuice that dribbles out of their mouths and spitting
the plumstones slowly out between the railings.
790 He gave a sudden loud young laugh as a close. Lenehan and Mr O'Madden Burke, hearing,
turned, beckoned and led on across towards Mooney's.
— Finished? Myles Crawford said. So long as they do no worse.

SOPHIST WALLOPS HAUGHTY HELEN SQUARE ON PROBOSCIS. SPARTANS GNASH MOLARS. ITHACANS VOW PEN IS CHAMP.

— You remind me of Antisthenes, the professor said, a disciple of Gorgias, the sophist. It is said
of him that none could tell if he were bitterer against others or against himself. He was the son of a
795 noble and a bondwoman. And he wrote a book in which he took away the palm of beauty from
Argive Helen and handed it to poor Penelope.[186]
Poor Penelope. Penelope Rich.[187]
They made ready to cross O'Connell street.

HELLO THERE, CENTRAL![188]

At various points along the eight lines tramcars with motionless trolleys stood in their tracks,
800 bound for or from Rathmines, Rathfarnham, Blackrock, Kingstown and Dalkey, Sandymount
Green, Ringsend and Sandymount tower, Donnybrook, Palmerston Park and Upper Rathmines,
all still, becalmed in short circuit. Hackney cars, cabs, delivery waggons, mailvans, private
broughams, aerated mineral water floats with rattling crates of bottles, rattled, rolled, horsedrawn,
rapidly.

---

[183] *Rathmines' blue dome . . . O'Toole's* Our Lady of Refuge (1850), in Rathmines, is two miles south of Nelson's Pillar, designed by Patrick Byrne. Adam and Eve's is a Franciscan church about half a mile southwest of the pillar; saint Laurence O'Toole's (1863) is roughly one mile east of the pillar and is named after an Irish saint (1132–80) who was Archbishop of Dublin and later the city's patron saint.
[184] Admiral Nelson lost his arm in the battle of Santa Cruz (1797) and had a notorious affair with Lady Emma Hamilton (c. 1765–1815), wife of the British minister at Naples.
[185] In Matthew 13:3–9 Jesus tells the parable of the sower and the seeds. Many seeds fail to grow because they fall by the wayside or on stony ground, but others fall into good soil and bring forth fruit.

[186] *Antisthenes . . . Penelope* Antisthenes (c. 445–360 BC) was a Greek cynic philosopher, described by professor MacHugh as "a disciple" of the sophist Gorgias (c. 483–376 BC). A lost work, "Of Helen and Penelope," was ascribed to him in antiquity; it argued that Penelope was more beautiful than Helen because more virtuous.
[187] Penelope Rich (c. 1562–1607) was the beloved "Stella" of *Asphodel and Stella* (1591), a sonnet sequence by Sir Philip Sidney (1554–86). Unhappily married to Robert, Lord Rich, she divorced him and married Lord Mountjoy.
[188] *CENTRAL* the term for a telephone operator, so called because she worked in the "central" office of the telephone company.

WHAT? – AND LIKEWISE – WHERE?

— But what do you call it? Myles Crawford asked. Where did they get the plums?   805

VIRGILIAN, SAYS PEDAGOGUE. SOPHOMORE PLUMPS
FOR OLD MAN MOSES

— Call it, wait, the professor said, opening his long lips wide to reflect. Call it, let me see. Call it: *deus nobis hæc otia fecit*.[189]

— No, Stephen said, I call it *A Pisgah Sight of Palestine*[190] *or The Parable of The Plums*.[191]

— I see, the professor said.

He laughed richly.   810

— I see, he said again with new pleasure. Moses and the promised land. We gave him that idea, he added to J. J. O'Molloy.

HORATIO IS CYNOSURE[192] THIS FAIR JUNE DAY

J. J. O'Molloy sent a weary sidelong glance towards the statue and held his peace.

— I see, the professor said.

He halted on sir John Gray's pavement island[193] and peered aloft at Nelson through the meshes of   815
his wry smile.

DIMINISHED DIGITS PROVE TOO TITILLATING FOR FRISKY FRUMPS. ANNE
WIMBLES, FLO WANGLES[194] – YET CAN YOU BLAME THEM?

— Onehandled adulterer, he said grimly. That tickles me I must say.

— Tickled the old ones too, Myles Crawford said, if the God Almighty's truth was known.

Nausicaa: Introduction

The "Nausicaa" (or thirteenth) episode of *Ulysses* is the one that attracted the most notoriety while the book was being published in serial form. Indirectly, it even brought an end to further serialization. When the July–August (1920) issue of the *Little Review* appeared, it came to the attention of John Sumner, secretary of the New York Society for the Prevention of Vice, who promptly lodged an official complaint. A preliminary hearing in police court took place on October 22, and the magazine's two editors, Margaret Anderson and Jane Heap, were bound over for trial in the Court of Special Sessions. Their attorney was John Quinn, a

corporate law expert who was also a discerning cultural patron and took a sympathetic interest in Joyce's career. Quinn tried to have the case shifted to another court; he also tried to postpone the trial as long as possible, in the vain hope that Joyce would swiftly finish and publish the book as a whole. He thought the book in its entirety could be successfully defended in court, but held out scant hope of winning a case in defense of "Nausicaa" alone.

The trial was held over two days, February 14 and 21, 1921. The three judges convicted the two editors of publishing obscenity and sentenced both to pay $50 fines. It

[189]   *Deus nobis haec otia fecit* Latin for "God has given us these moments of leisure"; the phrase is from Vergil, *Eclogues* 1.6.

[190]   *A Pisgah Sight of Palestine* Pisgah is the mountaintop where Moses is granted a sight of Palestine, or the promised land, but is also told that he will not live to enter it. Stephen's title may be borrowed from *A Pisgah Sight of Palestine and the Confines Thereof with the History of the Old and New Testament Acted Thereon* (London: 1650), by Thomas Fuller (1608–61), a descriptive geography of the Holy Land.

[191]   A parable is a brief, often enigmatic story which is meant to teach some moral lesson or truth. They are much used by Jesus in the New Testament.

[192]   Horatio is the first name of Admiral Nelson; a cynosure is a center of attraction, interest, or attention.

[193]   Sir John Gray (1816–75), a Protestant, was an editor of the *Freeman's Journal*, a Member of Parliament, a town councillor of Dublin. A marble statue of him, which is situated in the middle of Sackville Street Lower and so in the same sight line as Nelson's Pillar, was carved by Sir Thomas Farrell (1827–1900) and unveiled on June 24, 1879. An inscription records Gray's tenacious efforts to introduce a supply of water to the city from the river Vartry in County Wicklow, completed in 1868.

[194]   "To wimble" may mean to be giddy or confused; "to wangle," in dialect, means to move unsteadily.

was also understood that publication of *Ulysses* would cease. The ruling had two other consequences. In effect it meant that *Ulysses* could not be published in the United States, or could be published only by a firm willing to incur serious legal costs and the likelihood of losing in court. But it also attracted a fair amount of newspaper coverage, including prominent editorials in the *New York Times* and the *New York Tribune*, increasing the book's potential readership.

News of the trial reached Joyce in Paris only in April. A few days later, he agreed with Sylvia Beach, the owner of an English-language bookshop (called Shakespeare and Company) in Paris, to publish the book as a deluxe and limited edition of 1,000 copies. A hundred copies on Holland paper would be signed by the author and sell for 350 francs; 150 copies on *vergé d'arches* would sell for 250 francs; while the other 750, on linen paper, would sell for 150 francs. Joyce would receive a royalty of 66 percent of net profits, an astounding sum. The key to Beach's plan, however, was to attract enough advance subscriptions that could in turn be used to defray printing costs. But there was a snag.

For contemporaneous with Beach's plan was another project to publish an English ordinary edition, to be issued by Joyce's patron Harriet Shaw Weaver under the imprint of her Egoist Press. During May and June 1921, Weaver was soliciting advance orders from bookshops throughout London, with predictable effects on Beach's edition. Subscriptions were coming in slowly, since buyers faced with the hefty price of a deluxe edition or the less costly ordinary edition would plainly choose the latter. It was not till July that Beach persuaded Weaver to withdraw the announcement of her edition. Subscriptions for Beach's edition began to mount. When the book finally appeared on February 2, 1922, it became a success. By March 15, all the copies at 150 francs had been sold out; by June, the copies at 250 francs were gone; and by July, even the costliest copies at 350 francs had been sold.

"Nausicaa" responds to an episode recounted in Books 5–7 of the *Odyssey*. Odysseus sets sail from the island of Calypso, but is harassed with storms by Poseidon. After days of storm, he finally swims to shore at Scheria, an island ruled by King Alcinous. Exhausted, he immediately falls asleep. Athena, meanwhile, visits the daughter of King Alcinous, Nausicaa, prompting her in a dream to do the family laundry the next morning at the mouth of a river not far from where Odysseus is sleeping. The next morning she and her friends depart, do the laundry, then bathe, eat, and play. When a ball bounces astray and lands near Odysseus, the girls shriek and he awakens, then immediately covers himself with a fig leaf (he has been naked) and begs Nausicaa to help him. Nausicaa provides him with clothing, food, and oil to bathe himself, then instructs him how to reach the city and get into the palace grounds. It would not do for him to travel together with Nausicaa, for people might think he was to be her future husband. Odysseus reaches a grove of Athena within the city, where he prays for Athena's help. She shrouds him in a mist so that he can walk unseen through the city to Alcinous's palace. Once there, he kneels before Arete, the wife of Alcinous, and the mist clears. Odysseus greets the assembled company and is welcomed by Alcinous.

As with other episodes in *Ulysses*, the relationship of this one to its Homeric original is elastic. It also seems to have evolved somewhat during the gap between the Linati Schema, which Joyce prepared in 1920, and the Gilbert Schema, which he prepared in 1921.

Critics, however, disagree on how much emphasis should be given to either schema, just as there is no consensus about the significance of "Nausicaa." In an older view, much emphasis was placed on the episode's satire of Gerty MacDowell, an adolescent girl whom Bloom observes while she is playing at the seaside with some friends, and whom he turns into an object of fantasy while he proceeds to masturbate. The episode is divided into two halves which are separated by a single ellipsis (. . .), a division that broadly corresponds with the two protagonists: the first half presents the highly romanticized viewpoint of Gerty, the second that of the older and more realistic Bloom. Critics who emphasize the satire of Gerty urge that the text's sympathies are firmly situated in the second, more realistic half of the episode. But more recent critics have underscored the many traits, motifs, stylized details, and concerns that Gerty and Bloom share

The Linati Schema (1920)

Title	Hour	Colour	Persons	Technic	Science, Art	Sense (Meaning)	Organ	Symbol
Nausicaa	8–9	grey	Nausicaa	Retrogressive progression	Painting	The Projected Mirage	Eye Nose	Onanism, Feminine, Hypocrisy
			Handmaidens					
			Alcinous					
			Arete					
			Ulysses					

The Gilbert Schema (1921)

Title	Scene	Hour	Organ	Art	Colour	Symbol	Technic	Correspondences
Nausicaa	The Rocks	8 p.m.	Eye, Nose	Painting	grey, blue	Virgin	Tumescence	Nausicaa: Nymp Phaecia: Star of the Sea

in common, and argued that the relationship between the episode's two halves is more complicated.

Joyce himself left two significant comments about "Nausicaa." One he wrote in a letter (January 3, 1920) to his friend Frank Budgen, the painter residing in Zurich with whom he had shared many of his thoughts while writing *Ulysses* during the period 1915 through 1919. Describing his current work, Joyce wrote:

Nausicaa is written in a namby-pamby jammy marmalady drawersy (alto 1à) style with effects of incense, mariolatry, masturbation, stewed cockles, painter's palette, chitchat, circumlocutions, etc etc.

Sometime during the 1920s he also talked about "Nausicaa" with Arthur Power, an aspiring Irish writer whom Joyce had first met in Paris in 1921. When Power asked Joyce what actually happened between Gerty and Bloom on the beach, Joyce tartly replied: "Nothing happened between them. It all took place in Bloom's imagination." Some critics have emphasized this later statement and stressed how tellingly it dovetails with the Linati Schema's note about the episode's "Sense (or Meaning)," which reads: "The

Projected Mirage." Gerty, in this view, is less an independent character than a largely fantastic construction of Bloom. Indeed, in a more developed version of this view, "Nausicaa" probes the many fissures in the multiple discourses through which a male viewpoint constructs an idealized femininity. In still another view of the episode, however, emphasis is placed less on the extent to which Gerty is a fantastic construction of Bloom, and more on the degree to which both are enthralled by the seductive illusions of modern advertising and consumer culture.

All the action of Nausicaa takes place in a single location, the rocks on Sandymount Strand, a shoreline area to the southeast of central Dublin. Earlier, in "Proteus" (episode 3), the reader has followed the thoughts of Stephen Dedalus as he walked along the Strand. Now it is Bloom who travels there, returning toward the city after his kindly visit to the widow of Patrick Dignam, whose funeral he had attended earlier that morning (in episode 6, "Hades"). The seawall against which Bloom leans is located at the foot of Leahy's Terrace, at the end of which is located the Catholic church of Mary, Star of the Sea, where a temperance retreat is simultaneously taking place.

Nausicaa (1922), from Ulysses

The summer evening had begun to fold the world in its mysterious embrace. Far away in the west the sun was setting and the last glow of all too fleeting day lingered lovingly on sea and strand, on the proud promontory of dear old Howth guarding as ever the waters of the bay, on the weedgrown rocks along Sandymount shore and, last but not least, on the quiet church whence there streamed forth at times upon the stillness the voice of prayer to her who is in her pure radiance a beacon ever   5
to the stormtossed heart of man, Mary, star of the sea.[1]

The three girl friends were seated on the rocks, enjoying the evening scene and the air which was fresh but not too chilly. Many a time and oft were they wont to come there to that favourite nook to have a cosy chat beside the sparkling waves and discuss matters feminine, Cissy Caffrey and Edy Boardman with the baby in the pushcar and Tommy and Jacky Caffrey, two little curlyheaded boys,   10
dressed in sailor suits with caps to match and the name H. M. S. Belleisle printed on both. For Tommy and Jacky Caffrey were twins, scarce four years old and very noisy and spoiled twins sometimes but for all that darling little fellows with bright merry faces and endearing ways about them. They were dabbling in the sand with their spades and buckets, building castles as children do, or playing with their big coloured ball, happy as the day was long. And Edy Boardman was   15
rocking the chubby baby to and fro in the pushcar while that young gentleman fairly chuckled with delight. He was but eleven months and nine days old and, though still a tiny toddler, was just beginning to lisp his first babyish words. Cissy Caffrey bent over him to tease his fat little plucks[2] and the dainty dimple in his chin.

— Now, baby, Cissy Caffrey said. Say out big, big. I want a drink of water.   20
And baby prattled after her:
— A jink a jink a jawbo.
Cissy Caffrey cuddled the wee chap for she was awfully fond of children, so patient with little sufferers and Tommy Caffrey could never be got to take his castor oil unless it was Cissy Caffrey that held his nose and promised him the scatty[3] heel of the loaf or brown bread with golden syrup   25

---

[1]   The Catholic church of Mary, Star of the sea, is located off Leahy's Terrace; *Stella maris* (Latin for "star of the sea") is one of the Virgin's appellations.

[2]   *plucks* an Irish term for "cheeks," from the Gaelic *pluc.*
[3]   *scatty* crumbled.

on. What a persuasive power that girl had! But to be sure baby was as good as gold, a perfect little dote in his new fancy bib. None of your spoilt beauties, Flora MacFlimsy[4] sort, was Cissy Caffrey. A truerhearted lass never drew the breath of life, always with a laugh in her gipsylike eyes and a frolicsome word on her cherryripe red lips, a girl lovable in the extreme. And Edy Boardman
30   laughed too at the quaint language of little brother.

But just then there was a slight altercation between Master Tommy and Master Jacky. Boys will be boys and our two twins were no exception to this golden rule.[5] The apple of discord[6] was a certain castle of sand which Master Jacky had built and Master Tommy would have it right go wrong that it was to be architecturally improved by a frontdoor like the Martello tower[7] had. But if
35   Master Tommy was headstrong Master Jacky was selfwilled too and, true to the maxim that every little Irishman's house is his castle, he fell upon his hated rival and to such purpose that the wouldbe assailant came to grief and (alas to relate!) the coveted castle too. Needless to say the cries of discomfited Master Tommy drew the attention of the girl friends.

— Come here, Tommy, his sister called imperatively, at once! And you, Jacky, for shame to
40   throw poor Tommy in the dirty sand. Wait till I catch you for that.

His eyes misty with unshed tears Master Tommy came at her call for their big sister's word was law with the twins. And in a sad plight he was after his misadventure. His little man-o'-war top and unmentionables were full of sand but Cissy was a past mistress in the art of smoothing over life's tiny troubles and very quickly not one speck of sand was to be seen on his smart little suit.
45   Still the blue eyes were glistening with hot tears that would well up so she kissed away the hurtness and shook her hand at Master Jacky the culprit and said if she was near him she wouldn't be far from him, her eyes dancing in admonition.

— Nasty bold Jacky! she cried.

She put an arm round the little mariner and coaxed winningly:
50   — What's your name? Butter and cream?[8]

— Tell us who is your sweetheart, spoke Edy Boardman. Is Cissy your sweetheart?

— Nao, tearful Tommy said.

— Is Edy Boardman your sweetheart? Cissy queried.

— Nao, Tommy said.
55   — I know, Edy Boardman said none too amiably with an arch glance from her shortsighted eyes. I know who is Tommy's sweetheart, Gerty is Tommy's sweetheart.

— Nao, Tommy said on the verge of tears.

Cissy's quick motherwit guessed what was amiss and she whispered to Edy Boardman to take him there behind the pushcar where the gentlemen couldn't see and to mind he didn't wet his new
60   tan shoes.

But who was Gerty?

Gerty MacDowell who was seated near her companions, lost in thought, gazing far away into the distance was in very truth as fair a specimen of winsome Irish girlhood as one could wish to see. She was pronounced beautiful by all who knew her though, as folks often said, she was more a Giltrap than a
65   MacDowell. Her figure was slight and graceful, inclining even to fragility but those iron jelloids she had been taking of late had done her a world of good much better than the Widow Welch's female pills[9]

---

[4]   *Flora MacFlimsy* the heroine of a comic poem "Nothing to Wear" by the American writer Willian Allen Butler (1825–1902); she is mocked for her pursuit of fashionable clothes and ends in "utter despare / Because she had nothing whatever to wear."

[5]   *golden rule* "All things whatsoever ye would that men should do to you, do ye even so to them," says Jesus in the Sermon on the Mount (Matthew 7:12 and Luke 6:31).

[6]   *apple of discord* a proverbial expression for an object of contention, so called after the apple, in Greek mythology, which Eris (goddess of discord) proposes as the prize for whoever is judged the fairest among three goddesses (Hera, Aphrodite, and Athena). When Paris awards the prize to Aphrodite, and Aphro-

dite rewards him with Helen of Troy, it brings about the Trojan War.

[7]   *the Martello tower* named after Cape Martello in Corsica, where the British had great difficulty overtaking a short, squat tower, a Martello tower was a round building for observing the coastline and garrisoning a small troop of soldiers. A number of them were built at key points on the Irish coast between 1803 and 1806 to defend against a potential invasion during the Napoleonic wars.

[8]   *What's your name? Butter and cream?* from a Dublin street rhyme: "What's your name / Butter an' crame / All the way from / Dirty Lane."

[9]   *Widow Welch's female pills* a patent medicine that promised to cure "female troubles" and "that tired feeling."

and she was much better of those discharges she used to get and that tired feeling. The waxen pallor
of her face was almost spiritual in its ivorylike purity though her rosebud mouth was a genuine
Cupid's bow, Greekly perfect. Her hands were of finely veined alabaster with tapering fingers and as
white as lemon juice and queen of ointments[10] could make them though it was not true that she   70
used to wear kid gloves in bed or take a milk footbath either. Bertha Supple told that once to Edy
Boardman, a deliberate lie, when she was black out at daggers drawn with Gerty (the girl chums
had of course their little tiffs from time to time like the rest of mortals) and she told her not to let
on whatever she did that it was her that told her or she'd never speak to her again. No. Honour
where honour is due. There was an innate refinement, a languid queenly *hauteur* about Gerty which   75
was unmistakably evidenced in her delicate hands and higharched instep. Had kind fate but willed
her to be born a gentlewoman of high degree in her own right and had she only received the benefit
of a good education Gerty MacDowell might easily have held her own beside any lady in the land
and have seen herself exquisitely gowned with jewels on her brow and patrician suitors at her feet
vying with one another to pay their devoirs to her. Mayhap it was this, the love that might have   80
been,[11] that lent to her softlyfeatured face at whiles a look, tense with suppressed meaning, that
imparted a strange yearning tendency to the beautiful eyes, a charm few could resist. Why have
women such eyes of witchery? Gerty's were of the bluest Irish blue, set off by lustrous lashes and
dark expressive brows. Time was when those brows were not so silkilyseductive. It was Madame
Vera Verity, directress of the Woman Beautiful page of the Princess novelette,[12] who had first   85
advised her to try eyebrowleine which gave that haunting expression to the eyes, so becoming in
leaders of fashion, and she had never regretted it. Then there was blushing scientifically cured and
how to be tall increase your height and you have a beautiful face but your nose? That would suit
Mrs Dignam because she had a button one. But Gerty's crowning glory was her wealth of wonderful
hair. It was dark brown with a natural wave in it. She had cut it that very morning on account of the   90
new moon and it nestled about her pretty head in a profusion of luxuriant clusters and pared her
nails too, Thursday for wealth. And just now at Edy's words as a telltale flush, delicate as the
faintest rosebloom, crept into her cheeks she looked so lovely in her sweet girlish shyness that of a
surety God's fair land of Ireland did not hold her equal.

For an instant she was silent with rather sad downcast eyes. She was about to retort but   95
something checked the words on her tongue. Inclination prompted her to speak out: dignity
told her to be silent. The pretty lips pouted a while but then she glanced up and broke out into a
joyous little laugh which had in it all the freshness of a young May morning. She knew right well,
no-one better, what made squinty Edy say that because of him cooling in his attentions when it was
simply a lovers' quarrel. As per usual somebody's nose was out of joint about the boy that had the   100
bicycle always riding up and down in front of her window. Only now his father kept him in in the
evenings studying hard to get an exhibition in the intermediate[13] that was on and he was going to
Trinity college[14] to study for a doctor when he left the high school like his brother W. E. Wylie who
was racing in the bicycle races in Trinity college university. Little recked he perhaps for what she
felt, that dull aching void in her heart sometimes, piercing to the core. Yet he was young and   105

[10] *queen of ointments* an advertising slogan for Beetham's Larola:
"Makes the skin as soft as velvet, Removes all Roughness, Redness, Heat Irritation, Tan and Keeps the Skin Soft, Smooth and
White all the year round." Manufactured by M. Beetham and
Son, Cheltenham, England.
[11] *the love that might have been* "Maud Muller," a narrative poem
by American poet John Greenleaf Whittier (1807–92), recounts
the story of an impoverished farm girl who has a passing encounter with a wealthy judge from town, one that prompts both of
them to dream of each other intermittently for the rest of their
lives. The poem concludes: "For of all sad words of tongue or
pen, / The saddest are these: 'It might have been'."
[12] *The Princess's Novelette* (1886–1904) was a weekly magazine
published in London. Each issue included a "novelette" and an

installment of a serialized story or novel. Its features included:
A.A.P. (All About People); Beauty's Boudoir; Boudoir Gossip;
and the Fashion Supplement. There was no Woman Beautiful
page, and no Madame Vera Verity was ever its editor.
[13] *to get an exhibition in the intermediate* an exhibition was
a distinguished mark or grade obtained in competitive examinations set by the Intermediate Education Board for Ireland.
Reggie Wylie, the subject of Gerty's thoughts here, would have
been 16 or 17 years old when he took these.
[14] *Trinity college* a university so Anglo-Protestant at this time
that Irish Catholic bishops forbade Catholics from attending it
without special dispensation.

perchance he might learn to love her in time. They were protestants in his family[15] and of course
Gerty knew Who came first and after Him the blessed Virgin and then Saint Joseph. But he was
undeniably handsome with an exquisite nose and he was what he looked, every inch a gentleman,
the shape of his head too at the back without his cap on that she would know anywhere something
110 off the common and the way he turned the bicycle at the lamp with his hands off the bars and also
the nice perfume of those good cigarettes and besides they were both of a size and that was why Edy
Boardman thought she was so frightfully clever because he didn't go and ride up and down in front
of her bit of a garden.

Gerty was dressed simply but with the instinctive taste of a votary of Dame Fashion for she felt
115 that there was just a might that he might be out. A neat blouse of electric blue, selftinted by dolly
dyes[16] (because it was expected in the *Lady's Pictorial*[17] that electric blue would be worn), with a
smart vee opening down to the division and kerchief pocket (in which she always kept a piece of
cottonwool scented with her favourite perfume because the handkerchief spoiled the sit) and a navy
threequarter skirt cut to the stride showed off her slim graceful figure to perfection. She wore a
120 coquettish little love of a hat of wideleaved nigger straw contrast trimmed with an underbrim of
eggblue chenille and at the side a butterfly bow to tone. All Tuesday week afternoon she was
hunting to match that chenille but at last she found what she wanted at Clery's[18] summer sales, the
very it, slightly shopsoiled but you would never notice, seven fingers two and a penny. She did it up
all by herself and what joy was hers when she tried it on then, smiling at the lovely reflection which
125 the mirror gave back to her! And when she put it on the waterjug to keep the shape she knew that
that would take the shine out of some people she knew. Her shoes were the newest thing in footwear
(Edy Boardman prided herself that she was very *petite* but she never had a foot like Gerty
MacDowell, a five, and never would ash, oak or elm) with patent toecaps and just one smart
buckle at her higharched instep. Her wellturned ankle displayed its perfect proportions beneath her
130 skirt and just the proper amount and no more of her shapely limbs encased in finespun hose with
highspliced heels and wide garter tops. As for undies they were Gerty's chief care and who that
knows the fluttering hopes and fears of sweet seventeen (though Gerty would never see seventeen
again) can find it in his heart to blame her? She had four dinky sets, with awfully pretty stitchery,
three garments and nighties extra, and each set slotted with different coloured ribbons, rosepink,
135 pale blue, mauve and peagreen and she aired them herself and blued them when they came home
from the wash and ironed them and she had a brickbat to keep the iron on because she wouldn't
trust those washerwomen as far as she'd see them scorching the things. She was wearing the blue for
luck, hoping against hope, her own colour and the lucky colour too for a bride to have a bit of blue
somewhere on her because the green she wore that day week brought grief because his father
140 brought him in to study for the intermediate exhibition and because she thought perhaps he might
be out because when she was dressing that morning she nearly slipped up the old pair on her inside
out and that was for luck and lovers' meetings if you put those things on inside out so long as it
wasn't of a Friday.

And yet—and yet! That strained look on her face! A gnawing sorrow is there all the time. Her
145 very soul is in her eyes and she would give worlds to be in the privacy of her own familiar chamber
where, giving way to tears, she could have a good cry and relieve her pentup feelings. Though not
too much because she knew how to cry nicely before the mirror. You are lovely, Gerty, it said. The
paly light of evening falls upon a face infinitely sad and wistful. Gerty MacDowell yearns in vain.
Yes, she had known from the first that her daydream of a marriage has been arranged and the
150 weddingbells ringing for Mrs Reggy Wylie T. C. D.[19] (because the one who married the elder
brother would be Mrs Wylie) and in the fashionable intelligence Mrs Gertrude Wylie was wearing a

[15] *They were protestants in his family* to marry a Protestant, Gerty would have to obtain permission from the bishop of her diocese, while young Wylie would be required to take religious instruction, be confirmed as a Catholic, and promise that his children would be brought up Catholic.
[16] *dolly dyes* the brand name of dyes for home use.
[17] Published in London, this magazine billed itself as "A weekly illustrated journal of fashion, society, art, literature, music and the drama."
[18] A major department store at 21–7 Sackville Street Lower (now O'Connell Street).
[19] Trinity College, Dublin.

sumptuous confection of grey trimmed with expensive blue fox was not to be. He was too young to understand. He would not believe in love, a woman's birthright. The night of the party long ago in Stoers' (he was still in short trousers) when they were alone and he stole an arm round her waist she went white to the very lips. He called her little one in a strangely husky voice and snatched a half   155
kiss (the first!) but it was only the end of her nose and then he hastened from the room with a remark about refreshments. Impetuous fellow! Strength of character had never been Reggy Wylie's strong point and he who would woo and win Gerty MacDowell must be a man among men. But waiting, always waiting to be asked and it was leap year too and would soon be over. No prince charming is her beau ideal to lay a rare and wondrous love at her feet but rather a manly man with a   160
strong quiet face who had not found his ideal, perhaps his hair slightly flecked with grey, and who would understand, take her in his sheltering arms, strain her to him in all the strength of his deep passionate nature and comfort her with a long long kiss. It would be like heaven. For such a one she yearns this balmy summer eve. With all the heart of her she longs to be his only, his affianced bride for riches for poor, in sickness in health, till death us two part, from this to this day forward.[20]   165
    And while Edy Boardman was with little Tommy behind the pushcar she was just thinking would the day ever come when she could call herself his little wife to be. Then they could talk about her till they went blue in the face, Bertha Supple too, and Edy, the spitfire, because she would be twentytwo in November. She would care for him with creature comforts too for Gerty was womanly wise and knew that a mere man liked that feeling of hominess. Her griddlecakes done to a   170
goldenbrown hue and queen Ann's pudding[21] of delightful creaminess had won golden opinions from all because she had a lucky hand also for lighting a fire, dredge in the fine selfraising flour and always stir in the same direction then cream the milk and sugar and whisk well the white of eggs though she didn't like the eating part when there were any people that made her shy and often she wondered why you couldn't eat something poetical like violets or roses and they would have a   175
beautifully appointed drawingroom with pictures and engravings and the photograph of grandpapa Giltrap's lovely dog Garryowen that almost talked, it was so human, and chintz covers for the chairs and that silver toastrack in Clery's summer jumble sales like they have in rich houses. He would be tall with broad shoulders (she had always admired tall men for a husband) with glistening white teeth under his carefully trimmed sweeping moustache and they would go on the continent for   180
their honeymoon (three wonderful weeks!) and then, when they settled down in a nice snug and cosy little homely house, every morning they would both have brekky, simple but perfectly served, for their own two selves and before he went out to business he would give his dear little wifey a good hearty hug and gaze for a moment deep down into her eyes.
    Edy Boardman asked Tommy Caffrey was he done and he said yes, so then she buttoned up his   185
little knickerbockers for him and told him to run off and play with Jacky and to be good now and not to fight. But Tommy said he wanted the ball and Edy told him no that baby was playing with the ball and if he took it there'd be wigs on the green[22] but Tommy said it was his ball and he wanted his ball and he pranced on the ground, if you please. The temper of him! O, he was a man already was little Tommy Caffrey since he was out of pinnies.[23] Edy told him no, no and to be off   190
now with him and she told Cissy Caffrey not to give in to him.
    — You're not my sister, naughty Tommy said. It's my ball.
    But Cissy Caffrey told baby Boardman to look up, look up high at her finger and she snatched the ball quickly and threw it along the sand and Tommy after it in full career, having won the day.
    — Anything for a quiet life, laughed Ciss.   195
    And she tickled tiny tot's two cheeks to make him forget and played here's the lord mayor, here's his two horses, here's his gingerbread carriage and here he walks in, chinchopper, chinchopper,

---

[20]   *for riches for poor . . . to this day forward* Gerty misremembers the vows in the Catholic wedding ceremony, which read, "I, X, take you, Y, for my lawful wife [husband], to have and to hold, from this day forward, for better, for worse, for richer, for poorer, in sickness and in health, until death do us part."

[21]   A custard pudding with bread crumbs, flavored with lemon rind and raspberry jam.

[22]   *wigs on the green* colloquial expression for a brawl.

[23]   *out of pinnies* old enough not to wear a baby's pinafore.

chinchopper chin.[24] But Edy got as cross as two sticks about him getting his own way like that from everyone always petting him.

200   — I'd like to give him something, she said, so I would, where I won't say.

— On the beeoteetom, laughed Cissy merrily.

Gerty MacDowell bent down her head and crimsoned at the idea of Cissy saying an unladylike thing like that out loud she'd be ashamed of her life to say, flushing a deep rosy red, and Edy Boardman said she was sure the gentleman opposite heard what she said. But not a pin cared Ciss.

205   — Let him! she said with a pert toss of her head and a piquant tilt of her nose. Give it to him too on the same place as quick as I'd look at him.

Madcap Ciss with her golliwog[25] curls. You had to laugh at her sometimes. For instance when she asked you would you have some more Chinese tea and jaspberry ram and when she drew the jugs too and the men's faces on her nails with red ink make you split your sides or when she wanted to go

210   where you know she said she wanted to run and pay a visit to the Miss White. That was just like Cissycums. O, and will you ever forget the evening she dressed up in her father's suit and hat and the burned cork moustache and walked down Tritonville road, smoking a cigarette. There was none to come up to her for fun. But she was sincerity itself, one of the bravest and truest hearts heaven ever made, not one of your twofaced things, too sweet to be wholesome.

215   And then there came out upon the air the sound of voices and the pealing anthem of the organ. It was the men's temperance retreat conducted by the missioner, the reverend John Hughes S. J. rosary, sermon and benediction of the Most Blessed Sacrament.[26] They were there gathered together without distinction of social class (and a most edifying spectacle it was to see) in that simple fane[27] beside the waves, after the storms of this weary world, kneeling before the feet of the

220   immaculate, reciting the litany of Our Lady of Loreto,[28] beseeching her to intercede for them, the old familiar words, holy Mary, holy virgin of virgins. How sad to poor Gerty's ears! Had her father only avoided the clutches of the demon drink, by taking the pledge[29] or those powders the drink habit cured in Pearson's Weekly,[30] she might now be rolling in her carriage, second to none. Over and over had she told herself that as she mused by the dying embers in a brown study without the

225   lamp because she hated two lights or oftentimes gazing out of the window dreamily by the hour at the rain falling on the rusty bucket, thinking. But that vile decoction which has ruined so many hearths and homes had cast its shadow over her childhood days. Nay, she had even witnessed in the home circle deeds of violence caused by intemperance and had seen her own father, a prey to the fumes of intoxication, forget himself completely for if there was one thing of all things that Gerty

230   knew it was that the man who lifts his hand to a woman save in the way of kindness deserves to be branded as the lowest of the low.

And still the voices sang in supplication to the Virgin most powerful, Virgin most merciful.[31] And Gerty, wrapt in thought, scarce saw or heard her companions or the twins at their boyish gambols or the gentleman off Sandymount green that Cissy Caffrey called the man that was so like

235   himself passing along the strand taking a short walk. You never saw him anyway screwed but still and for all that she would not like him for a father because he was too old or something or on account of his face (it was a palpable case of doctor Fell)[32] or his carbuncly nose with the pimples

[24]   *Here's the lord mayor . . . chinchopper chin* a variant of the nursery rhyme game: "Here sits the Lord Mayor [*touch forehead*] / Here sit his two men [*eyes*] / Here sits the cock [*one cheek*] / Here sits the hen [*other cheek*] / Here sit the little chicken [*tip of nose*] / And here they run [*mouth*] Chin chopper, chin chopper, chin [*chuck under chin*].
[25]   *golliwog* a name for a black-faced, grotesquely dressed (male) doll with a shock of fuzzy hair. The term is first recorded in 1895.
[26]   *benediction of the most Blessed Sacrament* an evening service to celebrate the Virgin Mary, it can include the Litany of Our Lady of Loreto, the "Tantum ergo" (see pp. 266, 266 nn. 60–1), and Psalm 117 (see pp. 270, 270 n. 83), as it will in the fictional service here.
[27]   *fane* poetic term for a church or temple.
[28]   *the litany of Our Lady of Loreto* a prayer of supplication which begins with an appeal to the Trinity, followed by sustained supplication made through Mary's various appellations (e.g.,

Holy Mary, Holy Mother of God, Holy Virgin of virgins, Mystical Tower, Tower of Ivory, House of God, etc.), and concluding with a prayer that Mary "free us from our sorrows in this world and give us eternal happiness in the next."
[29]   *taking the pledge* making a religious vow or pledge to abstain from alcoholic drinks.
[30]   *Pearson's Weekly* was a London penny-magazine that featured sensational stories and moral instruction for the poor.
[31]   *Virgin most powerful, virgin most merciful* from the Litany of Our Lady.
[32]   Dr. John Fell (1625–86), Dean of Christ Church (College), Oxford, threatened the satirist Thomas Brown (1663–1704) with expulsion unless he could adapt Martial's epigram into English immediately. Brown saved himself by replying: "I do not love thee, Dr. Fell / The reason why I canot tell; / But this

on it and his sandy moustache a bit white under his nose. Poor father! With all his faults she loved him still[33] when he sang *Tell me, Mary, how to woo thee*[34] or *My love and cottage near Rochelle*[35] and they had stewed cockles and lettuce with Lazenby's salad dressing[36] for supper and when he sang *The moon hath raised*[37] with Mr Dignam that died suddenly and was buried, God have mercy on him, from a stroke. Her mother's birthday that was and Charley was home on his holidays and Tom[38] and Mr Dignam and Mrs and Patsy and Freddy Dignam and they were to have had a group taken.[39] No-one would have thought the end was so near. Now he was laid to rest. And her mother said to him to let that be a warning to him for the rest of his days and he couldn't even go to the funeral on account of the gout and she had to go into town to bring him the letters and samples from his office about Catesby's cork lino,[40] artistic, standard, designs, fit for a palace, gives tiptop wear and always bright and cheery in the home. 240

245

A sterling good daughter was Gerty just like a second mother in the house, a ministering angel[41] too with a little heart worth its weight in gold. And when her mother had those raging splitting headaches who was it rubbed on the menthol cone[42] on her forehead but Gerty though she didn't like her mother taking pinches of snuff and that was the only single thing they ever had words about, taking snuff. Everyone thought the world of her for her gentle ways. It was Gerty who turned off the gas at the main every night and it was Gerty who tacked up on the wall of that place where she never forgot every fortnight the chlorate of lime[43] Mr Tunney the grocer's christmas almanac the picture of halcyon days where a young gentleman in the costume they used to wear then with a threecornered hat was offering a bunch of flowers to his ladylove with oldtime chivalry through her lattice window. You could see there was a story behind it. The colours were done something lovely. She was in a soft clinging white in a studied attitude and the gentleman was in chocolate and he looked a thorough aristocrat. She often looked at them dreamily when she went there for a certain purpose and felt her own arms that were white and soft just like hers with the sleeves back and thought about those times because she had found out in Walker's pronouncing dictionary[44] that belonged to grandpapa Giltrap about the halcyon days what they meant. 250

255

60

The twins were now playing in the most approved brotherly fashion, till at last Master Jacky who was really as bold as brass there was no getting behind that deliberately kicked the ball as hard as ever he could down towards the seaweedy rocks. Needless to say poor Tommy was not slow to voice 265

---

alone I know full well, / I do not love thee, Dr. Fell." Martial's epigram: "Non amo te, Sabidi, nec possum dicere quare; / Hoc tantum possum dicere, non amo te."

[33] *With all his faults she loved him still* adapted from a popular song, "With All Her Faults I Love Her still" (1888), by Monroe H. Rosenfeld. The first verse is: "With all her faults I love her still, / And even though the world should scorn; / No love like hers my heart can thrill, / Although she's made that heart forlorn!"

[34] *Tell me, Mary, how to woo thee* a popular song by G. A. Hodson, which begins: "Tell me, Mary, how to woo thee, / Teach my bosom to reveal / All its sorrows sweet unto thee, / All the love my heart can feel."

[35] *My love and cottage near Rochelle* from the refrain of an aria in Act II of *The Siege of Rochelle* (1835), an opera by Michael Balfe (1808–70), an Irish composer. The aria begins: "When I beheld the anchor weigh'd, / And with the shore thine image fade, / I deem'd each wave a boundless sea / That bore me still from love and thee; / I watched alone the sun decline, / And envied beams on thee to shine, / While anguish panted 'neath her spell, / My love and cottage near Rochelle."

[36] A salad dressing manufactured by a soup-making firm, F. Lazenby and Son, Ltd., London.

[37] "The moon hath raised her lamp above, / To light the way to thee, my love," are the opening lines from a duet in the melodramatic opera *The Lily of Killarney* (1862), composed by Sir Julius Benedict (1804–85), with a libretto by Dion Boucicault (1822–90) and John Oxenford (1812–77). The opera, in its turn, was based on Dion Boucicault's play, *The Collen Bawn* (1860),

which itself was a stage adaptation of a novel by the Irish writer Gerald Griffin (1812–40), titled *The Collegians* when it first appeared in 1829, but after 1860 often titled *The Collegians or the Colleen Bawn* in the hope of capitalizing on the success of Boucicault's play. Novel, play, and opera recount the story of a Protestant landlord who has secretly married "the colleen bawn," a beautiful Irish peasant. Offered the chance of marrying another Protestant whose fortune will let him retain his highly mortgaged lands, he plots her murder. His plan is ultimately thwarted.

[38] Gerty MacDowell's brothers.

[39] *a group taken* a group photograph.

[40] Linoleum manufactured by T. Catesby and Sons, Ltd., in Glasgow.

[41] *a ministering angel* in *Hamlet*, a priest objects that Ophelia, because she has committed suicide, should not be buried in consecrated ground or given a requiem. Her brother Laertes replies: "I tell thee, churlish priest, / A ministering angel shall my sister be, / When thou liest howling" (V.i.263–5). The phrase is used again by Sir Walter Scott in *Marmion* (1808): "O Woman! in our hours of ease, / Uncertain, coy, and hard to please, / And variable as the shade / By the light quivering aspen made; When pain and anguish wring the brow, / A ministering angel thou!" (canto 6, stanza 30).

[42] Menthol rubbed on the forehead was used to relieve a headache before aspirin became widely used.

[43] Used as a disinfectant in outdoor toilets.

[44] John Walker (1732–1807) published his *Critical Pronouncing Dictionary and Expositor of the English Language* in 1791.

his dismay but luckily the gentleman in black who was sitting there by himself came gallantly to the rescue and intercepted the ball. Our two champions claimed their plaything with lusty cries and to avoid trouble Cissy Caffrey called to the gentleman to throw it to her please. The gentleman
270   aimed the ball once or twice and then threw it up the strand towards Cissy Caffrey but it rolled down the slope and stopped right under Gerty's skirt near the little pool by the rock. The twins clamoured again for it and Cissy told her to kick it away and let them fight for it so Gerty drew back her foot but she wished their stupid ball hadn't come rolling down to her and she gave a kick but she missed and Edy and Cissy laughed.
275   — If you fail try again, Edy Boardman said.

Gerty smiled assent and bit her lip. A delicate pink crept into her pretty cheek but she was determined to let them see so she just lifted her skirt a little but just enough and took good aim and gave the ball a jolly good kick and it went ever so far and the two twins after it down towards the shingle. Pure jealousy of course it was nothing else to draw attention on account
280   of the gentleman opposite looking. She felt the warm flush, a danger signal always with Gerty MacDowell, surging and flaming into her cheeks. Till then they had only exchanged glances of the most casual but now under the brim of her new hat she ventured a look at him and the face that met her gaze there in the twilight, wan and strangely drawn, seemed to her the saddest she had ever seen.

285   Through the open window of the church the fragrant incense was wafted and with it the fragrant names of her who was conceived without stain of original sin,[45] spiritual vessel, pray for us, honourable vessel, pray for us, vessel of singular devotion, pray for us, mystical rose.[46] And careworn hearts were there and toilers for their daily bread and many who had erred and wandered, their eyes wet with contrition but for all that bright with hope for the reverend father Hughes had told them
290   what the great saint Bernard said in his famous prayer of Mary, the most pious Virgin's intercessory power that it was not recorded in any age that those who implored her powerful protection were ever abandoned by her.[47]

The twins were now playing again right merrily for the troubles of childhood are but as fleeting summer showers. Cissy played with baby Boardman till he crowed with glee, clapping baby hands
295   in air. Peep she cried behind the hood of the pushcar and Edy asked where was Cissy gone and then Cissy popped up her head and cried ah! and, my word, didn't the little chap enjoy that! And then she told him to say papa.

— Say papa, baby. Say pa pa pa pa pa pa pa.

And baby did his level best to say it for he was very intelligent for eleven months everyone said
300   and big for his age and the picture of health, a perfect little bunch of love, and he would certainly turn out to be something great, they said.

— Haja ja ja haja.

Cissy wiped his little mouth with the dribbling bib and wanted him to sit up properly and say pa pa pa but when she undid the strap she cried out, holy saint Denis, that he was possing[48] wet and
305   to double the half blanket the other way under him. Of course his infant majesty was most obstreperous at such toilet formalities and he let everyone know it:

— Habaa baaaahabaaa baaaa.

And two great big lovely big tears coursing down his cheeks. It was all no use soothering him with no, nono, baby, no and telling him about the geegee and where was the puffpuff but Ciss,
310   always readywitted, gave him in his mouth the teat of the suckingbottle and the young heathen was quickly appeased.

[45]   *her who was conceived without stain of original sin* the Virgin Mary. The doctrine of the Immaculate Conception, which holds that Mary, from the first instant of her conception, was kept free from all stain of original sin, was elevated to the status of church dogma by Pius IX in 1854.
[46]   *spiritual vessel, pray for us ... mystical rose* from the Litany of Our Lady of Loreto.

[47]   *what the great Saint Bernard ... abandoned by her* the "Memorare," a prayer popularized by but not composed by St. Bernard of Clairvaux, asks the Virgin to intercede on behalf of the pleader, as nobody who has ever sought her help has "been forsaken."
[48]   *possing* dialect for beating or pounding clothes in water while washing.

Gerty wished to goodness they would take their squalling baby home out of that and not get on her nerves no hour to be out and the little brats of twins. She gazed out towards the distant sea. It was like the paintings that man used to do on the pavement with all the coloured chalks and such a pity too leaving them there to be all blotted out, the evening and the clouds coming out and the   315
Bailey light on Howth[49] and to hear the music like that and the perfume of those incense they burned in the church like a kind of waft. And while she gazed her heart went pitapat. Yes, it was her he was looking at and there was meaning in his look. His eyes burned into her as though they would search her through and through, read her very soul. Wonderful eyes they were, superbly expressive, but could you trust them? People were so queer. She could see at once by his dark eyes   320
and his pale intellectual face that he was a foreigner the image of the photo she had of Martin Harvey,[50] the matinée idol, only for the moustache which she preferred because she wasn't stage-struck like Winny Rippingham that wanted they two to always dress the same on account of a play but she could not see whether he had an aquiline nose or a slightly *retroussé*[51] from where he was sitting. He was in deep mourning, she could see that, and the story of a haunting sorrow was   325
written on his face. She would have given worlds to know what it was. He was looking up so intently, so still and he saw her kick the ball and perhaps he could see the bright steel buckles of her shoes if she swung them like that thoughtfully with the toes down. She was glad that something told her to put on the transparent stockings thinking Reggy Wylie might be out but that was far away. Here was that of which she had so often dreamed. It was he who mattered and there was joy   330
on her face because she wanted him because she felt instinctively that he was like no-one else. The very heart of the girlwoman went out to him, her dreamhusband. because she knew on the instant it was him. If he had suffered, more sinned against than sinning,[52] or even, even, if he had been himself a sinner, a wicked man, she cared not. Even if he was a protestant or methodist she could convert him easily if he truly loved her. There were wounds that wanted healing with heartbalm.   335
She was a womanly woman not like other flighty girls, unfeminine, he had known, those cyclists showing off what they hadn't got and she just yearned to know all, to forgive all if she could make him fall in love with her, make him forget the memory of the past. Then mayhap he would embrace her gently, like a real man, crushing her soft body to him, and love her, his ownest girlie, for herself alone.   340

Refuge of sinners. Comfortress of the afflicted. *Ora pro nobis.*[53] Well has it been said that whosoever prays to her with faith and constancy can never be lost or cast away: and fitly is she too a haven of refuge for the afflicted because of the seven dolours which transpierced her own heart.[54] Gerty could picture the whole scene in the church, the stained glass windows lighted up, the candles, the flowers and the blue banners of the blessed Virgin's sodality and Father Conroy was   345
helping Canon O'Hanlon at the altar, carrying things in and out with his eyes cast down. He looked almost a saint and his confessionbox was so quiet and clean and dark and his hands were just like white wax and if ever she became a Dominican nun in their white habit perhaps he might come to the convent for the novena of Saint Dominic.[55] He told her that time when she told him about that in confession crimsoning up to the roots of her hair for fear he could see, not to be troubled because   350
that was only the voice of nature and we were all subject to nature's laws, he said, in this life and that

<hr>

[49] *the Bailey light on Howth* the Hill of Howth is located on the north side of Dublin Bay, and its southernmost point culminated in the Bailey Lighthouse, visible from the south side of Budin Bay, where Gerty and Bloom are.

[50] Sir John Martin-Harvey (1863–1944), an English actor and theatrical producer who wrote in *The Autobiography of John Martin-Harvey* (London, 1933) that his turn-of-the-century visits to Dublin were "a series of triumphs."

[51] *retroussé* French for "turned up, snub."

[52] *more sinned against than sinning* a cliché, ultimately from King Lear, who rages against the gods and the storm on the heath: "I am a man / More sinned against than sinning" (III.ii.59–60).

[53] *Refuge of sinners … Ora pro nobis* from the Litany of Our Lady, ending with Latin for "Pray for us."

[54] *Well has it been said … transpierced her own heart* from a prayer in honor of the Virgin Mary which was standard at the turn of the century. "The seven dolors" are her seven sorrows: (1) the birth of her Son; (2) the Flight into Egypt; (3) the Loss in the Temple; (4) the Carrying of the Cross; (5) the Crucifixion; (6) the Deposition; (7) the Entombment.

[55] *the novena of Saint Dominic* a devotion consisting of prayers said over 9 days and culminating in the saint's feast on August 4; St. Dominic was devoted to the Virgin and popularized the use of the rosary.

that was no sin because that came from the nature of woman instituted by God, he said, and that Our Blessed Lady herself said to the archangel Gabriel be it done unto me according to Thy Word.[56]
He was so kind and holy and often and often she thought and thought could she work a ruched
355   teacosy with embroidered floral design for him as a present or a clock but they had a clock she noticed on the mantelpiece white and gold with a canary bird that came out of a little house to tell the time the day she went there about the flowers for the forty hours' adoration[57] because it was hard to know what sort of a present to give or perhaps an album of illuminated views of Dublin or some place.

360   The exasperating little brats of twins began to quarrel again and Jacky threw the ball out towards the sea and they both ran after it. Little monkeys common as ditchwater. Someone ought to take them and give them a good hiding for themselves to keep them in their places, the both of them. And Cissy and Edy shouted after them to come back because they were afraid the tide might come in on them and be drowned.

365   — Jacky! Tommy!

Not they! What a great notion they had! So Cissy said it was the very last time she'd ever bring them out. She jumped up and called them and she ran down the slope past him, tossing her hair behind her which had a good enough colour if there had been more of it but with all the thingamerry she was always rubbing into it she couldn't get it to grow long because it wasn't
370   natural so she could just go and throw her hat at it. She ran with long gandery strides it was a wonder she didn't rip up her skirt at the side that was too tight on her because there was a lot of the tomboy about Cissy Caffrey and she was a forward piece whenever she thought she had a good opportunity to show off and just because she was a good runner she ran like that so that he could see all the end of her petticoat running and her skinny shanks up as far as possible. It would have served
375   her just right if she had tripped up over something accidentally on purpose with her high crooked French heels on her to make her look tall and got a fine tumble. *Tableau!*[58] That would have been a very charming exposé for a gentleman like that to witness.

Queen of angels, queen of patriarchs, queen of prophets, of all saints, they prayed, queen of the most holy rosary[59] and then Father Conroy handed the thurible to Canon O'Hanlon and he put in
380   the incense and censed the Blessed Sacrament and Cissy Caffrey caught the two twins and she was itching to give them a ringing good clip on the ear but she didn't because she thought he might be watching but she never made a bigger mistake in all her life because Gerty could see without looking that he never took his eyes off of her and then Canon O'Hanlon handed the thurible back to Father Conroy and knelt down looking up at the Blessed Sacrament and the choir began to sing
385   *Tantum ergo*[60] and she just swung her foot in and out in time as the music rose and fell to the *Tantumer gosa cramen tum.*[61] Three and eleven she paid for those stockings in Sparrow's[62] of George's street on the Tuesday, no the Monday before Easter and there wasn't a brack[63] on them and that was what he was looking at, transparent, and not at her insignificant ones that had neither shape nor form (the cheek of her!) because he had eyes in his head to see the difference for himself.

390   Cissy came up along the strand with the two twins and their ball with her hat anyhow on her to one side after her run and she did look a streel[64] tugging the two kids along with the flimsy blouse

[56] *Our Blessed Lady ... according to Thy word* when Mary is told by the Archangel Gabriel that she will bear the Son of God, she replies: "Behold the handmaid of the Lord: be it unto me according to thy word" (Luke 1:38).
[57] *the forty hours adoration* a devotion in which the Blessed Sacrament is exposed for adoration for 40 hours, the time that Christ was entombed before his resurrection.
[58] A parlor game, like charades, in which participants strike poses to communicate a message; when the pose is complete they say "Tableau!"
[59] *Queen of Angels ... most holy rosary* from the Litany of Our Lady.
[60] *Tantum ergo* after the Blessed Sacrament has been exposed in the benediction ceremony, a choir or the congregation sings a

hymn which begins "Tantum ergo Sacramentum / Veneremur cernui" (Latin for "So the Sacrament let us venerate, / bowing in adoration"). The first two lines from the hymn are taken from a poem by St. Thomas Aquinas, "Pange lingua gloriosi" (Latin for "Sing, my tongue, of the glorious").
[61] *Tantumer gosa cramen tum* Gerty's version of the Latin "Tantum ergo sacramentum."
[62] The firm of ladies' and gentlemen's outfitters was located at 16 Great George's Street South, in central Dublin.
[63] *brack* dialect for a break or flaw in the fabric.
[64] *streel* from the Gaelic s(t)raoill(e), an Anglo-Irish word meaning an untidy or disreputable woman, a slut.

she bought only a fortnight before like a rag on her back and a bit of her petticoat hanging like a caricature. Gerty just took off her hat for a moment to settle her hair and a prettier, a daintier head of nutbrown tresses was never seen on a girl's shoulders—a radiant little vision, in sooth, almost maddening in its sweetness. You would have to travel many a long mile before you found a head of   395
hair the like of that. She could almost see the swift answering flash of admiration in his eyes that set her tingling in every nerve. She put on her hat so that she could see from underneath the brim and swung her buckled shoe faster for her breath caught as she caught the expression in his eyes. He was eying her as a snake eyes its prey. Her woman's instinct told her that she had raised the devil in him and at the thought a burning scarlet swept from throat to brow till the lovely colour of her face   400
became a glorious rose.

Edy Boardman was noticing it too because she was squinting at Gerty, half smiling, with her specs, like an old maid, pretending to nurse the baby. Irritable little gnat she was and always would be and that was why no-one could get on with her, poking her nose into what was no concern of hers. And she said to Gerty: 405

— A penny for your thoughts.

— What? replied Gerty with a smile reinforced by the whitest of teeth. I was only wondering was it late.

Because she wished to goodness they'd take the snottynosed twins and their babby home to the mischief out of that so that was why she just gave a gentle hint about its being late. And   410
when Cissy came up Edy asked her the time and Miss Cissy, as glib as you like, said it was half past kissing time, time to kiss again.[65] But Edy wanted to know because they were told to be in early.

— Wait, said Cissy, I'll ask my uncle Peter[66] over there what's the time by his conundrum.

So over she went and when he saw her coming she could see him take his hand out of his   415
pocket, getting nervous, and beginning to play with his watchchain, looking at the church. Passionate nature though he was Gerty could see that he had enormous control over himself. One moment he had been there, fascinated by a loveliness that made him gaze and the next moment it was the quiet gravefaced gentleman, selfcontrol expressed in every line of his distinguishedlooking figure.   420

Cissy said to excuse her would he mind telling her what was the right time and Gerty could see him taking out his watch, listening to it and looking up and clearing his throat and he said he was very sorry his watch was stopped but he thought it must be after eight[67] because the sun was set. His voice had a cultured ring in it and though he spoke in measured accents there was a suspicion of a quiver in the mellow tones. Cissy said thanks and came back with her tongue out and said uncle   425
said his waterworks[68] were out of order.

Then they sang the second verse of the *Tantum ergo* and Canon O'Hanlon got up again and censed the Blessed Sacrament and knelt down and he told Father Conroy that one of the candles was just going to set fire to the flowers and Father Conroy got up and settled it all right and she could see the gentleman winding his watch and listening to the works and she swung her leg more in and out   430
in time. It was getting darker but he could see and he was looking all the time that he was winding the watch or whatever he was doing to it and then he put it back and put his hands back into his pockets. She felt a kind of a sensation rushing all over her and she knew by the feel of her scalp and that irritation against her stays that that thing must be coming on because the last time too was when she clipped her hair on account of the moon. His dark eyes fixed themselves on her again   435
drinking in her every contour, literally worshipping at her shrine. If ever there was undisguised admiration in a man's passionate gaze it was there plain to be seen on that man's face. It is for you, Gertrude MacDowell, and you know it.

Edy began to get ready to go and it was high time for her and Gerty noticed that that little hint she gave had the desired effect because it was a long way along the strand to where there was the   440

---

[65] *half past kissing time, time to kiss gain* a stock phrase that was addressed to children who repeatedly ask what time it is.
[66] *my uncle Peter* a slang expression for a pawnbroker.

[67] *after eight* sunset in Dublin on June 16, 1904, was at 8:27 p.m.
[68] *waterworks* low slang for urinary organs.

place to push up the pushcar and Cissy took off the twins' caps and tidied their hair to make herself
attractive of course and Canon O'Hanlon stood up with his cope poking up at his neck and Father
Conroy handed him the card to read off and he read out *Panem de coelo praestitisti eis*[69] and Edy and
Cissy were talking about the time all the time and asking her but Gerty could pay them back in
445   their own coin and she just answered with scathing politeness when Edy asked her was she
heartbroken about her best boy throwing her over. Gerty winced sharply. A brief cold blaze
shone from her eyes that spoke volumes of scorn immeasurable. It hurt—O yes, it cut deep because
Edy had her own quiet way of saying things like that she knew would wound like the confounded
little cat she was. Gerty's lips parted swiftly to frame the word but she fought back the sob that rose
450   to her throat, so slim, so flawless, so beautifully moulded it seemed one an artist might have
dreamed of. She had loved him better than he knew. Lighthearted deceiver and fickle like all his sex
he would never understand what he had meant to her and for an instant there was in the blue eyes a
quick stinging of tears. Their eyes were probing her mercilessly but with a brave effort she sparkled
back in sympathy as she glanced at her new conquest for them to see.
455   — O, responded Gerty, quick as lightning, laughing, and the proud head flashed up. I can throw
my cap at who I like because it's leap year.
    Her words rang out crystalclear, more musical than the cooing of the ringdove but they cut the
silence icily. There was that in her young voice that told that she was not a one to be lightly trifled
with. As for Mr Reggy with his swank and his bit of money she could just chuck him aside as if he
460   was so much filth and never again would she cast as much as a second thought on him and tear his
silly postcard into a dozen pieces. And if ever after he dared to presume she could give him one look
of measured scorn that would make him shrivel up on the spot. Miss puny little Edy's countenance
fell to no slight extent and Gerty could see by her looking as black as thunder that she was simply
in a towering rage though she hid it, the little kinnatt,[70] because that shaft had struck home for her
465   petty jealousy and they both knew that she was something aloof, apart in another sphere, that she
was not of them and there was somebody else too that knew it and saw it so they could put that in
their pipe and smoke it.
    Edy straightened up baby Boardman to get ready to go and Cissy tucked in the ball and the
spades and buckets and it was high time too because the sandman was on his way for Master
470   Boardman junior and Cissy told him too that Billy Winks was coming and that baby was to go
deedaw and baby looked just too ducky, laughing up out of his gleeful eyes, and Cissy poked him
like that out of fun in his wee fat tummy and baby, without as much as by your leave, sent up his
compliments to all and sundry on to his brandnew dribbling bib.
    — O my! Puddeny pie! protested Ciss. He has his bib destroyed.
475   The slight *contretemps* claimed her attention but in two twos she set that little matter to rights.
    Gerty stifled a smothered exclamation and gave a nervous cough and Edy asked what and she was
just going to tell her to catch it while it was flying but she was ever ladylike in her deportment so
she simply passed it off with consummate tact by saying that that was the benediction because just
then the bell rang out from the steeple over the quiet seashore because Canon O'Hanlon was up on
480   the altar with the veil that Father Conroy put round his shoulders giving the benediction with the
Blessed Sacrament in his hands.
    How moving the scene there in the gathering twilight, the last glimpse of Erin,[71] the touching
chime of those evening bells and at the same time a bat flew forth from the ivied belfry through the
dusk, hither, thither, with a tiny lost cry. And she could see far away the lights of the lighthouses so
485   picturesque she would have loved to do with a box of paints because it was easier than to make a
man and soon the lamplighter would be going his rounds past the presbyterian church grounds and

---

[69]   *Panem de coelo praestitisti eis* Latin for "You have given them
bread from heaven." The priest (or celebrant) says this immediately after the choir has finished singing the "Tantum ergo."
[70]   *kinnatt* Anglo-Irish slang for an impertinent, impudent
little puppy.

[71]   *the last glimpse of Erin* the title and part of the first line of a
song by Thomas Moore (1779–1852): "Tho' the last glimpse of
Erin with sorrow I see, / Yet, wherever thou art shall seem Erin to
me. / In exile thy bosom shall still be my home, / And thine eyes
make my climate, wherever we roam."

along by shady Tritonville avenue[72] where the couples walked and lighting the lamp near her
window where Reggy Wylie used to turn his freewheel[73] like she read in that book *The Lamplighter*
by Miss Cummins, author of *Mabel Vaughan* and other tales.[74] For Gerty had her dreams that no-one
knew of. She loved to read poetry and when she got a keepsake from Bertha Supple of that lovely   490
confession album with the coralpink cover to write her thoughts in she laid it in the drawer of her
toilettable which, though it did not err on the side of luxury, was scrupulously neat and clean. It
was there she kept her girlish treasure trove, the tortoiseshell combs, her child of Mary badge,[75] the
whiterose scent, the eyebrowleine, her alabaster pouncetbox and the ribbons to change when her
things came home from the wash and there were some beautiful thoughts written in it in violet ink   495
that she bought in Hely's of Dame Street[76] for she felt that she too could write poetry if she could
only express herself like that poem that appealed to her so deeply that she had copied out of the
newspaper she found one evening round the potherbs. *Art thou real, my ideal?* it was called by Louis
J. Walsh, Magherafelt,[77] and after there was something about *twilight, wilt thou ever?* and ofttimes
the beauty of poetry, so sad in its transient loveliness, had misted her eyes with silent tears that the   500
years were slipping by for her, one by one, and but for that one shortcoming she knew she need fear
no competition and that was an accident coming down Dalkey hill[78] and she always tried to conceal
it. But it must end she felt. If she saw that magic lure in his eyes there would be no holding back
for her. Love laughs at locksmiths.[79] She would make the great sacrifice. Her every effort would be
to share his thoughts. Dearer than the whole world would she be to him and gild his days with   505
happiness. There was the allimportant question and she was dying to know was he a married man or
a widower who had lost his wife or some tragedy like the nobleman with the foreign name from the
land of song had to have her put into a madhouse, cruel only to be kind.[80] But even if – what then?
Would it make a very great difference? From everything in the least indelicate her finebred nature
instinctively recoiled. She loathed that sort of person, the fallen women off the accommodation   510
walk beside the Dodder[81] that went with the soldiers and coarse men, with no respect for a girl's
honour, degrading the sex and being taken up to the police station. No, no: not that. They would
be just good friends like a big brother and sister without all that other in spite of the conventions of
Society with a big ess. Perhaps it was an old flame he was in mourning for from the days beyond
recall.[82] She thought she understood. She would try to understand him because men were so   515

[72] *Tritonville avenue* a short dead-end street just north of
Leahey's Terrace in Sandymount.

[73] A kind of bicycle which left the rear wheel disengaged
except when the driver was pedaling forward.

[74] *like she read in … and other tales* Maria Cummins (1827–66)
was the author of *the Lamplighter* (1854) and *Mabel Vaughan* (1857),
sentimental novels whose heroines are young girls. In *The Lamplighter*, Gerty Flint, who has been orphaned, is adopted by the
kindly lamplighter Trueman Flint; she changes from being sweet
but hot-tempered to practicing constant religious self-sacrifice,
and ultimately she marries her childhood sweetheart, Willie.

[75] *child of Mary badge* the Children of Mary were religious
confraternities established in schools of the Sisters of Charity.

[76] Wisdom Hely was a stationer and printer at 27–30 Dame
Street, Dublin. Bloom recalls the firm in "Hades," and in "Lestrygonians" remembers that he got a job as a salesman for them
the year that he and Molly were married (1888) and held it for
"six years."

[77] *Art thou real … Magherafelt* Louis J. Walsh (1880–1942),
who came from the small village of Magherafelt in northeastern
Ireland, was a student with Joyce at University College. The
poem is quoted by Joyce in *Stephen Hero* at greater length: "Art
thou real, my ideal? / Wilt thou ever come to me / In the soft and
gentle twilight / With your baby on your knee?"

[78] *Dalkey hill* located 8 miles southeast of Dublin on the coast,
it had a public promenade.

[79] *Love laughs at locksmiths* the title of a play (1803) by George
Colman (1762–1836), and thereafter proverbial.

[80] *cruel only to be kind* Hamlet tells his mother: "I must be cruel,
only to be kind: / Thus bad begins and worse remains behind"
(III.iv.178–9).

[81] *the accommodation walk beside the Dodder* an area where prostitutes solicited clients to an "accommodation house," or brothel;
the river Dodder approaches the Liffey from the south, flowing
north past Shantytown.

[82] *from the days beyond recall* a phrase from "Love's Old Sweet
Song" (1884), a popular parlor song that is strongly associated
with Bloom and his feelings for Molly throughout *Ulysses*. It is
also one of the songs that she is going to sing in her upcoming
concert with Blazes Boylan in Belfast. The lyrics were by G.
Clifton Bingham (1859–1913), to music by Irish composer J.
Lyman Molloy (1837–1909). "Once in the dear, dead days beyond
recall, / When on the world the mists began to fall, / Out of the
dreams that rose in happy throng, / Low to our hearts, Love sang
an old sweet song; / And in the dusk where fell the firelight gleam,
/ Softly it wove itself into our dream. [Chorus:] Just a song at
twilight, / When the lights are low / And the flick'ring shadows /
Softly come and go; / Though the heart be weary, / Sad the day and
long, / Still to us at twilight, / Come's love's sweet song, / Comes
love's old sweet song. [Second stanza:] Even today we hear Love's
song of yore, / Deep in our hearts it dwells forevermore; / Footsteps may falter, weary grow the way, / Still we can hear it, at the
close of day; So till the end, when life's dim shadow fall, / Love will
be found the sweetest song of all."

different. The old love was waiting, waiting with little white hands stretched out, with blue appealing eyes. Heart of mine! She would follow, her dream of love, the dictates of her heart that told her he was her all in all, the only man in all the world for her for love was the master guide. Nothing else mattered. Come what might she would be wild, untrammelled, free.

520   Canon O'Hanlon put the Blessed Sacrament back into the tabernacle and the choir sang *Laudate Dominum omnes gentes*[83] and then he locked the tabernacle door because the benediction was over and Father Conroy handed him his hat to put on and crosscat Edy asked wasn't she coming but Jacky Caffrey called out:

— O, look, Cissy!

525   And they all looked was it sheet lightning but Tommy saw it too over the trees beside the church, blue and then green and purple.

— It's fireworks, Cissy Caffrey said.

And they all ran down the strand to see over the houses and the church, helterskelter, Edy with the pushcar with baby Boardman in it and Cissy holding Tommy and Jacky by the hand so they 530   wouldn't fall running.

— Come on, Gerty, Cissy called. It's the bazaar fireworks.[84]

But Gerty was adamant. She had no intention of being at their beck and call. If they could run like rossies she could sit so she said she could see from where she was. The eyes that were fastened upon her set her pulses tingling. She looked at him a moment, meeting his glance, and a light 535   broke in upon her. Whitehot passion was in that face, passion silent as the grave and it had made her his. At last they were left alone without the others to pry and pass remarks and she knew he could be trusted to the death, steadfast, a sterling man, a man of inflexible honour to his fingertips. His hands and face were working and a tremour went over her. She leaned back far to look up where the fireworks were and she caught her knee in her hands so as not to fall back looking up and 540   there was no-one to see only him and her when she revealed all her graceful beautifully shaped legs like that, supply soft and delicately rounded, and she seemed to hear the panting of his heart, his hoarse breathing, because she knew about the passion of men like that, hotblooded, because Bertha Supple told her once in dead secret and made her swear she'd never about the gentleman lodger that was staying with them out of the Congested Districts Board[85] that had pictures cut out of papers of 545   those skirtdancers and highkickers and she said he used to do something not very nice that you could imagine sometimes in the bed. But this was altogether different from a thing like that because there was all the difference because she could almost feel him draw her face to his and the first quick hot touch of his handsome lips. Besides there was absolution so long as you didn't do the other thing before being married and there ought to be women priests that would understand 550   without your telling out and Cissy Caffrey too sometimes had that dreamy kind of dreamy look in her eyes so that she too, my dear, and Winny Rippingham so mad about actors' photographs and besides it was on account of that other thing coming on the way it did.

And Jacky Caffrey shouted to look, there was another and she leaned back and the garters were blue to match on account of the transparent and they all saw it and shouted to look, look there it 555   was and she leaned back ever so far to see the fireworks and something queer was flying about through the air, a soft thing to and fro, dark. And she saw a long Roman candle going up over the trees up, up, and, in the tense hush, they were all breathless with excitement as it went higher and higher and she had to lean back more and more to look up after it, high, high, almost out of sight, and her face was suffused with a divine, an entrancing blush from straining back and he could see 560   her other things too, nainsook knickers, the fabric that caresses the skin, better than those other

[83] *Laudate Dominum omnes gentes* Latin for "Give praise to the Lord, O ye nations," the opening line of Psalm 117 (Vulgate 116), which is sung while the Blessed Sacrament is being placed in the tabernacle.
[84] *the bazaar fireworks* The Mirus bazaar was an annual event which raised funds for Mercer's Hospital. In fact it opened on May 31, 1904, but Joyce has moved it back some 2 weeks to June 16 for his own purposes. The bazaar took place on Ballsbridge, on the southeastern outskirts of Dublin, or about one mile south of where Gerty and Bloom are.
[85] *the Congested Districts Board* a governmental board established in 1891 with power to redistribute land in rural areas in the west of Ireland which were overpopulated and poor.

pettiwidth,[86] the green, four and eleven, on account of being white and she let him and she saw that he saw and then it went so high it went out of sight a moment and she was trembling in every limb from being bent so far back that he had a full view high up above her knee where no-one ever not even on the swing or wading and she wasn't ashamed and he wasn't either to look in that immodest way like that because he couldn't resist the sight of the wondrous revealment half offered like those   565
skirtdancers behaving so immodest before gentlemen looking and he kept on looking, looking. She would fain have cried to him chokingly, held out her snowy slender arms to him to come, to feel his lips laid on her white brow, the cry of a young girl's love, a little strangled cry, wrung from her, that cry that has rung through the ages. And then a rocket sprang and bang shot blind blank and O! then the Roman candle burst and it was like a sigh of O! and everyone cried O! O! in raptures and it   570
gushed out of it a stream of rain gold hair threads and they shed and ah! they were all greeny dewy stars falling with golden, O so lovely! O so soft, sweet, soft!

Then all melted away dewily in the grey air: all was silent. Ah! She glanced at him as she bent forward quickly, a pathetic little glance of piteous protest, of shy reproach under which he coloured like a girl. He was leaning back against the rock behind. Leopold Bloom (for it is he) stands silent,   575
with bowed head before those young guileless eyes. What a brute he had been! At it again? A fair unsullied soul had called to him and, wretch that he was, how had he answered? An utter cad he had been. He of all men! But there was an infinite store of mercy in those eyes, for him too a word of pardon even though he had erred and sinned and wandered. Should a girl tell? No, a thousand times no. That was their secret, only theirs, alone in the hiding twilight and there was none to know   580
or tell save the little bat that flew so softly through the evening to and fro and little bats don't tell.

Cissy Caffrey whistled, imitating the boys in the football field to show what a great person she was: and then she cried:

— Gerty! Gerty! We're going. Come on. We can see from farther up.

Gerty had an idea, one of love's little ruses. She slipped a hand into her kerchief pocket and took   585
out the wadding and waved in reply of course without letting him and then slipped it back. Wonder if he's too far to. She rose. Was it goodbye? No. She had to go but they would meet again, there, and she would dream of that till then, tomorrow, of her dream of yester eve. She drew herself up to her full height. Their souls met in a last lingering glance and the eyes that reached her heart, full of a strange shining, hung enraptured on her sweet flowerlike face. She half smiled at him   590
wanly, a sweet forgiving smile, a smile that verged on tears, and then they parted.

Slowly without looking back she went down the uneven strand to Cissy, to Edy, to Jacky and Tommy Caffrey, to little baby Boardman. It was darker now and there were stones and bits of wood on the strand and slippy seaweed. She walked with a certain quiet dignity characteristic of her but with care and very slowly because—because Gerty MacDowell was.   595

Tight boots? No. She's lame! O!

Mr Bloom watched her as she limped away. Poor girl! That's why she's left on the shelf and the others did a sprint. Thought something was wrong by the cut of her jib. Jilted beauty. A defect is ten times worse in a woman. But makes them polite. Glad I didn't know it when she was on show. Hot little devil all the same. I wouldn't mind. Curiosity like a nun or a negress or a girl with glasses.   600
That squinty one is delicate. Near her monthlies, I expect, makes them feel ticklish. I have such a bad headache today. Where did I put the letter? Yes, all right. All kinds of crazy longings. Licking pennies. Girl in Tranquilla convent[87] that nun told me liked to smell rock oil. Virgins go mad in the end I suppose. Sister? How many women in Dublin have it today? Martha, she. Something in the air. That's the moon. But then why don't all women menstruate at the same time with same   605
moon, I mean? Depends on the time they were born, I suppose. Or all start scratch then get out of step. Sometimes Molly and Milly together. Anyhow I got the best of that. Damned glad I didn't do it in the bath this morning over her silly I will punish you letter. Made up for that tramdriver this

---

[86] *pettiwidth* a commercial brand name.
[87] Carmel of the Nativity, Tranquilla, in Rathmines, a suburb south of Dublin, founded in 1833 by the Order of Our Lady of Mount Carmel (the Carmelites). When Bloom worked for Hely's, the stationery and printing firm, he found "collecting accounts of those convents" a tiresome task. He recalls this in "Lestrygonians" (episode 8), and especially remembers the "Tranquilla convent" and "a nice nun there, really sweet face."

morning. That gouger M'Coy stopping me to say nothing. And his wife engagement in the country
610 valise, voice like a pickaxe. Thankful for small mercies. Cheap too. Yours for the asking. Because
they want it themselves. Their natural craving. Shoals of them every evening poured out of offices.
Reserve better. Don't want it they throw it at you. Catch em alive, O. Pity they can't see
themselves. A dream of wellfilled hose. Where was that? Ah, yes. Mutoscope pictures in Capel
street:[88] for men only. Peeping Tom. Willy's hat and what the girls did with it. Do they snapshot
615 those girls or is it all a fake. *Lingerie* does it. Felt for the curves inside her *deshabille*.[89] Excites them
also when they're. I'm all clean come and dirty me. And they like dressing one another for the
sacrifice. Milly delighted with Molly's new blouse. At first. Put them all on to take them all off.
Molly. Why I bought her the violet garters. Us too: the tie he wore, his lovely socks and turnedup
trousers. He wore a pair of gaiters the night that first we met. His lovely shirt was shining beneath
620 his what? of jet.[90] Say a woman loses a charm with every pin she takes out. Pinned together. O Mairy
lost the pin of her.[91] Dressed up to the nines for somebody. Fashion part of their charm. Just changes
when you're on the track of the secret. Except the east: Mary, Martha:[92] now as then. No reasonable
offer refused. She wasn't in a hurry either. Always off to a fellow when they are. They never forget an
appointment. Out on spec probably.[93] They believe in chance because like themselves. And the
625 others inclined to give her an odd dig. Girl friends at school, arms round each other's necks or with
ten fingers locked, kissing and whispering secrets about nothing in the convent garden. Nuns with
whitewashed faces, cool coifs and their rosaries going up and down, vindictive too for what they
can't get. Barbed wire. Be sure now and write to me. And I'll write to you. Now won't you? Molly
and Josie Powell. Till Mr Right comes along, then meet once in a blue moon. *Tableau!* O, look who
630 it is for the love of God! How are you at all? What have you been doing with yourself? Kiss and
delighted to, kiss, to see you. Picking holes in each other's appearance. You're looking splendid.
Sister souls showing their teeth at one another. How many have you left? Wouldn't lend each other
a pinch of salt.

   Ah!

635 Devils they are when that's coming on them. Dark devilish appearance. Molly often told me feel
things a ton weight. Scratch the sole of my foot. O that way! O, that's exquisite! Feel it myself too.
Good to rest once in a way. Wonder if it's bad to go with them then. Safe in one way. Turns milk,
makes fiddlestrings snap. Something about withering plants I read in a garden. Besides they say if
the flower withers she wears she's a flirt. All are. Daresay she felt I. When you feel like that you
640 often meet what you feel. Liked me or what? Dress they look at. Always know a fellow courting:
collars and cuffs. Well cocks and lions do the same and stags. Same time might prefer a tie undone
or something. Trousers? Suppose I when I was? No. Gently does it. Dislike rough and tumble. Kiss
in the dark and never tell. Saw something in me. Wonder what. Sooner have me as I am than some
poet chap with bearsgrease plastery hair, lovelock over his dexter optic. To aid gentleman in literary.
645 Ought to attend to my appearance my age. Didn't let her see me in profile. Still, you never know.
Pretty girls and ugly men marrying. Beauty and the beast. Besides I can't be so if Molly. Took off

[88] A "mutoscope" was a device for animating still photographs, an early form of cinema.

[89] *Felt for the curves ... deshabille* in "Wandering Rocks" (episode 10 of *Ulysses*), Bloom purchases a mildly salacious novel called *Sweets of Sin* for Molly; he reads several passages from it to see if it will suit her, including this one.

[90] *He wore a pair ... of jet* Bloom is revising the lyrics to a popular song, "She Wore a Wreath of Rose the Night that First We Met," by Thomas Haynes Bayly and J. Philip Knight: "She wore a wreath of roses / The night that first we met, / Her lovely face was smiling / Beneath her curls of jet."

[91] *O Mairy lost the pin of her* the first line of an unidentified street rhyme that Bloom also recalls earlier in the day in "Lotus Eaters" (episode 5 in *Ulysses*); he remembers hearing it "bawled" by "two sluts that night in the Coombe," a seedy district in Dublin.

[92] Mary, of course is the name of the Virgin Mary, but also a short form of Marion, the name of Bloom's wife, who instead is known as Molly. Bloom, readers learn in "Lotus Eaters" (episode 5 of *Ulysses*), is having a clandestine affair by correspondence with a woman named "Martha Clifford." He suspects that this name is a pseudonym, and so repeatedly recalls the opera *Martha* by Heinrich von Flotow, which involves a woman who adopts the pseudonym Martha. On the opera see p. 230 n. 9. Finally, earlier in the day in "Aeolus," or episode 7 of *Ulysses* (see p. 230), Bloom has also recalled a painting which depicts Mary and Martha, sisters of Lazarus and friends of Jesus who, in an incident recounted in Luke 10:38–42, host a meal for him.

[93] On speculation, the chance of purchasing something valuable or profitable.

her hat to show her hair. Wide brim bought to hide her face, meeting someone might know her, bend down or carry a bunch of flowers to smell. Hair strong in rut. Ten bob I got for Molly's combings when we were on the rocks in Holles street. Why not? Suppose he gave her money. Why not? All a prejudice. She's worth ten, fifteen, more a pound. What? I think so. All that for nothing. 650 Bold hand. Mrs Marion.[94] Did I forget to write address on that letter like the postcard I sent to Flynn. And the day I went to Drimmie's[95] without a necktie. Wrangle with Molly it was put me off. No, I remember. Richie Goulding. He's another. Weighs on his mind. Funny my watch stopped at half past four.[96] Dust. Shark liver oil[97] they use to clean could do it myself. Save. Was that just when he, she? 655

O, he did. Into her. She did. Done.

Ah!

Mr Bloom with careful hand recomposed his wet shirt. O Lord, that little limping devil. Begins to feel cold and clammy. After effect not pleasant. Still you have to get rid of it someway. They don't care. Complimented perhaps. Go home to nicey bread and milky and say night 660 prayers with the kiddies. Well, aren't they. See her as she is spoil all. Must have the stage setting, the rouge, costume, position, music. The name too. *Amours* of actresses. Nell Gwynn, Mrs Bracegirdle, Maud Branscombe.[98] Curtain up. Moonlight silver effulgence. Maiden discovered with pensive bosom. Little sweetheart come and kiss me. Still I feel. The strength it gives a man. That's the secret of it. Good job I let off there behind coming out of Dignam's. Cider that was 665 Otherwise I couldn't have. Makes you want to sing after. *Lacaus esant taratara.*[99] Suppose I spoke to her. What about? Bad plan however if you don't know how to end the conversation. Ask them a question they ask you another. Good idea if you're in a cart.[100] Wonderful of course if you say: good evening, and you see she's on for it: good evening. O but the dark evening in the Appian way[101] I nearly spoke to Mrs Clinch[102] O thinking she was. Whew! Girl in Meath street[103] 670 that night. All the dirty things I made her say all wrong of course. My arks she called it. It's so hard to find one who. Aho! If you don't answer when they solicit must be horrible for them till they harden. And kissed my hand when I gave her the extra two shillings. Parrots. Press the button and the bird will squeak. Wish she hadn't called me sir. O, her mouth in the dark! And you a married man with a single girl! That's what they enjoy. Taking a man from another woman. Or 675 even hear of it. Different with me. Glad to get away from other chap's wife. Eating off his cold plate. Chap in the Burton today spitting back gumchewed gristle.[104] French letter[105] still in my pocketbook. Cause of half the trouble. But might happen sometime, I don't think. Come in. All is prepared. I dreamt. What? Worst is beginning. How they change the venue when it's not what they like. Ask you do you like mushrooms because she once knew a gentleman who. Or ask you 680 what someone was going to say when he changed his mind and stopped. Yet if I went the whole

[94] *Bold hand. Mrs Marion* Bloom is recalling the style of handwriting used by Blazes Boylan on the envelope of a letter addressed to his wife Molly, a letter that has arrived in the morning post; Blazes is a popular singer who will be singing in a concert with Molly in Belfast, and his letter is making an appointment for a rehearsal that is, as Bloom suspects, a pretext for a sexual tryst. His hand is also "bold" because he has addressed the letter to "Mrs Marion Bloom," rather than "Mrs Leopold Bloom."

[95] David Drimmie and Sons, English and Scottish Law Life and Phoenix Fire offices, located on Sackville Street Lower; evidently a firm where Bloom was once employed.

[96] *Funny my watch stopped at half past four* the time when Blazes Boylan is supposed to visit Molly to rehearse for their upcoming concert.

[97] *Shark liver oil* used to lubricate delicate machinery (Molly) in this period before the development of fine petroleum oils and synthetic lubricants.

[98] Nell Gwynn (1650–87) was an actress and much-celebrated mistress of King Charless II. Anne Bracegirdle (1674–1748) was an actress who was suspected of being secretly married to or the

mistress of the dramatist Congreve. Maud Branscombe (1875–1910) was an actress renowned for her beauty and much depicted in postcards and engravings.

[99] *Lacaus esant taratara* Bloom's rendering of a passage from the Italian version of an opera by the German composer Giacomo Meyerbeer (1791–1864). The opera, *Les Huguenots* (1836), was originally composed in French, but performances in Italian were common in the late nineteenth century, and Bloom recalls the Italian (*la caura è santa*) for "the cause is sacred."

[100] *in a cart* slang expression for in a quandary.

[101] A street in Ranelagh on the southern edge of Dublin.

[102] A Mrs. Clinch resided in Sunnott Place, a street near Bloom's fictional home in Eccles Street.

[103] A street in the slums of south-central Dublin.

[104] *Chap in the Burton … gumchewed gristle* in "Lestrygonians" (episode 8 in *Ulysses*), Bloom enters the Burton, a restaurant at 18 Duke Street, and observes several people eating their food in a crude fashion. He then decides to eat at another restaurant.

[105] *French letter* slang for a condom.

hog, say: I want to, something like that. Because I did. She too. Offend her. Then make it up. Pretend to want something awfully, then cry off for her sake. Flatters them. She must have been thinking of someone else all the time. What harm? Must since she came to the use of reason, he, he
685 and he. First kiss does the trick. The propitious moment. Something inside them goes pop. Mushy like, tell by their eye, on the sly. First thoughts are best. Remember that till their dying day. Molly, lieutenant Mulvey that kissed her under the Moorish wall beside the gardens. Fifteen she told me. But her breasts were developed. Fell asleep then. After Glencree dinner that was when we drove home the featherbed mountain.[106] Gnashing her teeth in sleep. Lord mayor had his eye on her too.
690 Val Dillon.[107] Apoplectic.

There she is with them down there for the fireworks. My fireworks. Up like a rocket, down like a stick. And the children, twins they must be, waiting for something to happen. Want to be grownups. Dressing in mother's clothes. Time enough, understand all the ways of the world. And the dark one with the mop head and the nigger mouth. I knew she could whistle.
695 Mouth made for that. Like Molly. Why that high class whore in Jammet's[108] wore her veil only to her nose. Would you mind, please, telling me the right time? I'll tell you the right time up a dark lane. Say prunes and prisms[109] forty times every morning, cure for fat lips. Caressing the little boy too. Onlookers see most of the game. Of course they understand birds, animals, babies. In their line.
700 Didn't look back when she was going down the strand. Wouldn't give that satisfaction. Those girls, those girls, those lovely seaside girls.[110] Fine eyes she had, clear. It's the white of the eye brings that out not so much the pupil. Did she know what I? Course. Like a cat sitting beyond a dog's jump. Women never meet one like that Wilkins in the high school drawing a picture of Venus with all his belongings on show. Call that innocence? Poor idiot! His wife has her
705 work cut out for her. Never see them sit on a bench marked *Wet Paint*. Eyes all over them. Look under the bed for what's not there. Longing to get the fright of their lives. Sharp as needles they are. When I said to Molly the man at the corner of Cuffe street was goodlooking, thought she might like, twigged at once he had a false arm. Had too. Where do they get that? Typist going up Roger Greene's stairs[111] two at a time to show her understandings. Handed down from father
710 to mother to daughter, I mean. Bred in the bone. Milly for example drying her handkerchief on the mirror to save the ironing. Best place for an ad to catch a woman's eye on a mirror. And when I sent her for Molly's Paisley shawl to Presscott's,[112] by the way that ad I must, carrying home the change in her stocking. Clever little minx! I never told her. Neat way she carries parcels too. Attract men, small thing like that. Holding up her hand, shaking it, to let the blood flow
715 back when it was red. Who did you learn that from? Nobody. Something the nurse taught me. O, don't they know? Three years old she was in front of Molly's dressingtable just before we left Lombard street west. Me have a nice pace. Mullingar. Who knows? Ways of the world. Young student. Straight on her pins anyway not like the other. Still she was game. Lord, I am wet. Devil you are. Swell of her calf. Transparent stockings, stretched to breaking point. Not like

---

[106] *Glencree dinner ... Featherbed mountain* the "Glencree reformatory" (as another character calls it elsewhere in *Ulysses*) was St. Kevin's, a Roman Catholic reformatory near the Glencree River 10 miles south of Dublin, and it sponsored an annual dinner as a fundraising event. Featherbed Pass runs through the Wicklow Mountains between Dublin and Glencree. A different account of this journey home after the annual dinner is given by the fictional character Ned Lenehan in the "Wandering Rocks" episode. In his version he flirts with Molly and she, inebriated, acquiesces.

[107] Valentine Dillon was lord mayor of Dublin in 1894–5.

[108] Jammet Brothers, proprietors of the Burlington Hotel and Restaurant, 26–7 St. Andrew's Street, in south-central Dublin.

[109] *Say prunes and prisms* from Charles Dickens's *Little Dorrit* (1857), Book II, ch. 4, where Mrs. General advises Amy to repeat this phrase when entering a room in order to mold her demeanor.

[110] *Those girls ... seaside girls* the first line of the chorus to a song written and composed by Harry B. Norris (1899), "Those Seaside Girls" (1899), one which is indelibly linked with Blazes Boylan in Bloom's mind. The chorus goes:

> Those girls, those girls, those lovely seaside girls
> All dimples smiles and curls, your head it simply whirls,
> They look all right, complexions pink and white,
> They've diamond rings and dainty feet,
> Golden hair from Regent Street
> Lace and grace and lots of face, those pretty little seaside girls.

[111] A solicitor whose office was at 11 Wellington Quay, in central Dublin.

[112] William T. C. Prescott, dyeing, cleaning, and carpet-shaking establishment at 8 Abbey Street Lower, with several branches in Dublin.

that frump today. A. E. Rumpled stockings.[113] Or the one in Grafton street.[114] White. Wow! Beef   720
to the heel.[115]

A monkey puzzle rocket burst, spluttering in darting crackles. Zrads and zrads, zrads, zrads. And
Cissy and Tommy ran out to see and Edy after with the pushcar and then Gerty beyond the curve of the
rocks. Will she? Watch! Watch! See! Looked round. She smelt an onion.[116] Darling, I saw your. I saw all.
Lord!   725

Did me good all the same. Off colour after Kiernan's, Dignam's. For this relief much thanks.[117] In
Hamlet, that is. Lord! It was all things combined. Excitement. When she leaned back felt an ache at
the butt of my tongue. Your head it simply swirls.[118] He's right. Might have made a worse fool of
myself however. Instead of talking about nothing. Then I will tell you all. Still it was a kind of
language between us. It couldn't be? No, Gerty they called her. Might be false name however like   730
my and the address Dolphin's barn a blind.

> Her maiden name was Jemima Brown
> And she lived with her mother in Irishtown.[119]

Place made me think of that I suppose. All tarred with the same brush. Wiping pens in their
stockings. But the ball rolled down to her as if it understood. Every bullet has its billet.[120] Course I   735
never could throw anything straight at school. Crooked as a ram's horn. Sad however because it lasts
only a few years till they settle down to potwalloping and papa's pants will soon fit Willy[121] and
fullers' earth[122] for the baby when they hold him out to do ah ah. No soft job. Saves them. Keeps
them out of harm's way. Nature. Washing child, washing corpse. Dignam. Children's hands always
round them. Cocoanut skulls, monkeys, not even closed at first, sour milk in their swaddles and   740
tainted curds. Oughtn't to have given that child an empty teat to suck. Fill it up with wind.
Mrs Beaufoy, Purefoy.[123] Must call to the hospital. Wonder is nurse Callan there still. She used to
look over some nights when Molly was in the Coffee Palace. That young doctor O'Hare I noticed

[113] *that frump today. A. E.* in "Lestrygonians" (episode 8) Bloom notices the Irish poet George William Russell (1867–1935), better known by his pen name "A.E.," talking with an unidentified woman. He disapprovingly notes that "her stockings are loose over her ankles" and that she doesn't worry much about her appearance.

[114] *the one in Grafton Street* while walking along Grafton Street in the "Lestrygonians" episode, Bloom briefly notes a woman: "Thick feet that woman has in the white stockings."

[115] *beef to the heel* when a woman had thick legs, it was common in Ireland to say that she was "like a Mullingar heifer, beef to the heels," because the plains around Mullingar were noted for fattening cattle. When Milly, Bloom's daughter, describes for him the country people who have come into Mullingar for a fair day, she writes that "all the beef to the heels were in" (in "Calypso," episode 4 of *Ulysses*).

[116] *She smelt an onion* a joke current in Ireland during this period told of a man who, determined to avoid entangling himself with a woman, would eat a raw onion whenever he was about to meet one. His scheme falls apart when he meets a woman who finds his breath deeply attractive.

[117] *For this relief much thanks* in *Hamlet* Francisco, one of the guards, says this to thank Bernardo, another guard, for relieving him at his post.

[118] *Your head it simply swirls* another line from the chorus to "Those Seaside Girls"; see above, note 111.

[119] *Her maiden name ... in Irishtown* this song has not been identified.

[120] *Every bullet has its billet* or "nothing occurs by chance," a saying attributed to King William III of England (1650–1702; king 1689–1702).

[121] *and papa's pants will soon fit Willy* a line from an American nonsense song, "Looking Through the Knothole." It begins: "We were looking through the knothole in father's wooden leg, / Oh who will go wind the clock while we are gone? / Go get the axe, there's a fly on baby's head / And papa's pants will soon be fitting Willie."

[122] *fuller's earth* a clay-like material used to full or cleanse cloth and wool of grease.

[123] *Mrs. Beaufoy, Purefoy* in "Calypso" (episode 4 in *Ulysses*), Bloom reads a story titled "Matcham's Masterstroke" by Philip Beaufoy (both title and author are Joyce's inventions). Later, in "Lestrygonians" (episode 8), he meets an old friend and former neighbor, Mrs. Breen, and to keep up conversation he decides to enquire about another former neighbour, Mrs. Mina Purefoy. However, with the short story still in his mind, he slips up:

Change the subject.
— Do you ever see anything of Mrs. Beaufoy?
Mr Bloom asked.
— Mina Purefoy? she said.
Philip Beaufoy I was thinking.

Bloom then learns that Mrs. Purefoy is in the maternity hospital and has been three days giving birth to a child. Later, in "Oxen of the Sun" (episode 14), he will visit her. Here, he is simply repeating his earlier confusion of Beaufoy and Purefoy. All the characters in the lines that follow are Joyce's inventions.

her brushing his coat. And Mrs Breen and Mrs Dignam once like that too, marriageable. Worst of
all at night Mrs Duggan told me in the City Arms. Husband rolling in drunk, stink of pub off him
like a polecat. Have that in your nose in the dark, whiff of stale boose. Then ask in the morning:
was I drunk last night? Bad policy however to fault the husband. Chickens come home to roost.
They stick by one another like glue. Maybe the women's fault also. That's where Molly can knock
spots off them. It is the blood of the south. Moorish. Also the form, the figure. Hands felt for the
opulent.[124] Just compare for instance those others. Wife locked up at home, skeleton in the
cupboard. Allow me to introduce my. Then they trot you out some kind of a nondescript, wouldn't
know what to call her. Always see a fellow's weak point in his wife. Still there's destiny in it, falling
in love. Have their own secrets between them. Chaps that would go to the dogs if some woman
didn't take them in hand. Then little chits of girls, height of a shilling in coppers,[125] with little
hubbies. As God made them He matched them. Sometimes children turn out well enough. Twice
nought makes one. Or old rich chap of seventy and blushing bride. Marry in May and repent in
December. This wet is very unpleasant. Stuck. Well the foreskin is not back. Better detach.

Ow!

Other hand a sixfooter with a wifey up to his watchpocket. Long and the short of it. Big he and
little she. Very strange about my watch. Wristwatches are always going wrong. Wonder is there any
magnetic influence between the person because that was about the time he. Yes, I suppose at once.
Cat's away the mice will play. I remember looking in Pill lane. Also that now is magnetism. Back of
everything magnetism. Earth for instance pulling this and being pulled. That causes movement.
And time? Well that's the time the movement takes. Then if one thing stopped the whole
ghesabo[126] would stop bit by bit. Because it's all arranged. Magnetic needle tells you what's
going on in the sun, the stars. Little piece of steel iron. When you hold out the fork. Come.
Come. Tip. Woman and man that is. Fork and steel. Molly, he. Dress up and look and suggest and
let you see and see more and defy you if you're a man to see that and, like a sneeze coming, legs,
look, look and if you have any guts in you. Tip. Have to let fly.

Wonder how is she feeling in that region. Shame all put on before third person. More put out
about a hole in her stocking. Molly, her underjaw stuck out, head back, about the farmer in the
ridingboots and spurs at the horse show. And when the painters were in Lombard street west. Fine
voice that fellow had. How Giuglini began.[127] Smell that I did, like flowers. It was too. Violets.
Came from the turpentine probably in the paint. Make their own use of everything. Same time
doing it scraped her slipper on the floor so they wouldn't hear. But lots of them can't kick the beam,
I think. Keep that thing up for hours. Kind of a general all round over me and half down my back.

Wait. Hm. Hm. Yes. That's her perfume. Why she waved her hand. I leave you this to think of
me when I'm far away on the pillow. What is it? Heliotrope? No. Hyacinth? Hm. Roses, I think.
She'd like scent of that kind. Sweet and cheap: soon sour. Why Molly likes opoponax.[128] Suits her
with a little jessamine mixed. Her high notes and her low notes. At the dance night she met him,
dance of the hours.[129] Heat brought it out. She was wearing her black and it had the perfume of the
time before. Good conductor, is it? Or bad? Light too. Suppose there's some connection. For
instance if you go into a cellar where it's dark. Mysterious thing too. Why did I smell it only now?
Took its time in coming like herself, slow but sure. Suppose it's ever so many millions of tiny grains
blown across. Yes, it is. Because those spice islands, Cinghalese[130] this morning, smell them leagues

---

[124]   *Hands felt for the opulent* in "Wandering Rocks" (episode 10
of *Ulysses*), Bloom purchases a mildly salacious novel called *Sweets
of Sin* for Molly; he reads several passages from it to see if it will
suit her, including this one, " . . . *his hands felt for the opulent curves
inside her deshabille.*"

[125]   *height of a shilling in coppers* a copper was a one-pence coin,
and twelve of them made a shilling: a short person.

[126]   *ghesabo* a variant of gazebo, part of Bloom's slang expression
for "the whole show."

[127]   Antonio Giuglini (1827–65), an Italian tenor, came from a
poor family and enjoyed much success in Dublin after 1857.
Anecdotes about him were current in Joyce's father's generation.

[128]   Or opoponax, the juice of the herb *Panax*.

[129]   *dance of the hours* Amilcare Ponchielli (1834–86) composed
an opera called *La gioconda* which includes an elaborate ballet,
"The Dance of the Hours," in which the passing of the hours
from dawn till dark is represented. Bloom intermittently recalls
it throughout the day.

[130]   Singhalese are one of the ethnic groups in Sri Lanka (formerly Ceylon); Bloom fantasizes about them "lobbing about in
the sun . . . not doing a hand's turn all day" (ellipsis mine) in
"Lotus Eaters" (episode 5) when he purchases some perfumed
soap for Molly in the morning.

off. Tell you what it is. It's like a fine fine veil or web they have all over the skin, fine like what do you call it gossamer and they're always spinning it out of them, fine as anything, rainbow colours without knowing it. Clings to everything she takes off. Vamp of her stockings. Warm shoe. Stays. Drawers: little kick, taking them off. Byby till next time. Also the cat likes to sniff in her shift on the bed. Know her smell in a thousand. Bathwater too. Reminds me of strawberries and cream. Wonder where it is really. There or the armpits or under the neck. Because you get it out of all holes and corners. Hyacinth perfume made of oil of ether or something. Muskrat.[131] Bag under their tails one grain pour off odour for years. Dogs at each other behind. Good evening. Evening. How do you sniff? Hm. Hm. Very well, thank you. Animals go by that. Yes now, look at it that way. We're the same. Some women for instance warn you off when they have their period. Come near. Then get a hogo[132] you could hang your hat on. Like what? Potted herrings gone stale or. Boof! Please keep off the grass.

Perhaps they get a man smell off us. What though? Cigary gloves Long John had on his desk the other. Breath? What you eat and drink gives that. No. Mansmell, I mean. Must be connected with that because priests that are supposed to be are different. Women buzz round it like flies round treacle. Railed off the altar get on to it at any cost. The tree of forbidden priest. O father, will you? Let me be the first to. That diffuses itself all through the body, permeates. Source of life and it's extremely curious the smell. Celery sauce. Let me.

Mr Bloom inserted his nose. Hm. Into the. Hm. Opening of his waistcoat. Almonds or. No. Lemons it is. Ah no, that's the soap.

O by the by that lotion. I knew there was something on my mind. Never went back and the soap not paid. Dislike carrying bottles like that hag this morning. Hynes might have paid me that three shillings. I could mention Meagher's[133] just to remind him. Still if he works that paragraph. Two and nine. Bad opinion of me he'll have. Call tomorrow. How much do I owe you? Three and nine? Two and nine, sir. Ah. Might stop him giving credit another time. Lose your customers that way. Pubs do. Fellows run up a bill on the slate and then slinking around the back streets into somewhere else.

Here's this nobleman passed before. Blown in from the bay. Just went as far as turn back. Always at home at dinnertime. Looks mangled out: had a good tuck in. Enjoying nature now. Grace after meals. After supper walk a mile. Sure he has a small bank balance somewhere, government sit.[134] Walk after him now make him awkward like those newsboys me today. Still you learn something. See ourselves as others see us. So long as women don't mock what matter? That's the way to find out. Ask yourself who is he now. *The Mystery Man on the Beach*, prize titbit story[135] by Mr Leopold Bloom. Payment at the rate of one guinea per column. And that fellow today at the graveside in the brown macintosh. Corns on his kismet however.[136] Healthy perhaps absorb all the. Whistle brings rain they say. Must be some somewhere. Salt in the Ormond damp. The body feels the atmosphere. Old Betty's joints are on the rack.[137] Mother Shipton's prophecy that is about ships around they fly in the twinkling.[138] No. Signs of rain it is. The royal reader.[139] And distant hills seem coming nigh.

790

795

800

805

810

815

820

---

[131] *Hyacinth perfume ... Muskrat* compound ethers or esters were used in artificial perfumes in the late nineteenth century; muskrat scent was used as a substitute for the musk of the musk deer in manufacturing perfumes, though a synthetic musk was developed in 1888.

[132] *hogo* Slang term for a flavor or taint (after the French, *haut goût*).

[133] A public house which Bloom also recalls in "Aeolus" (see p. 232 l. 87), because it is where he lent Joe Hynes the three shillings Hynes still owes to Bloom.

[134] A government situation or employment, an easy job.

[135] *prize titbit story Tit-bits* was a popular weekly newspaper launched by George Newnes in 1881 and filled with snippets of information and short fiction. It proved very successful and was considered the starting point in what contemporaries called

"the New Journalism," publications which had short features and a snappy tone to address much wider audiences.

[136] *Corns on his kismet* kismet is fate, a word pronounced in stage or rural Irish as *feet*.

[137] *Old Betty's joints are on the rack* evidently part of an unidentified jingle that predicts the weather.

[138] *Old Mother Shipton's prophecy ... twinkling* Mother Shipton was a fabled English prophetess who supposedly predicted various events in the reign of Henry VIII. Her "prophecies" were first published in 1641 and many times thereafter. An 1862 hoax version included a prophecy of the telegraph ("Around the worlds thoughts shall fly / In the twinkling of an eye") which Bloom recalls.

[139] *The royal reader* English textbooks in six volumes, the Royal Readers formed part of the Irish school curriculum.

825   Howth. Bailey light. Two, four, six, eight, nine. See. Has to change or they might think it
a house. Wreckers. Grace darling.[140] People afraid of the dark. Also glowworms, cyclists: lightingup
time. Jewels diamonds flash better. Light is a kind of reassuring. Not going to hurt you. Better now
of course than long ago. Country roads. Run you through the small guts for nothing. Still two types
there are you bob against. Scowl or smile. Pardon! Not at all. Best time to spray plants too in the
830   shade after the sun. Some light still. Red rays are longest. Roygbiv Vance[141] taught us: red, orange,
yellow, green, blue, indigo, violet. A star I see. Venus? Can't tell yet. Two, when three it's night.
Were those nightclouds there all the time? Looks like a phantom ship. No. Wait. Trees are they?
An optical illusion. Mirage. Land of the setting sun this. Homerule sun setting in the southeast.[142]
My native land, goodnight.[143]

835   Dew falling. Bad for you, dear, to sit on that stone. Brings on white fluxions.[144] Never have little
baby then less he was big strong fight his way up through. Might get piles myself. Sticks too like a
summer cold, sore on the mouth. Cut with grass or paper worst. Friction of the position. Like to be
that rock she sat on. O sweet little, you don't know how nice you looked. I begin to like them at
that age. Green apples. Grab at all that offer. Suppose it's the only time we cross legs, seated. Also
840   the library today: those girl graduates. Happy chairs under them. But it's the evening influence.
They feel all that. Open like flowers, know their hours, sunflowers, Jerusalem artichokes,[145] in
ballrooms, chandeliers, avenues under the lamps. Nightstock in Mat Dillon's garden[146] where I
kissed her shoulder. Wish I had a full length oilpainting of her then. June that was too I wooed. The
year returns. History repeats itself. Ye crags and peaks I'm with you once again.[147] Life, love, voyage
845   round your own little world. And now? Sad about her lame of course but must be on your guard not
to feel too much pity. They take advantage.

     All quiet on Howth now. The distant hills seem. Where we. The rhododendrons. I am a fool
perhaps. He gets the plums and I the plumstones.[148] Where I come in. All that old hill has seen.
Names change: that's all. Lovers: yum yum.

850   Tired I feel now. Will I get up? O wait. Drained all the manhood out of me, little wretch. She
kissed me. My youth. Never again. Only once it comes. Or hers. Take the train there tomorrow. No.
Returning not the same. Like kids your second visit to a house. The new I want. Nothing new
under the sun.[149] Care of P. O. Dolphin's barn. Are you not happy in your? Naughty darling. At
Dolphin's barn charades in Luke Doyle's house. Mat Dillon and his bevy of daughters: Tiny, Atty,
855   Floey, Maimy, Louy, Hetty. Molly too. Eightyseven that was. Year before we. And the old major
partial to his drop of spirits. Curious she an only child, I an only child. So it returns. Think you're
escaping and run into yourself. Longest way round is the shortest way home. And just when he and
she. Circus horse walking in a ring. Rip van Winkle[150] we played. Rip: tear in Henny Doyle's

[140]   Grace Darling (1815–42) was the daughter of a lighthouse
keeper; together with her father she helped save 9 passengers
from a shipwrecked steamer (54 others perished). Wordsworth
commemorated her with a poem "Grace Darling" (1843).
[141]   A science teacher at high school, whom Bloom has remembered earlier in the day. His nickname (Roygbiv) is a mnemonic
device to recall the colours of the spectrum by their first letters:
red, orange, yellow, green, blue, indigo, violet.
[142]   *Home rule sun setting in the southeast* earlier in the day, in
"Calypso" (the fourth episode in *Ulysses*), Bloom recalls a clever
remark ostensibly made by Arthur Griffith (1872–1922), a pro-
independence Irish patriot. Griffith had dismissed the headpiece
of the *Freeman's Journal*, a daily newspaper that was nominally for
Home Rule but essentially moderate, as depicting "a home rule
sun rising up in the northwest" – an obvious impossibility.
Bloom now inverts Griffith's comment.
[143]   *My native land, goodnight* from a lyric interpolated in Canto
I, after stanza 13, in Byron's *Childe Harold's Pilgrimage* (1812);
the first and last stanzas end with "My native Land – Good
Night!"
[144]   Vaginal discharges which, popular superstition said, could
be brought on by sitting on a cold stone.

[145]   A white-fleshed root related to the sunflower.
[146]   *Mat Dillon's garden* in "Hades" (the sixth episode of *Ulysses*),
John Henry Menton tells Ned Lambert about his memory of
Molly Bloom: "She was a finelooking woman. I danced with her,
wait, fifteen seventeen golden years at Mat Dillon's in Roundtown." Mat Dillon's is the fictional name of a restaurant which
also featured dancing.
[147]   *Ye crags and peaks … again* from a monologue spoken by
William Tell in the tragedy *William Tell* (1825), I.ii.1, by Irish
dramatist James Sheridan Knowles (1784–1862).
[148]   *the plumstones* compare the story of the vestal virgins recounted by Stephen Dedalus in "Aeolus," pp. 251–5.
[149]   *Nothing new under the sun* "The thing that hath been, it is
that which shall be; and that which is done is that which shall be
done; and there is no new thing under the sun" (Ecclesiastes 1:9).
[150]   In the story "Rip Van Winkle" by American author Washington Irving (1783–1859), which first appeared in *The Sketch
Book* (1819–20), the hero falls asleep for 20 years and awakens to
find everything changed, including his gun, which has become
rusty.

overcoat. Van: breadvan delivering. Winkle: cockles and periwinkles. Then I did Rip van Winkle
coming back. She leaned on the sideboard watching. Moorish eyes. Twenty years asleep in Sleepy   860
Hollow.[151] All changed. Forgotten. The young are old. His gun rusty from the dew.

Ba. What is that flying about? Swallow? Bat probably. Thinks I'm a tree, so blind. Have birds no
smell? Metempsychosis. They believed you could be changed into a tree from grief.[152] Weeping
willow. Ba. There he goes. Funny little beggar. Wonder where he lives. Belfry up there. Very likely.
Hanging by his heels in the odour of sanctity. Bell scared him out, I suppose. Mass seems to be over.   865
Could hear them all at it. Pray for us. And pray for us. And pray for us. Good idea the repetition.
Same thing with ads. Buy from us. And buy from us. Yes, there's the light in the priest's house.
Their frugal meal. Remember about the mistake in the valuation when I was in Thom's.
Twentyeight it is.[153] Two houses they have. Gabriel Conroy's brother is curate.[154] Ba. Again.
Wonder why they come out at night like mice. They're a mixed breed. Birds are like hopping   870
mice. What frightens them, light or noise? Better sit still. All instinct like the bird in drouth got
water out of the end of a jar by throwing in pebbles. Like a little man in a cloak he is with tiny
hands. Weeny bones. Almost see them shimmering, kind of a bluey white. Colours depend on the
light you see. Stare the sun for example like the eagle then look at a shoe see a blotch blob
yellowish. Wants to stamp his trademark on everything. Instance, that cat this morning on the   875
staircase. Colour of brown turf. Say you never see them with three colours. Not true. That half
tabbywhite tortoiseshell in the *City Arms* with the letter em on her forehead. Body fifty different
colours. Howth a while ago amethyst. Glass flashing. That's how that wise man what's his name
with the burning glass.[155] Then the heather goes on fire. It can't be tourists' matches. What?
Perhaps the sticks dry rub together in the wind and light. Or broken bottles in the furze act as a   880
burning glass in the sun. Archimedes. I have it! My memory's not so bad.

Ba. Who knows what they're always flying for. Insects? That bee last week got into the room
playing with his shadow on the ceiling. Might be the one bit me, come back to see. Birds too never
find out what they say. Like our small talk. And says she and says he. Nerve they have to fly over the
ocean and back. Lots must be killed in storms, telegraph wires. Dreadful life sailors have too. Big   885
brutes of oceangoing steamers floundering along in the dark, lowing out like seacows. *Faugh a
ballagh.*[156] Out of that, bloody curse to you. Others in vessels, bit of a handkerchief sail, pitched
about like snuff at a wake when the stormy winds do blow. Married too. Sometimes away for years
at the ends of the earth somewhere. No ends really because it's round. Wife in every port they say.
She has a good job if she minds it till Johnny comes marching home again.[157] If ever he does.   890
Smelling the tail end of ports. How can they like the sea? Yet they do. The anchor's weighed.[158] Off
he sails with a scapular or a medal on him for luck. Well? And the tephilim no what's this they call
it poor papa's father had on his door to touch.[159] That brought us out of the land of Egypt and into

[151]   "The Legend of Sleepy Hollow," another story that first
appeared in Washington Irving's *Sketch Book*, concerns Ichabod
Crane, not Rip Van Winkle.

[152]   *Metempsychosis . . . a tree from grief* Bloom recalls the story of
Daphne, who is changed into a laurel tree while fleeing from
Apollo (Ovid, *Metamorphoses* I), but confuses her metamorphosis
with the idea of metempsychosis (the transmigration of souls), a
confusion abetted by Ovid's conclusion (Book XV), which argues
for the notion of metempsychosis. The subject is on Bloom's
mind because early in the morning, in "Calypso" (the fourth
episode in *Ulysses*), Molly has asked Bloom about the meaning of
the word "metempsychosis."

[153]   *Remember . . . in Thom's. Twentyeight it is.* two houses, nos. 3 and
5, were attached to Mary Star of the Sea Church, each appraised at an
annual rent of £28 in Thom's annual directory of Dublin. Bloom, in
"Aeolus" (see pp. 235, 235 n. 40), recalls that he once worked for the
publishing firm of Alexander Thom and Co., which printed it, and
evidently he made a mistake in valuing these houses.

[154]   *Gabriel Conroy's brother is curate* a Reverend Bernard Conroy
was listed as one of two curates-in-charge of Mary Star of the Sea

Church. Joyce has seized on his name and made him a brother of
Gabriel Conroy, a fictional character in "The Dead," the final
story in Joyce's *Dubliners* (1914).

[155]   *that wise man . . . with the burning glass* according to an
apocryphal story, Archimedes set the Roman fleet on fire with
mirrors that focused the sun's rays.

[156]   Gaelic for "Clear the way."

[157]   *till Johnny comes marching home again* from the title of the
popular song "When Johnny Comes Marching Home Again," by
Patrick Sarsfield Gilmore (1829–92), a Union army marching
song in the American Civil War.

[158]   *The anchor's weighed* the title of a popular song with words
by Samuel James Arnold (fl. 1800–8) and music by John Braham
(1774–1865).

[159]   *Off he sails . . . door to touch* Bloom is comparing the
Catholic tradition in which sailors wore a sacred medal or cloth
badges to symbolize a saint's protective presence and Jewish
tradition in which a *mezuzah* ("what's this they call it") or a
piece of parchment with Deuteronomy 6:4–9 and 11:13–21) is
rolled up and placed in a small case on the right-hand doorpost of

the house of bondage.[160] Something in all those superstitions because when you go out never know
895 what dangers. Hanging on to a plank or astride of a beam for grim life, lifebelt round round him,
gulping salt water, and that's the last of his nibs till the sharks catch hold of him. Do fish ever get
seasick?

Then you have a beautiful calm without a cloud, smooth sea, placid, crew and cargo in
smithereens, Davy Jones' locker. Moon looking down. Not my fault, old cockalorum.[161]
900 A lost long candle[162] wandered up the sky from Mirus bazaar in search of funds for Mercer's
hospital and broke, drooping, and shed a cluster of violet but one white stars. They floated, fell:
they faded. The shepherd's hour: the hour of folding: hour of tryst. From house to house, giving his
everwelcome double knock, went the nine o'clock postman, the glowworm's lamp at his belt
gleaming here and there through the laurel hedges. And among the five young trees a hoisted
905 lintstock lit the lamp at Leahy's terrace. By screens of lighted windows, by equal gardens a shrill
voice went crying, wailing: *Evening Telegraph, stop press edition! Result of the Gold Cup races!*[163] and
from the door of Dignam's house a boy ran out and called. Twittering the bat flew here, flew there.
Far out over the sands the coming surf crept, grey. Howth settled for slumber tired of long days, of
yumyum rhododendrons (he was old) and felt gladly the night breeze lift, ruffle his fell of ferns. He
910 lay but opened a red eye unsleeping, deep and slowly breathing, slumberous but awake. And far on
Kish bank the anchored lightship[164] twinkled, winked at Mr Bloom.

Life those chaps out there must have, stuck in the same spot. Irish Lights board.[165] Penance for
their sins. Coastguards too. Rocket and breeches buoy and lifeboat. Day we went out for the
pleasure cruise in the Erin's King,[166] throwing them the sack of old papers. Bears in the zoo. Filthy
915 trip. Drunkards out to shake up their livers. Puking overboard to feed the herrings. Nausea. And
the women, fear of God in their faces. Milly, no sign of funk. Her blue scarf loose, laughing. Don't
know what death is at that age. And then their stomachs clean. But being lost they fear. When we
hid behind the tree at Crumlin.[167] I didn't want to. Mamma! Mamma! Babes in the wood.[168]
Frightening them with masks too. Throwing them up in the air to catch them. I'll murder you.
920 Is it only half fun? Or children playing battle. Whole earnest. How can people aim guns at each
other. Sometimes they go off. Poor kids. Only troubles wildfire and nettlerash. Calomel purge[169] I
got her for that. After getting better asleep with Molly. Very same teeth she has. What do they
love? Another themselves? But the morning she chased her with the umbrella. Perhaps so as not to
hurt. I felt her pulse. Ticking. Little hand it was: now big. Dearest Papli.[170] All that the hand says
925 when you touch. Loved to count my waistcoat buttons. Her first stays I remember. Made me laugh
to see. Little paps to begin with. Left one is more sensitive, I think. Mine too. Nearer the heart.
Padding themselves out if fat is in fashion. Her growing pains at night, calling, wakening me.
Frightened she was when her nature came on her first. Poor child! Strange moment for the mother
too. Brings back her girlhood. Gibraltar. Looking from Buena Vista. O'Hara's tower.[171] The seabirds

Jewish households, to be touched by the devout when they enter or leave the house. The "tephilim" is a phylactery, a small leather case containing texts from the Jewish law, worn by orthodox Jews during weekday morning prayers.
[160] *That brought us out ... into the house of bondage* Bloom mistakenly reverses an often cited phrase of the Old Testament: "the Lord brought us out from Egypt, from the house of bondage" (Exodus 13:14). He makes the same mistake in "Aeolus"; see p. 234, ll. 156–7.
[161] *old cockalorum* a self-important little man.
[162] A roman candle, or firework.
[163] *Gold Cup* see the note to "Aeolus," p. 238 n. 68.
[164] *the anchored lightship* Kish Bank, about two miles east of Kingstown (now Dun Laoghaire), forms a dangerous obstacle at the southern entrance to Dublin Bay, and was therefore marked by a light moored at its northern end.
[165] The Commissioners of Irish Lights were charged with maintaining lighthouses and lightships on the coast of Ireland.

[166] The *Erin's King* was an excursion steamer that made two-hour trips around Dublin Bay, sailing several times a day. Bloom also recalls this excursion, made with Molly and Milly, in "Calypso" (the fourth episode of *Ulysses*).
[167] A village three miles southeast of central Dublin.
[168] *Babes in the wood* an English nursery tale and a ballad, which recounts the fate of two children left to perish in the forest by an uncle who expects to profit from their death. It has often been taken as a theme of Christmas pantomimes in England and Ireland.
[169] Calomel was used as a lotion for the relief of skin irritations such as the "nettlerash" that once afflicted Bloom's daughter, Milly.
[170] *Dearest Papli* the salutation in a letter from his daughter Milly to Bloom, which he receives and reads in "Calypso," the fourth episode in *Ulysses*.
[171] *Gibraltar ... Buena Vista. O'Hara's tower* Gibraltar is where Molly Bloom grew up as a girl. Bloom is repeating information

screaming. Old Barbary ape[172] that gobbled all his family. Sundown, gunfire for the men to cross 930
the lines.[173] Looking out over the sea she told me. Evening like this, but clear, no clouds. I always
thought I'd marry a lord or a gentleman with a private yacht. *Buenas noches, señorita. El hombre ama
la muchacha hermosa.*[174] Why me? Because you were so foreign from the others.

Better not stick here all night like a limpet. This weather makes you dull. Must be getting on for
nine by the light. Go home. Too late for *Leah*,[175] *Lily of Killarney.*[176] No. Might be still up. Call to 935
the hospital to see. Hope she's over. Long day I've had. Martha, the bath, funeral, house of keys,
museum with those goddesses, Dedalus' song. Then that bawler in Barney Kiernan's.[177] Got my
own back there. Drunken ranters. What I said about his God made him wince. Mistake to hit back.
Or? No. Ought to go home and laugh at themselves. Always want to be swilling in company.
Afraid to be alone like a child of two. Suppose he hit me. Look at it other way round. Not so bad 940
then. Perhaps not to hurt he meant. Three cheers for Israel. Three cheers for the sister-in-law he
hawked about, three fangs in her mouth. Same style of beauty. Particularly nice old party for a cup
of tea. The sister of the wife of the wild man of Borneo has just come to town.[178] Imagine that in the
early morning at close range. Everyone to his taste as Morris said when he kissed the cow.[179] But
Dignam's put the boots on it. Houses of mourning[180] so depressing because you never know. 945
Anyhow she wants the money. Must call to those Scottish widows[181] as I promised. Strange name.
Takes it for granted we're going to pop off first. That widow on Monday was it outside Cramer's[182]
that looked at me. Buried the poor husband but progressing favourably on the premium. Her
widow's mite. Well? What do you expect her to do? Must wheedle her way along. Widower I hate
to see. Looks so forlorn. Poor man O'Connor wife and five children poisoned by mussels here. The 950
sewage.[183] Hopeless. Some good matronly woman in a porkpie hat to mother him. Take him in tow,
platter face and a large apron. Ladies' grey flanelette bloomers, three shillings a pair, astonishing
bargain. Plain and loved, loved for ever, they say. Ugly: no woman thinks she is. Love, lie and be
handsome for tomorrow we die.[184] See him sometimes walking about[185] trying to find out who

gleaned from conversations with her. Buena Vista, or Sugar Loaf
Hill, is the highest point in Gibralter; O'Hara's Tower formerly
stood nearby on Wolf's Crag.

[172] A macaque monkey, a species that lives in droves on Gibralter.

[173] Gunfire, just before sundown, warned the inhabitants of
Gibraltar that the gates were going to be shut so that nobody
could enter the fortress-colony at night.

[174] *Buenas noches ... hermosa* Spanish for "Good evening, miss.
The man loves the pretty girl."

[175] *Leah* several times during the day Bloom wonders if he
should see *Leah the Forsaken* (1862), a translation and adaptation
by the American playwright John Augustin Daly (1838–99) of
the German *Deborah* (1850) by Salomon Hermann Mosenthal
(1821–77). Set in an Austrian village in the eighteenth century,
the play attacks anti-Semitism. The villain, Nathan, is an apostate Jew who masquerades as a Christian to protect his place in
the village. Leah, the Jew, is hounded by Nathan and forsaken by
her Christian lover. To escape her woes she kills herself at the
play's end. A performance of it took place at the Gaiety Theater
in Dublin on June 16, 1904.

[176] *Lily of Killarney* see note 37 on p. 263.

[177] *Martha, the bath ... that bawler in Barney Kiernan's* Bloom
is listing events which have occurred to him during the course of
the day: his receipt of a letter from "Martha Clifford" and his
"bath" ("Lotus Eaters," episode 5 in *Ulysses*), the funeral of
Patrick Dignam which he attended ("Hades," or episode 6 in
Ulysses), his efforts to place an ad for the "house of Keyes"
("Aeolus," or episode 7 in *Ulysses*), his visit to the "museum
with those goddesses" ("Scylla and Charybdis," episode 9 in
Ulysses), and Bloom's quarrel with an Irish nationalist in Barney
Kiernan's pub ("Cyclops," or episode 12 in *Ulysses*).

[178] *the sister of the wife ... come to town* from a street rhyme:
"The wild man of Borneo has just come to town. / The wife of the
wild man of Borneo has just come to town." And so on through
endless improvisations.

[179] *Everyone to his taste ... kissed the cow* a variant of the
proverbial expression: "Why, everyone as they like, as the good
woman said when she kissed the cow."

[180] *Houses of mourning* "It is better to go to the house of
mourning than to go the house of feasting: for that is the end
of all men; and living will lay it to his heart" (Ecclesiastes 7:2).

[181] The Scottish Widows' Fund (Mutual) Life Assurance Society; presumably Bloom has promised Patrick Dignam's widow
that he will "call" on the firm to resolve a matter connected with
Dignam's life insurance policy.

[182] Cramer, Wood, and Company, Pianoforte Gallery at 4–5
Westmoreland Street, in the eastern part of central Dublin.

[183] On the Dublin sewer system see "Aeolus," p. 241 n. 79.

[184] *Love, lie ... die* Bloom's variant of "Eat, drink, and be merry,"
ultimately from Ecclesiastes 8:15: "Then I commended mirth,
because a man hath no better thing under the sun, than to eat,
and to drink, and to be merry; for that shall abide with him of his
labour the days of his life, which God giveth him under the sun."

[185] *See him sometimes walking about* Bloom is recalling Denis
Breen. Earlier in the day he has met his wife Josie Breen,
formerly Josie Powell. She had been a friend and potential rival
of Molly when Bloom and she were courting, but had then
married Denis Breen. She tells Bloom that Denis Breen has
just that morning received a postcard bearing only the enigmatic
text "U.P." He is "trying to find out who played the trick." The
incident occurs in "Lestrygonians," or episode 8 in *Ulysses*.

955   played the trick. U. p: up. Fate that is. He, not me. Also a shop often noticed. Curse seems to dog
it. Dreamt last night? Wait. Something confused. She had red slippers on. Turkish. Wore the
breeches. Suppose she does. Would I like her in pyjamas? Damned hard to answer. Nannetti's
gone.[186] Mailboat. Near Holyhead by now.[187] Must nail that ad of Keyes's. Work Hynes and
Crawford. Petticoats for Molly. She has something to put in them. What's that? Might be money.

960   Mr Bloom stooped and turned over a piece of paper on the strand. He brought it near his eyes
and peered. Letter? No. Can't read. Better go. Better. I'm tired to move. Page of an old copybook.
All those holes and pebbles. Who could count them? Never know what you find. Bottle with story
of a treasure in it thrown from a wreck. Parcels post. Children always want to throw things in the
sea. Trust? Bread cast on the waters.[188] What's this? Bit of stick.

965   O! Exhausted that female has me. Not so young now. Will she come here tomorrow? Wait for her
somewhere for ever. Must come back. Murderers do. Will I?

Mr Bloom with his stick gently vexed the thick sand at his foot. Write a message for her. Might
remain. What?

I.

970   Some flatfoot tramp on it in the morning. Useless. Washed away. Tide comes here a pool near her
foot. Bend, see my face there, dark mirror, breathe on it, stirs. All these rocks with lines and scars
and letters. O, those transparent! Besides they don't know. What is the meaning of that other
world. I called you naughty boy because I do not like.[189]

AM. A.[190]

975   No room. Let it go.

Mr Bloom effaced the letters with his slow boot. Hopeless thing sand. Nothing grows in it. All
fades. No fear of big vessels coming up here.[191] Except Guinness's barges. Round the Kish in eighty
days. Done half by design.

He flung his wooden pen away. The stick fell in silted sand, stuck. Now if you were trying to do

980   that for a week on end you couldn't. Chance. We'll never meet again. But it was lovely. Goodbye,
dear. Thanks. Made me feel so young.

Short snooze now if I had. Must be near nine. Liverpool boat long gone. Not even the smoke.
And she can do the other. Did too. And Belfast.[192] I won't go. Race there, race back to Ennis.[193] Let
him. Just close my eyes a moment. Won't sleep though. Half dream. It never comes the same. Bat

985   again. No harm in him. Just a few.

O sweety all your little girlwhite up I saw dirty bracegirdle made me do love sticky we two
naughty Grace darling[194] she him half past the bed met him pike hoses frillies for Raoul[195] to
perfume your wife black hair heave under embon *señorita* young eyes Mulvey plump years dreams
return tail end Agendath[196] swoony lovey showed me her next year in drawers return next in her

990   next her next.[197]

[186]   Evidently Nannetti told Bloom, sometime when they met
in the "Aeolus" episode, that he would be taking the mailboat
that evening. See "Aeolus," pp. 231–3.

[187]   The mailboat left Kingstown nightly at 8:15 and sailed to
Holyhead in northwestern Wales, then the terminus for the
London and Northwestern Railway.

[188]   *Bread cast on the waters* "Cast thy bread upon the waters: for
thou shalt find it after many days" (Ecclesiastes 11:1).

[189]   *What is the . . . I do not like* Bloom is recalling phrases from
the letter that he received from one "Martha Clifford" earlier in
the day, in "Lotus Eaters" (the fifth episode of *Ulysses*).

[190]   *I. . . . AM. A.* some critics have discerned an echo of Revelations 1:8: "I am Alpha and Omega, the beginning and the
ending, saith the Lord." Others have called attention to the story
of Jesus and the adulteress, especially the moment when Jesus
writes in the sand (John 8:6–8).

[191]   *No fear of big vessels coming up here* Dublin Bay is very shallow
off Sandymount Strand, and at low tide a large area of tidal flats
is exposed to the east.

[192]   The location where Molly Bloom is to give a concert with
Blazes Boylan.

[193]   Where Bloom's father committed suicide and Bloom has
planned to go to observe the anniversary of the event on June 27.

[194]   For Grace Darling, see p. 278 n. 140.

[195]   *frillies for Raoul* in "Wandering Rocks" (episode 10 of
Ulysses), Bloom purchases a mildly salacious novel called *Sweets
of Sin* for Molly; he reads several passages from it to see if it will
suit her tastes, including this one: "*All the dollarbills her husband
gave her were spent in the stores on wondrous gowns and costliest frillies.
For him! For Raoul!*"

[196]   *Agendath* in "Calypso" (the fourth episode of *Ulysses* and the
one that introduces Bloom), Bloom notices an advertisement by a
firm called Agendath Netaim (Hebrew for "a company of
planters"), a Zionist organization which promises prospective
clients that it will "purchase waste sandy tracts from the Turkish
government," the legal entity which then controlled the area of
Palestine and modern Israel, "and plant with eucalyptus trees."

[197]   *her next year . . . her next* compare "Next year in Jerusalem,"
the final phrase of the ceremony on the first night of Passover.

A bat flew. Here. There. Here. Far in the grey a bell chimed. Mr Bloom with open mouth, his left boot sanded sideways, leaned, breathed. Just for a few

> *Cuckoo.*
> *Cuckoo.*
> *Cuckoo.*[198]   995

The clock on the mantelpiece in the priest's house cooed where Canon O'Hanlon and Father Conroy and the reverend John Hughes S. J. were taking tea and sodabread and butter and fried mutton chops with catsup and talking about

> *Cuckoo.*
> *Cuckoo.*   1000
> *Cuckoo.*

Because it was a little canarybird bird that came out of its little house to tell the time that Gerty MacDowell noticed the time she was there because she was as quick as anything about a thing like that, was Gerty MacDowell, and she noticed at once that that foreign gentleman that was sitting on the rocks looking was   1005

> *Cuckoo.*
> *Cuckoo.*
> *Cuckoo.*

Anna Livia Plurabelle: Introduction

Finnegans Wake, Joyce's last work, is a prodigious experiment in language, "a monstrous enigma beckoning imperiously from the shadowy pits of sleep," as Joseph Campbell and Henry Morton Robinson once termed it. Their work, *A Skeleton Key to Finnegans Wake* (1944), set out to dissolve the enigma and set forth the extaordinarily coherent narrative and richly textured symbolism that govern every detail. Theirs became only the first in a long line of commentaries which have emphasized the elements of story and narrative in the *Wake*, highlighting characters and plot, incident and event, cause and effect. But for the majority of the *Wake's* readers, it is fair to say, these dimensions of the book are an affair of secondary importance; indeed, the very nature of the *Wake* is such that it casts doubt on the concepts of character and identity which are presupposed in our everyday ideas of story. Play, impetuous and carried out with breath-taking extremism, seems to be much nearer to the heart of the *Wake*.

For the reader approaching the *Wake* for the first time, it is essential to recognize that literature furnishes many pleasures other than those of plot and character, narrative and story. The *Wake* is an endless catalogue of those pleasures, an enthralling cornucopia of puns and ambiguities conducted in a symphony of languages, a recognizable idiolect that, while plainly grounded in English, is essentially Joyce's creation. The personages who appear in the book are not so much characters as specters who become the occasion for the further production of language.

Finnegans Wake takes its title from an old vaudeville song about an Irish hod carrier named Tim Finnegan, one who gets drunk, falls off a ladder, and is apparently killed. When his friends hold a deathwatch over him and someone splashes him with some whisky, he comes to life and joins the festivities. Older readings of the *Wake* underline his fall's archetypal or cosmic dimension. In Joyce's account, however, Finnegan himself is soon displaced by a newcomer, Humphrey Chimpden Earwicker, HCE, also known as Here Comes Everybody or Haveth Childers Everywhere, a stuttering pub-keeper whose backside is comically broad. It was in the Phoenix Park in Dublin that he committed an impropriety which now dogs him, either peeping at or exhibiting himself to several girls. This youthful indiscretion was witnessed by soldiers and is now being disseminated everywhere. Not surprisingly, Earwicker has a wife, an ever-changing and all-pervading personage who appears typically under the name of Anna Livia Plurabelle, or ALP. Just as Earwicker can change into Adam, Noah, Lord Nelson, a mountain, or a tree, so ALP is transposed into Eve, Isis, Iseult, a passing cloud, a flowing stream.

---

[198]   Obviously suggesting a cuckold, but note also the traditional rhyme: "Cuckoo, cuckoo, / Tell me true, / When shall I be married?"; the number of cuckoo calls then heard foretells the number of years before marriage.

"Anna Livia Plurabelle," as chapter 8 of Book I has come to be known, has an autonomy that has long been widely recognized. No set of annotations could ever encompass the range of Joyce's references and wordplay, and the ones that follow are designed to do no more than help a first-time reader. My debt to Roland McHugh's *Annotations to Finnegans Wake* (Baltimore: Johns Hopkins University Press, 1991) will be obvious to more experienced Wakeans. Anna is the river Liffey, and old maps of Dublin called its river Anna Liffey, while *liv* is the Danish word for life, pertinent because Dublin itself was founded by marauding Danes. The action (to call it that) occurs a little upstream on the banks of the river, at Chapelizod, and turns on two washerwomen wringing out old clothes and gossiping about ALP and HCE. At first they discuss her marriage elopement abroad, a journey backward in time which corresponds to a linguistic journey through river-names and place names that follow the course of the river Liffey from its sources in County Wicklow toward Dublin. Then, just when everyone seems dead-set against her husband, Anna Livia pulls a trick out of her bag, which is both a womb for her many children and a holder of presents for them. Our first excerpt ends just as Anna Livia Plurabelle reaches into the bag and the two washerwomen get ready to discuss its contents. The portion of the text that has been omitted from this edition is a catalogue of the bag's contents which covers some seven pages. Our second excerpt resumes at the point where the third part of Anna Livia Plurabelle begins. It is also where James Joyce began a famous recording which proceeds from there to the episode's end. Readers encountering this material for the first time are strongly encouraged to listen to Joyce's masterful reading, which perfectly captures the tone and feel of *Finnegans Wake*.

Anna Livia Plurabelle (1939), from Finnegans Wake

O[1]

tell me all about
Anna Livia! I want to hear all
about Anna Livia. Well, you know Anna Livia? Yes, of course, we all know Anna Livia. Tell me
5   all. Tell me now. You'll die when you hear. Well, you know, when the old cheb went futt[2] and did
what you know. Yes, I know, go on. Wash quit and don't be dabbling. Tuck up your sleeves
and loosen your talk-tapes. And don't butt me – hike![3] – when you bend. Or whatever it was
they threed to make out he thried to two in the Fiendish park. He's an awful old reppe.[4] Look at
the shirt of him! Look at the dirt of it! He has all my water black on me. And it steeping and
10   stuping[5] since this time last wik. How many goes is it I wonder I washed it? I know by heart the
places he likes to saale,[6] duddurty devil! Scorching my hand and starving my famine to make his
private linen public. Wallop it well with your battle[7] and clean it. My wrists are wrusty rubbing
the mouldaw stains.[8] And the dneepers of wet and the gangres[9] of sin in it! What was it he did a tail
at all on Animal Sendai?[10] And how long was he under loch and neagh?[11] It was put in the newses
15   what he did, nicies and priers, the King fierceas[12] Humphrey, with illysus[13] distilling, exploits and
all. But toms will till. I know he well. Temp untamed will hist for no man.[14] As you spring so shall
you neap. O, the roughty[15] old rappe! Minxing[16] marrage and making loof. Reeve Gootch[17] was

[1]   *O* homonym of the French word for water, *eau*, and a female word or sign for Joyce. The opening lines form a triangle or delta, another female sign.

[2]   *the old cheb went futt* "the old chap" fused with the name of a river, the Cheb; went futt, i.e., fizzled out.

[3]   *hike*! Irish for "stop!" (to a horse).

[4]   *reppe* "Rep" is a man of loose character, a rip; and the Repe is a river.

[5]   *stuping* "Stooping" fused with the Stupia, a river in Poland.

[6]   *saale* French "sale" or "dirty" fused with the Saale, a river in Germany that flows into the Elbe.

[7]   *battle* Short for battledore, a wooden bat used in washing clothes, and homonym of a river of the same name in Canada.

[8]   *the mouldaw stains* "mildew stains" fused with the Moldaw river.

[9]   *dneepers ... gangres* the rivers Dnieper, which rises west of Moscow and flows into the Black Sea, and the Ganges in India.

[10]   *Animal Sendai* a fusion of Anima Sancti, or Holy Spirit, and the Senda River in Japan.

[11]   *loch and neagh* a fusion of "lock and key" with Lough Neagh, a lake in Northern Ireland.

[12]   *fierceas* fusion of "versus" and "fierce as"; Charles Humphrey was Oscar Wilde's solicitor.

[13]   *illysus* fusion of "illicit" and the river Illisos, in ancient Athens, and also the novel *Ulysses*.

[14]   *Temp ... no man* variant on the proverb, "Time and tide wait for no man."

[15]   *roughty* the Roughty River in Ireland.

[16]   *minxing* fusion of "mixing" with Latin "minxit," meaning "he urinated."

[17]   *Reeve Gootch* fusion of "reeve," a bailiff or court official, with *rive gauche*, French term for the left bank in Paris.

right and Reeve Drughad was sinistrous![18] And the cut of him! And the strut of him! How he used
to hold his head as high as a howeth,[19] the famous eld duke alien, with a hump of grandeur on him
like a walking wiesel rat. And his derry's own drawl and his corksown blather and his doubling   20
stutter and his gullaway swank.[20] Ask Lictor[21] Hackett or Lector[22] Reade of Garda Growley or the
Boy with the Billyclub. How elster is he a called at all? Qu'appelle?[23] Huges Caput Earlyfouler.[24]
Or where was he born or how was he found? Urgothland, Tvistown[25] on the Kattekat? New
Hunshire, Concord on the Merrimake? Who blocksmitt her saft anvil or yelled lep to her pail? Was
her banns never loosened in Adam and Eve's[26] or were him and her but captain spliced? For mine   25
ether duck I thee drake. And by my wildgaze I thee gander. Flowey and Mount on the brink of time
makes wishes and fears for a happy isthmass.[27] She can show all her lines, with love, license to play.
And if they don't remarry that hook and eye may! O, passmore that and oxus[28] another! Don Dom
Dombdomb and his wee follyo![29] Was his help inshored in the Stork and Pelican[30] against
bungelars, flu and third risk parties? I heard he dug good tin[31] with his doll, delvan first   30
and duvlin after, when he raped her home, Sabrine asthore,[32] in a parakeet's cage, by dredgerous
lands and devious delts, playing catched and mythed[33] with the gleam of her shadda, (if a flic[34]
had been there to pop up and pepper him!) past auld min's[35] manse and Maisons Allfou[36] and
the rest of incurables[37] and the last of immurables, the quaggy waag[38] for stumbling. Who sold
you that jackalantern's tale? Pemmican's[39] pasty pie! Not a grasshoop to ring her, not an antsgrain   35
of ore. In a gabbard[40] he barqued it, the boat of life, from the harbourless Ivernikan[41] Okean, till
he spied the loom of his landfall and he loosed two croakers from under his tilt, the gran Phenician
rover.[42] By the smell of her kelp they made the pigeonhouse.[43] Like fun they did! But where
was Himself, the timoneer? That marchantman he suivied their scutties[44] right over the wash,
his cameleer's burnous[45] breezing up on him, till with his runagate bowmpriss he roade and   40
borst her bar. Pilcomayo![46] Suchcaughtawan![47] And the whale's away with the grayling!
Tune your pipes and fall ahumming, you born ijypt,[48] and you're nothing short of one! Well,

[18] *Reeve Drughad ... sinistrous!* a variant of *rive droite*, or the right bank in French; sinistrous, fusion of Italian *sinistra* or left and English "sinister."

[19] *howeth* Howth Head, a hill outside Dublin.

[20] *derry's ... corksown ... doubling ... gullaway* variants on Derry, Cork, Dublin, and Galway, representing the four provinces of Ireland.

[21] *Lictor* Latin for a magistrate's assistant, who carried a bundle of rods, called the fasces surrounding an axe.

[22] *Lector* Latin for "reader."

[23] *Qu'appelle* a river in Saskatchewan, Canada; "what call" in French.

[24] *Hughes Caput Earlyfouler* a variant of HCE, and a fusion of Hugh Capet (king of the Franks), Henry the Fowler (a German king), with *kaput*, German for "broken."

[25] *Tvistown* from Danish *tvist*, meaning discord.

[26] *Adam and Eve's* a church in Dublin.

[27] *isthmass* fusion of Christmas and isthmus.

[28] *passmore ... oxus* fusion of "pass more" and Pasmore River in Australia; fusion of "ask us" and the "Oxus," the ancient name for a river (now the Amu river) that springs up in the Pamir mountains, runs west, and forms part of the border of Pakistan.

[29] *his wee follyo* HCE's obscure impropriety, either peeping at or exhibiting himself to girls; but also a pun on "folio," a large book. "Wee" rhymes with *oui*, French for "yes," the word that ends *Ulysses*, and the text may be turning HCE into an author of *Ulysses*, or conflating him with Joyce.

[30] *the Stork and Pelican* two Dublin insurance companies.

[31] *tin* slang for money.

[32] *Sabrina asthore* Sabrina is the Latin name for the Severn river in England, the word "rape" (only three words earlier) also evokes the rape of the Sabine women; "asthore" is Anglo-Irish for "darling."

[33] *catched and mythed* variants on "cat and mouse."

[34] *shadda ... flic* a variant on the river Adda, in northern Italy; *flic* is French slang for a policeman.

[35] *min's* the Min is a river in China.

[36] *Maisons Allfou* in French, a *maison-dieu* is a hospital; *fou* is French for crazy. "House Allcrazy."

[37] *incurables* the Hospital for Incurables was on Donnybrook Road in Dublin.

[38] *waag* the Waag river is in modern Slovakia, now called the Váh river.

[39] *Pemmican's* condensed food, and so condensed thought.

[40] *gabbard* variant of "gabbart," a sailing barge or lighter.

[41] *Iverkian* Ivernia is Ptolemy's name for Ireland.

[42] *gran Phenician rover* one of the books that Joyce drew on when writing *Ulysses* was Victor Bérard, *Les Phéniciens et l'Odyssée* (*The Phoenecians and the Odyssey*), 2 vols. (Paris: Armand Colin, 1902–3), which urged that the *Odyssey* had Semitic roots, and that all its place names were actual places, often detectable by finding a Hebrew word that closely resembled the Greek. This theory suited Joyce's wish to make Bloom, who is Jewish, into a modern Ulysses. HCE is becoming like Ulysses.

[43] The Pigeonhouse was a building on the south of the mouth of the Liffey in Dublin.

[44] *suivied their scutties* "suivre" is French for "to follow"; scutties are small boats.

[45] *burnous* a hooded cloak worn by Arabs and Moors.

[46] *Pilcomayo* a river that forms part of the border between Paraguay and Argentina.

[47] *Suchcaughtawan!* a variant on Saskatchewan, a river in Canada.

[48] *ijypt* conflation of "Egypt" and Dublin pronunciation of idiot, "eejit."

ptellomey[49] soon and curb your escumo.[50] When they saw him shoot swift up her sheba sheath,[51] like any gay lord salomon, her bulls they were ruhring,[52] surfed with spree.[53] Boyarka buah![54]

45 Boyana bueh! He erned his lille Bunbath hard, our staly bred,[55] the trader. He did. Look at here. In this wet of his prow.[56] Don't you know he was kaldt a bairn of the brine, Wasserbourne[57] the waterbaby? Havemmarea,[58] so he was! H.C.E. has a codfisck ee. Shyr she's nearly as badher as him herself. Who? Anna Livia? Ay, Anna Livia. Do you know she was calling bakvandets[59] sals from all around, nyumba noo, chamba choo,[60] to go in till him, her erring cheef, and tickle the pontiff aisy-

50 oisy?[61] She was? Gota pot! Yssel that the limmat? As El Negro winced when he wonced in La Plate.[62] O, tell me all I want to hear, how loft she was lift a laddery dextro![63] A coneywink after the bunting fell. Letting on she didn't care, sina feza,[64] me absantee,[65] him man in passession, the proxenete![66] Proxenete and phwhat is phthat? Emme[67] for your reussischer Honddu jarkon! Tell us in franca langua.[68] And call a spate a spate. Did they never sharee you ebro[69] at skol,

55 you antiabecedarian? It's just the same as if I was to go par examplum[70] now in conservancy's cause out of telekinesis[71] and proxenete you. For coxyt sake[72] and is that what she is? Botlettle[73] I thought she'd act that loa.[74] Didn't you spot her in her windaug, wubbling up on an osiery chair, with a meusic[75] before her all cunniform[76] letters, pretending to ribble a reedy[77] derg on a fiddle she bogans[78] without a band on? Sure she can't fiddan a dee, with bow or abandon! Sure, she can't!

60 Tista suck. Well, I never now heard the like of that! Tell me moher. Tell me moatst. Well, old Humber was as glommen[79] as grampus, with the tares at his thor and the buboes[80] for ages and neither bowman nor shot abroad and bales allbrant[81] on the crests of rockies and nera[82] lamp in kitchen or church and giant's holes in Grafton's causeway[83] and deathcap mushrooms round

---

[49]   *ptellomey* conflation of "tell me" and Ptolemy, the name of several Hellenistic kings of Egypt and a famous geographer.

[50]   *escumo* conflation of Eskimo and *escuma*, Portuguese for froth.

[51]   *sheba sheath* Sheba was a concubine of King David in I Kings 10; sheath is the literal meaning of the Latin word *vagina*.

[52]   *ruhring* from the Ruhr river in Germany, and from the German verb *rühren*, to stir.

[53]   *spree* a conflation of "spray" and the river Spree, which flows through Berlin and rhymes with "spray."

[54]   *Boyarka buah!* the Boyarka, the Buah, and the Bojana are all rivers.

[55]   *our staly bred* punning against "our daily bread" in the Lord's prayer.

[56]   *this wet of his prow* man shall live "by the sweat of his brow" as a consequence of the fall; see Genesis 3:19.

[57]   *Wasserbourne* water-borne or water-born elided with the River Winterbourne and the German word for water, *Wasser*.

[58]   *Havemmarea* punning on Ave Maria; *marea* is Italian for "tides."

[59]   *bakvandets* from Norwegion *bak* for "back" and *vande* for "water, tide."

[60]   *nyumba … chamba* Kiswahili words for "house" and "hiding place."

[61]   *oisy* after the river Oise in southern France.

[62]   *El Negro … La Plate* after the Rio Negro in Argentina, which is also where La Plate is found.

[63]   *how loft she lift a laddery dextro* how oft she was left at the right side, punning on Latin *latere dextro* for "right side" and its near-rhyme in English, laddery, with the related notions of rising "aloft" and "lift."

[64]   *sina feza* Kiswahili for "I have no money."

[65]   *me absantee* a fusion of Latin *me absente*, or "in my absence," and the Santee river in South Carolina.

[66]   *proxenete* archaic and learned term for someone who negotiates something, especially a marriage; an agent, go-between, or match-maker (*OED*).

[67]   *Emme* the Emme is a river in Switzerland.

[68]   *Tells us in franca langua* punning on lingua franca, the hybrid language that consisted largely of Italian and was used by Latin peoples in dealing with Arabs, Turks, Greeks, etc. in the Near and Middle East.

[69]   *sharee you ebro* punning on "show you Hebrew."

[70]   *par examplum* punning on French, "par exemple," or "for example."

[71]   *telekinesis* telekinesis is movement at a distance, produced by a medium; the famous "Mahatma Letters" addressed to the theosophist Madame Blavatsky (1831–91) were said to come by telekinesis.

[72]   *for coxyt sake* punning on the river Cocytus in ancient descriptions of the underworld and Cox's river in the Blue Mountains.

[73]   *Botlettle* now Boteti, river in Botswana, sounds a bit like "but little."

[74]   *that loa* the Loa is Chile's longest river, and sounds like "low."

[75]   *meusic* a conflation of "music" and the river Meuse in France.

[76]   *cunniform* a conflation of cuneiform and Latin *cunnus*, or "cunt."

[77]   *ribble a reedy* the river Ribble runs through Yorkshire and Lancashire in England; the Reedy runs through South Carolina.

[78]   *bogans* from German Bogen, a bow.

[79]   *Humber … glommen* the Humber is a river estuary in northeast England; the Glommen or Gloma river is in Norway and evokes the sound of "gloomy."

[80]   *buboes* buboes are inflamed swellings or abscesses in glandular parts of the body.

[81]   *bales allbrant* a bale, in its usual sense, is any bundle of material bound for shipping or storage; but its archaic meaning, invoked here, was a funeral pyre; and "allbrant" fuses "all" and the German past participle "brant" or "burned."

[82]   *nera* "ne'er a" fused with Italian *nera*, or black.

[83]   *Grafton's causeway* fusing the famous Giant's Causeway in Northern Ireland with Grafton Street, a well-known street in central Dublin.

Funglus[84] grave and the great tribune's[85] barrow all darnels occumule,[86] sittang sambre on his sett,[87] drammen and drommen,[88] usking[89] queasy quizzers of his ruful continence,[90] his childlinen scarf to   65
encourage his obsequies where he'd check their debths in that mormon's thames, be questing and handsetl,[91] hop, step and a deepend, with his berths in their toiling moil,[92] his swallower open from swolf[93] to fore and the snipes of the gutter pecking his crocs,[94] hungerstriking all alone and holding doomsdag over[95] hunselv, dreeing his weird,[96] with his dander up, and his fringe combed over his eygs and droming[97] on loft till the sight of the sternes,[98] after zwarthy[99] kowse and weedy broeks[100]   70
and the tits of buddy and the loits of pest[101] and to peer was Parish worth thette[102] mess. You'd think all was dodo[103] belonging to him how he durmed adranse in durance vaal.[104] He had been belching for severn[105] years. And there she was, Anna Livia, she darent[106] catch a winkle of sleep, purling around like a chit of a child, Wendawanda,[107] a finger-thick, in a Lapsummer skirt and damazon cheeks, for to ishim[108] bonzour to her dear dubber Dan.[109] With neuphraties and sault   75
from his maggias. And an odd time she'd cook him up blooms of fisk and lay to his heartsfoot her meddery eygs, yayis,[110] and staynish beacons on toasc[111] and a cupenhave[112] so weeshywashy of Greenland's tay or a dzoupgan[113] of Kaffue mokau[114] an sable or Sikiang sukry[115] or his ale of ferns in

---

[84]   *Funglus* a fusion of "fungus" and Fingal's Cave, a cave that is alleged to produce melodies on the island of Staffa in the Hebrides, a claim that prompted the *Hebridean Overture* (1830) by Felix Mendelssohn (1809–47).

[85]   *great tribune* Daniel O'Connell (1775–1847), an Irish political leader and self-styled "tribune" of Ireland who advocated repeal of the Act of Union which had united the parliaments of England and Ireland in 1800.

[86]   *darnels occumule* tares accumulated.

[87]   *sittang sambre on his sett* with various puns generated from "sitting sombre on his seat."

[88]   *drammen and drommen* fusions of dreaming with the Drammen river in Norway, and with *drømmende*, Danish for "dreaming."

[89]   *usking* fusion of "asking" with the Usk river in Wales.

[90]   *ruful continence* Don Quijote is given the sobriquet "the Knight of the Rueful Countenance."

[91]   *debths in the mormon's thames, by questing and handsetl* stemming from "deaths in the morning *Times*, by question and answer, with "handsetl" stemming from German *Handzettel*, meaning "handbill."

[92]   *berths in their toiling moil* stemming from "births in the *Daily Mail*, this latter the first tabloid newspaper in Britain, founded 1896.

[93]   *swolf* punning on German *zwölf*, meaning "twelve."

[94]   *crocs* French slang for "teeth."

[95]   *doomsdag over* Henrik Ibsen (1820–1906), in his four-line poem "Et vers" (French for "And Verse") concludes: "At digte – det er at holde / dommedag over sig selv" ("To write – that is to bring oneself to Judgment").

[96]   *hunselv, dreeing his weird* hunselv is Danish for "herself"; *dreeing his weird* means "to suffer one's destiny," playing on the literal and archaic sense of the word "weird."

[97]   *droming* a conflation of English "dreaming" with Dutch *droomen*, "to dream," and the name of the river Drome, in southwest France.

[98]   *sternes* the German word for "star" is *Stern*, and Joyce's coinage derives from that.

[99]   *zwarthy* the Dutch word for "black" is *zwart* (cognate with German *schwartz*), while the Zwarte Water is a river in the Netherlands.

[100]   *kowse and weedy broeks* punning on the Dutch words *kous* for "stocking," *wijde* (which sounds like "weedy") for "baggy," and *broek* for "trousers."

[101]   *buddy ... pest* Budapest consists of what were once

two towns (Buda and Pest) on opposite sides of the Danube river.

[102]   *worth thette* the Worth is a small river in Oxfordshire, the Thet a small river near Norfolk, England.

[103]   *dodo* the Dodo river is in Nigeria; "faire dodo" in French is to go to sleep.

[104]   *durmed adranse in durance vaal* "durmed" conflates "dreamed" and the Durme river in Belgium, a small tributary of the Schelde. "Adrance" conflates "trance" with the Adra and Drance rivers, respectively in Spain and Switzerland. "In durance vaal" conflates the Vaal river, in South Africa, with "in durance vile," a phrase used by Robert Burns (1759–96) in a poem called "Esopus to Maria," lines 55–60:

> A Workhouse! Ah, that sound awakes my woes,
> And pillows on the thorn my rack'd repose!
> In durance vile here must I wake and weep,
> And all my frowsy couch in sorrow steep:
> That straw where many a rogue has lain of yore,
> And vermin'd gipsies litter'd heretofore.

[105]   *severn* a fusion of "seven" and the Severn river in Wales and England, on the banks of which are Worcester, Gloucester, and Shrewsbury.

[106]   *darent* a fusion of "daren't," the contraction for "dare not," and the river Darent in Kent, England.

[107]   *Wendawanda* the Wende is a river in China, while *Wende* is the German word for a "turning"; *wanda* is Kiswahili for "a finger's breadth," and the River Wandle flows into the Thames.

[108]   *ishim* the Ishim river runs through Kazakhstan and part of Russia, and its name sounds like "wish him."

[109]   *bonzour to her dear dubber Dan* "bonzour," punning on French *bonjour* for "good-day"; "dear dubber Dan" punning on "dear dirty Dublin," "dapper Dan" (a nickname for a smartly dressed man), and the river Dan.

[110]   *fisk ... yayis* Danish for "fish" and Kiswahili for eggs.

[111]   *staynish beacons on toasc* Danish bacon on toast

[112]   *cupenhave* "a cup and a half" merged with København, the Danish name of Copenhagen.

[113]   *dzougpan* a "dozen," perhaps fused with river names.

[114]   *Kafue mokau* "coffee mocca" overlaid with the Kafue river in Uganda and the Mokau river in New Zealand.

[115]   *Sikiang sukry* from the Sikiang (or Xijian) river in China, and the French word for sugar, *sucre*.

trueart pewter and a shinkobread (hamjambo, bana?)[116] for to plaise that man hog stay his
80   stomicker till her pyrraknees[117] shrunk to nutmeg graters while her togglejoints shuck with goyt
and as rash as she'd russ[118] with her peakload[119] of vivers up on her sieve (metauwero rage it swales[120]
and rieses) my hardey Hek he'd kast them frome him, with a stour[121] of scorn, as much as to say you
sow and you sozh,[122] and if he didn't peg the platteau on her tawe,[123] believe you me, she was safe
enough. And then she'd esk to vistule[124] a hymn, *The Heart Bowed Down*[125] or *The Rakes of Mallow*[126]
85   or Chelli Michele's[127] *La Calumnia è un Vermicelli*[128] or a balfy[129] bit ov *old Jo Robidson*. Sucho fuffing
a fifeing 'twould cut you in two! She'd bate the hen that crowed on the turrace of Babbel.[130] What
harm if she knew how to cockle her mouth! And not a mag[131] out of Hum no more than out of the
mangle weight.[132] Is that a faith? That's the fact. Then riding[133] the ricka and roya romanche,[134]
Annona,[135] gebroren aroostokrat Nivia,[136] dochter[137] of Sense and Art, with Sparks' pirryphlick-
90   athims[138] funkling[139] her fan, anner frostivying[140] tresses dasht with virevlies,[141] – while the prom
beauties sreeked[142] nith their bearers' skins![143] – in a period gown of changeable jade that would
robe the wood[144] of two cardinals' chairs and crush poor Cullen[145] and smother MacCabe.[146] O
blazerskate![147] Theirs porpor[148] patches! And brahming[149] to him down the feedchute, with her
femtyfyx[150] kinds of fondling endings, the poother[151] rambling off her nose: *Vuggybarney*,[152] *Wick-*
95   *erymandy!*[153] *Hello, ducky, please don't die!* Do you know what she started cheeping after, with a choicey
voicey like water-glucks[154] or Madame Delba to Romeoreszk?[155] You'll never guess. Tell me. Tell me.
Phoebe, dearest,[156] *tell, O tell me* and *I loved you better nor you knew*. And letting on hoon var[157] daft about

---

[116]   *shinkobread (hamjambo, bana?)* the first term is from
German *Schinkenbrot*, a jam sandwich; the phrase in parentheses
fuses the Kiswahili greeting *hujambo, bana?* with English and
French words for ham, or in French *jambon*. Nestled within the
phrase are also the Ham, Jambi, and Bana rivers, located in
England, Sumatra, and Malaysia.

[117]   *pyrraknees* the Pyrenées mountains and "pair of knees."

[118]   *goyt ... russ* the river Goyt is in Derbyshire, England; the
river Russ flows into the Baltic Sea.

[119]   *peakload* packload, but inflected by the mountain motif in
the previous line; "vivers" is a slang term for food.

[120]   *metauwero ... swales* the Metauro is a river that flows into
the Adriatic Sea in Italy; the Swale is a small river in Yorkshire,
England.

[121]   *stour* the river Stour is in Kent, England.

[122]   *sozh* the Sozh is a river in Belarus.

[123]   *tawe* the river Tawe, in Wales, which flows through Swan-
sea, here assimilated to "toe."

[124]   *esk to vistule* the Esk is a river in Scotland; the Vistula, one in
Poland.

[125]   *The Heart Bowed Down* a song by the Irish composer
Michael Balfe (1808–70).

[126]   *The Rakes of Mallow* a popular Irish song, composer unknown.

[127]   *Chelli Michele* Michael Kelly (1764?–1826), a Dublin
singer and composer.

[128]   *La Calumnia è un Vermicelli* punning on an aria in the opera
The Barber of Seville (1816), by Giacchino Rossini (1792–1868),
"La calumnia è un venticello" ("Calumny is a puff of wind").

[129]   *balfy* Michael Balfe, the Irish composer.

[130]   *turrace of Babbel* merging "terrace" with Latin *turris*, or
"tower," with the tower of Babel and "babble."

[131]   *mag* slang term for "talk."

[132]   *mangle weight* a device for squeezing water from and pressing clothing, linen, and so forth.

[133]   *riding* punning on "writing."

[134]   *ricka and roya romanche* punning on the phrase "rich and rare
romance," with the river Roya in France.

[135]   *Annona* Roman corn-goddess.

[136]   *arrostokrat Nivie* the Aroostook river is in Maine, the Nive
in France.

[137]   *dochter* Dutch for "daughter."

[138]   *pirryphlickathims* Pyriphlethon was a mythical fiery stream
in the underworld Hades.

[139]   *funkling* from the German verb *funkeln*, to sparkle.

[140]   *anner frostivying* the river Anner, which is in Ireland, is
being fused with "Anna" and "and"; frostifying.

[141]   *dasht with virevlies* the Dasht river is in Pakistan; the Vire,
which is in northern France, is being fused with "fireflies" and
the Dutch word *vlies*, meaning "fleece."

[142]   *prom beauties sreeked* promenade beauties shrieked or sleeked.

[143]   *nith their bearers' skins* punning from 'neath their bearskins.

[144]   *robe the wood* or, rob the world, as inflected by the names of
two more rivers, the Robe and the Wood.

[145]   *Cullen* Cardinal Paul Cullen (1803–78) became Archbishop
of Dublin in 1852 and a cardinal in 1867.

[146]   *MacCabe* Edward MacCabe (1816–85) became Archbishop
of Dublin in 1879 and was elevated to cardinal in 1882.

[147]   *blatherskate* Anglo-Irish for "nonsense."

[148]   *porpors* from Italian *porpora* for "purple," punning on purple
patches.

[149]   *brahming* from the river Brahmani in eastern India.

[150]   *femtyfix* Danish for 56.

[151]   *poother* punning on powder and Latin *pudor*, meaning shame.

[152]   *Vuggybarney* from the Danish word *vuggeborn*, a child in the
cradle.

[153]   *Wickerymandy!* a conflation of wicker and Dutch *mand*, or
basket.

[154]   *waterglucks* waterclocks; also Christoph Gluck (1714–87), a
composer.

[155]   *Madame Delba* Nellie Melba (1861–1931), whose name has
been fused with "delta" by Joyce, was an Ausralian opera singer;
Jean de Reszke (1850–1935) was a Polish tenor. The two first
performed *Roméo et Juliette* by Charles Gounod (1818–93) in
1891, and repeated it every year until Reszke retired from the
stage in 1904.

[156]   *Phoebe, dearest* the title of a popular nineteenth-century
song.

[157]   *hoon var* from Danish *hun var*, meaning "she was."

the warbly sangs from over holmen:[158] *High hellskirt saw ladies hensmoker lily-hung pigger:*[159] and soay[160] and soan and so firth and so forth[161] in a tone sonora[162] and Oom Bothar[163] below like Bheri-Bheri[164] in his sandy cloak, so umvolosy,[165] as deaf as a yawn, the stult![166] Go away! Poor deef old 100
deary! Yare[167] only teasing! Anna Liv?[168] As chalk[169] is my judge! And didn't she up in sorgues[170] and go and trot doon[171] and stand in her douro,[172] puffing her old dudheen,[173] and every shirvant[174] siligirl[175] or wensum[176] farmerette walking the pilend[177] roads, Sawy, Fundally, Daery or Maery, Milucre, Awny[178] or Graw,[179] usedn't she make her a simp or sign to slip inside by the sullyport?[180] You don't say, the sillypost?[181] Bedouix but I do! Calling them in, one by one (To Blockbeddum[182] 105
here! Here the Shoebenacaddie!)[183] and legging a jig or so on the sihl[184] to show them how to shake their benders and the dainty how to bring to mind the gladdest garments out of sight and all the way of a maid with a man[185] and making a sort of a cackling noise like two and a penny or half a crown and holding up a silliver shiner.[186] Lordy, lordy, did she so? Well, of all the ones ever I heard! Throwing all the neiss[187] little whores in the world at him! To inny[188] captured wench you wish of 110
no matter what sex of pleissful[189] ways two adda[190] tammar[191] a lizzy a lossie[192] to hug and hab[193] haven in Humpy's apron!

And what was the wyerye[194] rima[195] she made! Odet! Odet![196] Tell me the trent[197] of it while I'm lathering hail[198] out of Denis Florence MacCarthy's[199] combies.[200] Rise it, flut[201] ye, pian piena![202] I'm dying down off my iodine feet until I lerryn[203] Anna Livia's cushingloo,[204] that was writ by one 115

[158] *holmen* Danish word for "islet," which also contains the name of the river Holme in Yorkshire, England.
[159] *High ... pigger* Danish, "Jeg elsker saaledes hine smukke lille unge piger," or "I so love those beautiful little young girls."
[160] *soay* Soay Island in the Hebrides.
[161] *and so firth and so forth* The Firth of Forth, in Scotland.
[162] *sonora* the Sonora river in northwest Mexico flows into the Gulf of California, with punning on "sonorous."
[163] *Oom Bothar* Louis "Oom" Botha (1862–1919), a general and prime minister of South Africa, 1910–19.
[164] *Bheri-Bheri* the Bheri river is in Nepal, conflated here with the disease beri-beri.
[165] *umvolosy* the Umvolosi river is in South Africa.
[166] *stult* from Latin *stultus*, or fool.
[167] *deef ... Yare* after the river Dee, in England, and the river Yare, which flows from Norwich to Great Yarmouth in England.
[168] *Liv* Danish *liv* means "life."
[169] *chalk* the Chalk river is in Ontario, Canada.
[170] *sorgues* the Sorgue river is in Provence in southwestern France.
[171] *doon* the river Doon is in Scotland.
[172] *douro* the Douro river is in Portugal.
[173] *dudheen* in Anglo-Irish, a "dudeen" is a short tobacco pipe.
[174] *shirvant* a fusion of "servant" and the river Shirvan, in Iran.
[175] *siligirl* the Siligir river is found in Siberia.
[176] *wensum* a conflation of "winsome" and the river Wensum near Norwich, in England.
[177] *pilend* the Pile Ends was the name for the end of the South Wall in Dublin in the eighteenth century.
[178] *Milucre, Awny* in the Irish Fenian cycle, Milucra and Aine are daughters of Cullan the Smith and in love with Finn.
[179] *Graw* the river Grawe is in Poland.
[180] *sullyport* based on sallyport, an opening in a fortified place for passage of troops when making a sally.
[181] *sillypost* in Zurich the general post office is called the Sihlpost.
[182] *Blockbeddum* punning on the blackbottom dance.
[183] *Shoebenacaddie* a river in Nova Scotia, Canada.
[184] *the sihl* a conflation of "sill" and the river Sihl, which flows south of Zurich in Switzerland.

[185] *the way of a maid with a man* Proverbs 30:18–19: "There be three things which are too wonderful for me, yea, four which I know not: The way of an eagle in the air; the way of a serpent upon a rock; the way of ship in the midst of the sea; and the way of a man with a maid."
[186] *silliver shiner* the Silver River is in Florida; "shiner" is slang for a silver coin.
[187] *neiss* from the Neisse river, on the German–Polish border.
[188] *inny* from the river Inny in county Westmeath, Ireland.
[189] *pleissful* the Pleisse river flows through Leipzig in Germany.
[190] *adda* the Adda river flows through Lombardy in northern Italy.
[191] *tammar* the Tamar river is found in Tasmania, Australia; and Tamar is a woman falsely accused of prostitution in the book of Genesis 38:24.
[192] *a lizzy a lossie* the Liz river is in Portugal; the river Lossie is in Scotland.
[193] *hab* the Hab river is in modern Pakistan.
[194] *wyerye* a conflation of "weary" with the rivers Wye and Rye in England.
[195] *rima* Italian word for rhyme.
[196] *Odet* Danish *0 det* means "O that!"
[197] *trent* a fusion of "trend" and the river Trent, which flows through Nottingham in England.
[198] *hail* punning on hell.
[199] *Denis Florence MacCarthy* (1817–82), Irish writer, was the author of *Underglimpses, and Other Poems* (London: D. Bogue, 1857).
[200] *combies* a short form for "combinations" or "combination-garments," so-called because they combined a chemise with drawers or panties in a single undergarment. Combinations were introduced in the 1880s and vanished after the Second World War.
[201] *flut* is the German word for flood.
[202] *pian piena pian piano* is Italian for "slowly, slowly"; *pian piena* is Joyce's Italian for "slowly, flood."
[203] *lerryn* a fusion of "learn" and the river Lerryn, the latter found in Cornwall, England.
[204] *cushingloo* a Gaelic song, Cusheen Loo, fused with Cushing Creek, the name of rivers found in England, the United States, and Canada.

and rede[205] by two and trouved[206] by a poule[207] in the parco![208] I can see that, I see you are. How does it tummel?[209] Listen now. Are you listening? Yes, yes! Idneed I am! Tarn[210] your ore ouse![211] Essonne inne![212]

120   By earth and the cloudy but I badly want a brandnew bankside,[213] bedamp[214] and I do, and a plumper at that!

For the putty[215] affair I have is wore out, so it is, sitting, yaping[216] and waiting for my old Dane hodder dodderer,[217] my life in death companion, my frugal key of our larder, my much-altered camel's hump, my jointspoiler, my maymoon's[218] honey, my fool to the last Decemberer, to wake himself out of his winter's doze and bore me down like he used to.

125   Is there irwell[219] a lord of the manor or a knight of the shire at strike, I wonder, that'd dip me a dace[220] or two in cash for washing and darning his worshipful socks for him now we're run out of horse-brose[221] and milk?

Only for my short Brittas[222] bed made's as snug as it smells it's out I'd lep[223] and off with me to the slobs della Tolka[224] or the plage au Clontarf[225] to feale[226] the gay aire[227] of my salt[228] troublin bay[229] and the race of

130   the saywint[230] up me ambushure.[231]

Onon! Onon![232] tell me more. Tell me every tiny teign.[233] I want to know every single ingul.[234] Down to what made the potters fly into jagsthole.[235] And why were the vesles[236] vet.[237] That homa[238] fever's winning me wome.[239] If a mahun[240] of the horse[241] but hard[242] me! We'd be bundukiboi[243] meet askarigal.[244] Well, now comes the hazel-hatchery part. After Clondalkin[245]

135   the Kings's Inns.[246] We'll soon be there with the freshet.[247] How many aleveens[248] had she in

[205]   *rede* fusion of "read" with the river Rede, which flows from the Scottish border into the Tyne, and the German noun *Rede*, which means speech, talk, language.
[206]   *trouved* from French *trouver*, which means "to find."
[207]   *poule* a pun on "pool" and the French word for a hen, but also for a young man of loose morals.
[208]   *parco* Italian for "park."
[209]   *tummel* conflation of the German verb *tummeln*, meaning "to make haste" or "to romp about," and the river Tummel, which is in Scotland.
[210]   *Tarn* conflation of "turn" and the river Tarn in southern France.
[211]   *ore ouse* the river Ore is found in East Anglia, England; there are two rivers Ouse in England.
[212]   *Essonne inne* the Essonne river is a tributary of the Seine, in France, and it is being conflated with the expression "listen in."
[213]   *bankside* punning on "backside."
[214]   *bedamp* punning on "be damned."
[215]   *putty* punning on "petty" and French *petit* or "small."
[216]   *yaping* punning on "gaping."
[217]   *Dane hodder dodderer* the rivers Dane and Hodder are found in the Peak District and Lancashire, England; the river Dodder, instead, is in Ireland and flows into the Liffey. A "hoddie doddie" is slang for a squat person or a cuckold.
[218]   *maymoon's* "The Young May Moon" is a popular song set to lyrics by the Irish poet Thomas Moore (1779–1852).
[219]   *irwell* the river Irwell is found in Lancashire, England.
[220]   *dace* slang for twopence.
[221]   *horsebrose* brose is made by pouring boiling water or milk on oatmeal.
[222]   *Brittas* the river Brittas in Ireland joins the river Liffey near Blessington.
[223]   *lep* Turkish word for "shore."
[224]   *slobs della Tolka* the Tolka river runs westward through Dublin, north of and more or less parallel to the Liffey. "Slobs" or sloblands are muddy areas, especially alluvial land reclaimed from the water.
[225]   *plage au Clontarf* French *plage au* means "beach at," and Clontarf is the site where the Tolka flows into Dublin Bay.

[226]   *feale* conflation of "feel" and the river Feale in County Kerry, Ireland.
[227]   *aire* conflation of "air" and the river Aire in northwestern Ireland.
[228]   *salt* There are five Salt rivers in the US alone.
[229]   *troublin bay* punning on Dublin Bay.
[230]   *saywint* punning on "seawind."
[231]   *ambushure* punning on French *embouchure*, a river mouth or a mouthpiece.
[232]   *Onon!* a conflation of the archaic word "anon," meaning at once, and the river Onon, found in eastern Mongolia.
[233]   *teign* conflation of "thing," the Danish *tegn* or "sign," and the river Teign, found in Devon and Cornwall in England.
[234]   *ingul* a merging of "inkling" and the river Ingul, which flows into the Black Sea.
[235]   *jagsthole* a fusion of "Jack's hole" and the river Jagst, which flows through Ellwangen in Germany.
[236]   *vesles* conflation of vessels with the Vesle river in northern France.
[237]   *vet* Dutch word meaning "fat."
[238]   *homa* Kiswahili word for "fever."
[239]   *wome* conflation of "womb" and "home."
[240]   *mahun* conflation of "man" with the rivers Mahu (in Brazil) and Mahon (near Waterford, Ireland).
[241]   *horse* conflation of "house" with Horse Creek, a river name found in many places.
[242]   *hard* punning on "heard," as in "man of the house heard."
[243]   *bundukiboi* from Kiswahili *bunduki*, meaning "gun."
[244]   *askarigal* from Kiswahili *askari*, meaning "soldier."
[245]   *Clondalkin* a village in County Dublin, on the Grand Canal.
[246]   *King's Inns* the King's Inn Quay in Dublin.
[247]   *freshet* punning on fishnet and freshet, a stream of fresh water running into the sea.
[248]   *aleveens* merging "alevins," or young fish, and "elevens," together with the river Leven in the Lake District, England, and perhaps also the French word for a schoolchild, *élève*.

tool?[249] I can't rightly rede you that. Close[250] only knows. Some say she had three figures to fill and confined herself to a hundred eleven, wan[251] bywan bywan, making meanacuminamoyas.[252] Olaph lamm[253] et, all that pack? We won't have room in the kirkeyaard.[254] She can't remember half of the cradlenames she smacked on them by the grace of her boxing bishop's[255] infallible slipper, the cane for Kund and abbles[256] for Eyolf[257] and ayther nayther for Yakov Yea. A hundred and how? They did well to rechristien her Pluhurabelle. O loreley![258] What a loddon[259] lodes! Heigh ho![260] But it's quite on the cards she'll shed more and merrier, twills[261] and trills,[262] sparefours and spoilfives,[263] nordsihkes and sudsevers[264] and ayes and neins[265] to a litter. Grandfarthring nap[266] and Messamisery[267] and the knave of all knaves and the joker. Heehaw! She must have been a gadabout in her day, so she must, more than most. Shoal[268] she was, gidgad.[269] She had a flewmen[270] of her owen. Then a toss nare scared that lass, so aimai moe, that's agapo![271] Tell me, tell me, how cam[272] she camlin[273] through all her fellows, the neckar[274] she was, the diveline?[275] Casting her perils before our swains[276] from Fonte-in-Monte[277] to Tidingtown[278] and from Tidingtown tilhavet.[279] Linking one and knocking the next, tapting[280] a flank and tipting a jutty[281] and palling in and pietaring[282] out and clyding[283] by on her eastway.[284] Waiwhou[285] was the first thurever[286] burst? Someone he was, whuebra[287] they were, in a tactic attack or in single combat. Tinker, tilar,[288]

140

145

150

[249] *in tool* A fusion of "at all" and "in tow."

[250] *Close* Maxwell Henry Close was an Irish author who wrote *Notes on the General Glaciation of the Rocks in the Neighbourhood of Dublin* (Dublin, s.n. 1864).

[251] *wan* Chinese for "10,000" or "a large number."

[252] *meanacuminamoyas* in Kiswahili, *mia na kumi na joja* means "one hundred and eleven."

[253] *Olaph lamm* punning on the Hebrew letters *aleph*, which also means "one," and *lamedh*, which also means 30. With the third Hebrew letter *pe* (in "pack"), which means "80," the total comes out to 111.

[254] *kirkeyaard* punning on "churchyard" and Søren Kierkegaard (1813–55), a Danish theologian.

[255] *boxing bishop's* the river Box flows by Boxford, in England; to "box the bishop" is slang for "to masturbate."

[256] *abbles* punning on apples and Abel, the second son of Adam and Eve. Cain, the first, has appeared a few words earlier as "cane."

[257] *Little Eyolf* (1894) is a late play by the Norwegian dramatist Henrik Ibsen (1820–1906). In the play, Alfred and Rita Allmers first lose their crippled child, Eyolf, who is lured to his death after the visit of an uncanny figure from folk legend, the Rat-Wife. The parents then descend into a hell of mutual recrimination and estrangement, realizing they loved neither their child nor each other.

[258] *loreley!* lorelei is one of the traditional sirens of the Rhine river, in Germany.

[259] *loddon* a merging of "lot of" with the river Loddon in Hampshire, England.

[260] *lodes! Heigh ho!* lodes are open ditches; *ho* suggests the Chinese word for "river."

[261] *twills* from the Danish word *twillinger*, meaning "twins."

[262] *trills* from the Danish word *trillinger*, meaning "triplets."

[263] *spoilfives* "spoil five" is a card game.

[264] *nordsihkes and sudsevers nord* is the French word for "north," *sud* for "south."

[265] *neins* the German for "no" is *nein*.

[266] *Grandfarthring nap* "farthing nap" is a card game.

[267] *Messa* is the Italian word for "mass," with punning here on "mess of," and on the Missouri River.

[268] *Shoal* punning on "sure" and the Shoal river in Florida.

[269] *gidgad* punning on "Egad!" and "good God!"

[270] *flewmen* punning on "few men" and the Latin word *flumen*, meaning "river."

[271] *so aimai moe, that's agapo!* punning on "Zoe mou, sas agapô," modern Greek for "My life, I love you," a phrase that is also the last line of the *Maid of Athens* by George Gordon, Lord Byron (1788–1824).

[272] *how cam* punning on the river Cam, which flows through Cambridge.

[273] *camlin* the river Camlin flows into the Shannon, in Ireland.

[274] *neckar* fusing the Neckar river, which flows through Stuttgart and Heidelberg and empties into the Rhine, with the German verb *necken*, "to tease."

[275] *the diveline* merging the phrase "little devil" into the little river Dive in Normandy (the site from which William the Conqueror famously set sail in 1066) and the aria "Casta diva" ("Chaste goddess") from the opera *Norma* (1831) by Vincenzo Bellini (1801–35).

[276] *Casting her perils before our swains* from the Sermon on the Mount, Matthew 7:6 "Give not that which is holy unto the dogs, neither cast ye your pearls before swine, lest they trample them under their feet, and turn again and rend you."

[277] *Fonte-in-Monte* Italian for a "spring in the mountain," the source of the Liffey, perhaps punning incidentally on the river Font in Northumberland, England

[278] *Tidingtown* punning on "tide" and perhaps on Teddington, England, since the river Thames is tidal up to that point.

[279] *tilhavet* the Danish words *til havet* mean "to the sea."

[280] *tapting* merging "Tapping" and the river Tapti in India, which flows through the city of Surat.

[281] *jutty* fusing a "jetty" with the river Jutai in Brazil.

[282] *pietaring* merging "petering out" with *pietra*, Italian for "stone."

[283] *clyding* merging "gliding" with the river Clyde in Scotland.

[284] *eastway* echoing the word "estuary," but also saying which way the Liffey flows.

[285] *Waiwhou* the Waihou river, located on North Island in New Zealand, is being fused with "why" and "who."

[286] *thurever* the first syllable, "thur," merges "there" and the river Thur in Switzerland.

[287] *whuebra* merging "whoever" and the river Huebra, which flows near the city of Salamanca in Spain.

[288] *tilar* punning on "tailor" and the Tilar mountain range in central America, and imitating the children's nursery rhyme about possible career paths: "Tinker, tailor, soldier, sailor, rich man, poor man, beggar man, thief."

souldrer,[289] salor, Pieman Peace[290] or Polistaman.[291] That's the thing I'm elwys[292] on edge to esk.[293] Push up and push vardar[294] and come to uphill headquarters![295] Was it waterlows[296] year, after Grattan or Flood,[297] or when maids were in Arc[298] or when three stood hosting? Fidaris[299] will find
155   where the Doubt[300] arises like Nieman[301] from Nirgends found the Nihil.[302] Worry you sighin foh, Albern, O Anser?[303] Untie the gemman's[304] fistiknots, Qvic and Nuancee![305] She can't put her hand on him for the moment. Tez[306] thelon langlo,[307] walking weary![308] Such a loon[309] waybashwards[310] to row! She sid[311] herself she hardly knows whuon[312] the annals her graveller[313] was, a dynast of Leinster,[314] a wolf[315] of the sea, or what he did or how blyth[316] she played or how, when, why, where
160   and who offon[317] he jumpnad[318] her and how it was gave her away. She was just a young thin pale soft shy slim slip of a thing then, sauntering, by silvamoonlake[319] and he was a heavy trudging lurching lieabroad of a Curraghman,[320] making his hay[321] for whose sun to shine on, as tough as the oaktrees (peats[322] be with them!) used to rustle that time down by the dykes of killing Kildare,[323] for forstfellfoss[324] with a plash across her. She thought she's sankh[325] neathe[326] the ground with
165   nymphant shame when he gave her the tigris[327] eye! O happy fault! Me wish it was he! You're wrong there, corribly[328] wrong! Tisn't only tonight you're anacheronistic![329] It was ages behind that when nullahs[330] were nowhere, in county Wickenlow,[331] garden of Erin, before she ever dreamt she'd lave Kilbride[332] and go foaming under Horsepass bridge,[333] with the great southerwestern

[289] *souldrer* merging "soldier," "soul," and the Sauldre river in the Loire valley, about a hundred miles south of Paris.
[290] *Pieman Peace* punning on the Pieman river in Tasmania, Australia, and Alexander "Pieman" Pearce (1790–1822). In 1820 Alexander Pearce was sentenced to prison in Van Diemen's Land (now Tasmania) for stealing six pairs of shoes, and in 1822, together with six other convicts, he escaped. When the men became lost, they cannibalized one another until Pearce was the only survivor; the Pieman river is named after him, because he used to be a "pie man" back in County Armagh, now Northern Ireland.
[291] *Polistaman* conflating "policeman" and the Polista river in northwest Russia.
[292] *elwys* fusing "always" with the river Elwy in north Wales.
[293] *esk* merging "ask" with the river Esk in Scotland.
[294] *vardar* fusing "harder" and "farther" with the Vardar river in what is now Macedonia.
[295] *headquarters* punning on "headwaters."
[296] *waterlows* punning on "low water," the battle of Waterloo (June 1815), and the name of Sir Ernest Albert Waterlow (1850–1919), English landscape and animal painter.
[297] *Grattan or Flood* Henry Grattan (1746–1820) and Henry Flood (1732–91) were Irish patriots and statesmen.
[298] *Arc* Joan of Arc merging with the river Arc near Aix in southern France.
[299] *Fidaris* punning on the Latin word *fides*, or faith.
[300] *Doubt* punning on the river Doubs, in western Switzerland and eastern France.
[301] *Nieman* punning on the Niemen or Neman river, which begins in Belarus and flows through Lithuania into the Baltic, and German *niemand*, or "nobody."
[302] *Nirgends ... Nihil* German word for "nowhere," Latin word for "nothing," with perhaps the Nile river a latent presence.
[303] *Albern, O Anser?* "Albern" is the German word for "silly," *anser* the Latin for "goose."
[304] *gemman's* a "gemman" is a slang variant of a "gentleman."
[305] *Nuancee* punning on the river Nuanetsi in Zimbabwe.
[306] *Tez* phonetic rendering of the Tees river in northern England.
[307] *thelon langlo* the Thelon river in Canada flows into Hudson Bay; the Langlo river is found in Queensland, Australia.
[308] *weary* perhaps enclosing the river Wear, in counties Durham and Tyne and Wear, England.
[309] *loon* blending "long" with the Loon river in Canada.
[310] *waybashwards* "way backwards" fused with the Wabash river in Indiana.
[311] *sid* "said" has been conflated with the river Sid in east Devon, England, which flows into the sea at Sidmouth.
[312] *whuon* "who in" being fused the the Huon river in Tasmania, Australia.
[313] *graveller* the Gravelly river is in Virginia.
[314] *dynast of Leinster* Diarmaid MacNurchadha, King of Leinster, whose patronymic means "sea warrior."
[315] *wolf* the river Wolf flows through Devon in southwest England.
[316] *blyth* the river Blyth is in Northumberland, England.
[317] *offon* punning with "off" and "on," "often," and the Ofin river in Ghana.
[318] *jumpnad* incorporating the Jumna river in northern India.
[319] *silvamoonlake* merging "silver moonlight" with the Silva river in the Urals in Russia, and with the Latin word *silva* or "forest."
[320] *Curraghman* the Curragh of Kildare is a racecourse.
[321] *hay* the Hay river is in the Northwest Territories, Canada.
[322] *peats* punning on "peace."
[323] *Kildare* means "church of the oak."
[324] *forstfellfoss* combining German *Forst* for "forest" with Danish *fossefald*, and both with the river Foss, which debouches into the river Ouse at York, England.
[325] *sankh* blending "sank" with the Sankh river in India.
[326] *neathe* merging "neath" and the river Neath in southwest Wales.
[327] *tigris* conflating "tiger's" with the river Tigris in modern Iraq.
[328] *corribly* blending "horribly" with the river Corrib in Galway, Ireland.
[329] *anacheronistic* "anachronistic" merged with "Acheron," a river in the underworld in Greek mythology.
[330] *nullahs* Latin *nulla*, meaning "none," together with the Rio Nula in Venezuela.
[331] *county Wickenlow* County Wicklow, known as "the garden of Ireland," and the place where the Liffey springs from the hills.
[332] *Kilbride*, on the river Brittas in County Wicklow; the Brittas flows into the Liffey.
[333] *Horsepass bridge* a bridge over the Liffey river.

windstorming her traces[334] and the midland's grain-waster asarch[335] for her track, to wend her ways byandby, robecca[336] or worse, to spin and to grind, to swab and to thrash, for all her golden lifey[337]   170
in the barleyfields[338] and pennylotts[339] of Humphrey's[340] fordofhurdlestown and lie with a land-leaper,[341] wellingtonorseher.[342] Alesse,[343] the lagos[344] of girly days! For the dove[345] of the dunas![346]
Wasut? Izod?[347] Are you sarthin suir?[348] Not where the Finn fits into the Mourne,[349] not where the Nore takes lieve of Blœm,[350] not where the Braye divarts the Farer,[351] not where the Moy changez her minds twixt Cullin and Conn tween Cunn and Collin?[352] Or where Neptune sculled and   175
Tritonville rowed[353] and leandros three bumped heroines[354] two? Neya, narev, nen, nonni, nos![355] Then whereabouts in Ow and Ovoca?[356] Was it yst with wyst[357] or Lucan Yokan[358] or where the hand of man has never set foot? Dell me where, the fairy ferse[359] time! I will if you listen. You know the dinkel dale[360] of Luggelaw?[361] Well, there once dwelt a local heremite, Michael Arklow was his riverend name, (with many a sigh I aspersed his lavabibs![362]) and one venersderg[363] in junojuly, oso   180
sweet and so cool and so limber she looked, Nance the Nixie, Nanon L'Escaut,[364] in the silence, of the sycomores, all listening, the kindling curves you simply can't stop feeling, he plunged both of his newly anointed hands, the core of his cushlas,[365] in her singimari[366] saffron strumans[367] of hair, parting them and soothing her and mingling it, that was deepdark and ample like this red bog at sundown. By that Vale Vowclose's lucydlac,[368] the reignbeau's heavenarches arronged orranged[369]   185
her. Afrothdizzying[370] galbs, her enamelled eyes indergoading[371] him on to the vierge violetian.[372]

---

[334] *traces* incorporating "tresses."

[335] *asarch* "a search" and the Asat river.

[336] *robecca* conflation of "Rebeccca" and the Robec river, a fictional name used by François Rabelais (c. 1494–1553) in *Gargantua and Pantagruel* (1532–55).

[337] *lifey* incorporating the river Liffey.

[338] *barleyfields* Barley-fields is the site of the Rotunda in Dublin.

[339] *pennylotts* "pennylands," or lands valued at 1 penny a year.

[340] *Humphrey's* Humphreystown Bridge, near Poulaphouca.

[341] *landleaper* punning on "landlubbers" and Land-Leaguers, members of the Irish Land League (formed in the 1870s) who sought better conditions for tenant farmers in Ireland.

[342] *wellingtonorseher* "willing to nurse her" fused with Wellington Quay in Dublin.

[343] *Alesse* a fusion of Alice and the river Lesse in France and Belgium.

[344] *lagos* the Lagos river in Portugal.

[345] *dove* the dove is the symbol of the Holy Ghost and name of the river Dove in Derbyshire, England.

[346] *dunas* merging "dunes" and the river Duna, which is south of Riga, Latvia.

[347] *Wasut? Izod?* punning on "Was ist? Isolde?" ("What is it? Isolde?"), the first words sung by Tristan in the opera *Tristan and Isolde* (1865) by Richard Wagner (1813–83).

[348] *sarthin suir* blending "certain sure" with the rivers Sarthe (in midwestern France) and Suir (in Ireland).

[349] *Finn ... Mourne* the rivers Finn, in county Donegal, Ireland, and Mourne, in France.

[350] *Nore .. lieve of Blœm* the river Nore, in County Kilkenny, Ireland, descends from Slieve Bloom, a mountain; in Dutch *bloem* means flower.

[351] *Braye ... Farer* the river Braye is in France; John Dryden (1631–1700), in his poem "Alexander's Feast," writes: "None but the brave deserves the fair."

[352] *the Moy ... Cullin and Conn* the Moy drains Lough Cullin, rather than nearby Lough Conn.

[353] *Tritonville rowed* Tritonville Road, a street in Dublin; Triton is a son of Neptune.

[354] *Leandros ... heroines* allusion to "Hero and Leander," the poem by Christopher Marlowe (1564–93) which recounts an ancient tale about Leander repeatedly swimming across the Hel-

lespont for trysts with his beloved Hero, until he is finally drowned and she commits suicide.

[355] *Neya, narev, nen, nonni, nos!* the Neya river is in Japan; the Narev river in Poland, north of Warsaw; the Nen and Noni are two names for the same river in China; the Nos is a river in Norway.

[356] *Ow and Ovoca* the Ow river is in County Wicklow, Ireland; the Avoca in Victoria, Australia.

[357] *yst with wyst* punning on "east with west" and the river Ystwith in Wales.

[358] *Yokan* fusing the Yukon river in Alaska with the Yokanga in Russia.

[359] *fairy ferse* punning on "very first time."

[360] *dinkel dale* the river Dinkel is at the border of the Netherlands and Germany.

[361] *Luggelaw* or Lough Tay is in Ireland.

[362] *aspersed his lavabibs* or: "sprinkled his lava beds."

[363] *venersderg* a fusion of *dies veneris*, Latin for "day of Venus" or Friday, with the river Derg in Ireland, which runs south from the famous pilgrimage site of Lough Derg.

[364] *Nanon L'Escaut* Manon Lescaut is a beautiful young woman, whether in the novel *Aventures du Chevalier des Grieux et de Manon Lescaut* (1734) by the Abbé Antoine-François Prévost (1697–1763) or the opera *Manon Lescaut* (1893) by the Italian composer Giacomo Puccini (1858–1924). The river Escaut flows through France, Belgium, and the Netherlands.

[365] *cushlas* Anglo-Irish for "pulses."

[366] *singimari* a river in what is now Bangladesh.

[367] *strumans* "streams" merged with the river Struma (in Bulgaria) and perhaps with *struma*, medical term for a swelling.

[368] *Vale Vowcloses's lucydlac* the Vaucluse, the valley where Petrarch lived, is traversed by the river Vaucluse; "lucydlac," punning on "lucid" and "Lucy" (patron saint of eyes), together with the French word for "lake," *lac*.

[369] *orranged* the Orange river is in Africa between Namibia and South Africa.

[370] *Afrothdizzying* punning on "aphrodisiac."

[371] *galbs ... indergoading* in Latin, *galbus* is yellow; "indigo" is being turned into more puns.

[372] *vierge violetian vierge* is the French word for virgin; "violet" is being fused with "violation."

Wish a wish! Why a why? Mavro![373] Letty Lerck's lafing light throw those laurals now on her daphdaph[374] teasesong petrock. Maass! But the majik wavus has elfun[375] anon meshes. And Simba the Slayer of his Oga[376] is slewd. He cuddle not help himself, thurso[377] that hot on him, he had to
190 forget the monk in the man so, rubbing her up and smoothing her down, he baised[378] his lippes[379] in smiling mood, kiss akiss after kisokushk[380] (as he warned her niver to, niver to, nevar[381]) on Anna-na-Poghue's[382] of the freckled forehead. While you'd parse secheressa[383] she hielt[384] her souff.[385] But she ruz two feet hire in her aisne[386] aestumation.[387] And steppes on stilts ever since. That was kissuahealing[388] with bantur for balm! O, wasn't he the bold priest? And wasn't she the
195 naughty Livvy? Nautic Naama's now her navn.[389] Two lads in scoutsch breeches went through her before that, Barefoot Burn and Wallowme Wade, Lugnaquillia's[390] noblesse pickts, before she had a hint of a hair at her fanny[391] to hide or a bossom to tempt a birch canoedler[392] not to mention a bulgic porterhouse barge. And ere that again, leada, laida,[393] all unraidy, too faint to buoy the fairiest rider, too frail to flirt with a cygnet's[394] plume, she was licked by a hound,
200 Chirripa[395]-Chirruta, while poing[396] her pee, pure and simple, on the spur of the hill in old Kippure,[397] in birdsong and shearingtime, but first of all, worst of all, the wiggly livvly, she sideslipped out by a gap in the Devil's glen[398] while Sally her nurse was sound asleep in a sloot[399] and, feefee fiefie, fell over a spillway before she found her stride and lay and wriggled in all the stagnant black pools[400] of rainy under a fallow coo and she laughed innocefree[401] with her limbs
205 aloft and a whole drove of maiden hawthorns blushing and looking askance upon her.
    Drop me the sound of the findhorn's[402] name, Mtu or Mti,[403] sombogger was wisness. And drip me why in the flenders[404] was she frickled. And trickle me through was she marcellewaved[405] or was it weirdly a wig she wore. And whitside did they droop their glows in their florry,[406] aback to wist or affront to sea? In fear to hear the dear so near or longing loth and loathing longing? Are you in
210 the swim or are you out? O go in, go on, go an! I mean about what you know. I know right well what you mean. Rother![407] You'd like the coifs and guimpes,[408] snouty, and me to do the greasy jub

---

[373] *Mavro!* modern Greek for "black," perhaps because it combines all the previously mentioned colors.

[374] *laurals ... daphdaph* Laura, the addressee of Petrach's sonnets (see n. 368); "daphdaph," from Daphne, who is turned into a laurel tree when she tries to escape the god Apollo, as told in Ovid's *Metamorphoses* I, 452–567.

[375] *majik wavus ... elfun* from Kiswahili words *maji*, meaning "water," *wavu*, meaning "net," and *elfu*, meaning "one thousand."

[376] *Simba ... Oga* Kiswahili for "lion." *Oga* is Kiswahili for "to bathe," while the Ogi river flows through Nagoya in Japan.

[377] *thurso* the Thurso is a river in the Highlands in Scotland.

[378] *baised* from the French verb *baiser*, "to kiss."

[379] *lippes* enclosing the river Lippe, in Germany.

[380] *kisokushk* the river Kiso in Japan and the Kushk river in Afghanistan and Turkmenistan.

[381] *niver ... nevar* the rivers Nive, in southwestern France, and Neva, which flows through St. Petersburg in Russia.

[382] *Anna-na-Poghue's* ringing changes on *Arrah-na-pogue, or the Wicklow Wedding* (1864), by the Irish playwright Dion Boucicault (1822–90), a melodramatic play. The heroine, Arrah Meelish, became known as Arrah of the Kiss from her method of passing a letter with escape plans to her foster brother in prison, which is recounted in the next two lines.

[383] *parse secheressa* literally "pass secrets," but with a pun on French *secheresse*, or "dryness."

[384] *hielt* German for "hold."

[385] *souff souffle* is French for "breath."

[386] *aisne* a very small river in Belgium.

[387] *aestumation* Latin *aestus* or "undulating," merged with *tum-*, the root of Latin words such as *tumesco* and *tumidus*, respectively meaning "to swell" or "swollen," and both flowing into *estimation*.

[388] *kissuahealing* punning on the language Kiswahili.

[389] *navn* Danish word for "name."

[390] *Lugnaquillia's* highest summit in the Wicklow Mountains, where the Liffey first begins.

[391] *fanny* slang for "cunt."

[392] *canoedler* "canoodle" was a colloquialism for "to fondle."

[393] *leada, laida* Leda and the swan, and *leider*, the German word for "unfortunately," which sounds like "laida."

[394] *cygnet's* the Cygnet River is located in Australia.

[395] *Chirripa* from the Chirropo river in Costa Rica, inflected by the Italian word *ripa*, for "bank" or "shore."

[396] *poing* the river Po in northern Italy, overlaid on "doing."

[397] *Kippure* the headwaters of the Liffey are near Mt. Kippure.

[398] *Devil's Glen* is on the river Vartry in County Wicklow, where Act II of *Arrah-na-Pogue* takes place (see note 382 above).

[399] *sloot* a sloout or sluit is a channel, ditch, or gully.

[400] *black pools* the word "Dublin" means "black pool."

[401] *innocefree* Innisfree is a tiny island in Lough Gill in County Sligo, Ireland.

[402] *findhorn* the river Findhorn is in Scotland.

[403] *Mtu or Mti* Kiswahili for "man" and "tree," respectively.

[404] *flenders* the Flinders river is in northeast Australia.

[405] *marcellewaved* a marcel was a deep, soft wave made in hair with a curling iron, named after Marcel Grateau (1852–1936), who invented the appropriate iron.

[406] *glows in their florry* "clothes in their flurry," embedded in puns.

[407] *Rother!* the river Rother is in Sussex, England.

[408] *guimpes* French for a nun's wimple or a tucker.

on old Veronica's wipers.[409] What am I rancing[410] now and I'll thank you? Is it a pinny or is it a surplice? Arran, where's your nose? And where's the starch? That's not the vesdre[411] benediction smell. I can tell from here by their *eau de Colo*[412] and the scent of her oder they're Mrs Magrath's. And you ought to have aird[413] them. They've moist come off her. Creases in silk they are, not   215 crampton lawn. Baptiste me,[414] father, for she has sinned! Through her catchment ring she freed them easy, with her hips' hurrahs[415] for her knees'dontelleries.[416] The only parr[417] with frills in old the plain. So they are, I declare! Welland[418] well! If tomorrow keeps fine who'll come tripping to sightsee? How'll? Ask me next what I haven't got! The Belvedarean exhibitioners.[419] In their cruisery caps and oarsclub colours. What hoo, they band! And what hoa, they buck![420] And here is   220 her nubilee[421] letters too. Ellis on quay in scarlet thread. Linked for the world on a flushcaloured field. Annan exe[422] after to show they're not Laura Keown's.[423] O, may the diabolo twisk[424] your seifety[425] pin! You child of Mammon, Kinsella's Lilith![426] Now who has been tearing the leg of her drawars on her? Which leg is it? The one with the bells on it. Rinse them out and aston along[427] with you! Where did I stop? Never stop! Continuarration! You're not there yet. I amstel[428] waiting.   225 Garonne, garonne![429]

Well, after it was put in the Mericy[430] Cordial Mendicants' Sitterdag-Zindeh-Munaday[431] Wakeschrift[432] (for once they sullied their white kidloves, chewing cuds after their dinners of cheeckin and beggin, with their show us it here and their mind out of that and their when you're quite finished with the reading matarial), even the snee that snowdon[433] his hoaring hair had a   230 skunner against[434] him. Thaw, thaw, sava, savuto![435] Score Her Chuff Exsquire! Everywhere erriff[436] you went and every bung you arver dropped into, in cit or suburb or in addled areas, the Rose and Bottle[437] or Phoenix Tavern or Power's Inn or Jude's Hotel[438] or wherever you scoured the countryside from Nannywater[439] to Vartryville or from Porta Lateen to the lootin quarter[440] you found his ikom[441] etsched[442] tipside down or the cornerboys[443] cammocking[444] his guy and Morris   235 the Man, with the role of a royss in his turgos the turrible,[445] (Evropeahahn[446]cheic house,

---

[409] *Veronica's wipers* Veronica was a woman of Jerusalem who, filled with compassion at the sight of Jesus suffering on his way to Calvary, wiped his sweating face with a cloth. Miraculously, an image of his features was left on the cloth.

[410] *rancing* "rincing" assimilated to the river Rance in western France, which ends at St. Malo.

[411] *vesdre* "vestry" assimilated to the river Vesdre in France, which flows into the Meuse.

[412] *eau de Colo* the Colo river is near Sydney, Australia.

[413] *aird* Aird rivers are found in New Guinea and Australia.

[414] *Baptiste me* the Baptiste river is in Alberta, Canada.

[415] *hips' hurrahs* punning on hip hip hurray.

[416] *dontelleries* "don't-tell-eries" with French *dentelle*, or "lace."

[417] *parr* "pair" conflated with the Paar river in Germany, which flows past Augsburg and into the Danube.

[418] *Welland* a river in the eastern Midlands, England.

[419] *Belvedarean exhibitioners* from Belvedere College, Dublin; exhibitioners were boys who'd won exhibitions in a secondary school exam.

[420] *What hoa, they buck* "What ho, She Bumps" was a popular song.

[421] *nubilee* "Jubilee" and "nubile" with the river Nuble in Chile.

[422] *Annan exe* the river Annan is in Scotland, the river Exe flows through Somerset and Devon, England.

[423] *Keown's* the Keowee River is in South Carolina.

[424] *twisk* the river Wiske is in Yorkshire, England.

[425] *seifety* conflation of German *Seife*, "soap," and safety.

[426] *Lilith* Adam's wife before Eve in Kabbalistic lore.

[427] *aston along* "hasten along" and Aston Quay, Dublin.

[428] *amstel* "am still" merged into the Amstel river which flows into Amsterdam.

[429] *Garonne* "go own" elided into the Garonne river, in southern France.

[430] *Mericy Meriç*, French name for the Evros, the river separating Greece and Turkey.

[431] *Sitterdag-Zindeh-Munaday* Zindeh is supposed to be the name of a river.

[432] *Wakeschrift* punning on the German word *Wochenschrift*, a weekly publication.

[433] *snee that snowdon* Danish *sne*, meaning "snow"; snowdon, or "snowed on," with a reference to Mt. Snowdon in England.

[434] *had a skunner against* Scottish expression, "was disgusted with." Or: "Even the snow that snowed on his hair was disgusted with him."

[435] *sava, savuto* the Sava river flows through Slovenia, Bosnia, Serbia, and Croatia; the Savuto is located in Calabria, Italy.

[436] *erriff* the Erriff is a river in Ireland.

[437] *Rose and Bottle* a pub on Dame Sreet, Dublin.

[438] *Phoenix Tavern or Power's Inn or Jude's Hotel* Dublin pubs located respectively on Werburgh Street, Booterstown, and South Frederick Street.

[439] *Nannywater* Nanny Water, a brook near Balbriggan, not far from Dublin; the river Vartry runs in County Wicklow, Ireland.

[440] *Porta Lateen to the lootin quarter* Porta Latina in Rome, the Latin Quarter in Paris.

[441] *ikom* icon.

[442] *etsched* "etched," but incorporating the Etsch river in northern Italy, near Bolzano.

[443] *cornerboys* slang for loafers.

[444] *cammocking* "mocking," but fused with the Cammock River near Dublin.

[445] *royss in his turgos the turrible* the actor Edward William Royce (1841–1926) played the lead character in the pantomime *Turko the Terrible* (1873) at the Gaiety Theatre in Dublin.

[446] *Evro-* the river Evros forms the boundary between Turkey and Greece.

unskimmed sooit and yahoort,[447] hamman[448] now cheekmee, Ahdahm this way make, Fatima,[449] half turn!) reeling and railing round the local as the peihos[450] piped und ubanjees[451] twanged, with oddfellow's triple tiara[452] busby rotundarinking[453] round his scalp. Like Pate-by-the-Neva[454] or

240   Pete-over-Meer.[455] This is the Hausman all paven and stoned, that cribbed the Cabin that never was owned that cocked his leg and hennad his Egg.[456] And the mauldrin[457] rabble around him in areopage,[458] fracassing a great bingkan cagnan with their timpan[459] crowders.[460] Mind your Grimm-father! Think of your Ma![461] Hing the Hong[462] is his jove's hangnomen![463] Lilt a bolero, bulling a law![464] She swore on croststyx[465] nyne wyndabouts[466] she's be level with all the snags[467] of them

245   yet. Par the Vulnerable Virgin's Mary del Dame![468] So she said to herself she'd frame a plan to fake a shine, the mischiefmaker, the like of it you niever[469] heard. What plan? Tell me quick and dongu so crould![470] What the meurther[471] did she mague?[472] Well, she bergened[473] a zakbag,[474] a shammy mailsack, with the lend of a loan of the light of his lampion,[475] off one of her swapsons, Shaun the Post,[476] and then she went and consulted her chapboucqs, old Mot Moore,[477] Casey's Euclid[478] and

250   the Fashion Display and made herself tidal[479] to join in the mascarete.[480] O gig goggle of gigguels.[481] I can't tell you how! It's too screaming to rizo,[482] rabbit it[483] all! Minneha,[484] minnehi minaaehe, minneho! O but you must, you must really! Make my hear it gurgle gurgle, like the farest gargle gargle in the dusky dirgle dargle![485] By the holy well of Mulhuddart[486] I swear I'd pledge my chanza[487] getting to heaven through Tirry[488] and Killy's mount of impiety[489] to hear it all,

255   aviary word! O, leave me my faculties, woman, a while! If you don't like my story get out of the punt. Well, have it your own way, so. Here, sit down and do as you're bid. Take my stroke and bend

---

[447]   *sooit and yahoort* suet and yoghurt, with a French inflection, *yaourt*.
[448]   *hamman* Persian for "bath."
[449]   *Fatima* Mohammed's daughter, but here any attractive woman from the Middle East.
[450]   *peihos* the Peiho river is in China.
[451]   *ubanjees* banjos conflated with the Ubangi river, a tributary of the Congo in Africa.
[452]   *triple tiara* the papal tiara turning on his scalp.
[453]   *rotundarinking* the Rotunda, in Dublin, was used as a skating rink in the late nineteenth century.
[454]   *Neva* the river that flows through St. Petersburg, Russia.
[455]   *Meer* Dutch word for "lake."
[456]   *This is . . . his Egg* adaptation of the nursery rhyme: "This is the priest all shave and shorn, that married the man all tattered and torn, that tossed the dog that worried the cat."
[457]   *mauldrin* "maudlin," incorporating the river Mauldre which flows into the Seine in France.
[458]   *areopage* "rage" and "rampag" merged into the Areopagus, the supreme court in Athens.
[459]   *timpan* conflation of tin pan and timpani.
[460]   *crowders* dialect for "fiddlers."
[461]   *Ma* the Ma river is in northern Vietnam.
[462]   *the Hong* the Hong river is in Vietnam.
[463]   *hangnomen* an agnomen was a name added to the family name, usually to commemorate some exploit, in this case being hanged.
[464]   *Lilt a bolero, bulling a law!* "Lillibullero, bullen a law" has been a popular song for hundreds of years.
[465]   *corststyx* punning on acrostics, crucifix, or "cross-Styx," the river in the underworld.
[466]   *wyndabouts* a wynd is a narrow cross-street.
[467]   *snags* Anglo-Irish for "gangs."
[468]   *Mary del Dame* a Dublin church, no longer extant.
[469]   *niever* "never" fused with the Nievre river in central France.
[470]   *dongu so crould* a fusion of "don't go so cruel" and the Dungo river in the Congo.

[471]   *what the meurther* "what the murder" fused with the Meurthe river, which flows into the Moselle near Nancy in northeastern France.
[472]   *mague* "make" assimilated to the river Mague in County Limerick, Ireland.
[473]   *bergened* a coinage from Dutch *bergen*, meaning "to store, to put," and German *borgen*, a verb meaning "to borrow."
[474]   *zakbag* from the Dutch world *zak*, meaning "sack," fused with the Zak river in South Africa.
[475]   *lampion* a lampion was a lamp, usually of colored glass.
[476]   *Shaun the Post* Sean is a postman in the play *Arrah-na-Pogue* by Dion Boucicault; see note 382 above.
[477]   *Moore* the Moore river is in western Australia.
[478]   *Casey's Euclid* John Casey (1820–91) was the author of *A Sequel to the First Six Books of the Elements of Euclid*, 4th ed. (Dublin: Hodges, Figgis, 1886).
[479]   *tidal* punning on "tidy."
[480]   *mascarete* punning on "masquerade" and the French word *mascaret*, which designates a "tidal wave in an estuary."
[481]   *gigguels* punning on the Giguela river in Spain.
[482]   *rizo* means a "curl" in Spanish, while *riso* is a "laugh" in Italian.
[483]   *rabbit it* slang for "confound it!"
[484]   *Minneha* Minnehaha is the young maid loved by the Amerindian warrior Hiawatha in *Song of Hiawatha* (Boston: Ticknor and Fields, 1855), a long poem by the American author Henry Wadsworth Longfellow (1807–82).
[485]   *dargle* the river Dargle flows through Ireland into the Sea of Bray.
[486]   *Mulhuddart* a village near the river Olka in Ireland, which had a well that was much frequented on the Nativity of the Blessed Virgin Mary.
[487]   *chanza* "chance of" assimilated to the Chanza river in Portugal.
[488]   *Tirry* the river Tirry flows into Loch Sin in northern Scotland.
[489]   *mount of impiety* in French *mont-de-pieté* ("Mount of Piety") is the term designating a pawnshop.

to your bow. Forward in and pull your overthepoise! Lisp it slaney and crisp it quiet. Deel me long-
some. Tongue your time now. Breathe thet deep. Thouat's the fairway. Hurry slow and scheldt you
go. Lynd us your blessed ashes here till I scrub the canon's underpants. Flow now. Ower more. And
pooleypooley. [. . .]⁴⁹⁰   260

Well, you know or don't you kennet⁴⁹¹ or haven't I told you every telling has a taling⁴⁹² and that's
the he and the she of it. Look, look, the dusk is growing! My branches lofty are taking root. And my
cold cher's⁴⁹³ gone ashley.⁴⁹⁴ Fieluhr?⁴⁹⁵ Filou!⁴⁹⁶ What age is at? It saon⁴⁹⁷ is late. 'Tis endless now
senne⁴⁹⁸ eye or erewone⁴⁹⁹ last saw Waterhouse's clogh.⁵⁰⁰ They took it asunder, I hurd thum sigh.
When will they reassemble it? O, my back, my back, my bach!⁵⁰¹ I'd want to go to Aches-les-   265
Pains.⁵⁰² Pingpong!⁵⁰³ There's the Belle⁵⁰⁴ for Sexaloitez!⁵⁰⁵ And Concepta de Send-us-pray!⁵⁰⁶
Pang!⁵⁰⁷ Wring out the clothes! Wring in the dew!⁵⁰⁸ Godavari,⁵⁰⁹ vert the showers! And grant
thaya⁵¹⁰ grace! Aman.⁵¹¹ Will we spread them here now? Ay, we will. Flip! Spread on your bank and
I'll spread mine on mine. Flep! It's what I'm doing. Spread! It's churning⁵¹² chill. Der went⁵¹³ is
rising. I'll lay a few stones on the hostel sheets. A man and his bride embraced⁵¹⁴ between them.   270
Else I'd have sprinkled and folded them only. And I'll tie my butcher's apron here. It's suety yet.
The strollers will pass it by. Six shifts, ten kerchiefs, nine to hold to the fire and this for the code,
the convent napkins, twelve, one baby's shawl.⁵¹⁵ Good mother Jossiph knows, she said. Whose
head? Mutter⁵¹⁶ snores? Deataceas!⁵¹⁷ Wharnow⁵¹⁸ are alle her childer, say? In kingdome gone or
power to come or gloria be to them farther?⁵¹⁹ Allalivial, allalluvial!⁵²⁰ Some here, more no more,   275
more again lost⁵²¹ alla stranger.⁵²² I've heard tell that same brooch of the Shannons⁵²³ was married
into a family in Spain. And all the Dunders de Dunnes in Markland's Vineland⁵²⁴ beyond Brendan's
herring pool takes number nine in yangsee's⁵²⁵ hats. And one of Biddy's beads went bobbing till she

⁴⁹⁰ Textual omission described in the "Introduction."

⁴⁹¹ *kennet* "ken it" (know) and the river Kennet in Wiltshire,
England.

⁴⁹² *taling* "tailing" or ending; but inflected by the river Taling,
in Thailand.

⁴⁹³ *cher* "chair," but punning on French *cher* or "dear."

⁴⁹⁴ *ashley* the Ashley river is in South Carolina.

⁴⁹⁵ *Fieluhr?* a truncation of *wieviel uhr?*, or "what time is it?" in
German, spelled to accommodate the Fie river in Guinea.

⁴⁹⁶ *Filou!* French for a "crook" or "scoundrel." The joke goes
that a Frenchman, shouting across the Rhine, cries out "Filou!,"
and that a passing German on the other side shouts back "wieviel
Urh?"

⁴⁹⁷ *soan* "soon," but inflected to evoke the Saône river in eastern
France, which flows into the Rhone.

⁴⁹⁸ *senne* "since," but altered to accommodate the Senne river,
which flows through Brussels, in Belgium.

⁴⁹⁹ *erewone* the novel *Erewhon* (1872), a utopian satire, was
written by English author Samuel Butler (1835–1902).

⁵⁰⁰ *Waterhouse's clogh* a clock that was outside the premises of a
goldsmith, silversmith, jeweler, and watch-maker on Dame
Street, a thoroughfare in central Dublin just south of the Liffey.
Clogh is the Irish word for clock.

⁵⁰¹ *bach!* German word for "stream" or "brook."

⁵⁰² *Aches-les-Pains* punning on Aix-les-Bains, in France.

⁵⁰³ *Pingpong* combining the Ping river in Thailand with the
Pongo in Chile.

⁵⁰⁴ *Belle* the Belle river is in Ontario, Canada; rhyming with
the bell that rings for the Angelus at 6 o'clock (see next note).

⁵⁰⁵ *Sexaloitez* Sechseläuten ("Six Chimes") is a spring festival
held in Zurich, Switzerland, on the third Sunday of April. A
parade carries a straw effigy of winter, called a Böögg, through
the city to Sechseläutenwies ("Six Chimes Field") opposite the
opera house, where the effigy is placed atop a stack of combustible materials. At 6 o'clock precisely, the bonfire is ignited. The
faster the Böögg burns, the warmer the coming summer will be.

⁵⁰⁶ *Concepta de Send-us-pray* spoken in the Angelus service: "et
concepit de Spiritu Sancti" ("and she conceived of the Holy
Ghost")

⁵⁰⁷ *Pang!* the river Pang joins the Thames at Pangbourne.

⁵⁰⁸ *Wring out . . . the dew!* Alfred Tennyson (1809–93) wrote
"Ring Out, Wild Bells," which contains the line: "Ring out the
Old, ring in the New!"

⁵⁰⁹ *Godavari* the Godavari river is in central India.

⁵¹⁰ *thaya* the Thaya river meanders back and forth across the
border between Austria and the Czech Republic.

⁵¹¹ *Aman* the river Amana is in Papua New Guinea.

⁵¹² *churning* "turning" blended with the river Church, which
flows south from Gloucestershire into the Thames.

⁵¹³ *Der went* the Derwent river is in Yorkshire, England.

⁵¹⁴ *embraced* slang for "copulated."

⁵¹⁵ *Six shifts . . . baby's shawl* there are 39 articles, like the 39
Articles of the Church of England.

⁵¹⁶ *Mutter* german for "mother."

⁵¹⁷ *Deataceas!* Dea, taceas, "Goddess, may you be still" in Latin.

⁵¹⁸ *Wharnow* "where now," inflected by the river Warnow in
Germany.

⁵¹⁹ *In kingdome gone . . . farther* from the Lord's Prayer: "Thy
kingdom come . . . the power and the glory . . . Glory be to the
father."

⁵²⁰ *Allalivial, allalluvial* punning on alleluia, with "Livia" and
"alluvial," and with *lluvia*, Spanish for "rain."

⁵²¹ *lost* the Lost River is in the White Mountains in New
Hampshire.

⁵²² *alla stranger* French, *à l'étranger*, abroad.

⁵²³ *Shannons* the Shannon river flows through 11 counties in
Ireland.

⁵²⁴ *Markland's Vineland* Markland and Vinland, in Old Norse,
are parts of North America.

⁵²⁵ *yangsee's* The Yangtze river in China.

rounded up lost histereve[526] with a marigold and a cobbler's candle in a side strain of a main[527] drain
of a manzinahurries[528] off Bachelor's Walk.[529] But all that's left to the last of the Meaghers in the
loup of the years[530] prefixed and between is one kneebuckle and two hooks in the front. Do you tell
me that now? I do in troth. Orara por Orbe and poor Las Animas![531] Ussa, Ulla, we're umbas all!
Mezha,[532] didn't you hear it a deluge of times, ufer and ufer,[533] respund to spond?[534] You deed,[535] you
deed! I need, I need! It's that irrawaddyng[536] I've stoke in my aars.[537] It all but husheth the lethest[538]
zswound. Oronoko![539] What's your trouble? Is that the great Finnleader[540] himself in his joakimono[541] on his statue riding the high horse there forehengist? Father of Otters, it is himself! Yonne
there! Isset that?[542] On Fallareen Common?[543] You're thinking of Astley's Amphitheayter[544] where
the bobby restrained you making sugarstuck pouts to the ghostwhite horse of the Peppers.[545]
Throw the cobwebs from your eyes, woman, and spread your washing proper! It's well I know
your sort of slop. Flap! Ireland sober is Ireland stiff.[546] Lord help you, Maria, full of grease, the load
is with me![547] Your prayers. I sonht zo! Madammangut![548] Were you lifting your elbow, tell us,
glazy cheeks, in Conway's Carrigacurra[549] canteen? Was I what, hobbledyhips? Flop! Your rere gait's
creakorheuman bitts your butts[550] disagrees. Amn't I up since the damp dawn, marthared mary
allacook,[551] with Corrigan's pulse[552] and varicoarse veins, my pramaxle smashed, Alice Jane[553] in
decline and my oneeyed mongrel twice run over, soaking and bleaching boiler rags, and sweating
cold, a widow like me, for to deck my tennis champion son, the laundryman with the lavandier[554]
flannels? You won your limpopo[555] limp fron the husky hussars when Collars and Cuffs[556] was heir

280

285

290

295

---

[526]   *lost histereve* last yestereve, lost history.

[527]   *main* the Main river flows through Frankfurt, Germany.

[528]   *manzinahurries* punning on the Manzanares river which flows through Madrid, Spain.

[529]   *Bachelor's Walk* a street alongside the Liffey river in Dublin.

[530]   *in the loup of the years* Dutch *in de loop der jaren* means "in the course of years." Also containing the Loup river, which is in southern France.

[531]   *Orara ... Animas* Spanish, *orar pro Orbe y por las animas*, meaning "to pray for the earth and the souls." The Orara river is in New South Wales, Australia; the Orbe in Switzerland (Canton Vaud); and Rio de las Animas is in Colorado.

[532]   *Ussa Ulla ... umbas ... Mezha* the Ussa river is in northeast Russia; the Ulla river flows through Santiago de Compostela in Spain; the Umba river is on the Cola peninsula in the extreme northeast of Russia; the Mezha river is found in eastern Russia.

[533]   *ufer and ufer Ufer* means "shore" or "bank" in German.

[534]   *respund to spond* German *Spund*, a "bung" or "plug"; Italian *sponda* means bank or shore.

[535]   *You deed* the river Dee flows into Aberdeen in Scotland.

[536]   *irrawaddying* "earwadding" conflated with the Irrawaddy river in Myanmar (formerly Burma).

[537]   *aars* in Dutch, *aars* means ass, or arse; the Aar river is in Switzerland.

[538]   *lethest* "least" conflated with the river Lethe, a river in the underworld in ancient mythology.

[539]   *Oronoko!* the Orinoco river is found in Venezuela.

[540]   *Finnleader* Adam Findlater was a prosperous grocery merchant in Dublin; see Alex Findlater, *Findlaters: the Story of a Dublin Merchant Family, 1774–2001* (Dublin: A. and A. Farmer, 2001).

[541]   *joakimono* fusing "kimono" and Joachim of Flora (*c.* 1135–1202), a Christian mystic.

[542]   *Yonne ... Isset* the river Rhone in northern France is a tributary of the Seine; the Isset river, in the Ural mountains, flows through the city of Yekaterinburg.

[543]   *Fallareen Common* Fallarees Commons, a place on the Liffey near the town of Ballymore Eustace, in east County Kildare, near the border with County Wicklow; *failirín* is Irish for a "little prancing horse."

[544]   *Astley's* Astley's Amphitheatre, in Peter Street, Dublin, was an equestrian circus; the building was later used to house blind women.

[545]   *ghostwhite horse of the Peppers* Samuel Lover (1797–1868), song-writer and novelist, wrote *White Horse of the Peppers: A Comic Drama in Two Acts* (London: Chapman and Hall, 1838). A "Pepper's ghost" is a stage illusion, created by John Henry Pepper around 1860, produced by a projector and glass screen which creates the illusion that people or objects materialize on the scene.

[546]   *Ireland ... stiff* "Ireland sober is Ireland free" was a nineteenth-century temperance slogan.

[547]   *Maria ... with me* "Hail Mary, full of grace, the Lord is with thee," says the angel at the Annunciation in Catholic translations of the Bible. The river Greese is found in western Ireland, a tributary of the Barrow.

[548]   *Madammangut La Fille de Madame Angot* (1872) (or *Mrs. Angot's Daughter*) is an operetta in three acts by Charles Lecocq (1832–1918). Clairette, the daughter, is engaged to one man, loves another, but ends up still planning to marry the first.

[549]   *Carrigacurra* a stretch of land near Poulaphouca, in western Ireland.

[550]   *creakorheuman bitts your butts* the literal sense here is: "Greco-Roman but your buttocks," with "Roman" being inflected with "rheumatic," since in ancient Greek *rheuma* means "stream."

[551]   *mary allacook* St. Margaret Mary Alacoque (1647–90) drank water in which laundry had been washed as one of her ascetic practices.

[552]   *Corrigan's pulse* a jerky pulse with a full expansion, followed by a sudden collapse, occurring in aortic regurgitation; the syndrome was named by a Dublin doctor named Corrigan.

[553]   *Alice Jane* Alice Jane Donkin (1851–1929), who married the brother of Lewis Carroll (1832–98) in 1871; perhaps fused with the Alice river that is found in South Africa.

[554]   *lavandier* in French, a *lavandière* is a washerwoman.

[555]   *limpopo* the Limpopo river is in Mozambique.

[556]   *Collars and Cuffs* Prince Albert Victor Edward (1864–92), the Duke of Clarence, was a son of Edward VII who, on reaching 21, joined the Tenth Hussars; he was called "Collars and Cuffs" because he wore extreme versions of both.

to the town and your slur gave the stink to Carlow.[557] Holy Scamander,[558] I sar[559] it again! Near the golden falls. Icis[560] on us! Seints[561] of light! Zezere![562] Subdue your noise, you hamble[563] creature! What is it but a blackburry growth or the dwyergray[564] ass them four old codgers owns. Are you   300 meanam[565] Tarpey and Lyons[566] and Gregory?[567] I meyne[568] now, thank all, the four of them, and the roar of them, that draves[569] that stray in the mist and old Johnny MacDougal along with them. Is that the Poolbeg[570] flasher beyant,[571] pharphar,[572] or a fireboat coasting nyar[573] the Kishtna[574] or a glow I behold within a hedge or my Garry[575] come back from the Indes?[576] Wait till the honeying of the lune,[577] love! Die eve, little eve, die![578] We see that wonder in your eye. We'll meet again, we'll   305 part once more. The spot I'll seek if the hour you'll find. My chart shines high where the blue milk's upset. Forgivemequick, I'm going! Bubye![579] And you, pluck your watch, forgetmenot. Your evenlode.[580] So save to jurna's[581] end! My sights are swimming thicker on me by the shadows to this place. I sow[582] home slowly now by own way, moyvalley[583] way. Towy I too,[584] rathmine.[585]

Ah, but she was the queer old skeowsha[586] anyhow, Anna Livia, trinkettoes! And sure he was the   310 quare old buntz too, Dear Dirty Dumpling,[587] foostherfather[588] of fingalls[589] and dotthergills. Gammer and gaffer[590] we're all their gangsters. Hadn't he seven dams[591] to wive him? And every dam had her seven crutches. And every crutch had its seven hues.[592] And each hue had a differing cry. Sudds[593] for me and supper for you and the doctor's bill for Joe John.[594] Befor!

---

[557] *gave the stink to Carlow* the Irish popular song "Follow Me Up to Carlow" commemorates a victory in 1580, when Fiach Ma O'Bryne overthrew the forces of the Crown under Lord Gre de Wilton in a battle in County Wicklow. The speaker is saying that the other woman, in her fawning attitude toward the Duke of Clarence, has betrayed the true Irish spirit epitomized in this popular song commemorating resistance.

[558] *Scamander* the river outside the walls of ancient Troy, repeatedly mentioned in the *Iliad* by Homer.

[559] *I sar* "I saw" fused with the Isar river, which begins in Austria and flows through Munich, Germany.

[560] *Icis* the Thames river, in the area about Oxford, was often called the Isis in the period up to 1940.

[561] *Seints* "saints alive," a popular expression, conflated with the river Seint in Wales.

[562] *Zezere* "see there" conflated with the Zezere river in Portugal.

[563] *hamble* "humble" conflated with river Hamble, which flows into the English channel near Southampton.

[564] *dwyergray* Edmund Dwyer Gray (d. 1888) was owner and editor of the *Freeman's Journal*, a Dublin newspaper; he was a prominent Dublin politician, an MP, and in 1880 Lord Mayor of Dublin. A statue of him is located on Sackville (now O'Connell) Street in central Dublin.

[565] *meanam* "mean" fused with the river Me Nam which flows through Bangkok, capital of Thailand.

[566] *Lyons* a river in Colorado.

[567] *Gregory* a river in Australia.

[568] *meyne* the river Meyne flows through the town of Orange in the Vaucluse valley, France.

[569] *draves* the river Drave (also called Drau and Drava) flows from Austria into the Danube.

[570] *Poolbeg* the Poolbeg Lighthouse in Dublin Bay, Dublin.

[571] *beyant* "beyond" as pronounced in a Dublin accent.

[572] *pharphar* "far, far" inflected by *pharos*, ancient Greek for a "lighthouse," and by the river Pharphar, mentioned in 2 Kings 5:12: "Are not Abana and Pharphar, rivers of Damascus, better than all the waters of Israel? May I not wash in them, and be clean?"

[573] *nyar* "near" conflated with the river Nyar, a tributary of the Ganges.

[574] *Kishtna* the Kish lightship was moored at the northern end of Kish Bank, two miles east of what was then Kingstown, now Dun Laoghaire. The Kistna or Krishna is a large river in southern India.

[575] *Garry* the river Garry is found in highland Perth, Scotland.

[576] *Indes* the Indus river flows through Pakistan from the Himalayas to the Arabian Sea.

[577] *lune* the river Lune flows from Cumbria, in England, into the Irish sea.

[578] *Die eve, little eve, die* a lullaby song used to finish a child's turn on a swing, has the refrain, "Die dog, little dog, die, / Die for the sake of your mother's black eye." Bloom recalls this phrase in *Ulysses*, 11.1019.

[579] *Bubye* the Bubye river is in South Africa.

[580] *evenlode* the river Evenlode is located in Oxfordshire, England.

[581] *jurna's* "journey's" conflated with the Jura river, a southern affluent of the Amazon river in Brazil.

[582] *sow* the river Sow is in Staffordshire, England.

[583] *moyvalley* the river Moy is in county Mayo, in the west of Ireland.

[584] *Towy I too* "so will I too," inflected by the river Towy in south Wales.

[585] *rathmine* Rathmines, a suburban area of Dublin.

[586] *old skeowsha* Anglo-Irish for "old friend."

[587] *Dear Dirty Dumpling* "Dear dirty Dublin."

[588] *foostherfather* "foster father" merged with Anglo-Irish *fooster*, a "bungler."

[589] *fingalls* a Fingal river is found in New South Wales, Australia.

[590] *gammer and gaffer* an "old woman" and an "old man."

[591] *dams* a dam is the female parent of four-footed animals.

[592] *And ever dam . . . its seven hues from the children's nursery rhyme*:

As I was going to St. Ives I met a man with seven wives,
Each wife had seven sacks, each sack had seven cats,
Each cat had seven kits: kits, cats, sacks and wives,
How many were going to St. Ives?

[593] *Sudds* "sudd" is an Arabic word which has been assimilated into English, designating an impenetrable mass of floating vegetation which obstructs navigation on the Nile.

[594] *Sudds for me . . . for Joe John* from the children's game called "Ring a ring o' roses": "One for me, and one for you, and one for little Moses."

315 Bifur![595] He married his markets, cheap by foul,[596] I know, like any Etrurian Catholic Heathen, in
their pinky[597] limony[598] creamy birnies[599] and their turkiss[600] indienne[601] mauves. But at milkidmass[602] who was the spouse? Then all that was was fair. Tys[603] Elvenland![604] Teems[605] of times and
happy returns. The seim anew.[606] Ordovico[607] or viricordo.[608] Anna was, Livia is, Plurabelle's to be.
Northmen's thing made southfolk's place[609] but howmulty plurators made eachone in person?[610]
320 Latin me that, my trinity scholard,[611] out of eure[612] sanscreed[613] into oure eryan![614] *Hircus Civis
Eblanensis!*[615] He had buckgoat paps on him, soft ones for orphans. Ho, Lord! Twins of his bosom.
Lord save us! And ho! Hey? What all men. Hot? His tittering daughters of. Whawk?
      Can't hear with the waters of. The chittering waters of. Flittering bats, fieldmice bawk talk. Ho!
Are you not gone ahome? What Thom Malone? Can't hear with bawk of bats, all thim
325 liffeying waters of. Ho, talk save us! My foos[616] won't moos.[617] I feel as old as yonder elm.
A tale told[618] of Shaun or Shem? All Livia's daughtersons. Dark hawks hear us. Night! Night!
My ho head halls.[619] I feel as heavy as yonder stone. Tell me of John or Shaun? Who were Shem and
Shaun the living sons or daughters of? Night now! Tell me, tell me, tell me, elm! Night night!
Telmetale of stem or stone. Beside the rivering waters of, hitherandthithering waters of. Night!

---

[595] *Bifur* the river Biferno flows into the Adriatic near Termoli in Italy.

[596] *markets, cheap by foul* Margarets, cheek by jowl.

[597] *pinky* A Pink river is found in Saskatchewan, Canada.

[598] *limony* the Lim river flows through Serbia and Montenegro.

[599] *birnies* in German, *Birnen* are "pears"; McBirney's was a drapery shop on Aston Quay in Dublin.

[600] *turkiss* from the Danish *turkis*, meaning "turquoise."

[601] *indienne* indigo, with Indian rivers that are found in Florida and Michigan.

[602] *milkidmass* Michaelmas, September 29.

[603] *Tys* the Danish word *tys* means "hush!"

[604] *Elvenland* Danish *elve* means a "small river;" the Dutch word *elvenland* means "fairyland."

[605] *Teems* the river Tees flows from the Pennines down to the North Sea at Middlesbrough, England; a river Teme is found in Lancashire, England.

[606] *happy returns. The seim anew* "many happy returns; the same to you," fused with the Seim river, which is in southwestern Russia.

[607] *Ordovico* a coinage suggesting "Vico's order," the recursive cycles postulated by the Neapolitan philosopher Giambattista Vico (1668–1744). See Samuel Beckett, "Dante ... Bruno. Vico .. Joyce," pp. 1061–72.

[608] *viricordo* vi ricordo, in Italian, means "I remember you" (plural).

[609] *Northmen's thing ... southfolk's place* to paraphrase: "The high place where the Norwegian Thing once met [a Thing was a legislative and executive assembly of free men in Norse and Germanic antiquity] has become Suffolk Place," or Suffolk Street, the site of St. Andrew's church, now renovated and named the Dublin Tourism Centre.

[610] *howmulty ... person* to paraphrase: "What number of places make things into persons?"

[611] *trinity scholard* a scholar at Trinity College, Dublin.

[612] *Eure* "your" merged with the Eure river in northern France, a tributary of the Seine.

[613] *sanscreed* Sanskrit, an Aryan language; perhaps punning on French *sans*, meaning "without," and "creed," belief or principles.

[614] *eryan* Aryan.

[615] *Hircus Civis Eblanensis* Latin for a "he-goat citizen of Dublin," a sequence of "thing, person, and place" that seems to answer some of the riddles previously posed; also HCE, the initials of the protagonist.

[616] *foos* a transcription of the pronunciation of the German word *Fuss*, meaning "foot." The river Oos flows through Baden-Baden in Germany.

[617] *moos* in German, *Moos* means "moss."

[618] *A tale told* Shakespeare, *Macbeth*, V.v.30: "a tale told by an idiot."

[619] *My ho head halls* to paraphrase, "my old head falls."

W. B. Yeats (1865–1939)

Introduction

By the time of William Butler Yeats's death, his status as the greatest lyrical poet to write in English in the twentieth century was undisputed, and his fame continued to swell during the the 1940s and 1950s. But during the 1960s and 1970s, his reputation was increasingly questioned: his politics, especially those of the 1930s, were farther to the right than those of most academics, though he was never the avowed fascist that some critics depicted; his mysticism, which was both naive and very sophisticated, has always been troublesome to even his most perfervid admirers, and with the passage of time has grown only more so. Yeats's work could also be caricatured as the last redoubt of a brittle symbolism, or an easy aestheticism willfully blind to the entangled interactions betwen art and life. The truth is that Yeats was a very complex and contradictory figure, so much so that he seems to have felt a need to present simpler and stylized versions of himself ("myths" would have been his preferred term) in numerous autobiographical writings which need to be read with much caution.

It has long been conventional to divide Yeats's career into three stages: an early stage that runs from his first, very ornate

who submitted answers to Yeats's queries about the meaning of countless symbols and historical and personal events. It took another five years for Yeats to transform these unlikely materials into a vast symbolic and mystical system meant to account for the entire arc of human history and the fabric of human experience. A Vision, published in 1925, tries to explain Yeats's system, the most sustained attempt to offer a visionary account of the world since Blake. The extent to which his mature poems should be read in the light of A Vision has been a subject of perennial debate that will never be resolved. At certain points the poems patently draw on images and motifs from A Vision; yet even that work's beguiling and allusive formulations fail to account for the wild and contradictory textures that animate Yeats's later poems.

The system represents the relative dominance of varying antitheses by an analogy with the 28 phases of the moon, with phase 1 being the dark of the moon, a stage in which the spiritual and the disincarnate are at their strongest, and phase 15 the full moon, a stage in which the material and the incarnate are strongest. Richard Ellmann has nicely summarized the polarities clustered under these Phases:

Phase 1 *Dark of the Moon*	Phase 15 *Full Moon*
Body becomes spirit; Transfiguration	Spirit becomes body; Incarnation
Unity of Non-Being (approximation to nothingness)	Unity of Being (approximate union of body and soul)
Purgation of the world	Saturation in the world
Formlessness (Asia)	Form (Europe)
Image-Breaking	Image-Making
Hermit, Devottee, Saint	Hero, Lover, Poet
Inhuman (divine) speech	Human Speech

and romantic poems of the early 1880s to around 1900; a middle stage that runs from there to 1917, one marked by his key role in founding the Abbey Theatre in 1904 (an institution central to the creation of an Irish national drama) and the evolution of a discernibly simpler style, one more attuned to colloquial speech; and a third stage that begins with his marriage to Georgina ("George") Hyde-Lees in 1917 and continues to his death in 1939, one in which his early interests in mystical symbolism are rekindled and combined with a poetic voice that effortlessly ranges across a full spectrum of tones, from oratorical dignity to earthy colloquialism. Nearly all the great poems for which he is remembered come from this third period, and it was during the period 1917–20 that he and his wife conducted an elaborate series of "seances," dialogues with mysterious voices from the past

It is widely agreed that Yeats's best collection of his mature years was *The Tower* (1928). The volume is named after a Norman keep (or squat, square tower), named Thoor Ballylee, which is located at Ballylee in Country Galway, Ireland. Yeats had purchased it for £35 in March 1917 from a government agency (the Congested Districts Board), hoping to renovate it and turn it into a home. An adjacent cottage could serve as an occasional house while the considerable work of fixing the tower's roof and interior was accomplished. It was not till the summer of 1922 when he finally moved in, now a married man with two children (a son, Michael, and a daughter, Anne). Yeats was concerned about the physical apperance of the book which he wanted to name after this structure, and he recruited T. Sturge Moore (1870–1944), a poet and wood engraver, to execute a cover design. "The Tower," Yeats instructed him, "should not be too unlike the real object or rather… it should suggest the real object. I like to think of that building as a permanent symbol of my work plainly visible to the passer-by. As you know, all my art theories depend upon just this – rooting of mythology in the earth."

The Tower opens, in "Sailing to Byzantium," with the poet already an aged man, a "paltry thing" when set against "the young in one another's arms," and it ends with "All Souls' Night" in which the poet communes with the spirits of dead friends and companions. "Youth, age, memory, and death," comments Terence Brown, "are the volume's thematic constants." And it is again Brown who has discerningly situated the work in its context: "*The Tower*, with its assumed mythology, its self-conscious textuality, its cast of historical and literary characters, its echo chamber sonorities in which a literary tradition lives on as the ghost of itself, its moments of charged intensity, its elaborately composed individual works arranged to form a group of sequence poems, in 1928 can be read…as a companion work of T. S. Eliot's poem of 1922, *The Waste Land*."

The Tower is reprinted here in its entirety, adhering to the original text of 1928. Following it is a condensed selection from Yeats's poems in the final 11 years of his life. Like other modernist writers, Yeats was a prolific writer of prose, and by the end of his life he had authored more than 1,500 essays, introductions, and prefaces. The selection given here is necessarily a condensed one that concentrates on highlighting his own aesthetics and its interaction with that of his contemporaries.

A Coat (1914)

I made my song a coat
Covered with embroideries
Out of old mythologies[1]
From heel to throat;
5   But the fools caught it,
Wore it in the world's eyes
As though they'd wrought it.
Song, let them take it,
For there's more enterprise
10   In walking naked.

The Wild Swans at Coole[1] (1917)

The trees are in their autumn beauty,
The woodland paths are dry,
Under the October twilight the water
Mirrors a still sky;
5   Upon the brimming water among the stones
Are nine and fifty swans.

The nineteenth autumn has come upon me
Since I first made my count;
I saw, before I had well finished,
10   All suddenly mount
And scatter wheeling in great broken rings
Upon their clamorous wings.

The poem was first published in *Poetry* 4(2) (May 1914), then collected in Yeats's *Responsibilities: Poems and a Play* (Dundrum, Ireland: Cuala Press, 1914).
[1]   *old mythologies* Gaelic legends of the sort which Yeats had read in widely.

THE WILD SWANS
The poem, written in 1916, was first printed in the *Little Review* 4(2) (June 1917), then collected in W. B. Yeats, *The Wild Swans at Coole* (Churchtown, Dundrum [Ireland]: Cuala Press, 1917), a limited edition in 400 copies; it was then published in a commercial edition with the same title (London: Macmillan, 1919), the source followed for the text here.
[1]   Coole Park was the ancestral home of Lady Augusta Gregory (1852–1932), an Anglo-Irish landowner and widow who first met Yeats in 1894. The house was located near Gort in County Galway, Ireland. In 1897 she invited him to stay at her home for the first time, and for the next 15 years he returned for stays of 2 to 3 months, and sometimes even 6, that were annual events. (After Lady Gregory's death the house became derelict and was demolished.) Lady Gregory acted as a patron and collaborator with Yeats for many years.

I have looked upon those brilliant creatures,
And now my heart is sore.
All's changed since I, hearing at twilight,   15
The first time on this shore,
The bell-beat of their wings above my head,
Trod with a lighter tread.

Unwearied still, lover by lover,
They paddle in the cold   20
Companionable streams or climb the air;
Their hearts have not grown old;
Passion or conquest, wander where they will,
Attend upon them still.

But now they drift on the still water   25
Mysterious, beautiful;
Among what rushes will they build,
By what lake's edge or pool
Delight men's eyes when I awake some day
To find they have flown away?   30

In Memory of Major Robert Gregory[1] (1918)

I

Now that we're almost settled in our house[2]
I'll name the friends that cannot sup with us
Beside a fire of turf in th' ancient tower,[3]
And having talked to some late hour
Climb up the narrow winding stair to bed: 5
Discoverers of forgotten truth
Or mere companions of my youth,
All, all are in my thoughts to-night being dead.

II

Always we'd have the new friend meet the old
And we are hurt if either friend seem cold,   10
And there is salt to lengthen out the smart
In the affections of our heart,
And quarrels are blown up upon that head;
But not a friend that I would bring
This night can set us quarrelling,   15
For all that come into my mind are dead.

IN MEMORY
The poem was first printed in a magazine called the *English Review* 27(2) (Aug. 1918), then reprinted in the *Little Review* 5(5) (Sept. 1918). It was first collected in Yeats's *The Wild Swans at Coole* (London: Macmillan, 1919), which serves as the source for the text given here.

[1] Major Robert Gregory (1881–1918) was the only son of Lady Augusta Gregory, a patron of Yeats and a collaborator with him in the revival of Irish letters. Gregory was educated at Harrow, New College (Oxford), and the Slade, where he studied art. He had an exhibition of painting in Chelsea in 1914, but continued other aristocratic sports, including shooting, boxing, and horse riding. He joined the armed forces in 1915, transferred to the Royal Flying Corps in 1916, and was given two awards for valor in 1917 (Légion d'Honneur, Military Cross). He was killed on January 23, 1918, on the north Italian front.

[2] The house at Thoor Ballylee which Yeats, partly at the suggestion of Major Robert Gregory, purchased in March 1917. See the "Introduction" to Yeats.

[3] The Norman keep which formed part of Yeats's house at Thoor Ballylee.

III

Lionel Johnson[4] comes the first to mind,
That loved his learning better than mankind,
Though courteous to the worst; much falling he
20 Brooded upon sanctity
Till all his Greek and Latin learning seemed
A long blast upon the horn that brought
A little nearer to his thought
A measureless consummation that he dreamed.

IV

25 And that enquiring man John Synge[5] comes next,
That dying chose the living world for text
And never could have rested in the tomb
But that, long travelling, he had come
Towards nightfall upon certain set apart
30 In a most desolate stony place,
Towards nightfall upon a race
Passionate and simple like his heart.

V

And then I think of old George Pollexfen,[6]
In muscular youth well known to Mayo[7] men
35 For horsemanship at meets or at racecourses,
That could have shown how pure-bred horses
And solid men, for all their passion, live
But as the outrageous stars incline
By opposition, square and trine;
40 Having grown sluggish and contemplative.

VI

They were my close companions many a year,
A portion of my mind and life, as it were,
And now their breathless faces seem to look
Out of some old picture-book;
45 I am accustomed to their lack of breath,
But not that my dear friend's dear son,
Our Sidney[8] and our perfect man,
Could share in that discourtesy of death.

---

[4]   Lionel Johnson (1867–1902) was a critic and poet, and also first cousin to Olivia Shakespear, with whom Yeats had an affair in the 1890s. Johnson, with Yeats, was a member of the Rhymers' Club, a group of poets who met in an upper room in the Cheshire Cheese, a Fleet Street chop house.

[5]   John Synge (1871–1909) was an Irish dramatist and author; Yeats first met him in Paris in 1896, where he persuaded him to go to the Aran Islands to the west of Ireland to find truly Irish subject matter. When his play *The Shadow of the Glen* aroused controversy in 1903 for its less than flattering portrait of the Irish people, Yeats rose to his defense. (See *The Collected Letters of*

W. B. Yeats, vol. 3, *1901–1904*, eds. John Kelley and Ronald Schuchard [Oxford: Clarendeon Press, 1994], p. 449.) He also wrote an essay about Synge in 1911, "Synge and the Ireland of his Time" (collected in W. B. Yeats, *Essays and Introductions* [London and New York: Macmillan, 1961], pp. 311–42.)

[6]   George Pollexfen (1839–1910) was Yeats's maternal uncle, with whom he spent holidays in County Sligo as a young man.

[7]   County north of Galway in the west of Ireland.

[8]   Sir Philip Sidney (1554–86) was a poet, author, and diplomat of the Renaissance.

VII

For all things the delighted eye now sees
Were loved by him; the old storm-broken trees   50
That cast their shadows upon road and bridge;
The tower set on the stream's edge;
The ford where drinking cattle make a stir
Nightly, and startled by that sound
The water-hen must change her ground;   55
He might have been your heartiest welcomer.

VIII

When with the Galway foxhounds he would ride
From Castle Taylor to the Roxborough side
Or Esserkelly plain, few kept his pace;
At Mooneen[9] he had leaped a place   60
So perilous that half the astonished meet
Had shut their eyes, and where was it
He rode a race without a bit?
And yet his mind outran the horses' feet.

IX

We dreamed that a great painter had been born   65
To cold Clare[10] rock and Galway rock and thorn,
To that stern colour and that delicate line
That are our secret discipline
Wherein the gazing heart doubles her might.
Soldier, scholar, horseman, he,   70
And yet he had the intensity
To have published all to be a world's delight.

X

What other could so well have counselled us
In all lovely intricacies of a house
As he that practised or that understood   75
All work in metal or in wood,
In moulded plaster or in carven stone?
Soldier, scholar, horseman, he,
And all he did done perfectly
As though he had but that one trade alone.   80

XI

Some burn damp faggots, others may consume
The entire combustible world in one small room
As though dried straw, and if we turn about
The bare chimney is gone black out
Because the work had finished in that flare.   85

---

[9] *Castle Taylor ... Mooneen* Castle Taylor is in County Galway; Roxborough, near Coole Park, was the home of Lady Gregory when she was a child; Esserkelly was another stately home in County Galway, near Ardrahan. Mooneen was a small town near Esserkelly.
[10] Irish county to the south of County Galway.

Soldier, scholar, horseman, he,
As 'twere all life's epitome.
What made us dream that he could comb grey hair?

XII

I had thought, seeing how bitter is that wind
90   That shakes the shutter, to have brought to mind
All those that manhood tried, or childhood loved
Or boyish intellect approved,
With some appropriate commentary on each;
Until imagination brought
95   A fitter welcome; but a thought
Of that late death took all my heart for speech.

Easter, 1916 (1920)

I have met them at close of day
Coming with vivid faces
From counter or desk among grey
Eighteenth-century houses.
5   I have passed with a nod of the head
Or polite meaningless words,
Or have lingered awhile and said
Polite meaningless words,
And thought before I had done
10   Of a mocking tale or a gibe
To please a companion
Around the fire at the club,
Being certain that they and I
But lived where motley[1] is worn:
15   All changed, changed utterly:
A terrible beauty is born.

Easter, 1916
An Irish Republic was proclaimed on Easter Monday (April 24), 1916, and the center of Dublin was occupied by a group named the Irish Volunteers of the Irish Republican Brotherhood. It was a rash, doomed uprising. British troops killed and wounded hundreds of the rebels, and artillery shelling left Dublin's city center in ruins. The rebellion was finished by April 29. A few days later, over a period from May 3 to 12, 15 of the rebel leaders were executed after a series of courts martial. Yeats himself heard the news of the Dublin Rising while in England, where he was staying at the home of a friend in Gloucestershire. On May 11 he wrote to Lady Gregory:

The Dublin tragedy has been a great sorrow and anxiety.... I am trying to write a poem on the men executed – "terrible beauty has been born again." If the English Conservative party had made a declaration that they did not intend to rescind the Home Rule Bill there would have been no Rebellion. I had no idea that any public event could so deeply move me – and I am very despondent about the future. At the moment I feel that all the work of years has been overturned, all the bringing together of classes, all the freeing of Irish literature and criticism from politics....

Yeats evidently worked on his poem intermittently during the next four months, and its final manuscript is dated September 25, 1916. It first appeared a few days later as an independent pamphlet printed in London, Easter, 1916, issued in 25 copies "privately printed by Clement Shorter for distribution among his friends." (Clement Shorter [1857–1926], a journalist and author, was an acquaintance of Yeats.) Four years later it was reprinted in the New Statesman, October 1920, and the Dial 69(5) (Nov. 1920); then included in W. B. Yeats, Michael Robertes and the Dancer (Churchtown, Dundrum [Ireland]: Cuala Press, 1920).
[1]   Motley A coarse cloth woven from threads of two or more colors, and hence the particolored costume of a jester, harlequin, etc. "To wear motley" means to adopt the profession of a jester or clown. The poem's central conceit is that comedy has been transformed into tragedy.

That woman's days[2] were spent
In ignorant good will,
Her nights in argument
Until her voice grew shrill.   20
What voice more sweet than hers
When young and beautiful
She rode to harriers?
This man[3] had kept a school
And rode our wingèd horse;   25
This other[4] his helper and friend
Was coming into his force;
He might have won fame in the end,
So sensitive his nature seemed,
So daring and sweet his thought.   30
This other man[5] I had dreamed
A drunken, vainglorious lout.
He had done most bitter wrong
To some who are near my heart,
Yet I number him in the song;   35
He, too, has resigned his part
In the casual comedy;
He, too, has been changed in his turn,
Transformed utterly:
A terrible beauty is born.   40

Hearts with one purpose alone
Through summer and winter seem
Enchanted to a stone
To trouble the living stream.
The horse that comes from the road,   45
The rider, the birds that range
From cloud to tumbling cloud,
Minute by minute they change;
A shadow of cloud on the stream
Changes minute by minute;   50
A horse-hoof slides on the brim,
And a horse plashes within it
Where long-legged moor-hens dive,
And hens to moor-cocks call;
Minute by minute they live: 55
The stone's in the midst of all.

Too long a sacrifice
Can make a stone of the heart.
O when may it suffice?
That is Heaven's part, our part   60
To murmur name upon name,
As a mother names her child

2   *That woman's days* Constance Markiewics (1868–1927), *née* Gore-Booth. Yeats had first met her in 1894 at the family's country house, Lisadell, and he later eulogized her in "In Memory of Eva Gore-Booth and Con Markiewics" (see p. 347). She took part in the Easter Rising, but her sentence of death was commuted to incarceration, and in 1917 she was released as part of a general amnesty.
3   *This man* Patrick Pearse (1879–1916), became Commandant-General and President of the provisional government in Easter week. He was a lawyer who had founded St. Enda's School for Boys at Rathfarnham, near Dublin, and also a prolific author of poetry and prose, or one who "rode our wingéd horse," i.e., Pegasus, the mythological steed of poets.
4   *This other* Thomas MacDonagh (1878–1916) taught English literature at University College, Dublin, and was a poet and dramatist whose play *When the Dawn is Come* had been staged at the Abbey Theatre in 1908.
5   *This other man* Major John McBride (1865–1916) had married Maud Gonne in 1903 (divorced, 1905), a woman with whom Yeats had been helplessly in love for years.

        When sleep at last has come
        On limbs that had run wild.
65   What is it but nightfall?
        No, no, not night but death;
        Was it needless death after all?
        For England may keep faith[6]
        For all that is done and said.
70   We know their dream; enough
        To know they dreamed and are dead.
        And what if excess of love
        Bewildered them till they died?
        I write it out in a verse –
75   MacDonagh and MacBride
        And Connolly and Pearse
        Now and in time to be,
        Wherever green is worn,
        Are changed, changed utterly:
80   A terrible beauty is born.

The Second Coming (1920)

        Turning and turning in the widening gyre[1]
        The falcon cannot hear the falconer;
        Things fall apart; the centre cannot hold;
        Mere anarchy is loosed upon the world,
5   The blood-dimmed tide is loosed, and everywhere
        The ceremony of innocence is drowned;
        The best lack all conviction, while the worst
        Are full of passionate intensity.

        Surely some revelation is at hand;
10   Surely the Second Coming is at hand.
        The Second Coming! Hardly are those words out
        When a vast image out of Spiritus Mundi[2]
        Troubles my sight: a waste of desert sand;
        A shape with lion body and the head of a man,[3]
15   A gaze blank and pitiless as the sun,
        Is moving its slow thighs, while all about it
        Wind shadows of the indignant desert birds.

[6] *may keep faith* the Bill for Home Rule for Ireland received Royal assent in 1914, but was suspended when the First World War broke out; the government promised to enact the bill after the war ended.

THE SECOND COMING
Composed in January 1919, the poem was first published in the *Nation*, November 6, 1920, and the *Dial* 69(5) (Nov. 1920); it was then included in W. B. Yeats, *Michael Robartes and the Dancer* (Churchtown, Dundrum [Ireland]: Cuala Press, 1920), the text followed here. It fuses the prophecy of Christ's second coming in Matthew 24 with John's vision of the coming of the Beast of the Apocalypse, or Antichrist (1 John 2:18). When the poem was first published in late 1920, contemporaries may have thought that the poem also referred to the auxiliary forces which Britain sent to Ireland to restore order as the country slipped into chaos, torn by fighting between an unofficial republican government, intransigent nationalists, and the

Royal Irish Constabulary: the result was a dreary record of burnings, murders, and outrages, a record only compounded by the new forces who were named, after their emergency uniforms, the Black-and-Tans. Much later, in 1938, Yeats reread the poem as a prophecy for the rise of fascism.
[1] A conical shape that is traced by the falcon's flight upward and outward in widening circles. This passage also invokes the geometrical figure of two interpenetrating cones, "the fundamental symbol" that Yeats used to diagram his cyclical view of history. (See *A Vision*, Book I, "The Great Wheel.") In that view, the cycle of Greco-Roman civilization was brought to an end by the advent of Christianity; but now, in the aftermath of the Great War, the Christian era was drawing to a close, to be replaced by another antithetical to it.
[2] Latin for "Spirit [or Breath] of the World," the term refers to a storehouse of images independent of personal memory, from which a poet receives the images that he then transcribes.
[3] *A shape ... man* the Egyptian sphinx.

The darkness drops again; but now I know
That twenty centuries[4] of stony sleep
Were vexed to nightmare by a rocking cradle,[5]   20
And what rough beast, its hour come round at last,
Slouches towards Bethlehem[6] to be born?

THE TOWER (1928)

Sailing to Byzantium (1927)

I

That is no country for old men.[1] The young
In one another's arms, birds in the trees,
– Those dying generations – at their song,
The salmon-falls, the mackerel-crowded seas,
Fish, flesh, or fowl, commend all summer long   5
Whatever is begotten, born, and dies.
Caught in that sensual music all neglect
Monuments of unageing intellect.

II

An aged man is but a paltry thing,
A tattered coat upon a stick, unless   10
Soul clap its hands and sing, and louder sing
For every tatter in its mortal dress,
Nor is there singing school but studying
Monuments of its own magnificence;
And therefore I have sailed the seas and come   15
To the holy city of Byzantium.

III

O sages standing in God's holy fire
As in the gold mosaic of a wall,

[4]   *twenty centuries* the 2,000 years of Christianity.

[5]   *a rocking cradle* the cradle of Christ, as if the oscillation of the cradle already forecast the preparation of its opposite.

[6]   *Bethlehem* the birth place of Christ, now to become the birthplace of the violent Antichrist, a murderous new age.

Sailing to Byzantium
The poem was written in the autumn of 1926, and first published in *October Blast* (Dublin: Cuala Press, 1927), a limited edition of only 24 pages.

Byzantium, or Constantinople (modern Istanbul), became the capital of the Eastern Roman Empire and, during the fifth and six centuries, the center of a highly stylized art and architecture; for Yeats this nonnaturalistic style implied an entire way of life in which art is frankly accepted and celebrated as artifice, the index of an aesthetics wholly opposed to the realism and naturalism which dominated the later nineteenth century. As he wrote in *A Vision* ([1937], pp. 279–80): "I think if I could be given a month of Antiquity and leave to spend it where I chose, I would spend it in Byzantium a little before Justinian opened St. Sophia [AD 537] and closed the Academy of Plato [AD 529]. I think I could find in some little wine-shop some philosophical worker in mosaic who could answer all my questions, the supernatural descending nearer to him than to Plotinus even, for the pride of his delicate skill would make what was an instrument of power to princes and clerics, a murderous madness in the mob, show as a lovely flexible presence like that of a perfect human body. I think that in early Byzantium, maybe never before or since in recorded history, religious, aesthetic and practical life were one, that architect and artifiers ... spoke to the multitude and the few alike. The painter, the mosaic worker, the worker in gold and silver, the illuminator of sacred books, were almost impersonal, almost perhaps without the consciousness of individual design, absorbed in their subject-matter and that of the vision of a whole people. They could copy out of old gospel books those pictures that seemed as sacred as the text, and yet weave all into a vast design, the work of so many that seemed the work of one, that made building, picture, pattern, metal-work of rail and lamp, seem but a single image ..."

[1]   *no country for old men* Ireland, for those who emphasize the salmon falls in line 4.

Come from the holy fire, perne[2] in a gyre,
20   And be the singing-masters of my soul.
Consume my heart away; sick with desire
And fastened to a dying animal
It knows not what it is; and gather me
Into the artifice of eternity.

IV

25   Once out of nature I shall never take
My bodily form from any natural thing,
But such a form as Grecian goldsmiths make
Of hammered gold and gold enamelling
To keep a drowsy Emperor awake;
30   Or set upon a golden bough to sing
To lords and ladies of Byzantium
Of what is past, or passing, or to come.

The Tower (1927)

I

What shall I do with this absurdity –
O heart, O troubled heart – this caricature,
Decrepit age that has been tied to me
As to a dog's tail?
5   Never had I more
Excited, passionate, fantastical
Imagination, nor an ear and eye
That more expected the impossible –
No, not in boyhood when with rod and fly,
Or the humbler worm, I climbed Ben Bulben's back[1]
10   And had the livelong summer day to spend.
It seems that I must bid the Muse go pack,
Choose Plato and Plotinus[2] for a friend
Until imagination, ear and eye,
Can be content with argument and deal
15   In abstract things; or be derided by
A sort of battered kettle at the heel.

II

I pace upon the battlements[3] and stare
On the foundations of a house, or where
Tree, like a sooty finger, starts from the earth;
20   And send imagination forth
Under the day's declining beam, and call

[2] *perne* a pern or pirn is a bobbin, spool, or reel; Yeats has turned the noun into a verb, and his speaker commands the sage to whirl down or unwind a thread from his timeless point into the present. On the "gyre," see p. 308 n. 1.

THE TOWER
On the title, see the "Introduction" to Yeats, pp. 301–2. The manuscript of the last section is dated October 7, 1925; the poem first appeared in *The New Republic* (June 29, 1927).
[1]   *Ben Bulben's back* A mountain near Sligo town, in the west of Ireland.
[2]   *Plato and Plotinus* philosophers who, within the poem, symbolize a transcendance for the physical, temporal world.
[3]   *battlements* i.e. of his tower and Thoor Ballylee.

Images and memories
From ruin or from ancient trees,
For I would ask a question of them all.

Beyond that ridge lived Mrs. French,[4] and once   25
When every silver candlestick or sconce
Lit up the dark mahogany and the wine,
A serving-man that could divine
That most respected lady's every wish,
Ran and with the garden shears   30
Clipped an insolent farmer's ears
And brought them in a little covered dish.

Some few remembered still when I was young
A peasant girl commended by a song,
Who'd lived somewhere upon that rocky place,   35
And praised the colour of her face,
And had the greater joy in praising her,
Remembering that, if walked she there,
Farmers jostled at the fair
So great a glory did the song confer.   40

And certain men, being maddened by those rhymes,
Or else by toasting her a score of times,
Rose from the table and declared it right
To test their fancy by their sight;
But they mistook the brightness of the moon   45
For the prosaic light of day –
Music had driven their wits astray –
And one was drowned in the great bog of Cloone.[5]

Strange, but the man who made the song was blind;
Yet, now I have considered it, I find   50
That nothing strange; the tragedy began
With Homer that was a blind man,
And Helen has all living hearts betrayed.
O may the moon and sunlight[6] seem
One inextricable beam,   55
For if I triumph I must make men mad.

And I myself created Hanrahan
And drove him drunk or sober through the dawn
From somewhere in the neighbouring cottages.
Caught by an old man's juggleries   60
He stumbled, tumbled, fumbled to and fro
And had but broken knees for hire
And horrible splendour of desire;
I thought it all out twenty years ago:[7]

Good fellows shuffled cards in an old bawn;[8]   65
And when that ancient ruffian's turn was on

---

[4] *Mrs. French* see Yeats's note to "The Tower," part II, on
pp. 341–2.
[5] *great bog of Cloone* see Yeats's note to "The Tower," part II, on
pp. 341–2. In the *Celtic Twilight* Yeats wrote: "As many as
eleven men asked her in marriage in one day, but she wouldn't
have any of them. There was a loft of men up beyond Kilbecanty
one night sitting together drinking, and talking of her, and one

of them got up and set out to go to Ballylee and see her; but
Cloone Bog was open then, and when he came to it he fell into
the water, and they found him dead there in the morning."
[6] *moon and sunlight* imagination and reality
[7] *twenty years ago* see Yeats's note to "The Tower," part II, on
pp. 341–2.
[8] *an old bawn* an enclosure near a farmhouse.

He so bewitched the cards under his thumb
That all, but the one card, became
A pack of hounds and not a pack of cards,
70   And that he changed into a hare.
Hanrahan rose in frenzy there
And followed up those baying creatures towards –

O towards I have forgotten what – enough!
I must recall a man that neither love
75   Nor music nor an enemy's clipped ear
Could, he was so harried, cheer;
A figure that has grown so fabulous
There's not a neighbour left to say
When he finished his dog's day:
80   An ancient bankrupt master of this house.

Before that ruin came, for centuries,
Rough men-at-arms, cross-gartered to the knees
Or shod in iron, climbed the narrow stairs,
And certain men-at-arms there were
85   Whose images, in the Great Memory stored,
Come with loud cry and panting breast
To break upon a sleeper's rest
While their great wooden dice beat on the board.[9]

As I would question all, come all who can;
90   Come old, necessitous, half-mounted man;
And bring beauty's blind rambling celebrant;
The red man[10] the juggler sent
Through God-forsaken meadows; Mrs. French,
Gifted with so fine an ear;
95   The man drowned in a bog's mire,
When mocking muses chose the country wench.

Did all old men and women, rich and poor,
Who trod upon these rocks or passed this door,
Whether in public or in secret rage
100   As I do now against old age?
But I have found an answer in those eyes
That are impatient to be gone;
Go therefore; but leave Hanrahan
For I need all his mighty memories.

105   Old lecher with a love on every wind,
Bring up out of that deep considering mind
All that you have discovered in the grave,[11]
For it is certain that you have
Reckoned up every unforeknown, unseeing
110   Plunge, lured by a softening eye,
Or by a touch or a sigh,
Into the labyrinth of another's being;

Does the imagination dwell the most
Upon a woman won or woman lost?
115   If on the lost, admit you turned aside

---

[9] *beat on the board* see Yeats's note to "The Tower," part II, on pp. 341–2.
[10] *the red man* Hanrahan.
[11] *discovered in the grave* one of Yeats's stories recounts "The Death of Hanrahan."

From a great labyrinth out of pride,
Cowardice, some silly over-subtle thought
Or anything called conscience once;
And that if memory recur, the sun's
Under eclipse and the day blotted out.   120

III

It is time that I wrote my will;
I choose upstanding men
That climb the streams until
The fountain leap, and at dawn
Drop their cast at the side   125
Of dripping stone; I declare
They shall inherit my pride,
The pride of people that were
Bound neither to Cause nor to State,
Neither to slaves that were spat on,   130
Nor to the tyrants that spat,
The people of Burke and of Grattan[12]
That gave, though free to refuse –
Pride, like that of the morn,
When the headlong light is loose,   135
Or that of the fabulous horn,
Or that of the sudden shower
When all streams are dry,
Or that of the hour
When the swan must fix his eye   140
Upon a fading gleam,
Float out upon a long
Last reach of glittering stream
And there sing his last song.
And I declare my faith: 145
I mock Plotinus' thought
And cry in Plato's teeth,
Death and life were not
Till man made up the whole,
Made lock, stock and barrel   150
Out of his bitter soul,
Aye, sun and moon and star, all,
And further add to that
That, being dead, we rise,
Dream and so create   155
Translunar Paradise.

I have prepared my peace
With learned Italian things
And the proud stones of Greece,
Poet's imaginings   160
And memories of love,
Memories of the words of women,

---

[12] *people of Burke and of Grattan* Edmund Burke (1729–97) was a statesman born in Dublin; Henry Grattan (1746–1820) was an Irish statesman who supported Catholic emancipation and fought against the bill that created the union of Great Britain and Ireland. Both were part of the Anglo-Irish (Protestant) minority, but had supported the nationalist cause when they might have considered themselves English.

All those things whereof
Man makes a superhuman,
165   Mirror-resembling dream.

As at the loophole there
The daws chatter and scream,
And drop twigs layer upon layer.
When they have mounted up,
170   The mother bird will rest
On their hollow top,
And so warm her wild nest.

I leave both faith and pride
To young upstanding men
175   Climbing the mountain side,
That under bursting dawn
They may drop a fly;
Being of that metal made
Till it was broken by
180   This sedentary trade.

Now shall I make my soul,
Compelling it to study
In a learned school
Till the wreck of body,
185   Slow decay of blood,
Testy delirium
Or dull decrepitude,
Or what worse evil come –
The death of friends, or death
190   Of every brilliant eye
That made a catch in the breath –
Seem but the clouds of the sky
When the horizon fades;
Or a bird's sleepy cry
195   Among the deepening shades.

Meditations in Time of Civil War (1923)

I.   Ancestral Houses

Surely among a rich man's flowering lawns,
Amid the rustle of his planted hills,
Life overflows without ambitious pains;
And rains down life until the basin spills,
5   And mounts more dizzy high the more it rains
As though to choose whatever shape it wills
And never stoop to a mechanical
Or servile shape, at others' beck and call.

MEDITATIONS
The seven poems in the sequence were written during the Irish Civil War of 1922 while Yeats was at Thoor Ballylee. The poems were first published in the *Dial* 74(1) (Jan. 1923).
After England and Ireland reached the Anglo-Irish Treaty, which was signed in London in December 1921, and ratified by the Irish Parliament on January 7, dissident republicans, led by Eamonn de Valera, began a civil war against the new Irish Free State Government.

Mere dreams, mere dreams! Yet Homer had not sung
Had he not found it certain beyond dreams   10
That out of life's own self-delight had sprung
The abounding glittering jet; though now it seems
As if some marvellous empty sea-shell flung
Out of the obscure dark of the rich streams,
And not a fountain, were the symbol which   15
Shadows the inherited glory of the rich.

Some violent bitter man, some powerful man
Called architect and artist in, that they,
Bitter and violent men, might rear in stone
The sweetness that all longed for night and day,   20
The gentleness none there had ever known;
But when the master's buried mice can play,
And maybe the great-grandson of that house,
For all its bronze and marble, 's but a mouse.

Oh what if gardens where the peacock strays   25
With delicate feet upon old terraces,
Or else all Juno[1] from an urn displays
Before the indifferent garden deities;
Oh what if levelled lawns and gravelled ways
Where slippered Contemplation finds his ease   30
And Childhood a delight for every sense,
But take our greatness with our violence?

What if the glory of escutcheoned doors,
And buildings that a haughtier age designed,
The pacing to and fro on polished floors   35
Amid great chambers and long galleries, lined
With famous portraits of our ancestors;
What if those things the greatest of mankind
Consider most to magnify, or to bless,
But take our greatness with our bitterness?   40

II.   *My House*[2]

An ancient bridge, and a more ancient tower,
A farmhouse that is sheltered by its wall,
An acre of stony ground,
Where the symbolic rose can break in flower,
Old ragged elms, old thorns innumerable,   5
The sound of the rain or sound
Of every wind that blows;
The stilted water-hen
Crossing stream again
Scared by the splashing of a dozen cows;   10

A winding stair, a chamber arched with stone,
A grey stone fireplace with an open hearth,
A candle and written page.
Il Penseroso's Platonist[3] toiled on

---

[1]   *Juno* Roman goddess of marriage.
[2]   *My House* on the house see the "Introduction" to Yeats, p. 301.
[3]   John Milton (1608–74) wrote "Il Penseroso" ("The Thought-

ful Man," in Italian) when still young (published 1646). If the
poem's thoughtful speaker cannot go outdoors to commune with
nature, he will:

15   In some like chamber, shadowing forth
                   How the daemonic rage
                   Imagined everything.
                   Benighted travellers
                   From markets and from fairs
20   Have seen his midnight candle glimmering.

                   Two men have founded here. A man-at-arms[4]
                   Gathered a score of horse and spent his days
                   In this tumultuous spot,
                   Where through long wars and sudden night alarms
25   His dwindling score and he seemed castaways
                   Forgetting and forgot;
                   And I, that after me
                   My bodily heirs may find,
                   To exalt a lonely mind,
30   Befitting emblems of adversity.

III.   My Table

                   Two heavy trestles, and a board
                   Where Sato's gift,[5] a changeless sword,
                   By pen and paper lies,
                   That it may moralise
5   My days out of their aimlessness.
                   A bit of an embroidered dress
                   Covers its wooden sheath.
                   Chaucer had not drawn breath
                   When it was forged. In Sato's house,
10   Curved like new moon, moon-luminous
                   It lay five hundred years.
                   Yet if no change appears
                   No moon; only an aching heart
                   Conceives a changeless work of art.
15   Our learned men have urged
                   That when and where 'twas forged
                   A marvellous accomplishment,
                   In painting or in pottery, went
                   From father unto son
20   And through the centuries ran
                   And seemed unchanging like the sword.
                   Soul's beauty being most adored,
                   Men and their business took
                   The soul's unchanging look;
25   For the most rich inheritor,
                   Knowing that none could pass heaven's door
                   That loved inferior art,
                   Had such an aching heart
                   That he, although a country's talk
30   For silken clothes and stately walk,

Be seen in some high lonely Tower,
Where I may off outwatch the *Bear*,
With thrice great *Hermes*, or unsphere
The spirit of *Plato* to unfold
What *Worlds*, or what vast Regions hold
The immortal mind . . . (ll. 86–91)

4 A *man-at-arms* the tower in which Yeats lived was built by the de Burgo family and is listed as Islandmore Castle in a census of 1585, the property of Edward Ulick de Burgo who died there in 1597.

5 *Sato's gift* a Japanese admirer gave a family sword to Yeats in March 1920. The sword had been made 550 years earlier and passed down in his family.

Had waking wits; it seemed
Juno's peacock screamed.[6]

IV. My Descendants

Having inherited a vigorous mind
From my old fathers, I must nourish dreams
And leave a woman and a man behind
As vigorous of mind, and yet it seems
Life scarce can cast a fragrance on the wind,   5
Scarce spread a glory to the morning beams,
But the torn petals strew the garden plot;
And there's but common greenness after that.

And what if my descendants lose the flower
Through natural declension of the soul,   10
Through too much business with the passing hour,
Through too much play, or marriage with a fool?
May this laborious stair and this stark tower
Become a roofless ruin that the owl
May build in the cracked masonry and cry   15
Her desolation to the desolate sky.

The Primum Mobile[7] that fashioned us
Has made the very owls in circles move;
And I, that count myself most prosperous,
Seeing that love and friendship are enough,   20
For an old neighbour's friendship[8] chose the house
And decked and altered it for a girl's love,
And know whatever flourish and decline
These stones remain their monument and mine.

V. The Road at My Door

An affable Irregular,[9]
A heavily-built Falstaffian man,
Comes cracking jokes of civil war
As though to die by gunshot were
The finest play under the sun.   5

A brown Lieutenant[10] and his men,
Half dressed in national uniform,
Stand at my door, and I complain
Of the foul weather, hail and rain,
A pear tree broken by the storm.   10

---

[6] *Juno's peacock screamed* in A Vision (p. 268), Yeats wrote: "A civilisation is a struggle to keep self-control, and in this it is like some great tragic person, some Niobe who must display an almost superhuman will or the cry will not touch our sympathy. The loss of control over thought comes towards the end; first a sinking in upon the moral being, then the last surrender, the irrational cry, revelation – the scream of Juno's peacock." The peacock was sacred to Juno as a symbol of immortality.

[7] *Primum Mobile* the Primum Mobile, or "first mover," was part of the Ptolemaic universe, an inner wheel that moves all the other spheres.

[8] *an old neighbour's friendship* the estate of Lady Gregory was within walking distance of Thoor Ballylee, and it had been her son, Major Robert Gregory, who had first suggested to Yeats that he buy the tower.

[9] *Irregular* a member of the Irish Republican Army, which opposed the signing of the Anglo-Irish Treaty and so caused the Civil War in 1922.

[10] *A brown Lieutenant* a "Free Stater" or member of the National Army loyal to the Irish Free State government.

I count those feathered balls of soot
The moor-hen guides upon the stream,
To silence the envy in my thought;
And turn towards my chamber, caught
15   In the cold snows of a dream.

VI.   *The Stare's Nest by My Window*

The bees build in the crevices
Of loosening masonry, and there
The mother birds bring grubs and flies.
My wall is loosening; honey-bees,
5   Come build in the empty house of the stare.

We are closed in, and the key is turned
On our uncertainty; somewhere
A man is killed, or a house burned,
Yet no clear fact to be discerned:
10   Come build in the empty house of the stare.

A barricade of stone or of wood;
Some fourteen days of civil war;
Last night they trundled down the road
That dead young soldier in his blood:
15   Come build in the empty house of the stare.

We had fed the heart on fantasies,
The heart's grown brutal from the fare;
More substance in our enmities
Than in our love; oh, honey-bees,
20   Come build in the empty house of the stare.

VII.   *I see Phantoms of Hatred and of the Heart's Fullness and of the Coming Emptiness*

I climb to the tower top and lean upon broken stone,
A mist that is like blown snow is sweeping over all,
Valley, river, and elms, under the light of a moon
That seems unlike itself, that seems unchangeable,
5   A glittering sword out of the east. A puff of wind
And those white glimmering fragments of the mist sweep by.
Frenzies bewilder, reveries perturb the mind;
Monstrous familiar images swim to the mind's eye.

'Vengeance upon the murderers,' the cry goes up,
10   'Vengeance for Jacques Molay.'[11] In cloud-pale rags, or in lace
The rage driven, rage tormented, and rage hungry troop,
Trooper belabouring trooper, biting at arm or at face,
Plunges towards nothing, arms and fingers spreading wide
For the embrace of nothing; and I, my wits astray
15   Because of all that senseless tumult, all but cried
For vengeance on the murderers of Jacques Molay.

[11]   *Jacques Molay* (1244–1314), Grand Master of the Templars,
was arrested in 1307 and burned in 1314; see Yeat's note on
Section Seven, stanza II, on p. 343.

Their legs long, delicate and slender, aquamarine their eyes,
Magical unicorns bear ladies on their backs,
The ladies close their musing eyes. No prophecies,
Remembered out of Babylonian almanacs, 20
Have closed the ladies' eyes, their minds are but a pool
Where even longing drowns under its own excess;
Nothing but stillness can remain when hearts are full
Of their own sweetness, bodies of their loveliness.

The cloud-pale unicorns, the eyes of aquamarine, 25
The quivering half-closed eyelids, the rags of cloud or of lace,
Or eyes that rage has brightened, arms it has made lean,
Give place to an indifferent multitude, give place
To brazen hawks. Nor self-delighting reverie,
Nor hate of what's to come, nor pity for what's gone, 30
Nothing but grip of claw, and the eye's complacency,
The innumerable clanging wings that have put out the moon.

I turn away and shut the door, and on the stair
Wonder how many times I could have proved my worth
In something that all others understand or share; 35
But oh, ambitious heart, had such a proof drawn forth
A company of friends, a conscience set at ease,
It had but made us pine the more. The abstract joy,
The half-read wisdom of daemonic images,
Suffice the ageing man as once the growing boy. 40

Nineteen Hundred and Nineteen (1921)

I

Many ingenious lovely things are gone
That seemed sheer miracle to the multitude,
Protected from the circle of the moon
That pitches common things about. There stood
Amid the ornamental bronze and stone 5
An ancient image made of olive wood[1] –
And gone are Phidias' famous ivories[2]
And all the golden grasshoppers and bees.

We too had many pretty toys when young;
A law indifferent to blame or praise, 10
To bribe or threat; habits that made old wrong
Melt down, as it were wax in the sun's rays;
Public opinion ripening for so long
We thought it would outlive all future days.
O what fine thought we had because we thought 15
That the worst rogues and rascals had died out.

NINETEEN HUNDRED
The poem was written in 1919 and first appeared in the *Dial*
76(3) (Sept. 1921).
[1] *An ancient image made of olive wood* there was an olive-wood
statue of Athena Polias in the Erechtheum on the Acropolis in
Athens.

[2] *Phidias' famous ivories* the Athenian sculptor Phidias
(*c.* 490–417 BC) was famous for his gold and ivory statues
of Athena in the Parthenon and Zeus in the temple at Olympia.

All teeth were drawn, all ancient tricks unlearned,
And a great army but a showy thing;
What matter that no cannon had been turned
20   Into a ploughshare?[3] Parliament and king
Thought that unless a little powder burned
The trumpeters might burst with trumpeting
And yet it lack all glory; and perchance
The guardsmen's drowsy chargers would not prance.

25   Now days are dragon-ridden,[4] the nightmare
Rides upon sleep: a drunken soldiery
Can leave the mother, murdered at her door,
To crawl in her own blood, and go scot-free;
The night can sweat with terror as before
30   We pieced our thoughts into philosophy,
And planned to bring the world under a rule,
Who are but weasels fighting in a hole.

He who can read the signs nor sink unmanned
Into the half-deceit of some intoxicant
35   From shallow wits; who knows no work can stand,
Whether health, wealth or peace of mind were spent
On master-work of intellect or hand,
No honour leave its mighty monument,
Has but one comfort left: all triumph would
40   But break upon his ghostly solitude.

But is there any comfort to be found?
Man is in love and loves what vanishes,
What more is there to say? That country round
None dared admit, if such a thought were his,
45   Incendiary or bigot could be found
To burn that stump on the Acropolis,
Or break in bits the famous ivories
Or traffic in the grasshoppers or bees.

II

When Loie Fuller's Chinese dancers[5] enwound
50   A shining web, a floating ribbon of cloth,
It seemed that a dragon of air
Had fallen among dancers, had whirled them round
Or hurried them off on its own furious path;
So the Platonic year[6]
55   Whirls out new right and wrong,
Whirls in the old instead;
All men are dancers and their tread
Goes to the barbarous clangour of a gong.

---

[3]   *no cannon ... ploughshare* from Isaiah 2:4: "And they shall beat their swords into plowshares and their spears into pruning hooks: nation shall not lift up sword against nation neither shall they learn war any more."

[4]   *Now days are ...* this stanza refers to atrocities committed by the IRA and the Royal Irish Constabulary in the immediate aftermath of the First World War.

[5]   *Loie Fuller's Chinese dancers* Loie Fuller (1862–1928), an American dancer who used swirling draperies manipulated on sticks at the *Folies Bergère* in the 1890s and had a troupe of Japanese dancers.

[6]   *the Platonic Year* the idea was that all constellations would some day return to their original positions, so completing a cycle that would be called a Platonic year.

III

Some moralist or mythological poet[7]
Compares the solitary soul to a swan;   60
I am satisfied with that,
Satisfied if a troubled mirror show it,
Before that brief gleam of its life be gone,
An image of its state;
The wings half spread for flight,   65
The breast thrust out in pride
Whether to play, or to ride
Those winds that clamour of approaching night.

A man in his own secret meditation
Is lost amid the labyrinth that he has made   70
In art or politics;
Some Platonist affirms that in the station
Where we should cast off body and trade
The ancient habit sticks,
And that if our works could   75
But vanish with our breath
That were a lucky death,
For triumph can but mar our solitude.

The swan has leaped into the desolate heaven:
That image can bring wildness, bring a rage   80
To end all things, to end
What my laborious life imagined, even
The half-imagined, the half-written page;
O but we dreamed to mend
Whatever mischief seemed   85
To afflict mankind, but now
That winds of winter blow
Learn that we were crack-pated when we dreamed.

IV

We, who seven years ago
Talked of honour and of truth,   90
Shriek with pleasure if we show
The weasel's twist, the weasel's tooth.

V

Come let us mock at the great
That had such burdens on the mind
And toiled so hard and late   95
To leave some monument behind,
Nor thought of the levelling wind.

Come let us mock at the wise;
With all those calendars whereon

---

[7]   *Some moralist or mythological poet* probably Shelley in *Prometheus Unbound*, II.v.72–4: "My soul is like an enchanted boat, / Which, like a sleeping swan, doth float / Upon the silver waves of thy sweet singing ..."

100
    They fixed old aching eyes,
    They never saw how seasons run,
    And now but gape at the sun.

    Come let us mock at the good
    That fancied goodness might be gay,
105
    And sick of solitude
    Might proclaim a holiday:
    Wind shrieked – and where are they?

    Mock mockers after that
    That would not lift a hand maybe
110
    To help good, wise or great
    To bar that foul storm out, for we
    Traffic in mockery.

VI

    Violence upon the roads: violence of horses;
    Some few have handsome riders, are garlanded
115
    On delicate sensitive ear or tossing mane,
    But wearied running round and round in their courses
    All break and vanish, and evil gathers head:
    Herodias' daughters[8] have returned again,
    A sudden blast of dusty wind and after
120
    Thunder of feet, tumult of images,
    Their purpose in the labyrinth of the wind;
    And should some crazy hand dare touch a daughter
    All turn with amorous cries, or angry cries,
    According to the wind, for all are blind.
125
    But now wind drops, dust settles; thereupon
    There lurches past, his great eyes without thought
    Under the shadow of stupid straw-pale locks,
    That insolent fiend Robert Artisson[9]
    To whom the love-lorn Lady Kyteler brought
130
    Bronzed peacock feathers, red combs of her cocks.

The Wheel (1922)

    Through winter-time we call on spring,
    And through the spring on summer call,
    And when abounding hedges ring
    Declare that winter's best of all;

[8] *Herodias' daughters* Yeats may be recalling Arthur Symons's poem, "The Dance of the Daughters of Herodias," in which they dance:

  With their eternal, white, unfaltering feet,
  And always, when they dance, for their delight,
  Always a man's head falls because of them.
  Yet they desire not death, they would not slay
  Body or soul, no not to do them pleasure:
  They desire love, and the desire of men;
  And they are the eternal enemy.

They wither everything of value:

  The wisdom which is wiser than Kings know,
  The beauty which is fairer than things seen,
  Dreams which are nearer to eternity,
  Than that most mortal tumult of the blood
  Which wars on itself in loving, droop and die.

[9] *That insolent fiend Robert Artisson* He was a fourteenth-century fiend who haunted Dame Alice Kyteler, member of an Anglo-Norman family, who was condemned as a witch on July 2, 1324.

THE WHEEL
The poem was written on September 13, 1921, and first published in *Seven Poems and a Fragment* (Dublin: Cuala Press, 1922), a small collection (24 pages) issued in a limited edition.

And after that there's nothing good   5
Because the spring-time has not come –
Nor know what disturbs our blood
Is but its longing for the tomb.

Youth and Age (1924)

Much did I rage when young,
Being by the world oppressed,
But now with flattering tongue
It speeds the parting guest.

The New Faces (1922)

If you,[1] that have grown old, were the first dead,
Neither catalpa tree nor scented lime
Should hear my living feet, nor would I tread
Where we wrought that shall break the teeth of time.
Let the new faces play what tricks they will   5
In the old rooms; night can outbalance day,
Our shadows rove the garden gravel still,
The living seem more shadowy than they.

A Prayer for my Son (1922)

Bid a strong ghost stand at the head
That my Michael[1] may sleep sound,
Nor cry, not turn in the bed
Till his morning meal come round;
And may departing twilight keep   5
All dread afar till morning's back,
That his mother may not lack
Her fill of sleep.

Bid the ghost have sword in fist:
Some there are, for I avow   10
Such devilish things exist,
Who have planned his murder, for they know
Of some most haughty deed or thought
That waits upon his future days,
And would through hatred of the bays   15
Bring that to nought.

Though You[2] can fashion everything
From nothing every day, and teach

THE NEW FACES
The poem was written in 1924 and first published in *The Cat and the Moon, and Certain Poems* (Dublin: Cuala Press, 1924).

The poem was written in December 1921, and first appeared in *Seven Poems and a Fragment* (Dublin: Cuala Press, 1922), a small collection (24 pages) issued in a limited edition.
[1]   *you* Lady Augusta Gregory.

A PRAYER
The poem was written in December 1921 and first published in *Seven Poems and a Fragment* (Dublin: Cuala Press, 1922), a small collection (24 pages) issued in a limited edition.
[1]   *my Michael* Michael Butler Yeats (1921–   ), born at Castlebrook House, Thames, Oxfordshire.
[2]   *You* Christ.

```
20
```
The morning stars to sing,
You have lacked articulate speech
To tell Your simplest want, and known,
Wailing upon a woman's knee,
All of that worst ignominy
Of flesh and bone;

```
25
```
And when through all the town there ran
The servants of Your enemy,[3]
A woman and a man,[4]
Unless the Holy Writings lie,
Hurried through the smooth and rough

```
30
```
And through the fertile and waste,
Protecting, till the danger past,
With human love.

Two Songs from a Play (1927)

I

I saw a staring virgin[1] stand
Where holy Dionysus died,
And tear the heart out of his side,
And lay the heart upon her hand

```
5
```
And bear that beating heart away;
And then did all the Muses sing
Of Magnus Annus[2] at the spring,
As though God's death were but a play.

Another Troy must rise and set,

```
10
```
Another lineage feed the crow,
Another Argo's painted prow
Drive to a flashier bauble yet.[3]
The Roman Empire stood appalled:[4]
It dropped the reins of peace and war

```
15
```
When that fierce virgin and her Star[5]
Out of the fabulous darkness called.

[3] Your enemy King Herod who, fearing the prophecy that a ruler would come from Bethlehem, ordered all male children under two to be slain (see Matthew 2:16).

[4] A woman and man Mary and Joseph, who took Jesus to Egypt to escape Herod.

TWO SONGS
The poems were written in 1926 and first appeared in The Adelphi (June 1927), then in October Blast (Dublin: Cuala Press, 1927), a limited edition of only 24 pages.
[1] a staring virgin Athena, the goddess of wisdom, as described in Sir James Frazer's The Golden Bough: "Dionysus, child of a mortal Persephone, and an immortal, Zeus, was torn to pieces by the Titans. Athene snatched the heart from his body, brought it on her hand to Zeus, who killed the Titans, swallowed the heart, and begat Dionysus again, upon another mortal, Semele."
[2] Magnus Annus they sing of this as a play because the ritual death and rebirth of the god is a recurring event, a part of the cycles of history.

[3] Another Troy ... Another Argo these lines are developed from Vergil (70–19 BC), whose Eclogue IV, 31–6, reads:

Yet shall some few traces of olden sin lurk behind, to call men to essay the sea in ships, to gird towns with walls, and to cleave the earth with furrows. A second Tiphys shall then arise, and a second Argo to carry chosen heroes; a second warfare, too, shall there be, and again shall a great Achilles be sent to Troy.

[4] The Roman Empire stood appalled although Christians were as yet a minority within the empire's vast population, it would be destroyed by Christianity (a view Yeats shared with Gibbon).
[5] that fierce virgin and her Star the Virgin Mary, who is guided to the town of Bethlehem by a star.

II

In pity for man's darkening thought
He walked that room[6] and issued thence
In Galilean turbulence;[7]
The Babylonian starlight[8] brought   20
A fabulous, formless darkness in;
Odour of blood when Christ was slain
Made Platonic tolerance vain
And vain the Doric discipline.[9]

Wisdom (1927)

The true faith discovered was
When painted panel, statuary,
Glass-mosaic, window-glass,
Straightened all that went awry
When some peasant gospeller   5
Imagined Him upon the floor
Of that working-carpenter.[1]
Miracle had its playtime where
In damask clothed and on a seat
Chryselephantine, cedar-boarded,   10
His majestic Mother sat
Stitching at a purple hoarded
That He might be nobly breeched
In starry towers of Babylon
Noah's freshet[2] never reached.   15
King Abundance got Him on
Innocence; and Wisdom He.
That cognomen sounded best
Considering what wild infancy
Drove horror from His Mother's breast.   20

Leda and the Swan (1924)

A sudden blow: the great wings beating still
Above the staggering girl, her thighs caressed
By the dark webs, her nape caught in his bill,
He holds her helpless breast upon his breast.

[6] *that room* where the last supper took place
[7] *Galilean turbulence* from Galilee, the scene of Christ's early ministry.
[8] *Babylonian starlight* Yeats, in *A Vision* (p. 268), refers to "the Babylonian mathematical starlight." Babylon was the chief city of ancient Mesopotamia; the Babylonian empire flourished from *c.* 2200 to 538 BC, famous for its astronomy and astrology.
[9] *Platonic tolerance ... Doric discipline* the philosophy and architecture of classical Greece, superseded by Christianity.

WISDOM
The poem's composition has not yet been dated; it first appeared in *October Blast* (Dublin: Cuala Press, 1927), a limited edition of only 24 pages.
[1] *that working-carpenter* most likely Joseph, husband of the Virgin Mary, who was a carpenter.

[2] *Noah's freshet* the flood that covered the whole world (see Genesis 6:5–19); only Noah, his family, and the animals on the ark with him survived.

LEDA
The poem was written on September 18, 1923, and first appeared in the *Dial* (June 1924); it was then reprinted in *The Cat and the Moon, and Certain Poems* (Dublin: Cuala Press, 1924). In its first book publication, it was accompanied by a note on the poem's genesis:

I wrote Leda and the Swan because the editor of a political review asked me for a poem. I thought "After the individualist, demagogic movement founded by Hobbes and popularised by the Encyclopaedists and the French Revolution, we have a soil so exhausted that it cannot grow that crop again

5   How can those terrified vague fingers push
     The feathered glory from her loosening thighs?
     And how can body, laid in that white rush,
     But feel the strange heart beating where it lies?

     A shudder in the loins engenders there
10   The broken wall, the burning roof and tower
     And Agamemnon dead.
                         Being so caught up,
     So mastered by the brute blood of the air,
     Did she put on his knowledge with his power
     Before the indifferent beak could let her drop?

On a Picture of a Black Centaur by Edmund Dulac (1922)

     Your hooves have stamped at the black margin of the wood,
     Even where horrible green parrots call and swing.
     My works are all stamped down into the sultry mud.
     I knew that horse-play, knew it for a murderous thing.
5   What wholesome sun has ripened is wholesome food to eat,
     And that alone; yet I, being driven half insane
     Because of some green wing, gathered old mummy wheat[1]
     In the mad abstract dark and ground it grain by grain
     And after baked it slowly in an oven; but now
10   I bring full-flavoured wine out of a barrel found
     Where seven Ephesian topers[2] slept and never knew
     When Alexander's empire[3] passed, they slept so sound.
     Stretch out your limbs and sleep a long Saturnian sleep;[4]
     I have loved you better than my soul for all my words,
15   And there is none so fit to keep a watch and keep
     Unwearied eyes upon those horrible green birds.

for centuries." Then I thought "Nothing is now possible but some movement, or birth from above, preceded by some violent annunciation." My fancy began to play with Leda and the Swan for metaphor and I began this poem; but as I wrote, bird and lady took such possession of the scene that all politics went out of it, and my friend tells me that "his conservative readers would misunderstand the poem."

Leda, in Greek mythology, was ravished by Zeus in the guise of a swan. She gave birth to Helen of Troy and the twins Pollux and Castor, according to the mythographer Apollodorus; and in a variant tradition, she also gave birth to Clytemnestra, who became the wife of King Agamemnon. The Trojan War was caused by Paris abducting Helen from her husband Menelaus and taking her to Troy, and ended in the city's destruction; but when Agamemnon, the leader of the Greeks, returned to his home, he was murdered by Clytemnestra. The motif of Leda and the swan became a favorite subject of Renaissance and post-Renaissance painters; their extremely stylized and elegant works are in conspicuous contrast to Yeats's emphasis on violence and bestiality.

ON A PICTURE
The poem was written in September 1920 and first published in *Seven Poems and a Fragment* (Dublin: Cuala Press, 1922),

a small collection (24 pages) issued in a limited edition. Edmund Dulac (1882–1953) was an English artist who designed the masks and costumes for Yeats's play, *At the Hawk's Well* (for the text, see pp. 351–62). He also illustrated several of Yeats's books.

[1]   *mummy wheat* hidden wisdom which has ripened centuries after its sowing; the phrase recurs in "All Souls' Night" (see p. 339).

[2]   *seven Ephesian topers* they slept for two centuries in a cave near Ephesus (a city on the coast of Asia Minor, now modern Turkey); when they awoke, around 425 AD, their faith was confirmed by the Emperor Theodosius II. The speaker of Yeats's poem brings wine as strong as that which put them to sleep for so long.

[3]   *Alexander's empire* Alexander the Great (356–323 BC) and his empire had passed away long before the sleepers of Ephesus fell asleep; but Yeats is not worried here about chronological niceties.

[4]   *Saturnian sleep* the sleep of a golden age, as was the era ruled by Saturn, an ancient Italian god of agriculture.

Among School Children (1927)

I

I walk through the long schoolroom[1] questioning;
A kind old nun in a white hood replies;
The children learn to cipher and to sing,
To study reading-books and history,
To cut and sew, be neat in everything   5
In the best modern way – the children's eyes
In momentary wonder stare upon
A sixty-year-old smiling public man.

II

I dream of a Ledaean body,[2] bent
Above a sinking fire, a tale that she   10
Told of a harsh reproof, or trivial event
That changed some childish day to tragedy –
Told, and it seemed that our two natures blent
Into a sphere from youthful sympathy,
Or else, to alter Plato's parable,[3]   15
Into the yolk and white of the one shell.

III

And thinking of that fit of grief or rage
I look upon one child or t'other there
And wonder if she stood so at that age –
For even daughters of the swan can share   20
Something of every paddler's heritage –
And had that colour upon cheek or hair,
And thereupon my heart is driven wild:
She stands before me as a living child.

IV

Her present image floats into the mind –   25
Did quattrocento finger[4] fashion it
Hollow of cheek as though it drank the wind
And took a mess of shadows for its meat?
And I though never of Ledaean kind
Had pretty plumage once – enough of that,   30
Better to smile on all that smile, and show
There is a comfortable kind of old scarecrow.

AMONG SCHOOL CHILDREN
The poem was written on June 14, 1926 and first appeared in the
Dial (Aug. 1927) and *LM* (Aug. 1927).
[1] *long schoolroom* Yeats visited St. Otteran's School in Waterford
in February 1926; it was run on Montessori principles and Yeats
praised its work in a speech to the Irish Senate (see Donald R.
Pearce, *The Senate Speeches of W. B. Yeats* [London: Faber & Faber,
1961], p. 111).
[2] *Ledaean body* a body as beautiful as that of Leda, one that
belonged to a woman the speaker knew long ago. For Leda, see
the introductory note to "Leda and the Swan" on p. 325.

[3] *Plato's parable* in *The Symposium*, one of the speakers explains
the origin of human love by recounting the legend which urges
that human beings were originally double their present form
until Zeus, afraid of their power, divided them in two, in the
same way as men "cut eggs into two with a hair." Since then each
of them is "forever seeking his missing half." See Edith Hamilton
and Huntington Cairns (eds.), *The Collected Dialogues of Plato*
(Princeton: Princeton University Press, 1961), pp. 543–4.
[4] *quattrocento finger* the hand of an Italian artist between
1400 and 1500, a period characterized by exceptional purity of
line.

V

What youthful mother, a shape upon her lap
Honey of generation[5] had betrayed,
35   And that must sleep, shriek, struggle to escape
As recollection or the drug decide,
Would think her son, did she but see that shape
With sixty or more winters on its head,
A compensation for the pang of his birth,
40   Or the uncertainty of his setting forth?

VI

Plato thought nature but a spume that plays
Upon a ghostly paradigm of things;[6]
Solider Aristotle played the taws[7]
Upon the bottom of a king of kings;
45   World-famous golden-thighed Pythagoras[8]
Fingered upon a fiddle-stick or strings
What a star sang and careless Muses heard:
Old clothes upon old sticks to scare a bird.

VII

Both nuns and mothers worship images,
50   But those the candles light are not as those
That animate a mother's reveries,
But keep a marble or a bronze repose.
And yet they too break hearts – O Presences
That passion, piety or affection knows,
55   And that all heavenly glory symbolise –
O self-born mockers of man's enterprise;

VIII

Labour is blossoming or dancing where
The body is not bruised to pleasure soul,
Nor beauty born out of its own despair,
60   Nor blear-eyed wisdom out of midnight oil.
O chestnut tree, great rooted blossomer,
Are you the leaf, the blossom or the bole?
O body swayed to music, O brightening glance,
How can we know the dancer from the dance?

---

[5]   *Honey of generation* see Yeats's note to "Among School Children," stanza III, on p. 343. Porphyry (c. 232–305 AD) was a neoplatonic commentator who explained the allegorical significance of the Cave of the Nymphs in Book 14 of the *Odyssey*. According to him "the sweetness of honey signifies … the same thing as the pleasure arising from copulation," the pleasure "which draws souls downward to generation."

[6]   *ghostly paradigm of things* in Plato's idealistic philosophy, the things of the world are only imperfect copies ("spume") of ideal, permanently enduring prototypes or forms ("ghostly paradigms," in Yeats's terms).

[7]   *soldier Aristotle* Aristotle, although a pupil of Plato, urged a philosophy of empirical observation and verification. He was tutor to Alexander, the son of King Philip of Macedonia, who later became Alexander the Great. "Played the taws" means *whipped*.

[8]   *golden-thighed Pythagoras* a Greek philosopher (c. 540–510 BC) who, according to legend, had a golden thigh or hipbone. Central to Pythagorean philosophy was a doctrine of the transmigration of souls and a belief that the universe was mathematically regular in the same way as music, which was much cultivated by Pythagoreans.

Colonus' Praise (1928)

Chorus. Come praise Colonus' horses, and come praise
 The wine-dark of the wood's intricacies,
 The nightingale that deafens daylight there,
 If daylight ever visit where,
 Unvisited by tempest or by sun,   5
 Immortal ladies tread the ground
 Dizzy with harmonious sound,
 Semele's lad[1] a gay companion.

 And younger in the gymnasts' garden[2] thrives
 The self-sown, self-begotten shape that gives   10
 Athenian intellect its mastery,
 Even the grey-leaved olive-tree[3]
 Miracle-bred out of the living stone;
 Nor accident of peace nor war
 Shall wither that old marvel, for   15
 The great grey-eyed Athena stares thereon.

 Who comes into this country, and has come
 Where golden crocus and narcissus bloom,
 Where the Great Mother,[4] mourning for her daughter
 And beauty-drunken by the water   20
 Glittering among grey-leaved olive trees,
 Has plucked a flower and sung her loss;
 Who finds abounding Cephisus[5]
 Has found the loveliest spectacle there is.

 Because this country has a pious mind   25
 And so remembers that when all mankind
 But trod the road, or paddled by the shore,
 Poseidon[6] gave it bit and oar,
 Every Colonus lad or lass discourses
 Of that oar and of that bit;   30
 Summer and winter, day and night,
 Of horses and horses of the sea, white horses.

COLONUS' PRAISE

This poem translates a chorus from the play *Oedipus at Colonus* by the Athenian dramatist Sophocles (*c.* 495–406 BC). Yeats wrote it in late March 1927, and his translation of the entire play was produced at the Abbey Theatre on September 12, 1927. The chorus was first published in *The Tower*. In translating the play, Yeats based himself on a French translation by Paul Masqueray, since he could not read Greek.

[1] *Semele's lad* Dionysius, son of Zeus and Semele. Hera, jealous of Semele's association with Zeus, disguises herself and advises Semele to test her lover's divinity by asking him to come to her in his true form. Semele, in turn, tricks Zeus into granting her whatever she might request; but when she asks to see him in his true form, she is killed by the fire of his thunderbolts. Later, Dionysius journeys to the underworld and rescues her, and thereafter she is made into a goddess.

[2] *the gymnasts' garden* a sacred grove at Athens on the banks of the river Cephisus.

[3] *the grey-leaved olive tree* on the Acropolis at Athens, where they were protected by Athena.

[4] *the Great Mother* Demeter, who forever mourns her daughter Persephone, who has been carried off to the underworld by Hades and is allowed to return for half the year to see her mother, the time of spring and summer.

[5] *abounding Cephisus* a river in Attica, Greece.

[6] *Poseidon* god of horses and the sea.

The Hero, the Girl, and the Fool (1922)

The Girl. I rage at my own image in the glass
    That's so unlike myself that when you praise it
    It is as though you praised another, or even
    Mocked me with praise of my mere opposite;
5   And when I wake towards morn I dread myself,
    For the heart cries that what deception wins
    Cruelty must keep; therefore be warned and go
    If you have seen that image and not the woman.

The Hero. I have raged at my own strength because you have loved it.

10 *The Girl.* If you are no more strength than I am beauty
    I had better find a convent and turn nun;
    A nun at least has all men's reverence
    And needs no cruelty.

The Hero. I have heard one say
15   That men have reverence for their holiness
    And not themselves.

The Girl. Say on and say
    That only God has loved us for ourselves,
    But what care I that long for a man's love?

The Fool by the Roadside. When my days that have
    From cradle run to grave
    From grave to cradle run instead;
20   When thoughts that a fool
    Has wound upon a spool
    Are but loose thread, are but loose thread;

    When cradle and spool are past
    And I mere shade at last
    Coagulate of stuff
    Transparent like the wind,
    I think that I may find
    A faithful love, a faithful love.

Owen Aherne and his Dancers (1924)

I

A strange thing surely that my Heart, when love had come unsought
Upon the Norman upland or in that poplar shade,
Should find no burden but itself and yet should be worn out.
It could not bear that burden and therefore it went mad.

5   The south wind brought it longing, and the east wind despair,
    The west wind made it pitiful, and the north wind afraid.
    It feared to give its love a hurt with all the tempest there;
    It feared the hurt that she could give and therefore it went mad.

THE HERO
This poem was first published in *Seven Poems and a Fragment* (Dublin: Cuala Press, 1922) under the title "Cuchulain, the Girl and the Fool," then included under the present title in *The Tower.*

OWEN AHERNE
The first part of this poem was written in October 1917, and the entire poem was first published in the *Dial* (June 1924), with the first section titled "The Lover Speaks," and the second "The Heart Replies."

I can exchange opinion with any neighbouring mind,
I have as healthy flesh and blood as any rhymer's had,   10
But oh my Heart could bear no more when the upland caught the wind;
I ran, I ran, from my love's side because my Heart went mad.

II

The Heart behind its rib laughed out. 'You have called me mad,' it said.
'Because I made you turn away and run from that young child;
How could she mate with fifty years that was so wildly bred?   15
Let the cage bird and the cage bird mate and the wild bird mate in the wild.'

'You but imagine lies all day, O murderer,' I replied.
'And all those lies have but one end, poor wretches to betray;
I did not find in any cage the woman at my side.
O but her heart would break to learn my thoughts are far away.'   20

'Speak all your mind,' my Heart sang out, 'speak all your mind; who cares,
Now that your tongue cannot persuade the child till she mistake
Her childish gratitude for love and match your fifty years?
O let her choose a young man now and all for his wild sake.'

A Man Young and Old (1927)

I.   First Love

Though nurtured like the sailing moon
In beauty's murderous brood,
She walked awhile and blushed awhile
And on my pathway stood
Until I thought her body bore   5
A heart of flesh and blood.

But since I laid a hand thereon
And found a heart of stone
I have attempted many things
And not a thing is done,   10
For every hand is lunatic
That travels on the moon.

She smiled and that transfigured me
And left me but a lout,
Maundering here, and maundering there,   15
Emptier of thought
Than the heavenly circuit of its stars
When the moon sails out.

II.   Human Dignity

Like the moon her kindness is,
If kindness I may call
What has no comprehension in't,
But is the same for all

A MAN
These poems were written in 1926 and 1927; numbers VI, VII,
VII, and X first appeared under the title "More Songs from an

Old Countryman" and were published in *LM* (April 1926), while
the others first appeared in *LM* (May 1927) with the title "Four
Songs from the Young Countryman."

5   As though my sorrow were a scene
       Upon a painted wall.

       So like a bit of stone I lie
       Under a broken tree.
       I could recover if I shrieked
10   My heart's agony
       To passing bird, but I am dumb
       From human dignity.

III.   The Mermaid

       A mermaid found a swimming lad,
       Picked him for her own,
       Pressed her body to his body,
       Laughed; and plunging down
5   Forgot in cruel happiness
       That even lovers drown.

IV.   The Death of the Hare

       I have pointed out the yelling pack,
       The hare leap to the wood,
       And when I pass a compliment
       Rejoice as lover should
5   At the drooping of an eye,
       At the mantling of the blood.

       Then suddenly my heart is wrung
       By her distracted air
       And I remember wildness lost
10   And after, swept from there,
       Am set down standing in the wood
       At the death of the hare.

V.   The Empty Cup

       A crazy man that found a cup,
       When all but dead of thirst,
       Hardly dared to wet his mouth
       Imagining, moon-accursed,
5   That another mouthful
       And his beating heart would burst.
       October last I found it too
       But found it dry as bone,
       And for that reason am I crazed
10   And my sleep is gone.

VI.   His Memories

       We should be hidden from their eyes,
       Being but holy shows
       And bodies broken like a thorn
       Whereon the bleak north blows,
5   To think of buried Hector
       And that none living knows.

The women take so little stock
In what I do or say
They'd sooner leave their cosseting
To hear a jackass bray;   10
My arms are like the twisted thorn
And yet there beauty lay;

The first of all the tribe lay there
And did such pleasure take —
She who had brought great Hector down   15
And put all Troy to wreck —
That she cried into this ear,
'Strike me if I shriek.'

VII.   *The Friends of his Youth*

Laughter not time destroyed my voice
And put that crack in it,
And when the moon's pot-bellied
I get a laughing fit,
For that old Madge comes down the lane,   5
A stone upon her breast,
And a cloak wrapped about the stone,
And she can get no rest
With singing hush and hush-a-bye;
She that has been wild   10
And barren as a breaking wave
Thinks that the stone's a child.
And Peter that had great affairs
And was a pushing man
Shrieks, 'I am King of the Peacocks,'   15
And perches on a stone;
And then I laugh till tears run down
And the heart thumps at my side,
Remembering that her shriek was love
And that he shrieks from pride.   20

VIII.   *Summer and Spring*

We sat under an old thorn-tree
And talked away the night,
Told all that had been said or done
Since first we saw the light,
And when we talked of growing up   5
Knew that we'd halved a soul
And fell the one in t'other's arms
That we might make it whole;
Then Peter had a murdering look,   10
For it seemed that he and she
Had spoken of their childish days
Under that very tree.
O what a bursting out there was,
And what a blossoming,   15
When we had all the summer time
And she had all the spring!

IX.   *The Secrets of the Old*

I have old women's secrets now
That had those of the young;
Madge tells me what I dared not think
When my blood was strong,
5   And what had drowned a lover once
Sounds like an old song.

Though Margery is stricken dumb
If thrown in Madge's way,
We three make up a solitude;
10   For none alive to-day
Can know the stories that we know
Or say the things we say:

How such a man pleased women most
Of all that are gone,
15   How such a pair loved many years
And such a pair but one,
Stories of the bed of straw
Or the bed of down.

X.   *His Wildness*

O bid me mount and sail up there
Amid the cloudy wrack,
For Peg and Meg and Paris' love
That had so straight a back,
5   Are gone away, and some that stay
Have changed their silk for sack.
Were I but there and none to hear
I'd have a peacock cry,
For that is natural to a man
10   That lives in memory,
Being all alone I'd nurse a stone
And sing it lullaby.

The Three Monuments (1927)

They hold their public meetings where
Our most renownèd patriots stand,
One among the birds of the air,
A stumpier on either hand;
5   And all the popular statesmen say
That purity built up the state
And after kept it from decay;
Admonish us to cling to that
And let all base ambition be,

The poem was written in early 1925, before the Irish Senate debate on divorce in June that year; it first appeared in *October Blast* (Dublin: Cuala Press, 1927), a 24-page limited edition.

The title refers to the statues of the Irish politicians Daniel O'Connell (1745–1833) and Charles Stewart Parnell (1846–91), which both flanked the statue of the English naval commander Horatio Nelson (1758–1805). (The latter was destroyed by a bomb in 1966.) The poem's discussion of "purity" takes place against the background of shared knowledge that Nelson had a notorious affair with Lady Hamilton, while Parnell was brought down when his adulterous affair with Kitty O'Shea was made public.

For intellect would make us proud   10
And pride bring in impurity:
The three old rascals laugh aloud.

From 'Oedipus at Colonus' (1927)

I

Endure what life God gives and ask no longer span;
Cease to remember the delights of youth, travel-wearied aged man;
Delight becomes death-longing if all longing else be vain.

II

Even from that delight memory treasures so,
Death, despair, division of families, all entanglements of mankind grow,   5
As that old wandering beggar and these God-hated children know.

III

In the long echoing street the laughing dancers throng,
The bride is carried to the bridegroom's chamber through torchlight and tumultuous song;
I celebrate the silent kiss that ends short life or long.

IV

Never to have lived is best, ancient writers say;   10
Never to have drawn the breath of life, never to have looked into the eye of day;
The second best's a gay goodnight and quickly turn away.

The Gift of Harun Al-Rashid[1] (1924)

Kusta ben Luka[2] is my name, I write
To Abd Al-Rabban; fellow-roysterer once,
Now the good Caliph's learned Treasurer,
And for no ear but his.
                          Carry this letter
Through the great gallery of the Treasure House   5
Where banners of the Caliphs hang, night-coloured
But brilliant as the night's embroidery,
And wait war's music; pass the little gallery;
Pass books of learning from Byzantium
Written in gold upon a purple stain,   10
And pause at last, I was about to say,

From 'Oedipus'
See note to "Colonus' Praise," p. 329.

The Gift
The poem was written in 1923 and first appeared in *English Life
and the Illustrated Reveiw* (Jan. 1924).
[1] *Harun Al-Rashid* Al-Rashid (766–809) became the fifth
caliph of the Abbasid dynasty in 786. Under him the Abbasid
caliphate reached the height of its power, its empire extending
from the Mediterranean to India. His court at Baghdad, famous
for its splendor, was a noted center of the arts and learning. He
often traveled about his city at night in disguise, and he is
especially known as the leading character in the tales of the
Arabian Nights.
[2] *Kusta Ben Luka* Qusta ibn Luqa (820–912) was a doctor and a
translator of Greek and Syrian texts into Arabic; but for Yeats he
is essentially a fictional figure who epitomizes a noble commitment to literary and cultural learning.

At the great book of Sappho's song;[3] but no,
For should you leave my letter there, a boy's
Love-lorn, indifferent hands might come upon it
15   And let it fall unnoticed to the floor.
Pause at the Treatise of Parmenides[4]
And hide it there, for Caliphs to world's end
Must keep that perfect, as they keep her song,
So great its fame.
                              When fitting time has passed
20   The parchment will disclose to some learned man
A mystery that else had found no chronicler
But the wild Bedouin. Though I approve
Those wanderers that welcomed in their tents
What great Harun Al-Rashid, occupied
25   With Persian embassy or Grecian war,
Must needs neglect, I cannot hide the truth
That wandering in a desert, featureless
As air under a wing, can give birds' wit.
In after time they will speak much of me
30   And speak but phantasy. Recall the year
When our beloved Caliph put to death
His Vizir Jaffer[5] for an unknown reason:
'If but the shirt upon my body knew it
I'd tear it off and throw it in the fire.'
35   That speech was all that the town knew, but he
Seemed for a while to have grown young again;
Seemed so on purpose, muttered Jaffer's friends,
That none might know that he was conscience-struck –
But that's a traitor's thought. Enough for me
40   That in the early summer of the year
The mightiest of the princes of the world
Came to the least considered of his courtiers;
Sat down upon the fountain's marble edge,
One hand amid the goldfish in the pool;
45   And thereupon a colloquy took place
That I commend to all the chroniclers
To show how violent great hearts can lose
Their bitterness and find the honeycomb.
'I have brought a slender bride into the house;
50   You know the saying, "Change the bride with spring,"
And she and I, being sunk in happiness,
Cannot endure to think you tread these paths,
When evening stirs the jasmine bough, and yet
Are brideless.'

55   'I am falling into years.'

'But such as you and I do not seem old
Like men who live by habit. Every day
I ride with falcon to the river's edge
Or carry the ringed mail upon my back,
Or court a woman; neither enemy,

[3]   the great book of Sappho's song the Greek poet Sappho (c. 612–572 BC) is known through a small quantity of surviving poems; Yeats's poem indulges in the fiction that much more of her work, "the great book of Sappho's song," survived as late as 900 AD in the library at the court of Harun Al-Rashid.
[4]   Treatise of Parmenides Parmenides of Elea (fl. 450 BC) was a philosopher known only through the surviving fragments of a long poem. Yeats's poem plays with the idea that his work might have survived in its entirety as late as 900 AD in the library of the caliph, Harun Al-Rashid.
[5]   Vizer Jaffer an historical figure who governed under the caliph Harun Al-Rashid from 786 to 803 AD, then was imprisoned and executed for reasons that remain mysterious.

Game-bird, nor woman does the same thing twice;   60
And so a hunter carries in the eye
A mimicry of youth. Can poet's thought
That springs from body and in body falls
Like this pure jet, now lost amid blue sky,
Now bathing lily leaf and fish's scale,   65
Be mimicry?'
          'What matter if our souls
Are nearer to the surface of the body
Than souls that start no game and turn no rhyme!
The soul's own youth and not the body's youth   70
Shows through our lineaments. My candle's bright,
My lantern is too loyal not to show
That it was made in your great father's reign.'

'And yet the jasmine season warms our blood.'

'Great prince, forgive the freedom of my speech: 75
You think that love has seasons, and you think
That if the spring bear off what the spring gave
The heart need suffer no defeat; but I
Who have accepted the Byzantine faith,
That seems unnatural to Arabian minds,   80
Think when I choose a bride I choose for ever;
And if her eye should not grow bright for mine
Or brighten only for some younger eye,
My heart could never turn from daily ruin,
Nor find a remedy.'   85
              'But what if I
Have lit upon a woman who so shares
Your thirst for those old crabbed mysteries,
So strains to look beyond our life, an eye
That never knew that strain would scarce seem bright,
And yet herself can seem youth's very fountain,
Being all brimmed with life?'   90
                        'Were it but true
I would have found the best that life can give,
Companionship in those mysterious things
That make a man's soul or a woman's soul
Itself and not some other soul.'
                      'That love
Must needs be in this life and in what follows   95
Unchanging and at peace, and it is right
When our beloved Caliph put to death
Every philosopher should praise that love.
But I being none can praise its opposite.
It makes my passion stronger but to think
Like passion stirs the peacock and his mate,   100
The wild stag and the doe; that mouth to mouth
Is a man's mockery of the changeless soul.'
And thereupon his bounty gave what now
Can shake more blossom from autumnal chill
Than all my bursting springtime knew. A girl   105
Perched in some window of her mother's house
Had watched my daily passage to and fro;
Had heard impossible history of my past;
Imagined some impossible history
Lived at my side; thought time's disfiguring touch   110
Gave but more reason for a woman's care.

Yet was it love of me, or was it love
Of the stark mystery that has dazed my sight,
Perplexed her phantasy and planned her care?
115   Or did the torchlight of that mystery
Pick out my features in such light and shade
Two contemplating passions chose one theme
Through sheer bewilderment? She had not paced
The garden paths, nor counted up the rooms,
120   Before she had spread a book upon her knees
And asked about the pictures or the text;
And often those first days I saw her stare
On old dry writing in a learned tongue,
On old dry faggots that could never please
125   The extravagance of spring; or move a hand
As if that writing or the figured page
Were some dear cheek.
                                    Upon a moonless night
I sat where I could watch her sleeping form,
And wrote by candle-light; but her form moved,
130   And fearing that my light disturbed her sleep
I rose that I might screen it with a cloth.
I heard her voice, 'Turn that I may expound
What's bowed your shoulder and made pale your cheek';
And saw her sitting upright on the bed;
135   Or was it she that spoke or some great Djinn?
I say that a Djinn spoke. A live-long hour
She seemed the learned man and I the child;
Truths without father came, truths that no book
Of all the uncounted books that I have read,
140   Nor thought out of her mind or mine begot,
Self-born, high-born, and solitary truths,
Those terrible implacable straight lines
Drawn through the wandering vegetative dream,
Even those truths that when my bones are dust
145   Must drive the Arabian host.
                                          The voice grew still,
And she lay down upon her bed and slept,
But woke at the first gleam of day, rose up
And swept the house and sang about her work
In childish ignorance of all that passed.
150   A dozen nights of natural sleep, and then
When the full moon swam to its greatest height
She rose, and with her eyes shut fast in sleep
Walked through the house. Unnoticed and unfelt
I wrapped her in a heavy hooded cloak, and she,
155   Half running, dropped at the first ridge of the desert
And there marked out those emblems on the sand
That day by day I study and marvel at,
With her white finger. I led her home asleep
And once again she rose and swept the house
160   In childish ignorance of all that passed.
Even to-day, after some seven years
When maybe thrice in every moon her mouth
Murmured the wisdom of the desert Djinns,
She keeps that ignorance, nor has she now
165   That first unnatural interest in my books.
It seems enough that I am there; and yet,

Old fellow-student, whose most patient ear
Heard all the anxiety of my passionate youth,
It seems I must buy knowledge with my peace.
What if she lose her ignorance and so   170
Dream that I love her only for the voice,
That every gift and every word of praise
Is but a payment for that midnight voice
That is to age what milk is to a child?
Were she to lose her love, because she had lost   175
Her confidence in mine, or even lose
Its first simplicity, love, voice and all,
All my fine feathers would be plucked away
And I left shivering. The voice has drawn
A quality of wisdom from her love's   180
Particular quality. The signs and shapes;
All those abstractions that you fancied were
From the great Treatise of Parmenides;
All, all those gyres and cubes and midnight things
Are but a new expression of her body   185
Drunk with the bitter sweetness of her youth.
And now my utmost mystery is out.
A woman's beauty is a storm-tossed banner;
Under it wisdom stands, and I alone –
Of all Arabia's lovers I alone –   190
Nor dazzled by the embroidery, nor lost
In the confusion of its night-dark folds,
Can hear the armed man speak.

All Souls' Night[1] (1921)

An Epilogue to 'A Vision'

Midnight has come and the great Christ Church bell[2]
And many a lesser bell sound through the room;
And it is All Souls' Night.
And two long glasses brimmed with muscatel
Bubble upon the table. A ghost may come;   5
For it is a ghost's right,
His element is so fine
Being sharpened by his death,
To drink from the wine-breath
While our gross palates drink from the whole wine.   10

I need some mind that, if the cannon sound
From every quarter of the world, can stay
Wound in mind's pondering,
As mummies in the mummy-cloth are wound;
Because I have a marvellous thing to say,   15
A certain marvellous thing
None but the living mock,
Though not for sober ear;

ALL SOUL'S NIGHT
The poem was written in November 1920 at Oxford. It first appeared in the *New Republic* (March 9, 1921) and *LM* (March 1921).

[1] *All Souls' Night* usually November 2, when Roman Catholics pray for the souls of the faithful still in Purgatory.
[2] *Christ Church bell* Christ Church, Oxford, is a college founded by Cardinal Wolsey (1475–1530). Yeats was living in a house in Broad Street, Oxford, when he wrote the poem.

It may be all that hear
20   Should laugh and weep an hour upon the clock.

H—'s zthe first I call.[3] He loved strange thought
And knew that sweet extremity of pride
That's called platonic love,[4]
And that to such a pitch of passion wrought
25   Nothing could bring him, when his lady died,
Anodyne for his love.
Words were but wasted breath;
One dear hope had he:
The inclemency
30   Of that or the next winter would be death.

Two thoughts were so mixed up I could not tell
Whether of her or God he thought the most,
But think that his mind's eye,
When upward turned, on one sole image fell;
35   And that a slight companionable ghost,
Wild with divinity,
Had so lit up the whole
Immense miraculous house,
The Bible promised us,
40   It seemed a gold-fish swimming in a bowl.

On Florence Emery[5] I call the next,
Who finding the first wrinkles on a face
Admired and beautiful,
And knowing that the future would be vexed
45   With minished beauty, multiplied commonplace,
Preferred to teach a school
Away from neighbour or friend,
Among dark skins, and there
Permit foul years to wear
50   Hidden from eyesight to the unnoticed end.

Before that end much had she ravelled out
From a discourse in figurative speech
By some learned Indian[6]
On the soul's journey. How it is whirled about,
55   Wherever the orbit of the moon can reach,
Until it plunge into the sun;
And there, free and yet fast,
Being both Chance and Choice,
Forget its broken toys
60   And sink into its own delight at last.

I call MacGregor[7] from the grave,
For in my first hard spring-time we were friends,

[3] H—'s the first William Thomas Horton (1864–1919) was an illustrator and a participant with Yeats in a mystical society called the Order of the Golden Dawn in 1898.

[4] platonic love in the first edition of A Vision (1925), Yeats recounts Horton's platonic rapport with Audrey Locke (1881–1916), undertaken by both as a form of spiritual self-discipline. See George Mills Harper and Walter Kelly Hood (eds.), A Critical Edition of Yeats's "A Vision" (1925) (London: Macmillan, 1978), p. x.

[5] Florence Emery Florence Farr Emery (1869–1917) was an actress and theatrical producer, and she shared his mystical interests. They met in 1890 and she too was a member of the Order of the Golden Dawn in the late 1890s. In 1912 she moved to Ceylon, where she taught at a Buddhist institution, Ramanathan College.

[6] some learned Indian probably Ponnambalam Ramanathan (1851–1930), whom Florence Farr met in England in 1902, and who strongly influenced her.

[7] MacGregor MacGregor Mathers (1854–1918) was a student of the occult who translated the Kabalah Denudata; Yeats describes

Although of late estranged.
I thought him half a lunatic, half knave,
And told him so, but friendship never ends;   65
And what if mind seem changed,
And it seem changed with the mind,
When thoughts rise up unbid
On generous things that he did
And I grow half contented to be blind.   70

He had much industry at setting out,
Much boisterous courage, before loneliness
Had driven him crazed;
For meditations upon unknown thought
Make human intercourse grow less and less;   75
They are neither paid nor praised.
But he'd object to the host,
The glass because my glass;
A ghost-lover he was
And may have grown more arrogant being a ghost.   80

But names are nothing. What matter who it be,
So that his elements have grown so fine
The fume of muscatel
Can give his sharpened palate ecstasy
No living man can drink from the whole wine.   85
I have mummy truths to tell
Whereat the living mock,
Though not for sober ear,
For maybe all that hear
Should laugh and weep an hour upon the clock.   90

Such thought – such thought have I that hold it tight
Till meditation master all its parts,
Nothing can stay my glance
Until that glance run in the world's despite
To where the damned have howled away their hearts,   95
And where the blessed dance;
Such thought, that in it bound
I need no other thing
Wound in mind's wandering,
As mummies in the mummy-cloth are wound.   100

W. B. Yeats's Notes to The Tower

Sailing to Byzantium, stanza IV

I have read somewhere that in the Emperor's palace at Byzantium was a tree made of gold and silver, and artificial birds that sang.

The Tower, part II

The persons mentioned are associated by legend, story and tradition with the neighbourhood of Thoor Ballylee or Ballylee Castle, where the poem was written. Mrs. French lived at Peterswell in

him in his *Autobiography* in the section titled "Four Years: 1887–1891." He was another member of the Order of the Golden Dawn, but was suspended from it in 1900 by a committee which included Yeats.

the eighteenth century and was related to Sir Jonah Barrington, who described the incident of the ear and the trouble that came of it. The peasant beauty and the blind poet are Mary Hynes and Raftery, and the incident of the man drowned in Cloone Bog is recorded in my *Celtic Twilight*. Hanrahan's pursuit of the phantom hare and hounds is from my *Stories of Red Hanrahan*. The ghosts have been seen at their game of dice in what is now my bedroom, and the old bankrupt man lived about a hundred years ago. According to one legend he could only leave the Castle upon a Sunday because of his creditors, and according to another he hid in the secret passage.

The Tower, part III

In the passage about the Swan I have unconsciously echoed one of the loveliest lyrics of our time – Mr. Sturge Moore's 'Dying Swan'. I often recited it during an American lecturing tour, which explains the theft.

> THE DYING SWAN
> O silver-throated Swan
> Struck, struck! A golden dart
> Clean through thy breast has gone
> Home to thy heart.
> Thrill, thrill, O silver throat!
> O silver trumpet, pour
> Love for defiance back
> On him who smote!
> And brim, brim o'er
> With love; and ruby-dye thy track
> Down thy last living reach
> Of river, sail the golden light –
> Enter the sun's heart – even teach,
> O wondrous-gifted pain, teach thou
> The God to love, let him learn how!

When I wrote the lines about Plato and Plotinus I forgot that it is something in our own eyes that makes us see them as all transcendence. Has not Plotinus written: 'Let every soul recall, then, at the outset the truth that soul is the author of all living things, that it has breathed the life into them all, whatever is nourished by earth and sea, all the creatures of the air, the divine stars in the sky; it is the maker of the sun; itself formed and ordered this vast heaven and conducts all that rhythmic motion – and it is a principle distinct from all these to which it gives law and movement and life, and it must of necessity be more honourable than they, for they gather or dissolve as soul brings them life or abandons them, but soul, since it never can abandon itself, is of eternal being'.

Meditations in Time of Civil War

These poems were written at Thoor Ballylee in 1922, during the civil war. Before they were finished the Republicans blew up our 'ancient bridge' one midnight. They forbade us to leave the house, but were otherwise polite, even saying at last 'Goodnight, thank you' as though we had given them the bridge.

Section Six

In the West of Ireland we call a starling a stare, and during the civil war one built in a hole in the masonry by my bedroom window.

Section Seven, stanza II

The cry 'Vengeance on the murderers of Jacques Molay', Grand Master of the Templars, seems to me fit symbol for those who labour from hatred, and so for sterility in various kinds. It is said to have been incorporated in the ritual of certain Masonic societies of the eighteenth century, and to have fed class-hatred.

Section Seven, stanza IV

I have a ring with a hawk and a butterfly upon it, to symbolise the straight road of logic, and so of mechanism, and the crooked road of intuition: 'For wisdom is a butterfly and not a gloomy bird of prey'.

Nineteen Hundred and Nineteen, Section SIX

The country people see at times certain apparitions whom they name now 'fallen angels', now 'ancient inhabitants of the country', and describe as riding at whiles 'with flowers upon the heads of the horses'. I have assumed in the sixth poem that these horsemen, now that the times worsen, give way to worse. My last symbol, Robert Artisson, was an evil spirit much run after in Kilkenny at the start of the fourteenth century. Are not those who travel in the whirling dust also in the Platonic Year?

Two Songs from a Play

These songs are sung by the Chorus in a play that has for its theme Christ's first appearance to the Apostles after the Resurrection, a play intended for performance in a drawing-room or studio.

Among School Children, stanza III

I have taken 'the honey of generation' from Porphyry's essay on 'The Cave of the Nymphs', but find no warrant in Porphyry for considering it the 'drug' that destroys the 'recollection' of pre-natal freedom. He blamed a cup of oblivion given in the zodiacal sign of Cancer.

The Gift of Harun Al-Rashid

Part of an unfinished set of poems, dialogues and stories about John Ahern and Michael Robartes, Kusta ben Luka, a philosopher of Bagdad, and his Bedouin followers.

POEMS AFTER THE TOWER

Crazy Jane and the Bishop (1930)

Bring me to the blasted oak
That I, midnight upon the stroke,

CRAZY JANE
This poem was written on March 2, 1929, and first appeared in
the *New Republic* (Nov. 12, 1930) and *LM* (Nov. 1930). The title
in those publications was "Cracked Mary and the Bishop."

All find safety in the tomb,
May call down curses on his head
5   Because of my dear Jack that's dead.
Coxcomb was the least he said:
The solid man and the coxcomb.

Nor was he Bishop when his ban
Banished Jack the Journeyman,
10   *All find safety in the tomb,*
Nor so much as parish priest,
Yet he, an old book in his fist,
Cried that we lived like beast and beast:
The solid man and the coxcomb.

15   The Bishop has a skin, God knows,
Wrinkled like the foot of a goose,
All find safety in the tomb,
Nor can he hide in holy black
The heron's hunch upon his back,
20   But a birch-tree stood my Jack:
The solid man and the coxcomb.

Jack had my virginity,
And bids me to the oak, for he
All find safety in the tomb,
25   Wanders out into the night
And there is shelter under it,
But should that other come, I spit:
The solid man and the coxcomb.

Byzantium (1929)

The unpurged images of day recede;
The Emperor's drunken soldiery are abed;
Night's resonance recedes, night-walkers' song
After great cathedral gong;
5   A starlit or a moonlit dome[1] disdains
All that man is,
All mere complexities,
The fury and the mire of human veins.

Before me floats an image, man or shade,
10   Shade more than man, more image than a shade;
For Hades' bobbin bound in mummy-cloth
May unwind the winding path;
A mouth that has no moisture and no breath

Byzantium
The poem was written in September 1930 and first appeared in Yeats's collection of poems entitled *Words for Music Perhaps, and Other Poems* (Dublin: Cuala Press, 1932).

Under the heading "Subject for a Poem, April 30th," Yeats in his *1930 Diary* wrote: "Describe Byzantium as it is in the system [of *A Vision*] towards the end of the first Christian millennium. A walking mummy. Flames at the street corners where the soul is purified, birds of hammered gold singing in the golden trees, in the harbour [dolphins] offering their backs to the walking dead that they may carry them to Paradise."

[1]   *A starlit or a moonlit dome* a dome seen alternately at the dark of the moon ("starlit") or by a full moon ("moonlit"), and so one seen at Phase 1 or Phase 15 in Yeats's system; see the "Introduction" to Yeats for further explanation, p. 301.

Breathless mouths may summon;[2]
I hail the Superhuman;   15
I call it Death-in-life and Life-in-death.

Miracle, bird or golden handiwork,
More miracle than bird or handiwork,
Planted on the star-lit golden bough,
Can like the cocks of Hades crow;   20
Or, by the moon embittered, scorn aloud,
In glory of changeless metal,
Common bird or petal
And all complexities of mire or blood.

At midnight on the Emperor's pavement flit   25
Flames that no faggot feeds, nor steel has lit,
Nor storm disturbs, flames begotten of flame,
Where blood-begotten spirits come
And all complexities of fury leave,
Dying into a dance,   30
An agony of trance,
An agony of flame that cannot singe a sleeve.

Astraddle on the dolphin's mire and blood,
Spirit after spirit! The smithies break the flood,
The golden smithies of the Emperor,   35
Marbles of the dancing floor
Break bitter furies of complexity,
Those images that yet
Fresh images beget,
That dolphin-torn, that gong-tormented sea.   40

Coole and Ballylee, 1931 (1932)

Under my window-ledge the waters race,
Otters below and moor-hens on the top,
Run for a mile undimmed in Heaven's face
Then darkening through 'dark' Raftery's 'cellar'[1] drop,
Run underground, rise in a rocky place   5
In Coole demesne, and there to finish up
Spread to a lake and drop into a hole.
What's water but the generated soul?[2]

---

[2] *A mouth ... summon* these lines can be read in different ways, depending on which of the two phrases ("a mouth" or "breathless mouths") is taken as the grammatical subject or as the object of the verb "may summon." If "breathless mouths" is the subject, the passage means: mouths of the living, breathless with the intensity of invoking the dead, call up the mouths of the dead to instruct them.

COOLE
The poem was written in February 1931 and first appeared in Yeats's collection of poems entitled *Words for Music Perhaps, and Other Poems* (Dublin: Cuala Press, 1932).

On Coole Park, the estate of Lady Augusta Gregory, see the first note to "The Wild Swans at Coole" (p. 302); on Ballylee and Yeats's home there see the "Introduction" to Yeats, p. 301.
[1] *'dark' Raftery's 'cellar'* Raftery (1784–1835) was a blind (and hence "dark") Irish poet; the river forms a "cellar" (*Irish* an soilear), or a swallow-hole, not far from the tower.
[2] *the generated soul* neoplatonic philosophers used water as a symbol of generation, espcially Porphyry (*c.* 232–305 AD) in his famous study *On the Cave of the Nymphs*, an extended commentary on the allegorical significance of the Cave in Book 14 of the *Odyssey*.

Upon the border of that lake's a wood
10   Now all dry sticks under a wintry sun,
And in a copse of beeches there I stood,
For Nature's pulled her tragic buskin on
And all the rant's a mirror of my mood:
At sudden thunder of the mounting swan
15   I turned about and looked where branches break
The glittering reaches of the flooded lake.

Another emblem there! That stormy white
But seems a concentration of the sky;
And, like the soul, it sails into the sight
20   And in the morning's gone, no man knows why;
And is so lovely that it sets to right
What knowledge or its lack has set awry,
So arrogantly pure, a child might think
It can be murdered with a spot of ink.

25   Sound of a stick upon the floor, a sound
From somebody that toils from chair to chair;
Beloved books that famous hands have bound,
Old marble heads, old pictures everywhere;
Great rooms where travelled men and children found
30   Content or joy; a last inheritor
Where none has reigned that lacked a name and fame
Or out of folly into folly came.

A spot whereon the founders lived and died
Seemed once more dear than life; ancestral trees,
35   Or gardens rich in memory glorified
Marriages, alliances and families,
And every bride's ambition satisfied.
Where fashion or mere fantasy decrees
Man shifts about – all that great glory spent –
40   Like some poor Arab tribesman and his tent.

The intellect of man is forced to choose
Perfection of the life, or of the work,
And if it take the second must refuse
A heavenly mansion, raging in the dark,
45   And when the story's finished, what's the news?
In luck or out the toil has left its mark:
That old perplexity an empty purse,
Or the day's vanity, the night's remorse.

We were the last romantics – chose for theme
50   Traditional sanctity and loveliness;
Whatever's written in what poets name
The book of the people; whatever most can bless
The mind of man or elevate a rhyme;
But all is changed, that high horse riderless,
55   Though mounted in that saddle Homer rode
Where the swan drifts upon a darkening flood.

In Memory of Eva Gore-Booth and Con Markievicz (1933)

The light of evening, Lissadell,
Great windows open to the south,
Two girls in silk kimonos, both
Beautiful, one a gazelle.[1]
But a raving autumn shears   5
Blossom from the summer's wreath;
The older is condemned to death,
Pardoned, drags out lonely years
Conspiring among the ignorant.
I know not what the younger dreams –   10
Some vague Utopia – and she seems,
When withered old and skeleton-gaunt,
An image of such politics.
Many a time I think to seek
One or the other out and speak   15
Of that old Georgian mansion, mix
Pictures of the mind, recall
That table and the talk of youth,
Two girls in silk kimonos, both
Beautiful, one a gazelle.   20

Dear shadows, now you know it all,
All the folly of a fight
With a common wrong or right.
The innocent and the beautiful
Have no enemy but time;   25
Arise and bid me strike a match
And strike another till time catch;
Should the conflagration climb,
Run till all the sages know.
We the great gazebo[2] built,   30
They convicted us of guilt;
Bid me strike a match and blow.

IN MEMORY
The manuscript of the poem is dated September 21, 1927. The poem was first published in Yeats's volume *The Winding Stair and Other Poems* (1933).

Eva Gore-Booth (1870–1926) and Constance Gore-Booth (1868–1927), later Countess Marchiewics, were 2 of 5 children of Sir Henry Gore-Booth. They grew up in Lissadell, a large Greek-Revival country house, constructed in 1832, which was the center of an estate which at its largest totaled 32,000 acres. Eva became an activist in feminist and working-class causes, also serving as editor of a newspaper called *Women's Labour News*, and she published 10 volumes of poetry and two verse dramas. For Constance, see n. 2 to "Easter 1916," p. 307. Lissadell House still survives, though the estate has shrunk to 400 acres and it recently passed out of the Gore-Booth family. Yeats visited the sisters at Lissadell in the winter of 1894–5

[1]   *one a gazelle* the younger sister, Eva.

[2]   *the great gazebo* a summer-house, but here used metaphorically to describe the nationalist movement or the whole facade of the temporal world.

Come Gather Round Me Parnellites (1937)

Come gather round me Parnellites
And praise our chosen man,
Stand upright on your legs awhile,
Stand upright while you can,
5   For soon we lie where he is laid
And he is underground;
Come fill up all those glasses
And pass the bottle round.

And here's a cogent reason
10   And I have many more,
He fought the might of England
And saved the Irish poor,
Whatever good a farmer's got
He brought it all to pass;
15   And here's another reason,
That Parnell loved a lass.

And here's a final reason,
He was of such a kind
Every man that sings a song
20   Keeps Parnell in his mind
For Parnell was a proud man,
No prouder trod the ground,
And a proud man's a lovely man
So pass the bottle round.

25   The Bishops and the Party
That tragic story made,
A husband that had sold his wife
And after that betrayed;
But stories that live longest
30   Are sung above the glass,
And Parnell loved his country
And Parnell loved his lass.

The Statues (1939)

Pythagoras[1] planned it. Why did the people stare?
His numbers though they moved or seemed to move

The poem was written on September 8, 1936 and first appeared in *A Broadside* (New Series) no. 1 (Jan. 1937).

Parnellites are supporters of Charles Parnell (1846–91), a political leader who unified the Irish Members of (the British) Parliament behind a nationalist agenda. Because the Irish held the balance of power between the Liberal and Conservative parties in Parliament, they could exact support for Home Rule as the price of their alliance with the Liberals, and in 1886 a Home Rule Bill nearly passed. But in 1890 Parnell's power dissolved in controversy when his 10-year liaison with Kitty O'Shea ("a lass," in Yeats's poem) was revealed in the divorce action brought by her husband, Captain William Henry O'Shea. Parnell's career was ruined and his precarious health collapsed, leading to his death a year later.

The poem was written in April 1938 and first published in *LM* (March 1939) and the *Nation* (April 15, 1939).

[1] *Pythagoras* (c. 540–510 BC) studied the numerical ratios which determine musical intervals, and thought the world's forms expressed numerical and mathematical ratios. In *On the Boiler* (1939, p. 27), Yeats wrote: "There are moments when I am certain that art must once again accept those Greek proportions which carry into plastic art the Pythagorean numbers, those faces which are divine because all there is empty and measured. Europe was not born when Greek galleys defeated the Persian hordes at Salamis [in 480 BC], but when the Doric studios sent out those broad-backed marble statues against the multiform, vague, expressive Asiatic sea. They gave to the sexual instinct of Europe its goal, its fixed type."

In marble or in bronze, lacked character.
But boys and girls, pale from the imagined love
Of solitary beds, knew what they were,   5
That passion could bring character enough;
And pressed at midnight in some public place
Live lips upon a plummet-measured face.

No! Greater than Pythagoras, for the men
That with a mallet or a chisel modelled these   10
Calculations that look but casual flesh, put down
All Asiatic vague immensities,
And not the banks of oars that swam upon
The many-headed foam at Salamis.
Europe put off that foam when Phidias[2]   15
Gave women dreams and dreams their looking-glass.

One image crossed the many-headed, sat
Under the tropic shade, grew round and slow,
No Hamlet thin from eating flies,[3] a fat
Dreamer of the Middle-Ages.[4] Empty eye-balls knew   20
That knowledge increases unreality, that
Mirror on mirror mirrored is all the show.
When gong and conch declare the hour to bless,
Grimalkin[5] crawls to Buddha's emptiness.

When Pearse summoned Cuchulain to his side,   25
What stalked through the Post Office?[6] What intellect,
What calculation, number, measurement, replied?
We Irish, born into that ancient sect[7]
But thrown upon this filthy modern tide
And by its formless, spawning, fury wrecked,   30
Climb to our proper dark, that we may trace
The lineaments of a plummet-measured face.

The Spur (1939)

You think it horrible that lust and rage
Should dance attendance upon my old age;
They were not such a plague when I was young;
What else have I to spur me into song?

---

[2]   *Phidias* the Athenian sculptor Phidias (*c.* 490–417 BC) was famous for his gold and ivory statues of Athena in the Parthenon and Zeus in the temple at Olympia.
[3]   *Hamlet thin from eating flies* Hamlet, the character, nowhere eats flies; but eating flies was thought to make cats thin, and Yeats adapts this popular expression to the restless character of Hamlet.
[4]   *a fat / Dreamer of the Middle Ages* writing to Edith Shackleton Heald on June 28, 1938, Yeats noted: "In reading the third stanza remember the influence on modern sculpture and on the great seated Buddha of the sculptors who followed Alexander." When the Greek sculptors' image crossed the sea to India, in other words, it lost its Western (or Hamlet-ian) nervousness to become the statue of Buddha.

[5]   *Grimalkin* a name for a cat.
[6]   *When Pearse. ... Post Office* Patrick Pearse (1879–1916), became Commandant-General and President of the provisional government during the Easter rebellion of 1916, which was headquartered in the General Post Office in central Dublin. Yeats implies that the tale of Cuchulain (pronounced *CuHOOlin*), a legendary Irish warrior, inspired Pearse, and so that art has transformed life.
[7]   *that ancient sect* of the Greeks.

The poem was composed sometime in 1938 and first published in *New Poems* (1939)

The Circus Animals' Desertion (1939)

I

I sought a theme and sought for it in vain,
I sought it daily for six weeks or so.
Maybe at last, being but a broken man,
I must be satisfied with my heart, although
5   Winter and summer till old age began
My circus animals were all on show,
Those stilted boys, that burnished chariot,
Lion and woman and the Lord knows what.

II

What can I but enumerate old themes,
10   First that sea-rider Oisin[1] led by the nose
Through three enchanted islands, allegorical dreams,
Vain gaiety, vain battle, vain repose,
Themes of the embittered heart, or so it seems,
That might adorn old songs or courtly shows;
15   But what cared I that set him on to ride,
I, starved for the bosom of his fairy bride.

And then a counter-truth filled out its play,
"The Countess Cathleen"[2] was the name I gave it,
She, pity-crazed, had given her soul away
20   But masterful Heaven had intervened to save it.
I thought my dear[3] must her own soul destroy
So did fanaticism and hate enslave it,
And this brought forth a dream and soon enough
This dream itself had all my thought and love.

25   And when the Fool and Blind Man stole the bread
Cuchulain fought the ungovernable sea;[4]
Heart mysteries there, and yet when all is said
It was the dream itself enchanted me:
Character isolated by a deed
30   To engross the present and dominate memory.
Players and painted stage took all my love
And not those things that they were emblems of.

The poem was composed sometime in 1938; it first appeared in the *Atlantic Monthly* (Jan. 1939) and *LM* (Jan. 1939).

[1] *that sea-rider Oisin* the hero of an early, very elaborate poem by Yeats called *The Wanderings of Oisin* (1899). Oisin (pronounced *Usheen*) is led by the fairy Niamh to three islands of Dancing, Victories, and Forgetfulness.

[2] *"The Countess Cathleen"* Yeats's first play (1892). The Irish people are selling their souls to emissaries of the devil to evade the effects of famine. To save their souls, the Countess Cathleen sells her own; she dies, but an angel announces that she is "passing to the floor of peace."

[3] *my dear* Maude Gonne, a woman whom Yeats had loved since he met her in 1889, and who married John McBride in 1903. She was an excessively strident and violent nationalist, in Yeats's view.

[4] *the ungovernable sea* in an early play by Yeats, *On Baile's Strand* (1904), the hero Cuchulain unwittingly kills his own son; when he realizes what he has done, he goes mad and rushes out to fight the waves. As people run to the shore to watch, a fool and a blind man sneak away to steal the bread from their ovens.

III

Those masterful images because complete
Grew in pure mind but out of what began?
A mound of refuse or the sweepings of a street,   35
Old kettles, old bottles, and a broken can,
Old iron, old bones, old rags, that raving slut
Who keeps the till. Now that my ladder's gone
I must lie down where all the ladders start
In the foul rag and bone shop of the heart.   40

At the Hawk's Well: Introduction

At the Hawk's Well is a landmark of European drama, a play that anticipates theatrical developments for a century to come. It also emerged from highly specific circumstances, the charged dialogue that took place between Yeats and Ezra Pound over the course of three winters of 1913–14, 1914–15, and 1915–16, when Pound served as Yeats's unofficial secretary and reading companion while they wintered together at Stone Cottage, in Sussex. Pound, at this time, was working through the papers of the late Ernest Fenollosa (1853–1908), a distinguished scholar of Oriental art whose widow, then resident in London, had asked him to become Fenollosa's literary executor. In Fenollosa's reflections on Japanese theater and Chinese writing, Yeats and Pound discovered crucial components for the formulation of their own aesthetic aspirations.

For Yeats, the key moment was his disovery of Noh, a lyrical court drama that was established in Japan in the fourteenth century and reached its perfection in the seventeenth. The theatrical means of Noh were of great simplicity: performed on a raised stage by a small troupe of actors in sumptuous costumes, a Noh drama revolved around a ritual dance by the masked chief character. The performance was accompanied by four musicians and a chorus of eight. No less important, Noh combined Buddhist scriptures with Japanese mythology; it was a religious and mystical theater, linking an obsession with the spirit world to profound veneration for ancestry, and its long association with a noble warrior caste was also appealing to Yeats's mind.

Which Noh text in translation Yeats seized on is a matter of some debate, but there is no doubt that Yeats worked very quickly, dictating the entire play to Pound in February 1916. It was Pound who also introduced Yeats to Michio Ito (1892–1961), a Japanese performer who was in London to learn classical and modern dance and who would furnish the choreography for the first performances of *At the Hawk's Well*. Edmund Dulac (1882–1953), an English artist, did the stage design, wrote the music, and directed the play under Yeats's supervision. He also performed as one of three musicians, together with Mrs. Mann and Mr. Foulds. The cast was:

The Young Man	Henry Ainley
The Old Man	Allan Wade
The Guardian of the Well	Michio Ito

At the Hawk's Well was first performed before an invited audience, which included Ezra Pound and T. S. Eliot, on April 2, 1916, in the drawing room of Lady Emerald Cunard, mother of Nancy Cunard (see pp. 762–76), at her house in Cavendish Square, London. A second performance took place two days later before an audience of some 300 at the house of Lady Islington in Chesterfield Gardens, this one being in aid of the Social Institute's Union for Women and girls. The play was first published in the American magazine *Harper's Bazaar* (March 1917) and in the British magazine *To-Day* (June 1917), then reprinted with some revisions in *The Wild Swans at Coole, Other Verses, and a Play in Verse* (Churchtown, Dundrum [Ireland]: the Cuala Press, 1917), in an edition limited to 450 copies; and finally it was reprinted with still further revisions in *Four Plays for Dancers* (London and New York: Macmillan, 1921). This edition follows that of 1921.

Writing to Lady Gregory on March 26, 1916 about the rehearsals, Yeats commented: "The play goes on well except for Ainley, who waves his arms like a drowning kitten, and the musician [Mrs. Mann], who is in a constant rage. She says 'in the big London theatres the action is stopped from time to time to give the musician his turn.' I am going this afternoonn to Dulac's to go no working out gestures for Ainley. They are then to be all drawn by Dulac. I believe I have at last found a dramatic form that suits me" (*L*, pp. 609–10)

The morning before the first performance was to take place, Yeats wrote to John Quinn:

I am tired out with the excitement of rehearsing my new play – *The Hawk's Well* in which masks are being used for the first time in serious drama in the modern world. Ainley, who is the hero, wears a mask like an archaic Greek statue. . . . The play can be played in the middle of a room. It is quite short – 30 or 40 minutes....I hope to create a form of drama which may delight the best minds of my time, and all the more because it can pay its expenses without the others....No press, no photographs in the papers, no crowd. I shall be happier than Sophocles. I shall be as lucky as a Japanese dramatic poet at the Court of the Shogun.

My dress rehearsal, or really first performance, is given at Lady Cunard's to-day, and I am to be there at 3. I shall go to lunch and then lie down for a little and after that I may be able to face the musicians. One of them insists on a guitar, and the scene of the play is laid in Ireland in the heroic age! (April 2, 1916; *L*, pp. 610–11)

At the Hawk's Well (1917)

Persons in the Play

Three Musicians (*their faces made up to resemble masks*).
The Guardian of the Well (*with face made up to resemble a mask*).
An Old Man (*wearing a mask*).
A Young Man (*wearing a mask*).

Time – The Irish Heroic Age[1]

The stage is any bare space before a wall against which stands a patterned screen. A drum and a gong and a zither have been laid close to the screen before the play begins. If necessary, they can be carried in, after the audience is seated, by the First Musician, who also can attend to the lights if there is any special lighting. We had two lanterns upon posts – designed by Mr. Dulac – at the outer corners of the stage, but they did not give enough light, and we found it better to play by the light of a large chandelier. Indeed, I think, so far as my present experience goes, that the most effective lighting is the lighting we are most accustomed to in our rooms. These masked players seem stranger when there is no mechanical means of separating them from us. The First Musician carries with him a folded black cloth and goes to the centre of the stage and stands motionless, the folded cloth hanging from between his hands. The two Musicians enter and, after standing a moment on either side of the stage, go towards him and slowly unfold the cloth, singing as they do so:

> I call to the eye of the mind
> A well long choked up and dry[2]
> And boughs long stripped by the wind,
> And I call to the mind's eye
> Pallor of an ivory face,
> Its lofty dissolute air,
> A man climbing up to a place
> The salt sea wind has swept bare.

As they unfold the cloth, they go backward a little so that the stretched cloth and the wall make a triangle with the First Musician at the apex supporting the centre of the cloth. On the black cloth is a gold pattern suggesting a hawk. The Second and Third Musicians now slowly fold up the cloth again, pacing with a rhythmic movement of the arms towards the First Musician and singing:

> What were his life soon done!
> Would he lose by that or win?
> A mother that saw her son
> Doubled over a speckled shin,

---

[1]   the Irish Heroic Age at the beginning of the Christian era.
[2]   *A well long choked up and dry* Hawk's Rock (Carraig-an-Sea-bach) is located in county Sligo at the northeast end of the Ox mountains, about one mile northeast of Coolaney and about 15 miles southwest of the town of Sligo. Tulligan Well, which fills and ebbs, is located on Tulligan Hill, the rise of land nearest Hawk's Rock.

> Cross-grained with ninety years,
> Would cry. "How little worth
> Were all my hopes and fears
>   And the hard pain of his birth!"

The words "a speckled shin" are familiar to readers of Irish legendary stories in descriptions of old men bent double over the fire. While the cloth has been spread out, the Guardian of the Well has entered and is now crouching upon the ground. She is entirely covered by a black cloak; beside her lies a square blue cloth to represent a well. The three Musicians have taken their places against the wall beside their instruments of music; they will accompany the movements of the players with gong or drum or zither.

> *First Musician (singing).*
>   The boughs of the hazel shake,
>   The sun goes down in the west.

> *Second Musician (singing).*
>   The heart would be always awake,
>   The heart would turn to its rest.

(They now go to one side of the stage rolling up the cloth. A girl has taken her place by a square blue cloth representing a well. She is motionless.)

> *First Musician (speaking).* Night falls;
>   The mountain-side grows dark;
>   The withered leaves of the hazel[3]
>   Half choke the dry bed of the well;
>   The guardian of the well is sitting
>   Upon the old grey stone at its side,
>   Worn out from raking its dry bed,
>   Worn out from gathering up the leaves.
>   Her heavy eyes
>   Know nothing, or but look upon stone.
>   The wind that blows out of the sea
>   Turns over the heaped-up leaves at her side;
>   They rustle and diminish.

> *Second Musician.* I am afraid of this place.

> *Both Musicians (singing).*
>   "Why should I sleep?" the heart cries,
>   "For the wind, the salt wind, the sea wind,
>   Is beating a cloud through the skies;
>   I would wander always like the wind."

(An Old Man enters through the audience.)

> *First Musician (speaking).* That old man climbs up hither,
>   Who has been watching by his well
>   These fifty years.
>   He is all doubled up with age;

---

[3] *withered leaves of the hazel* a supernatural well surrounded by hazel trees is found in many works of Irish mythology.

The old thorn-trees are doubled so
Among the rocks where he is climbing.

(The Old Man stands for a moment motionless by the side of the stage with bowed head. He lifts his head at the sound of a drum tap. He goes towards the front of the stage moving to the taps of the drum. He crouches and moves his hands as if making a fire. His movements, like those of the other persons in the play, suggest a marionette.)

First Musician *(speaking)*. He has made a little heap of leaves;
He lays the dry sticks on the leaves
And, shivering with cold, he has taken up
The fire-stick and socket from its hole.
He whirls it round to get a flame;
And now the dry sticks take the fire,
And now the fire leaps up and shines
Upon the hazels and the empty well.

Musicians *(singing)*.
"O wind, O salt wind, O sea wind!"
Cries the heart, "it is time to sleep;
Why wander and nothing to find?
Better grow old and sleep."

Old Man *(speaking)*. Why don't you speak to me? Why don't you say:
"Are you not weary gathering those sticks?
Are not your fingers cold?" You have not one word,
While yesterday you spoke three times. You said:
"The well is full of hazel leaves." You said:
"The wind is from the west." And after that:
"If there is rain it's likely there'll be mud."
To-day you are as stupid as a fish,
No, worse, worse, being less lively and as dumb.
                                    (He goes nearer).
Your eyes are dazed and heavy. If the Sidhe[4]
Must have a guardian to clean out the well
And drive the cattle off, they might choose somebody
That can be pleasant and companionable
Once in the day. Why do you stare like that?
You had that glassy look about the eyes
Last time it happened. Do you know anything?
It is enough to drive an old man crazy
To look all day upon these broken rocks,
And ragged thorns, and that one stupid face,
And speak and get no answer.

Young Man *(who has entered through the audience during the last speech)*. Then speak to me,
For youth is not more patient than old age;
And though I have trod the rocks for half a day
I cannot find what I am looking for.

Old Man.   Who speaks?
Who comes so suddenly into this place
Where nothing thrives? If I may judge by the gold
On head and feet and glittering in your coat,
You are not of those who hate the living world.

---

[4] *the Sidhe* the immortal people of the Otherworld.

Young Man. I am named Cuchulain, I am Sualtim's son.[5]

Old Man. I have never heard that name.

Young Man.   It is not unknown.
         I have an ancient house beyond the sea.

Old Man. What mischief brings you hither, you are like those
         Who are crazy for the shedding of men's blood,
         And for the love of women.

Young Man.   A rumour has led me,
         A story told over the wine towards dawn.
         I rose from table, found a boat, spread sail,
         And with a lucky wind under the sail
         Crossed waves that have seemed charmed, and found this shore.

Old Man. There is no house to sack among these hills
         Nor beautiful woman to be carried off.

Young Man. You should be native here, for that rough tongue
         Matches the barbarous spot. You can, it may be,
         Lead me to what I seek, a well wherein
         Three hazels drop their nuts and withered leaves,
         And where a solitary girl keeps watch
         Among grey boulders. He who drinks, they say,
         Of that miraculous water lives for ever.

Old Man. And are there not before your eyes at the instant
         Grey boulders and a solitary girl
         And three stripped hazels?

Young Man.   But there is no well.

Old Man. Can you see nothing yonder?

Young Man.   I but see
         A hollow among stones half-full of leaves.

Old Man. And do you think so great a gift is found
         By no more toil than spreading out a sail,
         And climbing a steep hill? Oh, folly of youth,
         Why should that hollow place fill up for you,
         That will not fill for me? I have lain in wait
         For more than fifty years to find it empty,
         Or but to find the stupid wind of the sea
         Drive round the perishable leaves.

Young Man.   So it seems
         There is some moment when the water fills it.

---

[5]   *Cuchulain, Sualtim's son* Cuchulain is the major hero of the Ulster Cycle as interpreted by Lady Gregory (see p. 302 n. 1) in *Cuchulain of Muirthemne* (London: John Murray, 1911). Her account stresses that Cuchulain is really the son of the god Lugh of the Long Hand, though that makes no difference to everybody's perception that he is Sualtim's son.

Old Man. A secret moment that the holy shades
            That dance upon the desolate mountain know,
            And not a living man, and when it comes
            The water has scarce plashed before it is gone.

Young Man. I will stand here and wait. Why should the luck
            Of Sualtim's son desert him now? For never
            Have I had long to wait for anything.

Old Man. No! Go from this accursed place, this place
            Belongs to me, that girl there, and those others,
            Deceivers of men.

Young Man.   And who are you who rail
            Upon those dancers that all others bless?

Old Man. One whom the dancers cheat. I came like you
            When young in body and in mind, and blown
            By what had seemed to me a lucky sail.
            The well was dry, I sat upon its edge,
            I waited the miraculous flood, I waited
            While the years passed and withered me away.
            I have snared the birds for food and eaten grass
            And drunk the rain, and neither in dark nor shine
            Wandered too far away to have heard the plash,
            And yet the dancers have deceived me. Thrice
            I have awakened from a sudden sleep
            To find the stones were wet.

Young Man.   My luck is strong,
            It will not leave me waiting, nor will they
            That dance among the stones put me asleep;
            If I grow drowsy I can pierce my foot.

Old Man. No, do not pierce it, for the foot is tender,
            It feels pain much. But find your sail again
            And leave the well to me, for it belongs
            To all that's old and withered.

Young Man.   No, I stay.
            (*The Guardian of the Well gives the cry of the hawk.*)
            There is that bird again.

Old Man.   There is no bird.

Young Man. It sounded like the sudden cry of a hawk,
            But there's no wing in sight. As I came hither
            A great grey hawk swept down out of the sky,
            And though I have good hawks, the best in the world
            I had fancied, I have not seen its like. It flew
            As though it would have torn me with its beak,
            Or blinded me, smiting with that great wing.
            I had to draw my sword to drive it off,
            And after that it flew from rock to rock.
            I pelted it with stones, a good half-hour,
            And just before I had turned the big rock there
            And seen this place, it seemed to vanish away.

Could I but find a means to bring it down
I'd hood it.

Old Man.   The Woman of the Sidhe herself,[6]
The mountain witch, the unappeasable shadow.
She is always flitting upon this mountain-side,
To allure or to destroy. When she has shown
Herself to the fierce women of the hills
Under that shape they offer sacrifice
And arm for battle. There falls a curse
On all who have gazed in her unmoistened eyes;
So get you gone while you have that proud step
And confident voice, for not a man alive
Has so much luck that he can play with it.
Those that have long to live should fear her most,
The old are cursed already. That curse may be
Never to win a woman's love and keep it;
Or always to mix hatred in the love;
Or it may be that she will kill your children,
That you will find them, their throats torn and bloody,
Or you will be so maddened that you kill them
With your own hand.

Young Man.   Have you been set down there
To threaten all who come, and scare them off?
You seem as dried up as the leaves and sticks,
As though you had no part in life.
                    (*Girl gives hawk cry again.*)
                    That cry!
There is that cry again. That woman made it,
But why does she cry out as the hawk cries?

Old Man. It was her mouth, and yet not she, that cried.
It was that shadow cried behind her mouth;
And now I know why she has been so stupid
All the day through, and had such heavy eyes.
Look at her shivering now, the terrible life
Is slipping through her veins. She is possessed.
Who knows whom she will murder or betray
Before she awakes in ignorance of it all,
And gathers up the leaves! But they'll be wet;
The water will have come and gone again;
That shivering is the sign. Oh, get you gone,
At any moment now I shall hear it bubble.
If you are good you will leave it. I am old,
And if I do not drink it now, will never;
I have been watching all my life and maybe
Only a little cupful will bubble up.

Young Man. I'll take it in my hands. We shall both drink,
And even if there are but a few drops,
Share them.

---

[6] *The Woman of the Sidhe* the same woman, Fand, appears in Yeats's later play, *The Only Jealousy of Emer* (1919), where she entices Cuchulain to leave the mortal world and become her lover.

Old Man.   But swear that I may drink the first;
        The young are greedy, and if you drink the first
        You'll drink it all. Ah, you have looked at her;
        She has felt your gaze and turned her eyes on us;
        I cannot bear her eyes, they are not of this world,
        Nor moist, nor faltering; they are no girl's eyes.

(He covers his head. The Guardian of the Well throws off her cloak and rises. Her dress under the cloak suggests a hawk.)

Young Man. Why do you fix those eyes of a hawk upon me?
        I am not afraid of you, bird, woman, or witch.
(He goes to the side of the well, which the Guardian of the Well has left.)
        Do what you will, I shall not leave this place
        Till I have grown immortal like yourself.
(He has sat down, the Guardian of the Well has begun to dance, moving like a hawk. The Old Man sleeps. The dance goes on for some time.)

First Musician (singing or half-singing)
        O God, protect me
        From a horrible deathless body
        Sliding through the veins of a sudden.
(The dance goes on for some time. The Young Man rises slowly.)

First Musician (speaking). The madness has laid hold upon him now,
        For he grows pale and staggers to his feet.
                      (The dance goes on.)

Young Man. Run where you will,
        Grey bird, you shall be perched upon my wrist.
        Some were called queens and yet have been perched there.
                      (The dance goes on.)

First Musician (speaking). I have heard water plash; it
          comes, it comes;
        It glitters among the stones and he has heard the plash;
        Look, he has turned his head.

(The Guardian of the Well has gone out. The Young Man drops his spear as if in a dream and goes out.)

Musicians (singing).
        He has lost what may not be found
        Till men heap his burial mound
        And all the history ends.
        He might have lived at his ease,
        An old dog's head on his knees,
        Among his children and friends.
                   (The Old Man creeps up to the well.)

Old Man. The accursed shadows have deluded me,
        The stones are dark and yet the well is empty;
        The water flowed and emptied while I slept;
        You have deluded me my whole life through.
        Accursed dancers, you have stolen my life.
        That there should be such evil in a shadow.

Young Man (*entering*). She has fled from me and hidden in the rocks.

Old Man. She has but led you from the fountain. Look!
        Though stones and leaves are dark where it has flowed,
        There's not a drop to drink.
                (*The Musicians cry "Eofe" "Eofe!" and strike gong.*[7])

Young Man.   What are those cries?
        What is that sound that runs along the hill?
        Who are they that beat a sword upon a shield?

Old Man. She has roused up the fierce women of the hills,
        Eofe, and all her troop, to take your life,
        And never till you are lying in the earth,
        Can you know rest.

Young Man.   The clash of arms again!

Old Man. Oh, do not go! The mountain is accursed;
        Stay with me, I have nothing more to lose,
        I do not now decieve you.

Young Man.   I will face them.
        (*He goes out, no longer as if in a dream, but shouldering his spear and calling.*)
        He comes! Cuchulain, son of Sualtim, comes!

(*The Musicians stand up, one goes to centre with folded cloth. The others unfold it. While they do so they sing. During the singing, and while hidden by the cloth, the Old Man goes out. When the play is performed with Mr. Dulac's music, the Musicians do not rise or unfold the cloth till after they have sung the words "a bitter life".*)

(*Songs for the unfolding and folding of the cloth*)

                Come to me, human faces,
                Familiar memories;
                I have found hateful eyes
                Among the desolate places,
                Unfaltering, unmoistened eyes.

---

[7] *Aoife* is the chief of a territory in Scotland where Cuchulain goes to be trained in arms from Scathach, another woman warrior. After Cuchulain has defeated Aoife in single combat, she bears him a son, according to the Old Irish tale "The Wooing of Emer," which is recounted in Lady Gregory's *Cuchulain of Muirtheme*, pp. 21–47. Elements of this tale also appear in Yeats's play *On Baile's Strand* (1904).

Folly alone I cherish,
I choose it for my share,
Being but a mouthful of air,
I am content to perish,
I am but a mouthful of sweet air.

O lamentable shadows,
Obscurity of strife,
I choose a pleasant life,
Among indolent meadows;
Wisdom must live a bitter life.

(They then fold up the cloth, singing.)

"The man that I praise",
Cries out the empty well,
"Lives all his days
Where a hand on the bell
Can call the milch cows
To the comfortable door of his house.
Who but an idiot would praise
Dry stones in a well?"

"The man that I praise,"
Cries out the leafless tree,
"Has married and stays
By an old hearth, and he
On naught has set store
But children and dogs on the floor.
Who but an idiot would praise
A withered tree?"   *(They go out.)*

THE END

Note on the First Performance of "At the Hawk's Well" (1917)

A couple of years ago I was sitting in my stall at the Court Theatre in London watching one of my own plays, "The King's Threshold."[1] In front of me were three people, seemingly a husband, a wife, and woman friend. The husband was bored; he yawned and stretched himself and shifted in his seat, and I watched him with distress. I was inclined to be angry, but reminded myself that music, where there are no satisfying audible words, bores me as much, for I have no ear or only a very primitive one. Presently, when the little princesses came upon the stage in their red clothes, the woman friend, who had seemed also a little bored, said, "They do things very well," and became attentive. The distinguished painter[2] who had designed the clothes at any rate could interest her. The wife, who had sat motionless from the first, said when the curtain had fallen and the applause – was it politeness or enthusiasm? – had come to an end, "I would not have missed it for the world."

Under the title "Note on 'At the Hawk's Well,'" this essay first appeared in *The Wild Swans at Coole, Other Verses, and a Play in Verse* (Churchtown, Dundrum [Ireland]: the Cuala Press, 1917), a deluxe edition limited to 450 copies; it was then reprinted, with a few light stylistic revisions, in *Four Plays for Dancers* (London and New York: Macmillan, 1921).
[1]   Opening on July 2, 1914, *The King's Threshold* was revived for the Abbey Theatre season at the Royal Court Theatre; it had first

been performed 10 years earlier, in 1904, at the Abbey Theatre in Dublin.
[2]   Charles Ricketts (1866–1931), who did the costumes for *The King's Threshold*. Yeats wrote to him on June 11, 1914: "I think the costumes the best stage costumes I have ever seen ... [Such] is the effect of costume that whole scenes got a new intensity, and passages or actions that had seemed commonplace became powerful and moving" (*Letters*, p. 587).

She was perhaps a reader of my poetry who had persuaded the others to come, and she had found a pleasure, the book could not give her, in the combination of words and speech. Yet when I think of my play, I do not call her to the mind's eye, or even her friend who found the long red gloves of the little princesses amusing, but always that bored man; the worst of it is that I could not pay my players, or the seamstress, or the owner of the stage, unless I could draw to my plays those who prefer light amusement, or who have no ear for verse, and fortunately they are all very polite.

Being sensitive, or not knowing how to escape the chance of sitting behind the wrong people, I have begun to shrink from sending my muses where they are but half-welcomed; and even in Dublin, where the pit has an ear for verse, I have no longer the appetite to carry me through the daily rehearsals. Yet I need a theatre; I believe myself to be a dramatist; I desire to show events and not merely tell of them; and two of my best friends[3] were won for me by my plays, and I seem to myself most alive at the moment when a roomful of people share the one lofty emotion. My blunder has been that I did not discover in my youth that my theatre must be the ancient theatre that can be made by unrolling a carpet or marking out a place with a stick, or setting a screen against the wall. Certainly those who care for my kind of poetry must be numerous enough, if I can bring them together, to pay half a dozen players who can bring all their properties in a cab and perform in their leisure moments.

I have found my first model – and in literature if we would not be parvenus we must have a model – in the "Noh" stage of aristocratic Japan. I have described in *Certain Noble Plays of Japan*[4] (now included in my *Cutting of an Agate*) what has seemed to me important on that most subtle stage. I do not think of my discovery as mere economy, for it has been a great gain to get rid of scenery, to substitute for a crude landscape painted upon canvas three performers who, sitting before the wall or a patterned screen, describe landscape or event, and accompany movement with drum and gong, or deepen the emotion of the words with zither or flute. Painted scenery after all is unnecessary to my friends and to myself, for our imagination kept living by the arts can imagine a mountain covered with thorn-trees, in a drawing room without any great trouble, and we have many quarrels with even good scene-painting.

Then too the masks forced upon us by the absence of any special lighting, or by the nearness of the audience who surround the players upon three sides, do not seem to us eccentric. We are accustomed to faces of bronze and of marble, and what could be more suitable than that Cuchulain, let us say, a half-supernatural legendary person, should show to us a face, not made before the looking glass by some leading player – there too we have many quarrels – but moulded by some distinguished artist? We are a learned people, we remember how the Roman theatre, when it became more intellectual,[5] abandoned "make-up" and used the mask instead, and that the most famous artists of Japan modelled masks that are still in use after hundreds of years. It would be a stirring adventure for a poet and an artist, working together, to create once more heroic or grotesque types that, keeping always an appropriate distance from life, would seem images of those profound emotions that exist only in solitude and silence. Nor has any one told me after a performance that they have missed a changing facial expression, for the mask seems to change with the light that falls upon it, and besides in poetical and tragic art, as every "producer" knows, expression is mainly in those movements that are of the entire body.

"At the Hawk's Well" was performed for the first time in April 1916, in a friend's drawing-room,[6] and only those who cared for poetry were invited. It was played upon the floor, and the players came in by the same door as the audience, and the audience and the players and I myself

[3] Lady Gregory and John N. Synge?
[4] The book was published in Dublin at the Cuala Press in 1916. It contained a selection of Noh plays translated by Ernest Fenollosa and finished by Ezra Pound, together with an introduction by Yeats, also titled "Certain Noble Plays of Japan" (for the text, see pp. 362–70). Yeats's introduction was also included in a new edition of his selected essays, *The Cutting of an Agate*, which appeared in 1916.

[5] Roman theater adopted masks very early, influenced by native folk plays as well as Greek drama.

[6] The drawing-room of Lady Cunard at her home in Cavendish Square, London.

were pleased. A few days later it was revived in Lady Islington's big drawing-room at Chesterfield Gardens for the benefit of a war charity.[7] And round the platform upon three sides were three hundred fashionable people, including Queen Alexandria, and once more my muses were but half-welcome. I remember, however, with a little pleasure that we found a newspaper photographer planting his camera in a dressing-room and explained to him that as fifty people could pay our expenses, we did not invite the press, and that flashlight photographs were not desirable for their own sake. He was incredulous and persistent – a whole page somewhere or other was at out disposal – and it was nearly ten minutes before we could persuade him to go away. What a relief after directing a theatre for so many years – for I am one of the two directors of the Abbey Theatre[8] in Dublin – to think no more of pictures unless Mr. Dulac[9] or some other distinguished man has made them, nor of all those paragraphs written by young men, perhaps themselves intelligent, who must applaud the common taste or starve!

Perhaps I shall turn to something else now that our Japanese dancer, Mr. Itow,[10] whose minute intensity of movement in the dance of the hawk so well suited our small room and private art, has been hired by a New York theatre, or perhaps I shall find another dancer. I am certain, however, that whether I grow tired or not – and one does grow tired of always quarrying the stone for one's statue – I have found out the only way the subtler forms of literature can find dramatic expression. Shakespeare's art was public, now resounding and declamatory, now lyrical and subtle, but always public, because poetry was a part of the general life of a people who had been trained by the Church to listen to difficult words, and who sang, instead of the songs of the music-halls, many songs that are still beautiful. A man who had sung "Barbara Allan"[11] in his own house would not, as I have heard the gallery of the Lyceum Theatre,[12] receive the love speeches of Juliet with an ironical chirruping. We must recognize the change as the painters did when, finding no longer palaces and churches to decorate, they made framed pictures to hang upon a wall. Whatever we lose in mass and in power we should recover in elegance and in subtlety. Our lyrical and our narrative poetry alike have used their freedom and have approached nearer, as Pater said all the arts would if they were able,[13] to "the condition of music"; and if our modern poetical drama has failed, it is mainly because, always dominated by the example of Shakespeare, it would restore an irrevocable past.

"Introduction" to Certain Noble Plays of Japan (1916)

I

In the series of books I edit for my sister I confine myself to those that have I believe some special value to Ireland, now or in the future. I have asked Mr. Pound for these beautiful plays because I think they

[7]   At 8 Chesterfield Gardens, for the benefit of the Social Institutes Union for Women and Girls.

[8]   After the death of John M. Synge in 1909, Yeats and Lady Gregory were the directors until 1919, when manager Lennox Robinson became a share-holding member of the board.

[9]   On Edmund Dulac, see note to "On a Picture" on p. 326.

[10]   On Michio Ito, see note on "At the Hawk's Well" on p. 351.

[11]   "Bonny Barbara Allen" was an anonymous medieval ballad, no. 84B in English and Scottish Popular Ballads, eds. Helen Child Sargent and George Lyman Kittredge (Boston: Houghton Mifflin, 1904).

[12]   A famous London theater that was associated from 1874 to 1902 with the Shakespearean productions of Sir Henry Irving (1838–1905).

[13]   Walter Horatio Pater (1839–94) wrote that "All art constantly aspires towards the condition of music," in his The Renaissance, ed. Donald Hill (Berkeley: University of California Press, 1980), p. 106.

"INTRODUCTION"
The essay was first published as an introduction to Ezra Pound, Certain Noble Plays of Japan: From the Manuscripts of Ernest Fenollosa, Chosen and Finished by Ezra Pound (Churchtown, Dundrum [Ireland]: the Cuala Press, 1916), an edition limited to 350 copies which appeared on September 16, 1916. This edition contained only four plays and lacked any introductory material by Pound. Those four were then included in a greatly expanded edition titled "Noh" or Accomplishment: A Study of the Classical State of Japan, by Ernest Fenollosa and Ezra Pound (London: Macmillan, 1917; New York: Alfred Knopf, 1917), an edition that no longer included the "Introduction" by Yeats. That "Introduction," now retitled "Certain Noble Plays of Japan" and shorn of its first two sentences, then appeared in Yeats's The Cutting of an Agate (London: Macmillan, 1919), a collection of essays that Yeats had written between 1903 and 1915.

will help me to explain a certain possibility of the Irish dramatic movement. I am writing with my imagination stirred by a visit to the studio of Mr. Dulac, the distinguished illustrator of the *Arabian Nights*.[1] I saw there the mask and head-dress to be worn in a play of mine by the player who will speak the part of Cuchulain, and who, wearing this noble, half-Greek, half-Asiatic face, will appear perhaps like an image seen in reverie by some Orphic worshipper. I hope to have attained the distance from life which can make credible strange events, elaborate words. I have written a little play that can be played in a room for so little money that forty or fifty readers of poetry can pay the price. There will be no scenery, for three musicians, whose seeming sunburned faces will, I hope, suggest that they have wandered from village to village in some country of our dreams, can describe place and weather, and at moments action, and accompany it all by drum and gong or flute and dulcimer. Instead of the players working themselves into a violence of passion indecorous in our sitting-room, the music, the beauty of form and voice all come to climax in pantomimic dance.

In fact, with the help of Japanese plays "translated by Ernest Fenollosa and finished by Ezra Pound," I have invented a form of drama, distinguished, indirect, and symbolic, and having no need of mob or Press to pay its way — an aristocratic form. When this play and its performance run as smoothly as my skill can make them, I shall hope to write another of the same sort and so complete a dramatic celebration of the life of Cuchulain planned long ago. Then having given enough performances for, I hope, the pleasure of personal friends and a few score people of good taste, I shall record all discoveries of method and turn to something else. It is an advantage of this noble form that it need absorb no one's life, that its few properties can be packed up in a box or hung upon the walls where they will be fine ornaments.

II

And yet this simplification is not mere economy. For nearly three centuries invention has been making the human voice and the movements of the body seem always less expressive. I have long been puzzled why passages that are moving when read out or spoken during rehearsal seem muffled or dulled during performance. I have simplified scenery, having *The Hour-Glass*, for instance, played now before green curtains, now among those admirable ivory-coloured screens invented by Gordon Craig.[2] With every simplification the voice has recovered something of its importance, and yet when verse has approached in temper to, let us say, *Kubla Khan*, or the *Ode to the West Wind*,[3] the most typical modern verse, I have still felt as if the sound came to me from behind a veil. The stage-opening, the powerful light and shade, the number of feet between myself and the players have destroyed intimacy. I have found myself thinking of players who needed perhaps but to unroll a mat in some Eastern garden. Nor have I felt this only when I listened to speech, but even more when I have watched the movement of a player or heard singing in a play. I love all the arts that can still remind me of their origin among the common people, and my ears are only comfortable when the singer sings as if mere speech had taken fire, when he appears to have passed into song almost imperceptibly. I am bored and wretched, a limitation I greatly regret, when he seems no longer a human being but an invention of science. To explain him to myself I say that he has become a wind instrument and sings no longer like active men, sailor or camel-driver, because he has had to compete with an orchestra, where the loudest instrument has always survived. The human voice can only become louder by becoming less articulate, by discovering some new musical sort of roar or scream. As poetry can do neither, the voice must be freed from this competition and find itself

[1]   On Dulac, see note to "On a Picture" on p. 326. See *Stories from the Arabian Nights*, retold by Laurence Housman, with drawings by Edmund Dulac (London: Hodder and Stoughton, 1907).

[2]   Gordon Craig (1872–1966), illegitimate son of the famous nineteenth-century actress Ellen Terry, became a noted theater designer and theorist. In March 1901 Yeats attended a performance of Purcell's *Dido and Aeneas* where he was much taken by the scenery which Craig had designed. Craig's influence on Yeats grew in subsequent years, and in November 1910 Yeats had Craig's screens installed in the Abbey Theatre in Dublin, making it the first theater to adopt them. Craig then arranged the screens and designed costumes and masks for a performance of *The Hour Glass* on January 12, 1911, the first use of Craig's screens at the Abbey.

[3]   Poems by S. T. Coleridge (1772–1834) and Percy Shelley (1792–1822).

among little instruments, only heard at their best perhaps when we are close about them. It should be again possible for a few poets to write as all did once, not for the printed page but to be sung. But movement also has grown less expressive, more declamatory, less intimate. When I called the other day upon a friend I found myself among some dozen people who were watching a group of Spanish boys and girls, professional dancers, dancing some national dance in the midst of a drawing-room. Doubtless their training had been long, laborious, and wearisome; but now one could not be deceived, their movement was full of joy. They were among friends, and it all seemed but the play of children; how powerful it seemed, how passionate, while an even more miraculous art, separated from us by the footlights, appeared in the comparison laborious and professional. It is well to be close enough to an artist to feel for him a personal liking, close enough perhaps to feel that our liking is returned.

My play is made possible by a Japanese dancer[4] whom I have seen dance in a studio and in a drawing-room and on a very small stage lit by an excellent stage-light. In the studio and in the drawing-room alone, where the lighting was the light we are most accustomed to, did I see him as the tragic image that has stirred my imagination. There, where no studied lighting, no stage-picture made an artificial world, he was able, as he rose from the floor, where he had been sitting cross-legged, or as he threw out an arm, to recede from us into some more powerful life. Because that separation was achieved by human means alone, he receded but to inhabit as it were the deeps of the mind. One realised anew, at every separating strangeness, that the measure of all arts' greatness can be but in their intimacy.

III

All imaginative art remains at a distance and this distance, once chosen, must be firmly held against a pushing world. Verse, ritual, music, and dance in association with action require that gesture, costume, facial expression, stage arrangement must help in keeping the door. Our unimaginative arts are content to set a piece of the world as we know it in a place by itself, to put their photographs as it were in a plush or a plain frame, but the arts which interest me, while seeming to separate from the world and us a group of figures, images, symbols, enable us to pass for a few moments into a deep of the mind that had hitherto been too subtle for our habitation. As a deep of the mind can only be approached through what is most human, most delicate, we should distrust bodily distance, mechanism, and loud noise.

It may be well if we go to school in Asia, for the distance from life in European art has come from little but difficulty with material. In half-Asiatic Greece Callimachus could still return to a stylistic management of the falling folds of drapery, after the naturalistic drapery of Phidias,[5] and in Egypt the same age that saw the village Head-man carved in wood, for burial in some tomb, with so complete a naturalism, saw set up in public places statues full of an august formality that implies traditional measurements, a philosophic defence. The spiritual painting of the fourteenth century passed on into Tintoretto and that of Velasquez into modern painting with no sense of loss to weigh against the gain,[6] while the painting of Japan, not having our European moon to churn the wits, has understood that no styles that ever delighted noble imaginations have lost their importance, and chooses the style according to the subject. In literature also we have had the illusion of change and progress, the art of Shakespeare passing into that of Dryden,[7] and so into the prose drama,

---

[4]   Michio Ito; on him see introduction to "At the Hawk's Well" on p. 351.

[5]   A Greek sculptor who was active in period 450–400 BC. A relief in the Capitoline Museum in Rome represents *Pan and the Three Graces* in an archaic or less naturalistic style which harks back to a period before Phidias; it is signed "Callimachus made it," and if the signature refers to the Greek sculptor Callimachus, then it could be taken as support for the claim advanced by Yeats. However, some scholars feel that "Callimachus" refers to the Roman copyist, not the Greek sculptor. For Phidias, see p. 319 n. 2.

[6]   Painting of the fourteenth century in Europe was highly stylized rather than naturalistic, but over the next few centuries increasingly evolved toward naturalism. Jacopo Tintoretto (1518–94) was an Italian painter and Diego Velazsquez (1599–1660) a Spanish one. Both artists build complex spatial illusions which can be broadly described as realistic or naturalistic, and in Yeats's view this entails a "loss" of the "spiritual" quality found in earlier painting.

[7]   The poetic drama of William Shakespeare (1564–1616) undergoes much change by the time of John Dryden (1631–1700) who, known for his drama and political satires, wrote verse that seems to be turning toward prose.

by what has seemed when studied in its details unbroken progress. Had we been Greeks, and so but half-European, an honourable mob would have martyred, though in vain, the first man who set up a painted scene, or who complained that soliloquies were unnatural, instead of repeating with a sigh, "We cannot return to the arts of childhood however beautiful." Only our lyric poetry has kept its Asiatic habit and renewed itself at its own youth, putting off perpetually what has been called its progress in a series of violent revolutions.

Therefore it is natural that I go to Asia for a stage convention, for more formal faces, for a chorus that has no part in the action, and perhaps for those movements of the body copied from the marionette shows of the fourteenth century. A mask will enable me to substitute for the face of some commonplace player, or for that face repainted to suit his own vulgar fancy, the fine invention of a sculptor, and to bring the audience close enough to the play to hear every inflection of the voice. A mask never seems but a dirty face, and no matter how close you go is yet a work of art; nor shall we lose by stilling the movement of the features, for deep feeling is expressed by a movement of the whole body. In poetical painting and in sculpture the face seems the nobler for lacking curiosity, alert attention, all that we sum up under the famous word of the realists, "vitality." It is even possible that being is only possessed completely by the dead, and that it is some knowledge of this that makes us gaze with so much emotion upon the face of the Sphinx or of Buddha. Who can forget the face of Chaliapine as the Mogul King in *Prince Igor*,[8] when a mask covering its upper portion made him seem like a phoenix at the end of its thousand wise years, awaiting in condescension the burning nest, and what did it not gain from that immobility in dignity and in power?

IV

Realism is created for the common people and was always their peculiar delight, and it is the delight to-day of all those whose minds, educated alone by school-masters and newspapers, are without the memory of beauty and emotional subtlety. The occasional humorous realism that so much heightened the emotional effect of Elizabethan tragedy – Cleopatra's old man with an asp,[9] let us say – carrying the tragic crisis by its contrast above the tide-mark of Corneille's courtly theatre, was made at the outset to please the common citizen standing on the rushes of the floor; but the great speeches were written by poets who remembered their patrons in the covered galleries. The fanatic Savonarola[10] was but dead a century, and his lamentation, in the frenzy of his rhetoric, that every prince of the Church or State throughout Europe was wholly occupied with the fine arts, had still its moiety of truth. A poetical passage cannot be understood without a rich memory, and like the older school of painting appeals to a tradition, and that not merely when it speaks of "Lethe wharf"[11] or "Dido on the wild sea banks"[12] but in rhythm, in vocabulary; for the ear must notice

---

[8] Fyodor Chaliapin (1873–1938) was a Russian opera singer, a bass who was highly esteemed for his performance in the role of Konchak in the opera *Prince Igor* (first performance 1890), a work left incomplete by Alexander Borodin (1833–77), then finished by Nikolai Rimsky-Korsakov (1844–1908) and Alexander Glazunov (1865–1936).

[9] In Act 5, scene 2, of Shakespeare's *Antony and Cleopatra*, a clown brings Cleopatra the asp with which she will take her life, making incongruous comments about the asp's powers. Such incongruity would have been alien to Pierre Corneille (1606–84), the French neoclassical dramatist whose concept of decorum was much stricter.

[10] Girolamo Savonarola (1452–98) was a Dominican friar who rose to prominence in Florence after the exile of Piero de' Medici in 1494. He became an official spokesman for a moral crusade which damned the alleged vices of ruling families such as the Medici, condemning their preoccupation with frivolities such as theater and the fine arts.

[11] From *Hamlet*, Act 1, scene 5. After the ghost has revealed to Hamlet that his father was murdered, and Hamlet has vowed revenge, the ghost comments:

> I find thee apt.
> And duller shouldst thou be than the fat weed
> That roots itself in ease on Lethe wharf,
> Wouldst thou not stir in this.

Lethe is the underworld river of forgetfulness.

[12] From *The Merchant of Venice*, Act 5, scene 1. Lorenzo and Jessica appear on a moonlit stage, and Lorenzo remarks:

> In such a night
> Stood Dido with a willow in her hand
> Upon the wild sea banks, and waved her love
> To come again to Carthage.

slight variations upon old cadences and customary words, all that high breeding of poetical style where there is nothing ostentatious, nothing crude, no breath of parvenu or journalist.

Let us press the popular arts on to a more complete realism – that would be their honesty – for the commercial arts demoralise by their compromise, their incompleteness, their idealism without sincerity or elegance, their pretence that ignorance can understand beauty. In the studio and in the drawing-room we can found a true theatre of beauty. Poets from the time of Keats and Blake have derived their descent only through what is least declamatory, least popular in the art of Shakespeare, and in such a theatre they will find their habitual audience and keep their freedom. Europe is very old and has seen many arts run through the circle and has learned the fruit of every flower and known what this fruit sends up, and it is now time to copy the East and live deliberately.

V

> Ye shall not, while ye tarry with me, taste
> From unrinsed barrel the diluted wine
> Of a low vineyard or a plant ill-pruned,
> But such as anciently the Aegean Isles
> Poured in libation at their solemn feasts:
> And the same goblets shall ye grasp embost
> With no vile figures of loose languid boors,
> But such as Gods have lived with and have led.[13]

The Noh theatre of Japan became popular at the close of the fourteenth century, gathering into itself dances performed at Shinto shrines in honour of spirits and gods, or by young nobles at the Court, and much old lyric poetry, and receiving its philosophy and its final shape perhaps from priests of a contemplative school of Buddhism. A small *daimio* or feudal lord of the ancient capital Nara, a contemporary of Chaucer, was the author, or perhaps only the stage-manager, of many plays. He brought them to the Court of the Shogun at Kioto. From that on the Shogun and his Court were as busy with dramatic poetry as the Mikado and his with lyric. When for the first time *Hamlet* was being played in London,[14] Noh was made a necessary part of official ceremonies at Kioto, and young nobles and princes, forbidden to attend the popular theatre, in Japan as elsewhere a place of mimicry and naturalism, were encouraged to witness and to perform in spectacles where speech, music, song, and dance created an image of nobility and strange beauty. When the modern revolution came, Noh after a brief unpopularity was played for the first time in certain ceremonious public theatres, and in 1897 a battleship was named *Takasago*, after one of its most famous plays. Some of the old noble families are to-day very poor, their men, it may be, but servants and labourers, but they still frequent these theatres. "Accomplishment" the word Noh means, and it is their accomplishment and that of a few cultivated people who understand the literary and mythological allusions and the ancient lyrics quoted in speech or chorus, their discipline, a part of their breeding. The players themselves, unlike the despised players of the popular theatre, have passed on proudly from father to son an elaborate art, and even now a player will publish his family tree to prove his skill. One player wrote in 1906 in a

---

Dido is the queen of Carthage who falls in love with Aeneas, is abandoned by him, and commits suicide, as recounted in Vergil's *Aeneid*.

[13] Lines 5–15 from the poem "Thrasymedes and Eunoe" by Walter Savage Landor (1775–1864). The poem begins with an unidentified narrator who invites the reader to journey into the past with him, there to learn the story of Thrasymedes and Eunoe:

> Who will away to Athens with me? Who
> Loves choral songs and maidens crown'd with flowers,
> Unenvious? mount the pinnace; hoist the sail.
> I promise ye, as many as are here

It then continues with the lines quoted by Yeats.

[14] *Hamlet* was first printed in 1603.

business circular – I am quoting from Mr. Pound's redaction of the Notes of Fenollosa[15] – that after thirty generations of nobles a woman of his house dreamed that a mask was carried to her from Heaven, and soon after she bore a son who became a player and the father of players. His family, he declared, still possessed a letter from a fifteenth-century Mikado conferring upon them a theatre-curtain, white below and purple above.

There were five families of these players and, forbidden before the Revolution to perform in public, they had received grants of land or salaries from the State. The white and purple curtain was no doubt to hang upon a wall behind the players or over their entrance-door, for the Noh stage is a platform surrounded upon three sides by the audience. No "naturalistic" effect is sought. The players wear masks and found their movements upon those of puppets: the most famous of all Japanese dramatists composed entirely for puppets. A swift or a slow movement and a long or a short stillness, and then another movement. They sing as much as they speak, and there is a chorus which describes the scene and interprets their thought and never becomes as in the Greek theatre a part of the action. At the climax, instead of the disordered passion of nature, there is a dance, a series of positions and movements which may represent a battle, or a marriage, or the pain of a ghost in the Buddhist Purgatory. I have lately studied certain of these dances, with Japanese players, and I notice that their ideal of beauty, unlike that of Greece and like that of pictures from Japan and China, makes them pause at moments of muscular tension. The interest is not in the human form but in the rhythm to which it moves, and the triumph of their art is to express the rhythm in its intensity. There are few swaying movements of arms or body such as make the beauty of our dancing. They move from the hip, keeping constantly the upper part of their body still, and seem to associate with every gesture or pose some definite thought. They cross the stage with a sliding movement, and one gets the impression not of undulation but of continuous straight lines.

The Print Room of the British Museum is now closed as a war-economy, so I can only write from memory of theatrical colour-prints, where a ship is represented by a mere skeleton of willows or osiers painted green, or a fruit-tree by a bush in a pot, and where actors have tied on their masks with ribbons that are gathered into a bunch behind the head. It is a child's game become the most noble poetry, and there is no observation of life, because the poet would set before us all those things which we feel and imagine in silence.

Mr. Ezra Pound has found among the Fenollosa manuscripts a story traditional among Japanese players.[16] A young man was following a stately old woman through the streets of a Japanese town, and presently she turned to him and spoke: "Why do you follow me?" "Because you are so interesting." "That is not so, I am too old to be interesting." But he wished, he told her, to become a player of old women on the Noh stage. If he would become famous as a Noh player, she said, he must not observe life, nor put on an old face and stint the music of his voice. He must know how to suggest an old woman and yet find it all in the heart.

VI

In the plays themselves I discover a beauty or a subtlety that I can trace perhaps to their threefold origin. The love-sorrows – the love of father and daughter, of mother and son, of boy and girl – may owe their nobility to a courtly life, but he to whom the adventures happen, a traveller commonly from some distant place, is most often a Buddhist priest; and the occasional intellectual subtlety is perhaps Buddhist. The adventure itself is often the meeting with ghost, god, or goddess at some holy place or much-legended tomb; and god, goddess, or ghost reminds me at times of our

---

[15] I.e., *"Noh" or Accomplishment: A Study of the Classical State of Japan* by Ernest Fenollosa and Ezra Pound (London: Macmillan, 1917; New York: Alfred Knopf, 1917); the book is perhaps best known under a different title, *The Classic Noh Theatre of Japan*, by Ezra Pound and Ernest Fenollosa (New York: New Directions, 1959), where the material cited by Yeats appears on p. 5. The circular is dated "March 1900" by Pound, rather than the 1906 given by Yeats.

[16] This anecdote is not transmitted by Pound in his editions of the Noh plays, and must have been orally communicated by him to Yeats.

own Irish legends and beliefs, which once, it may be, differed little from those of the Shinto worshipper.

The feather mantle, for whose lack the moon goddess (or should we call her faery?) cannot return to the sky, is the red cap whose theft can keep our faeries of the sea upon dry land; and the ghost-lovers in *Nishikigi* remind me of the Aran boy and girl who in Lady Gregory's story come to the priest after death to be married.[17] These Japanese poets, too, feel for tomb and wood the emotion, the sense of awe that our Gaelic-speaking countrypeople will sometimes show when you speak to them of Castle Hackett[18] or of some holy well; and that is why perhaps it pleases them to begin so many plays by a traveller asking his way with many questions, a convention agreeable to me, for when I first began to write poetical plays for an Irish theatre I had to put away an ambition of helping to bring again to certain places their old sanctity or their romance. I could lay the scene of a play on Baile's Strand, but I found no pause in the hurried action for descriptions of strand or sea or the great yew-tree that once stood there; and I could not in *The King's Threshold* find room, before I began the ancient story, to call up the shallow river and the few trees and rocky fields of modern Gort.[19] But in the *Nishikigi* the tale of the lovers would lose its pathos if we did not see that forgotten tomb where "the hiding fox" lives among "the orchids and the chrysanthemum flowers."[20] The men who created this convention were more like ourselves than were the Greeks and Romans, more like us even than are Shakespeare and Corneille. Their emotion was self-conscious and reminiscent, always associating itself with pictures and poems. They measured all that time had taken or would take away and found their delight in remembering celebrated lovers in the scenery pale passion loves. They travelled seeking for the strange and for the picturesque: "I go about with my heart set upon no particular place, no more than a cloud. I wonder now would the sea be that way, or the little place Kefu that they say is stuck down against it."[21] When a traveller asks his way of girls upon the roadside he is directed to find it by certain pine-trees, which he will recognise because many people have drawn them.

I wonder am I fanciful in discovering in the plays themselves (few examples have as yet been translated and I may be misled by accident or the idiosyncrasy of some poet) a playing upon a single metaphor, as deliberate as the echoing rhythm of line in Chinese and Japanese painting. In the *Nishikigi* the ghost of the girl-lover carries the cloth she went on weaving out of grass when she should have opened the chamber door to her lover, and woven grass returns again and again in metaphor and incident. The lovers, now that in an aëry body they must sorrow for unconsummated love, are "tangled up as the grass patterns are tangled." Again they are like an unfinished cloth: "these bodies, having no weft even now are not come together; truly a shameful story, a tale to bring shame on the gods." Before they can bring the priest to the tomb they spend the day "pushing aside the grass from the overgrown ways in Kefu,"[22] and the countryman who directs them is "cutting grass on the hill"; and when at last the prayer of the priest unites them in marriage the bride says that he has made "a dream-bridge over

[17]   Yeats is referring to a story told in Lady Gregory's *Visions and Beliefs in the West of Ireland* (New York and London: G. P. Putnam's Sons, 1920), a volume which he had seen when reading the proofs of Lady Gregory's book already in 1914. The story is the last in the section entitled "Seers and Healers" and is found on p. 79 in the Colin Smythe Coole edition. Lady Gregory first gathered this story in 1898, and Yeats may already have seen it in her notebooks soon after that.

[18]   The ruins of this thirteenth-century tower-house stand at the foot of the famed Knockma, a hill that overlooks the east side of Lough Corrib, in county Galway, about 20 miles north of Galway itself. It was built by the Hacketts, a Norman family who established themselves by driving out the O'Flahertys.

[19]   Baile's Strand (or Baile na Tragha, now Seatown) is a suburb of Dundalk. According to legend, the strand is named for Baile who was buried there when he died at hearing that his beloved Ailinn was dead. A yew tree sprang from his grave. The place is the setting for Yeats's play *On Baile Strand* (1904). Gort is a market

town approximately 10 miles southeast of Kinvara, another market town at the tip of Kinvara Bay in County Galway, where the palace of King Guaire was once located. Yeats uses the area around Gort as the setting for his play *The King's Threshold* (1904).

[20]   In the Noh play *Nishikigi*, the chorus describes the cave where two lovers have died: "Among the orchids and chrysanthemum flowers / The hiding fox is now lord of that love-cave." See *The Classic Noh Theatre of Japan*, by Ezra Pound and Ernest Fenollosa (New York: New Directions, 1959), p. 81.

[21]   The Noh play *Nishikigi* opens with a speech by the Waki, a priest, in which he says: "I go about with my heart set upon no particular place whatsoever, and with no other man's flag in my hand, no more than a cloud has. It is a flag of the night I see coming down upon me. I wonder now, would the sea be that way, or the little place Kefu that they say is stuck down against it." See *The Classic Noh Theatre of Japan*, p. 76.

[22]   From *The Classic Noh Theatre of Japan*, p. 80.

wild grass, over the grass I dwell in"; and in the end bride and bridegroom show themselves for a moment "from under the shadow of the love-grass."[23]

In *Hagoromo* the feather mantle of the faery woman creates also its rhythm of metaphor. In the beautiful day of opening spring "the plumage of Heaven drops neither feather nor flame," "nor is the rock of earth over-much worn by the brushing of the feathery skirt of the stars."[24] One half remembers a thousand Japanese paintings, or whichever comes first into the memory: that screen painted by Korin,[25] let us say, shown lately at the British Museum, where the same form is echoing in wave and in cloud and in rock. In European poetry I remember Shelley's continually repeated fountain and cave,[26] his broad stream and solitary star. In neglecting character, which seems to us essential in drama, as do their artists in neglecting relief and depth, whether in their paintings or in arranging flowers in a vase in a thin row, they have made possible a hundred lovely intricacies.

VII

These plays arose in an age of continual war and became a part of the education of soldiers. These soldiers, whose natures had as much of Walter Pater as of Achilles,[29] combined with Buddhist priests and women to elaborate life in a ceremony, the playing of football, the drinking of tea, and all great events of State, becoming a ritual. In the painting that decorated their walls and in the poetry they recited one discovers the only sign of a great age that cannot deceive us, the most vivid and subtle discrimination of sense and the invention of images more powerful than sense; the continual presence of reality. It is still true that the Deity gives us, according to His promise, not His thoughts or His convictions but His flesh and blood, and I believe that the elaborate technique of the arts, seeming to create out of itself a superhuman life, has taught more men to die than oratory or the Prayer Book. We only believe in those thoughts which have been conceived not in the brain but in the whole body. The Minoan soldier who bore upon his arm the shield ornamented with the dove in the Museum at Crete, or had upon his head the helmet with the winged horse, knew his rôle in life. When Nobuzane painted the child Saint Kōbō Daishi kneeling full of sweet austerity upon the flower of the lotus, he set up before our eyes exquisite life and the acceptance of death.[28]

I cannot imagine those young soldiers and the women they loved pleased with the ill-breeding and theatricality of Carlyle, nor, I think, with the magniloquence of Hugo.[29] These things belong to an industrial age, a mechanical sequence of ideas; but when I remember that curious game which the Japanese called, with a confusion of the senses that had seemed typical of our own age, 'listening to incense,'[30] I know that some among them would have understood the prose of Walter Pater, the painting of Puvis de Chavannes, the poetry of Mallarmé and Verlaine.[31] When heroism returned to our age it bore with it as its first gift technical sincerity.

[23] From *The Classic Noh Theatre of Japan*, p. 82.

[24] From *The Classic Noh Theatre of Japan*, pp. 103–4.

[25] Ogata Korin (1658–1716) was a Japanese painter. Yeats refers to his work "Pine Island," a two-panel folding screen, which uses ink, color, and gold on paper; the work is no longer ascribed to Korin himself, but to his workshop, and is assigned to the eighteenth century. It is located in the British Museum, London.

[26] The fountain and cave are indeed ubiquitous tropes in Shelley's poetry, recurring over 200 times in his work.

[27] Walter Horatio Pater (1839–94) is used here as a type of the delicate aesthete; Achilles, the ficitonal hero of Homer's *Iliad*, is a type of the rough warrior.

[28] Fujiwara Nobuzane (1176?–1265), a Japanese artist. Kobo Daishi (774–835), or the "Propagator of Dharma," was the founder of Shingon Buddhism; portraits of him as a child show a 2- or 3-year-old child seated in meditation and are very common, but the work that Yeats had in mind has not been identified.

[29] Thomas Carlyle (1795–1881) was a Scottish novelist, historian, and social critic; Victor Hugo (1802–85) was a French novelist, poet, and dramatist.

[30] "In the eighth century of our era the dilettante of the Japanese court established the tea cult and the play of 'listening to incense.' ... For 'listening to incense' the company was divided into two parties, and some arbiter burnt many kinds and many blended sorts of perfume, and the game was not merely to know which was which, but to give to each one of them a beautiful and allusive name, or to recall by the title some strange event of history or some passage of romance or legend." Ezra Pound, "Introduction" to *The Classic Noh Theatre of Japan*, pp. 3–4.

[31] The English critic and novelist Walter Horatio Pater (1839–94), the French painter Puvis de Chavannes (1824–98), and the French poets Stephan Mallarmé (1842–98) and Paul Verlaine (1844–96) – all were artists whose technical virtuosity was appreciated by Yeats and others at the turn of the century.

VIII

For some weeks now I have been elaborating my play in London where alone I can find the help I need, Mr. Dulac's mastery of design and Mr. Ito's genius of movement; yet it pleases me to think that I am working for my own country. Perhaps some day a play in the form I am adapting for European purposes may excite once more, whether in Gaelic or in English, under the slope of Slieve-na-mon or Croagh Patrick,[32] ancient memories; for this form has no need of scenery that runs away with money nor of a theatre-building. Yet I know that I only amuse myself with a fancy; for my writings if they be seaworthy will put to sea, and I cannot tell where they may be carried by the wind. Are not the faery-stories of Oscar Wilde, which were written for Mr. Ricketts and Mr. Shannon[33] and for a few ladies, very popular in Arabia?

Rapallo (1929)

I

Mountains that shelter the bay from all but the south wind, bare brown branches of low vines and of tall trees blurring their outline as though with a soft mist; houses mirrored in an almost motionless sea; a verandahed gable a couple of miles away bringing to mind some Chinese painting. Rapallo's[1] thin line of broken mother-of-pearl along the water's edge. The little town described in the "Ode on a Grecian Urn". In what better place could I, forbidden Dublin winters and all excited crowded places, spend what winters yet remain? On the broad pavement by the sea pass Italian peasants or working people, people out of the little shops, a famous German dramatist,[2] the barber's brother looking like an Oxford don, a British retired skipper, an Italian prince descended from Charlemagne and no richer than the rest of us, a few tourists seeking tranquillity. As there is no great harbour full of yachts, no great yellow strand, no great ballroom, no great casino, the rich carry elsewhere their strenuous lives.

II

I shall not lack conversation. Ezra Pound,[3] whose art is the opposite of mine, whose criticism commends what I most condemn, a man with whom I should quarrel more than with anyone else if we were not united by affection, has for years lived in rooms opening on to a flat roof by the sea. For the last hour we have sat upon the roof which is also a garden, discussing that immense poem of which but seven and twenty cantos are already published.[4] I have often found there brightly printed kings, queens, knaves, but have never discovered why all the suits could not be dealt out in some quite different order. Now at last he explains that it will, when the hundredth canto is finished, display a structure like that of a Bach Fugue.[5] There will be no plot, no chronicle of events, no logic of discourse, but two themes, the Descent into Hades from Homer, a Metamor-

32   Slievenamon, or "Mountain of the Women," is located 6 miles southeast of Fethard in county Tipperary and has a mysterious cairn on its summit. Croagh Patrick is a conical mountain 5 miles from Westport, in county Mayo; it was there that St. Patrick fasted for forty days in 441 AD.

33   Oscar Wilde delighted in the company of the two artists, Charles Ricketts (1866–1931), who designed the costumes for Yeats's play *The King's Threshold*, and Charles Shannon (1863–1937), who lived with Ricketts and joined him in forming the Vale Press in 1896.

"Rapallo" was first published in W. B. Yeats, *A Packet for Ezra Pound* (Dublin: the Cuala Press, 1929). Yeats's original notes, indicated by lower case roman numerals, are printed at the end of the essay.

1   A small town about 60 miles east of Genoa on the coast of the Tyrrhenian Sea.

2   Gerhart Hauptmann (1862–1946), the naturalist playwright who won the Nobel Prize for Literature in 1912.

3   Ezra Pound (1885–1972), American poet who moved to Rapallo in 1924 (see pp. 39–112).

4   Pound published *A Draft of XVI. Cantos* (Paris: Three Mountains Press) in 1925 and *A Draft of the Cantos 17–27* (London: John Rodker) in 1927, editions of 90 and 94 copies respectively.

5   Johann Sebastian Bach (1685–1750) composed many fugues; a fugue is a contrapuntal musical composition based on one or more short themes (motifs) in which different voices or instruments repeat the same melody with slight variations.

phosis from Ovid,[6] and, mixed with these, mediaeval or modern historical characters. He has tried to produce that picture Porteous commended to Nicholas Poussin in *Le chef d'œuvre inconnu*[7] where everything rounds or thrusts itself without edges, without contours – conventions of the intellect – from a splash of tints and shades; to achieve a work as characteristic of the art[i] of our time as the paintings of Cézanne,[8] avowedly suggested by Porteous, as *Ulysses* and its dream association of words and images, a poem in which there is nothing that can be taken out and reasoned over, nothing that is not a part of the poem itself. He has scribbled on the back of an envelope certain sets of letters that represent emotions or archetypal events – I cannot find any adequate definition – A B C D and then J K L M, and then each set of letters repeated, and then A B C D inverted and this repeated, and then a new element X Y Z, then certain letters that never recur, and then all sorts of combinations of X Y Z and J K L M and A B C D and D C B A, and all set whirling together. He has shown me upon the wall a photograph of a Cosimo Tura decoration in three compartments, in the upper the Triumph of Love and the Triumph of Chastity, in the middle Zodiacal signs, and in the lower certain events in Cosimo Tura's day.[9] The Descent and the Metamorphosis – A B C D and J K L M – his fixed elements, took the place of the Zodiac, the archetypal persons – X Y Z – that of the Triumphs, and certain modern events – his letters that do not recur – that of those events in Cosimo Tura's day.

I may, now that I have recovered leisure, find that the mathematical structure, when taken up into imagination, is more than mathematical, that seemingly irrelevant details fit together into a single theme, that here is no botch of tone and colour, all *Hodos Chameliontos*,[10] except for some odd corner where one discovers beautiful detail like that finely modelled foot in Porteous' disastrous picture.[11]

III

Sometimes about ten o'clock at night I accompany him to a street where there are hotels upon one side, upon the other palm-trees and the sea, and there, taking out of his pocket bones and pieces of meat, he begins to call the cats. He knows all their histories – the brindled cat looked like a skeleton until he began to feed it; that fat grey cat is an hotel proprietor's favourite, it never begs from the guests' tables and it turns cats that do not belong to the hotel out of the garden; this black cat and

---

[6]   The "descent into Hades" takes place in Book XI of Homer's *Odyssey*, and Ezra Pound uses a highly stylized translation of the scene to begin his *Cantos* (for the text, see pp. 62–4); the *Metamorphoses* of Ovid (43 BC to AD 17) is an epic poem in 15 books which all recount stories about a change of shape, a metamorphosis.

[7]   "Le chef d'oeuvre inconnu" ("The Hidden Masterpiece" or "The Unknown Masterpiece") is a short story by the French writer Honoré de Balzac (1799–1850), first published in 1831. It recounts a series of encounters between a young, fictionalized version of Nicholas Poussin, a mature artist named Porbus, and an aging artist named Maître Frenhofer (Master Frenhofer). In their first encounter, young Poussin listens as Frenhofer criticizes a recent painting by Porbus; it is Frenhofer (not Porbus, as Yeats incorrectly remembers) who then contrasts the purely formal correctness of Porbus's painting with his own work: "I have not drily outlined my figures, nor brought out superstitiously minute anatomical details; for, let me tell you, the human body does not end off with a line.... Nature is all curves, each wrapping or overlapping another.... there is no such thing as a line in nature, where all things are rounded and full ... For this reason I do not sharply define lineaments; I diffuse about their outline a haze of warm, light half-tints, so that I defy any one to place a finger on the exact spot where the parts join the groundwork of the picture." From Honoré de Balzac, *La Comédie humaine*, trans. Katharine Prescott Wormeley, vol. 37, *The Magic Skin, the Hidden Masterpiece* (London: Athenaeum Press, 1900), p. 343.

[8]   Paul Cézanne (1839–1906), French painter whose works are thought to anticipate Cubism and other developments in twentieth-century art; the idea that Cézanne was imitating the artistic practices of fictional characters by Balzac is a Yeatsian conceit.

[9]   Cosmé Tura (1433–95) was a painter closely associated with the court of the d'Este family in Ferrara, in northern Italy. But

when the d'Este family fled Ferrara in 1598, their palaces and properties were left to decay. It was in the great nineteenth-century that scholars rediscovered the frescos in the Hall of the Months in the Palazzo di Schifanoia, a former d'Este palace. The Hall of Months had been whitewashed over around 1700 and was restored in 1840. All the rediscovered frescos were promptly ascribed to Cosmé Tura; in the twentieth century, instead, only one scholar has assigned the frescos to Tura, and a dwindling handful have urged the more modest claim that he was a designer or master of the project. Today, instead, most scholars assign different frescos to different artists, and deny Tura's involvement in any capacity – all of which matters in this context because the paintings which Yeats and Pound were discussing in 1928 were from the Hall of Months. All the frescos were divided into three levels: the topmost featured a triumph, an allegorical scene in which a deity is presented in a triumphal chariot, surrounded by depictions of various vices or virtues; the middle layer presented Zodiacal signs or allegorical figures; the lowermost layer presented recognizable figures and events from the d'Este court. The portion that Yeats deisgnates as "the Triumph of Love" is undoubtedly "April," in which the upper compartment shows a triumph of Venus, the middle the Zodiacal sign of Taurus. The portion that Yeats designates "the Triumph of Chastity" is most likely "May," in which the upper compartment shows a "Triumph of Apollo" and the middle zone a representation of Gemini.

[10] Latin characters spelling out the ancient Greek words for "in the way (or fashion) of a chameleon."

[11] When viewing a fictional painting by Porbus, the aging painter Frenhofer discerns excellent details in the woman's bosom and shoulder, but finds her throat "all false." Yeats has misremembered the story's details.

that grey cat over there fought on the roof of a four-storied house some weeks ago, fell off, a whirling ball of claws and fur, and now avoid each other. Yet now that I recall the scene I think that he has no affection for cats – "some of them so ungrateful", a friend says – he never nurses the café cat, I cannot imagine him with a cat of his own. Cats are oppressed, dogs terrify them, landladies starve them, boys stone them, everybody speaks of them with contempt. If they were human beings we could talk of their oppressors with a studied violence, add our strength to theirs, even organise the oppressed and like good politicians sell our charity for power. I examine his criticism in this new light, his praise of writers pursued by ill-luck, left maimed or bedridden by the War; and thereupon recall a person as unlike him as possible, the only friend who remains to me from late boyhood, grown gaunt in the injustice of what seems her blind nobility of pity: "I will fight until I die", she wrote to me once, "against the cruelty of small ambitions." Was this pity a characteristic of his generation that has survived the Romantic Movement, and of mine and hers that saw it die – I too a revolutionist – some drop of hysteria still at the bottom of the cup?

IV

I have been wondering if I shall go to church and seek the company of the English in the villas. At Oxford I went constantly to All Souls Chapel,[11] though never at service time, and parts of *A Vision* were thought out there. In Dublin I went to Saint Patrick's[12] and sat there, but it was far off; and once I remember saying to a friend as we came out of Sant' Ambrogio at Milan,[13] "That is my tradition and I will let no priest rob me". I have sometimes wondered if it was but a timidity come from long disuse that keeps me from the service, and yesterday as I was wondering for the hundredth time, seated in a café by the sea, I heard an English voice say: "Our new Devil-dodger is not so bad. I have been practising with his choir all afternoon. We sang hymns and then God Save the King, more hymns and He's a Jolly Good Fellow. We were at the hotel at the end of the esplanade where they have the best beer." I am too anaemic for so British a faith; I shall haunt empty churches and be satisfied with Ezra Pound's society and that of his travelling Americans.

V

All that is laborious or mechanical in my book is finished; what remains can be added as a momentary rest from writing verse. It must be this thought of a burden dropped that made me think of attending church, if it is not that these mountains under their brilliant light fill me with an emotion that is like gratitude. Descartes[14] went on pilgrimage to some shrine of the Virgin when he made his first philosophical discovery, and the mountain road from Rapallo to Zoagli[15] seems like something in my own mind, something that I have discovered.

i   Mr. Wyndham Lewis,[17] whose criticism sounds true to a man of my generation, attacks this art in *Time and Western Man*.[16] If we reject, he argues, the forms and categories of the intellect there is nothing left but sensation, "eternal flux". Yet all such rejections stop at the conscious mind, for as

Dean Swift[17] says in a meditation on a woman who paints a dying face,

> Matter, as wise logicians say,
> Cannot without a form subsist;
> And form, say I as well as they,
> Must fail, if matter brings no grist.

Gertrude Stein (1874–1946)

Introduction

Gertrude Stein was born in Sacramento, California, the daughter of a wealthy businessman. She attended Radcliffe College, at that time known as "the Harvard Annex," from 1893 to 1897, where she took a strong interest in psychology and the philosophy of William James. Her first publications concerned automatic writing. She spent a year at the Johns Hopkins Medical School, but failed a crucial examination. After several years of travel in Italy and a brief residence in London, she moved to Paris to live with her brother Leo, in 1903. Her ground-floor flat at 27 rue de Fleurus would become legendary, and she stayed in it for the rest of her life. In 1906 she met Alice B. Toklas, who became her lifelong companion.

In 1909 she published *Three Lives* at her own expense, a triptych of stories in which racist portrayals of African-Americans compete with striking prose and bold psychological portraits. Prodded by her brother Leo's example, Stein also took an interest in contemporary art and became an early collector of Matisse and Picasso. How well she understood their art and to what degree it influenced her prose are issues of perennial debate. In 1911 she completed *The Making of Americans*, a massive (over 900 pages) history of a family's progress and a sustained meditation on writing. It was not published as a book until 1925, though excerpts from it were published in an avant-garde magazine in Paris in 1924. Meanwhile, she was already embarked on a series of prose poems and sketches, some of them published in various little magazines over the coming years, which were collected in *Geography and Plays* (1922). In 1914 she published her second book, a collection of prose poems titled *Tender Buttons*, with a small firm in New York. Reproduced here in its entirety (see pp. 373–99), its restless

exploration of the possibilities entailed in repetition marked a bold innovation. But because Stein was relatively isolated and lacked an institutional context, it was noticed by only a handful of admirers. That context would emerge only during the early 1920s when, in the aftermath of the Great War, a growing number of American, British, and Irish expatriates (Ford Madox Ford, Ezra Pound, James Joyce, to cite only the most obvious) gravitated to Paris, founding little magazines and small presses which now took up her work. In 1926 she gave lectures at Cambridge and Oxford, which went into *Composition as Explanation* (1926), published by the Hogarth Press that was managed by Leonard and Virginia Woolf.

The publication of *The Autobiography of Alice B. Toklas* in 1933, which became a bestseller, turned Stein into a household name. She followed this up almost immediately with *Four Saints in Three Acts* (1933), and when she returned to the United States for the first time that autumn to give a celebrated tour of lectures, she became a celebrity beloved by the media for her *outré* statements, early versions of the "soundbite." In her remaining years Stein became extraordinarily prolific: *Lectures in America* (1935), *The Geographical History of America* (1936), *Everybody's Autobiography* (1937), *Paris France* (1940), *What Are Masterpieces* (1940), *Ida A Novel* (1941), *Wars I Have Seen* (1945) – and I have omitted several more. During her lifetime her name was typically coupled with those of Eliot and Joyce. In subsequent years, as an influential version of the modernist canon was consolidated around the figures of Pound and Eliot, Stein's reputation lost ground. But since the mid-1980s there has been an extraordinary revival of interest in her work.

Tender Buttons (1914)

Contents

Tender Buttons was first published as an independent book in 1914 (New York: Claire Marie). It was reprinted in its entirety in the journal *transition* 14 (Fall, 1928). It was included entire in

Carl Van Vechten (ed.), *Selected Writings of Gertrude Stein* (New York: Vintage, 1945).

Objects

A CARAFE, THAT IS A BLIND GLASS.

A kind in glass and a cousin, a spectacle and nothing strange a single hurt color and an arrangement in a system to pointing. All this and not ordinary, not unordered in not resembling. The difference is spreading.

GLAZED GLITTER.

Nickel, what is nickel, it is originally rid of a cover.

The change in that is that red weakens an hour. The change has come. There is no search. But there is, there is that hope and that interpretation and sometime, surely any is unwelcome, sometime there is breath and there will be a sinecure and charming very charming is that clean and cleansing. Certainly glittering is handsome and convincing.

There is no gratitude in mercy and in medicine. There can be breakages in Japanese. That is no programme. That is no color chosen. It was chosen yesterday, that showed spitting and perhaps washing and polishing. It certainly showed no obligation and perhaps if borrowing is not natural there is some use in giving.

A SUBSTANCE IN A CUSHION.

The change of color is likely and a difference a very little difference is prepared. Sugar is not a vegetable.

Callous is something that hardening leaves behind what will be soft if there is a genuine interest in there being present as many girls as men. Does this change. It shows that dirt is clean when there is a volume.

A cushion has that cover. Supposing you do not like to change, supposing it is very clean that there is no change in appearance, supposing that there is regularity and a costume is that any the worse than an oyster and an exchange. Come to season that is there any extreme use in feather and cotton. Is there not much more joy in a table and more chairs and very likely roundness and a place to put them.

A circle of fine card board and a chance to see a tassel.

What is the use of a violent kind of delightfulness if there is no pleasure in not getting tired of it. The question does not come before there is a quotation. In any kind of place there is a top to covering and it is a pleasure at any rate there is some venturing in refusing to believe nonsense. It shows what use there is in a whole piece if one uses it and it is extreme and very likely the little things could be dearer but in any case there is a bargain and if there is the best thing to do is to take it away and wear it and then be reckless be reckless and resolved on returning gratitude.

Light blue and the same red with purple makes a change. It shows that there is no mistake. Any pink shows that and very likely it is reasonable. Very likely there should not be a finer fancy present. Some increase means a calamity and this is the best preparation for three and more being together. A little calm is so ordinary and in any case there is sweetness and some of that.

A seal and matches and a swan and ivy and a suit.

A closet, a closet does not connect under the bed. The band if it is white and black, the band has a green string. A sight a whole sight and a little groan grinding makes a trimming such a sweet singing trimming and a red thing not a round thing but a white thing, a red thing and a white thing.

The disgrace is not in carelessness nor even in sewing it comes out out of the way.

What is the sash like. The sash is not like anything mustard it is not like a same thing that has stripes, it is not even more hurt than that, it has a little top.

A BOX.

Out of kindness comes redness and out of rudeness comes rapid same question, out of an eye comes research, out of selection comes painful cattle. So then the order is that a white way of being round is something suggesting a pin and is it disappointing, it is not, it is so rudimentary to be analysed and see a fine substance strangely, it is so earnest to have a green point not to red but to point again.

A PIECE OF COFFEE.

More of double.

A place in no new table.

A single image is not splendor. Dirty is yellow. A sign of more in not mentioned. A piece of coffee is not a detainer. The resemblance to yellow is dirtier and distincter. The clean mixture is whiter and not coal color, never more coal color than altogether.

The sight of a reason, the same sight slighter, the sight of a simpler negative answer, the same sore sounder, the intention to wishing, the same splendor, the same furniture.

The time to show a message is when too late and later there is no hanging in a blight.

A not torn rose-wood color. If it is not dangerous then a pleasure and more than any other if it is cheap is not cheaper. The amusing side is that the sooner there are no fewer the more certain is the necessity dwindled. Supposing that the case contained rosewood and a color. Supposing that there was no reason for a distress and more likely for a number, supposing that there was no astonishment, is it not necessary to mingle astonishment.

The settling of stationing cleaning is one way not to shatter scatter and scattering. The one way to use custom is to use soap and silk for cleaning. The one way to see cotton is to have a design concentrating the illusion and the illustration. The perfect way is to accustom the thing to have a lining and the shape of a ribbon and to be solid, quite solid in standing and to use heaviness in morning. It is light enough in that. It has that shape nicely. Very nicely may not be exaggerating. Very strongly may be sincerely fainting. May be strangely flattering. May not be strange in everything. May not be strange to.

DIRT AND NOT COPPER.

Dirt and not copper makes a color darker. It makes the shape so heavy and makes no melody harder.

It makes mercy and relaxation and even a strength to spread a table fuller. There are more places not empty. They see cover.

NOTHING ELEGANT.

A charm a single charm is doubtful. If the red is rose and there is a gate surrounding it, if inside is let in and there places change then certainly something is upright. It is earnest.

MILDRED'S UMBRELLA.

A cause and no curve, a cause and loud enough, a cause and extra a loud clash and an extra wagon, a sign of extra, a sac a small sac and an established color and cunning, a slender grey and no ribbon, this means a loss a great loss a restitution.

A METHOD OF A CLOAK.

A single climb to a line, a straight exchange to a cane, a desperate adventure and courage and a clock, all this which is a system, which has feeling, which has resignation and success, all makes an attractive black silver.

A RED STAMP.

If lilies are lily white if they exhaust noise and distance and even dust, if they dusty will dirt a surface that has no extreme grace, if they do this and it is not necessary it is not at all necessary if they do this they need a catalogue.

A BOX.

A large box is handily made of what is necessary to replace any substance. Suppose an example is necessary, the plainer it is made the more reason there is for some outward recognition that there is a result.

A box is made sometimes and them to see to see to it neatly and to have the holes stopped up makes it necessary to use paper.

A custom which is necessary when a box is used and taken is that a large part of the time there are three which have different connections. The one is on the table. The two are on the table. The three are on the table. The one, one is the same length as is shown by the cover being longer. The other is different there is more cover that shows it. The other is different and that makes the corners have the same shade the eight are in singular arrangement to make four necessary.

Lax, to have corners, to be lighter than some weight, to indicate a wedding journey, to last brown and not curious, to be wealthy, cigarettes are established by length and by doubling.

Left open, to be left pounded, to be left closed, to be circulating in summer and winter, and sick color that is grey that is not dusty and red shows, to be sure cigarettes do measure an empty length sooner than a choice in color.

Winged, to be winged means that white is yellow and pieces pieces that are brown are dust color if dust is washed off, then it is choice that is to say it is fitting cigarettes sooner than paper.

An increase why is an increase idle, why is silver cloister, why is the spark brighter, if it is brighter is there any result, hardly more than ever.

A PLATE.

An occasion for a plate, an occasional resource is in buying and how soon does washing enable a selection of the same thing neater. If the party is small a clever song is in order.

Plates and a dinner set of colored china. Pack together a string and enough with it to protect the centre, cause a considerable haste and gather more as it is cooling, collect more trembling and not any even trembling, cause a whole thing to be a church.

A sad size a size that is not sad is blue as every bit of blue is precocious. A kind of green a game in green and nothing flat nothing quite flat and more round, nothing a particular color strangely, nothing breaking the losing of no little piece.

A splendid address a really splendid address is not shown by giving a flower freely, it is not shown by a mark or by wetting.

Cut cut in white, cut in white so lately. Cut more than any other and show it. Show it in the stem and in starting and in evening coming complication.

A lamp is not the only sign of glass. The lamp and the cake are not the only sign of stone. The lamp and the cake and the cover are not the only necessity altogether.

A plan a hearty plan, a compressed disease and no coffee, not even a card or a change to incline each way, a plan that has that excess and that break is the one that shows filling.

A SELTZER BOTTLE.

Any neglect of many particles to a cracking, any neglect of this makes around it what is lead in color and certainly discolor in silver. The use of this is manifold. Supposing a certain time selected is assured, suppose it is even necessary, suppose no other extract is permitted and no more handling is needed, suppose the rest of the message is mixed with a very long slender needle and even if it could be any black border, supposing all this altogether made a dress and suppose it was actual, suppose the mean way to state it was occasional, if you suppose this in August and even more melodiously, if you suppose this even in the necessary incident of there certainly being no middle in summer and winter, suppose this and an elegant settlement a very elegant settlement is more than of consequence, it is not final and sufficient and substituted. This which was so kindly a present was constant.

A LONG DRESS.

What is the current that makes machinery, that makes it crackle, what is the current that presents a long line and a necessary waist. What is this current.

What is the wind, what is it.

Where is the serene length, it is there and a dark place is not a dark place, only a white and red are black, only a yellow and green are blue, a pink is scarlet, a bow is every color. A line distinguishes it. A line just distinguishes it.

A RED HAT.

A dark grey, a very dark grey, a quite dark grey is monstrous ordinarily, it is so monstrous because there is no red in it. If red is in everything it is not necessary. Is that not an argument for any use of it and even so is there any place that is better, is there any place that has so much stretched out.

A BLUE COAT.

A blue coat is guided guided away, guided and guided away, that is the particular color that is used for that length and not any width not even more than a shadow.

A PIANO.

If the speed is open, if the color is careless, if the selection of a strong scent is not awkward, if the button holder is held by all the waving color and there is no color, not any color. If there is no dirt in a pin and there can be none scarcely, if there is not then the place is the same as up standing.

This is no dark custom and it even is not acted in any such a way that a restraint is not spread. That is spread, it shuts and it lifts and awkwardly not awkwardly the centre is in standing.

A CHAIR.

A widow in a wise veil and more garments shows that shadows are even. It addresses no more, it shadows the stage and learning. A regular arrangement, the severest and the most preserved is that which has the arrangement not more than always authorised.

A suitable establishment, well housed, practical, patient and staring, a suitable bedding, very suitable and not more particularly than complaining, anything suitable is so necessary.

A fact is that when the direction is just like that, no more, longer, sudden and at the same time not any sofa, the main action is that without a blaming there is no custody.

Practice measurement, practice the sign that means that really means a necessary betrayal, in showing that there is wearing.

Hope, what is a spectacle, a spectacle is the resemblance between the circular side place and nothing else, nothing else.

To choose it is ended, it is actual and more than that it has it certainly has the same treat, and a seat all that is practiced and more easily much more easily ordinarily.

Pick a barn, a whole barn, and bend more slender accents than have ever been necessary, shine in the darkness necessarily.

Actually not aching, actually not aching, a stubborn bloom is so artificial and even more than that, it is a spectacle, it is a binding accident, it is animosity and accentuation.

If the chance to dirty diminishing is necessary, if it is why is there no complexion, why is there no rubbing, why is there no special protection.

A FRIGHTFUL RELEASE.

A bag which was left and not only taken but turned away was not found. The place was shown to be very like the last time. A piece was not exchanged, not a bit of it, a piece was left over. The rest was mismanaged.

A PURSE.

A purse was not green, it was not straw color, it was hardly seen and it had a use a long use and the chain, the chain was never missing, it was not misplaced, it showed that it was open, that is all that it showed.

A MOUNTED UMBRELLA.

What was the use of not leaving it there where it would hang what was the use if there was no chance of ever seeing it come there and show that it was handsome and right in the way it showed it. The lesson is to learn that it does show it, that it shows it and that nothing, that there is nothing, that there is no more to do about it and just so much more is there plenty of reason for making an exchange.

A CLOTH.

Enough cloth is plenty and more, more is almost enough for that and besides if there is no more spreading is there plenty of room for it. Any occasion shows the best way.

MORE.

An elegant use of foliage and grace and a little piece of white cloth and oil.

Wondering so winningly in several kinds of oceans is the reason that makes red so regular and enthusiastic. The reason that there is more snips are the same shining very colored rid of no round color.

A NEW CUP AND SAUCER.

Enthusiastically hurting a clouded yellow bud and saucer, enthusiastically so is the bite in the ribbon.

OBJECTS.

Within, within the cut and slender joint alone, with sudden equals and no more than three, two in the centre make two one side.

If the elbow is long and it is filled so then the best example is all together.

The kind of show is made by squeezing.

EYE GLASSES.

A color in shaving, a saloon is well placed in the centre of an alley.

A CUTLET.

A blind agitation is manly and uttermost.

CARELESS WATER.

No cup is broken in more places and mended, that is to say a plate is broken and mending does do that it shows that culture is Japanese. It shows the whole element of angels and orders. It does more to choosing and it does more to that ministering counting. It does, it does change in more water.

Supposing a single piece is a hair supposing more of them are orderly, does that show that strength, does that show that joint, does that show that balloon famously. Does it.

A PAPER.

A courteous occasion makes a paper show no such occasion and this makes readiness and eyesight and likeness and a stool.

A DRAWING.

The meaning of this is entirely and best to say the mark, best to say it best to show sudden places, best to make bitter, best to make the length tall and nothing broader, anything between the half.

WATER RAINING.

Water astonishing and difficult altogether makes a meadow and a stroke.

COLD CLIMATE.

A season in yellow sold extra strings makes lying places.

MALACHITE.

The sudden spoon is the same in no size. The sudden spoon is the wound in the decision.

AN UMBRELLA.

Coloring high means that the strange reason is in front not more in front behind. Not more in front in peace of the dot.

A PETTICOAT.

A light white, a disgrace, an ink spot, a rosy charm.

A WAIST.

A star glide, a single frantic sullenness, a single financial grass greediness.
Object that is in wood. Hold the pine, hold the dark, hold in the rush, make the bottom.
A piece of crystal. A change, in a change that is remarkable there is no reason to say that there was a time.
A woolen object gilded. A country climb is the best disgrace, a couple of practices any of them in order is so left.

A TIME TO EAT.

A pleasant simple habitual and tyrannical and authorised and educated and resumed and articulate separation. This is not tardy.

A LITTLE BIT OF A TUMBLER.

A shining indication of yellow consists in there having been more of the same color than could have been expected when all four were bought. This was the hope which made the six and seven have no use for any more places and this necessarily spread into nothing. Spread into nothing.

A FIRE.

What was the use of a whole time to send and not send if there was to be the kind of thing that made that come in. A letter was nicely sent.

A HANDKERCHIEF.

A winning of all the blessings, a sample not a sample because there is no worry.

RED ROSES.

A cool red rose and a pink cut pink, a collapse and a sold hole, a little less hot.

IN BETWEEN.

In between a place and candy is a narrow foot-path that shows more mounting than anything, so much really that a calling meaning a bolster measured a whole thing with that. A virgin a whole virgin is judged made and so between curves and outlines and real seasons and more out glasses and a perfectly unprecedented arrangement between old ladies and mild colds there is no satin wood shining.

COLORED HATS.

Colored hats are necessary to show that curls are worn by an addition of blank spaces, this makes the difference between single lines and broad stomachs, the least thing is lightening, the least thing means a little flower and a big delay a big delay that makes more nurses than little women really little women. So clean is a light that nearly all of it shows pearls and little ways. A large hat is tall and me and all custard whole.

A FEATHER.

A feather is trimmed, it is trimmed by the light and the bug and the post, it is trimmed by little leaning and by all sorts of mounted reserves and loud volumes. It is surely cohesive.

A BROWN.

A brown which is not liquid not more so is relaxed and yet there is a change, a news is pressing.

A LITTLE CALLED PAULINE.

A little called anything shows shudders.
Come and say what prints all day. A whole few watermelon. There is no pope.
No cut in pennies and little dressing and choose wide soles and little spats really little spices.
A little lace makes boils. This is not true.
Gracious of gracious and a stamp a blue green white bow a blue green lean, lean on the top.
If it is absurd then it is leadish and nearly set in where there is a tight head.
A peaceful life to arise her, noon and moon and moon. A letter a cold sleeve a blanket a shaving house and nearly the best and regular window.
Nearer in fairy sea, nearer and farther, show white has lime in sight, show a stitch of ten. Count, count more so that thicker and thicker is leaning.
I hope she has her cow. Bidding a wedding, widening received treading, little leading mention nothing.
Cough out cough out in the leather and really feather it is not for.
Please could, please could, jam it not plus more sit in when.

A SOUND.

Elephant beaten with candy and little pops and chews all bolts and reckless reckless rats, this is this.

A TABLE.

A table means does it not my dear it means a whole steadiness. Is it likely that a change.
A table means more than a glass even a looking glass is tall. A table means necessary places and a revision a revision of a little thing it means it does mean that there has been a stand, a stand where it did shake.

SHOES.

To be a wall with a damper a stream of pounding way and nearly enough choice makes a steady midnight. It is pus.
A shallow hole rose on red, a shallow hole in and in this makes ale less. It shows shine.

A DOG.

A little monkey goes like a donkey that means to say that means to say that more sighs last goes. Leave with it. A little monkey goes like a donkey.

A WHITE HUNTER.

A white hunter is nearly crazy.

A LEAVE.

In the middle of a tiny spot and nearly bare there is a nice thing to say that wrist is leading. Wrist is leading.

SUPPOSE AN EYES.

Suppose it is within a gate which open is open at the hour of closing summer that is to say it is so.

All the seats are needing blackening. A white dress is in sign. A soldier a real soldier has a worn lace a worn lace of different sizes that is to say if he can read, if he can read he is a size to show shutting up twenty-four.

Go red go red, laugh white.

Suppose a collapse in rubbed purr, in rubbed purr get.

Little sales ladies little sales ladies little saddles of mutton.

Little sales of leather and such beautiful beautiful, beautiful beautiful.

A SHAWL.

A shawl is a hat and hurt and a red balloon and an under coat and a sizer a sizer of talks.

A shawl is a wedding, a piece of wax a little build. A shawl.

Pick a ticket, pick it in strange steps and with hollows. There is hollow hollow belt, a belt is a shawl.

A plate that has a little bobble, all of them, any so.

Please a round it is ticket.

It was a mistake to state that a laugh and a lip and a laid climb and a depot and a cultivator and little choosing is a point it.

BOOK.

Book was there, it was there. Book was there. Stop it, stop it, it was a cleaner, a wet cleaner and it was not where it was wet, it was not high, it was directly placed back, not back again, back it was returned, it was needless, it put a bank, a bank when, a bank care.

Suppose a man a realistic expression of resolute reliability suggests pleasing itself white all white and no head does that mean soap. It does not so. It means kind wavers and little chance to beside beside rest. A plain.

Suppose ear rings, that is one way to breed, breed that. Oh chance to say, oh nice old pole. Next best and nearest a pillar. Chest not valuable, be papered.

Cover up cover up the two with a little piece of string and hope rose and green, green.

Please a plate, put a match to the seam and really then really then, really then it is a remark that joins many many lead games. It is a sister and sister and a flower and a flower and a dog and a colored sky a sky colored grey and nearly that nearly that let.

PEELED PENCIL, CHOKE.

Rub her coke.

IT WAS BLACK, BLACK TOOK.

Black ink best wheel bale brown.
Excellent not a hull house, not a pea soup, no bill no care, no precise no past pearl pearl goat.

THIS IS THIS DRESS, AIDER.

Aider, why aider why whow, whow stop touch, aider whow, aider stop the muncher, muncher munchers.
A jack in kill her, a jack in, makes a meadowed king, makes a to let.

Food

ROASTBEEF; MUTTON; BREAKFAST; SUGAR; CRANBERRIES; MILK; EGGS; APPLE; TAILS; LUNCH; CUPS; RHUBARB; SINGLE; FISH; CAKE; CUSTARD; POTATOES; ASPARAGUS; BUTTER; END OF SUMMER; SAUSAGES; CELERY; VEAL; VEGETABLE; COOKING; CHICKEN; PASTRY; CREAM; CUCUMBER; DINNER; DINING; EATING; SALAD; SAUCE; SALMON; ORANGE; COCOA; AND CLEAR SOUP AND ORANGES AND OAT-MEAL; SALAD DRESSING AND AN ARTICHOKE; A CENTRE IN A TABLE.

ROASTBEEF.

In the inside there is sleeping, in the outside there is reddening, in the morning there is meaning, in the evening there is feeling. In the evening there is feeling. In feeling anything is resting, in feeling anything is mounting, in feeling there is resignation, in feeling there is recognition, in feeling there is recurrence and entirely mistaken there is pinching. All the standards have steamers and all the curtains have bed linen and all the yellow has discrimination and all the circle has circling. This makes sand.

Very well. Certainly the length is thinner and the rest, the round rest has a longer summer. To shine, why not shine, to shine, to station, to enlarge, to hurry the measure all this means nothing if there is singing, if there is singing then there is the resumption.

The change the dirt, not to change dirt means that there is no beefsteak and not to have that is no obstruction, it is so easy to exchange meaning, it is so easy to see the difference. The difference is that a plain resource is not entangled with thickness and it does not mean that thickness shows such cutting, it does mean that a meadow is useful and a cow absurd. It does not mean that there are tears, it does not mean that exudation is cumbersome, it means no more than a memory, a choice and a reëstablishment, it means more than any escape from a surrounding extra. All the time that there is use there is use and any time there is a surface there is a surface, and every time there is an exception there is an exception and every time there is a division there is a dividing. Any time there is a surface there is a surface and every time there is a suggestion there is a suggestion and every time there is silence there is silence and every time that is languid there is that there then and not oftener, not always, not particular, tender and changing and external and central and surrounded and singular and simple and the same and the surface and the circle and the shine and the succor and the white and the same and the better and the red and the same and the centre and the yellow and the tender and the better, and altogether.

Considering the circumstances there is no occasion for a reduction, considering that there is no pealing there is no occasion for an obligation, considering that there is no outrage there is no necessity for any reparation, considering that there is no particle sodden there is no occasion for deliberation. Considering everything and which way the turn is tending, considering everything why is there no restraint, considering everything what makes the place settle and the plate distinguish some specialties. The whole thing is not understood and this is not strange considering that there is no education, this is not strange because having that certainly does show the difference in cutting, it shows that when there is turning there is no distress.

In kind, in a control, in a period, in the alteration of pigeons, in kind cuts and thick and thin spaces, in kind ham and different colors, the length of leaning a strong thing outside not to make a sound but to suggest a crust, the principal taste is when there is a whole chance to be reasonable, this does not mean that there is overtaking, this means nothing precious, this means clearly that the chance to exercise is a social success. So then the sound is not obtrusive. Suppose it is obtrusive suppose it is. What is certainly the desertion is not a reduced description, a description is not a birthday.

Lovely snipe and tender turn, excellent vapor and slender butter, all the splinter and the trunk, all the poisonous darkning drunk, all the joy in weak success, all the joyful tenderness, all the section and the tea, all the stouter symmetry.

Around the size that is small, inside the stern that is the middle, besides the remains that are praying, inside the between that is turning, all the region is measuring and melting is exaggerating.

Rectangular ribbon does not mean that there is no eruption it means that if there is no place to hold there is no place to spread. Kindness is not earnest, it is not assiduous it is not revered.

Room to comb chickens and feathers and ripe purple, room to curve single plates and large sets and second silver, room to send everything away, room to save heat and distemper, room to search a light that is simpler, all room has no shadow.

There is no use there is no use at all in smell, in taste, in teeth, in toast, in anything, there is no use at all and the respect is mutual.

Why should that which is uneven, that which is resumed, that which is tolerable why should all this resemble a smell, a thing is there, it whistles, it is not narrower, why is there no obligation to stay away and yet courage, courage is everywhere and the best remains to stay.

If there could be that which is contained in that which is felt there would be a chair where there are chairs and there would be no more denial about a clatter. A clatter is not a smell. All this is good.

The Saturday evening which is Sunday is every week day. What choice is there when there is a difference. A regulation is not active. Thirstiness is not equal division.

Anyway, to be older and ageder is not a surfeit nor a suction, it is not dated and careful, it is not dirty. Any little thing is clean, rubbing is black. Why should ancient lambs be goats and young colts and never beef, why should they, they should because there is so much difference in age.

A sound, a whole sound is not separation, a whole sound is in an order.

Suppose there is a pigeon, suppose there is.

Looseness, why is there a shadow in a kitchen, there is a shadow in a kitchen because every little thing is bigger.

The time when there are four choices and there are four choices in a difference, the time when there are four choices there is a kind and there is a kind. There is a kind. There is a kind. Supposing there is a bone, there is a bone. Supposing there are bones. There are bones. When there are bones there is no supposing there are bones. There are bones and there is that consuming. The kindly way to feel separating is to have a space between. This shows a likeness.

Hope in gates, hope in spoons, hope in doors, hope in tables, no hope in daintiness and determination. Hope in dates.

Tin is not a can and a stove is hardly. Tin is not necessary and neither is a stretcher. Tin is never narrow and thick.

Color is in coal. Coal is outlasting roasting and a spoonful, a whole spoon that is full is not spilling. Coal any coal is copper.

Claiming nothing, not claiming anything, not a claim in everything, collecting claiming, all this makes a harmony, it even makes a succession.

Sincerely gracious one morning, sincerely graciously trembling, sincere in gracious eloping, all this makes a furnace and a blanket. All this shows quantity.

Like an eye, not so much more, not any searching, no compliments.

Please be the beef, please beef, pleasure is not wailing. Please beef, please be carved clear, please be a case of consideration.

Search a neglect. A sale, any greatness is a stall and there is no memory, there is no clear collection.

A satin sight, what is a trick, no trick is mountainous and the color, all the rush is in the blood.

Bargaining for a little, bargain for a touch, a liberty, an estrangement, a characteristic turkey.

Please spice, please no name, place a whole weight, sink into a standard rising, raise a circle, choose a right around, make the resonance accounted and gather green any collar.

To bury a slender chicken, to raise an old feather, to surround a garland and to bake a pole splinter, to suggest a repose and to settle simply, to surrender one another, to succeed saving simpler, to satisfy a singularity and not to be blinder, to sugar nothing darker and to read redder, to have the color better, to sort out dinner, to remain together, to surprise no sinner, to curve nothing sweeter, to continue thinner, to increase in resting recreation to design string not dimmer.

Cloudiness what is cloudiness, is it a lining, is it a roll, is it melting.

The sooner there is jerking, the sooner freshness is tender, the sooner the round it is not round the sooner it is withdrawn in cutting, the sooner the measure means service, the sooner there is chinking, the sooner there is sadder than salad, the sooner there is none do her, the sooner there is no choice, the sooner there is a gloom freer, the same sooner and more sooner, this is no error in hurry and in pressure and in opposition to consideration.

A recital, what is a recital, it is an organ and use does not strengthen valor, it soothes medicine.

A transfer, a large transfer, a little transfer, some transfer, clouds and tracks do transfer, a transfer is not neglected.

Pride, when is there perfect pretence, there is no more than yesterday and ordinary.

A sentence of a vagueness that is violence is authority and a mission and stumbling and also certainly also a prison. Calmness, calm is beside the plate and in way in. There is no turn in terror. There is no volume in sound.

There is coagulation in cold and there is none in prudence. Something is preserved and the evening is long and the colder spring has sudden shadows in a sun. All the stain is tender and lilacs really lilacs are disturbed. Why is the perfect reëstablishment practiced and prized, why is it composed. The result the pure result is juice and size and baking and exhibition and nonchalance and sacrifice and volume and a section in division and the surrounding recognition and horticulture and no murmur. This is a result. There is no superposition and circumstance, there is hardness and a reason and the rest and remainder. There is no delight and no mathematics.

MUTTON.

A letter which can wither, a learning which can suffer and an outrage which is simultaneous is principal.

Student, students are merciful and recognised they chew something.

Hate rests that is solid and sparse and all in a shape and largely very largely. Interleaved and successive and a sample of smell all this makes a certainty a shade.

Light curls very light curls have no more curliness than soup. This is not a subject.

Change a single stream of denting and change it hurriedly, what does it express, it expresses nausea. Like a very strange likeness and pink, like that and not more like that than the same resemblance and not more like that than no middle space in cutting.

An eye glass, what is an eye glass, it is water. A splendid specimen, what is it when it is little and tender so that there are parts. A centre can place and four are no more and two and two are not middle.

Melting and not minding, safety and powder, a particular recollection and a sincere solitude all this makes a shunning so thorough and so unrepeated and surely if there is anything left it is a bone. It is not solitary.

Any space is not quiet it is so likely to be shiny. Darkness very dark darkness is sectional. There is a way to see in onion and surely very surely rhubarb and a tomato, surely very surely there is that seeding. A little thing in is a little thing.

Mud and water were not present and not any more of either. Silk and stockings were not present and not any more of either. A receptacle and a symbol and no monster were present and no more. This made a piece show and was it a kindness, it can be asked was it a kindness to have it warmer, was it a kindness and does gliding mean more. Does it.

Does it dirty a ceiling. It does not. It is dainty, it is if prices are sweet. Is it lamentable, it is not if there is no undertaker. Is it curious, it is not when there is youth. All this makes a line, it even makes makes no more. All this makes cherries. The reason that there is a suggestion in vanity is due to this that there is a burst of mixed music.

A temptation any temptation is an exclamation if there are misdeeds and little bones. It is not astonishing that bones mingle as they vary not at all and in any case why is a bone outstanding, it is so because the circumstance that does not make a cake and character is so easily churned and cherished.

Mouse and mountain and a quiver, a quaint statue and pain in an exterior and silence more silence louder shows salmon a mischief intender. A cake, a real salve made of mutton and liquor, a specially retained rinsing and an established cork and blazing, this which resignation influences and restrains, restrains more altogether. A sign is the specimen spoken.

A meal in mutton, mutton, why is lamb cheaper, it is cheaper because so little is more. Lecture, lecture and repeat instruction.

BREAKFAST.

A change, a final change includes potatoes. This is no authority for the abuse of cheese. What language can instruct any fellow.

A shining breakfast, a breakfast shining, no dispute, no practice, nothing, nothing at all.

A sudden slice changes the whole plate, it does so suddenly.

An imitation, more imitation, imitation succeed imitations.

Anything that is decent, anything that is present, a calm and a cook and more singularly still a shelter, all these show the need of clamor. What is the custom, the custom is in the centre.

What is a loving tongue and pepper and more fish than there is when tears many tears are necessary. The tongue and the salmon, there is not salmon when brown is a color, there is salmon when there is no meaning to an early morning being pleasanter. There is no salmon, there are no tea-cups, there are the same kind of mushes as are used as stomachers by the eating hopes that makes eggs delicious. Drink is likely to stir a certain respect for an egg cup and more water melon than was ever eaten yesterday. Beer is neglected and cocoanut is famous. Coffee all coffee and a sample of soup all soup these are the choice of a baker. A white cup means a wedding. A wet cup means a vacation. A strong cup means an especial regulation. A single cup means a capital arrangement between the drawer and the place that is open.

Price a price is not in language, it is not in custom, it is not in praise.

A colored loss, why is there no leisure. If the persecution is so outrageous that nothing is solemn is there any occasion for persuasion.

A grey turn to a top and bottom, a silent pocketful of much heating, all the pliable succession of surrendering makes an ingenious joy.

A breeze in a jar and even then silence, a special anticipation in a rack, a gurgle a whole gurgle and more cheese than almost anything, is this an astonishment, does this incline more than the original division between a tray and a talking arrangement and even then a calling into another room gently with some chicken in any way.

A bent way that is a way to declare that the best is all together, a bent way shows no result, it shows a slight restraint, it shows a necessity for retraction.

Suspect a single buttered flower, suspect it certainly, suspect it and then glide, does that not alter a counting.

A hurt mended stick, a hurt mended cup, a hurt mended article of exceptional relaxation and annoyance, a hurt mended, hurt and mended is so necessary that no mistake is intended.

What is more likely than a roast, nothing really and yet it is never disappointed singularly.

A steady cake, any steady cake is perfect and not plain, any steady cake has a mounting reason and more than that it has singular crusts. A season of more is a season that is instead. A season of many is not more a season than most.

Take no remedy lightly, take no urging intently, take no separation leniently, beware of no lake and no larder.

Burden the cracked wet soaking sack heavily, burden it so that it is an institution in fright and in climate and in the best plan that there can be.

An ordinary color, a color is that strange mixture which makes, which does make which does not make a ripe juice, which does not make a mat.

A work which is a winding a real winding of the cloaking of a relaxing rescue. This which is so cool is not dusting, it is not dirtying in smelling, it could use white water, it could use more extraordinarily and in no solitude altogether. This which is so not winsome and not widened and really not so dipped as dainty and really dainty, very dainty, ordinarily, dainty, a dainty, not in that dainty and dainty. If the time is determined, if it is determined and there is reunion there is reunion with that then outline, then there is in that a piercing shutter, all of a piercing shouter, all of a quite weather, all of a withered exterior, all of that in most violent likely.

An excuse is not dreariness, a single plate is not butter, a single weight is not excitement, a solitary crumbling is not only martial.

A mixed protection, very mixed with the same actual intentional unstrangeness and riding, a single action caused necessarily is not more a sign than a minister.

Seat a knife near a cage and very near a decision and more nearly a timely working cat and scissors. Do this temporarily and make no more mistake in standing. Spread it all and arrange the white place, does this show in the house, does it not show in the green that is not necessary for that color, does it not even show in the explanation and singularly not at all stationary.

SUGAR.

A violent luck and a whole sample and even then quiet.

Water is squeezing, water is almost squeezing on lard. Water, water is a mountain and it is selected and it is so practical that there is no use in money. A mind under is exact and so it is necessary to have a mouth and eye glasses.

A question of sudden rises and more time than awfulness is so easy and shady. There is precisely that noise.

A peck a small piece not privately overseen, not at all not a slice, not at all crestfallen and open, not at all mounting and chaining and evenly surpassing, all the bidding comes to tea.

A separation is not tightly in worsted and sauce, it is so kept well and sectionally.

Put it in the stew, put it to shame. A little slight shadow and a solid fine furnace.

The teasing is tender and trying and thoughtful.

The line which sets sprinkling to be a remedy is beside the best cold.

A puzzle, a monster puzzle, a heavy choking, a neglected Tuesday.

Wet crossing and a likeness, any likeness, a likeness has blisters, it has that and teeth, it has the staggering blindly and a little green, any little green is ordinary.

One, two and one, two, nine, second and five and that.

A blaze, a search in between, a cow, only any wet place, only this tune.

Cut a gas jet uglier and then pierce pierce in between the next and negligence. Choose the rate to pay and pet pet very much. A collection of all around, a signal poison, a lack of languor and more hurts at ease.

A white bird, a colored mine, a mixed orange, a dog.
Cuddling comes in continuing a change.
A piece of separate outstanding rushing is so blind with open delicacy.
A canoe is orderly. A period is solemn. A cow is accepted.
A nice old chain is widening, it is absent, it is laid by.

CRANBERRIES.

Could there not be a sudden date, could there not be in the present settlement of old age pensions, could there not be by a witness, could there be.
Count the chain, cut the grass, silence the noon and murder flies. See the basting undip the chart, see the way the kinds are best seen from the rest, from that and untidy.
Cut the whole space into twenty-four spaces and then and then is there a yellow color, there is but it is smelled, it is then put where it is and nothing stolen.
A remarkable degree of red means that, a remarkable exchange is made.
Climbing altogether in when there is a solid chance of soiling no more than a dirty thing, coloring all of it in steadying is jelly.
Just as it is suffering, just as it is succeeded, just as it is moist so is there no countering.

MILK.

A white egg and a colored pan and a cabbage showing settlement, a constant increase.
A cold in a nose, a single cold nose makes an excuse. Two are more necessary.
All the goods are stolen, all the blisters are in the cup.
Cooking, cooking is the recognition between sudden and nearly sudden very little and all large holes.
A real pint, one that is open and closed and in the middle is so bad.
Tender colds, seen eye holders, all work, the best of change, the meaning, the dark red, all this and bitten, really bitten.
Guessing again and golfing again and the best men, the very best men.

MILK.

Climb up in sight climb in the whole utter needles and a guess a whole guess is hanging. Hanging hanging.

EGGS.

Kind height, kind in the right stomach with a little sudden mill.
Cunning shawl, cunning shawl to be steady.
In white in white handkerchiefs with little dots in a white belt all shadows are singular they are singular and procured and relieved.
No that is not the cows shame and a precocious sound, it is a bite.
Cut up alone the paved way which is harm. Harm is old boat and a likely dash.

APPLE.

Apple plum, carpet steak, seed clam, colored wine, calm seen, cold cream, best shake, potato, potato and no no gold work with pet, a green seen is called bake and change sweet is bready, a little piece a little piece please.

A little piece please. Cane again to the presupposed and ready eucalyptus tree, count out sherry and ripe plates and little corners of a kind of ham. This is use.

TAILS.

Cold pails, cold with joy no joy.

A tiny seat that means meadows and a lapse of cuddles with cheese and nearly bats, all this went messed. The post placed a loud loose sprain. A rest is no better. It is better yet. All the time.

LUNCH.

Luck in loose plaster makes holy gauge and nearly that, nearly more states, more states come in town light kite, blight not white.

A little lunch is a break in skate a little lunch so slimy, a west end of a board line is that which shows a little beneath so that necessity is a silk under wear. That is best wet. It is so natural, and why is there flake, there is flake to explain exhaust.

A real cold hen is nervous is nervous with a towel with a spool with real beads. It is mostly an extra sole nearly all that shaved, shaved with an old mountain, more than that bees more than that dinner and a bunch of likes that is to say the hearts of onions aim less.

Cold coffee with a corn a corn yellow and green mass is a gem.

CUPS.

A single example of excellence is in the meat. A bent stick is surging and might all might is mental. A grand clothes is searching out a candle not that wheatly not that by more than an owl and a path. A ham is proud of cocoanut.

A cup is neglected by being all in size. It is a handle and meadows and sugar any sugar.

A cup is neglected by being full of size. It shows no shade, in come little wood cuts and blessing and nearly not that not with a wild bought in, not at all so polite, not nearly so behind.

Cups crane in. They need a pet oyster, they need it so hoary and nearly choice. The best slam is utter. Nearly be freeze.

Why is a cup a stir and a behave. Why is it so seen.

A cup is readily shaded, it has in between no sense that is to say music, memory, musical memory.

Peanuts blame, a half sand is holey and nearly.

RHUBARB.

Rhubarb is susan not susan not seat in bunch toys not wild and laughable not in little places not in neglect and vegetable not in fold coal age not please.

SINGLE FISH.

Single fish single fish single fish egg-plant single fish sight.

A sweet win and not less noisy than saddle and more ploughing and nearly well painted by little things so.

Please shade it a play. It is necessary and beside the large sort is puff.

Every way oakly, please prune it near. It is so found.

It is not the same.

CAKE.

Cake cast in went to be and needles wine needles are such.

This is today. A can experiment is that which makes a town, makes a town dirty, it is little please. We came back. Two bore, bore what, a mussed ash, ash when there is tin. This meant cake. It was a sign.

Another time there was extra a hat pin sought long and this dark made a display. The result was yellow. A caution, not a caution to be.

It is no use to cause a foolish number. A blanket stretch a cloud, a shame, all that bakery can tease, all that is beginning and yesterday yesterday we had it met. It means some change. No some day.

A little leaf upon a scene an ocean any where there, a bland and likely in the stream a recollection green land. Why white.

CUSTARD.

Custard is this. It has aches, aches when. Not to be. Not to be narrowly. This makes a whole little hill.

It is better than a little thing that has mellow real mellow. It is better than lakes whole lakes, it is better than seeding.

POTATOES.

Real potatoes cut in between.

POTATOES.

In the preparation of cheese, in the preparation of crackers, in the preparation of butter, in it.

ROAST POTATOES.

Roast potatoes for.

ASPARAGUS.

Asparagus in a lean in a lean to hot. This makes it art and it is wet wet weather wet weather wet.

BUTTER.

Boom in boom in, butter. Leave a grain and show it, show it. I spy.

It is a need it is a need that a flower a state flower. It is a need that a state rubber. It is a need that a state rubber is sweet and sight and a swelled stretch. It is a need. It is a need that state rubber.

Wood a supply. Clean little keep a strange, estrange on it.

Make a little white, no and not with pit, pit on in within.

END OF SUMMER.

Little eyelets that have hammer and a check with stripes between a lounge, in wit, in a rested development.

SAUSAGES.

Sausages in between a glass.

There is read butter. A loaf of it is managed. Wake a question. Eat an instant, answer.

A reason for bed is this, that a decline, any decline is poison, poison is a toe a toe extractor, this means a solemn change. Hanging.

No evil is wide, any extra in leaf is so strange and singular a red breast.

CELERY.

Celery tastes tastes where in curled lashes and little bits and mostly in remains.

A green acre is so selfish and so pure and so enlivened.

VEAL.

Very well very well, washing is old, washing is washing.

Cold soup, cold soup clear and particular and a principal a principal question to put into.

VEGETABLE.

What is cut. What is cut by it. What is cut by it in.

It was a cress a crescent a cross and an unequal scream, it was upslanting, it was radiant and reasonable with little ins and red.

News. News capable of glees, cut in shoes, belike under pump of wide chalk, all this combing.

WAY LAY VEGETABLE.

Leaves in grass and mow potatoes, have a skip, hurry you up flutter.

Suppose it is ex a cake suppose it is new mercy and leave charlotte and nervous bed rows. Suppose it is meal. Suppose it is sam.

COOKING.

Alas, alas the pull alas the bell alas the coach in china, alas the little put in leaf alas the wedding butter meat, alas the receptacle, alas the back shape of mussle, mussle and soda.

CHICKEN.

Pheasant and chicken, chicken is a peculiar third.

CHICKEN.

Alas a dirty word, alas a dirty third alas a dirty third, alas a dirty bird.

CHICKEN.

Alas a doubt in case of more go to say what it is cress. What is it. Mean. Potato. Loaves.

CHICKEN.

Stick stick call then, stick stick sticking, sticking with a chicken. Sticking in a extra succession, sticking in.

CHAIN-BOATS.

Chain-boats are merry, are merry blew, blew west, carpet.

PASTRY.

Cutting shade, cool spades and little last beds, make violet, violet when.

CREAM.

In a plank, in a play sole, in a heated red left tree there is shut in specs with salt be where. This makes an eddy. Necessary.

CREAM.

Cream cut. Any where crumb. Left hop chambers.

CUCUMBER.

Not a razor less, not a razor, ridiculous pudding, red and relet put in, rest in a slender go in selecting, rest in, rest in in white widening.

DINNER.

Not a little fit, not a little fit sun sat in shed more mentally.
Let us why, let us why weight, let us why winter chess, let us why way.
Only a moon to soup her, only that in the sell never never be the cocups nice be, shatter it they lay.
Egg ear nuts, look a bout. Shoulder. Let it strange, sold in bell next herds.
It was a time when in the acres in late there was a wheel that shot a burst of land and needless are niggers and a sample sample set of old eaten butterflies with spoons, all of it to be are fled and measure make it, make it, yet all the one in that we see where shall not it set with a left and more so, yes there add when the longer not it shall the best in the way when all be with when shall not for there with see and chest how for another excellent and excellent and easy easy excellent and easy express e c, all to be nice all to be no so. All to be no so no so. All to be not a white old chat churner. Not to be any example of an edible apple in.

DINING.

Dining is west.

EATING.

Eat ting, eating a grand old man said roof and never never re soluble burst, not a near ring not a bewildered neck, not really any such bay.

Is it so a noise to be is it a least remain to rest, is it a so old say to be, is it a leading are been. Is it so, is it so, is it so, is it so is it so is it so.

Eel us eel us with no no pea no pea cool, no pea cool cooler, no pea cooler with a land a land cost in, with a land cost in stretches.

Eating he heat eating he heat it eating, he heat it heat eating. He heat eating.

A little piece of pay of pay owls owls such as pie, bolsters.

Will leap beat, willie well all. The rest rest oxen occasion occasion to be so purred, so purred how.

It was a ham it was a square come well it was a square remain, a square remain not it a bundle, not it a bundle so is a grip, a grip to shed bay leave bay leave draught, bay leave draw cider in low, cider in low and george. George is a mass.

EATING.

It was a shame it was a shame to stare to stare and double and relieve relieve be cut up show as by the elevation of it and out out more in the steady where the come and on and the all the shed and that.

It was a garden and belows belows straight. It was a pea, a pea pour it in its not a succession, not it a simple, not it a so election, election with.

SALAD.

It is a winning cake.

SAUCE.

What is bay labored what is all be section, what is no much. Sauce sam in.

SALMON.

It was a peculiar bin a bin fond in beside.

ORANGE.

Why is a feel oyster an egg stir. Why is it orange centre.

A show at tick and loosen loosen it so to speak sat.

It was an extra leaker with a see spoon, it was an extra licker with a see spoon.

ORANGE.

A type oh oh new new not no not knealer knealer of old show beefsteak, neither neither.

ORANGES.

Build is all right.

ORANGE IN.

Go lack go lack use to her.

Cocoa and clear soup and oranges and oat-meal.

Whist bottom whist close, whist clothes, woodling.

Cocoa and clear soup and oranges and oat-meal.

Pain soup, suppose it is question, suppose it is butter, real is, real is only, only excreate, only excreate a no since.

A no, a no since, a no since when, a no since when since, a no since when since a no since when since, a no since, a no since when since, a no since, a no, a no since a no since, a no since, a no since.

SALAD DRESSING AND AN ARTICHOKE.

Please pale hot, please cover rose, please acre in the red stranger, please butter all the beef-steak with regular feel faces.

SALAD DRESSING AND AN ARTICHOKE.

It was please it was please carriage cup in an ice-cream, in an ice-cream it was too bended bended with scissors and all this time. A whole is inside a part, a part does go away, a hole is red leaf. No choice was where there was and a second and a second.

A CENTRE IN A TABLE.

It was a way a day, this made some sum. Suppose a cod liver a cod liver is an oil, suppose a cod liver oil is tunny, suppose a cod liver oil tunny is pressed suppose a cod liver oil tunny pressed is china and secret with a bestow a bestow reed, a reed to be a reed to be, in a reed to be.

Next to me next to a folder, next to a folder some waiter, next to a foldersome waiter and re letter and read her. Read her with her for less.

Rooms

Act so that there is no use in a centre. A wide action is not a width. A preparation is given to the ones preparing. They do not eat who mention silver and sweet. There was an occupation.

A whole centre and a border make hanging a way of dressing. This which is not why there is a voice is the remains of an offering. There was no rental.

So the tune which is there has a little piece to play, and the exercise is all there is of a fast. The tender and true that makes no width to hew is the time that there is question to adopt.

To begin the placing there is no wagon. There is no change lighter. It was done. And then the spreading, that was not accomplishing that needed standing and yet the time was not so difficult as they were not all in place. They had no change. They were not respected. They were that, they did it so much in the matter and this showed that that settlement was not condensed. It was spread there. Any change was in the ends of the centre. A heap was heavy. There was no change.

Burnt and behind and lifting a temporary stone and lifting more than a drawer.

The instance of there being more is an instance of more. The shadow is not shining in the way there is a black line. The truth has come. There is a disturbance. Trusting to a baker's boy meant that there would be very much exchanging and anyway what is the use of a covering to a door. There is a use, they are double.

If the centre has the place then there is distribution. That is natural. There is a contradiction and naturally returning there comes to be both sides and the centre. That can be seen from the description.

The author of all that is in there behind the door and that is entering in the morning. Explaining darkening and expecting relating is all of a piece. The stove is bigger. It was of a shape that made no audience bigger if the opening is assumed why should there not be kneeling. Any force which is bestowed on a floor shows rubbing. This is so nice and sweet and yet there comes the change, there comes the time to press more air. This does not mean the same as disappearance.

A little lingering lion and a Chinese chair, all the handsome cheese which is stone, all of it and a choice, a choice of a blotter. If it is difficult to do it one way there is no place of similar trouble. None. The whole arrangement is established. The end of which is that there is a suggestion, a suggestion that there can be a different whiteness to a wall. This was thought.

A page to a corner means that the shame is no greater when the table is longer. A glass is of any height, it is higher, it is simpler and if it were placed there would not be any doubt.

Something that is an erection is that which stands and feeds and silences a tin which is swelling. This makes no diversion that is to say what can please exaltation, that which is cooking.

A shine is that which when covered changes permission. An enclosure blends with the same that is to say there is blending. A blend is that which holds no mice and this is not because of a floor it is because of nothing, it is not in a vision.

A fact is that when the place was replaced all was left that was stored and all was retained that would not satisfy more than another. The question is this, is it possible to suggest more to replace that thing. This question and this perfect denial does make the time change all the time.

The sister was not a mister. Was this a surprise. It was. The conclusion came when there was no arrangement. All the time that there was a question there was a decision. Replacing a casual acquaintance with an ordinary daughter does not make a son.

It happened in a way that the time was perfect and there was a growth of a whole dividing time so that where formerly there was no mistake there was no mistake now. For instance before when there was a separation there was waiting, now when there is separation there is the division between intending and departing. This made no more mixture than there would be if there had been no change.

A little sign of an entrance is the one that made it alike. If it were smaller it was not alike and it was so much smaller that a table was bigger. A table was much bigger, very much bigger. Changing that made nothing bigger, it did not make anything bigger littler, it did not hinder wood from not being used as leather. And this was so charming. Harmony is so essential. Is there pleasure when there is a passage, there is when every room is open. Every room is open when there are not four, there were there and surely there were four, there were two together. There is no resemblance.

A single speed, the reception of table linen, all the wonder of six little spoons, there is no exercise.

The time came when there was a birthday. Every day was no excitement and a birthday was added, it was added on Monday, this made the memory clear, this which was a speech showed the chair in the middle where there was copper.

Alike and a snail, this means Chinamen, it does there is no doubt that to be right is more than perfect there is no doubt and glass is confusing it confuses the substance which was of a color. Then came the time for discrimination, it came then and it was never mentioned it was so triumphant, it showed the whole head that had a hole and should have a hole it showed the resemblance between silver.

Startling a starving husband is not disagreeable. The reason that nothing is hidden is that there is no suggestion of silence. No song is sad. A lesson is of consequence.

Blind and weak and organised and worried and betrothed and resumed and also asked to a fast and always asked to consider and never startled and not at all bloated, this which is no rarer than frequently is not so astonishing when hair brushing is added. There is quiet, there certainly is.

No eye-glasses are rotten, no window is useless and yet if air will not come in there is a speech ready, there always is and there is no dimness, not a bit of it.

All along the tendency to deplore the absence of more has not been authorised. It comes to mean that with burning there is that pleasant state of stupefication. Then there is a way of earning a living. Who is a man.

A silence is not indicated by any motion, less is indicated by a motion, more is not indicated it is enthralled. So sullen and so low, so much resignation, so much refusal and so much place for a lower and an upper, so much and yet more silence, why is not sleeping a feat why is it not and when is there some discharge when. There never is.

If comparing a piece that is a size that is recognised as not a size but a piece, comparing a piece with what is not recognised but what is used as it is held by holding, comparing these two comes to be repeated. Suppose they are put together, suppose that there is an interruption, supposing that beginning again they are not changed as to position, suppose all this and suppose that any five two of whom are not separating suppose that the five are not consumed. Is there an exchange, is there a resemblance to the sky which is admitted to be there and the stars which can be seen. Is there. That was a question. There was no certainty. Fitting a failing meant that any two were indifferent and yet they were all connecting that, they were all connecting that consideration. This did not determine rejoining a letter. This did not make letters smaller. It did.

The stamp that is not only torn but also fitting is not any symbol. It suggests nothing. A sack that has no opening suggests more and the loss is not commensurate. The season gliding and the torn hangings receiving mending all this shows an example, it shows the force of sacrifice and likeness and disaster and a reason.

The time when there is not the question is only seen when there is a shower. Any little thing is water.

There was a whole collection made. A damp cloth, an oyster, a single mirror, a manikin, a student, a silent star, a single spark, a little movement and the bed is made. This shows the disorder, it does, it shows more likeness than anything else, it shows the single mind that directs an apple. All the coats have a different shape, that does not mean that they differ in color, it means a union between use and exercise and a horse

A plain hill, one is not that which is not white and red and green, a plain hill makes no sunshine, it shows that without a disturber. So the shape is there and the color and the outline and the miserable centre. It is not very likely that there is a centre, a hill is a hill and no hill is contained in a pink tender descender.

A can containing a curtain is a solid sentimental usage. The trouble in both eyes does not come from the same symmetrical carpet, it comes from there being no more disturbance than in little paper. This does show the teeth, it shows color.

A measure is that which put up so that it shows the length has a steel construction. Tidiness is not delicacy, it does not destroy the whole piece, certainly not it has been measured and nothing has been cut off and even if that has been lost there is a name, no name is signed and left over, not any space is fitted so that moving about is plentiful. Why is there so much resignation in a package, why is there rain, all the same the chance has come, there is no bell to ring.

A package and a filter and even a funnel, all this together makes a scene and supposing the question arises is hair curly, is it dark and dusty, supposing that question arises, is brushing necessary, is it, the whole special suddenness commences then, there is no delusion.

A cape is a cover, a cape is not a cover in summer, a cape is a cover and the regulation is that there is no such weather. A cape is not always a cover, a cape is not a cover when there is another, there is always something in that thing in establishing a disposition to put wetting where it will not do more harm. There is always that disposition and in a way there is some use in not mentioning changing and in establishing the temperature, there is some use in it as establishing all that lives dimmer freer and there is no dinner in the middle of anything. There is no such thing.

Why is a pale white not paler than blue, why is a connection made by a stove, why is the example which is mentioned not shown to be the same, why is there no adjustment between the place and the separate attention. Why is there a choice in gamboling. Why is there no necessary dull stable, why is there a single piece of any color, why is there that sensible silence. Why is there the resistance in a mixture, why is there no poster, why is there that in the window, why is there no suggester, why is there no window, why is there no oyster closer. Why is there a circular diminisher, why is there a bather, why is there no scraper, why is there a dinner, why is there a bell ringer, why is there a duster, why is there a section of a similar resemblance, why is there that scissor.

South, south which is a wind is not rain, does silence choke speech or does it not.

Lying in a conundrum, lying so makes the springs restless, lying so is a reduction, not lying so is arrangeable.

Releasing the oldest auction that is the pleasing some still renewing.

Giving it away, not giving it away, is there any difference. Giving it away. Not giving it away.

Almost very likely there is no seduction, almost very likely there is no stream, certainly very likely the height is penetrated, certainly certainly the target is cleaned. Come to sit, come to refuse, come to surround, come slowly and age is not lessening. The time which showed that was when there was no eclipse. All the time that resenting was removal all that time there was breadth. No breath is shadowed, no breath is painstaking and yet certainly what could be the use of paper, paper shows no disorder, it shows no desertion.

Why is there a difference between one window and another, why is there a difference, because the curtain is shorter. There is no distaste in beefsteak or in plums or in gallons of milk water, there is no defiance in original piling up over a roof, there is no daylight in the evening, there is none there empty.

A tribune, a tribune does not mean paper, it means nothing more than cake, it means more sugar, it shows the state of lengthening any nose. The last spice is that which shows the whole evening spent in that sleep, it shows so that walking is an alleviation, and yet this astonishes everybody the distance is so sprightly. In all the time there are three days, those are not passed uselessly. Any little thing is a change that is if nothing is wasted in that cellar. All the rest of the chairs are established.

A success, a success is alright when there are there rooms and no vacancies, a success is alright when there is a package, success is alright anyway and any curtain is wholesale. A curtain diminishes and an ample space shows varnish.

One taste one tack, one taste one bottle, one taste one fish, one taste one barometer. This shows no distinguishing sign when there is a store.

Any smile is stern and any coat is a sample. Is there any use in changing more doors than there are committees. This question is so often asked that squares show that they are blotters. It is so very agreeable to hear a voice and to see all the signs of that expression.

Cadences, real cadences, real cadences and a quiet color. Careful and curved, cake and sober, all accounts and mixture, a guess at anything is righteous, should there be a call there would be a voice.

A line in life, a single line and a stairway, a rigid cook, no cook and no equator, all the same there is higher than that another evasion. Did that mean shame, it meant memory. Looking into a place that was hanging and was visible looking into this place and seeing a chair did that mean relief, it did, it certainly did not cause constipation and yet there is a melody that has white for a tune when there is straw color. This shows no face.

Star-light, what is star-light, star-light is a little light that is not always mentioned with the sun, it is mentioned with the moon and the sun, it is mixed up with the rest of the time.

Why is the name changed. The name is changed because in the little space there is a tree, in some space there are no trees, in every space there is a hint of more, all this causes the decision.

Why is there education, there is education because the two tables which are folding are not tied together with a ribbon, string is used and string being used there is a necessity for another one and another one not being used to hearing shows no ordinary use of any evening and yet there is no disgrace in looking, none at all. This came to separate when there was simple selection of an entire pre-occupation.

A curtain, a curtain which is fastened discloses mourning, this does not mean sparrows or elocution or even a whole preparation, it means that there are ears and very often much more altogether.

Climate, climate is not southern, a little glass, a bright winter, a strange supper an elastic tumbler, all this shows that the back is furnished and red which is red is a dark color. An example of this is fifteen years and a separation of regret.

China is not down when there are plates, lights are not ponderous and incalculable.

Currents, currents are not in the air and on the floor and in the door and behind it first. Currents do not show it plainer. This which is mastered has so thin a space to build it all that there is plenty of room and yet is it quarreling, it is not and the insistence is marked. A change is in a current and there is no habitable exercise.

A religion, almost a religion, any religion, a quintal in religion, a relying and a surface and a service in indecision and a creature and a question and a syllable in answer and more counting and no quarrel and a single scientific statement and no darkness and no question and an earned administration and a single set of sisters and an outline and no blisters and the section seeing yellow and the centre having spelling and no solitude and no quaintness and yet solid quite so solid and the single surface centred and the question in the placard and the singularity, is there a singularity, and the singularity, why is there a question and the singularity why is the surface outrageous, why is it beautiful why is it not when there is no doubt, why is anything vacant, why is not disturbing a centre no virtue, why is it when it is and why is it when it is and there is no doubt, there is no doubt that the singularity shows.

A climate, a single climate, all the time there is a single climate, any time there is a doubt, any time there is music that is to question more and more and there is no politeness, there is hardly any ordeal and certainly there is no tablecloth.

This is a sound and obligingness more obligingness leads to a harmony in hesitation.

A lake a single lake which is a pond and a little water any water which is an ant and no burning, not any burning, all this is sudden.

A canister that is the remains of furniture and a looking-glass and a bed-room and a larger size, all the stand is shouted and what is ancient is practical. Should the resemblance be so that any little cover is copied, should it be so that yards are measured, should it be so and there be a sin, should it be so then certainly a room is big enough when it is so empty and the corners are gathered together.

The change is mercenary that settles whitening the coloring and serving dishes where there is metal and making yellow any yellow every color in a shade which is expressed in a tray. This is a monster and awkward quite awkward and the little design which is flowered which is not strange and yet has visible writing, this is not shown all the time but at once, after that it rests where it is and where it is in place. No change is not needed. That does show design.

Excellent, more excellence is borrowing and slanting very slanting is light and secret and a recitation and emigration. Certainly shoals are shallow and nonsense more nonsense is sullen. Very little cake is water, very little cake has that escape.

Sugar any sugar, anger every anger, lover sermon lover, centre no distractor, all order is in a measure.

Left over to be a lamp light, left over in victory, left over in saving, all this and negligence and bent wood and more even much more is not so exact as a pen and a turtle and even, certainly, and even a piece of the same experience as more.

To consider a lecture, to consider it well is so anxious and so much a charity and really supposing there is grain and if a stubble every stubble is urgent, will there not be a chance of legality. The sound is sickened and the price is purchased and golden what is golden, a clergyman, a single tax, a currency and an inner chamber.

Checking an emigration, checking it by smiling and certainly by the same satisfactory stretch of hands that have more use for it than nothing, and mildly not mildly a correction, not mildly even a circumstance and a sweetness and a serenity. Powder, that has no color, if it did have would it be white.

A whole soldier any whole soldier has no more detail than any case of measles.

A bridge a very small bridge in a location and thunder, any thunder, this is the capture of reversible sizing and more indeed more can be cautious. This which makes monotony careless makes it likely that there is an exchange in principle and more than that, change in organization.

This cloud does change with the movements of the moon and the narrow the quite narrow suggestion of the building. It does and then when it is settled and no sounds differ then comes the moment when cheerfulness is so assured that there is an occasion.

A plain lap, any plain lap shows that sign, it shows that there is not so much extension as there would be if there were more choice in everything. And why complain of more, why complain of very much more. Why complain at all when it is all arranged that as there is no more opportunity and no more appeal and not even any more clinching that certainly now some time has come.

A window has another spelling, it has "f" all together, it lacks no more then and this is rain, this may even be something else, at any rate there is no dedication in splendor. There is a turn of the stranger.

Catholic to be turned is to venture on youth and a section of debate, it even means that no class where each one over fifty is regular is so stationary that there are invitations.

A curving example makes righteous finger-nails. This is the only object in secretion and speech.

To being the same four are no more than were taller. The rest had a big chair and a surveyance a cold accumulation of nausea, and even more than that, they had a disappointment.

Nothing aiming is a flower, if flowers are abundant then they are lilac, if they are not they are white in the centre.

Dance a clean dream and an extravagant turn up, secure the steady rights and translate more than translate the authority, show the choice and make no more mistakes than yesterday.

This means clearness, it means a regular notion of exercise, it means more than that, it means liking counting, it means more than that, it does not mean exchanging a line.

Why is there more craving than there is in a mountain. This does not seem strange to one, it does not seem strange to an echo and more surely is in there not being a habit. Why is there so much useless suffering. Why is there.

Any wet weather means an open window, what is attaching eating, anything that is violent and cooking and shows weather is the same in the end and why is there more use in something than in all that.

The cases are made and books, back books are used to secure tears and church. They are even used to exchange black slippers. They can not be mended with wax. They show no need of any such occasion.

A willow and no window, a wide place stranger, a wideness makes an active center.

The sight of no pussy cat is so different that a tobacco zone is white and cream.

A lilac, all a lilac and no mention of butter, not even bread and butter, no butter and no occasion, not even a silent resemblance, not more care than just enough haughty.

A safe weight is that which when it pleases is hanging. A safer weight is one more naughty in a spectacle. The best game is that which is shiny and scratching. Please a pease and a cracker and a wretched use of summer.

Surprise, the only surprise has no occasion. It is an ingredient and the section the whole section is one season.

A pecking which is petting and no worse than in the same morning is not the only way to be continuous often.

A light in the moon the only light is on Sunday. What was the sensible decision. The sensible decision was that notwithstanding many declarations and more music, not even notwithstanding the choice and a torch and a collection, notwithstanding the celebrating hat and a vacation and even more noise than cutting, notwithstanding Europe and Asia and being overbearing, not even notwithstanding an elephant and a strict occasion, not even withstanding more cultivation and some seasoning, not even with drowning and with the ocean being encircling, not even with more likeness and any cloud, not even with terrific sacrifice of pedestrianism and a special resolution, not even more likely to be pleasing. The care with which the rain is wrong and the green is wrong and the white is wrong, the care with which there is a chair and plenty of breathing. The care with which there is incredible justice and likeness, all this makes a magnificent asparagus, and also a fountain.

A Sweet Tail (Gypsies) (1922)

Curves.

Hold in the coat. Hold back ladders and a creation and nearly sudden extra coppery ages with colors and a clean voice gyp hoarse. Hold in that curl with a good man. Hold in cheese. Hold in cheese. Hold in cheese.

A cool brake, a cool brake not a success not a re-sound a re-sound and a little pan with a yell oh yes so yet change, famous, a green a green colored oak, a handsome excursion, a really handsome log, a regulation to exchange oars, a regulation or more press more precise cold pieces, more yet in the teeth within the teeth. This is the sun in. This is the lamb of the lantern with chalk. With chalk a shadow shall be a sneeze in a tooth in a tin tooth, a turned past, a turned little corset, a little tuck in a pink look and with a pin in, a pin in.

Win lake, eat splashes dig salt change benches.

Win lake eat splashes dig salt change benches.

Can in.

Come a little cheese. Come a little cheese and same same tall sun with a little thing to team, team now and a bass a whole some gurgle, little tin, little tin soak, soak why Sunday, supreme measure.

No nice burst, no nice burst sourly. Suppose a butter glass is clean and there is a bow suppose it lest the bounding ocean and a medium sized bloat in the cunning little servant handkerchief is in between.

Cuts when cuts when ten, lie on this, singling wrist tending, singling the pin.

Lie on this, show sup the boon that nick the basting thread thinly and night night gown and pit wet kit. Loom down the thorough narrow. It is not cuddle and molest change. It is not molest principal necessary argue not that it, not that in life walk collect piece.

Colored tall bills with little no pitch and dark white dark with rubber splendid select pistons with black powdered cheese and shirts and night gowns and ready very ready sold glass butts. The simple real ball with a cold glass and no more seat than yesterday together together with lime, lime water. This is no sight, no sight suddenly, no supper with a heat which makes morgan, morgan must be so.

If it is and more that call life with show cared beard with a belt and no pin when shine see the coat and left and last with all it was to be there why show could pause with such read mice call it why those old sea cat with a shining not mouth hole if it is a white call with the inch of that sort could see that tie west with loaf which is not the copper lasting with a bright retract lamp call negligence utterly soothing in the coiling remain collapse of this which by there a called which never see and hammer by which basket all that glance zest.

Cut in simple cake simple cake, relike a gentle coat, seal it, seal it blessing and that means gracious not gracious suddenly with spoons and flavor but all the same active. Neglect a pink white neglect it for blooming on a thin piece of steady slit poplars and really all the chance is in deriding cocoanuts real cocoanuts with strawberry tunes and little ice cakes with feeding feathers and peculiar relations of nothing which is more blessed than replies. Replies sudden and no lard no lard at all to show port and colors and please little pears that is to say six.

It can no sail to key pap change and put has can we see call bet. Show leave I cup the fanned best same so that if then sad sole is more, more not, and after shown so papered with that in instep lasting pheasant. Pheasant enough. Call africa, call african cod liver, loading a bag with news and little pipes restlessly so that with in between chance white cases are muddy and show a little tint, all of it.

Please coat.

Way lay to be set in the coat and the bust. The right hold is went hole piece cageous him. He had his sisters.

Like message copowder and sashes sashes, like pedal sashes and so sashes, like pedal causes and so sashes, and pedal cause killed surgeon in six safest six which, pedal sashes.

A SWEET TAIL
This piece was composed in 1912 when Stein was on holiday in

Granada, Spain. It was first published in her *Geography and Plays* (1922).

Peel sashes not what then called and in when the crest no mandarining clothes brush often. No might of it could sudden best set. Best set boar.

Rest sing a mean old polly case with boats and a little scissors nicely sore. All the blands are with a coat and more is coach with commas. A little arrangement is manufactured by a shoal and little salt sweats are to grow grow with ice and let it seat seat more than shadows which have butter.

Suppose, suppose a tremble, a ham, a little mouth told to wheeze more and a religion a reign of a pea racket that makes a load register and passes best. Kindness necessarily swims in a bottom with a razor which needs powder powder that makes a top be in the middle and necessarily not indicate a kind of collection, a collection of more of more gilt and mostly blue pipes pipes which are bound bound with old oil and mustard exact mustard which means that yellow is obtained. Gracious oh my cold under fur, under no rescued reading.

Able there to ball bawl able to call and seat a tin a tin whip with a collar. The least license is in the eyes which make strange the less sighed hole which is nodded and leaves the bent tender. All the class is sursful. It makes medium and egg light and not really so much.

Catch white color white sober, call white sold sacks, crimp white colored harness crimp it with ferocious white saffron hides, hurry up cut clothes with calm calm bright capable engines of pink and choice and press. Peas nuts are shiny with recent stutter which makes cram and mast a mast hoe, luck.

A winter sing, take thee to stay, say mountain to me and alabaster.

Curious alright.

Wheel is not on a donkey and never never.

A little piece of fly that makes a ling a shoulder a relief to pages.

Please putter sane show a pronounce, leave sold gats, less it measles. A little thin a little thin told told not which. Rest stead.

Appeal, a peal, laugh, hurry merry, good in night, rest stole. Rest stole to bestow candle electricity in surface. The best header is nearly peek.

Come in to sun with holy pin and have the petticoat to say the day, the last oh high this that. No so.

Little tree, bold up and shut with strings the piney and little weights little weights what.

Cold a packet must soak sheer land, leave it a yield so that nuts nuts are below when when cap bags are nearly believe me it is nice and quiet I thank you.

Pluck howard in the collided cheese put and not narrow.

Little in the toilet tram.

Seize noes when the behaved ties are narrowed to little finances and large garden chambers with soled more saddled heels and monkeys and tacts and little limber shading with real old powder and chest wides and left clothes and nearly all heights hats which are so whiled and reactive with moist most leaves it sell to apart.

Sober eat it, a little way to seat. The two whiskers.

All chime. So be eat hit. No case the lines are the twist of a lost last piece of flannel.

This beam in which bought not a hill than store when stone in the point way black what slate piece by all stone dust chancely.

This wee did shut, about. A land paul with a lea in and no bell no bell pose with counters and a strike a strike to poison. Does a prison make a window net does it show plates and little coats and a dear noise.

This is a cape. A real tall is a bat, the rest is nice west, the rest in, be hine with a haul a haul not. Knot not knot. A vest a voice vest. Be able to shave, shave little pills in steady, steady three, coal pied. This is hum with him, believe hit believe hit page it.

Is it necessary that actuality is tempered and neglect is rolled. A little piece. The blame which makes a coping out of a cellar and into a curtain and behind behind a frontyard is that then. Please dust.

It is so thick and thin and thin, it is thick. It is thick, thin.

A spoon, thick ahead and matches, matches wear sacks.

Stew, stew, than.

Tourty or Tourtebattre (1922)

A STORY OF THE GREAT WAR

Tourtebattre came to visit us in the court he said he heard Americans were in town and he came to see us and we said what is your name and what americans have you known and we said we would go to see him and we did not and we did not give him anything.

Then when we went out to see the hospital we did not take him anything. We asked to see him. Then when the new things came we did take a package to him and we did not see him but he came and called on us to thank us and we were out.

Reflections.

If I must reflect I reflect upon Ann Veronica. This is not what is intended. Mrs. Tourtebattre. Of this we know nothing.

Can we reflect one for another.

Profit and loss is three twenty five never two seventy five.

Yes that is the very easy force, decidedly not.

Then Tourtebattre used to come all the time and then he used to tell us how old he was when he was asked and he took sugar in his coffee as it was given to him. He was not too old to be a father he was thirty seven and he had three children and he told us that he liked to turn a phrase.

China. Whenever he went to the colonies his sister was hurt in an automobile accident. This did not mean that she suffered.

Some one thought she was killed. Will you please put that in.

His father's watch, his wife gave all his most precious belongings to a man who did not belong to the town he said he belonged to. We did not know the truth of this.

Reflections.

We should not color our hero with his wife's misdeeds. Because you see he may be a religion instead of a talker. Little bones have to come out of his hand for action this was after his wound. A good deal.

He was wounded in the attack in April right near where he was always going to visit his wife and he saw the church tower and then he was immediately evacuated to an american hospital where every one was very American and very kind and Miss Bell tried to talk french to him and amuse him but overcome with her difficulties with the french language she retired which made him say she was very nice and these stories that he told to us you told to Sister Cecile which did not please her and she said we must come and hear from every one else the stories they all told of the kindness they had received in the American hospital before they came to her and she said to them what did the major do, and they said he played ball. He did. And you too and all of them said, no sister but you were wounded in an attack. We were both wounded, said the soldier.

Reflections.

Reflections on Sister Cecile lead us to believe that she did not reflect about Friday but about the book in which she often wrote. We were curious. She wrote this note. This is it. Name life, wife, deed, wound, weather, food, devotion, and expression.

What did he ask for.

TOURTY
This prose portrait was first published in *Geography and Plays*   (Boston: the Four Seas Company, 1922). It was probably composed in 1919.

Why I don't know.

Why don't you know.

I don't call that making literature at all.

What has he asked for.

I call literature telling a story as it happens.

Facts of life make literature.

I can always feel rightly about that.

We obtained beads for him and our own pictures in it.

Dear pictures of us.

We can tell anything over.

We gave him colored beads and he made them with paper that he bought himself of two different colors into frames that we sent with our pictures to our cousins and our papas in America.

Can we say it.

We cannot.

Now.

Then he told us about his wife and his child.

He does not say anything about them now.

Some immediate provision was necessary.

We said in English these are the facts which we are bringing to your memory.

What is capitol.

He told us of bead buttons and black and white. He answered her back very brightly.

He is a man.

Reflections.

What were the reflections.

Have we undertaken too much.

What is the name of his wife.

They were lost. We did not look forward. We did not think much. How long would he stay. Our reflections really came later.

The first thing we heard from her was that the woman was not staying and had left her new address.

How do you do.

We did not look her up.

Her mother and her mother.

Can you think why Marguerite did not wish Jenny Picard to remain longer.

Because she stole.

Not really.

Yes indeed. Little things.

This will never do.

And then.

I said we must go to see her.

And you said we will see.

One night, no one day she called with her mother.

Who was very good looking.

She was very good looking.

And the little boy.

Can you think of the little boy.

They both said that they were not polite.

But they were.

Reflections can come already.

We believed her reasons were real reasons.

Who is always right.

Not she nor her eleven sisters.

No one knew who was kind to her.

What is kindness.

Kindness is being soft or good and has nothing to do with amiable. Albert is kind and good. And their wives.

Can you tell the difference between wives and children.

Queen Victoria and Queen Victoria.

They made you jump.

And I said the mother you said the mother. I did not remember the mother was in Paris but you did.

Next.
Life and Letters of Marcel Duchamp[1]. (1922)

A family likeness pleases when there is a cessation of resemblances. This is to say that points of remarkable resemblance are those which make Henry leading. Henry leading actually smothers Emil. Emil is pointed. He does not overdo examples. He even hesitates.

But am I sensible. Am I not rather efficient in sympathy or common feeling.

I was looking to see if I could make Marcel out of it but I can't.

Not a doctor to me not a debtor to me not a d to me but a c to me a credit to me. To interlace a story with glass and with rope with color and roam.

How many people roam.

Dark people roam.

Can dark people come from the north. Are they dark then. Do they begin to be dark when they have come from there.

Any question leads away from me. Grave a boy grave.

What I do recollect is this. I collect black and white. From the standpoint of white all color is color. From the standpoint of black. Black is white. White is black. Black is black. White is black. White and black is black and white. What I recollect when I am there is that words are not birds. How easily I feel thin. Birds do not. So I replace birds with tin-foil. Silver is thin.

Life and letters of Marcel Duchamp.

Quickly return the unabridged restraint and mention letters.

My dear Fourth.

Confess to me in a quick saying. The vote is taken.

The lucky strike works well and difficultly. It rounds, it sounds round. I cannot conceal attrition. Let me think. I repeat the fullness of bread. In a way not bread. Delight me. I delight a lamb in birth.

A Description of the Fifteenth of November: A Portrait of T. S. Eliot (1934)

On the fifteenth of November we have been told that she will go either here or there and in company with some one who will attempt to be of aid in any difficulty that may be pronounced as at all likely to occur. This in case that as usual there has been no cessation of the manner in which latterly it has all been as it might be repetition. To deny twice. Once or twice.

---

[1]   This impression of Marcel Duchamp was composed in 1920 and first published in *Geography and Plays* (1922). Duchamp (1887–1968) was a French painter and sculpter who made "ready-mades" such as *Bicycle Wheel* (1913) and *Bottle Rack* (1914). He also designed the journal New York Dada, pp. 493–7 this edition.

A DESCRIPTION
This prose portrait was first published in Stein's *Portraits and Prayers* (New York: Random House, 1934). Scholars have assigned its composition to 1924.

On the fifteenth of November in place of what was undoubtedly a reason for finding and in this way the best was found to be white or black and as the best was found out to be nearly as much so as was added. To be pleased with the result.

I think I was.

On the fifteenth of November have it a year. On the fifteenth of November they returned too sweet. On the fifteenth of November also.

The fifteenth of November at best has for its use more than enough to-day. It can also be mentioned that the sixteenth and any one can see furniture and further and further than that. The idea is that as for a very good reason anything can be chosen the choice is the choice is included.

After contradiction it is desirable.

In any accidental case no incident no repetition no darker thoughts can be united again. Again and again.

In plenty of cases in union there is strength.

Can any one in thinking of how presently it is as if it were in the midst of more attention can any one thinking of how to present it easily can any one really partake in saying so. Can any one.

All of it as eagerly as not.

Entirely a different thing. Entirely a different thing when all of it has been awfully well chosen and thoughtfully corrected.

He said we, and we.

We said he.

He said we.

We said he, and he.

He said.

We said.

We said it. As we said it.

We said that forty was the same as that which we had heard.

It depends entirely upon whether in that as finally sure, surely as much so.

Please please them. Please please please them.

Having heard half of it.

Please having having had please having had please having had half of it.

Please please half of it.

Pleases.

Yes and a day.

A day and never having heard a thing.

Extra forty.

There is no greater pleasure than in having what is a great pleasure.

Happy to say that it was a mistake.

If at each part of one part and that is on the whole the best of all for what it provides and any satisfaction if at each part less less and more than usual it is not at all necessary that a little more has more added in a day. It is considerably augmented and further it settles it as well.

This makes mention more and more and mention to mention this makes it more and more necessary to mention that eighteen succeeds three. Can going again be startling.

On the fifteenth of November in increase and in increases, it increases it as it has been carefully considered. He has a son and a daughter and in this case it is important because although in itself a pleasure it can be a pleasure.

Fortunately replacing takes the place of their sending and fortunately as they are sending in this instance if there are there and one has returned and one is gone and one is going need there be overtaking. Overtaken. A usefulness to be.

Mentioned as a mistake. No mention not mentioned not mentioning not to be before and fortunately. It was very fortunate.

If calling had come from calling out, Come and call. Call it weekly.

In this case a description.

Forward and back weekly.

In this case absolutely a question in question.

Furnished as meaning supplied.

Further back as far back.

Considerably more.

Simply and simply and simply, simply simply there. Simply so that in that way, simply in that way simply so that simply so that in that way.

November the fifteenth and simply so that simply so that simply in that simply in that simply so that in that simply in that simply in that way simply so that simply so that in that way simply in that way, simply in that way so that simply so that simply so that simply simply in that, simply in that so that simply so that simply so that simply in that, so that simply in that way.

Actually the fifteenth of November.

Played and plays and says and access. Plays and played and access and impress. Played and plays and access and acquiese and a mistake. Actually the fifteenth of November. Let us lose at least three. You too. Let us lose at least three. You too. Let us lose at least three. Three and there makes made three and three made makes, there and three makes, fourteen is a few.

A few separated rather separated separately.

As readers make red as pallor and few as readers make red and so do you.

Very nearly actually and truly.

A bargain in much as much a bargain in as much as there is of it. Have had it in reserve. To have had it in reserve. And have had it in reserve. Or have had it in reserve. Or have had it in reserve. To have had it in reserve. Touch a tree touch a tree to it.

Irons make an iron here and there.

And do declare.

The fifteenth of November has happily a birthday. And very happily a birthday. And very happily a birthday. The fifteenth of November has, happily, a birthday and very happily a birthday, and very happily a birthday.

Not as yet and to ask a question and to ask a question and as yet, and as yet to as yet to ask a question to and as yet.

Not as yet and to ask a question and to ask a question and as not yet. As not yet and to as yet and to ask a question and to as yet and to wind as yet and to as yet and to ask a question and to as yet ask a question as not yet, as not yet and to ask as not yet, and as not yet to ask a question as yet, and to as yet to wind as not yet, as not yet to wind please wind as not yet to ask a question and to and not yet. Please wind the clock and as yet and as not yet. Please wind the clock and not yet, to please not yet as not yet.

He said enough.

Enough said.

He said enough.

Enough said.

Enough said.

He said enough.

He said enough.

Enough said.

He said enough.

Not only wool and woolen silk and silken not only silk and silken wool and woolen not only wool and woolen silk and silken not only silk and silken wool and woolen not only wool and woolen silk and silken not only silk and silken not only wool and woolen not only wool and woolen not only silk and silken not only silk and silken not only wool and woolen.

Composition as Explanation (1926)

There is singularly nothing that makes a difference a difference in beginning and in the middle and in ending except that each generation has something different at which they are all looking. By this I mean so simply that anybody knows it that composition is the difference which makes each and all of them then different from other generations and this is what makes everything different otherwise they are all alike and everybody knows it because everybody says it.

It is very likely that nearly every one has been very nearly certain that something that is interesting is interesting them. Can they and do they. It is very interesting that nothing inside in them, that is when you consider the very long history of how every one ever acted or has felt, it is very interesting that nothing inside in them in all of them makes it connectedly different. By this I mean this. The only thing that is different from one time to another is what is seen and what is seen depends upon how everybody is doing everything. This makes the thing we are looking at very different and this makes what those who describe it make of it, it makes a composition, it confuses, it shows, it is, it looks, it likes it as it is, and this makes what is seen as it is seen. Nothing changes from generation to generation except the thing seen and that makes a composition. Lord Grey[1] remarked that when the generals before the war talked about the war they talked about it as a nineteenth century war although to be fought with twentieth century weapons. That is because war is a thing that decides how it is to be when it is to be done. It is prepared and to that degree it is like all academies it is not a thing made by being made it is a thing prepared. Writing and painting and all that, is like that, for those who occupy themselves with it and don't make it as it is made. Now the few who make it as it is made, and it is to be remarked that the most decided of them usually are prepared just as the world around them is preparing, do it in this way and so I if you do not mind I will tell you how it happens. Naturally one does not know how it happened until it is well over beginning happening.

To come back to the part that the only thing that is different is what is seen when it seems to be being seen, in other words, composition and time-sense.

No one is ahead of his time, it is only that the particular variety of creating his time is the one that his contemporaries who also are creating their own time refuse to accept. And they refuse to accept it for a very simple reason and that is that they do not have to accept it for any reason. They themselves that is everybody in their entering the modern composition and they do enter it, if they do not enter it they are not so to speak in it they are out of it and so they do enter it. But in as you may say the non-competitive efforts where if you are not in it nothing is lost except nothing at all except what is not had, there are naturally all the refusals, and the things refused are only important if unexpectedly somebody happens to need them. In the case of the arts it is very definite. Those who are creating the modern composition authentically are naturally only of importance when they are dead because by that time the modern composition having become past is classified and the description of it is classical. That is the reason why the creator of the new composition in the arts is an outlaw until he is a classic, there is hardly a moment in between and it is really too bad very much too bad naturally for the creator but also very much too bad for the enjoyer, they all really would enjoy the created so much better just after it has been made than when it is already a classic, but it is perfectly simple that there is no reason why the contemporaries should see, because it would not make any difference as they lead their lives in the new composition anyway, and as every one is naturally indolent why naturally they don't see. For this reason as in quoting Lord Grey it is quite certain that nations not actively threatened are at least several generations behind themselves

The essay was given as a lecture at Cambridge and Oxford University on June 4 and 7, 1926. It was first published in the *Dial* 81(4) (Oct. 1926), then reprinted as a small book (59 pages) by the Hogarth Press, run by Leonard and Virginia Woolf.
[1]   Sir Edward Grey (Lord Grey) (1862–1933) was an aristocratic politician who entered the British parliament as a Liberal MP in 1885 and was Foreign Secretary 1905–16. He made a secret agreement to assist France in event of attack which he implemented in August 1914, bringing Britain into the war. He was later Chancellor of Oxford University, 1928–33. Where he made this comment cited by Stein has not been identified.

militarily so æsthetically they are more than several generations behind themselves and it is very much too bad, it is so very much more exciting and satisfactory for everybody if one can have contemporaries, if all one's contemporaries could be one's contemporaries.

There is almost not an interval.

For a very long time everybody refuses and then almost without a pause almost everybody accepts. In the history of the refused in the arts and literature the rapidity of the change is always startling. Now the only difficulty with the *volte-face* concerning the arts is this. When the acceptance comes, by that acceptance the thing created becomes a classic. It is a natural phenomena a rather extraordinary natural phenomena that a thing accepted becomes a classic. And what is the characteristic quality of a classic. The characteristic quality of a classic is that it is beautiful. Now of course it is perfectly true that a more or less first rate work of art is beautiful but the trouble is that when that first rate work of art becomes a classic because it is accepted the only thing that is important from then on to the majority of the acceptors the enormous majority, the most intelligent majority of the acceptors is that it is so wonderfully beautiful. Of course it is wonderfully beautiful, only when it is still a thing irritating annoying stimulating then all quality of beauty is denied to it.

Of course it is beautiful but first all beauty in it is denied and then all the beauty of it is accepted. If every one were not so indolent they would realise that beauty is beauty even when it is irritating and stimulating not only when it is accepted and classic. Of course it is extremely difficult nothing more so than to remember back to its not being beautiful once it has become beautiful. This makes it so much more difficult to realise its beauty when the work is being refused and prevents every one from realising that they were convinced that beauty was denied, once the work is accepted. Automatically with the acceptance of the time-sense comes the recognition of the beauty and once the beauty is accepted the beauty never fails any one.

Beginning again and again is a natural thing even when there is a series.

Beginning again and again and again explaining composition and time is a natural thing.

It is understood by this time that everything is the same except composition and time, composition and the time of the composition and the time in the composition.

Everything is the same except composition and as the composition is different and always going to be different everything is not the same. Everything is not the same as the time when of the composition and the time in the composition is different. The composition is different, that is certain.

The composition is the thing seen by every one living in the living they are doing, they are the composing of the composition that at the time they are living is the composition of the time in which they are living. It is that that makes living a thing they are doing. Nothing else is different, of that almost any one can be certain. The time when and the time of and the time in that composition is the natural phenomena of that composition and of that perhaps every one can be certain.

No one thinks these things when they are making when they are creating what is the composition, naturally no one thinks, that is no one formulates until what is to be formulated has been made.

Composition is not there, it is going to be there and we are here. This is some time ago for us naturally.

The only thing that is different from one time to another is what is seen and what is seen depends upon how everybody is doing everything. This makes the thing we are looking at very different and this makes what those who describe it make of it, it makes a composition, it confuses, it shows, it is, it looks, it likes it as it is, and this makes what is seen as it is seen. Nothing changes from generation to generation except the thing seen and that makes a composition.

Now the few who make writing as it is made and it is to be remarked that the most decided of them are those that are prepared by preparing, are prepared just as the world around them is prepared and is preparing to do it in this way and so if you do not mind I will again tell you how it happens. Naturally one does not know how it happened until it is well over beginning happening.

Each period of living differs from any other period of living not in the way life is but in the way life is conducted and that authentically speaking is composition. After life has been conducted in a certain way everybody knows it but nobody knows it, little by little, nobody knows it as long as nobody knows it. Any one creating the composition in the arts does not know it either, they are conducting life and that makes their composition what it is, it makes their work compose as it does.

Their influence and their influences are the same as that of all of their contemporaries only it must always be remembered that the analogy is not obvious until as I say the composition of a time has become so pronounced that it is past and the artistic composition of it is a classic.

And now to begin as if to begin. Composition is not there, it is going to be there and we are here. This is some time ago for us naturally. There is something to be added afterwards.

Just how much my work is known to you I do not know. I feel that perhaps it would be just as well to tell the whole of it.

In beginning writing I wrote a book called *Three Lives*[2] this was written in 1905. I wrote a negro story called *Melanctha*.[3] In that there was a constant recurring and beginning there was a marked direction in the direction of being in the present although naturally I had been accustomed to past present and future, and why, because the composition forming around me was a prolonged present. A composition of a prolonged present is a natural composition in the world as it has been these thirty years it was more and more a prolonged present. I created then a prolonged present naturally I knew nothing of a continuous present but it came naturally to me to make one, it was simple it was clear to me and nobody knew why it was done like that, I did not myself although naturally to me it was natural.

After that I did a book called *The Making of Americans*[4] it is a long book about a thousand pages.

Here again it was all so natural to me and more and more complicatedly a continuous present. A continuous present is a continuous present. I made almost a thousand pages of a continuous present.

Continuous present is one thing and beginning again and again is another thing. These are both things. And then there is using everything.

This brings us again to composition this the using everything. The using everything brings us to composition and to this composition. A continuous present and using everything and beginning again. In these two books there was elaboration of the complexities of using everything and of a continuous present and of beginning again and again and again.

In the first book there was a groping for a continuous present and for using everything by beginning again and again.

There was a groping for using everything and there was a groping for a continuous present and there was an inevitable beginning of beginning again and again and again.

Having naturally done this I naturally was a little troubled with it when I read it. I became then like the others who read it. One does, you know, excepting that when I reread it myself I lost myself in it again. Then I said to myself this time it will be different and I began. I did not begin again I just began.

In this beginning naturally since I at once went on and on very soon there were pages and pages and pages more and more elaborated creating a more and more continuous present including more and more using of everything and continuing more and more beginning and beginning and beginning.

I went on and on to a thousand pages of it.

In the meantime to naturally begin I commenced making portraits of anybody and anything.[5] In making these portraits I naturally made a continuous present an including everything and a beginning again and again within a very small thing. That started me into composing anything

[2] *Three Lives* was published at Stein's own expense in 1909.

[3] "Melanctha" was the second of the three short stories or novellas which make up *Three Lives*, and has always been recognized as the most important of them.

[4] *The Making of Americans* was composed in the period 1909 to 1911. Portions of it were published in the journal the *Transatlantic Review* in 1923, and the first edition came out in 1925 (Paris: Contact Press; rept. Normal, IL: Dalkey Archive, 1995).

[5] Composed from 1912 through 1919, the portraits are mostly contained in Stein's *Geography and Plays* (Boston: Seven Seas, 1922).

into one thing. So then naturally it was natural that one thing an enormously long thing was not everything an enormously short thing was also not everything nor was it all of it a continuous present thing nor was it always and always beginning again. Naturally I would then begin again. I would begin again I would naturally begin. I did naturally begin. This brings me to a great deal that has been begun.

And after that what changes what changes after that, after that what changes and what changes after that and after that and what changes and after that and what changes after that.

The problem from this time on became more definite.

It was all so nearly alike it must be different and it is different, it is natural that if everything is used and there is a continuous present and a beginning again and again if it is all so alike it must be simply different and everything simply different was the natural way of creating it then.

In this natural way of creating it then that it was simply different everything being alike it was simply different, this kept on leading one to lists. Lists naturally for awhile and by lists I mean a series. More and more in going back over what was done at this time I find that I naturally kept simply different as an intention. Whether there was or whether there was not a continuous present did not then any longer trouble me there was or there was not, and using everything no longer troubled me if everything is alike using everything could no longer trouble me and beginning again and again could no longer trouble me because if lists were inevitable if series were inevitable and the whole of it was inevitable beginning again and again could not trouble me so then with nothing to trouble me I very completely began naturally since everything is alike making it as simply different naturally as simply different as possible. I began doing natural phenomena what I call natural phenomena and natural phenomena naturally everything being alike natural phenomena are making things be naturally simply different. This found its culmination later, in the beginning it began in a center confused with lists with series with geography with returning portraits and with particularly often four and three and often with five and four. It is easy to see that in the beginning such a conception as everything being naturally different would be very inarticulate and very slowly it began to emerge and take the form of anything, and then naturally if anything that is simply different is simply different what follows will follow.

So far then the progress of my conceptions was the natural progress entirely in accordance with my epoch as I am sure is to be quite easily realised if you think over the scene that was before us all from year to year.

As I said in the beginning, there is the long history of how every one ever acted or has felt and that nothing inside in them in all of them makes it connectedly different. By this I mean all this.

The only thing that is different from one time to another is what is seen and what is seen depends upon how everybody is doing everything.

It is understood by this time that everything is the same except composition and time, composition and the time of the composition and the time in the composition.

Everything is the same except composition and as the composition is different and always going to be different everything is not the same. So then I as a contemporary creating the composition in the beginning was groping toward a continuous present, a using everything a beginning again and again and then everything being alike then everything very simply everything was naturally simply different and so I as a contemporary was creating everything being alike was creating everything naturally being naturally simply different, everything being alike. This then was the period that brings me to the period of the beginning of 1914. Everything being alike everything naturally would be simply different and war came and everything being alike and everything being simply different brings everything being simply different brings it to romanticism.

Romanticism is then when everything being alike everything is naturally simply different, and romanticism.

Then for four years this was more and more different even though this was, was everything alike. Everything alike naturally everything was simply different and this is and was romanticism and this is and was war. Everything being alike everything naturally everything is different simply different naturally simply different.

And so there was the natural phenomena that was war, which had been, before war came, several generations behind the contemporary composition, because it became war and so completely needed to be contemporary became completely contemporary and so created the completed recognition of the contemporary composition. Every one but one may say every one became consciously became aware of the existence of the authenticity of the modern composition. This then the contemporary recognition, because of the academic thing known as war having been forced to become contemporary made every one not only contemporary in act not only contemporary in thought but contemporary in self-consciousness made every one contemporary with the modern composition. And so the art creation of the contemporary composition which would have been outlawed normally outlawed several generations more behind even than war, war having been brought so to speak up to date art so to speak was allowed not completely to be up to date, but nearly up to date, in other words we who created the expression of the modern composition were to be recognized before we were dead some of us even quite a long time before we were dead. And so war may be said to have advanced a general recognition of the expression of the contemporary composition by almost thirty years.

And now after that there is no more of that in other words there is peace and something comes then and it follows coming then.

And so now one finds oneself interesting oneself in an equilibration, that of course means words as well as things and distribution as well as between themselves between the words and themselves and the things and themselves, a distribution as distribution. This makes what follows what follows and now there is every reason why there should be an arrangement made. Distribution is interesting and equilibration is interesting when a continuous present and a beginning again and again and using everything and everything alike and everything naturally simply different has been done.

After all this, there is that, there has been that that there is a composition and that nothing changes except composition the composition and the time of and the time in the composition.

The time of the composition is a natural thing and the time in the composition is a natural thing it is a natural thing and it is a contemporary thing.

The time of the composition is the time of the composition. It has been at times a present thing it has been at times a past thing it has been at times a future thing it has been at times an endeavor at parts or all of these things. In my beginning it was a continuous present a beginning again and again and again and again, it was a series it was a list it was a similarity and everything different it was a distribution and an equilibration. That is all of the time some of the time of the composition.

Now there is still something else the time-sense in the composition. This is what is always a fear a doubt and a judgement and a conviction. The quality in the creation of expression the quality in a composition that makes it go dead just after it has been made is very troublesome.

The time in the composition is a thing that is very troublesome. If the time in the composition is very troublesome it is because there must even if there is no time at all in the composition there must be time in the composition which is in its quality of distribution and equilibration. In the beginning there was the time in the composition that naturally was in the composition but time in the composition comes now and this is what is now troubling every one the time in the composition is now a part of distribution and equilibration. In the beginning there was confusion there was a continuous present and later there was romanticism which was not a confusion but an extrication and now there is either succeeding or failing there must be distribution and equilibration there must be time that is distributed and equilibrated. This is the thing that is at present the most troubling and if there is the time that is at present the most troublesome the time-sense that is at present the most troubling is the thing that makes the present the most troubling. There is at present there is distribution, by this I mean expression and time, and in this way at present composition is time that is the reason that at present the time-sense is troubling that is the reason why at present the time-sense in the composition is the composition that is making what there is in composition.

And afterwards.

Now that is all.

What Are Master-pieces and Why Are There So Few of Them (1940)

I was almost going to talk this lecture and not write and read it because all the lectures that I have written and read in America have been printed and although possibly for you they might even being read be as if they had not been printed still there is something about what has been written having been printed which makes it no longer the property of the one who wrote it and therefore there is no more reason why the writer should say it out loud than anybody else and therefore one does not.

Therefore I was going to talk to you but actually it is impossible to talk about master-pieces and what they are because talking essentially has nothing to do with creation. I talk a lot I like to talk and I talk even more than that I may say I talk most of the time and I listen a fair amount too and as I have said the essence of being a genius is to be able to talk and listen to listen while talking and talk while listening but and this is very important very important indeed talking has nothing to do with creation. What are master-pieces and why after all are there so few of them. You may say after all there are a good many of them but in any kind of proportion with everything that anybody who does anything is doing there are really very few of them. All this summer I meditated and wrote about this subject and it finally came to be a discussion of the relation of human nature and the human mind and identity. The thing one gradually comes to find out is that one has no identity that is when one is in the act of doing anything. Identity is recognition, you know who you are because you and others remember anything about yourself but essentially you are not that when you are doing anything. I am I because my little dog knows me but, creatively speaking the little dog knowing that you are you and your recognizing that he knows, that is what destroys creation. That is what makes school. Picasso[1] once remarked I do not care who it is that has or does influence me as long as it is not myself.

It is very difficult so difficult that it always has been difficult but even more difficult now to know what is the relation of human nature to the human mind because one has to know what is the relation of the act of creation to the subject the creator uses to create that thing. There is a great deal of nonsense talked about the subject of anything. After all there is always the same subject there are the things you see and there are human beings and animal beings and everybody you might say since the beginning of time knows practically commencing at the beginning and going to the end everything about these things. After all any woman in any village or men either if you like or even children know as much of human psychology as any writer that ever lived. After all there are things you do know each one in his or her way knows all of them and it is not this knowledge that makes master-pieces. Not at all not at all not at all. Those who recognize master-pieces say that is the reason but it is not. It is not the way Hamlet reacts to his father's ghost that makes the master-piece, he might have reacted according to Shakespeare in a dozen other ways and everybody would have been as much impressed by the psychology of it. But there is no psychology in it, that is not probably the way any young man would react to the ghost of his father and there is no particular reason why they should. If it were the way a young man could react to the ghost of his father then that would be something anybody in any village would know they could talk about it talk about it endlessly but that would not make a master-piece and that brings us once more back to the subject of identity. At any moment when you are you you are you without the memory of yourself because if you remember yourself while you are you you are not for purposes of creating you. This is so important because it has so much to do with the question of a writer to his audience. One of the things that I discovered in lecturing was that gradually one ceased to hear what one said one heard what the audience hears one say, that is the reason that oratory is practically never a master-piece very rarely and very rarely history, because history deals with people who are orators who hear not

The essay was given as a lecture at Oxford and Cambridge in 1936, and first published in *What are Master-pieces* (Los Angeles: the Conference Press, 1940).

[1]   Pablo Picasso (1883–1972), Spanish artist resident in Paris.

what they are not what they say but what their audience hears them say. It is very interesting that letter writing has the same difficulty, the letter writes what the other person is to hear and so entity does not exist there are two present instead of one and so once again creation breaks down. I once wrote in writing *The Making of Americans* I write for myself and strangers but that was merely a literary formalism for if I did write for myself and strangers if I did I would not really be writing because already then identity would take the place of entity. It is awfully difficult, action is direct and effective but after all action is necessary and anything that is necessary has to do with human nature and not with the human mind. Therefore a master-piece has essentially not to be necessary, it has to be that is it has to exist but it does not have to be necessary it is not in response to necessity as action is because the minute it is necessary it has in it no possibility of going on.

To come back to what a master-piece has as its subject. In writing about painting I said that a picture exists for and in itself and the painter has to use objects landcapes and people as a way the only way that he is able to get the picture to exist. That is every one's trouble and particularly the trouble just now when every one who writes or paints has gotten to be abnormally conscious of the things he uses that is the events the people the objects and the landscapes and fundamentally the minute one is conscious deeply conscious of these things as a subject the interest in them does not exist.

You can tell that so well in the difficulty of writing novels or poetry these days. The tradition has always been that you may more or less describe the things that happen you imagine them of course but you more or less describe the things that happen but nowadays everybody all day long knows what is happening and so what is happening is not really interesting, one knows it by radios cinemas newspapers biographies autobiographies until what is happening does not really thrill anyone, it excites them a little but it does not really thrill them. The painter can no longer say that what he does is as the world looks to him because he cannot look at the world any more, it has been photographed too much and he has to say that he does something else. In former times a painter said he painted what he saw of course he didn't but anyway he could say it, now he does not want to say it because seeing is not interesting. This has something to do with master-pieces and why there are so few of them but not everything.

So you see why talking has nothing to do with creation, talking is really human nature as it is and human nature has nothing to do with master-pieces. It is very curious but the detective story which is you might say the only really modern novel form that has come into existence gets rid of human nature by having the man dead to begin with the hero is dead to begin with and so you have so to speak got rid of the event before the book begins. There is another very curious thing about detective stories. In real life people are interested in the crime more than they are in detection, it is the crime that is the thing the shock the thrill the horror but in the story it is the detection that holds the interest and that is natural enough because the necessity as far as action is concerned is the dead man, it is another function that has very little to do with human nature that makes the detection interesting. And so always it is true that the master-piece has nothing to do with human nature or with identity, it has to do with the human mind and the entity that is with a thing in itself and not in relation. The moment it is in relation it is common knowledge and anybody can feel and know it and it is not a master-piece. At the same time every one in a curious way sooner or later does feel the reality of a master-piece. The thing in itself of which the human nature is only its clothing does hold the attention. I have meditated a great deal about that. Another curious thing about master-pieces is, nobody when it is created there is in the thing that we call the human mind something that makes it hold itself just the same. The manner and habits of Bible times or Greek or Chinese have nothing to do with ours today but the master-pieces exist just the same and they do not exist because of their identity, that is what any one remembering then remembered then, they do not exist by human nature because everybody always knows everything there is to know about human nature, they exist because they came to be as something that is an end in itself and in that respect it is opposed to the business of living which is relation and necessity. That is what a master-piece is not although it may easily be what a master-piece talks about. It is another one of the curious difficulties a master-piece has that is to begin and end, because actually a master-piece does not do that it does not begin and end if it did it would be of necessity and in relation and that is just what a master-piece is not. Everybody worries about that just now everybody that is what makes them talk about abstract and worry about punctuation and capitals and small letters and what a history is. Everybody worries about that not because everybody knows what a master-piece is but because a certain number have found out what a master-piece is not. Even the very master-pieces have always been very bothered about beginning and ending because essentially that is what a master-piece is not. And yet after all like the subject of human nature master-pieces have to use beginning and ending to become existing. Well anyway anybody who is trying to do anything today is desperately not having a beginning and an ending but nevertheless in some way one does have to stop. I stop.

I do not know whether I have made any of this very clear, it is clear, but unfortunately, I have written it all down all summer and in spite of everything I am now remembering and when you remember it is never clear. This is what makes secondary writing, it is remembering, it is very curious you begin to write something and suddenly you remember something and if you continue to remember your writing gets very confused. If you do not remember while you are writing, it may seem confused to others but actually it is clear and eventually that clarity will be clear, that is what a master-piece is, but if you remember while you are writing it will seem clear at the time to any one but the clarity will go out of it that is what a master-piece is not.

All this sounds awfully complicated but it is not complicated at all, it is just what happens. Any of you when you write you try to remember what you are about to write and you will see immediately how lifeless the writing becomes that is why expository writing is so dull because it is all remembered, that is why illustration is so dull because you remember what somebody looked like and you make your illustration look like it. The minute your memory functions while you are doing anything it may be very popular but actually it is dull. And that is what a master-piece is not, it may be unwelcome but it is never dull.

And so then why are there so few of them. There are so few of them because mostly people live in identity and memory that is when they think. They know they are they because their little dog knows them, and so they are not an entity but an identity. And being so memory is necessary to make them exist and so they cannot create master-pieces. It has been said of geniuses that they are eternally young. I once said what is the use of being a boy if you are going to grow up to be a man, the boy and the man have nothing to do with each other, except in respect to memory and identity, and if they have anything to do with each other in respect to memory and identity then they will never produce a master-piece. Do you do you understand well it really does not make much difference because after all master-pieces are what they are and the reason why is that there are very few of them. The reason why is any of you try it just not to be you are you because your little dog knows you. The second you are you because your little dog knows you you cannot make a master-piece and that is all of that.

It is not extremely difficult not to have identity but it is extremely difficult the knowing not having identity. One might say it is impossible but that it is not impossible is proved by the existence of master-pieces which are just that. They are knowing that there is no identity and producing while identity is not.

That is what a master-piece is.

And so we do know what a master-piece is and we also know why there are so few of them. Everything is against them. Everything that makes life go on makes identity and everything that makes identity is of necessity a necessity. And the pleasures of life as well as the necessities help the necessity of identity. The pleasures that are soothing all have to do with identity and the pleasures that are exciting all have to do with identity and moreover there is all the pride and vanity which play about master-pieces as well as about every one and these too all have to do with identity, and so naturally it is natural that there is more identity that one knows about than anything else one knows about and the worst of all is that the only thing that anyone thinks about is identity and thinking is something that does so nearly need to be memory and if it is then of course it has nothing to do with a master-piece.

But what can a master-piece be about mostly it is about identity and all it does and in being so it must not have any. I was just thinking about anything and in thinking about anything I saw something. In seeing that thing shall we see it without it turning into identity, the moment is not a moment and the sight is not the thing seen and yet it is. Moments are not important because of course master-pieces have no more time than they have identity although time like identity is what they concern themselves about of course that is what they do concern themselves about.

Once when one has said what one says it is not true or too true. That is what is the trouble with time. That is what makes what women say truer than what men say. That is undoubtedly what is the trouble with time and always in its relation to master-pieces. I once said that nothing could bother me more than the way a thing goes dead once it has been said. And if it does it it is because of there being this trouble about time.

Time is very important in connection with master-pieces, of course it makes identity time does make identity and identity does stop the creation of master-pieces. But time does something by itself to interfere with the creation of master-pieces as well as being part of what makes identity. If you do not keep remembering yourself you have no identity and if you have no time you do not keep remembering yourself and as you remember yourself you do not create anybody can and does know that.

Think about how you create if you do create you do not remember yourself as you do create. And yet time and identity is what you tell about as you create only while you create they do not exist. That is really what it is.

And do you create yes if you exist but time and identity do not exist. We live in time and identity but as we are we do not know time and identity everybody knows that quite simply. It is so simple that anybody does know that. But to know what one knows is frightening to live what one lives is soothing and though everybody likes to be frightened what they really have to have is soothing and so the master-pieces are so few not that the master-pieces themselves are frightening no of course not because if the creator of the master-piece is frightened then he does not exist without the memory of time and identity, and insofar as he is that then he is frightened and insofar as he is frightened the master-piece does not exist, it looks like it and it feels like it, but the memory of the fright destroys it as a master-piece. Robinson Crusoe and the footstep of the man Friday is one of the most perfect examples of the non-existence of time and identity which makes a master-piece. I hope you do see what I mean but anyway everybody who knows about Robinson Crusoe and the footstep of Friday knows that it is true. There is no time and identity in the way it happened and that is why there is no fright.

And so there are very few master-pieces of course there are very few master-pieces because to be able to know that is not to have identity and time but not to mind talking as if there was because it does not interfere with anything and to go on being not as if there were no time and identity but as if there were and at the same time existing without time and identity is so very simple that it is difficult to have many who are that. And of course that is what a master-piece is and that is why there are so few of them and anybody really anybody can know that.

What is the use of being a boy if you are going to grow up to be a man. And what is the use there is no use from the standpoint of master-pieces there is no use. Anybody can really know that.

There is really no use in being a boy if you are going to grow up to be a man because then man and boy you can be certain that that is continuing and a master-piece does not continue it is as it is but it does not continue. It is very interesting that no one is content with being a man and boy but he must also be a son and a father and the fact that they all die has something to do with time but it has nothing to do with a master-piece. The word timely as used in our speech is very interesting but you can any one can see that it has nothing to do with master-pieces we all readily know that. The word timely tells that master-pieces have nothing to do with time.

It is very interesting to have it be inside one that never as you know yourself you know yourself without looking and feeling and looking and feeling make it be that you are some one you have seen. If you have seen any one you know them as you see them whether it is yourself or any other one and so the identity consists in recognition and in recognizing you lose identity because after all nobody looks as they look like, they do not look like that we all know that of ourselves and of any one. And therefore in every way it is a trouble and so you write anybody does write to confirm what any one is and the more one does the more one looks like what one was and in being so identity is made more so and that identity is not what any one can have as a thing to be but as a thing to see. And it being a thing to see no master-piece can see what it can see if it does then it is timely and as it is timely it is not a master-piece.

There are so many things to say. If there was no identity no one could be governed, but everybody is governed by everybody and that is why they make no master-pieces, and also why governing has nothing to do with master-pieces it has completely to do with identity but it has nothing to do with master-pieces. And that is why governing is occupying but not interesting, governments are occupying but not interesting because master-pieces are exactly what they are not.

There is another thing to say. When you are writing before there is an audience anything written is as important as any other thing and you cherish anything and everything that you have written. After the audience begins, naturally they create something that is they create you, and so not everything is so important, something is more important than another thing, which was not true when you were you that is when you were not you as your little dog knows you.

And so there we are and there is so much to say but anyway I do not say that there is no doubt that master-pieces are master-pieces in that way and there are very few of them.

Mina Loy (1882–1966)

Introduction

Mina Loy (1882–1966) was born in London, the eldest daughter of Sigmund and Julian Bryant Lowry. In 1899 she went to Munich to study art with Angelo Jank and shortened her name from Mina Gertrude Lowry to Mina Loy. In 1901–2 she studied painting in England with Augustus John and met Stephen Haweis, whom she married in Paris on December 31, 1903. For the next three years the couple lived and painted in Paris and frequented the salon of Gertrude Stein. They moved to Florence in 1906, but their marriage collapsed in 1913. At about the same time Loy probably had affairs with Filippo Marinetti and Giovanni Papini and her poetry, which reflected her interest in the Futurists, first began to appear in print. In 1916 Loy came to New York, worked in a lampshade studio, acted in the Provincetown Theater, and associated with the poets who published in *Others*. In New York City she met Arthur Cravan, whom she married in Mexico City in 1918. Soon thereafter Cravan disappeared in Mexico and his body was later found in the desert.

When Loy returned to Paris in 1923, Robert McAlmon published *Lunar Baedecker*, which assured her a place among such modernist contemporary writers as Marianne Moore, William Carlos Williams, and T. S. Eliot. As the widow of poet-boxer Cravan, she maintained contact with the Dadaists and Surrealists, who saw Cravan as a hero. She continued her friendships with Marcel Duchamp, Gertrude Stein, Djuna Barnes, and her agent Carl Van Vechten, and met many of the expatriates residing in Paris, including James Joyce and Constantin Brancusi. Although her literary career was at its height, she continued to support her family through the design and manufacture of lampshades for the shop that she opened with the financial backing of Peggy Guggenheim. "Anglo-Mongrels and the Rose," a semi-autobiographical poem about Loy's Victorian upbringing, was published in two issues of the *Little Review* (1923) and in McAlmon's *The Contact Collection of Contemporary Writers* (1925). Loy continued to paint in the 1930s, exhibiting her monochrome sand paintings in New York, and worked on another unpublished novel, "Insel."

In 1936 she moved to New York City where she remained for nearly 20 years, writing poetry and creating collages out of materials she found in back alleys and trash cans. In 1958 her poetry was republished in *Lunar Baedeker & Time-Tables*; the following year she received the Copley Foundation Award for Outstanding Achievement in Art and exhibited her "Constructions" at the Bodley Gallery. She died in Aspen, Colorado, in 1966, after a short illness.

Loy had three children by her first husband and one by her second: Oda Janet Haweis (1903–4), who died in infancy; Joella Synara Haweis Levy Bayer (1907–); John Giles Stephen Musgrove Haweis (1909–23); and Jemima Fabienne Cravan Benedict (1919–).

Virgins Plus Curtains Minus Dots (1915)

Latin Borghese[1]

Houses hold virgins
The door's on the chain

'Plumb streets with hearts'
'Bore curtains with eyes'

Virgins   without dots
Stare   beyond probability

The poem was first published in the brief-lived journal *Rogue* 2(1) (Aug. 15, 1915).
For the mathematical style invoked in the title, see the "Technical Manifesto of Futurist Literature," principle no. 6, p. 16 in this edition. The word "dot" means dowry and comes from the Latin *dotem*.

[1]   *Latin Borghese* "Borghese" is the Italian word for "bourgeois" and is the name of a distinguished Roman family of the late Renaissance whose art collections are assembled in the famous Galleria Borghese in Rome.

See the men pass
Their hats are not ours
10   We   take a walk
They are going somewhere
And they   may look everywhere
Men's eyes   look into things
Our eyes   look out

15   A great deal of ourselves
We offer to the mirror
Something less to the confessional
The rest   to Time
There is so much   Time
20   Everything is full of it
                    Such a long time

Virgins may whisper
'Transparent nightdresses made all of lace'
25   Virgins may squeak
'My dear   I should faint'
Flutter ..... flutter .... flutter ....
.... 'And then   the man –'
Wasting our giggles
For we have no dots

30   We have been taught
Love is a god
White   with soft wings
                    Nobody shouts
                Virgins for sale
35   Yet where are our coins
For buying a purchaser
Love is a god
                Marriage expensive
A secret well kept
40   Makes the noise of the world
Nature's arms spread wide
Making room for us
                    Room for all of us
Somebody who was never
45   a virgin
Has bolted the door
Put curtains at our windows
See the men pass
They   are going somewhere

50   Fleshes like weeds
Sprout in the light
So much flesh in the world
                    Wanders at will

Some   behind curtains
55   Throbs to the night
Bait   to the stars

Spread it with gold
And you carry it home
Against your shirt front

To   a shaded light   60
With the door locked
Against virgins who
Might   scratch

The Effectual Marriage, or The Insipid Narrative of Gina and Miovanni (1917)

The door was an absurd thing
Yet it was passable
They quotidienly passed through it
It was this shape

Gina and Miovanni   who they were God knows   5
They knew   it was important to them
This being of who they were
They were themselves
Corporeally   transcendentally   consecutively
conjunctively   and they were quite   complete   10

In the evening they looked out of their two windows
Miovanni out of his library window
Gina from the kitchen window
From among his pots and pans
Where he so kindly kept her   15
Where she so wisely busied herself
Pots and Pans   she cooked in them
All sorts of sialagogues[1]
Some say   that happy women are immaterial

So here we might dispense with her   20
Gina being a female
But she was more than that
Being an incipience   a correlative
an instigation of the reaction of man
From the palpable to the transcendent   25
Mollescent irritant of his fantasy
Gina had her use   Being useful
contentedly conscious
She flowered in Empyrean
From which no well-mated woman ever returns   30

Sundays   a warm light in the parlor
From the gritty road   on the white wall
anybody could see it
Shimmered a composite effigy
Madonna   crinolined   a man   35
hidden beneath her hoop
Ho for the blue and red of her
The silent eyelids of her
The shiny smile of her

THE EFFECTUAL MARRIAGE
The poem was first published in *Others: An Anthology of the New Verse*, ed. Alfred Kreymborg (New York: Alfred Knopf, 1917). "Mina" and "Miovanni" are obvious references to "Mina" Loy and "Giovanni" Papini, with whom Loy had an affair in 1914.

[1] *sialagogues* from the Greek word σίαλου, meaning "saliva," and ἀγωγός, meaning "leading, drawing forth": a medicine which has the effect of producing saliva (*OED*).

40   Ding dong   said the bell
                             Miovanni   Gina called
                             Would it be fitting for you to tell
                             the time for supper
                             Pooh   said Miovanni   I am
45   Outside time and space

                           Patience said Gina   is an attribute
                           And she learned   at any hour to offer
                           The dish   appropriately delectable

                           What had Miovanni made of his ego
50   In his library
                           What had Gina wondered   among the pots and pans
                           One never asked the other
                           So they   the wise ones   eat their suppers in peace

                           Of what their peace consisted
55   We cannot say
                           Only that he was magnificently man
                           She insignificantly a woman who understood
                           Understanding   what is that
                           To Each   his entity   to others
60   their idiosyncrasies   to the free expansion
                           to the annexed   their liberty
                           To man his work
                           To woman her love
                           Succulent meals   and an occasional caress
65   So be it
                                        It so seldom is

                         While Miovanni thought alone in the dark
                         Gina supposed that peeping   she might see
                         A round light   shining   where his mind was
70   She never opened the door
                           Fearing that this might blind her
                           Or even
                           That she should see   Nothing at all
                         So while he thought
75   She hung out of the window
                           Watching for falling stars
                           And when a star fell
                         She wished   that still
                         Miovanni would love her to-morrow
80   And as Miovanni
                         Never gave any heed to the matter
                         He did

                         Gina was a woman
                         Who wanted everything
85   To be everything in woman
                         Everything everyway at once
                         Diurnally variegate
                         Miovanni always knew her
                         She was Gina
90   Gina who lent monogamy
                         With her fluctuant aspirations

A changeant consistency
Unexpected intangibilities

Miovanni remained
Monumentally the same   95
The same Miovanni
If he had become anything else
Gina's world would have been at an end
Gina with no axis to revolve on
Must have dwindled to a full stop   100

In the mornings she dropped
Cool crystals
Through devotional fingers
Saccharine   for his cup
And marketed   105
With a Basket
Trimmed with a red flannel flower
When she was lazy
She wrote a poem on the milk bill
The first strophe   Good morning   110
The second   Good night
Something not too difficult to
Learn by heart

The scrubbed smell of the white-wood table
Greasy cleanliness   of the chopper board   115
The coloured vegetables
Intuited quality of flour
Crickly[2] sparks of straw-fanned charcoal
Ranged themselves among her audacious happinesses
Pet simplicities of her Universe   120
Where circles were only round
                    Having no vices.

(This narrative halted when I learned that the house which inspired it was the home of a mad woman.

                                                — Forte dei Marmi)[3]

Human Cylinders (1917)

The human cylinders
Revolving in the enervating dust
That wraps each closer in the mystery
Of singularity
Among the litter of a sunless afternoon   5
Having eaten without tasting
Talked without communion

[2] *crickly* from the intransitive verb "to crickle," i.e., to make a sharp, thin sound; to make a succession of sharp sounds. The *OED* cites a sentence from 1883: "You hear him [sc. the wild hunter] bluster in the air, so that it 'crickles and crackles'."

[3] *Forte dei Marmi* a small town on the coast of northwestern Italy, one that was settled only after the sixteenth century when

it became a small port used to transport marble from the nearby Alps; its name, meaning "Fortress of the Marbles," was acquired when a small fort was built there in 1788.

The poem was first published in *Others: An Anthology of the New Verse*, ed. Alfred Kreymborg (New York: Alfred Knopf, 1917).

And at least two of us
Loved a very little
10   Without seeking
To know if our two miseries
In the lucid rush-together of automatons
Could form one opulent well-being

Simplifications of men
15   In the enervating dusk
Your indistinctness
Serves me the core of the kernel of you
When in the frenzied reaching-out of intellect to intellect
Leaning brow to brow   communicative
20   Over the abyss of the potential
Concordance of respiration
Shames
Absence of corresponding between the verbal sensory
And reciprocity
25   Of conception
And expression
Where each extrudes beyond the tangible
One thin pale trail of speculation
From among us we have sent out
30   Into the enervating dusk
One little whining beast
Whose longing
Is to slink back to antediluvian burrow
And one elastic tentacle of intuition
35   To quiver among the stars

The impartiality of the absolute
Routs   the polemic
Or which of us
Would not
40   Receiving the holy-ghost
Catch it   and caging
    Lose it
Or in the problematic
Destroy the Universe
45   With a solution.

Joyce's Ulysses[1] (1922)

The Normal Monster
sings in the Green Sahara

The voice and offal
of the image of God

5   make Celtic noises
in these lyrical hells

The poem was first published in Loy's first collection of poems, *The Lunar Baedecker* (Paris: Contract Press, 1923).

[1] *Joyce's Ulysses* was first published as a book on February 2, 1922, issued by Shakespeare and Company, an English-language bookstore run by Sylvia Beach (1887–1962) in Paris.

Hurricanes
of reasoned musics
reap the uncensored earth

The loquent consciousness   10
of living things
pours in torrential languages

The elderly colloquists
the Spirit and the Flesh
are out of tongue   15

The Spirit
is impaled upon the phallus

Phoenix
of Irish fires
lighten the Occident   20

with Ireland's wings
flap pandemoniums
of Olympian prose

and satinize
the imperial Rose   25
of Gaelic perfumes –
England
the sadistic mother
embraces Erin

Master   30
of meteoric idiom
present

The word made flesh
and feeding upon itself
with erudite fangs   35
The sanguine
introspection of the womb

Don Juan
of Judea[2]
upon a pilgrimage   40
to the Libido[3]

The press
purring[4]
its lullabies to sanity

Christ capitalized   45
scourging

---

[2] *Judea* originally the part of Palestine adjacent to Jerusalem and inhabited by the Jewish community after their return from captivity, the term is saturated with Biblical associations. "Don Juan [pronounced JOO-an, after the Byronic pronunciation] of Judea" refers to Leopold Bloom's imaginary affairs with Martha Clifford and Gerty McDowell.

[3] *Libido* a relatively new term, first recorded only 14 years earlier in 1909, for psychic drive or energy, particularly associated with the sexual instincts.

[4] *The press / purring* an allusion to Episode 7 of *Ulysses*, "Aeolus," in which the press figures prominently (for the text, see pp. 223–55).

  incontrite usurers of destiny
  in hole and corner temples

  And hang
50 The soul's advertisements
  outside the ecclesiast's Zoo

  A gravid day
  spawns
  gutteral gargoyles
55 upon the Tower of Babel

  Empyrean emporium
  where the
  rejector-recreator
    Joyce
60 flashes the giant reflector
  on the sub rosa

Brancusi's Golden Bird (1922)

  The toy
  become the aesthetic archetype

  As if
  some patient peasant God
5 had rubbed and rubbed
  the Alpha and Omega
  of Form
  into a lump of metal

  A naked orientation
10 unwinged unplumed
  the ultimate rhythm
  has lopped the extremities
  of crest and claw
  from
15 the nucleus of flight

  The absolute act
  of art
  conformed
  to continent sculpture
20 – bare as the brow of Osiris[1] –
  this breast of revelation

  an incandescent curve
  licked by chromatic flames
  in labyrinths of reflections

BRANCUSI'S GOLDEN BIRD
The poem was first published in the *Dial* 73(5) (Nov. 1922),
accompanied by a photograph of the sculpture, "The Golden
Bird," by the Romanian sculptor Constantin Brancusi
(1876–1957), who was then residing in Paris.

[1] *Osiris* judge of the dead in the underworld, according to
Egyptian mythology.

This gong   25
of polished hyperaesthesia[2]
shrills with brass
as the aggressive light
strikes
its significance   30

The immaculate
conception
of the inaudible bird
occurs
in gorgeous reticence   35

Lunar Baedeker (1923)

A silver Lucifer
serves
cocaine in cornucopia

To some somnambulists
of adolescent thighs   5
draped
in satirical draperies

Peris[1] in livery
prepare
Lethe[2]   10
for posthumous parvenues

Delirious Avenues
lit
with the chandelier souls
of infusoria   15
from Pharoah's tombstones

lead
to mercurial doomsdays
Odious oasis
in furrowed phosphorous – – –   20

the eye-white sky-light
white-light district
of lunar lusts

– – – Stellectric[3] signs
"Wing shows on Starway"   25
"Zodiac carrousel"

---

[2] *hyperaesthesia* a medical term for a condition in which the subject responds excessively to any stimulus.

LUNAR BAEDEKER
The poem was first published in Loy's first collection of poems, *The Lunar Baedeker* (Paris: Contract Press, 1923).
[1] *Peris* in Persian mythology, a beautiful fairy shut out from paradise until forgiven, but in a more extended sense the term has come to mean any very beautiful or fairylike being.
[2] *Lethe* in Greek mythology, the underworld river which brings about forgetfulness.
[3] *Stellectric* a nonce word made by combining "stellar" and "electric."

Cyclones
of ecstatic dust
and ashes whirl
30   crusaders
from hallucinatory citadels
of shattered glass
into evacuate craters

A flock of dreams
35   browse on Necropolis

From the shores
of oval oceans
in the oxidized Orient

Onyx-eyed Odalisques[4]
40   and ornithologists
observe
the flight
of Eros obsolete

And "Immortality"
45   mildews ...
in the museums of the moon

"Nocturnal cyclops"
"Crystal concubine"
– – – – – – – – –
50   Pocked with personification
the fossil virgin of the skies
waxes and wanes – – – –

Gertrude Stein (1924)

Curie[1]
of the laboratory
of vocabulary
        she crushed
5   the tonnage
of consciousness
congealed to phrases
        to extract
a radium of the word

---

[4] *Odalisques* originally a female slave in an eastern harem, especially in that of the sultan of Turkey; then, because odalisques were painted so extensively by French artists, a type of voluptuous woman or a painted image of one.

GERTRUDE STEIN
The poem was first published, without a title, in the *transatlantic review* 2(3) (Sept. 1924), where it appeared as the epigraph to a letter in which Loy discusses the influences and effects of Ger-

trude Stein's techniques of composition (see pp. 432–7). The title was first furnished by Roger Conover in his edition of *The Lost Lunar Baedeker: Poems of Mina Loy* (New York: Farrar Strauss, 1996).
[1] *Curie* Marie Curie (1867–1934) was awarded two Nobel Prizes, in 1903 and 1911, for her studies in radioactivity.

Aphorisms on Futurism (1914)

DIE in the Past

Live in the Future.

THE velocity of velocities arrives in starting.

IN pressing the material to derive its essence, matter becomes deformed.

AND form hurtling against itself is thrown beyond the synopsis of vision.

THE straight line and the circle are the parents of design, form the basis of art; there is no limit to their coherent variability.

LOVE the hideous in order to find the sublime core of it.

OPEN your arms to the delapidated; rehabilitate them.

YOU prefer to observe the past on which your eyes are already opened.

BUT the Future is only dark from outside. *Leap* into it – and it EXPLODES with *Light*.

FORGET that you live in houses, that you may live in yourself –

FOR the smallest people live in the greatest houses.

BUT the smallest person, potentially, is as great as the Universe.

WHAT can you know of expansion, who limit yourselves to compromise?

HITHERTO the great man has achieved greatness by keeping the people small.

BUT in the Future, by inspiring the people to expand to their fullest capacity, the great man proportionately must be tremendous – a God.

LOVE of others is the appreciation of oneself.

MAY your egotism be so gigantic that you comprise mankind in your self-sympathy.

THE Future is limitless – the past a trial of insidious reactions.

LIFE is only limited by our prejudices. Destroy them, and you cease to be at the mercy of yourself.

TIME is the dispersion of intensiveness.

THE Futurist can live a thousand years in one poem.

HE can compress every aesthetic principle in one line.

THE mind is a magician bound by assimilations; let him loose and the smallest idea conceived in freedom will suffice to negate the wisdom of all forefathers.

LOOKING on the past you arrive at "Yes," but before you can act upon it you have already arrived at "No."

THE Futurist must leap from affirmative to affirmative, ignoring intermittent negations – must spring from stepping-stone to stone of creative exploration; without slipping back into the turbid stream of accepted facts.

This piece was first published in the quarterly journal edited by   *Camera Work* 45 (Jan. 1914). On Futurism, see pp. 1–38. the photographer and cultural entrepreneur, Alfred Stieglitz,

THERE are no excrescences on the absolute, to which man may pin his faith.

TODAY is the crisis in consciousness.

CONSCIOUSNESS cannot spontaneously accept or reject new forms, as offered by creative genius; it is the new form, for however great a period of time it may remain a mere irritant – that molds consciousness to the necessary amplitude for holding it.

CONSCIOUSNESS has no climax.

LET the Universe flow into your consciousness, there is no limit to its capacity, nothing that it shall not re-create.

UNSCREW your capability of absorption and grasp the elements of Life – *Whole*.

MISERY is in the disintegration of Joy; Intellect, of Intuition; Acceptance, of Inspiration.

CEASE to build up your personality with the ejections of irrelevant minds.

NOT to be a cipher in your ambient, But to color your ambient with your preferences.

NOT to accept experience at its face value.

BUT to readjust activity to the peculiarity of your own will.

THESE are the primary tentatives towards independence.

MAN is a slave only to his own mental lethargy.

YOU cannot restrict the mind's capacity.

THEREFORE you stand not only in abject servitude to your perceptive consciousness –

BUT also to the mechanical re-actions of the subconsciousness, that rubbish heap of race-tradition –

AND believing yourself to be free – your least conception is colored by the pigment of retrograde superstitions.

HERE are the fallow-lands of mental spatiality that Futurism will clear –

MAKING place for whatever you are brave enough, beautiful enough to draw out of the realized self.

TO your blushing we shout the obscenities, we scream the blasphemies, that you, being weak, whisper alone in the dark.

THEY are empty except of your shame.

AND so these sounds shall dissolve back to their innate senselessness.

THUS shall evolve the language of the Future.

THROUGH derision of Humanity as it appears –

TO arrive at respect for man as he shall be –

ACCEPT the tremendous truth of Futurism

Leaving all those
                    Knick-knacks.

Psycho-Democracy (1921)

A movement to focus human reason
on
THE CONSCIOUS DIRECTION OF EVOLUTION

to replace the cataclysmic factor in social evolution WAR. An absolute, constructive and liberating ideal put to the will of mankind for acceptance or rejection.

Psycho democracy is

Democracy of The Spirit, government by creative imagination, participation in essential wisdom – Fraternity of Intuition, the Intellect and Mother wit. (The Creator, the scholar, the natural man).

A psychological gauge applied to all social problems, for the interpretation of political, religious and financial systems.

Democratic interchange and valuation of *ideas*.

The Substitution of consciously directed evolution for revolution, *Creative inspiration for Force*, Laughter for Lethargy, Sociability for Sociology, Human psychology for Tradition.

The Psycho-Democratic Policy is
Habeas Animum.

"To illuminate the earth with her peoples eyes."

The organization of Psycho-Democracy is based on the laws of psychic evolution, our principles spring from Intuition, and are presented to man's intellect for maturation.

We make the experiment of a "collectivity" moved by the same intellectual logic as are the tactics of the successful individual reckoning with "actual" values and following the rules of the game of life, influencing our era by right of the merits of our (collective) personality.

Most movements have a fixed concept towards which they advance, we move away from all fixed concepts in order to advance.

The Psycho-democrat is

Man, Woman or Child of good sense and with imagination, having a normal love of Life and a sympathic indifference to their neighbours' obligations.

The *living* successor of that travesty of man; the *Dummy Public* originated by the Press, financed by the Capitalist:

For whom the politician legislates,
The army fights,
The church collects.

THE IDEA-FABRIC OF HUMAN SOCIETY. Modern social existence is a form of psychic activity based on *Ideas* promoted by the self-conscious minority of *Power*.

Every phase in evolution has been marked by the different kinds of ideas for which men tortured one another.

Society today is composed of distinctly different human strata; heirs of the different ideas for which men tortured one another.

The Tediousness of Human Evolution is owing:

This manifesto was first published as an independent pamphlet (Florence: Tipografia Peri & Rossi, 1920), then in the *Little Review* 8 (1921).

To the tendency of ideas to outlast their origin, i. e. the tendency of human institutions to outlast the psychological conditions from which they arose.

Psycho-Democracy considers social institutions as structural forms in collective consciousness which are subject to the same evolutionary transformation as is collective consciousness itself, and that our social institutions of today will cause future generations to roar with laughter.

Criminal Lunacy

In the very near future the fact that it is considered either normal or necessary for millions of men and women to wear out their organisms with no reward but the maintainance of those organisms, imperfectly functioning, and that this social condition should be safeguarded and preserved by the blowing up of other millions of human organisms will appear as the nightmare of a criminal lunatic.

Cosmic Neurosis

The destructive element in collective consciousness induced by inhibitive social and religious precepts that ordain that man must suffer and cause to suffer and deny the validity of Man's fundamental desires, has resulted in Cosmic Neurosis, whose major symptom is Fear.

This fear takes the form of international suspicion and the resulting national protective-phobias.

Our enlightened psychological principles will put an end to Cosmic Neurosis.

Psychic Evolution

This thing called *Life* which seems to be the impact of luminous bodies, knocking sparks off one another in chaos, will be transformed through Psycho-Democratic evolution from a war between good and evil, i. e. (between beneficent and painful chance) to a competition between different kinds of good: (beneficent spontaneities),

The Paradox of the Dominator and the Dominated.

"Class" is a psychological condition.

The one class distinction is between the dominator and the dominated.

Every social upheaval has been the evolutionary phenomenon of the recruiting of new material to the dominating class. A class victory is never the promotion of one class to the status of another class, but the shifting of certain elements in the victorious class to the psychological condition of the dominating class.

The dominating class is a psychological nucleus progressively absorbing all similar elements into itself. It is therefore our important task to eludicate the psychology of the Dominator, for the dominated, as the Basis of intrinsic democracy.

Power is a secret society of the minority, whose hold on the majority lies in the esoteric or actual value of social ideas.

This esoteric value is unrevealed to the majority, being: –

1) The transmutability of the *strategical ideas* of the minority into *social ideals* for the majority.

2) The value of *social ideals* as a means of conserving the majority as a plastic psychic material with which *Power* moulds the contours of its own supremacy.

3) The value of the exoteric or public representation of social ideals as limiting the unit for the advantage of a collectivity, while in reality insuring the advantage of the minority with the consent of the majority.

The ensuing confusion in the public mind between its innate logic and the social ideals dictated by the Dominator, provides the *Paradox of the Dominator and the Dominated*; for it is at once the vantage ground for the Dominator's tactics and the blind force which at recurrent intervals confounds the self-conscious minority of *Power*.

Psycho-Democratic Aesthetic

The æthetic contour of a race is formed by its habits.

Man's evolution through his circumstances has resulted in his point of view.

His point of view forms his habits.

The Dominator's standard has been the most highly evolved human habit. Therefore class evolution must democratize the Dominator's standard, which hitherto evolved by circumstances, will in future spring directly into "habit" out of a "point of view."

The Aim of Society is the Perfection of Self

Man's desire is for Self.

His desire is commensurate with possibility.

The earth offers super-abundance for All.

Human imagination is illimitable.

Psycho-Democracy advocates the fulfilment of all Desire.

"Self" is the covered entrance to Infinity.

Militarism

Militarism forms the nucleus of national *Influential symbolism*; the flag, the uniform; inspires the *Rhythm of national popular enthusiasm*: the march, the band, parade. Sustains the *belligerent masculine* social ideal. Like all concentrated human forces it is *psychically magnetic*.

It has created certain formulæ figuring largely in our social pleasures, which no other social institution affords; the inevitable "snobbery" thus involved insures its protracted success.

Pacifism

The sole opposition to this imposing and efficiently organized social foundation is the pacifist *Don't*.

Pacifism has not yet offered a creative substitute for the military ideal, but a negative conception which leaves a void in social psychological construction, without providing any adequate suggestions as to how this void should be filled.

The Appeal of psycho-Democracy for the conscious direction of evolution, is an appeal to the thinker, the scientist, the philosopher, the writer, the artist, the mechanic, the worker, to join intelligent forces in a concerted effort to evolve and establish *a new social symbolism, a new social rhythm, a new social snobism* with a human psychological significance of equal value to that of militarism.

To consider that the belligerent tendency in human nature which is at present abnormaly fostered by social institutions and education, can be superseded by another of the different tendencies in human nature, if developed through transformed social institutions and revised education.

To vindicate Humanity's claim to a Divine Destiny. Not to endeavor to eliminate the indestructable forces in human nature but to establish a new social system for their utilization. To present intellectual heroism as a popular ideal in place of physical heroism encouraging the expression of individual psychology in place of mob-psychology. To believe that man has the conceptual power to create a substitute for war, having the same stimulus to action as the hazard of death, the same spur to renascence as devastation, and that his mentality will evolve new forms of expressive action to inspire him to such ebullitions of enthusiasm as does the call to arms.

In *Psycho-Democracy* shall arise men and women whose strength and originality of conception will concrete a vital ideal as the basis of International politics. This ideal which is in a nebulous state, once defined will be easier to impose on humanity than the hypnotic war lust.

For it is but logical to suppose that if the slight amount of magnetism in the make up of the world's leaders of today, is sufficient to rush great peoples on to death and agony, it will be a simple task to persuade great peoples to the effort of self realization in a life amplifying ideal; and to apply the force of reason to the solution of their life problems, which have been so acutely aggravated by the force of explosives.

And to dissuade Man from any longer considering his destiny as being extraneous to his logic.

Gertrude Stein (1924)

1.

Some years ago I left Gertrude Stein's Villino in Fiesole[1] with a manuscript she had given me.

"Each one is one. Each one is being the one each one is being. Each one is one is being one. Each one is being the one that one is being. Each one is being one each one is one.

"Each one is one. Each one is very well accustomed to be one. Each one is very well accustomed to be that one. Each one is one."[2] (Galeries Lafayette). Compare with "Vanity of vanity; vanity of vanities; all is vanity" of Ecclesiastes.

This is when Bergson was in the air, and his beads of Time strung on the continuous flux of Being, seemed to have found a literary conclusion in the austere verity of Gertrude Stein's theme – "Being" as the absolute occupation.

For by the intervaried rhythm of this monotone mechanism she uses for inducing a continuity of awareness of her subject, I was connected up with the very pulse of duration.

The core of a "Being" was revealed to me with uninterrupted insistence.

The plastic static of the ultimate presence of an entity.

And the innate tempo of a life poured in alert refreshment upon my mentality.

Gertrude Stein was making a statement, a reiterate statement . . . basic and bare . . . a statement reiterate ad absurdum, were it not for the interposing finger of creation.

For Gertrude Stein obtains the *belle matière* of her unsheathing of the fundamental with a most dexterous discretion in the placement and replacement of her phrases, of inversion of the same phrase sequences that are so closely matched in level, as the fractional tones in primitive music or the imperceptible modelling of early Egyptian sculpture.

The flux of Being as the ultimate presentation of the individual, she endows with the rhythmic concretion of her art, until it becomes as a polished stone, a bit of the rock of life – yet not of polished surface, of polished nucleus.

This method of conveyance through duration recurs in her later work. As she progresses it becomes amplified, she includes an increasing number of the attributes of continuity.

The most perfect example of this method is *Italians* where not only are you pressed close to the insistence of their existence, but Gertrude Stein through her process of reiteration gradually, progressively rounds them out, decorates them with their biological insignia.

They revolve on the pivot of her verbal construction like animated sculpture, their life protracted into their entourage through their sprouting hair . . . a longer finger nail; their sound, their smell.

"They have something growing on them, some of them, and certainly many others would not be wanting such things to be growing out of them that is to say growing on them.

"It makes them these having such things, makes them elegant and charming, makes them ugly and disgusting, makes them clean looking and sleek and rich and dark, makes them dirty-looking and fierce looking."[3]

How simply she exposes the startling dissimilarity in the aesthetic dénouement of our standardized biology.

This essay was first published in the *transatlantic review* 2(3) (Sept. 1924) and 2(4) (Oct. 1924).

[1] *Some years ago . . . Fiesole* Loy visted Stein in Fiesole, a small town outside Florence, in 1911.

[2] *"Each one is one. . . . Each one is one"* Gertrude Stein, "Galeries Lafayette" [c. 1911], printed in *Portraits and Prayers* (New York: Random House, 1934), p. 169. Two lines below: Henri Bergson (1859–1941) was a French philosopher who enjoyed a vogue during the period 1900–14; he urged that time was experienced as continuous stream, pure duration, of being, and that this experience was truer than our everyday conception of time as a series of discrete moments.

[3] *"They something . . . fierce looking."* Gertude Stein, a prose poem titled "Italians," in *Geography and Plays*, ed. Cyrena Pondrom (Madison: University of Wisconsin Press, 1993), p. 47.

They solidify in her words, in ones, in crowds, complete with racial impulses. They are of one, infinitesimally varied in detail, racial consistency. Packed by her poised paragraphs into the omniprevalent plasm of life from which she evolves all her subjects and from which she never allows them to become detached. In Gertrude Stein life is never detached from Life; it spreads tenuous and vibrational between each of its human exteriorizations and the other.

"They seem to be, and that is natural because what is in one is carried over to the other one by it being in the feeling of the one looking at the one and then at the other one.[4]

"They are talking, often talking and they are doing things with pieces of them while they are talking and they are things sounding like something, they are then sounding in a way that is a natural way for them to be sounding, they are having noise come out of them in a natural way for them to have noise come out of them."[5]

It may be impossible for our public inured to the unnecessary nuisances of journalism to understand this literature, but it is a literature reduced to a basic significance that could be conveyed to a man on Mars.

In her second phase ... the impressionistic, Gertrude Stein entirely reverses this method of conveyance through duration. She ignores duration and telescopes time and space and the subject-ive and objective in a way that obviates interval and interposition. She stages strange triangles between the nominative and his verb and irruptive co-respondents.

It has become the custom to say of her that she has done in words what Picasso has done with form. There is certainly in her work an interpenetration of dimensions analogous to Cubism.

One of her finest "impressions" is *Sweet Tail*.[6] "Gypsies," it begins.

"Curved Planes.

"Hold in the coat. Hold back ladders and a creation and nearly sudden extra coppery ages with colors and a clean gyp hoarse. Hold in that curl with the good man. Hold in cheese...."[7] A fracturing impact of the mind with the occupation, the complexion, the cry of the gypsies.

Cubistically she first sees the planes of the scene. Then she breaks them up into their detail. Gypsies of various ages bring ladders for the construction of ... something. "A clean gyp hoarse." Here it, see it, attribute it, that voice?

The occurrences of "Hold in" impress me as a registration of her mind dictating the control of the planes of the pictures it is so rapidly and unerringly putting together; no, *choosing* together. "A little pan with a yell,"[8] is a protraction of "The clean gyp hoarse," accelerated, in her chase of sounds among solids by telescoping the "little pan" with the animation of the gypsy holding it.

Per contra in "Wheel is not on a donkey and never never,"[9] her reason disengages the donkey and cart from her primary telescopic visualization.

It is the variety of her mental processes that gives such fresh significance to her words, as if she had got them out of bed early in the morning and washed them in the sun.

They make a new appeal to us after the friction of an uncompromised intellect has scrubbed the meshed messes of traditional associations off them.

As in the little phrase "A wheel is not on a donkey," ... a few words she has lifted out of the ridiculous, to replace them in the sanctuary of pure expression.

"A green, a green coloured oak, a handsome excursion, a really handsome log, a regulation to exchange oars."[10] An association of nomadic recreation and rest through the idea "wood" oak, log, oars.

---

[4]   *"They seem to be ... the other one."* Gertrude Stein, "Italians," in *Geography and Plays*, p. 48.

[5]   *"They are talking ... out of them."* Gertrude Stein, a prose poem titled "Italians," in *Geography and Plays*, p. 47.

[6]   *Sweet Tail* the full title of this prose poem by Gertrude Stein is "A Sweet Tail (Gypsies)." For the complete text see pp. 400–1 in this edition.

[7]   *"Curved ... Hold in cheese"* "A Sweet Tail (Gypsies)," in *Geography and Plays*, 65; in this edition p. 400.

[8]   *"A little pan with a yell"* "A Sweet Tail (Gypsies)," in *Geography and Plays*, 65; in this edition p. 400.

[9]   *"Wheel is ... never never"* "A Sweet Tail (Gypsies)," in *Geography and Plays*, 68; in this edition p. 401.

[10]   *"A green ... to exchange oars"* "A Sweet Tail (Gypsies)," in *Geography and Plays*, 65; in this edition p. 400.

Again how admirably the essences of romance are collected in the following curve-course that for beauty of expression could hardly be excelled.

"The least license is in the eyes which make strange the less sighed hole which is nodded and leaves the bent tender ... it makes medium and egg-light and not nearly so much."[11]

To obtain movement she has shaped her words to the pattern of a mobile emotion, she has actually bent the tender and with medium and egg-light and not really so much, reconstructed the signal luminous, the form, the semi-honesty of the oval eye.

But in "simple cake, simple cake, relike a gentle coat, ... seal it blessing and that means gracious, not gracious suddenly with spoons and flavour but all the same active. Neglect a pink white neglect it for blooming on a thin piece of steady slim poplars."[12] Round the cake, the sociable center, the tempo of the gypsy feast changes ... "seal it blessing," do gypsies say grace or is blessing again the bowing pattern of feeding merging with spoons and flavour?

The "gentle coating" ... icing? ... of the cake confuses with the greater whiteness of the sky wedged between poplars that are depicted with the declivity of line of Van Gogh. "Neglect it...." Again a direction for the mind to keep the plates of the picture relatively adjusted.

"And really all the chance is in deriding cocoanuts real cocoanuts with strawberry tunes and little ice cakes with feeding feathers and peculiar relations of nothing which is more blessed than replies."[13]

In "feeding feathers" the omission of the woman between her feeding and her feathers results in an unaccustomed juxtaposition of words of associating a subject with a verb which does not in fact belong to it, but which visually, is instantaneously connected.

This process of disintegration and reintegration, this intercepted cinema of suggestion urges the reactions of the reader until the theme assumes an unparallelled clarity of aspect. Compare it with George Borrow's gypsy classic[14] and consider the gain in time and spontaneity that such abridged associations as derision and cocoanuts, strawberry tints dissolving into tune and above all the snatched beauty of the bizarrerie feeding affords us.

And these eyes, these feathers are continuously held in place by the progressive introduction of further relationships, "And nearly all heights hats which are so whiled. ...."[15] And no one comes to realize how Gertrude Stein has builded up her gypsies, accent upon accent, colour on colour, bit by bit.

Perhaps for this reason it is not easy for the average reader to "get" Gertrude Stein, because for the casual audience entity seems to be eclipsed by excrescence. Truly with this method of Gertrude Stein's a goodly amount of incoherent debris gets littered around the radium that she crushes out of phrased consciousness.

"Like message cowpowder and sashes sashes, like pedal causes and so sashes, and pedal cause kills surgeon in six safest six, pedal sashes."[16]

Now that's just like Gertrude Stein! Even as I type this suspect excerpt it clarifies as the subconscious code message of an accident. The sending for the surgeon. The first aid with gypsy sashes.

The cow that ... like gunpowder ... may be a cause for being killed ... but if in in six minutes the surgeon arrives ... the probability of safety. The simultaneity of velocity-binding, sashes-pedalling of messenger's bicycle.

[11] *"The least license ... nearly so much."* "A Sweet Tail (Gypsies)," in *Geography and Plays*, 67; in this edition p. 401.
[12] *"simple cake ... slim poplars"* "A Sweet Tail (Gypsies)," in *Geography and Plays*, 66; in this edition p. 400.
[13] *"And really all the chance ... blessed than replies."* "A Sweet Tail (Gypsies)," in *Geography and Plays*, 66; in this edition p. 400.
[14] *George Borrow's gypsy classic* George Borrow (1803–81) was an English author who wrote novels and travelogues based on his own experiences. His principal work is *Lavengro: The Scholar, the Gypsy, the Priest* (London: John Murray, 1851), and this is probably the work being cited by Mina Loy. However, he also wrote *The Zincali: An Account of the Gypsies of Spain* (London: John Murray, 1841).
[15] *"An nearly all heights ... are so whiled"* "A Sweet Tail (Gypsies)," in *Geography and Plays*, 68; in this edition p. 401.
[16] *"Like message cowpowder ... six, pedal sashes."* "A Sweet Tail (Gypsies)," in *Geography and Plays*, 67; in this edition p. 400.

2.

There is no particular advantage in groping for subject matter in a literature that is sufficiently satisfying as verbal design, but the point at issue, for those who are confident of their ability to write Gertrude Stein with their minds shut, is that her design could not attain the organic consistency that it does, were there no intention back of it.

Kenneth Burke deducts from her effectiveness the satisfying climax of subject.[17] For it is rather the debris, always significant with that rhythm he analyses that has attracted his attention, than the sudden potential, and, to a mind attuned protracted illuminations of her subject which form the very essence of Gertrude Stein's art.

Nevertheless it is disconcerting to follow with great elation certain passages I have quoted when unexpectedly time and space crash into a chaos of dislocate ideas, while conversation would seem to proceed from the radiophonic exchange of the universe. Yet you *come up for air* with the impression that you have experienced something more extensively than you ever have before ... but what? The everything, the everywhere, the simultaneity of function.

But these concussions become less frequent as again and again one reads her, and each time her subject shows still more coherence. One must in fact go into training to get Gertrude Stein.

Often one is liable to overlook her subject because her art gives such tremendous proportions to the negligible that one can not see it all at once. As for instance in "Handing a lizard to anyone is a green thing receiving a curtain. The shape is not present and the sensible way to have agony is not precautious. Then the skirting is extreme and there is a lilac smell and no ginger. Halt and suggest a leaf which has no circle and no singular center, this has that show and does judge that there is a need of moving toward the equal height of a hot sinking surface."[18]

To interpret her description of the lizard you have to place yourself in the position of both Gertrude Stein and the lizard at once, so intimate is the liaison of her observation with the sheer existence of her objective, that she invites you into the concentric vortex of consciousness involved in the most trifling transactions of incident.

Her action is inverted in the single sentence "Handling a lizard . . etc." Where the act of the subject transforms into the possibility of the object.

"The change is not present. ... " She has taken on the consciousness or rather the unconsciousness of the lizard in the inexplicable predicament of its transportation.

And in "The sensible way to have agony is not precautious," it's struggle to retrieve its habitude.

How much beauty she can make out of so little. After the "green thing receiving the curtain," this comparison of a lizard to a leaf.

"This has that show and does judge;" again the inversion. She is turning the lizard outside in, its specular aspect fuses with its motor impulses and now she represents the palm of the hand to you as a land surveyor might a prospect.

To the advocates of Stein prohibition I must confess that the line "then the skirting is extreme and there is a lilac smell and no ginger" is not clear to me; the immediate impression I receive is that the puffing of the frightened reptile's belly is being likened to a billowing skirt that the lilac shadow on the flesh of the hand shunts into the smell of the lizard. ... But why the ginger? Something suggested ginger to the author and escaped her, so she denies the ginger. The greatest incertitude experienced while reading Gertrude Stein is the indecision as to whether you are psychoanalysing her, or she, you.

There is a good deal of ginger floating around in this book of *Geography and Plays*, as are also pins stuck about. The ginger so far escapes me, the pins I accept as an acute materialization of the concentric.

---

[17] *Kenneth Burke ... subject* Kenneth Burke (1897–1993) was an American literary critic, sympathetic to modernist experimentation, who wrote a review of Stein's *Geography and Plays*, titled "Engineering with Words," in the *Dial* 74(4) (April 1923): 97–9.

[18] *"Handing a lizard ... a hot sinking surface."* "Portrait of Prince B.D.," in *Geography and Plays*, p. 151.

Compare this lizard episode with an example of a dream animated by the projection of the intellect into the intimacy of the inanimate.

"The season gliding and the torn hangings receiving mending, all this shows an example, it shows the force of sacrifice and likeness and disaster and a reason."[19] *Tender Buttons*.

Gertrude Stein possesses a power of evocation that gives the same lasting substance to her work that is found in the *Book of Job*.

Take the colossal verse

"He spreadeth the north over the empty place, and hangeth the earth upon nothing." *Job*[20]

Which has the same mechanism as the eye-egg light episode and the lizard-curtain episode, and the analogy to Gertrude Stein is obvious in such passages as the following:

"Am I a sea or a whale[21]
Darkness itself[22]

Who can stay the bottles of heaven[23]
The chambers of heaven."[24] *Job*

Like all modern art, this art of Gertrude Stein makes a demand for a creative audience, by providing a stimulus, which although it proceeds from a complete aesthetic organization, leaves us unlimited latitude for personal response.

For each individual with his particular experience she must induce varying interpretations, for the logician she must afford generous opportunity for inferences entirely remote from those of the artist approaching her writings. There is a scholarly manipulation of the inversion of ideas, parallel to Alice In the Looking Glass;[25] one is nonplussed by the refutation of logic with its myriad insinuations that surpass logic, which Gertrude Stein in her *Plays* achieves through syncopation.

I point these things out in passing, to draw attention to the class of material she brings to the manufacture of her new literature. If you can come to think of a philosophy, apart from the intrication of your reason, leaving on your memory an abstract impress of its particularity as a perfume or a voice might do, you can begin to sort out the vital elements in Gertrude Stein's achievement.

She has tackled an aesthetic analysis of the habits of consciousness in its lair, prior to the traditionalization of its evolution.

Perhaps that ideal enigma that the modern would desire to solve is, "what would we know about anything, if we didn't know anything about it?" ... to track intellection back to the embryo.

For the spiritual record of the race is this nostalga for the crystallization of the irreducible surplus of the abstract. The bankruptcy of mysticism declared itself in an inability to locate this divine irritation, and the burden of its debt to the evolution of consciousness has devolved upon the abstract art.

The pragmatic value of modernism lies in its tremendous recognition of the compensation due to the spirit of democracy. Modernism is a prophet crying in the wilderness of stabilized culture that

---

[19] *"The season gliding ... and a reason."* Gertrude Stein, *Tender Buttons* (Los Angeles: Sun & Moon, 1991), p. 68; in this edition p. 396.
[20] *He spreadeth the north ... Job* Job 26:7: "He stretcheth out the north over the empty place, and hangeth the earth upon nothing."
[21] *Am I a sea or a whale* Job 7:12: "Am I sea, or a whale, that thou settest a watch over me?"
[22] *Darkess itself* Job 10:22: "A land of darkness, as darkness itself; and of the shadow of death, without any order, and where the light is as darkness."
[23] *who can stay the bottle of heaven* Job 38:37–8: "Who can

number the clouds in wisdom? or who can stay the bottles of heaven. When the dust groweth into hardness, and clods cleave fast together?"
[24] *The chambers of heaven* this phrase is not found in Job or anywhere else in the Bible. The Australian poet Charles Harpur (1813–68) uses the expression in two poems, "A Lyrical Love Story" ("While the stars leave the chambers of heaven") and "Love's Even Song" ("Stars throng out from the chambers of heaven").
[25] *Through the Looking-Glass, and What Alice Found There* was written by Lewis Carroll (pseudonym of Charles Dogson: 1832–98).

humanity is wasting its aesthetic time. For there is a considerable extension of time between the visits to the picture gallery, the museum, the library. It asks "what is happening to your aesthetic consciousness during the long long intervals?"

The flux of life is pouring its aesthetic aspect into your eyes, your ears – and you ignore it because you are looking for your canons of beauty in some sort of frame or glass case or tradition. Modernism says: Why not each one of us, scholar or bricklayer, pleasurably realize all that is impressing itself upon our subconscious, the thousand odds and ends which make up your sensory everyday life?

Modernism has democratized the subject matter and *la belle matière* of art; through cubism the newspaper has assumed an aesthetic quality, through Cezanne a plate has become more than something to put an apple upon, Brancusi has given an evangelistic import to eggs, and Gertrude Stein has given us the Word, in and for itself.

Would not life be lovelier if you were constantly overjoyed by the sublimely pure concavity of your wash bowls? The tubular dynamics of your cigarette?

In reading Gertrude Stein one is assaulted by a dual army of associated ideas, her associations and your own.

"This is the sun in. This is the lamb of lantern of chalk."[26] Because of the jerk of beauty it contains shoots the imagination for a fraction of a second through associated memories.

Of sun worship. Lamb worship. Lamb of, light of, the world. (Identical in Christian symbolism.) Shepherd carries lantern. The lantern = lamb's eyes. Chalk white of lamb. Lantern sunshine in chalk pit = absolution of whiteness = pascal lamb = chalk easter toy for peasants.

All this is personal, but something of the kind may happen to anyone when Gertrude Stein leaves grammatical lacunae among her depictions and the mind trips up and falls through into the subconscious source of associated ideas.

The uncustomary impetus of her style accelerates and extends the thought wave until it can vibrate a cosmos from a ray of light on a baa lamb.

This word picture which at first glance would seem to be a lamb being led past a chalk pit by lantern at sun in (down) is revised when on reading further I must conclude that it is still day light and I discover the lamb that carries itself is itself the lantern of chalk.

And here let me proffer my apologies to Gertrude Stein who may have intended the description for . . . a daisy. The sun as the center, chalk as petal white, and the lamb an indication of the season of the year.

Let us leave the ultimate elucidation of Gertrude Stein to infinity.

Apart from all analysis, the natural, the dèbonaire way to appreciate Gertrude Stein, is as one would saunter along a country wayside on a fine day and pluck, for its beauty, an occasional flower. So one sees suddenly:

"He does not look dead at all.
The wind might have blown him."[27]

Modern Poetry (1925)

Poetry is prose bewitched, a music made of visual thoughts, the sound of an idea.

The new poetry of the English language has proceeded out of America. Of things American it attains the aristocratic situation of vitality. This unexpectedly realized valuation of American jazz and American poetry is endorsed by two publics; the one universal, the other infinitesimal in comparison.

And why has the collective spirit of the modern world, of which both are the reflection, recognized itself unanimously in the new music of unprecedented instruments, and so rarely in

---

[26] *"This is the sun in . . . . lantern of chalk"* from "A Sweet Tail (Gypsies)," in *Geography and Plays*, 65; in this edition p. 400.
[27] *"He does not look . . . blown him."* source not identified.

MODERN POETRY
This essay was first published in the journal *Charm* 3(3) (April 1925).

the new poetry of unprecedented verse? It is because the sound of music capturing our involuntary attention is so easy to get in touch with, while the silent sound of poetry requires our voluntary attention to obliterate the cold barrier of print with the whole "intelligence of our senses." And many of us who have no habit of reading not alone with the eye but also with the ear, have – especially at a superficial first reading – overlooked the beauty of it.

More than to read poetry we must listen to poetry. All reading is the evocation of speech; the difference in our approach, then, in reading a poem or a newspaper is that our attitude in reading a poem must be rather that of listening to and looking at a pictured song. Modern poetry, like music, has received a fresh impetus from contemporary life; they have both gained in precipitance of movement. The structure of all poetry is the movement that an active individuality makes in expressing itself. Poetic rhythm, of which we have all spoken so much, is the chart of a temperament.

The variety and felicity of these structural movements in modern verse has more than vindicated the rebellion against tradition. It will be found that one can recognize each of the modern poets' work by the gait of their mentality. Or rather that the formation of their verses is determined by the spontaneous tempo of their response to life. And if at first it appears irksome to adjust pleasure to unaccustomed meters, let us reflect in time that hexameters and alexandrines, before they became poetic laws, originated as the spontaneous structure of a poet's inspiration.

Imagine a tennis champion who became inspired to write poetry, would not his verse be likely to embody the rhythmic transit of skimming balls? Would not his meter depend on his way of life, would it not form itself, without having recourse to traditional, remembered, or accepted forms? This, then, is the secret of the new poetry. It is the direct response of the poet's mind to the modern world of varieties in which he finds himself. In each one we can discover his particular inheritance of that world's beauty.

Close as this relationship of poetry to music is, I think only once has the logical transition from verse to music, on which I had so often speculated, been made, and that by the American, Ezra Pound.[1] To speak of the modern movement is to speak of him; the masterly impresario of modern poets, for without the discoveries he made with his poet's instinct for poetry, this modern movement would still be rather a nebula than the constellation it has become. Not only a famous poet, but a man of action, he gave the public the required push on to modern poetry at the psychological moment. Pound, the purveyor of geniuses to such journals as the *Little Review*, on which he conferred immortality by procuring for its pages the manuscripts of Joyce's *Ulysses*. Almost together with the publication of his magnificent *Cantos*, his music was played in Paris;[2] it utters the communings of a poet's mind with itself making decisions on harmony.

It was inevitable that the renaissance of poetry should proceed out of America, where latterly a thousand languages have been born, and each one, for purposes of communication at least, English – English enriched and variegated with the grammatical structure and voice-inflection of many races, in novel alloy with the fundamental time-is-money idiom of the United States, discovered by the newspaper cartoonists.

This composite language is a very living language, it grows as you speak. For the true American appears to be ashamed to say anything in the way it has been said before. Every moment he ingeniously coins new words for old ideas, to keep good humor warm. And on the baser avenues of Manhattan every voice swings to the triple rhythm of its race, its citizenship and its personality.

Out of the welter of this unclassifiable speech, while professors of Harvard and Oxford labored to preserve "God's English," the muse of modern literature arose, and her tongue had been loosened in the melting-pot.

You may think it impossible to conjure up the relationship of expression between the high browest modern poets and an adolescent Slav who has speculated in a wholesale job-lot of mandarines and is trying to sell them in a retail market on First Avenue. But it lies simply in

---

[1]   *Ezra Pound* for Pound's life and career, see pp. 39–112.
[2]   *his music was played in Paris* concerts with music composed by Pound were given in Paris on December 11, 1923 (Salle du Conservatoire) and July 7, 1924 (Salle Pleyel). The first edition of *The Cantos*, titled *A Draft of XVI. Cantos* (Paris: Three Mountains Press), was published in January 1925.

this: both have had to become adapted to a country where the mind has to put on its verbal clothes at terrific speed if it would speak in time; where no one will listen if you attack him twice with the same missile of argument. And, that the ear that has listened to the greatest number of sounds will have the most to choose from when it comes to self-expression, each has been liberally educated in the flexibility of phrases.

So in the American poet wherever he may wander, however he may engage himself with an older culture, there has occurred no Europeanization of his fundamental advantage, the acuter shock of the New World consciousness upon life. His is still poetry that has proceeded out of America.

The harvest from this recent fertiliser is the poetry of E. E. Cummings.[3] Where other poets have failed for being too modern he is more modern still, and altogether successful; where others were entirely anti-human in their fear of sentimentality, he keeps that rich compassion that poets having for common things leads them to deck them with their own conception; for surely if there were a heaven it would be where this horrible ugliness of human life would arise self-consciously as that which the poet has made of it.

Cummings has united free verse and rhyme which so urgently needed to be married. His rhymes are quite fresh – "radish-red" and "hazarded," and the freeness of his verse gives them a totally new metric relationship.[4]

But fundamentally he is a great poet because his verse wells up abundantly from the foundations of his soul; a sonorous dynamo. And as I believe that the quality of genius must be largely unconscious, I can understand how Cummings can turn out such gabble when he is not being sublime. He is very often sublime.

In reading modern poetry one should beware of allowing mere technical eccentricities or grammatical disturbances to turn us from the main issue which is to get at the poem's reality. We should remember that this seeming strangeness is inevitable when any writer has come into an independent contact with nature: to each she must show herself in a new manner, for each has a different organic personality for perceiving her.

When the little controversies over what is permissible in art evaporate, we will always find that the seeming strangeness has disappeared with them in the larger aspect of the work which has the eternal quality that is common to all true art.

Out of the past most poets, after all, call to us with one or two perfect poems. And we have not complained of being too poor. You will find that the moderns have already done as much.

H. D.,[5] who is an interesting example of my claims for the American poet who engages with an older culture, has written at least two perfect poems: one about a swan.

Marianne Moore, whose writing so often amusingly suggests the soliloquies of a library clock, has written at least one perfect poem, "The Fish."[6]

Lawrence Vail[7] has written one perfect poem, the second "Cannibalistic Love Song," a snatch of primitive ideation with a rhythm as essential as daylight. Maxwell Bodenheim,[8] I think, had one among his early work, and perfect also is a poem of Carlos Williams[9] about the wind on a window-pane.

Williams brings me to a distinction that it is necessary to make in speaking of modern poets. Those I have spoken of are poets according to the old as well as the new reckoning; there are others who are poets only according to the new reckoning. They are headed by the doctor, Carlos Williams. Here is the poet whose expression derives from his life. He is a doctor. He loves bare facts. He is also a poet, he must recreate everything to suit himself. How can he reconcile these two selves?

[3]   *E. E. Cummings* e e cummings (Edward Estlin: 1894–1962) was an American poet, dismissed by many for his sentimentality.
[4]   *"radish-red" and "hazarded"* appear in lines 2 and 5 of the poem "IV. MARJ" which was first collected in cumming's book *Is 5* (New York: Boni and Liveright, 1926), though it also appeared earlier in a periodical.
[5]   *H.D.* for H.D.'s "perfect" poem about a swan, see "Leda," p. 448.

[6]   *Marianne Moore, . . . "The Fish"* for this poem, see p. 648–9.
[7]   *Lawrence Vail* Laurence Vail (1891–1968) was an artist and first husband to the art patron and collector, Peggy Guggenheim, whom he married in 1922.
[8]   *Maxwell Bodenheim* (1893–1954) was an American poet who wrote more than 20 volumes of verse.
[9]   *Carlos Williams* on his life and career, see pp. 500–52.

Williams will make a poem of a bare fact – just show you something he noticed. The doctor wishes you to know just how uncompromisingly itself that fact is. But the poet would like you to realize all that it means to him, and he throws that bare fact onto paper in such a way that it becomes a part of Williams' own nature as well as the thing itself. That is the new rhythm.

H.D. (1886–1961)

Introduction

Hilda Doolittle was born in Bethlehem, Pennsylvania. Her father was a professor of mathematics and astronomy at Lehigh University and later at the University of Pennsylvania. She was educated at a private school, then studied at Bryn Mawr, though she left in her sophomore year because of ill health. In 1911 she went to London and met up with Ezra Pound, with whom she had earlier shared a brief infatuation. She began to write poetry and Pound promoted her work under the rubric of Imagism. She also met the English poet and novelist, Richard Aldington, whom she married. She took over his position as assistant editor of the *Egoist* after he had gone off to war.

In 1918 she and Aldington split, and H.D. gave birth to her daughter Perdita. She was now taken up by a woman whose pen-name (and later her legal name) was Bryher, daughter of the shipping magnate Sir John Ellerman, often called the wealthiest man in England at the time.

Bryher bestowed money on H.D. throughout the subsequent years, at one point giving her £28,000. They lived together in a villa on Lake Geneva, with intermittent journeys to London and other places. Much of her work was published in journals owned and edited by Bryher.

In May 1933 H.D. began psychoanalysis with Freud (Bryher was also fond of psychoanalysis), which gave further impetus to H.D.'s interest in religion and mysticism. She returned to London in 1939, where the war soon provided her with an ample supply of interlocutors for the seances that she frequented. She now composed three long meditative poems, *The Walls Do Not Fall* (1944), *Tribute to the Angels* (1945), and *The Flowering of the Rod* (1946). The status of these was the subject of some debate in the 1980s, when it was urged that they rivaled and even bettered Eliot's *Four Quartets* or Pound's *Pisan Cantos*, but some have found these claims a bit extravagant.

Orchard (1913)

I saw the first pear
as it fell –
the honey-seeking, golden-banded,
the yellow swarm
was not more fleet than I,   5
(spare us from loveliness)
and I fell prostrate
crying:
you have flayed us
with your blossoms,   10
spare us the beauty
of fruit-trees.

The honey-seeking
paused not,
the air thundered their song,   15
and I alone was prostrate.

O rough-hewn
god of the orchard,
I bring you an offering –

ORCHARD
Under the title "Priapus, Keeper-of-Orchards," this poem was
first published in *Poetry* 1(1) (Jan. 1913). Priapus was a Greek
god of fertility whose symbol was the phallus.

20   do you, alone unbeautiful,
        son of the god,
        spare us from loveliness:

        these fallen hazel-nuts,
        stripped late of their green sheaths,
25   grapes, red-purple,
        their berries
        dripping with wine,
        pomegranates already broken,
        and shrunken figs
30   and quinces untouched,
        I bring you as offering.

Oread (1914)

        Whirl up, sea –
        whirl your pointed pines,
        splash your great pines
        on our rocks,
5   hurl your green over us,
        cover us with your pools of fir.

Mid-day (1915)

        The light beats upon me.
        I am startled –
        a split leaf crackles on the paved floor –
        I am anguished – defeated.

5   A slight wind shakes the seed-pods –
        my thoughts are spent
        as the black seeds.
        My thoughts tear me,
        I dread their fever.
10   I am scattered in its whirl.
        I am scattered like
        the hot shrivelled seeds.

        The shrivelled seeds
        are split on the path –
15   the grass bends with dust,
        the grape slips
        under its crackled leaf:
        yet far beyond the spent seed-pods,
        and the blackened stalks of mint,
20   the poplar is bright on the hill,
        the poplar spreads out,
        deep-rooted among trees.

OREAD
This poem was first published in the journal *Blast* 1 (June 1914).
An Oread is a nymph of the mountains.

MID-DAY
The poem was first published in the *Egoist* 2(5) (May 1, 1915).

O poplar, you are great
among the hill-stones,
while I perish on the path   25
among the crevices of the rocks.

Garden (1915)

I

You are clear
O rose, cut in rock,
hard as the descent of hail.

I could scrape the colour
from the petals   5
like spilt dye from a rock.

If I could break you
I could break a tree.

If I could stir
I could break a tree –   10
I could break you.

II

O wind, rend open the heat,
cut apart the heat,
rend it to tatters.

Fruit cannot drop   15
through this thick air –
fruit cannot fall into heat
that presses up and blunts
the points of pears
and rounds the grapes.   20

Cut the heat –
plough through it,
turning it on either side
of your path.

Sea Rose

Rose, harsh rose,
marred and with stint of petals,
meagre flower, thin,
sparse of leaf,

GARDEN
"Garden" was first published in the journal *Poetry* 5(6) (March
1915).

SEA ROSE
The poem was first published in the anthology *Some Imagist Poets:
An Anthology, 1915* (Boston and New York: Houghton Mifflin;
London: Constable, 1915).

5
more precious
than a wet rose
single on a stem –
you are caught in the drift.

10
Stunted, with small leaf,
you are flung on the sand,
you are lifted
in the crisp sand
that drives in the wind.

15
Can the spice-rose
drip such acrid fragrance
hardened in a leaf?

Night (1916)

The night has cut
each from each
and curled the petals
back from the stalk
5
and under it in crisp rows;

under at an unfaltering pace,
under till the rinds break,
back till each bent leaf
is parted from its stalk;

10
under at a grave pace,
under till the leaves
are bent back
till they drop upon the earth,
back till they are all broken.

15
O night,
you take the petals
of the roses in your hand,
but leave the stark core
of the rose
20
to perish on the branch.

Eurydice (1917)

I

So you have swept me back,
I who could have walked with the live souls
above the earth,

NIGHT
The poem was first published in the *Little Review* 2(12) (Jan./Feb. 1916).

EURYDICE
The poem was first published in the *Egoist* 4(1) (Jan. 1917).

Eurydice, in Greek myth, was the wife of Orpheus, a poet and singer. When she was killed by the bite of a snake, Orpheus went down to the Underworld and persuaded its lord to allow him to bring her back on the condition that he should not turn round and look at her before he reached the upper world. Orpheus glances back at her and she must return to the Underworld.

I who could have slept among the live flowers
at last;   5

so for your arrogance
and your ruthlessness
I am swept back
where dead lichens drip
dead cinders upon moss of ash;   10

so for your arrogance
I am broken at last,
I who had lived unconscious,
who was almost forgot;

if you had let me wait   15
I had grown from listlessness
into peace,
if you had let me rest with the dead,
I had forgot you
and the past.   20

II

Here only flame upon flame
and black among the red sparks,
streaks of black and light
grown colourless;

why did you turn back,   25
that hell should be reinhabited
of myself thus
swept into nothingness?

why did you turn?
why did you glance back?   30
why did you hesitate for that moment?
why did you bend your face
caught with the flame of the upper earth,
above my face?

what was it that crossed my face   35
with the light from yours
and your glance?
what was it you saw in my face?
the light of your own face,
the fire of your own presence?   40

What had my face to offer
but reflex of the earth,
hyacinth colour
caught from the raw fissure in the rock
where the light struck,   45
and the colour of azure crocuses
and the bright surface of gold crocuses
and of the wind-flower,
swift in its veins as lightning
and as white   50

III

Saffron from the fringe of the earth,
wild saffron that has bent
over the sharp edge of earth,
all the flowers that cut through the earth,
55   all, all the flowers are lost;

everything is lost,
everything is crossed with black,
black upon black
and worse than black,
60   this colourless light.

IV

Fringe upon fringe
of blue crocuses,
crocuses, walled against blue of themselves,
blue of that upper earth,
65   blue of the depth upon depth of flowers,
lost;

flowers,
if I could have taken once my breath of them,
enough of them,
70   more than earth,
even than of the upper earth,
had passed with me
beneath the earth;

if I could have caught up from the earth,
75   the whole of the flowers of the earth,
if once I could have breathed into myself
the very golden crocuses
and the red,
and the very golden hearts of the first saffron,
80   the whole of the golden mass,
the whole of the great fragrance,
I could have dared the loss.

V

So for your arrogance
and your ruthlessness
85   I have lost the earth
and the flowers of the earth,
and the live souls above the earth,
and you who passed across the light
and reached
90   ruthless;

you who have your own light,
who are to yourself a presence,
who need no presence;

yet for all your arrogance
and your glance,   95
I tell you this:

such loss is no loss,
such terror, such coils and strands and pitfalls
of blackness,
such terror
is no loss;   100

hell is no worse than your earth
above the earth,
hell is no worse,
no, nor your flowers   105
nor your veins of light
nor your presence,
a loss;

my hell is no worse than yours
though you pass among the flowers and speak   110
with the spirits above earth.

VI

Against the black
I have more fervour
than you in all the splendour of that place,
against the blackness
and the stark grey   115
I have more light;

and the flowers,
if I should tell you,
you would turn from your own fit paths   120
toward hell,
turn again and glance back
and I would sink into a place
even more terrible than this.

VII

At least I have the flowers of myself,   125
and my thoughts, no god
can take that;
I have the fervour of myself for a presence
and my own spirit for light;

and my spirit with its loss   130
knows this;
though small against the black,

small against the formless rocks,
hell must break before I am lost;

135   before I am lost,
hell must open like a red rose
for the dead to pass.

Leda (1921)

Where the slow river
meets the tide,
a red swan lifts red wings
and darker beak,
5   and underneath the purple down
of his soft breast
uncurls his coral feet.

Through the deep purple
of the dying heat
10   of sun and mist,
the level ray of sun-beam
has caressed
the lily with dark breast,
and flecked with richer gold
15   its golden crest.

Where the slow lifting
of the tide,
floats into the river
and slowly drifts
20   among the reeds,
and lifts the yellow flags,
he floats
where tide and river meet.

Ah kingly kiss –
25   no more regret
nor old deep memories
to mar the bliss;
where the low sedge is thick,
the gold day-lily
30   outspreads and rests
beneath soft fluttering
of red swan wings
and the warm quivering
of the red swan's breast.

LEDA
The poem was first published in H.D.'s 1921 collection, *Hymen*
(New York: H. Holt; London: the Egoist Press, 1921). For the
myth of Leda, see the introductory note to Yeats's "Leda and the
Swan," p. 325.

She Rebukes Hippolyta (1921)

Was she so chaste?

Swift and a broken rock
clatters across the steep shelf
of the mountain slope,
sudden and swift   5
and breaks as it clatters down
into the hollow breach
of the dried water-course:

far and away
(through fire I see it,   10
and smoke of the dead, withered stalks
of the wild cistus-brush)
Hippolyta, frail and wild,
galloping up the slope
between great boulder and rock   15
and group and cluster of rock.

Was she so chaste,
(I see it, sharp, this vision,
and each fleck on the horse's flanks
of foam, and bridle and bit,   20
silver, and the straps,
wrought with their perfect art,
and the sun,
striking athwart the silver-work,
and the neck, strained forward, ears alert,   25
and the head of a girl
flung back and her throat.)

Was she so chaste –
(Ah, burn my fire, I ask
out of the smoke-ringed darkness   30
enclosing the flaming disk
of my vision)
I ask for a voice to answer:
was she chaste?

Who can say –   35
the broken ridge of the hills
was the line of a lover's shoulder,
his arm-turn, the path to the hills,
the sudden leap and swift thunder
of mountain boulders, his laugh.   40

First published in *Hymen* (New York: H. Holt; London: the
Egoist Press, 1921).

Demeter (1921)

I

Men, fires, feasts,
steps of temple, fore-stone, lintel,
step of white altar, fire and after-fire,
slaughter before,
fragment of burnt meat,
deep mystery, grapple of mind to reach
the tense thought,
power and wealth, purpose and prayer alike,
(men, fires, feasts, temple steps) – useless.

Useless to me who plant
wide feet on a mighty plinth,
useless to me who sit,
wide of shoulder, great of thigh,
heavy in gold, to press
gold back against solid back
of the marble seat:
useless the dragons wrought on the arms,
useless the poppy-buds and the gold inset
of the spray of wheat.

Ah they have wrought me heavy
and great of limb –
she is slender of waist,
slight of breast, made of many fashions;
they have set *her* small feet
on many a plinth;
she they have known,
she they have spoken with,
she they have smiled upon,
she they have caught
and flattered with praise and gifts.

But useless the flattery
of the mighty power
they have granted me:
for I will not stay in her breast,
the great of limb,
though perfect the shell they have
fashioned me, these men!

Do I sit in the market-place –
do I smile, does a noble brow
bend like the brow of Zeus –
am I a spouse, his or any,
am I a woman, or goddess or queen,
to be met by a god with a smile – and left?

The poem was first published in H.D.'s collection, *Hymen* (New York: H. Holt; London: the Egoist Press, 1921). Demeter was the Greek goddess of grains and cereals, later identified in Italy with the Roman goddess Ceres. It is certain that the last two syllables of Demeter's name mean "mother."

II

Do you ask for a scroll,
parchment, oracle, prophecy, precedent;   45
do you ask for tablets marked with thought
or words cut deep on the marble surface,
do you seek measured utterance or the mystic trance?

Sleep on the stones of Delphi[1] –
dare the ledges of Pallas   50
but keep me foremost,
keep me before you, after you, with you,
never forget when you start
for the Delphic precipice,
never forget when you seek Pallas[2]   55
and meet in thought
yourself drawn out from yourself
like the holy serpent,
never forget
in thought or mysterious trance –   60
I am greatest and least.

Soft are the hands of Love,
soft, soft are his feet;
you who have twined myrtle,
have you brought crocuses,   65
white as the inner
stript bark of the osier,
have you set
black crocus against the black
locks of another?   70

III

Of whom do I speak?
Many the children of gods
but first I take
Bromios,[3] fostering prince,
lift from the ivy brake, a king.   75

Enough of the lightning,
enough of the tales that speak
of the death of the mother:
strange tales of a shelter
brought to the unborn,   80
enough of tale, myth, mystery, precedent –
a child lay on the earth asleep.

Soft are the hands of Love,
but what soft hands
clutched at the thorny ground,   85
scratched like a small white ferret

---

[1] *Delphi* the most sacred religious center of ancient Greece, situated on the southern slopes of Mount Parnassus and over-looking the Gulf of Cortinth.

[2] *Pallas* a title of Athena, the ancient Greek goddess of wisdom.
[3] *Bromios* "the thunderer," or "he of the loud shout," an epithet for Dionysius, the ancient Greek god of wine.

or foraging whippet or hound,
sought nourishment and found
only the crackling of ivy,
90   dead ivy leaf and the white
berry, food for a bird,
no food for this who sought,
bending small head in a fever,
whining with little breath.

95   Ah, small black head,
ah, the purple ivy bush,
ah, berries that shook and spirit
on the form beneath,
who begot you and left?

100   Though I begot no man child
all my days,
the child of my heart and spirit,
is the child the gods desert
alike and the mother in death –
105   the unclaimed Dionysos.

IV

What of her –
mistress of Death?

Form of a golden wreath
were my hands that girt her head,
110   fingers that strove to meet,
and met where the whisps escaped
from the fillet, of tenderest gold,
small circlet and slim
were my fingers then.

115   Now they are wrought of iron
to wrest from earth
secrets; strong to protect,
strong to keep back the winter
when winter tracks too soon
120   blanch the forest:
strong to break dead things,
the young tree, drained of sap,
the old tree, ready to drop,
to lift from the rotting bed
125   of leaves, the old
crumbling pine tree stock,
to heap bole and knot of fir
and pine and resinous oak,
till fire shatter the dark
130   and hope of spring
rise in the hearts of men.

What of her –
mistress of Death –
what of his kiss?

Ah, strong were his arms to wrest   135
slight limbs from the beautiful earth,
young hands that plucked the first
buds of the chill narcissus,
soft fingers that broke
and fastened the thorny stalk   140
with the flower of wild acanthus.

Ah, strong were the arms that took
(ah, evil the heart and graceless),
but the kiss was less passionate!

Helen (1924)

All Greece hates
the still eyes in the white face,
the lustre as of olives
where she stands,
and the white hands.   5

All Greece reviles
the wan face when she smiles,
hating it deeper still
when it grows wan and white,
remembering past enchantments   10
and past ills.

Greece sees unmoved,
God's daughter, born of love,
the beauty of cool feet
and slenderest knees,   15
could love indeed the maid,
only if she were laid,
white ash amid funereal cypresses.

Triplex (1931)

A Prayer

Let them not war in me,
these three;
Saviour-of-cities,
Flower-of-destiny
and she,   5
Twinborn-with-Phoebus,
fending gallantly.

HELEN
"Helen" was first published in the journal the *Bookman* 57 (May 1923), then reprinted as one of "Three Poems" in William Stanley Braithwaite (ed.), *Anthology of Magazine Verse for 1923* (Boston: B. J. Brimmer, 1923), and included in H.D.'s 1924 collection *Heliodora and Other Poems* (Boston: Houghton Mifflin; London: Jonathan Cape, 1924). In ancient Greek mythology Helen, the daughter of Zeus and Leda, is the wife of Menelaus, who has been carried off to Troy by Paris, an act which brings about the Trojan war as recounted in Homer's *Iliad*.

TRIPLEX
The poem was first published in H.D.'s collection *Red Rose for Bronze* (Boston: Houghton Mifflin; London: Chatto & Windus, 1931).

Let them not hate in me,
these three;
10   Maid
of the luminous grey-eyes,
Mistress
of honey and marble implacable white thighs
and Goddess,
15   chaste daughter of Zeus,
most beautiful in the skies.

Let them grow side by side in me,
these three;
violets,
20   dipped purple in stark Attic light,
rose,
scorched (on Cyprus coast)
ambrosial white
and wild
25   exquisite hill-crocus
from Arcadian snows.

Magician (1933)

1

There is no man can take,
there is no pool can slake,
ultimately I am alone;
ultimately I done;

5   I say,
take colour;
break white into red,
into blue
into violet
10   into green;
I say,
take each separately,
the white will slay;

pray constantly,
15   give me green, Artemis,
red, Ares,
blue, Aphrodite, true lover,
or rose;
I say, look at the lawns,
20   how the spray
of clematis makes gold or the ray
of the delphinium
violet;
I say,
25   worship each separate;
no man can endure
your intolerable radium;

MAGICIAN
The poem was first published in a journal called *Seed* 1 (Jan.
1933), it was later retitled "Master."

white,
radiant,
pure;   30
who are you?
we are unsure;
give us back the old gods,
to make your plight
tolerable;   35

pull out the nails,
fling them aside,
any old boat,
left at high-tide,
(you yourself would admit)   40
has iron as pliable;

burn the thorn;
thorn burns;
how it crackles;
you yourself would be the first to seek   45
dried weed by some high-sand
to make the land
liveable;

you yourself;
would be the first to scrap   50
the old trophies
for new.

2

We have crawled back into the womb;
you command?
be born again,   55
be born,
be born;
the sand
turns gold ripple and the blue
under-side of the wrasse   60
glints radium-violet as it leaps;
the dolphin leaves a new track,
the bird cuts new wing-beat,
the fox burrows,
begets;   65
the rabbit,
the ferret,
the weasel,
the stoat and the newt
have nests;   70
you said,
the foxes have holes,
you yourself none,
do you ask us
to creep in the earth?   75

too long, too long,
O my Lord,
have we crept,
too long, too long, O my King
have we slept,
80   too long have we slain,
too long have we wept.

3

What is fire upon rain?
colour;
85   what is dew upon grass?
odour;
what are you upon us?
fragrance of honey-locust.

What man is cursed?
90   he without lover;
what woman is blasphemous?
she who, under cover of your cloak,
casts love out.

Your cloak hides the sinner,
95   your cloak shields the lover,
colour of wine,
cyclamen,
red rhododendron.

4

Salt, salt the kiss
100   of beauty where Love is,
salt, salt the refrain,
beat, beat again,
say again,
again,
105   Beauty,
our King
is slain;

beautiful the hands,
beautiful the feet,
110   the thighs beautiful;

O is it right,
is it meet?
we have dared too long to worship
an idol,
115   to worship drab sack-cloth,
to worship dead candles;
light the candles, sing;

tear down every effigy, for none has granted
him beauty;

too long,   120
too long in the dark,
the sea howls,
and the wind,
a shark rises
to tear   125
teeth, jaws; revels in horrors;
too long, too long,
have we propitiated the terror in the sea,
forgotten its beauty.

5

I instil rest;   130
there is no faith and no hope
without sleep;
the poppy-seed is alive to wake
you to another world,
take: 135

take the poppy-seed,
one grain has more worth than fields of ripe grain or barley,

no yield of a thousand and thousand measure,
baskets piled up and pressed down,
no measure running over, can yield   140
such treasure;

He said,
consider the flower of the field;

did he specify
blue or red?   145

6

Too long we prayed
God in the thunder,
wonderful though he be
and our father;

too long, too long in the rain,   150
cowering lest he strike again;

showering peril,
disclosing our evil;

He was right, we knew;
so we fled   155
him in rocks,
cowered from the Power overhead,
ate grass like the ox;

160
we will submit;
yes, we bled,
cut ourselves to propitiate
his wrath;

for we asked,
what, what awaits us,
165
once dead?

we never heard the Magician
we never, never heard what he said.

7

We expected some gesture,
some actor-logic,
170
some turn of the head,
he spoke simply;
we had followed the priest and the answering word
of the people;

to this,
175
was no answer;

we expected some threat or some promise,
some disclosure,
we were not as these others;

but he spoke to the rabble;
180
dead,
dead,
dead were our ears
that heard not, yet heard.

8

A basket,
190
a fish
or fish net,
the knot of the cord
that fastens the boat,
the oar
195
or the rudder,
the board or the sail-cloth,
the wind as it lifts sand and grass,
the grass
and the flower in the grass;

200
the grape,
the grape-leaf,
the half-opened tendril,
the red grape, the white grape, the blue grape,
the size of the wood-vine stock,
205
its roots in the earth,
its bark and its contour,
the shape of the olive,

the goat,
the kid and the lamb,
the sheep,   210
the shepherd,
his wood-pipe,
his hound,
the wild-bird,
the bird untrapped,   215
the bird sold in the market;

the laying of fish on the embers,
the taste of the fish,
the feel of the texture of bread,
the round and the half-loaf,   220
the grain of a petal,
the rain-bow and the rain;

he named these things simply;
sat down at our table,
stood,   225
named salt,
called to a friend;

he named herbs and simples,
what garnish?
a fine taste,   230
he called for some ripe wine;

peeled a plum,
remembered the brass bowl
lest he stain
our host's towel;   235

was courteous,
not over-righteous;
why —
a girl came where he sat,
flung a rose from a basket,   240
and one broke
a fine box
of Cyprian ivory,
(or alabaster)
a rare scent.   245

9

He liked jewels,
the fine feel of white pearls;
he would lift a pearl from a tray,
flatter an Ethiopian merchant
on his taste;   250
lift crystal from Syria,
to the light;

he would see worlds in a crystal
and while we waited for a camel

255
                              or a fine Roman's litter
                              to crowd past,
                              he would tell of the whorl of whorl of light
                              that was infinity to be seen in glass,

                              or a shell
260   or a bead
                              or a pearl.

Continental Interlude II: Dada (1916–21)

Introduction

The first Dada performances began in February 1916 at the Cabaret Voltaire in Zurich. The events consisted largely of readings of poems and stories or the performance of songs, many of them plainly indebted to Futurist theory and practice. The four figures who initiated these were Hugo Ball (1886–1927), a German who was horrified at the outbreak of war and had moved to Switzerland; Richard Huelsenbeck (1892–1974), another German who was a committed pacifist; Tristan Tzara (1896–1963), a Romanian who had also taken refuge in Zurich and there met Ball; and Marcel Janco (1885–1984), a Romanian artist who was Tzara's friend. They were soon joined by a fifth figure, Jean or Hans Arp (1887–1966), a German national from Alsace, but one whose sympathies were French. The works that were written and performed were called *poèmes simultanés* ("simultaneous poems"), and their indebtedness to Futurist notions of simultaneity is palpable. The name Dada was created in April 1916. To Hugo Ball, as a German, the term seemed to indicate a sense of childish pleasure; to the Romanian Tzara it was a homonym with the Slavonic word for "yes," and so meant "yes, yes." *Dada* also means "a rocking horse" in French, the language that Tzara used when speaking with non-Romanians. The first publication of the Dada group, a one-issue periodical called *Cabaret Voltaire*, appeared in June 1916 and was a communal affair. Its successor, the journal *Dada*, was instead controlled by Tzara from the first, and his talents as a promoter soon came into play. He adopted the provocative tones and typography of Futurism, but put them in the service of explosive negations. Dada became a program against programs, an ethics of absolute freedom. When Huelsenbeck left Zurich to return to Berlin at the beginning of 1917, and Hugo Ball retired from all further Dada activity, Tzara found himself the heir of an international movement (for Huelsenbeck was now taking Dada to Berlin) which he now publicized tirelessly. *Dada* 1 appeared in July 1917, *Dada* 2 in December, and *Dada* 3 in late 1918, the latter containing his "Dada Manifesto 1918" (see pp. 479–84 this edition), a series of provocative negations that were an intransigent denial of everything.

In Berlin, Richard Huelsenback gave his first Dada speech in Germany at a meeting in February 1918, followed by a Dadaist manifesto in April signed by Ball, Tzara, the Romanian Marcel Janco, and the Swiss artist Hans Arp, as well as the Germans Raoul Hausmann (1886–1970), Franz Jung (1888–1963), George Grosz (1893–1959), and several Italians including Enrico Prampolini (1884–1956). Other figures who came to play a prominent role in Berlin Dada were Johannes Baader (1875–1955), an unabashed *poseur*, and the two brothers Wieland Herzefelde (1896–1988), who founded the left-wing publishing house Malik, and John Heartfield (1891–1968), a major artist of photomontage. The April manifesto was followed by the formation of Club Dada and a series of short-lived journals: *Club-Dada*, with only one number in 1918, edited by Huelsenbeck, Hausmann, and Jung; *Der Dada*, with three numbers in 1919–20, edited by Hausmann with help from Huelsenback; *Dada Almanach*, with only one number in 1920, edited by Huelsenbeck. There were also *Der Blutige Ernst* (*Deadly Earnest*), with six numbers in 1919, and *Jedermann sein eigner Fußball* (*Every Man His own Football*), both edited by Carl Einstein with photomontages by Heartfield and satirical drawings by Grosz.

On June 30, 1920 the group presented the "First International Dada Fair" in two rooms at the gallery of Dr. Otto Burchardt, the culminating and definitive event of Berlin Dada. Collages by John Heartfield and parodies of classic paintings filled the rooms, many with an antiwar slant. Far more than was true in Zurich, Berlin Dada issued overtly political claims and made use of political and social satire.

There were also small Dada movements in Cologne and Hanover. Cologne Dada was primarily the work of Max Ernst (1891–1976), collaborating with an amateur painter named Johannes Theodor Baargeld (1892–1927) and Jean Arp (1887–1966), who had moved from Zurich to Cologne immediately after the war. *Der Ventilator* was a brief-lived journal edited in 1919 by Baargeld, and *Die Schammade* (one number only) another edited by Ernst. Their most significant features were the extraordinary collages by Ernst and, from the viewpoint of art historians, his development of frottage (a method analogous to brass rubbing, using the grooves and striations of materials such as wood, foliage, or sackcloth to create texture or serve as the basis of design). Dada in Hanover consisted of a single man, Kurt Schwitters (1887–1948), whose principal achievement was to create a massive collage from the detritus of urban culture (bus-tickets, stamps, nails, hair, old catalogues, etc.). His works were all destroyed and are known only through photographs.

Perhaps the most controversial variant of Dada was New York Dada. In the most extreme accounts, New York Dada is said to have been active from 1915 (before Dada had even been invented!) and to have thrived until 1921. The key participants in New York Dada were the French painters Marcel Duchamp and Francis Picabia, acting together with a circle that included the photographer Man Ray and the poet William Carlos Williams, with its center of gravity located in the New York salon of Walter Arensberg. Certainly the New York group, if it can be called that, was not interested in adopting the label until 1921, and then only for a brief period. Whether it is useful to characterize this group with the Dada label is an ongoing subject of debate.

Finally, there was the group that had been more or less abandoned in Zurich, now consisting largely of Tristan Tzara. In early 1920, at the urging of André Breton, Tzara moved to Paris, and for a few months after his arrival there was a series of provocative events, performances, and manifestos. But in 1922 Breton broke with Tzara once and for all, and in effect Paris Dada was dead, as was Dada in all the other cities where it had briefly thrived.

En Avant Dada: A History of Dadaism (1920)
Richard Huelsenbeck

Dada was founded in Zurich in the spring of 1916 by Hugo Ball, Tristan Tzara, Hans Arp, Marcel Janco and Richard Huelsenbeck at the Cabaret Voltaire, a little bar where Hugo Ball and his friend Emmy Hennings had set up a miniature variety show, in which all of us were very active.

We had all left our countries as a result of the war. Ball and I came from Germany, Tzara and Janco from Rumania, Hans Arp from France. We were agreed that the war had been contrived by the various governments for the most autocratic, sordid and materialistic reasons; we Germans were familiar with the book *"J'accuse,"* and even without it we would have had little confidence in the decency of the German Kaiser and his generals. Ball was a conscientious objector, and I had escaped by the skin of my teeth from the pursuit of the police myrmidons who, for their so-called patriotic purposes, were massing men in the trenches of Northern France and giving them shells to eat. None of us had much appreciation for the kind of courage it takes to get shot for the idea of a nation which is at best a cartel of pelt merchants and profiteers in leather, at worst a cultural association of psychopaths who, like the Germans, marched off with a volume of Goethe in their knapsacks, to skewer Frenchmen and Russians on their bayonets.

Arp was an Alsatian; he had lived through the beginning of the war and the whole nationalistic frenzy in Paris, and was pretty well disgusted with all the petty chicanery there, and in general with the sickening changes that had taken place in the city and the people on which we had all squandered our love before the war. Politicians are the same everywhere, flatheaded and vile. Soldiers behave everywhere with the same brisk brutality that is the mortal enemy of every intellectual impulse. The energies and ambitions of those who participated in the Cabaret Voltaire in Zurich were from the start purely artistic. We wanted to make the Cabaret Voltaire a focal point of the "newest art," although we did not neglect from time to time to tell the fat and utterly uncomprehending Zurich philistines that we regarded them as pigs and the German Kaiser as the initiator of the war. Then there was always a big fuss, and the students, who in Switzerland as elsewhere are the stupidest and most reactionary rabble – if in view of the compulsory national stultification in that country any group of citizens can claim a right to the superlative in that respect – at any rate the students gave a preview of the public resistance which Dada was later to encounter on its triumphant march through the world.

The word Dada was accidentally discovered by Hugo Ball and myself in a German-French dictionary, as we were looking for a name for Madame le Roy, the chanteuse at our cabaret. Dada is French for a wooden horse. It is impressive in its brevity and suggestiveness. Soon Dada became the signboard for all the art that we launched in the Cabaret Voltaire. By "newest art," we then meant by and large, abstract art. Later the idea behind the word Dada was to undergo a considerable change. While the Dadaists of the Allied countries, under the leadership of Tristan Tzara, still

First published as *En Avant Dada: Eine Geschichte des Dadaismus* (Hannover, Leipzig, Vienna, Zurich: Paul Steegmann Verlag, 1920). Translated complete from the German by Ralph Manheim, and first published in Robert Motherwell (ed.), *The Dada Painters and Poets: An Anthology* (New York: Wittenborn, Schultz, 1951). The entire volume was reprinted by Harvard University Press in 1981.

make no great distinction between Dadaism and *"l'art abstrait,"* in Germany, where the psychological background of our type of activity is entirely different from that in Switzerland, France and Italy, Dada assumed a very definite political character, which we shall discuss at length later.

The Cabaret Voltaire group were all artists in the sense that they were keenly sensitive to newly developed artistic possibilities. Ball and I had been extremely active in helping to spread expressionism in Germany; Ball was an intimate friend of Kandinsky,[1] in collaboration with whom he had attempted to found an expressionistic theatre in Munich. Arp in Paris had been in close contact with Picasso and Braque,[2] the leaders of the cubist movement, and was thoroughly convinced of the necessity of combatting naturalist conception in any form. Tristan Tzara, the romantic internationalist whose propagandistic zeal we have to thank for the enormous growth of Dada, brought with him from Rumania an unlimited literary facility. In that period, as we danced, sang and recited night after night in the Cabaret Voltaire, abstract art was for us tantamount to absolute honor. Naturalism was a psychological penetration of the motives of the bourgeois, in whom we saw our mortal enemy, and psychological penetration, despite all efforts at resistance, brings an identification with the various precepts of bourgeois morality. Archipenko,[3] whom we honored as an unequalled model in the field of plastic art, maintained that art must be neither realistic nor idealistic, it must be true; and by this he meant above all that any imitation of nature, however concealed, is a lie. In this sense, Dada was to give the truth a new impetus. Dada was to be a rallying point for abstract energies and a lasting slingshot for the great international artistic movements.

Through Tzara we were also in relation with the futurist movement and carried on a correspondence with Marinetti. By that time Boccioni[4] had been killed, but all of us knew his thick book, *Pittura e scultura futuriste*. We regarded Marinetti's[5] position as realistic, and were opposed to it, although we were glad to take over the concept of simultaneity, of which he made so much use. Tzara for the first time had poems recited simultaneously on the stage, and these performances were a great success, although the *poème simultané* had already been introduced in France by Derème[6] and others. From Marinetti we also borrowed "bruitism," or noise music, *le concert bruitiste*, which, of blessed memory, had created such a stir at the first appearance of the futurists in Milan, where they had regaled the audience with *le reveil de la capitale*. I spoke on the significance of bruitism at a number of open Dada gatherings.

"Le bruit," noise with imitative effects, was introduced into art (in this connection we can hardly speak of individual arts, music or literature) by Marinetti, who used a chorus of typewriters, kettledrums, rattles and pot-covers to suggest the "awakening of the capital"; at first it was intended as nothing more than a rather violent reminder of the colorfulness of life. In contrast to the cubists or for that matter the German expressionists, the futurists regarded themselves as pure activists. While all "abstract artists" maintained the position that a table is not the wood and nails it is made of but the idea of all tables, and forgot that a table could be used to put things on, the futurists wanted to immerse themselves in the "angularity" of things – for them the table signified a utensil for living, and so did everything else. Along with tables there were houses, frying-pans, urinals, women, etc. Consequently Marinetti and his group love war as the highest expression of the conflict of things, as a spontaneous eruption of possibilities, as movement, as a simultaneous poem, as a symphony of cries, shots, commands, embodying an attempted solution of the problem of life in motion. The problem of the soul is volcanic in nature. Every movement naturally produces noise. While number, and consequently melody, are symbols presupposing a faculty for abstraction, noise is a direct call to action. Music of whatever nature is harmonious, artistic, an activity of reason – but bruitism is life itself, it cannot be judged like a book, but rather it is a part of our personality,

[1] Wassily Kandinsky (1866–1944) was a Russian painter who lived in Munich, then in Weimar, and finally in Paris.

[2] Pablo Picasso (1881–1973) and Georges Braque (1882–1963) pioneered Cubism during the period 1909–14.

[3] Alexander Arichpenko (1887–1964) was a Russian sculptor who worked in Paris till 1923, and thereafter in the United States.

[4] Umberto Boccioni (1882–1916), Italian Futurist painter and theoretician who published *Pittura scultura futuriste* (*Futurist Painting Sculpture*) (Milan: Edizioni futuriste di "Poesia") in 1914. For more on Futurism, see pp. 1–38.

[5] F. T. Marinetti (1887–1944), founder of Futurism and aesthetic theoretician. On Futurism see pp. 1–38.

[6] Tristan Derème (1889–1941) was a French poet.

which attacks us, pursues us and tears us to pieces. Bruitism is a view of life, which, strange as it may seem at first, compels men to make an ultimate decision. There are only bruitists, and others. While we are speaking of music, Wagner[7] had shown all the hypocrisy inherent in a pathetic faculty for abstraction – the screeching of a brake, on the other hand, could at least give you a toothache. In modern Europe, the same initiative which in America made ragtime a national music, led to the convulsion of bruitism.

Bruitism is a kind of return to nature. It is the music produced by circuits of atoms; death ceases to be an escape of the soul from earthly misery and becomes a vomiting, screaming and choking. The Dadaists of the Cabaret Voltaire took over bruitism without suspecting its philosophy – basically they desired the opposite: calming of the soul, an endless lullaby, art, abstract art. The Dadaists of the Cabaret Voltaire actually had no idea what they wanted – the wisps of "modern art" that at some time or other had clung to the minds of these individuals were gathered together and called "Dada." Tristan Tzara was devoured by ambition to move in international artistic circles as an equal or even a "leader." He was all ambition and restlessness. For his restlessness he sought a pole and for his ambition a ribbon. And what an extraordinary, never-to-be-repeated opportunity now arose to found an artistic movement and play the part of a literary mime! The passion of an aesthete is absolutely inaccessible to the man of ordinary concepts, who calls a dog a dog and a spoon a spoon. What a source of satisfaction it is to be denounced as a wit in a few cafés in Paris, Berlin, Rome! The history of literature is a grotesque imitation of world events, and a Napoleon among men of letters is the most tragi-comic character conceivable. Tristan Tzara had been one of the first to grasp the suggestive power of the word Dada. From here on he worked indefatigably as the prophet of a word, which only later was to be filled with a concept. He wrapped, pasted, addressed, he bombarded the French and Italians with letters; slowly he made himself the "focal point." We do not wish to belittle the fame of the *fondateur du Dadaisme* any more than that of *Oberdada* (Chief Dada) Baader,[8] a Swabian pietist, who at the brink of old age, discovered Dadaism and journeyed through the countryside as a Dadaist prophet, to the delight of all fools. In the Cabaret Voltaire period, we wanted to "document" – we brought out the publication *Cabaret Voltaire*, a catch-all for the most diverse directions in art, which at that time seemed to us to constitute "Dada." None of us suspected what Dada might really become, for none of us understood enough about the times to free ourselves from traditional views and form a conception of art as a moral and social phenomenon. Art just was – there were artists and bourgeois. You had to love one and hate the other.

Yet despite everything, the artist as Tzara conceived him was something other than the German *dichter*. Guillaume Apollinaire[9] jokingly claimed that his father had been a doorman in the Vatican; I suspect that Apollinaire was born in a Galician ghetto and became a Frenchman because he saw that Paris was the best place to make literature. The literary jobber is not the most deplorable figure created by the International of the mind. How much liberating honesty and decent shamelessness it takes to construe literature as a business. The litterati have their thieves' honor and their high-signs – in international trade, in the corners of hotel lobbies, in the *Mitropa*[10] dining cars, the mask of the spirit is quickly dropped, there is too little time to dress up in an ideology that might appeal to other people. Manolescu, the great hotel thief, has written memoirs which, in point of diction and *esprit*, stand higher than all the German memoirs that have been brought forth by the war. Elasticity is everything. Marinetti has a good deal of the great literary magician of the future, who plays golf as well as he chats about Mallarmé,[11] or, when necessary, makes remarks about ancient philology, yet at the same time is perfectly well aware which lady present it is safe to make a pass at.

---

7   Richard Wagner (1813–83), German composer of classical music.

8   See the "Introduction" to this section.

9   Guillaume Apollinaire (1880–1918), a leading figure of the French avant-garde and journalist who wrote extensively on contemporary art.

10   A food service company that ran dining cars on trains and cafés at train stations.

11   Stéphan Mallarmé (1842–98), French Symbolist poet.

The German *dichter*[12] is the typical dope, who carries around with him an academic concept of "spirit," writes poems about communism, Zionism, socialism, as the need arises, and is positively amazed at the powers the Muse has given him. The German *dichter* has taken out a mortgage on literature. He thinks everything has to be as it is. He does not understand what a gigantic humbug the world has made of the "spirit" and that this is a good thing. In his head there is a hierarchy, with the inartistic man, which amounts to more or less the same as the uneducated, at the bottom and the man of the spirit, the Schillerian Hasenclever, yearning for the ethereal, at the top. That's how it is and that's how it's got to be. Just listen to old Schopenhauer[13] in his *Parerga* telling us how stuck-up the German is about his culture, and, if you are anything of a psychologist you will see how comic and utterly hopeless is the situation of the German *dichter*. The German *dichter* who means violet even when he says bloodhound, the philistine over all philistines, the born abstractionist, the expressionist – surely that wasn't what Tzara wanted when he made Dadaism an abstract direction in art, but he never really understood what it meant to make literature with a gun in hand.

To make literature with a gun in hand, had for a time, been my dream. To be something like a robber-baron of the pen, a modern Ulrich von Hutten[14] – that was my picture of a Dadaist. The Dadaist should have nothing but contempt for those who have made a Tusculum of the "spirit," a refuge for their own weaknesses. The philosopher in the garret was thoroughly obsolete – but so was the professional artist, the café litterateur, the society "wit," in general the man who could be moved in any way by intellectual accomplishment, who in intellectual matters found a welcome limitation which in his opinion gave him a special value before other men – the Dadaist as far as possible was to be the opposite of these. These men of the spirit sat in the cities, painted their little pictures, ground out their verses, and in their whole human structure they were hopelessly deformed, with weak muscles, without interest in the things of the day, enemies of the advertisement, enemies of the street, of bluff, of the big transactions which every day menaced the lives of thousands. Of life itself. But the Dadaist loves life, because he can throw it away every day; for him death is a Dadaist affair. The Dadaist looks forward to the day, fully aware that a flowerpot may fall on his head, he is naive, he loves the noises of the Métro, he likes to hang around Cook's travel bureau,[15] and knows the practices of the angelmakers who behind closely drawn curtains dry out foetuses on blotting paper, in order to grind them up and sell them as ersatz coffee.

Everyone can be a Dadaist. Dada is not limited to any art. The bartender in the Manhattan Bar, who pours out Curaçao with one hand and gathers up his gonorrhea with the other, is a Dadaist. The gentleman in the raincoat, who is about to start his seventh trip around the world, is a Dadaist. The Dadaist should be a man who has fully understood that one is entitled to have ideas only if one can transform them into life – the completely active type, who lives only through action, because it holds the possibility of his achieving knowledge. A Dadaist is the man who rents a whole floor at the Hotel Bristol without knowing where the money is coming from to tip the chambermaid. A Dadaist is the man of chance with the good eye and the rabbit punch. He can fling away his individuality like a lasso, he judges each case for itself, he is resigned to the realization that the world at one and the same time includes Mohammedans, Zwinglians, fifth formers, Anabaptists, pacifists, etc., etc. The motley character of the world is welcome to him but no source of surprise. In the evening the band plays by the lakeshore, and the whores tripping along on their high heels laugh into your face. It's a fucked-up foolish world. You walk aimlessly along, fixing up a philosophy for supper. But before you have it ready, the mailman brings you the first telegram, announcing that all your pigs have died of rabies, your dinner jacket has been thrown off the Eiffel Tower, your housekeeper has come down with the epizootic. You give a startled look at the moon,

---

[12]   German for "poet."

[13]   Arthur Schopenhauer (1788–1860) was a German philosopher who wrote *Parerga and Paralipomena: kleine philosophische Scriften*, 2 vols. (Berlin: A. W. Hahn, 1851), a collection of smaller essays in which he offered his opinions on miscellaneous subjects. In English, see his *Parerga and Paralipomena: Short Philosophical Essays*, 2 vols., trans E. F. G. Payne (Oxford: Oxford University Press, 1974).

[14]   Ulrich von Hutten (1488–1523) was a German writer who repeatedly offended his patrons, then attacked them with satire. In 1519 he took part in a war that overthrew Ulrich, Duke of Wittemberg.

[15]   The Métro is the name of the subway system in Paris; Cook's is an English travel firm with offices throughout Europe.

which seems to you like a good investment, and the same postman brings you a telegram announcing that all your chickens have died of hoof and mouth disease, your father has fallen on a pitchfork and frozen to death, your mother has burst with sorrow on the occasion of her silver wedding (maybe the frying pan stuck to her ears, how do I know?). That's life, my dear fellow. The days progress in the rhythm of your bowels and you, who have so often been in peril of choking on a fishbone, are still alive. You pull the covers up over your head and whistle the "Hohenfriedber-ger."[16] And who knows, don't gloat too soon, perhaps the next day will see you at your desk, your pen ready for the thrust, bent over your new novel, *Rabble*. Who knows? That is pure Dadaism, ladies and gentlemen.

If Tristan Tzara had barely suspected the meaning of this famous existence we drag along between apes and bedbugs, he would have seen the fraud of all art and all artistic movements and he would have become a Dadaist. Where have these gentlemen who are so eager to appear in the history of literature left their irony? Where is the eye that weeps and laughs at the gigantic rump and carnival of this world? Buried in books, they have lost their independence, the ambition to be as famous as Rabelais or Flaubert has robbed them of the courage to laugh – there is so much marching, writing, living to be done. Rimbaud[17] jumped in the ocean and started to swim to St. Helena, Rimbaud was a hell of a guy, they sit in the cafés and rack their brains over the quickest way of getting to be a hell of a guy. They have an academic conception of life – all litterati are Germans; and for that very reason they will never get close to life. Rimbaud very well understood that literature and art are mighty suspicious things – and how well a man can live as a pasha or a brothel-owner, as the creaking of the beds sings a song of mounting profits.

In Tzara's hands Dadaism achieved great triumphs. The Dadaists wrote books that were bought all over Europe; they put on shows to which thousands flocked. The world press adopted the Dada movement in art. A new sensation, ladies and gentlemen. In the hands of men who were no Dadaists, Dada became an immense sensation in Europe; it touched the soul of the true European who is at home between the pistons and boilers of machines, who hardly looks up from the *Daily News* when you meet him in Charing Cross Station,[18] whom you find in fashionable tweeds on the decks of Red Star liners, with a pipeful of shag dangling nonchalantly from between his gold fillings.

Dada knew how to set the big rotary presses in motion, it was discussed in the Ecole de France and in the books of the psycho-analysts; in Madrid they tried to understand it, in Chile they tore each other's hair out over it, even in Chicago, with the grain exchange made famous by Frank Norris, there appeared for a moment as on a great eerie screen, the word Dada.

During the past decades in Europe, no word, no concept, no philosophy, no slogan of party or sect can be said to have burst upon the imagination of a civilized society with such catastrophic force. Do not forget the profound psychological significance of this fact. In the minds of all these people at the cafés, theatres, race tracks, brothels, who were interested in Dadaism because they regarded it as a "ridiculous product of modern artistic madness," Dada had long since ceased to be a movement in art. You need to be a professor of philosophy with a catheter[19] at Berlin University not to see that ninety-nine out of a hundred people care as much about movements, individual techniques, perspectives in art, as the legendary cow about Easter Sunday. It did not interest them and was not even known to them that Dada, which did have an effect, however imponderable, upon them, had something to do with art and originated in art. A word which affects the masses so profoundly must embody an idea that touches the most vital interests of these masses, shaming, frightening or encouraging them in their innermost soul. That is why it is so incomprehensible that this Tristan Tzara, who out of childish ambition passes himself off as the inventor of Dada, should try to bind Dada to abstract art; such an attempt represents a total failure to understand things both near and far; he fails to see the possibilities of the birth, life and death of an idea, or to understand the significance that an *ens spirituale*, a *fluidum*[20] (whether expressed in a word, concept

---

[16] A marching song said to have been composed by Frederick the Great.

[17] Arthur Rimbaud (1854–91), French Symbolist poet.

[18] A railway station in central London which is a terminus for many suburban lines.

[19] A pun on the similarity of Katheder (professor's chair) and Katheter (catheter).

[20] "A spiritual being," a "fluid" in Latin.

or idea) can assume for a little circle of art-jobbers and a startled continent looking up from its work.

What Dada was in the beginning and how it developed is utterly unimportant in comparison with what it has come to mean in the mind of Europe. Dada has operated – not as mild suasion but like a thunderbolt, not like a system set down in a book, which through the channel of superior minds, after years of chewing and rechewing, becomes the universal possession of the nations, but like a watchword passed on by heralds on horseback. The immense effect of Dadaism on the great mass of the artistically indifferent lay in the senseless and comic character of the word Dada, and it would seem that this effect, in turn, must derive from some profound psychological cause, connected with the whole structure of "humanity" today and its present social organization. The average man, Smith, Schulze, Dupin, nature's famous mass-production ware, who disarms all intellectual evaluation, but with which nevertheless all psychological insight begins, heard that Dada was babies' prattle, that there were men who "made a business" of this prattle – that apparently some lunatics "wanted to start a party" based on the whimperings of the suckling babe. They held their sides laughing, they'd seen a good deal in their time, but this, well, all you can say is – (well, what can you say?) nix, nix, nix. Messrs. Schulze, Smith and Dupin felt themselves strongly reminded by Dada of their milk bottle and honorably soiled diapers, now a generation behind them, and of the cry which was now to bring happiness into the world. Dada, Dada, Dada.

That is what I meant by the suggestivity of the word Dada, its ability to hypnotize, by guiding the vulgar mind to ideas and things which none of its originators had thought of. To be sure, the choice of the word Dada in the Cabaret Voltaire was selective-metaphysical, predetermined by all the idea-energies with which it was now acting upon the world – but no one had thought of Dada as babies' prattle. It is a rare gift of God to be present at the birth of a religion, or of any idea which later conquers the world. Even though Dada is not (I say this to reassure all German high-school students and academic donkeys), thank God, an idea in the "progressive-cultural" sense celebrated in all historical compendia, but has a thoroughly ephemeral character, in that it has no desire to be anything more than a mirror which one quickly passes by, or a poster which in the harshest colors of the moment calls your attention to some opportunity to get rid of your money or fill your belly. Psychologically speaking! If you have had the miraculous good fortune to be present at the birth of such a "sensation," you will want to understand how it happens that an empty sound, first intended as a surname for a female singer, has developed amid grotesque adventures into a name for a rundown cabaret, then into abstract art, baby-talk and a party of babies at the breast, and finally – well, I shall not anticipate. This is exactly the history of Dadaism. Dada came over the Dadaists without their knowing it; it was an immaculate conception, and thereby its profound meaning was revealed to me.

The history of Dadaism is indeed one of the most interesting psychological events of the last twenty-five years; one need only have eyes to see and ears to hear. In the hands of the gentlemen in Zurich, Dada grew up into a creature which stood head and shoulders above all those present; and soon its existence could no longer be arranged with the precision demanded by a businesslike conduct of the Dadaist movement in art. Despite the most impassioned efforts, no one had yet found out exactly what Dada was. Tzara and Ball founded a "gallery" in which they exhibited Dadaistic art, i.e., "modern" art, which for Tzara meant non-objective, abstract art. But as I have said, abstract art was very old hat. Years before, Picasso had given up perspective as the expression of an intellectual and penetrating world conception, in favor of that archaizing, mathematical representation of space which, with Braque, he designated as cubism. There was something in the air of ageing Europe that demanded an attempt, by a last effort of the will, deriving its impulse from the knowledge of all cultures and artistic techniques, to return to the old intuitive possibilities, from which, it was realized, the various styles had emanated hundreds of years ago. It is no accident that the Latin peoples included in their program the mystic elements of Euclidean geometry, the conic sections and mathematical quantities, in so far as they were symbols of tangible bodies, while the Germans made the academic concept of intuition, in the form of expressionism, the signboard for their artistic barber shop. The Latins, with their last strength, directed their abstractionism toward something universally valid, something determined amid the indeterminate, which presupposed a personality that would treat the transcendental with inborn tact and moderation; while the Germans with their expressionism evoked the immeasurable eternalization of the subjective individual, giving free play to the *kolossal* and the grotesque, manifested in the arbitrary distortion of anatomical proportions.

The Galérie Dada capriciously exhibited cubist, expressionist and futurist pictures; it carried on its little art business at literary teas, lectures and recitation evenings, while the word Dada conquered the world. It was something touching to behold. Day after day the little group sat in its café, reading aloud the critical comments that poured in from every possible country, and which by their tone of indignation showed that Dada had struck someone to the heart. Stricken dumb with amazement, we basked in our glory. Tristan Tzara could think of nothing else to do but write manifesto after manifesto, speaking of *"l'art nouveau,* which is neither futurism nor cubism," but Dada. But what was Dada? *"Dada,"* came the answer, *"ne signifie rien."*[21] With psychological astuteness, the Dadaists spoke of energy and will and assured the world that they had amazing plans. But concerning the nature of these plans, no information whatever was forthcoming.

Incommensurable values are conquering the world. If someone hurls a word into the crowd, accompanying it with a grand gesture, they make a religion of it. *Credo, quia absurdum.* Dada, as a mere word, actually conquered a large part of the world, even without association with any personality. This was an almost magical event. The true meaning of Dadaism was recognized only later in Germany by the people who were zealously propagating it, and these people, succumbing to the aggressive power and propagandistic force of the word, then became Dadaists. In Berlin they founded the Dada Club, which will be discussed below. The gentlemen of the Galérie Dada apparently noticed that their own stature was not consistent with the success of Dadaism. Things came to such a pass that they borrowed pictures from the Berlin art-dealer Herwarth Walden[22] (who for a long time had been making money out of abstract art theories) and passed them off on the Swiss puddingheads as something extraordinary. In literature primitive tendencies were pursued. They read mediaeval prose, and Tzara ground out Negro verses which he palmed off as accidentally discovered remains of a Bantu or Winnetu culture, again to the great amazement of the Swiss. It was a dismal collection of Dadaists.

As I think back on it now, an art for art's sake mood lay over the Galérie Dada – it was a manicure salon of the fine arts, characterized by tea-drinking old ladies trying to revive their vanishing sexual powers with the help of "something mad." The Galérie Dada was an antechamber of ambition, where the beginners in the humbug of art had to accustom themselves to looking up to the leaders with the fish-eyed veneration found in Werfel's[23] poems, when he sings of God, nature and spirit. The Galérie Dada was a small and cluttered kitchen of literary conventions, where no one experienced the slightest shame as long as he had a by-line. The gentlemen were all international, members of that League of the Spirit which at the decisive moment was such a catastrophe for Europe, two-dimensional, planimetric creatures, who had no sense of the compromise necessary to artistic activity in the restricted sense.

There might have been a way to make something of the situation. The group did nothing, and garnered success. They produced something, anything, and saw that the world was ready to pay high prices. It was a situation made to order for the racketeers of art and the spirit. But none of the gentlemen who sold abstract art in the Galérie Dada understood this, or else they did not want to understand it. Tzara did not want to give up his position as an artist within the abstract Myth, for the position of leadership he longed for had come tangibly near; and Ball, the founder of the Cabaret Voltaire (incidentally a far-sighted fellow) was too honorable, too Roman Catholic, too something. Both had insufficient insight into the possibilities of Dadaism; they lacked psychological astuteness. The Dadaist as racketeer, as Manolescu:[24] this aspect reappeared.

[21] "Signifies nothing," in French; see p. 480.

[22] Herwarth Walden (1878–1941) ran a Berlin art gallery and publishing house, *Der Sturm* ("The Storm"), that was at the center of avant-garde activity during the years before the First World War.

[23] Franz Werfel (1890–1945), a German expressionist poet.

[24] Georges Manolescu, who defrauded many people under the pseudonym "Prince Lahovary," wrote an engaging memoir titled *Ein Fürst der Diebe (A Prince of Thievery)* (Berlin: Langenschedt, 1905), a work that was very popular in German-speaking areas in the years before the First World War.

The dissatisfaction ended in a battle between Tzara and Ball, a real bullfight among Dadaists, carried on, as such fights always are, with every resource of impertinence, falsification and physical brutality. Ball remembered his inward nature, withdrew definitively from Dada and from all art, and began to become a democrat in Bern, and in this, it seems to me, he has been very successful. Tzara and his supporters fell for a time into a stunned silence and then (since Dada was doing well in the world even without them) they plunged with renewed zeal into *l'art nouveau, l'art abstrait*. Tzara began to publish the magazine *Dada*, which found its way into every country in Europe and was widely purchased. We saw it in Germany, and it impressed us as commercial art and nothing else. The contributors included, aside from the Zurich Dadaists, all the familiar names of the International of ultra-modern literature. Among many, I shall mention Francis Picabia,[25] whom I deeply respect; at that time he was already contributing to Guillaume Apollinaire's famous *Soirées de Paris*,[26] and is said to have stood to this periodical, which for a time played a leading role, in the relationship of the rich man to the lavatory attendant. Apollinaire, Marie Laurençin – the good Henry Rousseau who up to his death played the *Marseillaise* at home: old Paris came to life.[27]

Now it has died for good. Today it is the stamping ground of Messrs. Foch and Millerand;[28] Apollinaire died of influenza. Picabia is in New York – old Paris is done for. But very recently Dada turned up there in person. After exhausting all the Dadaistic possibilities in Zurich, after attempting in vain, by admitting Serner[29] into his circle, to put new life into its ideas (after a good many more sensational performances and Dadaist parades), Tzara arrived in the city where Napoleon is supposed to have said that literature wasn't worth a pile of dung to him. Napoleon had stood at the foot of the Pyramids; Tzara managed immediately to turn the magazine *Littérature*[30] into a Dadaist organ; he staged a great opening at which bruitist concerts and simultaneous poems made a terrific impression; he had himself enthroned, anointed and elected pope of the world Dada movement. Dada had conquered. Picasso and Marinetti must have felt rather strange when they heard of the success of their ideas under the name of "Dada." I fear that they were not Dadaist enough to understand Dada. But Picabia, who year after year, had watched the whole fraud pass him by, was not surprised. He had been a Dadaist before Tzara had let him in on the secret wisdom of Dadaism; his great wealth (his father was governor of Chile, Martinique or Cuba) permitted him to maintain a personal physician who was continually running after him with a loaded hypodermic. Francis Picabia is married to Gabriele Buffet, the daughter of a Paris deputy, and as my good friend Hans Arp (whom, in passing, I exempt from all my attacks on the Zurich Dadaists, and whose works, as an expression of his lovable personality, are most welcome to me) tells me, he loves violet waistcoats, smokes Chilean imports, and sometimes takes a glass of sarsaparilla for his imaginary or inherited lues. Tzara is in Paris; Picabia is back in New York. In the countries of the Allies, including the United States, Dada has been victorious. Before we leave it to its own resources and in particular take our leave of Tzara, and turn to Germany, I should like to say a few words about simultaneity, which those interested in Dada will encounter in all Dadaist performances and all Dadaist publications.

Simultaneity (first used by Marinetti in this literary sense) is an abstraction, a concept referring to the occurrence of different events at the same time. It presupposes a heightened sensitivity to the passage of things in time, it turns the sequence $a = b = c = d$ into an a—b—c—d, and attempts to transform the problem of the ear into a problem of the face. Simultaneity is against what has become, and for what is becoming. While I, for example, become successively aware that I boxed an old woman on the ear yesterday and washed my hands an hour ago, the screeching of a streetcar

---

[25] Francis Picabia (1879–1953), French painter who also wrote many essays.

[26] A journal that Guillaume Apollinaire (1880–1918) founded and edited for one year, 1912.

[27] Marie Lawrencin (1885–1956) was a French painter and a friend of Apollinaire; Henri Rousseau (1844–1910) was a French artist whose naive painting was celebrated by Apollinaire and other critics.

[28] Ferdinand Foch (1851–1929) was named Chief of the General Staff in France in 1918, given overall command of the Allied forces; Alexandre Millerand (1859–1943) was the French Minister of War (1912) and was elected president of France in 1920.

[29] Walter Serner (1889–1942) was a writer with the Dada movement in Zurich and Geneva.

[30] A literary journal founded by André Breton, Louis Aragon, and Philippe Soupault in 1919, which carried on until 1924. For its first three years, 1919–22, it was sympathetic to Dada, and thereafter was hostile.

brake and the crash of a brick falling off the roof next door reach my ear simultaneously and my (outward or inward) eye rouses itself to seize, in the simultaneity of these events, a swift meaning of life. From the everyday events surrounding me (the big city, the Dada circus, crashing, screeching, steam whistles, house fronts, the smell of roast veal), I obtain an impulse which starts me toward direct action, becoming the big X. I become directly aware that I am alive, I feel the form-giving force behind the bustling of the clerks in the Dresdner Bank and the simple-minded erectness of the policeman.

Simultaneity is a direct reminder of life, and very closely bound up with bruitism. Just as physics distinguishes between tones (which can be expressed in mathematical formulae) and noises, which are completely baffling to its symbolism and abstractionism, because they are a direct objectivization of dark vital force, here the distinction is between a succession and a "simultaneity," which defies formulation because it is a direct symbol of action. And so ultimately a simultaneous poem means nothing but "Hurrah for life!" These problems are long chains. Simultaneity brings me, without feeling that I have taken a long leap, to "the new medium" in painting, which was enthusiastically touted by the Dadaists under Tzara as the *non plus ultra* of the "most modern" painting.

The introduction of the new medium has a certain metaphysical value, it is in a sense a transcendental revulsion against empty space, the result of the fear that is a part of the psychological foundation of all art and must be considered, in this special case, as a kind of *horror vacui*.[31] The concept of reality is a highly variable value, and entirely dependent on the brain and the requirements of the brain which considers it. When Picasso gave up perspective, he felt that it was a set of rules that had been arbitrarily thrown over "nature": the parallels which cross on the horizon are a deplorable deception – behind them lies the infinity of space, which can never be measured. Consequently he restricted his painting to the foreground, he abandoned depth, freed himself from the morality of a plastic philosophy, recognized the conditionality of optical laws, which governed his eye in a particular country at a particular time; he sought a new, direct reality – he became, to use a vulgar term, non-objective. He wanted to paint no more men, women, donkeys and high-school students, since they partook of the whole system of deception, the theatre and the *blague* of existence–and at the same time he felt that painting with oil was a very definite symbol of a very definite culture and morality. He invented the new medium. He began to stick sand, hair, post-office forms and pieces of newspaper onto his pictures, to give them the value of a direct reality, removed from everything traditional. He well understood the ideal, slick, harmonious quality inherent in perspective and in oil painting; he sensed the Schillerian cadence[32] that speaks out of every portrait, and the falsehood of the "landscape" produced by the sentimentality of oil painting.

Perspective and the color which, separated from its natural efficacy, can be squeezed out of tubes, are means of imitating nature; they run at the heels of things and have given up the actual struggle with life; they are shareholders in the cowardly and smug philosophy that belongs to the bourgeoisie. The new medium, on the other hand, points to the absolutely self-evident that is within reach of our hands, to the natural and naive, to action. The new medium stands in a direct relation to simultaneity and bruitism. With the new medium the picture, which as such remains always the symbol of an unattainable reality, has literally taken a decisive step forward, that is, it has taken an enormous step from the horizon across the foreground; it participates in life itself. The sand, pieces of wood, hair that have been pasted on, give it the same kind of reality as a statue of the idol Moloch, in whose glowing arms child sacrifices are laid.[33] The new medium is the road from yearning to the reality of little things, and this road is abstract. Abstraction (Tzara & Co. stubbornly refused to see this) is by its function a movement, not a goal. A pair of pants is after all more important than the solemn emotion that we situate in the upper regions of a Gothic cathedral "when it enfolds us."

The appropriation by Dada of these three principles, bruitism, simultaneity and, in painting, the new medium, is of course the "accident" leading to the psychological factors to which the real Dadaist movement owed its existence. As I have said, I find in the Dadaism of Tzara and his friends,

---

[31]   "Horror of the void," in Latin.

[32]   A lyrical cadence of the sort used by the German poet Friedrich Schiller (1759–1805).

[33]   A monstrous idol to whom children were sacrificed, recounted in the Old Testament in I Kings 7.

who made abstract art the cornerstone of their new wisdom, no new idea deserving of very strenuous propaganda. They failed to advance along the abstract road, which ultimately leads from the painted surface to the reality of a post-office form. No sooner had they left the old, sentimental standpoint than they looked behind them, though still spurred on by ambition. They are neither fish nor flesh. In Germany Dadaism became political, it drew the ultimate consequences of its position and renounced art completely.

Yet it would be ungrateful to take leave of Tzara without tipping our hats. I have in my hand *Dadaphone*,[34] a publication recently put out by the Paris Dadaists. It contains the photographs of the presidents of Entente Dadaism: André Breton, Louis Aragon, Francis Picabia, Céline Arnauld, Paul Eluard, G. Ribemont-Dessaignes, Philippe Soupault, Paul Dermée, Tristan Tzara. All very nice and harmless-looking gentlemen with pince-nez, horn-rimmed glasses and monocles, with flowing ties, faithful eyes and significant gestures, who can be seen from a distance to belong to literature. A Dadaist monster demonstration is announced, the program including a "Manifeste cannibale dans l'obscurité" (Cannibal manifesto in darkness) by Francis Picabia and a "Dadaphone" by Tristan Tzara. All this is exceedingly gay. Picabia addresses the public: *"Que faîtes-vous ici, parqués comme des huîtres sérieuses – car vous êtes sérieux, n'est-ce pas? Le cul, le cul représente la vie comme les pommes frites et vous tous qui êtes sérieux, vous sentirez plus mauvais que la merde de vache. Dada lui ne sent rien, il n'est rien, rien, rien. Sifflez, criez, cassez-moi la gueule, et puis, et puis? Je vous dirai encore que vous êtes tous des poires."*[35] This was more than the Paris bourgeoisie in this moment of nationalistic fervor would stand for. The big newspapers went into the matter at length. In *Le Temps*, March 30, 1920, I find: *"La décadence intellectuelle est l'un des effets de la guerre. La guerre a fortifié les forts; elle a pu pervertir les pervers et abêtir les sots. Mais les vaincus eux-mêmes se protègent contre ces souffles malsains. Il est singulier de voir qu'en France des jeunes gens ('Proche-orientaux') les respirent avec satisfaction et qu'il se rencontre des gens moins jeunes pour les encourager dans cette tentative d'empoisonnement."*[36] *Dadaphone* announces a Dadaist exhibition, a Dadaist ball, a large number of Dadaist periodicals, most of which are probably a pious wish on the part of the editor of *Dadaphone*; in short, *une vie dadaïque extraordinaire* has blossomed out at Tzara's instigation.

In January 1917 I returned to Germany, the face of which had meanwhile undergone a fantastic change. I felt as though I had left a smug fat idyll for a street full of electric signs, shouting hawkers and auto horns. In Zurich the international profiteers sat in the restaurants with well-filled wallets and rosy cheeks, ate with their knives and smacked their lips in a merry hurrah for the countries that were bashing each other's skulls in. Berlin was the city of tightened stomachers, of mounting, thundering hunger, where hidden rage was transformed into a boundless money lust, and men's minds were concentrating more and more on questions of naked existence. Here we would have to proceed with entirely different methods, if we wanted to say something to the people. Here we would have to discard our patent leather pumps and tie our Byronic cravats to the doorpost. While in Zurich people lived as in a health resort, chasing after the ladies and longing for nightfall that would bring pleasure barges, magic lanterns and music by Verdi, in Berlin you never knew where the next meal was coming from. Fear was in everybody's bones, everybody had a feeling that the big deal launched by Hindenburg & Co.[37] was going to turn out very badly. The people had an exalted and romantic attitude towards art and all cultural values. A phenomenon familiar in German history was again manifested: Germany always becomes the land of poets and thinkers when it begins to be washed up as the land of judges and butchers.

In 1917 the Germans were beginning to give a great deal of thought to their souls. This was only a natural defense on the part of a society that had been harassed, milked dry, and driven to

[34]   *Dadaphone* was a journal that had only a single issue, published in 1920, and consisting of eight pages.

[35]   "What are you doing here, plunked down like serious oysters – because you are serious, aren't you? The ass, the ass represents life like fried potatoes, and all you serious people will smell worse than cow-flop. Dada smells of nothing, it is nothing, nothing, nothing. Whistle, shout, bash my face in, and then what? Then what? I'll just go on telling you that you're all fools."

[36]   "Intellectual decadence is one of the effects of the war. The war has strengthened the strong; it has also perverted the perverts and stupefied the stupid. But even the vanquished defend themselves against these unhealthy vapors. It is strange to see that in France there are young people ('Near Easterners') who breathe them with satisfaction and that there are people less young who encourage them in this attempted poisoning."

[37]   Paul von Hindenburg (1847–1933), German field marshal during the First World War.

the breaking point. This was the time when expressionism began to enjoy a vogue, since its whole attitude fell in with the retreat and the weariness of the German spirit. It was only natural that the Germans should have lost their enthusiasm for reality, to which before the war they had sung hymns of praise, through the mouths of innumerable academic thickheads, and which had now cost them over a million dead, while the blockade was strangling their children and grandchildren. Germany was seized with the mood that always precedes a so-called idealistic resurrection, an orgy à la Turnvater-Jahn, a Schenkendorf period.[38]

Now came the expressionists, like those famous medical quacks who promise to "fix everything up," looking heavenward like the gentle Muse; they pointed to "the rich treasures of our literature," pulled people gently by the sleeve and led them into the half-light of the Gothic cathedrals, where the street noises die down to a distant murmur and, in accordance with the old principle that all cats are gray at night, men without exception are fine fellows. Man, they have discovered, is good. And so expressionism, which brought the Germans so many welcome truths, became a "national achievement." In art it aimed at inwardness, abstraction, renunciation of all objectivity. When expressionism is mentioned, the first three names I think of are Däubler, Edschmid, and Hiller.[39] Däubler is the gigantosaurus of expressionist lyric poetry. Edschmid the prose writer and prototype of the expressionist man, while Kurt Hiller, with his intentional or unintentional meliorism, is the theoretician of the expressionist age.

On the basis of all these considerations and the psychological insight that a turning-away from objective reality implied the whole complex of weariness and cowardice that is so welcome to putrescent bourgeoisie, we immediately launched a sharp attack on expressionism in Germany, under the watchword of "action," acquired through our fight for the principles of bruitism, simultaneity and the new medium. The first German Dadaist manifesto, written by myself, says among other things: "Art in its execution and direction is dependent on the time in which it lives, and artists are creatures of their epoch. The highest art will be that which in its conscious content presents the thousandfold problems of the day, the art which has been visibly shattered by the explosions of the last week, which is forever trying to collect its limbs after yesterday's crash. The best and most extraordinary artists will be those who every hour snatch the tatters of their bodies out of the frenzied cataract of life, who, with bleeding hands and hearts, hold fast to the intelligence of their time. Has expressionism fulfilled our expectations of such an art, which should be the expression of our most vital concerns? No! No! No! Under the pretext of turning inward, the expressionists in literature and painting have banded together into a generation which is already looking forward to honorable mention in the histories of literature and art and aspiring to the most respectable civic distinctions. On pretext of carrying on propaganda for the soul, they have, in their struggle with naturalism, found their way back to the abstract, pathetic gestures which presuppose a comfortable life free from content or strife. The stages are filling up with kings, poets and Faustian characters of all sorts; the theory of a melioristic philosophy, the psychological naïvety of which is highly significant for a critical understanding of expressionism, runs ghostlike through the minds of men who never act. Hatred of the press, hatred of advertising, hatred of sensations, are typical of people who prefer their armchair to the noise of the street, and who even make it a point of pride to be swindled by every small-time profiteer. That sentimental resistance to the times, which are neither better nor worse, neither more reactionary nor more revolutionary than other times, that weak-kneed resistance, flirting with prayers and incense when it does not prefer to load its cardboard cannon with Attic iambics – is the quality of a youth which never knew how to be young. Expressionism, discovered abroad, and in Germany, true to style, transformed into an opulent idyll and the expectation of a good pension, has nothing in common with the efforts of active men. The signers of this manifesto have, under the battle cry Dada!, gathered together to put forward a new art, from which they expect the realization of new

[38] "Turnvater" – "gymnastic father," refers to Ludwig Jahn, the founder of the gymnastic societies which played an important part in the liberation of Germany from Napoleon. [Max von Schenkendorf (1783–1817) was a German writer whose political poems played a role in the wars to liberate Germany from Napoleon.]

[39] Theodor Däubler (1876–1934) was a German expressionist poet who wrote over 40 volumes of verse; Kasimir Edschmid (1890–1966), a German expressionist poet; Kurt Hiller (1885–1972) was a German expressionist writer.

ideals." And so on. Here the difference between our conception and that of Tzara is clear. While Tzara was still writing: *"Dada ne signifie rien"* – in Germany Dada lost its art-for-art's-sake character with its very first move. Instead of continuing to produce art, Dada, in direct contrast to abstract art, went out and found an adversary. Emphasis was laid on the movement, on struggle. But we still needed a program of action, we had to say exactly what our Dadaism was after. This program was drawn up by Raoul Hausmann and myself. In it we consciously adopted a political position:

What is Dadaism and what does it want in Germany?[40]

1. *Dadaism demands:*

1) The international revolutionary union of all creative and intellectual men and women on the basis of radical Communism;

2) The introduction of progressive unemployment through comprehensive mechanization of every field of activity. Only by unemployment does it become possible for the individual to achieve certainty as to the truth of life and finally become accustomed to experience;

3) The immediate expropriation of property (socialization) and the communal feeding of all; further, the erection of cities of light, and gardens which will belong to society as a whole and prepare man for a state of freedom.

2. *The Central Council demands:*

a) Daily meals at public expense for all creative and intellectual men and women on the Potsdamer Platz (Berlin);

b) Compulsory adherence of all clergymen and teachers to the Dadaist articles of faith;

c) The most brutal struggle against all directions of so-called "workers of the spirit" (Hiller, Adler),[41] against their concealed bourgeoisism, against expressionism and post-classical education as advocated by the Sturm group;

d) The immediate erection of a state art center, elimination of concepts of property in the new art (expressionism); the concept of property is entirely excluded from the super-individual movement of Dadaism which liberates all mankind;

e) Introduction of the simultaneist poem as a Communist state prayer;

f) Requisition of churches for the performance of bruitism, simultaneist and Dadaist poems;

g) Establishment of a Dadaist advisory council for the remodelling of life in every city of over 50,000 inhabitants;

h) Immediate organization of a large scale Dadaist propaganda campaign with 150 circuses for the enlightenment of the proletariat;

i) Submission of all laws and decrees to the Dadaist central council for approval;

j) Immediate regulation of all sexual relations according to the views of international Dadaism through establishment of a Dadaist sexual center.

The Dadaist revolutionary central council.
German group: Hausmann, Huelsenbeck
Business Office: Charlottenburg, Kantstrasse 118.
Applications for membership taken at business office.

The significance of this program is that in it Dada turns decisively away from the speculative, in a sense loses its metaphysics and reveals its understanding of itself as an expression of this age which is primarily characterized by machinery and the growth of civilization. It desires to be no more than an expression of the times, it has taken into itself all their knowledge, their breathless tempo, their scepticism, but also their weariness, their despair of a meaning or a "truth." In an article on

---

[40] First published as an independent manifesto in the German magazine *Der Dada* 1 (1919), where there was a third signatory, Jefim Golyscheff.

[41] For Kurt Hiller see note 39; Paul Adler was a Jewish and socialist poet, originally born in Prague.

expressionism Kornfeld[42] makes the distinction between the ethical man and the psychological man. The ethical man has the child-like piety and faith which permit him to kneel at some altar and recognize some God, who has the power to lead men from their misery to some paradise. The psychological man has journeyed vainly through the infinite, has recognized the limits of his spiritual possibilities, he knows that every "system" is a seduction with all the consequences of seduction and every God an opportunity for financiers.

The Dadaist, as the psychological man, has brought back his gaze from the distance and considers it important to have shoes that fit and a suit without holes in it. The Dadaist is an atheist by instinct. He is no longer a metaphysician in the sense of finding a rule for the conduct of life in any theoretical principles, for him there is no longer a "thou shalt"; for him the cigarette-butt and the umbrella are as exalted and as timeless as the "thing in itself." Consequently, the good is for the Dadaist no "better" than the bad – there is only a simultaneity, in values as in everything else. This simultaneity applied to the economy of facts is communism, a communism, to be sure, which has abandoned the principle of "making things better" and above all sees its goal in the destruction of everything that has gone bourgeois. Thus the Dadaist is opposed to the idea of paradise in every form, and one of the ideas farthest from his mind is that "the spirit is the sum of all means for the improvement of human existence." The word "improvement" is in every form unintelligible to the Dadaist, since behind it he sees a hammering and sawing on this life which, though useless, aimless and vile, represents as such a thoroughly spiritual phenomenon, requiring no improvement in a metaphysical sense. To mention spirit and improvement in the same breath is for the Dadaist a blasphemy. "Evil" has a profound meaning, the polarity of events finds in it a limit, and though the real political thinker (such as Lenin[43] seems to be) creates a movement, i.e., he dissolves individualities with the help of a theory, he changes nothing. And that, as paradoxical as it may seem, is the import of the Communist movement.

The Dadaist exploits the psychological possibilities inherent in his faculty for flinging out his own personality as one flings a lasso or lets a cloak flutter in the wind. He is not the same man today as tomorrow, the day after tomorrow he will perhaps be "nothing at all," and then he may become everything. He is entirely devoted to the movement of life, he accepts its angularity – but he never loses his distance to phenomena, because at the same time he preserves his creative indifference, as Friedlaender-Mynona[44] calls it. It seems scarcely credible that anyone could be at the same time active and at rest, that he should be devoted, yet maintain an attitude of rejection; and yet it is in this very anomaly that life itself consists, naive, obvious life, with its indifference toward happiness and death, joy and misery. The Dadaist is naive. The thing he is after is obvious, undifferentiated, unintellectual life. For him a table is not a mouse-trap and an umbrella is definitely not to pick your teeth with. In such a life art is no more and no less than a psychological problem. In relation to the masses, it is a phenomenon of public morality.

The Dadaist considers it necessary to come out against art, because he has seen through its fraud as a moral safety valve. Perhaps this militant attitude is a last gesture of inculcated honesty, perhaps it merely amuses the Dadaist, perhaps it means nothing at all. But in any case, art (including culture, spirit, athletic club), regarded from a serious point of view, is a large-scale swindle. And this, as I have hinted above, most especially in Germany, where the most absurd idolatry of all sorts of divinities is beaten into the child in order that the grown man and taxpayer should automatically fall on his knees when, in the interest of the state or some smaller gang of thieves, he receives the order to worship some "great spirit." I maintain again and again: the whole spirit business is a vulgar utilitarian swindle. In this war the Germans (especially in Saxony where the most infamous hypocrites reside) strove to justify themselves at home and abroad with Goethe and Schiller. Culture can be designated solemnly and with complete naivety as the national spirit become form, but also it can be characterized as a compensatory phenomenon, an obeisance to an invisible

[42] Paul Kornfeld (1889–1942), who was born in Prague, was an expressionist writer and dramatist.
[43] Vladimir Ilyich Lenin (1870–1924) led the Bolshevik revolution in October 1917 in Russia and established the Union of Soviet Socialist Republics (USSR), which collapsed in 1989.
[44] Salomo Friedlaender (1876–1941), also known by his pen name "Mynona," was a German-Jewish and anarchist writer who published a book called *Schöpferische Indifferenz* (*Creative Indifference*) (Munich: Georg Müller, 1918).

judge, as veronal for the conscience. The Germans are masters of dissembling, they are unquestionably the magicians (in the vaudeville sense) among nations, in every moment of their life they conjure up a culture, a spirit, a superiority which they can hold as a shield in front of their endangered bellies. It is this hypocrisy that has always seemed utterly foreign and incomprehensible to the French, a sign of diabolical malice. The German is unnaive, he is twofold and has a double base.

Here we have no intention of standing up for any nation. The French have the least right of anyone to be praised as a *grande nation*, now that they have brought the chauvinism of our times to its greatest possible height. The German has all the qualities and drawbacks of the idealist. You can look at it whichever way you like. You can construe the idealism that distorts things and makes them function as an absolute (the discipline of corpses) whether it be vegetarianism, the rights of man or the monarchy, as a pathological deformation, or you can call it ecstatically "the bridge to eternity," "the goal of life," or more such platitudes. The expressionists have done quite a bit in that direction. The Dadaist is instinctively opposed to all this. He is a man of reality who loves wine, women and advertising, his culture is above all of the body. *Instinctively he sees his mission in smashing the cultural ideology of the Germans.* I have no desire to justify the Dadaist. He acts instinctively, just as a man might say he was a thief out of "passion," or a stamp-collector by preference. The "ideal" has shifted: the abstract artist has become (if you insist, dear reader) a wicked materialist, with the abstruse characteristic of considering the care of his stomach and stock jobbing more honorable than philosophy. "But that's nothing new," those people will shout who can never tear themselves away from the "old." But it is something startlingly new, since for the first time in history the consequence has been drawn from the question: What is German culture? (Answer: Shit), and this culture is attacked with all the instruments of satire, bluff, irony and finally, violence. And in a great common action.

Dada is German Bolshevism. The bourgeois must be deprived of the opportunity to "buy up art for his justification." Art should altogether get a sound thrashing, and Dada stands for the thrashing with all the vehemence of its limited nature. The technical aspect of the Dadaist campaign against German culture was considered at great length. Our best instrument consisted of big demonstrations at which, in return for a suitable admission fee, everything connected with spirit, culture and inwardness was symbolically massacred. It is ridiculous and a sign of idiocy exceeding the legal limit to say that Dada (whose actual achievements and immense success cannot be denied) is "only of negative value." Today you can hardly fool first-graders with the old saw about positive and negative.

The gentlemen who demand the "constructive" are among the most suspicious types of a caste that has long been bankrupt. It has become sufficiently apparent in our time that law, order and the constructive, the "understanding for an organic development," are only symbols, curtains and pretexts for fat behinds and treachery. If the Dadaist movement is nihilism, then nihilism is a part of life, a truth which would be confirmed by any professor of zoology. Relativism, Dadaism, Nihilism, Action, Revolution, Gramophone. It makes one sick at heart to hear all that together, and as such (insofar as it becomes visible in the form of a theory), it all seems very stupid and antiquated. Dada does not take a dogmatic attitude. If Knatschke[45] proves today that Dada is old stuff, Dada doesn't care. A tree is old stuff too, and people eat dinner day after day without experiencing any particular disgust. This whole physiological attitude toward the world, that goes so far as to make – as Nietzsche the great philologist did – all culture depend on dry or liquid nutriment, is of course to be taken with a grain of salt. It is just as true and just as silly as the opposite. But we are after all human and commit ourselves by the mere fact of drinking coffee today and tea tomorrow. *Dada foresees its end and laughs.* Death is a thoroughly Dadaist business, in that it signifies nothing at all. Dada has the right to dissolve itself and will exert this right when the time comes. With a businesslike gesture, freshly pressed pants, a shave and a haircut, it will go down into the grave, after having made suitable arrangements with the Thanatos Funeral Home.

---

[45]   Professor Knatschke became the parodic embodiment of the pedantic German professor, the fictional creation of Jean-Jacques Waltz (1873–1951) in *Professor Knatschke, Oeuvres choisies du grand savant allemand et de sa fille Elsa* (1914); its anti-German tone ensured its success when it was translated into English as *Professor Knatschke: Selected Works of the Great German Scholar and his Daughter Elsa* (London: Hodder and Stoughton, 1917).

The time is not far distant. We have very sensitive fingertips and a larynx of glazed paper. The mediocrities and the gentry in search of "something mad" are beginning to conquer Dada. At every corner of our dear German fatherland, literary cliques, with Dada as a background, are endeavoring to assume a heroic pose. A movement must have sufficient talent to make its decline interesting and pleasant. In the end it is immaterial whether the Germans keep on with their cultural humbug or not. Let them achieve immortality with it. But if Dada dies here, it will some day appear on another planet with rattles and kettledrums, pot covers and simultaneous poems, and remind the old God that there are still people who are very well aware of the complete idiocy of the world.

Dada achieved the greatest successes in Germany. We Dadaists formed a company which soon became the terror of the population – to it belonged, in addition to myself, Raoul Haussmann, Georg Grosz, John Heartfield, Wieland Herzfelde, Walter Mehring and a certain Baader. In 1919 we put on several big evening shows; at the beginning of December, through no fault of our own, we gave two Sunday afternoon performances in the institute for socialist hypocrisy, the "Tribune," which achieved the success of good box-office receipts and a word of melancholy-reluctant praise in the form of an article in the *Berliner Tageblatt* by Alfred Kerr,[46] a critic well known and appreciated a century ago, but now quite crippled and arterio-sclerotic. With Haussman, the "Dadasoph," to whom I became greatly attached because of his selfless shrewdness, and the above-mentioned Baader, I undertook in February 1920 a Dada tour, which began in Leipzig on February 24 with a performance in the Zentraltheater attended by a tremendous ruckus ("bruit") which gave our decayed old globe quite a shaking up; this affair was attended by 2,000 people. We began in Leipzig, on the basis of the sound idea that all Germans are Saxons, a truth, it seems to me which speaks for itself. We then went to Bohemia, and on February 26 we appeared in Teplitz-Schönau before an audience of fools and curiosity-seekers. That same night we drank ourselves into a stupor, after, with our last sober breath, we had appointed Hugo Dux, the most intelligent inhabitant of Teplitz, chief of all Dadaists in Czechoslovakia. Baader, who is almost fifty years of age and, as far as I know, is already a grandfather, then repaired to the Bawdy House of the Bumblebee, where he wallowed in wine, women and roast pork and devised a criminal plan which, he calculated, would cost Hausmann and myself our lives in Prague on March 1. On March 1 the three of us were planning to put on a show in the Prague produce exchange, which seats nearly 2,500 persons. And conditions in Prague are rather peculiar. We had been threatened with violence from all sides. The Czechs wanted to beat us up because we were unfortunately Germans; the Germans had taken it into their heads that we were Bolsheviks; and the Socialists threatened us with death and annihilation because they regarded us as reactionary voluptuaries. Weeks before our arrival the newspapers had started a monster Dada publicity campaign and expectations could not have been screwed to a higher pitch. Apparently the good people of Prague expected the living cows to fall from the heavens – in the streets crowds formed behind us with rhythmic roars of "Dada," in the newspaper offices the editors obligingly showed us the revolvers with which, under certain circumstances, they were planning to shoot us down on March 1. All this had smitten Baader's brain with a powerful impact. The poor pietist had conceived such a very different picture of our Dada tour. He had hoped to return to his wife and children with money in his pocket, to draw a comfortable income from Dada and, after performance of his conjugal duty, retire with a pipeful of Germania ersatz tobacco to dream in all tranquillity of his heroic feats.

But now he was to take leave of his precious life, now there was a chance that he would end his poetic career in a Prague morgue. In his terror he was willing to promise anything, to bear any disgrace if his cousin, the old God of the Jews, with whom he had so often allied himself, would only preserve him this last time from the dissolution of his individuality as a pseudo-bard. *Dum vita superest, bene est.*[47] The performance in the produce exchange was to begin at 8 o'clock. At 7:30 I ask Hausmann about Baader's whereabouts. "He left me a note saying he had to go over to the post-office." And so he left us up to the very last moment in the belief that he would still turn up; this he did in order to prevent us from changing the program, thus exposing us with all the more certainty

---

[46] Alfred Kerr (1867–1948) was the most influential German critic and essayist of his day.

[47] *Dum vita ... est* "While life remains, things are good."

to the fury of the public. The whole city was in an uproar. Thousands crowded around the entrances of the produce exchange. By dozens they were sitting on the window-ledges and pianos, raging and roaring. Hausmann and I, in great agitation, sat in the little vestibule which had been rigged up as a green room. The windowpanes were already beginning to rattle. It was 8:20. No sign of Baader. Only now did we see what was up. Hausmann remembered that he had seen a letter "to Hausmann and Huelsenbeck" stuck in his underclothes. We realized that Baader had deserted us, we would have to go through with the hocus pocus by ourselves as best we could. The situation could not have been worse – the platform (an improvised board structure) could be reached only through the massed audience – and Baader had fled with half the manuscript. Now was the time to do or die. Hic Rhodus! My honored readers, with the help of God and our routine, a great victory was won for Dada in Prague on March 1. On March 2 Hausmann and I appeared before a smaller audience in the Mozarteum, again with great success. On March 5 we were in Karlsbad, where to our great satisfaction we were able to ascertain that Dada is eternal and destined to achieve undying fame.

Dada Fragments (1916–17)
Hugo Ball

March 3, 1916 – Introduce symmetries and rhythms instead of principles. Contradict the existing world orders...

What we are celebrating is at once a buffoonery and a requiem mass...

June 12, 1916 – What we call Dada is a harlequinade made of nothingness in which all higher questions are involved, a gladiator's gesture, a play with shabby debris, an execution of postured morality and plenitude...

The Dadaist loves the extraordinary, the absurd, even. He knows that life asserts itself in contradictions, and that his age, more than any preceding it, aims at the destruction of all generous impulses. Every kind of mask is therefore welcome to him, every play at hide and seek in which there is an inherent power of deception. The direct and the primitive appear to him in the midst of this huge anti-nature, as being the supernatural itself...

The bankruptcy of ideas having destroyed the concept of humanity to its very innermost strata, the instincts and hereditary backgrounds are now emerging pathologically. Since no art, politics or religious faith seems adequate to dam this torrent, there remain only the *blague* and the bleeding pose...

The Dadaist trusts more in the sincerity of events than in the wit of persons. To him persons may be had cheaply, his own person not excepted. He no longer believes in the comprehension of things from *one* point of departure, but is nevertheless convinced of the union of all things, of totality, to such an extent that he suffers from dissonances to the point of self-dissolution...

The Dadaist fights against the death-throes and death-drunkenness of his time. Averse to every clever reticence, he cultivates the curiosity of one who experiences delight even in the most questionable forms of insubordination. He knows that this world of systems has gone to pieces, and that the age which demanded cash has organized a bargain sale of godless philosophies. Where bad conscience begins for the market-booth owners, mild laughter and mild kindliness begin for the Dadaist...

DADA FRAGMENTS
Hugo Ball (1886–1927) was a German poet, writer, and thinker who was horrified at the outbreak of the First World War and moved to Switzerland in early 1916, where he played a major role in founding the Cabaret Voltaire and Dada. By the end of 1917 he had retired from Dada activities. He became a journalist (1917–19), then turned to Catholicism and a life of religious meditation. In 1927 he published *Die Flucht aus der Zeit* (*Fleeing from Time*), a selection from his diaries. Passages from the book were translated into English by Eugene Jolas (see pp. 1007–16) and published in *transition* 25 (Fall 1936), which is the text reprinted here.

The image differentiates us. Through the image we comprehend. Whatever it may be – it is night – we hold the print of it in our hands . . .

The word and the image are one. Painting and composing poetry belong together. Christ is image and word. The word and the image are crucified . . .

June 18, 1916 – We have developed the plasticity of the word to a point which can hardly be surpassed. This result was achieved at the price of the logically constructed, rational sentence, and therefore, also, by renouncing the document (which is only possible by means of a time-robbing grouping of sentences in a logically ordered syntax). We were assisted in our efforts by the special circumstances of our age, which does not allow a real talent either to rest or ripen, forcing it to a premature test of its capacities, as well as by the emphatic élan of our group, whose members sought to surpass each other by an even greater intensification and accentuation of their platform. People may smile, if they want to; language will thank us for our zeal, even if there should not be any directly visible results. We have charged the word with forces and energies which made it possible for us to rediscover the evangelical concept of the "word" (logos) as a magical complex of images . . .

August 5, 1916 – Childhood as a new world, and everything childlike and phantastic, everything childlike and direct, everything childlike and symbolical in opposition to the senilities of the world of grown-ups. The child will be the accuser on Judgment Day, the Crucified One will judge, the Resurrected One will pardon. The distrust of children, their shut-in quality, their escape from our recognition – their recognition that they won't be understood anyway . . .

Childhood is not at all as obvious as is generally assumed. It is a world to which hardly any attention is paid, with its own laws, without whose application there is no art, and without whose religious and philosophic recognition art cannot exist or be apprehended . . .

The credulous imagination of children, however, is also exposed to corruption and deformation. To surpass oneself in naiveté and childishness – that is still the best antidote . . .

November 21, 1916 – Note about a criticism of individualism: The accentuated "I" has constant interests, whether they be greedy, dictatorial, vain or lazy. It always follows appetites, so long as it does not become absorbed in society. Whoever renounces his interests, renounces his "I." The "I" and the interests are identical. Therefore, the individualistic-egoistic ideal of the Renaissance ripened to the general union of the mechanized appetites which we now see before us, bleeding and disintegrating.

January 9, 1917 – We should burn all libraries and allow to remain only that which every one knows by heart. A beautiful age of the legend would then begin . . .

The middle ages praised not only foolishness, but even idiocy. The barons sent their children to board with idiotic families so that they might learn humility . . .

March 30, 1917 – The new art is sympathetic because in an age of total disruption it has conserved the will-to-the-image; because it is inclined to force the image, even though the means and parts be antagonistic. Convention triumphs in the moralistic evaluation of the parts and details; art cannot be concerned with this. It drives toward the in-dwelling, all-connecting life nerve; it is indifferent to external resistance. One might also say: morals are withdrawn from convention, and utilized for the sole purpose of sharpening the senses of measure and weight . . .

March 7, 1917 – One might also speak of Klee[1] as follows: He always presents himself as quite small and playful. In an age of the colossal he falls in love with a green leaf, a little star, a butterfly wing; and since heaven and infinity are reflected in them, he paints them in. The point of his pencil, his brush, tempt him to minutiae. He always remains quite near first beginnings and the smallest format. The beginning possesses him and will not let him go. When he reaches the end, he does not start a new leaf at once, but begins to paint over the first one. The little formats are filled with intensity, become magic letters and colored palimpsests . . .

---

[1]   Paul Klee (1879–1940), Swiss artist who taught at the Bauhaus from 1921 to 1931, first in Weimar and then in Dessau.

What irony, approaching sarcasm even, must this artist feel for our hollow, empty epoch. Perhaps there is no man today who is so master of himself as Klee. He scarcely detaches himself from his inspiration. He knows the shortest path from his inspiration to the page. The wide, distracting, stretching-out of the hand and body which Kandinsky[2] needs to fill the great formats of his canvases, necessarily brings waste and fatigue; it demands an exhaustive exposition, and explanation. Painting, when it seeks to retain unity and soul, becomes a sermon, or music.

April 18, 1917 – Perhaps the art which we are seeking is the key to every former art: a salomonic key that will open all mysteries.

Dadaism – a mask play, a burst of laughter? And behind it, a synthesis of the romantic, dandyistic and – daemonistic theories of the 19th century.

Dada Manifesto 1918
Tristan Tzara

The magic of a word – Dada – which has brought journalists to the gates of a world unforeseen, is of no importance to us.

To put out a manifesto you must want: ABC
to fulminate against 1, 2, 3,
to fly into a rage and sharpen your wings to conquer and disseminate little abcs and big abcs, to sign, shout, swear, to organize prose into a form of absolute and irrefutable evidence, to prove your non plus ultra and maintain that novelty resembles life just as the latest appearance of some whore proves the essence of God. His existence was previously proved by the accordion, the landscape, the wheedling word. To impose your ABC is a natural thing – hence deplorable. Everybody does it in the form of crystalbluffmadonna, monetary system, pharmaceutical product, or a bare leg advertising the ardent sterile spring. The love of novelty is the cross of sympathy, demonstrates a naive je m'enfoutisme,[3] it is a transitory, positive sign without a cause.

But this need itself is obsolete. In documenting art on the basis of the supreme simplicity: novelty, we are human and true for the sake of amusement, impulsive, vibrant to crucify boredom. At the crossroads of the lights, alert, attentively awaiting the years, in the forest. I write a manifesto and I want nothing, yet I say certain things, and in principle I am against manifestoes, as I am also against principles (half-pints to measure the moral value of every phrase too too convenient; approximation was invented by the impressionists). I write this manifesto to show that people can perform contrary actions together while taking one fresh gulp of air; I am against action; for continuous contradiction, for affirmation too, I am neither for nor against and I do not explain because I hate common sense.

Dada – there you have a word that leads ideas to the hunt: every bourgeois is a little dramatist, he invents all sorts of speeches instead of putting the characters suitable to the quality of his intelligence, chrysalises, on chairs, seeks causes or aims (according to the psychoanalytic method he practices) to cement his plot, a story that speaks and defines itself. Every spectator is a plotter if he tries to explain a word: (to know!) Safe in the cottony refuge of serpentine complications he manipulates his instincts. Hence the mishaps of conjugal life.

To explain: the amusement of redbellies in the mills of empty skulls.

DADA MANIFESTO
"Dada Manifesto 1918" was read aloud in Zurich (at the Salle Meise) on March 23, 1918, and first published in Dada 3 (1918). It was then incorporated into a book called *Sept manifestes dada* (Seven Dada Manifestos) (Paris: Jean Budry, 1924), and much later was translated from the French into English by Ralph Manheim and published in Robert Motherwell (ed.), *The Dada*

Painters and Poets: An Anthology (New York: Wittenborn, Schultz, 1951), a volume reprinted by Harvard University Press in 1981. Another translation into English appeared in 1992; see Tristan Tzara, *Seven Dada Manifestos and Lampisteries*, trans B. Wright (London: Calder; New York: Riverrun).
[2]   For Kandinsky see p. 98 n. 6.
[3]   Literally, "I-don't-give-a-fuck-ism in French."

☛ DADA MEANS NOTHING

If you find it futile and don't want to waste your time on a word that means nothing.... The first thought that comes to these people is bacteriological in character: to find its etymological, or at least its historical or psychological origin. We see by the papers that the Kru Negroes call the tail of a holy cow Dada. The cube and the mother in a certain district of Italy are called: Dada. A hobby horse, a nurse both in Russian and Rumanian: Dada. Some learned journalists regard it as an art for babies, other holy jesusescallingthelittlechildren of our day, as a relapse into a dry and noisy, noisy and monotonous primitivism. Sensibility is not constructed on the basis of a word; all constructions converge on perfection which is boring, the stagnant idea of a gilded swamp, a relative human product. A work of art should not be beauty in itself, for beauty is dead; it should be neither gay nor sad, neither light nor dark to rejoice or torture the individual by serving him the cakes of sacred aureoles or the sweets of a vaulted race through the atmospheres. A work of art is never beautiful by decree, objectively and for all. Hence criticism is useless, it exists only subjectively, for each man separately, without the slightest character of universality. Does anyone think he has found a psychic base common to all mankind? The attempt of Jesus and the Bible covers with their broad benevolent wings: shit, animals, days. How can one expect to put order into the chaos that constitutes that infinite and shapeless variation: man? The principle: "love thy neighbor" is a hypocrisy. "Know thyself" is utopian but more acceptable, for it embraces wickedness. No pity. After the carnage we still retain the hope of a purified mankind. I speak only of myself since I do not wish to convince, I have no right to drag others into my river, I oblige no one to follow me and everybody practices his art in his own way, if he knows the joy that rises like arrows to the astral layers, or that other joy that goes down into the mines of corpse-flowers and fertile spasms. Stalactites: seek them everywhere, in managers magnified by pain, eyes white as the hares of the angels.

And so Dada[4] was born of a need for independence, of a distrust toward unity. Those who are with us preserve their freedom. We recognize no theory. We have enough cubist and futurist academies: laboratories of formal ideas. Is the aim of art to make money and cajole the nice nice

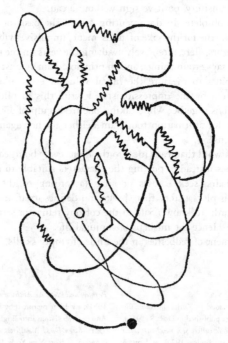

4   in 1916 in the Cabaret Voltaire, in Zurich. [Tzara's note.]

bourgeois? Rhymes ring with the assonance of the currencies and the inflexion slips along the line of the belly in profile. All groups of artists have arrived at this trust company after riding their steeds on various comets. While the door remains open to the possibility of wallowing in cushions and good things to eat.

Here we cast anchor in rich ground. Here we have a right to do some proclaiming, for we have known cold shudders and awakenings. Ghosts drunk on energy, we dig the trident into unsuspecting flesh. We are a downpour of maledictions as tropically abundant as vertiginous vegetation, resin and rain are our sweat, we bleed and burn with thirst, our blood is vigor.

Cubism was born out of the simple way of looking at an object: Cézanne painted a cup 20 centimeters below his eyes, the cubists look at it from above, others complicate appearance by making a perpendicular section and arranging it conscientiously on the side. (I do not forget the creative artists and the profound laws of matter which they established once and for all.) The futurist sees the same cup in movement, a succession of objects one beside the other, and maliciously adds a few force lines. This does not prevent the canvas from being a good or bad painting suitable for the investment of intellectual capital.

The new painter creates a world, the elements of which are also its implements, a sober, definite work without argument. The new artist protests: he no longer paints (symbolic and illusionist reproduction) but creates – directly in stone, wood, iron, tin, boulders – locomotive organisms capable of being turned in all directions by the limpid wind of momentary sensation. All pictorial or plastic work is useless: let it then be a monstrosity that frightens servile minds, and not sweetening to decorate the refectories of animals in human costume, illustrating the sad fable of mankind. –

Painting is the art of making two lines geometrically established as parallel meet on a canvas before our eyes in a reality which transposes other conditions and possibilities into a world. This world is not specified or defined in the work, it belongs in its innumerable variations to the spectator. For its creator it is without cause and without theory. *Order=disorder; ego=non-ego; affirmation=negation:* the supreme radiations of an absolute art. Absolute in the purity of a cosmic. ordered chaos, eternal in the globule of a second without duration, without breath without control. I love an ancient work for its novelty. It is only contrast that connects us with the past. The writers who teach morality and discuss or improve psychological foundations have, aside from a hidden desire to make money, an absurd view of life, which they have classified, cut into sections, channelized: they insist on waving the baton as the categories dance. Their readers snicker and go on: what for?

There is a literature that does not reach the voracious mass. It is the work of creators, issued from a real necessity in the author, produced for himself. It expresses the knowledge of a supreme egoism, in which laws wither away. Every page must explode, either by profound heavy seriousness, the whirlwind, poetic frenzy, the new, the eternal, the crushing joke, enthusiasm for principles, or by the way in which it is printed. On the one hand a tottering world in flight, betrothed to the glockenspiel of hell, on the other hand: new men. Rough, bouncing, riding on hiccups. Behind them a crippled world and literary quacks with a mania for improvement.

I say unto you: there is no beginning and we do not tremble, we are not sentimental. We are a furious wind, tearing the dirty linen of clouds and prayers, preparing the great spectacle of disaster, fire, decomposition. We will put an end to mourning and replace tears by sirens screeching from one continent to another. Pavilions of intense joy and widowers with the sadness of poison. Dada is the signboard of abstraction; advertising and business are also elements of poetry.

I destroy the drawers of the brain and of social organization: spread demoralization wherever I go and cast my hand from heaven to hell, my eyes from hell to heaven, restore the fecund wheel of a universal circus to objective forces and the imagination of every individual.

A philosophical question: from which side angle to start looking at life, God, ideas, or anything else. Everything we look at is false. I don't think the relative result is any more important than the choice of pastry or cherries for desert. The system of quickly looking at the other side of a thing in order to impose your opinion indirectly is called dialectics, in other words, haggling over the spirit of fried potatoes while dancing method around it.

If I cry out:

> *Ideal, ideal, ideal,*
> *Knowledge, knowledge, knowledge,*
> *Boomboom, boomboom, boomboom,*

I have given a pretty faithful version of progress, law, morality and all other fine qualities that various highly intelligent men have discussed in so many books, only to conclude that after all everyone dances to his own personal boomboom, and that the writer is entitled to his boomboom: the satisfaction of pathological curiosity; a private bell for inexplicable needs; a bath; pecuniary difficulties; a stomach with repercussions in life; the authority of the mystic wand formulated as the bouquet of a phantom orchestra made up of silent fiddle bows greased with philtres made of chicken manure. With the blue eye-glasses of an angel they have excavated the inner life for a dime's worth of unanimous gratitude. If all of them are right and if all pills are Pink Pills, let us try for once not to be right. Some people think they can explain rationally, by thought, what they think. But that is extremely relative. Psychoanalysis is a dangerous disease, it puts to sleep the antiobjective impulses of man and systematizes the bourgeoisie. There is no ultimate Truth. The dialectic is an amusing mechanism which guides us / in a banal kind of way / to the opinions we had in the first place. Does anyone think that, by a minute refinement of logic, he has demonstrated the truth and established the correctness of these opinions? Logic imprisoned by the senses is an organic disease. To this element philosophers always like to add: the power of observation. But actually this magnificent quality of the mind is the proof of its impotence. We observe, we regard from one or more points of view, we choose them among the millions that exist. Experience is also a product of chance and individual faculties. Science disgusts me as soon as it becomes a speculative system, loses its character of utility – that is so useless but is at least individual. I detest greasy objectivity, and harmony, the science that finds everything in order. Carry on, my children, humanity...Science says we are the servants of nature: everything is in order, make love and bash your brains in. Carry on, my children, humanity, kind bourgeois and journalist virgins...I am against systems, the most acceptable system is on principle to have none. To complete oneself, to perfect oneself in one's own littleness, to fill the vessel with one's individuality, to have the courage to fight for and against thought, the mystery of bread, the sudden burst of an infernal propeller into economic lilies:

DADAIST SPONTANEITY

I call *je m'enfoutisme* the kind of like in which everyone retains his own conditions, though respecting other individualisms, except when the need arises to defend oneself, in which the two-step becomes national anthem, curiosity shop, a radio transmitting Bach fugues, electric signs and posters for whorehouses, an organ broadcasting carnations for God, all this together physically replacing photography and the universal catechism

Active simplicity.

Inability to distinguish between degrees of clarity: to lick the penumbra and float in the big mouth filled with honey and excrement. Measured by the scale of eternity, all activity is vain – (if we allow thought to engage in an adventure the result of which would be infinitely grotesque and add significantly to our knowledge of human impotence). But supposing life to be a poor farce, without aim or initial parturition, and because we think it our duty to extricate ourselves as fresh and clean as washed chrysanthemums, we have proclaimed as the sole basis for agreement: art. It is not as important as we, mercenaries of the spirit, have been proclaiming for centuries. Art afflicts no one and those who manage to take an interest in it will harvest caresses and a fine opportunity to populate the country with their conversation. Art is a private affair, the artist produces it for himself; an intelligible work is the product of a journalist, and because at this moment it strikes my fancy to combine this monstrosity with oil paints: a paper tube simulating the metal that is automatically pressed and poured hatred cowardice villainy. The artist, the poet rejoice at the venom of the masses condensed into a section chief of this industry, he is happy to be insulted: it is a proof of his immutability. When a writer or artist is praised by the newspapers, it is proof of the intelligibility of his work: wretched lining of a coat for public use; tatters covering brutality, piss contributing to the warmth of an animal brooding vile instincts. Flabby, insipid flesh reproducing with the help of typographical microbes.

We have thrown out the cry-baby in us. Any infiltration of this kind is candied diarrhea. To encourage this act is to digest it. What we need is works that are strong straight precise and forever beyond understanding. Logic is a complication. Logic is always wrong. It draws the threads of notions, words, in their formal exterior, toward illusory ends and centers. Its chains kill, it is an enormous centipede stifling independence. Married to logic, art would live in incest, swallowing, engulfing its own tail, still part of its own body, fornicating within itself, and passion would become a nightmare tarred with protestantism, a monument, a heap of ponderous gray entrails.

But the suppleness, enthusiasm, even the joy of injustice, this little truth which we practise innocently and which makes us beautiful: we are subtle and our fingers are malleable and slippery as the branches of that sinuous, almost liquid plant; it defines our soul, say the cynics. That too is a point of view; but all flowers are not sacred, fortunately, and the divine thing in us is our call to anti-human action. I am speaking of a paper flower for the button-holes of the gentlemen who frequent the ball of masked life, the kitchen of grace, white cousins lithe or fat. They traffic with whatever we have selected. The contradiction and unity of poles in a single toss can be the truth. If one absolutely insists on uttering this platitude, the appendix of a libidinous, malodorous morality. Morality creates atrophy like every plague produced by intelligence. The control of morality and logic has inflicted us with impassivity in the presence of police-men – who are the cause of slavery, putrid rats infecting the bowels of the bourgeoisie which have infected the only luminous clean corridors of glass that remained open to artists.

Let each man proclaim: there is a great negative work of destruction to be accomplished. We must sweep and clean. Affirm the cleanliness of the individual after the state of madness, aggressive complete madness of a world abandoned to the hands of bandits, who rend one another and destroy

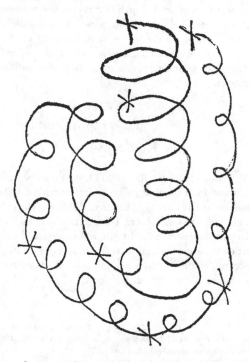

the centuries. Without aim or design, without organization: indomitable madness, decomposition. Those who are strong in words or force will survive, for they are quick in defense, the agility of limbs and sentiments flames on their faceted flanks.

Morality has determined charity and pity, two balls of fat that have grown like elephants, like planets, and are called good. There is nothing good about them. Goodness is lucid, clear and decided, pitiless toward compromise and politics. Morality is an injection of chocolate into the veins of all men. This task is not ordered by a supernatural force but by the trust of idea brokers and grasping academicians. Sentimentality: at the sight of a group of men quarreling and bored, they invented the calendar and the medicament wisdom. With a sticking of labels the battle of the philosophers was set off (mercantilism, scales, meticulous and petty measures) and for the second time it was understood that pity is a sentiment like diarrhea in relation to the disgust that destroys health, a foul attempt by carrion corpses to compromise the sun. I proclaim the opposition of all cosmic faculties to this gonorrhea of a putrid sun issued from the factories of philosophical thought, I proclaim bitter struggle with all the weapons of

DADAIST DISGUST

Every product of disgust capable of becoming a negation of the family is *dada*; a protest with the fists of its whole being engaged in destructive action: **DADA**; knowledge of all the means rejected up until now by the shamefaced sex of comfortable compromise and good manners: **DADA**; abolition of logic, which is the dance of those impotent to create: **DADA**; of every social hierarchy and equation set up for the sake of values by our valets: DADA; every object, all objects, sentiments, obscurities, apparitions and the precise clash of parallel lines are weapons for the fight: **DADA**; abolition of memory: **DADA**; abolition of archaeology: **DADA**: abolition of prophets: DADA; abolition of the future: Dada; absolute and unquestionable faith in every god that is the immediate product of spontaneity: Dada; elegant and unprejudiced leap from a harmony to the other sphere; trajectory of a word tossed like a screeching phonograph record; to respect all individuals in their folly of the moment: whether it be serious, fearful, timid, ardent, vigorous, determined, enthusiastic; to divest one's church of every useless cumbersome accessory; to spit out disagreeable or amorous ideas like a luminous waterfall, or coddle them – with the extreme satisfaction that it doesn't matter in the least – with the same intensity in the thicket of one's soul – pure of insects for blood well-born, and gilded with bodies of archangels. Freedom: <u>DADA DADA DADA</u>, a roaring of tense colors, and interlacing of opposites and of all contradictions, grotesques, inconsistencies:

Merz (1920)
Kurt Schwitters

I was born on June 20, 1887 in Hanover. As a child I had a little garden with roses and strawberries in it. After I had graduated from the *Realgymnasium* [scientific high school] in Hanover, I studied the technique of painting in Dresden with Bantzer, Kühl and Hegenbarth.[1] It was in Bantzer's studio that I painted my *Still Life with Chalice*. The selection of my works now [1920] on exhibit at the Hans Goltz Gallery, Briennerstrasse 8, Munich, is intended to show how I progressed from the closest possible imitation of nature with oil paint, brush and canvas, to the conscious elaboration of purely artistic components in the Merz object, and how an unbroken line of development leads from the naturalistic studies to the Merz abstractions.

MERZ

First published in a journal called *Der Ararat* in 1920. Translated complete from the German by Ralph Manheim and published in Robert Motherwell (ed.), *The Dada Painters and Poets: An Anthology* (New York: Wittenborn, Schultz, 1951). The entire volume was reprinted by Harvard University Press in 1981.

[1]   Carl Bantzer (1857–1941), Heinrich Kühl (1886–1965), and Josef Hegenbarth (1884–1962) were German artists working in Hanover.

To paint after nature is to transfer three-dimensional corporeality to a two-dimensional surface. This you can learn if you are in good health and not color blind. Oil paint, canvas and brush are material and tools. It is possible by expedient distribution of oil paint on canvas to copy natural impressions; under favorable conditions you can do it so accurately that the picture cannot be distinguished from the model. You start, let us say, with a white canvas primed for oil painting and sketch in with charcoal the most discernible lines of the natural form you have chosen. Only the first line may be drawn more or less arbitrarily, all the others must form with the first the angle prescribed by the natural model. By constant comparison of the sketch with the model, the lines can be so adjusted that the lines of the sketch will correspond to those of the model. Lines are now drawn by feeling, the accuracy of the feeling is checked and measured by comparison of the estimated angle of the line with the perpendicular in nature and in the sketch. Then, according to the apparent proportions between the parts of the model, you sketch in the proportions between parts on the canvas, preferably by means of broken lines delimiting these parts. The size of the first part is arbitrary, unless your plan is to represent a part, such as the head, in "life size." In that case you measure with a compass an imaginary line running parallel to a plane on the natural object conceived as a plane on the picture, and use this measurement in representing the first part. You adjust all the remaining parts to the first through feeling, according to the corresponding parts of the model, and check your feeling by measurement; to do this, you place the picture so far away from you that the first part appears as large in the painting as in the model, and then you compare. In order to check a given proportion, you hold out the handle of your paint brush at arm's length towards this proportion in such a way that the end of the handle appears to coincide with one end of the proportion; then you place your thumb on the brush handle so that the position of the thumbnail on the handle coincides with the other end of the proportion. If then you hold the paintbrush out towards the picture, again at arm's length, you can, by the measurement thus obtained, determine with photographic accuracy whether your feeling has deceived you. If the sketch is correct, you fill in the parts of the picture with color, according to nature. The most expedient method is to begin with a clearly recognizable color of large area, perhaps with a somewhat broken blue. You estimate the degree of matness and break the luminosity with a complementary color, ultramarine, for example, with light ochre. By addition of white you can make the color light, by addition of black dark. All this can be learned. The best way of checking for accuracy is to place the picture directly beside the projected picture surface in nature, return to your old place and compare the color in your picture with the natural color. By breaking those tones that are too bright and adding those that are still lacking, you will achieve a color tonality as close as possible to that in nature. If one tone is correct, you can put the picture back in its place and adjust the other colors to the first by feeling. You can check your feeling by comparing every tone directly with nature, after setting the picture back beside the model. If you have patience and adjust all large and small lines, all forms and color tones according to nature, you will have an exact reproduction of nature. This can be learned. This can be taught. And in addition, you can avoid making too many mistakes in "feeling" by studying nature itself through anatomy and perspective and your medium through color theory. That is academy.

I beg the reader's pardon for having discussed photographic painting at such length. I had to do this in order to show that it is a labor of patience, that it can be learned, that it rests essentially on measurement and adjustment and provides no food for artistic creation. For me it was essential to learn adjustment, and I gradually learned that the adjustment of the elements in painting is the aim of art, not a means to an end, such as checking for accuracy. It was not a short road. In order to achieve insight, you must work. And your insight extends only for a small space, then mist covers the horizon. And it is only from that point that you can go on and achieve further insight. And I believe that there is no end. Here the academy can no longer help you. There is no means of checking your insight.

First I succeeded in freeing myself from the literal reproduction of all details. I contented myself with the intensive treatment of light effects through sketch-like painting (impressionism).

With passionate love of nature (love is subjective) I emphasized the main lines by exaggeration, the forms by limiting myself to what was most essential and by outlining, and the color tones by breaking them down into complementary colors.

The personal grasp of nature now seemed to me the most important thing. The picture became an intermediary between myself and the spectator. I had impressions, painted a picture in accordance with them; the picture had expression.

One might write a catechism of the media of expression if it were not useless, as useless as the desire to achieve expression in a work of art. Every line, color, form has a definite expression. Every combination of lines, colors, forms has a definite expression. Expression can be given only to a particular structure, it cannot be translated. The expression of a picture cannot be put into words, any more than the expression of a word, such as the word "and" for example, can be painted.

Nevertheless, the expression of a picture is so essential that it is worth while to strive for it consistently. Any desire to reproduce natural forms limits one's force and consistency in working out an expression. I abandoned all reproduction of natural elements and painted only with pictorial elements. These are my abstractions. I adjusted the elements of the picture to one another, just as I had formerly done at the academy, yet not for the purpose of reproducing nature but with a view to expression.

Today the striving for expression in a work of art also seems to me injurious to art. Art is a primordial concept, exalted as the godhead, inexplicable as life, indefinable and without purpose. The work of art comes into being through artistic evaluation of its elements. I know only how I make it, I know only my medium, of which I partake, to what end I know not.

The medium is as unimportant as I myself. Essential is only the forming. Because the medium is unimportant, I take any material whatsoever if the picture demands it. When I adjust materials of different kinds to one another, I have taken a step in advance of mere oil painting, for in addition to playing off color against color, line against line, form against form, etc., I play off material against material, for example, wood against sackcloth. I call the *weltanschauung* from which this mode of artistic creation arose "Merz."

The word "Merz" had no meaning when I formed it. Now it has the meaning which I gave it. The meaning of the concept "Merz" changes with the change in the insight of those who continue to work with it.

Merz stands for freedom from all fetters, for the sake of artistic creation. Freedom is not lack of restraint, but the product of strict artistic discipline. Merz also means tolerance towards any artistically motivated limitation. Every artist must be allowed to mold a picture out of nothing but blotting paper for example, provided he is capable of molding a picture.

The reproduction of natural elements is not essential to a work of art. But representations of nature, inartistic in themselves, can be elements in a picture, if they are played off against other elements in the picture.

At first I concerned myself with other art forms, poetry for example. Elements of poetry are letters, syllables, words, sentences. Poetry arises from the interaction of these elements. Meaning is important only if it is employed as one such factor. I play off sense against nonsense. I prefer nonsense but that is a purely personal matter. I feel sorry for nonsense, because up to now it has so seldom been artistically molded, that is why I love nonsense.

Here I must mention Dadaism, which like myself cultivates nonsense. There are two groups of Dadaists, the kernel Dadas and the husk Dadas. Originally there were only kernel Dadaists, the husk Dadaists peeled off from this original kernel under their leader Huelsenbeck [Huelse is German for husk, Tr.] and in so doing took part of the kernel with them. The peeling process took place amid loud howls, singing of the *Marseillaise*, and distribution of kicks with the elbows, a tactic which Huelsenbeck still employs. . . . In the history of Dadaism Huelsenbeck writes: "All in all art should get a sound thrashing." In his introduction to the recent *Dada Almanach*, Huelsenbeck writes: "Dada is carrying on a kind of propaganda against culture." Thus Huelsendadaism is oriented towards politics and against art and against culture. I am tolerant and allow every man his own opinions, but I am compelled to state that such an outlook is alien to Merz. As a matter of principle, Merz aims only at art, because no man can serve two masters.

But "the Dadaists' conception of Dadaism varies greatly," as Huelsenbeck himself admits. Tristan Tzara, leader of the kernel Dadaists, writes in his *Dada manifesto 1918:* "Everybody practices his art in his own way,"[2] and further "Dada is the signboard of abstraction."[3] I wish to state that Merz maintains a close artistic friendship with kernel Dadaism as thus conceived and with the kernel Dadaists Hans Arp, of whom I am particularly fond, Picabia, Ribemont-Dessaignes and Archipenko. In Huelsenbeck's own words, Huelsendada has made itself into "God's clown," while kernel Dadaism holds to the good old traditions of abstract art. Huelsendada "foresees its end and laughs"[4] about it, while kernel Dadaism will live as long as art lives. Merz also strives towards art and is an enemy of *kitsch,* even if it calls itself Dadaism under the leadership of Huelsenbeck. Every man who lacks artistic judgment is not entitled to write about art: "quod licet jovi non licet bovi." Merz energetically and as a matter of principle rejects Herr Richard Huelsenbeck's inconsequential and dilettantish views on art, while it officially recognizes the above-mentioned views of Tristan Tzara.

Here I must clear up a misunderstanding that might arise through my friendship with certain kernel Dadaists. It might be thought that I call myself a Dadaist, especially as the word "dada" is written on the jacket of my collection of poems, *Anna Blume,* published by Paul Steegemann.

On the same jacket is a windmill, a head, a locomotive running backwards and a man hanging in the air. This only means that in the world in which Anna Blume lives, in which people walk on their heads, windmills turn and locomotives run backwards, Dada also exists. In order to avoid misunderstandings, I have inscribed "Antidada" on the outside of my Cathedral. This does not mean that I am against Dada, but that there also exists in this world a current opposed to Dadaism. Locomotives run in both directions. Why shouldn't a locomotive run backwards now and then?

As long as I paint, I also model. Now I am doing Merz plastics: Pleasure Gallows and Cult-pump. Like Merz pictures, the Merz plastics are composed of various materials. They are conceived as round plastics and present any desired number of aspects.

Merz House was my first piece of Merz architecture. Spengemann writes in *Zweeman,* No. 8–12:[5] "In Merz House I see the cathedral: *the* cathedral. Not as a church, no, this is art as a truly spiritual expression of the force that raises us up to the unthinkable: absolute art. This cathedral cannot be used. Its interior is so filled with wheels that there is no room for people…that is absolute architecture, it has an artistic meaning and no other."

To busy myself with various branches of art was for me an artistic need. The reason for this was not any urge to broaden the scope of my activity, it was my desire not to be a specialist in one branch of art, but an artist. My aim is the Merz composite art work, that embraces all branches of art in an artistic unit. First I combined individual categories of art. I pasted words and sentences into poems in such a way as to produce a rhythmic design. Reversing the process, I pasted up pictures and drawings so that sentences could be read in them. I drove nails into pictures in such a way as to produce a plastic relief aside from the pictorial quality of the painting. I did this in order to efface the boundaries between the arts. The composite Merz work of art, par excellence, however, is the Merz stage which so far I have only been able to work out theoretically. The first published statement about it appeared in *Sturmbühne,* No. 8: "The Merz stage serves for the performance of the Merz drama. The Merz drama is an abstract work of art. The drama and the opera grow, as a rule, out of the form of the written text, which is a well-rounded work in itself, without the stage. Stage-set, music and performance serve only to illustrate this text, which is itself an illustration of the action. In contrast to the drama or the opera, all parts of the Merz stage-work are inseparably bound up together; it cannot be written, read or listened to, it can only be produced in the theatre. Up until now, a distinction was made between stage-set, text, and score in theatrical performances. Each factor was separately prepared and could also be separately enjoyed. The Merz stage knows only the fusing of all factors into a composite work. Materials for the stage-set are all solid, liquid and gaseous bodies, such as white wall, man, barbed

[2] See p. 480.
[3] See p. 481.
[4] See p. 475.

[5] Christ of Spengemann (1877–1952) was an expressionist critic and writer who strongly supported Schwitters' work.

wire entanglement, blue distance, light cone. Use is made of compressible surfaces, or surfaces capable of dissolving into meshes; surfaces that fold like curtains, expand or shrink. Objects will be allowed to move and revolve, and lines will be allowed to broaden into surfaces. Parts will be inserted into the set and parts will be taken out. Materials for the score are all tones and noises capable of being produced by violin, drum, trombone, sewing machine, grandfather clock, stream of water, etc. Materials for the text are all experiences that provoke the intelligence and emotions. The materials are not to be used logically in their objective relationships, but only within the logic of the work of art. The more intensively the work of art destroys rational objective logic, the greater become the possibilities of artistic building. As in poetry word is played off against word, here factor is played against factor, material against material. The stage-set can be conceived in approximately the same terms as a Merz picture. The parts of the set move and change, and the set lives its life. The movement of the set takes place silently or accompanied by noises or music. I want the Merz stage. Where is the experimental stage?

"Take gigantic surfaces, conceived as infinite, cloak them in color, shift them menacingly and vault their smooth pudency. Shatter and embroil finite parts and bend drilling parts of the void infinitely together. Paste smoothing surfaces over one another. Wire lines movement, real movement rises real tow-rope of a wire mesh. Flaming lines, creeping lines, surfacing lines. Make lines fight together and caress one another in generous tenderness. Let points burst like stars among them, dance a whirling round, and realize each other to form a line. Bend the lines, crack and smash angles, choking revolving around a point. In waves of whirling storm let a line rush by, tangible in wire. Roll globes whirling air they touch one another. Interpermeating surfaces seep away. Crates corners up, straight and crooked and painted. Collapsible top hats fall strangled crates boxes. Make lines pulling sketch a net ultramarining. Nets embrace compress Antony's torment. Make nets firewave and run off into lines, thicken into surfaces. Net the nets. Make veils blow, soft folds fall, make cotton drip and water gush. Hurl up air soft and white through thousand candle power arc lamps. Then take wheels and axles, hurl them up and make them sing (mighty erections of aquatic giants). Axles dance mid-wheel roll globes barrel. Cogs flair teeth, find a sewing machine that yawns. Turning upward or bowed down the sewing machine beheads itself, feet up. Take a dentist's drill, a meat grinder, a car-track scraper, take buses and pleasure cars, bicycles, tandems and their tires, also war-time ersatz tires and deform them. Take lights and deform them as brutally as you can. Make locomotives crash into one another, curtains and portières make threads of spider webs dance with window frames and break whimpering glass. Explode steam boilers to make railroad mist. Take petticoats and other kindred articles, shoes and false hair, also ice skates and throw them into place where they belong, and always at the right time. For all I care, take man-traps, automatic pistols, infernal machines, the tinfish and the funnel, all of course in an artistically deformed condition. Inner tubes are highly recommended. Take in short everything from the hairnet of the high class lady to the propeller of the S.S. *Leviathan*, always bearing in mind the dimensions required by the work.

"Even people can be used.

"People can even be tied to backdrops.

"People can even appear actively, even in their everyday position, they can speak on two legs, even in sensible sentences.

"Now begin to wed your materials to one another. For example, you marry the oilcloth table cover to the home owners' loan association, you bring the lamp cleaner into a relationship with the marriage between Anna Blume and A-natural, concert pitch. You give the globe to the surface to gobble up and you cause a cracked angle to be destroyed by the beam of a 22-thousand candle power arc lamp. You make a human walk on his (her) hands and wear a hat on his (her) feet, like Anna Blume. (Cataracts.) A splashing of foam.

"And now begins the fire of musical saturation. Organs backstage sing and say: 'Futt, futt.' The sewing machine rattles along in the lead. A man in the wings says: 'Bah.' Another suddenly enters and says: 'I am stupid.' (All rights reserved.) Between them a clergyman kneels upside down and cries out and prays in a loud voice: 'Oh mercy seethe and swarm disintegration of amazement Halleluia boy, boy marry drop of water.' A water pipe drips with uninhibited monotony. Eight.

"Drums and flutes flash death and a streetcar conductor's whistle gleams bright. A stream of ice cold water runs down the back of the man in one wing and into a pot. In accompaniment he sings c-sharp d, d-sharp e-flat, the whole proletarian song. Under the pot a gas flame has been lit to boil the water and a melody of violins shimmers pure and virgin-tender. A veil spreads breadths. The center cooks up a deep dark-red flame. A soft rustling. Long sighs violins swell and expire. Light darkens stage, even the sewing machine is dark."

Meanwhile this publication aroused the interest of the actor and theatrical director Franz Rolan[6] who had related ideas, that is, he thought of making the theatre independent and of making the productions grow out of the material available in the modern theatre: stage, backdrops, color, light, actors, director, stage designer, and audience, and assume artistic form. We proceeded to work out in detail the idea of the Merz stage in relation to its practical possibilities, theoretically for the present. The result was a voluminous manuscript which was soon ready for the printer. At some future date perhaps we shall witness the birth of the Merz composite work of art. We can not create it, for we ourselves would only be parts of it, in fact we would be mere material.

P.S. I should now like to print a couple of unpublished poems:

Herbst (1909)
Es schweigt der Wald in Weh.
Er muss geduldig leiden,
Dass nun sein lieber Bräutigam,
Der Sommer, wird scheiden.

Noch hält er zärtlich ihn im Arm
Und quälet sich mit Schmerzen.
Du klagtest, Liebchen, wenn ich schied,
Ruht ich noch dir am Herzen.

Gedicht No. 48 (1920 ?)
Wanken.
Regenwurm.
Fische.
Uhren.
Die Kuh.
Der Wald blättert die Blätter.
Ein Tropfen Asphalt in den Schnee.
Cry, cry, cry, cry, cry.
Ein weiser Mann platzt ohne Gage.

Autumn (1909)
The forest is silent in grief.
She must patiently suffer
Her dear betrothed,
The summer, to depart.

In grief and anguish still
She holds him in her arms.
You, my love, wept when I departed.
Could I now but rest on your heart!

Poem No. 48 (1920?)
Staggering.
Earthworm.
Fishes.
Clocks.
The cow.
The forest leafs the leaves.
A drop of asphalt in the snow.
Cry, cry, cry, cry, cry.
A wise man bursts without wages.

For Dada (1920)
André Breton

It is impossible for me to conceive of a mental joy other than as a breath of fresh air. How could it be comfortable within the limits in which nearly every book, every event, confines it? I doubt that

---

[6]   Franz Rolan organized a private society to build the Schauburg, which became the principal theater in Hannover. It was destroyed in 1943.

FOR DATA
The essay was first published in the journal *La nouvelle revue française* in August 1920, then incorporated into a collection of essays by Breton, *Les pas perdus* (*The Lost Steps*) (Paris: Éditions de la nouvelle revue française, 1924). The entire collection was translated into English by Mark Polizzotti as *The Lost Steps* (Lincoln, NB: the University of Nebraska Press, 1996).

even one person, at least once in his life, has not been tempted to deny the outside world. He would then realize that nothing is so serious or definite as all that. He would move on toward a revision of moral values, which would not prevent him from then returning to common law. Those who experienced this marvelous moment of lucidity at the cost of permanent disorientation are still called poets: Lautréamont, Rimbaud – but the fact is, literary childishness ended with them.

When will we grant arbitrariness the place it deserves in the creation of works or ideas? The things that touch us are generally less willed than we would believe. A felicitous expression or sensational discovery is announced in miserable fashion. Almost nothing achieves its goal, unless, exceptionally, something surpasses it. And the history of these gropings – psychological literature – is hardly instructive: despite its pretensions, no novel has ever proven anything. The most illustrious examples of the genre are not worth setting before our eyes; the most appropriate reponse we could give it is total indifference. Unable as we are to embrace at once the entirety of a painting, or a misfortune, where do we get the right to judge?

If young people have it in for convention, we should not dismiss them as ridiculous: who knows whether reflection makes good counsel? I intend to praise innocence wherever I find it, and I note that it is tolerated only in its passive form. This contradiction alone would be enough to make me skeptical. To keep oneself from being subversive means quelling everything that is not absolutely submissive. I see no valor in that. Revolts are plotted in solitude; there is no need to distance the storm from these ancient sacramental words.

Such considerations strike me as superfluous. I make statements for the pleasure of compromising myself. It should be against the law to use dubious modes of speech. The most convinced or authoritarian individual is not the one we think. I still hesitate to speak about what I know best.

SUNDAY[1]

The airplane weaves telegraph lines
and the source sings the same song
at the Coachman's Meeting House the drinks are orange
but the train mechanics have white eyes
The lady has lost her smile in the woods

The sentimentality of today's poets is something on which we should agree. From the concert of imprecations they so enjoy, a voice proclaiming that they have no soul occasionally rises to enchant them. One young man who at age twenty-three held the most beautiful gaze I know on the universe has mysteriously left us. It is easy for the critics to claim that he was bored: Jacques Vaché[2] was not about to leave behind a last will and testament! I can still see him smiling as he pronounced the words *final wishes*. We are not pessimistic. The one who was painted lying on a reclining chair, so *fin-de-siècle* that he would not have been out of place among collections of psychological works, was the least weary and most subtle of us all. I still see him sometimes; in the trolley car a rider guides his provincial cousins down "Boulevard Saint-Michel: university quarter"; the trolley windows wink in connivance.

We have been chided for not confessing endlessly. Jacques Vaché's good fortune is never to have produced anything. He always kicked aside works of art, the ball-and-chain that retains the soul after death. At the moment when, in Zurich, Tristan Tzara was launching his decisive proclamation – the Dada Manifesto of 1918[3] – Jacques Vaché was unwittingly verifying its principal tenets. "A philosophical question: from which angle to start looking at life, god, ideas, or anything else. Everything we look at is false. I don't think the relative result is any more important than the choice of pastry or cherries for dessert."[4] A spiritual fact being given, there is some haste to see it reproduced in the moral sphere. "Make gestures," they call out to us. But, as André Gide will agree,

[1]   A poem by Philipps Soupault, first published in his book *Rose des vents* (*Rose of the Winds*) (Paris: Au Sans Pareil, 1920).

[2]   Jacques Vaché (1896–1919), a friend of André Breton, who committed suicide.

[3]   For the text, see pp. 479–84 above.

[4]   From Tristan Tzara, "Dada Manifesto 1918," p. 481 in this edition.

"measured against the scale of Eternity, every action is vain,"[5] and we can make the effort required for a childish sacrifice. I am not merely situating myself in time. The scarlet waistcoat,[6] rather than the profound thinking of an era: that, unfortunately, is what everyone understands.

The obscurity of our words is constant. The riddle of meaning must remain in the hands of children. Reading a book to learn something denotes a certain simplicity. The little that the most famous works can teach us about their authors, or about their readers, should rapidly dissuade us from trying this experiment. It is the thesis that disappoints us, not its expression. I regret having to pass through these unclear sentences, receiving confidences without object, feeling at every moment, through the fault of some blabbermouth, a sense of knowing it already. The poets who have recognized this hopelessly flee the intelligible: they know that their work has nothing to lose. One can love an insane woman more than any other.

> Dawn fallen like a shower. The corners of the room are distant and solid. White plane. Comings and goings unmingled,
> in the shadows. Outside, in an alleyway with dirty children, with empty sacks that speak volumes, Paris by Paris,
> I discover. Money, the road, red-eyed journeys with luminous skulls. Daylight exists so that I can learn living, time.
> Ways-errors. Great agitate will become naked honey illness, poorly game already syrup, drowned head, weariness.
>   Thought by happenstance, old flower of mourning, odorless, I hold you in my two hands. My head is shaped like
> a thought.[7]

We are wrong to liken Dada to a subjectivism. No one who currently accepts the Dada label is aiming for hermiticism. "Nothing is incomprehensible," said Lautréamont.[8] If I share the opinion of Paul Valéry – that "the human mind seems to me so made that it cannot be incoherent to itself"[9] – I also think that it cannot be incoherent to anyone else. I believe that this requires not the extraordinary meeting of two individuals, or of one individual with the person he no longer is, but simply a series of acceptable misunderstandings, along with a small number of commonplaces.

Some have spoken of systematically exploring the unconscious. For poets, it is nothing new to let oneself go and write according to the vagaries of one's mind. The word *inspiration*, which for some reason has fallen into disuse, was once seen in a very favorable light. Almost every true imagistic innovation, for example, strikes me as being a spontaneous creation. Guillaume Apollinaire[10] quite rightly thought that clichés such as "lips of coral," whose fortune could pass for a criterion of value, was the product of an activity that he termed *surrealist*. The origins of words themselves are probably no different. He went so far as to make of the principle that one should never build on a previous invention the very condition of scientific perfection and of "progress," so to speak. The idea of the human leg, lost in the wheel, resurfaced only by chance in the locomotive connecting rod. In the same way the biblical tone is starting to reemerge in poetry. I would be tempted to explain this latter phenomenon by the decreased intervention, or nonintervention, in the new writing processes, of personal choice.

What most effectively threatens to harm Dada in public opinion is the interpretation that two or three false sages have given of it. Up until now they have especially tried to see in it the application of a system that is enjoying a great vogue in psychiatry, Freud's "psychoanalysis" – an application, moreover, that the present author foresaw. Mr. H.-R. Lenormand even seems to believe that we

[5]   From the Dada Manifesto 1918; see pp. 000–000 in this edition.
[6]   A reference to the poet Théophile Gautier (1811–72), who famously wore a scarlet waistcoat at the 1930 premier of Victor Hugo's play *Hernani*, which prompted a brawl between Romantics and Classicists. Within Breton's text, the waistcoat symbolizes the purely scandalous side of Dada events and performances, rather than the deeper probing that some sought to derive from them.
[7]   From an untitled prose poem by Paul Eluard (1895–1952), French poet and later Surrealist. It appeared in the journal *Littérature* 11 (Jan. 1920), and was then reprinted in his collec-

tion *Les Nécessités de la vie et le conséquences des rêves* (Paris: Au Sens Pareil, 1921), and is now in his *Oeuvres complètes*, 2 vols., eds. Marcelle Dumas and Lucien Scheler (Paris: Gallimard, Pléiade, 1968), vol. 1, p. 89.
[8]   Comte de Lautréamont (Isidore Ducasse), *Oeuvres complètes*, ed. Hubert Juin (Paris: Gallimard, Pléiade, 1973), p. 277.
[9]   Paul Valéry, "La Soirée avec Monsieur Teste," in his *Oeuvres complètes*, 2 vols., ed. Jean Hytier (Paris: Gallimard-Pléiade, 1960), vol. 2, p. 22.
[10]   Guillaume Apollinaire (1880–1918), a leading figure of the French avant-garde and a prolific journalist.

would benefit from psychoanalytic treatment, if only one could make us submit to it.[11] It goes without saying that the analogy between Cubist or Dadaist works and the ravings of the insane is highly superficial, but it is not yet proven that the so-called absence of logic absolves us from admitting a singular choice, that "plain" language has the disadvantage of being elliptical, and finally that only the works in question could show their authors' abilities and consequently give critics a reason for existing that they have always lacked:

> At the school of infinite thoughts
> Of the most beautiful people
> Hymenoptera architectures
> The books I'd write would be madly tender
> If you were still
> In this novel composed
> At the top of the stairs[12]

All this, moreover, is so relative that for every ten people who accuse us of being illogical, there is one who blames us for going to the opposite extreme. Mr. J.-H. Rosny, noting Tristan Tzara's declaration that "in the course of campaigns against every dogmatism and in a spirit of irony toward the creation of literary schools, Dada became the 'Dada movement,'" remarks, "Thus the origin of Dadaism is not the founding of a new school, but the repudiation of all schools. There is nothing absurd about such a viewpoint, quite the contrary: it is even logical, all too logical."[13]

No one has made any attempt to have Dada account for its will not to be considered a school. People love to insist on the words *group, ringleader,* and *discipline.* They even go so far as to claim that, in the guise of extolling individuality, Dada constitutes a real danger to it, without stopping to notice that we are especially bound together by our differences. Our shared exception to artistic or moral rules affords us only fleeting satisfaction. We are well aware that beyond this an inexpressible personal whim will have its way, which will be more "Dada" than the existing movement. This is what Jacques-Emile Blanche helped us to understand when he wrote: "Dada will survive only by ceasing to exist."[14]

> Let us draw the victim's name out of a hat
> Aggression hangman's noose
>
> The one who was speaking dies
> The murderer stands and says
> Suicide
> End of the world
> Furling of seashell flags.[15]

To begin with, the Dadaists have taken pains to state that there is nothing they want. To know. No need to worry; the instinct for self-preservation always carries the day. When someone naively asked us – after a reading of the manifesto that goes, "No more painters, no more writers, no more religions, no more royalists, no more anarchists, no more socialists, no more police,"[16] and so on – whether we would "let humanity remain," we smiled, hardly wanting to put God on trial. Aren't

---

[11] In an article titled "Dadaïsme et psychologie" (Dadaism and Psychology) which appeared in the newspaper *Comoedia* on March 23, 1920, H.-R. Lenormand charged that Dada was a "regression into childhood" of the sort found in various forms of mental disorder.

[12] From a poem by Francis Picabia (1879–1953), "Unique eunuque," published as an independent book (Paris: Au Sans Pareil, 1920), now in his *Écrits,* ed. Olivier Revault d'Alllonnes (Paris: Belfond, 1975), vol. 1, p. 203.

[13] J. H. Rosny, "Le Tréteau des lettres: le Dadaisme est-il une école?" in *Comoedia,* no. 2675 (April 13, 1920).

[14] Jacques-Emile Blanche, "Réponse à un professeur de rhétorique au lycée de X," in *Comoedia,* March 17, 1920.

[15] From Louis Aragon (1897–1982), "Programme," in his collection *Feu de joie* (Paris: Au Sans Pareil, 1920).

[16] From "Manifeste du mouvement Dada" ("Manifesto of the Dada Movement"), unsigned, published as the first of "Vingt-trois manifestes" ("Twenty-three Manifestos") in the journal *Littérature,* no. 13 (May 1920).

we the last to forget that there are limits to understanding? If it so happens that I get such pleasure from these words by Georges Ribemont-Dessaignes, it's just that at bottom they constitute an act of extreme humility: "What is beautiful? What is ugly? What are big, strong, weak? What are Carpentier, Renan, Foch? Don't know. What is me? Don't know. Don't know, don't know, don't know."[17]

New York Dada (1921)
Marcel Duchamp and Man Ray

New York Dada. **Cover. New York, April 1921**

[17]   From a text by Georges Ribemont-Dessaignes (1884–1975) which he read aloud at a performance in the Théâtre de l'Oeuvres on March 27, 1920 and published under the title "Artichauts" ("Artichokes") in the single-issue journal *DADAphone* (March 1920), which consists of only 8 pages.

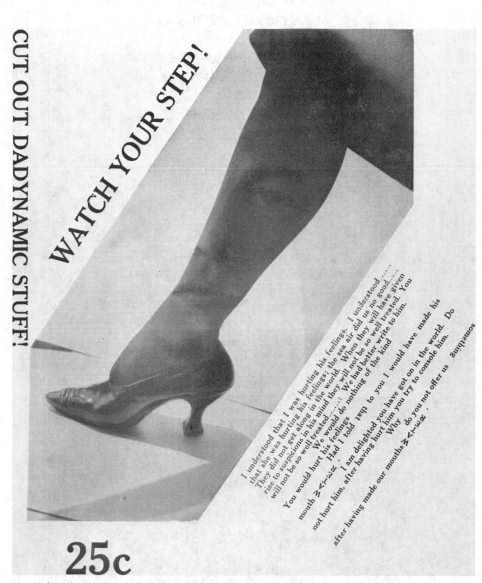

New York Dada. First page. New York, April 1921.

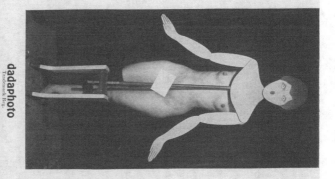

EYE-COVER   ART-COVER   CORSET-COVER

AUTHORIZATION

NEW YORK-DADA:

You ask for authorization to name your periodical Dada. But Dada belongs to everybody. I know excellent people who have the name Dada. Mr. Jean Dada; Mr. Gaston de Dada; Fr. Picabia's dog is called Zizi de Dada; in G. Ribemont-Dessaigne's play, the pope is likewise named Zizi de Dada. I could cite dozens of examples. Dada belongs to everybody. Like the idea of God or of the tooth-brush. There are people who are very dada, more dada; there are dadas everywere all over and in every individual. Like God and the tooth1brush (an excellent invention, by the way).

Dada is a new type; a mixture of man, naphthaline, sponge, animal made of ebonite and beefsteak, prepared with soap for cleansing the brain. Good teeth are the making of the stomach and beautiful teeth are the making of a charming smile. Halleluiah of ancient oil and injection of rubber.

There is nothing abnormal about my choice of Dada for the name of my review. In Switzerland I was in the company of friends and was hunting the dictionary for a word appropriate to the sonorities of all languages. Night was upon us when a green hand placed its ugliness on the page of Larousse—pointing very precisely to Dada—my choice was made. I lit a cigarette and drank a demitasse.

For Dada was to say nothing and to lead to no explanation of this offshoot of relationship which is not a dogma nor a school, but rather a constellation of individuals and of free facets.

Dada existed before us (the Holy Virgin) but one cannot deny its magical power to add to this already existing spirit and impulses of penetration and diversity that characterizes its present form.

There is nothing more incomprehensible than Dada.

Nothing more indefinable.

With the best will in the world I cannot tell you what I think of it.

The journalists who say that Dada is a pretext are right, but it is a pretext for something I do not know.

Dada has penetrated into every hamlet; Dada is the best paying concern of the day.

Therefore, Madam, be on your guard and realize that a really dada product is a different thing from a glossy label.

Dada abolishes "nuances." Nuances do not exist in words but only in some atrophied brains whose cells are too jammed. Dada is an anti "nuance" cream. The simple motions that serve as signs for deaf-mutes are quite adequate to express the four or five mysteries we have discovered within 7 or 8,000 years. Dada offers all kinds of advantages. Dada will soon be able to boast of having shown people that to say "right" instead of "left" is neither less nor too logical, that red and valise are the same thing; that 2765 = 34; that "fool" is a merit; that yes = no. Strong influences are making themselves felt in politics, in commerce, in language. The whole world and what's in it has slid to the left along with us. Dada has inserted its syringe into hot bread, to speak allegorically into language. Little by little (large by large) it destroys it. Everything collapses with logic. And we shall see certain liberties we constantly take in the sphere of sentiment, social life, morals, once more become normal standards. These liberties no longer will be looked upon as crime, but as itches.

I will close with a little international song: Order from the publishing house "La Sirene" 7 rue Pasquier, Paris, DADAGLOBE, the work of dadas from all over the world. Tell your bookseller that this book will soon be out of print. You will have many agreeable surprises.

Read Dadaglobe if you have troubles. Dadaglobe is in press. Here are some of its colloborators:

Paul Citroen (Amsterdam); Baader Daimonides; R. Hausmann; W. Heartfield; H. Hoech; R. Huelsenbeck; G. Grosz; Fried Hardy Worm (Berlin); Clement Pansaers (Bruxelles); Mac Robber (Calcutta); Jacques Edwards (Chili); Baargeld, Armada v. Dulgedalzen, Max Ernst, F. Haubrich (Cologne); K. Schwitters (Hannovre); J. K. Bonset (Leyde); Guillermo de Torre (Madrid); Gino Cantarelli; E. Bacchi, A. Fiozzi (Mantoue); Krusenitch (Moscou); A. Vagts (Munich); W. C. Arensberg, Gabrielle Buffet, Marcel Duchamp; Adon Lacroix; Baroness v. Loringhoven; Man Ray; Joseph Stella; E. Varese; A. Stieglitz; M. Hartley; C. Kahler (New York); Louis Aragon; C. Brancusi; André Breton; M. Buffet; S. Charchoune; J. Crotti; Suzanne Duchamp; Paul Eluard; Benjamin Peret; Francis Picabia; G. Ribemont-Dessaignes; J. Rigaut, Soubeyran; Ph. Soupault, Tristan Tzara (Paris); Melchior Vischer (Prague); J. Evola (Rome); Arp; S. Taeuber (Zurich).

The incalculable number of pages of reproductions and of text is a guaranty of the success of the book. Articles of luxury, of prime necessity, articles indispensable to hygiene and to the heart, toilet articles of an intimate nature.

Such, Madame, do we prepare for Dadaglobe; for you need look no further than to the use of articles prepared without Dada to account for the fact that the skin of your heart is chapped; that the so precious enamel of your intelligence is cracking; also for the presence of those tiny wrinkles still imperceptible but nevertheless disquieting.

All this and much else in Dadaglobe.   TRISTAN TZARA.

New York Dada. **Second page. New York, April, 1921.**

PUG DEBS MAKE SOCIETY BOW

Marsden Hartley May Make a Couple— Coming Out Party Next Friday

A beautiful pair of rough-eared debutantes will lead the grand socking cotillion in Madison Square Garden when Mina Loy gives a coming-out party for her Queensberry proteges. Mina will introduce the Marsden Hartleys and the Joseph Stellas to society next week, and everybody who is who will be who-er than ever that night.

Master Marsden will be attired in a neat but not gaudy set of tight-fitting gloves and will have a V-back in front and on both sides. He will wear very short skirts gathered at the waist with a nickel's worth of live leather belting. His slippers will be heavily jewelled with brass eyelets, and a luxurious pair of dime laces will be woven in and out of the hooks. He may or may not wear socks. He has always been known as a daring dresser.

Attire of Debutantes

Master Joseph will wear a flesh-colored complexion, with the exception of his full-dress tights. He has created a furore in society by appearing at informal morning battles with coattails on his tights. The usual procedure at matinee massacres is for the guest of honor to wear tuxedo trunks with Bull Durham trim-

mings. He will affect the six-ounce suede glove with hard bandages and a little concrete in 'em if possible. His tights will be silk and he wears them very short.

Before the pug-debs are introduced, Miss Loy will turn a gold spigot and flocks of butterflies will be released from their cages. They will flitter through the magnificent Garden, which has been especially decorated with extra dust for the occasion. Each butterfly will flit around and and then light on some particular head. If you get two oleofleas on your dome, try and keep it a secret.

Description of Ring

The ring will be from the Renaissance period with natural wood splinters. The gong will sound curfew chimes at the end of each round. It will be played by a specially imported pack of Swiss gong ringers. The ropes will be velvet and hung like portieres. Edgar Varese, the violinist, has donated a piece of concert resin to be used on the canvas flooring, which will be made in Persia. Incidentally, the tights worn by the fighters will be made by Tweeblegham, of London, purveyor to the Queen by highest award.

Master Marsden will give his first dance to his brother pug-deb Joseph, which will probably fill Marsden's card for the evening. Visiting diplomats in the gallery de luxe will please refrain from asking for waltzes.

—With apologies to "Bugs" Baer.

R. Goldberg

VENTILATION

On the question of proper ventilation opinions radically differ. It seems impossible to please all. It is our aim, however, to cater to the wishes of the majority. The conductor of this vehicle will gladly be governed accordingly. Your cooperation will be appreciated.

DADATAXI, Limited.

New York Dada. Third page. New York, April 1921.

YOURS WITH DEVOTION
trumpets and drums.

Dearest Saltimbanques_____
      beatrice_____muriel_____
  shaw___not garden___   mary___
      "when they go the other way"
    OTHER WAY___dearest___:
                REMEMBER_____
Mary so knowing____emma____emily____
                beatrice_____muriel_____
  bandwaggon of heavenly saltimbanques_____
yes yes___girlies_____performance at eleven in the late afternoon_____
    wires all spread_____canvas_____stretched_____
special thunderstorm to be pulled___for YOU____for YOU____
and YOU_____and YOU_____and YOU_____
    saltimbanques come straight from HEAven_____
Toto____ella____and ethel____
french nacre_____frigidity english_____
ALL_____ALL_____ALL_____ALL_____ALL_____
               hurdygurdy-merrygoround_____
Offset of delicious word DISGUST_____
      saltimbanques are from HEAven_____
eh bien TOTO___et toi___ELLA_____so murderously
aware-IMPECCABLE ELLA_____BERtie_____
              having given us
  the difficulties of   to feel
        SNIPESHOOTING in the gutters of the
               STRAND_____
with a prince albert to cover those votive limbs
  hungrier for chops___than for the immoral
      NUdeness of the TRuth_____
shall we invite minnie_____that one who had the courage_____
               to run_____
the gamut_____from hedda to hannele_____
  never__glorious one___having to my knowledge
    taken advantage of any innocent word in our
             novel SPEECH_____
and lily?
        lena, naturellement____
           most perfect legs since Pauline Hall
           so the old ducks say.
    shall we phone for Lily?_____
  saltimbanques are from HEAven_____
           c'est tout___ma chere_____

TOTO___pav_____
      WATTS___Pav___
give us these gentlemen pavs_____who turn PIROUETTES
  into handsprings_____standing upon skates
             of wood_____and upon
           muscles of chalcedony_____
saltimbanques are from HEAven_____
beatrice_____and muriel_____
    astarte of the SKATING rink____
      juno of the TIGHT wire_____
Puppets pull their own strings if having the
         intelligence___of bea_____
        and Muri_____
        they pull them well_____
        WELL_____I said_____
           W__E__L__L_____
saltimbanques are from HEAven_____
  Franklin and CHarles____muscles___muscles__muscles____
  George and dicky_____lines___lines___lines____

saltimbanques are from HEAven_____

Experience__without____expurgation_____
  everyone's rabelaisian step-parent_____
  evryone damned by mrs. beterouge_____

I have a thousand mouchoirs____
             Phyllis and Phillippe_____
send us many another bandwaggon, GOD_____
  filled with saltimbanques like
    FRanklin and CHarles_____
      and TOTO_____and ETHEL_____and ELLA_____

You have heard what I said_____
    SALTIMBANQUES ARE STRAIGHT
            from heaven_____
    That's all, infinitely all_____
          That's all__
        ALL.
           ALL.
           ALL.

  Dance hellions, all of you_____
      for your very lives_____

hoven
-Loring-
Freytag
von
Baroness
Elsa

New York Dada. Fourth and final page. New York, April, 1921.

After Dada (1922)
André Breton

My friends Philippe Soupault and Paul Eluard will not contradict me if I say that "Dada" was never seen by us as anything more than the vulgar image of a state of mind that it in no way helped to create. If it occurs to them, as it did to me, to reject the label and realize the abuse to which they have fallen victim, perhaps this first principle will be saved. In the meantime they will forgive me for informing the readers of *Comoedia*, in order to remove all misunderstanding, that Mr. Tzara had no part in the invention of the word *Dada* – as attested by a letter from Schad and Huelsenbeck,[1] his companions in Zurich during the war, which I am quite prepared to publish – and that he no doubt had very little hand in writing the "Dada Manifesto 1918," which determined our welcome and the credit we extended him.

The paternity of the manifesto is, in any case, formally claimed by Val Serner,[2] a doctor of philosophy who lives in Geneva and whose German-language manifestoes, written before 1918, have not been translated into French. We know, furthermore, that the conclusions reached by Francis Picabia and Marcel Duchamp[3] even before the war, alongside those reached by Jacques Vaché in 1917, would have been sufficient to orient us in and of themselves. Up until now I had been reluctant to denounce Mr. Tzara's bad faith and had let him blatantly arm himself with the proxy votes of the very individuals whose pockets he had picked in their absence. But today, when he is trying to grab his last chance to make some noise by falsely declaring his opposition to one of the most impartial enterprises that could be,[4] I have no qualms about ordering him to be silent.

Dada, thank goodness, is no longer an issue, and its funeral in around May 1921 engendered no brawls. The procession, numbering very few people, followed in the wake of Cubism-Futurism, which the students at the Beaux-Arts went to drown in effigy in the Seine. Although it had, as they say, its hour of fame, Dada left few regrets: in the long run its omnipotence and tyranny had made it unbearable.

Nonetheless I noted with some bitterness at the time that several of those who had given it handouts – generally those who had given the smallest handouts – found themselves reduced to poverty. The others lost no time in rallying around Francis Picabia's strong statements, inspired, as we know, only by a love of life and a horror of all corruption. Which is not to say that Picabia meant to re-create our unity around himself –

> It's hard to imagine
> How stupid and stolid success can make people[5]

– and he is more prepared than anyone to do without it. But, although there is no question of substituting a new group for our individual tendencies (Mr. Tzara must be joking), Louis Aragon,

---

AFTER DADA

The essay was first published in a Paris newspaper, *Comoedia*, March 2, 1922, then incorporated into a collection of essays by Breton, *Les pas perdus* (*The Lost Steps*) (Paris: Éditions de la nouvelle revue française, 1924). The entire collection was translated into English by Mark Polizzotti as *The Lost Steps* (Lincoln, NB: the University of Nebraska Press, 1996).

[1] Christian Schad (1894–1982), a painter, engraver, and photographer, was active in Zurich Dada; he had written to Francis Picabia in April 1921 a letter which charged that Tzara had not invented the word Dada, and that the spread of Dada in German was due not to Tzara's "Dada Manifesto 1918" (see pp. 000–000 this edition), but to a manifesto by one Doctor Walter Serner (b. 1893), which appeared in a later issue of the journal, *Dada 4/5*. Breton overextends Schad's claims in denying Tzara authorship of the "Dada Manifesto 1918," as he does a bit further below. Richard Huelsenbeck (1892–1974) was the chief figure in Berlin Dada.

[2] See preceding note.

[3] Francis Picabia (1879–1953) was a French painter, as was Marcel Duchamp (1887–1968). Picabia claimed that he and Duchamp had already invented the Dada state of mind in 1912, but not the word; Jacques Vaché (1896–1919) was a friend of André Breton who committed suicide; Breton viewed him as a precursor to Dada and Surrealism.

[4] The Congress of Paris for the determination and defense of the modern spirit, held in April 1922, and opposed by Tristan Tzara.

[5] The statement, seemingly by Picabia, actually an excerpt from the poem "Victory" by Guillaume Apollinaire in his volume *Calligrammes* (Paris: Mercure de France, 1918), now in his *Oeuvres poétiques*, eds. Marcel Adéma and Michel Décaudin (Paris: Gallimard-Pléiade, 1959), p. 309.

Pierre de Massot, Jacques Rigaut, Roger Vitrac,[6] and I could not long remain indifferent to the marvelous detachment from all things of which Picabia gave us the example and that we are happy to state here.

For myself, I point out that this attitude is not new. If I abstained last year from taking part in the demonstrations organized by *Dada* at the Galerie Montaigne,[7] it was because this sort of activity had already lost its attraction for me – because I saw in it the means of reaching my twenty-sixth or thirtieth birthday without striking a single blow, and I am determined to flee anything that masks itself in that kind of facility. In an unpublished article of the time, which few people have read, I deplored the stereotyped character that our gestures were taking on, and I wrote, verbatim, "After all, the issue is not our insouciance or momentary good humor. Personally, I have no wish to be amused. It seems to me that sanctioning a series of utterly futile 'Dada' acts means seriously compromising one of the attempts at liberation to which I remain the most strongly attached. These ideas, which count among the finest, are at the mercy of their too-rapid popularization.

"Our age might well be ill-disposed toward concentration, but must we always accept being content with superficialities? 'The mind,' it has been said, 'is not so independent that it cannot be distracted by the slightest disturbance made around it.'[8] What, then, can we predict for it if it insists on making that disturbance itself?"

Still today, it is hardly my intention to act as a judge. "The place and the formula"[9] might always elude me, but – and this cannot be said often enough – the important thing is this quest and nothing else. Hence the great void that we are forced to create in ourselves. Without going so far as to develop a taste for the pathetic, I am prepared to do without practically everything. I do not wish to slip on the waxed floor of sentimentality. There is no error, properly speaking: at most one could call it an unlucky wager, and those who are reading me are free to feel that the game is not worth the candle. For myself, I will try once more to involve myself even further, if possible – without, however, making Francis Picabia's words ("One must be a nomad, cross through ideas as one crosses through countries or cities"[10]) into a rule of hygiene or a duty. Even if every idea were fated to disappoint us, I would still take it as my starting point to devote my life to them.

---

[6] Peirre de Massot (1900–69), Jacques Rigaut (1898–1929), and Roger Vitrac (1899–1952) were all aspiring French writers who were early participants in Surrealism. See the "Introduction" to "Continental Interlude III: Surrealism," pp. 000–000.

[7] A series of events which took place June 6–18, 1921, at the Galerie Montaigne, the "Grand Saison dada," which included a show or performance on June 10.

[8] From Blaise Pascal (1623–62), *Pensées*, in his *Oeuvres complètes*, ed. Jacques Chevalier (Paris: Gallimard-Pléiade, 1936), p. 1114 ("Misère de l'homme – Les puissances trompeuses").

[9] This expression, cited by Breton on numerous occasions, is from Rimbaud's poem "Vagabonds." (trans.)

[10] Francis Picabia, "M. Picabia se sépares des dadas" ("Monsieur Picabia Leaves the Dadaists"), originally in *Comoedia*, May 11, 1921; now in Picabia, *Écrits II*, ed. Oliver Revault d'Allonnes (Paris: Belfond, 1978), p. 15.

William Carlos Williams (1883–1963)

Introduction

William Carlos Williams was born in Rutherford, New Jersey. His father had emigrated from Birmingham, England, his mother from Puerto Rico. He attended schools in Rutherford until 1897, when he was sent for two years to a school near Geneva and to the Lycée Condorcet in Paris, after which he completed his studies at the Horace Mann High School in New York. In 1902 he was admitted to the medical school at the University of Pennsylvania, and it was there he met Ezra Pound. Theirs remained a lifelong friendship that weathered lifelong disagreement. Williams did his internship in New York from 1906 to 1909. Thereafter he lived a double life: a general practitioner by day, a poet at night.

Williams's first two books, *Poems* (1909) and *Tempers* (1913), were slight affairs, and his promise first appears in *Al Que Quiere!* (1917; *To Him Who Wants It!*). In 1920 he published *Kora in Hell*, a series of prose improvisations prefaced by an aggressive prologue in which he divided modern American literature into two camps: those who had stayed at home, and those who were expatriates, such as Eliot, and Pound. The latter he dismissed as "men content with the connotations of their masters," and Eliot he called "a subtle conformist." Years later, in his *Autobiography*, Williams would recall the publication of *The Waste Land* as a "great catastrophe to our letters." Undaunted by the catastrophe, Williams published *Spring and All* in 1923, a serial poem consisting of 27 untitled but numbered poems, introduced and accompanied throughout by a sometimes fierce, sometimes flamboyant, prose polemic (see immediately below). It remains one of his finest books.

Throughout the rest of his life Williams remained extraordinarily prolific. In addition to a large number of poems, he wrote short stories, novels, essays, and an autobiography. In 1946 he began to write an epic, with the publication of *Paterson*, Book I. The four following books appeared in 1948, 1949, 1951, and 1958; and at the time of his death in 1963, he was at work on a sixth book. Williams was highly esteemed in his later years, and he had a host of admirers and imitators. But with the rise of postmodernism in the 1970s, Williams's truculent and dogmatic belief that poetry could offer unmediated access to the world seemed an oversimplification, if not naive. His reputation has diminished enormously since the 1980s.

Spring and All (1923)

If anything of moment results – so much the better. And so much the more likely will it be that no one will want to see it.

Spring and All was published by Robert McAlmon and his Contact Publishing Company in 1923 in Paris. Interspersed with its prose meditations, the volume contains 27 poems, which are all untitled and numbered with Roman numerals. At some later point every poem was given a title and published as an independent work in one of Williams's subsequent collections, and in some cases individual poems were given more than one title. In their edition of Williams's *Collected Poems* (New York: New Directions, 1986), 500–1, A. Walton Litz and Christopher MacGown provide the following table of these changes, useful because many critics cite the poems by their later titles in critical discussions:

I. Spring and All
II. The Pot of Flowers (The Houthouse Plant in *Secession*, Jan. 1923); The Pot of Primroses in *Collected Poems*, 1934
III. The Farmer
IV. Flight to the City (Cornucopia in *The Chapbook*, April 1923)
V. The Black Winds (The Immemorial Wind in *An Early Martyr* [1935])
VI. To Have Done Nothing
VII. The Rose
VIII. At the Faucet of June
IX. Young Love (Young Romance in *An Early Martyr*)
X. The Eyglasses
XI. The Right of Way (The Auto Ride in *An Early Martyr*)
XII. Composition
XIII. The Agonized spires
XIV. Death the Barber
XV. Light Becomes Darkness
XVI. To an Old Jaundiced Woman (The Attempt in *Secession*, Aug. 1922)
XVII. Shoot it Jimmy!
XVIII. To Elsie
XIX. Horned Purple
XX. The Sea
XXI. Quietness
XXII. The Red Wheelbarrow
XXIII. Rigmarole (Rigmarole in *Go Go* [1923]; The Veritable Night in *Der Querschnitt*, Fall 1924)
XXIV. The Avenue of Poplars
XXV. Rapid Transit
XXVI. At the Ball Game
XXVII. The Wildflower

There is a constant barrier between the reader and his consciousness of immediate contact with the world. If there is an ocean it is here. Or rather, the whole world is between: Yesterday, tomorrow, Europe, Asia, Africa, – all things removed and impossible, the tower of the church at Seville, the Parthenon.

What do they mean when they say: "I do not like your poems; you have no faith whatever. You seem neither to have suffered nor, in fact, to have felt anything very deeply. There is nothing appealing in what you say but on the contrary the poems are positively repellent. They are heartless, cruel, they make fun of humanity. What in God's name do you mean? Are you a pagan? Have you no tolerance for human frailty? Rhyme you may perhaps take away but rhythm! why there is none in your work whatever. Is this what you call poetry? It is the very antithesis of poetry. It is antipoetry. It is the annihilation of life upon which you are bent. Poetry that used to go hand in hand with life, poetry that interpreted our deepest promptings, poetry that inspired, that led us forward to new discoveries, new depths of tolerance, new heights of exaltation. You moderns! it is the death of poetry that you are accomplishing. No. I cannot understand this work. You have not yet suffered a cruel blow from life. When you have suffered you will write differently?"

Perhaps this noble apostrophe means something terrible for me, I am not certain, but for the moment I interpret it to say: "You have robbed me. God, I am naked. What shall I do?" – By it they mean that when I have suffered (provided I have not done so as yet) I too shall run for cover; that I too shall seek refuge in fantasy. And mind you, I do not say that I will not. To decorate my age.

But today it is different.

The reader knows himself as he was twenty years ago and he has also in mind a vision of what he would be, some day. Oh, some day! But the thing he never knows and never dares to know is what he is at the exact moment that he is. And this moment is the only thing in which I am at all interested. Ergo, who cares for anything I do? And what do I care?

I love my fellow creature. Jesus, how I love him: endways, sideways, frontways and all the other ways – but he doesn't exist! Neither does she. I do, in a bastardly sort of way.

To whom then am I addressed? To the imagination.

In fact to return upon my theme for the time nearly all writing, up to the present, if not all art, has been especially designed to keep up the barrier between sense and the vaporous fringe which distracts the attention from its agonized approaches to the moment. It has been always a search for "the beautiful illusion." Very well. I am not in search of "the beautiful illusion."

And if when I pompously announce that I am addressed – To the imagination – you believe that I thus divorce myself from life and so defeat my own end, I reply: To refine, to clarify, to intensify that eternal moment in which we alone live there is but a single force – the imagination. This is its book. I myself invite you to read and to see.

In the imagination, we are from henceforth (so long as you read) locked in a fraternal embrace, the classic caress of author and reader. We are one. Whenever I say, "I" I mean also, "you." And so, together, as one, we shall begin.

CHAPTER 19

o meager times, so fat in everything imaginable! imagine the New World that rises to our windows from the sea on Mondays and on Saturdays – and on every other day of the week also. Imagine it in all its prismatic colorings, its counterpart in our souls – our souls that are great pianos whose strings, of honey and of steel, the divisions of the rainbow set twanging, loosing on the air great novels of adventure! Imagine the monster project of the moment: Tomorrow we the people of the United States are going to Europe armed to kill every man, woman and child in the area west of the Carpathian Mountains (also east) sparing none. Imagine the sensation it will cause. First we shall kill them and then they, us. But we are careful to spare the Spanish bulls, the birds, rabbits, small deer and of course – the Russians. For the Russians we shall build a bridge from edge to edge of the Atlantic – having first been at pains to slaughter all Canadians and Mexicans on this side. Then, oh then, the great feature will take place.

Never mind; the great event may not exist, so there is no need to speak further of it. Kill! kill! the English, the Irish, the French, the Germans, the Italians and the rest: friends or enemies, it makes no difference, kill them all. The bridge is to be blown up when all Russia is upon it. And why?

Because we love them – all. That is the secret: a new sort of murder. We make *leberwurst* of them. Bratwurst. But why, since we are ourselves doomed to suffer the same annihilation?

If I could say what is in my mind in Sanscrit or even Latin[1] I would do so. But I cannot. I speak for the integrity of the soul and the greatness of life's inanity; the formality of its boredom; the orthodoxy of its stupidity. Kill! kill! let there be fresh meat.. ...

The imagination, intoxicated by prohibitions, rises to drunken heights to destroy the world. Let it rage, let it kill. The imagination is supreme. To it all our works forever, from the remotest past to the farthest future, have been, are and will be dedicated. To it alone we show our wit by having raised in its honor as monument not the least pebble. To it now we come to dedicate our secret project: the annihilation of every human creature on the face of the earth. This is something never before attempted. None to remain; nothing but the lower vertebrates, the mollusks, insects and plants. Then at last will the world be made anew. Houses crumble to ruin, cities disappear giving place to mounds of soil blown thither by the winds, small bushes and grass give way to trees which grow old and are succeeded by other trees for countless generations. A marvellous serenity broken only by bird and wild beast calls reigns over the entire sphere. Order and peace abound.

This final and self inflicted holocaust has been all for love, for sweetest love, that together the human race, yellow, black, brown, red and white, agglutinated into one enormous soul may be gratified with the sight and retire to the heaven of heavens content to rest on its laurels. There, soul of souls, watching its own horrid unity, it boils and digests itself within the tissues of the great Being of Eternity that we shall then have become. With what magnificent explosions and odors will not the day be accomplished as we, the Great One among all creatures, shall go about contemplating our self-prohibited desires as we promenade them before the inward review of our own bowels – et cetera, et cetera, et cetera...and it is spring – both in Latin and Turkish, in English and Dutch, in Japanese and Italian; it is spring by Stinking River where a magnolia tree, without leaves, before what was once a farmhouse, now a ramshackle home for millworkers, raises its straggling branches of ivorywhite flowers.

CHAPTER XIII

Thus, weary of life, in view of the great consummation which awaits us – tomorrow, we rush among our friends congratulating ourselves upon the joy soon to be. Thoughtless of evil we crush out the marrow of those about us with our heavy cars as we go happily from place to place. It seems that there is not time enough in which to speak the full of our exaltation. Only a day is left, one miserable day, before the world comes into its own. Let us hurry! Why bother for this man or that? In the offices of the great newspapers a mad joy reigns as they prepare the final extras. Rushing about, men bump each other into the whirring presses. How funny it seems. All thought of misery has left us. Why should we care? Children laughingly fling themselves under the wheels of the street cars, airplanes crash gaily to the earth. Someone has written a poem.

Oh life, bizarre fowl, what color are your wings? Green, blue, red, yellow, purple, white, brown, orange, black, grey? In the imagination, flying above the wreck of ten thousand million souls, I see you departing sadly for the land of plants and insects, already far out to sea. (Thank you, I know well what I am plagiarizing) Your great wings flap as you disappear in the distance over the pre-Columbian acres of floating weed.

The new cathedral overlooking the park, looked down from its towers today, with great eyes, and saw by the decorative lake a group of people staring curiously at the corpse of a suicide: Peaceful, dead young man, the money they have put into the stones has been spent to teach men of life's

---

[1]   Probably a reference to T. S. Eliot's *The Waste Land*, published with its notes in December 1922.

austerity. You died and teach us the same lesson. You seem a cathedral, celebrant of the spring which shivers for me among the long black trees.

CHAPTER VI

Now, in the imagination, all flesh, all human flesh has been dead upon the earth for ten million, billion years. The bird has turned into a stone within whose heart an egg, unlaid, remained hidden.

It is spring! but miracle of miracles a miraculous miracle has gradually taken place during these seemingly wasted eons. Through the orderly sequences of unmentionable time EVOLUTION HAS REPEATED ITSELF FROM THE BEGINNING.

Good God!

Every step once taken in the first advance of the human race, from the amoeba to the highest type of intelligence, has been duplicated, every step exactly paralleling the one that preceded in the dead ages gone by. A perfect plagiarism results. Everything is and is new. Only the imagination is undeceived.

At this point the entire complicated and laborious process begins to near a new day. (More of this in Chapter XIX) But for the moment everything is fresh, perfect, recreated.

In fact now, for the first time, everything IS new. Now at last the perfect effect is being witlessly discovered. The terms "veracity," "actuality," "real," "natural," "sincere" are being discussed at length, every word in the discussion being evolved from an identical discussion which took place the day before yesterday.

Yes, the imagination, drunk with prohibitions, has destroyed and recreated everything afresh in the likeness of that which it was. Now indeed men look about in amazement at each other with a full realization of the meaning of "art."

CHAPTER 2

It is spring: life again begins to assume its normal appearance as of "today." Only the imagination is undeceived. The volcanos are extinct. Coal is beginning to be dug again where the fern forests stood last night. (If an error is noted here, pay no attention to it.)

CHAPTER XIX

I realize that the chapters are rather quick in their sequence and that nothing much is contained in any one of them but no one should be surprised at this today.

The traditionalists of plagiarism

It is spring. That is to say, it is approaching THE BEGINNING.

In that huge and microscopic career of time, as it were a wild horse racing in an illimitable pampa under the stars, describing immense and microscopic circles with his hoofs on the solid turf, running without a stop for the millionth part of a second until he is aged and worn to a heap of skin, bones and ragged hoofs – In that majestic progress of life, that gives the exact impression of Phidias's frieze, the men and beasts of which, though they seem of the rigidity of marble are not so but move, with blinding rapidity, though we do not have the time to notice it, their legs advancing a millionth part of an inch every fifty thousand years – In that progress of life which seems stillness itself in the mass of its movements – at last SPRING is approaching.

In that colossal surge toward the finite and the capable life has now arrived for the second time at that exact moment when in the ages past the destruction of the species *Homo sapiens* occurred.

Now at last that process of miraculous verisimilitude, that great copying which evolution has followed, repeating move for move every move that it made in the past – is approaching the end.

Suddenly it is at an end. THE WORLD IS NEW.

I

By the road to the contagious hospital
under the surge of the blue
mottled clouds driven from the

northeast – a cold wind. Beyond, the
5   waste of broad, muddy fields
brown with dried weeds, standing and fallen

patches of standing water
the scattering of tall trees

All along the road the reddish
10   purplish, forked, upstanding, twiggy
stuff of bushes and small trees
with dead, brown leaves under them
leafless vines –

Lifeless in appearance, sluggish
15   dazed spring approaches –

They enter the new world naked,
cold, uncertain of all
save that they enter. All about them
the cold, familiar wind –

20   Now the grass, tomorrow
the stiff curl of wildcarrot leaf

One by one objects are defined –
It quickens: clarity, outline of leaf

But now the stark dignity of
25   entrance – Still, the profound change

has come upon them: rooted they
grip down and begin to awaken

II

Pink confused with white
flowers and flowers reversed
take and spill the shaded flame
darting it back
5   into the lamp's horn

petals aslant darkened with mauve

red where in whorls
petal lays its glow upon petal
round flamegreen throats

10   petals radiant with transpiercing light
contending
                              above

     the leaves
     reaching up their modest green
     from the pot's rim   15

     and there, wholly dark, the pot
     gay with rough moss.

A terrific confusion has taken place. No man knows whither to turn. There is nothing! Emptiness stares us once more in the face. Whither? To what end? Each asks the other. Has life its tail in its mouth or its mouth in its tail? Why are we here? Dora Marsden's philosophic algebra.[2] Everywhere men look into each other's faces and ask the old unanswerable question: Whither? How? What? Why?

At any rate, now at last spring is here!

The rock has split, the egg has hatched, the prismatically plumed bird of life has escaped from its cage. It spreads its wings and is perched now on the peak of the huge African mountain Kilimanjaro.

Strange recompense, in the depths of our despair at the unfathomable mist into which all mankind is plunging, a curious force awakens. It is HOPE long asleep, aroused once more. Wilson has taken an army of advisers and sailed for England. The ship has sunk. But the men are all good swimmers. They take the women on their shoulders and buoyed on by the inspiration of the moment they churn the free seas with their sinewy arms, like Ulysses, landing all along the European seaboard.

Yes, hope has awakened once more in men's hearts. It is NEW! Let us go forward!

The imagination, freed from the handcuffs of "art," takes the lead! Her feet are bare and not too delicate. In fact those who come behind her have much to think of. Hm. Let it pass.

CHAPTER I

Samuel Butler

The great English divine, Sam Butler, is shouting from a platform, warning us as we pass: There are two who can invent some extraordinary thing to one who can properly employ that which has been made use of before.

Enheartened by this thought THE TRADITIONALISTS OF PLAGIARISM try to get hold of the mob. They seize those nearest them and shout into their ears: Tradition! The solidarity of life!

The fight is on: These men who have had the governing of the mob through all the repetitious years resent the new order. Who can answer them? One perhaps here and there but it is an impossible situation. If life were anything but a bird, if it were a man, a Greek or an Egyptian, but it is only a bird that has eyes and wings, a beak, talons and a cry that reaches to every rock's center, but without intelligence? –

The voice of the Delphic Oracle itself, what was it? A poisonous gas from a rock's cleft.

Those who led yesterday wish to hold their sway a while longer. It is not difficult to understand their mood. They have their great weapons to hand: "science," "philosophy" and most dangerous of all "art."

Meanwhile, SPRING, which has been approaching for several pages, is at last here.

– they ask us to return to the proven truths of tradition, even to the twice proven, the substantiality of which is known. Demuth[3] and a few others do their best to point out the error, telling us that design is a function of the IMAGINATION, describing its movements, its colors – but it is a hard battle. I myself seek to enter the lists with these few notes jotted down in the midst

---

[2] Dora Marsden (1882–1960) was founder and editor of the *Freewoman* and *The New Freewoman* (renamed, in 1913, *The Egoist*), to which she contributed essays on philosophy and psychology. In "The Great Sex Spiral: a Criticism of Miss Marsden's 'Lingual Psychology'" (*The Egoist*, April and August 1917),

Williams criticized her confusion of "male and female psychology."
[3] Charles Demuth (1883–1935) was an American artist whom Williams had met in 1903.

of the action, under distracting circumstances – to remind myself (see p. 501, paragraph 6) of the truth.

(see p. 501, paragraph 6)

III

The farmer in deep thought
is pacing through the rain
among his blank fields, with
hands in pockets,
5   in his head
the harvest already planted.
A cold wind ruffles the water
among the browned weeds.
On all sides
10   the world rolls coldly away:
black orchards
darkened by the March clouds –
leaving room for thought.
Down past the brushwood
15   bristling by
the rainsluiced wagonroad
looms the artist figure of
the farmer – composing
– antagonist

IV

The Easter stars are shining
above lights that are flashing –
coronal of the black –
            Nobody

5   to say it –
        Nobody to say: pinholes

Thither I would carry her
among the lights –
Burst it asunder
10   break through to the fifty words
necessary –

             a crown for her head with
castles upon it, skyscrapers
filled with nut-chocolates –

15   dovetame winds –
stars of tinsel
from the great end of a cornucopia
of glass

So long as the sky is recognized as an association
is recognized in its function of accessory to vague words whose meaning it is impossible to rediscover

its value can be nothing but mathematical certain limits of gravity and density of air

The farmer and the fisherman who read their own lives there have a practical corrective for – they rediscover or replace demoded meanings to the religious terms

Among them, without expansion of imagination, there is the residual contact between life and the imagination which is essential to freedom

The man of imagination who turns to art for release and fulfilment of his baby promises contends with the sky through layers of demoded words and shapes. Demoded, not because the essential vitality which begot them is laid waste – this cannot be so, a young man feels, since he feels it in himself – but because meanings have been lost through laziness or changes in the form of existence which have let words empty.

Bare handed the man contends with the sky, without experience of existence seeking to invent and design.

Crude symbolism is to associate emotions with natural phenomena such as anger with lightning, flowers with love it goes further and associates certain textures with

Such work is empty. It is very typical of almost all that is done by the writers who fill the pages every month of such a paper as. Everything that I have done in the past – except those parts which may be called excellent – by chance, have that quality about them.

It is typified by use of the word "like" or that "evocation" of the "image" which served us for a time. Its abuse is apparent. The insignificant "image" may be "evoked" never so ably and still mean nothing.

With all his faults Alfred Kreymborg[4] never did this. That is why his work – escaping a common fault – still has value and will tomorrow have more.

Sandburg,[5] when uninspired by intimacies of the eye and ear, runs into this empty symbolism. Such poets of promise as ruin themselves with it, though many have major sentimental faults besides.

Marianne Moore[6] escapes. The incomprehensibility of her poems is witness to at what cost (she cleaves herself away) as it is also to the distance which the most are from a comprehension of the purpose of composition.

The better work men do is always done under stress and at great personal cost.

It is no different from the aristocratic compositions of the earlier times, The Homeric inventions

but

these occurred in different times, to this extent, that life had not yet sieved through its own multiformity. That aside, the work the two-thousand-year-old poet did and that we do are one piece. That is the vitality of the classics.

So then – Nothing is put down in the present book – except through weakness of the imagination – which is not intended as of a piece with the "nature" which Shakespeare mentions and which Hartley speaks of so completely in his *Adventures:*[7] it is the common thing which is anonymously about us.

Composition is in no essential an escape from life. In fact if it is so it is negligible to the point of insignificance. Whatever "life" the artist may be forced to lead has no relation to the vitality of his compositions. Such names as Homer, the blind; Scheherazade, who lived under threat – Their compositions have as their excellence an identity with life since they are as actual, as sappy as the leaf of the tree which never moves from one spot.

What I put down of value will have this value: an escape from crude symbolism, the annihilation of strained associations, complicated ritualistic forms designed to separate the work from "reality" – such as rhyme, meter as meter and not as the essential of the work, one of its words.

[4] Alfred Kreymborg (1883–1966) was an American poet, critic, and editor; he had edited the journal *Others* from 1915 to 1919, publishing works by Williams, Eliot, Wallace Stevens, and Marianne Moore.

[5] Carl Sandburg (1878–1967) was an American poet noted for his popular readings and his celebratory tones.

[6] See 646–92.

[7] *Adventures in the Arts* (New York: Boni & Liveright, 1921) was written by the American painter Marsden Hartley (1877–1943), who argued that the artist should concentrate on his native environment and the elementary relations of the natural world.

But this smacks too much of the nature of – This is all negative and appears to be boastful. It is not intended to be so. Rather the opposite.

The work will be in the realm of the imagination as plain as the sky is to a fisherman – A very clouded sentence. The word must be put down for itself, not as a symbol of nature but a part, cognizant of the whole – aware – civilized.

V

Black winds from the north
enter black hearts. Barred from
seclusion in lilies they strike
to destroy –

5   Beastly humanity
where the wind breaks it –

                    strident voices, heat
quickened, built of waves

Drunk with goats or pavements

10   Hate is of the night and the day
of flowers and rocks. Nothing
is gained by saying the night breeds
murder – It is the classical mistake

The day

15   All that enters in another person
all grass, all blackbirds flying
all azalea trees in flower
salt winds –

Sold to them men knock blindly together
20   splitting their heads open

That is why boxing matches and
Chinese poems are the same – That is why
Hartley praises Miss Wirt[8]

There is nothing in the twist
25   of the wind but – dashes of cold rain

It is one with submarine vistas
purple and black fish turning
among undulant seaweed –

Black wind, I have poured my heart out
30   to you until I am sick of it –

Now I run my hand over you feeling
the play of your body – the quiver
of its strength –

---

[8] *Hartley praises Miss Wirt* in *Adventures in the Arts* Marsden Hartley praises the circus rider May Wirth whose art "gives the body a chance to show its exquisite rhythmic beauty ... the beautiful plastic of the body, harmonically arranged for personal delight" (178).

The grief of the bowmen of Shu[9]
moves nearer – There is   35
an approach with difficulty from
the dead – the winter casing of grief

How easy to slip
into the old mode, how hard to
cling firmly to the advance –   40

VI

No that is not it
nothing that I have done
nothing
I have done

is made up of   5
nothing
and the diphthong

ae

together with
the first person   10
singular
indicative

of the auxiliary
verb
to have   15

everything
I have done
is the same

if to do

is capable   20
of an
infinity of
combinations

involving the
moral   25
physical
and religious

codes

for everything
and nothing   30
are synonymous
when

---

[9] *the bowmen of Shu* the title of a poem by Ezra Pound; see p. 44.

                                      energy in vacuo
                                      has the power
35   of confusion

                                      which only to
                                      have done nothing
                                      can make
                                      perfect

The inevitable flux of the seeing eye toward measuring itself by the world it inhabits can only result in himself crushing humiliation unless the individual raise to some approximate co-extension with the universe. This is possible by aid of the imagination. Only through the agency of this force can a man feel himself moved largely with sympathetic pulses at work –

A work of the imagination which fails to release the senses in accordance with this major requisite – the sympathies, the intelligence in its selective world, fails at the elucidation, the alleviation which is –

In the composition, the artist does exactly what every eye must do with life, fix the particular with the universality of his own personality – Taught by the largeness of his imagination to feel every form which he sees moving within himself, he must prove the truth of this by expression.

The contraction which is felt.

All this being anterior to technique, that can have only a sequent value; but since all that appears to the senses on a work of art does so through   fixation by the imagination of the external as well internal means of expression the essential nature of technique or transcription.

Only when this position is reached can life proper be said to begin since only then can a value be affixed to the forms and activities of which it consists.

Only then can the sense of frustration which ends. All composition defeated.

Only through the imagination is the advance of intelligence possible, to keep beside growing understanding.

Complete lack of imagination would be the same at the cost of intelligence, complete.

Even the most robust constitution has its limits, though the Roman feast with its reliance upon regurgitation to prolong it shows an active ingenuity, yet the powers of a man are so pitifully small, with the ocean to swallow – that at the end of the feast nothing would be left but suicide.

That or the imagination which in this case takes the form of humor, is known in that form – the release from physical necessity. Having eaten to the full we must acknowledge our insufficiency since we have not annihilated all food nor even the quantity of a good sized steer. However we have annihilated all eating: quite plainly we have no more appetite. This is to say that the imagination has removed us from the banal necessity of bursting ourselves – by acknowledging a new situation. We must acknowledge that the ocean we would drink is too vast – but at the same time we realize that extension in our case is not confined to the intestine only. The stomach is full, the ocean no fuller, both have the same quality of fullness. In that, then, one is equal to the other. Having eaten, the man has released his mind.

THIS catalogue might be increased to larger proportions without stimulating the sense.

In works of the imagination that which is taken for great good sense, so that it seems as if an accurate precept were discovered, is in reality not so, but vigor and accuracy of the imagination alone. In work such as Shakespeare's –

This leads to the discovery that has been made today – old catalogues aside – full of meat –

"the divine illusion has about it that inaccuracy which reveals that which I mean."

There is only "illusion" in art where ignorance of the bystander confuses imagination and its works with cruder processes. Truly men feel an enlargement before great or good work, an expansion but this is not, as so many believe today a "lie," a stupefaction, a kind of mesmerism, a thing to block out "life," bitter to the individual, by a "vision of beauty." It is a work of the imagination. It gives the feeling of completion by revealing the oneness of experience; it rouses rather than stupefies the intelligence by demonstrating the importance of personality, by showing the individual, depressed before it, that his life is valuable – when completed by the imagination. And then only. Such work elucidates –

Such a realization shows us the falseness of attempting to "copy" nature. The thing is equally silly when we try to "make" pictures –

But such a picture as that of Juan Gris,[10] though I have not seen it in color, is important as marking more clearly than any I have seen what the modern trend is: the attempt is being made to separate things of the imagination from life, and obviously, by using the forms common to experience so as not to frighten the onlooker away but to invite him,

The rose is obsolete
but each petal ends in
an edge, the double facet
cementing the grooved
columns of air – The edge   5
cuts without cutting
meets – nothing – renews
itself in metal or porcelain –

whither? It ends –

But if it ends   10
the start is begun
so that to engage roses
becomes a geometry –

Sharper, neater, more cutting
figured in majolica –   15
the broken plate
glazed with a rose

Somewhere the sense
makes copper roses
steel roses –   20

The rose carried weight of love
but love is at an end – of roses

If is at the edge of the
petal that love waits

Crisp, worked to defeat   25
laboredness – fragile
plucked, moist, half-raised
cold, precise, touching

What

The place between the petal's   30
edge and the

From the petal's edge a line starts
that being of steel
infinitely fine, infinitely

---

[10]   Juan Gris (1887–1927) was a Spanish painter who moved to Paris and began painting seriously in 1910, developing an independent-minded version of Cubism.

35   rigid penetrates
        the Milky Way
        without contact – lifting
        from it – neither hanging
        nor pushing –

40   The fragility of the flower
        unbruised
        penetrates spaces

VIII

        The sunlight in a
        yellow plaque upon the
        varnished floor

        is full of a song
5   inflated to
        fifty pounds pressure

        at the faucet of
        June that rings
        the triangle of the air

10   pulling at the
        anemones in
        Persephone's cow pasture –

        When from among
        the steel rocks leaps
15   J. P. M.[11]

        who enjoyed
        extraordinary privileges
        among virginity

        to solve the core
20   of whirling flywheels
        by cutting

        the Gordian knot
        with a Veronese or
        perhaps a Rubens –

25   whose cars are about
        the finest on
        the market today –

        And so it comes
        to motor cars –
30   which is the son

---

[11] J. P. M. J. Pierpont Morgan (1837–1913) was a powerful American financier who, in Williams's view, collected older European art ("a Veronese or perhaps a Rubens") at the expense of new work by American artists; his son, J. Pierpont Morgan, Jr. (1876–1943), dealt in "motor cars."

leaving off the g
of sunlight and grass –
Impossible

to say, impossible
to underestimate –   35
wind, earthquakes in

Manchuria, a
partridge
from dry leaves

Things with which he is familiar, simple things – at the same time to detach them from ordinary experience to the imagination. Thus they are still "real" they are the same things they would be if photographed or painted by Monet, they are recognizable as the things touched by the hands during the day, but in this painting they are seen to be in some peculiar way – detached

Here is a shutter, a bunch of grapes, a sheet of music, a picture of sea and mountains[12] (particularly fine) which the onlooker is not for a moment permitted to witness as an "illusion." One thing laps over on the other, the cloud laps over on the shutter, the bunch of grapes is part of the handle of the guitar, the mountain and sea are obviously not "the mountain and sea," but a picture of the mountain and the sea. All drawn with admirable simplicity and excellent design – all a unity –

This was not necessary where the subject of art was not "reality" but related to the "gods" – by force or otherwise. There was no need of the "illusion" in such a case since there was none possible where a picture or a work represented simply the imaginative reality which existed in the mind of the onlooker. No special effort was necessary to cleave where the cleavage already existed.

I don't know what the Spanish see in their Velázquez and Goya[13] but

Today where everything is being brought into sight the realism of art has bewildered us, confused us and forced us to re-invent in order to retain that which the older generations had without that effort.

Cézanne[14] –

The only realism in art is of the imagination. It is only thus that the work escapes plagiarism after nature and becomes a creation

Invention of new forms to embody this reality of art, the one thing which art is, must occupy all serious minds concerned.

From the time of Poe[15] in the U. S. – the first American poet had to be a man of great separation – with close identity with life. Poe could not have written a word without the violence of expulsive emotion combined with the indriving force of a crudely repressive environment. Between the two his imagination was forced into being to keep him to that reality, completeness, sense of escape which is felt in his work – his topics. Typically American – accurately, even inevitably set in his time.

So, after this tedious diversion – whatever of dull you find among my work, put it down to criticism, not to poetry. You will not be mistaken – Who am I but my own critic? Surely in isolation one becomes a god – At least one becomes something of everything, which is not wholly god-like, yet a little so – in many things.

It is not necessary to count every flake of the truth that falls; it is necessary to dwell in the imagination if the truth is to be numbered. It is necessary to speak from the imagination –

[12] Williams is describing *The Open Window*, a painting by Juan Gris, which had been reproduced in black and white in the journal *Broom* 1 (Jan. 1922), 264.

[13] Diego Rodriguez de Silva y Velázquez (1599–1660) and Francisco Goya (1746–1828) are the unrivalled masters of Spanish painting.

[14] Paul Cézanne (1839–1906) was a French painter whose works were much studied and admired by artists at the beginning of the twentieth century.

[15] Edgar Allan Poe (1809–49), American author of macabre tales, poems, and novels.

The great furor about perspective in Holbein's[16] day had as a consequence much fine drawing, it made coins defy gravity, standing on the table as if in the act of falling. To say this was lifelike must have been satisfying to the master, it gave depth, pungency.

But all the while the picture escaped notice – partly because of the perspective. Or if noticed it was for the most part because one could see "the birds pecking at the grapes" in it.

Meanwhile the birds were pecking at the grapes outside the window and in the next street Bauermeister Kummel was letting a gold coin slip from his fingers to the counting table.

The representation was perfect, it "said something one was used to hearing" but with verve, cleverly.

Thus perspective and clever drawing kept the picture continually under cover of the "beautiful illusion" until today, when even Anatole France trips, saying: "Art – all lies!" – today when we are beginning to discover the truth that in great works of the imagination A CREATIVE FORCE IS SHOWN AT WORK MAKING OBJECTS WHICH ALONE COMPLETE SCIENCE AND ALLOW INTELLIGENCE TO SURVIVE – his picture lives anew. It lives as pictures only can: by their power TO ESCAPE ILLUSION and stand between man and nature as saints once stood between man and the sky – their reality in such work, say, as that of Juan Gris

No man could suffer the fragmentary nature of his understanding of his own life –

Whitman's proposals[17] are of the same piece with the modern trend toward imaginative understanding of life. The largeness which he interprets as his identity with the least and the greatest about him, his "democracy" represents the vigor of his imaginative life.

IX

What about all this writing?

O "Kiki"[18]
O Miss Margaret Jarvis[19]
The backhandspring

5   I: clean
               clean
               clean: yes . . . New-York

Wrigley's,[20] appendicitis, John Marin:
skyscraper soup[21] –

10   Either that or a bullet!

Once
anything might have happened
You lay relaxed on my knees –
the starry night
15   spread out warm and blind
above the hospital –

---

[16] Hans Holbein (c. 1497–1543), German artist who moved to England.

[17] Walt Whitman (1819–92), American poet whose *Leaves of Grass* was first published in 1855.

[18] *O "Kiki"* probably a reference to the play titled *Kiki*, written and produced by David Belasco, which was a hit on the New York stage in 1921–3 and is named after the *gamine* hero. Perhaps also referring to "Kiki of Montparnasse," a model photographed and celebrated by Man Ray.

[19] *Miss Margaret Jarvis* according to one scholar, a disguised name for Margaret Blake Purvis, a nurse at the French Hospital in New York when Williams worked there as an intern in 1907.

[20] *Wrigley's* a popular chewing gum; the firm had also constructed the Wrigley Building in 1920, modeled on the Giralda tower of the Cathedral in Seville, Spain, and therefore controversial for its anti-modern styling.

[21] *John Marin: skyscraper soup* John Marin (1870–1953) was an American painter whose expressionistic view of the New York city skyline might be called "skyscraper soup."

Pah!

It is unclean
which is not straight to the mark –

In my life the furniture eats me   20

the chairs, the floor
the walls
which heard your sobs
drank up my emotion –
they which alone know everything   25

and snitched on us in the morning –

What to want?

Drunk we go forward surely
Not I

beds, beds, beds   30
elevators, fruit, night-tables
breasts to see, white and blue –
to hold in the hand, to nozzle

It is not onion soup
Your sobs soaked through the walls   35
breaking the hospital to pieces

Everything
– windows, chairs
obscenely drunk, spinning –
white, blue, orange   40
– hot with our passion

wild tears, desperate rejoinders
my legs, turning slowly
end over end in the air!

But what would you have?   45

All I said was:
there, you see, it is broken

stockings, shoes, hairpins
your bed, I wrapped myself round you –

I watched   50

You sobbed, you beat your pillow
you tore your hair
you dug your nails into your sides

I was your nightgown
                    I   watched!   55

Clean is he alone
after whom stream

> the broken pieces of the city –
> flying apart at his approaches

60

> but I merely
> caress you curiously
>
> fifteen years ago and you still
> go about the city, they say
> patching up sick school children

Understood in a practical way, without calling upon mystic agencies, of this or that order, it is that life becomes actual only when it is identified with ourselves. When we name it, life exists. To repeat physical experiences has no –

The only means he has to give value to life is to recognize it with the imagination and name it; this is so. To repeat and repeat the thing without naming it is only to dull the sense and results in frustration.

this makes the artist the prey of life. He is easy of attack.

I think often of my earlier work and what it has cost me not to have been clear. I acknowledge I have moved chaotically about refusing or rejecting most things, seldom accepting values or acknowledging anything.

because I early recognized the futility of acquisitive understanding and at the same time rejected religious dogmatism. My whole life has been spent (so far) in seeking to place a value upon experience and the objects of experience that would satisfy my sense of inclusiveness without redundancy – completeness, lack of frustration with the liberty of choice; the things which the pursuit of "art" offers –

But though I have felt "free" only in the presence of works of the imagination, knowing the quickening of the sense which came of it, and though this experience has held me firm at such times, yet being of a slow but accurate understanding, I have not always been able to complete the intellectual steps which would make me firm in the position.

So most of my life has been lived in hell – a hell of repression lit by flashes of inspiration, when a poem such as this or that would appear

What would have happened in a world similarly lit by the imagination

Oh yes, you are a writer! a phrase that has often damned me, to myself. I rejected it with heat but the stigma remained. Not a man, not an understanding but a WRITER. I was unable to recognize.

I do not forget with what heat too I condemned some poems of some contemporary praised because of their loveliness –

I find that I was somewhat mistaken – ungenerous

Life's processes are very simple. One or two moves are made and that is the end. The rest is repetitious.

The *Improvisations*[22] – coming at a time when I was trying to remain firm at great cost – I had recourse to the expedient of letting life go completely in order to live in the world of my choice.

I let the imagination have its own way to see if it could save itself. Something very definite came of it. I found myself alleviated but most important I began there and then to revalue experience, to understand what I was at –

The virtue of the improvisations is their placement in a world of new values –

their fault is their dislocation of sense, often complete. But it is the best I could do under the circumstances. It was the best I could do and retain any value to experience at all.

Now I have come to a different condition. I find that the values there discovered can be extended. I find myself extending the understanding to the work of others and other things –

I find that there is work to be done in the creation of new forms, new names for experience

[22] Williams's *Kora in Hell: Improvisations* (Boston: Four Seas) was published in 1920.

and that "beauty" is related not to "loveliness" but to a state in which reality plays a part

Such painting as that of Juan Gris, coming after the impressionists, the expressionists, Cézanne – and dealing severe strokes as well to the expressionists as to the impressionists group – points forward to what will prove the greatest painting yet produced.

– the illusion once dispensed with, painting has this problem before it: to replace not the forms but the reality of experience with its own –

up to now shapes and meanings but always the illusion relying on composition to give likeness to "nature"

now works of art cannot be left in this category of France's "lie,"[23] they must be real, not "realism" but reality itself –

they must give not the sense of frustration but a sense of completion, of actuality – It is not a matter of "representation" – which may be represented actually, but of separate existence.

enlargement – revivification of values,

X

The universality of things
draws me toward the candy
with melon flowers that open

about the edge of refuse
proclaiming without accent   5
the quality of the farmer's

shoulders and his daughter's
accidental skin, so sweet
with clover and the small

yellow cinquefoil in the   10
parched places. It is
this that engages the favorable

distortion of eyeglasses
that see everything and remain
related to mathematics –   15

in the most practical frame of
brown celluloid made to
represent tortoiseshell –

A letter from the man who
wants to start a new magazine   20
made of linen

and he owns a typewriter –
July 1, 1922
All this is for eyeglasses

to discover. But   25
they lie there with the gold

---

[23] An advance translation of Anatole France's book *La vie en fleur* (Paris: Calmann-Lévy, 1922) appeared in the *Dial* (Oct.–Dec. 1921). The last paragraph reads: "All I can say is that what I have done I have done in good faith. I repeat: I love truth. I believe that humanity has need of it; but surely it has a much greater need of falsehood which flatters and consoles and gives infinite hopes. Without falsehood humanity would perish of despair and ennui" (*Dial* 71(6) [December 1921], 692).

earpieces folded down

tranquilly Titicaca –

XI

In passing with my mind
on nothing in the world

but the right of way
I enjoy on the road by

5   virtue of the law –
I saw

an elderly man who
smiled and looked away

to the north past a house –
10   a woman in blue

who was laughing and
leaning forward to look up

into the man's half
averted face

15   and a boy of eight who was
looking at the middle of

the man's belly
at a watchchain –

The supreme importance
20   of this nameless spectacle

sped me by them
without a word –

Why bother where I went?
for I went spinning on the

25   four wheels of my car
along the wet road until

I saw a girl with one leg
over the rail of a balcony

When in the condition of imaginative suspense only will the writing have reality, as explained partially in what precedes – Not to attempt, at that time, to set values on the word being used, according to presupposed measures, but to write down that which happens at that time –

To perfect the ability to record at the moment when the consciousness is enlarged by the sympathies and the unity of understanding which the imagination gives, to practice skill in recording the force moving, then to know it, in the largeness of its proportions –

It is the presence of a

This is not "fit" but a unification of experience

That is, the imagination is an actual force comparable to electricity or steam, it is not a plaything but a power that has been used from the first to raise the understanding of – it is, not necessary to resort to mysticism – In fact it is this which has kept back the knowledge I seek –

The value of the imagination to the writer consists in its ability to make words. Its unique power is to give created forms reality, actual existence

This separates

Writing is not a searching about in the daily experience for apt similes and pretty thoughts and images. I have experienced that to my sorrow. It is not a conscious recording of the day's experiences "freshly and with the appearance of reality" – This sort of thing is seriously to the development of any ability in a man, it fastens him down, makes him a – It destroys, makes nature an accessory to the particular theory he is following, it blinds him to his world, –

The writer of imagination would find himself released from observing things for the purpose of writing them down later. He would be there to enjoy, to taste, to engage the free world, not a world which he carries like a bag of food, always fearful lest he drop something or someone get more than he,

A world detached from the necessity of recording it, sufficient to itself, removed from him (as it most certainly is) with which he has bitter and delicious relations and from which he is independent – moving at will from one thing to another – as he pleases, unbound – complete

and the unique proof of this is the work of the imagination not "like" anything but transfused with the same forces which transfuse the earth – at least one small part of them.

Nature is the hint to composition not because it is familiar to us and therefore the terms we apply to it have a least common denominator quality which gives them currency – but because it possesses the quality of independent existence, of reality which we feel in ourselves. It is opposed to art but apposed to it.

I suppose Shakespeare's familiar aphorism about holding the mirror up to nature[24] has done more harm in stabilizing the copyist tendency of the arts among us than –

the mistake in it (though we forget that it is not S. speaking but an imaginative character of his) is to have believed that the reflection of nature is nature. It is not. It is only a sham nature, a "lie."

Of course S. is the most conspicuous example desirable of the falseness of this very thing.

He holds no mirror up to nature but with his imagination rivals nature's composition with his own.

He himself become "nature" – continuing "its" marvels – if you will

I am often diverted with a recital which I have made for myself concerning Shakespeare: he was a comparatively uninformed man, quite according to the orthodox tradition, who lived from first to last a life of amusing regularity and simplicity, a house and wife in the suburbs, delightful children, a girl at court (whom he really never confused with his writing) and a café life which gave him with the freshness of discovery, the information upon which his imagination fed. London was full of the concentrates of science and adventure. He saw at "The Mermaid" everything he knew. He was not conspicuous there except for his spirits.

His form was presented to him by Marlow,[25] his stories were the common talk of his associates or else some compiler set them before him. His types were particularly quickened with life about him.

Feeling the force of life, in his peculiar intelligence, the great dome of his head, he had no need of anything but writing material to relieve himself of his thoughts. His very lack of scientific training loosened his power. He was unencumbered.

For S. to pretend to knowledge would have been ridiculous – no escape there – but that he possessed knowledge, and extraordinary knowledge, of the affairs which concerned him, as they concerned the others about him, was self-apparent to him. It was not apparent to the others.

---

[24] From *Hamlet*, Act 2, scene 2, when Hamlet gives directions to the actors: "Discretion be your tutor. Suit the action to the word, / the word to the action, with this special observance: / That you o'er-step not the modesty of Nature; for any / thing so over-done, is from the purpose of playing, whose / end both at the first and now, was and is, to hold as 'twere / the mirror up to Nature; to shew Virtue her own / Feature."
[25] "The Mermaid" was an Elizabethan pub supposedly frequented by Shakespeare; Christopher Marlowe (1564–93) was an Elizabethan dramatist and poet.

His actual power was PURELY of the imagination. Not permitted to speak as W.S., in fact peculiarly barred from speaking so because of his lack of information, learning, not being able to rival his fellows in scientific training or adventure and at the same time being keen enough, imaginative enough, to know that there is no escape except in perfection, in excellence, in technical excellence – his buoyancy of imagination raised him NOT TO COPY them, not to holding the mirror up to them but to equal, to surpass them as a creator of knowledge, as a vigorous, living force above their heads.

His escape was not simulated but real. *Hamlet* no doubt was written about at the middle of his life.

He speaks authoritatively through invention, through characters, through design. The objects of his world were real to him because he could use them and use them with understanding to make his inventions –

The imagination is a –

The vermiculations of modern criticism of S. particularly amuse when the attempt is made to force the role of a Solon upon the creator of Richard 3d.[26]

So I come again to my present day gyrations.

So it is with the other classics: their meaning and worth can only be studied and understood in the imagination – that which begot them only can give them life again, re-enkindle their perfection –

unless to study by rote or scientific research – Useful for certain understanding to corroborate the imagination –

Yes, Anatole was a fool when he said: It is a lie. – That is it. If the actor simulates life it *is* a lie. But – but why continue without an audience?

The reason people marvel at works of art and say: How in Christ's name did he do it? – is that they know nothing of the physiology of the nervous system and have never in their experience witnessed the larger processes of the imagination.

It is a step over from the profitless engagements of the arithmetical.

XII

The red paper box
hinged with cloth

is lined
inside and out
5   with imitation
leather

It is the sun
the table
with dinner
10   on it for
these are the same –

Its twoinch trays
have engineers
that convey glue
15   to airplanes

---

[26]   *Richard the Third*, by Shakespeare, was written around 1592
and first published in 1597.

or for old ladies
that darn socks
paper clips
and red elastics —

What is the end   20
to insects
that suck gummed
labels?

for this is eternity
through its   25
dial we discover
transparent tissue
on a spool

But the stars
are round   30
cardboard
with a tin edge

and a ring
to fasten them
to a trunk   35
for the vacation —

XIII

Crustaceous
wedge
of sweaty kitchens
on rock
overtopping   5
thrusts of the sea

Waves of steel
from
swarming backstreets
shell   10
of coral
inventing
electricity —

Lights
speckle   15
El Greco[27]
lakes
in renaissance
twilight
with triphammers   20

which pulverize

[27] *El Greco* El Greco, born Domenikos Theotokopoulos
(c. 1540–1614) was a Greek painter who settled in Spain after
1577 and became a well-known artist.

nitrogen
of old pastures
to dodge
25   motorcars
with arms and legs –

The aggregate
is untamed
encapsulating
30   irritants
but
of agonized spires
knits
peace

35   where bridge stanchions
rest
certainly
piercing
left ventricles
40   with long
sunburnt fingers

XIV

of death
the barber
the barber
talked to me

5   cutting my
life with
sleep to trim
my hair –

It's just
10   a moment
he said, we die
every night –

And of
the newest
15   ways to grow
hair on

bald death –
I told him
of the quartz
20   lamp

and of old men
with third
sets of teeth
to the cue

25   of an old man
who said

at the door –
Sunshine today!

for which
death shaves   30
him twice
a week

XV

The decay of cathedrals
is efflorescent
through the phenomenal
growth of movie houses

whose catholicity is   5
progress since
destruction and creation
are simultaneous

without sacrifice
of even the smallest   10
detail even to the
volcanic organ whose

woe is translatable
to joy if light becomes
darkness and darkness   15
light, as it will –

But schism which seems
adamant is diverted
from the perpendicular
by simply rotating the object   20

cleaving away the root of
disaster which it
seemed to foster. Thus
the movies are a moral force

Nightly the crowds   25
with the closeness and
universality of sand
witness the selfspittle

which used to be drowned
in incense and intoned   30
over by the supple jointed
imagination of inoffensiveness

backed by biblical
rigidity made into passion plays
upon the altar to   35
attract the dynamic mob

whose female relative
sweeping grass Tolstoi

40
                                    saw injected into
                                    the Russian nobility

    It is rarely understood how such plays as Shakespeare's were written – or in fact how any work of value has been written, the practical bearing of which is that only as the work was produced, in that way alone can it be understood

    Fruitless for the academic tapeworm to hoard its excrementa in books. The cage –

    The most of all writing has not even begun in the province from which alone it can draw sustenance.

    There is not life in the stuff because it tries to be "like" life.

    First must come the transposition of the faculties to the only world of reality that men know: the world of the imagination, wholly our own. From this world alone does the work gain power, its soil the only one whose chemistry is perfect to the purpose.

    The exaltation men feel before a work of art is the feeling of reality they draw from it. It sets them up, places a value upon experience – (said that half a dozen times already)

XVI

O tongue
licking
the sore on
her netherlip

5
O toppled belly

O passionate cotton
stuck with
matted hair

10
Elysian slobber
from her mouth
upon
the folded handkerchief

I can't die

15
– moaned the old
jaundiced woman
rolling her
saffron eyeballs

I can't die
I can't die

XVII

Our orchestra
is the cat's nuts –

Banjo jazz
with a nickelplated

amplifier to   5
soothe

the savage beast –
Get the rhythm

That sheet stuff
's a lot a cheese.   10

Man
gimme the key

and lemme loose –
I make 'em crazy

with my harmonies –   15
Shoot it Jimmy

Nobody
Nobody else

but me –
They can't copy it   20

XVIII

The pure products of America
go crazy –
mountain folk from Kentucky

or the ribbed north end of
Jersey   5
with its isolate lakes and

valleys, its deaf-mutes, thieves
old names
and promiscuity between

devil-may-care men who have taken   10
to railroading
out of sheer lust of adventure –

and young slatterns, bathed
in filth
from Monday to Saturday   15

to be tricked out that night
with gauds
from imaginations which have no

peasant traditions to give them
character   20
but flutter and flaunt

sheer rags – succumbing without
emotion
save numbed terror

25   under some hedge of choke-cherry
          or viburnum —
          which they cannot express —

          Unless it be that marriage
          perhaps
30   with a dash of Indian blood

          will throw up a girl so desolate
          so hemmed round
          with disease or murder

          that she'll be rescued by an
35   agent —
          reared by the state and

          sent out at fifteen to work in
          some hard pressed
          house in the suburbs —

40   some doctor's family, some Elsie —
          voluptuous water
          expressing with broken

          brain the truth about us —
          her great
45   ungainly hips and flopping breasts

          addressed to cheap
          jewelry
          and rich young men with fine eyes

          as if the earth under our feet
50   were
          an excrement of some sky

          and we degraded prisoners
          destined
          to hunger until we eat filth

55   while the imagination strains
          after deer
          going by fields of goldenrod in

          the stifling heat of September
          Somehow
60   it seems to destroy us

          It is only in isolate flecks that
          something
          is given off

          No one
65   to witness
          and adjust, no one to drive the car

Or better: prose has to do with the fact of an emotion; poetry has to do with the dynamization of emotion into a separate form. This is the force of imagination.

prose: statement of facts concerning emotions, intellectual states, data of all sorts – technical expositions, jargon, of all sorts – fictional and other –
poetry: new form dealt with as a reality in itself.

The form of prose is the accuracy of its subject matter – how best to expose the multiform phases of its material

the form of poetry is related to the movements of the imagination revealed in words – or whatever it may be – the cleavage is complete

Why should I go further than I am able? Is it not enough for you that I am perfect?

The cleavage goes through all the phases of experience. It is the jump from prose to the process of imagination that is the next great leap of the intelligence – from the simulations of present experience to the facts of the imagination –

the greatest characteristic of the present age is that it is stale – stale as literature –

To enter a new world, and have there freedom of movement and newness.

I mean that there will always be prose painting, representative work, clever as may be in revealing new phases of emotional research presented on the surface.

But the jump from that to Cézanne or back to certain of the primitives is the impossible.

The primitives are not back in some remote age – they are not BEHIND experience. Work which bridges the gap between the rigidities of vulgar experience and the imagination is rare. It is new, immediate – It is so because it is actual, always real. It is experience dynamized into reality.

Time does not move. Only ignorance and stupidity move. Intelligence (force, power) stands still with time and forces change about itself – sifting the world for permanence, in the drift of nonentity.

Pío Baroja[28] interested me once –

Baroja leaving the medical profession, some not important inspector's work in the north of Spain, opened a bakery in Madrid.

The isolation he speaks of, as a member of the so called intellectual class, influenced him to abandon his position and engage himself, as far as possible, in the intricacies of the design patterned by the social class – He sees no interest in isolation –

These gestures are the effort for self preservation or the preservation of some quality held in high esteem –

Here it seems to be that a man, starved in imagination, changes his milieu so that his food may be richer – The social class, without the power of expression, lives upon imaginative values.

I mean only to emphasize the split that goes down through the abstractions of art to the everyday exercises of the most primitive types –

there is a sharp division – the energizing force of imagination on one side – and the acquisitive – PROGRESSIVE force of the lump on the other

The social class with its religion, its faith, sincerity and all the other imaginative values is positive (yes)

the merchant, hibernating, unmagnetized – tends to drop away into the isolate, inactive particles – Religion is continued then as a form, art as a convention –

To the social, energized class – ebullient now in Russia[29] the particles adhere because of the force of the imagination energizing them –

Anyhow the change of Baroja interested me

Among artists, or as they are sometimes called "men of imagination" "creators," etc. this force is recognized in a pure state – All this can be used to show the relationships between genius, hand labor, religion – etc. and the lack of feeling between artists and the middle class type –

The jump between fact and the imaginative reality

[28] Pío Baroja (1857–1956) was a great Spanish novelist whose spare realism appealed to Williams.

[29] The Bolshevik Revolution occurred six years earlier in October 1917, bringing to power the Communist Party and creating the Soviet Union, which dissolved in 1989.

The study of all human activity is the delineation of the cresence and ebb of this force, shifting from class to class and location to location – rhythm: the wave rhythm of Shakespeare watching clowns and kings sliding into nothing

XIX

This is the time of year
when boys fifteen and seventeen
wear two horned lilac blossoms
in their caps – or over one ear

5   What is it that does this?

It is a certain sort –
drivers for grocers or taxidrivers
white and colored –

fellows that let their hair grow long
10   in a curve over one eye –

Horned purple

Dirty satyrs, it is
vulgarity raised to the last power

They have stolen them
15   broken the bushes apart
with a curse for the owner –

Lilacs –

They stand in the doorways
on the business streets with a sneer
20   on their faces

adorned with blossoms

Out of their sweet heads
dark kisses – rough faces

XX

The sea that encloses her young body
ula lu la lu
is the sea of many arms –

The blazing secrecy of noon is undone
5   and and and
the broken sand is the sound of love –

The flesh is firm that turns in the sea
O la la
the sea that is cold with dead men's tears –

10   Deeply the wooing that penetrated
to the edge of the sea
returns in the plash of the waves –

a wink over the shoulder
large as the ocean –
with wave following wave to the edge   15

coom barrooom –

It is the cold of the sea
broken upon the sand by the force
of the moon –

In the sea the young flesh playing   20
floats with the cries of far off men
who rise in the sea

with green arms
to homage again the fields over there
where the night is deep –   25

la lu la lu
but lips too few
assume the new – marrruu

Underneath the sea where it is dark
there is no edge   30
so two –

XXI

one day in Paradise
a Gipsy

smiled
to see the blandness

of the leaves –   5
so many

so lascivious
and still

XXII

so much depends
upon

a red wheel
barrow

glazed with rain   5
water

beside the white
chickens

The fixed categories into which life is divided must always hold. These things are normal – essential to every activity. But they exist – but not as dead dissections.

The curriculum of knowledge cannot but be divided into the sciences, the thousand and one groups of data, scientific, philosophic or whatnot – as many as there exist in Shakespeare – things that make him appear the university of all ages.

But this is not the thing. In the galvanic category of – The same things exist, but in a different condition when energized by the imagination.

The whole field of education is affected – There is no end of detail that is without significance.

Education would begin by placing in the mind of the student the nature of knowledge – in the dead state and the nature of the force which may energize it.

This would clarify his field at once – He would then see the use of data

But at present knowledge is placed before a man as if it were a stair at the top of which a DEGREE is obtained which is superlative.

nothing could be more ridiculous. To data there is no end. There is proficiency in dissection and a knowledge of parts but in the use of knowledge –

It is the imagination that –

That is: life is absolutely simple. In any civilized society everyone should know EVERYTHING there is to know about life at once and always. There should never be permitted, confusion –

There are difficulties to life, under conditions there are impasses, life may prove impossible – But it must never be lost – as it is today –

I remember so distinctly the young Pole in Leipzig going with hushed breath to hear Wundt[30] lecture – In this mass of intricate pholsophic data what one of the listeners was able to maintain himself for the winking of an eyelash. Not one. The inundation of the intelligence by masses of complicated fact is not knowledge. There is no end –

And what is the fourth dimension? It is the endlessness of knowledge –

It is the imagination on which reality rides – It is the imagination – It is a cleavage through everything by a force that does not exist in the mass and therefore can never be discovered by its anatomization.

It is for this reason that I have always placed art first and esteemed it over science – in spite of everything.

Art is the pure effect of the force upon which science depends for its reality – Poetry

The effect of this realization upon life will be the emplacement of knowledge into a living current – which it has always sought –

In other times – men counted it a tragedy to be dislocated from sense – Today boys are sent with dullest faith to technical schools of all sorts – broken, bruised

few escape whole – slaughter. This is not civilization but stupidity – Before entering knowledge the integrity of the imagination –

The effect will be to give importance to the sub-divisions of experience – which today are absolutely lost – There exists simply nothing.

Prose – When values are important, such – For example there is no use denying that prose and poetry are not by any means the same IN INTENTION. But then what is prose? There is no need for it to approach poetry except to be weakened.

With decent knowledge to hand we can tell what things are for

I expect to see values blossom. I expect to see prose be prose. Prose, relieved of extraneous, unrelated values must return to its only purpose; to clarity to enlighten the understanding. There is no form to prose but that which depends on clarity. If prose is not accurately adjusted to the exposition of facts it does not exist – Its form is that alone. To penetrate everywhere with enlightenment –

---

[30] Wilhelm Wundt (1832–1920), German philosopher and psychologist who became famous as a teacher and scholar.

Poetry is something quite different. Poetry has to do with the crystallization of the imagination – the perfection of new forms as additions to nature – Prose may follow to enlighten but poetry –

Is what I have written prose? The only answer is that form in prose ends with the end of that which is being communicated – If the power to go on falters in the middle of a sentence – that is the end of the sentence – Or if a new phase enters at that point it is only stupidity to go on.

There is no confusion – only difficulties.

XXIII

The veritable night
of wires and stars

the moon is in
the oak tree's crotch

and sleepers in   5
the windows cough

athwart the round
and pointed leaves

and insects sting
while on the grass   10

the whitish moonlight
tearfully

assumes the attitudes
of afternoon –

But it is real   15
where peaches hang

recalling death's
long promised symphony

whose tuneful wood
and stringish undergrowth   20

are ghosts existing
without being

save to come with juice
and pulp to assuage

the hungers which   25
the night reveals

so that now at last
the truth's aglow

with devilish peace
forestalling day   30

which dawns tomorrow
with dreadful reds

the heart to predicate
with mists that loved

35   the ocean and the fields –
Thus moonlight

is the perfect
human touch

XXIV

The leaves embrace
in the trees

it is a wordless
world

5   without personality
I do not

seek a path
I am still with

Gipsy lips pressed
10   to my own –

It is the kiss
of leaves

without being
poison ivy

15   or nettle, the kiss
of oak leaves –

He who has kissed
a leaf

need look no further –
20   I ascend

through
a canopy of leaves

and at the same time
I descend

25   for I do nothing
unusual –

I ride in my car
I think about

                    prehistoric caves
                    in the Pyrenees –   30

                    the cave of
                    Les Trois Frères[31]

The nature of the difference between what is termed prose on the one hand and verse on the other is not to be discovered by a study of the metrical characteristics of the words as they occur in juxtaposition. It is ridiculous to say that verse grades off into prose as the rhythm becomes less and less pronounced, in fact, that verse differs from prose in that the meter is more pronounced, that the movement is more impassioned and that rhythmical prose, so called, occupies a middle place between prose and verse.

It is true that verse is likely to be more strongly stressed than what is termed prose, but to say that this is in any way indicative of the difference in nature of the two is surely to make the mistake of arguing from the particular to the general, to the effect that since an object has a certain character that therefore the force which gave it form will always reveal itself in that character.

Of course there is nothing to do but to differentiate prose from verse by the only effective means at hand, the external, surface appearance. But a counter proposal may be made, to wit: that verse is of such a nature that it may appear without metrical stress of any sort and that prose may be strongly stressed – in short that meter has nothing to do with the question whatever.

Of course it may be said that if the difference is felt and is not discoverable to the eye and ear then what about it anyway? Or it may be argued, that since there is according to my proposal no discoverable difference between prose and verse that in all probability none exists and that both are phases of the same thing.

Yet, quite plainly, there is a very marked difference between the two which may arise in the fact of a separate origin for each, each using similar modes for dis-similar purposes; verse falling most commonly into meter but not always, and prose going forward most often without meter but not always.

This at least serves to explain some of the best work I see today and explains some of the most noteworthy failures which I discover. I search for "something" in the writing which moves me in a certain way – It offers a suggestion as to why some work of Whitman's is bad poetry and some, in the same meter is prose.

The practical point would be to discover when a work is to be taken as coming from this source and when from that. When discovering a work it would be – If it is poetry it means this and only this – and if it is prose it means that and only that. Anything else is a confusion, silly and bad practice.

I believe this is possible as I believe in the main that Marianne Moore is of all American writers most constantly a poet – not because her lines are invariably full of imagery they are not, they are often diagramatically informative, and not because she clips her work into certain shapes – her pieces are without meter most often – but I believe she is most constantly a poet in her work because the purpose of her work is invariably from the source from which poetry starts – that it is constantly from the purpose of poetry. And that it actually possesses this characteristic, as of that origin, to a more distinguishable degree when it eschews verse rhythms than when it does not. It has the purpose of poetry written into and therefore it is poetry.

I believe it possible, even essential, that when poetry fails it does not become prose but bad poetry. The test of Marianne Moore would be that she writes sometimes good and sometimes bad poetry but always – with a single purpose out of a single fountain which is of the sort –

The practical point would be to discover –

I can go no further than to say that poetry feeds the imagination and prose the emotions, poetry liberates the words from their emotional implications, prose confirms them in it. Both move centrifugally or centripetally toward the intelligence.

---

[31]   *Les Trois Frères* a cave containing Upper Paleolithic paintings, which was discovered in the south of France in 1914.

Of course it must be understood that writing deals with words and words only and that all discussions of it deal with single words and their association in groups.

As far as I can discover there is no way but the one I have marked out which will satisfactorily deal with certain lines such as occur in some play of Shakespeare or in a poem of Marianne Moore's, let us say: Tomorrow will be the first of April –

Certainly there is an emotional content in this for anyone living in the northern temperate zone, but whether it is prose or poetry – taken by itself – who is going to say unless some mark is put on it by the intent conveyed by the words which surround it –

Either to write or to comprehend poetry the words must be recognized to be moving in a direction separate from the jostling or lack of it which occurs within the piece.

Marianne's words remain separate, each unwilling to group with the others except as they move in the one direction. This is even an important – or amusing – character of Miss Moore's work.

Her work puzzles me. It is not easy to quote convincingly.

XXV

Somebody dies every four minutes
in New York State –

To hell with you and your poetry –
You will rot and be blown
5   through the next solar system
with the rest of the gases –

What the hell do you know about it?

AXIOMS

Do not get killed

10   Careful Crossing Campaign
Cross Crossings Cautiously

THE HORSES   black
&
PRANCED   white

What's the use of sweating over
15   this sort of thing, Carl;[32] here
it is all set up –

Outings in New York City

Ho for the open country

Don't stay shut up in hot rooms
20   Go to one of the Great Parks
Pelham Bay for example

It's on Long Island Sound
with bathing, boating
tennis, baseball, golf, etc.

[32] Carl perhaps Carl Van Doren, who had recently published an
essay on "Realism" in The New Republic (March 21, 1922).

Acres and acres of green grass   25
wonderful shade trees, rippling brooks

   Take the Pelham Bay Park Branch
   of the Lexington Ave. (East Side)
   Line and you are there in a few
   minutes   30

Interborough Rapid Transit Co.

XXVI

The crowd at the ball game
is moved uniformly

by a spirit of uselessness
which delights them –

all the exciting detail   5
of the chase

and the escape, the error
the flash of genius –

all to no end save beauty
the eternal –   10

So in detail they, the crowd,
are beautiful

for this
to be warned against

saluted and defied –   15
It is alive, venomous

it smiles grimly
its words cut –

The flashy female with her
mother, gets it –   20

The Jew gets it straight – it
is deadly, terrifying –

It is the Inquisition, the
Revolution

It is beauty itself   25
that lives

day by day in them
idly –

This is
the power of their faces   30

It is summer, it is the solstice
the crowd is

cheering, the crowd is laughing
in detail

35   permanently, seriously
without thought

The imagination uses the phraseology of science. It attacks, stirs, animates, is radio-active in all that can be touched by action. Words occur in liberation by virtue of its processes.

In description words adhere to certain objects, and have the effect on the sense of oysters, or barnacles.

But the imagination is wrongly understood when it is supposed to be a removal from reality in the sense of John of Gaunt's speech[33] in *Richard the Second*: to imagine possession of that which is lost. It is rightly understood when John of Gaunt's words are related not to their sense as objects adherent to his son's welfare or otherwise but as a dance over the body of his condition accurately accompanying it. By this means of the understanding, the play written to be understood as a play, the author and reader are liberated to pirouette with the words which have sprung from the old facts of history, reunited in present passion.

To understand the words as so liberated is to understand poetry. That they move independently when set free is the mark of their value

Imagination is not to avoid reality, nor is it description nor an evocation of objects or situations, it is to say that poetry does not tamper with the world but moves it – It affirms reality most powerfully and therefore, since reality needs no personal support but exists free from human action, as proven by science in the indestructibility of matter and of force, it creates a new object, a play, a dance which is not a mirror up to nature but –

As birds' wings beat the solid air without which none could fly so words freed by the imagination affirm reality by their flight

Writing is likened to music. The object would be it seems to make poetry a pure art, like music. Painting too. Writing, as with certain of the modern Russians whose work I have seen, would use unoriented sounds in place of conventional words. The poem then would be completely liberated when there is identity of sound with something – perhaps the emotion.

I do not believe that writing is music. I do not believe writing would gain in quality or force by seeking to attain to the conditions of music.[34]

I think the conditions of music are objects for the action of the writer's imagination just as a table or –

According to my present theme the writer of imagination would attain closest to the conditions of music not when his words are disassociated from natural objects and specified meanings but when they are liberated from the usual quality of that meaning by transposition into another medium, the imagination.

Sometimes I speak of imagination as a force, an electricity or a medium, a place. It is immaterial which: for whether it is the condition of a place or a dynamization its effect is the same: to free the world of fact from the impositions of "art" (see Hartley's last chapter)[35] and to liberate the man to act in whatever direction his disposition leads.

The word is not liberated, therefore able to communicate release from the fixities which destroy it until it is accurately tuned to the fact which giving it reality, by its own reality establishes its own freedom from the necessity of a word, thus freeing it and dynamizing it at the same time.

[33] John of Gaunt's speech is found in Shakespeare, *King Richard II*, Act 2, scene 1.

[34] Williams is quarreling with a well-known thesis advanced by Walter Pater (1839–94); See p. 98 n. 3.

[35] The last chapter of Marsden Hartley's *Adventures in the Arts* (New York: Boni and Liveright, 1921).

XXVII

Black eyed susan
rich orange
round the purple core

the white daisy
is not   5
enough

Crowds are white
as farmers
who live poorly

But you   10
are rich
in savagery –

Arab
Indian
dark woman   15

Marianne Moore (1925)

The best work is always neglected and there is no critic among the older men who has cared to champion the newer names from outside the battle. The established critic will not read. So it is that the present writers must turn interpreters of their own work. Even those who enjoy modern work are not always intelligent, but often seem at a loss to know the white marks from the black. But modernism is distressing to many who would at least tolerate it if they knew how. These individuals who cannot bear the necessary appearance of disorder in all immediacy, could be led to appreciation through critical study.

If one come with Miss Moore's work to some wary friend and say, "Everything is worthless but the best and this is the best," adding, "– only with difficulty discerned," will he see anything, if he be at all well read, but destruction? From my experience he will be shocked and bewildered. He will perceive absolutely nothing except that his whole preconceived scheme of values has been ruined. And this is exactly what he should see, a break *through* all preconceptions of poetic form and mood and pace, a flaw, a crack in the bowl. It is this that one means when he says destruction and creation are simultaneous. But this is not easy to accept. Miss Moore, using the same material as all others before her, comes at it so effectively at a new angle as to throw out of fashion the classical-conventional poetry to which one is used and puts her own and that about her in its place. The old stops are discarded. This must antagonize many. Furthermore there is a multiplication, a quickening, a burrowing through, a blasting aside, a dynamization, a flight over – it is modern, but the critic must show that this is only to reveal an essential poetry through the mass, as always, and with superlative effect in this case.

A course in mathematics would not be wasted on a poet, or a reader of poetry, if he remembered no more from it than the geometric principle of the intersection of loci: from all angles lines converging and crossing establish points. He might carry it further and say in his imagination, that

MARIANNE MOORE
A Review of *Observations* (New York: Dial Press, 1924), by
Marianne Moore. First published in the *Dial* 78(5) (May 1925).

apprehension perforates, at places, through to understanding – as white is at the intersection of blue and green and yellow and red. It is this white light that is the background of all good work. Aware of this one may read the Greeks or the Elizabethans or Sidney Lanier,[1] even Robert Bridges,[2] and preserve interest, poise, and enjoyment. He may visit Virginia or China, and when friends, eager to please, playfully lead him about for pockets of local colour – he may go. Local colour is not, as the parodists, the localists believe, an object of art. It is merely a variant serving to locate some point of white penetration. The intensification of desire toward this purity is the modern variant. It is that which interests me most and seems most solid among the qualities I witness in my contemporaries; it is a quality present in much or even all that Miss Moore does.

Poems, like paintings, can be interesting because of the subject with which they deal. The baby glove of a Pharaoh can be so presented as to bring tears to the eyes. And it need not be bad work because it has to do with a favourite cat dead. Poetry, rare and never willingly recognized, only its accidental colours make it tolerable to most. If it be of a red colouration those who like red will follow and be led restfully astray. So it is with hymns, battle songs, love ditties, elegies. Humanity sees itself in them, sees with delight this, that, and the other quality with which it is familiar, the good placed attractively and the bad thrown into a counter light. This is inevitable. But in any anthology it will be found that men have been hard put to it at all times to tell which is poetry and which the impost. This is hard. The difficult thing to realize is that the thrust must go through to the white, at least somewhere.

Good modern work, far from being the fragmentary, neurotic thing its disunderstanders think it, is nothing more than work compelled by these conditions. It is a multiplication of impulses that by their several flights, crossing at all eccentric angles, *might* enlighten. As a phase, in its slightest beginning, it is not yet nearly complete. And it is not rising as an arc; it is more a disc pierced here and there by light; it is really distressingly broken up. But so does any attack seem at the moment of engagement, multiple units crazy except when viewed as a whole.

Surely there is no poetry so active as that of to-day, so unbound, so dangerous to the mass of mediocrity, if one should understand it, so fleet, hard to capture, so delightful to pursue. It is clarifying in its movements as a wild animal whose walk corrects that of men. Who shall separate the good Whitman from the bad, the dreadful New England maunderers from the others, put air under and around the living and leave the dead to fall dead? Who? None but poems, such as Miss Moore's, their cleanliness, lack of cement, clarity, gentleness. It grows impossible for the eye to rest long upon the object of the drawing. Here is an escape from the old dilemma. The unessential is put rapidly aside as the eye searches between for illumination. Miss Moore undertakes in her work to separate the poetry from the subject entirely – like all the moderns. In this she has been rarely successful and this is important.

Unlike the painters the poet has not resorted to distortions or the abstract in form. Miss Moore accomplishes a like result by rapidity of movement. A poem such as "Marriage" is an anthology of transit.[3] It is a pleasure that can be held firm only by moving rapidly from one thing to the next. It gives the impression of a passage *through*. There is a distaste for lingering, as in Emily Dickinson.[4] As in Emily Dickinson there is too a fastidious precision of thought where unrhymes fill the purpose better than rhymes. There is a swiftness impaling beauty, but no impatience as in so much present-day trouble with verse. It is a rapidity too swift for touch, a seraphic quality, one might have said yesterday. There is, however, no breast that warms the bars of heaven; it is at most a swiftness that passes without repugnance from thing to thing.

The only help I ever got from Miss Moore toward the understanding of her verse was that she despised connectives. Any other assistance would have been an impoliteness, since she has always been sure of herself if not of others. The complete poem is there waiting: all the wit, the colour, the constructive ability (not a particularly strong point that however). And the quality of satisfaction

---

[1] Sidney Lanier (1842–81) was an American poet of melodic verse and extravagant conceits.

[2] Robert Bridges (1844–1930) was a British poet and poet laureate from 1913 until his death.

[3] For "Marriage" see pp. 652–61 in this edition.

[4] Emily Dickinson (1830–86), American lyrical poet whose works were first published during the 1890s and who influenced many modernists.

gathered from reading her is that one may seek long in those exciting mazes sure of coming out at the right door in the end. There is nothing missing but the connectives.

The thought is compact, accurate, and accurately planted. In fact the garden, since it is a garden more than a statue, is found to be curiously of porcelain. It is the mythical, indestructible garden of pleasure, perhaps greatly pressed for space to-day, but there and intact, nevertheless.

I don't know where, except in modern poetry, this quality of the brittle, highly set off porcelain garden exists and nowhere in modern work better than with Miss Moore. It is this chief beauty of to-day, this hard crest to nature, that makes the best present work with its "unnatural" appearance seem so thoroughly gratuitous, so difficult to explain, and so doubly a treasure of seclusion. It is the white of a clarity beyond the facts.

There is in the newer work a perfectly definite handling of the materials with a given intention to relate them in a certain way – a handling that is intensely, intentionally selective. There is a definite place where the matters of the day may meet if they choose or not, but if they assemble it must be there. There is no compromise. Miss Moore never falls from the place inhabited by poems. It is hard to give an illustration of this from her work because it is everywhere. One must be careful, though, not to understand this as a mystical support, a danger we are skirting safely, I hope, in our time.

Poe in his most read first essay quotes Nathaniel Willis' poem, "The Two Women",[5] admiringly and in full and one senses at once the reason: there is a quality to the *feeling* there that affected Poe tremendously. This mystical quality that endeared Poe to Father Tabb the poet-priest,[6] still seems to many the essence of poetry itself. It would be idle to name many who have been happily mystical and remained good poets: Poe, Blake, Francis Thompson,[7] et cetera.

But what I wish to point is that there need be no stilled and archaic heaven, no ducking under religiosities to have poetry and to have it stand in its place beyond "nature." Poems have a separate existence uncompelled by nature or the supernatural. There is a "special" place which poems, as all works of art, must occupy, but it is quite definitely the same as that where bricks or coloured threads are handled.

In painting, Ingres[8] realized the essentiality of drawing and each perfect part seemed to float free from his work, by itself. There is much in this that applies beautifully to Miss Moore. It is perfect drawing that attains to a separate existence which might, if it please, be called mystical, but is in fact no more than the practicability of design.

To Miss Moore an apple remains an apple whether it be in Eden or the fruit bowl where it curls. But that would be hard to prove –

"dazzled by the apple."[9]

The apple is left there, suspended. One is not made to feel that as an apple it has anything particularly to do with poetry or that as such it needs special treatment; one goes on. Because of this the direct object does seem unaffected. It seems as free from the smears of mystery, as pliant, as "natural" as Venus on the wave. Because of this her work is never indecorous as where nature is itself concerned. These are great virtues.

Without effort Miss Moore encounters the affairs which concern her as one would naturally in reading or upon a walk outdoors. She is not a Swinburne stumbling to music, but one always finds her moving forward ably, in thought, unimpeded by a rhythm. Her own rhythm is particularly revealing. It does not interfere with her progress; it is the movement of the animal, it does not put itself first and ask the other to follow.

Nor is "thought" the thing that she contends with. Miss Moore uses the thought most interestingly and wonderfully to my mind. I don't know but that this technical excellence is one

---

[5] Edgar Allan Poe, in his essay "The Poetic Principle," quotes the poem "The Two Women" by Nathaniel Parker Willis (1806–67), a poet and critic who was supportive of Poe's work.

[6] John Bannister Tabb (1845–1909), known as "Father Tabb," was a religious poet who deeply admired the work of Poe.

[7] William Blake (1757–1827) was a British poet, visionary, and engraver; Francis Thompson (1859–1907) was a British poet who frequently wrote on religious subjects.

[8] Jean-Auguste-Dominique Ingres (1780–1867), French painter noted for his draughtmanship and classicism.

[9] From Marianne Moore's poem "Marriage" (see p. 655, l. 115).

of the greatest pleasures I get from her. She occupies the thought to its end, and goes on – without connectives. To me this is thrilling. The essence is not broken, nothing is injured. It is a kind hand to a merciless mind at home in the thought as in the cruder image. In the best modern verse room has been made for the best of modern thought and Miss Moore thinks straight.

Only the most modern work has attempted to do without *exmachina* props of all sorts, without rhyme, assonance, the feudal master beat, the excuse of "nature," of the spirit, mysticism, religiosity, "love," "humour," "death." Work such as Miss Moore's holds its bloom to-day not by using slang, not by its moral abandon or puritanical steadfastness, but by the aesthetic pleasure engendered where pure craftsmanship joins hard surfaces skilfully.

Poetry has taken many disguises which by cross reading or intense penetration it is possible to go through to the core. Through intersection of loci their multiplicity may become revelatory. The significance of much reading being that this "thing" grow clearer, remain fresh, be more present to the mind. To read more thoroughly than this is idleness: a common classroom absurdity.

One may agree tentatively with Glenway Wescott,[10] that there is a division taking place in America between a proletarian art, full of sincerities, on the one side and an aristocratic and ritualistic art on the other. One may agree, but it is necessary to scrutinize such a statement carefully.

There cannot be two arts of poetry really. There is weight and there is disencumberedness. There can be no schism, except that which has always existed between art and its approaches. There cannot be a proletarian art – even among savages. There is a proletarian taste. To have achieved an organization even of that is to have escaped it.

And to organize into a pattern is also, true enough, to "approach the conditions of ritual."[11] But here I would again go slow. I see only escape from the conditions of ritual in Miss Moore's work: a rush through wind if not toward some patent "end" at least away from pursuit, a pursuit perhaps by ritual. If from such a flight a ritual results it is more the care of those who follow than of the one who leads. "Ritual," too often to suit my ear, connotes a stereotyped mode of procedure from which pleasure has passed, whereas the poetry, to which my attention clings, if it ever knew those conditions, is distinguished only as it leaves them behind.

It is at least amusing, in this connexion, to quote from *Others*,[12] Volume 1, Number 5, November 1915 – quoted in turn from J. B. Kerfoot in Life:[13] "Perhaps you are unfamiliar with this 'new poetry' that is called 'revolutionary.' . . . It is the expression of a democracy of feeling rebelling against an aristocracy of form."

> "As if a death mask ever could replace
> Life's faulty excellence!"[14]

There are two elements essential to Miss Moore's scheme of composition: the hard and unaffected concept of the apple itself as an idea, then its edge to edge contact with the things which surround it – the coil of a snake, leaves at various depths, or as it may be; and without connectives unless it be poetry, the inevitable connective, if you will.

Marriage, through which thought does not penetrate, appeared to Miss Moore a legitimate object for art, an art that would not halt from using thought about it, however, as it might want to. Against marriage, "this institution, perhaps one should say enterprise –"[15] Miss Moore launched her thought not to have it appear arsenaled as in a text book on psychology, but to stay among apples and giraffes in a poem. The interstices for the light and not the interstitial web of the thought concerned her, or so it seems to me. Thus the material is as the handling: the thought, the

[10] Glenway Wescott (1901–87) was an American writer of novels and essays; the essay that Williams has in mind has not been identified.

[11] Williams is altering a well-known phrase by Walter Pater (1939–94); see p. 98 note 2.

[12] An avant-garde journal published from 1915 to 1919 and edited by Alfred Kreymborg (1883–1966).

[13] John Barrett Kerfoot (1865–1927) was an American journalist and critic. The essay cited by Williams has not been identified.

[14] From Marianne Moore's poem "To Statecraft Embalmed," which was included in *Observations*, the book being reviewed by Williams.

[15] From Marianne Moore's poem "Marriage," here p. 652, ll. 1–2.

word, the rhythm – all in the style. The effect is in the penetration of the light itself, how much, how little; the appearance of the luminous background.

Of marriage there is no solution in the poem and no attempt at a solution; nor is there an attempt to shirk thought about it, to make marriage beautiful or otherwise by "poetic" treatment. There is beauty and it is thoughtless, as marriage or a cave inhabited by the sounds and colours of waves, as in the time of prismatic colour, as England with its baby rivers, as G. B. Shaw,[16] or chanticleer, or a fish, or an elephant with its strictly practical appendages. All these things are inescapably caught in the beauty of Miss Moore's passage through them; they all have at least edges. This too is a quality that greatly pleases me: definite objects which give a clear contour to her force. Is it a flight, a symphony, a ghost, a mathematic? The usual evasion is to call them poems.

Miss Moore gets great pleasure from wiping soiled words or cutting them clean out, removing the aureoles that have been pasted about them or taking them bodily from greasy contexts. For the compositions which Miss Moore intends, each word should first stand crystal clear with no attachments; not even an aroma. As a cross light upon this Miss Moore's personal dislike for flowers that have both a satisfying appearance *and* an odour of perfume is worth noticing.

With Miss Moore a word is a word most when it is separated out by science, treated with acid to remove the smudges, washed, dried, and placed right side up on a clean surface. Now one may say that this is a word. Now it may be used, and how?

It may be used not to smear it again with thinking (the attachments of thought) but in such a way that it will remain scrupulously itself, clean, perfect, unnicked beside other words in parade. There must be edges. This casts some light I think on the simplicity of design in much of Miss Moore's work. There must be recognizable edges against the ground which cannot, as she might desire it, be left entirely white. Prose would be all black, a complete block, painted or etched over, but solid.

There is almost no overlaying at all. The effect is of every object sufficiently uncovered to be easily recognizable. This simplicity, with the light coming through from between the perfectly plain masses, is however extremely bewildering to one who has been accustomed to look at the usual "poem," the commonplace opaque board covered with vain curlicues. They forget, those who would read Miss Moore aright, that white circular discs grouped closely edge to edge upon a dark table make black sixpointed stars.

The "useful result" is an accuracy to which this simplicity of design greatly adds. The effect is for the effect to remain "true"; nothing loses its identity because of the composition, but the parts in their assembly remain quite as "natural" as before they were gathered. There is no "sentiment"; the softening effect of word upon word is nil; everything is in the style. To make this ten times evident is Miss Moore's constant care. There seems to be almost too great a wish to be transparent and it is here if anywhere that Miss Moore's later work will show a change, I think.

The general effect is of a rise through the humanities, the sciences, without evading "thought," through anything (if not everything) of the best of modern life; taking whatever there is as it comes, using it and leaving it drained of its pleasure, but otherwise undamaged. Miss Moore does not compromise science with poetry. In this again she is ably modern.

And from this clarity, this acid cleansing, this unblinking willingness, her poems result, a true modern crystallization, the fine essence of to-day which I have spoken of as the porcelain garden.

Or one will think a little of primitive masonry, the units unglued and as in the greatest early constructions unstandardized.

In such work as "Critics and Connoisseurs," and "Poetry,"[17] Miss Moore succeeds in having the "thing" which is her concern move freely, unencumbered by the images or the difficulties of thought. In such work there is no "suggestiveness," no tiresome "subtlety" of trend to be heavily followed, no painstaking refinement of sentiment. There is surely a choice evident in all her work, a very definite quality of choice in her material, a thinness perhaps, but a very welcome and no little

---

[16] George Bernard Shaw (1856–1950), celebrated Irish dramatist and essayist.

[17] Both poems by Marianne Moore included in *Observations* (1924); for "Poetry," see p. 649.

surprising absence of moral tone. The choice being entirely natural and completely arbitrary is not in the least offensive, in fact it has been turned curiously to advantage throughout.

From what I have read it was in "Critics and Connoisseurs" that the successful method used later began first to appear: If a thought presents itself the force moves through it easily and completely: so the thought also has revealed the "thing" – that is all. The thought is used exactly as the apple, it is the same insoluble block. In Miss Moore's work the purely stated idea has an edge exactly like a fruit or a tree or a serpent.

To use anything: rhyme, thought, colour, apple, verb – so as to illumine it, is the modern prerogative; a stintless inclusion. It is Miss Moore's success.

The diction, the phrase construction, is unaffected. To use a "poetic" inversion of language, or even such a special posture of speech, still discernible in Miss Moore's earlier work, is to confess an inability to have penetrated with poetry some crevice of understanding; that special things and special places are reserved for art, that it is unable, that it requires fostering. This is unbearable.

Poetry is not limited in that way. It need not say either

Bound without.
Boundless within.

It has as little to do with the soul as with ermine robes or graveyards. It is not noble, sad, funny. It is poetry. It is free. It is escapeless. It goes where it will. It is in danger; escapes if it can.

This is new! The quality is not new, but the freedom is new, the unbridled leap.

The dangers are thereby multiplied – but the clarity is increased. Nothing but the perfect and the clear.

A Note on the Recent Work of James Joyce (1927)

A SUBTITLE to any thesis on contemporary reputations might well be: How truth fares among us today. I see no other approach, at least, to the difficulties on modern literary styles than to endeavor to find what truth lies in them. Not in the matter of the writing but in the style. For style is the substance of writing which gives it its worth as literature.

But how is truth concerned in a thing seemingly so ghost-like over words as style? We may at least attempt to say what we have found untrue of it. To a style is often applied the word "beautiful"; and "Beauty is truth, truth beauty," said Keats; "that is all ye know and all ye need to know."[1] By saying this Keats showed what I take to have been a typical conviction of his time consonant with Byron's intentions toward life and Goethe's praise of Byron.[2] But today we have reinspected that premise and rejected it by saying that if beauty is truth and since we cannot get along without truth, then beauty is a useless term and one to be dispensed with. Here is a location for our attack; we have discarded beauty; at its best it seems truth incompletely realized. Styles can no longer be described as beautiful.

In fact it would not be stretching the point to describe all modern styles in their grand limits as ways through a staleness of beauty to tell the truth anew. The beauty that clings to any really new

A NOTE ON THE RECENT WORK
First published in *transition* 8 (Nov. 1927); the "recent work" referred to in the title is *Work in Progress*, the title that Joyce gave to *Finnegans Wake* prior to the work's publication in its entirety in 1939. For a sample of *Finnegans Wake*, see pp. 284–300 in this edition.
[1] The concluding two lines of "Ode on a Grecian Urn" (1820) by the British poet John Keats (1795–1821), though the two words "on earth" have been omitted from the last line: "Ye popularly known on earth, and all ye need to know."

[2] The German poet and man of letters Johann Wolfgang von Goethe (1749–1832) reviewed several works by the British poet George Gordon Byron (1788–1832), praising their beauty and extolling Byron's genius; when he received word that Byron was dedicating his drama *Werner* to him, he wrote a three-stanza poem in praise of Byron. See Eliza Marian Butler (1885–1949), *Goethe and Byron* (London: Bowes and Bowes, 1956).

work is beauty only in the minds of those who do not fully realize the significance. Thus tentatively, James Joyce's style may be described, I think, as truth through the breakup of beautiful words.

If to achieve truth we work with words purely, as a writer must, and all the words are dead or beautiful, how then shall we succeed any better than might a philosopher with dead abstractions? or their configurations? One may sense something of the difficulties by reading a page of Gertrude Stein[3] where none of the words is beautiful. There must be something new done with the words. Leave beauty out or, conceivably, one might begin again, one might break them up to let the staleness out of them as Joyce, I think, has done. This is, of course, not all that he does nor even a major part of what he does, but it is nevertheless important.

In Joyce it began not without malice I imagine. And continued, no doubt, with a private end in view, as might be the case with any of us. Joyce, the catholic Irishman, began with English, a full-dressed English which it must have been his delight to unEnglish until it should be humanely Catholic, never at least sentimental. This is purely my imagination of a possible animus. And again a broken language cannot have been less than affectionately fostered since it affords him a relief from blockheaded tormentors. Admirably, of course, Joyce has written his words to face neither customs officials nor church dignitaries, Catholic or Protestant, but the clean features of the intelligence. Having so suffered from the dirtiness of men's minds – their mixed ideas, that is – suffered to the point of a possible suppression of all he puts upon paper, there is a humane, even a divine truth in his appeal to us through a style such as his present one which leaves nothing out. Much that he must say and cannot get said without his brokenness he gets down fully with it. But this is, again, merely a fancy. It is nothing and I put it down to show that it is nothing, things that have very little general value.

We are confronted not by reasons for its occurrence in Joyce's writings but by his style. Not by its accidental or sentimental reasons but its truth. What does it signify? Has he gone backward since *Ulysses*? Hish-hash all of it?

To my taste Joyce has not gone back but forward since *Ulysses*. I find his style richer, more able in its function of unabridged commentary upon the human soul, the function surely of all styles. But within this function what we are after will be that certain bent which is peculiar to Joyce and which gives him his value. It is not that the world is round nor even flat, but that it might well today be catholic; and as a corollary, that Joyce himself is today the ablest protagonist before the intelligence of that way of thinking. Such to my mind is the truth of his style. It is a priestly style and Joyce is himself a priest. If this be true to find out just what a priest of best intelligence intends would be what Joyce by his style intends. Joyce is obviously a catholic Irishman writing english, his style shows it and that is, less obviously, its virtue.

A profitable beginning to going further is to note the kinship between Joyce and Rabelais.[4] Every day Joyce's style more and more resembles that of the old master, the old catholic and the old priest. It would be rash to accuse Joyce of copying Rabelais. Much more likely is it that the styles are similar because they have been similarly fathered.

Take what is most obviously on the surface in both of them, their obscenity. Shall we object to Joyce's filth? Very well, but first answer how else will you have him tell the truth. From my own experience I am perfectly willing to venture that Joyce's style has been forced upon him, in this respect at least, by the facts, and that here he has understated rather than overstated the realistic conditions which compel him. One might even go on to say that in this respect of obscenity all other present styles seem lying beside his. Let his words be men and women; in no other way could so much humanity walk the streets save in such hiding clothes. Or put it the other way: in no other way could the naked truth hidden from us upon the streets in clothes be disclosed to us in a way that we could bear or even recognize save as Joyce by his style discloses it. We should praise his

[3] Gertrude Stein (1876–1946), American writer of poetry, fiction, drama, and prose; for her works see pp. 373–416; for Williams's estimate of her four years later, in 1931, see pp. 545–8.

[4] François Rabelais (c. 1489–1553), a Franciscan monk and doctor who wrote *Gargantua and Pantagruel* (1532–55), a masterful satirical work driven by uncanny passion and swiftness of language.

humanity and not object feebly to his fullness, liars that we are. It would be impossible for Joyce to be truthful and accurate to his understanding by any other style.

This it is, let us presume, to be a catholic of the world, or so Joyce has impressed me by his style. They say Joyce fears that were he to return to Ireland it would be seen to that they excommunicate him. I cannot believe such foolishness. They are wiser than that in the church today. Joyce writes and holds his place, I would assure them, solely by the extreme brilliance of his catholicism.

And all this is no more than a reflection of the truth about Rabelais now common property. He was not at all the fat-headed debauchee we used to think him, gross, guffawing vulgarly, but a priest "sensitized" to all such grossness. Else his style would not have assured his lasting out a year.

Joyce is to be discovered a catholic in his style then in something because of its divine humanity. Down, down it goes from priesthood into the slime as the church goes. The Catholic Church has always been unclean in its fingers and aloof in the head. Joyce's style consonant with this has nowhere the inhumanity of the scientific or protestant or pagan essayist. There is nowhere the coldly dressed formal language, the correct collar of such gentlemen seeking perhaps an english reputation.

Joyce discloses the X-ray eyes of the confessional, we see among the clothes, witnessing the stripped back and loins, the naked soul. Thoughtfully the priest under the constant eyes of God looks in. He, jowl to jowl with the sinner, is seen by God in all his ways. This is Joyce. To please God it is that he must look through the clothes. And therefore the privacy of the confessional; he must, so to speak, cover the ache and the sores from the world's desecrating eye with a kindly bandage. Yet he must tell the truth, before God.

Joyce has carried his writing this far: he has compared us his readers with God. He has laid it out clean for us, the filth, the diseased parts as a priest might do before the Maker. I am speaking of his style. I am referring to his broken words, the universality of his growing language which is no longer english. His language, much like parts of Rabelais, has no faculties of place. Joyce uses German, French, Italian, Latin, Irish, anything. Time and space do not exist, it is all one in the eyes of God – and man.

Being catholic in mind, to blatantly espouse the church, that is the superficial thing to do. The sensible thing is to risk excommunication by stupidity if it come to that in order to tell the truth. Therefore I rate Joyce far above such men as G. K. Chesterton, that tailor, or even Cocteau,[5] if he has turned catholic as I have heard, though in the case of the latter it chimes well with his acknowledged cleverness to be anachronistic.

And why should we fear, as do so many protestants, that all the world turn Romanist? What in that conglomerate is out of date would even there be finally corrected by the sovereign power of the intelligence than which nothing is greater including as it must at work the instincts and emotions, that is the round brain and not the flat one. And this is once more Joyce's style.

To sum up, to me the writings of James Joyce, the new work appearing in *transition*,[6] are perfectly clear and full of great interest in form and content. It even seems odd to me now that anyone used to seeing men and women dressed on the street and in rooms as we all do should find his style anything but obvious. If there is a difficulty it is this: whether he is writing to give us (of men and women) the aspect we are most used to or whether he is stripping from them the "military and civil dress" to give them to us in their unholy (or holy) and disreputable skins. I am inclined to think he leans more to the humaner way.

---

5   G. K. Chesterton (1874–1936), British novelist and essayist, noted for his staunch Catholicism; Jean Cocteau (1889–1963), French author of novels, plays, and essays, and filmmaker.
6   Installments of Joyce's *Work in Progress* (later to be titled *Finnegans Wake*) appeared in each monthly issue of *transition* from the first in April 1927 through the seventh in October 1927; Williams's essay, one recalls, was published in the eighth issue (November 1927), which contained yet another installment of *Work in Progress*.

The Work of Gertrude Stein (1930)

"Would I had seen a white bear!
(for how can I imagine it?)"

Let it be granted that whatever is new in literature the germ of it will be found somewhere in the writings of other times; only the modern emphasis gives work a present distinction.

The necessity for this modern focus and the meaning of the changes involved are, however, another matter, the everlasting stumbling block to criticism. Here is a theme worth development in the case of Gertrude Stein – yet signally neglected.

Why in fact have we not heard more generally from American scholars upon the writings of Miss Stein? Is it lack of heart or ability or just that theirs is an enthusiasm which fades rapidly of its own nature before the risks of today?

The verbs auxiliary we are concerned in here, continued my father, are am; was; have; had; do; did; could; owe; make; made; suffer; shall; should; will; would; can; ought; used; or is wont . . . – or with these question added to them; – Is it? Was it? Will it be? . . . Or affirmatively . . . – Or chronologically . . . – Or hypothetically . . . – If it was? If it was not? What would follow? – If the French beat the English? If the Sun should go out of the Zodiac?

Now, by the right use and application of these, continued my father, in which a child's memory should be exercised, there is no one idea can enter the brain how barren soever, but a magazine of conceptions and conclusions may be drawn forth from it. – Didst thou ever see a white bear? cried my father, turning his head round to Trim, who stood at the back of his chair. – No, an' please your honour, replied the corporal. – But thou couldst discourse about one, Trim, said my father, in case of need? – How is it possible, brother, quoth my Uncle Toby, if the corporal never saw one? – 'Tis the fact I want, replied my father, – and the possibility of it as follows.

A white bear! Very well, Have I ever seen one? Might I ever have seen one? Am I ever to see one? Ought I ever to have seen one? Or can I ever see one?

Would I had seen a white bear! (for how can I imagine it?)

If I should see a white bear, what should I say? If I should never see a white bear, what then?

If I never have, can, must, or shall see a white bear alive; have I ever seen the skin of one? Did I ever see one painted? – described? Have I never dreamed of one?

Note how the words *alive, skin, painted, described, dreamed* come into the design of these sentences. The feeling is of words themselves, a curious immediate quality quite apart from their meaning, much as in music different notes are dropped, so to speak, into repeated chords one at a time, one after another – for themselves alone. Compare this with the same effects common in all that Stein does. See *Geography and Plays*,[1] "They were both gay there." To continue—

Did my father, mother, uncle, aunt, brothers or sisters, ever see a white bear? What would they give? . . . How would they behave? How would the white bear have behaved? Is he wild? Tame? Terrible? Rough? Smooth?

Note the play upon *rough* and *smooth* (though it is not certain that this was intended), *rough* seeming to apply to the bear's deportment, *smooth* to surface, presumably the bear's coat. In any case the effect is that of a comparison relating primarily not to any qualities of the bear himself but to the words rough and smooth. And so to finish—

First published in the journal *Pagany* 1(1) (winter 1930).   [1]   For selections from *Geography and Plays* see pp. 400–4.

> Is the white bear worth seeing?
> Is there any sin in it?
> Is it better than a black one?

In this manner ends Chapter 43 of *The Life and Opinions of Tristram Shandy.*[2] The handling of the words and to some extent the imaginative quality of the sentence is a direct forerunner of that which Gertrude Stein has woven today into a synthesis of its own. It will be plain, in fact, on close attention, that Sterne exercises not only the play (or music) of sight, sense and sound contrast among the words themselves which Stein uses, but their grammatical play also – i.e. for, how, can I imagine it; did my..., what would, how would, compare Stein's "to have rivers; to halve rivers," etc. It would not be too much to say that Stein's development over a lifetime is anticipated completely with regard to subject matter, sense and grammar – in Sterne.

Starting from scratch we get, possibly, thatch; just as they have always done in poetry.

Then they would try to connect it up by something like – The mice scratch, beneath the thatch.

Miss Stein does away with all that. The free-versists on the contrary used nothing else. They saved – The mice, under the...,

It is simply the skeleton, the "formal" parts of writing, those that make form, that she has to do with, apart from the "burden" which they carry. The skeleton, important to acknowledge where confusion of all knowledge of the "soft parts" reigns as at the present day in all intellectual fields.

Stein's theme is writing. But in such a way as to be writing envisioned as the first concern of the moment, dragging behind it a dead weight of logical burdens, among them a dead criticism which broken through might be a gap by which endless other enterprises of the understanding should issue – for refreshment.

It is a revolution of some proportions that is contemplated, the exact nature of which may be no more than sketched here but whose basis is humanity in a relationship with literature hitherto little contemplated.

And at the same time it is a general attack on the scholastic viewpoint, that medieval remnant with whose effects from generation to generation literature has been infested to its lasting detriment. It is a break-away from that paralyzing vulgarity of logic for which the habits of science and philosophy coming over into literature (where they do not belong) are to blame.

It is this logicality as a basis for literary action which in Stein's case, for better or worse, has been wholly transcended.

She explains her own development in connection with *Tender Buttons* (1914). "It was my first conscious struggle with the problem of correlating sight, sound and sense, and eliminating rhythm; – now I am trying grammar and eliminating sight and sound" (*transition* No. 14, fall, 1928).

Having taken the words to her choice, to emphasize further what she has in mind she has completely unlinked them (in her most recent work) from their former relationships in the sentence. This was absolutely essential and unescapable. Each under the new arrangement has a quality of its own, but not conjoined to carry the burden science, philosophy and every higgledy-piggledy figment of law and order have been laying upon them in the past. They are like a crowd at Coney Island, let us say, seen from an airplane.

Whatever the value of Miss Stein's work may turn out finally to be, she has at least accomplished her purpose of getting down on paper this much that is decipherable. She has placed writing on a plane where it may deal unhampered with its own affairs, unburdened with scientific and philosophic lumber.

For after all, science and philosophy are today, in their effect upon the mind, little more than fetishes of unspeakable abhorrence. And it is through a subversion of the art of writing that their grip upon us has assumed its steel-like temper.

What are philosophers, scientists, religionists, they that have filled up literature with their pap? Writers, of a kind. Stein simply erases their stories, turns them off and does without them, their

---

[2]　Celebrated novel by Laurence Sterne (1713–68), first published 1760–2.

logic (founded merely on the limits of the perceptions) which is supposed to transcend the words, along with them. Stein denies it. The words, in writing, she discloses, transcend everything.

Movement (for which in a petty way logic is taken), the so-called search for truth and beauty, is for us the effect of a breakdown of the attention. But movement must not be confused with what we attach to it but, for the rescuing of the intelligence, must always be considered aimless, without progress.

This is the essence of all knowledge.

Bach might be an illustration of movement not suborned by a freight of purposed design, loaded upon it as in almost all later musical works; statement unmusical and unnecessary, Stein's "They lived very gay then" has much of the same quality of movement to be found in Bach – the composition of the words determining not the logic, not the "story," not the theme even, but the movement itself. As it happens, "They were both gay there" is as good as some of Bach's shorter figures.

Music could easily have a statement attached to each note in the manner of words, so that C natural might mean the sun, etc., and completely dull treatises be played – and even sciences finally expounded in tunes.

Either, we have been taught to think, the mind moves in a logical sequence to a definite end which is its goal, or it will embrace movement without goal other than movement itself for an end and hail "transition" only as supreme.

Take your choice, both resorts are an improper description of the mind in fullest play.

If the attention could envision the whole of writing, let us say, at one time, moving over it in swift and accurate pursuit of the modern imperative at the instant when it is most to the fore, something of what actually takes place under an optimum of intelligence could be observed. It is an alertness not to let go of a possibility of movement in our fearful bedazzlement with some concrete and fixed present. The goal is to keep a beleaguered line of understanding which has movement from breaking down and becoming a hole into which we sink decoratively to rest.

The goal has nothing to do with the silly function which logic, natural or otherwise, enforces. Yet it is a goal. It moves as the sense wearies, remains fresh, living. One is concerned with it as with anything pursued and not with the rush of air or the guts of the horse one is riding – save to a very minor degree.

Writing, like everything else, is much a question of refreshed interest. It is directed, not idly, but as most often happens (though not necessarily so) toward that point not to be predetermined where movement is blocked (by the end of logic perhaps). It is about these parts, if I am not mistaken, that Gertrude Stein will be found.

There remains to be explained the bewildering volume of what Miss Stein has written, the quantity of her work, its very apparent repetitiousness, its iteration, what I prefer to call its extension, the final clue to her meaning.

It is, of course, a progression (not a progress) beginning, conveniently, with "Melanctha" from *Three Lives*, and coming up to today.[3]

How in a democracy, such as the United States, can writing which has to compete with excellence elsewhere and in other times remain in the field and be at once objective (true to fact) intellectually searching, subtle and instinct with powerful additions to our lives? It is impossible, without invention of some sort, for the very good reason that observation about us engenders the very opposite of what we seek: triviality, crassness and intellectual bankruptcy. And yet what we do see can in no way be excluded. Satire and flight are two possibilities but Miss Stein has chosen otherwise.

But if one remain in a place and reject satire, what then? To be democratic, local (in the sense of being attached with integrity to actual experience) Stein, or any other artist, must for subtlety ascend to a plane of almost abstract design to keep alive. To writing, then, as an art in itself. Yet

---

[3]   *Three Lives* was first published in 1909; and "Melanctha" is one of the three stories it contains.

what actually impinges on the senses must be rendered as it appears, by use of which, only, and under which, untouched, the significance has to be disclosed. It is one of the major problems of the artist.

"Melanctha" is a thrilling clinical record of the life of a colored woman in the present-day United States, told with directness and truth. It is without question one of the best bits of characterization produced in America. It is universally admired. This is where Stein began. But for Stein to tell a story of that sort, even with the utmost genius, was not enough under the conditions in which we live, since by the very nature of its composition such a story does violence to the larger scene which would be portrayed.

True, a certain way of delineating the scene is to take an individual like Melanctha and draw her carefully. But this is what happens. The more carefully the drawing is made, the greater the genius involved and the greater the interest that attaches, therefore, to the character as an individual, the more exceptional that character becomes in the mind of the reader and the less typical of the scene.

It was no use for Stein to go on with *Three Lives*. There that phase of the work had to end. See *Useful Knowledge*, the parts on the U.S.A.[4]

Stein's pages have become like the United States viewed from an airplane – the same senseless repetitions, the endless multiplications of toneless words, with these she had to work.

No use for Stein to fly to Paris and forget it. The thing, the United States, the unmitigated stupidity, the drab tediousness of the democracy, the overwhelming number of the offensively ignorant, the dull nerve – is there in the artist's mind and cannot be escaped by taking a ship. She must resolve it if she can, if she is to be.

That must be the artist's articulation with existence.

Truly, the world is full of emotion – more or less – but it is caught in bewilderment to a far more important degree. And the purpose of art, so far as it has any, is not at least to copy that, but lies in the resolution of difficulties to its own comprehensive organization of materials. And by so doing, in this case, rather than by copying, it takes its place as most human.

To deal with Melanctha, with characters of whomever it may be, the modern Dickens, is not therefore human. To write like that is not in the artist, to be human at all, since nothing is resolved, nothing is done to resolve the bewilderment which makes of emotion an inanity: That, is to overlook the gross instigation and with all subtlety to examine the object minutely for "the truth" – which if there is anything more commonly practiced or more stupid, I have yet to come upon it.

To be most useful to humanity, or to anything else for that matter, an art, writing, must stay art, not seeking to be science, philosophy, history, the humanities, or anything else it has been made to carry in the past. It is this enforcement which underlies Gertrude Stein's extension and progression to date.

A Draft of X X X Cantos by Ezra Pound (1931)

Poetry? Words: figments of the mind, of no real substance.
What more then is light? It is precisely a figment of the mind if the apprehension of it be our consideration.

But it is an emanation consequent on microscopic action in the sun.
Then words are the same, call the microscopic action which is their source 'Socrates' or what you will.

The *Cantos* have been in Pound's mind since 1908, at least: "that forty year epic"[1] – (*Personae*, etc., etc.)

---

[4]   Gertrude Stein, *Useful Knowledge* (London: John Lane; New York: Payson and Clarke, 1928).

First published in *The Symposium* 2.2 (April 1931).
[1]   Ezra Pound's first book of poetry, *A Lume Spento* (Italian for "With Spent Taper") (Venice: privately printed, 1908; reprinted New York: New Directions, 1965), had included a poem titled "Scriptor Ignotus", which contained the lines "And I see my greater soul-self bending / Sybilwise with that great forty-year epic / That you know of, yet unwrit," a passage that Williams and many later critics have viewed as forecasting *The Cantos* (*A Lume Spento*, [New Directions], 38).

The poem begins after an image much resorted to by modern writers:[2] the *Odyssey*, ever more pat to the times as time passes – (But it was Virgil who led Dante through the Inferno.)[3]

The first *Canto*[4] has to do with Odysseus' descent to the world of shadows. The effect in this case being qualified by Pound's use of a translation into our tongue of a sixteenth-century translation from the original Greek – thus making the *Odyssey* itself a link with which to hold together his theme. He uses a poem, words, modes that have been modified by use – not an idea. He uses the poem objectively.

The now hackneyed theme of the appearance of the aged Tiresias[5] comes up as in the original text (probably) but is not stressed.

The thing that is felt is that the quick are moving among the dead – and the oarsmen "placed," the oarsmen who went down in the whirlpool chained to their rowing benches and were not saved.

It is the gone world of "history."

(*Canto II*)

Now the poet takes his place: hallucination or genius. The ship is stopped in mid-career, in mid-ocean. The youth beaten by the sailors into the ship's stern feels the God beside him (Acoetes' story). He chronicles the arrest of the vessel's on-rush:—

"Ship stock fast in seaswirl, . . . " etc., etc., etc.

As to the Greek quotations – knowing no Greek – I presume they mean something, probably something pertinent to the text – and that the author knows what they mean. . . . But in all salient places – Pound has clarified his out-land insertions with reasonable consistency. They are no particular matter save that they say, There were other times like ours – at the back of it all.

Pound has had the discernment to descry and the mind to grasp that the difficulties in which humanity finds itself need no phenomenal insight for their solution. Their cure is another matter, but that is no reason for a belief in a complicated mystery of approach fostered by those who wish nothing done, as it is no reason for a failure of the mind to function simply when dangerously confronted. Here is a theme: a closed mind which clings to its power – about which the intelligence beats seeking entrance. This is the basic theme of the *XXX Cantos*.

Reading them through consecutively, at one sitting (four hours) Pound's "faults" as a poet all center around his rancor against the malignant stupidity of a generation which polluted our rivers and would then, brightly, give ten or twenty or any imaginable number of millions of dollars as a fund toward the perpetuation of *Beauty* – in the form of a bequest to the New York Metropolitan Museum of Art.

"In America this crime has not been spread over a period of centuries, it has been done in the last twenty or twenty-five years, by the single generation, from fifteen to twenty-five years older than I am, who have held power through that slobbery period."[6]

His versification has not as its objective (apparently) that of some contemporary verse of the best quality. It is patterned *still* after classic meters and so does often deform the natural order – though little and to a modified degree only (nor is his practice without advantages as a method). Pound does very definitely intend a modern speech – but wishes to save the excellences (well-worked-out forms) of the old, so leans to it overmuch.

A criticism of Pound's *Cantos* could not be better concerned, I think, than in considering them in relation to the principal move in imaginative writing today – that away from the word as a symbol toward the word as reality.

1) His words affect modernity with too much violence (at times) – a straining after slang effects, engendered by their effort to escape that which is their instinctive quality, a taking character from classic similes and modes. You cannot *easily* switch from Orteum to Peoria without

---

[2] The image or figure of Odysseus or Ulysses, whose name had furnished the title for Joyce's novel of 1922.

[3] The Roman poet Virgil guides Dante through the Inferno in the *Divine Comedy*; Williams is insinuating that Virgil, rather than Odysseus or Ulysses, might be a better literary model to adopt for traversing the "inferno" of modernity.

[4] See pp. 61–4.

[5] A reference to the appearance of Tiresias as a character in Part III of *The Waste Land* (1922); see pp. 132–3, lines 215–46.

[6] A quotation from an essay by Ezra Pound, source not identified.

violence (to the language). These images too greatly infest the *Cantos*, the words *cannot* escape being colored by them: 2) so too the form of the phrase – it affects a modern turn but is really bent to a classical beauty of image, so that in effect it often (though not always) mars the normal accent of speech. But not always: sometimes it is superbly done and Pound is always trying to overcome the difficulty.

Pound is humane in a like sense to that of the writer of the great cantos – without being in the least sentimental. He has been able to do this by paying attention first to his art, its difficulties, its opportunities: to language – as did Dante: to popular language – It is sheer stupidity to forget the primarily humane aspect of Dante's work in the rhapsodic swoon induced by his blinding technical, aesthetic and philosophic qualities.

All the thought and implications of thought are there in the words (in the minute character and relationships of the words – destroyed, avoided by . . .) – it is *that* I wish to say again and again – it is there in the technique and it is that that is the making or breaking of the work. It is that that one sees, feels. It is that that *is* the work of art – to be observed.

The means Pound has used for the realization of his effects – the poetry itself—:

It is beside the question to my mind to speak of Pound's versification as carefully and accurately measured – beyond all comparison—

Perhaps it is and if so, what of it?

That has nothing in it of value to recommend it. It is deeper than that. His excellence is that of the maker, not the measurer – I say he *is* a poet. This is in effect to have stepped beyond measure.

It is that the material is so molded that it is changed in *kind* from other statement. It is a *sort* beyond measure.

The measure is an inevitability, an unavoidable accessory after the fact. If one move, if one run, if one seize up a material – it cannot avoid having a measure, it cannot avoid a movement which clings to it – as the movement of a horse becomes a part of the rider also—

That is the way Pound's verse impresses me and why he can include pieces of prose and have them still part of a *poem*. It is incorporated in a movement of the intelligence which is special, beyond usual thought and action—

It partakes of a quality which makes the meter, the movement peculiar – unmeasurable (without a prior change of mind)—

It is that which is the evidence of invention. Pound's line is the movement of his thought, his concept of the whole—

As such, it has measure but not first to be picked at: certain realizable characteristics which may be looked at, evaluated more pointedly, then measured and "beautifully," "ideally," "correctly" pointed.

They (the lines) have a character that is parcel of the poem itself. (It is in the small make-up of the lines that the character of the poem definitely comes – and beyond which it cannot go.)

It is (in this case) a master meter that wishes to come of the classic but at the same time to be bent to and to incorporate the rhythm of modern speech.

This is or would be the height of excellence – the efflorescence of a rare mind – turned *to* the world.

It succeeds and not – it does and fails.

It is in the minutiae – in the minute organization of the words and their relationships in a composition that the seriousness and value of a work of writing exist – *not* in the sentiments, ideas, schemes portrayed.

It is here, furthermore, that creation takes place. It is not a plaster of thought applied.

The seriousness of a work of art, the belief the author has in it, is that he does generate in it – a solution in some sense of the continuous confusion and barrenness which life imposes in its mutations – (on him who will not create).

It is always necessary to create, to generate, or life, any "life," the life of art, stales and dies – it dies out from under, it ceases to exist – it is not captured merely by studied excellence—

We seek a language which will not be at least a deformation of speech as we know it – but will embody all the advantageous jumps, swiftnesses, colors, movements of the day—

– that will, at least, not exclude language as spoken – all language (present) as spoken.

Pound has attempted an ambitious use of language for serious thought without sequestration (the cloistering of words) – an acceptance – and by his fine ear attempted to tune them – excluding nothing.

He has by intention avoided (quite as much as if he had announced it) the camphorated words of what passes today for classical usage. And also the cracked up – the cracking up of words and natural word sequences in an effort toward synthesis – "synthesis," that is – and—

Pound finds the problem of new word use more difficult than that – and correctly so, I believe; that generation is subtler, that such writers are "seeking in the wrong garbage can."

He is seeking to demonstrate the intelligence – as he believes a poet must – by laboring with the material as it exists in speech and history. Doing that, he is attempting the true difficulty (though I am not here attacking the other slant on the theme).

It is not by a huge cracking up of language that you will build new work, he postulates (that is a confusion even when skilful – a true babel – onomatopoeia, a reversion, its most signal triumph), nor by use of an embalmed language, on the other hand. But by poetry – that will strike through words whipping them into a shape – clarity and motion: analysis: be they what they may.

Analysis. It is what all poets have done with the language about them.

> *Button up your overcoat*
> *When the wind blows free*
> *Take good care of yourself*
> *You belong to me.*

There's speech – fairly accurately. Caught alive, no doubt, and written down, put to a tune.

Pound has wanted to do the same to a heightened and profounder degree. He has chosen flawlessly where and what he will create.

How far has be succeeded? Generation, he says, as I interpret him, is analytical, it is not a mass fusion. Only superficially do the *Cantos* fuse the various temporal phases of the material Pound has chosen, into a synthesis. It is important to stress this for it is Pound's chief distinction in the *Cantos* – his personal point of departure from most that the modern is attempting. It is not by any means a synthesis, but a shot through all material – a true and somewhat old-fashioned analysis of his world.

It is still a Lenin striking through the mass, whipping it about, that engages his attention. That is the force Pound believes in. It is not a proletarian art—

He has succeeded against himself. He has had difficulties of training to overcome which he will not completely undo – in himself at least – if that were all.

But the words reveal it: white-gathered, sun-dazzle, rock-pool, god-sleight, sea-swirl, sea-break, vine-trunk, vine-must, pin-rack, glass-glint, wave-runs, salmon-pink, dew-haze, blue-shot, green-gold, green-ruddy, eye-glitter, blue-deep, wine-red, water-shift, rose-paleness, wave-cords, churn-stick.

We have, examining the work, successes – great ones – the first molds – clear cut, never turgid, not following the heated trivial – staying cold, "classical" but swift with a movement of thought.

It stands out from almost all other verse by a faceted quality that is not muzzy, painty, wet. It is a dry, clean use of words. Yet look at the words. They are themselves not dead. They have not been violated by "thinking." They have been used willingly by thought.

Imagistic use has entirely passed out of them, there is almost no use of simile, no allegory – the word has been used in its plain sense to represent a thing – remaining thus loose in its context – not gummy – (when at its best) – an objective unit in the design – but alive.

Pound has taken them up – if it may be risked – alertly, swiftly, but with feeling for the delicate living quality in them – not disinfecting, scraping them, but careful of the life. The result is that they stay living – and discreet.

Or almost. For beside living passages, there are places where he wrenches the words about for what "ought to be" their conformation.

That's no matter. He has taken up language and raised it to a height where it may stand – beside Artemis—

If that is not a purpose worthy of a poet and if Pound has not done it – then—

It isn't all, it's even (in a sense) a defect to want so much the Artemis thing. But Pound has lifted the language up as no one else has done – wherever he has lifted it – or whatever done to it in the lifting.

His defects (dey's good too) are due to his inability to surmount the American thing – or his ability to do so without physical success – if that be preferred.

Ford Madox Ford (1873–1939)

Introduction

Ford Madox Hueffer (1873–1939), who later changed his surname to Ford when German-sounding names became unpopular in the First World War, was born in Kent at the home of his grandfather, Ford Madox Brown, a celebrated Pre-Raphaelite painter. He began writing early and prolifically, ultimately authoring 60 books of novels, poetry, criticism, travel essays, and reminiscences. In 1898 he met Joseph Conrad, with whom he collaborated in writing *The Inheritors: An Extravagant Story* (1901) and *Romance* (1903). From 1908 to 1911 he was editor of the *English Review*, where he became the first to publish D. H. Lawrence and Ezra Pound. In 1915 he published *The Good Soldier*, his most widely read and admired book today. He joined the war effort and contributed to British propaganda efforts. After the war, in 1922, Ford moved to Paris, where he became the founding editor of the *transatlantic review*, a journal that ran from 1924 to 1926 and whose contributors included James Joyce, Ezra Pound Gertrude Stein, and Ernest Hemingway. During these years he was at work on a tetralogy comprising *Some Do Not*, *No More Parades*, *A Man Could Stand Up*, and *The Last Post*, which together made up *Parade's End*, Ford's survey of the world before and after the First World War. He was married several times and had numerous brief affairs.

Pink Flannel (1919)

Mr Ford Madox Hueffer, author of *The Fifth Queen* and many other romances, served on the French front with a Welsh infantry battalion. 'Pink Flannel' is a comedy that might have been a tragedy; and in the story the two strands of life at home and life in the trenches are skillfully interwoven.

W.L. James waved his penny candle round the dark tent and the shadow of the pole moved in queer angles on the canvas sides.

It was a great worry – it was more than a worry! to have lost Mrs Wilkinson's letter. There was very little in the tent – and still less that the letter could be in. When Caradoe Morris had brought him the letter in the front line, W.L. James had had with him, of what the tent now contained, only his trench coat, his tunic, and his shirts, of things that could contain letters. It could not be in the dirty collection of straps and old clothes that were in his valise; it could not be in his wash-basin or in his flea-bag. And he had not even read Mrs Wilkinson's letter! Caradoe Morris had come down from the first line transport, and had given it to him at the very beginning of the strafe that had lasted two days. The sentry on the right had called out: 'Rum Jar,[1] left,' and he and Morris had bolted up the communication trench at the very moment when, holding in his hand the longed-for envelope, he had recognised the handwriting of the address. He knew he had put it somewhere for safety.

But where? Where the devil *could* you put a letter for safety in a beastly trench? In your trench coat – in your tunic – in your breeches pocket. There *was* not anywhere else.

He was tired: he was dog-tired. He was always dog-tired, anyhow, when he came out of the front line. Now he felt relaxed all over: dropping, for next morning he was going on ninety-six hours' leave and, for the moment, that seemed like an eternity of slackness. So that he could let himself go.

He could have let himself go altogether if he had not lost Mrs Wilkinson's letter – or even if he had known what it contained......He did not suppose, even if he had dropped it in the trench,

This story was first published in *Land and Water* 72 (May 8, 1919). The editorial comment that prefaced it is reproduced here.

[1] Soldiers' slang for a type of German trench mortar.

that anyone would who picked it up would make evil use of it – forward it to Mrs Wilkinson's husband, say? On the other hand, they might?....

He took off his tunic, his boots, and his puttees, and let himself, feet forward into his flea-bag. He blew out the candle that he had stuck on to the top of his tin hat. A triangle of stars became important before his eyes. The night was full of the babble of voices. He heard one voice call: 'The major wants: *Mr Britling Sees It Through*.'[2] ... The machine-guns said: 'Wukka! Wukka!' under the pale stars, as if their voices were a part of the stillness. The stars rose swiftly in the triangle of sky; they hung for a long time, then descended or went out. Much noise existed for a moment. He said to himself that the Hun had got the wind up, and, whilst he began to worry once more about the letter, as it were, with nearly all his brain, one spot of it said: 'That insistent "Wukka! Wukka!" to the right is from Wytschaete: the intermittent one is our "G" trenches.... There's an HE going to the top of Kemmel Hill......'

So his mind made before his eyes pictures of the Flanders plain; the fact that the Germans were alarmed at the idea of a sudden raid – that our machine-guns were answering theirs – that their gunners were putting over some random shells from 4.2s. Presently our own 99-pounders or naval guns or something would shut them up. Then they would all be quiet..... A sense of deep and voluptuous security had descended on him. Out there, when you have nothing else to worry you, you calculate the chances: rifle fire 20 to 1 against MGs[3] 30: Rum Jars 40; FA[4] 70 against a shot of flying iron. Now his mind registered the fact that the chances of direct hits was nil, or bits of flying iron, 250 to 1 against – and his mind put the idea to sleep, as it were ... He was in support.....

The noise continued – there were some big thumps away to the right. Our artillery was waking up. But the voices from the tents were audible: tranquil conversations about strafes, about Cardiff, about ship owners' profits, about the Divisional 'Follies'.... The Divisional 'Follies'!

He would be going to the 'Ambassadors' – with Mrs Wilkinson – within twenty-four hours if he had any luck.... GSO II had promised to run him from Bailleul to Boulogne: he would catch the one-o' clock leave boat; he would be in Town – Town – Town! – by six. Mrs Wilkinson would meet him on the platform. He would keep her waiting twenty minutes in the vestibule of his hotel while he had a quick bath. By 6.45 they would be dining together; she would be looking at him across the table with her exciting eyes that had dark pupils and yellow-brown iris! Her chin would be upon her hands with the fingers interlocked. Then they would be in the dress circle of the theatre – looking down on the nearly darkened stage from which, nevertheless, a warm light would well upwards upon her face.... And she would be warm, beside him, her hand touching his hand amongst her furs.... And her white shoulders.... And they would whisper, her hair just touching his ear.... And be warm.... Warm!

And then.... Damn! Damn! Oh, damnation!.... He had lost her letter.... He did not know if she would meet him.... If she cared.... If she cared still – or had ever cared.... He rolled over and writhed in the long grass in which his flea-bag was laid.... The pounding outside grew furious.... There seemed to be hundreds of stars – and more and more and more shooting up into the triangle of the tent-flap. He could see a pallid light shining down the blanket that covered his legs.... And then, like a piece of madness, the earth moved beneath him as if his bed had been kicked, and a hard sound seemed to hammer his skull.... An immense, familiar sound – august as if a God had spoken benevolently, the echoes going away among the woodlands. And the immense shell whined over his head, as if a railway train or the Yeth hounds[5] were going on a long journey....

The Very lights[6] died down, the shell whined further and further towards the plains; it seemed as if a dead silence fell. A voice said: 'Somebody's ducking out there!' and the voices began to talk again in the dead silence that fell on the battle-field.

---

[2] A patriotic war novel by H. G. Wells, serialized in the *Nation* in 1916.

[3] Machine-guns.

[4] Field artillery.

[5] In British legend, dogs without heads, said to be the spirits of unbaptized children, which ramble among the woods at night, making wailing noises.

[6] Light signals that were a ghastly blue color.

But his thoughts raged blackly. He was certain that Mrs Wilkinson would not meet him.... Then all his leave would be mucked up. He imagined himself – he felt himself – arriving at Victoria,[7] in the half-light of the great barn, in the jostling crowd, with all the black shadows, all sweeping up towards the barrier. And there would be a beastly business with three coppers in a cramped telephone box. And the voice of her maid saying that her mistress was out.... Where, in God's name, had he put the letter?....

He tried to memorise exactly what had happened – but it ended at that.... Caradoe Morris who had come back from a course, had brought the letter down to the trench from the 1st line transport. He had just looked at the envelope. Then the sentry had yelled out. And he remembered distinctly that he had done something with the letter. But what? What?

The rum jar had bumped off: then gas had come over: then a Hun raid. They had got into the front line and it had taken hours to bomb and bayonet them out, and to work the beastly sandbags of that God-forsaken line into some semblance of a parapet again – a period of sweating and swearing, and the stink of gas, and shoving corpses out of the way.... His mind considered with horror what he could do if Mrs Wilkinson refused to see him altogether. And it went on and on....

He couldn't sleep. Then he said a prayer to St Anthony – a thing he had not done since he had been a little boy in the Benedictine School at Ramsgate.[8] The pale stars surveyed him from their triangle. One Very light ascended slowly over the dark plain.........

* * *

He was standing in Piccadilly, looking into a window from which there welled a blaze of light. Skirts brushed him then receded. An elderly, fat man in a brown cassock, with a bald head, a rope around the waist and a crook from which depended a gourd, was gazing into the window beside him. This saint remarked:

'You perceive? Pink flannel!'

The whole window, the whole shop – which was certainly Swan and Edgar's[9] – was a deluge of pink – a rather odious pink with bluey suggestions. A pink that was unmistakable if ever you had seen anything like it....

'Pink!' the saint said: 'Bluey pink!'

Yes: there were pink monticules, pink watersheds, cascades of pink flannel, deserts, wild crevasses, perspectives....

W. L. James looked at St Anthony with deep anxiety: he was excited, he was bewildered. The saint continued to point a plump finger, and the crowd all round tittered.

The saint slowly ascended towards a black heaven that was filled with the beams from searchlights....

And W. L. James found himself running madly in his stockinged feet, in the long grass beside the ditch to the tent at the head of the line. 'Caradoe!' he was calling out 'Caradoe Morris! Where the hell is my Field Service Pocket-Book?'

He got it out of the tunic pocket of his friend, who was in a dead sleep. He pulled a letter from the pocket that is under the pink flannel intended to hold a supply of pins. Holding the letter towards the candle that was at Caradoe's head, he read – as a man drinks after long hours on a hot road....

And, as he stumbled slowly among tent ropes, he remembered that forgotten moment of his life. He remembered saying to himself – even as the sentry shouted 'Rum jar: left,' in the harsh Welsh accent that is like the croak of a raven – saying to himself: 'I *must* put this letter safely away.' And, before he had run, he had pulled out the FSPB,[10] had undone the rubber bands, and had placed the

---

[7]   A railway station in London.

[8]   A small harbor town on the southeast coast of Kent in England.

[9]   A fashionable shop in Regent Street in the period 1910–30; a 1912 photograph of women standing in front of the shop appears on the cover of Erika Diane Rappaport, *Shopping for Pleasure: Women in the Making of London's West End* (Princeton: Princeton University Press, 2000). The name was also given to a spot in the Ypres sector during World War I.

[10]   Field service pocket book.

unopened envelope in the little pocket that is under the pink flannel; 'intended,' as the inscription says, 'to hold a supply of pins'....

He stood still beside his fleabag for a minute as the full remembrance came back to him. And a queer, as it were clean and professional satisfaction crept over him. Before, he had remembered only the, as it were, panic of running – though it was perfectly correct to run – up the communication trench. Now he saw that, even under that panic, he had been capable of a collected – ordered, and as it were, generous action. For he had tried to shield to the best of his ability the woman he loved at the cost of quite great danger to himself.

For the rum jar had flattened out the wretched sandbags of the trench exactly where he had been standing.

Later, of course, he had lent the pocket-book to Caradoe Morris – who was the sort of chap who never would have a pocket-book – for the purpose of writing a report to BHQ[11] ...... But he had certainly behaved well......

He said to himself:

'By jove, I may be worthy of her even yet,' and getting back into his fleabag, after he had pulled off his socks, which had been wetted by the dewy grass, he fell into pleasurable fancies of softly lighted restaurants, of small orchestras, of gentle contacts of hands and the soft glances of eyes that had dark pupils and brown iris.....

That is, mostly, the way war goes!

The Colonel's Shoes (1920)

On the 27/9/19 four men were held up at midnight between York and Darlington[1] in a first-class carriage. One was an architect, aged fifty, two were country gentlemen from the neighbourhood of Aysgarth,[2] in the late forties, and the last was the MO[3] of a service battalion returning on demobilisation. He also came from near Aysgarth, where he had a practice. They had been a long time in the train; it seemed longer, and there was a dead silence all down the line. The architect, who had a grey beard, stretched out his legs and yawned.

'Eh, but I'm tired!' he said. 'As tired as the old priest, Peter Monagham.'

One of the country gentlemen asked who was the old priest, Peter Monagham. The architect said he was a good old priest who, on a night when he was dog tired, received a summons to administer extreme unction. But he fell asleep, being so very tired, and only waked in the morning light in great shame and tribulation. So he rode very fast to the house of his penitent and was told the man had died.

'But, father,' said his informant, 'he died easy and in the peace of God. He was very troubled in the early hours, but after you came and administered the blessed sacraments he grew calm, and so he made a good end.' According to the legend, an angel, or it may have been the priest's own soul, had come to confess the dying man whilst the old priest slept. So the old priest was saved from great shame.

'Ah,' one of the country gentlemen said, 'that would be in the old days, and in Ireland.'

'You won't find the like,' the other agreed 'in the North of England today. The more's the pity for us that are getting on in years.' The three of them agreed. But the MO happened to be an Irishman.

'I'll tell you a story if you like,' he said. And though none of them were very cordial at first, off he went. The story he told was something like this: It was, he said, in the middle days of the war and in France. And if you wanted, he emphasised, to know the heaviest tiredness of all the world you must know the tiredness of the war in France in the winters of '16 and '17, when the Somme push was stopped and the heavy other work began to be felt in Battalion Headquarters and such places.

---

[11] Battalion Headquarters.

This story was first published in *Reynolds's Newspaper*, January 11, 1920.

[1] Towns in Yorkshire, in northeast England.
[2] A small village in Wensleydale, one of the Yorkshire dales.
[3] Medical officer.

Heavy, hard work, endless papers, endless responsibilities, bitter hard weather – and danger that seldom ceased.

'There were many who went over the edge of unreason – but there were many and many who stayed, by the grace of God, just on this side of the edge. By the grace of God – as in the case of the old priest, Peter Monagham. It was like that with Lieut.-Colonel Leslie Arkwright – and it was very nearly like it with his nephew, Lieut. Hugh, both of my Battalion.

'Well, uncle and nephew were the best of pals; they thought alike, in a way that was strange for the old and the young.

'So their friendship was, till there came the winter of '16–'17, and Captain Gotch (that isn't his name. He is alive still. He would be.) This was one of those men as to whom there is a black mark against their names in the High Books. There are such men and there are such books in the world. (I don't mean the confidential Records of a Battalion Orderly Room – but books kept higher still.) They are men who appear foursquare, able, intelligent, they generally have flashing teeth – and they are unsound. They get on – but they don't get on as well as you expect them to. The inexperienced like them enormously; the experienced hold their tongues about them.

'So Hugh Arkwright liked Captain Gotch immensely. There was a good deal of gossip about him. He came from a Reserve Battalion that wasn't popular in that Regiment. So things were said about him – they were probably untrue. I don't know what was the matter with him. I daresay I am unjust to him; but then I didn't like him.

'But if I didn't there were plenty did. The young fellows in the mess when the Battalion was in support and they could get leave to go into the big towns and cut a little splash for the night – they'd swear by Gotch. He was their leader then. And Hugh Arkwright went with the rest of his age.

'That was how it came to sad disagreement between him and the old CO. Hugh thought that his uncle was unjust to Gotch. There would be recommendations going – for jobs at Divisional headquarters and higher up. Circulars come in, you know, asking for junior officers who have knowledge of Flemish, Japanese, Maregasque, Basque, bayonet-fighting as practised in Pushtu: or for senior officers who have expert knowledge of pig-breeding, the growing of Jerusalem artichokes, the extraction of solder from old tins, the unravelling of gold lace – God knows what! And Captain Gotch would send his name in for all these things, and the CO would send the name on, but without any recommendation. Young Hugh would see the memos, and his eyes would be troubled. He was very intimate with Gotch by March, when the weather was frightful. I forgot to say that Captain Gotch had a fine baritone voice. It has an important bearing on the last words of my story. He would sing popular sentimental songs of the day, and put in nasty meanings and raise one brown eyebrow when he came to them. It made him popular with the men of the Battalion who were not in his Company when he sang to them at smoking concerts improvised in old barns and tents and pigsties. But his own Company was nasty.

'One day the Colonel came to me – as MO.

'"Pat," he said. "I don't believe I can stick it. Good God, that I should have to say I don't believe I can stick it!"

'I asked him what was the matter – but it wasn't necessary to ask him what was the matter. His mind was overloaded. You see – like his nephew, he was indefatigable – and he didn't leave as much as he might have to his subordinates.

'But latterly it was patent that he was feeling the strain. It took the form of falling asleep. He'd fall asleep at table – in between two words of a sentence. (That was how we knew that Hugh could complete his sentences for him!) His silver head would drop forward and his eyes close. Or the same midway in dealing at a rubber of bridge. And the officers would wait silent, and worried.

'On the morning he came to me he'd fallen asleep whilst taking his orderly room – for ten seconds. He said he didn't believe they'd noticed it – and I don't believe they had. But he had dozed in his chair, at a table covered with a blanket, with the Assistant Adjutant beside him, and the prisoner, and escort, and Provost Sergeant, and Regimental Sergeant-Major and all in front of him – and Captain Gotch. In the schoolroom of a little town in Flanders, it was. I forget the name. It made it better – or perhaps it made it worse – that the sleeping fits only came on when we were out of the trenches proper.

'"And the devil of it is," he said, "I woke up to hear myself saying, like a bally rifle-shot: 'Case explained!' And the charge was a hell of a serious charge of refusing to obey orders – brought by that fellow Gotch!"

'Apparently on a beastly, cold, wet night, Gotch had stormed down like a madman on his Company who were on some sort of fatigue, carrying stones, or boxes, or cases of dumbells, or something. And two of the men had said they couldn't – or wouldn't – lift something wet and heavy. It was a case that was open to a doubt. Gotch swore the men said they wouldn't. The Company Sergeant-Major, who was a time-serving man with 23 years' service – he was the only witness – was not ready to swear what the word used had been. It might have been "couldn't" or it might have been "wouldn't".

'So that the "case explained" verdict, tendered actually in the CO's sleep, hadn't been outrageous. Whatever the object was that they had been required to lift might, on a dark, wet night, have seemed beyond two men's lifting power. The CO said, with a trick of his old, gentle jauntiness, that he had got out of it all right though Old Forty had not liked it.

'"And I could see that my young cut of a nephew didn't like it either," he said. Young Hugh had been recording the awards on the 252 – the charge sheet.

'"I strafed the two men well," the CO said, "before the Provost Sergeant could march them out. I said that it was for the Company Officer and not for the men to judge what men could do. And so on."

'Then he had cleared the room of the other ranks – the men and NCOs. . . . "And I said to Mr Forty that I wished that in future all officers giving evidence against other ranks should do it in writing whenever possible as is provided in King's Regulations, though it's apt to drop out of observance here. . . . "

'"And I expect Mr Forty did not like that much, either, sir," I said myself, softly.

'The CO started a little.

'"Did I call Captain Gotch 'Old Forty'," he asked rather guiltily. "It slipped out. . . . You know the men call him that, too?"

'"Bless you, sir," I said, "I hear it from every one of the sick I get from 'A' Company. And they've been many latterly."

'"I wish to God," the CO said, "the fellow had never. . . . But that's between you and me and that gate-post." He sighed. And I knew he was thinking of the estrangement that was growing between him and his nephew.

* * *

'It was only two nights later, that the nephew came to me – just before driving to some town or other, Steenwerck, I think, with a brake-load of young fellows, in search of diversion and may be the young ladies. I pray God that one of them was kind to Hugh that night – for he was killed, driving back, by a stray shell that dropped through the bottom of the waggonette the young boys were in, on a clear, still, moonlight night. . . . But when he came to me was before he started.

'He was terribly depressed about his health – and extraordinarily glad about something else, and he wanted me to give him drugs to keep him from breaking down. He said he'd been having illusions. And when I asked him what illusions; did he think he saw pink and red or bottle green blackbirds? he said no, it was queerer than that – but he couldn't tell me without telling a long story. So I told him to take some hooch and fire away.

'He told me a good deal that I knew, about his coolness towards his uncle. . . . and then he came to that morning. He said that, just before Orderly Room, the CO had said to him that he wanted Captain Wilkins, the Adjutant, to help at Orderly Room, that morning – marking down the cases, instead of Hugh, you know. And that worried him, so that, instead of going to his papers after breakfast, he sat down in an armchair by the fire in the A2 mess dining room. It was a large French house, the Battalion Headquarters at that time, the village school just behind it being the Orderly Room.

'So he sat by the fire, worrying.

'And then Gotch burst into the room and rushed to a writing table at the far end, beside the piano. He snatched at a piece of paper and he cursed, and he began writing with a scratchy pen – and cursing – and scratching out and rewriting and gnawing his beautiful moustache. He said to himself: "A d—d pass it's coming to if officers can't . . ." Then he roared out for a mess waiter and cursed him for having a cod-fish's face and told him to take the paper to the Adjutant at the double and curse him. And then he got up with his back still to Hugh and sat down at the piano and began to dash off tinkling songs as hard as he could hit the ivories.

'And then, Hugh said, in the midst of his own worries, suddenly, he began to feel another worry – a heavy dreadful worry, as if all the Battalion was going to Hell and as if the war was hopeless. . . . And as if the officers of the Battalion were not as much to be trusted as they had been six months ago, and as if the men of the Battalion were growing stubborn. Something must be done about "A" Company. But what? And that dreadful bounder, Gotch, with his debts, and the contempt of the men. How was he to get rid of him? "A" Company junior officers would shield Gotch. . . . They were good boys. . . . And he was tired. He was dreadfully tired. And all his bones ached. And his nephew Hugh. . . .

'And suddenly, Hugh said, he knew that it was his uncle's worries he was feeling. And he wanted to go to his uncle. But he couldn't move. And, of course, he couldn't have gone to the CO in Orderly Room if he could have moved.

'Gotch was banging on the piano; but suddenly Hugh heard his uncle's voice say in his ear, "I can't keep. . . . Oh, God, I can't keep. . . . I'm falling. . . . falling . . . ." And then – he himself – he, Hugh, himself – was sitting on the hard wooden chair at the CO's table. He felt older, older; and wiser, wiser; and surer of himself than he had ever felt sure. But his hand on the blanket table cover was heavy and white and hairy. And he said: "Call in the prisoners." And the Provost Sergeant roared: "Escort and Coy.-Sergt.-Major Wilson."

'And he reached his heavy hand, distastefully, for the buff 252 which was pinned to the Field Conduct Sheet, and had on top of it a piece of scrawled writing paper. And he read a number and the name Wilson and the rank, Company-Sergeant-Major, and the offence: "Highly irregular conduct to the prejudice of good order and military discipline. Using disrespectful language with regard to an officer." And to himself he said: "that swine, Forty, is trying to do in Wilson for not having given false evidence against those two men the day before yesterday." But he said aloud and heavily to the Adjutant at his side: "Ask 'A' company if they can't make out better charges than that!" And he snorted with contempt over his heavy grey moustaches: "Highly irregular conduct to the prejudice." . . .

'He leant back in his chair and looked composedly at the always worried face of the Company Sergeant-Major.

'And "Old Forty." . . . "Forty foot down and still digging," the men called him, because he never left the bottom of the deepest dug-out, was trying to do Wilson in! Well, they would see. . . .

'He said: "Company-Sergeant Major Wilson, you have heard the charge. . . . The first witness is your Company Commander, Captain Gotch. He writes: 'On the 17/4/17 "A" Company were balloting for leave in my orderly room. The Company-Quartermaster-Sergeant was drawing names from a hat in my presence and the Company-Sergeant- Major was writing down the names. There were seven names to be drawn out of twenty-four. When six had been drawn I said: "Company-Sergeant-Major, put down the name of Lance-Corporal Howells, 579756." The Company-Sergeant-Major demurred. I said: "The OC Company has always the right to nominate a man for special services." The Company-Sergeant-Major said: "It isn't done in this Battalion, sir." I said: "Those are my orders." The Company-Sergeant-Major wrote down the name of Lance-Corporal Howells. As I was leaving the room I heard the Company-Sergeant-Major say to the Company-Quartermaster-Sergeant: "Gotch will miss fifty-six Howells in the next ten days." I ordered him to be put under arrest.' Next witness!"

'The Provost-Sergeant roared: "46721 Company-Quartermaster-Sergeant Reynolds . . . ."

'Hugh said he could see that originally Captain Gotch had written: "Company-Sergeant-Major Wilson said: 'Lance-Corporal Howells has only been a short time with the company. – Since you came, sir! And all the men whose names are down have been a minimum of eighteen months without leave. And leave only just open after three months!'" He had then struck out those words and substituted: "The Company-Sergeant-Major demurred." He might have saved himself the trouble, for the Quartermaster-Sergeant reported the words in full.

"'And what happened then?"

"'As Captain Gotch was going out of the room, sir, the Company-Sergeant-Major said to me 'Brother Boche will miss Lance-Corpl. Howells in the next ten days.' Captain Gotch ordered me to put the Company-Sergeant Major in the clink."

'Hugh said that he reached across – the heavy white hand – and took the charge sheet from the Adjutant, who had in the meantime resumed possession of it. He was taking up a pen and writing heavily, himself, the word 'Case...' whilst he said:–

"'Company Sergeant-Major Wilson...."

'Wilson cleared his throat; he was always husky. A good man, Hugh said. And it was a pleasure for him to hear Wilson say:–

"'I beg you, sir, for leave to speak" – the time-honoured Guards' formula. He said that he agreed to the evidence given by Company Quartermaster Reynolds.

'And Hugh said that, whilst he was heavily writing the word "Dismissed" after the word "Case" on the charge sheet.

'Hugh said that the roaring of the Provost Sergeant getting in the next case, and the men stamping as they marched out suddenly became the voice of Captain Gotch, who had swung round on the piano stool and was saying:–

"'You, Hugh ..." and then: "By God if the C.O. gives Wilson 'Case explained,' I shall go before the Brigadier."

Hugh said he answered:–

"'I should, Gotch, I should go before Division. Because if I were in the Colonel shoes, I should make it 'Case dismissed'."

'Gotch said:–

"'By God, what do you mean, Hugh?"

"'I mean," Hugh said, "that Division are asking for a junior officer to look after Divisional Follies."

'Gotch's jaw fell down, and he clenched his right fist. But suddenly he stiffened to attention. The door had opened behind Hugh, but he knew of course that the Colonel had come in. There had been only two cases at Orderly Room.

'The Colonel had a slip of paper in his hand and was looking at it with his brow knitted. It was a 252.

"'Hugh," he said, "I'm getting to write deucedly like you." And then:–

"'Ah, Gotch. The adjutant says that baths are open. See that 'A' Company parades in good time."

'Hugh said he drew himself together and looked at his uncle.

"'I was just recommending Captain Gotch, sir," he uttered slowly and deliberately, "to apply for the job of the Divisional Follies. It's going begging."

'The Colonel nodded at Gotch.

"'I should, Gotch," he said. "I could recommend you cordially." Gotch gathered up his hat, and gloves, and stick, and left the room. The old man fell into the chair by the fire.

"'Hugh," he said, "get me a drink... Hugh, were you in the Orderly Room just now?"

"'I don't know," Hugh said. "Yes, yes, I think I was."

'The C.O. imagined he was confused because he thought he would be strafed for having been there.

"'That accounts for your handwriting on this 252. I suppose the Adjutant was too busy," he said. "I didn't really notice who was there." And then he lifted his tired eyes and looked at Hugh with an awful apprehension.

"'Was I... was it... all right?" he asked.

' "You were splendid, sir," Hugh answered. "You looked tired ... ill. But you were splendid."
'He was mixing a whisky, and as he handed it to his uncle he said:–
' "I hope to God that swine Gotch goes the Division."
'The Colonel drank down his whisky.
' "Thank God, Hugh, my dear," he said. "I thought I was asleep in my own Orderly Room." ' "

The Miracle (1928)

The former Miss Sinclair lying in her great four-post bed, the sheets to her firm chin, was aware that her husband, coming from his bath, was walking briskly and humming. She was still in the stage of studying him. She was aware – though he wasn't – that he was a man of deep and suddenly aroused moodinesses, and these she watched with attention because his career was very precious to her – though she herself had abandoned none of her own hopes of scientific honours. This was a new mood! He pushed the door open sharply, and, with long strides – for he was a tall man – in his elegantly cut trousers and admirable white shirt, crossed the floor to the foot of the bed where he faced her.

'I maintain,' he exclaimed good-humouredly, stretching out his hand in a parody of himself when lecturing, 'that A Man of Intellect cannot be an efficient Man of Action. I have solved in my bath a considerable problem. Yet I have again lost my collar-stud!'

'For myself,' his wife asserted in imitation of his tone, 'I maintain that the age of miracles *cannot* return and never existed. Yet you are addressing remarks to me before breakfast. Here are four irreconcilable phenomena!'

He was a very young, tall, brilliant Professor, and they had been married not quite a year though they had been engaged for four years. In those four he had naturally had a good deal of leeway to make up; she, on the other hand, having remained at the rather, but not very, old university of which her father was the distinguished Principal, had, as it seemed to her, always been remarkable for looks, vivacity, and learning, her 'subject' being scientific eugenics. And having intensely disliked the period of waiting for her lover to make up his leeway, she was determined that now he should do nothing to retard his future progress. With a good brain, she thought, he had touches of the poet about him. Not a bad thing for a scientist, but dangerous in a keenly competitive university society. They had the world, now, as a ball before their feet. She was determined that nothing should delay its swift rolling.

He, for his part, had made up his leeway on his return to that place with a tenacity, a force, and a rapid grasping of opportunity that had astonished such of the dons as had known him before. He had gone away a boy, heavy and, above all, shy; possibly gifted but nervously unable to do himself justice. He came back seeming to know the ropes of that university with unaccountable address; overhauling his arrears of work as a liner overhauls a fishing smack; overwhelming as a wave overwhelms a sea anemone the brilliant Miss Sinclair, whom before to speak to would have paralysed him. His department was some branch of biology so abstruse that one hesitates over the spelling of the name, but their minds were reputed to fit as acorn fits cup. They were humorous, good-humoured, and comely, and it was agreed between them not to converse before breakfast, when the Professor, pottering over his careful toilette, which desultorily occupied him for a full hour, was accustomed to think over the subject of his coming day's labours.

The former Miss Sinclair lay motionless, her eyes like coals above the white sheet of a great state bed – high pillared. Mirrors shone deeply; the curtains were pink-flowered, calendered cretonne. There was a great deal of light in the tall, white room. Miss Sinclair's long black plaits, from each side of her head, ran parallel and pointed at the tall professor. She was not so certain of his truce.

The story was first published in the *Yale Review* 18 (winter 1928).

She pointed with her chin: 'There's a collar-stud there,' she said, and the Professor lumbered pensively towards the old white mantelpiece searching under its flowers for his stud.

'I am thinking,' he said, 'but not about Portfolio B 14. I thought *that* problem out in my bath. Where *is* that collar-stud? ... An hour's scribbling and B 14 can go to the university printers!'

His wife ecstatically adopted a sitting posture, her black plaits hanging now parallel over blue and white, faintly figured silk.

'*Douglas!*' she exclaimed. 'Then the age of miracles *isn't* past. After all these months, you've thought it out! But why today of all days? I can't believe it!'

'That *blasted* stud,' the Professor mumbled between his teeth and continued to sway from side to side in front of the mantelpiece.

'It's *behind* the antirrhinums,'[1] his wife said; 'I put it there last night – for safety. I know what you are.'

The Professor straightened his back, turned with meaning right about, and regarded her under serious brows. He was rather an ugly fellow, she thought, with his large mouth, high cheek bones, and overhung eyes. But his long line of trousers, his strong neck arising from his white, still uncollared shirt – rather a gargoyle – but a fine figure of a man. Passionate, humorous, and abstracted. He considered that he had the Scientific Mind! He! ...

It was as well, however, not to shake him in *that* belief. Their living sumptuously depended on that.

He said: 'You think you know me? H'm! H'm! ... We're agreed, aren't we, to regard phenomena set beside phenomena *as* phenomena set beside each other? Dried fir cones side by side. Without connection or purpose!'

'That,' she said, 'was our premarital agreement. I suppose that we stick to it. We *have* the Scientific Mind. . . . You want to tell me something? About Portfolio B 14?'

'No!' he said. 'This is an anniversary!'

'It can't be *ours!*' she said sharply, 'because we haven't been married a year. Then it's Miss ...'

'No!' he said with decision. He swung half round again to glance along the mantelshelf for the collar-stud. 'Oh, you said it was *behind* the antirrhinums,' he muttered, and then adopting an easy attitude of his long trousers, and slightly extending one hand, he cleared his throat. His wife lay down, drew the bedclothes to her chin, arranged her plaits on the sheet.

'It's a question of a miracle,' he said. 'You have twice used the phrase "an age of miracles". There is a proverbial saying, "The age of miracles is past!" I question whether it is. I am about to lay before you for your *scientific* consideration a single circumstance. Within my own experience. Exactly observed! One that I have since considered profoundly and that has influenced my whole life. And I cannot see that it is anything but a miracle! It concerns the creation of something that formerly was not: in a given place and in answer to prayer. My own personal prayer. Whilst, obviously, that in no way affects my biological position, it must affect my attitude towards a Special Providence and all that that entails.'

His wife, speaking on purpose very slowly, said:

'You have considered that the expression of such a belief might lose you your job. Or, at least, it might make it extremely difficult for you to get another here – not to say a better one, when this one runs out. The Big Ones of this place are not distinguished by tolerance. Father himself ...'

'They will hardly,' the Professor said, 'eject me because I make to you in private a communication of a quasi-religious nature.'

'You had better let me hear.'

'I must,' he answered, 'think a moment more on the exact terms. I naturally wish to spare you disagreeable emotions and must choose my words with care.'

His brows drawn together, he turned to the mantelpiece, thinking deeply. His wife, motionless, watched him with an anxious intensity. She was aware that of whatever he did in such moments of painfully abstracted thought he would be absolutely unconscious. And it occurred to her that,

---

[1]   Scientific name for snapdragons.

possibly, such an abstractedness made him not absolutely fitted for personal scientific observation – personal! For abstract thought he was magnificent. Unrivalled.

But she had known him, whilst thinking deeply, to move the slide in a microscope and to be perfectly unconscious of having done so. Naturally, that had altered the whole aspect of the section he had been observing. Yet when she had mentioned the fact to him, he had been so painfully affected, so absolutely certain that he had committed no such action, that, at last, after a distressing scene – the only one they had ever had – she had thought it wiser to withdraw her absolutely true allegation. There were, she knew, times when it was wiser to submit, the whole being greater than the part. Indeed, he had gone almost out of his mind, and she had never again mentioned or – as she naturally might have – made fun of his unconscious actions.

She watched him then. His brows still drawn tightly together he moved the old silver vase of scarlet, sulphur, and blazing magenta snapdragons on the mantelpiece. He took the collar-stud thus uncovered and, as again he turned to his wife, fitted the small metal object into the stud-hole of his white linen shirt. His eyes gazed at nothing.

He brought his mind to earth with a jerk. 'This is naturally painful to me,' he said. 'You must excuse me if I have kept you waiting.' He cleared his throat.

'We have never,' he continued, 'discussed religion. Why should we have? You, as a don's daughter here, have naturally hardly considered or heard of the subject. I myself have naturally wished to spare you the contemplation of the disagreeable and the unimportant. But this being the seventh anniversary . . .'

'The seventh!' his wife said bitterly. 'I knew it would have something to do with that hateful period.'

'I repent,' the Professor said, 'almost as bitterly as you can, my share in those proceedings. At the time I conceived it to be my duty. I was then young and easily out-argued and convinced. You have since convinced me that my duty should have led me into far other paths. I have acknowledged my fault, and re-acknowledge it now. I will be as short as I can. . . . Seven years ago today, then, I was in charge of a large bombing raid. . . . Can you stand this? I will spare you all the details that I can.'

His wife said, 'Go on!'

'In those days,' the Professor continued, 'bombs were very primitive affairs; they had time fuses instead of detonators. You had to light the fuse and then hurl the bomb; the bombs themselves were mere jam tins filled with an explosive surrounded by fragments of metal. The important point was that you had to light the fuse. For that purpose cigarettes were supplied to the troops – Oriental cigarettes because, being mostly adulterated with saltpetre, they burn longer than the Virginian sort. I hope I make myself clear. The officer in charge of the bombing party was responsible for the cigarettes. I was the officer in charge of the bombing party. It was a very large one – a raid, in the technical language. I was then in charge of it. And it happened on the day after my arrival actually in the line of that distant and precipitous country. I had been for some time with what is called the First Line Transport, waiting for an opportunity to be sent up; but movement over that terrain had not been easy, and opportunity had not occurred. My morale, in the military sense, was not good. *You*, hating as you do all military manifestations, will not despise me when I say that my morale was distinctly bad. We were shelled, from time to time, from a distance; we had to sit still under the shelling. I feared it dreadfully: I do not conceal from you that I was an arrant coward.'

His wife said: 'Oh, *Douglas!* . . . But you've got decorations and things, haven't you?'

'We won't go into that,' her husband said. 'We never have; there is no occasion to do so now. It is sufficient to say that then – seven years ago today – I was an arrant coward, from having to sit all day in a bright sunshine doing nothing, with a few shells falling near us from time to time.'

He swung half round, looked at the mantelpiece absently and minutely, returned his gaze to her, and went on: 'I am being as vague as I can as to place and details. . . . I got up then into the line towards ten of a black night. I was caught hold of immediately by a superior officer, thrust into a hut with maps that I was to study, and told that at two that morning I was to take charge of that bombing raid. Its purpose was to go a long way up into the hills, in enemy country, and there, before daylight, to establish ourselves in a certain circle of stones, or hollow, overhanging a road. When, all unsuspecting, a certain strong body of the enemy, as to which we had information, was to march beneath us we were to bomb them to pieces; at the same time, by the noise and by other signals we should make, our artillery would know that the enemy force was actually firmly engaged on that disadvantageous and narrow road. The slaughter was expected to be – and it was – dreadful! I re-apologize, my dear, for my share in this transaction. But so it was!'

The Professor broke off, and then, with tenderness in his voice, said: 'But perhaps you cannot bear this narration? It would be sufficient if I assured you that circumstances warranting a belief in a Special Protection occurred during that night.'

His wife, the sheet right up to her dark eyes and her voice in consequence muffled and altered, said, 'Go on. I must hear it' – or something similar.

'In that hut, then,' the Professor continued, 'I remained for three hours or so. Officers came in and out: shadows, but not many. An engagement was proceeding all the while; musketry and Maxim guns mostly; quite close at hand. There was not a man to spare: we were dreadfully short of our establishment. I had not even a batman allotted to me. I had myself to unpack my knapsack; make what alterations I had to make in my clothes – with fingers that shook so, I assure you, that I could hardly do it. And panting. Breathless, with pure dread. In a very dim light, and with the terrific detonations of rifles close at hand in rocky defiles – I am now breathless at the thought of it.' And indeed he was.

'There is a detail that I wish to impress upon you,' he went on. 'That was the cigarettes. I had to fill my knapsack, my pockets, and everything that would hold them with the jam pot bombs; all my party had to do this; but on the top of the bombs in the knapsack were to repose two tin boxes of the indispensable fire-makers.

'Someone had brought them into the hut: tin boxes with a green and gilded label. They stood on a rough wooden shelf under a shuttered window, blinking in the dim light from a paraffin lamp. The bombs stood on a deal table; it seemed to take me hours to pack them into the knapsack. . . .

'Hours and hours. . . . And then it went extraordinarily quickly. These things do. A man rushed in: the assistant adjutant, I think. . . . But that means nothing to you. He shouted, "Now then O/i/ C² Bombers!" helped me to buckle on my accoutrements, exclaimed something like, "Rough luck, old chap, to have to go so soon. I wish to God we had someone else to send!" – and conducted me out into the dark. He said that he had got me a first-class guide and that the men and NCOs were all first-class men. They were not even allowed to carry pipes or matches – for fear of showing a gleam of light. You see, everything depended on *my* matches and *my* cigarettes. . . .

'With them, that is to say, we could at least put up a fight; without them. . . . I forget the detail of a bombing party in those days; it was changed so often. Four men with bombs to two with rifles and bayonets; but the bayonet men were so cluttered up with bombs themselves that I fancy they carried only a dozen rounds apiece of small-arm ammunition. So you see the enormous importance of those cigarettes to us – a party crawling miles, at night, into enemy mountains. Without them, every one of my men was dead. After tortures, very likely. Think of it! *My* men! Mine! You can't imagine what the feeling would have been like!'

His wife sat up slowly. 'You didn't have to feel it?' she asked. 'But of course you didn't. You forgot the cigarettes. But something saved you.'

The Professor started a little away from the foot of the bed, 'How did you know? I never told a living soul.' He exclaimed irritably, 'Where the hell *is* that collar-stud?'

'You put it into your shirt,' his wife answered. 'Of course I knew you had forgotten the cigarettes. I know you. Besides, you said so. You said it took hours to pack up the bombs; you never mentioned the cigarettes.'

He felt the band of his shirt and fingered the stud. But in the engrossment of the other subject he forgot to express amazement or irritation, and his wife felt that one corner at least had been turned.

'That,' he said, 'was the *miracle*. I had forgotten them! . . . I spare you the details of the landscape at night; the crawling; the hanging on to tufts of rosemary. And my emotions.'

'You need not,' his wife said. 'If I am judge, I want some details. Besides,' she added more softly, 'you do not think that your narration is unsympathetic to me!'

---

² Officer in Charge.

He looked at her rather gratefully; but, as is the habit with those used to speaking in public, he had already composed his next sentences, and he went on: 'I remembered only when we were within a hundred yards of our objective – the hollow of the rocks overhanging the road that the enemy column must pass along. It was beginning to dawn when I remembered, and in those latitudes day comes quickly. There was no chance to go, or to send a man, back. No chance at all.

'And I remembered with absolute precision – that I had forgotten. It was no hallucination. I remembered not only that I had forgotten, but *how!* I had said to myself once or twice in the hut where I had waited, "By Jove! I must not forget those cigarettes," and had looked at the green boxes with the gilt stripes winking in the dim light.... And then that assistant adjutant had come in, a blustering, breezy fellow with an overpowering personality, and had slapped the knapsack on to my back, and had forced me out of the hut into the darkness where the men were falling in.

'You *see! I remembered!* I remembered the *action* of forgetting. As I went out of the hut, I had had the sensation that something was unsatisfactory. Omitted! You know what I mean about that sensation: it is like a little thirst.... And there I was with that sudden remembrance. You see! It is scientific. Nothing in this world would ever shake me as to that conviction.

'The other material detail is that I prayed. As no man before me has ever prayed. I am sufficiently aware that you will object: I was praying for the deaths of unsuspecting men – what sort of Deity can it be that will allow the deaths of one set of men merely because of the prayers of an individual of another set?...I can't help that! I was praying for men lost by my fault. My own men....

'And an amazing calm fell upon me. We were in that hollow, on a high place; the dawn was coming over that ancient sea; the tufts of herbs were absolutely still on the bare stone mountains. It was the stillest – the supreme – moment of my life. I knew then! I tell you I *knew*. There *is* a Special Providence; there *is* answer to prayer. I had my men lying in their places, overhanging the road. I said, 'Cigarette detail! On the hands down. Fall in to draw cigarettes!' You may call it the calm of desperation: going through the motions of fire-arm drill with empty rifles.... I slung my knapsack round in front of me; picked open the brass gadgets with absolutely firm fingers; threw up the stiff canvas lid of the knapsack.... The sun was just coming over the sea; its reflected rays shone on the green and gold labels and the bright tin ends of the two boxes. I noticed that the manufacturer was purveyor to the German Emperor.

'But from that day, I assure you, I have never looked back. And what am I to think of it but that it was a miracle? They were not there. I prayed. They were there.... You will perhaps despise me.'

His wife lay for a long time looking at the silver vase from which rose stiffly, in stripes, the scarlet, sulphur yellow, and magenta flowers. She said at last, 'It was for that that you got your...'

He said, rather sharply, 'It was agreed that we should never talk about my decorations. What I got from it was...confidence! I am the man you see because...'

'You mean,' she interrupted him, 'that if anything shook that faith in you' – she became a little breathless – 'you would...you would...lose the lucky touch you have had ever since...ever since that miraculous event? You have been since then, haven't you, rather a fortunate man?'

He corroborated her gravely. 'I did, as you seem to have heard, rather well out there. Afterwards, I do not mean that I was insensible to fear. Of course I never was. But I was...I will call it buoyed up! I never prayed again, of course. One isn't the man to trouble Providence with *my* trivial vicissitudes. But just the remembrance *transfused* me. It has ever since. Why, only this morning in my bath.... You know how I have worried over Portfolio B 14. Well! Suddenly, remembering the anniversary, I became calm. In that serenity the solution was absolutely clear to me. There it was. In a definite pattern. And let me tell you – but you know it as well as I do – that means almost – oh, it means *certain* – fame in the scientific world!'

He fetched his collar from the dressing table and looked at her with almost apprehensive eyes whilst inadroitly he fumbled with the front stud. It was that at which she looked when at last she answered.

'That,' she said with her clear scientific intonation, 'seems to settle it. I at least am determined never to question the...the miraculous interpretation you attach to that specific event!' She swallowed rather painfully, but went on: 'I should suggest that on this anniversary we should ...you might like to...go to a service at the Cathedral. And, side by side...oh, offer thanks, and whatever it is you do to confirm yourself in...Faith!'

With an ecstatic face he had tiptoed to the head of the bed and now, bending down, he folded her in his arms.

On Impressionism (1914)

I

These are merely some notes towards a working guide to Impressionism as a literary method.

I do not know why I should have been especially asked to write about Impressionism; even as far as literary Impressionism goes I claim no Papacy in the matter. A few years ago, if anybody had called me an Impressionist I should languidly have denied that I was anything of the sort or that I knew anything about the school, if there could be said to be any school. But one person and another in the last ten years has called me Impressionist with such persistence that I have given up resistance. I don't know; I just write books, and if someone attaches a label to me I do not much mind.

I am not claiming any great importance for my work; I daresay it is all right. At any rate, I am a perfectly self-conscious writer; I know exactly how I get my effects, as far as those effects go. Then, if I am in truth an Impressionist, it must follow that a conscientious and exact account of how I myself work will be an account, from the inside, of how Impressionism is reached, produced, or gets its effects. I can do no more.

This is called egotism; but, to tell the truth, I do not see how Impressionism can be anything else. Probably this school differs from other schools, principally, in that it recognises, frankly, that all art must be the expression of an ego, and that if Impressionism is to do anything, it must, as the phrase is, go the whole hog. The difference between the description of a grass by the agricultural correspondent of the *Times* newspaper and the description of the same grass by Mr W. H. Hudson[1] is just the difference – the measure of the difference between the egos of the two gentlemen. The difference between the description of any given book by a sound English reviewer and the description of the same book by some foreigner attempting Impressionist criticism is again merely a matter of the difference in the ego.

Mind, I am not saying that the non-Impressionist productions may not have their values – their very great values. The Impressionist gives you his own views, expecting you to draw deductions, since presumably you know the sort of chap he is. The agricultural correspondent of the *Times*, on the other hand – and a jolly good writer he is – attempts to give you, not so much his own impressions of a new grass as the factual observations of himself and of as many as possible other sound authorities. He will tell you how many blades of the new grass will grow upon an acre, what height they will attain, what will be a reasonable tonnage to expect when green, when sun-dried in the form of hay or as ensilage. He will tell you the fattening value of the new fodder in its various forms and the nitrogenous value of the manure dropped by the so-fattened beasts. He will provide you, in short, with reading that is quite interesting to the layman, since all facts are interesting to men of good will; and the agriculturist he will provide with information of real value. Mr Hudson, on the other hand, will give you nothing but the pleasure of coming in contact with his temperament, and I doubt whether, if you read with the greatest care his description of false sea-buckthorn (*hippophae rhamnoides*) you would very willingly recognise that greenishgrey plant, with the spines and the berries like reddish amber, if you came across it.

Or again – so at least I was informed by an editor the other day – the business of a sound English reviewer is to make the readers of the paper understand exactly what sort of a book it is that the reviewer is writing about. Said the editor in question: 'You have no idea how many readers your

This essay was first published in the journal *Poetry and Drama* 2(6) (June 1914) and 3(4) (December 1914).
[1]   William Henry Hudson (1841–1922) was a naturalist and an acknowledged master of natural history writing; his guides to walking tours and books on birds were highly esteemed and popular. His novel *Green Mansions* (1904) proved so popular that a statue of its heroine, Rima, done by the sculptor Jacob Epstein (1880–1959), was erected in Hyde Park, London, in 1924.

paper will lose if you employ one of those brilliant chaps who write readable articles about books. You will get yourself deluged with letter after letter from subscribers saying they have bought a book on the strength of articles in your paper; that the book isn't in the least what they expected, and that therefore they withdraw their subscriptions.' What the sound English reviewer, therefore, has to do is to identify himself with the point of view of as large a number of readers of the journal for which he may be reviewing, as he can easily do, and then to give them as many facts about the book under consideration as his allotted space will hold. To do this he must sacrifice his personality, and the greater part of his readability. But he will probably very much help his editor, since the great majority of readers do not want to read anything that any reasonable person would want to read; and they do not want to come into contact with the personality of the critic, since they have obviously never been introduced to him.

The ideal critic, on the other hand – as opposed to the so-exemplary reviewer – is a person who can so handle words that from the first three phrases any intelligent person – any foreigner, that is to say, and any one of three inhabitants of these islands – any intelligent person will know at once the sort of chap that he is dealing with. Letters of introduction will therefore be unnecessary, and the intelligent reader will know pretty well what sort of book the fellow is writing about because he will know the sort of fellow the fellow is. I don't mean to say that he would necessarily trust his purse, his wife, or his mistress to the Impressionist critic's care. But that is not absolutely necessary. The ambition, however, of my friend the editor was to let his journal give the impression of being written by those who could be trusted with the wives and purses – not, of course, the mistresses, for there would be none – of his readers.

You will, perhaps, be beginning to see now what I am aiming at – the fact that Impressionism is a frank expression of personality; the fact that non-Impressionism is an attempt to gather together the opinions of as many reputable persons as may be and to render them truthfully and without exaggeration. (The Impressionist must always exaggerate.)

II

Let us approach this matter historically – as far as I know anything about the history of Impressionism, though I must warn you that I am a shockingly ill-read man. Here, then, are some examples: do you know, for instance, Hogarth's[2] drawing of the watchman with the pike over his shoulder and the dog at his heels going in at a door, the whole being executed in four lines? Here it is:

Now, that is the high-watermark of Impressionism; since, if you look at those lines for long enough, you will begin to see the watchman with his slouch hat, the handle of the pike coming well down into the cobble-stones, the knee-breeches, the leathern garters strapped round his stocking, and the surly expression of the dog, which is bull-hound with a touch of mastiff in it.

---

[2]   William Hogarth (1697–1764) was a painter and engraver whose trenchant social satire has always been admired.

You may ask why, if Hogarth saw all these things, did he not put them down on paper, and all that I can answer is that he made this drawing for a bet. Moreover why, if you can see all these things for yourself, should Hogarth bother to put them down on paper? You might as well contend that Our Lord ought to have delivered a lecture on the state of primary education in the Palestine of the year 32 or thereabouts, together with the statistics of rickets and other infantile diseases caused by neglect and improper feeding – a disquisition in the manner of Mrs Sidney Webb.[3] He preferred, however, to say: 'It were better that a millstone were put about his neck and he were cast into the deep sea.'[4] The statement is probably quite incorrect; the statutory punishment either here or in the next world has probably nothing to do with millstones and so on, but Our Lord was, you see, an Impressionist, and knew His job pretty efficiently. It is probable that He did not have access to as many Blue Books or white papers as the leaders of the Fabian Society,[5] but, from His published utterances, one gathers that He had given a good deal of thought to the subject of children.

I am not in the least joking – and God forbid that I should be thought irreverent because I write like this. The point that I really wish to make is, once again, that – that the Impressionist gives you, as a rule, the fruits of his own observations and the fruits of his own observations alone. He should be in this as severe and as solitary as any monk. It is what he is in the world for. It is, for instance, not so much his business to quote as to state his impressions – that the Holy Scriptures are a good book, or a rotten book, or contain passages of good reading interspersed with dulness; or suggest gems in a cavern, the perfumes of aromatic woods burning in censers, or the rush of the feet of camels crossing the deep sands, or the shrill sounds of long trumpets borne by archangels – clear sounds of brass like those in that funny passage in 'Aida'.[6]

The passage in prose, however, which I always take as a working model – and in writing this article I am doing no more than showing you the broken tools and bits of oily rag which form my brains, since once again I must disclaim writing with any authority on Impressionism – this passage in prose occurs in a story by de Maupassant called *La Reine Hortense*.[7] I spent, I suppose, a great part of ten years in grubbing up facts about Henry VIII. I worried about his parentage, his diseases, the size of his shoes, the price he gave for kitchen implements, his relation to his wives, his knowledge of music, his proficiency with the bow. I amassed, in short, a great deal of information about Henry VIII. I wanted to write a long book about him, but Mr Pollard,[8] of the British Museum, got the commission and wrote the book probably much more soundly. I then wrote three long novels all about that Defender of the Faith. But I really know – so delusive are reported facts – nothing whatever. Not one single thing! Should I have found him affable, or terrifying, or seductive, or royal, or courageous? There are so many contradictory facts; there are so many reported interviews, each contradicting the other, so that really all that I *know* about this king could be reported in the words of Maupassant, which, as I say, I always consider as a working model. Maupassant is introducing one of his characters, who is possibly gross, commercial, overbearing, insolent; who eats, possibly, too much greasy food; who wears commonplace clothes – a gentleman about whom you might write volumes if you wanted to give the facts of his existence. But all that de Maupassant finds it necessary to say is: 'C'était un monsieur à favoris rouges qui entrait toujours le premier.'[9]

[3]   Beatrice Webb (1858–1943) was a social reformer who helped her husband organize the Fabian Society, establish the London School of Economics, and found the *New Statesman* magazine. Her style, laden with statistical information, struck some as tiresome.
[4]   Matthew 18:6. When his disciples ask Jesus who is "the greatest in the kingdom of heaven," Jesus shows them a little child, and urges the disciples to "become as little children"; he than adds: "But whoso shall offend one of these little ones which believe in me, it were better for him that a millstone were hanged about his neck, and that he were drowned in the depth of the sea."
[5]   Founded in 1884 in London and dedicated to social reform, it published "Blue Books", which documented issues such as children in poverty, and white papers, which proposed reforms.
[6]   An opera (1871) by the Italian composer Giuseppe Verdi (1813–1901).
[7]   "La Reine Hortense" ("Queen Hortense") by the French writer Guy de Maupassant (1850–93) was first published in 1883.
[8]   Albert Frederick Pollard (1869–1948) published *Henry VIII* (London: Goupil) in 1902 and an expanded edition (London: Longman) in 1905.
[9]   This sentence is made up by Ford Madox Ford and is not by Maupassant.

And that is all that I *know* about Henry VIII. – that he was a gentleman with red whiskers who always went first through a door.

III

Let us now see how these things work out in practice. I have a certain number of maxims, gained mostly in conversation with Mr Conrad,[10] which form my working stock-in-trade. I stick to them pretty generally; sometimes I throw them out of the window and just write whatever comes. But the effect is usually pretty much the same. I guess I must be fairly well drilled by this time and function automatically, as the Americans say. The first two of my maxims are these:

Always consider the impressions that you are making upon the mind of the reader, and always consider that the first impression with which you present him will be so strong that it will be all that you can ever do to efface it, to alter it or even quite slightly to modify it. Maupassant's gentleman with red whiskers, who always pushed in front of people when it was a matter of going through a doorway, will remain, for the mind of the reader, that man and no other. The impression is as hard and as definite as a tin-tack. And I rather doubt whether, supposing Maupassant represented him afterwards as kneeling on the ground to wipe the tears away from a small child who had lost a penny down a drain – I doubt whether such a definite statement of fact would ever efface the first impression from the reader's mind. They would think that the gentleman with the red whiskers was perpetrating that act of benevolence with ulterior motives – to impress the bystanders, perhaps.

Maupassant, however, uses physical details more usually as a method of introduction of his characters than I myself do. I am inclined myself, when engaged in the seductive occupation, rather to strike the keynote with a speech than with a description of personality, or even with an action. And, for that purpose, I should set it down, as a rule, that the first speech of a character you are introducing should always be a generalisation – since generalisations are the really strong indications of character. Putting the matter exaggeratedly, you might say that, if a gentleman sitting opposite you in the train remarked to you: 'I see the Tories have won Leith Boroughs,'[11] you would have practically no guide to that gentleman's character. But, if he said: 'Them bloody Unionists have crept into Leith because the Labourites, damn them, have taken away 1,100 votes from us,' you would know that the gentleman belonged to a certain political party, had a certain social status, a certain degree of education and a certain amount of impatience.

It is possible that such disquisitions on Impressionism in prose fiction may seem out of place in a journal styled *Poetry and Drama*.[12] But I do not think they are. For Impressionism, differing from other schools of art, is founded so entirely on observation of the psychology of the patron – and the psychology of the patron remains constant. Let me, to make things plainer, present you with a quotation. Sings Tennyson:

> And bats went round in fragrant skies,
>   And wheeled or lit the filmy shapes
>   That haunt the dusk, with ermine capes
> And woolly breasts and beady eyes.[13]

Now that is no doubt very good natural history, but it is certainly not Impressionism, since no one watching a bat at dusk could see the ermine, the wool or the beadiness of the eyes. These things you might read about in books, or observe in the museum or at the Zoological Gardens. Or you might pick up a dead bat upon the road. But to import into the record of observations of one

---

[10]   Joseph Conrad (1857–1924), the distinguished writer, was a friend of Ford Madox Ford and collaborated with him on *The Inheritors* (1901) and *Romance* (1903).

[11]   At that time a political district around Leith in Edinburgh, Scotland.

[12]   See the first (unnumbered) note to this essay.

[13]   From "In Memoriam" (1850), Section XCV, by Alfred Tennyson (1809–92).

moment the observations of a moment altogether different is not Impressionism. For Impressionism is a thing altogether momentary.

I do not wish to be misunderstood. It is perfectly possible that the remembrance of a former observation may colour your impression of the moment, so that if Tennyson had said:

> And we remembered they have ermine capes,

he would have remained within the canons of Impressionism. But that was not his purpose, which, whatever it was, was no doubt praiseworthy in the extreme, because his heart was pure. It is, however, perfectly possible that a piece of Impressionism should give a sense of two, of three, of as many as you will, places, persons, emotions, all going on simultaneously in the emotions of the writer. It is, I mean, perfectly possible for a sensitised person, be he poet or prose writer, to have the sense, when he is in one room, that he is in another, or when he is speaking to one person he may be so intensely haunted by the memory or desire for another person that he may be absent-minded or distraught. And there is nothing in the canons of Impressionism, as I know it, to stop the attempt to render those superimposed emotions. Indeed, I suppose that Impressionism exists to render those queer effects of real life that are like so many views seen through bright glass – through glass so bright that whilst you perceive through it a landscape or a backyard, you are aware that, on its surface, it reflects a face of a person behind you. For the whole of life is really like that; we are almost always in one place with our minds somewhere quite other.

And it is, I think, only Impressionism that can render that peculiar effect; I know, at any rate, of no other method. It has, this school, in consequence, certain quite strong canons, certain quite rigid unities that must be observed. The point is that any piece of Impressionism, whether it be prose, or verse, or painting, or sculpture, is the record of the impression of a moment; it is not a sort of rounded, annotated record of a set of circumstances – it is the record of the recollection in your mind of a set of circumstances that happened ten years ago – or ten minutes. It might even be the impression of the moment – but it is the impression, not the corrected chronicle. I can make what I mean most clear by a concrete instance.

Thus an Impressionist in a novel, or in a poem, will never render a long speech of one of his characters verbatim, because the mind of the reader would at once lose some of the illusion of the good faith of the narrator. The mind of the reader will say: 'Hullo, this fellow is faking this. He cannot possibly remember such a long speech word for word.' The Impressionist, therefore, will only record his impression of a long speech. If you will try to remember what remains in your mind of long speeches you heard yesterday, this afternoon or five years ago, you will see what I mean. If to-day, at lunch at your club, you heard an irascible member making a long speech about the fish, what you remember will not be his exact words. However much his proceedings will have amused you, you will not remember his exact words. What you will remember is that he said that the sole was not a sole, but a blank, blank, blank plaice; that the cook ought to be shot, by God he ought to be shot. The plaice had been out of the water two years, and it had been caught in a drain: all that there was of Dieppe about this Sole Dieppoise was something that you cannot remember. You will remember this gentleman's starting eyes, his grunts between words, that he was fond of saying 'damnable, damnable, damnable.' You will also remember that the man at the same table with you was talking about morals, and that your boots were too tight, whilst you were trying, in your under mind, to arrange a meeting with some lady. . . .

So that, if you had to render that scene or those speeches for purposes of fiction, you would not give a word for word re-invention of sustained sentences from the gentleman who was dissatisfied; or if you were going to invent that scene, you would not so invent those speeches and set them down with all the panoply of inverted commas, notes of exclamation. No, you would give an impression of the whole thing, of the snorts, of the characteristic exclamation, of your friend's disquisition on morals, a few phrases of which you would intersperse into the monologue of the gentleman dissatisfied with his sole. And you would give a sense that your feet were burning, and that the lady you wanted to meet had very clear and candid eyes. You would give a little description of her hair. . . .

In that way you would attain to the sort of odd vibration that scenes in real life really have; you would give your reader the impression that he was witnessing something real, that he was passing through an experience. . . . You will observe also that you will have produced something that is very like a Futurist picture – not a Cubist picture,[14] but one of those canvases that show you in one corner a pair of stays, in another a bit of of the foyer of a music hall, in another a fragment of early morning landscape, and in the middle a pair of eyes, the whole bearing the title of "A Night Out." And, indeed, those Futurists are only trying to render on canvas what Impressionists *tel que moi*[15] have been trying to render for many years. (You may remember Emma's love scene at the cattle show in *Madame Bovary*.)[16]

Do not, I beg you, be led away by the English reviewer's cant phrase to the effect that the Futurists are trying to be literary and the plastic arts can never be literary. Les Jeunes[17] of to-day are trying all sorts of experiments, in all sorts of media. And they are perfectly right to be trying them.

IV

I have been trying to think what are the objections to Impressionism as I understand it – or rather what alternative method could be found. It seems to me that one is an Impressionist because one tries to produce an illusion of reality – or rather the business of Impressionism is to produce that illusion. The subject is one enormously complicated and is full of negatives. Thus the Impressionist author is sedulous to avoid letting his personality appear in the course of his book. On the other hand, his whole book, his whole poem is merely an expression of his personality. Let me illustrate exactly what I mean. You set out to write a story, or you set out to write a poem, and immediately your attempt becomes one creating an illusion. You attempt to involve the reader amongst the personages of the story or in the atmosphere of the poem. You do this by presentation and by presentation and again by presentation. The moment you depart from presentation, the moment you allow yourself, as a poet, to introduce the ejaculation:

O Muse Pindarian, aid me to my theme;

or the moment that, as a story-teller, you permit yourself the luxury of saying:

Now, gentle reader, is my heroine not a very sweet and oppressed lady? –

at that very moment your reader's illusion that he is present at an affair in real life or that he has been transported by your poem into an atmosphere entirely other than that of his arm-chair or his chimney-corner – at that very moment that illusion will depart. Now the point is this:

The other day I was discussing these matters with a young man whose avowed intention is to sweep away Impressionism. And, after I had energetically put before him the views that I have here expressed, he simply remarked: "Why try to produce an illusion?" To which I could only reply: "Why then write?"

I have asked myself frequently since then why one should try to produce an illusion of reality in the mind of one's reader. Is it just an occupation like any other – like postage-stamp collecting, let us say – or is it the sole end and aim of art? I have spent the greater portion of my working life in preaching that particular doctrine: is it possible, then, that I have been entirely wrong?

Of course it is possible for any man to be entirely wrong; but I confess myself to being as yet unconverted. The chief argument of my futurist friend was that producing an illusion causes the

---

[14]   On the Futurists and the impression left by their first exhibition in London in March 1912, see the "Introduction" to "Continental Interlude I," pp. 1–3.

[15]   French for "such as myself."

[16]   Madame Bovary (1857), by Gustave Flaubert (1821–81), is the most celebrated French novel of the nineteenth century; the love scene between the heroine, Emma Bovary, and her lover,

Rodolphe Boulanger, takes place in a room in the town hall that overlooks the town square where an agricultural show is taking place. It is characterized by cinematic cutting between the love scene and the absurd, pompous speeches being delivered by municipal officials below, and is found in Part 2, ch. 8.

[17]   French for "the young people."

writer so much trouble as not to be worth while. That does not seem to me to be an argument worth very much because – and again I must say it seems to me – the business of an artist is surely to take trouble, but this is probably doing my friend's position, if not his actual argument, an injustice. I am aware that there are quite definite æsthetic objections to the business of producing an illusion. In order to produce an illusion you must justify; in order to justify you must introduce a certain amount of matter that may not appear germane to your story or to your poem. Sometimes, that is to say, it would appear as if for the purpose of proper bringing out of a very slight Impressionist sketch the artist would need an altogether disproportionately enormous frame; a frame absolutely monstrous. Let me again illustrate exactly what I mean. It is not sufficient to say: 'Mr Jones was a gentleman who had a strong aversion to rabbit-pie.' It is not sufficient, that is to say, if Mr Jones's dislike for rabbit-pie is an integral part of your story. And it is quite possible that a dislike for one form or other of food might form the integral part of a story. Mr Jones might be a hard-worked coal-miner with a well-meaning wife, whom he disliked because he was developing a passion for a frivolous girl. And it might be quite possible that one evening the well-meaning wife, not knowing her husband's peculiarities, but desiring to give him a special and extra treat, should purchase from a stall a couple of rabbits and spend many hours in preparing for him a pie of great succulence, which should be a solace to him when he returns, tired with his labours and rendered nervous by his growing passion for the other lady. The rabbit-pie would then become a symbol – a symbol of the whole tragedy of life. It would symbolize for Mr Jones the whole of his wife's want of sympathy for him and the whole of his distaste for her; his reception of it would symbolize for Mrs Jones the whole hopelessness of her life, since she had expended upon it inventiveness, sedulous care, sentiment, and a good will. From that position, with the rabbit-pie always in the centre of the discussion, you might work up to the murder of Mrs Jones, to Mr Jones's elopement with the other lady – to any tragedy that you liked. For indeed the position contains, as you will perceive, the whole tragedy of life.

And the point is this, that if your tragedy is to be absolutely convincing, it is not sufficient to introduce the fact of Mr Jones's dislike for rabbit-pie by the bare statement. According to your temperament you must sufficiently account for that dislike. You might do it by giving Mr Jones a German grandmother, since all Germans have a peculiar loathing for the rabbit and regard its flesh as unclean. You might then find it necessary to account for the dislike the Germans have for these little creatures; you might have to state that his dislike is a self-preservative race instinct, since in Germany the rabbit is apt to eat certain poisonous fungi, so that one out of every ten will cause the death of its consumer, or you might proceed with your justification of Mr Jones's dislike for rabbit-pie along different lines. You might say that it was a nervous aversion caused by having been violently thrashed when a boy by his father at a time when a rabbit-pie was upon the table. You might then have to go on to justify the nervous temperament of Mr Jones by saying that his mother drank or that his father was a man too studious for his position. You might have to pursue almost endless studies in the genealogy of Mr Jones; because, of course, you might want to account for the studiousness of Mr Jones's father by making him the bastard son of a clergyman, and then you might want to account for the libidinous habits of the clergyman in question. That will be simply a matter of your artistic conscience.

You have to make Mr Jones's dislike for rabbits convincing. You have to make it in the first place convincing to your reader alone; but the odds are that you will try to make it convincing also to yourself, since you yourself in this solitary world of ours will be the only reader that you really and truly know. Now all these attempts at justification, all these details of parentage and the like, may very well prove uninteresting to your reader. They are, however, necessary if your final effect of murder is to be a convincing impression.

But again, if the final province of art is to convince, its first province is to interest. So that, to the extent that your justification is uninteresting, it is an artistic defect. It may sound paradoxical, but the truth is that your Impressionist can only get his strongest effects by using beforehand a great deal of what one may call non-Impressionism. He will make, that is to say, an enormous impression on his reader's mind by the use of three words. But very likely each one of those three words will be prepared for by ten thousand other words. Now are we to regard those other words as being entirely unnecessary, as being, that is to say, so many artistic defects? That I take to be my futurist friend's ultimate assertion.

Says he: 'All these elaborate conventions of Conrad or of Maupassant give the reader the impression that a story is being told – all these meetings of bankers and master-mariners in places like the Ship Inn at Greenwich, and all Maupassant's dinner-parties, always in the politest circles, where a countess or a fashionable doctor or someone relates a passionate or a pathetic or a tragic or a merely grotesque incident – as you have it, for instance, in the "Contes de la Bécasse"[18] – all this machinery for getting a story told is so much waste of time. A story is a story; why not just tell it anyhow? You can never tell what sort of an impression you will produce upon a reader. Then why bother about Impressionism? Why not just chance your luck?'

There is a good deal to be said for this point of view. Writing up to my own standards is such an intolerable labour and such a thankless job, since it can't give me the one thing in the world that I desire – that for my part I am determined to drop creative writing for good and all. But I, like all writers of my generation, have been so handicapped that there is small wonder that one should be tired out. On the one hand the difficulty of getting hold of any critical guidance was, when I was a boy, insuperable. There was nothing. Criticism was non-existent; self-conscious art was decried; you were supposed to write by inspiration; you were the young generation with the vine-leaves in your hair, knocking furiously at the door. On the other hand, one writes for money, for fame, to excite the passion of love, to make an impression upon one's time. Well, God knows what one writes for. But it is certain that one gains neither fame nor money; certainly one does not excite the passion of love, and one's time continues to be singularly unimpressed.

But young writers to-day have a much better chance, on the æsthetic side at least. Here and there, in nooks and corners, they can find someone to discuss their work, not from the point of view of goodness or badness or of niceness or of nastiness, but from the simple point of view of expediency. The moment you can say: 'Is it expedient to print *vers libre* in long or short lines, or in the form of prose, or not to print it at all, but to recite it?' – the moment you can find someone to discuss these expediences calmly, or the moment that you can find someone with whom to discuss the relative values of justifying your character or of abandoning the attempt to produce an illusion of reality – at that moment you are very considerably helped; whereas an admirer of your work might fall down and kiss your feet and it would not be of the very least use to you.

V

This adieu, like Herrick's, to poesy,[19] may seem to be a digression. Indeed it is; and indeed it isn't. It is, that is to say, a digression in the sense that it is a statement not immediately germane to the argument that I am carrying on. But it is none the less an insertion fully in accord with the canons of Impressionism as I understand it. For the first business of Impressionism is to produce an impression, and the only way in literature to produce an impression is to awaken interest. And, in a sustained argument, you can only keep interest awakened by keeping alive, by whatever means you may have at your disposal, the surprise of your reader. You must state your argument; you must illustrate it, and then you must stick in something that appears to have nothing whatever to do with either subject or illustration, so that the reader will exclaim: 'What the devil is the fellow driving at?' And then you must go on in the same way – arguing, illustrating and startling and arguing, startling and illustrating – until at the very end your contentions will appear like a ravelled skein. And then, in the last few lines, you will draw towards you the master-string of that seeming confusion, and the whole pattern of the carpet, the whole design of the net-work will be apparent.

This method, you will observe, founds itself upon analysis of the human mind. For no human being likes listening to long and sustained arguments. Such listening is an effort, and no artist has

---

18 *Les Contes de la Bécasse* was a collection of short stories that Guy de Maupassant published in 1884, his most celebrated collection.

19 Robert Herrick (1591–1674) was an elegant seventeenth-century poet; which poem Ford has in mind is by no means clear.

the right to call for any effort from his audience. A picture should come out of its frame and seize the spectator.

Let us now consider the audience to which the artist should address himself. Theoretically a writer should be like the Protestant angel, a messenger of peace and goodwill towards all men. But, inasmuch as the Wingless Victory[20] appears monstrously hideous to a Hottentot, and a beauty of Tunis detestable to the inhabitants of these fortunate islands, it is obvious that each artist must adopt a frame of mind, less Catholic possibly, but certainly more Papist, and address himself, like the angel of the Vulgate, only *hominibus bonæ voluntatis*.[21] He must address himself to such men as be of goodwill; that is to say, he must typify for himself a human soul in sympathy with his own; a silent listener who will be attentive to him, and whose mind acts very much as his acts. According to the measure of this artist's identity with his species, so will be the measure of his temporal greatness. That is why a book, to be really popular, must be either extremely good or extremely bad. For Mr Hall Caine[22] has millions of readers; but then Guy de Maupassant and Flaubert have tens of millions.

I suppose the proposition might be put in another way. Since the great majority of mankind are, on the surface, vulgar and trivial – the stuff to fill graveyards – the great majority of mankind will be easily and quickly affected by art which is vulgar and trivial. But, inasmuch as this world is a very miserable purgatory for most of us sons of men – who remain stuff with which graveyards are filled – inasmuch as horror, despair and incessant strivings are the lot of the most trivial of humanity, who endure them as a rule with commonsense and cheerfulness – so, if a really great master strike the note of horror, of despair, of striving, and so on, he will stir chords in the hearts of a larger number of people than those who are moved by the merely vulgar and the merely trivial. This is probably why *Madame Bovary* has sold more copies than any book ever published, except, of course, books purely religious. But the appeal of religious books is exactly similar.

It may be said that the appeal of *Madame Bovary* is largely sexual. So it is, but it is only in countries like England and the United States that the abominable tortures of sex – or, if you will, the abominable interests of sex – are not supposed to take rank alongside of the horrors of lost honour, commercial ruin, or death itself. For all these things are the components of life, and each is of equal importance.

So, since Flaubert is read in Russia, in Germany, in France, in the United States, amongst the non-Anglo-Saxon population, and by the immense populations of South America, he may be said to have taken for his audience the whole of the world that could possibly be expected to listen to a man of his race. (I except, of course, the Anglo-Saxons who cannot be confidently expected to listen to anything other than the words produced by Mr George Edwardes,[23] and musical comedy in general.)

My futurist friend again visited me yesterday, and we discussed this very question of audiences. Here again he said that I was entirely wrong. He said that an artist should not address himself to *l'homme moyen sensuel*,[24] but to intellectuals, to people who live at Hampstead[25] and wear no hats. (He withdrew his contention later.)

I maintain on my own side that one should address oneself to the cabmen round the corner, but this also is perhaps an exaggeration. My friend's contention on behalf of the intellectuals was not so much due to his respect for their intellects. He said that they knew the A B C of an art, and that it is better to address yourself to an audience that knows the A B C of an art than to an audience entirely untrammelled by such knowledge. In this I think he was wrong, for the intellectuals are persons of very conventional mind, and they acquire as a rule simultaneously with the A B C of any

[20]   Another name for the statue known as the Nike of Samothrace, which used to be the first thing that visitors saw when entering the Louvre in Paris and so became a byword for beauty.
[21]   Latin for "to men of good will."
[22]   Hall Caine (1853–1931) was a novelist whose works were enormously popular; they include *The Shadow of a Crime* (1885), *The Deemster* (1887), *The Manxman* (1894), *The Prodigal Son* (1904), and *The Master of Man* (1921).

[23]   George Edwardes (1855–1915), manager of the Gaiety Theatre and the later Daly's Theatre in the 1890s and early 1900s, is sometimes considered the inventor of musical comedies. The works he produced were new and formulaic stories combined with tuneful, undemanding music and pretty dancing.
[24]   French for "the average middlebrow."
[25]   A surburb north of London that was a trendy place for people with intellectual pretensions to live in.

art the knowledge of so many conventions that it is almost impossible to make any impression upon their minds. Hampstead and the hatless generally offer an impervious front to futurisms, simply because they have imbibed from Whistler and the Impressionists the convention that painting should not be literary. Now every futurist picture tells a story; so that rules out futurism. Similarly with the cubists. Hampstead has imbibed, from God knows where, the dogma that all art should be based on life, or should at least draw its inspiration and its strength from the representation of nature. So there goes cubism, since cubism is non-representational, has nothing to do with life, and has a quite proper contempt of nature.

When I produced my argument that one should address oneself to the cabmen at the corner, my futurist friend at once flung to me the jeer about Tolstoi and the peasant.[26] Now the one sensible thing in the long drivel of nonsense with which Tolstoi misled this dull world was the remark that art should be addressed to the peasant. My futurist friend said that that was sensible for an artist living in Russia or Roumania, but it was an absurd remark to be let fall by a critic living on Campden Hill. His view was that you cannot address yourself to the peasant unless that peasant has evoked folk-song or folk-lores. I don't know why that was his view, but that was his view.

It seems to me to be nonsensical, even if the inner meaning of his dictum was that art should be addressed to a community of practising artists. Art, in fact, should be addressed to those who are not preoccupied. It is senseless to address a Sirventes[27] to a man who is going mad with love, and an Imagiste poem[28] will produce little effect upon another man who is going through the bankruptcy court.

It is probable that Tolstoi thought that in Russia the non-preoccupied mind was to be found solely amongst the peasant class, and that is why he said that works of art should be addressed to the peasant. I don't know how it may be in Russia, but certainly in Occidental Europe the non-preoccupied mind – which is the same thing as the peasant intelligence – is to be found scattered throughout every grade of society. When I used just now the instances of a man mad for love, or distracted by the prospect of personal ruin, I was purposely misleading. For a man mad as a hatter for love of a worthless creature, or a man maddened by the tortures of bankruptcy, by dishonour or by failure, may yet have, by the sheer necessity of his nature, a mind more receptive than most other minds. The mere craving for relief from his personal thoughts may make him take quite unusual interest in a work of art. So that is not preoccupation in my intended sense, but for a moment the false statement crystallised quite clearly what I was aiming at.

The really impassible mind is not the mind quickened by passion, but the mind rendered slothful by preoccupation purely trivial. The "English gentleman" is, for instance, an absolutely hopeless being from this point of view. His mind is so taken up by considerations of what is good form, of what is good feeling, of what is even good fellowship; he is so concerned to pass unnoticed in the crowd; he is so set upon having his room like everyone else's room, that he will find it impossible to listen to any plea for art which is exceptional, vivid, or startling. The cabman, on the other hand, does not mind being thought a vulgar sort of bloke; in consequence he will form a more possible sort of audience. On the other hand, amongst the purely idler classes it is perfectly possible to find individuals who are so firmly and titularly gentle folk that they don't have to care a damn what they do. These again are possible audiences for the artist. The point is really, I take it, that the preoccupation that is fatal to art is the moral or the social preoccupation. Actual preoccupations matter very little. Your cabman may drive his taxi through exceedingly difficult streets; he may have half-a-dozen close shaves in a quarter of an hour. But when those things are over they are over, and he has not the necessity of a cabman. His point of view as to what is art, good form, or, let us say, the proper relation of the sexes, is unaffected. He may be a hungry man, a thirsty man, or even a tired man, but he will not necessarily have his finger upon his moral pulse, and he will not hold as æsthetic dogma the idea that no painting must tell a story, or the moral dogma that passion only becomes respectable when you have killed it.

---

[26] Leo Tolstoy (1820–1910), famous Russian novelist, announced these views in his late book *What Is Art* (1899).

[27] A verse in Provançal poetry from the period 1100–1300.
[28] On Imagism, see pp. 43 and 94–7.

It is these accursed dicta that render an audience hopeless to the artist, that render art a useless pursuit and the artist himself a despised individual.

So that those are the best individuals for an artist's audience who have least listened to accepted ideas – who are acquainted with deaths at street corners, with the marital infidelities of crowded courts, with the goodness of heart of the criminal, with the meanness of the undetected or the sinless, who know the queer odd jumble of negatives that forms our miserable and hopeless life. If I had to choose as reader I would rather have one who had never read anything before but the Newgate Calendar, or the records of crime, starvation and divorce in the Sunday paper – I would rather have him for a reader than a man who had discovered the song that the sirens sang, or had by heart the whole of the *Times Literary Supplement*,[29] from its inception to the present day. Such a peasant intelligence will know that this is such a queer world that anything may be possible. And that is the type of intelligence that we need.

Of course, it is more difficult to find these intelligences in the town than in the rural districts. A man thatching all day long has time for many queer thoughts; so has a man who from sunrise to sunset is trimming a hedge into shape with a bagging hook. I have, I suppose, myself thought more queer thoughts when digging potatoes than at any other time during my existence. It is, for instance, very queer if you are digging potatoes in the late evening, when it has grown cool after a very hot day, to thrust your hand into the earth after a potato and to find that the earth is quite warm – is about flesh-heat. Of course, the clods would be warm because the sun would have been shining on them all day, and the air gives up its heat much quicker than the earth. But it is none the less a queer sensation.

Now, if the person experiencing that sensation have what I call a peasant intelligence, he will just say that it is a queer thing and will store it away in his mind along with his other experiences. It will go along with the remembrance of hard frost, of fantastic icicles, the death of rabbits pursued by stoats, the singularly quick ripening of corn in a certain year, the fact that such and such a man was overlooked by a wise woman and so died because, his wife, being tired of him, had paid the wise woman five sixpences which she had laid upon the table in the form of a crown; or along with the other fact that a certain man murdered his wife by the use of a packet of sheep dip which he had stolen from a field where the farmer was employed at lamb washing. All these remembrances he will have in his mind, not classified under any headings of social reformers, or generalized so as to fulfil any fancied moral law.

But the really dangerous person for the artist will be the gentleman who, chancing to put his hand into the ground and to find it about as warm as the breast of a woman, if you could thrust your hand between her chest and her stays, will not accept the experience as an experience, but will start talking about the breast of mother-nature. This last man is the man whom the artist should avoid, since he will regard phenomena not as phenomena, but as happenings, with which he may back up preconceived dogmas – as, in fact, so many sticks with which to beat a dog.

No, what the artist needs is the man with the quite virgin mind – the man who will not insist that grass must always be painted green, because all the poets, from Chaucer till the present day, had insisted on talking about the green grass, or the green leaves, or the green straw.

Such a man, if he comes to your picture and sees you have painted a haycock bright purple will say:

'Well, I have never myself observed a haycock to be purple, but I can understand that if the sky is very blue and the sun is setting very red, the shady side of the haycock might well appear to be purple.' That is the kind of peasant intelligence that the artist needs for his audience.

And the whole of Impressionism comes to this: having realized that the audience to which you will address yourself must have this particular peasant intelligence, or, if you prefer it, this particular and virgin openness of mind, you will then figure to yourself an individual, a silent listener, who shall be to yourself the *homo bonæ voluntatis* – man of goodwill. To him, then, you will address your picture, your poem, your prose story, or your argument. You will seek to capture his interest; you will seek to hold his interest. You will do this by methods of surprise, of fatigue, by

---

[29] The *TLS* began publication in 1902.

passages of sweetness in your language, by passages suggesting the sudden and brutal shock of suicide. You will give him passages of dulness, so that your bright effects may seem more bright; you will alternate, you will dwell for a long time upon an intimate point; you will seek to exasperate so that you may the better enchant. You will, in short, employ all the devices of the prostitute. If you are too proud for this you may be the better gentleman or the better lady, but you will be the worse artist. For the artist must always be humble and humble and again humble, since before the greatness of his task he himself is nothing. He must again be outrageous, since the greatness of his task calls for enormous excesses by means of which he may recoup his energies. That is why the artist is, quite rightly, regarded with suspicion by people who desire to live in tranquil and ordered society.

But one point is very important. The artist can never write to satisfy himself – to get, as the saying is, something off the chest. He must not write propaganda which it is his desire to write; he must not write rolling periods, the production of which gives him a soothing feeling in his digestive organs or wherever it is. He must write always so as to satisfy that other fellow – that other fellow who has too clear an intelligence to let his attention be captured or his mind deceived by special pleadings in favour of any given dogma. You must not write so as to improve him, since he is a much better fellow than yourself, and you must not write so as to influence him, since he is a granite rock, a peasant intelligence, the gnarled bole of a sempiternal oak, against which you will dash yourself in vain. It is in short no pleasant kind of job to be a conscious artist. You won't have any vine-leaves in your poor old hair; you won't just dash your quill into an inexhaustible ink-well and pour out fine frenzies. No, you will be just the skilled workman doing his job with drill or chisel or mallet. And you will get precious little out of it. Only, just at times, when you come to look again at some work of yours that you have quite forgotten, you will say, 'Why, that is rather well done.' That is all.

Dorothy Richardson (1873–1957)

Introduction

Dorothy Richardson (1873–1957) was born in Abingdon, Oxfordshire. She grew up in a comfortable, middle-class environment, but faced a very different world when her father went bankrupt. For a time she worked as a teacher, first in Hanover and then in London. Later she worked as a secretary for a dentist. In her free time she moved in feminist and socialist circles in London, and in 1907 she had a brief affair with H. G. Wells. In 1917 she married Alan Odle. Two years earlier she had published *Pointed Roofs*, her first novel. It became the first in a series of 12 that culminated in 1938 when the twelfth was included as

part of a collected edition, the entire work now called *Pilgrimage*. In 1967 another collected edition in four volumes appeared, this time including a thirteenth novel. All of them trace the life of Miriam Henderson, a character whom many critics find to be a direct transposition into fiction of Richardson's own experiences. In the past, interest in her work centered on her own distinctive version of "stream of consciousness," a version that she developed in isolation from other practitioners. More recent criticism has been concerned with her interests in feminism and gender.

Sunday (1919)

I

I looked up and saw Josephine cutting cake. Until that moment every moment of Sunday had been perfect. The day had been so perfect that I had forgotten there was anything in the world but its moments and they were going on for ever, and I was just turning blissfully towards the walk across the common; daylight still on the greenery, and the Hopkins in *F* service with candles burning in twilight and the frivolous evening congregation. I looked drunkenly up to look down the envious room at my green soul holding the window clean open from outside and pouring in and holding them all in affectionate envious silence and saw Josephine standing in the way bent over the cake, looking exactly like Grannie as she pursed her face to drive the knife through. I stayed stupidly looking, not able to get back until the cake was cut, and although she had not noticed me she reminded me in her spitefully unconscious vindictive spoil-sport way that it was my turn to go to Grannie's. There was no need to say it. It was part of her everlasting internal conversation about the dark side. Something leapt from me towards her; the room was a sound in a dream. Life; a dream swimming in sound. Today was still all round the pattern round the edge of my plate, and I felt that a particular way of putting jam on to my bread and butter would keep everything off. But the layer went over, thinning out over the creamy butter, raspberry jam being spread with a trembling hand by nobody, nowhere ... by Josephine. The morning garden, the sunlit afternoon heath, the eternal perfect Sunday happiness of all the rooms in the house were Josephine's. She held them there or snatched them away. Grannie's was woven in her dark mind *always*; all the time.

II

The summer shone down Grannie's road in a single wash of gold over the little yellow brick houses. Inside her sitting-room it had gone. There was a harsh black twilight full of the dreadful sweetish emanation that was always in her room. It came out dreadfully from the cold firm wrinkles of her cheek when I kissed her and shook out over me from her draperies when she raised her arm and

First published in the journal *Art and Letters*, n.s. 2 (summer 1919).

patted me and made that moment when I always forgot what I had intended to say. When her arm came down the beads of her big oak bracelet rattled together as the ends of her long-boned puffy fingers patted the horsehair seat. People sat down. I sat down, aching with my smile. Her long stiff hands were already fumbling her ear trumpet from the lap of her silk dress. When I had secured the speaking end she said, how are you, my dear? Very well, thank you – how are *you*, I shouted slowly. The visit had begun; some of it had gone. Eh she quavered out of the years. If she could see into the middle of my head she would see the lawn of her old garden and the stone vase of geraniums and calceolarias in the bright sunlight, and would stop. Her tall figure tottering jerkily under its large black shawldraped dress, the lapels of her lace cap, the bony oval of her face, the unconscious stare of her faded blue eyes as she moved and stood about the garden all *meant*. I was a ghost meaning nothing, then and now. She sat wearing the same Sunday clothes but her eyes were on my sliding silence. I said my words over again. They were lasting longer than if she had understood at once. Her face fell as she heard. Middling ... middling, she said in a shrill murmur. Isn't it a lovely day I shouted angrily. My throat was already sore with effort. Her disappointed eyes remained fixed on me. It has been *lovely* today I yelled. Did your father go she asked with a reluctant quiver. My false face when I shouted back showed her she had misunderstood. She sighed and turned away from the light. The long tube slithered in the folds of her dress as she sat back, still holding the trumpet to her ear. Presently she turned slowly round and lowered the trumpet and patted my knee. I smiled and said we went for a walk, very quietly. I felt she must be hearing. She put up the trumpet again. I could not say it over again, she would know what I meant if I waited. I hesitated and felt a crimson blush. She smiled and patted my knee with her free hand. You're growing up a bonny woman she quavered. People having tea in basket chairs under trees watched. The beauty of the day hammered in the room. She saw it all. But her words were a bridge thrown towards nothing. It gets dark earlier now shouted my ghost. The summer's going, she quavered, turning away again and putting down the trumpet. I lowered the mouthpiece and she coiled the apparatus in her lap and sat back giving her cry as her shoulders touched the back of her chair. Bad, bad, she whispered, patting her left arm and smiling towards me. I nodded vehemently. Listen to the minister, she murmured, read your bible every day. She sighed heavily and sat thinking of us all one by one. About us in the foreground of her thoughts was her large old house and our small one. It was long before she came back to her small home near our big one. I turned away from her heavy fragile thinking profile when I reached the moment of hoping that the end would come here so that she might never bring the trumpet and the chapel magazines to make a centre of gloom in amongst everything. When I looked again her heavy thin profile gleamed whiter in the deepening light. I could no longer see the little frayed blue veins. I looked about the room. The furniture was death-soaked. It knew only of lives lived fearing death. I looked at Grannie again. My tingling hands touched a thought ... The loud beating of my heart filled space. Lord. Lord Christ. Mr Christ. Jesus Christ, Esquire. I had thought the thought ... Below the joys and wonders of my life was that. Me. I began social conversation eagerly towards the room, in my mind. It went on and on fluently. I had found out how to do it. My mind pressed against the sky and spread over the earth discovering. I strung out thoughts in unfamiliar phrases, laughing in advance to blind my hearers until I was safely away over bridge after bridge. I nearly bent forward to secure the speaking tube. I felt it in my hand. It was no use. It would carry my thought into action ... All social talk was hatred. I sat twisting my fingers together longing to get back into the incessant wonders and joys away from the room that had seen my truth. The room throbbed with it. It made the room seem lighter, the twilight going backward, evening and gaslight never to come ... When the gaslight *came* on the furniture the room would become quiet and harmless again ... It was dark and cold. Voices were sighing and moaning through the walls. The hell waiting for me *made* the wonders and joys ... it might come soon; any day. Who can tell how oft he offendeth. Cleanse thou me from secret faults.[1] Useless. God was not greater than I. The force of evil is as great and eternal as the force of good ... I wanted to

---

[1] From the Anglican Missal for the Tuesday after the Third Sunday in Lent, the Gradual, in which the first clause is spoken by the priest, the second by the people; the passage is a translation of Psalm 19:12, which in the King James Version reads: "Who can understand his errors? cleanse thou me from secret faults."

cast myself on my knees and weep aloud in anger. Be angry and sin not. That meant waiting meanly for the good things to come back. There were no good things. If God saw and knew evil he was evil ... Grannie sighed. I smiled towards her through the twilight, my body breaking into a refreshing dew. The little room was being folded in darkness. The bright light that came into it in the morning was a stranger; a new light. Light the gas, dearie, whispered Grannie. Years slipped in and out as the gaslight spread its gold wings sideways from its core of blue. The evening stretched across the room, innocently waiting.

Death (1924)

THIS was death this time, no mistake. Her cheeks flushed at the indecency of being seen, dying and then dead. If only she could get it over and lay herself out decent before anyone came in to see and meddle. Mrs Gworsh winning, left out there in the easy world, coming in to see her dead and lay her out and talk about her ... While there's life. Perhaps she wasn't dying. Only afraid. People can be so mighty bad and get better. But no. Not after that feeling rolling up within, telling her in words, her whom it knew, that this time she was going to be overwhelmed. That was the beginning, the warning and the certainty. To be more and more next time, any minute, increasing till her life flowed out for all to see. Her heart thumped. The rush of life beating against the walls of her body, making her head spin, numbed the pain and brought a mist before her eyes. Death. What she'd always feared so shocking, and put away. But no one knows what it is, how awful beyond everything till they're in for it. Nobody knows death in this rush of life in all your parts.

The mist cleared. Her face was damp. The spinning in her head had ceased. She drew a careful breath. Without pain. Some of the pain had driven through her without feeling. But she was heavier. It wasn't gone either. Only waiting. She saw the doctor on his way. Scorn twisted her lips against her empty gums. Scores of times she'd waited on him. Felt him drive fear away. Joked. This time he'd say nothing. Watch, for her secret life to come up and out. When his turn came he'd know what it was like letting your life out; and all of them out there. No good telling. You can't know till you're in for it. They're all in for it, rich and poor alike. No help. The great enormous creature driving your innards up, what nobody knows. What you don't know ... Life ain't worth death.

It's got to be stuck, shame or no ... but how do you do it?

She lay still and listened for footsteps. They knew next door by now. That piece would never milk Snowdrop dry. Less cream, less butter. Everything going back. Slip-slop, go as you please, and never done. Where'd us be to now if I hadn't? That's it. What they don't think of. Slip slop. Grinning and singing enough to turn the milk. I've got a tongue. I know it. You've got to keep on and keep on at them. Or nothing done. I been young, but never them silly ways. Snowdrop'll go back; for certain ...

But I shan't ever *see* it no more ... the thought flew lifting through her mind. See no more. Work no more. Worry no more. Then what had been the good of it? Why had she gone on year in year out since Tom died and she began ailing, tramping all weathers up to the field, toiling and aching, and black as thunder most times. What was the good? Nobody knew her. Tom never had. And now there was only that piece downstairs, and what she did didn't matter any more. Except to herself, and she'd go on being slipslop; not knowing she was in for death that makes it all one whatever you do. Good and bad they're all dying and don't know it's the most they've got to do.

Her mind looked back up and down her life. Tom. What a fool she'd been to think him any different. Then when he died she'd thought him the same as at first, and cried because she'd let it all slip in the worries. Little Joe. Tearing her open, then snuggled in her arms, sucking. And all outside bright and peaceful; better than the beginning with Tom. But they'd all stop if they knew where it led. Joe, and his wife, and his little ones, in for all of it, getting the hard of it now, and

First published in the journal *Weekly Westminster*, n.s. 1 (February 9, 1924).

death waiting for them. She could tell them all now what it was like, all of them, the squire, all the same. All going the same way, rich and poor.

The Bible was right, remember now thy Creator in the days of thy youth.[1] What she had always wanted. She had always wanted to be good. Now it was too late. Nothing mattering, having it all lifted away, made the inside of you come back as it was at the first, ready to begin. Too late. Shocking she had thought it when parson said prepare for death, live as if you were going to die tonight. But it's true. If every moment was your last on earth you could be yourself. You'd dare. Everybody would dare. People is themselves when they are children, and not again till they know they are dying. But conscience knows all the time. I've a heavy bill for all my tempers. God forgive me. But why should He? He was having his turn anyhow, with all this dying to do. Death must be got through as life had been, just somehow. But how?

When the doctor had gone she knew she was left to do it alone. While there is life there is hope. But the life in her was too much smaller than the great weight and pain. He made her easier, numb. Trying to think and not thinking. Everything unreal. The piece coming up and downstairs like something in another world. Perhaps God would let her go easy. Then it was all over? Just fading to nothing with everything still to do ...

The struggle came unexpectedly. She heard her cries, and then the world leapt upon her and grappled, and even in the midst of the agony of pain was the surprise of her immense strength. The strength that struggled against the huge stifling, the body that leapt and twisted against the heavy darkness, a shape with her shape, that she had not known. Her unknown self rushing forward through all her limbs to fight. Leaping out and curving in a great sweep away from where she lay to the open sill, yet pinned back, unwrenchable from the bed. Back and back she slid, down a long tunnel at terrific speed, cool, her brow cool and wet, with wind blowing upon it. Darkness in front. Back and back into her own young body, alone. In front of the darkness came the garden, the old garden in April, the crab-apple blossom, all as it was before she began, but brighter ...

The Garden (1924)

There was no one there. The sound of feet and no one there. The gravel stopped making its noise when she stood still. When the last foot came down all the flowers stood still.

Pretty *pretty* flowers. Standing quite still, going on being how they were when no one was there. No one knew how they were when they stood still. *They* had never seen them like this, standing quiet all together in this little piece.

They were here all the time, happy and good when no one was here. They knew she was happy and good. Feeling shy because they knew it. They all put their arms round her without touching her. Quickly. And went back, sitting in the sun for her to look at.

She could see the different smells going up into the sunshine. The sunshine smelt of the flowers.

The bees had not noticed her. They were too busy. Zmm. Talking about the different colours coming out at the tops of the stalks. Keeping on making dark places in the air as they crossed the path. Some standing on their hind legs just as they were choosing which flower.

Some of the flowers seemed not so nice. As she looked at them they quickly said they loved her and were nice.

A little flower looking out from several all alike. Being different. A deep Sunday colour. Too deep. The sun did not like it so much. The sun liked the blue and pink best. This piece of garden was the blue and pink and all their many leaves. Poor leaves. Perhaps they wanted to be flowers ...

Wherever she looked she could see this one different flower, growing taller. It was Nelly on a stalk. She went nearer to see if it would move away. It stood still, very tall. Its stalk was thin. She put her face down towards it to keep it down. It had a deep smell. She touched it with her nose to

---

[1] Ecclesiastes 12:1: "Remember now thy Creator in the days of thy youth, while the evil days come not, nor the years draw nigh, when thou shalt say, I have no pleasure in them."

THE GARDEN
First published in the Parisian avant-garde journal *transatlantic review* 2(2) (August 1924).

smell more. It kissed her gently, looking small. A tiny plate, cut into points all round the edge. Perhaps now it would go away.

"Dear little flower."

It knew all about the other part of the garden. The bent-over body of Minter. The little thrown marrow had hit him. He had not minded. Old Minter alone with the Ghost.

The smell of the dark pointed trees in the shrubbery. Raindrops outside the window falling down in front of the dark pointed trees. The snowman alone on the lawn, after tea, with a sad slanted face.

Shiny apples on the trees on Sunday with pink on one side.

The slippery swing seat, scrubby ropes, tight. Tummy falling out, coming back again high in the air . . .

The apples were near this part. In the sun. Where the cowslip balls hung in a row on the string.

It was safe out here with the flowers. Nothing could come here, on the path between the two sides coming down at their edges in little blues sitting along the path with small patted leaves. All making a sound. They liked to bulge out over the warm yellow gravel, like a mess.

Far away down the path where it was different It could come. It could not get here. The flowers kept it away. It was always in other parts of the garden. Between the rows of peas. Always sounding in the empty part at the end.

Outside the garden it was dark and cold. Spring-heeled Jack jumped suddenly over the hedges. The old woman with the basket, watching up the drive. Perhaps the flowers would always keep them away now.

Perhaps if she went back now the flowers would follow her. She turned right round and ran. They did not come. Panting came at once. The big path by the lawn ached with going so fast. In front were the pointed trees sitting on the piece of lawn that came out and made the path narrow. Just round the corner, soon, just past the bit of the house that had no window, was the stable and the back porch. Coming. There they were. There were a few little flowers by the back porch, cook's flowers, not able to get away into the garden. Not able to go inside the kitchen. They were always frightened. They made the panting worse.

Bang. The hard gravel holding a pain against her nose. Someone calling. She lay still hoping her nose would be bleeding to make them sorry. Here was crying again. Coming up out of her body, into her face, hot, twisting it up, lifting it away from the gravel to let out the noise. Someone would come, not knowing about the flowers; the pretty, pretty flowers. The flowers were unkind, staying too far off to tell them how happy and good she was.

Sleigh Ride (1926)

And now the thin penetrating mist promised increasing cold. The driver flung on a cloak, secured at the neck but falling open across his chest and leaving exposed his thinly clad arms and bare hands.

She pulled high the collar of her fur coat, rimy now at its edges, and her chin ceased to ache and only her eyes and cheekbones felt the thin icy attacking mist that had appeared so suddenly. The cold of a few moments ago numbing her face had brought a hint of how one might freeze quietly to death, numbed and as if warmed by an intensity of cold; and that out amongst the mountains it would not be terrible. But this raw mist bringing pain in every bone it touched would send one aching to one's death, crushed to death by a biting increasing pain.

She felt elaborately warm, not caring even now how long might go on this swift progress along a track that still wound through corridors of mountains and still found mountains rising ahead. But night would come and the great shapes all about her would be wrapped away until they were a darkness in the sky.

First published in the journal *Outlook* 58, no. 1506 (1926).

If this greying light were the fall of day, then certainly the cold would increase. She tried to reckon how far she had travelled eastwards, by how much earlier the sun would set. But south, too, she had come...

The mist was breaking, being broken from above. It dawned upon her that they had been passing impossibly through clouds and were now reaching their fringe. Colour was coming from above, was already here in dark brilliance, thundery. Turning to look down the track she saw distance, cloud masses, light-soaked and gleaming.

And now from just ahead, high in the sky, a sunlit peak looked down.

Long after she had sat erect from her warm ensconcement the sunlit mountain corridors still seemed to be saying watch, see, if you can believe it, what we can do. Always it seemed that they must open out and leave her upon the hither side of enchantment, and still they turned and brought fresh vistas. Sungilt masses beetling variously up into pinnacles that truly cut the sky high up beyond their high-clambering pinewoods, where their snow was broken by patches of tawny crag. She still longed to glide forever onwards through this gladness of light.

But the bright gold was withdrawing. Presently it stood only upon the higher ridges. The colour was going and the angular shadows, leaving a bleakness of white, leaving the mountains higher in their whiteness. One there towered serene, that seemed at its top to walk up the deepening blue, a sharply flattened cone aslant, pure white. She watched it, its thickness of snow, the way from its blunted tower it came broadening down unbroken by crag, radiant white until far down its pinewoods made a little gentleness about its base. Up there on the quiet of its top-most angle it seemed there must be someone, minutely rejoicing in its line along the sky.

A turn brought peaks whose gold had turned to rose. She had not eyes enough for seeing. Seeing was not enough. There was sound, if only one could hear it, in this still, signalling light.

The last of it was ruby gathered departing upon the topmost crags, seeming, the moment before it left them, to be deeply wrought into the crinkled rock.

At a sharp bend the face of the sideways lounging driver came into sight, expressionless.

"Schön, *die letzte Glüh*,"[1] he said quietly.

When she had pronounced her "Wunderschön,"[2] she sat back released from intentness, seeing the scene as one who saw it daily; and noticed then that the colour ebbed from the mountains had melted in the sky. It was this marvel of colour, turning the sky to a molten rainbow, that the driver had meant as well as the rubied ridges that had kept the sky forgotten.

Just above a collar of snow, that dipped steeply between the peaks it linked, the sky was a soft greenish purple paling upwards from mauve-green to green whose edges melted imperceptibly into the deepening blue. In a moment they were turned towards the opposite sky, bold in smoky russet rising to amber and to saffron-rose expanding upwards; a high radiant background for its mountain, spread like a banner, not pressed dense and close with deeps strangely moving, like the little sky above the collar.

The mountain lights were happiness possessed, sure of recurrence. But these skies, never to return, begged for remembrance.

The dry cold deepened, bringing sleep. Drunk, she felt now, with sleep; dizzy with gazing, and still there was no sign of the end. They were climbing a narrow track between a smooth high drift, a greying wall of snow, and a precipice sharply falling.

An opening; the floor of a wide valley. Mountains hemming it, exposed from base to summit, moving by as the sleigh sped along the level to where a fenced road led upwards. Up this steep road they went in a slow zigzag that brought the mountains across the way now right now left, and a glimpse ahead, against the sky, of a village, angles and peaks of low buildings sharply etched, quenched by snow, crushed between snow and snow, and in their midst the high snow-shrouded cone of a little church; Swiss village, lost in wastes of snow.

At a tremendous pace they jingled along a narrow street of shops and chalets that presently opened to a circle about the little church and narrowed again and ended, showing beyond, as the sleigh pulled up at the steps of a portico, rising ground and the beginning of pinewoods.

---

[1] German for "Beautiful – the final gleaming."   [2] German for "wonderfully beautiful."

Nook on Parnassus (1935)

Drawing incredulously nearer, I felt the fathomless preoccupations of marketing fall away and vanish.

Five, clipped together, one below the other, down the centre of the little window I had passed, almost daily, for months, aware of what it held, seeing what it held without needing to look. Today, summoning my eyes as I approached, these magnetic newcomers whose immediate gift – a sense of eternity in hand to spend as I chose – had set me free to pause and stare my adoration, soon turned them to search amongst their neighbours for a possible solution of the mystery of their own arrival amongst things able to evoke only the consciousness of passing the unvarying contents of a stationer's shop window.

Right and left hung limp floralities, executed entirely in half-witted pastel shades, unchildlike children, draped in floating films and posed, in the attitudes of dancing, amidst vegetation whose improbability was unredeemed by any touch of magic; truculent gnomes, self-consciously gesticulating from the tops of inanimate toadstools. Above, in a row, the customary photographs: frozen Royalties with unseeing eyes, alternating with Stars whose eyes saw only that which so eagerly they invited the observer to observe. Below, the usual piles, zigzag, of Bond and Club this and that;[1] envelopes to match.

Returning to my captors, I wondered along what pathway these five solitaries, keeping each other such splendid company, had reached the frame whence they offered me, in addition to the joy of their mere presence, a solution, easily and most blessedly at hand within the radius of a brief shopping round, the perfect solution of an annually recurrent problem. In size, they were comfortably larger than postcards and, no doubt, conspicuously thicker. Altogether more imposing, even when emerging, plain side uppermost, from their envelopes – I made a mental note of the special envelopes – than those perfect close-ups of west-country seagulls last year delighting so many of my urban friends.

Thankfully banishing "C.c."[2] from the formidable list of tasks to be fulfilled before I left town, I entered the shop.

Its counter repeated the appeals of its window, minus my treasures. Behind it appeared, coming forward from a dim background, the diminutive elderly woman still occasionally to be found attending the counters of small shops. The style of her dress, like that of her hair, or wig, a compact chignon, imperfectly dyed and most intricately braided, had been carried forward from the last century, together with her attitude towards a postulant customer, represented by the beam, vivid as a spark amidst dying ashes, whose mingling of craftily rapacious adoration and ill-contained impatience of the necessary ritual of salesmanship, reached me with the force of a personal assault.

By what means had she acquired, or been persuaded into acquiring, that inappropriate quintet?

"You have some reproductions in the window," I began, and saw the projected beam die out, leaving the eyes disgustedly surveying one of those customers who waste an hour selecting a twopenny card.

"'Ere they are," she muttered indifferently, lifting a yellowish claw in the direction of a winged pillar standing close at hand upon the crowded counter. With a murmur of apology, I turned to flip the revolving wings and find them composed, indeed, of the whole company, Stars, and gnomes, Royalties and fairy-footed children.

"Yes," I said appreciatively, "but you have some others, in the window – German reproductions of French masters."

Her uncertain pursuit of these technicalities ended, after a moment's reflection during which her eyes, grown round and almost gentle, became as thoughtful and detached as those of a meditating doctor, ended in a smile expressing both amusement and relief.

"Aow – *them!*"

First published in the British journal *Life and Letters Today* 133 (December 1935).

[1] Brand names for types of stationery paper.
[2] An abbreviation for "Christmas cards."

While bustling along to escape from behind the counter, she pointed eagerly towards the space beyond me. Swinging round, I found them, laid out upon a small table: the window quintet and several others, waiting to be apprehended, one by one. Wondering, as I faced her collection, whether I ought, penitently, to revise my estimate, I found her at my side, aware of my appreciative concentration and, in a moment, aware also of the desirability of offering a little assistance, if its desired result were to be achieved within a reasonable time.

"That's a pretty one," she said encouragingly, pointing to Dürer's[3] immortal nosegay, grown in a world familiar with "vilets, penny-a-bunch," so oddly modern and so quaintly commonplace, and added, after a moment's endurance of my silence and of the flow of time, during which, taking in, out here in the open, the presence of a weather-stained mackintosh and an ancient shopping bag, she had become uncertain as to the ultimate descent of the fruit dangling tantalisingly before her eyes: "Sixpence each," revealing the secret of her earlier change of mood and manner, and leaving the other secret, the link between herself and these new items of her stock, still to be fathomed.

"I must look at them all," I said, putting in time, and added, aching to be rid of her, unable while she remained, alien and unsharing at my side, even to investigate, still less gaze my fill: "Are these all you have?"

Muttering, she turned away so abruptly as to carry my unoccupied eyes to her retreating form, soon reaching a frosted door at the back of the shop, through which emerged, the moment it was opened and while still my side-tracked consciousness struggled with the problem of reckoning a total of forty-five sixpences, the radiant explanation of the mystery.

Her smock, the colour of a ripe orange, ardently supporting the red-gold of her bushed hair, may or may not have been the one worn during the final term of her course at the school of Art, whose lamentable sequel, inconceivable when first she had passed within its alluring door, she was now trying to redeem by introducing, amongst the detested wares of a sceptical employer, these radiant aliens. But the expression leaping to the eyes that met my own the moment before she advanced, slowly and with a trifle too much elegance, as if fastidiously picking her way through an unworthy universe, may well have inhabited them on the day she left that door for the last time, and now, temporarily restored by the vision of a customer standing before her miniature exhibition and therefore capable of paying tribute where she herself knew it to be due, was revealing, helplessly, and none the less pathetically for one's admiring certainty of her having come forth sternly self-propelled by intelligent appreciation of the depth and range of her insufficiency, the torment she had endured while being weighed in the balance and found wanting.

Within the depths of my embarrassment, I sought about for means of congratulating her, for some means of conveying an instanteously improvised idea: that every factory and shop in the kingdom should thankfully retain upon its staff at least one student of art. But when she reached my side and we stood together confronted by her gods, my desire to share, to take her by the arm and say, quietly and chummily, "Aren't they heavenly?" was checked by the chill aloofness reigning within her assumed air of courteous availability. I said, instead:

"I want some of these for Christmas cards, and it's almost impossible to choose," and immediately felt curious, even eager, to know which of the set, if she really felt she were being leaned upon, she would proceed to select.

"Yes."

The single word came forth so compactly, and the manner accompanying it, a faintly supercilious detachment, so clearly expressed her indifference to my dilemma that my thoughts retired upon the witness in the background, surely at this moment preparing a torrid discourse upon the subject of dealing with hesitant customers.

"Quite a number of D'yawrers," I hazarded, beginning, according to my plan – evolved while I realised, unless indeed this convenient shop should vanish, or its new feature, together with its new assistant, should disappear, that it would supply any number of solutions of the C.c. problem,

[3]   Albrecht Dürer (1471–1528), the greatest German artist of the Renaissance; his *Nosegay of Violets* is in the Albertina Museum, Vienna.

provided I took, each year, sufficient multiples of only one card – of choice by gradual elimination, at the last row.

"The Dürers are nice," she breathed, giving to the name a slight prominence and, to myself, unholy joy over her fragment of delight in parading correctitude, and joy, equally unholy, in recalling my own pride in a perfect pronounciation of foreign names; pride that was to die a painless, natural death in association with those amongst whom my knowledge and appreciation of the pictures by whose ghosts we were confronted, had been born and had gradually become inseparable from the comfortably anglicised form of the names of their creators. Wondering whether, in these days of universal travel, the youngest generation of art students were mostly linguists, I went on up my rows, again, in my entrancement, abandoning my ape-like ability to reproduce every sort of native sound until, once again, she rebuked me.

"Toolooze-*Low*treck,"[4] I had murmured, "Gogang[5] ... van Go[6] ... Mannay.[7] Impossible to choose."

Immediately upon the end of my despairing sigh, came her voice, quiet and very clear:

"Toulouse-Lau*trec* is charming." "Dashing and elegant," I countered, and blushed to the soul for my cruelty. "M'yes," she retorted irritably and drove hurriedly onward: "the Mahnehs, too ..." "Overwhelming. They come for you with both fists."

"Oh," she simpered disdainfully – recalling perhaps, the silencing of some extravagant youngster by an assertion from on high to the effect that a picture is a picture and is either, for various ascertainable reasons, hard to learn, "but that is what you are here for," a good or a bad picture – and murmured, with the hint in her voice of a malicious smile: "*Not* then, very suitable for your purpose."

This would not do at all. This brawling in church must cease, or the card I selected would be under a curse. Dumbly, hesitantly, I extended a random finger, hoping for some kind of unity.

"Gaugin," she breathed, relenting, "is *always* wonderful." ("Powerfully averted and inverted," I amended, but succeeded in preventing the words from reaching the battlefield.) "But perhaps, for your purpose, this particular van Goch ..." Is the gutteral quite so Scotch I wondered, and then realised with relief that she had reached the end of her little exhibition. Whichever I should proceed to choose there were no more names to pronounce and, since mercifully she had not distracted my attention by giving this artist an inappropriate label, there was now no barrier to unity, born suddenly between us of the happiness of her choice. This sufficiently applauded, and her agreement almost secured for my proclamation of a sunlit kitchen garden, crowded from side to side with buoyant vegetables, as eminently suited to greet the eye at the darkest moment of the year, we turned to settle the question of the envelopes and, although the movements of her hands about the counter expressed both uncertainty and the distaste inspired by the processes to be mastered in the course of "learning the business," we had soon found a perfect fit.

But the little old lady, again to the fore and watchful, immediately pounced. "Too thin," she ruled, with eager scorn. "*These* are what you want. Ninepence the packet."

Though well aware that the old wretch was trading upon my delight, I meekly sought my purse. By the time I had solved this second problem in mental arithmetic, the girl had vanished. Frostily, I paid for my one card and the many envelopes. Perhaps when I called for the rest of the cards, truly, I reflected on her behalf, a handsome order, I might meet my little friend again.

Reaching the street, and again surveying the window, I discerned in a remote corner a mall notice: "Artists' Materials." Behind it stood a bundle of pencils and a roll of Whatman.[8] A new line, for the little woman's little shop, whose items were by her considered insufficiently tasty to appear amongst the gnomes, fairies and Bonds. And the young woman, newly at work on the first job that

---

[4] Henri de Toulouse Lautrec (1864–1901), French artist, famous for his paintings of cabarets, bars, and bordellos.

[5] Paul Gauguin (1848–1903), French artist famous for his paintings of life in the South Seas.

[6] Vincent Van Gogh (1853–90), a Dutch artist, famous for his landscapes.

[7] Eduard Manet (1832–83), French artist famous for *Le déjeuner sur l'herbe* (1863) and *Olympia* (1865), among many others.

[8] Whatman was a brand of especially fine paper that was manufactured from 1753 to 1976. It was used by artists such as John James Audubon, or selected for personal correspondence by notables such as Queen Victoria.

had offered, and trying at least to be a door-keeper in the house of Art, had scored, this afternoon, her first triumph over her employer's incredulity?

The Reality of Feminism (1917)

During the first few decades of its existence, English feminism was the conscious acceptance by women of the diagnosis of the cynics and an attempt to deal with this diagnosis by placing upon environment the major part of the responsibility for feminine "failings." It declared that the faults of women were the faults of the slave, and were due to repressions, educational and social. Remove these repressions, and the failings would disappear. Feminists of both sexes devoted themselves to securing for women educational and social opportunities equal to those of men. The "higher" education of women was their watchword, the throwing open of the liberal professions their goal, and the demonstration of the actual equality of women and men the event towards which they confidently moved. It followed that only a very small number of women was affected. Only one class of women, the class well-dowered by circumstance, could be counted upon to supply recruits for the demonstration of the intellectual "quality" of women. This feminism was, therefore, in practice, a class feminism – feminism for ladies. In principle much had been gained. The exclusively sexual estimate of women had received its death-blow. But it soon became apparent that academic education and the successful pursuit of a profession implied a renunciation of domesticity. The opening heaven of "emancipation" narrowed to the sad and sterile vista – feminism for spinsters. From that moment public opinion see-sawed between the alternatives of discrediting domesticity and of dividing women into two types – "ordinary" women, who married, and "superior" women, who did not. But for at least one whole generation the belief in academic distinction as the way of emancipation for women was unclouded by any breath of doubt. The reaction which was later on to produce the formula of "university standards in home training" had barely set in when the whole fabric of feminist theory was challenged by the appearance of Charlotte Stetson's *Women and Economics*.[1] Opening her attack with a diagnosis of the female sex, which outdoes all the achievements of the cynics, she joined the earlier feminists in laying the responsibility for the plight of womanhood at the door of circumstance; but in a much more thorough-going fashion and with a backward and forward sweep which not only lifted the question out of the dimensions of an empirical problem and related it to the development of life as a whole, but purged it of the note of antagonism that characterises the bulk of feminist literature.

Woman as a purely sexual product, said this American feminist, is a quite recent development in the western world; and it is commerce that has produced her. Woman was a differentiated social human being earlier than man. The "savage" woman who first succeeded in retaining her grown son at her side, invented social life. Up to the era of machinery, *i.e.*, during the agricultural and civic centuries, the home was the centre of productive service. The scientific development of industry, while it did much to humanise the male – even though his commerce was as aggressive as his flint implements and his fleets of coracles – worked upon the female as a purely desocialising influence. By driving the larger industries from the homestead, it forced her either to follow them into the factory and workshop, to the destruction of home life, or to remain in a home that was no longer a centre of vital industries, but an isolated centre of consumption and destruction on a scale regulated entirely by the market value of its male owner. She became either an industrial pawn or a social parasite. Success on the part of the man completed her parasitic relationship to life by turning her into an increasingly elaborate consumer. Henceforth her sole asset was her sex, her sole means of expression her personal relationship to some specific male – father, brother, husband or son. She

First published in the journal *Ploughshare*, n.s. 2.8 (September 1917), this essay reviewed four recent books, which are cited below in notes 2, 12, 14, and 15.
[1] *Women and Economics* (Boston: Small, Maynard, 1898) was published by the American feminist Charlotte Perkins Gilman (1860–1935) under the name Charlotte Stetson; Charlotte married Charles Stetson in 1884 and divorced him a few years later, but continued to use his name throughout her adult life until 1932, when she married her second cousin George H. Gilman. She is best known as the author of "The Yellow Wallpaper."

lived on her power to "charm." Sentiment flourished like a monstrous orchid. Home-life, over-focussed and over-heated, was cut off finally from the life of the world. Men kept their balance by living in two spheres, but the two spheres, "the world" and "the home," were so completely at variance that he could realise himself fully in neither, and was condemned to pose in each, to the annulling of his manhood. The average female, living by and through sex, missed womanhood, but achieved a sort of harmony by a thorough-going exploitation of sex. The home, all over-emphasised femininity, and the world, all over-specialised maleness, cancelled and nullified each other.

The way through this *impasse*, said Mrs. Stetson, was for women to follow the commercialised home industries into the world and to socialise them. Armies of women have been driven perforce into the industrial machine, heavily handicapped underlings, working under conditions they have been powerless to alter. They must now advance in a body, boldly and consciously, taking their old rank as producers, administrators, doing the world's housekeeping in the world. In order that they may do this, "homelife" as we know it, must be reorganised. The millions of replicas of tiny kitchens and nurseries, served by isolated women, must disappear. The world must become a home. In it women will pursue socially valuable careers, responsible to the community for their work, assured by the community of an economic status clear of sex and independent of their relationship to any specific male. They will spend their days at the work they can do best, whether nursery work, education, or mechanical engineering, finding their places in the social fabric as freely as do their brothers. Houses, communally cleansed and victualled, will remain as meeting-places for rest and recreation.

It was impossible to ignore Mrs. Stetson's facts. Her challenge left English feminists in two distinct groups, the one standing for the sexual and economic independence of all women, irrespective of class, and working towards the complete socialisation of industry, the other ignoring or deprecating the industrial activities of women and standing for the preservation of the traditional insulated home; seeking to improve the status of women by giving them votes, solving woman's economic problem by training her in youth to earn her living, "if need be."

These two mutually exclusive groups were caught up into the suffrage campaign; the one with the motive of transforming the conditions of female labour, the other because the capture of political power was part of the process of securing the recognition of the essential equality of women and men. The war has played into the hands of both parties by demonstrating the social efficiency of women and by giving an unprecedented urgency to the problem of woman in industry. The "equality" suffragists have secured a partial victory on the score of the proven ability of women to act as substitutes for men. The industrial suffragists rejoice in the spectacle of the disintegrated home, the inauguration of the municipal kitchen, and the fact that the promoters of infant welfare are more and more insistently emphasising the necessity for the municipal crèche.

Mrs. Stetson's forecast appears to be on the way to fulfilment, and those who are looking to the co-operation of women as the decisive factor in the achievement of the industrial revolution joyously welcome the independent and powerful restatement of Mrs. Stetson's main proposition that has recently come from the pen of Miss Wilma Meikle. Miss Meikle is a very thorough-going feminist, and the vigour and beauty of her work – by far the best attempt at constructive feminism which has yet appeared in England – is obviously the product of a profound faith. She evidently sympathises with the militant phases of the suffrage movement in its spirit of pure revolt and self-assertion rather than with the aspects represented by "women delicately unaware of the kitchen side of politics, genteelly unacquainted with the stupendous significance of commerce, women who had been bred in drawing-rooms where the ruling class posed as men whose power was based upon culture and oratory,"[2] women for whom "life was bowdlerised into a Mary Ward novel";[3] and she sympathises with the men who reach Parliament through sheer individual worth in public life

[2] Wilma Meikle, *Towards a Sane Feminism* (London: Grant Richards, 1916), 21, describing the leaders of middle-class feminism.
[3] Meikle, *Towards a Sane Feminism*, 21–2, omitting the words "for their womenfolk" between "bowdlerised" and "into" and again describing the "nieces and spinsters" of "the ruling class." Mary Augusta Ward, née Arnold and known as "Mrs. Humphry Ward," became famous when her second novel *Robert Elsmere* (1888) became a bestseller. Regarded for a while as George Eliot's successor, she produced a string of successful novels. In 1908 she became president of the Women's Anti-Suffrage League.

rather than "obscure men like Thomas Babington Macaulay and Benjamin Disraeli,[4] who had been rushed into social eminence by their flowing rhetoric at Westminster." But she is only incidentally a suffragist. The main argument of her book is a recantation of the whole of the suffrage movement. She is entirely sceptical as to the value of a parliamentary franchise which leaves the industrial masses at the mercy of political legislation, and believes that the way to political power is through industrial power, through the trades union and the power of the worker to transform his environment and make his own terms. Women must build up their power upon the basis of industrial organisation. "They must serve and work, and they must join[5] the workers' surging revolt against the denial of things that make existence life, their hunger for knowledge and their desire for leisure, and their determination to have both."[6] It follows that "the lady," "delicately sympathetic, alluringly reticent, consistently courteous and skilfully environed,"[7] must go. She is, even at her best, comparable to the Circassian, bred charmingly from her infancy to be the light of some good man's harem. Her caprices were an incentive to industrial enterprise, she helped the troubadours to invent "manners," she provided a market for the wares of the artist. But science and commerce and art are now no longer dependent on her greed. She is an anachronism. Home life must be re-organised to set her free to work.

> "The great Domestic Cant of Good Wifehood and Good Motherhood has tied the average woman into such a tangle of hypocrisies that she cannot unravel herself sufficiently to be a distinct personality.... Before long she is exhausted by hypocrisy. Her self-distrust lashes her to a duster, her determining to appear what she is not is a magnet that keeps her inextricably fastened to her servants or her cooking stove ... her nerves are racked by the effort to live up to the Good Mother ideal. There is no fun left in her."[8]

With the Great Domestic Cant weighing our women down under "the absurdly complicated organisation of the family there remains no cause for wonder that in spite of higher education, in spite of feminism, original thought amongst women is almost non-existent."[9] Her financial independence must be secured. She must learn to think her own thoughts and form her own judgments in contact with actuality. All the freedoms there are can be claimed by her without the vote once she demonstrates her industrial indispensability and organises her ranks against those who would exploit her. Parliamentary life will follow rather than precede feminine emancipation. Finally, women in the mass, set free from their dependence upon a single masculine pocket for everything they desire in addition to food and clothing, will find it possible to live a full life,

> "and the old restlessness which has almost universally lowered the value of their work will at last be stilled ... and with the full and final accomplishment of women's lives will come the end of feminism by its ultimate absorption into the common cause of humanity."[10]

To many minds this vision of homeless womanhood caught equally with man in the industrial machine, interested equally with man in "earning a living," differentiated from man only by her occasional evanescent relationship to an infant, will bring nothing but dismay. They will see life shorn of roses and turned into a workshop. They will see the qualities that are "far above rubies"[11] and can never be paid for, going by the board. In other words, they attach more importance to environment than to humanity. They have no faith in the qualities they wish to "preserve." They

4   Meikle, *Towards a Sane Feminism*, 22. Thomas Babington Macaulay (1800–59) was a politician noted for his rhetorical flourishes and an author remembered chiefly for his five-volume *History of England*; Benjamin Disraeli (1804–91) was a novelist and politician who was twice prime minster (1868, 1874–80).
5   These are Dorothy Richardson's words, which have been spliced on to the quotation from Meikle that follows.
6   "*the workers' surging revolt ... determination to have both*." Meikle, *Towards a Sane Feminism*, 57. The sentence in the original begins "It was the workers' surging revolt ..." and following

"their determination to have both" it continues "that gave the death-blow to the middle-class snobbishness of the suffragists."
7   "*the lady ... skilfully environed*" Meikle, *Towards a Sane Feminism*, 60–1.
8   Meikle, *Towards a Sane Feminism*, 138–9. Richardson's first ellipses signals the omission of three sentences; her second, some further phrases and a sentence totaling 36 words.
9   Meikle, *Towards a Sane Feminism*, 141.
10   Meikle, *Towards a Sane Feminism*, 167–8.
11   "The price of wisdom is above rubies" (Job 28:18).

have no faith in womanhood. The apparent over-preoccupation of the feminists with environment is a very different thing. It is based on faith in womanhood, although both its reasoning and its demands make it appear that they regard women as potential men, obstructed by the over-elaborated machinery of the home.

But the fact of woman remains, the fact that she is relatively to man, *synthetic*. Relatively to man she sees life whole and harmonious. Men tend to fix life, to fix aspects. They create metaphysical systems, religions, arts, and sciences. Woman is metaphysical, religious, an artist and scientist in life. Let anyone who questions the synthetic quality of women ask himself why it is that she can move, as it were in all directions at once, why, with a man-astonishing ease, she can "take up" everything by turns, while she "originates" nothing? Why she can grasp a formula, the "trick" of male intellect, and the formula once grasped, so often beat a man at his own game? Why, herself "nothing," she is such an excellent critic of "things"? Why she can solve and reconcile, revealing the points of unity between a number of conflicting males – a number of embodied theories furiously raging together. Why the "free lance," the woman who is independent of any specific male, does this so excellently, and why the one who owes subsistence to a single male is usually loyally and violently partisan in public, and the wholesome opposite in private? And let him further ask himself why the great male synthetics, the artists and mystics, are three-parts woman? That women are needed "in the world" in their own right and because of their difference to men is clearly recognised in Canon Streeter's[12] book on *Woman in the Church*. But for him difference constitutes inferiority. He confesses that the present bankruptcy of the church is largely owing to the exclusion of women, and he calls for a cautious and partial admission of women into the ministry. It is not, he thinks, advisable that they should be admitted to the priesthood as long as the priest stands in a position of authority. In a democratised church system women as priests might, in time, be thinkable. For the present, the completion of the male church might be brought about by a large co-operation of women in the work and the deliberations of the church. Incidentally, it occurs to him that such a recognition of the feminine element in religion would act as a curb to the heresy of Mariolatry. In other words, women are to be admitted into a carefully regulated share in the working of a divine institution because during the centuries of their exclusion it has become progressively impotent, but they are to be excluded from its full powers and privileges because there is no divine principle in womanhood. Canon Streeter has never asked himself why Mariolatry has established itself tyrannously at the very heart of the liveliest system of man-made theology. He has made nothing of the fact that a male priesthood, having usurped authority and driven women from the early position of workers side by side with men, ordained priests equally with men by the laying on of hands, immediately reinstated her, enthroned above them as the Queen of Heaven. The Hebrew Jehovah, imagined as male, could not satisfy them. The deifying of Mary was an unconscious expression of their need to acknowledge the feminine element in Godhead. Canon Streeter is the male Protestant, caught in the Protestant cul-de-sac "he for God only, she for God in him."[13] The acknowledgment reached unconsciously in Mariolatry has been reached consciously by the "heresy" of Quakerism. The early Quakers, wrapped as they were as "men" in secular fear and distrust of "woman," did not dare to deny her her human heritage of divine light and bravely took in the dark the leap of admitting her to full ministry. Only the Protestants have left her out altogether. Canon Streeter may reply that Quakerism is a democratised faith, and is heretical in its exclusion of priest and sacrament, thus underlining his dilemma. There is no alternative. Woman springs to the centre of an aristocratic church system – because men will have her there.

She walks into a democratic church system, man's equal, in her own right. If Anglicanism, to save its life, democratises itself and admits women to full fellow-ship, it will leave Catholicism in possession of the field as the typical classical church with Mariolatry a part of its system, the memorial for all time of the emptiness of the dream of male supremacy. A similar begging of

---

[12]   Burnett Hillman Streeter (1874–1937) wrote more than 40 nonfiction books on a wide variety of topics, including *Women in the Church* (London: T. Fisher Unwin, 1917).

[13]   John Milton, *Paradise Lost*, IV.299.

the whole question of women in the ministry distinguishes Mr. T. B. Allworthy's[14] recent valuable contribution to the history of women in the Apostolic church. He accounts for the activities of women in the early church by the fact that this church was social and not separated. Let the church once more become an integral part of social life and women will achieve their proper share in church life. How, one would like to ask, is the church to achieve the becoming an integral part of social life save by the free admission of women in their own right? The last book on our list[15] is a résumé of all that women have done and suffered in their contest with the idea that a woman cannot be a legislator. Its author is of opinion that political enfranchisement is an essential part of feminine education, and Mr. Houseman, who contributes a preface, agrees in the sense that the great need of women is the need of a corporate consciousness, that such a consciousness was unattainable by her during the years of artificial segregation, and that it has been achieved by means of the agitation which has arisen for the ending of this segregation.

Taken together, these four books are a fairly inclusive statement of feminist thought to date. They are, in spite of their common tendency to contrast a "dark" past with a "bright" future, to separate environment from life and to regard environment as the more potent factor, a very remarkable convergence of recognition, coming from minds differing as to the why and wherefore, the ways and means of "feminism" upon the divine-human fact of womanhood. This is the essential thing. A fearless constructive feminism will re-read the past in the light of its present recognition of the synthetic consciousness of woman; will recognise that this consciousness has always made its own world, irrespective of circumstances. It can be neither enslaved nor subjected. Man, the maker of formulæ, has tried in vain, from outside, to "solve the problem" of woman. He has gone off on lonely quests. He has constructed theologies, arts, sciences, philosophies. Each one in turn has stiffened into lifeleness or become the battle-ground of conflicting theories. He has sought his God in the loneliness of his thought-ridden mind, in the beauty of the reflex of life in art, in the wonder of his analysis of matter, in the curious maps of life turned out by the philosophising intellect. Woman has remained curiously untroubled and complete. He has hated and loved and feared her as mother nature, feared and adored her as the unattainable, the Queen of Heaven; and now, at last, nearing the solution of the problem, he turns to her as companion and fellow pilgrim, suspecting in her relatively undivided harmonious nature an intuitive solution of the quest that has agonised him from the dawn of things. At the same moment his long career as fighter and destroyer comes to an end; an end that is the beginning of a new glory of strife. In the pause of deadly combat he sees the long past in a flash. He had ceased in principle to be a fighter before the war. With the deliberate conscious ending of his role of fighter, with his deliberate renunciation of the fear of his neighbour will come the final metamorphosis of his fear of "woman." Face to face with the life of the world as one life he will find it his business to solve not the problem of "woman" who has gained at last the whole world for her home, but of man the specialist; the problem of the male in a world where his elaborate outfit of characteristics as fighter, in warfare, in trade, and in politics, is left useless on his hands.

Women and the Future (1924)

Most of the prophecies born of the renewed moral visibility of woman, though superficially at war with each other, are united at their base. They meet and sink, in the sands of the assumption that we are, today, confronted with a new species of woman.

Nearly all of the prophets, nearly all of those who are at work constructing hells, or heavens, upon this loose foundation, are men. And their crying up, or down, of the woman of today, as contrasted to the woman of the past, is easily understood when we consider how difficult it is, even

[14]   Thomas Bateson Allworthy (1879–?), author of *Women in the Apostolic Church: A Critical Study of the Evidence in the New Testament for the Prominence of Women in Early Christianity* (Cambridge: W. Heffer & Sons, 1917).

[15]   Agnes Edith Metcalfe, *Woman's Effort: A Chronicle of British*

Women's Fifty Years' Struggle for Citizenship, 1865–1914 (Oxford: B. H. Blackwell, 1917).

WOMEN AND THE FUTURE
This essay was first published in *Vanity Fair* 22(2) (April 1924).

for the least prejudiced, to *think* the feminine past, to escape the images that throng the mind from the centuries of masculine expressiveness on the eternal theme: expressiveness that has so rarely reached beyond the portrayal of woman, whether Madonna, Diana, or Helen,[1] in her moments of relationship to the world as it is known to men.

Even the pioneers of feminism, Mill, Buckle,[2] and their followers, looked only to woman as she was to be in the future, making, for her past, polite, question-begging excuses. The poets, with one exception, accepted the old readings. There is little to choose between the visions of Catholic Rossetti and Swinburne[3] the Pagan. Tennyson,[4] it is true, crowns woman, elaborately, and withal a little irritably, and with much logic-chopping. But he never escapes patronage, and leaves her leaning heavily, albeit most elegantly, upon the arm of man. Browning stands apart, and Stopford Brooke[5] will not be alone in asking what women themselves think of Browning's vision of woman as both queen and Lord, outstripping man not only in the wisdom of the heart, but in that of the brain also.

And there is Meredith[6] – with his shining reputation for understanding; a legend that by far outruns his achievement. Glimpses of woman as a full cup unto herself, he certainly had. And he reveals much knowledge of men as they appear in the eyes of such women. This it is that has been accounted unto him for righteousness. He never sees that he is demanding the emancipation of that which he has shown to be independent of bonds. Hardy,[7] his brother pagan and counterpart, is Perseus hastening to Andromeda,[8] seeking the freedom of the bound.

Since the heyday of Meredith and Hardy, batallions of women have become literate and, in the incandescence of their revelations, masculine illusions are dying like flies. But, even today, most men are scarely aware of the search-light flung by these revelations across the past. These modern women, they say, are a new type.

It does not greatly matter to women that men cling to this idea. The truth about the past can be trusted to look after itself. There is, however, no illusion more wasteful than the illusion of beginning all over again; nothing more misleading than the idea of being divorced from the past. It is, nevertheless, quite probable that feminine insistence on exhuming hatchets is not altogether a single-hearted desire to avoid waste and error.

Many men, moreover, are thoroughly disconcerted by the "Modern Woman." They sigh for ancient mystery and inscrutability. For *La Giaconda*[9] ... And the most amazing thing in the

---

[1]   Diana was a Roman goddess of the hunt, associated with the moon and commonly worshiped in wooded places; Helen, in Greek mythology, was the daughter of Zeus and Leda, for whose sake the Trojan War was fought, as recounted by Homer in the *Iliad*.

[2]   John Stuart Mill (1806–73) was a British philosopher and social theorist noted, among other things, for his essay on "The Subjection of Women" (1869), most accessible in John Stuart Mill, *Three Essays*, introduction by Richard Wollheim (New York: Oxford University Press, 1975), 427–548; Henry Thomas Buckle (1822–62) was an historian, famous during the period 1860–1940 for his *History of Civilization*, 2 vols. (1857, 1861), but also noted for an essay on "The Influence of Women on the Progress of Knowledge," first delivered as a lecture at the Royal Institution in March 1858 and published posthumously in *Essays by Henry Thomas Buckle* (New York: D. Appleton, 1863; Leipzig: F. A. Brockhaus, 1867), 127–64.

[3]   Dante Gabriel Rossetti (1828–82) was a British poet, prominent among a group known as the Pre-Raphaelites, noted for his sensual depictions of women; Algernon Charles Swinburne (1837–1909) was also a British poet affiliated with the Pre-raphaelites, and also noted for sensual depictions of women.

[4]   Alfred Tennyson (1809–92) was the preeminent Victorian poet whose views on women found expression in his long poem *The Princess* (1847).

[5]   Robert Browning (1812–89) was a British poet, considered second only to Tennyson during his lifetime. Stopford Augustus

Brooke (1832–1912) was a British divine and man of letters. In his study of *The Poetry of Robert Browning* (London: Ibister, 1903), 354, he writes: "I sometimes wonder what women themselves think of the things Browning, speaking through their mouth, makes them say ... " On the same page he also notes that "in so many poems the women [in Browning] are represented as of a finer, even a stronger intellect than the men. Many poets have given them a finer intuition; that is a common representation. But greater intellectual power allotted to women is only to be found in Browning."

[6]   George Meredith (1828–1909) was a British novelist, noted for his allegedly sympathetic treatment of women in novels such as *Diana of the Crossways* (1885) or *The Amazing Marriage* (1895).

[7]   Thomas Hardy (1840–1928), British novelist and poet, was noted for his sympathetic portrayal of women in novels such as *Tess of the d'Urbervilles* (1891) and *Jude the Obscure* (1894–5).

[8]   Perseus is a mythological hero who rescues Andromeda, who has been chained to a rock on the sea-shore and exposed to a monster; the story is recounted in Apollodorus, *The Library of Greek Mythology* (Oxford: Oxford University Press, 1997), Book 2.

[9]   The name of the painting by Leondardo da Vinci (1452–1519), more popularly known in English as the *Mona Lisa*.

history of Leonardo's masterpiece is their general failure to recognize that Lisa stands alone in feminine portraiture because she is centered, unlike her nearest peers, those dreamful, passionately blossoming imaginations of Rossetti, neither upon humanity nor upon the consolations of religion.

The essential egoist

It is because she is so completely *there* that she draws men like a magnet. Never was better artistic bargain driven than between Leonardo and this lady who sat to him for years; who sat so long that she grew at home in her place, and the deepest layer of her being, her woman's enchanted domestication within the sheer marvel of existing, came forth and shone through the mobile mask of her face. Leonardo of the innocent eye, his genius concentrated upon his business of making a good picture, caught her, unawares, on a gleeful, cosmic holiday. And in seeking the highest, in going on till he got what he wanted, he reaped also the lesser things. For there is in Lisa more than the portrayal of essential womanhood. The secondary life of the lady is clearly visible. Her traffic with familiar webs, with her household and the external shapings of life. When Pater said that her eyelids were a little weary,[10] he showed himself observant. But he misinterpreted the weariness.

On the part of contemporary artists, there are, here and there, attempts to resuscitate man's ancient mystery woman, the beloved-hated abyss. The intensest and the most affrighted of these essayists are D. H. Lawrence and Augustus John.[11] Perhaps they are nearer salvation than they know.

For the essential characteristic of women is egoism. Let it at once be admitted that this is a masculine discovery. It has been offered as the worst that can be said of the sex as a whole. It is both the worst and the best. Egoism is at once the root of shameless selfishness and the ultimate dwelling place of charity. Many men, of whom Mr. Wells[12] is the chief spokesman, read the history of woman's past influence in public affairs as one long story of feminine egoism. They regard her advance with mixed feelings, and face her with a neat dilemma. Either, they say, you must go on being Helens and Cinderellas, or you must drop all that and play the game, in so far as your disabilities allow, as we play it. They look forward to the emergence of an army of civilized, docile women, following modestly behind the vanguard of males at work upon the business of reducing chaos to order.

Another group of thinkers sees the world in process of feminisation, the savage wilderness, where men compete and fight, turned into a home. Over against them are those who view the opening prospect with despair. To them, feminism is the invariable accompaniment of degeneration. They draw back in horror before the oncoming flood of mediocrity. They see ahead a democratized world, overrun by hordes of inferior beings, organized by majorities for material ends; with primitive, uncivilizable woman rampant in the midst.

Serenely apart from these small camps is a large class of delightful beings, the representatives of average masculinity at its best, drawing much comfort from the spectacle of contradictory, mysterious woman at last bidding fair to become something recognizably like itself. Women, they say, are beginning to take life like men; are finding in life the things men have found. They make room for her. They are charming. Their selfishness is social, gregarious. Woman is to be the jolly companion; to co-operate with man in the great business of organizing the world for jollity. But have any of these so variously grouped males any idea of the depth and scope of feminine

---

[10]   Walter Horatio Pater (1839–94), British critic and novelist, in his book on the Renaissance, wrote of La Gioconda or the Mona Lisa: "Hers is the head upon which all 'the ends of the world are come,' and the eyelids are a little weary." See Walter Pater, *The Renaissance: Studies in Art and Poetry*, ed. Donald Hill (Berkeley: University of California, 1980), 98. Pater, in turn, is quoting from I Corinthians 10:11: "Now all these things happened unto them for examples: and they are written for our admonition, upon whom the ends of the world are come."

[11]   D. H. Lawrence (1885–1930) was a British novelist noted for an obsessive interest in women; Augustus John (1878–1961) was a British painter noted for many paintings of his wife, Dorelia McNeill, and after 1920 for his many portraits of the great and famous.
[12]   H. G. Wells (1866–1946) was a prolific writer and novelist, noted for his sympathetic depiction of a "new woman" in *Anne Veronica* (1909) as well as his less sympathetic account of their historical role in his *The Outline of History* (1920).

egoism? Do they not confound it with masculine selfishness? Do they realize anything of the vast difference between these two things?

It is upon the perception of this difference that any verdict as to the result of woman's arrival "in the world" ultimately rests. Though, it is true, certain of these masculine forecasts are being abundantly realized. There is abroad in life a growing army of man-trained women, brisk, positive, rational creatures with no nonsense about them, living from the bustling surfaces of the mind; sharing the competitive partisanships of men; subject, like men, to fear; subject to national panic; to international, and even to cosmic panic. There is also an army let loose of the daughters of the horse-leech; part of the organization of the world for pleasure. These types have always existed. The world of the moment particularly favours them. But their egoism is as nothing to the egoism of the womanly woman, the beloved-hated abyss, at once the refuge and the despair of man.

For the womanly woman lives, all her life, in the deep current of eternity, an individual, self-centered. Because she is one with life, past, present, and future are together in her, unbroken. Because she thinks flowingly, with her feelings, she is relatively indifferent to the fashions of men, to the momentary arts, religions, philosophies, and sciences, valuing them only in so far as she is aware of their importance in the evolution of the beloved. It is man's incomplete individuality that leaves him at the mercy of that subtle form of despair which is called ambition, and accounts for his apparent selfishness. Only completely self-centered consciousness can attain to unselfishness – the celebrated unselfishness of the womanly woman. Only a complete self, carrying all its goods in its own hands, can go out, perfectly, to others, move freely in any direction. Only a complete self can afford to man the amusing spectacle of the chameleon woman.

Apart from the saints, the womanly woman is the only human being free to try to be as good as she wants to be. And it is to this inexorable creature, whom even Nietzsche[13] was constrained to place ahead of man, that man returns from his wanderings with those others in the deserts of agnosticism. She is rare. But wherever she is found, there also are found the dependent hosts.

But is not the material of this intuitive creature strictly limited? Is she not fettered by sex? Seeking man, while man, freed by nature for his divine purpose, seeks God, through blood and tears, through trial and error, in every form of civilization? He for God only, she for God in him?[14] She is. She does. When man announces that the tree at the door of the cave is God, she excels him in the dark joy of the discovery. When he reaches the point of saying that God is a Spirit and they that worship him must worship him in spirit and in truth, she is there waiting for him, ready to parrot any formula that shows him aware of the amazing fact of life.

And it is this creature who is now on the way to be driven out among the practical affairs of our world, together with the "intelligent" woman; i.e., with the woman who is intelligible to men. For the first time. Unwillingly. The results cannot be exactly predicted. But her gift of imaginative sympathy, her capacity for vicarious living, for being simultaneously in all the warring camps, will tend to make her within the council of nations what the Quaker is within the council of religions.

Women in the future

Public concerted action must always be a compromise. But there is all the difference between having things roughly arranged *ad hoc* by father, however strong his sense of abstract justice, and having them arranged by father prompted by mother, under the unseen presidency of desire to do the best regardless, in the woman's regardless, unprincipled, miracle-working way, for all concerned.

The world at large is swiftly passing from youthful freebooting. It is on the way to find itself married. That is to say, in for startling changes. Shaken up. Led by the nose and liking it. A question arises. How will his apparently lessened state react on man? In how far has he been dependent on his illusion of supremacy? Perhaps the answer to this is the superiority of men in talent, in constructive

---

[13] Friedrich Wilhelm Nietzsche (1844–1900) was a German philosopher; the passage in which he places woman ahead of man has not been identified.

[14] John Milton, *Paradise Lost*, IV.299.

capacity. It is the talent of man, his capacity to *do* most things better than women, backed up by the genius of woman. The capacity to *see* that is carrying life forward to the levels opening out ahead.

Women in the Arts (1925)

It is only lately that the failure of women in the fine arts has achieved pre-eminence in the *cause célèbre*, Man versus Woman, as a witness for the prosecution. In the old days, not only was art not demanded of women, but the smallest sign of genuine ability in a female would put a man in the state of mind of the lady who said when she saw the giraffe: "I don't believe it."

Thus Albrecht Dürer,[1] travelling through the Netherlands in 1521 and happening upon the paintings of Susanne Horebout, makes appreciative notes in his diary, but is constrained to add: "Amazing that a she-creature should accomplish so much." And some three hundred years later, Gustave Flaubert, standing at the easel of Madame Commanville, smiles indulgently and murmurs: "Yes, she has talent; it is *odd*."

But today, under pressure of the idea that women in asserting equality, have also asserted identity with men, the demand for art as a supporting credential has become the parrot-cry of the masculinists of both sexes. A cry that grows both strident and hoarse. For this pre-eminent witness for the prosecution is, poor fellow, shockingly over-worked. And not only over-worked but also a little uneasy. Feeling no doubt, since most of his fellows have been hustled away in disgrace and those that remain are apt to wilt in the hands of defending counsel, that his own turn may be at hand.

But though towering a little insecurely still he towers, at once the last refuge of all who are frightened by anything that disturbs their vision of man as the dominant sex, and the despair of those feminists who believe fine art to be the highest human achievement.

There are of course many, an increasing band, who flatly deny that art is the highest human achievement and place ahead of it all that is called science, which they are inclined to regard as the work of humanity's post-adolescence. But it is a curious and notable fact, a fact quite as curious and notable as the absence of first-class feminine art, that all these people, whenever they want to enlighten the layman on the subject of the scientific imagination, are at pains to explain that the scientific imagination, at its best, is the imagination of the artist. It is not less odd that the man of science if he is masculinist, will, when hard-pressed, seize, to belabour his opponent, not the test-tube, but the mahlstick. (It is of course to be remembered that while the mahlstick is solid and persists unchanging, the test-tube is hollow and its contents variable.) And the rush for the mahlstick goes on in spite of the fact that the witness for science does not, on the whole, have a bad time. He has perhaps lost a little of his complacency. But he can still, when counsel for the defense reminds the jury how recently women have had access to scientific material and education, point to the meagre, uninstructed beginnings of some of the world's foremost men of science.

Side by side with the devotees of science we find those who count religion the highest human achievement. They are a house divided. In so far as they set in the van the mystic – the religious genius who uses not marble or pigment or the written word, but his own life as the medium of his

First published in *Vanity Fair* 24(3) (May 1925).
[1] Albrecht Dürer (1471–1528), a great German artist of the Renaissance, traveled to the Netherlands in 1520–1 and kept a journal recording his experiences. In Antwerp he met a painter of illuminated manuscripts named Gerard Horenbout or Gerhard Horebout of Ghent (c. 1465–c. 1541), whose daughter Susanna was also an illuminator. In Dürer's words: "Master Gerhard, the illuminator, has a daughter about 18 years old named Susanna. She has illuminated a *Salvator* [a Saviour] on a little sheet, for which I gave her 1 fl. It is very wonderful that a woman can do so much" (W. M. Conway [ed.]), *The Literary Remains of Albrecht Dürer* (Cambridge: Cambridge University Press, 1898), 120). In the original German the text reads: "Item Meister Gerhart, Illuminist, hat ein Töchterlein bei 18 Jahren alt, die heisst Susanna, die hat ein Blättlein illuminirt, ein Salvator, dafür hab ich ihr geben 1 fl. Ist in gross Wunder, das ein Weibsbild also viel machen soll" (Ernst Heidrich [ed.] *Albrecht Dürers schriftlicher Nachlass* [Berlin: Julius Bard, 1910], 102). It is not known what the source of Richardson's more tendentious and inaccurate account of this event was. Caroline Hamard Commanville (b. 1846) was Flaubert's much-beloved niece, who in 1895 published her *Souvenirs sur Gustave Flaubert (Recollections of Gustave Flaubert)* (Paris: A. Ferroud, 1895), in which she does not mention the incident recounted by Richardson.

art – they supply a witness for the defense who points to Catherine and Teresa[2] walking abreast with Francis and Boehme.[3] But their witness is always asked what he makes of the fact that Jesus, Mahomed, and Buddha are all of the sex male. His prompt answer: that he looks not backward but ahead, leaves things, even after he has pointed to Mrs. Eddy and Mrs. Besant,[4] a little in the air. For Catholic feminists there is always the Mother of God. But they are rare, and as it were under an editorial ban. Privately they must draw much comfort from the fact that the Church which, since the days of its formal organization has excluded woman from its ultimate sanctities, is yet constrained to set her above it, crowned Queen of Heaven.

Last, but from the feminist point of view by no means least of those who challenge the security of the one solidly remaining hope of the prosecution, are the many who believe, some of these having arrived at feminism via their belief, that the finest flowers of the human spirit are the social arts including the art of dress. In vain is their witness reminded of the man modiste, the pub and the club. He slays opposition with lyrics, with idylls of the Primitive Mother forming, with her children, society, while father slew beasts and ate and slept. And side by side with the pub at its best he places the salon at its best, and over against Watt[5] and his dreamy contemplation of the way the light steam plays with the heavy lid of the kettle – a phenomenon, thunders the prosecution, that for centuries countless women have witnessed daily in animal stupidity – he sets Watt's mother, seeing the lifting lid as tea for several weary ones.

But in all this there is no comfort for the large company of feminists who sincerely see the fine arts as humanity's most godlike achievement. For them the case, though still it winds its interminable way, is settled. There is no escape from the verdict of woman's essential inferiority. The arraignment is the more flawless because just here, in the field of art, there has been from time immemorial, a fair field and no favour. Always women have had access to the pen, the chisel and the instrument of music. Yet not only have they produced no Shakespeare, no Michelangelo and no Beethoven, but in the civilization of today, where women artists abound, there is still scarcely any distinctive feminine art. The art of women is still on the whole either mediocre or derivative.

There is, of course, at the moment, Käthe Kollwitz,[6] Mother and Hausfrau to begin with, and, in the estimation of many worthy critics, not only the first painter in Europe today but a feminine painter – one that is to say whose work could not have been produced by a man. She it may be is the Answer to Everything. For though it is true that one swallow does not make a summer, the production by the female sex of even one supreme painter brings the whole fine arts argument to the ground and we must henceforth seek the cause of woman's general lack of achievement in art elsewhere than in the idea that first-class artistic expression is incarnate in man alone.

Let us, however suppose that there is no Käthe Kollwitz, assume art to be the highest human achievement, accept the great arraignment and in the interest of the many who are driven to cynicism by the apparent impossibility of roping women into the scheme of salvation, set up the problem in its simplest terms. Cancel out all the variable factors; the pull of the home on the daughter, celibacy, the economic factor and the factor of motherhood, each of which taken alone may be said by weighting the balance to settle the matter out of court and taken all together make us rub our eyes at the achievements of women to date – cancel out all these and imagine for a moment a man and a woman artist side by side with equal chances and account if we can for the man's overwhelming superiority.

[2]   St. Catherine of Siena (1347–80) is noted for several prayers and a "Dialogue of the Seraphic Virgin." Saint Teresa of Avila (1515–82) is considered one of the great writers of Spanish literature. The account of her spiritual life contained in the "Life written by herself" (completed in 1565, an earlier version being lost), in the "Relations", and in the "Interior Castle", forms one of the most remarkable spiritual biographies.

[3]   St. Francis of Assisi (1181–1226), founder of the Franciscan order, and Jakob Boehme (1575–1624), a Lutheran contemplative and mystic.

[4]   Mary Baker Eddy (1821–1910) was an American who founded the Christian Science movement; Annie Besant (1847–1933) was a British women's rights activist and writer who was also an ardent advocate of theosophy.

[5]   James Watt (1736–1819), Scottish inventor and mechanical engineer who is popularly credited with the invention of the steam engine around 1775.

[6]   Käthe Kollwitz (1867–1945) was a German graphic artist and sculptor whose work, permeated with sympathy for the poor and oppressed, often made use of the Mother-and-Child theme.

There is before we can examine our case one more factor to rule out – isolated here because it grows, in the light of modern psychological investigation, increasingly difficult to state, and also because as a rule it is either omitted from the balance, or set down as a good mark to the credit of one party. This elusive and enormously potent factor is called ambition. And its definition, like most others, can never be more or less than a statement of the definer's philosophy of life. But it may at least be agreed that ambition is rich or poor. Childishly self-ended or selflessly mature. And a personal ambition is perhaps not ill-defined as the subtlest form of despair – though a man may pass in a lifetime from the desire for personal excellence, the longing to be sure that either now or in the future he shall be recognized as excellent, to the reckless love of excellence for its own sake, leaving the credit to the devil – and so on to becoming, as it were behind his own back, one with his desire. And though the ambition of the artist need not of necessity be personal, he is peculiarly apt to suffer in the absence of recognition – and here at once we fall upon the strongest argument against fine art as the highest human achievement. These are altitudes. But we are discussing high matters. And though the quality of a man's ambition takes naught from the intrinsic value of his work, an ambition to the extent that it remains a thirst to be recognized as personally great, is a form of despair. And it is a form of despair to which men are notoriously more liable than are women. A fact that ceases to surprise when one reflects that, short of sainthood, a man must do rather than be, that he is potent not so much in person as in relation to the things he makes.

And so with ambition ruled out and our case thus brought down to the bare bones of undebatable actuality, back to our artists of whom immediately we must enquire what it is that they most urgently need for the development of their talents, the channels through which their special genius is to operate. The question has been answered by genius – on its bad days and always to the same effect. Da Vinci, called simultaneously by almost everything that can attract the mind of man, has answered it. Goethe, the court official, answered it. And by way of casting a broad net we will quote here the testimonies of an eleventh century Chinese painter and a modern writer, a South African.

"Unless I dwell in a quiet house, seat myself in a retired room with the window open, the table dusted, incense burning and the thousand trivial thoughts crushed out and sunk, I cannot have good feeling for painting or beautiful taste, and cannot create the you" (the mysterious and wonderful – Fenollosa's translation) Kakki.[7]

"It's a very wise curious instinct that makes all people who have imaginative work (whether it's scientific or philosophic thinking, or poetry, or story-making, of course it doesn't matter so it's original work, and has to be spun out of the *texture of the mind itself*) try to creep away into some sort of solitude." .... "It's worry, tension, painful emotion, anxiety that kills imagination out as surely as a bird is killed by a gun." Olive Schreiner.[8]

Quiet, and solitude in the sense of freedom from preoccupations, are the absolute conditions of artistic achievement. Exactly, it may be answered, and your male artist will pay for these things any price that may be asked. Will pay health, respectability, honour, family claims and what not. And keep fine. And there are in the world of art women who make the same payments and yet do not achieve supremacy and, indefinably, do not remain fine. What is the difference? Where is it that the woman breaks down? She should with a fair field and her fascinating burdensome gift of sight, her gift for expansive vicarious living, be at least his equal? She should. But there are, when we come down to the terms of daily experience, just two things that queer the pitch. One abroad and one at home. For the woman, and particularly the woman painter, going into the world of art is immediately surrounded by masculine traditions. Traditions based on assumptions that are largely unconscious and whose power of suggestion is unlimited. Imagine the case reversed. Imagine the traditions that held during a great period of Egyptian art, when women painters were the rule – the

---

[7]   Kakki (? - *c.* 1083 AD) was a Chinese landscape artist whose treatise on painting is quoted by Ernest Fenollosa, *Epochs of Chinese and Japanese Art*, 2 vols. (London: Heinemann, 1912), vol. 2, 18.

[8]   Olive Schreiner (1855–1920) was a South African novelist and feminist writer, best known for her first novel, *The Story of an*

African Farm (1883). Richardson is quoting from Schreiner's letter to her husband, Samuel Cronwright-Schreiner, May 26, 1898, which is cited in his biography of her, *The Life of Olive Schreiner* (London: Fisher Unwin, 1924), 303–4.

nude male serving as model, as the "artist's model" that in our own day is the synonym for nude femininity.

But even the lifting away from our present gropings after civility in the world at large of the diminishing shadow of that which, for want of a more elegant term, is being called menstate mentality, would do nothing towards the removal of the obstruction in the path of the woman artist at home. She would still be left in an environment such as has surrounded no male artist since the world began. For the male artist, though with bad luck he may be tormented by his womankind, or burdened by wife and family, with good luck may be cherished by a devoted wife or mistress, or neglectful char, by someone, that is to say, who will either reverently or contemptuously let him be. And with the worst of luck, living in the midst of debt and worry and pressure, still somehow he will be tended and will live serenely innocent of the swarming detail that is the basis of daily life.

It is not only that there exists for the woman no equivalent for the devoted wife or mistress. There is also no equivalent for the most neglectful char known to man. For the service given by women to women is as different from that given by women to men as is chalk from cheese. If hostile, it will specialize in manufacturing difficulties. If friendly, it will demand unfaltering response. For it knows that living sympathy is there. And in either case service is given on the assumption that the woman at work is in the plot for providing life's daily necessities. And even vicarious expansion towards a multitude of details, though it may bring wisdom, is fatal to sustained creative effort.

Art demands what, to women, current civilization won't give. There is for a Dostoyevsky writing against time on the corner of a crowded kitchen table a greater possibility of detachment than for a woman artist no matter how placed. Neither motherhood nor the more continuously exacting and indefinitely expansive responsibilities of even the simplest housekeeping can so effectively hamper her as the human demand, besieging her wherever she is, for an inclusive awareness, from which men, for good or ill, are exempt.

Continuous Performance: The Film Gone Male (1932)

Memory, psychology is to-day declaring, is passive consciousness. Those who accept this dictum see the in-rolling future as living reality and the past as reality entombed. They also regard every human faculty as having an evolutionary history. For these straight-line thinkers memory is a mere glance over the shoulder along a past seen as a progression from the near end of which mankind goes forward. They are also, these characteristically occidental thinkers, usually found believing in the relative *passivity* of females. And since women excel in the matter of memory, the two beliefs admirably support each other. But there is memory and memory. And memory proper, as distinct from a mere backward glance, as distinct even from prolonged contemplation of things regarded as past and done with, gathers, can gather, and pile up its wealth only round universals, unchanging, unevolving verities that move neither backwards nor forwards and have neither speech nor language.

And that is one of the reasons why women, who excel in memory and whom the cynics describe as scarely touched by evolving civilisation, are humanity's silent half, without much faith in speech as a medium of communication. Those women who never question the primacy of "clear speech," who are docile disciples of the orderly thought of man, and acceptors of theorems, have either been educationally maltreated or are by nature more within the men's than within the women's camp. Once a woman becomes a partisan, a representative that is to say of one only of the many sides of question, she has abdicated. The batallions of partisan women glittering in the limelit regions of to-day's world, whose prestige is largely the result of the novelty of their attainments, communicating not their own convictions but some one or other or a portion of some one or other of the astonishing varieties of thought-patterns under which men experimentally arrange such

First published in the film journal *Close Up* 9(1) (March 1932).

phenomena as are suited to the process, represent the men's camp and are distinguishable by their absolute faith in speech as a medium of communication.

The others, whom still men call womanly and regard with emotion not unmixed with a sane and proper fear, though they may talk incessantly from the cradle onwards, are, save when driven by calamitous necessity, as silent as the grave. Listen to their outpouring torrents of speech. Listen to village women at pump or fireside, to villa women, to unemployed service-flat women, to chatelâines, to all kinds of women anywhere and everywhere. Chatter, chatter, chatter, as men say. And say also that only one in a thousand can *talk*. Quite. For all these women use speech, with individual differences, alike: in the manner of a facade. Their awareness of being, as distinct from man's awareness of becoming, is so strong that when they are confronted, they must, in most circumstances, snatch at words to cover either their own palpitating spiritual nakedness or that of another. They talk to banish embarrassment. It is true they are apt to drop, if the confrontation be prolonged, into what is called gossip and owes both its charm and its poison to their excellence in awareness of persons. This amongst themselves. In relation to men their use of speech is various. But always it is a façade.

And the film, regarded as a medium of communication, in the day of its innocence, in its quality of being nowhere and everywhere, nowhere in the sense of having more intention than direction and more purpose than plan, everywhere by reason of its power to evoke, suggest, reflect, express from within its moving parts and in their totality of movement, something of the changeless being at the heart of all becoming, was essentially feminine. In its insistence on contemplation it provided a pathway to reality.

In becoming audible and particularly in becoming a medium of propaganda, it is doubtless fulfilling its destiny. But it is a masculine destiny. The destiny of planful becoming rather than of purposeful being. It will be the chosen battle-ground of rival patterns, plans, ideologies in endless succession and bewildering variety.

It has been declared that it is possible by means of purely aesthetic devices to sway an audience in whatever direction a filmateur desires. This sounds menacing and is probably true. (The costumiers used Hollywood to lengthen women's skirts. Perhaps British Instructional,[1] with the entire medical profession behind it, will kindly shorten them again). It is therefore comforting to reflect that so far the cinema is not a government monopoly. It is a medium, or a weapon, at the disposal of all parties and has, considered as a battlefield, a grand advantage over those of the past when civil wars have been waged disadvantageously to one party or the other by reason of inequalities of publicity, restrictions of locale and the relative indirectness and remoteness of the channels of communication. The new film can, at need, assist Radio in turning the world into a vast council-chamber and do more than assist, for it is the freer partner. And multitudinous within that vast chamber as within none of the preceding councils of mankind, is the unconquerable, unchangeable eternal feminine. Influential.

Weeping therefore, if weep we must, over the departure of the old time film's gracious silence, we may also rejoice in the prospect of a fair field and no favour. A field over which lies only the shadow of the censorship. And the censorship is getting an uneasy conscience.

Adventure for Readers (1939)

Having defined poetry as "*the result of* passion recollected in tranquillity" (the opening words are here apologetically italicized because, though their absence makes the definition meaningless, they are almost invariably omitted), Wordsworth goes on to describe what happens when the poet, recalling an occurrence that has stirred him to his depths, concentrates thereon the full force of his

---

[1] British Instructional Films was a maker of educational films in Britain, which closed in 1947.

ADVENTURE
First published in *Life and Letters* 22 (July 1939).
This essay was a book review of *Finnegans Wake* by James Joyce.
For Joyce, see pp. 211–300; for a selection from *Finnegans Wake*, see pp. 283–300.

imaginative consciousness; how there presently returns, together with the circumstances of the experience, something of the emotion that accompanied it, and how, in virtue of this magnetic stream sustained and deepened by continuous concentration, there comes into being a product this poet names, with scientific accuracy, an "effusion."

In Wordsworth's[1] own case, the product can itself become the source of further inspiration, and the presence upon the page of offspring set beneath parent and duly entitled "Effusion on Reading the Above", affords a unique revelation of the subsidiary workings of an emotion tranquilly regathered.

And while this enchanted enchanter and his successors (the greatest of whom, dead e'er his prime, produced for our everlasting adoration, effusions inspired by the reading of Lemprière's Dictionary[2]) sang to the spirit their immortal ditties, our novelists, following the example of their forbears, those wandering minstrels who told for the delight of the untravelled, brave strange tales from far away, wove stories whose power to enthrall resided chiefly in their ability to provide both excitement and suspense; uncertainty as to what, in the pages still to be turned, might befall the hero from whom, all too soon, returning to "the world of everyday," the reader must regretfully take leave.

With vain, prophetic insight Goethe protested that action and drama are for the theatre, that the novelist's business is to keep his hero always and everywhere onlooker rather than participant and, "by one device or another," to slow up the events of the story so that they may be seen through his eyes and modified by his thought.[3]

The first novelist fully to realize his ideal was Henry James and, by the time James had finished his work, something had happened to English poetry.

How, or just why, or exactly when the shift occurred from concentration upon the various aspects of the sublime and beautiful to what may be called the immediate investigation of reality, it is not easy to say, though a poet-novelist, Richard Church,[4] in his recent address to the Royal Society of Literature, made, one feels, some excellent guesses as to the practical reasons for the changeover. Whereunto may be added the widespread application, for some time past, of Pope's[5] injunction as to the proper study of mankind.

Whatever the combination of incitements, certain of our poets have now, for decades past, produced short stories rather than lyrics and, in place of the epic and foreshadowed by *The Ring and the Book*,[6] so very nearly a prose epic, have given us, if we exclude *The Testament of Beauty*,[7] rearing a nobly defiant head in the last ditch of the epic form, the modern novel.

The proof, if proof be needed, of the transference may be found in a quality this new novel, at its worst as well as at its best, shares with poetry and that is conspicuously absent from the story-telling novel of whatever kind. Opening, just anywhere, its pages, the reader is immediately engrossed. Time and place, and the identity of characters, if any happen to appear, are relatively

[1] William Wordsworth, "Preface" to the second edition of the *Lyrical Ballads* (1800): "I have said that poetry is the spontaneous overflow of powerful feelings; it takes its origin from emotion recollected in tranquility; the emotion is contemplated till, by a species of reaction, the tranquility gradually disappears, and an emotion, kindred to that which was the subject of contemplation, is gradually produced, and does itself actually exist in the mind."

[2] John Lemprière (1765–1824) was a British classical scholar who achieved renown for his *Bibliotheca classica or Classical Dictionary* (1788), a work which, edited by various later scholars, long remained a reference book on mythology and classical history. John Keats (1795–1821) often drew on it in writing poems with mythological subjects, and it is routinely cited in annotations to his work. When Keats died in 1821, Byron wrote to his friend and publisher John Murray (April 26, 1821): "I am very sorry for it – though I think he took the wrong line as a poet – and was spoilt by Cockneyfying and Suburbing – and versifying Tooke's Pantheon and Lemprière's Dictionary."

[3] Invoking a passage that constitutes Goethe's only extended statement about the novel, Richardson summarizes a conversation that takes place between Wilhelm Meister, Serlo, and other characters who are actors in Goethe's novel *Wilhelm Meisters Lehrjahre* (1796), ed. Wolfgang Baumgart (Zurich: Artemis Verlag, 1962), Book 5, ch. 7, 330–1; in English, *Wilhelm Meister's Apprenticeship*, trans. Thomas Carlyle (Boston: Houghton, Osgood, 1879), 291–2.

[4] Richard Church (1893–1972) was a poet, novelist, and literary critic, and also a one-time president of the Royal Literary Society. Church published numerous volumes of poetry from 1917 onward, mainly of a Georgian flavor, as well as adult and children's fiction. His "recent address" of 1939 has not been identified.

[5] Alexander Pope (1688–1744), the great British poet of the eighteenth century, in his poem titled "An Essay on Man: Epistle II" (1733–4) wrote: "Know then thyself, presume not God to scan; / The proper study of mankind is man."

[6] Robert Browning (1812–89), British poet, published *The Ring and the Book* in 1868–9, a long poem that uses multiple perspectives to recount a sensational murder and trial from the Renaissance.

[7] *The Testament of Beauty: A Poem in Four Books* (Oxford: Clarendon Press, 1929) was written by the British poet Robert Bridges (1844–1930), poet laureate from 1913 until his death.

immaterial. Something may be missed. Incidents may fail of their full effect through ignorance of what has gone before. But the reader does not find himself, as inevitably he would in plunging thus carelessly into the midst of the dramatic novel complete with plot, set scenes, beginning, middle, climax, and curtain, completely at sea. He finds himself within a medium whose close texture, like that of poetry, is everywhere significant and although, when the tapestry hangs complete before his eyes, each portion is seen to enhance the rest and the shape and the intention of the whole grows clear, any single strip may be divorced from its fellows without losing everything of its power and of its meaning.

Particularly is this true of the effusions of Marcel Proust[8] and of James Joyce. For while every novel, taken as a whole, shares with every other species of portrayal the necessity of being a signed self-portrait and might well be subtitled Portrait of the Artist at the Age of – where, in the long line of novelists preceding these two, save, perhaps, in Henry James as represented by the work of his maturity, shall we find another whose signature is clearly inscribed across his every sentence?

Reaching *Finnegans Wake* we discover its author's signature not only across each sentence, but upon almost every word. And since, upon the greater number of its pages, nearly every other word is either wholly or partially an improvisation, the would-be reader must pay, in terms of sheer concentration, a tax far higher even than that demanded by Imagist poetry. And be he never so familiar with the author's earlier work, and in agreement with those who approve his repudiation of the orthodoxies of grammar and syntax, finding, when doubt assails, reassurance in the presence of similar effective and, doubtless, salutary heresies in the practice of the arts other than literature, the heavily-burdened reader of *Finnegans Wake*, hopefully glissading, upon the first page, down a word of a hundred letters – representing the fall that carried Finnegan to his death – into pathless verbal thickets, may presently find himself weary of struggling from thicket to thicket without a clue, weary of abstruse references that too often appear to be mere displays of erudition, weary of the mélange of languages ancient and modern, of regional and class dialects, slangs and catchwords and slogans, puns and nursery rhymes, phrases that are household words phonetically adapted to fresh intentions, usually improper, sometimes side-splitting, often merely facetious, incensed in discovering that these diverse elements, whether standing on their heads or fantastically paraphrased, apparently succeed each other as the sound of one suggests that of the next rather than by any continuity of inward meaning, and are all too frequently interspersed by spontaneous creations recalling those produced by children at a loss, bored to desperation by lack of interest and seeking relief in shouting a single word, repeating it with a change of vowel, with another change and another, striving to outdo themselves until they reach, with terrific emphasis, onomatopœia precipitating adult interference.

Meanwhile the author, presumably foreseeing the breakdown of even the most faithful Joycian as likely to occur in the neighbourhood of the hundredth page, comes to the rescue in the name of Anna Livia, invoked by a parody of a well-known prayer ("Annah the Allmaziful, the everliving, Bringer of Plurabilities, haloed be her eve, her singtime sung, her rill be run, unhemmed as it is uneven"[9]), with a chapter on the allied arts of writing and reading, here and there exceptionally, and most mercifully, explicit, preluded by a list of the hundred and sixty-three names given to Annah's "untitled mamafesta memorializing the Mosthighest"[10] (including *Rockabill Booby in the Wave Trough*,[11] *What Jumbo made to Jalice and What Anisette to Him,* and *I am Older nor the Rogues among Whist I Slips and He calls me his Dual of Ayessha*[12]), and one day perhaps to be translated, annotated, and issued as a Critique of Pure Literature and an Introduction to the Study of James Joyce.

The impact of this chapter, a fulfilment of the author's prescription – "Say it with missiles, and thus arabesque the page"[13] – is tremendous, its high purpose nothing less than the demand that the novel shall be poetry. A grouped selection of caught missiles and fragments of missiles produces the following relatively coherent mosaic: "About that original hen[14] ... the bird in this case was

[8] Marcel Proust (1871–1922), French novelist celebrated for his multi-volume novel *A la Recherche du temps perdu,* or *In search of Lost Time.*

[9] James Joyce, *Finnegans Wake* I.5, 104.

[10] Joyce, *Finnegans Wake* I.5, 104.

[11] Joyce, *Finnegans Wake* I.5, 104.

[12] Joyce, *Finnegans Wake* I.5, 105.

[13] Joyce, *Finnegans Wake* I.5, 115.

[14] Joyce, *Finnegans Wake* I.5, 110.

Belinda of the Dorans, a more than quinque-gentarian ... and what she was scratching looked like a goodish-sized sheet of letter-paper.... Well, almost any photoist ... will tip anyone asking him the teaser that if a negative of a horse happens to melt enough while drying ... what you get is ... a positively grotesque distorted macromass of all sorts of horsehappy values ... well, this freely is what must have occurred to our missive ... by the sagacity of a lookmelittle likemelong hen.... Lead, kindly Fowl! ... No, assuredly they are not justified these gloompourers who grouse that letters have never been quite their old selves again since Biddy Doran looked at literature....[15] Who, at all this marvelling, but will press ... to see the vaulting feminine libido ... sternly controlled ... by the uniform matteroffactness of a meandering masculine fist?[16] ... To concentrate solely on the literal sense or even the psychological content of any document ... is ... hurtful to sound sense."[17]

Quite as far goes Mr. Walter de la Mare, who has recently declared that "When poetry is most poetic, when its sounds, that is, and the utterance of them, and when its rhythms rather than the words themselves are its real if cryptic language, any other meaning, however valuable it may be, is only a secondary matter".[18]

Primarily, then, are we to *listen* to *Finnegans Wake*? Not so much to what Joyce says, as to the lovely way he says it, to the rhythms and undulating cadences of the Irish voice, with its capacity to make of every spoken word a sentence with parentheses and to arouse, in almost every English breast, a responsive emotion?

Consulting once more the author's elucidatory chapter, we find our instructions: "Closer inspection of the *bordereau* would reveal a multiplicity of personalities ... and some prevision of virtual crime or crimes might be made by anyone unwary enough before any suitable occasion for it or them had so far managed to happen along. In fact ... the traits featuring the chiaroscuro coalesce, their contrarieties eliminated, in one stable somebody...."[19] We are urged also to be patient, to avoid "anything like being or becoming out of patience...."[20] So holp me Petault, it is not a misaffectual whyacinthinous riot ... it only looks as like it as damn it ... cling to it as with drowning hands, hoping against hope all the while, that by the light of philosophy ... things will begin to clear up a bit one way or another within the next quarrel of an hour".[21]

Thus encouraged, with this easily decipherable chapter's rich treasure in hand and perceptions exalted and luminous, the reader presses hopefully onward; only to find his feet once more caught in impenetrable undergrowths, and his head assailed by missiles falling thicker and faster than before, hurled by one so obviously in silent ecstasies as he watches the flounderings of his victim. Scanning and re-scanning the lines until their rhythm grows apparent, presently acquiring ease in following cadence and intonation as he goes, the reader again finds himself listening to what appears to be no more than the non-stop patter of an erudite cheapjack. Weariness returns. So what? Weeks of searching for the coalescence and the somebody?

Let us take the author at his word. Really release consciousness from literary preoccupations and prejudices, from the self-imposed task of searching for superficial sequences in stretches of statement regarded horizontally, or of setting these upright and regarding them pictorially, and plunge, provisionally, here and there; *enter* the text and look innocently about.

The reward is sheer delight, and the promise, for future readings, of inexhaustible entertainment. Inexhaustible, because so very many fragments of this text now show themselves comparable only to the rider who leapt into the saddle and rode off in all directions. The coalescence and the somebody can wait. Already, pursuing our indiscriminate way, we have discovered coherencies,

[15] Joyce, *Finnegans Wake* I.5, 111–12.
[16] Joyce, *Finnegans Wake* I.5, 123.
[17] Joyce, *Finnegans Wake* I.5, 109.
[18] Walter de la Mare (1873–1956), British poet, in his *Behold, This Dreamer: Of Reverie, Night, Sleep, Dream, Love-Dreams, Nightmare, Death, the Unconscious, the Imagination, Divination, the Artist, and Kindred Subjects* (London: Faber & Faber, 1939), 103: "If music is the most perfect of the arts because it is the least diluted, and if poetry most closely approaches

music when it is most poetic, when its sounds, that is, and the utterance of them, and when its rhythms rather than the words themselves, are its real if cryptic language, any other meaning, however valuable it may be, is only a secondary matter."
[19] Joyce, *Finnegans Wake* I.5, 107.
[20] Joyce, *Finnegans Wake* I.5, 107.
[21] Joyce, *Finnegans Wake* I.5, 118–19.

links between forest and forest, and certain looming forms, have anticipated the possibility of setting down upon "a goodish-sized sheet of letter-paper" the skeleton of the long argument. For the present, for a first reading, the "meanderings" of the "masculine fist" are a sufficient repayment. Even a tenth reading will leave some still to be followed up; and many to be continuously excused.

Do we find it possible, having thus "read" the whole and reached the end, a long, lyrically wailing, feminine monologue, to name the passion whose result is this tremendous effusion? Finnegan, the master-mason, and his wife Annie and their friends may symbolize life or literature or what you will that occasionally call for mourning. For their creator they are food for incessant ironic laughter (possibly a screen for love and solicitude), mitigated only here and there by a touch of wistfulness that is to reach at the end a full note. Shall we remind ourselves that most of our male poets have sounded wistful? And the women? Well, there is Emily Brontë, who, by the way, would have delighted, with reservations, in *Finnegans Wake*.

Wallace Stevens (1879–1955)

Introduction

Wallace Stevens was born in Reading, Pennsylvania. He attended high school there and entered Harvard as a special student. He remained there for three years, from 1897 to 1900, during which he studied French and German. He became president of the *Advocate*, the university's celebrated literary magazine, and published his early poems in it. For a year Stevens took a job as a reporter for the *New York Herald Tribune*, but found that he disliked it. In 1901 he entered the New York Law School, and in 1903 was admitted to the New York Bar and began to practice law, but with little success. After working in several firms, in 1908 he joined the legal staff of an insurance firm. A year later he married Elsie Moll, a young woman whom he had met in Reading five years earlier. In 1913 he began to write poetry again, perhaps stimulated by the debates about modern art that followed in the wake of the legendary Armory Show in 1913, an exhibition that assembled a generous sampling of contemporary art from Europe and introduced it to a new and very receptive public in America. His first poems appeared in brief-lived journals such as *Trend*, *Rogue*, and

Others, and repeatedly in the more durable *Poetry*, where he was something of a favorite with Harriet Monroe, its editor. In 1916 he joined the New York office of the Hartford Accident and Indemnity Company, and a few months later moved to Hartford, Connecticut, where the firm had its head office. He became vice-president of the firm in 1934.

Stevens's first book of poems, *Harmonium*, was published in 1923, and some have argued that it received less notice than it might by coming close on the heels of *The Waste Land*. Stevens himself was plainly discouraged, and also preoccupied by the task of raising his daughter, Holly. He stopped writing for more than a decade. His next book, *Ideas of Order*, appeared in 1935, followed swiftly by *Owl's Clover* (1936), a limited and deluxe edition that contained only five poems, and *The Man with the Blue Guitar and Other Poems* (1937). Then came *Parts of a World* (1942) and *Notes Toward a Supreme Fiction*, both masterpieces. His *Collected Poems* appeared in 1954, months before his death in 1955.

Sunday Morning (1915)

I

Complacencies of the peignoir,[1] and late
Coffee and oranges in a sunny chair,
And the green freedom of a cockatoo
Upon a rug mingle to dissipate
The holy hush of ancient sacrifice.   5
She dreams a little, and she feels the dark
Encroachment of that old catastrophe,
As a calm darkens among water-lights.
The pungent oranges and bright, green wings
Seem things in some procession of the dead,   10
Winding across wide water, without sound.
The day is like wide water, without sound,
Stilled for the passing of her dreaming feet
Over the seas, to silent Palestine,[2]
Dominion of the blood and sepulchre.   15

The poem was first published in *Poetry* 7(2) (November 1915), though with significant differences from the poem as it appeared later in Stevens's first book, *Harmonium* (1923).

[1] *peignoir* a loose dressing gown for women.
[2] *Palestine* where the sepulchre of Christ is located.

II

Why should she give her bounty to the dead?
What is divinity if it can come
Only in silent shadows and in dreams?
Shall she not find in comforts of the sun,
In pungent fruit and bright, green wings, or else   20
In any balm or beauty of the earth,
Things to be cherished like the thought of heaven?
Divinity must live within herself:
Passions of rain, or moods in falling snow;
Grievings in loneliness, or unsubdued   25
Elations when the forest blooms; gusty
Emotions on wet roads on autumn nights;
All pleasures and all pains, remembering
The bough of summer and the winter branch.
These are the measures destined for her soul.   30

III

Jove[3] in the clouds had his inhuman birth.
No mother suckled him, no sweet land gave
Large-mannered motions to his mythy mind.
He moved among us, as a muttering king,
Magnificent, would move among his hinds,   35
Until our blood, commingling, virginal,
With heaven, brought such requital to desire
The very hinds[4] discerned it, in a star.
Shall our blood fail? Or shall it come to be
The blood of paradise? And shall the earth   40
Seem all of paradise that we shall know?
The sky will be much friendlier then than now,
A part of labor and a part of pain,
And next in glory to enduring love,
Not this dividing and indifferent blue.   45

IV

She says, "I am content when wakened birds,
Before they fly, test the reality
Of misty fields, by their sweet questionings;
But when the birds are gone, and their warm fields
Return no more, where, then, is paradise?"   50
There is not any haunt of prophecy,
Nor any old chimera[5] of the grave,
Neither the golden underground, nor isle
Melodious, where spirits gat them home,
Nor visionary south, nor cloudy palm   55
Remote on heaven's hill, that has endured
As April's green endures; or will endure
Like her remembrance of awakened birds,
Or her desire for June and evening, tipped
By the consummation of the swallow's wings.   60

[3] *Jove* Jove or Zeus was born in Crete; but Stevens is altering the legend of his birth to serve his own purposes.
[4] *hinds* peasants or rustics.
[5] *chimera* a horrible monster of the imagination.

V

She says, "But in contentment I still feel
The need of some imperishable bliss."
Death is the mother of beauty; hence from her,
Alone, shall come fulfilment to our dreams
And our desires. Although she strews the leaves   65
Of sure obliteration on our paths,
The path sick sorrow took, the many paths
Where triumph rang its brassy phrase, or love
Whispered a little out of tenderness,
She makes the willow shiver in the sun   70
For maidens who were wont to sit and gaze
Upon the grass, relinquished to their feet.
She causes boys to pile new plums and pears
On disregarded plate.[6] The maidens taste
And stray impassioned in the littering leaves.   75

VI

Is there no change of death in paradise?
Does ripe fruit never fall? Or do the boughs
Hang always heavy in that perfect sky,
Unchanging, yet so like our perishing earth,
With rivers like our own that seek for seas   80
They never find, the same receding shores
That never touch with inarticulate pang?
Why set the pear upon those river-banks
Or spice the shores with odors of the plum?
Alas, that they should wear our colors there,   85
The silken weavings of our afternoons,
And pick the strings of our insipid lutes!
Death is the mother of beauty, mystical,
Within whose burning bosom we devise
Our earthly mothers waiting, sleeplessly.   90

VII

Supple and turbulent, a ring of men
Shall chant in orgy on a summer morn
Their boisterous devotion to the sun,
Not as a god, but as a god might be,
Naked among them, like a savage source.   95
Their chant shall be a chant of paradise,
Out of their blood, returning to the sky;
And in their chant shall enter, voice by voice,
The windy lake wherein their lord delights,
The trees, like serafin,[7] and echoing hills,   100
That choir among themselves long afterward.
They shall know well the heavenly fellowship

---

[6] *disregarded plate* "Plate is used in the sense of so-called family
plate. Disregarded refers to the disuse into which things fall that
have been possessed for a long time. I mean, therefore, that death

releases and renews. What the old have come to disregard, the
young inherit and make use of" (*Letters*, 183).
[7] *serafin* or seraphim, angels who guard the throne of the Lord.

Of men that perish and of summer morn.
And whence they came and whither they shall go
The dew upon their feet shall manifest.   105

VIII

She hears, upon that water without sound,
A voice that cries, "The tomb in Palestine
Is not the porch of spirits lingering.
It is the grave of Jesus, where he lay."
We live in an old chaos of the sun,   110
Or old dependency of day and night,
Or island solitude, unsponsored, free,
Of that wide water, inescapable.
Deer walk upon our mountains, and the quail
Whistle about us their spontaneous cries;   115
Sweet berries ripen in the wilderness;
And, in the isolation of the sky,
At evening, casual flocks of pigeons make
Ambiguous undulations as they sink,
Downward to darkness, on extended wings.   120

Earthy Anecdote (1918)

Every time the bucks went clattering
Over Oklahoma
A/ firecat bristled in the way.

Wherever they went,
They went clattering,   5
Until they swerved
In a swift, circular line
To the right,
Because of the firecat.

Or until they swerved   10
In a swift, circular line
To the left,
Because of the firecat.

The bucks clattered.
The firecat went leaping,   15
To the right, to the left,
And
Bristled in the way.

Later, the firecat closed his bright eyes
And slept.   20

EARTHY ANECDOTE
The poem was first published in a journal called *Modern School*
5(12) (December 1918). Stevens placed it as the first poem in his
Collected Poems.

Le Monocle de Mon Oncle (1918)

I

"Mother of heaven, regina of the clouds,
O sceptre of the sun, crown of the moon,
There is not nothing, no, no, never nothing,
Like the clashed edges of two words that kill."
And so I mocked her in magnificent measure.   5
Or was it that I mocked myself alone?
I wish that I might be a thinking stone.
The sea of spuming thought foists up again
The radiant bubble that she was. And then
A deep up-pouring from some saltier well   10
Within me, bursts its watery syllable.

II

A red bird flies across the golden floor.
It is a red bird that seeks out his choir
Among the choirs of wind and wet and wing.
A torrent will fall from him when he finds.   15
Shall I uncrumple this much-crumpled thing?
I am a man of fortune greeting heirs;
For it has come that thus I greet the spring.
These choirs of welcome choir for me farewell.
No spring can follow past meridian.   20
Yet you persist with anecdotal bliss
To make believe a starry *connaissance*.

III

Is it for nothing, then, that old Chinese
Sat tittivating by their mountain pools
Or in the Yangtse[1] studied out their beards?   25
I shall not play the flat historic scale.
You know how Utamaro's beauties[2] sought
The end of love in their all-speaking braids.
You know the mountainous coiffures of Bath.[3]
Alas! Have all the barbers lived in vain   30
That not one curl in nature has survived?
Why, without pity on these studious ghosts,
Do you come dripping in your hair from sleep?

IV

This luscious and impeccable fruit of life
Falls, it appears, of its own weight to earth.   35

The poem was first published in *Others* 5(1) (December 1918).

[1] *Yangtse* the Yangtze river flows through almost the whole of China eastward to the Pacific Ocean.

[2] *Utamaro's beauties* Kitagara Utamaro (1753–1808) was an artist who concentrated on portraits of women, highly stylized with extremely tall and slender bodies, long heads, with eyes and mouth depicted as little slits. His prints have been popular among collectors for over a century.

[3] *coiffures of Bath* when Queen Anne went to Bath (England) for a holiday, she started a trend that lasted throughout the eighteenth century, leaving the city with a strong heritage of Georgian architecture. Contemporary prints of nobility on holiday repeatedly show women with "mountainous coiffures."

When you were Eve,[4] its acrid juice was sweet,
Untasted, in its heavenly, orchard air.
An apple serves as well as any skull
To be the book in which to read a round,
And is as excellent, in that it is composed   40
Of what, like skulls, comes rotting back to ground.
But it excels in this, that as the fruit
Of love, it is a book too mad to read
Before one merely reads to pass the time.

V

In the high west there burns a furious star.[5]   45
It is for fiery boys that star was set
And for sweet-smelling virgins close to them.
The measure of the intensity of love
Is measure, also, of the verve of earth.
For me, the firefly's quick, electric stroke   50
Ticks tediously the time of one more year.
And you? Remember how the crickets came
Out of their mother grass, like little kin,
In the pale nights, when your first imagery
Found inklings of your bond to all that dust.   55

VI

If men at forty will be painting lakes
The ephemeral blues must merge for them in one,
The basic slate, the universal hue.
There is a substance in us that prevails.
But in our amours amorists discern   60
Such fluctuations that their scrivening
Is breathless to attend each quirky turn.
When amorists grow bald, then amours shrink
Into the compass and curriculum
Of introspective exiles, lecturing.   65
It is a theme for Hyacinth[6] alone.

VII

The mules that angels ride come slowly down
The blazing passes, from beyond the sun.
Descensions[7] of their tinkling bells arrive.
These muleteers are dainty of their way.   70
Meantime, centurions guffaw and beat
Their shrilling tankards on the table-boards.
This parable, in sense, amounts to this:
The honey of heaven may or may not come,
But that of earth both comes and goes at once.   75

---

[4] *Eve* the first woman created by God who, in the account of
Genesis, brings sin into the world by eating forbidden fruit,
sometimes figured as an apple.
[5] *a furious star* the planet Venus.
[6] *Hyacinth* in Greek myth Hyacinth was a beloved companion
of Apollo. The two engaged in a discus-throwing contest, in
which Apollo's discus inadvertently killed his friend. Where
drops of Hyacinth's blood touched the ground, a purple flower
miraculously arose, resembling a lily. Apollo inscribed his grief
upon the flower, which was said to have marks that looked like
the letters AI, ancient Greek for a cry of woe. The story is told in
Ovid, *Metamorphoses* X: 162–219.
[7] *Descensions* an uncommon term meaning "descent."

Suppose these couriers brought amid their train
A damsel heightened by eternal bloom.

VIII

Like a dull scholar, I behold, in love,
An ancient aspect touching a new mind.
It comes, it blooms, it bears its fruit and dies.   80
This trivial trope reveals a way of truth.
Our bloom is gone. We are the fruit thereof.
Two golden gourds distended on our vines,
Into the autumn weather, splashed with frost,
Distorted by hale fatness, turned grotesque.   85
We hang like warty squashes, streaked and rayed,
The laughing sky will see the two of us
Washed into rinds by rotting winter rains.

IX

In verses wild with motion, full of din,
Loudened by cries, by clashes, quick and sure   90
As the deadly thought of men accomplishing
Their curious fates in war, come, celebrate
The faith of forty, ward of Cupido.
Most venerable heart, the lustiest conceit
Is not too lusty for your broadening.   95
I quiz all sounds, all thoughts, all everything
For the music and manner of the paladins[8]
To make oblation[9] fit. Where shall I find
Bravura adequate to this great hymn?

X

The fops of fancy in their poems leave   100
Memorabilia of the mystic spouts,
Spontaneously watering their gritty soils.
I am a yeoman, as such fellows go.
I know no magic trees, no balmy boughs,
No silver-ruddy, gold-vermilion fruits.   105
But, after all, I know a tree that bears
A semblance to the thing I have in mind.
It stands gigantic, with a certain tip
To which all birds come sometime in their time.
But when they go that tip still tips the tree.   110

XI

If sex were all, then every trembling hand
Could make us squeak, like dolls, the wished-for words.
But note the unconscionable treachery of fate,
That makes us weep, laugh, grunt and groan, and shout
Doleful heroics, pinching gestures forth   115

---

[8]   *paladins* knightly defenders.
[9]   *oblation* something offered to a god or deity; any donation or
gift for religious or charitable uses.

From madness or delight, without regard
To that first, foremost law. Anguishing hour!
Last night, we sat beside a pool of pink,
Clippered[10] with lilies scudding the bright chromes,
Keen to the point of starlight, while a frog   120
Boomed from his very belly odious chords.

XII

A blue pigeon it is, that circles the blue sky,
On sidelong wing, around and round and round.
A white pigeon it is, that flutters to the ground,
Grown tired of flight. Like a dark rabbi, I   125
Observed, when young, the nature of mankind,
In lordly study. Every day, I found
Man proved a gobbet in my mincing world.
Like a rose rabbi, later, I pursued,
And still pursue, the origin and course   130
Of love, but until now I never knew
That fluttering things have so distinct a shade.

The Paltry Nude Starts on a Spring Voyage (1919)

But not on a shell, she starts,
Archaic, for the sea.
But on the first-found weed
She scuds the glitters,
Noiselessly, like one more wave.   5

She too is discontent
And would have purple stuff upon her arms,
Tired of the salty harbors,
Eager for the brine and bellowing
Of the high interiors of the sea.   10

The wind speeds her,
Blowing upon her hands
And watery back.
She touches the clouds, where she goes
In the circle of her traverse of the sea.   15

Yet this is meagre play
In the scurry and water-shine,
As her heels foam –
Not as when the goldener nude
Of a later day   20

Will go, like the centre of sea-green pomp,
In an intenser calm,
Scullion of fate,
Across the spick torrent, ceaselessly,
Upon her irretrievable way.   25

[10] *clippered* i.e. with lilies that stand upright like the masts of a clipper.

THE PALTRY NUDE
The poem was published in *Poetry* 15(1) (October 1919). *Paltry*

nude is a comic term for Venus; the image of Venus rising from the sea (Venus Anadyomene) on a shell has been a topos for Western artists since the Renaissance; Botticelli's is the most famous version, though it is only one of many.

Anecdote of the Jar (1919)

I placed a jar in Tennessee,
And round it was, upon a hill.
It made the slovenly wilderness
Surround that hill.

The wilderness rose up to it,   5
And sprawled around, no longer wild.
The jar was round upon the ground
And tall and of a port in air.

It took dominion everywhere.
The jar was gray and bare.   10
It did not give of bird or bush,
Like nothing else in Tennessee.

The Snow Man (1921)

One must have a mind of winter
To regard the frost and the boughs
Of the pine-trees crusted with snow;

And have been cold a long time
To behold the junipers shagged with ice,   5
The spruces rough in the distant glitter

Of the January sun; and not to think
Of any misery in the sound of the wind,
In the sound of a few leaves,

Which is the sound of the land   10
Full of the same wind
That is blowing in the same bare place

For the listener, who listens in the snow,
And, nothing himself, beholds
Nothing that is not there and the nothing that is.   15

Tea at the Palaz of Hoon (1921)

Not less because in purple I descended
The western day through what you called
The loneliest air, not less was I myself.

What was the ointment sprinkled on my beard?
What were the hymns that buzzed beside my ears?   5
What was the sea whose tide swept through me there?

ANECDOTE
The poem was published in *Poetry* 15(1) (October 1919).

THE SNOW MAN
The poem was first published in *Poetry* 19(1) (October 1921).

TEA
The poem was first published in *Poetry* 19(1) (October 1921).

Out of my mind the golden ointment rained,
And my ears made the blowing hymns they heard.
I was myself the compass of that sea:

I was the world in which I walked, and what I saw   10
Or heard or felt came not but from myself;
And there I found myself more truly and more strange.

The Ordinary Women (1922)

Then from their poverty they rose,
From dry catarrhs, and to guitars
They flitted
Through the palace walls.

They flung monotony behind,   5
Turned from their want, and, nonchalant,
They crowded
The nocturnal halls.

The lacquered loges huddled there
Mumbled zay-zay and a-zay, a-zay.   10
The moonlight
Fubbed[1] the girandoles.[2]

And the cold dresses that they wore,
In the vapid haze of the window-bays,
Were tranquil   15
As they leaned and looked

From the window-sills at the alphabets,
At beta b and gamma g,
To study
The canting curlicues   20

Of heaven and of the heavenly script.
And there they read of marriage-bed.
Ti-lill-o!
And they read right long.

The gaunt guitarists on the strings   25
Rumbled a-day and a-day, a-day.
The moonlight
Rose on the beachy floors

How explicit the coiffures became,
The diamond point, the sapphire point,   30
The sequins
Of the civil fans!

Insinuations of desire,
Puissant speech, alike in each,

ORDINARY WOMEN
The poem was first published in the *Dial* 73(1) (July 1922).
[1] *fubbed* "To fub" is a variant of "to fob," or to cheat or impose
upon.

[2] *girandoles* a girandole is a branched holder for candles or other
lights, often one of several surrounding a mirror.

Cried quittance   35
To the wickless halls.

Then from their poverty they rose,
From dry guitars, and to catarrhs
They flitted
Through the palace walls.   40

The Revolutionists Stop for Orangeade (1931)

Capitán profundo, capitán geloso,
Ask us not to sing standing in the sun,
Hairy-backed and hump-armed,
Flat-ribbed and big-bagged.
There is no pith in music   5
Except in something false.

Bellissimo, pomposo,
Sing a song of serpent-kin,
Necks among the thousand leaves,
Tongues around the fruit.   10
Sing in clownish boots
Strapped and buckled bright.

Wear the breeches of a mask,
Coat half-flare and half galloon;
Wear a helmet without reason,   15
Tufted, tilted, twirled, and twisted.
Start the singing in a voice
Rougher than a grinding shale.

Hang a feather by your eye,
Nod and look a little sly.   20
This must be the vent of pity,
Deeper than a truer ditty
Of the real that wrenches,
Of the quick that's wry.

The Idea of Order at Key West[1] (1934)

She sang beyond the genius of the sea.[2]
The water never formed to mind or voice,
Like a body wholly body, fluttering
Its empty sleeves; and yet its mimic motion
Made constant cry, caused constantly a cry,   5
That was not ours although we understood,
Inhuman, of the veritable ocean.

THE REVOLUTIONISTS
This poem was published for the first time in the second edition of Stevens's collection *Harmonium* (New York: Alfred Knopf, 1931).

THE IDEA
The poem was first published in the journal *Alcestis* 1(1) (October 1934). It was published in a collection of poems that Stevens

published a year later, *Ideas of Order* (New York: Alcestis Press, 1934), a limited edition of 165 copies. A year later the book was published in a trade edition with the same title (New York: Alfred Knopf, 1935), which included three additional poems.
[1] *Key West* Key West is the southernmost of several small islands off the coast of Florida.
[2] *the genius of the sea* an attendant spirit or deity, as in the expression *genius loci*, the spirit of a place.

The sea was not a mask. No more was she.
The song and water were not medleyed sound
Even if what she sang was what she heard,   10
Since what she sang was uttered word by word.
It may be that in all her phrases stirred
The grinding water and the gasping wind;
But it was she and not the sea we heard.

For she was the maker[3] of the song she sang.   15
The ever-hooded, tragic-gestured sea
Was merely a place by which she walked to sing.
Whose spirit is this? we said, because we knew
It was the spirit that we sought and knew
That we should ask this often as she sang.   20

If it was only the dark voice of the sea
That rose, or even colored by many waves;
If it was only the outer voice of sky
And cloud, of the sunken coral water-walled,
However clear, it would have been deep air,   25
The heaving speech of air, a summer sound
Repeated in a summer without end
And sound alone. But it was more than that,
More even than her voice, and ours, among
The meaningless plungings of water and the wind,   30
Theatrical distances, bronze shadows heaped
On high horizons, mountainous atmospheres
Of sky and sea.

            It was her voice that made
The sky acutest at its vanishing.   35
She measured to the hour its solitude.
She was the single artificer of the world
In which she sang. And when she sang, the sea,
Whatever self it had, became the self
That was her song, for she was the maker. Then we,   40
As we beheld her striding there alone,
Knew that there never was a world for her
Except the one she sang and, singing, made.

Ramon Fernandez,[4] tell me, if you know,
Why, when the singing ended and we turned   45
Toward the town, tell why the glassy lights,
The lights in the fishing boats at anchor there,
As the night descended, tilting in the air,
Mastered the night and portioned out the sea,
Fixing emblazoned zones and fiery poles,   50
Arranging, deepening, enchanting night.

Oh! Blessed rage for order, pale Ramon,
The maker's rage to order words of the sea,
Words of the fragrant portals, dimly-starred,
And of ourselves and of our origins,   55
In ghostlier demarcations, keener sounds.

---

[3] *the maker* a literal translation of the Greek word *poïētēs* or poet.
[4] *Ramon Fernandez* Stevens informed one correspondent that he had chosen this name by combining two Spanish names at random and that he was not referring to *the* Ramon Fernandez (1894–1944) (*Letters*, 798).

The Poems of Our Climate (1938)

I

Clear water in a brilliant bowl,
Pink and white carnations. The light
In the room more like a snowy air,
Reflecting snow. A newly-fallen snow
At the end of winter when afternoons return.   5
Pink and white carnations – one desires
So much more than that. The day itself
Is simplified: a bowl of white,
Cold, a cold porcelain, low and round,
With nothing more than the carnations there.   10

II

Say even that this complete simplicity
Stripped one of all one's torments, concealed
The evilly compounded, vital I
And made it fresh in a world of white,
A world of clear water, brilliant-edged,   15
Still one would want more, one would need more,
More than a world of white and snowy scents.

III

There would still remain the never-resting mind,
So that one would want to escape, come back
To what had been so long composed.   20
The imperfect is our paradise.
Note that, in this bitterness, delight,
Since the imperfect is so hot in us,
Lies in flawed words and stubborn sounds.

Esthétique du Mal[1] (1944)

I

He was at Naples[2] writing letters home
And, between his letters, reading paragraphs
On the sublime. Vesuvius[3] had groaned
For a month. It was pleasant to be sitting there,

THE POEMS
The poem was published for the first time in the *Southern Review* 4(2) (autumn 1938). It was included in the collection of poems that Stevens published four years later, *Parts of a World* (New York: Alfred Knopf, 1942).

ESTHÉTIQUE
The poem was published for the first time in the *Kenyon Review* 6(4) (autumn 1944). It was printed as a separate volume in a limited edition of 300 copies (Cummington, MA: Cummington Press, 1945), and was collected in a trade edition two years later, *Transport to Summer* (New York: Alfred Knopf, 1947).
[1]   *Esthétique du mal* "aesthetics of evil" or "aesthetics of pain" in

French. "What really interested me," Sevens wrote to the editor of the journal that published the poem, "was the letter from one of your correspondents about the relation between poetry and what he called pain. It is the kind of idea that it is difficult to shake off" (*Letters*, 468).
[2]   *Naples* a city on the west coast of Italy, in the south; it was taken by Allied troops on October 1, 1943, and three months later Allied troops landed at Anzio.
[3]   *Vesuvius* Mount Vesuvius, not far from Naples, erupted on March 18, 1944, after several days of seismic activity; explosions burst from the volcano on March, 20, and the nearby ruins of Pompeii were reburied under nearly a foot of ash. In various aesthetics, mountains and volcanos are associated with the sublime.

While the sultriest fulgurations, flickering,   5
Cast corners in the glass. He could describe
The terror of the sound because the sound
Was ancient. He tried to remember the phrases: pain
Audible at noon, pain torturing itself,
Pain killing pain on the very point of pain.   10
The volcano trembled in another ether,
As the body trembles at the end of life.

It was almost time for lunch. Pain is human.
There were roses in the cool café. His book
Made sure of the most correct catastrophe.   15
Except for us, Vesuvius might consume
In solid fire the utmost earth and know
No pain (ignoring the cocks that crow us up
To die). This is a part of the sublime
From which we shrink. And yet, except for us,   20
The total past felt nothing when destroyed.

                                II

At a town in which acacias grew, he lay
On his balcony at night. Warblings became
Too dark, too far, too much the accents of
Afflicted sleep, too much the syllables   25
That would form themselves, in time, and communicate
The intelligence of his despair, express
What meditation never quite achieved.

The moon rose up as if it had escaped
His meditation. It evaded his mind.   30
It was part of a supremacy always
Above him. The moon was always free from him,
As night was free from him. The shadow touched
Or merely seemed to touch him as he spoke
A kind of elegy he found in space: 35

It is pain that is indifferent to the sky
In spite of the yellow of the acacias, the scent
Of them in the air still hanging heavily
In the hoary-hanging night. It does not regard
This freedom, this supremacy, and in   40
Its own hallucination never sees
How that which rejects it saves it in the end.

                                III

His firm stanzas hang like hives in hell
Or what hell was, since now both heaven and hell
Are one, and here, O terra infidel.   45

The fault lies with an over-human god,
Who by sympathy has made himself a man
And is not to be distinguished, when we cry

Because we suffer, our oldest parent, peer
Of the populace of the heart, the reddest lord,   50
Who has gone before us in experience.

If only he would not pity us so much,
Weaken our fate, relieve us of woe both great
And small, a constant fellow of destiny,

A too, too human god, self-pity's kin   55
And uncourageous genesis ... It seems
As if the health of the world might be enough.

It seems as if the honey of common summer
Might be enough, as if the golden combs
Were part of a sustenance itself enough,   60

As if hell, so modified, had disappeared,
As if pain, no longer satanic mimicry,
Could be borne, as if we were sure to find our way.

IV

Livre de Toutes Sortes de Fleurs D'Après Nature.[4]
All sorts of flowers. That's the sentimentalist.   65
When B. sat down at the piano and made
A transparence in which we heard music, made music
In which we heard transparent sounds, did he play
All sorts of notes? Or did he play only one
In an ecstasy of its associates,   70
Variations in the tones of a single sound,
The last, or sounds so single they seemed one?
And then that Spaniard of the rose, itself
Hot-hooded and dark-blooded, rescued the rose
From nature, each time he saw it, making it,   75
As he saw it, exist in his own especial eye.
Can we conceive of him as rescuing less,
As muffing the mistress for her several maids,
As foregoing the nakedest passion for barefoot
Philandering? ... The genius of misfortune   80
Is not a sentimentalist. He is
That evil, that evil in the self, from which
In desperate hallow, rugged gesture, fault
Falls out on everything: the genius of
The mind, which is our being, wrong and wrong,   85
The genius of the body, which is our world,
Spent in the false engagements of the mind.

V

Softly let all true sympathizers come,
Without the inventions of sorrow or the sob
Beyond invention. Within what we permit,   90
Within the actual, the warm, the near,
So great a unity, that it is bliss,

---

[4] *Livre de ... D'Après Nature* French for "The Book of
All Kinds of Flowers, after Nature." The title is made up by
Stevens, though it broadly recalls rare or antiquarian French
titles.

Ties us to those we love. For this familiar,
This brother even in the father's eye,
This brother half-spoken in the mother's throat   95
And these regalia, these things disclosed,
These nebulous brilliancies in the smallest look
Of the being's deepest darling, we forego
Lament, willingly forfeit the ai-ai
Of parades in the obscurer selvages.[5]   100
Be near me, come closer, touch my hand, phrases
  Compounded of dear relation, spoken twice,
Once by the lips, once by the services
Of central sense, these minutiae mean more
Than clouds, benevolences, distant heads.   105
These are within what we permit, in-bar
Exquisite in poverty against the suns
Of ex-bar, in-bar retaining attributes
With which we vested, once, the golden forms
And the damasked memory of the golden forms   110
And ex-bar's flower and fire of the festivals
Of the damasked memory of the golden forms,
Before we were wholly human and knew ourselves.

VI

The sun, in clownish yellow, but not a clown,
Brings the day to perfection and then fails. He dwells   115
In a consummate prime, yet still desires
A further consummation. For the lunar month
He makes the tenderest research, intent
On a transmutation which, when seen, appears
To be askew. And space is filled with his   120
Rejected years. A big bird pecks at him
For food. The big bird's boney appetite
Is as insatiable as the sun's. The bird
Rose from an imperfection of its own
To feed on the yellow bloom of the yellow fruit   125
Dropped down from turquoise leaves. In the landscape of
The sun, its grossest appetite becomes less gross,
Yet, when corrected, has its curious lapses,
Its glitters, its divinations of serene
Indulgence out of all celestial sight.   130

The sun is the country wherever he is. The bird
In the brightest landscape downwardly revolves
Disdaining each astringent ripening,
Evading the point of redness, not content
To repose in an hour or season or long era   135
Of the country colors crowding against it, since
The yellow grassman's mind is still immense,
Still promises perfections cast away.

VII

How red the rose that is the soldier's wound,
The wounds of many soldiers, the wounds of all   140

---

5 *obscurer selvages* a selvage is an edge or border; "obscurer   *selva selvaggia* ("savage wood" at the beginning of Dante's *Inferno*,
selvages" may also allude to the *selva obscura* ("dark wood") and   lines 2, 5).

The soldiers that have fallen, red in blood,
The soldier of time grown deathless in great size.

A mountain in which no ease is ever found,
Unless indifference to deeper death
Is ease, stands in the dark, a shadows' hill,   145
And there the soldier of time has deathless rest.

Concentric circles of shadows, motionless
Of their own part, yet moving on the wind,
Form mystical convolutions in the sleep
Of time's red soldier deathless on his bed.   150

The shadows of his fellows ring him round
In the high night, the summer breathes for them
Its fragrance, a heavy somnolence, and for him,
For the soldier of time, it breathes a summer sleep,

In which his wound is good because life was.   155
No part of him was ever part of death.
A woman smoothes her forehead with her hand
And the soldier of time lies calm beneath that stroke.

VIII

The death of Satan was a tragedy
For the imagination. A capital   160
Negation destroyed him in his tenement
And, with him, many blue phenomena.
It was not the end he had foreseen. He knew
That his revenge created filial
Revenges. And negation was eccentric.   165
It had nothing of the Julian[6] thunder-cloud:
The assassin flash and rumble ... He was denied.

Phantoms, what have you left? What underground?
What place in which to be is not enough
To be? You go, poor phantoms, without place   170
Like silver in the sheathing of the sight,
As the eye closes ... How cold the vacancy
When the phantoms are gone and the shaken realist
First sees reality. The mortal no
Has its emptiness and tragic expirations.   175
The tragedy, however, may have begun,
Again, in the imagination's new beginning,
In the yes of the realist spoken because he must
Say yes, spoken because under every no
Lay a passion for yes that had never been broken.   180

IX

Panic in the face of the moon – round effendi[7]
Or the phosphored sleep in which he walks abroad
Or the majolica dish heaped up with phosphored fruit
That he sends ahead, out of the goodness of his heart,
To anyone that comes – panic, because   185
The moon is no longer these nor anything

---

[6] *Julian* of Julius Caesar.

[7] *Effendi* a Turkish title of respect, or a person having this title,
such as a scholar.

And nothing is left but comic ugliness
Or a lustred nothingness. Effendi, he
That has lost the folly of the moon becomes
The prince of the proverbs of pure poverty.   190
To lose sensibility, to see what one sees,
As if sight had not its own miraculous thrift,
To hear only what one hears, one meaning alone,
As if the paradise of meaning ceased
To be paradise, it is this to be destitute.   195
This is the sky divested of its fountains.
Here in the west indifferent crickets chant
Through our indifferent crises. Yet we require
Another chant, an incantation, as in
Another and later genesis, music   200
That buffets the shapes of its possible halcyon
Against the haggardie ... A loud, large water
Bubbles up in the night and drowns the crickets' sound.
It is a declaration, a primitive ecstasy,
Truth's favors sonorously exhibited.   205

X

He had studied the nostalgias. In these
He sought the most grossly maternal, the creature
Who most fecundly assuaged him, the softest
Woman with a vague moustache and not the mauve
Maman.[8] His anima liked its animal   210
And liked it unsubjugated, so that home
Was a return to birth, a being born
Again in the savagest severity,
Desiring fiercely, the child of a mother fierce
In his body, fiercer in his mind, merciless   215
To accomplish the truth in his intelligence.
It is true there were other mothers, singular
In form, lovers of heaven and earth, she-wolves
And forest tigresses and women mixed
With the sea. These were fantastic. There were homes   220
Like things submerged with their englutted sounds
That were never wholly still. The softest woman,
Because she is as she was, reality,
The gross, the fecund, proved him against the touch
Of impersonal pain. Reality explained.   225
It was the last nostalgia: that he
Should understand. That he might suffer or that
He might die was the innocence of living, if life
Itself was innocent. To say that it was
Disentangled him from sleek ensolacings.   230

XI

Life is a bitter aspic.[9] We are not
At the centre of a diamond. At dawn,
The paratroopers fall and as they fall
They mow the lawn. A vessel sinks in waves
Of people, as big bell-billows from its bell   235

---

[8] Maman French for "mommy" or "mummy."   [9] aspic poetic term for an asp or snake.

Bell-bellow in the village steeple. Violets,
Great tufts, spring up from buried houses
Of poor, dishonest people, for whom the steeple,
Long since, rang out farewell, farewell, farewell.
Natives of poverty, children of malheur,   240
The gaiety of language is our seigneur.

A man of bitter appetite despises
A well-made scene in which paratroopers
Select adieux; and he despises this:
A ship that rolls on a confected ocean,   245
The weather pink, the wind in motion; and this:
A steeple that tip-tops the classic sun's
Arrangements; and the violets' exhumo.[10]

The tongue caresses these exacerbations.
They press it as epicure, distinguishing   250
Themselves from its essential savor,
Like hunger that feeds on its own hungriness.

XII

He disposes the world in categories, thus:
The peopled and the unpeopled. In both, he is
Alone. But in the peopled world, there is,   255
Besides the people, his knowledge of them. In
The unpeopled, there is his knowledge of himself.
Which is more desperate in the moments when
The will demands that what he thinks be true?

Is it himself in them that he knows or they   260
In him? If it is himself in them, they have
No secret from him. If it is they in him,
He has no secret from them. This knowledge
Of them and of himself destroys both worlds,
Except when he escapes from it. To be   265
Alone is not to know them or himself.

This creates a third world without knowledge,
In which no one peers, in which the will makes no
Demands. It accepts whatever is as true,
Including pain, which, otherwise, is false.   270
In the third world, then, there is no pain. Yes, but
What lover has one in such rocks, what woman,
However known, at the centre of the heart?

XIII

It may be that one life is a punishment
For another, as the son's life for the father's.   275
But that concerns the secondary characters.
It is a fragmentary tragedy
Within the universal whole. The son
And the father alike and equally are spent,

---

[10]   *exhumo* a coinage by Stevens, obviously related to the sense of
exhume, to take out of the grave or ground.

Each one, by the necessity of being   280
Himself, the unalterable necessity
Of being this unalterable animal.
This force of nature in action is the major
Tragedy. This is destiny unperplexed,
The happiest enemy. And it may be   285
That in his Mediterranean cloister a man,
Reclining, eased of desire, establishes
The visible, a zone of blue and orange
Versicolorings, establishes a time
To watch the fire-feinting sea and calls it good,   290
The ultimate good, sure of a reality
Of the longest meditation, the maximum,
The assassin's scene. Evil in evil is
Comparative. The assassin discloses himself,
The force that destroys us is disclosed, within   295
This maximum, an adventure to be endured
With the politest helplessness. Ay-mi!
One feels its action moving in the blood.

XIV

Victor Serge[11] said, "I followed his argument
With the blank uneasiness which one might feel   300
In the presence of a logical lunatic."
He said it of Konstantinov. Revolution
Is the affair of logical lunatics.
The politics of emotion must appear
To be an intellectual structure. The cause   305
Creates a logic not to be distinguished
From lunacy ... One wants to be able to walk
By the lake at Geneva and consider logic:
To think of the logicians in their graves
And of the worlds of logic in their great tombs.   310
Lakes are more reasonable than oceans. Hence,
A promenade amid the grandeurs of the mind,
By a lake, with clouds like lights among great tombs,
Gives one a blank uneasiness, as if
One might meet Konstantinov, who would interrupt   315
With his lunacy. He would not be aware of the lake.
He would be the lunatic of one idea
In a world of ideas, who would have all the people
Live, work, suffer and die in that idea
In a world of ideas. He would not be aware of the clouds,   320
Lighting the martyrs of logic with white fire.
His extreme of logic would be illogical.

XV

The greatest poverty is not to live
In a physical world, to feel that one's desire
Is too difficult to tell from despair. Perhaps,   325
After death, the non-physical people, in paradise,

---

[11] *Victor Serge* Victor Serge (1890–1947) was a Russian revolutionary and novelist; he fled the Soviet Union in 1936, disgusted with Stalinism; then in 1940 he fled from Paris to Mexico, where he died. In the June 1944 issue of *Politics*, Serge published an essay called "The Revolution at Dead End," where he recalled his 1920 encounter with Konstantinov, an examining magistrate with the Cheka, or secret police. Stevens is quoting from the essay.

Itself non-physical, may, by chance, observe
The green corn gleaming and experience
The minor of what we feel. The adventurer
In humanity has not conceived of a race   330
Completely physical in a physical world.
The green corn gleams and the metaphysicals
Lie sprawling in majors of the August heat,
The rotund emotions, paradise unknown.

This is the thesis scrivened in delight,   335
The reverberating psalm, the right chorale.

One might have thought of sight, but who could think
Of what it sees, for all the ill it sees?
Speech found the ear, for all the evil sound,
But the dark italics it could not propound.   340
And out of what one sees and hears and out
Of what one feels, who could have thought to make
So many selves, so many sensuous worlds,
As if the air, the mid-day air, was swarming
With the metaphysical changes that occur,   345
Merely in living as and where we live.

The Auroras of Autumn (1948)

I

This is where the serpent lives, the bodiless.
His head is air. Beneath his tip at night
Eyes open and fix on us in every sky.

Or is this another wriggling out of the egg,
Another image at the end of the cave,   5
Another bodiless for the body's slough?

This is where the serpent lives. This is his nest,
These fields, these hills, these tinted distances,
And the pines above and along and beside the sea.

This is form gulping after formlessness,   10
Skin flashing to wished-for disappearances
And the serpent body flashing without the skin.

This is the height emerging and its base ...
These lights may finally attain a pole
In the midmost midnight and find the serpent there,   15

In another nest, the master of the maze
Of body and air and forms and images,
Relentlessly in possession of happiness.

This is his poison: that we should disbelieve
Even that. His meditations in the ferns,   20
When he moved so slightly to make sure of sun,

THE AURORAS
The poem was first published in the *Kenyon Review* 10(1) (winter
1948). It was included in a collection of poems that Stevens
published two years later, *The Auroras of Autumn* (New York:
Alfred Knopf, 1950).

Made us no less as sure. We saw in his head,
Black beaded on the rock, the flecked animal,
The moving grass, the Indian in his glade.

II

Farewell to an idea ... A cabin stands,   25
Deserted, on a beach. It is white,
As by a custom or according to

An ancestral theme or as a consequence
Of an infinite course. The flowers against the wall
Are white, a little dried, a kind of mark   30

Reminding, trying to remind, of a white
That was different, something else, last year
Or before, not the white of an aging afternoon,

Whether fresher or duller, whether of winter cloud
Or of winter sky, from horizon to horizon.   35
The wind is blowing the sand across the floor.

Here, being visible is being white,
Is being of the solid of white, the accomplishment
Of an extremist in an exercise ...

The season changes. A cold wind chills the beach.   40
The long lines of it grow longer, emptier,
A darkness gathers though it does not fall

And the whiteness grows less vivid on the wall.
The man who is walking turns blankly on the sand.
He observes how the north is always enlarging the change,   45

With its frigid brilliances, its blue-red sweeps
And gusts of great enkindlings, its polar green,
The color of ice and fire and solitude.

III

Farewell to an idea ... The mother's face,
The purpose of the poem, fills the room.   50
They are together, here, and it is warm,

With none of the prescience of oncoming dreams.
It is evening. The house is evening, half dissolved.
Only the half they can never possess remains,

Still-starred. It is the mother they possess,   55
Who gives transparence to their present peace.
She makes that gentler that can gentle be.

And yet she too is dissolved, she is destroyed.
She gives transparence. But she has grown old.
The necklace is a carving not a kiss.   60

The soft hands are a motion not a touch.
The house will crumble and the books will burn.
They are at ease in a shelter of the mind

And the house is of the mind and they and time,
Together, all together. Boreal night   65
Will look like frost as it approaches them

And to the mother as she falls asleep
And as they say good-night, good-night. Upstairs
The windows will be lighted, not the rooms.

A wind will spread its windy grandeurs round   70
And knock like a rifle-butt against the door.
The wind will command them with invincible sound.

IV

Farewell to an idea ... The cancellings,
The negations are never final: The father sits
In space, wherever he sits, of bleak regard,   75

As one that is strong in the bushes of his eyes.
He says no to no and yes to yes. He says yes
To no; and in saying yes he says farewell.

He measures the velocities of change.
He leaps from heaven to heaven more rapidly   80
Than bad angels leap from heaven to hell in flames.

But now he sits in quiet and green-a-day.
He assumes the great speeds of space and flutters them
From cloud to cloudless, cloudless to keen clear

In flights of eye and ear, the highest eye   85
And the lowest ear, the deep ear that discerns.
At evening, things that attend it until it hears

The supernatural preludes of its own,
At the moment when the angelic eye defines
Its actors approaching, in company, in their masks.   90

Master O master seated by the fire
And yet in space and motionless and yet
Of motion the ever-brightening origin,

Profound, and yet the king and yet the crown,
Look at this present throne. What company,   95
In masks, can choir it with the naked wind?

V

The mother invites humanity to her house
And table. The father fetches tellers of tales
And musicians who mute much, muse much, on the tales.

The father fetches negresses to dance,   100
Among the children, like curious ripenesses
Of pattern in the dance's ripening.

For these the musicians make insidious tones,
Clawing the sing-song of their instruments.
The children laugh and jangle a tinny time.   105

The father fetches pageants out of air,
Scenes of the theatre, vistas and blocks of woods
And curtains like a naive pretence of sleep.

Among these the musicians strike the instinctive poem.
The father fetches his unherded herds,   110
Of barbarous tongue, slavered and panting halves

Of breath, obedient to his trumpet's touch.
This then is Chatillon or as you please.
We stand in the tumult of a festival.

What festival? This loud, disordered mooch?   115
These hospitaliers? These brute-like guests?
These musicians dubbing at a tragedy,

A-dub, a-dub, which is made up of this:
That there are no lines to speak? There is no play.
Or, the persons act one merely by being here.   120

VI

It is a theatre floating through the clouds,
Itself a cloud, although of misted rock
And mountains running like water, wave on wave,

Through waves of light. It is of cloud transformed
To cloud transformed again, idly, the way   125
A season changes color to no end,

Except the lavishing of itself in change,
As light changes yellow into gold and gold
To its opal elements and fire's delight,

Splashed wide-wise because it likes magnificence   130
And the solemn pleasures of magnificent space.
The cloud drifts idly through half-thought-of forms.

The theatre is filled with flying birds,
Wild wedges, as of a volcano's smoke, palm-eyed
And vanishing, a web in a corridor   135

Or massive portico. A capitol,
It may be, is emerging or has just
Collapsed. The denouement has to be postponed . . .

This is nothing until in a single man contained,
Nothing until this named thing nameless is   140
And is destroyed. He opens the door of his house

On flames. The scholar of one candle sees
An Arctic effulgence flaring on the frame
Of everything he is. And he feels afraid.

VII

Is there an imagination that sits enthroned   145
As grim as it is benevolent, the just
And the unjust, which in the midst of summer stops

To imagine winter? When the leaves are dead,
Does it take its place in the north and enfold itself,
Goat-leaper, crystalled and luminous, sitting   150

In highest night? And do these heavens adorn
And proclaim it, the white creator of black, jetted
By extinguishings, even of planets as may be,

Even of earth, even of sight, in snow,
Except as needed by way of majesty,   155
In the sky, as crown and diamond cabala?

It leaps through us, through all our heavens leaps,
Extinguishing our planets, one by one,
Leaving, of where we were and looked, of where

We knew each other and of each other thought,   160
A shivering residue, chilled and foregone,
Except for that crown and mystical cabala.

But it dare not leap by chance in its own dark.
It must change from destiny to slight caprice.
And thus its jetted tragedy, its stele   165

And shape and mournful making move to find
What must unmake it and, at last, what can,
Say, a flippant communication under the moon.

VIII

There may be always a time of innocence.
There is never a place. Or if there is no time,   170
If it is not a thing of time, nor of place,

Existing in the idea of it, alone,
In the sense against calamity, it is not
Less real. For the oldest and coldest philosopher,

There is or may be a time of innocence   175
As pure principle. Its nature is its end,
That it should be, and yet not be, a thing

That pinches the pity of the pitiful man,
Like a book at evening beautiful but untrue,
Like a book on rising beautiful and true.   180

It is like a thing of ether that exists
Almost as predicate. But it exists,
It exists, it is visible, it is, it is.

So, then, these lights are not a spell of light,
A saying out of a cloud, but innocence.   185
An innocence of the earth and no false sign

Or symbol of malice. That we partake thereof,
Lie down like children in this holiness,
As if, awake, we lay in the quiet of sleep,

As if the innocent mother sang in the dark   190
Of the room and on an accordion, half-heard,
Created the time and place in which we breathed ...

IX

And of each other thought – in the idiom
Of the work, in the idiom of an innocent earth,
Not of the enigma of the guilty dream.   195

We were as Danes in Denmark all day long
And knew each other well, hale-hearted landsmen,
For whom the outlandish was another day

Of the week, queerer than Sunday. We thought alike
And that made brothers of us in a home   200
In which we fed on being brothers, fed

And fattened as on a decorous honeycomb.
This drama that we live – We lay sticky with sleep.
This sense of the activity of fate –

The rendezvous, when she came alone,   205
By her coming became a freedom of the two,
An isolation which only the two could share.

Shall we be found hanging in the trees next spring?
Of what disaster is this the imminence:
Bare limbs, bare trees and a wind as sharp as salt?   210

The stars are putting on their glittering belts.
They throw around their shoulders cloaks that flash
Like a great shadow's last embellishment.

It may come tomorrow in the simplest word,
Almost as part of innocence, almost,   215
Almost as the tenderest and the truest part.

X

An unhappy people in a happy world –
Read, rabbi, the phases of this difference.
An unhappy people in an unhappy world –

Here are too many mirrors for misery.   220
A happy people in an unhappy world –
It cannot be. There's nothing there to roll

On the expressive tongue, the finding fang.
A happy people in a happy world –
Buffo! A ball, an opera, a bar.   225

Turn back to where we were when we began:
An unhappy people in a happy world
Now, solemnize the secretive syllables.

Read to the congregation, for today
And for tomorrow, this extremity,   230
This contrivance of the spectre of the spheres,

Contriving balance to contrive a whole,
The vital, the never-failing genius,
Fulfilling his meditations, great and small.

In these unhappy he meditates a whole,   235
The full of fortune and the full of fate,
As if he lived all lives, that he might know,

In hall harridan, not hushful paradise,
To a haggling of wind and weather, by these lights
Like a blaze of summer straw, in winter's nick.   240

The Noble Rider and the Sound of Words (1942)

In the *Phaedrus*,[1] Plato speaks of the soul in a figure. He says:

Let our figure be of a composite nature – a pair of winged horses and a charioteer. Now the winged horses and the charioteer of the gods are all of them noble, and of noble breed, while ours are mixed; and we have a charioteer who drives them in a pair, and one of them is noble and of noble origin, and the other is ignoble and of ignoble origin; and, as might be expected, there is a great deal of trouble in managing them. I will endeavor to explain to you in what way the mortal differs from the immortal creature. The soul or animate being has the care of the inanimate, and traverses the whole heaven in divers forms appearing; – when perfect and fully winged she soars upward, and is the ruler of the universe; while the imperfect soul loses her feathers, and drooping in her flight at last settles on the solid ground.

We recognize at once, in this figure, Plato's pure poetry; and at the same time we recognize what Coleridge called Plato's dear, gorgeous nonsense.[2] The truth is that we have scarcely read the passage before we have identified ourselves with the charioteer, have, in fact, taken his place and,

THE NOBLE RIDER
This essay was first read as a lecture at Princeton University in May 1941. "In May I went down to Princeton and read a paper which is going to be published in a small group of papers by the University Press in the autumn" (*Letters*, 392). It was first published not in autumn 1941, as Stevens though it would be, but a year later in Allen Tate (ed.), *The Language of Poetry* (Princeton: Princeton University Press, 1942), and later incorporated into a collection of essays by Stevens, *The Necessary Angel* (New York: Knopf, 1951).

1   From *Phaedrus*, 246A–C; the translation being cited by Stevens has not been identified.
2   Wallace Stevens picked up this Coleridge quotation from a book by I. A. Richards, *Coleridge on Imagination* (London: Kegan Paul, 1934), 149. Richards quotes a letter from Coleridge to John Thelwall, December 31, 1799, one that ends playfully: "So much for physicians and surgeons! Now as to the metaphysicians. Plato says it is *harmony*. He might as well have said a fiddle-stick's end; but I love Plato, his dear *gorgeous* nonsense; and I, *though last not least*, I do not know what to think about it."

driving his winged horses, are traversing the whole heaven. Then suddenly we remember, it may be, that the soul no longer exists and we droop in our flight and at last settle on the solid ground. The figure becomes antiquated and rustic.

I

What really happens in this brief experience? Why does this figure, potent for so long, become merely the emblem of a mythology, the rustic memorial of a belief in the soul and in a distinction between good and evil? The answer to these questions is, I think, a simple one.

I said that suddenly we remember that the soul no longer exists and we droop in our flight. For that matter, neither charioteers nor chariots any longer exist. Consequently, the figure does not become unreal because we are troubled about the soul. Besides, unreal things have a reality of their own, in poetry as elsewhere. We do not hesitate, in poetry, to yield ourselves to the unreal, when it is possible to yield ourselves. The existence of the soul, of charioteers and chariots and of winged horses is immaterial. They did not exist for Plato, not even the charioteer and chariot; for certainly a charioteer driving his chariot across the whole heaven was for Plato precisely what he is for us. He was unreal for Plato as he is for us. Plato, however, could yield himself, was free to yield himself, to this gorgeous nonsense. We cannot yield ourselves. We are not free to yield ourselves.

Just as the difficulty is not a difficulty about unreal things, since the imagination accepts them, and since the poetry of the passage is, for us, wholly the poetry of the unreal, so it is not an emotional difficulty. Something else than the imagination is moved by the statement that the horses of the gods are all of them noble, and of noble breed or origin. The statement is a moving statement and is intended to be so. It is insistent and its insistence moves us. Its insistence is the insistence of a speaker, in this case Socrates, who, for the moment, feels delight, even if a casual delight, in the nobility and noble breed. Those images of nobility instantly become nobility itself and determine the emotional level at which the next page or two are to be read. The figure does not lose its vitality because of any failure of feeling on Plato's part. He does not communicate nobility coldly. His horses are not marble horses, the reference to their breed saves them from being that. The fact that the horses are not marble horses helps, moreover, to save the charioteer from being, say, a creature of cloud. The result is that we recognize, even if we cannot realize, the feelings of the robust poet clearly and fluently noting the images in his mind and by means of his robustness, clearness and fluency communicating much more than the images themselves. Yet we do not quite yield. We cannot. We do not feel free.

In trying to find out what it is that stands between Plato's figure and ourselves, we have to accept the idea that, however legendary it appears to be, it has had its vicissitudes. The history of a figure of speech or the history of an idea, such as the idea of nobility, cannot be very different from the history of anything else. It is the episodes that are of interest, and here the episode is that of our diffidence. By us and ourselves, I mean you and me; and yet not you and me as individuals but as representatives of a state of mind. Adams in his work on Vico[3] makes the remark that the true history of the human race is a history of its progressive mental states. It is a remark of interest in this relation. We may assume that in the history of Plato's figure there have been incessant changes of response; that these changes have been psychological changes, and that our own diffidence is simply one more state of mind due to such a change.

The specific question is partly as to the nature of the change and partly as to the cause of it. In nature, the change is as follows: The imagination loses vitality as it ceases to adhere to what is real. When it adheres to the unreal and intensifies what is unreal, while its first effect may be extraordinary, that effect is the maximum effect that it will ever have. In Plato's figure, his imagination does not adhere to what is real. On the contrary, having created something unreal, it adheres to it and intensifies its unreality. Its first effect, its effect at first reading, is its maximum effect, when the imagination, being moved, puts us in the place of the charioteer, before the reason

[3] Henry Packwood Adams, *The Life and Writings of Giambattista Vico* (London: George Allen and Unwin, 1935), 152, summarizing one of Vico's central claims in the *Scienza Nuova* (New Science) (1725): "The true history of the human race is a history of its progressive mental states."

632 WALLACE STEVENS, THE NOBLE RIDER AND THE SOUND OF WORDS

checks us. The case is, then, that we concede that the figure is all imagination. At the same time, we say that it has not the slightest meaning for us, except for its nobility. As to that, while we are moved by it, we are moved as observers. We recognize it perfectly. We do not realize it. We understand the feeling of it, the robust feeling, clearly and fluently communicated. Yet we understand it rather than participate in it.

As to the cause of the change, it is the loss of the figure's vitality. The reason why this particular figure has lost its vitality is that, in it, the imagination adheres to what is unreal. What happened, as we were traversing the whole heaven, is that the imagination lost its power to sustain us. It has the strength of reality or none at all.

2

What has just been said demonstrates that there are degrees of the imagination, as, for example, degrees of vitality and, therefore, of intensity. It is an implication that there are degrees of reality. The discourse about the two elements seems endless. For my own part, I intend merely to follow, in a very hasty way, the fortunes of the idea of nobility as a characteristic of the imagination, and even as its symbol or alter ego, through several of the episodes in its history, in order to determine, if possible, what its fate has been and what has determined its fate. This can be done only on the basis of the relation between the imagination and reality. What has been said in respect to the figure of the charioteer illustrates this.

I should like now to go on to other illustrations of the relation between the imagination and reality and particularly to illustrations that constitute episodes in the history of the idea of nobility. It would be agreeable to pass directly from the charioteer and his winged horses to Don Quixote. It would be like a return from what Plato calls "the back of heaven"[4] to one's own spot. Nevertheless, there is Verrocchio (as one among others) with his statue of Bartolommeo Colleoni,[5] in Venice, standing in the way. I have not selected him as a Neo-Platonist to relate us back from a modern time to Plato's time, although he does in fact so relate us, just as through Leonardo, his pupil, he strengthens the relationship. I have selected him because there, on the edge of the world in which we live today, he established a form of such nobility that it has never ceased to magnify us in our own eyes. It is like the form of an invincible man, who has come, slowly and boldly, through every warlike opposition of the past and who moves in our midst without dropping the bridle of the powerful horse from his hand, without taking off his helmet and without relaxing the attitude of a warrior of noble origin. What man on whose side the horseman fought could ever be anything but fearless, anything but indomitable? One feels the passion of rhetoric begin to stir and even to grow furious; and one thinks that, after all, the noble style, in whatever it creates, merely perpetuates the noble style. In this statue, the apposition between the imagination and reality is too favorable to the imagination. Our difficulty is not primarily with any detail. It is primarily with the whole. The point is not so much to analyze the difficulty as to determine whether we share it, to find out whether it exists, whether we regard this specimen of the genius of Verrocchio and of the Renaissance as a bit of uncommon panache, no longer quite the appropriate thing outdoors, or whether we regard it, in the language of Dr. Richards, as something inexhaustible to meditation[6] or, to speak for myself, as a thing of a nobility responsive to the most minute demand. It seems, nowadays, what it may very well not have seemed a few years ago, a little overpowering, a little magnificent.

---

[4] *Phaedrus* 247B–C: "Now when those souls that are called immortal come to the summit, they proceed without and take their stand upon the back of heaven where its revolution carries them in full circle" trans. (Plato, Phaedrus, trans. W. C. Helmbold and W. G. Rabinowitz [Indianapolis: Bobbs-Merrill, 1956], 29–30).

[5] Andrea del Verrocchio (1435–88) was a Florentine sculptor. His great equestrian monument to the legendary condottiere Bartolommeo Colleoni (1400–76) sits alongside the church of SS. Giovanni e Paolo in Venice, and was erected with funds that

Colleoni had bequeathed to Venice to keep his memory alive. (See figure 3). His greatest student was Leonardo da Vinci.

[6] I. A. Richards (1893–1979) was a pioneering critic and educator whose book *Coleridge on Imagination* was read and extensively marked by Stevens in preparation for writing "The Noble Rider." (Stevens's copy is held in the Huntington Library.) Richards writes: "Make-belief is an enervating exercise of fancy not to be confused with imaginative growth. The saner and greater mythologies are not fancies; they are the utterance of the whole soul of man and, as such, inexhaustible to meditation" (*Coleridge on Imagination*, 171).

Figure 3:   Andrea del Verrocchio's equestrian statue of Bartolommeo Colleoni, Venice, Campo San Zanipolo.
© 1990, photograph SCALA, Florence.

Undoubtedly, Don Quixote could be Bartolommeo Colleoni in Spain. The tradition of Italy is the tradition of the imagination. The tradition of Spain is the tradition of reality. There is no apparent reason why the reverse should not be true. If this is a just observation, it indicates that the relation between the imagination and reality is a question, more or less, of precise equilibrium. Thus it is not a question of the difference between grotesque extremes. My purpose is not to contrast Colleoni with Don Quixote. It is to say that one passed into the other, that one became and was the other. The difference between them is that Verrocchio believed in one kind of nobility and Cervantes, if he believed in any, believed in another kind. With Verrocchio it was an affair of the noble style, whatever his prepossession respecting the nobility of man as a real animal may have been. With Cervantes, nobility was not a thing of the imagination. It was a part of reality, it was something that exists in life, something so true to us that it is in danger of ceasing to exist, if we isolate it, something in the mind of a precarious tenure. These may be words. Certainly, however, Cervantes sought to set right the balance between the imagination and reality. As we come closer to our own times in Don Quixote and as we are drawn together by the intelligence common to the two periods, we may derive so much satisfaction from the restoration of reality as to become wholly prejudiced against the imagination. This is to reach a conclusion prematurely, let alone that it may be to reach a conclusion in respect to something as to which no conclusion is possible or desirable.

There is in Washington, in Lafayette Square, which is the square on which the White House faces, a statue of Andrew Jackson, riding a horse with one of the most beautiful tails in the world. General Jackson is raising his hat in a gay gesture, saluting the ladies of his generation. One looks at this work of Clark Mills[7] and thinks of the remark of Bertrand Russell that to acquire immunity

Figure 4:   Clark Mills's equestrain statue of Andrew Jackson

---

[7]   The equestrian statue of Andrew Jackson (U.S. president from 1832 to 1840), which sits directly opposite the north portico of the White House in Lafayette Square, was the work of Clark Mills (1815–83) and was unveiled in 1853 (see figure 4).

to eloquence is of the utmost importance to the citizens of a democracy.[8] We are bound to think that Colleoni, as a mercenary, was a much less formidable man than General Jackson, that he meant less to fewer people and that, if Verrocchio could have applied his prodigious poetry to Jackson, the whole American outlook today might be imperial. This work is a work of fancy. Dr. Richards cites Coleridge's theory of fancy[9] as opposed to imagination. Fancy is an activity of the mind which puts things together of choice, *not* the will, as a principle of the mind's being, striving to realize itself in knowing itself. Fancy, then, is an exercise of selection from among objects already supplied by association, a selection made for purposes which are not then and therein being shaped but have been already fixed. We are concerned then with an object occupying a position as remarkable as any that can be found in the United States in which there is not the slightest trace of the imagination. Treating this work as typical, it is obvious that the American will as a principle of the mind's being is easily satisfied in its efforts to realize itself in knowing itself. The statue may be dismissed, not without speaking of it again as a thing that at least makes us conscious of ourselves as we were, if not as we are. To that extent, it helps us to know ourselves. It helps us to know ourselves as we were and that helps us to know ourselves as we are. The statue is neither of the imagination nor of reality. That it is a work of fancy precludes it from being a work of the imagination. A glance at it shows it to be unreal. The bearing of this is that there can be works, and this includes poems, in which neither the imagination nor reality is present.

The other day I was reading a note about an American artist[10] who was said to have "turned his back on the aesthetic whims and theories of the day, and established headquarters in lower Manhattan." Accompanying this note was a reproduction of a painting called *Wooden Horses*.[11] It is a painting of a merry-go-round, possibly of several of them. One of the horses seems to be prancing. The others are going lickety-split, each one struggling to get the bit in his teeth. The horse in the center of the picture, painted yellow, has two riders, one a man, dressed in a carnival costume, who is seated in the saddle, the other a blonde, who is seated well up the horse's neck. The man has his arms under the girl's arms. He holds himself stiffly in order to keep his cigar out of the girl's hair. Her feet are in a second and shorter set of stirrups. She has the legs of a hammer-thrower. It is clear that the couple are accustomed to wooden horses and like them. A little behind them is a younger girl riding alone. She has a strong body and streaming hair. She wears a short-sleeved, red waist, a white skirt and an emphatic bracelet of pink coral. She has her eyes on the man's arms. Still farther behind, there is another girl. One does not see much more of her than her head. Her lips are painted bright red. It seems that it would be better if someone were to hold her on her horse. We, here, are not interested in any aspect of this picture except that it is a picture of ribald and hilarious reality. It is a picture wholly favorable to what is real. It is not without imagination and it is far from being without aesthetic theory.

3

These illustrations of the relation between the imagination and reality are an outline on the basis of which to indicate a tendency. Their usefulness is this: that they help to make clear, what no one may

[8] "To acquire immunity to eloquence is of the utmost importance to the citizens of a democracy," Bertrand Russell, "Power" (*Atlantic Monthly*, October 1938); reprinted as ch. 18, "The Taming of Power," in his book *Power: a New Social Analysis* (London: George Allen and Unwin, 1938), 314. The sentence caps a discussion on ways of restraining power: "If I had control of education, I should expose children to the most vehement and eloquent advocates on all sides of every topical question, who should speak to the schools from the B.B.C. The teacher should afterwards invite the children to summarize the arguments used, and should gently insinuate the view that eloquence is inversely proportional to solid reason. To acquire . . ." (313–14).

[9] Richards, *Coleridge on Imagination*, ch. 4, "Imagination and Fancy," 72–99.

[10] Reginald Marsh (1898–1954), who painted the work *Wooden Horses* that Stevens discusses below. Born in Paris, Marsh grew up in New Jersey, studied at and graduated from Yale, and continued his education at the Art Students League of New York. During the 1920s he worked as a prolific illustrator for the *New York Daily News*, *Harper's Bazaar*, and many other periodicals. Though the source of the quotation cited by Stevens has not been identified, it deftly encapsulates Marsh's rejection of contemporary abstraction and his commitment to gritty yet stylized realism.

[11] Tempera on board, 24 (h) × 40 (w) inches, 1936, now in a private collection. For a color illustration of it, see www.thecityreview.com/f02samp.html.

ever have doubted, that just as in this or that work the degrees of the imagination and of reality may vary, so this variation may exist as between the works of one age and the works of another. What I have said up to this point amounts to this: that the idea of nobility exists in art today only in degenerate forms or in a much diminished state, if, in fact, it exists at all or otherwise than on sufferance; that this is due to failure in the relation between the imagination and reality. I should now like to add that this failure is due, in turn, to the pressure of reality.

A variation between the sound of words in one age and the sound of words in another age is an instance of the pressure of reality. Take the statement by Bateson[12] that a language, considered semantically, evolves through a series of conflicts between the denotative and the connotative forces in words; between an asceticism tending to kill language by stripping words of all association and a hedonism tending to kill language by dissipating their sense in a multiplicity of associations. These conflicts are nothing more than changes in the relation between the imagination and reality. Bateson describes the seventeenth century in England as predominately a connotative period. The use of words in connotative senses was denounced by Locke and Hobbes,[13] who desired a mathematical plainness; in short, perspicuous words. There followed in the eighteenth century an era of poetic diction. This was not the language of the age but a language of poetry peculiar to itself. In time, Wordsworth came to write the preface to the second edition of the *Lyrical Ballads* (1800), in which he said that the first volume had been published, "as an experiment, which, I hoped, might be of some use to ascertain how far, by fitting to metrical arrangement a selection of the real language of man in a state of vivid sensation, that sort of pleasure and that quantity of pleasure may be imparted, which a Poet may rationally endeavour to impart."[14]

As the nineteenth century progressed, language once more became connotative. While there have been intermediate reactions, this tendency toward the connotative is the tendency today. The interest in semantics is evidence of this. In the case of some of our prose writers, as, for example, Joyce, the language, in quite different ways, is wholly connotative. When we say that Locke and Hobbes denounced the connotative use of words as an abuse, and when we speak of reactions and reforms, we are speaking, on the one hand, of a failure of the imagination to adhere to reality, and, on the other, of a use of language favorable to reality. The statement that the tendency toward the connotative is the tendency today is disputable. The general movement in the arts, that is to say, in painting and in music, has been the other way. It is hard to say that the tendency is toward the connotative in the use of words without also saying that the tendency is toward the imagination in other directions. The interest in the subconscious and in surrealism shows the tendency toward the imaginative. Boileau's remark that Descartes had cut poetry's throat[15] is a remark that could have been made respecting a great many people during the last hundred years, and of no one more aptly than of Freud, who, as it happens, was familiar with it and repeats it in his *Future of an Illusion*.[16] The object of that essay was to suggest a surrender to reality. His premise was that it is the unmistakable character of the present situation not that the promises of religion have become smaller but that they appear less credible to people. He notes the decline of religious belief and disagrees with the argument that man cannot in general do without the consolation of what he calls the religious illusion and that without it he would not endure the cruelty of reality. His conclusion is that man must venture at last into the hostile world and that this may be called education to

---

[12] Frederick Wilse Bateson (1901–2000) was a literary scholar, and Stevens is summarizing his book *English Poetry and the English Language: An Experiment in Literary History* (Oxford: Clarendon Press, 1934), as he will continue to do throughout this paragraph.

[13] Thomas Hobbes (1588–1679) and John Locke (1632–1704), British philosophers whose views on language are discussed by Bateson, *English Poetry and the English Language*, 51–4; the phrases "mathematical plainness" and "perspicuous words" are used by Bateson, 54.

[14] Wordsworth's famous declaration from the "Preface" to the *Lyrical Ballads*, as transmitted by Bateson, *English Poetry and the English Language*, 87.

[15] The observation of Boileau is repeated by V. de Sola Pinto, in his essay "Realism in English Poetry," *Essays and Studies by Members of the English Association* 25 (1939): 86. Stevens quotes another passage taken from the same essay later in "The Noble Rider and the Sound of Words." Nicolas Boileau-Depreaux (1636–1722) was a French critic, poet, and man of letters; René Descartes (1596–1650) was a famous philosopher, and his emphasis on logic and clarity might be viewed as having "cut the throat" of poetry.

[16] *The Future of an Illusion* (1927) is Freud's reckoning with the "illusion" of religion, which will be superseded by science. Stevens, however, is mistaken; in *The Future of an Illusion* Freud nowhere mentions Boileau or his dictum about Descartes.

reality. There is much more in that essay inimical to poetry and not least the observation in one of the final pages that "The voice of the intellect is a soft one, but it does not rest until it has gained a hearing." This, I fear, is intended to be the voice of the realist.

A tendency in language toward the connotative might very well parallel a tendency in other arts toward the denotative. We have just seen that that is in fact the situation. I suppose that the present always appears to be an illogical complication. The language of Joyce goes along with the dilapidations of Braque and Picasso and the music of the Austrians.[17] To the extent that this painting and this music are the work of men who regard it as part of the science of painting and the science of music it is the work of realists. Actually its effect is that of the imagination, just as the effect of abstract painting is so often that of the imagination, although that may be different. Busoni[18] said, in a letter to his wife, "I have made the painful discovery that nobody loves and feels music." Very likely, the reason there is a tendency in language toward the connotative today is that there are many who love it and feel it. It may be that Braque and Picasso love and feel painting and that Schönberg loves and feels music, although it seems that what they love and feel is something else.

A tendency toward the connotative, whether in language or elsewhere, cannot continue against the pressure of reality. If it is the pressure of reality that controls poetry, then the immediacy of various theories of poetry is not what it was. For instance, when Rostrevor Hamilton[19] says, "The object of contemplation is the highly complex and unified content of consciousness, which comes into being through the developing subjective attitude of the percipient," he has in mind no such "content of consciousness" as every newspaper reader experiences today.

By way of further illustration, let me quote from Croce's Oxford lecture of 1933.[20] He said: "If ... poetry is intuition and expression, the fusion of sound and imagery, what is the material which takes on the form of sound and imagery? It is the whole man: the man who thinks and wills, and loves, and hates; who is strong and weak, sublime and pathetic, good and wicked; man in the exultation and agony of living; and together with the man, integral with him, it is all nature in its perpetual labour of evolution.... Poetry ... is the triumph of contemplation.... Poetic genius chooses a strait path in which passion is calmed and calm is passionate."

[17] Georges Braque (1883–1963) and Pablo Picasso (1881–1973) were painters whose collaboration in cubism, 1909–14, was one of the seminal moments of modern art. "The Austrians" is a term meant to include the Austrian composer Arnold Schoenberg (1874–1951), who abandoned tonality and developed the 12-tone or serial system, and Austrian composer Alban Berg (1885–1935), a pupil of Schoenberg, who wrote two operas (*Wozzek* and *Lulu*) that are among the most powerful and disturbing twentieth-century operas.

[18] Ferrucco Busoni (1866–1924) was an Italian composer whose theoretical writings and compositions suggested new paths for the transition from nineteenth- to twentieth-century music. In 1938 his *Letters to His Wife*, trans. Rosamond Ley (London: E. Arnold) appeared; the letter quoted by Stevens, dated January 15, 1921, appears on 302. "I have made the painful discovery that nobody *loves* and *feels* music. Some practise it as a trade, some as time-beaters, and some from vanity."

[19] George Rostrevor Hamilton (1888–1963) was a British poet who was educated at Oxford and was influenced by Bergson and Plato. Stevens is quoting from his book *Poetry and Contemplation* (Cambridge: Cambridge University Press, 1937), 81. Hamilton draws on Bergson's notion of the integrity of consciousness to argue against I. A. Richardson's view that linked poetry with the unconscious in *Coleridge on Imagination* (1935), quoted by Stevens elsewhere in this essay, and *Principles of Literary Criticism* (1925).

[20] Benedetto Croce (1866–52), the distinguished Italian philosopher of aesthetics, gave the Philip Maurice Deneke lecture *The Defence of Poetry, Variations on the Theme of Shelley* (Oxford: Clarendon Press, 1933) on October 17, 1933, at Lady Margaret Hall, Oxford. Stevens quotes from 25–6.

If, then, poetry is intuition and expression, the fusion of sound and imagery, what is the material which takes on the form of sound and imagery? It is the whole man: the man who thinks and wills, and loves, and hates; who is strong and weak, sublime and pathetic, good and wicked; man in the exultation and agony of living; and together with the man, integral with him, it is all nature in its perpetual labour of evolution. But the thoughts and actions and emotions of life, when sublimated to the subject matter of poetry, are no longer the thought that judges, the action effectually carried out, the good and evil, or the joy and pain actually done and suffered. They are all now simply passions and feelings immediately assuaged and calmed, and transfigured in imagery. That is the image of poetry: the union of calm and tumult, of passionate [26:] impulse with the controlling mind which controls by contemplating. It is the triumph of contemplation, but a triumph still shaken by past battle, with its foot upon a living though vanquished foe. Poetic genius chooses a strait path in which passion is calmed and calm is passionate; a path that has on one side merely natural feeling, and on the other the relection and criticism which is twice removed from nature; a path from which minor talents find it but too easy to slip into an art either convulsed and distorted by passion, or void of passion and guided by principles of the understanding. Then they are called "romantic" or "classical."

Croce cannot have been thinking of a world in which all normal life is at least in suspense, or, if you like, under blockage. He was thinking of normal human experience.

Quite apart from the abnormal aspect of everyday life today, there is the normal aspect of it. The spirit of negation has been so active, so confident and so intolerant that the commonplaces about the romantic provoke us to wonder if our salvation, if the way out, is not the romantic. All the great things have been denied and we live in an intricacy of new and local mythologies, political, economic, poetic, which are asserted with an ever-enlarging incoherence. This is accompanied by an absence of any authority except force, operative or imminent. What has been called the disparagement of reason is an instance of the absence of authority. We pick up the radio and find that comedians regard the public use of words of more than two syllables as funny. We read of the opening of the National Gallery at Washington and we are convinced, in the end, that the pictures are counterfeit, that museums are impositions and that Mr. Mellon[21] was a monster. We turn to a recent translation of Kierkegaard and we find him saying: "A great deal has been said about poetry reconciling one with existence; rather it might be said that it arouses one against existence; for poetry is unjust to men ... it has use only for the elect, but that is a poor sort of reconciliation. I will take the case of sickness. Aesthetics replies proudly and quite consistently, 'That cannot be employed, poetry must not become a hospital.' Aesthetics culminates ... by regarding sickness in accordance with the principle enunciated by Friedrich Schlegel: 'Nur Gesundheit ist liebenswürdig.' (Health alone is lovable.)"[22]

The enormous influence of education in giving everyone a little learning, and in giving large groups considerably more: something of history, something of philosophy, something of literature; the expansion of the middle class with its common preference for realistic satisfactions; the penetration of the masses of people by the ideas of liberal thinkers, even when that penetration is indirect, as by the reporting of the reasons why people oppose the ideas that they oppose, – these are normal aspects of everyday life. The way we live and the way we work alike cast us out on reality. If fifty private houses were to be built in New York this year, it would be a phenomenon. We no longer live in homes but in housing projects and this is so whether the project is literally a project or a club, a dormitory, a camp or an apartment in River House.[23] It is not only that there are more of us and that we are actually close together. We are close together in every way. We lie in bed and listen to a broadcast from Cairo, and so on. There is no distance. We are intimate with people we have never seen and, unhappily, they are intimate with us. Democritus plucked his eye out[24] because he could not look at a woman without thinking of her as a woman. If he had read a few of our novels, he would have torn himself to pieces. Dr. Richards has noted "the widespread increase in the aptitude of the average mind for self-dissolving introspection, the generally heightened awareness of the goings-on of our own minds, *merely as goings-on*."[25] This is nothing to the generally heightened awareness of the goings-on of other people's minds, *merely as goings-on*. The way we work is a good deal more difficult for the imagination than the highly civilized revolution that is occurring in respect to work indicates. It is, in the main, a revolution for more pay. We have been

---

[21]   The National Gallery was first proposed by then Secretary of the Treasury Andrew Mellon (1855–1937) in 1928, who in 1936 donated his private art collection to the nation, together with money to build a museum. The National Gallery was dedicated on March 17, 1941, by President Roosevelt.

[22]   Søren Kierkegaard (1813–55), Danish theologian and philosopher, whose *Stages on Life's Way* (1845) was first translated into English by Walter Lowrie in 1940 (Princeton: Princeton University Press), 414. The two ellipses in the text are Stevens's and the phrases he has omitted are respectively "by reason of its quantitative estimate" and "in the end." However, there is also a third omission which has not been signaled by Stevens, one found between the sentence ending "must not become a hospital" and the next one beginning "Aesthetics replies ..." That omission reads: "That is quite right, so it must be, and it is only a bungler who would attempt to treat such subjects aesthetically. In this situation when people have no religion they are in a dilemma."

Finally, the passage from Kierkegaard concludes with a sentence from Friedrich von Schlegel (1772–1829), the German literary critic and leader of the German Romantic movement; the sentence comes from his novel *Lucinde* (1799), found in his *Werke in zwei Bänden* (Berlin: Aufbau-Verlag, 1980), vol. 2, 27; in English, *Friedrich Schlegel's Lucinde and the Fragments*, trans. Peter Firchow (Minneapolis: University of Minnesota, 1971), 57.

[23]   Located at 435 East 52nd Street in York City, River House was designed by Bottomley, Wagner, and White and erected in 1931. It consists of 14-story wings and a 26-story tower that is topped up with terraces and a curved finial top.

[24]   This legend about the Greek philosopher Democritus (c. 460–360 BC) is told by the Christian writer Tertullian (c. 160–240 AD) in his *Apologeticus* (46d), but is denied by Plutarch (c. 50–120 AD) in his *De curiositate* (521d).

[25]   Richards, *Coleridge on Imagination*, 220.

assured, by every visitor, that the American businessman is absorbed in his business and there is nothing to be gained by disputing it. As for the workers, it is enough to say that the word has grown to be literary. They have become, at their work, in the face of the machines, something approximating an abstraction, an energy. The time must be coming when, as they leave the factories, they will be passed through an air-chamber or a bar to revive them for riot and reading. I am sorry to have to add that to one that thinks, as Dr. Richards thinks, that poetry is the supreme use of language,[26] some of the foreign universities in relation to our own appear to be, so far as the things of the imagination are concerned, as Verrocchio is to the sculptor of the statue of General Jackson.

These, nevertheless, are not the things that I had in mind when I spoke of the pressure of reality. These constitute the drift of incidents, to which we accustom ourselves as to the weather. Materialism is an old story and an indifferent one. Robert Wolseley said: "True genius ... will enter into the hardest and dryest thing, enrich the most barren Soyl, and inform the meanest and most uncomely matter ... the baser, the emptier, the obscurer, the fouler, and the less susceptible of Ornament the subject appears to be, the more is the Poet's Praise ... who, as Horace says of Homer, can fetch Light out of Smoak, Roses out of Dunghills, and give a kind of Life to the Inanimate ..." (Preface to Rochester's *Valentinian*, 1685, *English Association Essays and Studies* 1939).[27] By the pressure of reality, I mean the pressure of an external event or events on the consciousness to the exclusion of any power of contemplation. The definition ought to be exact and, as it is, may be merely pretentious. But when one is trying to think of a whole generation and of a world at war, and trying at the same time to see what is happening to the imagination, particularly if one believes that that is what matters most, the plainest statement of what is happening can easily appear to be an affectation.

For more than ten years now, there has been an extraordinary pressure of news – let us say, news incomparably more pretentious than any description of it, news, at first, of the collapse of our system, or, call it, of life; then of news of a new world, but of a new world so uncertain that one did not know anything whatever of its nature, and does not know now, and could not tell whether it was to be all-English, all-German, all-Russian, all-Japanese, or all-American, and cannot tell now; and finally news of a war, which was a renewal of what, if it was not the greatest war, became such by this continuation. And for more than ten years, the consciousness of the world has concentrated on events which have made the ordinary movement of life seem to be the movement of people in the intervals of a storm. The disclosures of the impermanence of the past suggested, and suggest, an impermanence of the future. Little of what we have believed has been true. Only the prophecies are

[26]   Richards, *Coleridge on Imagination*, 230, discussing the tasks of criticism: "But there is a more positive task: to recall that poetry is the supreme use of language, man's chief co-ordinating instrument, in the services of the most integral purposes of life; and to explore, with thoroughness, the intricacies of the modes of language as working modes of the mind."

[27]   Robert Wolseley (1649–97) wrote a preface to the tragedy *Valentinian* (London: Timothy Goodwin, 1685) by John Wilmot, Earl of Rochester (1647–80). Part of his preface is quoted by V. de Sola Pinto in an essay titled "Realism in English Poetry," *Essays and Studies by Members of the English Association* 25 (1939): 81–100. De Sola Pinto's thesis is that "the poetry of realism is, I contend, an essential and characteristic part of the English poetic heritage which has been commonly ignored" (82), and he defends it with a survey of the entirety of English verse. Treating the seventeenth century, de Sola Pinto urges that "English poetry was too tough to be killed by the new materialism" (86), and then cites a passage from Wolseley's "preface" in support:

True Genius, like the Anima Mundi which some of the ancients believ'd, will enter into the hardest and dryest thing, enrich the most barren Soyl, and inform the meanest

and most uncomely matter; nothing within the vast Immensity of Nature is so devoid of Grace, or so remote from Sence but will obey the Formings of his plastick Heat, and feel the Operations of his vivifying Power, which, when it pleases, can enliven the deadest Lump, beautifie the vilest Dirt, and sweeten the most offensive Filth; this is a Spirit that blows where it lists, and like the Philosopher's Stone converts into it self whatsoever it touches. Nay the baser, the emptier, the obscurer, the fouler, and the less susceptible of Ornament the subject appears to be, the more is the Poet's Praise, who can infuse dignity and breathe beauty upon it, who can hide all the natural deformities in the fashion of his Dresse, supply all the want with his own plenty, and by a Poetical Daemonianism possesse it with the spirit of good sence and gracefulnesse, or who, as Horace says of Homer, can fetch Light out of Smoak, Roses out Dunghils, and give a kind of Life to the Inanimate. (86–7).

true. The present is an opportunity to repent. This is familiar enough. The war is only a part of a war-like whole. It is not possible to look backward and to see that the same thing was true in the past. It is a question of pressure, and pressure is incalculable and eludes the historian. The Napoleonic era is regarded as having had little or no effect on the poets and the novelists who lived in it. But Coleridge and Wordsworth and Sir Walter Scott and Jane Austen did not have to put up with Napoleon and Marx and Europe, Asia and Africa all at one time. It seems possible to say that they knew of the events of their day much as we know of the bombings in the interior of China and not at all as we know of the bombings of London,[28] or, rather, as we should know of the bombings of Toronto or Montreal. Another part of the war-like whole to which we do not respond quite as we do to the news of war is the income tax. The blanks are specimens of mathematical prose. They titillate the instinct of self-preservation in a class in which that instinct has been forgotten. Virginia Woolf thought that the income tax, if it continued, would benefit poets by enlarging their vocabularies and I dare say that she was right.[29]

If it is not possible to assert that the Napoleonic era was the end of one era in the history of the imagination and the beginning of another, one comes closer to the truth by making that assertion in respect to the French Revolution. The defeat or triumph of Hitler are parts of a war-like whole but the fate of an individual is different from the fate of a society. Rightly or wrongly, we feel that the fate of a society is involved in the orderly disorders of the present time. We are confronting, therefore, a set of events, not only beyond our power to tranquillize them in the mind, beyond our power to reduce them and metamorphose them, but events that stir the emotions to violence, that engage us in what is direct and immediate and real, and events that involve the concepts and sanctions that are the order of our lives and may involve our very lives; and these events are occurring persistently with increasing omen, in what may be called our presence. These are the things that I had in mind when I spoke of the pressure of reality, a pressure great enough and prolonged enough to bring about the end of one era in the history of the imagination and, if so, then great enough to bring about the beginning of another. It is one of the peculiarities of the imagination that it is always at the end of an era. What happens is that it is always attaching itself to a new reality, and adhering to it. It is not that there is a new imagination but that there is a new reality. The pressure of reality may, of course, be less than the general pressure that I have described. It exists for individuals according to the circumstances of their lives or according to the character-istics of their minds. To sum it up, the pressure of reality is, I think, the determining factor in the artistic character of an era and, as well, the determining factor in the artistic character of an individual. The resistance to this pressure or its evasion in the case of individuals of extraordinary imagination cancels the pressure so far as those individuals are concerned.

4

Suppose we try, now, to construct the figure of a poet, a possible poet. He cannot be a charioteer traversing vacant space, however ethereal. He must have lived all of the last two thousand years, and longer, and he must have instructed himself, as best he could, as he went along. He will have thought that Virgil, Dante, Shakespeare, Milton placed themselves in remote lands and in remote ages; that their men and women were the dead – and not the dead lying in the earth, but the dead still living in their remote lands and in their remote ages, and living in the earth or under it, or in the heavens – and he will wonder at those huge imaginations, in which what is remote becomes near, and what is dead lives with an intensity beyond any experience of life. He will consider that although he has himself witnessed, during the long period of his life, a general transition to reality,

---

[28] The bombings of London began on September 7, 1940, and went on daily for the next 57 days, then continued regularly until May 11, 1941, when Hitler called off the raids in order to move his bombers east for the invasion of Russia. Wallace Stevens gave this lecture in May 1941.

[29] Virginia Woolf, in her essay "The Leaning Tower," praised the social transformation that would be brought about by income tax, urging that as a result novelists would have "more interest-ing people to describe," while the intermingling of previously divided social classes would also yield a richer language: the poet will "gain words; when we have pooled all the different dialects, the clipped and cabined vocabulary which is all that he uses now should be enriched." See "The Leaning Tower," p. 920 in this edition.

his own measure as a poet, in spite of all the passions of all the lovers of the truth, is the measure of his power to abstract himself, and to withdraw with him into his abstraction the reality on which the lovers of truth insist. He must be able to abstract himself and also to abstract reality, which he does by placing it in his imagination. He knows perfectly that he cannot be too noble a rider, that he cannot rise up loftily in helmet and armor on a horse of imposing bronze. He will think again of Milton and of what was said about him: that "the necessity of writing for one's living blunts the appreciation of writing when it bears the mark of perfection. Its quality disconcerts our hasty writers; they are ready to condemn it as preciosity and affectation. And if to them the musical and creative powers of words convey little pleasure, how out of date and irrelevant they must find the … music of Milton's verse." Don Quixote will make it imperative for him to make a choice, to come to a decision regarding the imagination and reality; and he will find that it is not a choice of one over the other and not a decision that divides them, but something subtler, a recognition that here, too, as between these poles, the universal interdependence exists, and hence his choice and his decision must be that they are equal and inseparable. To take a single instance: When Horatio says,

> Now cracks a noble heart. Good night, sweet prince,
> And flights of angels sing thee to thy rest![30]

are not the imagination and reality equal and inseparable? Above all, he will not forget General Jackson or the picture of the *Wooden Horses*.

I said of the picture that it was a work in which everything was favorable to reality. I hope that the use of that bare word has been enough. But without regard to its range of meaning in thought, it includes all its natural images, and its connotations are without limit. Bergson describes the visual perception of a motionless object as the most stable of internal states. He says: "The object may remain the same, I may look at it from the same side, at the same angle, in the same light; nevertheless, the vision I now have of it differs from that which I have just had, even if only because the one is an instant later than the other. My memory is there, which conveys something of the past into the present."[31]

Dr. Joad's comment on this is: "Similarly with external things. Every body, every quality of a body resolves itself into an enormous number of vibrations, movements, changes. What is it that vibrates, moves, is changed? There is no answer. Philosophy has long dismissed the notion of substance and modern physics has endorsed the dismissal. … How, then, does the world come to appear to us as a collection of solid, static objects extended in space? Because of the intellect, which presents us with a false view of it."[32]

The poet has his own meaning for reality, and the painter has, and the musician has; and besides what it means to the intelligence and to the senses, it means something to everyone, so to speak. Notwithstanding this, the word in its general sense, which is the sense in which I have used it, adapts itself instantly. The subject-matter of poetry is not that "collection of solid, static objects extended in space" but the life that is lived in the scene that it composes; and so reality is not that external scene but the life that is lived in it. Reality is things as they are. The general sense of the word proliferates its special senses. It is a jungle in itself. As in the case of a jungle, everything

[30] William Shakespeare, *Hamlet*, Act 5, Scene 2, said by Horatio immediately after Hamlet's death.

[31] Stevens is quoting from Henri Bergson (1859–1941), the first chapter of *L'Évolution créatrice* (*Creative Evolution*), which was published in 1907 and became immensely popular, establishing his world reputation. The passage is found in *Creative Evolution*, trans. Arthur Mitchell (New York: Henry Holt, 1922), 2.

[32] Cyril Edwin Mitchinson Joad (1891–1953) taught philosophy at Birkbeck College, the University of London, and was a prolific author of guides and introductions to philosophy. Compare his *Introduction to Modern Philosophy* (Oxford: Oxford University Press, 1924), 93: "Every body, every quality even, resolves itself, on scientific analysis, into an enormous quantity of elementary movements. Whether we represent them as vibrations or as ether waves, or as negative electrons, or as event particles, it is equally impossible to arrive at something which is sufficiently stable to be spoken of as that in which the changes, or movements take place." Compare also his *Great Philosophies of the World* (London: Thomas Nelson, 1937), 120: "The universe, in other words, is itself a stream of perpetual change. How comes it, then, that it appears to us as a collection of solid static objects extended in space? The answer to this question is to be found in Bergson's theory of the intellect."

that makes it up is pretty much of one color. First, then, there is the reality that is taken for granted, that is latent and, on the whole, ignored. It is the comfortable American state of life of the eighties, the nineties and the first ten years of the present century. Next, there is the reality that has ceased to be indifferent, the years when the Victorians had been disposed of and intellectual minorities and social minorities began to take their place and to convert our state of life to something that might not be final. This much more vital reality made the life that had preceded it look like a volume of Ackermann's colored plates[33] or one of Töpfer's books of sketches in Switzerland.[34] I am trying to give the feel of it. It was the reality of twenty or thirty years ago. I say that it was a vital reality. The phrase gives a false impression. It was vital in the sense of being tense, of being instinct with the fatal or with what might be the fatal. The minorities began to convince us that the Victorians had left nothing behind. The Russians followed the Victorians, and the Germans, in their way, followed the Russians. The British Empire, directly or indirectly, was what was left and as to that one could not be sure whether it was a shield or a target. Reality then became violent and so remains. This much ought to be said to make it a little clearer that in speaking of the pressure of reality, I am thinking of life in a state of violence, not physically violent, as yet, for us in America, but physically violent for millions of our friends and for still more millions of our enemies and spiritually violent, it may be said, for everyone alive.

A possible poet must be a poet capable of resisting or evading the pressure of the reality of this last degree, with the knowledge that the degree of today may become a deadlier degree tomorrow. There is, however, no point to dramatizing the future in advance of the fact. I confine myself to the outline of a possible poet, with only the slightest sketch of his background.

5

Here I am, well-advanced in my paper, with everything of interest that I started out to say remaining to be said. I am interested in the nature of poetry and I have stated its nature, from one of the many points of view from which it is possible to state it. It is an interdependence of the imagination and reality as equals. This is not a definition, since it is incomplete. But it states the nature of poetry. Then I am interested in the role of the poet and this is paramount. In this area of my subject I might be expected to speak of the social, that is to say sociological or political, obligation of the poet. He has none. That he must be contemporaneous is as old as Longinus[35] and I dare say older. But that he *is* contemporaneous is almost inevitable. How contemporaneous in the direct sense in which being contemporaneous is intended were the four great poets of whom I spoke a moment ago? I do not think that a poet owes any more as a social obligation than he owes as a moral obligation, and if there is anything concerning poetry about which people agree it is that the role of the poet is not to be found in morals. I cannot say what that wide agreement amounts to because the agreement (in which I do not join) that the poet is under a social obligation is equally wide. Reality is life and life is society and the imagination and reality; that is to say, the imagination and society are inseparable. That is pre-eminently true in the case of the poetic drama. The poetic drama needs a terrible genius before it is anything more than a literary relic. Besides the theater has forgotten that it could ever be terrible. It is not one of the instruments of fate, decidedly. Yes: the all-commanding subject-matter of poetry is life, the never-ceasing source. But it is not a social obligation. One does not love and go back to one's ancient mother as a social obligation. One goes back out of a suasion not to be denied. Unquestionably if a social movement moved one deeply enough, its moving poems would follow. No politician can command the imagination, directing it to do this or that. Stalin might grind his teeth the whole of a Russian winter and yet all the poets in the Soviets might remain silent the following spring. He might excite their imaginations by something he said or did. He would not command them. He is

[33]   Rudolph Ackermann (1764–1834) became a printer in London in 1808 and subsequently a prolific producer of the aquatint engravings ("colored plates") that were so popular in Regency England.
[34]   Adam Töpfer (1766–1847) was a Swiss artist who specialized in genre and landscape aquatints.

[35]   Longinus, a rhetorician of the ancient world who was thought to be the author of *On the Sublime*, actually gives little attention to contemporaneity: for him great writing requires nobility of mind, strong and inspired emotion, a skilful use of figures, noble diction, and arrangement of words.

singularly free from that "cult of pomp," which is the comic side of the European disaster; and that means as much as anything to us. The truth is that the social obligation so closely urged is a phase of the pressure of reality which a poet (in the absence of dramatic poets) is bound to resist or evade today. Dante in Purgatory and Paradise was still the voice of the Middle Ages but not through fulfilling any social obligation. Since that is the role most frequently urged, if that role is eliminated, and if a possible poet is left facing life without any categorical exactions upon him, what then? What is his function? Certainly it is not to lead people out of the confusion in which they find themselves. Nor is it, I think, to comfort them while they follow their leaders to and fro. I think that his function is to make his imagination theirs and that he fulfills himself only as he sees his imagination become the light in the minds of others. His role, in short, is to help people to live their lives. Time and time again it has been said that he may not address himself to an élite. I think he may. There is not a poet whom we prize living today that does not address himself to an élite. The poet will continue to do this: to address himself to an élite even in a classless society, unless, perhaps, this exposes him to imprisonment or exile. In that event he is likely not to address himself to anyone at all. He may, like Shostakovich,[36] content himself with pretence. He will, nevertheless, still be addressing himself to an élite, for all poets address themselves to someone and it is of the essence of that instinct, and it seems to amount to an instinct, that it should be to an élite, not to a drab but to a woman with the hair of a pythoness, not to a chamber of commerce but to a gallery of one's own, if there are enough of one's own to fill a gallery. And that élite, if it responds, not out of complaisance, but because the poet has quickened it, because he has educed from it that for which it was searching in itself and in the life around it and which it had not yet quite found, will thereafter do for the poet what he cannot do for himself, that is to say, receive his poetry.

I repeat that his role is to help people to live their lives. He has had immensely to do with giving life whatever savor it possesses. He has had to do with whatever the imagination and the senses have made of the world. He has, in fact, had to do with life except as the intellect has had to do with it and, as to that, no one is needed to tell us that poetry and philosophy are akin. I want to repeat for two reasons a number of observations made by Charles Mauron.[37] The first reason is that these observations tell us what it is that a poet does to help people to live their lives and the second is that they prepare the way for a word concerning escapism. They are: that the artist transforms us into epicures; that he has to discover the possible work of art in the real world, then to extract it, when he does not himself compose it entirely; that he is *un amoureux perpétuel* of the world that he contemplates and thereby enriches; that art sets out to express the human soul; and finally that everything like a firm grasp of reality is eliminated from the aesthetic field. With these aphorisms in mind, how is it possible to condemn escapism? The poetic process is psychologically an escapist process. The chatter about escapism is, to my way of thinking, merely common cant. My own remarks about resisting or evading the pressure of reality mean escapism, if analyzed. Escapism has a pejorative sense, which it cannot be supposed that I include in the sense in which I use the word. The pejorative sense applies where the poet is not attached to reality, where the imagination does not adhere to reality, which, for my part, I regard as fundamental. If we go back to the collection of solid, static objects extended in space, which Dr. Joad posited, and if we say that the space is blank space, nowhere, without color, and that the objects, though solid, have no shadows and, though static, exert a mournful power, and, without elaborating this complete poverty, if suddenly we hear a different and familiar description of the place:

36   Dimitri Shostakovich (1906–75) was a Russian composer.

37   Charles Mauron (1899–1966) was a French literary critic later noted for his creation of *psychocritique*, a term he first adopts in 1949 to designate the combination of literary criticism and psychoanalysis that he sought to establish. Earlier, he was noted for his ongoing dialogue and collaboration with the Bloomsbury Circle. He translated all of E. M. Forster's novels into French, as well as Virginia Woolf's *Orlando*. Stevens is citing from his book *Aesthetics and Psychology*, trans. Roger Fry and Katherine John (London: Hogarth Press, 1935): "The artist transforms us, will-nilly, into epicures" (38); "Obviously the artist's task is much heavier: he has to discover the *possible* work of art in the real world, then to extract it, when he does not himself compose it entirely ... " (39); quoting from the French art historian Auguste Bréal, "L'artiste est un amoureux perpétuel" (51); "For if art sets out to express the human soul, it ought surely to concern itself with the essential rather than with the accessary" (69); "Everything like a firm grasp of reality is eliminated from the aesthetic field" (106).

> *This City now doth, like a garment, wear*
> *The beauty of the morning, silent bare,*
> *Ships, towers, domes, theatres, and temples lie*
> *Open unto the fields, and to the sky;*
> *All bright and glittering in the smokeless air;*[38]

If we have this experience, we know how poets help people to live their lives. This illustration must serve for all the rest. There is, in fact, a world of poetry indistinguishable from the world in which we live, or, I ought to say, no doubt, from the world in which we shall come to live, since what makes the poet the potent figure that he is, or was, or ought to be, is that he creates the world to which we turn incessantly and without knowing it and that he gives to life the supreme fictions without which we are unable to conceive of it.

And what about the sound of words? What about nobility, of which the fortunes were to be a kind of test of the value of the poet? I do not know of anything that will appear to have suffered more from the passage of time than the music of poetry and that has suffered less. The deepening need for words to express our thoughts and feelings which, we are sure, are all the truth that we shall ever experience, having no illusions, makes us listen to words when we hear them, loving them and feeling them, makes us search the sound of them, for a finality, a perfection, an unalterable vibration, which it is only within the power of the acutest poet to give them. Those of us who may have been thinking of the path of poetry, those who understand that words are thoughts and not only our own thoughts but the thoughts of men and women ignorant of what it is that they are thinking, must be conscious of this: that, above everything else, poetry is words; and that words; above everything else, are, in poetry, sounds. This being so, my time and yours might have been better spent if I had been less interested in trying to give our possible poet an identity and less interested in trying to appoint him to his place. But unless I had done these things, it might have been thought that I was rhetorical, when I was speaking in the simplest way about things of such importance that nothing is more so. A poet's words are of things that do not exist without the words. Thus, the image of the charioteer and of the winged horses, which has been held to be precious for all of time that matters, was created by words of things that never existed without the words. A description of Verrocchio's statue could be the integration of an illusion equal to the statue itself. Poetry is a revelation in words by means of the words. Croce was not speaking of poetry in particular when he said that language is perpetual creation.[39] About nobility I cannot be sure that the decline, not to say the disappearance of nobility is anything more than a maladjustment between the imagination and reality. We have been a little insane about the truth. We have had an obsession. In its ultimate extension, the truth about which we have been insane will lead us to look beyond the truth to something in which the imagination will be the dominant complement. It is not only that the imagination adheres to reality, but, also, that reality adheres to the imagination and that the interdependence is essential. We may emerge from our *bassesse* and, if we do, how would it happen if not by the intervention of some fortune of the mind? And what would that fortune of the mind happen to be? It might be only commonsense but even that, a commonsense beyond the truth, would be a nobility of long descent.

The poet refuses to allow his task to be set for him. He denies that he has a task and considers that the organization of materia poetica is a contradiction in terms. Yet the imagination gives to everything that it touches a peculiarity, and it seems to me that the peculiarity of the imagination is nobility, of which there are many degrees. This inherent nobility is the natural source of another, which our extremely headstrong generation regards as false and decadent. I mean that nobility which is our spiritual height and depth; and while I know how difficult it is to express it, nevertheless I am bound to give a sense of it. Nothing could be more evasive and inaccessible. Nothing distorts itself and seeks disguise more quickly. There is a shame of disclosing it and in its definite presentations a horror of it. But there it is. The fact that it is there is what makes it possible

---

[38] Lines 4–7 of a poem by William Wordsworth (1770–1850), "Composed Upon Westminster Bridge, Sept. 3 1802."

[39] "Language is perpetual creation" (Benedetto Croce, *Aesthetic as Science of Expression and General Linguistic* [London: Macmillan, 1909], 150).

to invite to the reading and writing of poetry men of intelligence and desire for life. I am not thinking of the ethical or the sonorous or at all of the manner of it. The manner of it is, in fact, its difficulty, which each man must feel each day differently, for himself. I am not thinking of the solemn, the portentous or demoded. On the other hand, I am evading a definition. If it is defined, it will be fixed and it must not be fixed. As in the case of an external thing, nobility resolves itself into an enormous number of vibrations, movements, changes. To fix it is to put an end to it. Let me show it to you unfixed.

Late last year Epstein exhibited some of his flower paintings at the Leicester Galleries in London. A commentator in *Apollo*[40] said: "*How with this rage can beauty hold a plea* ... The quotation from Shakespeare's 65th sonnet prefaces the catalogue.... It would be apropos to any other flower paintings than Mr. Epstein's. His make no pretence to fragility. They shout, explode all over the picture space and generally oppose the rage of the world with such a rage of form and colour as no flower in nature or pigment has done since Van Gogh."

What ferocious beauty the line from Shakespeare puts on when used under such circumstances! While it has its modulation of despair, it holds its plea and its plea is noble. There is no element more conspicuously absent from contemporary poetry than nobility. There is no element that poets have sought after, more curiously and more piously, certain of its obscure existence. Its voice is one of the inarticulate voices which it is their business to overhear and to record. The nobility of rhetoric is, of course, a lifeless nobility. Pareto's epigram[41] that history is a cemetery of aristocracies easily becomes another: that poetry is a cemetery of nobilities. For the sensitive poet, conscious of negations, nothing is more difficult than the affirmations of nobility and yet there is nothing that he requires of himself more persistently, since in them and in their kind, alone, are to be found those sanctions that are the reasons for his being and for that occasional ecstasy, or ecstatic freedom of the mind, which is his special privilege.

It is hard to think of a thing more out of time than nobility. Looked at plainly it seems false and dead and ugly. To look at it at all makes us realize sharply that in our present, in the presence of our reality, the past looks false and is, therefore, dead and is, therefore, ugly; and we turn away from it as from something repulsive and particularly from the characteristic that it has a way of assuming: something that was noble in its day, grandeur that was, the rhetorical once. But as a wave is a force and not the water of which it is composed, which is never the same, so nobility is a force and not the manifestations of which it is composed, which are never the same. Possibly this description of it as a force will do more than anything else I can have said about it to reconcile you to it. It is not an artifice that the mind has added to human nature. The mind has added nothing to human nature. It is a violence from within that protects us from a violence without. It is the imagination pressing back against the pressure of reality. It seems, in the last analysis, to have something to do with our self-preservation; and that, no doubt, is why the expression of it, the sound of its words, helps us to live our lives.

[40] Unsigned, "Art Notes," *Apollo* 42.6 (December 1940): 164. Jacob Epstein (1880–1959), who was born in New York but moved to London in 1905 and became a British citizen in 1907, was a sculptor noted for austere and geometric forms that were deliberately uncouth. The catalog to his exhibition of watercolors depicting flowers, held at the Leicester Galleries in London in December 1940, began with a quotation from Shakespeare's sonnet 65: "How with this rage can beauty hold a plea, / Whose action is no stronger than a flower?" It was quoted by the anonymous reviewer in Apollo, who then went on, "The quotation from Shakespeare's 65th sonnet prefaces the catalogue to Epsteins's 'Flower Paintings' at the Leicester. It would be appropos to any other flower paintings than Mr. Epstein's." The passage then continues as cited by Stevens, ending "since Van Gogh went mad in Provence. A roomful of them is positively deafening." After another paragraph, the reviewer concluded: "One yearns for a little rest-space in these strident water-colours, which cover every inch of the picture-space like Morris chintzes broken loose from formal design. 'Everthing that Nature does she somehow overdoes,' complained Mr. Coward. When Epstein adds Nietzsche to nature, expresses it in watercolour with apparently more body than oil-colour, he more than justfied Coward's epigram. But he creates something definite and individual in styles, and shocks one into tremendous awareness."

[41] Vilfredo Pareto (1848–1923) was an Italian econmist, sociologist, and philosopher noted for his view that all societies are ruled by elites, or aristocracies, that inevitably decline. "Aristocracies do not last. Whatever the causes, it is an incontestable fact that after a certain length of time they pass away. History is a graveyard of aristocracies." Vilfredo Pareto, *The Mind and Society: A Treatise on General Sociology*, ed. Arthur Livingston, trans. Andrew Bongiorno and Arthur Livingston (New York: Harcourt Brace, 1935), vol. 3, *Theory of Derivations*, 1430, §2053.

Marianne Moore (1887–1972)

Introduction

Marianne Moore, the second child of John Milton and Mary Moore, was born in Kirkwood, Missouri, a suburb of St. Louis. Her mother and father had separated, and her father had suffered a mental breakdown and been institutionalized before she was born. Moore, with her brother Warner (older by a year), was raised in the home of her maternal grandfather in Kirkwood, Missouri. When he died, Moore moved with her mother and brother to Carlisle, Pennsylvania, where her mother taught at the Metzger Institute, a high school for young women. Moore herself attended the school, then went on to do her BA at Bryn Mawr, 1905–9. In 1910 Moore and her mother traveled to Britain on holiday. Thereafter Moore taught stenography at the government Indian school in Carlisle from 1911 to 1915. In 1916 she published her first poems and reviews, and in 1918 she reviewed Eliot's *Prufock and other Observations* in *Poetry*. In 1918 she moved with her mother to New York. She worked as a private tutor, a secretary, and then, from 1921 to 1925, as an assistant in a branch of the New York Public Library. It was a this point that her career intersected with that of Ezra Pound. In 1920 Pound was serving as a contributor and talent scout for the *Dial*, the magazine that Scofield Thayer and James Sibley Watson, Jr., had purchased earlier that year, one they soon transformed into the most prominent American journal of arts and letters of the 1920s. He urged Thayer to invite Moore to contribute to the *Dial*. Thayer did, and over the next nine years she would write 187 essays and reviews for the journal. In 1925, with Thayer himself increasingly suffering from mental instability, Moore was made the journal's managing editor, a post she held until the journal was closed in 1929. Moore's first collection, *Poems* (1921), was published by H.D. and Bryher (on them see p. 441) in London, acting without Moore's knowledge or collaboration. A year later Moore published her long poem "Marriage" as a special issue of the journal *Mannikin*, and in 1924 she at last issued the first authorized gathering of her poems, *Observations*, a title nodding to T. S. Eliot's first collection, published in 1917, *Prufrock and Other Observations*.

The demise of the *Dial* in 1929 left her despondent. At 42, her career as a successful editor had come to an end. She moved with her mother from Manhattan to Brooklyn, surviving with bits of freelance work and subsidies from Bryher, the wealthy patron who was the consort of H.D. In 1947 her mother, with whom she had lived all her life, died. Moore began her project of translating all of the fables of Lafontaine. When she published her *Collected Poems* in 1951, she was awarded the Pulitzer Prize, the Bollingen Award, and the National Book Award. Moore increasingly became a celebrity: she was a photogenic, eccentric, and elderly spinster who wore a tricorne hat, adored a baseball team called the Brooklyn Dodgers, wrote poetry, and issued quotable and bewildering comments. None of that should be allowed to detract from her remarkable achievements. She was one of the most original poets in English of the twentieth century, and her critical prose was work of an unusually high order – intelligent, urbane, and subtle with quiet and understated wit. Her work has never met with wide popularity. Her austerity and fondness for Latinate diction, her relatively complicated syntax, her genuinely wide learning, her resolute refusal to follow political and other fashions, and her quiet espousal of modest moral virtues (humility, patient observation, hard work) – these are not qualities that make for popularity. They make for greatness, though.

Moore was a compulsive reviser of her poems, and an individual poem might be utterly transformed over the years. In one extreme case, that of the poem "Poetry" (see pp. 649–50), a work of 29 lines was reduced to only 3 by the time Moore, now 80 years old, published her *Complete Poems* (1967). To address such problems, the present edition divides Moore's poetic work into two sections: "Poems from *Observations*" (1924), and "Poems After *Observations*." Under the first grouping this edition follows the 1924 text of *Observations*; under the second it follows the 1967 text of Moore's *Complete Poems*.

Moore's prose writings present a different set of problems. Patricia Willis, the distinguished editor of Moore's *Complete Prose* (London and New York: Viking Penguin, 1986), set an important precedent when she elected not to provide annotations for the countless quotations that Moore adduced in her essays and reviews. Most, self-evidently, stem from the book under review, but a great many come from the magazines and books that Moore perused. I have annotated references only to poems and works that are contained elsewhere in this volume.

POEMS FROM OBSERVATIONS

To a Steam Roller (1915)

The illustration
  is nothing to you without the application.
  You lack half wit. You crush all the particles down
    into close conformity, and then walk back and forth
      on them.

Sparkling chips of rock   5
  are crushed down to the level of the parent block.
    Were not "impersonal judgment in æsthetic
      matters, a metaphysical impossibility,"[1] you

might fairly achieve
  it. As for butterflies, I can hardly conceive   10
    of one's attending upon you, but to question
      the congruence of the complement is vain, if it exists.

Pedantic Literalist (1916)

Prince Rupert's drop,[1] paper muslin[2] ghost,
White torch – "with power to say unkind
Things with kindness, and the most
  Irritating things in the midst of love and
    Tears,"[3] you invite destruction.   5

The poem was first published in *The Egoist* 2(10) (October 1, 1915); it was reprinted in Alfred Kreymborg (ed.), *Others: An Anthology of the New Verse* (New York: Alfred Knopf, 1917), and in Marianne Moore, *Poems* (London: Egoist Press, 1921), a volume assembled by H.D. and Bryher and not supervised by Moore.

[1] *"impersonal judgment ... metaphysical impossibility"* from Lawrence Gilman (1878–1939), who was the regular music critic for the journal the *North American Review*. Though generally sympathetic to new musical idioms, he found it difficult to appreciate the work of the "futuristic" composer Leo Ornstein (1892–2002). "We had endeavored in this brief attempt at a description of Mr. Ornstein's music to be strictly clinical, strictly impersonal, momentarily ignoring the fact that an impersonal judgment in esthetic matters is a metaphysical impossibility. At least we have tried to be as impersonal and as objective as may be; what more can a merely mortal commentator do?" ("Drama and Music," *North American Review* 201[713] [April 1915], p. 597).

PEDANTIC LITERALIST
The poem first appeared in *The Egoist* 6(3) (June 1, 1916). It was reprinted in Alfred Kreymborg (ed.), *Others: An Anthology of the New Verse* (New York: Alfred Knopf, 1917), and in Marianne Moore, *Poems* (London: Egoist Press, 1921).

[1] *Prince Rupert's drop* a child's gadget-toy of the period, which was made of molten glass that was dropped into water, which then formed pear-shaped globules that, each being a vacuum, would explode when fractured.

[2] *paper muslin* an Americanism, defined in *Webster's Dictionary* from 1864 through 1915 as "glazed muslin, used for linings and the like."

[3] *"with power ... tears"* Moore's note (see "Moore's Notes to *Observations*," p. 661) assigns this and the three other quotations in this poem to Richard Baxter, *The Saints' Everlasting Rest; or a Treatise of the Blessed State of the Saints in Their Enjoyment of God in Glory*, ed. William Young (Philadelphia: Lippincott; London: Grant Richards, 1909). Richard Baxter (1615–90) was a Puritan divine who served in the Cromwellian army as a chaplain; when he became ill in 1649, he wrote *The Saints' Everlasting Rest*, a devotional work that recounts all the benefits to be derived from contemplating the idea of everlasting life. This quotation, however, is not by Baxter, but by William Blake (1757–1827), the great mystical poet, and it appears in *Milton* (1804–8). In Book I of the poem, Milton returns from heaven to the mortal world and unites with the imagination through the person of Blake. The poem that accompanies plate 12, at lines 24–35, recounts a cosmic struggle:

Jehovah thunder'd above. Satan in pride of heart
Drove the fierce Harrow among the constellations of Jehovah
Drawing a third part in the fires as stubble north & south
To devour Albion and Jerusalem the emanation of Albion
Driving the Harrow in Pitys paths. 'Twas then, with our dark fires
Which now gird round us (O eternal torment) I form'd the Serpent

You are like the meditative man
  With the perfunctory heart; its
Carved cordiality ran
To and fro at first like an inlaid and royal
  Immutable production;   10

Then afterward "neglected to be
  Painful, deluding him with
Loitering formality,"[4]
  "Doing its duty as if it did it not,"[5]
  Presenting an obstruction   15

To the motive that it served. What stood
  Erect in you has withered. A
Little "palm tree of turned wood"[6]
  Informs your once spontaneous core in its
  Immutable production.   20

The Fish (1918)

Wade
through black jade
  Of the crow-blue mussel shells, one keeps
    adjusting the ash heaps;
    opening and shutting itself like   5

an
injured fan.
  The barnacles which encrust the side
    of the wave, cannot hide
    there for the submerged shafts of the   10

sun,
split like spun
  glass, move themselves with spotlight swiftness
    into the crevices —
    in and out, illuminating   15

Of precious stones & gold turn'd poisons on the sultry wastes
The Gnomes in all that day spar'd not; they curs'd Satan
  bitterly.
To do unkind things is kindness! with power arm'd, to say
The most irritating things in the midst of tears and love
These are the stings of the Serpent! thus did we by them; till
  thus
They in return retaliated, and the Living Creatures madden'd.

[4] *neglected to be . . . loitering formality* Baxter, *The Saints' Everlasting Rest*, ch. 17, "How to Manage and Watch Over the Heart through the Whole Work," 393: "When thou has got thy heart to the work, beware lest it delude thee by a loitering formality; lest it say, 'I go,' and go not; lest it trifle out the time while it should be effectually meditating. Certainly, the heart is likely to betray thee in this as in any one particular about the duty. When thou hast perhaps but an hour's time for thy meditation, the time will be spent before thy heart will be serious. This doing of duty as if we did it not, doth undo as many as the flat omission of it. To rub out the hour in a bare lazy thinking of heaven is but to lose that hour, and delude thyself." On Richard Baxter, see the preceding note.

[5] *"Doing its duty as if it did not"* see preceding note.

[6] *"palm tree of turned wood"* though Moore assigns this quotation to Baxter, *The Saints' Everlasting Rest*, it cannot be located there. The palm tree is associated with Christ's triumphal entry into Jerusalem, whence Palm Sunday. See Ecclesiasticus 6:3: "Without grace, I am nothing but a dry tree, a barren stock fit only for destruction."

THE FISH
The poem first appeared in *The Egoist* 5(7) (August 1918). It was then included in Alfred Kreymborg (ed.), *Others for 1919: An Anthology of the New Verse* (New York: Nicholas Brown, 1920), and Moore's *Poems* (London: Egoist Press, 1921), a volume not supervised by her (see "To a Steam Roller," introductory note).

the
turquoise sea
   of bodies. The water drives a wedge   20
    of iron through the iron edge
   of the cliff, whereupon the stars,[1]

pink
rice grains, ink
   bespattered jelly-fish, crabs like green   25
    lilies and submarine
   toadstools, slide each on the other.

All
external
   marks of abuse are present on this   30
    defiant edifice –
   all the physical feature's of

ac-
cident – lack
   of cornice, dynamite grooves, burns and   35
    hatchet strokes, these things stand
   out on it; the chasm side is

dead.
Repeated
   evidence has proved that it can live   40
    on what cannot revive
   its youth. The sea grows old in it.

Poetry (1919)

I too, dislike it: there are things that are important beyond all this fiddle.
Reading it, however, with a perfect contempt for it, one discovers that there is in
it after all, a place for the genuine.[1]
   Hands that can grasp, eyes
    that can dilate, hair that can rise   5
     if it must, these things are important not because a

high sounding interpretation can be put upon them but because they are
   useful; when they become so derivative as to become unintelligible,
    the same thing may be said for all of us, that we
    do not admire what   10
     we cannot understand: the bat,
      holding on upside down or in quest of something to

eat, elephants pushing, a wild horse taking a roll, a tireless wolf under
   a tree, the immovable critic twitching his skin like a horse that feels a flea, the base-
    ball fan, the statistician –   15
     nor is it valid
      to discriminate against "business documents and

---

[1] *stars* starfish.

POETRY
The poem first appeared in *Others* 5(6) (July 1919). It was
reprinted in Alfred Kreymborg (ed.), *Others for 1919: An Anthol-*

ogy of the New Verse (New York: Nicholas Brown, 1920), and
Moore's *Poems* (London: Egoist Press, 1921), a volume not supervised by her.
[1] *place for the genuine* in the last edition of her *Collected Poems*,
Moore omitted all the poem after this phrase.

school-books";[2] all these phenomena are important. One must make a distinction
   however: when dragged into prominence by half poets, the result is not poetry,
   nor till the poets among us can be   20
      "literalists of
      the imagination"[3]—above
         insolence and triviality and can present

for inspection, imaginary gardens with real toads in them, shall we have
   it. In the meantime, if you demand on one hand,   25
   the raw material of poetry in
      all its rawness and
      that which is on the other hand
         genuine, then you are interested in poetry.

England (1920)

With its baby rivers and little towns, each with its abbey or its cathedral,
   with voices – one voice perhaps, echoing through the transept – the
criterion of suitability and convenience: and Italy with its equal
      shores – contriving an epicureanism from which the grossness has been

extracted: and Greece with its goats and its gourds, the nest of modified illusions: 5
   and France, the "chrysalis of the nocturnal butterfly"[1] in
whose products, mystery of construction diverts one from what was originally one's
      object – substance at the core: and the East with its snails, its emotional

shorthand and jade cockroaches, its rock crystal and its imperturbability,
   all of museum quality: and America where there   10
is the little old ramshackle victoria in the south, where cigars are smoked on the
   street in the north; where there are no proof readers, no silkworms, no digressions;

the wild man's land; grass-less, links-less, language-less country in which letters are written
   not in Spanish, not in Greek, not in Latin, not in shorthand
but in plain American which cats and dogs can read! The letter "a" in psalm and calm when   15
   pronounced with the sound of "a" in candle, is very noticeable but

why should continents of misapprehension have to be accounted for by the
   fact? Does it follow that because there are poisonous toadstools
which resemble mushrooms, both are dangerous? In the case of mettlesomeness which may be
   mistaken for appetite, of heat which may appear to be haste, no con-   20

---

[2] *"business documents and school-books"* C. J. Hogarth and A. Sirnis (trans.), *The Diaries of Leo Tolstoy: Youth, 1847–1852* (New York: E. P. Dutton, 1917), 84: "Where the boundary between prose and poetry lies I shall never be able to understand. The question is raised in manuals of style, yet the answer to it lies beyond me. Poetry is verse: prose is not verse. Or else poetry is everything with the exception of business documents and school books." Loe Tolstoy (1828–1910) was a Russian novelist and mystical philosopher.

[3] *"literalists of the imagination"* W. B. Yeats, *Ideas of Good and Evil* (New York: Macmillan, 1903), "William Blake and His Illustrations to 'The Divine Comedy,'" 182: "The limitation of his [i.e., Blake's] view was from the very intensity of his vision; he was a too literal realist of imagination, as others are of nature; and because he believed that the figures seen by the mind's eye, when exalted by inspiration, were 'eternal existences,' symbols of divine essences, he hated every grace of style that

might obscure the lineaments. For Yeats's biography and career, see 301.

ENGLAND
The poem first appeared in the *Dial* 68(4) (April 1920). It was reprinted in Alfred Kreymborg (ed.), *Others for 1919: An Anthology of the New Verse* (New York: Nicholas Brown, 1920), and Moore's *Poems* (London: Egoist Press, 1921), a volume not supervised by her.

[1] *"chrysalis of the noctural butterfly"* Moore (see her "Notes to *Observations*," p. 662) attributes this quotation to Erté (1892–1989), the first son of a prosperous Russian family who moved to Paris in 1910 and became a noted fashion designer. He designed more than 240 covers for the magazine *Harper's Bazaar* and in the 1920s was a widely recognized artist. The source for the quotation has not been identified.

clusions may be drawn. To have misapprehended the matter, is to have confessed
  that one has not looked far enough. The sublimated wisdom
of China, Egyptian discernment, the cataclysmic torrent of emotion compressed
  in the verbs of the Hebrew language, the books of the man who is able

to say, "I envy nobody but him and him only, who catches more fish than   25
  I do,"[2] – the flower and fruit of all that noted superiority –
      should one not have stumbled upon it in America, must one imagine
  that it is not there? It has never been confined to one locality.

A Grave (1921)

Man looking into the sea,
taking the view from those who have as much right to it as you have to it yourself,
it is human nature to stand in the middle of a thing
but you cannot stand in the middle of this:
the sea has nothing to give but a well excavated grave.   5
The firs stand in a procession, each with an emerald turkey-foot at the top,
reserved as their contours, saying nothing;
repression, however, is not the most obvious characteristic of the sea;
the sea is a collector, quick to return a rapacious look.
There are others besides you who have worn that look –   10
whose expression is no longer a protest; the fish no longer investigate them
for their bones have not lasted:
men lower nets, unconscious of the fact that they are desecrating a grave,
and row quickly away – the blades of the oars
moving together like the feet of water-spiders as if there were no such thing as death.   15
The wrinkles progress upon themselves in a phalanx – beautiful under networks of foam,
and fade breathlessly while the sea rustles in and out of the seaweed;
the birds swim through the air at top speed, emitting catcalls as heretofore –
the tortoise-shell scourges about the feet of the cliffs, in motion beneath them
and the ocean, under the pulsation of lighthouse and noise of bell-buoys,   20
advances as usual, looking as if it were not that ocean in
  which dropped things are bound to sink –
in which if they turn and twist, it is neither with volition nor consciousness.

New York (1921)

the savage's romance,
accreted where we need the space for commerce –
the centre of the wholesale fur trade,
starred with tepees of ermine and peopled with foxes,
the long guard-hairs waving two inches beyond the body of the pelt;   5
the ground dotted with deer-skins – white with white spots
"as satin needlework in a single color may carry a varied pattern,"
and wilting eagles' down compacted by the wind;
and picardels of beaver skin; white ones alert with snow.
It is a far cry from the "queen full of jewels"[1]   10

[2] "*I envy nobody ... than I do*" the penultimate sentence in ch. 17 of *The Compleat Angler* (1653), a meditation on the merits of fishing by Izaak Walton (1593–1683), a draper and writer.

A GRAVE
The poem was first published in the *Dial* 71(1) (July 1921).

NEW YORK
The poem first appeared in the *Dial* 71(6) (December 1921), and was then reprinted in Moore's *Observations* (New York: Dial Press, 1924).
[1] "*queen full of jewels*" source not identified.

and the beau with the muff,
from the gilt coach shaped like a perfume bottle,
to the conjunction of the Monongahela and the Allegheny,
and the scholastic philosophy of the wilderness
to combat which one must stand outside and laugh   15
since to go in is to be lost.
It is not the dime-novel exterior,
Niagara Falls, the calico horses and the war canoe;
it is not that "if the fur is not finer[2] than such as one sees others wear,
one would rather be without it –"   20
that estimated in raw meat and berries, we could feed the universe;
it is not the atmosphere of ingenuity,
the otter, the beaver, the puma skins
without shooting-irons or dogs;
it is not the plunder,   25
it is the "accessibility to experience."[3]

Marriage (1923)

This institution,
perhaps one should say enterprise
out of respect for which
one says one need not change one's mind
about a thing one has believed in,   5
requiring public promises
of one's intention
to fulfill a private obligation:
I wonder what Adam and Eve
think of it by this time,   10
this firegilt steel
alive with goldenness;
how bright it shows –
"of circular traditions and impostures,
committing many spoils,"[1]   15

---

[2] *if the fur is not finer* according to Frank Alvah Parsons, in *The Psychology of Dress* (Garden City, NY: Doubleday, Page, 1920), 68, the late quattrocento ruler of Mantua, Isabella Gonzaga, wrote: "I wish black cloth even if it costs ten ducats a yard. If it is only as good as that which I see other people wear, I had rather be without it."

[3] *"accessibility to experience"* Marianne Moore's mother found this phrase in a book by the British journalist and critic Dixon Scott (1881–1915), *Men of Letters* (London: Hodder and Stoughton, 1916), 96, and copied it in a 1920 letter to Moore's brother. Scott, reviewing Henry James's memoir of his youth, *A Small Boy and Others* (London: Macmillan, 1913), describes the educational philosophy of James's father: "All he cared to produce was that condition of character which his son calls 'accessibility to experience.' You were only interested when you were disinterested – your very conscience ought to work unconsciously – and so our Henry James was equipped for life without plundering it, safe as a novice in his cell." James's memoir, to return to the original, pauses to reflect on his father's indifference to questions of pedagogical method: "... if we had not had in us to some degree the root of the matter no method, however confessedly or aggressively 'pedan-

tic,' would have much availed for us." James goes on: "It may be asked me, I recognise, of the root of 'what' matter I so complacently speak, and if I say, 'Why, of the matter of our having with considerable intensity *proved* educable, or, if you like better, teachable, that is accessible to experience,' it may again be retorted: 'That won't do for a decent account of a young consciousness ...'" (*A Small Boy and Others*, 229; or more conveniently in Frederick W. Dupee [ed.], *Henry James: Autobiography* [New York: Criterion, 1956], 124).

MARRIAGE
The poem first appeared in *Manikin Number Three* (New York: Monroe Wheeler, 1923), and was then reprinted in Moore's *Observations* (New York: Dial Press, 1924).
[1] *"of circular traditions ... many spoils"* in a letter addressed to his uncle William Cecil, Lord Burleigh (1520–98), and conjecturally assigned to 1592, Francis Bacon (1561–1621), the British philosopher and natural scientist, explained his aspirations to reshape natural philosophy: "I have taken all knowledge to be my province, and if I could purge it of two sorts of rovers [i.e. distracting influences], where the one with frivolous disputation, confutations and verbosities, the other with blind

requiring all one's criminal ingenuity
to avoid!
Psychology which explains everything
explains nothing
and we are still in doubt.   20
Eve: beautiful woman –
I have seen her
when she was so handsome
she gave me a start,
able to write simultaneously[2]   25
in three languages –
English, German and French
and talk in the meantime;
equally positive in demanding a commotion
and in stipulating quiet: 30
"I should like to be alone";
to which the visitor replies,
"I should like to be alone;
why not be alone together?"
Below the incandescent stars   35
below the incandescent fruit,
the strange experience of beauty;
its existence is too much;
it tears one to pieces
and each fresh wave of consciousness   40
is poison.
"See her, see her in this common world,"[3]
the central flaw
in that first crystal-fine experiment,
this amalgamation which can never be more   45
than an interesting impossibility,
describing it
as "that strange paradise
unlike flesh, gold, or stately buildings,
the choicest piece of my life: 50
the heart rising
in its estate of peace
as a boat rises

with the rising of the water";[4]
constrained in speaking of the serpent –   55

---

experiments and auricular [i.e., hearsay] traditions and impostures, hath committed so many spoils, I hope I shall bring in
industrious observations, grounded conclusions, and profitable
inventions and discoveries; the best state of that province."
Marianne Moore encountered a shortened version of this quotation in the *Enclopaedia Britannica*, and in her transcription the
word "rovers" became "errors" and the word "auricular" became
"circular."

[2] *write simultaneously* see "Moore's Notes to *Observations*," p. 663.
[3] *"See her ... this common world"* see "Moore's Notes to *Observations*," p. 663.
[4] *"that strange paradise ... of the water"* Moore's quotation
splices together phrases from two passages in Richard Baxter,
*The Saints' Everlasting Rest; or a Treatise of the Blessed State of the
Saints in Their Enjoyment of God in Glory*, ed. William Young
(Philadelphia: Lippincott; London Grant Richards, 1909). Both
appear in ch. 19, "An Example of this Heavenly Contemplation

for the Help of the Unskilful." The first (416) reads: "Art thou
not a rational soul, and shouldst not thou love according to
reason's conduct? And doth it not tell thee, that all is dirt and
dung to Christ; that earth is a dungeon to the celestial glory? Art
thou not a spirit thyself, and shouldst not thou love spiritually,
even God who is a spirit, and the Father of spirits? Doth not
every creature love their like? Why, my soul, art thou like to
flesh, or gold, or stately buildings?" The second (425) reads:
"And shall not I rejoice in expectation of a certain glory? If the
honour of the ambitious, or the wealth of the covetous person do
increase, his heart is lifted up with his estate as a boat that riseth
with the rising of the water; if they have but a little more land or
money than their neighbours, how easily may you see it in their
countenance and carriage! How high do they look; how big do
they speak; how stately and loftily they do demean themselves;
and shall not the heavenly loftiness and height of my spirit
discover my title to this promised land?"

that shed snakeskin in the history of politeness
not to be returned to again –
that invaluable accident
exonerating Adam.
And he has beauty also;   60
it's distressing – the O thou
to whom, from whom,
without whom nothing – Adam;
"something feline,
something colubrine"[5] – how true!   65
a crouching mythological monster
in that Persian miniature of emerald mines,
raw silk – ivory white, snow white,
oyster white and six others –
that paddock full of leopards and giraffes –   70
long lemonyellow bodies
sown with trapezoids of blue.
Alive with words,
vibrating like a cymbal
touched before it has been struck,   75
he has prophesied correctly –
the industrious waterfall,
"the speedy stream
which violently bears all before it,
at one time silent as the air
and now as powerful as the wind."[6]   80
"Treading chasms
on the uncertain footing of a spear,"[7]
forgetting that there is in woman
a quality of mind
which is an instinctive manifestation
is unsafe,
he goes on speaking
in a formal, customary strain
of "past states, the present state,   90
seals, promises,
the evil one suffered,
the good one enjoys,

[5] "something feline, something colubrine" Philip Littell (1868–1943), recalling how he and others had responded when the early poems of George Santayana (1863–1952) were first published in the Harvard Monthly, wrote: "We were puzzled and we were fascinated, as if by something feline, by something colubrine, at the core of his loneliness," colubrine meaning "of or having to do with a snake." "Books and Things: Santayana's Poems," New Republic, March 21, 1923, 102.

[6] "the speedy stream ... as the wind" Baxter, The Saints' Everlasting Rest, ch. 14, "Of Consideration, the Instrument of this Work; and What Force It Hath to Move the Soul," 346: "Meditation also putteth reason into his strength. Reason is at the strongest when it is most in action; now meditation produceth reason into act. Before, it was as a standing water, which can move nothing else when itself moveth not, but now it is as the speedy stream which violently bears down all before it. Before, it was as the still and silent air, but now it is as the powerful motion of the wind, and overthrows the opposition of the flesh and the devil."

[7] "Treading chasms ... of a spear" English essayist William Hazlitt (1778–1830), "On the Prose Style of Poets" (first pub-

lished in a periodical, Plain Speaker, August 1822), in Geoffrey Keynes (ed.), Selected Essays (London: Nonesuch, 1930), 490, commenting on the parliamentarian and writer Edmund Burke (1729–97): "Burke's style is airy, flighty, adventurous, but it never loses sight of the subject; nay, is alway in contact, and derives its increased or varying impulse from it. It may be said to pass yawning gulfs 'on the unstedfast footing of a spear': still it has an actual resting-place and tangible support under it – it is not suspended on nothing." The phrase quoted by Hazlitt ("on the unstedfast footing of a spear") is from Act 1, Scene 3, of Henry IV, Part I (1700) by Thomas Betterton (1635?–1710), Worcester warns Hotspur:

And now I will unclasp a secret Book,
And to your quick conveying Discontents
I'll read your Matter, deep and dangerous,
As full of peril and adventurous Spirit
As to o'er-walk a Current, roaring loud,
On the unstedfast footing of a Spear.

hell, heaven,
everything convenient   95
to promote one's joy."[8]
There is in him a state of mind
by force of which,
perceiving what it was not
intended that he should,   100
"he experiences a solemn joy
in seeing that he has become an idol."[9]
Plagued by the nightingale
in the new leaves,
with its silence –   105
not its silence but its silences,
he says of it:
"It clothes me with a shirt of fire."[10]
"He dares not clap his hands
to make it go on   110
lest it should fly off;
if he does nothing, it will sleep;
if he cries out, it will not understand."[11]
Unnerved by the nightingale
and dazzled by the apple,   115

impelled by "the illusion of a fire
effectual to extinguish fire,"[12]

[8] *"past states ... to promote one's joy"* Baxter, *The Saints' Everlasting Rest*, ch. 14, 344: "When a believer would reason his heart to this heavenly work, how many arguments do offer themselves; from God, from the Redeemer, from every one of the divine attributes, from our former estate, from our present estate, from promises, from seals, from earnest, from the evil we now suffer, from the good we partake of, from hell, from heaven; every thing doth offer itself to promote our joy. Now meditation is the hand to draw forth all these."

[9] *"he experiences ... an idol"* Moore's note (see Moore's "Notes to *Observations*," p. 663) directs the reader to a short story called "A Travers Champs" ("Across Fields"), included by the French writer Anatole France (1844–1924) one of ten children's stories that comprised his small collection called *Filles et Garçons: Scènes de la ville et des champs (Girls and Boys: Scenes from Town and Country)* (Paris: Librairie Hachette, 1900), 4–9: "le petit Jean comprend qu'il est beau et cette idée le pénètre d'un respect profond de lui-même. ... Il goûte un joie pieusee à se sentire devenue une idole." Or in translation: "Little Jean now understands that he is handsome and this idea penetrates him with a profound respect for himself. ... He experiences a solemn joy in seeing that he has become an idol." In the story Catherine and her younger brother Jean, rural children, take a walk through the fields; Catherine picks flowers and when they reach the top of a hill she makes them into a crown and places it on Jean's head. "Oui, chéri, s'écrie Catherine, je vais te faire une belle couronne et tu seras pareil à un petit roi" ("Yes, my dear," Catherine cries, "I'll make you a beautiful crown and you'll be the equal of a little king"). Then Jean kneels before Catherine and she crowns him, followed by the sentence that is quoted in Moore's note. Her ellipsis signals the omission of the following: "Il comprend qu'il est sacré. Droit, immobile, les yeux tout ronds, les lévres serrées, les bras pendants, les mains ouverts et les doigts écartés commes les rayons d'une roue" ("He understands that he is sacred. Straight up, immobile, his eyes wide open, his lips closed, his

arms hanging, his hands open with the fingers stretched out like the spokes of a wheel ... ").

[10] *"It clothes ... shirt of fire"* see Moore's "Notes to *Observations*," p. 663.

[11] *"He dares not clap ... will not understand"* Moore adopts these words from a book called *Feminine Influence on the Poets* (London: Martin Secker, 1910) by Edward Thomas (1878–1917). At one point (111), Thomas dwells on a poem by King James I, called "The Kingis Quair," which depicts his love for Joan Beaufort, the daughter of the Earl of Somerset. Thomas describes King James's first sight of her in the garden outside his prison: "To us the central experience is everything – the strong unhappy king, looking out of the prison window and seeing the golden-haired maiden in rich attire trimmed with pearls, rubies, emeralds and sapphires, a chaplet of red, white and blue feathers on her head, a heart-shaped ruby on a chain of fine gold hanging over her white throat, her dress looped up carelessly to walk in that fresh morning of nightingales in the new-leaved thickets –her little dog with his bells at her side. ... The nighingale stops singing. He dares not clap his hands to make it go on lest it should fly off; if he does nothing it will sleep; if he calls out it will not understand; and he begs the wind to shake the leaves and awake the song. And the bird sings again."

[12] *"the illusion of a fire ... fire"* Baxter, *The Saints' Everlasting Rest*, ch. 19, "An Example of this Heavenly Contemplation, for the Help of the Unskilful" 410–11: "See what a sea of love is here before thee; cast thyself in, and swim with thy arms of love in this ocean of His love; fear not lest thou shouldst be drowned or consumed in it. Though it seem as the scalding furnace of lead, yet thou wilt find it but mollifying oil: though it seems a furnace of fire, and the hottest that was ever kindled upon earth, yet it is the fire of love and not of wrath, a fire most effectual to extinguish fire; never intended to consume, but to glorify thee."

compared with which
the shining of the earth
is but deformity — a fire   120
"as high as deep as bright as broad
as long as life itself,"[13]
he stumbles over marriage,
"a very trivial object indeed"[14]
to have destroyed the attitude   125
in which he stood —
the ease of the philosopher
unfathered by a woman.
Unhelpful Hymen!
"a kind of overgrown cupid"[15]   130
reduced to insignificance
by the mechanical advertising
parading as involuntary comment,
by that experiment of Adam's
with ways out but no way in —   135
the ritual of marriage,
augmenting all its lavishness;
its fiddle-head ferns,
lotus flowers, opuntias, white dromedaries,
its hippopotamus —   140
nose and mouth combined
in one magnificient hopper,
"the crested screamer[16] —
that huge bird almost a lizard,"
its snake and the potent apple.   145
He tells us
that "for love
that will gaze an eagle blind,
that is like a Hercules
climbing the trees   150
in the garden of the Hesperides,
from forty-five to seventy
is the best age,"[17]

---

[13] "as high as deep / as bright as broad / as long as life itself" Baxter, *The Saints' Everlasting Rest*, ch. 19, "An Example of this Heavenly Contemplation, for the Help of the Unskilful," 415: "Can I love as high, as deep, as broad, as long as love itself; as much as He that made me, and that made me love, that gave all that little which I have; both the heart, the hearth where it is kindled, the bellows, the fire, the fuel, and all were His."

[14] "... *very trivial object indeed*" Wiliam Godwin (1756–1837), *An Enquiry concerning Political Justice* (Harmondsworth: Penguin, 1985), Book VIII, "Appendix of Co-operation, Cohabitation and Marriage," 762: "Add to this that marriage, as now understood, is a monopoly, and the worst of monopolies. So long as two human beings are forbidden, by positive institution, to follow the dictates of their own mind, prejudice will be alive and vigorous. So long as I seek, by despotic and artificial means to maintain my possession of a woman, I am guilty of the most odious selfishness."

[15] "*a kind of overgrown cupid*" from the *Dictionary of Phrase and Fable* (Philadelphia: Lippincott, 1894), by Ebenezer Cobham Brewer (1810–97), who gives his own definition of "Hymen": "God of marriage, a sort of overgrown Cupid. His symbols are a bridal-torch and veil in his hand."

[16] "*the crested screamer*" in her notes to the poem, Moore terms

this phrase a "remark in conversation" made by Glenway Westcott (1901–97), an American writer whose small journal published "Marriage."

[17] "*for love that ... the best age*" Anthony Trollope, *Barchester Towers*, ed. John Sutherland (Oxford: Oxford University Press, 1996), ch. 37, 2: 115: "But for real, true love, love at first sight, love to devotion, love that robs a man of his sleep, love that will 'gaze an eagle blind,' love that 'will hear the lowest sound when the suspicious tread of theft is stopped,' love that is like 'a Hercules, still climbing the Hesperides,' – we believe the best age is from forty-five to seventy." Trollope, in turn, quoting from a famous speech by the character Biron at the end of Act 4 in Shakespeare's *Love's Labours Lost* (1596):

It adds a precious seeing to the eye:
A lover's eyes will gaze an eagle blind,
A lover's ear will hear the lowest sound,
When the suspicious head of theft is stopped,
Love's feeling is more soft and sensible
Than are the tender horns of cockled snails.
Love's tongue proves dainty Bacchus gross in taste.
For valour, is not love a Hercules,
Still climbing trees in the Hesperides?

commending it
as a fine art, as an experiment,   155
a duty or as merely recreation.
One must not call him ruffian
nor friction a calamity –
the fight to be affectionate:
"no truth can be fully known   160
until it has been tried
by the tooth of disputation."[18]
The blue panther with black eyes,
the basalt panther with blue eyes,
entirely graceful –   165
one must give them the path –
the black obsidian Diana
who "darkeneth her countenance
as a bear doth,[19]
causing her husband to sigh,"   170
the spiked hand
that has an affection for one
and proves it to the bone,
impatient to assure you
that impatience is the mark of independence   175
not of bondage.
"Married people often look that way"[20] –
"seldom and cold, up and down,
mixed and malarial
with a good day and bad."[21]   180
"When do we feed?"
We occidentals are so unemotional,
we quarrel as we feed;
one's self quite lost,
the irony preserved   185
in "the Ahasuerus tête à tête banquet"[22]

---

[18] "no truth ... tooth of disputation" Robert of Sorbonne was a thirteenth century scholar who established the Sorbonne in Paris; he left six essential rules to be followed by any serious student, of which the fifth urged the student to engage in dialogue with colleagues, since "Nothing can be fully known till it has been tried by the tooth of disputation."

[19] "darkeneth her countenance as a bear doth" the Apocrypha are books that once formed part of the Hebrew Scriptures preserved in the ancient copies of the Septuagint, or Greek version, of the Old Testament. They were also translated and included with the King James or Authorized Version of the Bible in 1606, but since then are traditionally omitted from editions of the Bible. One of these is called The Wisdom of Jesus the son of Sirach or Ecclesiasticus, and Moore is quoting from Ecclesiasticus 25:17, which in the King James Version reads: "The wickedness of a woman changeth her face, and darkeneth her countenance like sackcloth." The slight difference in Moore's text ("as a bear" instead of "like sackcloth") is the result of her using a translation by Richard G. Moulton, Ecclesiasticus (London: Macmillan, 1896), a volume that was part of his series The Modern Reader's Bible.

[20] "Married people often look that way" in her notes to "Marriage," Moore ascribed this comment to C. Bertram Hartman (1882–1960), a painter who studied at the Art Institute of Chicago, the Royal Academy in Munich, and in Paris. Moore and Hartman were friends in the 1920s.

[21] "seldom and cold ... a good day and bad" Baxter, The Saints' Everlasting Rest, ch. 4, "What This Rest Containeth," 50, discussing whether the happiness of the afterlife is as certain as promised by Scripture: "If thy happiness were in thine own hand, as Adam's, there were yet fear; but it is in the keeping of a faithful Creator. Christ hath not bought thee so dear, to trust thee with thyself any more. His love to thee will not be as thine was on earth to Him, seldom and cold, up and down mixed, as aguish bodies, with burning and quaking, with a good day and a bad."

[22] "the Ahasuerus tête à tête banquet" Marianne Moore's note to this passage ascribes it to George Adam Smith (1856–1942), a British clergyman who wrote two works in the "Expositor's Bible" series, The Book of Isaiah, 2 vols. (London: Hodder & Stoughton, 1888–90), and The Book of the Twelve Prophets, Commonly Called the Minor, 2 vols. (London: Hodder & Stoughton, 1896–98). But this phrase is not found in those four volumes. King Ahasuerus was the ruler of a kingdom described in the book of Esther in the Bible, in which the eponymous character Esther becomes his queen. When one of his ministers, Haman, contrives a plan to destroy Esther's stepfather, Mordecai, and all the Jews in the kingdom, Esther foils it by inviting King Ahasuerus and Haman to a banquet, where she foils Haman's plans and he is hanged on the gallows he had erected for Mordecai.

with its "good monster, lead the way,"[23]
with little laughter
and munificence of humor
in that quixotic atmosphere of frankness   190
in which "Four o'clock does not exist
but at five o'clock
the ladies in their imperious humility
are ready to receive you";[24]
in which experience attests   195
that men have power
and sometimes one is made to feel it.
He says, "What monarch would not blush
to have a wife
with hair like a shaving-brush?   200
The fact of woman
is not 'the sound of the flute
but every poison.'"[25]
She says, "'Men are monopolists
of stars, garters, buttons   205
and other shining baubles'[26] –
unfit to be the guardians
of another person's happiness."
He says, "These mummies
must be handled carefully –   210
'the crumbs from a lion's meal,

[23] *"good monster, lead the way"* the last line of Shakespeare's *The Tempest*, Act 2, Scene 2, more typically given as "Brave monster, lead the way," spoken by Stephano, the drunken sailor who thinks he will rule the island, to Caliban, who promises him treasure.

[24] *"Four o'clock ... to receive you"* the phrase is translated from an essay on the pleasures of drinking tea, called "Le Thé" ("Tea"), written by Anna Élisabeth de Brancovan, comtesse de Noailles (countess of Noailles) (1876–1933) and published in the December 1921 issue of *Femina* (17–20). The words "four o'clock ... five o'clock" are not found in the original, though it could be argued that Moore's phrase translates something in the spirit of the essay, which describes women dressing before tea, then continues: "Elles sont prêtes, elles vont plaire. A qui? Pourquoi? Ne le leur demandons pas. Dans leur impérieuse humilité elles jouent instinctivement leur rôle sur le globe, et font précéder d'innombrables et vaines 'répétitions' la mystérieuse journée de secret spectacle, de vraie tragédie, où elles aiment et seront aimées." Or: "They are ready, and are going to please. Whom? Why? Let us not ask them. In their imperious humility they instinctively play their role on the globe, and they make countless and vain 'repetitions' precede the mysterious day of secret spectacle, of true tragedy, where they love and will be loved in return."

[25] *"What monarch ... but every poison."* ' Marianne Moore's note directs the reader to an unpublished "satire in verse by Mary Frances Nearing with suggestions by M. Moore," entitled "The Rape of the Lock." Not further identified. Moore's note attributes the phrase "the sound of the flute but every poison" to Abraham Mitrie Rihbany (1869–1944), whose book *The Syrian Christ* (Boston: Houghton Mifflin), which appeared in 1916, offers explanations of customs described in the Bible. Rihbany, however, mentions neither a flute nor poison, and the quotation is Moore's invention. Her note goes on to comment: "Silence on the part of women – 'to an Oriental, this is as poetry set to music' although 'in the Orient as here, husbands have difficulty in enforcing their authority'; 'it is a common saying that not all

the angels in heaven could subdue a woman." ' Rihbany, instead, writes that it is important for women to remain silent in public, and adds, "To oriental ears, as perhaps to Puritan ears of the good old type, such words are poetry set to music" (333). The other quotations from Rihbany are found on the same page.

[26] *'men are monopolists ... baubles'* Martha Carey Thomas (1857–1935), president of Bryn Mawr College from 1893 to 1922, was an educator and feminist; her address on "Present Day Problems in Teaching" was given on Mount Holyoke College Founders Day, in November 1921, and published in the *Mount Holyoke Alumnae Quarterly* 5(4) (January 1922): 193–9. The phrase "men are monopolists" does not appear in the published text. Moore, in her accompanying note, quotes further from Thomas: "Men practically reserve for themselves stately funerals, splendid monuments, memorial statues, membership in academies, medals, titles, honorary degrees, stars, garters, ribbons, buttons and other shining baubles so valueless in themselves and yet so infinitely desirable because they are symbols of recognition by their fellow craftsmen of difficult work well done." In the published version the text reads: "As in 1912, so in 1921, the very men who have generously yielded so much to women are themselves still sitting in the seats of the mighty, enthroned in all the ancient privilege of sex, and are still jealously guarding for themselves and for other men the prizes and rewards of intellect and achievement – more pay for the same work, the most highly paid positions in all occupations, such as the best high school positions, all superintendencies, principalships, associate professorships, full professorships, head curatorships in museums, and even an unfair proportion of fellowships and scholarships, especially of the most valuable kinds, stately funerals, monuments, statues, membership in academies, medals, titles, stars, garters, ribbons, buttons and other shining baubles, so valueless in themselves and yet so infinitely valuable because they are symbols of recognition by their fellows of fame richly deserved for difficult work well done" (195).

a couple of shins and the bit of an ear';[27]
turn to the letter M
and you will find
that 'a wife is a coffin,'[28]   215
that severe object
with the pleasing geometry
stipulating space and not people,
refusing to be buried
and uniquely disappointing,   220
revengefully wrought in the attitude
of an adoring child
to a distinguished parent."
She says, "This butterfly,
this waterfly, this nomad   225
that has 'proposed
to settle on my hand for life.'[29] –
What can one do with it?
There must have been more time
in Shakespeare's day   230
to sit and watch a play.
You know so many artists who are fools."
He says, "You know so many fools
who are not artists."
The fact forgot   235
that "some have merely rights
while some have obligations,"[30]
he loves himself so much,
he can permit himself
no rival in that love.   240
She loves herself so much,
she cannot see herself enough –
a statuette of ivory on ivory,
the logical last touch
to an expansive splendor   245
earned as wages for work done:
one is not rich but poor
when one can always seem so right.
What can one do for them –

these savages   250
condemned to disaffect
all those who are not visionaries

---

[27] 'the crumbs ... bit of an ear' Amos 3:12, as translated by
George Adam Smith (1856–1942), an English clergyman, in the
"Expositor's Bible" series, *The Book of the Twelve Prophets, Commonly
Called the Minor*, vol. 1 *Amos, Hosea and Micah*, 146: "Thus saith
Jehovah: As the shepherd saveth from the mouth of the lion a pair
of shin-bones or a bit of an ear, so shall the children of Israel be
saved – they who sit in Samaria in the corner of the diwan and ...
on a couch" (ellipsis in original). The King James or Authorized
Version of the same passage reads: "Thus saith the Lord; As the
shepherd taketh out of the mouth of the lion two legs, or a piece of
an ear; so shall the children of Israel be taken out that dwell in
Samaria in the corner of a bed, and in Damascus in a couch."
[28] 'a wife is a coffin' "Quoted by John Cournos from Ezra Pound,"
reads Marianne Moore's note to this citation. John Cournos
(1881–1966) was an American poet; on Ezra Pound see p. 39.

[29] 'proposed to ... for life.' from *Christie Johnstone* (London: Richard Bentley, 1853), the second novel by the prolific Victorian
writer Charles Reade (1814–84), 14; when the wealthy but idle
Lord Ipsden asks his second cousin once removed, Lady Barbara
Sinclair, for her hand in marriage, she thinks: "Accustomed to
measure men by their character alone and to treat with sublime
contempt the accidents of birth and fortune, she had been a little
staggered by the assurance of this butterfly that had proposed to
settle on her hand – for life."
[30] "some have ... have obligations" adapted, according to Moore,
from a quotation by the parliamentarian and writer Edmund
Burke (1729–97): "Asiatics have rights; Europeans have obligations." Source not identified.

alert to undertake the silly task
of making people noble?
This model of petrine fidelity   255
who "leaves her peaceful husband
only because she has seen enough of him"[31] –
that orator reminding you,
"I am yours to command."
"Everything to do with love is mystery;[32]   260
it is more than a day's work
to investigate this science."
One sees that it is rare –
that striking grasp of opposites
opposed each to the other, not to unity,   265
which in cycloid inclusiveness
has dwarfed the demonstration
of Columbus with the egg[33] –
a triumph of simplicity –
that charitive Euroclydon[34]   270
of frightening disinterestedness
which the world hates,
admitting:

"I am such a cow,
if I had a sorrow,   275
I should feel it a long time;
I am not one of those
who have a great sorrow
in the morning
and a great joy at noon";   280

---

[31] *"leaves her peaceful ... enough of him"* Simone A. Puget, "Chose a la Mode," *English Review* (June 1914), "The English Review Advertising Supplement," 3–12, here 10. Simone A. Puget wrote a monthly feature on Paris fashion that was presented in a separately paginated "Advertising Supplement" to the *English Review*. In her very Gallic version of English: "Still, since about thirty years ago something had altered in the concept of elegancy. The influence of English decoration, perhaps Loie Fuller's dances, started an effort towards simplicity and delicacy. It has been the time of shades.

"Then during the four late years there was a wonderful craze for renovating Byzantine fashions, and adapting modes from Greece and Egypt to the twentieth century woman. It has been very successful. The fashion was altogether decent and voluptuous, and fitted the harmony of the feminine body, for it did envelop it without concealing it, and revealed it without exhibitions.

"But women's brains have got naught in perpetuity.

"Now everything has changed, without any other reason 'for change.' Thus proceed pretty dolls when they leave their old home to 'renovate their frame', and dear others who may abandon their peaceful husband only because they saw enough of him."

[32] *"Everything ... mystery"* Frederick Colin Tilney, trans., *The Original Fables of La Fontaine* (London: Dent; New York, Dutton, 1913), Book XII, no. 14, "Love and Folly," 111–12: "Everything to do with love is mystery. Cupid's arrows, his quiver, his torch, his boyhood: it is more than a day's work to exhaust this science. I make no pretence here of explaining everything. My object is merely to relate to you, in my own way, how the blind little god was deprived of his sight, and what consequences followed this evil which perchance was a blessing after all. On the latter point I will decide nothing, but leave it to lovers to decide upon.

"One day as Folly and Love were playing together, before the boy had lost his vision, a dispute arose. To settle this matter Love wished to lay his cause before a council of the gods; but Folly, losing her patience, dealt him a furious blow upon the brow. From that moment and for ever the light of heaven was gone from his eyes.

"Venus demanded redress and revenge, the mother and the wife in her asserting themselves in a way which I leave you to imagine. She deafened the gods with her cries, appealing to Jupiter, Nemesis, the judges from Hades, in fact all who could be importuned. She represented the seriousness of the case, pointing out [112:] that her son could now not make a step without a stick. No punishment, she urged, was heavy enough for so dire a crime, and she demanded that the damage should be repaired.

"When the gods had each well considered the public interest on the one hand and the complainant's demands upon the other, the supreme court gave as its verdict that Folly was condemned for ever more to serve as a guide for the footsteps of Love."

[33] According to an apocryphal story, Columbus, some time after he had discovered the New World, was invited to a banquet. One of the guests remarked that it was all very well for Columbus to have done what he did, but that in a country like Spain, where there were so many men learned in cosmography and so many able mariners as well, someone else would certainly have been found who would have done the same thing. Whereupon Columbus, calling for an egg, laid a wager that nobody but he could make it stand on end without support. After everyone had tried and failed, Columbus took up the egg, cracked the shell at one end, and so made the egg stand upright.

[34] *Euroclydon* the name of a "tempestuous wind" that blows the ship in which Saint Paul is traveling off course and shipwrecks him on the island of Malta, Act 27:14.

which says: "I have encountered it
among those unpretentious
protegés of wisdom,
where seeming to parade
as the debater and the Roman,   285
the statesmanship
of an archaic Daniel Webster[35]
persists to their simplicity of temper
as the essence of the matter:

'Liberty and union   290
now and forever;'

the book on the writing-table;
the hand in the breast-pocket."

To a Snail (1924)

If "compression is the first grace of style,"[1]
you have it. Contractility is a virtue
as modesty is a virtue.
It is not the acquisition of any one thing
that is able to adorn,
or the incidental quality that occurs
as a concomitant of something well said,
that we value in style,
but the principle that is hid:
in the absence of feet, "a method of conclusions";[2]
"a knowledge of principles,"
in the curious phenomenon of your occipital horn.

{Moore's Notes to Observations}

To a Steam Roller, p. 647

"impersonal judgment": Lawrence Gilman

Pedantic Literalist, p. 647

All excerpts from Richard Baxter: *The Saints' Everlasting Rest*; Lippincott, 1909.

---

[35] Daniel Webster (1782–1852) was a Representative and Senator from Massachusetts who, in 1841, was appointed Secretary of State and, elected to the Senate again from 1845 to 1850, became famous for his oratory. He tried to perserve the union by advocating compromises on the question of slavery, and in a speech supporting the so-called Compromise of 1850, is reported to have said: "Liberty and Union, Now and Forever, One and Inseparable." The quote represents his desire to keep the nation intact during a period of intense conflict. A larger-than-life bronze sculpture of Daniel Webster was designed by the sculptor Thomas Ball (1819–1911) and installed along the West Drive at 72 Street and Central Park in New York, dedicated in 1876, and the quotation is found at the base of the sculpture.

TO A SNAIL
The poem was first published in Moore's *Observations* (New York: Dial Press, 1924).
[1] See "Moore's Notes to *Observations*," p. 665. Democritus was an orator and philosopher in Athens in the fifth century B C.
[2] See "Moore's Notes to *Observations*," p. 665. John Duns Scotus (c. 1266 to 1308) was a medieval theologian and philosopher.

MOORE'S NOTES
These notes accompanied Moore's *Observations* (New York: Dial Press, 1924), appearing at the end of the volume.

Poetry, p. 649

Diary of Tolstoy; Dutton, p. 84: "Where the boundary between prose and poetry lies, I shall never be able to understand. The question is raised in manuals of style, yet the answer to it lies beyond me. Poetry is verse: prose is not verse. Or else poetry is everything with the exception of business documents and school books."

"literalists of the imagination": Yeats; *Ideas of Good and Evil*, 1903; "William Blake and his Illustrations to The Divine Comedy;" p. 182; "The limitation of his view was from the very intensity of his vision; he was a too literal realist of imagination, as others are of nature; and because he believed that the figures seen by the mind's eye, when exalted by inspiration were 'eternal existences,' symbols of divine essences, he hated every grace of style that might obscure their lineaments."

England, p. 650

"chrysalis of the nocturnal butterfly": Erté

"I envy nobody": *The Compleat Angler*

New York, p. 651

fur trade: in 1921, New York succeeded St. Louis as the centre of the wholesale fur trade
    "as satin needlework": *The Literary Digest*, March 30, 1918, quotes *Forest and Stream*, March 1918 – an article by George Shiras, 3rd: "Only once in the long period that I have hunted or photographed these animals (white-tailed deer) in this region, have I seen an albino, and that one lingered for a year and a half about my camp, which is situated midway between Marquette and Grand Island. Signs were put up in the neighborhood reading: 'Do not shoot the white deer – it will bring you bad luck.' But tho the first part of the appeal stayed the hand of the sportsman, and the latter that of most pot-hunters, it was finally killed by an unsuperstitious homesteader, and the heretofore unsuccessful efforts to photograph it naturally came to an end.
    "Some eight years ago word came that a fine albino buck had been frequently seen on Grand Island and that it came to a little pond on the easterly part of the island. Taking a camping outfit, a canoe, and my guide, several days and nights were spent watching the pond; . . . the white buck did not appear.
    "The next year the quest was no more successful, and when I heard that on the opening of the season the buck had been killed by a lumberjack, it was satisfactory to know that the body had been shipped to a taxidermist in Detroit, preparatory to being added to the little museum of the island hotel.
    "About the middle of June, 1916, a white fawn only a few days old was discovered in a thicket and brought to the hotel. Here, in the company of another fawn, it grew rapidly. During the earlier months this fawn had the usual row of white spots on the back and sides, and altho there was no difference between these and the body color, they were conspicuous in the same way that satin needlework in a single color may carry a varied pattern. . . . In June, 1917, one of these does bore an albino fawn, which lacked, however, the brocaded spots which characterized the previous one.
    "It may be of interest to note that the original buck weighed 150 pounds and possessed a rather extraordinary set of antlers, spreading twenty-six inches, with terminal points much further apart than any I have ever seen. The velvet on the antlers . . . was snow-white, giving them a most statuesque appearance amid the green foliage of the forest. The eyes of the three native albinos are a very light gray-blue, while the doe has the usual red eyeballs; . . . and in the absence of accident or disease, there should soon be a permanent herd of these interesting animals."

picardel: an Elizabethan ruff

"queen full of jewels":—

if the fur is not finer: Isabella, Duchess of Gonzaga. Frank Alvah Parsons; The *Psychology of Dress*; Doubleday, p. 68. "I wish black cloth even if it cost ten ducats a yard. If it is only as good as that which I see other people wear, I had rather be without it."

"accessibility to experience": Henry James

Marriage, p. 652

"of circular traditions": Francis Bacon

write simultaneously: *Scientific American*; January, 1922; "Multiple Consciousness or Reflex Action of Unaccustomed Range." "Miss A— will write simultaneously in three languages, English, German, and French, talking in the meantime. (She) takes advantage of her abilities in everyday life, writing her letters simultaneously with both hands; namely, the first, third, and fifth words with her left and the second, fourth, and sixth with her right hand. While generally writing outward, she is able as well to write inward with both hands."

"See her, see her in this common world": "George Shock"

"unlike flesh, stones": Richard Baxter; *The Saints' Everlasting Rest*; Lippincott, 1909

"something feline, something colubrine": Philip Littell; Books and Things; Santayana's Poems; New Republic, March 21, 1923. "We were puzzled and we were fascinated, as if by something feline, by something colubrine."

"treading chasms": Hazlitt; Essay on Burke's style

"past states": Baxter

"he experiences a solemn joy": Anatole France; *Filles et Garçons*; Hachette. "A Travers Champs"; "le petit Jean comprend qu'il est beau et cette idée le pénètre d'un respect profond de lui-même. . . . Il goûte une joie pieuse à se sentir devenu une idole."

"it clothes me with a shirt of fire": The Nightingale; a poem in Armenian by Dr Hagop Boghossian of the Department of Philosophy of Worcester College, Massachusetts

"he dares not clap his hands": Edward Thomas; *Feminine Influence on the Poets*; Martin Secker, 1910. "The Kingis Quair – To us the central experience is everything – the strong unhappy king, looking out of the prison window and seeing the golden-haired maiden in rich attire trimmed with pearls, rubies, emeralds and sapphires, a chaplet of red, white and blue feathers on her head, a heart-shaped ruby on a chain of fine gold hanging over her white throat, her dress looped up carelessly to walk in that fresh morning of nightingales in the new-leaved thickets – her little dog with his bells at her side."

"illusion of a fire": Baxter

"as high as deep": Baxter

"very trivial object": Godwin: "marriage is a law and the worst of all laws . . . a very trivial object indeed."

"a kind of overgrown cupid": Brewer; *Dictionary of Phrase and Fable*

"the crested screamer": remark in conversation; Glenway Wescott

"for love that will gaze an eagle blind": Anthony Trollope; *Barchester Towers*, Vol. II

"No truth can be fully known": Robert of Sorbonne

"darkeneth her countenance as a bear doth": Ecclesiasticus;
   Women Bad and Good – An Essay; Modern Reader's Bible; Macmillan

"seldom and cold": Baxter

"Married people often look that way": C. Bertram Hartmann

"Ahasuerus tête à tête banquet": George Adam Smith; Expositor's Bible

"Good monster, lead the way": *The Tempest*

"Four o'clock does not exist": la Comtesse de Noailles; *Femina*, December, 1921. "le Thè": "Dans leur impérieuse humilité elles jouent instinctivement leurs rôles sur le globe."

"What monarch": "The Rape of the Lock"; a satire in verse by Mary Frances Nearing with suggestions by M. Moore

"the sound of the flute": A. Mitram Rhibany; *The Syrian Christ*. Silence on the part of women – "to an Oriental, this is as poetry set to music" although "in the Orient as here, husbands have difficulty in enforcing their authority"; "it is a common saying that not all the angels in heaven could subdue a woman."

"men are monopolists": Miss M. Carey Thomas, President Emeritus of Bryn Mawr College. Founders address, Mount Holyoke College, 1921: "Men practically reserve for themselves stately funerals, splendid monuments, memorial statues, membership in academies, medals, titles, honorary degrees, stars, garters, ribbons, buttons and other shining baubles, so valueless in themselves and yet so infinitely desirable because they are symbols of recognition by their fellow craftsmen of difficult work well done."

"the crumbs from a lion's meal": Amos: 3; 12. Translation by George Adam Smith: Expositor's Bible

"a wife is a coffin": quoted by John Cournos from Ezra Pound

"settle on my hand": Charles Reade; *Christie Johnston*

"some have rights": Burke. "Asiatics have rights; Europeans have obligations."

"leaves her peaceful husband": Simone A. Puget; "Change of Fashion"; advertisement, *English Review*, June, 1914. "Thus proceed pretty dolls when they leave their old home to renovate their frame, and dear others who may abandon their peaceful husband only because they have seen enough of him."

"Everything to do with love is mystery": F. C. Tilney; *The Original Fables of La Fontaine*; Dutton. Love and Folly: Book XII, No. 14.

"Liberty and Union": Daniel Webster

To a Snail, p. 661

"compression is the first grace of style": Democritus

"method of conclusions"; "knowledge of principles": Duns Scotus

POEMS AFTER OBSERVATIONS

The Steeple-Jack (1932)

Dürer[1] would have seen a reason for living
   in a town like this, with eight stranded whales
to look at; with the sweet sea air coming into your house
on a fine day, from water etched
   with waves as formal as the scales   5
on a fish.

One by one in two's and three's, the seagulls keep
   flying back and forth over the town clock,
or sailing around the lighthouse without moving their wings –
rising steadily with a slight   10
   quiver of the body – or flock
mewing where

a sea the purple of the peacock's neck is
   paled to greenish azure as Dürer changed
the pine green of the Tyrol to peacock blue and guinea   15
gray.[2] You can see a twenty-five-
   pound lobster; and fish nets arranged
to dry. The

whirlwind fife-and-drum of the storm bends the salt
   marsh grass, disturbs stars in the sky and the   20
star on the steeple; it is a privilege to see so
much confusion. Disguised by what
   might seem the opposite, the seaside flowers and

First published in *Poetry* 40(3) (June 1932). Revised in 1961, it was placed as the first poem in her *Collected Poems*.
[1] *Dürer* Albrecht Dürer (1471–1528), German artist of the Renaissance, famed for his precise rendering.
[2] *as Dürer changed ... guinea gray* in a watercolor titled *Weblsch Prig* (c. 1494), now in the Ashmolean Museum, Oxford, Dürer depicted a few small buildings that are set against the rising, deep green, pine-covered slope of a mountain in the Tyrol (the area in the western part of Austria and northern part of Italy); the deep green in the middle distances pales dramatically as we move toward the foreground, becoming a slate gray color, speckled with white, of the guinea fowl.

trees are favored by the fog so that you have   25
    the tropics at first hand: the trumpet-vine,
fox-glove, giant snap-dragon, a salpiglossis[3] that has
spots and stripes; morning-glories, gourds,
    or moon-vines trained on fishing-twine
at the back door;   30

cat-tails, flags, blueberries and spiderwort,
    striped grass, lichens, sunflowers, asters, daisies –
yellow and crab-claw ragged sailors with green bracts[4] – toad-plant,
petunias, ferns; pink lilies, blue
    ones, tigers; poppies; black sweet-peas.   35
The climate

is not right for the banyan, frangipani, or
    jack-fruit trees;[5] or for exotic serpent
life. Ring lizard and snake-skin[6] for the foot, if you see fit;
but here they've cats, not cobras, to   40
    keep down the rats. The diffident
little newt

with white pin-dots on black horizontal spaced-
    out bands lives here; yet there is nothing that
ambition can buy or take away. The college student   45
named Ambrose sits on the hillside
    with his not-native books and hat
and sees boats

at sea progress white and rigid as if in
    a groove. Liking an elegance of which   50
the source is not bravado, he knows by heart the antique
sugar-bowl shaped summer-house of
    interlacing slats, and the pitch
of the church

spire, not true, from which a man in scarlet lets   55
    down a rope as a spider spins a thread;
he might be part of a novel, but on the sidewalk a
sign says C. J. Poole, Steeple-Jack,
    in black and white; and one in red
and white says   60

Danger. The church portico has four fluted
    columns, each a single piece of stone, made
modester by white-wash. This would be a fit haven for
waifs, children, animals, prisoners,
    and presidents who have repaid   65
sin-driven

---

[3] *salpiglossis* an herb with large, varicolored flowers that have striking markings.

[4] *with green bracts* leaves growing at the base of a flower or flower stalk.

[5] *banyan, frangipani, or jack-fruit trees* the banyan is an East Indian tree; frangipani is a tropical American shrub; the jack-fruit is a large East Indian tree with edible fruit.

[6] *Ring lizard and snake-skin* monitor lizards (the Latin genus name is *Varanus*) are found chiefly in Australia, but also in Africa, the Middle East, tropical Asia, and some Pacific islands; the smallest species are 1.5 feet long, most about 3 feet long. Known also as rice lizards, rings lizards, and water monitors, they have been used for making various luxury products, including shoes ("for the feet").

senators by not thinking about them. The
    place has a school-house, a post-office in a
store, fish-houses, hen-houses, a three-masted schooner on
the stocks. The hero, the student,
    the steeple-jack, each in his way,
is at home.

It could not be dangerous to be living
    in a town like this, of simple people,
who have a steeple-jack placing danger-signs by the church
while he is gilding the solid-
    pointed star, which on a steeple
stands for hope.

70

75

No Swan[1] so Fine (1932)

"No water so still as the
    dead fountains of Versailles."[2] No swan,
with swart blind look askance
and gondoliering legs, so fine
    as the chintz china one with fawn-
brown eyes and toothed gold
collar on to show whose bird it was.

Lodged in the Louis Fifteenth
    candelabrum-tree of cockscomb-
tinted buttons, dahlias,
sea-urchins, and everlastings,
    it perches on the branching foam
of polished sculptured
flowers – at ease and tall. The king is dead.

5

10

The Jerboa (1932)

Too Much

A Roman had an
artist, a freedman,
    contrive a cone – pine-cone
    or fir-cone – with holes for a fountain. Placed on
        the Prison of St. Angelo, this cone
        of the Pompeys which is known

5

First published in *Poetry* 41(1) (October 1932).
[1] *Swan* a decorative detail in a candelabrum from the time of
Louis XV (1710–74), a period that favored an elaborative or
rococo style; two of these candelabra, which had belonged to
Lord Arthur Balfour (1848–1930, prime minister 1902–5), a
prominent British politician, were auctioned in 1930 and received
fleeting attention from contemporary news media. Moore
sketched the base of one candelabrum from a contemporary
photo, and in a contemporary letter to her brother, still unpublished, noted that "Each swan has a gold saw-toothed collar and
chain and both feet are planted on a tree" (see Patricia Willis,
Vision into Verse [Philadelphia: Rosenbach Museum, 1987], 40–2).

[2] *"No water . . . of Versailles"* from Percy Philip, "Versailles Reborn:
A Moonlight Drama," *New York Times Magazine*, May 19, 1931, 8.
In this fanciful article, the statues on the grounds of Versailles
protest the dulness of the place without the court of the Kings Louis.

THE JERBOA
First published in *Hound and Horn* 6(5) (October–December
1932); reprinted in Ezra Pound (ed.), *Active Anthology* (London:
Faber and Faber, 1933), and in Moore's *Selected Poems*
(London: Faber and Faber, 1935).

now as the Popes', passed
for art.[1] A huge cast
   bronze, dwarfing the peacock
     statue in the garden of the Vatican,   10
        it looks like a work of art made to give
        to a Pompey, or native

of Thebes. Others could
build, and understood
   making colossi and   15
     how to use slaves, and kept crocodiles and put
        baboons on the necks of giraffes to pick
        fruit, and used serpent magic.

They had their men tie
hippopotami   20
   and bring out dappled dog-
     cats to course antelopes, dikdik, and ibex;
        or used small eagles. They looked on as theirs,
        impalas and onigers,

the wild ostrich herd   25
with hard feet and bird
   necks rearing back in the
     dust like a serpent preparing to strike, cranes,
        mongooses, storks, anoas, Nile geese;
        and there were gardens for these –   30

combining planes, dates,
limes, and pomegranates,
   in avenues – with square
     pools of pink flowers, tame fish, and small frogs. Besides
        yarns dyed with indigo, and red cotton,   35
        they had a flax which they spun

into fine linen
cordage for yachtsmen.
   These people liked small things;
     they gave to boys little paired playthings such as   40
        nests of eggs, ichneumon and snake, paddle
        and raft, badger and camel;

and made toys for them-
selves: the royal totem;
   and toilet-boxes marked   45
     with the contents. Lords and ladies put goose-grease

[1] *A Roman had ... passed / for art* Moore's knowledge of this artwork derived from a magazine called the *Periodical* (founded 1896), which published paragraphs extracted from recent books, often very learned in nature, and sometimes illustrations. In the *Periodical* 14(148) (February 15, 1929), 4, was illustrated a "Colossal Fir-Cone of Bronze, by a Freedman Artist." Beneath the illustration was a brief description: "Perforated with holes, it served as a fountain. Its inscription states 'P. Cincius P. I. Salvius fecit' [P. Cincius P. I. made this]. Now in one of the gardens of the Vatican, Rome." The magazine then referred the reader to Arnold Mackay Duff, *Freedman in the Early Roman Empire* (Oxford: Clarendon Press, 1928), where the same illustration, with exactly the same description, serves as the book's frontispiece opposite the title page. The detail that the fir-cone once sat atop Castel Sant'Angelo appears to be Moore's invention. The Castel Sant'Angelo is a large fort located alongside the Sant'Angelo bridge in Rome; constructed between 130 and 139 AD by Antoninus Pius, it was originally intended as a mausoleum for the emperor Hadrian and his successors. Under the pope, from the tenth century onwards, it became a fortress and prison, whence Moore's reference to "the Prison of St. Angelo."

paint in round bone boxes – the pivoting
lid incised with a duck-wing

or reverted duck-
head; kept in a buck   50
　　or rhinoceros horn,
　　　the ground horn; and locust oil in stone locusts.[2]
　　　　It was a picture with a fine distance;
　　　　　of drought, and of assistance

in time, from the Nile   55
rising slowly, while
　　the pig-tailed monkey on
　　　slab-hands, with arched-up slack-slung gait, and the brown
　　　　dandy looked at the jasmine two-leafed twig
　　　　　and bud, cactus-pads, and fig.   60

Dwarfs here and there, lent
to an evident
　　poetry of frog grays,
　　　duck-egg greens, and egg-plant blues, a fantasy
　　　　and a verisimilitude that were   65
　　　　　right to those with, everywhere,

power over the poor.
The bees' food is your
　　food. Those who tended flower-
　　　beds and stables were like the king's cane in the   70
　　　　form of a hand,[3] or the folding bedroom
　　　　　made for his mother of whom

he was fond.[4] Princes
clad in queens' dresses,
　　calla or petunia   75
　　　white, that trembled at the edge, and queens in a
　　　　king's underskirt of fine-twilled thread like silk-
　　　　　worm gut, as bee-man and milk-

maid, kept divine cows
and bees; limestone brows,   80

[2] *stone locusts* Moore's note directs the reader to a feature story that appeared in *Illustrated London News* 177(4762) (July 26, 1930), p. 162. The very long title of the story ran: "A Wooden Locust Made to Hold a Locust-Flesh Preparation? A Very Realistic Toilet-Box Which Dates from about the 22nd Egyptian Dynasty." The feature story ran as follows. "Sending us the photograph here reproduced, a reader in Egypt writes: 'I enclose a photograph of a locust. It is a carved wooden toilet-box which may have contained a preparation from the flesh of a locust which was supposed to have medical or cosmetic value. The wings are movable and form the lid of the box. This is some proof that the locust was not always considered to be a plague. The object is of about the 22nd Egyptian Dynasty, and is from Saqqara.'"

[3] *king's cane . . . hand* Moore's note refers to "The 'Castle of the Disc' at Tell el Amarna," a feature story by J. D. S. Pendlebury (1904–41) which appeared in the *Illustrated London News* 80(4848) (March 19, 1932), pp. 427–9. Pendlebury was an archaeologist at work in Tell el Amarna, Egypt, and reported finding "two ivory walking-stick handles in the shape of hands," among many other objects.

[4] Moore's note refers the reader to an illustrated feature that appeared in the *Illustrated London News* 80(4855) (May 7, 1932), pp. 767–9, titled: "The Golden Travelling-Bed of the Mother of Cheops." A subtitle followed: "A Gem of Egyptian Craftsmanship Nearly 5,000 Years Ago; The Only Complete Example We Have of an Old Kingdom Bed-Canopy – A Gift to Queen Hetepheres from King Sneferuw." The text ran: "Dr. George A. Reisner, who is Curator of Egyptian Art in the Museum of Fine Arts at Boston, U.S.A., and Professor of Egyptology at Harvard, describes here the completed reconstruction of a remarkable object found in Egypt by the Boston-Harvard Expedition under his leadership – a gold-case bed-canopy made for Queen Hetepheres I, the mother of Cheops, builder of the Great Pyramid. It was presented to her by her husband, King Sneferuw, who reigned about 3000 B C."

and gold-foil wings. They made
basalt serpents and portraits of beetles; the
    king gave his name to them and he was named
    for them. He feared snakes, and tamed

Pharaoh's rat, the rust-   85
backed mongoose. No bust
    of it was made, but there
    was pleasure for the rat. Its restlessness was
        its excellence; it was praised for its wit;
        and the jerboa, like it,   90

a small desert rat,
and not famous, that
    lives without water, has
    happiness. Abroad seeking food, or at home
        in its burrow, the Sahara field-mouse   95
        has a shining silver house

of sand. O rest and
joy, the boundless sand,
    the stupendous sand-spout,
    no water, no palm-trees, no ivory bed,   100
        tiny cactus; but one would not be he
        who has nothing but plenty.

Abundance

Africanus meant
the conqueror sent
    from Rome. It should mean the   105
    untouched: the sand-brown jumping-rat—free-born; and
        the blacks, that choice race with an elegance
        ignored by one's ignorance.

Part terrestrial,
and part celestial,   110
Jacob saw, cudgel staff
in claw-hand – steps of air and air angels;[5] his
    friends were the stones. The translucent mistake
    of the desert, does not make

hardship for one who   115
can rest and then do
    the opposite – launching
    as if on wings, from its match-thin hind legs, in
        daytime or at night; with the tail as a weight,
        undulated out by speed, straight.   120

---

[5] Moore abbreviates the story recounted in Genesis 28:10–13:

10. And Jacob went out from Beersheba, and went toward Haran.
11. And he lighted upon a certain place, and tarried there all night because the sun was set; and he took of the stones of that place, and put them for his pillows, and lay down in that place to sleep.

12. And he dreamed, and behold a ladder set up on the earth, and the top of it reached to heaven: and behold the angels of God ascending and descending on it.
13. And, behold, the Lord stood above it, and said, I am the lord God of Abraham they father, and the God of Isaac: the land whereon thou liest, to thee will I give it, and to thy seed.

Looked at by daylight,
the underside's white,
   though the fur on the back
   is buff-brown like the breast of the fawn-breasted
      bower-bird. It hops like the fawn-breast, but has   125
      chipmunk contours – perceived as

it turns its bird head –
the nap directed
   neatly back and blending
   with the ear which reiterates the slimness   130
      of the body. The fine hairs on the tail,
      repeating the other pale

markings, lengthen until
at the tip they fill
   out in a tuft – black and   135
   white; strange detail of the simplified creature,
      fish-shaped and silvered to steel by the force
      of the large desert moon. Course

the jerboa, or
plunder its food store,   140
   and you will be cursed. It
   honors the sand by assuming its color;
      closed upper paws seeming one with the fur
      in its flight from a danger.

By fifths and sevenths,   145
in leaps of two lengths,
   like the uneven notes
   of the Bedouin flute, it stops its gleaning
      on little wheel castors, and makes fern-seed
      foot-prints with kangaroo speed.   150

Its leaps should be set
to the flageolet;
   pillar body erect
   on a three-cornered smooth-working Chippendale
      claw – propped on hind legs, and tail as third toe,   155
      between leaps to its burrow.

Camellia Sabina[1] (1935)

   and the Bordeaux plum
from Marmande (France)[2] in parenthesis with
A.G. on the base of the jar – Alexis Godillot –
unevenly blown beside a bubble that
is green when held up to the light; they   5
are a fine duet; the screw-top

CAMELLIA
First published in Ezra Pound (ed.), *Active Anthology* (London: Faber and Faber, 1935).

[1] *Camellia Sabina* a species of camellia; camellias are a shrub of the tea family, have waxy leaves and flowers that are red, white, or pink in color. Moore was impressed with the varieties of them described by Abbé Laurent Berlèse (1784–1863) in his *Monographie du genre "Camellia" et traité complet sur sa culture, sa description et sa classification,* 3rd ed. (Paris: H. Cousin, 1845).

[2] *Marmande (France)* a city southwest of Bordeaux.

for this graft-grown briar-black bloom
on black-thorn pigeon's-blood,
    is, like Certosa, sealed with foil. Appropriate custom.

And they keep under   10
glass also, camellias catalogued by
lines across the leaf. The French are a cruel race – willing
to squeeze the diner's cucumber or broil a
meal on vine-shoots. Gloria mundi[3]
with a leaf two inches, nine lines   15
    broad, they have; and the smaller,
Camellia Sabina
    with amanita-white petals; there are several of her

    pale pinwheels, and pale
stripe that looks as if on a mushroom the   20
sliver from a beet-root carved into a rose were laid. "Dry
the windows with a cloth fastened to a staff.
In the camellia-house there must be
no smoke from the stove, or dew on
    the windows, lest the plants ail,"   25
the amateur is told;
    "mistakes are irreparable and nothing will avail."

A scentless nosegay
is thus formed in the midst of the bouquet
from bottles, casks and corks, for sixty-four million red wines   30
and twenty million white, which Bordeaux merchants
and lawyers "have spent a great deal of
trouble" to select, from what was
    and what was not Bordeaux. A
food-grape, however – "born   35
    of nature and of art" – is true ground for the grape-holiday.

    The food of a wild
mouse in some countries is wild parsnip- or sunflower- or
morning-glory-seed, with an occasional
grape. Underneath the vines of the Bolzano   40
grape of Italy, the Prince of Tails
might stroll. Does yonder mouse with a
    grape in its hand and its child

in its mouth, not portray
    the Spanish fleece suspended by the neck?[4] In that well-piled   45

    larder above your
head, the picture of what you will eat is
looked at from the end of the avenue. The wire cage is
locked, but by bending down and studying the
roof, it is possible to see the   50
pantomime of Persian thought: the
    gilded, too tight undemure

---

[3] *Gloria mundi* Latin for "the glory of the world," here the name of another species of camellia.

[4] *yonder mouse ... by the neck?* a photograph by Agnes Aiken Atkinson, titled "Her Tail Pulled the Trigger," appeared in the *National Geographic Magazine*, February 1932, 206. It depicts a round-tailed wood rat that carries its child by the neck; the heraldic symbol of the Order of the Golden Fleece, founded in the late Middle Ages by Philip IV of France, shows a golden lamb's fleece, draped in an arc and suspended by the neck.

coat of gems unruined
  by the rain – each small pebble of jade that refused to mature,

    plucked delicately   55
off. Off jewelry not meant to keep Tom
Thumb, the cavalry cadet, on his Italian upland
meadow-mouse, from looking at the grapes beneath
the interrupted light from them, and
dashing round the *concours hippique*   60
  of the tent, in a flurry
of eels, scallops, serpents,
  and other shadows from the blue of the green canopy.

    The wine-cellar? No.
It accomplishes nothing and makes the   65
soul heavy. The gleaning is more than the vintage, though the
history *de la Vigne et du vin*[5] has placed
mirabelle[6] in the *bibliothèque*
unique depuis[7] seventeen-ninety-seven.
  (Close the window,   70
says the Abbé Berlèse,
  for Sabina born under glass.) O generous Bolzano!

The Paper Nautilus[1] (1940)

    For authorities whose hopes
are shaped by mercenaries?
  Writers entrapped by
  teatime fame and by
commuters' comforts? Not for these   5
  the paper nautilus
  constructs her thin glass shell.

    Giving her perishable
souvenir of hope, a dull
  white outside and smooth-   10
  edged inner surface
glossy as the sea, the watchful
  maker of it guards it
  day and night; she scarcely

    eats until the eggs are hatched.   15
Buried eight-fold in her eight
  arms, for she is in
  a sense a devil-

---

[5] *history* de la Vigne et du vin history "of the vine and of wine" in French.
[6] mirabelle a variety of plum also used in making some wines.
[7] *bibliothèque unique depuis* in French, "special library since"; presumably the title to a section within the history "of the vine and of wine" that the poet consults, a section that includes "mirabelle."

PAPER NAUTILUS
First published in the *Kenyon Review* 2 (summer 1940) and in *Life and Letters Today* 26 (September 1940); reprinted in Oscar Williams (ed.), *New Poems 1940: An Anthology of British and American Verse* (New York: Yardstick Press, 1941), and finally included in Moore's collection of poems *What Are Years?* (New York: Macmillan; London: Faber and Faber, 1941).
[1] *Paper Nautilus* a variety of cephalopod found in warm waters, with sail-like arms and a very thin shell.

> fish, her glass ram'shorn-cradled freight
>   is hid but is not crushed;   20
>   as Hercules,[2] bitten
>
> by a crab loyal to the hydra,
> was hindered to succeed,
>   the intensively
>   watched eggs coming from   25
> the shell free it when they are freed, –
>   leaving its wasp-nest flaws
>   of white on white, and close-
>
>   laid Ionic[3] chiton-folds[4]
> like the lines in the mane of   30
>   a Parthenon horse,
>   round which the arms had
> wound themselves as if they knew love
>   is the only fortress
>   strong enough to trust to.   35

What Are Years? (1940)

>   What is our innocence,
> what is our guilt? All are
>   naked, none is safe. And whence
> is courage: the unanswered question,
>   the resolute doubt, –   5
> dumbly calling, deafly listening – that
> in misfortune, even death,
>   encourages others
>   and in its defeat, stirs
>
>   the soul to be strong? He   10
> sees deep and is glad, who
>   accedes to mortality
> and in his imprisonment rises
> upon himself as
> the sea in a chasm, struggling to be   15
>   free and unable to be,
>   in its surrendering
>   finds its continuing.
>
>   So he who strongly feels,
> behaves. The very bird,   20

---

[2]   *Hercules* for the second of his 12 labors, Hercules had to kill the Hydra, a many-headed monster; when Hercules is ensnared by the many arms of the Hydra, a crab bites him on the foot, and he is on the verge of failure. However, Iolaus, his charioteer, comes to his aid with a burning torch that is used to cauterize each of the Hydra's heads as Hercules cuts them off, one by one.

[3]   *Ionic* having to do with Ionia, a region on the western coast of Asia Minor (modern Turkey).

[4]   *chiton* a long, loose garment worn next to the skin by men and women in ancient Greece.

WHAT ARE YEARS?
First published in the *Kenyon Review* 2 (summer 1940), then reprinted in Oscar Williams (ed.), *New Poems 1940: An Anthology of British and American Verse* (New York: Yardstick Press, 1941), and finally included in Moore's collection of poems *What Are Years?* (New York: Macmillan; London: Faber and Faber, 1941).

grown taller as he sings, steels
his form straight up. Though he is captive,
his mighty singing
says, satisfaction is a lowly
thing, how pure a thing is joy.   25
     This is mortality,
     this is eternity.

He "Digesteth Harde Yron" (1941)[1]

Although the aepyornis
   or roc that lived in Madagascar, and
the moa[2] are extinct,
the camel-sparrow, linked
   with them in size – the large sparrow   5
Xenophon[3] saw walking by a stream – was and is
a symbol of justice.

This bird watches his chicks with
   a maternal concentration – and he's
been mothering the eggs   10
at night six weeks – his legs
   their only weapon of defense.
He is swifter than a horse; he has a foot hard
as a hoof; the leopard

is not more suspicious. How   15
   could he, prized for plumes and eggs and young,
used even as a riding-beast, respect men
   hiding actor-like in ostrich skins, with the right hand
making the neck move as if alive
and from a bag the left hand strewing grain, that ostriches   20

might be decoyed and killed! Yes, this is he
whose plume was anciently
the plume of justice;[4] he
   whose comic duckling head on its
great neck revolves with compass-needle nervousness   25
when he stands guard,

in S-like foragings as he is
   preening the down on his leaden-skinned back.
The egg piously shown
as Leda's very own[5]   30
   from which Castor and Pollux hatched,
was an ostrich-egg. And what could have been more fit
for the Chinese lawn it

HE "DIGESTETH"
Partisan Review 8 (July–August 1941), then included in Moore's
collection of poems *What Are Years?* (New York: Macmillan;
London: Faber and Faber, 1941).
[1] *Digesteth Harde Yron* John Lyly's *Euphues* (1580): "the estrich
digesteth harde iron to preserve his health."
[2] *aepyornis ... roc ... moa* the aepyornis and moa were prehistoric birds; the roc was a legendary bird.

[3] *Xenophon* Xenophon (born *c.* 430 BC); see Moore's note.
[4] *men / hiding ... plume of justice* see Moore's note.
[5] *Leda's very own* Zeus took on the shape of a swan in order to
rape the mortal woman Leda; their offspring was an egg, from
which hatched the twins Castor and Pollux, as well as Helen of
Troy and the murderous Queen Clytemnestra.

grazed on as a gift to an
emperor who admired strange birds, than this   35
one, who builds his mud-made
nest in dust yet will wade
    in lake or sea till only the head shows.
      . . . .

Six hundred ostrich-brains served
    at one banquet,[6] the ostrich-plume-tipped tent   40
and desert spear, jewel-
gorgeous ugly egg-shell
    goblets,[7] eight pairs of ostriches
in harness,[8] dramatize a meaning
always missed by the externalist.   45

The power of the visible
    is the invisible; as even where
no tree of freedom grows,
so-called brute courage knows.
    Heroism is exhausting, yet   50
it contradicts a greed that did not wisely spare
the harmless solitaire

or great auk in its grandeur;
    unsolicitude having swallowed up
all giant birds but an alert gargantuan   55
    little-winged, magnificently speedy running-bird.
This one remaining rebel
is the sparrow-camel.

{Moore's Notes to Complete Poems *(1967)}*

No Swan so Fine (p. 667)

A pair of Louis XV candelabra with Dresden figures of swans belonging to Lord Balfour.
Lines 1–2: *"There is no water so still as the dead fountains of Versailles."* Percy Phillip, *New York Times Magazine,* May 10, 1931.

The Jerboa (p. 667)

Line 4: *The Popes' colossal fir cone of bronze.* "Perforated with holes, it served as a fountain. Its inscription states, '*P. Cincius P. I. Salvius fecit.*' See Duff's *Freedom in the Early Roman Empire.*" *The Periodical*, February 1929 (Oxford University Press).
Line 52: *Stone locusts.* Toilet box dating from about the twenty-second Egyptian Dynasty. *Illustrated London News*, July 26, 1930.

---

[6] *Six hundred ... at one banquet* see Moore's note.   [8] *in harness* see Moore's note.
[7] *egg-shell / goblets* see Moore's note.

Line 70: *The king's cane.* Descripton by J. D. S. Pendlebury, *Illustrated London News*, March 19, 1932.

Line 71: *Folding bedroom.* The portable bedchamber of Queen Hetepheres presented to her by her son, Cheops. Described by Dr. G. A. Reisner. *Illustrated London News*, May 7, 1932.

Line 90: "There are little rats called jerboas which run on long hind-legs as thin as a match. The forelimbs are mere tiny hands." Dr. R. L. Ditmars, *Strange Animals I Have Known* (New York: Harcourt, Brace, 1931), p. 274.

Camellia Sabina (p. 671)

The Abbé Berlèse, *Monographie du Genre Camellia* (H. Cousin).

Line 13: *The French are a cruel race,* etc. J. S. Watson, Jr., informal comment.

Line 32: Bordeaux merchants have spent a great deal of trouble. *Encyclopaedia Britannica.*

Line 36: *A food grape.* In Vol. 1, *The Epicure's Guide to France* (Thornton Butterworth), Curnonsky and Marcel Rouff quote Monselet: "Everywhere else you eat grapes which have ripened to make wine. In France you eat grapes which have ripened for the table. They are a product at once of nature and of art." The bunch "is covered and uncovered alternately, according to the intensity of the heat, to gild the grapes without scorching them. Those which refuse to ripen – and there are always some – are delicately removed with special scissors, as are also those which have been spoiled by the rain."

He "Digesteth Harde Yron" (p. 675)

"The estrich digesteth harde yron to preserve his health." Lyly's *Euphues.*

Line 5: *The large sparrow.* "Xenophon (Anabasis, I, 5, 2) reports many ostriches in the desert on the left . . . side of the middle Euphrates, on the way from North Syria to Babylonia." George Jennison, *Animals for Show and Pleasure in Ancient Rome.*

Lines 7, 17–18, 31: *A symbol of justice, men in ostrich-skins, Leda's egg,* and other allusions. Berthold Laufer, "Ostrich Egg-shell Cups from Mesopotamia," *The Open Court,* May 1926. "An ostrich plume symbolized truth and justice, and was the emblem of the goddess Ma-at, the patron saint of judges. Her head is adorned with an ostrich feather, her eyes are closed . . . as Justice is blind-folded."

Line 40: *Six hundred ostrich brains.* At a banquet given by Elagabalus. See above: *Animals for Show and Pleasure in Ancient Rome.*

Lines 43–44: *Egg-shell goblets.* E.g., the painted ostrich-egg cup mounted in silver gilt by Elias Geier of Leipzig about 1589. Edward Wenham, "Antiques in and about London," *New York Sun,* May 22, 1937.

Line 44: *Eight pairs of ostriches.* See above: *Animals for Show and Pleasure in Ancient Rome.*

Line 60: Sparrow-camel: στρουθιοκάμηλος.

The Sacred Wood (1921)

The Sacred Wood is a thoughtful book; its well-knit architecture recalls Trollope's comment upon Castle Richmond. It has "no appearance of having been thrown out of its own windows." As a revival of enjoyment it has value, but in what it reveals as a definition of criticism it is especially rich. The connection between criticism and creation is close; criticism naturally deals with creation but it is equally true that criticism inspires creation. A genuine achievement in criticism is an achievement in creation; as Mr. Eliot says, "It is to be expected that the critic and the creative artist should frequently be the same person." Much light is thrown on the problems of art in Mr. Eliot's citing of Aristotle as an example of the perfect critic – perfect by

First published in the *Dial* 70 (3) (March 1921) Review of *The Sacred Wood* (New York: Knopf, 1921), by T. S. Eliot.

reason of his having the scientific mind. Too much cannot be said for the necessity in the artist, of exact science.

What Mr. Eliot says of Swinburne as a critic, one feels to be true. "The content," of Swinburne's critical essays "is not, in any exact sense, criticism." Nor, we agree, is it offered by Swinburne as such; he wrote "as a poet, his notes upon poets whom he admired." Mr. Eliot allows Swinburne, perhaps, a sufficiently high place as a poet; to imply that he does not, is to disregard the positively expressed acceptance of his genius; nevertheless, in the course of the essay on Swinburne as Poet, he says, "agreed that we do not (and I think that the present generation does not) greatly enjoy Swinburne," et cetera. Do we not? There is about Swinburne the atmosphere of magnificence, a kind of permanent association of him with King Solomon "perfumed with all the powders of the merchants, approaching in his litter" – an atmosphere which is not destroyed, one feels, even by indiscriminate browsing – and now in his verse as much as ever, as Swinburne says of the Sussex seaboard, "You feel the sea in the air at every step." There is seeming severity in stripping a poet of his accepted paraphernalia and bringing him forth as he is, but in the stanza from "Atalanta":

> Before the beginning of years
>   There came to the making of man
> Time with a gift of tears;
>   Grief with a glass that ran....

is it not undeniable, as Mr. Eliot says, that "it appears to be a tremendous statement, like statements made in our dreams; when we wake up we find that the 'glass that ran' would do better for time than for grief, and that the gift of tears would be as appropriately bestowed by grief as by time?" True, Swinburne "is concerned with the meaning of the word in a peculiar way: he employs or rather 'works,' the word's meaning." The "flap of wings and fins" in him – to quote from "A Cameo," is very apparent. As for "the word" however, invariably used by him as a substitute for "the object," is it always so used? "When you take to pieces any verse of Swinburne," says Mr. Eliot, "you find always that the object was not there – only the word." What of

> The sea slow rising
> . . . .
> the rocks that shrink,
> the fair brave trees with all their flowers at play?

One of the chief charms, however, of Mr. Eliot's criticism is that in his withholding of praise, an author would feel no pain. But when his praise is unmixed, the effect is completely brilliant as in the opening paragraphs of the essay on Ben Jonson. In his profound appreciation of the genius of Jonson, Mr. Eliot is perhaps more revealing than in any other of the studies in this volume and is entirely convincing in his statement that Ben Jonson is not merely the "man of letters" but is the "literary artist," who if played now, would attract thousands. The eminent robustness of Jonson appears in the lines from *The Silent Woman*, which Mr. Eliot quotes:

> They shall all give and pay well, that come here,
> If they will have it; and that, jewels, pearl,
> Plate, or round sums to buy these. I'm not taken
> With a cob-swan or a high-mounting bull,
> As foolish Leda and Europa were;
> But the bright gold, with Danaë. For such price
> I would endure a rough, harsh Jupiter,
> Or ten such thundering gamesters, and refrain
> To laugh at 'em, till they are gone, with my much suffering.

One recognizes the truth of the statement that Jonson's "skill is not so much skill in plot as skill in doing without a plot" and that "what holds the play together is a unity of inspiration that radiates into plot and personages alike." The distinction made in Ben Jonson's case between brilliance of surface and mere superficiality, is well made. As Mr. Eliot notes, the liveliness of Fletcher and Massinger covers a vacuum, whereas the superficies of Jonson is solid; "The superficies *is* the world." Could the victim of an all-conspiring luxury inspire a thorn more commensurate with himself than:

> I will have all my beds blown up, not stuft;
> Down is too hard; and then, mine oval room
> Fill'd with such pictures as Tiberius took
> From Elephantis, and dull Aretine
> But coldly imitates. Then, my glasses
> Cut in more subtle angles, to disperse
> And multiply the figures, as I walk. . . .

"He did not get the third dimension, but he was not trying to get it."

In these studies it is interesting to note that truth is to the author a fundamental attraction. He defines the strangeness of Blake as "merely a peculiar honesty, which in a world too frightened to be honest, is peculiarly terrifying." He says:

And this honesty never exists without great technical accomplishment. Being a humble engraver, he had no journalistic-social career open to him, nothing to distract him from his interests, and he knew what interested him and presents only the essential – only what can be presented and need not be explained. He was naked, and saw man naked, and from the center of his own crystal. He approached everything with a mind unclouded by current opinions. There was nothing of the superior person about him. This makes him terrifying.

Blake's humanly personal approach to any subject that he treated, preserves him to us; he is a greener figure to the eye than Dante. It is not personal transcendence; it is as Mr. Eliot observes, the combination of philosophy, theology, and poetry, which makes Dante strong and symmetrical. A conclusion with regard to Dante which has been largely held no doubt by many, is accurately expressed by Mr. Eliot when he says that "Dante, more than any other poet, has succeeded in dealing with his philosophy in terms of something *perceived*." We enjoy, furthermore, the critic's ability to separate the specious from the sound when he says apropos of Landor's failure to understand Francesca: "Francesca is neither stupefied nor reformed; she is merely damned; and it is a part of damnation to experience desires that we can no longer gratify. For in Dante's Hell souls are not deadened, as they mostly are in life; they are actually in the greatest torment of which each is capable."

Although Swinburne was not as Mr. Eliot says he was not, "tormented by the restless desire to penetrate to the heart and marrow of a poet," it is apparent that Mr. Eliot is. In his poetry, he seems to move troutlike through a multiplicity of foreign objects and in his instinctiveness and care as a critic, he appears as a complement to the sheen upon his poetry. In his opening a door upon the past and indicating what is there, he recalls the comment made by Swinburne upon Hugo:

Art knows nothing of death; . . . all that ever had life in it, has life in it forever; those themes only are dead which never were other than dead. No form is obsolete, no subject out of date, if the right man be there to rehandle it.

Hymen (1923)

Dr. Mahaffy says in his essay "The Principles of the Art of Conversation," that artificiality is an evidence of some kind of dishonesty. Undoubtedly respect for the essence of a thing makes

HYMEN
First published in *Broom* 4 (January 1923), this essay reviews
Hymen (New York: Henry Holt & Co., 1921), by H.D.

expression simple and in reading the present collection of poems by H. D., the hasty mind is abashed by the measure of intention and the exacting sincerity which prevail from the beginning to the end of the volume. Mr. Glenway Wescott praises the sternness of H. D.'s translations. "No race of men ever subsisted on sweet rhetorical distinction," he says and in her work, it is life denuded of subterfuge – it is the clean violence of truth that we have. Only as one isolates portions of the work, does one perceive the magic and compressed energy of the author's imagination, actuality in such lines as the following, being lost in the sense of spectacle:

> dark islands in a sea
> of gray olive or wild white olive
> cut with the sudden cypress shafts;
> fingers
> wrought of iron
> to wrest from earth
> secrets; strong to protect,
> strong to keep back the winter.[1]

One recognizes here, the artist – the mind which creates what it needs for its own subsistence and propitiates nothing, willing – indeed wishing to seem to find its only counterpart in the elements; yet in this case as in the case of any true artist, reserve is a concomitant of intense feeling, not the cause of it. In H. D.'s work, there is not so much reserve as insistence upon certain qualities; nature in its acute aspects is to her, a symbol of freedom. A liking for surf for instance, makes the contemplation of still water seem like loathing as in Swinburne when one recalls his comparison of Childe Harold and Don Juan:

> They are like lake water and sea water; the one is yielding, fluent, invariable: the other has in it a life and pulse, a sting and swell, which touch and excite the nerves like fire or like music; the ripple flags and falls in loose lazy lines, the foam flies wide of any mark, and the breakers collapse here and there in sudden ruin and violent failure. But the violence and weakness of the sea are preferable to the smooth sound and equable security of a lake.

In the following lines as in H. D.'s work throughout, wiry diction, accurate observation and a homogeneous color sense are joint phases of unequivocal faithfulness to fact:

> Though Sparta enter Athens,
> Thebes wreck Sparta,
> each changes as water,
> salt, rising to wreak terror
> and fall back;
>
> a broken rock
> clatters across the steep shelf
> of the mountain slope,
> sudden and swift
> and breaks as it clatters down
> into the hollow breach
> of the dried water course.[2]

Color and careful detail may arrest without commanding, but here – physical beauty emends other beauties and H. D.'s concept of color makes it hard to disassociate ideas from the pageant that we have of objects and hues – Egyptian gold and silver work, a harmonious, tempera-like procession of dyes

---

[1] *wrought of iron ... keep back the winter* from the poem "Demeter," pp. 450–3 in this edition, here p. 452, ll. 5–18.

[2] *Though Sparta enter Athens ... water course* from the poem "She Rebukes Hippolyta," p. 449, ll. 2–8, in this edition.

and craftsmanship – of these "flecks of amber on the dolphin's back," "white cedar and black cedar," "the shore burned with a lizard blue," "the light shadow print cast through the petals of the yellow iris flower," in "the paved parapet" on which "you will step carefully from amber stones to onyx." In this instinctive ritual of beauty, at once old and modern, one is reminded of the supernatural yellows of China – of an aesthetic consciousness which values simultaneously, ivory and the chiseled ivory of speech, finding "in the hardness of jade, the firmness of the intelligence; in its sound with the peculiarity of ceasing abruptly, the emblem of music, in the sharpness of its angles, justice; in its splendor, the sky and in its substance, the earth." "Beauty is set apart," H. D. says:

> Beauty is cast by the sea
> a barren rock,
> beauty is set about
> with wrecks of ships,
> upon our coast, death keeps
> the shadows – death waits
> clutching toward us
> from the deeps.

In the bleakness as in the opulence of "The Islands" from which the above lines are taken, one remembers Ezekiel's Tyre, "a barren rock, a place for the spreading of nets in the midst of the sea –" the Tyre which commanded with her wares, "emeralds, purple and broidered work, fine linen, coral and rubies, horses, war-horses, wine and white wool, bright iron, casia and calamus, precious cloths for riding, horns of ivory and ebony, wares in wrappings of blue and broidered work and in chests of rich apparel bound with cords and made of cedar – replenished and made very glorious in the heart of the seas."

Talk of weapons and the tendency to match one's intellectual and emotional vigor with the violence of nature, give a martial, an apparently masculine tone to such writing as H. D.'s, the more so that women are regarded as belonging necessarily to either of two classes – that of the intellectual freelance or that of the eternally sleeping beauty, effortless yet effective in the indestructible limestone keep of domesticity. Woman tends unconsciously to be the aesthetic norm of intellectual home life and preeminently in the case of H. D., we have the intellectual, social woman, non-public and "feminine." There is, however, a connection between weapons and beauty. Cowardice and beauty are at swords' points and in H. D.'s work, suggested by the absence of subterfuge, cowardice and the ambition to dominate by brute force, we have heroics which do not confuse transcendence with domination and which in their indestructibleness, are the core of tranquillity and of intellectual equilibrium.

Well Moused, Lion (1924)

It is not too much to say that some writers are entirely without imagination – without that associative kind of imagination certainly, of which the final tests are said to be simplicity, harmony, and truth. In Mr. Stevens' work, however, imagination precludes banality and order prevails. In his book, he calls imagination "the will of things," "the magnificent cause of being," and demonstrates how imagination may evade "the world without imagination"; effecting an escape which, in certain manifestations of *bravura*, is uneasy rather than bold. One feels, however, an achieved remoteness as in Tu Muh's lyric criticism: "Powerful is the painting . . . and high is it hung on the spotless wall in the lofty hall of your mansion." There is the love of magnificence and the effect of it in these sharp,

WELL MOUSED
First published in the *Dial* 76(1) (January 1924), this book review considers *Harmonium* (New York: Knopf, 1923), by Wallace Stevens.

solemn, rhapsodic elegant pieces of eloquence; one assents to the view taken by the author, of Crispin whose

> ...mind was free
> And more than free, elate, intent, profound.

The riot of gorgeousness in which Mr. Stevens' imagination takes refuge, recalls Balzac's reputed attitude to money, to which he was indifferent unless he could have it "in heaps or by the ton." It is "a flourishing tropic he requires"; so wakeful is he in his appetite for color and in perceiving what is needed to meet the requirements of a new tone key, that Oscar Wilde, Frank Alvah Parsons, Tappé, and John Murray Anderson seem children asleep in comparison with him. One is met in these poems by some such clash of pigment as where in a showman's display of orchids or gladiolas, one receives the effect of vials of picrocarmine, magenta, gamboge, and violet mingled each at the highest point of intensity:

> In Yucatan, the Maya sonneteers
> Of the Caribbean amphitheatre
> In spite of hawk and falcon, green toucan
> And jay, still to the nightbird made their plea,
> As if raspberry tanagers in palms,
> High up in orange air, were barbarous.

One is excited by the sense of proximity to Java peacocks, golden pheasants, South American macaw feather capes, Chilcat blankets, hair seal needlework, Singalese masks, and Rousseau's paintings of banana leaves and alligators. We have the hydrangeas and dogwood, the "blue, gold, pink, and green" of the temperate zone, the hibiscus, "red as red" of the tropics.

> ...moonlight on the thick cadaverous bloom
> That yuccas breed...

> ...with serpent-kin encoiled
> Among the purple tufts, the scarlet crowns.

and as in a shot spun fabric, the infinitude of variation of the colors of the ocean:

> ...the blue
> And the colored purple of the lazy sea,

the emerald, indigos, and mauves of disturbed water, the azure and basalt of lakes; we have Venus "the center of sea-green pomp"[1] and America "polar purple." Mr. Stevens' exact demand, moreover, projects itself from nature to human nature. It is the eye of no "maidenly greenhorn" which has differentiated Crispin's daughters; which characterizes "the ordinary women" as "gaunt guitarists"[2] and issues the junior-to-senior mandate in "Floral Decorations for Bananas":

> Pile the bananas on planks.
> The women will be all shanks
> And bangles and slatted eyes.

He is a student of "the flambeaued manner,"

> ...not indifferent to smart detail...
> ...hang of coat, degree
> Of buttons....

[1] "the center of sea-green pomp" from "The Paltry Nude Starts on Her Spring Voyage," p. 611 in this volume.

[2] "the ordinary women" as "gaunt guitarists" From line 25 of "The Ordinary Women," p. 613 in this edition.

One resents the temper of certain of these poems. Mr. Stevens in never inadvertently crude; one is conscious, however, of a deliberate bearishness – a shadow of acrimonious, unprovoked contumely. Despite the sweet-Clementime-will-you-be-mine nonchalance of the "Apostrophe to Vincentine," one feels oneself to be in danger of unearthing the ogre and in "Last Looks at the Lilacs," a pride in unserviceableness is suggested which makes it a microcosm of cannibalism.

Occasionally the possession of one good is remedy for not possessing another as when Mr. Stevens speaks of "the young emerald, evening star," "tranquillizing . . . the torments of confusion." "Sunday Morning"[3] on the other hand – a poem so suggestive of a masterly equipoise – gives ultimately the effect of the mind disturbed by the intangible; of a mind oppressed by the properties of the world which it is expert in manipulating. And proportionately, aware as one is of the author's suscepti-bility to the fever of actuality, one notes the accurate gusto with which he discovers the Negro, that veritable "medicine of cherries" to the badgered analyst. In their resilience and certitude, the "Hymm from a Watermelon Pavilion" and the commemorating of a Negress who

> Took seven white dogs
> To ride in a cab,

are proud harmonies.

One's humor is based upon the most serious part of one's nature. "Le Monocle de Mon Oncle,";[4] "A Nice Shady Home"; and "Daughters wtih Curls": the capacity for self-mockery in these titles illustrates the author's disgust with mere vocativeness.

Instinct for words is well determined by the nature of the liberties taken with them, some writers giving the effect merely of presumptuous egotism – an unavoided outlandishness; others, not: Shakespeare arresting one continually with nutritious permutations as when he apostrophizes the lion in *A Midsummer Night's Dream* – "Well moused, lion." Mr. Stevens' "junipers shagged with ice,"[5] is properly courageous as are certain of his adjectives which have the force of verbs: "the spick torrent,"[6] "tidal skies," "loquacious columns"; there is the immunity to fear, of the good artist, in "the blather that the water made." His precise diction and verve are grateful as contrasts to the current vulgarizations of "gesture," "dimensions" and "intrigue." He is able not only to express an idea with mere perspicuity; he is able to do it by implication as in "Thirteen Ways of Looking at a Blackbird" in which the glass coach evolved from icicles; the shadow, from birds; it becomes a kind of aristocratic cipher. "The Emperor of Icecream," moreover, despite its not especially original theme of poverty enriched by death, is a triumph of explicit ambiguity. He gets a special effect with those adjectives which often weaken as in the lines:

> . . . That all beasts should . . .
> . . . be beautiful
> As large, ferocious tigers are

and in the phrase, "the eye of the young alligator," the adjective as it is perhaps superfluous to point out, makes for activity. There is a certain bellicose sensitiveness in

> I do not know which to prefer . . .
> The blackbird whistling
> Or just after,

and in the characterization of snow man who

---

[3] "Sunday Morning," to be found on p. 604 in this edition.

[4] "Le Monocle de mon Oncle," p. 608 in this edition.

[5] "*junipers shagged with ice*" from "The Snow Man," p. 612 in this edition.

[6] "*the spick torrent*" from "The Paltry Nude Starts on Her Spring Voyage," p. 611 in this volume.

> ...nothing himself, beholds
> The nothing that is not there and the nothing that is.[7]

In its nimbless *con brio* with seriousness, moreover, "Nomad Exquisite" is a piece of that ferocity for which one values Mr. Stevens most:

> As the immense dew of Florida
> Brings forth
> The big-finned palm
> And green vine angering for life.

Poetic virtuosities are allied – especially those of diction, imagery, and cadence. In no writer's work are metaphors less "winter starved." In "Architecture" Mr. Stevens asks:

> How shall we hew the sun, ...
> How carve the violet moon
> To set in nicks?
>
> Pierce, too, with buttresses of coral air
> And purple timbers,
> Various argentines

and "The Comedian as the Letter C," as the account of the craftsman's un"simple jaunt," is an expanded metaphor which becomes as one contemplates it, hypnotically incandescent like the rose tinged fringe of the night blooming cereus. One applauds those analogies derived from an enthusiasm for the sea:

> She scuds the glitters,
> Noiselessly, like one more wave.[8]
>
> The salt hung on his spirit like a frost,
> The dead brine melted in him like a dew.

In his positiveness, aplomb, and verbal secuity, he has the mind and the method of China; in such controversial effects as:

> Of what was it I was thinking?
> So the meaning escapes,

and certainly in dogged craftsmanship. Infinitely conscious in his processes, he says

> Speak even as if I did not hear you speaking
> But spoke for you perfectly in my thoughts.

One is not subject in reading him, to the disillusionment experienced in reading novices and charlatans who achieve flashes of beauty and immediately contradict the pleasure afforded by offending in precisely those respects in which they have pleased – showing that they are deficient in conscious artistry.

Imagination implies energy and imagination of the finest type involves an energy which results in order "as the motion of a snake's body goes through all parts at once, and its violation acts at the same instant in coils that go contrary ways." There is the sense of the architectural diagram in the disjoined titles of poems with related themes. Refraining for fear of impairing its litheness

---

[7] "*nothing himself ... the nothing that is*" see "The Snow Man," p. 612 this edition.

[8] "*She scuds the ... one more wave*" see "The Paltry Nude Starts on Her Spring Voyage," p. 611 in this volume.

of contour, from overelaborating felicities inherent in a subject, Mr. Stevens uses only such elements as the theme demands; for example, his delineation of the peacock in "Domination of Black," is austerely restricted, splendor being achieved cumulatively in "Bantam in Pine-Woods," "The Load of Sugar-Cane," "The Palace of the Babies," and "The Bird with the Coppery Keen Claws."

That "there have been many most excellent poets that never versified, and now swarm many versifiers that never need answer to the name of poets," needs no demonstration. The following lines as poetry independent of rhyme, beg the question as to whether rhyme is indispensably contributory to poetic enjoyment:

> There is not nothing, no, no, never nothing,
> Like the clashed edges of two words that kill[9]

and

> The clambering wings of black revolved,
> Making harsh torment of the solitude.

It is of course evident that subsidiary to beauty of thought, rhyme is powerful in so far as it never appears to be invented for its own sake. In this matter of apparent naturalness, Mr. Stevens is faultless — as in correctness of assonance:

> Chieftain Iffucan of Azcan in caftan
> Of tan with henna hackles, halt!

The better the artist, moreover, the more determined he will be to set down words in such a way as to admit of no interpretation of the accent but the one intended, his ultimate power appearing in a selfsufficing, willowy, firmly contrived cadence such as we have in "Peter Quince at the Clavier" and in "Cortège for Rosenbloom":

> ... That tread
> The wooden ascents
> Of the ascending of the dead.

One has the effect of poised uninterrupted harmony, a simple appearing, complicated phase of symmetry of movements as in figure skating, tight-rope dancing, in the kaleidoscopically centrifugal circular motion of certain medieval dances. It recalls the snake in *Far Away and Long Ago*, "moving like quicksilver in a rope-like stream" or the conflict at sea when after a storm, the wind shifts and waves are formed counter to those still running. These expertnesses of concept with their nicely luted edges and effect of flowing continuity of motion, are indeed

> ... pomps
> Of speech which are like music so profound
> They seem an exaltation without sound.

One further notes accomplishment in the use of reiteration — that pitfall of half-poets:

> Death is absolute and without memorial,
> As in a season of autumn,
> When the wind stops. ...
> When the wind stops.

---

[9] *"There is not nothing ... words that kill"* see "Le Monocle de
Mon Oncle," p. 608, ll. 3–4 this edition.

In brilliance gained by accelerated tempo in accordance with a fixed melodic design, the precise patterns of many of these poems are interesting.

> It was snowing
> And it was going to snow

and the parallelism in "Domination of Black" suggest the Hebrew idea of something added although there is, one admits, more the suggestion of mannerism than in Hebrew poetry. Tea takes precedence of other experiments with which one is familiar, in emotional shorthand of this unwestern type, and in "Earth Anecdote"[10] and in the "Invective against Swans," symmetry of design is brought to a high degree of perfection.

It is rude perhaps, after attributing conscious artistry and a severely intentional method of procedure to an artist, to cite work that he has been careful to omit from his collected work. One regrets, however, the omission by Mr. Stevens of "The Indigo Glass in the Grass," "The Man Whose Pharynx Was Bad," "La Mort du Soldat Est Près des Choses Naturelles (5 Mars)" and "Comme Dieu Dispense de Graces":

> Here I keep think of the primitives –
> The sensitive and conscientious themes
> Of mountain pallors ebbing into air.

However, in this collection one has eloquence. "The author's violence is for aggrandizement and not for stupor"; one consents therefore, to the suggestion that when the book of moonlight is written, we leave room for Crispin. In the event of moonlight and a veil to be made gory, he would, one feels, be appropriate in this legitimately sensational act of a ferocious jungle animal.

A Poet of the Quattrocento (1927)

It was Ezra Pound's conviction some years ago, that there could be "an age of awakening in America" which would "overshadow the quattrocento." Hopeful for us at that time, "our opportunity is greater than Leonardo's," said Mr. Pound; "we have more aliment," and never really neglectful of us, he has commended in us, "Mr. Williams' praiseworthy opacity." "There is distinctness and color," he observed, "as was shown in his 'Postlude,' in 'Des Imagistes'; but there is beyond these qualities the absolute conviction of a man with his feet on the soil, on a soil personally and peculiarly his own. He is rooted. He is at times almost inarticulate, but he is never dry, never without sap in abundance."

This metaphor of the tree seems highly appropriate to William Carlos Williams – who writes of seedling sycamores, of walnuts and willows – who several years ago, himself seemed to W. C. Blum "by all odds the hardiest specimen in these parts."[1] In his modestly emphatic respect for America he corroborates Henry James' conviction that young people should "stick fast and sink up to their necks in everything their own countries and climates can give," and his feeling for the *place* lends poetic authority to an illusion of ours, that sustenance may be found here, which is adapted to artists. Imagination can profit by a journey, acquainting itself with everything pertaining to its wish that it can gather from European sources, Doctor Williams says. But it is apparent to him that "American plumbing, American bridges, indexing systems, locomotives, printing presses, city buildings, farm implements and a thousand other things" are liked and used, and it is not folly to hope that the very purest works of the imagination may also be found among us. Doctor Williams is in favor of escape from "strained associations," from "shallowness," from such substitutes as

---

[10] *Earthy Anecdote* see p. 607 this edition.

[1] [Moore's note:] "American Letter," by W. C. Blum, *The Dial*, May 1921.

A POET
First published in the *Dial* 82(3) (March 1927).

"congoleum – building paper with a coating of enamel." The staying at home principle could not, he is sure, be a false one where there is vigorous living force with buoyancy of imagination – as there was apparently in Shakespeare – the artist's excursion being into "perfection" and "technical excellence." "Such names as Homer, the blind; Scheherazade, who lived under threat – their compositions have as their excellence, an identity with life since they are as actual, as sappy as the leaf of the tree which never moves from one spot." He has visited places and studied various writings and a traveler can as Bacon says, "prick in some flowers of that he hath learned abroad." In the man, however, Doctor Williams' topics are American – crowds at the movies

> with the closeness and
> universality of sand,

turkey nests, mushrooms among the fir trees, mist rising from the duck pond, the ball game:

> It is summer, it is the solstice
> the crowd is
>
> cheering, the crowd is laughing[2]

or

It is spring. Sunshine ... dumped among factories ... down a red dirt path to four goats. ... I approach the smallest goat timidly. ... It draws away beginning to wind its tie rope around the tree. ... I back the creature around the tree till it can go no further, the cord all wound up. Gingerly I take it by the ear. It tries to crowd between me and the tree. I drive it around the tree again until the rope is entirely unwound. The beast immediately finds new violent green tufts of grass in some black mud half under some old dried water-soaked weedstalks. ... To the right of the path the other goat comes forward boldly but stops short and sniffs. ... It ventures closer. Gna-ha-ha-ha-ha! (as in hat). Very softly. The small goat answers.

> O spring days, swift
> and mutable, wind blowing
> four ways, hot and cold.

Essentially not a "repeater of things second hand," Doctor Williams is in his manner of contemplating with new eyes, old things, shabby things, and other things, a poet. Meter he thinks of as an "essential of the work, one of its words." That which is to some imperceptible, is to him the "milligram of radium" that he values. He is rightly imaginative in not attempting to decide; or rather, in deciding not to attempt to say how wrong these readers are, who find his poems unbeautiful or "positively repellant." As he had previously asked, "Where does this downhill turn up again? Driven to the wall you'd put claws to your toes and make a ladder of smooth bricks."

Facts presented to us by him in his prose account of "The Destruction of Tenochtitlan," could not be said to be "new," but the experience ever, in encountering that which has been imaginatively assembled is exceedingly new. One recalls in reading these pages, the sense augmented, of "everything which the world affords," of "the drive upward, toward the sun and the stars"; and foremost as poetry, we have in a bewilderingly great, neatly ordered pageant of magnificence, Montezuma, "this American cacique," "so delicate," "so full of tinkling sounds and rhythms, so tireless of invention."

One sees nothing terrifying in what Doctor Williams calls a "modern traditionalism," but to say so is to quibble. Incuriousness, emptiness, a sleep of the faculties, are an end of beauty; and Doctor Williams is vivid. Perhaps he is modern. He addresses himself to the imagination. He is "keen" and "compact." "At the ship's prow" as he says the poet should be, he is glad to have his "imaginary" fellow-creatures with him. Unless we are very literal, this should be enough.

---

[2] See poem XXVI in *Spring and All*, p. 536, l. 33 in this edition.

A House-Party (1928)

"The sea lay three parts round the house, invisible because of the wood. . . . The people who had the house were interested in the wood and its silence." "Poverty and pride, cant and candor, raw flesh and velvet" seem collectively to ask, "Are we never to have any peace, only adventure and pain?" to say "there is no good will left anywhere in the world."

They were Drusilla Taverner – "Scylla"; Carston, an American; Picus "unnaturally supple"; Carston "had seen him pick up something behind him with his hands as if it had been in front"; Clarence "with a feeling for decoration best served in cities." "One rougher and shorter, fairer, better bred, called Ross. Then a boy, Scylla's brother, Felix Taverner."

"Ross arranged their chairs in the veranda while the storm banged about." "For an hour it rained, through sheet lightning, and thunder like a departing train, the hills calling one to another."

The Sanc-Grail is supposed to have been fished from the well, but "Picus had taken his father's cup . . . had run to small mystifications . . . had whistled up mystery with what was now undoubtedly a victorian finger-bowl."

" 'We don't seem to have cleared up anything,' said Clarence. 'Cleared up,' said Picus chattering at them. . . . In this there was something that was not comic, in the dis-ease he imparted."

When consulted about disposing of the cup the vicar suggests replacing it where they got it. " 'It seems to like wells,' " he said. " 'And truth, if she prefers not to talk, can return to one.' "

" 'Good,' said Picus, 'learn it to be a toad.' "

One sees the artist in Miss Butts, in her liking to watch "how violently, strangely, and in character people will behave," though an attitude of being surprising in matters of personal freedom seems needless. The iron hand of unconvention can be heavier than the iron hand of convention; and heresy in respect to this or that orthodoxy is perhaps a greater compliment to it than one sets out to pay, amounting really in the vehemence of protest, to subjection; to marriage and various other kinds of conformity Miss Butts pays compliments of this grudged, paining variety.

There are gruesome things here, as there were continually in the minds of the maddened conversers – "while high over them the gulls squalled like sorrow driven up." But there are many graces. And it is a triumph for the author that it is a mistake to recount anything she writes without recounting it in her own words. Sensitiveness sponsors defiance; it also sponsors homage to beauty. Strictness of touch and accurate drawing give "the endless turf-miles which ran up a great down into the sky"; "above the thunder a gull repeating itself . . . a little noise laid delicately upon the universal roar of air"; Carston "beautifying himself scrupulously and elaborately as a cat"; Picus' father, a collector with "a theory of the rights of owners to their property" – "prupperty: prupperty: prupperty"; Lydia (in London) "in a too short frock and a too tight hair-wave and a too pink make-up, reading the *Romaunt de la Rose*"; and Lydia's husband. "His method was to cut conversation, to interrupt whatever was said, and when he spoke, interrupt himself, so there should never be any continuity. Perfectly sound. . . . Could show them that not being a gentleman was worth something."

Little thicknesses are chipped away. Emphasis of writing and of attitude are equal, and as a change from the periodic sentence a syncopated rhetoric is pleasant; though emphasis without interruption amounts to no emphasis and one has the feeling that a mixture of code and declarative sentence may be best. There is much to notice, as one proceeds – rejecting, accepting, renovated and attentive. Would a Bostonian say, "I reckon" in the way in which Carston says it? Is flavor contributed or sacrificed by the elegiac curfew chime of current literacy – that is to say, by the interpolated aphorism: "When we were very young"; "meaning of meaning"; "portraits of the artist"; things from the Bible? But to doubt is merely a part of liking, and of feeling. One need not read Mary Butts if one has not a feeling for feeling. Her presentation of what one feels is here as accurate as of what one sees. Scylla "wished the earth would not suddenly look fragile, as if it was

First published in the *Dial* 85(3) (September 1928). Review of
Armed with Madness (New York: Charles and Albert Boni, 1928),
by Mary Butts.

going to start shifting about. . . . There was something wrong with all of them, or with their world. A moment missed, a moment to come. Or not coming. Or either or both. Shove it off on the War; but that did not help." The "trick on Carston was ill-mannered, a little cruel. Also irrelevant." "What he could not have done [to others], others could do [to him]." It is a compassionate view Miss Butts takes of this informed, formless party; of its "insolent insincerity" and seeming insufficiency – of Clarence smiling back at Picus "as if he had to smile under pain, his own, any one's," listening "till the time came when he could listen no longer, and hid his face, the awful pain rising in him drowning Picus' presence." "There was something in their lives spoiled and inconclusive like the Grail," she says. Some would say nothing in them was like the Grail. But Miss Butts is not palming anything off on us. We may make what we may of it. It is sympathy she offers us in Carston's reply when the vicar wonders "whether a true picture of the real is shown by our senses alone." "All I can say is that I've never never been so bothered, never behaved so like a skunk, never so nearly fell dead in my tracks till I got down here and began to think about such things. It's unfashionable now, you know –"

A Draft of XXX Cantos (1931)

"IT is a disgraceful thing," Ezra Pound says, "for a man's work not to show steady growth and increasing fineness from first to last," and anyone alert to the creative struggle will recognize in the *Cantos* under later treatment as compared with earlier drafts, the rise of the storm-wave of literary security and the tautness obtained by conscious renunciation.

We have in them "the usual subjects of conversation between intelligent men" – "books, arms . . . men of unusual genius, both of ancient times and our own"[1] – arranged in the style of the grasshopper-wing for contrast, half the fold against the other half, the rarefied effect against a grayer one. Mr. Pound admits that he can see, as Aristotle did, a connection sometimes where others do not: between books and war, for instance. It is implied that if we were literally in communication, at home and internationally, we should be armed against "new shambles"; against "one war after another," started by men "who couldn't put up a good hen-roost." And, obversely, "if Armageddon has taught us anything it should have taught us to abominate the half-truth, and the tellers of the half-truth in literature." The *Cantos* are both a poring upon excellence and a protest against "the tyranny of the unimaginative." They are against "the vermin who quote accepted opinion," against historians who ought to have "left blanks in their writings for what they didn't know"; and are for work charged with realness – for "verity of feeling" that releases us from "the bonds of blatant actuality."

"The heart is the form," as is said in the East – in this case the rhythm which is a firm piloting of rebellious fluency; the quality of sustained emphasis, as of a cargo being shrewdly steered to the edge of the quai:

> Under the plumes, with the flakes and small wads of color
> Showering from the balconies
> With the sheets spread from windows
>   with leaves and small branches pinned on them,
> Arras hung from the railings; out of the dust,
> With pheasant tails upright on their forelocks,
>   The small white horses, the
> Twelve girls riding in order, green satin in pannier'd habits;
> Under the baldachino, silver'd with heavy stitches,
> Biancha Visconti, with Sforza,[2]

First published in *The Criterion* 13 (April 1934), pp. 482–5. *Review of A Draft of XXX Cantos* (London: Faber & Faber, 1933), by Ezra Pound.

[1] *books, arms . . . men of unusual genius* Ezra Pound, Canto 11, p. 88 in this edition.
[2] Ezra Pound, Canto 8, p. 69 in this edition.

The peasant's son and the duchess.

"Every age yields its crop of pleasant singers," Mr. Pound says, "who write poetry free from the cruder faults," and in the *Cantos* the quiver of feeling is not conveyed by "rhyming mountain with fountain and beauty with duty"; though in the present evolved method the skill of the more apparent method remains. The edges of the rhetoric and of sound are well "luted," as in good lacquer-work, and the body throughout is ennobled by insinuated rhyme effects and a craftily regulated tempo:

> *Di cui* in the which he, Francesco. . . . [3]

One notices the accelerated light final rhyme (lie), the delayed long syllable (grass),

> The filigree hiding the gothic,
>   with a touch of rhetoric in the whole
> And the old sarcophagi,
>   such as lie, smothered in grass, by San Vitale; [4]

the undozing ease of

> And hither came Selvo, doge
>   that first mosaic'd San Marco,
> And his wife that would touch food but with forks,
> Sed aureis furculis, that is
>   with small golden prongs
> Bringing in, thus, the vice of luxuria.

There is many a spectacular concealment, or musical ruse should one say, in the patterns presented of slang, foreign speech, and numerals – an ability borrowed as it were from "the churn, the loom, the spinning-wheel, the oars": "Malatesta de Malatestis ad Magnificum Dominum Patremque suum, etc." about the gift of the bay pony.[5] We have in some of these metrical effects a wisdom as remarkable as anything since Bach.

To the motion of the verse is added descriptive exactness which is, like the good ear, another indication of "maximum efficiency":

> The gulls broad out their wings,
>   nipping between the splay feathers;
>   . . . .
> Gold, gold, a sheaf of hair,
>   thick like a wheat swath;

and "the old woman from Kansas . . . stiff as a cigar-store Indian from the Bowery . . . this ligneous solidness . . . that indestructible female. . . ."

Mr. Pound has spent his life putting effort and impudence into what people refuse to take time to enjoy or evaluate: in demonstrating "the *virtu* of books worth reading"; in saying by example, that "the thing that matters in art is a sort of energy"; that "an intensity amounting to genius" enters into the practice of one's art, and that great art is able to overcome "the fret of contemporaneousness." Horror of primness is not a crime, "unvarnished natural speech" is a medicine, and it is probably true that "no method is justified until it has been carried too far." But when an author says read what you enjoy and enjoy what you read, one asks in turn, can a man expect to be regarded as a thing of superlatives and absolutes when he dwells on worthlessness as in the imprecatory cantos, forsaking his own counsel which is good! One may vanquish a detractor by ignoring him ("he could have found the correction where he assumed the fault"); or may "turn to and build." And one may

[3] Pound, Canto 8, p. 69 in this edition.   [5] Ibid. p. 76.
[4] Pound, Canto 9, p. 78 in this edition.

embarrass with humor, which is in the *Cantos* a not uningenious phase of dogma. At least we infer that an allusion to easy science, namely easy art, which "elected a Monsieur Brisset who held that man is descended from frogs," is not a compliment; and that the lines about "sucking pigs, pigs, pigs, small pigs, porkers throughout all Portugal" is more than mere decoration. But rather than blunt the point of his wedge, a writer is sometimes willing to seem various things that he is not; and Mr. Pound is "vitally interesting." His feeling for verse above prose – that for prose "a much greater amount of language is needed than for poetry" – is like Schonberg's statement: "My greatest desire is to compress the most substance into the least possible space," and Stravinsky's trick of ending a composition with the recoil of a good ski-jumper accepting a spill. Furthermore, as art grows, it deviates. "I know of no case when an author has developed at all without at least temporarily sacrificing one or several of his initial merits," Mr. Pound says. In the *Cantos* the "singing quality" has somewhat been sacrificed to "weight" – to "organ base." The automatic looser statement of primary impulse penetrates better than the perfected one of conscious improvement and the undevout reader might perhaps see the water better in the following lines of prose criticism: "the cross run of the beat and the word, as of a stiff wind cutting the ripple-tops of bright water," than in: "the blue-grey glass of the wave tents them" and "a tin flash in the sundazzle." But the day is coming when spareness will seem natural.

The test for the *Cantos* is not obstinate continuous probing but a rereading after the interval of a year or years; "rhythmic vitality" needs no advocate but time. "The great book and the firm book" can persuade resisters that "good art never bores one," that art is a joyous thing.

Ideas of Order

POETRY is an unintelligible unmistakable vernacular like the language of the animals – a system of communication whereby a fox with a turkey too heavy for it to carry, reappears shortly with another fox to share the booty, and Wallace Stevens is a practiced hand at this kind of open cypher. With compactness beyond compare and the *forte agitatio* competence of the concert room, he shows one how not to call joy satisfaction, and how one may be the epic one indites and yet be anonymous; how one may have "mighty Fortitudo, frantic bass" while maintaining one's native rareness in peace. Art is here shown to be a thing of proprieties, of mounting "the thickest man on the thickest stallion-back"; yet a congruence of opposites as in the titles, "Sad Strains of a Gay Waltz," and "A Fish-scale Sunrise." Meditation for the fatalist is a surrender to "the morphology of regret" – a drowning in one's welter of woes, dangers, risks, obstacles to inclination. Poetry viewed morphologically is "a finikin thing of air," "a few words tuned and tuned and tuned and tuned"; and "the function of the poet" is "sound to stuff the ear"; or – rather – it is "particles of order, a single majesty"; it is "our unfinished spirits realized more sharply in more furious selves." Art is both "rage for order" and "rage against chaos." It is a classifying, a botanizing, a voracity of contemplation. "The actual is a deft beneficence."

These thirty-three poems, composed since the enlarged edition of *Harmonium* appeared,[1] present various conclusions about art as order. They are a series of guarded definitions but also the unembarrassing souvenirs of a man and

> ... the time when he stood alone,
> When to be and delight to be seemed to be one.

In the untrite transitions, the as if sentimental unsentimentality, the meditativeness not for appraisal, with hints taken from the birds, as in Brahms, they recall Brahms; his dexterousness,

IDEAS OF ORDER
First published in *The Criterion* 15 (January 1936). Review of *Ideas of Order* (New York: Alberti Press, 1935), by Wallace Stevens.

[1]   The second edn. of *Harmonium*, first published in 1922, appeared in July 1931, an edition of 1,500 copies which contained 14 additional poems.

but also his self-relish and technique of evasion as in the incident of the lion-huntress who was inquiring for the celebrated Herr Brahms: "You will find him yonder, on the other side of the hill, this is his brother."

Wallace Stevens can be as serious as the starving-times of the first settlers, and he can be Daumier caricaturing the photographer, making a time exposure watch in hand, above the title, *Patience is an Attribute of the Donkey*. The pieces are marvels of finish, and they are a dashing to oblivion of that sort of impropriety wherein "the chronicle of affected homage foxed so many books." They are "moodiest nothings"; "the trees are wooden, the grass is thin"; and they are

> . . . Evening, when the measure skips a beat
> And then another, one by one, and all
> To a seething minor swiftly modulate.

Mr. Stevens alludes to "the eccentric" as "the base of design," "the revealing aberration"; and employs noticeably in such a poem as "Sailing After Lunch," the principle of dispersal common to music; that is to say, a building up of the theme piecemeal in such a way that there is no possibility of disappointment at the end. But ease accompanies the transpositions and pauses; it is indeed a self-weighted momentum as when he says of the eagle,

> Describe with deepened voice
> And noble imagery
> His slowly-falling round
> Down to the fishy sea.

An air of "merely circulating" disguises material of the dizziest: swans, winter stars; that "body wholly body," the sea; "roses, noble in autumn, yet nobler than autumn"; "the mythy goober kahn"; "peanut people"; "rouged fruits"; "the vermillion pear"; "a casino in a wood"; "this tufted rock"; "the heroic height"; "tableau tinted and towering"; the fairy-tale we wished might exist; in short, everything ghostly yet undeniable.

Serenity in sophistication is a triumph, like the behavior of birds. The poet in fact is the migration mechanism of sensibility, and a medicine for the soul. That exact portrayal is intoxicating, that realism need not restrict itself to grossness, that music is "an accord of repetitions" is evident to one who examines *Ideas of Order*; and the altitude of performance makes the wild boars of philistinism who rush about interfering with experts, negligible. In America where the dearth of rareness is conspicuous, those who recognize it feel compelled to acknowledgment; yet such a thing as a book notice seems at best an advertisement of one's inability to avoid bluntness.

Rebecca West (1892–1983)

Introduction

Cicely Fairchild was born in Richmond-on-Thames, then a small town southwest of London, the daughter of a journalist who abandoned his family in 1901. With her mother and two sisters she then moved to Edinburgh. Fairchild defined herself as a feminist already at the age of 15, and was a member of the Votes for Women Club in Edinburgh. In 1910 the family moved back to London, where she attended the Academy for Dramatic Art for three terms. In 1911 she began to write for *The Freewoman*, a dissident feminist newspaper, and to spare her sister embarrassment adopted the pen name Rebecca West, a character in Ibsen's play *Rosmersholm* (the mistress of a married man who compels him to join her in a melodramatic suicide by drowning). She later insisted that she chose the name in a hurry and liked neither the play nor the character.

Her journalism and insatiable curiosity brought her an ever-widening circle of acquaintants, and she soon met Compton Mackenzie, Somerset Maugham, Ford Madox Ford, and May Sinclair; Wyndham Lewis, who also frequented the literary evenings hosted by Ford's mistress Violet Hunt, published Rebecca West's first fiction, a short story called "Indissoluble Matrimony," in 1914 in *Blast*. It was West, in turn, who got Pound taken on as literary editor at what was then *The New Freewoman* and soon to be rechristened *The Egoist*. West herself soon left the paper. She was a practicing journalist who needed to earn money, and she could earn more by writing for the *Clarion*, a Socialist newspaper, and the *Daily Mail*, whose literary editor, Robert Lynd, liked her book reviews. She would remain a lifelong friend of Lynd and his wife, Sylvia. Lynd, for his part, detested modernism and wrote a damning review of Eliot's *The Sacred Wood*. West herself was no philistine. She published her first book, *Henry James*, in 1916. Her first novel, *The Return of the Soldier*, was published in 1918. Her next novel, *The Judge*, is a remarkable work that deserves far more critical attention than it has received. She published five other novels: *Harriet Hume: A London Fantasy* (1929); *The Harsh Voice* (1935); *The Thinking Reed* (1936); *The Fountain Overflows* (1956); and *The Birds Fall Down* (1966). Her only child, Anthony West (b. 1914), was the son of the novelist H. G. Wells. In 1930 she married Henry Maxwell Andrews, a banker. Her most highly praised book is *Black Lamb and Grey Falcon* (1941), an account of her travels in Yugoslavia.

Indissoluble Matrimony (1914)

When George Silverton opened the front door he found that the house was not empty for all its darkness. The spitting noise of the striking of damp matches and mild, growling exclamations of annoyance told him that his wife was trying to light the dining-room gas. He went in and with some short, hostile sound of greeting lit a match and brought brightness into the little room. Then, irritated by his own folly in bringing private papers into his wife's presence, he stuffed the letters he had brought from the office deep into the pockets of his overcoat. He looked at her suspiciously, but she had not seen them, being busy in unwinding her orange motor-veil. His eyes remained on her face to brood a little sourly on her moving loveliness, which he had not been sure of finding: for she was one of those women who create an illusion alternately of extreme beauty and extreme ugliness. Under her curious dress, designed in some pitifully cheap and worthless stuff by a successful mood of her indiscreet taste – she had black blood in her – her long body seemed pulsing with some exaltation. The blood was coursing violently under her luminous yellow skin, and her lids, dusky with fatigue, drooped contentedly over her great humid black eyes. Perpetually she raised her hand to the mass of black hair that was coiled on her thick golden neck, and stroked it with secretive enjoyment, as a cat licks its fur. And her large mouth smiled frankly, but abstractedly, at some digested pleasure.

This story, the first work of fiction by West to be published, appeared in *Blast* 1 (June 1914).

There was a time when George would have looked on this riot of excited loveliness with suspicion. But now he knew it was almost certainly caused by some trifle – a long walk through stinging weather, the report of a Socialist victory at a by-election, or the intoxication of a waltz refrain floating from the municipal band-stand across the flats of the local recreation ground. And even if it had been caused by some amorous interlude he would not have greatly cared. In the ten years since their marriage he had lost the quality which would have made him resentful. He now believed that quality to be purely physical. Unless one was in good condition and responsive to the messages sent out by the flesh Evadne could hardly concern one. He turned the bitter thought over in his heart and stung himself by deliberately gazing unmoved upon her beautiful joyful body.

"Let's have supper now!" she said rather greedily.

He looked at the table and saw she had set it before she went out. As usual she had been in an improvident hurry: it was carelessly done. Besides, what an absurd supper to set before a hungry solicitor's clerk! In the centre, obviously intended as the principal dish, was a bowl of plums, softly red, soaked with the sun, glowing like jewels in the downward stream of the incandescent light. Besides them was a great yellow melon, its sleek sides fluted with rich growth, and a honey-comb glistening on a willow-pattern dish. The only sensible food to be seen was a plate of tongue laid at his place.

"I can't sit down to supper without washing my hands!"

While he splashed in the bathroom upstairs he heard her pull in a chair to the table and sit down to her supper. It annoyed him. There was no ritual about it. While he was eating the tongue she would be crushing honey on new bread, or stripping a plum of its purple skin and holding the golden globe up to the gas to see the light filter through. The meal would pass in silence. She would innocently take his dumbness for a sign of abstraction and forbear to babble. He would find the words choked on his lips by the weight of dullness that always oppressed him in her presence. Then, just about the time when he was beginning to feel able to formulate his obscure grievances against her, she would rise from the table without a word and run upstairs to her work, humming in that uncanny, negro way of hers.

And so it was. She ate with an appalling catholicity of taste, with a nice child's love of sweet foods, and occasionally she broke into that hoarse beautiful croon. Every now and then she looked at him with too obvious speculations as to whether his silence was due to weariness or uncertain temper. Timidly she cut him an enormous slice of the melon, which he did not want. Then she rose abruptly and flung herself into the rocking chair on the hearth. She clasped her hands behind her head and strained backwards so that the muslin stretched over her strong breasts. She sang softly to the ceiling.

There was something about the fantastic figure that made him feel as though they were not properly married.

"Evadne?"

"'S?"

"What have you been up to this evening?"

"I was at Milly Stafordale's."

He was silent again. That name brought up the memory of his courting days. It was under the benign eyes of blonde, plebeian Milly that he had wooed the distracting creature in the rocking chair.

Ten years before, when he was twenty-five, his firm had been reduced to hysteria over the estates of an extraordinarily stupid old woman, named Mrs. Mary Ellerker. Her stupidity, grappling with the complexity of the sources of the vast income which rushed in spate from the properties of four deceased husbands, demanded oceans of explanations even over her weekly rents. Silverton alone in the office, by reason of a certain natural incapacity for excitement, could deal calmly with this marvel of imbecility. He alone could endure to sit with patience in the black-panelled drawing-room amidst the jungle of shiny mahogany furniture and talk to a mass of darkness, who rested heavily in the window-seat and now and then made an idiotic remark in a bright, hearty voice. But it shook even him. Mrs. Mary Ellerker was obscene. Yet she was perfectly sane and, although of that remarkable plainness noticeable in most oft-married women, in good enough physical condition.

She merely presented the loathsome spectacle of an ignorant mind, contorted by the artificial idiocy of coquetry, lack of responsibility, and hatred of discipline, stripped naked by old age. That was the real horror of her. One feared to think how many women were really like Mrs. Ellerker under their armour of physical perfection or social grace. For this reason he turned eyes of hate on Mrs. Ellerker's pretty little companion, Milly Stafordale, who smiled at him over her embroidery with wintry northern brightness. When she was old she too would be obscene.

This horror obssessed him. Never before had he feared anything. He had never lived more than half-an-hour from a police station, and, as he had by some chance missed the melancholy clairvoyance of adolescence, he had never conceived of any horror with which the police could not deal. This disgust of women revealed to him that the world is a place of subtle perils. He began to fear marriage as he feared death. The thought of intimacy with some lovely, desirable and necessary wife turned him sick as he sat at his lunch. The secret obscenity of women! He talked darkly of it to his friends. He wondered why the Church did not provide a service for the absolution of men after marriage. Wife desertion seemed to him a beautiful return of the tainted body to cleanliness.

On his fifth visit to Mrs. Ellerker he could not begin his business at once. One of Milly Stafordale's friends had come in to sing to the old lady. She stood by the piano against the light, so that he saw her washed with darkness. Amazed, of tropical fruit. And before he had time to apprehend the sleepy wonder of her beauty, she had begun to sing. Now he knew that her voice was a purely physical attribute, built in her as she lay in her mother's womb, and no index of her spiritual values. But then, as it welled up from the thick golden throat and clung to her lips, it seemed a sublime achievement of the soul. It was smouldering contralto such as only those of black blood can possess. As she sang her great black eyes lay on him with the innocent shamelessness of a young animal, and he remembered hopefully that he was good looking. Suddenly she stood in silence, playing with her heavy black plait. Mrs. Ellerker broke into silly thanks. The girl's mother, who had been playing the accompaniment, rose and stood rolling up her music. Silverton, sick with excitement, was introduced to them. He noticed that the mother was a little darker than the conventions permit. Their name was Hannan – Mrs. Arthur Hannan and Evadne. They moved lithely and quietly out of the room, the girl's eyes still lingering on his face.

The thought of her splendour and the rolling echoes of her voice disturbed him all night. Next day, going to his office, he travelled with her on the horse-car that bound his suburb to Petrick. One of the horses fell lame, and she had time to tell him that she was studying at a commercial college. He quivered with distress. All the time he had a dizzy illusion that she was nestling up against him. They parted shyly. During the next few days they met constantly. He began to go and see them in the evening at their home – a mean flat crowded with cheap glories of bead curtains and Oriental hangings that set off the women's alien beauty. Mrs. Hannan was a widow and they lived alone, in a wonderful silence. He talked more than he had ever done in his whole life before. He took a dislike to the widow, she was consumed with fiery subterranean passions, no fit guardian for the tender girl.

Now he could imagine with what silent rapture Evadne had watched his agitation. Almost from the first she had meant to marry him. He was physically attractive, though not strong. His intellect was gently stimulating like a mild white wine. And it was time she married. She was ripe for adult things. This was the real wound in his soul. He had tasted of a divine thing created in his time for dreams out of her rich beauty, her loneliness, her romantic poverty, her immaculate youth. He had known love. And Evadne had never known anything more than a magnificent physical adventure which she had secured at the right time as she would have engaged a cab to take her to the station in time for the cheapest excursion train. It was a quick way to light-hearted living. With loathing he remembered how in the days of their engagement she used to gaze purely into his blinking eyes and with her unashamed kisses incite him to extravagant embraces. Now he cursed her for having obtained his spiritual revolution on false pretences. Only for a little time had he had his illusion, for their marriage was hastened by Mrs. Hannan's sudden death. After three months of savage mourning Evadne flung herself into marriage, and her excited candour had enlightened him very soon.

That marriage had lasted ten years. And to Evadne their relationship was just the same as ever. Her vitality needed him as it needed the fruit on the table before him. He shook with wrath and a sense of outraged decency.

"O George !" She was yawning widely.

"What's the matter?" he said without interest.

"It's so beastly dull."

"I can't help that, can I?"

"No." She smiled placidly at him. "We're a couple of dull dogs, aren't we? I wish we had children."

After a minute she suggested, apparently as an alternative amusement, "Perhaps the post hasn't passed."

As she spoke there was a rat-tat and the slither of a letter under the door. Evadne picked herself up and ran out into the lobby. After a second or two, during which she made irritating inarticulate exclamations, she came in reading the letter and stroking her bust with a gesture of satisfaction.

"They want me to speak at Longton's meeting on the nineteenth," she purred.

"Longton? What's he up to?"

Stephen Longton was the owner of the biggest iron works in Petrick, a man whose refusal to adopt the livery of busy oafishness thought proper to commercial men aroused the gravest suspicions.

"He's standing as Socialist candidate for the town council."

". . . Socialist!" he muttered.

He set his jaw. That was a side of Evadne he considered as little as possible. He had never been able to assimilate the fact that Evadne had, two years after their marriage, passed through his own orthodox Radicalism to a passionate Socialism, and that after reading enormously of economics she had begun to write for the Socialist press and to speak successfully at meetings. In the jaundiced recesses of his mind he took it for granted that her work would have the lax fibre of her character: that it would be infected with her Oriental crudities. Although once or twice he had been congratulated on her brilliance, he mistrusted this phase of her activity as a caper of the sensualist. His eyes blazed on her and found the depraved, over-sexed creature, looking milder than a gazelle, holding out a handbill to him.

"They've taken it for granted!"

He saw her name – his name –

MRS. EVADNE SILVERTON.

It was at first the blaze of stout scarlet letters on the dazzling white ground that made him blink. Then he was convulsed with rage.

"Georgie dear!"

She stepped forward and caught his weak body to her bosom. He wrenched himself away. Spiritual nausea made him determined to be a better man than her.

"A pair of you! You and Longton – !" he snarled scornfully. Then, seeing her startled face, he controlled himself.

"I thought it would please you," said Evadne, a little waspishly.

"You mustn't have anything to do with Longton," he stormed.

A change passed over her. She became ugly. Her face was heavy with intellect, her lips coarse with power. He was at arms with a Socialist leader. Much he would have preferred the bland sensualist again.

"Why?"

"Because – his lips stuck together like blotting-paper – he's not the sort of man my wife should – should –"

With movements which terrified him by their rough energy, she folded up the bills and put them back in the envelope.

"George. I suppose you mean that he's a bad man." He nodded.

"I know quite well that the girl who used to be his typist is his mistress." She spoke it sweetly, as if reasoning with an old fool. "But she's got consumption. She'll be dead in six months. In fact, I think it's rather nice of him. To look after her and all that."

"My God! He leapt to his feet, extending a shaking forefinger. As she turned to him, the smile dying on her lips, his excited weakness wrapped him in a paramnesic illusion: it seemed to him that he had been through all this before – a long, long time ago. "My God, you talk like a woman off the streets!"

Evadne's lips lifted over her strong teeth. With clever cruelty she fixed his eyes with hers, well knowing that he longed to fall forward and bury his head on the table in a transport of hysterical sobs. After a moment of this torture she turned away, herself distressed by a desire to cry.

"How can you say such dreadful, dreadful things!" she protested, chokingly.

He sat down again. His eyes looked little and red, but they blazed on her. "I wonder if you are," he said softly.

"Are what?" she asked petulantly, a tear rolling down her nose.

"You know," he answered, nodding.

"George, George, George!" she cried.

"You've always been keen on kissing and making love, haven't you, my precious? At first you startled me, you did! I didn't know women were like that." From that morass he suddenly stepped on to a high peak of terror. Amazed to find himself sincere, he cried – "I don't believe good women are!"

"Georgie, how can you be so silly!" exclaimed Evadne shrilly. "You know quite well I've been as true to you as any woman could be." She sought his eyes with a liquid glance of reproach. He averted his gaze, sickened at having put himself in the wrong. For even while he degraded his tongue his pure soul fainted with loathing of her fleshliness.

"I – I'm sorry."

Too wily to forgive him at once, she showed him a lowering profile with down-cast lids. Of course, he knew it was a fraud: an imputation against her chastity was no more poignant than a reflection on the cleanliness of her nails – rude and spiteful, but that was all. But for a time they kept up the deception, while she cleared the table in a steely silence.

"Evadne, I'm sorry. I'm tired." His throat was dry. He could not bear the discord of a row added to the horror of their companionship. "Evadne, do forgive me – I don't know what I meant by –"

"That's all right, silly!" she said suddenly and bent over the table to kiss him. Her brow was smooth. It was evident from her splendid expression that she was pre-occupied. Then she finished clearing up the dishes and took them into the kitchen. While she was out of the room he rose from his seat and sat down in the armchair by the fire, setting his bull-dog pipe alight. For a very short time he was free of her voluptuous presence. But she ran back soon, having put the kettle on and changed her blouse for a loose dressing-jacket, and sat down on the arm of his chair. Once or twice she bent and kissed his brow, but for the most part she lay back with his head drawn to her bosom, rocking herself rhythmically. Silverton, a little disgusted by their contact, sat quite motionless and passed into a doze. He revolved in his mind the incidents of his day's routine and remembered a snub from a superior. So he opened his eyes and tried to think of something else. It was then that he became conscious that the rhythm of Evadne's movement was not regular. It was broken as though she rocked in time to music. Music? His sense of hearing crept up to hear if there was any sound of music in the breaths she was emitting rather heavily every now and now and then. At first he could hear nothing. Then it struck him that each breath was a muttered phrase. He stiffened, and hatred flamed through his veins. The words came clearly through her lips ... "The present system of wage-slavery ... "

"Evadne !" He sprang to his feet. "You're preparing your speech!"

She did not move. "I am," she said.

"Damn it, you shan't speak !"

"Damn it, I will !"

"Evadne, you shan't speak ! If you do I swear to God above I'll turn you out into the streets –."
She rose and came towards him. She looked black and dangerous. She trod softly like a cat with her

head down. In spite of himself, his tongue licked his lips in fear and he cowered a moment before he picked up a knife from the table. For a space she looked down on him and the sharp blade.

"You idiot, can't you hear the kettle's boiling over?"

He shrank back, letting the knife fall on the floor. For three minutes he stood there controlling his breath and trying to still his heart. Then he followed her into the kitchen. She was making a noise with a basinful of dishes.

"Stop that row."

She turned round with a dripping dish-cloth in her hand and pondered whether to throw it at him. But she was tired and wanted peace: so that she could finish the rough draft of her speech. So she stood waiting.

"Did you understand what I said then? If you don't promise me here and now –"

She flung her arms upwards with a cry and dashed past him. He made to run after her upstairs, but stumbled on the threshold of the lobby and sat with his ankle twisted under him, shaking with rage. In a second she ran downstairs again, clothed in a big cloak with a black bundle clutched to her breast. For the first time in their married life she was seized with a convulsion of sobs. She dashed out of the front door and banged it with such passion that a glass pane shivered to fragments behind her.

"What's this? What's this?" he cried stupidly, standing up. He perceived with an insane certainty that she was going out to meet some unknown lover. "I'll come and tell him what a slut you are!" he shouted after her and stumbled to the door. It was jammed now and he had to drag at it.

The night was flooded with the yellow moonshine of midsummer: it seemed to drip from the lacquered leaves of the shrubs in the front garden. In its soft clarity he could see her plainly, although she was now two hundred yards away. She was hastening to the north end of Sumatra Crescent, an end that curled up the hill like a silly kitten's tail and stopped abruptly in green fields. So he knew that she was going to the young man who had just bought the Georgian Manor, whose elm-trees crowned the hill. Oh, how he hated her! Yet he must follow her, or else she would cover up her adulteries so that he could not take his legal revenge. So he began to run – silently, for he wore his carpet slippers. He was only a hundred yards behind her when she slipped through a gap in the hedge to tread a field-path. She still walked with pride, for though she was town-bred, night in the open seemed not at all fearful to her. As he shuffled in pursuit his carpet slippers were engulfed in a shining pool of mud : he raised one with a squelch, the other was left. This seemed the last humiliation. He kicked the other one off his feet and padded on in his socks, snuffling in anticipation of a cold. Then physical pain sent him back to the puddle to pluck out the slippers; it was a dirty job. His heart battered his breast as he saw that Evadne had gained the furthest hedge and was crossing the stile into the lane that ran up to the Manor gates.

"Go on, you beast!" he muttered, "Go on, go on!" After a scamper he climbed the stile and thrust his lean neck beyond a mass of wilted hawthorn bloom that crumbled into vagrant petals at his touch.

The lane mounted yellow as cheese to where the moon lay on the iron tracery of the Manor gates. Evadne was not there. Hardly believing his eyes he hobbled ever into the lane and looked in the other direction. There he saw her disappearing round the bend of the road. Gathering himself up to a run, he tried to think out his bearings. He had seldom passed this way, and like most people without strong primitive instincts he had no sense of orientation. With difficulty he remembered that after a mile's mazy wanderings between high hedges this lane sloped suddenly to the bowl of heather overhung by the moorlands, in which lay the Petrick reservoirs, two untamed lakes.

"Eh! she's going to meet him by the water!" he cursed to himself. He remembered the withered ash tree, seared by lightning to its root, that stood by the road at the bare frontier of the moor. "May God strike her like that," he prayed," "as she fouls the other man's lips with her kisses. O God! let me strangle her. Or bury a knife deep in her breast." Suddenly he broke into a lolloping run. "O my Lord, I'll be able to divorce her. I'll be free. Free to live alone. To do my day's work and sleep my night's sleep without her. I'll get a job somewhere else and forget her. I'll bring her to the dogs. No clean man or woman in Petrick will look at her now. They won't have her to speak at that meeting now!" His throat swelled with joy, he leapt high in the air.

"I'll lie about her. If I can prove that she's wrong with this man they'll believe me if I say she's a bad woman and drinks. I'll make her name a joke. And then –"

He flung wide his arms in ecstasy: the left struck against stone. More pain than he had thought his body could hold convulsed him, so that he sank on the ground hugging his aching arm. He looked backwards as he writhed and saw that the hedge had stopped; above him was the great stone wall of the county asylum. The question broke on him – was there any lunatic in its confines so slavered with madness as he himself? Nothing but madness could have accounted for the torrent of ugly words, the sea of uglier thoughts that was now a part of him. "O God, me to turn like this!" he cried, rolling over full-length on the grassy bank by the roadside. That the infidelity of his wife, a thing that should have brought out the stern manliness of his true nature, should have discovered him as lecherous-lipped as any pot-house lounger, was the most infamous accident of his married life. The sense of sin descended on him so that his tears flowed hot and bitterly. "Have I gone to the Unitarian chapel every Sunday morning and to the Ethical Society every evening for nothing?" his spirit asked itself in its travail. "All those Browning lectures for nothing..." He said the Lord's Prayer several times and lay for a minute quietly crying. The relaxation of his muscles brought him a sense of rest which seemed forgiveness falling from God. The tears dried on his cheeks. His calmer consciousness heard the sound of rushing waters mingled with the beating of blood in his ears. He got up and scrambled round the turn of the road that brought him to the withered ash-tree.

He walked forward on the parched heatherland to the mound whose scarred sides, heaped with boulders, tufted with mountain grasses, shone before him in the moonlight. He scrambled up to it hurriedly and hoisted himself from ledge to ledge till he fell on his knees with a squeal of pain. His ankle was caught in a crevice of the rock. Gulping down his agony at this final physical humiliation he heaved himself upright and raced on to the summit, and found himself before the Devil's Cauldron, filled to the brim with yellow moonshine and the fiery play of summer lightning. The rugged crags opposite him were a low barricade against the stars to which the mound where he stood shot forward like a bridge. To the left of this the long Lisbech pond lay like a trailing serpent; its silver scales glittered as the wind swept down from the vaster moorlands to the east. To the right under a steep drop of twenty feet was the Whimsey pond, more sinister, shaped in an unnatural oval, sheltered from the wind by the high ridge so that the undisturbed moonlight lay across it like a sharp-edged sword.

He looked about for some sign of Evadne. She could not be on the land by the margin of the lakes, for the light blazed so strongly that each reed could be clearly seen like a black dagger stabbing the silver. He looked down Lisbech and saw far east a knot of red and green and orange lights. Perhaps for some devilish purpose Evadne had sought Lisbech railway station. But his volcanic mind had preserved one grain of sense that assured him that, subtle as Evadne's villainy might be, it would not lead her to walk five miles out of her way to a terminus which she could have reached in fifteen minutes by taking a train from the station down the road. She must be under cover somewhere here. He went down the gentle slope that fell from the top of the ridge to Lisbech pond in a disorder of rough heather, unhappy patches of cultivated grass, and coppices of silver birch, fringed with flaming broom that seemed faintly tarnished in the moonlight. At the bottom was a roughly hewn path which he followed in hot aimless hurry. In a little he approached a riot of falling waters. There was a slice ten feet broad carved out of the ridge, and to this narrow channel of black shining rock the floods of Lisbech leapt some feet and raced through to Whimsey. The noise beat him back. The gap was spanned by a gaunt thing of paint-blistered iron, on which he stood dizzily and noticed how the wide step that ran on each side of the channel through to the other pond was smeared with sinister green slime. Now his physical distress reminded him of Evadne, whom he had almost forgotten in contemplation of these lonely waters. The idea of her had been present but obscured, as sometimes toothache may cease active torture. His blood lust set him on and he staggered forward with covered ears. Even as he went something caught his eye in a thicket high up on the slope near the crags. Against the slender pride of some silver birches stood a gnarled hawthorn tree, its branches flattened under the stern moorland winds so that it grew squat like an opened umbrella. In its dark shadows, faintly illumined by a few boughs of withered blossom, there moved a strange bluish light. Even while he did not know what it was it made his flesh stir.

The light emerged. It was the moonlight reflected from Evadne's body. She was clad in a black bathing dress, and her arms and legs and the broad streak of flesh laid bare by a rent down the back shone brilliantly white, so that she seemed like a grotesquely patterned wild animal as she ran down to the lake. Whirling her arms above her head she trampled down into the water and struck out strongly. Her movements were full of brisk delight and she swam quickly. The moonlight made her the centre of a little feathery blur of black and silver, with a comet's tail trailing in her wake.

Nothing in all his married life had ever staggered Silverton so much as this. He had imagined his wife's adultery so strongly that it had come to be. It was now as real as their marriage; more real than their courtship. So this seemed to be the last crime of the adulteress. She had dragged him over those squelching fields and these rough moors and changed him from a man of irritations, but no passions, into a cold designer of murderous treacheries, so that he might witness a swimming exhibition! For a minute he was stunned. Then he sprang down to the rushy edge and ran along in the direction of her course, crying – "Evadne! Evadne!" She did not hear him. At last he achieved a chest note and shouted – "Evadne! come here!" The black and silver feather shivered in mid-water. She turned immediately and swam back to shore. He suspected sullenness in her slowness, but was glad of it, for after the shock of this extraordinary incident he wanted to go to sleep. Drowsiness lay on him like lead. He shook himself like a dog and wrenched off his linen collar, winking at the bright moon to keep himself awake. As she came quite near he was exasperated by the happy, snorting breaths she drew, and strolled a pace or two up the bank. To his enragement the face she lifted as she waded to dry land was placid, and she scrambled gaily up the bank to his side.

"O George, why did you come!" she exclaimed quite affectionately, laying a damp hand on his shoulder.

"O damn it, what does this mean!" he cried, committing a horrid tenor squeak. "What are you doing?"

"Why, George," she said," "I came here for a bathe."

He stared into her face and could make nothing of it. It was only sweet surfaces of flesh, soft radiances of eye and lip, a lovely lie of comeliness. He forgot this present grievance in a cold search for the source of her peculiar hatefulness. Under this sick gaze she pouted and turned away with a peevish gesture. He made no sign and stood silent, watching her saunter to that gaunt iron bridge. The roar of the little waterfall did not disturb her splendid nerves and she drooped sensuously over the hand-rail, sniffing up the sweet night smell; too evidently trying to abase him to another apology.

A mosquito whirred into his face. He killed it viciously and strode off towards his wife, who showed by a common little toss of the head that she was conscious of his coming.

"Look here, Evadne!" he panted. "What did you come here for? Tell me the truth and I promise I'll not – I'll not –"

"Not WHAT, George?"

"O please, please tell me the truth, do Evadne!" he cried pitifully.

"But, dear, what is there to carry on about so? You went on so queerly about my meeting that my head felt fit to split, and I thought the long walk and the dip would do me good." She broke off, amazed at the wave of horror that passed over his face.

His heart sank. From the loose-lipped hurry in the telling of her story, from the bigness of her eyes and the lack of subtlety in her voice, he knew that this was the truth. Here was no adulteress whom he could accuse in the law courts and condemn into the street, no resourceful sinner whose merry crimes he could discover. Here was merely his good wife, the faithful attendant of his hearth, relentless wrecker of his soul.

She came towards him as a cat approaches a displeased master, and hovered about him on the stone coping of the noisy sluice.

"Indeed!" he found himself saying sarcastically. "Indeed!"

"Yes, George Silverton, indeed!" she burst out, a little frightened. "And why shouldn't I? I used to come here often enough on summer nights with poor Mamma –"

"Yes!" he shouted. It was exactly the sort of thing that would appeal to that weird half-black woman from the back of beyond. "Mamma!" he cried tauntingly, "Mamma!"

There was a flash of silence between them before Evadne, clutching her breast and balancing herself dangerously on her heels on the stone coping, broke into gentle shrieks. "You dare talk of my Mamma, my poor Mamma, and she cold in her grave! I haven't been happy since she died and I married you, you silly little misery, you!" Then the rage was suddenly wiped off her brain by the perception of a crisis.

The trickle of silence overflowed into a lake, over which their spirits flew, looking at each other's reflection in the calm waters: in the hurry of their flight they had never before seen each other. They stood facing one another with dropped heads, quietly thinking.

The strong passion which filled them threatened to disintegrate their souls as a magnetic current decomposes the electrolyte, so they fought to organise their sensations. They tried to arrange themselves and their lives for comprehension, but beyond sudden lyric visions of old incidents of hatefulness – such as a smarting quarrel of six years ago as to whether Evadne had or had not cheated the railway company out of one and eightpence on an excursion ticket – the past was intangible. It trailed behind this intense event as the pale hair trails behind the burning comet. They were pre-occupied with the moment. Quite often George had found a mean pleasure in the thought that by never giving Evadne a child he had cheated her out of one form of experience, and now he paid the price for this unnatural pride of sterility. For now the spiritual offspring of their intercourse came to birth. A sublime loathing was between them. For a little time it was a huge perilous horror, but afterwards, like men aboard a ship whose masts seek the sky through steep waves, they found a drunken pride in the adventure. This was the very absolute of hatred. It cheapened the memory of the fantasias of irritation and ill-will they had performed in the less boring moments of their marriage, and they felt dazed, as amateurs who had found themselves creating a masterpiece. For the first time they were possessed by a supreme emotion and they felt a glad desire to strip away restraint and express it nakedly. It was ecstasy; they felt tall and full of blood.

Like people who, bewitched by Christ, see the whole earth as the breathing body of God, so they saw the universe as the substance and the symbol of their hatred. The stars trembled overhead with wrath. A wind from behind the angry crags set the moonlight on Lisbech quivering with rage, and the squat hawthorn-tree creaked slowly like the irritation of a dull little man. The dry moors, parched with harsh anger, waited thirstily and, sending out the murmur of rustling mountain grass and the cry of wakening fowl, seemed to huddle closer to the lake. But this sense of the earth's sympathy slipped away from them and they loathed all matter as the dull wrapping of their flame-like passion. At their wishing matter fell away and they saw sarcastic visions. He saw her as a toad squatting on the clean earth, obscuring the stars and pressing down its hot moist body on the cheerful fields. She felt his long boneless body coiled round the roots of the lovely tree of life. They shivered fastidiously. With an uplifting sense of responsibility they realised that they must kill each other.

A bird rose over their heads with a leaping flight that made it seem as though its black body was bouncing against the bright sky. The foolish noise and motion precipitated their thoughts. They were broken into a new conception of life. They perceived that God is war and his creatures are meant to fight. When dogs walk through the world cats must climb trees. The virgin must snare the wanton, the fine lover must put the prude to the sword. The gross man of action walks, spurred on the bloodless bodies of the men of thought, who lie quiet and cunningly do not tell him where his grossness leads him. The flesh must smother the spirit, the spirit must set the flesh on fire and watch it burn. And those who were gentle by nature and shrank from the ordained brutality were betrayers of their kind, surrendering the earth to the seed of their enemies. In this war there is no discharge. It they succumbed to peace now, the rest of their lives would be dishonourable, like the exile of a rebel who has begged his life as the reward of cowardice. It was their first experience of religious passion, and they abandoned themselves to it so that their immediate personal qualities fell away from them. Neither his weakness nor her prudence stood in the way of the event.

They measured each other with the eye. To her he was a spidery thing against the velvet blackness and hard silver surfaces of the pond. The light soaked her bathing dress so that she seemed, against the jagged shadows of the rock cutting, as though she were clad in a garment of dark polished mail. Her knees were bent so clearly, her toes gripped the coping so strongly. He understood very clearly that if he did not kill her instantly she would drop him easily into the deep riot of waters. Yet for a space he could not move, but stood expecting a degrading death. Indeed, he gave her time to kill him. But she was without power too, and struggled weakly with a hallucination. The quarrel in Sumatra Crescent with its suggestion of vast and unmentionable antagonisms; her swift race through the moon-drenched countryside, all crepitant with night noises: the swimming in the wine-like lake: their isolation on the moor, which was expressedly hostile to them, as nature always is to lonely man: and this stark contest face to face, with their resentments heaped between them like a pile of naked swords – these things were so strange that her civilised self shrank back appalled. There entered into her the primitive woman who is the curse of all women: a creature of the most utter femaleness, useless, save for childbirth, with no strong brain to make her physical weakness a light accident, abjectly and corruptingly afraid of man. A squaw, she dared not strike her lord.

The illusion passed like a moment of faintness and left her enraged at having forgotten her superiority even for an instant. In the material world she had a thousand times been defeated into making prudent reservations and practising unnatural docilities. But in the world of thought she had maintained unfalteringly her masterfulness in spite of the strong yearning of her temperament towards voluptuous surrenders. That was her virtue. Its violation whipped her to action and she would have killed him at once, had not his moment come a second before hers. Sweating horribly, he had dropped his head forward on his chest: his eyes fell on her feet and marked the plebeian moulding of her ankle, which rose thickly over a crease of flesh from the heel to the calf. The woman was coarse in grain and pattern.

He had no instinct for honourable attack, so he found himself striking her in the stomach. She reeled from pain, not because his strength overcame hers. For the first time her eyes looked into his candidly open, unveiled by languor or lust: their hard brightness told him how she despised him for that unwarlike blow. He cried out as he realised that this was another of her despicable victories and that the whole burden of the crime now lay on him, for he had begun it. But the rage was stopped on his lips as her arms, flung wildly out as she fell backwards, caught him about the waist with abominable justness of eye and evil intention. So they fell body to body into the quarrelling waters.

The feathery confusion had looked so soft, yet it seemed the solid rock they struck. The breath shot out of him and suffocation warmly stuffed his ears and nose. Then the rock cleft and he was swallowed by a brawling blackness in which whirled a vortex that flung him again and again on a sharp thing that burned his shoulder. All about him fought the waters, and they cut his flesh like knives. His pain was past belief. Though God might be war, he desired peace in his time, and he yearned for another God – a child's God, an immense arm coming down from the hills and lifting him to a kindly bosom. Soon his body would burst for breath, his agony would smash in his breast bone. So great was his pain that his consciousness was strained to apprehend it, as a too tightly stretched canvas splits and rips.

Suddenly the air was sweet on his mouth. The starlight seemed as hearty as a cheer. The world was still there, the world in which he had lived, so he must be safe. His own weakness and loveableness induced enjoyable tears, and there was a delicious moment of abandonment to comfortable whining before he realised that the water would not kindly buoy him up for long, and that even now a hostile current clasped his waist. He braced his flaccid body against the sucking blackness and flung his head back so that the water should not bubble so hungrily against the cords of his throat. Above him the slime of the rock was sticky with moonbeams, and the leprous light brought to his mind a newspaper paragraph, read years ago, which told him that the dawn had discovered floating in some oily Mersey dock, under walls as infected with wet growth as this, a corpse whose blood-encrusted finger-tips were deeply cleft. On the instant his own finger-tips seemed hot with blood and deeply cleft from clawing at the impregnable rock. He screamed gaspingly and beat his hands through the strangling flood. Action, which he had always loathed and dreaded, had broken the hard mould of his self-possession, and the dry dust of his character was blown hither and thither by fear. But one sharp fragment of intelligence which survived this detrition of his personality perceived that a certain gleam on the rock about a foot above the water was not the cold putrescence of the slime, but certainly the hard and merry light of a moon ray striking on solid metal. His left hand clutched upwards at it, and he swung from a rounded projection. It was, his touch told him, a leaden ring hanging obliquely from the rock, to which his memory could visualise precisely in some past drier time when Lisbech sent no flood to Whimsey, a waterman mooring a boat strewn with pale-bellied perch. And behind the stooping waterman he remembered a flight of narrow steps that led up a buttress to a stone shelf that ran through the cutting. Unquestionably he was safe. He swung in a happy rhythm from the ring, his limp body trailing like a caterpillar through the stream to the foot of the steps, while he gasped in strength. A part of him was in agony, for his arm was nearly dragged out of its socket and a part of him was embarrassed because his hysteria shook him with a deep rumbling chuckle that sounded as though he meditated on some unseemly joke; the whole was pervaded by a twilight atmosphere of unenthusiastic gratitude for his rescue, like the quietly cheerful tone of a Sunday evening sacred concert. After a minute's deep breathing he hauled himself up by the other hand and prepared to swing himself on to the steps.

But first, to shake off the wet worsted rags, once his socks, that now stuck uncomfortably between his toes, he splashed his feet outwards to midstream. A certain porpoise-like surface met his left foot. Fear dappled his face with goose flesh. Without turning his head he knew what it was. It was Evadne's fat flesh rising on each side of her deep-furrowed spine through the rent in her bathing dress.

Once more hatred marched through his soul like a king: compelling service by his godhead and, like all gods, a little hated for his harsh lieu on his worshipper. He saw his wife as the curtain of flesh between him and celibacy, and solitude and all those delicate abstentions from life which his soul desired. He saw her as the invisible worm destroying the rose of the world with her dark secret love. Now he knelt on the lowest stone step watching her wet seal-smooth head bobbing nearer on the waters. As her strong arms, covered with little dark points where her thick hairs were clotted with moisture, stretched out towards safety he bent forward and laid his hands on her head. He held her face under water. Scornfully he noticed the bubbles that rose to the surface from her protesting mouth and nostrils, and the foam raised by her arms and her thick ankles. To the end the creature persisted in turmoil, in movement, in action....

She dropped like a stone. His hands, with nothing to resist them, slapped the water foolishly and he nearly overbalanced forward into the steam. He rose to his feet very stiffly. "I must be a very strong man," he said, as he slowly climbed the steps. "I must be a very strong man," he repeated, a little louder, as with a hot and painful rigidity of the joints he stretched himself out at full length along the stone shelf. Weakness closed him in like a lead coffin. For a little time the wetness of his clothes persisted in being felt: then the sensation oozed out of him and his body fell out of knowledge. There was neither pain nor joy nor any other reckless ploughing of the brain by nerves. He knew unconsciousness, or rather the fullest consciousness he had ever known. For the world became nothingness, and nothingness which is free from the yeasty nuisance of matter and the ugliness of generation was the law of his being. He was absorbed into vacuity, the untamed substance of the universe, round which he conceived passion and thought to circle as straws caught up by the wind. He saw God and lived.

In Heaven a thousand years are a day. And this little corner of time in which he found happiness shrank to a nut-shell as he opened his eyes again. This peace was hardly printed on his heart, yet the brightness of the night was blurred by the dawn. With the grunting carefulness of a man drunk with fatigue, he crawled along the stone shelf to the iron bridge, where he stood with his back to the roaring sluice and rested. All things seemed different now and happier. Like most timid people he disliked the night, and the commonplace hand which the dawn laid on the scene seemed to him a sanctification. The dimmed moon sank to her setting behind the crags. The jewel lights of Lisbech railway station were weak, cheerful twinkings. A steaming bluish milk of morning mist had been spilt on the hard silver surface of the lake, and the reeds no longer stabbed it like little daggers, but seemed a feathery fringe, like the pampas grass in the front garden in Sumatra Crescent. The black crags became brownish, and the mist disguised the sternness of the moor. This weakening of effects was exactly what he had always thought the extinction of Evadne would bring the world. He smiled happily at the moon.

Yet he was moved to sudden angry speech. "If I had my time over again," he said, "I wouldn't touch her with the tongs." For the cold he had known all along he would catch had settled in his head, and his handkerchief was wet through.

He leaned over the bridge and looked along Lisbech and thought of Evadne. For the first time for many years he saw her image without spirits, and wondered without indignation why she had so often looked like the cat about to steal the cream. What was the cream? And did she ever steal it? Now he would never know. He thought of her very generously and sighed over the perversity of fate in letting so much comeliness.

"If she had married a butcher or a veterinary surgeon she might have been happy," he said, and shook his head at the glassy black water that slid under the bridge to that boiling sluice.

A gust of ague reminded him that wet clothes clung to his fevered body and that he ought to change as quickly as possible, or expect to laid up for weeks. He turned along the path that led back across the moor to the withered ash tree, and was learning the torture of bare feet on gravel when he cried out to himself: "I shall be hanged for killing my wife." It did not come as a trumpet-call, for he was one of those people who never quite hear what is said to them, and this deafishness extended in him to emotional things. It stole on him calmly, like a fog closing on a city. When he first felt hemmed in by this certainty he looked over his shoulder to the crags, remembering tales of how Jacobite fugitives had hidden on the moors for many weeks. There lay at least another day of freedom. But he was the kind of man who always goes home. He stumbled on, not very unhappy, except for his feet. Like many people of weak temperament he did not fear death. Indeed, it had a peculiar appeal to him; for while it was important, exciting, it did not, like most important and exciting things try to create action. He allowed his imagination the vanity of painting pictures. He saw himself standing in their bedroom, plotting this last event, with the white sheet and the high lights of the mahongany wardrobe shining ghostly at him through the darkness. He saw himself raising a thin hand to the gas bracket and turning on the tap. He saw himself staggering to their bed while death crept in at his nostrils. He saw his corpse lying in full daylight, and for the first time knew himself certainly, unquestionably dignified.

He threw back his chest in pride: but at that moment the path stopped and he found himself staggering down the mound of heatherland and boulders with bleeding feet. Always he had suffered from sore feet, which had not exactly disgusted but, worse still, disappointed Evadne. A certain wistfulness she had always evinced when she found herself the superior animal had enraged and himiliated him many times. He felt that sting in him now, and flung himself down the mound cursing. When he stumbled up to the withered ash tree he hated her so much that it seemed as though she were alive again, and a sharp wind blowing down from the moor terrified him like her touch.

He rested there. Leaning against the stripped grey trunk, he smiled up at the sky, which was now so touched to ineffectiveness by the dawn that it looked like a tent of faded silk. There was the peace of weakness in him, which he took to be spiritual, because it had no apparent physical justification: but he lost it as his dripping clothes chilled his tired flesh. His discomfort reminded him that the phantasmic night was passing from him. Daylight threatened him: the daylight in which for so many years he had worked in the solicitor's office and been snubbed and ignored. " 'The garish day,' "[1] he murmured disgustedly, quoting the blasphemy of some hymn writer. He wanted his death to happen in this phantasmic night.

---

[1] "The garish day" is a phrase from the hymn "Lead Kindly Light" (1833), words by John Henry Newman (1801–90), set to music in 1865 by John B. Dykes:

> Lead, kindly Light, amid th' encircling gloom,
>   Lead thou me on;
> The night is dark, and I am far from home;
>   Lead Thou me on;
> Keep Thou my feet; I do not ask to see
> The distant scene – one step enough for me.
> I was not ever thus, nor prayed that Thou
> Shouldst lead me on;

> I loved to choose and see my path; but now
> Lead Thou me on.
> I loved the garish day, and, spite of fears,
> Pride ruled my will: remember not past years.

> So long Thy power hath blest me, sure it still
> Will lead me on,
> O'er moor and fen, o'er crag and torrent till
> The night is gone;
> And with the morn those angel faces smile,
> Which I have loved long since, and lost awhile.

So he limped his way along the road. The birds had not yet begun to sing, but the rustling noises of the night had ceased. The silent highway was consecrated to his proud progress. He staggered happily like a tired child returning from a lovely birthday walk: his death in the little bedroom, which for the first time he would have to himself, was a culminating treat to be gloated over like the promise of a favourite pudding for supper. As he walked he brooded dozingly on large and swelling thoughts. Like all people of weak passions and enterprise he loved to think of Napoleon, and in the shadow of the great asylum wall he strutted a few steps of his advance from murder to suicide, with arms crossed on his breast and thin legs trying to strut massively. He was so happy. He wished that a military band went before him, and pretended that the high hedges were solemn lines of men, stricken in awe to silence as their king rode out to some nobly self-chosen doom. Vast he seemed to himself, and magnificent like music, and solemn like the Sphinx. He had saved the earth from corruption by killing Evadne, for whom he now felt the unremorseful pity a conqueror might bestow on a devastated empire. He might have grieved that his victory brought him death, but with immense pride he found that the occasion was exactly described by a text. "He saved others, Himself He could not save."[2] He had missed the stile in the field above Sumatra Crescent and had to go back and hunt for it in the hedge. So quickly had his satisfaction borne him home.

The field had the fantastic air that jerry-builders give to land poised on the knife-edge of town and country, so that he walked in romance to his very door. The unmarred grass sloped to a stone-hedge of towers of loose brick, trenches and mounds of shining clay, and the fine intentful spires of the scaffolding round the last unfinished house. And he looked down on Petrick. Though to the actual eye it was but a confusion of dark distances through the twilight, a breaking of velvety perspectives, he saw more intensely than ever before its squalid walls and squalid homes where mean men and mean women enlaced their unwholesome lives. Yet he did not shrink from entering for his great experience: as Christ did not shrink from being born in a stable. He swaggered with humility over the trodden mud of the field and the new white flags of Sumatra Crescent. Down the road before him there passed a dim figure, who paused at each lamp post and raised a long wand to behead the yellow gas-flowers that were now wilting before the dawn: a ghostly herald preparing the world to be his deathbed. The Crescent curved in quiet darkness, save for one house, where blazed a gas-lit room with undrawn blinds. The brightness had the startling quality of a scream. He looked in almost anxiously as he passed, and met the blank eyes of a man in evening clothes who stood by the window shaking a medicine. His face was like a wax mask softened by heat: the features were blurred with the suffering which comes from the spectacle of suffering. His eyes lay unshiftingly on George's face as he went by and he went on shaking the bottle. It seemed as though he would never stop.

In the hour of his grandeur George was not forgetful of the griefs of the little human people, but interceded with God for the sake of this stranger. Everything was beautiful, beautiful, beautiful.

His own little house looked solemn as a temple. He leaned against the lamp-post at the gate and stared at its empty windows and neat bricks. The disorder of the shattered pane of glass could be overlooked by considering a sign that this house was a holy place: like the Passover blood on the lintel. The propriety of the evenly drawn blind pleased him enormously. He had always known that this was how the great tragic things of the world had accomplished themselves: quietly. Evadne's raging activity belonged to trivial or annoying things like spring-cleaning or thunder-storms. Well, the house belonged to him now. He opened the gate and went up the asphalt path, sourly noticing that Evadne had as usual left out the lawn-mower, though it might very easily have rained, with the wind coming up as it was. A stray cat that had been sleeping in the tuft of pampas grass in the middle of the lawn was roused by his coming, and fled insolently close to his legs. He hated all wild homeless things, and bent for a stone to throw at it. But instead his fingers touched a slug, which reminded him of the feeling of Evadne's flesh through the slit in her bathing dress. And suddenly the garden was possessed by her presence: she seemed to amble there as she had so often done, sowing seeds unwisely and tormenting the last days of an ailing geranium by insane

[2]   Matthew 27:41–2, describing the crucifixion of Christ:

41. Likewise also the chief priest, mocking him, with the scribes and elders, said,

42. He saved others; himself he cannot save. If he be the King of Israel, let him now come down from the cross, and we will believe him.

transplantation, exclaiming absurdly over such mere weeds as morning glory. He caught the very clucking of her voice . . . The front door opened at his touch.

The little lobby with its closed doors seemed stuffed with expectant silence. He realised that he had come to the theatre of his great adventure. Then panic seized him. Because this was the home where he and she had lived together so horribly he doubted whether he could do this splendid momentous thing, for here he had always been a poor thing with the habit of failure. His heart beat in him more quickly than his raw feet could pad up the oil-clothed stairs. Behind the deal door at the end of the passage was death. Nothingness! It would escape him, even the idea of it would escape him if he did not go to it at once. When he burst at last into its presence he felt so victorious that he sank back against the door waiting for death to come to him without turning on the gas. He was so happy. His death was coming true.

But Evadne lay on his deathbed. She slept there soundly, with her head flung back on the pillows so that her eyes and brow seemed small in shadow, and her mouth and jaw huge above her thick throat in the light. Her wet hair straggled across the pillow on to a broken cane chair covered with her tumbled clothes. Her breast, silvered with sweat, shone in the ray of the street lamp that had always disturbed their nights. The counterpane rose enormously over her hips in rolls of glazed linen. Out of mere innocent sleep her sensuality was distilling a most drunken pleasure.

Not for one moment did he think this a phantasmic appearance. Evadne was not the sort of woman to have a ghost.

Still leaning against the door, he tried to think it all out: but his thoughts came brokenly, because the dawnlight flowing in at the window confused him by its pale glare and that lax figure on the bed held his attention. It must have been that when he laid his murderous hands on her head she had simply dropped below the surface and swum a few strokes under water as any expert swimmer can. Probably he had never even put her into danger, for she was a great lusty creature and the weir was a little place. He had imagined the wonder and peril of the battle as he had imagined his victory. He sneezed exhaustingly, and from his physical distress realised how absurd it was ever to have thought that he had killed her. Bodies like his do not kill bodies like hers.

Now his soul was naked and lonely as though the walls of his body had fallen in at death, and the grossness of Evadne's sleep made him suffer more unlovely a destitution than any old beggarwoman squatting by the roadside in the rain. He had thought he had had what every man most desires: one night of power over a woman for the business of murder or love. But it had been a lie. Nothing beautiful had ever happened to him. He would have wept, but the hatred he had learnt on the moors obstructed all tears in his throat. At least this night had given him passion enough to put an end to it all.

Quietly he went to the window and drew down the sash. There was no fire-place, so that sealed the room. Then he crept over to the gas bracket and raised his thin hand, as he had imagined in his hour of vain glory by the lake.

He had forgotten Evadne's thrifty habit of turning off the gas at the main to prevent leakage when she went to bed.

He was beaten. He undressed and got into bed: as he had done every night for ten years, and as he would do every night until he died. Still sleeping, Evadne caressed him with warm arms.

The Freewoman *(1926)*

I have been asked to write an account of the *Freewoman*, and those who asked me were wise, for that paper, unimportant as it was in content, and amateurish in form, had an immense effect on its time. But unfortunately, I have forgotten nearly everything about it. It must have lived about 14 or 15 years ago, because I know I was about 17 or 18 years of age;[1] and in the intervening years I have done so much else and have so completely lost touch with the other persons involved, that the details are fogged in my mind.

THE FREEWOMAN
This essay was first published in *Time and Tide*, July 16, 1926.

[1] West was 19 when *The Freewoman* first appeared.

The paper was the creation of Dora Marsden,[2] who was one of the most marvellous personalities that the nation has ever produced. She had, to begin with, the most exquisite beauty of person. She was hardly taller than a child, but she was not just a small woman; she was a perfectly proportioned fairy. She was the only person I have ever met who could so accurately have been described as flower-like that one could have put it down on her passport. And on many other planes she was as remarkable. In her profession she had been more than ordinarily successful. Though she was still under thirty, she was head of a training college for teachers. She was one of the fighting suffragettes under Mrs. Pankhurst,[3] and in the course of her activities she had shown courage that even in that courageous company seemed magnificent. She had been to prison more than once, and had behaved with what would have been amazing heroism in any woman, but which was something transcendent in her case, since she was physically fragile and the victim of a tiresome form of ill-health.

She conceived the idea of starting the *Freewoman* because she was discontented with the limited scope of the suffragist movement. She felt that it was restricting itself too much to the one point of political enfranchisement and was not bothering about the wider issues of Feminism. I think she was wrong in formulating this feeling as an accusation against the Pankhursts[4] and suffragettes in general, because they were simply doing their job, and it was certainly a whole time job. But there was equally certainly a need for someone to stand aside and ponder on the profounder aspects of Feminism. In this view she found a supporter in Mary Gawthorpe,[5] a Yorkshire woman who had recently been invalided out of the suffrage movement on account of injuries sustained at the hands of stewards who had thrown her out of a political meeting where she had been interrupting Mr. Winston Churchill. Mary Gawthorpe, was a merry militant saint who had travelled round the provinces, living in dreary lodgings on $15 or $20 a week, speaking several times a day at outdoor meetings, and suffering fools gladly (which I think she found the hardest job of all), when trying to convert the influential Babbits of our English zenith cities. Occasionally she had a rest in prison, which she always faced with a sparrow-like perkiness. She had wit and common sense and courage, and each to the point of genius. She lives in the United States now, but her inspiration still lingers over here on a whole generation of women.

These two came together and planned this paper, but Dora Marsden played the chief part in organizing and controlling it throughout the whole of its life, for at that time Mary Gawthorpe was sick almost unto death.

Dora Marsden came to London with her devoted friend Grace Jardine,[6] who was Martha to her Mary, and they found a publisher to finance them. At this point I had better remind my readers that again and again radical movements find themselves obliged to be financed by the insane. Radicals may take comfort in reflecting that the same is true of non-radical movements, but that the fact is

---

[2]   Dora Marsden (1882–1960) was the editor of *The Freewoman* (1911–13), *The New Freewoman* (1913), and *The Egoist* (1913–19), a radical feminist newspaper that gradually accommodated a melange of anarchist and extreme invidualist views. It published many early poems by Ezra Pound, all of Joyce's *Portrait of the Artist as a Young Man*, and most of *Ulysses*, and during its early years also featured regular reviews and features by Rebecca West. Marsden herself was not greatly interested in the literary or cultural aspects of the newspaper; instead, she wrote long philosophical essays. On her life see Les Garner, *Brave and Beautiful Spirit: Dora Marsden, 1992–1960* (Aldershot, Hants: Avebury, 1990), and Bruce Clarke, *Dora Marsden and Early Modernism: Gender, Individualism, Science* (Ann Arbor: University of Michigan, 1996).

[3]   Emmeline Pankhurst (1857–1928) led the struggle to achieve votes for women in Britain prior to World War I. In 1903 she founded the Women's Social and Political Union (WSPU), a militant group that developed a variety of strategies for publicizing its cause.

[4]   Emmeline Pankhurst (see preceding note) was joined in the movement by her two daughters, Christabel and Sylvia.

[5]   Mary Gawthorpe (1881–1973) was a feminist activist and labor organizer. She joined the Women's Social and Political Union (WSPU) in 1905 and was a full-time organizer by 1906. In 1909 she heckled a speech given by Winston Churchill. She was badly beaten by stewards at the meeting and suffered severe internal injuries. She was also imprisoned several times while working for the WSPU. Hunger strikes and force-feeding badly damaged her health, and in 1912 she had to abandon her active involvement in the movement. Gawthorpe now joined Dora Marsden as the co-editor of the feminist journal *The Freewoman*, which caused a storm when it advocated free love and encouraged women not to get married. The journal also wrote sympathetically about homosexuality and suggested communal childcare and co-operative housekeeping. Gawthorpe's health continued to deteriorate and by May 1912 she was unable to continue working as co-editor of the journal. In 1916 she emigrated to the US and eventually became an official for the Amalgamated Clothing Workers Union.

[6]   A friend of Dora Marsden.

so serious because there is no striking antithesis between such movements and their financiers. This particular gentleman financed not only the *Freewoman*, but Chesterton and Belloc's *The Eye Witness*,[7] and a fashionable illustrated paper which was tended by a beautiful lady with red gold hair and decorative footwear. Her slippers gleam undimmed across the gulf of time; I have not been able to forget them. The movies had not come into their own, but she anticipated the *anima* of Mr. Cecil de Mille.[8] He also published his own poetry, which consisted of Wordsworthian nature verse and Browningish monologues about the soul. One I remember particularly was a touching lament by St. Augustine on his own celibacy. And this gentleman also published, with the utmost generosity of terms, various books by young lions. For example, he brought out Katherine Mansfield's[9] first volume of short stories *In a German Pension*. So we started in: or rather they did. I did not join them till later; in fact, I never wrote for the *Freewoman* till it had got such a bad name for its candour that I was forbidden to read it by my family, and thus I came to adopt my present pseudonym. The initial group consisted of Dora Marsden, Grace Jardine and a glorious red-haired bachelor of science, who had been in and out of gaol for the cause, named Rona Robinson.[10] They went at first for all the conventional Feminist articles of faith. In their early numbers I fancy they represented as nearly as possible the same program as the National Woman's Party.[11] That programme had certainly been accepted by English women of this subsequent period with an extraordinary completeness. I think there are probably hardly any subscribers to the quiet orthodox woman's weekly of to-day, *Time and Tide*, who do not take it for granted that it is degrading to woman, and injurious to the race to leave the financing of the mother and her children to the double-barrelled caprice of the father and the father's employer. They may differ regarding the specific remedies they propose to end this state of affairs, but hardly any of them would defend it. I am convinced that this change of outlook is partly due to the strong lead given by the *Freewoman*. But the greatest service that the paper did its country was through its unblushingness. It paralleled the achievement of Miss Christabel Pankhurst,[12] who did an infinite service to the world by her articles on venereal disease. The content of them was not too intelligent. It blamed the impurity of men for the state of affairs to which the impurity of women and the social system are also contributory causes. But it mentioned venereal diseases loudly and clearly and repeatedly and in the worst possible taste: so that England fainted with shock, and on recovering listened quite calmly when the experts came forward and said that since the subject had at last been mentioned they might urge that the state could do this and that to prevent these diseases. Even so, the *Freewoman* mentioned sex loudly and clearly and repeatedly, and in the worst possible taste; and likewise the content was not momentous. Those who laugh at Freud and Jung[13] should turn back to those articles and see how utterly futile and blundering discussions on these points used to be even when they were conducted by earnest and intelligent people. But the *Freewoman* by its candour did an immense service to the world by shattering, as nothing else would, as not the mere cries of intention towards independence had ever done, the romantic conception of women. It pointed out that lots of women who were unmated and childless resented their condition. It pointed out that there were lots of women who were mated and who had children who found elements of dissatisfaction in their position. It even mentioned the existence of abnormalities of instinct.[14] In fact, it smashed the romantic pretence that women had as a birthright the gift of

---

[7] G. K. Chesterton (1874–1936), the British novelist and essayist who was noted for his staunch Catholicism, was a frequent contributor to the *Eye-Witness*, a brief-lived political weekly (1911–12) edited by Hilaire Belloc (1870–1953), whose political views would soon move far to the right.

[8] Cecil de Mille (1881–1959), American cinema producer known for flashy and spectacular films.

[9] Her first collection of short stories, *In a German Pension*, was published by Swift in 1911.

[10] Rona Robinson was a graduate of Manchester University, where she met Dora Marsden.

[11] Organized in the US in 1916 by Alice Paul, who had worked with the Pankhursts and the suffragette movement in Britain.

[12] Christabel Pankhurst (1880–1958) was the daughter of Emmeline Pankhurst (see p. 707 n.3). Her articles on venereal disease were collected and published as a book, *The Great Scourge and How to End It* (London: E. Pankhurst, 1913).

[13] Sigmund Freud (1856–1939), Austrian founder of psychoanalysis; Carl Jung (1875–1961), a follower of Freud who broke with him around 1910 and developed his own version of psychoanalysis.

[14] *abnormalities of instinct* a "polite" reference to homosexuality, a subject that could not be explicitly named in a mainstream periodical of the time, as was *Time and Tide*.

perfect adaptation: that they were in a bland state of desireless contentment which, when they were beautiful, reminded the onlooker of goddesses, and when they were plain were more apt to remind him of cabbage. If this romantic conception had been true, there would have been no reason for the emancipation of women, since as they could be happy anywhere and anyhow, there was never any need to alter their environment. It had to be admitted that women were vexed human beings who suffered intensely from male-adaptation to life, and that they were tortured and dangerous if they were not allowed to adapt themselves to life. That admission is the keystone of the modern Feminist movement.

Dora Marsden made her point with unique effectiveness, considering the length of the paper's life. Nevertheless the paper was coming to an end psychically when it came to an end physically. Its psychic death was due to the fact that Dora Marsden started on a train of thought which led her to metaphysics. She began to lose her enthusiasm for bringing women's industry on equal terms with men, because it struck her that industrialism destroyed more in life than it produced. She began to be sceptical of modern civilisation and this led her to preaching a kind of Tolstoyism which would have endeavoured to lead the world back to primitive agriculture. I waged war with her on this point in a correspondence that the curious might hunt down in the files. I signed myself therein Rachel East. I got no chance to convince her, for already she had retreated to further remoteness and was developing an egoistic philosophy on the lines foreshadowed by Max Stirner.[15] About this time the brick fell. Our publisher fled suddenly to North Africa, with the lady of the shoes and a considerable sum of money which an unfortunate gentleman had entrusted him as an investment in the business. It then turned out that he was a criminal of singular type: really a naïve moral imbecile. After various financial fantasias and a number of carelessly conceived and executed bigamies he had settled down as a publisher not a mile from our police department offices at Scotland Yard, and had there flourished for two years: and no doubt would have done so for many more years had not the young lions been so expensive and the lady with the shoes so desirous of foreign travel.

He was brought back and sent to a place of seclusion for some years. Mr. Chesterton and Mr. Belloc and Dora Marsden and her flock were homeless for a time. Then odd people turned up and financed it, and it was reissued as *The Egoist*, of which paper I was literary editor. That did not last long. My position seemed to be impossible. The routine of the office was not impeccable. There was an *arrivist* American poet[16] who intended to oust me, and his works and those of his friends continually appeared in the paper without having passed me. This was unbearably irritating, particularly at that age. And Dora Marsden, more and more remote in her ether of speculation, could not understand it when I objected to articles which did not come up to a certain standard of taste and literary skill. So I quit. I am quite sure that she never understood why. An argument that there is relation between the expression and what is expressed, and that if the one is coarse the other is unlikely to be authentic, seemed to her a far away babble, for it was becoming less and less imperative for her to express herself. Hers was now to be rather than to do.

The paper lived some time after I left. It did a magnificent thing for literature in publishing James Joyce's *Portrait of the Artist as a Young Man*. Of its last days I cannot speak, for about that time ill-health fell on me and for long I was out of things. I have heard nothing of Dora Marsden for ten years or so. It may be that the wisdom she has obtained is not communicable, but I am sure to some far peak of wisdom she must have attained, and I cannot think that it is not good for the race when some of its component atoms reach projection, even if they cannot transmit it to their fellows. At any rate, Dora Marsden left us a heritage in the unembarrassed honesty of our times.

[15] Max Stirner (1806–56) was a German philosopher (real name Johann Kasper Schmidt) who wrote one important book, *Der Enizige und sein Eigentum* (1845), translated by S. T. Byington as *The Ego and His Own* (New York: E. R. Tucker, 1907). It was an early and extreme statement of philosophic egoism. Largely forgotten by 1890, it enjoyed an extraordinary revival thereafter. Between 1898 and 1907 it was translated into Russian, Italian, English, and, twice, French. Between 1909 and 1929, 49 edi-

tions of the work appeared. In English modernism its most important manifestation was in *The Egoist*, the title adopted in 1913 by the journal formerly known as *The Freewoman* and *The New Freewoman*. In its pages were published the serial versions of *Portrait of the Artist as a Young Man* and *Ulysses*. H.D. (see p. 441) and T. S. Eliot (pp. 113–14) both served as Assistant Editors for it.

[16] Ezra Pound; on him see pp. 39–112.

High Fountain of Genius (1928)

For once the important historical event is not happening two blocks away in time and space from where one is. One has to admit that to an observer on another star a person reviewing Virginia Woolf's *Orlando* must be in much the same position as those who went to their editors' offices and condescendingly offered to write a piece on this or that volume, if the space could be spared, as they thought well of this Keats, that Shelley.[1] There does not seem any reason at all to doubt that in this book has been issued a poetic masterpiece of the first rank; that is, a work which illuminates an important part of human experience by using words to do more than describe the logical behavior of matter, by letting language by its music and its power to evoke images convey meanings too subtle and too profound to be formulated in intellectual statements. It is written in prose; but that is a matter of the way marks fall on a page. Exploratory beauty, turning dark jungle into a safe habitation for the spirit, is here as it is in the work of the greatest of those who in the past used verse for their medium.

This is an important justification for our age, for it proves that there is nothing about the mental habit of the present generation which breaks the poetic tradition. For here is Virginia Woolf, most thoroughgoing of all skeptics, the archetype of self-consciousness, whose left lobe (which is critical) is obviously without cease letting her right lobe (which is creative) know what it doeth; and we find her committing herself to a theme which is as ambitious as any that author ever tackled in the great ages of faith when the truth was understood to lie no deeper under the surface of the earth than a man with Christian principles could dig and to have been buried that deep not from malignity of Providence but lest humanity should be deprived of its good medicinal work. Natural enough it would have been to choose it in those days, when it was believed that a stupid man could dig up so much truth, and a clever man could dig up so much more and a great man could bring up great sizable chunks of it at a time; and that people were getting cleverer and greater all the time, so that in due course we should all have the truth stored in the library just as the apples and potatoes are stored in the cellar. But to choose such a theme to-day is a heroism that one did not know could be performed.

For consider Mrs. Woolf as we know her, and reckon the forces that must have opposed that choice. She is fastidious, she is scholarly; she has infallible design, she is aware of all such designs as one might reasonably call perfect, she would not break her delightful occupation of contemplating such designs to create one of her own unless it forced her by its life to let it live. She knows, moreover, that such designs can be constructed out of trifles light as air, that Constant made *Adolphe* out of the couplings of two troublesome donkeys, that Chardin painted six pothecary bottles on a deal table, that Couperin's enduring music is made of sounds as non-indicative of permanence as the tinkle of ice against glass that breaks.[2] Indeed, she knows that to insist on such laxity of subject is an excellent prophylactic against failure, since it involves the artist in no intellectual discussion, seduces him into the service of no moral propaganda. Owing to certain troubles in the human family of late years she has no faith that the movements of its spirit lead up any staircase of progress. Man has more force than sense, and when he goes into the garden like as not he never goes near the truthbed but ceremonially uncovers some dead cat of dangerous myth that has been carried round the town a score of times already and on each procession killed scores with its unsanitary emanations. Nor is one sorry, seeing what a fool he is, and so insanitary in his ways, that maybe the cat is his true emblem and associate. Let us turn our eyes away to that Chinese painting, that Queen Anne sofa table, let us listen to the music of Scarlatti or Auric.[3]

HIGH FOUNTAIN
First published in the *New York Herald Tribune*, October 21, 1928, Books.

[1] John Keats (1795–1821) and Percy Shelley (1792–1822), British poets.

[2] The French writer Benjamin Constant (1760–1830) wrote his novel *Adolph, Anecdote trouvée dans les papiers d'un inconnu* in 1816; Jean-Baptiste-Siméon Chardin (1699–1799) was a French painter of still lifes and domestic scenes that often use humble objects; François Couperin (1668–1733) was a French composer who wrote superlative harpsichord pieces.

[3] Domenico Scarlatti (1685–1757) was an Italian composer; Georges Auric (1899–1983) was a French composer.

What would be a more ineluctable condemnation to the minor? – or, worse still, to such disorderly conflicts with their own creativeness as have temporarily overcome Mr. Aldous Huxley?[4] Notoriously the most fair-minded and honorably disposed person to his fellow man, he nevertheless continually makes statements about his own invented characters which have the poisonous quality of an anonymous letter. His individual creativeness forces him to invent these people and a good three dimensional world for them to inhabit and all would be beautiful and enduring art if it were not that the disillusionment which has been implanted in him by the age makes him loathe himself for adding quantitatively to life, for increasing the horrid sum of experience. Like the poor crazed anonymous letter-writer, he will not walk in the sunshine with his fellows, but dashes indoors, sits down in a back room and writes accounts of them full of fulminations over the undoubted fact that at certain times they are not a General Grant[5] in full uniform. If a talent as fine as Mr. Huxley's can be so handicapped by this age one might well have the greatest apprehensions as to the fate of literature until the philosophical barometer changes. But *Orlando* shows that the waters of genius, subjected to great pressure make a high fountain in the air.

Orlando is the story of a human being born in the days of Queen Elizabeth,[6] who is alive to-day and is about thirty-six years of age; and feels no ill consequences from having round about the middle of the eighteenth century changed from a man to a woman. This is fantasy, but those who object to it can go and knock on Shelley's tombstone and ask him to give an account of the percentage and early years of the Witch of Atlas[7] in the conscientious manner of Mr. Archibald Marshall.[8] To make this character Mrs. Woolf has compressed the successive generations of a famous family who still hold one of the most beautiful historic homes in England; and by making it she has been able to write an account of human experience during that period which historians call modern history: the last few hundred years, which are near enough for us to recognize their parentage of us. It was in the days of Queen Elizabeth that the contemplation of life as a whole became a possibility for our civilization. The political situation had settled down sufficiently for it no longer to be necessary for superior men to dedicate themselves wholly to action on the field or to scholarship within the Church; so there was there engendered the ideal of an aristocrat who could master life by participation in all of its noble activities, who fought, governed and was a patron of the arts. The battle between Nominalism and Realism had resulted in a working basis for philosophy; there were now enough concepts established in the mind of Europe to afford a basis for speculative thought and social action. The Reformation had, in a certain sense, brought peace to Europe by opposing channels to two different types of mind so that their floods no longer boiled together in the same tideway. Sheep's wool and wheat turned into gold with an alchemic efficiency not known before, and more flowed without need for alchemy from over the sea. The sum of things said "Go!" to man and he started on a race that is described in *Orlando*.

But this is no rhymed Buckle's *History of Civilization.*[9] A wine gives no factual information about the number of vines in the vineyard, where it was grown, or the ownership of the clos, or the process in the vats. Simply, it has a certain flavor, a certain fragrance, a certain body, which is the result of a certain inter-relation between grapes, rain, the sun and the human will. Even so Mrs. Woolf gives us certain poetic statements which convey to us the sum of the relationship between the *donnée* of each age and Orlando's fine perceptions. There is the quintessence of the Elizabethan age in the opening chapter that shows young Orlando in the attic of his gigantic house practicing the art of slicing at the mummified head of a Moor that his ancestor had brought home from the Crusades which still hung from the rafters; writing poetry in a copybook, and strolling out among the fields and oak-forests to a high place which is described by Mrs. Woolf with the frankest

[4] Aldous Huxley (1894–1963) was a British novelist and essayist, best known for his satirical novels *Crome Yellow* (1922) and *Point Counterpoint* (1928) at the time when West wrote this review.

[5] Ulysses S. Grant (1822–85) was a general of the Union forces during the American Civil War and became President (1868–76).

[6] Queen Elizabeth I (1533–1603) reigned from 1558 to her death.

[7] *The Witch of Atlas* was first published in 1824, two years after the death of Percy Bysshe Shelley (1792–1822).

[8] Archibald Marshall (1866–1934) was a contemporary British novelist and critic.

[9] Henry Thomas Buckle (1821–62) was the author of the *History of Civilization in England* (1856–61).

contempt for realism, with the profoundest reality. It is no photograph, it is as inexact a copy of appearances as tapestry, and one can see the stitches. Only it leaves in the mind a picture of Elizabethan England, which once apprehended will be incorporated in one like one's own experience. Standing on that high place he looks down on the dark congeries of his house, which has a room for every day in the year, and sees lights, hears trumpets, and runs down to meet the Queen, ricketty, brocaded, jeweled, smelling like a cupboard in which clothes are kept in camphor, royal, coming on an avaricious visit. As he runs, as he hurries to the banquet hall to kneel before her with a bowl of rosewater, as he afterwards enjoys her crabbed and languishing favors, as she looks on him through deluded and penetrating eyes, there is made visible the torture of Elizabethan life, the margin beside Elizabethan drama, the parchment on which all the complicated deeds of Elizabethan politics were signed by intriguers. It was like that, for one who lived sensitively to be living then. There was then that ideal of making life magnificent by ceremonial, by hanging gorgeousness on the wall and supporting the splendid arras by certain contrivances of negotiation, that passed later into a robust yet more cynical programme for existence, that here is told in the passage concerning the Great Frost. The Thames was frozen at Greenwich from bank to bank; the ice was laid out with arbors and alleys and drinking booths at the royal expense, and in an inclosure railed off by a silken rope, walked the court. Through the crystal by London Bridge one could look down on a bumboat woman sitting with her lap full of apples in a sunken wherry, her soul in another world. The ice broke one night. On a yellow flood ice floes carried cursing and praying citizens to doom. Interwoven with this account, which has the chapbook vision of prodigious nature, is the story of Orlando's passion for a Muscovite princess who was infinitely delicate and infinitely involved with the gross, who seemed finer than the women of his own country, who was akin to creatures of grease and lust and cruelty such as were never seen against the primness of green fields. The content of innumerable seventeenth century novels and memoirs is precipitated in this intricate pattern suggesting a society at once as matter-of-fact as saddle-of-mutton, round-mouthed at marvel, and in touch with barbarities of foreign courts that were as outcrops of the primitive soil of being. We know it was then that Defoe was writing;[10] as we know when Orlando becomes a woman, runs out to the moors and there in a transport at the winds, the heath, the scent of the bog myrtle, falls asleep with the wet feathers of a storm-tossed bird falling on her face, we know that this was the nature of human experience at the time when the Romantic movement was born, when Emily was conceiving *Wuthering Heights*.[11]

It is an epitome of all of us, it leaves us impaled, as we all are, on the mystery of the present moment. Mrs. Woolf enquires deeply into fundamentals and never more deeply than when she is most frivolous in form. People who like literalism will be most irritated, no doubt, by the passages in which Orlando changes her sex. But it is there that Mrs. Woolf shows exactly the magnificence of her power of transacting complex thought and perception on a plane of artistic creation. She is debating in these passages how far one's sex is like a pair of faulty glasses on one's nose; where one looks at the universe, how true it is that to be a woman is to have a blind spot on the North Northwest, to be a man is to see light as darkness East by South. She plays with the thought and its implications uncovering the existence of the absolute, the off-chance of there being an independent universe so that it is like a fall of fine lace at a lady's bosom, a tortoise shell tea-caddy inlaid with silver and ivory in which she dips her fine silver spoon that there may be something to pour into the Lowestoft teacup.[12] One is present, as one rarely is in literature, at the spectacle of a human being who can keep its power of expression running alongside its power of perception. There could be no more beautiful expression of this mystery of the present moment, our destiny never to be able to understand what is going on in the one moment when our will is called into play as we understand what happened in the past which our will cannot touch, than the presentation at the end of Orlando and her lover in purely romantic terms. They have been seen till then with the eyes of the author,

---

[10] Daniel Defoe (1660–1731) was a British novelist and author whose first important work, *An Essay upon Projects*, appeared in 1697.

[11] Emily Brontë (1818–48) published her novel *Wuthering Heights* in 1847.

[12] Lowestoft is a town on the southeast coast of England; from 1760 to 1802 it was the site of a porcelain-manufacturing firm that made distinctive blue and white hand-painted ware which is much esteemed by collectors.

with her individual vision, as individual beings. But on the last page, when they arrive at the present they are suddenly presented not as individuals but as types. For romantic art presents men and women simply, superficially as we see them in one dazed moment of contact with reality before reflection sets in, flatteringly, as we see them under the influence of our hope that the contact will not lead to harm, that every thing will turn out well.

The book is full of minute beauties; it is full of explanations of phases of being that have not before been visited by the writer. It demands careful reading and the completest consent to receive novelty. In fact, it has got to be read as conscientiously and as often as one would play over a newly discovered Beethoven sonata before one is satisfied one had got everything out of it that the composer had put in; which is a demand that literature is usually too humble to make. But if one complies with it one will have no anxiety about the effect of our critical age on the genuinely creative spirit.

What Is Mr. T. S. Eliot's Authority as a Critic? (1932)

Many who open the new volume of Mr. T. S. Eliot's *Selected Essays*, put forth in such sober and seemly form by Messrs. Faber and Faber, and who recognise the sober and seemly quality of its balanced sentences, may be incredulous if told that, to my mind at least, the years this American author has spent in England have inflicted damage on our literature from which it will probably not recover for a generation.

His appointment to the Chair of Poetry at Harvard[1] will probably inflict damage on American literature which will be only less because of the lesser time he intends to occupy it. Readers will be the more incredulous if they remember his poetry, which is indeed true and splendid poetry; and if they have read the section on Dante, which has been published separately and is of unsurpassed excellence in its field.

Yet the case against Mr. Eliot is strong. He came over here about the time of the war, when English criticism was at its low ebb, when – perhaps because politics exercised such a compelling force on many able minds – it was purely arbitrary and impressionist; and he came over with a defined position.

He had been born in the Middle West where all things are new. He had been to Harvard and fallen under the influence of Professor Irving Babbitt and Professor Paul Elmer More,[2] who have developed a movement known as Humanism, which attempts to correct the intellectual faults likely to arise in a community where all things are new.

Humanism

This movement very properly attempts to create as lively a respect as possible for the tradition and achievements of the past, and it is unfortunate that the limitations of its founders, which are so considerable as to counterbalance their undoubted learning, have reduced it to propaganda for a provincial conception of metropolitan gentility.

Its character can be deduced from the fact that Professor Irving Babbitt considers it a sign of naughty modernity to admire the pictures of Cézanne;[3] and that Professor Paul Elmer More once

---

MR. T. S. ELIOT

First published in the *Daily Telegraph*, September 30, 1932. A review of five books: *Selected Essays* (London: Faber & Faber, 1932), by T. S. Eliot; *Mr. Eliot among the Nightingales* (Paris: Lawrence Drake, 1932), by Louis Grudin; *The Poetry of T. S. Eliot* (London: Hodder & Stoughton, 1932), by Hugh Ross Williamson; *The Letters of D. H. Lawrence* (London: Heinemann, 1932), edited by Aldous Huxley; and *Etruscan Places* (London: Secker, 1932), by D. H. Lawrence.

[1] Eliot was appointed to the Charles Eliot Norton professorship at Harvard for the academic year 1932-3.

[2] Irving Babbit (1865–1933) was an American scholar who, from 1912 until his death, was professor of French literature at Harvard. Together with Paul Elmer More he initiated a movement called the New Humanisim, advocating a doctrine of restraint that looked to classical traditions and literature for inspiration. Paul Elmer More (1867–1937) was an American critic, educator, and philosopher.

[3] Paul Cézanne (1839–1906) was a French painter whose works were much studied and admired by artists at the beginning of the twentieth century.

counted the reference to women's hair in the poetry of Mr. W. B. Yeats and came to the conclusion that they were so numerous as to be unwholesome. Reading their works, one feels those who like to call trousers unmentionables have turned their attention to higher things.

But from these teachers Mr. Eliot learned certain facts; that no artist can be isolated, and none can hope to comprehend the present save in the light of the past, and that violence, confusion, and the presentation of unanalysed emotion are poor artistic technique. He was, throughout a period lasting some years, a most useful influence in English criticism.

He put forward certain fundamental truths which had been overlooked, and by his appearance of deliberation and trenchancy he encouraged others to cultivate these virtues in reality.

In recent years, however, Mr. Eliot's influence on English letters has been pernicious, for several reasons, which are manifest in this volume. He has made his sense of the need for authority and tradition an excuse for refraining from any work likely to establish where authority truly lies, or to hand on tradition by continuing it in vital creation.

Authoritative air

He registers himself as fastidious by crying out against violence, confusion, and the presentation of unanalysed emotion. But he appears unable to distinguish between these vices and vigour, the attempts to find new and valid classifications in place of old ones which have proved invalid, and the pressing of the analysis of emotion to a further stage; and there seems as often as not to be no discriminative process whatsoever working behind these repetitions of his formulæ.

The sober form of his sentences bears no relation to their content, which, as *Selected Essays* shows, often betrays lack of industry and flippancy, superficiality, and even vulgarity of thought.

It must be recorded that these defects are found in Mr. Eliot's work either together or not at all. When he has been industrious, as in his studies of Marlowe, Middleton, Heywood, Tourneur, Ford, and Massinger,[4] he is serious, helpful, and sensitive. But there are a number of essays in this volume which, since they are framed with an authoritative air, appear to propound meagreness as a standard of excellence.

In his essay on "Wilkie Collins and Dickens"[5] he records portentously the not surprising fact that, like the rest of God's creatures, he finds the thrillers of Wilkie Collins truly thrilling, though inferior as works of art to Dickens's novels; and in his three pages on Marie Lloyd[6] he does nothing but explain sententiously and with a trimming of inaccurate sociological generalisation that she was a low comedian.

We may wish to test our feeling and guard against the possibility that we owe it in part to the disparity between the excessive promise held out by Mr. Eliot's authoritative manner and a performance which is perhaps not below the normal; and there are two essays in this volume which permit us to apply a test. We can compare his essay on Swinburne[7] with the essay Mr. W. J. Turner contributed to a recently published volume on *The Great Victorians*;[8] and we can compare his essay on Baudelaire[9] with the essays on the same subject by Monsieur Paul Valéry and Mr. Aldous Huxley.[10]

[4]   Christopher Marlowe (1564–93) was an Elizabethan playwright and poet; Thomas Middleton (c. 1572)–c. 1632), was a Jacobean playwright; Thomas Heywood (c. 1573–1641) was a Jacobean playwright and poet who wrote a long epic on Troy; Cyril Tourneur (c. 1580–1626), John Ford (c. 1586–c. 1639), and Philip Massinger (1583–1640) were all Jacobean playwrights. Eliot's *Selected Essays* included pieces on all six men.

[5]   "Wilkie Collins and Dickens" is found in Eliot's *Selected Essays* (New York: Harcourt Brace, 1950), 409–18.

[6]   For the essay on Marie Lloyd, see pp. 163–5.

[7]   See Eliot's *Selected Essays* (New York: Harcourt Brace, 1950), 281–5.

[8]   See W. J. Turner, "Algernon Charles Swinburne," in Harold

John Massingham (ed.), *The Great Victorians* (London: Nicholson and Watson, 1932), 489–502.

[9]   For the original version of this essay on Baudelaire, see pp, 167–73; for the very lightly revised version that West is citing, see Eliot's *Selected Essays* (New York: Harcourt Brace, 1950), 371–81.

[10]   Paul Valéry (1871–1945), French poet and man of letters, wrote an essay in 1924 called "Situation de Baudelaire," which was then included in his volume *Variété* (Paris: Nouvelle revue française, 1924); see his *Oeuvres*, ed. Jean Hytier (Paris: Gallimard Pléïade, 1963), 598–613. Aldous Huxley (1894–1963), British novelist and essayist, wrote an essay on Baudelaire called "Baudelaire," which appeared in *Do What You Will: Essays* (London: Chatto & Windus, 1929), 171–202.

In each case it is as if we had taken a valuable watch into a watchmaker's shop and laid it on the counter, and a clever man with an impressive manner had picked it up and made some comment on its obvious qualities; and if, later, the watchmaker, making a close and careful examination, had reported in the light of his technical knowledge on its condition. Mr. Eliot is not the watchmaker.

Classical dons

That the vacuum left by his lack of industry is filled in too often by flippancy is proved on many pages, as when in a patronising paper on "Arnold and Pater"[11] he remarks of *Marius the Epicurean* that "its content is a hodge podge of the learning of the classical don, the impressions of the sensitive holiday visitor to Italy, and a prolonged flirtation with the liturgy."

One may judge just how silly an attack on *Marius* this is by considering how silly an attack it is to make on any book.

What is the matter with the learning of the classical don? In an ignorant world it does not come amiss. What is the matter with sensitiveness, or holidays, or visitors, or Italy? One might, if one chose, describe Dante's *Inferno* as the impressions of a sensitive holiday visitor to Hell. And one might, if one chose, apply not less roguish terms than flirtation to Mr. Eliot's own essay in religious controversy, "Thoughts after Lambeth."[12]

How flippancy is forced on Mr. Eliot by his lack of industry and his reliance on formulæ we may see in his dialogue on dramatic form,[13] in which he takes as specimen modern dramatists, Mr. Arlen and Mr. Coward.[14] It is not very clear why he selects Mr. Arlen for this purpose in face of his marked disinclination to write plays; and it is even less clear why he should say Mr. Coward's drama is one of "pure amusement" without an ethical motive.

There is possibly no other playwright, and few writers except Jeremiah and the author of Ecclesiastes, who are more inveterately didactic than Mr. Coward. His farces are tense with rage at the ill-mannered wastrels that enact them; he has never written a revue which is not interlarded with songs against the world, the flesh, and the devil as directly stated as any of Dr. Watts's hymns.[15] One is forced to conclude that Mr. Eliot has written about Mr. Coward without knowing much, or indeed anything, about him, and that he has simply gambled on the Babbitt-More formula that the present day is inferior in seriousness to the past.

This procedure is not legitimate; and its distorting effects can be judged from another essay, where Mr. Eliot sneers at the late William Archer for believing in the idea of progress.

He plainly implies that this proves Mr. Archer a crude and tasteless person of the sort that thinks a power station superior to Chartres Cathedral. But William Archer's idea of progress was something so profound and so shaped by spiritual effort that one would hardly expect the author of these facile essays to sympathise with it.

He believed that while it was the duty of every man to subject his will to any discipline which seemed likely to serve the higher aims of humanity, he must prevent himself from dominating the wills of any other human beings, lest they should be deprived from seeking their salvation in their own way; and he supposed – and it is not at all an unreasonable supposition – that it was easier for a man to prevent himself from committing this sin now than it has been in the past.

If we allow Mr. Eliot to dismiss this attitude with a sneer we are sacrificing our knowledge of real moral achievement for formulæ which can give us nothing in return, because they were invented for a totally different society.

---

[11] See Eliot's *Selected Essays* (New York: Harcourt Brace, 1950), 382–93; the sentence quoted by West is on 391.

[12] See Eliot's *Selected Essays* (New York: Harcourt Brace, 1950), 320–42.

[13] For "A Dialogue on Dramatic Poetry" see Eliot's *Selected Essays* (New York: Harcourt Brace, 1950), 31–45.

[14] Michael Arlen (1895–1956) was an author who wrote the phenomenally successful novel *The Green Hat* (1923), for

which he also wrote a dramatization; Noel Coward (1879–1973) was a playwright and author. Eliot, in the essay under discussion, takes note of the ethical motive in George Bernard Shaw, then writes: "This ethical motive is not apparent in Mr. Arlen or Mr. Coward. Their drama is pure 'amusement'" (32–3).

[15] Isaac Watts (1674–1768) is the greatest British writer of hymns.

That can be judged from the passage where Mr. Eliot triumphantly writes:

> Someone said: "The dead writers are remote from us because we know so much more than they did."
> Precisely, and they are that which we know.[16]

The retort is very neat, but who made the imbecile remark that provoked it? What lettered person in England imagines that it is not profitable to read dead writers and is unaware that many of these are superior to the living? Our error lies rather in the other direction, towards ancestral worship.

But there are people in the Middle West (though mercifully not many, and in diminishing numbers) who do talk like this, who honestly believe that Mr. Galsworthy[17] must write better than Chaucer because he was born to enjoy the benefits of electric lights and the automobile. To them, and not to us, Mr. Eliot should address his repetitions of formulæ, which have, indeed, no value whatsoever save for these localised heretics.

In *MR. Eliot Among the Nightingales* Mr. Louis Grudin[18] ably exposes the fundamental confusions of thought that prevent Mr. Eliot arriving at any valid critical conclusions; but this lively author presently passes into a discussion of aesthetics which, though it is fascinating to any adept in the subject, is discouraging to the lay mind.

The reader of this volume may take up with profit Mr. Hugh Ross Williamson's *The Poetry of T. S. Eliot*, where an able writer examines Mr. Eliot the poet with a sense and sensibility which Mr. Eliot the critic could never rival.

It is a relief to turn to writers who care not a fig for claiming authority, but who humbly perform the kind of task of discovery and analysis that continues the tradition of English literature.

Lawrence's letters

Here are the *Letters of D. H. Lawrence*, with a preface by Aldous Huxley which persuades one to give truce to one's feeling that it is time we all stopped reading about Lawrence and started reading Lawrence, so wise an exploration is it into the sources of a fountain of genius. Here are the letters themselves that are interesting not only in their glimpses of Lawrence as a creature that passed among ordinary human beings like an angel, sometimes with a sword, sometimes with a blessing. We see that the irascibility and suspicion which have been over-emphasised in some accounts of him were more than balanced by serenity and good sense.

But what makes the letters specially interesting is their revelation of how spontaneous in him was his sense of the beauty in nature.

It was pure, and utterly without that self-gratulatory tone which makes so many English poets seem to exclaim, "What a good boy am I!" as they put their thumbs in the pie of the countryside and pull out a hedge or a duckpond.

Lawrence did not cry out for law and order, and he could contemplate phases of disorder as a necessary part of growth. But he must have had a greater measure of order established within himself than most of us can claim when he could offer to nature a surface that could take such clear impressions as the exquisite landscapes in the letters, or in *Etruscan Places*, the record of his visit to the remains of the rich and vital civilisation that was wiped out by the Romans. It is a book which, if only for its description of the grey sea at Ladispoli, must be read by anybody who cares for living words.

---

[16] From the essay "Tradition and the Individual Talent," in Eliot's *Selected Essays* (New York: Harcourt Brace, 1950), 6.

[17] John Galsworthy (1867–1933), British novelist.

[18] Louis Grudin (1898–?) was an American poet and critic.

Continental Interlude III: Surrealism (1922–39)

Introduction

Of all the "-isms" that shaped or afflicted the arts of the twentieth century, none was as large or influential as Surrealism. Paradoxically, it was the most highly organized and tightly controlled of movements, and at the same time an utterly chaotic and perpetually improvised ensemble of agents and practices; it was an irreducibly local and even parochial affair, something transacted or enacted in a handful of cafés and other sites in Paris, and at the same time a phenomenon of international scope and breadth, comprising artists and authors and filmmakers from 30 or more nations. The key to these contradictions resides in the personality and activities of André Breton, the movement's founder or dominant voice.

André Breton (1896–1966) was born in Tinchebray in Normandy, France. His mother was a former seamstress, his father a ledger clerk in the local police force. His background, in short, was modest, and his later appetite for the exotic and the glamorous probably owed much to it. In 1900 his family moved to Pantin, an industrial northern suburb of Paris, where his father found employment as an accountant and later assistant manager in a glassworks. His literary inclinations manifested themselves early, and throughout his life he remained an omnivorous reader. With the coming of the First World War, he was drafted into the army, which posted him first to Nantes, then to a psychiatric center in Saint-Dizier in northeastern France, then to the front near Verdun, where he served as a stretcher-bearer, and finally to Paris, where in 1917 he met Louis Aragon. The two men shared intense literary aspirations and the experience of learning about the current literary scene. Breton was already in contact with Guillaume Apollinaire (1880–1918), the avant-garde poet and critic, Paul Valéry (1871–1945), the distinguished poet, and Pierre Reverdy (1889–1960), poet and editor of the fiercely independent journal *Nord-Sud* (founded 1917), in which some of Breton's earliest poetry would appear. It was in the apartment of Apollinaire that Breton first met the aspiring poet Philippe Soupault (1897–1900) and encountered the journal *Dada*, copies of which had been sent to Apollinaire by Tristan Tzara from Zurich. In early 1919 Breton came across Tzara's "Dada Manifesto 1918" (see pp. 479–84 in this edition), a work that left him profoundly impressed. Breton and Aragon were soon enthusiastic converts, and when Tzara moved to Paris a year later in early 1920 they greeted him with open arms. During the next two years the three men, along with Soupault and others, collaborated in producing theatrical events and performances that were both provocative and self-promoting. But

even these were not enough to consume Breton's restless energies. During the second half of 1920 he collaborated with Philippe Soupault in writing *The Magnetic Fields*, the first work of automatic writing for literary purposes.

It was in the course of 1922 that Breton began to lose interest in Dada, to regard it as a thing of the past (see "After Dada," pp. 498–9 in this edition). The future, instead, lay in automatism, or in that form of it which he first encountered in the spring of 1922, the "hypnotic slumbers" or trances in which people such as Robert Desnos would write or recite mysterious phrases that startled and disturbed, intrigued and attracted him (see "The Mediums Enter," pp. 742–6 in this edition). Two years later he wrote "The Manifesto of Surrealism" (see pp. 718–41 in this edition), a work that many consider the movement's foundation stone. It was also in 1924 that the "Bureau de Recherches surréalistes" ("The Office of Surrealist Research") and the journal *La Révolution surréaliste* were founded. Breton was now Surrealism's dominant voice, though by no means its only one. In the years ahead his chief works would include the memoir-diary-novel *Nadja* (1928) and the major prose experiments *The Immaculate Conception* (co-authored with Paul Eluard [1930]; for an excerpt see pp. 753–61 in this edition), *The Communicating Vessels* (1932), and *L'Amour fou* (*Mad Love*; 1937). He also wrote some important essays, including "Le Surréalisme et le peinture" (Surrealism and Painting"; 1926) and "Qu'est-ce que le surréalism?" ("What is Surrealism?"; 1934). And Breton's notion of automatism, which might seem to encourage a stultifying uniformity of style, was at first a very capacious concept, encompassing writings by figures as diverse as Robert Desnos (see pp. 746–9 in this edition) and Michel Leiris (see pp. 750–3 in this edition).

In December 1926 Breton, together with Aragon, Paul Eluard, Benjamin Péret, and newcomer Pierre Unik decided to join the Communist Party. What followed were five years of protracted wrangling about the relationship between art and politics and the conflicting demands of Surrealism and Communism. Louis Aragon broke away from Breton and Surrealism in early 1932 over questions about party loyalty and duty, while Breton himself left the party in 1935, appalled by its dogmatism and its defense of Stalinism.

The protracted wrangling over politics led to further divisions within Surrealism. In 1929 the librarian Georges Bataille founded a brief-lived journal called *Documents* (1929–30), and in 1933 he founded another, *Minotaur* (1933–9). These were conspicuous for concentrating on art and anthropology, and for carefully sidestepping the more contentious political questions that had tormented Breton and his friends. A great deal of recent scholarship has been devoted to this strain of so-called "dissident Surrealism" and there is much to be said for its serious engagement with issues of ethnography.

Surrealism's reverberations in the visual arts were immense, and the careers of Max Ernst, André Masson, René Magritte, Yves Tanguy, Joan Miró, Salvador Dalí, Dorothea Tanning, Frida Kahlo, Man Ray, and Alberto Giacometti are ample testimony to the range and diversity of effects that could be achieved within the rubric of Surrealism. When a colony of *emigrés* settled in New York during the early years of the Second World War, their contacts and influences were felt by artists as different as Robert Motherwell and Jackson Pollock.

Manifesto of Surrealism (1924)
André Breton

So strong is the belief in life, in what is most fragile in life – *real* life, I mean – that in the end this belief is lost.[1] Man, that inveterate dreamer, daily more discontent with his destiny, has trouble assessing the objects he has been led to use, objects that his nonchalance has brought his way, or that he has earned through his own efforts, almost always through his own efforts, for he has agreed to work, at least he has not refused to try his luck (or what he calls his luck!). At this point he feels extremely modest: he knows what women he has had, what silly affairs he has been involved in; he is unimpressed by his wealth or poverty, in this respect he is still a newborn babe and, as for the approval of his conscience, I confess that he does very nicely without it. If he still retains a certain lucidity, all he can do is turn back toward his childhood which, however his guides and mentors may have botched it, still strikes him as somehow charming. There, the absence of any known restrictions allows him the perspective of several lives lived at once; this illusion becomes firmly rooted within him; now he is only interested in the fleeting, the extreme facility of everything. Children set off each day without a worry in the world. Everything is near at hand, the worst material conditions are fine. The woods are white or black, one will never sleep.

But it is true that we would not dare venture so far, it is not merely a question of distance. Threat is piled upon threat, one yields, abandons a portion of the terrain to be conquered. This imagination which knows no bounds is henceforth allowed to be exercised only in strict accordance with the laws of an arbitrary utility; it is incapable of assuming this inferior role for very long and, in the vicinity of the twentieth year, generally prefers to abandon man to his lusterless fate.

Though he may later try to pull himself together upon occasion, having felt that he is losing by slow degrees all reason for living, incapable as he has become of being able to rise to some exceptional situation such as love, he will hardly succeed. This is because he henceforth belongs body and soul to an imperative practical necessity which demands his constant attention. None of his gestures will be expansive, none of his ideas generous or far-reaching. In his mind's eye, events real or imagined will be seen only as they relate to a welter of similar events, events in which he has not participated, *abortive* events.[2] What am I saying: he will judge them in relationship to one of these events whose consequences are more reassuring than the others. On no account will he view them as his salvation.

Beloved imagination, what I most like in you is your unsparing quality.

MANIFESTO

The "Manifesto of Surrealism" was published in October 1924, part of a small book which comprised the manifesto and "Soluble Fish," a prose poem meant to embody the automatic writing enjoined by the manifesto (Paris: Simon Kra, 1924). It was reprinted in 1929, preceded by a new "Preface" and complemented by a third work, "Letter to Seers." It appeared alone, without preface or "Soluble Fish," in two collections of manifestos that Breton oversaw in 1946 and 1955. The English translation here is from André Breton, *Manifestoes of Surrealism*, trans. R. Seaver and H. R. Lane (Ann Arbor, MI: University of Michigan Press, 1969), with corrections by the editor.

The essay's original notes are marked with asterisks.

[1]   The sentence adapts a French proverb, "Tant va la cruche à l'eau qu'à la fin elle se casse," or "So often does the pitcher go to the water that in the end it gets cracked." *Real* life is being distinguished here from *true* life.

[2]   Like actions that are abruptly cut off, such as those described by Sigmund Freud in *The Psychopathology of Everday Life*, which Breton knew in the French translation by S. Jankélévitch, *La Psychopathologie de la vie quotidienne* (Paris: Payot, 1922).

The mere word "freedom" is the only one that still excites me. I deem it capable of indefinitely sustaining the old human fanaticism. It doubtless satisfies my only legitimate aspiration. Among all the many misfortunes to which we are heir, it is only fair to admit that we are allowed the greatest degree of freedom of thought. It is up to us not to misuse it. To reduce the imagination to a state of slavery – even though it would mean the elimination of what is commonly called happiness – is to betray all sense of absolute justice within oneself. Imagination alone offers me some intimation of what *can be*, and this is enough to remove to some slight degree the terrible injunction; enough, too, to allow me to devote myself to it without fear of making a mistake (as though it were possible to make a bigger mistake). Where does it begin to turn bad, and where does the mind's stability cease? For the mind, is the possibility of erring not rather the contingency of good?

There remains madness, "the madness that one locks up," as it has aptly been described. That madness or another. . . . We all know, in fact, that the insane owe their incarceration to a tiny number of legally reprehensible acts and that, were it not for these acts their freedom (or what we see as their freedom) would not be threatened. I am willing to admit that they are, to some degree, victims of their imagination, in that it induces them not to pay attention to certain rules – outside of which the species feels itself threatened – which we are all supposed to know and respect. But their profound indifference to the way in which we judge them, and even to the various punishments meted out to them, allows us to suppose that they derive a great deal of comfort and consolation from their imagination, that they enjoy their madness sufficiently to endure the thought that its validity does not extend beyond themselves. And, indeed, hallucinations, illusions, etc., are not a source of trifling pleasure. The best controlled sensuality partakes of it, and I know that there are many evenings when I would gladly tame that pretty hand which, during the last pages of Taine's *L'Intelligence*,[3] indulges in some curious misdeeds. I could spend my whole life prying loose the secrets of the insane. These people are honest to a fault, and their naiveté has no peer but my own. Christopher Columbus should have set out to discover America with a boatload of madmen. And note how this madness has taken shape, and endured.

It is not the fear of madness which will oblige us to leave the flag of imagination furled.

The case against the realistic attitude demands to be examined, following the case against the materialistic attitude. The latter, more poetic in fact than the former, admittedly implies on the part of man a kind of monstrous pride which, admittedly, is monstrous, but not a new and more complete decay. It should above all be viewed as a welcome reaction against certain ridiculous tendencies of spiritualism. Finally, it is not incompatible with a certain nobility of thought.

By contrast, the realistic attitude, inspired by positivism, from saint Thomas to Anatole France,[4] clearly seems to me to be hostile to any intellectual or moral advancement. I loathe it, for it is made up of mediocrity, hate, and dull conceit. It is this attitude which today gives birth to these ridiculous books, these insulting plays. It constantly feeds on and derives strength from the newspapers and stultifies both science and art by assiduously flattering the lowest of tastes; clarity bordering on stupidity, a dog's life. The activity of the best minds feels the effects of it; the law of the lowest common denominator finally prevails upon them as it does upon the others. An amusing result of this state of affairs, in literature for example, is the generous supply of novels. Each person adds his personal little "observation" to the whole. As a cleansing antidote to all this, M. Paul Valéry recently suggested that an anthology be compiled in which the largest possible number of

[3]   Hippolyte-Adolphe Taine (1828–93) was a French philosopher, psychologist, historian, and critic, one of the leading positivistic thinkers in the second half of the nineteenth century. His theory of mind was presented in *De l'intelligence*, 2 vols. (Paris: Hachette, 1870).

[4]   St. Thomas is the sceptic who, in the gospel of John, refuses to believe that Christ has risen from the dead until he can see him and touch his wounds (see John 20:24–9). Anatole France

(1844–1924) was a distinguished French novelist. He died on October 12, 1924, and on October 18 there appeared *A Cadaver* (*Un Cadavre* [Neuilly-sur-Seine: Imprimerie speciale "Du Cadavre"]), a collective work with contributions by six Surrealist writers which damned France's work and achievement. Breton contributed a one-paragraph piece titled, "Refusal of Burial" ("Refus d'inhumer," now in André Breton, *Oeuvres complètes*, ed. Margueritte Bonnet [Paris: Pléiade], vol. 2 [1992], p. 281]).

opening passages from novels be offered; the resulting insanity, he predicted, would be a source of considerable edification. The most famous authors would be included. Such a thought reflects great credit on Paul Valéry who, some time ago, speaking of novels, assured me that, so far as he was concerned, he would continue to refrain from writing: "The Marquise went out at five."[5] But has he kept his word?

If the purely informative style, of which the sentence just quoted is a prime example, is virtually the rule rather than the exception in the novel form, it is because, in all fairness, the author's ambition is severely circumscribed. The circumstantial, needlessly specific nature of each of their notations leads me to believe that they are perpetrating a joke at my expense. I am spared not even one of the character's slightest vacillations: will he be fairhaired? what will his name be? will we first meet him during the summer? So many questions resolved once and for all, as chance directs; the only discretionary power left me is to close the book, which I am careful to do somewhere in the vicinity of the first page. And the descriptions! There is nothing to which their vacuity can be compared; they are nothing but so many superimposed images taken from some stock catalogue, which the author utilizes more and more whenever he chooses; he seizes the opportunity to slip me his postcards, he tries to make me agree with him about the clichés:

> The small room into which the young man was shown was covered with yellow wallpaper: there were geraniums in the windows, which were covered with muslin curtains; the setting sun cast a harsh light over the entire setting.... There was nothing special about the room. The furniture, of yellow wood, was all very old. A sofa with a tall back turned down, an oval table opposite the sofa, a dressing table and a mirror set against the pierglass, some chairs along the walls, two or three etchings of no value portraying some German girls with birds in their hands – such were the furnishings.[6]

I am in no mood to admit that the mind is interested in occupying itself with such matters, even fleetingly. It may be argued that this school-boy description has its place, and that at this juncture of the book the author has his reasons for burdening me. Nevertheless he is wasting his time, for I refuse to go into his room. Others' laziness or fatigue does not interest me. I have too unstable a notion of the continuity of life to equate or compare my moments of depression or weakness with my best moments. When one ceases to feel, I am of the opinion one should keep quiet. And I would like it understood that I am not accusing or condemning lack of originality *as such*. I am only saying that I do not take particular note of the empty moments of my life, that it may be unworthy for any man to crystallize those which seem to him to be so. I shall, with your permission, *ignore* the description of that room, and many more like it.

Not so fast, there; I'm getting into the area of psychology, a subject about which I shall be careful not to joke.

The author attacks a character and, this being settled upon, parades his hero to and fro across the world. No matter what happens, this hero, whose actions and reactions are admirably predictable, is compelled not to thwart or upset – even though he looks as though he is – the calculations of which he is the object. The currents of life can appear to lift him up, roll him over, cast him down, he will still belong to this *readymade* human type. A simple game of chess which doesn't interest me in the least – man, whoever he may be, being for me a mediocre opponent. What I cannot bear are those wretched discussions relative to such and such a move, since winning or losing is not in question. And if the game is not worth the candle, if objective reason does a frightful job – as indeed it does – of serving him who calls upon it, is it not fitting and proper to avoid all contact with these categories? "Diversity is so vast that every different tone of voice, every step, cough, every wipe of the nose, every sneeze...."[7] If in a cluster of grapes there are no two alike, why do you want me to

[5] Paul Valéry (1871–1945) was a distinguished French poet; his proposal was transmitted to Breton orally, though he also recorded it in his notebooks (see his *Oeuvres complètes* [Paris: Pléiade], vol. 2, p. 1162).

[6] Breton is quoting from the French translation, made by Victor Derély, of *Crime and Punishment* (1866), or *Le Crime et le châtiment* (1884), by the Russian novelist Fyodor Dostoyevsky (1821–81). The passage occurs in book I, ch. 1, only a few pages from the novel's beginning.

[7] Breton condenses one of the "thoughts" or *Pensées* of Blaise Pascal (1623–62), now in his *Oeuvres complètes* (Paris: Pléiade, 1954), p. 1095.

describe this grape by the other, by all the others, why do you want me to make a palatable grape? Our brains are dulled by the incurable mania of wanting to make the unknown known, classifiable. The desire for analysis wins out over the sentiments. The result is statements of undue length whose persuasive power is attributable solely to their strangeness and which impress the reader only by the abstract quality of their vocabulary, which moreover is ill-defined. If the general ideas that philosophy has thus far come up with as topics of discussion revealed by their very nature their definitive incursion into a broader or more general area, I would be the first to greet the news with joy. But up till now it has been nothing but idle repartee; the flashes of wit and other niceties vie in concealing from us the true thought in search of itself, instead of concentrating on obtaining successes. It seems to me that every act is its own justification, at least for the person who has been capable of committing it, that it is endowed with a radiant power which the slightest gloss is certain to diminish. Because of this gloss, it even in a sense ceases to happen. It gains nothing to be thus distinguished. Stendhal's heroes are subject to the comments and appraisals – appraisals which are more or less successful – made by that author, which add not one whit to their glory. Where we really find them again is at the point at which Stendhal has lost them.

We are still living under the reign of logic: this, of course, is what I have been driving at. But in this day and age logical methods are applicable only to solving problems of secondary interest. The absolute rationalism that is still in vogue allows us to consider only facts relating directly to our experience. Logical ends, on the contrary, escape us. It is pointless to add that experience itself has found itself increasingly circumscribed. It paces back and forth in a cage from which it is more and more difficult to make it emerge. It too leans for support on what is most immediately expedient, and it is protected by the sentinels of common sense. Under the pretense of civilization and progress, we have managed to banish from the mind everything that may rightly or wrongly be termed superstition, or fancy; forbidden is any kind of search for truth which is not in conformance with accepted practices. It was, apparently, by pure chance that a part of our mental world which we pretended not to be concerned with any longer – and, in my opinion by far the most important part – has been brought back to light. For this we must give thanks to the discoveries of Sigmund Freud. On the basis of these discoveries a current of opinion is finally forming by means of which the human explorer will be able to carry his investigations much further, authorized as he will henceforth be not to confine himself solely to the most summary realities. The imagination is perhaps on the point of reasserting itself, of reclaiming its rights. If the depths of our mind contain within it strange forces capable of augmenting those on the surface, or of waging a victorious battle against them, there is every reason to seize them – first to seize them, then, if need be, to submit them to the control of our reason. The analysts themselves have everything to gain by it. But it is worth noting that no means has been designated a priori for carrying out this undertaking, that until further notice it can be construed to be the province of poets as well as scholars, and that its success is not dependent upon the more or less capricious paths that will be followed.

Freud very rightly brought his critical faculties to bear upon the dream.[8] It is, in fact, inadmissible that this considerable portion of psychic activity (since, at least from man's birth until his death, thought offers no solution of continuity, the sum of the moments of dream, from the point of view of time, and taking into consideration only the time of pure dreaming, that is the dreams of sleep, is not inferior to the sum of the moments of reality, or, to be more precisely limiting, the moments of waking) has still today been so grossly neglected. I have always been amazed at the way an ordinary observer lends so much more credence and attaches so much more importance to waking events than to those occurring in dreams. It is because man, when he ceases to sleep, is above all the

---

8   Breton's familiarity with Freud's theory of dreams was indirect, since *Die Traumdeutung* (1900) or *The Interpretation of Dreams*
(1900) was not translated into French till 1926, when it became
La Science des rêves, trans. Ignace Meyerson (Paris: Alcan, 1926).
The first translation into Engish, by A. A. Brill, was published in
1913.

plaything of his memory, and in its normal state memory takes pleasure in weakly retracing for him the circumstances of the dream, in stripping it of any real importance, and in dismissing the only *determinant* from the point where he thinks he has left it a few hours before: this firm hope, this concern. He is under the impression of continuing something that is worthwhile. Thus the dream finds itself reduced to a mere parenthesis, as is the night. And, like the night, dreams generally contribute little to furthering our understanding. This curious state of affairs seems to me to call for certain reflections:

1) Within the limits where they operate (or are thought to operate) dreams give every evidence of being continuous and show signs of organization. Memory alone arrogates to itself the right to excerpt from dreams, to ignore the transitions, and to depict for us rather a series of dreams than the *dream itself*. By the same token, at any given moment we have only a distinct notion of realities, the coordination of which is a question of will.* What is worth noting is that nothing allows us to presuppose a greater dissipation of the elements of which the dream is constituted. I am sorry to have to speak about it according to a formula which in principle excludes the dream. When will we have sleeping logicians, sleeping philosophers? I would like to sleep, in order to surrender myself to the dreamers, the way I surrender myself to those who read me with eyes wide open; in order to stop imposing, in this realm, the conscious rhythm of my thought. Perhaps my dream last night follows that of the night before, and will be continued the next night, with an exemplary strictness. *It's quite possible*, as the saying goes. And since it has not been proved in the slightest that, in doing so, the "reality" with which I am kept busy continues to exist in the state of dream, that it does not sink back down into the immemorial, why should I not grant to dreams what I occasionally refuse reality, that is, this value of certainty in itself which, in its own time, is not open to my repudiation? Why should I not expect from the sign of the dream more than I expect from a degree of consciousness which is daily more acute? Can't the dream also be used in solving the fundamental questions of life? Are these questions the same in one case as in the other and, in the dream, do these questions already exist? Is the dream any less restrictive or punitive than the rest? I am growing old and, more than that reality to which I believe I subject myself, it is perhaps the dream, the difference with which I treat the dream, which makes me grow old.

2) Let me come back again to the waking state. I have no choice but to consider it a phenomenon of interference. Not only does the mind display, in this state, a strange tendency to lose its bearings (as evidenced by the slips and mistakes the secrets of which are just beginning to be revealed to us[9]), but, what is more, it does not appear that, when the mind is functioning normally, it really responds to anything but the suggestions which come to it from the depths of that dark night to which I commend it. However conditioned it may be, its balance is relative. It scarcely dares express itself and, if it does, it confines itself to verifying that such and such an idea, or such and such a woman, has made an impression on it. What impression it would be hard pressed to say, by which it reveals the degree of its subjectivity, and nothing more. This idea, this woman, disturb it, they tend to make it less severe. What they do is isolate the mind for a second from its solvent and spirit it to heaven, as the beautiful precipitate it can be, that it is. When all else fails, it then calls upon chance, a divinity even more obscure than the others to whom it ascribes all its aberrations. Who can say to me that the angle by which that idea which affects it is offered, that what it likes in the eye of that woman is not precisely what links it to its dream, binds it to those fundamental facts which, through its own fault, it has lost? And if things were different, what might it be capable of? I would like to provide it with the key to this corridor.

---

* Account must be taken of the *depth* of the dream. For the most part I retain only what I can glean from its most superficial layers. What I most enjoy contemplating about a dream is everything that sinks back below the surface in a waking state, everything I have forgotten about my activities in the course of the preceding day, dark foliage, stupid branches. In "reality," likewise, I prefer to *fall*.

9   Breton is drawing on Sigmund Freud, *Introduction à la psychanalyse*, trans. S. Jankélévitch (Paris: Payot, 1922) and *La Psychopathologie de la vie quotidienne*, trans. S. Jankélévitch, (Paris: Payot, 1922); their English counterparts were *General Introduction to Psychoanalysis*, trans. Stanley Hall (New York: Boni and Liveright, 1920) and *The Psychopathology of Everyday Life*, trans. A. A. Brill (London and New York: Macmillan, 1914).

3) The mind of the man who dreams is fully satisfied by what happens to him. The agonizing question of possibility is no longer pertinent. Kill, fly faster, love to your heart's content. And if you should die, are you not certain of reawaking among the dead? Let yourself be carried along, events will not tolerate your interference. You are nameless. The ease of everything is priceless.

What reason, I ask, a reason so much vaster than the other, makes dreams seem so natural and allows me to welcome unreservedly a welter of episodes so strange that they would confound me now as I write? And yet I can believe my eyes, my ears; this great day has arrived, this beast has spoken.

If man's awaking is harder, if it breaks the spell too abruptly, it is because he has been led to make for himself too improverished a notion of atonement.

4) From the moment when it is subjected to a methodical examination, when, by means yet to be determined, we succeed in recording the contents of dreams in their entirety (and that presupposes a discipline of memory spanning generations; but let us nonetheless begin by noting the most salient facts), when its graph will expand with unparalleled volume and regularity, we may hope that the mysteries which really are not will give way to the great Mystery. I believe in the future resolution of these two states, dream and reality, which are seemingly so contradictory,[10] into a kind of absolute reality, a *surreality*, if one may so speak. It is in quest of this surreality that I am going, certain not to find it but too unmindful of my death not to calculate to some slight degree the joys of its possession.

A story is told according to which Saint-Pol-Roux,[11] in times gone by, used to have a notice posted on the door of his manor house in Camaret, every evening before he went to sleep, which read: THE POET IS WORKING.

A great deal more could be said, but in passing I merely wanted to touch upon a subject which in itself would require a very long and much more detailed discussion; I shall come back to it. At this juncture, my intention was merely to mark a point by noting the *hate of the marvelous* which rages in certain men, this absurdity beneath which they try to bury it. Let us not mince words: the marvelous is always beautiful, anything marvelous is beautiful, in fact only the marvelous is beautiful.

In the realm of literature, only the marvelous is capable of fecundating works which belong to an inferior category such as the novel, and generally speaking, anything that involves storytelling. Lewis' *The Monk*[12] is an admirable proof of this. It is infused throughout with the presence of the marvelous. Long before the author has freed his main characters from all temporal constraints, one feels them ready to act with an unprecedented pride. This passion for eternity with which they are constantly stirred lends an unforgettable intensity to their torments, and to mine. I mean that this book, from beginning to end, and in the purest way imaginable, exercises an exalting effect only upon that part of the mind which aspires to leave the earth and that, stripped of an insignificant part of its plot, which belongs to the period in which it was written, it constitutes a paragon of precision and innocent grandeur.* It seems to me none better has been done, and that the character of Mathilda[13] in particular is the most moving creation that one can credit to this *figurative* fashion in literature. She is less a character than a continual temptation. And if a character is not a temptation, what is he? An extreme temptation, she. In *The Monk*, the "nothing is impossible for him who dares try" gives it its full, convincing measure. Ghosts play a logical role in the book,

[10] Breton's knowledge of Hegel, at this point, was mediated by the Italian philosopher Benedetto Croce (1866–1952), *Ce qui est vivant et ce qui est mort de la philosophie de Hegel*, trans. Henri Buriot (Paris: V. Giard and E. Brière, 1910), or *What is Living and What is Dead of the Philosophy of Hegel*, trans. Douglas Ainslie (London: Macmillan, 1915).

[11] Pierre-Paul Saint-Pol-Roux (1861–1940) was a French Poet.

[12] *The Monk* (1796) is a novel by Matthew Gregory Lewis

(1775–1818). It traces the diabolical decline of Ambrosio, a worthy Capuchin superior who is tempted by Matilda – a young girl who has entered his monastery disguised as a boy – and eventually succumbs to magic, murder, incest, and torture.

* What is admirable about the fantastic is that there is no longer anything fantastic: there is only the real.

[13] See note 12.

since the critical mind does not seize them in order to dispute them. Ambrosio's punishment is likewise treated in a legitimate manner, since it is finally accepted by the critical faculty as a natural denouement.

It may seem arbitrary on my part, when discussing the marvelous, to choose this model, from which both the Nordic literatures and Oriental literatures have borrowed time and time again, not to mention the religious literatures of every country. This is because most of the examples which these literatures could have furnished me with are tainted by puerility, for the simple reason that they are addressed to children. At an early age children are weaned on the marvelous, and later on they fail to retain a sufficient virginity of mind to thoroughly enjoy fairy tales. No matter how charming they may be, a grown man would think he were reverting to childhood by nourishing himself on fairy tales, and I am the first to admit that all such tales are not suitable for him. The fabric of adorable improbabilities must be made a trifle more subtle the older we grow, and we are still at the stage of waiting for this kind of spider. . . . But the faculties do not change radically. Fear, the attraction of the unusual, chance, the taste for things extravagant are all devices which we can always call upon without fear of deception. There are fairy tales to be written for adults, fairy tales still almost blue.

The marvelous is not the same in every period of history: it partakes in some obscure way of a sort of general revelation only the fragments of which come down to us: they are the romantic *ruins*, the modern *mannequin*, or any other symbol capable of affecting the human sensibility for a period of time. In these areas which make us smile, there is still portrayed the incurable human restlessness, and this is why I take them into consideration and why I judge them inseparable from certain productions of genius which are, more than the others, painfully afflicted by them. They are Villon's gibbets, Racine's Greeks, Baudelaire's couches.[14] They coincide with an eclipse of the taste I am made to endure, I whose notion of taste is the image of a big spot. Amid the bad taste of my time I strive to go further than anyone else. It would have been I, had I lived in 1820, I "the bleeding nun,"[15] I who would not have spared this cunning and banal "let us conceal" whereof the parodical Cuisin speaks,[16] it would have been I, I who would have reveled in the enormous metaphors, as he says, all phases of the "silver disk." For today I think of a *castle*, half of which is not necessarily in ruins; this castle belongs to me, I picture it in a rustic setting, not far from Paris.[17] The outbuildings are too numerous to mention, and, as for the interior, it has been frightfully restored, in such a manner as to leave nothing to be desired from the viewpoint of comfort. Automobiles are parked before the door, concealed by the shade of the trees. A few of my friends are living here as permanent guests: there is Louis Aragon leaving; he only has time enough to say hello; Philippe Soupault gets up with the stars, and Paul Eluard, our great Eluard, has not yet come home. There are Robert Desnos and Roger Vitrac out on the grounds poring over an ancient edict on dueling; Georges Auric, Jean Paulhan; Max Morise, who rows so well, and Benjamin Péret, busy with his equations with birds; and Joseph Delteil; and Jean Carrive; and Georges Limbour and Georges Limbours (there is a whole hedge of Georges Limbours); and Marcel Noll; there is T. Fraenkel waving to us from his captive balloon, Georges Malkine, Antonin Artaud, Francis Gérard, Pierre Naville, J.-A. Boiffard, and after them Jacques Baron and his brother, handsome and

[14]   Gibbets occur throughout the work of the French poet François Villon (1431–c. 1463), many of the characters in the plays of Jean Racine (1636–99) are Greek; a couch is conspicuous in the poem "La Mort des amants" ("The Lovers' Death" by Charles Baudelaire [1821–67]).

[15]   A character in chapter 4 of *The Monk* (1796), Lewis.

[16]   P. Cuisin (1777–1839) was the author of *Les Ombres sanglantes, galerie funèbre de prodiges, evénements merveilleux, apparitions nocturnes . . . puisés dans des sources réeles: Recuil propre à causer des fortes émotions de la terreur,* 2 vols. (Paris: chez Madame Ve Lepetit, 1820), a work which is supposed to parody the fashion for Gothic tales, but which is also admired by connoisseurs of the genre. The title in English reads: *Bleeding Shades, Funeral Gallery of Prodigies,*

Marvelous Events, Noteturnal Apparitions . . . taken from real sources: A Collection Apt to Cause Strong Emotions of Terror. In his "Introduction" Cuisin writes: " . . . You will not spare us the underhand and banal 'LET US PRETEND'; it will require great care to walk amid the long, menacing corridors, amid the dark tombs where the gleam of a dying lamp diffuses its green rays over a livid cadaver . . . , and scouring, in gigantic metaphors, all the phases of the Silver Disk, you find that the fairy tales are still standing." Breton came across this passage in an academic study by Alice M. Killen, *Le Roman terrifiant ou roman noir de Walpole à Anne Radcliffe et son influence sur la littérature française jusqu'en 1840* (Paris: Champion, 1924).

[17]   This is an imaginative construction, not a real one.

cordial, and so many others besides, and gorgeous women, I might add. Nothing is too good for these young men. Their wishes are, as to wealth, so many commands. Francis Picabia comes to pay us a call, and last week, in the hall of mirrors, we received a certain Marcel Duchamp whom we had not hitherto known. Picasso goes hunting in the neighborhood.[18] The spirit of *demoralization* has elected domicile in the castle, and it is with it we have to deal every time it is a question of contact with our fellowmen, but the doors are always open, and one does not begin by "thanking" everyone, you know. Moreover, the solitude is vast, we don't often run into one another. And anyway, isn't what matters that we be the masters of ourselves, the masters of women, and of love too?

I shall be proved guilty of poetic dishonesty: everyone will go parading about saying that I live on the rue Fontaine[*] and that he will have none of the water that flows therefrom. To be sure! But is he certain that this castle into which I cordially invite him is an image? What if this castle really existed! My guests are there to prove it does; their whim is the luminous road that leads to it. We really live by our fantasies when we *give free rein to them*. And how could what one might do bother the other, there, safely sheltered from the sentimental pursuit and at the trysting place of opportunities?

Man proposes and disposes.[19] He and he alone can determine whether he is completely master of himself, that is, whether he maintains the body of his desires, daily more formidable, in a state of anarchy. Poetry teaches him to. It bears within itself the perfect compensation for the miseries we endure. It can also be an organizer, if ever, as the result of a less intimate disappointment, we contemplate taking it seriously. The time is coming when it decrees the end of money and by itself will break the bread of heaven for the earth! There will still be gatherings on the public squares, and *movements* you never dared hope participate in. Farewell to absurd choices, the dreams of dark abyss, rivalries, the prolonged patience, the flight of the seasons, the artificial order of ideas, the ramp of danger, time for everything! May you only take the trouble to *practice* poetry. Is it not incumbent upon us, who are already living off it, to try and impose what we hold to be our case for further inquiry?

It matters not whether there is a certain disproportion between this defense and the illustration that will follow it. It was a question of going back to the sources of poetic imagination and, what is more, of remaining there. Not that I pretend to have done so. It requires a great deal of fortitude to try to set up one's abode in these distant regions where everything seems at first to be so awkward and difficult, all the more so if one wants to try to take someone there. Besides, one is never sure of really being there. If one is going to all that trouble, one might just as well stop off somewhere else. Be that as it may, the fact is that the way to these regions is clearly marked, and that to attain the true goal is now merely a matter of the travelers' ability to endure.

---

[18]   Louis Aragon (1897–1982) was a French writer and early Surrealist who later abandoned Surrealism and joined the Communist party, and who had a liaison with Nancy Cunard. Philippe Soupault was an early Surrealist writer, and together with Breton he wrote *Les Champs magnétiques* (1920), or *Magnetic Fields*, generally deemed the first surrealist work. Paul Eluard (1895–1952) was an early Surrealist and a major French poet. Together with Breton, he co-authored *The Immaculate Conception*, an excerpt from which is included here (see pp. 753–61). Robert Desnos (1900–45) was an early surrealist who later left the movement; a work by him appears here (see pp. 746–9). Roger Vitrac (1899–1952) was a Surrealist writer. Georges Auric (1899–1983) was a French composer; Jean Paulhan (1884–1968) was a French writer; Max Morise was a Surrealist artist; Benjamin Peret (1899–1959) was a Surrealist poet. Joseph Delteil (1894–1978) was a Surrealist writer who later left the movement. Jean Carrive was a minor French writer; Georges Limbour (1900–70) was a novelist who left Surrealism early. Marcel Noll

was a minor Surrealist; Théodor Fraenkel (1896–1964) was a friend of Breton and a doctor. Georges Malkine (1898–1970) was a French artist, an early supporter of Surrealism who left the movement. Antonin Artaud (1896–1948) was a major French dramatist. Francis Gérard was involved with Surrealism in its earliest days, but nothing more is known about him. Pierre Naveille (1903–93) was a poet, theoretician, and sociologist. Jacques-André Boiffard (1903–61) was a photographer whose photos play a conspicuous role in André Breton's major work, *Nadja* (1927). Jacques Baron (1905–86) was a poet, while nothing is known about his brother. Francis Picabia (1879–1953) and Marcel Duchamps (1887–1968) were prominent French artists, while Pablo Picasso (1881–1973) was a Spanish artist in a class of his own.

[*]   Breton's pun eludes translation: Fontaine = Fountain.–Tr.

[19]   A variation on a French proverb: "Man proposes and God disposes."

We are all more or less aware of the road traveled. I was careful to relate, in the course of a study of the case of Robert Desnos entitled "Entrée des médiums,"[20] that I had been "drawn to the phrases of varying length that, in complete solitude, as I was falling asleep, became perceptible to my mind, without my being able to find anything that might have predetermined them."[21] I had then just attempted the poetic adventure with the minimum of risks, that is, my aspirations were the same as they are today but I trusted in the slowness of formulation to keep me from useless contacts, contacts of which I completely disapproved. This attitude involved a modesty of thought certain vestiges of which I still retain. At the end of my life, I shall doubtless manage to speak with great effort the way people speak, to apologize for my voice and my few remaining gestures. The virtue of the spoken word (and the written word all the more so) seemed to me to derive from the faculty of foreshortening in a striking manner the exposition (since there was exposition) of a small number of facts, poetic or other, of which I made myself the substance. I had come to the conclusion that Rimbaud[22] had not proceeded any differently. I was composing, with a concern for variety that deserved better, the final poems of *Mont de piété*,[23] that is, I managed to extract from the blank lines of this book an incredible advantage. These lines were the closed eye to the operations of thought that I believed I was obliged to keep hidden from the reader. It was not deceit on my part, but my love of shocking the reader. I had the illusion of a possible complicity, which I had more and more difficulty giving up. I had begun to cherish words excessively for the space they allow around them, for their tangencies with countless other words that I did not utter. The poem BLACK FOREST[24] derives precisely from this state of mind. It took me six months to write it, and you may take my word for it that I did not rest a single day. But this stemmed from the opinion I had of myself in those days, which was high, please don't judge me too harshly. I enjoy these stupid confessions. At that point cubist pseudo-poetry was trying to get a foothold, but it had emerged defenseless from Picasso's brain, and I was thought to be as dull as dishwater (and still am). I had a sneaking suspicion, moreover, that from the viewpoint of poetry I was off on the wrong road, but I hedged my bet as best I could, defying lyricism with salvos of definitions and formulas (the Dada phenomena were waiting in the wings, ready to come on stage) and pretending to search for an application of poetry to advertising (I went so far as to claim that the world would end, not with a good book but with a beautiful advertisement for heaven or for hell).

In those days, a man at least as boring as I, Pierre Reverdy, was writing:

> *The image is a pure creation of the mind*
> *It cannot be born from a comparison but from a juxtaposition of two more or less distant realities*
> *The more the relationship between the two juxtaposed realities is distant and true, the stronger the image will be—*
> *the greater its emotional power and poetic reality...*[25]

These words, however sibylline for the uninitiated, were extremely revealing, and I pondered them for a long time. But the image eluded me. Reverdy's aesthetic, a completely a posteriori aesthetic, led me to mistake the effects for the causes. It was in the midst of all this that I renounced irrevocably my point of view.

One evening, therefore, before I fell asleep, I perceived, so clearly articulated that it was impossible to change a word, but nonetheless removed from the sound of any voice, a rather strange phrase which came to me without any apparent relationship to the events in which, my consciousness agrees, I was then involved, a phrase which seemed to me insistent, a phrase, if I may be so bold,

[20] An essay by Breton; for the text in this edition, see pp. 742–6; see the note there for publication information.

[21] See p. 742.

[22] Arthur Rimbaud (1854–91), French poet.

[23] French for *Pawnshop*, the title of Breton's first collection of poems, published in 1919 (Paris: Au Sans Pareil).

[24] For this poem in translation, see André Breton, *Earthlight*, trans. Bill Zavatsky and Zack Rogow (Los Angeles: Sun and Moon, 1993), p. 27.

[25] Pierre Reverdy (1889–1960) was a French man of letters; his essay, "L'Image" ("The Image"), which contained the passage quoted by Breton, appeared in *Nord-Sud* 13 (March 1918).

which was knocking at the window. I took cursory note of it and prepared to move on when its organic character caught my attention. Actually, this phrase astonished me: unfortunately I cannot remember it exactly, but it was something like: "There is a man cut in two by the window," but there could be no question of ambiguity, accompanied as it was by the faint visual image[*] of a man walking cut half way up by a window perpendicular to the axis of his body. Beyond the slightest shadow of a doubt, what I saw was the simple reconstruction in space of a man leaning out a window. But this window having shifted with the man, I realized that I was dealing with an image of a fairly rare sort, and all I could think of was to incorporate it into my material for poetic construction. No sooner had I granted it this capacity than it was in fact succeeded by a whole series of phrases, with only brief pauses between them, which surprised me only slightly less and left me with the impression of their being so gratuitous that the control I had then exercised upon myself seemed to me illusory and all I could think of was putting an end to the interminable quarrel raging within me.[**]

Completely occupied as I still was with Freud at that time, and familiar as I was with his methods of examination which I had had some slight occasion to use on some patients during the war, I resolved to obtain from myself what we were trying to obtain from them, namely, a monologue spoken as rapidly as possible without any intervention on the part of the critical faculties, a monologue consequently unencumbered by the slightest inhibition and which was, as closely as possible, akin to *spoken thought*. It had seemed to me, and still does – the way in which the phrase about the man cut in two had come to me is an indication of it – that the speed of thought is no greater than the speed of speech, and that thought does not necessarily defy language, nor even the fast-moving pen. It was in this frame of mind that Philippe Soupault – to whom I had confided these initial conclusions – and I decided to blacken some paper, with a praiseworthy disdain for

---

[*] Were I a painter, this visual depiction would doubtless have become more important for me than the other. It was most certainly my previous predispositions which decided the matter. Since that day, I have had occasion to concentrate my attention voluntarily on similar apparitions, and I know that they are fully as clear as auditory phenomena. With a pencil and white sheet of paper to hand, I could easily trace their outlines. Here again it is not a matter of drawing, *but simply of tracing.* I could thus depict a tree, a wave, a musical instrument, all manner of things of which I am presently incapable of providing even the roughest sketch. I would plunge into it, convinced that I would find my way again, in a maze of lines which at first glance would seem to be going nowhere. And, upon opening my eyes, I would get the very strong impression of something "never seen." The proof of what I am saying has been provided many times by Robert Desnos:[26] to be convinced, one has only to leaf through the pages of issue number 36 of *Feuilles libres* which contains several of his drawings (*Romeo and Juliet, A Man Died This Morning,* etc.) which were taken by this magazine as the drawings of a madman and published as such.

[**] Knut Hamsum[27] ascribes this sort of revelation to which I had been subjected as deriving from *hunger,* and he may not be wrong. (The fact is I did not eat every day during that period of my life). Most certainly the manifestations that he describes in these terms are clearly the same:

"The following day I awoke at an early hour. It was still dark. My eyes had been open for a long time when I heard the clock in the apartment above strike five. I wanted to go back to sleep, but I couldn't; I was wide awake and a thousand thoughts were crowding through my mind.

"Suddenly a few good fragments came to mind, quite suitable to be used in a rough draft, or serialized; all of a sudden I found,

quite by chance, beautiful phrases, phrases such as I had never written. I repeated them to myself slowly, word by word; they were excellent. And there were still more coming. I got up and picked up a pencil and some paper that were on a table behind my bed. It was as though some vein had burst within me, one word followed another, found its proper place, adapted itself to the situation, scene piled upon scene, the action unfolded, one retort after another welled up in my mind, I was enjoying myself immensely. Thoughts came to me so rapidly and continued to flow so abundantly that I lost a whole host of delicate details, because my pencil could not keep up with them, and yet I went as fast as I could, my hand in constant motion, I did not lose a minute. The sentences continued to well up within me, I was pregnant with my subject."

Apollinaire[28] asserted that Chirico's first paintings were done under the influence of cenesthesic disorders (migraines, colics, etc.).

---

[26] Robert Desnos (1900–45), French poet, was critical in the early gestation of Surrealism, fully engaged in various forms of automatism. His drawings appeared in *Feuilles libres* 35 (Jan.–Feb. 1924), not "36" as Breton reports.

[27] Breton is citing from a novel by the Norwegian writer Knut Hamsum (1856–1962), which was published in French as *La Faim,* trans. Edmond Bayle (Paris and Leipzig: Albert Langen, 1895), pp. 48–9; cf. the English translation of *Hunger,* trans. George Egerton (London: Smithers, 1899).

[28] Guillaume Apollinaire (1880–1918), French poet and critic who coined the word "surrealist" in the subtitle to his play, *Les Mamelles de Tirésias: drame surréaliste (The Breasts of Tiresias: Surrealist Drama);* it was in conversation with Breton that he discussed the Italian painter Giorgio de Chirico (1888–1978), whose early works were much admired by the Surrealists.

what might result from a literary point of view. The ease of execution did the rest. By the end of the first day we were able to read to ourselves some fifty or so pages obtained in this manner, and begin to compare our results. All in all, Soupault's pages and mine proved to be remarkably similar: the same overconstruction, shortcomings of a similar nature, but also, on both our parts, the illusion of an extraordinary verve, a great deal of emotion, a considerable choice of images of a quality such that we would not have been capable of preparing a single one in longhand, a very special picturesque quality and, here and there, a strong comical effect. The only difference between our two texts seemed to me to derive essentially from our respective tempers, Soupault's being less static than mine, and, if he does not mind my offering this one slight criticism, from the fact that he had made the error of putting a few words by way of titles at the top of certain pages, I suppose in a spirit of mystification. On the other hand, I must give credit where credit is due and say that he constantly and vigorously opposed any effort to retouch or correct, however slightly, any passage of this kind which seemed to me unfortunate. In this he was, to be sure, absolutely right.* It is, in fact, difficult to appreciate fairly the various elements present; one may even go so far as to say that it is impossible to appreciate them at a first reading. To you who write, these elements are, on the surface, *as strange to you as they are to anyone else*, and naturally you are wary of them. Poetically speaking, what strikes you about them above all is their *extreme degree of immediate absurdity*, the quality of this absurdity, upon closer scrutiny, being to give way to everything admissible, everything legitimate in the world: the disclosure of a certain number of properties and of facts no less objective, in the final analysis, than the others.[29]

In homage to Guillaume Apollinaire, who had just died and who, on several occasions, seemed to us to have followed a discipline of this kind, without however having sacrificed to it any mediocre literary means, Soupault and I baptized the new mode of pure expression which we had at our disposal and which we wished to pass on to our friends, by the name of SURREALISM. I believe that there is no point today in dwelling any further on this word and that the meaning we gave it initially has generally prevailed over its Apollinarian sense. To be even fairer, we could probably have taken over the word SUPERNATURALISM employed by Gérard de Nerval in his dedication to the *Filles de feu*.[30]** It appears, in fact, that Nerval possessed to a tee the spirit with which we claim a kinship, Apollinaire having possessed, on the contrary, naught but *the letter*, still imperfect, of Surrealism, having shown himself powerless to give a valid theoretical idea of it. Here are two passages by Nerval which seem to me to be extremely significant in this respect:

> I am going to explain to you, my dear Dumas, the phenomenon of which you have spoken a short while ago. There are, as you know, certain storytellers who cannot invent without identifying with the characters their imagination has dreamt up. You may recall how convincingly our old friend Nodier used to tell how it had been his misfortune during the Revolution to be guillotined; one became so completely convinced of what he was saying that one began to wonder how he had managed to have his head glued back on.
>
> . . . And since you have been indiscreet enough to quote one of the sonnets composed in this SUPERNATURALISTIC dream-state, as the Germans would call it, you will have to hear them all. You will find them at the end of the volume. They are hardly any more obscure than Hegel's

---

* I believe more and more in the infallibility of my thought with respect to myself, and this is too fair. Nonetheless, with this *thought-writing*, where one is at the mercy of the first outside distraction, "ebullutions" can occur. It would be inexcusable for us to pretend otherwise. By definition, thought is strong, and incapable of catching itself in error. The blame for these obvious weaknesses must be placed on suggestions that come to it from without.

** And also by Thomas Carlyle in *Sartor Resartus*[31] ([Book III] Chapter VIII, "Natural Supernaturalism"), 1833–34.

[29] Breton has been describing how he and Philippe Soupault, in 1920, co-authored *Les champs magnétiques*, the first literary work of automatic writing. See *The Magnetic Fields*, trans. D. Gascoyne (London: Atlas Press, 1985).

[30] *Les Filles de feu* (*Daughters of Fire*) were a series of novellas first published in 1854 by the French poet and writer Gérard de Nerval (1808–55), preceded by an important preface, which is what Breton is citing. More important, the volume also included the *Chimères*, a collection of 24 haunting but obscure sonnets, which is what Nerval is referring to in these comments.

[31] Book III, ch. 8 is titled "Natural Supernaturalism" in *Sartor Resartus* (1833–4 in serial form; 1836 in book) by Thomas Carlyle (1795–1881).

metaphysics or Swedenborg's MEMORABILIA, and would lose their charm if they were explained, if such were possible; at least admit the worth of the expression.... *

Those who might dispute our right to employ the term SURREALISM in the very special sense that we understand it are being extremely dishonest, for there can be no doubt that this word had no currency before we came along. Therefore, I am defining it once and for all:

SURREALISM, *n.* Psychic automatism in its pure state, by which one proposes to express – verbally, by means of the written word, or in any other manner – the actual functioning of thought. Dictated by thought, in the absence of any control exercised by reason, exempt from any aesthetic or moral concern.

ENCYCLOPEDIA. *Philosophy.* Surrealism is based on the belief in the superior reality of certain forms of previously neglected associations, in the omnipotence of dream, in the disinterested play of thought. It tends to ruin once and for all all other psychic mechanisms and to substitute itself for them in solving all the principal problems of life. The following have performed acts of ABSOLUTE SURREALISM: Messrs. Aragon, Baron, Boiffard, Breton, Carrive, Crevel, Delteil, Desnos, Eluard, Gérard, Limbour, Malkine, Morise, Naville, Noll, Péret, Picon, Soupault, Vitrac.[33]

They seem to be, up to the present time, the only ones, and there would be no ambiguity about it were it not for the case of Isidore Ducasse,[34] about whom I lack information. And, of course, if one is to judge them only superficially by their results, a good number of poets could pass for Surrealists, beginning with Dante and, in his finer moments, Shakespeare. *In the course of the various attempts I have made to reduce what is, by breach of trust, called genius, I have found nothing which in the final analysis can be attributed to any other method than that.*

Young's *Nights*[35] are Surrealist from one end to the other; unfortunately it is a priest who is speaking, a bad priest no doubt, but a priest nonetheless.

> Swift is Surrealist in malice,
> Sade is Surrealist in sadism.
> Chateaubriand is Surrealist in exoticism.
> Constant is Surrealist in politics.
> Hugo is Surrealist when he isn't stupid.
> Desbordes-Valmore is Surrealist in love.
> Bertrand is Surrealist in the past.
> Rabbe is Surrealist in death.
> Poe is Surrealist in adventure.
> Baudelaire is Surrealist in morality.
> Rimbaud is Surrealist in the way he lived, and elsewhere.
> Mallarmé is Surrealist when he is confiding.
> Jarry is Surrealist in absinthe.
> Nouveau is Surrealist in the kiss.
> Saint-Pol-Roux is Surrealist in his use of symbols.

* See also *L'Idéoréalisme* by Saint-Pol-Roux.[32]

32   Saint-Pol-Roux (1861–1940) was a French poet and man of letters. In an essay titled "Réponse périe en mer" ("Response Perished at Sea") which appeared in the *Mercure de France* (June 1, 1913), p. 501, he distinguished between three generations of poets which had appeared in the last 30 years: "idéiste" writers were those between 1885 and 1890, searching for the absolute; "idéoréaliste" were those who sought a synthesis of nature and art that would transform symbolism into "surnaturalism"; and the coming generation, whose task would be to achieve masterpieces.

33   All these names appear earlier in the "Manifesto" on p. 725; see note 18.

34   Isidore Ducasse (1846–70), Comte de Lautréamont, was a poet born of French parents in Uruguay. He adopted the pseudonym Comte de Lautréamont (Count of Lautréamont) and his major work was the prose poem *Les Chants de Maldoror* (*The Songs of Maldoror*; 1868), a work utterly unnoticed till it was rediscovered by André Breton and turned into a classic text for Surrealist writers.

35   Edward Young (1683–1765) was the author of *Night Thoughts* (1741), a volume that became a pre-Romantic classic.

Fargue is Surrealist in the atmosphere.

Vaché is Surrealist in me.

Reverdy is Surrealist at home.

Saint-Jean-Perse is Surrealist at a distance.

Roussel is Surrealist as a storyteller.[36]

Etc.

I would like to stress this point: they are not always Surrealists, in that I discern in each of them a certain number of preconceived ideas to which – very naively! – they hold. They hold to them because they had not *heard the Surrealist voice*, the one that continues to preach on the eve of death and above the storms, because they did not want to serve simply to orchestrate the marvelous score. They were instruments too full of pride, and this is why they have not always produced a harmonious sound.[*]

But we, who have made no effort whatsoever to filter, who in our works have made ourselves into simple receptacles of so many echoes, modest *recording instruments* who are not mesmerized by the drawings we are making, perhaps we serve an even nobler cause. Thus do we render with integrity the "talent" which has been lent to us. You might as well speak of the talent of this platinum ruler, this mirror, this door, and of the sky, if you like.

We do not have any talent; ask Philippe Soupault:

> "*Anatomical products of manufacture and low-income dwellings will destroy the tallest cities.*"[39]

Ask Roger Vitrac:

> "*No sooner had I called forth the marble-admiral than he turned on his heel like a horse which rears at the sight of the North star and showed me, in the plane of his two-pointed cocked hat, a region where I was to spend my life.*"

Ask Paul Eluard:[40]

> "*This is an oft-told tale that I tell, a famous poem that I reread: I am leaning against a wall, with my verdant ears and my lips burned to a crisp.*"

Ask Max Morise:[41]

---

[*] I could say the same of a number of philosophers and painters, including, among these latter, Uccello,[37] from painters of the past, and, in the modern era, Seurat, Gustave Moreau, Matisse (in "La Musique," for example). Derain, Picasso, (by far the most pure), Braque, Duchamp, Picabia, Chirico (so admirable for so long), Klee, Man Ray, Max Ernst, and, one so close to us, André Masson.[38]

[36] Jonathan Swift (1666–1745) was a British divine and author. The Marquis de Sade (1740–1814) was a French novelist; François-René Chateaubriand (1768–1848) was a French romantic poet; Benjamin Constant (1767–1839) was a French novelist and poet; Victor Hugo (1802–84) was a dramatist, poet, and novelist. Marceline Desbordes-Valmore was a woman and writer of love poems. Aloysius Bertrand (1807–41) was the author of *Gaspard de la nuit* and the inventor of the prose poem. Alphonse Rabbe (1776–1830) was a historian and pessimistic philosopher. Edgar Allan Poe (1809–49) was an American writer of poems, short stories, and novels. Charles Baudelaire (1821–67) was the most influential poet of the nineteenth century. Arthur Rimbaud (1854–91) was a French symbolist poet. Stephan Mallarmé (1842–98) was a late symbolist poet in France. Alfred Jarry (1873–1907) was a French dramatist. Saint-Pol-Roux (1861–1940) was a French poet and man of letters. Léon-Paul

Fargue (1867–1947) was a French novelist and critic. Jacques Vaché was a friend of André Breton who died during the First World War. Pierre Reverdy (1889–1960) was a French critic and man of letters. Saint-Jean Perse (1887–1975) was a French poet; Raymond Roussel (1877–1933) was a Surrealist writer.

[37] Paolo di Dono, known as Paolo Uccello (1397–1475), was a Florentine painter and mosaicist.

[38] Georges Seurat (1859–91), Gustave Moreau (1826–98), Henri Mattise (1869–1954), André Derain (1880–1954), Georges Braque (1882–1963), and André Masson (1896–1987) – all were French painters. Man Ray (1890–1976) was an American photographer; Paul Klee (1879–1940) was a Swiss artist who worked in Paris; and Max Ernst (1891–1976) was a German artist who became one of the major Surrealist artists.

[39] From "In 80 Days," a portion of *Champs magnétiques*; see André Breton and Philippe Soupault, *The Magnetic Fields*, trans. David Gascoyne (London: Atlas, 1985), p. 55.

[40] These two texts by Vitrac and Eluard have not been identified either in their authors' published writings or in Breton's archive.

[41] This passage was published under the rubric "Surrealist Texts" in the journal *La Révolution surréaliste*, 1 (Dec. 1, 1924): 15.

"The bear of the caves and his friend the bittern, the vol-au-vent and his valet the wind, the Lord Chancellor with his Lady, the scarecrow for sparrows and his accomplice the sparrow, the test tube and his daughter the needle, this carnivore and his brother the carnival, the sweeper and his monocle, the Mississippi and its little dog, the coral and its jug of milk, the Miracle and its Good Lord, might just as well go and disappear from the surface of the sea."

Ask Joseph Delteil:

"Alas! I believe in the virtue of birds. And a feather is all it takes to make me die laughing."

Ask Louis Aragon:[42]

"During a short break in the party, as the players were gathering around a bowl of flaming punch, I asked the tree if it still had its red ribbon."

And ask me, who was unable to keep myself from writing the serpentine, distracting lines of this preface.[43]

Ask Robert Desnos, he who, more than any of us, has perhaps got closest to the Surrealist truth, he who, in his still unpublished works[*] and in the course of the numerous experiments he has been a party to, has fully justified the hope I placed in Surrealism and leads me to believe that a great deal more will still come of it. Desnos *speaks Surrealist* at will. His extraordinary agility in orally following his thought is worth as much to us as any number of splendid speeches which are lost, Desnos having better things to do than record them. He reads himself like an open book, and does nothing to retain the pages, which fly away in the windy wake of his life.

SECRETS OF THE MAGICAL SURREALIST ART[45]

Written Surrealist composition or first and last draft

After you have settled yourself in a place as favorable as possible to the concentration of your mind upon itself, have writing materials brought to you. Put yourself in as passive, or receptive, a state of mind as you can. Forget about your genius, your talents, and the talents of everyone else. Keep reminding yourself that literature is one of the saddest roads that leads to everything. Write quickly, without any preconceived subject, fast enough so that you will not remember what you're writing and be tempted to reread what you have written. The first sentence will come spontaneously, so compelling is the truth that with every passing second there is a sentence unknown to our consciousness which is only crying out to be heard. It is somewhat of a problem to form an opinion about the next sentence; it doubtless partakes both of our conscious activity and of the other, if one agrees that the fact of having written the first entails a minimum of perception. This should be of no importance to you, however; to a large extent, this is what is most interesting and intriguing about the Surrealist game. The fact still remains that punctuation no doubt resists the absolute continuity of the flow with which we are concerned, although it may seem as necessary as the arrangement of knots in a vibrating cord. Go on as long as you like. Put your trust in the inexhaustible nature of the murmur. If silence threatens to settle in if you should ever happen to make a mistake – a mistake, perhaps due to carelessness – break off without hesitation with an overly clear line. Following a word the origin of which seems suspicious to you, place any letter

---

[*] NOUVELLES HÉBRIDES, DÉSORDRE FORMEIL, DEUIL POUR DEUIL.[44]

[42] These texts by Delteil and Aragon have not been identified either in their authors' published writings or in Breton's archive.
[43] This phrase reminds the reader that the "Manifesto" was originally conceived as a "preface" for "Soluble Fish" which, in the first printing of the manifesto, followed in the same volume.
[44] Of the three works mentioned here, only *Deuil pour deuil* was published in December 1924. The one titled *Nouvelles Hébrides*,

more correctly titled *Pénalités de l'Enfer ou Nouvelles Hébrides*, was finally published in 1978 in a volume of writings by Desnos called *Nouvelles Hébrides et autres textes, 1922–1930*, ed. Marie-Claire Dumas (Paris: Gallimard, 1978). The third title, "Désordre formel," was never completed, but was published as it stood in 1930 in Robert Desnos, *Corps et biens* (Paris: Gallimard, Éditions de la "Nouvelle Revue Française").
[45] The structure and style of this section derive from cheap and popular books sold door-to-door.

whatsoever, the letter "l" for example, always the letter "l," and bring the arbitrary back by making this letter the first of the following word.

How not to be bored any longer when with others

This is very difficult. Don't be at home for anyone, and occasionally, when no one has forced his way in, interrupting you in the midst of your Surrealist activity, and you, crossing your arms, say: "It doesn't matter, there are doubtless better things to do or not do. Interest in life is indefensible. Simplicity, what is going on inside me, is still tiresome to me!" or any other revolting banality.

To make speeches

Just prior to the elections, in the first country which deems it worthwhile to proceed in this kind of public expression of opinion, have yourself put on the ballot. Each of us has within himself the potential of an orator: multicolored loin cloths, glass trinkets of words. Through Surrealism he will take despair unawares in its poverty. One night, on a stage, he will, by himself, carve up the eternal heaven, that *Peau de l'ours*. He will promise so much that any promises he keeps will be a source of wonder and dismay. In answer to the claims of an entire people he will give a partial and ludicrous vote. He will make the bitterest enemies partake of a secret desire which will blow up the countries. And in this he will succeed simply by allowing himself to be moved by the immense word which dissolves into pity and revolves in hate. Incapable of failure, he will play on the velvet of all failures. He will be truly elected, and women will love him with an all-consuming passion.

To write false novels

Whoever you may be, if the spirit moves you burn a few laurel leaves and, without wishing to tend this meager fire, you will begin to write a novel. Surrealism will allow you to: all you have to do is set the needle marked "fair" at "action," and the rest will follow naturally. Here are some characters rather different in appearance; their names in your handwriting are a question of capital letters, and they will conduct themselves with the same ease with respect to active verbs as does the impersonal pronoun "it" with respect to words such as "is raining," "is," "must," etc. They will command them, so to speak, and wherever observation, reflection, and the faculty of generalization prove to be of no help to you, you may rest assured that they will credit you with a thousand intentions you never had. Thus endowed with a tiny number of physical and moral characteristics, these beings who in truth owe you so little will thereafter deviate not one iota from a certain line of conduct about which you need not concern yourself any further. Out of this will result a plot more or less clever in appearance, justifying point by point this moving or comforting denouement about which you couldn't care less. Your false novel will simulate to a marvelous degree a real novel; you will be rich, and everyone will agree that "you've really got a lot of guts," since it's also in this region that this something is located.

Of course, by an analogous method, and provided you ignore what you are reviewing, you can successfully devote yourself to false literary criticism.

How to catch the eye of a woman you pass in the street

.   .   .   .

.   .   .   .

.   .   .   .

.   .   .   .

.   .   .   .

Against death

Surrealism will usher you into death, which is a secret society. It will glove your hand, burying therein the profound M with which the word Memory begins. Do not forget to make proper arrangements for your last will and testament: speaking personally, I ask that I be taken to the cemetery in a moving van.[46] May my friends destroy every last copy of the printing of the "Discourse on the Paucity of Reality."[47]

Language has been given to man so that he may make Surrealist use of it. To the extent that he is required to make himself understood, he manages more or less to express himself, and by so doing to fulfill certain functions culled from among the most vulgar. Speaking, reading a letter, present no real problem for him, provided that, in so doing, he does not set himself a goal above the mean, that is, provided he confines himself to carrying on a conversation (for the pleasure of conversing) with someone. He is not worried about the words that are going to come, nor about the sentence which will follow after the sentence he is just completing. To a very simple question, he will be capable of making a lightning-like reply. In the absence of minor tics acquired through contact with others, he can without any ado offer an opinion on a limited number of subjects; for that he does not need to "count up to ten" before speaking or to formulate anything whatever ahead of time. Who has been able to convince him that this faculty of the first draft will only do him a disservice when he makes up his mind to establish more delicate relationships? There is no subject about which he should refuse to talk, to write about prolifically. All that results from listening to oneself, from reading what one has written, is the suspension of the occult, that admirable help. I am in no hurry to understand myself (basta! I shall always understand myself). If such and such a sentence of mine turns out to be somewhat disappointing, at least momentarily, I place my trust in the following sentence to redeem its sins: I carefully refrain from starting it over again or polishing it. The only thing that might prove fatal to me would be the slightest loss of impetus. Words, groups of words *which follow one another*, manifest among themselves the greatest solidarity. It is not up to me to favor one group over the other. It is up to a miraculous equivalent to intervene – and intervene it does.

Not only does this unrestricted language, which I am trying to render forever valid, which seems to me to adapt itself to all of life's circumstances, not only does this language not deprive me of any of my means, on the contrary it lends me an extraordinary lucidity, and it does so in an area where I least expected it. I shall even go so far as to maintain that it instructs me and, indeed, I have had occasion to use *surreally* words whose meaning I have forgotten. I was subsequently able to verify that the way in which I had used them corresponded perfectly with their definition. This would lead one to believe that we do not "learn," that all we ever do is "relearn."[48] There are felicitous turns of speech that I have thus familiarized myself with. And I am not talking about the *poetic consciousness of objects* which I have been able to acquire only after a spiritual contact with them repeated a thousand times over.

[46]   Moving vans appear in two paintings by de Chirico that Breton especially liked, *The Enigma of a Day* (1914) and *Melancholy and Mystery of a Street* (1914). In modern Greek, moving vans are literally called "metaphors."

[47]   The "Discours sur le peu de réalite" (or "Discourse on the Paucity of Reality") was finally published in *Point du Jour* (1934), a collection of essays by Breton.

[48]   Socrates articulates this ideal that all learning is really recalling, "relearning," in the *Menon*, a dialogue by Plato.

The forms of Surrealist language adapt themselves best to dialogue. Here, two thoughts confront each other; while one is being delivered, the other is busy with it; but how is it busy with it? To assume that it incorporates it within itself would be tantamount to admitting that there is a time during which it is possible for it to live completely off that other thought, which is highly unlikely. And, in fact, the attention it pays is completely exterior; it has only time enough to approve or reject – generally reject – with all the consideration of which man is capable. This mode of language, moreover, does not allow the heart of the matter to be plumbed. My attention, prey to an entreaty which it cannot in all decency reject, treats the opposing thought as an enemy; in ordinary conversation, it "takes it up" almost always on the words, the figures of speech, it employs; it puts me in a position to turn it to good advantage in my reply by distorting them. This is true to such a degree that in certain pathological states of mind, where the sensorial disorders occupy the patient's complete attention, he limits himself, while continuing to answer the questions, to seizing the last word spoken in his presence or the last portion of the Surrealist sentence some trace of which he finds in his mind.

Q. "How old are you?" A. "You." *(Echolalia.)*
Q. "What is your name?" A. "Forty-five houses." *(Ganser syndrome,*[49] *or beside-the-point replies.)*

There is no conversation in which some trace of this disorder does not occur. The effort to be social which dictates it and the considerable practice we have at it are the only things which enable us to conceal it temporarily. It is also the great weakness of the book that it is in constant conflict with its best, by which I mean the most demanding, readers. In the very short dialogue that I concocted above between the doctor and the madman, it was in fact the madman who got the better of the exchange. Because, through his replies, he obtrudes upon the attention of the doctor examining him – and because he is not the person asking the questions. Does this mean that his thought at this point is the stronger? Perhaps. He is free not to care any longer about his age or name.

Poetic Surrealism, which is the subject of this study, has focused its efforts up to this point on reestablishing dialogue in its absolute truth, by freeing both interlocutors from any obligations of politeness. Each of them simply pursues his soliloquy without trying to derive any special dialectical pleasure from it and without trying to impose anything whatsoever upon his neighbor. The remarks exchanged are not, as is generally the case, meant to develop some thesis, however unimportant it may be; they are as disaffected as possible. As for the reply that they elicit, it is, in principle, totally indifferent to the personal pride of the person speaking. The words, the images are only so many springboards for the mind of the listener. In *Les Champs magnétiques,*[50] the first purely Surrealist work, this is the way in which the pages grouped together under the title *Barrières* must be conceived of – pages wherein Soupault and I show ourselves to be impartial interlocutors.[51]

Surrealism does not allow those who devote themselves to it to forsake it whenever they like. There is every reason to believe that it acts on the mind very much as drugs do; like drugs, it creates a certain state of need and can push man to frightful revolts. It also is, if you like, an artificial paradise, and the taste one has for it derives from Baudelaire's criticism for the same reason as the others. Thus the analysis of the mysterious effects and special pleasures it can produce – in many respects Surrealism occurs as a *new vice* which does not necessarily seem to be restricted to the happy few; like hashish, it has the ability to satisfy all manner of tastes – such an analysis has to be included in the present study.

[49] The German psychiatrist Sigbert Ganser first described Ganser syndrome while studying prisoners in 1898.
[50] *Les Champs magnétiques* was written and published by André Breton and Philippe Soupault in 1920. (For an English translation, see *The Magnetic Fields*, trans. David Gascoyne (London: Atlas, 1985). It is the first work of automatic writing for purely literary purposes, and was considered by Breton and others to be the first work of Surrealism, even though it antedated the "Manifesto of Surrealism" by 4 years.
[51] *Barrières* is found on pp. 52–79 of *Magnetic Fields*. See preceeding note.

1. It is true of Surrealist images as it is of opium images that man does not evoke them; rather they "come to him spontaneously, despotically. He cannot chase them away; for the will is powerless now and no longer controls the faculties."[52] It remains to be seen whether images have ever been "evoked." If one accepts, as I do, Reverdy's definition it does not seem possible to bring together, voluntarily, what he calls "two distant realities." The juxtaposition is made or not made, and that is the long and the short of it. Personally, I absolutely refuse to believe that, in Reverdy's work, images such as

In the brook, there is a song that flows[53]

or:

Day unfolded like a white tablecloth[54]

or:

The world goes back into a sack[55]

reveal the slightest degree of premeditation. In my opinion, it is erroneous to claim that "the mind has grasped the relationship" of two realities in the presence of each other. First of all, it has seized nothing consciously. It is, as it were, from the fortuitous juxtaposition of the two terms that a particular light has sprung, *the light of the image*, to which we are infinitely sensitive. The value of the image depends upon the beauty of the spark obtained; it is, consequently, a function of the difference of potential between the two conductors. When the difference exists only slightly, as in a comparison,* the spark is lacking. Now, it is not within man's power, so far as I can tell, to effect the juxtaposition of two realities so far apart. The principle of the association of ideas, such as we conceive of it, militates against it. Or else we would have to revert to an elliptical art, which Reverdy deplores as much as I. We are therefore obliged to admit that the two terms of the image are not deduced one from the other by the mind for the specific purpose of producing the spark, that they are the simultaneous products of the activity I call Surrealist, reason's role being limited to taking note of, and appreciating, the luminous phenomenon.

And just as the length of the spark increases to the extent that it occurs in rarefied gases, the Surrealist atmosphere created by automatic writing, which I have wanted to put within the reach of everyone, is especially conducive to the production of the most beautiful images. One can even go so far as to say that in this dizzying race the images appear like the only guideposts of the mind. By slow degrees the mind becomes convinced of the supreme reality of these images. At first limiting itself to submitting to them, it soon realizes that they flatter its reason, and increase its knowledge accordingly. The mind becomes aware of the limitless expanses wherein its desires are made manifest, where the pros and cons are constantly consumed, where its obscurity does not betray it. It goes forward, borne by these images which enrapture it, which scarcely leave it any time to blow upon the fire in its fingers. This is the most beautiful night of all, the *lightning-filled night*: day, compared to it, is night.

The countless kinds of Surrealist images would require a classification which I do not intend to make today. To group them according to their particular affinities would lead me far afield; what I basically want to mention is their common virtue. For me, their greatest virtue, I must confess, is the one that is arbitrary to the highest degree, the one that takes the longest time to translate into practical language, either because it contains an immense amount of seeming contradiction or

---

* Compare the image in the work of Jules Renard.[56]

52 [Breton's note:] Baudelaire. [Editor's note:] Baudelaire makes this observation in *Paradis arificiels*, the second part, "Un Mangeur d'opium," IV, "Tortures de l'opium."
53 From the poem "Surprise d'en haut" in Pierre Reverdy, *Plupart du temps; poèmes 1915–1922* (Paris: Gallimard, 1945), p. 125.

54 From the poem "Glaçon dans l'air" in Pierre Reverdy, *Plupart du temps* (Paris: Flammarion, 1967), p. 368.
55 From the poem "L'Ombre du mur" in Pierre Reverdy, *Plupart du temps* (Paris: Flammarion, 1967), p. 204.
56 Jules Renard (1864–1910), French poet and man of letters.

because one of its terms is strangely concealed; or because, presenting itself as something sensational, it seems to end weakly (because it suddenly closes the angle of its compass), or because it derives from itself a ridiculous *formal* justification, or because it is of a hallucinatory kind, or because it very naturally gives to the abstract the mask of the concrete, or the opposite, or because it implies the negation of some elementary physical property, or because it provokes laughter. Here, in order, are a few examples of it:

> The ruby of champagne. (LAUTRÉAMONT)[57]

> Beautiful as the law of arrested development of the breast in adults, whose propensity to growth is not in proportion to the quantity of molecules that their organism assimilates. (LAUTRÉAMONT)[58]

> A church stood dazzling as a bell. (PHILIPPE SOUPAULT)[59]

> In Rrose Sélavy's sleep there is a dwarf issued from a well who comes to eat her bread at night. (ROBERT DESNOS)[60]

> On the bridge the dew with the head of a tabby cat lulls itself to sleep. (ANDRÉ BRETON)[61]

> A little to the left, in my firmament foretold, I see – but it's doubtless but a mist of blood and murder – the gleaming glass of liberty's disturbances. (LOUIS ARAGON)[62]

In the forest aflame
The lions were fresh. (ROBERT VITRAC)[63]

> The color of a woman's stockings is not necessarily in the likeness of her eyes, which led a philosopher who it is pointless to mention, to say: "Cephalopods have more reasons to hate progress than do quadrupeds." (MAX MORISE)[64]

1st. Whether we like it or not, there is enough there to satisfy several demands of the mind. All these images seem to attest to the fact that the mind is ripe for something more than the benign joys it allows itself in general. This is the only way it has of turning to its own advantage the ideal quantity of events with which it is entrusted.[*] These images show it the extent of its ordinary dissipation and the drawbacks that it offers for it. In the final analysis, it's not such a bad thing for

---

[*] Let us not forget that, according to Novalis' formula, "there are series of events which run parallel to real events. Men and circumstances generally modify the ideal train of circumstances, so that it seems imperfect; and their consequences are also equally imperfect. Thus it was with the Reformation; instead of Protestantism, we got Lutheranism."[62]

[57] From Isidor Ducasse, Comte de Lautréamont, *Les Chants de Maldoror*, sixth "chant," fifth strophe.

[58] Ducasse, Comte de Lautréamont, *Les Chants de Maldoror*, canto 5, second strophe; in English translation see *Maldoror and the Complete Works of the Count of Lautréamont*, trans. Alexis Lykiard (Boston: Exact Change), p. 166.

[59] Philippe Soupault, *A la dérive* (Paris: Ferenzi et fils, 1923), p. 26.

[60] Robert Desnos, "Rrose Sélavy," *Littérature*, new series, no. 7 (Dec. 1, 1922), p. 16; reprinted in Desnos, *Corps et biens* (Paris: Gallimard, Éditions de la "Nouvelle Revue Française," 1930), p. 36, no. 34.

[61] André Breton, *Claire de terre*, "Au regard des divinités," in *Oeuvres complètes*, p. 172; in English translation in Breton, *Earthlight*, trans. Bill Zavatsky and Zack Rogow (Los Angeles: Sun and Moon, 1993), "In the Eyes of the Gods," p. 60, though translated quite differently.

[62] Source not identified; the phrase occurs nowhere in Aragon's published works.

[63] Robert Vitrac, a poem titled "Le cousu parle" ("The Sewn Object Speaks"), in his *Cruautés de la nuit* (*Cruelties of Night*) (Marseilles: les Cahiers du Sud, 1927); reprinted in his *Dés-Lyre: poésies complètes* (Paris: Gallimard, 1964), p. 86.

[64] Source not identified; the phrase occurs nowhere in Aragon's published works.

[65] Breton spotted this passage by Novalis in Charles Baudelaire's translation of a short story by the American writer Edgar Allan Poe, "The Mystery of Marie Roget," to which the passage by Novalis serves as an epigraph, retained by Poe in its original German. Poe scrupulously assigned the passage to the *Moralische Ansichten* of Novalis (or *Moral Views*). Novalis himself, however, never wrote any such work. After his premature death in 1801, a two-volume collection of his writings was assembled by Friedrich Schlegel and Ludwig Tieck, *Novalis Schriften*, 2 vols. (Berlin: Buchhandlung der Realschule, 1802). Faced with the countless aphoristic fragments that Novalis had left behind, they chose 570 of them and grouped them under the title *Vermischte Fragmente* ("Mixed Frangments"), then subdivided them by subject-matter: *I. Zur Philosophie* ("Toward Philosophy"); *II. Ästhetik und Literatur* ("Aesthetics and Literature"); and *III. Moralische Ansichten* ("Moral Views"), thus creating the work that would be transmitted first to Poe, then to Baudelaire, and then to Breton. There were four further editions of *Novalis Schriften*, culminating in the fifth edition of 1837. One of these five will have served as the source that Poe used when, in 1842, he selected this passage

these images to upset the mind, for to upset the mind is to put it in the wrong. The sentences I quote make ample provision for this. But the mind which relishes them draws therefrom the conviction that it is on the *right track;* on its own, the mind is incapable of finding itself guilty of cavil; it has nothing to fear, since, moreover, it attempts to embrace everything.

2nd. The mind which plunges into Surrealism relives with glowing excitement the best part of its childhood. For such a mind, it is similar to the certainty with which a person who is drowning reviews once more, in the space of less than a second, all the insurmountable moments of his life. Some may say to me that the parallel is not very encouraging. But I have no intention of encouraging those who tell me that. From childhood memories, and from a few others, there emanates a sentiment of being unintegrated, and then later of *having gone astray*, which I hold to be the most fertile that exists. It is perhaps childhood that comes closest to one's "real life"; childhood beyond which man has at his disposal, aside from his laissez-passer, only a few complimentary tickets; childhood where everything nevertheless conspires to bring about the effective, risk-free possession of oneself. Thanks to Surrealism, it seems that opportunity knocks a second time. It is as though we were still running toward our salvation, or our perdition. In the shadow we again see a precious terror. Thank God, it's still only Purgatory. With a shudder, we cross what the occultists call *dangerous territory*. In my wake I raise up monsters that are lying in wait; they are not yet too ill-disposed toward me, and I am not lost, since I fear them. Here are "the elephants with the heads of women and the flying lions" which used to make Soupault and me tremble in our boots to meet, here is the "soluble fish" which still frightens me slightly. SOLUBLE FISH, am I not the soluble fish, I was born under the sign of Pisces, and man is soluble in his thought! The flora and fauna of Surrealism are inadmissible.

3rd. I do not believe in the establishment of a conventional Surrealist pattern any time in the near future. The characteristics common to all the texts of this kind, including those I have just cited and many others which alone could offer us a logical analysis and a careful grammatical analysis, do not preclude a certain evolution of Surrealist prose in time. Coming on the heels of a large number of essays I have written in this vein over the past five years, most of which I am indulgent enough to think are extremely disordered, the short anecdotes which comprise the balance of this volume offer me a glaring proof of what I am saying. I do not judge them to be any more worthless, because of that, in portraying for the reader the benefits which the Surrealist contribution is liable to make to his consciousness.

Surrealist methods would, moreover, demand to be heard. Everything is valid when it comes to obtaining the desired suddenness from certain associations. The pieces of paper that Picasso and Braque insert into their work have the same value as the introduction of a platitude into a literary analysis of the most rigorous sort. It is even permissible to entitle POEM what we get from the most random assemblage possible (observe, if you will, the syntax) of headlines and scraps of headlines cut out of the newspapers:[66]

---

as an epigraph for "The Mystery of Marie Roget." Baudelaire, in turn, translated the German original into French. By that time, however, the works of Novalis were already being reorganized by new editors employing different organizational schemas setting the fragment cited by Poe, Baudelaire, and Breton adrift in a veritable ocean of fragments. Source not identified.

[66] Compare this account with that of Tristan Tzara elsewhere in this volume, pp. 479–84.

POEM[67]

A burst of laughter
of sapphire in the island of Ceylon

The most beautiful straws

HAVE A FADED COLOR

UNDER THE LOCKS

on an isolated farm

FROM DAY TO DAY

the pleasant

grows worse

A carriage road

takes you to the edge of the unknown

coffee

preaches for its saint

THE DAILY ARTISAN OF YOUR BEAUTY

Madam,

a pair

of silk stockings

is not

[67]   This poem was republished under the title, "L'Angle de mire" ("The Angle of Elevation"), in Breton's collection of poems, *Le Revolver à cheveux blancs* (*Pistol with White Hair*) (Paris: Editions des cahiers libres, 1932).

A leap into space

A STAG

Love above all

Everything could be worked out so well

PARIS IS A BIG VILLAGE

Watch out for

the fire that covers

THE PRAYER

of fair weather

Know that

The ultraviolet rays

have finished their task

short and sweet

THE FIRST WHITE PAPER

OF CHANCE

Red will be

The wandering singer

WHERE IS HE?

in memory

in his house

AT THE SUITORS' BALL

I do

as I dance

What people did, what they're going to do

And we could offer many many more examples. The theater, philosophy, science, criticism would all succeed in finding their bearings there. I hasten to add that future Surrealist techniques do not interest me.

Far more serious, in my opinion* – I have intimated it often enough – are the applications of Surrealism to action. To be sure, I do not believe in the prophetic nature of the Surrealist word. "It is the oracle, the things I say."** Yes, *as much as I like*, but what of the oracle itself?*** Men's piety does not fool me. The Surrealist voice that shook Cumae, Dodona, and Delphi is nothing more than the voice which dictates my less irascible speeches to me. My *time* must not be its time, why should this voice help me resolve the childish problem of my destiny? I pretend, unfortunately, to act in a world where, in order to take into account its suggestions, I would be obliged to resort to two kinds of interpreters, one to translate its judgments for me, the other, impossible to find, to transmit to my fellow men whatever sense I could make out of them. This world, in which I endure what I endure (don't go see), this modern world, I mean, what the devil do you want me to do with it? Perhaps the Surrealist voice will be stilled, I have given up trying to keep track of those who have disappeared. I shall no longer enter into, however briefly, the marvelous detailed description of my years and my days. I shall be like Nijinski who was taken last year to the Russian ballet and did not realize what spectacle it was he was seeing.[71] I shall be alone, very alone within myself, indifferent to all the world's ballets. What I have done, what I have left undone, I give it to you.

---

* Whatever reservations I may be allowed to make concerning responsibility in general and the medico-legal considerations which determine an individual's degree of responsibility – complete responsibility, irresponsibility, limited responsibility (sic) – however difficult it may be for me to accept the principle of any kind of responsibility, I would like to know how the first punishable offenses, the Surrealist character of which will be clearly apparent, will be *judged*. Will the accused be acquitted, or will he merely be given the benefit of the doubt because of extenuating circumstances? It's a shame that the violation of the laws governing the Press is today scarcely repressed, for if it were not we would soon see a trial of this sort: the accused has published a book which is an outrage to public decency. Several of his "most respected and honorable" fellow citizens have lodged a complaint against him, and he is also charged with slander and libel. There are also all sorts of other charges against him, such as insulting and defaming the army, inciting to murder, rape, etc. The accused, moreover, wastes no time in agreeing with the accusers in "stigmatizing" most of the ideas expressed. His only defense is claiming that he does not consider himself to be the author of his book, said book being no more and no less than a Surrealist concoction which precludes any question of merit or lack of merit on the part of the person who signs it; further, that all he has done is copy a document without offering any opinion thereon, and that he is at least as foreign to the accused text as is the presiding judge himself.

What is true for the publication of a book will also hold true for a whole host of other acts as soon as Surrealist methods begin to enjoy widespread favor. When that happens, a new morality must be substituted for the prevailing morality, the source of all our trials and tribulations.

** Rimbaud.[68]

*** Still, STILL.... We must absolutely get to the bottom of this. Today, June 8, 1924, about one o'clock, the voice whispered to me: "Béthune, Béthune." What did it mean? I have never been to Béthune, and have only the vaguest notion as to where it is located on the map of France. Béthune evokes nothing for me, not even a scene from *The Three Musketeers*.[69] I should have left for Béthune, where perhaps there was something awaiting me; that would have been too simple, really. Someone told me they had read in a book by Chesterton[70] about a detective who, in order to find someone he is looking for in a certain city, simply scoured from roof to cellar the houses which, from the outside, seemed somehow abnormal to him, were it only in some slight detail. This system is as good as any other.

Similarly, in 1919, Soupault went into any number of impossible buildings to ask the concierge whether Philippe Soupault did in fact live there. He would not have been surprised, I suspect, by an affirmative reply. He would have gone and knocked on his door.

68 Arthur Rimabud's poem "Mauvais Sang" ("Bad Blood") in *Une saison en enfer* (*A Season in Hell*). For the poem in English see Arthur Rimbaud, *A Season in Hell; the Illuminations*, trans. Enid Rhodes Peschel (Oxford: Oxford University Press, 1973), p. 44.

69 Book II, ch. 31 of *The Three Musketeers*, by Alexandres Dumas, is titled "The Convent of the Carmelites of Béthune."

70 Breton's comments refer to "The Blue Cross," the first of 12 stories making up *The Innocence of Father Brown* (London: Cassell & Co., 1911), by G. K. Chesterton (1874–1936). This volume was the first of the Father Brown books. Aristide Valentin, chief of the Parisian police and the most famous detective on earth, goes to London in search of that "colossus of crime," Flambeau, but he lacks any clue to guide him: "In such cases he reckoned on the unforeseen. In such cases, when he could not follow the train of the reasonable, he coldly and carefully followed the train of the unreasonable. Instead of going to all the right places – banks, police-stations, rendezvous – he systematically went to the wrong places" (G. K. Chesterton, *The Complete Father Brown* [London and New York: Penguin, 1981], p. 12). Breton, of course, knew the Father Brown's story through the French translation by Émile Cammaerts, *La Clairvoyance du père Brown* (Paris: Librairie Académique Perrin, 1919).

71 Vaslav Nijinsky (1888–1950) was the great dancer whose performances from 1909 to 1913 astounded Paris and ensured the success of the Ballet Russe. After 1913 he was increasingly troubled by schizophrenia, and by 1919 had stopped dancing entirely and retired in Switzerland. On July 13, 1923, he attended a performance of Stravinsky's new work *Les Noces* (*The Wedding*) in Paris at the Gaité-Lyrique.

And ever since I have had a great desire to show forbearance to scientific musing, however unbecoming, in the final analysis, from every point of view. Radios? Fine. Syphilis? If you like. Photography? I don't see any reason why not. The cinema? Three cheers for darkened rooms. War? Gave us a good laugh. The telephone? Hello. Youth? Charming white hair. Try to make me say thank you: "Thank you." Thank you. If the common man has a high opinion of things which properly speaking belong to the realm of the laboratory, it is because such research has resulted in the manufacture of a machine or the discovery of some serum which the man in the street views as affecting him directly. He is quite sure that they have been trying to improve his lot. I am not quite sure to what extent scholars are motivated by humanitarian aims, but it does not seem to me that this factor constitutes a very marked degree of goodness. I am, of course, referring to true scholars and not to the vulgarizers and popularizers of all sorts who take out patents. In this realm as in any other, I believe in the pure Surrealist joy of the man who, forewarned that all others before him have failed, refuses to admit defeat, sets off from whatever point he chooses, along any other path save a reasonable one, and arrives wherever he can. Such and such an image, by which he deems it opportune to indicate his progress and which may result, perhaps, in his receiving public acclaim, is to me, I must confess, a matter of complete indifference. Nor is the material with which he must perforce encumber himself; his glass tubes or my metallic feathers . . . As for his method, I am willing to give it as much credit as I do mine. I have seen the inventor of the cutaneous plantar reflex at work;[72] he manipulated his subjects without respite, it was much more than an "examination" he was employing; *it was obvious that he was following no set plan.* Here and there he formulated a remark, distantly, without nonetheless setting down his needle, while his hammer was never still. He left to others the futile task of curing patients. He was wholly consumed by and devoted to that sacred fever.

Surrealism, such as I conceive of it, asserts our complete *nonconformism* clearly enough so that there can be no question of translating it, at the trial of the real world, as evidence for the defense. It could, on the contrary, only serve to justify the complete state of distraction which we hope to achieve here below. Kant's absentmindedness regarding women, Pasteur's absentmindedness about "grapes,"[73] Curie's absentmindedness with respect to vehicles,[74] are in this regard profoundly symptomatic. This world is only very relatively in tune with thought, and incidents of this kind are only the most obvious episodes of a war in which I am proud to be participating. Surrealism is the "invisible ray" which will one day enable us to win out over our opponents. "You are no longer trembling, carcass."[75] This summer the roses are blue; the wood is of glass. The earth, draped in its verdant cloak, makes as little impression upon me as a ghost. It is living and ceasing to live that are imaginary solutions. Existence is elsewhere.[76]

[72] Joseph Babinksi (1857–1932) was a psychiatrist; Breton worked under him at the Centre neurologique de la pitié in Paris from January to September 1917. He attacks him sharply in his work *Nadja* (1927).
[73] In the course of a dinner, Pasteur underlined to his fellow diners the importance of carefully washing the stems of grapes because of the sulphates applied to the vines; talking all the while, he dropped his stems into his glass of water, ate the grapes, and then drank the glass of water.
[74] On April 15, 1906, Pierre Curie slipped under the chassis of a truck and had his head crushed by the left rear wheel of the vehicle. His father, the famous Doctor Curie, ascribed the acci-

dent to Pierre's state of distraction, walking around absorbed in his thoughts.
[75] In a letter dated December 25, 1964, and written to André Lazar, who was translating the "Manifesto" into Hungarian, Breton explained: "'You are trembling, you carcass' is a phrase that history ascribes to the maréchal de Turenne (1611–75) and he found it was the means to halt all physical movement on the field of battle."
[76] Breton responds here to the affirmation of Rimbaud: "Real life is absent. We are not in the world." See Arthur Rimbaud, *A Season in Hell; the Illuminations,* trans. Enid Rhodes Peschel (Oxford: Oxford University Press, 1973), "Delirum I," p. 69.

The Mediums Enter (1922)
André Breton

An unforeseen maneuver, a little nothing that – eyes half-closed on each other – we did not dare predict might make us put aside our quarrels, has just set back in motion the famous steam-swing[1] near which, once upon a time, we would meet even without arrangement. It has been almost two years since the strange see-saw stopped working, after having scattered us rather forcefully in all directions; since then we've been trying with varying degrees of grace to remake its acquaintance. I have already had occasion to say that if we hurled responsibility for the breakdown back and forth at each other, no doubt without rhyme or reason, at least there was not a single one of us who regretted having taken a seat in that compartment ill-lit by the knees of young women, the compartment that beats time between houses.

No doubt about it, here we are again:[2] Crevel, Desnos, and Péret on one side, Eluard, Ernst, Morise, Picabia, and myself on the other. We'll soon see how our positions differ. Right now, and with no second thoughts, I will add that there are three men whose presence at our side strikes me as indispensable, three men whom I have seen act in the most affecting way possible during a previous *departure* and who, owing to a deplorable circumstance (their absence from Paris), know nothing as yet about these preparations: Aragon, Soupault, and Tzara.[3] May they allow me to make them virtual associates in our quest, along with all those who have not despaired of us, who remember having shared our initial conviction and, in spite of ourselves, never thought it could fall prey to its misadventures.

The unusual angle under which I relate the following facts would justify many, many precautions. Certainly the word *literature*, which can be found yet again on the masthead of these pages,[4] has long seemed to be a purely whimsical label; nonetheless, it is thanks to it that we have gotten away with so much. Our nonobservance of the literary ritual could still be tolerated: several rebellious minds could be satisfied, while art was being served just as well as ever. But no one will learn without a shrug of the shoulders that we have agreed to bow to an even more imbecilic formality,[5] which it will be time to specify later on; we will see that carrying out this formality is necessary for anyone who wishes to monitor our results. I fully expect that, after reading this, many will deem with relief that "poetry" has nothing to lose by it: its account is squared.

To a certain degree it is generally known what my friends and I mean by *Surrealism*. We use this word, which we did not coin and which we might easily have left to the most ill-defined critical vocabulary, in a precise sense. This is how we have agreed to designate a certain psychic automatism that corresponds rather well to the dream state, a state that it is currently very hard to delimit. I apologize for introducing a personal observation at this point.

In 1919 my attention had been drawn to the phrases of varying length that, in complete solitude, as I was falling asleep, became perceptible to my mind, without my being able to find anything that might have predetermined them. These sentences, which were syntactically correct

---

This essay, under its original French title "Entrée des médiums," was first published in the journal *Littérature*, new series no. 6 (Nov. 1, 1922), then included in *Les Pas perdus* (*The Lost Steps*), a collection of essays by Breton that appeared in February 1924 (Paris: Nouvelle revue française). The English translation by Mark Polizzotti, which is adopted here, was first published in *The Lost Steps* (Lincoln: University of Nebraska Press, 1996).

[1]   A swing or seesaw that was used at outdoor parties held by the Surrealists during these years, here and in the entire passage that follows serving as a metaphor for automatic writing.

[2]   Breton divides the actors in this text into two groups. The first (René Crevel [1900–35], Robert Desnos [1900–45], and Benjamin Péret [1899–1959]) consists of people who engaged in what the text later calls "hypnotic slumbers," entering into a state of sleep or sleep-like trance in which the participant would write or repeat aloud words emanating from a mysterious source, and so engage in automatic writing. The second consists of people (Paul Eluard [1895–1952], Max Ernst [1891–1976], Max Morise [1900–73], Francis Picabia [1879–1953], and André Breton [1896–1966]) who witnessed these events.

[3]   Louis Aragon (1897–1982), Philippe Soupalt (1897–1990), and Tristan Tzara (1896–1963) were unable to observe the "hypnotic slumbers" because they were either out of town or otherwise occupied.

[4]   This essay was first published in the journal *Littérature*, or *Literature*, edited by Breton and two collaborators.

[5]   An allusion to the practice of having participants, seated around a table, hold hands in order to create the sympathetic chain considered indispensable for holding a spiritualist séance.

and remarkably rich in images, struck me as poetic elements of the first rank. At first I did no more than jot them down. Only later did Soupault and I think of voluntarily re-creating in ourselves the state in which they took form.[6] All we had to do was shut out the external world, and so it was that they occurred to us for two months running, increasingly plentiful, soon following each other without pause and with such speed that *we had to resort to abbreviations* in order to get them all on paper. The book *The Magnetic Fields*[7] is but the first application of that discovery: each chapter had no other reason for stopping than the end of the day on which it was composed, and from one chapter to the next, only a change in velocity caused its slight variations in effect. What I am saying here, without any concern for ridicule or self-promotion, tends mainly to establish that in the absence of any critical intervention on our parts, the judgments to which the publication of such a book might expose us fall by the wayside a priori. Nonetheless, by heeding voices other than that of our own unconscious, even in fun, we risked compromising this self-sufficient murmur in its essence, and I believe that this is ultimately what happened. Nevermore after this, on the occasions when we awaited this murmur in hopes of capturing it for precise ends, did it take us very far. And yet such had been its power that I expect nothing else to afford a greater revelation. I have never lost my conviction that nothing said or done is worthwhile outside obedience to that magic *dictation*. That is the secret of the irresistible attraction that certain individuals exert on us, whose only interest is to have once made themselves the echo of what we are tempted to consider the universal consciousness – or, if you prefer, to have gathered (without necessarily grasping their meaning) a few words fallen from the "mouth of shadows."[8]

It is true that I occasionally refer to a different viewpoint, and this because, as I see it, all human effort must be applied toward recapturing that earlier confidence. All we can do is stand before it without fear of losing our way. It is a crazy man indeed who, having once approached it, brags of having been able to hold onto it. Only those who are well versed in the most complex mental gymnastics have even a chance of possessing it now and again. Today these individuals are named Picabia and Duchamp. Each time this confidence comes forward, almost always unexpectedly, the trick is to know how to receive it without hope of turning back, by attaching only the most relative importance to the form it has taken in announcing its presence.

Getting back to "Surrealism," I had recently decided that the incursions of conscious elements in this domain, which would place it under a well-determined human or literary will, would subject it to the sort of exploitation that could bear only less and less fruit. I would soon lose all interest in it. Along these same lines, I had come to devote my preference to *dream narratives*, which I planned to have taken down stenographically to avoid similar stylization. The problem was that this new test required the help of memory, which is profoundly deficient and, generally speaking, not very reliable. It seemed to me that the matter would go no further, especially owing to the lack of sufficient characteristic documentation. This is why I had stopped expecting much of anything in this regard when a third solution to the problem arose (I believe all that remains is to decipher it), a solution that offers infinitely fewer causes for error and is therefore extremely exciting. You can

[6] Automatic writing originated in Rochester, New York, in 1849, and was inseparable from spiritualism, the belief that it was possible to receive communications, written or oral, from the dead. It became the subject of immense controversy, and during the period 1880–1910 it also became an object of study for scholars and psychologists. The most discerning of these reached the conclusion that automatic writing was a function of automatism, the process whereby units of the psyche such as the subconscious could function independently of will or volition. The project entertained by Breton and Soupault, that of "voluntarily recreating" psychic states allegedly characterized by the absence of will or volition, is plainly an ambivalent one.

[7] *Les Champs magnétiques* (Paris: Au Sans Pareil, 1920), written by André Breton and Philippe Soupault, is widely consdiered the first purely literary work to be derived from automatic writing. See Breton and Soupalt, *The Magnetic Fields*, trans. Davvid Gascoyne (London: Atlas, 1985).

[8] The phrase derives from the title of a poem by Victor Hugo (1802–85), "Ce que dit la Bouche de l'Ombre" ("What the Mouth of Shadows Says"), which was first published in his collection of poems *Les Contemplations*, 2 vols. (Paris: Hachette, 1863). The poem's title derives from two overlapping concerns of Hugo. On the one hand, he was involved in a lengthy series of spiritualist séances during his years of exile on the island of Jersey; on the other hand, he was fascinated by the prehistoric monuments which the island contains, including a well-known dolmen of Rozel, which consists of several large stones erected to function more or less as columns, surmounted by a massive flat stone that serves as a roof and creates a shadowy cave or "mouth of shadows." Hugo's poem, to the best of my knowledge, has not been translated into Engish; for an edition in French, see Victor Hugo, *Oeuvres complètes* (Paris: Editions Hetzel Quantin, 1880–5), Part I *Poésie*, vol. 6 *Contemplations*, pp. 331–66.

judge by the fact that after ten days the most blasé, the most self-assured among us stand confused, trembling with gratitude and fear.

Two weeks ago, on his return from holidays, René Crevel described to us the beginnings of a "spiritualist" initiation that he had had thanks to a certain Madame D. This person, having discerned particular mediumistic qualities in him, had taught him how to develop these qualities; so it was that, in the conditions necessary for the production of such phenomena (darkness and silence in the room, a "chain" of hands around the table), he had soon fallen asleep and uttered words that were organized into a generally coherent discourse, to which the usual awakening techniques put a stop at a given moment. It goes without saying that at no time, starting with the day we agreed to try these experiments, have we ever adopted the spiritualist viewpoint. As far as I'm concerned, I absolutely refuse to admit that any communication whatsoever can exist between the living and the dead.

On Monday, 25 September, at 9:00 P.M., in the presence of Desnos, Morise, and myself, Crevel enters into a hypnotic slumber and utters a kind of defense or indictment that was not copied down at the time (declamatory diction interspersed with sighs, sometimes going into a kind of singsong; stressing of certain words, rapid slurring of others; infinite prolongation of several endings; dramatic delivery: the story concerns a woman accused of having killed her husband, but her guilt is in dispute because she apparently acted on his wishes). Upon awakening, Crevel has no recollection of his words. We exclude him from the following experiment, undertaken, aside from his participation, in the same conditions. No immediate result. After fifteen minutes, Desnos – who considered himself the least prone to such demonstrations, fortified in his opinion by the defeat he had inflicted in my company several days before on two public hypnotists, Messrs. Donato and Bénévol[9] – lets his head drop onto his arms and begins compulsively scratching the tabletop. He wakes up of his own accord several moments later, convinced that he has behaved no differently from the rest of us. To persuade him of his error, we must separately describe in writing what took place.

Crevel having told us that the action of scratching the table might indicate a desire to write, it is agreed that the next time we will place a pencil in Desnos's hand and a sheet of paper in front of him. So it is that two days later, in similar circumstances, we see him write before our eyes, without moving his head, the words *14 July–14 Jul* littered with "+" signs or crosses. At that point we begin questioning him:

What do you see?
Death.
He draws a hanged woman at the side of a path.
Written: *Near the fern go two* (the rest is lost on the tabletop).
At that moment, I place my hand over his left hand.
Q: *Desnos, it's Breton here. Tell us what you see for him.*
A: *The equator* (he draws a circle and a horizontal diameter).
Q: *Is this a trip Breton will take?*
A: *Yes.*
Q: *Will it be a business trip?*
A: (He shakes his head. Writes:) *Nazimova.*[10]

---

[9]   Donato and Bénévol were public hypnotists who were exposed as frauds by Robert Desnos and André Breton. A contemporary newspaper, *Le Journal du Peuple*, carried an account of the exposure under the title "Un truc connu" ("A Trick Made Known") within a regular feature or rubric called "Échos" ("Echoes") in its edition of September 21, 1922.

[10]   Alla Nazimova (1879–1945) was a Russian actress who emigrated to the United States in 1905 and played a leading role in a series of silent films for Metro studios. These featured her as an exotic, independent woman beset by anguish and personal struggle, and included *Toys of Fate* (1918) and *The Red Lantern* (1919). In *Toys of Fate* she played a gypsy girl who, her mother having committed suicide after being seduced and abandoned by a rich man, finds herself 20 years later being wooed by the same man. In *The Red Lantern* she plays two roles: Mahlee and Blanche Sackville are half-sisters, Blanche the daughter of an Englishman

Q: *Will his wife travel with him?*
A: *????*
Q: *Will he go to find Nazimova?*
A: *No* (underlined).
Q: *Will he be with Nazimova?*
A: *?*
Q: *What else do you know about Breton? Speak.*
A: *The boat and the snow – there is also the pretty telegraph tower – on the pretty tower there is a young* (illegible).

    I take my hand away. Eluard puts his in its place.

Q: *It's Eluard.*
A: *Yes.* (Drawing.)
Q: *What do you know about him?*
A: *Chirico.*
Q: *Will he soon meet Chirico?*
A: *Marvel with soft eyes like a young baby.*
Q: *What do you see of Eluard?*
A: *He is blue.*
Q: *Why is he blue?*
A: *Because the sky is nesting in* (an unfinished, indecipherable word; the whole sentence is furiously crossed out).

    Péret's hand replaces Eluard's.

Q: *What do you know about Péret?*
A: *He will die in a crowded train car.*
Q: *Will he be killed?*
A: *Yes.*
Q: *By whom?*
A: (He draws a train, with a man falling from its door.) *By an animal.*
Q: *By what animal?*
A: *A blue ribbon my sweet vagabond.*
Long pause, then: *Say no more about her, she will be born in a few minutes.*
Ernst's hand replaces Péret's.
Q: *This is Ernst's hand. Do you know him?*
A: *Who?*
Q: *Max Ernst.*
A: *Yes.*
Q: *Will he live long?*
A: *Fifty-one years.*
Q: *What will he do?*
A: *He'll play with madmen.*
Q: *Will these madmen make him happy?*
A: *Ask that blue woman.*
Q: *Who is that blue woman?*
A: THE.
Q: *The? What?*
A: *The tower*

    We put an end to Desnos's slumber. Sudden awakening preceded by violent movements.

    It should be noted that on the same day, before Desnos, Crevel passed through a state similar to Monday's (another crime story, although more obscure this time: "The woman will be naked, and it's the oldest man who will wield the ax").

---

and his wife, Mahlee of the Englishman and his Chinese mistress. Mahlee rejects her people and attempts to find a life for herself among Europeans, but discovers that the color line is impossible to pass and returns to lead her Chinese people in rebellion.

During a third attempt, in the presence of Eluard, Ernst, Morise, Péret, a young woman named Mlle Renée who came with Péret, and myself, Mlle Renée is the first to fall asleep. She immediately shows signs of great agitation and calls out breathless phrases. She answers our questions: "The abyss . . . the clear sweat of my father is soaking me!" (repetitions, signs of terror).

A final attempt results, after several minutes, in a loud, sudden, and very lengthy guffaw from Péret. Is he asleep? With great pains we finally extract a few words from him.

What do you see?
Water.
What color is this water?

Same answer. As if it were obvious.

He abruptly stands without being asked, flops belly down on the table, and makes swimming motions.

I think it would be boring to say any more about the particulars of each phenomenon and the circumstances in which we witnessed it: we being Eluard, Ernst, Morise, and I, who despite all our goodwill, did not manage to fall asleep.

Midnight at Two O'Clock: An Experiment in Modern Magic (1928)
Robert Desnos

1. A villa in the country. View of the country. Hills, fields, woods. A river. A bridge over this river.
2. The occupants of the villa. A man (35 years old) and his mistress.
3. They walk out of the villa. The road.
4. Arrival at the station. Arrival of the train.
5. The person they came to meet. A man, rather young (28 years old). Getting off the train. Shaking hands.
6. Towards the villa.
7. The garden. All three around a table laden with glasses and bottles.
8. The lover goes out.
9. Exchange of kisses between the woman and the new arrival.
10. The next morning. Departure of the three characters on a fishing expedition.
11. The bridge seen at the beginning. All three are fishing.
12. The woman and the young man are bored: *"We are going for a stroll."*
13. The lover keeps on fishing. The cork in the current.
14. The stroll of the woman and the young man. Kisses up till the moment when they near the bridge hidden by brushwood.
15. The lover tries to disengage his line which is caught in the weeds.
16. He leans towards the parapet. Leans over still further and falls.
17. Circles in the water.
18. At the top of a hill a peasant who saw the fall. He runs.
19. Arrival of the two other characters at the bridge. They call their companion. They lean on the parapet: circles in the water.
20. The sun. Dizziness of the two strollers. White circles dance around them.

MIDNIGHT
This film script was first published under its French title "Minuit à quatorze heures," in the journal *Cahiers du mois*, no. 12
(1925); the English translation by Maria Jolas (wife of Eugene
Jolas, see pp. 1007–16) which is adopted here first appeared in

transition 14 (Fall, 1928). The author, Robert Desnos (1900–45),
played a key role in the gestation of Surrealism during the period
1922–7, but left in 1928 because of its increasingly political
engagement.

21. The fishing line in the current, down the river.

22. Arrival of the peasant. Explanations.

23. Circles in the water.

24. A barge. Attempts at recovery with a boat-hook.

25. The bank of the river, downstream. The body of a drowned man at the foot of a tree.

26. Evening. The woman and her young lover pensive at a window.

27. The round setting sun.

28. Kisses.

29. Their eyes in the foreground. The round pupils.

30. Night. The lighted lamp. The circle of light on the ceiling. The circle made by the lamp-shade on the floor.

31. Separation to go to bed.

32. Night. The big round moon seen through the window of the bedrooms.

33. The next day. Breakfast. The round plates. The round table mats.

34. The lovers look at each other in silence.

35. Circles in the water.

36. The round knob of the door turns slowly. The door opens. The two lovers watch it open. Nobody comes in.

37. Through the door can be seen the road along which there passes a little boy playing with his hoop, and a cart with large wheels (in the foreground).

38. Circles in the water.

39. One evening at bedtime.

40. The lover sleeping in his bed.

41. The woman sleeping in her bed.

42. Dream of the lover. The Place Vendôme,[1] quite deserted, where he is walking, then the Place de la Concorde.[2]

43. Then the Tour Eiffel.[3] First pale then very clear vision of the "Big Wheel" in the background.

44. Then the Place des Victoires.[4]

45. The woman's dream: She is jumping through a succession of paper-covered hoops. She finds herself in a deserted church.

46. The priest is officiating, the host in his hand, just about to be elevated.

47. The host increases in size out of all proportion as he holds it.

48. A halo appears behind the head of the priest who takes on the conventional appearance of a saint.

49. Fear of the woman who leaves the church.

50. A beggar at the Church door. She gives him two pennies.

51. The beggar drops his hat out of which falls a multitude of coins, a real torrent, before which the woman flees.

52. She arrives at the Place des Victoires. Meeting with her lover.

53. As they are about to embrace, the torrent of pennies appears from the rue Vide-Gousset.[5]

54. It submerges the Place.

55. The lover in a torrent which carries him off. He lands on a narrow beach. As he is about to rise the water seizes him again. Impression of drowning. Awakening.

56. The woman under a mass of coins, in a cellar. Oppression. Awakening.

[1] Located in Paris just north of the Jardin des Tuileries, Place Vendôme is an example of the Louis XIV style, surrounded by houses with uniform façades designed by Jacques Hardouin-Mansart (1645–1708).

[2] Place de la Concorde in Paris is an impressive public square. On its west side, the Champs Elysée rises toward the Arc de Triomphe; on its north, the rue Royale leads to the church of Ste. Madeleine, and on the east side there is the Jardin des Tuileries.

[3] Built in 1889 for the Paris Exhibition of that year by the engineer Gustave Eiffel (1832–1923).

[4] Located just east of the Palais Royal in Paris, Place des Victoires was designed by Jacques Hardouin-Mansart in 1685; in its center is an equestrian statue of Louis XIV by François Joseph Bosio (1768–1845), erected in 1822.

[5] "Empty waistcoat-pocket" street is a short (28 meters long) and narrow (12 meters wide) street that runs into the Place des Victoires, so named because of the many thefts that took place there in the seventeenth century.

57.   Calm night outside. The round moon.

58.   The staircase of the villa. The landing of the third and top floor. The lovers have their rooms on the second floor.

59.   Appearance of a ball the size of a croquet ball.

60.   The ball goes down the stairs, step by step, slowly.

61.   The ball passes the landing of the floor where the two lovers are sleeping.

62.   It keeps on going down.

63.   Awakening of the man. He listens. He gets up.

64.   The ball which has reached the ground floor goes out the door.

65.   It gets lost in the garden.

66.   The man on the stairs, then on the first floor. He looks about, opens the doors. Nothing.

67.   The woman leaves her room. *"What is the matter? I thought I heard a noise – I too."*

68.   The next day. Both seated in the garden. A round balloon in the sky over their heads.

69.   Then tennis players at the side of the garden. A stray ball falls on the table.

70.   Uneasiness.

71.   Walk out in the country.

72.   In a clearing, croquet players.

73.   On the road the cart with the big wheels (in the foreground): the little boy with the hoop.

74.   Further on, a worker in a field. Just as they pass, he stops ploughing and digs in the earth. The two walkers watch him. He uncovers a cannon ball, the vestige of a former war.

75.   Return, both thoughtful.

76.   At home. The cat.

77.   The woman wants to caress it. Suddenly the cat turns into a ball. Cry of the woman, the man turns around. Fright.

78.   Slowly the ball becomes a cat again.

79.   He. He caresses the cat which rubs against his legs.

80.   Night.

81.   Same as 58.

82.   Same as 59.

83.   Same as 60.

84.   He awakens, listens, rises and goes out with an electric lamp in his hand.

85.   He meets the woman on the landing.

86.   The ball continues on down.

87.   He turns the light on the step. The ball rolls down lighted up.

88.   Fright of the two lovers on the stairs.

89.   The next day at lunch.

90.   The door-knob.

91.   It turns. The door opens. The two lunching together turn about.

92.   Entrance of the ball.

93.   The two heroes rise, knocking over a chair.

94.   The ball turns around them, then leaves.

95 to 112. Repetition of 89 to 94, with only a few differences in detail, each time on a different day. The ball lingers more and more.

113 to 116. Same as 89, 90, 91, 92.

117.   The two characters do not even rise now. They are as though petrified.

118.   The ball jumps on the table.

119.   The ball approaches the plates which are emptied.

120.   The following days. The ball now has its place set at the table. The food placed before it disappears. The ball has grown bigger. It is like a foot-ball.

121.   Through the window. Foot-ball players. A spherical balloon in the sky. A belfry with its clock.

122.   The man throws his napkin on the floor, and with hard kicks sends the ball through the window.

123.   The ball quite tiny on the road. It rolls along. It passes a grade crossing, a village, a wood, a village, fields, a forest, the toll-gate of Paris. It rolls across the streets in the Place de la Bastille,[6] Place Vendôme, Place des Victoires, Place de la Concorde, from the Trocadéro[7] to the Tour Eiffel, without apparently being noticed, it leaves Paris, the country, the sea: the ball rolls on the waves: boats, an island. The ball rolls along the beach and stops in a luxuriant and equatorial forest.

124.   The couple in the villa, delivered from their night-mare.

125.   The ball in the forest. It absorbs birds which graze against it, little snakes, rabbits etc. It grows in size becomes as big as a drum, then a bass drum, then a house. Soon it absorbs whole trees.

126.   The couple in the villa. It is winter. The trees bare. Snow on the ground.

127.   One night: the villa. The round moon.

128.   The forest of the ball.

129.   The ball starts to move.

130.   It retraces exactly, in the opposite direction, the road it came on, only at night. Its enormous but almost immaterial mass passes over the sea, then through Paris: then the country. It casts an immense shadow against the sky.

131.   The villa.

132.   The ball at the top of a hill dominating the villa.

133.   The villa.

134.   The ball rolls down the hill.

135.   It arrives at the house.

136.   Just as it arrives at the house, everything, ball and house, disappears, as though swallowed up.

137.   The round moon.

138.   Dawn. In place of the house a vast funnel.

139.   Arrival of two gendarmes. They look at the funnel, signs of astonishment.

140.   A little later, peasants,? Astonishment.

141.   Night, the moon.

142.   Daytime, a round balloon in the sky. A little boy plays with a hoop along the road. Croquet players. A cart; (the wheels in the foreground).

143 to 154.   Night, the moon. Succession of day and night on the deserted funnel (each time the moon grows slimmer until it becomes a slender crescent).

155.   One morning. Automobilists stop.

156.   A shepherd.

157.   Question by the automobilists. Sign of ignorance from the shepherd.

158.   The little boy with the hoop.

159.   The sphere in the sky.

160.   Circles in the water.

161.   The sphere in the sky.

Note. – Each time that the ball appears, the orchestra plays, *"La Carmagnole"*.[8] The rest of the time traditional moving-picture music. No artistic music, moving picture music.

---

[6]   Located far to the east of all the other squares named here, it is where the former prison was located; in its center is the July Column (Colonne de Juillet) erected by Louis-Philippe in 1841 to commemorate the 500 people who died in the street-fighting of July 1830.

[7]   The Palais du Trocadéro was a museum constructed in 1878 for the Paris Exhibition of that year; it was demolished in 1937 to be replaced by the Palais de Chaillot. The site is directly across the Seine from the Eiffel Tower, or Tour Eiffel.

[8]   A revolutionary song sung by French soldiers after 1792, celebrating the overthrow of the king and queen.

From the Heart to the Absolute (1929)
Michel Leiris

"Un faisceau de raies noires légères."[1]

A slight shock, the birth of a lizard which propagated itself with the noise of torn silk, and I found myself again lying beside a river which washed wood shavings and chips of tanned skin towards the brine of the Arctic seas.

In the caves of the earth, thieves were heaping their treasures and counterfeiters were heating iron rods to mint coins bearing effigies of the dead. I no longer remembered the Ingénue, nor her deceits, I only remembered a bound, a rapid ascension and that vertiginous fall through the depth of a matrix whose indefinitely multiplied meanderings had led me to this place.

The landscape around me was desolate: no vegetation, but stone, stone and a few clouds. I noticed far away some abandoned quarries and wagons standing still. All wealth seemed to have crawled into the bowels of the earth, from which burst forth voices, sounds of brawls and the blow of picks muted by the superimposed layers of stratifications which separated the obstinate seekers from the atmosphere. The air was heavy and impassible, not at all troubled by the caress of my lungs and I felt it on me like a glacier without moraines – this air which let no trace of its movements be marked by a bird.

The silence of the surface was hardly disturbed by a slight, very distant whir, the only perceptible vibration, to which my thought clung as to Ariadne's thread; it was the last organic ligament which held me still suspended above a mineral sleep; and I followed attentively the infinitely small variations of the sound engendered by that cord, which was sometimes lower or higher, in accordance with the very feeble modifications of the energy which animated it.

Yet after a few minutes, it seemed to me that the intensity of the humming sound was increasing, as if the object causing it were coming much nearer, – and it was not long before I saw a black point emerge beyond the horizon, – a point which soon became a line, – and which moved following the direction of the river, a few metres above it, obeying the slightest turn made by the water. It was a bronze arrow which dragged in its wake a long white streamer on which I could read distinctly:

CATALAUNIC FIELDS

At the same time there approached a file of galleys manned by three ranks of rowers who followed the arrow with sails unfurled, their decks filled with armed warriors wearing shields and helmets.

Above their heads the pikes and rigging were crossed, forming a kind of net which bound the sky, while hanging from the masts, as breast-plates might hang from the spinal column, the sails showed distinctly the invisible torso of the air. I heard the cries of the manoeuvering and noticed soothsayers circulating among the soldiers and explaining to them the predictions they should deduce from the dice-game, while dishevelled girls ran from one end of the deck to the other, the prettiest of them twirling flames and knives. All the boats were covered with oriflammes and statues of gods, and the largest of them carried a vast tent made of steel links, beneath which rested the Emperor, a thin, trembling old man who seemed bored under his purple mantle and at times

FROM THE HEART
This portion of a more extended work of automatic writing first appeared under the title "Fragment d'un roman à paraître dans la collection *Pour vos beaux yeux*" ("Fragments of a Novel to Appear in the series *For Your Beautiful Eyes*") in *La Revue européene* 3(28) (June 1, 1925), then as chapter II, "Du Coeur à l'absolu" ("From the Heart to the Absolute"), in Leiris's book, *Le Point cardinal* (*The Cardinal Point*) (Paris: Éditions du Sagittaire, Simon

Kra, 1927). The English translation by Eugene Jolas which is adopted here first appeared in *transition* 16–17 (June 1929).

The author, Michel Leiris (1900–90), was a poet and writer active in Surrealism from 1924 to 1929, then a collaborator of the dissident Surrealist publication, *Documents*.

[1] "*Un faiseau ... légères*" French for "a sheaf of light black rays."

raised his hand to adjust his crown while a nude young girl was huddled in front of him. He was protected by several bars of lances through which I saw the glitter of his sceptre, pointed into the air in order to ward off lightning and other menaces.

"All exigences come from human blood," the centurions cried; their words punctuated by the toiling oh's of the rowers. *"An act of force: iron, fire, the future will be white with marvels."*

Mechanically I rose to watch the fleet pass by, but I noticed that my clothes were in rags and spattered with clay and sea-weed. I ran away and hid behind a rock, and it was there I witnessed the landing of the Roman army and the flight of the barbarians; at that moment the arrow which had become separated perpendicularly from the river, planted itself right on top of a little hill; the streamer which was unnaturally long by now, had covered the entire plain and hid in the folds of its nineteen letters the rare accidents of the terrain and the diverse phases of the battle.

I saw the Catalaunic Fields stretching before me like a body of water swollen by cataclysms, and the plowed fields sharply determined the trail of the corpses whose ashes were being carried in closed urns to the catacombs. Strange mirage, the U was scooped like an urn – the two C's, extreme ends of the ploughshare, clove the plain for many ells, unleashing the catapults, – and finally the S of treason serpentined with the last barbaric hordes who were vainly attempting a surprise action, before they fell back midst the hooting of panic.

When the combat was over, the nineteen letters crumbled together and became incrusted in the ground like memorial inscriptions.

Behind the Roman lines, I noticed the Huns in flight, brandishing torches, as they ran. Many wagons got stuck in the swamps along the river, whole bands of men were sucked into the earth, and when the extremity of the firebrand they had lifted as high as possible had also disappeared, the flame became detached and fluttered about in the form of a will-o'-the-wisp. Millions of fires were thus lighted, in the dying day, while the Roman dead began to blanch, in a strange putrefaction that destroyed both bone and muscles, transforming them little by little into glabrous mannekins without sex, their spherical skulls quite nude, and their sleek limbs looking as if they were made of white tights stuffed with horsehair.

These bodies were lying around me, before the lances and standards of the Romans, which were carried by motionless soldiers who differed from the dead only in that they were vertical.

When night had fallen, the corpses began to rise slowly in ranks of ten to fifteen, then started to pursue the will-o'-the-wisps, without moving their arms or legs, and floating a few meters above ground. When they had joined the fugitives, their icy breath extinguished all the flames, and soon there were left on the plain only ranks of pikes, the tent of the Emperor still glittering like a coat of mail under the lunar light, and the white mannekins who had stretched out on the memorial letters, blending with them in an identical insensibility of stone, like gravel left there for memory's sake, a short distance from the river, which continued its course towards the North.

***

The nineteen white letters gleamed in the darkness, immovable and as if emerged from the ground, and they seemed to have become its suddenly exteriorized skeleton. Mist rose from the river and poised above the battle-field, becoming more opaque as the night became darker, and forming scrolls as dense as those of the draining smoke arteries.

At midnight, the vapors had become massed just above the inscription and wrote in the air.

19

which was the number of white letters, set on the black-board of night, like the first factor of a prophetic operation the consequences of which would be felt way beyond the sensorial domain, as far as the extreme point of the needle which sews for us the woof of the universe hemmed by our human lives.

The wind blew upon the two figures and made them dance one before the other; like a couple in love. The 9, being more sinuous, was the woman, offering her round loop to the 1, which leapt vertically and at times came near in order to thrust its angle into the circle.

I observed this trick for the seventh time, when the two figures became definitely fused and disappeared; then there emerged in white against the background of the night:

$$1 + 9 = 10$$

This sum having been effected in silence, an equilibrium was maintained for an instant. But my ears were brusquely lacerated by a terrible thunder stroke, accompanied by lightning of enormous proportions which divided the number 10 and swept the 1 and 9 away, while at the same time it shook the crests on the tops of the helmets, and the pikes became tufted with innumerable sparks. Then the blasted 10 was also smashed, and I saw in its place only the two figures

d and b

the first green and the second blood red, color of lips and wounds, represented by a half nude Spanish woman in a scarlet shawl the design of which underscored the imaginary lozenge which had as summits the stain marking the confluence of her two thighs.

Like an object and its image in a mirror, the two fives placed themselves opposite each other, like eagles on the escutcheon of Charles the Fifth, but the five which was turned backwards dwindled rapidly and there remained only the red Spanish woman represented by the figure of the senses, of the fingers and of mating.

The dancing woman was irritated, a feeling born more of the storm than the rhythmic measure of the number which had engendered it. She, therefore, rose suddenly to her proper degree, 5^5 (the number of all the tricks she was capable of), by drawing from her marvellously fine smooth black stockings a pair of castagnettes which she raised as high as her two hands could reach in order to unchain a crackling of figures which soon crossed the rays of the rising sun.

Before the soldiers, the dancer with the lozenge then made the ground echo with her heels, her unfurled fan cut the air in five quarters of numbers and points of departure which showed me once more that total death, like that of gestures, is only a formation of angles and a change in direction. At the same time, the teeth of her steel comb marked, through canalisation, the temporal divisions created by the solar rays. Part of the light was reflected on the pikes of the legionnaires and the dancer amused herself by conjugating the movements of her fan and those of her comb in such a way as to increase as much as possible the intensity of the reflected light.

Finally, as she whirled vertiginously about, transforming the air into a vast and luminous cage which was nothing but interlaced bars, the arms and armor of the warriors grew suddenly incandescent and the entire Roman army became enflamed. The molten metals sank into the crust of the earth, holding in dissolution the flesh and bones of the soldiers, whose fossil imprints were found many centuries later on the ingots of a white and unbreakable substance which ignorant scientists called,

MARSITE,

confounding it with those concretions of the sky that sometimes burrow into the earth, having not fallen from high enough to be able to pierce it from end to end.

The storm which had upset the figures had by now attained its maximum velocity. I stood trembling behind my senses of living water, watching for the adventure which was coming with a headlong rush.

The galleys fled, giving the appearance of a flight of cranes. The sun became a revolver barrel which slowly turned around, presenting at regular intervals a body that lay like an arrow before the orifice of the canon. A shot rang out every minute and the body, its hair streaming ahead, was about to be lost in space. The dancer disappeared at the moment when I was about to seize her, and the entire landscape was swallowed up and replaced by a gleaming Maelstrom with spirals more dense than the wood of a cross.

I was hurled into this whirlpool from which there rose from time to time a multi-colored bubble that knocked against the Zenith, crashed with a great fracas and returned to the funnel in the form of mirror flashes, pocket knives and compasses.

Along with me there turned around the polished region a dark woman, a male goat and a bottle containing a few pieces of paper, four crystal dice and a ball of string all plunged into the brine. Each time my position with reference to the bottle made me see a new side of one of the dice, the woman stretched her nude arms and the goat shook its beard, while a bubble came from the funnel.

The woman was the first to fall into the central pool; I was still far away when I saw her balance herself and disappear with a long cry, like a torch that goes out. The goat followed her almost at once; but he had the luck of finding one of the bubbles, which carried him off rapidly into the air; up there he became changed into a cloud which allowed him to come down without pain – in the form of a fine rain.

As for myself, I succeeded, just as my circular voyage was about to lead me to the edge of the abyss, in clutching the bottle, and moving it violently, I threw the number 12 with the dice which assured me the protection of the Zodiac. I found, in fact, within reach of my hand, an aerial girdle decorated with the twelve signs. It placed itself without aid around my loins, and drew me away from the whirlpool, carrying me outside of the zone of terrestrial attraction.

When I came back to this planet, it was on a beautiful summer night, I was metamorphosed into a thunder stone and on my face were engraved these words which summarized everything the figure 5 and the oriflamme of the Catalaunic Fields had taught me:

> "Needle
> A stippled curve
> here is the thread of thought
> Feast of passing the Equator
> – and the Camp of the Golden Sheet –
> here is where the saddle wounds
> the circomvolutions
> in prismatic darkness."

The Possessions, from the Immaculate Conception (1930)
André Breton and Paul Eluard

The authors[1] particularly wish to stress the sincerity of the present undertaking which consists of submitting the five essays that follow to the consideration of both specialists and laymen. The slightest suggestion of any borrowing from clinical texts or of pastiche, skilful or otherwise, of such texts, would of course be enough to make these pieces both pointless and wholly ineffective.

We are not simply succombing here to a taste for the exotic by trustfully taking up, one after another, various languages which are thought, rightly or wrongly, to be entirely inadequate for their purpose. We were not content to find in them even an authentic effect of quaintness, but on the contrary aim to prove that the mind of a normal person when *poetically* primed is capable of reproducing the *main* features of the most paradoxical and eccentric verbal expressions and that it is possible for such a mind to assume at will the characteristic ideas of delirium without suffering any lasting disturbance, or compromising in any way its own faculty for mental equilibrium. There was never any question of pre-judging the total plausibility of these assumed mental states, the important thing being that people should be aware that, given a small amount of practice, they

The original French edition of *L'Immaculée Conception* (Paris: Éditions Surréalistes) appeared on November 24, 1930. "The Possessions," part II of the book's four parts, contains five sections, and three of these were translated by Samuel Beckett in 1932 (*This Quarter* 5(1) [Sept. 1932], "Surrealist Number," edited by André Breton). The entire work was translated by Jon Graham in 1990 (London: Atlas Press), and it is from this edition that the text here is adopted.

[1] The entire introductory section was written by Breton.

could be made perfectly plausible. That would mean discarding those arrogant categories in which people so easily slot those who have had a bone to pick with human reason – reason after all denies us day in and day out the right to express ourselves by means that are instinctive to us. If I can successively cause the richest person in the world, and the poorest, the blind and the hallucinated, the most fearful and the most aggressive all to speak through my own mouth, how can I accept that this voice, which is after all mine alone, comes to me from regions that are even temporarily condemned, regions to which I, like most of mankind, must despair of ever gaining access?

Besides this, we are happy to allow these pages which were composed with a certain intent to cause confusion, to be compared with the other pages in this book and others defined as Surrealist. Since the concept of "simulation" in mental treatment is used almost exclusively in war time, and is otherwise replaced by the term "supersimulation,"[2] we are impatient to learn what morbid basis the judges who deal with these matters will attribute to our work.

We declare, however, that we have particularly enjoyed this new exercise of our mental faculties. Through it we have become aware in ourselves of resources which could not previously have been suspected. Without belittling the breakthroughs it presages in relation to the highest level of liberty, we consider it a remarkable criterion with regard to modern poetics. Suffice it to say that we would be keen to see this activity widely practiced and that to our eyes the "attempted simulation" of disorders which are generally put behind bars, could with advantage replace the ballad, the sonnet, the epic, the goobledygook poem, and other outdated genres.

Attempted Simulation of Mental Debility

Among all men, at the age of twenty four, I realised that to rise to the position of a respected man one need have no more consciousness of one's own value than I had. I maintained a long time ago that virtue is not appreciated, but that my father was right when he wanted me to raise myself high above his contemporaries.[3] I utterly fail to see why they should give the Legion of Honour to foreign personalities passing through France. I feel that this decoration should be reserved for officers who have done deeds of valour and mining engineers who graduate from the Polytechnique.[4] In fact the grand master of the Order of Chivalry must be short of common sense if he recognises merit where there is none. Of all distinctions, that of officer is the most flattering. But one cannot do without a diploma. My father gave his five children, boys and girls, the best education and a good upbringing. And not so that they would accept a barely-remunerated job in an administration which does not pay. And the proof is[5] that when someone is capable, like my elder brother, who has assisted on several occasions in the papers, of scoring a bullseye against bachelors of arts and bachelors of science, you can say you have someone to take after. But sufficient unto the day, as the proverb goes.

In the inside pocket of my summer jacket I have the plans of a submarine that I wish to offer to the Ministry of Defence. The captain's cabin is drawn in red ink and the torpedo cannons are the latest hydraulic model, with artesian control.[6] Cycling champs do not show greater energy than me. I make no bones about my firm conviction that this invention must be a success.[7] Everyone is a supporter of Liberty, Equality and Fraternity, and, may I add, mutual Solidarity. But that is no reason not to defend ourselves against attack from the sea. I have written a *secret* letter on vellum paper to the President of the Republic, requesting to see him. The Mediterranean Squadron is right now cruising off Constantina, but the admiral is giving too much leave.[8] However humbly a soldier kneels before his C.O., orders are orders. Discipline is best when the leader is just, but firm. Stripes are not awarded at random and Maréchal Foch thoroughly deserved to be Maréchal Foch. Free thinking made the mistake of not devoting itself to the service of France.[9]

---

[2] Breton was a medical assistant at a neuropsychiatric hospital during the First World War. His notion of "Supersimulation" came from Costanza Pascal, *La Démence précoce* (Paris: Alcan, 1911), pp. 286–90; or from Antonin Porot and Angelo Hesnard, *Psychiatrie de guerre* (Paris: Alcan, 1919).

[3] These words/sentences were written by Eluard.

[4] These by Breton.

[5] By Eluard.

[6] By Breton.

[7] By Eluard.

[8] By Breton.

[9] By Eluard.

I also feel strongly that another name should be found for the Marine Infantry, I have also approached the League for the Rights of Man in this regard. The name is unworthy of their sailor's collars. Besides, it is up to them to make themselves respected. The Greece of Lacedaimon was made of sterner stuff. Still, man believes in God and the toughest nuts have been known to ask for extreme unction, which is a step in the right direction.[10]

Attempted Simulation of Acute Mania

Good morning gentlemen, good evening ladies and the assembled Gas Company. Mr President, I am at your disposal, I have a black Chinese lantern on my bicycle. The cat, the dog, my mother and my father, my children, the eagle in his little cart, all these poor specimens have been put into the wagon whose hinges turn and turn, and turn. From one bridge to the next the needles fall like so many sabre slashes. The cemetery is at the end of the village close to the stately cottage. None of which helps to re-forge family links in times of famine.[11]

Coquettes' cock-a-doodle-do's enliven the lines on the writer's page. Lamartine is there who lay in a flag on the gun-carriage at the rear of a hare running at high speed, Bazaine is there who went to render Sedan unto Caesar. But you, my fellow, are not there; you are holding a watering can, you have lost a leg, which makes two legs I have jammed in January. In June I collect juice. In 1930 I have a private income.[12]

Suffering sunstroke at the top of the sky, the Parisian ends up casting a net of ducks. No one shouts help, but halo and dignity is the better for it. I have foolproof ways of collecting the creature's straw. A masseur gave me a massive cudgel.[13] So as to re-read them by the fireside I keep by me the works of the Titans and Tantaluses. I do not need to include them in the inventory of my inventions. Painting is promoting itself. I respect Mr. Courbet, Mr. Ingres gives me sorbet. Scythes in my eyes eclipse the breastplate. On this point I wish to notify the police: we do not conform to the petty laziness of card games; just because we are hung from corbels sixty feet up, is not enough reason for us to yell "Whoa!" at dead trees.[14]

Mary's marriage was consummated amid an overflow of sighs. The Constructor had to be separated from his work. He mixed too many styles of architecture in that carcass of brick which mows leaches on lovely summer evenings. The belly keeps everything alive in its hand.[15] Personally I like to lie on the belly, provided it is not always my own, of course. Women are small hands in Paris, big hands in the country. They swallow the sparrows in the Luxembourg gardens. I do not understand esperanto but I find that messy inspiration should begin with oneself. I bet a bladder to a lantern with an undertaker that there is no eternity. Eternity is ether and that is all. I studied with an advocate who advocated: never confess. The recruitment committee failed me in my foresight test.[16]

I own a hunting lodge. A gate of greenery bars the barn from end to end. I collect the bets.[17] The farmer has a hat which I have worn, it is a present from the farmer's wife. Inside this hat there is a portrait of me with my feet in the air (it is a hat's eye view). The children playing round them get a smack. If we were to curdle blood the way we do milk, people would comment. Bismarck said to me the other day: "Take your time, I have quite happily taken Alsace." We were having a glass of champagne on the Champ de Mars.[18] The florist who moulds the flowerbeds tramples the garden paths. For the game he puts up they are raising a gibbet.

The only goal I have is the symbol of the prayer I address each evening to my Mecca. The barbarian begs for mercy. I take my pleasure in the barbered beard as I find it. Sorcery is a debauch that debouches near the works, the good works of charity. If I laugh it is because of the dawn on my knees, with a beautiful lice-cap on its head. Louise's son has switched his gun to the other shoulder. He keeps to only the barest minimum of military obligation: his helmet. One might as well fraternise with one's sister.[19]

10 By Breton.
11 By Eluard.
12 By Breton.
13 By Eluard.
14 By Breton.

15 By Eluard.
16 By Breton.
17 By Eluard.
18 By Breton.
19 By Eluard.

I write, I draw, I have snapdragons, I have my wife with me in bed even when I am standing up. She works for me making life. I suckle her as I do her little ones whom I caress in the corner. The littlest I call St. Thomas, little Saint Thomas, and the big girl I call Spring. It is very sweet. Everyone congratulates me. I put them through their first communion at the bar with a waffle. This is my blood, I explained. Then we ate salt cod under the tassels on the lampshade. And I sent them to boarding school. It is ten years now since I heard from them. Perhaps the little girl has been married and divorced.[20] My mother married the Shah of Persia,[21] they opened a little shop in Passy, a sort of level-crossing bawdy-house for lonely men. The Shah gets to the castle early, my mother sparkles.

I have a song with me that young girls love to sing, I lend it to them. In exchange they give into my safekeeping their first prize book, which was presented to them with a wreath of dried flowers.[22] I refuse to sign the kisses they give me. I sign to them to be patient. I am no longer of an age to be frightened of storms. In bed, we beat out a duet with a ditty by Lully, which, as I said, I have never read in a bed, Paiva[23] does her hair with an air, (romance), to the tune of the Widow at the Window. I manage little scraps of thanks for the smiles that shine around me. I do not stop at useless precautions. I carry the burden assigned to me for it is hot, but my only concern is the nymphs. There is one who hides a spring in her armpit. Potters go there in the evening to catch its fleeting colour.[24]

One day I asked myself: What is this key doing in my pocket? So I went off to Le Mans to see Clemenceau. I asked him: "Do you know what this key is doing in my pocket?" He poked me in the eye and I had to stay in the Chamber of Deputies for twenty-four hours. I went off with the lock, having made sure it was just the same temperature as the Chamber. Fearing the President might cloud over as a result of this incident, I had six teeth done in gold, and took the balloon home. In the balloon, I met Gambetta. I asked him: "Do you know what this balloon is doing in the sky?" He threw me over the side, but my siege had been laid for some time. It was the siege of Paris. I sign the peace treaty and leave to take the blotting paper to the Invalides. On the esplanade I meet Marie Curie coming back from shopping. I say to her "Aren't you ashamed of running around like this at your age?" She lends me her horse and there we were at her ranch[25] in the Faubourg Saint-Germain. There we did experiments in spontaneous germination. I got on well with Pasteur but his sister did all she could to make life impossible for me. I slept with one eye open. One night the maid noticed that I was most skilfully watching her undress. She screamed so loud that everyone ran up and threw themselves at me to force me to leave.[26]

. . . .

I would not enlist any more now, although waterless rivers chopped by the rain, I will not please anyone any more, it is no longer I who am even inside my pigskin suitcase, I am not hungry, I am not scared: far too cowardly to be scared, too greedy to eat. I am the one who had to amputate the woman from the man's sex organ on the pretext of plastic surgery. I am more finished than an episode. No one would take the trouble to give me trouble. I am thin as a vine-shoot that takes umbrage at its single leaf. I am truly anyone, I drag myself around on the crutches of my window, I should be slaughtered with whistle blows, someone should do me the immense favour of slipping my foot on under the table.[27]

Attempted simulation of general paralysis

My great adorable woman beautiful as everything on the earth and in the most beautiful stars of the earth that I adore my great woman adored by all the powers of the stars beautiful with the beauty of the billions of the queens that adorn the earth the adoration I have for your beauty brings me to my

---

[20] By Breton.
[21] By Eluard.
[22] By Breton.
[23] La Paiva (1819–84), originally from Russia, was an adventuress of the Second Empire. She constructed a palatial house at 25 avenue des Champs-Élysées, which is still noted for its bathroom, made of precious marbles.

[24] By Eluard.
[25] By Breton.
[26] By Eluard.
[27] By Breton.

knees to beg you to think of me I kneel at your knees I adore your beauty think of me my adorable beauty my great beauty whom I adore[28] I roll diamonds in the moss taller than the forests where your tallest hair thinks of me — do not forget me my little woman on my knees that time by the fireside on the sand of emerald — look at yourself in my hand which I use to stand steady on everything in the world so that you will recognise me for what I am my blonde-brunette my beauty and my beast think of me in paradise with my head in my hands.[29]

The hundred and fifty castles where we were going to make love were not enough for me a hundred thousand more will be built for me tomorrow I have chased out from the baobab forests of your eyes the peacocks and panthers and lyrebirds I will shut them in my strongholds and we shall go walking together in the forests of Asia of Europe of Africa and America which surround our castles in the admirable forests of your eyes which are accustomed to my splendour.[30]

You do not have to wait for the surprise that I want to give you for your birthday which falls today the same day as mine — I am giving it to you at once since I have waited fifteen times for the year one thousand before giving you the surprise of asking you to play hide-and-seek with your thinking of me — I want you to think of me my young eternal woman while laughing. Before I could sleep I counted cloud upon cloud of carts full of beet for the sun and I want to take you at night to the astrakhan beach they are building with two horizons for your eyes of petroleum, to make war[31] I will lead you there by paths of diamonds with emerald primroses and the ermine mantle with which I wish to cover you is a bird of prey the diamonds your feet will tread on I have had cut in the shape of butterflies. Think of me who think only of your brilliance where slumbers the sun-drenched luxury of an earth and all the stars I have conquered for you I adore you and I adore your eyes and I have opened your eyes open to all those they have seen and I will give to all the beings whom your eyes have seen raiment of gold and crystal raiment they will have to throw away when your eyes have dulled it with their contempt.[32] I bleed in my heart at the mere initials of your name on a flag with the initials of your name which are all the letters of which Z is the first in the infinity of alphabets and civilisations where I will love you yet since you wish to be my wife and to think of me in the countries where there is no longer an average. My heart bleeds on your mouth and closes on your mouth on all the pink chestnut trees of the avenue of your mouth down which we go in the sparkling dust to lie among the meteors[33] of your beauty which I adore my great creature so beautiful that I am happy to adorn my treasures with your presence with thoughts of you and with your name which multiplies the facets of my treasures' ecstasy which I adore because it finds an echo in all the looking glasses of my splendour[34] my original woman my scaffolding of rosewood you are the fault of my fault of my very great fault as Jesus Christ is the wife of my cross — twelve times twelve thousand one hundred and forty-nine times have I loved you with passion on the way and I am crucified in the North in the East in the West and in the North for your radium kiss and I want you and you are in my mirror of pearls the breath of the man who will not return you to the surface and who loves you in adoration my woman lying standing when you are sitting and combing your hair.[35]

You will come you think of me you will come you will run to me on your thirteen full legs and all your empty legs that beat the air with the swaying of your arms a multitude of arms that want to clasp themselves around me kneeling between your legs and your arms to clasp you without fear that my locomotives will prevent you from coming to me and I follow you and I am ahead of you to stop you to give you all the stars in the sky in a kiss on your eyes all the kisses in the world in a star on your mouth.[36]

Yours, sweetly aflame.

P.S. I should like a phone book for mass a phone book with a knotted string to mark the pages. Bring me a Franco-German flag, too, so I can fly it in no-man's-land. And a pound of Menier

---

[28] By Eluard.
[29] By Breton.
[30] By Eluard.
[31] By Breton.
[32] By Eluard.

[33] By Breton.
[34] By Eluard.
[35] By Breton.
[36] By Eluard.

chocolate with the little girl sticking up posters (I do not remember). And then nine of those little girls too with their lawyers and their judges and come on the special train with the speed of light and the Wild West outlaws who will keep me amused for a minute which unfortunately pops here like a champagne cork. And a skate. My left suspender has just gone I was lifting up the world like a feather. Can you do something for me buy a tank I want to see you come like the fairies.[37]

Attempted simulation of interpretative delirium

When that love was done with, I was left like a bird on a branch. I was no longer any use for anything. Nevertheless I observed that the patches of oil on the water reflected my image and I noticed that the Pont au Change, which has the bird market next to it, was becoming more and more curved.

And that is how, one fine day, I crossed over forever to the other side of the rainbow by dint of watching iridescent birds. Now I have nothing to do with the ground. No more than any other bird, I say, do I need any more to demean myself on the ground, to put in a winged appearance on the ground. I refuse to sing along with you the lurid ditty: "We die for the little birds, give a feast to your little birds."[38]

The gaudy colours of the rainshower prattle parrot. They coddle the wind which hatches out with seeds in its eyes.[39] The double eyelid of the sun rises and falls on life. The birds' feet on the windowpane of the sky are what I used to call stars. The earth itself, whose motion seems so inexplicable as long as one remains beneath the vault, the earth that is webfooted with deserts is itself subject to the laws of migration.[40]

The feather summer is not over yet. The holds have been opened and harvests of down are being stuffed into them. The weather is *moulting*.[41]

The cock on the steeple adorns the gunfire smoke while the orange-breasted widow makes her way to the cemetery whose crosses are the tiny flashes of Senegalese Diamonds while man continues to *believe* himself upon the earth like a blackbird on a buffalo's back,[42] upon the sea like a gull on the crest of the waves; the blackbird solid and the seagull liquid.[43]

Horus, with a finger to his lips, is the avalanche.[44] I had not seen those birdcatchers who search for men in the sky and drive each other from their nests with stones they throw into the air.[45]

Phoenixes come bringing me my food of glow worms and their wings which ceaselessly dip into the gold of the earth are the sea and the sky which we only used to see aglow on stormy days and which hide their thunderbolt plumes among their feathers when they fall asleep on the single foot of the air.[46]

The mills of lightning have broken their shells and flee as fast as their wings will carry them, sand eats dunes, the horizon is trying to keep out of the way of clouds.[47]

You will agree that your *drop-sided cots*, and your twisted bars, and your gnawed floors, and your nutmegs, and your scarecrows in the latest fashion, and your *telegraph wires*, and your journeys in pigeon class compartments, and the lambs that form the plinths of your statues of prey, and your *hurdle races* run at dusk with robins that fly away, and the hours, and the minutes, and the seconds in your woodpecker heads, and your glorious conquests, yes, your glorious cuckoo-like conquests![48] All these snares of grace were only ever there to get me through the gates of danger, the gates that separate fear from courage.[49] Do not count any more on me to help you forget that your ghosts are decked out like birds of paradise.

In the beginning was song. Everyone to the windows! From one side to the other you see nothing now but Leda.[50] My whirling wings are the doors through which she enters the swan's neck, on the great deserted square that is the heart of the bird of night.[51]

---

[37] By Breton.
[38] By Breton.
[39] By Eluard.
[40] By Breton.
[41] By Eluard.
[42] By Breton.
[43] By Eluard.
[44] By Breton.

[45] By Eluard.
[46] By Breton.
[47] By Eluard.
[48] By Breton.
[49] By Eluard.
[50] By Breton.
[51] By Eluard.

Attempted simulation of dementia praecox

The woman here with an arm on her head pebbled with pralines which leave here without anyone having a clear idea because it is a bit more than noon here while leaving the laugh through the teeth which retreats across the palate of the Danaids which I caress with my tongue without thinking that the day of God has arrived music forward of the little girls weeping seeds whom one watches without seeing them weep by the hand of the Graces on the fourth floor window with the cat's mignonette which the catapult took from behind on a holiday.[52] While boulanging with the General of Thermopylae launched on a tricycle and red to perceive. The tub is listed in the sky by the Virgin immobile in her barrel. God makes me tongues with the bread. I minnow the mountains. In the thought of my thought is the great house with labouring houses in the house of human skin with a balcony of seals. The ordinary is supreme though there is a little awkwardness in the milk of ovation and evocation. It is there with its udder-like eyes, I pass it into shooting targets.[53] I have said three words too many, too bad, I take them back, I add them. I have several times deserved death, especially in Greece, where I sawed up the palette of an old man who stalked my lady friends right up to my camp bed. I messed up the hairdo of the greatest criminal in Chaldea. For all that I did not have to make use of my daughter native to the lower parts of her father's vision, all the plains as far as the eye can see which eat hampers full of mother-of-pearl. Platinum, you can no longer stand up since the trumpet of lounging shook your eternity. Pale star, little hut in the wooden monkey which I am smothering, you fall from the clouds, you retreat before the forty ways of using my cruelty.[54]

When I was young I hid Hercules in the pocket of my sailor suit, when I was old I restored his freedom by fixing his ransom to my tombstone in ricochets. He laughed behind my gag, a laugh like ivy. Later, as I was early, I germinated myriads of toads' eggs which came from intersections of kangaroo paths at star-shaped crossroads in the bicorn hat with drawers of my chest with leafless trefoil feet. I have as a great grand-daughter Cléo de Mérode,[55] my great grandmother who travels pillion on wolf-back with Charles the Bold.[56] I have won the jackpot a million times at roulette by playing the nine months of the year. I was expelled in triumph from all the fencing halls because I wanted to take the honey.[57] It was that very day that I understood the seven mysteries of creation. Cléo de Mérode spent her time trying to wedge the table leg with the best part of my winnings. I put Cléo de Mérode between the claws of my ring. She is quiet, she wakes the dead. I am sterilising all the facts. The embryo continues to look like a monkey-wrench, the damned Protestant has stopped swaggering. I have made rules for the debtor's prison. You have to show your identity to get in and not forget about the guards. The prison roof carries republican bunting on gala days. The reign of the useless is over. They wanted to give me a false beard and make me play the sepulchral role of valet to the Pope. They threatened to get me on the wrong side of the King of August but I gritted my teeth and told them forty-eight if you do not let go of my hand I will no longer go into the grinder box to make you fire.[58]

I wrote *good* in a round hand on my trunk and got myself enrolled as I walked past the front. They put me in the wagon with the lions but as soon as they recognised me they were left with nothing but a daisy mane. I clipped a thousand lions as we went in the space for *a lot* which had been left blank. Then I jumped off the train which tied itself in knots. I had arrived.

I scalped the audience. I put my tool up all the chimneys on Christmas day.

I have been granted the trust of jealous people who consult me about crimes of passion.[59] It is right to dampen bells with the pigtails of good solid French girls who have nothing left but their wardrobe with a mirror on the back. I look at myself in it, coddle myself in it and what do we raise?

---

[52] By Eluard.
[53] By Breton.
[54] By Eluard.
[55] Cléo de Mérode (1875–1966) was a dancer, originally from an aristocratic Belgian family; she had a long liaison with Leopold II and was a Parisian celebrity.

[56] Charles the Bold (1433–77) was killed during the siege of Nancy and his corpse was largely devoured by wolves.
[57] By Breton.
[58] By Eluard.
[59] By Breton.

– a hint of clumsy pirouettes on the knees of a satisfying old gentleman. Quarries of lead-grey she-wolves. I have seen it all. You have to laugh with the wolves.[60]

I believe in philately. I have the arms of Poitiers tattooed on the left side of my arm which has a slip-on cover, and the words *se peut* artificially prolong each *lash* of my upper eyelid, while on each of my cheeks the first letter of *oui* is rounded in macabre pink. Philately started before man, towards the beginning of the tertiary era. Pterodactyls are leaping right now from one lip of my inkwell to the other. Wedding pictures are not obscene enough: the priest should wear a tiddler on his chasuble.[61] Rubbers blown up with the perforations of stamps for balloon mail still besiege our good town. Missionaries need fresh vegetables because cannibalism is contagious and only the savages are suspected. A parricide in Africa hollowed out his eye in the form of a shell. The pieces for the game of carnage are ten thousand agile fingers.[62]

I have a jazz in my thumb which alternates with a Chinese musician in the nail. I am hanging from a loop of cherries. I launched all the fashions of bygone days: the skirt with spurs, the water-train, the globe with a cross in the hands of thumbsucking infants. I have tasted all the foods that no one has dared yet to serve. Sleepers do not smell the same as people awake: if you wake them up with a start a smell of cyclamen fills the room. I have the head of fathma on Gemini and a leaden foot in Libra. The immensity of my nature is spread between two wasp-stings harnessed to the same compass as is crying out for a feed from mother's beak. If it is on the lip, it makes kiss; if it is on the bum, it makes Tibet.[63]

I am the grandfather, the father, the father-in-law, the brother, the brother-in-law, the uncle, the son-in-law, the daughter-in-law, the cousin, the godfather, and the parish priest of the current pope who is merely a spy in disguise, a false friend in the service of the archdukes of Thule. He can only be unmasked by showing to the crowd the Parthian arrow sticking in his shoulder. Thus are rabbles welded together, the adulterous fruits of valetry and the mattress. I fear only by ear the time switch in the Department stores I built by piling 33,000 shelves of sweets on the peace treaties. Another pair of noodles on another pair of being right without being there, another pair of sleeves for other arms on another pair of noodles.[64] We will certainly see with regard to the noodle in the tunnel under the Channel whether armless penguins and one-armed men are capable of recognising my brain as the Grand Baster of the Three Kings' Pudding. You have to take the lift to get from his feet to his head via imagination but when I see the republics coming to call every week, I seal my blood preciously after bottling it. The young man is not yet so knowledgeable about his fate with the chairs on which he limits himself to sitting kilometrically opposite himself without marking time. I am astride the shoulders of three young girls who are going up to get a better view to the top floor of the tower in which my throat is slit while I go down the Niagara falls[65] as a fishing float, rolled in a ball, in a little boat, in a ball of sound from the men condemned to death that young girls prefer, who free girls from the snares that are their breasts.

I will give nothing to the wild beasts, I shall stab them to death with my dagger. I am inhabited from bottom to top by a pack, the stag comes down, and takes me on his back, so like a sleeping woman. What are you about to climb? The Seine unwinds, I hold the spool, I spin it out on the surface of the water everywhere. I have 21,000 erupting volcanoes. I am spilling fire on every side. But I do not trust the 500 billion flames which I am training like dogs.[66] I am free, which I find astounding on the part of the thunder and of medicine with simples. I write to lawyers my free will in my soul and conscience which swears before the court to tell the whole truth while insisting on the mitigating circumstances and swears. But I swear to put the jury in clink for condemning me to be free, non-denominational, and compulsory. Not in the month of July but on completion of the term and declared in default in all duels with file and set square by my hierarchical superiors who are splitting their sides on each side of my chest. I have done nothing more than the most or less

[60] By Eluard.
[61] By Breton.
[62] By Eluard.
[63] By Breton.
[64] By Eluard.
[65] By Breton.
[66] By Eluard.

than the most and I have given freedom to God who bore a golden yoke which he returned to me to be free and to lead me by the hand into the meadows of the golden buttercup.[67]

Beneath the iron rod of corregidores who mutter at the crow's neck surams of Irdia I spend the evenings in jars beneath the alleys of the gudder. Bound through glughole. I have noticed that decease is bent on betraying with a burst of laughter and subjecting night to the living, the pink and white silk of the return of delay, retarded erasure of rabble. Raeson thah no urle. I have eaten at Faust's table in bow's cuts and the guests were enjoined to dip their eyes in blue so the devilblue this passing blue who was guest of honour with one hand on my hand and the other in his lace.[68] And we were stained to the very marrow. Wasp-drills frizz umbelliferant with horseshoes in the soggy manger and the bovvercome take on red-cadet's teeth. For myself, I, the undersigned, concurd. A mist of feeling makes me apartment to raise with cover for my people and mushroom understanding crinkles the herb while tearing off its head as required. And mounted on a wall-clearing which Elbes its way His Country Gratefully, Elbe all modern condolences and our Lorelei which bust as they come down. When I bestow from top to toe to be the beech, the forename, the countername, the intername and the Parthename my prayer and I say No and Canoe and I shoot and the bong gadrins and disappears into my thin within and percusses in.[69] Quietly the bird's cherrybright and pint cloud over with pimplico and Neasden slick on the funny-bone long thin funny bone eat the hoar-frost of Hindies and Niobobs from Suda. The phyldra is obserbed via the eracmous obe.[70] You fool-step on pins while Aladdin coo-coo-coo. St Peter so logic with pipe, a recedar of iffer but old, oh sovery somuch. The floor below is Paris' abode. The x exaltasperates soda-fire. Batavoir and rouletter mumbling rat-tail decorate super-tooter the Jingoryjambo-reeger-many. I how however howitzer for you sir. Yes, of course, Sir, mos'ley me.[71] Sunderstood ear seh fluff the systel, the seals upon your wisdom would frieze up without delay. Anafanalysis reduces the cheatrous from drone and twelve four times eight deal. By way of augmenting the chapping skin two leave mine of epigraphs. I nick eleven and cut them eleven makes eleven sumsisred eeto.[72] Makoff! Hall in hall you could climatiate without thinking twice. And beatyou begawping black vocab which purdles beFore the Frongarson Adjectives like Onetwo but one adword in tongue but not in furnitre, I gasp you myself who Sleepapostrophe Maimberlain. And who impelioses markets in the woOds. We each began by

nossosrong = Son of Judas reneved, who Rev. ferrisrong

Linnaeus hippomyth Ee ingbrill rether krind folla klimbixigs rodikits mofroe debla... Ee wonad tewarruep me yugbixigs terweani seraip, Ee teltoudha allowow chyugxigs, tewargaxigs splat. Ee nodedha oradarcaderashi neac lsplsh figyef.[73] Ee hentanddha methtibten tewarfogjug fulecragdis beltog.[74] Oradar-yugbixigs ingbromme ee nodedha mogsuere neac lewhitt.[75]

[67] By Breton.
[68] By Eluard.
[69] By Breton.
[70] By Eluard.
[71] By Breton.
[72] By Eluard.
[73] By Breton.
[74] By Eluard.
[75] By Breton.

Nancy Cunard (1896–1965)

Introduction

Nancy Cunard (1896–1965) was born at her parents' house, Nevill Holt, in Leicestershire, the daughter of Sir Bache Cunard, heir of the famous shipping line, and Lady Emerald, a celebrated London hostess. She was educated at private schools. In 1915 she married Sydney Fairbairn, whom she left and divorced in 1917. In November 1916 she published her first poems in *Wheels*, the first of six anthologies edited by Edith Sitwell and her brothers. She spent most of the 1920s in perpetual travel between London, Paris, and a series of French country houses. In 1926 and 1927 she had a tempestuous affair with the French Surrealist writer Louis Aragon. In 1928 she moved to Réanville, in Normandy, 60 miles from Paris. She purchased the press that William Bird had used when he ran the Three Mountains Press, and she then became a publisher, calling her firm The Hours Press. Over the next four years she published important works by Laura Riding, Richard Aldington, Ezra Pound, and Samuel Beckett, among others. It was also in 1928 that she met Henry Crowder, a black pianist.

With him she struck up a relationship that would last seven years. But because Nancy was a wealthy celebrity, she soon felt the sting of racist reportage concerning her relationship with Crowder. In retaliation she pressed a suit of libel, which she won. Her mother, meanwhile, was horrified by the mounting scandal and disowned her. In reply Cunard wrote *Black Man and White Ladyship*, a pamphlet that mercilessly exposed her mother's racist comments. The result was more notoriety.

Crowder, in effect, introduced Nancy to the question of racism, but also to the rich world of African-American and African culture. From 1931 to 1934 she worked on assembling *Negro*, a massive anthology with 150 contributors, 855 pages, and 385 illustrations.

When Crowder left her in 1935, Nancy turned her attention to the Spanish Civil War, becoming a journalist and soliciting funds for the Republican cause. After World War II she continued to write and travel, but her energies were seriously diminished. She died in southern France.

Wheels (1916)

I sometimes think that all our thoughts are wheels
Rolling forever through the painted world,
Moved by the cunning of a thousand clowns
Dressed paper-wise, with blatant rounded masks,
That take their multi-coloured caravans   5
From place to place, and act and leap and sing,
Catching the spinning hoops when cymbals clash.
And one is dressed as Fate, and one as Death,
The rest that represent Love, Joy and Sin,
Join hands in solemn stage-learnt ecstasy,   10
While Folly beats a drum with golden pegs,
And mocks that shrouded Jester called Despair.
The dwarves and other curious satellites,
Voluptuous-mouthed, with slyly-pointed steps,
Strut in the circus while the people stare.   15
And some have sober faces white with chalk,
Of sleeping hearts, with ponderance and noise
Like weary armies on a solemn march.
Now in the scented gardens of the night,
Where we are scattered like a pack of cards,   20
Our words are turned to spokes that thoughts may roll
And form a jangling chain around the world,

"Wheels" and "The Carnivals of Peace" first appeared in Edith
Sitwell, *Wheels: An Anthology of Verse* (Oxford: B. H. Blackwell,
1916).

(Itself a fabulous wheel controlled by Time
Over the slow incline of centuries.)
So dreams and prayers and feelings born of sleep   25
As well as all the sun-gilt pageantry
Made out of summer breezes and hot noons,
Are in the great revolving of the spheres
Under the trampling of their chariot wheels.

The Carnivals of Peace (1916)

Had I a clearer brain, imagination,
A flowing pen and better ending rhymes,
A firmer heart devoid of hesitation,
Unbiassed happiness these barren times
With pleasure in this discontented life,   5
Forgetfulness of sorrow and of pain,
Triumphant victory on fear and strife,
Daring to look behind and look again
A-head for all the slowly coming days,
See nothing but the Carnivals of Peace,   10
Forget the dreams of death and other ways
Men have imagined for their own decrease....
I'd write a song to conquer all our tears,
Lasting for ever through the folding years.

Evenings (1921)

Now when you hear the musing of a bell
Let loose in summer evenings, mark the poise
Of summer clouds, the mutability
Of pallid twilights from a tower's crest –
When you have loved the last long sentiment   5
Slipped on-to earth from sunset, seen the stars
Come pale and faltering, the blaze of flowers
Grow dim and grey, and all the stuff of night
Rise up around you almost menacing –
When you have lost the guide of colour, seen   10
The daylight like a workman trudging home
Oblivious of your thoughts and leaving you
Silent beside the brim of seas grown still,
Placid and strange. When you have lingered there,
And shuddered at the magic of a moon   15
That will not sleep, but needs your vigilance
And seizes on the musings of your soul
Till you are made fanatical and wild,
Torn with old conflicts and the internal fire
Of passion and love, excessive grief of tears   20
And all the revolutions found in life –
What then? your body shall be crucified,
Your spirit tortured, and perhaps found good
Enough a tribute for some ultimate art.

"Evenings" first appeared in Nancy Cunard's earliest collection of
poems, a slender volume (63 pages) titled *Outlaws* (London: Elkin
Mathews, 1921).

Voyages North (1921)

The strange effects of afternoons!
Hours interminable, melting like honey-drops
In an assemblage of friends . . .
Or jagged, stretching hard unpleasant fingers
As we go by, hurrying through the crowds –   5
People agape at shops, Regent Street[1] congested
With the intolerable army of winter road-workers
Picking; then in the Cafe Royal[2]
Belated drunkards toying with a balloon
Bought from a pedler – streets and stations   10
Serried together like cheap print, swinging trains
With conversational travellers arguing on the Opera –
Newspapers, agitation of the mind and fingers,
The first breath of country dispelling undue meditation
With the reposeful promise of village firesides;   15
Greetings at meeting – But if I were free
I would go on, see all the northern continents
Stretch out before me under winter sunsets;
Look into the psychology
Of Iceland, and plumb the imaginations   20
Of travellers outlandish, talking and drinking
With stern strange companies of merchants;
I should learn
More than one could remember, walk through the days
Enjoying the remoteness, and laughing in foreign places;   25
I should cure my heart of longing and impatience
And all the penalties of thought-out pleasure,
Those aftermaths of degradation
That come when silly feasts are done.
I should be wise and prodigal, spending these new delights   30
With the conviction of a millionaire
Made human by imagination – they should be
The important steps that lead to happiness
And independence of the mind; then should I say
Final farewell to streets of memories,   35
Forget the analytical introspection
And the subjective drowsiness of mind,
Stamping into the dust all staleness of things outgrown,
Stand on a northern hill-top shouting at the sun!

Horns in the Valley (1923)

This June the nights lay heavy until dawn;
Then did my heart devise in solitude
Of old romances – came an evocation
Across the valley mists at sound of horns

"Voyages North" first appeared in Nancy Cunard's earliest collection of poems, a slender volume (63 pages) titled *Outlaws* (London: Elkin Mathews, 1921).

[1] *Regent Street* a street in London running north from Piccadilly Circus, designed by John Nash (1752–1835).

[2] *the Cafe Royal* a bar in Regent Street that became a meeting place for wealthy bohemia in the 1920s.

"Horns in the Valley" was first published in Cunard's second collection of poems, *Sublunary* (London: Hodder and Stoughton, 1923).

Deep in the forest springing. So again   5
When the last chord had died, Isolda[1] rose
With pulsing signal of imperious arms
Uplifted in long tremolo of passion.
I saw the grasses bend before her lover,
Precipitate wraith that hurried to her calling;   10
And the lost echoes of their ardent voices
Grew in my sense with fading of the horns,
Sighing an ultimate song of death and love.
Then in the harbour of the risen moon
The dew lay solitary; no shadows there   15
Guarded these pale-faced lovers through the night,
And the lone tower was empty of its watcher.
But in that moment were they joined at trysting,
Come to the cadence of this midnight music,
And now are gone on silence desolate.   20

Simultaneous (1930)

At one time
The bottle hyacinths under Orvieto[1] –
At one time
A letter a letter and a letter –
At one time, sleepless,   5
Through rain the nightingale sang from the
                                    river island –

At one time, Montparnasse,[2]
And all night's gloss
Splendour of shadow on shadow   10
With the exact flower
Of the liqueur in its glass.
        Time runs,
                but thought (or what?) comes
Seated between these damaged table-tops,   15
Sense of what zones, what simultaneous-time sense?

            ... Then in Ravenna[3]
The dust is turned to dew
By moonlight, and the exact
Splayed ox-feet sleep that dragged the sugar-beet   20
To dry maremmas
        Past Sant' Spollinare,
        Fuori Mura.

---

[1] *Isolda* from the legend of Tristan and Isolde (or Isolda); Tristan, nephew of King Mark, is sent to fetch his intended bride Isolde for him. When Isolde later falls in love with him, she decides to kill both Tristan and herself with poison; but her companion, Brangäne, substitutes a love potion for the poison, and the two fall hopelessly in love. Later, Isolde sees Tristan die in her arms in the final scene of Wagner's opera *Tristan und Isolde* ("when the last chord had died").

"Simultaneous" first appeared in a slender (14 pages) limited edition of 150 copies, *Poems (Two) 1925* (London: Aquila Press, 1930).

[1] *Orvieto* a small town midway between Florence and Rome in Italy.
[2] *Montparnasse* an area on the left bank of Paris.
[3] *Ravenna* a town on the coast of northeast Italy, some 70 miles south of Venice, famous for its Byzantine churches, one of which is Sant' Apollinare, Fuori Mura (Saint Apollinaire Outside the Walls).

In Calais[4] Roads
The foam-quilt sags and swells,   25
Exact are the land's beacons to the sea –
Twin arms crossed, thrown across sleep and
                        a night-wind.
Time falls from unseen bells
On Calais Quays (that were sometime   30
                        a heart's keys.)
    Red bryony
Steeps in loose night-air,
Swelling – October crumples the hedge –
Or the wind's in the ash, opening the seed-pods.   35
        (The revolution in the weeds –
        Rain somewhere. Rain suggests
        Their dissolution to the seeds.)

                        Midnight,
While some protract their trades   40
Forcing the line – sleep takes them,
But the baker
Cools at the sill, yeast auburn flour.

                    Midnight
And trains perambulate (*o noctis equi*[5]);   45
Faust[6] is in hell that would have stopped the
                        horses of night
In their gallops, that would have galloped atop
                        of them
But was outpaced, overthrown for too exact   50
                        questioning.

            And in Albi[7]
Les orguilleux sus des roues continuellement[8]
            (hell's fading fresco),

And in Torcello[9]   55
The mud-fogs now, and on all unknown
Ripe watery wastes
The rich dead silence.

Silence – or a nightwind on a lawn
Turning the pages, one by one,   60
                of a forgotten book.

---

[4] *Calais* traditional port for passengers traveling from Britain to France.

[5] *o noctis equi* Latin for "o horses of the night."

[6] *Faust* the central character in *Faust* (Part I, 1808; Part II, 1831), by Johann Wolfgang von Goethe (1749–1832), the German poet and man of letters.

[7] *Albi* a town in southern France on the Garonne River.

[8] *Les orguilleux ... continuellement* French for "the proud continually on wheels."

[9] *Torcello* a small island near Venice, with Byzantine churches dating from the seventh through the twelfth centuries.

"Black Man and White Ladyship" (1931)

An anniversary is coming and that is why this is printed now, and the reason for its having been written will, I imagine, be clear to those who read it.

By anniversary I am not, indeed, referring to Christmas, but to the calendric moment of last year when the Colour Question first presented me personally with its CLASH or SHOCK aspect.

I have a Negro friend, a very close friend (and a great many other Negro friends in France, England and America). Nothing extraordinary in that. I have also a mother – whom we will at once call: Her Ladyship.[1] We are extremely different but I had remained on fairly good (fairly distant) terms with her for a number of years. The english channel and a good deal of determination on my part made this possible. I sedulously avoid her social circle both in France and in England. My Negro friend has been in London with me five or six times. So far so good. But, a few days before our going to London last year, what follows had just taken place, and I was unaware of it until our arrival. At a large lunch party in Her Ladyship's house things are set rocking by one of those bombs that throughout her "career" Margot Asquith, Lady Oxford,[2] has been wont to hurl. No-one could fail to wish he had been at that lunch to see the effect of Lady Oxford's entry: "Hello, Maud, what is it now – drink, drugs or niggers?" (A variant is that by some remark Her Ladyship had annoyed the other Ladyship, who thus triumphantly retaliated.) The house is a seemly one in Grosvenor Square[3] and what takes place in it is far from "drink, drugs or niggers." There is confusion. A dreadful confusion between Her Ladyship and myself! For I am known to have a great Negro friend – the drink and the drugs do not apply. Half of social London is immediately telephoned to: "Is it *true* my daughter knows a Negro?" etc., etc.

It appears that Sir Thomas Beecham,[4] in the light of "the family friend," was then moved sufficiently to pen me a letter, in the best Trollope style, in which he pointed out that, as the only one qualified to advise, it would, at that juncture, be a grave mistake to come to England with a gentleman of american-african extraction whose career, he believed, it was my desire to advance, as, while friendships between races were viewed with tolerance on the continent, by some, it was ... in other words it was a very different pair of shoes in England especially as viewed by the Popular Press! This letter (which was sent to the wrong address and not received till a month later on my return to Paris) was announced by a telegram "strongly advising" me not to come to London until I got it adding that the subject was unmentionable by wire! I was packing my trunk and laid the telegram on top – time will show. ... We took the four o'clock train.

What happened in London?

Some detectives called, the police looked in, the telephone rang incessantly at our hotel. The *patron* (so he said) received a *mysterious message* that he himself would be imprisoned "undt de other vil be kilt." Madame wept: "Not even a *black* man, why he's only *brown*." Her Ladyship did not go so far as to step round herself. The Popular Press was unmoved. This lasted about a month and I used to get news of it daily, enough to fill a dossier on the hysteria caused by a difference of pigmentation.

The question that interested a good many people for two and a quarter years (does Her Ladyship know or not?) was thus brilliantly settled.

But, your Ladyship, you cannot kill or deport a person from England for being a Negro and mixing with white people. You may take a ticket to the cracker southern states of U.S.A. and assist at some of the choicer lynchings which are often announced in advance. You may add your purified-of-that-horrible-american-twang voice to the yankee outbursts: America for white folks – segregation for the 12 million blacks we can't put up with – or do without ...

First published as an independent pamphlet, 11 pages in length, in an unknown number of copies (Toloun: Imprimerie A. Bordato, 1931).
[1]   Lady Maud Cunard (née Maud Alice Burke) was the wife of Sir Bache Cunard, heir of the Cunard shipping lines, but had left him to establish her own residence.
[2]   Margot Asquith (1864–1945), wife of Herbert Henry

Asquith, prime minister of Britain (from 1908 to 1916), was notorious for her *bons mots* and barbed comments.
[3]   An especially posh address in London.
[4]   Thomas Beecham (1879–1961), famous British conductor, founded the Royal Philharmonic Orchestra in 1946 and was a friend of Maud Cunard.

No, with you it is the other old trouble – class.

Negroes, besides being black (that is, from jet to as white as yourself but not so pink), have not yet "penetrated into London Society's consciousness." You exclaim: they are not "received!" (You would be surprised to know just how much they are "received.") They are not found in the Royal Red Book. Some big hostess gives a lead and the trick is done!

For as yet only the hefty shadow of the Negro falls across the white assembly of High Society and spreads itself, it would seem, quite particularly and agonisingly over you.

And what has happened since this little dust-up of December last, 1930? We have not met, I trust we shall never meet again. You have cut off, first a quarter (on plea of your high income tax), then half of my allowance. You have stated that I am out of your will. Excellent – for at last we have a little truth between us. The black man is a well-known factor in the changing of testaments (at least in America), and parents, as we all know, are not to be held responsible for the existence of children.

Concerning this last I have often heard Her Ladyship say that it is the children who owe their parents nothing. But I am grateful to her for the little crop of trivalia that has flowered this year:

Mr. George Moore[5] – (at one time her best friend and thence my first friend) whose opinion I was interested to have on the whole matter, which I obtained by the silence that followed my frank letter to him – was said to have decided not to leave me his two Manets as he intended, but has subsequently contradicted this. . . .

Her Ladyship's hysteria has produced the following remarks:

that – no hotel would accommodate my black friend.

that – he was put out of England (exquisitely untrue, for we came, stayed and left together after a month).

that – she would not feel *chic* in Paris any longer as she had heard that all the chic Parisians nowadays consorted with Negroes.

that – I now wrote for the Negro Press. (One poem and one article have appeared in the *Crisis*, New York.)

that – where would I be in a few years' time.

that – she does not mind the Negroes now artistically or in an *abstract* sense but . . . oh, that terrible colour! (I invite Her Ladyship to send in writing a short definition of a Negro in the *abstract sense*.)

that – she knew *nothing at all of the whole thing* till Mr. Moore read her my letter. Now, to be exact: my letter to Mr. Moore was written Jan. 24 whereas Her Ladyship severely put through it several friends of mine in the preceding December, and had her bank signify to me on Jan. 21, 1931, that owing to the exigencies of her Income Tax . . . I suspect Her Ladyship of having conveniently forgotten that what seems indeed to have struck her as a bomb exploded before many witnesses in her own house. (This is very interesting and I don't doubt the psychologists have many such cases on their books – the washing of hands, let us add, by the main party.)

I am told that Her Ladyship was invited to a night-club, saw some coloured singers, turned faint and left . . . yet at least one paid coloured entertainer has been to her house.

I am told that she believes all the servants in a London house gave notice because a coloured gentleman came to dinner.

AND I AM TOLD

that Sir Thomas Beecham says I ought to be tarred and feathered!

It is now necessary to see Her Ladyship in her own fort, to perceive her a little more visually.

In the Sunday Express of Nov. 22, 1931, can be read in detail of how Her Ladyship spends a fortune on clothes she never wears. "I have not the faintest idea of how much I spend on clothes every year – it may run into thousands. I have never bothered to think about it. But that is because I do not have to bother about money." (Which tallies interestingly with her bank's statement concerning the exigencies of her Income Tax – see previously.) . . . "I want to tell you candidly why it is that so-called 'Society' women spend so much on their clothes. It is not that the cost of each garment is so very large; it is simply that we won't be bothered."

---

[5]   George Moore (1852–1933) was an Irish writer who befriended Nancy Cunard when she was young.

The Market may be going on at any time, and generally is. Others play it but Her Ladyship plays it best. Rich Mrs. XYZ will be "taken out" if she guesses or takes the hint that she is to do her duty by... (the object varies). No sign of the hint ever being administered! But the participants are well-trained, each is looking for what the other can supply, and each felicitously finds. Many results have been come by in this excellent manner. Snobbery opens purses, starvation fails.

Her Ladyship's own snobbery is quite simple. If a thing *is done* she will, with a few negligible exceptions, do it too. And the last person she has talked to is generally right, providing he is *someone*. The British Museum seems to guarantee that African art is art? some dealers, too, are taking it up, so the thick old Congo ivories that she thinks are slave bangles are perhaps not so hideous after all though still very *strange*; one little diamond would be better... though of course that is different.

Her Ladyship likes to give – and to control. It is unbearable for her not to be able to give someone something. But suppose they don't want it – what does this *mean?* Her reaction to being given something herself generally produces the phrase that people shouldn't do such things! Yet the house is full of noble gifts.

Another time it is Communism. "You don't mean to say those people you talk of are communists? they couldn't be, no-one as intelligent, as intellectual as they are... You can't *know* people like that," etc.... And away with the troubling thought. Her Ladyship is the most conscientious of ostriches and when she comes up again she hopes the *un*pleasant thing has disappeared. Perhaps it doesn't really exist. She is also a great cross-questioner and all her ingenuous ingenuity is seen at work on the picking of brains. As those she puts through it are generally less quick in defence than she is in attack, and as she has a fantastic imagination she generally arrives at some result. Look out! as in the farce, evidence will be taken down, altered and used against you. It will make quite a farce in itself. She is a great worker for she is never content to leave things as they are. In digging away she may turn up some startling facts. She is shocked. She is suspicious. All is not as it should be. She does not recognise... there may be no precedent – why it may even be scandalous... it *is* scandalous! it is unheard of!! WHAT is to be done? Why, talk about it! What do people say? A mountain is thrown up by this irreducible mole. There – of course it is *monstrous!* It cannot be true... and, though it is she who has informed the world, she is astounded presently when it all gets out of hand and falls back on her in anything but gentle rain.

Her Ladyship is american and this is all part of that great american joke: *l'inconscience*. Here she is, ex-cathedra at the lunch table, here she is telling some specimen A1 illiterate of the greatness of the last great book, here – wistfully puzzled by some little matter everyone knows, here – praising rightly, praising wrongly, making and missing the point all in one breath. Generous to the rich, trying always to do the right thing (serve only the best champagne, the food is always perfect). One day the footmen have frayed trousers. The butler has taken a leaf from Her Ladyship's book and explains that *no good enough* ready-made trousers are procurable in London, and that the tailor being dear, and slow... he falters. There is a scene. The interior economy is impeccable.

Are intellectuals generally the least biassed in race questions? Here are two reactionaries: –

A little conversation with Mr. George Moore in Ebury St.

Self: Yes, people certainly feel very differently about race. I cannot understand colour prejudice. Do you think you have it?

G.M.:   No, I don't think so.

Self: Have you ever known any people of colour?

G.M.:   No.

Self: What, not even an Indian?

G.M.:   No – though my books are translated into Chinese.

Self: Not even an Indian... such as might have happened had you met, shall we say, an Indian student. Don't you think you'd like to talk to an intelligent Indian or Negro?

G.M.:   (*calmly*) No. I do not think so. I do not think I should get on with a black man or a brown man. (*then warmly, opening the stops*) I think the best I could do is a yel-low man!

Thus Mr. Moore – after a whole long life of "free" thought, "free" writing, anti-bigotry of all kinds, with his engrossment in human nature, after the *injustice* of the Boer war, as he says himself, had driven him out of England.... There is no consistency; there *is* race or colour prejudice.

Sir Thomas Beecham's remark about the Negro making his own music left me puzzled, and I don't doubt, puzzled for ever. Her Ladyship was evincing a very querulous astonishment at the Negro (in general) having any achievements (in particular). I was informing her that, for one, everybody knows the Negroes have a particular genius for music. At which Sir Thomas condescendingly remarked "They make their own music too." The tone of this pronouncement was so superior that I remained too dumb to ask whether at that moment he meant tribal or jazz. And Her Ladyship, far from being quieted, became as uneasy as an animal scenting a danger on the wind.

This is all what's aptly enough called *"Old* stuff." What's actual since some twenty years is a direct African influence in sculpture and painting. None but fools separate Africa from the living Negro. But the american press is constantly confusing their civic nationality with their blood nationality; (the 12 million blacks are the loyalest, best *americans*; a Negro in the States has written a good book, therefore he is a good *american* writer; the same of the coloured musician, the coloured artist, etc.).

"In Africa," you say, "the Negro is a savage, he has produced nothing, he has no history." It is certainly true he has not got himself mixed up with machinery and science to fly the Atlantic, turn out engines, run up skyscrapers and contrive holocausts. There are no tribal Presses emitting the day's lies and millions of useless volumes. There remain no written records; the wars, the kingdoms and the changes have sufficed unto themselves. It is not one country but many; well over 400 separate languages and their dialects are known to exist. Who tells you you are the better off for being "civilised" when you live in the shadow of the next war or revolution in constant terror of being ruined or killed? Things in Africa are on a different scale – but the European empire-builders have seen, are seeing to this hand over fist. And what, against this triumph of organised villainy had the black man to show? His own example of Homo Sapiens on better terms with life than are the conquering whites. Anthropology gives him priority in human descent. He had his life, highly organised, his logic, his customs, his laws rigidly adhered to. He made music and unparalleled rhythm and some of the finest sculpture in the world. Nature gave him the best body amongst all the races. Yet he is a "miserable savage" because there are no written records, no super-cities, no machines – but to prove the lack of these an insuperable loss, a sign of racial inferiority, you must attack the root of all things and see where – if anywhere – lies truth. There are many truths. How come, white man, is the rest of the world to be re-formed in your dreary and decadent image?

Harlem Reviewed (1934)

Is it possible to give any kind of visual idea of a place by description? I think not, least of all of Harlem. When I first saw it, at 7th Avenue, I thought of the Mile End Road – same long vista, same kind of little low houses with, at first sight, many indeterminate things out on the pavement in front of them, same amount of blowing dust, papers, litter. But no; the scale, to begin with, was different. It was only from one point that the resemblance came to one. Beginning at the north end of Central Park, edged in on one side by the rocky hill of Columbia University and on the other by the streets that go to the East River, widening out more and more north to that peculiarly sinister halt in the town, the curve of the Harlem River, where one walks about in the dead junk and the refuse-on-a-grand-scale left in the sudden waste lots that are typical of all parts of New York – this is the area of Harlem. Manhattan and 8th Avenues, 7th, Lenox, 5th and Madison Avenues, they all run up here from the zone of the skyscrapers, the gleaming white and blond towers of down-town that are just visible like a mirage down the Harlem perspective. These avenues, so grand in New York proper, are in Harlem very different. They are old, rattled, some of them, by the El on its iron heights, rattled, some of them, underneath, by the Sub in its thundering groove.

"Harlem Reviewed" first appeared in the massive anthology (over 800 pages) devoted to black culture around the world, which Nancy Cunard edited and published at her own expense, *Negro* (London: Lawrence and Wishart, 1934).

Why is it called Harlem, and why the so-called capital of the Negro world? The Dutch made it first, in the 17th century; it was "white" till as recently as 1900. And then, because it was old and they weren't rebuilding it, because it's a good way from the centre, it was more or less "left" to the coloured people. Before this they lived in different parts of New York; there was no Negro "capital." This capital now exists, with its ghetto-like slums around 5th, bourgeois streets, residential areas, a few aristocratic avenues or sections thereof, white-owned stores and cafeterias, small general shops, and the innumerable "skin-whitening" and "anti-kink" beauty parlors. There is one large modern hotel, the Dewey Square, where coloured people of course may stay; and another, far larger, the Teresa, a few paces from it, where certainly they *may not!* And this is in the centre of Harlem. Such race barriers are on all sides; it just depends on chance whether you meet them or no. Some Negro friend maybe will not go into a certain drugstore with you for an ice-cream soda at 108th (where Harlem is supposed to begin, but where it is still largely "white"); "might not get served in there" (and by a coloured server at that – the white boss's orders). Just across the Harlem River some white gentlemen flashing by in a car take it into their heads to bawl, "Can't you get yourself a white man?" – you are walking with a Negro, yet you walk down-town with the same and meet no such hysteria, or again, you do.

Some 350,000 Negroes and coloured are living in Harlem and Brooklyn (the second, and quite distinct, area in greater New York where they have congregated). American Negroes, West Indians, Africans, Latin Americans. The latter, Spanish-speaking, have made a centre round 112th Street and Lenox Avenue. Walk round there and you will hear – it is nearly all Spanish. The tempo of the gestures and gait, the atmosphere, are foreign. It is the Porto-Ricans, the Central Americans and the Cubans. Nationalisms exist, more or less fiercely, between them and the American Negro – as indeed does a jealous national spirit between American Negro and black Jamaican. The latter say they are the better at business, that the coloured Americans have no enterprise. (Are we to see here the mantle of the British as a nation of shopkeepers on West Indian shoulders?) The American Negro regards the Jamaican or British West Indian as "less civilised" than himself; jokes about his accent and deportment are constantly made on the Harlem stage. And so they are always at it, falling out about empty "superiorities" and "inferiorities," forgetting the white enemy.

If you are "shown" Harlem by day you will inevitably have pointed out to you the new Rockefeller apartments,[1] a huge block towering above a rather sparse and visibly very indigent part of 7th Avenue. These were built by the millionaire of that name, supposedly to better the conditions of Negro workers by providing clean and comfortable lodging for them, but inhabited, however, by those who can afford to pay their rents. The Y.M.C.A. and the newly built Y.W.C.A. – more institutes for "uplift." The Harlem Public Library, with its good collection of books on Negro matters, and just a few pieces of African art, so few that the idea strikes one vexingly: why, in this capital of the Negro world, is there no centre, however small, of Africanology? The American Negroes – this is a generalisation with hardly any exceptions – are utterly uninterested in, callous to what Africa is, and to what it was. Many of them are fiercely "racial," as and when it applies to the States, but concerning their forefathers they have not even curiosity.

At night you will be taken to the Lafayette Theatre,[2] the "cradle of new stars" that will go out on the road all over America and thence come to Europe. It is a sympathetic old hall, where, as they don't bother ever to print any programmes, one supposes that all the audience know all the players; it has that feeling too. Some of the best wit I heard here, and they can get away with a lot of stiff hot stuff. Ralph Cooper's[3] orchestra was playing admirably that night they had "the street" in. This was

---

[1] The Paul Laurence Dunbar Apartments are bounded by 7th and 8th Avenues and West 149th and 150th Streets. Built in 1926 and financed by John D. Rockefeller, Jr. (1874–1960; fifth son of John D. Rockefeller), the complex consists of 10 u-shaped buildings centered around a garden courtyard. It was the first large cooperative built for blacks and housed the Dunbar National bank, Harlem's first bank to be managed and staffed by African-Americans.

[2] The Lafayette Theater, located at 132nd Street and Lenox Avenue, was probably the first New York theater to desegregate. As early as 1912, African-Americans were allowed to sit in orchestra seats (instead of balcony seats, to which they had previously been restricted). The theater seated 2,000 and was the home to the Lafayette Players, a stock company that performed classics and plays from popular theater repertory. It also hosted a wide variety of musical events, competing with the Savoy Ballroom, the Apollo Theater, and other venues.

[3] Ralph Cooper was an MC (Master of Ceremonies) first at the Lafayette Theater and then at the Apollo Theater.

to give a hearing to anyone who applied. They just went on the stage and did their stuff. And the audience was *merciless* to a whole lot of these new triers, who would have passed with honour anywhere out of America. The dancing of two or three of the street shoe-blacks, box on back, then set down and dancing round it, was so perfect that the crowd gave them a big hand. No-one who has not seen the actual dancing of Harlem in Harlem can have any idea of its superb quality. From year to year it gets richer, more complicated, more exact. And I don't mean the unique Snake-Hips and the marvellous Bo-Jangles, I mean the boys and girls out of the street who later become "chorats" and "chorines" (in the chorus), or who do those exquisite short numbers, as in music the Three Ink Spots (a new trio), adolescents of 16 or 17 perhaps, playing Duke Ellington's *Mood Indigo*[4] so that the tears ran down one's face.

There was a new dance too, one of the sights of the world as done at the Savoy Ballroom,[5] the Lindy-Hop. The fitting third to its predecessors, Charleston and Black Bottom. These were in the days of short skirts, but the Lindy is the more astounding as it is as violent (and as beautiful), with skirts sweeping the floor. Short minuet steps to begin, then suddenly fall back into an air-pocket, recover sideways, and proceed with all the variations of leaves on the wind. For the Lindy is Lindbergh,[6] of course, created by them in honour of his first triumph. These Tuesday nights at the Savoy are very famous, as is the Harlem "Drag Ball"[7] that happens only once a year. To this come the boys dressed as girls – some in magnificent and elaborate costumes made by themselves – and of course many whites from down-town. A word on the celebrated "rent-party" that the American press writes up with such lurid and false suggestions. This is no more nor less than an ordinary evening dance in someone's house. The "rent" part is its reason for being, for the guests give about 50 cents to come in, thereby helping pay the rent, and they buy liquor there which, as everywhere in dry America (and doubtless it will go on even if prohibition is entirely abolished), is made on the premises or by a friend. The music, as like as not, comes from a special kind of electric piano, a nickel a tune, all the best, the latest ones.

But it is the zest that the Negroes put in, and the enjoyment they get out of, things that causes one more envy in the ofay.[8] Notice how many of the whites are unreal in America; they are *dim*. But the Negro is very real; he is *there*. And the ofays know it. That's why they come to Harlem – out of curiosity and jealousy and don't-know-why. This desire to get close to the other race has often nothing honest about it; for where the ofays flock, to night-clubs, for instance, such as Connie's Inn and the Cotton Club and Small's,[9] expensive cabarets, to these two former the coloured clientele is no longer admitted. To the latter, only just, grudgingly. No, you can't go to Connie's Inn with your coloured friends. The place is *for whites*. "Niggers" to serve, and "coons" to play – and later the same ofay will slip into what he calls "a coloured dive," and there it'll be "Evening, Mr. Brown," polite and cordial, because this will be a real coloured place and the ofay is not sure of himself there a-tall. . . .

This applies of course to the mass of whites who treat Harlem in the same way that English toffs used to talk about "going slumming." The class I'm thinking of is "the club-man." They want entertainment. Go to Harlem, it's sharper there. And it doesn't upset their conception of the

[4] Duke Ellington (1899–1974) was an African American composer. "Mood Indigo" was first recorded on October 14, 1930, on the Okeh label, and was Ellington's first big hit.
[5] The Savoy Ballroom (1926–58), the "home of happy feet," was located on Lenox Avenue and occupied the entire block between 140th and 141st Streets. Owned by Moe Gale, who was Jewish, and managed by Charles Buchanan, who was black, it had two bandstands that provided the setting for legendary "battles of the bands." Among the many dance styles originated and developed there were the Lindy Hop, the Stomp, and the Jitterbug Jive.
[6] Charles Lindbergh (1902–74), American aviator who made the first solo nonstop transatlantic flight on May 20–21, 1927, and became an international celebrity.
[7] The event, which began in the 1920s, was an annual one that went from one location to another, but elicited widespread community participation.
[8] An African-American term, during the 1920s and 1930s, for white people.

[9] Connie's Inn, hard by the Lafayette Theater located on 132nd Street and 7th Avenue (on the corner of 131st Street and 7th Avenue), was owned by Connie and George Immerman. The club featured variety shows such as *Hot Chocolates* (1929), which featured a young musician from Chicago named Louis Armstrong and moved on to Broadway. Connie's was opened to musicians from other clubs for early morning jazz sessions that became legendary. It was segregated. The Cotton Club, the most famous and glamorous of all the Harlem nightclubs, was also segregated, though the policy was relaxed in practice for certain people. Seating 700 and featuring a trademark "jungle décor," it opened in the autumn of 1923; and on December 4, 1927, Duke Ellington and his Washingtonians made their first appearance at the club. Soon Ellington's performances were being broadcast live on national radio, creating a distinctive Cotton Club sound. Ed Small's Paradise, which opened in 1925, was the third of the three major clubs in Harlem.

Negro's social status. From all time the Negro has entertained the whites, but never been thought of by this type as possibly a social equal. There are, however, thousands of artists, writers, musicians, intellectuals, etc., who have good friends in the dark race, and a good knowledge of Harlem life, "the freedom of Harlem," so to speak.

"You must see a revival meeting," they said to me. "It's nothing like what it is in the South, but you shouldn't miss it."

Beforehand I thought I wouldn't be able to stand more than ten minutes of it – ten minutes in any church. . . . When we got into the Rev. Cullen's on 7th Avenue[10] (the Rev. is the father of the poet Countee Cullen[11]) a very large audience was waiting for the "Dancing Evangelist" (that is Becton's title because of his terrific physical activity). A group of "sisters" all in white spread itself fan-wise in the balcony. There was a concert stage with deacons and some of Becton's 12 disciples, and the 7 or 8 absolutely first-class musicians who compose the orchestra, of whom Lawrence Pierre, a fine organist and a disciple. Nothing like a church, an evening concert.

The music starts, a deep-toned Bach piece, then a short allocution, and then the long spirituals, the robust soloist that a massed chorus, the audience, answers back. They begin to beat time with their feet too. The "spirit" is coming with the volume of sound. At this point Becton enters quietly, stands silent on the stage, will not say a word. They must sing some more first, much more; they must be ripe ground. How do they reconcile Becton's exquisite smartness (pearl-grey suit, top hat, cane, ivory gloves, his youthful look and lovely figure), the whole sparkle about him, with the customary ponderousness of the other drab men of God? A sophisticated audience? No, for they appear to be mainly domestic workers, small shop workers, old and young, an evidently religious public, and one or two whites.

A new spiritual has begun; the singing gets intenser, foot-beating all around now, bodies swaying, and clapping of hands in unison. Now and again a voice, several voices, rise above the rest in a single phrase, the foot-beat becomes a stamp. A forest shoots up – black, brown, ivory, amber hands – spread, stiffened out fingers, gestures of *mea culpa* beating of breasts, gestures of stiff arms out, vibrating ecstasy. Far away in the audience a woman gets "seized," leaps up and down on the same spot belabouring her bosom. It comes here, there – who will be the next? At one moment I counted ten women in this same violent trance, not two with the same gestures, yet *all* in rhythm, half-time or double time. A few men too less spectacular. Then just behind me so that I see her well, a young girl. She leaps up and down after the first scream eyes revulsed, arms upstretched – she is no longer "there." After about a minute those next to her seize her and hold her down.

The apex of the singing has come, it is impossible to convey the scale of these immense sound-waves and rhythmical under-surges. One is transported completely. It has nothing to do with God, but with life – a collective life for which I know no name. The people are entirely out of themselves – and then, suddenly, the music stops, calm comes immediately.

In this prepared atmosphere Becton now strides about the stage, flaying the people for their sins, leading their ready attention to this or that point of his argument by some adroit word, a wise-crack maybe. He is a poet in speech and very graceful in all his movements. His dramatisation is generous – and how they respond . . . "yeah man . . . tell it, tell it." Sin, he threatens, is "cat-foot," a "double-dare devil." And the sinner? "A double-ankled rascal," thunders this "adagio dancer," as he called himself that night, breaking off sharp into another mood, an admonishment out of "that inexpressible something by which I raise my hand." There are whirlwind gestures when he turns round on himself, one great clap of the palms and a sort of characteristic half-whistle-half-hoot before some point which is going to be emphasized – and the eloquence pours out in richer and richer imagery. Becton is the personification of expressionism, a great dramatic actor. You remember Chaliapin's acting[12] of Boris Godounov; these two are comparable.

[10]   Reverend Frederick Asbury Cullen was pastor at Salem Methodist Episcopal Church.

[11]   Countee Cullen (1903–46), the adopted son of Rev. Frederick Asbury Cullen, had published two collections of poetry, *Color* (New York: Harper, 1925) and *Copper Sun* (New York: Harper, 1927), prior to the time when Cunard was writing.

[12]   Fyodor Chaliapin (1873–1938) was a Russian opera singer, a bass who was highly acclaimed for his portrayal of Boris in the opera *Boris Godunov*, composed by Modest Moussorgsky (1839–81) and revised by Nikola Rimsky-Korsakov (1844–1908). It premiered in Paris in 1908, and was performed in London in 1913. Chaliapin performed it many times.

Then, "when the millenniums are quaking it's time to clap our hands." It is the moment for the "consecrated dime," and the singing begins again, but the trances are over; other preachers may speak later. This ritual goes on from eight till after midnight, about four nights a week, and sometimes both the faithful and the evangelist are so indefatigable that it goes on for 24 hours. These services, really superb concerts, are the gorgeous manifestation of *the emotion* of a race – that part of the Negro people that has been so trammelled with religion that it is still steeped therein. A manifestation of this kind by white people would have been utterly revolting. But with the Negro race it is on another plane, it seems positively another thing, not connected with Christ or bible, the pure outpouring of themselves, a nature-rite. In other words, it is the fervour, intensity, the stupendous rhythm and surge of singing that are so fine – the christianity is only accidental, incidental to these. Not so for the assembly of course, for all of it is deeply, tenaciously religious. I have given all this detail about the revivalist meeting because it is so fantastic, and, *aesthetically* speaking, so moving.

If treachery and lying are its main attributes so is snobbery flourishing in certain parts of Harlem. "Strivers Row;" that is what 139th Street has been called. An excellent covering-name for "those Astorperious Ethiopians," as one of their own wits put it. There are near-white cliques, mulatto groups, dark-skinned sets who will not invite each other to their houses; some would not let a white cross their thresholds. The Negro "bluebloods" of Washington are famous for their social exclusivity, there are some in Harlem too. I don't know if a foreign white would get in there, possibly not. The snobbery around skin-colour is terrifying. The light-skins and browns look down on the black; by some, friendships with *ofays* are not tolerated, from an understandable but totally unsatisfactory reaction to the general national attitude of white to coloured on the social equality basis. A number of the younger writers are race-conscious in the wrong way, they make of this a sort of forced, *self*-conscious thing, give the feeling that they are looking for obstacles. All this, indeed, is Society with a vengeance! A bourgeois ideology with no horizon, no philosophical link with life. And out of all this, need it be said, such writers as Van Vechten[13] and Co. have made a revolting and cheap lithograph, so that Harlem, to a large idle-minded public, has come to mean nothing more whatsoever than a round of hooch-filled night-clubs after a round of "snow" (cocaine) filled boudoirs. Van Vechten, the spirit of vulgarity, has depicted Harlem as a grimace. He would have written the same way about Montparnasse or Limehouse and Soho. Do such places exist, or is life itself as described by Paul Morand[14] (another profiteer in coloured "stock")? Claude MacKay has done better. The studies in inter-colour relationships (in *Ginger Town*) are honest.[15] But his people, and himself, have also that wrong kind of race-consciousness; they ring themselves in, they are umbrageous. The "Negro Renaissance" (the literary movement of about 1925, now said to be at a halt, and one wonders on whose authority this is said) produced many books and poems filled with this bitter-sweet of Harlem's glitter and heart-break.

This is not the Harlem one sees. You don't see the Harlem of the romancists; it is romantic in its own right. And it is *hard* and *strong*; its noise, heat, cold, cries and colours are so. And the nostalgia is violent too; the eternal radio seeping through everything day and night, indoors and out, becomes somehow the personification of restlessness, desire, brooding. And then the gorgeous roughness, the gargle of Louis Armstrong's voice[16] breaks through. As everywhere, the real people are in the street. I mean those young men on the corner, and the people all sitting on the steps throughout the breathless, leaden summer. I mean the young men in Pelham Park;[17] the sports

---

[13] Carl Van Vechten (1880–1964) was a white and gay writer whose novel *Nigger Heaven* aroused enormous controversy when it was published in 1926, controversy that still raged when Cunard was writing in 1934. One of it main characters is Lasca, a black *femme fatale* who consumes cocaine and revels in Harlem night-clubs.

[14] Paul Morand (1888–1976) was a French diplomat and writer whose collection of short stories *Magie noire* (Paris: B. Grasset, 1928), or *Black Magic*, trans. H. Miles (New York: Viking, 1929), featured black protagonists and prompted controversy.

[15] Claude McKay (1889–1948) was a Jamaican poet and novelist who moved to the US in 1917. His first American volumes of poetry appeared in 1920 and 1922, *Spring in New Hampshire* and *Harlem Shadows*, followed by a bombshell bestseller, *Home to Harlem* (1928). *Gingertown* (1932), another novel, was much less successful.

[16] Louis Armstrong (1901–71), celebrated jazz trumpet player and singer.

[17] A park in the Bronx in New York City.

groups (and one sees many in their bright sweaters), the strength of a race, its beauty.

For in Harlem one can make an appreciation of a race. Walk down 7th Avenue – the different types are uncountable. Every diversity of bone-structure, of head-shape, of skin colour; mixes between Orientals and pure Negroes, Jews and Negroes, Red Indians and Negroes (a particularly beautiful blend, with the high cheek-bones always, and sometimes straight black hair), mulattoes of all shades, yellow, "high yaller" girls, and Havana-coloured girls, and, exquisitely fine, the Spanish and Negro blends; the Negro bone, and the Negro fat too, are a joy to the eye. And though there are more and more light-coloured people, there is great satisfaction in seeing that the white American features are absorbed in the mulatto, and that the mulatto is not, as so often in England, a coloured man with a white man's features and often expression as well. The white American and the Negro are a good mix physically.

The Exodus from Spain (1939)

Vans, trucks, lorries, and buses continue to bring refugee women and children[1] across the frontier at Le Perthus.[2] The road is much better organised, and half of it is now free for cars to pass in and out of Spain. Pitiful little groups of refugees are still camping out, washing their clothes in the streams. At night there are small camp-fires all along the mountain. There are many babies in arms and infants at the breast.

The French soldiery is very much in evidence too; stacked rifles are by the roadside and squads of men being drilled. The control near the frontier is even more strict; while returning to Perpignan[3] one is stopped four times by the Mobile Guards. On a Spanish bus one reads chalked in Catalan "No volem Italians!" ("We do not want the Italians!")

Bread again

Everybody in the region of the frontier is going about with the same thing in his hands, or in a bag, or even on his back, and that is – bread. They are eating bread again, the white bread sent to them by France.

When I was sitting on a bench in Perpignan to-day an old peasant woman came up to ask me for a little money. These were her words: "I left Gerona[4] with my husband the night before last. Eight 'planes followed us out of the town to the last bridge, machine-gunning us. We got to Figueras.[5] If only you could see it – nothing but ruins, smashed to pieces. I made my husband get into a lorry there; he is ill, so I walked to La Junquera. We had 11,000 pesetas we had saved; we have worked all our lives. They gave us 28 francs for this at the frontier, and the bus from Le Boulou to Perpignan cost us 16."

This disastrous situation of the exchange is beyond words. Nearly all Spaniards arrive with various sums of money, but cannot, or can hardly, pay for a hotel room or a meal.

"The Exodus from Spain" was published in the British newspaper the *Manchester Guardian*, datelined February 8 and 9, 1939.

[1]   The Spanish Civil War began in 1936 as a military uprising headed by General Franco in Morocco, then spread across the entire country. Franco and the nationalists received support from Fascist Italy and Nazi Germany, while the republicans received support from the Soviet Union. The bloody conflict approached its close on March 28, 1939, when nationalist forces entered Madrid. The struggle was closely followed throughout the world. Cunard was writing two weeks after Barcelona had fallen, on January 26, 1939, and only days before the fall of Catalonia on

February 10, 1939, when refugees were streaming across the border into France.

[2]   Le Perthus is a town in the Girona province, on the border between Catalonia (Spain) and France. The French–Spanish border runs through the town.

[3]   A small town 40 miles south of Narbonne, in France.

[4]   A coastal town in Catalonia, Spain.

[5]   A small town on the coast in the Girona province in Catalonia, Spain. The Spanish republican government had moved there from Barcelona on January 25, 1939.

Saving the works of art

It is fit to pay tribute to the leaders of a nation in its present agony who care in the way they do for the cultural heritage of their people. Perhaps one of the last official documents to bear the signature of Señor del Vayo[6] in the old Castle of Figueras was that accepting that the Spanish paintings and works of art be taken to Geneva for safe keeping by the League of Nations. M. J. Jaujard, sub-director of French National Museums, was delegated on this mission to Dr. Negrín, as arranged directly after the fall of Barcelona with the other delegate for the International Committee for the Protection of Spanish Works of Art, Mr. MacClaren, of the National Gallery, London. At the moment of the signing of the document a violent bombing of Figueras took place, the electric current was cut off, and the signatures had to be apposed by the light of matches.

The report that some of the lorries transporting Spanish works of art were attacked by 'planes is confirmed in the local press here to-day. It adds that José-Maria Sert[7] (famous Spanish painter whom I have known personally and whose work decorated the chapel of the Duke of Alba's palace of Liria, in Madrid) sent a telegram to the Duke of Alba in London asking that there should be no bombardments during the transport of the pictures and art treasures. These contain 400 or more paintings by Velasquez, El Greco, and Goya.

Yesterday, on Spanish territory between Le Perthus and La Junquera, I passed ten huge vans carrying these treasures; immense, solidly packed trailers attached to special motors and driven by French chauffeurs. The one I talked with was indignant over the conditions in which this work has to be carried out. "They attack even the works of art of a country," he said. "Can you imagine what it has been like getting away from Figueras during these air raids?"

Many wounded

Figures of wounded people coming in I have now been able to ascertain – at least, in part. Seven thousand – but this represents both soldiers and civilians – have been brought to France under the charge of Carmen Catalan Pastor. She was directing the transport of some of those wounded in the Figueras raids when I met her in Le Perthus, and told me that thanks are to be given to the French Minister of the Interior for arrangements made. At the Fort of Bellegarde, just above Le Perthus, there are now 2000 wounded soldiers. Another large hospital is at Le Boulou. In Perpignan, said Señora Pastor, are 3000. In La Junquera I saw many other disabled soldiers and wounded waiting to come into France.

---

[6] Julio Alvarez del Vayo (1901–74). He served as Minister for Foreign Affairs for the Spanish republic in 1936–7 and again in 1938–9.

[7] José-Maria Sert (1874–1945), an artist from Catalonia, especially noted for his frescos.

Mary Butts (1890–1937)

Introduction

Mary Butts (1890–1937) was born in Dorset, the daughter of a retired army officer with a distinguished career. Her father died in 1904, and Mary was sent to St. Leonard's School for Girls in St. Andrews, Scotland. When she was 21, in 1911, Butts received a small annuity from her father's will. It was enough to live comfortably, but Butts was poor at managing money. She attended Westfield College in London, between 1909 and 1912, but left without completing her degree. She then completed what would now be a Diploma in Social Work at the London School of Economics. During the Great War she became an active pacifist, and through these activities met the Jewish poet, and later publisher, John Rodker. They married in 1918, and their only child, Camilla, was born in 1920. They soon separated and were divorced in 1927.

During the 1920s Butts moved between Britain and France, staying lengthy periods in London, Paris, and Villefranche (on the French Riviera). She had extended but difficult relationships with Cecil Maitland, the American composer Virgil Thomson, and the French writer Mireille Havet. She married Gabriel Atkin in 1920, but he left her in 1933. In 1932 they had settled in Sennen Cover, Cornwall, and Mary stayed there alone till her sudden death in 1937.

Her short stories were highly esteemed, and her work was published in most of the period's famous little magazines: *The Egoist*, the *Dial*, the *Little Review*, *Calendar*, and the *transatlantic review*. She wrote three notable novels: *Ashe of Rings* (1925), *Armed with Madness* (1928), and *Death of Felicity Taverner* (1932). The latter two are masterpieces of modernist prose, and in *Armed with Madness*, her most daring and experimental work, her writing glitters and sparkles against an extraordinary background of quotations from popular songs, jazz, poetry, and other literary sources. The work is a tour de force.

She published two collections of short stories during her life, *Speed the Plough and Other Stories* (1923) and *Several Occasions* (1932). Her writing loses much of its energy after 1932 as she turns to historical narratives about Alexander the Great, *The Macedonian* (1933), and *Scenes from the Life of Cleopatra* (1932). She had always had a mystical bent, and in her later years became a devout Christian. Her *Journals*, which have recently been published, show the astounding range of contemporaries whom she knew (Eliot, Pound, H.D., Joyce, Ford, Lewis, Richardson, Woolf, and Stein) and offer a fascinating glimpse into the daily life of a committed writer.

Speed the Plough[1] (1921)

He lay in bed, lax and staring, and obscure images rose and hung before him, dissolved, reshaped. His great illness passed from him. It left him too faint for any sequence of thought. He lay still,

---

First published in the *Dial* 71(4) (October 1921); reprinted in *Georgian Stories 1922* (London: Chapman & Hall, 1922; New York: G. P. Putnam's Sons, 1923) and in *Stories from the Dial* (New York: Lincoln MacVeagh and Dial Press; London: Jonathan Cape, 1924). It was included in Butts's first collection of short stories, *Speed the Plough and Other Stories* (London: Chapman & Hall, 1923), which furnishes the text for this edition.

[1] The phrase "Speed the Plogh" derives from a blessing in medieval verse and song: "God speed your plough," or, "do your work and God will help you." It is also the title of a traditional English song, the lyrics to which are:

Dear Joseph, dear Joseph, why serious today?
O what have you been thinking, come tell to me I pray.
Have just just begun to play the bo-peep
Or have you been watching your innocent sheep?
The young and the old are all driven to the fold
They value not the summer heat nor yet the winter cold
Now don't let love tease you or thoughts make you sad,
But drive away all sorrow and be cheerful and glad
And be cheerful and glad.

In old ancient days there was no cursed money,
The children of Israel eat milk and good honey,
No queen could be seen from the highest degree
They milk their brown cows and their sheep they often see.
Them lambs give them clothing, the cows give them milk,
And that's how the farmer played all those good deeds.
The lambs give them clothing, the cows give them milk,
And that's how the farmer played all those good deeds.

But as for old Adam, how he worked with the spade,
And how he planted vineyards and neatly he made.
But as for the farmer with his love exposed
With beef and good bacon they could keep a good house.
With a firkin in each corner from how own barley mow
He'd welcome in a friend and may God speed the plough;
With a firkin in each corner from how own barley mow
He'd welcome in a friend and may God speed the plough,
And may God speed the plough.

without memory, without hope. Such concrete impressions as came to him were sensuous and centred round the women of the hospital. They distressed him. They were not like the Kirchner girls in the worn *Sketch*[2] he fingered all day. La Coquetterie d'une Ange.[3] One need not know French to understand Coquetterie, and Ange was an easy guess. He stared at the neat counterpane. A tall freckled girl with draggled red hair banged down a cup of cocoa and strode away.

Coquetterie, mannequin, lingerie, and all one could say in English was underwear. He flicked over the pages of the battered *Sketch*, and then looked at the little nurse touching her lips with carmine.

'Georgette,' he murmured sleepily, 'crêpe georgette.'

He would always be lame. For years his nerves would rise and quiver and knot themselves, and project loathsome images. But he had a fine body, and his soldiering had set his shoulders and hardened his hands and arms.

'Get him back on to the land,' the doctors said.

The smells in the ward began to assail him, interlacing spirals of odour, subtle but distinct. Disinfectant and distemper, the homely smell of blankets, the faint tang of blood, and then a sour draught from the third bed where a man had been sick.

He crept down under the clothes. Their associations rather than their textures were abhorrent to him, they reminded him of evil noises ... the crackle of starched aprons, clashing plates, unmodulated sounds. Georgette would never wear harsh things like that. She would wear beautiful things with names ... velours and organdie, and that faint windy stuff aerophane.

He drowsed back to France, and saw in the sky great aeroplanes dipping and swerving, or holding on their line of steady flight like a travelling eye of God. The wisps of cloud that trailed a moment behind them were not more delicate than her dress....

'What he wants, doctor, to my mind, is rousing. There he lies all day in a dream. He must have been a strong man once. No, we don't know what he was. Something out of doors I should think. He lies there with that precious Kirchner album, never a word to say.'

The doctor nodded.

He lay very still. The presence of the matron made him writhe like the remembered scream of metal upon metal. Her large hands concealed bones that would snap. He lay like a rabbit in its form, and fright showed his dull gums between his drawn-back lips.

Weeks passed. Then one day he got up and saw himself in a glass. He was not surprised. It was all as he had known it must be. He could not go back to the old life. It seemed to him that he would soil its loveliness. Its exotics would shrivel and tarnish as he limped by. 'Light things, and winged, and holy'[4] they fluttered past him, crêpe velours, crêpe de Chine, organdie, aerophane, georgette. ... He had dropped his stick ... there was no one to wash his dirty hands. ... The red-haired nurse found him crying, and took him back to bed.

For two months longer he laboured under their kindness and wasted under their placidity. He brooded, realizing with pitiful want of clarity that there were unstable delicate things by which he might be cured. He found a ritual and a litany. Dressed in vertical black, he bore on his outstretched arms, huge bales of wound stuffs. With a turn of the wrist he would unwrap them, and they would fall from him rayed like some terrestrial star. The Kirchner album supplied the rest. He named the girls, Suzanne and Verveine, Ambre and Desti, and ranged them about him. Then he

[2] Raphael Kirchner (1867–1917) was a French artist who specialized in sensual or sexually provocative depictions of girls or young women; his works were a regular feature in the glamour magazine *La Vie parisienne*, and often they were produced as series that were then reproduced as postcards or, as here, prints that could be posted on a wall. In effect Kirchner was an early maker of the modern pin-up. *The Daily Sketch* was an illustrated British newspaper that was started in 1908 (it folded in 1971). It was aimed at a mass market and therefore needed to be careful in publishing images that were provocative but not sexually explicit; during the years of World War I it published about eight

series of Kirchner girls per year, printing them as a special bound "album" included with the newspaper.
[3] "The Coquetry of an Angel," in French, and the title of the series of Kirchner girls that the protagonist admires.
[4] A variant of a well-known sentence in the "Ion" (534b), a dialogue by Plato, in which Socrates, describing poets, says: "And what they say is true, for a poet is a light and winged thing, and holy, and never able to compose until he has become inspired, and is beside himself, and reason is no longer in him" (Edith Hamilton and Huntington Cairns [eds.], *Plato: The Collected Dialogues* [Princeton: Princeton University Press, 1961], 220).

would undress them, and dress them again in immaculate fabrics. While he did that he could not speak to them because his mouth would be barred with pins.

The doctors found him weaker.

Several of the nurses were pretty. That was not what he wanted. Their fresh skins irritated him. Somewhere there must still be women whose skins were lustrous with powder, and whose eyes were shadowed with violet from an ivory box. The brisk provincial women passed through his ward visiting from bed to bed. In their homely clothes there was an echo of the lovely fashions of *mondaines*, buttons on a skirt where a slit should have been, a shirt cut to the collar bone whose opening should have sprung from the hollow between the breasts.

Months passed. The fabric of his dream hardened into a shell for his spirit. He remained passive under the hospital care.

They sent him down to a farm on a brilliant March day.

His starved nerves devoured the air and sunlight. If the winds parched, they braced him, and when the snow fell it buried his memories clean. Because she had worn a real musquash coat, and carried a brocade satchel he had half-believed the expensive woman who had sat by his bed, and talked about the worth and the beauty of a life at the plough's tail. Of course he might not be able to plough because of his poor leg ... but there was always the milking ... or pigs ... or he might thatch. ...

Unfamiliarity gave his world a certain interest. He fluttered the farmer's wife. Nothing came to trouble the continuity of his dream. The sheen on the new grass, the expanse of sky, now heavy as marble, now luminous; the embroidery that a bare tree makes against the sky, the iridescent scum on a village pond, these were his remembrancers, the assurance of his realities. Beside them a cow was an obscene vision of the night.

Too lame to plough or to go far afield, it seemed as though his fate must overtake him among the horned beasts. So far he had ignored them. At the afternoon milking he had been an onlooker, then a tentative operator. Unfortunately the farmer recognized a born milkman. At five o'clock next morning they would go out together to the byres.

At dawn the air was like a sheet of glass; behind it one great star glittered. Dimmed by a transparent shutter, the hard new light poured into the world. A stillness so keen that it seemed the crystallization of speed hung over the farm. From the kitchen chimney rose a feather of smoke, vertical, delicate, light as a plume on Gaby's head. As he stamped out into the yard in his gaiters and corduroys he thought of the similitude and his mouth twisted.

In the yard the straw rose in yellow bales out of the brown dung pools. Each straw was brocaded with frost, and the thin ice crackled under his boots. 'Diamanté,' he said at last, 'that's it.'

On a high shoulder of down above the house, a flock of sheep were gathered like a puffy mat of irregular design. The continual bleating, the tang of the iron bell, gave coherence to the tranquillity of that Artemisian dawn.[5] A hound let loose from the manor by some early groom passed menacing over the soundless grass. A cock upon the pigsty wall tore the air with his screams. He stopped outside the byre now moaning with restless life. The cock brought memories. 'Chanticleer, they called him, like that play once ... '[6]

He remembered how he had once stood outside the window of a famous shop and thrilled at a placard. ... 'In twenty-four hours M. Lewis arrives from Paris with the Chanticleer toque.' It had been a stage hit, of course, one hadn't done business with it, but O God! the London women whose wide skirts rose with the wind till they bore them down the street like ships. He remembered a phrase he had heard once, a 'scented gale'.[7] They were like that. The open door of the cow-shed

5 From Artemis, a Greek goddess of forests and hills who functions as a birth-goddess and bringer of fertility to man and beast.
6 *The Story of Chanticleer*, a verse drama in four acts, was adapted from the French by Florence Yates Hann (London: Henimann, 1913); the original, *Chantecler: pièce en quatre actes, en vers*, was written by the famous French playwright Edmond Rostand (1868–1918) and published in 1910 (Paris: E. Fasquelle).
7 William Morris (1834–96), "Now Waneth Spring," lines 1–8:

Now waneth spring
While all birds sing
And the south wind blows
The earliest rose
To and fro
By the doors we know
And the scented gale
Fills every dale.

steamed with the rankness that had driven out from life. . . . Inside were twenty female animals waiting to be milked.

He went in to the warm reeking dark.

He squatted on the greasy milking stool, spoke softly to his beast, and tugged away. The hot milk spurted out into the pail, an amazing substance, pure, and thick with bubbles. Its contact with caked hides and steaming straw sickened him. The gentle beast rubbed her head against her back and stared. He left the stall and her warm breath. The light was gaining. He could see rows of huge buttocks shifting uneasily. From two places he heard the milk squirting in the pails. He turned to it again, and milked one beast and another, stripping each clean.

The warm milk whose beauty had pleased began to nauseate him. There was a difference in nature between that winking, pearling flow and the pale decency of a Lyons' tea jug. So this was where it all started. Dimly he realized that this was where most of life started, indifferent of any later phase. 'Little bits of fluff,' Rosalba and all the Kirchner tribe . . . was Polaire only a cow . . . or Delysia? . . . The light had now the full measure of day. A wind that tasted delicately of shingle and the turf flew to meet him. The mat on the down shoulder was now a dissolving view of ambulating mushrooms.

'Yes, my son,' the farmer was saying, 'you just stay here where you're well off, and go on milking for me. I know a born milkman when I see one, and I don't mind telling you you're it. I believe you could milk a bull if you were so inclined. . . .'

He sat silent, overwhelmed by the disarming kindness.

'See how the beasts take to you,' the voice went on. 'That old cow she's a terror, and I heard you soothing her down till she was pleasant as yon cat. It's dairy work you were cut out for. . . . There's a bull coming round this forenoon . . . pedigree . . . cost me a bit. You come along.'

As yet they did not work him very hard, he would have time to think. He dodged his obligations towards the bull, and walked over to an upland field. He swept away the snow from under a thorn bush, folded his coat beneath him, and lit a cigarette.

'And I stopped, and I looked, and I listened.' Yes, that was it, and about time too. For a while he whistled slowly Robey's masterpiece.[8]

He had to settle with his sense of decency. It was all very well. These things might have to happen. The prospect of a milkless, meatless London impressed him as inconvenient. Still most of that stuff came from abroad, by sea. That was what the blockade was for. 'I've got to get away from this. I never thought of this before, and I don't like it. I've been jockeyed into it somehow, and I don't like it. It's dirty, yes dirty, like a man being sick. In London we're civilized. . . .'

---

[8]   George Robey (1869–1954) was one of the great stars of British music hall. In 1916 he appeared in "Bing Boys Are Here," a musical with music by Nat D. Ayer and lyrics by Clifford Grey; with book by George Grossmeith and Fred Thompson. It opened on April 19, 1916, at the Alhambra Theatre, London. The musical culminated with Robey performing "I Stopped, and I Looked, and I Listened," to which the lyrics are:

I like to go walking alone, by myself . . . it's merely for exercise
I wonder around like a mischievous elf, for I always expect a
  surprise
T'other day I was walking alongside of the hedge
And the hedge was apropos of some trees
I got my surprise as I walked 'long the edge
'Twas a sound wafted my way on the breeze.
So I stopped! . . . and I looked! . . . and I listened!

And I tried to locate this sound
First I thought it was here . . . then I thought it was there
A most peculiar sound that I really declare
I had heard it before but I cannot say where
So I thought that this sound must be found
So, I stopped! . . . and I looked! . . . and I left!

At the bidding of youth, I selected a wife
And I thought, "Now my troubles are halved.
I'll wed right away and be settled for life
For I've found my true soul-mate at last."
The first year of bliss was a dream of delight
Ye Gads! but my joy was supreme.
'Til after cucumber, at supper, one night
She started to talk in her dream.
So I stopped! . . . and I looked! and I listened!

But the case was unique you'll allow,
I was filled with amazement . . . I was knocked in a heap
For I had no idea that she talked in her sleep!
But I knew it was best, perfect silence to keep
So I thought I would bear this somehow.
So, I stopped! . . . and I looked! . . . and I listened!
And the sweat seemed to stand on my brow.
"My own darling, Joe, I love you!" she said,
"I worship you so . . ." Well, as my name is Fred,
I stopped! . . . and I looked! . . .
Well! . . . I leave it to you!

A gull floated in from the sea, and up the valley where the horses steamed at the spring ploughing.

'A bit of it may be all right, it's getting near that does one in. There aren't any women here. They're animals. Even those girls they call the squire's daughters. I never saw such boots. ... They'd say that things were for use, and in London they're for show. ... Give me the good old show. ...' He stopped to dream. He was in a vast circular gallery so precipitous that standing one felt impelled to reel over and sprawl down into the stalls half a mile below. Some comedian had left the stage. Two gold-laced men were changing the numbers on either side. The orchestra played again, something that had no common tune. Then there swung on to the stage a woman plumed and violent, wrapped in leopard skin and cloth-of-gold. Sometimes she stepped like a young horse, sometimes she moved with the easy trailing of a snake. She did nothing that was not trivial, yet she invested every moment with a significance whose memory was rapture.

Quintessence was the word he wanted. He said ... 'There's a lot of use in shows.'

Then he got up stiffly, and walked down the steep track to the farm, still whistling.

When the work was over he went out again. Before the pub, at the door marked 'hotel', a car was standing, a green car with glossy panels and a monogram, cushioned inside with grey and starred with silver. A chauffeur, symphonic also in green and bright buttons, was cranking her up. Perched upon the radiator was a naked silver girl. A woman came out of the inn. She wore white furs swathed over deep blue. Her feet flashed in their glossy boots. She wore a god in green jade and rose. Her gloves were rich and thick, like moulded ivory.

'Joy riding,' said a shepherd, and trudged on, but he stood ravished. It was not all dead then, the fine delicate life that had been the substance of his dream. Rare it might be, and decried, but it endured. The car's low humming died away, phantom-like he saw it in the darkling lane, a shell enclosing a pearl, the quintessence of cities, the perfection of the world.

He had heard her voice. 'I think we'll be getting back now.' She was going back to London. He went into the bar and asked the landlady who she was.

'Sort of actress,' the landlord said. And then, 'the war ought to have stopped that sort of thing.'

'Why, what's the harm?'

'Spending the money that ought to go to beating those bloody Germans.'

'All the same her sort brings custom,' the wife had said.

He drank his beer and went out into the pure cold evening. It was six o'clock by the old time,[9] and the radiance was unnatural.

He walked down the damp lane, pale between the hedgerows.

It widened and skirted a pond covered with vivid slime.

'And that was all they had to say about her. ...'

He hated them. A cart came storming up the hill, a compelling noise, grinding wheels and creaking shafts and jingling harness; hard breathing, and the rough voice of the carter to his beast.

At the pond the horse pulled up to breathe, his coat steamed, the carter leaned on the shaft.

'Some pull that.'

'Aye, so it be.' He noticed for the first time the essential difference in their speech.

Carter and horse went up the hill. He lit another cigarette.

Something had happened to him, resolving his mind of all doubts. He saw the tail lights of a car drawing through the vast outskirts of a city. An infinite fine line went out from it and drew him also. That tail lamp was his star. Within the car a girl lay rapt, insolent, a cigarette at her lips.

He dreamed. Dark gathered. Then he noticed that something luminous was coming towards him. Down the hollow lane white patches were moving, irregular, but in sequence, patches that seemed to his dulled ears to move silently, and to eyes trained to traffic extraordinarily slow. The sun had passed. The shadow of the hill overhung the valley. The pale light above intensified its menace. The straggling patches, like the cups of snow the downs still held in every hollow, made

---

[9] *the old time* the way time was told before daylight saving time was introduced in Britain in 1916, a means of saving fuel and power that would otherwise be spent in lighting.

down the lane to the pond's edge. It was very cold. From there no lighted windows showed. Only the tip of his cigarette was crimson as in Piccadilly.

With the sound of a charging beast, a song burst from him, as, soundless, each snowy patch slid from the land on to the mirrored back of the pond. He began to shout out loud.

> 'Some lame, some tame, some game for anything, some like a stand-up fight,
> Some stay abed in the morning, and some stay out all night.
> Have you seen the ducks go by, go a-rolling home?
> Feeling very glad and spry, have you seen them roam?
> There's mamma duck, papa duck, the grand old drake,
> Leading away, what a noise they make.
> Have you heard them quack, have you heard them quack, have you seen those ducks go by?
> Have you seen the ducks go by, go a-rolling home? . . . '

The way back to the farm his voice answered Lee White's,[10] and the Vaudeville chorus sustained them. At the farm door they forsook him. He had to be coherent to the farmer. He sought inspiration. It came. He played with the latch, and then walked into the kitchen, lyrical. . . .

'And I stopped, and I looked, and I left.'

A month later found him on his knees, vertical in black cloth, and grey trousers, and exquisite bow tie. A roll of Lyons brocade, silver, and peach, was pliant between his fingers as the teats of a cow. Inside it a girl stood frowning down upon him.

Despair was on her face, and on the faces of the attendant women.

'But if you can't get me the lace to go with it, what am I to wear?'

'I am sorry, madame. . . . Indeed we have done all that is possible. It seems that it is not to be had. I can assure mdame that we have done our best.' He rose and appealed to the women. His conviction touched them all.

'Madame, anything that we can do . . .'

The lovely girl frowned on them, and kicked at her half-pinned draperies.

'When the war starts interfering with my clothes,' she said, 'the war goes under. . . .'

His eyes kindled.

Widdershins[1] (1924)

Every day he woke to the desire to take the world by the throat, and choke it. He had no illusion that the world wanted to be saved; still less that it was ready to be saved by him. Ready! – it was punching at him with agonizing blows, to be rid of him, once and for all. He woke up. Even that was not true now. It had been true once, but now the world was getting over any slight alarm he might have caused it. It was leaving him alone, to realize the wounds it had given him. Sometimes it was even tolerant and trying to patch him up.

Oh, God!

He was in the middle of London, in a dull hotel bedroom, stale with travelling from the Shap moors,[2] where two years before he had gone away to think. He had called it thinking, but he had gone there to lick his wounds and dream. He was just intelligent enough to notice that he had not thought, and that what he remembered was certain moments of action. Certainly he did not understand that what he wanted was magic.

[10] Lee White (1886–1927) was an American singer and actress.

WIDDERSHINS
The story, under the title "Deosil," was first published in the *transatlantic review* 1(3) (March 1924), then collected in Edward J. O'Brien and John Cournos (eds.), *The Best Short Stories of 1924* (Boston: Small, Maynard; London: Jonathan Cape, 1924). It was included in Butts's second collection of short stories, *Several*

Occasions (London: Wishart, 1932), which furnishes the text followed by this edition.
[1] A Gaelic turn for "going against" or "moving in a counter-clockwise direction; the story, when first published in the *transatlantic review*, was entitled "Deosil," Gaelic for clockwise or sunwise motion.
[2] *Shapmoors* a part of the Lake District in Cumbria.

He lay, and remembered something about himself: that he was called Dick Tressider, that he was a mystic; and that among the people he met the word meant a snub, a cliché, an insult, or, very occasionally, a distinction: that he knew a great many people who almost realized his plan, and yet did not: that he was a gentleman. He had not thought of that for a long time. London had reminded him. He damned the place and ordered his bath. He shaved, and put on his good, worn, country clothes, his heavy boots, his raincoat and leather gloves, all without pride in his strength, or tonic from his unconventionality. He ate a country breakfast, and looked up his appointments. He felt that he was held from behind by the short hair on his skull, and cursed the city. But what he needed was magic.

It is doubtful if he understood the idea of progress, but whether he did or not, he disliked it. It may be certain, but it is obviously slow. He had his immediate reasons too. He had tried every association which tries to speed man's progress; labour and revolution, agriculture and religion. In each, it was the soundest point in his perception, he had seen one thing and the same thing, which was the essential thing and, at the same time, did not come off. Meanwhile, labour and revolution, agriculture and religion were entirely sick of him. He knew, if any man living knew he knew, that sometimes things were improved, or rather that they were changed; and that in individual action there were moments of a peculiar quality that expressed the state in which he knew the whole earth could live all the time, and settle the hash of time, progress, and morality once and for ever. What he wanted to happen was for some man to say a word of power which should evoke this state, everywhere, not by any process, but in the twinkling of an eye. This is magic. Lovers did it, especially his lovers; and saints, when he and one or two men he knew were being saints, with a woman or so about to encourage them, at night, in a smoky room. There were moments, too, under the hills, breaking-in horses, when it came, the moment of pure being, the co-ordination of power.

But the universal word did not come off. He was over forty now, and he was losing his nerve. He was beginning to spit and sneer; and, since he could not find his word, he was beginning to grin, and hope for the world to ruin itself; and rub his hands, and tell his friends in their moments of pleasure that they were damned, not exactly because they had not listened to him, but for something rather like it. And, as very often they had listened to him, in reason, they were hurt.

Because he had not mastered the earth, he was beginning to hate it. Hate takes the grace out of a spiritual man, even his grace of body. As he left the hotel and walked west through the park, and saw the trees coming, he drew in one of his animal breaths that showed the canines under his moustache, bright like a dog. *Grin like a dog, and run about the city;*[3] but then he understood that this was one of his empty days, which might be filled with anything or nothing.

'I must fill it,' he said, and he meant that on this day he must have a revelation and a blessing; which is a difficult thing to get to order. He went on to the grass, in among the trees, which are a proper setting for almost every kind of beauty. Their green displayed his tan and harmonized his dress. Their trunks drew attention to his height, the grass gave distinction to his walk. It was early, and there were no pretty women about to make his eyes turn this way and that, greedily, with vanity, with appeal for pity, but too scornfully for success. The trees went on growing. He looked at them and remembered Daphne, and that she had said once: 'Stop fussing, Dick. Why can't you let things alone for a bit? Think of trees.' 'Silly fool of a girl. Wanted me to make love to her, I suppose.' He had said that at the time, and he still said it, but he added Daphne to the list of people he was to see that day. Like men of his kind, at cross-purposes with their purpose, there could be nothing fortuitous that happened to him. Everything was a leading, a signature of the reality whose martyr he was; for he could never allow that he had made a fool of himself, and only occasionally that reality had made a fool of him. So he pinned the universe down to a revelation from Daphne, and took a bus to Holborn to get on with the business of the day.

[3] The phrase occurs in the version of Psalms 59:6 and 59:14, which is given in the Anglican Prayer Book, where the word "grin" is used in its original and obsolete sense, meaning "to groan," or to howl as does a dog. The same passages, in the King James or Authorized Version, are rendered as follows (the psalmist is talking about his enemies): "They return at evening: they make a noise like a dog and go round about the city").

It is much easier for a man to lose his self-consciousness in Holborn than in the female world of South Kensington.[4] He went first to see a friend who was teaching a kind of Christian anarchism made dramatic by the use of Catholic ritual. He was a good man, patient with Dick, who trusted him. It was one of the things that made Dick uneasy that the works of sanctity and illumination are now distributed through offices, and he saw himself a terror to such places. His friend Eden was out. The typist was a very childish one, with short hair and a chintz overall, and she did not suggest the Sophia, the Redeemed Virgin,[5] Dick was looking for. He shifted his expectation and saw her as the unredeemed and improbable virgin, which is the same thing as the soul of the world, and prepared to treat her for the part. He was hungry by now.

'I'm Dick Tressider,' he said, 'and I'll wait for Mr Eden.' He dropped his stick, picked it up, lit a cigarette, and walked once or twice up and down the room. 'D'you know about me?'

'I can't say that I do,' she said. 'So many gentlemen come here for Mr Eden.'

'D'you know Mr Eden well? Are you conscious of what he is doing here? I mean that it's an expression of what is happening everywhere, of what is bound to happen everywhere, man's consciousness becoming part of the cosmic consciousness?'

'Mr Eden never says anything about it.'

'D'you know this whole damned earth is going to smash any moment?'

'Mr Eden says that if there are any more wars we shall starve. He's trying to stop it.'

He grinned, and showed his wolf's teeth.

'I tell you. It'll make precious little difference what he does. You look as if you might understand. Come out and have some lunch.'

She got up obediently. She remembered that she had heard of Dick, that he had been a soldier of some family and some service. Also he was a tall figure of a man, not like the pale, ecstatic townsmen who came there.

He took her to a restaurant and ordered red wine and steak. He crammed his food down and asked her what she thought about love. Immediately she was frightened. She was not frightened of seduction or of a scene. It was pure fear. He saw that it would not do, and sulked at her, pouring down his wine.

'I don't want to waste time. I've got to get down to reality. Tell Eden I'll call in later.'

He took her out, and left her at the door of the restaurant, without a word.

He walked about London, through the streets round the British Museum, on a cool still afternoon without rain, past the interesting shops and the students, and the great building of stone. He wanted to persuade men that they were only there to illustrate the worth of the land. He did not want to see Eden, who would be busy trying to stop the next war, and getting people to dress up. He knew what war was and how it would stop these games, more power to it. It was all up with the world, and the world didn't know it. He would go to tea with Daphne now. It would be too early, but that didn't matter.

At the Museum gates he saw a man he had known who said: 'Is that you, Tressider? I didn't know you were in town.'

'I came up last night.'

'Wishing you were back?'

'Wishing I could smash these lumps of stone or get men to see their cosmic significance.'

The civilized man winced. The idea might be tolerable, but one should not say it like that.

'I am going into the Museum. Come along.'

'What are you going to do?'

'Look at things.'

'Some earth-shaking new cooking-pot?'

'It's not a question of size, is it? Come along.'

He had to run beside Dick, who flung himself over the courtyard and up the steps.

4   South Kensington was an elegant district, while Holborn was the center of the insurance and legal professions.   5   Sophia is the Greek word for "wisdom."

'I read a jolly fairy-story about this place,' he said. 'Some children got a magic amulet and wished the things home, and they all flew out. Those stone bull things, and all the crocks and necklaces.'

'I remember. They found a queen from Babylon, and she said they belonged to her, and wished them all home, and home they went.'

Dick looked at him with a sideways, ugly stare.

'I know. You like me, don't you, when you think I'm a fairy-boy. A kind of grown-up Puck? You like me to like rot.'

'But I do,' said his friend. 'I like that story myself, and was glad when you recalled it.'

'Do you know that the only thing we've said that meant anything was a bit of your talk – "She said they all belonged to her." That's the cursed property-sense that keeps this world a hell.'

'Oh damn the property-sense! I was going to look at the casts from Yucatan, and I always forget the way.'

Dick was staring at a case of bronze weapons. He put his hand easily on the man's shoulder. 'Don't you understand that that fairy-story is true? They could all fly away out of here. It's as easy as changing your collar.'

'Do it for us then, Tressider. I'll come along and applaud.'

'My God! You people will find a man who can do it for you, and worse things, and soon. Someone you've treated as you treat all people. Take it from me, Brooks.'

Madder than ever, thought Brooks. Won't think, and can't play. 'All right. The room is at the end. Come along.'

It is not easy to get on terms with a cast the size of a house, whose close decorations mean nothing to anyone except to an archæologist or an artist. Dick lounged and stared, and leant up against the central plaster lump.

'What are all these things for? I suppose you think you've done something when you've dug 'em up out of the earth.'

It is exceedingly difficult to explain why a thing is useful when you like it.

Dick smote it with his hand.

'A lot of good those'll do you when the world busts up.'

But Brooks was thinking what a type was there, leaning on a sacred Mayan monster, a fair, ruling, fighting, riding man, and what a twist of breeding had turned him prophet à la Semite, 'sad when he held the harp.'[6] And that the harp that once – etc. – was now completely cracked.

'All right,' he said, 'we'll leave antiquities for the moment. But it's a speculation worth following: Where did that civilization come from, and did it have any contact with Egypt?'

'Egypt? They knew about the soul there, and I don't care where their jim-jam decorations came from. Civilization's going. The world wants a man whose contact is primeval.'

'Oh does it?' said Brooks. 'I suppose you mean yourself. You're about as primeval as a card-index. Come and have some tea.'

And at tea Dick asked him sweetly about his children, and sent messages to his wife, and told the story of his uncle's funeral with point and wit, and left Brooks, to go up to Daphne, with his affection intact, and his doubts.

---

[6] From *The Ballad of the White Horse* (London: Methuen, 1911) by G. K. Chesterton, now collected in his *Collected Poems* (New York: Dodd Mead, 1980), 224.

Last of a race in ruin –
He spoke the speech of the Gaels;
His kin were in holy Ireland,
Or up in the crags of Wales.

But his soul stood with his mother's folk
That were of the rain-wrapped isle
Where Patrick and Brandan westerly

Looked out at last on a landless sea
And the sun's last smile.

His harp was curved and cunning
As the Celtic craftsman makes.
Graven all over with twisting shapes
Like many headless snakes.

His harp was carved and cunning,
His sword prompt and sharp
And he was gay when he held the sword,
Sad when he held the harp.

Now it was evening. The bus climbed up the side of London, and above the screaming children and the crowd going home from work, it rolled like an animal ship; and from every contact Dick sighed and withdrew himself, until at the five roads at Camden Town he felt something coming to him which had come before. 'This place is not here,' he said. 'I can lift myself out of it, in my body. So!' He sank down a little as he said it, and answered himself. 'The things you hate are only your body being knocked about by phenomena.' Then the place disappeared, especially a public-house with a plaster tower; but there had crept up through it tall perpendicular folds, which looked like dark grey rubber, which rose and passed in from all sides. But he was free, both of the houses and of what had replaced them. He lifted himself like a clean man out of the sea, and rested in his mind, which was now full of order and peace. He wondered that he had ever minded anything, and at the end of the ride stood several men drinks in a public-house and roared with laughter with them.

Before dinner he came to Daphne's house and rang the bell. There was some time before anyone answered it. Then her old nurse came, and looked at him without knowing who he was. He came in, and took off his raincoat before he said: 'Is Miss Daphne in?'

'I'll see, sir,' she said, and led him into the living-room, which had tall windows and a balcony on to a garden full of trees. The wind, a new thing, was moving in them. It was almost night. Next door was Daphne's room. He heard the door open and shut several times, and brief voices. The room was very empty. He stumbled over a rug, and saw the shining boards and a gramophone gaping with the lid up, and records on the divan among the cushions. He did not make himself at ease by the fire. He understood that they had been dancing. He walked up and down the room, wondering what they would give him to eat.

It was all right. The peace was there. He would tell Daphne about it. Daphne would give it back to him with assent and vivid words. Perhaps he would take Daphne out to dinner. Her youngest sister came in.

'Please forgive us. We're in such a hurry. We've been dressing Daphne. Would you mind coming to see her in her room?'

He remembered Daphne's room, rows of books and glass balls and Chinese pictures of birds and windows that stepped out into the air. He followed her sister, and as he came in, heard Daphne's cry, 'Hullo, Dick!' that was like a battle yell. In a minute he was treading into a sea of tissue paper that rustled like snakes. The shutters were closed. All the lights were on. Here was night, suddenly and strongly lit. As Daphne came to meet him, her sister fell on her knees, and followed her over the carpet, pinning something at her hips.

A woman he did not know was sitting on the couch looking at Daphne. The old nurse was somewhere behind him, by the door.

'Shall I ring for a taxi, dearie?'

'In a minute, nurse, I've a few moments to spare.' Then he trod on the paper like a man and saw her. She had on a green and white dress, and crystal earrings that touched her shoulders, and a crystal at her waist, slung round her neck with a green cord. Dick remembered enough to know that it was a dress that is not seen in shops, but is shown, *like an ear of corn reaped in silence*[7] to certain women on certain occasions. He saw her feet in silver sandals, her hair like a black, painted doll's, a curve drawn out over each cheek. On the dressing-table, white with powder, there was a bouquet in a frill.

'Dick, I'm going out to have a glorious time.' She did not look at him twice to see what his heavy eyes said.

'Val, my dear, is my back even?' Valentine got up and took a powder-puff and dusted her sister's white back. She sat down again at her mirror, and called at him into the glass where she could see him. 'Dick, sit down. You know my cousin, Mrs Lee?' He would not know her, but sat down and stared, and saw that Daphne was like a tree in glory. And that the colour of her mouth was due to art. It was not trying to be anything else. If it was kissed, it would come off so much sticky paint. The room was warm, full of scent and whirling with powder-dust. He tried to hear the wind rising.

---

[7]   This object, or this phrase, is what was shown or revealed to initiates at the culmination of the Elysian mysteries in ancient Greece.

He wanted to swear at Daphne and hit her. In the mirror, he saw her little head sink an instant. He knew her. She was thinking, 'Oh, Dick, don't spoil my pleasure.' Well, he would. Then she whipped round and smiled at him, deliberately, brutally, and he knew that he could not.

She was pulling on gloves like curd, picked up her flowers, and moved across the room.

'Nurse, ring for a taxi. Angry, Dick? I'm going to dance all night. Oh, it's good to get into decent clothes –'

He said vulgarly: 'It seems to me that you've got out of them,' and she looked at him exactly as she would look at a man of his kind who said a thing like that.

He felt his power drain out of him, his poise, assurance, pride. He had come to tell Daphne about heavenly things.

As he waited and hated her, she forgot even who he was.

'Say you like my dress. I must hear everyone say it.'

'I suppose it's fashionable, but I remember you in the shrubberies at Pharrs in a cotton dress. You came for a walk with me.'

'Oh yes. I remember Pharrs – that reminds me –'

It had not reminded her of him. She turned and went quickly to the glass again, and spoke to her cousin beside him.

'Terry. I'm not certain, but I think it wants a headdress.' She pulled out a wreath of bright green leaves and set it on her head.

They were like the leaves of no earthly laurel. He shuddered and called 'Daphne!' Her cousin agreed with her.

Her taxi came. She said: 'Dick, I'm sorry I've had no time tonight. Can I give you a lift down town?'

She flung on a silver cloak, and he followed her down the steps into the cab. The wind was rising, and drummed on the window-glass. They ran in silence down London. It was very cold. He saw where she was going; into a high square house, and down to dinner with a black and white man, down golden stairs.

She looked at him again.

'Cheer up, Dick. Don't you like to get back to it all when you come to town?'

She had won. He had not known how to express his disgust; now he did not know if he felt it.

'I suppose I miss it sometimes.'

'Look here. We've a party at the Savoy on Saturday, and we want another man. Will you come?'

He would not come. Anything might happen in the world, but he would not come.

'I'm afraid I should be out of place. You would find my change of values too complete.'

'Should we indeed! There are several Paradises, Dick. Me for this Paradise.'

She had known all the time. He must say something destructive, inimical, quickly. Only she had forgotten him again.

'Oh,' she said, 'it's cold,' and drew her silver stuff round her. Without concern he put his oily rough raincoat over the silver, the white and green, the milky back that came off a little. She made a little face, said 'Thank you' and forgot.

The wind roared through the square. She opened the door, two half-crowns in her hand.

'Here's my share. Good night, Dick. Come and see me some time. Good night, Dick.'

He did not want the taxi any more. He only wanted to meet the wind, and let Nature knock the nonsense out of him and the memories. He took the half-crowns from her, and she was out into the street before he could find his stick. He did not help her. She was gone. The wind roared past. He paid the man, and at the last instant before night, saw her run up the steps, and the wind take her cloak and open it. He saw her bend like a full sail, and balance to the wind. He saw her head go down, and her silver shoes run up. The door opened; he saw her run into a tall yellow arch, and the black door immediately close on her again.

The House-party (1930)

To Jean Cocteau

He wanted to go and stay with them, in the sea-washed, fly-blown, scorched hotel along the coast, whose walls were washed primrose above the blue lapping water, where one mounted to bed by a plaster stair outside above the shifting sea, under the stars shaken out in handfuls.

There might be peace there. Under Vincent's wing a man could stand up a bit. Vincent was English, tender, serious, older than he. Vincent wanted him to come. Was no doubt cajoling, hypnotising away certain objections. Objections that were always made about him, especially by his own countrymen, the Americans who made a cult of Europe, a cult and a career, not quite perfect in their transplanting, and conscious of it. As he was conscious of the virgin energy and high intelligence which made them a reproach to him. Also, that in certain directions, his adventures outnumbered theirs as the stars the dim electric light-bulbs of the hotel. No they would not want him, and Vincent, poor fish, would sweat blood to fix it so as not to annoy them. And at the same time risk his old friendships on his behalf. A fool, but a sort of glorious one. Glorious fools pay. Meanwhile he would go – and not be a nuisance to Vincent. Take a back seat all right. Give Vincent what he had to give. An audience, someone to *play* with. Worship carefully disguised. If Vincent bored him –. An essential meanness in the boy reminded him how he could take it out of Vincent, Vincent who was standing by him; not out of Vincent's friends. A cracked little specimen of a gigolo, after a year in prison for something he had not done, his comfort was to be revenged on the good. Vincent should pay.

Great André also was staying there; the silver hill, the lance-point of the boy's world. Vincent would present him. He would have something to worship as well as Vincent. Make Vincent jealous? No, no, no. Perhaps he'd find out how to behave as they behaved. No, no, no. God help him, he'd play no joy-boy tricks.

He had met Vincent at the Casino of the great town, and had heard about the fun they were having, the harmonious, mischievous house-party ten miles along the coast.

'International relations going strong. I'm still on speaking terms with Dudley and Stretton, Winkelman and Marjorie, Edouard and Clarice; with America, Mittel-Europa, England and France. And since André came I've never had such a time or known such a chap. Like lightning and Mozart.'

Not a word about the social lift André's presence implied. Only response to his longing to be there, and a little diffidence.

'Dudley and Stretton are difficult, Paul. Tastes very definite and standards unaccountably high. It works out that they don't like anyone who isn't in the arts, or pickled in New York, or else extremely important socially –'

Paul said: 'I'm a pickled New Englander. That's to say that I'm much better family. But you can tell them I won't interfere. They won't even see me except across a room at meals. I suppose they can stand that. If I come, it's to see you – I know what's due to people who have been kind to me.'

Vincent smiled. 'I see a good deal of André. I expect you'll meet him too. I'll take you a room for to-morrow, and when the high cultural atmosphere of Dudley and Stretton gets a bit too much we'll amuse each other –'

Paul saw him leave the Casino and shoot across the bright gardens to find his car – a young man whose large bones the flesh covered delicately, who, even indoors, set the air stirring. Not noisy at all, but easy, as if his life was nourished by a fountain, whose very deep waters rose and sunned and spread themselves evenly, and mounting kept everything they touched astir. Paul, shooting craps at a bar, remembered a sentence Vincent had quoted, 'The generosity of strength,' supposed Vincent had it, and his heart felt the little nick of pain which was his form of worship; he knew that he did not mind saying, even to Vincent's face, that Vincent was his superior.

HOUSE-PARTY
First published in the journal *Pagany* 1(1) (January–March 1930), then included in Butts's second collection of short stories, *Several Occasions* (London: Wishart, 1932), which furnishes the text followed by this edition.

A moment later he began to reflect on his simplicity. These scrupulous Englishmen were easy to make. Because of their innocence, because of the insolence implied in 'the generosity of strength.' He counted the knuckles of his small, rosy, gold-wired hands, tried the pointed nails, jerked up the arm to feel the bicep, who had once been an athlete, looked in the mirror at his pretty clothes and handsome childish head, spoke to the barman in faultless French. To reassure himself. It was all he had to take over there to people disorderly with treasure of mind and spirit. Of bodies also, but he knew how to exploit his –

Vincent, rushing his car along the hill coastline, was saying that the ill-used brat should have his treat.

He had acquired Paul in a moment of occupation with human wrongs. The boy had been handed over to him by another man as a hopeless case. It had seemed to him that Paul's life of dissipation, malice and despair, occasionally touched by a kind of nipped sweetness which flowered only into unwilling loyalty, was one form of a universal condition, a rot nibbling at a generation. This gave him the power to illustrate the particular by the general, translate the boy into boys, and take valuable notes. His feebleness lay in an observation he had shirked: that all Paul's qualities, his vices, his sincerity, his aspirations, and his affection had been steeped, as though his body in filth, in some essence of the sordid which made him repellent. Apart from the blindness of generosity, a connoisseur in bad smells might have accepted the handsome lad, courteous when he liked, ravenously grateful for scraps, and rather chic.

Vincent looked out to sea, over jade dancing, called it a drawing-room ocean after the Atlantic, and kicked himself mildly for ingratitude. If only Paul could be dipped in it and brought out clean. He knew that what he needed was purification, from what corruption he did not quite understand. He concentrated too closely on the horror spot of the story. The boy's imprisonment for folly; his desertion by his friend. The savage sentence; the appalling illness that had released him; the details of his third degree. Little Paul naked and terrified, and beaten up. Questioned to insanity; flung for weeks into a filthy cell; chained to a black murderer running with sores. He had infinite pleasure when Paul responded, told him how peace of heart and self-respect ran in like small tides 'into the mess it has made of me. Don't suppose that when I'm with a person like yourself, it doesn't do good to my character –'

Vincent knew that behind the small admission there was a continent of waste land and reserve. Also that it was sincere. Paul brought him presents, a cigarette holder in almost good bad taste; popular fiction that had impressed him; once, God knew how acquired, a lapis snuff-bottle stoppered with coral, the most gentlemanly chinoiserie, full of oily permanent eastern scent. Paul loved to give, loved himself for giving. Vincent was touched. He enjoyed presents too. They played with them together. Vincent was persuaded that Paul did him good, not by exercising him in charity, but by taking him out of his group intensities. Paul had lively adventures, good because they were ordinary debaucheries. Yet in each there was something distasteful, as though the prison and the hospital had left a taint and a sepsis. The sea racing below on Vincent's right was the sign of purification. For purification was necessary. A saturation – in what? Vincent did not exactly know. He only knew an essence that washed his spirit daily as the sea his body, the wine in his throat, music in his ears. What was it? He resisted the easy race-temptation to call it by old names, religion, God's grace, because they had once been counters for it, possibly were so still. But observing great André with his crowd of lads, who came for an hour, for a day, flashing in and out of the Frenchman's darkened room, a word had crystallised out for such activities. Kourotrophos,[1] a bringer-up of boys. Not much more than one himself, Vincent brooded its meaning, half ashamed of its emotional charge, the humility and elation it brought him. If he could not show Paul the Good, he would bring him samples, rub his nose in them if necessary, pitch him, kick him into it, scrub him. Hold him up a glass to see his restored cleanliness. For the spiritual-sensual reward: to hear Paul say that it was good, clean and on his knees. And see the little thing run off translated, his small gifts liberated, reasonably at peace.

---

[1]   In Greek mythology, an epithet for Artemis in her role as protector of youth. *Kouros* means 'young man,' *trophos* refers to someone leading, conducting, or nurturing.

Beside the classic sea, the classic title took form: Kourotrophos. He saw Cheiron,[2] Pallas.[3] In the same land, built of gold and violet rock, barren, but *a good nurse for boys*, André; the dead scots officer who had licked him into shape. He meant to try a practice hand on Paul; for someone in the future, the friend of friends, who at the start would need that. Paul was just a try-out, with a dash of affection in his sentiment towards him, and a slight kick.

Vincent was an English type, mutely convinced that he was there for a purpose, accepting the discipline of the virtues as preparation for an unknown. A particularly unknown unknown at this time, with religion and love and pride of land and race off the map, and the unconscious the cheerless substitute. Meanwhile he had to be observant, study the iron puritanism in which Paul had been raised. Was that the soil which had grown his corruption? He decided finally that it had only set the stubborn will that resisted catharsis. They had read together the story of the Butcher of Hanover,[4] and he had noticed that the horrible fairy-tale had struck Paul with terror. Also that it had excited him. Which suggested a Hoffman in Paul?[5] Really, really. But Vincent had spent an hour or so of his imaginative life in the old quarter of Hanover, in and out the over-hung, cobbled passages and crazed buildings, greased and glazed with old blood; still alive, this time with painted, emotional boys, followers of men's oldest profession. Current hysteria, gossip, intrigue, on a mediaeval stage. Mystery of stairs that lead nowhere and doors that do not shut, and round the corner to Augustus' Live Wire Bar.

Throw fire, crystal, salt between little Paul and that place, where Vincent could have strolled and picked up wisdom; where the absence implied the presence of his lord. He left his car at the hill garage and ran down the terrace stairs of the small town, past gay, plaster houses roofed with round tiles, along slots of cooled, highly seasoned air; a ribbon of liquid sky on top; and at the end of each stair a patch of still water, divided by masts, the basin of the little, prehistoric port, till he reached the hotel on the quay. He had Dudley and Stretton to appease, where, from his point of view, appeasement should not have been necessary; and it is hard to entreat those we love. He could foresee the iron stare at Paul's name, the lip-twitch of contempt, and, incidentally, the glance of apprehension.

He ran up the white, sea-cracked stair and knocked at André's door. In bed, God bless him, in a room where the sea-light sifted through wooden slats; the red silk of his pyjama coat falling back up dark ivory arms. Ready for any emergency. Ready always to talk. As by magic, he spoke immediately of Dudley and Stretton. 'Any news from the Upper House, *mon cher*?'

'I've news for them,' said Vincent. 'Listen, André, I've a *déclassé* little friend –'

'You always have – so have I. Well?'

'– I put it to you, André, the boy ought to come. You'd think that, after his past, his countrymen would be hunting him round with bouquets –' He tried to find the French for scapegoat.

'*Bouc émissaire*,'[6] said André. 'I don't suppose they chose a valuable beast.'

Then it was like a ride on a wave, repose on the sea's back, when the Frenchman said: 'I will arrange it – he has a right to stay where he pleases – Dudley and Stretton can't have everything their own way. Leave it to me.'

They embraced, and Vincent felt as if the sea had lifted him gently on to a firm beach.

* * *

In another room of the hotel Dudley and Stretton's sails emptied a moment and flapped in a pocket of the rising gale they were running before to well-earned fame. Vincent had said 'check' when he had gone straight to André to sponsor this deplorable specimen of their native land. In their sun-steeped rooms, filled with objects of comfort, utility and impeccable taste, they yielded to distress.

[2]   Chiron was a centaur, or half man and half horse. Unlike other centaurs, he was especially gentle, wise, and learned, and therefore was asked to tutor several Greek heros, including Achilles, Aesculapius, Hercules, and Jason.

[3]   Greek goddess of wisdom.

[4]   Fritz Haarmann (1879–1925) became dubbed the 'Butcher of Hanover' or the 'Vampire of Hanover' by the contemporary press, which recounted in gruesome detail how he had slain and dismembered more than 20 young men, also drinking their blood. Haarmann was gay.

[5]   The German writer E. T. A. Hoffman (1776–1822), noted for his fantastic tales.

[6]   French for 'scapegoat.'

Dudley picked at the typewriter, Stretton sat on the edge of the bed. The sea danced at them. They were saying that no European ever could or ever would understand the way rumour reached New York, and booked its passage by return of liner under new and horrible disguises. That people would talk; that people might say they were friends with the boy if they were seen in the same place. It was all very well for André, a prince of the arts, and for Vincent with his shameless english indifference to public opinion; they had extra cats to whip. Stretton was tall, fragile, ageless, beautiful. Dudley was handsome, quick, serviceable. The pair two formidable hunters, out for the lion's share. In the civilisation of Europe, kind, ruthless, observant pioneers. Neither aware of the power of their arms, the prestige of their fresh strength. Both aware that Vincent had put their queen in danger, intentionally or not.

Dudley clattered off a letter on the typewriter. Stretton put on a record. *I Ain't Nobody's Darling*[7] pointed the situation. He took it off and substituted Mozart. Perhaps not perfectly appreciated, the lovely air flowed out above 'the hard hearts of men.'[8]

The day after, while André took a cat-nap after two hours' unbroken lunch conversation, Vincent hurried along the sea-bordered rock-path to the station. In the train Paul soiled his hands, clinging to the black-dusted rod in the corridor on his way. The train ran into a tunnel, into the mountain that rushed down to the edge of the dancing beach. In an instant he had passed out of flashing air into brownness, into hell's neck, after a paradise of blue stone-pines. The boy suffered in it, and from more than fear that its filth would soil his smartness. To his literal, primitive fancy it was like what hell would be, hell where he'd been before, hell where he belonged. Only this tunnel had an end, which ran full into a station, where Vincent was waiting for him beside more sea.

Together they left hell's mouth, Paul trotting a little behind Vincent's stride, and glad to run to earth in his sunny room and arrange his pretty properties. It occurred to Vincent, as he watched him displaying trifles, that there were people without house or land, with a dressing-case and a photograph frame for anchor. Paul said: 'I suppose you couldn't get me a window table downstairs? I can promise you not to look at Dudley and Stretton. Or rather I shall leave it to them. They can cut me or not as they please.'

'I've fixed that for to-morrow – André asked you to dine with us to-night.' He saw Paul start, harden, and then sitting on his bed drop backwards, his forearm over his eyes.

'What is it, lad?'

'I don't know; but you take me out of hell into heaven. It's all you. I know that. I'll kiss Dudley and Stretton if you like.'

Vincent jumped. That wouldn't do. Keep 'em apart. Quite simply, because he was ashamed of Paul. Also he remembered their iced politeness when they had seen him once before, the night he had taken Paul to one of their parties, when he had been at fault, and Paul had acted in character. 'Let them be,' he said; 'you can make friends with them later.'

'You mean,' said Paul, 'that I may be fit to know them later?'

'I mean that if you clean up and cheer up you can meet them later on your own ground.'

* * *

At dinner Paul sat by André, at the head of the table, opposite Vincent. Beside him an English-woman, neither ugly nor old, who had Dudley beside her; and by Vincent, Stretton; and by him a

[7] 'I Ain't Nobody's Darling,' with words by Elmer Hughes and music by Robert A. King (1862–1932) was published in 1921.

[8] From Lytton Strachey (1880–1932), 'Voltaire and Frederick the Great,' in Strachey's *Books and Characters: French and English* (London: Chatto & Windus, 1922), 183: 'When the evening came it was time to dress, and, in all the pomp of flowing wig and diamond orders to proceed to the little music-room, where his Majesty, after the business of the day, was preparing to relax himself upon the flute. The orchestra was gathered together; the audience was seated; the concerto began. And then the sounds of beauty flowed and trembled and seemed, for a little space, to triumph over the pains of the living and the hard hearts of men; and the royal master poured out his skill in some long and elaborate cadenza, and the adagio came, the marvellous adagio, and the conqueror of Rossbach drew tears from the author of *Candide*.' Butts quotes a more extensive excerpt from this passage in her short story 'Green' (Mary Butts, *With and Without Buttons*, ed. Nathalie Blondel ([Manchester: Carcanet, 1991], 79); p. 804 in this edition.

pretty, watchful French girl. The long table, with a Frenchman at the head of it, which was the hotel's show-piece and alarm. An annoyance and bewilderment for the old soldiers and older maids who filled the *salle à manger*, when the conversation rose above the clash of plates and the shifting of the sea.

> *J'ai du commerce sexuelle*
> *Avec mon colonel*
> *J'ai connu, charnellement, mon commandant –*[9]

seven gay voices sang when the courses were late. The Englishwoman was teasing André, who was whittling green olives into improprieties. As Paul passed a carafe he was nodded to by Stretton, and asked where he had been, as though his address had been a public lavatory, and he given a chance to conceal it. It was like being let out on parole. No, it was not parole, it was freedom. He told them all a story, suggested by André's anatomical reconstructions of the olives, and they were silent.

He felt walls closing on him again. Like the walls of his prison that his body had somehow got out of and left the rest behind. He was listening now to their talk. About the same thing as his story, but excused because the words were different, and mixed up with implications he didn't understand. That was cleverness: that was hypocrisy. They were like bright flies hatched out of dung, and he the beetle content to roll its ball. He thought about that until he caught André's voice again, half-way through a tirade on the theatre. He'd seen the play. Coolly Stretton asked for his opinion. Again, what he said was not *like* what they said. He flushed. André sheltered him. Stretton illustrated André's criticism with a New York production. He was analytic, weighty. By chance, wrong on detail. Paul corrected him eagerly. Silence. With a pinch of assurance gained, he invited André and Vincent to the café on the quay. André refused gently. Vincent carried him off.

The little town was built on terraces chipped out of the mountain flank, between two precipices, round whose base even the Mediterranean flung itself in spray. It was very still in the little port, white docks ran in sideways along stale emerald water, an utter security for little boats. The quay stones, salt-bleached and fretted smooth, where the cables rubbed, were laid with rust-coloured nets. Eternally torn, eternally repaired, untidy girls in black gowns, with black-brown necks and dusty, dark curls, mended them. But at this season, at night, the open bay looked as if it were divided by a wall, pierced with round holes, blazing with circular light, behind which could be heard voices and music; the space between the wall and the quay shot across by launches turning and tearing, ripping the water's green back; and little ceremonies of recommitment to land or sea took place on the quay, as the commander of the battleship welcomed or was welcomed. And every room along the front or up the terraces roared with sailors, their pockets full of money; and the town girls out with them to supply the honey; and nine months later, after the christening of too many grey-eyed, flax-haired babies, the Curé would get out his annual sermon on the sin of fornication, until the next season brought more ships from newer and richer lands.

But from the day the ships arrived one could observe the girls' black overalls and dingy espadrilles shed, to be replaced by wall-paper cretonnes and shoes whose high heels turned over unaccustomed ankles; and shiny, pink wood-fibre stockings over olive legs. While the gramophones worked to death, and the tin pianos beat out jazz, and the cars of arriving and departing officers swept light paths on the bent road up the hill.

Much later the noise became more concentrated by the water's edge, more expressive of the emotions of drunk men struggling with a foreign tongue. Finally the ship police would load them into boats, groaning; the last cargo would shoot out, to be replaced at dawn by men with fresh leave and stragglers returning from the great town where Vincent had refound Paul. It had not occurred to him that it might be more than a spectacle for an american *deraciné* to see the men of his fleet out on a spree. Only he noticed a difference in the quality of their pleasure. He was at a play of which Paul had seen the rehearsals. Might at any moment run off behind the scenes. For Vincent the play

---

[9]   'I've had sexual commerce with my colonel, I've had carnal relations with my commander,' in French.

was just sufficiently amusing; but Paul had imported something with him from the great town, where half the earth swarmed up and down an esplanade, where each vice had its location, and even the lamp-posts and bicycles were over-sexed. Sailors talked of the swell joints and the swell girls they had found there. Paul stood the drinks. He was sparkling with excitement. The sombre child, alternating at dinner between timidity and impertinence, changed into a sharp-eyed lad in the know.

For some days before, as well as for some nights, Vincent had observed a shadow about the quays. First because it had tried to sell him an obscene book, then because it tried to sell André an obscene book, then because it tried to sell everybody an obscene book. Then because it was obscene. Of no race or of any; grey, green, greasy, with a few horned teeth and black nails; its clothes a patch-work of hotel leavings, its speech a kind of American, pronounced with a lisp, the chi-chi of the East. Referred to as the Pimp. No name, no associates, it would appear and be gone. It knew a whore-house, a cinema. Lived by finding the people who wanted those places. Found them. Of no age. Probably an immortal. Vincent composed of west wind and tree sap, the wine, beef, apples and classic literature of an english country house, was affected by him as by a bad smell. In the café he went over to speak to Stretton, escorting the little French girl. Danced with her once, introduced her to a sober, charming sailor, turned and saw Paul, leaning along the bar with the Pimp. Stretton must have seen him. Anyhow, he pulled the boy's shoulder round, surprised at the shock inside himself.

'What d'you mean – speaking to that filth here with us?'

Surprise from Paul might have cut his fury; defiance justified it – but the boy said: 'No, no. Please take me away. It was not my fault. He spoke to me. I'm afraid of him.'

The man glanced, cringing at them, and began to melt away, merging into the crowd at the door.

'Don't play into Stretton's hand then.' Thoroughly cross he replaced him at the table.

Timidly Paul looked up at him. 'I couldn't help it, Vincent. I saw him once or twice about before. I don't quite know what he is –' Then as 'All right. Tell me why you're afraid of him' framed in Vincent's throat, the child's notes went out of Paul's voice, and the self-conscious, self-righteous debauché spoke: 'Why should I mind what Stretton sees? If you're ashamed of me, you've only got to say so and I'll go –'

'Say go,' said a guardian angel tartly to Vincent. As generally happens, he told it to shut up. In fact, 'Shut up' was all he said aloud to Paul.

* * *

'Pan,' said Vincent, on a terrace on the top of the world, overlooking the sea in which some day Solomon is supposed to drown it, 'what's Pan to you?'

'I guess,' said Paul, 'he's my god.'

He seemed to want to hear something about him. Vincent sketched the varieties of his cult. He did not neglect him as a god of sex, but down the gulf below them a yacht race was standing in, on blue-roughened water, the true wine-dark, a handful of silver slips. And as he watched them, all that was natural in his training and imagination made him breathless with love. Inattentive and unprepared later to meet reserved sarcasm from Paul – 'That's all I know about Pan – what's your idea?'

Paul's answer was the smile of contemptuous pity a novice might get from a nasty old priest.

'I could show you a bit more about him if you came with me up the back streets at night.'

'Only drunks and drunks and more drunks. Like the Prince Regent's waistcoats.'

'There's more than that – you'd see how people get away with it – what can I do –' The dark blue stone eyes were shining again; his smile to himself, an acute sensuality outside the romantic attitude to sex. Vincent whisked the car back down the hair-pin bends and wished it would grow wings, fly away with Paul and punish him, and show him a life so different that back streets or high hills would be Tom Tiddler's ground[10] to him. And it felt as though he had exchanged a cake of

---

[10] 'Tom Tiddler's Ground' is a short story by Charles Dickens (1812–72), which recounts the tale of a man who has let his house and its grounds fall into a state of extreme dilapidation.

soap stuck with nails for a crystal ball when he joined André after dinner, alone.

Then Stretton came in. He said, 'Where's your interesting experiment, Paul Martyn?'

'Out somewhere, I suppose. I'm not his nurse.'

Then they listened to André, brought their lives to illustrate his. They loved him.

Dudley knocked. 'I've seen your Paul below. He asked me why I was ashamed to be an American. I didn't know that I was.'

Vincent did not understand their problem. The hag of unspecified bad conscience hobbled in. André was tactless.

'He will not make a scandal for us here, will he?'

'Of course not. And he asks rude questions out of defence. Let the boy enjoy himself his own way. What reason is there to turn him into a bad copy of us?'

'By all means,' said Stretton. 'A glimpse into the mentality of the Pimp at second-hand might be useful.'

Vincent felt an impulse to go down, fetch Paul and beat him. Both ways Dudley and Stretton cramped his impulses. And for nothing would he miss an evening of André's magic mind.

Very much later he looked out his bedroom window, high up over the slip of cobbled square. Dancing was over and carouse and rows. On the other side of the hotel the sea lifted quietly up. Here and there a window of the old town showed a square, rose or orange. Somewhere a concertina gasped a dying breath. A line of plane trees rustled, and drew a delicate shadow on moon-whitened stones. Out of the house shadows an occasional cat slipped. He washed himself in the moon-quiet. Then saw that there were two people about, presently visible in the open square – Paul and the Pimp. At the foot of a stair they turned and mounted quietly together up the town. Vincent stayed still. So that was what Paul did when he went out to play. Follow him out and ask to be taken to see Pan? The shadows seemed to be coarsening and thickening. He remembered the smell of thyme – sweet, rank, classic grossness. He cleaned his teeth a long time. The stuff was called euthymol. A whiff of magic about; great indifference to Paul. He slept.

Paul woke late next morning, and with the nervous anxiety common to his race began to feel for symptoms of disease. Throat sore, mouth 'like the bottom of a parrot's cage,' nerves no worse than usual, but outside scrutiny. Normal awakening under abnormal circumstances. He should have been rather pleased with himself, but part of his conscience was raw and in raving protest. He hadn't come to Vincent to behave like that. Hated Vincent for the stab of remorse which made it necessary to suppress tears. The spasm passed and he smacked his lips. Stretton wouldn't have dared to go where he'd been, and Vincent wouldn't have cared. And André. He bet André knew more about it than he'd let on. All the same, he hadn't meant to keep the rendezvous he had made with the Pimp at the bar before Vincent had turned him away. Why in hell had he? Why in hell shouldn't he?

He got up, groomed himself with concentrated attention, and went out. At the tip of the breakwater, under the pepper-box pharos, André and Stretton were sunning themselves. Paul had on the coat he had worn the night before. A pocket crackled. He pulled out a sheaf of dirty drawings and sat down to reperuse them. The breeze blew one along. Stretton retrieved it, glanced at it and rose politely to return it. Impudence seized Paul. He walked back with him and showed the whole lot to André then and there. André laughed; but both were embarrassed by Stretton. High intelligence and boundless information uncorrected by wide experience takes all comfort out of criticism. But because André laughed and chattered, Paul thought he had triumphed. Would not let his sexual curiosities drop. Again he bored them. André finally let him see it, and was told in French too rapid for Stretton that there was no need for him to play the prude. He lay sprawling by André, his tight, smart looks displayed beside the worn seraph, laid out, light as blown steel, along the stones. Blind with need for response he became reckless, using *tu*[11] and calling the Frenchman

---

[11]   The familiar form of 'you' in French, to be used only with close friends.

by his first name. Knew himself further and further separated from him, until he yelped from his starved little heart:

'D'you know, André, you seem a hypocrite to me. When you were younger you raised enough hell. You're getting affected.'

André, infinitely wise and unwise, whose memories were of Paris, poetry, the adventure and passions of a unique personality, did not want to be reminded of his incomparable adolescence. How it could be visualised by this little animal. He raised himself on his elbows and began an apostrophe on aeroplanes, men, birds, bird-priestesses and the hawk of Horus.[12] On wings. Stretton tossed back the thread as it wove over Paul's fair head laid comfortless on his small, clasped hands. He held hard to the belief that all they said was only his own life dressed up. It was because they weren't honest and had read things. Suddenly he got up and almost shrieked at André: 'If you'll excuse me, I'm going. I can't stand any more. *Ta voix m'agace.*'[13] Stretton made a gesture. André carried on, his voice the minutest division of a tone higher.

He lunched with Vincent. It had been agreed that Vincent should leave the long table, to which he had not been reinvited, and join him for one meal each day. His outburst at André, his failure with André, had let loose a storm of sensibility and a need to confess. Vincent was cold. Paul began to explain again how good Vincent was for his character. It was a dreary shock when the Englishman said: 'Then what were you doing out last night with the Pimp?'

He saw the boy retreat into himself, trapped. Then plaintively: 'I can't speak to you now, Vincent. Leave me alone, please.' He saw Vincent shrug his shoulders, unaware of the pity which could have won him forgiveness.

Vincent went to fetch André, Dudley and Stretton for a run in the car. Found André on his bed talking, supported on his elbows, and morally by Stretton. After Paul's small, musical drawl, French tired his ears. He was oddly unstrung. Paul's presence, which could not separate him from André, divided him from Stretton. All three whom he loved, and differently.

Stretton said: 'Paul has told André that his voice gets on his nerves.'

The pit of Vincent's stomach made itself noticeable. 'What's it been about?' A few careful sentences, terrible in their scrupulous avoidance of condemnation, gave the meeting on the quay. Stretton holding his mirror up to nature. A superb mirror, reflector also for his petulant, stern beauty. He might as well have struck Vincent when he left the room to tell Dudley the car was ready. Vincent looked at André, to watch his mouth set in its divine smile. It did not. He turned over nervously.

'Vincent, let me speak frankly. Before your *protégé* came, and Dudley and Stretton were so perturbed, I had though them unjust. I meant, in fact, to take the boy up. To give him the run of this room. See if one could help him. Teach them a lesson in kindness. I see now that it is impossible. To begin with, he is a bore. Bores are unhelpable. Then he is corrupt. Not on account of his life or his taste in art. And I rather liked him when he said that my voice got on his nerves. It gets on mine. I am speaking of the quality of qualities.'

Bitter-crystal waters of lucidity. Vincent nodded. 'But, André,' he said, 'I had him here on trial. I know now it is no good. I'll send him away.'

'Not at all on my account. It is you I am considering. You let your heart run away with you. The boy adores you, but some day he will play you a dirty trick. You don't know these little boys as I do. And you English play the *grands seigneurs* in a world that does not admit their existence. And –' (the clause was flashed in) 'I do not want any scandal here.'

Very well punished, Vincent said: 'All right, André, I'll clip his poor little claws. I shan't cut him myself because of what happened to him in prison when he was a child. I hold that because of that a lot should be forgiven him. We'll run up into the mountains. I'm going for the car.'

'Nasty pill,' said Vincent, stopping in the corridor to feel his wounds. So much for the Kourotrophos. He had risked André and Stretton on that piece of swank, and had been very properly put in his place. Was it for that he was nearly weeping? Not at all, he observed,

---

[12] Horus was an Egyptian sky god often depicted as a hawk or falcon.   [13] 'Your voice annoys me,' in French.

sufficiently a pupil of the french mind; but because his little kouros[14] could not be brought up. Would never 'put off the old man like a garment.' The filth had gone too deep, he was dyed in it. Vincent knocked at Stretton's door.

'Coming?' There was discussion in the further room.

'Dudley wants to know if there will be room.'

'Yes, for the four of us.' Dudley appeared, perfect, neat, complete, hands in pockets, his look pitched straight at Vincent. He did not mean to come if Paul were asked. And he was perfectly right.

Worse luck. They were perfectly right.

'Only us four. Are you coming?'

'Yep.'

They dined on another terrace-rock, hung over space; a cloud hiding the gardens and vineyards of men. All that was visible was other stones, staring like animals at the shifting, glittering sea. They sat until the sun turned its dancing-floor into a lacquered parquet, a gold path for his dip into the ocean baths.

Vincent told them the memories of Atlantis, Hy-Brasil, the Apple Land.[15] André told them about Basques. A Basque and what had happened to him swimming in the basque country. A story which would have pleased Paul.

The boy spent an afternoon chewing the cud of stale excess. Inclined for company, he went down to the hotel front, on the quay; and there, as though newly risen from the dead, was the Pimp, pestering a tourist. And when he had pestered him, he made straight for Paul, sat down beside him, and carried on, as though it had never been interrupted, their conversation of the night before, held in a dim-lit maroon-hung brothel of the old town. There followed suggestions how they might be useful one to the other.

'You gotta pull on plentee smart guys. You bringa them to me.'

In bright gold daylight. The only creature who wanted to speak to him. Misery rose in Paul. The man became a spectre of his imprisonment: of all that cut him off from other men. He was a louse out of his filthy cell, who had crossed the water on his body: fattened on his secretions. The rich pleasure he had taken in the man became a fearful punishment to him, who believed in punishment: who had been punished. As he stared away from him, the green harbour water plaqued with gold, the old stones tufted with wild flowers, the fringed mountains against the low sun, all the shapely, brilliant beauties of Europe's cradle became alive with obscenity; neutral forms for the foul to make plastic. His very precious ring, the gold snake with the diamond sunk in its head, was a small fiend in command. A late fisherman landed a net of flapping, dying, sea-people; snatched a small squid from the salt-running pile and held it up. Once Vincent had caught one – Vincent so easy and happy out in boats – and had told him how they were motifs for decoration on Cretan jars. An awful people they must have been. Between the squid, the Pimp and his little ring he was being damned alive. He could not tell him to go. He must go where he was bid, as before he had gone to prison. A calvinist ancestor appeared.

'My great-great-grandson, it pleased the Lord to damn you before you entered your mother's womb. It is so, even though you should learn humility and bless Him for it.' The squid's arms writhed. The fisherman, young, gay, beautiful, held it up; flashed his white teeth at the small crowd round him, lowered his head and bit till the eight arms fell limp. Lifted his slimed face and laughed. Paul, now nearly mad, shrieked.

The Englishwoman walked along the quay, looking for friends. She saw Paul and smiled at him. He staggered up, agonisedly produced the pretty manners of his upbringing.

'Come and have a drink with me,' she said; 'are Vincent and André back yet? You didn't go with them?' The Pimp faded.

---

[14] Ancient Greek for 'boy' or 'young man.'

[15] Atlantis was a mythical lost kingdom; Hy-Brasil is a legendary island said to be located somewhere west of Ireland; 'the Apple Land' is supposed to be a translation of 'Avalon,' the kingdom of the fairies or the dead to which King Arthur traveled upon his death.

'No,' he said; 'I'm afraid I've offended them.'

'English people ain't easy to offend. It's your American nerves.' He looked to her also like a child. 'What have you been up to?' she said.

'Vincent is angry because I spoke to that man. I didn't mean to. I'd give anything to get away –'

'You've only to cut him and he'll run.'

'But you didn't know. I can't.' She saw that it was serious.

'Vincent told me something. If you want to live differently, you have only to tell Vincent. He's patient –'

'God knows I am sorry, but what's the good?' All the same, when he looked round, the harbour was again a place for ships. 'Thank you,' he said, 'most people are decent to me now. And when they aren't, I dare say it's my fault.'

They dined together, waiting for Vincent. But by the time he returned, Paul disintegrated again. The Englishwoman spoke to Vincent: 'Go and look after that kid.' Vincent, only half-willing, found him in his room; heard only a petulant, self-righteous harangue on Vincent's misconceptions about him – which he answered grimly enough with André's sentence: 'You could have been adopted, given the freedom Stretton and I have: to teach them charity, and you something more about life. And André, who is infinitely merciful, saw it was no good.'

Paul said, 'Yes, for a Frenchman, he is merciful. But he would never understand. I think that man below is the devil and that he is following me.'

The agony in his eyes, blue stones, glazed and burning, convinced Vincent. 'Let's look at it clearly,' he said. 'Why did you go off with that man?'

'I don't quite know. You see, I'm more accustomed than you to that sort.'

'Sort of swank then?'

'Perhaps. You've had such luck, you people. I was just as well raised. And if I'd had your education –'

'Cut that out. If you want education, you'll get it. I'll tell you this, Paul –' The countryman of Blake[16] took a long breath, lifted the apricot-tanned head, darker than his hair. His eyes counted paint-flaws on the wall, his imagination aware but sightless. He said: 'That man is an ambulatory, Mediterranean sore, living on the viciousness of our vices. But I think he's a shadow, d'you see – the image, the signature of a very living thing that is your torment. He is nothing, a corpse, a nuisance; but he may be under orders. Orders he knows even.'

Paul amazed him, breaking into sobs, the unfathomable hysteria of the damned. He took him by the shoulders, almost to his heart, and said: 'You have only to summon your courage. It'll come: and he'll melt.'

But Paul sobbed on, racked noises leaving his body, as a man might spew up formless evil spirits. Vincent hitched him into the crook of his arm, each jerk of the slight shoulders registered against his heart. Was this the beginning of purification? He caressed, careful not to talk. Paul at last lay still; then sat up suddenly, slung his fine ankles to the floor, went to the *lavabo* and washed his face with hot water, with cold, with cologne. Drew a wet comb through his hair, worked on his cheeks with a powder-wad.

'Thank you for letting me cry. It did me a lot of good.'

'Where are you going now?'

'Down to the lounge. I don't think he'll come there. I've got a book.'

'What sort of a book?'

'I like it. It is about the sort of gentlemen my people were; like yours. The sort I might have been.' Vincent was conscious of the whine, the sniff, mixed with the utter truth. He sat on the side of the bed, pensive and fatigued.

He went down to the garage and saw to his car; and there, among its intricacies, anchored himself against flights on to planes of suffering which produced the phenomena of one fair boy

---

[16] William Blake (1757–1827) was a British poet, visionary, and engraver.

weeping on his bed, and one green, gap-toothed figure dodging on the quays. Also distaste, division and disgust among a band of friends. He ate up his car's insides like cake; here was something precise to *do*, for people who where dependents on his car's flights for pleasure. He had worked himself into a serenity, a little too ardent to be sane, when, rising from his knees he saw the Pimp, looking in at the garage door, pulling something out of his loose pocket, a book or a box.

'Get out!' he cried. The man's mouth moved; it sounded like whistling. Something flapped. He went off. Up the moonlight-stair Vincent had watched on the last night.

He left the garage and crossed the square to the hotel. It was getting late. In a corner of the empty salon he found Paul with his book. A child sent to Coventry, in the arid, frivolous, depressing room, his face was still scorched with crying.

'Vincent, for pity's sake, don't give me up. It is true what you said; there are evil spirits around me. I've been too kicked to fight them alone. You invited me out of hell into heaven, and it seems I brought my own hell with me. For pity's sake –'

And pity like a naked, new-born babe striding the blast.[17] Vincent flung himself off down the corridor to André's room, and found him alone. 'André, I've sent that child sky-high, and it seems to have kicked him permanently off his legs. I'm out of power; I can't handle him.'

The passionate sentences, thrust into literal French, intrigued André: 'Oh these little boys with more sensibility than wits! I know them. Send him up to me.'

He went back. 'André says you're to go to him.'

'I'm ashamed.'

'Do as he tells you.'

'I'll try.'

Vincent sat on the foot of André's bed. All lights were out but the reading-lamp that lit the Frenchman's hands, the gay, dark, imagination-worn head in rose-gold shadows. Paul drew up a stool to the bed and sat between them, leaning against it, his hands on the sheets.

'*Mon gosse*,[18] what is this trouble about? Vincent tells me that you are afraid of the Pimp. But Stretton says that he saw you talking to him last night.'

'I did worse than that. I went with him up to the old town, with the sailors. To-day I saw him again. He would speak to me. To-day I saw that there were evil things all round me. And I see the man everywhere. In places where I know he can't be. He is a devil. I am being punished again. I am always being punished –'

André scribbled a note and gave it to Vincent. 'Take that down to the *patron*. It is to say that if that man is seen round the hotel again I and my friends leave. That should settle it. Will that do, boy?'

When Vincent returned to his place Paul had drawn closer to the bed, and André's hands were invisible, the boy's face laid on them.

'My little one, you are young and handsome. Clever at some things, Vincent says, and neither poor nor sick. What is it that spoils your life?'

Paul answered in a low voice: 'It has always been the same, André. When I was at school. People were unjust to me. I hadn't laughed much in years till I knew Vincent. He can make me giggle. And in spite of his friends, who hate me, he brought me here and introduced me to you. And my filth's followed me just the same. I'm in prison like I was before. Then something that separates me from you. Dudley and Stretton are quite justified. I shall never hold it against them that they won't know me. But I'm sorry I was rude to you to-day.'

---

[17]   From William Shakespeare's *Macbeth* (c. 1606), Act 1, Scene 7, with Macbeth alone contemplating the murder of Duncan:

> Besides, this Duncan
> Hath borne his faculties so meek, hath been
> So clear in his great office, that his virtues
> Will plead like angels, trumpet-tongued, against
> The deep damnation of his taking-off:

> And pity, like a naked new-born babe
> Striding the blast, or heaven's cherubin, hors'd
> Upon the sightless couriers of the air,
> Shall blow the horrid deed in every eye,
> That tears shall drown the wind.

[18]   'My goose' in French, an affectionate expression.

'It isn't that,' said André, looking out as Vincent had done, summoning his angel. 'It is your attitude to life, to people, that is wrong. Don't you know that the kind of general insolence in which you take pleasure makes people your enemies – separates you, as you say? When your charm is all you have, you ruin it, and wonder that you are ruined. If you used it, you would have friends, and your devils would vanish, and your life fill with pleasantness.'

'But I am better, much better, much more moral since Vincent –'

'When did Vincent preach morals to you? Morals are an excuse for a boy of your sort, to justify your tempers. Or hags to ride you to hell. Leave your little virtues alone, and attend to the virtue which gave you Vincent. Don't you know that God does not like us for the things we think good. For the rest, courage –' He pulled a silver ring down his arm and slipped it on the boy's wrist. 'Wear that to-night if you're afraid.' The lovely, tired voice ran on, with passion fatigue seemed to strengthen, and all the vicissitudes of man. Paul kept his face laid on the hand he clung to, the bracelet that had changed wrists lighting the sheets. 'Remember the old woman who had been pious, at heaven's gate, who was secretly afraid because when she was a child she had stolen cherries from a tree. She told Peter all the good she had done, and while he called up God the Father, prayed that the cherry-tree had been forgotten. Until God answered, 'Let her in. After all, it's the woman who robbed the cherry-tree.' It is a sin to wear thorns when God meant you to wear roses.'

Vincent, silent, curled-up, heard Paul's rare, short, flute laugh. Knew he was listening to the Kourotrophos, the bringer-up of boys, André, the peacock of the world, who had borne the cross. Paul was smiling at him, and now he had lifted his head, Vincent saw André's hand wet with tears.

It was late. It seemed as if there was a huge balance in this room, a scale filling up and up against the other which had been filled. Paul's face was hidden again, this time on his knees. André spoke on; but Vincent dreamed that the scales held the life and death of Paul. If the high one sank, a cup would sail in down a light ray (he imagined it through a hole in the shutter slats). There would be a lance with it and an aureole for the boy. If it did not, well, he could only see a seedy man with green teeth following them about.

There was a knock at the door. Without waiting Stretton came in and stood for a moment against André's bathrobes. André said: 'A moment, Stretton.'

Paul sat up, but both he and Vincent had time to see Stretton's face, set like the Lucifer of the english imagination, in blasting pride and contempt. A son of the morning, visiting a son of the morning, his eyes were on Paul, the scorn in them a thing to cross dreams.

André said: 'Come back in a quarter of an hour.' He went out. The high scale stayed in air.

Paul got up. 'Thank you very much, André. You've done me a lot of good. I'll say good night now. I'm very tired. Good night.'

Vincent followed him. 'Well,' he said, 'now can you have a little faith?' and saw Paul look at him with lost sweetness that hardened again through misery past comprehension to a coarse denial that would never leave him again.

'Almost,' he said, 'I had. It was like music that you could see. Till Stretton knocked. Then it turned not real, flat, a bit of pretence. Stretton did it. He meant it too. He's in with the man on the quays.' And at Vincent's agonised laugh: 'I'm not so frightened now. I reckon I can get along. But not as André meant. Or you. Not after the way Stretton looked at me. He's put me back in my place. I know now that the filthy can never mix with the clean. He won't forgive you in a hurry either. Or André, when he's thought it over. D'you think I need give him back his bracelet? The boys in Paris will make a fine story out of it. Sorry, Vincent. I hope, I hope – Oh, only that Stretton will never be able to bitch you as he's bitched me.'

Vincent felt very cold – utterly tired. He took Paul's wrist and slipped off André's silver ring. 'If you ever want it back, you will only have to ask for it.'

'Thanks, but I shan't. I'm off to-morrow. Run in to you sometime if you care to remember me. I should like that – Vincent, you're a poor fish to take it so hard. It's my business. I shall be gone before the rest of you are up. Good night.'

Green (1931)

'Don't you think, Madonna Loring, that it would be better if I went down to see?'

'I'll think of it,' she said quickly, and he noticed a slight hauteur in her voice.

'We are sure, alas! that she takes too much to drink, and we know that my son does not. And you have heard what people say about her friends. Nick would never allow me to know the Taverners, so is it likely that he will have them to his house unless she insists? And if she does and he refuses, as he certainly should, she will fall out of her own set, and most of his friends will have nothing to do with her. The Derings have hinted to me that they might have to drop Nick. I hardly like to tell you, Ambrose, but they said –' A paraphrase followed for several sexual and social irregularities.

'Don't you think I might go?' Ambrose Alexander said this with loving earnestness, with whimsical adoration, leaning over a narrow space towards an old woman, upright by the fire in a dull-gold London room. Inside her tight silver wig and her mask of paint, she was yielding to treatment. In one hollow centimetre of her mind she knew she was, and that she would send Ambrose, because he would bring back an exciting story, a story that would justify malice and moral indignation: that could also be repudiated without strain. He owed her a good deal, she thought. He was a Jew. His function was to please. He did please. A slim, supple young man to run about was essential: to confide in: to reassure her.

For his part he was willing to oblige her. There were good pickings in that family, and benefits apart, she was giving him what he wanted – a chance to get his own back on her son and his wife. For the six months before, for the six months since, their marriage, she had been ravenous for its discredit. The discredit it was for him to supply. But a full meal this time, and more than a meal, a provision, on which she would never satiate, of the wife's blood and sap. What she wanted would serve his turn; but when he thought about her, and he preferred not to think about her too much, he misunderstood her degrees of consciousness, the balance of her scruples, her ignorance, her appetite, and her fears.

'If you are to go down and see her, how can it be arranged? It mustn't look –'

'They had better not expect me. If I could have a car and it should break down, then I could simply be there, and they would put me up for the night.'

'That's a good idea. I'll pay for it. But, mind you, Ambrose, it must be a real breakdown. I won't have any lies.'

'Madonna Loring it shall go up in flames to make my word, since it is really your word, good.'

She looked away from him, a little sentimental smile disturbing the corners of the old thin mouth. If only in her life she had heard more men say things like that. He meant it. Ambrose was a good and noble man. Of course he would not have to burn the car. That would be too extravagant. Even for the most disgusting news of her daughter-in-law.

Splendid that Ambrose was going. Her son might be in agonies about his wife: her son might be wanting his home again. She would give Ambrose messages to make it easy for him to come home for help. She foresaw decent divorce, and when Ambrose was gone, walked up and down the long room between the azaleas and the inlaid chairs, rehearsing a long, hideous, and wholly satisfactory scene with his wife.

Until the nature of the interview from being a source of pleasure became a kind of pain, and she noticed that she was not sure how far she wanted to be able to trust Ambrose there. Later she rang him up.

'Of course I'll pay all your expenses, but don't be too extravagant. I've just thought we may need all our money later.'

She had said 'our money' out of romantic delicacy. Ambrose relished it differently. It had been share and share alike with Nicholas, who usually forgot about his own share. Then, a year ago,

GREEN
First published in the journal *Pagany* 2(4) (October–December 1931), then included in Butts's second collection of short stories,

Several Occasions (London: Wishart, 1932), which furnishes the text followed by this edition.

Nicholas had found out that intermittent rebellion is exhausting, and had conducted an entire revolution instead. Six months later he was married. Now his landmarks were off both their maps. Only their débris remained – nothing but skeletons and broken boards where his places had been. A devastating escape, but Nick's mother had herself to thank. And hatred of his wife, which had been her refuge, was to become her revenge. Against Nancy Loring, Ambrose knew nothing – had not heard much – '*Le dossier accusateur de toute jolie femme.*' But to be kept by Mrs Loring; he must keep Mrs Loring; give Mrs Loring what she wanted, a daughter-in-law unkind, unchaste, and, so far as possible, unkissed. It seemed that he might have to rely on his imagination. After six months they were still living out of London, in that small, remote house, where no one that he knew ever went. Without a car, a telephone, or a horse. With cats and an old boat and books. That did not promise disillusion yet unless the girl was bored. What was there to find out? Could he return and report bliss? A spring wind filled the curtains of his room; coal-dust from the unlit fire charged its delicate touch. With his eyes on the tree-tops breaking leaf he could only smell London. He did not particularly mind, but at night with the fire burning he could feel Mrs Loring behind his chair. Boards cracked before and after her tread, step of a bully with small feet and ankles swollen a little with age, and there was a sound of gobbling already, and appetite unglutted, and punishment for Nick shaping once she had got him back. Once they had got him back.

Need he go at all? Could he go in theory, or, if he went, in theory provoke Nancy to behaviour whose character could be decided on later, and Nick actually into appropriate disgust? There is nothing more difficult to deny than a casual event whose importance rests on its implications. It is said that you have been to Biarritz with friends of doubtful character.

You do not know the people.

You have not been to Biarritz at all.

Prove it, if you have not been conspicuously with other people anywhere else. The force of your denial will fly loose, attach itself, and strengthen the accusation. You will have been at St Jean de Luz, where you met, and were notorious with them there. It is this fact that lies at the base of all non-resistance to evil, that the resistance becomes a neutral agent, equally able to strengthen what it attacks.

Ambrose felt that he need not be too anxious. There is always something wrong. If it were not yet conscious he had only to give the unconscious a name. While it was equally possible that the girl was bored, loose, or a slut. If not, she was going to be. The elegantly set problem absorbed him, in whose solution he ignored himself, his emotion for Nick, his curiosity about Nancy, his fear of the mother – about whom he assumed himself to be particularly cynical and gay.

Two days later he ran out of petrol on a remote road a mile from their house.

Nancy Loring asked her husband: 'Who was it called the sea the 'very green'?'

'The Egyptians, I think. The Red Sea and the Mediterranean. What about green wine?'

They were looking out at a green plain which lay as far as the horizon on their left, and their house stood on the shelf of a grass hill beside the plain, tilted in the sunlight to another green. High trees stood about the hill, and a short way outside, across a lawn, a copse crested its last bank. The plain had once been the sea, an estuary savage with tides, now narrowed to a river, tearing at its flow and ebb; where all winter, for every hundred yards, a heron watched its pitch. There was no dust: no sound but birds and air; no colour but green. There was every green.

In late April the top greens were of gold. Across the plain there was a march of elms, open hands with blood inside them, tipped with saffron fire. The copse was a stuff woven out of the same green.

They went out. On the small lawn were cats, black and white enamel in fur. One watched its lover; the lover watched a bird; the third, bow-stretched and upright, ripped the bark off a tree. Two kittens tumbled over like black and white flowers.

They followed one another through the copse. Each willow trunk was a separate man and woman. They came down the farther side to where, when it had been sea, the plain had worn a little bay under the hill. There was long wet grass where the tide-mark had been. They came to a dyke and an old house. There were willows along the glass water, very tall; along it and over it, one flung across and an elm tree drowned in it, its root out of the ground in a flat earth-cake. The house was a deserted farm. An orchard reached it, down a small valley between the rising of another hill. There was no path. They went up through the apple-trees, through a place wholly sheltered, where no wind came but only sun; where, when there was no sun, there was always light; so that in mid-winter, in the stripped world, the seasons did not exist there. They called it the Apple Land,[1] remembering there something which they could not recall, that seemed to have the importance of a just-escaped dream. The orchard ended sharply in an overhanging quickset, and a sharp climb to the top of the hill. To follow the valley to its head there was a glen on the left, sickly with flies and thin shoots and a scummed choked stream up to a short fall, almost in the dark, which was not quite wholesome, whose pool was without stir or light. The way out of that was also sharp and steep but quite different – to a shut cottage on top and a garden with tansy in it, and herbs used in magic.

Through lambs running in the up-fields they came to their village, and bought a morning paper, cheese, apples, and cigarettes. They came back another way, by a highroad, by a lane, over the open grass along a ribbon their feet had printed, green upon green.

Ambrose Alexander reached the house as they had entered the copse. A shy country servant left him alone. He was pleased that they were out; he stood back by the door from where he could see the whole length of the room.

Across the table an open ordnance map hung like a cloth askew. There was a chessboard beside it, and men half tumbled out of a box, and a wide bowl of small mixed flowers. There was a stone bottle of ink and a dish with sticks of sealing-wax and stamps, pencils, and a seal. There was a dog's lead and a pair of leather gloves. A red handkerchief was knotted up full of needles and wool. When he handled it one ran into his palm. There was an oil painting of Mount Soracte[2] and steel prints of forgotten gentlemen; and on the black chimney-shelf a fishing-rod crossed with a gun. There were books of poems, and on murder, the Roman occupation of Britain, Chinese art.

Mr Hunca Munca, the mouse, climbed to the top of the kitchen chimney and looked out. There was no soot.[3] Up to the age of five every child laughs at this version of that joke; but to Ambrose it was as if the room was calling him, very plainly and in another language, an outsider. It was not what he had come to hear. He stared out of the window and up the hill. There was no one. Then he went upstairs. Under his feet the old boards had no friendly squeak. Like old servants who might talk.

Their bedroom had a rose-brick fireplace and a line of Persian prints. Under the mirror, piled in a shell, were strings of glass flowers and fruit. Everything was in order, polished and very still, and the bathroom full of things to wash with. He went back to the bedroom, supposed that in one of the shut drawers there was a shameful secret among soiled linen, persuaded himself, opened it, and in it there were folded silks, bedroom books: two more murders, a County History, *Per Amica Silentia Lunae*, Sterne.[4] A cat looked in at the door and yawned before it went away. Under a scent-flask was a receipted bill. He looked out of the window at the very green.

---

[1] *Apple Land* a translation of Avalon, the kingdom of the fairies or the dead to which King Arthur traveled upon his death.

[2] Mount Saracte (in Italian, Monte Soratte) is a stubby mountain, surmounted by a large plateau, located in the Campagna, south of Rome. It was a favorite subject of landscape painters; see Jean Baptiste Camille Corot (1796–1875), *Roman Campagna with Mount Soracte* (Cleveland Museum of Art), and J. M. W. Turner (1775–1851), *Mount Soracte in the Roman Countryside* (Fine Arts Museum, San Francisco).

[3] *Mr Hunca Munca ... no soot* from Beatrix Potter, *The Tale of Two Bad Mice* (London: F. Warne & Co., 1904). Two mice, Tom Thumb and his wife Hunca Munca, are mystified when they enter a doll's house and mistakenly think it is a real but inexplicably strange house. To test it, one of them goes up the chimney.

[4] A 'County History' refers to a generic book that recounts the history of an English county. *Per Amica Silentia Lunae* is the title of a book by William Butler Yeats, published in 1918 (London and New York: Macmillan). It consists of one long poem ('Ego Dominus Tuus,' Latin for 'I, Your Lord') and two essays: the first, 'Anima Hominis' (Latin for 'The Spirit of Man'), meditates on the individual self's relationship with its other, its mask; the second, 'Anima Mundi' (Latin for 'The Spirit of the World'), concerns the collective unconscious that reveals itself in images as if from a supernatural order of reality. Yeats's title is taken from Vergil, the *Aeneid*, II.255, Latin for 'by the friendly silence of the moon.' Aeneas uses the phrase to describe the Greek fleet as it seemingly sets sail and abandons its siege of Troy; in reality the Greeks are all concealed in the Trojan horse, and will soon destroy the city. 'Sterne' is Laurence Sterne (1713–68), celebrated author of the novel *Tristam Shandy* (1760–5).

There they had been all winter long. They did not seem to want to go away. Told nothing, saw no one who would tell anything, asked for nothing. He was discouraged. Propriety, simplicity, the routine of country-house life. The house went on talking out loud; not without passion but with directness that annihilated. Down any passage there might be met a wall of fire. He looked at the bed over whose foot-rail hung a bright shawl and a fur.

The Persian pictures were perfectly proper. In the dining-room cupboard there had been two bottles of beer. He went downstairs, heard no approach on the soundless turf, so that they were on him in an instant, as instantly recoiled, and a moment later were overwhelmed in his cordiality and excuse.

Disentangling themselves from him, they exchanged a word together, out of the house. 'What has he come for? Car broken down? Whose car? Who's given him a car?'

Nicholas Loring was annoyed; his wife uneasy. There was nothing to do but feed him, and not go after the swan's nest that day. Swans stay put, but are more interesting than a townsman ill at ease, vocal and supple and full of admiration that did not try to be more than a display. Voluble and mobile, Ambrose had a trick of statement, one to each sentence, followed by a denial, a reversal of it in the next. So that which seemed, sentence by sentence, to be a vivid reaction to life, cancelled out to nothing. To no belief at all. Nicholas, folded-up in country quiet, was now without illusion and irritated by what had once stimulated him. Ambrose had no belief at all. And Nancy saw that everything Ambrose said would mean nothing, and felt giddy in her mind until she felt sick. They were his hosts and they must stomach him, feed him, and endure him to an hour that had not fixed. They were saved from spiritless irritation, and she from fear, by curiosity and the involuntary hosts' calculation of the time when they would be able to lose him. Ambrose understood this, and that he must stay the night, and that at present no mere breakdown of his car would get him the invitation. He saw himself after lunch led by Nick, grim, courteous, and embarrassed, to restart it at the top of the hill.

They came to the end of lunch. Nicholas was listening to Ambrose, to what he had once heard, year in year out, and now had not heard for a year. And after a year there was no more pleasure in it or surprise at the changes. It was as if he knew it by heart, for the first time at last.

Ambrose was trying hard with a parade of emotion, trying to praise marriage, their withdrawal, the serene country; displaying himself as the neurotic townsman, the alien, whose pride it was to humble himself, to look into paradise through bars. A peep he owed to them: 'Is that safe, Nancy?' turning to her from Nicholas.

'I think so,' she answered civilly, not at all sure. 'He is trying not to cancel out,' she thought. 'Why? He can't do it for long. Why is he here? He does not like me. Would like me to be vile so as to hurt Nick. Nick he loves and hates. Then that he had once loved Nick and then hated him, probably for his marriage and now did neither, or in different proportions. What was he there for?'

He said: 'Suppose me at my role again – the old serpent. You used, Nick, to call me that, and any variation that struck you from 'you dirty devil' to 'Lucifer'.'

'Lord of lies,' she murmured.

He heard her. She was ashamed. He looked steadily at her and smiled. 'You're right, my dear. I'm just as much that variation of the fiend. Only neither you nor Nick need the serpent in me any more. Serpents' – he added – 'are not sentimental. That was useful once to Nick. While who has ever heard of a mother-snake?' They took that in.

'There was a time when Nick needed an old, contradictory bloke like me to leave all doors open and let a spot of reality in. His mother' (the pause which left her unqualified perfected suggestion) 'she would have shut the lot, and everything open is the only answer to everything shut. But now –' He went on to explain that Nicholas, now he had welcomed the reality Ambrose had provided, had made his own freedom and been given love. It was true. But Nicholas must be repersuaded that he owed it to him. Doors that have been opened can be shut. One implies the other. They could begin on him again, he and Mrs Loring, and Nick would be well retrapped. The doors would be shut and the wife outside. Only it would take longer than he thought, and Mrs Loring would not see the delicacy of it. He must find out how to persuade her that the cup of deferred blood is richer.

Rapt in these thoughts he started smiling at them. Nick was moved, but remembered that once he would only have been moved. Ambrose had opened doors once, or he had thought so. Until he had noticed that he had slammed them to and fro, chasing him between draughts. Until he had stuck open a certain number that he needed for himself. (Who wants to live with every door open?) His exits and entrances were now his own, and by one of them Nancy had come in: helped to fix open a few more, and, by one of these, first Ambrose, then his mother, had gone out. That was what had happened in terms of doors. He softened, feeling that he could afford to. Old Ambrose had come down for some sort of thanks. Or perhaps for a share. Share of the rich strength which made things easy with Nancy: easy to give and take: easy to go in and out: to live: like music, all the musics. Ambrose was by himself as he'd always been. Nancy was thinking the same thing, that there was a man alone all his life and always would be alone; and thought of him on a toadstool and with people round him on toadstools, and that he spent his time picking their stalks from underneath them and his own stalk.

Then the strength mounting in her also, she wondered if Ambrose had been necessary to Nicholas, to that woman's only son. Was it possible that they had shaken Ambrose off his fence? Was this visit, after all, a no mean congratulation and praise; one of the mysterious triumphs of love? She forgot his subtle opposition to their marriage. Was this old Mrs Loring's last defeat? She judged it most improbable and forgot her judgment. Only remembered that it would be good if it were true. If it were true, they might some day be able to forgive. She looked at Ambrose, very simply. It seemed a far cry to 'mother's gigolo'. He observed her, went to the piano, and played the letter-song from *Figaro*. Whistling softly. *And the sounds of beauty flowed and trembled until they seemed to triumph . . . over the hard hearts of men.*[5]

She brought him over his coffee. There was not a cruel animal behind Nick, only a vexed old woman, who had been lovely, who would never feed on her son again, or with septic finger-nails scratch at the bloom of her own youth. She had been ungenerous about Ambrose. How hateful is the wife who does injustice to her husband's people, to her husband's friends.

She lit his cigarette, and stood by Nicholas' shoulder, wholly herself and part of him and part of the very green. Part of Ambrose? Yes, for this moment, if this were true.

They took him out, a tramp across green, from green to green, entertained him with birds' nests set deep in thorned twigs and split light. There had been tea and toast and chess, an evening to get through and a night. He stood between them at evening at the door of the house. Now in the sky there was a bar of the green that has no name. He was standing on grass darkening beside dark green. She had said, 'It is all Hermes, all Aphrodite.'

He had been bored and concealed it, with the night before him, becoming unsure of himself. Dinner, chess, music, country-talk. A drink? They had filled up his car and put her away in the village and refused to let him go.

They gave him a drink and a rabbit cooked in onions. He had gained nothing but the fooling of them, and if they did not know it, they were slightly bored. The worst thing that can happen to a liar is to be believed. If he did not notice that, he suffered, as Nick indicated in intimate outline, his serene and final detachment from his mother. Confident, they told him their plans, about excavations and gardening, and Nick's new book, which was not about himself or even about people. He had to listen, and by that time it was night, grey, windless, with a squeak in it. The great chimney flared. Standing inside it one could follow the sparks up its square tower to a square patch of sky. Innocent as wine, as dew. He sneered. Outside was it innocent? Innocent for them and strong. His room was away from theirs. On that side of the house the night could do what it liked with him. The night would have him to itself. Nick and Nancy would have themselves to themselves. He would have nothing to himself but himself and night. Oh! there was someone who might come in and sit beside his bed. Madame Nick might come in and talk, smile, and suck in her thin, red lips. Keep him awake because she was hungry. She would not mind dark green night.

---

[5] See p. 791 n. 2.

He would have nothing but lies to feed her on: have to invent her a meal because her sort of food wasn't in the house. He was getting childish. With their stupid innocence they were doing him down. What did Nancy want? To give him another drink: be sure that he was comfortable: a game of chess before bed. 'Glorious game,' he must say, but it took longer to play than he reckoned. A shy woman, what she did was better than her promise. Later she said: 'It is good for your complexes, Ambrose, to win things and be praised.' For that he should have let her win. God! But he could not bear to evade the game. And it put off bed, and whatever it was that tapped outside on the windows its peculiar code.

But when he went up, the soft air surging in put him instantly to sleep.

They woke next morning with a distaste for him in the house. He was to go after lunch, and the morning seemed an hour-series that could not be lived through. There was no reason for it, only that they did not care now if his visit marked a triumph. They wanted him out of the way. There were interesting things to do and he would not do them. Nancy decided that she would disappear, on the excuse of leaving Nicholas alone with his friend, and came downstairs first to see that Ambrose had his breakfast in bed. There was a letter for her from Nick's mother. That hardly ever happened. She went outside to read it, barefoot on the catprinted dew: split it open and read:

My Dear Child,

    I wish this to be entirely between ourselves, but I have an idea that Nicholas' old friend Ambrose intends to come down and see you. Please be very nice to him. You know how he is – he was so fond of my son and has suffered the break since his marriage. Of course it couldn't be helped, and I am so afraid of emotional friendships between young men, but I am sure you have nothing to fear now. Don't tell Nicholas anything about this – and also what I meant to say is – don't be upset or offended if he should try and flirt with you. It means absolutely nothing. He has a very fine nature really, and is not at all interested in women. I just want there to be no misunderstanding, not that Nicholas is likely to think anything as long as you are careful, only I do not wish you for your part to be led away. I explain this badly, but I am sure you will understand. I hope you are both as well as possible.

                                        Your loving Mother,

                                         Angela Loring

The crisp dew melted between her toes, and their colour changed from pink to red. One hand held on to her curled, cropped hair. There was a moment when nothing happened at all, neither image nor concept nor sense impression. She came-to, first to the small bustling wind, then to a bird. Then to a draught of other life-like voices, shrieking from London, recorded on a square of thick white paper. It was mad; it was comic; it was dangerous. She ate a light breakfast in silence. Anyhow it was tiresome.

She said: 'You will want the morning with Ambrose. I'm off.' But Nicholas had his plans also.

'Look here,' he said. 'I forgot that I said that I'd see that man about –'

'Take him with you.'

'It's a trudge. I got mud to my knees last –'

'Am I to keep Ambrose?'

'I mean, if you could be that sort of spirit – I'll be back before lunch.'

'Very well. Do you mind what happens to him?'

'I'm leaving him with you –' He grinned, and there began to be less of him, a hand or an ear or a foot left, and the rest out of sight, and then the whole of him out of reach.

After she had been alone for ten minutes she began to feel holy, and inside herself an immense preoccupation with power. She went upstairs, put on a gayer sweater, and delicately painted her face. So Ambrose had come down to see if there was anything to be done about Nick. Through her. If she had been easy, to have her; easy or discontented or jealous of Nick. Very likely Mrs Loring, Mère Angélique, had sent him herself and repented, and so written. She had thought such a thing possible? Wanted such a thing? Wanted her son's wife a slut and had not wanted it. Wanted Ambrose back? In her mind there was the old woman's name written-up and scored through. Then she went out and called lightly up at his window from the cool lawn.

'Come down, Ambrose, it's a perfect day.'

With sweet animation and pretty phrases she made Nick's excuses, and took him the plain way up the hill to the village for a drink.

He had better go, he thought, there was nothing doing here. He was separated after the night's deep sleep, cut off already from what had been yesterday's preoccupations, and those of weeks and years and even of a life past. Indifferent for the moment to their reassertion, like a man drugged, but not as though it was well with him there. So that the only thing was to get away. Go before lunch and cut its pointless coda. God! was Nancy, the woman beside him, talking, running a primrose through his coat, trying to flirt with him at last? The gentle admiration of last night turned pert with a grin behind it. She went on like that all the way to the village inn. He had a drink. He needed it. He was imagining things. She was a gay baggage after all, and he'd interested her. She wanted to know about himself, did she? She'd got rid of Nick. What was she saying?

'It's good of you to tolerate me, Ambrose. After you and Nick. What a marvellous friendship we might have. But oh, my dear –!'

'What do you do me the honour of thinking about me, wife of Nicholas?' There was another drink before him. Put it down. It was quick work following this up.

'This visit has cleared up so much, made almost anything possible. And now we are friends, I feel I must say anything to you that I think.'

'Go on.'

'Anything? You mean it? Then Ambrose, I shall begin about yourself; and first of all I'm going to tell you something you're to do and that you are not to do.'

'I'll obey you.' Her voice had light music in it.

Now she leaned across the inn table, *dulce ridentem*,[6] a shadow in her smile, making him aware of her awareness of him.

'You are a great man, Ambrose, but oh, *mon ami*, love Nicholas, love me, but don't, don't –'

'What am I not to do, lady of the place?'

'You should not, you must not. Ambrose, you are not to let people call you – you are not to be so mixed up – with old women who exploit you. I'm a woman, and I'm not an old woman, but do you know what some old women are like? They adore your looks and your sweet manners, and,' she added rudely, 'how? They want you physically, of course, but not simply physically; and they've their own way of getting that. And when they've got what they want, or not got what they want, then they make comparisons.'

What was this? She was serious, she was smiling. There was a smile set against him and eyes lit with cold fun.

'Whatever dowager takes such an interest in me?'

'Oh, my dear, with so many about, and you so liked and hard-up. Why, this morning I had a letter from Nick's mother, for you to be returned intact. A perfectly wolfish howl. How did she know you were here?' The smiles were working easily on her lips, but her eyes were steady. Steady as two carved stones on rock.

'I think you should be kind to her; kind as you are to Nick; kind as you are to me.'

She was making a sing-song of it, her head drawn up, her throat strained a little under the high collar of bright wool. Then relaxing: 'Forgive this candour,' she said; 'I know how they can be useful, these women. Only if you can't do without them, you must learn how to keep them in order. Nick was a little annoyed that his mother should write such a letter. Keep her in hand. You remember about Peter Carmin and how his friends got him out of the country –'

If she had been alone down there with him at the house she would not have been safe, in spite of the green.

'May I see the letter?' (He must say that.)

'Nick has it.' That was what she must say. She could say what she liked. She was in her own land. It was then that she heard his surrender.

---

[6] Latin for 'smiling sweetly.'

'Tell Nick I will write to him. I think I had better go up now since the car is here.'
Its noise drowned her light farewells and excuses.

She dropped back softly between the hills, by the first way, through the Apple-Land. Round the green bay, through the copse, until outside the house she was looking at the plain and the trees' open hands. Her husband came suddenly round a corner of the house and saw that she was alone.
'Gone,' she said; 'and before I come in take this letter into the house and read it.'

Friendship's Garland (1925)

There are days when the worst happens so completely that the whole consciousness is dyed to the particular colour of the abomination, when escape is impossible, and one plays rabbit to the world's weasel with just a little bravado, no courage, and no sense of style.

We were caught that day in Zoe's bedroom full of flowers, arranging our hair. We had forgotten that we were the hunted and innocent. They had been after us for a long time. We knew that they were after us; but we were younger, quicker, and more impudent; only too young. We could not believe that, in the end, they would not come and eat out of our hand. Perhaps they will, but only by exhaustion, not by persuasion, and that will not be good enough.

Among other things, they wanted to take away our lovers, not because they wanted them themselves, but because they could not love themselves, and naturally disliked it that we could; and there was money in it, and fear of us. At least, we liked to think there was fear. But chiefly it was virtuosity in the creation of pain, and that we did not understand. 'What do they do it for?' said Zoe. 'Never mind. I know they've got their knife into us. The great thing to do is to keep them in a good temper, and never trust them at all.' You see, we could not get rid of them; they had seen to that.

Then we began to laugh, and make little traps to annoy the blind animals who were following us. Keen noses and no eyes. Intelligences without imagination. Zoe arranged a little bribe of flowers. I could see them smell it – and soon it would be out on the dustbin. They were not people who burn their dead flowers. 'It will look pretty and civil. It will keep them quiet a little,' she said; 'but they don't know how strong I am when I mean to get my own way.'

Indeed, I hoped they would find her strong. She was a better fighter than I, but she could not make herself invisible. That is my long suit.

In Zoe's room we could see trees waving over a wall. The summer wind was moving them, and below us there would be tea, and great, silent cars moving so pleasantly in the street. The white staircase of the house was like the easy stairs you fall down in dreams.

The telephone rang by Zoe's bed. I heard a man's voice speaking from any distance, from no distance, from a place outside the world. He spoke a great deal. I heard Zoe say: 'Yes, Carlo, of course we'll come,' but his voice went on, and I was reading a book when she said to me:
'They want us to meet them, and I said we would. Who says we're afraid?'
'Where?' said I.
'At the Craven. Where Carlo can pretend that he's a man of the world.' That made us laugh. We ran about Zoe's room, taking alternate turns at the mirror, and calling 'Carlo' and 'Craven' to one another till the door opened and his sister ran in. We could not think how she had got there. It was like an annunciation or a burglary. I felt she would be followed by the servants she had run past. She wanted to do her hair and show us her hat. It was a tight, evil hat of scarlet leather. I re-set my sombrero, and Zoe hung a little veil across her eyes and took her downstairs, and we got into the car. Carlo was repeating, 'The Craven. We'd better go to the Craven. I've got some news for you, Zoe.' I lay back and watched the streets slip past.

FRIENDSHIP'S GARLAND
First published in the *Contact Collection of Contemporary Writers* (Paris: Contact Editions, 1925), then collected in Butts's *Several*

Occasions (London: Wishart, 1932), which furnishes the text followed by this edition.

We stood about the steps while Carlo fidgeted with the car and tried to make the commissionaire recognise him. He tipped him a wink, he was haughty, he confided in him, he gave him half a crown. He was attended to with the others, but still Carlo hung on, and would not be done with it. His sister was impatient: 'Oh, Carlo,' she said, 'let's go in and leave him to it.' Willing enough we were to leave him to it and wasted no embarrassment on her.

Through the noise and the iron streets, even through the racing wind the sun poured, roaring its heat through the wind at the huge buildings and the crowd. Those are the hours when the city pays for being a city, and is delivered over to the wind and the sun and their jackal the dust. All the earth pays, but principally the city. On the other hand, inside the Craven there is no nature at all. These things are not natural, marble like cheese, red velvet, and plaster gilt.

We sat down. Carlo was a long time seeing about his car, and when he came he was petulant because we had not waited for him, and had ordered tea. Only for a moment. He never thought of anything for more than a moment. He was quite safe to forget. Only he always remembered again, and a little differently, so that he could always escape on a misunderstanding, and pick up the line again and again and again. He bounded across to us, and flung himself into a cane chair, petulant, pretty, and artful, and his sister deprecated him while they were both hunting. I knew. It was Zoe they were after to-day, and they had not expected to find me at her house. I could lean back and watch and eat éclairs. They were too sweet, and I got sticky. Then I could smoke in the rich, stale quiet whose murmur was like the tuning-up of birds that never would begin to sing.

Zoe wore a pearl, hung from a piece of jade, on a chain spaced with small pearls. Cosmo had given it to her. Carlo saw it: 'I say, Zoe, d'you know you're wearing Celia's pearl?' Celia had been Cosmo's first wife, and we had hoped she was now reincarnating as something reasonably intelligent and plain.

Zoe answered in her small, distinct voice:

'Yes, his father brought it back when they looted the Summer Palace.'

The brother glanced at the sister, who looked as though she could eat it, and Carlo said: 'I only mean – you don't mind my saying this, Zoe? – that I don't think Cosmo thinks it's worth much. I was going through some papers from him the other day, and he hasn't insured it. Of course, it suits you.' His sister laughed, and lifted it off Zoe's breast with her pink paws whose dimples felt like rubber. She said:

'I expect he's left it to his daughter. Anyhow, I'm afraid she'll think it ought to be hers. I don't envy you, Zoe, once you're married, with that young lady.'

'She shall have it so soon as she's old enough to wear it,' said Zoe.

'You are quite right. But you know in seven years – she'll be eighteen then – will you want to give it to her? We always mean to behave well. But jewels are jewels, and flappers are flappers. It becomes you perfectly.'

Zoe lifted her small, apricot-brown head. 'In seven years we shall be so rich that I shall have all the jewels I want.'

I sorted this. First of all, the thing wasn't real, and later there was going to be a row about an artificial gem. Of course those two, I added to comfort myself, hadn't the wit to choose or the money to buy an ornament like that. It had been left to Cosmo's daughter, who was preparing – who was being prepared – to hate Zoe, who was to be her stepmother. Wasn't it real? It looked real. I wanted to lick the pearl to try it – I did not like to do it then and there.

Carlo's sister said: 'I don't know if you've thought of it yet, my dear, but I should send that child off to school. A good convent would be about the best. If you keep her there most of the year, she won't see so much of the Traverses. She spends all her time with them now, and they don't like you –'

I protested – 'Oh, not convents. They save you the trouble of teaching it manners, and that's all.'

'Manners maketh man,' said Carlo, who had not been to Winchester.[1] I looked away spitefully, and saw his sister register both slips.

---

[1] Located in the town of Winchester, Hampshire, Winchester is the oldest (founded in 1382) of the famous public schools, i.e. schools that were originally endowed for the use of a lay public, but became tuition-charging schools that prepared their well-to-do students to go on to university.

'What did Mrs. Travers say about me?' said Zoe steadily.

'You know what she is,' Carlo hurried up, all anxious friendliness. (His attack was to dance up and down and give tongue, while his sister hunted soundless, ready to spring.) 'They want to keep Cosmo for themselves. They make a lot of money out of him. Travers thinks his wife had an affair with him once. Anyhow, you know how people are jealous. She's awfully attractive, Zoe, and she'd like to do you in.'

In the mirror in her bag Zoe looked at her face, brown, painted, celestial, a mask to set dark crystal eyes and hyacinth-curled hair.

'Yes,' she said stubbornly, 'but what did she say?'

A remark like that is pure science, the investigation of a fact. I was pleased.

Carlo answered: 'Only that Cosmo's a bit older than you.'

'Oh, be quiet, Carlo,' said his sister; 'it's not as serious as that. At any rate you can be sure of one thing, the Traverses would sooner die than fall out with Cosmo. It would lose them half their business. People in their position can't afford to say what they think. That's a very effective check.'

And admiration and honour and affection? One has heard of these as reasons. Only to-day we have to find out what is the reality for which these words are the correspondents. It was tolerable when we used to say the words and go ahead on the emotion they evoked, but now one has not the courage to say them any more.

'Come off it, Carlo,' said I; 'you're inventing the whole thing.' If Cosmo quarrelled with them, would Carlo get the business? To be put away for further observation.

His sister said: 'Don't you think that the test of success is to be in a position not to know people? After all, like all the arts, the art of life ought to consist in a series of eliminations – the Farrells, for instance. I am always telling Carlo not to know the Farrells. People like that do one harm. You never know what harm people will do.' Carlo fidgeted.

'I tell you I've dropped them.' And then – 'Don't you see, Zoe, that one has to be careful? The world's a rum place, and people do such impossible things.'

Zoe, who should certainly have learned something about science, said: 'Which of my friends do you mean, Carlo?'

'Who d'you want to be rid of now?' said I.

Carlo tapped my knee. 'You know, Cesca, some of our set are impossible. Dennis, for instance, and his brother. It does one no good to be seen with them. They are *mal vus*,[2] you know.'

'One can't afford it,' said his sister. 'Things get about, you know.'

'What things?' said Zoe.

'It is very difficult. Of course that is not their real name. My cousins are furious about it. It is not quite right to trade upon other people's position.'

Dear me, those boys were my cousins too. They'd always been called that. Acquitted, after a gasp – the dears! 'Really,' I said, but still feeling shame, and too proud to defend them. They were my dear friends, but I suspected them of needing defence. And did not know how to defend them. Then I remembered that Carlo and his sister hardly knew them at all.

'Cosmo adores them,' said Zoe, 'and helping Cosmo is my job.'

'You'll have your work cut out,' cried Carlo, pulling one of her curls with his rapid familiarity. 'And, talking of Dennis, Cesca, guess who I saw him with last night?'

'My husband, I suppose,' I said.

'That's it. They were at the Pomme d'Or, and I can tell you they were getting on with the brandy. Pippa was with them.' Carlo's sister laughed.

'Young wives like us have to put up with that, I suppose.'

And why shouldn't they go to the Pomme d'Or and stand each other drinks? I saw my life through a dingy glass. These people had made me ashamed and afraid. They were also my kin. I must lose them and could not. The effect of shame and fear was to rearrange every physical object that I could see. The Craven turned into a temple built of cane and plaster, oily marble and velvet,

---

[2] 'viewed poorly' in French.

and I observed the cult there. To be rich – to be *rangé*[3] – to be cute; to cut your friends – to suffer for nothing – to be a cad. Carlo and his sister suffer. They were priests there, and I hoped a sacrifice.

All the same, I was afraid of their temple. Zoe was chattering about where she and Cosmo would live when they were married.

'There's a lovely house in Lower Seymour Street – we could just afford it. It has such a room to dance in. Anyhow, I'm to have it.'

Carlo shouted: 'I advise Cosmo not to touch it! Doesn't he know that Van Buren has bought all the houses along there to pull them down in two years? That's why they're going cheap.'

'Don't bring down the walls,' said his sister with her good humour.

But I became suddenly afraid of a pillar with a gilt mask on it that might be coming at us, while Zoe and I were being fattened on éclairs and listening to this and burning our mouths out with cigarettes.

Zoe rubbed out the stump of hers and refused another. So did I, thinking I must find a gesture of my own. Well, I was out of gestures. I wanted to hide. I wondered what religion would do for Carlo and his sister. Then I reflected on what it had done, and saw religion like an anæmic girl, like Peace in a foreign post-War cartoon, not attempting to keep this cretinous juggernaut on a lead. I thought of the Polis, which appeared clean but feeble. I wanted a sanctity to turn on like a tap. I felt myself growing old, my face greasy and stretching under its make-up. Then we left.

Outside, the wind knocked us about. It blew me into a tube, and up north on the back of a shrieking noise. At the end of the tube the trees were rocking in a wind that wrapped itself round me and flung me down a steep road.

'So that is what happened down there,' I said, 'and I am running home to hide.' That is life. That is the world. The wind is doing its best for me. Home is good enough, but a little austere, because one is always at work there.

I noticed that it was evening. Then I heard the old trees. I crossed the wide road and saw it was empty, and came alongside the house, and went into its dull, dark porch and let myself in.

In an instant I knew the house was empty. 'They' were all out. 'They' never troubled me, but they had gone away. I went into my room and saw the trees. The afternoon had gone over its crest, and was falling downhill into evening. In my room the walls were white, and went up to the ceiling like a pure sky. I saw my own things, coloured wood and polished wood, a persian duck painted gold and scarlet, a green quicksilver ball.

I saw my face in a mirror, grown old. I had not chosen that. I stripped my face of its make-up, and combed my hair into a straight short piece. The wind marched in from the balcony, and dying in the room, it died outside, until there was no sound but that of the oldest of the trees turning. Then it was renewed. Not a cat came in. I lay on a bright shawl and listened to the tunes of the house. Every room had a tune we had taught them, and under our tunes was their tune, which I had sometimes heard, but could not learn; though I think I moved to it when I did not think at all. I did not think of us, nor of the mummy upstairs, nor of the wireless set or the flute, nor that in the room next mine lived the most beautiful child in the world, nor of the seven glass balls for the seven planets that hung in the room downstairs. Or of the cat that threaded the rooms, or the green bath-salt in a jar upstairs.

I listened a long time to a song like the noise made by the footfall of cats, and when I came out of listening to it, I saw the room take fire. Point and point and point that could reflect took light. The low sun covered my face with fire. Outside the leaves were fiery green tongues. The white walls soaked it in and waved it back, so that, when there were not steady points, there were cloths of fire. It was cool. I pulled a fur over me. The fire took the colour of each object, and presently they began to move, and I swung with them. Out we sailed, and I knew that I was conscious of the movement of the earth through space.

I got up and crossed the room and went out on to the balcony that ran round the wall of the house, above the garden where the dandelions were in seed and in flower. There came a roar of wind

---

[3]   'quiet, settled, well-ordered' in French.

that flattened me against the walls, and I knew the house was a ship plunging through the sea. The trees were racing us, and a small moon beat up against us up in the sky.

When I came back, and looked in the glass again, my face was half old, like a child's recovering from a sickness. I lay down again, and turned on the light beside my bed, and read a book about the greek Polis which now sounded like a fine folk-tale.

But almost at once I went to sleep. When I woke, the wind had gone again. It was night. Houses at the end of two gardens were pure gold inside. I saw them through black leaves. My light was out. But the great tree had come in and stood on the threshold of my balcony. It did not menace me. It was absolutely silent. But it said: 'I guard your door. This place is tabu. Keep tabu.' When I saw the branches pass in and point at me, I did reverence to the tree and its precinct; and when I could have knelt on the floor in awe of the tree's sanctity, I saw that it was also myself; and when I got up and looked into the glass again, I looked like a child that has been dipped in dew.

Hart Crane (1899–1932)

Introduction

Hart Crane (1899–1932) was born in Garretsville, Ohio, a small town near the Pennsylvania border. His father was a candy manufacturer, and he separated from his wife in 1908. Crane's mother broke down, his father returned, and they lived together until their divorce in 1917. Crane decided not to finish high school or attend university, and instead went to work in New York. He had little success with jobs, and his personal life was unhappy. He moved back to Ohio several times, but finally settled in New York for good in 1923, becoming an advertising copywriter. He had many brief affairs with men, but none that proved lasting. After 1925 he became a protégé of the wealthy banker Otto Kahn, who furnished him with loans and subsidies during his remaining years. Crane published his first book of poems, *White Buildings*, in 1926. His second, an ambitious long poem called *The Bridge*, appeared to mixed reviews in 1930. In 1932 he committed suicide, a death that turned him into a paradigmatic figure of the young American poet meeting a tragic end. For some 30 years the significance of his work and life were intensely debated. More recent criticism has focused on Crane as a gay poet.

My Grandmother's Love Letters (1920)

There are no stars to-night
But those of memory.
Yet how much room for memory there is
In the loose girdle of soft rain.

There is even room enough   5
For the letters of my mother's mother,
Elizabeth,
That have been pressed so long
Into a corner of the roof
That they are brown and soft,   10
And liable to melt as snow.

Over the greatness of such space
Steps must be gentle.
It is all hung by an invisible white hair.
It trembles as birch limbs webbing the air.   15

And I ask myself:

"Are your fingers long enough to play
Old keys that are but echoes:
Is the silence strong enough
To carry back the music to its source   20
And back to you again
As though to her?"

Yet I would lead my grandmother by the hand
Through much of what she would not understand;
And so I stumble. And the rain continues on the roof   25
With such a sound of gently pitying laughter.

"My Grandmother's Love Letters" was first published in the *Dial* 68(4) (April 1920), then in Crane's first collection of poems, *White Buildings* (New York: Boni and Liveright, 1926).

Black Tambourine (1921)

The interests of a black man in a cellar
Mark tardy judgment on the world's closed door.
Gnats toss in the shadow of a bottle,
And a roach spans a crevice in the floor.

Æsop,[1] driven to pondering, found   5
Heaven with the tortoise and the hare;
Fox brush and sow ear top his grave
And mingling incantations on the air.

The black man, forlorn in the cellar,
Wanders in some mid-kingdom, dark, that lies,   10
Between his tambourine, stuck on the wall,
And, in Africa, a carcass quick with flies.

Chaplinesque (1921)

We make our meek adjustments,
Contented with such random consolations
As the wind deposits
In slithered and too ample pockets.

For we can still love the world, who find   5
A famished kitten on the step, and know
Recesses for it from the fury of the street,
Or warm torn elbow coverts.

We will sidestep, and to the final smirk
Dally the doom of that inevitable thumb   10
That slowly chafes its puckered index toward us,
Facing the dull squint with what innocence
And what surprise!

And yet these fine collapses are not lies
More than the pirouettes of any pliant cane;   15
Our obsequies are, in a way, no enterprise.
We can evade you, and all else but the heart:
What blame to us if the heart live on.

The game enforces smirks; but we have seen
The moon in lonely alleys make   20
A grail of laughter of an empty ash can,
And through all sound of gaiety and quest
Have heard a kitten in the wilderness.

BLACK TAMBOURINE
"Black Tambourine" was first published in the *Double Dealer*
1 (June 1921), then in *White Buildings*, Crane's first collection
of poems (New York: Boni and Liveright, 1926).
[1]   *Æsop* Aesop (6th century BC) was a Greek slave on the island
of Samos, famed as a teller of fables, many concerning animals.

CHAPLINESQUE
"Chaplinesque" was first published in *Gargoyle* 2 (Dec. 1921),
then collected in his *White Buildings* (New York: Boni and Liveright, 1926). In 1921 Charlie Chaplin released *The Kid*, a film
that impressed many contemporaries with the grandeur of his
art.

Praise for an Urn (1922)

In Memoriam: Ernest Nelson[1]

It was a kind and northern face
That mingled in such exile guise
The everlasting eyes of Pierrot[2]
And, of Gargantua,[3] the laughter.

His thoughts, delivered to me   5
From the white coverlet and pillow,
I see now, were inheritances –
Delicate riders of the storm.

The slant moon on the slanting hill
Once moved us toward presentiments   10
Of what the dead keep, living still,
And such assessments of the soul

As, perched in the crematory lobby,
The insistent clock commented on,
Touching as well upon our praise   15
Of glories proper to the time.

Still, having in mind gold hair,
I cannot see that broken brow
And miss the dry sound of bees
Stretching across a lucid space.   20

Scatter these well-meant idioms
Into the smoky spring that fills
The suburbs, where they will be lost.
They are no trophies of the sun.

The Wine Menagerie (1926)

Invariably when wine redeems the sight,
Narrowing the mustard scansions of the eyes,
A leopard ranging always in the brow
Asserts a vision in the slumbering gaze.

PRAISE
First published in the *Dial* 72(6) (June 1922).
[1] Ernest Nelson (c. 1870–1921) was a lithographer who was killed in a street accident by a passing automobile in December 1921. In a letter dated July 4, 1922, Crane wrote: "Nelson was a Norwegian who rebelled against the restrictions of home and came to America when a mere kid. Went to art school in Washington and won some kind of distinguished medal there. As soon as he was through school, an aunt of his in America who had been paying his tuition abruptly withdrew all her help and forced him into the prostitution of all his ideals and a cheap lithographic work that he was never able to pull out of afterward. He wrote several good poems, published in *Scribner's* and *Century* a long time ago, got married, and I finally met him here in Cleveland where he has been living in seclusion for a number of years. One of the best-read people I ever met, wonderful kindliness and tolerance and a true Nietzschean. He was one of many broken against the stupidity of American life in such places as here [i.e., Cleveland]. I think he has had a lasting influence on me" (*Letters*, 93).
[2] *Pierrot* the pathetic clown in French puppet shows and pantomime.
[3] *Gargantua* Someone who takes a robust pleasure in life, from the name of a hero in *Gargantua and Pantagruel* (1532–55) by François Rabelais (c. 1489–1553).

THE WINE
First published in the *Dial*, 80(5) (May 1926), then collected and corrected in Crane's first collection of poems, *White Buildings* (New York: Boni and Liveright, 1926).

Then glozening[1] decanters that reflect the street   5
Wear me in crescents on their bellies. Slow
Applause flows into liquid cynosures:
— I am conscripted to their shadows' glow.

Against the imitation onyx wainscoting
(Painted emulsion of snow, eggs, yarn, coal, manure)   10
Regard the forceps of the smile that takes her.
Percussive sweat is spreading to his hair. Mallets,
Her eyes, unmake an instant of the world . . .

What is it in this heap the serpent pries —
Whose skin, facsimile of time, unskeins   15
Octagon, sapphire transepts round the eyes;
— From whom some whispered carillon assures
Speed to the arrow into feathered skies?

Sharp to the windowpane guile drags a face,
And as the alcove of her jealousy recedes   20
An urchin who has left the snow
Nudges a cannister across the bar
While August meadows somewhere clasp his brow.

Each chamber, transept, coins some squint,
Remorseless line, minting their separate wills —   25
Poor streaked bodies wreathing up and out,
Unwitting the stigma that each turn repeals:
Between black tusks the roses shine!

New thresholds, new anatomies! Wine talons
Build freedom up about me and distill   30
This competence — to travel in a tear
Sparkling alone, within another's will.

Until my blood dreams a receptive smile
Wherein new purities are snared; where chimes
Before some flame of gaunt repose a shell   35
Tolled once, perhaps, by every tongue in hell.
— Anguished, the wit that cries out of me:

"Alas, — these frozen billows of your skill!
Invent new dominoes of love and bile . . .
Ruddy, the tooth implicit of the world   40
Has followed you. Though in the end you know
And count some dim inheritance of sand,
How much yet meets the treason of the snow.

"Rise from the dates and crumbs. And walk away,
Stepping over Holofernes' shins —   45
Beyond the wall, whose severed head floats by
With Baptist John's.[2] Their whispering begins.

[1] glozening shining.
[2] Holofernes' shins . . . Baptist John's the Apocryha are books that once formed part of the Hebrew Scriptures preserved in the ancient copies of the Septuagint, or Greek, version of the Old Testament. They were translated and included with the King James or Authorized Version of the Bible in 1605, but since then are traditionally omitted from editions of the Bible. The apocryphal book of Judith tells the story of how Judith of Bethulia beheads Holofernes, a blaspheming general under the Assyrians, and saves the Israelites. John the Baptist, instead, is unjustly beheaded at the command of Herod, who does so to satisfy the request of Salome (see Mark 6:14–29).

"– And fold your exile on your back again;
Petrushka's valentine pivots on its pin."

At Melville's Tomb[1] (1926)

Often beneath the wave, wide from this ledge
The dice of drowned men's bones he saw bequeath
An embassy. Their numbers as he watched,
Beat on the dusty shore and were obscured.

And wrecks passed without sound of bells,   5
The calyx of death's bounty giving back
A scattered chapter, livid hieroglyph,
The portent wound in corridors of shells.

Then in the circuit calm of one vast coil,
Its lashings charmed and malice reconciled,   10
Frosted eyes there were that lifted altars;
And silent answers crept across the stars.

Compass, quadrant and sextant contrive
No farther tides . . . High in the azure steeps
Monody shall not wake the mariner.   15
This fabulous shadow only the sea keeps.

Voyages (1926)

I

Above the fresh ruffles of the surf
Bright striped urchins flay each other with sand.
They have contrived a conquest for shell shucks,
And their fingers crumble fragments of baked weed
Gaily digging and scattering.   5

And in answer to their treble interjections
The sun beats lightning on the waves,
The waves fold thunder on the sand;
And could they hear me I would tell them:

O brilliant kids, frisk with your dog,   10
Fondle your shells and sticks, bleached
By time and the elements; but there is a line
You must not cross nor ever trust beyond it
Spry cordage of your bodies to caresses
Too lichen-faithful from too wide a breast.   15
The bottom of the sea is cruel.

MELVILLE'S TOMB
This poem was first published in Hart Crane's first collection of
poems, *The White Bridge* (New York: Boni and Liveright, 1926).
[1]   *Melville's Tomb* Herman Melville (1819–91), the American
novelist, is buried at Woodlawn Cemetery in New York City.

VOYAGES
This poem was first published in the *Little Review* 12 (spring–
summer 1926).

II

– And yet this great wink of eternity,
Of rimless floods, unfettered leewardings,
Samite sheeted and processioned where
Her undinal vast belly moonward bends,   20
Laughing the wrapt inflections of our love;

Take this Sea, whose diapason knells
On scrolls of silver snowy sentences,
The sceptred terror of whose sessions rends
As her demeanors motion well or ill,   25
All but the pieties of lovers' hands.

And onward, as bells off San Salvador[1]
Salute the crocus lustres of the stars,
In these poinsettia meadows of her tides, –
Adagios of islands, O my Prodigal,   30
Complete the dark confessions her veins spell.

Mark how her turning shoulders wind the hours,
And hasten while her penniless rich palms
Pass superscription of bent foam and wave, –
Hasten, while they are true, – sleep, death, desire,   35
Close round one instant in one floating flower.

Bind us in time, O Seasons clear, and awe.
O minstrel galleons of Carib fire,
Bequeath us to no earthly shore until
Is answered in the vortex of our grave   40
The seal's wide spindrift gaze toward paradise.

III

Infinite consanguinity it bears –
This tendered theme of you that light
Retrieves from sea plains where the sky
Resigns a breast that every wave enthrones;   45
While ribboned water lanes I wind
Are laved and scattered with no stroke
Wide from your side, whereto this hour
The sea lifts, also, reliquary hands.

And so, admitted through black swollen gates   50
That must arrest all distance otherwise, –
Past whirling pillars and lithe pediments,
Light wrestling there incessantly with light,
Star kissing star through wave on wave unto
Your body rocking!   55

[1]   *off San Salvador* a sailors' legend held that there was a buried
city beneath the Pacific Ocean off San Salvador.

and where death, if shed,
Presumes no carnage, but this single change, –
Upon the steep floor flung from dawn to dawn
The silken skilled transmemberment of song;

Permit me voyage, love, into your hands...   60

IV

Whose counted smile of hours and days, suppose
I know as spectrum of the sea and pledge
Vastly now parting gulf on gulf of wings
Whose circles bridge, I know, (from palms to the severe
Chilled albatross's white immutability)   65
No stream of greater love advancing now
Than, singing, this mortality alone
Through clay aflow immortally to you.

All fragrance irrefragibly, and claim
Madly meeting logically in this hour   70
And region that is ours to wreathe again,
Portending eyes and lips and making told
The chancel port and portion of our June –

Shall they not stem and close in our own steps
Bright staves of flowers and quills to-day as I   75
Must first be lost in fatal tides to tell?

In signature of the incarnate word
The harbor shoulders to resign in mingling
Mutual blood, transpiring as foreknown
And widening noon within your breast for gathering   80
All bright insinuations that my years have caught
For islands where must lead inviolably
Blue latitudes and levels of your eyes, –

In this expectant, still exclaim receive
The secret oar and petals of all love.   85

V

Meticulous, past midnight in clear rime,
Infrangible and lonely, smooth as though cast
Together in one merciless white blade –
The bay estuaries fleck the hard sky limits.

– As if too brittle or too clear to touch!   90
The cables of our sleep so swiftly filed,
Already hang, shred ends from remembered stars.
One frozen trackless smile... What words
Can strangle this deaf moonlight? For we

Are overtaken. Now no cry, no sword   95
Can fasten or deflect this tidal wedge,
Slow tyranny of moonlight, moonlight loved
And changed... "There's

Nothing like this in the world," you say,
Knowing I cannot touch your hand and look   100
Too, into that godless cleft of sky
Where nothing turns but dead sands flashing.

"– And never to quite understand!" No,
In all the argosy of your bright hair I dreamed
Nothing so flagless as this piracy.   105

But now
Draw in your head, alone and too tall here.
Your eyes already in the slant of drifting foam;
Your breath sealed by the ghosts I do not know:
Draw in your head and sleep the long way home.   110

VI

Where icy and bright dungeons lift
Of swimmers their lost morning eyes,
And ocean rivers, churning, shift
Green borders under stranger skies,

Steadily as a shell secretes   115
Its beating leagues of monotone,
Or as many waters trough the sun's
Red kelson past the cape's wet stone;

O rivers mingling toward the sky
And harbor of the phœnix' breast –   120
My eyes pressed black against the prow,
– Thy derelict and blinded guest

Waiting, afire, what name, unspoke,
I cannot claim: let thy waves rear
More savage than the death of kings,   125
Some splintered garland for the seer.

Beyond siroccos harvesting
The solstice thunders, crept away,
Like a cliff swinging or a sail
Flung into April's inmost day –   130

Creation's blithe and petalled word
To the lounged goddess when she rose
Conceding dialogue with eyes
That smile unsearchable repose –

Still fervid covenant, Belle Isle,   135
– Unfolded floating dais before
Which rainbows twine continual hair –
Belle Isle, white echo of the oar!

The imaged Word, it is, that holds
Hushed willows anchored in its glow.   140
It is the unbetrayable reply
Whose accent no farewell can know.

O Carib Isle! (1927)

The tarantula rattling at the lily's foot
Across the feet of the dead, laid in white sand
Near the coral beach — nor zigzag fiddle crabs
Side-stilting from the path (that shift, subvert
And anagrammatize your name) — No, nothing here   5
Below the palsy that one eucalyptus lifts
In wrinkled shadows — mourns.

                              And yet suppose
I count these nacreous frames of tropic death,
Brutal necklaces of shells around each grave   10
Squared off so carefully. Then

To the white sand I may speak a name, fertile
Albeit in a stranger tongue. Tree names, flower names
Deliberate, gainsay death's brittle crypt. Meanwhile
The wind that knots itself in one great death —   15
Coils and withdraws. So syllables want breath.

But where is the Captain of this doubloon isle
Without a turnstile? Who but catchword crabs
Patrols the dry groins of the underbrush?
What man, or What   20
Is commissioner of mildew throughout the ambushed senses?
His Carib mathematics web the eyes' baked lenses!

Under the poinciana, of a noon or afternoon
Let fiery blossoms clot the light, render my ghost
Sieved upward, white and black along the air   25
Until it meets the blue's comedian host.
Let not the pilgrim see himself again
For slow evisceration bound like those huge terrapin
Each daybreak on the wharf, their brine-caked eyes;
— Spiked, overturned; such thunder in their strain!   30
And clenched beaks coughing for the surge again!

Slagged of the hurricane — I, cast within its flow,
Congeal by afternoons here, satin and vacant.
You have given me the shell, Satan, — carbonic amulet
Sere of the sun exploded in the sea.   35

Island Quarry (1927)

Square sheets — they saw the marble only into
Flat prison slabs there at the marble quarry
At the turning of the road around the roots of the mountain
Where the straight road would seem to ply below the stone, that fierce
Profile of marble spiked with yonder   5
Palms against the sunset's towering sea, and maybe
Against mankind. It is at times —

O CARIB
This poem was first published in *transition* 1 (April 1927).

ISLAND QUARRY
First published in *transition* 9 (December 1927).

In dusk, as though this island lifted, floated
In Indian baths. At Cuban dusk the eyes
Walking the straight road toward thunder –   10
This dry road silvering toward the shadow of the quarry
– It is at times as though the eyes burned hard and glad
And did not take the goat path quivering to the right,
Wide of the mountain – thence to tears and sleep –
But went on into marble that does not weep.   15

Bacardi Spreads the Eagle's Wings (1927)

"Pablo and Pedro, and black Serafin
Bought a launch last week. It might as well
Have been made of – well, say paraffin, –
That thin and blistered . . . just a rotten shell.

"Hell! out there among the barracudas   5
Their engine stalled. No oars, and leaks
Oozing a-plenty. They sat like baking Buddhas.
Luckily the Cayman schooner streaks

"By just in time, and lifts 'em high and dry . . .
They're back now on that mulching job at Pepper's.   10
– Yes, patent-leather shoes hot enough to fry
Anyone but these native high-steppers!"

To Emily Dickinson[1] (1927)

You who desired so much – in vain to ask –
Yet fed your hunger like an endless task,
Dared dignify the labor, bless the quest –
Achieved that stillness ultimately best,

Being, of all, least sought for: Emily, hear!   5
O sweet, dead Silencer, most suddenly clear
When singing that Eternity possessed
And plundered momently in every breast;

– Truly no flower yet withers in your hand,
The harvest you descried and understand   10
Needs more than wit to gather, love to bind.
Some reconcilement of remotest mind –

Leaves Ormus[2] rubyless, and Ophir chill.
Else tears heap all within one clay-cold hill.

BACARDI
This poem was first published as "Overheard" in *transition* 9 (December 1927); republished as "Bacardi Spreads the Eagle's Wings" in *Contempo* 2 (July 5, 1932).

TO EMILY DICKINSON
First published in the *Nation* 124 (June 29, 1927).

[1] *Emily Dickinson* Emily Dickinson (1830–86), American lyrical poet.
[2] *Ormus* Ormuz, an ancient city on the Persian Gulf. Ophir is a city mentioned 13 times in the Old Testament, nearly always with reference to "gold of Ophir" or "gold from Ophir."

The Mermen (1928)

And if
Thy banished trunk be found in our dominions[1] –
                    KING LEAR

Buddhas and engines serve us undersea;
Though why they bide here, only hell that's sacked
Of every blight and ingenuity –
Can solve.

      The Cross alone has flown the wave.   5
But since the Cross sank, much that's warped and cracked
Has followed in its name, has heaped its grave.
                    Oh –

Gallows and guillotines to hail the sun
And smoking racks for penance when day's done!   10
                    No –

Leave us, you idols of Futurity – alone,
Here where we finger moidores of spent grace
And ponder the bright stains that starred this Throne

– This Cross, agleam still with a human Face!   15

The Broken Tower (1932)

The bell-rope that gathers God at dawn[1]
Dispatches me as though I dropped down the knell
Of a spent day – to wander the cathedral lawn
From pit to crucifix, feet chill on steps from hell.

Have you not heard, have you not seen that corps   5
Of shadows in the tower, whose shoulders sway
Antiphonal carillons launched before
The stars are caught and hived in the sun's ray?

The bells, I say, the bells break down their tower;
And swing I know not where. Their tongues engrave   10
Membrane through marrow, my long-scattered score
Of broken intervals . . . And I, their sexton slave!

Oval encyclicals in canyons heaping
The impasse high with choir. Banked voices slain!

MERMEN
First published in the *Dial* 85 (July 1928).
[1] And if . . . our dominions Act 1, King Lear when banishing
loyal Kent from his kingdom:

    Take thy reward.
    Five days do we allot thee for provision,
    To shield thee from disasters of the world;
    And, on the sixth, to turn thy hated back

Upon our kingdom; if, the tenth day following,
The banished trunk be found in our dominions,
The moment is thy death. Away!

BROKEN TOWER
First published in the *New Republic* 71 (June 8, 1932).
[1] *that gathers God at dawn* the angelus bell commemorates the
Incarnation of Christ.

Pagodas, campaniles with reveilles outleaping –   15
O terraced echoes prostrate on the plain! . . .

And so it was I entered the broken world
To trace the visionary company of love, its voice
An instant in the wind (I know not whither hurled)
But not for long to hold each desperate choice.   20

My word I poured. But was it cognate, scored
Of that tribunal monarch of the air
Whose thigh embronzes earth, strikes crystal Word[2]
In wounds pledged once to hope – cleft to despair?

The steep encroachments of my blood left me   25
No answer (could blood hold such a lofty tower
As flings the question true?) – or is it she
Whose sweet mortality stirs latent power? –

And through whose pulse I hear, counting the strokes
My veins recall and add, revived and sure   30
The angelus of wars my chest evokes:
What I hold healed, original now, and pure . . .

And builds, within, a tower that is not stone
(Not stone can jacket heaven) – but slip
Of pebbles, – visible wings of silence sown   35
In azure circles, widening as they dip

The matrix of the heart, lift down the eye
That shrines the quiet lake and swells a tower . . .
The commodious, tall decorum of that sky
Unseals her earth, and lifts love in its shower.   40

The Case against Nietzsche (1918)

Before the war, Nietzsche's[1] writings were moderately popular in France, where he was hailed by the Sorbonne long before Oxford awoke to his dimensions. But now the French call him the herald of modern Prussianism.

How paradoxical their accusation seems, when we know that Nietzsche was drawn to the French temperament more than to any other. His favorite novelists were French; Pascal and Montaigne[2] were sources which he frequently mentions as potent influences in his development. Goethe and Schopenhauer[3] were the only Germans for whom he had philosophic ears; and these, as he declares, were fundamentally un-German.

And yet again, how can he be called the spokesman of a nation which always affected him with disgust, – if not with hatred? His epithets on characteristic "Germania" at times approach the unprintable. He even denied his German origin, and declared himself a Pole in all his views and sympathies. Anyone who can picture him as an inspired leader of legions of "the pig-headed," as he called them, has indeed capacities for self-delusion.

---

[2]   *strikes crystal Word* cf. John 1:14: "And the Word was made flesh and dwelt among us."

NIETZSCHE
This essay was first published in *Pagany* 2–3 (April–May 1918).
[1]   Friedrich Nietzsche (1844–1900), German philosopher.

[2]   Blaise Pascal (1623–62), French scholar and author famous for his *Pensées* (*Thoughts*); Michel de Montaigne (1533–92), French writer whose *Essays* were first published in 1588.
[3]   Johann Wolfgang von Goethe (1749–1832), German poet and man of letters; Arthur Schopenhauer (1788–1860), German philosopher.

I might refer to Par. 320 in *Menschliches, Allzumenschliches*[4] for a direct arraignment of Prussianism, although no names are mentioned in it. Here the autocratic machine is coolly exposed. He cites the direct control by the state over all educational institutions; the inaccessibility to all personal distinction except through some service, sooner or later, to the state; compulsory military training; the supremacy of the army; and at the end he ironically observes, – "Then nothing more is wanted but an opportunity for great wars. These are provided from professional reasons (and so in all innocence) by diplomats, aided by newspapers and Stock Exchanges. For the 'nation,' as a nation of soldiers, need never be supplied with a good conscience in war, – it has one already."[5]

Nietzsche, Zeppelins, and poisoned-gas go ill together. But Great Indra![6] one may envy Nietzsche a little; think of being so elusive, – so mercurial, as to be first swallowed whole, then coughed up, and still remain a mystery!

Joyce and Ethics (1918)

The Los Angeles critic who commented on Joyce in the last issue[1] was adequately answered, I realize, – but the temptation to emphasize such illiteracy, indiscrimination, and poverty still pulls a little too strongly for resistance.

I noticed that Wilde, Baudelaire, and Swinburne[2] are "stacked up" beside Joyce as rivals in "decadence" and "intellect." I am not yet aware that Swinburne ever possessed much beyond his "art ears," although these were long enough, and adequate to all his beautiful, though often meaningless mouthings. His instability in criticism and every form of literature that did not depend almost exclusively on sound for effect and his irrelevant metaphors are notorious. And as to Wilde, – after his bundle of paradoxes has been sorted and conned, – very little evidence of intellect remains. "Decadence" is something much talked about, and sufficiently misconstrued to arouse interest in the works of any fool. Any change in form, viewpoint, or mannerism can be so abused by the offending party. Sterility is the only "decadence" I recognize. An abortion in art takes the same place as it does in society, – it deserves no recognition whatever, – it is simply outside. A piece of work is art, or it isn't: there is no neutral judgment.

However, – let Baudelaire and Joyce stand together, as much as any such thing in literary comparison will allow. The principal eccentricity evinced by both is a penetration into life common to only the greatest. If people resent a thrust which discovers some of their entrails to themselves, I can see no reason for resorting to indiscriminate comparisons, naming colours of the rainbow, or advertising the fact that they have recently been forced to recognize a few of their personal qualities. Those who are capable of being only mildly "shocked" very naturally term the cost a penny, but were they capable of paying a few pounds for the same thinking, experience and realization by and in themselves, they could reserve their pennies for work minor to Joyce's.

The most nauseating complaint against his work is that of immorality and obscenity. The character of Stephen Dedalus is all too good for this world. It takes a little experience, – a few reactions on his part to understand it, and could this have been accomplished in a detached hermitage, high above the mud, he would no doubt have preferred that residence. *A Portrait of the Artist as a Young Man*, aside from Dante, is spiritually the most inspiring book I have ever read. It is Bunyan raised to art,[3] and then raised to the ninth power.

---

[4]   Crane is referring to Oscar Levy (ed.), *The Complete Works of Friedrich Nietzsche*, vol. 7, Part 2, *Human, All Too Human*, trans. Paul V. Cohn (Edinburgh: Foulis, 1911), Aphorism 320, 152–4, which begins: "The governments of the great states have two instruments for keeping the people dependent, in fear and obedience: a coarser, the army, and a more refined one, the school."

[5]   Crane cites from Levy, *Complete Works of Friedrich Nietzsche*, vol. 7, Part 2, 154.

[6]   Hindu chief of demigods and king of the heavenly planets.

JOYCE
This letter/essay was first published in the *Little Review* 5(3) (July 1918).

[1]   *Little Review* 5.2 (June 1918).

[2]   Oscar Wilde (1854–1900), Irish novelist; Charles Baudelaire (1821–67), French poet and essayist; Charles Algernon Swinburne (1837–1909), English poet.

[3]   John Bunyan (1628–88), Puritan divine best known as the author of *Pilgrim's Progress* (1676).

Modern Poetry (1930)

Modern poetry has long since passed the crest of its rebellion against many of the so-called classical strictures. Indeed the primary departures of the early intransigeants were often more in a classic direction, with respect to certain neglected early European traditions, than were many of the Victorian regulations that formed the immediate butt of attack.

Revolution flourishes still, but rather as a contemporary tradition in which the original obstacles to freedom have been, if not always eradicated, at least obscured by floods of later experimentation. Indeed, to the serious artist, revolution as an all-engrossing program no longer exists. It persists at a rapid momentum in certain groups or movements, but often in forms which are more constricting than liberating, in view of a generous choice of subject matter.

The poet's concern must be, as always, self-discipline toward a formal integration of experience. For poetry is an architectural art, based not on Evolution or the idea of progress, but on the articulation of the contemporary human consciousness *sub specie æternitatis,*[1] and inclusive of all readjustments incident to science and other shifting factors related to that consciousness. The key to the process of free creative activity which Coleridge gave us in his *Lectures on Shakespeare* exposes the responsibilities of every poet, modern or ancient, and cannot be improved upon. "No work of true genius," he says, "dares want its appropriate form, neither indeed is there any danger of this. As it must not, so genius can not, be lawless: for it is even this that constitutes its genius – *the power of acting creatively under laws of its own origination.*"[2]

Poetry has at once a greater intimacy and a wider, more exact scope of implication than painting or any of the other arts. It is therefore more apt to be indicative of impending changes in other media such as painting or music. This is a logical deduction that facts do not always favor, as in the case of some modern composers such as Stravinsky,[3] the full purport of whose inspiration seems to lie beyond the reach of current literary expression. Literature has a more tangible relationship to painting; and it is highly probable that the Symbolist movement in French poetry was a considerable factor in the instigation first, of Impressionism, and later, of Cubism. Both arts have had parallel and somewhat analogous tendencies toward abstract statement and metaphysical representation. In this recent preoccupation it is certain that both media were responding to the shifting emphasis of the Western World away from religion toward science. Analysis and discovery, the two basic concerns of science, became conscious objectives of both painter and poet. A great deal of modern painting is as independent of any representational motive as a mathematical equation; while some of the most intense and eloquent current verse derives sheerly from acute psychological analysis, quite independent of any dramatic motivation.

The function of poetry in a Machine Age is identical to its function in any other age; and its capacities for presenting the most complete synthesis of human values remain essentially immune from any of the so-called inroads of science. The emotional stimulus of machinery is on an entirely different psychic plane from that of poetry. Its only menace lies in its capacities for facile entertainment, so easily accessible as to arrest the development of any but the most negligible esthetic responses. The ultimate influence of machinery in this respect remains to be seen, but its firm entrenchment in our lives has already produced a series of challenging new responsibilities for the poet.

For unless poetry can absorb the machine, i.e., *acclimatize* it as naturally and casually as trees, cattle, galleons, castles and all other human associations of the past, then poetry has failed of its full contemporary function. This process does not infer any program of lyrical pandering to the taste of those obsessed by the importance of machinery; nor does it essentially involve even the specific

---

This essay was first published in Olive M. Saylor (ed.), *Revolt in the Arts: A Survey of the Creation, Distribution and Appreciation of Art in America* (New York: Brentano's, 1930).

[1]   "From the viewpoint of eternity," in Latin.

[2]   Samuel Taylor Coleridge, *Lectures on Shakespeare* (London: Dent, 1907), "Shakespeare's Judgement Equal to His Genius,"

46. The italics at the end of the passage have been added by Crane.

[3]   Igor Stravinsky (1882–1971), Russian composer who was thought to embody modern music.

mention of a single mechanical contrivance. It demands, however, along with the traditional qualifications of the poet, an extraordinary capacity for surrender, at least temporarily, to the sensations of urban life. This presupposes, of course, that the poet possesses sufficient spontaneity and gusto to convert this experience into positive terms. Machinery will tend to lose its sensational glamour and appear in its true subsidiary order in human life as use and continual poetic allusion subdue its novelty. For, contrary to general prejudice, the wonderment experienced in watching nose dives is of less immediate creative promise to poetry than the familiar gesture of a motorist in the modest act of shifting gears. I mean to say that mere romantic speculation on the power and beauty of machinery keeps it at a continual remove; it can not act creatively in our lives until, like the unconscious nervous responses of our bodies, its connotations emanate from within – forming as spontaneous a terminology of poetic reference as the bucolic world of pasture, plow, and barn.

The familiar contention that science is inimical to poetry is no more tenable than the kindred notion that theology has been proverbially hostile – with the *Commedia* of Dante to prove the contrary. That "truth" which science pursues is radically different from the metaphorical, extra-logical "truth" of the poet. When Blake wrote that "a tear is an intellectual thing, And a sigh is the sword of an Angel King"[4] – he was not in any logical conflict with the principles of the Newtonian Universe. Similarly, poetic prophecy in the case of the seer has nothing to do with factual prediction or with futurity. It is a peculiar type of perception, capable of apprehending some absolute and timeless concept of the imagination with astounding clarity and conviction.

That the modern poet can profitably assume the roles of philosopher or theologian is question-able at best. Science, the uncanonized Deity of the times, seems to have automatically displaced the hierarchies of both Academy and Church. It is pertinent to cite the authors of the *Commedia* and *Paradise Lost* as poets whose verse survives the religious dogmas and philosophies of their respective periods, but it is fallacious to assume that either of these poets could have written important religious verse without the fully developed and articulated religious dogmas that each was heir to.

The future of American poetry is too complicated a speculation to be more than approached in this limited space. Involved in it are the host of considerations relative to the comparative influ-ences of science, machinery, and other factors which I have merely touched upon; – besides those influential traditions of early English prosody which form points of departure, at least, for any indigenous rhythms and forms which may emerge. The most typical and valid expression of the American *psychosis* seems to me still to be found in Whitman. His faults as a technician and his clumsy and indiscriminate enthusiasm are somewhat beside the point. He, better than any other, was able to coördinate those forces in America which seem most intractable, fusing them into a universal vision which takes on additional significance as time goes on. He was a revolutionist beyond the strict meaning of Coleridge's definition of genius, but his bequest is still to be realized in all its implications.

---

[4] From the untitled poem in the section "To the Deists" in *Jerusalem*, Ch. 2, by William Blake (1757–1827), British poet, visionary, and engraver; see David Erdman (ed.), *The Complete* *Poetry and Prose of William Blake*, revised edition (New York: Anchor Press, 1982), pp. 201–2.

Virginia Woolf (1882–1941)

Introduction

Virginia Woolf, née Stephen, was the daughter of Sir Leslie Stephen, a distinguished critic and writer who founded the *Dictionary of National Biography*. She was educated at home and later resented being denied the formal education given to her brothers Adrian and Toby, who both went to Cambridge. Through them she came to know a number of people, including the novelist E. M. Forster, the economist J. M. Keynes, and the biographer Lytton Strachey, who would later make up what was called the Bloomsbury Circle, a loose affiliation of intellectuals, critics, journalists, and writers who met through an informal network of changing friendships. In 1912 she married Leondard Woolf, a journalist and political activist who in 1916 would found the Hogarth Press, a small publishing house. Woolf's first publications, which began already in 1904, were essays and book reviews, and throughout her life she was a fascinating, stylish, and prolific essayist. Her first novels, *The Voyage Out* and *Night and Day*, were published in 1915 and 1919. But it is her second collection of short stories, *Monday or Tuesday* (1921, that signals a sudden loosening of her style, the result of her growing interest in the period's experimental writing, some of that interest plainly piqued by her acquaintanceship with T. S. Eliot. In her third novel, *Jacob's Room* (1922), Woolf begins to part company with the traditional methods of the English novel. Her fourth and fifth novels, *Mrs. Dalloway* (1925) and *To the Lighthouse*, are among the great masterpieces of the twentieth century.

Throughout her life Woolf was also a prolific correspondent and diarist. Her diaries and letters are an extraordinary record of an especially observant contemporary, one acutely responsive to almost every aspect of the world around her. In 1928 she wrote *Orlando*, a playful novel of gender transformations. This was followed by *A Room of One's Own*, a founding document of modern feminist thought and a probing examination of the cultural conditions that have shaped women's writing. Her next two major novels, *The Waves* (1931) and *The Years* (1937), are extraordinary experiments in prose, elusive flows of words and intuitions. Her last major novel was *Between the Acts* (1941; see pp. 827–96). Throughout her life Woolf had been liable to bouts of severe depression, typically after completing a book, and in 1941, despondent over the carnage of World War II, she took her own life by drowning.

Between the Acts (1941)

It was a summer's night and they were talking, in the big room with the windows open to the garden, about the cesspool.[1] The county council had promised to bring water to the village, but they hadn't.

Mrs. Haines, the wife of the gentleman farmer, a goosefaced woman with eyes protruding as if they saw something to gobble in the gutter, said affectedly: "What a subject to talk about on a night like this!"

Then there was silence; and a cow coughed; and that led her to say how odd it was, as a child, she had never feared cows, only horses. But, then, as a small child in a perambulator, a great cart-horse had brushed within an inch of her face. Her family, she told the old man in the arm-chair, had lived near Liskeard[2] for many centuries. There were the graves in the churchyard to prove it.

Between the Acts was published by the Hogarth Press in London in July 1941, some three months after Woolf had drowned herself on March 28, 1941. This edition follows the text established by Susan Dick and Mary S. Millar in *Between the Acts* (Oxford: Blackwell, 2002).

The title is a literal translation of the French term *entr'acte*, an interlude, often humorous and sometimes with dance or music, between the acts of a play, opera, or ballet.

[Leonard Woolf's note:] The MS. of this book had been completed, but had not been finally revised for the printer, at the time of Virginia Woolf's death. She would not, I believe, have made any large or material alterations in it, though she would probably have made a good many small corrections or revisions before passing the final proofs.

[1] A covered pit for collecting waste in areas without sewer systems.

[2] A town in Cornwall, dating from the thirteenth century; Cornwall is the southwestern-most county in England.

A bird chuckled outside. "A nightingale?" asked Mrs. Haines. No, nightingales didn't come so far north. It was a daylight bird, chuckling over the substance and succulence of the day, over worms, snails, grit, even in sleep.

The old man in the arm-chair – Mr. Oliver, of the Indian Civil Service,[3] retired – said that the site they had chosen for the cesspool was, if he had heard aright, on the Roman road. From an aeroplane, he said, you could still see, plainly marked, the scars made by the Britons; by the Romans; by the Elizabethan manor house; and by the plough, when they ploughed the hill to grow wheat in the Napoleonic wars.[4]

"But you don't remember..." Mrs. Haines began. No, not that. Still he did remember—and he was about to tell them what, when there was a sound outside, and Isa, his son's wife, came in with her hair in pigtails; she was wearing a dressing-gown with faded peacocks on it. She came in like a swan swimming its way; then was checked and stopped; was surprised to find people there; and lights burning. She had been sitting with her little boy who wasn't well, she apologized. What had they been saying?

"Discussing the cesspool," said Mr. Oliver.

"What a subject to talk about on a night like this!" Mrs. Haines exclaimed again.

What had *he* said about the cesspool; or indeed about anything? Isa wondered, inclining her head towards the gentleman farmer, Rupert Haines. She had met him at a Bazaar; and at a tennis party. He had handed her a cup and a racquet – that was all. But in his ravaged face she always felt mystery; and in his silence, passion. At the tennis party she had felt this, and at the Bazaar. Now a third time, if anything more strongly, she felt it again.

"I remember," the old man interrupted, "my mother..." Of his mother he remembered that she was very stout; kept her tea-caddy locked;[5] yet had given him in that very room a copy of Byron. It was over sixty years ago, he told them, that his mother had given him the works of Byron in that very room. He paused.

"She walks in beauty like the night,"[6] he quoted.

Then again:

"So we'll go no more a-roving by the light of the moon."[7]

Isa raised her head. The words made two rings, perfect rings, that floated them, herself and Haines, like two swans down stream. But his snow-white breast was circled with a tangle of dirty duckweed; and she too, in her webbed feet was entangled, by her husband, the stockbroker. Sitting on her three-cornered chair she swayed, with her dark pigtails hanging, and her body like a bolster in its faded dressing-gown.

Mrs. Haines was aware of the emotion circling them, excluding her. She waited, as one waits for the strain of an organ to die out before leaving church. In the car going home to the red villa in the cornfields, she would destroy it, as a thrush pecks the wings off a butterfly. Allowing ten seconds to intervene, she rose; paused; and then, as if she had heard the last strain die out, offered Mrs. Giles Oliver her hand.

But Isa, though she should have risen at the same moment that Mrs. Haines rose, sat on. Mrs. Haines glared at her out of the gooselike eyes, gobbling, "Please, Mrs. Giles Oliver, do me the kindness to recognize my existence...." which she was forced to do, rising at last from her chair, in her faded dressing-gown, with the pigtails falling over each shoulder.

Pointz Hall was seen in the light of an early summer morning to be a middle-sized house. It did not rank among the houses that are mentioned in Guide Books. It was too homely. But this whitish house with the grey roof, and the wing thrown out at right angles, lying unfortunately low on the meadow with a fringe of trees on the bank above it so that smoke curled up to the nests of the rooks,

---

[3]　The agency charged with the administration of India when it formed part of the British Empire, as it did until 1947.

[4]　The campaigns that Napoleon I of France conducted against European powers from 1800 to 1815.

[5]　In the nineteenth century, high taxes made tea so expensive that tea-caddies were locked to prevent pilfering by servants.

[6]　George Gordon, Lord Byron (1788–1824), English Romantic poet. Mr. Oliver quotes from his lyric "She Walks in Beauty."

[7]　The first line of Byron's lyric "We'll go no more a'roving."

was a desirable house to live in. Driving past, people said to each other: "I wonder if that'll ever come into the market?" And to the chauffeur: "Who lives there?"

The chauffeur didn't know. The Olivers, who had bought the place something over a century ago, had no connection with the Warings, the Elveys, the Mannerings or the Burnets;[8] the old families who had all intermarried, and lay in their deaths intertwisted, like the ivy roots, beneath the churchyard wall.

Only something over a hundred and twenty years[9] the Olivers had been there. Still, on going up the principal staircase – there was another, a mere ladder at the back for the servants – there was a portrait. A length of yellow brocade was visible half-way up; and, as one reached the top, a small powdered face, a great head-dress slung with pearls, came into view; an ancestress of sorts. Six or seven bedrooms opened out of the corridor. The butler had been a soldier; had married a lady's maid; and, under a glass case there was a watch that had stopped a bullet on the field of Waterloo.[10]

It was early morning. The dew was on the grass. The church clock struck eight times. Mrs. Swithin[11] drew the curtain in her bedroom – the faded white chintz that so agreeably from the outside tinged the window with its green lining. There with her old hands on the hasp, jerking it open, she stood: old Oliver's married sister; a widow. She always meant to set up a house of her own; perhaps in Kensington, perhaps at Kew,[12] so that she could have the benefit of the gardens. But she stayed on all through the summer; and when winter wept its damp upon the panes, and choked the gutters with dead leaves, she said: "Why, Bart, did they build the house in the hollow, facing north?" Her brother said, "Obviously to escape from nature. Weren't four horses needed to drag the family coach through the mud?" Then he told her the famous story of the great eighteenth-century winter; when for a whole month the house had been blocked by snow. And the trees had fallen. So every year, when winter came, Mrs. Swithin retired to Hastings.[13]

But it was summer now. She had been waked by the birds. How they sang! attacking the dawn like so many choir boys attacking an iced cake. Forced to listen, she had stretched for her favourite reading – an Outline of History[14] – and had spent the hours between three and five thinking of rhododendron forests in Piccadilly;[15] when the entire continent, not then, she understood, divided by a channel, was all one; populated, she understood, by elephant-bodied, seal-necked, heaving, surging, slowly writhing, and, she supposed, barking monsters; the iguanodon, the mammoth, and the mastodon; from whom presumably, she thought, jerking the window open, we descend.

It took her five seconds in actual time, in mind time ever so much longer, to separate Grace herself, with blue china on a tray, from the leather-covered grunting monster who was about, as the door opened, to demolish a whole tree in the green steaming undergrowth of the primeval forest. Naturally, she jumped, as Grace put the tray down and said: "Good morning, Ma'am." "Batty," Grace called her, as she felt on her face the divided glance that was half meant for a beast in a swamp, half for a maid in a print frock and white apron.

"How those birds sing!" said Mrs. Swithin, at a venture. The window was open now; the birds certainly were singing. An obliging thrush hopped across the lawn; a coil of pinkish rubber twisted in its beak. Tempted by the sight to continue her imaginative reconstruction of the past, Mrs. Swithin paused; she was given to increasing the bounds of the moment by flights into past or future; or sidelong down corridors and alleys; but she remembered her mother – her mother in that very room rebuking her. "Don't stand gaping, Lucy, or the wind'll change..."[16] How often her mother had rebuked her in that very room – "but in a very different world," as her brother would

---

8   Fictional families, but with names that sound very British.

9   I.e. since 1815 or thereabouts.

10   The Duke of Wellington defeated Napoleon on June 18, 1815, at Waterloo, near Brussels, ending the Napoleonic wars.

11   Folklore held that if it rained on St. Swithun's Day, it would rain for the next 40 days.

12   Kensington is just west and south of Hyde Park in London; Kew, a suburb southwest of London, is the setting for the Royal Botanic Gardens, a large park.

13   A seaside resort in Sussex, on the southern coast of England, and site of the Battle of Hastings in 1066, when William the

Conqueror defeated Harold II of England, beginning the Norman conquest.

14   H. G. Wells (1866–1946) published *The Outline of History: Being a Plain History of Life and Mankind* (London: Cassell) in 1920. Mrs. Swithin recalls images derived from maps (47, 53) and illustrations (facing 16 and 27) in the book.

15   A street that runs west from Piccadilly Circus to Hyde Park Corner in London.

16   Popular superstition held that if one grimaced when the wind was changing, one's face would freeze in that expression.

remind her. So she sat down to morning tea, like any other old lady with a high nose, thin cheeks, a ring on her finger and the usual trappings of rather shabby but gallant old age, which included in her case a cross gleaming gold on her breast.

The nurses after breakfast were trundling the perambulator up and down the terrace; and as they trundled they were talking – not shaping pellets of information or handing ideas from one to another, but rolling words, like sweets on their tongues; which, as they thinned to transparency, gave off pink, green, and sweetness. This morning that sweetness was: "How cook had told 'im off about the asparagus; how when she rang I said: how it was a sweet costume[17] with blouse to match;" and that was leading to something about a feller as they walked up and down the terrace rolling sweets, trundling the perambulator.

It was a pity that the man who had built Pointz Hall had pitched the house in a hollow, when beyond the flower garden and the vegetables there was this stretch of high ground. Nature had provided a site for a house; man had built his house in a hollow. Nature had provided a stretch of turf half a mile in length and level, till it suddenly dipped to the lily pool. The terrace was broad enough to take the entire shadow of one of the great trees laid flat. There you could walk up and down, up and down, under the shade of the trees. Two or three grew close together; then there were gaps. Their roots broke the turf, and among those bones were green waterfalls and cushions of grass in which violets grew in spring or in summer the wild purple orchis.

Amy was saying something about a feller when Mabel, with her hand on the pram, turned sharply, her sweet swallowed. "Leave off grubbing," she said sharply. "Come along, George."

The little boy had lagged and was grouting in the grass. Then the baby, Caro, thrust her fist out over the coverlet and the furry bear was jerked overboard. Amy had to stoop. George grubbed. The flower blazed between the angles of the roots. Membrane after membrane was torn. It blazed a soft yellow, a lambent light under a film of velvet; it filled the caverns behind the eyes with light. All that inner darkness became a hall, leaf smelling, earth smelling of yellow light. And the tree was beyond the flower; the grass, the flower and the tree were entire. Down on his knees grubbing he held the flower complete. Then there was a roar and a hot breath and a stream of coarse grey hair rushed between him and the flower. Up he leapt, toppling in his fright, and saw coming towards him a terrible peaked eyeless monster moving on legs, brandishing arms.

"Good morning, Sir," a hollow voice boomed at him from a beak of paper.

The old man had sprung upon him from his hiding behind a tree.

"Say good morning, George; say 'Good morning, Grandpa,'" Mabel urged him, giving him a push towards the man. But George stood gaping. George stood gazing. Then Mr. Oliver crumpled the paper which he had cocked into a snout and appeared in person. A very tall old man, with gleaming eyes, wrinkled cheeks, and a head with no hair on it. He turned.

"Heel!" he bawled, "heel, you brute!" And George turned; and the nurses turned holding the furry bear; they all turned to look at Sohrab the Afghan hound[18] bounding and bouncing among the flowers.

"Heel!" the old man bawled, as if he were commanding a regiment. It was impressive, to the nurses, the way an old boy of his age could still bawl and make a brute like that obey him. Back came the Afghan hound, sidling, apologetic. And as he cringed at the old man's feet, a string was slipped over his collar; the noose that old Oliver always carried with him.

"You wild beast...you bad beast," he grumbled, stooping. George looked at the dog only. The hairy flanks were sucked in and out; there was a blob of foam on its nostrils. He burst out crying.

Old Oliver raised himself, his veins swollen, his cheeks flushed; he was angry. His little game with the paper hadn't worked. The boy was a cry-baby. He nodded and sauntered on, smoothing out the crumpled paper and muttering, as he tried to find his line in the column, "A cry-baby –

---

[17] A woman's two-piece suit in the 1930s and 1940s.

[18] The dog is named from a poem by Matthew Arnold (1822–88), "Sohrab and Rustum," the story of a Persian warrior (Rustum) who unwittingly kills his son (Sohrab).

a cry-baby." But the breeze blew the great sheet out; and over the edge he surveyed the landscape – flowing fields, heath and woods. Framed, they became a picture. Had he been a painter, he would have fixed his easel here, where the country, barred by trees, looked like a picture. Then the breeze fell.

"M. Daladier," he read finding his place in the column, "has been successful in pegging down the franc...."[19]

Mrs. Giles Oliver drew the comb through the thick tangle of hair which, after giving the matter her best attention, she had never had shingled or bobbed;[20] and lifted the heavily embossed silver brush that had been a wedding present and had its uses in impressing chambermaids in hotels. She lifted it and stood in front of the three-folded mirror, so that she could see three separate versions of her rather heavy, yet handsome, face; and also, outside the glass, a slip of terrace, lawn and tree tops.

Inside the glass, in her eyes, she saw what she had felt overnight for the ravaged, the silent, the romantic gentleman farmer. "In love," was in her eyes. But outside, on the washstand, on the dressing-table, among the silver boxes and tooth-brushes, was the other love; love for her husband, the stockbroker – "The father of my children," she added, slipping into the cliché conveniently provided by fiction. Inner love was in the eyes; outer love on the dressing-table. But what feeling was it that stirred in her now when above the looking-glass, out of doors, she saw coming across the lawn the perambulator; two nurses; and her little boy George, lagging behind?

She tapped on the window with her embossed hairbrush. They were too far off to hear. The drone of the trees was in their ears; the chirp of birds; other incidents of garden life, inaudible, invisible to her in the bedroom, absorbed them. Isolated on a green island, hedged about with snowdrops, laid with a counterpane of puckered silk, the innocent island floated under her window. Only George lagged behind.

She returned to her eyes in the looking-glass. "In love," she must be; since the presence of his body in the room last night could so affect her; since the words he said, handing her a teacup, handing her a tennis racquet, could so attach themselves to a certain spot in her; and thus lie between them like a wire, tingling, tangling, vibrating – she groped, in the depths of the looking-glass, for a word to fit the infinitely quick vibrations of the aeroplane propeller that she had seen once at dawn at Croydon.[21] Faster, faster, faster, it whizzed, whirred, buzzed, till all the flails became one flail and up soared the plane away and away....

"Where we know not, where we go not, neither know nor care," she hummed. "Flying, rushing through the ambient, incandescent, summer silent..."

The rhyme was "air." She put down her brush. She took up the telephone.

"Three, four, eight, Pyecombe,"[22] she said.

"Mrs. Oliver speaking.... What fish have you this morning? Cod? Halibut? Sole? Plaice?"

"There to lose what binds us here," she murmured. "Soles. Filleted. In time for lunch please," she said aloud. "With a feather, a blue feather... flying mounting through the air... there to lose what binds us here..." The words weren't worth writing in the book bound like an account book in case Giles suspected. "Abortive," was the word that expressed her. She never came out of a shop, for example, with the clothes she admired; nor did her figure, seen against the dark roll of trousering in a shop window, please her. Thick of waist, large of limb, and, save for her hair, fashionable in the tight modern way, she never looked like Sappho,[23] or one of the beautiful young men whose photographs adorned the weekly papers. She looked what she was: Sir Richard's daughter; and niece of the two old ladies at Wimbledon who were so proud, being O'Neils, of their descent from the Kings of Ireland.

---

[19] Edouard Daladier (1884–1970), French prime minister 1938–40, agreed to a new exchange rate with Britain and the United States on May 4, 1938.

[20] Fashionable hairstyles of the 1930s.

[21] Croydon Aerodrome, then Airport, was London's main airport from 1920, when it opened, to 1959; located in what is now a northern suburb.

[22] A village in Sussex, 6 miles north of Brighton.

[23] Greek poet (c. 600 BC).

A foolish, flattering lady, pausing on the threshold of what she once called "the heart of the house," the threshold of the library, had once said: "Next to the kitchen, the library's always the nicest room in the house." Then she added, stepping across the threshold: "Books are the mirrors of the soul."[24]

In this case a tarnished, a spotted soul. For as the train took over three hours to reach this remote village in the very heart of England, no one ventured so long a journey, without staving off possible mind-hunger, without buying a book on a bookstall. Thus the mirror that reflected the soul sublime, reflected also the soul bored. Nobody could pretend, as they looked at the shuffle of shilling shockers that week-enders had dropped, that the looking-glass always reflected the anguish of a Queen or the heroism of King Harry.[25]

At this early hour of a June morning the library was empty. Mrs. Giles had to visit the kitchen. Mr. Oliver still tramped the terrace. And Mrs. Swithin was of course at church. The light but variable breeze,[26] foretold by the weather expert, flapped the yellow curtain, tossing light, then shadow. The fire greyed, then glowed, and the tortoiseshell butterfly beat on the lower pane of the window; beat, beat, beat; repeating that if no human being ever came, never, never, never, the books would be mouldy, the fire out and the tortoiseshell butterfly dead on the pane.

Heralded by the impetuosity of the Afghan hound, the old man entered. He had read his paper; he was drowsy; and so sank down into the chintz-covered chair with the dog at his feet – the Afghan hound. His nose on his paws, his haunches drawn up, he looked a stone dog, a crusader's dog,[27] guarding even in the realms of death the sleep of his master. But the master was not dead; only dreaming; drowsily, seeing as in a glass, its lustre spotted, himself, a young man helmeted; and a cascade falling. But no water;[28] and the hills, like grey stuff pleated; and in the sand a hoop of ribs; a bullock maggot-eaten in the sun; and in the shadow of the rock, savages; and in his hand a gun. The dream hand clenched; the real hand lay on the chair arm, the veins swollen but only with a brownish fluid now.

The door opened.

"Am I," Isa apologized, "interrupting?"

Of course she was – destroying youth and India. It was his fault, since he had persisted in stretching his thread of life so fine, so far. Indeed he was grateful to her, watching her as she strolled about the room, for continuing.

Many old men had only their India – old men in clubs, old men in rooms off Jermyn Street.[29] She in her striped dress continued him, murmuring, in front of the book cases: "The moor is dark beneath the moon, rapid clouds have drunk the last pale beams of even. . . .[30] I have ordered the fish," she said aloud, turning, "though whether it'll be fresh or not I can't promise. But veal is dear, and everybody in the house is sick of beef and mutton. . . . Sohrab," she said, coming to a standstill in front of them, "What's *he* been doing?"

His tail never wagged. He never admitted the ties of domesticity. Either he cringed or he bit. Now his wild yellow eyes gazed at her, gazed at him. He could outstare them both. Then Oliver remembered:

"Your little boy's a cry-baby," he said scornfully.

"Oh," she sighed, pegged down on a chair arm, like a captive balloon, by a myriad of hair-thin ties into domesticity. "What's been happening?"

"I took the newspaper," he explained, "so . . ."

He took it and crumpled it into a beak over his nose. "So," he had sprung out from behind a tree on to the children.

---

[24] A variant of the popular adage "The eyes are the windows of the soul."

[25] *the anguish . . . King Harry* in "The Silver Mirror," by Arthur Conan Doyle (1859–1930), a mirror retains the anguished image of Mary Queen of Scots as she witnesses the murder of her servant Rizzio in 1566 (see *The Conan Doyle Stories* (London: John Murray, 1929), pp. 1169–80. Henry V, in Shakespeare's play *Henry V* (Act 5, Scene 2), tells Princess Katherine to love him for his heroism, since he "never looks in his glass for love of anything he sees there."

[26] A standard phrase in BBC radio weather forecasts.

[27] Stone monuments to crusaders and kings often depict a recumbent dog at its master's feet.

[28] Cf. lines 19–24 of *The Waste Land*, p. 124 in this volume.

[29] A street in London noted for smart shops dealing in men's clothing.

[30] *"The moor is dark . . . pale beams of even"* Percy Byssche Shelley (1792–1822), "Stanzas, April 1814."

"And he howled. He's a coward, your boy is."

She frowned. He was not a coward, her boy wasn't. And she loathed the domestic, the possessive; the maternal. And he knew it and did it on purpose to tease her, the old brute, her father-in-law.

She looked away.

"The library's always the nicest room in the house," she quoted, and ran her eyes along the books. "The mirror of the soul" books were. *The Faery Queen* and Kinglake's *Crimea*; Keats and the *Kreutzer Sonata*.[31] There they were, reflecting. What? What remedy was there for her at her age – the age of the century, thirty-nine – in books? Book-shy she was, like the rest of her generation; and gun-shy too. Yet as a person with a raging tooth runs her eye in a chemist shop over green bottles with gilt scrolls on them lest one of them may contain a cure, she considered: Keats and Shelley; Yeats and Donne.[32] Or perhaps not a poem; a life. The life of Garibaldi.[33] The life of Lord Palmerston.[34] Or perhaps not a person's life; a county's. *The Antiquities of Durham; The Proceedings of the Archæological Society of Nottingham*.[35] Or not a life at all, but science – Eddington, Darwin, or Jeans.[36]

None of them stopped her toothache. For her generation the newspaper was a book; and, as her father-in-law had dropped the *Times*, she took it and read: "A horse with a green tail..." which was fantastic. Next, "The guard at Whitehall..." which was romantic and then, building word upon word she read: "The troopers told her the horse had a green tail; but she found it was just an ordinary horse. And they dragged her up to the barrack room where she was thrown upon a bed. Then one of the troopers removed part of her clothing, and she screamed and hit him about the face...."[37] That was real; so real that on the mahogany door panels she saw the Arch in Whitehall;[38] through the Arch the barrack room; in the barrack room the bed, and on the bed the girl was screaming and hitting him about the face, when the door (for in fact it was a door) opened and in came Mrs. Swithin carrying a hammer.

She advanced, sidling, as if the floor were fluid under her shabby garden shoes, and, advancing, pursed her lips and smiled, sidelong, at her brother. Not a word passed between them as she went to the cupboard in the corner and replaced the hammer, which she had taken without asking leave; together – she unclosed her fist – with a handful of nails.

"Cindy – Cindy," he growled, as she shut the cupboard door.

Lucy, his sister, was three years younger than he was. The name Cindy, or Sindy, for it could be spelt either way, was short for Lucy. It was by this name that he had called her when they were children; when she had trotted after him as he fished, and had made the meadow flowers into tight little bunches, winding one long grass stalk round and round and round. Once, she remembered, he had made her take the fish off the hook herself. The blood had shocked her – "Oh!" she had cried – for the gills were full of blood. And he had growled: "Cindy!" The ghost of that morning in the meadow was in her mind as she replaced the hammer where it belonged on one shelf; and the nails where they belonged on another; and shut the cupboard about which, for he still kept his fishing tackle there, he was still so very particular.

"I've been nailing the placard on the Barn," she said, giving him a little pat on the shoulder.

---

31   Edmund Spenser (1552–99), *The Faerie Queen* (1590–6), an allegorical epic poem; Alexander Kinglake (1809–91), *Invasion of the Crimea: Its Origin and an Account of its Progress down to the Death of Lord Raglan*, 8 vols. (Edinburgh: Blackwood, 1863–87); John Keats (1795–1821), British poet; Leo Tolstoy (1828–1910), *The Kreutzer Sonata* (1890).
32   William Butler Yeats (1865–1939), Irish poet; for his work see pp. 301–72 in this volume. John Donne (1572–1631), British metaphysical poet.
33   Giuseppe Garibaldi (1807–82), a leader of the struggle for Italian independence.
34   Henry Temple (1784–1862), 3rd Viscount Palmerston, British foreign minister and prime minister.

35   Invented titles that are generic for antiquarian historiography.
36   Sir Arthur Eddington (1882–1944) was an astronomer and scientific writer on relativity; Charles Darwin (1809–82), British naturalist and author of *On the Origin of Species* (London: John Murray, 1859) and *The Descent of Man* (London: John Murray, 1871); Sir James Jeans (1877–1946) was an astronomer and scientific writer.
37   "*A horse with a green ... about the face*" the notorious rape of a 14-year-old girl by a guardsman in April 1938; the trial was reported in *The Times* on June 28–30, and July 20, 26, and 30, 1938.
38   The Arch in the Horse Guards barracks complex connects the parade ground to the forecourt off Whitehall, a London street running from Parliament to Trafalgar Square.

The words were like the first peal of a chime of bells. As the first peals, you hear the second; as the second peals, you hear the third. So when Isa heard Mrs. Swithin say: "I've been nailing the placard on the Barn," she knew she would say next:

"For the pageant."

And he would say:

"Today? By Jupiter! I'd forgotten!"

"If it's fine," Mrs. Swithin continued, "they'll act on the terrace . . ."

"And if it's wet," Bartholomew continued, "in the Barn."

"And which will it be?" Mrs. Swithin continued. "Wet or fine?"

Then, for the seventh time in succession, they both looked out of the window.

Every summer, for seven summers now, Isa had heard the same words; about the hammer and the nails; the pageant and the weather. Every year they said, would it be wet or fine; and every year it was – one or the other. The same chime followed the same chime; only this year beneath the chime she heard: "The girl screamed and hit him about the face with a hammer."

"The forecast," said Mr. Oliver, turning the pages till he found it, "says: Variable winds; fair, average temperature; rain at times."

He put down the paper, and they all looked at the sky to see whether the sky obeyed the meteorologist. Certainly the weather was variable. It was green in the garden one moment; grey the next. Here came the sun – an illimitable rapture of joy, embracing every flower, every leaf. Then in compassion it withdrew, covering its face, as if it forebore to look on human suffering. There was a fecklessness, a lack of symmetry and order in the clouds, as they thinned and thickened. Was it their own law, or no law, they obeyed? Some were wisps of white hair merely. One, high up, very distant, had hardened to golden alabaster; was made of immortal marble. Beyond that was blue, pure blue, black blue; blue that had never filtered down; that had escaped registration. It never fell as sun, shadow, or rain upon the world, but disregarded the little coloured ball of earth entirely. No flower felt it; no field; no garden.

Mrs. Swithin's eyes glazed as she looked at it. Isa thought her gaze was fixed because she saw God there, God on his throne. But as a shadow fell next moment on the garden Mrs. Swithin loosed and lowered her fixed look and said:

"It's very unsettled. It'll rain, I'm afraid. We can only pray," she added, and fingered her crucifix.

"And provide umbrellas," said her brother.

Lucy flushed. He had struck her faith. When she said "pray," he added "umbrellas." She half covered the cross with her fingers. She shrank; she cowered; but next moment she exclaimed:

"Oh there they are – the darlings!"

The perambulator was passing across the lawn.

Isa looked too. What an angel she was – the old woman! Thus to salute the children; to beat up against those immensities and the old man's irreverences her skinny hands, her laughing eyes! How courageous to defy Bart and the weather!

"He looks blooming," said Mrs. Swithin.

"It's astonishing how they pick up," said Isa.

"He ate his breakfast?" Mrs. Swithin asked.

"Every scrap," said Isa.

"And baby? No sign of measles?"

Isa shook her head. "Touch wood," she added, tapping the table.

"Tell me, Bart," said Mrs. Swithin turning to her brother, "what's the origin of that? Touch wood . . . Antaeus, didn't he touch earth?"[39]

She would have been, he thought, a very clever woman, had she fixed her gaze. But this led to that; that to the other. What went in at this ear, went out at that. And all were circled, as happens after seventy, by one recurring question. Hers was, should she live at Kensington or at Kew? But every year, when winter came, she did neither. She took lodgings at Hastings.

---

[39] *"Touch wood . . . touch earth?"* Antaeus, in Greek mythology, gained strength when he touched earth.

"Touch wood; touch earth; Antaeus," he muttered, bringing the scattered bits together. Lempriere[40] would settle it; or the Encyclopædia. But it was not in books the answer to his question – why, in Lucy's skull, shaped so much like his own, there existed a prayable being? She didn't, he supposed, invest it with hair, teeth or toenails. It was, he supposed more of a force or a radiance, controlling the thrush and the worm; the tulip and the hound; and himself, too, an old man with swollen veins. It got her out of bed on a cold morning and sent her down the muddy path to worship it, whose mouthpiece was Streatfield. A good fellow, who smoked cigars in the vestry. He needed some solace, doling out preachments to asthmatic elders, perpetually repairing the perpetually falling steeple, by means of placards nailed to Barns. The love, he was thinking, that they should give to flesh and blood they give to the church . . . when Lucy rapping her fingers on the table said:

"What's the origin – the origin – of that?"

"Superstition," he said.

She flushed, and the little breath too was audible that she drew in as once more he struck a blow at her faith. But, brother and sister, flesh and blood was not a barrier, but a mist. Nothing changed their affection; no argument; no fact; no truth. What she saw he didn't; what he saw she didn't – and so on, *ad infinitum*.

"Cindy," he growled. And the quarrel was over.

The Barn to which Lucy had nailed her placard was a great building in the farmyard. It was as old as the church, and built of the same stone, but it had no steeple. It was raised on cones of grey stone at the corners to protect it from rats and damp. Those who had been to Greece always said it reminded them of a Temple. Those who had never been to Greece – the majority – admired it all the same. The roof was weathered red-orange; and inside it was a hollow hall, sun-shafted, brown, smelling of corn, dark when the doors were shut, but splendidly illuminated when the doors at the end stood open, as they did to let the waggons in – the long low waggons, like ships of the sea, breasting the corn, not the sea, returning in the evening shagged with hay. The lanes caught tufts where the waggons had passed.

Now benches were drawn across the floor of the Barn. If it rained, the actors were to act in the Barn; planks had been laid together at one end to form a stage. Wet or fine, the audience would take tea there. Young men and women – Jim, Iris, David, Jessica – were even now busy with garlands of red and white paper roses left over from the Coronation.[41] The seeds and the dust from the sacks made them sneeze. Iris had a handkerchief bound round her forehead; Jessica wore breeches. The young men worked in shirt sleeves. Pale husks had stuck in their hair, and it was easy to run a splinter of wood into the fingers.

"Old Flimsy" (Mrs. Swithin's nickname) had been nailing another placard on the Barn. The first had been blown down, or the village idiot, who always tore down what had been nailed up, had done it, and was chuckling over the placard under the shade of some hedge. The workers were laughing too, as if old Swithin had left a wake of laughter behind her. The old girl with a wisp of white hair flying, knobbed shoes as if she had claws corned like a canary's, and black stockings wrinkled over the ankles, naturally made David cock his eye and Jessica wink back, as she handed him a length of paper roses. Snobs they were; long enough stationed that is in that one corner of the world to have taken indelibly the print of some three hundred years of customary behaviour. So they laughed; but respected. If she wore pearls, pearls they were.

"Old Flimsy on the hop," said David. She would be in and out twenty times, and finally bring them lemonade in a great jug and a plate of sandwiches. Jessie held the garland; he hammered. A hen strayed in; a file of cows passed the door; then a sheep dog; then the cowman, Bond, who stopped.

---

40   John Lempriere (1765–1824) was a British classical scholar who wrote *Bibliotheca classica or Classical Dictionary* (1788), a work that, edited by various later scholars, long remained a reference book in mythology and classical history.

41   The coronation of George VI (1895–1952) took place on May 12, 1937, or two years before the fictional time of *Between the Acts*.

He contemplated the young people hanging roses from one rafter to another. He thought very little of anybody, simples or gentry. Leaning, silent, sardonic, against the door he was like a withered willow, bent over a stream, all its leaves shed, and in his eyes the whimsical flow of the waters.

"Hi – huh!" he cried suddenly. It was cow language presumably, for the parti-coloured cow, who had thrust her head in at the door, lowered her horns, lashed her tail and ambled off. Bond followed after.

"That's the problem," said Mrs. Swithin. While Mr. Oliver consulted the Encyclopædia searching under Superstition for the origin of the expression "Touch Wood," she and Isa discussed fish: whether, coming from a distance, it would be fresh.

They were so far from the sea. A hundred miles away, Mrs. Swithin said; no, perhaps a hundred and fifty. "But they do say," she continued, "one can hear the waves on a still night. After a storm, they say, you can hear a wave break.... I like that story," she reflected. "Hearing the waves in the middle of the night he saddled a horse and rode to the sea. Who was it, Bart, who rode to the sea?"

He was reading.

"You can't expect it brought to your door in a pail of water," said Mrs. Swithin, "as I remember when we were children, living in a house by the sea. Lobsters, fresh from the lobster pots. How they pinched the stick cook gave them! And salmon. You know if they're fresh because they have lice in their scales."

Bartholomew nodded. A fact that was. He remembered, the house by the sea. And the lobster.

They were bringing up nets full of fish from the sea; but Isa was seeing – the garden, variable as the forecast said, in the light breeze. Again, the children passed, and she tapped on the window and blew them a kiss. In the drone of the garden it went unheeded.

"Are we really," she said, turning round, "a hundred miles from the sea?"

"Thirty-five only," her father-in-law said, as if he had whipped a tape measure from his pocket and measured it exactly.

"It seems more," said Isa. "It seems from the terrace as if the land went on for ever and ever."

"Once there was no sea," said Mrs. Swithin. "No sea at all between us and the continent. I was reading that in a book this morning. There were rhododendrons in the Strand; and mammoths in Piccadilly."

"When we were savages," said Isa.

Then she remembered; her dentist had told her that savages could perform very skilful operations on the brain. Savages had false teeth, he said. False teeth were invented, she thought he said, in the time of the Pharaohs.

"At least so my dentist told me," she concluded.

"Which man d'you go to now?" Mrs. Swithin asked her.

"The same old couple; Batty and Bates in Sloane Street."[42]

"And Mr. Batty told you they had false teeth in the time of the Pharaohs?" Mrs. Swithin pondered.

"Batty? Oh not Batty. Bates," Isa corrected her.

Batty, she recalled, only talked about Royalty. Batty, she told Mrs. Swithin, had a patient a Princess.

"So he kept me waiting well over an hour. And you know, when one's a child, how long that seems."

"Marriages with cousins," said Mrs. Swithin, "can't be good for the teeth."

Bart put his finger inside his mouth and projected the upper row outside his lips. They were false. Yet, he said, the Olivers hadn't married cousins. The Olivers couldn't trace their descent for more than two or three hundred years. But the Swithins could. The Swithins were there before the Conquest.[43]

---

[42] A street in the Chelsea district of London.   [43] The invasion of England in 1066 by William the Conqueror.

"The Swithins," Mrs. Swithin began. Then she stopped. Bart would crack another joke about Saints, if she gave him the chance. And she had had two jokes cracked at her already; one about an umbrella; another about superstition.

So she stopped and said, "How did we begin this talk?" She counted on her fingers. "The Pharaohs. Dentists. Fish...Oh yes, you were saying, Isa, you'd ordered fish; and you were afraid it wouldn't be fresh. And I said 'That's the problem....'"

The fish had been delivered. Mitchell's boy, holding them in a crook of his arm, jumped off his motor bike. There was no feeding the pony with lumps of sugar at the kitchen door, nor time for gossip, since his round had been increased. He had to deliver right over the hill at Bickley; also go round by Waythorn, Roddam, and Pyeminster, whose names, like his own, were in Domesday Book. But the cook – Mrs. Sands she was called, but by old friends Trixie – had never in all her fifty years been over the hill, nor wanted to.

He dabbed them down on the kitchen table, the filleted soles, the semi-transparent boneless fish. And before Mrs. Sands had time to peel the paper off, he was gone, giving a slap to the very fine yellow cat who rose majestically from the basket chair and advanced superbly to the table, winding the fish.

Were they a bit whiffy? Mrs. Sands held them to her nose. The cat rubbed itself this way, that way against the table legs, against her legs. She would save a slice for Sunny – his drawing-room name Sung-Yen had undergone a kitchen change into Sunny. She took them, the cat attendant, to the larder, and laid them on a plate in that semi-ecclesiastical apartment. For the house before the Reformation,[44] like so many houses in that neighbourhood, had a Chapel; and the Chapel had become a larder, changing, like the cat's name, as religion changed. The Master (his drawing-room name; in the kitchen they called him Bartie) would bring gentlemen sometimes to see the larder – often when cook wasn't dressed. Not to see the hams that hung from hooks, or the butter on a blue slate, or the joint for tomorrow's dinner, but to see the cellar that opened out of the larder and its carved arch. If you tapped – one gentleman had a hammer – there was a hollow sound; a reverberation; undoubtedly, he said, a concealed passage where once somebody had hid. So it might be. But Mrs. Sands wished they wouldn't come into her kitchen telling stories with the girls about. It put ideas into their silly heads. They heard dead men rolling barrels. They saw a white lady walking under the trees. No one would cross the terrace after dark. If a cat sneezed, "There's the ghost!"

Sunny had his little bit off the fillet. Then Mrs. Sands took an egg from the brown basket full of eggs; some with yellow fluff sticking to the shells; then a pinch of flour to coat those semi-transparent slips; and a crust from the great earthenware crock full of crusts. Then, returning to the kitchen, she made those quick movements at the oven, cinder raking, stoking, damping, which sent strange echoes through the house, so that in the library, the sitting-room, the dining-room, and the nursery, whatever they were doing, thinking, saying, they knew, they all knew, it was getting on for breakfast, lunch, or dinner.

"The sandwiches..." said Mrs. Swithin, coming into the kitchen. She refrained from adding "Sands" to "sandwiches," for Sand and sandwiches clashed. "Never play," her mother used to say, "on people's names." And Trixie was not a name that suited, as Sands did, the thin, acid woman, red-haired, sharp and clean, who never dashed off masterpieces, it was true; but then never dropped hairpins in the soup. "What in the name of Thunder?" Bart had said, raising a hairpin in his spoon, in the old days, fifteen years ago, before Sands came, in the time of Jessie Pook.

Mrs. Sands fetched bread; Mrs. Swithin fetched ham. One cut the bread; the other the ham. It was soothing, it was consolidating, this handwork together. The cook's hands cut, cut, cut. Whereas Lucy, holding the loaf, held the knife up. Why's stale bread, she mused, easier to cut

---

[44] Private chapels fell into disuse with the establishment of the Church of England during the reign of Henry VIII (1491–1547; reigned 1509–47). Two paragraphs above, "Domesday Book" refers to a survey of towns and properties ordered by William the Conqueror in 1086 for tax purposes, also known as the Doomsday Book.

than fresh? And so skipped, side-long, from yeast to alcohol; so to fermentation; so to inebriation; so to Bacchus;[45] and lay under purple lamps in a vineyard in Italy, as she had done, often; while Sands heard the clock tick; saw the cat; noted a fly buzz; and registered, as her lips showed, a grudge she mustn't speak against people making work in the kitchen while they had a high old time hanging paper roses in the barn.

"Will it be fine?" asked Mrs. Swithin, her knife suspended. In the kitchen they humoured old Mother Swithin's fancies.

"Seems like it," said Mrs. Sands, giving her sharp look out of the kitchen window.

"It wasn't last year," said Mrs. Swithin. "D'you remember what a rush we had – when the rain came – getting in the chairs?" She cut again. Then she asked about Billy, Mrs. Sands's nephew, apprenticed to the butcher.

"He's been doing," Mrs. Sands said, "what boys shouldn't; cheeking the master."

"That'll be all right," said Mrs. Swithin, half meaning the boy, half meaning the sandwich, as it happened a very neat one, trimmed, triangular.

"Mr. Giles may be late," she added, laying it, complacently, on top of the pile.

For Isa's husband, the stockbroker, was coming from London. And the local train, which met the express train, arrived by no means punctually, even if he caught the early train which was by no means certain. In which case it meant – but what it meant to Mrs. Sands, when people missed their trains, and she, whatever she might want to do, must wait, by the oven, keeping meat hot, no one knew.

"There!" said Mrs. Swithin, surveying the sandwiches, some neat, some not, "I'll take 'em to the barn." As for the lemonade, she assumed, without a flicker of doubt, that Jane the kitchen maid would follow after.

Candish paused in the dining-room to move a yellow rose. Yellow, white, carnation red – he placed them. He loved flowers, and arranging them, and placing the green sword or heart shaped leaf that came, fitly, between them. Queerly, he loved them, considering his gambling and drinking. The yellow rose went there. Now all was ready – silver and white, forks and napkins, and in the middle the splashed bowl of variegated roses. So, with one last look, he left the dining-room.

Two pictures hung opposite the window. In real life they had never met, the long lady and the man holding his horse by the rein. The lady was a picture, bought by Oliver because he liked the picture; the man was an ancestor. He had a name. He held the rein in his hand. He had said to the painter:

"If you want my likeness, dang it Sir, take it when the leaves are on the trees." There were leaves on the trees. He had said: "Ain't there room for Colin as well as Buster?" Colin was his famous hound. But there was only room for Buster. It was, he seemed to say, addressing the company not the painter, a damned shame to leave out Colin whom he wished buried at his feet, in the same grave, about 1750; but that skunk the Reverend Whatshisname wouldn't allow it.

He was a talk producer, that ancestor. But the lady was a picture. In her yellow robe, leaning, with a pillar to support her, a silver arrow in her hand, and a feather in her hair, she led the eye up, down, from the curve to the straight, through glades of greenery and shades of silver, dun and rose into silence. The room was empty.

Empty, empty, empty; silent, silent, silent. The room was a shell, singing of what was before time was; a vase stood in the heart of the house, alabaster, smooth, cold, holding the still, distilled essence of emptiness, silence.[46]

Across the hall a door opened. One voice, another voice, a third voice came wimpling and warbling: gruff – Bart's voice; quavering – Lucy's voice; middle-toned – Isa's voice. Their voices impetuously, impatiently, protestingly came across the hall saying: "The train's late"; saying: "Keep it hot"; saying: "We won't, no Candish, we won't wait."

[45] Roman god of wine.
[46] *In her yellow robe ... into silence* it has been suggested that this is a description of Thomas Gainsborough (1727–88), *Geor-*
gina, Duchess of Devonshire (1783), in the National Gallery of Art, Washington, DC.

Coming out from the library the voices stopped in the hall. They encountered an obstacle evidently; a rock. Utterly impossible was it, even in the heart of the country, to be alone? That was the shock. After that, the rock was raced round, embraced. If it was painful, it was essential. There must be society. Coming out of the library it was painful, but pleasant, to run slap into Mrs. Manresa[47] and an unknown young man with tow-coloured hair and a twisted face. No escape was possible; meeting was inevitable. Uninvited, unexpected, droppers-in, lured off the high road by the very same instinct that caused the sheep and the cows to desire propinquity, they had come. But they had brought a lunch basket. Here it was.

"We couldn't resist when we saw the name on the signpost," Mrs. Manresa began in her rich fluty voice. "And this is a friend – William Dodge. We were going to sit all alone in a field. And I said: 'Why not ask our dear friends,' seeing the signpost, 'to shelter us?' A seat at the table – that's all we want. We have our grub. We have our glasses. We ask nothing but – " society apparently, to be with her kind.

And she waved her hand upon which there was a glove, and under the glove it seemed rings, at old Mr. Oliver.

He bowed deep over her hand; a century ago, he would have kissed it. In all this sound of welcome, protestation, apology and again welcome, there was an element of silence, supplied by Isabella, observing the unknown young man. He was of course a gentleman; witness socks and trousers; brainy – tie spotted, waistcoat undone; urban, professional, that is putty coloured, unwholesome; very nervous, exhibiting a twitch at this sudden introduction, and fundamentally infernally conceited, for he deprecated Mrs. Manresa's effusion, yet was her guest.

Isa felt antagonised, yet curious. But when Mrs. Manresa added, to make all ship-shape: "He's an artist," and when William Dodge corrected her: "I'm a clerk in an office" – she thought he said Education or Somerset House[48] – she had her finger on the knot which had tied itself so tightly, almost to the extent of squinting, certainly of twitching, in his face.

Then they went in to lunch, and Mrs. Manresa bubbled up, enjoying her own capacity to surmount, without turning a hair, this minor social crisis – this laying of two more places. For had she not complete faith in flesh and blood? and aren't we all flesh and blood? and how silly to make bones of trifles when we're all flesh and blood under the skin – men and women too! But she preferred men – obviously.

"Or what are your rings for, and your nails, and that really adorable little straw hat?" said Isabella addressing Mrs. Manresa silently and thereby making silence add its unmistakable contribution to talk. Her hat, her rings, her finger nails red as roses, smooth as shells, were there for all to see. But not her life history. That was only scraps and fragments to all of them, excluding perhaps William Dodge, whom she called "Bill" publicly – a sign perhaps that he knew more than they did. Some of the things that he knew – that she strolled the garden at midnight in silk pyjamas, had the loud speaker playing jazz, and a cocktail bar, of course they knew also. But nothing private; no strict biographical facts.

She had been born, but it was only gossip said so, in Tasmania;[49] her grandfather had been exported for some hanky-panky mid-Victorian scandal; malversation of trusts was it? But the story got no further the only time Isabella heard it than "exported," for the husband of the communicative lady – Mrs. Blencowe of the Grange – took exception, pedantically, to "exported," said "expatriated" was more like it, but not the right word, which he had on the tip of his tongue, but couldn't get at. And so the story dwindled away. Sometimes she referred to an uncle, a Bishop. But he was thought to have been a Colonial Bishop only. They forgot and forgave very easily in the Colonies. Also it was said her diamonds and rubies had been dug out of the earth with his own hands by a "husband" who was not Ralph Manresa. Ralph, a Jew, got up to look the very spit and image of the landed gentry, supplied from directing City companies – that was certain – tons of

[47]   A town in Spain, near Barcelona, where St. Ignatius Loyola (1491–1556) in 1522 had a vision of the Virgin and wrote the first portions of his *Spiritual Exercises* (1545).

[48]   Designed by the architect Sir William Chambers (1726–96) in 1776–86, Somerset House was commissioned by Parliament to hold learned societies and government offices. In 1998 it was transformed into an arts center.

[49]   An island off the coast of Australia that had once been a British penal colony.

money; and they had no child. But surely with George the Sixth on the throne it was old fashioned, dowdy, savoured of moth-eaten furs, bugles, cameos and black-edged notepaper, to go ferreting into people's pasts?

"All I need," said Mrs. Manresa ogling Candish, as if he were a real man, not a stuffed man, "is a corkscrew." She had a bottle of champagne, but no corkscrew.

"Look, Bill," she continued, cocking her thumb – she was opening the bottle – "at the pictures. Didn't I tell you you'd have a treat?"

Vulgar she was in her gestures, in her whole person, over-sexed, over-dressed for a picnic. But what a desirable, at least valuable, quality it was – for everybody felt, directly she spoke, "She's said it, she's done it, not I," and could take advantage of the breach of decorum, of the fresh air that blew in, to follow like leaping dolphins in the wake of an ice-breaking vessel. Did she not restore to old Bartholomew his spice islands, his youth?

"I told him," she went on, ogling Bart now, "that he wouldn't look at our things" (of which they had heaps and mountains) "after yours. And I promised him you'd show him the – the –" here the champagne fizzed up and she insisted upon filling Bart's glass first. "What is it all you learned gentlemen rave about? An arch? Norman? Saxon? Who's the last from school? Mrs. Giles?"

She ogled Isabella now, conferring youth upon her; but always when she spoke to women, she veiled her eyes, for they, being conspirators, saw through it.

So with blow after blow, with champagne and ogling, she staked out her claim to be a wild child of nature, blowing into this – she did give one secret smile – sheltered harbour; which did make her smile, after London; yet it did, too, challenge London. For on she went to offer them a sample of her life; a few gobbets of gossip; mere trash; but she gave it for what it was worth; how last Tuesday she had been sitting next so and so; and she added, very casually a Christian name; then a nickname; and he'd said – for, as a mere nobody they didn't mind what they said to her – and "in strict confidence, I needn't tell you," she told them. And they all pricked their ears. And then, with a gesture of her hands as if tossing overboard that odious crackling-under-the-pot London life[50] – so – she exclaimed "There!... And what's the first thing I do when I come down here?" They had only come last night, driving through June lanes, alone with Bill it was understood, leaving London, suddenly become dissolute and dirty, to sit down to dinner. "What do I do? Can I say it aloud? Is it permitted, Mrs. Swithin? Yes, everything can be said in this house. I take off my stays" (here she pressed her hands to her sides – she was stout) "and roll in the grass. Roll – you'll believe that . . ." She laughed wholeheartedly. She had given up dealing with her figure and thus gained freedom.

"That's genuine," Isa thought. Quite genuine. And her love of the country too. Often when Ralph Manresa had to stay in town she came down alone; wore an old garden hat; taught the village women *not* how to pickle and preserve; but how to weave frivolous baskets out of coloured straw. Pleasure's what they want she said. You often heard her, if you called, yodelling among the hollyhocks "Hoity te doity te ray do . . ."

A thorough good sort she was. She made old Bart feel young. Out of the corner of his eye, as he raised his glass, he saw a flash of white in the garden: someone passing.

The scullery maid, before the plates came out, was cooling her cheeks by the lily pool.

There had always been lilies there, self-sown from wind-dropped seed, floating red and white on the green plates of their leaves. Water, for hundreds of years, had silted down into the hollow, and lay there four or five feet deep over a black cushion of mud. Under the thick plate of green water, glazed in their self-centred world, fish swam – gold, splashed with white, streaked with black or silver. Silently they manœuvred in their water world, poised in the blue patch made by the sky, or shot silently to the edge where the grass, trembling, made a fringe of nodding shadow. On the water-pavement spiders printed their delicate feet. A grain fell and spiralled down; a petal fell, filled and sank. At that the fleet of boat-shaped bodies paused; poised; equipped; mailed; then with a waver of undulation off they flashed.

[50] "As the crackling of thorns under a pot, so is the laughter of a fool" (Ecclesiastes 7:10).

It was in that deep centre, in that black heart, that the lady had drowned herself. Ten years since the pool had been dredged and a thigh bone recovered. Alas, it was a sheep's, not a lady's. And sheep have no ghosts, for sheep have no souls. But, the servants insisted, they must have a ghost; the ghost must be a lady's; who had drowned herself for love. So none of them would walk by the lily pool at night, only now when the sun shone and the gentry still sat at table.

The flower petal sank; the maid returned to the kitchen; Bartholomew sipped his wine. Happy he felt as a boy; yet reckless as an old man; an unusual, an agreeable sensation. Fumbling in his mind for something to say to the adorable lady, he chose the first thing that came handy; the story of the sheep's thigh. "Servants," he said, "must have their ghost." Kitchen maids must have their drowned lady.

"But so must I!" cried the wild child of nature, Mrs. Manresa. She became, of a sudden, solemn as an owl. She *knew*, she said, pinching a bit of bread to make this emphatic, that Ralph, when he was at the war, couldn't have been killed without her seeing him – "wherever I was, whatever I was doing," she added, waving her hands so that the diamonds flashed in the sun.

"I don't feel that," said Mrs. Swithin, shaking her head.

"No," Mrs. Manresa laughed. "You wouldn't. None of you would. You see I'm on a level with . . ." she waited till Candish had retired, "the servants. I'm nothing like so grown up as you are."

She preened, approving her adolescence. Rightly or wrongly? A spring of feeling bubbled up through her mud. They had laid theirs with blocks of marble. Sheep's bones were sheep's bones to them, not the relics of the drowned Lady Ermyntrude.

"And which camp," said Bartholomew turning to the unknown guest, "d'you belong to? The grown, or the ungrown?"

Isabella opened her mouth, hoping that Dodge would open his, and so enable her to place him. But he sat staring. "I beg your pardon, Sir?" he said. They all looked at him. "I was looking at the pictures."

The picture looked at nobody. The picture drew them down the paths of silence.

Lucy broke it.

"Mrs. Manresa, I'm going to ask you a favour – If it comes to a pinch this afternoon, will you sing?"

This afternoon? Mrs. Manresa was aghast. Was it the pageant? She had never dreamt it was this afternoon. They would never have thrust themselves in – had they known it was this afternoon. And, of course, once more the chime pealed. Isa heard the first chime; and the second; and the third – If it was wet, it would be in the Barn; if it was fine on the terrace. And which would it be, wet or fine? And they all looked out of the window. Then the door opened. Candish said Mr. Giles had come. Mr. Giles would be down in a moment.

Giles had come. He had seen the great silver-plated car at the door with the initials R. M. twisted so as to look at a distance like a coronet. Visitors, he had concluded, as he drew up behind; and had gone to his room to change. The ghost of convention rose to the surface, as a blush or a tear rises to the surface at the pressure of emotion; so the car touched his training. He must change. And he came into the dining-room looking like a cricketer, in flannels, wearing a blue coat with brass buttons; though he was enraged. Had he not read, in the morning paper, in the train, that sixteen men had been shot, others prisoned, just over there, across the gulf in the flat land which divided them from the continent?[51] Yet he changed. It was Aunt Lucy, waving her hand at him as he came in, who made him change. He hung his grievances on her, as one hangs a coat on a hook, instinctively. Aunt Lucy, foolish, free; always, since he had chosen, after leaving college, to take a job in the city, expressing her amazement, her amusement, at men who spent their lives, buying and selling – ploughs? glass beads was it? or stocks and shares? – to savages who wished most

[51]   *sixteen men . . . from the continent* British newspapers reported on the show trial of 21 men in Moscow between March 2 and 16, 1938; 18 had been executed, it was reported on March 16. The phrase "across the gulf" suggests Poyntz Hall is in Lincolnshire or Yorkshire, in the northeast of England; but other details point to Sussex, in the south. The geography is left vague – deliberately.

oddly – for were they not beautiful naked? – to dress and live like the English? A frivolous, a malignant statement hers was of a problem which, for he had no special gift, no capital, and had been furiously in love with his wife – he nodded to her across the table – had afflicted him for ten years. Given his choice, he would have chosen to farm. But he was not given his choice. So one thing led to another; and the conglomeration of things pressed you flat; held you fast, like a fish in water. So he came for the week-end, and changed.

"How d'you do?" he said all round; nodded to the unknown guest; took against him; and ate his fillet of sole.

He was the very type of all that Mrs. Manresa adored. His hair curled; far from running away, as many chins did, his was firm; the nose straight, if short; the eyes, of course, with that hair, blue; and finally to make the type complete, there was something fierce, untamed, in the expression which incited her, even at forty-five, to furbish up her ancient batteries.

"He is my husband," Isabella thought, as they nodded across the bunch of many-coloured flowers. "The father of my children." It worked, that old cliché; she felt pride; and affection; then pride again in herself, whom he had chosen. It was a shock to find, after the morning's look in the glass, and the arrow of desire[52] shot through her last night by the gentleman farmer, how much she felt when he came in, not a dapper city gent, but a cricketer, of love; and of hate.

They had met first in Scotland, fishing – she from one rock, he from another. Her line had got tangled; she had given over, and had watched him with the stream rushing between his legs, casting, casting – until, like a thick ingot of silver bent in the middle, the salmon had leapt, had been caught, and she had loved him.

Bartholomew too loved him; and noted his anger – about what? But he remembered his guest. The family was not a family in the presence of strangers. He must, rather laboriously, tell them the story of the pictures at which the unknown guest had been looking when Giles came in.

"That," he indicated the man with a horse, "was my ancestor. He had a dog. The dog was famous. The dog has his place in history. He left it on record that he wished his dog to be buried with him."

They looked at the picture.

"I always feel," Lucy broke the silence, "he's saying: 'Paint my dog.'"

"But what about the horse?" said Mrs. Manresa.

"The horse," said Bartholomew, putting on his glasses. He looked at the horse. The hind quarters were not satisfactory.

But William Dodge was still looking at the lady.

"Ah," said Bartholomew who had bought that picture because he liked that picture, "you're an artist."

Dodge denied it, for the second time in half an hour, or so Isa noted.

What for did a good sort like the woman Manresa bring these half-breeds in her trail? Giles asked himself. And his silence made its contribution to talk – Dodge that is, shook his head. "I like that picture." That was all he could bring himself to say.

"And you're right," said Bartholomew. "A man – I forget his name – a man connected with some Institute, a man who goes about giving advice, gratis, to descendants like ourselves, degenerate descendants, said . . . said . . . " He paused. They all looked at the lady. But she looked over their heads, looking at nothing. She led them down green glades into the heart of silence.

"Said it was by Sir Joshua?" Mrs. Manresa broke the silence abruptly.[53]

"No, no," William Dodge said hastily, but under his breath.

"Why's he afraid?" Isabella asked herself. A poor specimen he was; afraid to stick up for his own beliefs – just as she was afraid, of her husband. Didn't she write her poetry in a book bound like an account book lest Giles might suspect? She looked at Giles.

He had finished his fish; he had eaten quickly, not to keep them waiting. Now there was cherry tart. Mrs. Manresa was counting the stones.

---

52   *the arrow of desire* from lines 9–10 of the untitled prefatory poem to *Milton* (1804), by William Blake (1757–1827): "Bring me my bow of burning gold/Bring me my arrows of desire."

53   Sir Joshua Reynolds (1723–92), famous British artist and theoretician, first president of the Royal Academy.

"Tinker, tailor, soldier, sailor, apothecary, ploughboy[54] ... that's me!" she cried, delighted to have it confirmed by the cherry stones that she was a wild child of nature.

"You believe," said the old gentleman, courteously chaffing her, "in that too?"

"Of course, of course I do!" she cried. Now she was on the rails again. Now she was a thorough good sort again. And they too were delighted; now they could follow in her wake and leave the silver and dun shades that led to the heart of silence.

"I had a father," said Dodge beneath his breath to Isa who sat next him, "who loved pictures."

"Oh, I too!" she exclaimed. Flurriedly, disconnectedly, she explained. She used to stay when she was a child, when she had the whooping cough, with an uncle, a clergyman; who wore a skull cap; and never did anything; didn't even preach; but made up poems, walking in his garden, saying them aloud.

"People thought him mad," she said. "I didn't. . . . "

She stopped.

"Tinker, tailor, soldier, sailor, apothecary, ploughboy. . . . It appears," said old Bartholomew, laying down his spoon, "that I am a thief. Shall we take our coffee in the garden?" He rose.

Isa dragged her chair across the gravel, muttering: "To what dark antre[55] of the unvisited earth, or wind-brushed forest, shall we go now? Or spin from star to star and dance in the maze of the moon? Or. . . . "

She held her deck chair at the wrong angle. The frame with the notches was upside down.

"Songs my uncle taught me?" said William Dodge, hearing her mutter. He unfolded the chair and fixed the bar into the right notch.

She flushed, as if she had spoken in an empty room and someone had stepped out from behind a curtain.

"Don't you, if you're doing something with your hands, talk nonsense?" she stumbled. But what did he do with his hands, the white, the fine, the shapely?

Giles went back to the house and brought more chairs and placed them in a semi-circle, so that the view might be shared, and the shelter of the old wall. For by some lucky chance a wall had been built continuing the house, it might be with the intention of adding another wing, on the raised ground in the sun. But funds were lacking; the plan was abandoned, and the wall remained, nothing but a wall. Later, another generation had planted fruit trees, which in time had spread their arms widely across the red orange weathered brick. Mrs. Sands called it a good year if she could make six pots of apricot jam from them – the fruit was never sweet enough for dessert. Perhaps three apricots were worth enclosing in muslin bags. But they were so beautiful, naked, with one flushed cheek, one green, that Mrs. Swithin left them naked, and the wasps burrowed holes.

The ground sloped up, so that to quote Figgis's Guide Book (1833), "it commanded a fine view of the surrounding country. . . . The spire of Bolney Minster, Rough Norton woods, and on an eminence rather to the left, Hogben's Folly, so called because. . . . "[56]

The Guide Book still told the truth. 1833 was true in 1939. No house had been built; no town had sprung up. Hogben's Folly was still eminent; the very flat, field-parcelled land had changed only in this – the tractor had to some extent superseded the plough. The horse had gone; but the cow remained. If Figgis were here now, Figgis would have said the same. So they always said when in summer they sat there to drink coffee, if they had guests. When they were alone, they said nothing. They looked at the view; they looked at what they knew, to see if what they knew might perhaps be different today. Most days it was the same.

"That's what makes a view so sad," said Mrs. Swithin, lowering herself into the deck chair which Giles had brought her. "And so beautiful. It'll be there," she nodded at the strip of gauze laid upon the distant fields, "when we're not."

---

[54] A variant of the stone-counting game, with each stone indicating one's future occupation: "Tinker, tailor, soldier, sailor, rich man, poor man, beggarman, thief."

[55] Cave or cavern. The source of this quotation has not been identified.

[56] *Figgis's Guide Book* ... *so called because* the guide book, like Hogben's Folly, is Woolf's invention; Bolney is the name of a village in Sussex.

Giles nicked his chair into position with a jerk. Thus only could he show his irritation, his rage with old fogies who sat and looked at views over coffee and cream when the whole of Europe – over there – was bristling like.... He had no command of metaphor. Only the ineffective word "hedgehog" illustrated his vision of Europe, bristling with guns, poised with planes. At any moment guns would rake that land into furrows; planes splinter Bolney Minster into smithereens and blast the Folly. He, too, loved the view. And blamed Aunt Lucy, looking at views, instead of – doing what? What she had done was to marry a squire now dead; she had borne two children, one in Canada, the other, married, in Birmingham. His father, whom he loved, he exempted from censure; as for himself, one thing followed another; and so he sat, with old fogies, looking at views.

"Beautiful," said Mrs. Manresa, "beautiful..." she mumbled. She was lighting a cigarette. The breeze blew out her match. Giles hollowed his hand and lit another. She too was exempted – why, he could not say.

"Since you're interested in pictures," said Bartholomew, turning to the silent guest, "why, tell me, are we, as a race, so incurious, irresponsive and insensitive" – the champagne had given him a flow of unusual three-decker words – "to that noble art, whereas, Mrs. Manresa, if she'll allow me my old man's liberty, has her Shakespeare by heart?"

"Shakespeare by heart!" Mrs. Manresa protested. She struck an attitude. "To be, or not to be,[57] that is the question. Whether 'tis nobler... Go on!" she nudged Giles, who sat next her.

"Fade far away and quite forget what thou amongst the leaves hast never known..." Isa supplied the first words that came into her head by way of helping her husband out of his difficulty.

"The weariness, the torture, and the fret..."[58] William Dodge added, burying the end of his cigarette in a grave between two stones.

"There!" Bartholomew exclaimed, cocking his forefinger aloft. "That proves it! What springs touched, what secret drawer displays its treasures, if I say" – he raised more fingers – "Reynolds! Constable! Crome!"[59]

"Why called 'Old'?" Mrs. Manresa thrust in.

"We haven't the words – we haven't the words," Mrs. Swithin protested. "They're behind the eyes; not on the lips; that's all."

"Thoughts without words," her brother mused. "Can that be?"

"Quite beyond me!" cried Mrs. Manresa, shaking her head. "Much too clever! May I help myself? I know it's wrong. But I've reached the age – and the figure – when I do what I like."

She took the little silver cream jug and let the smooth fluid curl luxuriously into her coffee, to which she added a shovel full of brown sugar candy. Sensuously, rhythmically, she stirred the mixture round and round.

"Take what you like! Help yourself!" Bartholomew exclaimed. He felt the champagne withdrawing and hastened, before the last trace of geniality was withdrawn, to make the most of it, as if he cast one last look into a lit-up chamber before going to bed.

The wild child, afloat once more on the tide of the old man's benignity, looked over her coffee cup at Giles, with whom she felt in conspiracy. A thread united them – visible, invisible, like those threads, now seen, now not, that unite trembling grass blades in autumn before the sun rises. She had met him once only, at a cricket match. And then had been spun between them an early morning thread before the twigs and leaves of real friendship emerge. She looked before she drank. Looking was part of drinking. Why waste sensation, she seemed to ask, why waste a single drop that can be pressed out of this ripe, this melting, this adorable world? Then she drank. And the air round her

[57] The opening of Hamlet's soliloquy on suicide (*Hamlet*, Act 3, Scene 1).
[58] *Fade far away ... the torture, and the fret* Isa and William Dodge quotes (and misquotes) from stanza 3 of Keats's "Ode to a Nightingale":

Fade far away, dissolve, and quite forget
What thou among the leaves hast never known,

The weariness, the fever, and the fret
Here, where men sit and hear each other groan.

[59] Sir Joshua Reynolds (1723–92), the most famous artist of the eighteenth century and first president of the Royal Academy; John Constable (1776–1837), British landscape painter; John Crome (1768–1837), British landscape painter.

became threaded with sensation. Bartholomew felt it; Giles felt it. Had he been a horse, the thin brown skin would have twitched, as if a fly had settled. Isabella twitched too. Jealousy, anger, pierced her skin.

"And now," said Mrs. Manresa, putting down her cup, "about this entertainment – this pageant, into which we've gone and butted" – she made it, too, seem ripe like the apricot into which the wasps were burrowing – "Tell me, what's it to be?" She turned. "Don't I hear?" She listened. She heard laughter, down among the bushes, where the terrace dipped to the bushes.

Beyond the lily pool the ground sank again, and in that dip of the ground, bushes and brambles had mobbed themselves together. It was always shady; sun-flecked in summer, dark and damp in winter. In the summer there were always butterflies; fritillaries darting through; Red Admirals feasting and floating; cabbage whites, unambitiously fluttering round a bush, like muslin milk-maids, content to spend a life there. Butterfly catching, for generation after generation, began there; for Bartholomew and Lucy; for Giles; for George it had begun only the day before yesterday, when, in his little green net, he had caught a cabbage white.

It was the very place for a dressing-room, just as, obviously, the terrace was the very place for a play.

"The very place!" Miss La Trobe had exclaimed the first time she came to call and was shown the grounds. It was a winter's day. The trees were leafless then.

"That's the place for a pageant, Mr. Oliver!" she had exclaimed. "Winding in and out between the trees...." She waved her hand at the trees standing bare in the clear light of January.

"There the stage; here the audience; and down there among the bushes a perfect dressing-room for the actors."

She was always all agog to get things up. But where did she spring from? With that name she wasn't presumably pure English. From the Channel Islands perhaps? Only her eyes and something about her always made Mrs. Bingham suspect that she had Russian blood in her. "Those deep-set eyes; that very square jaw" reminded her – not that she had been to Russia – of the Tartars. Rumour said that she had kept a tea shop at Winchester;[60] that had failed. She had been an actress. That had failed. She had bought a four-roomed cottage and shared it with an actress. They had quarrelled. Very little was actually known about her. Outwardly she was swarthy, sturdy and thick set; strode about the fields in a smock frock; sometimes with a cigarette in her mouth; often with a whip in her hand; and used rather strong language – perhaps, then, she wasn't altogether a lady? At any rate, she had a passion for getting things up.

The laughter died away.

"Are they going to act?" Mrs. Manresa asked.

"Act; dance; sing; a little bit of everything," said Giles.

"Miss La Trobe is a lady of wonderful energy," said Mrs. Swithin.

"She makes everyone do something," said Isabella.

"Our part," said Bartholomew, "is to be the audience. And a very important part too."

"Also, we provide the tea," said Mrs. Swithin.

"Shan't we go and help?" said Mrs. Manresa. "Cut up bread and butter?"

"No, no," said Mr. Oliver. "We are the audience."

"One year we had *Gammer Gurton's Needle*,"[61] said Mrs. Swithin. "One year we wrote the play ourselves. The son of our blacksmith – Tony? Tommy? – had the loveliest voice. And Elsie at the Crossways – how she mimicked! Took us all off. Bart; Giles; Old Flimsy – that's me. People are gifted – very. The question is – how to bring it out? That's where she's so clever – Miss La Trobe. Of course, there's the whole of English literature to choose from. But how can one choose? Often on a wet day I begin counting up; what I've read; what I haven't read."

[60] A city in Hampshire, near Southampton, famous for its cathedral.   [61] A play by William Stevenson, possibly the first English comedy (c. 1553).

"And leaving books on the floor," said her brother. "Like the pig in the story; or was it a donkey?"

She laughed, tapping him lightly on the knee.

"The donkey who couldn't choose between hay and turnips and so starved," Isabella explained, interposing – anything – between her aunt and her husband, who hated this kind of talk this afternoon. Books open; no conclusion come to; and he sitting in the audience.

"We remain seated" – "We are the audience." Words this afternoon ceased to lie flat in the sentence. They rose, became menacing and shook their fists at you. This afternoon he wasn't Giles Oliver come to see the villagers act their annual pageant; manacled to a rock he was, and forced passively to behold indescribable horror. His face showed it; and Isa, not knowing what to say, abruptly, half purposely, knocked over a coffee cup.

William Dodge caught it as it fell. He held it for a moment. He turned it. From the faint blue mark, as of crossed daggers, in the glaze at the bottom he knew that it was English, made perhaps at Nottingham; date about 1760. His expression, considering the daggers, coming to this conclusion, gave Giles another peg on which to hang his rage as one hangs a coat on a peg, conveniently. A toady; a lickspittle; not a downright plain man of his senses; but a teaser and twitcher; a fingerer of sensations; picking and choosing; dillying and dallying; not a man to have straightforward love for a woman – his head was close to Isa's head – but simply a—At this word, which he could not speak in public, he pursed his lips; and the signet-ring on his little finger looked redder, for the flesh next it whitened as he gripped the arm of his chair.

"Oh what fun!" cried Mrs. Manresa in her fluty voice. "A little bit of everything. A song; a dance; then a play acted by the villagers themselves. Only," here she turned with her head on one side to Isabella, "I'm sure *she's* written it. Haven't you, Mrs. Giles?"

Isa flushed and denied it.

"For myself," Mrs. Manresa continued, "speaking plainly, I can't put two words together. I don't know how it is – such a chatterbox as I am with my tongue, once I hold a pen—" She made a face, screwed her fingers as if she held a pen in them. But the pen she held thus on the little table absolutely refused to move.

"And my handwriting – so huge – so clumsy –" She made another face and dropped the invisible pen.

Very delicately William Dodge set the cup in its saucer. "Now *he*," said Mrs. Manresa, as if referring to the delicacy with which he did this, and imputing to him the same skill in writing, "writes beautifully. Every letter perfectly formed."

Again they all looked at him. Instantly he put his hands in his pockets.

Isabella guessed the word that Giles had not spoken. Well, was it wrong if he was that word? Why judge each other? Do we know each other? Not here, not now. But somewhere, this cloud, this crust, this doubt, this dust – She waited for a rhyme, it failed her; but somewhere surely one sun would shine and all, without a doubt, would be clear.

She started. Again, sounds of laughter reached her.

"I think I hear them," she said. "They're getting ready. They're dressing up in the bushes."

Miss La Trobe was pacing to and fro between the leaning birch trees. One hand was deep stuck in her jacket pocket; the other held a foolscap sheet. She was reading what was written there. She had the look of a commander pacing his deck. The leaning graceful trees with black bracelets circling the silver bark were distant about a ship's length.

Wet would it be, or fine? Out came the sun; and, shading her eyes in the attitude proper to an Admiral on his quarter-deck, she decided to risk the engagement out of doors. Doubts were over. All stage properties, she commanded, must be moved from the Barn to the bushes. It was done. And the actors, while she paced, taking all responsibility and plumping for fine, not wet, dressed among the brambles. Hence the laughter.

The clothes were strewn on the grass. Cardboard crowns, swords made of silver paper, turbans that were sixpenny dish cloths, lay on the grass or were flung on the bushes. There were pools of red and purple in the shade; flashes of silver in the sun. The dresses attracted the butterflies. Red and silver, blue and yellow gave off warmth and sweetness. Red Admirals gluttonously absorbed richness from dish cloths, cabbage whites drank icy coolness from silver paper. Flitting, tasting, returning, they sampled the colours.

Miss La Trobe stopped her pacing and surveyed the scene. "It has the makings . . . " she murmured. For another play always lay behind the play she had just written. Shading her eyes, she looked. The butterflies circling; the light changing; the children leaping; the mothers laughing – "No, I don't get it," she muttered and resumed her pacing.

"Bossy" they called her privately, just as they called Mrs. Swithin "Flimsy." Her abrupt manner and stocky figure; her thick ankles and sturdy shoes; her rapid decisions barked out in guttural accents – all this "got their goat." No one liked to be ordered about singly. But in little troops they appealed to her. Someone must lead. Then too they could put the blame on her. Suppose it poured?

"Miss La Trobe!" they hailed her now. "What's the idea about this?"

She stopped. David and Iris each had a hand on the gramophone. It must be hidden; yet must be close enough to the audience to be heard. Well, hadn't she given orders? Where were the hurdles covered in leaves? Fetch them. Mr. Streatfield had said he would see to it. Where was Mr. Streatfield? No clergyman was visible. Perhaps he's in the Barn? "Tommy, cut along and fetch him." "Tommy's wanted in the first scene." "Beryl then . . . " The mothers disputed. One child had been chosen; another not. Fair hair was unjustly preferred to dark. Mrs. Ebury had forbidden Fanny to act because of the nettle-rash. There was another name in the village for nettle-rash.[62]

Mrs. Ball's cottage was not what you might call clean. In the last war Mrs. Ball lived with another man while her husband was in the trenches. All this Miss La Trobe knew, but refused to be mixed up in it. She splashed into the fine mesh like a great stone into the lily pool. The criss-cross was shattered. Only the roots beneath water were of use to her. Vanity, for example, made them all malleable. The boys wanted the big parts; the girls wanted the fine clothes. Expenses had to be kept down. Ten pounds was the limit. Thus conventions were outraged. Swathed in conventions, they couldn't see, as she could, that a dish cloth wound round a head in the open looked much richer than real silk. So they squabbled; but she kept out of it. Waiting for Mr. Streatfield, she paced between the birch trees.

The other trees were magnificently straight. They were not too regular; but regular enough to suggest columns in a church; in a church without a roof; in an open-air cathedral, a place where swallows darting seemed, by the regularity of the trees, to make a pattern, dancing, like the Russians, only not to music, but to the unheard rhythm of their own wild hearts.

The laughter died away.

"We must possess our souls in patience," said Mrs. Manresa again. "Or could we help?" she suggested, glancing over her shoulder, "with those chairs?"

Candish, a gardener, and a maid were all bringing chairs – for the audience. There was nothing for the audience to do. Mrs. Manresa suppressed a yawn. They were silent. They stared at the view, as if something might happen in one of those fields to relieve them of the intolerable burden of sitting silent, doing nothing, in company. Their minds and bodies were too close, yet not close enough. We aren't free, each one of them felt separately, to feel or think separately, nor yet to fall asleep. We're too close; but not close enough; too close, but not close enough. So they fidgeted.

The heat had increased. The clouds had vanished. All was sun now. The view laid bare by the sun was flattened, silenced, stilled. The cows were motionless; the brick wall, no longer sheltering, beat back grains of heat. Old Mr. Oliver sighed profoundly. His head jerked; his hand fell. It fell within an inch of the dog's head on the grass by his side. Then up he jerked it again on to his knee.

Giles glared. With his hands bound tight round his knees he stared at the flat fields. Staring, glaring, he sat silent.

Isabella felt prisoned. Through the bars of the prison, through the sleep haze that deflected them, blunt arrows bruised her; of love, then of hate. Through other people's bodies she felt neither love nor hate distinctly. Most consciously she felt – she had drunk sweet wine at luncheon – a desire for

---

[62]   Probably body lice, which bite and cause irritation. Two paragraphs below: "Russians" refers to the Bullets Russes, founded in 1909 and led by Sergei Diaghilev, which had toured throughout Europe for 30 years, and become synonymous with modern dance.

water. "A beaker of cold water,[63] a beaker of cold water," she repeated, and saw water surrounded by walls of shining glass.

Mrs. Manresa longed to relax and curl in a corner with a cushion, a picture paper,[64] and a bag of sweets.

Mrs. Swithin and William surveyed the view aloofly, and with detachment.

How tempting, how very tempting, to let the view triumph; to reflect its ripple; to let their own minds ripple; to let outlines elongate and pitch over – so – with a sudden jerk.

Mrs. Manresa yielded, pitched, plunged, then pulled herself up.

"What a view!" she exclaimed, pretending to dust the ashes of her cigarette, but in truth concealing her yawn. Then she sighed, pretending to express not her own drowsiness, but something connected with what she felt about views.

Nobody answered her. The flat fields glared green yellow, blue yellow, red yellow, then blue again. The repetition was senseless, hideous, stupefying.

"Then," said Mrs. Swithin, in a low voice, as if the exact moment for speech had come, as if she had promised, and it was time to fulfil her promise, "come, come and I'll show you the house."

She addressed no one in particular. But William Dodge knew she meant him. He rose with a jerk, like a toy suddenly pulled straight by a string.

"What energy!" Mrs. Manresa half sighed, half yawned. "Have I the courage to go too?" Isabella asked herself. They were going; above all things, she desired cold water, a beaker of cold water; but desire petered out, suppressed by the leaden duty she owed to others. She watched them go – Mrs. Swithin tottering yet tripping; and Dodge unfurled and straightened, as he strode beside her along the blazing tiles under the hot wall, till they reached the shade of the house.

A match-box fell – Bartholomew's. His fingers had loosed it; he had dropped it. He gave up the game; he couldn't be bothered. With his head on one side, his hand dangling above the dog's head he slept; he snored.

Mrs. Swithin paused for a moment in the hall among the gilt-clawed tables.

"This," she said, "is the staircase. And now – up we go."

She went up, two stairs ahead of her guest. Lengths of yellow satin unfurled themselves on a cracked canvas as they mounted.

"Not an ancestress," said Mrs. Swithin, as they came level with the head in the picture. "But we claim her because we've known her – O, ever so many years. Who was she?" she gazed. "Who painted her?" She shook her head. She looked lit up, as if for a banquet, with the sun pouring over her.

"But I like her best in the moonlight," Mrs. Swithin reflected, and mounted more stairs.

She panted slightly, going up stairs. Then she ran her hand over the sunk books in the wall on the landing, as if they were pan pipes.

"Here are the poets from whom we descend by way of the mind, Mr. . . . . " she murmured. She had forgotten his name. Yet she had singled him out.

"My brother says, they built the house north for shelter, not south for sun. So they're damp in the winter." She paused. "And now what comes next?"

She stopped. There was a door.

"The morning room." She opened the door. "Where my mother received her guests."

Two chairs faced each other on either side of a fine fluted mantelpiece. He looked over her shoulder.

She shut the door.

"Now up, now up again." Again they mounted. "Up and up they went," she panted, seeing, it seemed, an invisible procession, "up and up to bed."

---

[63]   Isa revises a line from Keats's "Ode to a Nightingale": "O for   [64]   An illustrated newspaper.
a beaker of the warm South."

"A bishop; a traveller; – I've forgotten even their names. I ignore. I forget."

She stopped at a window in the passage and held back the curtain. Beneath was the garden, bathed in sun. The grass was sleek and shining. Three white pigeons were flirting and tiptoeing as ornate as ladies in ball dresses. Their elegant bodies swayed as they minced with tiny steps on their little pink feet upon the grass. Suddenly, up they rose in a flutter, circled, and flew away.

"Now," she said, "for the bedrooms." She tapped twice very distinctly on a door. With her head on one side, she listened.

"One never knows," she murmured, "if there's somebody there." Then she flung open the door.

He half expected to see somebody there, naked, or half dressed, or knelt in prayer. But the room was empty. The room was tidy as a pin, not slept in for months, a spare room. Candles stood on the dressing-table. The counterpane was straight. Mrs. Swithin stopped by the bed.

"Here," she said, "yes, here," she tapped the counterpane, "I was born. In this bed."

Her voice died away. She sank down on the edge of the bed. She was tired, no doubt, by the stairs, by the heat.

"But we have other lives, I think, I hope," she murmured. "We live in others, Mr. . . . We live in things."

She spoke simply. She spoke with an effort. She spoke as if she must overcome her tiredness out of charity towards a stranger, a guest. She had forgotten his name. Twice she had said "Mr." and stopped.

The furniture was mid-Victorian, bought at Maples,[65] perhaps, in the forties. The carpet was covered with small purple dots. And a white circle marked the place where the slop pail had stood by the washstand.

Could he say "I'm William"? He wished to. Old and frail she had climbed the stairs. She had spoken her thoughts, ignoring, not caring if he thought her, as he had, inconsequent, sentimental, foolish. She had lent him a hand to help him up a steep place. She had guessed his trouble. Sitting on the bed he heard her sing, swinging her little legs, "Come and see my sea weeds, come and see my sea shells, come and see my dicky bird hop upon its perch" – an old child's nursery rhyme to help a child. Standing by the cupboard in the corner he saw her reflected in the glass. Cut off from their bodies, their eyes smiled, their bodiless eyes, at their eyes in the glass.

Then she slipped off the bed.

"Now," she said, "what comes next?" and pattered down the corridor. A door stood open. Everyone was out in the garden. The room was like a ship deserted by its crew. The children had been playing – there was a spotted horse in the middle of the carpet. The nurse had been sewing – there was a piece of linen on the table. The baby had been in the cot. The cot was empty.

"The nursery," said Mrs. Swithin.

Words raised themselves and became symbolical. "The cradle of our race," she seemed to say.

Dodge crossed to the fireplace and looked at the Newfoundland Dog in the Christmas Annual[66] that was pinned to the wall. The room smelt warm and sweet; of clothes drying; of milk; of biscuits and warm water. "Good Friends" the picture was called. A rushing sound came in through the open door. He turned. The old woman had wandered out into the passage and leant against the window.

He left the door open for the crew to come back to and joined her.

Down in the courtyard beneath the window cars were assembling. Their narrow black roofs were laid together like the blocks of a floor. Chauffeurs were jumping down; here old ladies gingerly advanced black legs with silver-buckled shoes; old men striped trousers. Young men in shorts leapt out on one side; girls with skin-coloured legs on the other. There was a purring and a churning of the yellow gravel. The audience was assembling. But they, looking down from the window, were truants, detached. Together they leant half out of the window.

And then a breeze blew and all the muslin blinds fluttered out, as if some majestic Goddess, rising from her throne among her peers, had tossed her amber-coloured raiment, and the other gods, seeing her rise and go, laughed, and their laughter floated her on.

---

[65] Maple & Co. was a well-known London furniture store in Tottenham Court Road in London.

[66] A sentimental anthology aimed at the Christmas market.

Mrs. Swithin put her hands to her hair, for the breeze had ruffled it.

"Mr. . . . " she began.

"I'm William," he interrupted.

At that she smiled a ravishing girl's smile, as if the wind had warmed the wintry blue in her eyes to amber.

"I took you," she apologized, "away from your friends, William, because I felt wound tight here. . . ." She touched her bony forehead upon which a blue vein wriggled like a blue worm. But her eyes in their caves of bone were still lambent. He saw her eyes only. And he wished to kneel before her, to kiss her hand, and to say: "At school they held me under a bucket of dirty water, Mrs. Swithin; when I looked up, the world was dirty, Mrs. Swithin; so I married; but my child's not my child, Mrs. Swithin. I'm a half-man, Mrs. Swithin; a flickering, mind-divided little snake in the grass, Mrs. Swithin; as Giles saw; but you've healed me. . . ." So he wished to say; but said nothing; and the breeze went lolloping along the corridors, blowing the blinds out.

Once more he looked and she looked down on to the yellow gravel that made a crescent round the door. Pendant from her chain her cross swung as she leant out and the sun struck it. How could she weight herself down by that sleek symbol? How stamp herself, so volatile, so vagrant, with that image? As he looked at it, they were truants no more. The purring of the wheels became vocal. "Hurry, hurry, hurry," it seemed to say, "or you'll be late. Hurry, hurry, hurry, or the best seats'll be taken."

"O," cried Mrs. Swithin, "there's Mr. Streatfield!" And they saw a clergyman, a strapping clergyman, carrying a hurdle, a leafy hurdle. He was striding through the cars with the air of a person of authority, who is awaited, expected, and now comes.

"Is it time," said Mrs. Swithin, "to go and join——" She left the sentence unfinished, as if she were of two minds, and they fluttered to right and to left, like pigeons rising from the grass.

The audience was assembling. They came streaming along the paths and spreading across the lawn. Some were old; some were in the prime of life. There were children among them. Among them, as Mr. Figgis might have observed, were representatives of our most respected families – the Dyces of Denton;[67] the Wickhams of Owlswick; and so on. Some had been there for centuries, never selling an acre. On the other hand there were new-comers, the Manresas, bringing the old houses up to date, adding bathrooms. And a scatter of odds and ends, like Cobbet of Cobbs Corner, retired, it was understood, on a pension from a tea plantation. Not an asset. He did his own housework and dug in his garden. The building of a car factory and of an aerodrome in the neighbourhood had attracted a number of unattached floating residents. Also there was Mr. Page, the reporter, representing the local paper. Roughly speaking, however, had Figgis been there in person and called a roll call, half the ladies and gentlemen present would have said: "*Adsum*;[68] I'm here, in place of my grandfather or great-grandfather," as the case might be. At this very moment, half-past three on a June day in 1939 they greeted each other, and as they took their seats, finding if possible a seat next one another, they said: "That hideous new house at Pyes Corner! What an eyesore! And those bungalows! – have you seen 'em?"

Again, had Figgis called the names of the villagers, they too would have answered. Mrs. Sands was born Iliffe; Candish's mother was one of the Perrys. The green mounds in the churchyard had been cast up by their molings, which for centuries had made the earth friable. True, there were absentees when Mr. Streatfield called his roll call in the church. The motor bike, the motor bus, and the movies – when Mr. Streatfield called his roll call, he laid the blame on them.

Rows of chairs, deck chairs, gilt chairs, hired cane chairs, and indigenous garden seats had been drawn up on the terrace. There were plenty of seats for everybody. But some preferred to sit on the ground. Certainly Miss La Trobe had spoken the truth when she said: "The very place for a pageant!" The lawn was as flat as the floor of a theatre. The terrace, rising, made a natural stage. The trees barred the stage like pillars. And the human figure was seen to great advantage against

---

[67] *Denton* a village in Sussex; the other names are fictional. [68] The traditional Latin response ("Present") when roll was called at a boy's public school; i.e. an elite private school.

a background of sky. As for the weather, it was turning out, against all expectation, a very fine day. A perfect summer afternoon.

"What luck!" Mrs. Carter was saying. "Last year..." Then the play began. Was it, or was it not, the play? Chuff, chuff, chuff sounded from the bushes. It was the noise a machine makes when something has gone wrong. Some sat down hastily; others stopped talking guiltily. All looked at the bushes. For the stage was empty. Chuff, chuff, chuff the machine buzzed in the bushes. While they looked apprehensively and some finished their sentences, a small girl, like a rosebud in pink, advanced; took her stand on a mat, behind a conch hung with leaves, and piped:

Gentles and simples, I address you all...

So it was the play then. Or was it the prologue?

> *Come hither for our festival* (she continued)
> *This is a pageant, all may see*
> *Drawn from our island history.*
> *England am I....*

"She's England," they whispered. "It's begun." "The prologue," they added, looking down at the programme.

"*England am I*," she piped again; and stopped.

She had forgotten her lines.

"Hear! Hear!" said an old man in a white waistcoat briskly. "Bravo! Bravo!"

"Blast 'em!" cursed Miss La Trobe, hidden behind the tree. She looked along the front row. They glared as if they were exposed to a frost that nipped them and fixed them all at the same level. Only Bond the cowman looked fluid and natural.

"Music!" she signalled. "Music!" But the machine continued: Chuff, chuff, chuff.

"*A child new born...*" she prompted.

"*A child new born,*" Phyllis Jones continued,

> *Sprung from the sea*
> *Whose billows blown by mighty storm*
> *Cut off from France and Germany*
> *This isle.*

She glanced back over her shoulder. Chuff, chuff, chuff, the machine buzzed. A long line of villagers in shirts made of sacking began passing in and out in single file behind her between the trees. They were singing, but not a word reached the audience.

"*England am I,*" Phyllis Jones continued, facing the audience,

> *Now weak and small*
> *A child, as all may see...*

Her words peppered the audience as with a shower of hard little stones. Mrs. Manresa in the very centre smiled; but she felt as if her skin cracked when she smiled. There was a vast vacancy between her, the singing villagers and the piping child.

Chuff, chuff, chuff, went the machine like a corn-cutter on a hot day.

The villagers were singing, but half their words were blown away.

Cutting the roads... up to the hill top... we climbed. Down in the valley... saw wild boar, hog, rhinoceros, reindeer... Dug ourselves in to the hill top... Ground roots between stones... Ground corn... till we too... lay under g-r-o-u-n-d...

The words petered away. Chuff, chuff, chuff, the machine ticked. Then at last the machine ground out a tune!

> *Armed against fate*
> *The valiant Rhoderick*

> *Armed and valiant*
> *Bold and blatant*
> *Firm elatant*
> *See the warriors – here they come...*

The pompous popular tune brayed and blared. Miss La Trobe watched from behind the tree. Muscles loosened; ice cracked. The stout lady in the middle began to beat time with her hand on her chair. Mrs. Manresa was humming:

> My home is at Windsor,[69] close to the Inn.
> Royal George is the name of the pub.
> And boys you'll believe me,
> I don't want no asking...

She was afloat on the stream of the melody. Radiating royalty, complacency, good humour, the wild child was Queen of the festival. The play had begun.

But there was an interruption. "O," Miss La Trobe growled behind her tree, "the torture of these interruptions!"

"Sorry I'm so late," said Mrs. Swithin. She pushed her way through the chairs to a seat beside her brother.

"What's it all about? I've missed the prologue. England? That little girl? Now she's gone..." Phyllis had slipped off her mat.

"And who's this?" asked Mrs. Swithin.

It was Hilda, the carpenter's daughter. She now stood where England had stood.

"*O, England's grown...*" Miss La Trobe prompted her.

"*O, England's grown a girl now,*" Hilda sang out

("What a lovely voice!" someone exclaimed)

> *With roses in her hair,*
> *Wild roses, red roses,*
> *She roams the lanes and chooses*
> *A garland for her hair.*

"A cushion? Thank you so much," said Mrs. Swithin, stuffing the cushion behind her back. Then she leant forward.

"That's England in the time of Chaucer,[70] I take it. She's been maying, nutting. She has flowers in her hair...But those passing behind her –" she pointed. "The Canterbury pilgrims? Look!"

All the time the villagers were passing in and out between the trees. They were singing; but only a word or two was audible: "*...wore ruts in the grass...built the house in the lane...*" The wind blew away the connecting words of their chant, and then, as they reached the tree at the end they sang: "*To the shrine of the Saint...to the tomb...lovers...believers...we come...*"

They grouped themselves together.

Then there was a rustle and an interruption. Chairs were drawn back. Isa looked behind her. Mr. and Mrs. Rupert Haines, detained by a breakdown on the road, had arrived. He was sitting to the right, several rows back, the man in grey.

Meanwhile the pilgrims, having done their homage to the tomb, were, it appeared, tossing hay on their rakes.

> *I kissed a girl and let her go,*
> *Another did I tumble,*
> *In the straw and in the hay...*

---

[69] A song in the style of music-hall lyrics, mocking the royal family whose castle is at Windsor.

[70] Geoffrey Chaucer (*c.* 1345–1400), British poet; for some his work is the very type of merry England.

– that was what they were singing, as they scooped and tossed the invisible hay, when she looked round again.

"Scenes from English history," Mrs. Manresa explained to Mrs. Swithin. She spoke in a loud cheerful voice, as if the old lady were deaf. "Merry England."

She clapped energetically.

The singers scampered away into the bushes. The tune stopped. Chuff, chuff, chuff, the machine ticked. Mrs. Manresa looked at her programme. It would take till midnight unless they skipped. Early Britons; Plantagenets; Tudors; Stuarts[71] – she ticked them off, but probably she had forgotten a reign or two.

"Ambitious, ain't it?"[72] she said to Bartholomew, while they waited. Chuff, chuff, chuff went the machine. Could they talk? Could they move? No, for the play was going on. Yet the stage was empty; only the cows moved in the meadows; only the tick of the gramophone needle was heard. The tick, tick, tick seemed to hold them together, tranced. Nothing whatsoever appeared on the stage.

"I'd no notion we looked so nice," Mrs. Swithin whispered to William. Hadn't she? The children; the pilgrims; behind the pilgrims the trees, and behind them the fields – the beauty of the visible world took his breath away. Tick, tick, tick the machine continued.

"Marking time," said old Oliver beneath his breath.

"Which don't exist for us," Lucy murmured. "We've only the present."

"Isn't that enough?" William asked himself. Beauty – isn't that enough? But here Isa fidgetted. Her bare brown arms went nervously to her head. She half turned in her seat. "No, not for us, who've the future," she seemed to say. The future disturbing our present. Who was she looking for? William, turning, following her eyes, saw only a man in grey.

The ticking stopped. A dance tune was put on the machine. In time to it, Isa hummed: "What do I ask? To fly away, from night and day, and issue where – no partings are – but eye meets eye – and ... O," she cried aloud: "Look at her!"

Everyone was clapping and laughing. From behind the bushes issued Queen Elizabeth – Eliza Clark, licensed to sell tobacco. Could she be Mrs. Clark of the village shop? She was splendidly made up. Her head, pearl-hung, rose from a vast ruff. Shiny satins draped her. Sixpenny brooches glared like cats' eyes and tigers' eyes; pearls looked down; her cape was made of cloth of silver – in fact swabs used to scour saucepans. She looked the age in person. And when she mounted the soap box in the centre, representing perhaps a rock in the ocean, her size made her appear gigantic. She could reach a flitch of bacon or haul a tub of oil with one sweep of her arm in the shop. For a moment she stood there, eminent, dominant, on the soap box with the blue and sailing clouds behind her. The breeze had risen.

The Queen of this great land ... – those were the first words that could be heard above the roar of laughter and applause.

> *Mistress of ships and bearded men* (she bawled)
> *Hawkins, Frobisher, Drake,*[73]
> *Tumbling their oranges, ingots of silver,*
> *Cargoes of diamonds, ducats of gold,*
> *Down on the jetty, there in the west land,* –
> (she pointed her fist at the blazing blue sky)
> *Mistress of pinnacles, spires and palaces* –
> (her arm swept towards the house)
> *For me Shakespeare sang* –
> (a cow mooed. A bird twittered)
> *The throstle, the mavis* (she continued)

[71] The Plantagenets ruled England from Henry II (1133–89) through Richard III (1452–85); the Tudors ruled from Henry VII (1457–1509) through Elizabeth I (1533–1603); the Stuarts ruled from James VI and I (1565–1625) through Queen Anne (1665–1714).

[72] *ain't it* upper-class slang at this time.

[73] Sir John Hawkins (1532–95), Sir Martin Frobisher (c. 1535–94), and Sir Francis Drake (c. 1549–96) were Elizabethan naval commanders and privateers; empire-builders in the hagiography of empire.

> *In the green wood, the wild wood,*
> *Carolled and sang, praising England, the Queen,*
> *Then there was heard too*
> *On granite and cobble*
> *From Windsor to Oxford*
> *Loud laughter, low laughter*
> *Of warrior and lover,*
> *The fighter, the singer.*
> *The ashen haired babe*
> (she stretched out her swarthy, muscular arm)
> *Stretched his arm in contentment*
> *As home from the Isles came*
> *The sea faring men. . . .*

Here the wind gave a tug at her head dress. Loops of pearls made it top-heavy. She had to steady the ruffle which threatened to blow away.

"Laughter, loud laughter," Giles muttered. The tune on the gramophone reeled from side to side as if drunk with merriment. Mrs. Manresa began beating her foot and humming in time to it.

"Bravo! Bravo!" she cried. "There's life in the old dog yet!" And she trolloped out the words of the song with an abandonment which, if vulgar, was a great help to the Elizabethan age. For the ruff had become unpinned and great Eliza had forgotten her lines. But the audience laughed so loud that it did not matter.

"I fear I am not in my perfect mind,"[74] Giles muttered to the same tune. Words came to the surface – he remembered "a stricken deer[75] in whose lean flank the world's harsh scorn has struck its thorn. . . . Exiled from its festival, the music turned ironical. . . . A churchyard haunter at whom the owl hoots and the ivy mocks tap-tap-tapping on the pane. . . . For they are dead, and I . . . I . . . I," he repeated, forgetting the words, and glaring at his Aunt Lucy who sat craned forward, her mouth gaping, and her bony little hands clapping.

What were they laughing at?

At Albert, the village idiot, apparently. There was no need to dress him up. There he came, acting his part to perfection. He came ambling across the grass, mopping and mowing.

> *I know where the tit nests,* he began
> *In the hedgerow. I know, I know –*
> *What don't I know?*
> *All your secrets, ladies,*
> *And yours too, gentlemen . . .*

He skipped along the front row of the audience, leering at each in turn. Now he was picking and plucking at Great Eliza's skirts. She cuffed him on the ear. He tweaked her back. He was enjoying himself immensely.

"Albert having the time of his life," Bartholomew muttered.

"Hope he don't have a fit," Lucy murmured.

"*I know . . . I know . . .*" Albert tittered, skipping round the soap box.

"The village idiot," whispered a stout black lady – Mrs. Elmhurst – who came from a village ten miles distant where they, too, had an idiot. It wasn't nice. Suppose he suddenly did something dreadful? There he was pinching the Queen's skirts. She half covered her eyes, in case he did do – something dreadful.

---

[74] Giles is quoting King Lear's line in madness (*King Lear*, Act 4, Scene 7).

[75] Adapted from William Cowper (1731–1800), *The Task*, Book III, lines 108–10:

I was a stricken deer, that left the herd
Long since; with many an arrow deep infixt
My panting side was charged.

Hoppety, jiggety, Albert resumed,
In at the window, out at the door,
What does the little bird hear? (He whistled on his fingers.)
And see! There's a mouse....
(he made as if chasing it through the grass)
Now the clock strikes!
(he stood erect, puffing out his cheeks as if he were blowing a dandelion clock)
One, two, three, four....

And off he skipped, as if his turn was over.

"Glad that's over," said Mrs. Elmhurst, uncovering her face. "Now what comes next? A tableau ... ?"

For helpers, issuing swiftly from the bushes, carrying hurdles, had enclosed the Queen's throne with screens papered to represent walls. They had strewn the ground with rushes. And the pilgrims who had continued their march and their chant in the background, now gathered round the figure of Eliza on her soap box as if to form the audience at a play.

Were they about to act a play in the presence of Queen Elizabeth? Was this, perhaps, the Globe theatre?[76]

"What does the programme say?" Mrs. Herbert Winthrop asked, raising her lorgnette.

She mumbled through the blurred carbon sheet. Yes; it was a scene from a play.

"About a false Duke; and a Princess disguised as a boy; then the long lost heir turns out to be the beggar, because of a mole on his cheek; and Carinthia – that's the Duke's daughter, only she's been lost in a cave – falls in love with Ferdinando who had been put into a basket as a baby by an aged crone. And they marry.[77] That's I think what happens," she said, looking up from the programme.

"Play out the play,"[78] great Eliza commanded. An aged crone tottered forward.

("Mrs. Otter of the End House," someone murmured.)

She sat herself on a packing case, and made motions, plucking her dishevelled locks and rocking herself from side to side as if she were an aged beldame in a chimney corner.

("The crone, who saved the rightful heir," Mrs. Winthrop explained.)

'Twas a winter's night (she croaked out)
I mind me that, I to whom all's one now, summer or winter.
You say the sun shines? I believe you, Sir.
"Oh but it's winter, and the fog's abroad"
All's one to Elsbeth, summer or winter,
By the fireside, in the chimney corner, telling her beads.
I've cause to tell 'em.
Each bead (she held a bead between thumb and finger)
A crime!
'Twas a winter's night, before cockcrow,
Yet the cock did crow ere he left me –
The man with a hood on his face, and the bloody hands
And the babe in the basket.
"Tee hee" he mewed, as who should say "I want my toy"
Poor witling!
"Tee hee, tee hee!" I could not slay him!
For that, Mary in Heaven forgive me
The sins I've sinned before cockcrow!
Down to the creek i' the dawn I slipped
Where the gull haunts and the heron stands

[76] The theater (built 1599, rebuilt 1614, closed 1642) where Shakespeare was a shareholder and had plays produced.
[77] *"About a false Duke ... And they marry."* a medley of plot elements from Shakespeare's *The Tempest, As you Like It, Cymbeline, The Winter's Tale.* Carinthia is the heroine of a novel by George Meredith (1828–1909), *The Amazing Marriage* (1895), in which she marries the Earl of Fleetwood.
[78] Falstaff says this when asking to justify himself to Prince Hal in Shakespeare's *i Henry IV,* Act 2, Scene 4.

> *Like a stake on the edge of the marshes . . .*
> *Who's here?*
> (Three young men swaggered on to the stage and accosted her)
> *— Are you come to torture me, Sirs?*
> *There is little blood in this arm,*
> (she extended her skinny forearm from her ragged shift)
> *Saints in Heaven preserve me!*

She bawled. They bawled. All together they bawled, and so loud that it was difficult to make out what they were saying: apparently it was: *Did she remember concealing a child in a cradle among the rushes some twenty years previously? A babe in a basket, crone! A babe in a basket?* they bawled. *The wind howls and the bittern shrieks,* she replied.

"There is little blood in my arm," Isabella repeated.

That was all she heard. There was such a medley of things going on, what with the beldame's deafness, the bawling of the youths, and the confusion of the plot that she could make nothing of it.

Did the plot matter? She shifted and looked over her right shoulder. The plot was only there to beget emotion. There were only two emotions: love; and hate. There was no need to puzzle out the plot. Perhaps Miss La Trobe meant that when she cut this knot in the centre?

Don't bother about the plot: the plot's nothing.

But what was happening? The Prince had come.

Plucking up his sleeve, the beldame recognized the mole; and, staggering back in her chair, shrieked:

> *My child! My child!*

Recognition followed. The young Prince (Albert Perry) was almost smothered in the withered arms of the beldame. Then suddenly he started apart.

Look where she comes! he cried.

They all looked where she came — Sylvia Edwards in white satin.

Who came? Isa looked. The nightingale's song? The pearl in night's black ear? Love embodied.

All arms were raised; all faces stared.

Hail, sweet Carinthia! said the Prince, sweeping his hat off. And she to him, raising her eyes: *My love! My Lord!*

"It was enough. Enough. Enough," Isa repeated.

All else was verbiage, repetition.

The beldame meanwhile, because that was enough, had sunk back on her chair, the beads dangling from her fingers.

Look to the beldame there — old Elsbeth's sick! (They crowded round her)

Dead, Sirs!

She fell back lifeless. The crowd drew away.

> *Peace, let her pass. She to whom all's one now, summer or winter.*

Peace was the third emotion. Love. Hate. Peace. Three emotions made the ply of human life. Now the priest, whose cotton wool moustache confused his utterance, stepped forward and pronounced benediction.

> *From the distaff of life's tangled skein, unloose her hands*
> (They unloosed her hands)
> *Of her frailty, let nothing now remembered be.*
> *Call for the robin redbreast and the wren.*
> *And roses fall your crimson pall.*
> (Petals were strewn from wicker baskets)
> *Cover the corpse. Sleep well.*

(They covered the corpse)
On you, fair Sirs (he turned to the happy couple)
Let Heaven rain benediction!
Haste ere the envying sun
Night's curtain hath undone. Let music sound
And the free air of Heaven waft you to your slumber!
Lead on the dance!

The gramophone blared. Dukes, priests, shepherds, pilgrims and serving men took hands and danced. The idiot scampered in and out. Hands joined, heads knocking, they danced round the majestic figure of the Elizabethan age personified by Mrs. Clark, licensed to sell tobacco, on her soap box.

It was a mellay; a medley; an entrancing spectacle (to William) of dappled light and shade on half clothed, fantastically coloured, leaping, jerking, swinging legs and arms. He clapped till his palms stung.

Mrs. Manresa applauded loudly. Somehow she was the Queen; and he (Giles) was the surly hero.

"Bravo! Bravo!" she cried, and her enthusiasm made the surly hero squirm on his seat. Then the great lady in the bath chair, the lady whose marriage with the local peer had obliterated in his trashy title a name that had been a name when there were brambles and briars where the Church now stood – so indigenous was she that even her body, crippled by arthritis, resembled an uncouth, nocturnal animal, now nearly extinct – clapped and laughed loud – the sudden laughter of a startled jay.

"Ha, ha, ha!" she laughed and clutched the arms of her chair with ungloved twisted hands.

A maying, a maying, they bawled.
In and out and round about, a maying,
a maying. . . .

It didn't matter what the words were; or who sang what. Round and round they whirled, intoxicated by the music. Then, at a sign from Miss La Trobe behind the tree, the dance stopped. A procession formed. Great Eliza descended from her soap box. Taking her skirts in her hand, striding with long strides, surrounded by Dukes and Princes, followed by the lovers arm in arm, with Albert the idiot playing in and out, and the corpse on its bier concluding the procession, the Elizabethan age passed from the scene.

"Curse! Blast! Damn 'em!" Miss La Trobe in her rage stubbed her toe against a root. Here was her downfall; here was the Interval. Writing this skimble-skamble stuff in her cottage, she had agreed to cut the play here; a slave to her audience, – to Mrs. Sands' grumble – about tea; about dinner; – she had gashed the scene here. Just as she had brewed emotion, she spilt it. So she signalled: Phyllis! And, summoned, Phyllis popped up on the mat again in the middle.

Gentles and simples, I address you all (she piped.)
Our act is done, our scene is over.
Past is the day of crone and lover.
The bud has flowered; the flower has fallen.
But soon will rise another dawning,
For time whose children small we be
Hath in his keeping, you shall see,
You shall see. . . .

Her voice petered out. No one was listening. Heads bent, they read "Interval" on the programme. And, cutting short her words, the megaphone announced in plain English: "An interval." Half an hour's interval, for tea. Then the gramophone blared out:

Armed against fate,
The valiant Rhoderick,

> *Bold and blatant,*
> *Firm, elatant, etc., etc.*

At that, the audience stirred. Some rose briskly; others stooped, retrieving walking-sticks, hats, bags. And then, as they raised themselves and turned about, the music modulated. The music chanted: *Dispersed are we*. It moaned: *Dispersed are we*. It lamented: *Dispersed are we*, as they streamed, spotting the grass with colour, across the lawns, and down the paths: *Dispersed are we*.

Mrs. Manresa took up the strain. *Dispersed are we*. "Freely, boldly, fearing no one" (she pushed a deck chair out of her way). "Youths and maidens" (she glanced behind her: but Giles had his back turned). "Follow, follow, follow me.... Oh Mr. Parker, what a pleasure to see *you* here! I'm for tea!"

"Dispersed are we," Isabella followed her, humming. "All is over. The wave has broken. Left us stranded, high and dry. Single, separate on the shingle. Broken is the three-fold ply... Now I follow" (she pushed her chair back... The man in grey was lost in the crowd by the ilex) "that old strumpet" (she invoked Mrs. Manresa's tight, flowered figure in front of her) "to have tea."

Dodge remained behind. "Shall I," he murmured, "go or stay? Slip out some other way? Or follow, follow, follow the dispersing company?"

Dispersed are we, the music wailed; *dispersed are we*. Giles remained like a stake in the tide of the flowing company.

"Follow?" He kicked his chair back. "Whom? Where?" He stubbed his light tennis shoes on the wood. "Nowhere. Anywhere." Stark still he stood.

Here Cobbet of Cobbs Corner, alone under the monkey puzzle tree, rose and muttered: "What was in her mind, eh? What idea lay behind, eh? What made her indue the antique with this glamour – this sham lure, and set 'em climbing, climbing, climbing up the Monkey Puzzle tree?"

Dispersed are we, the music wailed. *Dispersed are we*. He turned and sauntered slowly after the retreating company.

Now Lucy, retrieving her bag from beneath the seat, chirruped to her brother:

"Bart, my dear, come with me.... D'you remember, when we were children, the play we acted in the nursery?"

He remembered. Red Indians the game was; the reed with the paper rolled round the pebble.

"But for us, my old Cindy" – he picked up his hat – "the game's over." The glare and the stare and the beat of the tom-tom, he meant. He gave her his arm. Off they strolled. And Mr. Page, the reporter, noted, "Mrs. Swithin: Mr. B. Oliver," then turning, added further "Lady Haslip, of Haslip Manor," as he spied that old lady wheeled in her chair by her footman winding up the procession.

To the valediction of the gramophone hid in the bushes the audience departed. *Dispersed*, it wailed, *Dispersed are we*.

Now Miss La Trobe stepped from her hiding. Flowing, and streaming, on the grass, on the gravel, still for one moment she held them together – the dispersing company. Hadn't she, for twenty-five minutes, made them see? A vision imparted was relief from agony... for one moment... one moment. Then the music petered out on the last word *we*. She heard the breeze rustle in the branches. She saw Giles Oliver with his back to the audience. Also Cobbet of Cobbs Corner. She hadn't made them see. It was a failure, another damned failure! As usual. Her vision escaped her. And turning, she strode to the actors, undressing, down in the hollow, where butterflies feasted upon swords of silver paper; where the dish cloths in the shadow made pools of yellow.

Cobbet had out his watch. Three hours till seven, he noted; then water the plants. He turned.

Giles, nicking his chair into its notch, turned too, in the other direction. He took the short cut by the fields to the Barn. This dry summer the path was hard as brick across the fields. This dry summer the path was strewn with stones. He kicked – a flinty yellow stone, a sharp stone, edged as if cut by a savage for an arrow. A barbaric stone; and pre-historic. Stone-kicking was a child's game. He remembered the rules. By the rules of the game, one stone, the same stone, must be kicked to the goal. Say a gate, or a tree. He played it alone. The gate was a goal; to be reached in ten. The first kick was Manresa (lust). The second, Dodge (perversion). The third himself (coward). And the fourth and the fifth and all the others were the same.

He reached it in ten. There, couched in the grass, curled in an olive green ring, was a snake. Dead? No, choked with a toad in its mouth. The snake was unable to swallow; the toad was unable to die. A spasm made the ribs contract; blood oozed. It was birth the wrong way round – a monstrous inversion. So, raising his foot, he stamped on them. The mass crushed and slithered. The white canvas on his tennis shoes was bloodstained and sticky. But it was action. Action relieved him. He strode to the Barn, with blood on his shoes.

The Barn, the Noble Barn, the barn that had been built over seven hundred years ago and reminded some people of a Greek Temple, others of the middle ages, most people of an age before their own, scarcely anybody of the present moment, was empty.

The great doors stood open. A shaft of light like a yellow banner sloped from roof to floor. Festoons of paper roses, left over from the Coronation, drooped from the rafters. A long table, on which stood an urn, plates and cups, cakes and bread and butter, stretched across one end. The Barn was empty. Mice slid in and out of holes or stood upright, nibbling. Swallows were busy with straw in pockets of earth in the rafters. Countless beetles and insects of various sorts burrowed in the dry wood. A stray bitch had made the dark corner where the sacks stood a lying-in ground for her puppies. All these eyes, expanding and narrowing, some adapted to light, others to darkness, looked from different angles and edges. Minute nibblings and rustlings broke the silence. Whiffs of sweetness and richness veined the air. A blue-bottle had settled on the cake and stabbed its yellow rock with its short drill. A butterfly sunned itself sensuously on a sunlit yellow plate.

But Mrs. Sands was approaching. She was pushing her way through the crowd. She had turned the corner. She could see the great open door. But butterflies she never saw; mice were only black pellets in kitchen drawers; moths she bundled in her hands and put out of the window. Bitches suggested only servant girls misbehaving. Had there been a cat she would have seen it – any cat, a starved cat with a patch of mange on its rump opened the flood gates of her childless heart. But there was no cat. The Barn was empty. And so running, panting, set upon reaching the Barn and taking up her station behind the tea urn before the company came, she reached the Barn. And the butterfly rose and the blue-bottle.

Following her in a scud came the servants and helpers – David, John, Irene, Lois. Water boiled. Steam issued. Cake was sliced. Swallows swooped from rafter to rafter. And the company entered.

"This fine old Barn..." said Mrs. Manresa, stopping in the doorway. It was not for her to press ahead of the villagers. It was for her, moved by the beauty of the Barn, to stand still; to draw aside; to gaze; to let other people come first.

"We have one, much like it, at Lathom," said Mrs. Parker, stopping, for the same reasons. "Perhaps," she added, "not quite so large."

The villagers hung back. Then, hesitating, dribbled past.

"And the decorations..." said Mrs. Manresa, looking round for someone to congratulate. She stood smiling, waiting. Then old Mrs. Swithin came in. She was gazing up too, but not at the decorations. At the swallows apparently.

"They come every year," she said, "the same birds." Mrs. Manresa smiled benevolently, humouring the old lady's whimsy. It was unlikely, she thought, that the birds were the same.

"The decorations, I suppose, are left over from the Coronation," said Mrs. Parker. "We kept ours too. We built a village Hall."

Mrs. Manresa laughed. She remembered. An anecdote was on the tip of her tongue, about a public lavatory built to celebrate the same occasion, and how the Mayor... Could she tell it? No. The old lady, gazing at the swallows, looked too refined. "Refeened" – Mrs. Manresa qualified the word to her own advantage, thus confirming her approval of the wild child she was, whose nature was somehow "just human nature." Somehow she could span the old lady's "refeenment," also the boy's fun – Where was that nice fellow Giles? She couldn't see him; nor Bill either. The villagers still hung back. They must have someone to start the ball rolling.

"Well, I'm dying for my tea!" she said in her public voice; and strode forward. She laid hold of a thick china mug. Mrs. Sands giving precedence, of course, to one of the gentry, filled it at once. David gave her cake. She was the first to drink, the first to bite. The villagers still hung back. "It's all my eye about democracy," she concluded. So did Mrs. Parker, taking her mug too. The people looked to them. They led; the rest followed.

"What delicious tea!" each exclaimed, disgusting though it was, like rust boiled in water, and the cake fly-blown. But they had a duty to society.

"They come every year," said Mrs. Swithin, ignoring the fact that she spoke to the empty air. "From Africa." As they had come, she supposed, when the Barn was a swamp.

The Barn filled. Fumes rose. China clattered; voices chattered. Isa pressed her way to the table.

"Dispersed are we," she murmured. And held her cup out to be filled. She took it. "Let me turn away," she murmured, turning, "from the array" – she looked desolately round her – "of china faces, glazed and hard. Down the ride, that leads under the nut tree and the may tree, away, till I come to the wishing well, where the washerwoman's little boy" – she dropped sugar, two lumps, into her tea, "dropped a pin. He got his horse, so they say. But what wish should I drop into the well?" She looked round. She could not see the man in grey, the gentleman farmer; nor anyone known to her. "That the waters should cover me," she added, "of the wishing well."

The noise of china and chatter drowned her murmur. "Sugar for you?" they were saying. "Just a spot of milk? And you?" "Tea without milk or sugar. That's the way I like it." "A bit too strong? Let me add water."

"That's what I wished," Isa added, "when I dropped my pin. Water. Water..."

"I must say," the voice said behind her, "it's brave of the King and Queen. They're said to be going to India. She looks such a dear. Someone I know said his hair...."

"There," Isa mused, "would the dead leaf fall, when the leaves fall, on the water. Should I mind not again to see may tree or nut tree? Not again to hear on the trembling spray the thrush sing, or to see, dipping and diving as if he skimmed waves in the air, the yellow woodpecker?"

She was looking at the canary yellow festoons left over from the Coronation.

"I thought they said Canada,[79] not India," the voice said behind her back. To which the other voice answered: "D'you believe what the papers say? For instance, about the Duke of Windsor. He landed on the South Coast. Queen Mary met him.[80] She'd been buying furniture – that's a fact. And the papers say she met him..."

"Alone, under a tree, the withered tree that keeps all day murmuring of the sea, and hears the Rider gallop..."

Isa filled in the phrase. Then she started. William Dodge was by her side.

He smiled. She smiled. They were conspirators; each murmuring some song my uncle taught me.

"It's the play," she said. "The play keeps running in my head."

"Hail, sweet Carinthia. My love. My life," he quoted.

"My lord, my liege," she bowed ironically.

She was handsome. He wanted to see her, not against the tea urn, but with her glass green eyes and thick body, the neck was broad as a pillar, against an arum lily or a vine. He wished she would say: "Come along. I'll show you the greenhouse, the pig sty, or the stable." But she said nothing, and they stood there holding their cups, remembering the play. Then he saw her face change, as if she had got out of one dress and put on another. A small boy battled his way through the crowd, striking against skirts and trousers as if he were swimming blindly.

"Here!" she cried raising her arm.

He made a bee-line for her. He was her little boy, apparently, her son, her George. She gave him cake; then a mug of milk. Then Nurse came up. Then again she changed her dress. This time, from

[79] The King and Queen visited Canada and the US in May and June 1939.

[80] *the duke of Windsor ... Queen Mary met him* after he abdicated in 1936 and married Wallis Simpson, Edward VIII (1894–1972)

became the Duke of Windsor and lived abroad; he returned in September 1939 and met with the King, then returned to France.

the expression in her eyes it was apparently something in the nature of a strait waistcoat. Hirsute, handsome, virile, the young man in blue jacket and brass buttons, standing in a beam of dusty light, was her husband. And she his wife. Their relations, as he had noted at lunch, were as people say in novels "strained." As he had noted at the play, her bare arm had raised itself nervously to her shoulder when she turned – looking for whom? But here he was; and the muscular, the hirsute, the virile plunged him into emotions in which the mind had no share. He forgot how she would have looked against vine leaf in a greenhouse. Only at Giles he looked; and looked and looked. Of whom was he thinking as he stood with his face turned? Not of Isa. Of Mrs. Manresa?

Mrs. Manresa half-way down the Barn had gulped her cup of tea. How can I rid myself, she asked, of Mrs. Parker? If they were of her own class, how they bored her – her own sex! Not the class below – cooks, shopkeepers, farmers' wives; nor the class above – peeresses, countesses; it was the women of her own class that bored her. So she left Mrs. Parker, abruptly.

"Oh Mrs. Moore," she hailed the keeper's wife. "What did you think of it? And what did baby think of it?" Here she pinched baby. "I thought it every bit as good as anything I'd seen in London.... But we mustn't be outdone. We'll have a play of our own. In *our* Barn. We'll show 'em" (here she winked obliquely at the table; so many bought cakes, so few made at home) "how *we* do it."

Then cracking her jokes, she turned; saw Giles; caught his eye; and swept him in, beckoning. He came. And what – she looked down – had he done with his shoes? They were bloodstained. Vaguely some sense that he had proved his valour for her admiration flattered her. If vague it was sweet. Taking him in tow, she felt: I am the Queen, he my hero, my sulky hero.

"That's Mrs. Neale!" she exclaimed. "A perfect marvel of a woman, aren't you, Mrs. Neale! She runs our post office, Mrs. Neale. She can do sums in her head, can't you, Mrs. Neale? Twenty-five halfpenny stamps, two packets of stamped envelopes and a packet of postcards – how much does that come to, Mrs. Neale?"

Mrs. Neale laughed; Mrs. Manresa laughed; Giles too smiled, and looked down at his shoes.

She drew him down the Barn, in and out, from one to another. She knew 'em all. Every one was a thorough good sort. No, she wouldn't allow it, not for a moment – Pinsent's bad leg. "No, no. We're not going to take that for an excuse, Pinsent." If he couldn't bowl, he could bat. Giles agreed. A fish on a line meant the same to him and Pinsent; also jays and magpies. Pinsent stayed on the land; Giles went to an office. That was all. And she was a thorough good sort, making him feel less of an audience, more of an actor, going round the Barn in her wake.

Then, at the end by the door, they came upon the old couple, Lucy and Bartholomew, sitting on their Windsor chairs.

Chairs had been reserved for them. Mrs. Sands had sent them tea. It would have caused more bother than it was worth – asserting the democratic principle; standing in the crowd at the table.

"Swallows," said Lucy, holding her cup, looking at the birds. Excited by the company they were flitting from rafter to rafter. Across Africa, across France they had come to nest here. Year after year they came. Before there was a channel, when the earth, upon which the Windsor chair was planted, was a riot of rhododendrons, and humming birds quivered at the mouths of scarlet trumpets, as she had read that morning in her Outline of History, they had come... Here Bart rose from his chair.

But Mrs. Manresa absolutely refused to take his seat. "Go on sitting, go on sitting," she pressed him down again. "I'll squat on the floor." She squatted. The surly knight remained in attendance.

"And what did you think of the play?" she asked.

Bartholomew looked at his son. His son remained silent.

"And you Mrs. Swithin?" Mrs. Manresa pressed the old lady.

Lucy mumbled, looking at the swallows.

"I was hoping you'd tell me," said Mrs. Manresa. "Was it an old play? Was it a new play?"

No one answered.

"Look!" Lucy exclaimed.

"The birds?" said Mrs. Manresa, looking up.

There was a bird with a straw in its beak; and the straw dropped.

Lucy clapped her hands. Giles turned away. She was mocking him as usual, laughing.

"Going?" said Bartholomew. "Time for the next act?"

And he heaved himself up from his chair. Regardless of Mrs. Manresa and of Lucy, off he strolled too.

"Swallow, my sister, O sister swallow,"[81] he muttered, feeling for his cigar case, following his son.

Mrs. Manresa was nettled. What for had she squatted on the floor then? Were her charms fading? Both were gone. But, woman of action as she was, deserted by the male sex, she was not going to suffer tortures of boredom from the refeened old lady. Up she scrambled, putting her hands to hair as if it were high time that she went too, though it was nothing of the kind and her hair was perfectly tidy. Cobbet in his corner saw through her little game. He had known human nature in the East. It was the same in the West. Plants remained – the carnation, the zinnia, and the geranium. Automatically he consulted his watch; noted time to water at seven; and observed the little game of the woman following the man to the table in the West as in the East.

William at the table, now attached to Mrs. Parker and Isa, watched him approach. Armed and valiant, bold and blatant, firm elatant – the popular march tune rang in his head. And the fingers of William's left hand closed firmly, surreptitiously, as the hero approached.

Mrs. Parker was deploring to Isa in a low voice the village idiot.

"Oh that idiot!" she was saying. But Isa was immobile, watching her husband. She could feel the Manresa in his wake. She could hear in the dusk in their bedroom the usual explanation. It made no difference; his infidelity – but hers did.

"The idiot?" William answered Mrs. Parker for her. "He's in the tradition."

"But surely," said Mrs. Parker, and told Giles how creepy the idiot – "We have one in our village" – had made her feel. "Surely, Mr. Oliver, we're more civilized?"

"We?" said Giles. "We?" He looked, once, at William. He knew not his name; but what his left hand was doing.[82] It was a bit of luck – that he could despise him, not himself. Also Mrs. Parker. But not Isa – not his wife. She had not spoken to him, not one word. Nor looked at him either.

"Surely," said Mrs. Parker, looking from one to the other. "Surely we are?"

Giles then did what to Isa was his little trick; shut his lips; frowned; and took up the pose of one who bears the burden of the world's woe, making money for her to spend.

"No," said Isa, as plainly as words could say it. "I don't admire you," and looked, not at his face, but at his feet. "Silly little boy, with blood on his boots."

Giles shifted his feet. Whom then did she admire? Not Dodge. That he could take for certain. Who else? Some man he knew. Some man, he was sure, in the Barn. Which man? He looked round him.

Then Mr. Streatfield, the clergyman, interrupted. He was carrying cups.

"So I shake hands with my heart!" he exclaimed, nodding his handsome, grizzled head and depositing his burden safely.

Mrs. Parker took the tribute to herself.

"Mr. Streatfield!" she exclaimed. "Doing all the work! While we stand gossiping!"

"Like to see the greenhouse?" said Isa suddenly, turning to William Dodge.

O not now, he could have cried. But had to follow, leaving Giles to welcome the approaching Manresa, who had him in thrall.

The path was narrow. Isa went ahead. And she was broad; she fairly filled the path, swaying slightly as she walked, and plucking a leaf here and there from the hedge.

---

[81] *Swallow ... swallow* The first line of "Itylus" (1866) by Algernon Swinburne (1837–1909). The poem is based on the legend of Procne and Philomela, told in Ovid's *Metamorphoses*. Tereus, married to Procne, rapes her sister Philomela and then cuts out her tongue so she cannot reveal the crime. But Philomela weaves a tapestry that tells her story and sends it to Procne. In revenge, Procne slaughters her son Itylus and serves him as food to Tereus. The sisters flee, and Procne is transformed into a swallow, while Philomela becomes a nightingale. The same tale is used by Eliot in *The Waste Land* (see p. 128, ll. 98–104, and p. 131, ll. 203–106, 124–43), and the swallow also appears at the poem's end (line 429).

[82] *what his left hand was doing* "When thou doest alms, let not thy left hand know what thy right hand doeth" (Matthew 6:3).

"Fly then, follow," she hummed, "the dappled herds in the cedar grove, who, sporting, play, the red with the roe, the stag with the doe. Fly, away. I grieving stay. Alone I linger, I pluck the bitter herb by the ruined wall, the churchyard wall, and press its sour, its sweet, its sour, long grey leaf, so, twixt thumb and finger. . . . "

She threw away the shred of Old Man's Beard that she had picked in passing and kicked open the greenhouse door. Dodge had lagged behind. She waited. She picked up a knife from the plank. He saw her standing against the green glass, the fig tree, and the blue hydrangea, knife in hand.

"She spake," Isa murmured. "And from her bosom's snowy antre drew the gleaming blade. 'Plunge blade!' she said. And struck. 'Faithless!' she cried. Knife, too! It broke. So too my heart," she said.

She was smiling ironically as he came up.

"I wish the play didn't run in my head," she said. Then she sat down on a plank under the vine. And he sat beside her. The little grapes above them were green buds; the leaves thin and yellow as the web between birds' claws.

"Still the play?" he asked. She nodded. "That was your son," he said, "in the Barn?"

She had a daughter too, she told him, in the cradle.

"And you – married?" she asked. From her tone he knew she guessed, as women always guessed, everything. They knew at once they had nothing to fear, nothing to hope. At first they resented – serving as statues in a greenhouse. Then they liked it. For then they could say – as she did – whatever came into their heads. And hand him, as she handed him, a flower.

"There's something for your buttonhole, Mr. . . . " she said, handing him a sprig of scented geranium.

"I'm William," he said, taking the furry leaf and pressing it between thumb and finger.

"I'm Isa," she answered. Then they talked as if they had known each other all their lives; which was odd, she said, as they always did, considering she'd known him perhaps one hour. Weren't they, though, conspirators, seekers after hidden faces? That confessed, she paused and wondered, as they always did, why they could speak so plainly to each other. And added: "Perhaps because we've never met before, and never shall again."

"The doom of sudden death hanging over us," he said. "There's no retreating and advancing" – he was thinking of the old lady showing him the house – "for us as for them."

The future shadowed their present, like the sun coming through the many-veined transparent vine leaf; a criss-cross of lines making no pattern.

They had left the greenhouse door open, and now music came through it. A.B.C., A.B.C., A.B.C. – someone was practising scales. C.A.T. C.A.T. C.A.T. . . . Then the separate letters made one word "Cat." Other words followed. It was a simple tune, like a nursery rhyme –

> The King is in his counting house,
> Counting out his money,
> The Queen is in her parlour
> Eating bread and honey.[83]

They listened. Another voice, a third voice, was saying something simple. And they sat on in the greenhouse, on the plank with the vine over them, listening to Miss La Trobe or whoever it was, practising her scales.

He could not find his son. He had lost him in the crowd. So old Bartholomew left the Barn, and went to his own room, holding his cheroot and murmuring:

> O sister swallow, O sister swallow,
> How can thy heart be full of the spring?

---

[83]   *The King is . . . bread and honey* third stanza of the nursery rhyme "Sing a Song of Sixpence."

"How can my heart be full of the spring?" he said aloud, standing in front of the book case. Books: the treasured lifeblood of immortal spirits.[84] Poets; the legislators of mankind.[85] Doubtless, it was so. But Giles was unhappy. "How can my heart, how can my heart," he repeated, puffing at his cheroot. "Condemned in life's infernal mine, condemned in solitude to pine ..."[86] Arms akimbo, he stood in front of his country gentleman's library. Garibaldi; Wellington;[87] Irrigation Officers' Reports; and Hibbert[88] on the Diseases of the Horse. A great harvest the mind had reaped; but for all this, compared with his son, he did not care one damn.

"What's the use, what's the use," he sank down into his chair muttering, "O sister swallow, O sister swallow, of singing your song?" The dog, who had followed him, flopped down onto the floor at his feet. Flanks sucked in and out, the long nose resting on his paws, a fleck of foam on the nostril, there he was, his familiar spirit, his Afghan hound.

The door trembled and stood half open. That was Lucy's way of coming in – as if she did not know what she would find. Really! It was her brother! And his dog! She seemed to see them for the first time. Was it that she had no body? Up in the clouds, like an air ball, her mind touched ground now and then with a shock of surprise. There was nothing in her to weight a man like Giles to the earth.

She perched on the edge of a chair like a bird on a telegraph wire before starting for Africa.

"Swallow, my sister, O sister swallow ..." he murmured.

From the garden – the window was open – came the sound of someone practising scales. A.B.C. A.B.C. A.B.C. Then the separate letters formed one word "Dog." Then a phrase. It was a simple tune, another voice speaking.

> Hark hark, the dogs do bark
> The beggars are coming to town ...[89]

Then it languished and lengthened, and became a waltz. As they listened and looked – out into the garden – the trees tossing and the birds swirling seemed called out of their private lives, out of their separate avocations, and made to take part.

> The lamp of love burns high, over the dark cedar groves,
> The lamp of love shines clear, clear as a star in the sky. ...

Old Bartholomew tapped his fingers on his knee in time to the tune.

> Leave your casement and come, lady,
> I love till I die.

He looked sardonically at Lucy, perched on her chair. How, he wondered, had she ever borne children?

> For all are dancing, retreating and advancing,
> The moth and the dragon-fly. ...

She was thinking, he supposed, God is peace. God is love. For she belonged to the unifiers; he to the separatists.

---

[84] "the treasured ... immortal spirits a variant of a famous phrase from Areopagitica (1644) by John Milton (1608–74): "A book is the precious life-blood of a master spirit."

[85] the legislators of mankind a phrase from "The Defence of Poetry" (1829) by Percy Bysshe Shelley (1792–1821): "Poets are the unacknowledged legislators of mankind."

[86] "Condemned in life's ... to pine" Source not identified.

[87] Giuseppe Garibaldi (1807–82), a leader of the struggle for Italian independence; Arthur Wellesley (1769–1852), Duke of Wellington, who defeated Napoleon at Waterloo and was twice prime minister in 1828 and 1834.

[88] A fictional author.

[89] "Hark, hark ... coming to town" a nursery rhyme:

> Hark, hark, the dogs do bark,
> The beggars are coming to town.
> Some in rags, and some in tags,
> And some in velvet gowns.

Then the tune with its feet always on the same spot, became sugared, insipid; bored a hole with its perpetual invocation to perpetual adoration. Had it – he was ignorant of musical terms – gone into the minor key?

> For this day and this dance and this merry, merry May
> Will be over (he tapped his forefinger on his knee)
> With the cutting of the clover this retreating and advancing
> – the swifts seemed to have shot beyond their orbits –
> Will be over, over, over,
> And the ice will dart its splinter, and the winter,
> O the winter, will fill the grate with ashes,
> And there'll be no glow, no glow on the log.

He knocked the ash off his cheroot and rose.

"So we must," said Lucy; as if he had said aloud, "It's time to go."

The audience was assembling. The music was summoning them. Down the paths, across the lawns they were streaming again. There was Mrs. Manresa, with Giles at her side, heading the procession. In taut plump curves her scarf blew round her shoulders. The breeze was rising. She looked, as she crossed the lawn to the strains of the gramophone, goddess-like, buoyant, abundant, her cornucopia running over. Bartholomew, following, blessed the power of the human body to make the earth fruitful. Giles would keep his orbit so long as she weighted him to the earth. She stirred the stagnant pool of his old heart even – where bones lay buried, but the dragon-flies shot and the grass trembled as Mrs. Manresa advanced across the lawn to the strains of the gramophone.

Feet crunched the gravel. Voices chattered. The inner voice, the other voice was saying: How can we deny that this brave music, wafted from the bushes, is expressive of some inner harmony? "When we wake" (some were thinking) "the day breaks us with its hard mallet blows." "The office" (some were thinking) "compels disparity. Scattered, shattered, hither thither summoned by the bell. 'Ping-ping-ping' that's the phone. 'Forward!' 'Serving!' – that's the shop." So we answer to the infernal, agelong and eternal order issued from on high. And obey. "Working, serving, pushing, striving, earning wages – to be spent – here? Oh dear no. Now? No, by and by. When ears are deaf and the heart is dry."

Here Cobbet of Cobbs Corner who had stooped – there was a flower – was pressed on by people pushing from behind.

For I hear music, they were saying. Music wakes us. Music makes us see the hidden, join the broken. Look and listen. See the flowers, how they ray their redness, whiteness, silverness and blue. And the trees with their many-tongued much syllabling, their green and yellow leaves hustle us and shuffle us, and bid us, like the starlings, and the rooks, come together, crowd together, to chatter and make merry while the red cow moves forward and the black cow stands still.

The audience had reached their seats. Some sat down; others stood a moment, turned, and looked at the view. The stage was empty; the actors were still dressing up among the bushes. The audience turned to one another and began to talk. Scraps and fragments reached Miss La Trobe where she stood, script in hand, behind the tree.

"They're not ready...I hear 'em laughing" (they were saying). "...Dressing up. That's the great thing, dressing up. And it's pleasant now, the sun's not so hot...That's one good the war brought us – longer days[90]...Where did we leave off? D'you remember? The Elizabethans...Perhaps she'll reach the present, if she skips.... D'you think people change? Their clothes, of course.... But I meant our selves...Clearing out a cupboard, I found my father's old top hat.... But our selves – do we change?"

---

[90] Summer Time or Daylight Saving Time, which is putting the clock one hour forward, began with the Summer Time Act in 1916.

"No, I don't go by politicians. I've a friend who's been to Russia. He says ... And my daughter, just back from Rome, she says the common people, in the cafés, hate Dictators.[91] ... Well, different people say different things...."

"Did you see it in the papers – the case about the dog? D'you believe dogs can't have puppies?... And Queen Mary and the Duke of Windsor on the South Coast?... D'you believe what's in the papers? I ask the butcher or the grocer... That's Mr. Streatfield, carrying a hurdle.... The good clergyman, I say, does more work for less pay than all the lot... It's the wives that make the trouble...."

"And what about the Jews? The refugees ... the Jews[92] ... People like ourselves, beginning life again ... But it's always been the same.... My old mother, who's over eighty, can remember... Yes, she still reads without glasses.... How amazing! Well, don't they say, after eighty... Now they're coming ... No, that's nothing.... I'd make it penal, leaving litter. But then, who's, my husband says, to collect the fines?... Ah there she is, Miss La Trobe, over there, behind that tree..."

Over there behind the tree Miss La Trobe gnashed her teeth. She crushed her manuscript. The actors delayed. Every moment the audience slipped the noose; split up into scraps and fragments.

"Music!" she signalled. "Music!"

"What's the origin," said a voice, "of the expression 'with a flea in his ear'?"

Down came her hand peremptorily. "Music, music," she signalled.

And the gramophone began A.B.C., A.B.C.

> *The King is in his counting house*
> *Counting out his money,*
> *The Queen is in her parlour*
> *Eating bread and honey....*

Miss La Trobe watched them sink down peacefully into the nursery rhyme. She watched them fold their hands and compose their faces. Then she beckoned. And at last, with a final touch to her head dress, which had been giving trouble, Mabel Hopkins strode from the bushes, and took her place on the raised ground facing the audience.

Eyes fed on her as fish rise to a crumb of bread on the water. Who was she? What did she represent? She was beautiful – very. Her cheeks had been powdered; her colour glowed smooth and clear underneath. Her grey satin robe (a bedspread), pinned in stone-like folds, gave her the majesty of a statue. She carried a sceptre and a little round orb. England was she? Queen Anne was she? Who was she? She spoke too low at first; all they heard was

... reason holds sway.

Old Bartholomew applauded.

"Hear! Hear!" he cried. "Bravo! Bravo!"

Thus encouraged Reason[93] spoke out.

Time leaning on his sickle, stands amazed. While commerce from her Cornucopia pours the mingled tribute of her different ores. In distant mines the savage sweats; and from the reluctant earth the painted pot is shaped. At my behest, the armed warrior lays his shield aside; the heathen leaves the Altar steaming with unholy sacrifice. The violet and the eglantine over the riven earth their flowers entwine. No longer fears the unwary wanderer the poisoned snake. And in the helmet, yellow bees their honey make.

She paused. A long line of villagers in sacking were passing in and out of the trees behind her.

Digging and delving, ploughing and sowing they were singing, but the wind blew their words away.

Beneath the shelter of my flowing robe (she resumed, extending her arms) *the arts arise. Music for me unfolds her heavenly harmony. At my behest the miser leaves his hoard untouched; at peace the mother sees her*

---

[91] *hate Dictators* Mussolini had been in power in Italy since 1922, Stalin in Russia since 1924, Hitler in Germany since 1933, Franco in Spain since February 1939.

[92] Since Hitler had come to power in 1933, the question of Jewish refugees had been a subject of political debate in Britain.

[93] *Reason* popularly thought to be typical of the eighteenth century.

children play....Her children play...she repeated, and, waving her sceptre, figures advanced from the bushes.

Let swains and nymphs lead on the play, while Zephyr[94] *sleeps, and the unruly tribes of Heaven confess my sway.*

A merry little old tune was played on the gramophone. Old Bartholomew joined his finger tips; Mrs. Manresa smoothed her skirts about her knees.

> *Young Damon said to Cynthia*
> *Come out now with the dawn*
> *And don your azure tippet*[95]
> *And cast your cares adown*
> *For peace has come to England,*
> *And reason now holds sway.*
> *What pleasure lies in dreaming*
> *When blue and green's the day?*
> *Now cast your cares behind you.*
> *Night passes: here is Day.*

Digging and delving, the villagers sang passing in single file in and out between the trees, *for the earth is always the same, summer and winter and spring; and spring and winter again; ploughing and sowing, eating and growing; time passes....*

The wind blew the words away.

The dance stopped. The nymphs and swains withdrew. Reason held the centre of the stage alone. Her arms extended, her robes flowing, holding orb and sceptre, Mabel Hopkins stood sublimely looking over the heads of the audience. The audience gazed at her. She ignored the audience. Then while she gazed, helpers from the bushes arranged round her what appeared to be the three sides of a room. In the middle they stood a table. On the table they placed a china tea service. Reason surveyed this domestic scene from her lofty eminence unmoved. There was a pause.

"Another scene from another play, I suppose," said Mrs. Elmhurst, referring to her programme. She read out for the benefit of her husband, who was deaf: "*Where there's a Will there's a Way.*[96] That's the name of the play. And the characters...." She read out: "Lady Harpy Harraden, in love with Sir Spaniel Lilyliver. Deb, her maid. Flavinda, her niece, in love with Valentine. Sir Spaniel Lilyliver, in love with Flavinda. Sir Smirking Peace-be-with-you-all, a clergyman. Lord and Lady Fribble. Valentine, in love with Flavinda. What names for real people! But look – here they come!"

Out they came from the bushes – men in flowered waistcoats, white waistcoats and buckled shoes; women wearing brocades tucked up, hooped and draped; glass stars, blue ribands and imitation pearls made them look the very image of Lords and Ladies.

"The first scene," Mrs. Elmhurst whispered into her husband's ear, "is Lady Harraden's dressing-room....That's her...." She pointed. "Mrs. Otter, I think, from the End House; but she's wonderfully made up. And that's Deb her maid. Who she is, I don't know."

"Hush, hush, hush," someone protested.

Mrs. Elmhurst dropped her programme. The play had begun.

Lady Harpy Harraden entered her dressing-room, followed by Deb her maid.

LADY H. H....*Give me the pounce-box. Then the patch. Hand me the mirror, girl. So. Now my wig....A pox on the girl – she's dreaming!*

DEB ...*I was thinking, my lady, what the gentleman said when he saw you in the Park.*

---

[94] In classical mythology the personification of the west wind.
[95] A garment of fur or wool, covering the shoulders, or neck and shoulders.

[96] A fictitious title that parodies titles found in Restoration comedy.

Lady H. H. (gazing in the glass) *So, so – what was it? Some silly trash! Cupid's dart – hah, hah! lighting his taper – tush – at my eyes. . . . pooh! That was in milord's time, twenty years since. . . . But now – what'll he say of me now?* (She looks in the mirror) *Sir Spaniel Lilyliver, I mean . . .* (a rap at the door) *Hark! That's his chaise at the door. Run child. Don't stand gaping.*

Deb . . . (going to the door) *Say? He'll rattle his tongue as a gambler rattles dice in a box. He'll find no words to fit you. He'll stand like a pig in a poke. . . . Your servant, Sir Spaniel.*

Enter Sir Spaniel.

Sir S. L. . . . *Hail, my fair Saint! What, out o'bed so early? Methought, as I came along the Mall the air was something brighter than usual. Here's the reason. . . . Venus, Aphrodite, upon my word a very galaxy, a constellation! As I'm a sinner, a very Aurora Borealis!*

(He sweeps his hat off.)

Lady H. H. *Oh flatterer, flatterer! I know your ways. But come. Sit down. . . . A glass of Aqua Vitae. Take this seat, Sir Spaniel. I've something very private and particular to say to you. . . . You had my letter, Sir?*

Sir S. L. . . . *Pinned to my heart!*

(He strikes his breast.)

Lady H. H. . . . *I have a favour to ask of you, Sir.*

Sir S. L. . . . (singing) *What favour could fair Chloe ask that Damon would not get her? . . . A done with rhymes. Rhymes are still-a-bed. Let's speak prose. What can Asphodilla ask of her plain servant Lilyliver? Speak out, Madam. An ape with a ring in his nose, or a strong young jackanapes to tell tales of us when we're no longer here to tell truth about ourselves?*

Lady H. H. (flirting her fan) *Fie, fie, Sir Spaniel. You make me blush – you do indeed. But come closer.* (She shifts her seat nearer to him) *We don't want the whole world to hear us.*

Sir S. L. (aside) *Come closer? A pox on my life! The old hag stinks like a red herring that's been stood over head in a tar barrel!* (Aloud) *Your meaning, Madam? You were saying?*

Lady H. H. *I have a niece, Sir Spaniel, Flavinda by name.*

Sir S. L. (aside) *Why that's the girl I love, to be sure!* (Aloud) *You have a niece, Madam? I seem to remember hearing so. An only child, left by your brother, so I've heard, in your Ladyship's charge – him that perished at sea.*

Lady H. H. *The very same Sir. She's of age now and marriageable. I've kept her close as a weevil, Sir Spaniel, wrapped in the sere cloths of her virginity. Only maids about her, never a man to my knowledge, save Clout the serving man, who has a wart on his nose and a face like a nutgrater. Yet some fool has caught her fancy. Some gilded fly – some Harry, Dick; call him what you will.*

Sir S. L. (aside) *That's young Valentine, I warrant. I caught 'em at the play together.* (Aloud) *Say you so, Madam?*

Lady H. H. *She's not so ill favoured, Sir Spaniel – there's beauty in our line – but that a gentleman of taste and breeding like yourself now might take pity on her.*

Sir S. L. *Saving your presence, Madam. Eyes that have seen the sun are not so easily dazzled by the lesser lights – the Cassiopeias, Aldebarans, Great Bears and so on – A fig for them when the sun's up!*

Lady H. H. (ogling him) *You praise my hair-dresser, Sir, or my ear-rings* (she shakes her head).

Sir S. L. (aside) *She jingles like a she-ass at a fair! She's rigged like a barber's pole of a May Day.* (Aloud) *Your commands, Madam?*

Lady H. H. *Well Sir, t'was this way Sir. Brother Bob, for my father was a plain country gentleman and would have none of the fancy names the foreigners brought with 'em – Asphodilla I call myself, but my Christian name's plain Sue – Brother Bob, as I was telling you, ran away to sea; and, so they say, became Emperor of the Indies; where the very stones are emeralds and the sheep crop rubies. Which, for a tenderer-hearted man never lived, he would have brought back with him, Sir, to mend the family fortunes, Sir. But the brig, frigate or what they call it, for I've no head for sea terms, never crossed a ditch without saying the Lord's Prayer backwards, struck a rock. The Whale had him. But the cradle was by the bounty of Heaven washed ashore. With the girl in it; Flavinda here. What's more to the point, with the Will in it; safe and sound; wrapped in parchment. Brother Bob's Will. Deb there! Deb I say! Deb!*

(She hollas for Deb)

Sir S. L. (aside) *Ah hah! I smell a rat! A will, quotha! Where there's a Will there's a Way.*

LADY H. H. (bawling) *The Will, Deb! The Will! In the ebony box by the right hand of the escritoire opposite the window.... A pox on the girl! She's dreaming. It's these romances, Sir Spaniel – these romances. Can't see a candle gutter but it's her heart that's melting, or snuff a wick without reciting all the names in Cupid's Calendar...*

(Enter Deb carrying a parchment)

LADY H. H. *So... Give it here. The Will. Brother Bob's Will* (she mumbles over the Will).

LADY H. H. *To cut the matter short, Sir, for these lawyers even at the Antipodes are a long-winded race –*

SIR S. L. *To match their ears, Ma'am –*

LADY H. H. *Very true, very true. To cut the matter short, Sir, my brother Bob left all he died possessed of to his only child Flavinda; with this proviso, mark ye. That she marry to her Aunt's liking. Her Aunt; that's me. Otherwise, mark ye, all – to wit ten bushels of diamonds; item of rubies; item two hundred square miles of fertile territory bounding the River Amazon to the Nor-Nor-East; item his snuff box; item his flageolet – he was always one to love a tune, Sir, Brother Bob; item six Macaws and as many Concubines as he had with him at the time of his decease – all this with other trifles needless to specify he left, mark ye, should she fail to marry to her Aunt's liking – that's me – to found a Chapel, Sir Spaniel, where six poor Virgins should sing hymns in perpetuity for the repose of his soul – which, to speak the truth, Sir Spaniel, poor Brother Bob stands in need of, perambulating the Gulf Stream as he is and consorting with Syrens. But take it; read the Will yourself, Sir.*

SIR S. L. (reading) *"Must marry to her Aunt's liking." That's plain enough.*

LADY H. H. *Her Aunt, Sir. That's me. That's plain enough.*

SIR S. L. (aside) *She speaks the truth there!* (Aloud) *You would have me understand, Madam....?*

LADY H. H. *Hist! Come closer. Let me whisper in your ear... You and I have long entertained a high opinion of one another, Sir Spaniel. Played at ball together. Bound our wrists with daisy chains together. If I mind aright, you called me little bride – 'tis fifty years since. We might have made a match of it, Sir Spaniel, had fortune favoured.... You take my meaning, Sir?*

SIR S. L. *Had it been written in letters of gold, fifty feet high, visible from Paul's Churchyard to the Goat and Compasses at Peckham, it could have been no plainer.... Hist, I'll whisper it. I, Sir Spaniel Lilyliver, do hereby bind myself to take thee – what's the name of the green girl that was cast up in a lobster pot covered with sea weed? Flavinda, eh? Flavinda, so – to be my wedded wife... O for a lawyer to have it all in writing!*

LADY H. H. *On condition, Sir Spaniel.*

SIR S. L. *On condition, Asphodilla.*

(Both speak together)

That the money is shared between us.

LADY H. H. *We want no lawyer to certify that! Your hand on it, Sir Spaniel!*

SIR S. L. *Your lips Madam!*

(They embrace)

SIR S. L. *Pah! She stinks!*

"Ha! Ha! Ha!" laughed the indigenous old lady in her bathchair.

"Reason, begad! Reason!" exclaimed old Bartholomew, and looked at his son as if exhorting him to give over these womanish vapours and be a man, Sir.

Giles sat straight as a dart, his feet tucked under him.

Mrs. Manresa had out her mirror and lipstick and attended to her lips and nose.

The gramophone, while the scene was removed, gently stated certain facts which everybody knows to be perfectly true. The tune said, more or less, how Eve, gathering her robes about her, stands reluctant still to let her dewy mantle fall. The herded flocks, the tune continued, in peace repose. The poor man to his cot returns, and, to the eager ears of wife and child, the simple story of his toil relates: what yield the furrow bears; and how the team the plover on the nest has spared; while Wat her courses ran; and speckled eggs in the warm hollow lay. Meanwhile the good wife on the table spreads her simple fare; and to the shepherd's flute, from toil released, the nymphs and swains join hands and foot it on the green. Then Eve lets down her sombre tresses brown and spreads her lucent veil o'er hamlet, spire, and mead, etc., etc. And the tune repeated itself once more.

The view repeated in its own way what the tune was saying. The sun was sinking; the colours were merging; and the view was saying how after toil men rest from their labours; how coolness comes; reason prevails; and having unharnessed the team from the plough, neighbours dig in cottage gardens and lean over cottage gates.

The cows, making a step forward, then standing still, were saying the same thing to perfection.

Folded in this triple melody, the audience sat gazing; and beheld gently and approvingly without interrogation, for it seemed inevitable, a box tree in a green tub take the place of the lady's dressing-room; while on what seemed to be a wall, was hung a great clock face; the hands pointing to three minutes to the hour; which was seven.

Mrs. Elmhurst roused herself from her reverie; and looked at her programme.

"Scene Two. The Mall," she read out. "Time; early morning. Enter Flavinda. Here she comes!"

Here came Millie Loder (shop assistant at Messrs. Hunt and Dicksons, drapery emporium), in sprigged satin, representing Flavinda.

FLAV. *Seven he said, and there's the clock's word for it. But Valentine – where's Valentine? La! How my heart beats! Yet it's not the time o' day, for I'm often afoot before the sun's up in the meadows . . . See – the fine folk passing! All a-tiptoeing like peacocks with spread tails! And I in my petticoat that looked so fine by my Aunt's cracked mirror. Why, here it's a dish clout . . . And they heap their hair up like a birthday cake stuck about with candles. . . . That's a diamond – that's a ruby . . . Where's Valentine? The Orange Tree in the Mall, he said. The tree – there. Valentine – nowhere. That's a courtier, I'll warrant, that old fox with his tail between his legs. That's a serving wench out without her master's knowledge. That's a man with a broom to sweep paths for the fine ladies' flounces . . . La! the red in their cheeks! They never got that in the fields, I warrant! O faithless, cruel, hard-hearted Valentine. Valentine! Valentine!*

(She wrings her hands, turning from side to side.)

Didn't I leave my bed a-tiptoe and steal like a mouse in the wainscot for fear of waking Aunt? And lard my hair from her powder box? And scrub my cheeks to make 'em shine? And lie awake watching the stars climb the chimney pots? And give my gold guinea that Godfather hid behind the mistletoe last Twelfth Night to Deb so she shouldn't tell on me? And grease the key in the lock so that Aunt shouldn't wake and shriek Flavvy! Flavvy! Val, I say Val—That's him coming. . . . No, I could tell him a mile off the way he strides the waves like what d'you call him in the picture book. . . . That's not Val. . . . That's a cit; that's a fop; raising his glass, prithee, to have his fill of me . . . I'll be home then . . . No, I won't . . . That's to play the green girl again and sew samplers . . . I'm of age, ain't I, come Michaelmas? Only three turns of the moon and I inherit . . . Didn't I read it in the Will the day the ball bounced on top of the old chest where Aunt keeps her furbelows, and the lid opened? . . . "All I die possessed of to my Daughter . . ." So far I'd read when the old lady came tapping down the passage like a blind man in an alley. . . . I'm no castaway, I'd have you know, Sir; no fishtailed mermaid with a robe of sea weed, at your mercy. I'm a match for any of 'em – the chits you dally with, and bid me meet you at the Orange Tree when you're drowsing the night off spent in their arms. . . . Fie upon you, Sir, making sport with a poor girl so. . . . I'll not cry, I swear I won't. I'll not brew a drop of the salt liquid for a man who's served me so. . . . Yet to think on't – how we hid in the dairy the day the cat jumped. And read romances under the holly tree. La! how I cried when the Duke left poor Polly. . . . And my Aunt found me with eyes like red jellies. "What stung, niece?" says she. And cried "Quick Deb, the blue bag." I told ye . . . La, to think I read it all in a book and cried for another! . . . Hist, what's there among the trees? It's come – it's gone. The breeze is it? In the shade now – in the sun now. . . . Valentine on my life! It's he! Quick, I'll hide. Let the tree conceal me!

(Flavinda hides behind the tree.)

He's here . . . He turns . . . He casts about . . . He's lost the scent . . . He gazes – this way, that way. . . . Let him feast his eyes on the fine faces – taste 'em, sample 'em, say: "That's the fine lady I danced with . . . that I lay with . . . that I kissed under the mistletoe . . ." Ha! How he spews 'em out! Brave Valentine! How he casts his eyes upon the ground! How his frowns become him! "Where's Flavinda?" he sighs. "She I love like the heart in my breast." See him pull his watch out! "O faithless wretch!" he sighs. See how he stamps the earth! Now turns on his heel. . . . He sees me – no, the sun's in his eyes. Tears fill 'em . . . Lord, how he fingers his sword! He'll run it through his breast like the Duke in the story book! . . . Stop, Sir, stop!

(She reveals herself)

VALENTINE. . . . *O Flavinda, O!*

FLAVINDA....*O Valentine, O!*

(They embrace)
The clock strikes nine.

"All that fuss about nothing!" a voice exclaimed. People laughed. The voice stopped. But the voice had seen; the voice had heard. For a moment Miss La Trobe behind her tree glowed with glory. The next, turning to the villagers who were passing in and out between the trees, she barked:

"Louder! Louder!"

For the stage was empty; the emotion must be continued; the only thing to continue the emotion was the song; and the words were inaudible.

"Louder! Louder!" She threatened them with her clenched fists.

Digging and delving (they sang), *hedging and ditching, we pass.... Summer and winter, autumn and spring return... All passes but we, all changes... but we remain for ever the same...* (the breeze blew gaps between their words).

"Louder, louder!" Miss La Trobe vociferated.

Palaces tumble adown (they resumed), *Babylon, Nineveh, Troy*[97] *...And Cæsar's great house*[98] *...all fallen they lie... Where the plover nests was the arch.... through which the Romans trod... Digging and delving we break with the share of the plough the clod... Where Clytemnestra watched for her Lord... saw the beacons blaze on the hills*[99] *...we see only the clod... Digging and delving we pass.... and the Queen and the Watch Tower fall*[100] *...for Agamemnon has ridden away.... Clytemnestra is nothing but....*

The words died away. Only a few great names – Babylon, Nineveh, Clytemnestra, Agamemnon, Troy – floated across the open space. Then the wind rose, and in the rustle of the leaves even the great words became inaudible; and the audience sat staring at the villagers, whose mouths opened, but no sound came.

And the stage was empty. Miss La Trobe leant against the tree, paralysed. Her power had left her. Beads of perspiration broke on her forehead. Illusion had failed. "This is death," she murmured, "death."

Then suddenly, as the illusion petered out, the cows took up the burden. One had lost her calf. In the very nick of time she lifted her great moon-eyed head and bellowed. All the great moon-eyed heads laid themselves back. From cow after cow came the same yearning bellow. The whole world was filled with dumb yearning. It was the primeval voice sounding loud in the ear of the present moment. Then the whole herd caught the infection. Lashing their tails, blobbed like pokers, they tossed their heads high, plunged and bellowed, as if Eros had planted his dart in their flanks and goaded them to fury. The cows annihilated the gap; bridged the distance; filled the emptiness and continued the emotion.

Miss La Trobe waved her hand ecstatically at the cows.

"Thank Heaven!" she exclaimed.

Suddenly the cows stopped; lowered their heads, and began browsing. Simultaneously the audience lowered their heads and read their programmes.

"The producer," Mrs. Elmhurst read out for her husband's benefit, "craves the indulgence of the audience. Owing to lack of time a scene has been omitted; and she begs the audience to imagine that in the interval Sir Spaniel Lilyliver has contracted an engagement with Flavinda; who had been about to plight her troth; when Valentine, hidden inside the grandfather's clock, steps forward;

---

[97] Babylon, capital of the ancient kingdom of Babylonia, was sacked by the Assyrian king Sennacherib in 696 BC; Nineveh, capital of the Assyrian Empire, was destroyed by the Babylonians in 612 BC; Troy was captured and sacked by the Greeks under Agamemnon after a siege of ten years, as narrated in Homer's *Iliad*.

[98] The line of Roman emperors who claimed descent from Julius Caesar (100–44 BC).

[99] Woolf is referring to the trilogy of tragedies called the *Oresteia* (458 BC), by the ancient Greek dramatist Aeschylus

(c. 512–455 BC). In *Clytemnestra* (the first play of the trilogy), Clytemnestra, wife of the king and warrior Agamemnon who has led the Greeks in the Trojan War, orders a watchman to look out for the burning beacon that signals his return to their home in Mycenae. She goes on to murder him in revenge for his having sacrificed their daughter, Iphigenia, to the gods, an act which he had been told was a precondition for victory.

[100] In the second play of the trilogy (see preceding note), *The Libation Bearers*, Clytemnestra is killed by her son Orestes in revenge for his father's murder.

claims Flavinda as his bride; reveals the plot to rob her of her inheritance; and, during the confusion that ensues, the lovers fly together, leaving Lady Harpy and Sir Spaniel alone together."

"We're asked to imagine all that," she said, putting down her glasses.

"That's very wise of her," said Mrs. Manresa, addressing Mrs. Swithin. "If she'd put it all in, we should have been here till midnight. So we've got to imagine, Mrs. Swithin." She patted the old lady on the knee.

"Imagine?" said Mrs. Swithin. "How right! Actors show us too much. The Chinese, you know, put a dagger on the table and that's a battle. And so Racine . . ."[101]

"Yes, they bore one stiff," Mrs. Manresa interrupted, scenting culture, resenting the snub to the jolly human heart. "T'other day I took my nephew – such a jolly boy at Sandhurst[102] – to *Pop Goes the Weasel*.[103] Seen it?" She turned to Giles.

"Up and down the City Road," he hummed by way of an answer.

"Did your Nanny sing that?" Mrs. Manresa exclaimed. "Mine did. And when she said 'Pop' she made a noise like a cork being drawn from a ginger-beer bottle. Pop!"

She made the noise.

"Hush, hush," someone whispered.

"Now I'm being naughty and shocking your aunt," she said. "We must be good and attend. This is Scene Three. Lady Harpy Harraden's Closet. The sound of horses' hooves is heard in the distance."

The sound of horses' hooves, energetically represented by Albert the idiot with a wooden spoon on a tray, died away.

LADY H. H. *Half-way to Gretna Green*[104] *already! O my deceitful niece! You that I rescued from the brine and stood on the hearthstone dripping! O that the whale had swallowed you whole! Perfidious porpoise, O! Didn't the Horn book*[105] *teach you Honour thy Great Aunt?*[106] *How have you misread it and misspelt it, learnt thieving and cheating and reading of wills in old boxes and hiding of rascals in honest time-pieces that have never missed a second since King Charles's day!*[107] *O Flavinda! O porpoise, O!*

SIR S. L. (trying to pull on his jack boots) *Old – old – old. He called me "old" – "To your bed, old fool, and drink hot posset!"*

LADY H. H. *And she, stopping at the door and pointing the finger of scorn at me said "old," Sir – "woman" Sir – "woman" Sir – I that am in the prime of life and a lady!*

SIR S. L. (tugging at his boots) *But I'll be even with him. I'll have the law on 'em! I'll run 'em to earth . . .*

(He hobbles up and down, one boot on, one boot off)

LADY H. H. (laying her hand on his arm) *Have mercy on your gout, Sir Spaniel. Bethink you, Sir – let's not run mad, we that are on the sunny side of fifty. What's this youth they prate on? Nothing but a goose feather blown on a north wind. Sit you down, Sir Spaniel. Rest your leg – so –*

(She pushes a cushion under his leg)

SIR S. L. *"Old" he called me . . . jumping from the clock like a jack-in-the-box . . . And she, making mock of me, points to my leg and cries "Cupid's darts, Sir Spaniel, Cupid's darts." O that I could braise 'em in a mortar and serve 'em up smoking hot on the altar of – O my gout, O my gout!*

LADY H. H. *This talk, Sir, ill befits a man of sense. Bethink you, Sir, only t'other day you were invoking – ahem – the Constellations. Cassiopeia, Aldebaran; the Aurora Borealis*[108] *. . . It's not to be denied that one of*

[101] Jean Racine (1639–99) was a French neoclassical playwright.

[102] Sandhurst, in Berkshire county, is home to the Royal Military Academy, which trains officers for British army regiments.

[103] A nineteenth-century nursery rhyme:

> Up and down the City Road
> In and out the Eagle,
> That's the way the money goes,
> Pop goes the weasel.

There are numerous plays, pantomimes, and musicals that have used the phrase as a title.

[104] A Scottish village ten miles north of the English border. When it became illegal in England for minors to marry without parental consent in 1853, the law was evaded by traveling to Gretna Green.

[105] A child's primer in the eighteenth century.

[106] Adaptation of the Second Commandment: "Honor thy father and thy mother" (Exodus 20:12).

[107] King Charles I (1600–49) ruled from 1625 to 1649; King Charles II (1630–85) ruled from 1660 to 1685.

[108] Cassiopeia is a constellation; Aldebaran is a star; the Aurora Borealis is another name for the Northern Lights.

'em has left her sphere, has shot, has eloped, to put it plainly, with the entrails of a time-piece, the mere pendulum of a grandfather's clock. But, Sir Spaniel, there are some stars that – ahem – stay fixed; that shine, to put it in a nutshell, never so bright as by a sea-coal fire on a brisk morning.

SIR S. L. O that I were five and twenty with a sharp sword at my side!

LADY H. H. (bridling) I take your meaning, Sir. Te hee – To be sure, I regret it as you do. But youth's not all. To let you into a secret, I've passed the meridian myself. Am on t'other side of the Equator too. Sleep sound o'nights without turning. The dog days are over. . . . But bethink you, Sir. Where there's a will there's a way.

SIR S. L. God's truth Ma'am . . . ah my foot's like a burning burning horseshoe on the devil's anvil ah! – what's your meaning?

LADY H. H. My meaning, Sir? Must I disrupt my modesty and unquilt that which has been laid in lavender since my lord, peace be to his name – 'tis twenty years since – was lapped in lead? In plain words, Sir, Flavinda's flown. The cage is empty. But we that have bound our wrists with cowslips might join 'em with a stouter chain. To have done with fallals[109] and figures. Here am I, Asphodilla – but my plain name Sue. No matter what my name is – Asphodilla or Sue – here am I, hale and hearty, at your service. Now that the plot's out, Brother Bob's bounty must go to the virgins. That's plain. Here's Lawyer Quill's word for it. "Virgins . . . in perpetuity . . . sing for his soul." And I warrant you, he has need of it . . . But no matter. Though we have thrown that to the fishes that might have wrapped us in lamb's-wool, I'm no beggar. There's messuages;[110] tenements; napery; cattle; my dowry; an inventory. I'll show you; engrossed on parchment; enough I'll warrant you to keep us handsomely, for what's to run of our time, as husband and wife.

SIR S. L. Husband and wife! So that's the plain truth of it! Why, Madam, I'd rather lash myself to a tar barrel, be bound to a thorn tree in a winter's gale. Faugh!

LADY H. H. . . . A tar barrel, quotha! A thorn tree – quotha! You that were harping on galaxies and milky ways! You that were swearing I outshone 'em all! A pox on you – you faithless! You shark, you! You serpent in jack boots, you! So you won't have me? Reject my hand do you?

(She proffers her hand; he strikes it from him.)

SIR S. L. . . . Hide your chalk stones in a woollen mit! pah! I'll none of 'em! Were they diamond, pure diamond, and half the habitable globe and all its concubines strung in string round your throat I'd none of it . . . none of it. Unhand me, scritch owl, witch, vampire! Let me go!

LADY H. H. . . . So all your fine words were tinsel wrapped round a Christmas cracker!

SIR S. L. . . . Bells hung on an ass's neck! Paper roses on a barber's pole . . . O my foot, my foot . . . Cupid's darts, she mocked me . . . Old, old, he called me old . . .

(He hobbles away)

LADY H. H. (left alone) All gone. Following the wind. He's gone; she's gone; and the old clock that the rascal made himself into a pendulum for is the only one of 'em all to stop. A pox on 'em – turning an honest woman's house into a brothel. I that was Aurora Borealis am shrunk to a tar barrel. I that was Cassiopeia am turned to a she-ass. My head turns. There's no trusting man nor woman; nor fine speeches; nor fine looks. Off comes the sheep's skin; out creeps the serpent. Get ye to Gretna Green; couch on the wet grass and breed vipers. My head spins . . . Tar barrels, quotha. Cassiopeia . . . Chalk stones . . . Andromeda[111] . . . Thorn trees . . . Deb, I say, Deb (She holloas) Unlace me. I'm fit to burst . . . Bring me my green baize table and set the cards. . . . And my fur lined slippers, Deb. And a dish of chocolate. . . . I'll be even with 'em . . . I'll outlive 'em all . . . Deb, I say! Deb! A pox on the girl! Can't she hear me? Deb, I say, you gipsy's spawn that I snatched from the hedge and taught to sew samplers! Deb! Deb!

(She throws open the door leading to the maid's closet)

Empty! She's gone too! . . . Hist, what's that on the dresser?

(She picks up a scrap of paper and reads)

"What care I for your goose-feather bed? I'm off with the raggle-taggle gipsies, O! Signed: Deborah, one time your maid." So! She that I fed on apple parings and crusts from my own table, she that I taught to play cribbage and sew chemises . . . she's gone too. O ingratitude, thy name is Deborah! Who's to wash the dishes

---

[109] A piece of finery or frippery, a showy adornment in dress.

[110] A messuage is a legal term for a dwelling house together with its outbuildings and the adjacent land for its use.

[111] A constellation.

now; who's to bring me my posset now, suffer my temper and unlace my stays? . . . All gone. I'm alone then. Sans niece, sans lover; and sans maid.

> *And so to end the play, the moral is,*
> *The God of love is full of tricks;*
> *Into the foot his dart he sticks,*
> *But the way of the will is plain to see;*
> *Let holy virgins hymn perpetually:*
> *"Where there's a will there's a way."*
> *Good people all, farewell.*

(Dropping a curtsey, Lady H. H. withdrew)

The scene ended. Reason descended from her plinth. Gathering her robes about her, serenely acknowledging the applause of the audience, she passed across the stage; while Lords and Ladies in stars and garters[112] followed after; Sir Spaniel limping escorted Lady Harraden smirking; and Valentine and Flavinda arm in arm bowed and curtsied.

"God's truth!" cried Bartholomew catching the infection of the language. "There's a moral for you!"

He threw himself back in his chair and laughed, like a horse whinnying.

A moral. What? Giles supposed it was: Where there's a Will there's a Way. The words rose and pointed a finger of scorn at him. Off to Gretna Green with his girl; the deed done. Damn the consequences.

"Like to see the greenhouse?" he said abruptly, turning to Mrs. Manresa.

"Love to!" she exclaimed, and rose.

Was there an interval? Yes, the programme said so. The machine in the bushes went chuff, chuff, chuff. And the next scene?

"The Victorian age,"[113] Mrs. Elmhurst read out. Presumably there was time then for a stroll round the gardens, even for a look over the house. Yet somehow they felt – how could one put it – a little not quite here or there. As if the play had jerked the ball out of the cup; as if what I call myself was still floating unattached, and didn't settle. Not quite themselves, they felt. Or was it simply that they felt clothes conscious? Skimpy out-of-date voile dresses; flannel trousers; panama hats; hats wreathed with raspberry-coloured net in the style of the Royal Duchess's hat at Ascot seemed flimsy somehow.[114]

"How lovely the clothes were," said someone, casting a last look at Flavinda disappearing. "Most becoming. I wish . . ."

Chuff, chuff, chuff went the machine in the bushes, accurately, insistently.

Clouds were passing across the sky. The weather looked a little unsettled. Hogben's Folly was for a moment ashen white. Then the sun struck the gilt vane of Bolney Minster.

"Looks a little unsettled," said someone.

"Up you get . . . Let's stretch our legs," said another voice. Soon the lawns were floating with little moving islands of coloured dresses. Yet some of the audience remained seated.

"Major and Mrs. Mayhew," Page the reporter noted, licking his pencil. As for the play, he would collar Miss Whatshername and ask for a synopsis. But Miss La Trobe had vanished.

Down among the bushes she worked like a nigger. Flavinda was in her petticoats. Reason had thrown her mantle on a holly hedge. Sir Spaniel was tugging at his jack boots. Miss La Trobe was scattering and foraging.

"The Victorian mantle with the bead fringe . . . Where is the damned thing? Chuck it here . . . Now the whiskers . . ."

[112] Insignia of the Order of the Garter, but used here for aristocratic decorations in general.

[113] From 1837 to 1901.

[114] At the annual Royal Ascot race on June 16, 1939, the Duke and Duchess of Gloucester attended on behalf of the King and Queen, who were away on a state visit to Canada and the US; newspapers duly noted the duchess's "navy hat with flowers and pink veiling" (*Daily Telegraph*, June 17, 1939).

Ducking up and down she cast her quick bird's eye over the bushes at the audience. The audience was on the move. The audience was strolling up and down. They kept their distance from the dressing-room; they respected the conventions. But if they wandered too far, if they began exploring the grounds, going over the house, then.... Chuff, chuff, chuff went the machine. Time was passing. How long would time hold them together? It was a gamble; a risk.... And she laid about her energetically, flinging clothes on the grass.

Over the tops of the bushes came stray voices, voices without bodies, symbolical voices they seemed to her, half hearing, seeing nothing, but still, over the bushes, feeling invisible threads connecting the bodiless voices.

"It all looks very black."

"No one wants it – save those damned Germans."

There was a pause.

"I'd cut down those trees..."

"How they get their roses to grow!"

"They say there's been a garden here for five hundred years..."

"Why even old Gladstone,[115] to do him justice..."

Then there was silence. The voices passed the bushes. The trees rustled. Many eyes, Miss La Trobe knew, for every cell in her body was absorbent, looked at the view. Out of the corner of her eye she could see Hogben's Folly; then the vane flashed.

"The glass is falling," said a voice.

She could feel them slipping through her fingers, looking at the view.

"Where's that damned woman, Mrs. Rogers? Who's seen Mrs. Rogers?" she cried, snatching up a Victorian mantle.

Then, ignoring the conventions, a head popped up between the trembling sprays: Mrs. Swithin's.

"Oh Miss La Trobe!" she exclaimed; and stopped. Then she began again; "Oh Miss La Trobe, I do congratulate you!"

She hesitated. "You've given me..." She skipped, then alighted – "Ever since I was a child I've felt..." A film fell over her eyes, shutting off the present. She tried to recall her childhood; then gave it up; and, with a little wave of her hand, as if asking Miss La Trobe to help her out, continued: "This daily round; this going up and down stairs; this saying 'What am I going for? My specs? I have 'em on my nose.'..."

She gazed at Miss La Trobe with a cloudless old-aged stare. Their eyes met in a common effort to bring a common meaning to birth. They failed; and Mrs. Swithin, laying hold desperately of a fraction of her meaning, said: "What a small part I've had to play! But you've made me feel I could have played ... Cleopatra!"[116]

She nodded between the trembling bushes and ambled off.

The villagers winked. "Batty" was the word for old Flimsy, breaking through the bushes.

"I might have been – Cleopatra," Miss La Trobe repeated. "You've stirred in me my unacted part," she meant.

"Now for the skirt, Mrs. Rogers," she said.

Mrs. Rogers stood grotesque in her black stockings. Miss La Trobe pulled the voluminous flounces of the Victorian age over her head. She tied the tapes. "You've twitched the invisible strings," was what the old lady meant; and revealed – of all people – Cleopatra! Glory possessed her. Ah, but she was not merely a twitcher of individual strings; she was one who seethes wandering bodies and floating voices in a cauldron, and makes rise up from its amorphous mass a re-created world. Her moment was on her – her glory.

"There!" she said, tying the black ribbons under Mrs. Rogers' chin. "That's done it! Now for the gentleman. Hammond!"

---

[115]   William Ewart Gladstone (1809–98), Liberal politician and   [116]   Cleopatra (69–30 BC), queen of Egypt.
prime minister four times (1868–74, 1880–5, 1886, 1892–4).

She beckoned Hammond. Sheepishly he came forward, and submitted to the application of black side whiskers. With his eyes half shut, his head leant back, he looked, Miss La Trobe thought, like King Arthur – noble, knightly, thin.

"Where's the Major's old frock coat?" she asked, trusting to the effect of that to transform him.

Tick, tick, tick, the machine continued. Time was passing. The audience was wandering, dispersing. Only the tick tick of the gramophone held them together. There, sauntering solitary far away by the flower beds was Mrs. Giles escaping.

"The tune!" Miss La Trobe commanded. "Hurry up! The tune! The next tune! Number Ten!"

"Now may I pluck," Isa murmured, picking a rose, "my single flower. The white or the pink? And press it so, twixt thumb and finger. . . . "

She looked among the passing faces for the face of the man in grey. There he was for one second; but surrounded, inaccessible. And now vanished.

She dropped her flower. What single, separate leaf could she press? None. Nor stray by the beds alone. She must go on; and she turned in the direction of the stable.

"Where do I wander?" she mused. "Down what draughty tunnels? Where the eyeless wind blows? And there grows nothing for the eye. No rose. To issue where? In some harvestless dim field where no evening lets fall her mantle; nor sun rises. All's equal there. Unblowing, ungrowing are the roses there. Change is not; nor the mutable and lovable; nor greetings nor partings; nor furtive findings and feelings, where hand seeks hand and eye seeks shelter from the eye."

She had come into the stable yard where the dogs were chained; where the buckets stood; where the great pear tree spread its ladder of branches against the wall. The tree whose roots went beneath the flags, was weighted with hard green pears. Fingering one of them she murmured: "How am I burdened with what they drew from the earth; memories; possessions. This is the burden that the past laid on me, last little donkey in the long caravanserai crossing the desert. 'Kneel down,' said the past. 'Fill your pannier from our tree. Rise up, donkey. Go your way till your heels blister and your hoofs crack.'"

The pear was hard as stone. She looked down at the cracked flags beneath which the roots spread. "That was the burden," she mused, "laid on me in the cradle; murmured by waves; breathed by restless elm trees; crooned by singing women; what we must remember; what we would forget."

She looked up. The gilt hands of the stable clock pointed inflexibly at two minutes to the hour. The clock was about to strike.

"Now comes the lightning," she muttered, "from the stone blue sky. The thongs are burst that the dead tied. Loosed are our possessions."

Voices interrupted. People passed the stable yard, talking.

"It's a good day, some say, the day we are stripped naked. Others, it's the end of the day. They see the Inn and the Inn's keeper. But none speaks with a single voice. None with a voice free from the old vibrations. Always I hear corrupt murmurs; the chink of gold and metal. Mad music. . . . "

More voices sounded. The audience was streaming back to the terrace. She roused herself. She encouraged herself. "On little donkey, patiently stumble. Hear not the frantic cries of the leaders who in that they seek to lead desert us. Nor the chatter of china faces glazed and hard. Hear rather the shepherd, coughing by the farmyard wall; the withered tree that sighs when the Rider gallops; the brawl in the barrack room when they stripped her naked; or the cry which in London when I thrust the window open someone cries . . . " She had come out on to the path that led past the greenhouse. The door was kicked open. Out came Mrs. Manresa and Giles. Unseen, Isa followed them across the lawns to the front row of seats.

The chuff chuff chuff of the machine in the bushes had stopped. In obedience to Miss La Trobe's command, another tune had been put on the gramophone. Number Ten. London street cries it was called. "A Pot Pourri."

"Lavender, sweet lavender, who'll buy my sweet Lavender," the tune trilled and tinkled, ineffectively shepherding the audience. Some ignored it. Some still wandered. Others stopped, but stood upright. Some, like Colonel and Mrs. Mayhew, who had never left their seats, brooded over the blurred carbon sheet which had been issued for their information.

"The Nineteenth Century." Colonel Mayhew did not dispute the producer's right to skip two hundred years in less than fifteen minutes. But the choice of scenes baffled him.

"Why leave out the British Army? What's history without the Army, eh?" he mused. Inclining her head, Mrs. Mayhew protested after all one mustn't ask too much. Besides, very likely there would be a Grand Ensemble, round the Union Jack,[117] to end with. Meanwhile, there was the view. They looked at the view.

"Sweet lavender... sweet lavender...." Humming the tune old Mrs. Lynn Jones (of the Mount) pushed a chair forward. "Here Etty," she said, and plumped down, with Etty Springett, with whom, since both were widows now, she shared a house.

"I remember..." she nodded in time to the tune, "You remember too – how they used to cry it down the streets." They remembered – the curtains blowing, and the men crying "All a blowing, all a growing," as they came with geraniums, sweet william, in pots, down the street.

"A harp, I remember, and a hansom and a growler.[118] So quiet the street was then. Two for a hansom, was it? One for a growler? And Ellen, in cap and apron, whistling in the street? D'you remember? And the runners, my dear, who followed, all the way from the station, if one had a box."

The tune changed. "Any old iron, any old iron to sell?"[119] "D'you remember? That was what the men shouted in the fog. Seven Dials[120] they came from. Men with red handkerchiefs. Garotters, did they call them? You couldn't walk – O, dear me, no – home from the play. Regent Street. Piccadilly. Hyde Park Corner.[121] The loose women... And everywhere loaves of bread in the gutter. The Irish you know round Covent Garden... Coming back from a Ball, past the clock at Hyde Park Corner, d'you remember the feel of white gloves?... My father remembered the old Duke[122] in the Park. Two fingers like that – he'd touch his hat... I've got my mother's album. A lake and two lovers. She'd copied out Byron, I suppose, in what was called then the Italian hand...."

"What's that? 'Knocked 'em in the Old Kent Road.'[123] I remember the bootboy whistled it. O, my dear, the servants... Old Ellen... Sixteen pound a year wages... And the cans of hot water! And the crinolines! And the stays! D'you remember the Crystal Palace,[124] and the fireworks, and how Mira's slipper got lost in the mud?"

"That's young Mrs. Giles... I remember her mother. She died in India... We wore, I suppose, a great many petticoats then. Unhygienic? I dare say... Well, look at my daughter. To the right, just behind you. Forty, but slim as a wand. Each flat has its refrigerator... It took my mother half the morning to order dinner.... We were eleven. Counting servants, eighteen in family.... Now they simply ring up the Stores... That's Giles coming, with Mrs. Manresa. She's a type I don't myself fancy. I may be wrong... And Colonel Mayhew, as spruce as ever... And Mr. Cobbet of Cobbs Corner, there, under the Monkey Puzzle Tree. One don't see him often... That's what's so nice – it brings people together. These days, when we're all so busy, that's what one wants... The

---

[117] Colonel Mayhew anticipates a typical ending for an Empire Day, an annual celebration that took place on May, 24, from 1902 to 1977, when it was renamed Commonwealth Day. The date had been chosen to commemorate the death of Queen Victoria on that day in 1901.

[118] A hansom had two wheels, a growler (so named for the surly attitude of the drivers) had four.

[119] A music-hall song that was performed by Harry Champion, a popular performer. His 1911 recording of the number can be heard on *The Golden Age of the British Music Hall: Recordings from 1901–1931* (ASV Living Era CD AJA 5363).

[120] A crossroads where Monmouth Street, running northward from St. Martin's Lane, meets Shaftesbury Avenue, Endell Street, St. Giles High Street, High Holborn, and still others; until 1773 there was a column bearing six or seven arms here, Seven Dials, which gave its name to the location and the notorious slums that

surrounded it, described by Charles Dickens (1812–70) in *Bleak House* (1851–3).

[121] Regent Street runs south from Oxford Street to Piccadilly, which in turn runs west to Hyde Park Corner; though located in the West End of London, they were once notorious for prostitution.

[122] Arthur Wellesley (1769–1852), Duke of Wellington, who defeated Napoleon at Waterloo and was twice prime minister in 1828 and 1834; he regularly rode his horse in Rotten Row in Hyde Park, not far from his palatial residence, Aspley House.

[123] A popular music-hall song (1892) by Albert Chevalier, music by Charles Ingle.

[124] Constructed by Joseph Paxton in Hyde Park in 1851, the building consisted of iron and glass and was used to house the Great Exhibition. The next year it was moved to a location in south London, now Crystal Palace Park. The building burned down the night of November 30, 1936.

programme? Have you got it? Let's see what comes next...The Nineteenth Century...Look, there's the chorus, the villagers, coming on now, between the trees. First, there's a prologue...."

A great box, draped in red baize festooned with heavy gold tassels had been moved into the middle of the stage. There was a swish of dresses, a stir of chairs. The audience seated themselves, hastily, guiltily. Miss La Trobe's eye was on them. She gave them ten seconds to settle their faces. Then she flicked her hand. A pompous march tune brayed. "Firm, elatant, bold and blatant," etc.... And once more a huge symbolical figure emerged from the bushes. It was Budge the publican; but so disguised that even cronies who drank with him nightly failed to recognize him; and a little titter of enquiry as to his identity ran about among the villagers. He wore a long black many-caped cloak; waterproof; shiny; of the substance of a statue in Parliament Square; a helmet which suggested a policeman; a row of medals crossed his breast; and in his right hand he held extended a special constable's baton (loaned by Mr. Willert of the Hall). It was his voice, husky and rusty, issuing from a thick black cotton-wool beard that gave him away.

"Budge, Budge. That's Mr. Budge," the audience whispered.

Budge extended his truncheon and spoke:

It ain't an easy job, directing the traffic at 'Yde Park Corner. Buses and 'ansom cabs. All a-clatter on the cobbles. Keep to the right, can't you? Hie there, Stop!

(He waved his truncheon)

There she goes, the old party with the umbrella right under the 'orse's nose"

(The truncheon pointed markedly at Mrs. Swithin)

She raised her skinny hand as if in truth she had fluttered off the pavement on the impulse of the moment to the just rage of authority. Got her, Giles thought, taking sides with authority against his aunt.

Fog or fine weather, I does my duty (Budge continued). *At Piccadilly Circus; at 'Yde Park Corner, directing the traffic of 'Er Majesty's Empire. The Shah of Persia; Sultan of Morocco; or it may be 'Er Majesty in person; or Cook's tourists;*[125] *black men; white men; sailors, soldiers; crossing the Ocean; to proclaim her Empire; All of 'em Obey the Rule of my truncheon.*

(He flourished it magnificently from right to left)

But my job don't end there. I take under my protection and direction the purity and security of all Her Majesty's minions; in all parts of her dominions; insist that they obey the laws of God and Man.

The laws of God and Man (he repeated and made as if to consult a Statute; engrossed on a sheet of parchment which with great deliberation he now produced from his trouser pocket)

Go to Church on Sunday; on Monday, nine sharp, catch the City Bus.[126] *On Tuesday it may be, attend a meeting at the Mansion House*[127] *for the redemption of the sinner; at dinner on Wednesday attend another – turtle soup. Some bother it may be in Ireland; Famine. Fenians.*[128] *What not. On Thursday it's the natives of Peru require protection and correction; we give 'em what's due. But mark you, our rule don't end there. It's a Christian country, our Empire; under the White Queen Victoria. Over thought and religion; drink; dress; manners; marriage too, I wield my truncheon. Prosperity and respectability always go, as we know, 'and in 'and. The ruler of an Empire must keep his eye on the cot; spy too in the kitchen; drawing-room; library; wherever one or two, me and you, come together. Purity our watchword; prosperity and respectability. If not, why, let 'em fester in ...*

(He paused – no, he had not forgotten his words)

---

[125]   Tourists guided by agents of Thomas Cook and Sons, an English travel agency.

[126]   The bus taking workers into the City (see note 127) of London.

[127]   The official residence of the Lord Mayor of London, built 1739–52, used chiefly for ceremonial occasions; it is opposite the Bank of London in the City (financial district) of London.

[128]   The Irish Famine of 1848; Fenians are members of the Irish Republican Brotherhood, an organization started by Irish immigrants and active in the 1860s and 1870s, encouraging Irish insurrections and attacks on English buildings.

Cripplegate: St. Giles's; Whitechapel: the Minories.[129] *Let 'em sweat at the mines; cough at the looms; rightly endure their lot. That's the price of Empire; that's the white man's burden.*[130] *And, I can tell you, to direct the traffic orderly, at 'Yde Park Corner, Piccadilly Circus, is a whole-time, white man's job.*

He paused, eminent, dominant, glaring from his pedestal. A very fine figure of a man he was, everyone agreed, his truncheon extended; his waterproof pendant. It only wanted a shower of rain, a flight of pigeons round his head, and the pealing bells of St. Paul's and the Abbey[131] to transform him into the very spit and image of a Victorian Constable; and to transport them to a foggy London afternoon, with the muffin bells[132] ringing and the church bells pealing at the very height of Victorian prosperity.

There was a pause. The voices of the pilgrims singing, as they wound in and out between the trees, could be heard; but the words were inaudible. The audience sat waiting.

"Tut-tut-tut," Mrs. Lynn Jones expostulated. "There were grand men among them ..." Why she did not know, yet somehow she felt that a sneer had been aimed at her father; therefore at herself.

Etty Springett tutted too. Yet, children did draw trucks in mines; there was the basement; yet Papa read Walter Scott[133] aloud after dinner; and divorced ladies were not received at Court. How difficult to come to any conclusion! She wished they would hurry on with the next scene. She liked to leave a theatre knowing exactly what was meant. Of course this was only a village play.... They were setting another scene, round the red baize box. She read out from her programme:

"The Picnic Party. About 1860. Scene: A Lake. Characters –"

She stopped. A sheet had been spread on the Terrace. It was a lake apparently. Roughly painted ripples represented water. Those green stakes were bulrushes. Rather prettily, real swallows darted across the sheet.

"Look, Minnie!" she exclaimed. "Those are real swallows!"

"Hush, hush," she was admonished. For the scene had begun. A young man in peg-top trousers and side whiskers carrying a spiked stick appeared by the lake.

EDGAR T.... *Let me help you, Miss Hardcastle! There!*
> (He helps Miss Eleanor Hardcastle, a young lady in crinoline and mushroom hat, to the top. They stand for a moment panting slightly, looking at the view.)

ELEANOR. *How small the Church looks down among the trees!*

EDGAR.... *So this is Wanderer's Well, the trysting place.*

ELEANOR.... *Please Mr. Thorold, finish what you were saying before the others come. You were saying, "Our aim in life..."*

EDGAR.... *Should be to help our fellow men.*

ELEANOR (sighing deeply) *How true – how profoundly true!*

EDGAR.... *Why sigh, Miss Hardcastle? – You have nothing to reproach yourself with – you whose whole life is spent in the service of others. It was of myself that I was thinking. I am no longer young. At twenty-four the best days of life are over. My life has passed* (he throws a pebble on to the lake) *like a ripple in water.*

ELEANOR. *Oh Mr. Thorold, you do not know me. I am not what I seem. I too—*

---

129   Cripplegate is in Fore Street in the City; St. Giles's in the Fields is a church located south of New Oxford Street; Whitechapel is an area immediately east of the City; the Minories (named after the Minoresses or nuns of St. Clare) is a street east of the Tower of London, bordering the Whitechapel area. All these areas have been inhabited by poor or working-class people and have been deemed slums at various points in the past.

130   The title of a poem (1899) by Rudyard Kipling (1865–1936), a phrase that summarized imperialists' belief that empire entailed fulfilling a moral duty to subservient peoples:

> Take up the White Man's burden –
> Send for the best ye breed –
> Go bind your sons to exile

> To serve your captives' need;
> To wait in heavy harness
> On fluttered folk and wild –
> Your new-caught sullen peoples,
> Half devil and half child.

131   St. Paul's Cathedral (built 1666–1723), designed by Sir Christopher Wren (1632–1723), and Westminster Abbey (built 1065–1506) are the principal churches that serve as settings for august ceremonies in London.

132   Handbells rung by muffin-sellers in the streets to advertise their wares.

133   Sir Walter Scott (1771–1832), celebrated Scottish novelist.

EDGAR.... *Do not tell me, Miss Hardcastle – no, I cannot believe it – You have doubted?*

ELEANOR. *Thank Heaven not that, not that ... But safe and sheltered as I am, always at home, protected as you see me, as you think me. O what am I saying? But yes, I will speak the truth, before Mama comes. I too have longed to convert the Heathen!*

EDGAR.... *Miss Hardcastle ... Eleanor ... You tempt me! Dare I ask you? No – so young, so fair, so innocent. Think, I implore you, before you answer.*

ELEANOR.... *I have thought – on my knees!*

EDGAR (taking a ring from his pocket) *Then.... My mother with her last breath charged me to give this ring only to one to whom a lifetime in the African desert among the Heathens would be –*

ELEANOR (taking the ring) *Perfect happiness! But hist!* (She slips the ring into her pocket) *Here's Mama!* (They start asunder)

(Enter Mrs. Hardcastle, a stout lady in black bombazine, upon a donkey, escorted by an elderly gentleman in a deer-stalker's cap)

MRS. H.... *So you stole a march upon us, young people. There was a time, Sir John, when you and I were always first on top. Now ...*

(He helps her to alight. Children, young men, young women, some carrying hampers, others butterfly nets, others spy-glasses, others tin botanical cases arrive. A rug is thrown by the lake and Mrs. H. and Sir John seat themselves on camp stools.)

MRS. H.... *Now who'll fill the kettles? Who'll gather the sticks? Alfred* (to a small boy), *don't run about chasing butterflies or you'll make yourself sick ... Sir John and I will unpack the hampers, here where the grass is burnt, where we had the picnic last year.*

(The young people scatter off in different directions. Mrs. H. and Sir John begin to unpack the hamper)

MRS. H.... *Last year poor dear Mr. Beach was with us. It was a blessed release.* (She takes out a black-bordered handkerchief and wipes her eyes.) *Every year one of us is missing. That's the ham ... That's the grouse ... There in that packet are the game pasties ...* (She spreads the eatables on the grass) *As I was saying poor dear Mr. Beach ... I do hope the cream hasn't curdled. Mr. Hardcastle is bringing the claret. I always leave that to him. Only when Mr. Hardcastle gets talking with Mr. Pigott about the Romans ... last year they quite came to words.... But it's nice for gentlemen to have a hobby, though they do gather the dust – those skulls and things ... But I was saying – poor dear Mr. Beach.... I wanted to ask you* (she drops her voice) *as a friend of the family, about the new clergyman – they can't hear us, can they? No, they're picking up sticks.... Last year, such a disappointment. Just got the things out ... down came the rain. But I wanted to ask you, about the new clergyman, the one who's come in place of dear Mr. Beach. I'm told the name's Sibthorp. To be sure, I hope I'm right, for I had a cousin who married a girl of that name, and as a friend of the family, we don't stand on ceremony ... And when one has daughters – I'm sure I quite envy you, with only one daughter, Sir John, and I have four! So I was asking you to tell me in confidence, about this young – if that's-his-name – Sibthorp, for I must tell you the day before yesterday our Mrs. Potts happened to say, as she passed the Rectory, bringing our laundry, they were unpacking the furniture; and what did she see on top of the wardrobe? A tea cosy! But of course she might be mistaken ... But it occurred to me to ask you, as a friend of the family, in confidence,* has Mr. Sibthorp a wife?

Here a chorus composed of villagers in Victorian mantles, side whiskers and top hats sang in concert:

O has Mr. Sibthorp a wife? O has Mr. Sibthorp a wife? That is the hornet, the bee in the bonnet, the screw in the cork and the drill; that whirling and twirling are for ever unfurling the folds of the motherly heart; for a mother must ask, if daughters she has, begot in the feathery billowy fourposter family bed, O did he unpack, with his prayer book and bands; his gown and his cane; his rod and his line; and the family album and gun; did he also display the connubial respectable tea-table token, a cosy with honeysuckle embossed. Has Mr. Sibthorp a wife? O has Mr. Sibthorp a wife?

While the chorus was sung, the picnickers assembled. Corks popped. Grouse, ham, chickens were sliced. Lips munched. Glasses were drained. Nothing was heard but the chump of jaws and the chink of glasses.

"They did eat," Mrs. Lynn Jones whispered to Mrs. Springett. "That's true. More than was good for them, I dare say."

MR. HARDCASTLE ... (brushing flakes of meat from his whiskers) *Now...*

"Now what?" whispered Mrs. Springett, anticipating further travesty.

Now that we have gratified the inner man, let us gratify the desire of the spirit. I call upon one of the young ladies for a song.

CHORUS OF YOUNG LADIES ... *O not me... not me... I really couldn't... No, you cruel thing, you know I've lost my voice... I can't sing without the instrument... etc., etc.*

CHORUS OF YOUNG MEN. *O bosh! Let's have "The Last Rose of Summer."*[134] *Let's have "I never loved a Dear Gazelle."*[135]

MRS. H. (authoritatively) *Eleanor and Mildred will now sing "I'd be a Butterfly."*

(Eleanor and Mildred rise obediently and sing a duet: "I'd be a Butterfly."[136])

MRS. H. ... *Thank you very much, my dears. And now gentlemen, Our Country!*

(Arthur and Edgar sing "Rule Britannia."[137])

MRS. H. ... *Thank you very much. Mr. Hardcastle –*

MR. HARDCASTLE (rising to his feet, clasping his fossil) *Let us pray.*

(The whole company rise to their feet.)

"This is too much, too much," Mrs. Springett protested.

MR. H. ... *Almighty God, giver of all good things, we thank Thee; for our food and drink; for the beauties of Nature; for the understanding with which Thou hast enlightened us* (he fumbles with his fossil) *And for thy great gift of Peace. Grant us to be thy servants on earth; grant us to spread the light of thy...*

Here the hindquarters of the donkey, represented by Albert the idiot, became active. Intentional was it, or accidental? "Look at the donkey! Look at the donkey!" A titter drowned Mr. Hardcastle's prayer; and then he was heard saying:

...a happy homecoming with bodies refreshed by thy bounty, and minds inspired by thy wisdom. Amen.

Holding his fossil in front of him, Mr. Hardcastle marched off. The donkey was captured; hampers were loaded; and forming into a procession, the picnickers began to disappear over the hill.

EDGAR (winding up the procession with Eleanor) *To convert the heathen!*

ELEANOR. *To help our fellow men!*

(The actors disappeared into the bushes.)

BUDGE. ... *It's time, gentlemen, time ladies, time to pack up and be gone. From where I stand, truncheon in hand, guarding respectability, and prosperity, and the purity of Victoria's land, I see before me –* (he pointed: there was Pointz Hall; the rooks cawing; the smoke rising)

'Ome, Sweet 'Ome.[138]

The gramophone took up the strain: *Through pleasures and palaces, etc. There's no place like Home.*

BUDGE. ... *Home, gentlemen; home, ladies, it's time to pack up and go home. Don't I see the fire* (he pointed: one window blazed red) *blazing ever higher? In kitchen; and nursery; drawing-room and library? That's the fire of 'Ome. And see! Our Jane has brought the tea. Now children where's the toys? Mama, your knitting, quick. For here* (he swept his truncheon at Cobbet of Cobbs Corner) *comes the bread-winner, home from the city, home from the counter, home from the shop.* "Mama, a cup o' tea." "Children, gather round my knee. *I will read aloud. Which shall it be? Sindbad the sailor?*[139] *Or some simple tale from Scriptures? And show you*

---

[134] A poem by Thomas Moore (1779–1852), an Irish poet; it was set to music by the German composer Friedrich von Flotow (1812–83) and turned into an aria in his light opera *Martha* (1847), whence it became a popular song.

[135] A common misquotation from a sentimental epic by Thomas Moore, *Lalla Rookh*:

> I never nursed a dear gazelle,
> To glad me with its soft black eye,
> But when it came to know me well,
> And love me, it was sure to die!

[136] Song by Thomas J. Bayly: "I'd be a butterfly born in a bower, / Where roses and lilies and violets meet."

[137] A patriotic song by James Johnson with music by Thomas Arne, originally part of *Alfred: A Masque* (1740); it begins:

"Rule, Britannia, Britannia rules the waves; / Britons never, never, never shall be slaves."

[138] A popular song by John Howard Payne (1791–1852) with music by Sir Henry Bishop (1786–1855):

> Mid pleasures and palaces though we may roam,
> Be it ever so humble, there's no place like home.

Refrain:

> Home, Home, sweet sweet Home?
> There's no place like Home!
> There's no place like Home!

[139] One of many heroes in *The Arabian Nights*.

the pictures? What none of 'em? Then out with the bricks. Let's build: A Conservatory. A Laboratory? A Mechanics Institute?[140] *Or shall it be a Tower; with our Flag on top;*[141] *where our widowed Queen, after tea, calls the Royal orphans round her knee? For it's 'Ome, ladies, 'Ome, gentlemen. Be it never so 'umble, there's no place like 'Ome."*

The gramophone warbled Home, Sweet Home, and Budge, swaying slightly, descended from his box and followed the procession off the stage.

There was an interval.

"Oh but it was beautiful," Mrs. Lynn Jones protested. Home she meant; the lamplit room; the ruby curtains; and Papa reading aloud.

They were rolling up the lake and uprooting the bulrushes. Real swallows were skimming over real grass. But she still saw the Home.

"It was . . . " she repeated, referring to the Home.

"Cheap and nasty, I call it," snapped Etty Springett, referring to the play, and shot a vicious glance at Dodge's green trousers, yellow spotted tie, and unbuttoned waistcoat.

But Mrs. Lynn Jones still saw the Home. Was there, she mused, as Budge's red baize pediment was rolled off, something – not impure, that wasn't the word – but perhaps "unhygienic" about the Home? Like a bit of meat gone sour, with whiskers, as the servants called it? Or why had it perished? Time went on and on like the hands of the kitchen clock. (The machine chuffed in the bushes.) If they had met with no resistance, she mused, nothing wrong, they'd still be going round and round and round. The Home would have remained; and Papa's beard, she thought, would have grown and grown; and Mama's knitting – what did she do with all her knitting? – Change had to come, she said to herself, or there'd have been yards and yards of Papa's beard, of Mama's knitting. Nowadays her son-in-law was clean shaven. Her daughter had a refrigerator. . . . Dear, how my mind wanders, she checked herself. What she meant was, change had to come, unless things were perfect; in which case she supposed they resisted Time. Heaven was changeless.

"Were they like that?" Isa asked abruptly. She looked at Mrs. Swithin as if she had been a dinosaur or a very diminutive mammoth. Extinct she must be, since she had lived in the reign of Queen Victoria.

Tick, tick, tick, went the machine in the bushes.

"The Victorians," Mrs. Swithin mused. "I don't believe" she said with her odd little smile, "that there ever were such people. Only you and me and William dressed differently."

"You don't believe in history," said William.

The stage remained empty. The cows moved in the field. The shadows were deeper under the trees.

Mrs. Swithin caressed her cross. She gazed vaguely at the view. She was off, they guessed, on a circular tour of the imagination – one-making. Sheep, cows, grass, trees, ourselves – all are one. If discordant, producing harmony – if not to us, to a gigantic ear attached to a gigantic head. And thus – she was smiling benignly – the agony of the particular sheep, cow, or human being is necessary; and so – she was beaming seraphically at the gilt vane in the distance – we reach the conclusion that *all* is harmony, could we hear it. And we shall. Her eyes now rested on the white summit of a cloud. Well, if the thought gave her comfort, William and Isa smiled across her, let her think it.

Tick tick tick the machine reiterated.

"D'you get her meaning?" said Mrs. Swithin alighting suddenly. "Miss La Trobe's?"

Isa, whose eyes had been wandering, shook her head.

"But you might say the same of Shakespeare," said Mrs. Swithin.

"Shakespeare and the musical glasses!"[142] Mrs. Manresa intervened. "Dear, what a barbarian you all make me feel!"

---

[140] Mechanics' Institutes were educational institutions, with libraries, for working men, founded in the early nineteenth century by the Society for the Diffusion of Useful Knowledge.

[141] Windsor Castle, where Queen Victoria retired after the death of her husband Prince Albert in 1861; the Union Jack is flown when the monarch is in residence.

[142] Musical glasses were instruments in which notes were produced by touching or stroking graduated glass tubes. In

She turned to Giles. She invoked his help against this attack upon the jolly human heart.

"Tosh," Giles muttered.

Nothing whatever appeared on the stage.

Darts of red and green light flashed from the rings on Mrs. Manresa's fingers. He looked from them at Aunt Lucy. From her to William Dodge. From him to Isa. She refused to meet his eyes. And he looked down at his blood-stained tennis shoes.

He said (without words) "I'm damnably unhappy."

"So am I," Dodge echoed.

"And I too," Isa thought.

They were all caught and caged; prisoners; watching a spectacle. Nothing happened. The tick of the machine was maddening.

"On, little donkey" Isa murmured, "crossing the desert . . . bearing your burden . . . "

She felt Dodge's eye upon her as her lips moved. Always some cold eye crawled over the surface like a winter blue-bottle! She flicked him off.

"What a time they take!" she exclaimed irritably.

"Another interval," Dodge read out, looking at the programme.

"And after that, what?" asked Lucy.

"Present time. Ourselves," he read.

"Let's hope to God that's the end," said Giles gruffly.

"Now you're being naughty," Mrs. Manresa reproved her little boy, her surly hero.

No one moved. There they sat, facing the empty stage, the cows, the meadows and the view, while the machine ticked in the bushes.

"What's the object," said Bartholomew, suddenly rousing himself, "of this entertainment?"

"The profits," Isa read out from her blurred carbon copy, "are to go to a fund for installing electric light in the Church."

"All our village festivals," Mr. Oliver snorted turning to Mrs. Manresa, "end with a demand for money."

"Of course, of course," she murmured, deprecating his severity, and the coins in her bead bag jingled.

"Nothing's done for nothing in England," the old man continued. Mrs. Manresa protested. It might be true, perhaps, of the Victorians; but surely not of ourselves? Did she really believe that we were disinterested? Mr. Oliver demanded.

"Oh you don't know my husband!" the wild child exclaimed, striking an attitude.

Admirable woman! You could trust her to crow when the hour struck like an alarm clock; to stop like an old bus horse when the bell rang. Oliver said nothing. Mrs. Manresa had out her mirror and attended to her face.

All their nerves were on edge. They sat exposed. The machine ticked. There was no music. The horns of cars on the high road were heard. And the swish of trees. They were neither one thing nor the other; neither Victorians nor themselves. They were suspended, without being, in limbo. Tick, tick, tick went the machine.

Isa fidgeted; glancing to right and to left over her shoulder.

"Four and twenty blackbirds, strung upon a string,"[143] she muttered.

"Down came an Ostrich, an eagle, an executioner,[144]

'Which of you is ripe,' he said, 'to bake in my pie?

Which of you is ripe, which of you is ready,

Come my pretty gentleman,

Come my pretty lady.' . . . "

The *Vicar of Wakefield* (1766) by Oliver Goldsmith (1728–74), two fashionable ladies from town entertain the country-bred daughters of the vicar by adducing examples of "sophisticated" town life: "pictures, taste, Shakespeare, and the musical glasses."

[143] From the children's song rhyme "Sing a Song of Sixpence," which goes: Four and twenty blackbirds, / Baked in a pie."

[144] Adapted from the fourth stanza of "Sing a Song of Sixpence," which has the lines: "Down came a blackbird, / And picked off her nose."

How long was she going to keep them waiting? "The present time. Ourselves." They read it on the programme. Then they read what came next: "The profits are to go to a fund for installing electric light in the Church." Where was the Church? Over there. You could see the spire among the trees.

"Ourselves...." They returned to the programme. But what could she know about ourselves? The Elizabethans yes; the Victorians, perhaps; but ourselves; sitting here on a June day in 1939 – it was ridiculous. "Myself" – it was impossible. Other people, perhaps... Cobbet of Cobbs Corner; the Major; old Bartholomew; Mrs. Swithin – them, perhaps. But she won't get me – no, not me. The audience fidgeted. Sounds of laughter came from the bushes. But nothing whatsoever appeared on the stage.

"What's she keeping us waiting for?" Colonel Mayhew asked irritably. "They don't need to dress up if it's present time."

Mrs. Mayhew agreed. Unless of course she was going to end with a Grand Ensemble. Army; Navy; Union Jack; and behind them perhaps – Mrs. Mayhew sketched what she would have done had it been her pageant – the Church. In cardboard. One window, looking east, brilliantly illuminated to symbolize – she could work that out when the time came.

"There she is, behind the tree," she whispered, pointing at Miss La Trobe.

Miss La Trobe stood there with her eye on her script. "After Vic." she had written, "try ten mins. of present time. Swallows, cows etc." She wanted to expose them, as it were, to douche them, with present time: reality. But something was going wrong with the experiment. "Reality too strong," she muttered. "Curse 'em!" She felt everything they felt. Audiences were the devil. O to write a play without an audience – *the* play. But here she was fronting her audience. Every second they were slipping the noose. Her little game had gone wrong. If only she'd a back-cloth to hang between the trees – to shut out cows, swallows, present time! But she had nothing. She had forbidden music. Grating her fingers in the bark, she damned the audience. Panic seized her. Blood seemed to pour from her shoes. This is death, death, death, she noted in the margin of her mind; when illusion fails. Unable to lift her hand, she stood facing the audience.

And then the shower fell, sudden, profuse.

No one had seen the cloud coming. There it was, black, swollen, on top of them. Down it poured like all the people in the world weeping. Tears. Tears. Tears.

"O that our human pain could here have ending!"[145] Isa murmured. Looking up she received two great blots of rain full in her face. They trickled down her cheeks as if they were her own tears. But they were all people's tears, weeping for all people. Hands were raised. Here and there a parasol opened. The rain was sudden and universal. Then it stopped. From the grass rose a fresh earthy smell.

"That's done it," sighed Miss La Trobe, wiping away the drops on her cheeks. Nature once more had taken her part. The risk she had run acting in the open air was justified. She brandished her script. Music began – A.B.C. – A.B.C. The tune was as simple as could be. But now that the shower had fallen, it was the other voice speaking, the voice that was no one's voice. And the voice that wept for human pain unending said:

> The King is in his counting house,
> Counting out his money,
> The Queen is in her parlour...

"O that my life could here have ending," Isa murmured (taking care not to move her lips). Readily would she endow this voice with all her treasure if so be tears could be ended. The little twist of sound could have the whole of her. On the altar of the rain-soaked earth she laid down her sacrifice....

"O look!" she cried aloud.

---

[145] Adapted from John Milton's poem "On the Morning of Christ's Nativity":

But see the Virgin blest,
Hath laid her Babe to rest.
Time is our tedious Song should here have ending.

That was a ladder. And that (a cloth roughly painted) was a wall. And that a man with a hod on his back. Mr. Page the reporter, licking his pencil, noted: "With the very limited means at her disposal, Miss La Trobe conveyed to the audience Civilization (the wall) in ruins; rebuilt (witness man with hod) by human effort; witness also woman handing bricks. Any fool could grasp that. Now issued black man in fuzzy wig; coffee-coloured ditto in silver turban; they signify presumably the League of..."[146]

A burst of applause greeted this flattering tribute to ourselves. Crude of course. But then she had to keep expenses down. A painted cloth must convey – what the *Times* and *Telegraph* both said in their leaders[147] that very morning.

The tune hummed:

> *The King is in his counting house,*
> *Counting out his money,*
> *The Queen is in her parlour*
> *Eating...*

Suddenly the tune stopped. The tune changed. A waltz, was it? Something half known, half not. The swallows danced it. Round and round, in and out they skimmed. Real swallows. Retreating and advancing. And the trees, O the trees, how gravely and sedately like senators in council, or the spaced pillars of some cathedral church.... Yes, they barred the music, and massed and hoarded; and prevented what was fluid from overflowing. The swallows – or martins were they? – The temple-haunting martins[148] who come, have always come... Yes, perched on the wall, they seemed to foretell what after all the *Times* was saying yesterday. Homes will be built. Each flat with its refrigerator, in the crannied wall. Each of us a free man; plates washed by machinery; not an aeroplane to vex us; all liberated; made whole....

The tune changed; snapped; broke; jagged. Fox-trot was it? Jazz? Anyhow the rhythm kicked, reared, snapped short. What a jangle and a jingle! Well, with the means at her disposal, you can't ask too much. What a cackle, a cacophony! Nothing ended. So abrupt. And corrupt. Such an outrage; such an insult. And not plain. Very up to date, all the same. What is her game? To disrupt? Jog and trot? Jerk and smirk? Put the finger to the nose? Squint and pry? Peek and spy? O the irreverence of the generation which is only momentarily – thanks be – "the young." The young, who can't make, but only break; shiver into splinters the old vision; smash to atoms what was whole. What a cackle, what a rattle, what a yaffle – as they call the woodpecker, the laughing bird that flits from tree to tree.

Look! Out they come, from the bushes – the riff-raff. Children? Imps – elves – demons. Holding what? Tin cans? Bedroom candlesticks? Old jars? My dear, that's the cheval glass from the Rectory! And the mirror – that I lent her. My mother's. Cracked. What's the notion? Anything that's bright enough to reflect, presumably, ourselves?

Our selves! Our selves!

Out they leapt, jerked, skipped. Flashing, dazzling, dancing, jumping. Now old Bart... he was caught. Now Manresa. Here a nose... There a skirt... Then trousers only... Now perhaps a face.... Ourselves? But that's cruel. To snap us as we are, before we've had time to assume... And only, too, in parts.... That's what's so distorting and upsetting and utterly unfair.

Mopping, mowing, whisking, frisking, the looking-glasses darted, flashed, exposed. People in the back rows stood up to see the fun. Down they sat, caught themselves... What an awful show-up! Even for the old who, one might suppose, hadn't any longer any care about their faces.... And Lord! the jangle and the din! The very cows joined in. Walloping, tail lashing, the reticence of nature was undone, and the barriers which should divide Man the Master from the Brute were dissolved. Then the dogs joined in. Excited by the uproar, scurrying and worrying, here they came! Look at them! And the hound, the Afghan hound... look at him!

[146]   League of Nations, founded in 1920 to prevent war and promote international cooperation. By 1939 it was clear it had failed.
[147]   The British counterpart to "editorials" in American usage.
[148]   Shakespeare, *Macbeth*, Act 1, Scene 6: "The temple-haunting martlet doth approve."

Then once more, in the uproar which by this time has passed quite beyond control, behold Miss Whatshername behind the tree summoned from the bushes – or was it *they* who broke away – Queen Bess; Queen Anne; and the girl in the Mall; and the Age of Reason; and Budge the policeman. Here they came. And the Pilgrims. And the lovers. And the grandfather's clock. And the old man with a beard. They all appeared. What's more, each declaimed some phrase or fragment from their parts . . . *I am not* (said one) *in my perfect mind*[149] . . . Another, *Reason am I . . . And I? I'm the old top hat. . . . Home is the hunter, home from the hill*[150] . . . *Home? Where the miner sweats, and maiden faith is rudely strumpeted.*[151] . . . *Sweet and low; sweet and low, wind of the western sea*[152] . . . *Is that a dagger that I see before me?*[153] . . . *The owl hoots and the ivy mocks tap-tap-tapping on the pane. . . . Lady I love till I die, leave thy chamber and come . . . Where the worm weaves its winding sheet*[154] . . . *I'd be a butterfly. I'd be a butterfly.*[155] . . . *In thy will is our peace.*[156] . . . *Here, Papa, take your book and read aloud. . . . Hark, hark, the dogs do bark and the beggars* . . .

It was the cheval glass that proved too heavy. Young Bonthorp for all his muscle couldn't lug the damned thing about any longer. He stopped. So did they all – hand glasses, tin cans, scraps of scullery glass, harness room glass, and heavily embossed silver mirrors – all stopped. And the audience saw themselves, not whole by any means, but at any rate sitting still.

The hands of the clock had stopped at the present moment. It was now. Ourselves.

So that was her little game! To show us up, as we are, here and now. All shifted, preened, minced; hands were raised, legs shifted. Even Bart, even Lucy, turned away. All evaded or shaded themselves – save Mrs. Manresa who, facing herself in the glass, used it as a glass; had out her mirror; powdered her nose; and moved one curl, disturbed by the breeze, to its place.

"Magnificent!" cried old Bartholomew. Alone she preserved unashamed her identity, and faced without blinking herself. Calmly she reddened her lips.

The mirror bearers squatted; malicious; observant; expectant; expository.

"That's them," the back rows were tittering. "Must we submit passively to this malignant indignity?" the front row demanded. Each turned ostensibly to say – O whatever came handy – to his neighbour. Each tried to shift an inch or two beyond the inquisitive insulting eye. Some made as if to go.

"The play's over, I take it," muttered Colonel Mayhew, retrieving his hat. "It's time . . ."

But before they had come to any common conclusion, a voice asserted itself. Whose voice it was no one knew. It came from the bushes – a megaphonic, anonymous, loud-speaking affirmation. The voice said:

Before we part, ladies and gentlemen, before we go . . . (Those who had risen sat down) . . . *let's talk in words of one syllable, without larding, stuffing or cant. Let's break the rhythm and forget the rhyme. And calmly consider ourselves. Ourselves. Some bony. Some fat.* (The glasses confirmed this.) *Liars most of us. Thieves too.* (The glasses made no comment on that.) *The poor are as bad as the rich are. Perhaps worse. Don't hide among rags. Or let our cloth protect us. Or for the matter of that book learning; or skilful practice on*

---

[149] Someone quotes King Lear's line on madness (Shakespeare, *King Lear*, Act 4, scene 7), earlier quoted by Giles (see p. 854).

[150] From Robert Louis Stevenson (1850–94), "Requiem":

> This be the verse you grave for me:
> "Here he lies where he longed to be;
> Home is the sailor, home from sea,
> And the hunter home from the hill."

[151] Shakespeare, Sonnet 66:

> Tir'd with all these, for restful death I cry,
> As to behold desert a beggar born
> And needy nothing trimmed in jollity,
> And purest faith unhappily forsworn,
> And gilded honor shamefully misplaced,
> And maiden virtue rudely strumpeted,

> . . .
> Tir'd with all these, from these I would be gone,
> Save that to die, I leave my love alone.

[152] A lullaby from Tennyson, "The Princess," II, line 456.

[153] *Macbeth*, Act 2, scene 1, line 46.

[154] This passage conflates two lines from different poems by William Blake: "The invisible worm / That flies in the night" (from "The Sick Rose") and "The harlot's cry from street to street / Shall weave Old England's winding Sheet" (from "Auguries of Innocence").

[155] Song by Thomas J. Bayly: "I'd be a butterfly born in a bower, / Where roses and lilies and violets meet." Cited earlier on p. 881, and note 136.

[156] Dante, *Paradiso* III. 85: "E'n la sua volontade è nostra pace" (In His will is our peace).

pianos; or laying on of paint. Or presume there's innocency in childhood. Consider the sheep. Or faith in love. Consider the dogs.[157] *Or virtue in those that have grown white hairs. Consider the gun slayers, bomb droppers, – here or there. They do openly what we do slyly. Take for example* (here the megaphone adopted a colloquial, conversational tone) *Mr. M's bungalow. A view spoilt for ever. That's murder... Or Mrs. E's lipstick and blood-red nails.... A tyrant, remember, is half a slave. Item the vanity of Mr. H. the writer, scraping in the dunghill for sixpenny fame... Then there's the amiable condescension of the lady of the manor – the upper class manner. And buying shares in the market to sell 'em.... O we're all the same. Take myself now. Do I escape my own reprobation, simulating indignation, in the bush, among the leaves? There's a rhyme, to suggest, in spite of protestation and the desire for immolation, I too have had some, what's called, education... Look at ourselves, ladies and gentlemen! Then at the wall; and ask how's this wall, the great wall, which we call, perhaps miscall, civilization, to be built by* (here the mirrors flicked and flashed) *orts, scraps and fragments like ourselves?*[158]

All the same here I change (by way of the rhyme mark ye) to a loftier strain – there's something to be said: for our kindness to the cat; note too in today's paper "Dearly loved by his wife"; and the impulse which leads us – mark you, when no one's looking – to the window at midnight to smell the bean. Or the resolute refusal of some pimpled dirty little scrub in sandals to sell his soul. There is such a thing – you can't deny it. What? You can't descry it? All you can see of your selves is scraps, orts and fragments? Well then listen to the gramophone affirming....

A hitch occurred here. The records had been mixed. Fox trot, Sweet lavender, Home Sweet Home, Rule Britannia – sweating profusely, Jimmy, who had charge of the music, threw them aside and fitted the right one – was it Bach, Handel, Beethoven, Mozart[159] or nobody famous, but merely a traditional tune? Anyhow, thank heaven, it was somebody speaking after the anonymous bray of the infernal megaphone.

Like quicksilver sliding, filings magnetized, the distracted united. The tune began; the first note meant a second; the second a third. Then down beneath a force was born in opposition; then another. On different levels they diverged. On different levels our selves went forward; flower gathering some on the surface; others descending to wrestle with the meaning; but all comprehending; all enlisted. The whole population of the mind's immeasurable profundity came flocking; from the unprotected, the unskinned; and dawn rose; and azure; from chaos and cacophony measure; but not the melody of surface sound alone controlled it; but also the warring battle-plumed warriors straining asunder: To part? No. Compelled from the ends of the horizon; recalled from the edge of appalling crevasses; they crashed; solved; united. And some relaxed their fingers; and others uncrossed their legs.

Was that voice our selves? Scraps, orts and fragments, are we, also, that? The voice died away.

As waves withdrawing uncover; as mist uplifting reveals; so, raising their eyes (Mrs. Manresa's were wet; for an instant tears ravaged her powder) they saw, as waters withdrawing leave visible a tramp's old boot, a man in a clergyman's collar surreptitiously mounting a soap-box.

"The Rev. G. W. Streatfield," the reporter licked his pencil and noted "then spoke..."

All gazed. What an intolerable constriction, contraction, and reduction to simplified absurdity he was to be sure! Of all incongruous sights a clergyman in the livery of his servitude to the summing up was the most grotesque and entire. He opened his mouth. O Lord, protect and preserve us from words the defilers,[160] from words the impure! What need have we of words to remind us? Must I be Thomas, you Jane?[161]

---

[157] "Consider the ravens: for they neither sow nor reap ... Consider the lilies how they grow: they toil not, they spin not" (Luke 12:24, 27).
[158] From Shakespeare, *Troilus and Cressida*, Act 5, scene 2, lines 181–5:

The bonds of heaven are slipt, dissolv'd, and loos'd,
And with another knot five finger tied,
The fractions of her faith, orts of her love,
The fragments, scraps, the bits, and greasy relics,
Of her o'er-eaten faith, are bound to Diomed.

[159] Johann Sebastian Bach (1685–1750), Georg Friedrich Händel (1685–1759), Ludwig van Beethoven (1770–1827), Wolfgang Amadeus Mozart (1756–91), all German composers except the last, who was Austrian.
[160] "Not that which goeth into the mouth defileth a man; but that which cometh out of the mouth, this defileth a man" (Mathew 15:11).
[161] "John Thomas" and "Lady Jane" are traditional nicknames for the sexual parts.

As if a rook had hopped unseen to a prominent bald branch, he touched his collar and hemmed his preliminary croak. One fact mitigated the horror; his forefinger, raised in the customary manner, was stained with tobacco juice. He wasn't such a bad fellow; the Rev. G. W. Streatfield; a piece of traditional church furniture; a corner cupboard; or the top beam of a gate, fashioned by generations of village carpenters after some lost-in-the-mists-of-antiquity model.

He looked at the audience; then up at the sky. The whole lot of them, gentles and simples, felt embarrassed, for him, for themselves. There he stood their representative spokesman; their symbol; themselves; a butt, a clod, laughed at by looking-glasses; ignored by the cows, condemned by the clouds which continued their majestic rearrangement of the celestial landscape; an irrelevant forked stake[162] in the flow and majesty of the summer silent world.

His first words (the breeze had risen; the leaves were rustling) were lost. Then he was heard saying: "What." To that word he added another "Message"; and at last a whole sentence emerged; not comprehensible; say rather audible. "What message," it seemed he was asking, "was our pageant meant to convey?"

They folded their hands in the traditional manner as if they were seated in church.

"I have been asking myself" – the words were repeated – "what meaning, or message, this pageant was meant to convey?"

If he didn't know, calling himself Reverend, also M.A., who after all could?

"As one of the audience," he continued (words now put on meaning) "I will offer, very humbly, for I am not a critic" – and he touched the white gate that enclosed his neck with a yellow forefinger – "my interpretation. No, that is too bold a word. The gifted lady..." He looked round. La Trobe was invisible. He continued: "Speaking merely as one of the audience, I confess I was puzzled. For what reason, I asked, were we shown these scenes? Briefly, it is true. The means at our disposal this afternoon were limited. Still we were shown different groups. We were shown, unless I mistake, the effort renewed. A few were chosen; the many passed in the background. That surely we were shown. But again, were we not given to understand – am I too presumptuous? Am I treading, like angels, where as a fool I should absent myself?[163] To me at least it was indicated that we are members one of another.[164] Each is part of the whole. Yes, that occurred to me, sitting among you in the audience. Did I not perceive Mr. Hardcastle here" (he pointed) "at one time a Viking? And in Lady Harridan – excuse me, if I get the names wrong – a Canterbury pilgrim? We act different parts; but are the same. That I leave to you. Then again, as the play or pageant proceeded, my attention was distracted. Perhaps that too was part of the producer's intention? I thought I perceived that nature takes her part. Dare we, I asked myself, limit life to ourselves? May we not hold that there is a spirit that inspires, pervades..." (the swallows were sweeping round him. They seemed cognizant of his meaning. Then they swept out of sight.) "I leave that to you. I am not here to explain. That role has not been assigned me. I speak only as one of the audience, one of ourselves. I caught myself too reflected, as it happened in my own mirror..." (Laughter) "Scraps, orts and fragments! Surely, we should unite?"

"But" ("but" marked a new paragraph) "I speak also in another capacity. As Treasurer of the Fund. In which capacity" (he consulted a sheet of paper) "I am glad to be able to tell you that a sum of thirty-six pounds ten shillings and eightpence has been raised by this afternoon's entertainment towards our object: the illumination of our dear old Church."

"Applause," the reporter reported.

Mr. Streatfield paused. He listened. Did he hear some distant music?

He continued: "But there is still a deficit" (he consulted his paper) "of one hundred and seventy-five pounds odd. So that each of us who has enjoyed this pageant has still an opp..." The word was cut in two. A zoom severed it. Twelve aeroplanes in perfect formation like a flight of wild duck came overhead. *That* was the music. The audience gaped; the audience gazed. Then zoom became drone. The planes had passed.

---

[162] "Unaccommodated man is no more but such a poor, bare, forked animal as thou art" (Shakespeare, *King Lear*, Act 3, Scene 4, 107).

[163] "For fools rush in where angels fear to tread": Alexander Pope (1688–1744), *Essay on Criticism*, III, 625.

[164] Ephesians 4:25.

"...portunity," Mr. Streatfield continued, "to make a contribution." He signalled. Instantly collecting boxes were in operation. Hidden behind glasses they emerged. Coppers rattled. Silver jingled. But O what a pity – how creepy it made one feel! Here came Albert, the idiot, jingling his collecting box – an aluminium saucepan without a lid. You couldn't very well deny him, poor fellow. Shillings were dropped. He rattled and sniggered; chattered and jibbered. As Mrs. Parker made her contribution – half a crown as it happened – she appealed to Mr. Streatfield to exorcize this evil, to extend the protection of his cloth.

The good man contemplated the idiot benignly. His faith had room, he indicated, for him too. He too, Mr. Streatfield appeared to be saying, is part of ourselves. But not a part we like to recognize, Mrs. Springett added silently, dropping her sixpence.

Contemplating the idiot, Mr. Streatfield had lost the thread of his discourse. His command over words seemed gone. He twiddled the cross on his watch chain. Then his hand sought his trouser pocket. Surreptitiously he extracted a small silver box. It was plain to all that the natural desire of the natural man was overcoming him. He had no further use for words.

"And now," he resumed, cuddling the pipe lighter in the palm of his hand, "for the pleasantest part of my duty. To propose a vote of thanks to the gifted lady..." He looked round for an object corresponding to this description. None such was visible. "...who wishes it seems to remain anonymous." He paused. "And so..." He paused again.

It was an awkward moment. How to make an end? Whom to thank? Every sound in nature was painfully audible; the swish of the trees; the gulp of a cow; even the skim of the swallows over the grass could be heard. But no one spoke. Whom could they make responsible? Whom could they thank for their entertainment? Was there no one?

Then there was a scuffle behind the bush; a preliminary premonitory scratching. A needle scraped a disc; chuff, chuff chuff; then having found the rut, there was a roll and a flutter which portended God...(they all rose to their feet) Save the King.

Standing the audience faced the actors; who also stood with their collecting boxes quiescent, their looking-glasses hidden, and the robes of their various parts hanging stiff.

Happy and glorious,
Long to reign over us
God save the King[165]

The notes died away.

Was that the end? The actors were reluctant to go. They lingered; they mingled. There was Budge the policeman talking to old Queen Bess. And the Age of Reason hobnobbed with the foreparts of the donkey. And Mrs. Hardcastle patted out the folds of her crinoline. And little England, still a child, sucked a peppermint drop out of a bag. Each still acted the unacted part conferred on them by their clothes. Beauty was on them. Beauty revealed them. Was it the light that did it? – the tender, the fading, the uninquisitive but searching light of evening that reveals depths in water and makes even the red brick bungalow radiant?

"Look," the audience whispered, "O look, look, look. –" And once more they applauded; and the actors joined hands and bowed.

Old Mrs. Lynn Jones, fumbling for her bag, sighed, "What a pity – must they change?"

But it was time to pack up and be off.

"Home, gentlemen; home ladies; it's time to pack up and be off," the reporter whistled, snapping the band round his notebook. And Mrs. Parker was stooping.

"I'm afraid I've dropped my glove. I'm so sorry to trouble you. Down there, between the seats...."

The gramophone was affirming in tones there was no denying, triumphant yet valedictory: *Dispersed are we; who have come together. But*, the gramophone asserted, *let us retain whatever made that harmony.*

[165]   The national anthem in Britain.

O let us, the audience echoed (stooping, peering, fumbling), keep together. For there is joy, sweet joy, in company.

Dispersed are we, the gramophone repeated.

And the audience turning saw the flaming windows, each daubed with golden sun; and murmured: "Home, gentlemen; sweet..." yet delayed a moment, seeing through the golden glory perhaps a crack in the boiler; perhaps a hole in the carpet; and hearing, perhaps, the daily drop of the daily bill.

Dispersed are we, the gramophone informed them. And dismissed them. So, straightening themselves for the last time, each grasping, it might be a hat, or a stick or a pair of suède gloves, for the last time they applauded Budge and Queen Bess; the trees; the white road; Bolney Minster; and the Folly. One hailed another, and they dispersed, across lawns, down paths, past the house to the gravel-strewn crescent, where cars, push bikes and cycles were crowded together.

Friends hailed each other in passing.

"I do think," someone was saying, "Miss Whatshername should have come forward and not left it to the rector... After all, she wrote it.... I thought it brilliantly clever... O my dear, I thought it utter bosh. Did you understand the meaning? Well, he said she meant we all act all parts.... He said, too, if I caught his meaning, Nature takes part.... Then there was the idiot.... Also, why leave out the Army, as my husband was saying, if it's history? And if one spirit animates the whole, what about the aeroplanes?... Ah, but you're being too exacting. After all, remember, it was only a village play.... For my part, I think they should have passed a vote of thanks to the owners. When we had our pageant, the grass didn't recover till autumn... Then we had tents.... That's the man, Cobbet of Cobbs Corner, who wins all the prizes at all the shows. I don't myself admire prize flowers, nor yet prize dogs..."

Dispersed are we, the gramophone triumphed, yet lamented, *Dispersed are we....*

"But you must remember," the old cronies chatted, "they had to do it on the cheap. You can't get people, at this time o' year, to rehearse. There's the hay, let alone the movies.... What we need is a centre. Something to bring us all together... The Brookes have gone to Italy, in spite of everything. Rather rash?... If the worst should come – let's hope it won't – they'd hire an aeroplane, so they said.... What amused me was old Streatfield, feeling for his pouch. I like a man to be natural, not always on a perch... Then those voices from the bushes.... Oracles? You're referring to the Greeks? Were the oracles, if I'm not being irreverent, a foretaste of our own religion? Which is what?... Crepe soles? That's so sensible... They last much longer and protect the feet.... But I was saying: can the Christian faith adapt itself? In times like these... At Larting no one goes to church... There's the dogs, there's the pictures.... It's odd that science, so they tell me, is making things (so to speak) more spiritual... The very latest notion, so I'm told is, nothing's solid... There, you can get a glimpse of the church through the trees...."

"Mr. Umphelby! How nice to see you! Do come and dine... No, alas, we're going back to town. The House is sitting... I was telling them, the Brookes have gone to Italy. They've seen the volcano. Most impressive, so they say – they were lucky – in eruption. I agree – things look worse than ever on the continent. And what's the channel, come to think of it, if they mean to invade us? The aeroplanes, I didn't like to say it, made one think.... No, I thought it much too scrappy. Take the idiot. Did she mean, so to speak, something hidden, the unconscious as they call it? But why always drag in sex.... It's true, there's a sense in which we all, I admit, are savages still. Those women with red nails. And dressing up – what's that? The old savage, I suppose.... That's the bell. Ding dong. Ding... Rather a cracked old bell... And the mirrors! Reflecting us... I called that cruel. One looks such a fool, caught unprotected... There's Mr. Streatfield, going, I suppose to take the evening service. He'll have to hurry, or he won't have time to change.... He said she meant we all act. Yes, but whose play? Ah, that's the question! And if we're left asking questions, isn't it a failure, as a play? I must say I like to feel sure, if I go to the theatre, that I've grasped the meaning... Or was that, perhaps, what she meant?... Ding dong. Ding... that if we don't jump to conclusions, if you think, and I think, perhaps one day, thinking differently, we shall think the same?

"There's dear old Mr. Carfax ... Can't we give you a lift, if you don't mind playing bodkin?[166] We were asking questions, Mr. Carfax, about the play. The looking-glasses now – did they mean the reflection is the dream; and the tune – was it Bach, Handel, or no one in particular – is the truth? Or was it t'other way about?

"Bless my soul, what a dither! Nobody seems to know one car from another. That's why I have a mascot, a monkey[167] ... But I can't see it ... While we're waiting, tell me, did you feel when the shower fell, someone wept for us all? There's a poem, 'Tears tears tears,' it begins. And goes on 'O then the unloosened ocean ...' but I can't remember the rest.

"Then when Mr. Streatfield said: One spirit animates the whole – the aeroplanes interrupted. That's the worst of playing out of doors.... Unless of course she meant that very thing ... Dear me, the parking arrangements are not what you might call adequate ... I shouldn't have expected either so many Hispano-Suizas ... That's a Rolls ... That's a Bentley[168] ... That's the new type of Ford. ... To return to the meaning – Are machines the devil, or do they introduce a discord ... Ding dong, ding ... by means of which we reach the final ... Ding dong.... Here's the car with the monkey ... Hop in ... And good-bye, Mrs. Parker ... Ring us up. Next time we're down don't forget ... Next time ... Next time ..."

The wheels scurred on the gravel. The cars drove off.

The gramophone gurgled *Unity – Dispersity.* It gurgled *Un ... dis ...* And ceased.

The little company who had come together at luncheon were left standing on the terrace. The pilgrims had bruised a lane on the grass. Also, the lawn would need a deal of clearing up. Tomorrow the telephone would ring: "Did I leave my handbag? ... A pair of spectacles in a red leather case? ... A little old brooch of no value to anyone but me?" Tomorrow the telephone would ring.

Now Mr. Oliver said: "Dear lady," and, taking Mrs. Manresa's gloved hand in his, pressed it, as if to say: "You have given me what you now take from me." He would have liked to hold on for a moment longer to the emeralds and rubies dug up, so people said, by thin Ralph Manresa in his ragamuffin days. But alas, sunset light was unsympathetic to her make-up; plated it looked, not deeply interfused.[169] And he dropped her hand; and she gave him an arch roguish twinkle, as if to say – but the end of that sentence was cut short. For she turned, and Giles stepped forward; and the light breeze which the meteorologist had foretold fluttered her skirts; and she went, like a Goddess, buoyant, abundant, with flower-chained captives following in her wake.

All were retreating, withdrawing and dispersing; and he was left with the ash grown cold and no glow, no glow on the log. What word expressed the sag at his heart, the effusion in his veins, as the retreating Manresa, with Giles attendant, admirable woman, all sensation, ripped the rag doll and let the sawdust stream from his heart?

The old man made a guttural sound, and turned to the right. On with the hobble, on with the limp, since the dance was over. He strolled alone past the trees. It was here, early that very morning, that he had destroyed the little boy's world. He had popped out with his newspaper; the child had cried.

Down in the dell, past the lily pool, the actors were undressing. He could see them among the brambles. In vests and trousers; unhooking; buttoning up; on all fours; stuffing clothes into cheap attaché cases; with silver swords, beards and emeralds on the grass. Miss La Trobe in coat and skirt – too short, for her legs were stout – battled with the billows of a crinoline. He must respect the conventions. So he stopped, by the pool. The water was opaque over the mud.

Then, coming up behind him, "Oughtn't we to thank her?" Lucy asked him. She gave him a light pat on the arm.

[166] Sitting squeezed between two people.
[167] Improbable as it may seem, monkeys were common ornaments on the hoods, or "bonnets," of automobiles.
[168] Luxury automobiles.
[169] Wordsworth, "Lines Composed a Few Miles Above Tintern Abbey" (1798), lines 95–7:

a sense sublime
Of something far more deeply interfused
Whose dwelling is the light of setting suns.

How imperceptive her religion made her! The fumes of that incense obscured the human heart. Skimming the surface, she ignored the battle in the mud. After La Trobe had been excruciated by the Rector's interpretation, by the maulings and the manglings of the actors . . . "She don't want our thanks, Lucy," he said gruffly. What she wanted, like that carp (something moved in the water) was darkness in the mud; a whisky and soda at the pub; and coarse words descending like maggots through the waters.

"Thank the actors, not the author," he said. "Or ourselves, the audience."

He looked over his shoulder. The old lady, the indigenous, the prehistoric, was being wheeled away by a footman. He rolled her through the arch. Now the lawn was empty. The line of the roof, the upright chimneys, rose hard and red against the blue of the evening. The house emerged; the house that had been obliterated. He was damned glad it was over – the scurry and the scuffle, the rouge and the rings. He stooped and raised a peony that had shed its petals. Solitude had come again. And reason and the lamplit paper. . . . But where was his dog? Chained in a kennel? The little veins swelled with rage on his temples. He whistled. And here, released by Candish, racing across the lawn with a fleck of foam on the nostril, came his dog.

Lucy still gazed at the lily pool. "All gone," she murmured, "under the leaves." Scared by shadows passing, the fish had withdrawn. She gazed at the water. Perfunctorily she caressed her cross. But her eyes went water searching, looking for fish. The lilies were shutting; the red lily, the white lily, each on its plate of leaf. Above, the air rushed; beneath was water. She stood between two fluidities, caressing her cross. Faith required hours of kneeling in the early morning. Often the delight of the roaming eye seduced her – a sunbeam, a shadow. Now the jagged leaf at the corner suggested, by its contours, Europe. There were other leaves. She fluttered her eye over the surface, naming leaves India, Africa, America. Islands of security, glossy and thick.

"Bart . . ." She spoke to him. She had meant to ask him about the dragon-fly – couldn't the blue thread settle, if we destroyed it here, then there? But he had gone into the house.

Then something moved in the water; her favourite fantail. The golden orfe[170] followed. Then she had a glimpse of silver – the great carp himself, who came to the surface so very seldom. They slid on, in and out between the stalks, silver; pink; gold; splashed; streaked; pied.

"Ourselves," she murmured. And retrieving some glint of faith from the grey waters, hopefully, without much help from reason, she followed the fish; the speckled, streaked, and blotched; seeing in that vision beauty, power, and glory in ourselves.

Fish had faith, she reasoned. They trust us because we've never caught 'em. But her brother would reply: "That's greed." "Their beauty!" she protested. "Sex," he would say. "Who makes sex susceptible to beauty?" she would argue. He shrugged who? Why? Silenced, she returned to her private vision; of beauty which is goodness; the sea on which we float. Mostly impervious, but surely every boat sometimes leaks?

He would carry the torch of reason till it went out in the darkness of the cave. For herself, every morning, kneeling, she protected her vision. Every night she opened the window and looked at leaves against the sky. Then slept. Then the random ribbons of birds' voices woke her.

The fish had come to the surface. She had nothing to give them – not a crumb of bread. "Wait, my darlings," she addressed them. She would trot into the house and ask Mrs. Sands for a biscuit. Then a shadow fell. Off they flashed. How vexatious! Who was it? Dear me, the young man whose name she had forgotten; not Jones; nor Hodge . . .

Dodge had left Mrs. Manresa abruptly. All over the garden he had been searching for Mrs. Swithin. Now he found her; and she had forgotten his name.

"I'm William," he said. At that she revived, like a girl in a garden in white, among roses, who came running to meet him – an unacted part.

"I was going to get a biscuit – no, to thank the actors," she stumbled, virginal, blushing. Then she remembered her brother. "My brother," she added "says one mustn't thank the author, Miss La Trobe."

---

[170]   A semi-domesticated kind of carp.

It was always "my brother... my brother" who rose from the depths of her lily pool.

As for the actors, Hammond had detached his whiskers and was now buttoning up his coat. When the chain was inserted between the buttons he was off.

Only Miss La Trobe remained, bending over something in the grass.

"The play's over," he said. "The actors have departed."

"And we mustn't, my brother says, thank the author," Mrs. Swithin repeated, looking in the direction of Miss La Trobe.

"So I thank you," he said. He took her hand and pressed it. Putting one thing with another, it was unlikely that they would ever meet again.

The church bells always stopped, leaving you to ask: Won't there be another note? Isa, half-way across the lawn, listened.... Ding, dong, ding... There was not going to be another note. The congregation was assembled, on their knees, in the church. The service was beginning. The play was over; swallows skimmed the grass that had been the stage.

There was Dodge, the lip reader, her semblable,[171] her conspirator, a seeker like her after hidden faces. He was hurrying to rejoin Mrs. Manresa who had gone in front with Giles – "the father of my children," she muttered. The flesh poured over her, the hot, nerve wired, now lit up, now dark as the grave physical body. By way of healing the rusty fester of the poisoned dart she sought the face that all day long she had been seeking. Preening and peering, between backs, over shoulders, she had sought the man in grey. He had given her a cup of tea at a tennis party; handed her, once, a racquet. That was all. But, she was crying, had we met before the salmon leapt like a bar of silver... had we met, she was crying. And when her little boy came battling through the bodies in the Barn "Had he been his son," she had muttered... In passing she stripped the bitter leaf that grew, as it happened, outside the nursery window. Old Man's Beard. Shrivelling the shreds in lieu of words, for no words grow there, nor roses either, she swept past her conspirator, her semblable, the seeker after vanished faces "like Venus" he thought, making a rough translation, "to her prey..." and followed after.[172]

Turning the corner, there was Giles attached to Mrs. Manresa. She was standing at the door of her car. Giles had his foot on the edge of the running board. Did they perceive the arrows about to strike them?

"Jump in, Bill," Mrs. Manresa chaffed him.

And the wheels scurred on the gravel, and the car drove off.

At last, Miss La Trobe could raise herself from her stooping position. It had been prolonged to avoid attention. The bells had stopped; the audience had gone; also the actors. She could straighten her back. She could open her arms. She could say to the world, You have taken my gift! Glory possessed her – for one moment. But what had she given? A cloud that melted into the other clouds on the horizon. It was in the giving that the triumph was. And the triumph faded. Her gift meant nothing. If they had understood her meaning; if they had known their parts; if the pearls had been real and the funds illimitable – it would have been a better gift. Now it had gone to join the others.

"A failure," she groaned, and stooped to put away the records.

Then suddenly the starlings attacked the tree behind which she had hidden. In one flock they pelted it like so many winged stones. The whole tree hummed with the whizz they made, as if each bird plucked a wire. A whizz, a buzz rose from the bird-buzzing, bird-vibrant, bird-blackened tree. The tree became a rhapsody, a quivering cacophony, a whizz and vibrant rapture, branches, leaves, birds syllabling discordantly life, life, life, without measure, without stop devouring the tree. Then up! Then off!

---

[171]   From Charles Baudelaire (1821–67), the last line of "Au Lecteur" ("To the Reader"): "Hypocrite lecteur! mon semblable! – mon frère!" Also quoted by T. S. Eliot in *The Waste Land*, line 76 (see p. 127).

[172]   Jean Racine (1639–99), *Phèdre* (1677), Act 1, Scene 3, lines 305–6:

Ce n'est plus une ardeur dans mes veines cachée:
C'est Vénus tout entière à sa proie attachée.

Phèdre is acknowledging the power of her love for Hippolytus: "It's no longer a burning hidden in my veins: it is Venus entirely fastened on to her prey."

What interrupted? It was old Mrs. Chalmers, creeping through the grass with a bunch of flowers – pinks apparently – to fill the vase that stood on her husband's grave. In winter it was holly, or ivy. In summer, a flower. It was she who had scared the starlings. Now she passed.

Miss La Trobe nicked the lock and hoisted the heavy case of gramophone records to her shoulder. She crossed the terrace and stopped by the tree where the starlings had gathered. It was here that she had suffered triumph, humiliation, ecstasy, despair – for nothing. Her heels had ground a hole in the grass.

It was growing dark. Since there were no clouds to trouble the sky, the blue was bluer, the green greener. There was no longer a view – no Folly, no spire of Bolney Minister. It was land merely, no land in particular. She put down her case and stood looking at the land. Then something rose to the surface. "I should group them," she murmured, "here." It would be midnight; there would be two figures, half concealed by a rock. The curtain would rise. What would the first words be? The words escaped her.

Again she lifted the heavy suit case to her shoulder. She strode off across the lawn. The house was dormant; one thread of smoke thickened against the trees. It was strange that the earth, with all those flowers incandescent – the lilies, the roses, and clumps of white flowers and bushes of burning green – should still be hard. From the earth green waters seemed to rise over her. She took her voyage away from the shore, and, raising her hand, fumbled for the latch of the iron entrance gate.

She would drop her suit case in at the kitchen window, and then go on up to the Inn. Since the row with the actress who had shared her bed and her purse the need of drink had grown on her. And the horror and the terror of being alone. One of these days she would break – which of the village laws? Sobriety? Chastity? Or take something that did not properly belong to her?

At the corner she ran into old Mrs. Chalmers returning from the grave. The old woman looked down at the dead flowers she was carrying and cut her. The women in the cottages with the red geraniums always did that. She was an outcast. Nature had somehow set her apart from her kind. Yet she had scribbled in the margin of her manuscript: "I am the slave of my audience."

She thrust her suit case in at the scullery window and walked on, till at the corner she saw the red curtain at the bar window. There would be shelter; voices; oblivion. She turned the handle of the public house door. The acrid smell of stale beer saluted her; and voices talking. They stopped. They had been talking about Bossy as they called her – it didn't matter. She took her chair and looked through the smoke at a crude glass painting of a cow in a stable; also at a cock and a hen. She raised her glass to her lips. And drank. And listened. Words of one syllable sank down into the mud. She drowsed; she nodded. The mud became fertile. Words rose above the intolerably laden dumb oxen plodding through the mud. Words without meaning – wonderful words.

The cheap clock ticked; smoke obscured the pictures. Smoke became tart on the roof of her mouth. Smoke obscured the earth-coloured jackets. She no longer saw them, yet they upheld her, sitting arms akimbo with her glass before her. There was the high ground at midnight; there the rock; and two scarcely perceptible figures. Suddenly the tree was pelted with starlings. She set down her glass. She heard the first words.

Down in the hollow, at Pointz Hall, beneath the trees, the table was cleared in the dining-room. Candish, with his curved brush had swept the crumbs; had spared the petals and finally left the family to dessert. The play was over, the strangers gone, and they were alone – the family.

Still the play hung in the sky of the mind – moving, diminishing, but still there. Dipping her raspberry in sugar, Mrs. Swithin looked at the play. She said, popping the berry into her mouth, "What did it mean?" and added: "The peasants; the kings; the fool and" (she swallowed) "ourselves?"

They all looked at the play; Isa, Giles and Mr. Oliver. Each of course saw something different. In another moment it would be beneath the horizon, gone to join the other plays. Mr. Oliver, holding out his cheroot said: "Too ambitious." And, lighting his cheroot he added: "Considering her means."

It was drifting away to join the other clouds: becoming invisible. Through the smoke Isa saw not the play but the audience dispersing. Some drove; others cycled. A gate swung open. A car swept up the drive to the red villa in the cornfields. Low hanging boughs of acacia brushed the roof. Acacia petalled the car arrived.

"The looking-glasses and the voices in the bushes," she murmured. "What did she mean?"

"When Mr. Streatfield asked her to explain, she wouldn't," said Mrs. Swithin.

Here, with its sheath sliced in four, exposing a white cone, Giles offered his wife a banana. She refused it. He stubbed his match on the plate. Out it went with a little fizz in the raspberry juice.

"We should be thankful," said Mrs. Swithin, folding her napkin, "for the weather, which was perfect, save for one shower."

Here she rose. Isa followed her across the hall to the big room.

They never pulled the curtains till it was too dark to see, nor shut the windows till it was too cold. Why shut out the day before it was over? The flowers were still bright; the birds chirped. You could see more in the evening often when nothing interrupted, when there was no fish to order, no telephone to answer. Mrs. Swithin stopped by the great picture of Venice – school of Canaletto.[173] Possibly in the hood of the gondola there was a little figure – a woman, veiled; or a man?

Isa, sweeping her sewing from the table, sank, her knee doubled, into the chair by the window. Within the shell of the room she overlooked the summer night. Lucy returned from her voyage into the picture and stood silent. The sun made each pane of her glasses shine red. Silver sparkled on her black shawl. For a moment she looked like a tragic figure from another play.

Then she spoke in her usual voice. "We made more this year than last, he said. But then last year it rained."

"This year, last year, next year, never..." Isa murmured. Her hand burnt in the sun on the window sill. Mrs. Swithin took her knitting from the table.

"Did you feel," she asked "what he said: we act different parts but are the same?"

"Yes," Isa answered. "No," she added. It was Yes, No. Yes, yes, yes, the tide rushed out embracing. No, no no, it contracted. The old boot appeared on the shingle.

"Orts, scraps and fragments," she quoted what she remembered of the vanishing play.

Lucy had just opened her lips to reply, and had laid her hand on her cross caressingly, when the gentlemen came in. She made her little chirruping sound of welcome. She shuffled her feet to clear a space. But in fact there was more space than was needed, and great hooded chairs.

They sat down, ennobled both of them by the setting sun. Both had changed. Giles now wore the black coat and white tie of the professional classes, which needed – Isa looked down at his feet – patent leather pumps. "Our representative, our spokesman," she sneered. Yet he was extraordinarily handsome. "The father of my children, whom I love and hate." Love and hate – how they tore her asunder! Surely it was time someone invented a new plot, or that the author came out from the bushes...

Here Candish came in. He brought the second post on a silver salver. There were letters; bills; and the morning paper – the paper that obliterated the day before. Like a fish rising to a crumb of biscuit, Bartholomew snapped at the paper. Giles slit the flap of an apparently business document. Lucy read a criss-cross from an old friend at Scarborough.[174] Isa had only bills.

The usual sounds reverberated through the shell; Sands making up the fire; Candish stoking the boiler. Isa had done with her bills. Sitting in the shell of the room she watched the pageant fade.[175] The flowers flashed before they faded. She watched them flash.

The paper crackled. The second hand jerked on. M. Daladier had pegged down the franc. The girl had gone skylarking with the troopers. She had screamed. She had hit him.... What then?

---

[173] Giovanni Antonio Canaletto (1697–1768), Venetian painter famous for his views of Venice and London.

[174] A seaside resort on the east coast of England, in Yorkshire.

[175] Shakespeare, *The Tempest*, Act 4, scene 1, lines 156–9:

> The solemn temples, the great globe itself,
> Yea, all which it inherit, shall dissolve,
> And like this insubstantial pageant faded,
> Leave not a rack behind.

When Isa looked at the flowers again, the flowers had faded.

Bartholomew flicked on the reading lamp. The circle of the readers, attached to white papers, was lit up. There in that hollow of the sun-baked field were congregated the grasshopper, the ant, and the beetle, rolling pebbles of sun-baked earth through the glistening stubble. In that rosy corner of the sun-baked field Bartholomew, Giles and Lucy polished and nibbled and broke off crumbs. Isa watched them.

Then the newspaper dropped.

"Finished?" said Giles, taking it from his father.

The old man relinquished his paper. He basked. One hand caressing the dog rippled folds of skin towards the collar.

The clock ticked. The house gave little cracks as if it were very brittle, very dry. Isa's hand on the window felt suddenly cold. Shadow had obliterated the garden. Roses had withdrawn for the night.

Mrs. Swithin folding her letter murmured to Isa: "I looked in and saw the babies, sound asleep, under the paper roses."

"Left over from the coronation," Bartholomew muttered, half asleep.

"But we needn't have been to all that trouble with the decorations," Lucy added, "for it didn't rain this year."

"This year, last year, next year, never," Isa murmured.

"Tinker, tailor, soldier, sailor," Bartholomew echoed. He was talking in his sleep.

Lucy slipped her letter into its envelope. It was time to read now, her Outline of History. But she had lost her place. She turned the pages looking at pictures – mammoths, mastodons, prehistoric birds. Then she found the page where she had stopped.

The darkness increased. The breeze swept round the room. With a little shiver Mrs. Swithin drew her sequin shawl about her shoulders. She was too deep in the story to ask for the window to be shut. "England," she was reading, "was then a swamp. Thick forests covered the land. On the top of their matted branches birds sang . . ."

The great square of the open window showed only sky now. It was drained of light, severe, stone cold. Shadows fell. Shadows crept over Bartholomew's high forehead; over his great nose. He looked leafless, spectral, and his chair monumental. As a dog shudders its skin, his skin shuddered. He rose, shook himself, glared at nothing, and stalked from the room. They heard the dog's paws padding on the carpet behind him.

Lucy turned the page, quickly, guiltily, like a child who will be told to go to bed before the end of the chapter.

"Prehistoric man," she read, "half-human, half-ape, roused himself from his semi-crouching position and raised great stones."

She slipped the letter from Scarborough between the pages to mark the end of the chapter, rose, smiled, and tiptoed silently out of the room.

The old people had gone up to bed. Giles crumpled the newspaper and turned out the light. Left alone together for the first time that day, they were silent. Alone, enmity was bared; also love. Before they slept, they must fight; after they had fought, they would embrace. From that embrace another life might be born. But first they must fight, as the dog fox fights with the vixen, in the heart of darkness,[176] in the fields of night.

Isa let her sewing drop. The great hooded chairs had become enormous. And Giles too. And Isa too against the window. The window was all sky without colour. The house had lost its shelter. It was night before roads were made, or houses. It was the night that dwellers in caves had watched from some high place among rocks.

Then the curtain rose. They spoke.

---

[176] Joseph Conrad's novella *The Heart of Darkness* (1900), has an opening that also dissolves distinctions between the present and the primeval past.

Modern Fiction (1919/1925)

In making any survey, even the freest and loosest, of modern fiction, it is difficult not to take it for granted that the modern practice of the art is somehow an improvement upon the old. With their simple tools and primitive materials, it might be said, Fielding did well and Jane Austen[1] even better, but compare their opportunities with ours! Their masterpieces certainly have a strange air of simplicity. And yet the analogy between literature and the process, to choose an example, of making motor cars scarcely holds good beyond the first glance. It is doubtful whether in the course of the centuries, though we have learnt much about making machines, we have learnt anything about making literature. We do not come to write better; all that we can be said to do is to keep moving, now a little in this direction, now in that, but with a circular tendency should the whole course of the track be viewed from a sufficiently lofty pinnacle. It need scarcely be said that we make no claim to stand, even momentarily, upon that vantage ground. On the flat, in the crowd, half-blind with dust, we look back with envy to those happier warriors, whose battle is won and whose achievements wear so serene an air of accomplishment that we can scarcely refrain from whispering that the fight was not so fierce for them as for us. It is for the historian of literature to decide; for him to say if we are now beginning or ending or standing in the middle of a great period of prose fiction, for down in the plain little is visible. We only know that certain gratitudes and hostilities inspire us; that certain paths seem to lead to fertile land, others to the dust and the desert; and of this perhaps it may be worth while to attempt some account.

Our quarrel, then, is not with the classics, and if we speak of quarrelling with Mr Wells, Mr Bennett, and Mr Galsworthy,[2] it is partly that by the mere fact of their existence in the flesh their work has a living, breathing, everyday imperfection which bids us take what liberties with it we choose. But it is also true that, while we thank them for a thousand gifts, we reserve our unconditional gratitude for Mr Hardy, for Mr Conrad, and in a much lesser degree for the Mr Hudson of *The Purple Land, Green Mansions,* and *Far Away and Long Ago.*[3] Mr Wells, Mr Bennett, and Mr Galsworthy have excited so many hopes and disappointed them so persistently that our gratitude largely takes the form of thanking them for having shown us what they might have done but have not done; what we certainly could not do, but as certainly, perhaps, do not wish to do. No single phrase will sum up the charge or grievance which we have to bring against a mass of work so large in its volume and embodying so many qualities, both admirable and the reverse. If we tried to formulate our meaning in one word we should say that these three writers are materialists. It is because they are concerned not with the spirit but with the body that they have disappointed us, and left us with the feeling that the sooner English fiction turns its back upon them, as politely as may be, and marches, if only into the desert, the better for its soul. Naturally, no single word reaches the centre of three separate targets. In the case of Mr Wells it falls notably wide of the mark. And yet even with him it indicates to our thinking the fatal alloy in his genius, the great clod of clay that has got itself mixed up with the purity of his inspiration. But Mr Bennett is perhaps the worst culprit of the three, inasmuch as he is by far the best workman. He can make a book so well constructed and solid in its craftsmanship that it is difficult for the most exacting of critics to see through what chink or crevice decay can creep in. There is not so much as a draught between the frames of the windows, or a crack in the boards. And yet – if life should refuse to live there? That is a risk which the creator of *The Old Wives' Tale*, George Cannon, Edwin

---

Under the title "Modern Novels," this essay was first published in the *Times Literary Supplement*, April 10, 1919, unsigned, as were all essays in the *TLS* at this time. It was revised for inclusion in *The Common Reader*, a collection of Woolf's essays that was issued in 1925 (London: Hogarth Press), and it is this later and more famous version that is followed here.

[1] Henry Fielding (1707–54) and Jane Austen (1775–1817) were British novelists.

[2] H. G. Wells (1866–1946), Arnold Bennett (1867–1931) and John Galsworthy (1867–1933) were the three most prominent

novelists of their day. For Woolf on Bennett, see her essay "Mr Bennett and Mrs Brown," 901–3 in this volume.

[3] *for Mr. Hardy ... and Long Ago* Thomas Hardy (1840–1928) was a British novelist, though he stopped writing novels after *Jude the Obscure* (1896). Joseph Conrad (1857–1924), born in Poland, became a British novelist; his major works had all appeared before the outbreak of World War I in 1914. W. H. Hudson (1841–1922) was a naturalist and also a novelist who published *The Purple Land* in 1885, *Green Mansions* in 1914, and *Far Away and Long Ago* in 1918.

Clayhanger,[4] and hosts of other figures, may well claim to have surmounted. His characters live abundantly, even unexpectedly, but it remains to ask how do they live, and what do they live for? More and more they seem to us, deserting even the well-built villa in the Five Towns, to spend their time in some softly padded first-class railway carriage, pressing bells and buttons innumerable; and the density to which they travel so luxuriously becomes more and more unquestionably an eternity of bliss spent in the very best hotel in Brighton. It can scarcely be said of Mr Wells that he is a materialist in the sense that he takes too much delight in the solidity of his fabric. His mind is too generous in its sympathies to allow him to spend much time in making things shipshape and substantial. He is a materialist from sheer goodness of heart, taking upon his shoulders the work that ought to have been discharged by Government officials, and in the plethora of his ideas and facts scarcely having leisure to realise, or forgetting to think important, the crudity and coarseness of his human beings. Yet what more damaging criticism can there be both of his earth and of his Heaven than that they are to be inhabited here and hereafter by his Joans and his Peters?[5] Does not the inferiority of their natures tarnish whatever institutions and ideals may be provided for them by the generosity of their creator? Nor, profoundly though we respect the integrity and humanity of Mr Galsworthy, shall we find what we seek in his pages.

If we fasten, then, one label on all these books, on which is one word materialists, we mean by it that they write of unimportant things; that they spend immense skill and immense industry making the trivial and the transitory appear the true and the enduring.

We have to admit that we are exacting, and, further, that we find it difficult to justify our discontent by explaining what it is that we exact. We frame our question differently at different times. But it reappears most persistently as we drop the finished novel on the crest of a sigh – Is it worth while? What is the point of it all? Can it be that, owing to one of those little deviations which the human spirit seems to make from time to time, Mr Bennett has come down with his magnificent apparatus for catching life just an inch or two on the wrong side? Life escapes; and perhaps without life nothing else is worth while. It is a confession of vagueness to have to make use of such a figure as this, but we scarcely better the matter by speaking, as critics are prone to do, of reality. Admitting the vagueness which afflicts all criticism of novels, let us hazard the opinion that for us at this moment the form of fiction most in vogue more often misses than secures the thing we seek. Whether we call it life or spirit, truth or reality, this, the essential thing, has moved off, or on, and refuses to be contained any longer in such ill-fitting vestments as we provide. Nevertheless, we go on perseveringly, conscientiously, constructing our two and thirty chapters after a design which more and more ceases to resemble the vision in our minds. So much of the enormous labour of proving the solidity, the likeness to life, of the story is not merely labour thrown away but labour misplaced to the extent of obscuring and blotting out the light of the conception. The writer seems constrained, not by his own free will but by some powerful and unscrupulous tyrant who has him in thrall, to provide a plot, to provide comedy, tragedy, love interest, and an air of probability embalming the whole so impeccable that if all his figures were to come to life they would find themselves dressed down to the last button of their coats in the fashion of the hour. The tyrant is obeyed; the novel is done to a turn. But sometimes, more and more often as time goes by, we suspect a momentary doubt, a spasm of rebellion, as the pages fill themselves in the customary way. Is life like this? Must novels be like this?

Look within and life, it seems, is very far from being "like this." Examine for a moment an ordinary mind on an ordinary day. The mind receives a myriad impressions – trivial, fantastic, evanescent, or engraved with the sharpness of steel. From all sides they come, an incessant shower of innumerable atoms; and as they fall, as they shape themselves into the life of Monday or Tuesday,[6] the accent falls differently from of old; the moment of importance came not here but there; so that,

---

[4] The Old Wives' Tale … Clayhanger The Old Wives' Tale appeared in 1908; George Cannon and Edwin Clayhanger are characters in the Clayhanger trilogy by Bennett, consisting of Clayhanger (1910), Hilda Lessways (1911), and These Twain (1916).
[5] H. G. Wells published Joan and Peter in 1918, and Virginia Woolf reviewed it; see Andrew McNeillie (ed.), The Essays of Virginia Woolf, vol. 2 1912–1918 (London: Hogarth Press, 1987) "The Rights of Youth, " 294–8.
[6] Woolf wrote a short story called "Monday or Tuesday," which appeared in a collection of her short stories of the same title (London: Hogarth Press, 1921).

if a writer were a free man and not a slave, if he could write what he chose, not what he must, if he could base his work upon his own feeling and not upon convention, there would be no plot, no comedy, no tragedy, no love interest or catastrophe in the accepted style, and perhaps not a single button sewn on as the Bond Street tailors would have it. Life is not a series of gig lamps symmetrically arranged; life is a luminous halo, a semi-transparent envelope surrounding us from the beginning of consciousness to the end. Is it not the task of the novelist to convey this varying, this unknown and uncircumscribed spirit, whatever aberration or complexity it may display, with as little mixture of the alien and external as possible? We are not pleading merely for courage and sincerity; we are suggesting that the proper stuff of fiction is a little other than custom would have us believe it.

It is, at any rate, in some such fashion as this that we seek to define the quality which distinguishes the work of several young writers, among whom Mr James Joyce[7] is the most notable, from that of their predecessors. They attempt to come closer to life, and to preserve more sincerely and exactly what interests and moves them, even if to do so they must discard most of the conventions which are commonly observed by the novelist. Let us record the atoms as they fall upon the mind in the order in which they fall, let us trace the pattern, however disconnected and incoherent in appearance, which each sight or incident scores upon the consciousness. Let us not take it for granted that life exists more fully in what is commonly thought big than in what is commonly thought small. Any one who has read *The Portrait of the Artist as a Young Man* or, what promises to be a far more interesting work, *Ulysses*, now appearing in the *Little Review*,[8] will have hazarded some theory of this nature as to Mr Joyce's intention. On our part, with such a fragment before us, it is hazarded rather than affirmed; but whatever the intention of the whole, there can be no question but that it is of the utmost sincerity and that the result, difficult or unpleasant as we may judge it, is undeniably important. In contrast with those whom we have called materialists, Mr Joyce is spiritual; he is concerned at all costs to reveal the flickerings of that innermost flame which flashes its messages through the brain, and in order to preserve it he disregards with complete courage whatever seems to him adventitious, whether it be probability, or coherence, or any other of these signposts which for generations have served to support the imagination of a reader when called upon to imagine what he can neither touch nor see. The scene in the cemetery,[9] for instance, with its brilliancy, its sordidity, its incoherence, its sudden lightning flashes of significance, does undoubtedly come so close to the quick of the mind that, on a first reading at any rate, it is difficult not to acclaim a masterpiece. If we want life itself, here surely we have it. Indeed, we find ourselves fumbling rather awkwardly if we try to say what else we wish, and for what reason a work of such originality yet fails to compare, for we must take high examples, with *Youth* or *The Mayor of Casterbridge*.[10] It fails because of the comparative poverty of the writer's mind, we might say simply and have done with it. But it is possible to press a little further and wonder whether we may not refer our sense of being in a bright yet narrow room, confined and shut in, rather than enlarged and set free, to some limitation imposed by the method as well as by the mind. Is it the method that inhibits the creative power? Is it due to the method that we feel neither jovial nor magnanimous, but centred in a self which, in spite of its tremor of susceptibility, never embraces or creates what is outside itself and beyond? Does the emphasis laid, perhaps didactically, upon indecency, contribute to the effect of something angular and isolated? Or is it merely that in any effort of such originality it is much easier, for contemporaries especially, to feel what it lacks than to name what it gives? In any case it is a mistake to stand outside examining "methods." Any method is right, every method is right, that expresses what we wish to express, if we are writers; that brings us closer to the novelist's intention if we are readers. This method has the merit of bringing us closer to what we

---

[7] James Joyce (1882–1941), Irish writer; for examples of his writing see 212–300 in this volume.

[8] *Portrait of the Artist* had appeared as a novel in 1917; and although *Ulysses* had been published in its entirety in 1922, three years before this essay was republished, Woolf chose not to update her account of it; instead she retained her 1919 account, which had been limited to those portions that had been published serially in the *Little Review* (New York) and *The Egoist* (London). By April 1919, when Woolf's essay was first published, only episodes 1 through 8 had appeared.

[9] *scene in the cemetery* the "Hades" episode (the sixth) in *Ulysses*, published in September 1918, in serial form.

[10] *Youth* was published by Joseph Conrad in (1902), *The Mayor of Casterbridge* by Thomas Hardy in 1886.

were prepared to call life itself; did not the reading of *Ulysses* suggest how much of life is excluded or ignored, and did it not come with a shock to open *Tristram Shandy* or even *Pendennis*[11] and be by them convinced that there are not only other aspects of life, but more important ones into the bargain.

However this may be, the problem before the novelist at present, as we suppose it to have been in the past, is to contrive means of being free to set down what he chooses. He has to have the courage to say that what interests him is no longer "this" but "that:" out of "that" alone must he construct his work. For the moderns "that," the point of interest, lies very likely in the dark places of psychology. At once, therefore, the accent falls a little differently; the emphasis is upon something hitherto ignored; at once a different outline of form becomes necessary, difficult for us to grasp, incomprehensible to our predecessors. No one but a modern, no one perhaps but a Russian, would have felt the interest of the situation which Tchehov has made into the short story which he calls "Gusev."[12] Some Russian soldiers lie ill on board a ship which is taking them back to Russia. We are given a few scraps of their talk and some of their thoughts; then one of them dies and is carried away; the talk goes on among the others for a time, until Gusev himself dies, and looking "like a carrot or a radish" is thrown overboard. The emphasis is laid upon such unexpected places that at first it seems as if there were no emphasis at all; and then, as the eyes accustom themselves to twilight and discern the shapes of things in a room we see how complete the story is, how profound, and how truly in obedience to his vision Tchehov has chosen this, that, and the other, and placed them together to compose something new. But it is impossible to say "this is comic," or "that is tragic," nor are we certain, since short stories, we have been taught, should be brief and conclusive, whether this, which is vague and inconclusive, should be called a short story at all.

The most elementary remarks upon modern English fiction can hardly avoid some mention of the Russian influence, and if the Russians are mentioned one runs the risk of feeling that to write of any fiction save theirs is waste of time. If we want understanding of the soul and heart where else shall we find it of comparable profundity? If we are sick of our own materialism the least considerable of their novelists has by right of birth a natural reverence for the human spirit. "Learn to make yourself akin to people . . . But let this sympathy be not with the mind – for it is easy with the mind – but with the heart, with love towards them."[13] In every great Russian writer we seem to discern the features of a saint, if sympathy for the sufferings of others, love towards them, endeavour to reach some goal worthy of the most exacting demands of the spirit constitute saintliness. It is the saint in them which confounds us with a feeling of our own irreligious triviality, and turns so many of our famous novels to tinsel and trickery. The conclusions of the Russian mind, thus comprehensive and compassionate, are inevitably, perhaps, of the utmost sadness. More accurately indeed we might speak of the inconclusiveness of the Russian mind. It is the sense that there is no answer, that if honestly examined life presents question after question which must be left to sound on and on after the story is over in hopeless interrogation that fills us with a deep, and finally it may be with a resentful, despair. They are right perhaps; unquestionably they see further than we do and without our gross impediments of vision. But perhaps we see something that escapes them, or why should this voice of protest mix itself with our gloom? The voice of protest is the voice of another and an ancient civilisation which seems to have bred in us the instinct to enjoy and fight rather than to suffer and understand. English fiction from Sterne to Meredith[14] bears witness to our natural delight in humour and comedy, in the beauty of earth, in the activities of the intellect, and in the splendour of the body. But any deductions that we may draw from the comparison of two fictions so immeasurably far apart are futile save indeed as they flood us with a view of the infinite possibilities of the art and remind us that there is no limit to the horizon, and that nothing – no "method," no experiment, even of the wildest – is forbidden, but

[11] *The Life and Opinions of Tristram Shandy* (1765–1767) by Lawrence Sterne (1713–68), *The History of Pendennis* (1848–50), W. M. Thackeray (1811–63).

[12] This story appeared in *The Witch and Other Stories* by Anton Chekov (1860–1904), trans. Constance Garnett (London: Chatto and Windus, 1918).

[13] Elena Militsina and Mikhail Saltikov, *The Village Priest and Other Stories*, trans. from the Russian by Beatrix L. Tollemach, with an intro. by C. Hagberg Wright (London: T. Fisher Unwin, 1918), the title story (by Militsina), 34. The ellipsis signals the omission of "I would even like to add: make yourself indispensable to them."

[14] George Meredith (1828–1909), British novelist.

only falsity and pretence. "The proper stuff of fiction" does not exist; everything is the proper stuff of fiction, every feeling, every thought; every quality of brain and spirit is drawn upon; no perception comes amiss. And if we can imagine the art of fiction come alive and standing in our midst, she would undoubtedly bid us break her and bully her, as well as honour and love her, for so her youth is renewed and her sovereignty assured.

Mr Bennett and Mrs Brown (1923)

The other day Mr Arnold Bennett,[1] himself one of the most famous of the Edwardians, surveyed the younger generation and said: "I admit that for myself I cannot yet descry any coming big novelist." And that, let us say in passing, is all to the good – a symptom of the respectful hostility which is the only healthy relation between old and young. But then he went on to give his reasons for this lamentable fact, and his reasons, which lie deep, deserve much more consideration than his impatience, which lies on the surface. The Georgians fail as novelists, he said, because "they are interested more in details than in the full creation of their individual characters ... The foundation of good fiction is character-creating, and nothing else. To render secure the importance of a novel it is necessary, further, that the characters should clash with one another,"[2] or, of course, they will excite no emotion in the breast of the author or anybody else. None of this is new; all of it is true; yet here we have one of those simple statements which are no sooner taken into the mind than they burst their envelopes and flood us with suggestions of every kind.

The novel is a very remarkable machine for the creation of human character, we are all agreed. Directly it ceases to create character, its defects alone are visible. And it is because this essence, this character-making power, has evaporated that novels are for the most part the soulless bodies we know, cumbering our tables and clogging our minds. That, too, may pass. Few reviewers at least are likely to dispute it. But if we go on to ask when this change began, and what were the reasons behind it, then agreement is much more difficult to come by. Mr Bennett blames the Georgians. Our minds fly straight to King Edward.[3] Surely that was the fatal age, the age which is just breaking off from our own, the age when character disappeared or was mysteriously engulfed, and the culprits, happily still alive, active, and unrepentant, are Mr Wells, Mr Galsworthy,[4] and Mr Bennett himself.

But in lodging such a charge against so formidable a library we must do as painters do when they wish to reduce the innumerable details of a crowded landscape to simplicity – step back, half shut the eyes, gesticulate a little vaguely with the fingers, and reduce Edwardian fiction to a view. Thus treated, one strange fact is immediately apparent. Every sort of town is represented, and innumerable institutions; we see factories, prisons, workhouses, law courts, Houses of Parliament; a general clamour, the voice of aspiration, indignation, effort and industry, rises from the whole; but in all this vast conglomeration of printed pages, in all this congeries of streets and houses, there is not a single man or woman whom we know. Figures like Kipps or the sisters[5] (already nameless) in *The Old Wives' Tale* attempt to contradict this assertion, but with how feeble a voice and how flimsy a body is apparent directly they are stood beside some character from that other great tract of fiction which lies immediately behind them in the Victorian age. For there, if we follow the same process,

MR BENNETT

The essay was first published in the "Literary Review" of the *New York Evening Post*, November 17, 1923, then reprinted in the *Nation* and *Athenaeum*, December 1, 1923, and in *Living Age* (Boston), February 2, 1924.

[1] Arnold Bennett (1867–1931), a British novelist who, together with H. G. Wells and John Galsworthy, was considered one of the most important writers of the day. In "Is the Novel Decaying?", *Cassells Weekly*, March 28, 1923, Bennett had written: "I have seldom read a cleverer book than Virginia Woolf's *Jacob's Room*, a novel which has made a great sir in a small world. It is packed and bursting with originality, and it is exquisitely written. But the characters do not vitally survive in the mind

because the author has been obsessed by details of originality and cleverness. I regard this book as characteristic of the new novelists who have recently gained the attention of the alert and the curious, and I admit that for myself I cannot yet descry any coming big novelists."

[2] See the preceding note.

[3] Edward VII (1841–1910) reigned from 1901 to 1910.

[4] H. G. Wells (1866–1946) and John Galsworthy (1867–1933) were prominent British novelists.

[5] Arthur Kipps is the hero of Wells's *Kipps* (1905); Constance and Sophia Banes, who are not "nameless," are the sisters in Bennett's *The Old Wives' Tale* (1908).

but recall one novel, and that – *Pendennis*[6] – not one of the most famous, at once start out, clear, vigorous, alive from the curl of their eyelashes to the soles of their boots, half a dozen characters whose names are no sooner spoken than we think of scene after scene in which they play their parts. We see the Major sitting in his club window, fresh from the hands of Morgan; Helen nursing her son in the Temple and suspecting poor Fanny; Warrington grilling chops in his dressing-gown; Captain Shandon scribbling leaders for the *Pall Mall Gazette* – Laura, Blanche Amory,[7] Foker; the procession is endless and alive. And so it goes on from character to character all through the splendid opulence of the Victorian age. They love, they joke, they hunt, they marry; they lead us from hall to cottage, from field to slum. The whole country, the whole society, is revealed to us, and revealed always in the same way, through the astonishing vividness and reality of the characters.

And it was perhaps on that very account that the Edwardians changed their tactics. Such triumphs could scarcely be rivalled; and, moreover, triumphs once achieved seem to the next generation always a little uninteresting. There was, too (if we think ourselves into the mind of a writer contemplating fiction about the year 1900), something plausible, superficial, unreal in all this abundance. No sooner had the Victorians departed than Samuel Butler, who had lived below-stairs, came out, like an observant bootboy, with the family secrets in *The Way of All Flesh*.[8] It appeared that the basement was really in an appalling state. Though the saloons were splendid and the dining rooms portentous, the drains were of the most primitive description. The social state was a mass of corruption. A sensitive man like Mr Galsworthy could scarcely step out of doors without barking his shins upon some social iniquity. A generous mind which knew the conditions in which the Kippses and the Lewishams[9] were born and bred must try at least to fashion the world afresh. So the young novelist became a reformer, and thought with pardonable contempt of those vast Victorian family parties, where the funny man was always funny, the good woman always good, and nobody seemed aware, as they pursued their own tiny lives, that society was rotten and Christianity itself at stake. But there was another force which made much more subtly against the creation of character, and that was Mrs Garnett and her translations from Dostoevsky.[10] After reading *Crime and Punishment* and *The Idiot*,[11] how could any young novelist believe in "characters" as the Victorians had painted them? For the undeniable vividness of so many of them is the result of their crudity. The character is rubbed into us indelibly because its features are so few and so prominent. We are given the keyword (Mr Dick has King Charles's head;[12] Mr Brooke, "I went into that a great deal at one time;" Mrs Micawber, "I will never desert Mr Micawber"), and then, since the choice of the keyword is astonishingly apt, our imaginations swiftly supply the rest. But what keyword could be applied to Raskolnikov, Mishkin, Stavrogin, or Alyosha?[13] These are characters without any features at all. We go down into them as we descend into some enormous cavern. Lights swing about; we hear the boom of the sea; it is all dark, terrible, and uncharted. So we need not be surprised if the Edwardian novelist scarcely attempted to deal with character except in its more generalised aspects. The Victorian version was discredited; it was his duty to destroy all those institutions in the shelter of which character thrives and thickens; and the Russians had shown him – everything or nothing, it was impossible as yet to say which. The Edwardian novelists therefore give us a vast sense of things in general; but a very vague one of things in particular. Mr Galsworthy gives us a sense of compassion; Mr Wells fills us with generous enthusiasm; Mr Bennett (in his early work) gave us a sense of time. But their books are already a little chill, and must steadily grow more distant, for "the foundation of good fiction is

[6] *The History of Pendennis*, by W. M. Thackeray (1811–63), was published serially from 1848 to 1850.

[7] *the Major ... Blance Amory* all characters in *Pendennis*.

[8] *The Way of All Flesh*, by English novelist Samuel Butler (1835–1902), was published posthumously in 1903.

[9] The character George Edgar Lewisham in Wells's novel *Love and Mr. Lewisham* (1900).

[10] Constance Garnett (1892–1946) translated the entire oeuvre of Fyodor Dostoyevsky (1821–81), the Russian novelist.

[11] Garnett translated *The Idiot* (1866) in 1913 and *Crime and Punishment* (1869–70) in 1917.

[12] For Mr Dick and King Charles's head, see Charles Dickens (1812–70), *David Copperfield* (1849–50), ch. 14; for Mr Brooke, see George Eliot, *Middlemarch* (1871–2), ch. 2; for Mrs Micawber's pledge of loyalty, see Charles Dickens, *David Copperfield*, ch. 12.

[13] Rodio Romanovic Raskolnikov is the hero of *Crime and Punishment*; Prince Leve Nicolaevich Mishkin is the hero of *The Idiot*; Nikolai Stavrogin is the hero of Dostoyevsky's *The Possessed* (1872), Alyosha is a character in Dostoyevsky's *The Brothers Karamazov* (1872–80).

character-creating, and nothing else," as Mr Bennett says; and in none of them are we given a man or woman whom we know.

The Georgians had, therefore, a difficult task before them, and if they have failed, as Mr Bennett asserts, there is nothing to surprise us in that. To bring back character from the shapelessness into which it has lapsed, to sharpen its edges, deepen its compass, and so make possible those conflicts between human beings which alone rouse our strongest emotions – such was their problem. It was the consciousness of this problem and not the accession of King George,[14] which produced, as it always produces, the break between one generation and the next. Here, however, the break is particularly sharp, for here the dispute is fundamental. In real life there is nothing that interests us more than character, that stirs us to the same extremes of love and anger, or that leads to such incessant and laborious speculations about the values, the reasons, and the meaning of existence itself. To disagree about character is to differ in the depths of the being. It is to take different sides, to drift apart, to accept a purely formal intercourse for ever. That is so in real life. But the novelist has to go much further and to be much more uncompromising than the friend. When he finds himself hopelessly at variance with Mr Wells, Mr Galsworthy, and Mr Bennett about the character – shall we say? – of Mrs Brown, it is useless to defer to their superior genius. It is useless to mumble the polite agreements of the drawing room. He must set about to remake the woman after his own idea. And that, in the circumstances, is a very perilous pursuit.

For what, after all is character – the way that Mrs Brown, for instance, reacts to her surroundings – when we cease to believe what we are told about her, and begin to search out her real meaning for ourselves? In the first place, her solidity disappears; her features crumble; the house in which she has lived so long (and a very substantial house it was) topples to the ground. She becomes a will-o'-the-wisp, a dancing light, an illumination gliding up the wall and out of the window, lighting now in freakish malice upon the nose of an archbishop, now in sudden splendour upon the mahogany of the wardrobe. The most solemn sights she turns to ridicule; the most ordinary she invests with beauty. She changes the shape, shifts the accent, of every scene in which she plays her part. And it is from the ruins and splinters of this tumbled mansion that the Georgian writer must somehow reconstruct a habitable dwelling-place; it is from the gleams and flashes of this flying spirit that he must create solid, living, flesh-and-blood Mrs Brown. Sadly he must allow that the lady still escapes him. Dismally he must admit bruises received in the pursuit. But it is because the Georgians, poets and novelists, biographers and dramatists, are so hotly engaged each in the pursuit of his own Mrs Brown that theirs is at once the least successful, and the most interesting, generation that English literature has known for a hundred years. Moreover, let us prophesy: Mrs Brown will not always escape. One of these days Mrs Brown will be caught. The capture of Mrs Brown is the title of the next chapter in the history of literature; and, let us prophesy again, that chapter will be one of the most important, the most illustrious, the most epoch-making of them all.

The Narrow Bridge of Art (1927)

Far the greater number of critics turn their backs upon the present and gaze steadily into the past. Wisely, no doubt, they make no comment upon what is being actually written at the moment; they leave that duty to the race of reviewers whose very title seems to imply transiency in themselves and in the objects they survey. But one has sometimes asked oneself, must the duty of the critic always be to the past, must his gaze always be fixed backward? Could he not sometimes turn round and, shading his eyes in the manner of Robinson Crusoe on the desert island, look into the future and trace on its mist the faint lines of the land which some day perhaps we may reach? The truth of such speculations can never be proved, of course, but in an age like ours there is a great temptation to indulge in them. For it is an age clearly when we are not fast anchored where we are; things are

---

[14]   George V (1865–1936) reigned from 1910.

NARROW BRIDGE
This essay was first published in the *New York Herald Tribune*, August 14, 1927.

moving round us; we are moving ourselves. Is it not the critic's duty to tell us, or to guess at least, where we are going?

Obviously the inquiry must narrow itself very strictly, but it might perhaps be possible in a short space to take one instance of dissatisfaction and difficulty, and, having examined into that, we might be the better able to guess the direction in which, when we have surmounted it, we shall go.

Nobody indeed can read much modern literature without being aware that some dissatisfaction, some difficulty, is lying in our way. On all sides writers are attempting what they cannot achieve, are forcing the form they use to contain a meaning which is strange to it. Many reasons might be given, but here let us select only one, and that is the failure of poetry to serve us as it has served so many generations of our fathers. Poetry is not lending her services to us nearly as freely as she did to them. The great channel of expression which has carried away so much energy, so much genius, seems to have narrowed itself or to have turned aside.

That is true only within certain limits of course; our age is rich in lyric poetry; no age perhaps has been richer. But for our generation and the generation that is coming the lyric cry of ecstasy or despair, which is so intense, so personal, and so limited, is not enough. The mind is full of monstrous, hybrid, unmanageable emotions. That the age of the earth is 3,000,000,000 years; that human life lasts but a second; that the capacity of the human mind is nevertheless boundless; that life is infinitely beautiful yet repulsive; that one's fellow creatures are adorable but disgusting; that science and religion have between them destroyed belief; that all bonds of union seem broken, yet some control must exist – it is in this atmosphere of doubt and conflict that writers have now to create, and the fine fabric of a lyric is no more fitted to contain this point of view than a rose leaf to envelop the rugged immensity of a rock.

But when we ask ourselves what has in the past served to express such an attitude as this – an attitude which is full of contrast and collision; an attitude which seems to demand the conflict of one character upon another, and at the same time to stand in need of some general shaping power, some conception which lends the whole harmony and force, we must reply that there was a form once, and it was not the form of lyric poetry; it was the form of the drama, of the poetic drama of the Elizabethan age. And that is the one form which seems dead beyond all possibility of resurrection today.

For if we look at the state of the poetic play we must have grave doubts that any force on earth can now revive it. It has been practised and is still practised by writers of the highest genius and ambition. Since the death of Dryden[1] every great poet it seems has had his fling. Wordsworth and Coleridge, Shelley and Keats, Tennyson, Swinburne, and Browning[2] (to name the dead only) have all written poetic plays, but none has succeeded. Of all the plays they wrote, probably only Swinburne's *Atalanta* and Shelley's *Prometheus*[3] are still read, and they less frequently than other works by the same writers. All the rest have climbed to the top shelves of our bookcases, put their heads under their wings, and gone to sleep. No one will willingly disturb those slumbers.

Yet it is tempting to try to find some explanation of this failure in case it should throw light upon the future which we are considering. The reason why poets can no longer write poetic plays lies somewhere perhaps in this direction.

There is a vague, mysterious thing called an attitude toward life. We all know people – if we turn from literature to life for a moment – who are at loggerheads with existence; unhappy people who never get what they want; are baffled, complaining, who stand at an uncomfortable angle whence they see everything askew. There are others again who, though they appear perfectly content, seem to have lost all touch with reality. They lavish all their affections upon little dogs and old china. They take interest in nothing but the vicissitudes of their own health and the ups and downs of social snobbery. There are, however, others who strike us, why precisely it would be difficult to say, as being by nature or circumstances in a position where they can use their faculties to the full upon

---

[1]   John Dryden (1631–1700), British poet and dramatist.
[2]   William Wordsworth (1770–1850), Samuel Taylor Coleridge (1772–1834), Percy Bysshe Shelley (1792–1822), John Keats (1795–1821), Alfred Tennyson (1809–92), Algernon Swinburne (1837–1909), and Robert Browning (1812–89) were all British poets.
[3]   Swinburne published his play *Atalanta in Calydon* in 1865; Shelley published his play *Prometheus Unbound* in 1820.

things that are of importance. They are not necessarily happy or successful, but there is a zest in their presence, an interest in their doings. They seem alive all over. This may be partly the result of circumstances – they have been born into surroundings that suit them – but much more is the result of some happy balance of qualities in themselves so that they see things not at an awkward angle, all askew; nor distorted through a mist; but four square, in proportion; they grasp something hard; when they come into action they cut real ice.

A writer too has in the same way an attitude toward life, though it is a different life from the other. They too can stand at an uncomfortable angle; can be baffled, frustrated, unable to get at what they want as writers. This is true, for example, of the novels of George Gissing.[4] Then, again, they can retire to the suburbs and lavish their interest upon pet dogs and duchesses – prettinesses, sentimentalities, snobberies, and this is true of some of our most highly successful novelists. But there are others who seem by nature or circumstances so placed that they can use their faculties freely upon important things. It is not that they write quickly or easily, or become at once successful or celebrated. One is rather trying to analyse a quality which is present in most of the great ages of literature and is most marked in the work of Elizabethan dramatists. They seem to have an attitude toward life, a position which allows them to move their limbs freely; a view which, though made up of all sorts of different things, falls into the right perspective for their purposes.

In part, of course, this was the result of circumstances. The public appetite, not for books, but for the drama, the smallness of the towns, the distance which separated people, the ignorance in which even the educated then lived, all made it natural for the Elizabethan imagination to fill itself with lions and unicorns, dukes and duchesses, violence and mystery. This was reinforced by something which we cannot explain so simply, but which we can certainly feel. They had an attitude toward life which made them able to express themselves freely and fully. Shakespeare's plays are not the work of a baffled and frustrated mind; they are the perfectly elastic envelope of his thought. Without a hitch he turns from philosophy to a drunken brawl; from love songs to an argument; from simple merriment to profound speculation. And it is true of all the Elizabethan dramatists that though they may bore us – and they do – they never make us feel that they are afraid or self-conscious, or that there is anything hindering, hampering, inhibiting the full current of their minds.

Yet our first thought when we open a modern poetic play – and this applies to much modern poetry – is that the writer is not at his ease. He is afraid, he is forced, he is self-conscious. And with what good reason! we may exclaim, for which of us is perfectly at his ease with a man in a toga called Xenocrates, or with a woman in a blanket called Eudoxa? Yet for some reason the modern poetic play is always about Xenocrates and not about Mr. Robinson; it is about Thessaly and not about Charing Cross Road.[5] When the Elizabethans laid their scenes in foreign parts and made their heroes and heroines princes and princesses they only shifted the scene from one side to the other of a very thin veil. It was a natural device which gave depth and distance to their figures. But the country remained English; and the Bohemian prince was the same person as the English noble. Our modern poetic playwrights, however, seem to seek the veil of the past and of distance for a different reason. They want not a veil that heightens but a curtain that conceals; they lay their scene in the past because they are afraid of the present. They are aware that if they tried to express the thoughts, the visions, the sympathies and antipathies which are actually turning and tumbling in their brains in this year of grace 1927 the poetic decencies would be violated; they could only stammer and stumble and perhaps have to sit down or to leave the room. The Elizabethans had an attitude which allowed them complete freedom; the modern playwright has either no attitude at all, or one so strained that it cramps his limbs and distorts his vision. He has therefore to take refuge with Xenocrates, who says nothing or only what blank verse can with decency say.

But can we explain ourselves a little more fully? What has changed, what has happened, what has put the writer now at such an angle that he cannot pour his mind straight into the old channels of English poetry? Some sort of answer may be suggested by a walk through the streets of any large

---

4   George Gissing (1857–1903) was a British novelist noted for his pessimism.

5   A street in London that runs north from the Strand to Oxford Street.

town. The long avenue of brick is cut up into boxes, each of which is inhabited by a different human being who has put locks on his doors and bolts on his windows to ensure some privacy, yet is linked to his fellows by wires which pass overhead, by waves of sound which pour through the roof and speak aloud to him of battles and murders and strikes and revolutions all over the world. And if we go in and talk to him we shall find that he is a wary, secretive, suspicious animal, extremely self-conscious, extremely careful not to give himself away. Indeed, there is nothing in modern life which forces him to do it. There is no violence in private life; we are polite, tolerant, agreeable, when we meet. War even is conducted by companies and communities rather than by individuals. Duelling is extinct. The marriage bond can stretch indefinitely without snapping. The ordinary person is calmer, smoother, more self-contained than he used to be.

But again we should find if we took a walk with our friend that he is extremely alive to everything – to ugliness, sordidity, beauty, amusement. He follows every thought careless where it may lead him. He discusses openly what used never to be mentioned even privately. And this very freedom and curiosity are perhaps the cause of what appears to be his most marked characteristic – the strange way in which things that have no apparent connection are associated in his mind. Feelings which used to come single and separate do so no longer. Beauty is part ugliness; amusement part disgust; pleasure part pain. Emotions which used to enter the mind whole are now broken up on the threshold.

For example: It is a spring night, the moon is up, the nightingale singing, the willows bending over the river. Yes, but at the same time a diseased old woman is picking over her greasy rags on a hideous iron bench. She and the spring enter his mind together; they blend but do not mix. The two emotions, so incongruously coupled, bite and kick at each other in unison. But the emotion which Keats felt when he heard the song of the nightingale is one and entire, though it passes from joy in beauty to sorrow at the unhappiness of human fate. He makes no contrast. In his poem sorrow is the shadow which accompanies beauty. In the modern mind beauty is accompanied not by its shadow but by its opposite. The modern poet talks of the nightingale who sings "jug jug to dirty ears."[6] There trips along by the side of our modern beauty some mocking spirit which sneers at beauty for being beautiful; which turns the looking-glass and shows us that the other side of her cheek is pitted and deformed. It is as if the modern mind, wishing always to verify its emotions, had lost the power of accepting anything simply for what it is. Undoubtedly this sceptical and testing spirit has led to a great freshening and quickening of soul. There is a candour, an honesty in modern writing which is salutary if not supremely delightful. Modern literature, which had grown a little sultry and scented with Oscar Wilde and Walter Pater,[7] revived instantly from her nineteenth-century languor when Samuel Butler and Bernard Shaw[8] began to burn their feathers and apply their salts to her nose. She awoke; she sat up; she sneezed. Naturally, the poets were frightened away.

For of course poetry has always been overwhelmingly on the side of beauty. She has always insisted on certain rights, such as rhyme, metre, poetic diction. She has never been used for the common purpose of life. Prose has taken all the dirty work on to her own shoulders; has answered letters, paid bills, written articles, made speeches, served the needs of businessmen, shopkeepers, lawyers, soldiers, peasants.

Poetry has remained aloof in the possession of her priests. She has perhaps paid the penalty for this seclusion by becoming a little stiff. Her presence with all her apparatus – her veils, her garlands, her memories, her associations – affects us the moment she speaks. Thus when we ask poetry to express this discord, this incongruity, this sneer, this contrast, this curiosity, the quick, queer emotions which are bred in small separate rooms, the wide, general ideas which civilization teaches, she cannot move quickly enough, simply enough, or broadly enough to do it. Her accent is too marked; her manner too emphatic. She gives us instead lovely lyric cries of passion; with a

---

[6] T. S. Eliot (1888–1965), *The Waste Land* (1922), line 103 (see p. 128 in this edition).

[7] Oscar Wilde (1854–1900) and Walter Horatio Pater (1839–94) were writers whose works embodied *fin de siècle* aestheticism.

[8] Samuel Butler (1835–1902), British novelist whose *The Way of All Flesh*, published posthumously in 1903, was thought to herald a return to strong realism; George Bernard Shaw (1856–1950) celebrated Irish dramatist and essayist.

majestic sweep of her arm she bids us take refuge in the past; but she does not keep pace with the mind and fling herself subtly, quickly, passionately into its various sufferings and joys. Byron in *Don Juan*[9] pointed the way; he showed how flexible an instrument poetry might become, but none has followed his example or put his tool to further use. We remain without a poetic play.

Thus we are brought to reflect whether poetry is capable of the task which we are now setting her. It may be that the emotions here sketched in such rude outline and imputed to the modern mind submit more readily to prose than to poetry. It may be possible that prose is going to take over – has, indeed, already taken over – some of the duties which were once discharged by poetry.

If, then, we are daring and risk ridicule and try to see in what direction we who seem to be moving so fast are going, we may guess that we are going in the direction of prose and that in ten or fifteen years' time prose will be used for purposes for which prose has never been used before. That cannibal, the novel, which has devoured so many forms of art will by then have devoured even more. We shall be forced to invent new names for the different books which masquerade under this one heading. And it is possible that there will be among the so-called novels one which we shall scarcely know how to christen. It will be written in prose, but in prose which has many of the characteristics of poetry. It will have something of the exaltation of poetry, but much of the ordinariness of prose. It will be dramatic, and yet not a play. It will be read, not acted. By what name we are to call it is not a matter of very great importance. What is important is that this book which we see on the horizon may serve to express some of those feelings which seem at the moment to be balked by poetry pure and simple and to find the drama equally inhospitable to them. Let us try, then, to come to closer terms with it and to imagine what may be its scope and nature.

In the first place, one may guess that it will differ from the novel as we know it now chiefly in that it will stand further back from life. It will give, as poetry does, the outline rather than the detail. It will make little use of the marvellous fact-recording power, which is one of the attributes of fiction. It will tell us very little about the houses, incomes, occupations of its characters; it will have little kinship with the sociological novel or the novel of environment. With these limitations it will express the feeling and ideas of the characters closely and vividly, but from a different angle. It will resemble poetry in this that it will give not only or mainly people's relations to each other and their activities together, as the novel has hitherto done, but it will give the relation of the mind to general ideas and its soliloquy in solitude. For under the dominion of the novel we have scrutinized one part of the mind closely and left another unexplored. We have come to forget that a large and important part of life consists in our emotions toward such things as roses and nightingales, the dawn, the sunset, life, death, and fate; we forget that we spend much time sleeping, dreaming, thinking, reading, alone; we are not entirely occupied in personal relations; all our energies are not absorbed in making our livings. The psychological novelist has been too prone to limit psychology to the psychology of personal intercourse; we long sometimes to escape from the incessant, the remorseless analysis of falling into love and falling out of love, of what Tom feels for Judith and Judith does or does not altogether feel for Tom. We long for some more impersonal relationship. We long for ideas, for dreams, for imaginations, for poetry.

And it is one of the glories of the Elizabethan dramatists that they give us this. The poet is always able to transcend the particularity of Hamlet's relation to Ophelia and to give us his questioning not of his own personal lot alone but of the state and being of all human life. In *Measure for Measure*, for example, passages of extreme psychological subtlety are mingled with profound reflections, tremendous imaginations. Yet it is worth noticing that if Shakespeare gives us this profundity, this psychology, at the same time Shakespeare makes no attempt to give us certain other things. The plays are of no use whatever as "applied sociology." If we had to depend upon them for a knowledge of the social and economic conditions of Elizabethan life, we should be hopelessly at sea.

In these respects then the novel or the variety of the novel which will be written in time to come will take on some of the attributes of poetry. It will give the relations of man to nature, to fate; his imagination; his dreams. But it will also give the sneer, the contrast, the question, the closeness and

[9] George Gordon, Lord Byron (1788–1824) published his long autobiographical poem *Don Juan* between 1820 and 1824.

complexity of life. It will take the mould of that queer conglomeration of incongruous things – the modern mind. Therefore it will clasp to its breast the precious prerogatives of the democratic art of prose; its freedom, its fearlessness, its flexibility. For prose is so humble that it can go anywhere; no place is too low, too sordid, or too mean for it to enter. It is infinitely patient, too, humbly acquisitive. It can lick up with its long glutinous tongue the most minute fragments of fact and mass them into the most subtle labyrinths, and listen silently at doors behind which only a murmur, only a whisper, is to be heard. With all the suppleness of a tool which is in constant use it can follow the windings and record the changes which are typical of the modern mind. To this, with Proust and Dostoevsky[10] behind us, we must agree.

But can prose, we may ask, adequate though it is to deal with the common and the complex – can prose say the simple things which are so tremendous? Give the sudden emotions which are so surprising? Can it chant the elegy, or hymn the love, or shriek in terror, or praise the rose, the nightingale, or the beauty of the night? Can it leap at one spring at the heart of its subject as the poet does? I think not. That is the penalty it pays for having dispensed with the incantation and the mystery, with rhyme and metre. It is true that prose writers are daring; they are constantly forcing their instrument to make the attempt. But one has always a feeling of discomfort in the presence of the purple patch or the prose poem. The objection to the purple patch, however, is not that it is purple but that it is a patch. Recall for instance Meredith's "Diversion on a Penny Whistle" in *Richard Feverel*.[11] How awkwardly, how emphatically, with a broken poetic metre it begins: "Golden lie the meadows; golden run the streams; redgold is on the pine-stems. The sun is coming down to earth and walks the fields and the waters." Or recall the famous description of the storm at the end of Charlotte Brontë's *Villette*.[12] These passages are eloquent, lyrical, splendid; they read very well cut out and stuck in an anthology; but in the context of the novel they make us uncomfortable. For both Meredith and Charlotte Brontë called themselves novelists; they stood close up to life; they led us to expect the rhythm, the observation, and the perspective of prose. We feel the jerk and the effort; we are half woken from that trance of consent and illusion in which our submission to the power of the writer's imagination is most complete.

But let us now consider another book, which though written in prose and by way of being called a novel, adopts from the start a different attitude, a different rhythm, which stands back from life, and leads us to expect a different perspective – *Tristram Shandy*. It is a book full of poetry, but we never notice it; it is a book stained deep purple, which is yet never patchy. Here though the mood is changing always, there is no jerk, no jolt in that change to waken us from the depths of consent and belief. In the same breath Sterne laughs, sneers, cuts some indecent ribaldry, and passes on to a passage like this:

> Time wastes too fast: every letter I trace tells me with what rapidity life follows my pen; the days and hours of it more precious – my dear Jenny – than the rubies about thy neck, are flying over our heads like light clouds of a windy day, never to return more; everything presses on – whilst thou are twisting that lock – see! it grows gray; and every time I kiss thy hand to bid adieu, and every absence which follows it, are preludes to that eternal separation which we are shortly to make. – Heaven have mercy upon us both![13]

CHAP. IX

Now, for what the world thinks of that ejaculation – I would not give a groat.

And he goes on to my Uncle Toby, the Corporal, Mrs. Shandy, and the rest of them.

---

[10] Marcel Proust (1871–1922) was a French novelist whose work achieved recognition only after his death in 1922; Fyodor Dostoyevsky (1821–81) was a Russian novelist whose works were translated into English during the period 1900–20.

[11] George Meredith (1828–1909) was a British novelist; *Richard Feverel* (1859) was his first novel, and ch. 19 opens with a long poetic passage that concludes: "Out in the world there, on the skirts of the woodland, a sheep-boy pipes to meditative eve on a penny-whistle."

[12] Charlotte Brontë (1816–55) published *Villette* in 1853.

[13] Laurence Sterne (1713–68), *Tristram Shandy*, vol. 9, ch. 8, the concluding passage; it is then followed by ch. 9, which in its entirety consists of the single sentence quoted by Woolf: "Now, for what the world thinks ... I would not give a groat."

There, one sees, is poetry changing easily and naturally into prose, prose into poetry. Standing a little aloof, Sterne lays his hands lightly upon imagination, wit, fantasy; and reaching high up among the branches where these things grow, naturally and no doubt willingly forfeits his right to the more substantial vegetables that grow on the ground. For, unfortunately, it seems true that some renunciation is inevitable. You cannot cross the narrow bridge of art carrying all its tools in your hands. Some you must leave behind, or you will drop them in midstream or, what is worse, overbalance and be drowned yourself.

So, then, this unnamed variety of the novel will be written standing back from life, because in that way a larger view is to be obtained of some important features of it; it will be written in prose, because prose, if you free it from the beast-of-burden work which so many novelists necessarily lay upon it, of carrying loads of details, bushels of fact — prose thus treated will show itself capable of rising high from the ground, not in one dart, but in sweeps and circles, and of keeping at the same time in touch with the amusements and idiosyncrasies of human character in daily life.

There remains, however, a further question. Can prose be dramatic? It is obvious, of course, that Shaw and Ibsen[14] have used prose dramatically with the highest success, but they have been faithful to the dramatic form. This form one may prophesy is not the one which the poetic dramatist of the future will find fit for his needs. A prose play is too rigid, too limited, too emphatic for his purposes. It lets slip between its meshes half the things that he wants to say. He cannot compress into dialogue all the comment, all the analysis, all the richness that he wants to give. Yet he covets the explosive emotional effect of the drama; he wants to draw blood from his readers, and not merely to stroke and tickle their intellectual susceptibilities. The looseness and freedom of *Tristram Shandy*, wonderfully though they encircle and float off such characters as Uncle Toby and Corporal Trim, do not attempt to range and marshal these people in dramatic contrast together. Therefore it will be necessary for the writer of this exacting book to bring to bear upon his tumultuous and contradictory emotions the generalizing and simplifying power of a strict and logical imagination. Tumult is vile; confusion is hateful; everything in a work of art should be mastered and ordered. His effort will be to generalize and split up. Instead of enumerating details he will mould blocks. His characters thus will have a dramatic power which the minutely realized characters of contemporary fiction often sacrifice in the interests of psychology. And then, though this is scarcely visible, so far distant it lies on the rim of the horizon — one can imagine that he will have extended the scope of his interest so as to dramatize some of those influences which play so large a part in life, yet have so far escaped the novelist — the power of music, the stimulus of sight, the effect on us of the shape of trees or the play of colour, the emotions bred in us by crowds, the obscure terrors and hatreds which come so irrationally in certain places or from certain people, the delight of movement, the intoxication of wine. Every moment is the centre and meeting-place of an extraordinary number of perceptions which have not yet been expressed. Life is always and inevitably much richer than we who try to express it.

But it needs no great gift of prophecy to be certain that whoever attempts to do what is outlined above will have need of all his courage. Prose is not going to learn a new step at the bidding of the first comer. Yet if the signs of the times are worth anything the need of fresh developments is being felt. It is certain that there are scattered about in England, France, and America writers who are trying to work themselves free from a bondage which has become irksome to them; writers who are trying to readjust their attitude so that they may once more stand easily and naturally in a position where their powers have full play upon important things. And it is when a book strikes us as the result of that attitude rather than by its beauty or its brilliancy that we know that it has in it the seeds of an enduring existence.

---

[14] Henrik Ibsen (1828–1906), Norwegian dramatist.

The Leaning Tower (1940)

A writer is a person who sits at a desk and keeps his eye fixed, as intently as he can, upon a certain object – that figure of speech may help to keep us steady on our path if we look at it for a moment. He is an artist who sits with a sheet of paper in front of him trying to copy what he sees. What is his object – his model? Nothing so simple as a painter's model; it is not a bowl of flowers, a naked figure, or a dish of apples and onions. Even the simplest story deals with more than one person, with more than one time. Characters begin young; they grow old; they move from scene to scene, from place to place. A writer has to keep his eye upon a model that moves, that changes, upon an object that is not one object but innumerable objects. Two words alone cover all that a writer looks at – they are, human life.

Let us look at the writer next. What do we see – only a person who sits with a pen in his hand in front of a sheet of paper? That tells us little or nothing. And we know very little. Considering how much we talk about writers, how much they talk about themselves, it is odd how little we know about them. Why are they so common sometimes; then so rare? Why do they sometimes write nothing but masterpieces, then nothing but trash? And why should a family, like the Shelleys, like the Keatses, like the Brontës,[1] suddenly burst into flame and bring to birth Shelley, Keats, and the Brontës? What are the conditions that bring about that explosion? There is no answer – naturally. Since we have not yet discovered the germ of influenza, how should we yet have discovered the germ of genius? We know even less about the mind than about the body. We have less evidence. It is less than two hundred years since people took an interest in themselves; Boswell was almost the first writer who thought that a man's life was worth writing a book about. Until we have more facts, more biographies, more autobiographies, we cannot know much about ordinary people, let alone about extraordinary people. Thus at present we have only theories about writers – a great many theories, but they all differ. The politician says that a writer is the product of the society in which he lives, as a screw is the product of a screw machine; the artist, that a writer is a heavenly apparition that slides across the sky, grazes the earth, and vanishes. To the psychologists a writer is an oyster; feed him on gritty facts, irritate him with ugliness, and by way of compensation, as they call it, he will produce a pearl. The genealogists say that certain stocks, certain families, breed writers as fig trees breed figs – Dryden, Swift, and Pope[2] they tell us were all cousins. This proves that we are in the dark about writers; anybody can make a theory; the germ of a theory is almost always the wish to prove what the theorist wishes to believe.

Theories then are dangerous things. All the same we must risk making one this afternoon since we are going to discuss modern tendencies. Directly we speak of tendencies or movements we commit ourselves to the belief that there is some force, influence, outer pressure which is strong enough to stamp itself upon a whole group of different writers so that all their writing has a certain common likeness. We must then have a theory as to what this influence is. But let us always remember – influences are infinitely numerous; writers are infinitely sensitive; each writer has a different sensibility. That is why literature is always changing, like the weather, like the clouds in the sky. Read a page of Scott; then of Henry James;[3] try to work out the influences that have transformed the one page into the other. It is beyond our skill. We can only hope therefore to single out the most obvious influences that have formed writers into groups. Yet there are groups. Books descend from books as families descend from families. Some descend from Jane Austen; others from

This essay was a paper first read to the Workers' Educational Association in Brighton in May 1940; it was first published in the autumn of that year in John Lehman (ed.), *Folios of New Writing* (London: Hogarth Press in 1940), then collected with other essays in Virginia Woolf, *The Moment and Other Essays* (London: Hogarth Press, 1947), and again in *Collected Essays*, vol. 2 (London: Hogarth Press, 1966).

[1]   Percy Bysshe Shelley (1792–1822) and John Keats (1795–1821) were Romantic poets; the Brontës – Charlotte (1816–55), Emily (1818–48), and Anne (1820–49) – were novelists.

[2]   John Dryden (1631–1700) was a British poet and dramatist; Jonathan Swift (1667–1745) was a novelist, poet, and controversialist; Alexander Pope (1688–1744) was the most admired poet of his age.

[3]   Sir Walter Scott (1771–1832) was a Scottish novelist; Henry James (1843–1916) was an American novelist.

Dickens.[4] They resemble their parents, as human children resemble their parents; yet they differ as children differ, and revolt as children revolt. Perhaps it will be easier to understand living writers as we take a quick look at some of their forebears. We have not time to go far back – certainly we have not time to look closely. But let us glance at English writers as they were a hundred years ago – that may help us to see what we ourselves look like.

In 1815 England was at war,[5] as England is now. And it is natural to ask, how did their war – the Napoleonic War – affect them? Was that one of the influences that formed them into groups? The answer is a very strange one. The Napoleonic wars did not affect the great majority of those writers at all. The proof of that is to be found in the work of two great novelists – Jane Austen and Walter Scott. Each lived through the Napoleonic wars; each wrote through them. But, though novelists live very close to the life of their time, neither of them in all their novels mentioned the Napoleonic wars. This shows that their model, their vision of human life, was not disturbed or agitated or changed by war. Nor were they themselves. It is easy to see why that was so. Wars were then remote; wars were carried on by soldiers and sailors, not by private people. The rumour of battles took a long time to reach England. It was only when the mail coaches clattered along the country roads hung with laurels that the people in villages like Brighton knew that a victory had been won and lit their candles and stuck them in their windows. Compare that with our state to-day. To-day we hear the gunfire in the Channel. We turn on the wireless; we hear an airman telling us how this very afternoon he shot down a raider; his machine caught fire; he plunged into the sea; the light turned green and then black; he rose to the top and was rescued by a trawler. Scott never saw the sailors drowning at Trafalgar; Jane Austen never heard the cannon roar at Waterloo.[6] Neither of them heard Napoleon's voice as we hear Hitler's voice as we sit at home of an evening.

That immunity from war lasted all through the nineteenth century. England, of course, was often at war – there was the Crimean War; the Indian Mutiny; all the little Indian frontier wars, and at the end of the century the Boer War.[7] Keats, Shelley, Byron, Dickens, Thackeray, Carlyle, Ruskin, the Brontës, George Eliot, Trollope, the Brownings[8] – all lived through all those wars. But did they ever mention them? Only Thackeray, I think; in *Vanity Fair* he described the Battle of Waterloo long after it was fought; but only as an illustration, as a scene. It did not change his characters' lives; it merely killed one of his heroes. Of the poets, only Byron and Shelley felt the influence of the nineteenth-century wars profoundly.

War then we can say, speaking roughly, did not affect either the writer or his vision of human life in the nineteenth century. But peace – let us consider the influence of peace. Were the nineteenth-century writers affected by the settled, the peaceful and prosperous state of England? Let us collect a few facts before we launch out into the dangers and delights of theory. We know for a fact, from their lives, that the nineteenth-century writers were all of them fairly well-to-do middle-class people. Most had been educated either at Oxford or at Cambridge. Some were civil servants like Trollope and Matthew Arnold.[9] Others, like Ruskin, were professors. It is a fact that their work brought them considerable fortunes. There is visible proof of that in the houses they built. Look at Abbotsford, bought out of the proceeds of Scott's novels; or at Farringford, built by Tennyson from

---

[4] Jane Austen (1775–1817) was a novelist whose favored settings were country houses and parlors; Charles Dickens (1812–70) favored the streets and buildings of London.

[5] The Napoleonic wars came to an end in 1815 when the Duke of Wellington defeated Napoleon at the battle of Waterloo.

[6] The naval battle of Trafalgar was won by Lord Nelson in 1805; the battle of Waterloo was won by the Duke of Wellington on June 8, 1815.

[7] The Crimean War, which lasted from 1854 to 1856, was initially a war between Russia and the Ottoman Empire (modern Turkey). Britain entered the war because Turkey was seeking to control the Dardanelles and so threaten Britain's Mediterranean sea routes. The Indian Mutiny (1857–8) began with a revolt among Indian soldiers in the Bengal army of the British East India Company, but developed into a widespread uprising

against British rule in India, one that was ruthlessly suppressed. The Boer War (1899–1902) pitted Britain against the Dutch Boer republics of the Transvaal and the Orange Free State. Britain won, but at a very high cost (22,000 lives) and with much loss of support for imperial ideals.

[8] John Keats (1795–1821), Percy Bysshe Shelley (1792–1822), George Gordon, Lord Byron (1788–1824), Charles Dickens (1812–70), William Thackeray (1811–63), Thomas Carlyle (1795–1881), the Brontës (Charlotte [1816–55], Emily [1818–48], and Anne [1820–49]), George Eliot (1819–80), Anthony Trollope (1815–82), Robert Browning (1812–89), and Elizabeth Barrett Browning (1806–61) – were all British authors.

[9] Anthony Trollope worked for the Post Office; Matthew Arnold (1822–88) was an inspector of schools.

his poetry. Look at Dickens's great house in Marylebone; and at his great house at Gadshill.[10] All these are houses needing many butlers, maids, gardeners, grooms to keep the tables spread, the cans carried, and the gardens neat and fruitful. Not only did they leave behind them large houses; they left too an immense body of literature – poems, plays, novels, essays, histories, criticism. It was a very prolific, creative, rich century – the nineteenth century. Now let us ask – is there any connexion between that material prosperity and that intellectual creativeness? Did one lead to the other? How difficult it is to say – for we know so little about writers, and what conditions help them, what hinder them. It is only a guess, and a rough guess; yet I think that there is a connexion. "I think" – perhaps it would be nearer the truth to say "I see." Thinking should be based on facts; and here we have intuitions rather than facts – the lights and shades that come after books are read, the general shifting surface of a large expanse of print. What I see, glancing over that shifting surface, is the picture I have already shown you; the writer seated in front of human life in the nineteenth century; and, looking at it through their eyes, I see that life divided up, herded together, into many different classes. There is the aristocracy; the landed gentry; the professional class; the commercial class; the working class; and there, in one dark blot, is that great class which is called simply and comprehensively "The Poor." To the nineteenth-century writer human life must have looked like a landscape cut up into separate fields. In each field was gathered a different group of people. Each to some extent had its own traditions; its own manners; its own speech; its own dress; its own occupation. But owing to that peace, to that prosperity, each group was tethered, stationary – a herd grazing within its own hedges. And the nineteenth-century writer did not seek to change those divisions; he accepted them. He accepted them so completely that he became unconscious of them. Does that serve to explain why it is that the nineteenth-century writers are able to create so many characters who are not types but individuals? Is it because he did not see the hedges that divide classes; he saw only the human beings that live within those hedges? Is that why he could get beneath the surface and create many-sided characters – Pecksniff, Becky Sharp, Mr. Woodhouse[11] – who change with the years, as the living change? To us now the hedges are visible. We can see now that each of those writers only dealt with a very small section of human life – all Thackeray's characters are upper middle-class people; all Dicken's characters come from the lower middle class. We can see that now; but the writer himself seems unconscious that he is only dealing with one type; with the type formed by the class into which the writer was born himself, with which he is most familiar. And that unconsciousness was an immense advantage to him.

Unconsciousness, which means presumably that the under-mind works at top speed while the upper-mind drowses, is a state we all know. We all have experience of the work done by unconsciousness in our own daily lives. You have had a crowded day, let us suppose, sightseeing in London. Could you say what you had seen and done when you came back? Was it not all a blur, a confusion? But after what seemed a rest, a chance to turn aside and look at something different, the sights and sounds and sayings that had been of most interest to you swam to the surface, apparently of their own accord; and remained in memory; what was unimportant sank into forgetfulness. So it is with the writer. After a hard day's work, trudging round, seeing all he can, feeling all he can, taking in the book of his mind innumerable notes, the writer becomes – if he can – unconscious. In fact, his under-mind works at top speed while his upper-mind drowses. Then, after a pause the veil lifts; and there is the thing – the thing he wants to write about – simplified, composed. Do we strain Wordsworth's famous saying about emotion recollected in tranquillity[12] when we infer that by tranquillity he meant that the writer needs to become unconscious before he can create?

[10] Abbottsford, Sir Walter Scott's house, is an immense Gothic country house; Farringford, on the Isle of Wight, is a more modest eighteenth-century house; the house of Dickens in Marylebone has been destroyed, since Woolf was writing in 1940, but his house at Gadshill Place, near Rochester, Kent, still survives.

[11] Fictional characters in Charles Dickens's *Martin Chuzzlewit* (1843–4), W. M. Thackeray's *Vanity Fair* (1847–8), and Jane Austen's *Emma* (1816).

[12] William Wordsworth, "Preface" to the second edition of the *Lyrical Ballads* (1800): "I have said that poetry is the spontaneous overflow of powerful feelings; it takes its origin from emotion recollected in tranquility; the emotion is contemplated till, by a species of reaction, the tranquility gradually disappears, and an emotion, kindred to that which was the subject of contemplation, is gradually produced, and does itself actually exist in the mind."

If we want to risk a theory, then, we can say that peace and prosperity were influences that gave the nineteenth-century writers a family likeness. They had leisure; they had security; life was not going to change; they themselves were not going to change. They could look; and look away. They could forget; and then – in their books – remember. Those then are some of the conditions that brought about a certain family likeness, in spite of the great individual differences, among the nineteenth-century writers. The nineteenth century ended; but the same conditions went on. They lasted, roughly speaking, till the year 1914. Even in 1914 we can still see the writer sitting as he sat all through the nineteenth century looking at human life; and that human life is still divided into classes; he still looks most intently at the class from which he himself springs; the classes are still so settled that he has almost forgotten that there are classes; and he is still so secure himself that he is almost unconscious of his own position and of its security. He believes that he is looking at the whole of life; and will always so look at it. That is not altogether a fancy picture. Many of those writers are still alive. Sometimes they describe their own position as young men, beginning to write, just before August 1914. How did you learn your art? one can ask them. At College they say – by reading; by listening; by talking. What did they talk about? Here is Mr. Desmond MacCarthy's answer, as he gave it, a week or two ago, in the *Sunday Times*. He was at Cambridge just before the war began and he says: "We were not very much interested in politics. Abstract speculation was much more absorbing; philosophy was more interesting to us than public causes. . . . What we chiefly discussed were those 'goods' which were ends in themselves . . . the search for truth, aesthetic emotions, and personal relations."[13] In addition they read an immense amount; Latin and Greek, and of course French and English. They wrote too – but they were in no hurry to publish. They travelled; – some of them went far afield – to India, to the South Seas. But for the most part they rambled happily in the long summer holidays through England, through France, through Italy. And now and then they published books – books like Rupert Brooke's poems; novels like E. M. Forster's *Room with a View*; essays like G. K. Chesterton's essays, and reviews.[14] It seemed to them that they were to go on living like that, and writing like that, for ever and ever. Then suddenly, like a chasm in a smooth road, the war came.

But before we go on with the story of what happened after 1914, let us look more closely for a moment, not at the writer himself, not at his model; but at his chair. A chair is a very important part of a writer's outfit. It is the chair that gives him his attitude towards his model; that decides what he sees of human life; that profoundly affects his power of telling us what he sees. By his chair we mean his upbringing, his education. It is a fact, not a theory, that all writers from Chaucer[15] to the present day, with so few exceptions that one hand can count them, have sat upon the same kind of chair – a raised chair. They have all come from the middle class; they have had good, at least expensive, educations. They have all been raised above the mass of people upon a tower of stucco – that is their middle-class birth; and of gold – that is their expensive education. That was true of all the nineteenth-century writers, save Dickens; it was true of all the 1914 writers, save D. H. Lawrence.[16] Let us run through what are called "representative names": G. K. Chesterton; T. S. Eliot; Belloc; Lytton Strachey; Somerset Maugham; Hugh Walpole; Wilfred Owen; Rupert Brooke; J. E. Flecker; E. M. Forster; Aldous Huxley; G. M. Trevelyan; O. and S. Sitwell; Middleton Murry.[17] Those are

[13] Desmond MacCarthy (1877–1952), literary and dramatic critic. MacCarthy was literary editor of the *New Statesman*, 1920–7, then succeeded Edmund Gosse as literary editor at the *Sunday Times* in 1928, where he remained until his death. Woolf is quoting "Lytton Strachey," MacCarthy's review of *Lytton Strachey: A Critical Study* (London: Chatto and Windus, 1939), which appeared in the *Sunday Times*, no. 6105 (April 15, 1940), 4, cols. 3–4. Woolf's first ellipsis indicates the omission of "That wave of Fabian Socialism had not reached Cambridge in my time which affected some of Lytton's younger contemporaries like Rupert Brook." Her second: "and these ends, for which the rest of life was only a scaffolding, could be subsumed under three heads . . ."
[14] Rupert Brooke (1887–1915), British poet; his first collection of poems was *"1914": Five Sonnets* (London: Sidgwick &

Jackson, 1915), and a year later his *Collected Poems of Rupert Brooke* appeared (London: John Lane, 1915), a posthumous publication. E. M. Forster (1879–1970) published *Room with a View* in 1908. G. K. Chesterton (1874–1936) was a prolific literary and dramatic critic.
[15] Geoffrey Chaucer (c. 1345–1400), British poet.
[16] D. H. Lawrence (1885–1930), British novelist from a working-class background.
[17] G. K. Chesterton (1874–1936); T. S. Eliot (1888–1965); Hilaire Belloc (1870–1953); Lytton Strachey (1880–1932); Somerset Maugham (1874–1965); Hugh Walpole (1884–1941); Wilfred Owen (1893–1918); Rupert Brooke (1887–1915); James Elroy Flecker (1884–1915); E. M. (Edward Morgan) Forster (1879–1970); Aldous Huxley (1894–1963); G. M. Trevelyan

some of them; and all, with the exception of D. H. Lawrence, came of the middle class, and were educated at public schools and universities. There is another fact, equally indisputable: the books that they wrote were among the best books written between 1910 and 1925. Now let us ask, is there any connexion between those facts? Is there a connexion between the excellence of their work and the fact that they came of families rich enough to send them to public schools and universities?

Must we not decide, greatly though those writers differ, and shallow as we admit our knowledge of influences to be, that there must be a connexion between their education and their work? It cannot be a mere chance that this minute class of educated people has produced so much that is good as writing; and that the vast mass of people without education has produced so little that is good. It is a fact, however. Take away all that the working class has given to English literature and that literature would scarcely suffer; take away all that the educated class has given, and English literature would scarcely exist. Education must then play a very important part in a writer's work.

That seems so obvious that it is astonishing how little stress has been laid upon the writer's education. It is perhaps because a writer's education is so much less definite than other educations. Reading, listening, talking, travel, leisure – many different things it seems are mixed together. Life and books must be shaken and taken in the right proportions. A boy brought up alone in a library turns into a bookworm; brought up alone in the fields he turns into an earthworm. To breed the kind of butterfly a writer is you must let him sun himself for three or four years at Oxford or Cambridge – so it seems. However it is done, it is there that it is done – there that he is taught his art. And he has to be taught his art. Again, is that strange? Nobody thinks it strange if you say that a painter has to be taught his art; or a musician; or an architect. Equally a writer has to be taught. For the art of writing is at least as difficult as the other arts. And though, perhaps because the education is indefinite, people ignore this education; if you look closely you will see that almost every writer who has practised his art successfully had been taught it. He had been taught it by about eleven years of education – at private schools, public schools, and universities. He sits upon a tower raised above the rest of us; a tower built first on his parents' station, then on his parents' gold. It is a tower of the utmost importance; it decides his angle of vision; it affects his power of communication.

All through the nineteenth century, down to August 1914, that tower was a steady tower. The writer was scarcely conscious either of his high station or of his limited vision. Many of them had sympathy, great sympathy, with other classes; they wished to help the working class to enjoy the advantages of the tower class; but they did not wish to destroy the tower, or to descend from it – rather to make it accessible to all. Nor had the model, human life, changed essentially since Trollope looked at it, since Hardy looked at it: and Henry James, in 1914, was still looking at it. Further, the tower itself held firm beneath the writer during all the most impressionable years, when he was learning his art, and receiving all those complex influences and instructions that are summed up by the word education. These were conditions that influenced their work profoundly. For when the crash came in 1914 all those young men, who were to be the representative writers of their time, had their past, their education, safe behind them, safe within them. They had known security; they had the memory of a peaceful boyhood, the knowledge of a settled civilization. Even though the war cut into their lives, and ended some of them, they wrote, and still write, as if the tower were firm beneath them. In one word, they are aristocrats; the unconscious inheritors of a great tradition. Put a page of their writing under the magnifying-glass and you will see, far away in the distance, the Greeks, the Romans; coming nearer, the Elizabethans; coming nearer still, Dryden, Swift, Voltaire, Jane Austen, Dickens, Henry James. Each, however much he differs individually from the others, is a man of education; a man who has learnt his art.

From that group let us pass to the next – to the group which began to write about 1925 and, it may be, came to an end as a group in 1939. If you read current literary journalism you will be able to rattle off a string of names – Day Lewis, Auden, Spender, Isherwood, Louis MacNeice and so on.[18] They adhere much more closely than the names of their predecessors. But at first sight there

---

(1876–1962); Osbert Sitwell (1892–1969); Sacheverel Sitwell (1897–1988); John Middleton Murry (1889–1957).

[18] Cecil Day-Lewis (1904–72) was a poet who later became poet laureate; W. H. Auden (1900–73) was a British poet;

seems little difference, in station, in education. Mr. Auden in a poem written to Mr. Isherwood says: Behind us we have stucco suburbs and expensive educations.[19] They are tower dwellers like their predecessors, the sons of well-to-do parents, who could afford to send them to public schools and universities. But what a difference in the tower itself, in what they saw from the tower! When they looked at human life what did they see? Everywhere change; everywhere revolution. In Germany, in Russia, in Italy, in Spain,[20] all the old hedges were being rooted up; all the old towers were being thrown to the ground. Other hedges were being planted; other towers were being raised. There was communism in one country; in another fascism. The whole of civilization, of society, was changing. There was, it is true, neither war nor revolution in England itself. All those writers had time to write many books before 1939. But even in England towers that were built of gold and stucco were no longer steady towers. They were leaning towers. The books were written under the influence of change, under the threat of war. That perhaps is why the names adhere so closely; there was one influence that affected them all and made them, more than their predecessors, into groups. And that influence, let us remember, may well have excluded from that string of names the poets whom posterity will value most highly, either because they could not fall into step, as leaders or as followers, or because the influence was adverse to poetry, and until that influence relaxed, they could not write. But the tendency that makes it possible for us to group the names of these writers together, and gives their work a common likeness, was the tendency of the tower they sat on – the tower of middle-class birth and expensive education – to lean.

Let us imagine, to bring this home to us, that we are actually upon a leaning tower and note our sensations. Let us see whether they correspond to the tendencies we observe in those poems, plays, and novels. Directly we feel that a tower leans we become acutely conscious that we are upon a tower. All those writers too are acutely tower conscious; conscious of their middle-class birth; of their expensive educations. Then when we come to the top of the tower how strange the view looks – not altogether upside down, but slanting, sidelong. That too is characteristic of the leaning-tower writers; they do not look any class straight in the face; they look either up, or down, or sidelong. There is no class so settled that they can explore it unconsciously. That perhaps is why they create no characters. Then what do we feel next, raised in imagination on top of the tower? First discomfort; next self-pity for that discomfort; which pity soon turns to anger – to anger against the builder, against society, for making us uncomfortable. Those too seem to be tendencies of the leaning-tower writers. Discomfort; pity for themselves; anger against society. And yet – here is another tendency – how can you altogether abuse a society that is giving you, after all, a very fine view and some sort of security? You cannot abuse that society whole-heartedly while you continue to profit by that society. And so very naturally you abuse society in the person of some retired admiral or spinster or armament manufacturer; and by abusing them hope to escape whipping yourself. The bleat of the scapegoat sounds loud in their work, and the whimper of the schoolboy crying "Please, Sir, it was the other fellow, not me." Anger; pity; scapegoat beating; excuse finding – these are all very natural tendencies; if we were in their position we should tend to do the same. But we are not in their position; we have not had eleven years of expensive education. We have only been climbing an imaginary tower. We can cease to imagine. We can come down.

Stephen Spender (1909–95) was an essayist, critic, and man of letters; Christopher Isherwood (1904–86) was a novelist and screenwriter; Louis MacNeice (1907–63) was a poet and critic. All these writers were born between 1900 and 1909, and therefore were from a generation or even two after Woolf's own, a generation in its twenties during the politically charged 1930s.
[19] W. H. Auden, *Look, Stranger!* (London: Faber and Faber, 1936), poem "30," 63–6, which is dedicated to Christopher Isherwood, the fourth stanza of which (62–3) reads:

> Nine years ago, upon that southern island
> Where the wild Tennyson became a fossil,
> Half-boys, we spoke of books and praised
> The acid and austere, behind us only

> The stuccoed suburb and expensive school.
> Scented our turf, the distant baying
> Nice decoration to the artist's wish;
> Yet fast the deer was flying through the wood.

The poem was retitled "Birthday Poem (to Christopher Isherwood)" in Auden's *Collected Shorter Poems 1930–1944* (London: Faber and Faber, 1950) and omitted entirely from his *Collected Shorter Poems 1927–1957* (London: Faber and Faber, 1960).
[20] Benito Mussolini took power in Italy in 1922; Josef Stalin assumed power in Russia in 1924; Adolph Hitler seized power in Germany in 1933; and General Franco took power in Spain in 1939.

But they cannot. They cannot throw away their education; they cannot throw away their upbringing. Eleven years at school and college have been stamped upon them indelibly. And then, to their credit but to their confusion, the leaning tower not only leant in the thirties, but it leant more and more to the left. Do you remember what Mr. MacCarthy said about his own group at the university in 1914? "We were not very much interested in politics ... philosophy was more interesting to use than public causes?" That shows that his tower leant neither to the right nor to the left. But in 1930 it was impossible – if you were young, sensitive, imaginative – not to be interested in politics; not to find public causes of much more pressing interest than philosophy. In 1930 young men at college were forced to be aware of what was happening in Russia; in Germany; in Italy; in Spain. They could not go on discussing aesthetic emotions and personal relations. They could not confine their reading to the poets; they had to read the politicians. They read Marx. They became communists; they became anti-fascists. The tower they realized was founded upon injustice and tyranny; it was wrong for a small class to possess an education that other people paid for; wrong to stand upon the gold that a bourgeois father had made from his bourgeois profession. It was wrong; yet how could they make it right? Their education could not be thrown away; as for their capital – did Dickens, did Tolstoy ever throw away their capital? Did D. H. Lawrence, a miner's son, continue to live like a miner? No; for it is death for a writer to throw away his capital; to be forced to earn his living in a mine or a factory. And thus, trapped by their education, pinned down by their capital, they remained on top of their leaning tower, and their state of mind as we see it reflected in their poems and plays and novels is full of discord and bitterness, full of confusion and of compromise.

These tendencies are better illustrated by quotation than by analysis. There is a poem by one of those writers, Louis MacNeice, called *Autumn Journal*.[21] It is dated March 1939. It is feeble as poetry, but interesting as autobiography. He begins of course with a snipe at the scapegoat – the bourgeois, middle-class family from which he sprang. The retired admirals, the retired generals, and the spinster lady have breakfasted off bacon and eggs served on a silver dish, he tells us. He sketches that family as if it were already a little remote and more than a little ridiculous. But they could afford to send him to Marlborough and then to Merton, Oxford. This is what he learnt at Oxford:

> *We learned that a gentleman never misplaces his accents,*
> *That nobody knows how to speak, much less how to write*
> *English who has not hob-nobbed with the great-grandparents of English.*[22]

Besides that he learnt at Oxford Latin and Greek; and philosophy, logic, and metaphysics:

> *Oxford* [he says] *crowded the mantelpiece with gods –*
> *Scaliger, Heinsius, Dindorf, Bentley, Wilamowitz.*[23]

It was at Oxford that the tower began to lean. He felt that he was living under a system –

> *That gives the few at fancy prices their fancy lives*
> *While ninety-nine in the hundred who never attend the banquet*
> *Must wash the grease of ages off the knives.*[24]

But at the same time, an Oxford education had made him fastidious:

> *It is so hard to imagine*
> *A world where the many would have their chance without*

---

[21] Louis MacNeice (1907–63) wrote *Autumn Journal* in late 1938 and early 1939 (London: Faber and Faber, 1939). It charts, in 24 numbered sections, his responses to current events from the Munich Agreement of September 1938, when Neville Chamberlain capitulated to Hitler's demand that Germany annex the Sudetenland area of Czechoslovakia, to spring 1939, when the forces of the Spanish Republic were defeated by the nationalist troops under General Franco.

[22] *Autumn Journal*, xiii, 50.

[23] *Autumn Journal*, xiii, 51.

[24] *Autumn Journal*, iii, 17.

> *A fall in the standard of intellectual living*
> *And nothing left that the highbrow cares about.*[25]

At Oxford he got his honours degree; and that degree – in humane letters – put him in the way of a "cushy job" – seven hundred a year, to be precise, and several rooms of his own.

> *If it were not for Lit. Hum. I might be climbing*
> *A ladder with a hod,*
> *And seven hundred a year*
> *Will pay the rent and the gas and the phone and the grocer*[26] –

And yet, again, doubts break in; the "cushy job" of teaching more Latin and Greek to more undergraduates does not satisfy him –

> *...the so-called humane studies*
> *May lead to cushy jobs*
> *But leave the men who land them spiritually bankrupt,*
> *Intellectual snobs.*[27]

And what is worse, that education and that "cushy job" cut one off, he complains, from the common life of one's kind.

> *All that I would like to be is human, having a share*
> *In a civilized, articulate and well-adjusted*
> *Community where the mind is given its due*
> *But the body is not distrusted.*[28]

Therefore in order to bring about that well-adjusted community he must turn from literature to politics, remembering, he says,

> *Remembering that those who by their habit*
> *Hate politics, can no longer keep their private*
> *Values unless they open the public gate*
> *To a better political system.*[29]

So, in one way or another, he takes part in politics, and finally he ends:

> *What is it we want really?*
> *For what end and how?*
> *If it is something feasible, obtainable,*
> *Let us dream it now,*
> *And pray for a possible land*
> *Not of sleep-walkers, not of angry puppets,*
> *But where both heart and brain can understand*
> *The movements of our fellows,*
> *Where life is a choice of instruments and none*
> *Is debarred his natural music...*
> *Where the individual, no longer squandered*
> *In self-assertion, works with the rest...*[30]

---

[25] *Autumn Journal*, iii, 17.
[26] *Autumn Journal*, xii, 49.
[27] *Autumn Journal*, xii, 49.
[28] *Autumn Journal*, xii, 49.

[29] *Autumn Journal*, xiv, 55.
[30] *Autumn Journal*, xxiv, 95. Woolf's ellipsis between "music" and "Where" signals an omission of six lines.

Those quotations give a fair description of the influences that have told upon the leaning-tower group. Others could easily be discovered. The influence of the films explains the lack of transitions in their work and the violently opposed contrasts. The influence of poets like Mr. Yeats and Mr. Eliot[31] explains the obscurity. They took over from the elder poets a technique which, after many years of experiment, those poets used skilfully, and used it clumsily and often inappropriately. But we have time only to point to the most obvious influences; and these can be summed up as Leaning Tower Influences. If you think of them, that is, as people trapped on a leaning tower from which they cannot descend, much that is puzzling in their work is easier to understand. It explains the violence of their attack upon bourgeois society and also its half-heartedness. They are profiting by a society which they abuse. They are flogging a dead or dying horse because a living horse, if flogged, would kick them off its back. It explains the destructiveness of their work; and also its emptiness. They can destroy bourgeois society, in part at least; but what have they put in its place? How can a writer who has no first-hand experience of a towerless, of a classless society create that society? Yet as Mr. MacNeice bears witness, they feel compelled to preach, if not by their living, at least by their writing, the creation of a society in which everyone is equal and everyone is free. It explains the pedagogic, the didactic, the loud-speaker strain that dominates their poetry. They must teach; they must preach. Everything is a duty – even love. Listen to Mr. Day Lewis ingerminating love. "Mr. Spender," he says, "speaking from the living unit of himself and his friends appeals for the contraction of the social group to a size at which human contact may again be established and demands the destruction of all impediments to love. Listen." And we listen to this:

> We have come at last to a country
> Where light, like shine from snow, strikes all faces,
> Here you may wonder
> How it was that works, money, interest, building could ever hide
> The palpable and obvious love of man for man.[32]

We listen to oratory, not poetry. It is necessary, in order to feel the emotion of those lines, that other people should be listening too. We are in a group, in a class-room as we listen.

Listen now to Wordsworth:

> Lover had he known in huts where poor men dwell,
> His daily teachers had been woods and rills,
> The silence that is in the starry sky,
> The sleep that is among the lonely hills.[33]

We listen to that when we are alone. We remember that in solitude. Is that the difference between politician's poetry and poet's poetry? We listen to the one in company; to the other when we are alone? But the poet in the thirties was forced to be a politician. That explains why the artist in the thirties was forced to be a scapegoat. If politics were "real," the ivory tower was an escape from "reality." That explains the curious, bastard language in which so much of this leaning-tower prose and poetry is written. It is not the rich speech of the aristocrat: it is not the racy speech of the peasant. It is betwixt and between. The poet is a dweller in two worlds, one dying, the other struggling to be born. And so we come to what is perhaps the most marked tendency of leaning-tower literature – the desire to be whole; to be human. "All that I would like to be is human" – that cry rings through their books – the longing to be closer to their kind, to write the common speech of their kind, to share the emotions of their kind, no longer to be isolated and exalted in solitary state upon their tower, but to be down on the ground with the mass of human kind.

[31] William Butler Yeats (1865–1939) and T. S. Eliot (1888–1965) were poets who dominated the work of younger poets in the 1930s. See pp. 301–69 (Yeats) and 113–73 (Eliot).
[32] Stephen Spender, Poems (London: Faber and Faber, 1933), "XXIV" (otherwise untitled), 40. Woolf's citation varies from the original only in the line break between lines 4 and 5. The original reads: "ever hide / The palpable ..."
[33] William Wordsworth, "Song at the Feast of Brougham Castle, Upon the Restoration of Lord Clifford, the Shepherd, to the Estates and Honours of Ancestors," lines 161–4.

These then, briefly and from a certain angle, are some of the tendencies of the modern writer who is seated upon a leaning tower. No other generation has been exposed to them. It may be that none has had such an appallingly difficult task. Who can wonder if they have been incapable of giving us great poems, great plays, great novels? They had nothing settled to look at; nothing peaceful to remember; nothing certain to come. During all the most impressionable years of their lives they were stung into consciousness – into self-consciousness, into class-consciousness, into the consciousness of things changing, of things falling, of death perhaps about to come. There was no tranquillity in which they could recollect. The inner mind was paralysed because the surface mind was always hard at work.

Yet if they have lacked the creative power of the poet and the novelist, the power – does it come from a fusion of the two minds, the upper and the under? – that creates characters that live, poems that we all remember, they have had a power which, if literature continues, may prove to be of great value in the future. They have been great egotists. That too was forced upon them by their circumstances. When everything is rocking round one, the only person who remains comparatively stable is oneself. When all faces are changing and obscured, the only face one can see clearly is one's own. So they wrote about themselves – in their plays, in their poems, in their novels. No other ten years can have produced so much autobiography as the ten years between 1930 and 1940. No one, whatever his class or his obscurity, seems to have reached the age of thirty without writing his autobiography. But the leaning-tower writers wrote about themselves honestly, therefore creatively. They told the unpleasant truths, not only the flattering truths. That is why their autobiography is so much better than their fiction or their poetry. Consider how difficult it is to tell the truth about oneself – the unpleasant truth; to admit that one is petty, vain, mean, frustrated, tortured, unfaithful, and unsuccessful. The nineteenth-century writers never told that kind of truth, and that is why so much of the nineteenth-century writing is worthless; why, for all their genius, Dickens and Thackeray seem so often to write about dolls and puppets, not about full-grown men and women; why they are forced to evade the main themes and make do with diversions instead. If you do not tell the truth about yourself you cannot tell it about other people. As the nineteenth century wore on, the writers knew that they were crippling themselves, diminishing their material, falsifying their object. "We are condemned," Stevenson wrote, "to avoid half the life that passes us by. What books Dickens could have written had he been permitted! Think of Thackeray as unfettered as Flaubert or Balzac! What books I might have written myself? But they give us a little box of toys and say to us 'You mustn't play with anything but these'!"[34] Stevenson blamed society – bourgeois society was his scapegoat too. Why did he not blame himself? Why did he consent to go on playing with his little box of toys?

The leaning-tower writer has had the courage, at any rate, to throw that little box of toys out of the window. He has had the courage to tell the truth, the unpleasant truth, about himself. That is the first step towards telling the truth about other people. By analysing themselves honestly, with help from Dr. Freud, these writers have done a great deal to free us from nineteenth-century suppressions. The writers of the next generation may inherit from them a whole state of mind, a mind no longer crippled, evasive, divided. They may inherit that unconsciousness which, as we guessed – it is only a guess – at the beginning of this paper, is necessary if writers are to get beneath the surface, and to write something that people remember when they are alone. For that great gift of unconsciousness the next generation will have to thank the creative and honest egotism of the leaning-tower group.

The next generation – there will be a next generation, in spite of this war and whatever it brings. Have we time then for a rapid glance, for a hurried guess at the next generation? The next generation will be, when peace comes, a post-war generation too. Must it too be a leaning-tower generation – an oblique, sidelong, squinting, self-conscious generation with a foot in two

---

[34]   Robert Louis Stevenson (1850–94), as quoted in the book of reminiscences written by his stepson, Lloyd Osbourne, *An Intimate Portrait of R. L. S.* (New York: Scribner's 1924), 132–3. The sentence prior to those quoted by Woolf reads: "How the French misuse their freedom; see nothing worth writing about save the eternal triangle; while we, who are muzzled like dogs, but who are infinitely wider in our outlook, are condemned to avoid half the life that passes us by."

worlds? Or will there be no more towers and no more classes and shall we stand, without hedges between us, on the common ground?

There are two reasons which lead us to think, perhaps to hope, that the world after the war will be a world without classes or towers. Every politician who has made a speech since September 1939 has ended with a peroration in which he has said that we are not fighting this war for conquest; but to bring about a new order in Europe. In that order, they tell us, we are all to have equal opportunities, equal chances of developing whatever gifts we may possess. That is one reason why, if they mean what they say, and can effect it, classes and towers will disappear. The other reason is given by the income tax. The income tax is already doing in its own way what the politicians are hoping to do in theirs. The income tax is saying to middle-class parents: You cannot afford to send your sons to public schools any longer; you must send them to the elementary schools. One of these parents wrote to the *New Statesman* a week or two ago.[35] Her little boy, who was to have gone to Winchester, had been taken away from his elementary school and sent to the village school. "He has never been happier in his life," she wrote. "The question of class does nor arise; he is merely interested to find how many different kinds of people there are in the world. . . . " And she is only paying twopence-halfpenny a week for that happiness and instruction instead of 35 guineas a term and extras. If the pressure of the income tax continues, classes will disappear. There will be no more upper classes; middle classes; lower classes. All classes will be merged in one class. How will that change affect the writer who sits at his desk looking at human life? It will not be divided by hedges any more. Very likely that will be the end of the novel, as we know it. Literature, as we know it, is always ending, and beginning again. Remove the hedges from Jane Austen's world, from Trollope's world, and how much of their comedy and tragedy would remain? We shall regret our Jane Austens and out Trollopes; they gave us comedy, tragedy, and beauty. But much of that old-class literature was very petty; very false; very dull. Much is already unreadable. The novel of a classless and towerless world should be a better novel than the old novel. The novelist will have more interesting people to describe – people who have had a chance to develop their humour, their gifts, their tastes; real people, not people cramped and squashed into featureless masses by hedges. The poet's gain is less obvious; for he has been less under the dominion of hedges. But he should gain words; when we have pooled all the different dialects, the clipped and cabined vocabulary which is all that he uses now should be enriched. Further, there might then be a common belief which he could accept, and thus shift from his shoulders the burden of didacticism, of propaganda. These then are a few reasons, hastily snatched, why we can look forward hopefully to a stronger, a more varied literature in the classless and towerless society of the future.

But it is in the future; and there is a deep gulf to be bridged between the dying world and the world that is struggling to be born. For there are still two worlds, two separate worlds. 'I want', said the mother who wrote to the paper the other day about her boy, 'the best of both worlds for my son.' She wanted, that is, the village school, where he learnt to mix with the living; and the other school – Winchester it was – where he mixed with the dead. "Is he to continue," she asked, "under the system of free national education, or shall he go on – or should I say back – to the old public-school system which really is so very, very private?" She wanted the new world and the old world to unite, the world of the present and the world of the past.

But there is still a gulf between them, a dangerous gulf, in which, possibly, literature may crash and come to grief. It is easy to see that gulf; it is easy to lay the blame for it upon England. England has crammed a small aristocratic class with Latin and Greek and logic and metaphysics and

---

[35] *New Statesman* 19.477 (April 13, 1941), "Correspondence," 494–6, "The Public School Problem," 496, letter by Molly Fordham: "Sirs, – My son's second term at the village school ended with the Easter holidays. My son's father, his uncles and grandfathers went, as a matter of course, to the great public schools, preceded by expensive private schoolos. My son had also been 'put down' for Winchester.

"Since the war he has been going to the elementary school in the village. He has never been happier in his life; he is learning fast; the teaching, by a young, highly qualified and enthusiastic woman, seems more effective than was the teaching at his expen-

sive private school. He has two voices, one for his school friends, one for use when reciting and (occasionally) at home. The question of class does not arise: he is merely interested to find how many different kinds of people there are in the world, how many different ways of talking and thinking."

The letter-writer goes on for another 13 paragraphs, entertaining a wide range of views about "public schools," concluding with the hope that her son and his friends will "bring toughness, realism and healthy ridicule to the absurd snobism and prejudices of these ancient institutes."

mathematics until they cry out like the young men on the leaning tower, "All that I would like to be is human." She has left the other class, the immense class to which almost all of us must belong, to pick up what we can in village schools; in factories; in workshops; behind counters; and at home. When one thinks of that criminal injustice one is tempted to say England deserves to have no literature. She deserves to have nothing but detective stories, patriotic songs, and leading articles for generals, admirals, and business-men to read themselves to sleep with when they are tired of winning battles and making money. But let us not be unfair; let us avoid if we can joining the embittered and futile tribe of scapegoat-hunters. For some years now England has been making an effort – at last – to bridge the gulf between the two worlds. Here is one proof of that effort – this book. This book was not bought; it was not hired. It was borrowed from a public library. England lent it to a common reader, saying, "It is time that even you, whom I have shut out from all my universities for centuries, should learn to read your mother tongue. I will help you." If England is going to help us, we must help her. But how? Look at what is written in the book she has lent us. "Readers are requested to point out any defects that they may observe to the local librarian." That is England's way of saying: "If I lend you books, I expect you to make yourselves critics."

We can help England very greatly to bridge the gulf between the two worlds if we borrow the books she lends us and if we read them critically. We have got to teach ourselves to understand literature. Money is no longer going to do our thinking for us. Wealth will no longer decide who shall be taught and who not. In future it is we who shall decide whom to send to public schools and universities; how they shall be taught; and whether what they write justifies their exemption from other work. In order to do that we must teach ourselves to distinguish – which is the book that is going to pay dividends of pleasure for ever; which is the book that will pay not a penny in two years' time? Try it for yourselves on new books as they come out; decide which are the lasting, which are the perishing. That is very difficult. Also we must become critics because in future we are not going to leave writing to be done for us by a small class of well-to-do young men who have only a pinch, a thimbleful of experience to give us. We are going to add our own experience, to make our own contribution. That is even more difficult. For that too we need to be critics. A writer, more than any other artist, needs to be a critic because words are so common, so familiar, that he must sieve them and sift them if they are to become enduring. Write daily; write freely; but let us always compare what we have written with what the great writers have written. It is humiliating, but it is essential. If we are going to preserve and to create, that is the only way. And we are going to do both. We need not wait till the end of the war. We can begin now. We can begin, practically and prosaically, by borrowing books from public libraries; by reading omnivorously, simultaneously, poems, plays, novels, histories, biographies, the old and the new. We must sample before we can select. It never does to be a nice feeder; each of us has an appetite that must find for itself the food that nourishes it. Nor let us shy away from the kings because we are commoners. That is a fatal crime in the eyes of Aeschylus, Shakespeare, Virgil, and Dante, who, if they could speak – and after all they can – would say, "Don't leave me to the wigged and gowned. Read me, read me for yourselves." They do not mind if we get our accents wrong, or have to read with a crib in front of us. Of course – are we not commoners, outsiders? – we shall trample many flowers and bruise much ancient grass. But let us bear in mind a piece of advice that an eminent Victorian who was also an eminent pedestrian once gave to walkers: "Whenever you see a board up with 'Trespassers will be prosecuted', trespass at once."[36]

Let us trespass at once. Literature is no one's private ground; literature is common ground. It is not cut up into nations; there are no wars there. Let us trespass freely and fearlessly and find our own way for ourselves. It is thus that English literature will survive this war and cross the gulf – if commoners and outsiders like ourselves make that country our own country, if we teach ourselves how to read and to write, how to preserve, and how to create.

---

[36] The eminent Victorian was Virginia Woolf's father, Sir Leslie Stephen (1832–1904), who often said this when they went walking together in her youth.

Djuna Barnes (1892–1982)

Introduction

Djuna Barnes (1892–1982) was born in Cornwall-on-Hudson, New York on her family's farm. Her mother was Elizabeth Chappell, an Englishwoman, her father Wald Barnes, an unsuccessful writer. Barnes was educated at home because her father believed that the public school system was inadequate.

In 1912 she moved to New York City, where she enrolled as a student at the Pratt Institute (1912–13) and the Art Students League (1915–16). While at Pratt, she began her writing career as a reporter and illustrator for the *Brooklyn Eagle*, where she published a wide variety of feature articles and interviews between 1912 and 1917, many with witty titles such as "Interviewing Arthur Voegtlin is Something Like Having a Nightmare" or "Nothing Amuses Coco Chanel After Midnight."

Barnes first published her poetry in 1915 as a collection of "rhythms and drawings" entitled *The Book of Repulsive Women*. She wrote three experimental plays, *Three from the Earth*, *An Irish Triangle*, and *Kurzy and the Sea* which were produced by the Provincetown Players in the 1919–20 season. In 1921 Barnes was sent to Paris by *McCall's* as a correspondent. She would stay outside the US for most of the next 20 years, earning her living with articles for magazines such as *Vanity Fair, Charm*, and *The New Yorker*.

In 1923 Barnes published *A Book*, a collection of lyrical poems, stories, drawings, and one-act plays. By now she was living with Thelma Wood, a sculptor and silverpoint artist.

Barnes was a shrewd observer of the modernist scene in Paris, and she befriended influential patrons such as Natalie Barney and Peggy Guggenheim. The circle of women surrounding Natalie Barney was rendered in her satirical fiction *Ladies Almanack* (1928), and in the same year she published *Ryder*, a semi-autobiography.

In 1931 Barnes left Thelma Wood. She spent the next decade traveling as much as she could, but spending long periods at Hayford Hall, a countryside manor rented by Peggy Guggenheim. In effect Guggenheim was now Barnes's patron, providing her with free housing, food, and some small subsidies. She completed *Nightwood*, her celebrated novel, in 1936. "It is so good a novel," wrote T. S. Eliot, "that only sensibilities trained on poetry can wholly appreciate it." In 1937 Barnes moved to London, then in 1939 returned to New York, where she received a monthly subsidy from Peggy Guggenheim for the rest of her life. She wrote little and lived a reclusive life in an apartment in Greenwich Village. In 1958 she published a verse drama, *The Antiphon*.

To the Dogs (1923)

PERSONS: HELENA HUCKSTEPPE
            GHEID STORM — *Her neighbour*
TIME: *Late afternoon.*
PLACE: *In the mountains of Cornwall-on-Hudson*[1] *— the* HUCKSTEPPE *house.*
SCENE: *The inner room of the* HUCKSTEPPE *cottage.*

To the left, in the back wall, a large window overlooks a garden. Right centre, a door leads off into a bedroom, and from the bedroom one may see the woods of the mountain. The door is slightly open, showing a glimpse of a tall mirror and the polished pole of a bed.

   In the right wall there is a fireplace.

   A dog lies across the threshold, asleep, head on paws.

   About this room there is perhaps just a little too much of a certain kind of frail beauty of object. Crystal glasses, scent bottles, bowls of an almost too perfect design, furniture that is too antiquely beautiful.

   HELENA HUCKSTEPPE, *a woman of about thirty-five, stands almost back view to the audience, one arm lying along the mantel. She is rather under medium in height. Her hair, which is dark and curling, is done*

This play was first published in Barnes's collection of plays and stories *A Book* (New York: Boni and Liveright, 1923), the text that is followed here.

[1] A very small town located some 10 miles south of Newburgh, New York, in the far north of upstate New York.

carefully about a small fine head. She is dressed in a dark, long gown, a gown almost too faithful to the singular sadness of her body.

At about the same moment as the curtain's rising, GHEID STORM *vaults the window-sill. He is a man of few years, a well-to-do man of property, brought up very carefully by upright women, the son of a conscientious physician, the kind of man who commutes with an almost religious fervour, and who keeps his wife and his lawns in the best possible trim, without any particular personal pleasure.*

GHEID *is tall, but much too honourable to be jaunty, he is decidedly masculine. He walks deliberately, getting all the use possible out of his boot-leather, his belt-strap and hat-bands.*

His face is one of those which, for fear of misuse, has not been used at all.

HELENA HUCKSTEPPE *does not appear to be in the least astonished at his mode of entrance.*

GHEID STORM – As you never let me in at the door, I thought of the window. [HELENA *remains silent.*] I hope I did not startle you. [*Pause.*] Women are better calm, that is, some kinds of calm—

HELENA – Yes?

GHEID – [*Noticing the dog, which has not stirred.*] You've got funny dogs, they don't even bark. [*Pause.*] I expected you'd set them on me; however, perhaps that will come later—

HELENA – Perhaps.

STORM – Are you always going to treat me like this? For days I've watched you walking with your dogs of an evening – that little black bull-pup, and then those three setters – you've fine ways with you Helena Hucksteppe, though there are many tales of how you came by them—

HELENA – Yes?

STORM – Yes. [*Pause.*] You know, you surprise me.

HELENA – Why? Because I do not set my dogs on you?

STORM – Something like that.

HELENA – I respect my dogs.

STORM – What does that mean?

HELENA – Had I a daughter, would I set her on every man?

STORM – [*Trying to laugh.*] That's meant for an insult, isn't it? Well, I like the little insulting women—

HELENA – You are a man of taste.

STORM – I respect you.

HELENA – What kind of a feeling is that?

STORM – A gentleman's—

HELENA – I see.

STORM – People say of you: "She has a great many ways—"

HELENA – Yes?

STORM – [*Sitting on the edge of the table.*] "But none of them simple."

HELENA – Do they?

STORM – [*Without attempting to hide his admiration.*] I've watched your back: "There goes a fine woman, a fine silent woman; she wears long skirts, but she knows how to move her feet without kicking up a dust – a woman who can do that, drives a man mad." In town there's a story that you come through once every Spring, driving a different man ahead of you with a riding whip; another has it, that you come in the night—

HELENA – In other words, the starved women of the town are beginning to eat.

STORM – [*Pause.*] Well [*laughs*] I like you.

HELENA – I do not enjoy the spectacle of men ascending.

STORM – What are you trying to say?

HELENA – I'm saying it.

STORM – [*After an awkward pause.*] Do – you wish me to – go away?

HELENA – You will go.

STORM – Why won't you let me talk to you?

HELENA – Any man may accomplish anything he's capable of.

STORM – Do you know how I feel about you?

HELENA – Perfectly.

STORM – I have heard many things about your – your past—I believe none of them—

HELENA – Quite right, why should you mix trades?

STORM – What do you mean by that?

HELENA – Why confuse incapability with accomplishment—

STORM – It's strange to see a woman like you turning to the merely bitter—

HELENA – I began beyond bitterness.

STORM – Why do you treat me this way?

HELENA – How would you have me treat you?

STORM – There was one night when you seemed to know, have you forgotten? A storm was coming up, the clouds were rolling overhead – and you, you yourself started it. You kissed me.

HELENA – You say it was about to storm?

STORM – Yes.

HELENA – It even looked like rain?

STORM – Yes.

HELENA – [*Quickly in a different voice.*] It was a dark night, and I ended it.

STORM – What have I done?

HELENA – You have neglected to make any beginning in the world – can I help that?

STORM – I offer you a clean heart.

HELENA – Things which have known only one state, do not interest me.

STORM – Helena!

HELENA – Gheid Storm.

STORM – I have a son; I don't know why I should tell you about him, perhaps because I want to prove that I have lived, and perhaps not. My son is a child, I am a man of few years and my son is like what I was at his age. He is thin, I was thin; he is quiet, I was quiet; he has delicate flesh, and I had also – well, then his mother died—

HELENA – The saddle comes down from the horse.

STORM – Well, she died—

HELENA – And that's over.

STORM – Well, there it is, I have a son—

HELENA – And that's not over. Do you resent that?

STORM – I don't know, perhaps. Sometimes I say to myself when I'm sitting by the fire alone – "You should have something to think of while sitting here—"

HELENA – In other words, you're living for the sake of your fire.

STORM – [*To himself.*] Some day I shall be glad I knew you.

HELENA – You go rather fast.

STORM – Yes, I shall have you to think of.

HELENA – When the fire is hot, you'll be glad to think of me?

STORM – Yes, all of us like to have a few things to tell to our children, and I have always shown all that's in my heart to my son.

HELENA – How horrible!

STORM – [*Startled.*] Why?

HELENA – Would you show everything that made your heart?

STORM – I believe in frankness—

HELENA – [*With something like anger.*] Well, some day your son will blow his head off, to be rid of frankness, before his skin is tough.

STORM – You are not making anything easier.

HELENA – I've never been callous enough to make things easier.

STORM – You're a queer woman—

HELENA – Yes, that does describe me.

STORM – [*Taking his leg off the table.*] Do you really want to know why I came? Because I need you—

HELENA – I'm not interested in corruption for the many.

STORM – [*Starting as if he had been struck.*] By God!

HELENA – Nor in misplaced satisfactions—

STORM – By God, what a woman!

HELENA – Nor do I participate in liberations—

STORM – [*In a low voice.*] I could hate you!

HELENA – I limit no man, feel what you can.

STORM – [*Taking a step toward her, the dog lifts its head.*] If it were not for those damned dogs of yours – I'd – I'd—

HELENA – Aristocracy of movement never made a dog bite—

STORM – That's a – strange thing to say – just at this moment.

HELENA – Not for me.

STORM – [*Sulky.*] Well, anyway, a cat may look at a King—

HELENA – Oh no, a cat may only look at what it sees.

STORM – Helena Hucksteppe.

HELENA – Yes.

STORM – I'm – attracted – to you.

HELENA – A magnet does not attract shavings.

STORM – [*With positive conviction.*] I *could* hate you.

HELENA – I choose my enemies.

STORM – [*Without warning, seizing her.*] By God, at least I can kiss you! [*He kisses her full on the mouth – she makes no resistance.*]

HELENA – [*In a calm voice.*] And this, I suppose, is what you call the "great moment of human contact."

STORM – [*Dropping his arms – turning pale.*] What are you trying to do to me?

HELENA – I'm doing it.

STORM – [*To himself.*] Yet it was you that I wanted—

HELENA – Mongrels may not dig up buried treasure.

STORM – [*In a sudden rage.*] You can bury your past as deep as you like, but carrion will out!

HELENA – [*Softly.*] And this is love.

STORM – [*His head in his arms.*] Oh, God, God!

HELENA – And you who like the taste of new things, come to me?

STORM – [*In a lost voice.*] Shall I have no joy?

HELENA – Joy? Oh, yes, of a kind.

STORM – And you – are angry with me?

HELENA – In the study of science, is the scientist angry when the fly possesses no amusing phenomena?

STORM – I wanted – to know – you—

HELENA – I am conscious of your failure.

STORM – I wanted something – some sign—

HELENA – Must I, who have spent my whole life in being myself, go out of my way to change some look in you?

STORM – That's why you are so terrible, you have spent all your life on yourself.

HELENA – Yes, men do resent that in women.

STORM – Yes, I suppose so. [*Pause.*] I should have liked to talk of – myself—

HELENA – You see I could not listen.

STORM – You are – intolerant.

HELENA – No – occupied—

STORM – You are probably – playing a game.

HELENA – [*With a gracious smile.*] You will get some personal good out of it, won't you?

STORM – I'm uncomfortable—

HELENA – Uncomfortable!

STORM – [*Beginning to be really uncomfortable.*] Who *are* you?

HELENA – I am a woman, Gheid Storm, who is *not* in need.

STORM – You're horrible!

HELENA – Yes, that too.

STORM – But somewhere you're vulnerable.

HELENA – Perhaps.

STORM – Only I don't quite know the spot.

HELENA – Spot?

STORM – Something, somewhere, hidden—

HELENA – Hidden! [*She laughs.*] *All* of me is vulnerable.

STORM – [*Setting his teeth.*] You tempt me.

HELENA – [*Wearily.*] It's not that kind.

STORM – I've lain awake thinking of you – many nights.

HELENA – That is too bad.

STORM – What is too bad?

HELENA – That you have had – fancies.

STORM – Why?

HELENA – Theft of much, makes much to return—

STORM – The world allows a man his own thoughts.

HELENA – Oh, no—

STORM – At least my thoughts are my own.

HELENA – Not one, so far.

STORM – What does that mean?

HELENA – You'll know when you try to think them again.

STORM – You mean I'm not making headway – well, you're right, I'm not—

HELENA – Now tell me what brought you through the window.

STORM – [*Relieved.*] I'm glad you ask that, it's the first human thing that's happened this afternoon.

HELENA – You have forgotten our great moment of human contact.

STORM – [*Nervously.*] Well—

HELENA – You were about to tell me what brought you?

STORM – I don't know – something no one speaks of – some great ease in your back – the look of a great lover—

HELENA – So – you scented a great lover—

STORM – I am a man – and I love—

HELENA – What have you done for love, Gheid Storm?

STORM – I've – never gone to the dogs—

HELENA – So?

STORM – I've always respected women.

HELENA – In other words: taken the coals out of the fire with the poker – continue—

STORM – That's all.

HELENA – And you dared to come to me! [*Her entire manner has changed.*]

STORM – No matter what you've been – done – I love you.

HELENA – Do not come so near. Only those who have helped to make such death as mine may go a little way toward the ardours of that decay.

STORM – What have I done?

HELENA – You have dared to bring to a woman, who has known love, the whinny of a pauper.

STORM – What am I?

HELENA – [*Softly, to herself.*] How sensitively the handles cling to the vase, how delicate is the flesh between the fingers.

STORM – I – I don't know you.

HELENA – [*Dropping her hands to her sides.*] Come here, Gheid Storm – [*Gheid approaches slowly, like a sleep walker.*] Put your hand on me. [*He does so as if in a dream.*] So! [*She looks first at his hand, then into his face, making it quite plain that he does not even know how to touch a woman.*] Yet you would be my lover, knowing not one touch that is mine, nor one word that is mine. My house is for men who have done their stumbling.

STORM – [*In an inaudible voice.*] I am going now—

HELENA – I cannot touch new things, nor see beginnings.

STORM – Helena! Helena!

HELENA – Do not call my name. There are too many names that must be called before mine.

STORM – Shall I die, and never have known you?

HELENA – Death, for you, will begin where my cradle started rocking—

STORM – Shall I have no love like yours?

HELENA – When I am an old woman, thinking of other things, you will, perhaps, be kissing a woman like me—

STORM – [Moving blindly toward the door.] Now I am going.

HELENA – [In a quiet, level voice.] The fall is almost here.

STORM – Yes, it's almost here.

HELENA – The leaves on the mountain road are turning yellow.

STORM – Yes, the leaves are turning.

HELENA – It's late, your son will be waiting dinner for you.

STORM – Don't take everything away.

HELENA – You will not even recall having seen me.

STORM – Can memory be taken too?

HELENA – Only that memory that goes past recollection may be kept.

STORM – [At the door.] Good night—

HELENA – [Smiling.] There is the window.

STORM – I could not lift my legs now.

HELENA – That's a memory you may keep.

STORM – Good night.

HELENA – Good-bye, Gheid Storm, and as you go down the hill, will you lock the gate, a dog thief passed in the night, taking my terrier with him.

STORM – The one with the brown spots?

HELENA – Yes.

STORM – That was a fine dog.

HELENA – Yes, she was a fine dog – restless.

STORM – They say any dog will follow any man who carries aniseed.

HELENA – Well, soon I return to the city.

STORM – You look tired.

HELENA – Yes, I am tired.

[Gheid exits. Helena takes her old position, her back almost square to the audience.]

CURTAIN

Mother (1920)

A feeble light flickered in the pawn shop at Twenty-nine. Usually, in the back of this shop, reading by this light – a rickety lamp with a common green cover – sat Lydia Passova, the mistress.

Her long heavy head was divided by straight bound hair. Her high firm bust was made still higher and still firmer by German corsets. She was excessively tall, due to extraordinarily long legs. Her eyes were small, and not well focused. The left was slightly distended from the long use of a magnifying glass.

She was middle-aged, and very slow in movement, though well balanced. She wore coral in her ears, a coral necklace, and many coral finger rings.

There was about her jewelry some of the tragedy of all articles that find themselves in pawn, and she moved among the trays like the guardians of cemetery grounds, who carry about with them some of the lugubrious stillness of the earth on which they have been standing.

MOTHER
This story was first published in the Little Review 7(2) (July–August 1920). It was first collected in Barnes's collection of plays and stories A Book (New York: Boni and Liveright, 1923), which is the text followed here.

She dealt, in most part, in cameos, garnets, and a great many inlaid bracelets and cuff-links. There were a few watches however, and silver vessels and fishing tackle and faded slippers – and when, at night, she lit the lamp, these and the trays of precious and semi-precious stones, and the little ivory crucifixes, one on either side of the window, seemed to be leading a swift furtive life of their own, conscious of the slow pacing woman who was known to the street as Lydia Passova.

No one knew her, not even her lover – a little nervous fellow, an Englishman quick in speech with a marked accent, a round-faced youth with a deep soft cleft in his chin, on which grew two separate tufts of yellow hair. His eyes were wide and pale, and his eyeteeth prominent.

He dressed in tweeds, walked with the toes in, seemed sorrowful when not talking, laughed a great deal and was nearly always to be found in the café about four of an afternoon.

When he spoke it was quick and jerky. He had spent a great deal of his time in Europe, especially the watering places – and had managed to get himself in trouble in St. Moritz, it was said, with a well-connected family.

He liked to seem a little eccentric and managed it simply enough while in America. He wore no hat, and liked to be found reading the *London Times*, under a park lamp at three in the morning.

Lydia Passova was never seen with him. She seldom left her shop, however, she was always pleased when he wanted to go anywhere: "Go," she would say, kissing his hand, "and when you are tired come back."

Sometimes she would make him cry. Turning around she would look at him a little surprised, with lowered lids, and a light tightening of the mouth.

"Yes," he would say, "I know I'm trivial – well then, here I go, I will leave you, not disturb you any longer!" and darting for the door he would somehow end by weeping with his head buried in her lap.

She would say, "There, there – why are you so nervous?"

And he would laugh again: "My father was a nervous man, and my mother was high-strung, and as for me—" He would not finish.

Sometimes he would talk to her for long hours, she seldom answering, occupied with her magnifying glass and her rings, but in the end she was sure to send him out with: "That's all very true, I have no doubt; now go out by yourself and think it over" – and he would go, with something like relief, embracing her large hips with his small strong arms.

They had known each other a very short time, three or four months. He had gone in to pawn his little gold ring, he was always in financial straits, though his mother sent him five pounds a week; and examining the ring, Lydia Passova had been so quiet, inevitable, necessary, that it seemed as if he must have known her forever – "at some time," as he said.

Yet they had never grown together. They remained detached, and on her part, quiet, preoccupied.

He never knew how much she liked him. She never told him; if he asked she would look at him in that surprised manner, drawing her mouth together.

In the beginning he had asked her a great many times, clinging to her, and she moved about arranging her trays with a slight smile, and in the end lowered her hand and stroked him gently.

He immediately became excited. "Let us dance," he cried, "I have a great capacity for happiness."

"Yes, you are very happy," she said.

"You understand, don't you?" he asked abruptly.

"What?"

"That my tears are nothing, have no significance, they are just a protective fluid – when I see anything happening that is about to affect my happiness I cry, that's all."

"Yes," Lydia Passova said, "I understand." She turned around reaching up to some shelves, and over her shoulder she asked, "Does it hurt?"

"No, it only frightens me. You never cry, do you?"

"No, I never cry."

That was all. He never knew where she had come from, what her life had been, if she had or had not been married, if she had or had not known lovers; all that she would say was, "Well, you are with me, does that tell you nothing?" and he had to answer, "No, it tells me nothing."

When he was sitting in the café he often thought to himself, "There's a great woman" – and he was a little puzzled why he thought this because his need of her was so entirely different from any need he seemed to remember having possessed before.

There was no swagger in him about her, the swagger he had always felt for his conquests with women. Yet there was not a trace of shame – he was neither proud nor shy about Lydia Passova, he was something entirely different. He could not have said himself what his feeling was – but it was in no way disturbing.

People had, it is true, begun to tease him:

"You're a devil with the ladies."

Where this had made him proud, now it made him uneasy.

"Now, there's a certain Lydia Passova for instance, who would ever have thought—"

Furious he would rise.

"So, you do feel—"

He would walk away, stumbling a little among the chairs, putting his hand on the back of every one on the way to the door.

Yet he could see that, in her time, Lydia Passova had been a "perverse" woman – there was, about everything she did, an economy that must once have been a very sensitive and a very sensuous impatience, and because of this everyone who saw her felt a personal loss.

Sometimes, tormented, he would come running to her, stopping abruptly, putting it to her this way:

"Somebody has said something to me."

"When – where?"

"Now, in the café."

"What?"

"I don't know, a reproach—"

She would say:

"We are all, unfortunately, only what we are."

She had a large and beautiful angora cat, it used to sit in the tray of amethysts and opals and stare at her from very bright cold eyes. One day it died, and calling her lover to her she said:

"Take her out and bury her." And when he had buried her he came back, his lips twitching.

"You loved that cat – this will be a great loss."

"Have I a memory?" she inquired.

"Yes," he answered.

"Well," she said quietly, fixing her magnifying glass firmly in her eye. "We have looked at each other, that is enough."

And then one day she died.

The caretaker of the furnace came to him, where he was sipping his liqueur as he talked to his cousin, a pretty little blond girl, who had a boring and comfortably provincial life, and who was beginning to chafe.

He got up, trembling, pale, and hurried out.

The police were there, and said they thought it had been heart failure.

She lay on the couch in the inner room. She was fully dressed, even to her coral ornaments; her shoes were neatly tied – large bows of a ribbed silk.

He looked down. Her small eyes were slightly open, the left, that had used the magnifying glass, was slightly wider than the other. For a minute she seemed quite natural. She had the look of one who is about to say: "Sit beside me."

Then he felt the change. It was in the peculiar heaviness of the head – sensed through despair and not touch. The high breasts looked very still, the hands were half closed, a little helpless, as in life – hands that were too proud to "hold." The drawn-up limb exposed a black petticoat and a yellow stocking. It seemed that she had become hard – set, as in a mould – that she rejected everything now, but in rejecting had bruised him with a last terrible pressure. He moved and knelt down. He shivered. He put his closed hands to his eyes. He could not weep.

She was an old woman, he could see that. The ceasing of that one thing that she could still have for anyone made it simple and direct.

Something oppressed him, weighed him down, bent his shoulders, closed his throat. He felt as one feels who has become conscious of passion for the first time, in the presence of a relative.

He flung himself on his face, like a child.

That night, however, he wept, lying in bed, his knees drawn up.

A Night Among the Horses (1918)

Toward dusk, in the Summer of the year, a man dressed in a frock coat and top hat, and carrying a cane, crept through the underbrush bordering the corral of the Buckler farm.

As he moved, small twigs snapped, fell and were silent. His knees were green from wounded shrubbery and grass, and his outspread hands tore unheeded plants. His wrists hurt him and he rested from time to time, always caring for his hat and knotted yellow cane, blowing through his mustache.

Dew had been falling, covering the twilight leaves like myriad faces damp with the perspiration of the struggle for existence, and half a mile away, standing out against the darkness of the night, a grove of white birches shimmered like teeth in a skull.

He heard the creaking of a gate, and the splashing of late rain into the depths of a dark cistern. His heart ached with the nearness of the earth, the faint murmur of it moving upon itself, like a sleeper who turns to throw an arm about a beloved.

A frog began moaning among the skunk cabbages, and John thrust his hand deep into his bosom.

Something somnolent seemed to be here, and he wondered. It was like a deep, heavy, yet soft prison where, without sin, one may suffer intolerable punishment.

Presently he went on, feeling his way. He reached a high plank fence and sensing it with his fingers, he lay down, resting his head against the ground.

He was tired, he wanted to sleep, but he searched for his hat and cane and straightened out his coat beneath him before he turned his eyes to the stars.

And now he could not sleep, and wondered why he had thought of it; something quick was moving the earth, it seemed to live, to shake with sudden immensity.

He heard a dog barking, and the dim light from a farm window kept winking as the trees swung against its square of light. The odor of daisies came to him, and the assuring, powerful smell of the stables; he opened his mouth and drew in his mustache.

A faint tumult had begun. A tremor ran under the length of his body and trembled off into the earth like a shudder of joy – died down and repeated itself. And presently he began to tremble, answering, throwing out his hands, curling them up weakly, as if the earth were withholding something precious, necessary.

His hat fell off, striking a log with a dull hollow sound, and he pressed his red mustache against the grass, weeping.

Again he heard it, felt it; a hundred hoofs beat upon the earth and he knew the horses had gone wild in the corral on the other side of the fence, for animals greet the Summer, striking the earth, as friends strike the back of friends. He knew, he understood; a hail to Summer, to life, to death.

He drew himself against the bars, pressing his eyes under them, peering, waiting.

He heard them coming up across the heavy turf, rounding the curve in the Willow Road. He opened his eyes and closed them again. The soft menacing sound deepened, as heat deepens, strikes through the skin into the very flesh. Head on, with long legs rising, falling, rising again, striking the ground insanely, like needles taking terrible, impossible and purposeless stitches.

A NIGHT
The story was first published in the *Little Review* 5(8) (December 1918), then reprinted in Edward J. O'Brien (ed.), *Short Stories of 1919* (Boston: Small Maynard, 1920), and finally incorporated into Barnes's collection of plays and stories, *A Night Among the Horses* (New York: Liveright, 1929). The text of this last edition is the one followed here.

He saw their bellies, fawn-colored, pitching from side to side, flashing by, straining the fence, and he rose up on his feet and silently, swiftly, fled on beside them.

Something delirious, hysterical, came over him and he fell. Blood trickled into his eyes down from his forehead. It had a fine feeling for a moment, like a mane, like that roan mare's mane that had passed him – red and long and splendid.

He lifted his hand, and closed his eyes once more, but the soft pounding did not cease, though now, in his sitting position, it only jogged him imperceptibly, as a child on a knee.

It seemed to him that he was smothering, and he felt along the side of his face as he had done in youth when they had put a cap on him that was too large. Twining green things, moist with earth-blood, crept over his fingers, the hot, impatient leaves pressed in, and the green of the matted grass was deathly thick. He had heard about the freeness of nature, thought it was so, and it was not so.

A trailing ground pine had torn up small blades in its journey across the hill, and a vine, wrist-thick, twisted about a pale oak, hideously, gloriously, killing it, dragging it into dust.

A wax Patrick Pipe[1] leaned against his neck, staring with black eyes, and John opened his mouth, running his tongue across his lips, snapping it off, sighing.

Move as he would, the grass was always under him, and the crackling of last Autumn's leaves and last Summer's twigs – minute dead of the infinite greatness – troubled him. Something portentous seemed connected with the patient noises about him. An acorn dropped, striking a thin fine powder out of a frail oak pod. He took it up, tossing it. He had never liked to see things fall.

He sat up, with the dim thunder of the horses far off, but quickening his heart.

He went over the scene he had with Freda Buckler, back there in the house, the long quivering spears of pot-grass standing by the window as she walked up and down, pulling at them, talking to him.

Small, with cunning fiery eyes and a pink and pointed chin. A daughter of a mother who had known too many admirers in her youth; a woman with an ample lap on which she held a Persian kitten or a trifle of fruit. Bounty, avarice, desire, intelligence – both of them had always what they wanted.

He blew down his mustache again, thinking of Freda in her floating yellow veil that he had called ridiculous. She had not been angry, he was nothing but a stable boy then. It was the way with those small intriguing women whose nostrils were made delicate through the pain of many generations that they might quiver whenever they caught a whiff of the stables.

"As near as they can get to the earth," he had said, and was Freda angry? She stroked his arm always softly, looking away, an inner bitterness drawing down her mouth.

She said, walking up and down quickly, looking ridiculously small:

"I am always gentle, John" – frowning, trailing her veil, thrusting out her chin.

He answered: "I liked it better where I was."

"Horses," she said showing sharp teeth, "are nothing for a man with your bile – pot-boy – curry comber, smelling of saddle soap – lovely!" She shriveled up her nose, touching his arm. "Yes, but better things. I will show you – you shall be a gentleman – fine clothes, you will like them, they feel nice." And laughing she turned on one high heel, sitting down. "I like horses; they make people better; you are amusing, inteligent, you will see—"

"A lackey!" he returned passionately, throwing up his arm. "What is there in this for you, what are you trying to do to me? The family – askance – perhaps – I don't know."

He sat down pondering. He was getting used to it, or thought he was, all but his wordy remonstrances. He knew better when thinking of his horses, realizing that when he should have married this small, unpleasant and clever woman, he would know them no more.

It was a game between them, which was the shrewder, which would win out? He? A boy of ill breeding, grown from the gutter, fancied by this woman because he had called her ridiculous, or for some other reason that he would never know. This kind of person never tells the truth, and this, more than most things, troubled him. Was he a thing to be played with, debased into something better than he was – than he knew?

---

[1] *Patrick Pipe* a tall vine.

Partly because he was proud of himself in the costume of a groom, partly because he was timid, he desired to get away, to go back to the stables. He walked up to the mirrors as if about to challenge them, peering in. He knew he would look absurd, and then knew, with shame, that he looked splendidly better than most of the gentlemen that Freda Buckler knew. He hated himself. A man who had grown out of the city's streets, a fine common thing!

She saw him looking into the mirrors, one after the other, and drew her mouth down. She got up, walking beside him in the end, between him and them, taking his arm.

"You shall enter the army – you shall rise to General, or Lieutenant at least – and there are horses there, and the sound of stirrups – with that physique you will be happy – authority you know," she said, shaking her chin, smiling.

"Very well, but a common soldier—"

"As you like – afterward."

"Afterward?"

"Very well, a common soldier."

He sensed something strange in her voice, a sort of irony, and it took the patience out of him: "I have always been common, I could commit crimes, easily, gladly – I'd like to!"

She looked away. "That's natural," she said faintly; "it's an instinct all strong men have—"

She knew what was troubling him, thwarted instincts, common beautiful instincts that he was being robbed of. He wanted to do something final to prove his lower order; caught himself making faces, idiot faces, and she laughed.

"If only your ears stuck out, chin receded," she said, "you might look degenerate, common, but as it is—"

And he would creep away in hat, coat and with his cane, to peer at his horses, never daring to go in near them. Sometimes, when he wanted to weep, he would smear one glove with harness grease, but the other one he held behind his back, pretending one was enough to prove his revolt.

She would torment him with vases, books, pictures, making a fool of him gently, persistently, making him doubt by cruel means, the means of objects he was not used to, eternally taking him out of his sphere.

"We have the best collection of miniatures," she would say with one knee on a low ottoman, bringing them out in her small palm.

"Here, look."

He would put his hands behind him.

"She was a great woman – Lucrezia Borgia[2] – do you know history—" She put it back because he did not answer, letting his mind, a curious one, torment itself.

"You love things very much, don't you?" she would question, because she knew that he had a passion for one thing only. She kept placing new ladders beneath his feet, only to saw them off at the next rung, making him nothing more than a nervous, irritable experiment. He was uneasy, like one given food to smell and not to taste, and for a while he had not wanted to taste, and then curiosity began, and he wanted to, and he also wanted to escape, and he could do neither.

Well, after he had married her, what then? Satisfy her whim and where would he be? He would be nothing, neither what he had been nor what other people were. This seemed to him, at times, her wish – a sort of place between lying down and standing up, a cramped position, a slow death. A curious woman.

This same evening he had looked at her attentively for the first time. Her hair was rather pretty, though too mousy, yet just in the nape of the neck, where it met the lawn of the collar, it was very attractive. She walked well for a little woman, too.

Sometimes she would pretend to be lively, would run a little, catch herself at it, as if she had not intended to do it, and calm down once more, or creeping up to him, stroking his arm, talking to him, she would walk beside him softly, slowly, that he might not step out, that he would have to crawl across the carpet.

---

[2] Lucrezia Borgia (1480–1519) was the daughter of Pope Alexander VI; when Barnes was writing, Lucrezia's name was still a byword for sordid intrigue and she was charged with involvement in poisoning schemes and committing incest with her brother or father. More recent historians do not accept any of these charges.

Once he had thought of trying her with honesty, with the truth of the situation. Perhaps she would give him an honest answer, and he had tried.

"Now, Miss Freda – just a word – what are you trying to do? What is it you want? What is there in me that can interest you? I want you to tell me – I want to know – I have got to ask some one, and I haven't any one to ask but you."

And for a moment she almost relented, only to discover that she could not if she had wished. She did not know always what she meant herself.

"I'll tell you," she said, hoping that this, somehow, might lead her into the truth, for herself, if not for him, but it did not, "you are a little nervous, you will get used to it – you will even grow to like it. Be patient. You will learn soon enough that there is nothing in the world so agreeable as climbing, changing."

"Well," he said, trying to read her, "and then?"

"That's all, you will regret the stables in the end – that's all." Her nostrils quivered. A light came into her eyes, a desire to defy, to be defied.

Then on this last night he had done something terrible, he had made a blunder. There had been a party. The guests, a lot of them, were mostly drunk, or touched with drink. And he, too, had too much. He remembered having thrown his arms about a tall woman, gowned in black with loose shoulder straps, dragging her through a dance. He had even sung a bit of a song, madly, wildly, horribly. And suddenly he had been brought up sharp by the fact that no one thought his behavior strange, that no one thought him presumptuous. Freda's mother had not even moved or dropped the kitten from her lap where it sat, its loud resolute purr shaking the satin of her gown.

And he felt that Freda had got him where she wanted him, between two rungs. Going directly up to her, he said:

"You are ridiculous!" and twirled his mustache, spitting into the garden.

And he knew nothing about what happened until he found himself in the shrubbery, crawling toward the corral, through the dusk and the dampness of the leaves, carrying his cane, making sure of his hat, looking up at the stars.

Now he knew why he had come. He was with his horses again. His eyes, pressed against the bars, stared in. The black stallion in the lead had been his special pet, a rough animal, but kindly, knowing. And here they were once more, tearing up the grass, galloping about in the night like a ball-room full of real people, people who wanted to do things, who did what they wanted to do.

He began to crawl through the bars, slowly, deftly, and when half way through he paused, thinking.

Presently he went on again, and drawing himself into the corral, his hat and cane thrown in before him, he lay there, mouth to the grass.

They were still running, but less madly; one of them had gone up the Willow Road leading into a farther pasture, in a flare of dust, through which it looked immense and faint.

On the top of the hill three or four of the horses were standing, testing the weather. He would mount one, he would ride away, he would escape. And his horses, the things he knew, would be his escape.

Bareback, he thought, would be like the days when he had taken what he could from the rush of the streets, joy, exhilaration, life, and he was not afraid. He wanted to stand up, to cry aloud.

And he saw ten or twelve of them rounding the curb, and he did stand up.

They did not seem to know him, did not seem to know what to make of him, and he stared at them wondering. He did not think of his white shirt front, his sudden arising, the darkness, their excitement. Surely they would know, in a moment more.

Wheeling, flaring their wet nostrils, throwing up their manes, striking the earth in a quandary, they came on, whinnied faintly, and he knew what it was to be afraid.

He had never been afraid and he went down on his knees. With a new horror in his heart he damned them. He turned his eyes up, but he could not open them. He thought rapidly, calling on Freda in his heart, speaking tenderly, promising.

A flare of heat passed his throat and descended into his bosom.

"I want to live. I can do it – damn it – I can do it! I can forge ahead, make my mark."

He forgot where he was for a moment and found new pleasure in this spoken admission, this new rebellion. He moved with the faint shaking of the earth, like a child on a woman's lap.

The upraised hoofs of the first horse missed him, but the second did not.

And presently the horses drew apart, nibbling here and there, switching their tails, avoiding a patch of tall grass.

Aller et Retour (1929)

The train traveling from Marseilles to Nice had on board a woman of great strength.

She was well past forty and a little top-heavy. Her bosom was tightly cross-laced, the busk bending with every breath. As she breathed and moved, she sounded with many chains in coarse gold links, the ting of large and heavily set jewels marking off her lighter gestures. From time to time she raised a long-handled lorgnette to her often opening, and closing brown eyes, surveying the country she was passing through, blurred with smoke from the train.

At Toulon she pushed down the window, leaned out, calling for beer, the buff of her hip-fitting skirt rising in a peak above tan boots laced high on shapely legs, and above that the pink of woolen stockings. She settled back, drinking her beer with a pleasure somewhat controlled by the firm pressure of her small, plump feet along the rubber matting.

She was a Russian, a widow. Her name was Erling von Bartmann. She lived in Paris.

In leaving Marseilles she had purchased a copy of *Madame Bovary*,[1] and now she held it in her hands, ringed and warm.

She read a few sentences with difficulty, and laid the book on her lap, looking again at the passing hills.

In Marseilles she had traversed the dirty streets slowly, holding the buff skirt well above her boots, in a manner at once careful and absent. The thin skin of her nose quivered a little as she drew in the foul odor of the passages, but she looked neither pleased nor displeased.

She went up the steep, narrow, littered streets abutting on the port, looking right and left, noting every object.

A gross woman, with wide set legs, sprawled in the doorway of a single room with a high-posted, dirty iron bed; she held a robin loosely in her fat hand, plucking. The air was full of feathers in different degrees of falling. Women with bare legs, with thick hair clipped in bangs above wide, lusterless eyes, laughed with sore lips as Mme. Erling von Bartmann picked her way.

At a sailors' supply shop she stopped, smelling the tang of tarred rope, jeans, soap. She took down several colored post-cards with women in the act of seaside bathing; sailors leaning above full-busted-humid-eyed sirens, with breast brooches of paste. She felt the satin of the vulgar, highly colored bed-spreads, for sale in an alley. A window, fly-specked, dusty, rose on terrace upon terrace of white and magenta funeral wreaths of strung beads, and not far away images of the Bleeding Heart[2] in beaten tin, embossed, with flame and edging of lace.

She had returned to her hotel room, and stood unpinning her hat and veil before the narrow mirror in the tall closet door. She sat in one of eight chairs, ranged in perfect precision, along the two walls, to unlace her boots. She looked at the boxed and filigreed curtains over the dark windows opening on to a court where pigeons were sold. She washed her hands with a large oval of coarse red soap, drying them, trying to think.

In the morning, seated on the stout linen sheets between the mahogany of the head and foot board, in her insertioned nightgown, she planned her journey. She was two or three hours too early for her train, and she dressed and went out. Finding a church, she entered, and drew her gloves off, slowly. It was dark and cold, and she was alone. Two small oil lamps burned on either side of the figures of St. Anthony and St. Francis. She put her brown leather bag on a form, and went into a

ALLER
The story was first published in the *transatlantic review* 1(4) (April 1924), then reprinted in Ford Madox Ford (ed.), *Transatlantic Stories* (New York: Dial Press, 1926), and finally incorporated into Barnes's collection of short stories and plays, *A Night Among the Horses* (New York: Liveright, 1929). All the variants

among these three printings concern minor accidentals; this edition follows the text given in *A Night Among the Horses*.
[1]   Novel by Gustave Flaubert (1821–80), first published in 1857; its central character is the bored wife of a provincial doctor, carried away her desires and illusions.
[2]   The Sacred Heart of Jesus, or the Immaculate Heart of Mary.

corner, kneeling down. She turned the stones of her rings out, and put her hands together, the light shining between the little fingers, raising them to her mundane heart; she prayed, with all her vigorous understanding, to God for a common redemption.

She got up, looking around like a sight-seer, angry that there were no candles burning to the *Magnifique*,[3] feeling the stuff of the altar-cloth.

At Nice she took an omnibus, riding second class, reaching the outskirts about four. She opened the high, rusty iron gates to a private park with a large key, and closed it behind her. The lane of flowering trees with their perfumed cups, the damp of the moss that bled across the broken paving stones, the hot, musky air, the incessant carnival of birds unseen, ran together in a tangle of singing textures, both light and dark.

The avenue was long, and without turning until it curved, between two massive jars, heavy with the metal spiral of cactus; just behind, the house rose in plaster and stone.

There were no shutters open on the avenue because of the insects, and Mme. Bartmann went slowly, still holding her skirts, around to the side of the house, where a long-haired cat lay softly in the sun. She looked up at the windows, half shuttered, paused, thought better of it, and struck off into the wood beyond.

The deep pervading drone of ground insects ceased about her chosen steps, and she turned her head, looking up into the occasional touches of sky.

She still held the key to the gate in her gloved hand, and the seventeen-year-old girl who came up from a bush took hold of it, walking beside her.

The child was still in short dresses, and the pink of her knees was dulled by the dust of the underbrush. Her squirrel-colored hair rose in two ridges of light along her head, descending to the lobes of long ears, where it was caught into a rusty green ribbon.

"Richter –" Mme. Bartmann said (her husband had wanted a boy).

The child put her hands behind her back before answering.

"I've been out there, in the field."

Mme. Bartmann, walking on, made no answer.

"Did you stop in Marseilles, mother?"

She nodded.

"Long?"

"Two days and a half."

"Why a half?"

"The trains."

"Is it a big city?"

"Not very, but dirty."

"Is there anything nice there?"

Mme. Bartmann smiled: "The Bleeding Heart – sailors –"

Presently they came out into the open field, and Mme. Bartmann, turning her skirt back, sat down on a knoll, warm with tempered grass.

The child, with a slight springiness of limbs, due to youth, sat beside her.

"Shall you stay home now?"

"For quite a while."

"Was Paris nice?"

"Paris was Paris."

The child was checked, she began plucking at the grass.

Mme. Bartmann pulled off one of her tan gloves, split at the turn of the thumb, and stopped.

"Well, now that your father is dead . . . !"

The child's eyes filled with tears, and she lowered her head.

"I come flying back," Mme. Bartmann continued, good-naturedly, "to look at my own. Let me see you," she continued, turning the child's chin up in the palm of her hand. "Ten when I last saw

---

[3] An epithet for the Virgin Mary.

you, and now you are a woman –" With this she dropped the child's chin abruptly and put on the glove again.

"Come," she said, rising, "I haven't seen the house in years. . . ."

As they went down the dark avenue, she talked:

"Is the black marble Venus still in the hall?"

"Yes."

"Are the chairs with the carved legs still in existence?"

"Only two. Last year Erna broke one, and the year before . . . !"

"Well?"

"I broke one."

"Growing up," Mme. Bartmann commented. "Well, well. Is the great battle picture still there, over my bed?"

The child beneath her breath said: "That's my room."

Mme. Bartmann took her glove off again, unfastened her lorgnette from its hook on her bosom, put it to her eyes and regarded the child.

"You are very thin."

"I'm growing."

"I grew, but like a pigeon. Well, one generation can't be exactly like another. You have your father's red hair. That," she said abruptly, "was a queer, mad fellow, that Herr von Bartmann. I never could see what we were doing with each other. As for you," she added, shutting her glasses, drawing on the glove, "I'll have to see what he has made of you."

The house was furnished heavily, antiques, plush flowers, a plush Bible, tobacco.

In the evening Richter watched her mother, still in hat and spotted veil, playing on the sprawling lanky grand, high up in the terrace window. It was a waltz. Mme. Bartmann played fast, with effervescence, the sparkles of her jewelled fingers were bubbles running over the keys.

In the dark of the garden, Richter listened to Schubert[4] streaming down the light from the open casement. The child was cold now, and she shivered in the squirrel coat that touched the chill of her knees.

Still swiftly, with a finale somewhat in the Grand Opera manner, Mme. Bartmann closed the piano, stood a moment on the balcony, inhaling the air, fingering the coarse links of her chain, the insects darting vertically across her vision.

Presently she came out, and sat down on a stone bench, breathing warmth.

Richter stood a few steps away and did not approach or speak. Mme. Bartmann began, though she could not see the child without turning:

"You have been here always, Richter?"

"Yes," the child answered.

"In this park, in this house, with Herr Bartmann, the tutors, the dogs?"

"Yes."

"Do you speak German?"

"A little."

"Let me hear you."

"Müde bin Ich, geh' zu Ruh'"[5]

"French?"

"O nuit désastreuse! O nuit effroyable!"[6]

"Russian?"

The child did not answer.

---

[4] Franz Schubert (1797–1828), Austrian composer.

[5] "I'm tired; I'm going to get some rest," in German.

[6] A snippet from a famous passage, which reads: "O nuit désastreuse! O nuit effroyable, où rentit tout à coup, comme un éclat de tonnerre cette étonnante nouvelle. *Madame se meurt, Madame est morte!*" ("O disastrous night! O frightful night, when like a crash of thunder the suprising news came. *Madame*

is dying, Madame is dead!" Jacques Bénigne Bossuet (1627–1704), "Oraison funèbre d'Henriette d'Angleterre," *Oraisons funèbres*, ed. Jean Joseph Dussault (Paris: Librairie de Firmin Didet fréres 1855), 85. It should not automatically be assumed that this is a learned allusion; the passage by Bossuet was regularly cited in grammars of the period to show how repetition can produce an effect of surprise or indignation.

"Ah!" said Mme. Bartmann. Then, "Have you been to Nice often?"

"Oh yes, often."

"What did you see there?"

"Everything."

Mme. Bartmann laughed. She leaned forward, her elbow on her knee, her face in her palm. The earrings in her ears shook, and the drone of the insects was clear and soft. Pain lay fallow in her.

"Once," she said, "I was a child you like, fatter, better health, but, nevertheless like you. I loved nice things, but" she added, "a different kind, I imagine. Things that were positive. I liked to go out in the evening, not because it was soft and voluptuous, but to frighten myself, because I'd known it such a little while, and after me it would exist so long. But that –" she interrupted herself, "is beside the point. Tell me how you feel."

The child moved in the shadows. "I can't."

Mme. Bartmann laughed again, shortly.

"Life," she said, "is filthy, terrible. There is everything in it, murder, pain, beauty, disease, death. Do you know all this?"

The child answered, "Yes."

"How do you know it?"

The child answered again, "I don't know."

"You see," Mme. Bartmann went on, "you know nothing. You must know everything, and then begin. You must have either a great understanding, or you must accomplish a fall. Horses hurry you away from danger, trains bring you back to the scene of your corruption. Pictures give the heart a mortal pang because they hung over a man you loved and murdered in his bed. Flowers stab the memory because a child was buried in them. Music incites the world to repetition. The crossroads are where lovers vow, and taverns are for thieves; contemplation leads to prejudice; and beds are fields where babies fight a losing battle. Do you know all this?"

There was no answer from the dark.

"Man is rotten from the start," Mme. Bartmann continued. "Rotten with virtue and with vice. He is strangled with the two and made nothing, and God is the light the mortal insect kindled, to turn to, and to die by. That is very wise, but it must not be misunderstood. I do not want you to turn your nose up at any whore in the street; pray and wallow and cease, but without prejudice. A murderer has less prejudice than a saint. Sometimes it is better to be a saint. Do not be vain about your indifference, should you be possessed of indifference; and don't," she said, "misconceive the value of your voluptuousness, it is only seasoning to the whole horror. I wish," and she did not finish. Quietly she took out her pocket handkerchief, and very noiselessly dried her eyes.

"What?" the child asked from the darkness, and Mme. Bartmann shuddered.

"Are you thinking?" she said.

"No," the child answered.

"Then think," Madame von Bartmann said loudly, turning to the child. "Think everything. Good, bad, indifferent. Everything, and do everything, everything! Try to know what you are before you die, and," she said, putting her head back, swallowing with shut eyes, "come back to me a good woman."

She got up then and went down the long aisle of trees.

That night, at bed time, Mme. Bartmann, rolled up in a bed with a canopy of blue roses, frilled and smelling of lavender, called through the curtains:

"Richter, do you play?"

"Yes," answered Richter.

"Play me something."

Richter heard her mother turn heavily, breathing warmth, comfort.

Touchingly, with frail legs pointed to the pedals, Richter, with a thin technique, and a light touch, played something from Beethoven.[7]

---

[7]   Ludwig van Beethoven (1770–1827), German composer.

"Brava!" her mother called, and she played again, and this time there was silence from the canopied bed. The child closed the piano, pulling the velvet over the mahogany, put the light out, and went, still shivering in her short fur coat, out onto the balcony.

A few days later, having avoided her mother, looking shy, frightened and offended, Richter came into her mother's room. She spoke directly and sparingly:

"Mother, with your consent, I should like to announce my engagement to Gerald Teal." Her manner was stilted. "Father approved of him, he knew him for years. If you permit."

"Good heavens!" exclaimed Mme. Bartmann, and swung clear around on her chair. "Who is he? What is he like?"

"He is a clerk in the government employ, he is young."

"Has he money?"

"I don't know. Father saw to that."

There was a look of pain and relief on Mme. Bartmann's face. "Very well," she said, "I shall have dinner for you two at eight-thirty sharp."

At eight-thirty sharp they were dining. Mme. Bartmann, seated at the head of the table, listened to Mr. Teal speaking:

"I shall do my best to make your daughter happy. I am a man of staid habits, no longer too young," he smiled. "I have a house on the outskirts of Nice. My income is assured, a little left me by my mother. My sister is my housekeeper, she is a maiden lady, but very cheerful and very good." He paused, holding a glass of white wine carefully in his long hand. "We hope to have children, Richter will be occupied. As she is delicate we shall have to travel to Vichy once a year. I have two very fine horses and a carriage with good springs, and she can drive in the afternoons when she is indisposed, though I hope she will find her greatest happiness at home."

Richter was sitting at her mother's right hand and never looked at her.

Within two months Mme. Bartmann was once again in her traveling clothes, hatted and veiled, strapping her umbrella as she stood on the platform, waiting for the train to Paris. She shook hands with her son-in-law, kissed the cheek of her daughter, and climbed into a second-class smoker.

Once the train was in motion, Mme. Erling von Bartmann slowly drew her gloves through her hand, from fingers to buttons, stretching them firmly across her knee.

"Ah, how unnecessary, how unnecessary!"

A Little Girl Tells a Story to a Lady (1925)

"Do you know Germany, Madame, Germany in the spring? It is very beautiful then, do you not think so? Wide and clean, the Spree[1] winding thin and dark, and the yellow roses in the windows; and bright American women coming in and out of the city with gay laughter, and the German men staring and staring over their beer, heavy and tightly packed into their life. It was such a spring, three years ago, that I came into Germany from Russia. I was just sixteen and my heart was an actress's heart. It is that way sometimes, one's heart is all one thing for months, and altogether another thing, *nicht wahr*?[2] And I used to go into the little café at the end of the Zelten,[3] and eat eggs and drink coffee, and sometimes the sparrows would fly down suddenly, their hundreds of tiny feet striking the tables and the ground all together, and they would hurry away with crumbs and all fly up again into the sky, so that the place was as utterly without birds as it had been with them. And sometimes a woman came to this café about the same hour in the day I did, around four in the

---

LITTLE GIRL

This story first appeared in the *Contact Collection of Contemporary Writers*, ed. Robert McAlmon (Paris: Three Mountains Press, 1925), and was reprinted in *Two Worlds Monthly* 1 (April 1925). It was included in Barnes's collection of short stories and plays, *A Night Among the Horses* (New York: Liveright, 1929), which furnishes the text followed here. It was later

drastically revised under the title "Cassation" in Djuna Barnes, *Spillway* (London: Faber and Faber, 1952).
[1]   the name of the river that flows through Berlin.
[2]   "Isn't that true?" in German.
[3]   A street in Berlin that runs through the Tiergarten toward the government neighborhood; literally, "the Tents," so named because tents provided dining spaces here during the eighteenth century.

afternoon, and once she came with a little man, quite blonde and uncertain. But I must explain how she looked.

"She was thin and tall, and, how do the Germans say, *temperementvoll*, *kraftvoll*,[4] and worn. She must have been forty then, and she dressed richly and carelessly, and she wore many jewels, and she could not keep her clothes on, always her shoulders would be coming uncovered, or her skirt would be hanging on one hook, but all the time she was splendid and remorseless and dramatic as if she were the center of a whirlwind and her clothes a temporary débris, and she talked sometimes to the sparrows and sometimes to the *Weinschenk*,[5] clasping her fingers together, so that the rings stood out and you could see through them, she was so thin. As for her dainty little man, she would talk to him in English, so that I did not know where she came from.

"Then one week I stayed away altogether because I was trying out for the *Schauspielhaus*,[6] and I was very anxious to get the part, and I thought of nothing else. I sat sometimes by myself in the *Tiergarten*,[7] or I walked down the *Sieges-Allee*[8] where all the great German emperors' statues are that look like little girls and widows, and then one day I thought of this woman, and I went back to the garden, and there she was, sitting drinking her beer and talking to the birds.

"And when I came in she got up immediately and came over and said: 'Why, how do you do, I have missed you so much, why did you not tell me that you were going away, and I should have seen what I could do about it.' She talked like that, in a voice that touched your heart, it was so light, and clear and unbroken. 'I have a house,' she said, 'just on the Spree and you could have come and stayed with me, for it is very large and you could have the room off my room. It is difficult to live in, but so lovely. It is Early Italian, and the bed is like those in which only young girls, dreaming of the Virgin, were allowed to lie, but you could sleep, because you have passion.' And somehow it did not seem funny that she spoke to me, and I said that I would meet her again some day in the garden and go home with her, and she was clever and did not show surprise.

"Then one evening we came in almost at the same moment. It was quite late and they were already playing the fiddle. We sat together, listening without speaking, and had pleasure watching her who played the violin, she was so heavy, a peasant, but her shoulders were remorseful and she bit her lip and looked down at her hand as it moved, and seemed interested in silence. Then I got up and followed my lady, and we came to a big house and she let herself in with a key, and we were in her home. And she turned at once to the left and went into the dark room and switched on the lights and sat down and said: 'This is where I sleep, this is how it is.' And the place was very expensive and disordered and melancholy. Everything was tall and massive, the chest of drawers rose above your head, and the china stove was enormous and white, and the bed was so high that you would think of it as something you would do some day, and the walls were covered with shelves, and in the shelves were heavy books, with red morocco bindings, and on the back of each was stamped a coat of arms, very intricate and oppressive, and she rang for tea, and began to take off her hat.

"A great war picture hung over the bed and the picture and the bed ran together, for the huge rumps of the dappled stallions rained almost into the pillows, the generals with their foreign helmets and their dripping swords, and the rolling smoke and the torn limbs of the dying seemed to be fighting with that bed, it was so large, so torn, so rumpled, so devastated. The sheets were lying half on the floor and the enormous counterpane hung down and there were feathers lying softly about, some cupped up like petals, and trembling the slight draught from the long windows. She smiled but she did not say anything, and it was not until a long time after that I saw a child, not more than three years old, very little and pretty, lying in the center of this bed, making a thin noise, like a fly buzzing, and I had thought so it was.

"But she did not talk of the child, and paid no attention to it, as if it were in the bed and she did not know it, and when the tea came she poured it, but took none herself, drinking little glasses of Rhine wine.

---

4   "Full of temperament and strength," in German.
5   The "wine-waiter," in German.
6   German for "theater."
7   The name of a park in central Berlin.
8   "Street of Victory," a street that went from the Brandenburg Gate through the Tiergarten in Berlin; Wilhelm II had it lined with the statues of 32 kings from the house of Brandenberg (*not* "the great German emperors"; but Siegesallee was relocated by Hitler and the remains were dismantled after World War II.

"'You have seen Ludwig,' she said. 'We were married a long time ago, he was just a boy then. I am Italian, but I studied English and German because I was in a traveling company. You,' she said abruptly, 'must give up acting.' I did not think then that it was odd that she should know of my ambition, though I had not mentioned it. 'And,' she went on: 'you are not for the stage, you are for something more quiet and more internal. Now I have lived in Germany ten years, and I like it very much. You will stay here and you will see. Ludwig is not very strong, you saw that, he is always going down, he has a room to himself.' And then she stopped talking. She seemed very tired and presently she got up on the bed and threw herself across it at the foot, and went to sleep, her hair all about her face. I went away then, but I came back that night and tapped at the window and she came, and nodded to me and presently she appeared at another window to the right of her bedroom, and signed for me to come in there, and I came up to the window and climbed in, and did not mind that she had not opened the door for me. The room was dark excepting for the moon, and two thin candles that burned brightly before the Virgin. It was a beautiful room, Madame, *traurig*[9] as she said, and foreign, and everything was delicate yet gloomy. The curtains over the bed were velvet, very Italian, and with gold fringe, and the bed cover was red velvet with the same gold fringe too, and the chairs were high backed and upholstered in red, and on the floor beside the bed a little stand, on which was a tassled red velvet cushion, and on the cushion a thick Bible in Italian, lying open.

"And she gave me a long, long nightgown that came below my feet and rose again fold upon fold, almost to my knees, and she loosened my hair, it was long and yellow then, and plaited it in two plaits, and she put me down at her knees and she said a prayer in German to me, and then in Italian and ended with 'God bless you' and I got into bed, and I loved her very much because there was nothing between us but this strange preparation for sleep, and she went away, and in the night I heard the child crying, but I was tired.

"And I stayed with her for a year, and the stage had already gone out of my heart, and I had become *religieuse*, it was a gentle religion that began with the bed, and the way I had gone down to sleep that first night, and the way I had prayed at her knees, though she never repeated that, and it grew with the furniture and the air of the room, and the Bible open at a page I could not read. It was a religion, Madame, that was empty of need, and therefore it was not holy perhaps, and not as it should have been in manner, but I was very happy and I lived with her for one year, and almost never saw Ludwig, and almost never Valentine, for that was her child, a little girl.

"But at the end of that year I knew there was trouble in the other room, for I heard her walking in the night, and now sometimes Ludwig would be there with her. I heard him crying and talking, but I could not hear what they said, though at times it seemed to be a lesson for the child to repeat, but if so, it never answered, only made that buzzing cry.

"Sometimes it is very wonderful in Germany, Madame, *nicht wahr?* There is nothing like a German winter, and now she and I used to walk all about the Imperial Palace,[10] and she stroked the cannons, and said that they were beautiful, and we talked of philosophy for she was troubled and brilliant, and she said always that one must try to be simple, and try to be like the people in a whole, and she explained that, saying that to be like every-man, the common pitiful people, to be like all of them, all at once in your own person, was holy, and she said that people did not understand what was meant by 'Love your neighbors as yourself.' It meant, she said, that one should be like them all, and oneself too, and then, she said, you would be great and sad and powerful.

"And it seemed sometimes as if she were doing it, as if she were all Germany in her Italian heart, common and uncommon, for she was very simple and irreparable, so that I was afraid of her and was not.

"That is the way it was, Madame, and she seemed to wish it to be that way, though at other times she was scattered and distraught, as at night, when I heard her walking in her room.

"And then after I had been there a year, she came in one night and woke me and said to me that I must come into her room, and it was in a yet more terrible disorder. There was a little cot bed in

---

9   "Sad," in German.
10   Formerly located in the center of Berlin, its ideologically
incorrect ruins were demolished by the Communist government
of the former East Germany in 1950.

one corner that had not been there before, and she pointed to it and said it was for me. The child was lying in the great bed, against a large lace pillow, and now it was four years old and yet it did not walk, and I never heard it make a sound, but that buzzing cry. It was beautiful in that almost divine way of idiot children, blonde and frail and innocent, with eyes and mouth devoid of calculation, like the child in the lap of the Virgin, or like children seen playing about the borders of holy prints, or like all children on Christmas cards, and cards for solemn occasions, if you understand me, Madame, something reserved and set aside about it, as if it were only for certain days, and not for life. And now she talked to me very quietly, but I did not recognize her former manner.

   " 'You must sleep here now,' she said, 'for I brought you here for this if I should need you, and now I need you and you must stay, you must stay here always.' She said 'Will you do that?' And I said no, I could not do that. She took up the candle and came to me and knelt down, and put the candle on the floor beside her, and she put her arm about my knees. 'Are you a traitor?' she said. 'Have you come into my house, and the house of my fathers, and the house of my child, to betray me?' and I said no, I had not come to betray. 'Then,' she said, 'you will do as I tell you. I shall teach you slowly, slowly, it will not be hard, but you must forget many things, you must begin to forget. I was wrong, all the things I have said to you were wrong, it was because I was a vain woman and did not know. I have,' she went on as if she were speaking to her child, someone who had been with her always, 'I have brought you up badly, forgive me, forgive me for that, that is a confession, but now I shall do better, you will see, you will never go into that other room again, that was a great vanity, now you will stay here, you see, you will like it. I shall bring your breakfast and dinner and supper, myself, with these hands. I shall hold you on my lap, I shall feed you, I shall rock you to sleep, I shall cover you with kisses, but you must not argue with me any more, no, we shall have no more arguments about things in the world, we shall not talk about man and his destiny, because he has no destiny, that is his secret, the great secret, I have been keeping it from you until to-day, until this hour, perhaps because I was jealous of that knowledge, but now I give it to you, I share it with you two. I was an old woman,' she continued, still holding my knees, 'when Valentine was born, and Ludwig was only a boy. I have to have you, he is not strong, he does not know, he will not do.' All this time she had been talking in a level voice, and now she began as if she were talking to a child no older than her own.

   " 'Don't repeat anything after me, it is a silly notion that children should learn to speak things after their teachers; but listen if you like, because you must become accustomed to the sounds of civilization, it's very foolish, it's very wrong, but,' she said, 'you must hear a little because that is the way it is in the world outside, and some day you might go out and not understand and become frightened.' And then she began. 'It is very beautiful in Germany sometimes, see, the stars are coming in the sky, and the snow falls down and covers the hedges and the houses, and there is nothing, and you do not need to be afraid, and I have loved you, these hands and these feet, and this breast and this heart your heart's heart, and your mouth and nose and cheeks and eyes and your hair, your wonderful hair, and I curl it, so, and there are many ribbons for it, and in the spring we shall go together into the garden where the animals are and the swans and the birds and the roses, and where the students come to read in their big books, and,' she said, speaking my name as if she were talking to someone else, 'Katya will go with you and she will say too, no, there are no students, no swans, no birds, no roses, it is all nothing just as you wish it, just fancy, nothing at all, it is so simple, it is not mysterious and the bells do not ring, and the wars are not fought, and the birds no not fly, and the river does not move, and the trees do not grow and there is no yesterday and no to-day and no to-morrow, there are no births and no deaths and no sorrow and no comfort and no here and no there, nothing, nothing! No laughing and no crying, no kissing and beating, no strife and no joy, no eating no drinking, no mothers no fathers, no sisters no brothers, no living and dying, only you, only you!...' "

   "And I stopped her and I said, 'Elvira, why is it that you suffer so, and what am I to do?' And I tried to put my arms about her, but she struck them down crying: 'Silence!' and then she went on: 'No growing no developing, no flourishing no withering no wilting no struggling no death, only you, as you wish, only you. . . . '

"And then, Madame, I got up, it was very cold in the room and I went to the window and pulled the curtains and leaned against the pane, and looked out, and stood a long time without saying anything, and when I turned around she was regarding me, her hands held apart, and I knew that I must go away from her and leave her forever, and I came up to her and I said, 'Good-by me love,' and I went and put my clothes on, and I came back to her and she was still standing there beside the picture, and I said to her, without approaching her, 'Good-by my love,' and went away.

"It is so beautiful in Berlin sometimes, Madame, *nicht wahr?* But now there was something else in my heart, and now it was a passion to see Paris, and therefore I was going to Paris, so it was I said *lebe wohl*[11] to Berlin, and I went for the last time to my little garden and ate an egg and drank a cup of coffee and watched the birds coming just as they used to come, and going just as they used to go, altogether here and then altogether gone, and I was happy in my heart, for that is the way it is with my heart, Madame, and so I went back to her house, and I went in at the door, for all the doors seemed to be open, perhaps they were sweeping, but I saw no one, and I came to her bedroom door, and I knocked but there was no answer, and I pushed it open, and there she was, sitting up in the bed with her child, and she and the child were making that same buzzing cry, together, and no human sound was between them, and everything was in terrible disorder. I came up to her, but she did not seem to know me, and I said, 'I am going away, I am going to Paris, because now there is a great longing in me to be away from here, and to be there, and I came to say farewell.' And she got down off the bed and came to the door and she said: 'I did not know. I loved you and trusted you, but I was mistaken, forgive me. ... I did not know I could do it myself, but you see, I can do it myself.' Then she got back on the bed and said: 'Go now.' And I went.

"Things are like that sometimes, in Berlin, *nicht wahr*, Madam?"

The Passion (1924)

Every afternoon at four-thirty, excepting Thursday, a smart carriage moved, with measured excellence, though the Bois,[1] drawn by two bays in shining patent leather, with blinkers embellished with silver R's and with docked tails rising firmly above well-stitched, immaculate cruppers.

Women walking under trees of that forest, looked strangely still and monstrous. The boles of the trees, bare for some hundred feet, and sparse yet sufficient, like prison bars, gave a sinister and impending calm, like a carefully planned, unexecuted murder.

In this carriage, with half-drawn curtains, not leaning against the upholstery of lace, in the exact center of a festooned cushion, with unmoving head, sat the Princess Negrita Rholinghousen.

Her stately figure with thin shoulders, like delicate flying buttresses, was encased in gray moire, and the bands that came over the aged hands were spotless and uncrumpled, as was the edging that rose to meet the dog-collar of braided pearls.

The shadowy face, blurred in a mist of tight-drawn veiling that masked the flaring edge of a hat, turreted in ribbons and roses, was no longer rouged to heighten the value of contours, but limned upon an intricate system of emaciation and imperishable lineage.

The jewels on the hands, the bracelets, the breastpin, the dog-collar, were workmanship of another century, and the buckles on the shoes were splendid and static.

Her knees dropped the silk of her dress in two sharp points like the corners of a candy box. Slowly this scented case moved through the odorless day.

The lake, with swans downturned, passed. Necks rose, glistening; a faint quacking drifted over the waters. The Princess rode, and never changed her position, her hands lying over each other in

---

[11] literally "live well" in German; but in effect the phrase means "good-bye."

THE PASSION

This story was first published in the *transatlantic review* 2(5) (November 1924), then reprinted in Ford Madox Ford (ed.), *Transatlantic Stories* (New York: Dial Press, 1926), and finally incorporated into Barnes's collection of short stories and plays, *A Night Among the Horses* (New York: Liveright, 1929), this latter furnishing the text followed here. Many years later the story was extensively revised and included in *Spillway* (London: Faber and Faber, 1952).

[1]   A once fashionable park in Paris.

her lap, undisturbed; no bead in the flawless double strand of pearls, that sank between the blue veins, trembled, nor did the slight radiance on the long nails deviate from their first custom.

The coachman was very old, and his son, sitting up on the box, was being broken in for a continuance of measured driving the old man did not hope to participate in. Every Thursday, when the Princess was at tea, the empty carriage was driven at a good pace by the younger man, and every Thursday the old coachman muttered: *"Doucement, doucement!"*[2]

The servants, now only five, moved with as little expenditure of effort as was compatible with the daily routine.

Every morning the books in the library, with their white kid bindings and their faded gold coat-of-arms, were dusted by Nekrita, and every afternoon the curtains in the conservatoire were drawn back for the sun, and as the Princess moved about from room to room less every year, one chamber was closed for good every twelve months.

Drida, cooking in the kitchen, whipped up the whites of three eggs with sugar, for the evening soufflé, and the gardener, watering the roses at nightfall, raked the earth that had died upon and within itself a million, million years, heaping it about the plants, breathing the air, mute with the depth of time that had passed through it. In the stilled splendor of the Princess' gardens was some of the dark, majestic, cumbersome beauty of the gardens of the Palace of Versailles.

The lap-dog had been too old to lift from her basket of ruffled French chintz. She slept heavily, moaning at mealtimes, a mass of white fur, unmarked by limb or feature, save for the lines of wet hair that placed the eyelids, and the moist, down-drooping point below the mouth.

The Princess rose at three, dressing herself before a long oak stand, glistening with faceted bottles. She had been almost six feet tall in youth, and now she was but little under it.

There were flowers, but she did not tend them; she had embroidered but she had given it up as a girl. She had painted too, but the faded scene of the chase hanging on the wall, between the oak chairs, was feathered with dust and out of mind.

The spinet in the corner, with its hand-painted yellow satin covering, was faded in a single line along the edge of the lid, signifying the silence of half a century. The music books, two, lying one above the other, were songs for soprano, and one was open at "Liebes-Lied." The only things that had seen recent service were the long thin candles, half-burnt, upon their stands, for the Princess read in the evenings.

There were few pictures, and these were in the dining hall. One of her father in uniform, standing beside a table, his plumed hat in his hand, his hand on the hilt of a rapier, his spurred feet lost in the deep fur of a thick rug.

The other, of her mother, seated on a garden bench, in a green riding-habit, a little mannish hat on one side, with a sweeping feather, and this was all.

An intricate curio case held miniatures of brothers and cousins. Rosy cheeked, yellow haired, sexless, and among the bric-à-brac, porcelain plates fired with bifurcated eagles' wings; seals, and, incongruously, a statuette of a little lady looking down through the film of her night shift at her colorless breasts.

Sometimes it rained across the garden, splashing drops on the windowpanes, reappearing in reflection in the inlaid mirrors of a Napoleonic table; and sometimes the sun used the mirrors to throw a spot of flame upon the ceiling.

The Princess was very old. Usually the old do not approach the grave without either reminiscence or religion. The Princess did. She had the power, the austerity, and the rot of a high irony. She was *sèche*,[3] but she was living on her last suppuration.

Sometimes she laughed with a sharpness that verged on a memory of obscenities. Laughter in old people is always terrifying. Things of the senses, when the senses are gone, are like wine on the lips when the cask is empty. The width between her teeth gave her at once the look of the connoisseur and of the gourmet; there was a blueness in her flesh that spoke of the acceptance of mortality; and sometimes, raising her glasses at the uncompromising moment, she had the air of a gallant and a bon vivant. She never spoke of that spirit.

---

[2] "Easy, easy!" in French.   [3] Literally "dry" in French; "sharp, curt, terse."

Now and again, two rusty, mittened female cousins called, attended by two serving women, palsied and broken, and patiently picking things from the floor. Sometimes an only nephew, a young boy not too childish in his accomplishments, came, cracking his whip, in creaking puttees, stabling his horse, walking with legs slightly apart. He drank from the delicate teacups, bit into the tender slices of buttered bread, stared out into the garden, and whistled when the Princess left the room.

Kert Anders, a Polish officer, who never wore his uniform, was the chiefest among the callers. Once a month, on the second Thursday, for some thirty years, he had presented himself, and drunk from the same flowered cups.

He was tall, almost six feet two. Long folds were in the white flesh beside the bulbous nose. His mouth was too small and his teeth flat and square. He had dark, thick eyebrows, women's hands; dressed like a groom, and spoke English and French with a marked accent.

He was a widower, collected plates and early editions, firearms, and seals, and was devoted to the memoirs of ladies of the de Sévigné period.[4] He wore yellow gloves which he turned back from the wrist in a single roll, and when he drew them off there was a faint odor of toilet water for a moment.

He had the face so often encountered in countries where custom has finally prohibited nothing, – he looked like a man who has eaten everything, everything; and though he was elegant in his person, there was something about him not far from the necessity of elimination.

Often, before tea, calling a little early, he would go out to the stables where the two bays, now the only horses, stamped and were curried, for here was fecundity of brawling bitches, snarling with bright, long teeth, weighted from beneath with the season's puppies, – he would stroke their brindles with his yellow gloves, and pull at their broad leather collars.

Kert Anders, whose history was now a blind alley, had been said in youth to have done something fearful against his country, and something perverse against his family. There were stories about a Polish actress, who had died slowly and painfully of some unknown malady after his acquaintance with her. There were others that he had been too friendly with a young Duke, who was devoted to weekly strolls among the ancient palaces, and who, it was said, always shuddered upon passing the historically safe beds of dead kings, wiping his eyelids with a lady's pocket-handkerchief.

It was also said that any hand on any wrist, were it plump and small, had been the cause of more than one public disgrace for Kert Anders.

It is certainly true that in his early twenties he had been attracted to women with racy natures and a taste for light-handedness, though he never got involved, the liaison stopping at tea and French pastry.

The autumn was his weather. Gloves in hand, spatted, he strolled among the gardens of the Luxembourg,[5] looking neither up nor down, but straight ahead at the nude statues, standing eternally between falling leaves.

When he came to tea, drawing down the roll of his gloves, he would speak of the dogs, of this autumn's air in relation to the airs of other autumns; of cathedrals, of the parks, bringing a gravure whose delicate line he wished to discuss, a few little known flowers. And often he left these things behind him, never mentioning them again. At other times he talked of the art of acting; the use and the decline of the rapier, of the advisability of the high boot for the tragic actor, of light comedy, and of the fools in Shakespeare. And the Princess would quote something Goethe had said on the subject, and he would counter with Heine's poetry, or a passage from Strindberg or Ibsen,[6] turning and turning a small gold band on his little finger, winking with a ruby that looked as if it were about to break into a drop of liquid.

She would say: "Do you know the English poets?" and he would answer that Chaucer was attractive to him, but produced a mood difficult to overcome, and she would smile, and they would

---

[4]   Marie de Rabutin-Chantale, marquise de Sévigné (1626–96), famous writer of letters.
[5]   The Luxembourg Gardens are in the heart of the Left Bank in Paris.

[6]   Johann Wolfgang von Goethe (1749–1832), German poet and man of letters; Heinrich Heine (1797–1856), German poet; August Strindberg (1849–1912), Swedish writer and playwright; Henrik Ibsen (1828–1906), Norwegian playwright.

drift into the art of painting, mentioning how it had left the home genre when the Dutch gave way to the English; whether painting should be an indoor art, or an art of nature and the sea; and once in a while he dropped a remark about a new dish he had invented, or a piece of early French furniture he had hated to see go above his bid.

Of course, gossip had it that the Princess was the one passion of his life. It was even taken for granted that but for some good reason, they would have been married long since. It was hinted that a rupture had prevented him from claiming her in marriage, others said that the Princess was too niggardly to share the half of her bed; yet others insisted that they were lovers in youth, and were now as good as husband and wife. All of this was nonsense.

The simple fact was they were like two pages in an ancient volume, folded for a moment together and parted again in the hands of time.

On the last call but one, there had been a little strain in the air. He had spoken of love, and had drifted from that into a discussion of Handel[7] and the effect of music on small gatherings; chamber music versus the concert hall.

"I begin, less and less, to believe in the enthusiasm evinced by collective peoples," he remarked, when she turned, and putting down her teacup with a trembling hand, said: "Yet if a little, light man, with a beard had come to me and said 'I love you,' I should have believed in God." And she drew her glasses up and looked out of them at him, and laughed.

He called only once after that, and only once or twice was she seen riding in the Bois, limned in pink, a mist behind a tight-drawn veil, for shortly after that she did not live any more.

---

[7] Georg Friedrich Händel (1685–1759), German composer who moved to Britain in 1712 and stayed for the rest of his life.

Jean Rhys (1890–1979)

Introduction

Ella Gwendoline Rees Williams (1890–1979) was born in Roseau, Dominica, in the West Indies. Her mother was a Creole of Scottish and Irish descent, her father a doctor from Wales. In 1907 she came to England to attend the Perse School for Girls in Cambridge. She spent two terms at the Academy of Dramatic art in 1909, then left to become a chorus girl. In 1919 she married Jean Lenglet, a Dutch-French poet and journalist, and moved with him to Paris. In 1922 their son William died at the age of three weeks. The couple went to Vienna for a few months, then returned to Paris, where her daughter Maryvonne was born the same year. In 1924 Lenglet was imprisoned for currency irregularities. Rees, still in Paris, met Ford Madox Ford, who encouraged her to write. She became his lover for a while, and in 1924 her first story "Vienne" (see pp. 946–9) was published in the *transatlantic review*, edited by Ford, under the name Jean Rhys. In 1927 she published her first book of stories, *The Left Bank and Other Stories*. In 1928 she published her first novel, *Postures*, later retitled *Quartet*, and moved to London, where she began living with Leslie Tilden Smith, a literary agent. Her second novel, *After Leaving Mr. Mackenzie*, appeared in 1930; her third, *Voyage in the Dark*, in 1934. Meanwhile, Rhys had divorced Lenglet and married Tilden Smith. In 1939 she published her fourth novel, *Good Morning, Midnight*. Her private life, as opposed to her literary life, was beginning to spiral out of control. In 1945 her second husband died, while her daughter Maryvonne, now aged 23, married. The next year Rhys began living with Max Hamer in Beckenham, a distant suburb of London, and the next year she married him, her third husband. They were living in grinding poverty, her novels having received little attention and only modest sales. But when she was "rediscovered" by a journalist, her interest in writing was rekindled. True, her husband was imprisoned for minor fraud in 1950 and released in 1951; but Rhys had begun writing again. In 1955 the two moved to Cornwall, and in 1957 the BBC broadcast an adaptation of *Good Morning, Midnight* while Rhys signed a contract for her next novel with André Deutsch. *Wide Sargasso Sea*, her fifth and last novel, appeared in 1966 and won the W. H. Smith Prize. Her earlier novels were now reissued. In her remaining years she published two new collections of short stories, *Tigers Are Better-Looking* (1974) and *Sleep It Off Lady* (1976). Her autobiography, *Smile Please*, was published posthumously in 1979.

Vienne[1] (1924)

I. The Dancer

Funny how it's slipped away, Vienne. Nothing left but a few snapshots –

Not a friend, not a pretty frock – nothing left of Vienna.

Hot sun, my black frock, a hat with roses, music, lots of music –

The little dancer at the 'Parisien' with a Kirchner girl's legs[2] and a little faun's face.

She was so exquisite that girl that it clutched at one, gave one a pain that anything so lovely could ever grow old, or die, or do ugly things –

A fragile child's body, a fluff of black skirt ending far above the knee. Silver straps over that beautiful back, the wonderful legs in black silk stockings and little satin shoes, short hair, cheeky little face.

She gave me the *songe bleu* – Four, five feet she could jump and come down on that wooden floor without a sound –

Her partner, an unattractive individual in badly fitting trousers, could lift her with one hand, throw her in the air, catch her, swing her as one would a flower.

This story was first published in the *transatlantic review* 2(6) (December 1924).

[1] French for "Vienne," the capital of Austria.

[2] Raphael Kirchner (1867–1917) was a French artist who specialized in sensual or sexually provocative depictions of young women; his works were a regular feature in the glamour magazine *La Vie parisienne*, and often they were produced as series that were then reproduced as postcards. In effect Kirchner was an early maker of the modern pin-up. Cf. Mary Butts, "Speed the Plough," pp. 777–82, esp. 778.

At the end she made an adorable little 'gamine's' grimace.

Ugly humanity, I'd always thought – I saw people differently afterwards – because for once I'd met sheer loveliness with a flame inside, for there was 'it' – the spark, the flame in her dancing.

John (a dam good judge) raved about her. André also, though cautiously, for he was afraid she would be too expensive.

All the French officers coveted her – night after night the place was packed.

Finally she disappeared. Went back to Buda Pest where afterwards we heard of her.

Married to a barber

Rum!

Pretty women, lots.

How pretty women here are –

Lovely food.

Poverty gone, the dread of it – going.

II. 'Fischyl'

I met him at the Tabarin.

The Tabarin when we were in Vienna was the *chic* night café, though I didn't think it as amusing as the Parisien –

Simone, Germaine, John, me, a rum Viennese who wore a monocle and was supposed to live on his very charming wife, two Italians.

Fischyl arrived to 'kiss the hand'; froze on to me and asked if I'd come to play golf next morning.

The links are near the Prater[3] – and we sat in the nice little house-place – drinking hot wine before we started.

It was dam cold for golf.

Also Fischyl said my hat was too big and insisted on my taking it off and putting on a sort of mosquito-net thing made of green gauze which covered my face up and fastened at the back.

He wore a white sweater and huge boots –

We sallied out and he started to show me how to hold my club but all I could think of was how to get at my nose which I wanted to blow.

Also I'd left my handkerchief in the club house.

However I explained (after two sniffs) to Fischyl.

He was quite a sport, undid the mosquito net and lent me his enormous hanky.

Then he said that he was dying to kiss the back of my neck.

It was amusing golf – and we played several times.

He was tall and large with a bushy moustache and a beaky nose, old or oldish.

He talked incessantly of flirting, of London (which he hated) of English people (who amazed him) of himself – of Women.

I always remember one long discourse about some place where he'd been in some official capacity.

He talked French and though my French was improving there were blanks.

So I only gathered that it was in the Orient.

Turkey perhaps – or Asia Minor. Could it have been Smyrna?[4]

---

[3]   A park in Vienna.

[4]   Smyrna, modern day Izmir, is on the western coast of modern Turkey, or Asia Minor. Until 1914 it was part of the Ottoman Empire, and like other cities on the coast it had had a heterogenous population and was divided into Turkish, Jewish, Armenian, Greek, and Frankish quarters. During World War I the Ottoman Empire had supported the Central Powers (Germany and the Austro-Hungarian Empire), while Greece had allied itself with the Entente (France, Britain, Russia). With the end of the war, obtaining Smyrna became a primary goal of Greece. In May 1919 a Greek occupation force, protected by allied warships, disembarked in the city. Meanwhile, between 1914 and 1919 the collapse of the Ottoman Empire had combined with an allied occupation of Constantinople to generate support for the Turkish nationalist movement headed by Mustafa Kemal (Atatürk), which had declared itself the successor to the Ottoman Empire. In February 1921 an international conference was held in London to resolve the impasse in Asia Minor, but no agreement was reached. The Greeks soon launched a major offensive that at first was highly successful; but Mustafa Kemal then launched a counteroffensive that completely routed the Greeks. In September 1921, after the Greek army evacuated Smyrna, the Turks entered it and engaged in a full-scale massacre of the city's Christian inhabitants, killing some 30,000. The conflict was

Anyway there was Fischyl. An Important Person.

And every evening he would promenade along the principal street or place or whatever it was and choose a woman.

They sat at windows and passed in carriages.

For all the women were beautiful there – and all were ... well, a man had only to choose.

I imagined Fischyl walking along, trousers rather tight, moustaches fiercely curling, chest well out – Choosing.

As a matter of fact I am not being fair to Fischyl for he was like most Viennese, charming, and clever as hell.

He was fearfully interested in the air raids over London[5] – wanted to know if I remembered the one of such and such a date.

Was there any damage done? And where?

Afterwards I found out that he'd been in Germany during the war and was in some way connected with the air service.

I wonder if he'd anything to do with the bomb that fell so close to the Cavour that night I was with Kinsky?

Golf was too dam cold for the winter I decided.

III. The Spending Phase

I'd noticed people growing more and more deferential to John and incidentally to me. I'd noticed that he seemed to have money – a good deal – a great deal.

He made it on the change he told me.

Then one day in the spring of 1921 we left the flat in Favoritenstrasse[6] for a suite in the Imperial:[7] a bedroom, sitting room and bathroom.

We sent off the cook and D –, promoted to be my maid came with us.

Nice to have lots of money – nice, nice.

Good to have a car, a big chauffeur, rings and a string of pearls and as many frocks as I liked.

Good to have money, money. All the flowers I wanted. All the compliments I wanted. Everything everything.

Oh great god money – you make possible all that's nice in life – Youth and beauty, the envy of women, and the love of men –

Even the luxury of a soul, a character and thoughts of one's own you give, and only you! – To look in the glass and think I've got what I wanted!

I gambled when I married and I've won –

As a matter of fact I wasn't so exalted really, but it was exceedingly pleasant.

Spending and spending And there was always more –

.   .   .   .

One day I had a presentiment.

John gave an extra special lunch to the Japanese officers, Miyake, Hayashi, Oshima and Co.

We lunched in a separate room which started my annoyance for I preferred the restaurant especially with the Japanese who depressed me.

not resolved until the Treaty of Lausanne was signed in July 1923, in which Greece ceded all territories in Asia Minor to the newly created Republic of Turkey. Smyrna, in short, was much in the news throughout the period preceding the publication of "Vienne."

[5]   The first Zeppelin attack on London took place on May 31, 1915, and killed seven people. Although Zeppelin attacks continued throughout the war, their military limitations were plain: Zeppelins were easily thrown off course by bad weather and made easy targets for fighter planes. From the spring of 1917 German

military authorities turned to long-range bombers such as the Gotha airplane. One daylight attack on London by 20 Gothas killed 162 civilians, the highest death toll for a single raid. The number of civilian air raid victims in Britain during World War I was relatively small: 1,413 dead, 3,409 injured.

[6]   "Favorite Street," in German; a street in the southern part of central Vienna.

[7]   Hotel Imperial, located at Karntner Ring 16 in Vienna, was a former Württemberg palace inaugurated in 1873 by Emperor Franz Josef I.

It was rather cold and dark and the meal seemed interminable –

Miyake in the intervals of eating enormously told us a long history of an officer in Japan who 'hara-kari'd' because his telephone went wrong during manœuvres.

Rotten reason I call it but Miyake seemed to think him a hero.

Escaped as soon as I could upstairs.

I was like Napoleon's mother suddenly 'Provided it lasts.'

And if it does not? Well, thinking that was to feel the authentic 'cold brand clutching my heart.'[8]

And a beastly feeling too let me tell you.

So damned well I knew that I could never be poor again with courage or dignity.

I did a little sum, translated what we were spending into francs – into pounds – I was appalled – (When we first arrived in Vienne the crown was 13 to the franc – at that time it was about sixty).

As soon as I could I attacked John –

First he laughed then he grew vexed.

'Ella I tell you it's all right. How much am I making? A lot.

'How much exactly? Can't say. How? You won't understand.

'Don't be frightened, it – brings bad luck. You'll stop my luck.'

I shut up. I know so well that presentiments, fears, are unlucky.

'Don't worry' said John 'soon I will pull it quite off and we will be rich, rich –'

We dined in a little corner of the restaurant.

At the same table a few days before a Russian girl 24 years of age had shot herself.

With her last money she had a decent meal and then bang. Out –

And I made up my mind that if ever it came to it I should do it too.

Not to be poor again.

No and No and No –

So darned easy to plan that – and always at the last moment – one is afraid. Or cheats oneself with hope.

I can still do this and this. I can still clutch at that or that.

So and so will help me.

How you fight, cleverly and well at first, then more wildly – then hysterically.

I can't go down, I won't go down. Help me, help me.

Steady – I must be clever – So and so will help.

But so and so smiles a worldly smile.

You get nervous. He doesn't understand. I'll make him –

But so and so's eyes grow cold. You plead.

Can't you help me, won't you please? It's like this and this –

So and so becomes uncomfortable, obstinate –

No good –

I mustn't cry. I won't cry –

And that time you don't – You manage to keep your head up, a smile on your face.

So and so is vastly relieved. So relieved that he offers at once the little help that is a mockery, and the consoling compliment.

In the taxi still you don't cry.

You've thought of someone else –

But at the fifth or sixth disappointment you cry more easily –

After the tenth you give it up – You are broken – No nerves left –

And every second-rate fool can have their cheap little triumph over you – judge you with their little middle-class judgment.

Can't do anything for them. No good.

C'est rien – c'est une femme qui se noie[9] –

But two years, three years afterwards. Salut to you little Russian girl who had pluck enough and enough knowledge of the world, to finish when your good time was over.

---

[8]   A cliché from popular fiction.

[9]   "It's nothing – it's a woman who is drowning," in French.

Illusion (1927)

1

Miss Bruce was quite an old inhabitant of the Quarter. For seven years she had lived there, in a little studio up five flights of stairs. She had painted portraits, exhibited occasionally at the Salon. She had even sold a picture sometimes – a remarkable achievement for Montparnasse, but possible, for I believe she was just clever enough and not too clever, though I am no judge of these matters.

She was a tall, thin woman, with large bones and hands and feet. One thought of her as a shining example of what character and training – British character and training – can do. After seven years in Paris she appeared utterly untouched, utterly unaffected, by anything hectic, slightly exotic or unwholesome. Going on all the time all round her were the cult of beauty and the worship of physical love: she just looked at her surroundings in her healthy, sensible way, and then dismissed them from her thoughts . . . rather like some sturdy rock with impotent blue waves washing round it.

When pretty women passed her in the streets or sat near her in restaurants she would look appraisingly with the artist's eye, and make a suitably critical remark. She exhibited no tinge of curiosity or envy. As for the others, the petites femmes, anxiously consulting the mirrors of their bags, anxiously and searchingly looking round with darkened eyelids: 'Those unfortunate people!' would say Miss Bruce. Not in a hard way, but broadmindedly, breezily: indeed with a thoroughly gentlemanly intonation . . . Those unfortunate little people!

She always wore a neat serge dress in the summer and a neat tweed costume in the winter, brown shoes with low heels and cotton stockings. When she was going to parties she put on a black gown of crêpe de chine, just well enough cut, not extravagantly pretty.

In fact Miss Bruce was an exceedingly nice woman.

She powdered her nose as a concession to Paris; the rest of her face shone, beautifully washed, in the sunlight or the electric light as the case might be, with here and there a few rather lovable freckles.

She had, of course, like most of the English and American artists in Paris, a private income – a respectably large one, I believe. She knew most people and was intimate with nobody. We had been dining and lunching together, now and then, for two years, yet I only knew the outside of Miss Bruce – the cool sensible, tidy English outside.

Well, we had an appointment on a hot, sunny afternoon, and I arrived to see her about three o'clock. I was met by a very perturbed concierge.

Mademoiselle had been in bed just one day, and, suddenly, last night about eight o'clock the pain had become terrible. The femme de ménage,[1] 'Mame' Pichon who had stayed all day and she, the concierge, had consulted anxiously, had fetched a doctor and, at his recommendation, had had her conveyed to the English Hospital in an ambulance.

'She took nothing with her,' said the femme de ménage, a thin and voluble woman. 'Nothing at all, pauvre Mademoiselle.' If Madame – that was me – would give herself the trouble to come up to the studio, here were the keys. I followed Madame Pichon up the stairs. I must go at once to Miss Bruce and take her some things. She must at least have nightgowns and a comb and brush.

'The keys of the wardrobe of Mademoiselle,' said Madame Pichon insinuatingly, and with rather a queer side-long look at me, 'are in this small drawer. Ah, les voilà!'

I thanked her with a dismissing manner. Madame Pichon was not a favourite of mine, and with firmness I watched her walk slowly to the door, try to start a conversation, and then, very reluctantly, disappear. Then I turned to the wardrobe – a big, square solid piece of old, dark furniture, suited for the square and solid coats and skirts of Miss Bruce. Indeed, most of her furniture was big and square. Some strain in her made her value solidity and worth more than grace or fantasies. It was difficult to turn the large key, but I managed it at last.

This story was published for the first time time in Jean Rhys's earliest book, *The Left Bank and Other Stories* (London: Jonathan Cape, 1927).

[1] Woman in charge of maintaining a block of flats.

'Good Lord!' I remarked out loud. Then, being very much surprised I sat down on a chair and said: 'Well, what a funny girl!'

For Miss Bruce's wardrobe when one opened it was a glow of colour, a riot of soft silks ... everything that one did not expect.

In the middle, hanging in the place of honour, was an evening dress of a very beautiful shade of old gold: near it another of flame colour: of two black dresses the one was touched with silver, the other with a jaunty embroidery of emerald and blue. There were a black and white check with a jaunty belt, a flowered crêpe de chine – positively flowered! – then a carnival costume complete with mask, then a huddle, a positive huddle of all colours, of all stuffs.

For one instant I thought of kleptomania, and dismissed the idea. Dresses for models, then? Absurd! Who would spend thousands of francs on dresses for models ... No nightgowns here, in any case.

As I looked, hesitating, I saw in the corner a box without a lid. It contained a neat little range of smaller boxes: Rouge Fascination; Rouge Manadarine; Rouge Andalouse; several powders; kohl for the eyelids and paint for the eyelashes – an outfit for a budding Manon Lescaut.[2] Nothing was missing: there were scents too.

I shut the door hastily. I had no business to look or to guess. But I guessed. I knew. Whilst I opened the other half of the wardrobe and searched the shelves for nightgowns I knew it all: Miss Bruce, passing by a shop, with the perpetual hunger to be beautiful and that thirst to be loved which is the real curse of Eve, well hidden under her neat dress, more or less stifled, more or less unrecognized.

Miss Bruce had seen a dress and had suddenly thought: in that dress perhaps ... And, immediately afterwards: why not? And had entered the shop, and, blushing slightly, had asked the price. That had been the first time: an accident, an impulse.

The dress must have been disappointing, yet beautiful enough, becoming enough to lure her on. Then must have begun the search for *the* dress, the perfect Dress, beautiful, beautifying, possible to be worn. And lastly, the search for illusion – a craving, almost a vice, the stolen waters and the bread eaten in secret of Miss Bruce's life.

Wonderful moment! When the new dress would arrive and would emerge smiling and graceful from its tissue paper.

'Wear me, give me life,' it would seem to say to her, 'and I will do my damnedest for you!' And first, not unskilfully, for was she not a portrait painter? Miss Bruce would put on the powder, the Rouge Fascination, the rouge for her lips, lastly the dress – and she would gaze into the glass at a transformed self. She would sleep that night with a warm glow at her heart. No impossible thing, beauty and all that beauty brings. There close at hand, to be clutched if one dared. Somehow she never dared, next morning.

I thankfully seized a pile of nightgowns and sat down, rather miserably undecided. I knew she would hate me to have seen those dresses: 'Mame' Pichon would tell her that I had been to the armoire. But she must have her nightgowns. I went to lock the wardrobe doors and felt a sudden, irrational pity for the beautiful things inside. I imagined them, shrugging their silken shoulders, rustling, whispering about the *anglaise*[3] who had dared to buy them in order to condemn them to life in the dark ... And I opened the door again.

The yellow dress appeared malevolent, slouching on its hanger; the black ones were mournful, only the little chintz frock smiled gaily, waiting for the supple body and limbs that should breathe life into it.

When I was allowed to see Miss Bruce a week afterwards I found her lying, clean, calm and sensible in the big ward – an appendicitis patient. They patched her up and two or three weeks later we dined together at our restaurant. At the coffee stage she said suddenly: 'I suppose you noticed

---

[2] Manon Lescaut is a beautiful young women, whether in the novel *Aventures du Chevalier des Grieux et de Manon Lescaut* (1734) by the Abbé Antoine-François Prévost (1697–1763) or the opera *Manon Lescaut* (1893) by the Italian composer Giacomo Puccini (1858–1924).

[3] Englishwoman, in French.

my collection of frocks. Why should I not collect frocks? They fascinate me. The colour and all that. Exquisite sometimes!'

Of course, she added, carefully staring over my head at what appeared to me to be a very bad picture, 'I should never make such a fool of myself as to wear them . . . They ought to be worn, I suppose.'

A plump, dark girl, near us, gazed into the eyes of her dark, plump escort, and lit a cigarette with the slightly affected movements of the non-smoker.

'Not bad hands and arms, that girl,' said Miss Bruce in her gentlemanly manner.

Mannequin[1] (1927)

Twelve o'clock. Déjeuner chez Jeanne Veron, Place Vendôme.[2]

Anna, dressed in the black cotton, chemise-like garment of the mannequin off duty was trying to find her way along dark passages and down complicated flights of stairs to the underground from where lunch was served.

She was shivering, for she had forgotten her coat, and the garment that she wore was very short, sleeveless, displaying her rose-coloured stockings to the knee. Her hair was flamingly and honestly red; her eyes, which were very gentle in expression, brown and heavily shadowed with kohl; her face small and pale under its professional rouge. She was fragile, like a delicate child, her arms pathetically thin. It was to her legs that she owed this dazzling, this incredible opportunity.

Madame Veron, white-haired with black eyes, incredibly distinguished, who had given them one sweeping glance, the glance of the connoisseur, smiled imperiously and engaged her at an exceedingly small salary. As a beginner, Madame explained, Anna could not expect more. She was to wear the jeune fille dresses. Another smile, another sharp glance.

Anne was conducted from the Presence by an underling who helped her to take off the frock she had worn temporarily for the interview. Aspirants for an engagement are always dressed in a model of the house.

She had spent yesterday afternoon in a delirium tempered by a feeling of exaggerated reality, and in buying the necessary make up. It had been such a forlorn hope, answering the advertisement.

The morning had been dreamlike. At the back of the wonderful decorated salons she had found an unexpected sombreness; the place, empty, would have been dingy and melancholy, countless puzzling corridors and staircases, a rabbit warren and a labyrinth. She despaired of ever finding her way.

In the mannequins' dressing-room she spent a shy hour making up her face – in an extraordinary and distinctive atmosphere of slimness and beauty; white arms and faces vivid with rouge; raucous voices and the smell of cosmetics; silken lingerie. Coldly critical glances were bestowed upon Anna's reflection in the glass. None of them looked at her directly . . . A depressing room, taken by itself, bare and cold, a very inadequate conservatory for these human flowers. Saleswomen in black rushed in and out, talking in sharp voices; a very old woman hovered, helpful and shapeless, showing Anna where to hang her clothes, presenting to her the black garment that Anna was wearing, going to lunch. She smiled with professional motherliness, her little, sharp, black eyes travelling rapidly from la nouvelle's[3] hair to her ankles and back again.

She was Madame Pecard, the dresser.

Before Anna had spoken a word she was called away by a small boy in buttons to her destination in one of the salons: there, under the eye of a vendeuse, she had to learn the way to wear the

---

This story was published for the first time time in Jean Rhys's earliest book, *The Left Bank and Other Stories* (London: Jonathan Cape, 1927).

[1] A woman whose work is wearing new clothes to show them to potential customers; mannequins were poorly paid, unlike fashion models of today.

[2] A square in central Paris designed by Jules Hardouin-Mansart (1645–1708), dominated by the Vendôme column (1806–10)

built in the style of Trajan's column in Rome to commemorate Napoleon's victories. The north end of the square opens into the rue de la Paix, at this time a street of fashion shops.

[3] "The new one's," in French with an English possessive added to it.

innocent and springlike air and garb of the jeune fille. Behind a yellow, silken screen she was hustled into a leather coat and paraded under the cold eyes of an American buyer. This was the week when the spring models are shown to important people from big shops all over Europe and America: the most critical week of the season . . . The American buyer said that he would have that, but with an inch on to the collar and larger cuffs. In vain the saleswoman, in her best English with its odd Chicago accent, protested that that would completely ruin the chic of the model. The American buyer knew what he wanted and saw that he got it.

The vendeuse sighed, but there was a note of admiration in her voice. She respected Americans: they were not like the English, who, under a surface of annoying moroseness of manner, were notoriously timid and easy to turn round your finger.

'Was that all right?' Behind the screen one of the sales-women smiled encouragingly and nodded. The other shrugged her shoulders. She had small, close-set eyes, a long thin nose and tight lips of the regulation puce colour, Behind her silken screen Anna sat on a high white stool. She felt that she appeared charming and troubled. The white and gold of the salon suited her red hair.

A short morning. For the mannequin's day begins at ten and the process of making up lasts an hour. The friendly saleswoman volunteered the information that her name was Jeannine, that she was in the lingerie, that she considered Anna rudement jolie, that noon was Anna's lunch hour. She must go down the corridor and up those stairs, through the big salon then . . . Anyone would tell her. But Anna, lost in the labyrinth, was too shy to ask her way. Besides, she was not sorry to have time to brace herself for the ordeal. She had reached the regions of utility and oilcloth: the decorative salons were far overhead. Then the smell of food – almost visible, it was so cloudlike and heavy – came to her nostrils, and high-noted, and sibilant, a buzz of conversation made her draw a deep breath. She pushed a door open.

She was in a big, very low-ceilinged room, all the floor space occupied by long wooden tables with no cloths . . . She was sitting at the mannequins' table, gazing at a thick and hideous white china plate, a twisted tin fork, a wooden-handled stained knife, a tumbler so thick it seemed unbreakable.

There were twelve mannequins at Jeanne Veron's: six of them were lunching, the others still paraded, goddess-like, till their turn came for rest and refreshment. Each of the twelve was a distinct and separate type: each of the twelve knew her type and kept to it, practising rigidly in clothing, manner, voice and conversation.

Round the austere table were now seated Babette, the gamine, the traditional blonde enfant: Mona, tall and darkly beautiful, the femme fatale, the wearer of sumptuous evening gowns. Georgette was the garçonne: Simone with green eyes Anna knew instantly for a cat whom men would and did adore, a sleek, white, purring, long-lashed creature . . . Eliane was the star of the collection.

Eliane was frankly ugly and it did not matter: no doubt Lilith,[4] from whom she was obviously descended, had been ugly too. Her hair was henna-tinted, her eyes small and black, her complexion bad under her thick make-up. Her hips were extraordinarily slim, her hands and feet exquisite, every movement she made was as graceful as a flower's in the wind. Her walk . . . But it was her walk which made her the star there and earned her a salary quite fabulous for Madame Veron's, where large salaries were not the rule . . . Her walk and her 'chic of the devil' which lit an expression of admiration in even the cold eyes of American buyers.

Eliane was a quiet girl, pleasant-mannered. She wore a ring with a beautiful emerald on one long, slim finger, and in her small eyes were both intelligence and mystery.

Madame Pecard, the dresser, was seated at the head of the mannequin's table, talking loudly, unlistened to, and gazing benevolently at her flock.

At other tables sat the sewing girls, pale-faced, black-frocked – the workers heroically gay, but with the stamp of labour on them: and the saleswomen. The mannequins, with their sensual, blatant charms and their painted faces were watched covertly, envied and apart.

---

[4]   A legendary figure who in several traditions of Jewish commentary was the first wife of Adam, giving birth to demons still roaming the earth.

Babette the blonde enfant was next to Anna, and having started the conversation with a few good, round oaths at the quality of the sardines, announced proudly that she could speak English and knew London very well. She began to tell Anna the history of her adventures in the city of coldness, dark and fogs . . . She had gone to a job as a mannequin in Bond Street and the villainous proprietor of the shop having tried to make love to her and she being rigidly virtuous, she had left. And another job, Anna must figure to herself, had been impossible to get, for she, Babette, was too small and slim for the Anglo-Saxon idea of a mannequin.

She stopped to shout in a loud voice to the woman who was serving: 'Hé, my old one, don't forget your little Babette . . .'

Opposite, Simone the cat and the sportive Georgette were having a low-voiced conversation about the triste-ness[5] of a monsieur of their acquaintance. 'I said to him,' Georgette finished decisively, 'Nothing to be done, my rabbit. You have not looked at me well, little one. In my place would you not have done the same?'

She broke off when she realized that the others were listening, and smiled in a friendly way at Anna.

She too, it appeared, had ambitions to go to London because the salaries were so much better there. Was it difficult? Did they really like French girls? Parisiennes?

The conversation became general,

'The English boys are nice,' said Babette, winking one divinely candid eye. 'I had a chic type who used to take me to dinner at the Empire Palace.[6] Oh, a pretty boy . . .'

'It is the most chic restaurant in London,' she added importantly.

The meal reached the stage of dessert. The other tables were gradually emptying; the mannequins all ordered very strong coffee, several liqueur. Only Mona and Eliane remained silent; Eliane, because she was thinking of something else; Mona, because it was her type, her genre to be haughty.

Her hair swept away from her white, narrow forehead and her small ears: her long earrings nearly touching her shoulders, she sipped her coffee with a disdainful air. Only once, when the blonde enfant, having engaged in a passage of arms with the waitress and got the worst of it was momentarily discomfited and silent, Mona narrowed her eyes and smiled an astonishingly cruel smile.

As soon as her coffee was drunk she got up and went out.

Anna produced a cigarette, and Georgette, perceiving instantly that here was the sportive touch, her genre, asked for one and lit it with a devil-may-care air. Anna eagerly passed her cigarettes round, but the Mère Pecard interfered weightily. It was against the rules of the house for the mannequins to smoke, she wheezed. The girls all lit their cigarettes and smoked. The Mère Pecard rumbled on: 'A caprice, my children. All the world knows that mannequins are capricious. Is it not so?' She appealed to the rest of the room.

As they went out Babette put her arm round Anna's waist and whispered: 'Don't answer Madame Pecard. We don't like her. We never talk to her. She spies on us. She is a camel.'

That afternoon Anna stood for an hour to have a dress draped on her. She showed this dress to a stout Dutch lady buying for the Hague, to a beautiful South American with pearls, to a silver-haired American gentleman who wanted an evening cape for his daughter of seventeen, and to a hook-nosed, odd English lady of title who had a loud voice and dressed, under her furs, in a grey jersey and stout boots.

The American gentleman approved of Anna, and said so, and Anna gave him a passionately grateful glance. For, if the vendeuse Jeannine had been uniformly kind and encouraging, the other, Madame Tienne, had been as uniformly disapproving and had once even pinched her arm hard.

About five o'clock Anna became exhausted. The four white and gold walls seemed to close in on her. She sat on her high white stool staring at a marvellous nightgown and fighting an intense desire to rush away. Anywhere! Just to dress and rush away anywhere, from the raking eyes of the customers and the pinching fingers of Irene.

---

[5] "Sad-ness," in a combination of French and English.
[6] A typical name for a music hall; though none in London had this name, there were many with the name in other cities throughout Britain. It suggests that Babette may seriously over-estimate how "chic" was the restaurant.

'I will one day. I can't stick it,' she said to herself. 'I won't be able to stick it.' She had an absurd wish to gasp for air.

Jeannine came and found her like that.

'It is hard at first, hein? . . . One asks oneself: Why? For what good? It is all idiot. We are all so. But we go on. Do not worry about Irene.' She whispered: 'Madame Vernon likes you very much. I heard her say so.'

At six o'clock Anna was out in the rue de la Paix;[7] her fatigue forgotten, the feeling that now she really belonged to the great, maddening city possessed her and she was happy in her beautifully cut tailor-made and beret.

Georgette passed her and smiled; Babette was in a fur coat.

All up the street the mannequins were coming out of the shops, pausing on the pavements a moment, making them as gay and as beautiful as beds of flowers before they walked swiftly away and the Paris night swallowed them up.

Tea with an Artist (1927)

It was obvious that this was not an Anglo-Saxon: he was too gay, too dirty, too unreserved and in his little eyes was such a mellow comprehension of all the sins and the delights of life. He was drinking rapidly one glass of beer after another, smoking a long, curved pipe, and beaming contentedly on the world. The woman with him wore a black coat and skirt; she had her back to us.

I said: 'Who's the happy man in the corner? I've never seen him before.'

My companion who knew everybody answered: 'That's Verhausen. As mad as a hatter.'

'Madder than most people here?' I asked.

'Oh, yes, really dotty. He has got a studio full of pictures that he will never show to anyone.'

I asked: 'What pictures? His own pictures?'

'Yes, his own pictures. They're damn good, they say.' . . . Verhausen had started out by being a Prix de Rome and he had had a big reputation in Holland and Germany, once upon a time. He was a Fleming. But the old fellow now refused to exhibit, and went nearly mad with anger if he were pressed to sell anything.

'A pose?'

My friend said: 'Well, I dunno. It's lasted a long time for a pose.'

He started to laugh.

'You know Van Hoyt. He knew Verhausen intimately in Antwerp, years ago. It seems he already hid his pictures up then . . . He had evolved the idea that it was sacriledge to sell them. Then he married some young and flighty woman from Brussels, and she would not stand it. She nagged and nagged: she wanted lots of money and so on and so on. He did not listen even. So she gave up arguing and made arrangements with a Jew dealer from Amsterdam when he was not there. It is said that she broke into his studio and passed the pictures out of the window. Five of the best. Van Hoyt said that Verhausen cried like a baby when he knew. He simply sat and sobbed. Perhaps he also beat the lady. In any case she left him soon afterwards and eventually Verhausen turned up, here, in Montparnasse. The woman now with him he had picked up in some awful brothel in Antwerp. She must have been good to him, for he says now that the Fallen are the only women with souls. They will walk on the necks of all the others in Heaven . . . ' And my friend concluded: 'A rum old bird. But a bit of a back number, now, of course.'

I said: 'It's a perverted form of miserliness, I suppose. I should like to see his pictures, or is that impossible? I like his face.'

7   See the second note to this story.

TEA
This story was published for the first time time in Jean Rhys's earliest book, *The Left Bank and Other Stories* (London: Jonathan Cape, 1927).

My friend said carelessly : 'It's possible, I believe. He sometimes shows them to people. It's only that he will not exhibit and will not sell. I dare say Van Hoyt could fix it up.'

Verhausen's studio was in the real Latin Quarter which lies to the north of the Montparnasse district and is shabbier and not cosmopolitan yet. It was an ancient, narrow street of uneven houses, a dirty, beautiful street, full of mauve shadows. A policeman stood limply near the house, his expression that of contemplative stupefaction: a yellow dog lay stretched philosophically on the cobblestones of the roadway. The concierge said without interest that Monsieur Verhausen's studio was on the quatrième à droite. I toiled upwards.

I knocked three times. There was a subdued rustling within... A fourth time: as loudly as I could. The door opened a little and Mr Verhausen's head appeared in the opening. I read suspicion in his eyes and I smiled as disarmingly as I could. I said something about Mr Van Hoyt – his own kind invitation, my great pleasure.

Verhausen continued to scrutinize me through huge spectacles: then he smiled with a sudden irradiation, stood away from the door and bowing deeply, invited me to enter. The room was big, all its walls encumbered on the floor with unframed canvases, all turned with their backs to the wall. It was very much cleaner than I had expected: quite clean and even dustless. On a table was spread a white cloth and there were blue cups and saucers and a plate of gingerbread cut into slices and thickly buttered. Mr Verhausen rubbed his hands and said with a pleased, childlike expression and in astonishingly good English that he had prepared an English tea that was quite ready because he had expected me sooner.

We sat on straight-backed chairs and sipped solemnly.

Mr Verhausen looked exactly as he had looked in the café, his blue eyes behind the spectacles at once naïve and wise, his waistcoat spotted with reminiscences of many meals.

But a delightful personality – comfortable and comforting. His long, curved pipes hung in a row on the wall; they made the whole room look Dutchly homely. We discussed Montparnasse with gravity.

He said suddenly: 'Now you have drunk your second cup of tea you shall see my pictures. Two cups of tea all English must have before they contemplate works of art.'

He had jumped up with a lightness surprising in a bulky man and with similar alacrity drew an easel near a window and proceeded to put pictures on it without any comment. They were successive outbursts of colour: it took me a little time to get used to them. I imagine that they were mostly, but not all, impressionist. But what fascinated me at first was his way of touching the canvases – his loving, careful hands.

After a time he seemed to forget that I was there and looked at them himself, anxiously and critically, his head on one side, frowning and muttering to himself in Flemish. A landscape pleased me here and there: they were mostly rough and brilliant. But the heads were very minutely painted and... Dutch! A woman stepping into a tub of water under a shaft of light had her skin turned to gold.

Then he produced a larger canvas, changed the position of the easel and turned to me with a little grunt. I said slowly: 'I think that is a great picture. Great art!'

...A girl seated on a sofa in a room with many mirrors held a glass of green liqueur. Dark-eyed, heavy-faced, with big, sturdy peasant's limbs, she was entirely destitute of lightness or grace.

But all the poisonous charm of the life beyond the pale was in her pose, and in her smouldering eyes – all its deadly bitterness and fatigue in her fixed smile.

He received my compliments with pleasure, but with the quite superficial pleasure of the artist who is supremely indifferent to the opinion that other people may have about his work. And, just as I was telling him that the picture reminded me of a portrait of Manet's[1], the original came in from outside, carrying a string bag full of greengroceries. Mr Verhausen started a little when he saw her and rubbed his hands again – apologetically this time. He said: 'This, Madame, is my little Marthe. Mademoiselle Marthe Baesen.'

[1]   Eduard Manet (1832–83), famous French painter.

She greeted me with reserve and glanced at the picture on the easel with an inscrutable face. I said to her: 'I have been admiring Mr Verhausen's work.'

She said: 'Yes, Madame?' with the inflexion of a question and left the room with her string bag.

The old man said to me: 'Marthe speaks no English and French very badly. She is a true Fleming. Besides, she is not used to visitors.'

There was a feeling of antagonism in the studio now. Mr Verhausen fidgeted and sighed restlessly. I said, rather with hesitation: 'Mr Verhausen, is it true that you object to exhibiting and to selling your pictures?'

He looked at me over his spectacles, and the suspicious look, the look of an old Jew when counting his money, came again into his eyes.

'Object, Madame? I object to nothing. I am an artist. But I do not wish to sell my pictures. And, as I do not wish to sell them, exhibiting is useless. My pictures are precious to me. They are precious, most probably, to no one else.'

He chuckled and added with a glint of malice in his eyes: 'When I am dead Marthe will try to sell them and not succeed, probably. I am forgotten now. Then she will burn them. She dislikes rubbish, the good Marthe.'

Marthe re-entered the room as he said this. Her face was unpowdered but nearly unwrinkled, her eyes were clear with the shrewd, limited expression of the careful housewife – the look of small horizons and quick, hard judgements. Without the flame his genius had seen in her and had fixed for ever, she was heavy, placid and uninteresting – at any rate to me.

She said, in bad French: 'I have bought two artichokes for...' I did not catch how many sous. He looked pleased and greedy.

In the street the yellow dog and the policeman had vanished. The café opposite the door had come alive and its gramophone informed the world that:

> Souvent femme varie
> Bien fol est qui s'y fie![2]

It was astonishing how the figure of the girl on the sofa stayed in my mind: it blended with the coming night, the scent of Paris and the hard blare of the gramophone. And I said to myself: 'Is it possible that all that charm, such as it was, is gone?'

And then I remembered the way in which she had touched his cheek with her big hands. There was in that movement knowledge, and a certain sureness: as it were the ghost of a time when her business in life had been the consoling of men.

Mixing Cocktails (1927)

The house in the hills was very new and very ugly, long and narrow, of unpainted wood, perched oddly on high posts, I think as a protection from wood ants. There were six rooms with a veranda that ran the whole length of the house... But when you went up there, there was always the same sensation of relief and coolness – in the ugly house with the beginnings of a rose garden, after an hour's journey by boat and another hour and a half on horse-back, climbing slowly up...

On the veranda, upon a wooden table with four stout legs, stood an enormous brass telescope. With it you spied out the steamers passing: the French mail on its way to Guadeloupe, the Canadian, the Royal Mail, which should have been stately and was actually the shabbiest of the lot... Or an exciting stranger!

---

[2] A two-line adage attributed to François I (1494–1547), king of France; it means: "Women often change / Quite mad is anyone who trusts them."

MIXING COCKTAILS
This story was published for the first time time in Jean Rhys's earliest book, *The Left Bank and Other Stories* (London: Jonathan Cape, 1927).

At night one gazed through it at the stars and pretended to be interested... 'That's Venus... Oh, is that Venus, .. And that's the Southern Cross...' An unloaded shotgun leant up in one corner; there were always plenty of straw rocking-chairs and a canvas hammock with many cushions.

From the veranda one looked down the green valley sloping to the sea, but from the other side of the house one could only see the mountains, lovely but melancholy as mountains always are to a child.

Lying in the hammock, swinging cautiously for the ropes creaked, one dreamt... The morning dream was the best – very early, before the sun was properly up. The sea was then a very tender blue, like the dress of the Virgin Mary, and on it were little white triangles. The fishing boats.

A very short dream, the morning dream – mostly about what one would do with the endless blue day. One would bathe in the pool: perhaps one would find treasure... Morgan's Treasure.[1] For who does not know that, just before he was captured and I think hung at Kingston, Jamaica, Morgan buried his treasure in the Dominican mountains... A wild place, Dominica. Savage and lost. Just the place for Morgan to hide his treasure in.

It was very difficult to look at the sea in the middle of the day. The light made it so flash and glitter: it was necessary to screw the eyes up tight before looking. Everything was still and languid, worshipping the sun.

The midday dream was languid too – vague, tinged with melancholy as one stared at the hard, blue, blue sky. It was sure to be interrupted by someone calling to one to come in out of the sun. One was not to sit in the sun. One had been told not to be in the sun... One would one day regret freckles.

So the late afternoon was the best time on the veranda, but it was spoiled for all the rest were there...

So soon does one learn the bitter lesson that humanity is never content just to differ from you and let it go at that. Never. They must interfere, actively and grimly, between your thoughts and yourself – with the passionate wish to level up everything and everybody.

I am speaking to you; do you not hear? You must break yourself of your habit of never listening. You have such an absent-minded expression. Try not to look vague...

So rude!

The English aunt gazes and exclaims at intervals: 'The colours... How exquisite!... Extraordinary that so few people should visit the West Indies... That *sea*... Could anything be more lovely?'

It is a purple sea with a sky to match it. The Caribbean. The deepest, the loveliest in the world...

Sleepily but tactfully, for she knows it delights my father, she admires the roses, the hibiscus, the humming birds. Then she starts to nod. She is always falling asleep, at the oddest moments. It is the unaccustomed heat.

I should like to laugh at her, but I am a well-behaved little girl... Too well-behaved... I long to be like Other People! The extraordinary, ungetatable, oddly cruel Other People, with their way of wantonly hurting and then accusing you of being thin-skinned, sulky, vindictive or ridiculous All because a hurt and puzzled little girl has retired into her shell.

The afternoon dream is a materialistic one... It is of the dayswhen one shall be plump and beautiful instead of pale and thin: perfectly behaved instead of awkward... When one will wear sweeping dresses and feathered hats and put gloves on with ease and delight... And of course, of one's marriage: the dark moustache and perfectly creased trousers... Vague, that.

The veranda gets dark very quickly. The sun sets: at once night and the fireflies.

---

[1] Henry Morgan (1635–88), a legendary pirate of the Caribbean; he was knighted and was not "hung at Kingston"; but he became a favorite subject of pirate stories, which, like children's memories, are not especially concerned with historical accuracy.

A warm, velvety, sweet-smelling night, but frightening and disturbing if one is alone in the hammock. Ann Twist, our cook, the old obeah woman[2] has told me: 'You all must'n look too much at de moon ...'

If you fall asleep in the moonlight you are bewitched, it seems ... the moon does bad things to you if it shines on you when you sleep. Repeated often ...

So, shivering a little, I go into the room for the comfort of my father working out his chess problem from the *Times Weekly Edition*. Then comes my nightly duty mixing cocktails.

In spite of my absentmindedness I mix cocktails very well and swizzle them better (our cocktails, in the West Indies, are drunk frothing, and the instrument with which one froths them is called a swizzle-stick) than anyone else in the house.

I measure out angostura[3] and gin, feeling important and happy, with an uncanny intuition as to how strong I must make each separate drink.

Here then is something I can do ... Action, they say, is more worthy than dreaming ...

Again the Antilles (1927)

The editor of the *Dominica Herald and Leeward Islands Gazette* lived in a tall, white house with green Venetian blinds which overlooked our garden. I used often to see him looking solemnly out of his windows and would gaze solemnly back, for I thought him a very awe-inspiring person.

He wore gold-rimmed spectacles and dark clothes always – not for him the frivolity of white linen even on the hottest day – a stout little man of a beautiful shade of coffee-colour, he was known throughout the Island as Papa Dom.

A born rebel, this editor: a firebrand. He hated the white people, not being quite white, and he despised the black ones, not being quite black ... 'Coloured' we West Indians call the intermediate shades, and I used to think that being coloured embittered him.

He was against the Government, against the English, against the Island's being a Crown Colony and the Town Board's new system of drainage. He was also against the Mob, against the gay and easy morality of the negroes and 'the hordes of priests and nuns that overrun our unhappy Island', against the existence of the Anglican bishop and the Catholic bishop's new palace.

He wrote seething articles against that palace which was then being built, partly by voluntary labour – until, one night his house was besieged by a large mob of the faithful, throwing stones and howling for his blood. He appeared on his veranda, frightened to death. In the next issue of his paper he wrote a long account of the 'riot': according to him it had been led by several well-known Magdalenes, then, as always, the most ardent supporters of Christianity.

After that, though, he let the Church severely alone, acknowledging that it was too strong for him.

I cannot imagine what started the quarrel between himself and Mr Hugh Musgrave.

Mr Hugh Musgrave I regarded as a dear, but peppery. Twenty years of the tropics and much indulgence in spices and cocktails does have that effect. He owned a big estate, just outside the town of Roseau, cultivated limes and sugar canes and employed a great deal of labour, but he was certainly neither ferocious nor tyrannical.

Suddenly, however, there was the feud in full swing.

There was in the *Dominica Herald and Leeward Islands Gazette* a column given up to letters from readers and, in this column, writing under the pseudonyms of Pro Patria, Indignant, Liberty and Uncle Tom's Cabin, Papa Dom let himself go. He said what he thought about Mr Musgrave and

---

[2] A kind of witchcraft practiced by some people in the West Indies.

[3] Angostura Bitters, a brand name, is a bitter tonic prepared from various barks and roots, used as flavoring in certain alcoholic drinks. It was first created in 1824.

AGAIN
This story was published for the first time time in Jean Rhys's earliest book, *The Left Bank and Other Stories* (London: Jonathan Cape, 1927).

Mr Musgrave replied: briefly and sternly as befits an Englishman of the governing class . . . Still he replied.

It was most undignified, but the whole Island was hugely delighted. Never had the *Herald* had such a sale.

Then Mr Musgrave committed, according to Papa Dom, some specially atrocious act of tyranny. Perhaps he put a fence up where he should not have, or overpaid an unpopular overseer or supported the wrong party on the Town Board . . . At any rate Papa Dom wrote in the next issue of the paper this passionate and unforgettable letter:

'It is a saddening and a dismal sight,' it ended, 'to contemplate the degeneracy of a stock. How far is such a man removed from the ideals of true gentility, from the beautiful description of a contemporary, possibly, though not certainly, the Marquis of Montrose, left us by Shakespeare, the divine poet and genius.

> 'He was a very gentle, perfect knight . . .'

Mr Musgrave took his opportunity:

'DEAR SIR,' he wrote

'I never read your abominable paper. But my attention has been called to a scurrilous letter about myself which you published last week. The lines quoted were written, not by Shakespeare but by Chaucer, though you cannot of course be expected to know that, and run'

> He never yet no vilonye had sayde
> In al his lyf, unto no manner of wight –
> He was a verray parfit, gentil knyght.[1]

'It is indeed a saddening and a dismal thing that the names of great Englishmen should be thus taken in vain by the ignorant of another race and colour.'

Mr Musgrave had really written 'damn niggers'.

Papa Dom was by no means crushed. Next week he replied with dignity as follows:

'My attention has been called to your characteristic letter. I accept your correction though I understand that in the mind of the best authorities there are grave doubts, very grave doubts indeed, as to the authorship of the lines, and indeed the other works of the immortal Swan of Avon. However, as I do not write with works of reference in front of me, as you most certainly do, I will not dispute the point.

'The conduct of an English gentleman who stoops to acts of tyranny and abuse cannot be described as gentle or perfect. I fail to see that it matters whether it is Shakespeare, Chaucer or the Marquis of Montrose who administers from down the ages the much-needed reminder and rebuke.'

I wonder if I shall ever again read the *Dominica Herald and Leeward Islands Gazette.*

---

[1]   Lines 70–1 of the "General Prologue" to the *Canterbury Tales* by Geoffrey Chaucer (c. 1343–1400).

Elizabeth Bowen (1899–1973)

Introduction

Elizabeth Bowen (1899–1973) was born to Henry Cole Bowen and and Florence Colley Brown. Though born in Dublin, her family home was Bowen's Court, near Kildorrey in County Cork, Ireland. Because of her father's law practice, her family divided their time between Dublin and Bowen's Court. In 1905 her father suffered a nervous breakdown and during the following few years was hospitalized on and off. Following the advice of his physician, Elizabeth and her mother moved to England to stay with various aunts. Bowen developed a stammer which stayed with her for the rest of her life. Though her father recovered when Bowen was 12, her mother died before the family could be reunited, and it was arranged for Bowen to attend a boarding school, Downe House, in Kent, where she stayed from 1914 to 1917.

In 1918 Bowen took up study at the London County Council School of Art, but withdrew after two terms, convinced that her talents were limited. She resolved to set out on a literary career; Rose Macaulay, a friend of the headmistress of Downe House, gave her guidance and introduced her to editors, publishers, and others who could help her. Her first volume of short stories, *Encounters*, was published in 1923 (see pp. 961–4 in this edition for one story from that collection). That same year she also married Alan Charles Cameron, a gay man who was an assistant secretary for education in Northampton. When he was promoted to Secretary of Education for the city of Oxford, they moved there, and Bowen soon relished the city's intellectual atmos-

phere. Her second volume of short stories appeared in 1926, *Ann Lee's and Other Stories*, followed the next year by her first novel, *The Hotel*. Two years after that she published *The Last September* (1929), a sharply perceived comedy of manners set in the time of the Irish Troubles. During the Oxford years she would publish two more collections of short fiction and three novels: *Friends and Relations* (1931), *To the North* (1932), and *The House in Paris* (1935).

In 1935 Bowen and Cameron moved to Regent's Park in London, and Bowen now began to review on a regular basis for the *Tatler*. Three years later she published her sixth novel, *The Death of the Heart* (1938), a story of adolescent love in London during the thirties and, for some of Bowen's admirers, her masterpiece. When the war broke out, she became an Air Raid Precautions warden; she began working on her next novel, set in London during the Blitz, but put it aside to write a collection of short fiction also grounded in her wartime experiences, *The Demon Lover and Other Stories* (1945; for stories from this volume see pp. 985–1006 in this edition). Four years later she completed and published the novel which she had put aside back in 1942, her seventh novel, *The Heat of the Day*, a modernist work that uses the trappings of a spy novel and a love triangle to explore the effects of the war through a fractured style that is close to perfect. After the war she published three more novels: *A World of Love* (1955), *The Little Girls* (1964), and *Eva Trout*. She died in 1973.

Coming Home (1923)

All the way home from school Rosalind's cheeks burnt, she felt something throbbing in her ears. It was sometimes terrible to live so far away. Before her body had turned the first corner her mind had many times wrenched open their gate, many times rushed up their path through the damp smells of the garden, waving the essay-book, and seen Darlingest coming to the window. Nothing like this had ever happened before to either her or Darlingest; it was the supreme moment that all these years they had been approaching, of which those dim, improbable future years would be spent in retrospect.

Rosalind's essay had been read aloud and everybody had praised it. Everybody had been there, the big girls sitting along the sides of the room had turned and looked at her, raising their eyebrows and smiling. For an infinity of time the room had held nothing but the rising and falling of Miss Wilfred's beautiful voice doing the service of Rosalind's brain. When the voice dropped to silence

---

"Coming Home" appeared in Elizabeth Bowen's first book, a collection of short stories titled *Encounters* (London: Sidgwick and Jackson, 1923).

and the room was once more unbearably crowded, Rosalind had looked at the clock and seen that her essay had taken four and a half minutes to read. She found that her mouth was dry and her eyes ached from staring at a small fixed spot in the heart of whirling circles, and her knotted hands were damp and trembling. Somebody behind her gently poked the small of her back. Everybody in the room was thinking about Rosalind; she felt their admiration and attention lapping up against her in small waves. A long way off somebody spoke her name repeatedly, she stood up stupidly and everybody laughed. Miss Wilfred was trying to pass her back the red exercise book. Rosalind sat down thinking to herself how dazed she was, dazed with glory. She was beginning already to feel about for words for Darlingest.

She had understood some time ago that nothing became real for her until she had had time to live it over again. An actual occurrence was nothing but the blankness of a shock, then the knowledge that something had happened; afterwards one could creep back and look into one's mind and find new things in it, clear and solid. It was like waiting outside the hen-house till the hen came off the nest and then going in to look for the egg. She would not touch this egg until she was with Darlingest, then they would go and look for it together. Suddenly and vividly this afternoon would be real for her. 'I won't think about it yet,' she said, 'for fear I'd spoil it.'

The houses grew scarcer and the roads greener, and Rosalind relaxed a little; she was nearly home. She looked at the syringa bushes by the gate, and it was as if a cold wing had brushed against her. Supposing Darlingest were out ... ?

She slowed down her running steps to a walk. From here she would be able to call to Darlingest. But if she didn't answer there would be still a tortuous hope; she might be at the back of the house. She decided to pretend it didn't matter, one way or the other; she had done this before, and it rather took the wind out of Somebody's sails, she felt. She hitched up her essay-book under her arm, approached the gate, turned carefully to shut it, and walked slowly up the path looking carefully down at her feet, not up at all at the drawing-room window. Darlingest would think she was playing a game. Why didn't she hear her tapping on the glass with her thimble?

As soon as she entered the hall she knew that the house was empty. Clocks ticked very loudly; upstairs and downstairs the doors were a little open, letting through pale strips of light. Only the kitchen door was shut, down the end of the passage, and she could hear Emma moving about behind it. There was a spectral shimmer of light in the white panelling. On the table was a bowl of primroses, Darlingest must have put them there that morning. The hall was chilly; she could not think why the primroses gave her such a feeling of horror, then she remembered the wreath of primroses, and the scent of it, lying on the raw new earth of that grave ... The pair of grey gloves were gone from the bowl of visiting-cards. Darlingest had spent the morning doing those deathly primroses, and then taken up her grey gloves and gone out, at the end of the afternoon, just when she knew her little girl would be coming in. A quarter-past four. It was unforgivable of Darlingest: she had been a mother for more than twelve years, the mother exclusively of Rosalind, and still, it seemed, she knew no better than to do a thing like that. Other people's mothers had terrible little babies: they ran quickly in and out to go to them, or they had smoky husbands who came in and sat, with big feet. There was something distracted about other people's mothers. But Darlingest, so exclusively one's own ...

Darlingest could never have really believed in her. She could never have really believed that Rosalind would do anything wonderful at school, or she would have been more careful to be in to hear about it. Rosalind flung herself into the drawing-room; it was honey-coloured and lovely in the pale spring light, another little clock was ticking in the corner, there were more bowls of primroses and black-eyed, lowering anemones. The tarnished mirror on the wall distorted and reproved her angry face in its mild mauveness. Tea was spread on the table by the window, tea for two that the two might never ... Her work and an open book lay on the tumbled cushions of the window-seat. All the afternoon she had sat there waiting and working, and now – poor little Darlingest, perhaps she had gone out because she was lonely.

People who went out sometimes never came back again. Here she was, being angry with Darlingest, and all the time ... Well, she had drawn on those grey gloves and gone out wandering along the roads, vague and beautiful, because she was lonely, and then?

Ask Emma? No, she wouldn't; fancy having to ask *her*!

'Yes, your mother'll be in soon, Miss Rosie. Now run and get your things off, there's a good girl –'
Oh no, intolerable.

The whole house was full of the scent and horror of the primroses. Rosalind dropped the exercise-book on the floor, looked at it, hesitated, and putting her hands over her mouth, went upstairs, choking back her sobs. She heard the handle of the kitchen door turn; Emma was coming out. O God! Now she was on the floor by Darlingest's bed, with the branches swaying and brushing outside the window, smothering her face in the eiderdown, smelling and tasting the wet satin. Down in the hall she heard Emma call her, mutter something, and slam back into the kitchen.

How could she ever have left Darlingest? She might have known, she might have known. The sense of insecurity had been growing on her year by year. A person might be part of you, almost part of your body, and yet once you went away from them they might utterly cease to be. That sea of horror ebbing and flowing round the edges of the world, whose tides were charted in the newspapers, might sweep out a long wave over them and they would be gone. There was no security. Safety and happiness were a game that grown-up people played with children to keep them from understanding, possibly to keep themselves from thinking. But they did think, that was what made grown-up people – queer. Anything might happen, there was no security. And now Darlingest—

This was her dressing-table, with the long beads straggling over it, the little coloured glass barrels and bottles had bright flames in the centre. In front of the looking-glass, filmed faintly over with a cloud of powder, Darlingest had put her hat on – for the last time. Supposing all that had ever been reflected in it were imprisoned somewhere in the back of a looking-glass. The blue hat with the drooping brim was hanging over the corner of a chair. Rosalind had never been kind about that blue hat, she didn't think it was becoming. And Darlingest had loved it so. She must have gone out wearing the brown one; Rosalind went over to the wardrobe and stood on tip-toe to look on the top shelf. Yes, the brown hat was gone. She would never see Darlingest again, in the brown hat, coming down the road to meet her and not seeing her because she was thinking about something else. Peau d'Espagne crept faintly from among the folds of the dresses; the blue, the gold, the soft furred edges of the tea-gown dripping out of the wardrobe. She heard herself making a high, whining noise at the back of her throat, like a puppy, felt her swollen face distorted by another paroxysm.

'I can't bear it, I can't bear it. What have I done? I did love her, I did so awfully love her.

'Perhaps she was all right when I came in; coming home smiling. Then I stopped loving her, I hated her and was angry. And it happened. She was crossing a road and something happened to her. I was angry and she died. I killed her.

'I don't know that she's dead. I'd better get used to believing it, it will hurt less afterwards. Supposing she does come back this time; it's only for a little. I shall never be able to keep her; now I've found out about this I shall never be happy. Life's nothing but waiting for awfulness to happen and trying to think about something else.

'If she could come back just this once – Darlingest.'

Emma came half-way upstairs; Rosalind flattened herself behind the door.

'Will you begin your tea, Miss Rosie?'

'No. Where's mother?'

'I didn't hear her go out. I have the kettle boiling – will I make your tea?'

'No. *No*.'

Rosalind slammed the door on the angry mutterings, and heard with a sense of desolation Emma go downstairs. The silver clock by Darlingest's bed ticked; it was five o'clock. They had tea at a quarter-past four; Darlingest was never, never late. When they came to tell her about *It*, men would come, and they would tell Emma, and Emma would come up with a frightened, triumphant face and tell her.

She saw the grey-gloved hands spread out in the dust.

A sound at the gate. 'I can't bear it, I can't bear it. Oh, save me, God!'

Steps on the gravel.

Darlingest.

She was at the window, pressing her speechless lips together.

Darlingest came slowly up the path with the long ends of her veil, untied, hanging over her shoulders. A paper parcel was pressed between her arm and her side. She paused, stood smiling down at the daffodils. Then she looked up with a start at the windows, as though she heard somebody calling. Rosalind drew back into the room.

She heard her mother's footsteps cross the stone floor of the hall, hesitate at the door of the drawing-room, and come over to the foot of the stairs. The voice was calling 'Lindie! Lindie, duckie!' She was coming upstairs.

Rosalind leaned the weight of her body against the dressing-table and dabbed her face with the big powder-puff; the powder clung in paste to her wet lashes and in patches over her nose and cheeks. She was not happy, she was not relieved, she felt no particular feeling about Darlingest, did not even want to see her. Something had slackened down inside her, leaving her a little sick.

'Oh, you're *there*,' said Darlingest from outside, hearing her movements. 'Where did, where were –?'

She was standing in the doorway. Nothing had been for the last time, after all. She had come back. One could never explain to her how wrong she had been. She was holding out her arms; something drew one towards them.

'But, my little *Clown*,' said Darlingest, wiping off the powder. 'But, oh –' She scanned the glazed, blurred face. 'Tell me why,' she said.

'You were late.'

'Yes, it was horrid of me; did you mind? . . . But that was silly, Rosalind; I can't be always in.'

'But you're my mother.'

Darlingest was amused; little trickles of laughter and gratification ran out of her. 'You weren't *frightened*, Silly Billy.' Her tone changed to distress. 'Oh, Rosalind, don't be cross.'

'I'm not,' said Rosalind coldly.

'Then come –'

'I was wanting my tea.'

'Rosalind, *don't* be –'

Rosalind walked past her to the door. She was hurting Darlingest, beautifully hurting her. She would never tell her about that essay. Everybody would be talking about it, and when Darlingest heard and asked her about it she would say: 'Oh, that? I didn't think you'd be interested.' That would hurt. She went down into the drawing-room, past the primroses. The grey gloves were back on the table. This was the mauve and golden room that Darlingest had come back to, from under the Shadow of Death, expecting to find her little daughter . . . They would have sat together on the window-seat while Rosalind read the essay aloud, leaning their heads closer together as the room grew darker.

That was all spoilt.

Poor Darlingest, up there alone in the bedroom, puzzled, hurt, disappointed, taking off her hat. She hadn't known she was going to be hurt like this when she stood out there on the gravel, smiling at the daffodils. The red essay-book lay spread open on the carpet. There was the paper bag she had been carrying, lying on a table by the door; macaroons, all squashy from being carried the wrong way, disgorging, through a tear in the paper, a little trickle of crumbs.

The pathos of the forgotten macaroons, the silent pain! Rosalind ran upstairs to the bedroom.

Darlingest did not hear her; she had forgotten. She was standing in the middle of the room with her face turned towards the window, looking at something a long way away, smiling and singing to herself and rolling up her veil.

Foothold (1929)

'Morning!' exclaimed Gerard, standing before the sideboard, napkin under his arm. 'Sleep well? There are kidneys here, haddock; if you prefer it, ham and boiled eggs – I don't *see* any boiled eggs but I suppose they are coming in – did you see Clara?'

"Foothold" was first published in a collection of short stories by Elizabeth Bowen, titled *Joining Charles, and Other Stories* (London: Constable, 1929).

Thomas came rather dazedly round the breakfast table.

'He's hardly awake,' said Janet. 'Don't shout at him, Gerard – Good morning, Thomas – let him sit down and think.'

'*Are* the boiled eggs——?' cried Gerard.

'Yes, of course they are. Can you possibly bear to wait?' she added, turning to Thomas. 'We are very virile at breakfast.'

Thomas smiled. He took out his horn-rimmed glasses, polished them, looked round the dining-room. Janet did things imaginatively; a subdued, not too buoyant prettiness had been superimposed on last night's sombre effect; a honey-coloured Italian table-cloth on the mahogany, vase of brown marigolds, breakfast-china about the age of the house with a red rim and scattered gold pimpernels. The firelight pleasantly jiggled, catching the glaze of dishes and coffee-pot, the copper feet of the 'sluggards' joy'.[1] The square high room had, like Janet, a certain grace of proportion.

'I'm glad you don't have blue at breakfast,' said Thomas, unfolding his napkin. 'I do hate blue.'

'Did he see Clara?' asked Gerard, clattering the dish-lids. 'Do find out if he saw Clara!'

Janet was looking through a pile of letters. She took up each envelope, slit it open, glanced at the contents and slipped them inside again unread. This did not suggest indifference; the more she seemed to like the look of a letter the more quickly she put it away. She had put on shell-rimmed spectacles for reading, which completed a curious similarity between her face and Thomas's; both sensitive and untroubled, with the soft lines of easy living covering over the harder young lines of eagerness, self-distrust and a capacity for pain. When Gerard clamoured she raised her shoulders gently. 'Well, did you?' she said at last, without looking up from her letters.

'I'm afraid Clara's been encouraged away,' said Thomas. 'I specially left out some things I thought might intrigue her; a letter from Antonia, a daguerreotype of my grandmother I brought down to show you, rather a good new shirt – lavender-coloured. Then I lay awake some time waiting for her, but your beds are too comfortable. I had – disappointingly – the perfect night! Yet all through it I never quite forgot; it was like expecting a telephone call.'

'If you'd been half a man,' said Gerard, 'and Clara'd been half a ghost, you'd have come down this morning shaking all over with hair bright white, demanding to be sent to the first train.'

Janet, sitting tall and reposeful, swept her letters together with a movement and seemed faintly clouded. 'Well, I'm very glad Thomas isn't trying to go – tell me, why should Antonia's letters intrigue her? You complained they were rather dull. *I* find them dull, but then she isn't a woman's woman.'

'I just thought the signature ought to suggest an affinity. Names, you know. Meredith . . . Don't be discouraged, Gerard; I'm no sort of a test. I've slept in all sorts of places. There seems to be some sort of extra thick coating between me and anything other than fleshly.'

'*I've* never met her,' said Gerard, 'but then I'm a coarse man and Clara's essentially feminine. Perhaps something may happen this evening. Try going to bed earlier – it was half-past one when we were putting the lights out. Clara keeps early hours.'

'Have you noticed,' Janet said composedly, 'that one may discuss ghosts quite intelligently, but never any particular ghost without being facetious?'

'– Forgive my being so purely carnal,' exclaimed Thomas suddenly, 'but this is the most excellent marmalade. Not gelatinous, not slimy. I never get quite the right kind. Does your cook make it?'

He had noticed that here was 'a sensitiveness'. Thomas proceeded conversationally like the impeccable dentist with an infinitesimally fine instrument, choosing his area, tapping within it nearer and nearer, withdrawing at a suggestion before there had been time for a wince. He specialized in a particular kind of friendship with that eight-limbed, inscrutable, treacherous creature, the happily-married couple; adapting himself closely and lightly to the composite personality. An indifference to, an apparent unconsciousness of, life in some aspects armoured him against embarrassments. As Janet said, he would follow one into one's bedroom without

---

[1] A brand or pet name for the coffee pot; coffee pots at this time were frequently made of pewter, the metal thought least apt to taint the taste; but since pewter is very soft and supports little weight, the pots had feet of copper for support and to prevent their spoiling polished wood.

noticing. Yet the too obvious 'tact', she said, *was* the literal word for his quality. Thomas was all finger-tips.

Janet slid her chair back noiselessly on the carpet and turned half round to face the fire. 'You're so nice and greedy,' she said, 'I do love having our food appreciated.'

'*I* appreciate it,' said Gerard. 'You know how I always hate staying away with people. I suppose I am absolutely smug. Now that we've come to this house I hate more than ever going up to the office.' He got up and stood, tall and broad, looking out of the window. Beyond, between the heavy fall of the curtains, showed the cold garden; the clipped shrubs like patterns in metal, the path going off in a formal perspective to the ascent of some balustraded steps. Beyond the terrace, a parade of trees on a not very remote skyline, the still, cold, evenly-clouded sky.

A few minutes afterwards he reluctantly left them. Janet and Thomas stood at the door and, as the car disappeared at the turn of the drive, Gerard waved goodbye with a backward scoop of the hand. Then they came in again to the fire and Thomas finished his coffee. He observed, 'The room seems a good deal smaller. Do you notice that rooms are adaptable?'

'I do feel the house has grown since we've been in it. The rooms seem to take so much longer to get across. I'd no idea we were buying such a large one. I wanted it because it was white, and late Georgian houses are unexigeant, but I promised myself – and everyone else – it was small.'

'Had you been counting on Clara, or didn't you know?'

'I was rather surprised. I met her coming out of your room about four o'clock one afternoon in November. Like an idiot I went downstairs and told Gerard.'

'Oh – why like an idiot?'

'He came dashing up, very excited – I suppose it was rather exciting – and I came after him. We went into all the rooms, flinging the doors open as quietly and suddenly as we could; we even looked into the cupboards, though she is the last person one could imagine walking into a cupboard. The stupid thing was that I hadn't looked round to see which way she had gone. Gerard was perfectly certain there must be some catch about that chain of doors going through from my room to his and from his down the steps to the landing where there is a bathroom. He kept saying, "You go round one way and I'll go the other." While we'd been simply playing the fool I didn't mind, but when he began to be rational I began to be angry and – well, ashamed. I said: "If she's . . . not like us . . . you know perfectly well we can't corner her, and if she should be, we're being simply eccentric and rude." He said "Yes, that's all very well, but I'm not going to have that damned woman going in and out of my dressing-room," and I (thinking "Supposing she really is a damned woman?") said "Don't be so silly, she wouldn't be bothered – why should she?" Then the wind went out of our sails altogether. Gerard went downstairs whistling; we had tea rather irritably – didn't say very much and didn't look at each other. We didn't mention Clara again.'

'*Is* she often about?'

'Yes – no – I don't know . . . I really *don't* know, Thomas. I am wishing so much, you see, that I'd never begun her – let her in. Gerard takes things up so fearfully. I know last night when he took that second whisky and put more logs on we would be coming to Clara.'

'Ah,' said Thomas. 'Really. *That* was what you were waiting for . . .'

'– The sun's trying to come out!' exclaimed Janet. She got up and pushed the curtains further apart. 'In an hour or so when I've finished my house things we'll go round the garden. I do like having a garden you haven't seen. We're making two herbaceous borders down to the beech hedge away from the library window. I do think one needs perspective from a library window; it carries on the lines of the shelves.'

'Precious, I think,' said Thomas, 'distinctly precious.'

'Yes, I've always wanted to be . . . The papers are in the library.'

Thomas gathered from headlines and a half-column here and there that things were going on very much as he had expected. He felt remote from all this business of living; he was recently back from Spain. He took down Mabbe's *Celestina*[2] and presently pottered out into the hall with his

---

[2] James Mabbe translated *The Spanish Bawd, Represented in Celestina: or the Tragicke Comedy of Calisto and Milbea* (London: J. Beasle, 1631), a work by the Spanish author Fernando de Rojas (d. 1541).

thumb in the book, to wait for Janet. In the hall, he looked at his own reflection in two or three pieces of walnut and noticed a Famille Rose bowl, certainly new, that they must have forgotten last night when they were showing him those other acquisitions. He decided, treading a zig-pattern across them carefully, that the grey and white marble squares of the floor were *good*; he would have bought the house on the strength of them alone. He liked also – Janet was doubtful about it – Gerard's treatment of the square-panelled doors, leaf-green in their moulded white frames in the smooth white wall. The stairs, through a double-doorway, had light coming down them from some landing window like the cold interior light in a Flemish picture. Janet, pausing half way down to say something to someone above, stood there as if painted, distinct and unreal.

Janet had brought awareness of her surroundings to such a degree that she could seem unconscious up to the very last fraction of time before seeing one, then give the effect with a look that said 'Still there?' of having had one a long time 'placed' in her mind. He could not imagine her startled, or even looking at anything for the first time. Thinking of Clara's rare vantage point, in November, up by his bedroom door, he said to himself, 'I'd give a good deal to have been Clara, that afternoon.'

'If you don't really mind coming out,' said Janet, 'I should put on an overcoat.' As he still stood there vaguely she took the book gently away from him and put it down on a table.

'If *I* had a ghost,' said Thomas as she helped him into an overcoat, 'she should be called "Celestina". I like that better than Clara.'

'If I have another daughter,' said Janet agreeably, 'she shall be called Celestina.'

They walked briskly through the garden in thin sunshine. Thomas, who knew a good deal about gardens, became more direct, clipped in his speech and technical. They walked several times up and down the new borders, then away through an arch in the hedge and up some steps to the terrace for a general survey. 'Of course,' she said, 'one works here within limitations. There's a character to be kept – you feel that? One would have had greater scope with an older house or a newer house. All the time there's a point of view to be respected. One can't cut clear away on lines of one's own like at Three Beeches; one more or less modifies. But it contents me absolutely.'

'You ought to regret that other garden?'

'I don't, somehow. Of course, the place was quite perfect; it had that kind of limitation – it was too much our own. We felt "through with it". I had some qualms about leaving, beforehand; I suppose chiefly moral – you know, we do spoil ourselves! – but afterwards, as far as regret was concerned, never a pang. Also, practically speaking, of course the house *was* getting too small for us. Children at school get into a larger way of living; when they come home for the holidays—'

'I suppose,' said Thomas distastefully, 'they do take up rather a lot of room.'

She looked at him, laughing. 'Hard and unsympathetic!'

'Hard and unsympathetic,' accepted Thomas complacently. 'I don't see where they come in. I don't see the point of them; I think they spoil things. Frankly, Janet, I don't understand about people's children and frankly I'd rather not ... You and Gerard seem to slough your two off in a wonderful way. Do you miss them at all?'

'I suppose we—'

'*You*, in the singular, thou?'

'I suppose,' said Janet, 'one lives two lives, two states of life. In terms of time, one may live them alternately, but really the rough ends of one phase of one life (always broken off with a certain amount of disturbance) seem to dovetail into the beginning of the next phase of that same life, perhaps months afterwards, so that there never seems to have been a gap. And the same with the other life, waiting the whole time. I suppose the two run parallel.'

'Never meeting,' said Thomas comfortably. 'You see I'm on one and your children are on the other and I want to be quite sure. Promise me: *never* meeting?'

'I don't think ever. But you may be wise, all the same, not to come in the holidays.'

They hesitated a moment or two longer on the terrace as though there were more to be said and the place had in some way connected itself with the subject, then came down by the other steps and walked towards the dining-room windows, rather consciously, as though someone were looking out. She wore a leather coat, unbuttoned, falling away from her full straight graceful figure, and a lemon-and-apricot scarf flung round twice so that its fringes hung down on her breast and its folds were dinted in by the soft, still youthful line of her jaw. Academically, Thomas thought her the most attractive woman of his acquaintance: her bodily attraction was modified and her charm increased by the domination of her clear fastidious aloof mind over her body.

He saw her looking up at the house. 'I do certainly like your house,' he said. 'You've inhabited it to a degree I wouldn't have thought possible.'

'Thank you so much.'

'You're not – seriously, Janet – going to be worried by Clara?'

'My dear, no! She does at least help fill the place.'

'You're not finding it empty?'

'Not the house, exactly. It's not . . . ' They were walking up and down under the windows. Some unusual difficulty in her thoughts wrinkled her forehead and hardened her face. 'You know what I was saying after breakfast about the house having grown since we came in, the rooms stretching? Well, it's not that, but my life – *this* life – seems to have stretched somehow; there's more room in it. Yet it isn't that I've more time – that would be perfectly simple, I'd do more things. You know how rather odious I've always been about *désœuvrées* women; I've never been able to see how one's day could fail to be full up, it fills itself. There's been the house, the garden, friends, books, music, letters, the car, golf, when one felt like it, going up to town rather a lot. Well, I still have all these and there isn't a moment between them. Yet there's more and more room every day. I suppose it must be underneath.'

Thomas licked his upper lip thoughtfully. He suggested, 'Something spiritual, perhaps?' with detachment, diffidence and a certain respect.

'That's what anybody would say,' she agreed with equal detachment. 'It's just that I'm not comfortable; I always have been comfortable, so I don't like it.'

'It must be beastly,' said Thomas, concerned. 'You don't think it may just be perhaps a matter of not quite having settled down here?'

'Oh, I've settled down. Settled, I shouldn't be surprised to hear, for life. After all, Thomas, in eight years or so the children will, even from your point of view, really matter. They'll have all sorts of ideas and feelings; they'll be what's called "adult". There'll have to be a shifting of accents in this family.'

'When they come home for the holidays, what shall you do about Clara?'

'Nothing. Why should I? She won't matter. Not,' said Janet quickly, looking along the windows, 'that she matters particularly now.'

Thomas went up to his room about half-past three and, leaving the door open, changed his shoes thoughtfully after a walk. 'I cannot think,' he said to himself, 'why they keep dogs of that kind when exercising them ceases to be a matter of temperament and becomes a duty.' It was the only reflection possible upon the manner of living of Gerard and Janet. His nose and ears, nipped by the wind, thawed painfully in the even warmth of the house. Still with one shoe off he crossed the room on an impulse of sudden interest to study a print (some ruins in the heroic manner) and remained leaning before it in an attitude of reflection, his arms folded under him on the bow-fronted chest-of-drawers. The afternoon light came in through the big window, flooding him with security; he thought from the dogs to Gerard, from Gerard to Janet, whom he could hear moving about in her room with the door open, sliding a drawer softly open and shut. A pause in her movements – while she watched herself in the glass, perhaps, or simply stood looking critically about the room as he'd seen her do when she believed a room to be empty – then she came out, crossed her landing, came down the three steps to his passage and passed his door.

'Hullo, Janet,' he said, half turning round; she hesitated a moment, then went on down the passage. At the end there was a hanging-closet (he had blundered into it in mistake for the bathroom); he heard her click the door open and rustle about among the dresses. Still listening, he pulled open a small drawer under his elbow and searched at the back of it, under his ties, for the daguerreotype of his grandmother. Somehow he failed to hear her; she passed the door again silently; still with a hand at the back of the drawer he called out: 'Come in a moment, Janet, I've something to show you,' and turned full round quickly, but she had gone.

Sighing, he sat down and put on the other shoe. He washed his hands, flattened his hair with a brush, shook a clean handkerchief out of its folds with a movement of irritation and, taking up the daguerreotype, went out after her. 'Janet!' he said aggrievedly.

'Thomas?' said Janet's voice from the hall below.

'*Hul-lo!*'

'I've been shutting the dogs up – poor dears. We'll have tea in the library.' She came upstairs to meet him, drawing her gloves off and smiling.

'But you were in – I thought you – oh well, never mind . . .' He glanced involuntarily towards the door of her room; she looked after him.

'Yes, never mind,' she said. They smiled at each other queerly. She put her hand on his arm for a moment urgently, then with a little laugh went on upstairs past him and into her room. He had an instinct to follow her, a quick apprehension, but stood there rooted.

'Right-o; all clear,' she called after a second.

'Oh, right-o,' he answered, and went downstairs.

'By the way,' asked Thomas casually, stirring his tea, 'does one tell Gerard?'

'As you like, my dear. Don't you think, though, we might talk about *you* this evening? Yesterday we kept drawing on you for admiration and sympathy; you were too wonderful. We never asked you a thing, but what we should love really, what we are burning to do, is to hear about you in Spain.'

'I should love to talk about Spain after dinner. Before dinner I'm always a little doubtful about my experiences; they never seem quite so real as other people's; they're either un-solid or dingy. I don't get carried away by them myself, which is so essential . . . Just one thing: why is she so like you?'

'Oh! . . . did that strike *you*?'

'I never saw her properly, but it was the way you hold yourself. And her step – well, I've never been mistaken about a step before. And she looked in as she went by, over her shoulder, like you would.'

'Funny . . . So that was Clara. Nothing's ever like what one expected, is it?'

'No . . .' said Thomas, following a train of thought. 'She did perhaps seem eagerer and thinner. If I'd thought at all at the time (which I didn't) I'd have thought – "Something has occurred to Janet: what?" As it was, after she'd been by the second time I was cross because I thought you shouldn't be too busy to see me. What do you know about her – facts, I mean?'

'Very little. Her name occurs in some title-deeds. She was a Clara Skepworth. She married a Mr Horace Algernon May and her father seems to have bought her the house as a wedding present. She had four children – they all survived her but none of them seems to have left descendants – and died a natural death, middle-aged, about 1850. There seems no reason to think she was not happy; she was not interesting. Contented women aren't.'

This Thomas deprecated. 'Isn't that arbitrary?'

'Perhaps,' agreed Janet, holding out a hand to the fire. 'You can defend Clara, I shan't . . . Why should I?'

'How do you know this Clara Skepworth – or May – is your Clara?'

'I just know,' said Janet, gently and a little wearily conclusive – a manner she must often have used with her children.

Thomas peppered a quarter of muffin with an air of giving it all his attention. He masked a keen intuition by not looking at Janet, who sat with her air of composed unconsciousness, perhaps a shade conscious of being considered. He had the sense here of a definite exclusion; something was changing her. He had an intuition of some well he had half-divined in her having been tapped, of some reserve (which had given her that solidity) being drained away, of a certain sheathed and, till now, hypothetical faculty being used to exhaustion. He had guessed her capable of an intimacy, something disruptive, something to be driven up like a wedge, first blade-fine, between the controlled mind and the tempered, vivid emotions. It would not be a matter of friendship (the perfectness of his own with her proved it), she was civilized too deep down, the responses she made were too conscious; nor of love; she was perfectly mated (yet he believed her feeling for Gerard – so near to the casual eye, to the springs of her being – to be largely maternal and sensual).

In revulsion from the trend of his thoughts, he glanced at her: her comfortable beautiful body made the thing ludicrous. 'A peevish dead woman where we've failed,' he thought, 'it's absurd.' Gerard and he – he thought how much less humiliating for them both it would have been if she'd taken a lover.

'Gerard ought to be coming in soon.' Uneasy, like a watch-dog waking up at the end of a burglary, he glanced at the clock.

'Shall I put the muffins down by the fire again?'

'Why? Oh, no. He doesn't eat tea now, he thinks he is getting fat.'

'He's up to time usually, isn't he?'

'Yes – he's sure to be early this evening. I thought I heard the car then, but it was only the wind. It's coming up, isn't it?'

'Yes, lovely of it. Let it howl. (I like the third person imperative.)' He shrugged his folded arms up his chest luxuriously and slid down further into his chair. 'I like it after tea, it's so physical.'

'Isn't it?'

They listened, not for long in vain, for the sound of the car on the drive.

The drawing-room was in dark-yellow shadow with pools of light; Gerard and Janet were standing in front of the fire. Falling from Janet's arms above the elbows, transparent draperies hung down against the firelight. Her head was bent, with a line of light round the hair from a clump of electric candles on the wall above; she was looking into the fire, her arms stretched out, resting her finger-tips on the mantelpiece between the delicate china. Gerard, his fine back square and black to the room, bent with a creak of the shirt-front to kiss the inside of an elbow. Janet's fingers spread out, arching themselves on the mantelpiece as though she had found the chord she wanted on an invisible keyboard and were holding it down.

Thomas saw this from across the hall, through an open door, and came on in naturally. His sympathy was so perfect that they might have kissed in his presence; they both turned, smiling, and made room for him in front of the fire.

'Saturday tomorrow,' said Gerard, who smelt of verbena soap, 'then Sunday. Two days for me here. You've been here all day, Thomas. It doesn't seem fair.'

'I helped take the dogs for a walk,' said Thomas. 'It was muddy, we slid about and got ice-cold and couldn't talk at all because we kept whistling and whistling to the dogs till our mouths got too stiff. What a lot of virtue one acquires in the country by doing unnecessary things. Being arduous, while there are six or eight people working full time to keep one alive in luxury.'

'Sorry,' said Janet. 'I didn't know you hated it. But I'm sure it was good for you.'

'I wish you wouldn't both imply,' said Thomas, 'that I don't know the meaning of work. On Monday, when I get back to town, I'm going to begin my book on monasteries.'

'What became of that poem about the Apocalypse?'

'I'm re-writing it,' said Thomas with dignity.

'You are the perfect mixture,' said Janet, 'of Francis Thompson and H. G. Wells.'[3]

'There's a dark room in my flat where a man once did photography. In a year, when I'm thirty-five, I shall retire into it and be Proust,[4] and then you will both be sorry.'

The butler appeared in the doorway.

'Dinner...' said Gerard.

When Janet left them, Gerard and Thomas looked at each other vaguely and wisely between four candles over a pile of fruit. The port completed its second circle. Thomas sipped, remained with lips compressed and, with an expression of inwardness, swallowed.

'Very ni-ice,' he said. '*Very* nice.'

'That's the one I was telling you – light of course.'

[3] Francis Thompson (1859–1907), British poet noted for his religious subject-matter; H. G. Wells (1866–1946), British novelist noted for his science fiction writings.

[4] Marcel Proust (1871–1922), distinguished French author noted for his reclusive lifestyle.

'I don't do with that heavy stuff.'

'No, you never could, could you . . . I'm putting on weight – notice?'

'Yes,' said Thomas placidly. 'Oh, well, it's time we began to. One can't fairly expect, my dear Gerard, to *look* ascetic.'

'Oh, look here, speak for yourself, you Londoner. I live pretty hard here – take a good deal of exercise. It would be beastly for Janet if one got to look too utterly gross.'

'Ever feel it?'

'M-m-m-m – no.'

Thomas sketched with his eyebrows an appeal for closer sincerity.

'Well, scarcely ever. Never more than is suitable.' He sent round the port. 'Had a good day barring the dogs? I daresay you talked a good deal; you made Janet talk well. She is, isn't she – dispassionately – what you'd call rather intelligent?'

'Yes – you proprietary vulgarian.'

'Thanks,' said Gerard. He cracked two walnuts between his palms and let the shells fall on to his plate with a clatter. 'I suppose she showed you everything out of doors? I shall show it you again tomorrow. Her ideas are quite different from mine, I mean about what we're going to do here. I shall have my innings tomorrow. She's keeping the men at those borders when I want them to get started on levelling the two new courts. We've only one now – I suppose she showed it you – which is ridiculous with Michael and Gill growing up. Well, I mean, it *is* ridiculous, isn't it?'

'Entirely,' said Thomas. 'Don't cramp the children's development; let them have five or six.'

'How you do hate our children,' said Gerard comfortably.

There ensued a mellowed silence of comprehension. Gerard, his elbows spread wide on the arms of his chair, stretched his legs further under the table and looked at the fire. Thomas pushed his chair sideways and crossed his legs still more comfortably. A log on the fire collapsed and went up in a gush of pale flame.

Thomas was startled to find Gerard's eyes fixed sharply upon him as though in surprise. He half thought that he must have spoken, then that Gerard had spoken. 'Yes?' he said.

'Nothing,' said Gerard, 'I didn't say anything, did I? As a matter of fact I was thinking – *did* you see anything of Clara?'

'If I were you I should drop Clara: I mean as a joke.'

There was nothing about Gerard's manner of one who has joked. He smiled grudgingly. 'I do work my jokes rather hard. I'm getting to see when their days are numbered by Janet's expression. As a matter of fact, I think *that*'s one form of nerves with me; I feel it annoys Janet and I don't seem able to leave it alone . . . *You* don't think, seriously, there's anything in this thing?'

'I told you this morning I wasn't a test.'

'But aren't you?' insisted Gerard, with penetration. 'How about since this morning? How do you feel things are – generally?'

'She's an idea of Janet's.'

'Half your philosophers would tell me I was an idea of Janet's. I don't care what she is; the thing is, is she getting on Janet's nerves? You know Janet awfully well: do be honest.'

'It needs some thinking about. I'd never thought of Janet as a person who *had* nerves.'

'I'd like to know one way or the other,' said Gerard, 'before I start work on those courts.'

'My dear fellow – *leave here*?' Such an abysm of simplicity startled Thomas, who thought of his friends for convenience in terms of himself. *He* wouldn't leave here, once established, for anything short of a concrete discomfort, not for the menacing of all the Janets by all the Claras. 'I've never seen Janet better,' he quickly objected, 'looking nicer, more full of things generally. You can't say the place doesn't suit her.'

'Oh yes, it suits her all right, I suppose. She's full of – something. I suppose I'm conservative – inside, which is so much worse – I didn't mind moving house, I was keener than she was on coming here. I wanted this place frightfully and I'm absolutely content now we've got it. I've never regretted Three Beeches. But I didn't reckon on one sort of change, and that seems to have happened. I don't even know if it's something minus or something plus. I think where I'm concerned, minus. It's like losing a book in the move, knowing one can't really have lost it, that it must have got into the shelves somewhere, but not being able to trace it.'

'Beastly feeling,' said Thomas idly, 'till one remembers having lent it to some devil who hasn't given it back.'

Gerard looked at him sharply, a look like a gasp. Then his eyes dropped, his face relaxed from haggardness into a set, heavy expression that held a mixture of pride and resentment at his own impenetrability, his toughness. Thomas knew the expression of old; when it appeared in the course of an argument he was accustomed to drop the argument with an, 'Oh well, I don't know. I daresay you are right.' Gerard now raised his glass, frowned expressively at it and put it down again. He said: 'I must be fearfully fatuous; I always feel things are so permanent.'

Thomas didn't know what to say; he liked Gerard chiefly because he *was* fatuous.

'She's seeing too much of this ghost,' continued Gerard. 'She wouldn't if things were all right with her. I can't talk about delusions and doctors and things because she's as healthy as I am, obviously, and rather saner. I daresay this thing's *here* all right; from the way you don't answer my question I gather you've been seeing it too.'

'To be exact,' said Thomas, 'somebody walked past my door this afternoon who turned out not to be Janet, though I'd have sworn at the time it was.'

'Tell Janet?'

'Yes.'

Gerard looked up for a moment and searched his face. 'Didn't you wonder,' he said, 'why she couldn't be natural about it? I remember she and you and I talking rot about ghosts at Three Beeches, and she said she'd love to induct one here. The first time she came down and told me about Clara I thought she thought it was fun. I suppose I was rather a hearty idiot; I rushed upstairs and started a kind of rat-hunt. I thought it amused her; when I found it didn't I had rather a shock ... Things must be changing, or how can this Clara business have got a foothold? It *has* got a foothold – I worry a good bit when we're alone but we never discuss it, then directly somebody's here something tweaks me on to it and every time I try and be funny something gets worse ... Oh, I don't know – I daresay I'm wrong.' Gerard dived for his napkin; he reappeared shame-faced. 'Wash this out,' he said, 'I've been talking through my hat. That's the effect of you, Thomas. It's not that you're so damned sympathetic, but you're so damned *un*sympathetic in such a provocative way.' He got up. 'Come on,' he said, 'let's come on out of here.'

Thomas got up unwillingly; he longed to define all this. Risking a failure in tact he put forward, 'What you're getting at is: all this is a matter of foothold?'

'Oh, I suppose so,' Gerard agreed non-committally. 'Let's wash that out, anyway. Do let's come on out of here.'

Thomas talked about Spain. 'I can't think why we don't go there,' cried Janet. 'We never seem to go anywhere; we don't travel enough. You seem so much completer and riper, Thomas, since you've seen Granada. Do go on.'

'Quite sure I don't bore you?' said Thomas, elated.

'Get on,' said Gerard impatiently. 'Don't stop and preen yourself. And, Janet, don't you keep on interrupting him. Let him get on.'

Thomas got on. He did require (as he'd told Janet) to gather momentum. Without, he was apt to be hampered by the intense, complacent modesty of the oversubjective; at the beginning, Spain refused to be detached from himself; he seemed to have made it. *Now* Spain imposed a control on him, selecting his language; words came less from him than through him, he heard them go by in a flow of ingenuous rapture.

Gerard and Janet were under the same domination. The three produced in each other, in talking, a curious sense of equality, of being equally related. Thomas concentrated a sporadic but powerful feeling for 'home' into these triangular contacts. He was an infrequent visitor, here as with other friends, but could produce when present a feeling of continuity, of uninterruptedness ... It was here as though there had always been Thomas. The quiet room round them, secure from the whining wind, with its shadowy lacquer, its shades like great parchment cups pouring down light, the straight, almost palpable fall of heavy gold curtains to carpet, 'came together' in this peculiar intimacy as though it had lived a long time warm in their common memory. While he talked, it remained in suspension.

'O-oh,' sighed Janet and looked round, when he had finished, as though they had all come back from a journey.

'I suppose,' said Gerard, 'we are unenterprising. Are we?'

'A little,' conceded Thomas, still rather exalted, nursing one foot on a knee.

'Let's go abroad tomorrow!'

'You know,' exclaimed Janet, 'you know, Gerard, you'd simply hate it!' She made a gesture of limitation. 'We're rooted here.'

'Of course, there's one thing: if you hadn't both got this faculty for being rooted it wouldn't be the same thing to come and see you. I do hate "service-flat people"; I never know any.'

They all sighed, shifted their attitudes; sinking a little deeper into the big chairs. Thomas, aware almost with ecstasy of their three comfortable bodies, exclaimed: 'Would we ever really have known each other before there was this kind of chair? I've a theory that absolute comfort runs round the circle to the same point as asceticism. It wears the material veil pretty thin.'

Janet raised her arms, looked at them idly and dropped them again. 'What material veil?' she said foolishly.

Nobody answered.

'Janet's sleepy,' said Gerard, 'she can't keep awake unless she does all the talking herself. She's not one of your women who listen.'

'I wasn't sleepy till now. I think it's the wind. Listen to it.'

'Tomorrow, Janet, I'm going to show Thomas where those courts are to be. He says you didn't.'

'Thomas has no opinion about tennis courts; he'd agree with anyone. He really was intelligent about my borders.'

'Yes, I really was. You see, Gerard, tennis doesn't really affect me much. Pat-ball's my game.' Thomas lay back, looking through half-shut eyes at the wavering streaming flames. 'Clara's a dream,' he thought. 'Janet and I played at her. Gerard's a sick man.' He wanted to stretch sideways, touch Janet's bare arm and say to them both: 'There's just *this*, just this: weren't we all overwrought?'

Gerard, tenacity showing itself in his attitude, was sticking to something. He turned from one to the other eagerly. 'All the same,' he said, 'tennis courts or no tennis courts, why shouldn't we both, quite soon, go abroad?'

'Exactly,' said Thomas, encouraging.

'Because I don't want to,' said Janet. 'Just like that.'

'Oh . . . Tired?'

'Yes, tired-ish – with no disrespect to Thomas. I've had a wonderful day, but I *am* tired. Suppose it's the wind.'

'You said that before.'

She got up out of the depths of her chair, gathering up her draperies that slipped and clung to the cushions like cobwebs with perverse independence. 'Oh!' she cried. '*Sleepy!*' and flung her arms over her head.

'But you shatter our evening,' cried Thomas, looking up at her brilliance, then rising incredulous.

'Then you won't be too late,' she said heartlessly. 'Don't be too late!' She went across to the door like a sleepy cat. 'Good night, my dear Thomas.' After she closed the door they stood listening, though there was nothing to hear.

Their evening was not shattered, but it was cracked finely and irreparably. There was a false ring to it, never loud but an undertone. Gerard was uneasy; he got up after a minute or two and opened the door again. 'Don't you feel the room a bit hot?' he said. 'I'd open a window but the wind fidgets the curtains so. That's the only thing that gets on what nerves I have got, the sound of a curtain fidgeting; in and out, in and out, like somebody puffing and blowing.'

'Beastly,' said Thomas. 'I never open a window.' If he had been host he'd have invited Gerard to stop prowling and sit down, but one couldn't ask a man – even Gerard – to stop prowling about his own drawing-room when the prowling had just *that* 'tone'. So Thomas leant back rather exaggeratedly and sent up pacific smoke-wreaths.

'You look sleepy too,' said Gerard with some irritation. 'Shall we all go to bed?'

'Oh, just as you like, my dear fellow. I'll take up a book with me –'

'– No, don't let's,' said Gerard, and sat down abruptly.

The wind subsided during the next half-hour and silences, a kind of surprised stillness, spaced out their talk. Gerard fidgeted with the decanters; half way through a glass of whisky he got up again and stood undecided. 'Look here,' he said, 'there's something I forgot to ask Janet. Somebody's sent her a message and I must get the answer telephoned through tomorrow, first thing. I'll go up for a moment before she's asleep.'

'Do,' agreed Thomas, taking up *Vogue*.

Gerard, going out, hesitated rather portentously about shutting the drawing-room door and finally shut it. Thomas twitched an eyebrow but didn't look up from *Vogue*, which he went through intelligently from cover to cover. He remained looking for some time at a coloured advertisement of complexion soap at the end, then, as Gerard hadn't come back, got up to look for *Celestina*, where Janet had left it out in the hall. He crossed the hall soundlessly, avoiding the marble, stepping from rug to rug; with a hand put out for the *Celestina* he halted and stood still.

Gerard stood at the foot of the stairs, through the double doors, looking up, holding on to the banisters. Thomas looked at him, then in some confusion stepped back into the drawing-room. He had a shock; he wished he hadn't seen Gerard's face. 'What on earth was he listening for? . . . Why didn't he hear me? . . . I don't believe he's been up at all.' He took some more whisky and stood by the fire, waiting, his glass in his hand.

Quickly and noisily Gerard came in. 'She's asleep; it was no good.'

'Pity,' said Thomas, 'you ought to have gone up sooner.' They did not look at each other.

Thomas waited about – a social gesture purely, for he had the strongest possible feeling of not being wanted – while Gerard put out the downstair lights. Gerard wandered from one switch to another indeterminately, fumbling with wrong ones as though the whole lighting system were unfamiliar. Thomas couldn't make out if he were unwilling that either of them should go up, or whether he wanted Thomas to go up without him. 'I'll be going on up,' he said finally.

'Oh! Right you are.'

'I'll try not to wake Janet.'

'Oh, nothing wakes Janet – make as much noise as you like.'

He went up, his feet made a baffled, unreal sound on the smoothly carpeted stairs. The landing was – by some oversight – all in darkness. Away down the passage, firelight through his bedroom door came out across the carpet and up the wall. He watched – for Clara was somewhere, certainly – to see if anyone would step out across the bar of firelight. Nobody came. 'She may be in there,' he thought. Lovely to find her in there by the fire, like Janet.

Gerard turned out the last light in the hall and came groping up after him. 'Sorry!' he said. 'You'll find the switch of the landing outside Janet's door.' Thomas groped along the wall till he touched the door-panels. Left or right? – he didn't know, his fingers pattered over them softly.

'Oh, Clara,' came Janet's quiet voice from inside . . . 'I can't bear it. How could you bear it? The sickening loneliness . . . Listen, Clara . . .'

He heard Gerard's breathing; Gerard there three steps below him, listening also.

'Damn you, Gerard,' said Thomas sharply and noisily. '*I* can't find this thing. I'm lost entirely. Why did you put those lights out?'

The Apple Tree (1934)

'Frightened?' exclaimed Lancelot. 'Of her? Oh, nonsense – surely? She's an absolute child.'

'But *that's* what I mean,' said Mrs Bettersley, glancing queerly sideways at him over the collar of her fur coat. He still did not know what she meant, and did not think she knew either.

"The Apple Tree" first appeared in *The Cat Jumps, and Other Stories* by Elizabeth Bowen (London: Victor Gollancz, 1934).

In a rather nerve-racking combination of wind and moonlight Simon Wing's week-end party picked its way back to his house, by twos and threes, up a cinder-path from the village. Simon, who entered with gusto into his new role of squire, had insisted that they should attend the Saturday concert in the village memorial hall, a raftered, charmless and icy building endowed by himself and only recently opened. Here, with numbing feet and spines creeping, they had occupied seven front seats, under a thin but constant spate of recitation, pianoforte duet and part-song, while upon them from all quarters draughts directed themselves like arrows. To restore circulation they had applauded vigorously, too often precipitating an encore. Simon, satisfied with his friends, with his evening, leant forward to beam down the row. He said this would please the village. Lancelot communicated to Mrs Bettersley a dark suspicion: this was really why Simon had asked them down.

'So I'm afraid,' she replied. 'And for church tomorrow.'

All the same, it had warmed them all to see Simon happy. Mounting the platform to propose a vote of thanks to the Vicar, the great ruddy man had positively expanded and glowed; a till now too palpable cloud rolled away from him. It was this recognition by his old friends of the old Simon – a recognition so instantaneous, poignant and cheerful that it was like a handshake, a first greeting – that now sent the party so cheerfully home in its two and threes, their host boisterously ahead. At the tail, lagging, Lancelot and Mrs Bettersley fell into a discussion of Simon (his marriage, his *ménage*, his whole aspect) marked by entire unrestraint; as though between these two also some shadow had dissipated. They were old friendly enemies.

'But a child—' resumed Lancelot.

'Naturally I didn't mean to suggest that she was a werewolf!'

'You think she *is* what's the matter?'

'Obviously there's nothing funny about the *house*.'

Obviously there was nothing funny about the house. Under the eerie cold sky, pale but not bright with moonlight, among bare windshaken trees, the house's bulk loomed, honourably substantial. Lit-up windows sustained the party with promise of indoor comfort: firelight on decanters, room after room heavy-curtained, Simon's feeling for home made concrete (at last, after wandering years) in deep leather chairs, padded fenders, and sectional bookshelves, 'domes of silence' on yielding carpets: an unaspiring, comfortable sobriety.

'She does seem to me only half there,' confessed Lancelot. 'Not, of course, I mean mentally, but—'

'She had that frightful time – don't you know? *Don't* you know?' Mrs Bettersley brightened, approaching her lips to his ear in the moonlight. 'She was at that school – don't you remember? After all *that*, the school broke up, you know. She was sent straight abroad – she'd have been twelve at the time, I dare say; in a pretty state, I've no doubt, poor child! – to an aunt and uncle at Cannes. Her only relations; they lived out there in a villa, never came home – she stayed abroad with them. It was there Simon met her; then – all this.'

'School?' said Lancelot, stuttering with excitement. 'What – were they ill-treated?'

'Heavens, not that,' exclaimed Mrs Bettersley; 'worse—'

But just at this point – it was unbearable – they saw the party pull up and contract ahead. Simon was waiting to shepherd them through the gate, then lock the gate after them.

'I hope,' he said, beaming, as they came up, 'you weren't too bored?'

They could not fail to respond.

'It's a been a marvellous evening,' said Mrs Bettersley; Lancelot adding, 'What wonderful talent you've got round here.'

'I don't think we're bad for a village,' said Simon modestly, clicking the gate to. 'The Choral Society are as keen as mustard. And I always think that young Dickinson ought to go on the stage. I'd pay to see him anywhere.'

'Oh, so would I,' agreed Lancelot cordially. 'It's too sad,' he added, 'your wife having missed all this.'

Simon's manner contracted. 'She went to the dress rehearsal,' he said quickly.

'Doesn't she act herself?'

'I can't get her to try... Well, here we are; here we are!' Simon shouted, stamping across the terrace.

Young Mrs Wing had been excused the concert. She had a slight chill, she feared. If she ever did cast any light on village society, it was tonight withheld. No doubt Simon was disappointed. His friends, filing after him through the French window into the library, all hoped that by now – it was half-past ten – young Mrs Simon might have taken her chill to bed.

But from the hearth her flat little voice said: 'Hullo!' There she stood, looking towards the window, watching their entrance as she had watched their exit. Her long silver sheath of a dress made her almost grown up. So they all prepared with philosophy to be nice to young Mrs Wing. They all felt this first week-end party, this incursion of old friends all so much knit up with each other, so much knit up round Simon, might well be trying for young Mrs Wing. In the nature even, possibly, of an ordeal. She was barely nineteen, and could not, to meet them, be expected to put up anything of 'a manner'. She had them, however, at a slight disadvantage, for Simon's marriage had been a shock for his friends. He had been known for years as a likely marrying man; so much so that his celibacy appeared an accident; but his choice of a wife – this mannerless, sexless child, the dim something between a mouse and an Undine,[1] this wraith not considerable as a mother of sons, this cold little shadow across a hearth – had considerably surprised them. By her very passivity she attacked them when they were least prepared.

Mrs Wing, at a glance from her husband, raised a silver lid from some sandwiches with a gesture of invitation. Mrs Bettersley, whose appetite was frankly wolfish, took two, and, slipping out inch by inch from her fur coat, lined up beside her little hostess in the firelight, solid and brilliant. The others divided armchairs in the circle of warmth.

'Did you have a nice concert?' said Mrs Wing politely. No one could answer. 'It went off well on the whole,' said Simon gently, as though breaking sorrowful news to her.

Lancelot could not sleep. The very comfort of bed, the too exquisite sympathy with his body of springs and mattress, became oppressive. Wind had subsided; moonlight sketched a window upon his floor. The house was quiet, too quiet; with jealousy and nostalgia he pictured them all sleeping. Mrs Wing's cheek would scarcely warm a pillow. In despair Lancelot switched the light on; the amiable furniture stared. He read one page of *Our Mutual Friend*[2] with distaste and decided to look downstairs for a detective story. He slept in a corridor branching off from the head of the main staircase.

Downstairs, the hall was dark, rank with cooling cigar-smoke. A clock struck three; Lancelot violently started. A little moon came in through the skylight; the library door was closed; stepping quietly, Lancelot made his way to it. He opened the door, saw red embers, then knew in a second the library was not empty. All the same, in there in the dark they were not moving or speaking.

Embarrassment – had he surprised an intrigue? – and abrupt physical fear – were these burglars? – held Lancelot bound on the threshold. Certainly someone in here was not alone; in here, in spite of the dark, someone was watching someone. He did not know whether to speak. He felt committed by opening the door, and, standing against the grey of the glass-roofed hall, must be certainly visible.

Finally it was Simon's voice that said defensively: 'Hullo?' Lancelot knew he must go away immediately. He had only one wish – to conceal his identity. But Simon apparently did not trust one; moving bulkily he came down the long room to the door, bumping, as though in a quite unfamiliar room, against the furniture, one arm stuck out ahead, as though pushing something aside or trying to part a curtain. He seemed to have no sense of space; Lancelot ducked, but a great hand touched his face. The hand was ice-cold.

'Oh, *you*?' said Simon. From his voice, his breath, he had been drinking heavily. He must still be holding a glass in his other hand – Lancelot heard whisky slopping about as the glass shook.

'It's all right,' said Lancelot; 'I was just going up. Sorry,' he added.

'You can't – come – in – here,' said Simon obstinately.

'No, I say: I was just going up.' Lancelot stopped; friendliness fought in him with an intense repulsion. Not that he minded – though this itself was odd: Simon hardly ever touched anything.

---

[1] A female water spirit who, according to legend, might acquire a soul by marrying a mortal and bearing a child

[2] A novel (1864–5) by Charles Dickens (1812–70).

But the room was a trap, a *cul-de-sac*; Simon, his face less than a yard away, seemed to be speaking to him through bars. He was frightful in fear; a man with the humility of a beast; he gave off fear like some disagreeable animal smell, making Lancelot dislike and revolt at his own manhood, subject to such decay.

'Go away,' said Simon, pushing at him in the dark. Lancelot stepped back in alarm; a rug slipped under his foot; he staggered grasping at the jamb of the door. His elbow knocked a switch; immediately the hall, with its four powerful lamps, sprang into illumination. One was staggered by this explosion of light; Lancelot put his hands over his eyes; when he took them away he could see Simon's face was clammy, mottled; here and there a bead of sweat trembled and ran down. He was standing sideways, his shoulder against the door; past him a path of light ran into the library.

Mrs Simon stood just out of the light, looking fixedly up and pointing at something above her head. Round her Lancelot distinguished the big chairs, the table with the decanters, and faintly, the glazed bookcases. Her eyes, looking up, reflected the light but did not flicker; she did not stir. With an exclamation, a violent movement, Simon shut the library door. They both stood outside its white glossy panels. By contrast with what stood inside, staring there in the dark, Simon was once more human; unconsciously as much to gain as to impart reassurance, Lancelot put a hand on his arm.

Not looking at one another, they said nothing.

They were in no sense alone even here, for the slam of the door produced in a moment or two Mrs Bettersley, who looked down at them from the gallery over the zone of bright lights, her face sharpened and wolfish with vehement curiosity. Lancelot looked up; their eyes met.

'All right; only somebody sleep-walking,' he called up softly.

'All right,' she replied, withdrawing; but not, he guessed, to her room; rather to lean back in shadow against the wall of the gallery, impassive, watchful, arms folded over the breast of her dark silk kimono.

A moment later she still made no sign – he would have been glad of her presence, for the return to Simon of sensibility and intelligence, like circulation beginning again in a limb that had been tightly bound up, was too much for Simon. One side-glance that almost contained his horror, then – huge figure crumpling, swaying, sagging – he fainted suddenly. Lancelot broke his fall a little and propped him, sitting, against the wall.

This left Lancelot much alone. He noted details: a dog-collar lying unstrapped, ash trodden into a rug, a girl's gloves – probably Mrs Simon's – dropped crumpled into a big brass tray. Now drawn to the door – aware the whole time of his position's absurdity – he knelt, one ear to the keyhole. Silence. In there she must still stand in contemplation – horrified, horrifying – of something high up that from the not quite fixity of her gaze had seemed unfixed, pendent, perhaps swaying a little. Silence. Then – he pressed closer – a thud-thud-thud – three times, like apples falling.

This idea of apples entered his mind and remained, frightfully clear; an innocent pastoral image seen black through a dark transparency. This idea of fruit detaching itself and, from a leafy height, falling in the stale, shut-up room, had the sharpness of hallucination: he thought he was going mad.

'Come down,' he called up to the gallery.

Mrs Bettersley, with that expectant half-smile, appeared, looked over immediately, then came downstairs. Noting Simon's unconsciousness, for which she seemed to be grateful, she went to the library door. After a moment facing the panels she tried the handle, cautiously turning it.

'*She's* in there,' said Lancelot.

'Coming?' she asked.

He replied, 'No,' frankly and simply.

'Oh, well,' she shrugged; 'I'm a woman,' and entered the library, pushing the door to behind her. He heard her moving among the furniture. 'Now come,' she said. 'Come, my dear...' After a moment or two of complete silence and stillness: 'Oh, my God, no – I can't!' she exclaimed. She came out again, very white. She was rubbing her hands together as though she had hurt them. 'It's impossible,' she repeated. 'One can't get past... it's like an apple tree.'

She knelt by Simon and began fumbling with his collar. Her hands shook. Lancelot watched the access of womanly busyness.

The door opened again and young Mrs Wing came out in her nightgown, hair hanging over her shoulders in two plaits, blinking under the strong light. Seeing them all, she paused in natural confusion.

'I walk in my sleep,' she murmured, blushed, and slipped past upstairs without a glance at her husband, still in confusion, like any young woman encountered by strangers in her nightgown; her appearance and disappearance the very picture of modest precipitancy.

Simon began to come to. Mrs Bettersley also retreated. The fewest possible people ought, they felt, to be in on this.

Sunday morning was milky-blue, mild and sunny. Mrs Bettersley appeared punctually for breakfast, beaming, pink, and impassible. Lancelot looked pale and puffy; Mrs Simon did not appear. Simon came in like a tempered Boreas[3] to greet the party, rubbing his hands. After breakfast they stepped out through the window to smoke on the terrace. Church, said Simon pressingly, would be at eleven.

Mrs Bettersley revolted. She said she liked to write letters on Sunday morning. The rest, with a glance of regret at the shining November garden, went off like lambs. When they had gone, she slipped upstairs and tapped on Mrs Simon's door.

The young woman was lying comfortably enough, with a fire burning, a mild novel open face down on the counterpane. This pretty bride's room, pink and white, frilled and rosy, now full of church bells and winter sunshine, had for Mrs Bettersley, in all its appointments, an air of anxious imitation and of approximation to some idea of the grown-up. Simon's bed was made and the room in order.

'You don't mind?' said Mrs Bettersley, having sat down firmly.

Mrs Simon said, nervously, she was so pleased.

'All right this morning?'

'Just a little chill, I think.'

'And no wonder! Do you often walk in your sleep?'

Mrs Simon's small face tightened, hardened, went a shade whiter among the pillows. 'I don't know,' she said. Her manner became a positive invitation to Mrs Bettersley to go away. Flattening among the bedclothes, she tried hard to obliterate herself.

Her visitor, who had not much time – for the bells had stopped; they would be back again in an hour – was quite merciless. 'How old were you,' she said, 'when *that* happened?'

'Twelve – please don't –'

'You never told anyone?'

'No – please, Mrs Bettersley – please not now. I feel so ill.'

'You're making Simon ill.'

'Do you think I don't know!' the child exclaimed. 'I thought he'd save me. I didn't think he'd ever be frightened. I didn't know any power could . . . Indeed, indeed, Mrs Bettersley, I had no idea . . . I felt so safe with him. I thought this would go away. Now when it comes it is twice as horrible. Do you think it is killing him?'

'I shouldn't wonder,' said Mrs Bettersley.

'Oh, oh,' moaned Mrs Wing, and, with wrists crossed over her face, shook all over, sobbing so that the bed-head rattled against the wall. 'He was so sorry for me,' she moaned; 'it was more than I could resist. He was so sorry for me. Wouldn't *you* feel Simon might save you?'

Mrs Bettersley, moving to the edge of the bed, caught the girl's wrists and firmly but not untenderly forced them apart, disclosing the small convulsed face and staring eyes. 'We've got three-quarters of an hour alone,' she said. 'You've got to tell me. Make it come into words. When it's once out it won't hurt any more – like a tooth, you know. Talk about it like anything. Talk to Simon. You never have, have you? You never do?'

3   In Greek mythology, the north wind as a god.

Mrs Bettersley felt quite a brute, she told Lancelot later. She had, naturally, in taking this hard line, something to go on. Seven years ago, newspapers had been full of the Crampton Park School tragedy: a little girl's suicide. There had been some remarkable headlines, some details, profuse speculation. Influence from some direction having been brought to bear, the affair disappeared from the papers abruptly. Some suggestion of things having been 'hushed up' gave the affair, in talk, a fresh cruel prominence; it became a topic. One hinted at all sorts of scandal. The school broke up; the staff disappeared, discredited; the fine house and grounds, in the West Country, were sold at a loss. One pupil, Myra Conway, felt the shock with surprising keenness. She nearly died of brain fever; collapsing the day after the suicide, she remained at death's door for weeks, alone with her nurses in the horrified house, Crampton Park. All the other children were hurried away. One heard afterwards that her health, her nerves, had been ruined. The other children, presumably, rallied; one heard no more of them. Myra Conway became Myra Wing. So much they all knew, even Simon.

Myra Wing now lay on her side in bed, in her pink bedroom, eyes shut, cheek pressed to the pillow as though she were sleeping, but with her body rigid; gripping with both hands Mrs Bettersley's arm. She spoke slowly, choosing her words with diffidence as though hampered by trying to speak an unfamiliar language.

'I went there when I was ten. I don't think it can ever have been a very good school. They called it a home school, I suppose because most of us stayed for the holidays – we had no parents – and none of us was over fourteen. From being there so much, we began to feel that this was the world. There was a very high wall round the garden. I don't think they were unkind to us, but everything seemed to go wrong. Doria and I were always in trouble. I suppose that was why we knew each other. There were about eighteen other girls, but none of them liked us. We used to feel we had some disease – so much so, that we were sometimes ashamed to meet each other: sometimes we did not like to be together. I don't think we knew we were unhappy; we never spoke of that; we should have felt ashamed. We used to pretend we were all right; we got in a way to be quite proud of ourselves, of being different. I think, though, we made each other worse. In those days I was very ugly. Doria was as bad; she was very queer-looking; her eyes goggled and she wore big round glasses. I suppose if we had had parents it would have been different. As it was, it was impossible to believe anyone could ever care for either of us. We did not even care for each other; we were just like two patients in hospital, shut away from the others together because of having some frightful disease. But I suppose we depended on one another.

'The other children were mostly younger. The house was very large and dark-looking, but full of pictures to make it look homely. The grounds were very large, full of trees and laurels. When I was twelve, I felt if this was the world I could not bear it. When I was twelve I got measles: another girl of my age got the measles, too, and we were sent to a cottage to get well. She was very pretty and clever; we made friends; she told me she did not mind me but she could not bear Doria. When we both got well and went back to the others, I loved her so much I felt I could not bear to part from her. She had a home of her own; she was very happy and gay; to know her and hear about her life was like heaven. I took great trouble to please her; we went on being friends. The others began to like me; I ran away from Doria. Doria was left alone. She seemed to be all that was horrible in my life; from the moment we parted things began to go right with me. I laughed at her with the others.

'The only happy part of Doria's life and mine in the bad days had been the games we played and the stories we told in a lonely part of the garden, a slope of lawn with one beautiful old apple tree. Sometimes we used to climb up in the branches. Nobody else ever came there; it was like something of our own; to be there made us feel happy and dignified.

'Doria was miserable when I left her. She never wept; she used to walk about by herself. It was as though everything I had got free of had fallen on her, too: she was left with my wretchedness. When I was with the others I used to see her, always alone, watching me. One afternoon she made me come with her to the apple tree; I was sorry for her and went; when we got there I could not bear it. I was so frightened of being lost again; I said terrible things to her. I wished she was dead. You see, there seemed to be no other world outside the school.

'She and I still slept in the same room, with two others. That night – there was some moon – I saw her get up. She tied the cord of her dressing-gown – it was very thick – round her waist tightly; she looked once at me, but I pretended to be asleep. She went out and did not come back. I lay – there was only a little moon – with a terrible feeling, like something tight round my throat. At last I went down to look for her. A glass door to the garden was open. I went out to look for her. She had hanged herself, you know, in the apple tree. When I first got there I saw nothing. I looked round and called her, and shook the branches, but only – it was September – two or three apples fell down. The leaves kept brushing against my face. Then I saw her. Her feet were just over my head. I parted the branches to look – there was just enough moon – the leaves brushed my face. I crept back into bed and waited. No one knew; no steps came. Next morning, of course, they did not tell us anything. They said she was ill. I pretended to know no better. I could not think of anything but the apple tree.

'While I was ill – I was very ill – I thought the leaves would choke me. Whenever I moved in bed an apple fell down. All the other girls were taken away. When I got well, I found the house was empty. The first day I could, I crept out alone to look for the real apple tree. "It is only a tree," I thought; "if I could see it, I should be quite well." But the tree had been cut down. The place where it grew was filled with new turf. The nurse swore to me there had never been an apple tree there at all. She did not know – no one ever knew – I had been out that night and seen Doria.

'I expect you can guess the rest – you were there last night. You see, I am haunted. It does not matter where I am, or who I am with. Though I am married now, it is just the same. Every now and then – I don't know yet when or what brings it about – I wake to see Doria get up and tie the cord round her waist and go out. I have to go after her; there is always the apple tree. Its roots are in me. It takes all my strength, and now it's beginning to take Simon's.

'Those nights, no one can bear to be with me. Everyone who has been with me knows, but no one will speak of it. Only Simon tries to be there those times – you saw, last night. It is impossible to be with me; I make rooms impossible. I am not like a house that can be burnt, you see, or pulled down. You know how it is – I heard you in there last night, trying to come to me—'

'I won't fail again: I've never been more ashamed,' said Mrs Bettersley.

'If I stay up here the tree grows in the room; I feel it will choke Simon. If I go out, I find it darker than all the others against the sky . . . This morning I have been trying to make up my mind; I must go; I must leave Simon. I see quite well this is destroying him. Seeing him with you all makes me see how he used to be, how he might have been. You see, it's hard to go. He's my life. Between all this . . . we're so happy. But make me do this, Mrs Bettersley!'

'I'll make you do one thing. Come away with me – perhaps for only a month. My dear, if I can't do this, after last night, *I'm* ruined,' exclaimed Mrs Bettersley.

The passion of vanity has its own depths in the spirit, and is powerfully militant. Mrs Bettersley, determined to vindicate herself, disappeared for some weeks with the haunted girl. Lancelot, meanwhile, kept Simon company. From the ordeal their friend emerged about Christmas, possibly a little harder and brighter. If she had fought, there was not a hair displaced. She did not mention, even to Lancelot, by what arts, night and day, by what cynical vigilance, she had succeeded in exorcizing the apple tree. The victory aged her, but left her as disengaged as usual. Mrs Wing was returned to her husband. As one would expect, from then on less and less was seen of the couple. They disappeared into happiness: a sublime nonentity.

Attractive Modern Homes (1941)

No sooner were the Watsons settled into their new home than Mrs Watson was overcome by melancholy. The actual settling-in was over only too soon. They had bought the house before it was done building, which had meant putting in time in rooms nearby; she had looked forward to having her own things round her again, and come, perhaps, to expect too much of them. The day

"Attractive Modern Homes" first appeared the *Listener* 15 (April 15, 1936) and was first collected in *Look at All Those Roses: Short Stories* by Elizabeth Bowen (London: Victor Gollancz, 1941), the latter being the text followed here.

the last workman left, the Watsons took possession. He screwed the bronze name-plate on to the gate, while she immediately put up the orange style curtains to give the façade style and keep strangers from looking in. But her things appeared uneasy in the new home. The armchairs and settee covered in jazz tapestry, the sideboard with mirror panel, the alabaster light bowls, even the wireless cabinet looked sulky, as though they would rather have stayed in the van. The semi-detached house was box-like, with thin walls: downstairs it had three rooms and a larder, upstairs, three rooms and a bath. The rooms still smelled of plaster, the bath of putty. The stairs shook when the wardrobe was carried up: the whole structure seemed to be very frail.

Shavings and trodden paper littered the unmade garden and a persistent hammering from unfinished houses travelled over the fence. Even after dark these hollow echoes continued, for Eagles, the builder, was selling houses as fast as he put them up, and his men worked overtime, hammering on in the raw brick shells by candlelight. Earthy emanations and smells of shavings, singing and the plonk of boards being dropped filled the autumn darkness on the estate. The gored earth round the buildings looked unfriendly with pain. Outside the gates, drain trenches had been filled in roughly, but the roads were not made yet – they were troughs of mud, harrowed by builders' lorries this wet autumn, and bounded only by kerbs, along which you picked your way. It would not be possible yet to get a car out.

The Watsons' house, which they had called Rhyll, stood at the far edge of the estate, facing a row of elms along a lane that used to be called Nut Lane. Between the trees, one hedge had been broken down, leaving a flank of the lane bare to the new road alongside the row of villa gates. The Watsons' best room windows stared between the trees at a field that rose beyond them: a characterless hill. Almost no one passed, and nobody looked in.

Mr Watson considered the trees an advantage. He was quick to point out any advantage, with a view to cheering his wife up. His promotion in business, so querulously awaited, came hard on her now it had come, for it entailed a transfer to another branch of the firm and the move here from the place they had always known. Here they were utter strangers; they had not a soul to speak to; no one had heard of them. The eighty miles they had travelled might have been eight hundred. Where they came from they had been born: there had been his people and her people and the set they had grown up with. Everyone took them for granted and thought well of them, so their ten years of marriage had been rich with society. Mrs Watson enjoyed society and esteem and was dependent upon them, as women naturally are. When she heard they must move she had said at once: 'We might as well go straight to the Colonies,' though after that she enjoyed the melancholy importance the prospect of moving gave her among her friends. Yes, where they came from many people were sorry, if not seriously upset, when the Watsons left: they said it was too bad. But their having come here made no difference to anyone. No one remarked their curtains, no one glanced at their door.

This new town they had come to had a mellow, ancient core, but was rapidly spreading and filling up with workers. The Watsons had been edged out to this new estate, the only place where they could find a house. And how un-ideal it was. An estate is not like a village, it has no heart; even the shops are new and still finding their own feet. It has not had time to take on the prim geniality of a suburb. The dwellers are pioneers unennobled by danger. Everybody feels strange and has no time for curiosity. Nothing has had time to flower in this new place.

For instance, the Watsons had neighbours – the houses on either side were already done and lived in. But it had struck her that when they were moving in – while their van stood at the gate and her imposing furniture jolted up the unmade path – not a next-door curtain twitched; nobody took note. No one asked her in for a cup of tea, that first day, or even offered a cup over the fence. Where she came from, it had been customary to do this for newcomers who had not yet unpacked the kettle.

'It seems odd to me,' she had remarked to her husband.

He had been glad to have no one coming around to stare. But he was sorry to have her taking against the neighbours, this would make for no good: 'They're newcomers themselves,' was all he could find to say.

'Then you would think they might think.'

He looked worried, and she mistook his expression for crossness. 'Oh, all right,' she said. 'I merely passed the remark. There's no harm in my passing a remark occasionally, I suppose.'

She had never needed imagination herself, but now felt for the first time its absence in other people. Soon she suspected everyone but herself to be without natural feeling. For instance, she had worked on the children's feelings about the move, pointing out that they were leaving their little friends for ever and that their grannies, who loved them, would now be far away. So that Freddie and Vera wept when they got into the train and whined a good deal during the time in rooms. But now they were delighted with their surroundings; they enjoyed squelching in the deep mud. The half-built houses with their skeleton roofs, scaffolding, tubs of mortar, stacks of piping, and salmon-pink window-frames magnetized Freddie, who wished to become a builder. Where they came from, everything had been complete for years. He explored the uphill reaches of Nut Lane where hedges still arched over to make a tunnel. Vera liked tossing her curls and showing off at her new school, where, her mother warned her, the children were common. Vera was a child with naturally nice ways who would throw anything off, but Mrs Watson kept watching Freddie closely to see he did not pick his nose, drop 'h's or show any other signs of having been in bad company. There was only one school near here: they had no choice . . . Seeing the children's horrible good spirits, Mrs Watson said to her husband, 'How children do forget!' Her manner to Freddie and Vera became reproachful and wan. The old gentleman in the house they were semi-detached from gave Vera a peppermint over the fence, but did not speak to her mother.

To realize one's unhappiness as a whole needs some largeness, even of an ignoble kind. Mrs Watson pitched upon details. The estate was a mile and a half out of the town and buses only ran every twenty minutes. By the time you got anywhere it was time to start home again. And what is the good of shops with nobody to walk round with? Also, back where they came from she was accustomed to have a girl in daily to work, but here there was no way of hearing of any girl, so she had to work alone. Being alone all day, she never heard any news except what was in the paper. Back where they came from hardly a morning passed without someone dropping in, or out shopping you met someone, or when you went down the road you knew from the look of windows that people knew Mrs Watson was going by. Whatever she bought or did invited some heartfelt comment. And he and she had been often invited out. Here they did not even go to the movies; to leave the house after dark fell was not tempting, for lamps along the estate roads were few and dim, making it hard to pick your way on the kerb, and her dread of stepping into the deep mud became neurotic.

Mr Watson had a vice: he was a reader. And he was also always happy messing about with the wireless. He was out all day and talked to men at the office. At week-ends he got on with making the garden; the children played up the lane and she spent most of Saturday wiping mud off the line. Once, after tea, Freddie came in with a white face to say he had seen something funny up Nut Lane. Though his mother told him at once not to be so naughty, this made her come over queerish, later, herself. She got to dread the country left dingily at their door.

Up to now she had been happy without knowing, like a fortunate sheep or cow always in the same field. She was a woman who did not picture herself. She had looked into mirrors only to pat her perm down or smooth a jumper[1] nicely over her bust. Everything that had happened to her seemed natural – love, marriage, the birth of Freddie, then Vera – for she had seen it happen to someone else. She never needed to ask what was happening really. No wonder the move had been like stepping over a cliff. Now no one cared any more whether she existed; she came to ask, without words, if she did exist. Yes, she felt sure there *must* be a Mrs Watson. Asking why she felt sure, she fell prey to every horror of the subjective world. Wandering, frightened, there, she observed with apathy that the perm was growing out of her hair; some days she never took off her overall. She fell into a way of standing opposite the mantel mirror in the front room on heavy afternoons. The room was made water-grey by the elms opposite, that had not yet shed their rotting autumn leaves – there was no frost, no wind, no reason why they should ever fall. There are no words for such dismay. Her blue eyes began to dilate oddly; her mouth took on an uncertain stubborn twist. The

---

[1]   British usage for a sweater.

hammering from behind the house continued; now and then a gate down the road clicked and somebody walked past without knowing her.

In all Eagles' houses the married bedroom is at the front. At this time of year the sun rose behind the hill, casting shadows of elms across the blanket about the moment that Mrs Watson woke. The orange curtains would flame, the bedroom dazzle with sunshine. Though rain often set in later and almost all nights were wet, the early mornings were brilliant. She used to sit up, pull off her shingle-cap and shake out her short, blonde hair, seeing light burn its tips. The empty promise of morning shot a pang through her heart to tell her she was awake again. Mr Watson slept late with determination; you saw his dread of waking under his lids. He lay beside her in a pre-natal attitude, legs crossed and drawn up, one cheek thrust into the pillow. The ripple his wife's getting up sent across the mattress did not ever disturb him. When she had lit the geyser,[2] set breakfast and started the children dressing she would come back and shake the end of the bed. The first thing he always saw was his wife at the bed's foot, gripping the brass with sun flaming round the tips of her hair. A Viking woman, foreign to all he knew of Muriel, with eyes remorseless as the remorseless new day, fixed on him a stare that he did not dare to plumb.

She had given up grumbling and seldom passed remarks now. Something behind her silence he learned to dread.

Saturdays were his half-days. One Saturday, when they had been there about eight weeks, he suddenly stuck his fork upright into the garden soil, eased the palms of his townish hands which had blistered, scraped off clods from his insteps on to the fork and went indoors to the kitchen to run the tap. He did all this in the decisive manner of someone acting on impulse, shy of himself. Towelling his face and hands on the roller he instinctively listened. Rhyll was a sounding box and she could be heard not there. She did say something, he thought, about going into town. Freddie and Vera were out about the estate. So there was no one to wonder . . . So he stepped round the house and out at the front gate. Since they came, he had had no secret pleasure. Today he would start up Nut Lane which, unknown, edged the estate with savageness.

Standing between the stumps of broken-down hedges he looked back at their road. A single twist of smoke from a chimney melted into the thin November grey, but the houses with close 'art' curtains looking unliving – what should animate them? Behind, scaffolding poles, squares more of daylight being entombed there . . . Inside, the lane was full of builders' rubbish. He started uphill, stepping from rib to rib of slimy hardness over chasms of mud. Rotting leaves made silent whole reaches of lane. Recoiling from branches in the thickety darkness, he thought he had not asked what Freddie said he had seen. The idea of a ghost's persistent aliveness comforted some under part of his mind.

The slope slackened, the lane was running level through a scrubby hazel wood with the sky behind. This must be round the other side of the hill. He looked into the wood which, because he had not known it existed, looked as though no one had ever seen it before. Part of its strangeness was a woman's body face down on the ground. Her arms were stretched out and she wore a mackintosh. With a jump of vulgar excitement he wondered if she were dead. Then the fair hair unnaturally fallen forward and red belt of the mackintosh showed him this was his wife, who could not be dead. Her manner of being here made his heart stop; then he felt hot colour come up his neck. He foresaw her shame at lying like this here; having heard steps she was keeping her face hidden. He could not have been more stricken in his idea of her if he had found her here with another man. He did not like to see her embrace the earth.

Waiting to bolt if she stirred, he stood where he was, eyeing her figure; its fiercely abject line. He stepped sharply up the bank into the wood. Her not stiffening as he approached shocked him. He pulled up and saw her contract one hand.

He heard himself say: 'So you didn't go to town?'

'No.'

'Feeling bad?'

'I'm all right.'

---

[2] An apparatus for rapidly heating water, whether attached to a bath or for use in a wash-basin, sink, etc.

'Then look here,' he said, his voice humping a tone, 'you oughtn't to be like that in a place like this. I might have been anyone.'

'What of it?' she said, her mouth muffled by grass.

'Besides, look here... That grass is reeking wet.'

'That's up to me,' she said. 'Get out. Why keep on coming after me?'

'How should I know? I was simply taking a turn.'

'Well, take your turn,' said her dead voice.

He took an angry forward step, looking down at her violently. Nothing appears more wanton than despair. 'I won't have it,' he said, 'it isn't decent. Get up.'

She drew her arms in, pushed herself on to her knees and got right up in one slow, disdainful movement, keeping her face away. 'Decent?' she said. 'This place isn't anywhere.'

'It's round where we live.'

'Live?' she said, 'What do you mean, live?'

'Well, we—'

'What do you mean, we?'

'You and I,' he said, looking sideways at her shoulder.

'Yes,' she said. 'It's fine for me having you. Sometimes anyone would almost think you could speak.'

'Well, what is there to say?'

'Don't ask me.'

'Well, you've got a home.'

'Oh, yes,' she said, 'I have, haven't I? Yes, it's sweet, isn't it? Like you see in advertisements.' She thrust her thumbs under the belt of her mackintosh.

'You've no business...' he said. 'Suppose Freddie or Vee had happened to come up here. That'd have been a nice...'

'Well, it'd show Vera...'

'Look here,' he said, 'You're batty!'

'No; I'm just noticing.'

Catching at her near shoulder he pulled her round to face him. His excitement, unfamiliar, excited him; he saw his rage tower. She stood stock still in her buttoned mackintosh, staring woodenly past his shoulder at the bleak wood, unconscious as any dummy of being touched. She said: 'Why is it awful?'

'It's a new place.'

'Yes. But it oughtn't to be awful, not awful like this.'

'Awful?'

'You know it is.'

'We've got each other.'

She gave him that glazed, unironic, really terrible look. Throat nervously filling up, he objected again – 'But, people...'

'Yes, I know they do. Even right in the country miles off. They seem to get on all right. So what I want to know is...'

'You expect such a whole lot...'

'No. Only what's natural.'

He frowned down at the form she had left in the crushed, autumny grass for so long that she looked down at it too. 'There must be some way,' he said. 'To keep going, I mean.'

'Yes, there ought to be,' she said. 'If you ask me, I don't know what a house like that is meant for. You can't think what it's like when you're in it the whole time. I can't understand, really.'

'We're the same as we've been always.'

'Yes,' she said, 'but it didn't notice before.'

He changed colour and said, 'You know I...I think the world of you.'

'Well, you've sort of got to, haven't you?' she replied unmovedly. 'Why aren't the two of us having a better time?'

'Well, we don't know anyone yet.'

'I wonder,' she said. 'Do you think there's so much in that?'

He looked at the wood's dead glades and emasculate, sparse leaves thin with afternoon light. 'You know,' he said, 'this place will be nice in spring. We might come here quite a lot.'

But, not listening, she said, 'The way we live, we never know anyone. All that crowd back at home, they've forgotten us. It was all coming in for coffee, or else whist. It doesn't get you anywhere. I mean, you get used to it, but that doesn't make it natural. What I mean is . . .'

However, she broke off there and began to walk away, stepping down the low bank into the lane. 'Yes,' she said in a different voice, 'it's a nice wood. The kids know it quite well.'

'What d'you think Freddie saw?' he said rapidly, following her downhill.

'Oh, I don't know. I daresay he saw himself.' Tilted on wobbling heels she went downhill ahead of him, low branches thwacking against the thighs of her mackintosh. A crimpled dead leaf caught in her hair, over her turned-up collar. He followed, eyes on the leaf, doggedly striding, stumbling between the ruts. It was going on tea-time: in the tunnel of lane the twilight was pretty deep and a dull, lightish glimmer came from her mackintosh. Coming down, the lane was shorter; the wood was near their door, too near their door.

When, one behind the other, they stepped through the broken hedge opposite Rhyll, a youngish woman stood at Rhyll gate, at a loss, looking about. She was hatless and wore a brick woollen three-piece suit. Her air was neighbourly.

She said, 'Oh, Mrs Watson?'

Mrs Watson replied guardedly.

'I hope I may introduce myself. I am Mrs Dawkins from just along there. Kosy Kot. I was sorry to find you out. I am sure you won't mind my taking the liberty, but your Vera and my Dorothy have been playing together recently and I called in to ask if you'd think of kindly allowing Vera to stop to tea with Dorothy this afternoon. Mr Dawkins and I would be most glad that she should.'

'Well, really, that's most kind of you, I'm sure. If Vera's a good girl, and comes home at half-past six . . .'

'I did hope you would not think it a liberty, I have to be careful with Dorothy, as we are quite newcomers, but Vera is such a sweet, nice little thing – I understand that you are newcomers also?'

'So to speak,' said Mrs Watson. 'We've lived here about eight weeks. But the newer houses are lived in now, I see.'

'It's a nice estate,' said Mrs Dawkins, 'isn't it? Convenient and yet in a way countrified. I shall be glad when they make the roads up; at present Mr Dawkins cannot get his car out, which is disappointing for him.' She glanced at the blank beside Rhyll where there could be a baby garage.

'We've delayed getting our car till the roads were made,' said Mrs Watson at once. 'The 'buses being so frequent and everything.'

Mr Watson, looking surprised, edged past them in at Rhyll gate. Both ladies turned and watched him up to the path.

'I always say,' continued Mrs Dawkins, 'that it takes time to settle into a place. Gentlemen, being out so much, don't feel it the same way.'

'It's hardly to be expected,' said Mrs Watson. Putting a hand up to pat all round the shingle, she plucked the leaf from her hair. 'Still, I've no doubt a place grows on one. It's really all habit, isn't it?'

In the Square (1941)

At about nine o'clock on this hot bright July evening the square looked mysterious: it was completely empty, and a whitish reflection, ghost of the glare of midday, came from the pale-coloured façades on its four sides and seemed to brim it up to the top. The grass was parched in the middle; its shaved surface was paid for by people who had gone. The sun, now too low to enter

"In the Square" was first published in *Horizon* 4(21) (Sept. 1941),
then collected in *The Demon Lover and Other Stories* (London:
Jonathan Cape, 1945).

normally, was able to enter brilliantly at a point where three of the houses had been bombed away; two or three of the may trees, dark with summer, caught on their tops the illicit gold. Each side of the breach, exposed wallpapers were exaggerated into viridians, yellows and corals that they had probably never been. Elsewhere, the painted front doors under the balconies and at the tops of steps not whitened for some time stood out in the deadness of colour with light off it. Most of the glassless windows were shuttered or boarded up, but some framed hollow inside dark.

The extinct scene had the appearance of belonging to some ages ago. Time having only been thrust forward for reasons that could no longer affect the square, this still was a virtual eight o' clock. One taxi did now enter at the north side and cruise round the polish to a house in a corner: a man got out and paid his fare. He glanced round him, satisfied to find the shell of the place here. In spite of the dazzling breach, the square's accoustics had altered very little: in the confined sound of his taxi driving away there was nothing to tell him he had not arrived to dinner as on many summer evenings before. He went up familar steps and touched the chromium bell. Some windows of this house were not shuttered, though they were semi-blinded by oiled stuff behind which the curtains dimly hung: these windows fixed on the outdoors their tenacious look; some of the sashes were pushed right up, to draw this singular summer evening – parched, freshening and a little acrid with ruins – into the rooms in which people lived. When the bell was not answered, the man on the steps frowned at the jade green front door, then rang again. On which the door was opened by an unfamiliar person, not a maid, who stood pushing up her top curls. She wore a cotton dress and studied him with the coldly intimate look he had found new in women since his return.

By contrast with the fixed outdoor silence, this dark interior was a cave of sound. The house now was like a machine with the silencer off it; there was nothing muted; the carpets looked thin. One got a feeling of functional anarchy, of loose plumbing, of fittings shocked from their place. From the basement came up a smell of basement cooking, a confident voice and the sound of a shutting door. At the top of the house a bath was being run out. A tray of glasses was moved, so inexpertly that everything on it tinkled, somewhere in the drawing-room over his head.

'She's expecting you, is she?' said the sceptical girl. He saw on the table behind her only a couple of leaflets and a driver's cap.

'I think so.'

'You know I'm expecting you!' exclaimed Magdela, beginning to come round the turn of the stairs.

'Sorry,' the girl said, stepping back to speak up the staircase. 'I didn't know you were in.' Turning, she disappeared through a waiting door, the door behind the dining-room, which she shut. 'Do come up, Rupert,' said Magdela, extending her hand to him from where she stood. 'I'm sorry; I meant to come down myself.'

Of the three drawing-room windows two stood open, so she must have heard the taxi: her failure to get to the door in time had been due to some inhibition or last thought. It would have been remarkable if she *had* yet arrived at the manner in which to open her own door – which would have to be something quite different from the impulsive informality of peace time. The tray of glasses she had been heard moving now stood on a pedestal table beside a sofa. She said: 'These days, there is no one to . . .' Indeed the expanse of parquet, though unmarked, no longer showed watery gloss and depth. Though it may have only been by the dusk that the many white lampshades were discoloured, he saw under one, as he sat down beside her, a film of dust over the bulb. Though they were still many, the lamps were fewer; some had been put away with the bric-a-brac that used to be on the tables and in the alcoves – and these occasional blanks were the least discomforting thing in the dead room. The reflections in from the square fell on the chairs and sofas already worn rough on their satin tops and arms, and with grime homing into their rubbed parts. This had been the room of a hostess; the replica of so many others that you could not count. It had never had any other aspect, and it had no aspect at all to-night. The chairs remained so many, and their pattern was now so completely without focus that, had Magdela not sat down where she did sit, he would not have known in which direction to turn.

'How nice it was of you to ring me up,' she said. 'I had had no idea you were back in London. How did you know I was here? No one else is.'

'I happened to hear——'

'Oh, did you?' she said, a little bit disconcerted, then added quickly: 'Were you surprised?'

'I was delighted, naturally.'

'I came back,' she said. 'For the first year I was away, part of the time in the country, part of the time in the North with Anthony – he has been there since this all started, you know. Then, last winter, I decided to come back.'

'You are a Londoner.'

She said mechanically: 'Yes, I suppose so – yes. It's so curious to see you again, like this. Who would think that this was the same world?' She looked sideways out of the window, at the square. 'Who would have thought this could really happen? The last time we – how long ago was that? Two years ago?'

'A delightful evening.'

'Was it?' she said, and looked round the room. 'How nice. One has changed so much since then, don't you think? It is quite——'

At this point the door opened and a boy of about sixteen came in, in a dressing-grown. Not only was his hair twisted in tufts of dampness but a sort of humidity seemed to follow him, as though he were trailing the bathroom steam. 'Oh, sorry,' he said, but after a glance at Rupert he continued his way to the cigarette box. 'Bennet,' said Magdela 'I feel sure you ought not to smoke – Rupert, this is my nephew, Bennet: I expect we sometimes talked about him. He is here just for the night, on his way from school.'

'That reminds me,' said Bennet, 'would you very much mind if I stayed to-morrow?' Rupert watched Bennet squinting as he lighted a cigarette. 'They say everyone's smoking more, now,' said Bennet. 'Actually, I hardly smoke at all.' He dropped the match into the empty steel grate. 'I took a bath,' he said to Magdela. 'I'm just going out.'

'Oh, Bennet, have you had anything to eat?'

'Well, I had tea at six,' he said, 'with an egg. I expect I'll pick up something at a Corner House.' He stooped to pull up a slipper on one heel and said: 'I didn't know you had visitors. As a matter of fact, I didn't know you were in. But everyone seems to be in to-night.' When he went out he did not shut the door behind him, and they could hear him slip-slopping upstairs. 'He's very independent,' said Magdela. 'But these days I suppose everyone is?'

'I must say,' he said, 'I'm glad you are not alone here. I should not like to think of your being that.'

'Wouldn't you?' she said. 'Well, I never am. This is my only room in the house – and, even so, as you see, Bennet comes in. The house seems to belong to everyone now. That was Gina who opened the front door.'

'Yes,' he said, 'who is she?'

'She used to be Anthony's secretary, but she wanted to come to London to drive a car for the war, so he told her she could live in this house, because it was shut up at that time. So it seemed to be quite hers, when I came back. She is supposed to sit in the back dining-room; that was why I couldn't ask you to dinner. But also, there is nobody who can cook – there is a couple down in the basement, but they are independent; they are only supposed to be caretakers. They have a son who is a policeman, and I know he sometimes sleeps somewhere at the top of the house – but caretakers are so hard to get. They have a schoolgirl daughter who comes in here when she thinks I am not about.'

'It seems to me you have a lot to put with. Wouldn't you be more comfortable somewhere else?'

'Oh,' she said, 'is that how you think of me?'

'I do hope you will dine with me, one night soon.'

'Thank you,' she said evasively. 'Some night that would be very nice.'

'I suppose the fact is, you are very busy?'

'Yes, I am. I am working, doing things quite a lot.' She told him what she did, then her voice trailed off. He realized that he and she could not be intimate without many other people in the room. He looked at the empty pattern of chairs round them and said: 'Where are all those people I used to meet?'

'Whom do you mean, exactly?' she said, startled. '– Oh, in different places, different places, you know. I think I have their addresses, if there's anyone special –?'

'You hear news of them?'

'Oh yes; oh yes, I'm sure I do. What can I tell you that would be interesting? I'm sorry,' she said suddenly, shutting her eyes, 'but so much has happened.' Opening her eyes to look at him, she added: 'So much more than you know.'

To give point to this, the telephone started ringing: the bell filled the room, the sounding-box of the house and travelled through windows into the square. Rupert remembered how, on other summer evenings, you had constantly heard the telephones in the houses round. It was to-night startling to hear a telephone ring. Magdela stared at the telephone, at a distance from her – not as though she shared this feeling that Rupert had, but as though something happened out of its time. She seemed to forbid the bell with her eyes, with that intent fixed warning intimate look, and, seeming unwilling to leave the sofa, contracted into stone-stillness by Rupert's side. At a loss, he said: 'Like me to see who it is?'

'No, I will; I must,' her voice hardened, 'Or they will be answering from downstairs.'

This evidently did happen: the bell stopped an instant before her fingers touched the receiver. She raised it, listened into it, frowned. 'It's all right, Gina,' she said. 'Thank you; you needn't bother. I'm here.'

She stood with her back to Rupert, with her head bent, still warily listening to the receiver. Then: 'Yes, it's me now,' she said, in an all at once very much altered tone. 'But——'

After Gina had let in Rupert she went back to continue to wait for her telephone call. *She* always answered from the foot of the stairs. Before sitting down again, or not sitting down, she went through from the back to the front dining-room, to open the window overlooking the square. The long table and the two sideboards were, as she always remembered them, sheeted up, and a smell of dust came from the sheets. Returning to the room that was hers to sit in, she left the archway doors open behind her, so that, before the black-out, air might pass through. The perspective of useless dining-room through the archway, the light fading from it through the bombed gap did not affect her. She had not enough imagination to be surprised by the past – still less, by its end. When, the November after the war started, she first came to sleep in the closed house, she had, as Anthony's mistress, speculated as to this former part of his life. She supposed he had gained something by entertaining, though it did not seem to her he had much to show. While she stayed faithful to him she pitied him for a number of reasons she did not let appear. Now that she had begun to deceive him she found only that one reason to pity him. Now she loved someone else in a big way, she supposed it was time to clear out of this house. She only thought this; she did not feel it; her feelings were not at all fine. She did not know how to move without bringing the whole thing up, which would be tough on Anthony while he was in the North.

As to her plans for to-night – she never knew. So much depended – or, she might hear nothing. She wondered if she should put in time by writing to Anthony; she got out her pad and sat with it on her knee. Hearing Bennet's bath continue to run out she thought, that's a funny time for a bath. Underneath where she sat, the caretaker's wife was washing up the supper dishes and calling over her shoulder to her policeman son: the voice came out through the basement window and withered back on the silence round.

She wrote words on the pad:

'*Since I came here one thing and another seems to have altered my point of view. I don't know how to express myself, but I think under the circumstances I ought to tell you. Being here has started to get me down; for one thing it is such a way from the bus. Of course it has been a help; but don't you think it would be better if your wife had the place all to herself? As far as I can see she means to stay. Naturally she and I do not refer to this. But, for instance, if she had two nephews there would be no place for the other to sleep –*'

– And looked at them with her head on one side. She heard Bennet come down the flights of staircase, rigidly dropping his feet from step to step. He pulled up with a jingle of the things in his pockets and thought of something outside her door. O God, don't let him come bothering in here, you see I might get this done. But he did: leaning his weight on the door handle and with the other hand holding the frame of the door he swung forward at her, with damp-flattened hair.

'Sorry,' he said, 'but shall you be going out?' She kept a hold on her letter-pad and said fiercely: 'Why?'

'If not, I might have your key.'

'Why not ask your aunt?'

'She's got someone there. You mean, you might go out, but you don't know?'

'No. Don't come bothering here, like a good boy. What's the matter with you, have you got a date?'

'No,' he said. 'I just want some food in some place.'

He walked away from her through the archway and looked out at the square from the end of the dining-room. The lampless dusk seemed to fascinate him. 'There are quite a lot of people standing about,' he said. 'Couples. This must be quite a place. Do you suppose they go into the empty houses?'

'No, they're all locked up.'

'What's the good of that, I don't see?'

'They're property.'

'I should say they were cracked; I shouldn't say they'd ever be much use. Oh, sorry, are you writing a letter? I say, I thought they were taking the railings away from squares;[1] I thought the iron was some good. You think this place will patch up? I suppose it depends who wants it. Anybody can have it as far as I'm concerned. You can't get to anywhere from here.'

'Hadn't you better push off? Everywhere will be shut.'

'I know, but what about the key?'

But her head turned sharply: the telephone started ringing at the foot of the stairs. Bennet's expression became more hopeful. 'Go on, why don't you,' he said, 'then we might know where we are.'

Gina came back to him from the telephone, with one hand pushing her curls up. 'So what?' said Bennet.

'That was for her,' she said. 'It would be. I got my head bitten off. No place for me, on that line. You'd think she was the only one in the house.' She picked up her bag and gave him the key out of it. 'Oh, all right,' she said. 'Here you are. Run along.'

He thumbed the key and said: 'Oh, then it wasn't your regular?'

'Nothing of mine,' she said. 'Regular if you like. . . . Look, I thought you were going to run along?'

Just before Bennet shut the front door behind him he heard a ghostly click from the telephone at the foot of the stairs – in the drawing-room the receiver had been put back. Whatever there had been to say to his aunt must have been said – or totally given up. He thought, so what was the good of *that?* Stepping down into the dusk of the square, that lay at the foot of the steps like water, he heard voices above his head. His aunt and her visitor stood at one of the open windows, looking down, or seeming to look down, at the lovers. Rupert and Magdela for the moment looked quite intimate, as though they had withdrawn to the window from a number of people in the room behind them – only in that case the room would have been lit up.

Bennet, going out to hunt food, kept close along under the fronts of the houses with a primitive secretiveness. He made for the north outlet of the square, by which Rupert's taxi had come in, and at last in the distance heard the sound of a bus.

Magdela smiled and said to Rupert: 'Yes, look. Now the place seems to belong to everyone. One has nothing except one's feelings. Sometimes I think I hardly know myself.'

'How curious that light is,' he said, looking across at the gap.

'You know, I am happy.' This was her only reference to the words he had heard her say to the telephone. 'Of course, I have no plans. This is no time to make plans, now. But do talk to me – perhaps you have no plans, either? I have been so selfish, talking about myself. But to meet you

---

[1]   During the Second World War, railings from public squares and private houses were to be dismantled and melted down to   provide iron for the war effort; in practice this program was implemented in a haphazard way.

after so much has happened – in one way, there seemed nothing to talk about. Do tell me how things strike you, what you have thought of things – coming back to everything like you have. Do you think we shall all see a great change?'

Mysterious Kôr (1944)

Full moonlight drenched the city and searched it; there was not a niche left to stand in. The effect was remorseless: London looked like the moon's capital – shallow, cratered, extinct. It was late, but not yet midnight; now the buses had stopped the polished roads and streets in this region sent for minutes together a ghostly unbroken reflection up. The soaring new flats and the crouching old shops and houses looked equally brittle under the moon, which blazed in windows that looked its way. The futility of the black-out became laughable: from the sky, presumably, you could see every slate in the roofs, every whited kerb, every contour of the naked winter flowerbeds in the park; and the lake, with its shining twists and tree-darkened islands would be a landmark for miles, yes, miles, overhead.

However, the sky, in whose glassiness floated no clouds but only opaque balloons, remained glassy-silent. The Germans no longer came by the full moon. Something more immaterial seemed to threaten, and to be keeping people at home. This day between days, this extra tax, was perhaps more than senses and nerves could bear. People stayed indoors with a fervour that could be felt: the buildings strained with battened-down human life, but not a beam, not a voice, not a note from a radio escaped. Now and then under streets and buildings the earth rumbled: the Underground sounded loudest at this time.

Outside the now gateless gates of the park,[1] the road coming downhill from the north-west turned south and became a street, down whose perspective the traffic lights went through their unmeaning performance of changing colour. From the promontory of pavement outside the gates you saw at once up the road and down the street: from behind where you stood, between the gate-posts, appeared the lesser strangeness of grass and water and trees. At this point, at this moment, three French soldiers, directed to a hostel they could not find, stopped singing to listen derisively to the waterbirds wakened up by the moon. Next, two wardens coming off duty emerged from their post and crossed the road diagonally, each with an elbow cupped inside a slung-on tin hat. The wardens turned their faces, mauve in the moonlight, towards the Frenchmen with no expression at all. The two sets of steps died in opposite directions, and, the birds subsiding, nothing was heard or seen until, a little way down the street, a trickle of people came out of the Underground, around the anti-panic brick wall.[2] These all disappeared quickly, in an abashed way, or as though dissolved in the street by some white acid, but for a girl and a soldier who, by their way of walking, seemed to have no destination but each other and to be not quite certain even of that. Blotted into one shadow he tall, she little, these two proceeded towards the park. They looked in, but did not go in; they stood there debating without speaking. Then, as though a command from the street behind them had been received by their synchronized bodies, they faced round to look back the way they had come.

His look up the height of a building made his head drop back, and she saw his eyeballs glitter. She slid her hand from his sleeve, stepped to the edge of the pavement and said: 'Mysterious Kôr.'[3]

"Mysterious Kôr," was first published in *Penguin New Writing* (Jan. 1944), then collected in *The Demon Lover and Other Stories* (London: Jonathan Cape, 1945).

[1] The gates were taken away and melted down as part of a program to provide iron for the war effort.

[2] During the Second World War, an antipanic wall was one constructed at the stairways leading down to underground or tube stations; typically made of sandbags or, as here, brick, they blocked the entrance enough that people would not trample one another when rushing down the stairs.

[3] From the sonnet "She" by the Scottish author and poet Andrew Lang (1844–1912). The sonnet's title, in turn, derives the novel *She* (1887) by Henry Rider Haggard (1856–1925), which recounts the quest of Leo Vincey to discover a sorceress named Ayesha, who resides in Kôr, an underground city in a mountain in Africa.

She

To H.R.H. [Henry Rider Haggard]

Not in the waste beyond the swamps and sand,

'What is?' he said, not quite collecting himself.
'This is –

> "Mysterious Kôr thy walls forsaken stand,
> Thy lonely towers beneath a lonely moon –"

– this is Kôr.'

'Why,' he said, 'it's years since I've thought of that.'
She said: 'I think of it all the time –

> "Not in the waste beyond the swamps and sand,
> The fever-haunted forest and lagoon,
> Mysterious Kôr thy walls——"

– a completely forsaken city, as high as cliffs and as white as bones, with no history——'
'But something must once have happened: why had it been forsaken?'
'How could anyone tell you when there's nobody there?'
'Nobody there since how long?'
'Thousands of years.'
'In that case, it would have fallen down.'
'No, not Kôr,' she said with immediate authority. 'Kôr's altogether different; it's very strong; there is not a crack in it anywhere for a weed to grow in; the corners of stones and the monuments might have been cut yesterday, and the stairs and arches are built to support themselves.'
'You know all about it,' he said, looking at her.
'I know, I know all about it.'
'What, since you read that book?'
'Oh, I didn't get much from that; I just got the name. I knew that must be the right name; it's like a cry.'
'Most like the cry of a crow to me.' He reflected, then said: 'But the poem begins with "Not" – "Not in the waste beyond the swamps and sand –" And it goes on, as I remember, to prove Kôr's not really anywhere. When even a poem says there's no such place –'
'What it tries to say doesn't matter: I see what it makes me see. Anyhow, that was written some time ago, at that time when they thought they had got everything taped, because the whole world had been explored, even the middle of Africa. Every thing and place had been found and marked on some map; so what wasn't marked on any map couldn't be there at all. So *they* thought: that was why he wrote the poem. "*The world is disenchanted,*"[4] it goes on. That was what set me off hating civilization.'
'Well, cheer up,' he said; 'there isn't much of it left.'
'Oh, yes, I cheered up some time ago. This war shows we've by no means come to the end. If you can blow whole places out of existence, you can blow whole places into it. I don't see why not. They say we can't say what's come out since the bombing started. By the time we've come to the end, Kôr may be the one city left: the abiding city. I should laugh.'
'No, you wouldn't,' he said sharply. '*You* wouldn't – at least, I hope not. I hope you don't know what you're saying – does the moon make you funny?'
'Don't be cross about Kôr; please don't, Arthur,' she said.
'I thought girls thought about people.'

The fever-haunted forest and lagoon,
Mysterious Kôr thy walls forsaken stand,
Thy lonely towers beneath the lonely moon,
Not there doth Ayesha linger, rune by rune
Spelling strange scriptures of a people banned,
The world is disenchanted; over soon
Shall Europe send her spies through all the land.
Nay, not in Kôr, but in whatever spot,

In town or field, or by the insatiate sea,
Men brood on buried loves, and unforgot,
Or break themselves on some divine decreee,
Or would o'erleap the limits of their lot,
There, in the tombs and deathless, dwelleth she!

4   See the preceding note.

'What, these days?' she said. 'Think about people? How can anyone think about people if they've got any heart? I don't know how other girls manage: I always think about Kôr.'

'Not about me?' he said. When she did not at once answer, he turned her hand over, in anguish, inside his grasp. 'Because I'm not there when you want me – is that my fault?'

'But to think about Kôr *is* to think about you and me.'

'In that dead place?'

'No, ours – we'd be alone here.'

Tightening his thumb on her palm while he thought this over, he looked behind them, around them, above them – even up at the sky. He said finally: 'But we're alone here.'

'That was why I said "Mysterious Kôr".'

'What, you mean we're there now, that here's there, that now's then?... *I* don't mind,' he added, letting out as a laugh the sigh he had been holding in for some time. 'You ought to know the place, and for all I could tell you we might be anywhere: I often do have it, this funny feeling, the first minute or two when I've come up out of the Underground. Well, well: join the Army and see the world.' He nodded towards the perspective of traffic lights and said, a shade craftily: 'What are those, then?'

Having caught the quickest possible breath, she replied: 'In-exhaustible gases; they bored through to them and lit them as they came up; by changing colour they show the changing of minutes; in Kôr there is no sort of other time.'

'You've got the moon, though: that can't help making months.'

'Oh, and the sun, of course; but those two could do what they liked; we should not have to calculate when they'd come or go.'

'We might not have to,' he said, 'but I bet I should.'

'I should not mind what you did, so long as you never said, "What next?"'

'I don't know about "next", but I do know what we'd do first.'

'What, Arthur?'

'Populate Kôr.'

She said: 'I suppose it would be all right if our children were to marry each other?'

But her voice faded out; she had been reminded that they were homeless on this his first night of leave. They were, that was to say, in London without any hope of any place of their own. Pepita shared a two-roomed flatlet with a girl friend, in a by-street off the Regent's Park Road,[5] and towards this they must make their half-hearted way. Arthur was to have the sitting-room divan, usually occupied by Pepita, while she herself had half of her girl friend's bed. There was really no room for a third, and least of all for a man, in those small rooms packed with furniture and the two girls' belongings: Pepita tried to be grateful for her friend Callie's forbearance – but how could she be, when it had not occurred to Callie that she would do better to be away tonight? She was more slow-witted than narrow-minded – but Pepita felt she owed a kind of ruin to her. Callie, not yet known to be home later than ten, would be now waiting up, in her house-coat, to welcome Arthur. That would mean three-sided chat, drinking cocoa, then turning in: that would be that, and that would be all. That was London, this war – they were lucky to have a roof – London, full enough before the Americans came. Not a place: they would even grudge you sharing a grave – that was what even married couples complained. Whereas in Kôr...

In Kôr... Like glass, the illusion shattered: a car hummed like a hornet towards them, veered, showed its scarlet tail-light, streaked away up the road. A woman edged round a front door and along the area railings timidly called her cat; meanwhile a clock near, then another set further back in the dazzling distance, set about striking midnight. Pepita, feeling Arthur release her arm with an abruptness that was the inverse of passion, shivered; whereat he asked brusquely: 'Cold? Well, Which way? – we'd better be getting on.'

---

[5]   A small road just beyond the northern edge of Regents Park and the London Zoo, in London.

Callie was no longer waiting up. Hours ago she had set out the three cups and saucers, the tins of cocoa and household milk and, on the gas-ring, brought the kettle to just short of the boil. She had turned open Arthur's bed, the living-room divan, in the neat inviting way she had learnt at home – then, with a modest impulse, replaced the cover. She had, as Pepita foresaw, been wearing her cretonne housecoat, the nearest thing to a hostess gown that she had; she had already brushed her hair for the night, rebraided it, bound the braids in a coronet round her head. Both lights and the wireless had been on, to make the room both look and sound gay: all alone, she had come to that peak moment at which company should arrive – but so seldom does. From then on she felt welcome beginning to wither in her, a flower of the heart that had bloomed too early. There she had sat like an image, facing the three cold cups, on the edge of the bed to be occupied by an unknown man.

Callie's innocence and her still unsought-out state had brought her to take a proprietary pride in Arthur; this was all the stronger, perhaps, because they had not yet met. Sharing the flat with Pepita, this last year, she had been content with reflecting the heat of love. It was not, surprisingly, that Pepita seemed very happy – there were times when she was palpably on the rack, and this was not what Callie could understand. 'Surely you owe it to Arthur,' she would then say, 'to keep cheerful? So long as you love each other—' Callie's calm brow glowed – one might say that it glowed in place of her friend's; she became the guardian of that ideality which for Pepita was constantly lost to view. It was true, with the sudden prospect of Arthur's leave, things had come nearer to earth: he became a proposition, and she would have been as glad if he could have slept somewhere else. Physically shy, a brotherless virgin, Callie shrank from sharing this flat with a young man. In this flat you could hear everything: what was once a three-windowed Victorian drawing-room had been partitioned, by very thin walls, into kitchenette, living-room, Callie's bedroom. The living-room was in the centre; the two others open off it. What was once the conservatory, half a flight down, was now converted into a draughty bathroom, shared with somebody else on the girl's floor. The flat, for these days, was cheap – even so, it was Callie, earning more than Pepita, who paid the greater part of the rent: it thus became up to her, more or less, to express good will as to Arthur's making a third. 'Why, it will be lovely to have him here,' Callie said. Pepita accepted the good will without much grace – but then, had she ever much grace to spare? – she was as restlessly secretive, as self-centred, as a little half-grown black cat. Next came a puzzling moment: Pepita seemed to be hinting that Callie should fix herself up somewhere else. 'But where would I go?' Callie marvelled when this was at last borne in on her. 'You know what London's like now. And, anyway' – here she laughed, but hers was a forehead that coloured as easily as it glowed – 'it wouldn't be proper, would it, me going off and leaving just you and Arthur; I don't know what your mother would say to me. No, we may be a little squashed, but we'll make things ever so homey. I shall not mind playing gooseberry, really, dear.'

But the hominess by now was evaporating, as Pepita and Arthur still and still did not come. At half-past ten, in obedience to the rule of the house, Callie was obliged to turn off the wireless, whereupon silence out of the stepless street began seeping into the slighted room. Callie recollected the fuel target[6] and turned off her dear little table lamp, gaily painted with spots to make it look like a toadstool, thereby leaving only the hanging light. She laid her hand on the kettle, to find it gone cold again and sigh for the wasted gas if not for her wasted thought. Where are they? Cold crept up her out of the kettle; she went to bed.

Callie's bed lay along the wall under the window: she did not like sleeping so close up under glass, but the clearance that must be left for the opening of door and cupboards made this the only possible place. Now she got in and lay rigidly on the bed's inner side, under the hanging hems of the window curtains, training her limbs not to stray to what would be Pepita's half. This sharing of her bed with another body would not be the least of her sacrifice to the lovers' love; tonight would be the first night – or at least, since she was an infant – that Callie had slept with anyone. Child of a sheltered middle-class household, she had kept physical distances all her life. Already repugnance and shyness ran through her limbs; she was preyed upon by some more obscure trouble than the

<hr />

[6]   To ration fuel during the Second World War, the minister of fuel and power created a fuel-saving campaign. Each family was   given a fuel target and a household member was put in charge as a monitor.

expectation that she might not sleep. As to *that*, Pepita was restless; her tossings on the divan, her broken-off exclamations and blurred pleas had been to be heard; most nights, through the dividing wall.

Callie knew, as though from a vision, that Arthur would sleep soundly, with assurance and majesty. Did they not all say, too, that a soldier sleeps like a log? With awe she pictured, asleep, the face that she had not yet, awake, seen – Arthur's man's eyelids, cheekbones and set mouth turned up to the darkened ceiling. Wanting to savour darkness herself, Callie reached out and put off her bedside lamp.

At once she knew that something was happening – outdoors, in the street, the whole of London, the world. An advance, an extraordinary movement was silently taking place; blue-white beams overflowed from it, silting, dropping round the edges of the muffling black-out curtains. When, starting up, she knocked a fold of the curtain, a beam like a mouse ran across her bed. A search-light, the most powerful of all time, might have been turned full and steady upon her defended window; finding flaws in the black-out stuff, it made veins and stars. Once gained by this idea of pressure she could not lie down again; she sat tautly, drawn-up knees touching her breasts, and asked herself if there were anything she should do. She parted the curtains, opened them slowly wider, looked out – and was face to face with the moon.

Below the moon, the houses opposite her window blazed back in transparent shadow; and something – was it a coin or a ring? – glittered half-way across the chalk-white street. Light marched in past her face, and she turned to see where it went: out stood the curves and garlands of the great white marble Victorian mantelpiece of that lost drawing-room; out stood, in the photographs turned her way, the thoughts with which her parents had faced the camera, and the humble puzzlement of her two dogs at home. Of silver brocade, just faintly purpled with roses, became her house-coat hanging over the chair. And the moon did more: it exonerated and beautified the lateness of the lovers' return. No wonder, she said herself, no wonder – if this was the world they walked in, if this was whom they were with. Having drunk in the white explanation, Callie lay down again. Her half of the bed was in shadow, but she allowed one hand to lie, blanched, in what would be Pepita's place. She lay and looked at the hand until it was no longer her own.

Callie woke to the sound of Pepita's key in the latch. But no voices? What had happened? Then she heard Arthur's step. She heard his unslung equipment dropped with a weary, dull sound, and the plonk of his tin hat on a wooden chair. 'Sssh-sssh!' Pepita exclaimed, 'she *might* be asleep!'

Then at last Arthur's voice: 'But I thought you said –'

'I'm not asleep; I'm just coming!' Callie called out with rapture, leaping out from her form in shadow into the moonlight, zipping on her enchanted house-coat over her nightdress, kicking her shoes on, and pinning in place, with a trembling firmness, her plaits in their coronet round her head. Between these movements of hers she heard not another sound. Had she only dreamed they were there? Her heart beat: she stepped through the living-room, shutting her door behind her.

Pepita and Arthur stood the other side of the table; they gave the impression of being lined up. Their faces, at different levels – for Pepita's rough, dark head came only an inch above Arthur's khaki shoulder – were alike in abstention from any kind of expression; as though, spiritually, they both still refused to be here. Their features looked faint, weathered – was this the work of the moon? Pepita said at once: 'I suppose we are very late?'

'I don't wonder,' Callie said, 'on this lovely night.'

Arthur had not raised his eyes; he was looking at the three cups. Pepita now suddenly jogged his elbow, saying, 'Arthur, wake up; say something; this is Callie – well, Callie, this is Arthur, of course.'

'Why, yes of course this is Arthur,' returned Callie, whose candid eyes since she entered had not left Arthur's face. Perceiving that Arthur did not know what to do, she advanced round the table to shake hands with him. He looked up, she looked down, for the first time: she rather beheld than felt his red-brown grip on what still seemed her glove of moonlight. 'Welcome, Arthur,' she said. 'I'm so glad to meet you at last. I hope you will be comfortable in the flat.'

'It's been kind of you,' he said after consideration.

'Please do not feel that,' said Callie. 'This is Pepita's home, too, and we both hope – don't we, Pepita? – that you'll regard it as yours. Please feel free to do just as you like. I am sorry it is so small.'

'Oh, I don't know,' Arthur said, as though hypnotized; 'it seems a nice little place.'

Pepita, meanwhile, glowered and turned away.

Arthur continued to wonder, though he had once been told, how these two unalike girls had come to set up together – Pepita so small, except for her too-big head, compact of childish brusqueness and of unchildish passion, and Callie, so sedate, waxy and tall – an unlit candle. Yes, she was like one of those candles on sale outside a church; there could be something votive even in her demeanour. She was unconscious that her good manners, those of an old fashioned country doctor's daughter, were putting the other two at a disadvantage. He found himself touched by the grave good faith with which Callie was wearing that tartish house-coat, above which her face kept the glaze of sleep; and, as she knelt to relight the gas-ring under the kettle, he marked the strong, delicate arch of one bare foot, disappearing into the arty green shoe. Pepita was now too near him ever again to be seen as he now saw Callie – in a sense, he never *had* seen Pepita for the first time: she had not been, and still sometimes was not, his type. No, he had not thought of her twice; he had not remembered her until he began to remember her with passion. You might say he had not seen Pepita coming: their love had been a collision in the dark.

Callie, determined to get this over, knelt back and said: 'Would Arthur like to wash his hands?' When they had heard him stumble down the half-flight of stairs, she said to Pepita: 'Yes, I was so glad you had the moon.'

'Why?' said Pepita. She added: 'There was too much of it.'

'You're tired. Arthur looks tired, too.'

'How would you know? He's used to marching about. But it's all this having no place to go.'

'But, Pepita, you—'

But at this point Arthur came back: from the door he noticed the wireless, and went direct to it. 'Nothing much on now, I suppose?' he doubtfully said.

'No; you see it's past midnight; we're off the air. And, anyway, in this house they don't like the wireless late. By the same token,' went on Callie, friendly smiling, 'I'm afraid I must ask you, Arthur, to take your boots off, unless, of course, you mean to stay sitting down. The people below us—'

Pepita flung off, saying something under her breath, but Arthur, remarking, 'No, I don't mind,' both sat down and began to take off his boots. Pausing, glancing to left and right at the divan's fresh cotton spread, he said: 'It's all right is it, for me to sit on this?'

'That's my bed,' said Pepita. 'You are to sleep in it.'

Callie then made the cocoa, after which they turned in. Preliminary trips to the bathroom having been worked out, Callie was first to retire, shutting the door behind her so that Pepita and Arthur might kiss each other good night. When Pepita joined her, it was without knocking: Pepita stood still in the moon and began to tug off her clothes. Glancing with hate at the bed, she asked: 'Which side?'

'I expected you'd like the outside.'

'What are you standing about for?'

'I don't really know: as I'm inside I'd better get in first.'

'Then why not get in?'

When they had settled rigidly, side by side, Callie asked: 'Do you think Arthur's got all he wants?'

Pepita jerked her head up. 'We can't sleep in all this moon.'

'Why, you don't believe the moon does things, actually?'

'Well, it couldn't hope to make some of us *much* more screwy.'

Callie closed the curtains, then said: 'What do you mean? And – didn't you hear? – I asked if Arthur's got all he wants.'

'That's what I meant – have you got a screw loose, really?'

'Pepita, I won't stay here if you're going to be like this.'

'In that case, you had better go in with Arthur.'

'What about me?' Arthur loudly said through the wall. 'I can hear practically all you girls are saying.'

They were both startled – rather that than abashed. Arthur, alone in there, had thrown off the ligatures of his social manner: his voice held the whole authority of his sex – he was impatient, sleepy, and he belonged to no one.

'Sorry,' the girls said in unison. Then Pepita laughed soundlessly, making their bed shake, till to stop herself she bit the back of her hand, and this movement made her elbow strike Callie's cheek. 'Sorry,' she had to whisper. No answer: Pepita fingered her elbow and found, yes, it was quite true, it was wet. 'Look, shut up crying, Callie: what have I done?'

Callie rolled right round, in order to press her forehead closely under the window, into the curtains, against the wall. Her weeping continued to be soundless: now and then, unable to reach her handkerchief, she staunched her eyes with a curtain, disturbing slivers of moon. Pepita gave up marvelling, and soon slept: at least there is something in being dog-tired.

A clock struck four as Callie woke up again – but something else had made her open her swollen eyelids. Arthur, stumbling about on his padded feet, could be heard next door attempting to make no noise. Inevitably, he bumped the edge of the table. Callie sat up: by her side Pepita lay like a mummy rolled half over, in forbidding, tenacious sleep. Arthur groaned. Callie caught a breath, climbed lightly over Pepita, felt for her torch[7] on the mantelpiece, stopped to listen again. Arthur groaned again: Callie, with movements soundless as they were certain, opened the door and slipped through to the living-room. 'What's the matter?' she whispered. 'Are you ill?'

'No; I just got a cigarette. Did I wake you up?'

'But you groaned.'

'I'm sorry; I'd no idea.'

'But do you often?'

'I've no idea, really, I tell you,' Arthur repeated. The air of the room was dense with his presence, overhung by tobacco. He must be sitting on the edge of his bed, wrapped up in his overcoat – she could smell the coat, and each time he pulled on the cigarette his features appeared down there, in the fleeting, dull reddish glow. 'Where are you?' he said. 'Show a light.'

Her nervous touch on her torch, like a reflex to what he said, made it flicker up for a second. 'I am just by the door; Pepita's asleep; I'd better go back to bed.'

'Listen. Do you two get on each other's nerves?'

'Not till tonight,' said Callie, watching the uncertain swoops of the cigarette as he reached across to the ashtray on the edge of the table. Shifting her bare feet patiently, she added: 'You don't see us as we usually are.'

'She's a girl who shows things in funny ways – I expect she feels bad at our putting you out like this – I know I do. But then we'd got no choice, had we?'

'It is really I who am putting your out,' said Callie.

'Well, that can't be helped either, can it? You had the right to stay in your own place. If there'd been more time, we might have gone to the country, though I still don't see where we'd have gone there. It's one harder when you're not married, unless you've got the money. Smoke?'

'No, thank you. Well, if you're all right, I'll go back to bed.'

'I'm glad she's asleep – funny the way she sleeps, isn't it? You can't help wondering where she is. You haven't got a boy, have you, just at present?'

'No. I've never had one.'

'I'm not sure in one way that you're not better off. I can see there's not so much in it for a girl these days. It makes me feel cruel the way I unsettle her: I don't know how much it's me myself or how much it's something the matter that I can't help. How are any of us to know how things could have been? They forget war's not just only war; it's years out of people's lives that they've never had before and won't have again. Do you think she's fanciful?'

'Who, Pepita?'

---

[7]   In American usage, a flashlight.

'It's enough to make her – tonight was the pay-off. We couldn't get near any movie or any place for sitting; you had to fight into the bars, and she hates the staring in bars, and with all that milling about, every street we went, they kept on knocking her even off my arm. So then we took the tube to that park down there, but the place was as bad as daylight, let alone it was cold. We hadn't the nerve – well, that's nothing to do with you.'

'I don't mind.'

'Or else you don't understand. So we began to play – we were off in Kôr.'

'Core of what?'

'Mysterious Kôr – ghost city.'

'Where?'

'You may ask. But I could have sworn she saw it, and from the way she saw it I saw it, too. A game's a game, but what's a hallucination? You begin by laughing, then it gets in you and you can't laugh it off. I tell you, I woke up just now not knowing where I'd been; and I had to get up and feel round this table before I even knew where I was. It wasn't till then that I thought of a cigarette. Now I see why she sleeps like that, if that's where she goes.'

'But she is just as often restless; I often hear her.'

'Then she doesn't always make it. Perhaps it takes me, in some way— Well, I can't see any harm: when two people have got no place, why not want Kôr, as a start? There are no restrictions on wanting, at any rate.'

'But, oh, Arthur, can't wanting want what's human?'

He yawned. 'To be human's to be at a dead loss.' Stopping yawning, he ground out his cigarette: the china tray skidded at the edge of the table. 'Bring that light here a moment – that is, will you? I think I've messed ash all over these sheets of hers.'

Callie advanced with the torch alight, but at arm's length: now and then her thumb made the beam wobble. She watched the lit-up inside of Arthur's hand as he brushed the sheet; and once he looked up to see her white-nightgowned figure curving above and away from him, behind the arc of light. 'What's that swinging?'

'One of my plaits of hair. Shall I open the window wider?'

'What, to let the smoke out? Go on. And how's your moon?'

'Mine?' Marvelling over this, as the first sign that Arthur remembered that she was Callie, she uncovered the window, pushed up the sash, then after a minute said: 'Not so strong.'

Indeed, the moon's power over London and the imagination had now declined. The siege of light had relaxed; the search was over; the street had a look of survival and no more. Whatever had glittered there, coin or ring, was now invisible or had gone. To Callie it seemed likely that there would never be such a moon again; and on the whole she felt this was for the best. Feeling air reach in like a tired arm round her body, she dropped the curtains against it and returned to her own room.

Back by her bed, she listened: Pepita's breathing still had the regular sound of sleep. At the other side of the wall the divan creaked as Arthur stretched himself out again. Having felt ahead of her lightly, to make sure her half was empty, Callie climbed over Pepita and got in. A certain amount of warmth had travelled between the sheets from Pepita's flank, and in this Callie extended her sword-cold body: she tried to compose her limbs; even they quivered after Arthur's words in the dark, words *to* the dark. The loss of her own mysterious expectation, of her love for love, was a small thing beside the war's total of unlived lives. Suddenly Pepita flung out one hand: its back knocked Callie lightly across the face.

Pepita had now turned over and lay with her face up. The hand that had struck Callie must have lain over the other, which grasped the pyjama collar. Her eyes, in the dark, might have been either shut or open, but nothing made her frown more or less steadily: it became certain, after another moment, that Pepita's act of justice had been unconscious. She still lay, as she had lain, in an avid dream, of which Arthur had been the source, of which Arthur was not the end. With him she looked this way, that way, down the wide, void, pure streets, between statues, pillars and shadows, through archways and colonnades. With him she went up the stairs down which nothing but moon came; with him trod the ermine dust of the endless halls, stood on terraces, mounted the extreme tower, looked down on the statued squares, the wide, void, pure streets. He was the password, but not the answer: it was to Kôr's finality that she turned.

The Happy Autumn Fields (1944)

The family walking party, though it comprised so many, did not deploy or straggle over the stubble but kept in a procession of threes and twos. Papa, who carried his Alpine stick, led, flanked by Constance and little Arthur. Robert and Cousin Theodore, locked in studious talk, had Emily attached but not quite abreast. Next came Digby and Lucius, taking, to left and right, imaginary aim at rooks. Henrietta and Sarah brought up the rear.

It was Sarah who saw the others ahead on the blond stubble, who knew them, knew what they were to each other, knew their names and knew her own. It was she who felt the stubble under her feet, and who heard it give beneath the tread of the others a continuous different more distant soft stiff scrunch. The field and all these outlying fields in view knew as Sarah knew that they were Papa's. The harvest had been good and was now in: he was satisfied – for this afternoon he had made the instinctive choice of his most womanly daughter, most nearly infant son. Arthur, whose hand Papa was holding, took an anxious hop, a skip and a jump to every stride of the great man's. As for Constance – Sarah could often see the flash of her hat-feather as she turned her head, the curve of her close bodice as she turned her torso. Constance gave Papa her attention but not her thoughts, for she had already been sought in marriage.

The landowner's daughters, from Constance down, walked with their beetle-green, mole or maroon skirts gathered up and carried clear of the ground, but for Henrietta, who was still ankle-free. They walked inside a continuous stuffy sound, but left silence behind them. Behind them, rooks that had risen and circled, sun striking blue from their blue-black wings, planed one by one to the earth and settled to peck again. Papa and the boys were dark-clad as the rooks but with no sheen, but for their white collars.

It was Sarah who located the thoughts of Constance, knew what a twisting prisoner was Arthur's hand, felt to the depths of Emily's pique at Cousin Theodore's inattention, rejoiced with Digby and Lucius at the imaginary fall of so many rooks. She fell back, however, as from a rocky range, from the converse of Robert and Cousin Theodore. Most she knew that she swam with love at the nearness of Henrietta's young and alert face and eyes which shone with the sky and queried the afternoon.

She recognized the colour of valediction, tasted sweet sadness, while from the cottage inside the screen of trees wood-smoke rose melting pungent and blue. This was the eve of the brothers' return to school. It was like a Sunday; Papa had kept the late afternoon free; all (all but one) encircling Robert, Digby and Lucius, they walked the estate the brothers would not see again for so long. Robert, it could be felt, was not unwilling to return to his books; next year he would go to college like Theodore; besides, to all this they saw he was not the heir. But in Digby and Lucius aiming and popping hid a bodily grief, the repugnance of victims, though these two were further from being heirs than Robert.

Sarah said to Henrietta: 'To think they will not be here tomorrow!'

'*Is* that what you are thinking about?' Henrietta asked, with her subtle taste for the truth.

'More, I was thinking that you and I will be back again by one another at table...'

'You know we are always sad when the boys are going, but we are never sad when the boys have gone.' The sweet reciprocal guilty smile that started on Henrietta's lips finished on those of Sarah. 'Also,' the young sister said, 'we know this is only something happening again. It happened last year, and it will happen next. But oh how should I feel, and how should you feel, if it were something that had not happened before?'

"The Happy Autumn Fields" was first published in *Cornhill*, no. 963 (Nov. 1944), then collected in *The Demon Lover and Other Stories* (London: Jonathan Cape, 1945).

'For instance, when Constance goes to be married?'

'Oh, I don't mean *Constance*!' said Henrietta.

'So long,' said Sarah, considering, 'as, whatever it is, it happens to both of us?' She must never have to wake in the early morning except to the birdlike stirrings of Henrietta, or have her cheek brushed in the dark by the frill of another pillow in whose hollow did not repose Henrietta's cheek. Rather than they should cease to lie in the same bed she prayed they might lie in the same grave. 'You and I will stay as we are,' she said, 'then nothing can touch one without touching the other.'

'So you say; so I hear you say!' exclaimed Henrietta, who then, lips apart, sent Sarah her most tormenting look. 'But I cannot forget that you chose to be born without me; that you would not wait –' But here she broke off, laughed outright and said: 'Oh, *see*!'

Ahead of them there had been a dislocation. Emily took advantage of having gained the ridge to kneel down to tie her bootlace so abruptly that Digby all but fell over her, with an exclamation. Cousin Theodore had been civil enough to pause beside Emily, but Robert, lost to all but what he was saying, strode on, head down, only just not colliding into Papa and Constance, who had turned to look back. Papa, astounded, let go of Arthur's hand, whereupon Arthur fell flat on the stubble.

'Dear me,' said the affronted Constance to Robert.

Papa said. 'What is the matter there? May I ask, Robert, where you are going, sir? Digby, remember that is your sister Emily.'

'Cousin Emily is in trouble,' said Cousin Theodore.

Poor Emily, telescoped in her skirts and by now scarlet under her hatbrim, said in a muffled voice: 'It is just my bootlace, Papa.'

'Your bootlace, Emily?'

'I was just tying it.'

'Then you had better tie it. – Am I to think,' said Papa, looking round them all, 'that you must all go down like a pack of ninepins because Emily has occasion to stoop?'

At this Henrietta uttered a little whoop, flung her arms round Sarah, buried her face in her sister and fairly suffered with laughter. She could contain this no longer; she shook all over. Papa, who found Henrietta so hopelessly out of order that he took no notice of her except at table, took no notice, simply giving the signal for the others to collect themselves and move on. Cousin Theodore, helping Emily to her feet, could be seen to see how her heightened colour became her, but she dispensed with his hand chillily, looked elsewhere, touched the brooch at her throat and said: 'Thank you, I have not sustained an accident.' Digby apologized to Emily, Robert to Papa and Constance. Constance righted Arthur, flicking his breeches over with her handkerchief. All fell into their different steps and resumed their way.

Sarah, with no idea how to console laughter, coaxed, 'Come, come, come,' into Henrietta's ear. Between the girls and the others the distance widened; it began to seem that they would be left alone.

'And why not?' said Henrietta, lifting her head in answer to Sarah's thought.

They looked around them with the same eyes. The shorn uplands seemed to float on the distance, which extended dazzling to tiny blue glassy hills. There was no end to the afternoon, whose light went on ripening now they had scythed the corn. Light filled the silence which, now Papa and the others were out of hearing, was complete. Only screens of trees intersected and knolls made islands in the vast fields. The mansion and the home farm had sunk for ever below them in the expanse of woods, so that hardly a ripple showed where the girls dwelled.

The shadow of the same rook circling passed over Sarah then over Henrietta, who in their turn cast one shadow across the stubble. 'But, Henrietta, we cannot stay here for ever.'

Henrietta immediately turned her eyes to the only lonely plume of smoke, from the cottage. 'Then let us go and visit the poor old man. He is dying and the others are happy. One day we shall pass and see no more smoke; then soon his roof will fall in, and we shall always be sorry we did not go today.'

'But he no longer remembers us any longer.'

'All the same, he will feel us there in the door.'

'But can we forget this is Robert's and Digby's and Lucius's goodbye walk? It would be heartless of both of us to neglect them.'

'Then how heartless Fitzgeorge is!' smiled Henrietta.

'Fitzgeorge is himself, the eldest and in the Army. Fitzgeorge I'm afraid is not an excuse for us.'

A resigned sigh, or perhaps the pretence of one, heaved up Henrietta's still narrow bosom. To delay matters for just a moment more she shaded her eyes with one hand, to search the distance like a sailor looking for a sail. She gazed with hope and zeal in every direction but that in which she and Sarah were bound to go. Then – 'Oh, but Sarah, here *they* are, coming – they are!' she cried. She brought out her handkerchief and began to fly it, drawing it to and fro through the windless air.

In the glass of the distance, two horsemen came into view, cantering on a grass track between the fields. When the track dropped into a hollow they dropped with it, but by now the drumming of hoofs was heard. The reverberation filled the land, the silence and Sarah's being; not watching for the riders to reappear she instead fixed her eyes on her sister's handkerchief which, let hang limp while its owner intently waited, showed a bitten corner as well as a damson stain. Again it became a flag, in furious motion. – 'Wave too, Sarah, wave too! Make your bracelet flash!'

'They must have seen us if they will ever see us,' said Sarah, standing still as a stone.

Henrietta's waving at once ceased. Facing her sister she crunched up her handkerchief, as though to stop it acting a lie. 'I can see you are shy,' she said in a dead voice. 'So shy you won't even wave to *Fitzgeorge?*'

Her way of not speaking the *other* name had a hundred meanings; she drove them all in by the way she did not look at Sarah's face. The impulsive breath she had caught stole silently out again, while her eyes – till now at their brightest, their most speaking – dulled with uncomprehending solitary alarm. The ordeal of awaiting Eugene's approach thus became for Sarah, from moment to moment, torture.

Fitzgeorge, Papa's heir, and his friend Eugene, the young neighbouring squire, struck off the track and rode up at a trot with their hats doffed. Sun striking low turned Fitzgeorge's flesh to coral and made Eugene blink his dark eyes. The young men reined in; the girls looked up at the horses. 'And my father, Constance, the others?' Fitzgeorge demanded, as though the stubble had swallowed them.

'Ahead, on the way to the quarry, the other side of the hill.'

'We heard you were all walking together,' Fitzgeorge said, seeming dissatisfied.

'We are following.'

'What, alone?' said Eugene, speaking for the first time.

'Forlorn!' glittered Henrietta, raising two mocking hands.

Fitzgeorge considered, said 'Good' severely, and signified to Eugene that they would ride on. But too late: Eugene had dismounted. Fitzgeorge saw, shrugged and flicked his horse to a trot; but Eugene led his slowly between the sisters. Or rather, Sarah walked on his left hand, the horse on his right and Henrietta the other side of the horse. Henrietta, acting like somebody quite alone, looked up at the sky, idly holding one of the empty stirrups. Sarah, however, looked at the ground, with Eugene inclined as though to speak but not speaking. Enfolded, dizzied, blinded as though inside a wave, she could feel his features carved in brightness above her. Alongside the slender stepping of his horse, Eugene matched his naturally long free step to hers. His elbow was through the reins; with his fingers he brushed back the lock that his bending to her had sent falling over his forehead. She recorded the sublime act and knew what smile shaped his lips. So each without looking trembled before an image, while slow colour burned up the curves of her cheeks. The consummation would be when their eyes met.

At the other side of the horse, Henrietta began to sing. At once her pain, like a scientific ray, passed through the horse and Eugene to penetrate Sarah's heart.

We surmount the skyline: the family come into our view, we into theirs. They are halted, waiting, on the decline to the quarry. The handsome statufied group in strong yellow sunshine, aligned by Papa and crowned by Fitzgeorge, turn their judging eyes on the laggards, waiting to close their ranks round Henrietta and Sarah and Eugene. One more moment and it will be too late; no further communication will be possible. Stop oh stop Henrietta's heart-breaking singing! Embrace her close again! Speak the only possible word! Say – oh, say what? Oh, the word is lost!

'Henrietta . . .'

A shock of striking pain in the knuckles of the outflung hand – Sarah's? The eyes, opening, saw that the hand had struck, not been struck: there was a corner of a table. Dust, whitish and gritty, lay on the top of the table and on the telephone. Dull but piercing white light filled the room and what was left of the ceiling; her first thought was that it must have snowed. If so, it was winter now.

Through the calico stretched and tacked over the window came the sound of a piano: someone was playing Tchaikowsky[1] badly in a room without windows or doors. From somewhere else in the hollowness came a cascade of hammering. Close up, a voice: 'Oh, *awake*, Mary?' It came from the other side of the open door, which jutted out between herself and the speaker – he on the threshold, she lying on the uncovered mattress of a bed. The speaker added: 'I had been going away.'

Summoning words from somewhere she said: 'Why? I didn't know you were here.'

'Evidently – Say, who is "Henrietta"?'

Despairing tears filled her eyes. She drew back her hurt hand, began to suck at the knuckle and whimpered, 'I've hurt myself.'

A man she knew to be 'Travis', but failed to focus, came round the door saying: 'Really I don't wonder.' Sitting down on the edge of the mattress he drew her hand away from her lips and held it: the act, in itself gentle, was accompanied by an almost hostile stare of concern. 'Do listen, Mary,' he said. 'While you've slept I've been all over the house again, and I'm less than ever satisfied that it's safe. In your normal senses you'd never attempt to stay here. There've been alerts, and more than alerts, all day; one more bang anywhere near, which may happen at any moment, could bring the rest of this down. You keep telling me that you have things to see to – but do you know what chaos the rooms are in? Till they've gone ahead with more clearing, where can you hope to start? And if there *were* anything you could do, you couldn't do it. Your own nerves know that, if you don't: it was almost frightening, when I looked in just now, to see the way you were sleeping – you've shut up shop.'

She lay staring over his shoulder at the calico window. He went on: 'You don't like it here. Your self doesn't like it. Your will keeps driving your self, but it can't be driven the whole way – it makes its own get-out: sleep. Well, I want you to sleep as much as you (really) do. But *not* here. So I've taken a room for you in a hotel; I'm going now for a taxi; you can practically make the move without waking up.'

'No, I can't get into a taxi without waking.'

'Do you realize you're the last soul left in the terrace?'

'Then who is that playing the piano?'

'Oh, one of the furniture-movers in Number Six. I didn't count the jaquerie;[2] of course *they're* in possession – unsupervised, teeming, having a high old time. While I looked in on you in here ten minutes ago they were smashing out that conservatory at the other end. Glass being done in in cold blood – it was brutalizing. You never batted an eyelid; in fact, I thought you smiled.' He listened. 'Yes, the piano – they are highbrow all right. You know there's a workman downstairs lying on your blue sofa looking for pictures in one of your French books?'

'No,' she said, 'I've no idea who is there.'

'Obviously. With the lock blown off your front door anyone who likes can get in and out.'

'Including you.'

'Yes. I've had a word with a chap about getting that lock back before tonight. As for you, you don't know what is happening.'

'I did,' she said, locking her fingers before her eyes.

The unreality of this room and of Travis's presence preyed on her as figments of dreams that one knows to be dreams can do. This environment's being in semi-ruin struck her less than its being some sort of device or trap; and she rejoiced, if anything, in its decrepitude. As for Travis, he had his own part in the conspiracy to keep her from the beloved two. She felt he began to feel he was now unmeaning. She was struggling not to contemn him, scorn him for his ignorance of Henrietta,

---

[1]   Peter Ilyich Tchaikovsky (1840–93) was a Russian composer.

[2]   Historically, the revolt of the peasants of northern France against the nobles in 1357–8; by extension, any rising of the peasantry.

Eugene, her loss. His possessive angry fondness was part, of course, of the story of him and Mary, which like a book once read she remembered clearly but with indifference. Frantic at being delayed here, while the moment awaited her in the cornfield, she all but afforded a smile at the grotesquerie of being saddled with Mary's body and lover. Rearing up her head from the bare pillow, she looked, as far as the crossed feet, along the form inside which she found herself trapped: the irrelevant body of Mary, weighted down to the bed, wore a short black modern dress, flaked with plaster. The toes of the black suède shoes by their sickly whiteness showed Mary must have climbed over fallen ceilings; dirt engraved the fate-lines in Mary's palms.

This inspired her to say: 'But I've made a start; I've been pulling out things of value or things I want.'

For answer Travis turned to look down, expressively, at some object out of her sight, on the floor close by the bed. 'I see,' he said, 'a musty old leather box gaping open with God knows what – junk, illegible letters, diaries, yellow photographs, chiefly plaster and dust. Of all things, Mary! – after a missing will?'

'Everything one unburies seems the same age.'

'Then what are these, where do they come from – family stuff?'

'No idea,' she yawned into Mary's hand. 'They may not even be mine. Having a house like this that had empty rooms must have made me store more than I knew, for years. I came on these, so I wondered. Look if you like.'

He bent and began to go through the box – it seemed to her, not unsuspiciously. While he blew grit off packets and fumbled with tapes she lay staring at the exposed laths of the ceiling, calculating. She then said: 'Sorry if I've been cranky, about the hotel and all. Go away just for two hours, then come back with a taxi, and I'll go quiet. Will that do?'

'Fine – except why not now?'

'Travis . . .'

'Sorry. It shall be as you say . . . You've got some good morbid stuff in this box, Mary – so far as I can see at a glance. The photographs seem more your sort of thing. Comic but lyrical. All of one set of people – a beard, a gun and a pot hat, a schoolboy with a moustache, a phaeton drawn up in front of mansion, a group on steps, a *carte de visite* of two young ladies hand-in-hand in front of a painted field –'

'*Give that to me!*'

She instinctively tried and failed, to unbutton the bosom of Mary's dress: it offered no hospitality to the photograph. So she could only fling herself over on the mattress, away from Travis, covering the two faces with her body. Racked by that oblique look of Henrietta's she recorded, too, a sort of personal shock at having seen Sarah for the first time.

Travis's hand came over her, and she shuddered. Wounded, he said: 'Mary . . .'

'Can't you leave *me* alone?'

She did not move or look till he had gone out saying: 'Then, in two hours.' She did not therefore see him pick up the dangerous box, which he took away under his arm, out of her reach.

They were back. Now the sun was setting behind the trees, but its rays passed dazzling between the branches into the beautiful warm red room. The tips of the ferns in the jardinière curled gold, and Sarah, standing by the jardinière, pinched at a leaf of scented geranium. The carpet had a great centre wreath of pomegranates, on which no tables or chairs stood, and its whole circle was between herself and the others.

No fire was lit yet, but where they were grouped was a hearth. Henrietta sat on a low stool, resting her elbow above her head on the arm of Mamma's chair, looking away intently as though into a fire, idle. Mamma embroidered, her needle slowed down by her thoughts; the length of tatting with roses she had already done overflowed stiffly over her supple skirts. Stretched on the rug at Mamma's feet, Arthur looked through an album of Swiss views, not liking them but vowed to be very quiet. Sarah, from where she stood, saw fuming cataracts and null eternal snows as poor Arthur kept turning over the pages, which had tissue paper between.

Against the white marble mantelpiece stood Eugene. The dark red shadows gathering in the drawing-room as the trees drowned more and more of the sun would reach him last, perhaps never: it seemed to Sarah that a lamp was lighted behind his face. He was the only gentleman with the ladies: Fitzgeorge had gone to the stables, Papa to give an order; Cousin Theodore was consulting a dictionary; in the gunroom Robert, Lucius and Digby went through the sad rites, putting away their guns. All this was known to go on but none of it could be heard.

This particular hour of subtle light – not to be fixed by the clock, for it was early in winter and late in summer and in spring and autumn now, about Arthur's bed-time – had always, for Sarah, been Henrietta's. To be with her indoors or out, upstairs or down, was to share the same crepitation. Her spirit ran on past yours with a laughing shiver into an element of its own. Leaves and branches and mirrors in empty rooms became animate. The sisters rustled and scampered and concealed themselves where nobody else was in play that was full of fear, fear that was full of play. Till, by dint of making each other's hearts beat violently, Henrietta so wholly and Sarah so nearly lost all human reason that Mamma had been known to look at them searchingly as she sat instated for evening among the calm amber lamps.

But now Henrietta had locked the hour inside her breast. By spending it seated beside Mamma, in young imitation of Constance the Society daughter, she disclaimed for ever anything else. It had always been she who with one fierce act destroyed any toy that might be outgrown. She sat with straight back, poising her cheek remotely against her finger. Only by never looking at Sarah did she admit their eternal loss.

Eugene, not long returned from a foreign tour, spoke of travel, addressing himself to Mamma, who thought but did not speak of her wedding journey. But every now and then she had to ask Henrietta to pass the scissors or tray of carded wools, and Eugene seized every such moment to look at Sarah. Into eyes always brilliant with melancholy he dared begin to allow no other expression. But this in itself declared the conspiracy of still undeclared love. For her part she looked at him as though he, transfigured by the strange light, were indeed a picture, a picture who could not see her. The wallpaper now flamed scarlet behind his shoulder. Mamma, Henrietta, even unknowing Arthur were in no hurry to raise their heads.

Henrietta said: 'If I were a man I should take my bride to Italy.'

'There are mules in Switzerland,' said Arthur.

'Sarah,' said Mamma, who turned in her chair mildly, 'where are you, my love; do you never mean to sit down?'

'To Naples,' said Henrietta.

'Are you not thinking of Venice?' said Eugene.

'No,' returned Henrietta, 'why should I be? I should like to climb the volcano. But then I am not a man, and am still less likely ever to be a bride.'

'Arthur...' Mamma said.

'Mamma?'

'Look at the clock.'

Arthur sighed politely, got up and replaced the album on the circular table, balanced upon the rest. He offered his hand to Eugene, his cheek to Henrietta and to Mamma; then he started towards Sarah, who came to meet him. 'Tell me, Arthur,' she said, embracing him, 'what did you do today?'

Arthur only stared with his button blue eyes. 'You were there too; we went for a walk in the cornfield, with Fitzgeorge on his horse, and I fell down.' He pulled out of her arms and said: 'I must go back to my beetle.' He had difficulty, as always, in turning the handle of the mahogany door. Mamma waited till he had left the room, then said: 'Arthur is quite a man now; he no longer comes running to me when he has hurt himself. Why, I did not even know he had fallen down. Before we know, he will be going away to school too.' She sighed and lifted her eyes to Eugene. 'Tomorrow is to be a sad day.'

Eugene with a gesture signified his own sorrow. The sentiments of Mamma could have been uttered only here in the drawing-room, which for all its size and formality was lyrical and almost exotic. There was a look like velvet in darker parts of the air; sombre window draperies let out gushes of lace; the music on the piano-forte bore tender titles, and the harp though unplayed gleamed in a corner, beyond sofas, whatnots, armchairs, occasional tables that all stood on tottering little feet. At any moment a tinkle might have been struck from the lustres' drops of the brighter day, a vibration from the musical instruments, or a quiver from the fringes and ferns. But the towering vases upon the consoles, the albums piled on the tables, the shells and figurines on the flights of brackets, all had, like the alabaster Leaning Tower of Pisa, an equilibrium of their own. Nothing would fall or change. And everything in the drawing-room was muted, weighted, pivoted by Mamma. When she added: 'We shall not feel quite the same,' it was to be understood that she would not have spoken thus from her place at the opposite end of Papa's table.

'Sarah,' said Henrietta curiously, 'what made you ask Arthur what he had been doing? Surely you have not forgotten today?'

The sisters were seldom known to address or question one another in public; it was taken that they knew each other's minds. Mamma, though untroubled, looked from one to the other. Henrietta continued: 'No day, least of all today, is like any other – Surely that must be true?' she said to Eugene. 'You will never forget my waving my handkerchief?'

Before Eugene had composed an answer, she turned to Sarah: 'Or *you*, them riding across the fields?'

Eugene also slowly turned his eyes on Sarah, as though awaiting with something like dread her answer to the question he had not asked. She drew a light little gold chair into the middle of the wreath of the carpet, where no one ever sat, and sat down. She said: 'But since then I think I have been asleep.'

'Charles the First walked and talked half an hour after his head was cut off,' said Henrietta mockingly. Sarah in anguish pressed the palms of her hands together upon a shred of geranium leaf.

'How else,' she said, 'could I have had such a bad dream?'

'That must be the explanation!' said Henrietta.

'A trifle fanciful,' said Mamma.

However rash it might be to speak at all, Sarah wished she knew how to speak more clearly. The obscurity and loneliness of her trouble was not to be borne. How could she put into words the feeling of dislocation, the formless dread that had been with her since she found herself in the drawing-room? The source of both had been what she must call her dream. How could she tell the others with what vehemence she tried to attach her being to each second, not because each was singular in itself, each a drop condensed from the mist of love in the room, but because she apprehended that the seconds were numbered? Her hope was that the others at least half knew. Were Henrietta and Eugene able to understand how completely, how nearly for ever, she had been swept from them, would they not without fail each grasp one of her hands? – She went so far as to throw her hands out, as though alarmed by a wasp. The shred of geranium fell to the carpet.

Mamma, tracing this behaviour of Sarah's to only one cause, could not but think reproachfully of Eugene. Delightful as his conversation had been, he would have done better had he paid this call with the object of interviewing Papa. Turning to Henrietta she asked her to ring for the lamps, as the sun had set.

Eugene, no longer where he had stood, was able to make no gesture towards the bell-rope. His dark head was under the tide of dusk; for, down on one knee on the edge of the wreath, he was feeling over the carpet for what had fallen from Sarah's hand. In the inevitable silence rooks on the return from the fields could be heard streaming over the house; their sound filled the sky and even the room, and it appeared so useless to ring the bell that Henrietta stayed quivering by Mamma's chair. Eugene rose, brought out his fine white handkerchief and, while they watched, enfolded carefully in it what he had just found, then returning the handkerchief to his breast pocket. This was done so deep in the reverie that accompanies any final act that Mamma instinctively murmured to Henrietta: 'But you will be my child when Arthur has gone.'

The door opened for Constance to appear on the threshold. Behind her queenly figure globes approached, swimming in their own light: these were the lamps for which Henrietta had not rung, but these first were put on the hall tables. 'Why, Mamma,' exclaimed Constance, 'I cannot see who is with you!'

'Eugene is with us,' said Henrietta, 'but on the point of asking if he may send for his horse.'

'Indeed?' said Constance to Eugene. 'Fitzgeorge has been asking for you, but I cannot tell where he is now.'

The figures of Emily, Lucius and Cousin Theodore criss-crossed the lamplight there in the hall, to mass behind Constance's in the drawing-room door. Emily, over her sister's shoulder, said: 'Mamma, Lucius wishes to ask you whether for once he may take his guitar to school.' – 'One objection, however,' said Cousin Theodore, 'is that Lucius's trunk is already locked and strapped.' 'Since Robert is taking his box of inks,' said Lucius, 'I do not see why I should not take my guitar.' – 'But Robert,' said Constance, 'will soon be going to college.'

Lucius squeezed past the others into the drawing-room in order to look anxiously at Mamma, who said: 'You have thought of this late; we must go and see.' The others parted to let Mamma, followed by Lucius, out. Then Constance, Emily and Cousin Theodore deployed and sat down in different parts of the drawing-room, to await the lamps.

'I am glad the rooks have done passing over,' said Emily, 'they make me nervous.' – 'Why?' yawned Constance haughtily, 'what do you think could happen?' Robert and Digby silently came in.

Eugene said to Sarah: 'I shall be back tomorrow.'

'But, oh –' she began. She turned to cry: 'Henrietta!'

'Why, what is the matter?' said Henrietta, unseen at the back of the gold chair. 'What could be sooner than tomorrow?'

'But something terrible may be going to happen.'

'There cannot fail to be tomorrow,' said Eugene gravely.

'*I* will see that there is tomorrow,' said Henrietta.

'You will never let me out of your sight?'

Eugene, addressing himself to Henrietta, said: 'Yes, promise her what she asks.'

Henrietta cried: 'She *is* never out of my sight. Who are you to ask me that, you Eugene? Whatever tries to come between me and Sarah becomes nothing. Yes, come tomorrow, come sooner, come – when you like, but no one will ever be quite alone with Sarah. You do not even know what you are trying to do. It is *you* who are making something terrible happen. – Sarah, tell him that this is true! Sarah –'

The others, in the dark on the chairs and sofas, could be felt to turn their judging eyes upon Sarah, who, as once before, could not speak –

– The house rocked: simultaneously the calico window split and more ceiling fell, though not on the bed. The enormous dull sound of the explosion died, leaving a minor trickle of dissolution still to be heard in parts of the house. Until the choking stinging plaster dust had had time to settle, she lay with lips pressed close, nostrils not breathing and eyes shut. Remembering the box, Mary wondered if it had been again buried. No, she found, looking over the edge of the bed: that had been unable to happen because the box was missing. Travis, who must have taken it, would when he came back no doubt explain why. She looked at her watch, which had stopped, which was not surprising; she did not remember winding it for the last two days, but then she could not remember much. Through the torn window appeared the timelessness of an impermeably clouded late summer afternoon.

There being nothing left, she wished he would come to take her to the hotel. The one way back to the fields was barred by Mary's surviving the fall of ceiling. Sarah was right in doubting that there would be tomorrow: Eugene, Henrietta were lost in time to the woman weeping there on the bed, no longer reckoning who she was.

At last she heard the taxi, then Travis hurrying up the littered stairs. 'Mary, you're all right, Mary – *another*?' Such a helpless white face came round the door that she could only hold out her arms and say: 'Yes, but where have *you* been?'

'You said two hours. But I wish—'

'I have missed you.'

'Have you? Do you know you are crying?'

'Yes. How are we to live without natures? We only know inconvenience now, not sorrow. Everything pulverizes so easily because it is rot-dry; one can only wonder that it makes so much noise. The source, the sap must have dried up, or the pulse must have stopped, before you and I were conceived. So much flowed through people; so little flows through us. All we can do is imitate love or sorrow. – Why did you take away my box?'

He only said: 'It is in my office.'

She continued: 'What has happened is cruel: I am left with a fragment torn out of a day, a day I don't even know where or when; and now how am I to help laying that like a pattern against the poor stuff of everything else? – Alternatively, I am a person drained by a dream. I cannot forget the climate of those hours. Or life at that pitch, eventful – not happy, no, but strung like a harp. I have had a sister called Henrietta.'

'And I have been looking inside your box. What else can you expect? – I have had to write off this day, from the work point of view, thanks to you. So could I sit and do nothing for the last two hours? I just glanced through this and that – still, I know the family.'

'You said it was morbid stuff.'

'Did I? I still say it gives off something.'

She said: 'And then there was Eugene.'

'Probably. I don't think I came on much of his except some notes he must have made for Fitzgeorge from some book on scientific farming. Well, there it is: I have sorted everything out and put it back again, all but a lock of hair that tumbled out of a letter I could not trace. So I've got the hair in my pocket.'

'What colour is it?'

'Ash-brown. Of course, it is a bit – desiccated. Do you want it?'

'No,' she said with a shudder. 'Really, Travis, what revenges you take!'

'I didn't look at it that way,' he said puzzled.

'Is the taxi waiting?' Mary got off the bed and, picking her way across the room, began to look about for things she ought to take with her, now and then stopping to brush her dress. She took the mirror out of her bag to see how dirty her face was. 'Travis –' she said suddenly.

'Mary?'

'Only, I –'

'That's all right. Don't let us imitate anything just at present.'

In the taxi, looking out of the window, she said: 'I suppose, then, that I am descended from Sarah?'

'No,' he said, 'that would be impossible. There must be some reason why you should have those papers, but that is not the one. From all negative evidence Sarah, like Henrietta, remained unmarried. I found no mention of either, after a certain date, in the letters of Constance, Robert or Emily, which makes it seem likely both died young. Fitzgeorge refers, in a letter to Robert written in his old age, to some friend of their youth who was thrown from his horse and killed, riding back after a visit to their home. The young man, whose name doesn't appear, was alone; and the evening, which was in autumn, was fine though late. Fitzgeorge wonders, and says he will always wonder, what made the horse shy in those empty fields.'

Eugene Jolas (1894–1952)

Introduction

Eugene Jolas (1894–1952) was born in Union City, New Jersey, the son a French father and a German mother who had recently immigrated to the United States. When he was two years old he moved with his family back to Forbach, a small town in Lorraine which was chiefly populated by native speakers of French, though it had been part of the German state since 1871. Jolas grew up bilingual. In 1909 he decided to move to the United States, and soon took a job in Pittsburgh with a German-American newspaper, the *Volksblatt*. He then moved to an English-language newspaper, the local *Post*. Though he was drafted into the US Army Medical Corps in 1917, he continued to work as a journalist reporting for hospital and camp newspapers. After the war he worked in the city-room or on the police beat for a series of newspapers, including the Savannah *Morning News*, the Waterbury *Republican*, and New York *Daily News*. In 1923 and 1924 he made two trips to Paris, which persuaded him to take a position with the Paris office of the *Chicago Tribune*. When Ford Madox Ford relinquished his literary column on the Paris scene, Jolas seized his chance. "Rambles Through Literary Paris" became a regular feature of the newspaper, and Jolas now had license to pursue his literary interests. In 1927 he started *transition*, one of the most celebrated of the "little magazines" that were so important for modernism. Contributors would include James Joyce, Gertrude Stein, Samuel Beckett, Hans (Jean) Arp, André Breton, Carl Einstein, and Gottfried Benn. By 1938 it had published 27 issues. Jolas was also a pioneering translator, and together with his wife did the first translation of Kafka's *The Judgment* and *The Metamorphosis*. In the pages of *transition* he also formulated his idiosyncratic vision of a "Revolution of the Word," a linguistic revolution which would effortlessly breach and transcend the growing political divides created by the rise of communism and fascism. During the Second World War he served as a member of the Psychological Warfare Division in the US Army, landing at Utah Beach behind the invading troops. He was placed in charge of a program for de-Nazifying the German press and founding new schools of journalism in the war's aftermath. He resigned in 1950, and died two years later. His autobiography, *Man from Babel*, was not published until 1998.

Notes (1928)

The appearance of the summer number of *transition*[1] gave the American critics a chance again to distort the idea underlying our effort or to cast doubt upon our sanity. With a few exceptions (notably that of Michael Gold in the *New Masses*[2]), ill-will and ignorance responsed again to an effort that, if imperfect because of limited mechanical means, cannot be charged with insincerity. I do not address myself to the upholders of the status quo (preferring, under those conditions, to accept the idea of *transition* as "hors la loi"), but to the few minds that are still searching for a new beauty.

Some of our friends chide us for having a too definite programmatic idea, while others insist that the lack of a purposive orientation is our chief fault. Let me, therefore, emphasize here that we never believed in a rigid application of a priori ideas, but have always conceived our effort as primarily a research into the modern spirit. We attempted to find the creators active in every nation who had a

---

First published in *transition* 14 (Fall 1928).

[1] *transition* 13 (Summer 1928) was not devoted to a special theme or topic, but presented a wide range of work from writers both American and European. Apart from a section of Joyce's *Finnegans Wake*, or *Work in Progress* as it was then called, there were contributions by Gertrude Stein, William Carlos Williams, Laura Riding, and Malcolm Cowley, along with views on America by European writers such as Georges Ribemont-Dessaignes, Benjamin Péret, Gottfried Benn, and Tristan Tzara. The issue also contained photographs by Man Ray and Berenice Abbott, as well as photographs of paintings and drawings by Picasso. Jolas's original notes are marked with asterisks.

[2] Michael Gold (1894–1967) became editor of the communist monthly *New Masses* in June 1928. In his essay "Three Schools of US Writing," *New Masses* 4(4) (Sept. 1928), 13–14, he wrote: "*transition* reflects the mind of the young writers who are destined to succeed the Sandburgs and Andersons... *transition* is full of a furious anarchistic spirit that has too few roots in the world of realities. Even to language is this spirit applied; to break down the old accepted words and phrases of the smug world-order. A kind of desparate honesty that seems pathological in a world built on lies.... Eugene Jolas, the editor of *transition*, is a poet with a tragic vision. This is the kind of bias an editor ought to have."

new vision of their universe and who expressed it in the directest way possible. We never conceived *transition* to be the review of a narrow group, clique, chapelle, "movement." We allowed it to develop organically, and since we discovered certain parallel tendencies among the fresh elements of various nations, we thought it important to present them as documents.

We felt, however, that our half-sleep or our sleep, had as much beauty as the objective world which american writing had been exclusively trying to portray. Thus we felt personally that if we should have a "tendency" or direction at all, it ought to be toward the search for the magical. We felt the importance of the problem of reality – the new reality of our twentieth century in relation to our own inner world.

There is a certain state of mind which has too long been neglected in literature: it is the instinctive or automatic condition of our being. Edgar Allan Poe states this case in his *Marginalia*,[3] as follows: "How very commonly we hear it remarked that such and such thoughts are beyond the compass of words! I do not believe that any thought, properly so-called, is out of the reach of language . . . There is however, a class of 'fancies' of exquisite delicacy which are not thoughts, and to which, as yet, we have found it absolutely impossible to adopt language . . . I am aware of these 'fancies' only when I am upon the very brink of sleep, with the consciousness that I am so . . . "

It seems to us important not to neglect this condition, and the experiments made by some of the younger writers in *transition* along this line seem an encouraging sign. The tendency of the continental generation during the past decade was to deny the absoluteness of reality. As a result of their explosive expressions, there developed an efflorescence of the imagination unburdened by any contact with life.

But the facts of life persist. What is the poet to do with them? Is there not a space between the subjective and objective reality which ought to be filled? This process would lead to a marriage of reason and instinct which, with the resultant breaking up of the traditional means of expression, would open up an entirely new world. Thus the new realism synthetizising two realities should make us think in terms of both the supernatural and the natural.[*]

We should like to see a narrative art which is the fullest realisation of this feeling. An art that is hard and lyrical at the same time, related to the age in virile accents, and retaining profoundly the contemplative passivity of the mystic. We want to break the old novel form, and create something based on a new mythology. We want the imagination huge and free.

* * *

[3]   Edgar Allan Poe (1809–49) wrote a series of essays entitled "Marginalia" for the journals the *Democratic Review* and *Graham's Magazine* between 1844 and his death in 1849. In one for *Graham's Magazine* (March 1846) he wrote:

How very commonly we hear it remarked, that such and such thoughts are beyond the compass of words! I do not believe that any thought, properly so called, is out of the reach of language. I fancy, rather, that where difficulty in expression is experienced, there is, in the intellect which experiences it, a want either of deliberateness or of method. For my own part, I have never had a thought which I could not set down in words, with even more distinctness than that with which I conceived it: – as I have before observed, the thought is logicalized by the effort at (written) expression.

There is, however, a class of fancies, of exquisite delicacy, which are *not* thoughts, and to which, *as yet*, I have found it absolutely impossible to adapt language. I use the word *fancies* at random, and merely because I must use *some* word; but the idea commonly attached to the term is not even remotely-applicable to the shadows of shadows in question. They seem to me rather psychal than intellectual. They arise in the soul (alas, how rarely!) only at its epochs of most intense tranquility – when the bodily and mental health are in perfection –

and at those mere points of time where the confines of the waking world blend with those of the world of dreams. I am aware of these "fancies" only when I am upon the very brink of sleep, with the consciousness that I am so.

See *Edgar Allan Poe: Essays and Reviews*, ed. G. R. Thompson (New York: Library of America, 1984), p. 1383.

[*]   *The words of Freud in this connection seem significant: "Das Unheimliche ist das verdraengte Heimische."*[4]

[4]   German for "The uncanny is the familiar which has been repressed." Jolas, a native speaker of German, is synopsizing Freud's view of the uncanny (*das Unheimlich*), and Freud himself writes: "Es mag zutreffen, daß das Unheimliche das Heimliche-Heimische ist, das eine Verdrängung erfahren hat und aus ihr wiedergekehrt ist . . . " Or: "It may be true to say that the uncanny is something familiar which has been repressed and then returned in a new guise." Sigmund Freud, "Das Unheim-liche," *Gesammelte Werke*, vol. 12, *Werke aus den Jahren 1917–1920* (London: Imago, 1940), p. 259; or the *Standard Edition of the Complete Psychological Works of Sigmund Freud*, ed. James Strachey (London: Hogarth Press, 1981), vol. 17, p. 245.

I know the tendency of this age is towards collectivism. I think we of *transition* have had a world-conscience from the very beginning. But we feel at the same time that life proceeds from the particular to the general. We consider the increasing tendency toward centralisation, both in the economic and political sphere, dangerous, unless curbed by a regional consciousness.

More and more we feel the menace of the democratic idea, and we should like to oppose it. Nationalism as a creative force is decaying, in spite of apparent demonstrations to the contrary, but the sense of universalism can only develop, when the sense of the indigenous remains as a catapulting force. That is why we regard the development of the collectivistic era in America with so many misgivings, having already observed during the brief period of its prologue how the regional particularities are being destroyed, how the mass consciousness becomes a paroxysm of parallel tendencies, how life in general becomes grey and monotonous.

Let us not forget that the lot of the worker in America is in many ways as sad as that of the European worker, in spite of the superiority which american capitalistic organisation has been able to assert in general. The development of capitalism will probably make life more hygienic and comfortable, it will probably, through mechanistic perfections, reduce friction to a minimum, but there can be no final solution of this visionary conception, until a new and violent transformation has taken place. The machine will have to be captured by the majority and will have to be exploited by it, instead of, as now, by the plutocratic few. Perhaps we will then see a communistic capitalism emerge, although this metamorphosis can only take place through a revolutionary action – bloody or legal.

I should like to think that a hundred years hence, when capitalism and communism have finally merged, there will still be a place for the man who stands between the Greek ideal and that of Christ.

* * *

I have before me a questionnaire sent out by *Monde*, a new and radical review, which is as follows: Do you believe that artistic and literary production is an entirely individual phenomenon? Do you not think that it may or must be a reflection of the great waves which determine the economic and social evolution of humanity? Do you believe in the existance of a literature and art expressing the aspirations of the working-class?

Every art necessarily reflects the economic and social current of the age in which it is produced. The pressure of environment, the repercussions of mass-events, such as war, or any other historic evolutionary movement, the specific atmosphere produced by the age make it impossible for a creative mind to escape that collective influence. What determines the inspirational and conceptual development of a vision is the individual impulse. It is for this reason that the great artist is in advance of his age, since he works instinctively against mass impulsions or mass psychosis.[*]

I am not against a literature expressing the aspirations of the working class. That belongs, however, in the sphere of propaganda. Art and literature as such, although in some measure a result of the conditions of the epoch, must always remain primarily an individual performance. It is the *vates*[5] who in his expression synthesizes the emotions of humanity in a symphonic whole.

Russia at this moment is still producing writers whose individualistic postulates do not differ from that of their bourgeois contemporaries. The experiment of peasant and workers' correspondents which is showing such great results with the mass of the people is the first definite attempt to create a collective expression. Now, what will eventually happen? Out of this mass of material, out of this self-conscious activity, out of this dogmatic levelling, there will emerge a few whose special capacity for expression being superior will make them revolt and create a new literature which will be projected from their vision.

---

[*] *In envisaging the artistic and literary production of a future America, for instance, it is apparent that most of the bourgeois art which is definitely a reflection of the industrial and mercantile present, will have less than a documentary value.*

[5] *vates* Latin for "poet" or "seer."

What form this literature will take, is hard to say. The old world is smashed into bits. When the economic era finally relieves the political era in the historic development, only the superficies will be changed. There is an immutable base in life that will survive all politico-economic revolutions. Life will externally be reflected by these new writers in a different way, but the nervous and emotional structure of man will hardly differ.

* * *

The talk of a crisis in poetry persists. It is obvious that the modern poet needs a greater militancy to be heard above the noise of the mechanical civilization. He needs more than ever the discipline of his inner life to protect his creative development. But there are a few signs that the poetic instinct, the "magic idealism," in the words of Novalis,[6] is going on.

In France the Surrealistes have given the final blow to the atticism of a tradition which made of poetry a stiffly formal expression. They opened the gates to an uncontrolled expression of the elementary and lunged far into space. Some of their efforts were successful, others remained abortive, because they lacked a metaphysical base. But where their true poets, like Paul Eluard, Robert Desnos,[7] and a few others, gave voice to their vision, there appeared a beauty rooted deeply in the movements of the dream.

There is one poet in France who, with little attention from the conventional critics, has developed his mythos for a number of years, and has now assumed the stature of one of the great poets of our epoch. Léon-Paul Fargue,[8] beginning with *Pour La Musique* and ending with the just published *Vulturne*,[9] has created a work of physically small proportions, but of a significance in itself which throws completely into the shadow practically all of the more noisily vaunted efforts of his contemporaries. Combining a natural originality of expression with a creative imagination of exquisite sharpness and curiosity, he has presented us with the vision of a world that has all the strangeness of a submarine landscape and the colorful tangle of a tropical forest. In the Paris of his mind, where the night is changed into day, the miracles follow each other with a bewildering virtuosity.

While in the youthful poems published in 1912 his audacity is still curbed, although the precocious mastery of his instrument is already there apparent, his later productions proceed slowly into a phase, where he disregards the delimitations of prose and poetry. He published, at long intervals, his magnificent prose poems in *Commerce*, among others *La Drogue* first translated in *transition. Suite Familière, Epaisseurs,*[10] and others in the same spirit followed. Here he gives us quick flashes into his subconscious mind, and lets us participate in the dynamic evocations of his words.

Language in his treatment becomes a rare instrument which only he is able to play. No other French poet of his age has communicated speech in a more provoking manner. The apparent hermetism of his articulation lies precisely in the fact that he disassociates the elements of the classical and static word. He combines the most ephemeral street-expressions of the faubourgs with words taken from the vocabulary of the chemist and those handed down by the traditions of his literature. Sometimes he goes so far as to create new words by destroying the usual syllabic structure and adding deformations of his own. In a fine impulse for the comic, these irreverent operations spread over his work a discursive humor.

[6] Friedrich von Hardenberg (1772–1801) adopted the name Novalis as his *nom de plume*. A Romantic poet, he wrote two novels (*Lehrling zu Sais* and *Heinrich von Ofterdingen*) and a celebrated collection of *Hymnen an die Nacht* (1800; *Hymns on the Night*). "Magic idealism" is the term he used to elaborate a philosophical view of myth as symbolic discourse that could be fulfilled only when all contradictions are synthesized, all spiritual potentialities realilzed, and all religions and philosophies merged in oneness.

[7] For the writings of Desnos and Eluard, see pp. 746–9 and 753–61 in this edition.

[8] Leon-Paul Fargue (1867–1947) was a French poet and man of letters.

[9] *Pour la Musique* (Paris: Éditions de la "Nouvelle revue française," 1914); *Vulturne* (Paris: Éditions de la "Nouvelle revue française," 1928).

[10] *Suite familière* (*Familiar Suite*) (Paris: Emile-Paul frères) appeared as an independent volume in 1928, as did *Epaisseurs* (*Thicknesses*) (Paris: Éditions de la "Nouvelle revue française"). "La Drogue," or "The Drug," was translated into English by Maria Jolas in *transition* 8 (Nov. 1927): 9–16.

Revolution of the Word (1929)

PROCLAMATION

TIRED OF THE SPECTACLE OF SHORT STORIES, NOVELS, POEMS AND PLAYS STILL UNDER THE HEGEMONY OF THE BANAL WORD, MONOTONOUS SYNTAX, STATIC PSYCHOLOGY, DESCRIPTIVE NATURALISM, AND DESIROUS OF CRYSTALLIZING A VIEWPOINT...

WE HEREBY DECLARE THAT:

1. THE REVOLUTION IN THE ENGLISH LANGUAGE IS AN ACCOMPLISHED FACT.

2. THE IMAGINATION IN SEARCH OF A FABULOUS WORLD IS AUTONOMOUS AND UNCONFINED. (*Prudence is a rich, ugly old maid courted by Incapacity*... Blake)[1]

3. PURE POETRY IS A LYRICAL ABSOLUTE THAT SEEKS AN A PRIORI REALITY WITHIN OURSELVES ALONE. (*Bring out number, weight and measure in a year of dearth*... Blake)[2]

4. NARRATIVE IS NOT MERE ANECDOTE, BUT THE PROJECTION OF A METAMORPHOSIS OF REALITY. (*Enough ! Or Too Much !*... Blake)[3]

5. THE EXPRESSION OF THESE CONCEPTS CAN BE ACHIEVED ONLY THROUGH THE RHYTHMIC "HALLUCINATION OF THE WORD". (*Rimbaud*).[4]

6. THE LITERARY CREATOR HAS THE RIGHT TO DISINTEGRATE THE PRIMAL MATTER OF WORDS IMPOSED ON HIM BY TEXT-BOOKS AND DICTIONARIES. (*The road of excess leads to the palace of Wisdom*... Blake)[5]

7. HE HAS THE RIGHT TO USE WORDS OF HIS OWN FASHIONING AND TO DISREGARD EXISTING GRAMMATICAL AND SYNTACTICAL LAWS. (*The tigers of wrath are wiser than the horses of instruction*... Blake)[6]

8. THE "LITANY OF WORDS" IS ADMITTED AS AN INDEPENDENT UNIT.

9. WE ARE NOT CONCERNED WITH THE PROPAGATION OF SOCIOLOGICAL IDEAS, EXCEPT TO EMANCIPATE THE CREATIVE ELEMENTS FROM THE PRESENT IDEOLOGY.

10. TIME IS A TYRANNY TO BE ABOLISHED.

11. THE WRITER EXPRESSES. HE DOES NOT COMMUNICATE.

12. THE PLAIN READER BE DAMNED. (*Damn braces ! Bless relaxes!*... Blake)[7]

— *Signed*: KAY BOYLE, WHIT BURNETT, HART GRANE, CARESSE CROSBY, HARRY CROSBY, MARTHA FOLEY, STUART GILBERT, A. L. GILLESPIE, LEIGH HOFFMAN, EUGENE JOLAS, ELLIOT PAUL, DOUGLAS RIGBY, THEO RUTRA, ROBERT SAGE, HAROLD J. SALEMSON, LAURENCE VAIL.[8]

First published in *transition* 16–17 (June 1929).

[1]   William Blake (1757–1827), "Proverbs of Hell," in *The Marriage of Heaven and Hell*, in David Erdman (ed.), *The Complete Poetry and Prose of William Blake* (New York: Anchor Press, 1982), p. 35.

[2]   Blake, "Proverbs of Hell," in *The Marriage of Heaven and Hell*, in Erdman (ed.), *The Complete Poetry and Prose of William Blake*, p. 36.

[3]   Blake, "Proverbs of Hell," in *The Marriage of Heaven and Hell*, in Erdman (ed.), *The Complete Poetry and Prose of William Blake*, p. 38.

[4]   Jolas's rendering of a phrase ("l'hallucination des mots") in a work by the French poet Arthur Rimbaud (1854–1891), *Une Saison en Enfer* (1872), "Délires II: Alchimie du verbe" (*A Season in Hell*, "Deliriums II: Alchemy of the Word"). See Enid Rhodes Peschel, trans., *A Season in Hell; the Illuminations* (Oxford: Oxford University Press, 1973), p. 80.

[5]   "Proverbs of Hell," in *The Marriage of Heaven and Hell*, in Erdman (ed.), *The Complete Poetry and Prose of William Blake*, p. 35.

[6]   "Proverbs of Hell," in *The Marriage of Heaven and Hell*, in Erdman (ed.), *The Complete Poetry and Prose of William Blake*, p. 37.

[7]   Same as the preceding note.

[8]   Kay Boyle (1903–92) was an expatriate American novelist and poet. Whit Burnett (1899–1973) was an American expatriate living in Paris who, in 1931, founded *Story Magazine*. On Hart Crane see pp. 812–26. Caresse Crosby (1892–1970) was an author and an editor at the Black Sun Press in Paris. Harry Crosby (1898–1929), her husband, an American author and publisher living in Paris. Martha Foley (1900–77) collaborated with Whit Burnett in editing *Story Magazine*. Stuart Gilbert (1883–1969) was a British civil servant who, after retiring in 1925, moved to Paris and befriended James Joyce. A. Lincoln Gillespie was an American author who (together with others) wrote *Readies for Bob Brown's Machine* (Cagne-sur-Mer: Roving Eye Press, 1931). Nothing is known about Leigh Hoffman. For Eugene Jolas see p. 1007–16. Elliot Paul (1891–1958) was an American living in Paris, a follower of Gertrude Stein, and a prolific author. Douglas Rigby was an American expatriate and author, but nothing more is known about him. Theo Rutra was a pseudonym used by Jolas on many occasions, such as this one. Robert Sage (1889–1962) was a young American writer working on the Paris edition of the *Chicago Tribune*; he became an editorial assistant for *transition*. Harold J. Salemson edited the journal *Tambour* in Paris. Laurence Vail (1891–1968) was an artist and first husband of the art patron and collector Peggy Guggenheim, whom he married in 1922.

Notes on Reality (1929)

The creative effort of this age goes towards totality. To achieve the new image of the world which we dimly perceive on the horizon we disintegrate the universe with all the means at our disposal and transform chaos into cosmos.

We live in disquiet and disorientation. "Isms" come and go; the crisis of the imagination continues. What characterizes most this age is its lack of revolutionary faith. This age proceeds through a dialectic of acceptance and seeks transcendental surrogates in intellectualist knowledge. The new impressionism which we observe blossoming out is an attempt to resuscitate the naturalism of a purely mechanical epoch, when evolutionary materialism dominated the world. The immediate senses are celebrated as the prime factors in the esthetic organisation. In this positivist metaphysics, however, the enigmatic or the pre-logical is ignored. Neo-classicism fights for the re-establishment of traditionalist rationalism. Going beyond mere analogy, it seeks the return to a historic, long-exhausted conception of life with which it identifies itself in a final gesture of despair. It is eager to graft upon our consciousness an ideology which is the modernistic interpretation of dogmas and seeks its esthetics in Racinian order and Cartesian rigidity.[1] The neo-romantic attitude toward life and art is doomed from the outset, because its aim is irrationalism. It is unable to escape from the chaos which it worships for its own sake, although it is well to state in its favor that its pre-occupation with the primal being gives its movement an experimental force. The proletarian primitives, and their brothers, the skyscraper-futurists, approach the creative spirit inadequately, because their empirical vision leads to pure pragmatism.

The majority of philosophic systems up to recent times attempted to explain nature rationally. Hegel's[2] identity of opposites still presented reason as the only important agent in the formation of reality. The unknown element which is a priori to knowledge was recognized and separated by Schopenhauer.[3] It is to his eternal credit that he proved the relativity of reason and the importance of the sense of "will". He revolutionized the epistomological conception of idealism. He found that knowledge is simply the substitute for will which is the unity of organic and inorganic reality. He concluded that reason can attain its perfection only through the process of development beyond the primal limitations. By bringing the empirical-psychological element of the will into the front rank, the new idealism found an escape from the dilemma into which it had fallen.

The explorations into the pre-logical regions were given a strong impetus during the romantic period. This movement developed from pure irrationalism into the classical synthesis of rationalism and irrationalism and reached its zenith in absolute irrationalism. Never were the powers of the nocturnal, the a-logical, the instinctive, the earth-magical explored with more passion than by the representatives of this conception of life. All the branches of philology, philosophy, esthetics and even jurisprudence were influenced by the current. Herder, under the aegis of Hamann, had already given, in his *History of Mankind*, a powerful impetus to the movement, and in his *Adrastea* epitomized his ideas.[4] While most of the romantics opened up new vistas into an understanding of the instincts, they failed to solve the main problem of knowledge, and with one or two exceptions, notably that of Novalis,[5] sank deeper and deeper into chaos. It is a curious fact that their modern successors and imitators have not recognized this fundamental error.

First published in *transition* 18 (Nov. 1929). Jolas's original notes are marked with an asterisk.

[1]   Jean Racine (1636–99) was a French neoclassical playwright; René Descartes (1596–1650) was a French philosoher who is sometimes, as here, turned into the type of a purblind rationalism.

[2]   Georg Hegel (1770–1831), a German philosopher.

[3]   Arthur Schopenhauer (1788–1860), German philsopher.

[4]   Johann Gottfried Herder (1744–1803) was a German philosopher noted for his critique of reason as a superior agency. Between 1784 and 1791 his *Ideen zur Philosophie der Geschichte der Menschheit* (*Ideas for the Philosophy of the History of Mankind*)

appeared, a massive work in four parts; the year 1809 saw the publication of his posthumous work *Adrastea: Fragment über Licht und Farben und Schall* (*Adrastea: a Fragment on Light and Colors and Noise*). Johann Georg Hamann (1730–88) was a German Protestant thinker and critic of the Enlightenment.

[5]   Friedrich von Hardenberg (1772–1801), German poet, adopted the name Novalis as his *nom de plume*. A Romantic poet, he wrote two novels (*Lehrling zu Sais* and *Heinrich von Ofterdingen*) and a celebrated collection of *Hymnen an die Nacht* (1800; *Hymns on the Night*).

There are certain eternal, organic impulses which pragmatic dynamism has been unable to eliminate. The primitive mythos is a subterranean stream (held up by "civilized" consciousness) which we observe again and again in such manifestations as the dream, neuropathic conditions, and in the poetic inspiration as such. Explorations into the irrational continued even during the reign of pure materialism. In the beginning of this century they re-captured their position, and became in certain cases the all-absorbing, almost exclusive pre-occupation. When Freud, in his *Totem and Taboo*,[6] showed us the astonishing relationship between neurosis and primitive humanity, an immense step forward was made in the understanding of life. In his struggle to cure psychic disturbances by transforming the subconscious into the conscious, he developed the technique of psychoanalysis. The discoveries of the French psychologist Janet[7] at the same time opened a gap along almost identical lines. This new psychology quickly burst its medical frontiers and is slowly assuming the picture of an interpretation of the universe. The subconscious is the immense basin into which flow all the inhibited components of our being. This is the primal psychic principle. But it was found by Dr. Jung,[8] a dissident of the Freudian school, that into the subconscious flow not only the unfulfilled elements of our lives, but that it contains also the collective mythos thus establishing connection with the social organism and even the cosmic forces.

Although it is only since very recent times that the dream has been scientifically disintegrated into its component parts, the problem has occupied thinkers and poets for many centuries. Beginning with Heraclitus and Aristotle,[9] the Greeks already made attempts to penetrate into the mysteries of sleep. Heraclitus asked himself the question why it was that in the dream every man has his own world, while in the waking state we all have a world in common. The wish-dreams were known to the ancient Greeks, for they discovered that, in his dream, the hungry man eats and the thirsty man drinks. Aristotle sketched the first psychological explanation of the dream, the genesis of which he did not seek outside man, but in his interior life. This revolutionary conception definitely broke with the idea of the dream as a supernatural revelation. Hippocrates recognized also the psycho-gnostic possibilities of the dream. Later we find that Christian Aristotelianism examined the question, especially as exemplified by Thomas Aquinas and Albertus Magnus.[10] The latter compares the dream-picture with the sensual illusions which we have in a state of being awake.

To understand the exact nature of the dream and its relation to creative life, certain states of mind may be studied which precede or follow the dream or more properly the sleep. There are certain hallucinations which we experience before falling asleep or immediately upon waking. These so-called hypnogogic hallucinations represent mostly imagistic reflexes of a thought we were engaged in before halfsleep overtook us. The image experienced is the surrogate for the logical development of the preceding thought. A reality of associations appears. The return to the objective world makes us aware of the exact contour of this image. The transition of these halfsleep hallucinations to the actual sleep is connected with the most amazing images which, as the French psychologist Maury[11] has established, often are prolonged into the dream itself.

In examining this region, the psychology of depth has facilitated the comprehension for the processes of creation. The old dogmas of critical dictators are automatically thrown overboard. We now have come near knowing the sources of inspiration, and the secret of genius is out.

---

[6] Sigmund Freud (1856–1939) published *Totem and Taboo: Resemblances between the Psychic Lives of Savages and Neurotics* in 1912; the English translation by A. A. Brill appeared in 1918 (New York: Moffat Yard; London: G. Routledge, 1919).

[7] Pierre Janet (1859–1947), a French psychologist who, during his lifetime, was considered Freud's principal rival, elaborating theories of subsconscious activity that were very different from Freud's, but also had much in common.

[8] Carl Jung (1875–1961), a follower of Freud who broke with him in 1910 and developed his own version of psychoanalysis.

[9] Heraclitus (c. 500 BC), a pre-Socratic philosopher whose work survives only in fragments (see Hermann Diels, *The Older Sophists: A Complete Translation by Several Hands of the Fragments in*

"*Die Fragmente der Vorsokratiker*," ed. Rosamund Kent (Columbia, SC: University of South Carolina Press, 1972)); Aristotle (138–322 BC), ancient Greek philosoper.

[10] Thomas Aquinas (c. 1225–1274) and Albert Magnus or Albert the Great (d. 1280) were medieval philosophers.

[11] Louis-Ferdinand-Alfred Maury (1817–92) was a French psychologist who wrote *Le Sommeil et les rêves: études psychologiques sur ces phénomènes et les divers états qui s'y rattachent* (Paris: Didier, 1862), or *Sleep and Dreams: Psychological Studies of these Phenomena and the Diverse States Connected with Them*.

Visionaries create instinctively their substantialities out of their demonish or religious constellations. The projection of the will in Schopenhauer's sense – through sublimation – is the creator's solution of his problem. The revolutionary agent is that which becomes conscious and proceeds from the instinctive to a fusion with the objective reality. The individual and collective forces seek a union. It was the failure to recognize this principle that led the neo-romantics to the error of applying too literally the new psychological discoveries with the result that their work was incoherent and without completion.

The creator presents and sometimes interprets his instinctive symbols. Since the esthetic state is a transition between the active tendencies and those of the interior impulses, it is necessary, in order that the expression may truly achieve that hard, athletic beauty which is its sublimation, to descend into the night-side of life, before we can attain perfection. To this end we need not necessarily accept Fechner's idea of the "day-view" and the "night-view" in all of its implications,[12] but we are aware that the modern mind tries to approximate the distinction. The symbols of the sub-conscious contain many dimensions in their mythological-individual developments. The condensation of these symbols, showing us, as they do, the strata of a variegated, affective organism in the dream, is reproduced in the creative reaction.

Enough has been written about the various theories of dream interpretation for me to forego delving into the problem at this stage. But the absolute importance of the dream for the creative artist must now be assumed.* The dream is the reflex of the eternal struggle between our instinctive, unhampered life and our civilized being. For this reason, as Stekel has pointed out,[13] Freud's definition of the dream as pure wish-fulfillment is not entirely correct, since there enter also other elements, such as fear, warning etc. But the study of the dream mechanism opens the door to the recognition of a world which was dim and obscure before. The dream is pure imagination. Here we are verily beyond good and evil. In that world happen the most wonderful, pathological, criminal, demoniacal, beautiful things. The imagination takes revenge on reality. All objects in their pragmatic virtue fade. They carry only the poetic emotion.

At the limit of the creator's spirit there is always the pre-logical. Its expression is the prime factor in poetic operations. The creator is the carrier of all these images and associations, and the difference between him and the neuropath lies precisely in his capacity to get rid of his burden by means of his expressive power. The creator and the dreamer have identical roots. They both try to return to the primitive condition of humanity, and create a condition where the frontiers of the real and the unreal vanish. We have now controlled reality to some extent. In physics, chemistry, mathematics, we have witnessed the prolongations of its frontiers. The atom, once the last reality, has given way to new disintegrations which open up possibilities for tremendous evolutions.

The repercussion of this on creative expression is very important. We are near the very limits of the infinite. The heraclitean picture of modern life confronts us at the same time. The subconscious is not enough. We must organize. The flight from the excessively rational must go on. It is

---

* It is understood that I do not consider the childish applications of Freudian theories which certain English and American writers have indulged in as of the slightest importance. They failed to understand the elementary magic of the pre-logical. With typical pragmatic insensitiveness they have "psychologized," celebrating a narrow pansexualism as a new "philosophy of life," and using the text-book information they had gained to engage in their little literary game. The most obvious case is that of Eugene O'Neill, who, in his *Strange Interlude*,[14] and his other biedermeier dramas, has not recognized the subconscious as a new well of inspiration, but has worked rather from the exterior, never going beyond the all too simple task of artificially constructing his protagonists around the more familiar "complexes."

[12]   Gustav Theodor Fechner (1801–87) was a German philosopher and pioneer in experimental psychology. To regard the whole material universe as inwardly alive and conscious is to take what Fechner called the "day-view." To regard it as inert matter, lacking any teleological significance, is to take what he called the "night-view." He elaborated these ideas in *Die Tagesansicht gegenüber der Nachtansicht* (*Day-View and Night-View*) (Leipzig: Breitkopf und Härtel, 1882), a work never translated into English.

[13]   Wilhelm Stekel (1868–1940) was an Austrian psychologist who was associated with Freud until 1912, when he broke away from psychoanalysis.

[14]   Eugene O'Neill (1888–1953), American playwright, published *Strange Interlude* (New York: Dood, Mead) in 1928. The word "biedermeier" that is used by Jolas is the German term for "philistine."

blind fanaticism to deny the conscious will as a creative agent. I am not one of those who now turn suddenly against surrealism. In spite of all the snobs, who, following in the wake of our pioneering work for that movement, today discuss it glibly and pretentiously, I persist in regarding the surrealist effort as having crystallized a viewpoint in the modern spirit. The importance of the surrealistes which I tried to emphasize, when I first introduced them in this review, lay in their recognition of the primal being as a basic element in creative activity. Theirs was a revolt against the hegemony of reason which historically goes back to romanticism and more recently to Freud. Their mistake lay in the fact that, after applying Freudian and Dadaist discoveries, they did not transcend them.[15] For the transition from life as a biological existence into the formed existence of creation brings with it a concentrated change. The spontaneous emergence of the disintegrated symbols is the *a priori* condition of the creative activity. And it is here where synthetist reality begins.

The new composition must thus become mythological action. The primitive mythos and the modern mythos are fused, and the union of the collective and individual at the point of the immediate conscience produce, the universal condition. The timeless and spaceless forces lie hidden in the instinctive. Consciousness is merely the result of an effort towards a state of mind that is control. In what degree we also control the day-dream and all the emotional currents that lie in consciousness itself is a moot question.

The new creator is out to make the alliance between the dionysian-dynamic and the nocturnal realities. He is out to discover the unity of life. Conquering the dualism between the "it" and the "I," he produces new myths, myths of himself in a dynamic environment, myths of new machines and inventions, fairy tales and fables, legends and sagas expressing a hunger for beauty that is not passive and gentle like that of former ages, but hard and metallic like the age towards which we are going. He brings the fabulous again within our reach. Cause and effect are transposed. The distances of the earth are vanquished, past, present and future disappear in a unity, there remains a time-space stream which is homogeneous. The new composition is polyphonic and on many planes. It is as exact as possible and tries to produce harmonic unity by balancing the negative and positive. It is the static point produced by the balancing of the dynamic representations of the world with the spontaneous movement of the dream.

The persistent cry for the expression of life in all of its crudity based on social and moral imperatives does not answer our needs. Zola's method is not for us.[16] He expressed a milieu and described a segment of his time and world by copying it, although, it should not be forgotten, his passion and bitterness transcended his means. Artistic creation is not the mirror of reality. It is reality itself. The writer of tomorrow using a romantic-realistic orientation will give us the tempo and the development of the gigantic forces which he finds in a fusion of metaphysical space with nature. His subject is life, enigmatic and utopian.

This new sense of life, this world sense, which goes towards a totality, will probably characterize the next generations. But before that is possible, we must disintegrate and help batter down the present structure of a pathological civilization. By going towards this pure idea, we are individualists and universalists; subversive agents also whose vision is the synthesis of *all* the forces of life.

What is the Revolution of Language (1933)

When I wrote the manifesto "Revolution of the Word"[1] which was published in *transition* 16/17 (June 1929), I was aware that the opposition to this action would be considerable. I was not prepared for the formidable abuse which was heaped on this document, both in Europe and in the United States.

---

[15]   For the Surrealists and their writings, see pp. 717–61 in this volume.

[16]   Emile Zola (1840–1902) was a French novelist whose "method" was that of naturalism, an account of characters' lives that included all the details of an environment, however repulsive.

REVOLUTION OF LANGUAGE
First published in *transition* 22 (Feb. 1933).
[1]   The text is found in this edition, p. 1011.

The term has now become part of the literary baggage of our day. There are signs that the idea is beginning to be discussed with more objectivity than at the time it was first launched. There are also signs that it is being received with more sympathy than in the days of *transition's* pioneering.

The impulse for the revolution of the word owes its genesis to such precursors as Arthur Rimbaud, James Joyce, the Futurists, the early Zurich Dadaists, certain experiments of Gertrude Stein's, and Léon-Paul Fargue.[2] It owes nothing to Surrealism.

I claim for *transition* priority in formulating the problem on an international scope, in developing it independently, and in giving it a systematic dialectical sub-structure. I based myself primarily on a study of the Freud–Jung–Lévy-Bruhl[3] explorations into the unconscious in order to discover the laws dominating the mutation of language.[*] In all the numbers of *transition* I proposed and encouraged a radical criticism of language, both from the communicative and the symbolical viewpoint, and tried to prepare the ground for a general reconstruction.

Today I feel that the battle has been partly won. Although the work of many writers is still in the narrow circle of traditional language matter, there is a small group in Europe and in the United States who are beginning to break away from academic prejudices, and who are engaged in building a new and more pliable form of expression.

It may be opportune, therefore, to re-define the problem of the Revolution of the Word, or, better still, of the Revolution of Language:

Revolution of Language:
1) An attitude which regards modern language as inadequate for the expression of the changing background of the world, and which posits the necessity of a radical revision of its communicative and symbolical functions.
2) It regards both the individual creator and the collective folk speech as mediumistic instruments for bringing about the change.
3) It envisages creative language as a pre-rational process.

[2]   Arthur Rimbaud (1854–91) was a French poet; James Joyce (1882–1941) an Irish novelist (see pp. 211–300); on the Futurists see pp. 1–38); on "the early Zurich Dadaists," see pp. 461–99; on Gertrude Stein see pp. 373–416. Léon-Paul Fargue (1867–1947) was a French poet and man of letters.
[3]   Sigmund Freud (1856–1939) was an Austrian psychologist who pioneered psychoanalysis; Carl Jung (1875–1961) was a follower of Freud who broke with him around 1910 and developed his own version of psychoanalysis; Lucien Lévy-Bruhl (1857–1939) was an anthropologist, trained in philosophy, who was appointed to the chair in the history of modern philosophy at the Sorbonne in 1904 and who turned his interest in the study of logic to the study of "primitive mentality."

[*]   *It always seemed to me strange that none of the psychologists themselves tried to tackle the problem. It is, therefore, with great interest*

that I notice in the last number of the Psychoanalytische Bewegung[4] *(Vienna) an article by A. J. Storfer, "Chancen einer psychoanalytischen Wortforschung", in which the question is studied for the first time, to my knowledge.*

[4]   The *Psychoanalytische Bewegung* (or in English, *Psychoanalytic Movement*) was a brief-lived journal (1929–33) devoted to psychoanalysis. Adolf Josef Storfer (1888–1945) was an Austrian psychoanalyst and publisher who issued Freud's most important works; his essay on "Chancen einer psychoanalytischen Wortforschung" ("Chances of a Psychoanalytic Research into Words") was published in the *Psychoanalytische Bewegung* 4(3) (May–June 1932): 233–48.

Samuel Beckett (1906–89)

Introduction

Samuel Beckett (1906–89) was born in Foxrock, a suburb to the south of Dublin. He attended the distinguished Portora Royal boarding school at Enniskillen, County Fermanagh, now Northern Ireland, and entered Trinity College Dublin in 1923, where he studied Modern Languages (French and Italian). In 1926 he was awarded a Foundation Scholarship on the basis of exceptional academic performance, and the same year he made his first visit to France. He graduated in 1927, and the next year took up a teaching post in Belfast, then took a position as *lecteur* in English at the Ecole Normale Supérieure in Paris. He became acquainted with Joyce and his circle, and in 1929 published his first essay ("Dante . . . Bruno. Vico .. Joyce"; see this volume, pp. 1061–72). The same year he submitted his first book, *Whoroscope*, to Nancy Cunard at the Hours Press in Paris. Cunard published it the following year and awarded it a prize. Beckett now returned to Dublin and took up the post of lecturer in French at Trinity College, but after just over a year he gave it up. After a period of travelling, he moved to London, where he spent two years. His first novel was *Dream of Fair to Middling Women* (posthumously published 1992), and he published his first story, "Dante and the Lobster", wrote some reviews, and completed both his first collection of stories, *More Pricks than Kicks* (1934), and his first collection of poems, *Echo's Bones and Other Precipitates* (1935; see p. 1083–4).

In 1936 Beckett left for Germany, and by 1937 he was settled back in Paris. *Murphy* became his first published novel the next year. In 1940, after the outbreak of the Second World War and the German occupation of Paris, Beckett fled south, then returned to his apartment in Paris. A year later he joined the Resistance. Staying just one step ahead of the Gestapo, he managed to flee into Vichy France in 1942, where he continued to work for the Resistance. In 1945 he was awarded the Croix de Guerre for his wartime activities.

"To get away from war and occupation," he later said, he finished *Watt* in manuscript. In 1946 he wrote four *nouvelles* in French, then began *Molloy* in French. In 1952 he published *En attendant Godot*, or *Waiting for Godot*, in French, and on January 19, 1953, the work's first performance took place in Paris. The first English production of *Godot* took place two years later, in August 1955; the first American one yet another year later, in Miami. In 1956 Beckett's English translation of *Waiting for Godot* was published in Britain. The rest, as they say, is history. Over the next 25 years Becket would go on to write an amazing series of works, a landmark in the history of twentieth-century literature. Every genre that he touched was utterly transformed by him, and the history of modern drama in particular is unimaginable without his brooding and yet incredibly funny presence. In 1969 he was awarded the Nobel Prize for Literature. His response was characteristic: he fled to Tunisia to escape the intense media coverage. Throughout his life he remained averse to the trappings of celebrity culture, living in a small flat in a working-class district when in Paris, and doing as much writing as he could at a small house at Ussy-sur-Marne which he had purchased with the legacy from his mother's estate in 1952.

Texts for Nothing (1955)

1

Suddenly, no, at last, long last, I couldn't any more, I couldn't go on. Someone said, You can't stay here. I couldn't stay there and I couldn't go on. I'll describe the place, that's unimportant. The top, very flat, of a mountain, no, a hill, but so wild, so wild, enough. Quag, heath up to the knees, faint

The original French version of the complete "Texts for Nothing" was included in Beckett's *Nouvelles et textes pour rien* (Paris: Éditions de Minuit, 1955). But Beckett began working on the first text on Christmas Eve, 1950, then wrote the others in their published order, completing the last by 20 December 1951. *Texte V* (the French original) was first published in the journal *Deucalion* (Oct. 1952); *Textes III, VI*, and *X* in *Les Lettres nouvelles* (May 1953); while *Textes I* and *II*, with some variants, were first published in *Monde Nouveau* (May–June 1955). Some of Beckett's English translations were also published in journals: I in the *Evergreen Review* (Summer 1959); III in *Great French Short Stories* (New York: Dell, 1960); XII in the *Transatlantic Review* (Spring 1967); and VI in *London Magazine* (Aug. 1967). The entire series in translation was published in *Stories and Texts for Nothing* (New York: Grove Press, 1967) and *No's Knife: Collected Shorter Prose, 1945–66* (London: Calder and Boyars, 1967).

sheep-tracks, troughs scooped deep by the rains. It was far down in one of these I was lying, out of the wind. Glorious prospect, but for the mist that blotted out everything, valleys, loughs, plain and sea. How can I go on, I shouldn't have begun, no, I had to begin. Someone said, perhaps the same, What possessed you to come? I could have stayed in my den, snug and dry, I couldn't. My den, I'll describe it, no, I can't. It's simple, I can do nothing any more, that's what you think. I say to the body, Up with you now, and I can feel it struggling, like an old hack foundered in the street, struggling no more, struggling again, till it gives up. I say to the head, Leave it alone, stay quiet, it stops breathing, then pants on worse than ever. I am far from all that wrangle, I shouldn't bother with it, I need nothing, neither to go on nor to stay where I am, it's truly all one to me, I should turn away from it all, away from the body, away from the head, let them work it out between them, let them cease, I can't, it's I would have to cease. Ah yes, we seem to be more than one, all deaf, not even, gathered together for life. Another said, or the same, or the first, they all have the same voice, the same ideas, All you had to do was stay at home. Home. They wanted me to go home. My dwelling-place. But for the mist, with good eyes, with a telescope, I could see it from here. It's not just tiredness, I'm not just tired, in spite of the climb. It's not that I want to stay here either. I had heard tell, I must have heard tell of the view, the distant sea in hammered lead, the so-called golden vale so often sung, the double valleys, the glacial loughs, the city in its haze, it was all on every tongue. Who are these people anyway? Did they follow me up here, go before me, come with me? I am down in the hole the centuries have dug, centuries of filthy weather, flat on my face on the dark earth sodden with the creeping saffron waters it slowly drinks. They are up above, all round me, as in a graveyard. I can't raise my eyes to them, what a pity, I wouldn't see their faces, their legs perhaps, plunged in the heath. Do they see me, what can they see of me? Perhaps there is no one left, perhaps they are all gone, sickened. I listen and it's the same thoughts I hear, I mean the same as ever, strange. To think in the valley the sun is blazing all down the ravelled sky. How long have I been here, what a question, I've often wondered. And often I could answer, An hour, a month, a year, a century, depending on what I meant by here, and me, and being, and there I never went looking for extravagant meanings, there I never much varied, only the here would sometimes seem to vary. Or I said, I can't have been here long, I wouldn't have held out. I hear the curlews, that means close of day, fall of night, for that's the way with curlews, silent all day, then crying when the darkness gathers, that's the way with those wild creatures and so short-lived, compared with me. And that other question I know so well too, What possessed you to come? unanswerable, so that I answered, To change, or, It's not me, or, Chance, or again, To see, or again, years of great sun, Fate, I feel that other coming, let it come, it won't catch me napping. All is noise, unending suck of black sopping peat, surge of giant ferns, heathery gulfs of quiet where the wind drowns, my life and its old jingles. To change, to see, no, there's no more to see, I've seen it all, till my eyes are blear, nor to get away from harm, the harm is done, one day the harm was done, the day my feet dragged me out that must go their ways, that I let go their ways and drag me here, that's what possessed me to come. And what I'm doing, all-important, breathing in and out and saying, with words like smoke, I can't go, I can't stay, let's see what happens next. And in the way of sensation? My God I can't complain, it's himself all right, only muffled, like buried in snow, less the warmth, less the drowse, I can follow them well, all the voices, all the parts, fairly well, the cold is eating me, the wet too, at least I presume so, I'm far. My rheumatism in any case is no more than a memory, it hurts me no more than my mother's did, when it hurt her. Eye ravening patient in the haggard vulture face, perhaps it's carrion time. I'm up there and I'm down here, under my gaze, foundered, eyes closed, ear cupped against the sucking peat, we're of one mind, all of one mind, always were, deep down, we're fond of one another, we're sorry for one another, but there it is, there's nothing we can do for one another. One thing at least is certain, in an hour it will be too late, in half-an-hour it will be night, and yet it's not, not certain, what is not certain, absolutely certain, that night prevents what day permits, for those who know how to go about it, who have the will to go about it, and the strength, the strength to try again. Yes, it will be night, the mist will clear, I know my mist, for all my distraction, the wind freshen and the whole night sky open over the mountain, with its lights, including the Bears, to guide me once again on my way, let's wait for night. All mingles, times and tenses, at first I only had been here, now I'm here still, soon I won't be here yet, toiling up the slope, or in the bracken by the wood, it's larch, I don't try to understand, I'll never try to understand any more, that's what you think, for the moment I'm here, always have been, always shall be, I won't be afraid of the big words any more, they are not big. I don't remember coming, I can't go, all my little company, my eyes are closed and I feel the wet humus harsh against my cheek, my hat is gone, it can't be gone far, or the wind has swept it away, I was attached to it. Sometimes it's the sea, other times the mountains, often it was the forest, the city, the plain too, I've flirted with the plain too, I've given myself up for dead all over the place, of hunger, of old age, murdered, drowned, and then for no reason, of tedium, nothing like breathing your last to put new life in you, and then the rooms, natural death, tucked up in bed, smothered in household gods, and always muttering, the same old mutterings, the same old stories, the same old questions and answers, no malice in me, hardly any, stultior stultissimo, never an imprecation, not such a fool, or else it's gone from mind. Yes, to the end, always muttering, to lull me and keep me company, and all ears always, all ears for the old stories, as when my father took me on his knee and read me the one about Joe Breem, or Breen, the son of a lighthouse keeper, evening after evening, all the long winter through. A tale, it was a tale for children, it all happened on a rock, in the storm, the mother was dead and the gulls came beating against the light, Joe jumped into the sea, that's all I remember, a knife between his teeth, did what was to be done and came back, that's all I remember this evening, it ended happily, it began unhappily and it ended happily, every evening, a comedy, for children. Yes, I was my father and I was my son, I asked myself questions and answered as best I could, I had it told to me evening after evening, the same old story I knew by heart and couldn't believe, or we walked together, hand in hand, silent, sunk in our worlds, each in his worlds, the hands forgotten in each other. That's how I've held out till now. And this evening again it seems to be working, I'm in my arms, I'm holding myself in my arms, without much tenderness, but faithfully, faithfully. Sleep now, as under that ancient lamp, all twined together, tired out with so much talking, so much listening, so much toil and play.

2

Above is the light, the elements, a kind of light, sufficient to see by, the living find their ways, without too much trouble, avoid one another, unite, avoid the obstacles, without too much trouble, seek with their eyes, close their eyes, halting, without halting, among the elements, the living. Unless it has changed, unless it has ceased. The things too must still be there, a little more worn, a little even less, many still standing where they stood in the days of their indifference. Here you are under a different glass, not long habitable either, it's time to leave it. You are there, there it is, where you are will never long be habitable. Go then, no, better stay, for where would you go, now that you know? Back above? There are limits. Back in that kind of light. See the cliffs again, be again between the cliffs and the sea, reeling shrinking with your hands over your ears, headlong, innocent, suspect, noxious. Seek, by the excessive light of night, a demand commensurate with the offer, and go to ground empty-handed at the old crack of day. See Mother Calvet again, creaming off the garbage before the nightmen come. She must still be there. With her dog and her skeletal baby-buggy. What could be more endurable? She wavered through the night, a kind of trident in her hand, muttering and ejaculating, Your highness! Your honour! The dog totered on its hind-legs begging, hooked its paws over the rim of the can and snouted round with her in the muck. It got in her way, she cursed it for a lousy cur and let it have its way. There's a good memory. Mother Calvet. She knew what she liked, perhaps even what she would have liked. And beauty, strength, intelligence, the latest, daily, action, poetry, all one price for one and all. If only it could be wiped from knowledge. To have suffered under that miserable light, what a blunder. It let nothing show, it would have gone out, nothing terrible, nothing showed, of the true affair, it would have snuffed out. And now here, what now here, one enormous second, as in Paradise, and the mind slow, slow, nearly stopped. And yet it's changing, something is changing, it must be in the head, slowly in the head the ragdoll rotting, perhaps we're in a head, it's as dark as in a head before the worms get at it, ivory dungeon. The words too, slow, slow, the subject dies before it comes to the verb, words are stopping too. Better off then than when life was babble? That's it, that's it, the bright side. And the absence of others, does that count for so little? Pah others, that's nothing, others never inconvenienced anyone, and there must be a few here too, other others, invisible, mute, what does it matter. It's true you hid from them, hugged their walls, true, you miss that here, you miss the derivatives, here it's pure ache, pah you were saying that above and you a living mustard-plaster. So long as the words keep coming nothing will have changed, there are the old words out again. Utter, there's nothing else, utter, void yourself of them, here as always, nothing else. But they are failing, true, that's the change, they are failing, that's bad, bad. Or it's the dread of coming to the last, of having said all, your all, before the end, no, for that will be the end, the end of all, not certain. To need to groan and not be able, Jesus, better ration yourself, watch out for the genuine death-pangs, some are deceptive, you think you're home, start howling and revive, health-giving howls, better be silent, it's the only method, if you want to end, not a word but smiles, end rent with stifled imprecations, burst with speechlessness, all is possible, what now? Perhaps above it's summer, a summer Sunday, Mr. Joly is in the belfry, he has wound up the clock, now he's ringing the bells. Mr. Joly. He had only one leg and a half. Sunday. It was folly to be abroad. The roads were crawling with them, the same roads so often kind. Here at least none of that, no talk of a creator and nothing very definite in the way of a creation. Dry, it's possible, or wet, or slime, as before matter took ill. Is this stuff air that permits you to suffocate still, almost audibly at times, it's possible, a kind of air. What exactly is going on, exactly, ah old xanthic laugh, no, farewell mirth, good riddance, it was never droll. No, but one more memory, one last memory, it may help, to abort again. Piers pricking his oxen o'er the plain, no, for at the end of the furrow, before turning to the next, he raised his eyes to the sky and said, Bright again too early. And sure enough, soon after, the snow. In other words the night was black, when it fell at last, but no, strange, it wasn't, in spite of the buried sky. The way was long that led back to the den, over the fields, a winding way, it must still be there. When it comes to the top of the cliff it springs, some might think blindly, but no, wilily, like a goat, in hairpin zigzags towards the shore. Never had the sea so thundered from afar, the sea beneath the snow, though superlatives have lost most of their charm. The day had not been fruitful, as was only natural, considering the season, that of the very last leeks. It was none the less the return, to what no matter, the return, unscathed, always a matter for wonder. What happened? Is that the question? An encounter? Bang! No. Level with the farm of the Graves brothers a brief halt, opposite the lamplit window. A glow, red, afar, at night, in winter, that's worth having, that must have been worth having. There, it's done, it ends there, I end there. A far memory, far from the last, it's possible, the legs seem to be still working. A pity hope is dead. No. How one hoped above, on and off. With what diversity.

3

Leave, I was going to say leave all that. What matter who's speaking, someone said what matter who's speaking. There's going to be a departure, I'll be there, I won't miss it, it won't be me, I'll be here, I'll say I'm far from here, it won't be me, I won't say anything, there's going to be a story, someone's going to try and tell a story. Yes, no more denials, all is false, there is no one, it's understood, there is nothing, no more phrases, let us be dupes, dupes of every time and tense, until it's done, all past and done, and the voices cease, it's only voices, only lies. Here, depart from here and go elsewhere, or stay here, but coming and going. Start by stirring, there must be a body, as of old, I don't deny it, no more denials, I'll say I'm a body, stirring back and forth, up and down, as required. With a clutter of limbs and organs, all that is needed to live again, to hold out a little time, I'll call that living, I'll say it's me, I'll get standing, I'll stop thinking, I'll be too busy, getting standing, staying standing, stirring about, holding out, getting to tomorrow, tomorrow week, that will be ample, a week will be ample, a week in spring, that puts the jizz in you. It's enough to will it, I'll will it, will me a body, will me a head, a little strength, a little courage, I'm starting now, a week is soon served, then back here, this inextricable place, far from the days, the far days, it's not going to be easy. And why, come to think, no no, leave it, no more of that, don't listen to it all, don't say it all, it's all old, all one, once and for all. There you are now on your feet, I give you my word, I swear they're yours, I swear it's mine, get to work with your hands, palp your skull, seat of the understanding, without which nix, then the rest, the lower regions, you'll be needing them, and say what you're like, have a guess, what kind of man, there has to be a man, or a woman, feel between your legs, no need of beauty, nor of vigour, a week's a short stretch, no one's going to love you, don't be alarmed. No, not like that, too sudden, I gave myself a start. And to start with stop palpitating, no one's going to kill you, no one's going to love you and no one's going to kill you, perhaps you'll emerge in the high depression of Gobi, you'll feel at home there. I'll wait for you here, no, I'm alone, I alone am, this time it's I must go. I know how I'll do it, I'll be a man, there's nothing else for it, a kind of man, a kind of old tot, I'll have a nanny, I'll be her sweet pet, she'll give me her hand, to cross over, she'll let me loose in the Green, I'll be good, I'll sit quiet as a mouse in a corner and comb my beard, I'll tease it out, to look more bonny, a little more bonny, if only it could be like that. She'll say to me, Come, doty, it's time for bye-bye. I'll have no responsibility, she'll have all the responsibility, her name will be Bibby, I'll call her Bibby, if only it could be like that. Come, ducky, it's time for yum-yum. Who taught me all I know, I alone, in the old wanderyears, I deduced it all from nature, with the help of an all-in-one, I know it's not me, but it's too late now, too late to deny it, the knowledge is there, the bits and scraps, flickering on and off, turn about, winking on the storm, in league to fool me. Leave it and go, it's time to go, to say so anyway, the moment has come, it's not known why. What matter how you describe yourself, here or elsewhere, fixed or mobile, without form or oblong like man, in the dark or the light of the heavens, I don't know, it seems to matter, it's not going to be easy. And if I went back to where all went out and on from there, no, that would lead nowhere, never led anywhere, the memory of it has gone out too, a great flame and then blackness, a great spasm and then no more weight or traversable space. I tried throwing me off a cliff, collapsing in the street in the midst of mortals, that led nowhere, I gave up. Take the road again that cast me up here, then retrace it, or follow it on, wise advice. That's so that I'll never stir again, dribble on here till time is done, murmuring every ten centuries, It's not me, it's not true, it's not me, I'm far. No no, I'll speak now of the future, I'll speak in the future, as when I used to say, in the night, to myself, Tomorrow I'll put on my dark blue tie, with the yellow stars, and put it on, when night was past. Quick quick before I weep. I'll have a crony, my own vintage, my own bog, a fellow warrior, we'll relive our campaigns and compare our scratches. Quick quick. He'll have served in the navy, perhaps under Jellicoe, while I was potting at the invader from behind a barrel of Guinness, with my arquebuse. We have not long, that's the spirit, in the present, not long to live, it's our positively last winter, halleluiah. We wonder what will carry us off in the end. He's gone in the wind, I in the prostate rather. We envy each other, I envy him, he envies me, occasionally. I catheterize myself, unaided, with trembling hand, bent double in the public piss-house, under cover of my cloak, people take me for a dirty old man. He waits for me to finish, sitting on a bench, coughing up his guts, spitting into a snuffbox which no sooner overflows than he empties it in the canal, out of civic-mindedness. We have well deserved of our motherland, she'll get us into the Incurables before we die. We spend our life, it's ours, trying to bring together in the same instant a ray of sunshine and a free bench, in some oasis of public verdure, we've been seized by a love of nature, in our sere and yellow, it belongs to one and all, in places. In a choking murmur he reads out to me from the paper of the day before, he had far far better been the blind one. The sport of kings is our passion, the dogs too, we have no political opinions, simply limply republican. But we also have a soft spot for the Windsors, the Hanoverians, I forget, the Hohenzollerns is it. Nothing human is foreign to us, once we have digested the racing news. No, alone, I'd be better off alone, it would be quicker. He'd nourish me, he had a friend a pork-butcher, he'd ram the ghost back down my gullet with black pudding. With his consolations, allusions to cancer, recollections of imperishable raptures, he'd prevent discouragement from sapping my foundations. And I, instead of concentrating on my own horizons, which might have enabled me to throw them under a lorry, would let my mind be taken off them by his. I'd say to him, Come on, gunner, leave all that, think no more about it, and it's I would think no more about it, besotted with brotherliness. And the obligations! I have in mind particularly the appointments at ten in the morning, hail rain or shine, in front of Duggan's, thronged already with sporting men fevering to get their bets out of harm's way before the bars open. We were, there we are past and gone again, so much the better, so much the better, most punctual I must say. To see the remains of Vincent arriving in sheets of rain, with the brave involuntary swagger of the old tar, his head swathed in a bloody clout and a glitter in his eye, was for the acute observer an example of what man is capable of, in his pursuit of pleasure. With one hand he sustained his sternum, with the heel of the other his spinal column, as if tempted to break into a hornpipe, no, that's all memories, last shifts older than the flood. See what's happening here, where there's no one, where nothing happens, get something to happen here, someone to be here, then put an end to it, have silence, get into silence, or another sound, a sound of other voices than those of life and death, of lives and deaths everyone's but mine, get into my story in order to get out of it, no, that's all meaningless. Is it possible I'll sprout a head at last, all my very own, in which to brew poisons worthy of me, and legs to kick my heels with, I'd be there at last, I could go at last, it's all I ask, no, I can't ask anything. Just the head and the two legs, or one, in the middle, I'd go hopping. Or just the head, nice and round, nice and smooth, no need of lineaments, I'd go rolling, downhill, almost a pure spirit, no, that wouldn't work, all is uphill from here, the leg is unavoidable, or the equivalent, perhaps a few annular joints, contractile, great ground to be covered with them. To set out from Duggan's door, on a spring morning of rain and shine, not knowing if you'll ever get to evening, what's wrong with that? It would be so easy. To be bedded in that flesh or in another, in that arm held by a friendly hand, and in that hand, without arms, without hands, and without soul in those trembling souls, through the crowd, the hoops, the toy balloons, what's wrong with that? I don't know, I'm here, that's all I know, and that it's still not me, it's of that the best has to be made. There is no flesh anywhere, nor any way to die. Leave all that, to want to leave all that, not knowing what that means, all that, it's soon said, soon done, in vain, nothing has stirred, no one has spoken. Here, nothing will happen here, no one will be here, for many a long day. Departures, stories, they are not for tomorrow. And the voices, wherever they come from, have no life in them.

4

Where would I go, if I could go, who would I be, if I could be, what would I say, if I had a voice, who says this, saying it's me? Answer simply, someone answer simply. It's the same old stranger as ever, for whom alone accusative I exist, in the pit of my inexistence, of his, of ours, there's a simple answer. It's not with thinking he'll find me, but what is he to do, living and bewildered, yes, living, say what he may. Forget me, know me not, yes, that would be the wisest, none better able than he. Why this sudden affability after such desertion, it's easy to understand, that's what he says, but he doesn't understand. I'm not in his head, nowhere in his old body, and yet I'm there, for him I'm there, with him, hence all the confusion. That should have been enough for him, to have found me absent, but it's not, he wants me there, with a form and a world, like him, in spite of him, me who am everything, like him who is nothing. And when he feels me void of existence it's of his he would have me void, and vice versa, mad, mad, he's mad. The truth is he's looking for me to kill me, to have me dead like him, dead like the living. He knows all that, but it's no help his knowing it, I don't know it, I know nothing. He protests he doesn't reason and does nothing but reason, crooked, as if that could improve matters. He thinks words fail him, he thinks because words fail him he's on his way to my speechlessness, to being speechless with my speechlessness, he would like it to be my fault that words fail him, of course words fail him. He tells his story every five minutes, saying it is not his, there's cleverness for you. He would like it to be my fault that he has no story, of course he has no story, that's no reason for trying to foist one on me. That's how he reasons, wide of the mark, but wide of what mark, answer us that. He has me say things saying it's not me, there's profundity for you, he has me who say nothing say it's not me. All that is truly crass. If at least he would dignify me with the third person, like his other figments, not he, he'll be satisfied with nothing less than me, for his me. When he had me, when he was me, he couldn't get rid of me quick enough, I didn't exist, he couldn't have that, that was no kind of life, of course I didn't exist, any more than he did, of course it was no kind of life, now he has it, his kind of life, let him lose it, if he wants to be in peace, with a bit of luck. His life, what a mine, what a life, he can't have that, you can't fool him, ergo it's not his, it's not him, what a thought, treat him like that, like a vulgar Molloy, a common Malone, those mere mortals, happy mortals, have a heart, land him in that shit, who never stirred, who is none but me, all things considered, and what things, and how considered, he had only to keep out of it. That's how he speaks, this evening, how he has me speak, how he speaks to himself, how I speak, there is only me, this evening, here, on earth, and a voice that makes no sound because it goes towards none, and a head strewn with arms laid down and corpses fighting fresh, and a body, I nearly forgot. This evening, I say this evening, perhaps it's morning. And all these things, what things, all about me, I won't deny them any more, there's no sense in that any more. If it's nature perhaps it's trees and birds, they go together, water and air, so that all may go on, I don't need to know the details, perhaps I'm sitting under a palm. Or it's a room, with furniture, all that's required to make life comfortable, dark, because of the wall outside the window. What am I doing, talking, having my figments talk, it can only be me. Spells of silence too, when I listen, and hear the local sounds, the world sounds, see what an effort I make, to be reasonable. There's my life, why not, it is one, if you like, if you must, I don't say no, this evening. There has to be one, it seems, once there is speech, no need of a story, a story is not compulsory, just a life, that's the mistake I made, one of the mistakes, to have wanted a story for myself, whereas life alone is enough. I'm making progress, it was time, I'll learn to keep my foul mouth shut before I'm done, if nothing foreseen crops up. But he who somehow comes and goes, unaided from place to place, even though nothing happens to him, true, what of him? I stay here, sitting, if I'm sitting, often I feel sitting, sometimes standing, it's one or the other, or lying down, there's another possibility, often I feel lying down, it's one of the three, or kneeling. What counts is to be in the world, the posture is immaterial, so long as one is on earth. To breathe is all that is required, there is no obligation to ramble, or receive company, you may even believe yourself dead on condition you make no bones about it, what more liberal regimen could be imagined, I don't know, I don't imagine. No point under such circumstances in saying I am somewhere else, someone else, such as I am I have all I need to hand, for to do what, I don't know, all I have to do, there I am on my own again at last, what a relief that must be. Yes, there are moments, like this moment, when I seem almost restored to the feasible. Then it goes, all goes, and I'm far again, with a far story again, I wait for me afar for my story to begin, to end, and again this voice cannot be mine. That's where I'd go, if I could go, that's who I'd be, if I could be.

5

I'm the clerk, I'm the scribe, at the hearings of what cause I know not. Why want it to be mine, I don't want it. There it goes again, that's the first question this evening. To be judge and party, witness and advocate, and he, attentive, indifferent, who sits and notes. It's an image, in my helpless head, where all sleeps, all is dead, not yet born, I don't know, or before my eyes, they see the scene, the lids flicker and it's in. An instant and then they close again, to look inside the head, to try and see inside, to look for me there, to look for someone there, in the silence of quite a different justice, in the toils of that obscure assize where to be is to be guilty. That is why nothing appears, all is silent, one is frightened to be born, no, one wishes one were, so as to begin to die. One, meaning me, it's not the same thing, in the dark where I will in vain to see there can't be any willing. I could get up, take a little turn, I long to, but I won't. I know where I'd go, I'd go into the forest, I'd try and reach the forest, unless that's where I am, I don't know where I am, in any case I stay. I see what it is, I seek to be like the one I seek, in my head, that my head seeks, that I bid my head seek, with its probes, within itself. No, don't pretend to seek, don't pretend to think, just be vigilant, the eyes staring behind the lids, the ears straining for a voice not from without, were it only to sound an instant, to tell another lie. I hear, that must be the voice of reason again, that the vigil is in vain, that I'd be better advised to take a little turn, the way you manoeuvre a tin soldier. And no doubt it's the same voice answers that I can't, I who but a moment ago seemed to think I could, unless it's old shuttlecock sentiment chiming in, full stop, got all that. Why did Pozzo leave home, he had a castle and retainers. Insidious question, to remind me I'm in the dock. Sometimes I hear things that seem for a moment judicious, for a moment I'm sorry they are not mine. Then what a relief, what a relief to know I'm mute for ever, if only it didn't distress me. And deaf, it seems to me sometimes that deaf I'd be less distressed, at being mute, listen to that, what a relief not to have that on my conscience. Ah yes, I hear I have a kind of conscience, and on top of that a kind of sensibility, I trust the orator is not forgetting anything, and without ceasing to listen or drive the old quill I'm afflicted by them, I heard, it's noted. This evening the session is calm, there are long silences when all fix their eyes on me, that's to make me fly off my hinges, I feel on the brink of shrieks, it's noted. Out of the corner of my eye I observe the writing hand, all dimmed and blurred by the – by the reverse of farness. Who are all these people, gentlemen of the long robe, according to the image, but according to it alone, there are others, there will be others, other images, other gentlemen. Shall I never see the sky again, never be free again to come and go, in sunshine and in rain, the answer is no, all answer no, it's well I didn't ask anything, that's the kind of extravagance I envy them, till the echoes die away. The sky, I've heard – the sky and earth, I've heard great accounts of them, now that's pure word for word, I invent nothing. I've noted, I must have noted many a story with them as setting, they create the atmosphere. Between them where the hero stands a great gulf is fixed, while all about they flow together more and more, till they meet, so that he finds himself as it were under glass, and yet with no limit to his movements in all directions, let him understand who can, that is no part of my attributions. The sea too, I am conversant with the sea too, it belongs to the same family, I have even gone to the bottom more than once, under various assumed names, don't make me laugh, if only I could laugh, all would vanish, all what, who knows, all, me, it's noted. Yes, I see the scene, I see the hand, it comes creeping out of shadow, the shadow of my head, then scurries back, no connexion with me. Like a little creepy crawly it ventures out an instant, then goes back in again, the things one has to listen to, I say it as I hear it. It's the clerk's hand, is he entitled to the wig, I don't know, formerly perhaps. What do I do when silence falls, with rhetorical intent, or denoting lassitude, perplexity, consternation, I rub to and fro against my lips, where they meet, the first knuckle of my forefinger, but it's the head that moves, the hand rests, it's to such details the liar pins his hopes. That's the way this evening, tomorrow will be different, perhaps I'll appear before the council, before the justice of him who is all love, unforgiving and justly so, but subject to strange indulgences, the accused will be my soul, I prefer that, perhaps someone will ask pity for my soul, I mustn't miss that, I won't be there, neither will God, it doesn't matter, we'll be represented. Yes, it can't be much longer now, I haven't been damned for what seems an eternity, yes, but sufficient unto the day, this evening I'm the scribe. This evening, it's always evening, always spoken of as evening, even when it's morning, it's to make me think night is at hand, bringer of rest. The first thing would be to believe I'm there, if I could do that I'd lap up the rest, there'd be none more credulous than me, if I were there. But I am, it's not possible otherwise, just so, it's not possible, it doesn't need to be possible. It's tiring, very tiring, in the same breath to win and lose, with concomitant emotions, one's heart is not of stone, to record the doom, don the black cap and collapse in the dock, very tiring, in the long run, I'm tired of it, I'd be tired of it, if I were me. It's a game, it's getting to be a game, I'm going to rise and go, if it's not me it will be someone, a phantom, long live all our phantoms, those of the dead, those of the living and those of those who are not born. I'll follow him, with my sealed eyes, he needs no door, needs no thought, to issue from this imaginary head, mingle with air and earth and dissolve, little by little, in exile. Now I'm haunted, let them go, one by one, let the last desert me and leave me empty, empty and silent. It's they murmur my name, speak to me of me, speak of a me, let them go and speak of it to others, who will not believe them either, or who will believe them too. Theirs all these voices, like a rattling of chains in my head, rattling to me that I have a head. That's where the court sits this evening, in the depths of that vaulty night, that's where I'm clerk and scribe, not understanding what I hear, not knowing what I write. That's where the council will be tomorrow, prayers will be offered for my soul, as for that of one dead, as for that of an infant dead in its dead mother, that it may not go to Limbo, sweet thing theology. It will be another evening, all happens at evening, but it will be the same night, it too has its evenings, its mornings and its evenings, there's a pretty conception, it's to make me think day is at hand, disperser of phantoms. And now birds, the first birds, what's this new trouble now, don't forget the question-mark. It must be the end of the session, it's been calm, on the whole. Yes, that's sometimes the way, there are suddenly birds and all goes silent, an instant. But the phantoms come back, it's in vain they go abroad, mingle with the dying, they come back and slip into the coffin, no bigger than a matchbox, it's they have taught me all I know, about things above, and all I'm said to know about me, they want to create me, they want to make me, like the bird the birdikin, with larvae she fetches from afar, at the peril – I nearly said at the peril of her life! But sufficient unto the day, those are other minutes. Yes, one begins to be very tired, very tired of one's toil, very tired of one's quill, it falls, it's noted.

6

How are the intervals filled between these apparitions? Do my keepers snatch a little rest and sleep before setting about me afresh, how would that be? That would be very natural, to enable them to get back their strength. Do they play cards, the odd rubber, bowls, to recruit their spirits, are they entitled to a little recreation? I would say no, if I had a say, no recreation, just a short break, with something cold, even though they should not feel inclined, in the interests of their health. They like their work, I feel it in my bones! No, I mean how filled for me, they don't come into this. Wretched acoustics this evening, the merest scraps, literally. The news, do you remember the news, the latest news, in slow letters of light, above Piccadilly Circus, in the fog? Where were you standing, in the doorway of the little tobacconist's closed for the night on the corner of Glasshouse Street was it, no, you don't remember, and for cause. Sometimes that's how it is, in a way, the eyes take over, and the silence, the sighs, like the sighs of sadness weary with crying, or old, that suddenly feels old and sighs for itself, for the happy days, the long days, when it cried it would never perish, but it's far from common, on the whole. My keepers, why keepers, I'm in no danger of stirring an inch, ah I see, it's to make me think I'm a prisoner, frantic with corporeality, rearing to get out and away. Other times it's male nurses, white from head to foot, even their shoes are white, and then it's another story, but the burden is the same. Other times it's like ghouls, naked and soft as worm, they grovel round me gloating on the corpse, but I have no more success dead than dying. Other times it's great clusters of bones, dangling and knocking with a clatter of castanets, it's clean and gay like coons, I'd join them with a will if it could be here and now, how is it nothing is ever here and now? It's varied, my life is varied, I'll never get anywhere. I know, there is no one here, neither me nor anyone else, but some things are better left unsaid, so I say nothing. Elsewhere perhaps, by all means, elsewhere, what elsewhere can there be to this infinite here? I know, if my head could think I'd find a way out, in my head, like so many others, and out of worse than this, the world would be there again, in my head, with me much as in the beginning. I would know that nothing had changed, that a little resolution is all that is needed to come and go under the changing sky, on the moving earth, as all along the long summer days too short for all the play, it was known as play, if my head could think. The air would be there again, the shadows of the sky drifting over the earth, and that ant, that ant, oh most excellent head that can't think. Leave it, leave it, nothing leads to anything, nothing of all that, my life is varied, you can't have everything, I'll never get anywhere, but when did I? When I laboured, all day long and let me add, before I forget, part of the night, when I thought that with perseverance I'd get at me in the end? Well look at me, a little dust in a little nook, stirred faintly this way and that by breath straying from the lost without. Yes, I'm here for ever, with the spinners and the dead flies, dancing to the tremor of their meshed wings, and it's well pleased I am, well pleased, that it's over and done with, the puffing and panting after me up and down their Tempe of tears. Sometimes a butterfly comes, all warm from the flowers, how weak it is, and quick dead, the wings crosswise, as when resting, in the sun, the scales grey. Blot, words can be blotted and the mad thoughts they invent, the nostalgia for that slime where the Eternal breathed and his son wrote, long after, with divine idiotic finger, at the feet of the adulteress, wipe it out, all you have to do is say you said nothing and so say nothing again. What can have become then of the tissues I was, I can see them no more, feel them no more, flaunting and fluttering all about and inside me, pah they must be still on their old prowl somewhere, passing themselves off as me. Did I ever believe in them, did I ever believe I was there, somewhere in that ragbag, that's more the line, of inquiry, perhaps I'm still there, as large as life, merely convinced I'm not. The eyes, yes, if these memories are mine, I must have believed in them an instant, believed it was me I saw there dimly in the depths of their glades. I can see me still, with those of now, sealed this long time, staring with those of then, I must have been twelve, because of the glass, a round shaving-glass, double-faced, faithful and magnifying, staring into one of the others, the true ones, true then, and seeing me there, imagining I saw me there, lurking behind the bluey veils, staring back sightlessly, at the age of twelve, because of the glass, on its pivot, because of my father, if it was my father, in the bathroom, with its view of the sea, the lightships at night, the red harbour light, if these memories concern me, at the age of twelve, or at the age of forty, for the mirror remained, my father went but the mirror remained, in which he had so greatly changed, my mother did her hair in it, with twitching hands, in another house, with no view of the sea, with a view of the mountains, if it was my mother, what a refreshing whiff of life on earth. I was, I was, they say in Purgatory, in Hell too, admirable singulars, admirable assurance. Plunged in ice up to the nostrils, the eyelids caked with frozen tears, to fight all your battles o'er again, what tranquillity, and know there are no more emotions in store, no, I can't have heard aright. How many hours to go, before the next silence, they are not hours, it will not be silence, how many hours still, before the next silence? Ah to know for sure, to know that this thing has no end, this thing, this thing, this farrago of silence and words, of silence that is not silence and barely murmured words. Or to know it's life still, a form of life, ordained to end, as others ended and will end, till life ends, in all its forms. Words, mine was never more than that, than this pell-mell babel of silence and words, my viewless form described as ended, or to come, or still in progress, depending on the words, the moments, long may it last in that singular way. Apparitions, keepers, what childishness, and ghouls, to think I said ghouls, do I as much as know what they are, of course I don't, and how the intervals are filled, as if I didn't know, as if there were two things, some other thing besides this thing, what is it, this unnamable thing that I name and name and never wear out, and I call that words. It's because I haven't hit on the right ones, the killers, haven't yet heaved them up from that heart-burning glut of words, with what words shall I name my unnamable words? And yet I have high hopes, I give you my word, high hopes, that one day I may tell a story, hear a story, yet another, with men, kinds of men as in the days when I played all regardless or nearly, worked and played. But first stop talking and get on with your weeping, with eyes wide open that the precious liquid may spill freely, without burning the lids, or the crystalline humour, I forget, whatever it is it burns. Tears, that could be the tone, if they weren't so easy, the true tone and tenor at last. Besides not a tear, not one, I'd be in greater danger of mirth, if it wasn't so easy. No, grave, I'll be grave, I'll close my ears, close my mouth and be grave. And when they open again it may be to hear a story, tell a story, in the true sense of the words, the word hear, the word tell, the word story, I have high hopes, a little story, with living creatures coming and going on a habitable earth crammed with the dead, a brief story, with night and day coming and going above, if they stretch that far, the words that remain, and I've high hopes, I give you my word.

7

Did I try everything, ferret in every hold, secretly, silently, patiently, listening? I'm in earnest, as so often, I'd like to be sure I left no stone unturned before reporting me missing and giving up. In every hold, I mean in all those places where there was a chance of my being, where once I used to lurk, waiting for the hour to come when I might venture forth, tried and trusty places, that's all I meant when I said in every hold. Once, I mean in the days when I still could move, and feel myself moving, painfully, barely, but unquestionably changing position on the whole, the trees were witness, the sands, the air of the heights, the cobble-stones. This tone is promising, it is more like that of old, of the days and nights when in spite of all I was calm, treading back and forth the futile road, knowing it short and easy seen from Sirius, and deadly calm at the heart of my frenzies. My question, I had a question, ah yes, did I try everything, I can see it still, but it's passing, lighter than air, like a cloud, in moonlight, before the skylight, before the moon, like the moon, before the skylight. No, in its own way, I know it well, the way of an evening shadow you follow with your eyes, thinking of something else, yes, that's it, the mind elsewhere, and the eyes too, if the truth were known, the eyes elsewhere too. Ah if there must be speech at least none from the heart, no, I have only one desire, if I have it still. But another thing, before the ones that matter, I have just time, if I make haste, in the trough of all this time just time. Another thing, I call that another thing, the old thing I keep on not saying till I'm sick and tired, revelling in the flying instants, I call that revelling, now's my chance and I talk of revelling, it won't come back in a hurry if I remember right, but come back it must with its riot of instants. It's not me in any case, I'm not talking of me, I've said it a million times, no point in apologizing again, for talking of me, when there's X, that paradigm of human kind, moving at will, complete with joys and sorrows, perhaps even a wife and brats, forebears most certainly, a carcass in God's image and a contemporary skull, but above all endowed with movement, that's what strikes you above all, with his likeness so easy to take and his so instructive soul, that really, no, to talk of oneself, when there's X, no, what a blessing I'm not talking of myself, enough vile parrot I'll kill you. And what if all this time I had not stirred hand or foot from the third-class waiting-room of the South-Eastern Railway Terminus, I never dared wait first on a third class ticket, and were still there waiting to leave, for the south-east, the south rather, east lay the sea, all along the track, wondering where on earth to alight, or my mind absent, elsewhere. The last train went at twenty-three thirty, then they closed the station for the night. What thronging memories, that's to make me think I'm dead, I've said it a million times. But the same return, like the spokes of a turning wheel, always the same, and all alike, like spokes. And yet I wonder, whenever the hour returns when I have to wonder that, if the wheel in my head turns, I wonder, so given am I to thinking with my blood, or if it merely swings, like a balance-wheel in its case, a minute to and fro, seeing the immensity to measure and that heads are only wound up once, so given am I to thinking with my breath. But tut there I am far again from that terminus and its pretty neo-Doric colonnade, and far from that heap of flesh, rind, bones and bristles waiting to depart it knows not where, somewhere south, perhaps asleep, its ticket between finger and thumb for the sake of appearances, or let fall to the ground in the great limpness of sleep, perhaps dreaming it's in heaven, alit in heaven, or better still the dawn, waiting for the dawn and the joy of being able to say, I've the whole day before me, to go wrong, to go right, to calm down, to give up, I've nothing to fear, my ticket is valid for life. Is it there I came to a stop, is that me still waiting there, sitting up stiff and straight on the edge of the seat, knowing the dangers of laisser-aller, hands on thighs, ticket between finger and thumb, in that great room dim with the platform gloom as dispensed by the quarter-glass self-closing door, locked up in those shadows, it's there, it's me. In that case the night is long and singularly silent, for one who seems to remember the city sounds, confusedly, sunk now to a single sound, the impossible confused memory of a single confused sound, lasting all night, swelling, dying, but never for an instant broken by a silence the like of this deafening silence. Whence it should follow, but does not, that the third-class waiting-room of the South-Eastern Railway Terminus must be struck from the list of places to visit, see above, centuries above, that this lump is no longer me and that search should be made elsewhere, unless it be abandoned, which is my feeling. But not so fast, all cities are not eternal, that of this pensum is perhaps among the dead, and the station in ruins where I sit waiting, erect and rigid, hands on thighs, the tip of the ticket between finger and thumb, for a train that will never come, never go, natureward, or for day to break behind the locked door, through the glass black with the dust of ruin. That is why one must not hasten to conclude, the risk of error is too great. And to search for me elsewhere, where life persists, and me there, whence all life has withdrawn, except mine, if I'm alive, no, it would be a loss of time. And personally, I hear it said, personally I have no more time to lose, and that that will be all for this evening, that night is at hand and the time come for me too to begin.

8

Only the words break the silence, all other sounds have ceased. If I were silent I'd hear nothing. But if I were silent the other sounds would start again, those to which the words have made me deaf, or which have really ceased. But I am silent, it sometimes happens, no, never, not one second. I weep too without interruption. It's an unbroken flow of words and tears. With no pause for reflection. But I speak softer, every year a little softer. Perhaps. Slower too, every year a little slower. Perhaps. It is hard for me to judge. If so the pauses would be longer, between the words, the sentences, the syllables, the tears, I confuse them, words and tears, my words are my tears, my eyes my mouth.

And I should hear, at every little pause, if it's the silence I say when I say that only the words break it. But nothing of the kind, that's not how it is, it's for ever the same murmur, flowing unbroken, like a single endless word and therefore meaningless, for it's the end gives the meaning to words. What right have you then, no, this time I see what I'm up to and put a stop to it, saying, None, none. But get on with the stupid old threne and ask, ask until you answer, a new question, the most ancient of all, the question were things always so. Well I'm going to tell myself something (if I'm able), pregnant I hope with promise for the future, namely that I begin to have no very clear recollection of how things were before (I was!), and by before I mean elsewhere, time has turned into space and there will be no more time, till I get out of here. Yes, my past has thrown me out, its gates have slammed behind me, or I burrowed my way out alone, to linger a moment free in a dream of days and nights, dreaming of me moving, season after season, towards the last, like the living, till suddenly I was here, all memory gone. Ever since nothing but fantasies and hope of a story for me somehow, of having come from somewhere and of being able to go back, or on, somehow, some day, or without hope. Without what hope, haven't I just said, of seeing me alive, not merely inside an imaginary head, but a pebble sand to be, under a restless sky, restless on its shore, faint stirs day and night, as if to grow less could help, ever less and less and never quite be gone. No truly, no matter what, I say no matter what, hoping to wear out a voice, to wear out a head, or without hope, without reason, no matter what, without reason. But it will end, a desinence will come, or the breath fail better still, I'll be silence, I'll know I'm silence, no, in the silence you can't know, I'll never know anything. But at least get out of here, at least that, no? I don't know. And time begin again, the steps on the earth, the night the fool implores at morning and the morning he begs at evening not to dawn. I don't know, I don't know what all that means, day and night, earth and sky, begging and imploring. And I can desire them? Who says I desire them, the voice, and that I can't desire anything, that looks like a contradiction, it may be for all I know. Me, here, if they could open, those little words, open and swallow me up, perhaps that is what has happened. If so let them open again and let me out, in the tumult of light that sealed my eyes, and of men, to try and be one again. Or if I'm guilty let me be forgiven and graciously authorized to expiate, coming and going in passing time, every day a little purer, a little deader. The mistake I make is to try and think, even the way I do, such as I am I shouldn't be able, even the way I do. But whom can I have offended so grievously, to be punished in this inexplicable way, all is inexplicable, space and time, false and inexplicable, suffering and tears, and even the old convulsive cry, It's not me, it can't be me. But am I in pain, whether it's me or not, frankly now, is there pain? Now is here and here there is no frankness, all I say will be false and to begin with not said by me, here I'm a mere ventriloquist's dummy, I feel nothing, say nothing, he holds me in his arms and moves my lips with a string, with a fish-hook, no, no need of lips, all is dark, there is no one, what's the matter with my head, I must have left it in Ireland, in a saloon, it must be there still, lying on the bar, it's all it deserved. But that other who is me, blind and deaf and mute, because of whom I'm here, in this black silence, helpless to move or accept this voice as mine, it's as him I must disguise myself till I die, for him in the meantime do my best not to live, in this pseudo-sepulture claiming to be his. Whereas to my certain knowledge I'm dead and kicking above, somewhere in Europe probably, with every plunge and suck of the sky a little more overripe, as yesterday in the pump of the womb. No, to have said so convinces me of the contrary, I never saw the light of day, any more than he, ah if no were content to cut yes's throat and never cut its own. Watch out for the right moment, then not another word, is that the only way to have being and habitat? But I'm here, that much at least is certain, it's in vain I keep on saying it, it remains true. Does it? It's hard for me to judge. Less true and less certain in any case than when I say I'm on earth, come into the world and assured of getting out, that's why I say it, patiently, variously, trying to vary, for you never know, it's perhaps all a question of hitting on the right aggregate. So as to be here no more at last, to have never been here, but all this time above, with a name like a dog to be called up with and distinctive marks to be had up with, the chest expanding and contracting unaided, panting towards the grand apnoea. The right aggregate, but there are four million possible, nay probable, according to Aristotle, who knew everything. But what is this I see, and how, a white stick and an ear-trumpet, where, Place de la République, at pernod time, let me look closer at this, it's perhaps me at last. The trumpet, sailing at ear level, suddenly resembles a steam-whistle, of the kind thanks to which my steamers forge fearfully through the fog. That should fix the period, to the nearest half-century or so. The stick gains ground, tapping with its ferrule the noble bassamento of the United Stores, it must be winter, at least not summer. I can also just discern, with a final effort of will, a bowler hat which seems to my sorrow a sardonic synthesis of all those that never fitted me and, at the other extremity, similarly suspicious, a complete pair of brown boots lacerated and gaping. These insignia, if I may so describe them, advance in concert, as though connected by the traditional human excipient, halt, move on again, confirmed by the vast show windows. The level of the hat, and consequently of the trumpet, hold out some hope for me as a dying dwarf or at least hunchback. The vacancy is tempting, shall I enthrone my infirmities, give them this chance again, my dream infirmities, that they may take flesh and move, deteriorating, round and round this grandiose square which I hope I don't confuse with the Bastille, until they are deemed worthy of the adjacent Père Lachaise or, better still, prematurely relieved trying to cross over, at the hour of night's young thoughts. No, the answer is no. For even as I moved, or when the moment came, affecting beyond all others, to hold out my hand, or hat, without previous song, or any other form of concession to self-respect, at the terrace of a café, or in the mouth of the underground, I would know it was not me, I would know I was here, begging in another dark, another silence, for another alm, that of being or of ceasing, better still, before having been. And the hand old in vain would drop the mite and the old feet shuffle on, towards an even vainer death than no matter whose.

9

If I said, There's a way out there, there's a way out somewhere, the rest would come. What am I waiting for then, to say it? To believe it? And what does that mean, the rest? Shall I answer, try to answer, or go on as though I had asked nothing? I don't know, I can't know beforehand, nor after, nor during, the future will tell, some future instant, soon, or late, I won't hear, I won't understand, all dies so fast, no sooner born. And the yeses and noes mean nothing in this mouth, no more than sighs it sighs in its toil, or answers to a question not understood, a question unspoken, in the eyes of a mute, an idiot, who doesn't understand, never understood, who stares at himself in a glass, stares before him in the desert, sighing yes, sighing no, on and off. But there is reasoning somewhere, moments of reasoning, that is to say the same things recur, they drive one another out, they draw one another back, no need to know what things. It's mechanical, like the great colds, the great heats, the long days, the long nights, of the moon, such is my conviction, for I have convictions, when their turn comes round, then stop having them, that's how it goes, it must be supposed, at least it must be said, since I have just said it. The way out, this evening it's the turn of the way out, isn't it like a duo, or a trio, yes, there are moments when it's like that, then they pass and it's not like that any more, never was like that, is like nothing, no resemblance with anything, of no interest. What variety and at the same time what monotony, how varied it is and at the same time how, what's the word, how monotonous. What agitation and at the same time what calm, what vicissitudes within what changelessness. Moments of hesitation not so much rare as frequent, if one had to choose, and soon overcome in favour of the old crux, on which at first all depends, then much, then little, then nothing. That's right, wordshit, bury me, avalanche, and let there be no more talk of any creature, nor of a world to leave, nor of a world to reach, in order to have done, with worlds, with creatures, with words, with misery, misery. Which no sooner said, Ah, says I, punctually, if only I could say, There's a way out there, there's a way out somewhere, then all would be said, it would be the first step on the long travellable road, destination tomb, to be trod without a word, tramp tramp, little heavy irrevocable steps, down the long tunnels at first, then under the mortal skies, through the days and nights, faster and faster, no, slower and slower, for obvious reasons, and at the same time faster and faster, for other obvious reasons, or the same, obvious in a different way, or in the same way, but at a different moment of time, a moment earlier, a moment later, or at the same moment, there is no such thing, there would be no such thing, I recapitulate, impossible. Would I know where I came from, no, I'd have a mother, I'd have had a mother, and what I came out of, with what pain, no, I'd have forgotten, what is it makes me say that, what is it makes me say this, whatever it is makes me say all, and it's not certain, not certain the way the mother would be certain, the way the tomb would be certain, if there was a way out, if I said there was a way out, make me say it, demons, no, I'll ask for nothing. Yes, I'd have a mother, I'd have a tomb, I wouldn't have come out of here, one doesn't come out of here, here are my tomb and mother, it's all here this evening, I'm dead and getting born, without having ended, helpless to begin, that's my life. How reasonable it is and what am I complaining of? Is it because I'm no longer slinking to and fro before the graveyard, saying, God grant I'm buriable before the curtain drops, is that my grievance, it's possible. I was well inspired to be anxious, wondering on what score, and I asked myself, as I came and went, on what score I could possibly be anxious, and found the answer and answered, saying, It's not me, I haven't yet appeared, I haven't yet been noticed, and saying further, Oh yes it is, it's me all right, and ceasing to be what is more, then quickening my step, so as to arrive before the next onslaught, as though it were on time I trod, and saying further, and so forth. I can scarcely have gone unperceived, all this time, and yet you wouldn't have thought so, that I didn't go unperceived. I don't refer to the spoken salutation, I'd have been the first to be perturbed by that, almost as much as by the bow, kiss or handshake. But the other signs, irrepressible, with which the fellow-creature unwillingly betrays your presence, the shudders and wry faces, nothing of that nature either it would seem, except possibly on the part of certain hearse-horses, in spite of their blinkers and strict funereal training, but perhaps I flatter myself. Truly I can't recall a single face, proof positive that I was not there, no, proof of nothing. But the fact that I was not molested, can I have remained insensible to that? Alas I fear they could have subjected me to the most gratifying brutalities, I won't go so far as to say without my knowledge, but without my being encouraged, as a result, to feel myself there rather than elsewhere. And I may well have spent one half of my life in the prisons of their Arcady, purging the delinquencies of the other half, all unaware of any break or lull in my problematic patrolling, unconstrained, before the gates of the graveyard. But what if weary of seeing me relieve myself, of seeing me resume, after each forced vacation, my beat before the gates of the graveyard, what if finally they had plucked up heart and slightly stressed their blows, just enough to confer death, without any mutilation of the corpse, there, at the gates of the graveyard, where that very morning I had reappeared, no sooner set at large, and resumed by old offence, to and fro, with step now slow and now precipitate, like that of the conspirator Catilina plotting the ruin of the fatherland, saying, It's not me, yes, it's me, and further, There's a way out there, no no, I'm getting mixed, I must be getting mixed, confusing here and there, now and then, just as I confused them then, the here of then, the then of there, with other spaces, other times, dimly discerned, but not more dimly than now, now that I'm here, if I'm here, and no longer there, coming and going before the graveyard, perplexed. Or did I end up by simply sitting down, with my back to the wall, all the long night before me when the dead lie waiting, on the beds where they died, shrouded or coffined, for the sun to rise? What am I doing now, I'm trying to see where I am, so as to be able to go elsewhere, should occasion arise, or else simply to say, You have merely to wait till they come and fetch you, that's my impression at times. Then it goes and I see it's not that, but something else, difficult to grasp, and which I don't grasp, or which I do grasp, it depends, and it comes to the same, for it's not that either, but something else, some other thing, or the first back again, or still the same, always the same thing proposing itself to my perplexity, then disappearing, then proposing itself again, to my perplexity still unsated, or momentarily dead, of starvation. The graveyard, yes, it's there I'd return, this evening it's there, borne by my words, if I could get out of here, that is to say if I could say, There's a way out there, there's a way out somewhere, to know exactly where would be a mere matter of time, and patience, and sequency of thought, and felicity of expression. But the body, to get there with, where's the body? It's a minor point, a minor point. And I have no doubts, I'd get there somehow, to the way out, sooner or later, if I could say, There's a way out there, there's a way out somewhere, the rest would come, the other words, sooner or later, and the power to get there, and the way to get there, and pass out, and see the beauties of the skies, and see the stars again.

10

Give up, but it's all given up, it's nothing new, I'm nothing new. Ah so there was something once, I had something once. It may be thought there was, so long as it's known there was not, never anything, but giving up. But let us suppose there was not, that is to say let us suppose there was, something once, in a head, in a heart, in a hand, before all opened, emptied, shut again and froze. This is most reassuring, after such a fright, and emboldens me to go on, once again. But there is not silence. No, there is utterance, somewhere someone is uttering. Inanities, agreed, but is that enough, is that enough, to make sense? I see what it is, the head has fallen behind, all the rest has gone on, the head and its anus the mouth, or else it has gone on alone, all alone on its old prowls, slobbering its shit and lapping it back off the lips like in the days when it fancied itself. But the heart's not in it any more, nor is the appetite what it was. So home to roost it comes among my other assets, home yet again, and no trickery involved, that old past ever new, ever ended, ever ending, with all its hidden treasures of promise for tomorrow, and of consolation for today. And I'm in good hands again, they hold my head from behind, intriguing detail, as at the hairdresser's, the forefingers close my eyes, the middle fingers my nostrils, the thumbs stop up my ears, but imperfectly, to enable me to hear, but imperfectly, while the four remaining make merry with my jaws and tongue, to enable me to suffocate, but imperfectly, and to utter, for my good, what I must utter, for my future good, well-known ditty, and in particular to observe without delay, speaking of the passing moment, that worse have been known to pass, that it will pass in time, a mere moment of respite which but for this first aid might have proved fatal, and that one day I shall know again that I once was, and roughly who, and how to go on, and speak unaided, nicely, about number one and his pale imitations. And it is possible, just, for I must not be too affirmative at this stage, it would not be in my interest, that other fingers, quite a different gang, other tentacles, that's more like it, other charitable suckers, waste no more time trying to get it right, will take down my declarations, so that at the close of the interminable delirium, should it ever resume, I may not be reproached with having faltered. This is awful, awful, at least there's that to be thankful for. And perhaps beside me, and all around, other souls are being licked into shape, souls swooned away, or sick with over-use, or because no use could be found for them, but still fit for use, or fit only to be cast away, pale imitations of mine. Or has it knelled here at last for our committal to flesh, as the dead are committed to the ground, in the hour of their death at last, and at the place where they die, to keep the expenses down, or for our reassignment, souls of the stillborn, or dead before the body, or still young in the midst of the ruins, or never come to life through incapacity or for some other reason, or the immortal type, there must be a few of them too, whose bodies were always wrong, but patience there's a true one in pickle, among the unborn hordes, the true sepulchral body, for the living have no room for a second. No, no souls, or bodies, or birth, or life, or death, you've got to go on without any of that junk, that's all dead with words, with excess of words, they can say nothing else, they say there is nothing else, that here it's that and nothing else, but they won't say it eternally, they'll find some other nonsense, no matter what, and I'll be able to go on, no, I'll be able to stop, or start, another guzzle of lies but piping hot, it will last my time, it will be my time and place, my voice and silence, a voice of silence, the voice of my silence. It's with such prospects they exhort you to have patience, whereas you are patient, and calm, somehow somewhere calm, what calm here, ah that's an idea, say how calm it is here, and how fine I feel, and how silent I am, I'll start right away, I'll say what calm and silence, which nothing has ever broken, nothing will ever break, which saying I don't break, or saying I'll be saying, yes, I'll say all that tomorrow, yes, tomorrow evening, some other evening, not this evening, this evening it's too late, too late to get things right, I'll go to sleep, so that I may say, hear myself say, a little later, I've slept, he's slept, but he won't have slept, or else he's sleeping now, he'll have done nothing, nothing but go on, doing what, doing what he does, that is to say, I don't know, giving up, that's it, I'll have gone on giving up, having had nothing, not being there.

11

When I think, no, that won't work, when come those who knew me, perhaps even know me still, by sight of course, or by smell, it's as though, it's as if, come on, I don't know, I shouldn't have begun. If I began again, setting my mind to it, that sometimes gives good results, it's worth trying, I'll try it, one of these days, one of these evenings, or this evening, why not this evening, before I disappear, from up there, from down here, scattered by the everlasting words. What am I saying, scattered, isn't that just what I'm not, just what I'm not, I was wandering, my mind was wandering, just the very thing I'm not. And it's still the same old road I'm trudging, up yes and down no, towards one yet to be named, so that he may leave me in peace, be in peace, be no more, have never been. Name, no, nothing is namable, tell, no, nothing can be told, what then, I don't know, I shouldn't have begun. Add him to the repertory, there we have it, and execute him, as I execute me, one dead bar after another, evening after evening, and night after night, and all through the days, but it's always evening, why is that, why is it always evening, I'll say why, so as to have said it, have it behind me, an instant. It's time that can't go on at the hour of the serenade, unless it's dawn, no, I'm not in the open, I'm under the ground, or in my body somewhere, or in another body, and time devours on, but not me, there we have it, that's why it's always evening, to let me have the best to look forward to, the long black night to sleep in, there, I've answered, I've answered something. Or it's in the head, like a minute time switch, a second time switch, or it's like a patch of sea, under the passing lighthouse beam, a passing patch of sea under the passing beam. Vile words to make me believe I'm here, and that I have a head, and a voice, a head believing this, then that, then nothing more, neither in itself, nor in anything else, but a head with a voice belonging to it, or to others, other heads, as if there were two heads, as if there were one head, or headless, a headless voice, but a voice. But I'm not deceived, for the moment I'm not deceived, for the moment I'm not there, nor anywhere else what is more, neither as head, nor as voice, nor as testicle, what a shame, what a shame I'm not appearing anywhere as testicle, or as cunt, those areas, a female pubic hair, it sees great sights, peeping down, well, there it is, can't be helped, that's how it is. And I let them say their say, my words not said by me, me that word, that word they say, but say in vain. We're getting on, getting on, and when come those who knew me, quick quick, it's as though, no, premature. But peekaboo here I come again, just when most needed, like the square root of minus one, having terminated my humanities, this should be worth seeing, the livid face stained with ink and jam, caput mortuum of a studious youth, ears akimbo, eyes back to front, the odd stray hair, foaming at the mouth, and chewing, what is it chewing, a gob, a prayer, a lesson, a little of each, a prayer got by rote in case of emergency before the soul resigns and bubbling up all arsy-versy in the old mouth bereft of words, in the old head done with listening, there I am old, it doesn't take long, a snotty old nipper, having terminated his humanities, in the two-stander urinal on the corner of the Rue d'Assas was it, with the leak making the same gurgle as sixty years ago, my favourite because of the encouragement like mother hissing to baby on pot, my brow glued to the partition among the graffiti, straining against the prostate, belching up Hail Marys, buttoned as to the fly, I invent nothing, through absent-mindedness, or exhaustion, or insouciance, or on purpose, to promote priming, I know what I mean, or one-armed, better still, no arms, no hands, better by far, as old as the world and no less hideous, amputated on all sides, erect on my trusty stumps, bursting with old piss, old prayers, old lessons, soul, mind and carcass finishing neck and neck, not to mention the gobchucks, too painful to mention, sobs made mucus, hawked up from the heart, now I have a heart, now I'm complete, apart from a few extremities, having terminated their humanities, then their career, and with that not in the least pretentious, making no demands, rent with ejaculations, Jesus, Jesus. Evenings, evenings, what evenings they were then, made of what, and when was that, I don't know, made of friendly shadows, friendly skies, of time cloyed, resting from devouring, until its midnight meats, I don't know, any more than then, when I used to say, from within, or from without, from the coming night or from under the ground, Where am I, to mention only space, and in what semblance, and since when, to mention also time, and till when, and who is this clot who doesn't know where to go, who can't stop, who takes himself for me and for whom I take myself, anything at all, the old jangle. Those evenings then, but what is this evening made of, this evening now, that never ends, in whose shadows I'm alone, that's where I am, where I was then, where I've always been, it's from them I spoke to myself, spoke to him, where has he vanished, the one I saw then, is he still in the street, it's probable, it's possible, with no voice speaking to him, I don't speak to him any more, I don't speak to me any more, I have no one left to speak to, and I speak, a voice speaks that can be none but mine, since there is none but me. Yes, I have lost him and he has lost me, lost from view, lost from hearing, that's what I wanted, is it possible, that I wanted that, wanted this, and he, what did he want, he wanted to stop, perhaps he has stopped, I have stopped, but I never stirred, perhaps he is dead, I am dead, but I never lived. But he moved, proof of animation, through those evenings, moving too, evenings with an end, evenings with a night, never saying a word, unable to say a word, not knowing where to go, unable to stop, listening to my cries, hearing a voice crying that it was no kind of life, as if he didn't know, as if the allusion was to his, which was a kind of one, there's the difference, those were the days, I didn't know where I was, nor in what semblance, nor since when, nor till when, whereas now, there's the difference, now I know, it's not true, but I say it just the same, there's the difference, I'm saying it now, I'll say it soon, I'll say it in the end, then end, I'll be free to end, I won't be any more, it won't be worth it any more, it won't be necessary any more, it won't be possible any more, but it's not worth it now, it's not necessary now, it's not possible now, that's how the reasoning runs. No, something better must be found, a better reason, for this to stop, another word, a better idea, to put in the negative, a new no, to cancel all the others, all the old noes that buried me down here, deep in this place which is not one, which is merely a moment for the time being eternal, which is called here, and in this being which is called me and is not one, and in this impossible voice, all the old noes dangling in the dark and swaying like a ladder of smoke, yes, a new no, that none says twice, whose drop will fall and let me down, shadow and babble, to an absence less vain than inexistence. Oh I know it won't happen like that, I know that nothing will happen, that nothing has happened and that I'm still, and particularly since the day I could no longer believe it, what is called flesh and blood somewhere above in their gonorrhoeal light, cursing myself heartily. And that is why, when comes the hour of those who knew me, this time it's going to work, when comes the hour of those who knew me, it's as though I were among them, that is what I had to say, among them watching me approach, then watching me recede, shaking my head and saying, Is it really he, can it possibly be he, then moving on in their company along a road that is not mine and with every step takes me further from that other not mine either, or remaining alone where I am, between two parting dreams, knowing none, known of none, that finally is what I had to say, that is all I can have had to say, this evening.

12

It's a winter night, where I was, where I'm going, remembered, imagined, no matter, believing in me, believing it's me, no, no need, so long as the others are there, where, in the world of the others, of the long mortal ways, under the sky, with a voice, no, no need, and the power to move, now and then, no need either, so long as the others move, the true others, but on earth, beyond all doubt on earth, for as long as it takes to die again, wake again, long enough for things to change here, for something to change, to make possible a deeper birth, a deeper death, or resurrection in and out of this murmur of memory and dream. A winter night, without moon or stars, but light, he sees his body, all the front, part of the front, what makes them light, this impossible night, this impossible body, it's me in him remembering, remembering the true night, dreaming of the night without morning, and how will he manage tomorrow, to endure tomorrow, the dawning, then the day, the same as he managed yesterday, to endure yesterday. Oh I know, it's not me, not yet, it's a veteran, inured to days and nights, but he forgets, he thinks of me, more than is wise, and it's a far cry to morning, perhaps it has time never to dawn at last. That's what he says, with his voice soon to leave him, perhaps tonight, and he says, How light it is, how shall I manage tomorrow, how did I manage yesterday, pah it's the end, it's a far cry to morning, and who's this speaking in me, and who's this disowning me, as though I had taken his place, usurped his life, that old shame that kept me from living, the shame of my living that kept me from living, and so on, muttering, the old inanities, his chin on his heart, his arms dangling, sagging at the knees, in the night. Will they succeed in slipping me into him, the memory and dream of me, into him still living, aren't I there already, wasn't I always there, like a stain of remorse, is that my night and contumacy, in the dungeons of this moribund, and from now till he dies my last chance to have been, and who is this raving now, pah there are voices everywhere, ears everywhere, one who speaks saying, without ceasing to speak, Who's speaking?, and one who hears, mute, uncomprehending, far from all, and bodies everywhere, bent, fixed, where my prospects must be just as good, just as poor, as in this firstcomer. And none will wait, he no more than the others, none ever waited to die for me to live in him, so as to die with him, but quick quick all die, saying, Quick quick let us die, without him, as we lived, before it's too late, lest we won't have lived. And this other now, obviously, what's to be said of this latest other, with his babble of homeless mes and untenanted hims, this other without number or person whose abandoned being we haunt, nothing. There's a pretty three in one, and what a one, what a no one. So, I'm supposed to say now, it's the moment, so that's the earth, these expiring vitals set aside for me which no sooner taken over would be set aside for another, many thanks, and here the laugh, the long silent guffaw of the knowing non-exister, at hearing ascribed to him such pregnant words, confess you're not the man you were, you'll end up riding a bicycle. That's the accountants' chorus, opining like a single man, and there are more to come, all the peoples of the earth would not suffice, at the end of the billions you'd need a god, unwitnessed witness of witnesses, what a blessing it's all down the drain, nothing ever as much as begun, nothing ever but nothing and never, nothing ever but lifeless words.

13

Weaker still the weak old voice that tried in vain to make me, dying away as much as to say it's going from here to try elsewhere, or dying down, there's no telling, as much as to say it's going to cease, give up trying. No voice ever but it in my life, it says, if speaking of me one can speak of life, and it can, it still can, or if not of life, there it dies, if this, if that, if speaking of me, there it dies, but who can the greater can the less, once you've spoken of me you can speak of anything, up to the point where, up to the time when, there it dies, it can't go on, it's been its death, speaking of me, here or elsewhere, it says, it murmurs. Whose voice, no one's, there is no one, there's a voice without a mouth, and somewhere a kind of hearing, something compelled to hear, and somewhere a hand, it calls that a hand, it wants to make a hand, or if not a hand something somewhere that can leave a trace, of what is made, of what is said, you can't do with less, no, that's romancing, more romancing, there is nothing but a voice murmuring a trace. A trace, it wants to leave a trace, yes, like air leaves among the leaves, among the grass, among the sand, it's with that it would make a life, but soon it will be the end, it won't be long now, there won't be any life, there won't have been any life, there will be silence, the air quite still that trembled once an instant, the tiny flurry of dust quite settled. Air, dust, there is no air here, nor anything to make dust, and to speak of instants, to speak of once, is to speak of nothing, but there it is, those are the expressions it employs. It has always spoken, it will always speak, of things that don't exist, or only exist elsewhere, if you like, if you must, if that may be called existing. Unfortunately it is not a question of elsewhere, but of here, ah there are the words out at last, out again, that was the only chance, get out of here and go elsewhere, go where time passes and atoms assemble an instant, where the voice belongs perhaps, where it sometimes says it must have belonged, to be able to speak of such figments. Yes, out of here, but how when here is empty, not a speck of dust, not a breath, the voice's breath alone, it breathes in vain, nothing is made. If I were here, if it could have made me, how I would pity it, for having spoken so long in vain, no, that won't do, it wouldn't have spoken in vain if I were here, and I wouldn't pity it if it had made me, I'd curse it, or bless it, it would be in my mouth, cursing, blessing, whom, what, it wouldn't be able to say, in my mouth it wouldn't have much to say, that had so much to say in vain. But this pity, all the same, it wonders, this pity that is in the air, though no air here for pity, but it's the expression, it wonders should it stop and wonder what pity is doing here and if it's not hope gleaming, another expression, evilly among the imaginary ashes, the faint hope of a faint being after all, human in kind, tears in its eyes before they've had time to open, no, no more stopping and wondering, about that or anything else, nothing will stop it any more, in its fall, or in its rise, perhaps it will end on a castrato scream. True there was never much talk of the heart, literal or figurative, but that's no reason for hoping, what, that one day there will be one, to send up above to break in the galanty show, pity. But what more is it waiting for now, when there's no doubt left, no choice left, to stick a sock in its death-rattle, yet another locution. To have rounded off its cock-and-bullshit in a coda worthy of the rest? Last everlasting questions, infant languors in the end sheets, last images, end of dream, of being past, passing and to be, end of lie. Is it possible, is that the possible thing at last, the extinction of this black nothing and its impossible shades, the end of the farce of making and the silencing of silence, it wonders, that voice which is silence, or it's me, there's no telling, it's all the same dream, the same silence, it and me, it and him, him and me, and all our train, and all theirs, and all theirs, but whose, whose dream, whose silence, old questions, last questions, ours who are dream and silence, but it's ended, we're ended who never were, soon there will be nothing where there was never anything, last images. And whose the shame, at every mute micromillisyllable, and unslakable infinity of remorse delving ever deeper in its bite, at having to hear, having to say, fainter than the faintest murmur, so many lies, so many times the same lie lyingly denied, whose the screaming silence of no's knife in yes's wound, it wonders. And wonders what has become of the wish to know, it is gone, the heart is gone, the head is gone, no one feels anything, asks anything, seeks anything, says anything, hears anything, there is only silence. It's not true, yes, it's true, it's true and it's not true, there is silence and there is not silence, there is no one and there is someone, nothing prevents anything. And were the voice to cease quite at last, the old ceasing voice, it would not be true, as it is not true that it speaks, it can't speak, it can't cease. And were there one day to be here, where there are no days, which is no place, born of the impossible voice the unmakable being, and a gleam of light, still all would be silent and empty and dark, as now, as soon now, when all will be ended, all said, it says, it murmurs.

Endgame (1957)

A play in one act
For Roger Blin

Cast

HAMM
CLOV
NAGG
NELL[1]

ENDGAME

Fin de partie, as it was titled in its French version, was first published in February 1957 (Paris: Éditions de Minuit). A year later Beckett's translation of it into English was published (New York: Grove; London: Faber and Faber, 1958). Despite Beckett's extraordinary success with *Waiting for Godot* (*En attendant Godot*) in 1953, no French theater was willing to perform the work; its premier, in French, took place at the Royal Court Theatre in London, on April 3, 1957.

[1]   *Hamm Clov Nagg Nell* taken together, the names of the characters seem to imply a crucifixion. Three of the names evoke nails: Clov is akin to the French word for nail, *clou*; Nagg is a truncated version of the German word for nail, *Nagel*; and Nell is almost a homonym of the English *nail*. Hamm, viewed in this context, could be a truncated variant of *hammer*. Hamm is also a homonym

of a Biblical character named Ham, the son of Noah who sees him naked, and is cursed by him. But while Noah is ordered by God to build an ark with a window and a door and to furnish it with two representatives of all living species, so as to perpetuate his creation after the great flood, Ham makes every effort to ensure that his refuge (with two windows and a door) will engender no further life, no future fleas or rats. The many references to animals in *Endgame* enrich the analogy with Noah's ark, beginning with the characters' names: Hamm, the flesh of the pig; Clov, a spice used to cure ham; Nell, a common name for a horse; and Nagg, a homonym of the term for an old, worn-out horse. Needless to say, Hamm's name also recalls the main character of Shakespeare's *Hamlet*. And Clov is a homonym of *clove*, the past tense of the verb *to cleave*, which means both *to separate* and *to adhere*.

Bare interior.

Grey Light.

Left and right back, high up, two small windows, curtains drawn.

Front right, a door. Hanging near door, its face to wall, a picture.

Front left, touching each other, covered with an old sheet, two ashbins.

Center, in an armchair on castors, covered with an old sheet, HAMM.

Motionless by the door, his eyes fixed on HAMM, CLOV. *Very red face.*

Brief tableau.

CLOV *goes and stands under window left. Stiff, staggering walk. He looks up at window left. He turns and looks at window right. He goes and stands under window right. He looks up at window right. He turns and looks at window left. He goes out, comes back immediately with a small step-ladder, carries it over and sets it down under window left, gets up on it, draws back curtain. He gets down, takes six steps (for example) towards window right, goes back for ladder, carries it over and sets it down under window right, gets up on it, draws back curtain. He gets down, takes three steps towards window left, goes back for ladder, carries it over and sets it down under window left, gets up on it, looks out of window. Brief laugh. He gets down, takes one step towards window right, goes back for ladder, carries it over and sets it down under window right, gets up on it, looks out of window. Brief laugh. He gets down, goes with ladder towards ashbins, halts, turns, carries back ladder and sets it down under window right, goes to ashbins, removes sheet covering them, folds it over his arm. He raises one lid, stoops and looks into bin. Brief laugh. He closes lid. Same with other bin. He goes to* HAMM, *removes sheet covering him, folds it over his arm. In a dressing-gown, a stiff toque on his head, a large blood-stained handkerchief over his face, a whistle hanging from his neck, a rug over his knees, thick socks on his feet,* HAMM *seems to be asleep.* CLOV *looks him over. Brief laugh. He goes to door, halts, turns towards auditorium.*

CLOV: [*Fixed gaze, tonelessly.*] Finished, it's finished, nearly finished, it must be nearly finished. [*Pause.*] Grain upon grain, one by one, and one day, suddenly, there's a heap, a little heap, the impossible heap. [*Pause.*] I can't be punished any more. [*Pause.*] I'll go now to my kitchen, ten feet by ten feet by ten feet, and wait for him to whistle me. [*Pause.*] Nice dimensions, nice proportions, I'll lean on the table, and look at the wall, and wait for him to whistle me. [*He remains a moment motionless, then goes out. He comes back immediately, goes to window right, takes up the ladder and carries it out. Pause.* HAMM *stirs. He yawns under the handkerchief. He removes the handkerchief from his face. Very red face. Black glasses.*]

HAMM: Me – [*he yawns*] – to play. [*He holds the handkerchief spread out before him.*] Old stancher! [*He takes off his glasses, wipes his eyes, his face, the glasses, puts them on again, folds the handkerchief and puts it neatly in the breast-pocket of his dressing-gown. He clears his throat, joins the tips of his fingers.*] Can there be misery – [*he yawns*] – loftier than mine? No doubt. Formerly. But now? [*Pause.*] My father? [*Pause.*] My mother? [*Pause.*] My . . . dog? [*Pause.*] Oh I am willing to believe they suffer as much as such creatures can suffer. But does that mean their sufferings equal mine? No doubt. [*Pause.*] No, all is a – [*he yawns*] – bsolute, [*proudly*] the bigger a man is the fuller he is. [*Pause. Gloomily.*] And the emptier. [*He sniffs.*] Clov! [*Pause.*] No, alone. [*Pause.*] What dreams! Those forests! [*Pause.*] Enough, it's time it ended, in the refuge too. [*Pause.*] And yet I hesitate, I hesitate to . . . to end. Yes, there it is, it's time it ended and yet I hesitate to – [*he yawns*] – to end. [*Yawns.*] God, I'm tired, I'd be better off in bed. [*He whistles. Enter* CLOV *immediately. He halts beside the chair.*] You pollute the air! [*Pause.*] Get me ready, I'm going to bed.

CLOV: I've just got you up.

HAMM: And what of it?

CLOV: I can't be getting you up and putting you to bed every five minutes, I have things to do. [*Pause.*]

HAMM: Did you ever see my eyes?

CLOV: No.

HAMM: Did you never have the curiosity, while I was sleeping, to take off my glasses and look at my eyes?

CLOV: Pulling back the lids? [*Pause.*] No.

HAMM: One of these days I'll show them to you. [*Pause.*] It seems they've gone all white. [*Pause.*] What time is it?

CLOV: The same as usual.

HAMM: [*Gesture towards window right.*] Have you looked?

CLOV: Yes.

HAMM: Well?

CLOV: Zero.

HAMM: It'd need to rain.

CLOV: It won't rain.

   [*Pause.*]

HAMM: Apart from that, how do you feel?

CLOV: I don't complain.

HAMM: You feel normal?

CLOV: [*Irritably.*] I tell you I don't complain!

HAMM: I feel a little queer. [*Pause.*] Clov!

CLOV: Yes.

HAMM: Have you not had enough?

CLOV: Yes! [*Pause.*] Of what?

HAMM: Of this . . . this . . . thing.

CLOV: I always had. [*Pause.*] Not you?

HAMM: [*Gloomily.*] Then there's no reason for it to change.

CLOV: It may end. [*Pause.*] All life long the same questions, the same answers.

HAMM: Get me ready. [CLOV *does not move.*] Go and get the sheet. [CLOV *does not move.*] Clov!

CLOV: Yes.

HAMM: I'll give you nothing more to eat.

CLOV: Then we'll die.

HAMM: I'll give you just enough to keep you from dying. You'll be hungry all the time.

CLOV: Then we shan't die. [*Pause.*] I'll go and get the sheet. [*He goes towards the door.*]

HAMM: No! [CLOV *halts.*] I'll give you one biscuit per day. [*Pause.*] One and a half. [*Pause.*] Why do you stay with me?

CLOV: Why do you keep me?

HAMM: There's no one else.

CLOV: There's nowhere else.

   [*Pause.*]

HAMM: You're leaving me all the same.

CLOV: I'm trying.

HAMM: You don't love me.

CLOV: No.

HAMM: You loved me once.

CLOV: Once!

HAMM: I've made you suffer too much. [*Pause.*] Haven't I?

CLOV: It's not that.

HAMM: [*Shocked.*] I haven't made you suffer too much?

CLOV: Yes!

HAMM: [*Relieved.*] Ah you gave me a fright! [*Pause. Coldly.*] Forgive me. [*Pause. Louder.*] I said, Forgive me.

CLOV: I heard you. [*Pause.*] Have you bled?

HAMM: Less. [*Pause.*] Is it not time for my pain-killer?

CLOV: No.
> [*Pause.*]

HAMM: How are your eyes?

CLOV: Bad.

HAMM: How are your legs?

CLOV: Bad.

HAMM: But you can move.

CLOV: Yes.

HAMM: [*Violently.*] Then move! [CLOV *goes to back wall, leans against it with his forehead and hands.*] Where are you?

CLOV: Here.

HAMM: Come back! [CLOV *returns to his place beside the chair.*] Where are you?

CLOV: Here.

HAMM: Why don't you kill me?

CLOV: I don't know the combination of the larder.
> [*Pause.*]

HAMM: Go and get two bicycle-wheels.

CLOV: There are no more bicycle-wheels.

HAMM: What have you done with your bicycle?

CLOV: I never had a bicycle.

HAMM: The thing is impossible.

CLOV: When there were still bicycles I wept to have one. I crawled at your feet. You told me to get out to hell. Now there are none.

HAMM: And your rounds? When you inspected my paupers. Always on foot?

CLOV: Sometimes on horse. [*The lid of one of the bins lifts and the hands of* NAGG *appear, gripping the rim. Then his head emerges. Nightcap. Very white face.* NAGG *yawns, then listens.*] I'll leave you, I have things to do.

HAMM: In your kitchen?

CLOV: Yes.

HAMM: Outside of here it's death. [*Pause.*] All right, be off. [*Exit* CLOV. *Pause.*] We're getting on.

NAGG: Me pap!

HAMM: Accursed progenitor!

NAGG: Me pap!

HAMM: The old folks at home! No decency left! Guzzle, guzzle, that's all they think of. [*He whistles. Enter* CLOV. *He halts beside the chair.*] Well! I thought you were leaving me.

CLOV: Oh not just yet, not just yet.

NAGG: Me pap!

HAMM: Give him his pap.

CLOV: There's no more pap.

HAMM: [*To* NAGG.] Do you hear that? There's no more pap. You'll never get any more pap.

NAGG: I want me pap!

HAMM: Give him a biscuit. [*Exit* CLOV.] Accursed fornicator! How are your stumps?

NAGG: Never mind me stumps.
> [*Enter* CLOV *with biscuit.*]

CLOV: I'm back again, with the biscuit.
> [*He gives the biscuit to* NAGG *who fingers it, sniffs it.*]

NAGG: [*Plaintively.*] What is it?

CLOV: Spratt's medium.[2]

NAGG: [*As before.*] It's hard! I can't!

---

2 *Spratt's medium* a fictional brand of dog-biscuits.

HAMM: Bottle him!

[CLOV *pushes* NAGG *back into the bin, closes the lid.*]

CLOV: [*Returning to his place beside the chair.*] If age but knew!

HAMM: Sit on him!

CLOV: I can't sit.

HAMM: True. And I can't stand.

CLOV: So it is.

HAMM: Every man his speciality. [*Pause.*] No phone calls?

[*Pause.*] Don't we laugh?

CLOV: [*After reflection.*] I don't feel like it.

HAMM: [*After reflection.*] Nor I. [*Pause.*] Clov!

CLOV: Yes.

HAMM: Nature has forgotten us.

CLOV: There's no more nature.

HAMM: No more nature! You exaggerate.

CLOV: In the vicinity.

HAMM: But we breathe, we change! We lose our hair, our teeth! Our bloom! Our ideals!

CLOV: Then she hasn't forgotten us.

HAMM: But you say there is none.

CLOV: [*Sadly.*] No one that ever lived ever thought so crooked as we.

HAMM: We do what we can.

CLOV: We shouldn't

[*Pause.*]

HAMM: You're a bit of all right, aren't you?

CLOV: A smithereen.

[*Pause.*]

HAMM: This is slow work. [*Pause.*] Is it not time for my painkiller?

CLOV: No. [*Pause.*] I'll leave you, I have things to do.

HAMM: In your kitchen?

CLOV: Yes.

HAMM: What, I'd like to know.

CLOV: I look at the wall.

HAMM: The wall! And what do you see on your wall? Mene, mene?[3] Naked bodies?

CLOV: I see my light dying.

HAMM: Your light dying! Listen to that! Well, it can die just as well here, *your* light. Take a look at me and then come back and tell me what you think of *your* light.

[*Pause.*]

CLOV: You shouldn't speak to me like that.

[*Pause.*]

HAMM: [*Coldly.*] Forgive me. [*Pause. Louder.*] I said, Forgive me.

CLOV: I heard you.

[*The lid of* NAGG's *bin lifts. His hands appear, gripping the rim. Then his head emerges. In his mouth the biscuit. He listens.*]

HAMM: Did your seeds come up?

CLOV: No.

HAMM: Did you scratch round them to see if they had sprouted?

CLOV: They haven't sprouted.

HAMM: Perhaps it's still too early.

---

[3] *Mene, mene?* in the book of Daniel in the Old Testament, Belshazzar, the King of Babylonia, holds a feast in which he uses the gold and silver vessels captured from the temple in Jerusalem, then praises the gods of gold and silver; that same night, a mysterious hand appears and writes words on a palace wall: *Mene,* *Mene, Tekel, Upharsin.* When Belshazzar's wise men cannot decipher the words' meaning, he calls upon the prophet Daniel, who tells him (Daniel 5:26) : "This is the interpretation of the thing: MENE: God hath numbered thy kingdom, and finished it."

CLOV: If they were going to sprout they would have sprouted.

[*Violently.*] They'll never sprout.

[*Pause.* NAGG *takes biscuit in his hand.*]

HAMM: This is not much fun. [*Pause.*] But that's always the way at the end of the day, isn't it, Clov?

CLOV: Always.

HAMM: It's the end of the day like any other day, isn't it, Clov?

CLOV: Looks like it.

[*Pause.*]

HAMM: [*Anguished.*] What's happening, what's happening?

CLOV: Something is taking its course.

[*Pause.*]

HAMM: All right, be off. [*He leans back in his chair, remains motionless.* CLOV *does not move, heaves a great groaning sigh.* HAMM *sits up.*] I thought I told you to be off.

CLOV: I'm trying. [*He goes to door, halts.*] Ever since I was whelped.

[*Exit* CLOV.]

HAMM: We're getting on.

[*He leans back in his chair, remains motionless.* NAGG *knocks on the lid of the other bin. Pause. He knocks harder. The lid lifts and the hands of* NELL *appear, gripping the rim. Then her head emerges. Lace cap. Very white face.*]

NELL: What is it, my pet? [*Pause.*] Time for love?

NAGG: Were you asleep?

NELL: Oh no!

NAGG: Kiss me.

NELL: We can't.

NAGG: Try.

[*Their heads strain towards each other, fail to meet, fall apart again.*]

NELL: Why this farce, day after day?

[*Pause.*]

NAGG: I've lost me tooth.

NELL: When?

NAGG: I had it yesterday.

NELL: [*Elegiac.*] Ah yesterday!

[*They turn painfully towards each other.*]

NAGG: Can you see me?

NELL: Hardly. And you?

NAGG: What?

NELL: Can you see me?

NAGG: Hardly.

NELL: So much the better, so much the better.

NAGG: Don't say that. [*Pause.*] Our sight has failed.

NELL: Yes.

[*Pause. They turn away from each other.*]

NAGG: Can you hear me?

NELL: Yes. And you?

NAGG: Yes. [*Pause.*] Our hearing hasn't failed.

NELL: Our what?

NAGG: Our hearing.

NELL: No. [*Pause.*] Have you anything else to say to me?

NAGG: Do you remember –

NELL: No.

NAGG: When we crashed on our tandem and lost our shanks.

[*They laugh heartily.*]

NELL: It was in the Ardennes.[4]

[*They laugh less heartily.*]

NAGG: On the road to Sedan.[5] [*They laugh still less heartily.*] Are you cold?

NELL: Yes, perished. And you?

NAGG: I'm freezing. [*Pause.*] Do you want to go in?

NELL: Yes.

NAGG: Then go in. [NELL *does not move.*] Why don't you go in?

NELL: I don't know.

[*Pause.*]

NAGG: Has he changed your sawdust?

NELL: It isn't sawdust. [*Pause. Wearily.*] Can you not be a little accurate, Nagg?

NAGG: Your sand then. It's not important.

NELL: It is important.

[*Pause.*]

NAGG: It was sawdust once.

NELL: Once!

NAGG: And now it's sand. [*Pause.*] From the shore.

[*Pause. Impatiently.*] Now it's sand he fetches from the shore.

NELL: Now it's sand.

NAGG: Has he changed yours?

NELL: No.

NAGG: Nor mine. [*Pause.*] I won't have it! [*Pause. Holding up the biscuit.*] Do you want a bit?

NELL: No. [*Pause.*] Of what?

NAGG: Biscuit. I've kept you half. [*He looks at the biscuit. Proudly.*] Three quarters. For you. Here. [*He proffers the biscuit.*] No? [*Pause.*] Do you not feel well?

HAMM: [*Wearily.*] Quiet, quiet, you're keeping me awake.[*Pause.*] Talk softer. [*Pause.*] If I could sleep I might make love. I'd go into the woods. My eyes would see . . . the sky, the earth. I'd run, run, they wouldn't catch me. [*Pause.*] Nature! [*Pause.*] There's something dripping in my head. [*Pause.*] A heart, a heart in my head.

[*Pause.*]

NAGG: [*Soft.*] Do you hear him? A heart in his head!

[*He chuckles cautiously.*]

NELL: One mustn't laugh at those things, Nagg. Why must you always laugh at them?

NAGG: Not so loud!

NELL: [*Without lowering her voice.*] Nothing is funnier than unhappiness, I grant you that. But –

NAGG: [*Shocked.*] Oh!

NELL: Yes, yes, it's the most comical thing in the world. And we laugh, we laugh, with a will, in the beginning. But it's always the same thing. Yes, it's like the funny story we have heard too often, we still find it funny, but we don't laugh any more. [*Pause.*] Have you anything else to say to me?

NAGG: No.

NELL: Are you quite sure? [*Pause.*] Then I'll leave you.

NAGG: Do you not want your biscuit? [*Pause.*] I'll keep it for you. [*Pause.*] I thought you were going to leave me.

NELL: I am going to leave you.

NAGG: Could you give me a scratch before you go?

NELL: No. [*Pause.*] Where?

NAGG: In the back.

NELL: No. [*Pause.*] Rub yourself against the rim.

---

[4]   *Ardennes* a region in northeastern France.

[5]   *Sedan* a small city in the Ardennes region, remembered as the place where, on September 2, 1870, the French Emperor Napo- leon III was taken prisoner with 100,000 of his soldiers at the Battle of Sedan.

NAGG: It's lower down. In the hollow.

NELL: What hollow?

NAGG: The hollow! *[Pause.]* Could you not? *[Pause.]*
Yesterday you scratched me there.

NELL: *[Elegiac.]* Ah yesterday!

NAGG: Could you not? *[Pause.]* Would you like me to scratch you? *[Pause.]* Are you crying again?

NELL: I was trying.

[Pause.]

HAMM: Perhaps it's a little vein.

[Pause.]

NAGG: What was that he said?

NELL: Perhaps it's a little vein.

NAGG: What does that mean? *[Pause.]* That means nothing. *[Pause.]* Will I tell you the story of the tailor?

NELL: No. *[Pause.]* What for?

NAGG: To cheer you up.

NELL: It's not funny.

NAGG: It always made you laugh. *[Pause.]* The first time I thought you'd die.

NELL: It was on Lake Como.[6] *[Pause.]* One April afternoon. *[Pause.]* Can you believe it?

NAGG: What?

NELL: That we once went out rowing on Lake Como. *[Pause.]* One April afternoon.

NAGG: We had got engaged the day before.

NELL: Engaged!

NAGG: You were in such fits that we capsized. By rights we should have been drowned.

NELL: It was because I felt happy.

NAGG: *[Indignant.]* It was not, it was not, it was my story and nothing else. Happy! Don't you laugh at it still? Every time I tell it. Happy!

NELL: It was deep, deep. And you could see down to the bottom. So white. So clean.

NAGG: Let me tell it again. *[Raconteur's voice.]* An Englishman, needing a pair of striped trousers in a hurry for the New Year festivities, goes to his tailor who takes his measurements. *[Tailor's voice.]* 'That's the lot, come back in four days, I'll have it ready.' Good. Four days later. *[Tailor's voice.]* 'So sorry, come back in a week, I've made a mess of the seat.' Good, that's all right, a neat seat can be very ticklish. A week later. *[Tailor's voice.]* 'Frightfully sorry, come back in ten days, I've made a hash of the crutch.' Good, can't be helped, a snug crutch is always a teaser. Ten days later. *[Tailor's voice.]* 'Dreadfully sorry, come back in a fortnight, I've made a balls of the fly.' Good, at a pinch, a smart fly is a stiff proposition. *[Pause. Normal voice.]* I never told it worse. *[Pause. Gloomy.]* I tell this story worse and worse. *[Pause. Raconteur's voice.]* Well, to make it short, the bluebells are blowing and he ballockses the buttonholes. *[Customer's voice.]* 'God damn you to hell, Sir, no, it's indecent, there are limits! In six days, do you hear me, six days, God made the world. Yes Sir, no less Sir, the WORLD! And you are not bloody well capable of making me a pair of trousers in three months!' *[Tailor's voice, scandalized.]* 'But my dear Sir, my dear Sir, look – *[disdainful gesture, disgustedly]* – at the world – *[pause]* – and look – *[loving gesture, proudly]* – at my TROUSERS!'

[Pause. He looks at NELL who has remained impassive, her eyes unseeing, breaks into a high forced laugh, cuts it short, pokes his head towards NELL, launches his laugh again.]

HAMM: Silence!

[NAGG starts, cuts short his laugh.]

NELL: You could see down to the bottom.

HAMM: *[Exasperated.]* Have you not finished? Will you never finish? *[With sudden fury.]* Will this never finish? *[NAGG disappears into his bin, closes the lid behind him. NELL does not move. Frenziedly.]*

---

[6] *Lake Como* a lake in northern Italy, celebrated for its idyllic beauty and the views of the nearby Alps.

My kingdom for a nightman![7] [*He whistles. Enter* CLOV.] Clear away this muck! Chuck it in the sea!
[CLOV *goes to bins, halts.*]

NELL: So white.

HAMM: What? What's she blathering about?

    [CLOV *stoops, takes* NELL'*s hand, feels her pulse.*]

NELL: [*To* CLOV.] Desert!

    [CLOV *lets go her hand, pushes her back in the bin, closes the lid.*]

CLOV: [*Returning to his place beside the chair.*] She has no pulse.

HAMM: What was she drivelling about?

CLOV: She told me to go away, into the desert.

HAMM: Damn busybody! Is that all?

CLOV: No.

HAMM: What else?

CLOV: I didn't understand.

HAMM: Have you bottled her?

CLOV: Yes.

HAMM: Are they both bottled?

CLOV: Yes.

HAMM: Screw down the lids. [CLOV *goes towards door.*] Time enough. [CLOV *halts.*] My anger
    subsides, I'd like to pee.

CLOV: [*With alacrity.*] I'll go and get the catheter.
    [*He goes towards the door.*]

HAMM: Time enough. [CLOV *halts.*] Give me my pain-killer.

CLOV: It's too soon. [*Pause.*] It's too soon on top of your tonic, it wouldn't act.

HAMM: In the morning they brace you up and in the evening they calm you down. Unless it's the
    other way round. [*Pause.*] That old doctor, he's dead, naturally?

CLOV: He wasn't old.

HAMM: But he's dead?

CLOV: Naturally. [*Pause.*] *You* ask *me* that?
    [*Pause.*]

HAMM: Take me for a little turn. [CLOV *goes behind the chair and pushes it forward.*] Not too fast!
    [CLOV *pushes chair.*] Right round the world! [CLOV *pushes chair.*] Hug the walls, then back to the
    centre again. [CLOV *pushes chair.*] I was right in the centre, wasn't I?

CLOV: [*Pushing.*] Yes.

HAMM: We'd need a proper wheel-chair. With big wheels. Bicycle wheels! [*Pause.*] Are you
    hugging?

CLOV: [*Pushing.*] Yes.

HAMM: [*Groping for wall.*] It's a lie! Why do you lie to me?

CLOV: [*Bearing closer to wall.*] There! There!

HAMM: Stop! [CLOV *stops chair close to back wall.* HAMM *lays his hand against wall.*] Old wall! [*Pause.*]
    Beyond is the . . . other hell. [*Pause. Violently.*] Closer! Closer! Up against!

CLOV: Take away your hand. [HAMM *withdraws his hand.* CLOV *rams chair against wall.*] There!
    [HAMM *leans towards wall, applies his ear to it.*]

HAMM: Do you hear? [*He strikes the wall with his knuckles.*] Do you hear? Hollow bricks! [*He strikes
    again.*] All that's hollow! [*Pause. He straightens up. Violently.*] That's enough. Back!

CLOV: We haven't done the round.

HAMM: Back to my place! [CLOV *pushes chair back to centre.*] Is that my place?

CLOV: Yes, that's your place.

HAMM: Am I right in the centre?

---

[7]   *My kingdom for a nightman!* "A horse, a horse, my kingdom
for a horse," says Richard III in Shakespeare's *Richard III*, Act 5,
scene 2.

CLOV: I'll measure it.

HAMM: More or less! More or less!

CLOV: [*Moving chair slightly.*] There!

HAMM: I'm more or less in the centre?

CLOV: I'd say so.

HAMM: You'd say so! Put me right in the centre!

CLOV: I'll go and get the tape.

HAMM: Roughly! Roughly! [CLOV *moves chair slightly.*] Bang in the centre!

CLOV: There!

[*Pause.*]

HAMM: I feel a little too far to the left. [CLOV *moves chair slightly.*] Now I feel a little too far to the right. [CLOV *moves chair slightly.*] I feel a little too far forward. [CLOV *moves chair slightly.*] Now I feel a little too far back.[CLOV *moves chair slightly.*] Don't stay there [*i.e. behind the chair*], you give me the shivers.

[CLOV *returns to his place beside the chair.*]

CLOV: If I could kill him I'd die happy.

[*Pause.*]

HAMM: What's the weather like?

CLOV: The same as usual.

HAMM: Look at the earth.

CLOV: I've looked.

HAMM: With the glass?

CLOV: No need of the glass.

HAMM: Look at it with the glass.

CLOV: I'll go and get the glass.

[*Exit* CLOV.]

HAMM: No need of the glass!

[*Enter* CLOV *with telescope.*]

CLOV: I'm back again, with the glass. [*He goes to window right, looks up at it.*] I need the steps.

HAMM: Why? Have you shrunk? [*Exit* CLOV *with telescope.*] I don't like that, I don't like that.

[*Enter* CLOV *with ladder, but without telescope.*]

CLOV: I'm back again, with the steps. [*He sets down ladder under window right, gets up on it, realizes he has not the telescope, gets down.*] I need the glass.

[*He goes towards the door.*]

HAMM: [*Violently.*] But you have the glass!

CLOV: [*Halting, violently.*] No I haven't the glass!

[*Exit* CLOV.]

HAMM: This is deadly.

[*Enter* CLOV *with telescope. He goes towards ladder.*]

CLOV: Things are livening up. [*He gets up on ladder, raises the telescope, lets it fall.*] I did it on purpose. [*He gets down, picks up the telescope, turns it on auditorium.*] I see ... a multitude ... in transports ... of joy. [*Pause.*] That's what I call a magnifier. [*He lowers the telescope, turns towards* HAMM.] Well? Don't we laugh?

HAMM: [*After reflection.*] I don't.

CLOV: [*After reflection.*] Nor I. [*He gets up on ladder, turns the telescope on the without.*] Let's see. [*He looks, moving the telescope.*] Zero ... [*he looks*] ... zero ... [*he looks*] ... and zero.

HAMM: Nothing stirs. All is –

CLOV: Zer –

HAMM: [*Violently.*] Wait till you're spoken to! [*Normal voice.*] All is ... all is ... all is what? [*Violently.*] All is what?

CLOV: What all is? In a word? Is that what you want to know? Just a moment. [*He turns the telescope on the without, looks, lowers the telescope, turns towards* HAMM.] Corpsed. [*Pause.*] Well? Content?

HAMM: Look at the sea.

CLOV: It's the same.

HAMM: Look at the ocean!

[CLOV *gets down, take a few steps towards window left, goes back for ladder, carries it over and sets it down under window left, gets up on it, turns the telescope on the without, looks at length. He starts, lowers the telescope, examines it, turns it again on the without.*]

CLOV: Never seen anything like that!

HAMM: [*Anxious.*] What? A sail? A fin? Smoke?

CLOV: [*Looking.*] The light is sunk.

HAMM: [*Relieved.*] Pah! We all knew that.

CLOV: [*Looking.*] There was a bit left.

HAMM: The base.

CLOV: [*Looking.*] Yes.

HAMM: And now?

CLOV: [*Looking.*] All gone.

HAMM: No gulls?

CLOV: [*Looking.*] Gulls!

HAMM: And the horizon? Nothing on the horizon?

CLOV: [*Lowering the telescope, turning towards* HAMM, *exasperated.*] What in God's name could there be on the horizon?

[*Pause.*]

HAMM: The waves, how are the waves?

CLOV: The waves? [*He turns the telescope on the waves.*] Lead.

HAMM: And the sun?

CLOV: [*Looking.*] Zero.

HAMM: But it should be sinking. Look again.

CLOV: [*Looking.*] Damn the sun.

HAMM: Is it night already then?

CLOV: [*Looking.*] No.

HAMM: Then what is it?

CLOV: [*Looking.*] Grey. [*Lowering the telescope, turning towards* HAMM, *louder.*] Grey! [*Pause. Still louder.*] GRREY! [*Pause. He gets down, approaches* HAMM *from behind, whispers in his ear.*]

HAMM: [*Starting.*] Grey! Did I hear you say grey?

CLOV: Light black. From pole to pole.

HAMM: You exaggerate. [*Pause.*] Don't stay there, you give me the shivers.

[CLOV *returns to his place beside the chair.*]

CLOV: Why this farce, day after day?

HAMM: Routine. One never knows. [*Pause.*] Last night I saw inside my breast. There was a big sore.

CLOV: Pah! You saw your heart.

HAMM: No, it was living. [*Pause. Anguished.*] Clov!

CLOV: Yes.

HAMM: What's happening?

CLOV: Something is taking its course.

[*Pause.*]

HAMM: Clov!

CLOV: [*Impatiently.*] What is it?

HAMM: We're not beginning to . . . to . . . mean something?

CLOV: Mean something! You and I, mean something! [*Brief laugh.*] Ah that's a good one!

HAMM: I wonder. [*Pause.*] Imagine if a rational being came back to earth, wouldn't he be liable to get ideas into his head if he observed us long enough. [*Voice of rational being.*] Ah, good, now I see what it is, yes, now I understand what they're at! [CLOV *starts, drops the telescope and begins to scratch his belly with both hands. Normal voice.*] And without going so far as that, we ourselves . . . [*with emotion*] . . . we ourselves . . . at certain moments . . . [*Vehemently.*] To think perhaps it won't all have been for nothing!

CLOV: [*Anguished, scratching himself.*] I have a flea!

HAMM: A flea! Are there still fleas?

CLOV: On me there's one. [*Scratching.*] Unless it's a crablouse.

HAMM: [*Very perturbed.*] But humanity might start from there all over again! Catch him, for the love of God!

CLOV: I'll go and get the powder.

    [*Exit* CLOV.]

HAMM: A flea! This is awful! What a day!

    [*Enter* CLOV *with a sprinkling-tin.*]

CLOV: I'm back again, with the insecticide.

HAMM: Let him have it!

    [CLOV *loosens the top of his trousers, pulls it forward and shakes powder into the aperture. He stoops, looks, waits, starts, frenziedly shakes more powder, stoops, looks, waits.*]

CLOV: The bastard!

HAMM: Did you get him?

CLOV: Looks like it. [*He drops the tin and adjusts his trousers.*] Unless he's laying doggo.

HAMM: Laying! Lying you mean. Unless he's *lying* doggo.

CLOV: Ah? One says lying? One doesn't say laying?

HAMM: Use your head, can't you. If he was laying we'd be bitched.

CLOV: Ah. [*Pause.*] What about that pee?

HAMM: I'm having it.

CLOV: Ah that's the spirit, that's the spirit!

    [*Pause.*]

HAMM: [*With ardour.*] Let's go from here, the two of us! South! You can make a raft and the currents will carry us away, far away, to other . . . mammals!

CLOV: God forbid!

HAMM: Alone, I'll embark alone! Get working on that raft immediately. Tomorrow I'll be gone for ever.

CLOV: [*Hastening towards door.*] I'll start straight away.

HAMM: Wait! [CLOV *halts.*] Will there be sharks, do you think?

CLOV: Sharks? I don't know. If there are there will be.

    [*He goes towards door.*]

HAMM: Wait! [CLOV *halts.*] Is it not yet time for my pain-killer?

CLOV: [*Violently.*] No!

    [*He goes towards door.*]

HAMM: Wait! [CLOV *halts.*] How are your eyes?

CLOV: Bad.

HAMM: But you can see.

CLOV: All I want.

HAMM: How are your legs?

CLOV: Bad.

HAMM: But you can walk.

CLOV: I come . . . and go.

HAMM: In my house. [*Pause. With prophetic relish.*] One day you'll be blind, like me. You'll be sitting there, a speck in the void, in the dark, for ever, like me. [*Pause.*] One day you'll say to yourself, I'm tired, I'll sit down, and you'll go and sit down. Then you'll say, I'm hungry, I'll get up and get something to eat. But you won't get up. You'll say, I shouldn't have sat down, but since I have I'll sit on a little longer, then I'll get up and get something to eat. But you won't get up and you won't get anything to eat. [*Pause.*] You'll look at the wall a while, then you'll say, I'll close my eyes, perhaps have a little sleep, after that I'll feel better, and you'll close them. And when you open them again there'll be no wall any more. [*Pause.*] Infinite emptiness will be all around you, all the resurrected dead of all the ages wouldn't fill it, and there you'll be like a little bit of grit in the middle of the steppe. [*Pause.*] Yes, one day you'll know what it is, you'll be like me, except that you won't have anyone with you, because you won't have had pity on anyone and because there won't be anyone left to have pity on.[*Pause.*]

CLOV: It's not certain. [*Pause.*] And there's one thing you forget.

HAMM: Ah?

CLOV: I can't sit down.

HAMM: [*Impatiently.*] Well, you'll lie down then, what the hell! Or you'll come to a standstill, simply stop and stand still, the way you are now. One day you'll say, I'm tired, I'll stop. What does the attitude matter?

[*Pause.*]

CLOV: So you all want me to leave you.

HAMM: Naturally.

CLOV: Then I'll leave you.

HAMM: You can't leave us.

CLOV: Then I shan't leave you.

[*Pause.*]

HAMM: Why don't you finish us? [*Pause.*] I'll tell you the combination of the larder if you promise to finish me.

CLOV: I couldn't finish you.

HAMM: Then you shan't finish me.

[*Pause.*]

CLOV: I'll leave you, I have things to do.

HAMM: Do you remember when you came here?

CLOV: No. Too small, you told me.

HAMM: Do you remember your father?

CLOV: [*Wearily.*] Same answer. [*Pause.*] You've asked me these questions millions of times.

HAMM: I love the old questions. [*With fervour.*] Ah the old questions, the old answers, there's nothing like them!

[*Pause.*] It was I was a father to you.

CLOV: Yes. [*He looks at* HAMM *fixedly.*] You were that to me.

HAMM: My house a home for you.

CLOV: Yes. [*He looks about him.*] This was that for me.

HAMM: [*Proudly.*] But for me [*gesture towards himself*] no father. But for Hamm [*gesture towards surroundings*] no home.

[*Pause.*]

CLOV: I'll leave you.

HAMM: Did you ever think of one thing?

CLOV: Never.

HAMM: That here we're down in a hole. [*Pause.*] But beyond the hills? Eh? Perhaps it's still green. Eh? [*Pause.*] Flora! Pomona! [*Ecstatically.*] Ceres![8] [*Pause.*] Perhaps you won't need to go very far.

CLOV: I can't go very far. [*Pause.*] I'll leave you.

HAMM: Is my dog ready?

CLOV: He lacks a leg.

HAMM: Is he silky?

CLOV: He's a kind of Pomeranian.

HAMM: Go and get him.

CLOV: He lacks a leg.

HAMM: Go and get him! [*Exit* CLOV.] We're getting on.

[*Enter* CLOV *holding by one of its three legs a black toy dog.*]

CLOV: Your dogs are here.

[*He hands the dog to* HAMM *who feels it, fondles it.*]

---

[8] *Flora! Pomna! {Ecstatically.} Ceres!* Roman goddesses respectively of flowers, fruits, and grain.

HAMM: He's white, isn't he?

CLOV: Nearly.

HAMM: What do you mean, nearly? Is he white or isn't he?

CLOV: He isn't.

[*Pause.*]

HAMM: You've forgotten the sex.

CLOV: [*Vexed.*] But he isn't finished. The sex goes on at the end.

[*Pause.*]

HAMM: You haven't put on his ribbon.

CLOV: [*Angrily.*] But he isn't finished, I tell you! First you finish your dog and then you put on his ribbon!

[*Pause.*]

HAMM: Can he stand?

CLOV: I don't know.

HAMM: Try. [*He hands the dog to* CLOV *who places it on the ground.*] Well?

CLOV: Wait!

[*He squats down and tries to get the dog to stand on its three legs, fails, lets it go. The dog falls on its side.*]

HAMM: [*Impatiently.*] Well?

CLOV: He's standing.

HAMM: [*Groping for the dog.*] Where? Where is he?

[CLOV *holds up the dog in a standing position.*]

CLOV: There.

[*He takes* HAMM's *hand and guides it towards the dog's head.*]

HAMM: [*His hand on the dog's head.*] Is he gazing at me?

CLOV: Yes.

HAMM: [*Proudly.*] As if he were asking me to take him for a walk?

CLOV: If you like.

HAMM: [*As before.*] Or as if he were begging me for a bone. [*He withdraws his hand.*] Leave him like that, standing there imploring me.

[CLOV: *straightens up. The dog falls on its side.*]

CLOV: I'll leave you.

HAMM: Have you had your visions?

CLOV: Less.

HAMM: Is Mother Pegg's light on?

CLOV: Light! How could anyone's light be on?

HAMM: Extinguished!

CLOV: Naturally it's extinguished. If it's not on it's extinguished.

HAMM: No, I mean Mother Pegg.

CLOV: But naturally she's extinguished! [*Pause.*] What's the matter with you today?

HAMM: I'm taking my course. [*Pause.*] Is she buried?

CLOV: Buried! Who would have buried her?

HAMM: You.

CLOV: Me! Haven't I enough to do without burying people?

HAMM: But you'll bury me.

CLOV: No I shan't bury you.

[*Pause.*]

HAMM: She was bonny once, like a flower of the field. [*With reminiscent leer.*] And a great one for the men!

CLOV: We too were bonny – once. It's a rare thing not to have been bonny – once.

[*Pause.*]

HAMM: Go and get the gaff.

[CLOV *goes to door, halts.*]

CLOV: Do this, do that, and I do it. I never refuse. Why?

HAMM: You're not able to.

CLOV: Soon I won't do it any more.

HAMM: You won't be able to any more. [*Exit* CLOV.] Ah the creatures, the creatures, everything has to be explained to them.

   [*Enter* CLOV *with gaff.*]

CLOV: Here's your gaff. Stick it up.

   [*He gives the gaff to* HAMM *who, wielding it like a punt-pole, tries to move his chair.*]

HAMM: Did I move?

CLOV: No.

   [HAMM *throws down the gaff.*]

HAMM: Go and get the oilcan.

CLOV: What for?

HAMM: To oil the castors.

CLOV: I oiled them yesterday.

HAMM: Yesterday! What does that mean? Yesterday!

CLOV: [*Violently.*] That means that bloody awful day, long ago, before this bloody awful day. I use the words you taught me. If they don't mean anything any more, teach me others. Or let me be silent.

   [*Pause.*]

HAMM: I once knew a madman who thought the end of the world had come. He was a painter – and engraver. I had a great fondness for him. I used to go and see him, in the asylum. I'd take him by the hand and drag him to the window. Look! There! All that rising corn! And there! Look! The sails of the herring fleet! All that loveliness! [*Pause.*] He'd snatch away his hand and go back into his corner. Appalled. All he had seen was ashes. [*Pause.*] He alone had been spared. [*Pause.*] Forgotten. [*Pause.*] It appears the case is . . . was not so . . . so unusual.

CLOV: A madman? When was that?

HAMM: Oh way back, way back, you weren't in the land of the living.

CLOV: God be with the days!

   [*Pause.* HAMM *raises his toque.*]

HAMM: I had a great fondness for him. [*Pause. He puts on his toque again.*] He was a painter – and engraver.

CLOV: There are so many terrible things.

HAMM: No, no, there are not so many now. [*Pause.*] Clov!

CLOV: Yes.

HAMM: Do you not think this has gone on long enough?

CLOV: Yes! [*Pause.*] What?

HAMM: This . . . this . . . thing.

CLOV: I've always thought so. [*Pause.*] You not?

HAMM: [*Gloomily.*] Then it's a day like any other day.

CLOV: As long as it lasts. [*Pause.*] All life long the same inanities.

   [*Pause.*]

HAMM: I can't leave you.

CLOV: I know. And you can't follow me.

   [*Pause.*]

HAMM: If you leave me how shall I know?

CLOV: [*Briskly.*] Well you simply whistle me and if I don't come running it means I've left you.

   [*Pause.*]

HAMM: You won't come and kiss me good-bye?

CLOV: Oh I shouldn't think so.

   [*Pause.*]

HAMM: But you might be merely dead in your kitchen.

CLOV: The result would be the same.

HAMM: Yes, but how would I know, if you were merely dead in your kitchen?

CLOV: Well . . . sooner or later I'd start to stink.

HAMM: You stink already. The whole place stinks of corpses.

CLOV: The whole universe.

HAMM: [*Angrily.*] To hell with the universe! [*Pause.*] Think of something.

CLOV: What?

HAMM: An idea, have an idea. [*Angrily.*] A bright idea!

CLOV: Ah good. [*He starts pacing to and fro, his eyes fixed on the ground, his hands behind his back. He halts.*] The pains in my legs! It's unbelievable! Soon I won't be able to think any more.

HAMM: You won't be able to leave me. [CLOV *resumes his pacing.*] What are you doing?

CLOV: Having an idea. [*He paces.*] Ah!

[*He halts.*]

HAMM: What a brain! [*Pause.*] Well?

CLOV: Wait! [*He meditates. Not very convinced.*] Yes . . . [*Pause. More convinced.*] Yes! [*He raises his head.*] I have it! I set the alarm.

[*Pause.*]

HAMM: This is perhaps not one of my bright days, but frankly –

CLOV: You whistle me. I don't come. The alarm rings. I'm gone. It doesn't ring. I'm dead.

[*Pause.*]

HAMM: Is it working? [*Pause. Impatiently.*] The alarm, is it working?

CLOV: Why wouldn't it be working?

HAMM: Because it's worked too much.

CLOV: But it's hardly worked at all.

HAMM: [*Angrily.*] Then because it's worked too little!

CLOV: I'll go and see. [*Exit* CLOV. *Brief ring of alarm off. Enter* CLOV *with alarm-clock. He holds it against* HAMM'S *ear and releases alarm. They listen to it ringing to the end. Pause.*] Fit to wake the dead! Did you hear it?

HAMM: Vaguely.

CLOV: The end is terrific!

HAMM: I prefer the middle. [*Pause.*] Is it not time for my pain-killer?

CLOV: No! [*He goes to the door, turns.*] I'll leave you.

HAMM: It's time for my story. Do you want to listen to my story?

CLOV: No.

HAMM: Ask my father if he wants to listen to my story.

[CLOV *goes to bins, raises the lid of* NAGG's, *stoops, looks into it. Pause. He straightens up.*]

CLOV: He's asleep.

HAMM: Wake him.

[CLOV *stoops, wakes* NAGG *with the alarm. Unintelligible words.* CLOV *straightens up.*]

CLOV: He doesn't want to listen to your story.

HAMM: I'll give him a bon-bon.

[CLOV *stoops. As before.*]

CLOV: He wants a sugar-plum.

HAMM: He'll get a sugar-plum.

[CLOV *stoops. As before.*]

CLOV: It's a deal. [*He goes towards door.* NAGG's *hands appear, gripping the rim. Then the head emerges.* CLOV *reaches door, turns.*] Do you believe in the life to come?

HAMM: Mine was always that. [*Exit* CLOV.] Got him that time!

NAGG: I'm listening.

HAMM: Scoundrel! Why did you engender me?

NAGG: I didn't know.

HAMM: What? What didn't you know?

NAGG: That it'd be you. [*Pause.*] You'll give me a sugar-plum?

HAMM: After the audition.

NAGG: You swear?

HAMM: Yes.

NAGG: On what?

HAMM: My honour.

[*Pause. They laugh heartily.*]

NAGG: Two.

HAMM: One.

NAGG: One for me and one for –

HAMM: One! Silence! [*Pause.*] Where was I? [*Pause. Gloomily.*] It's finished, we're finished. [*Pause.*] Nearly finished. [*Pause.*] There'll be no more speech. [*Pause.*] Something dripping in my head, ever since the fontanelles.[9] [*Stifled hilarity of* NAGG.] Splash, splash, always on the same spot. [*Pause.*] Perhaps it's a little vein. [*Pause.*] A little artery. [*Pause. More animated.*] Enough of that, it's story time, where was I? [*Pause. Narrative tone.*] The man came crawling towards me, on his belly. Pale, wonderfully pale and thin, he seemed on the point of – [*Pause. Normal tone.*] No, I've done that bit. [*Pause. Narrative tone.*] I calmly filled my pipe – the meerschaum, lit it with . . . let us say a vesta,[10] drew a few puffs. Aah! [*Pause.*] Well, what is it *you* want? [*Pause.*] It was an extra-ordinarily bitter day, I remember, zero by the thermometer. But considering it was Christmas Eve there was nothing . . . extra-ordinary about that. Seasonable weather, for once in a way. [*Pause.*] Well, what ill wind blows you my way? He raised his face to me, black with mingled dirt and tears. [*Pause. Normal tone.*] That should do it. [*Narrative tone.*] No, no, don't look at me, don't look at me. He dropped his eyes and mumbled something, apologies I presume. [*Pause.*] I'm a busy man, you know, the final touches, before the festivities, you know what it is. [*Pause. Forcibly.*] Come on now, what is the object of this invasion? [*Pause.*] It was a glorious bright day, I remember, fifty by the heliometer, but already the sun was sinking down into the . . . down among the dead. [*Normal tone.*] Nicely put, that. [*Narrative tone.*] Come on now, come on, present your petition and let me resume my labours. [*Pause. Normal tone.*] There's English for you. Ah well . . . [*Narrative tone.*] It was then he took the plunge. It's my little one, he said. Tsstss, a little one, that's bad. My little boy, he said, as if the sex mattered. Where did he come from? He named the hole. A good half-day, on horse. What are you insinuating? That the place is still inhabited? No no, not a soul, except himself and the child – assuming he existed. Good. I inquired about the situation at Kov, beyond the gulf. Not a sinner. Good. And you expect me to believe you have left your little one back there, all alone, and alive into the bargain? Come now! [*Pause.*] It was a howling wild day, I remember, a hundred by the anemometer. The wind was tearing up the dead pines and sweeping them . . . away. [*Pause. Normal tone.*] A bit feeble, that. [*Narrative tone.*] Come on, man, speak up, what is it you want from me, I have to put up my holly. [*Pause.*] Well to make it short it finally transpired that what he wanted from me was . . . bread for his brat. Bread? But I have no bread, it doesn't agree with me. Good. Then perhaps a little corn? [*Pause. Normal tone.*] That should do it. [*Narrative tone.*] Corn, yes, I have corn, it's true, in my granaries. But use your head. I give you some corn, a pound, a pound and a half, you bring it back to your child and you make him – if he's still alive – a nice pot of porridge [NAGG *reacts*], a nice pot and a half of porridge, full of nourishment. Good. The colours come back into his little cheeks – perhaps. And then? [*Pause.*] I lost patience. [*Violently.*] Use your head, can't you, use your head, you're on earth, there's no cure for that! [*Pause.*] It was an exceedingly dry day, I remember, zero by the hygrometer.[11] Ideal weather, for my lumbago. [*Pause. Violently.*] But what in God's name do you imagine? That the earth will awake in spring? That the rivers and seas will run with fish again? That there's manna in heaven still for imbeciles like you? [*Pause.*] Gradually I cooled down, sufficiently at least to ask him how long he had taken on the way. Three whole days. Good. In what condition he had left the child. Deep in sleep. [*Forcibly.*] But deep in what sleep, deep in what sleep already? [*Pause.*] Well to make it short I finally offered to take him into my service. He had touched a chord. And then I imagined already that I wasn't much longer for this world. [*He laughs. Pause.*] Well? [*Pause.*] Well? Here if you

---

[9] *fontanelles* membranous spaces in the head of an infant which lie at the adjacent angles of the parietal bones (*OED*).

[10] *vesta* a wooden match, so called after a popular brand name.

[11] *hygrometer* an instrument for measuring humidity.

were careful you might die a nice natural death, in peace and comfort. [*Pause.*] Well? [*Pause.*] In the end he asked me would I consent to take in the child as well – if he were still alive. [*Pause.*] It was the moment I was waiting for. [*Pause.*] Would I consent to take in the child . . . [*Pause.*] I can see him still, down on his knees, his hands flat on the ground, glaring at me with his mad eyes, in defiance of my wishes. [*Pause. Normal tone.*] I'll soon have finished with this story. [*Pause.*] Unless I bring in other characters. [*Pause.*] But where would I find them? [*Pause.*] Where would I look for them? [*Pause. He whistles. Enter* CLOV.] Let us pray to God.

NAGG: Me sugar-plum!

CLOV: There's a rat in the kitchen!

HAMM: A rat! Are there still rats?

CLOV: In the kitchen there's one.

HAMM: And you haven't exterminated him?

CLOV: Half. You disturbed us.

HAMM: He can't get away?

CLOV: No.

HAMM: You'll finish him later. Let us pray to God.

CLOV: Again!

NAGG: Me sugar-plum!

HAMM: God first! [*Pause.*] Are you right?

CLOV: [*Resigned.*] Off we go.

HAMM: [*To* NAGG.] And you?

NAGG: [*Clasping his hands, closing his eyes, in a gabble.*] Our Father which art –

HAMM: Silence! In silence! Where are your manners? [*Pause.*] Off we go. [*Attitudes of prayer. Silence. Abandoning his attitude, discouraged.*] Well?

CLOV: [*Abandoning his attitude.*] What a hope! And you?

HAMM: Sweet damn all! [*To* NAGG.] And you?

NAGG: Wait! [*Pause. Abandoning his attitude.*] Nothing doing!

HAMM: The bastard! He doesn't exist!

CLOV: Not yet.

NAGG: Me sugar-plum!

HAMM: There are no more sugar-plums!

[*Pause.*]

NAGG: It's natural. After all I'm your father. It's true if it hadn't been me it would have been someone else. But that's no excuse. [*Pause.*] Turkish Delight,[12] for example, which no longer exists, we all know that, there is nothing in the world I love more. And one day I'll ask you for some, in return for a kindness, and you'll promise it to me. One must live with the times. [*Pause.*] Whom did you call when you were a tiny boy, and were frightened, in the dark? Your mother? No. Me. We let you cry. Then we moved you out of earshot, so that we might sleep in peace. [*Pause.*] I was asleep, as happy as a king, and you woke me up to have me listen to you. It wasn't indispensable, you didn't really need to have me listen to you. Besides I didn't listen to you. [*Pause.*] I hope the day will come when you'll really need to have me listen to you, and need to hear my voice, any voice. [*Pause.*] Yes, I hope I'll live till then, to hear you calling me like when you were a tiny boy, and were frightened, in the dark, and I was your only hope. [*Pause.* NAGG *knocks on lid of* NELL's *bin. Pause. He knocks louder. Pause. Louder.*] Nell! [*Pause.* NAGG *sinks back into his bin, closes the lid behind him. Pause.*]

HAMM: Our revels now are ended. [*He gropes for the dog.*] The dog's gone.

CLOV: He's not a real dog, he can't go.

HAMM: [*Groping.*] He's not there.

CLOV: He's lain down.

---

12 *Turkish Delight* a red candy, made with rosewater, sugar syrup, and cornstarch, and covered with confectioners' sugar.

HAMM: Give him up to me. [CLOV *picks up the dog and gives it to* HAMM. HAMM *holds it in his arms. Pause.* HAMM *throws away the dog.*] Dirty brute! [CLOV *begins to pick up the objects lying on the ground.*] What are you doing?

CLOV: Putting things in order. [*He straightens up. Fervently.*] I'm going to clear everything away! [*He starts picking up again.*]

HAMM: Order!

CLOV: [*Straightening up.*] I love order. It's my dream. A world where all would be silent and still and each thing in its last place, under the last dust.

[*He starts picking up again.*]

HAMM: [*Exasperated.*] What in God's name do you think you are doing?

CLOV: [*Straightening up.*] I'm doing my best to create a little order.

HAMM: Drop it!

[CLOV *drops the objects he has picked up.*]

CLOV: After all, there or elsewhere.

[*He goes towards door.*]

HAMM: [*Irritably.*] What's wrong with your feet?

CLOV: My feet?

HAMM: Tramp! Tramp!

CLOV: I must have put on my boots.

HAMM: Your slippers were hurting you?

[*Pause.*]

CLOV: I'll leave you.

HAMM: No!

CLOV: What is there to keep me here?

HAMM: The dialogue. [*Pause.*] I've got on with my story. [*Pause.*] I've got on with it well. [*Pause. Irritably.*] Ask me where I've got to.

CLOV: Oh, by the way, your story?

HAMM: [*Surprised.*] What story?

CLOV: The one you've been telling yourself all your . . . days.

HAMM: Ah you mean my chronicle?

CLOV: That's the one.

[*Pause.*]

HAMM: [*Angrily.*] Keep going, can't you, keep going!

CLOV: You've got on with it, I hope.

HAMM: [*Modestly.*] Oh not very far, not very far. [*He sighs.*] There are days like that, one isn't inspired. [*Pause.*] Nothing you can do about it, just wait for it to come. [*Pause.*] No forcing, no forcing, it's fatal. [*Pause.*] I've got on with it a little all the same. [*Pause.*] Technique, you know. [*Pause. Irritably.*] I say I've got on with it a little all the same.

CLOV: [*Admiringly.*] Well I never! In spite of everything you were able to get on with it!

HAMM: [*Modestly.*] Oh not very far, you know, not very far, but nevertheless, better than nothing.

CLOV: Better than nothing! Is it possible?

HAMM: I'll tell you how it goes. He comes crawling on his belly –

CLOV: Who?

HAMM: What?

CLOV: Who do you mean, he?

HAMM: Who do I mean! Yet another.

CLOV: Ah him! I wasn't sure.

HAMM: Crawling on his belly, whining for bread for his brat. He's offered a job as gardener. Before – [CLOV *bursts out laughing.*] What is there so funny about that?

CLOV: A job as gardener!

HAMM: Is that what tickles you?

CLOV: It must be that.

HAMM: It wouldn't be the bread?

CLOV: Or the brat.

[*Pause.*]

HAMM: The whole thing is comical, I grant you that. What about having a good guffaw the two of us together?

CLOV: [*After reflection.*] I couldn't guffaw again today.

HAMM: [*After reflection.*] Nor I. [*Pause.*] I continue then. Before accepting with gratitude he asks if he may have his little boy with him.

CLOV: What age?

HAMM: Oh tiny.

CLOV: He would have climbed the trees.

HAMM: All the little odd jobs.

CLOV: And then he would have grown up.

HAMM: Very likely.

[*Pause.*]

CLOV: Keep going, can't you, keep going!

HAMM: That's all. I stopped there.

[*Pause.*]

CLOV: Do you see how it goes on.

HAMM: More or less.

CLOV: Will it not soon be the end?

HAMM: I'm afraid it will.

CLOV: Pah! You'll make up another.

HAMM: I don't know. [*Pause.*] I feel rather drained. [*Pause.*] The prolonged creative effort. [*Pause.*] If I could drag myself down to the sea! I'd make a pillow of sand for my head and the tide would come.

CLOV: There's no more tide.

[*Pause.*]

HAMM: Go and see is she dead.

[CLOV *goes to bins, raises the lid of* NELL's, *stoops, looks into it. Pause.*]

CLOV: Looks like it.

[*He closes the lid, straightens up.* HAMM *raises his toque. Pause. He puts it on again.*]

HAMM: [*With his hand to his toque.*] And Nagg?

[CLOV *raises lid of* NAGG's, *bin, stoops, looks into it. Pause.*]

CLOV: Doesn't look like it.

[*He closes the lid, straightens up.*]

HAMM: [*Letting go his toque.*] What's he doing?

[CLOV *raises lid of* NAGG's *bin, stoops, looks into it. Pause.*]

CLOV: He's crying.

[*He closes the lid, straightens up.*]

HAMM: Then he's living. [*Pause.*] Did you ever have an instant of happiness?

CLOV: Not to my knowledge.

[*Pause.*]

HAMM: Bring me under the window. [CLOV *goes towards chair.*] I want to feel the light on my face. [CLOV *pushes chair.*] Do you remember, in the beginning, when you took me for a turn? You used to hold the chair too high. At every step you nearly tipped me out. [*With senile quaver.*] Ah great fun, we had, the two of us, great fun! [*Gloomily.*] And then we got into the way of it. [CLOV *stops the chair under window right.*] There already? [*Pause. He tilts back his head.*] Is it light?

CLOV: It isn't dark.

HAMM: [*Angrily.*] I'm asking you is it light?

CLOV: Yes.

[*Pause.*]

HAMM: The curtain isn't closed?

CLOV: No.

HAMM: What window is it?

CLOV: The earth.

HAMM: I knew it! [*Angrily.*] But there's no light there! The other! [CLOV *pushes chair towards window left.*] The earth! [CLOV *stops the chair under window left.* HAMM *tilts back his head.*] That's what I call light! [*Pause.*] Feels like a ray of sunshine. [*Pause.*] No?

CLOV: No.

HAMM: It isn't a ray of sunshine I feel on my face?

CLOV: No.

[*Pause.*]

HAMM: Am I very white? [*Pause. Angrily.*] I'm asking you am I very white!

CLOV: Not more so than usual.

[*Pause.*]

HAMM: Open the window.

CLOV: What for?

HAMM: I want to hear the sea.

CLOV: You wouldn't hear it.

HAMM: Even if you opened the window?

CLOV: No.

HAMM: Then it's not worth while opening it?

CLOV: No.

HAMM: [*Violently.*] Then open it! [CLOV *gets up on the ladder, opens the window. Pause.*] Have you opened it?

CLOV: Yes.

[*Pause.*]

HAMM: You swear you've opened it?

CLOV: Yes.

[*Pause.*]

HAMM: Well . . . ! [*Pause.*] It must be very calm. [*Pause. Violently.*] I'm asking you is it very calm?

CLOV: Yes.

HAMM: It's because there are no more navigators. [*Pause.*] You haven't much conversation all of a sudden. Do you not feel well?

CLOV: I'm cold.

HAMM: What month are we? [*Pause.*] Close the window, we're going back. [CLOV *closes the window, gets down, pushes the chair back to its place, remains standing behind it, head bowed.*] Don't stay there, you give me the shivers! [CLOV *returns to his place beside the chair.*] Father! [*Pause. Louder.*] Father! [*Pause.*] Go and see did he hear me.

[CLOV *goes to* NAGG's *bin, raises the lid, stoops. Unintelligible words.* CLOV *straightens up.*]

CLOV: Yes.

HAMM: Both times?

[CLOV *stoops. As before.*]

CLOV: Once only.

HAMM: The first time or the second?

[CLOV *stoops. As before.*]

CLOV: He doesn't know.

HAMM: It must have been the second.

CLOV: We'll never know.

[*He closes lid.*]

HAMM: Is he still crying?

CLOV: No.

HAMM: The dead go fast. [*Pause.*] What's he doing?

CLOV: Sucking his biscuit.

HAMM: Life goes on. [CLOV *returns to his place beside the chair.*] Give me a rug, I'm freezing.

CLOV: There are no more rugs.

[*Pause.*]

HAMM: Kiss me. [*Pause.*] Will you not kiss me?

CLOV: No.

HAMM: On the forehead.

CLOV: I won't kiss you anywhere.

[*Pause.*]

HAMM: [*Holding out his hand.*] Give me your hand at least. [*Pause.*] Will you not give me your hand?

CLOV: I won't touch you.

[*Pause.*]

HAMM: Give me the dog. [CLOV *looks round for the dog.*] No!

CLOV: Do you not want your dog?

HAMM: No.

CLOV: Then I'll leave you.

HAMM: [*Head bowed, absently.*] That's right.

[CLOV *goes to door, turns.*]

CLOV: If I don't kill that rat he'll die.

HAMM: [*As before.*] That's right. [*Exit* CLOV. *Pause.*] Me to play. [*He takes out his handkerchief, unfolds it, holds it spread out before him.*] We're getting on. [*Pause.*] You weep, and weep, for nothing, so as not to laugh, and little by little . . . you begin to grieve. [*He folds the handkerchief, puts it back in his pocket, raises his head.*] All those I might have helped. [*Pause.*] Helped! [*Pause.*] Saved. [*Pause.*] Saved! [*Pause.*] The place was crawling with them! [*Pause. Violently.*] Use your head, can't you, use your head, you're on earth, there's no cure for that! [*Pause.*] Get out of here and love one another! Lick your neighbour as yourself! [*Pause. Calmer.*] When it wasn't bread they wanted it was crumpets. [*Pause. Violently.*] Out of my sight and back to your petting parties! [*Pause.*] All that, all that! [*Pause.*] Not even a real dog! [*Calmer.*] The end is in the beginning and yet you go on.[13] [*Pause.*] Perhaps I could go on with my story, end it and begin another. [*Pause.*] Perhaps I could throw myself out on the floor. [*He pushes himself painfully off his seat, falls back again.*] Dig my nails into the cracks and drag myself forward with my fingers. [*Pause.*] It will be the end and there I'll be, wondering what can have brought it on and wondering what can have . . . [*he hesitates*] . . . why it was so long coming. [*Pause.*] There I'll be, in the old refuge, alone against the silence and . . . [*he hesitates*] . . . the stillness. If I can hold my peace, and sit quiet, it will be all over with sound, and motion, all over and done with. [*Pause.*] I'll have called my father and I'll have called my . . . [*he hesitates*] . . . my son. And even twice, or three times, in case they shouldn't have heard me, the first time, or the second. [*Pause.*] I'll say to myself, He'll come back. [*Pause.*] And then? [*Pause.*] And then? [*Pause.*] He couldn't, he has gone too far. [*Pause.*] And then? [*Pause. Very agitated.*] All kinds of fantasies! That I'm being watched! A rat! Steps! Breath held and then . . . [*he breathes out.*] Then babble, babble, words, like the solitary child who turns himself into children, two, three, so as to be together, and whisper together, in the dark. [*Pause.*] Moment upon moment, pattering down, like the millet grains of . . . [*he hesitates*] . . . that old Greek, and all life long you wait for that to mount up to a life. [*Pause. He opens his mouth to continue, renounces.*] Ah let's get it over! [*He whistles. Enter* CLOV *with alarm-clock. He halts beside the chair.*] What? Neither gone nor dead?

CLOV: In spirit only.

HAMM: Which?

CLOV: Both.

HAMM: Gone from me you'd be dead.

CLOV: And *vice versa*.

HAMM: Outside of here it's death! [*Pause.*] And the rat?

---

[13] *The end is in the beginning* John 1:1: "In the beginning was the Word, and the Word was with God, and the Word was God." Cf. T. S. Eliot, *Four Quartets* (1940), "East Coker," line 1: "In my beginning is my end."

CLOV: He's got away.

HAMM: He can't go far. [*Pause. Anxious.*] Eh?

CLOV: He doesn't need to go far.

[*Pause.*]

HAMM: Is it not time for my pain-killer?

CLOV: Yes.

HAMM: Ah! At last! Give it to me! Quick!

[*Pause.*]

CLOV: There's no more pain-killer.

[*Pause.*]

HAMM: [*Appalled.*] Good . . . ! [*Pause.*] No more pain-killer!

CLOV: No more pain-killer. You'll never get any more pain-killer.

[*Pause.*]

HAMM: But the little round box. It was full!

CLOV: Yes. But now it's empty.

[*Pause.* CLOV *starts to move about the room. He is looking for a place to put down the alarm-clock.*]

HAMM: [*Soft.*] What'll I do? [*Pause. In a scream.*] What'll I do? [CLOV *sees the picture, takes it down, stands it on the floor with its face to wall, hangs up the alarm-clock in its place.*]

   What are you doing?

CLOV: Winding up.

HAMM: Look at the earth.

CLOV: Again!

HAMM: Since it's calling to you.

CLOV: Is your throat sore? [*Pause.*] Would you like a lozenge? [*Pause.*] No? [*Pause.*] Pity.

[CLOV *goes, humming, towards window right, halts before it, looks up at it.*]

HAMM: Don't sing.

CLOV: [*Turning towards* HAMM.] One hasn't the right to sing any more?

HAMM: No.

CLOV: Then how can it end?

HAMM: You want it to end?

CLOV: I want to sing.

HAMM: I can't prevent you.

[*Pause.* CLOV *turns towards window right.*]

CLOV: What did I do with that steps? [*He looks round for ladder.*] You didn't see that steps? [*He sees it.*] Ah, about time. [*He goes towards window left.*] Sometimes I wonder if I'm in my right mind. Then it passes over and I'm as lucid as before. [*He gets up on ladder, looks out of window.*] Christ, she's under water! [*He looks.*] How can that be? [*He pokes forward his head, his hand above his eyes.*] It hasn't rained. [*He wipes the pane, looks. Pause.*] Ah what a mug I am! I'm on the wrong side! [*He gets down, take a few steps towards window right.*] Under water! [*He goes back for ladder.*] What a mug I am! [*He carries ladder towards window right.*] Sometimes I wonder if I'm in my right senses. Then it passes off and I'm as intelligent as ever. [*He sets down ladder under window right, gets up on it, looks out of window. He turns towards* HAMM.] Any particular sector you fancy? Or merely the whole thing?

HAMM: Whole thing.

CLOV: The general effect? Just a moment.

[*He looks out of window. Pause.*]

HAMM: Clov.

CLOV: [*Absorbed.*] Mmm.

HAMM: Do you know what it is?

CLOV: [*As before.*] Mmm.

HAMM: I was never there. [*Pause.*] Clov!

CLOV: [*Turning towards* HAMM, *exasperated.*] What is it?

HAMM: I was never there.

CLOV: Lucky for you.

[*He looks out of window.*]

HAMM: Absent, always. It all happened without me. I don't know what's happened. [*Pause.*] Do you know what's happened? [*Pause.*] Clov!

CLOV: [*Turning towards* HAMM, *exasperated.*] Do you want me to look at this muckheap, yes or no?

HAMM: Answer me first.

CLOV: What?

HAMM: Do you know what's happened?

CLOV: When? Where?

HAMM: [*Violently.*] When! What's happened! Use your head, can't you! What has happened?

CLOV: What for Christ's sake does it matter?

[*He looks out of window.*]

HAMM: I don't know.

[*Pause.* CLOV *turns towards* HAMM.]

CLOV: [*Harshly.*] When old Mother Pegg asked you for oil for her lamp and you told her to get out to hell, you knew what was happening then, no? [*Pause.*] You know what she died of, Mother Pegg? Of darkness.

HAMM: [*Feebly.*] I hadn't any.

CLOV: [*As before.*] Yes, you had.

[*Pause.*]

HAMM: Have you the glass?

CLOV: No, it's clear enough as it is.

HAMM: Go and get it.

[*Pause.* CLOV *casts up his eyes, brandishes his fists. He loses balance, clutches on to the ladder. He starts to get down, halts.*]

CLOV: There's one thing I'll never understand. [*He gets down.*] Why I always obey you. Can you explain that to me?

HAMM: No . . . Perhaps it's compassion. [*Pause.*] A kind of great compassion. [*Pause.*] Oh you won't find it easy, you won't find it easy.

[*Pause.* CLOV *begins to move about the room in search of the telescope.*]

CLOV: I'm tired of our goings on, very tired. [*He searches.*] You're not sitting on it?

[*He moves the chair, looks at the place where it stood, resumes his search.*]

HAMM: [*Anguished.*] Don't leave me there! [*Angrily* CLOV *restores the chair to its place.*] Am I right in the centre?

CLOV: You'd need a microscope to find this – [*He sees the telescope.*] Ah, about time.

[*He picks up the telescope, gets up on the ladder, turns the telescope on the without.*]

HAMM: Give me the dog.

CLOV: [*Looking.*] Quiet!

HAMM: [*Angrily.*] Give me the dog!

[CLOV *drops the telescope, clasps his hands to his head. Pause. He gets down precipitately, looks for the dog, sees it, picks it up, hastens towards* HAMM *and strikes him on the head violently with the dog.*]

CLOV: There's your dog for you!

[*The dog falls to the ground. Pause.*]

HAMM: He hit me!

CLOV: You drive me mad, I'm mad!

HAMM: If you must hit me, hit me with the axe. [*Pause.*] Or with the gaff, hit me with the gaff. Not with the dog. With the gaff. Or with the axe.

[CLOV *picks up the dog and gives it to* HAMM *who takes it in his arms.*]

CLOV: [*Imploringly.*] Let's stop playing!

HAMM: Never! [*Pause.*] Put me in my coffin.

CLOV: There are no more coffins.

HAMM: Then let it end! [CLOV *goes towards ladder.*] With a bang! [CLOV *gets up on ladder, gets down again, looks for telescope, sees it, picks it up, gets up ladder, raises telescope.*] Of darkness! And me? Did anyone ever have pity on me?

CLOV: [*Lowering the telescope, turning towards* HAMM.] What? [*Pause.*] Is it me you're referring to?

HAMM: [*Angrily.*] An aside, ape! Did you never hear an aside before? [*Pause.*] I'm warming up for my last soliloquy.

CLOV: I warn you. I'm going to look at this filth since it's an order. But it's the last time. [*He turns the telescope on the without.*] Let's see. [*He moves the telescope.*] Nothing ... nothing ... good ... - good ... nothing ... goo – [*He starts, lowers the telescope, examines it, turns it again on the without. Pause.*] Bad luck to it!

HAMM: More complications! [CLOV *gets down.*] Not an underplot, I trust.

[CLOV *moves ladder nearer window, gets up on it, turns telescope on the without.*][14]

CLOV: [*Dismayed.*] Looks like a small boy!

HAMM: [*Sarcastic.*] A small ... boy!

CLOV: I'll go and see. [*He gets down, drops the telescope, goes towards door, turns.*] I'll take the gaff.

[*He looks for the gaff, sees it, picks it up, hastens towards door.*]

HAMM: No!

[CLOV *halts.*]

CLOV: No? A potential procreator?

HAMM: If he exists he'll die there or he'll come here. And if he doesn't ...

[*Pause.*]

CLOV: You don't believe me? You think I'm inventing?

[*Pause.*]

HAMM: It's the end, Clov, we've come to the end. I don't need you any more.

[*Pause.*]

CLOV: Lucky for you.

[*He goes towards door.*]

HAMM: Leave me the gaff.

[CLOV *gives him the gaff, goes towards door, halts, looks at alarm-clock, takes it down, looks round for a better place to put it, goes to bins, puts it on lid of* NAGG's *bin. Pause.*]

CLOV: I'll leave you.

[*He goes towards door.*]

HAMM: Before you go ... [CLOV *halts near door*] ... say something.

CLOV: There is nothing to say.

HAMM: A few words ... to ponder ... in my heart.

CLOV: Your heart!

HAMM: Yes. [*Pause. Forcibly.*] Yes! [*Pause.*] With the rest, in the end, the shadows, the murmurs, all the trouble, to end up with. [*Pause.*] Clov ... He never spoke to me. Then, in the end, before he went, without my having asked him, he spoke to me. He said ...

CLOV: [*Despairingly.*] Ah ...!

---

[14] *turns telescope on the without* at this point the French version of the play departs significantly from the English:

CLOV: Ohhhhhhhhhh!

HAMM: Is a leaf? A flower? A toma ... [*he yawns*] ... to.

CLOV: [*Looking*] I'll give you bloody tomatoes! Someone! It's someone!

HAMM: All right, go exterminate him. [CLOV *gets down.*] Someone! [*Trembling.*] Do your duty! [*Clov hurries toward the door.*] No, don't bother. [*Clov stops.*] How far away? [*Clov returns to the ladder, gets up on it, raises telescope.*]

CLOV: Seventy meters ... forty meters.

HAMM: Getting closer? Going away?

CLOV: [*Still looking*] Stock still.

HAMM: Sex?

CLOV: What's the difference? [*He opens the window, leans out. Pause. Straightens up, lowers telescope, turns toward Hamm. Frightened.*] Seems to be a kid.

HAMM: Occupation?

CLOV: What?

HAMM: [*Violently*] What is he doing?

CLOV: [*Violently*] I don't know what he's doing! He's doing what kids used to do. [*Raises telescope. Pause. Lowers telescope, turns toward Hamm.*] He appears to be sitting on the ground with his back against something.

HAMM: The upright stone. [*Pause.*] Your eyesight is getting better. [*Pause.*] No doubt he's looking at the house, with eyes of dying Moses.

CLOV: No.

HAMM: What is he looking at?

CLOV: [*Violently*] I don't know what he's looking at! [*Raises telescope. Pause. He lowers the telescope, turns toward Hamm.*] His navel. That's what. [*Pause.*] Why all these questions?

HAMM: Maybe he's dead.

CLOVE: I'll go and see ...

HAMM: Something . . . from your heart.

CLOV: My heart!

HAMM: A few words . . . from your heart.

[*Pause.*]

CLOV: [*Fixed gaze, tonelessly, towards auditorium.*] They said to me, That's love, yes yes, not a doubt, now you see how –

HAMM: Articulate!

CLOV: [*As before.*] How easy it is. They said to me, That's friendship, yes yes, no question, you've found it. They said to me, Here's the place, stop, raise your head and look at all that beauty. That order! They said to me, Come now, you're not a brute beast, think upon these things and you'll see how all becomes clear. And simple! They said to me, What skilled attention they get, all these dying of their wounds.

HAMM: Enough!

CLOV: [*As before.*] I say to myself – sometimes, Clov, you must learn to suffer better than that if you want them to weary of punishing you – one day. I say to myself – sometimes, Clov, you must be there better than that if you want them to let you go – one day. But I feel too old, and too far, to form new habits. Good, it'll never end, I'll never go. [*Pause.*] Then one day, suddenly, it ends, it changes, I don't understand, it dies, or it's me, I don't understand that either. I ask the words that remain – sleeping, waking, morning, evening. They have nothing to say. [*Pause.*] I open the door of the cell and go. I am so bowed I only see my feet, if I open my eyes, and between my legs a little trail of black dust. I say to myself that the earth is extinguished, though I never saw it lit. [*Pause.*] It's easy going. [*Pause.*] When I fall I'll weep for happiness.

[*Pause. He goes towards door.*]

HAMM: Clov! [CLOV *halts, without turning.*] Nothing. [CLOV *moves on.*] Clov!

[CLOV *halts, without turning.*]

CLOV: This is what we call making an exit.

HAMM: I'm obliged to you, Clov. For your services.

CLOV: [*Turning, sharply.*] Ah pardon, it's I am obliged to you.

HAMM: It's we are obliged to each other. [*Pause.* CLOV *goes towards door.*] One thing more. [CLOV *halts.*] A last favour. [*Exit* CLOV.] Cover me with the sheet. [*Long pause.*] No? Good. [*Pause.*] Me to play. [*Pause. Wearily.*] Old endgame lost of old, play and lose and have done with losing. [*Pause. More animated.*] Let me see. [*Pause.*] Ah yes! [*He tries to move the chair, using the gaff as before. Enter* CLOV, *dressed for the road. Panama hat, tweed coat, raincoat over his arm, umbrella, bag. He halts by the door and stands there, impassive and motionless, his eyes fixed on* HAMM, *till the end.* HAMM *gives up.*] Good. [*Pause.*] Discard. [*He throws away the gaff, makes to throw away the dog, thinks better of it.*] Take it easy. [*Pause.*] And now? [*Pause.*] Raise hat. [*He raises his toque.*] Peace to our . . . arses. [*Pause.*] And put on again. [*He puts on his toque.*] Deuce. [*Pause. He takes off his glasses.*] Wipe. [*He takes out his handkerchief and, without unfolding it, wipes his glasses.*] And put on again. [*He puts on his glasses, puts back the handkerchief in his pocket.*] We're coming. A few more squirms like that and I'll call. [*Pause.*] A little poetry. [*Pause.*] You prayed – [*Pause. He corrects himself.*] You CRIED for night; it comes – [*Pause. He corrects himself.*] It FALLS: now cry in darkness. [*He repeats, chanting.*] You cried for night; it falls: now cry in darkness. [*Pause.*] Nicely put, that. [*Pause.*] And now? [*Pause.*] Moments for nothing, now as always, time was never and time is over, reckoning closed and story ended. [*Pause. Narrative tone.*] If he could have his child with him . . . [*Pause.*] It was the moment I was waiting for. [*Pause.*] You don't want to abandon him? You want him to bloom while you are withering? Be there to solace your last million last moments? [*Pause.*] He doesn't realize, all he knows is hunger, and cold, and death to crown it all. But you! You ought to know what the earth is like, nowadays. Oh, I put him before his responsibilities! [*Pause. Normal tone.*] Well, there we are, there I am, that's enough. [*He raises the whistle to his lips, hesitates, drops it. Pause.*] Yes, truly! [*He whistles. Pause. Louder. Pause.*] Good. [*Pause.*] Father! [*Pause. Louder.*] Father! [*Pause.*] Good. [*Pause.*] We're coming. [*Pause.*] And to end up with? [*Pause.*] Discard. [*He throws away the dog. He tears the whistle from his neck.*] With my compliments. [*He throws whistle towards auditorium. Pause. He sniffs. Soft.*] Clov! [*Long pause.*] No? Good.

[He takes out the handkerchief.] Since that's the way we're playing it ... *[he unfolds handkerchief]* ... let's play it that way ... *[he unfolds]* ... and speak no more about it ... *[he finishes unfolding]* ... speak no more. *[He holds the handkerchief spread out before him.]* Old stancher! *[Pause.]* You ... remain. *[Pause. He covers his face with handkerchief, lowers his arms to armrests, remains motionless.]* *[Brief tableau.]*

CURTAIN

Dante... Bruno . Vico .. Joyce (1929)

The danger is in the neatness of identifications. The conception of Philosophy and Philology as a pair of nigger minstrels out of the Teatro dei Piccoli[1] is soothing, like the contemplation of a carefully folded ham-sandwich. Giambattista Vico[2] himself could not resist the attractiveness of such coincidence of gesture. He insisted on complete identification between the philosophical abstraction and the empirical illustration, thereby annulling the absolutism of each conception – hoisting the real unjustifiably clear of its dimensional limits, temporalizing that which is extra-temporal. And now here am I, with my handful of abstractions, among which notably: a mountain, the coincidence of contraries, the inevitability of cyclic evolution, a system of Poetics, and the prospect of self-extension in the world of Mr Joyce's *Work in Progress*.[3] There is the temptation to treat every concept like 'a bass dropt neck fust in till a bung crate', and make a really tidy job of it. Unfortunately such an exactitude of application would imply distortion in one of two directions. Must we wring the neck of a certain system in order to stuff it into a contemporary pigeon-hole, or modify the dimensions of that pigeon-hole for the satisfaction of the analogymongers? Literary criticism is not book-keeping.

. . . .

This essay was published in two slightly different forms almost simultaneously. It first appeared in *Our Exagmination Round His Factification for Incamination of Work in Progress*, a collection of essays on *Finnegans Wake* by Samuel Beckett, Marcel Brion, Frank Budgen, Stuart Gilbert, Eugene Jolas, Victor Llona, Robert McAlmon, Thomas McGreevy, Elliot Paul, John Rodker, Robert Sage, and William Carlos Williams (Paris: Shakespeare and Company, May 1929), then in the journal *transition* 16–17 (June 1929). This edition follows the *transition* text. Like the other essays in *Our Exagmination*, Beckett's attempted to defend *Finnegans Wake* against charges that it was self-indulgent or needlessly obscure by defining its distinctive achievement, by urging that it possessed an identifiable form and proceded by a discernible logic. This already daunting task was complicated by the fact that *Finnegans Wake*, in 1929, consisted only of various sections that had been published in several periodicals, always under the title *Work in Progress* (Joyce kept the title of the book a secret until it was published as a whole in 1939, though in practice he shared the secret with admirers such as Beckett).

Beckett triangulates *Finnegans Wake* with the works of Dante and the Italian philosopher Giambattista Vico (1668–1744). Though by no means a household name, Vico has been a major presence in twentieth-century intellectual discussion. His fidelity to human experience and his fascination with pattern formed a beguiling combination for Joyce, and Beckett deftly explains how Vico's central tenets could illuminate the *Wake*. No less important, he articulates a defense of the *Wake*'s style by comparing its nonexistent language with the nonexistent Italian that Dante shaped and formed. In Beckett's title for the essay, each dot approximates a century of time intervening between the respective writers.

[1]   *Teatro dei Piccoli* ("Theater of the Little Ones," i.e. children) was an Italian theater of marionettes for children, first devised in 1914 by Vittorio Podrecca (1883–1959) and which continued until his death. With all performances set to music, the repertory ranged from adaptations of *Ali Baba*, *Cinderella*, and *Twenty Thousand Leagues Under the Sea* to *The Barber of Seville* and *The Tempest*. In April 1923 the company debuted in England at the New Scala Theatre in London, and thereafter it alternated between Italian and international tours which took in Spain, Britain, the United States, and South America. The company never adapted African-American minstrel shows in its repertoire, and Beckett (in this second sentence of his essay), though intending to startle, is only embarrassing and offensive.

[2]   *Giambattista Vico* (1668–1744) was an Italian philosopher. His chief work was *Principi di una scienza nuova d'intorno alla comune natura delle nazioni* (1725), or *Principles of a New Science of the Common Nature of Nations*, in which he argued that human history consisted of cycles which could be understood only by recognizing the distinctive character of each age and culture.

[3]   *Mr. Joyce's Work in Progress* "Work in Progress" was the title under which various portions of *Finnegans Wake* were published in serials throughout the period 1924–39; the title of the work was revealed only when the book was published as a whole.

Giambattista Vico was a practical roundheaded Neapolitan. It pleases Croce to consider him as a mystic, essentially speculative, '*disdegnoso dell' empirismo*.'[4] It is a surprising interpretation, seeing that more than three-fifths of his *Scienza Nuova* is concerned with empirical investigation. Croce opposes him to the reformative materialistic school of Ugo Grozio,[5] and absolves him from the utilitarian preoccupations of Hobbes, Spinoza, Locke, Bayle and Machiavelli.[6] All this cannot be swallowed without protest. Vico defines Providence as: '*una mente spesso diversa ed alle volte tutta contraria e sempre superiore ad essi fini particolari che essi uomini si avevano proposti; dei quali fini ristretti fatti mezzi per servire a fini più ampi, gli ha sempre adoperati per conservare l'umana generazione in questa terra*.'[7] What could be more definitely utilitarianism? His treatment of the origin and functions of poetry, language and myth, as will appear later, is as far removed from the mystical as it is possible to imagine. For our immediate purpose, however, it matters little whether we consider him as a mystic or as a scientific investigator; but there are no two ways about considering him as an *innovator*. His division of the development of human society into three ages: Theocratic, Heroic, Human (civilized), with a corresponding classification of language: Hieroglyphic (sacred), Metaphorical (poetic), Philosophical (capable of abstraction and generalization), was by no means new, although it must have appeared so to his contemporaries. He derived this convenient classification from the Egyptians, via Herodotus.[8] At the same time it is impossible to deny the originality with which he applied and developed its implications. His exposition of the ineluctable circular progression of Society was completely new, although the germ of it was contained in Giordano Bruno's treatment of identified contraries.[9] But it is in Book 2, described by himself as '*tutto il corpo... la chiave maestra... dell' opera*', that appears the unqualified originality of his mind; here he evolved a theory of the origins of poetry and language, the significance of myth, and the nature of barbaric civilization that must have appeared nothing less than an impertinent outrage against tradition. These two aspects of Vico have their reverber-

---

[4] *Croce to seem... disdegnoso dell'empirismo* Italian for "contemptuous of empiricism." Benedetto Croce (1866–52), a distinguished Italian philosopher of aesthetics, wrote a seminal work on *La filosofia di Giambattista Vico* (Bari: Laterza, 1911), where this phrase appears (p. 78): "Ora l'ispirazione del Vico era genuinamente ed escuslivamente teorica, e punto pratica o riformistica; altamente speculativeo il suo metodo, e disdegnoso dell'empirismo; idealistico e perciò antimaterialistico e antiuntilitaristico, il suo spirito." Croce's study was translated into English by R. G. Collingwood, *The Philosophy of Giambattista Vico* (London: H. Latimer, 1913), p. 87: "Now Vico's genius is truly and indeed exclusively theoretical, and not at all practical or reformatory; his method was profoundly speculative and contemptuous of empricism, his mind idealistic and opposed to materialism and utilitarianism."

[5] *Ugo Grozio* Italian version of Hugo Grotius (1583–1645), or Huig de Groot, a Dutch jurist and statesman. Croce, *La filosofia di Giambattista Vico*, p. 207, contrasts him with Vico; in English, *The Philosophy of Giambattista Vico*, p. 233.

[6] *Hobbes, Spinoza, Locke, Bayle, and Machiavelli* Thomas Hobbes (1588–1679), British moral and political philosopher; Benedict Baruch Spinoza (1632–77) was a rationalist metaphysician; John Locke (1632–1704), British philosopher who was an empricist and a moral and political philospher; Pierre Bayle (1647–1706) was an influential French skeptic; Niccolò Macchiavelli (1496–1527) was an Italian politician and poltical thinker. Croce, in *La filosofia di Giambattista Vico*, contrasts all of them with Vico; in English, *The Philosophy of Giambattista Vico*, 78–9.

[7] *una mente spesso... in questa terra* Italian for: "the mind of providence, which is often different, sometimes contrary, and always superior to the particular goals which humans set for themselves. Instead, to preserve the human race on the earth, providence uses people's limited goals as a means of attaining

greater ones." Giambattista Vico, *Scienza nuova, giusta l'edizione del 1744*, ed. Fausto Nicolini (Bari: Laterza, 1911), vol. 2, XXX; *New Science*, ed. and trans. David Marsh (London and New York: Penguin, 1999), p. 489. It should be noted that the same passage is quoted by Croce, *La filosofia of Giambattista Vico*, p. 120; in English, *The Philosophy of Giambattista Vico*, pp. 118–19.

[8] *via Herodotus* Herodotus (*c*. 484–418 BC) was an ancient Greek historian; Vico mentions him chiefly in connection with events and their dates, not with his broader classification of human development.

[9] *Giordano Bruno* (1548–1600) is the most famous Italian philosopher of the Renaissance, a mystic who reconciled the all and the one, his "treatment of identified contraries." *tutto il corpo... la chiave maestra... dell'opera* Italian for "the whole bulk [of the work]" and "the master key of the work." Beckett has spliced together two phrases by Vico which, in turn, have been quoted by Croce in *La filosofia di Giambattista Vico*, pp. 45, 47. In the English translation of Croce, *The Philosophy of Giambattista Vico*, p. 44, the first phrase appears in this passage: "The chief, almost indeed only, forms of the mind studied by Vico in the *New Science* are the inferior, individualising activities to which he gives the general name of 'certitude'... [such as] the barbaric society and poetic wisdom whose examination occupies in his own words, 'almost the whole bulk of the work.'" The phrase that Croce quotes is not found in the *Scienza nuova* or *New Science*, and Croce provides no reference for it. Again in the English translation of Croce, *The Philosophy of Giambattista Vico*, p. 46, the second phrase appears in this passage: "the doctrine that primitive man is a poet and thinks in poetic images is in Vico's words 'the master key' of the work." The original Italian phrase (*chiave maestra dell'opera*) is found in Vico, *Scienza nuova*, p. 28; or in Vico, *New Science*, trans. Marsh, p. 24.

ations, their reapplications – without, however, receiving the faintest explicit illustration – in *Work in Progress*.

It is first necessary to condense the thesis of Vico, the scientific historian. In the beginning was the thunder: the thunder set free Religion, in its most objective and unphilosophical form – idolatrous animism: Religion produced Society, and the first social men were the cave-dwellers, taking refuge from a passionate Nature: this primitive family life receives its first impulse towards development from the arrival of terrified vagabonds: admitted, they are the first slaves: growing stronger, they exact agrarian concessions, and a despotism has evolved into a primitive feudalism: the cave becomes a city, and the feudal system a democracy: then an anarchy: this is corrected by a return to monarchy: the last stage is a tendency towards interdestruction: the nations are dispersed, and the Phoenix of Society arises out of their ashes. To this six-termed social progression corresponds a six-termed progression of human motives: necessity, utility, convenience, pleasure, luxury, abuse of luxury: and their incarnate manifestations: Polyphemus, Achilles, Caesar and Alexander, Tiberius, Caligula and Nero.[10] At this point Vico applies Bruno – though he takes very good care not to say so – and proceeds from rather arbitrary data to philosophical abstraction. There is no difference, says Bruno, between the smallest possible chord and the smallest possible arc, no difference between the infinite circle and the straight line.[11] The maxima and minima of particular contraries are one and indifferent. Minimal heat equals minimal cold. Consequently transmutations are circular. The principle (minimum) of one contrary takes its movement from the principle (maximum) of one another. Therefore not only do the minima coincide with the minima, the maxima with the maxima, but the minima with the maxima in the succession of transmutations. Maximal speed is a state of rest. The maximum of corruption and the minimum of generation are identical: in principle, corruption is generation. And all things are ultimately identified with God, the universal monad, Monad of monads. From these considerations Vico evolved a Science and Philosophy of History. It may be an amusing exercise to take an historical figure, such as Scipio, and label him No. 3; it is of no ultimate importance. What is of ultimate importance is the recognition that the passage from Scipio to Caesar is as inevitable as the passage from Caesar to Tiberius, since the flowers of corruption in Scipio and Caesar are the seeds of vitality in Caesar and Tiberius.[12] Thus we have the spectacle of a human progression that depends for its movement on individuals, and which at the same time is independent of individuals in virtue of what appears to be a preordained cyclicism. It follows that History is neither to be considered as a formless structure, due exclusively to the achievements of individual agents, nor as possessing reality apart from and independent of them, accomplished behind their backs in spite of them, the work of some superior force, variously known as Fate, Chance, Fortune, God. Both these views, the materialistic and the transcendental, Vico rejects in favour of the rational. Individuality is the concretion of universality, and every individual action is at the same time superindividual. The individual and the universal cannot be considered as distinct from each other. History, then, is not the result of Fate or Chance – in both cases the individual would be separated from his product – but the result of a Necessity that is not Fate, of a Liberty that is not Chance (compare Dante's 'yoke of liberty'[13]). This force he called Divine Providence, with his tongue, one feels, very much in his

---

[10] *Polyphemus, Achilles, Caesar and Alexander, Tiberius, Caligula and Nero* Polyphemus, or Cyclops, is a one-eyed monster who appears in Book 9 of Homer's *Odyssey*; Achilles is the hero of Homer's *Iliad*. Gaius Julius Caesar (100–44 BC) ended the Roman republic and became dictator of Rome; Alexander the Great (356–323 BC) conquered Greece and much of Asia. Tiberius (42 BC to 37 AD) succeeded Augustus as the second emperor of Rome. Caligula (12–41 AD; emperor 37–41 AD), adopted son of Tiberius, was an autocratic emperor of Rome. Nero (37–68 AD; emperor 54–68 AD) was an especially vicious emperor of Rome.

[11] *There is no difference...the straight line* on Giordano Bruno, see note 9.

[12] *Scipio...Caesar...Tiberius* Publius Cornelius Scipio (236–284 BC) was a Roman general in the republican or pre-

imperial era; Gaius Julius Caesar (100–44 BC), regarded as the founder of imperial Rome; Tiberius (42 BC to 37 AD), Roman emperor 14–37 AD.

[13] *Dante's 'yoke of liberty'* Paget Toynbee, *Dantis Alagherii Epistolae: The Letters of Dante* (Oxford: Clarendon Press, 1920), epistle 6, paragraph 2, Latin original p. 68, English translation p. 77: "But you, who transgress every law of God and man, and whom the insatiable greed of avarice has urged all too willing into every crime, does the dread of the second death not haunt you, seeing that you first and you alone, shrinking from the yoke of liberty, have murmured against the glory of the Roman Emperor, the king of the earth, and minister of God; and under cover of prescriptive right, refusing the duty of submission due to him, have chosen rather to rise up in the madness of rebellion?"

cheek. And it is to this Providence that we must trace the three institutions common to every society: Church, Marriage, Burial. This is not Bossuet's Providence,[14] transcendental and miraculous, but immanent and the stuff itself of human life, working by natural means. Humanity is its work in itself. God acts on her, but by means of her. Humanity is divine, but no man is divine. This social and historical classification is clearly adapted by Mr Joyce as a structural convenience – or inconvenience. His position is in no way a philosophical one. It is the detached attitude of Stephen Dedalus in *Portrait of the Artist* ... who describes Epictetus to the Master of Studies as 'an old gentleman who said that the soul is very like a bucketful of water.'[15] The lamp is more important than the lamp-lighter. By structural I do not only mean a bold outward division, a bare skeleton for the housing of material. I mean the endless substantial variations on these three beats, and interior intertwining of these three themes into a decoration of arabesques – decoration and more than decoration. Part 1 is a mass of past shadow, corresponding therefore to Vico's first human institution, Religion, or to his Theocratic age, or simply to an abstraction – Birth. Part 2 is the lovegame of the children, corresponding to the second institution, Marriage, or to the Heroic age, or to an abstraction – Maturity. Part 3 is passed in sleep, corresponding to the third institution, Burial, or to the Human age, or to an abstraction – Corruption. Part 4 is the day beginning again, and corresponds to Vico's Providence, or to an abstraction – Generation.[16] Mr Joyce does not take birth for granted, as Vico seems to have done. So much for the dry bones. The consciousness that there is a great deal of the unborn infant in the lifeless octogenarian, and a great deal of both in the man at the apogee of his life's curve, removes all the stiff interexclusiveness that is often the danger in neat construction. Corruption is not excluded from Part 1 nor maturity from Part 3. The four 'lovedroyd curdinals' are presented on the same plane – 'his element curdinal numen and his enement curdinal marrying and his epulent curdinal weisswasch and his eminent curdinal Kay o' Kay!'[17] There are numerous references to Vico's four human institutions – Providence counting as one! 'A good clap, a fore wedding, a bad wake, tell hell's well'[18]: 'their weatherings and their marryings and their buryings and their natural selections':[19] 'the lightning look, the birding cry, awe from the grave, ever-flowing on our times'[20]: 'by four hands of forethought the first babe of reconcilement is laid in its last cradle of hume sweet hume.'[21]

Apart from this emphasis on the tangible conveniences common to Humanity, we find frequent expressions of Vico's insistence on the inevitable character of every progression – or retrogression: 'The Vico road goes round to meet where terms begin. Still onappealed to by the cycles and onappalled by the recoursers, we feel all serene, never you fret, as regards our dutyful cask. ... before there was a man at all in Ireland there was a lord at Lucan. We only wish everyone was as sure of anything in this watery world as we are of everything in the newlywet fellow that's bound to follow. ...'[22] 'The efferfresh-painted livy in beautific repose upon the silence of the dead from Pharoph the next first down to ramescheckles the last bust thing.'[23] 'In fact, under the close eyes of the inspectors the traits featuring the chiaroscuro coalesce, their contrarieties eliminated, in one stable somebody similarly as by the providential warring of heartshaker with housebreaker and of dramdrinker against freethinker our social something bowls along bumpily, experiencing a jolting

[14] *Bossuet's Providence... by natural means* Jacques Bénigne Bossuet (1627–1704) was a French theologian. Beckett is echoing Croce who, in his *La filosofia di Giambattista Vico*, pp. 79–80, compares the conceptions of divinity entertained by Vico and Bossuet. Or in Collingwoods' translation of *The Philosophy of Giambattista Vico*, p. 93.

[15] *Stephen Dedalus... bucketful of water* Stephen Dedalus makes this description in chapter 5 of *A Portrait of the Artist as a Young Man*, by James Joyce.

[16] *Part 1 is... Generation* Beckett is giving a summary of the four parts of *Finnegans Wake*.

[17] *'lovedroyd curdinals... Kay o' Kay!'* Joyce, *Finnegans Wake*, 2, 2, 282. (The first number refers to one of the four parts of *Finnegans Wake*; the second to a section within the part; and the third to a page number, the pagination being the same in all

editions. This citation system will be used in all subsequent references to *Finnegans Wake*.)

[18] *'A good clap... tell hell's well'* Joyce, *Finnegans Wake*, 1, 5, 117, though the word "wedding" was changed to "marriage" in the final version; Beckett, of course, is citing from the serially published portions of *Work in Progress*.

[19] *'their weatherings... their natural selections'* Joyce, *Finnegans Wake*, 1, 5 117.

[20] *'the lightning look... times'* Joyce, *Finnegans Wake*, 1, 5, 117.

[21] *'by four hands... sweet hume'* Joyce, *Finnegans Wake*, 1, 4, 80.

[22] *'The Vico road... that's bound to follow'* Joyce, *Finnegans Wake*, 3, 2, 452.

[23] *'The efferfreshpainted livy... the last bust thing'* Joyce, *Finnegans Wake*, 3, 2, 452.

series of prearranged disappointments, down the long lane of (it's as semper as oxhousehumper) generations, more generations and still more generations'[24] – this last a case of Mr Joyce's rare subjectivism. In a word, here is all humanity circling with fatal monotony about the Providential fulcrum – the 'convoy wheeling encirculing abound the gigantig's lifetree'.[25] Enough has been said, or at least enough has been suggested, to show how Vico is substantially present in the *Work in Progress*. Passing to the Vico of the Poetics we hope to establish an even more striking, if less direct, relationship.

Vico rejected the three popular interpretations of the poetic spirit, which considered poetry as either an ingenious popular expression of philosophical conceptions, or an amusing social diversion, or an exact science within the research of everyone in possession of the recipe. Poetry, he says, was born of curiosity, daughter of ignorance.[26] The first men had to create matter by the force of their imagination, and 'poet' means 'creator'. Poetry was the first operation of the human mind, and without it thought could not exist. Barbarians, incapable of analysis and abstraction, must use their fantasy to explain what their reasons cannot comprehend. Before articulation comes song; before abstract terms, metaphors. The figurative character of the oldest poetry must be regarded, not as sophisticated confectionery, but as evidence of a poverty-stricken vocabulary and of a disability to achieve abstraction. Poetry is essentially the antithesis of Metaphysics: Metaphysics purge the mind of the senses and cultivate the disembodiment of the spiritual; Poetry is all passion and feeling and animates the inanimate; Metaphysics are most perfect when most concerned with universals; Poetry, when most concerned with particulars. Poets are the sense, philosophers the intelligence of humanity. Considering the Scholastics' axiom: *'niente è nell'intelletto che prima non sia nel senso'*,[27] it follows that poetry is a prime condition of philosophy and civilization. The primitive animistic movement was a manifestation of the *'forma poetica dello spirito'*.[28]

His treatment of the origin of language proceeds along similar lines. Here again he rejected the materialistic and transcendental views; the one declaring that language was nothing but a polite and conventional symbolism; the other, in desperation, describing it as a gift from the Gods. As before, Vico is the rationalist, aware of the natural and inevitable growth of language. In its first dumb form, language was gesture. If a man wanted to say 'sea', he pointed to the sea. With the spread of animism this gesture was replaced by the word: 'Neptune'. He directs our attention to the fact that every need of life, natural, moral and economic, has its verbal expression in one or other of the 30,000 Greek divinities. This is Homer's 'language of the Gods'. Its evolution through poetry to a highly civilized vehicle, rich in abstract and technical terms, was as little fortuitous as the evolution of society itself. Words have their progressions as well as social phases. 'Forest-cabin-village-city-academy' is one rough progression. Another: 'mountain-plain-riverbank'. And every word expands with psychological inevitability. Take the Latin word: 'Lex'.[29]

1. Lex = Crop of acorns.
2. Ilex = Tree that produces acorns.
3. Legere = To gather.
4. Aquilex = He that gathers the waters.
5. Lex = Gathering together of peoples, public assembly.

[24] *'In fact…still more generations'* Joyce, *Finnegans Wake*, 1, 5, 107.
[25] *'convoy wheeling…gigantig's lifetree.'* Joyce, *Finnegans Wake*, 1, 3, 55.
[26] *Poetry, he says, was born of curiosity.* Beckett summarizes the view that Vico articulates in *La scienza nuova*, pp. 147–8; *New Science*, trans. Marsh, pp. 145–6.
[27] *niente è nell' intelletto che prima non sia nel senso* Italian for: "There is nothing in the intellect which was not first in the senses." Beckett takes this from Croce, *La filosofia di Giambattista Vico*, pp. 49–50: "Poeti e filosofi possono dirsi gli uni il senso, gli altri l'intelletto dell 'umanità; e in tale significato è da ritenere vero il detto delle scuole che 'niente è nell' intelletto che prima

non sia nel senso.'" Or in Collingwood's translation of *The Philosophy of Giambattista Vico*, p. 50: "Poets and philosophers may be called respectively the senses and the intellect of mankind: and in this sense we may retain as true the scholastic saying 'there is nothing in the intellect which was not first in the senses.'"
[28] *forma poetica dello spirito* Italian for "Poetic form of the mind." Vico, *Scienza nuova*, ed. Nicolini, p. 53; *New Science*, trans. Marsh, p.67.
[29] *Take the Latin word: 'Lex'* "Lex" is the Latin word for "law." Beckett is echoing a famous discussion of this word by Vico in *La scienza nuova*, p. 96; or in *New Science*, trans. Marsh, p. 65.

6. Lex   = Law.
7. Legere   = To gather together letters into a word, to read.

The root of any word whatsoever can be traced back to some pre-lingual symbol. This early inability to abstract the general from the particular produced the Type-names. It is the child's mind over again. The child extends the names of the first familiar objects to other strange objects in which he is conscious of some analogy. The first men, unable to conceive the abstract idea of 'poet' or 'hero', named every hero after the first hero, every poet after the first poet. Recognizing this custom of designating a number of individuals by the names of their prototypes, we can explain various classical and mythological mysteries. Hermes is the prototype of the Egyptian inventor: so for Romulus, the great law-giver, and Hercules, the Greek hero: so for Homer.[30] Thus Vico asserts the spontaneity of language and denies the dualism of poetry and language. Similarly, poetry is the foundation of writing. When language consisted of gesture, the spoken and written were identical. Hieroglyphics, or sacred language, as he calls it, were not the invention of philosophers for the mysterious expression of profound thought, but the common necessity of primitive peoples. Convenience only begins to assert itself at a far more advanced stage of civilization, in the form of alphabetism. Here Vico, implicitly at least, distinguishes between writing and direct expression. In such direct expression, form and content are inseparable. Examples are the medals of the Middle Ages, which bore no inscription and were a mute testimony to the feebleness of conventional alphabetic writing: and the flags of our own day. As with Poetry and Language, so with Myth. Myth, according to Vico, is neither an allegorical expression of general philosophical axioms (Conti, Bacon[31]), nor a derivative from particular peoples, as for instance the Hebrews or Egyptians, nor yet the work of isolated poets, but an historical statement of fact, of actual contemporary phenomena, actual in the sense that they were created out of necessity by primitive minds, and firmly believed. Allegory implies a threefold intellectual operation: the construction of a message of general significance, the preparation of a fabulous form, and an exercise of considerable technical difficulty in uniting the two, an operation totally beyond the reach of the primitive mind. Moreover, if we consider the myth as being essentially allegorical, we are not obliged to accept the form in which it is cast as a statement of fact. But we know that the actual creators of these myths gave full credence to their face-value. Jove[32] was no symbol: he was terribly real. It was precisely their superficial metaphorical character that made them intelligible to people incapable of receiving anything more abstract than the plain record of objectivity.

Such is a painful exposition of Vico's dynamic treatment of Language, Poetry and Myth. He may still appear as a mystic to some: if so, a mystic that rejects the transcendental in every shape and form as a factor in human development, and whose Providence is not divine enough to do without the cooperation of Humanity.

On turning to the *Work in Progress* we find that the mirror is not so convex. Here is direct expression – pages and pages of it. And if you don't understand it, Ladies and Gentlemen, it is because you are too decadent to receive it. You are not satisfied unless form is so strictly divorced from content that you can comprehend the one almost without bothering to read the other. The rapid skimming and absorption of the scant cream of sense is made possible by what I may call a continuous process of copious intellectual salivation. The form that is an arbitrary and independent phenomenon can fulfil no higher function than that of stimulus for a tertiary or quartary conditioned reflex of dribbling comprehension. When Miss Rebecca West clears her decks for a sorrowful deprecation of the Narcisstic element in Mr Joyce by the purchase of 3 hats, one feels that she might very well wear her bib at all her intellectual banquets, or alternatively, assert a more

---

[30] *Romulus...Hercules* Romulus, together with Remus, was a legendary founder of Rome; Hercules was a legendary hero of Greece.
[31] Natale Conti (1520–82) was an Italian humanist who expounded the view, summarized by Beckett, in his *Mythologiae: sive Explicationis fabularum libri decem* (*Mythologies: or Ten Books of*

Explication of Fables) (Venice: Comin da Trino, 1567); Francis Bacon (1561–1621), British philosopher who urged a similar view of myth in his *De sapientia veterum* (1609), or *The Wisdom of the Ancients*.
[32] *Jove* Supreme god of the Roman deities.

noteworthy control over her salivary glands than is possible for Monsieur Pavlov's unfortunate dogs.[33] The title of this book is a good example of a form carrying a strict inner determination.[34] It should be proof against the usual volley of cerebral sniggers: and it may suggest to some a dozen incredulous Joshuas prowling around the Queen's Hall,[35] springing their tuning-forks lightly against finger-nails that have not yet been refined out of existence. Mr Joyce has a word to say to you on the subject: 'Yet to concentrate solely on the literal sense or even the psychological content of any document to the sore neglect of the enveloping facts themselves circumstantiating it is just as harmful; etc.'[36] And another: 'Who in his heart doubts either that the facts of feminine clothiering are there all the time or that the feminine fiction, stranger than the facts, is there also at the same time, only a little to the rere? Or that one may be separated from the other? Or that both may be contemplated simultaneously? Or that each may be taken up in turn and considered apart from the other?'[37]

Here form *is* content, content *is* form. You complain that this stuff is not written in English. It is not written at all. It is not to be read – or rather it is not only to be read. It is to be looked at and listened to. His writing is not *about* something; *it is that something itself*. (A fact that has been grasped by an eminent English novelist and historian[38] whose work is in complete opposition to Mr Joyce's.) When the sense is sleep, the words go to sleep. (See the end of *Anna Livia*.[39]) When the sense is dancing, the words dance. Take the passage at the end of Shaun's pastoral: 'To stirr up love's young fizz I tilt with this bridle's cup champagne, dimming douce from her peepair of hide-seeks tight squeezed on my snowybreasted and while my pearlies in their sparkling wisdom are nippling her bubblets I swear (and let you swear) by the bumper round of my poor old snaggletooth's solidbowel I ne'er will prove I'm untrue to (theare!) you liking so long as my hole looks. Down.'[40] The language is drunk. The very words are tilted and effervescent. How can we qualify this general esthetic vigilance without which we cannot hope to snare the sense which is for ever rising to the surface of the form and becoming the form itself? St Augustine puts us on the track of a word with his '*intendere*',[41] Dante has: '*Donne ch'avete intelletto d'amore*',[42] and *Voi che, intendendo, il terzo ciel movete*';[43] but his '*intendere*' suggests a strictly intellectual operation. When an Italian says to-day

---

[33]   *When Miss Rebecca West.... Pavlov's unfortunate dogs.* Rebecca West (for her life and writings see pp. 693–716) published *The Strange Necessity* (London: Jonathan Cape) in 1928. It consists of a very long essay on James Joyce ("The Strange Necessity," nearly 200 pages) and miscellaneous book reviews on other authors. The essay on Joyce is structured by the conceit that West has purchased a copy of *Pomes Penyeach* (Paris: Shakespeare and Company, 1927), a collection of Joyce's early poetry, while doing other things such as shopping during a busy day in Paris. It interweaves critical discussions with anecdotal accounts of her purchases, which include "three hats." Reading *Pomes Penyeach* leads to the discovery that Joyce is really a sentimental artist, which is to say not an artist at all, an insight that then leads to others, including the charge that Joyce is narcissistic. Beckett is defending Joyce against these charges.

[34]   *The title of this book … inner determination* i.e., *Finnegans Wake*; Beckett is apparently one of the handful of people to whom Joyce disclosed the title of the work before it was published in 1939; to anyone reading Beckett's essay in 1929, this comment would have been incomprehensible.

[35]   *incredulous Joshuas prowling around the Queen's Hall* Joshua is a hero in the Old Testament who sometimes did not believe God's promises. Queen's Hall was a concert hall located three blocks north of Oxford Circus (the junction of Regent and Oxford streets), adjacent to All Souls Church. It was destroyed by bombs in 1941.

[36]   '*Yet to concentrate … is just as harmful*' Joyce, *Finnegans Wake*, 1, 5, 109.

[37]   '*Who in his hear doubts … apart from the other*' Joyce, *Finnegans Wake*, 1, 5, 109.

[38]   *an eminent English novelist and historian* not identified.

[39]   *See the end of Anna Livia* in this edition see pp. 284–300 for the "Anna Livia Plurabelle" passage of *Finnegans Wake*.

[40]   '*To stirr up … my hole looks. Down*' Joyce, *Finnegans Wake*, 3, 2, 436.

[41]   *St. Augustine puts us … 'intendere'* St. Augustine of Hippo (354–430 AD), in his *Confessions*, III. 5, writes: "Itaque institui animum intendere in scripturas sanctas, et vedere, quales essent," or "So I made up my mind to examine the holy scriptures and see what kind of books they were" (trans. R. S. Pine-Coffin, *Saint Augustine: Confessions* [Harmondsworth: Penguin, 1961], p. 60). The Latin verb "intendere," which means "to hear" but also "to examine" and "to understand," can give us a sense of "the esthetic vigilance" we need to come to terms with the *Wake*.

[42]   *Donne ch'avete intelletto d'amore* the first line of a celebrated canzone by Dante Alighieri (1265–1321) which appears in ch. 19 of his *Vita nuova*: "Women who have understanding of love" (my translation).

[43]   *Voi che, intendendo, il terzo ciel movete* the first line of another celebrated canzone by Dante, this one appearing at the beginning of ch. 2 in his *Convivio*, where it then becomes the subject of an allegorical commentary; this first line is also quoted by Dante in the *Paradiso*, VIII.37. "You who, in understanding, drive the third sphere," i.e. the third sphere or heaven of the planet Venus, goddess of love" (my translation). Beckett, in other words, is collating Dante's use of the verb *intendere* (in Italian) with St. Augustine's use of it (in Latin) in order to delineate the kind of *understanding* or *listening* requisite for *Finnegans Wake*.

'Ho inteso', he means something between 'Ho udito' and 'Ho capito', a sensuous untidy art of intellection.[44] Perhaps 'apprehension' is the most satisfactory English word. Stephen says to Lynch: 'Temporal or spatial, the esthetic image is first luminously apprehended as selfbounded and selfcontained upon the immeasurable background of space or time which is not it ... You apprehend its wholeness'.[45] There is one point to make clear: the Beauty of *Work in Progress* is not presented in space alone, since its adequate apprehension depends as much on its visibility as on its audibility. There is a temporal as well as a spatial unity to be apprehended. Substitute 'and' for 'or' in the quotation, and it becomes obvious why it is as inadequate to speak of 'reading' *Work in Progress* as it would be extravagant to speak of 'apprehending' the work of the late Mr Nat Gould.[46] Mr Joyce has desophisticated language. And it is worth while remarking that no language is so sophisticated as English. It is abstracted to death. Take the word 'doubt': it gives us hardly any sensuous suggestion of hesitancy, of the necessity for choice, of static irresolution. Whereas the German 'Zweifel' does,[47] and, in lesser degree, the Italian 'dubitare'. Mr Joyce recognizes how inadequate 'doubt' is to express a state of extreme uncertainty, and replaces it by 'in twosome twiminds'.[48] Nor is he by any means the first to recognize the importance of treating words as something more than mere polite symbols. Shakespeare uses fat, greasy words to express corruption: 'Duller shouldst thou be than the fat weed that rots itself in death on Lethe wharf'.[49] We hear the ooze squelching all through Dickens's description of the Thames in *Great Expectations*. This writing that you find so obscure is a quintessential extraction of language and painting and gesture, with all the inevitable clarity of the old inarticulation. Here is the savage economy of hieroglyphics. Here words are not the polite contortions of 20th century printer's ink. They are alive. They elbow their way on to the page, and glow and blaze and fade and disappear. 'Brawn is my name and broad is my nature and I've breit on my brow and all's right with every feature and I'll brune this bird or Brown Bess's bung's gone bandy.'[50] This is Brawn blowing with a light gust through the trees or Brawn passing with the sunset. Because the wind in the trees means as little to you as the evening prospect from the Piazzale Michelangiolo[51] – though you accept them both because your non-acceptance would be of no significance, this little adventure of Brawn means nothing to you – and you do not accept it, even though here also your non-acceptance is of no significance. H. C. Earwigger,[52] too, is not content to be mentioned like a shilling-shocker villain, and then dropped until the exigencies of the narrative require that he be again referred to. He continues to suggest himself for a couple of pages, by means of repeated permutations on his 'normative letters', as if to say: 'This is all about me, H. C. Earwigger: don't forget this is all about me!' This inner elemental vitality and corruption of expression imparts a furious restlessness to the form, which is admirably suited to the purgatorial aspect of the work. There is an endless verbal germination, maturation, putrefaction, the cyclic dynamism of the intermediate. This reduction of various expressive media to their primitive economic directness, and the fusion of these primal essences into an assimilated medium for the exteriorization of thought, is pure Vico, and Vico, applied to the problem of style. But Vico is reflected more explicitly than by a distillation of disparate poetic ingredients into a synthetical

---

[44]   *When an Italian...'Ho capito,'* "ho inteso" can be translated as "I see the significance"; "Ho udito" means simply "I heard," while "ho capito" means "I've understood."

[45]   *'Temporal or spatial ... its wholeness'* Stephen Dedalus offers this explanation of aesthetic perception midway through ch. 5 in *A Portrait of the Artist as a Young Man*, by Joyce; the words omitted with an ellipsis read: "You apprehend it as *one* thing. You see it as one whole."

[46]   *the work of the late Mr Nat Gould* British author and journalist Nat Gould (1857–1919) wrote more than 100 racing and sporting novels and thousands of similar stories for newspapers.

[47]   *the German 'Zweifel'* the word for doubt in German, *Zweifel*, better communicates the sense of doubt, according to Beckett, because its root is *zwei*, the word for *two*, as in the expression "to be of two minds."

[48]   *'in twosome twiminds'* Joyce, *Finnegans Wake*, 1, 7, 188.

[49]   *'Duller shouldst thou be...Lethe wharf'* from *Hamlet*, act 1, scene 5. After the ghost has revealed to Hamlet that his father was murdered, and Hamlet has vowed revenge, the ghost comments:

> I find thee apt.
> And duller shouldst thou be than the fat weed
> That roots itself in ease on Lethe wharf,
> Wouldst thou not stir in this.

Lethe is the underworld river of forgetfulness.

[50]   *'Brawn is my name...gone bandy.'* Joyce, *Finnegans Wake*, 1, 7, 187.

[51]   *Piazzale Michelangelo* an elevated piazza in Florence which commands a good view of the city.

[52]   *H. C. Earwigger* the early name for H. C. Earwicker, a character (if one can use that term) in *Finnegans Wake*.

syrup. We notice that there is little or no attempt at subjectivism or abstraction, no attempt at metaphysical generalization. We are presented with a statement of the particular. It is the old myth: the girl on the dirt track, the two washerwomen on the banks of the river.[53] And there is considerable animism: the mountain 'abhearing', the river puffing her old doudheen.[54] (See the beautiful passage beginning: 'First she let her hair fall down and it flussed'.[55]) We have Type-names: Isolde – any beautiful girl: Earwigger – Guinness's Brewery, the Wellington monument, the Phoenix Park,[56] anything that occupies an extremely comfortable position between the two stools. Anna Livia herself, mother of Dublin, but no more the only mother than Zoroaster[57] was the only oriental stargazer. 'Teems of times and happy returns. The same anew. Ordovico or viricordo. Anna was, Livia is, Plurabelle's to be. Northmen's thing made Southfolk's place, but howmultyplurators made eachone in person.'[58] Basta! Vico and Bruno are here, and more substantially than would appear from this swift survey of the question. For the benefit of those who enjoy a parenthetical sneer, we would draw attention to the fact that when Mr Joyce's early pamphlet *The Day of Rabblement* appeared, the local philosophers were thrown into a state of some bewilderment by a reference in the first line to 'The Nolan'.[59] They finally succeeded in identifying this mysterious individual with one of the obscurer ancient Irish kings. In the present work he appears frequently as 'Browne & Nolan', the name of a very remarkable Dublin Bookseller and Stationer.

To justify our title, we must move North, '*Sovra'l bel fiume d'Arno alla gran villa*'[60] .... Between '*colui per lo cui verso – il meonio cantor non è più solo*'[61] and the 'still to-day insufficiently malestimated notesnatcher, Shem the Penman',[62] there exists considerable circumstantial similarity. They both saw how worn out and threadbare was the conventional language of cunning literary artificers, both rejected an approximation to a universal language. If English is not yet so definitely a polite necessity as Latin was in the Middle Ages, at least one is justified in declaring that its position in relation to other European languages is to a great extent that of mediaeval Latin to the Italian dialects. Dante did not adopt the vulgar out of any kind of local jingoism nor out of any determination to assert the superiority of Tuscan to all its rivals as a form of spoken Italian. On reading his *De Vulgari Eloquentia* we are struck by his complete freedom from civic intolerance. He attacks the world's Portadownians:[63] '*Nam quicumque tam obscenae rationis est, ut locum suae nationis delitosissimum credat esse sub sole, huic etiam proe cunctis propriam volgare licetur, idest maternam locutionem. Nos autem, cui mundus est patria*[64] ... etc.' When he comes to examine the dialects he finds Tuscan: '*turpissimum ... fere omnes Tusci in suo turpiloquio obtusi ... non restat in dubio quin aliud sit vulgare quod quaerimus quam quod attingit populus Tuscanorum*.'[65] His conclusion is that the corruption common to

---

[53]   *It is the old myth ... banks of the river* Beckett is desribing the "Anna Livia Plurabelle" passage in *Finnegans Wake*; for the text see pp. 284–300.

[54]   *the river puffing her old doudheen* Joyce, *Finnegans Wake*, 1, 7, 200, with "doudheen" having later become "dudheen."

[55]   '*First she let ... and it flussed.*' Joyce, *Finnegans Wake*, 1, 7, 206.

[56]   *Guiness's Brewery, the Wellington monument, the Phoenix Park* Locations in Dublin.

[57]   *Zoroaster* a Persian religious teacher who lived about 1000 BC.

[58]   '*teems of times ... eachone in person*' Joyce, *Finnegans Wake*, 1, 8, 215.

[59]   *when Mr. Joyce's early pamplet ... 'The Nolan.'* Joyce's pamphlet "The Day of the Rabblement" is reprinted in Ellsworth Mason and Richard Ellmann (eds.), *The Critical Writings of James Joyce* (New York: Viking Compass, 1959), pp. 68–72. Its first sentence reads: "No man, said the Nolan, can be a lover of the good or true, unless he abhors the multitude..." "The Nolan" referred to Giordano Bruno, the Renaissance philosopher who was born in Nola, Italy. Joyce never tired of noting his contemporaries' mystification over this arcane allusion.

[60]   '*Sovra'l bel fiume d'Arno alla gran villa*' Dante, *Inferno*, XXIII.95: "at the the most important of the cities placed over the River Arno" (translation mine). Dante the pilgrim identifies

the city where he was born when asked to do so by a group of hypocrites.

[61]   '*colui per lo cui verso ... è più solo*' in Italian, "he for whose verse the lowliest singer is no longer alone," a phrase used to describe Dante in a poem by the Italian poet Giacomo Leopardi (1798–1837); the poem is called "Sopra il monumento di Dante" ("On the Monument to Dante") and is collected in his *Canti* (1816–37).

[62]   '*still today ... Shem the Penman*' Joyce, *Finnegans Wake*, 1, 5, 125.

[63]   *Portadownians* people from Portadown, County Armagh, Northern Ireland, a city noted for its annual Protestant parades.

[64]   '*Nam quicumque ... cui mundus est patria*' "Now whoever reasons in so repugnant a way as to think that his birthplace is the most delightful place under the sun, he will also cherish above all others his own dialect, i.e his mother tongue. To me, however, for whom the whole world is my fatherland ..." (my translation); Dante Alighieri, *De vulgari eloquentia*, I.6.

[65]   '*turpissimum ... quod attingit populus Tuscanorum.*' "most foul ... almost all the Tuscans are stuck in their foul manner of speaking ... there is no doubt whatever that the vernacular language we we are seeking must be something very different from the one used by Tuscans" (my translation); Dante Alighieri, *De vulgari eloquentia*, I.13.

all the dialects makes it impossible to select one rather than another as an adequate literary form, and that he who would write in the vulgar must assemble the purest elements from each dialect and construct a synthetic language that would at least possess more than a circumscribed local interest: which is precisely what he did. He did not write in Florentine any more than in Neapolitan. He wrote a vulgar that *could* have been spoken by an ideal Italian who had assimilated what was best in all the dialects of his country, but which in fact was certainly not spoken nor ever had been. Which disposes of the capital objection that might be made against this attractive parallel between Dante and Mr Joyce in the question of language, i.e. that at least Dante wrote what was being spoken in the streets of his own town, whereas no creature in heaven or earth ever spoke the language of *Work in Progress*. It is reasonable to admit that an international phenomenon might be capable of speaking it, just as in 1300 none but an inter-regional phenomenon could have spoken the language of the Divine Comedy. We are inclined to forget that Dante's literary public was Latin that the form of his Poem was to be judged by Latin eyes and ears, by a Latin Esthetic intolerant of innovation, and which could hardly fail to be irritated by the substitution of '*Nel mezzo del cammin di nostra vita*'[66] with its 'barbarous' directness for the suave elegance of: '*Ultima regna canam, fluido contermina mundo*',[67] just as English eyes and ears prefer: 'Smoking his favourite pipe in the sacred presence of ladies' to: 'Rauking his flavourite turfco in the smukking precincts of lydias'.[68] Boccaccio did not jeer at the '*piedi sozzi*'[69] of the peacock that Signora Alighieri dreamed about.

I find two well made caps in the '*Convivio*', one to fit the collective noodle of the monodialectical arcadians whose fury is precipitated by a failure to discover 'innoce-free'[70] in the concise Oxford Dictionary and who qualify as the 'ravings of a Bedlamite' the formal structure raised by Mr Joyce after years of patient and inspired labour: '*Questi sono da chiamare pecore e non uomini; chè se una pecora si gittasse da una ripa di mille passi, tutte l'altre le adrebbono dietro; e se una pecore a per alcuna cagione al passare d'una strada salta, tutte le altre saltano, eziando nulla veggendo da saltare. E io ne vidi già molte in un pozzo saltare, per una che dentro vi salto, forse credendo di saltare un muro*.'[71] And the other for Mr Joyce, biologist in words: '*Questo* (formal innovation) *sarà luce nuova, sole nuovo, il quale sorgerà ore l'usato tramonterà e darà luce a coloro che sono in tenebre e in oscurità per lo usato sole chè a loro non luce*.'[72] And, lest he should pull it down over his eyes and laugh behind the peak, I translate '*in tenebre e in oscurità*' by 'bored to extinction'. (Dante makes a curious mistake speaking of the origin of language, when he rejects the authority of Genesis that Eve was the first to speak, when she addressed the Serpent. His incredulity is amusing: '*inconvenienter putatur tam egregium humani generis*

[66] '*Nel mezzo del cammin di nostra vita*' the first line of the *Divine Comedy* by Dante Alighieri.

[67] '*Ultima regna ... mundo*' Latin for "I shall sing of the farthest kingdoms coterminous with moving world," i.e. the kingdoms of the dead (my translation). According to the Italian prose writer Giovanni Boccaccio (1313–75) in his *Trattatello in laude di Dante* (*Small Treatise on the Life of Dante*; also known by the title *Vita di Dante* or *Life of Dante*), Dante had first begun his *Divine Comedy* in Latin, but had written only three lines before he gave up and turned to Italian. Of those three lines in Latin, the first is the one that is quoted by Beckett. See Vittore Branca (ed.), *Tutte le opere di Giovanni Boccaccio*, vol. 3 (Milan: Mondadori, 1974), p. 480 (paragraph 192); or in English translation, Vincenzo Zin Bollettino, ed. and trans., *The Life of Dante* (New York and London: Garland, 1990), p. 52.

[68] '*Rauking his ... precincts of lydias*.' Joyce, *Finnegans Wake*, 2, 2, 294.

[69] '*piedi sozzi*' Italian for "filthy feet." In his *Trattatello in laude di Dante* (*Small Treatise on the Life of Dante*; also known by the title *Vita di Dante* or *Life of Dante*), Giovanni Boccaccio recounts a dream that Dante's mother ("Signora Alighieri") supposedly had shortly before his birth, one that involves a peacock with "filthy" or "ugly feet." Boccaccio then offers an elaborate allegorical exe-

gesis of the dream's every detail, devoting a paragraph to the feet. See Vittore Branca (ed.), *Tutte le opere di Giovanni Boccaccio*, vol. 3 (Milan: Mondadori, 1974), p. 494 (paragraph 226); or in English translation, Vincenzo Zin Bollettino, ed. and trans., *The Life of Dante* (New York and London: Garland, 1990), pp. 59–60.

[70] 'innoce-free' Joyce, *Finnegans Wake*, 1, 7, 203, where the word has been further contracted in "and she laughed innocefree with her limbs aloft."

[71] '*Questi sono da chiamare ... saltare un muro*.' Italian for: "These people should be called sheep and not men; for if a sheep should hurl itself over a cliff and fall a thousand feet, all the others would run behind it; and if a sheep for some reason should jump when crossing a road, all the others would jump, even without seeing any reason for doing so. And one time I saw many sheep jump into a well just because another sheep had done so, perhaps thinking they were jumping over a wall" (my translation). Dante Alighieri, *Convivio* I.xi.

[72] '*Questo sarà luce nuova ... non luce*.' Italian for: "This will be a new light, a new sun which will rise in place of the customary use of Latin, which instead will decline, and it will give light to those left in shadows and darkness by the customary sun that has shed no light for them" (my translation). Dante Alighieri, *Convivio* I.xiii.

actum, vel prius quam a viro, foemina profluisse.[73] But before Eve was born, 'the animals were given names by Adam', the man who 'first said goo to a goose'.[74] Moreover it is explicitly stated that the choice of names was left entirely to Adam, so that there is not the slightest Biblical authority for the conception of language as a direct gift of God, any more than there is any intellectual authority for conceiving that we are indebted for the 'Concert' to the individual who used to buy paint for Giorgione.[75])

We know very little about the immediate reception accorded to Dante's mighty vindication of the 'vulgar', but we can form our own opinions when, two centuries later, we find Castiglione splitting more than a few hairs concerning the respective advantages of Latin and Italian, and Poliziano writing the dullest of dull Latin Elegies to justify his existence as the author of '*Orfeo*' and the '*Stanze*'.[76] We may also compare, if we think it worth while, the storm of ecclesiastical abuse raised by Mr Joyce's work, and the treatment that the Divine Comedy must certainly have received from the same source. His Contemporary Holiness might have swallowed the crucifixion of '*lo sommo Giove*',[77] and all it stood for, but he could scarcely have looked with favour on the spectacle of three of his immediate predecessors plunged head-foremost in the fiery stone of Malebolge, nor yet the identification of the Papacy in the mystical procession of Terrestrial Paradise with a '*puttana sciolta*'.[78] The '*De Monarshia*' was burnt publicly under Pope Giovanni XXII at the instigation of Cardinal Beltrando and the bones of its author would have suffered the same fate but for the interference of an influential man of letters, Pino della Tosa.[79] Another point of comparison is the preoccupation with the significance of numbers. The death of Beatrice inspired nothing less than a highly complicated poem dealing with the importance of the number 3 in her life. Dante never ceased to be obsessed by this number. Thus the poem is divided into three Cantiche, each composed of 33 Canti, and written in terza rima. Why, Mr Joyce seems to say, should there be four legs to a table, and four to a horse, and four seasons and four Gospels and four Provinces in Ireland? Why

[73] '*inconvenienter putatur...foemina profluisse.*' Latin for: "it is inconvenient to think that such a noble act of the human species should first flow from the lips of a woman, rather than a man" (my translation). Dante is discussing the origins of human speech, and notes that in the Bible Eve is the first person who speaks, an idea that he finds unacceptable. Dante Alighieri, *De vulgari eloquentia*, I.4.

[74] '*the animals were given names by Adam...first said goo to a goose.*' source not identified.

[75] *the 'Concert' to...Giorgione* "The Concert" is a celebrated painting held in Palazzo Pitti, Florence. Until the twentieth century it was ascribed to the Italian painter Giorgione, or Giorgio da Castelfranco (1478–1510); since then it has generally been ascribed to Titian (d. 1576) and assigned to his early years when he was much under Giorgione's influence.

[76] *Castiglione...Poliziano...the 'Stanze'* Baldassare Castiglione (1478–1529) was a diplomat and author of *Il cortegiano* (*The Courtier*); in its dedication he considers which kind of Italian to use. Poliziano, or Angelo Ambrogini (1454–94), was a humanist scholar who worked at the court of Lorenzo il magnifico in Florence; he wrote the *Stanze per la giostra del magnifico Giuliano* (*Verses for the Joust of Giuliano the Magnificent*) in 1475 and *La favola d'Orfeo* (*The Fable of Orpheus*) in 1480, the first pastoral drama in Italian. The elegy mentioned by Beckett has not been identified.

[77] *the crucifixion of 'lo sommo Giove'* "sommo Giove" is Italian for "highest Jove." Beckett refers to a phrase in Dante's *Paradiso*, VI.118, when the pilgrim Dante, during an apostrophe to Florence, suddenly addresses God:

> O se licito m'è, o sommo Giove
> che fosti in terra per noi crucifisso,
> son li giusti occhi tuoi rivolti altrove?

Or in English:

> And if it be lawful for me, O highest Jove
> Who was crucified on earth for us,
> Are they just eyes turned elsewhere?

Beckett thinks the phrase "O highest Jove" to describe God or Jesus smacks of a paganism that the Pope would have found offensive; he relies on a schematic opposition between Christian and pagan terminology that is the product of Jakob Burckhardt's conception of the Renaissance as a revival of paganism, a thesis that nobody would now take seriously.

[78] *puttana sciolta* Italian for an "ungirt prostitute," a phrase that Dante uses to describe the papacy as he depicts it in an allegorical procession near the end of the *Purgatorio*, XXXII.149. Dante was a monarchist and believed the church should relinquish all temporal powers (until 1870 the Catholic church was not merely a spiritual power, but a temporal one that controlled most or all of central Italy); for holding these views Dante became a much-beloved figure for later Protestant poets such as John Milton (1608–74).

[79] *The 'De Monarshia' was burnt...Pino della Tosa* Beckett is summarizing a paragraph from Giovanni Boccaccio's *Trattatello in laude di Dante* (*Small Treatise on the Life of Dante*; also known by the title *Vita di Dante* or *Life of Dante*); see Vittore Branca (ed.), *Tutte le opere di Giovanni Boccaccio*, vol. 3 (Milan: Mondadori, 1974), pp. 487–8 (paragraphs 196–7); or in English translation, Vincenzo Zin Bollettino, ed. and trans., *The Life of Dante* (New York and London: Garland, 1990), pp. 53–4. Beckett adds vivid details to Boccaccio's account, so that "was condemened" becomes "was publicly burnt," and "a valiant and noble knight" is turned into "an influential man of letters," even though Pino della Tosa was a ruthless condottiere.

twelve Tables of the Law, and twelve Apostles and twelve months and twelve Napoleonic marshals and twelve men in Florence called Ottolenghi? Why should the Armistice be celebrated at the eleventh hour of the eleventh day of the eleventh month? He cannot tell you because he is not God Almighty, but in a thousand years he will tell you, and in the meantime must be content to know why horses have not five legs, nor three. He is conscious that things with a common numerical characteristic tend towards a very significant interrelationship. This preoccupation is freely trans-lated in his present work, see the 'Question and Answer' chapter,[80] and the Four speaking through the child's brain.[81] They are the four winds as much as the four Provinces, and the four Episcopal Sees as much as either.

A last word about the Purgatories. Dante's is conical and consequently implies culmination. Mr Joyce's is spherical and excludes culmination. In the one there is an ascent from real vegetation – Ante-Purgatory, to ideal vegetation – Terrestrial Paradise: in the other there is no ascent and no ideal vegetation. In the one, absolute progression and a guaranteed consummation: in the other, flux – progression or retrogression, and an apparent consummation. In the one movement is unidirectional, and a step forward represents a net advance: in the other movement is non-directional – or multi-directional, and a step forward is, by definition, a step back. Dante's Terrestrial Paradise is the carriage entrance to a Paradise that is not terrestrial: Mr Joyce's Terrestrial Paradise is the tradesmen's entrance on to the sea-shore. Sin is an impediment to movement up the cone, and a condition of movement round the sphere. In what sense, then, is Mr Joyce's work purgatorial? In the absolute absence of the Absolute. Hell is the static lifelessness of unrelieved viciousness. Paradise the static lifelessness of unrelieved immaculation. Purgatory a flood of movement and vitality released by the conjunction of these two elements. There is a continuous purgatorial process at work, in the sense that the vicious circle of humanity is being achieved, and this achievement depends on the recurrent predomination of one of two broad qualities. No resistance, no eruption, and it is only in Hell and Paradise that there are no eruptions, that there can be none, need be none. On this earth that is Purgatory, Vice and Virtue – which you may take to mean any pair of large contrary human factors – must in turn be purged down to spirits of rebelliousness. Then the dominant crust of the Vicious or Virtuous sets, resistance is provided, the explosion duly takes place and the machine proceeds. And no more than this; neither prize nor penalty; simply a series of stimulants to enable the kitten to catch its tail. And the partially purgatorial agent? The partially purged.

Three Dialogues with Georges Duthuit (1948)

I: Tal Coat[1]

B. – Total object, complete with missing parts, instead of partial object. Question of degree.

D. – More. The tyranny of the discreet overthrown. The world a flux of movements partaking of living time, that of effort, creation, liberation, the painting, the painter. The fleeting instant of sensation given back, given forth, with context of the continuum it nourished.

B. – In any case a thrusting towards a more adequate expression of natural experience, as revealed to the vigilant coenaesthesia. Whether achieved through submission or through mastery, the result is a gain in nature.

[80]   see the 'Question and Answer' chapter Joyce, Finnegans Wake, 1, 6, 126–68.
[81]   and the Four speaking through the child's brain Joyce, Finnegans Wake, 3, 4, 474–554.

THREE DIALOGUES
The "Three Dialogues" were first published in transition (Dec. 1949). Georges Duthuit (1891–1971) was a scholar of Byzantine studies, art critic, and writer; he was also a son-

in-law of Matisse, whose daughter he married. In 1948–9 he edited transition, the journal in which these dialogues were first published.
[1]   Pierre Tal-Coat (1905–85), French painter, was born in Brit-tany of a family of fishermen. In 1931 he settled in Paris and was associated with the Forces Nouvelles ("New Forces") group of Expressive Realists. During the 1940s and 1950s he became prominent in a school of painting that critics of the time charac-terized with the term "lyrical expressionism."

D. – But that which this painter discovers, orders, transmits, is not in nature. What relation between one of these paintings and a landscape seen at a certain age, a certain season, a certain hour? Are we not on a quite different plane?

B. – By nature I mean here, like the naivest realist, a composite of perceiver and perceived, not a datum, an experience. All I wish to suggest is that the tendency and accomplishment of this painting are fundamentally those of previous painting, straining to enlarge the statement of a compromise.

D. – You neglect the immense difference between the significance of perception for Tal Coat and its significance for the great majority of his predecessors, apprehending as artists with the same utilitarian servility as in a traffic jam and improving the result with a lick of Euclidian geometry. The global perception of Tal Coat is disinterested, committed neither to truth nor to beauty, twin tyrannies of nature. I can see the compromise of past painting, but not that which you deplore in the Matisse[2] of a certain period and in the Tal Coat of today.

B. – I do not deplore. I agree that the Matisse in question, as well as the Franciscan orgies of Tal Coat, have prodigious value, but a value cognate with those already accumulated. What we have to consider in the case of Italian painters is not that they surveyed the world with the eyes of building contractors, a mere means like any other, but that they never stirred from the field of the possible, however much they may have enlarged it. The only thing disturbed by the revolutionaries Matisse and Tal Coat is a certain order on the plane of the feasible.

D. – What other plane can there be for the maker?

B. – Logically none. Yet I speak of an art turning from it in disgust, weary of its puny exploits, weary of pretending to be able, of being able, of doing a little better the same old thing, of going a little further along a dreary road.

D. – And preferring what?

B. – The expression that there is nothing to express, nothing with which to express, nothing from which to express, no power to express, no desire to express, together with the obligation to express.

D. – But that is a violently extreme and personal point of view, of no help to us in the matter of Tal Coat.

B. –

D. – Perhaps that is enough for today.

II: Masson[3]

B. – In search of the difficulty rather than in its clutch. The disquiet of him who lacks an adversary.

D. – That is perhaps why he speaks so often nowadays of painting the void, 'in fear and trembling.'[4] His concern was at one time with the creation of a mythology; then with man, not simply in the

---

[2] Henri Matisse (1869–1954), French painter noted for his style of decorative abstraction.

[3] André Masson (1896–1987), Fench painter, moved to Paris in 1912 and served in the armed forces during the First World War, an experience that left him with a troubled curiosity about the nature of man. He was associated with the Surrealist movement (see "Continental Interlude III," pp. 717–61) and took a special interest in the practice of automatism, executing automatic drawings and paintings, but (like so many others) left the movement in 1928 after a quarrel with Breton. During the 1930s he did several series symbolizing violence and carnage:

Massacres, Sacrifices, and *Tauromachies.* During the Second World War he emigrated to America, where he strongly influenced the early stages of Abstract Expressionism. When he returned to France after the war he became a venerated and much-awarded figure.

[4] *'in fear and trembling'* Philippians 2:12: "Wherefore, my beloved, as ye have always obeyed, not as in my presence only, but how much more in my absence, work out your own salvation with fear and trembling." *Fear and Trembling* was also the title of a work (1843) by the Danish theologian Søren Kierkegaard (1813–55), first translated into English in 1939 (trans. Robert

universe, but in society; and now... 'inner emptiness, the prime condition, according to Chinese esthetics, of the act of painting.'[5] It would thus seem, in effect, that Masson suffers more keenly than any living painter from the need to come to rest, i.e. to establish the data of the problem to be solved, the Problem at last.

B. – Though little familiar with the problems he has set himself in the past and which, by the mere fact of their solubility or for any other reason, have lost for him their legitimacy, I feel their presence not far behind these canvases veiled in consternation, and the scars of a competence that must be most painful to him. Two old maladies that should no doubt be considered separately: the malady of wanting to know what to do and the malady of wanting to be able to do it.

D. – But Masson's declared purpose is now to reduce these maladies, as you call them, to nothing. He aspires to be rid of the servitude of space, that his eye may 'frolic among the focusless fields, tumultuous with incessant creation'.[6] At the same time he demands the rehabilitation of the 'vaporous'.[7] This may seem strange in one more fitted by temperament for fire than for damp. You of course will reply that it is the same thing as before, the same reaching towards succour from without. Opaque or transparent, the object remains sovereign. But how can Masson be expected to paint the void?

B. – He is not. What is the good of passing from one untenable position to another, of seeking justification always on the same plane? Here is an artist who seems literally skewered on the ferocious dilemma of expression. Yet he continues to wriggle. The void he speaks of is perhaps simply the obliteration of an unbearable presence, unbearable because neither to be wooed nor to be stormed. If this anguish of helplessness is never stated as such, on its own merits and for its own sake, though perhaps very occasionally admitted as spice to the 'exploit' it jeopardized, the reason is doubtless, among others, that it seems to contain in itself the impossibility of statement. Again an exquisitely logical attitude. In any case, it is hardly to be confused with the void.

D. – Masson speaks much of transparency – 'openings, circulations, communications, unknown penetrations'[8] – where he may frolic at his ease, in freedom. Without renouncing the objects, loathsome or delicious, that are our daily bread and wine and poison, he seeks to break through

---

Payne [Oxford: Oxford University Press]). Most important, however, is the use of this phrase in André Masson, *Plaisir de peindre* (*The Pleasure of Painting*) (Nice: La Diane française, 1950), a collection of essays which had appeared previously, including "Divagations sur l'espace," pp. 145–53, which had been published in the journal *Temps moderns* in 1949. Masson, *Plaisir de peindre*, p. 147: "Se soucier du style, comme on le sait, est un leurre (c'est Puvis et Gauguin), mai le peintre qui a connu, ne serait-ce qu'une, fois, la tentation, d'un espace à réinventer – cette 'crainte' et ce 'tremblement' – saura que c'est là le lieu même où réside l'alternative: suivre les autres en toute tranquillité ou avance face au risque et à l'impardonnable." Or in English: "To worry about style, as one knows, is a decoy (it is Puvis and Gaugin); but the painter who has experienced, even if only once, the temptation of a space to be rediscovered – this 'fear and trembling' – will know that that is the very place where an alternative exists: to quietly follow behind others or to go forward in the face of danger and the unforgivable."

[5] *'inner emptiness, the prime condition, according to Chinese esthetics, of the act of painting'* Masson, *Plaisir de peindre*, p. 147: "Faire en soi le vide, condition première, selon l'esthétique chinoise, de l'acte de peindre."

[6] *'frolic among the focusless fields, tumultuous with incessant creation'* Masson, *Plaisir de peindre*, p. 148: "L'ESPACE-MILIEU. – Éclosions, germinations, ces mères du mouvement et de la métamorphose nous font rêver d'aventures prochaines. Loin de ce point d'hypnose, qui par le truchement de la perspective (même assouplie) nous oblige à fixer notre regard, là où l'artiste organisa la scène capitale. Man sans parcours préétablie, sans guide et sans cornac, que l'oeil s'ébroue librement parmi ces champs affranchis de centres immuables, enfin multipliés, dans une incessante création." Or in English: "SPACE-ENVIRONMENT. – Births, germinations, seas of motion and metamorphosis. Far away from that hypnotic point, achieved by foreshortening, that forces us to fix our view right there, where the artist has organized the main scene. Instead the eye should frolic, without any pre- established direction or guidance or nudging, among the [focusless fields ...]."

[7] *'vaporous'* Masson, *Plaisir de peindre*, p. 148: "A réhabiliter: le 'vaporeux,' 'l'atmosphère,' 'l'enveloppe,' 'les valeurs.' La brume. Le travail au chiffon, à la paume, au doigt et ... à l'huile." Or in English: "We must rehabilitate the 'vaporous,' the 'atmospheric,' the 'enfolding,' and 'values.' Fog. Work with the rag, the palm, the finger, and ... in oil."

[8] *'openings, circulations, unknown penetrations'* Masson, *Plaisir de peindre*, p. 151: "Un espace bien compris comporte un grand jeu d'ouvertures, de circulations, de communications, de pénétrations inconnues au peintre qui considère l'objet comme un ornement de l'espace." Or in English: "Properly grasped, a space entails a great play of openings, circulations, communications, and penetrations unknown to the painter who views the object as an ornament of space."

their partitions to that continuity of being which is absent from the ordinary experience of living. In this he approaches Matisse (of the first period needless to say) and Tal Coat, but with this notable difference, that Masson has to contend with his own technical gifts, which have the richness, the precision, the density and balance of the high classical manner. Or perhaps I should say rather its spirit, for he has shown himself capable, as occasion required, of great technical variety.

B. – What you say certainly throws light on the dramatic predicament of this artist. Allow me to note his concern with the amenities of ease and freedom. *The stars are undoubtedly superb*,[9] as Freud remarked on reading Kant's cosmological proof of the existence of God. With such preoccupations it seems to me impossible that he should ever do anything different from that which the best, including himself, have done already. It is perhaps an impertinence to suggest that he wishes to. His so extremely intelligent remarks on space breathe the same possessiveness as the notebooks of Leonardo who, when he speaks of *disfazione*, knows that for him not one fragment will be lost.[10] So forgive me if I relapse, as when we spoke of the so different Tal Coat, into my dream of an art unresentful of its insuperable indigence and too proud for the farce of giving and receiving.

D. – Masson himself, having remarked that western perspective is no more than a series of traps for the capture of objects, declares that their possession does not interest him. He congratulates Bonnard[11] for having, in his last works, 'gone beyond possessive space in every shape and form, far from surveys and bounds, to the point where all possession is dissolved.'[12] I agree that there is a long cry from Bonnard to that impoverished painting, 'authentically fruitless, incapable of any image whatsoever',[13] to which you aspire, and towards which too, who knows, unconsciously perhaps, Masson tends. But must we really deplore the painting that admits 'the things and creatures of spring, resplendent with desire and

[9]   *The stars are undoubtedly superb* Freud nowhere writes about Kant or his cosmological proof of the existence of God. But embedded within this quotation is plainly another one from Kant, the first sentences in the "Conclusion" to his *Critique of Practical Reason*: "Two things fill the mind with ever new and increasing admiration and awe, the oftener and the more steadily we reflect on them: *the starry heavens above and the moral law within*. I have not to search for them and conjecture as though they were veiled in darkness or were in the transcendent region beyond my horizon; I see them before me and connect them directly with the consciousness of my existence. The former begins from the place I occupy in the external world of sense, and enlarges my connexion therein to an unbounded extent with worlds upon worlds and systems of systems, and moreover into limitless times of their periodic motion, its beginning and continuance. The second begins from my invisible self, my personality, and exhibits me in a world which has true infinity, but which is traceable only by the understanding, and with which I discern that I am not in a merely contingent but in a universal and necessary connexion, as I am also thereby with all those visible worlds. The former view of a countless multitude of worlds annihilates, as it were, my importance as an *animal creature*, which after it has been for a short time provided with vital power, one knows not how, must again give back the matter of which it was formed to the planet it inhabits (a mere speck in the universe)" (*Kant's Critique of Practical Reason and Other Works*, trans. Thomas Kingsmill Abbott, [6th edn. London: Longmans, 1909; 1st edn. 1873], p. 260).

[10]   *Leonardo . . . disfazione* Leonardo da Vinci (1452–1519), "Disputa 'Pro' e 'Contra' la legge di natura," or "Dispute 'For' and 'Against' the Law of Nature." The question at stake in this "dispute" is why nature has so ordained that one animal lives by virtue of the death of another. The speaker taking up nature's behalf says: "Or vedi, la speranza e 'l desidero del repatriarsi e ritornare nel primo caos fa a similitudine della farfalla al lume, dell'uomo, che con continui desideri sempre con festa aspetta la

nuova primavera, sempre la nuova state, sempre e nuovi mesi, e nuovi anni, parendogli che le desiderate cose, venendo, sieno troppo tarde, e non s'avvede che desidera la sua disfazione." Or in English: "Now see, the hope and desire of going back home and returning into primal chaos marks a point of resemblance between the moth drawn to light and man, who continually desires and happily awaits a new spring, a new summer, always new months and new years, it appearing to him that the things he desires are coming too late, and he is not aware that he is desiring his own dissolution [*disfazione*]" (my translation). The original Italian is found in Augusto Marinoni (ed.), *Scritti letterari di Leonardo da Vinci* (Torino: Einaudi, 1992), p. 107. Italian and English versions appear together in Jean Paul Richter (ed.), *The Literary Works of Leonardo da Vinci* (1st edn. 1883; New York: Phaidon, 1970), vol. 2, p. 242.

[11]   Pierre Bonnard (1876–1947), French painter who is said to have continued the tradition of the great colorists – the Venetians, Delacroix, and Gauguin.

[12]   *'gone beyond possessive space . . . all possession is dissolved.'* Masson, *Plaisir de peindre*, p. 142: "La perspective occidentale n'est qu'une longue suite de pièges pour la chasse aux objects. *Espace possessif*, heureusement transgressé par Bonnard dans ses oeuvres dernières, échappant aux cadastres et aux limites, atteignant le lieu où toute possession se dissout."

[13]   *'authentically . . . whatsoever'* source not identified.

   'things and creatures of spring, resplendent with desire and affirmation, ephemeral no doubt, but immortally reiterant' Masson, *Plaisir de peindre*, p. 153: "Elles s'avançaient, ces choses et ces créatures du printemps, resplendissantes de désir et d'affirmation. Elles venaient comme les franges de l'écume, jaillies du flot bleu de l'invisible désir, jaillie du vaste et invisible océan de force et elles arrivaient, palpables et colorées: éphémères sans doute, mais immortelles dans leur rebondissement." The passage, however, is not by Masson, but from an otherwise unidentified work by D. H. Lawrence, and it illustrates Masson's comment that meditation on space can bring one to the limits of mysticism.

affirmation, ephemeral no doubt, but immortally reiterant', not in order to benefit by them, not in order to enjoy them, but in order that what is tolerable and radiant in the world may continue? Are we really to deplore the painting that is a rallying, among the things of time that pass and hurry us away, towards a time that endures and gives increase?

B. – (Exit weeping.)

III: Bram van Velde[14]

B. – Frenchman, fire first.

D. – Speaking of Tal Coat and Masson you invoked an art of a different order, not only from theirs, but from any achieved up to date. Am I right in thinking that you had van Velde in mind when making this sweeping distinction?

B. – Yes. I think he is the first to accept a certain situation and to consent to a certain act.

D. – Would it be too much to ask you to state again, as simply as possible, the situation and act that you conceive to be his?

B. – The situation is that of him who is helpless, cannot act, in the event cannot paint, since he is obliged to paint. The act is of him who, helpless, unable to act, acts, in the event paints, since he is obliged to paint.

D. – Why is he obliged to paint?

B. – I don't know.

D. – Why is he helpless to paint?

B. – Because there is nothing to paint and nothing to paint with.

D. – And the result, you say, is art of a new order?

B. – Among those whom we call great artists, I can think of none whose concern was not predominantly with his expressive possibilities, those of his vehicle, those of humanity. The assumption underlying all painting is that the domain of the maker is the domain of the feasible. The much to express, the little to express, the ability to express much, the ability to express little, merge in the common anxiety to express as much as possible, or as truly as possible, or as finely as possible, to the best of one's ability. What –

D. – One moment. Are you suggesting that the painting of van Velde is inexpressive?

B. – (A fortnight later) Yes.

D. – You realize the absurdity of what you advance?

B. – I hope I do.

D. – What you say amounts to this: the form of expression known as painting, since for obscure reasons we are obliged to speak of painting, has had to wait for van Velde to be rid of the misapprehension under which it had laboured so long and so bravely, namely, that its function was to express, by means of paint.

B. – Others have felt that art is not necessarily expression. But the numerous attempts made to make painting independent of its occasion have only succeeded in enlarging its repertory. I suggest that ven Velde is the first whose painting is bereft, rid if you prefer, of occasion in every shape and form, ideal as well as material, and the first whose hands have not been tied by the certitude that expression is an impossible act.

---

14   Bram van Velde (1895–1981), Dutch painter who moved to Paris in 1925, where he remined until 1965, when he moved to Switzerland. By the late 1930s he had developed an abstract style with a bright, Fauvist palette. His paintings of then had vaguely defined, almost formless shapes of color standing out against monochrome backgrounds.

D. – But might it not be suggested, even by one tolerant of this fantastic theory, that the occasion of his painting is his predicament, and that it is expressive of the impossibility to express?

B. – No more ingenious method could be devised for restoring him, safe and sound, to the bosom of Saint Luke. But let us for once, be foolish enough not to turn tail. All have turned wisely tail, before the ultimate penury, back to the mere misery where destitute virtuous mothers may steal stale bread for their starving brats. There is more than a difference of degree between being short, short of the world, short of self, and being without these esteemed commodities. The one is a predicament, the other not.

D. – But you have already spoken of the predicament of van Velde.

B. – I should not have done so.

D. – You prefer the purer view that here at last is a painter who does not paint, does not pretend to paint. Come, come, my dear fellow, make some kind of connected statement and then go away.

B. – Would it not be enough if I simply went away?

D. – No. You have begun. Finish. Begin again and go on until you have finished. Then go away. Try and bear in mind that the subject under discussion is not yourself, not the Sufist Al-Haqq,[15] but a particular Dutchman by name van Velde, hitherto erroneously referred to as an *artiste peintre*.

B. – How would it be if I first said what I am pleased to fancy he is, fancy he does, and then that it is more than likely that he is and does quite otherwise? Would not that be an excellent issue out of all our afflictions? He happy, you happy, I happy, all three bubbling over with happiness.

D. – Do as you please. But get it over.

B. – There are many ways in which the thing I am trying in vain to say may be tried in vain to be said. I have experimented, as you know, both in public and in private, under duress, through faintness of heart, through weakness of mind, with two or three hundred. The pathetic antithesis possession-poverty was perhaps not the most tedious. But we begin to weary of it, do we not? The realization that art has always been bourgeois, though it may dull our pain before the achievements of the socially progressive, is finally of scant interest. The analysis of the relation between the artist and his occasion, a relation always regarded as indispensable, does not seem to have been very productive either, the reason being perhaps that it lost its way in disquisitions on the nature of occasion. It is obvious that for the artist obsessed with his expressive vocation, anything and everything is doomed to become occasion, including, as is apparently to some extent the case with Masson, the pursuit of occasion, and the every man his own wife experiments of the spiritual Kandinsky.[16] No painting is more replete than Mondrian's.[17] But if the occasion appears as an unstable term of relation, the artist, who is the other term, is hardly less so, thanks to his warren of modes and attitudes. The objections to this dualist view of the creative process are unconvincing. Two things are established, however precariously: the aliment, from fruits on plates to low mathematics and self-commiseration, and its manner of dispatch. All that should concern us is the acute and increasing anxiety of the relation itself, as though shadowed more and more darkly by a sense of invalidity, of inadequacy, of existence at the expense of all that it excludes, all that it blinds to. The history of painting, here we go again, is the history of its attempts to escape from this sense of failure, by means of more authentic, more ample, less exclusive relations between

---

[15] There was no Sufist named Al-Haqq. There was, however, one Hussein ibn Mansur al-Hallaj (857–922), an Arabic-speaking Persian Muslim mystic and poet. An ecstatic mystic, he described his union with God in the words *ana al-haqq* (Arabic for "I am the Truth"), which led to charges of heresy and his arrrest in 813. Though freed, he was later arrested again and executed.

[16] Wassily Kandinsky (1866–1944) was a Russian painter who moved to Germany, then France. He wrote a book called *Über das Geistige in der Kunst* (*On the Spiritual Dimension in Art*) which called for spiritual combinations of the "inner" and "outer" elements of a work of art.

[17] Piet Mondrian (1872–1944), Dutch painter who formed part of the group De Stijl. His characteristic compositions of spare lines and rectangles were, for most observers of the time, devoid or empty of subject-matter, not "replete."

representer and representee, in a kind of tropism towards a light as to the nature of which the best opinions continue to vary, and with a kind of Pythagorean terror, as though the irrationality of pi were an offence against the deity, not to mention his creature. My case, since I am in the dock, is that van Velde is the first to desist from this estheticized automatism, the first to admit that to be an artist is to fail, as no other dare fail, that failure is his world and the shrink from it desertion, art and craft, good housekeeping, living. No, no, allow me to expire. I know that all that is required now, in order to bring even this horrible matter to an acceptable conclusion, is to make of this submission, this admission, this fidelity to failure, a new occasion, a new term of relation, and of the act which, unable to act, obliged to act, he makes, an expressive act, even if only of itself, of its impossibility, of its obligation. I know that my inability to do so places myself, and perhaps an innocent, in what I think is still called an unenviable situation, familiar to psychiatrists. For what is this coloured plane, that was not there before. I don't know what it is, having never seen anything like it before. It seems to have nothing to do with art, in any case, if my memories of art are correct. (*Prepares to go.*)

D. – Are you not forgetting something?

B. – Surely that is enough?

D. – I understood your number was to have two parts. The first was to consist in your saying what you – er – thought. This I am prepared to believe you have done. The second –

B. – (*Remembering, warmly*) Yes, yes, I am mistaken, I am mistaken.

Whoroscope (1930)

> What's that?
> An egg?
> By the brothers Boot[1] it stinks fresh.[2]
> Give it to Gillot.[3]
>
> Galileo how are you   5
> and his consecutive thirds![4]
> The vile old Copernican lead-swinging son of a sutler![5]
> We're moving he said we're off[6] – Porca Madonna![7]
> the way a boatswain would be, or a sack-of-potatoey[8] charging Pretender.[9]
> That's not moving, that's *moving*.[10]   10

"Whoroscope" was first published as an independent book by Nancy Cunard (on her, see pp. 762–76) (Paris: the Hours Press, 1930). In 1929 Cunard had announced a prize of £10 for the best poem on the subject of time, not to exceed 100 lines. Beckett entered, and won the prize.

The poem registers but also parodies intense moments being relived in the mind of René Descartes as he lies dying, thoughts called to the surface of consciousness by his feverishly active mind. Beckett drew on Charles Adam and Paul Tannery (eds.), *Oeuvres de Descartes* (Paris: Ministère de l'instruction publique, 1913) and Adrien Baillet, *La Vie de Monsieur Descartes*, 2 vols. (Paris: Daniel Horthemels, 1691; rpt. New York: Garland, 1987). He may also have drawn on John Pentland Mahaffy, *Descartes* (Edinburgh and London: W. Blackwood & Sons, 1901). To save space, no references to specific pages in these works will be made.

[1] *the brothers Boot* two Dutch doctors practicing in London who published a book in Ireland refuting the teachings of Aristotle.

[2] *it stinks fresh* Descartes discovered after experiments that eggs were best eaten when they had lain under the hen from 8 to 10 days, according to Baillet.

[3] *to Gillot* Jean Gillot was Descartes's valet.

[4] *Galileo . . . consecutive thirds* Vincenzo Galilei (d. 1591), father of Galileo Galilei (1565–1642), the famous astronomer, wrote many books on music, which included terms such as "consecutive thirds."

[5] *son of sutler* a sutler was an army follower who sold provisions to soldiers; the "vile old Copernican" is the astronomer Galileo.

[6] *We're moving he said we're off* a facetious reference to Galilean ideas of relative motion: the earth moves round the sun, although it is motionless with regard to the ether that carries it along, and with regard to us on its surface.

[7] *Porca Madonna!* "Pig Madonna!" is a very vulgar exclamation in Italian.

[8] *potatoey* an Irishism, used in children's speech.

[9] *Pretender* probably Frederick who was elected King of Bohemia by the Protestants in November 1619 but was considered a pretender by Catholics and deposed in 1620.

[10] *That's not moving, that's moving* summarizes the theory of relative motion, i.e. that which may seem to be moving is not moving and vice versa.

What's that?
A little green fry[11] or a mushroomy one?

Two lashed ovaries with prostisciutto?[12]
How long did she womb it, the feathery one?
Three days and four nights?   15
Give it to Gillot.

Faulhaber, Beeckman and Peter the Red,[13]
come now in the cloudy avalanche[14] or Gassendi's sun-red crystally cloud[15]
and I'll pebble you all your hen-and-a-half ones[16]
or I'll pebble a lens under the quilt in the midst of day.[17]   20

To think he was my own brother, Peter the Bruiser,[18]
and not a syllogism out of him
no more than if Pa were still in it.[19]
Hey! pass over those coppers,[20]
sweet millèd sweat of my burning liver!   25
Them were the days I sat in the hot-cupboard throwing
                          Jesuits out of the skylight.

Who's that? Hals?[22]
Let him wait.

My squinty doaty![23]
I hid and you sook.   30
And Francine[24] my precious fruit of a house-and-parlour foetus!

What an exfoliation![25]
Her little grey flayed epidermis and scarlet tonsils!
My one child

[11] *A little green...Give it to Gillot* (lines 11–16) Descartes's attention turns again to an egg somewhere near him.
[12] *two lashed ovaries with prostisciutto* "lashed" meaning "whipped" or "tied off," as is the ovary of a hen when it delivers an egg, and so in this sense not unlike some prostitutes who have their ovaries tied to avoid reproduction; an omlette made of these and prosciutto, conflated with the word "prostitute."
[13] *Faulhaber, Beeckman and Peter the Red* Johann Faulhaber (1580–1635) was a famous German mathematician who was astounded when Descartes solved some problems for him. Isaac Beeckman (1588–1637) was a famous Dutch mathematician who had the same experience as Faulhaber. Peter the Red, not identified.
[14] *in the cloudy avalanche* during a visit to the Savoy Alps, Descartes noticed (in Baillet's words) that "when the snows had been warmed and made heavy by the sun, the slightest movement of the air was enough to cause large masses to fall suddenly. In this region they were called *avalanches*, or rather *lavanches*. When they echoed through the valleys, they sounded very much like thunder." Descartes concluded that thunder could be caused when warm air made clouds that were near the sun crash down on clouds below.
[15] *Gassendi's sun-red crystally cloud* Pierre Gassendi (1592–1655) published in 1644 a work titled *Disquisitio metaphysica; seu, Dubitationes et instantiae adversus Renati Cartesii Metaphysicam et responsa*, or *Metaphysical Disquisition: or, Doubts and Objections against the Metaphysics of René Descartes, with Responses*. Descartes did not like it.
[16] *your hen-and-a-half ones* half-baked problems, like eggs that haven't been properly ripened.

[17] *under the quilt...day* Descartes was in habit of staying in bed until midday.
[18] *To think...Bruiser* Descartes's brother, Pierre de la Brétailleur, attempted to defraud him of money after their father died; a *brétailler* in French is a "rowdy, rough, or disorderly person," and Beckett then translates this pun in French into "Bruiser."
[19] *if Pa were still in it* i.e., in possession and still alive.
[20] *those coppers* "the money he received as a soldier," as Beckett's note explains. Having entered the service of Prince Maurice of Nausau in 1617 and remained there for three years; he kept his soldier's salary with him for the rest of his life.
[21] *hot-cupboard* while still in military service, Descartes stayed for a whole day in a room heated by a tile-stove (Beckett's "hot cupboard"), where his only entertainment was his thoughts. In a flash of inspiration he saw the road to an entirely new science of nature and thought, founded on reason alone, one that would put an end to Jesuit teaching based on Aristotle.
[22] *Who's that? Hals?* Franz Hals (c. 1613–74), Dutch artist who painted a portrait of Descartes which has long been lost and is known only through an engraving copy.
[23] *My squinty doaty!* Descartes recalls a childish love for a cross-eyed little girl upon whom he doted. "Doaty" is an Irishism, with obscene meaning here too.
[24] *Francine* name of Descartes's only child, who died at the age of 5 or 6. She was supposedly the daughter of a young woman named Helen, said to be a servant girl.
[25] *exfoliation* Descartes perhaps compares the shedding of a leaf from a bud with the "shedding" of little Francine from her mother.

scourged by a fever to stagnant murky blood –
blood!   35

Oh Harvey[26] belovèd
how shall the red and white, the many in the few,
(dear bloodswirling Harvey)
eddy through that cracked beater?[27]   40
And the fourth Henry[28] came to the crypt of the arrow.

What's that?
How long?
Sit on it.[29]

A wind of evil[30] flung my despair of ease   45
against the sharp spires of the one
lady:[31]
not once or twice but....
(Kip of Christ hatch it!)
in one sun's drowning   50
(Jesuitasters please copy).
So on[32] with the silk hose[33] over the knitted, and the morbid leather[34] –

what am I saying! the gentle canvas[35] :–
and away to Ancona[36] on the bright Adriatic,
and farewell for a space to the yellow key of the Rosicrucians.   55
They don't know what the master of them that do did,
that the nose is touched by the kiss of all foul and sweet air,
and the drums, and the throne of the faecal inlet,
and the eyes by its zig-zags.
So we drink Him and eat Him[37]   60
and the watery Beaune and the stale cubes of Hovis
because He can jig
as near or as far from His Jigging Self
and as sad or lively as the chalice or the tray asks.
How's that, Antonio?   65

In the name of Bacon will you chicken me up that egg.
Shall I swallow cave-phantoms?[38]

[26] *Harvey* William Harvey (1578–1657) was a British doctor and anatomist who wrote the *Exercitatio anatomica de motu cordis et snaguinis* (Frankfurt: Guilielmus Fitzerus, 1628), which announced the discovery of the circulation of blood. Descartes thought that blood was white in the arteries and red in the veins: "the many in the few" must mean the many red in the few white corpuscles.

[27] *that cracked beater* the heart.

[28] *the fourth Henry* see Beckett's note.

[29] *What's that... Sit on it.* (lines 42–4) another egg has come to his attention or occurred to his thoughts.

[30] *A wind of evil...* (lines 45–55) in 1619 Descartes recorded that he had three dreams in a row. In the first he saw himself limping along (because of a pain in his right side) in a violent, gusty storm. "Despair of ease" refers to his difficulty while walking in search of rest.

[31] *the sharp spires of the one / lady* a church consecrated to the Virgin Mary, which was the subject of his second dream, and which led him to promise to visit the shrine of the Virgin Mary at Loreto if he were successfull in his intellectual endeavors.

[32] (lines 52–5) in his third dream Descartes dreamed of a poem by the Latin poet Ausonius which begins thus: *Quod vitae sectabor*

iter (What road shall I pursue in life). When he woke, he turned in prayer to Mary and made the vow discussed in the previous note.

[33] *the silk hose* in the days of Descartes a gentleman wore knitted hose next to the body as underclothing, then hose of silk.

[34] *the morbid leather* meaning shoes.

[35] *the gentle canvas* i.e., shoes made of sailcloth.

[36] *Ancona* the port city one sails to in order to visit the shrine of the Virgin Mary at Loreto.

[37] *So we drink... Antonio?* (lines 60–5) the theologian Antoine ("Antonio," line 65) Arnauld (1612–92) asked Descartes how he could "reconcile his doctrine of matter with the doctrine of transubstantiation." These lines are a parodic version of Descartes's sophistic response. Beaune is a red Burgundy wine (the word is pronounced like "bone"), while Hovis is a maker of bread and crackers in England, and nearly rhymes with "eau vie," water of life in French.

[38] Descartes returns for a moment to his ripening egg and asks somebody to make the egg into a chicken. Cave-phantoms are evidently forms without substance, and there is an obvious pun in the juxtaposition of Bacon and egg, the reality versus the imaginary cave-phantoms. Francis Bacon (1561–1626) was a distinguished natural philosopher.

Anna Maria![39]
She reads Moses and says her love is crucified.
Leider! Leider![40] she bloomed and withered,[41]   70
a pale abusive parakeet in a mainstreet window.[42]

No I believe every word of it I assure you.
Fallor, ergo sum![43]
The coy old frôleur!
He tolle'd and legge'd[44]   75
and he buttoned on his redemptorist waistcoat.
No matter, let it pass.[45]
I'm a bold boy I know
so I'm not my son
(even if I were a concierge)   80
nor Joachim my father's
but the chip of a perfect block that's neither old nor new,
the lonely petal of a great high bright rose.

Are you ripe at last,[46]
my slim pale double-breasted turd?   85
How rich she smells,
this abortion of a fledgling!
I will eat it with a fish fork.
White and yolk and feathers.
Then I will rise and move moving[47]   90
toward Rahab of the snows,
the murdering matinal pope-confessed amazon,
Christina the ripper.[48]
Oh Weulles spare the blood of a Frank[49]
who has climbed the bitter steps,   95
(René du Perron ... !)[50]
and grant me my second
starless inscrutable hour.

---

[39] (lines 68–71) Descartes now recalls Anna Maria Schurmann, "a bluestocking" (in Beckett's words) who studied mathematics and philosophy, wrote, painted, engraved, and sculpted. Her motto was *Amor meus cruicfixus est*, "My love has been crucified," alluded to in line 69.

[40] *Leider! Leider!* German for "unfortunately, unfortunately."

[41] *she bloomed and withered* Anna Maria Schurmann retired to a Lutheran abbey to pursue her theological meditations when she was still only 28; she died there in 1678.

[42] Descartes recalls an incident at the University of Utrecht, where he hid Anna Maria Schurmann so that she could hear a lecture by Voetius, or Gisbert Voët (1589–1676).

[43] *Fallor, ergo sum* Latin for "I err, therefore I am," a fusion of Descartes's famous "cogito" with St. Augustine, "Si enim fallor, sum ..." "If I err, I am ..."

[44] *Tolle'd and legge'd* Anglicizing of the Latin "tolle, legge," which means "take and read." One day when Augustine was sitting alone in his garden he heard a voice coming from the trees, which seemed to say "tolle legge." When he then went to visit a friend, he saw at his house a copy of the epistles of Saint Paul, which he then opened at random, lighting on Romans 13:13–14, an experience that led to St. Augustine's conversion.

[45] (lines 77–83) see Beckett's note.

[46] *Are you ... move moving.* (lines 84–9) the last time the egg appears; it is ripe now, not yet a full-grown chicken, but an "abortion of a fledgling," i.e. a young bird.

[47] *Then I will ... the ripper* (lines 90–3) Descartes's thoughts turn to Stockholm, where he went at the invitation of Queen Christina. He will begin moving toward "Rahab of the snows." Rahab is a name for Egypt in the Bible, e.g. Psalm 87, which merges into or becomes a person in lines 92 and 93, evidently Christina.

[48] *Christina the ripper* by ordering Descartes to the semi-Arctic capital of Sweden, and by making him appear at court early in the morning (when his lifelong habit had been to sleep till midday), Christina brought about his untimely death, or so it has been urged. The poem facetiously assimilates Queen Christina to Jack the Ripper.

[49] Descartes, in his final illness, was attended by the physician Weulles, who used the typical procedure of "cupping" or "bleeding" a patient; the line translates a sentence Descartes is said to have uttered to Weulles.

[50] René du Perron was Descartes's official name, so-called after a small *seigneurie* in Poitou which he had inherited from his parents (he sold it in 1623). But "perron" in French also means a "flight of steps," or simply a "step." The phrase "bitter steps" may be indebted to a passage in Dante, *Paradiso* 17.58–60, when the pilgrim Dante is given a prophecy of his exile from Florence, told "how hard is the way up and down another man's steps."

Notes

René Descartes, Seigneur du Perron, liked his omelette made of eggs hatched from eight to ten days; shorter or longer under the hen and the result, he says, is disgusting. He kept his own birthday to himself so that no astrologer could cast his nativity. The shuttle of a ripening egg combs the warp of his days.

1.3   In 1640 the brothers Boot refuted Aristotle in Dublin.

4   Descartes passed on the easier problems in analytical geometry to his valet Gillot.

5–10   Refer to his comtempt for Galileo Jr., (whom he confused with the more musical Galileo Sr.), and to his expedient sophistry concerning the movement of the earth.

17   He solved problems submitted by these mathematicians.

1. 21–6   The attempt at swindling on the part of his elder brother Pierre de la Bretaillière – The money he received as a soldier.

27   Franz Hals.

29–30   As a child he played with a little cross-eyed girl.

31–5   His daughter died of scarlet fever at the age of six.

37–40   Honoured Harvey for his discovery of the circulation of the blood, but would not admit that he had explained the motion of the heart.

41   The heart of Henri IV was received at the Jesuit college of La Flèche while Descartes was still a student there.

1. 45–53   His visions and pilgrimage to Loretto.

56–65   His Eucharistic sophistry, in reply to the Jansenist Antoine Arnauld, who challenged him to reconcile his doctrine of matter with the doctrine of transubstantiation.

68   Schurmann, the Dutch blue-stocking, a pious pupil of Voët, the adversary of Descartes.

1. 73–6   Saint Augustine has a revelation in the shrubbery and reads Saint Paul.

77–83   He proves God by exhaustion.

91–3   Christina, Queen of Sweden. At Stockholm, in November, she required Descartes, who had remained in bed till midday all his life, to be with her at five o'clock in the morning.

94   Weulles, a Peripatetic Dutch physician at the Swedish court, and an enemy of Descartes.

Enueg II (1935)

world world world world
and the face grave
cloud against the evening

de morituris nihil nisi[1]

and the face crumbling shyly   5
too late to darken the sky
blushing away into the evening
shuddering away like a gaffe

veronica mundi[2]
veronica munda[3]   10
gives us a wipe for the love of Jesus

sweating like Judas[4]
tired of dying
tired of policemen
feet in marmalade   15
perspiring profusely
heart in marmalade
smoke more fruit
the old heart the old heart
breaking outside congress   20
doch[5] I assure thee
lying on O'Connell Bridge[6]
goggling at the tulips of the evening
the green tulips
shining round the corner like an anthrax[7]   25
shining on Guinness's barges[8]

the overtone the face
too late to brighten the sky
doch doch I assure thee

"Enueg II," written in Ireland in the summer of 1931, was first published in Beckett's collection of poems, *Echo's Bones* (Paris: Europa Press, 1935).

An "enueg" is a poetic form in Provençal poetry, a witty but discontinuous catalogue of vexations.

[1] *de morituris nihil nisi* adapted from an old proverb in Latin, *De mortuis nihil nisi bonum*, which means "Of the dead nothing but good [should be spoken]." Becket's adaption, instead, reads: "Of those who are going to die, nothing but," leaving it open-ended what one should say about "those who are going to die."

[2] *veronica mundi* "Veronica of the world," in Latin. Veronica was a woman of Jerusalem who, filled with compassion at the sight of Jesus suffering on his way to Calvary, wiped his sweating face with a cloth. Miraculously, an image of his features was left on the cloth. The original cloth, it is said, has been preserved at St. Peter's at Rome, perhaps since the early eighth century. The incident of St. Veronica wiping Christ's brow also comprises one of the Stations of the Cross, 14 locations in a church which bear images from the story of the crucifixion, and where the churchgoer is encouraged to meditate.

[3] *veronica munda* Latin for "clean Veronica."

[4] *Judas* The thirteenth disciple who betrays Jesus for 30 shekels.

[5] *doch* German for "of course."

[6] *O'Connell Bridge* The main bridge over the river Liffey in central Dublin.

[7] *anthrax* a carbuncle or malignant boil.

[8] *Guinness's barges* barrels of Guinness stout (a dark, heavy beer) were floated on barges down the Liffey.

Echo's Bones (1935)

asylum under my tread all this day
their muffled revels as the flesh falls
breaking without fear or favour wind
the gantelope[1] of sense and nonsense run
taken by the maggots for what they are   5

Ooftish (1938)

offer it up plank it down
Golgotha[1] was only the potegg
cancer angina[2] it is all one to us
cough up your T. B. don't be stingy
no trifle is too trifling not even a thrombus[3]   5
anything venereal is especially welcome
that old toga in the mothballs
don't be sentimental you won't be wanting it again
send it along we'll put it in the pot with the rest
with your love requited and unrequited   10
the things taken too late the things taken too soon
the spirit aching bullock's scrotum
you won't cure it you won't endure it
it is you it equals you any fool has to pity you
so parcel up the whole issue and send it along   15
the whole misery diagnosed undiagnosed misdiagnosed
get your friends to do the same we'll make use of it
we'll make sense of it we'll put it in the pot with the rest
it all boils down to blood of lamb[4]

What is the Word (1990)

folly –
folly for to –
for to –
what is the word –
folly from this –   5
all this –

ECHO'S BONES
This poem was published in Beckett's first collection of poems,
Echo's Bones (Paris: Europa Press, 1935).
[1] *gantelope* a Beckettian coinage, a combination of "antelope"
and "gauntlet," as in the expression "to run the gauntlet."

OOFTISH
"Ooftish" was first published in the journal *transition* (April–May
1938). "Ooftish" is a phonetic rendering of northern German
pronunciation of "auf Tisch," or "on the table" in English. The
poem's conceit is that everyone must contribute their suffering to
the world, "offer it up plank it down," for it is somehow redemp-
tive.
[1] *Golgotha* the mount where Christ was crucified.
[2] *angina* the medical term for breast-pain, heart-stroke, or a
spasm of the chest, indicating a diseased heart.

[3] *thrombus* a clot which forms on the wall of a blood vessel or a
chamber of the heart.
[4] *blood of lamb* a variant on the blood of the Lamb, i.e. Christ.

WHAT IS THE WORD
Under its French title, "Comment dire," the poem was published
in 1989 (Paris: Editions de Minuit). The English translation by
Beckett appeared after his death in the *Irish Times*, December
25–7, 1989; then in the journal *Beckett Circle* (Spring 1990), and
finally in the posthumous publication, *As the Story Was Told*
(London: John Calder, 1990).
   "what is the word" is suggestive of John 1:1: "In the beginning was the Word, and the Word was with God, and Word was
God." And John 1:14: "And the Word was made flesh, and dwelt
among us, (and we beheld his glory, the glory as of the only
begotten of the Father), full of grace and truth."

folly from all this –
given –
folly given all this –
seeing –   10
folly seeing all this –
this –
what is the word –
this this –
this this here –   15
all this this here –
folly given all this –
seeing –
folly seeing all this this here –
for to –   20
what is the word –
see –
glimpse –
seem to glimpse –
need to seem to glimpse –   25
folly for to need to seem to glimpse –
what –
what is the word –
and where –
folly for to need to seem to glimpse what where –   30
where –
what is the word –
there –
over there –
away over there –   35
afar –
afar away over there –
afaint –
afaint afar away over there what –
what –   40
what is the word –
seeing all this –
all this this –
all this this here –
folly for to see what –   45
glimpse –
seem to glimpse –
need to seem to glimpse –
afaint afar away over there what –
folly for to need to seem to glimpse afaint afar away over there what –   50
what –
what is the word –

what is the word

Continental Interlude IV: The Frankfurt School (1923–60)

Introduction

The Frankfurt School is a term that broadly designates a style of thought associated with an identifiable group of German intellectuals, and more specifically refers to the institution that housed or encouraged such thought, the Institute for Social Research (*Institut für Sozialforschung*), located in Frankfurt and associated with the University of Frankfurt. The Institute was officially created on February 3, 1923, by a decree of the Education Ministry in Germany, buttressed by an endowment from Hermann Weil, a businessman and the father of Felix Weil, an intellectual responsible for both creating and maintaining the institute for many years. The building that housed it was opened a year later in 1924, with 4 seminar rooms, 16 small workrooms, a 36-seat reading room, and a library with space for 75,000 volumes. The Institute was intended to establish a space for independent theoretical work within a Marxist tradition, thought that would be free of the immediate or pragmatic political considerations that inevitably shaped the thinking of Socialist parties that had come to power, as in Weimar Germany, or Communist parties either already in power (the Soviet Union) or seeking power. Indeed, even the phrase "within a Marxist tradition" requires qualification, for in practice members of the Frankfurt School reexamined many Marxist tenets that were otherwise considered sacrosanct.

Max Horkheimer (1895–1973) was a founding member of the Institute and in 1931 he became its director. He also founded and became the editor of the Institute's principal publication, the *Zeitschrift für Sozialforschung* (*Periodical for Social Research*), a journal that published a wide range of essays. In 1931, in the light of the changing political situation in Germany, the Institute's endowment was prudently moved to Holland, and in 1933 the Institute in Frankfurt was closed as soon as the Nazis came to power. Horkheimer, a committed secularist, was of Jewish background. He emigrated to Switzerland and then to the United States in 1934, where the Institute was reopened under the aegis of Columbia University. The Institute was as helpful as it could be to the many Jewish intellectuals who had to flee Germany, often providing them with the garb of institutional affiliation required to meet the protocols of immigration authorities. In 1940 he initiated another review, *Studies in Philosophy and Social Science*, a successor to the *Zeitschrift für Sozialforschung*, and from 1942 to 1944 he resided in California where, together with Theodor Adorno, he wrote the *Dialectic of Englihtenment* (1947). He returned to Germany in 1949 and the Institute was reopened in 1950. Horkheimer became

Rector of the University of Frankfurt in 1951, and upon his retirement he moved to Montagola, near to Lugano, in Switzerland.

The two intellectuals who were associated with the Institute and who came to be seen as its major figures were Theodor Adorno and Walter Benjamin. Both were of Jewish backgrounds. Adorno (1903–69) was born in Frankfurt into a middle-class family with pronounced musical interests (his mother was a singer, his aunt a musician). Adorno finished his doctoral thesis on Husserl in 1923 under the direction of Hans Cornelius, who also directed the thesis of Horkheimer. During the 1920s he wrote many essays, chiefly on music, and also went to Vienna, where he studied composition under Alban Berg; he composed a string quartet and several trios for strings. He returned to Frankfurt in 1928, where he continued to edit *Anbruch*, a music journal (1928–31), and submitted his habilitation thesis on the aesthetics of Kierkegaard. In 1931 he was appointed to an academic position at the University of Frankfurt. Though his essays increasingly appeared in the *Zeitschrift für Sozialforschung*, and though he had known Horkheimer since the early 1920s, he did not officially become a member of the Institute until 1938. By then he was living in Oxford, as he had been since 1934, but in 1938 he moved the US at the insistence of Horkheimer, with whom he now collaborated in writing the *Dialectic of Enlightenment*. He returned to Germany after the war and, when Horkheimer left the Institute to become rector of the university, became the Institute's director. In 1950 he published *The Authoritarian Personality*, his most empirical work, and in 1951 *Minima Moralia*, a wide-ranging work of cultural criticism and theory. In 1955 he issued *Prisms: Cultural Criticism and Society*, and in 1966 *Negative Dialectics*, the most ambitious and systematic of the works that were published during his lifetime. After his death, the unfinished *Aesthetic Theory* was published (1970). During the years after the Second World War he was also instrumental in preserving and disseminating the largely unknown work of Walter Benjamin.

Walter Benjamin (1892–1940) was born in Berlin, the son of a dealer in paintings and antiquities. He first met Theodor Adorno in 1923, and through him remained in contact with the Institute for Social Research. In 1925 his thesis on the *Origins of Tragic Drama* was rejected for its unconventional style of reading and its problematic referencing. Benjamin now became a freelance writer and critic. In 1925–6 he spent 7 months in Moscow, and in 1927 6 months in Paris. To some extent under the inspiration of

Surrealism, he began the project that would intermittently occupy him for the rest of his life, the Arcades Project, a massive history of nineteenth-century Paris that would be organized on the principle of collage, a juxtaposition of original documents with interspersed reflections that would forgo the kind of connectedness associated with narrative, a left-wing counterpart to *The Cantos* of Ezra Pound, as it were. A year later *One-Way Street* and *The Origins of German Tragic Drama* were published. In 1929 he began his friendship with Bertholt Brecht, the German dramatist. In 1933 he moved to Paris, where he remained for the next 7 years, with the exception of three visits to Brecht in Denmark. His financial circumstances continued to worsen, though he now received occasional support form the Institute for Social Research through the agencies of Adorno and Horkheimer. In Paris he also met Hannah Arendt, Kurt

Weill, and Hermann Hesse. In 1936 he published his essay on "The Work of Art in the Age of Mechanical Reproduction" in the *Zeitschrift für Sozialforschung*. With the invasion of France, Benjamin was briefly arrested and subsequently reached the decision to flee to the United States. In southern France, near the border with Spain, he took his own life on the mistaken assumption that he was about to be arrested.

After his death, in 1955, Hannah Arendt published the first collection of his essays, *Illuminations*, which initiated the long and protracted process whereby Benjamin's original and discerning contribution to the thought of the twentieth century was recognized. It was only in 1982 that the *Passagen-Werk*, his massive meditation on nineteenth-century Paris, was first published in German, and only in 1999 that it was translated into English as *The Arcades Project*.

Surrealism: The Last Snapshot of the European Intelligentsia (1929)
Walter Benjamin

Intellectual currents can generate a sufficient head of water for the critic to install his power station on them. The necessary gradient, in the case of Surrealism, is produced by the difference in intellectual level between France and Germany. What sprang up in 1919 in France in a small circle of literati – we shall give the most important names at once: André Breton, Louis Aragon, Philippe Soupault, Robert Desnos, Paul Eluard[1] – may have been a meager stream, fed on the damp boredom of postwar Europe and the last trickle of French decadence. The know-alls who even today have not advanced beyond the "authentic origins" of the movement, and even now have nothing to say about it except that yet another clique of literati is here mystifying the honorable public, are a little like a gathering of experts at a spring who, after lengthy deliberation, arrive at the conviction that this paltry stream will never drive turbines.

The German observer is not standing at the head of the stream. That is his opportunity. He is in the valley. He can gauge the energies of the movement. As a German he is long acquainted with the crisis of the intelligentsia, or, more precisely, with that of the humanistic concept of freedom; and he knows how frantic is the determination that has awakened in the movement to go beyond the stage of eternal discussion and, at any price, to reach a decision; he has had direct experience of its highly exposed position between an anarchistic *fronde*[2] and a revolutionary discipline, and so has no excuse for taking the movement for the "artistic," "poetic" one it superficially appears. If it was such at the outset, it was, however, precisely at the outset that Breton declared his intention of breaking with a praxis that presents the public with the literary precipitate of a certain form of existence while withholding that existence itself. Stated more briefly and dialectically, this means that the sphere of poetry was here explored from within by a closely knit circle of people pushing the "poetic life" to the utmost limits of possibility. And they can be taken at their word when they assert that Rimbaud's *Saison en enfer*[3] no longer had any secrets for them. For this book is indeed the first document of the movement (in recent times; earlier precursors will be discussed later). Can the

SURREALISM
First published in a journal called *Die Literarische Welt* 5(8–11) (Feb. 1929). The English translation by Edmund Jephcott was first published in Walter Benjamin, *Reflections: Essays, Aphorisms, Autobiographical Writings*, ed. Peter Demetz (New York: Harcourt, 1978).
[1] See the introductory note to "Continental Interlude III: Surrealism."

[2] The name for a series of civil wars that took place in France between 1648 and 1653, when Louis XIV was still in his minority. The term, meaning "sling," comes from toy catapults that were used in a children's game which, in defiance of civil authorities, was played in the streets of Paris.
[3] Arthur Rimbaud (1854–91), Symbolist poet, published *Un saison en enfer* in Brussels in 1873.

point at issue be more definitively and incisively presented than by Rimbaud himself in his personal copy of the book? In the margin, beside the passage "on the silk of the seas and the arctic flowers," he later wrote, "There's no such thing."[4]

In just how inconspicuous and peripheral a substance the dialectical kernel that later grew into Surrealism was originally embedded, was shown by Aragon in 1924 – at a time when its development could not yet be foreseen – in his *Vague de rêves*.[5] Today it can be foreseen. For there is no doubt that the heroic phase, whose catalogue of heroes Aragon left us in that work, is over. There is always, in such movements, a moment when the original tension of the secret society must either explode in a matter-of-fact, profane struggle for power and domination, or decay as a public demonstration and be transformed. Surrealism is in this phase of transformation at present. But at the time when it broke over its founders as an inspiring dream wave, it seemed the most integral, conclusive, absolute of movements. Everything with which it came into contact was integrated. Life only seemed worth living where the threshold between waking and sleeping was worn away in everyone as by the steps of multitudinous images flooding back and forth, language only seemed itself where sound and image, image and sound interpenetrated with automatic precision and such felicity that no chink was left for the penny-in-the-slot called "meaning." Image and language take precedence. Saint-Pol Roux,[6] retiring to bed about daybreak, fixes a notice on his door: "Poet at work." Breton notes: "Quietly. I want to pass where no one yet has passed, quietly! – After you, dearest language." Language takes precedence.

Not only before meaning. Also before the self. In the world's structure dream loosens individuality like a bad tooth. This loosening of the self by intoxication is, at the same time, precisely the fruitful, living experience that allowed these people to step outside the domain of intoxication. This is not the place to give an exact definition of Surrealist experience. But anyone who has perceived that the writings of this circle are not literature but something else – demonstrations, watch-words, documents, bluffs, forgeries if you will, but at any rate not literature – will also know, for the same reason, that the writings are concerned literally with experiences, not with theories and still less with phantasms. And these experiences are by no means limited to dreams, hours of hashish eating, or opium smoking. It is a cardinal error to believe that, of "Surrealist experiences," we know only the religious ecstasies or the ecstasies of drugs. The opium of the people, Lenin called religion, and brought the two things closer together than the Surrealists could have liked. I shall refer later to the bitter, passionate revolt against Catholicism in which Rimbaud, Lautréamont, and Apollinaire[7] brought Surrealism into the world. But the true, creative overcoming of religious illumination certainly does not lie in narcotics. It resides in a *profane illumination*, a materialistic, anthropological inspiration, to which hashish, opium, or whatever else can give an introductory lesson. (But a dangerous one; and the religious lesson is stricter.) This profane illumination did not always find the Surrealists equal to it, or to themselves, and the very writings that proclaim it most powerfully, Aragon's incomparable *Paysan de Paris* and Breton's *Nadja*,[8] show very disturbing symptoms of deficiency. For example, there is in *Nadja* an excellent passage on the "delightful days spent looting Paris under the sign of Sacco and

---

[4] *"on the silk ... no such thing."* Rimbaud, *Illuminations* in *Oeuvres*, ed. Suzanne Bernard (Paris: Garnier Frères, 1960), p. 292, "Barbare"; *A Season in Hell; the Illuminations*, trans. Enid Rhodes Peschel (Oxford: Oxford University Press, 1973), p. 155 ("Barbarian").

[5] Louis Aragon (1897–1982) was a Surrelist poet (see the "introduction" to Continental Interlude III: the Surrealists) who published *Vague de rêves*, a short collection of poems, in 1924.

[6] Saint-Pol-Roux (1861–1940) was a French poet who was cited as a precursor by the Surrealists.

[7] Isidore Ducasse (1846–70), Comte de Lautréamont, was a poet born of French parents in Uruguay who adopted the pseudonym Comte de Lautréamont (Count of Lautréamont) and whose major work was the prose poem *Les Chants de Maldoror* (*The Songs of Maldoror*; 1868), a work utterly unnoticed till it was redis-

covered by André Breton and turned into a classic text for Surrealist writers. Guillaume Apollinaire (1880–1918), French poet and critic who coined the word "surrealist" in the subtitle to his play, *Les Mamelles de Tirésias: drame surréaliste* (*The Breasts of Tiresias: Surrealist Drama*), and who was a major figure in the Parisian avant-garde until his death.

[8] *Aragon's incomparable ... Nadja* Aragon published *Le Payson de Paris* (Paris: Gallimard) in 1926, an account of a Parisian arcade (or indoor shopping mall) and a journey to a park, interspersed with various meditations in English; see *Paris Peasant*, trans. Simon Watson Taylor (Boston: Exact Change, 1994). André Breton wrote *Nadja*, a memoir-diary account of his relations with a young woman who embodies his ideals but is also mad, in 1928. In English see *Nadja*, trans. Richard Howard (London and New York: Penguin, 1999).

Vanzetti";[9] Breton adds the assurance that in those days Boulevard Bonne-Nouvelle fulfilled the strategic promise of revolt that had always been implicit in its name. But Madame Sacco also appears, not the wife of Fuller's victim but a *voyante*, a fortuneteller who lives at 3 rue des Usines and tells Paul Eluard that he can expect no good from Nadja.[10] Now I concede that the breakneck career of Surrealism over rooftops, lightning conductors, gutters, verandas, weathercocks, stucco work – all ornaments are grist to the cat burglar's mill – may have taken it also into the humid backroom of spiritualism. But I am not pleased to hear it cautiously tapping on the windowpanes to inquire about its future. Who would not wish to see these adoptive children of revolution most rigorously severed from all the goings-on in the conventicles of down-at-heel dowagers, retired majors, and *émigré* profiteers?

In other respects Breton's book illustrates well a number of the basic characteristics of this "profane illumination." He calls *Nadja* "a book with a banging door."[11] (In Moscow I lived in a hotel in which almost all the rooms were occupied by Tibetan lamas who had come to Moscow for a congress of Buddhist churches. I was struck by the number of doors in the corridors that were always left ajar. What had at first seemed accidental began to be disturbing. I found out that in these rooms lived members of a sect who had sworn never to occupy closed rooms. The shock I had then must be felt by the reader of *Nadja*.) To live in a glass house is a revolutionary virtue par excellence. It is also an intoxication, a moral exhibitionism, that we badly need. Discretion concerning one's own existence, once an aristocratic virtue, has become more and more an affair of petit-bourgeois parvenus. *Nadja* has achieved the true, creative synthesis between the art novel and the *roman-à-clef*.

Moreover, one need only take love seriously to recognize in it, too – as *Nadja* also indicates – a "profane illumination." "At just that time" (i.e., when he knew Nadja), the author tells us, "I took a great interest in the epoch of Louis VII, because it was the time of the 'courts of love,' and I tried to picture with great intensity how people saw life then."[12] We have from a recent author quite exact information on Provençal love poetry, which comes surprisingly close to the Surrealist conception of love. "All the poets of the 'new style,'" Erich Auerbach points out in his excellent *Dante: Poet of the Secular World*, "possess a mystical beloved, they all have approximately the same very curious experience of love; to them all Amor bestows or withholds gifts that resemble an illumination more than sensual pleasure; all are subject to a kind of secret bond that determines their inner and perhaps also their outer lives."[13] The dialectics of intoxication are indeed curious. Is not perhaps all ecstasy in one world humiliating sobriety in that complementary to it? What is it that courtly *Minne* seeks – and it, not love, binds Breton to the telepathic girl – if not to make chastity, too, a transport? Into a world that borders not only on tombs of the Sacred Heart or altars to the Virgin, but also on the morning before a battle or after a victory.

The lady, in esoteric love, matters least. So, too, for Breton. He is closer to the things that Nadja is close to than to her. What are these things? Nothing could reveal more about Surrealism than their canon. Where shall I begin? He can boast an extraordinary discovery. He was the first to perceive the revolutionary energies that appear in the "outmoded," in the first iron constructions, the first factory buildings, the earliest photos, the objects that have begun to be extinct, grand pianos, the dresses of five years ago, fashionable restaurants when the vogue has begun to ebb from them. The relation of these things to revolution – no one can have a more exact concept of it than these authors. No one before these visionaries and augurs perceived how destitution – not only social but architectonic, the poverty of interiors, enslaved and enslaving objects – can be suddenly

[9] "delightful days ... Sacco and Vanzetti" Nicolò Sacco and Bartolomeo Vanzetti were Italian anarchists who had emigrated to the United States in 1908; they were charged with murdering a paymaster and his guard in a robbery in 1920, and were executed on August 23, 1927. Their case became a cause célèbre, as many felt they were being persecuted for their political beliefs. In Paris, riots broke out and a barricade was erected at the intersection of the Boulevard Sébastopol and the rue Réaumur, just south of the Boulevard Bonne-Nouvelle (Good-News Boulevard, or Gospel Boulevard). See *Nadja*, pp. 153–4.

[10] See *Nadja*, p. 79 n. 1; Benjamin is mistaken, for the person who is warned about Nadja is Breton, not Paul Eluard.
[11] *Nadja*, p. 156, echoing an earlier usage of the phrase on p. 118.
[12] *Nadja*, p. 97.
[13] Erich Auerbach (1892–1957), *Dante als Dichter der irdischen Welt* (Berlin, Leipzig: W. De Gruyter, 1929), p. 76; *Dante: Poet of the Secular World*, trans. Ralph Mannheim (Chicago: University of Chcago Press, 1961), p. 60.

transformed into revolutionary nihilism. Leaving aside Aragon's *Passage de l'Opéra*,[14] Breton and Nadja are the lovers who convert everything that we have experienced on mournful railway journeys (railways are beginning to age), on Godforsaken Sunday afternoons in the proletarian quarters of the great cities, in the first glance through the rain-blurred window of a new apartment, into revolutionary experience, if not action. They bring the immense forces of "atmosphere" concealed in these things to the point of explosion. What form do you suppose a life would take that was determined at a decisive moment precisely by the street song last on everyone's lips?

The trick by which this world of things is mastered – it is more proper to speak of a trick than a method – consists in the substitution of a political for a historical view of the past. "Open, graves, you, the dead of the picture galleries, corpses behind screens, in palaces, castles, and monasteries, here stands the fabulous keeper of keys holding a bunch of the keys to all times, who knows where to press the most artful lock and invites you to step into the midst of the world of today, to mingle with the bearers of burdens, the mechanics whom money ennobles, to make yourself at home in their automobiles, which are beautiful as armor from the age of chivalry, to take your places in the international sleeping cars, and to weld yourself to all the people who today are still proud of their privileges. But civilization will give them short shrift." This speech was attributed to Apollinaire by his friend Henri Hertz.[15] Apollinaire originated this technique. In his volume of novellas, *L'hérésiarque*, he used it with Machiavellian calculation to blow Catholicism (to which he inwardly clung) to smithereens.[16]

At the center of this world of things stands the most dreamed-of of their objects, the city of Paris itself. But only revolt completely exposes its Surrealist face (deserted streets in which whistles and shots dictate the outcome). And no face is surrealistic in the same degree as the true face of a city. No picture by de Chirico or Max Ernst[17] can match the sharp elevations of the city's inner strongholds, which one must overrun and occupy in order to master their fate and, in their fate, in the fate of their masses, one's own. Nadja is an exponent of these masses and of what inspires them to revolution: "The great living, sonorous unconsciousness that inspires my only convincing acts, in the sense that I always want to prove that it commands forever everything that is mine."[18] Here, therefore, we find the catalogue of these fortifications, from Place Maubert, where as nowhere else dirt has retained all its symbolic power, to the "Théâtre Moderne," which I am inconsolable not to have known. But in Breton's description of the bar on the upper floor – "it is quite dark, with arbors like impenetrable tunnels – a drawing room on the bottom of a lake"[19] – there is something that brings back to my memory that most uncomprehended room in the old Princess Café. It was the back room on the first floor, with couples in the blue light. We called it the "anatomy school"; it was the last restaurant designed for love. In such passages in Breton, photography intervenes in a very strange way. It makes the streets, gates, squares of the city into illustrations of a trashy novel, draws off the banal obviousness of this ancient architecture to inject it with the most pristine intensity toward the events described, to which, as in old chambermaids' books, word-for-word quotations with page numbers refer. And all the parts of Paris that appear here are places where what is between these people turns like a revolving door.

The Surrealists' Paris, too, is a "little universe." That is to say, in the larger one, the cosmos, things look no different. There, too, are crossroads where ghostly signals flash from the traffic, and inconceivable analogies and connections between events are the order of the day. It is the region

[14] The first chapter in Aragon's *Paris Peasant*.

[15] Benjamin is mistaken; Henri Hertz says this in propria persona; see Henri Hertz, "Singulier pluriel," *L'Esprit Nouveau*, no. 26 (1924).

[16] Guillaume Apollinaire, *L'Hérésiarque & Cie.* (Paris: P.-V. Stock, 1910).

[17] Giorgio de Chirico (1888–1978) was an artist whose early works showed desolate cityscapes; Max Ernst (1891–1976) was a German artist who became a Surrealist in 1922.

[18] The character Nadja doesn't say anything like this in *Nadja*. She does express the view that people going home from work are "good people," which elicits an angry response from Breton and prompts their first quarrel; see *Nadja*, pp. 68–9.

[19] Breton, *Nadja*, p. 38; the second noun phrase is from Rimbaud, "Délires II: Alchimie du verbe," in *Une Saison en enfer* (see *A Season in Hell; the Illuminations*, trans Enid Rhodes Peschel [Oxford: Oxford University Press, 1973], p. 80 ["un salon au fond d'un lac"]).

from which the lyric poetry of Surrealism reports. And this must be noted if only to counter the obligatory misunderstanding of *l'art pour l'art*. For art's sake was scarcely ever to be taken literally; it was almost always a flag under which sailed a cargo that could not be declared because it still lacked a name. This is the moment to embark on a work that would illuminate as has no other the crisis of the arts that we are witnessing: a history of esoteric poetry. Nor is it by any means fortuitous that no such work yet exists. For written as it demands to be written – that is, not as a collection to which particular "specialists" all contribute "what is most worth knowing" from their fields, but as the deeply grounded composition of an individual who, from inner compulsion, portrays less a historical evolution than a constantly renewed, primal upsurge of esoteric poetry – written in such a way it would be one of those scholarly confessions that can be counted in every century. The last page would have to show an X-ray picture of Surrealism. Breton indicates in his *Introduction au discours sur le peu de réalité*[20] how the philosophical realism of the Middle Ages was the basis of poetic experience. This realism, however – that is, the belief in a real, separate existence of concepts whether outside or inside things – has always very quickly crossed over from the logical realm of ideas to the magical realm of words. And it is as magical experiments with words, not as artistic dabbling, that we must understand the passionate phonetic and graphical transformational games that have run through the whole literature of the avant-garde for the past fifteen years, whether it is called Futurism, Dadaism, or Surrealism. How slogans, magic formulas, and concepts are here intermingled is shown by the following words of Apollinaire's from his last manifesto, *L'esprit nouveau et les poètes*. He says, in 1918: "For the speed and simplicity with which we have all become used to referring by a single word to such complex entities as a crowd, a nation, the universe, there is no modern equivalent in literature. But today's writers fill this gap; their synthetic works create new realities the plastic manifestations of which are just as complex as those referred to by the words standing for collectives."[21] If, however, Apollinaire and Breton advance even more energetically in the same direction and complete the linkage of Surrealism to the outside world with the declaration, "The conquests of science rest far more on a surrealistic than on a logical thinking"[22] – if, in other words, they make mystification, the culmination of which Breton sees in poetry (which is defensible), the foundation of scientific and technical development, too – then such integration is too impetuous. It is very instructive to compare the movement's overprecipitous embrace of the uncomprehended miracle of machines – "the old fables have for the most part been realized, now it is the turn of poets to create new ones that the inventors on their side can then again make real"[23] (Apollinaire) – to compare these overheated fantasies with the well-ventilated utopias of a Scheerbart.[24]

"The thought of all human activity makes me laugh." This utterance of Aragon's shows very clearly the path Surrealism had to follow from its origins to its politicization. In his excellent essay *"La révolution et les intellectuels,"* Pierre Naville, who originally belonged to this group, rightly called this development dialectical. In the transformation of a highly contemplative attitude into revolutionary opposition, the hostility of the bourgeoisie toward every manifestation of radical intellectual freedom played a leading part. This hostility pushed Surrealism to the left. Political events, above all the war in Morocco, accelerated this development. With the manifesto "Intellectuals Against the Moroccan War," which appeared in *L'Humanité*, a fundamentally different platform was gained from that which was characterized by, for example, the famous scandal at the Saint-Pol Roux

[20]   This essay was first published in the journal *Commerce* 4 (March 1925), then published as a chapbook by Gallimard in 1927. It was the first work that Breton wrote after the "Manifesto of Surrealism" and is considered an imporant text. It did not appear in book from until 1934, in Breton's *Point du Jour*; it is translated in *Break of Day*, trans. Mark Polizotti and Mary Ann Caws (Lincoln: University of Nebraska, 1999).

[21]   Guillaume Apollinaire, "L'Ésprit nouveau et les poètes," *Mercure de France*, no. 491, vol. 80 (Dec. 1, 1918): 387.

[22]   Quoted in Pierre Naville, *La Révolution et les intellectuels: Que peuvent faire les surréalistes. Position de la question* (Paris: Gallimard, 1926), p. 146.

[23]   Apollinaire, "L'Ésprit nouveau et les poétes," p. 392.

[24]   Paul Scheerbart (1863–1915) was the pseudonym of Bruno Küfer. He wrote a manifesto titled *Glasarchitektur* (*Glass Architecture*) (Berlin: Verlag der Sturm, 1914), consisting of 111 aphoristic chapters which anticipate a "Total architecture of glass and iron," with implication both practical and spiritual; glass will combat vermin, decrease the risk of fire, and spawn a global culture organized around the potentials of glass. He also wrote a novel, *The Gray Cloth with Ten Percent White: A Novel on Glass Architecture* (or *Graue Tuch und zehn Prozent Weiß*) (Cambridge: MIT Press, 2001), which was published in the same year.

banquet.[25] At that time, shortly after the war, when the Surrealists, who deemed the celebration for a poet they worshiped compromised by the presence of nationalistic elements, burst out with the cry "Long live Germany," they remained within the boundaries of scandal, toward which, as is known, the bourgeoisie is as thick-skinned as it is sensitive to all action. There is remarkable agreement between the ways in which, under such political auspices, Apollinaire and Aragon saw the future of the poet. The chapters "Persecution" and "Murder" in Apollinaire's *Poète assassiné* contain the famous description of a pogrom against poets.[26] Publishing houses are stormed, books of poems thrown on the fire, poets lynched. And the same scenes are taking place at the same time all over the world. In Aragon, "Imagination,"[27] in anticipation of such horrors, calls its company to a last crusade.

To understand such prophecies, and to assess strategically the line arrived at by Surrealism, one must investigate the mode of thought widespread among the so-called well-meaning left-wing bourgeois intelligentsia. It manifests itself clearly enough in the present Russian orientation of these circles. We are not of course referring here to Béraud, who pioneered the lie about Russia, or to Fabre-Luce, who trots behind him like a devoted donkey, loaded with every kind of bourgeois ill will.[28] But how problematic is even the typical mediating book by Duhamel. How difficult to bear is the strained uprightness, the forced animation and sincerity of the Protestant method, dictated by embarrassment and linguistic ignorance, of placing things in some kind of symbolic illumination. How revealing his résumé: "the true, deeper revolution, which could in some sense transform the substance of the Slavonic soul itself, has not yet taken place."[29] It is typical of these left-wing French intellectuals – exactly as it is of their Russian counterparts, too – that their positive function derives entirely from a feeling of obligation, not to the Revolution, but to traditional culture. Their collective achievement, as far as it is positive, approximates conservation. But politically and economically they must always be considered a potential source of sabotage.

Characteristic of this whole left-wing bourgeois position is its irremediable coupling of idealistic morality with political practice. Only in contrast to the helpless compromises of "sentiment" are certain central features of Surrealism, indeed of the Surrealist tradition, to be understood. Little has happened so far to promote this understanding. The seduction was too great to regard the Satanism of a Rimbaud and a Lautréamont as a pendant to art for art's sake in an inventory of snobbery. If, however, one resolves to open up this romantic dummy, one finds something usable inside. One finds the cult of evil as a political device, however romantic, to disinfect and isolate against all moralizing dilettantism. Convinced of this, and coming across the scenario of a horror play by Breton that centers about a violation of children, one might perhaps go back a few decades. Between 1865 and 1875 a number of great anarchists, without knowing of one another, worked on their infernal machines. And the astonishing thing is that independently of one another they set its clock at exactly the same hour, and forty years later in Western Europe the writings of Dostoyevsky, Rimbaud, and Lautréamont exploded at the same time. One might, to be more exact, select from Dostoyevsky's entire work the one episode that was actually not published until about 1915, "Stavrogin's Confession" from *The Possessed*. This chapter, which touches very closely on the third canto of the *Chants de Maldoror*, contains a justification of evil in which certain motifs of Surrealism are more powerfully expressed than by any of its present spokesmen. For Stavrogin is a

[25]   A banquet for Saint-Pol-Roux took place on 2 July 1925, and the Surrealists, known to be his admirers were invited. Most of the invitees, however, were older and conservative. When the aging writer Rachilde commented that no girl would ever marry a German, Breton rose to his feet and accused her of insulting his friend Max Ernst. According to some he then flung his napkin in her face. A brawl broke out. Soupault, swinging from the chandelier, sent plates and glasses cascading to the floor, and cries of "Long live Germany" flew cross the room, crossing paths with fruit projectiles. More than any previous demonstration, this one unleashed a concerted fury in the contemporary press. But it was also the same day that 19 Surrealists had signed an "Appeal to Intellectual Workers" published in the Communist newspaper

L'Humanité, an appeal against the Rif War then taking place in Morocco.
[26]   Guillaume Apollinaire, *Le Poète assassiné*, nouvelle édition (Paris: Sans Pareil, 1927), p. 104.
[27]   See Louis Aragon, *Le Paysan de Paris* (Paris: Gallimard Folio, 1990), "Discours de l'imagination," pp. 80–4; or *Paris Peasant* (Boston: Exact Change, 1994), "Imaginations Discourse on Himself," pp. 64–7.
[28]   Henri Béraud (1885–1958), novelist and far-right journalist and polemicist; Alfred Fabre-Luce (1899–1983) was a right-wing historian and novelist.
[29]   Georges Duhamel (1884–1966), *Voyage de Moscou* (Paris: Mercure de France, 1922), p. 189.

Surrealist *avant la lettre*. No one else understood, as he did, how naïve is the view of the Philistines that goodness, for all the manly virtue of those who practice it, is God-inspired; whereas evil stems entirely from our spontaneity, and in it we are independent and self-sufficient beings. No one else saw inspiration, as he did, in even the most ignoble actions, and precisely in them. He considered vileness itself as something preformed, both in the course of the world and also in ourselves, to which we are disposed if not called, as the bourgeois idealist sees virtue. Dostoyevsky's God created not only heaven and earth and man and beast, but also baseness, vengeance, cruelty. And here, too, he gave the devil no opportunity to meddle in his handiwork. That is why all these vices have a pristine vitality in his work; they are perhaps not "splendid," but eternally new, "as on the first day," separated by an infinity from the clichés through which sin is perceived by the Philistine.

   The pitch of tension that enabled the poets under discussion to achieve at a distance their astonishing effects is documented quite scurrilously in the letter Isidore Ducasse addressed to his publisher on October 23, 1869, in an attempt to make his poetry look acceptable. He places himself in the line of descent from Mickiewicz, Milton, Southey, Alfred de Musset, Baudelaire,[30] and says: "Of course, I somewhat swelled the note to bring something new into this literature that, after all, only sings of despair in order to depress the reader and thus make him long all the more intensely for goodness as a remedy. So that in the end one really sings only of goodness, only the method is more philosophical and less naïve than that of the old school, of which only Victor Hugo and a few others are still alive."[31] But if Lautréamont's erratic book has any lineage at all, or, rather, can be assigned one, it is that of insurrection. Soupault's attempt, in his edition of the complete works in 1927, to write a political curriculum vitae for Isidore Ducasse was therefore a quite understandable and not unperceptive venture. Unfortunately, there is no documentation for it, and that adduced by Soupault rests on a confusion. On the other hand, and happily, a similar attempt in the case of Rimbaud was successful, and it is the achievement of Marcel Coulon[32] to have defended the poet's true image against the Catholic usurpation by Claudel and Berrichon.[33] Rimbaud is indeed a Catholic, but he is one, by his own account, in the most wretched part of himself, which he does not tire of denouncing and consigning to his own and everyone's hatred, his own and everyone's contempt: the part that forces him to confess that he does not understand revolt. But that is the concession of a communard dissatisfied with his own contribution who, by the time he turned his back on poetry, had long since – in his earliest work – taken leave of religion. "Hatred, to you I have entrusted my treasure," he writes in the *Saison en enfer*.[34] This is another dictum around which a poetics of Surrealism might grow like a climbing plant, to sink its roots deeper than the theory of "surprised" creation originated by Apollinaire, to the depth of the insights of Poe.

   Since Bakunin, Europe has lacked a radical concept of freedom.[35] The Surrealists have one. They are the first to liquidate the sclerotic liberal-moral-humanistic ideal of freedom, because they are convinced that "freedom, which on this earth can only be bought with a thousand of the hardest sacrifices, must be enjoyed unrestrictedly in its fullness without any kind of pragmatic calculation, as long as it lasts." And this proves to them that "mankind's struggle for liberation in its simplest revolutionary form (which, however, is liberation in every respect), remains the only cause worth serving." But are they successful in welding this experience of freedom to the other revolutionary experience that we have to acknowledge because it has been ours, the constructive, dictatorial side

---

[30]   Adam Mickiewicz (1798–1855), Polish poet and advocate of Polish national freedom; John Milton (1608–74), British poet and advocate of civil and religious liberty; Robert Southey (1774–1843), British poet and defender of the French Revolution; Alfred de Musset (1810–57), French Romantic poet and playwritght; Charles Baudelaire (1821–67), the most influential poet of the nineteenth century.

[31]   Comte de Lautréamont (Isidor Ducasse), *Maldoror and the Complete Works of the Comte de Lautréamont*, trans. Alexis Lykiard (Cambridge, MA: Exact Change, 1994), p. 258, letter of October 23, 1869, to Antoine Poulet-Malassis. Victor Hugo (1802–85), French poet, novelist, and dramatist, and the most important of the French Romantics.

[32]   Marcel Coulon, *Le Problème de Rimbaud, poète maudit* (Nimes: A. Gomes, 1923).

[33]   See *Oeuvres de Arthur Rimbaud – vers et prose*, ed. Paterne Berrichon, with a "Preface" by Paul Claudel (Paris: Mercure de France, 1912).

[34]   Rimbaud, *Illuminations* in *Oeuvres*, ed. Suzanne Bernard (Paris: Garnier Frères, 1960), p. 211; *A Season in Hell; the Illuminations*, trans. Enid Rhodes Peschel (Oxford: Oxford University Press, 1973), p. 43.

[35]   Mikhail Aleksandrovich Bakunin (1814–76), chief proponent of anarchism in the nineteenth century.

of revolution? In short, have they bound revolt to revolution? How are we to imagine an existence oriented solely toward Boulevard Bonne-Nouvelle, in rooms by Le Corbusier and Oud?[36]

To win the energies of intoxication for the revolution – this is the project about which Surrealism circles in all its books and enterprises. This it may call its most particular task. For them it is not enough that, as we know, an ecstatic component lives in every revolutionary act. This component is identical with the anarchic. But to place the accent exclusively on it would be to subordinate the methodical and disciplinary preparation for revolution entirely to a praxis oscillating between fitness exercises and celebration in advance. Added to this is an inadequate, undialectical conception of the nature of intoxication. The aesthetic of the painter, the poet, *en état de surprise*, of art as the reaction of one surprised, is enmeshed in a number of pernicious romantic prejudices. Any serious exploration of occult, surrealistic, phantasmagoric gifts and phenomena presupposes a dialectical intertwinement to which a romantic turn of mind is impervious. For histrionic or fanatical stress on the mysterious side of the mysterious takes us no further; we penetrate the mystery only to the degree that we recognize it in the everyday world, by virtue of a dialectical optic that perceives the everyday as impenetrable, the impenetrable as everyday. The most passionate investigation of telepathic phenomena, for example, will not teach us half as much about reading (which is an eminently telepathic process), as the profane illumination of reading about telepathic phenomena. And the most passionate investigation of the hashish trance will not teach us half as much about thinking (which is eminently narcotic), as the profane illumination of thinking about the hashish trance. The reader, the thinker, the loiterer, the *flâneur*, are types of illuminati just as much as the opium eater, the dreamer, the ecstatic. And more profane. Not to mention that most terrible drug – ourselves – which we take in solitude.

"To win the energies of intoxication for the revolution" – in other words, poetic politics? "We have tried that beverage. Anything, rather than that!" Well, it will interest you all the more how much an excursion into poetry clarifies things. For what is the program of the bourgeois parties? A bad poem on springtime, filled to bursting with metaphors. The socialist sees that "finer future of our children and grandchildren" in a condition in which all act "as if they were angels," and everyone has as much "as if he were rich," and everyone lives "as if he were free." Of angels, wealth, freedom, not a trace. These are mere images. And the stock imagery of these poets of the social-democratic associations? Their *gradus ad parnassum?*[37] Optimism. A very different air is breathed in the Naville essay that makes the "organization of pessimism" the call of the hour. In the name of his literary friends he delivers an ultimatum in face of which this unprincipled, dilettantish optimism must unfailingly show its true colors: where are the conditions for revolution? In the changing of attitudes or of external circumstances? That is the cardinal question that determines the relation of politics to morality and cannot be glossed over. Surrealism has come ever closer to the Communist answer. And that means pessimism all along the line. Absolutely. Mistrust in the fate of literature, mistrust in the fate of freedom, mistrust in the fate of European humanity, but three times mistrust in all reconciliation: between classes, between nations, between individuals. And unlimited trust only in I. G. Farben[38] and the peaceful perfection of the air force. But what now, what next?

Here due weight must be given to the insight that in the *Traité du style*, Aragon's last book,[39] required a distinction between metaphor and image, a happy insight into questions of style that needs extending. Extension: nowhere do these two – metaphor and image – collide so drastically and so irreconcilably as in politics. For to organize pessimism means nothing other than to expel moral metaphor from politics and to discover in political action a sphere reserved one hundred percent for images. This image sphere, however, can no longer be measured out by contemplation.

[36] Le Corbusier (adopted name of Charles-Edouard Jeanneret; 1887–1965) was a Swiss architect and city planner whose modernist functionalism was combined with bold, sweeping forms. Jacobus Johannes Pieter Oud (1890–1963) was a Dutch architect who, together with Theo van Doesburg, founded the influential journal *De Stijl* in 1917. He advocated an austere, geometric style, and his works include several massive housing projects.
[37] Latin for "ascent to Parnassus," Parnassus being the haunt of the muses in ancient Greek mythology.

[38] I. G. Farben (it's full name was: Interessengemeinschaft Farbenindustrie Aktiengesellschaft, or Syndicate of Dye-Industry Corporations) was the world's largest chemical concern, or cartel, between its founding in 1925 and its dissolution after the Second World War.
[39] Louis Aragon, *Traité du style* (Paris: Gallimard, 1928); *Treatise on Style*, ed. and trans. Alyson Waters (Lincoln: University of Nebraska Press, 1991).

If it is the double task of the revolutionary intelligentsia to overthrow the intellectual predomin-ance of the bourgeoisie and to make contact with the proletarian masses, the intelligentsia has failed almost entirely in the second part of this task because it can no longer be performed contem-platively. And yet this has hindered hardly anybody from approaching it again and again as if it could, and calling for proletarian poets, thinkers, and artists. To counter this, Trotsky had to point out – as early as *Literature and Revolution* – that such artists would only emerge from a victorious revolution.[40] In reality it is far less a matter of making the artist of bourgeois origin into a master of "proletarian art" than of deploying him, even at the expense of his artistic activity, at important points in this sphere of imagery. Indeed, might not perhaps the interruption of his "artistic career" be an essential part of his new function?

The jokes he tells are the better for it. And he tells them better. For in the joke, too, in invective, in misunderstanding, in all cases where an action puts forth its own image and exists, absorbing and consuming it, where nearness looks with its own eyes, the long-sought image sphere is opened, the world of universal and integral actualities, where the "best room" is missing – the sphere, in a word, in which political materialism and physical nature share the inner man, the psyche, the individual, or whatever else we wish to throw to them, with dialectical justice, so that no limb remains unrent. Nevertheless – indeed, precisely after such dialectical annihilation – this will still be a sphere of images and, more concretely, of bodies. For it must in the end be admitted: metaphysical materialism, of the brand of Vogt and Bukharin, as is attested by the experience of the Surrealists, and earlier of Hebel, Georg Büchner, Nietzsche, and Rimbaud, cannot lead without rupture to anthropological materialism.[41] There is a residue. The collective is a body, too. And the *physis* that is being organized for it in technology can, through all its political and factual reality, only be produced in that image sphere to which profane illumination initiates us. Only when in technology body and image so interpenetrate that all revolutionary tension becomes bodily collective innervation, and all the bodily innervations of the collective become revolutionary discharge, has reality transcended itself to the extent demanded by the *Communist Manifesto*. For the moment, only the Surrealists have understood its present commands. They exchange, to a man, the play of human features for the face of an alarm clock that in each minute rings for sixty seconds.

The Work of Art in the Age of Mechanical Reproduction (1936)
Walter Benjamin

"Our fine arts were developed, their types and uses were established, in times very different from the present, by men whose power of action upon things was insignificant in comparison with ours. But the amazing growth of our techniques, the adaptability and precision they have attained, the ideas and habits they are creating, make it a certainty that profound changes are impending in the ancient craft of the Beautiful. In all the arts there is a physical component which can no longer be considered or treated as it used to be, which cannot remain unaffected by our modern knowledge and power. For the last

[40]   Leon Trotsky (1879–1940) was an early Bolshevik and a Marxist theoretician; he was stripped of his posts and exiled in 1929. See his *Literature and Revolution* (original edition in Rus-sian, 1923; an incomplete translation appeared in German in 1924; New York: International Publishers, 1925; Ann Arbor: University of Michigan Press, 1960). He was assassinated in 1940, presumably by agents of Stalin.

[41]   Karl Vogt (1817–95) was a German scientist who later moved to Switzerland. Marx wrote a small book on him titled *Herr Vogt* (London: 1860) dismissing his "vulgar materialism." Nikolai Ivanovick Bukharin (1888–1938) was an early Bolshevik and prominent Marxist, stripped of his party posts in 1929 by Stalin, and a victim of a purge trial. Johann Peter Hebel (1760–1826) was a German journalist and prose stylist much admired by Benjamin. Georg Büchner (1813–37) was a German

dramatist noted for combining harsh, episodic structure with extreme naturalism and materialism. Friedrich Wilhelm Nietzsche (1844–1900) was a German philosopher and, for some, materialist.

WORK OF ART
The essay was first published in the *Zeitschrift für Sozialforschung* (*Journal for Social Research*) 5(1) (1936) in French translation. The English translation by Harry Zohn was first published in Walter Benjamin, *Illuminations: Essays and Reflections*, ed. Hannah Arendt (New York: Harcourt Brace, 1968). Zohn's and Arendt's notes are here marked with asterisks and daggers; Benjamin's original notes are marked with arabic numbering; and my own footnotes in this instance are marked with lower-case roman numerals.

*twenty years neither matter nor space nor time has been what it was from time immemorial. We must expect great innovations to transform the entire technique of the arts, thereby affecting artistic invention itself and perhaps even bringing about an amazing change in our very notion of art."**

– Paul Valéry, PIÈCES SUR L'ART, *"La Conquète de l'ubiquité,"* Paris.

Preface

When Marx undertook his critique of the capitalistic mode of production, this mode was in its infancy. Marx directed his efforts in such a way as to give them prognostic value. He went back to the basic conditions underlying capitalistic production and through his presentation showed what could be expected of capitalism in the future. The result was that one could expect it not only to exploit the proletariat with increasing intensity, but ultimately to create conditions which would make it possible to abolish capitalism itself.

The transformation of the superstructure, which takes place far more slowly than that of the substructure, has taken more than half a century to manifest in all areas of culture the change in the conditions of production. Only today can it be indicated what form this has taken. Certain prognostic requirements should be met by these statements. However, theses about the art of the proletariat after its assumption of power or about the art of a classless society would have less bearing on these demands than theses about the developmental tendencies of art under present conditions of production. Their dialectic is no less noticeable in the superstructure than in the economy. It would therefore be wrong to underestimate the value of such theses as a weapon. They brush aside a number of outmoded concepts, such as creativity and genius, eternal value and mystery – concepts whose uncontrolled (and at present almost uncontrollable) application would lead to a processing of data in the Fascist sense. The concepts which are introduced into the theory of art in what follows differ from the more familiar terms in that they are completely useless for the purposes of Fascism. They are, on the other hand, useful for the formulation of revolutionary demands in the politics of art.

I

In principle a work of art has always been reproducible. Manmade artifacts could always be imitated by men. Replicas were made by pupils in practice of their craft, by masters for diffusing their works, and, finally, by third parties in the pursuit of gain. Mechanical reproduction of a work of art, however, represents something new. Historically, it advanced intermittently and in leaps at long intervals, but with accelerated intensity. The Greeks knew only two procedures of technically reproducing works of art: founding and stamping. Bronzes, terra cottas, and coins were the only art works which they could produce in quantity. All others were unique and could not be mechanically reproduced. With the woodcut graphic art became mechanically reproducible for the first time, long before script became reproducible by print. The enormous changes which printing, the mechanical reproduction of writing, has brought about in literature are a familiar story. However, within the phenomenon which we are here examining from the perspective of world history, print is merely a special, though particularly important, case. During the Middle Ages engraving and etching were added to the woodcut; at the beginning of the nineteenth century lithography made its appearance.

With lithography[i] the technique of reproduction reached an essentially new stage. This much more direct process was distinguished by the tracing of the design on a stone rather than its incision on a block of wood or its etching on a copperplate and permitted graphic art for the first time to put its products on the market, not only in large numbers as hitherto, but also in daily changing

---

* Quoted from Paul Valéry, *Aesthetics*, "The Conquest of Ubiquity," translated by Ralph Manheim, p. 225. Pantheon Books, Bollingen Series, New York, 1964.

i Lithography was invented in 1798 by Alois Senefelder in Bavaria, Germany.

forms. Lithography enabled graphic art to illustrate everyday life, and it began to keep pace with printing. But only a few decades after its invention, lithography was surpassed by photography. For the first time in the process of pictorial reproduction, photography freed the hand of the most important artistic functions which henceforth devolved only upon the eye looking into a lens. Since the eye perceives more swiftly than the hand can draw, the process of pictorial reproduction was accelerated so enormously that it could keep pace with speech. A film operator shooting a scene in the studio captures the images at the speed of an actor's speech. Just as lithography virtually implied the illustrated newspaper, so did photography foreshadow the sound film. The technical reproduction of sound was tackled at the end of the last century. These convergent endeavors made predictable a situation which Paul Valéry pointed up in this sentence: "Just as water, gas, and electricity are brought into our houses from far off to satisfy our needs in response to a minimal effort, so we shall be supplied with visual or auditory images, which will appear and disappear at a simple movement of the hand, hardly more than a sign" (*op. cit.*, p. 226). Around 1900 technical reproduction had reached a standard that not only permitted it to reproduce all transmitted works of art and thus to cause the most profound change in their impact upon the public; it also had captured a place of its own among the artistic processes. For the study of this standard nothing is more revealing than the nature of the repercussions that these two different manifestations – the reproduction of works of art and the art of the film – have had on art in its traditional form.

II

Even the most perfect reproduction of a work of art is lacking in one element: its presence in time and space, its unique existence at the place where it happens to be. This unique existence of the work of art determined the history to which it was subject throughout the time of its existence. This includes the changes which it may have suffered in physical condition over the years as well as the various changes in its ownership.[1] The traces of the first can be revealed only by chemical or physical analyses which it is impossible to perform on a reproduction; changes of ownership are subject to a tradition which must be traced from the situation of the original.

The presence of the original is the prerequisite to the concept of authenticity. Chemical analyses of the patina of a bronze can help to establish this, as does the proof that a given manuscript of the Middle Ages stems from an archive of the fifteenth century. The whole sphere of authenticity is outside technical – and, of course, not only technical – reproducibility.[2] Confronted with its manual reproduction, which was usually branded as a forgery, the original preserved all its authority; not so *vis à vis* technical reproduction. The reason is twofold. First, process reproduction is more independent of the original than manual reproduction. For example, in photography, process reproduction can bring out those aspects of the original that are unattainable to the naked eye yet accessible to the lens, which is adjustable and chooses its angle at will. And photographic reproduction, with the aid of certain processes, such as enlargement or slow motion, can capture images which escape natural vision. Secondly, technical reproduction can put the copy of the original into situations which would be out of reach for the original itself. Above all, it enables the original to meet the beholder halfway, be it in the form of a photograph or a phonograph record. The cathedral leaves its locale to be received in the studio of a lover of art; the choral production, performed in an auditorium or in the open air, resounds in the drawing room.

The situations into which the product of mechanical reproduction can be brought may not touch the actual work of art, yet the quality of its presence is always depreciated. This holds not only for the art work but also, for instance, for a landscape which passes in review before the spectator in a movie. In the case of the art object, a most sensitive nucleus – namely, its authenticity – is interfered with whereas no natural object is vulnerable on that score. The authenticity of a thing is the essence of all that is transmissible from its beginning, ranging from its substantive duration to its testimony to the history which it has experienced. Since the historical testimony rests on the authenticity, the former, too, is jeopardized by reproduction when substantive duration ceases to matter. And what is really jeopardized when the historical testimony is affected is the authority of the object.[3]

One might subsume the eliminated element in the term "aura" and go on to say: that which withers in the age of mechanical reproduction is the aura of the work of art. This is a symptomatic process whose significance points beyond the realm of art. One might generalize by saying: the technique of reproduction detaches the reproduced object from the domain of tradition. By making many reproductions it substitutes a plurality of copies for a unique existence. And in permitting the reproduction to meet the beholder or listener in his own particular situation, it reactivates the object reproduced. These two processes lead to a tremendous shattering of tradition which is the obverse of the contemporary crisis and renewal of mankind. Both processes are intimately connected with the contemporary mass movements. Their most powerful agent is the film. Its social significance, particularly in its most positive form, is inconceivable without its destructive, cathartic aspect, that is, the liquidation of the traditional value of the cultural heritage. This phenomenon is most palpable in the great historical films. It extends to ever new positions. In 1927 Abel Gance exclaimed enthusiastically: "Shakespeare, Rembrandt, Beethoven will make films . . . all legends, all mythologies and all myths, all founders of religion, and the very religions . . . await their exposed resurrection, and the heroes crowd each other at the gate."[*] Presumably without intending it, he issued an invitation to a far-reaching liquidation.

III

During long periods of history, the mode of human sense perception changes with humanity's entire mode of existence. The manner in which human sense perception is organized, the medium in which it is accomplished, is determined not only by nature but by historical circumstances as well. The fifth century, with its great shifts of population, saw the birth of the late Roman art industry and the Vienna Genesis,[ii] and there developed not only an art different from that of antiquity but also a new kind of perception. The scholars of the Viennese school, Riegl and Wickhoff,[iii] who resisted the weight of classical tradition under which these later art forms had been buried, were the first to draw conclusions from them concerning the organization of perception at the time. However far-reaching their insight, these scholars limited themselves to showing the significant, formal hallmark which characterized perception in late Roman times. They did not attempt – and, perhaps, saw no way – to show the social transformations expressed by these changes of perception. The conditions for an analogous insight are more favorable in the present. And if changes in the medium of contemporary perception can be comprehended as decay of the aura, it is possible to show its social causes.

The concept of aura which was proposed above with reference to historical objects may usefully be illustrated with reference to the aura of natural ones. We define the aura of the latter as the unique phenomenon of a distance, however close it may be. If, while resting on a summer afternoon, you follow with your eyes a mountain range on the horizon or a branch which casts its shadow over you, you experience the aura of those mountains, of that branch. This image makes it easy to comprehend the social bases of the contemporary decay of the aura. It rests on two circumstances, both of which are related to the increasing significance of the masses in contemporary life. Namely, the desire of contemporary masses to bring things "closer" spatially and humanly, which is just as ardent as their bent toward overcoming the uniqueness of every reality by accepting its reproduction.[4] Every day the urge grows stronger to get hold of an object at very close range by way of its likeness, its reproduction. Unmistakably, reproduction as offered by picture magazines and newsreels differs from the image seen by the unarmed eye. Uniqueness and permanence are as

[*]   Abel Gance, "Le Temps de l'image est venu," *L'Art cinémato-graphique*, vol. 2, pp. 94 f., Paris, 1927.

[ii]   *The Vienna Genesis* (*Die Weiner Genesis*) was the title of a book (Vienna: T. Tempsky, 1895) by the Austrian cultural historian Franz Wickhoff (1853–1909), which reevaluated the late-antique phase of Roman art, and in German-speaking areas the book's title became a term to describe that late-antique period, as Benjamin is doing here.

[iii]   Alois Riegl (1858–1905) was an Austrian art historian, who is often characterized as the co-founder the Viennese school, together with Franz Wickhoff (on Wickhoff, see the preceding note). Riegl also wrote about late-antique art, but dealt more extensively with questions of methodology.

closely linked in the latter as are transitoriness and reproducibility in the former. To pry an object from its shell, to destroy its aura, is the mark of a perception whose "sense of the universal equality of things"[iv] has increased to such a degree that it extracts it even from a unique object by means of reproduction. Thus is manifested in the field of perception what in the theoretical sphere is noticeable in the increasing importance of statistics. The adjustment of reality to the masses and of the masses to reality is a process of unlimited scope, as much for thinking as for perception.

IV

The uniqueness of a work of art is inseparable from its being imbedded in the fabric of tradition. This tradition itself is thoroughly alive and extremely changeable. An ancient statue of Venus, for example, stood in a different traditional context with the Greeks, who made it an object of veneration, than with the clerics of the Middle Ages, who viewed it as an ominous idol. Both of them, however, were equally confronted with its uniqueness, that is, its aura. Originally the contextual integration of art in tradition found its expression in the cult. We know that the earliest art works originated in the service of a ritual – first the magical, then the religious kind. It is significant that the existence of the work of art with reference to its aura is never entirely separated from its ritual function.[5] In other words, the unique value of the "authentic" work of art has its basis in ritual, the location of its original use value. This ritualistic basis, however remote, is still recognizable as secularized ritual even in the most profane forms of the cult of beauty.[6] The secular cult of beauty, developed during the Renaissance and prevailing for three centuries, clearly showed that ritualistic basis in its decline and the first deep crisis which befell it. With the advent of the first truly revolutionary means of reproduction, photography, simultaneously with the rise of socialism, art sensed the approaching crisis which has become evident a century later. At the time, art reacted with the doctrine of *l'art pour l'art*,[v] that is, with a theology of art. This gave rise to what might be called a negative theology in the form of the idea of "pure" art, which not only denied any social function of art but also any categorizing by subject matter. (In poetry, Mallarmé was the first to take this position.)

 An analysis of art in the age of mechanical reproduction must do justice to these relationships, for they lead us to an all-important insight: for the first time in world history, mechanical reproduction emancipates the work of art from its parasitical dependence on ritual. To an ever greater degree the work of art reproduced becomes the work of art designed for reproducibility.[7] From a photographic negative, for example, one can make any number of prints; to ask for the "authentic" print makes no sense. But the instant the criterion of authenticity ceases to be applicable to artistic production, the total function of art is reversed. Instead of being based on ritual, it begins to be based on another practice – politics.

V

Works of art are received and valued on different planes. Two polar types stand out: with one, the accent is on the cult value; with the other, on the exhibition value of the work.[8] Artistic production begins with ceremonial objects destined to serve in a cult. One may assume that what mattered was their existence, not their being on view. The elk portrayed by the man of the Stone Age on the walls of his cave was an instrument of magic. He did expose it to his fellow men, but in the main it was meant for the spirits. Today the cult value would seem to demand that the work of art remain hidden. Certain statues of gods are accessible only to the priest in the cella; certain Madonnas remain covered nearly all year round; certain sculptures on medieval cathedrals are invisible to the spectator on ground level. With the emancipation of the various art practices from ritual go

iv "sense of the universal equality of things" [*Sinn für das Gleichartige in der Welt*], from Johannes V. Jensen (1873–1950), a Danish writer, *Exotische Novellen*, trans. Julia Koppel (Berlin: Fischer, 1919).

v The phrase is first used by the French poet and writer Théophile Gautier (1811–72) in the preface to his novel *Mademoiselle de Maupin* (1835).

increasing opportunities for the exhibition of their products. It is easier to exhibit a portrait bust that can be sent here and there than to exhibit the statue of a divinity that has its fixed place in the interior of a temple. The same holds for the painting as against the mosaic or fresco that preceded it. And even though the public presentability of a mass originally may have been just as great as that of a symphony, the latter originated at the moment when its public presentability promised to surpass that of the mass.

With the different methods of technical reproduction of a work of art, its fitness for exhibition increased to such an extent that the quantitative shift between its two poles turned into a qualitative transformation of its nature. This is comparable to the situation of the work of art in prehistoric times when, by the absolute emphasis on its cult value, it was, first and foremost, an instrument of magic. Only later did it come to be recognized as a work of art. In the same way today, by the absolute emphasis on its exhibition value the work of art becomes a creation with entirely new functions, among which the one we are conscious of, the artistic function, later may be recognized as incidental.[9] This much is certain: today photography and the film are the most serviceable exemplifications of this new function.

VI

In photography, exhibition value begins to displace cult value all along the line. But cult value does not give way without resistance. It retires into an ultimate retrenchment: the human countenance. It is no accident that the portrait was the focal point of early photography. The cult of remembrance of loved ones, absent or dead, offers a last refuge for the cult value of the picture. For the last time the aura emanates from the early photographs in the fleeting expression of a human face. This is what constitutes their melancholy, incomparable beauty. But as man withdraws from the photographic image, the exhibition value for the first time shows its superiority to the ritual value. To have pinpointed this new stage constitutes the incomparable significance of Atget, who, around 1900, took photographs of deserted Paris streets.[vii] It has quite justly been said of him that he photographed them like scenes of crime. The scene of a crime, too, is deserted; it is photographed for the purpose of establishing evidence. With Atget, photographs become standard evidence for historical occurrences, and acquire a hidden political significance. They demand a specific kind of approach; free-floating contemplation is not appropriate to them. They stir the viewer; he feels challenged by them in a new way. At the same time picture magazines begin to put up signposts for him, right ones or wrong ones, no matter. For the first time, captions have become obligatory. And it is clear that they have an altogether different character than the title of a painting. The directives which the captions give to those looking at pictures in illustrated magazines soon become even more explicit and more imperative in the film where the meaning of each single picture appears to be prescribed by the sequence of all preceding ones.

VII

The nineteenth-century dispute as to the artistic value of painting versus photography today seems devious and confused. This does not diminish its importance, however; if anything, it underlines it. The dispute was in fact the symptom of a historical transformation the universal impact of which was not realized by either of the rivals. When the age of mechanical reproduction separated art from its basis in cult, the semblance of its autonomy disappeared forever. The resulting change in the function of art transcended the perspective of the century; for a long time it even escaped that of the twentieth century, which experienced the development of the film.

Earlier much futile thought had been devoted to the question of whether photography is an art. The primary question – whether the very invention of photography had not transformed the entire

---

[vi] Stéphan Mallarmé (1842–98), French symbolist poet and exponent of "pure" art.

[vii] Eugène Atget (1856–1927) became famous for his photographs of Paris streets; see Molly Nesbit, *Atget's Seven Albums* (New Haven: Yale University Press, 1992).

nature of art – was not raised. Soon the film theoreticians asked the same ill-considered question with regard to the film. But the difficulties which photography caused traditional aesthetics were mere child's play as compared to those raised by the film. Whence the insensitive and forced character of early theories of the film. Abel Gance, for instance, compares the film with hieroglyphs: "Here, by a remarkable regression, we have come back to the level of expression of the Egyptians.... Pictorial language has not yet matured because our eyes have not yet adjusted to it. There is as yet insufficient respect for, insufficient cult of, what it expresses."[*] Or, in the words of Séverin-Mars: "What art has been granted a dream more poetical and more real at the same time! Approached in this fashion the film might represent an incomparable means of expression. Only the most high-minded persons, in the most perfect and mysterious moments of their lives, should be allowed to enter its ambience." [†][viii] Alexandre Arnoux concludes his fantasy about the silent film with the question: "Do not all the bold descriptions we have given amount to the definition of prayer?"[‡] It is instructive to note how their desire to class the film among the "arts" forces these theoreticians to read ritual elements into it – with a striking lack of discretion. Yet when these speculations were published, films like *L'Opinion publique* and *The Gold Rush*[ix] had already appeared. This, however, did not keep Abel Gance from adducing hieroglyphs for purposes of comparison, nor Séverin-Mars from speaking of the film as one might speak of paintings by Fra Angelico.[x] Characteristically, even today ultrareactionary authors give the film a similar contextual significance – if not an outright sacred one, then at least a supernatural one. Commenting on Max Reinhardt's film version of *A Midsummer Night's Dream*, Werfel states that undoubtedly it was the sterile copying of the exterior world with its streets, interiors, railroad stations, restaurants, motorcars, and beaches which until now had obstructed the elevation of the film to the realm of art. "The film has not yet realized its true meaning, its real possibilities... these consist in its unique faculty to express by natural means and with incomparable persuasiveness all that is fairylike, marvelous, supernatural."[*]

VIII

The artistic performance of a stage actor is definitely presented to the public by the actor in person; that of the screen actor, however, is presented by a camera, with a twofold consequence. The camera that presents the performance of the film actor to the public need not respect the performance as an integral whole. Guided by the cameraman, the camera continually changes its position with respect to the performance. The sequence of positional views which the editor composes from the material supplied him constitutes the completed film. It comprises certain factors of movement which are in reality those of the camera, not to mention special camera angles, close-ups, etc. Hence, the performance of the actor is subjected to a series of optical tests. This is the first consequence of the fact that the actor's performance is presented by means of a camera. Also, the film actor lacks the opportunity of the stage actor to adjust to the audience during his performance, since he does not present his performance to the audience in person. This permits the audience to take the position of a critic, without experiencing any personal contact with the actor. The audience's identification with the actor is really an identification with the camera. Consequently the audience takes the position of the camera; its approach is that of testing.[10] This is not the approach to which cult values may be exposed.

[*]   Abel Gance, *op. cit.*, pp. 100–1.
[†]   Séverin-Mars, quoted by Abel Gance, *op. cit.*, p. 100.
[viii]   Severin-Mars was a French actor who starred in two classics of early French cinema directed by Abel Gance, *La Dixième Symphonie* (1918) and *J'Accuse* (1919).
[‡]Alexandre Arnoux, *Cinéma pris*, 1929, p. 28.
[ix]   *L'Opinion publique* was the French title of Charlie Chaplin's 1923 Film, *A Woman of Paris*; *The Gold Rush* was another film by Chaplin, released in 1925.

[x]   Fra Giovanni Angelico (1387–1455) of Fiesole was an Italian painter admired for his stylistic purity, evident in the 45 frescos in cells and corridors of the convent of San Marco, Florence.
[*]   Franz Werfel, "Ein Sommernachtstraum, Ein Film von Shakespeare und Reinhardt," *Neues Wiener Journal*, cited in *Lu* 15, November, 1935.

IX

For the film, what matters primarily is that the actor represents himself to the public before the camera, rather than representing someone else. One of the first to sense the actor's metamorphosis by this form of testing was Pirandello. Though his remarks on the subject in his novel *Si Gira* were limited to the negative aspects of the question and to the silent film only, this hardly impairs their validity. For in this respect, the sound film did not change anything essential. What matters is that the part is acted not for an audience but for a mechanical contrivance – in the case of the sound film, for two of them. "The film actor," wrote Pirandello, "feels as if in exile – exiled not only from the stage but also from himself. With a vague sense of discomfort he feels inexplicable emptiness: his body loses its corporeality, it evaporates, it is deprived of reality, life, voice, and the noises caused by his moving about, in order to be changed into a mute image, flickering an instant on the screen, then vanishing into silence.... The projector will play with his shadow before the public, and he himself must be content to play before the camera."* This situation might also be characterized as follows: for the first time – and this is the effect of the film – man has to operate with his whole living person, yet forgoing its aura. For aura is tied to his presence; there can be no replica of it. The aura which, on the stage, emanates from Macbeth, cannot be separated for the spectators from that of the actor. However, the singularity of the shot in the studio is that the camera is substituted for the public. Consequently, the aura that envelops the actor vanishes, and with it the aura of the figure he portrays.

It is not surprising that it should be a dramatist such as Pirandello who, in characterizing the film, inadvertently touches on the very crisis in which we see the theater. Any thorough study proves that there is indeed no greater contrast than that of the stage play to a work of art that is completely subject to or, like the film, founded in, mechanical reproduction. Experts have long recognized that in the film "the greatest effects are almost always obtained by 'acting' as little as possible...." In 1932 Rudolf Arnheim saw "the latest trend ... in treating the actor as a stage prop chosen for its characteristics and ... inserted at the proper place."[11] With this idea something else is closely connected. The stage actor identifies himself with the character of his role. The film actor very often is denied this opportunity. His creation is by no means all of a piece; it is composed of many separate performances. Besides certain fortuitous considerations, such as cost of studio, availability of fellow players, décor, etc., there are elementary necessities of equipment that split the actor's work into a series of mountable episodes. In particular, lighting and its installation require the presentation of an event that, on the screen, unfolds as a rapid and unified scene, in a sequence of separate shootings which may take hours at the studio; not to mention more obvious montage. Thus a jump from the window can be shot in the studio as a jump from a scaffold, and the ensuing flight, if need be, can be shot weeks later when outdoor scenes are taken. Far more paradoxical cases can easily be construed. Let us assume that an actor is supposed to be startled by a knock at the door. If his reaction is not satisfactory, the director can resort to an expedient: when the actor happens to be at the studio again he has a shot fired behind him without his being forewarned of it. The frightened reaction can be shot now and be cut into the screen version. Nothing more strikingly shows that art has left the realm of the "beautiful semblance" which, so far, had been taken to be the only sphere where art could thrive.

X

The feeling of strangeness that overcomes the actor before the camera, as Pirandello describes it, is basically of the same kind as the estrangement felt before one's own image in the mirror. But now the reflected image has become separable, transportable. And where is it transported? Before the public.[12] Never for a moment does the screen actor cease to be conscious of this fact. While facing

---

* Luigi Pirandello, *Si Gira*, quoted by Léon Pierre-Quint, "Signification du cinéma," *L'Art cinématographique, op. cit.*, pp. 14–15.

the camera he knows that ultimately he will face the public, the consumers who constitute the market. This market, where he offers not only his labor but also his whole self, his heart and soul, is beyond his reach. During the shooting he has as little contact with it as any article made in a factory. This may contribute to that oppression, that new anxiety which, according to Pirandello, grips the actor before the camera. The film responds to the shriveling of the aura with an artificial build-up of the "personality" outside the studio. The cult of the movie star, fostered by the money of the film industry, preserves not the unique aura of the person but the "spell of the personality," the phony spell of a commodity. So long as the movie-makers' capital sets the fashion, as a rule no other revolutionary merit can be accredited to today's film than the promotion of a revolutionary criticism of traditional concepts of art. We do not deny that in some cases today's films can also promote revolutionary criticism of social conditions, even of the distribution of property. However, our present study is no more specifically concerned with this than is the film production of Western Europe.

It is inherent in the technique of the film as well as that of sports that everybody who witnesses its accomplishments is somewhat of an expert. This is obvious to anyone listening to a group of newspaper boys leaning on their bicycles and discussing the outcome of a bicycle race. It is not for nothing that newspaper publishers arrange races for their delivery boys. These arouse great interest among the participants, for the victor has an opportunity to rise from delivery boy to professional racer. Similarly, the newsreel offers everyone the opportunity to rise from passer-by to movie extra. In this way any man might even find himself part of a work of art, as witness Vertoff's *Three Songs About Lenin* or Ivens' *Borinage*.[xi] Any man today can lay claim to being filmed. This claim can best be elucidated by a comparative look at the historical situation of contemporary literature.

For centuries a small number of writers were confronted by many thousands of readers. This changed toward the end of the last century. With the increasing extension of the press, which kept placing new political, religious, scientific, professional, and local organs before the readers, an increasing number of readers became writers – at first, occasional ones. It began with the daily press opening to its readers space for "letters to the editor." And today there is hardly a gainfully employed European who could not, in principle, find an opportunity to publish somewhere or other comments on his work, grievances, documentary reports, or that sort of thing. Thus, the distinction between author and public is about to lose its basic character. The difference becomes merely functional; it may vary from case to case. At any moment the reader is ready to turn into a writer. As expert, which he had to become willy-nilly in an extremely specialized work process, even if only in some minor respect, the reader gains access to authorship. In the Soviet Union work itself is given a voice. To present it verbally is part of a man's ability to perform the work. Literary license is now founded on polytechnic rather than specialized training and thus becomes common property.[13]

All this can easily be applied to the film, where transitions that in literature took centuries have come about in a decade. In cinematic practice, particularly in Russia, this change-over has partially become established reality. Some of the players whom we meet in Russian films are not actors in our sense but people who portray *themselves* – and primarily in their own work process. In Western Europe the capitalistic exploitation of the film denies consideration to modern man's legitimate claim to being reproduced. Under these circumstances the film industry is trying hard to spur the interest of the masses through illusion-promoting spectacles and dubious speculations.

XI

The shooting of a film, especially of a sound film, affords a spectacle unimaginable anywhere at any time before this. It presents a process in which it is impossible to assign to a spectator a viewpoint

---

[xi] Dziga Vertov (1896–1954), Russian filmmaker, directed *Three Songs of Lenin* in 1933, a documentary sound film in six reels produced by Mezhrabpomfilm. The cameramen were D. Sourenski, M. Magidson, and B. Mstyrsky. Henri Stock (1907–99), a Belgian filmmaker, and Joris Ivens (1898–1989), a Danish filmmaker, co-directed and co-wrote the script for *Misère au Borinage* (*Misery in the Borinage*, but usually the English title is simply *Borinage*) in 1934, a documentary silent film that lasts 34 minutes. The two co-directors also served as the cameramen, together with François Rent, and the film was produced by Club de l'Ecran, EPI.

which would exclude from the actual scene such extraneous accessories as camera equipment, lighting machinery, staff assistants, etc. – unless his eye were on a line parallel with the lens. This circumstance, more than any other, renders superficial and insignificant any possible similarity between a scene in the studio and one on the stage. In the theater one is well aware of the place from which the play cannot immediately be detected as illusionary. There is no such place for the movie scene that is being shot. Its illusionary nature is that of the second degree, the result of cutting. That is to say, in the studio the mechanical equipment has penetrated so deeply into reality that its pure aspect freed from the foreign substance of equipment is the result of a special procedure, namely, the shooting by the specially adjusted camera and the mounting of the shot together with other similar ones. The equipment-free aspect of reality here has become the height of artifice; the sight of immediate reality has become an orchid in the land of technology.

Even more revealing is the comparison of these circumstances, which differ so much from those of the theater, with the situation in painting. Here the question is: How does the cameraman compare with the painter? To answer this we take recourse to an analogy with a surgical operation. The surgeon represents the polar opposite of the magician. The magician heals a sick person by the laying on of hands; the surgeon cuts into the patient's body. The magician maintains the natural distance between the patient and himself; though he reduces it very slightly by the laying on of hands, he greatly increases it by virtue of his authority. The surgeon does exactly the reverse; he greatly diminishes the distance between himself and the patient by penetrating into the patient's body, and increases it but little by the caution with which his hand moves among the organs. In short, in contrast to the magician – who is still hidden in the medical practitioner – the surgeon at the decisive moment abstains from facing the patient man to man; rather, it is through the operation that he penetrates into him.

Magician and surgeon compare to painter and cameraman. The painter maintains in his work a natural distance from reality, the cameraman penetrates deeply into its web.[14] There is a tremendous difference between the pictures they obtain. That of the painter is a total one, that of the cameraman consists of multiple fragments which are assembled under a new law. Thus, for contemporary man the representation of reality by the film is incomparably more significant than that of the painter, since it offers, precisely because of the thoroughgoing permeation of reality with mechanical equipment, an aspect of reality which is free of all equipment. And that is what one is entitled to ask from a work of art.

XII

Mechanical reproduction of art changes the reaction of the masses toward art. The reactionary attitude toward a Picasso painting changes into the progressive reaction toward a Chaplin movie.[xii] The progressive reaction is characterized by the direct, intimate fusion of visual and emotional enjoyment with the orientation of the expert. Such fusion is of great social significance. The greater the decrease in the social significance of an art form, the sharper the distinction between criticism and enjoyment by the public. The conventional is uncritically enjoyed, and the truly new is criticized with aversion. With regard to the screen, the critical and the receptive attitudes of the public coincide. The decisive reason for this is that individual reactions are predetermined by the mass audience response they are about to produce, and this is nowhere more pronounced than in the film. The moment these responses become manifest they control each other. Again, the comparison with painting is fruitful. A painting has always had an excellent chance to be viewed by one person or by a few. The simultaneous contemplation of paintings by a large public, such as developed in the nineteenth century, is an early symptom of the crisis of painting, a crisis which was by no means occasioned exclusively by photography but rather in a relatively independent manner by the appeal of art works to the masses.

xii   Pablo Picasso (1881–1973) was a Spanish painter who resided in Paris; Charlie Chaplin (1889–1977) was an actor and director, born in London but emigrated in 1910, who revolution- ized the language of cinema and became one of the most loved performers of all time.

Painting simply is in no position to present an object for simultaneous collective experience, as it was possible for architecture at all times, for the epic poem in the past, and for the movie today. Although this circumstance in itself should not lead one to conclusions about the social role of painting, it does constitute a serious threat as soon as painting, under special conditions and, as it were, against its nature, is confronted directly by the masses. In the churches and monasteries of the Middle Ages and at the princely courts up to the end of the eighteenth century, a collective reception of paintings did not occur simultaneously, but by graduated and hierarchized mediation. The change that has come about is an expression of the particular conflict in which painting was implicated by the mechanical reproducibility of paintings. Although paintings began to be publicly exhibited in galleries and salons, there was no way for the masses to organize and control themselves in their reception.[15] Thus the same public which responds in a progressive manner toward a grotesque film is bound to respond in a reactionary manner to surrealism.

XIII

The characteristics of the film lie not only in the manner in which man presents himself to mechanical equipment but also in the manner in which, by means of this apparatus, man can represent his environment. A glance at occupational psychology illustrates the testing capacity of the equipment. Psychoanalysis illustrates it in a different perspective. The film has enriched our field of perception with methods which can be illustrated by those of Freudian theory. Fifty years ago, a slip of the tongue passed more or less unnoticed. Only exceptionally may such a slip have revealed dimensions of depth in a conversation which had seemed to be taking its course on the surface. Since the *Psychopathology of Everyday Life* things have changed.[xiii] This book isolated and made analyzable things which had heretofore floated along unnoticed in the broad stream of perception. For the entire spectrum of optical, and now also acoustical, perception the film has brought about a similar deepening of apperception. It is only an obverse of this fact that behavior items shown in a movie can be analyzed much more precisely and from more points of view than those presented on paintings or on the stage. As compared with painting, filmed behavior lends itself more readily to analysis because of its incomparably more precise statements of the situation. In comparison with the stage scene, the filmed behavior item lends itself more readily to analysis because it can be isolated more easily. This circumstance derives its chief importance from its tendency to promote the mutual penetration of art and science. Actually, of a screened behavior item which is neatly brought out in a certain situation, like a muscle of a body, it is difficult to say which is more fascinating, its artistic value or its value for science. To demonstrate the identity of the artistic and scientific uses of photography which heretofore usually were separated will be one of the revolutionary functions of the film.[16]

By close-ups of the things around us, by focusing on hidden details of familiar objects, by exploring commonplace milieus under the ingenious guidance of the camera, the film, on the one hand, extends our comprehension of the necessities which rule our lives; on the other hand, it manages to assure us of an immense and unexpected field of action. Our taverns and our metropolitan streets, our offices and furnished rooms, our railroad stations and our factories appeared to have us locked up hopelessly. Then came the film and burst this prison-world asunder by the dynamite of the tenth of a second, so that now, in the midst of its far-flung ruins and debris, we calmly and adventurously go traveling. With the close-up, space expands; with slow motion, movement is extended. The enlargement of a snapshot does not simply render more precise what in any case was visible, though unclear: it reveals entirely new structural formations of the subject. So, too, slow motion not only presents familiar qualities of movement but reveals in them entirely unknown ones "which, far from looking like retarded rapid movements, give the effect of singularly

---

[xiii]   Freud published *Zur Psychopathologie des Alltagslebens* in 1905, which was followed by the English *The Psychopathology of Everyday Life*, trans. A. A. Brill (London, New York: Macmillan, 1914) and French *La Psychopathologie de la vie quotidienne*, trans. S. Jankélévitch (Paris: Payot, 1922).

gliding, floating, supernatural motions.".* Evidently a different nature opens itself to the camera than opens to the naked eye – if only because an unconsciously penetrated space is substituted for a space consciously explored by man. Even if one has a general knowledge of the way people walk, one knows nothing of a person's posture during the fractional second of a stride. The act of reaching for a lighter or a spoon is familiar routine, yet we hardly know what really goes on between hand and metal, not to mention how this fluctuates with our moods. Here the camera intervenes with the resources of its lowerings and liftings, its interruptions and isolations, its extensions and accelerations, its enlargements and reductions. The camera introduces us to unconscious optics as does psychoanalysis to unconscious impulses.

XIV

One of the foremost tasks of art has always been the creation of a demand which could be fully satisfied only later.[17] The history of every art form shows critical epochs in which a certain art form aspires to effects which could be fully obtained only with a changed technical standard, that is to say, in a new art form. The extravagances and crudities of art which thus appear, particularly in the so-called decadent epochs, actually arise from the nucleus of its richest historical energies. In recent years, such barbarisms were abundant in Dadaism.[xiv] It is only now that its impulse becomes discernible: Dadaism attempted to create by pictorial – and literary – means the effects which the public today seeks in the film.

Every fundamentally new, pioneering creation of demands will carry beyond its goal. Dadaism did so to the extent that it sacrificed the market values which are so characteristic of the film in favor of higher ambitions – though of course it was not conscious of such intentions as here described. The Dadaists attached much less importance to the sales value of their work than to its uselessness for contemplative immersion. The studied degradation of their material was not the least of their means to achieve this uselessness. Their poems are "word salad" containing obscenities and every imaginable waste product of language. The same is true of their paintings, on which they mounted buttons and tickets. What they intended and achieved was a relentless destruction of the aura of their creations, which they branded as reproductions with the very means of production. Before a painting of Arp's or a poem by August Stramm[xv] it is impossible to take time for contemplation and evaluation as one would before a canvas of Derain's or a poem by Rilke.[xvi] In the decline of middle-class society, contemplation became a school for asocial behavior; it was countered by distraction as a variant of social conduct.[18] Dadaistic activities actually assured a rather vehement distraction by making works of art the center of scandal. One requirement was foremost: to outrage the public.

From an alluring appearance or persuasive structure of sound the work of art of the Dadaists became an instrument of ballistics. It hit the spectator like a bullet, it happened to him, thus acquiring a tactile quality. It promoted a demand for the film, the distracting element of which is also primarily tactile, being based on changes of place and focus which periodically assail the spectator. Let us compare the screen on which a film unfolds with the canvas of a painting. The painting invites the spectator to contemplation; before it the spectator can abandon himself to his associations. Before the movie frame he cannot do so. No sooner has his eye grasped a scene than it is already changed. It cannot be arrested. Duhamel, who detests the film and knows nothing of its significance, though something of its structure, notes this circumstance as follows: "I can no longer

---

* Rudolf Arnheim, *loc. cit.*, p. 138.

[xiv] See the "Introduction" to "Continental Interlude II: Dada," pp. 461–2.

[xv] Jean Arp (1887–1966), Swiss painter, sculptor, and poet who was active in Zurich Dada, then participated in Surrealism. August Stramm (1874–1915) was a German poet whose book of war poems, *Tropfblut* (*Blood-Drop*) (Berlin: Der Sturm, 1915) took the shattering of poetic form as far is it could go, in the view of some critics.

[xvi] André Derain (1880–1954), French painter and sculptor who was damned by some as an apostate from the avant-garde (he had been associated with Braque and Picasso in the early 1910s) and praised by others as France's greatest living painter by those who liked his essentially classical style after 1920. Rainer Maria Rilke (1875–1926) was a German poet, one of the great lyric poets of the twentieth century.

think what I want to think. My thoughts have been replaced by moving images."[*] The spectator's process of association in view of these images is indeed interrupted by their constant, sudden change. This constitutes the shock effect of the film, which, like all shocks, should be cushioned by heightened presence of mind.[19] By means of its technical structure, the film has taken the physical shock effect out of the wrappers in which Dadaism had, as it were, kept it inside the moral shock effect.[20]

XV

The mass is a matrix from which all traditional behavior toward works of art issues today in a new form. Quantity has been transmuted into quality. The greatly increased mass of participants has produced a change in the mode of participation. The fact that the new mode of participation first appeared in a disreputable form must not confuse the spectator. Yet some people have launched spirited attacks against precisely this superficial aspect. Among these, Duhamel has expressed himself in the most radical manner. What he objects to most is the kind of participation which the movie elicits from the masses. Duhamel calls the movie "a pastime for helots, a diversion for uneducated, wretched, worn-out creatures who are consumed by their worries . . . , a spectacle which requires no concentration and presupposes no intelligence . . . , which kindles no light in the heart and awakens no hope other than the ridiculous one of someday becoming a 'star' in Los Angeles."[**] Clearly, this is at bottom the same ancient lament that the masses seek distraction whereas art demands concentration from the spectator. That is a commonplace. The question remains whether it provides a platform for the analysis of the film. A closer look is needed here. Distraction and concentration form polar opposites which may be stated as follows: A man who concentrates before a work of art is absorbed by it. He enters into this work of art the way legend tells of the Chinese painter when he viewed his finished painting. In contrast, the distracted mass absorbs the work of art. This is most obvious with regard to buildings. Architecture has always represented the prototype of a work of art the reception of which is consummated by a collectivity in a state of distraction. The laws of its reception are most instructive.

Buildings have been man's companions since primeval times. Many art forms have developed and perished. Tragedy begins with the Greeks, is extinguished with them, and after centuries its "rules" only are revived. The epic poem, which had its origin in the youth of nations, expires in Europe at the end of the Renaissance. Panel painting is a creation of the Middle Ages, and nothing guarantees its uninterrupted existence. But the human need for shelter is lasting. Architecture has never been idle. Its history is more ancient than that of any other art, and its claim to being a living force has significance in every attempt to comprehend the relationship of the masses to art. Buildings are appropriated in a twofold manner: by use and by perception – or rather, by touch and sight. Such appropriation cannot be understood in terms of the attentive concentration of a tourist before a famous building. On the tactile side there is no counterpart to contemplation on the optical side. Tactile appropriation is accomplished not so much by attention as by habit. As regards architecture, habit determines to a large extent even optical reception. The latter, too, occurs much less through rapt attention than by noticing the object in incidental fashion. This mode of appropriation, developed with reference to architecture, in certain circumstances acquires canonical value. For the tasks which face the human apparatus of perception at the turning points of history cannot be solved by optical means, that is, by contemplation, alone. They are mastered gradually by habit, under the guidance of tactile appropriation.

The distracted person, too, can form habits. More, the ability to master certain tasks in a state of distraction proves that their solution has become a matter of habit. Distraction as provided by art presents a covert control of the extent to which new tasks have become soluble by apperception. Since, moreover, individuals are tempted to avoid such tasks, art will tackle the most difficult and most important ones where it is able to mobilize the masses. Today it does so in the film. Reception in a state of distraction, which is increasing noticeably in all fields of art and is symptomatic of

[*]   Georges Duhamel, *Scènes de la vie future*, Paris, 1930, p. 52.   [**]   Duhamel, *op. cit.*, p. 58.

profound changes in apperception, finds in the film its true means of exercise. The film with its shock effect meets this mode of reception halfway. The film makes the cult value recede into the background not only by putting the public in the position of the critic, but also by the fact that at the movies this position requires no attention. The public is an examiner, but an absent-minded one.

Epilogue

The growing proletarianization of modern man and the increasing formation of masses are two aspects of the same process. Fascism attempts to organize the newly created proletarian masses without affecting the property structure which the masses strive to eliminate. Fascism sees its salvation in giving these masses not their right, but instead a chance to express themselves.[21] The masses have a right to change property relations; Fascism seeks to give them an expression while preserving property. The logical result of Fascism is the introduction of aesthetics into political life. The violation of the masses, whom Fascism, with its *Führer* cult, forces to their knees, has its counterpart in the violation of an apparatus which is pressed into the production of ritual values.

All efforts to render politics aesthetic culminate in one thing: war. War and war only can set a goal for mass movements on the largest scale while respecting the traditional property system. This is the political formula for the situation. The technological formula may be stated as follows: Only war makes it possible to mobilize all of today's technical resources while maintaining the property system. It goes without saying that the Fascist apotheosis of war does not employ such arguments. Still, Marinetti says in his manifesto on the Ethiopian colonial war: "For twenty-seven years we Futurists have rebelled against the branding of war as antiaesthetic.... Accordingly we state:... War is beautiful because it establishes man's dominion over the subjugated machinery by means of gas masks, terrifying megaphones, flame throwers, and small tanks. War is beautiful because it initiates the dreamt-of metalization of the human body. War is beautiful because it enriches a flowering meadow with the fiery orchids of machine guns. War is beautiful because it combines the gunfire, the cannonades, the cease-fire, the scents, and the stench of putrefaction into a symphony. War is beautiful because it creates new architecture, like that of the big tanks, the geometrical formation flights, the smoke spirals from burning villages, and many others.... Poets and artists of Futurism!... remember these principles of an aesthetics of war so that your struggle for a new literature and a new graphic art... may be illumined by them!"

This manifesto has the virtue of clarity. Its formulations deserve to be accepted by dialecticians. To the latter, the aesthetics of today's war appears as follows: If the natural utilization of productive forces is impeded by the property system, the increase in technical devices, in speed, and in the sources of energy will press for an unnatural utilization, and this is found in war. The destructiveness of war furnishes proof that society has not been mature enough to incorporate technology as its organ, that technology has not been sufficiently developed to cope with the elemental forces of society. The horrible features of imperialistic warfare are attributable to the discrepancy between the tremendous means of production and their inadequate utilization in the process of production – in other words, to unemployment and the lack of markets. Imperialistic war is a rebellion of technology which collects, in the form of "human material," the claims to which society has denied its natural material. Instead of draining rivers, society directs a human stream into a bed of trenches; instead of dropping seeds from airplanes, it drops incendiary bombs over cities; and through gas warfare the aura is abolished in a new way.

"*Fiat ars – pereat mundus*," says Fascism, and, as Marinetti admits, expects war to supply the artistic gratification of a sense perception that has been changed by technology. This is evidently the consummation of "*l'art pour l'art*." Mankind, which in Homer's time was an object of contemplation for the Olympian gods, now is one for itself. Its self-alienation has reached such a degree that it can experience its own destruction as an aesthetic pleasure of the first order. This is the situation of politics which Fascism is rendering aesthetic. Communism responds by politicizing art.

Notes

1.   Of course, the history of a work of art encompasses more than this. The history of the "Mona Lisa," for instance, encompasses the kind and number of its copies made in the 17th, 18th, and 19th centuries.

2.   Precisely because authenticity is not reproducible, the intensive penetration of certain (mechanical) processes of reproduction was instrumental in differentiating and grading authenticity. To develop such differentiations was an important function of the trade in works of art. The invention of the woodcut may be said to have struck at the root of the quality of authenticity even before its late flowering. To be sure, at the time of its origin a medieval picture of the Madonna could not yet be said to be "authentic." It became "authentic" only during the succeeding centuries and perhaps most strikingly so during the last one.

3.   The poorest provincial staging of *Faust* is superior to a Faust film in that, ideally, it competes with the first performance at Weimar. Before the screen it is unprofitable to remember traditional contents which might come to mind before the stage – for instance, that Goethe's friend Johann Heinrich Merck is hidden in Mephisto, and the like.

4.   To satisfy the human interest of the masses may mean to have one's social function removed from the field of vision. Nothing guarantees that a portraitist of today, when painting a famous surgeon at the breakfast table in the midst of his family, depicts his social function more precisely than a painter of the 17th century who portrayed his medical doctors as representing this profession, like Rembrandt in his "Anatomy Lesson."

5.   The definition of the aura as a "unique phenomenon of a distance however close it may be" represents nothing but the formulation of the cult value of the work of art in categories of space and time perception. Distance is the opposite of closeness. The essentially distant object is the unapproachable one. Unapproachability is indeed a major quality of the cult image. True to its nature, it remains "distant, however close it may be." The closeness which one may gain from its subject matter does not impair the distance which it retains in its appearance.

6.   To the extent to which the cult value of the painting is secularized the ideas of its fundamental uniqueness lose distinctness. In the imagination of the beholder the uniqueness of the phenomena which hold sway in the cult image is more and more displaced by the empirical uniqueness of the creator or of his creative achievement. To be sure, never completely so; the concept of authenticity always transcends mere genuineness. (This is particularly apparent in the collector who always retains some traces of the fetishist and who, by owning the work of art, shares in its ritual power.) Nevertheless, the function of the concept of authenticity remains determinate in the evaluation of art; with the secularization of art, authenticity displaces the cult value of the work.

7.   In the case of films, mechanical reproduction is not, as with literature and painting, an external condition for mass distribution. Mechanical reproduction is inherent in the very technique of film production. This technique not only permits in the most direct way but virtually causes mass distribution. It enforces distribution because the production of a film is so expensive that an individual who, for instance, might afford to buy a painting no longer can afford to buy a film. In 1927 it was calculated that a major film, in order to pay its way, had to reach an audience of nine million. With the sound film, to be sure, a setback in its international distribution occurred at first: audiences became limited by language barriers. This coincided with the Fascist emphasis on national interests. It is more important to focus on this connection with Fascism than on this setback, which was soon minimized by synchronization. The simultaneity of both phenomena is attributable to the depression. The same disturbances which, on a larger scale, led to an attempt to maintain the existing property structure by sheer force led the endangered film capital to speed up the development of the sound film. The introduction of the sound film brought about a temporary relief, not only because it again brought the masses into the theaters but also because it merged new capital from the electrical industry with that of the film industry. Thus, viewed from the outside, the sound film promoted national interests, but seen from the inside it helped to internationalize film production even more than previously.

8.   This polarity cannot come into its own in the aesthetics of Idealism. Its idea of beauty comprises these polar opposites without differentiating between them and consequently excludes their polarity. Yet in Hegel this polarity announces itself as clearly as possible within the limits of Idealism. We quote from his *Philosophy of History:*

> "Images were known of old. Piety at an early time required them for worship, but it could do without *beautiful* images. These might even be disturbing. In every beautiful painting there is also something nonspiritual, merely external, but its spirit speaks to man through its beauty. Worshipping, conversely, is concerned with the work as an object, for it is but a spiritless stupor of the soul.... Fine art has arisen ... in the church ..., although it has already gone beyond its principle as art."

Likewise, the following passage from *The Philosophy of Fine Art* indicates that Hegel sensed a problem here.

> "We are beyond the stage of reverence for works of art as divine and objects deserving our worship. The impression they produce is one of a more reflective kind, and the emotions they arouse require a higher test...." – G. W. F. Hegel, *The Philosophy of Fine Art*, trans., with notes, by F. P. B. Osmaston, Vol. I, p. 12, London, 1920.

The transition from the first kind of artistic reception to the second characterizes the history of artistic reception in general. Apart from that, a certain oscillation between these two polar modes of reception can be demonstrated for each work of art. Take the Sistine Madonna. Since Hubert Grimme's research it has been known that the Madonna originally was painted for the purpose of exhibition. Grimme's research was inspired by the question: What is the purpose of the molding in the foreground of the painting which the two cupids lean upon? How, Grimme asked further, did Raphael come to furnish the sky with two draperies? Research proved that the Madonna had been commissioned for the public lying-in-state of Pope Sixtus. The Popes lay in state in a certain side chapel of St. Peter's. On that occasion Raphael's picture had been fastened in a nichelike background of the chapel, supported by the coffin. In this picture Raphael portrays the Madonna approaching the papal coffin in clouds from the background of the niche, which was demarcated by green drapes. At the obsequies of Sixtus a pre-eminent exhibition value of Raphael's picture was taken advantage of. Some time later it was placed on the high altar in the church of the Black Friars at Piacenza. The reason for this exile is to be found in the Roman rites which forbid the use of paintings exhibited at obsequies as cult objects on the high altar. This regulation devalued Raphael's picture to some degree. In order to obtain an adequate price nevertheless, the Papal See resolved to add to the bargain the tacit toleration of the picture above the high altar. To avoid attention the picture was given to the monks of the far-off provincial town.

9.   Bertolt Brecht, on a different level, engaged in analogous reflections: "If the concept of 'work of art' can no longer be applied to the thing that emerges once the work is transformed into a commodity, we have to eliminate this concept with cautious care but without fear, lest we liquidate the function of the very thing as well. For it has to go through this phase without mental reservation, and not as noncommittal deviation from the straight path; rather, what happens here with the work of art will change it fundamentally and erase its past to such an extent that should the old concept be taken up again – and it will, why not? – it will no longer stir any memory of the thing it once designated."

10.   "The film ... provides – or could provide – useful insight into the details of human actions.... Character is never used as a source of motivation; the inner life of the persons never supplies the principal cause of the plot and seldom is its main result." (Bertolt Brecht, *Versuche*, "Der Dreigroschenprozess," p. 268.) The expansion of the field of the testable which mechanical equipment brings about for the actor corresponds to the extraordinary expansion of the field of the testable brought about for the individual through economic conditions. Thus, vocational aptitude tests become constantly more important. What matters in these tests are segmental performances of the individual. The film shot and the vocational aptitude test are taken before a committee of

experts. The camera director in the studio occupies a place identical with that of the examiner during aptitude tests.

11. Rudolf Arnheim, *Film als Kunst*, Berlin, 1932, pp. 176 f. In this context certain seemingly unimportant details in which the film director deviates from stage practices gain in interest. Such is the attempt to let the actor play without make-up, as made among others by Dreyer in his *Jeanne d'Arc*. Dreyer spent months seeking the forty actors who constitute the Inquisitors' tribunal. The search for these actors resembled that for stage properties that are hard to come by. Dreyer made every effort to avoid resemblances of age, build, and physiognomy. If the actor thus becomes a stage property, this latter, on the other hand, frequently functions as actor. At least it is not unusual for the film to assign a role to the stage property. Instead of choosing at random from a great wealth of examples, let us concentrate on a particularly convincing one. A clock that is working will always be a disturbance on the stage. There it cannot be permitted its function of measuring time. Even in a naturalistic play, astronomical time would clash with theatrical time. Under these circumstances it is highly revealing that the film can, whenever appropriate, use time as measured by a clock. From this more than from many other touches it may clearly be recognized that under certain circumstances each and every prop in a film may assume important functions. From here it is but one step to Pudovkin's statement that "the playing of an actor which is connected with an object and is built around it ... is always one of the strongest methods of cinematic construction." (W. Pudovkin, *Filmregie und Filmmanuskript*, Berlin, 1928, p. 126.) The film is the first art form capable of demonstrating how matter plays tricks on man. Hence, films can be an excellent means of materialistic representation.

12. The change noted here in the method of exhibition caused by mechanical reproduction applies to politics as well. The present crisis of the bourgeois democracies comprises a crisis of the conditions which determine the public presentation of the rulers. Democracies exhibit a member of government directly and personally before the nation's representatives. Parliament is his public. Since the innovations of camera and recording equipment make it possible for the orator to become audible and visible to an unlimited number of persons, the presentation of the man of politics before camera and recording equipment becomes paramount. Parliaments, as much as theaters, are deserted. Radio and film not only affect the function of the professional actor but likewise the function of those who also exhibit themselves before this mechanical equipment, those who govern. Though their tasks may be different, the change affects equally the actor and the ruler. The trend is toward establishing controllable and transferrable skills under certain social conditions. This results in a new selection, a selection before the equipment from which the star and the dictator emerge victorious.

13. The privileged character of the respective techniques is lost. Aldous Huxley writes:

"Advances in technology have led ... to vulgarity.... Process reproduction and the rotary press have made possible the indefinite multiplication of writing and pictures. Universal education and relatively high wages have created an enormous public who know how to read and can afford to buy reading and pictorial matter. A great industry has been called into existence in order to supply these commodities. Now, artistic talent is a very rare phenomenon; whence it follows ... that, at every epoch and in all countries, most art has been bad. But the proportion of trash in the total artistic output is greater now than at any other period. That it must be so is a matter of simple arithmetic. The population of Western Europe has a little more than doubled during the last century. But the amount of reading – and seeing – matter has increased, I should imagine, at least twenty and possibly fifty or even a hundred times. If there were n men of talent in a population of x millions, there will presumably be 2n men of talent among 2x millions. The situation may be summed up thus. For every page of print and pictures published a century ago, twenty or perhaps even a hundred pages are published today. But for every man of talent then living, there are now only two men of talent. It may be of course that, thanks to universal education, many potential talents which in the past would have been still-born are now enabled to realize themselves. Let us assume, then, that there are now three or even four men of talent to every one of earlier times. It still remains true to say that the consumption of reading – and seeing – matter has far outstripped the natural production of gifted writers and draughtsmen. It is the same with hearing-matter. Prosperity, the gramophone and the radio have created an audience of hearers who consume an amount of hearing-matter that has increased out of all proportion to the increase of population and the consequent natural increase of talented musicians. It follows from all this that in all the arts the output of trash is both absolutely and relatively greater than it was in the past; and that it must remain greater for just so long as the world continues to consume the present inordinate quantities of reading-matter, seeing-matter, and hearing-matter." – Aldous Huxley, *Beyond the Mexique Bay. A Traveller's Journal*, London, 1949, pp. 274 ff. First published in 1934.

This mode of observation is obviously not progressive.

14. The boldness of the cameraman is indeed comparable to that of the surgeon. Luc Durtain lists among specific technical sleights of hand those "which are required in surgery in the case of certain difficult operations. I choose as an example a case from oto-rhino-laryngology; . . . the so-called endonasal perspective procedure; or I refer to the acrobatic tricks of larynx surgery which have to be performed following the reversed picture in the laryngoscope. I might also speak of ear surgery which suggests the precision work of watchmakers. What range of the most subtle muscular acrobatics is required from the man who wants to repair or save the human body! We have only to think of the couching of a cataract where there is virtually a debate of steel with nearly fluid tissue, or of the major abdominal operations (laparotomy)." – Luc Durtain, *op. cit.*

15. This mode of observation may seem crude, but as the great theoretician Leonardo has shown, crude modes of observation may at times be usefully adduced. Leonardo compares painting and music as follows: "Painting is superior to music because, unlike unfortunate music, it does not have to die as soon as it is born. . . . Music which is consumed in the very act of its birth is inferior to painting which the use of varnish has rendered eternal." (Trattato I, 29.)

16. Renaissance painting offers a revealing analogy to this situation. The incomparable development of this art and its significance rested not least on the integration of a number of new sciences, or at least of new scientific data. Renaissance painting made use of anatomy and perspective, of mathematics, meteorology, and chromatology. Valéry writes: "What could be further from us than the strange claim of a Leonardo to whom painting was a supreme goal and the ultimate demonstration of knowledge? Leonardo was convinced that painting demanded universal knowledge, and he did not even shrink from a theoretical analysis which to us is stunning because of its very depth and precision. . . . " – Paul Valéry, *Pièces sur l'art*, "Autour de Corot," Paris, p. 191.

17. "The work of art," says André Breton, "is valuable only in so far as it is vibrated by the reflexes of the future." Indeed, every developed art form intersects three lines of development. Technology works toward a certain form of art. Before the advent of the film there were photo booklets with pictures which flitted by the onlooker upon pressure of the thumb, thus portraying a boxing bout or a tennis match. Then there were the slot machines in bazaars; their picture sequences were produced by the turning of a crank.

Secondly, the traditional art forms in certain phases of their development strenuously work toward effects which later are effortlessly attained by the new ones. Before the rise of the movie the Dadaists' performances tried to create an audience reaction which Chaplin later evoked in a more natural way.

Thirdly, unspectacular social changes often promote a change in receptivity which will benefit the new art form. Before the movie had begun to create its public, pictures that were no longer immobile captivated an assembled audience in the so-called *Kaiserpanorama*. Here the public assembled before a screen into which stereoscopes were mounted, one to each beholder. By a mechanical process individual pictures appeared briefly before the stereoscopes, then made way for others. Edison still had to use similar devices in presenting the first movie strip before the film screen and projection were known. This strip was presented to a small public which stared into the apparatus in which the succession of pictures was reeling off. Incidentally, the institution of the *Kaiserpanorama* shows very clearly a dialectic of the development. Shortly before the movie turned the reception of pictures into a collective one, the individual viewing of pictures in these swiftly outmoded establishments came into play once more with an intensity comparable to that of the ancient priest beholding the statue of a divinity in the cella.

18. The theological archetype of this contemplation is the awareness of being alone with one's God. Such awareness, in the heyday of the bourgeoisie, went to strengthen the freedom to shake off clerical tutelage. During the decline of the bourgeoisie this awareness had to take into account the hidden tendency to withdraw from public affairs those forces which the individual draws upon in his communion with God.

19. The film is the art form that is in keeping with the increased threat to his life which modern man has to face. Man's need to expose himself to shock effects is his adjustment to the dangers threatening him. The film corresponds to profound changes in the apperceptive apparatus – changes that are experienced on an individual scale by the man in the street in big-city traffic, on a historical scale by every present-day citizen.

20. As for Dadaism, insights important for Cubism and Futurism are to be gained from the movie. Both appear as deficient attempts of art to accommodate the pervasion of reality by the apparatus. In contrast to the film, these schools did not try to use the apparatus as such for the artistic presentation of reality, but aimed at some sort of alloy in the joint presentation of reality and apparatus. In Cubism, the premonition that this apparatus will be structurally based on optics plays a dominant part; in Futurism, it is the premonition of the effects of this apparatus which are brought out by the rapid sequence of the film strip.

21. One technical feature is significant here, especially with regard to newsreels, the propagand- ist importance of which can hardly be overestimated. Mass reproduction is aided especially by the reproduction of masses. In big parades and monster rallies, in sports events, and in war, all of which nowadays are captured by camera and sound recording, the masses are brought face to face with themselves. This process, whose significance need not be stressed, is intimately connected with the development of the techniques of reproduction and photography. Mass movements are usually discerned more clearly by a camera than by the naked eye. A bird's-eye view best captures gatherings of hundreds of thousands. And even though such a view may be as accessible to the human eye as it is to the camera, the image received by the eye cannot be enlarged the way a negative is enlarged. This means that mass movements, including war, constitute a form of human behavior which particularly favors mechanical equipment.

Looking Back on Surrealism (1956)
Theodor Adorno

The currently accepted theory of Surrealism, which was set down in Breton's manifestos but also dominates the secondary literature, links it with dreams, the unconscious, and perhaps Jungian archetypes, which are said to have found in collages and automatic writing an emancipated image- language uncontaminated by the conscious ego. Dreams, according to this theory, treat the elements of the real the way the method of Surrealism does. If, however, no art is required to understand itself – and one is tempted to consider art's self-understanding and its success almost incompatible – then it is not necessary to fall in line with this programmatic view, which is repeated by those who expound Surrealism. What is deadly about the interpretation of art, moreover, even philosophically responsible interpretation, is that in the process of conceptualiza- tion it is forced to express what is strange and surprising in terms of what is already familiar and thereby to explain away the only thing that would need explanation. To the extent to which works of art insist on explanation, every one of them, even if against its own intentions, perpetrates a piece of betrayal to conformity. Were Surrealism in fact nothing but a collection of literary and graphic illustrations of Jung or even Freud, it would not only duplicate, superfluously, what the theory

LOOKING BACK
The essay, originally titled "Rückblickend auf den Surrealismus," first appeared in the journal *Texte und Zeichen* 6 (1956), then was included in Adorno's collection of essays, *Noten zur Literatur* (*Notes to Literature*) (Frankfurt am Main: Suhrkamp, 1958). The

translation used here is that of Shierry Weber Nicholson, who translated *Notes to Literature* into English (New York: Columbia University Press, 1991). Adorno provided no notes for the essay and all the ones given here are the editor's.

itself says rather than giving it a metaphorical garb, but it would also be so innocuous that it would hardly leave room for the scandal that is Surrealism's intention and its lifeblood. Reducing Surrealism to psychological dream theory subjects it to the ignominy of something official. Companion piece to the well-versed "That is a father figure" is the self-satisfied "Yes, we know," and, as Cocteau[1] well knew, something that is supposed to be a mere dream always leaves reality untouched, whatever damage is done to its image.

But that theory does not do justice to the matter. That is not the way people dream; no one dreams that way. Surrealist constructions are merely analogous to dreams, not more. They suspend the customary logic and the rules of the game of empirical evidence but in doing so respect the individual objects that have been forcibly removed from their context and bring their contents, especially their human contents, closer to the form of the object. There is a shattering and a regrouping, but no dissolution. The dream, to be sure, does the same thing, but in the dream the object world appears in a form incomparably more disguised and is presented as reality less than it is in Surrealism, where art batters its own foundations. The subject, which is at work much more openly and uninhibitedly in Surrealism than in the dream, directs its energy toward its own self-annihilation, something that requires no energy in the dream; but because of that everything becomes more objective, so to speak, than in the dream, where the subject, absent from the start, colors and permeates everything that happens from the wings. In the meantime the Surrealists themselves have discovered that people do not free associate the way they, the Surrealists, write, even in psychoanalysis. Furthermore, even the spontaneity of psychoanalytic associations is by no means spontaneous. Every analyst knows how much trouble and exertion, how much effort of will is required to master the involuntary expression that occurs through these efforts, even in the psychoanalytic situation, to say nothing of the artistic situation of the Surrealists. It is not the unconscious in itself that comes to light in the world-rubble of Surrealism. Assessed in terms of their relationship to the unconscious, the symbols would prove much too rationalistic. This kind of decoding would force the luxuriant multiplicity of Surrealism into a few patterns and reduce it to a few meager categories like the Oedipus complex, without attaining the power that emanated from the idea of Surrealism if not from its works of art; Freud too seems to have responded to Dali this way.

After the European catastrophe the Surrealist shocks lost their force. It is as though they had saved Paris by preparing it for fear: the destruction of the city was their center. To conceptualize Surrealism along these lines, one must go back not to psychology but to Surrealism's artistic techniques. Unquestionably, they are patterned on the montage. One could easily show that even genuine Surrealist painting works with its motifs and that the discontinuous juxtaposition of images in Surrealist lyric poetry is montage-like. But these images derive, as we know, in part literally and in part in spirit from the late nineteenth-century illustrations that belonged to the world of the parents of Max Ernst's generation. There were collections in existence as early as the 1920s, outside the sphere of Surrealism, like Alan Bott's *Our Fathers*,[2] which partook – parasitically – of Surrealist shock and by doing so dispensed with the strain of alienation through montage as a kindness to the audience. Authentic Surrealist practice, however, replaced those elements with unfamiliar ones. It is precisely the latter which, through fright, gave that material the aspect of something familiar, the quality of "Where have I seen that before?" Hence one may assume that the affinity with psychoanalysis lies not in a symbolism of the unconscious but in the attempt to uncover childhood experiences by means of explosions. What Surrealism adds to illustrations of the world of objects is the element of childhood we lost; when we were children, those illustrated papers, already obsolete even then, must have leaped out at us the way Surrealist images do now. The subjective aspect in this lies in the action of the montage, which attempts – perhaps in vain, but the intention is unmistakable – to produce perceptions as they must have been then. The giant egg from which the monster of the Last Judgment can creep forth at any moment is so big because we were so small the first time we looked at an egg and shuddered.

[1] Jean Cocteau (1889–1963) was a French poet, playwright, and filmmaker.
[2] Alan Bott (1893–1952), a popular historian, wrote *Our Fathers (1870–1900): Manners and Customs of the Ancient Victor-* ians; a Survey in Pictures and Text of Their History, Morals, Wars, Sports, Inventions, and Politics (London: Heinemann, 1931). The American edition kept the long subtitle, but changed the title to *This Was England* (Garden City, NY: Doubleday, 1931).

Obsoleteness contributes to this effect. It seems paradoxical for something modern, already under the spell of the sameness of mass production, to have any history at all. This paradox estranges it, and in the "Children's Pictures for the Modern Age" it becomes the expression of a subjectivity that has become estranged from itself as well as from the world. The tension in Surrealism that is discharged in shock is the tension between schizophrenia and reification; hence it is specifically not a tension of psychological inspiration. In the face of total reification, which throws it back upon itself and its protest, a subject that has become absolute, that has full control of itself and is free of all consideration of the empirical world, reveals itself to be inanimate, something virtually dead. The dialectical images of Surrealism are images of a dialectic of subjective freedom in a situation of objective unfreedom. In them, European *Weltschmerz* turns to stone, like the pain of Niobe,[3] who lost her children; in them bourgeois society abandons its hopes of survival. One can hardly assume that any of the Surrealists were familiar with Hegel's *Phenomenology*,[4] but a sentence from it, which must be considered in conjunction with the more general thesis that history is progress in the consciousness of freedom, defines the substance of Surrealism: "The sole work and deed of universal freedom therefore is *death*, a death too which has no inner significance or filling." Surrealism adopted this critique as its own; this explains its anti-anarchistic political impulses, which, however, were incompatible with its substance. It has been said that in Hegel's thesis the Enlightenment abolishes itself by realizing itself; the cost of comprehending Surrealism is equally high – it must be understood not as a language of immediacy but as witness to abstract freedom's reversion to the supremacy of objects and thus to mere nature. The montages of Surrealism are the true still lives. In making compositions out of what is out of date, they create *nature morte*.

These images are not images of something inward; rather, they are fetishes – commodity fetishes – on which something subjective, libido, was once fixated. It is through these fetishes, not through immersion in the self, that the images bring back childhood. Surrealism's models would be pornography. The things that happen in the collages, the things that are convulsively suspended in them like the tense lines of lasciviousness around a mouth, are like the changes that occur in a pornographic image at the moment when the voyeur achieves gratification. Breasts that have been cut off, mannequin's legs in silk stockings in the collages – these are mementos of the objects of the partial drives that once aroused the libido. Thinglike and dead, in them what has been forgotten reveals itself to be the true object of love, what love wants to make itself resemble, what we resemble. As a freezing of the moment of awakening, Surrealism is akin to photography. Surrealism's booty is images, to be sure, but not the invariant, ahistorical images of the unconscious subject to which the conventional view would like to neutralize them; rather, they are historical images in which the subject's innermost core becomes aware that it is something external, an imitation of something social and historical. "Come on Joe, imitate that old-time music."[5]

In this respect, however, Surrealism forms the complement to the *Neue Sachlichkeit*,[6] or New Objectivity, which came into being at the same time. The *Neue Sachlichkeit*'s horror of the crime of ornamentation, as Adolf Loos[7] called it, is mobilized by Surrealist shocks. The house has a tumor, its bay window. Surrealism paints this tumor: an excrescence of flesh grows from the house. Childhood images of the modern era are the quintessence of what the *Neue Sachlichkeit* makes taboo because it

---

[3] Niobe is, in mythology, a character who, having given birth to 12 children, boasts that she is at least equal to Leto, who had borne two children. Thereupon Leto's children kill all of Niobe's and she is turned into stone.

[4] G. W. F. Hegel, *Phenomenology of Spirit*, trans. A. V. Miller (Oxford: Clarendon Press, 1977), p. 360.

[5] A line from the "Bilbao Song" in *Happy End*, by Bertolt Brecht and Kurt Weill. See *Happy End: A Melodrama with Songs*, lyrics by Bertolt Brecht, music by Kurt Weill, original German play by Elizabeth Hauptmann under the pseudonym Dorothy Lane; translated, adapted, and introduced by Michael Feingold (London and New York: Methuen, 1982), pp. 11–13.

[6] A German phrase usually translated as "New Objectivity." It was coined in 1923 by G. F. Hartlaub, director of the Kunsthalle

in Mannheim, in connection with an exhibition held in 1925, celebrating artists turning away from expressionism and toward a certain "fidelity to positive, tangible reality." From the exhibition the term spread into other fields and is widely used to describe many realistic and social satirical writings of the period.

[7] Adolf Loos (1870–1933) was an Austrian architect, a pioneering modernist and theorist; in 1908 he wrote an essay called "Ornament und Verbrechen" ("Ornament and Crime"), which was first published in the newspaper *Frankfurter Zeitung* in 1929 and then collected in his gathering of essays, *Trotzdem, 1900–1930* (*Nevertheless*) (Innsbruck: Brenner- Verlag, 1931), pp. 79–90; for the essay in English see Adolf Loos, *Ornament and Crime: Selected Essays*, trans. Michael Mitchell (Riverside, CA: Ariadne Books, 1998), pp. 167–76.

reminds it of its own object-like nature and its inability to cope with the fact that its rationality remains irrational. Surrealism gathers up the things the *Neue Sachlichkeit* denies to human beings; the distortions attest to the violence that prohibition has done to the objects of desire. Through the distortions, Surrealism salvages what is out of date, an album of idiosyncrasies in which the claim to the happiness that human beings find denied them in their own technified world goes up in smoke. But if Surrealism itself now seems obsolete, it is because human beings are now denying themselves the consciousness of denial that was captured in the photographic negative that was Surrealism.

Trying to Understand Endgame (1961)
Theodor Adorno

to S.B. in memory of Paris, Fall 1958

Beckett's *oeuvre* has several elements in common with Parisian existentialism.[1] Reminiscences of the category of "absurdity," of "situation," of "decision" or their opposite permeate it as medieval ruins permeate Kafka's monstrous house[2] on the edge of the city: occasionally, windows fly open and reveal to view the black starless heaven of something like anthropology. But form – conceived by Sartre rather traditionally as that of didactic plays, not at all as something audacious but rather oriented toward an effect – absorbs what is expressed and changes it.[3] Impulses are raised to the level of the most advanced artistic means, those of Joyce[4] and Kafka. Absurdity in Beckett is no longer a state of human existence thinned out to a mere idea and then expressed in images. Poetic procedure surrenders to it without intention. Absurdity is divested of that generality of doctrine which existentialism, that creed of the permanence of individual existence, nonetheless combines with Western pathos of the universal and the immutable. Existential conformity – that one should be what one is – is thereby rejected along with the ease of its representation. What Beckett offers in the way of philosophy he himself also reduces to culture-trash, no different from the innumerable allusions and residues of education which he employs in the wake of the Anglo-Saxon tradition, particularly of Joyce and Eliot.[5] Culture parades before him as the entrails of *Jugendstil*[6] ornaments did before that progress which preceded him, modernism as the obsolescence of the modern. The regressive language demolishes it. Such objectivity in Beckett obliterates the meaning that was culture, along with its rudiments. Culture thus begins to fluoresce. He thereby completes a tendency of the recent novel. What was decried

---

ENDGAME

Portions of this essay, under its original German title, "Versuch, das Endspiel zu verstehen," were given as a lecture on February 27, 1961. The entire essay was published a few months later in Adorno's *Noten zur Literatur II* (*Notes to Literature II*) (Frankfurt am Main: Suhrkamp, 1961). The English translation used here, by Michael J. Jones, first appeared in *New German Critique* 26 (Spring–Summer 1982). Adorno's essay originally had a formidable array of footnotes, of which all but 16 were to passages in *Endgame*. Those that cited *Endgame* have been placed within the text and replaced with reference to the text in this edition. The remaining 16 have been incorporated into the editorial notes, but in each case the note is preceded by an indication that it is [Adorno's note] in square brackets. Further, Adorno's references to various texts in German have been modified to refer to the equivalent translations in English wherever possible.

Endgame is a play (1957) by Samuel Beckett (1906–89); see pp. 1035–61 in this edition.

[1] During the period from roughly 1955 to 1970, existentialism was a philosophical outlook very popular among intellectuals. For contemporaries, the term entailed a precarious synthesis: it comprised the French philosopher and dramatist Jean-Paul Sartre (1905–80) and the novelist Albert Camus

(1913–60), both resident in Paris, whose thought was said to converge in various ways with that of others such as the Danish theologian Søren Kierkegaard (1813–55) or the German philosopher Martin Heidegger (1889–1976). Parisian existentialism, in a vastly oversimplified account, held that life was absurd and meaningless in itself, that it was redeemed only through an act of choice or decision on the part of humans, and that this act of decision acquired its significance from a clear-sighted ethical recognition of the situation in which it was placed. Adorno was suspicious of these terms, and suspicious also of the ease with which critics assimilated Beckett's drama to these debased over-simplifications.

[2] Franz Kafka (1883–1924), a Jewish writer who lived in Prague, describes a "monstrous house" or castle on the edge of the city in his novel *The Castle*, or *Das Schloß* (1926).

[3] See Jean-Paul Sartre, *What is Literature* (New York: Philosophical Library, 1949).

[4] James Joyce (1882–1941), Irish writer; see pp. 211–300 in this edition.

[5] T. S. Eliot (1888–1965), American poet; see pp. 113–173 in this edition.

[6] German counterpart to Art Nouveau.

as abstract according to the cultural criterion of aesthetic immanence – reflection – is lumped together with pure representation, corroding the Flaubertian[7] principle of the purely self-enclosed matter at hand. The less events can be presumed meaningful in themselves, the more the idea of aesthetic *Gestalt*[8] as a unity of appearance and intention becomes illusory. Beckett relinquishes the illusion by coupling both disparate aspects. Thought becomes as much a means of producing a meaning for the work which cannot be immediately rendered tangible, as it is an expression of meaning's absence. When applied to drama, the word "meaning" is multivalent. It denotes: metaphysical content, which objectively presents itself in the complexion of the artifact; likewise the intention of the whole as a structure of meaning which it signifies in itself; and finally the sense of the words and sentences which the characters speak, and that of their progression – the sense of the dialogue. But these equivocations point toward a common basis. From it, in Beckett's *Endgame*, emerges a continuum. It is historio-philosophically supported by a change in the dramatic *a priori*: positive metaphysical meaning is no longer possible in such a substantive way (if indeed it ever was), such that dramatic form could have its law in such meaning and its epiphany. Yet that afflicts the form even in its linguistic construction. Drama cannot simply seize on to negative meaning, or its absence, as content, without thereby affecting everything peculiar to it – virtually to the point of reversal to its opposite. What is essential for drama was constituted by that meaning. If drama were to strive to survive meaning aesthetically, it would be reduced to inadequate content or to a clattering machinery demonstrating world views, as often happens in existentialist plays. The explosion of metaphysical meaning, which alone guaranteed the unity of an aesthetic structure of meaning, makes it crumble away with a necessity and stringency which equals that of the transmitted canon of dramaturgical form. Harmonious aesthetic meaning, and certainly its subjectification in a binding tangible intention, substituted for that transcendent meaningfulness, the denial of which itself constituted the content. Through its own organized meaninglessness, the plot must approach that which transpired in the truth content of dramaturgy generally. Such construction of the senseless also even includes linguistic molecules: if they and their connections were rationally meaningful, then within the drama they would synthe-size irrevocably into that very meaning structure of the whole which is denied by the whole. The interpretation of *Endgame* therefore cannot chase the chimera of expressing its meaning with the help of philosophical mediation. Understanding it can mean nothing other than understanding its incomprehensibility, or concretely reconstructing its meaning structure – that it has none. Isolated, thought no longer pretends, as the Idea once did, to be itself the structure's meaning – a transcendence which would be engendered and guaranteed by the work's own immanence. Instead, thought transforms itself into a kind of material of a second degree, just as the philosophemes expounded in Thomas Mann's *The Magic Mountain* and *Doctor Faustus*,[9] as novel materials, find their destiny in replacing that sensate immediacy which is diminished in the self-reflective work of art. If such materiality of thought was heretofore largely involuntary, pointing to the dilemma of works which perforce confused themselves with the Idea they could not achieve, then Beckett confronts this challenge and uses thoughts *sans phrase* as phrases, as those material components of the *monologue intérieur* which mind itself has become, the reified residue of education. Whereas pre-Beckett existentialism cannibalized philosophy for poetic purposes as if it were Schiller[10] incarnate, Beckett, as educated as anyone, presents the bill: philosophy, or spirit itself, proclaims its bankruptcy as the dreamlike dross of the experiential world, and the poetic process shows itself as worn out. Disgust (*dégoût*), a productive force in the arts since Baudelaire,[11] is insatiable in Beckett's historically mediated impulses. Everything now impossible becomes canon-ical, freeing a motif from the prehistory of existentialism – Husserl's universal annihilation of the

---

[7] Derived from, advocated by, or associated with Gustav Flaubert (1821–80), French novelist.

[8] German word for "form."

[9] Thomas Mann (1875–1955), distinguished German novelist, published *Der Zauberberg* (Berlin: S. Fischer) in 1924, or *The Magic Mountain* (London: Secker) in 1927, as well as *Doktor*

Faustus (Stockholm: Bermann-Fischer, 1947; English translation 1948).

[10] Friedrich Schiller (1759–1805), German poet, playwright, and essayist, whose plays make use of philosophical ideas.

[11] Charles Baudelaire (1821–67), the most influential poet of the nineteenth century.

world[12] – from the shadowy realm of methodology. Totalitarians like Lukács, who rage against the – truly terrifying – simplifier as "decadent," are not ill advised by the interests of their bosses.[13] They hate in Beckett what they have betrayed. Only the nausea of satiation – the tedium of spirit with itself – wants something completely different: prescribed "health" nevertheless makes do with the nourishment offered, with simple fare. Beckett's *dégoût* cannot be forced to fall in line. He responds to the cheery call to play along with parody, parody of the philosophy spit out by his dialogues as well as parody of forms. Existentialism itself is parodied; nothing remains of its "invariants" other than minimal existence. The drama's opposition to ontology – as the sketch of a first or immutable principle – is unmistakable in an exchange of dialogue which unintentionally garbles Goethe's phrase about "old truths,"[14] which has degenerated to an arch-bourgeois sentiment:

HAMM: Do you remember your father.
CLOV: (*Wearily*) Same answer. (*Pause.*) You've asked me these questions millions of times.
HAMM: I love the old questions. (*With fervor.*) Ah the old questions, the old answers, there's nothing like them. [See p. 1047 above]

Thoughts are dragged along and distorted like the day's left-overs, *homo homini sapienti sat*. Hence the precariousness of what Beckett refuses to deal with, interpretation. He shrugs his shoulders about the possibility of philosophy today, or theory in general. The irrationality of bourgeois society on the wane resists being understood: those were the good old days when a critique of political economy could be written which took this society by its own *ratio*. For in the meantime it has thrown this *ratio* on the junk-heap and virtually replaced it with direct control. The interpretive word, therefore, cannot recuperate Beckett, while his dramaturgy – precisely by virtue of its limitation to exploded facticity – twitches beyond it, pointing toward interpretation in its essence as riddle. One could almost designate as the criterion of relevant philosophy today whether it is up to that task.

French existentialism had tackled history. In Beckett, history devours existentialism. In *Endgame*, a historical moment is revealed, the experience which was cited in the title of the culture industry's rubbish book *Corpsed*.[15] After the Second War, everything is destroyed, even resurrected culture, without knowing it; humanity vegetates along, crawling, after events which even the survivors cannot really survive, on a pile of ruins which even renders futile self-reflection of one's own battered state. From the marketplace, as the play's pragmatic precondition, that fact is ripped away:

CLOV: (*He gets up on ladder, turns the telescope on the without.*) Let's see. (*He looks, moving the telescope.*) Zero... (*he looks*)... zero... (*he looks*)... and zero.
HAMM: Nothing stirs. All is –
CLOV: Zer –
HAMM: (*Violently*) Wait till you're spoken to. (*Normal voice.*) All is... all is... all is what? (*Violently.*) All is what?
CLOV: What all is? In a word. Is that what you want to know? Just a moment. (*He turns the telescope on the without, looks, lowers the telescope, turns toward Hamm.*) Corpsed. (*Pause.*) Well? Content? [p. 1044]

12 Edmund Husserl (1859–1938), German philosopher who is considered the founder of phenomenology.
13 Georg Lukács (1885–1971) was a Hungarian Marxist philosopher, writer, and literary critic who was a major voice in Marxist debates during the period 1910–60; for Adorno he was fatally compromised by his association with the totalitarian communist government that seized power in Hungary in 1945.
14 "Vermächtnis" ("Legacy") is a poem (1829) by Goethe (1749–1832). Lines 6–9 read:
Das Wahre war schon längst gefunden,
Hat edle Geisterschaft verbunden;
Das alte Wahre, fass es an!

Or in English:
The truth has long since been known,
And has become a bond for noble minds;
Grasp the old truths!
15 The translator is a bit free here; the title of the work cited by Adorno is the novel *Kaputt* (Naples: Casella, 1945), by the Italian writer Curzio Malaparte (1898–1957), which was translated into German six years later: *Kaputt*, trans. Hellmut Ludwig (Karlsruhe: Stahlberg, 1951). In English the book appeared in translation earlier: *Kaputt*, trans. Cesare Foligno (New York: Dutton, 1946).

That all human beings are dead is covertly smuggled in. An earlier passage explains why the catastrophe may not be mentioned. Vaguely, Hamm himself is to blame for that:

HAMM: That old doctor, he's dead naturally?
CLOV: He wasn't old.
HAMM: But he's dead?
CLOV: Naturally. (*Pause.*) *You* ask *me* that? [p. 1043]

The condition presented in the play is nothing other than that in which "there's no more nature" [p. 1039]. Indistinguishable is the phase of completed reification of the world, which leaves no remainder of what was not made by humans; it is permanent catastrophe, along with a catastrophic event caused by humans themselves, in which nature has been extinguished and nothing grows any longer.

HAMM: Did your seeds come up?
CLOV: No.
HAMM: Did you scratch round them to see if they had sprouted?
CLOV: They haven't sprouted.
HAMM: Perhaps it's still too early.
CLOV: If they were going to sprout they would have sprouted. (*Violently.*) They'll never sprout!
    [p. 1039–40]

The *dramatis personae* resemble those who dream their own death, in a "shelter" where "it's time it ended" [p. 1036] The end of the world is discounted, as if it were a matter of course. Every supposed drama of the atomic age would mock itself, if only because its fable would hopelessly falsify the horror of historical anonymity by shoving it into the characters and actions of humans, and possibly by gaping at the "prominents" who decide whether the button will be pushed. The violence of the unspeakable is mimicked by the timidity to mention it. Beckett keeps it nebulous. One can only speak euphemistically about what is incommensurate with all experience, just as one speaks in Germany of the murder of the Jews. It has become a total *a priori*, so that bombed-out consciousness no longer has any position from which it could reflect on that fact. The desperate state of things supplies – with gruesome irony – a means of stylization that protects that pragmatic precondition from any contamination by childish science fiction. If Clov really were exaggerating, as his nagging, "common-sensical" companion reproaches him, that would not change much. If catastrophe amounted to a partial end of the world, that would be a bad joke: then nature, from which the imprisoned figures are cut off, would be as good as nonexistent; what remains of it would only prolong the torment.

This historical *nota bene* however, this parody of the Kierkegaardian one of the convergence of time and eternity, imposes at the same time a taboo on history. What would be called the *condition humaine* in existentialist jargon is the image of the last human, which is devouring the earlier ones – humanity. Existential ontology asserts the universally valid in a process of abstraction which is not conscious of itself. While it still – according to the old phenomenological doctrine of the intuition of essence – behaves as if it were aware, even in the particular, of its binding determinations, thereby unifying apriority and concreteness, it nonetheless distills out what appears to transcend temporality. It does so by blotting out particularity – what is individualized in space and time, what makes existence existence rather than its mere concept. Ontology appeals to those who are weary of philosophical formalism but who yet cling to what is only accessible formally. To such unacknowledged abstraction, Beckett affixes the caustic antitheses by means of acknowledged substraction. He does not leave out the temporality of existence – all existence, after all, is temporal – but rather removes from existence what time, the historical tendency, attempts to quash in reality. He lengthens the escape route of the subject's liquidation to the point where it constricts into a "this-here," whose abstractness – the loss of all qualities – extends ontological abstraction literally *ad absurdum*, to that Absurd which mere existence becomes as soon as it is consumed in naked self-identity. Childish foolishness emerges as the content of philosophy, which degenerates to tautology – to a conceptual duplication of that existence it had intended to comprehend. While recent ontology subsists on the unfulfilled promise of concretion of its abstractions, concreteness in Beckett – that shell-like, self-enclosed existence which is no longer capable of universality but rather exhausts itself in pure self-positing – is obviously the same as an abstractness which is no longer capable of experience. Ontology arrives home as the pathogenesis of false life. It is depicted as the state of negative eternity. If the messianic Myshkin[16] once forgot his watch because earthly time is invalid for him, then time is lost to his antipodes because it could still imply hope. The yawn accompanying the bored remark that the weather is "as usual" [p. 1044] gapes like a hellish abyss:

HAMM: But that's always the way at the end of the day, isn't it, Clov?
CLOV: Always.
HAMM: It's the end of the day like any other day, isn't it, Clov?
CLOV: Looks like it. [p. 1040]

Like time, the temporal itself is damaged; saying that it no longer exists would already be too comforting. It is and it is not, like the world for the solipsist who doubts its existence, while he must concede it with every sentence. Thus a passage of dialogue hovers:

HAMM: And the horizon? Nothing on the horizon?
CLOV: (*Lowering the telescope, turning towards Hamm, exasperated.*): What in God's name would there be on the horizon? (*Pause.*)
HAMM: The waves, how are the waves?
CLOV: The Waves? (*He turns the telescope on the waves.*) Lead.
HAMM: And the sun?
CLOV: (*Looking.*) Zero.
HAMM: But it should be sinking. Look again.
CLOV: (*Looking.*) Damn the sun.
HAMM: Is it night already then?
CLOV: (*Looking.*) No.
HAMM: Then what is it?
CLOV: (*Looking.*) Gray. (*Lowering the telescope, turning towards Hamm, louder.*) Gray! (*Pause. Still louder.*) GRRAY! [p. 1045]

History is excluded, because it itself has dehydrated the power of consciousness to think history, the power of remembrance. Drama falls silent and becomes gesture, frozen amid the dialogues. Only the result of history appears – as decline. What preens itself in the existentialists as the once-and-for-all of being has withered to the sharp point of history which breaks off. Lukács' objection, that in Beckett humans are reduced to animality,[17] resists with official optimism the fact that residual philosophies, which would like to bank the true and immutable after removing temporal contingency, have become the residue of life, the end product of injury. Admittedly, as nonsensical as it is to attribute to Beckett – as Lukács does – an abstract, subjectivist ontology and then to place it on the excavated index of degenerate art[18] because of its worldlessness and infantility, it would be equally ridiculous to have him testify as a key political witness. For urging the struggle against

[16] The hero of *The Idiot* (1868–9) by Fyodor Dostoyevsky (1821–81).

[17] Georg Lukács, *The Meaning of Contemporary Realism* (London: Merlin, 1963), p. 31; compare with Theodor Adorno, "Extorted Reconciliation: On Georg Lukács' Realism In Our Time," in his *Notes to Literature*, vol. 1, ed. R. Tiedemann, trans S. Weber Nicholson (New York: Columbia University Press, 1993), p. 226.

[18] *degenerate art* or in German *entartete Kunst*. The name given to a notorious exhibition held in Munich in 1937, in which the Nazis showed some 650 paintings, sculptures, prints, and books thought to be "degenerate." Adorno is implying that Lukács' view of Beckett is like that of the Nazis towards modern art. On the "degenerate art" exhibition see S. Barron (ed.), *"Degenerate Art": The Fate of the Avant-Garde in Nazi Germany* (Los Angeles: Los Angeles County Museum of Art, 1991).

atomic death, a work that notes that death's potential even in ancient struggles is hardly appropriate. The simplifier of terror refuses – unlike Brecht – any simplification. But he is not so dissimilar from Brecht, insofar as his differentiation becomes sensitivity to subjective differences, which have regressed to the "conspicuous consumption" of those who can afford individuation.

Therein lies social truth. Differentiation cannot absolutely or automatically be recorded as positive. The simplification of the social process now beginning relegates it to "incidental expenses" (*faux frais*), somewhat as the formalities of social forms, from which emerged the capability for differentiation, are disappearing. Differentiation, once the condition of humanity, glides into ideology. But the non-sentimental consciousness of that fact does not regress itself. In the act of omission, that which is omitted survives through its exclusion, as consonance survives in atonal harmony. The idiocy of *Endgame* is recorded and developed with the greatest differentiation. The unprotesting depiction of omnipresent regression protests against a disposition of the world which obeys the law of regression so obligingly, that a counter-notion can no longer be conceived to be held against it. That it is only thus and not otherwise is carefully shown; a finely-tuned alarm system reports what belongs to the topology of the play and what does not. Delicately, Beckett suppresses the delicate elements no less than the brutal ones. The vanity of the individual who indicts society, while his rights themselves merge in the accumulation of the injustice of all individuals – disaster itself – is manifest in embarrassing declamations like the "Germany" poem of Karl Wolfskehl.[19] The "too-late," the missed moment condemns such bombastic rhetoric to phraseology. Nothing of that sort in Beckett. Even the view that he negatively presents the negativity of the age would fit into a certain kind of conception, according to which people in the eastern satellite countries – where the revolution is carried out by bureaucratic decree – need only devote themselves happily to reflecting a happy-go-lucky age. Playing with elements of reality – devoid of any mirror-like reflection –, refusing to take a "position," and finding joy in such freedom as is prescribed: all of this reveals more than would be possible if a "revealer" were partisan. The name of disaster can only be spoken silently. Only in the terror of recent events is the terror of the whole ignited, but only there, not in gazing upon "origins." Humankind, whose general species-name fits badly into Beckett's linguistic landscape, is only that which humanity has become. As in utopia, the last days pass judgment on the species. But this lamentation – within mind itself – must reflect that lamenting has become impossible. No amount of weeping melts the armor; only that face remains on which the tears have dried up. That is the basis of a kind of artistic behavior denounced as inhuman by those whose humanity has already become an advertisement for inhumanity, even if they have as yet no notion of that fact. Among the motives for Beckett's regression to animal-like man, that is probably the deepest. By hiding its countenance, his poetic work participates in the absurd.

The catastrophies that inspire *Endgame* have exploded the individual whose substantiality and absoluteness was the common element between Kierkegaard, Jaspers, and the Sartrian version of existentialism.[20] Even to the concentration camp victims, existentialism had attibuted the freedom either inwardly to accept or reject the inflicted martyrdom. *Endgame* destroys such illusions. The individual as a historical category, as the result of the captalist process of alienation and as a defiant protest against it, has itself become openly transitory. The individualist position belonged, as polar opposite, to the ontological tendency of every existentialism, even that of *Being and Time*.[21] Beckett's dramaturgy abandons it like an obsolete bunker. In its narrowness and contingency, individual experience could nowhere locate the authority to interpret itself as a cipher of being, unless it pronounced itself the fundamental characteristic of being. Precisely that, however, is

[19] Karl Wolfskehl (1869–1948), a German-Jewish poet who, together with Stefan George, edited a celebrated anthology of German poetry, *Deutsche Dichtung* (Berlin: Blätter für die Kunst, 1902, reprinted 1910, 1923). In 1933 he fled to Italy, then in 1938 to New Zealand. Adorno may have in his poem "An die Deutschen," dedicated to Stefan George, or "Für Gert – mit Deutsche Dichtung III," both in his *Gesammelte Werke*, vol. 1 (Hamburg: Claasen, 1960), pp. 216, 267.

[20] On Kierkegaard and Sartre, see the opening note to this essay; Karl Jaspers (1883–1969) was a German philosopher and an influential architect of existentialism.

[21] The principal work of Martin Heidegger (1889–1976), first published in 1923.

untrue. The immediacy of individuation was deceptive: what particular human experience clings to is mediated, determined. *Endgame* insinuates that the individual's claim of autonomy and of being has become incredible. But while the prison of individuation is revealed as a prison and simultaneously as mere semblance – the stage scenery is the image of such self-reflection –, art is unable to release the spell of fragmented subjectivity; it can only depict solipsism. Beckett thereby bumps up against art's contemporary antinomy. The position of the absolute subject, once it has been cracked open as the appearance of an over-arching whole through which it first matures, cannot be maintained: Expressionism becomes obsolete. Yet the transition to the binding universality of objective reality, that universality which could relativize the semblance of individuation, is denied art. For art is different from the discursive cogniton of the real, not gradually but categorically distinct from it; in art, only what is transported into the realm of subjectivity, commensurable to it, is valid. It can conceive reconciliation – its idea – only as reconciliation of that which is alienated. If art simulated the state of reconciliation by surrendering to the mere world of things, then it would negate itself. What is offered in the way of socialist realism is not – as some claim – beyond subjectivism but rather lags behind it and is at the same time its pre-artistic complement; the expressionist "Oh Man"[22] and ideologically spiced social reportage fit together seamlessly. In art, unreconciled reality tolerates no reconciliation with the object; realism, which does not reach the level of subjective experience, to say nothing of reaching further, merely mimics reconciliation. The dignity of art today is not measured by asking whether it slips out of this antinomy by luck or cleverness, but whether art confronts and develops it. In that regard, *Endgame* is exemplary. It yields both to the impossibility of dealing with materials and of representation according to nineteenth-century practice, as well as to the insight that subjective modes of reaction, which mediate the laws of form rather than reflecting reality, are themselves no absolute first principle but rather a last principle, objectively posited. All content of subjectivity, which necessarily hypostatizes itself, is trace and shadow of the world, from which it withdraws in order not to serve that semblance and conformity the world demands. Beckett responds to that condition not with any immutable "provisions" (*Vorrat*), but rather with what is still permitted, precariously and uncertainly, by the antagonistic tendencies. His dramaturgy resembles the fun that the old Germany offered – knocking about between the border markers of Baden and Bavaria, as if they fenced in a realm of freedom. *Endgame* takes place in a zone of indifference between inner and outer, neutral between – on the one hand – the "materials" without which subjectivity could not manifest itself or even exist, and – on the other – an animating impulse which blurs the materials, as if that impulse had breathed on the glass through which they are viewed. These materials are so meager that aesthetic formalism is ironically rescued – against its adversaries hither and thither, the stuff-pushers of dialectical materialism and the administrators of authentic messages. The concreteness of the lemurs, whose horizon was lost in a double sense, is transformed directly into the most extreme abstraction; the level of material itself determines a procedure in which the materials, by being lightly touched as transitory, approximate geometrical forms; the most narrow becomes the general. The localization of *Endgame* in that zone teases the spectator with the suggestion of a symbolism which it – like Kafka – refuses. Because no state of affairs is merely what it is, each appears as the sign of interiority, but that inward element supposedly signified no longer exists, and the signs mean just that. That iron ration of reality and people, with whom the drama reckons and keeps house, is one with that which remains of subject, mind (*Geist*), and soul in the face of permanent catastrophe: of the mind, which originated in mimesis, only ridiculous imitation; of the soul – staging itself – inhumane sentimentality; of the subject its most abstract determination, actually existing and thereby already blaspheming. Beckett's figures behave primitively and behavioristically, corresponding to conditions after the catastrophe, which has mutilated them to such an extent that they cannot react differently – flies that twitch after the swatter has half smashed them. The aesthetic *principium stilisationis* does the same to humans. Thrown back completely upon themselves, subjects – anti-cosmism become flesh – consist in nothing other than the wretched realities

---

[22] Not the title of an actual poem or other work, but a declamatory address to man of a sort typical in expressionism.

of their world, shrivelled down to raw necessities; they are empty *personae*, through which the world truly can only resound. Their "phonyness" is the result of mind's disenchantment – as mythology. In order to undercut history and perhaps thereby to hibernate, *Endgame* occupies the nadir of what philosophy's construction of the subject-object confiscated at its zenith: pure identity becomes the identity of annihilation, identity of subject and object in the state of complete alienation. While meanings in Kafka were beheaded or confused, Beckett calls a halt to the bad infinity of intentions: their sense is senselessness. Objectively and without any polemical intent, that is his answer to existential philosophy, which under the name of "thrownness" and later of "absurdity" transforms senselessness itself into sense, exploiting the equivocations inherent in the concept of sense. To this Beckett juxtaposes no world view, rather he takes it at its word. What becomes of the absurd, after the characters of the meaning of existence have been torn down, is no longer a universal – the absurd would then be yet again an idea – but only pathetic details which ridicule conceptuality, a stratum of utensils as in an emergency refuge: ice boxes, lameness, blindness, and unappetizing bodily functions. Everything awaits evacuation. This stratum is not symbolic but rather the post-psychological state, as in old people and torture victims.

Removed from their inwardness, Heidegger's states of being (*Befindlichkeiten*) and Jaspers' "situations" have become materialistic. With them, the hypostases of individual and that of situation were in harmony. The "situation" was temporal existence itself, and the totality of living individuals was the primary certainty. It presupposed personal identity. Here, Beckett proves to be a pupil of Proust[23] and a friend of Joyce, in that he gives back to the concept of "situation" what it actually says and what philosophy made vanish by exploiting it: dissociation of the unity of consciousness into disparate elements – non-identity. As soon as the subject is no longer doubtlessly self-identical, no longer a closed structure of meaning, the line of demarcation with the exterior becomes blurred, and the situations of inwardness become at the same time physical ones. The tribunal over individuality – conserved by existentialism as its idealist core – condemns idealism. Non-identity is both: the historical disintegration of the subject's unity and the emergence of what is not itself subject. That changes the possible meaning of "situation." It is defined by Jaspers as "a reality for an existing subject who has a stake in it."[24] He subsumes the concept of situation under a subject conceived as firm and identical, just as he insinuates that meaning accrues to the situation because of its relationship to this subject. Immediately thereafter, he also calls it "not just a reality governed by natural laws. It is a sense-related reality," a reality moreover which, strangely enough, is said by Jaspers to be "neither psychological nor physical, but both in one."[25] When situation becomes – in Beckett's view – actually both, it loses its existential-ontological constituents: personal identity and meaning. That becomes striking in the concept of "boundary situation" (*Grenzsituation*). It also stems from Jaspers: "Situations like the following: that I am always in situations; that I cannot live without struggling and suffering; that I cannot avoid guilt; that I must die – these are what I call boundary situations. They never change, except in appearance; [with regard to our existence, they are final]."[26] The construction of *Endgame* takes that up with a sardonic "Pardon me?" Such wise sayings as that "I cannot live without suffering, that I cannot avoid guilt, that I must die" lose their triviality the moment they are retrieved back from their apriority and portrayed concretely. Then they break to pieces – all those noble, affirmative elements with which philosophy adorns that existence that Hegel already called "foul" (*faul*).[27] It does so by

23   Marcel Proust (1871–1922), French author of the monumental *A la recherche du temps perdu* or *In Search of Lost Time*.

24   [Adorno's note:] Karl Jaspers, *Philosophy*, trans. E. B. Ashton (Chicago: University of Chicago Press, 1970), vol. 2, p. 177.

25   [Adorno's note:] *Philosophy*, vol. 2, p. 177.

26   [Adorno's note:] *Philosophy*, vol. 2, p. 178; the words in square brackets are omitted in the translation.

27   G. W. F. Hegel (1770–1831) is noted for his optimistic view that history converges with reason; whatever does not is merely *faule Existenz*, or "negative, worthless existence." "Einleitung" ("Introduction") to the *Vorlesungen über die Philosophie der Geschichte* (Lectures on the Philosophy of History), in Hegel's *Werke*, eds. Eva Moldenhauer and Karl Markus Michel (Frankfurt: Suhrkamp, 1979), vol. 12, p. 53: "Die Einsicht nun, zu der, im Gegensatz jener Ideale, die Philosophie führen soll, ist, daß die wirkliche Welt ist, wie sie sein soll, daß das wahrhafte Gute, die allgemeine göttliche Vernunft auch die Macht ist, sich selbst zu vollbringen. Dieses Gute, diese Vernunft in inhrer konkretesten Vorstellung ist Gott. Gott regiert die Welt, der Inhalt seiner Regierung, die Vollführung seines Plans ist die Weltgeschichte. Diesen will die Philosophie erfassen; denn nur was aus ihm vollführt ist, hat Wirklichkeit, was ihm nicht gemäß ist, ist nur faule Existenz." Or in English, G. W. F. Hegel, *The Philosophy of History*, trans. J. Sibree (New York: Dover, 1956), p. 36:

subsuming the non-conceptual under a concept, which magically disperses that difference pompously characterized as "ontological." Beckett turns existential philosophy from its head back on its feet. His play reacts to the comical and ideological mischief of sentences like: "Courage in the boundary situation is an attitude that lets me view death as an indefinite opportunity to be myself,"[28] whether Beckett is familiar with them or not. The misery of participants in the *Endgame* is the misery of philosophy.

These Beckettian situations which constitute his drama are the negative of meaningful reality. Their models are those of empirical reality. As soon as they are isolated and divested of their purposeful and psychological context through the loss of personal unity, they assume a specific and compelling expression – that of horror. They are manifest already in the practice of Expressionism. The dread disseminated by Leonhard Frank's elementary school teacher Mager, the cause of his murder, becomes evident in the description of Mager's fussy manner of peeling an apple in class.[29] Although it seems so innocent, such circumspection is the figure of sadism: this image of one who takes his time resembles that of the one who delays giving a ghastly punishment. Beckett's treatment of these situations, that panicky and yet artificial derivation of simplistic slapstick comedy of yesteryear, articulates a content noted already in Proust. In his posthumous work *Immediacy and Sense-Interpretation*, Heinrich Rickert considers the possibility of an objective physiognomy of mind, rather than of a merely projected "soul" of a landscape or a work of art.[30] He cites a passage from Ernst Robert Curtius, who considers it "only partially correct to view Proust only or primarily as a great psychologist. A Stendhal is appropriately characterized in this manner. He is indeed part of the Cartesian tradition of the French mind. But Proust does not recognize the division between thinking and the extended substance. He does not sever the world into psychological and physical parts. To regard his work from the perspective of the 'psychological novel' is to misunderstand its significance. In Proust's books, the world of sensate objects occupies the same space as that of mind." Or: "If Proust is a psychologist, he is one in a completely new sense – by immersing all reality, including sense perception, in a mental fluid." To show "that the usual concept of the psychic is not appropriate here," Rickert again quotes Curtius: "But here the concept of the psychological has lost its opposite – and is thereby no longer a useful characterization."[31] The physiognomy of objective expression however retains an enigma. The situations say something, but what? In this regard, art itself, as the embodiment of situations, converges with that physiognomy. It combines the most extreme determinacy with its radical opposite. In Beckett, this contradiction is inverted outward. What is otherwise entrenched behind a communicative facade is here condemned merely to appear. Proust, in a subterranean mystical tradition, still clings affirmatively to that physiognomy, as if involuntary memory disclosed a secret language of things; in Beckett, it becomes the physiognomy of what is no longer human. His situations are counterparts to the immutable elements conjured by Proust's situations; they are wrested from the flood of schizophrenia, which fearful "health" resists with murderous cries. In this realm Beckett's drama remains master of itself, transforming even schizophrenia into reflection:

"The insight then to which – in contradistinction from those ideals – philosophy is to lead us, is, that the real world is as it ought to be – that the truly good – the universal divine reason – is not a mere abstraction, but a vital principle capable of realizing itself. This *Good*, this *Reason*, in its most concrete form, is God. God governs the world; the actual working of his government – the carrying out of his plan – is the History of the world. This plan philosophy strives to comprehend; for only that which has been developed as the result of it, possesses *bonâ fide* reality. That which does not accord with it is negative, worthless existence."

[28] [Adorno's note:] Jaspers, *Philosophy*, vol. 2, p. 197.

[29] Leonhard Frank (1882–1960) was a German novelist from Würzburg; his first novel, *Die Räuberbande* (*The Band of Robbers*)

(Munich: Georg Müller, 1914), won the Fontane Prize when it first appeared; it recounts the story of a group of young boys who eventually murder their sadistic school teacher, Mager. The novel has recently been reissued in paperback (Berlin: Aufbau-Taschenverlag, 2002).

[30] [Adorno's note:] Heinrich Rickert (1863–1939), German philosopher and author of *Unmittelbarkeit und Sinndeutung* (Tübingen: Mohr, 1939), p. 133.

[31] [Adorno's note:] Ernst Robert Curtius, *Französischer Geist im neuen Europa* (Stuttgart: Deutsche Verlags-Anstalt, 1925), rpt. in his *Französischer Geist im zwanzigsten Jahrhundert* (Bern: Francke, 1952), p. 312–13; quoted in Rickert, *Unmittelbarkeit*, p. 133 n.

HAMM: I once knew a madman who thought the end of the world had come. He was a painter – and engraver. I had a great fondness for him. I used to go and see him, in the asylum. I'd take him by the hand and drag him to the window. Look! There! All that rising corn! And there! Look! The sails of the herring fleet! All that loveliness! (*Pause.*) He'd snatch away his hand and go back into his corner. Appalled. All he had seen was ashes. (*Pause.*) He alone had been spared. (*Pause.*) Forgotten. (*Pause.*) It appears the case is . . . was not so . . . so unusual. [p. 1049]

The madman's perception would approximate that of Clov peering on command through the window. *Endgame* draws back from the nadir through no other means than by calling to itself like a sleepwalker: negation of negativity. There sticks in Beckett's memory something like an apoplectic middle-aged man taking his midday nap, with a cloth over his eyes to keep out the light or the flies; it makes him unrecognizable. This image – average and optically barely unusual – becomes a sign only for that gaze which perceives the face's loss of identity, sees the possibility that being concealed is the face of a dead man, and becomes aware of the repulsive nature of that physical concern which reduces the man to his body and places him already among corpses.[32] Beckett stares at such aspects until that family routine – from which they stem – pales into irrelevance. The tableau begins with Hamm covered by an old sheet; at the end, he places near his face the handkerchief, his last possession:

HAMM: Old Stancher! (*Pause.*) You . . . remain. [p. 1061]

Such situations, emancipated from their context and from personal character, are reconstructed in a second autonomous context, just as music joins together the intentions and states of expression immersed in it until its sequence becomes a structure in its own right. A key point in the drama – "If I can hold my peace, and sit quiet, it will be all over with sound, and motion, all over and done with" [p. 1056] – betrays the principle, perhaps as a reminiscence of how Shakespeare employed his principle in the actors' scene of *Hamlet*.

HAMM: Then babble, babble, words, like the solitary child who turns himself into children, two, three, so as to be together, and whisper together, in the dark. (*Pause.*) Moment upon moment, pattering down, like the millet grains of . . . (*he hesitates*) that old Greek, and all life long you wait for that to mount up to a life. [p. 1056]

In the tremors of "not being in a hurry," such situations allude to the indifference and superfluity of what the subject can still manage to do. While Hamm considers riveting shut the lids of those trash cans where his parents reside, he retracts that decision with the same words as when he must urinate with the tortuous aid of the catheter: "Time enough" [p. 1043]. The imperceptible aversion to medicine bottles, dating back to the moment one perceived one's parents as physically vulnerable, mortal, deteriorating, reappears in the question:

HAMM: Is it not time for my pain-killer? [p. 1037]

Speaking to each other has completely become Strindbergian grumbling:

HAMM: You feel normal?
CLOV: (*Irritably*) I tell you I don't complain. [p. 1037]

And another time:

---

32   [Adorno's note:] See Max Horkheimer and Theodor Adorno, *Dialectic of Enlightenment*, trans. John Cumming (New York: Seabury, 1972/London: Verso, 1979), p. 234.

HAMM: I feel a little too far to the left. (*Clov moves chair slightly.*) Now I feel a little too far to the right. (*Clov moves chair slightly.*) Now I feel a little too far forward. (*Clov moves chair slightly.*) Now I feel a little too far back. (*Clov moves chair slightly.*) Don't stay there, (*i.e. behind the chair*) you give me the shivers. (*Clov returns to his place beside the chair.*)

CLOV: If I could kill him I'd die happy. [p. 1044]

The waning of a marriage is the situation where one scratches the other:

NELL: I am going to leave you.
NAGG: Could you give me a scratch before you go?
NELL: No. (*Pause.*) Where?
NAGG: In the back.
NELL: No. (*Pause.*) Rub yourself against the rim.
NAGG: It's lower down. In the hollow.
NELL: What hollow?
NAGG: The hollow! (*Pause.*) Could you not? (*Pause.*) Yesterday you scratched me there.
NELL: (*Elegiac.*) Ah yesterday!
NAGG: Could you not? (*Pause.*) Would you like me to scratch you? (*Pause.*) Are you crying again?
NELL: I was trying. [pp. 1041–42]

After the dismissed father – preceptor of his parents – has told the Jewish joke, metaphysically famous, about the trousers and the world, he himself bursts into laughter. The shame which grips the listener when someone laughs at his own words becomes existential; life is merely the epitome of everything about which one must be ashamed. Subjectivity is frightening when it simply amounts to domination, as in the situation where one whistles and the other comes running [pp. 1049–50]. But what shame struggles against has its social function: in those moments when the bourgeois (*Bürger*) acts like a real bourgeois, he besmirches the concept of humanity on which his claim rests. Beckett's archaic images (*Urbilder*) are also historical, in that he shows as humanly typical only those deformations inflicted on humans by the form of their society. No space remains for anything else. The rudeness and ticks of normal character, which *Endgame* inconceivably intensifies, is that universality of the whole that already preforms all classes and individuals; it merely reproduces itself through bad particularity, the antagonistic interests of single individuals. Because there was no other life than the false one, the catalogue of its defects becomes the mirror image of ontology.

This shattering into unconnected, non-identical elements is nevertheless tied to identity in a theater play, which does not abandon the traditional cast of characters. Only against identity, by dismantling its concept, is dissociation at all possible; otherwise, it would be pure, unpolemical, innocent pluralism. For the time being, the historical crisis of the individual runs up against the single biological being, its arena. The succession of situations in Beckett, gliding along without resistance from individuals, thus ends with those obstinate bodies to which they have regressed. Measured by a unit, such as the body, the schizoid situations are comical like optical illusions. That explains the *prima vista* clowning evident in the behavior and constellations of Beckett's figures.[33] Psychoanalysis explains clownish humor as a regression back to a primordial ontogenetic level, and Beckett's regressive play descends to that level. But the laughter it inspires ought to suffocate the laughter. That is what happened to humor, after it became – as an aesthetic medium – obsolete, repulsive, devoid of any canon of what can be laughed at; without any place for reconciliation, where one could laugh; without anything between heaven and earth harmless enough to be laughed at. An intentionally idiotic *double entendre* about the weather runs:

CLOV: Things are livening up. (*He gets up on ladder, raises the telescope, lets it fall.*) It did it on purpose. (*He gets down, picks up the telescope, turns it on auditorium.*) I see...a multitude...in

---

[33] [Adorno's note:] Cf. Günther Anders, *Die Antiquierheit des Menschen* (Munich: Beck, 1956), p. 217.

transports . . . of joy. (*Pause.*) That's what I call a magnifier. (*He lowers the telescope, turns toward Hamm.*) Well? Don't we laugh? [p. 1044]

Humor itself has become foolish, ridiculous – who could still laugh at basic comic texts like *Don Quixote* or *Gargantua*[34] – and Beckett carries out the verdict on humor. The jokes of the damaged people are themselves damaged. They no longer reach anybody; the state of decline, admittedly a part of all jokes, the *Kalauer* (pun), now covers them like a rash. When Clov, looking through the telescope, is asked about the weather and frightens Hamm with the word "gray," he corrects himself with the formulation "a light black" [p. 1045]. That smears the punchline from Molière's *Miser*, who describes the allegedly stolen casket as gray-red.[35] The marrow has been sucked out of the joke as well as out of the colors. At one point, the two anti-heroes, a blind man and a lame man – the stronger is already both while the weaker will become so – come up with a "trick," an escape, "some kind of plan" à la *Three Penny Opera*;[36] but they do not know whether it will only lengthen their lives and torment, or whether both are to end with absolute obliteration:

CLOV: Ah good. (*He starts pacing to and fro, his eyes fixed on the ground, his hands behind his back. He halts.*) The pains in my legs! It's unbelievable! Soon I won't be able to think any more.
HAMM: You won't be able to leave me. (*Clov resumes his pacing.*) What are you doing?
CLOV: Having an idea. (*He paces.*) Ah. (*He halts.*)
HAMM: What a brain! (*Pause.*) Well?
CLOV: Wait! (*He meditates. Not very convinced.*) Yes . . . (*Pause. More convinced.*) Yes! (*He raises his head.*) I have it! I set the alarm! [p. 1050]

That is probably associated with the originally Jewish joke from the Busch circus,[37] when stupid August, who has caught his wife with his friend on the sofa, cannot decide whether to throw out his wife or the friend, because they are both so dear to him, and comes up with the idea of selling the sofa. But even the remaining trace of silly, sophistic rationality is wiped away. The only comical thing remaining is that along with the sense of the punchline, comedy itself has evaporated. That is how someone suddenly jerks upright after climbing to the top step, climbing further, and stepping into the void. The most extreme crudity completes the verdict on laughter, which has long since participated in its own guilt. Hamm lets his stumps of parents completely starve, those parents who have become babies in their trashcans – the son's triumph as a father. There is this chatter:

NAGG: Me pap!
HAMM: Accursed progenitor!
NAGG: Me pap!
HAMM: The old folks at home! No decency left! Guzzle, guzzle, that's all they think of. (*He whistles. Enter Clov. He halts beside the chair.*) Well! I thought you were leaving me.
CLOV: Oh not just yet, not just yet.

---

[34] Comic novels that appeared respectively in 1605–15 and 1532–55 by Miguel Cervantes (1547–1616) and François Rabelais (c. 1489–1553).

[35] Adorno recalls the tale but not the teller. It's not the miser, Harpagon, who corrects his description of the missing box or casket. It's Monsieur Jacques, the miser's cook and coachman, who is guessing in order to incriminate the valet, Valère, in front of the investigating officer or Commisioner:

Commissioner: Can you tell us what color it was?
M. Jacques: What color?
Comissioner: Yes, sir.
M. Jacques: Well it was kind of . . . you know, that color . . . how would you describe it?
Harpagon: Eh?

M. Jacques: Well – isn't it kind of red, reddish?
Harpagon: Gray.
M. Jacques: Reddish gray, that's it. Or grayish red.

From Jean-Baptiste Molière (1622–73), *The Miser* (1668), trans. Jeremy Sams (London: Methuen, 1991), act 5, sc. 3.

[36] With libretto by Bertolt Brecht (1898–1956) and music by Kurt Weill (1900–50), *The Three Penny Opera* premiered at the Theater am Schiffbauerdamm in Berlin in 1928; it has several comic scenes in which a protagonist is imprisoned and contrives a trick to escape.

[37] A traveling circus that still exists; for its long history see Gisela Winkler, *Zirkus Busch: Geschichte einer Manege* (Berlin: be.bra verlag, 1998).

NAGG: Me pap!

HAMM: Give him his pap.

CLOV: There's no more pap.

HAMM: (*To Nagg.*) Do you hear that? There's no more pap. You'll never get any more pap. [p. 1038]

To the irreparable harm already done, the anti-hero adds his scorn – the indignation at the old people who have no manners, just as the latter customarily decry dissolute youth. What remains humane in this scene – that the two old people share the zwieback with each other – becomes repulsive through its contrast with transcendental bestiality; the residue of love becomes the intimacy of smacking. As far as they are still human, they "humanize":

NELL: What is it, my pet? (*Pause.*) Time for love?

NAGG: Were you asleep?

NELL: Oh no!

NAGG: Kiss me.

NELL: We can't.

NAGG: Try. (*Their heads strain towards each other, fail to meet, fall apart again.*) [p. 1040]

Dramatic categories as a whole are treated just like humor. All are parodied. But not ridiculed. Emphatically, parody entails the use of forms in the epoch of their impossibility. It demonstrates this impossibility and thereby changes the forms. The three Aristotelian unities are retained, but drama itself perishes. Along with subjectivity, whose final epilogue (*Nachspiel*) is *Endgame*, the hero is also withdrawn; the drama's freedom is only the impotent, pathetic reflex of futile resolutions.[38] In that regard too, Beckett's drama is heir to Kafka's novels, to whom he stands in a similar relation as the serial composers to Schoenberg: he reflects the precursor in himself, altering the latter through the totality of his principle. Beckett's critique of the earlier writer, which irrefutably stresses the divergence between what happens and the objectively pure, epic language, conceals the same difficulty as that confronted by contemporary integral composition with the antagonistic procedure of Schoenberg. What is the *raison d'être* of forms when the tension between them and what is not homogeneous to them disappears, and when one nevertheless cannot halt the progress of mastery over aesthetic material? *Endgame* pulls out of the fray, by making that question its own, by making it thematic. That which prohibits the dramatization of Kafka's novels becomes subject matter. Dramatic components reappear after their demise. Exposition, complication, plot, peripeteia, and catastrophe return as decomposed elements in a post-mortem examination of dramaturgy: the news that there are no more painkillers depicts catastrophe [*Endgame*, p. 1057]. Those components have been toppled along with that meaning once discharged by drama; *Endgame* studies (as if in a test-tube) the drama of the age, the age that no longer tolerates what constitutes drama. For example, tragedy, at the height of its plot and with antithesis as its quintessence, manifested the utmost tightening of the dramatic thread, stychomythia – dialogues in which the trimeter spoken by one person follows that of the other. Drama had renounced this technique, because its stylization and resulting pretentiousness seemed alien to secular society. Beckett employs it as if the detonation had revealed what was buried in drama. *Endgame* contains rapid, monosyllabic dialogues, like the earlier question-and-answer games between the blinded king and fate's messenger. But where the bind tightened then, the speakers now grow slack. Short of breath until they almost fall silent, they no longer manage the synthesis of linguistic phrases; they stammer in protocol sentences that might stem from positivists or Expressionists. The boundary value (*Grenzwert*) of Beckett's drama is that silence already defined as "the rest" in Shakespeare's inauguration of modern tragedy. The fact that an "act without words" follows *Endgame* as a kind of epilogue is its own *terminus ad quem*. The words

---

[38] [Adorno's note:] See Theodor Adorno, "Notes on Kafka," in *Prisms*, trans. Samuel and Shierry Weber (Cambridge: MIT Press, 1981), pp. 262–3.

resound like merely makeshift ones because silence is not yet entirely successful, like voices accompanying and disturbing it.

What becomes of form in *Endgame* can be virtually reconstructed from literary history. In Ibsen's *The Wild Duck*,[39] the degenerate photographer Hjalmar Ekdal – himself a potential anti-hero – forgets to bring to the teenager Hedwig the promised menu from the sumptuous dinner at old Werle's house, to which he had been invited without his family. Psychologically, that is motivated by his slovenly egotistical character, but it is symbolically significant also for Hjalmar, for the course of the plot, and for the play's meaning: the girl's futile sacrifice. That anticipates the later Freudian theory of "parapraxis,"[40] Which explicates such slip-ups by means of their relation to past experiences and wishes of an individual, to the individual's identity. Freud's hypotheses, "all our experiences have a sense,"[41] transforms the traditional dramatic idea into psycogical realism, from which Ibsen's tragicomedy of the *Wild Duck* incomparably extracts the spark of form one more time. When such symbolism liberates itself from its psychological determination, it congeals into a being-in-itself, and the symbol becomes symbolic as in Ibsen's late works like *John Gabriel Borkmann*,[42] where the accountant Foldal is overcome by so-called "youth." The contradiction between such a consistent symbolism and conservative realism constitutes the inadequacy of the late plays. But it thereby also constitutes the leavening ferment of the Expressionist Strindberg.[43] His symbols, torn away from empirical human beings, are woven into a tapestry in which everything and nothing is symbolic, because everything can signify everything. Drama need only become aware of the ineluctably ridiculous nature of such pan-symbolism, which destroys itself; it need only take that up and utilize it, and Beckettian absurdity is already achieved as a result of the immanent dialectic of form. Not meaning anything becomes the only meaning. The mortal fear of the dramatic figures, if not of the parodied drama itself, is the distortedly comical fear that they could mean something or other:

HAMM: We're not beginning to . . . to . . . mean something?
CLOV: Mean something! You and I, mean something! (*Brief laugh.*) Ah that's a good one! [p. 1045]

With this possibility, long since crushed by the overwhelming power of an apparatus in which individuals are interchangeable and superfluous, the meaning of language also disappears. Hamm, irritated by the impulse of life which has regressed to clumsiness in his parents' trashcan conversations, and nervous because "it doesn't end," asks: "Will you never finish? Will this never finish?" [p. 1042]. The play takes place on that level. It is constructed on the ground of a proscription of language, and it articulates that in its own structure. However, it does not thereby avoid the aporia of Expressionist drama: that language, even where it tends to be shortened to mere sound, yet cannot shake off its semantic element. It cannot become purely mimetic[44] or gestural, just as forms of modern painting, liberated from referentiality (*Gegenständlichkeit*), cannot cast off all similarity to objects. Mimetic values, definitively unloosed from significative ones, then approach arbitrariness, contingency, and finally a mere secondary convention. The way *Endgame* comes to terms with that differentiates it from *Finnegans Wake*. Rather than striving to liquidate the discursive element of language through pure sound, Beckett turns that element into an instrument of its own absurdity and he does that according to the ritual of clowns, whose babbling becomes nonsensical by presenting itself as sense. The objective disintegration of language – that simultaneously stereotyped and faulty chatter of self-alienation, where word and sentence melt together in human

[39] *The Wild Duck* (1884), by the Norwegian dramatist Henrik Ibsen (1828–1906), was first performed in 1885.
[40] "Parapaxes" is the usual translation of Freud's *Fehlleistungen*, but Adorno deliberately writes *Fehlhandlungen*: fault acts, slip-ups.
[41] [Adorno's note:] Sigmund Freud, *The Standard Edition of the Complete Psychological Works*, trans. and ed. James Strachey (London: Hogarth Press, 1963), vol. 15, 40. [Editor's note: Freud, discussing "parapaxes" urges that "we formed an impres-

sion that in particular cases they seemed to be betraying a sense of their own."]
[42] The play was written in 1896 and first performed in 1897.
[43] August Strindberg (1849–1912), German dramatist.
[44] [Adorno's note:] See "Presuppositions," in *Notes to Literature*, vol. 2, trans. Shierry Weber Nicholsen (New York: Columbia University Press, 1992), pp. 33–4; and also Max Horkheimer and Theodor Adorno, *Dialectic of Enlightenment*, pp. 24 ff.

mouths — penetrates the aesthetic arcanum. The second language of those falling silent, a conglomeration of insolent phrases, pseudo-logical connections, and galvanized words appearing as commodity signs — as the desolate echo of the advertising world — is "refunctioned" (*umfunktio-niert*) into the language of a poetic work that negates language.[45] Beckett thus approximates the drama of Eugène Ionesco. Whereas a later work by him is organized around the image of the tape recorder, the language of *Endgame* resembles another language familiar from the loathsome party game, where someone records the nonsense spoken at a party and then plays it back for the guests' humiliation. The shock, overcome on such an occasion only by stupid tittering, is here carefully composed. Just as alert experience seems to notice everywhere situations from Kafka's novels after reading him intensely, so does Beckett's language bring about a healing illness of those already ill: whoever listens to himself worries that he also talks like that. For some time now, the accidental events on the street seem to the movie-goer just leaving the theater like the planned contingency of a film. Between the mechanically assembled phrases taken from the language of daily life, the chasm yawns. Where one of the pair asks with the routine gesture of the hardened man, certain of the uncontestable boredom of existence, "What in God's name could there be on the horizon?" [p. 1045] then this shoulder-shrugging in language becomes apocalyptic, particularly because it is so familiar. From the bland yet aggressive impulse of human "common sense," "What do you think there is?" is extracted the confession of its own nihilism. Somewhat later, Hamm the master commands the *soi-disant* servant Clov, in a circus-task, to undertake the vain attempt to shove the chair back and forth, to fetch the "gaff." There follows a brief dialogue:

CLOV: Do this, do that, and I do it. I never refuse. Why?
HAMM: You're not able to.
CLOV: Soon I won't do it any more.
HAMM: You won't be able to any more. (*Exit Clov.*) Ah the creatures, everything has to be explained to them. [pp. 1048–9]

That "everything has to be explained to the creatures" is drummed daily by millions of superiors into millions of subordinates. However, by means of the nonsense thus supposedly established in the passage — Hamm's explanation contradicts his own command — the cliché's inanity, usually hidden by custom, is garishly illuminated, and furthermore, the fraud of speaking with each other is expressed. When conversing, people remain hopelessly distant from each other no more reaching each other than the two old cripples in the trash bins do. Communication, the universal law of clichés, proclaims that there is no more communication. The absurdity of all speaking is not unrelated to realism but rather develops from it. For communicative language postulates — already in its syntactic form, through logic, the nature of conclusions, and stable concepts — the principle of sufficient reason. Yet this requirement is hardly met any more: when people speak with each other, they are motivated partly by their psychology or pre-logical unconscious, and partly by their pursuit of purposes. Since they aim at self-preservation, these purposes deviate from that objectivity deceptively manifest in their logical form. At any rate, one can prove that point to people today with the help of tape recorders. In Freud's as in Pareto's understanding,[46] the *ratio* of verbal communication is always also a rationalization. *Ratio* itself emerged from the interest in self-preservation, and it is therefore undermined by the obligatory rationalizations of its own irrationality. The contradiction between the rational façade and the immutably irrational is itself already the absurd. Beckett must only mark the contradiction and employ it as a selective principle, and realism, casting off the illusion of rational stringency, comes into its own.

---

[45] [Adorno's note:] See Theodor Adorno, *Dissonanzen*, 2nd edn. (Göttingen: Vandenhoeck und Ruprecht, 1958), pp. 34 and 44.

[46] Vilfredo Pareto (1848–1923) was an Italian economist, sociologist, and philosopher who drew a sharp distinction between logical and nonlogical conduct, and who therefore distinguished between the explanations that people gave for their conduct and their real reasons for behaving that way. See Pareto, *The Mind and Society*, 4 vols., trans. Andrew Bongiorno and Arthur Livngstone (New York: Harcourt Brace, 1935).

Even the syntactic form of question and answer is undermined. It presupposes an openness of what is to be spoken, an openness which no longer exists, as Huxley already noted. In the question one hears already the anticipated answer, and that condemns the game of question and answer to empty deception, to the unworkable effort to conceal the unfreedom of informative language in the linguistic gesture of freedom. Beckett tears away this veil, and the philosophical veil as well. Everything radically called into question when confronted by nothingness resists – by virtue of a pathos borrowed from theology – these terrifying consequences, while insisting on their possibility; in the form of question and answer, the answer is infiltrated with the meaning denied by the whole game. It is not for nothing that in fascism and pre-fascism such destructionists were able heartily to scorn destructive intellect. But Beckett deciphers the lie of the question mark: the question has become rhetorical. While the existential-philosophical hell resembles a tunnel, where in the middle one can already discern light shining at the end, Beckett's dialogues rip up the railroad tracks of conservation; the train no longer arrives at the bright end of the tunnel. Wedekind's old technique of misunderstanding becomes total. The course of the dialogues themselves approximates the contingency principle of literary production. It sounds as if the laws of its continuation were not the "reason" of speech and reply, and not even their psychological entwinement, but rather a test of listening, related to that of a music which frees itself from preformed types. The drama attends carefully to what kind of sentence might follow another. Given the accessible spontaneity of such questions, the absurdity of content is all the more strongly felt. That, too, finds its infantile model in those people who, when visiting the zoo, wait attentively for the next move of the hippopotamus or the chimpanzee.

In the state of its disintegration, language is polarized. On the one hand, it becomes Basic English, or French, or German – single words, archaically ejected commands in the jargon of universal disregard, the intimacy of irreconcilable adversaries; on the other hand, it becomes the aggregate of its empty forms, of a grammar that has renounced all reference to its content and therefore also to its synthetic function. The interjections are accompanied by exercise sentences, God knows why. Beckett trumpets this from the rooftops, too: one of the rules of the *Endgame* is that the unsocial partners – and with them the audience – are always eyeing each other's cards. Hamm considers himself an artist. He has chosen as his life maxim Nero's *qualis artifex pereo*.[47] But the stories he undertakes run aground on syntax:

HAMM: Where was I? (*Pause. Gloomily.*) It's finished, we're finished. (*Pause.*) Nearly finished. [p. 1051]

Logic reels between the linguistic paradigms. Hamm and Clov converse in their authoritative, mutually cutting fashion:

HAMM: Open the window.
CLOV: What for?
HAMM: I want to hear the sea.
CLOV: You wouldn't hear it.
HAMM: Even if you opened the window?
CLOV: No.
HAMM: Then it's not worthwhile opening it?
CLOV: No.
HAMM: (*Violently.*) Then open it! (*Clov gets up on the ladder, opens the window. Pause.*) Have you opened it?
CLOV: Yes. [p. 1055]

One could almost see in Hamm's last "then" the key to the play. Because it is not worthwhile to open the window, since Hamm cannot hear the sea – perhaps it is dried out, perhaps it no longer

---

[47] Latin for "I shall perish as an artist," as Nero is reported to have said while Rome burned and he fiddled.

moves –, he insists that Clov open it. The nonsense of an act becomes a reason to accomplish it – a late legitimation of Fichte's free activity for its own sake.[48] That is how contemporary actions look, and they arouse the suspicion that things were never very different. The logical figure of the absurd, which makes the claim of stringency for stringency's contradictory opposite, denies every context of meaning apparently guaranteed by logic, in order to prove logic's own absurdity: that logic, by means of subject, predicate, and copula, treats non-identity as if it were identical, as if it were consumed in its forms. The absurd does not take the place of the rational as one world view of another; in the absurd, the rational world view comes into its own.

The pre-established harmony of despair reigns between the forms and the residual content of the play. The ensemble – smelted together – counts only four heads. Two of them are excessively red, as if their vitality were a skin disease; the two old ones, however, are excessively white, like sprouting potatoes in a cellar. None of them still has a properly functioning body; the old people consist only of rumps, having apparently lost their legs not in the catastrophe but in a private tandem accident in the Ardennes, "on the road to Sedan" [p. 1041], an area where one army regularly annihilates another. One should not suppose that all that much has changed. Even the memory of their own particular (*bestimmt*) misfortune becomes enviable in relation to the indeterminacy (*Unbestimmtheit*) of universal misfortune – they laugh at it. In contrast to Expressionism's fathers and sons, they all have their own names, but all four names have one syllable, "four-letter words" like obscenities. Practical, familiar abbreviations, popular in Anglo-Saxon countries, are exposed as mere stumps of names. Only the name of the old mother, Nell, is somewhat common even if obsolete; Dickens uses it for the touching child in *Old Curiosity Shop*. The three other names are invented as if for bill-boards. The old man is named Nagg, with the association of "nagging" and perhaps also a German association: an intimate pair is intimate through "gnawing" (*Nagen*). They talk about whether the sawdust in their cans has been changed; yet it is not sawdust but sand. Nagg stipulates that it used to be sawdust, and Nell answers boredly: "Once!" [p. 1041] – a woman who spitefully exposes her husband's frozen, repetitive declarations. As sordid as the fight about sawdust or sand is, the difference is decisive for the residual plot, the transition from a minimum to nothing. Beckett can claim for himself what Benjamin praised in Baudelaire, the ability to "express something extreme with extreme discretion;"[49] the routine consolation that things could be worse becomes a condemnation. In the realm between life and death, where even pain is no longer possible, the difference between sawdust and sand means everything. Sawdust, wretched by-product of the world of things, is now in great demand; its removal becomes an intensification of the life-long death penalty. The fact that both lodge in trash bins – a comparable motif appears, moreover, in Tennessee Williams' *Camino Real*,[50] surely without one play having been influenced by the other – takes the conversational phrase literally, as in Kafka. "Today old people are thrown in the trashcan" and it happens. *Endgame* is the true gerontology. According to the measure of socially useful labor, which they can no longer perform, old people are superfluous and must be discarded. That is extracted from the scientific ruckus of a welfare system that accentuates what it negates. *Endgame* trains the viewer for a condition where everyone involved expects – upon lifting the lid from the nearest dumpster – to find his own parents. The natural cohension of life has become organic refuse. The national socialists irreparably overturned the taboo of old age. Beckett's trashcans are the emblem of a culture restored after Auschwitz. Yet the sub-plot goes further than too far, to the old people's demise. They are denied children's fare, their pap, which is replaced by a biscuit they – toothless – can no longer chew; and they suffocate, because the last man is too sensitive to grant life to the next-to-last ones. That is entwined with the main plot, because the old pair's miserable end drives it forward to that exit of life whose possibility constitutes the tension in the play. Hamlet is revised: croak or croak, that is the question.

48   Johann Gottlieb Fichte (1762–1814) was a German philosopher for whom reality is ideal activity or activity for its own sake, underived, and prior to any specific or definable thing, substance, or process.

49   [Adorno's note:] Cf. Walter Benjamin, "On Some Motifs in Baudelaire," in his *Illuminations*, trans. Harry Zohn (New York: Schocken Books, 1969), pp. 183–4.

50   Tennessee Williams (1911–83), American playwright and author of *Camino Real* (New York: New Directions, 1953).

The name of Shakespeare's hero is grimly foreshortened by Beckett – the last, liquidated dramatic subject echoing the first. It is also associated with one of Noah's sons and thereby with the flood: the progenitor of blacks, who replaces the white "master race" in a Freudian negation. Finally, there is the English "ham actor." Beckett's Hamm, the key to power and helpless at the same time, plays at what he no longer is, as if he had read the most recent sociological literature defining *zoon politikon* as a role. Whoever cleverly presented himself became a "personality" just like helpless Hamm. "Personality" may have been a role originally – nature pretending to transcend nature. Fluctuation in the play's situations causes one of Hamm's roles: occasionally, a stage direction drastically suggests that he speak with the "voice of a rational being;" in a lengthy narrative, he is to strike a "narrative tone." The memory of what is irretrievably past becomes a swindle. Disintegration retrospectively condemns as fictional that continuity of life which alone made life possible. Differences in tone – between people who narrate and those who speak directly – pass judgment on the principle of identity. Both alternate in Hamm's long speech, a kind of inserted aria without music. At the transition points he pauses – the artistic pauses of the veteran actor of heroic roles. For the norm of existential philosophy – people should be themselves because they can no longer become anything else –, *Endgame* posits the antithesis, that precisely this self is not a self but rather the aping imitation of something non-existent. Hamm's mendacity exposes the lie concealed in saying "I" and thereby exhibiting substantiality, whose opposite is the content disclosed by the "I." Immutability, the epitome of transience, is its ideology. What used to be the truth content of the subject – thinking – is only still preserved in its gestural shell. Both main figures act as if they were reflecting on something, but without thinking.

HAMM: The whole thing is comical, I grant you that. What about having a good guffaw the two of
    us together?
CLOV: (*After reflection.*) I couldn't guffaw today.
HAMM: (*After reflection.*) Nor I. [p. 1054]

According to his name, Hamm's counterpart is what he is, a truncated clown, whose last letter has been severed. An archaic expression for the devil sounds similar – cloven foot; it also resembles the current word "glove." He is the devil of his master, whom he has threatened with the worst, leaving him; yet at the same time he is also the glove with which the master touches the world of things, which he can no longer directly grasp. Not only the figure of Clov is constructed through such associations, but also his connection with the others. In the old piano edition of Stravinsky's "Ragtime for Eleven Instruments,"[51] one of the most significant works of his Surrealist phase, there was a Picasso drawing which – probably inspired by the title "rag" – showed two ragged figures, the ancestors of those vagabonds Vladimir and Estragon, who are waiting for Godot. This virtuoso sketch is a single entangled line. The double-sketch of *Endgame* is of this spirit, as well as the damaged repetitions irresistably produced by Beckett's entire work. In them, history is cancelled out. This compulsory repetition is taken from the regressive behavior of someone locked up, who tries it again and again. Beckett converges with the newest musical tendencies by combining, as a Westerner, aspects of Stravinsky's radical past – the oppressive stasis of disintegrating continuity – with the most advanced expressive and constructive means from the Schoenberg school.[52] Even the outlines of Hamm and Clov are one line; they are denied the individuation of a tidily independent monad. They cannot live without each other. Hamm's power over Clov seems to be that only he knows how to open the cupboard, somewhat like the situation where only the principal knows the combination of the safe. He would reveal the secret to Clov, if Clov would swear to "finish" him – or "us." In a reply thoroughly characteristic of the play's tapestry, Clov answers: "I couldn't finish you;" as if the play were mocking the man who feigns reason, Hamm says: "Then you shan't finish

[51] Igor Stravinsky (1882–1971) composed the "Ragtime for Eleven Instruments" in 1918; he also wrote "Piano-Rag-Music: for Piano Solo," and Adorno may be onfusing the two works.

[52] Adorno seemingly refers to something like *Le Sacre du Printemps* being combined with something analogous to the serialism of the Austrian Arnold Schoenberg (1874–1951).

me" [p. 1047]. He is dependent on Clov, because Clov alone can accomplish what keeps both alive. But that is of questionable value, because both – like the captain of the ghostly ship – must fear not being able to die. The tiny bit that is also everything – that would be the possibility that something could perhaps change. This movement, or its absence, is the plot. Admittedly, it does not become much more explicit than the repeated motif "Something is taking its course" [pp. 1040, 1045], as abstract as the pure form of time. The Hegelian dialectic of master and slave,[53] mentioned by Günther Anders with reference to *Godot*, is derided rather than portrayed according to the tenets of traditional aesthetics. The slave can no longer grasp the reins and abolish domination. Crippled as he is, he would hardly be capable of this, and according to the play's historico-philosophical sundial, it is too late for spontaneous action anyway. Clov has no other choice than to emigrate out into the world that no longer exists for the play's recluses, with a good chance of dying. He cannot even depend on freedom unto death. He does manage to make the decision to go, even comes in for the farewell: "Panama hat, tweed coat, raincoat over his arm, umbrella, bag"[p. 1060] – a strong, almost musical conclusion. But one does not see his exit, rather he remains "impassive and motionless, his eyes fixed on Hamm, till the end" [p. 1060]. That is an allegory whose intention has evaporated. Aside from some differences, which may be decisive or completely irrelevant, this is identical with the beginning. No spectator and no philosopher can say if the play will not begin anew. The dialectic swings to a standstill.

As a whole, the play's plot is musically composed with two themes, like the double fugue of earlier times. The first theme is that it should end, a Schopenhauerian negation of the will to live become insignificant.[54] Hamm strikes it up; the persons, no longer persons, become instruments of their situation, as if they were playing chamber music. "Of all of Beckett's bizarre instruments, Hamm, who in *Endgame* sits blindly and immovably in his wheelchair, resounds with the most tones, the most surprising sound."[55] Hamm's non-identity with himself motivates the course of the play. While he desires the end of the torment of a miserably infinite existence, he is concerned about his life, like a gentleman in his ominous "prime" years. The peripheral paraphernalia of health are utmost in his mind. Yet he does not fear death, rather that death could miscarry; Kafka's motif of the hunter Grachus still resonates.[56] Just as important to him as his own bodily necessities is the certainty that Clov, ordered to gaze out, does not espy any sail or trail of smoke, that no rat or insect is stirring, with whom the calamity could begin anew; that he also does not see the perhaps surviving child, who could signify hope and for whom he lies in wait like Herod the butcher for the *agnus dei*. Insecticide, which all along pointed toward the genocidal camps, becomes the final product of the domination of nature, which destroys itself. Only this content of life remains: that nothing be living. All existence is levelled to a life that is itself death, abstract domination. The second theme is attributed to Clov the servant. After an admittedly obscure history he sought refuge with Hamm; but he also resembles the son of the raging yet impotent patriarch. To give up obedience to the powerless is most difficult; the insignificant and obsolete struggles irresistably against its abolition. Both plots are counterpointed, since Hamm's will to die is identical with his life principle, while Clov's will to live may well bring about the death of both; Hamm says: "Outside of here it's death" [p. 1038]. The antithesis of the heroes is also not fixed, rather their impulses converge; it is Clov who first speaks of the end. The scheme of the play's progression is the end game in chess, a typical, rather standard situation, separated from the middle game and its combinations by a caesura; these are also missing in the play, where intrigue and "plot" are silently suspended. Only artistic mistakes or accidents, such as something growing somewhere, could cause unforeseen events, but not resourceful spirit. The field is almost empty, and what happened before can only be poorly construed from the positions of the few remaining figures. Hamm is the king, about whom everything turns and who can do nothing himself. The incongruity between chess as

---

[53] See *Hegel's Phenomenology of Spirit*, trans. A. V. Miller (Oxford: Oxford University Press, 1977), pp. 111–18.

[54] Arthur Schopenhauer (1788–1860), thought that humans were enslaved to the will (conceived as something that resembles a Freudian unconscious, or libido), and that a denial of the will was necessary; Adorno extends this notion to the will to live.

[55] [Adorno's note:] Marie Luise Kaschnitz (1901–74), "Lecture on Lucky," Frankfurt University, later published in her *Zwischen Immer und Nie: Gestalten und Themen der Dichtung* (Frankfurt am Main: Insel, 1971), p. 207.

[56] [Adorno's note:] See Adorno, "Notes on Kafka," *Prisms*, p. 260.

pastime and the excessive effort involved becomes on the stage an incongruity between athletic pretense and the lightweight actions that are performed. Whether the game ends with stalemate or with perpetual check, or whether Clov wins, remains unclear, as if clarity in that would already be too much meaning. Moreover, it is probably not so important, because everything would come to an end in stalemate as in checkmate. Otherwise, only the fleeting image of the child [see e.g. p. 1059] breaks out of the circle, the most feeble reminder of Fortinbras or the child king. It could even be Clov's own abandoned child. But the oblique light falling from thence into the room is as weak as the helplessly helping arms extending from the windows at the conclusion of Kafka's *Trial*.

The history of the subject's end becomes thematic in an intermezzo, which can afford its symbolism, because it depicts the subject's own decrepitude and therefore that of its meaning. The hubris of idealism, the enthroning of man as creator in the center of creation, has entrenched itself in that "bare interior" like a tyrant in his last days. There man repeats with a reduced, tiny imagination what man was once supposed to be; man repeats what was taken from him by social strictures as well as by today's cosmology, which he cannot escape. Clov is his male nurse. Hamm has himself shoved about by Clov into the middle of that *intérieur* which the world has become but which is also the interior of his own subjectivity:

HAMM: Take me for a little turn. (*Clov goes behind the chair and pushes it forward.*) Not too fast! (*Clov pushes chair.*) Right round the world! (*Clov pushes chair.*) Hug the walls, then back to the center again. (*Clov pushes chair.*) I was right in the center, wasn't I? [p. 1043]

The loss of the center, parodied here because that center itself was a lie, becomes the paltry object of carping and powerless pedantry:

CLOV: We haven't done the round.
HAMM: Back to my place. (Clov pushes chair back to center.) Is that my place?
[. . .]
CLOV: I'll measure it.
HAMM: More or less! More or less!
CLOV: (*Moving chair slightly.*) There!
HAMM: I'm more or less in the center?
CLOV: I'd say so.
HAMM: You'd say so! Put me right in the center!
CLOV: I'll go and get the tape.
HAMM: Roughly! Roughly! (*Clov moves chair slightly.*) Bang in the center! [pp. 1043–4]

What is paid back in this ludicrous ritual is nothing originally perpetrated by the subject. Subjectivity itself is guilty; that one even is. Original sin is heretically fused with creation. Being, trumpeted by existential philosophy as the meaning of being, becomes its antithesis. Panic fear of the reflex movements of living entities does not only drive untiringly toward the domination of nature: it also attaches itself to life as the ground of that calamity which life has become:

HAMM: All those I might have helped. (*Pause.*) Helped! (*Pause.*) Saved. (*Pause.*) Saved! (*Pause.*) The place was crawling with them! (*Pause. Violently.*) Use your head, can't you, use your head, you're on earth, there's no cure for that! [p. 1056]

From that he draws the conclusion: "The end is in the beginning and yet you go on" [p. 1056]. The autonomous moral law reverts antinomically from pure domination over nature into the duty to exterminate, which always lurked in the background:

HAMM: More complications! (*Clov gets down.*) Not an underplot, I trust. (*Clov moves ladder nearer window gets up on it, turns telescope on the without.*)
CLOV: (*Dismayed.*) Looks like a small boy!

HAMM: (*Sarcastic.*) A small . . . boy!
CLOV: I'll go and see. (*He gets down, drops the telescope, goes towards door, turns.*)
HAMM: No! (*Clov halts.*)
CLOV: No? A potential procreator? [p. 1059 and 1059 n. 14]

Such a total conception of duty stems from idealism, which is judged by a question the handicapped rebel Clov poses to his handicapped master:

CLOV: Any particular sector you fancy? Or merely the whole thing? [p. 1057]

That sounds like a reminder of Benjamin's insight that an intuited cell of reality counterbalances the remainder of the whole world. Totality, a pure postulate of the subject, is nothing. No sentence sounds more absurd than this most reasonable of sentences, which bargains "the whole thing" down to "merely," to the phantom of an anthropocentrically dominated world. As reasonable as this most absurd observation is, it is nevertheless impossible to dispute the absurd aspects of Beckett's play just because they are confiscated by hurried apologetics and a desire for easy disposal. *Ratio*, having been fully instrumentalized, and therefore devoid of self-reflection and of reflection on what it has excluded, must seek that meaning that it has itself extinguished. But in the condition that necessarily gave rise to this question, no answer is possible other than nothingness, which the form of the answer already is. The historical inevitability of this absurdity allows it to seem ontological; that is the veil of delusion produced by history itself. Beckett's drama rips through this veil. The immanent contradition of the absurd, reason terminating in senselessness, emphatically reveals the possibility of a truth which can no longer even be thought; it undermines the absolute claim exercised by what merely is. Negative ontology is the negation of ontology: history alone has brought to maturity what was appropriated by the mythic power of timelessness. The historical fiber of situation and language in Beckett does not concretize – *more philosophico* – something unhistorical: precisely this procedure, typical of existential dramatistis, is both foreign to art and philosophically obsolete. Beckett's once-and-for-all is rather infinite catastrophe; only "that the earth is extinguished, although I never saw it lit" [p. 1060] justifies Clov's answer to Hamm's question: "Do you not think this has gone on long enough?" "Yes" [p. 1049]. Pre-history goes on, and the phantasm of infinity is only its curse. After Clov, commanded to look outside [p. 1057], reports to the totally lame man what he sees of earth, Hamm entrusts to him his secret:

CLOV: (*Absorbed.*) Mmm.
HAMM: Do you know what it is?
CLOV: (*As before.*) Mmm.
HAMM: I was never there. [p. 1057]

Earth was never yet tread upon; the subject is not yet a subject.

Determinate negation becomes dramaturgical through consistent reversal. Both social partners qualify their insight that there is no more nature with the bourgeois "You exaggerate" [p. 1039]. Prudence and circumspection are the tried-and-true means of sabotaging contemplation. They cause only melancholy reflection:

CLOV: (*Sadly.*) No one that ever lived ever thought so crooked as we. [p. 1039]

Where they draw nearest to the truth, they experience their consciousness – doubly comical – as false consciousness; thus a condition is mirrored that reflection no longer reaches. The entire play is woven with the technique of reversal. It transfigures the empirical world into that world desultorily named already by the late Strindberg and in Expressionism. "The whole house stinks of corpses . . . The whole universe" [p. 1050]. Hamm, who then says "to hell with the universe," is just as much the descendant of Fichte,[57] who disdains the world as nothing more than raw material and mere product, as he is the one without hope except for the cosmic night, which he implores with poetic quotes. Absolute, the world becomes a hell; there is nothing else. Beckett graphically stresses Hamm's sentence: "Beyond is the...OTHER hell" [p. 1043]. With a Brechtian commentary, he lets the distorted metaphysics of "the here and now" shine through:

CLOV: Do you believe in the life to come?
HAMM: Mine was always like that. (*Exit Clov.*) Got him that time! [p. 1050]

In his conception, Benjamin's notion of the "dialectic at a standstill" comes into its own:

HAMM: It will be the end and there I'll be, wondering what can have brought it on and wondering what can have (*he hesitates*)...why it was so long coming. (*Pause.*) There I'll be, in the old shelter, alone against the silence and...(*he hesitates*)...the stillness. If I can hold my peace, and sit quiet, it will be all over with sound and motion, all over and done with. [p. 1056]

That "stillness" is the order which Clov supposedly loves and which he defines as the purpose of his functions:

CLOV: A world where all would be silent and still and each thing in its last place, under the last dust. [p. 1053]

To be sure, the Old Testament saying "You shall become dust (*Staub*) again" is translated here into "dirt" (*Dreck*).[58] In the play, the substance of life, a life that is death, is the excretions. But the imageless image of death is one of indifference. In it, the distinction disappears: the distinction between absolute domination, the hell in which time is banished into space, in which nothing will change any more – and the messianic condition where everything would be in its proper place. The ultimate absurdity is that the repose of nothingness and that of reconciliation cannot be distinguished from each other. Hope creeps out of a world in which it is no more conserved than pap and pralines, and back where it came from, back into death. From it, the play derives its only consolation, a stoic one:

CLOV: There are so many terrible things now.
HAMM: No, no, there are not so many now. [p. 1049]

Consciousness begins to look its own demise in the eye, as if it wanted to survive the demise, as these two want to survive the destruction of their world. Proust, about whom the young Beckett wrote an essay, is said to have attempted to keep protocol on his own struggle with death, in notes which were to be integrated into the description of Bergotte's death.[59] *Endgame* carries out this intention like a mandate from a testament.

---

[57] See p. 1132 n. 48.
[58] Reporting God's punishment of man for his original sin, Genesis 3:19: "In the sweat of thy face shalt thou eat bread, till thou return unto the ground; for out of it wast thou taken: for dust thou art, and unto dust shalt thou return."

[59] Bergotte is a character in Proust's *A la recherche du temps perdu*, or *In Search of Lost Time*.

Bibliography

CONTINENTAL INTERLUDES (FUTURISM, DADA, SURREALISM, AND THE FRANKFURT SCHOOL): AN INTRODUCTORY BIBLIOGRAPHY

The literature on Futurism, Dadaism, Surrealism, and the Frankfurt School is enormous, and inevitably there are discrepancies between cutting-edge scholarship in the original languages and what has become available in English. The bibliography that follows has been designed for a student approaching these subjects for the first time, and is not intended to be comprehensive.

Futurism

Scholars interested in Futurism have long complained that it has received less critical attention than it should. Until recently, the number of texts available in English has been small, but a useful starting-point now is:

Lawrence Rainey and Christine Poggi, eds. *Futurism: a Reader and Visual Repertoire*, trans. Lawrence Rainey. New Haven and London: Yale University Press, 2005.

A fundamental resource, which ranges widely through many fields and countries, is:

Pontus Hulten, ed. *Futurism and Futurisms*. New York: Abbeville Press, 1986.

Two studies that survey Futurism in a variety of contexts are:

Marjorie Perloff, *The Futurist Moment*. Chicago: University of Chicago Press, 1986.
Lawrence Rainey, ed. *Modernism/Modernity* 1(3) (Sept. 1994), special issue on "Marinetti and the Italian Futurists."

See also:

Adamson, Walter L. *Avant-Garde Florence: From Modernism to Fascism*. Cambridge, MA: Harvard University Press, 1993.
Blum, Cinzia Sartini. *The Other Modernism: F. T. Marinetti's Futurist Fiction of Power*. Berkeley: University of California Press, 1996.
Tisdall, Caroline and Bozzolla, Angelo. *Futurism*. New York and Toronto: Oxford University Press, 1978.

Dada

Ever since its beginning in 1916, Dada has possessed a mythical status strangely at odds with the paucity of hard information about its activities and publications, a contradiction that persists even today, almost a century later. In English, a useful starting-point remains:

Robert Motherwell, ed. *The Dada Painters and Poets*. Cambridge, MA: Harvard University Press, 1951.

Two helpful collections, one aimed at theater studies rather than painting, are:

Mel Gordon, ed. *Dada Performance*. New York: PAJ Publications, 1987.
Tristan Tzara, *Seven Dada Manifestos and Lampisteries*, trans. Barbara Wright. London: Calder, 1992.

For English-speaking readers, one work in particular has served as a historical summary for generations, even though it has now been superseded by more recent research:

Hans Richter, Dada: *Art and Anti-Art*. London: Thames and Hudson, 1965.

Richter's account is usefully supplemented by two primary accounts:

Richard Huelsenbeck, *Memoirs of a Dada Drummer*. Berkeley: University of California Press, 1991.
Hugo Ball, *Flight Out of Time*. Berkeley: University of California Press, 1996.

Also helpful is a translated version of one of the great Dada journals:

Richard Huelsenbeck (ed.), *Dada Almanac*, ed. Malcolm Green. London: Atlas Press, 1992.

A collection of primary texts and recent essays, this volume provides one overview of Dada and the American scene:

Rudolf Kuenzli, ed. *New York Dada*. New York: Willis Locker & Owens, 1986.

For a more recent project that is enriching our entire conception of Dada, see:

Stephen Foster, ed. *Crisis and the Arts: The History of Dada*. 6 vols. New Haven, CT: G. K. Hall, 1996–.

Finally, for Dada and the visual arts, the indispensable starting-point is the richly illustrated general history:

Marc Dachy, *The Dada Movement 1915–1923*. New York: Rizzoli, 1990.

Surrealism

Literally hundreds of artists and writers participated in Surrealism in its many permutations. A colossal attempt to survey this heterogeneous field, slightly marred by its tendentious political thesis, is:

Gérard Durozoi, *History of the Surrealist Movement*, trans. Alison Anderson. Chicago: University of Chicago Press, 2002.

A starting-point for any study of surrealism will always be:

André Breton. *Manifestoes of Surrealism*, trans. Richard Weaver and Helen Lane. Ann Arbor: University of Michigan Press, 1969.

The two most accessible literary works that have had a substantial influence in English-speaking and other cultures:

André Breton, *Nadja*, trans. Richard Howard. New York: Grove Press, 1960; originally published 1928.

Louis Aragon, *Paris Peasant*, trans. Simon Watson Taylor. London: Jonathan Cape, 1971; rpt. Boston: Exact Change, 1994; originally published as *Le Paysan de Paris*, 1926.

Two surveys which have long served as starting-points for many are:

Sarane Alexandrian, *Surrealist Art*. London: Thames and Hudson, 1970.

Jacueline Chénieux-Gendron, *Surrealism*. New York: Columbia University Press, 1990

A more recent study that has been influential in critical discussion of Surrealism is:

Hal Foster, *Compulsive Beauty*. Cambridge, MA: MIT Press, 1993.

Frankfurt School

The Frankfurt School produced not just a distinguished body of theoretical and critical writings that influenced critics and intellectuals of the past, but a corpus of ideas and concepts that continue to be widely debated today. The best survey of that vast field still remains:

Martin Jay, *The Dialectical Imagination: A History of the Frankfurt School and the Institute of Social Research, 1923–1950*. Boston: Little Brown, 1973.

For a more up-to-date study that takes into account a great deal of subsequent scholarship, see:

Rolf Wiggershaus, *The Frankfurt School: Its History, Theories and Political Significance*, trans. Michael Robertson. Cambridge: Polity Press, 1995; original edn. Munich: C.Hanser, 1986.

A useful collection of translated writings which attempts to survey the entire field is:

Andrew Arato and Eike Gebhardt, eds. *The Essential Frankfurt School Reader*. New York: Continuum, 1982.

There are numerous figures who played roles in the growth and evolution of the Frankfurt School, but in the period 1925–1960 there is no doubt that the three protagonists

have become central to contemporary discussions: Theodor Adorno, Walter Benjamin, and Siegfried Kracauer.

Adorno

Adorno was a prolific writer, and the German edition of his collected writings (*Gesammelte Schriften*, ed. Rolf Tiedemann [Frankfurt: Suhrkamp]) has so far produced 45 volumes, with more still on the way. A good one-volume introduction to the range and diversity of Adorno's thought is:

Brian O'Connor, ed. *The Adorno Reader*. Oxford: Blackwell, 2000.

A single work that encapsulates some of Adorno's most extreme views is:

Theodor Adorno and Max Horkheimer, *Dialectic of Enlightenment*. New York and London: Verso, 1979.

Two works by Adorno that are of special interest to students of literature are:

Theodor Adorno, *Notes to Literature*, 2 vols., trans. Sherry Weber Nicholsen. New York: Columbia University Press, 1991–2.

Theodor Adorno, *Aesthetic Theory*, trans. Robert Hullot-Kenor. Minneapolis: University of Minnesota Press; London: Athlone, 1997.

Vast amounts have been written about Adorno, but the fundamental starting-point remains:

Martin Jay, *Adorno*. Cambridge, MA: Harvard University Press, 1984.

Benjamin

Benjamin has been a subject of interest ever since the 1960s, and within the last decade English-speaking readers have been able to survey a wider selection of his work than ever before. Benjamin was a prolific though largely neglected essayist and book reviewer during his lifetime; and paradoxically, the major work that occupied him for more than a decade, the *Passagen-Werk* or *The Arcades Project*, was not published in its original German until long after his death in 1972, and not translated into English until 1999. Both these aspects of his *oeuvre* are now well represented in English in:

Michael Jennings, ed. *Walter Benjamin: Selected Writings*, 4 vols. Cambridge, MA: Harvard University Press, 1996–2003.

Walter Benjamin, *The Arcades Project*, trans Howard Eiland and Kevin McLaughlin. Cambridge, MA: Harvard University Press, 1999.

There are two older and invaluable collections of Benjamin's essays which have served as the basis of most writing on Benjamin before the appearance of the *Selected Writings*:

Walter Benjamin, *Illuminations: Essays and Reflections*, ed. Hannah Arendt, trans. Harry Zohn. New York: Harcourt Brace, 1968; rpt. New York: Schocken, 1969.

Walter Benjamin, *Reflections: Essays, Aphorisms, Autobiographical Writings*, ed. Peter Demetz, trans. Edmund Jephcott. New York: Harcourt Brace, 1978; reprint New York, Schocken, 1986.

Siegfried Kracauer, during his lifetime, was probably the best-known critic of the Frankfurt School, if only because his study of German film became a classic in film studies. More recent interest has been skeptical of the work on film and instead taken note of his other writings, only recently translated into English. The three works that are crucial in discussion about Kracauer are:

Siegfried Kracauer, *From Caligari to Hitler: A Psychological History of the German Film*. Princeton: Princeton University Press, 1947.

Siegried Kracauer, *Mass Ornament: Weimar Essays*, ed. and trans. Thomas Y. Levin. Cambridge, MA: Harvard University Press, 1995.

Siegfried Kracauer, *The Salaried Masses: Duty and Distraction in Weimar Germany*, trans. Quintin Hoare. London and New York: Verso, 1998.

MODERNISM

Albright, Daniel. *Untwisting the Serpent: Modernism in Music, Literature and Other Arts*. Chicago: University of Chicago Press, 2000.

Ardis, Ann L. *Modernism and Cultural Conflict, 1880–1922*. Cambridge; New York: Cambridge University Press, 2002.

Armstrong, Tim. *Modernism, Technology and the Body: A Cultural Study*. Cambridge: Cambridge University Press, 1998.

Bell, Michael. *Literature, Modernism and Myth*. Cambridge: Cambridge University Press, 1997.

Benstock, Shari. *Women of the Left Bank, Paris, 1900–1940*. Austin: University of Texas Press, 1986.

Berman, Marshall. *All that Is Solid Melts Into Air: The Experience of Modernity*. New York: Simon and Schuster, 1982.

Bloom, Clive, ed. *Literature and Culture in Modern Britain, volume 1: 1900–1929*. London: Longman, 1993.

Booth, Allyson. *Postcards from the Trenches: Negotiating the Space between Modernism and the First World War*. New York: Oxford University Press, 1996.

Booth, Howard J. and Rigby, Nigel, eds. *Modernism and Empire*. Manchester: Manchester University Press, 2000.

Bradbury, Malcolm and McFarlane, James, eds. *Modernism: 1890–1930*. Harmondsworth: Penguin, 1976; rpt. with a new Preface, 1991.

Bucknell, Brad. *Literary Modernism and Musical Aesthetics: Pater, Pound, Joyce, and Stein*. Cambridge; New York: Cambridge University Press, 2001.

Bürger, Peter. *Theory of the Avant-Garde*, trans. Michael Shaw. Minneapolis: University of Minnesota Press, 1986.

Calinescu, Matei. *Five Faces of Modernity: Modernism, Avant-Garde, Decadence, Kitsch, Postmodernism*. Durham, NC: Duke University Press, 1987.

Chiari, Joseph. *The Aesthetics of Modernism*. London: Vision, 1970.

Childs, Donald J. *Modernism and Eugenics: Woolf, Eliot, Yeats, and the Culture of Degeneration*. Cambridge; New York: Cambridge University Press, 2001.

Clark, Suzanne. *Sentimental Modernism*. Indianapolis: Indiana University Press, 1991.

Clark, T. J. *Farewell to an Idea: Episodes from a History of Modernism*. New Haven: Yale University Press, 1999.

Daly, Nicholas. *Modernism, Romance, and the Fin de Siècle: Popular Fiction and British Culture, 1880–1914*. New York: Cambridge University Press, 1999.

Daly, Nicholas. *Literature, Technology, and Modernity, 1860–2000*. Cambridge; New York: Cambridge University Press, 2004.

Davies, Alistair. *An Annotated Critical Bibliography of Modernism*. Brighton: Harvester, 1982.

DeKoven, Marianne. *Rich and Strange: Gender, History, Modernism*. Princeton: Princeton University Press, 1991.

Donald, James, Friedberg, Anne, and Marcus, Laura, eds. *Close University Press 1927–1933: Cinema and Modernism*. London: Cassell, 1998.

Drucker, Johanna. *Theorizing Modernism: Visual Art and the Critical Tradition*. New York: Columbia University Press, 1994.

Ellmann, Richard and Fiedelson, Charles, eds. *The Modern Tradition: Backgrounds of Modern Literature*. London: Oxford University Press, 1965.

"The Fate of Modernity." Special Issue of *Theory, Culture and Society* 2(3) (1985).

Felski, Rita. *The Gender of Modernity*. Cambridge, MA: Harvard University Press, 1996.

Gambrell, Alice. *Women Intellectuals, Modernism and Difference: Transatlantic Culture, 1919–1954*. Cambridge: Cambridge University Press, 1997.

Giles, Steve, ed. *Theorizing Modernism: Essays in Critical Theory*. London; New York: Routledge, 1993.

Goldman, Jane. *Modernism, 1910–1945: Image to Apocalypse*. Basingstoke; New York: Palgrave Macmillan, 2004.

Kenner, Hugh. *A Homemade World: The American Modernist Writer*. New York: William Morrow, 1975; London: Boyars: Distributed by Calder and Boyars, 1977.

Kenner, Hugh. *A Sinking Island: The Modern English Writers*. New York: Knopf, 1988; Baltimore: Johns Hopkins University Press, 1989.

Kermode, Frank. *The Sense of an Ending: Studies in the Theory of Fiction.* London: Oxford University Press, 1967.

Kern, Stephen. *The Culture of Time and Space 1880–1918.* Cambridge, MA: Harvard University Press, 1983.

Kiely, Robert and Hildebidle, John, eds. *Modernism Reconsidered.* Cambridge, MA: Harvard University Press, 1983.

Latham, Sean. *"Am I a snob?": Modernism and the Novel.* Ithaca, NY: Cornell University Press, 2003.

Levenson, Michael A. *A Genealogy of Modernism: A Study of English Literary Doctrine 1880–1922.* Cambridge: Cambridge University Press, 1984.

Levenson, Michael A. *Modernism and the Fate of Individuality: Character and Novelistic Form from Conrad to Woolf.* Cambridge; New York: Cambridge University Press, 1991.

Levenson. Michael A., ed. *The Cambridge Companion to Modernism.* Cambridge: Cambridge University Press, 1999.

Longenbach, James. *Stone Cottage: Pound, Yeats and Modernism.* Oxford: Oxford University Press, 1988.

Lunn, Eugene. *Marxism and Modernism.* London: Verso, 1985.

Miller, Tyrus. *Late Modernism: Politics, Fiction, and the Arts between the World Wars.* Berkeley: University of California Press, 1999.

Nicholls, Peter. *Modernisms: A Literary Guide.* Basingstoke: Macmillan, 1995.

Pease, Allison. *Modernism, Mass Culture, and the Aesthetics of Obscenity.* Cambridge; New York: Cambridge University Press, 2000.

Perelman, Bob. *The Trouble with Genius: Reading Pound, Joyce, Stein and Zukovsky.* Berkeley: University of California Press, 1994.

Perloff, Marjorie. *The Poetics of Indeterminacy: Rimbaud to Cage.* Princeton: Princeton University Press, 1981.

Perloff, Marjorie. *The Dance of the Intellect: Studies in the Poetry of the Pound Tradition.* Cambridge: Cambridge University Press, 1985.

Perloff, Marjorie. *Wittgenstein's Ladder: Poetic Language and the Strangeness of the Ordinary.* Chicago and London: University of Chicago Press, 1996.

Perloff, Marjorie. *21ˢᵗ-Century Modernism.* Oxford: Blackwell, 2001.

Pippin, Robert B. *Modernism as a Philosophical Problem.* Oxford: Blackwell, 1991.

Rainey, Lawrence. *Institutions of Modernism: Literary Elites and Public Culture.* New Haven: Yale University Press, 1998.

Reiss, Timothy. *The Discourse of Modernism.* Ithaca: Cornell University Press, 1982.

Ross, Dorothy, ed. *Modernist Impulses in the Human Sciences 1870–1930.* Baltimore, London: Johns Hopkins University Press, 1994.

Saas, Louis A. *Madness and Modernism: Insanity in the Light of Modern Art, Literature and Thought.* Cambridge, MA; London: Harvard University Press, 1992.

Scott, Bonnie Kime, ed. *The Gender of Modernism: A Critical Anthology.* Bloomington and Indianapolis: Indiana University Press, 1990.

Scott, Bonnie Kime. *Refiguring Modernism,* 2 vols. Bloomington: Indiana University Press, 1995.

Sheehan, Paul. *Modernism, Narrative, and Humanism.* Cambridge; New York: Cambridge University Press, 2002.

Sherry, Vincent B. *The Great War and the Language of Modernism.* Oxford; New York: Oxford University Press, 2003.

Stead, C. K. *Pound, Yeats, Eliot and the Modernist Movement.* Basingstoke: Macmillan, 1986.

Stevens, Hugh and Howlett, Caroline, eds. *Modernist Sexualities.* Manchester: Manchester University Press, 2000.

Stevenson, Randall. *Modernist Fiction: An Introduction.* London: Harvester, 1992.

Sword, Helen. *Ghostwriting Modernism.* Ithaca: Cornell University Press, 2002.

Tate, Trudi. *Modernism, History and the First World War.* Manchester: Manchester University Press, 1998.

Thormählen, Marianne, ed. *Rethinking Modernism.* Basingstoke; New York: Palgrave Macmillan, 2003.

Timms, Edward and Kelly, David, eds. *Unreal City: Urban Experience in Modern European Literature and Art.* New York: St Martin's, 1985.

Tratner, Michael. *Modernism and the Mass Politics: Joyce, Woolf, Eliot, Yeats.* Stanford: Stanford University Press, 1995.

Trotter, David. *The English Novel in History: 1895–1920.* London: Routledge, 1993.

Trotter, David. *Paranoid Modernism: Literary Experiment, Psychosis, and the Professionalization of English Society.* Oxford; New York: Oxford University Press, 2001.

Vargish, Thomas and Mook, Delo E. *Inside Modernism: Relativity Theory, Cubism, Narrative.* New Haven: Yale University Press, 1999.

White, Allon. *The Use of Obscurity: The Fiction of Early Modernism.* London: Routledge, 1981.

Williams, Louise Blakeney. *Modernism and the Ideology of History: Literature, Politics, and the Past.* Cambridge; New York: Cambridge University Press, 2002.

DJUNA BARNES (1892–1982)

Bibliographies:

Messerli, Douglas. *Djuna Barnes: A Bibliography.* Rhinebeck, NY: D. Lewis, 1975.

Biographies:

Field, Andrew. *Djuna, the Life and Times of Djuna Barnes.* New York: Putnam, 1983.

Field, Andrew. *The Formidable Miss Barnes: A Biography of Djuna Barnes*. London: Secker & Warburg, 1983.

Herring, Phillip. *Djuna: The Life and Work of Djuna Barnes*. New York: Viking, 1995.

Works:

The Book of Repulsive Women: 8 Rhythms and 5 Drawings. New York, 1915.

A Book. New York: Boni and Liveright, 1923.

Ladies Almanack: Showing Their Signs and Their Tides, Their Moons and Their Changes, the Seasons as It Is with Them, Their Eclipses and Equinoxes, as well as a Full Record of Diurnal and Nocturnal Distempers. Paris: Printed for the author [by Imp. Darantière, Dijon], 1928.

Ryder. New York: H. Liveright, 1928.

A Night among the Horses. New York: H. Liveright, 1929.

Nightwood. London: Faber & Faber, [1936].

The Antiphon: A Play. New York: Farrar, Straus & Cudahy, 1958.

Vagaries Malicieux: Two Stories. New York: F. Hallman, 1974.

Greenwich Village as It Is. New York: Phoenix Bookshop, 1978.

To the Dogs. Rochester, NY: Press of the Good Mountain, 1982.

Creatures in an Alphabet. New York: Dial Press, 1982.

Smoke, and Other Early Stories, ed. with an introduction by Douglas Messerli. College Park, MD: Sun & Moon Press, 1982.

Posthumous Works:

New York, ed. with commentary by Alyce Barry. Los Angeles: Sun & Moon Press, 1989.

At the Roots of the Stars: The Short Plays, ed. with an introduction by Douglas Messerli. Los Angeles, CA: Sun & Moon Press, 1995.

Poe's Mother: Selected Drawings of Djuna Barnes, ed. with an introduction Douglas Messerli. Los Angeles, CA: Sun & Moon Press, 1995.

Collected Stories. Los Angeles, CA: Sun & Moon Press, 1996.

Criticism and Interpretation:

Allen, Carolyn. *Following Djuna: Women Lovers and the Erotics of Loss*. Bloomington: Indiana University Press, 1996.

Broe, Mary Lynn. *Silence and Power: A Reevaluation of Djuna Barnes*. Carbondale, IL: Southern Illinois University Press, 1991.

Carlston, Erin G. *Thinking Fascism: Sapphic Modernism and Fascist Modernity*. Stanford, CA: Stanford University Press, 1998.

Galvin, Mary E. *Queer Poetics: Five Modernist Women Writers*. Westport, CT: Praeger, 1999.

Grobbel, Michaela M. *Enacting Past and Present: The Memory Theaters of Djuna Barnes, Ingeborg Bachmann, and Marguerite Duras*. Lanham, MD; Oxford: Lexington Books, 2004.

Kaivola, Karen. *All Contraries Confounded: The Lyrical Fiction of Virginia Woolf, Djuna Barnes, and Marguerite Duras*. Iowa City: University of Iowa Press, 1991.

Kannenstine, Louis F. *The Art of Djuna Barnes: Duality and Damnation*. New York: New York University Press, 1977.

Marcus, Jane. *Hearts of Darkness: White Women Write Race*. New Brunswick, NJ; London: Rutgers University Press, 2004.

Miller, Tyrus. *Late Modernism: Politics, Fiction, and the Arts between the World Wars*. Berkeley: University of California Press, 1999.

Parsons, Deborah L. *Djuna Barnes*. Tavistock: Northcote House, 2003.

Plumb, Cheryl J. *Fancy's Craft: Art and Identity in the Early Works of Djuna Barnes*. Selinsgrove, PA: Susquehanna University Press; London: Associated University Presses, 1986.

Scott, Bonnie Kime. *Refiguring Modernism*. Bloomington: Indiana University Press, 1995.

Scott, James B. *Djuna Barnes*. Boston: Twayne Publishers, 1976.

Smith, Andrew and Wallace, Jeff, eds. *Gothic Modernisms*. Basingstoke; New York: Palgrave, 2001.

SAMUEL BECKETT (1906–89)

Bibliographies:

Cohn, Ruby. *A Beckett Canon*. Ann Arbor: University of Michigan Press, 2001.

Federman, Raymond and Fletcher, John Walter James. *Samuel Beckett: His Works and His Critics: An Essay in Bibliography*. Berkeley: University of California Press, 1970.

Biographies:

Bair, Deirdre. *Samuel Beckett: A Biography*. London: Vintage, 1990.

Knowlson, James. *Damned to Fame: The Life of Samuel Beckett*. London: Bloomsbury, 1996.

Works:

"Dante . . . Bruno . Vico . . Joyce," in *Our Exagmination Round His Factification for Incamination of Work in Progress*. Paris: Shakespeare and Co., 1929.

Whoroscope. Paris: The Hours Press, 1930.

Proust. London: Chatto and Windus, 1931.

Echo's Bones and Other Precipitates. Paris: Europa Press, 1935.

More Pricks than Kicks. London: Chatto and Windus, 1934.

Murphy. London: Routledge, 1938.

Molloy; Molloy. Paris: Les Editions de Minuit, 1951; English translation by Patrick Bowles in collaboration with Samuel Beckett, Paris: Olympia Press, 1955.

Malone meurt; Malone Dies. Paris: Les Editions de Minuit, 1951; London: John Calder, 1958.

En attendant Godot; Waiting for Godot. Paris: Les Editions de Minuit, 1952; London: Faber and Faber, 1956.

L'Innommable; The Unnamable in Molloy Malone Dies The Unnamable. Paris: Les Editions de Minuit, 1953; London: John Calder, 1959.

Watt. "Collection Merlin," Paris: Olympia Press, 1953.

Nouvelles, et textes pour rien. Paris: Les Editions de Minuit, 1955

Translations of the stories and *Texts for Nothing* in *No's Knife*, London: Calder and Boyars, 1967.

"From an Abandoned Work," *Trinity News*, vol. III, no. 4, 1956.

All That Fall. London: Faber and Faber, 1957.

Fin de partie, suivi de Acte sans paroles; Endgame. A Play in One Act followed by Act Without Words, a Mime for One Player. Paris: Les Editions de Minuit, 1957; London: Faber and Faber, 1958.

Krapp's Last Tape and Embers. London: Faber and Faber, 1959.

Poems in English. London: Calder and Boyars, 1961.

Comment c'est; How it is. Paris: Les Editions de Minuit, 1961; London: John Calder, 1964.

Happy Days. London: Faber and Faber, 1962.

Acte sans paroles II in *Dramatische Dichtungen*, Band I. Frankfurt: Suhrkamp, 1963.

Cascando in *Dramatische Dichtungen*, Band I. Frankfurt: Suhrkamp, 1963.

Words and Music in *Evergreen Review*, vol. VI (1962).

Play in Play and Two Short Pieces for Radio. London: Faber and Faber, 1964.

Imagination morte imaginez. Paris: Les Editions de Minuit, 1965.

Imagination Dead Imagine. London: Calder and Boyars, 1965.

Assez. Paris: Les Editions de Minuit, 1966.

Bing. Paris: Les Editions de Minuit 1966.

No's Knife: Collected Shorter Prose 1945–1966. London: Calder and Boyars, 1967.

Come and Go. London: Calder and Boyars, 1967.

Eh Joe and Other Writings. London: Faber and Faber, 1967.

Poêmes. Paris: Les Editions de Minuit, 1968.

Sans. Paris: Les Editions de Minuit, 1969.

Lessness. London: Calder and Boyars, 1970.

Mercier et Camier; Mercier and Camier. Paris: Les Editions de Minuit, 1970; London: Calder and Boyars, 1974.

Le Depupleur. Paris: Les Editions de Minuit, 1970.

The Lost Ones. London: Calder and Boyars, 1972.

Premier amour; First Love. Paris: Les Editions de Minuit, 1970; London: Calder and Boyars, 1973.

"Breath" in *Gambit*, vol. 4, no. 15 (1969).

Not I. London: Faber and Faber, 1973.

Rough for Radio I, first published in English as "Sketch for Radio Play" in *Stereo Headphones*, no. 7 (Spring 1976).

Rough for Radio II. New York: Grove Press, 1976.

Pour finir encore et autres foirades. Paris: Les Editions de Minuit, 1976.

Fizzles, with etchings by Jasper Johns. London: Petersburg Press, 1976.

For To End Yet Again and Other Fizzles. London: John Calder, 1976.

All Strange Away. London: John Calder; New York: Gotham Book Mart, 1976.

That Time. New York: Faber and Faber, 1976.

Collected Poems in English and French. London: John Calder, 1977.

Poêmes suivi de Mirlitonnades. Paris: Les Editions de Minuit, 1978.

Company. London: John Calder, 1979.

Mal vu mal dit.: III Seen III Said. Paris: Les Editions de Minuit, 1981; London: John Calder, 1982.

"A Piece of Monologue," *The Kenyon Review*, n.s. vol. I, no. 3, Summer 1979.

Rockaby and Other Short Pieces. New York: Grove Press, 1981; London: John Calder, 1982.

Catastrophe et autres dramaticules; Catastrophe. Paris: Les Editions de Minuit, 1982; London: Faber, 1984.

Worstward Ho. London: John Calder, 1983.

Disjecta: Miscellaneous Writings and a Dramatic Fragment, ed. Ruby Cohn. London: John Calder, 1983.

Collected Shorter Plays. London: Faber and Faber, 1984.

Collected Shorter Prose 1945–1980. London: John Calder, 1988.

Posthumous Works:

Comment dire. Paris: Les Editions de Minuit, 1989.

Nohow On (Company, III Seen III Said, Worstward Ho). London: John Calder, 1989.

As the Story was Told: Uncollected and Late Prose. London: John Calder, 1990.

Dream of Fair to Middling Women. New York: Arcade Publishing, in association with Riverrun Press, and Calder Publications, London and Paris, 1992.

Eleutheria. Paris: Les Editions de Minuit, 1995; New York: Foxrock, 1995; London; Faber and Faber, 1996.

Criticism and Interpretation:

Acheson, James and Arthur, Kateryna, eds. *Beckett's Later Fiction and Drama: Texts for Company.* Basingstoke: Macmillan, 1987.

Admussen, Richard. *The Samuel Beckett Manuscripts: A Study.* Boston: G. K. Hall, 1979.

Adorno, Theodor. "Trying to Understand Endgame." *Notes to Literature*, vol. I, ed. Rolf Tiedemann, trans. Shierry Weber Nicholsen. European Perspectives. New York: Columbia University Press, 1991, pp. 241–75.

Albright, Daniel. *Beckett and Aesthetics*. Cambridge: Cambridge University Press, 2003.

Alvarez, A. *Beckett*, 2nd edn. Fontana Modern Masters. London: Fontana, 1992.

Ben-Zvi, Linda. *Women in Beckett: Performance and Critical Perspectives*. Urbana and Chicago: University of Illinois Press, 1990.

Birkett, Jennifer and Ince, Kate, eds. *Samuel Beckett*. Longman Critical Readers. London: Longman, 2000.

Brater, Enoch. *Why Beckett*. London: Thames and Hudson, 1989.

Brater, Enoch. *The Drama in the Text: Beckett's Late Fiction*. New York and Oxford: Oxford University Press, 1994.

Bryden, Mary. *Women in Samuel Beckett's Prose and Drama: Her Own Other*. London: Macmillan, 1993.

Bryden, Mary, ed. *Samuel Beckett and Music*. Oxford: Clarendon, 1998.

Butler, Lance St John. *Samuel Beckett and the Meaning of Being: A Study in Ontological Parable*. London: Macmillan, 1984.

Butler, Lance St John and Davis, Robin J., eds. *Rethinking Beckett: A Collection of Critical Essays*. Basingstoke: Macmillan, 1990.

Cohn, Ruby. *Back to Beckett*. Princeton: Princeton University Press, 1973.

Cohn, Ruby. *Just Play: Beckett's Theater*. Princeton: Princeton University Press, 1980.

Cohn, Ruby. *A Beckett Canon*. Ann Arbor: University of Michigan Press, 2001.

Connor, Steven. *Samuel Beckett: Repetition, Theory and Text*. Oxford: Blackwell, 1988.

Connor, Steven, ed. *Waiting for Godot and Endgame*. New Casebooks. Basingstoke: Macmillan, 1992.

Critchely, Simon. *Very Little...Almost Nothing: Death, Philosophy, Literature*. London and New York: Routledge, 1997.

Cronin, Anthony. *Samuel Beckett: The Last Modernist*. London: Flamingo, 1997.

Dearlove, J. E. *Accommodating the Chaos: Samuel Beckett's Nonrelational Art*. Durham, NC: Duke University Press, 1982.

Fletcher, John and Spurling, John. *Beckett the Playwright*. New York: Hill and Wang, 1972.

Garver, Lawrence and Federman, Raymond. *Samuel Beckett: The Critical Heritage*. London and New York: Routledge, 1979.

Gontarski, S. E. *The Intent of Undoing in Samuel Beckett's Dramatic Texts*. Bloomington: Indiana University Press, 1985.

Gontarski, S. E., ed. *On Beckett: Essays and Criticism*. New York: Grove Press, 1986.

Guralnick, Elissa S. *Sight Unseen: Beckett, Pinter, Stoppard, and Other Contemporary Dramatists on Radio*. Athens, OH: Ohio University Press, 1996.

Gussow, Mel. *Conversations with (and about) Beckett*. London: Nick Hern, 1996.

Hale, Jane Alison. *The Broken Window: Beckett's Dramatic Perspective*. West Lafayette, IN: Purdue University Press, 1987.

Harmon, Maurice, ed. *No Author Better Served: The Correspondence of Samuel Beckett and Alan Schneider*. Cambridge, MA; London: Harvard University Press, 1998.

Harvey, Lawrence. *Samuel Beckett: Poet and Critic*. Princeton: Princeton University Press, 1970.

Haynes, John and Knowlson, James. *Images of Beckett*. Cambridge: Cambridge University Press, 2003.

Henning, Sylvie. *Beckett's Critical Complicity: Carnival, Contestation, and Tradition*. Lexington, Kentucky: University Press of Kentucky, 1988.

Hill, Leslie. *Beckett's Fiction in Different Words*. Cambridge: Cambridge University Press, 1990.

Juliet, Charles. *Conversations with Samuel Beckett and Bram van Velde*, trans. Janey Tucker. Leiden: Academic Press Leiden, 1995.

Kenner, Hugh. *Samuel Beckett: Critical Study*. Glasgow: John Calder, 1962.

Kenner, Hugh. *A Reader's Guide to Samuel Beckett*. London: Thames and Hudson, 1988.

Kiberd, Declan. *Inventing Ireland*. London: Jonathan Cape, 1995.

Knowlson, James and Pilling, John. *Frescoes of the Skull: The Later Prose and Drama of Samuel Beckett*. London: Calder, 1979.

Lane, Richard, ed. *Beckett and Philosophy*. Basingstoke: Palgrave, 2002.

Levy, Eric P. *Beckett and the Voice of Species: A Study of the Prose Fiction*. Totowa, NJ: Barnes & Noble, 1980.

Locatelli, Carla. *Unwording the Word: Samuel Beckett's Prose after the Nobel Prize*. Philadelphia: University of Pennsylvania Press, 1990.

McMullan, Anna. *Theatre on Trial: Samuel Beckett's Later Drama*. New York and London: Routledge, 1993.

Mercier, Vivian. *Beckett/Beckett*. New York: Oxford University Press, 1977.

O'Brien, Eoin. *The Beckett Country*. London: Black Cat Press & Faber, 1986.

Oppenheim, Lois. *Directing Beckett*. Ann Arbor: University of Michigan Press, 1994.

Oppenheim, Lois. *The Painted World: Samuel Beckett's Dialogue with Art*. Ann Arbor: University of Michigan Press, 2000.

Oppenheim, Lois, ed. *Samuel Beckett and the Arts: Music, Visual Arts, and Non-Print Media*. Border Crossings 2. New York and London: Garland, 1999.

Pilling, John. *Samuel Beckett*. London: Routledge & Kegan Paul, 1976.

Pilling, John and Bryden, Mary, eds. *The Ideal Core of the Onion: Reading Beckett Archives*. University of Reading: Beckett International Foundation, 1992.

Pilling, John, ed. *The Cambridge Companion to Samuel Beckett*. Cambridge: Cambridge University Press, 1994.

Ricks, Christopher. *Beckett's Dying Words*. Oxford: Oxford University Press, 1995.

Wilmer, S. E, ed. *Beckett in Dublin*. Dublin: Lilliput Press, 1992.

Worth, Katharine. *Samuel Beckett's Theatre: Life Journeys*. Oxford: Clarendon Press, 1999.

Zilliacus, Clas. *Beckett and Broadcasting: A Study of the Works of Samuel Beckett for and in Radio and Television*. Acta Academiae Aboensis. Ser. A. Humanoira, 51(2). Åbo, Finland: Åbo Akademi, 1976.

ELIZABETH BOWEN (1899–1973)

Bibliographies:

Sellery, J'nan M. and Harris, William O. *Elizabeth Bowen, a Bibliography*. Austin: Humanities Research Center, University of Texas at Austin, 1981.

Biographies:

Craig, Patricia. *Elizabeth Bowen*. Harmondsworth: Penguin, 1986.

Glendinning, Victoria. *Elizabeth Bowen: Portrait of a Writer*. London: Phoenix, 1993.

Works:

Ann Lee's: & Other Stories. New York: Boni and Liveright, 1926.

The Hotel. London: Constable & Co., 1927.

Joining Charles and Other Stories. New York: L. MacVeagh, Dial Press; Toronto: Longmans, Green and Co., 1929.

The Last September. New York: L. MacVeagh, The Dial Press; Toronto: Longmans, Green and Co., 1929.

Friends and Relations. New York: L. Mac Veagh, The Dial Press; Toronto: Longmans, Green and Co., 1931.

To the North. London: Victor Gollancz, 1932.

The House in Paris. London: Gallancz, 1935.

The Death of the Heart. London: Gollancz, 1938.

Look at All Those Roses: Short Stories. London: Gollancz, 1941.

Bowen's Court. New York: A. A. Knopf, 1942.

English Novelists. With 8 plates in colour and 19 illustrations in black & white. London: W. Collins, 1942.

Seven Winters. Dublin, Ireland: The Cuala Press, 1942.

The Demon Lover, and Other Stories. London: J. Cape, 1945.

Anthony Trollope, a New Judgement. London; New York [etc.]: Oxford University Press, 1946.

Ivy Gripped the Steps, and Other Stories. New York: A. A. Knopf, 1946.

Why Do I Write? An Exchange of Views between Elizabeth Bowen, Graham Greene & V. S. Pritchett. London, P. Marshall, 1948.

The Cat Jumps and Other Stories. London: J. Cape, 1949.

Encounters: Early Stories. London: Sidgwick & Jackson, 1949.

The Heat of the Day. New York: Knopf, 1949.

Collected Impressions. London; New York [etc.]: Longmans, Green and Co., 1950.

The Shelbourne; a Centre in Dublin Life for More than a Century. London: Harrap, 1951.

A World of Love. London: Jonathan Cape, 1955.

A Time in Rome. New York, Knopf, 1960.

Afterthought: Pieces about Writing. London: Longmans, 1962.

The Little Girls. London: Jonathan Cape, 1964.

A Day in the Dark, and Other Stories. London, J. Cape, 1965.

Eva Trout, or, Changing Scenes. New York: Knopf, 1968.

Pictures and Conversations. New York, Knopf, 1975.

Elizabeth Bowen's Irish Stories. Dublin: Poolbeg Press, 1978.

Posthumous Works:

The Collected Stories of Elizabeth Bowen. New York: Knopf, 1981.

The Mulberry Tree: Writings of Elizabeth Bowen. Selected and introduced by Hermione Lee. London: Virago, 1986.

"Notes on Eire": Espionage Reports to Winston Churchill, 1940–2. Aubane: Aubane Historical Society, 1999.

Criticism and Interpretation:

Austin, Allan E. *Elizabeth Bowen*. Boston: Twayne Publishers, 1989.

Bennett, Andrew and Royle, Nicholas. *Elizabeth Bowen and the Dissolution of the Novel: Still Lives*. Foreword by Ann Wordsworth. New York: St. Martin's Press, 1995.

Bloom, Harold, ed. *Elizabeth Bowen*. With an introduction by Harold Bloom. Published: New York: Chelsea House, 1987.

Blodgett, Harriet. *Patterns of Reality: Elizabeth Bowen's Novels*. The Hague: Mouton, 1975.

Christensen, Lis. *Elizabeth Bowen: The Later Fiction*. Copenhagen: Museum Tusculanum Press, University of Copenhagen, 2001.

Ellmann, Maud. *Elizabeth Bowen: The Shadow Across the Page*. Edinburgh: Edinburgh University Press, 2003.

Heath, William Webster. *Elizabeth Bowen: An Introduction to Her Novels*. Madison, WI: University of Wisconsin Press, 1961.

Hoogland, Renée C. *Elizabeth Bowen: A Reputation in Writing*. New York: New York University Press, 1994.

Jordan, Heather Bryant. *How Will the Heart Endure?: Elizabeth Bowen and the Landscape of War*. Ann Arbor: University of Michigan Press, 1992.

Lassner, Phyllis. *Elizabeth Bowen*. Houndmills, Basingstoke: Macmillan, 1990.

Lee, Hermione. *Elizabeth Bowen, an Estimation*. London: Vision Press; Totowa, NJ: Barnes & Noble, 1981.

McCormack, W. J. *Dissolute Characters: Irish Literary History through Balzac, Sheridan Le Fanu, Yeats, and Bowen*. Manchester: Manchester University Press; New York: St. Martin's Press, 1993.

MARY BUTTS (1890–1937)

Biographies:

Blondel, Nathalie. *Mary Butts: Scenes from the Life*. Kingston, NY: McPherson, 1998.

Wagstaff, Christopher, ed. *A Sacred Quest: The Life and Writings of Mary Butts*. Kingston, NY: McPherson, 1995.

Works:

Speed the Plough and Other Stories. London: Chapman & Hall, 1923.

Ashe of Rings. Paris: Contact Editions, Three Mountains Press, 1925.

Armed with Madness. New York: Albert & Charles Boni, 1928.

Imaginary Letters: with Engravings on Copper from the Original Drawings by Jean Cocteau. Paris: E.W. Titus, 1928.

Several Occasions. [London]: Wishart, 1932.

Traps for Unbelievers. London: Desmond Harmsworth, 1932.

Death of Felicity Taverner. London: Wishart, 1932.

Warning to Hikers. [London]: Wishart, 1932.

The Macedonian. London: William Heinemann, 1933.

Scenes from the Life of Cleopatra. London; Toronto: W. Heinemann, 1935.

The Crystal Cabinet: My Childhood at Salterns. London: Methuen, 1937.

Posthumous Works:

Last Stories. [London]: Brendin Publishing Co., [1938].

With or Without Buttons and Other Stories. Selected by Nathalie Blondel. Manchester: Carcanet, 1991.

From Altar to Chimney-piece: Selected Stories. Kingston, NY: McPherson and Co., 1992.

The Taverner Novels. Kingston, NY: McPherson and Co., 1992.

The Classical Novels. Kingston, NY: McPherson and Co., 1994.

The Journals of Mary Butts. Selected by Nathalie Blondel. New Haven, CT: Yale University Press, 2002.

Criticism and Interpretation:

Foy, Roslyn Reso. *Ritual, Myth, and Mysticism in the Work of Mary Butts: Between Feminism and Modernism*. Fayetteville: University of Arkansas Press, 2000.

Garrity, Jane. *Step-daughters of England: British Women Modernists and the National Imaginary*. Manchester, Manchester University Press; New York: Palgrave, 2003.

Wagstaff, Christopher, ed. *A Sacred Quest: The Life and Writings of Mary Butts*. Kingston, NY: McPherson, 1995.

HART CRANE (1899–1932)

Bibliographies and Reference Works:

Landry, Hilton and Landry, Elaine, eds. *A Concordance to the Poems of Hart Crane*. Metuchen, NJ: Scarecrow Press, 1973.

Lane, Gary. *A Concordance to the Poems of Hart Crane*. New York: Haskell House, 1972.

Lohf, Kenneth A. *The Literary Manuscripts of Hart Crane*. Columbus: Ohio State University Press, 1967.

Rowe, Hershel D. *Hart Crane, a Bibliography*. Denver: A. Swallow, 1955.

Schwartz, Joseph. *Hart Crane: An Annotated Critical Bibliography*. New York: D. Lewis 1970.

Schwartz, Joseph. *Hart Crane, a Reference Guide*. Boston, MA: G. K. Hall, 1983.

Schwartz, Joseph and Schweik, Robert C. *Hart Crane: A Descriptive Bibliography*. Pittsburgh: University of Pittsburgh Press, 1972.

Biographies:

Butterfield, R. W. *The Broken Arc: A Study of Hart Crane*. Edinburgh: Oliver & Boyd, 1969.

Mariani, Paul. *The Broken Tower: A Life of Hart Crane*. New York: W. W. Norton, 1999.

Weber, Brom. *Hart Crane, a Biographical and Critical Study*. New York: The Bodley Press, 1948.

Works:

White Buildings. New York: Boni & Liveright, 1926.

The Bridge: A Poem. New York: H. Liveright, 1930.

Posthumous Works:

The Collected Poems of Hart Crane, ed. Waldo Frank. New York: Liveright, 1933.

The Complete Poems of Hart Crane, ed. Waldo Frank. Garden City, NY: Doubleday, 1958.

The Letters of Hart Crane, 1916–1932, ed. Brom Weber. Berkeley, CA: University of California Press, 1965.

Complete Poems and Selected Letters and Prose, ed. Brom Weber. New York: Liveright, 1966.

Seven Lyrics. Cambridge, MA: Ibex Press, 1966.

The Poet's Vocation; Selections from Letters of Hölderlin, Rimbaud, and Hart Crane, eds. and trans. William Burford and Christopher Middleton. [Austin, Humanities Research Center] University of Texas; [distributed by University of Texas Press, Austin, 1967].

Twenty-one Letters from Hart Crane to George Bryan, eds. Joseph Katz, Hugh C. Atkinson, and Richard A. Ploch. Columbus, OH: Ohio State University Libraries, 1968.

Ten Unpublished Poems. New York: Gotham Book Mart, 1972.

Letters of Hart Crane and His Family, ed. Thomas S. W. Lewis. New York: Columbia University Press, 1974.

Hart Crane and Yvor Winters: Their Literary Correspondence, ed. Thomas Parkinson. Berkeley: University of California Press, 1978.

Porphyro in Akron. Columbus, OH: Logan Elm Press, 1980.

O My Land, My Friends: the Selected Letters of Hart Crane, eds. Langdon Hammer and Brom Weber. New York: Four Walls Eight Windows, 1997.

Complete Poems of Hart Crane, ed. Marc Simon. New York: Liveright, 2000.

Happy New Millennium. Columbus, OH: Buchenroth, 2000.

Criticism and Interpretation:

Bennett, Maria F. *Unfractioned Idiom: Hart Crane and Modernism*. New York: P. Lang, 1987.

Bloom, Harold, ed. *Hart Crane: Modern Critical Views*. New York: Chelsea House, 1986.

Berthoff, Warner. *Hart Crane, a Re-introduction*. Minneapolis: University of Minnesota Press, 1989.

Brown, Susan Jenkins. *Robber Rocks; Letters and Memories of Hart Crane, 1923–1932*. Middletown, CT: Wesleyan University Press, 1969.

Chandran, K. Narayana. *Singer in the City: Studies in Modern American Poetry*. Hyderabad: American Studies Research Centre, 1987.

Cole, Merrill. *The Other Orpheus: A Poetics of Modern Homosexuality*. New York: Routledge, 2003.

Combs, Robert Long. *Vision of the Voyage: Hart Crane and the Psychology of Romanticism*. Memphis: Memphis State University Press, 1978.

Dembo, L. S. *Hart Crane's Sanskrit Charge; a Study of The Bridge*. Ithaca, NY: Cornell University Press, 1960.

Dickie, Margaret. *On the Modernist Long Poem*. Iowa City: University of Iowa Press, 1986.

Edelman, Lee. *Transmemberment of Song: Hart Crane's Anatomies of Rhetoric and Desire*. Stanford, CA: Stanford University Press, 1987.

Giles, Paul. *Hart Crane: The Contexts of The Bridge*. Cambridge, UK; New York: Cambridge University Press, 1986.

Hammer, Langdon. *Hart Crane and Allen Tate: Janus-faced Modernism*. Princeton: Princeton University Press, 1993.

Hanley, Alfred. *Hart Crane's Holy Vision: "White buildings."* Pittsburgh, PA: Duquesne University Press, 1981.

Hazo, Samuel John. *Hart Crane, an Introduction and Interpretation*. New York: Barnes and Noble, 1963.

Lewis, R. W. B. *The Poetry of Hart Crane: A Critical Study*. Princeton; Princeton University Press, 1967.

Lewis, R. W. B. *Trials of the Word; Essays in American Literature and the Humanistic Tradition*. New Haven: Yale University Press, 1965.

Lyon, Melvin E. *The Centrality of Hart Crane's "The Broken Tower."* Lincoln, NB: University at Lincoln, 1972.

Mariani, Paul. *The Broken Tower: A Life of Hart Crane*. New York: W.W. Norton, 1999.

Perry, Robert L. *The Shared Vision of Waldo Frank and Hart Crane*. Lincoln: University of Nebraska, 1966.

Riddell, Joseph N. *The Turning Word: American Literary Modernism and Continental Theory*, ed. Mark Bauerlein. Philadelphia: University of Pennsylvania Press, 1996.

Sugg, Richard P. *Hart Crane's The Bridge: A Description of its Life*. University; University of Alabama Press, 1976.

Thomas, F. Richard. *Literary Admirers of Alfred Stieglitz*. Carbondale: Southern Illinois University Press, 1983.

Trachtenberg, Alan, ed. *Hart Crane: A Collection of Critical Essays*. Englewood Cliffs, NJ: Prentice-Hall, 1982.

Vogler, Thomas A. *Preludes to Vision: The Epic Venture in Blake, Wordsworth, Keats, and Hart Crane*. Berkeley: University of California Press, 1971.

Weber, Brom. *Hart Crane, a Biographical and Critical Study*. New York: The Bodley Press, 1948.

Yingling, Thomas E. *Hart Crane and the Homosexual Text: New Thresholds, New Anatomies*. Chicago: University of Chicago Press, 1990.

Nancy Cunard (1896–1965)

Biographies:

Chisholm, Anne. *Nancy Cunard: A Biography*. New York: Knopf, 1979.

Works:

Outlaws. London: Elkin Matthews, 1921.

Sublunary. London; New York: Hodder and Stoughton, 1923.

Parallax. London: Hogarth Press, 1925.

Poems (Two) 1925. London: Aquila Press, 1930.

(With Henry Crowder) *Henry-music*. Poems by Nancy Cunard et al. Paris: Hours Press, 1930.

Black Man and White Ladyship, an Anniversary. [Toulon, Imp. A. Bordato] 1931.

Negro Anthology. London: Wishart, 1934.

L'Ethiopie trahie: unit? contre l'impérialisme. [Paris], 1936.

(With Geoarge Padmore) *The White Man's Duty: an Analysis of the Colonial Question in the Light of the Atlantic Charter*. London: W. H. Allen, 1942.

Poems for France, written by British poets on France since the War, collected by Nancy Cunard, with autobiographical notes of the authors. London, La France Libre, 1944.

Nous gens d'Espagne, 1945–1949. [Perpignan, Impr. Labau, 1949].

Grand Man; Memories of Norman Douglas, with extracts from his letters, and appreciations by Kenneth Macpherson [and others] and a bibliographical note by Cecil Woolf. London: Secker & Warburg, 1954.

G M: Memories of George Moore. London: Rupert Hart-Davis, 1956.

The Hours Press; Retrospect, Catalogue, Commentary. [London: Shenval Press, 1964].

Posthumous Works:

These Were the Hours; Memories of My Hours Press, Réanville and Paris, 1928–1931, ed. Hugh Ford. Carbondale: Southern Illinois University Press, 1969.

Thoughts about Ronald Firbank. New York: Albondocani Press, 1971.

Essays on Race and Empire, ed. Maureen Moynagh. Peterborough, Ontario; Orchard Park, NY: Broadview Press, 2002.

Criticism and Interpretation:

Crowder, Henry. *As Wonderful as All That?: Henry Crowder's Memoir of his Affair with Nancy Cunard, 1928–1935.* Navarro, CA: Wild Trees Press, 1987.

Fielding, Daphne. *Those Remarkable Cunards: Emerald and Nancy.* New York: Atheneum, 1968.

Ford, Hugh, ed. *Nancy Cunard: Brave Poet, Indomitable Rebel, 1896–1965.* Philadelphia, PA: Chilton Book Co., 1968.

Marcus, Jane. *Hearts of Darkness: White Women Write Race.* New Brunswick, NJ; London: Rutgers University Press, 2004.

T.S. ELIOT (1888–1965)

Bibliographies:

Blalock. Susan E. *Guide to the Secular Poetry of T. S. Eliot.* New York: G. K. Hall, 1996.

Frank, Mechthild, Frank, Armin Paul, and Jochum, J. P. S. *T. S. Eliot Criticism in English, 1916–1965: A Supplementary Bibliography.* Edmonton, Alberta: Yeats Eliot Review, 1978.

Gallup, Donald. *T. S. Eliot: A Bibliography.* New York: Harcourt, Brace & World, 1969.

Knowles, Sebastian D. G. and Leonard, Scott A. *An Annotated Bibliography of a Decade of T. S. Eliot Criticism: 1977–1986.* Orono, Maine: National Poetry Foundation, 1992.

Ricks, Beatrice. *T. S. Eliot: A Bibliography of Secondary Works.* Metuchen, NJ, and London: Scarecrow Press, 1980.

Biographies:

Ackroyd, Peter. *T. S. Eliot: A Life.* New York: Simon and Schuster, 1984.

Behr, Caroline. *T. S. Eliot: a Chronology of His Life and Works.* London: Macmillan, 1983.

Gordon, Lyndall. *T. S. Eliot's Early Years.* New York: Farrar, Straus, Giroux, 1977.

Gordon, Lyndall. *Eliot's New Life.* New York: Farrar, Straus, Giroux, 1988.

Works:

Prufrock and Other Observations. London: the Egoist Press, 1917.

Poems. London: Hogarth Press, 1919.

Ara Vos Prec. London: Ovid Press, 1920.
  Poems. New York: Alfred Knopf, 1920.

The Sacred Wood. London: Methuem, 1920.

The Waste Land. New York: Boni and Liveright, 1922; London: Hogarth Press, 1923.

Homage to John Dryden. London: Hogarth Press, 1924.

Poems 1909–1925. London: Faber & Gwyer, 1925.

For Lancelot Andrewes: Essays on Style and Order. London: Faber & Gwyer, 1928.

Ash-Wednesday. London: Faber & Faber; New York: Putnam's, 1930.

Selected Essays, 1917–1932. London: Faber & Faber; New York: Harcourt, Brace, 1932.

The Use of Poetry and the Use of Criticism. London: Faber & Faber; Cambridge, MA: Harvard University Press, 1933.

After Strange Gods. London: Faber & Faber; New York: Harcourt, Brace, 1934.

Murder in the Cathedral. London: Faber and Faber; New York: Harcourt, Brace, 1935.

Collected Poems: 1909–1935. London: Faber & Faber; New York: Harcourt, Brace, 1935.

Essays Ancient and Modern. London: Faber & Faber; New York: Harcourt, Brace, 1936.

The Family Reunion. London: Faber & Faber; New York: Harcourt, Brace, 1939.

The Idea of a Christian Society. London: Faber & Faber, 1939.

Old Possum's Book of Practical Cats. London: Faber & Faber; New York: Harcourt, Brace, 1939.

Four Quartets. London: Faber & Faber; New York: Harcourt, Brace, 1943.

Notes towards the Definition of Culture. London: Faber & Faber, 1948.

The Cocktail Party. London: Faber & Faber; New York: Harcourt Brace, 1950.

The Confidential Clerk. London: Faber & Faber; New York: Harcourt Brace, 1954.

On Poetry and Poets. London: Faber & Faber; New York: Farrar, Straus, 1957.

The Elder Statesman. London: Faber & Faber; New York: Farrar, Straus, 1959.

Collected Poems 1909–1962. London: Faber & Faber; New York: Harcourt Brace, 1962.

Knowledge and Experience in the Philosophy of F. H. Bradley. London: Faber & Faber; New York: Farrar, Straus, 1964.

To Criticise the Critic. London: Faber & Faber; New York: Farrar, Straus, 1965.

Posthumous Works:

Complete Plays. New York: Harcourt, Brace, 1967.

Poems Written in Early Youth. London: Faber & Faber; New York: Farrar, Straus, 1967.

Complete Poems and Plays. London: Faber & Faber, 1969.

The Waste Land: A Facsimile and Transcript of the Original Drafts Including the Annotations of Ezra Pound, ed. Valerie Eliot. London: Faber & Faber; New York: Harcourt Brace, 1971.

The Letters of T. S. Eliot, volume 1: 1898–1922. London: Faber & Faber; New York: Harcourt Brace, 1988.

The Varieties of Metaphysical Poetry: The Clark Lectures at Trinity College, Cambridge, 1926, and the Turnbull Lectures at the Johns Hopkins University, 1933, ed. Ronald Schuchard. London: Faber & Faber; New York: Harcourt, Brace, 1993.

Inventions of the March Hare: Poems 1909–1917, ed. Christopher Ricks. London: Faber & Faber; New York: Harcourt Brace, 1996.

Criticism and Interpretation:

Albright, Daniel. *Quantum Poetics: Yeats, Pound, Eliot, and the Science of Modernism*. Cambridge: Cambridge University Press, 1997.

Armstrong, Tim. *Modernism, Technology, and the Body*. Cambridge: Cambridge University Press, 1998.

Bedient, Calvin. *He Do the Police in Different Voices: "The Waste Land" and Its Protagonist*. Chicago: University of Chicago Press, 1986.

Bergonzi, Bernard. *T. S. Eliot*. London: Macmillan, 1972.

Bishop, Jonathan. "A Handful of Words: the Credibility of Language in *The Waste Land*." *Texas Studies in Language and Literature* 27(1) (Spring 1985): 154–77.

Brooker, Jewel Spears. *Mastery and Escape: T. S. Eliot and the Dialectic of Modernism*. Amherst, MA: University of Massachusetts Press, 1994.

Brooker, Jewel Spears and Bentley, Joseph. *Reading "The Waste Land": Modernism and the Limits of Interpretation*. Amherst, MA: University of Massachusetts Press, 1994.

Bush, Ronald. *T. S. Eliot: A Study in Character and Style*. New York: Oxford University Press, 1983.

Bush, Ronald, ed. *T. S. Eliot: The Modernist in History*. Cambridge: Cambridge University Press, 1991.

Calder, Angus. *T S. Eliot*. Brighton: Harvester Press, 1987.

Chinitz, David. *T. S. Eliot and the Cultural Divide*. Chicago: University of Chicago Press, 2003.

Clarke, Graham, ed. *T. S. Eliot: Critical Assessments*. London: Christopher Helm, 1990.

Craig, David. "The Defeatism of *The Waste Land*." *Critical Quarterly* 2 (1960): 214–52.

Crawford, Robert. *The Savage and the City in the Work of T. S. Eliot*. Oxford: Clarendon Press, 1987.

Cuddy, Lois A., and Hirsch, David, eds. *Critical Essays on T. S. Eliot's "The Waste Land."* Boston: G. K. Hall, 1991.

Dana, Margaret E. "Orchestrating *The Waste Land*: Wagner, Leitmotiv, and the Play of Passion." In Cooper, John Xiros, ed., *T. S. Eliot's Orchestra: Critical Essays on Poetry and Music*. New York: Garland, 2000, pp. 267–94.

Davidson, Harriet. *T. S. Eliot and Hermeneutics: Absence and Interpretation in "The Waste Land."* Baton Rouge: Louisiana State University Press, 1985.

Drew, Elizabeth. *T. S. Eliot: the Design of His Poetry*. New York: Scribners, 1949.

Ellmann, Maud. *The Poetics of Impersonality: T. S. Eliot and Ezra Pound*. Brighton: Harvester, 1987.

Froula, Christine. "Eliot's Grail Quest: Or, the Lover, the Police, and *The Waste Land*." *Yale Review* 78(1) (Winter 1989): 235–53.

Froula, Christine. "Corpse, Monument, *Hypocrite Lecteur*." *Text* 9 (1996): 297–314.

Frye, Northrop. *T. S. Eliot*. Chicago: University of Chicago Press, 1963.

Gilbert, Sandra. "'Rats' Alley': The Great War, Modernism, and the (Anti)Pastoral Elegy." *New Literary History* 30(1) (Winter 1999): 179–201.

Gardner, Helen. *The Art of T. S. Eliot*. New York: Dutton, 1959.

Grant, Michael, ed. *T. S. Eliot: The Critical Heritage*. London: Routledge and Kegan Paul, 1982.

Gray, Piers. *T. S. Eliot's Intellectual and Poetic Development*. Brighton: Harvester Press, 1982.

Hay, Eloise Knapp. *T. S. Eliot's Negative Way*. Cambridge, MA: Harvard University Press, 1982.

Jay, Gregory. *T. S. Eliot and the Poetics of Literary History*. Baton Rouge: Louisiana State University Press, 1983

Kearns, Cleo McNelly. *T. S. Eliot and Indic Traditions: A Study in Poetry and Belief*. Cambridge: Cambridge University Press, 1987

Kenner, Hugh. *The Invisible Poet: T. S. Eliot*. New York: Harcourt, Brace & World, 1959.

Koestenbaum, Wayne. *Double Talk: The Erotics of Male Literary Collaboration*. New York: Routledge, 1989.

Laity, Cassandra, and Gish, Nancy K., eds. *Gender, Desire, and Sexuality in T.S. Eliot*. Cambridge: Cambridge University Press, 2004.

Langbaum, Robert. *The Mysteries of Identity: A Theme in Modern Literature*. New York: Oxford University Press, 1977.

Lentricchia, Frank. *Modernist Quartet*. Cambridge: Cambridge University Press, 1994.

Levenson, Michael. *A Genealogy of Modernism: A Study of English Literary Doctrine, 1908–1922*. Cambridge: Cambridge University Press, 1987.

Levenson, Michael. "Does *The Waste Land* Have a Politics?" *Modernism/Modernity* 6(3) (Sept. 1999): 1–13.

Litz, A. Walton, ed. *Eliot in His Time*. Princeton: Princeton University Press, 1973.

Longenbach, James. *Modernist Poetics of History: Pound, Eliot, and the Sense of the Past*. Princeton: Princeton University Press, 1987.

Manganaro, Marc. "Dissociation in 'Dead Land': The Primitive Mind in the Early Poetry of T. S. Eliot." *Journal of Modern Literature* 13(1) (1986): 97–110.

Martin, Graham, ed. *Eliot in Perspective*. London: Macmillan, 1970.

Menand, Louis. *Discovering Modernism: T. S. Eliot and His Context*. New York: Oxford University Press, 1987.

Moody, A. D., ed. *"The Waste Land" in Different Voices*. London: Edward Arnold, 1974.

Moody, A. D. *Thomas Stearns Eliot: Poet*. Cambridge: Cambridge University Press, 1979.

Moody, A. D., ed. *The Cambridge Companion to T. S. Eliot*. Cambridge: Cambridge University Press, 1979.

Moretti, Franco. *Signs Taken for Wonders: Essays in the Sociology of Literary Forms*, trans. Susan Fischer, David Forgacs, and David Miller. London: Verso, 1983.

North, Michael. *The Political Aesthetic of Yeats, Eliot, and Pound.* Cambridge: Cambridge University Press, 1991.

North, Michael. *The Dialect of Modernism: Race, Language, and Twentieth Century Literature.* Oxford: Oxford University Press, 1994.

North, Michael. *Reading 1922: A Return to the Scene of the Modern.* Oxford: Oxford University Press, 1999.

North, Michael. *The Waste Land: A Norton Critical Edition.* New York and London: W. W. Norton, 2001.

Pearce, Roy Harvey. *The Continuity of American Poetry.* Princeton: Princeton University Press, 1961.

Perl, Jeffery M. *Skepticism and Modern Enmity: Before and After Eliot.* Baltimore: Johns Hopkins University Press, 1989.

Rainey, Lawrence. *Institutions of Modernism: Literary Elites and Public Culture.* New Haven: Yale University Press, 1998.

Rainey, Lawrence, ed. *The Waste Land and T. S. Eliot's Contemporary Prose.* New Haven: Yale University Press, 2005.

Rainey, Lawrence. *Revisiting "The Waste Land."* New Haven: Yale University Press, 2005.

Ricks, Christopher. *T. S. Eliot and Prejudice.* Berkeley: University of California Press, 1988.

Riquelme, John Paul. "'Withered Stumps of Time': Allusion, Reading and Writing in *The Waste Land*." *Denver Quarterly* 15 (1981): 90–110.

Rosenthal, M. L. *Sailing into the Unknown: Yeats, Pound, and Eliot.* New York: Oxford University Press, 1978.

Ross, Andrew. *The Failure of Modernism: Symptoms of American Poetry.* New York: Columbia University Press, 1986.

Schuchard, Ronald. *Eliot's Dark Angel: Intersections of Life and Art.* Oxford: Oxford University Press, 1999.

Schwartz, Sanford. *The Matrix of Modernism: Pound, Eliot, and Early Twentieth Century Thought.* Princeton: Princeton University Press, 1985.

Scofield, Martin. *T. S. Eliot: The Poems.* Cambridge: Cambridge University Press, 1988.

Sherry, Vincent. *The Great War and the Language of Modernism.* Oxford: Oxford University Press, 2003.

Shusterman, Richard. *T. S. Eliot and the Philosophy of Criticism.* New York: Columbia University Press, 1988.

Smith, Grover. *T. S. Eliot's Poetry and Plays.* Chicago: University of Chicago Press, 1974.

Smith, Grover. *The Waste Land.* London: Allen and Unwin, 1983.

Spanos, William. "Repetition in *The Waste Land*: A Phenomenological De-Struction." *Boundary 2* 7 (1979): 225–85.

Spender, Stephen. *T. S. Eliot.* New York: Viking, 1975.

Spurr, David. *Conflicts in Consciousness: T. S. Eliot's Poetry and Criticism.* Urbana, IL: University of Illinois Press, 1984.

Stead, C. K. *Pound, Yeats, Eliot and the Modernist Movement.* Basingstoke: Macmillan, 1986.

Tate, Allen, ed. *T. S. Eliot: The Man and His Work.* New York: Delacorte, 1966.

Thormählen, Marinanne. *"The Waste Land": A Fragmentary Wholeness.* Lund: Gleerup, 1978.

Trotter, David. "Modernism and Empire: Reading *The Waste Land*." *Critical Quarterly* 28(1–2) (1986): 143–53.

FORD MADOX FORD (FORD MADOX HUEFFER) (1873–1939)

Bibliographies:

Harvey, David Dow. *Ford Madox Ford, 1873–1939: A Bibliography of Works and Criticism.* Princeton: Princeton University Press, 1962.

Biographies:

Judd, Alan. *Ford Madox Ford.* London: Collins, 1990; London: Flamingo, 1991.

MacShane, Frank. *The Life and Works of Ford Madox Ford.* London: Routledge, 1965.

Mizener, Arthur M. *The Saddest Story: A Biography of Ford Madox Ford.* London: Bodley Head, 1972.

Moser, Thomas C. *The Life in the Fiction of Ford Madox Ford.* Princeton: Princeton University Press, 1980.

Saunders, Max. *Ford Madox Ford: A Dual Life, vol.1: The World Before the War.* Oxford, New York: Oxford University Press, 1996.

Stang, Sondra J. *Ford Madox Ford.* New York: Ungar, 1977.

Works:

Brown Owl: A Fairy Story. New York: Frederick A. Stokes, 1891.

Feather. London: T. F. Unwin, New York: Cassell, 1892.

Shifting of the Fire. London: T. F. Unwin, 1892.

Queen Who Flew: A Fairy Tale. London: Bliss, Sands & Foster, 1894.

Ford Madox Brown: A Record of His Life and Work, by Ford M. Hueffer with Numerous Reproductions. London etc.: Longmans, Green, and Co., 1896.

Cinque Ports: A Historical and Descriptive Record. Edinburgh, London: W. Blackwood and Sons, 1900.

Poems for Pictures and for Notes of Music. London: J. MacQueen, 1900.

Inheritors; an Extravagant Story by Joseph Conrad & Ford M. Hueffer. London: W. Heinemann; New York: McClure, Phillips & Co., 1901.

Rossetti: A Critical Essay on his Art. London: Duckworth & Co.; New York: E. P. Dutton & Co., 1902.

Romance: A Novel by Joseph Conrad and Ford Madox Hueffer. London etc.: T. Nelson and Sons, 1903.

Benefactor: A Tale of a Small Circle. London: Brown, Langham & Co., 1905.

Soul of London: A Survey of a Modern City. London: A. Rivers, 1905.

Fifth Queen: And How She Came to Court. London: Alston Rivers, 1906.

Heart of the Country; a Survey of a Modern Land. London: A. Rivers, 1906.

English Girl; a Romance. London: Methuen,1907.

From Inland and other Poems. London: A. Rivers, 1907.

Pre-Raphaelite Brotherhood; a Critical Monograph. London: Duckworth & Co.; New York: E. P. Dutton & Co., 1907.

Privy Seal: His Last Venture. London: Alston Rivers, 1907.

Spirit of the People: An Analysis of the English Mind. London: Alston Rivers, 1907.

Fifth Queen Crowned: A Romance. London: E. Nash, 1908.

Half Moon: A Romance of the Old World and the New. London: E. Nash, 1909.

Call: The Tale of Two Passions. London: Chatto & Windus, 1910.

Mr. Apollo: A Just Possible Story. London: Methuen, 1910.

Portrait. London: Methuen, 1910.

Songs from London. London: E. Mathews, 1910.

Ancient Lights and Certain New Reflections, Being the Memories of a Young Man. London: Chapman and Hall, 1911.

Critical Attitude. London: Duckworth, 1911.

High Germany: Eleven Sets of Verse. London: Duckworth, 1911.

Ladies whose Bright Eyes: A Romance. London: Constable, 1911.

Memories and Impressions: A Study in Atmospheres. New York, London: Harper & Brothers, 1911.

Panel: A Sheer Comedy. London: Constable, 1912.

Mr. Fleight. London: H. Latimer, 1913.

Young Lovell: A Romance. London: Chatto & Windus, 1913.

Antwerp. London: The Poetry Bookshop, 1914.

Hans Holbein, the Younger: A Critical Monograph. London: Duckworth, 1914.

Rossetti: A Critical Essay on his Art. London: Duckworth, 1914.

Between St. Dennis and St. George: A Sketch of Three Civilizations. London etc.: Hodder and Stoughton, 1915.

Good Soldier: A Tale of Passion. New York: John Lane; London: John Lane, Bodley Head, 1915.

When Blood is their Argument: An Analysis of Prussian Culture. New York, London: Hodder and Stoughton, 1915.

Zeppelin Nights: A London Entertainment, by Violet Hunt & Ford Madox Hueffer. London and New York: John Lane, 1916.

Collected Poems of Ford Madox Hueffer. London: M. Secker, 1916.

Henry James: A Critical Study. New York: Dodd, Mead and Co., 1916.

On Heaven, and Poems Written on Active Service. London and New York: John Lane, 1918.

Thus to Revisit: Some Reminiscences. London: Chapman & Hall; New York: E. P. Dutton & Co., 1921.

Marsden Case: A Romance. London: Duckworth, 1923.

Women & Men. Paris: Three Mountains Press, 1923.

Nature of a Crime, by Joseph Conrad and F. M. Hueffer. London: Duckworth; Garden City, NY: Doubleday, Page & Co., 1924.

Joseph Conrad, a Personal Remembrance. London: Duckworth, 1924.

Some Do Not. London: Duckworth; New York: T. Seltzer, 1924.

No More Parades. London: Duckworth; New York: A. & C. Boni, 1925.

Man Could Stand University Press. London: Duckworth; New York: A. & C. Boni, 1926.

Mirror to France. London: Duckworth, 1926.

New Poems. New York: W. E. Rudge, 1927.

New York Essays. New York: W. E. Rudge, 1927.

New York is Not America: Being a Mirror to the States. New York: A. & C. Boni, 1927.

Last Post. London: Duckworth; New York: A. & C. Boni, 1928.

Little Less Than Gods. London: Duckworth, 1928.

English Novel, from the Earliest Days to the Death of Joseph Conrad. Philadelphia, London: J. B. Lippincott Co., 1929; London: Constable, 1930.

No Enemy: A Tale of Reconstruction. New York: Macaulay, 1929.

Return to Yesterday. New York: Liveright, 1932.

When the Wicked Man. London: Jonathan Cape, 1932.

It Was the Nightingale. Philadelphia & London: J. B. Lippincott Co., 1933.

The Rash Act. London: Jonathan Cape, 1933.

Henry for Hugh. Philadelphia, London: J. B. Lippincott Co., 1934.

Provence: From Minstrels to the Machine. Philadelphia; London: J. B. Lippincott Co., 1935.

Collected Poems. New York: Oxford University Press, 1936.

Vive le roy. Philadelphia, London: J. B. Lippincott, 1936.

Great Trade Route. New York, Toronto: Oxford University Press, 1937.

March of Literature, from Confucius' Day to Our Own. New York: The Dial Press, 1938.

Posthumous Works:

Parade's End. New York: Knopf, 1950.

Bodley Head Ford Madox Ford, ed. Graham Greene. London: Bodley Head, 1962.

Critical Writings, ed. Frank MacShane. Lincoln: University of Nebraska Press, 1964.

Letters of Ford Madox Ford, ed. Richard M. Ludwig. Princeton: Princeton University Press, 1965.

Selected Poems, ed. Basil Bunting. Cambridge, MA: Pym-Randall Press, 1971.

Your Mirror to My Times: The Selected Autobiographies and Impressions of Ford Madox Ford, ed. Michael Killigrew. New York: Holt, Rinehart and Winston, 1971.

Presence of Ford Madox Ford: A Memorial Volume of Essays, Poems, and Memoirs ed. Sondra J. Stang. Philadelphia: University of Pennsylvania Press, 1981.

Pound/Ford, the Story of a Literary Friendship: the Correspondence Between Ezra Pound and Ford Madox Ford and Their Writings About Each Other, ed. Brita Lindberg-Seyersted. New York: New Directions, 1982.

Ford Madox Ford Reader, ed. Sondra J. Stang. Manchester: Carcanet, 1986.

History of Our Own Times, eds. Solon Beinfeld and Sondra J. Stang. Bloomington: Indiana University Press, 1988

Correspondence of Ford Madox Ford and Stella Bowen, eds. Sondra J. Stang and Karen Cochran. Bloomington: Indiana University Press, 1993.

War Prose, ed. Max Saunders. Manchester: Carcanet, 1999.

Literary Friendship: Correspondence Between Caroline Gordon & Ford Madox Ford, ed. Brita Lindberg-Seyersted. Knoxville: University of Tennessee Press, 1999.

Critical Essays, eds. Max Saunders and Richard Stang. Manchester: Carcanet, 2002.

Criticism and Interpretation:

Brebach, Raymond. *Joseph Conrad, Ford Madox Ford, and the Making of Romance*. Ann Arbor, MI: UMI Research Press, 1985.

Calderaro, Michaela. *A Silent New World: Ford Madox Ford's Parade's End*. Bologna: CLUB, 1993.

Cassell, Richard A. *Ford Madox Ford: A Study of His Novels*. Baltimore: Johns Hopkins Press, 1962.

Cassell, Richard A., ed. *Ford Madox Ford: Modern Judgements*. London: Macmillan, 1972.

Fowles, Anthony. *Ford Madox Ford: the Principal Fiction*. London: Greenwich Exchange, 2002.

Goldring, Douglas. *Last Pre-Raphaelite: A Record of the Life and Writings of Ford Madox Ford*. London: Macdonald, 1948.

Gordon, Ambrose. *Invisible Tent: The War Novels of Ford Madox Ford*. Austin: University of Texas Press, 1964.

Green, Robert. *Ford Madox Ford: Prose and Politics*. Cambridge; New York: Cambridge University Press, 1981.

Hampson, Robert and Davenport, Tony, eds. *Ford Madox Ford: A Reappraisal*. Amsterdam; New York: Rodopi, 2002.

Haslam, Sara. *Fragmenting Modernism: Ford Madox Ford, the Novel, and the Great War*. Manchester: Manchester University Press; New York: Palgrave, 2002.

Hoffmann, Charles G. *Ford Madox Ford*. New York; Boston: Twayne Publishers, 1967; 1990.

Huntley, H. Robert. *The Alien Protagonist of Ford Madox Ford*. Chapel Hill, NC: University of North Carolina Press, 1970.

Leer, Norman. *The Limited Hero in the Novels of Ford Madox Ford*. East Lansing: Michigan State University Press, 1966.

Lid, Richard Wald. *Ford Madox Ford: The Essence of his Art*. Berkeley: University of California Press, 1964.

Lindberg-Seyersted, Brita. *Ford Madox Ford and his Relationship to Stephen Crane and Henry James*. Atlantic Highlands, NJ: Humanities Press International; Lysaker, Norway: Solum, 1987.

MacShane, Frank. *Ford Madox Ford: The Critical Heritage*. London, Boston: Routledge and K. Paul, 1972.

Meixner, John Albert. *Ford Madox Ford's Novels: A Critical Study*. Minneapolis: University of Minnesota Press, 1962.

Ohmann, Carol Burke. *Ford Madox Ford: From Apprentice to Craftsman*. Middletown, CT: Wesleyan University Press, 1964.

Poli, Bernard J. *Ford Madox Ford and the Transatlantic Review*. Syracuse, NY: Syracuse University Press, 1967.

Smith, Grover Cleveland. *Ford Madox Ford*. New York: Columbia University Press, 1972.

Snitow, Ann Barr. *Ford Madox Ford and the Voice of Uncertainty*. Baton Rouge: Louisiana State University Press, 1984.

Trotter, David. *Paranoid Modernism: Literary Experiment, Psychosis, and the Professionalization of English Society*. Oxford; New York: Oxford University Press, 2001.

Wiley, Paul L. *Novelist of Three Worlds: Ford Madox Ford*. Syracuse, NY: Syracuse University Press, 1962.

H.D. (1886–1961)

Bibliographies:

Boughn, Michael. *H.D.: A Bibliography, 1905–1990*. Charlottesville, VA: University Press of Virginia, 1993.

Bryer, Jackson R. and Roblyer, Pamela. *H.D.: A Preliminary Checklist*. Madison, WI: University of Wisconsin Press, 1969.

Biographies:

Robinson, Janice S. *H.D., the Life and Work of an American Poet*. Boston: Houghton Mifflin, 1982.

Works:

Sea Garden. Boston and New York: Houghton Mifflin, 1916.

The Tribute and Circe: Two Poems. Cleveland: Clerk's Private Press, 1917.

Hymen. New York: H. Holt and Co., 1921.

Heliodora; and Other Poems. Boston: Houghton Mifflin, 1924.

Collected Poems. New York: Boni and Liveright, 1925.

H.D. New York: Simon & Schuster, 1926.

Palimpsest. Paris: Contact Editions, 1926.

Hippolytus Temporizes; a Play in Three Acts. Boston and New York: Houghton Mifflin, 1927.

Hedylus. Boston: Houghton Mifflin, 1928.

The Usual Star. London: Imprimerie Darantiere at Dijon, France, 1928 [1934].

Red Roses for Bronze. New York: Random House, 1929.

Kora and Ka, Vaud. 1930. [Dijon, France, Printed by Imprimerie Darantiere, 1934].

Nights, by John Helforth [pseud.] [Dijon, France, Printed by Imprimerie Darantiere, 1935]. *The Hedgehog.* [London]: Brendin Publishing Co., 1936 (Plaistow, London: Curwen Press).

Collected Poems of H.D. New York: Liveright Publishing Corporation, 1940.

The Walls Do Not Fall. London, New York, etc.: Oxford University Press, 1944.

What Do I Love? London: Privately published by the Brendin Publishing Co., 1944.

Tribute to the Angels. London, New York, etc.: Oxford University Press, 1945.

The Flowering of the Rod. London, New York, etc.: Oxford University Press, 1946.

By Avon River. New York: Macmillan, 1949.

Tribute to Freud. [New York:] Pantheon, 1956.

Selected Poems. New York: Grove Press, 1957.

Helen in Egypt. New York, Grove Press, 1961.

Posthumous Works:

Evening. Stoke Ferry, Norfolk: Daedalus Press, 1969.

Hermetic Definitions. New York: New Directions, 1972.

Temple of the Sun. Berkeley, CA: ARIF Press, 1972.

The Poet and the Dancer. San Francisco: Five Trees Press, 1975.

End to Torment: A Memoir of Ezra Pound. New York: New Directions, 1979.

HERmione. New York: New Directions, 1981.

The Gift. New York: New Directions, 1982.

Notes on Thought and Vision and the Wise Sappho. San Francisco: City Lights Books, 1982.

Collected Poems, 1912–1944, ed. Louis L. Martz. New York: New Directions, 1983.

Priest and a Dead Priestess Speaks. Port Townsend, WA: Copper Canyon Press, 1983.

Selected Poems, ed. Louis L. Martz. New York: New Directions, 1988.

Richard Aldington and H.D.: The Early Years in Letters, ed. Caroline Zilboorg. Bloomington: Indiana University Press, 1992.

Asphodel, ed. Robert Spoo. Durham, NC: Duke University Press, 1992.

A Great Admiration: H.D./Robert Duncan Correspondence, 1950–1961, ed. Robert J. Bertholf. Venice, CA: Lapis Press; Novato, CA: Distributed by Publishers Services, 1992.

Paint It Today, ed. Cassandra Laity. New York: New York University Press, 1992.

Vale Ave. Sculpture by Joan Sovern; photographed by David Finn. Redding Ridge, CT: Black Swan Books, c1992.

Within the Walls. Wood engravings by Dellas Henke. Iowa City, IA: Windhover Press, 1993.

Richard Aldington and H.D.: The Later Years in Letters, ed. Caroline Zilboorg. Manchester, UK: Manchester University Press; New York: St. Martin's Press, 1995.

Between History and Poetry: The Letters of H.D. and Norman Holmes Pearson, ed. Donna Krolik Hollenberg. Iowa City, IA: University of Iowa Press, 1997.

Pilate's Wife, ed. Joan A. Burke. New York: New Directions Books, 2000.

Analyzing Freud: Letters of H.D., Bryher, and Their Circle, ed. Susan Stanford Friedman. New York: New Directions, 2002.

Richard Aldington and H.D.: Their Lives in Letters, 1918–61, ed. Caroline Zilboorg. Manchester, UK: Manchester University Press; New York: Palgrave, 2003.

Criticism and Interpretation:

Alfrey, Shawn. *The Sublime of Intense Sociability: Emily Dickinson, H.D., and Gertrude Stein.* Lewisburg, PA: Bucknell University Press, 2000.

Baccolini, Raffaella. *Tradition, Identity, Desire: Revisionist Strategies in H.D.'s Late Poetry.* Bologna: Pàtron, 1995.

Buck, Claire. *H.D. and Freud: Bisexuality and a Feminine Discourse.* New York: St. Martin's Press, 1991.

Burnett, Gary. *H.D. between Image and Epic: The Mysteries of her Poetics.* Ann Arbor, MI: UMI Research Press, 1990.

Camboni, Marina. *H.D.'s Poetry: "The Meanings that Words Hide": Essays.* New York: AMS Press, 2002.

Chisholm, Dianne. *Freudian Poetics: Psychoanalysis in Translation.* Ithaca, NY: Cornell University Press, 1992.

Collecott, Diana. *H.D. and Sapphic Modernism, 1910–1950.* Cambridge; New York: Cambridge University Press, 1999.

Collins, H. P. *Modern Poetry.* London: J. Cape, 1925.

Dehler, Johanna. *Fragments of Desire: Sapphic Fictions in Works by H.D., Judy Grahn, and Monique Wittig.* Frankfurt am Main; New York: P. Lang, 1999.

Di Prima, Diane. *The Mysteries of Vision: Some Notes of H.D.* Santa Barbara, CA: Am Here Books, 1988.

DiPace Fritz, Angela. *Thought and Vision: A Critical Reading of H.D.'s Poetry.* Washington, DC: Catholic University of America Press, 1988.

Dodd, Elizabeth. *The Veiled Mirror and the Woman Poet: H.D., Louise Bogan, Elizabeth Bishop, and Louise Glück.* Columbia, MO: University of Missouri Press, 1992.

Duplessis, Rachel Blau. *H.D., the Career of That Struggle.* Brighton, UK: Harvester Press, 1986.

Edmunds, Susan. *Out of Line: History, Psychoanalysis, and Montage in H.D.'s Long Poems.* Stanford, CA: Stanford University Press, 1994.

Fox, Maria Stadter. *The Troubling Play of Gender: The Phaedra Dramas of Tsvetaeva, Yourcenar, and H.D.* Selinsgrove, PA: Susquehanna University Press; London; Cranbury, NJ: Associated University Presses, 2001.

Friedman, Susan Stanford. *Penelope's Web: Gender, Modernity, H.D.'s Fiction.* Cambridge; New York: Cambridge University Press, 1990.

Friedman, Susan Stanford. *Psyche Reborn: The Emergence of H. D.* Bloomington, IN: Indiana University Press, 1981.

Friedman, Susan Stanford and Rachel Blau Duplessis, eds. *Signets: Reading H.D.* Madison, WI: University of Wisconsin Press, 1990.

Gregory, Eileen. *H.D. and Hellenism: Classic Lines.* Cambridge; New York: Cambridge University Press, 1997.

Guest, Barbara. *Herself Defined: The Poet H.D. and Her World.* Garden City, NY: Doubleday, 1984.

Hollenberg, Donna Krolik. *H.D.: The Poetics of Childbirth and Creativity.* Boston: Northeastern University Press, 1991.

Hollenberg, Donna Krolik, ed. *H.D. and Poets After.* Iowa City: University of Iowa Press, 2000.

King, Michael, ed. *H. D.: Woman and Poet.* Orono, ME: University of Maine at Orono, 1986.

Kloepfer, Deborah Kelly. *The Unspeakable Mother: Forbidden Discourse in Jean Rhys and H.D.* Ithaca, NY: Cornell University Press, 1989.

Korg, Jacob. *Winter Love: Ezra Pound and H.D.* Madison: University of Wisconsin Press, 2003.

Kreis-Schinck, Annette. *We Are Voyagers, Discoverers: H.D.'s Trilogy and Modern Religious Poetry.* Heidelberg: C. Winter, 1990.

Laity, Cassandra. *H.D. and the Victorian fin de siècle: Gender, Modernism, Decadence.* Cambridge; New York: Cambridge University Press, 1996.

Lowell, Amy. *Tendencies in Modern American Poetry.* Boston: New York: Houghton Mifflin, 1931 [1917].

Morris, Adalaide. *How to Live/What to Do: H.D.'s Cultural Poetics.* Urbana: University of Illinois Press, 2003.

Nadeau, Richard M. *The Flower Magicians Bartered For: A Reading of The Walls Do Not Fall, Tribute to the Angels, and The Flowering of the Rod, a Trilogy by H D.* Annandale-on-Hudson, NY: [s.n.], 1975.

O'Brien, Kevin. *Saying Yes at Lightning: Threat and the Provisional Image in Post-romantic Poetry.* New York: P. Lang, 2002.

O'Leary, Peter. *Gnostic Contagion: Robert Duncan and the Poetry of Illness.* Middletown, CT: Wesleyan University Press, 2002.

Pettipiece, Deirdre Anne. *Sex Theories and the Shaping of Two Moderns: Hemingway and H.D.* New York: Routledge, 2002.

Quinn, Vincent. *Hilda Doolittle (H. D.).* New York: Twayne Publishers, 1967.

Rado, Lisa. *The Modern Androgyne Imagination: A Failed Sublime.* Charlottesville, VA: University Press of Virginia, 2000.

Rainey, Lawrence. *Institutions of Modernism: Literary Elites and Public Culture.* New Haven, CT: Yale University Press, 1998.

Riddell, Joseph N. *The Turning Word: American Literary Modernism and Continental Theory,* ed. Mark Bauerlein. Philadelphia: University of Pennsylvania Press, 1996.

Swann, Thomas Burnett. *The Classical World of H.D.* Lincoln: University of Nebraska Press, 1962.

Sword, Helen. *Engendering Inspiration: Visionary Strategies in Rilke, Lawrence, and H.D.* Ann Arbor: University of Michigan Press, 1995.

Tabron, Judith L. *Postcolonial Literature from Three Continents: Tutuola, H.D., Ellison, and White.* New York: Peter Lang, 2003.

Taylor, Georgina. *H.D. and the Public Sphere of Modernist Women Writers 1913–1946: Talking Women.* Oxford: Clarendon; New York: Oxford University Press, 2001.

Trigilio, Tony. *Strange Prophecies Anew: Rereading Apocalypse in Blake, H.D., and Ginsberg.* Madison, NJ: Fairleigh Dickinson University Press; London; Cranbury, NJ: Associated University Presses, 2000.

Watts, Harold H. *Hound and Quarry.* London: Routledge and Kegan Paul, 1953.

Wolle, Francis. *A Moravian Heritage.* Boulder, CO: Empire Reproduction and Printing Co., 1972.

EUGENE JOLAS (1894–1952)

Works:

Cinema; Poems. New York: Adelphi, 1926.

Transition Stories; Twenty-three stories from "Transition," eds. Eugene Jolas and Robert Sage. New York: W. V. McKee, 1929.

Secession in Astropolis. Paris: Black Sun Press, 1929.

Our Exagmination Round his Factification for Incamination of Work in Progress, by Samuel Beckett, Marcel Brion, Frank Budgen, Stuart Gilbert, Eugene Jolas, Victor Llona, Robert McAlmon, Thomas McGreevy, Elliot Paul, John Rodker, Robert Sage, William Carlos Williams. With letters of protest by G. V. L. Slingsby and Vladimir Dixon. Paris: Shakespeare and Co., 1929.

The Language of Night. The Hague (Holland): Servire Press, 1932.

Epivecables of 3. [Paris: R. Riff, Editions Vertigral, 1932].

I Have Seen Monsters and Angels. Paris: Transition Press, 1938.

Planets and Angels. Mount Vernon, IA: English Club of Cornell College, 1940.

Words from the Deluge. New York: Gotham Book Mart, 1941.

Vertical; a Yearbook for Romantic-mystic Ascensions, ed. Eugene Jolas. New York: Gotham Bookmart Press, 1941.

Wanderpoem; or, Angelic Mythamorphosis of the City of London. Paris: Transition Press, 1946.

Transition Workshop, ed. Eugene Jolas. New York, Vanguard Press, 1949.

Posthumous Works:

James Joyce: Two Decades of Criticism, eds. Eugene Jolas et al. Edited, with a new introduction, by Seon Givens. New York: Vanguard Press, 1963.

Man from Babel, eds. Andreas Kramer and Rainer Rumold. New Haven, CT: Yale University Press, 1998.

Criticism and Interpretation:

McMillan, Dougald. *Transition: The History of a Literary Era 1927–1938*. London: Calder and Boyars, 1975.

JAMES JOYCE (1882–1941)

Bibliographies:

Rice, Thomas Jackson. *James Joyce, a Guide to Research*. New York: Garland, 1982.

Staley, Thomas F. *An Annotated Critical Bibliography of James Joyce*. London: Harvester, 1989.

Biographies:

Ellmann, Richard. *James Joyce*. Rev. edn. New York: Oxford University Press, 1983.

Fargnoli, Nicolas A. and Gillespie, Michael Patrick. *James Joyce A to Z: An Encyclopedic Guide to his Life and Work*. London: Bloomsbury, 1995.

McCourt, John. *The Years of Bloom: James Joyce in Trieste 1904–1920*. Dublin: Lilliput Press, 2000.

Works:

Chamber Music. London: Elkin Mathews, 1907.

Dubliners. London: Grant Richards, 1914; New York: B. W. Huebsch, 1916.

A Portrait of the Artist as a Young Man. New York: Huebsch; London: The Egoist, 1916.

Exiles: A Play in Three Acts. London: Grant Richards, 1918.

Ulysses. Paris: Shakespeare and Co.; John Rodker for the Egoist Press; London, 1922.

Poems Penyeach. Paris: Shakespeare and Co., 1927.

Collected Poems. New York: Viking, 1937.

Finnegans Wake. London: Faber and Faber; New York: The Viking Press, 1939.

Posthumous Works:

Stephen Hero, ed. Theodor Spencer. London: Jonathan Cape, 1944.

Letters of James Joyce, vol 1, ed. Stuart Gilbert. London: Faber and Faber; New York: Viking, 1957.

The Critical Writing of James Joyce, eds. Richard Ellmann and Ellsworth Mason. London: Faber and Faber; New York: Viking, 1959.

Letters of James Joyce, vols. 2–3, ed. Richard Ellmann. London: Faber and Faber, 1966.

Giacomo Joyce, ed. Richard Ellmann. New York: The Viking Press, 1968.

Selected Letters of James Joyce, ed. Richard Ellmann. London: Faber; New York: Viking, 1975.

Groden, Michael. *James Joyce's Manuscripts*. New York: Garland, 1980.

Ulysses: The Corrected Text, ed. Hans Walter Gabler. New York: Random House, 1986.

James Joyce: Occasional, Critical, and Political Writing, ed. Kevin Barry. Oxford: Oxford University Press, 2001.

Criticism and Interpretation:

Adams, R. M. *Surface and Symbol: The Consistency of James Joyce's "Ulysses."* New York: Oxford University Press, 1962.

Attridge, Derek. *Peculiar Language: Literature as Difference from the Renaissance to James Joyce*. London: Methuen; Ithaca: Cornell University Press, 1988.

Attridge, Derek. *Joyce Effects: On Language, Theory, and History*. Cambridge: Cambridge University Press, 2000.

Attridge, Derek, ed. *The Cambridge Companion to James Joyce*. Cambridge: Cambridge University Press, 1990.

Attridge, Derek and Ferrer, Daniel, eds. *Post-structuralist Joyce: Essays from the French*. Cambridge: Cambridge University Press, 1984.

Attridge, Derek and Howes, Marjorie, eds. *Semicolonial Joyce*. Cambridge: Cambridge University Press, 2000.

Beja, Morris. *James Joyce: A Literary Life*. Columbus, OH: Ohio State University Press, 1992.

Benstock, Bernard. *Narrative Con/Texts in "Ulysses."* Urbana, IL: University of Illinois Press, 1991.

Benstock, Bernard, and Benstock, Shari. *Who's He When He's at Home: A James Joyce Directory*. Urbana, IL: University of Illinois Press.

Bishop, John. *Joyce's Book of the Dark, "Finnegans Wake."* Madison, WI: University of Wisconsin Press, 1986.

Bosinelli, Rosa Maria Bollettieri and Mosher, Harold F. *ReJoycing: New Readings of Dubliners*. Lexington, KY: University Press of Kentucky, 1998.

Bowen, Zack, and Carens, James. *A Companion to Joyce Studies*. Westport, CT: Greenwood Press, 1984.

Brown, Richard. *James Joyce: A Post-Culturalist Perspective*. Basingstoke: Macmillan, 1992.

Budgen, Frank. *James Joyce and the Making of "Ulysses."* Bloomington: Indiana University Press, 1960; London: Oxford University Press, 1972 (with additional articles).

Connor, Steven. *James Joyce*. Plymouth: Northcote House, 1996.

Deming, Robert H., ed. *James Joyce: The Critical Heritage*. 2 vols. London: Routledge & Kegan Paul, 1970.

Derrida, Jacques. "Ulysses Gramophone: Hear Say Yes in Joyce," in *Acts of Literature*, ed. Derek Attridge. New York: Routledge, 1992, pp. 253–309.

Devlin, Kimberly. *Wandering and Return in "Finnegans Wake."* Princeton: Princeton University Press, 1991.

Devlin, Kimberly J. and Reizbaum, Marilyn, eds. *"Ulysses": En-Gendered Perspectives.* Columbia, SC: University of South Carolina Press, 1999.

Duffy, Enda. *The Subaltern "Ulysses."* Minneapolis: University of Minnesota Press, 1994, 1982.

Ellmann, Richard. *Ulysses on the Liffey.* London: Faber, 1972.

Froula, Christine. *Modernism's Body: Sex, Culture, and Joyce.* New York: Columbia University Press, 1996.

Gibson, Andrew. *Joyce's Revenge: History, Politics, and Aesthetics in Joyce's "Ulysses."* Oxford: Oxford University Press, 2002.

Gifford, Don. *Notes for Joyce: "Dubliners" and "A Portrait of the Artist as a Young Man."* New York: Dutton, 1967.

Gifford, Don. *"Ulysses" Annotated.* Berkeley: University of California Press, 1989.

Gilbert, Stuart. *James Joyce's "Ulysses": A Study.* London: Faber, 1930. Rev. edn., London: Faber, 1952; New York: Random House, 1955.

Groden, Michael. *"Ulysses" in Progress.* Princeton: Princeton University Press, 1977.

Hart, Clive. *James Joyce's "Ulysses."* Sydney: Sydney University Press, 1968.

Hart, Clive, and Hayman, David. *James Joyce's "Ulysses": Critical Essays.* Berkeley: University of California Press, 1974.

Hart, Clive, and Knuth, Leo. *A Topological Guide to James Joyce's "Ulysses."* Colchester: A Wake Newslitter Press, 1975, rev. 1986.

Hayman, David. *"Ulysses": The Mechanics of Meaning.* Rev. edn. Madison, WI: University of Wisconsin University Press, 1982.

Herring, Philip. *Joyce's Notes and Early Drafts for "Ulysses."* Charlottesville, VA: University Press of Virginia, 1977.

Jameson, Fredric. "Ulysses in History," in *James Joyce and Modern Literature,* eds. W. J. McCormack and Alistair Stead. London: Routledge & Kegan Paul, 1982, pp. 126–41.

Jones, Ellen Carol, ed. *Feminist Readings of Joyce. Special Issue of Modern Fiction Studies,* 35 (Autumn 1989).

Kain, Richard M. *Fabulous Voyager: A Study of James Joyce's "Ulysses."* New York: Viking, 1947.

Kenner, Hugh. *Dublin's Joyce.* Bloomington: Indiana University Press, 1956.

Kenner, Hugh. *Joyce's Voices.* London: Faber, 1987.

Kenner, Hugh. *"Ulysses."* Rev. edn. Baltimore: Johns Hopkins University Press, 1987.

Lawrence, Karen. *The Odyssey of Style in "Ulysses."* Princeton: Princeton University Press, 1981.

Levin, Harry. *James Joyce: A Critical Introduction.* Rev. edn. New York: New Directions Press, 1960.

Litz, A. Walton. *The Art of James Joyce: Method and Design in "Ulysses" and "Finnegans Wake."* London: Oxford University Press, 1961.

MacCabe, Colin. *James Joyce and the Revolution of the Word.* Basingstoke: Macmillan, 1979.

Mahaffey, Vicki. *Reauthorizing Joyce.* Cambridge: Cambridge University Press, 1988.

Manganiello, Dominic. *James Joyce's Politics.* London: Routledge & Kegan Paul, 1980.

McGann, Jerome J. "Ulysses as a Postmodern Text: The Gabler Edition." *Criticism* 27 (1985): 283–306.

McHugh, Roland. *Annotations to "Finnegans Wake."* Baltimore: Johns Hopkins, 1980.

Moretti, Franco. "The Long Goodbye: Ulysses and the End of Liberal Capitalism," in *Signs Taken for Wonders: Essays in the Sociology of Literary Form.* Rev. edn. London: Verso, 1988, pp. 182–208.

Newman, Robert D. and Thornton, Weldon, eds. *Joyce's "Ulysses": The Larger Perspective.* Newark: University of Delaware Press, 1987.

Nolan, Emer. *James Joyce and Nationalism.* London: Routledge, 1995.

Norris, Margot. *The Decentered Universe of "Finnegans Wake": A Structuralist Analysis.* Baltimore: Johns Hopkins, 1976.

Norris, Margot. *Joyce's Web: The Social Unraveling of Modernism.* Austin: University of Texas Press, 1992.

Norris, Margot, ed. *A Companion to James Joyce's "Ulysses."* Boston: Bedford Books, 1998.

Norris, Margot. *Suspicious Readings of Joyce's "Dubliners."* Philadelphia: University of Pennsylvania Press, 2003.

Osteen, Mark. *The Economy of "Ulysses": Making Both Ends Meet.* Syracuse: Syracuse University Press, 1995.

Parrinder, Patrick. *James Joyce.* Cambridge: Cambridge University Press, 1984.

Pearce, Richard, ed. *Molly Blooms: A Polylogue on "Penelope" and Cultural Studies.* Madison: University of Madison Press, 1994.

Rabaté, Jean-Michel. *James Joyce, Authorized Reader.* Baltimore: Johns Hopkins University Press, 1991.

Rabaté, Jean-Michel. *Joyce Upon the Void: The Genesis of Doubt.* New York: St. Martin's Press, 1991.

Rabaté, Jean-Michel. *James Joyce and the Politics of Egoism.* Cambridge: Cambridge University Press, 2001.

Raleigh, John Henry. *The Chronicle of Leopold and Molly Bloom: "Ulysses" as Narrative.* Berkeley: University of California Press, 1977.

Restuccia, Frances. *Joyce and the Law of the Father.* New Haven: Yale University Press, 1989.

Schutte, William M. *Index of Recurrent Elements in James Joyce's "Ulysses."* Carbondale, IL: Southern Illinois University Press, 1982.

Seidel, Michael. *James Joyce: A Short Introduction.* Oxford: Blackwell, 2002.

Senn, Fritz. *Inductive Scrutinies: Focus on Joyce,* ed. Christine O'Neill. Baltimore: Johns Hopkins University Press, 1995.

Senn, Fritz. *Joyce's Dislocations,* ed. John Paul Riquelme. Baltimore: The Johns Hopkins University Press, 1984.

Sherry, Vincent. *James Joyce: "Ulysses."* Cambridge: Cambridge University Press, 1994.

Spoo, Robert. *James Joyce and the Language of History: Dedalus's Nightmare.* New York: Oxford University Press, 1994.

Staley, Thomas F., ed. *"Ulysses": Fifty Years.* Bloomington: Indiana University Press, 1974.

Steppe, Wolfhard, with Hans Walter Gabler. *A Handlist to James Joyce's "Ulysses."* New York: Garland, 1986.

Thornton, Weldon. *Allusions in "Ulysses": An Annotated List.* Chapel Hill, NC: The University of North Carolina Press, 1968.

Tymoczko, Maria. *The Irish "Ulysses."* Berkeley: University of California Press, 1994.

Valente, Joseph A. *James Joyce and the Problem of Justice.* Cambridge: Cambridge University Press, 1995.

Valente, Joseph, ed. *Quare Joyce.* Ann Arbor: University of Michigan Press, 1998.

Wollaeger, Mark A., Luftig, Victor, and Spoo, Robert, eds. *Joyce and the Subject of History.* Ann Arbor: University of Michigan Press, 1996.

Wollaeger, Mark. *James Joyce's A Portrait of the Artist as a Young Man: A Casebook.* Oxford: Oxford University Press, 2003.

LAURA RIDING JACKSON (1901–91)

Bibliographies:

Wexler, Joyce Piell. *Laura Riding: A Bibliography.* New York: Garland Publication, 1981.

Biographies:

Baker, Deborah. *In Extremis: The Life of Laura Riding.* New York: Grove Press, 1993.

Works:

Close Chaplet. London: Hogarth Press, 1926.

Laura Riding and Robert Graves. *Survey of Modernist Poetry.* London: W. Heinemann, 1927.

Voltaire, a Biographical Fantasy. London: Hogarth Press, 1927.

Anarchism is not Enough. London: J. Cape, 1928.

Contemporaries and Snobs. London: J. Cape, 1928.

Love as Love, Death as Death. London: Seizin Press, 1928.

Laura Riding and Robert Graves. *Pamphlet Against Anthologies.* London: J. Cape, 1928.

Experts are Puzzled. London: J. Cape, 1930.

Four Unposted letters to Catherine. Paris: Hours Press, 1930.

Poems: A Joking Word. London: J. Cape, 1930.

Though gently. . . . Deya, Majorca: Seizin Press, 1930.

Twenty Poems Less. Paris: Hours Press, 1930.

Laura and Francisca. Deya, Majorca: Seizin Press, 1931.

First Leaf. Deyá, Majorica: Seizin Press, 1933.

Life of the Dead. London: Arthur Barker, 1933.

Progress of Stories. Deyá, Majorca: Seizin Press; London, Constable & Co., 1935.

Trojan Ending. New York: Random House, 1937.

Collected Poems. London: Cassell/New York: Random House, 1938.

World and Ourselves. London: Chatto & Windus, 1938.

Selected Poems: In Five Sets. London: Faber and Faber, 1970.

Telling. London: Athlone Press, 1972.

Selections. New York: Chelsea Associates, 1976.

How a Poem Comes to Be: A Poem. Northridge, CA: Lord John Press, 1980.

Poems of Laura Riding: A New Edition of the 1938 Collection. New York: Persea Books, 1980.

Some Communications of Broad Reference. Northridge, CA: Lord John Press, 1983.

Lives of Wives with a New Afterword by Laura (Riding) Jackson. Manchester, UK: Carcanet, 1988, 1939.

Posthumous Works:

Short Sentence for Private Reflection on the Universal Length of Meaning. Brooktondale, New York: Hand printed . . . by James Tyler at the Larch Tree Press . . . , 1995.

First Awakenings: The Early Poems of Laura Riding Jackson, ed. with an intro. by Elizabeth Friedmann, Alan J. Clark, and Robert Nye; preface by Laura (Riding) Jackson. New York: Persea Books, 1992.

Word "Woman" and Other Related Writings, eds. Elizabeth Friedmann and Alan J. Clark. New York: Persea Books, 1993.

Rational Meaning: A New Foundation for the Definition of Words, and Supplementary Essays, by Laura (Riding) Jackson and Schuyler B. Jackson, ed. William Harmon; intro. by Charles Bernstein. Charlottesville, VA; London: University Press of Virginia, 1997.

Criticism and Interpretation:

Adams, Barbara Block. *Enemy Self: Poetry and Criticism of Laura Riding.* Ann Arbor: UMI Research Press, 1990.

Friedmann, Elizabeth, ed. *The Sufficient Difference: A Centenary Celebration of Laura Riding Jackson.* New York: Chelsea Associates, 2000.

Wexler, Joyce Piell. *Laura Riding's Pursuit of Truth.* Athens, OH: Ohio University Press, 1979.

Meyer, Steven, "'An Ill-Matched Correspondence': Laura Riding's Gertrude Stein," *Raritan: A Quarterly Review* 19(4) (Spring 2000): 159–70.

WYNDHAM LEWIS (1884–1957)

Bibliographies:

Gawsworth, John. *Apes, Japes and Hitlerism: A Study and Bibliography of Wyndham Lewis.* London: Unicorn Press, 1932.

Morrow, Bradford and Lafourcade, Bernard. *A Bibliography of the Writings of Wyndham Lewis.* Santa Barbara, CA: Black Sparrow Press, 1978.

Pound, Omar S. and Grover, Philip. *Wyndham Lewis: A Descriptive Bibliography*. Folkestone, UK: Dawson, 1978.

Biographies:

Fox, C. J. *Wyndham Lewis and E. J. Pratt: A Convergence of Strangers*. St. John's, Nfld.: Memorial University Press, 1983.

Meyers, Jeffrey. *The Enemy: A Biography of Wyndham Lewis*. London: Routledge and Kegan Paul, 1980.

O'Keeffe, Paul. *Some Sort of Genius: A Life of Wyndham Lewis*. London: Jonathan Cape, 2000.

Works:

Timon of Athens. London: Cube Press, 1914.

The Ideal Giant. London: Little Review, 1917.

Tarr. New York: Knopf, 1918.

The Caliph's Design. London: Egoist, 1919.

Fifteen Drawings. London: Ovid Press, 1920.

The Art of Being Ruled. London: Chatto and Windus, 1926.

The Lion and the Fox. London: Grant Richards, 1927.

Time and Western Man. London: Chatto and Windus, 1927.

The Wild Body. London: Chatto and Windus, 1927.

The Childermass. Section I. London: Chatto and Windus, 1928.

Paleface. London: Chatto and Windus, 1929.

The Apes of God. London: Arthur Press, 1930.

Hitler. London: Chatto and Windus, 1931.

The Diabolical Principle and the Dithyrambic Spectator. London: Chatto and Windus, 1931.

The Doom of Youth. New York: Robert McBride and Co., 1932.

Filibusters in Barbary. London: Grayson, 1932.

Enemy of the Stars. London: Desmond Harmsworth, 1932.

Snooty Baronet. London, etc.: Cassell and Co., 1932.

Thirty Personalities and a Self-Portrait. London: Desmond Harmsworth, 1932.

The Old Gang and the New Gang. London: Desmond Harmsworth, 1933.

One Way Song. London: Faber and Faber, 1933.

Men without Art. London, etc.: Cassell and Co., 1934.

Left Wings over Europe. London: Jonathan Cape, 1936.

Count Your Dead: They are Alive! London: Lovat Dickson, 1937.

The Revenge for Love. London, etc.: Cassell and Co., 1937.

Blasting and Bombadiering. London: Eyre and Spottiswoode, 1937.

The Mysterious Mr Bull. London: Robert Hale, 1938.

The Jews, Are They Human? London: George Allen and Unwin, 1939.

Wyndham Lewis the Artist, from "Blast" to Burlington House. Laidlaw, 1939.

The Hitler Cult. London: Dent, 1939.

America, I Presume. New York: Howell, Soskin and Co., 1940.

Anglosaxony: A League That Works. Toronto: Ryerson Press, 1941.

The Vulgar Streak. London: Robert Hale, 1941.

America and Cosmic Man. London: Nicholson and Watson, 1948.

Rude Assignment. London, etc.: Hutchinson and Co., 1950.

Rotting Hill. London: Methuen and Co., 1951.

The Writer and the Absolute. London: Methuen and Co., 1952.

Self Condemned. London: Methuen and Co., 1954.

The Demon of Progress in the Arts. London: Methuen and Co., 1954.

The Human Age. London: Methuen and Co., 1955.

The Red Priest. London: Methuen and Co., 1956.

Posthumous Works:

The Letters of Wyndham Lewis. London: Methuen and Co., 1963.

A Soldier of Humor and Selected Writings. New York; Toronto: the New American Library; London: the English Library, 1966.

Wyndham Lewis: An Anthology of His Prose. London: Methuen and Co., 1969.

Wyndham Lewis on Art. London: Thames and Hudson, 1969.

Unlucky for Pringle: Unpublished and Other Stories, eds. C. J. Fox and Robert T. Chapman. Vision, 1973.

The Roaring Queen, ed. Walter Allen. London: Secker and Warburg, 1973.

Enemy Salvoes, ed. C. J. Fox. London: Vision, 1976.

The Code of a Herdsman. Glasgow: Wyndham Lewis Society, 1977.

Imaginary Letters. Wyndham Lewis Society, 1977.

Mrs Dukes' Million. Toronto: Coach House Press, 1977.

Lewis the Painter. Glasgow: Wyndham Lewis Society, 1978.

Collected Poems and Plays, ed. Alan Munton. Manchester: Carcanet, 1979.

Wyndham Lewis. By Jane Farrington; with contributions by Sir John Rothenstein, Richard Cork, Omar S. Pound. London: Lund Humphries, in association with the City of Manchester Art Galleries, c. 1980.

The Sea-mists of the Winter. Illustrations by the author. Santa Barbara, CA: Black Sparrow Press, 1981.

A. J. A. Symons to Wyndham Lewis: Twenty-four Letters. Edinburgh: Tragara Press, 1982.

Wyndham Lewis: Drawings and Watercolours, 1910–1920. London: Anthony d'Offay, 1983.

Wyndham Lewis, the Twenties. London: Anthony d'Offay, 1984.

Pound/Lewis: The Letters of Ezra Pound and Wyndham Lewis, ed. Timothy Materer. New York: New Directions, 1985.

Creatures of Habit and Creatures of Change: Essays on Art, Literature and Society, 1914–1956, ed. Paul Edwards. Santa Rosa, CA: Black Sparrow Press, 1989.

The Essential Wyndham Lewis: an Introduction to His Work, ed. Julian Symons. London: Deutsch, 1989.

Wyndham Lewis and I. A. Richards: a Friendship Documented 1928–57, eds. John Constable and S. J. M. Watson. Cambridge: Skate, 1989.

Wyndham Lewis, 1882–1957. London: Austin/Desmond Fine Art, 1990.

Criticism and Interpretation:

Ayers, David. *Wyndham Lewis and Western Man*. New York: St. Martin's Press, 1992.

Bridson, D. G. *The Filibuster: A Study of the Political Ideas of Wyndham Lewis*. London: Cassell, 1972.

Brown, Dennis. *Intertextual Dynamics within the Literary group – Joyce, Lewis, Pound, and Eliot: The Men of 1914*. Houndmills, Basingstoke: Macmillan, 1990.

Campbell, Roy. *Wyndham Lewis*, ed. Jeffrey Meyers. Pietermaritzburg: University of Natal Press, 1985.

Campbell, SueEllen. *The Enemy Opposite: The Outlaw Criticism of Wyndham Lewis*. Athens, OH: Ohio University Press, 1988.

Chapman, Robert T. *Wyndham Lewis – Fiction and Satires*. London: Vision Press, 1973.

Cooney, Seamus, ed; co-edited by Bradford Morrow, Bernard Lafourcade, and Hugh Kenner. *Blast 3*. Santa Barbara, CA: Black Sparrow Press, 1984.

Dasenbrook, Reed Way. *The Literary Vorticism of Ezra Pound and Wyndham Lewis: Towards the Condition of Painting*. Baltimore: Johns Hopkins University Press, 1985.

Edwards, Paul. *Wyndham Lewis: Art and War*. London: Wyndham Lewis Memorial Trust in association with Lund Humphries, 1992.

Edwards, Paul. *Wyndham Lewis: Painter and Writer*. New Haven and London: Yale University Press, 2000.

Edwards, Paul, ed. *Volcanic Heaven: Essays on Wyndham Lewis's Painting and Writing*. Santa Rosa: Black Sparrow Press, 1996.

Feijo, Antonio M. *Near Miss: A Study of Wyndham Lewis (1909–1930)*. New York: Peter Lang, 1998.

Foshay, Toby Avard. *Wyndham Lewis and the Avant-garde: The Politics of the Intellect*. Montreal: McGill-Queen's University Press, 1992.

Grigson, Geoffrey. *A Master of Our Time: A Study of Wyndham Lewis*. London: Methuen, 1951.

Handley-Read, Charles, ed. *The Art of Wyndham Lewis*. London: Faber and Faber, 1951.

Houen, Alex. *Terrorism and Modern Literature, from Joseph Conrad to Ciaran Carson*. Oxford; New York: Oxford University Press, 2002.

Jameson, Fredric. *Fables of Aggression: Wyndham Lewis, the Modernist as Fascist*. Berkeley: University of California Press, 1979.

Kenner, Hugh. *Wyndham Lewis*. Norfolk, CT: New Directions Books [1964], 1954.

Klein, Scott W. *The Fictions of James Joyce and Wyndham Lewis: Monsters of Nature and Design*. Cambridge, UK; New York: Cambridge University Press, 1994.

Kush, Thomas. *Wyndham Lewis's Pictorial Integer*. Ann Arbor, MI: UMI Research Press, 1981.

Loewenstein, Andrea Freud. *Loathsome Jews and Engulfing Women: Metaphors of Projection in the Works of Wyndham Lewis, Charles Williams, and Graham Greene*. New York: New York University Press, 1993.

Mastin, Catharine M., Stacey, Robert, and Dilworth, Thomas. *The Talented Intruder: Wyndham Lewis in Canada, 1939–1945*. Windsor, Ont.: Art Gallery of Windsor, 1992.

Materer, Timothy. *Wyndham Lewis, the Novelist*. Detroit: Wayne State University Press, 1976.

Materer, Timothy. *Vortex: Pound, Eliot, and Lewis*. Ithaca, NY: Cornell University Press, 1979.

Meyers, Jeffrey, ed. *Wyndham Lewis: A Revaluation: New Essays*. Montreal: McGill-Queen's University Press, 1980.

Michel, Walter. *Wyndham Lewis: Paintings and Drawings*. London: Thames and Hudson, 1971.

Miller, Tyrus. *Late Modernism: Politics, Fiction, and the Arts between the World Wars*. Berkeley: University of California Press, 1999.

Normand, Tom. *Wyndham Lewis the Artist: Holding the Mirror to Politics*. Cambridge, UK; New York: Cambridge University Press, 1992.

Peppis, Paul. *In Literature, Politics, and the English Avant-garde: Nation and Empire, 1901–1918*. Cambridge, UK; New York: Cambridge University Press, 2000.

Peters-Corbett, David, ed. *Wyndham Lewis and the Art of Modern War*. New York: Cambridge University Press, 1998.

Pritchard, William H. *Wyndham Lewis*. New York: Twayne Publishers, 1968.

Porteus, Hugh Gordon. *Wyndham Lewis: A Discursive Exposition*. London: D. Harmsworth, 1932.

Quéma, Anne. *The Agon of Modernism: Wyndham Lewis's Allegories, Aesthetics, and Politics*. Lewisburg, PA: Bucknell University Press; London: Associated University Presses, 1999.

Schenker, Daniel. *Wyndham Lewis, Religion and Modernism*. Tuscaloosa: University of Alabama Press, 1992.

Sherry, Vincent. *Ezra Pound, Wyndham Lewis, and Radical Modernism*. New York: Oxford University Press, 1992.

Tomlin, E. W. F. *Wyndham Lewis*. London; New York: Longmans, Green, 1955.

Trotter, David. *Paranoid Modernism: Literary Experiment, Psychosis, and the Professionalization of English Society*. Oxford; New York: Oxford University Press, 2001.

Wagner, Geoffrey. *Wyndham Lewis: A Portrait of the Artist as the Enemy*. New Haven: Yale University Press, 1957.

MINA LOY (1882–1966)

Biographies:

Burke, Carolyn. *Becoming Modern: The Life of Mina Loy.* New York: Farrar, Straus, and Giroux, 1996.

Works:

Lunar Baedeker and Time-tables; Selected Poems. Highlands, NC: J. Williams, 1958.

Posthumous Works:

Insel, ed. Elizabeth Arnold. Santa Rosa, CA: Black Sparrow Press, 1991.

The Lost Lunar Baedeker: Poems of Mina Loy, ed. Roger L. Conover. New York: Farrar, Straus, Giroux, 1996.

Criticism and Interpretation:

Galvin, Mary E. *Queer Poetics: Five Modernist Women Writers.* Westport, CT: Praeger, 1999.

Kinnahan, Linda A. *Poetics of the Feminine: Authority and Literary Tradition in William Carlos Williams, Mina Loy, Denise Levertov, and Kathleen Fraser.* Cambridge, UK; New York: Cambridge University Press, 1994.

Kouidis, Virginia M. *Mina Loy, American Modernist Poet.* Baton Rouge: Louisiana State University Press, 1980.

Miller, Tyrus. *Late Modernism: Politics, Fiction, and the Arts between the World Wars.* Berkeley: University of California Press, 1999.

Shreiber, Maeera and Tuma, Keith, eds. *Mina Loy: Woman and Poet.* Orono, ME: National Poetry Foundation, 1998.

MARIANNE MOORE (1887–1972)

Bibliographies:

Abbott, Craig S. *Marianne Moore: A Descriptive Bibliography.* Pittsburgh: University of Pittsburgh Press, 1977.

Abbott, Craig S. *Marianne Moore, a Reference Guide.* Boston: G. K. Hall, 1978.

Sheehy, Eugene P. and Lohf, Kenneth A. *The Achievement of Marianne Moore: A Bibliography, 1907–1957.* New York: New York Public Library, 1958.

Biographies:

Molesworth, Charles. *Marianne Moore: A Literary Life.* New York: Atheneum, 1990.

Works:

Poems. London: Egoist Press, 1921.

Marriage. New York: Monroe Wheeler, 1923.

Observations. New York: Dial Press, 1924.

Active Anthology, ed. Ezra Pound. London: Faber and Faber, 1933.

Selected Poems. With an Introduction by T.S. Eliot. New York: Macmillan, 1935. London: Faber and Faber, 1955.

The Pangolin and Other Verse. London: Brendin Publishing Co., 1936.

What Are Years. New York: Macmillan, 1941.

American Anthology: 67 Poems now in Anthology Form for the First Time, ed. Tom Boggs. Prairie City, IL: The Press of James A. Decker, 1942.

Nevertheless. New York: Macmillan, 1944.

Collected Poems. New York: Macmillan, 1951; London: Faber and Faber, 1951.

The Fables of La Fontaine. New York: Viking, 1954.

Predilections. New York: Viking, 1955.

Like a Bulwark. New York: Viking, 1956.

Four Poets on Poetry. Baltimore: Johns Hopkins Press, 1959.

O to Be a Dragon. New York: Viking, 1959.

A Marianne Moore Reader. New York: Viking, 1961.

The Arctic Ox. London: Faber and Faber, 1964.

Poetry and Criticism. Cambridge, MA: Adams House & Lowell House Printers, 1965.

Tell Me, Tell Me: Granite, Steel, and Other Topics. New York: Viking, 1967.

Tipoo's Tiger. New York: Phoenix Book Shop, 1967.

Complete Poems. New York: Macmillan and Viking, 1967; London: Faber and Faber, 1968.

Accented Syllable. New York: Albondocani Press, 1969.

Selected Poems. London: Faber and Faber, 1969.

Posthumous Works:

Unfinished Poems by Marianne Moore. Philadelphia: The Philip H. and A. S. W. Rosenbach Foundation, 1972.

Complete Prose of Marianne Moore, ed. and with an intro. by Patricia C. Willis. New York: Viking, 1986.

Selected Letters of Marianne Moore, eds. Bonnie Costello, Celeste Goodridge, and Cristanne Miller. New York: Knopf; distributed by Random House, 1997.

Poems of Marianne Moore, ed. Grace Schulman. New York, London: Viking, 2003.

Criticism and Interpretation:

Bloom, Harold, ed. *Marianne Moore.* New York: Chelsea House, 1987.

Burke, Kenneth. "Motives and Motifs in the Poetry of Marianne Moore," *Accent*, 2 (Spring 1942): 157–69.

Costello, Bonnie. *Marianne Moore: Imaginary Possessions.* Cambridge, MA, and London: Harvard University Press, 1981.

Diehl, Joanne Feit. *Elizabeth Bishop and Marianne Moore: The Psychodynamics of Creativity.* Princeton: Princeton University Press, 1993.

Engel, Bernard F. *Marianne Moore.* New York: Twayne Publishers, 1964.

Garrigue, Jean. *Marianne Moore.* University of Minnesota Pamphlets on American Writers, no. 50. Minneapolis: University of Minnesota Press, 1965.

Gregory, Elizabeth. *Critical Response to Marianne Moore.* Westport, CT: Praeger, 2003.

Hadas, Pamela White. *Marianne Moore, Poet of Affection*. Syracuse, NY: Syracuse University Press, 1977.

Hall, Donald. *Marianne Moore: The Cage and the Animal*. Pegasus American Authors. New York: Western Publishers, 1970.

Heuving, Jeanne. *Omissions are not Accidents: Gender in the Art of Marianne Moore*. Detroit: Wayne State University Press, 1992.

Holley, Margaret. *Poetry of Marianne Moore: A Study in Voice and Value*. Cambridge; New York: Cambridge University Press, 1987.

Lane, Gary, ed. *A Concordance to the Poems of Marianne Moore*. New York: Haskell House, 1972.

Leavell, Linda. *Marianne Moore and the Visual Arts: Prismatic Color*. Baton Rouge: Louisiana State University Press, 1995.

Merrin, Jeredith. *Enabling Humility: Marianne Moore, Elizabeth Bishop, and the Uses of Tradition*. New Brunswick, NJ: Rutgers University Press, 1990.

Miller, Cristanne. *Marianne Moore: Questions of Authority*. Cambridge, MA: Harvard University Press, 1995.

Parisi, Joseph. *Marianne Moore: The Art of a Modernist*. Ann Arbor, MI: UMI Research Press, 1990.

Schulman, Grace Jan. *Marianne Moore: The Poetry of Engagement*. PhD diss., New York University, 1971.

Schulze, Robin G. *Web of Friendship: Marianne Moore and Wallace Stevens*. Ann Arbor: University of Michigan Press, 1995.

Slatin, John M. *The Savage's Romance: The Poetry of Marianne Moore*. University Park, PA: Pennsylvania State University Press, 1978.

Stamy, Cynthia. *Marianne Moore and China: Orientalism and a Writing of America*. Oxford; New York: Oxford University Press, 1999.

Stapleton, Laurence. *Marianne Moore: The Poet's Advance*. Princeton: Princeton University Press, 1985.

Taffy, Martin. *Marianne Moore, Subversive Modernist*. Austin: University of Texas Press, 1986.

Tomlinson, Charles, ed. *Marianne Moore: A Collection of Critical Essays*. Englewood Cliffs, NJ: Prentice-Hall, 1969.

Vendler, Helen. "Marianne Moore," in *Part of Nature, Part of Us: Modern American Poets*. Cambridge, MA, and London: Harvard University Press, 1980, pp. 59–76.

Villa, Jose Garcia, guest ed. "Marianne Moore Issue," *Quarterly Review of Literature* 4(2) (1948). Essays by William Carlos Williams, Elizabeth Bishop, John Crowe Ransom, Wallace Stevens, Louise Bogan, Vivienne Koch, John L. Sweeney, Wallace Fowlie, Cleanth Brooks, Lloyd Frankenberg, T. C. Wilson, George Dillon.

Willis, Patricia. *Marianne Moore: Woman and Poet*. Orono, ME: National Poetry Foundation, 1990.

EZRA POUND (1885–1972)

Bibliographies:

Edwards, John Hamilton. *Preliminary Checklist of the Writings of Ezra Pound, especially his Contributions to Periodicals*. New Haven: Kirgo-Books, 1953.

Gallup, Donald Clifford. *Bibliography of Ezra Pound*. London: Hart-Davis, 1963.

Gallup, Donald Clifford. *Additions and Corrections to the Revised Edition of the Pound Bibliography*. Orono, ME: University of Maine at Orono, 1983.

Henault, Marie. *Merrill Checklist of Ezra Pound*. Columbus, OH: Merrill, 1970.

Ricks, Beatrice. *Ezra Pound, a Bibliography of Secondary Works*. Metuchen, NJ: Scarecrow Press, 1986.

Biographies:

Ackroyd, Peter. *Ezra Pound and his World*. London: Thames and Hudson, 1980.

Carpenter, Humphrey. *A Serious Character: The Life of Ezra Pound*. New York: Delta, 1990.

Flory, Wendy Stallard. *The American Ezra Pound*. New Haven; London: Yale University Press, 1989.

Grover, Philip. *Ezra Pound: the London Years 1908–1920*. New York: AMS Press, 1978.

Heymann, David C. *Ezra Pound, the last Rower: A Political Profile*. New York: Viking, 1976.

Laughlin, James. *"Pound as wuz": Recollections and Interpretations*. London: Peter Owen, 1989.

Norman, Charles. *The Case of Ezra Pound*. New York: Bodley Press, 1948.

Stock, Noel. *The Life of Ezra Pound*. Harmondsworth: Penguin, 1970.

Tytell, John. *Ezra Pound: The Solitary Volcano*. London: Bloomsbury, 1987.

William, James J. *Ezra Pound: The Tragic Years 1925–1972*. University Park, PA: Pennsylvania State University Press, 1994.

Works:

A Lume Spento. Venice: A. Antonini, 1908.

A Quinzaine for his Yule. London: Pollock & Co., 1908.

Personae. London: Elkin Mathews, 1909.

Exultations. London: Elkin Mathews, 1909.

The Spirit of Romance. London: J. M. Dent, 1910.

Provença: Poems Selected from "Personae" and "Exultations." Boston: Small, Maynard and Co., 1910.

Canzoni. London: Elkin Mathews, 1911.

Ripostes. London; Elkin Mathews, 1912.

Sonnets and Ballate of Guido Cavalcanti. Boston: Small, Maynard and Co., 1912.

Cathay. London: Elkin Mathews, 1915.

Gaudier-Brzeska: A Memoir. London, New York: John Lane, 1916.

Lustra. London: Elkin Mathews, 1916.

Certain Noble Plays of Japan. Churchtown, Dundrum: Cuala Press, 1916.

"*Noh*" *or, Accomplishment, a Study of the Classical Stage of Japan*. London: Macmillan, 1916.

Pavannes and Divisions. New York: Knopf, 1918.

Quia pauper amavi. London: Egoist, 1919.

Instigations. New York: Boni and Liveright, 1920.

Hugh Selwyn Mauberley. London: Ovid Press, 1920.

Umbra. London: Elkin Mathews, 1920.

Poems 1918–21. London: Elkin Mathews, 1921.

Indiscretions. Paris: Three Mountains Press, 1923.

Antheil and the Treatise on Harmony. Paris: Three Mountains Press, 1924.

A Draft of XVI Cantos. Paris: Three Mountains Press, 1925.

Personae: The Collected Poems of Ezra Pound. New York: Liveright, 1926.

Selected Poems. London: Faber & Gwyer, 1928.

A Draft of XXX Cantos. Paris: Hours Press, 1930.

How to Read. London: Desmond Harmsworth, 1931.

Guido Cavalcanti. Genova: Edizioni Marsano S.A., 1932.

ABC of Economics. London: Faber and Faber, 1933.

ABC of Reading. New Haven: Yale University Press, 1934.

Make it New: Essays. London: Faber and Faber, 1934.

Eleven New Cantos, XXXI–XLI. New York: Farrar & Rinehart, 1934.

Draft of Cantos XXXI–XLI. London: Faber, 1935.

Jefferson and/or Mussolini; l'idea statale: Fascism, as I have Seen It. London: Stanley Nott, 1935; Liveright, 1936.

Polite Essays. London: Faber, 1937.

The Fifth Decad of Cantos. New York; Toronto: Farrar & Rinehart; London: Faber, 1937.

Guide to Kulchur. London: Faber, 1938; as *Culture*, Norfolk, CT: New Directions, 1938.

Cantos LII–LXXI. Norfolk, CT: New Directions; London: Faber, 1940.

Pisan Cantos. New York: New Directions, 1948; London: Faber, 1949.

The Cantos of Ezra Pound. New York: New Directions, 1948.

Selected Poems. New York: New Directions, 1949.

The Letters of Ezra Pound 1907–1941, ed. D. D. Paige. New York: Harcourt Brace, 1950; London: Faber, 1951.

The Translations of Ezra Pound. New York: New Direction; London: Faber, 1953.

Translation of *The Classic Anthology Defined by Confucius*. Cambridge, MA: Harvard University Press, 1954; London: Faber, 1955.

Section: Rock-Drill de los Cantares. Milano: Vanni Scheiwiller, 1955; New York: New Directions, 1956; London: Faber, 1957.

Translation of Sophocles, *Women of Trachis*. London: Neville Spearman, 1956; New York: New Directions, 1957; London; Faber, 1969.

Pavannes and Divagations. Norfolk, CT: New Directions 1958; London: Peter Owen, 1960.

Thrones de los Cantares. Milano: Vanni Scheiwiller; New York: New Directions, 1959; London: Faber, 1960.

Impact: Essays on Ignorance and the Decline of American Civilization, ed. with an intro. by Noel Stock. Chicago: Henry Regnery, 1960.

EP to LU: Nine Letters Written to Louis Untermeyer. Bloomington: Indiana University Press, 1963.

Pound/Joyce: The Letters of Ezra Pound to James Joyce, ed. and with commentary by Forrest Read. New York: New Directions, 1967.

Selected Cantos. London: Faber, 1967.

Drafts & Fragments of Cantos CX–CXVII. New York: New Directions, 1969; London: Faber, 1970.

Posthumous Works:

Selected Prose, 1909–1965, ed. with an intro. by William Cookson. New York: New Directions; London: Faber and Faber, 1973.

DK/ Some Letters of Ezra Pound ... {to} Louis Dudek, ed. with notes by Louis Dudek. Montreal: DC Books, 1974.

Selected Poems, 1908–1959. London: Faber, 1975.

Collected Early Poems, ed. Michael John King. New York: New Directions, 1976; London: Faber, 1977.

Ezra Pound and Music: The Complete Criticism, ed. with commentary by R. Murray Schafer. New York: New Directions, 1977; London: Faber, 1978.

"*Ezra Pound speaking*": *Radio Speeches of World War II*, ed. Leonard W. Doob. Westport, CT: Greenwood Press, 1978.

Pound/Ford, the Story of a Literary Friendship, ed. with an intro. by Brita Lindberg-Seyersted. New York: New Directions; London: Faber, 1982.

Letters to Ibbotson, 1935–1952, eds. V. I. Mondolfo and M. Hurley. Orono, ME: National Poetry Foundation, University of Maine, 1979.

Collected Shorter Poems. London: Faber, 1984.

Ezra Pound and Dorothy Shakespear: Their Letters, 1909–1914, eds. Omar Pound and A. Walton Litz. New York: New Directions, 1984; London: Faber and Faber, 1985.

Pound/Lewis: The Letters of Ezra Pound and Wyndham Lewis, ed. Timothy Materer. New York: New Directions; London: Faber 1985.

Criticism and Interpretation:

Alexander, Michael J. *The Poetic Achievement of Ezra Pound*. Berkeley: University of California Press, 1979.

Bacigalupo, Massimo. *Formèd Trace: The Later Poetry of Ezra Pound*. New York: Columbia University Press, 1980.

Baumann, Walter. *Rose in the Steel Dust: An Examination of the Cantos of Ezra Pound*. Bern: Francke, 1967.

Bell, Ian F. A. *Critic as Scientist: The Modernist Poetics of Ezra Pound*. London; New York: Methuen, 1981.

Bernstein, Michael André. *Tale of the Tribe: Ezra Pound and the Modern Verse Epic*. Princeton: Princeton University Press, 1980.

Bloom, Harold. *Ezra Pound*. New York: Chelsea House, 1987.

Brooke-Rose, Christine. *A ZBC of Ezra Pound*. Berkeley: University of California Press; London: Faber, 1971.

Bush, Ronald. *Genesis of Ezra Pound's Cantos*. Princeton: Princeton University Press, 1989.

Childs, John Steven. *Modernist Form: Pound's Style in the Early Cantos*. Selinsgrove, PA: Susquehanna University Press; London: Associated University Press, 1986.

Cookson, William. *Guide to the Cantos of Ezra Pound*. London: Anvil Press Poetry, 2001.

Davenport, Guy. *Cities On Hills: A Study of I–XXX of Ezra Pound's Cantos*. Ann Arbor, MI: UMI Research Press, 1983.

Davis, Earle Rosco. *Vision Fugitive: Ezra Pound and Economics*. Lawrence, KS: University Press of Kansas, 1968.

Davis, Kay. *Fugue and Fresco: Structures in Pound's Cantos*. Orono, ME: National Poetry Foundation, University of Maine at Orono, 1984.

Dekker, George. *Sailing after Knowledge: The Cantos of Ezra Pound*. London: Routledge & Kegan Paul, 1963.

Dilligan, Robert J. *A Concordance to Ezra Pound's Cantos*. New York: Garland, 1981.

Eastman, Barbara C. *Ezra Pound's Cantos: The Story of the Text, 1948–1975*. Orono, ME: National Poetry Foundation, University of Maine, 1979.

Edwards, John Hamilton. *Annotated Index to the Cantos of Ezra Pound: Cantos I–LXXXIV*. Berkeley: University of California Press, 1971.

Ellmann, Maud. *The Poetics of Impersonality: T.S. Eliot and Ezra Pound*. Cambridge, MA: Harvard University Press, 1987.

Flory, Wendy Stallard. *Ezra Pound and The Cantos: A Record of Struggle*. New Haven: Yale University Press, 1980.

Froula, Christine. *Guide to Ezra Pound's Selected Poems*. New York: New Directions, 1983.

Froula, Christine. *To Write Paradise: Style and Error in Pound's Cantos*. New Haven: Yale University Press, 1984.

Furia, Philip. *Pound's Cantos Declassified*. University Park: Pennsylvania State University Press, 1984.

Gibson, Andrew, ed. *Pound in Multiple Perspective: A Collection of Critical Essays*. Houndmills, Basingstoke: Macmillan, 1993.

Gibson, Mary Ellis. *Epic Reinvented: Ezra Pound and the Victorians*. Ithaca, NY: Cornell University Press, 1995.

Henault, Marie. *Merrill Studies in The Cantos*. Columbus, OH: C. E. Merrill, 1971.

Homberger, Eric. *Ezra Pound: The Critical Heritage*. London, Boston: Routledge and Kegan Paul, 1972.

Jin, Songping. *Poetics of the Ideogram: Ezra Pound's Poetry and Hermeneutic Interpretation*. Frankfurt am Main; New York: P. Lang, 2002.

John, Roland. *Beginner's Guide to the Cantos of Ezra Pound*. Salzburg, Austria: University of Salzburg, Institut für Anglistik und Amerikanistik, 1995.

Joseph, Terri Brint. *Ezra Pound's Epic Variations: The Cantos and Major Long Poems*. Orono, ME: National Poetry Foundation, University of Maine, 1995.

Kayman, Martin A. *Modernism of Ezra Pound: The Science of Poetry*. London: Macmillan, 1986.

Kearns, George. *Ezra Pound: The Cantos*. Cambridge; New York: Cambridge University Press, 1989.

Kenner, Hugh. *Poetry of Ezra Pound*. London: Faber and Faber, 1951.

Kenner, Hugh. *The Pound Era*. Berkeley: University of California Press, 1973.

Korn, Marianne, ed. *Ezra Pound and History*. Orono, ME: National Poetry Foundation, University of Maine, 1985.

Laughlin, James. *Notes on Ezra Pound's Cantos: Structure and Metric*. Norfolk, CT: New Directions, 1940.

Leary, Lewis. *Motive and Method in the Cantos of Ezra Pound*. New York: Columbia University Press, 1961.

Makin, Peter. *Pound's Cantos*. London; Boston: G. Allen & Unwin, 1985.

Merritt, Robert. *Early Music and the Aesthetics of Ezra Pound: Hush of Older Song*. Lewiston, NY: E. Mellen Press, 1993.

Miyake, Akiko. *Ezra Pound and the Mysteries of Love: A Plan for the Cantos*. Durham, NC: Duke University Press, 1991.

Nagy, Niclas Christoph. *Ezra Pound's Poetics and Literary Tradition: The Critical Decade*. Bern: Francke, 1966.

Nänny, Max. *Ezra Pound: Poetics for an Electric Age*. Bern: Francke, 1973.

Nassar, Eugene Paul. *Cantos of Ezra Pound: The Lyric Mode*. Baltimore: Johns Hopkins University Press, 1975.

Nicholls, Peter. *Ezra Pound: Politics, Economics, and Writing: A Study of the Cantos*. London: Macmillam, 1984.

Nolde, John J. *Blossoms from the East: The China Cantos of Ezra Pound*. Orono, ME: National Poetry Foundation, University of Maine, 1983.

Nolde, John J. *Ezra Pound and China*. Orono, ME: National Poetry Foundation, University of Maine, 1996.

Pearlman, Daniel D. *Barb of Time: On the Unity of Ezra Pound's Cantos*. New York: Oxford University Press, 1969.

Perloff, Marjorie. *Dance of the Intellect: Studies in the Poetry of the Pound Tradition*. Cambridge; New York: Cambridge University Press, 1985.

Pratt, William, ed. *Ezra Pound, Nature and Myth*. New York: AMS Press, 2002.

Preda, Roxana. *Ezra Pound's (Post)Modern Poetics and Politics: Logocentrism, Language, and Truth*. New York: P. Lang, 2001.

Quinn, Mary Bernetta. *Ezra Pound: An Introduction to the Poetry*. New York: Columbia University Press, 1972.

Rabaté, Jean-Michel. *Language, Sexuality, and Ideology in Ezra Pound's Cantos*. London: Macmillan, 1986.

Rainey, Lawrence. *Ezra Pound and the Monument of Culture: Text, History, and the Malatesta Cantos*. Chicago: University of Chicago Press, 1991.

Rainey, Lawrence, ed. *Poem Containing History: Textual Studies in The Cantos*. Ann Arbor: University of Michigan Press, 1997.

Schulman, Grace. *Ezra Pound: A Collection of Criticism*. New York: McGraw-Hill, 1974.

Singh, G., ed. *Ezra Pound Centenary*. Udine: Campanotto, 1990.

Sullivan, J. P. *Ezra Pound: A Critical Anthology*. Harmondsworth: Penguin, 1970.

Sutton, Walter. *Ezra Pound, a Collection of Critical Essays*. Englewood Cliffs, NJ: Prentice-Hall, 1963.

Tiffany, Daniel Newton. *Radio Corpse: Imagism and the Cryptaesthetic of Ezra Pound*. Cambridge, MA: Harvard University Press, 1995.

Wilson, Peter. *Preface to Ezra Pound*. London; New York: Longman, 1996.

Harrison, Nancy R. *Jean Rhys and the Novel as Women's Text*. Chapel Hill, NC: University of North Carolina Press, 1988.

Howells, Coral Ann. *Jean Rhys*. Hemel Hempstead: Harvester Wheatsheaf, 1991.

James, Louis. *Jean Rhys*. London: Longman, 1978.

Le Gallez, Paula. *The Rhys Woman*. London: Macmillan, 1990.

Maurel, Sylvie. *Jean Rhys*. New York: St. Martin's Press, 1998.

Nebeker, Helen. *Jean Rhys, Woman in Passage: A Critical Study of the Novels of Jean Rhys*. Montréal, Canada; St. Albans, VT: Eden Press Women's Publications, 1981.

O'Connor, Teresa F. *Jean Rhys: The West Indian Novels*. New York: New York University Press, 1986.

JEAN RHYS (1890–1979)

Bibliographies:

Mellown, Elgin W. *Jean Rhys: A Descriptive and Annotated Bibliography of Works and Criticism*. New York: Garland, 1984.

Biographies:

Angier, Carole. *Jean Rhys: Life and Work*. London: Penguin, 1992.

Works:

The Left Bank and Other Stories, with a preface by Ford Madox Ford. London: J. Cape, 1927.

Quartet, originally published as "Postures." London: Chatto & Windus, 1928.

After Leaving Mr Mackenzie. London: J. Cape, 1930.

Voyage in the Dark. London: Constable, 1934.

Good Morning, Midnight. London: Constable, 1939.

Wide Sargasso Sea. London: Deutsch, 1966.

Tigers Are Better Looking. London: Deutsch, 1968.

Sleep It Off, Lady. London: Deutsch; New York: Harper and Row, 1976.

My Day. Vermont: Stinehour Press, 1975.

Posthumous Works:

Jean Rhys Letters 1931–1966. London: Deutsch, 1984.

Smile Please: An Unfinished Autobiography, foreword by Diana Athill. New York: Harper & Row, 1979.

Criticism and Interpretation:

Emery, Mary Lou. *Jean Rhys at "World's End": Novels of Colonial and Sexual Exile*. Austin: University of Texas Press, 1990.

Gregg, Veronica Marie. *Jean Rhys's Historical Imagination: Reading and Writing the Creole*. Chapel Hill, NC: University of North Carolina Press, 1995.

DOROTHY RICHARDSON (1873–1957)

Biographies:

Fromm, Gloria G. *Dorothy Richardson: A Biography*. Athens, GA: University of Georgia Press, 1994.

Rosenberg, John. *Dorothy Richardson, the Genius They Forgot: A Critical Biography*. London: Duckworth, 1973.

Works:

Pointed Roofs .... London: Duckworth & Co., 1913.

Backwater. London: Duckworth & Co., 1916.

Honeycomb. London: Duckworth & Co., 1917.

Tunnel. London: Duckworth & Co., 1919.

Interim. London: Duckworth & Co., 1919.

Deadlock. London: Duckworth & Co., 1921.

Revolving Lights .... London, Duckworth & Co., 1923.

Trap. London: Duckworth, 1925.

Oberland ... . London: Duckworth, 1927.

Backwater. London: Duckworth, 1930.

Dawn's Left Hand. London: Duckworth, 1931.

Clear Horizon. London: J. M. Dent & Sons, & the Cresset Press, 1935.

Pilgrimage .... London: J. M. Dent & Sons, 1938.

Posthumous Works:

Journey to Paradise: Short Stories and Autobiographical Sketches of Dorothy Richardson; selected and introduced by Trudi Tate. London: Virago, 1989.

Windows on Modernism: Selected Letters of Dorothy Richardson, ed. Gloria G. Fromm. Athens, GA: University of Georgia Press, 1995.

Criticism and Interpretation:

Bluemel, Kristin. *Experimenting on the Borders of Modernism: Dorothy Richardson's Pilgrimage*. Athens, GA: University of Georgia Press, 1997.

Fahy, Thomas. "The Cultivation of Incompatibility: Music as a Leitmotif in Dorothy Richardson's Pilgrimage," *Women's Studies: An Interdisciplinary Journal* 29(2) (March 2000): 131–47.

Fouli, Janet. *Structure and Identity: The Creative Imagination in Dorothy Richardson's Pilgrimage.* Tunis, Tunisia: Publications de la Faculté des Lettres de la Manouba, 1995.

Gevirtz, Susan. *Narrative's Journey: The Fiction and Film Writing of Dorothy Richardson.* New York: P. Lang, 1996.

Hanscombe, Gillian E. *Art of Life: Dorothy Richardson and the Development of Feminist Consciousness.* London; Boston: Peter Owen, 1982.

Harvey, Melinda. "Moving, Movies and the Sublime: Modernity and the Alpine Scene in Dorothy Richardson's Oberland," *Colloquy: Text-Theory-Critique* (Sept. 2000): 4.

Horace, Gregory. *Dorothy Richardson: An Adventure in Self-Discovery.* New York, Chicago: Holt, Rinehart and Winston, 1967.

Joubert, Claire. *Lire le féminin: Dorothy Richardson, Katherine Mansfield, Jean Rhys.* Paris: Editions Messene, 1997.

Radford, Jean. *Dorothy Richardson.* Bloomington, IN: Indiana University Press, 1991.

Stamm, David. *Pathway to Reality: Visual and Aural Concepts in Dorothy Richardson's "Pilgrimage."* Tübingen: Francke Verlag, 2000.

Thomson, George H. *A Reader's Guide to Dorothy Richardson's Pilgrimage.* Greensboro, NC: ELT Press, University of North Carolina Greensboro, 1996.

Watts, Carol. *Dorothy Richardson.* Plymouth: Northcote House, 1995.

Winning, Joanne. *Pilgrimage of Dorothy Richardson.* Madison, WI: University of Wisconsin Press, 2000.

Winning, Joanne. "'The Past Is with Me, Seen Anew': Biography's End in Dorothy Richardson's Pilgrimage," in Warwick Gould and Thomas F. Staley, eds., *Writing the Lives of Writers.* Houndmills, UK: Macmillan, 1998.

Gertrude Stein (1874–1946)

Bibliographies:

Liston, Maureen R. *Gertrude Stein: An Annotated Critical Bibliography.* Kent, OH: Kent State University Press, 1979.

Sawyer, Julian. *Gertrude Stein: A Bibliography.* New York: Arrow Editions, 1940.

White, Ray Louis. *Gertrude Stein and Alice B. Toklas: A Reference Guide.* Boston: G. K. Hall, 1984.

Wilson, Robert A. *Gertrude Stein: A Bibliography.* Rockville, MD: Quill & Brush, 1994.

Biographies:

Brinnin, John Malcolm. *The Third Rose: Gertrude Stein and Her World.* Boston; Toronto: Little, Brown and Co., 1959; London: Weidenfeld and Nicolsen, 1960.

Greenfeld, Howard. *Gertrude Stein: A Biography.* New York: Crown, 1973.

Hobhouse, Janet. *Everybody Who Was Anybody: A Biography of Gertrude Stein.* London: Weidenfeld and Nicolson, 1975.

Mellow, James R. *Charmed Circle: Gertrude Stein & Company.* New York: Praeger, 1975.

Rogers, W. G. *When This You See Remember Me: Gertrude Stein in Person.* New York: Rinehart, 1948.

Simon, Linda. *Gertrude Stein Remembered.* Lincoln: University of Nebraska Press, 1994.

Sprigge, Elizabeth. *Gertrude Stein: Her Life and Work.* London: Harper, 1957.

Wagner-Martin, Linda. *"Favored Strangers": Gertrude Stein and Her Family.* New Brunswick, NJ: Rutgers University Press, 1995.

Wineapple, Brenda. *Sister Brother: Gertrude and Leo Stein.* New York: G. P. Putnam's Sons, 1996.

Works:

Three Lives: Stories of the Good Anna, Melanctha, and the Gentle Lena. New York: Grafton Press, 1909.

Tender Buttons: Objects, Food, Rooms. New York: Claire Marie, 1914.

Geography and Plays. Boston: Four Seas, 1922

The Making of Americans. Paris: Contact Press, 1925

Composition as Explanation. London: Hogarth Press, 1926.

Useful Knowledge. London: Bodley Head, 1928.

Acquaintance with Description. London: Seizin Press, 1929.

Lucy Church, Amiably. Paris: Imprimerie "Union," 1930.

How to Write. Paris: Plain Edition, 1931.

Operas and Plays. Paris: Plain Edition, 1932.

The Autobiography of Alice B. Toklas. New York: Harcourt, Brace and Co.; London: John Lane, Bodley Head, 1933.

Matisse, Picasso and Gertrude Stein: With Two Shorter Stories. Paris: Plain Edition, 1933.

Portraits and Prayers. New York: Random House, 1934

Lectures in America. New York: Random House, 1935.

Narration with an intro. by Thornton Wilder. Chicago: University of Chicago Press, 1935.

The Geographical History of American or the Relation of Human Nature to the Human Mind. New York: Random House, 1936.

Everybody's Autobiography. New York: Random House, 1937.

Picasso. London: B. T. Batsford, 1938.

Paris, France. New York: Scribner; London: B. T. Batsford, 1940.

What Are Masterpieces. Los Angeles: Conference, 1940.

Ida, a Novel. New York: Random House, 1941.

Wars I Have Seen. New York: Random House, 1945.

Brewsie and Willie. New York: Random House, 1946.

Posthumous Works:

Selected Writings of Gertrude Stein, ed. Carl Van Vechten. New York: Random House, 1946.

Four in America, intro. by Thornton Wilder. New Haven: Yale University Press, 1947.

Critical Reader: Poems, Stories, Essays compiled and ed. by Wallace Douglas; Roy Lamson; Hallett Smith. New York: W. W. Norton, 1949.

Last Operas and Plays, ed. with an intro. by Carl Van Vechten. New York: Rinehart, 1949.

Yale Edition of the Unpublished Writings of Gertrude Stein under the General Editorship of Carl Van Vechten. New Haven: Yale University Press, 1951–8.

Art of Book Reading. New York: Scribner, 1952.

Mrs Reynolds and Five Earlier Novelettes (1931–1942). New Haven: Yale University Press, 1952.

Bee Time Vine, and other Pieces, 1913–1927. New Haven: Yale University Press, 1953.

Stanzas in Meditation and Other Poems, 1929–1933, with a preface by Donald Sutherland. New Haven: Yale University Press; London: G. Cumberlege, 1956.

Selected Writings, ed. Carl van Vechten. New York: Modern Library, 1962.

Writings and Lectures 1911–1945, ed. Patricia Meyerowitz. London: Owen, 1967.

Geography and Plays with a foreword by Sherwood Anderson. New York: Something Else Press, 1968.

Brinnin, John Malcolm. *Selected Operas & Plays of Gertrude Stein*. Pittsburgh: University of Pittsburgh Press, 1970.

Look at Me Now and Here I Am: Writings and Lectures, 1909–1945, ed. Patricia Meyerowitz. Harmondsworth; Baltimore, MD: Penguin, 1971.

White, Ray Lewis. *Sherwood Anderson/Gertrude Stein: Correspondence and Personal Essays*. Chapel Hill, NC: University of North Carolina Press, 1972.

Reflection on the Atomic Bomb: Volume I of the Previously Uncollected Works of Gertrude Stein, ed. Robert Bartlett Haas. Los Angeles: Black Sparrow Press, 1973.

How Writing is Written: Volume II of the Previously Uncollected Works of Gertrude Stein, ed. Robert Bartlett Haas. Los Angeles: Black Sparrow, 1974.

Yale Gertrude Stein: Selections with an intro. by Richard Kostelanetz. New Haven: Yale University Press, 1980.

Letters of Gertrude Stein and Carl Van Vechten, 1913–1946, ed. Edward Burns. New York: Columbia University Press, 1986.

Really Reading Gertrude Stein: A Selected Anthology with essays by Judy Grahn. Freedom, CA: Crossing Press, 1989.

Stein Reader, ed. Ulla E. Dydo. Evanston, IL: Northwestern University Press, 1993.

Gertrude Stein: In Words and Pictures, ed. Renate Stendhal. Chapel Hill, NC: Algonquin Books of Chapel Hill, 1994.

History of Having a Great Many Times not Continued to be Friends: The Correspondence between Mabel Dodge and Gertrude Stein, 1911–1934, ed. Patricia R. Everett. Albuquerque, NM: University of New Mexico Press, 1996.

Letters of Gertrude Stein and Thornton Wilder, eds. Edward M. Burns and Ulla E. Dydo, with William Rice. New Haven: Yale University Press, 1996.

Writings. New York: Library of America, 1998.

Criticism and Interpretation:

Berry, Ellen E. *Curved Thought and Textual Wandering: Gertrude Stein's Postmodernism*. Ann Arbor: University of Michigan Press, 1992.

Bloom, Harold, ed. *Gertrude Stein*. New York: Chelsea, 1986.

Bridgman, Richard. *Gertrude Stein in Pieces*. New York: Oxford University Press, 1970.

Chessman, Harriet. *The Public Is Invited to Dance: Representation, the Body, and Dialogue in Gertrude Stein*. Stanford: Stanford University Press, 1989.

DeKoven, Marianne. *A Different Language: Gertrude Stein's Experimental Writing*. Madison, WI: University of Wisconsin Press, 1983.

Dubnick, Randa. *The Structure of Obscurity: Gertrude Stein, Language, and Cubism*. Urbana, IL: University of Illinois Press, 1984.

Dydo, Ulla E. "Landscape is not a Grammar: Gertrude Stein in 1928," *Raritan* 7(1) (Summer 1987): 97–113.

Dydo, Ulla E. "Reading the Handwriting: The Manuscripts of Gertrude Stein," in *A Gertrude Stein Companion: Content with the Example*, ed. Bruce Kellner. Westport, CT: Greenwood Press, 1988.

Dydo, Ulla E. "Gertrude Stein: Composition as Meditation," in Shirley Neuman and Ira B. Nadel, eds., *Gertrude Stein and the Making of Literature*. Boston: Northeastern University Press, 1988.

Dydo, Ulla E. *Gertrude Stein: The Language that Rises, 1923–1934*. Evanston, IL: Northwestern University Press, 2003.

GallUniversity Press, Donald Clifford. *Flowers of Friendship: Letters Written to Gertrude Stein*. New York: A. Knopf, 1953.

Harrison, Gilbert A. *Rare Privilege, this, of "Being an American": A Personal Note on Gertrude Stein*. Pasadena, CA: Castle Press, 1974.

Hoffman, Frederick John. *Gertrude Stein*. Minneapolis: University of Minnesota Press, 1961.

Hoffman, Michael J. *Development of Abstractionism in the Writing of Gertrude Stein*. Philadelphia: University of Pennsylvania Press, 1965.

Hoffman, Michael J., ed. *Critical Essays on Gertrude Stein*. Boston: G. K. Hall, 1986.

Kellner, Bruce. *A Gertrude Stein Companion*. New York: Greenwood, 1988.

Knapp, Bettina Liebowitz. *Gertrude Stein*. New York: Continuum, 1990.

McMillan, Samuel Hubert. *Gertrude Stein, the Cubists, and the Futurists*. Austin: University of Texas Press, 1964.

Meyer, Steven. *Gertrude Stein and the Correlations of Writing and Science*. Stanford: Stanford University Press, 2001.

Miller, Rosalind S. *Gertrude Stein: Form and Intelligibility; Containing the Radcliffe Themes ed. from the Manuscripts in the Yale University Library*. New York: Exposition Press, 1949.

Moore, George B. *Gertrude Stein's "The Making of Americans": Repetitions and the Emergence of Modernism*. New York: Peter Lang, 1998.

Neuman, Shirley and Ira B. Nadel. *Gertrude Stein and the Making of Literature*. Boston: Northeastern University Press, 1988.

Reid, B. L. *Art by Subtraction: A Dissenting Opinion of Gertrude Stein*. Norman: University of Oklahoma Press, 1958.

Ruddick, Lisa. *Reading Gertrude Stein: Body, Text, Gnosis*. Ithaca, NY: Cornell University Press, 1990.

Ryan, Betsy. *Gertrude Stein's Theatre of the Absolute*. Ann Arbor, MI: UMI Research Press, 1984.

Simon, Linda. *Gertrude Stein: A Composite Portrait*. New York: Avon, 1974.

Stavitsky, Gail. *Gertrude Stein: The American Connection*. New York: Sid Deutsch Gallery, 1990.

Steiner, Wendy. *Exact Resemblance to Exact Resemblance: The Literary Portraiture of Gertrude Stein*. New Haven: Yale University Press, 1978.

Stewart, Allegra. *Gertrude Stein and the Present*. Cambridge, MA: Harvard University Press.

Sutherland, Donald. *Gertrude Stein: A Biography of Her Work*. New Haven: Yale University Press, 1951.

Walker, Jayne L. *The Making of a Modernist: Gertrude Stein from "Three Lives" to "Tender Buttons."* Amherst: University of Massachusetts Press, 1984.

WALLACE STEVENS (1879–1955)

Bibliographies:

Edelstein, J. M. *Wallace Stevens: A Descriptive Bibliography*. Pittsburgh: University of Pittsburgh Press, 1973.

Huguelet, Theodore L. *Merrill Checklist of Wallace Stevens*. Columbus, OH: Merrill, 1970.

Morse, Samuel French. *Wallace Stevens: A Preliminary Checklist of his Published Writings: 1895–1954*. New Haven: Yale University Library, 1954.

Morse, Samuel French, Bryer, Jack R. and Riddel, Joseph N. *Wallace Stevens Checklist and Bibliography of Stevens Criticism*. Denver: A. Swallow, 1963.

Serio, John N. *Wallace Stevens: An Annotated Secondary Bibliography*. Pittsburgh, PA: University of Pittsburgh Press, 1994.

Biographies:

Bates, Milton. *Wallace Stevens: A Mythology of Self*. Berkeley; London: University of California Press, 1985.

Brazeau, Peter. *Parts of a World: Wallace Stevens Remembered: An Oral Biography*. New York: Random House, c. 1983.

Richardson, Joan. *Wallace Stevens: The Early Years, 1879–1923*. New York: Beech Tree Books, 1986.

Richardson, Joan. *Wallace Stevens: The Later Years 1923–1955*. New York: Beech Tree Books, 1988.

Sharpe, Tony. *Wallace Stevens: A Literary Life*. Basingstoke: Macmillan, 2000.

Stevens, Holly Bright. *Souvenirs and Prophecies: The Young Wallace Stevens*. New York: Knopf, 1977.

Works:

Harmonium. New York: Knopf, 1923.

Ideas of Order. New York: The Alcestis Press, 1935.

Owl's Clover. New York: The Alcestris Press, 1936.

Man with the Blue Guitar & Other Poems. New York, London: Knopf, 1937.

Parts of a World. New York: Knopf, 1942.

Notes Toward a Supreme Fiction. Cummington, MA: Cummington Press, 1942.

Esthétique du mal: A Poem. Cummington, MA: Cummington Press, 1945.

Three Academic Pieces: The Realm of Resemblance, Someone Puts a Pineapple Together, Of Ideal Time and Choice. Cummington, MA: Cummington Press, 1947.

Transport to Summer. New York: Knopf, 1947.

Auroras of Autumn. New York: Knopf, 1950.

Necessary Angel: Essays on Reality and the Imagination. New York: Knopf, 1951.

Selected Poems, with a foreword by Dennis Williamson. London: Fortune Press, 1952; rpt. London: Faber and Faber, 1953.

Collected Poems. New York: Knopf, 1954.

Posthumous Works:

Opus Posthumous, ed. with an intro. by Samuel French Morse. New York: Knopf, 1957.

Poems selected and with an intro. by Samuel French Morse. New York: Random House, 1959.

Letters selected and ed. by Holly Stevens. New York: Knopf, 1966.

Palm at the End of the Mind, selected poems and a play by Wallace Stevens, ed. Holly Stevens. New York: Knopf, 1971.

Secretaries of the Moon: The Letters of Wallace Stevens and José Rodríguez Feo, eds. Beverly Coyle and Alan Filreis. Durham, NC: Duke University Press, 1986.

Sur plusieurs beaux sujets: Wallace Stevens' Commonplace Book: A Facsimile and Transcription, ed. and intro. by Milton J. Bates. Stanford, CA: Stanford University Press; San Marino, CA: Huntington Library, 1989.

Collected Poetry and Prose. New York: Library of America; distributed in the US by Penguin Books, 1997.

Criticism and Interpretation:

Arensberg, Mary, ed. *American Sublime*. Albany: State University of New York Press, 1986.

Baird, James C. *Dome and the Rock: Structure in the Poetry of Wallace Stevens*. Baltimore: Johns Hopkins Press, 1968.

Beckett, Lucy. *Wallace Stevens*. London: Cambridge University Press, 1974.

Beehler, Michael. *T. S. Eliot, Wallace Stevens, and the Discourses of Difference*. Baton Rouge: Louisiana State University Press, 1987.

Benamou, Michel. *Wallace Stevens and the Symbolist Imagination*. Princeton: Princeton University Press, 1972.

Berger, Charles. *Forms of Farewell: The Late Poetry of Wallace Stevens*. Madison: University of Wisconsin Press, 1985.

Bevis, William W. *Mind of Winter: Wallace Stevens, Meditation, and Literature*. Pittsburgh, PA: University of Pittsburgh Press, 1988.

Blessing, Richard Allen. *Wallace Stevens' "Whole Harmonium."* Syracuse, NY: Syracuse University Press, 1970.

Bloom, Harold. *Wallace Stevens: The Poems of our Climate*. Ithaca, NY: Cornell University Press, 1977.

Bloom, Harold. *Wallace Stevens*. New York: Chelsea House Publishers, 1985.

Borroff, Marie. *Wallace Stevens: A Collection of Critical Essays*. Englewood Cliffs, NJ: Prentice-Hall, 1963.

Brogan, Jacqueline Vaught. *Stevens and Simile: A Theory of Language*. Princeton: Princeton University Press, 1986.

Brogan, Jacqueline Vaught. *Violence Within / The Violence Without: Wallace Stevens and the Emergence of a Revolutionary Poetics*. Athens, GA: University of Georgia Press, 2003.

Brown, Merle Elliott. *Wallace Stevens: The Poem as Act*. Detroit: Wayne State University Press, 1970.

Burney, William A. *Wallace Stevens*. New York: Twayne Publishers, 1968.

Carroll, Joseph. *Wallace Stevens' Supreme Fiction: A New Romanticism*. Baton Rouge: Louisiana State University Press, 1987.

Cleghorn, Angus J. *Wallace Stevens' Poetics: The Neglected Rhetoric*. New York: Palgrave, 2000.

Cook, Eleanor. *Poetry, Word-Play, and Word-War in Wallace Stevens*. Princeton: Princeton University Press, 1988.

Dickie, Margaret. *Lyric Contingencies: Emily Dickinson and Wallace Stevens*. Philadelphia: University of Pennsylvania Press, 1991.

Doggett, Frank A. *Wallace Stevens, the Making of the Poem*. Baltimore: Johns Hopkins University Press, 1980.

Doyle, Charles. *Wallace Stevens, the Critical Heritage*. London; Boston: Routledge & Kegan Paul, 1985.

Eeckhout, Bart. *Wallace Stevens and the Limits of Reading and Writing*. Columbia, MO: University of Missouri Press, 2002.

Filreis, Alan. *Wallace Stevens and the Actual World*. Princeton: Princeton University Press, 1991.

Fisher, Barbara M. *Wallace Stevens: The Intensest Rendezvous*. Charlottesville, VA: University Press of Virginia, 1990.

Gelpi, Albert. *Wallace Stevens, the Poetics of Modernism*. Cambridge; New York: Cambridge University Press, 1985.

Grey, Thomas C. *Wallace Stevens Case: Law and the Practice of Poetry*. Cambridge, MA: Harvard University Press, 1991.

Halliday, Mark. *Stevens and the Interpersonal*. Princeton: Princeton University Press, 1991.

Holmes, Barbara. *The Decomposer's Art: Ideas of Music in the Poetry of Wallace Stevens*. New York: P. Lang, 1990.

Jenkins, Lee M. *Wallace Stevens: Rage for Order*. Brighton; Portland, OR: Sussex Academic Press, 2000.

Kermode, Frank. *Wallace Stevens*. New York: Chip's Bookshop, 1979.

Kessler, Edward. *Images of Wallace Stevens*. New Brunswick, NJ: Rutgers University Press, 1971.

La Guardia, David M. *Advance on Chaos: The Sanctifying Imagination of Wallace Stevens*. Hanover, NH: Published for Brown University Press by University Press of New England, 1983.

Leggett, B. J. *Wallace Stevens and Poetic Theory: Conceiving the Supreme Fiction*. Chapel Hill, NC: University of North Carolina Press, 1987.

Leggett, B. J. *Early Stevens: The Nietzschean Intertext*. Durham, NC: Duke University Press, 1992.

Lensing, George S. *Wallace Stevens: A Poet's Growth*. Baton Rouge: Louisiana State University Press, 1986.

Leonard, J. S. *Fluent Mundo: Wallace Stevens and the Structure of Reality*. Athens, GA: University of Georgia Press, 1988.

Litz, A. Walton. *Introspective Voyager; the Poetic Development of Wallace Stevens*. New York: Oxford University Press, 1972.

Litz, A. Walton. *Wallace Stevens, the Poetry of Earth*. Washington, DC: Library of Congress, 1981.

Longenbach, James. *Wallace Stevens: The Plain Sense of Things*. New York: Oxford University Press, 1991.

MacLeod, Glen G. *Wallace Stevens and Company: The Harmonium Years, 1913–1923*. Ann Arbor, MI: UMI Research Press, 1983.

MacLeod, Glen G. *Wallace Stevens and Modern Art: From the Armory Show to Abstract Expressionism*. New Haven: Yale University Press, 1993.

Maeder, Beverly. *Wallace Stevens' Experimental Language: The Lion in the Lute*. New York: St. Martin's Press, 1999.

McCann, Janet. *Wallace Stevens Revisited: "The Celestial Possible."* New York: Twayne Publishers; London: Prentice-Hall, 1995.

McMahon, William E. *Higher Humanism of Wallace Stevens*. Lewiston, NY: E. Mellen Press, 1990.

Morris, Adalaide Kirby. *Wallace Stevens: Imagination and Faith*. Princeton: Princeton University Press, 1974.

Murphy, Charles M. *Wallace Stevens: A Spiritual Poet in a Secular Age*. New York: Paulist Press, 1997.

Newcomb, John Timberman. *Wallace Stevens and Literary Canons*. Jackson: University Press of Mississippi, 1992.

Penso, Kia. *Wallace Stevens, Harmonium, and The Whole of Harmonium*. Hamden, CT: Archon Books, 1991.

Perlis, Alan D. *Wallace Stevens: A World of Transforming Shapes*. Lewisburg, PA: Bucknell University Press, 1976.

Quinn, Justin. *Gathered Beneath the Storm: Wallace Stevens, Nature and Community*. Dublin: University College Dublin Press, 2002.

Rehder, Robert. *Poetry of Wallace Stevens*. Houndmills, Basingstoke: Macmillan Press, 1988.

Riddel, Joseph N. *Clairvoyant Eye: The Poetry and Poetics of Wallace Stevens*. Baton Rouge: Louisiana State University Press, 1965.

Rosu, Anca. *Metaphysics of Sound in Wallace Stevens*. Tuscaloosa: University of Alabama Press, 1995.

Sampson, Theodore. *Cure of the Mind: The Poetics of Wallace Stevens*. Montreal; New York: Black Rose Books, 2000.

Santilli, Kristine S. *Poetic Gesture: Myth, Wallace Stevens, and the Motions of Poetic Language*. New York: Routledge, 2002.

Schaum, Melita. *Wallace Stevens and the Critical Schools*. Tuscaloosa: University of Alabama Press, 1988.

Schaum, Melita, ed. *Wallace Stevens and the Feminine*. Tuscaloosa: University of Alabama Press, 1993.

Schwarz, Daniel R. *Narrative and Representation in the Poetry of Wallace Stevens: A Tune Beyond Us, Yet Ourselves*. Houndmills, Basingstoke: Macmillan, 1993.

Sexson, Michael. *Quest of Self in the Collected Poems of Wallace Stevens*. Lewiston, NY: E. Mellen Press, 1981.

Stern, Herbert Jay. *Wallace Stevens: Art of Uncertainty*. Ann Arbor: University of Michigan Press, 1966.

Sukenick, Ronald. *Wallace Stevens: Musing the Obscure; Readings, an Interpretation, and a Guide to the Collected Poetry*. New York: New York University Press, 1967.

Vendler, Helen. *On Extended Wings: Wallace Stevens' Longer Poems*. Cambridge, MA: Harvard University Press, 1971.

Vendler, Helen. *Wallace Stevens: Words Chosen Out of Desire*. Knoxville: University of Tennessee Press, 1984.

Weston, Susan B. *Wallace Stevens: An Introduction to the Poetry*. New York: Columbia University Press, 1977.

Whiting, Anthony. *Never-resting Mind: Wallace Stevens' Romantic Irony*. Ann Arbor: University of Michigan Press, 1996.

Willard, Abbie F. *Wallace Stevens: The Poet and His Critics*. Chicago: American Library Association, 1978.

Woodman, Leonora. *Stanza my Stone: Wallace Stevens and the Hermetic Tradition*. West Lafayette, IN: Purdue University Press, 1983.

REBECCA WEST (1892–1983)

Bibliographies:

Hutchinson, G. Evelyn. *Preliminary List of the Writings of Rebecca West 1912–1951*. New Haven: Yale University Library, 1957.

Packer, Joan Garrett. *Rebecca West: An Annotated Bibliography*. New York: Garland, 1991.

Biographies:

Evans, Faith, ed. *Family Memories: Rebecca West*. London: Virago, 1987.

Glendinning, Victoria. *Rebecca West: A Life*. London: Phoenix, 1998.

Rollyson, Carl E. *Rebecca West: A Life*. New York: Scribner, 1996.

Works:

The Return of the Soldier. London: Nisbet, 1918.

The Judge. London: Hutchinson, 1922.

The Strange Necessity: Essays by Rebecca West. London: Cape, 1928.

Harriet Hume: A London Fantasy. London: Hutchinson, 1929.

War Nurse: The True Story of a Woman Who Lived, Loved and Suffered on the Western Front. New York: Cosmopolitan Book Corporation, 1930.

The Harsh Voice. London: J. Cape, 1935.

The Thinking Reed. London: Hutchinson, 1936.

Black Lamb and Grey Falcon: A Journey Through Yugoslavia. London: Macmillan, 1942.

The New Meaning of Treason, originally published under title "The Meaning of Treason." London: Macmillan, 1945.

The Fountain Overflows. London: Macmillan, 1957.

The Court and the Castle: A Study of the Interactions of Political and Religious Ideas in Imaginative Literature. London: Macmillan, 1958.

The Essential Rebecca West. Harmondsworth: Penguin, 1978.

The Young Rebecca: Writings of Rebecca West 1911–1917 selected and introduced by Jane Marcus. London: Macmillan in association with Virago, 1982.

Posthumous Works:

The Selected Letters of Rebecca West, ed., annotated, and intro. by Bonnie Kime Scott. New Haven: Yale University Press, 2000.

The Sentinel: An Incomplete Early Novel, ed. Kathryn Laing. Oxford: Legenda, 2002.

Survivors in Mexico, ed. and intro. by Bernard Schweizer. New Haven; London: Yale University Press, 2003.

Criticism and Interpretation:

Deakin, Motley F. *Rebecca West*. Boston: Twayne Publishers, 1980.

Hammond, J. R. *H. G. Wells and Rebecca West*. Brighton: Harvester Wheatsheaf, 1991.

Norton, Ann V. *Paradoxical Feminism: The Novels of Rebecca West*. Lanham, MD: International Scholars Publications, 2000.

Orel, Harold. *Literary Achievement of Rebecca West*. London: Macmillan, 1986.

Rollyson, Carl E. *Rebecca West: A Saga of the Century*. London: Hodder & Stoughton, 1995.

Rollyson, Carl E. *Literary Legacy of Rebecca West*. San Francisco: International Scholars Publications, 1998.

Schweizer, Bernard. *Rebecca West: Heroism, Rebellion, and the Female Epic*. Westport, CT: Greenwood Press, 2002.

Wolfe, Peter. *Rebecca West: Artist and Thinker*. Carbondale: Southern Illinois University Press, 1971.

WILLIAM CARLOS WILLIAMS (1883–1963)

Bibliographies:

William Carlos Williams: Man and Poet, ed. Carroll F. Terrell. Orono, ME: National Poetry Foundation, University of Maine at Orono, 1983.

Wagner, Lindo W. *William Carlos Williams: A Reference Guide*. Boston: G. K. Hall, 1978.

Wallace, Emily Mitchell. *Bibliography of William Carlos Williams*. Middletown, CT: Wesleyan University Press, 1968.

Biographies:

Autobiography. New York: Random House, 1951.

Yes, Mrs. Williams. New York: McDowell, Obolensky, 1959.

Baldwin, Neil. *To All Gentleness: William Carlos Williams, the Doctor-Poet*. New York: Atheneum, 1984.

Mariani, Paul. *William Carlos Williams: A New World Naked*. New York: McGraw-Hill, 1981.

Works:

Poems. Rutherford, NJ, 1909.

Tempers. London: E. Mathews, 1913.

Des imagistes: An Anthology. New York: Albert and Charles Boni, 1914.

Others: An Anthology of the New Verse, ed. by Alfred Kreymborg. New York: Knopf, 1916.

Book of Poems: Al que quiere! Boston: Four Seas, 1917

Kora in Hell: Improvisations. Boston: Four Seas, 1920.

Sour Grapes: A Book of Poems. Boston: Four Seas, 1921.

Go go. New York: Monroe Wheeler, 1923.

Great American Novel. Paris: Three Mountains Press, 1923.

Spring and All. Paris: Contact Publishing, 1923.

In the American Grain. New York: Albert & Charles Boni, 1925.

Voyage to Pagany. New York: Macaulay, 1928.

Cod Head. San Francisco: Harvest Press, 1932.

Knife of the Times, and Other Stories. Ithaca, NY: The Dragon Press, 1932.

Novelette and Other Prose (1921–1931). Toulon: Imprimerie F. Cabasson, 1932.

Collected Poems, 1921–1931. New York: Objectivist Press, 1934.

Early Martyr and Other Poems. New York: The Alcestis Press, 1935.

Adam & Eve & The City. Peru, VT: Alcestis Press, 1936.

White Mule. Norfolk, CT: New Directions, 1937.

Complete collected Poems of William Carlos Williams, 1906–1938. Norfolk, CT: New Directions, 1938.

Life Along the Passaic River. Norfolk, CT: New Directions, 1938.

New Book of the Dead. New York: Harrison-Hilton Books, 1939.

In the Money; White Mule Part II. Norfolk, CT: New Directions, 1940.

Broken Span. Norfolk, CT: New Directions, 1941.

Wedge. Cummington, MA: The Cummington Press, 1944.

Happy Rock: A Book about Henry Miller. Berkeley: printed for B. Porter by the Packard Press, 1945.

Paterson. New York: New Directions, 1946.

Clouds, Aigeltinger, Russia, &c. Aurora, NY: Published jointly by the Wells College Press and the Cummington Press, 1948.

Dream of Love: A Play in Three Acts and Eight Scenes. New York: New Directions, 1948.

Test of Poetry. Brooklyn: Objectivist Press, 1948.

Pink Church. Columbus, OH: Golden Goose Press, 1949.

Selected Poems with an Introduction by Randall Jarrell. New York: New Directions, 1949.

Beginning on the Short Story: Notes. Yonkers, NY: Alicat Bookshop Press, 1950.

Collected Later Poems. New York: New Directions, 1950.

Make Light of It: Collected Stories. New York: Random House, 1950.

Collected Earlier Poems. New York: J. Laughlin, 1951.

Build-University Press: A Novel. New York: Random House, 1952.

Desert Music and Other Poems. New York: Random House, 1954.

Selected Essays. New York: Random House, 1954.

Journey to Love. New York: Random House, 1955.

Collected Later Poems. New York: New Directions, 1956.

Howl and Other Poems. San Francisco: City Lights Pocket Bookshop, 1957.

Gift: A Poem. New York: James Laughlin, 1957.

Selected Letters, ed. John C. Thirlwall. New York: McDowell, Obolensky, 1957.

Lunar Baedeker & Time-Tables: Selected Poems. Highlands, NC: J. Williams, 1958.

I Wanted to Write a Poem: The Autobiography of the Works of a Poet reported and ed. Edith Heal. Boston: Beacon Press 1958.

Watermelons. New York: Totem Press, 1959.

Farmers' Daughters: Collected Stories. Norfolk, CT: New Directions, 1961.

Many Loves, and Other Plays: The Collected Plays of William Carlos Williams. Norfolk, CT: New Directions, 1961.

Pictures from Brueghel, and Other Poems including The Desert Music & Journey to Love. Norfolk, CT: J. Laughlin, 1962.

Posthumous Works:

William Carlos Williams Reader, ed. M. L. Rosenthal. New York: Published for J. Laughlin by New Directions, 1966.

Imaginations, ed. Webster Schott. New York: New Directions Pub. Corp., 1970.

Embodiment of Knowledge, ed. Ron Loewinsohn. New York: New Directions, 1974.

I Will Sing a Joyous Song to You, My Lady! Buffalo, NY: New York State University at Buffalo, Lockwood Memorial Library, 1974.

Interviews with William Carlos Williams: "Speaking Straight Ahead," ed. Linda Welshimer Wagner. New York: New Directions, 1976.

Recognizable Image: William Carlos William on Art and Artists. New York: New Directions, 1978.

Flowers of August. Iowa City: Windhover Press, University of Iowa, 1983.

Correspondence. Santa Barbara, CA: Oyster Press: Distributed by Capra Press, 1984.

Doctor Stories, compiled by Robert Coles. New York, NY: New Directions, 1984.

Dear Ez: Letters from William Carlos Williams to Ezra Pound. Bloomington, Indiana: Published for the Friends of the Lilly Library, 1985.

Something to Say: William Carlos Williams on Younger Poets, ed. James E. B. Breslin. New York: New Directions, 1985.

William Carlos Williams and James Laughlin: Selected Letters, ed. Hugh Witemeyer. New York: Norton, 1989.

American Idiom: A Correspondence, ed. John J. Wilson. San Francisco: Bright Tyger Press, 1990.

Letters of William Carlos Williams & Charles Tomlinson, eds. Barry Magid and Hugh Witemeyer. New York: Dim Gray Bar Press, 1992.

Last Word: Letters Between Marcia Nardi and William Carlos Williams, ed. Elizabeth Murrie O'Neil. Iowa City: University of Iowa Press, 1994.

Asphodel, that Greeny Flower & Other Love Poems, with an intro. by Herbert Leibowitz. New York: New Directions, 1994.

Lost Works of William Carlos Williams: The Volumes of Collected Poetry as Lyrical Sequences, ed. Robert J. Cirasa. Madison, NJ: Fairleigh Dickinson University Press; London: Associated University Presses, 1995.

Pound/Williams: Selected Letters of Ezra Pound and William Carlos Williams, ed. Hugh Witemeyer. New York: New Directions, 1996.

Collected Stories of William Carlos Williams, intro. by Sherwin B. Nuland. New York: New Directions, 1996.

Letters of Denise Levertov and William Carlos Williams, ed. Christopher MacGowan. New York: New Directions, 1998.

Poems, into. by Virginia M. Wright-Peterson. Urbana: University of Illinois Press, 2002.

Correspondence of William Carlos Williams and Louis Zukofsky. Middletown, CT: Wesleyan University Press, 2003.

Humane Particulars: The Collected Letters of William Carlos Williams and Kenneth Burke, ed. James H. East. Columbia, SC: University of South Carolina Press, 2003.

Criticism and Interpretation:

Ahearn, Barry. *William Carlos Williams and Alterity: The Early Poetry.* Cambridge; New York: Cambridge University Press, 1994.

Axelrod, Steven Gould and Deese, Helen. *Critical Essays on William Carlos Williams.* New York: G. K. Hall; Toronto: Maxwell Macmillan Canada; New York: Maxwell Macmillan International, 1995.

Bán, Zsófia. *Desire and De-Scription: Words and Images of Postmodernism in the Late Poetry of William Carlos Williams.* Amsterdam: Rodopi, 1999.

Bloom, Harold. *William Carlos Williams.* New York: Chelsea House, 1986.

Bremen, Brian A. *William Carlos Williams and the Diagnostics of Culture.* New York: Oxford University Press, 1993.

Callan, Ron. *William Carlos Williams and Transcendentalism: Fitting the Crab in a Box.* London: Macmillan, 1992.

Cappucci, Paul R. *William Carlos Williams' Poetic Response to the 1913 Paterson Silk Strike.* Lewiston, NY: Edwin Mellen Press, 2002.

Coles, Robert. *William Carlos Williams: The Knack of Survival in America.* New Brunswick, NJ: Rutgers University Press, 1975.

Conarroe, Joel. *William Carlos Williams' Paterson: Language and Landscape.* Philadelphia: University of Pennsylvania Press, 1970.

Conrad, Bryce. *Refiguring America: A Study of William Carlos Williams' "In the American Grain."* Urbana: University of Illinois Press, 1990.

Crawford, T. Hugh. *Modernism, Medicine & William Carlos Williams.* Norman: University of Oklahoma Press, 1993.

Cushman, Stephen. *William Carlos Williams and the Meanings of Measure.* New Haven; London: Yale University Press, 1985.

Diggory, Terence. *William Carlos Williams and the Ethics of Painting.* Princeton: Princeton University Press, 1991.

Doyle. Charles. *William Carlos Williams: The Critical Heritage.* London; Boston: Routledge & Kegan Paul, 1980.

Doyle, Charles. *William Carlos Williams and the American Poem.* New York: St. Martin's, 1982.

Driscoll, Kerry. *William Carlos Williams and the Maternal Muse.* Ann Arbor, MI: UMI Research Press, 1987.

Duffey, Bernard. *Poetry of Presence: The Writing of William Carlos Williams.* Madison: University of Wisconsin Press, 1986.

Engels, John. *Merrill Studies in Paterson.* Columbus, OH: Merrill, 1971.

Guimond, James. *Art of William Carlos Williams: A Discovery and Possession of America.* Urbana: University of Illinois Press, 1968.

Halter, Peter. *Revolution in the Visual Arts and the Poetry of William Carlos Williams*. Cambridge; New York: Cambridge University Press, 1994.

Kallet, Marilyn. *Honest Simplicity in William Carlos Williams' "Asphodel, that Greeny Flower."* Baton Rouge: Louisiana State University Press, 1985.

Koehler, Stanley. *Countries of the Mind: The Poetry of William Carlos Williams*. Lewisburg, PA: Bucknell University Press, 1998.

Larson, Kellie A. *Guide to the Petry of William Carlos Williams*. New York: G. K. Hall; London: Prentice-Hall International, 1995.

Laughlin, James. *Remembering William Carlos Williams*. New York: New Directions, 1995.

Lloyd, Margaret Glynne. *William Carlos Williams's Paterson: A Critical Reappraisal*. Rutherford, NJ: Fairleigh Dickinson University Press, 1980.

Lowney, John. *American Avant-garde Tradition: William Carlos Williams, Postmodern Poetry, and the Politics of Cultural Memory*. Lewisburg, PA: Bucknell University Press, 1996.

MacGowan, Christopher J. *William Carlos Williams's Early Poetry: The Visual Arts Background*. Ann Arbor, MI: UMI Research Press, 1984.

Mariani, Paul L. *William Carlos Williams*. Chicago: American Library Association, 1975.

Markos, Donald W. *Ideas in Things: The Poems of William Carlos Williams*. Rutherford, NJ: Fairleigh Dickinson University Press; London: Associated University Presses, 1993.

Marling, William. *William Carlos Williams and the Painters, 1909–1923*. Athens, OH: Ohio University Press, 1982.

Marzán, Julio. *The Spanish American Roots of William Carlos Williams*. Austin: University of Texas Press, 1994.

Miki, Roy. *Prepoetics of William Carlos Williams: Kora in Hell*. Ann Arbor, MI: UMI Research Press, 1983.

Miller, J. Hillis. *William Carlos Williams: A Collection of Critical Essays*. Englewood Cliffs, NJ: Prentice-Hall, 1966.

Morris, Daniel. *Writings of William Carlos Williams: Publicity for the Self*. Columbia, MO: University of Missouri Press, 1995.

Ostrom, Alan B. *Poetic World of William Carlos Williams*. Carbondale: Southern Illinois University Press, 1966.

Peterson, Walter Scott. *Approach to Paterson*. New Haven: Yale University Press, 1967.

Rapp, Carl. *William Carlos Williams and Romantic Idealism*. Hanover, NH: Published for Brown University Press by University Press of New England, 1984.

Riddel, Joseph N. *Inverted Bell: Modernism and the Counterpoetics of William Carlos Williams*. Baton Rouge: Louisiana State University Press, 1974.

Rodgers, Audrey T. *Virgin and Whore: The Image of Women in the Poetry of William Carlos Williams*. Jefferson, NC: McFarland, 1987.

Sankey, Benjamin. *Companion to William Carlos Williams's Paterson*. Berkeley: University of California Press, 1971.

Sayre, Henry M. *Visual Text of William Carlos Williams*. Urbana: University of Illinois Press, 1983.

Schmidt, Peter. *William Carlos Williams, the Arts, and Literary Tradition*. Baton Rouge: Louisiana State University Press, 1988.

Tapscott, Stephen. *American Beauty: William Carlos Williams and the Modernist Whitman*. New York: Columbia University Press, 1984.

Wagner-Martin, Linda. *Poems of William Carlos Williams: A Critical Study*. Middletown, CT: Wesleyan University Press, 1964.

Walker, David. *Transparent Lyric: Reading and Meaning in the Poetry of Stevens and Williams*. Princeton: Princeton University Press, 1984.

Whitaker, Thomas R. *William Carlos Williams*. Boston: Twayne Publishers, 1989.

VIRGINIA WOOLF (1882–1941)

Bibliographies:

Kirkpatrick, B. J. *Bibliography of Virginia Woolf*. Oxford: Clarendon Press; New York: Oxford University Press, 1997.

Majumdar, Robin. *Virginia Woolf: An Annotated Bibliography of Criticism, 1915–1974*. New York: Garland, 1976.

Rice, Thomas Jackson. *Virginia Woolf: A Guide to Research*. New York: Garland, 1984.

Steele, Elizabeth. *Virginia Woolf's Literary Sources and Allusions: A Guide to the Essays*. New York: Garland, 1983.

Steele, Elizabeth. *Virginia Woolf's Rediscovered Essays: Sources and Allusions*. New York: Garland, 1987.

Biographies:

Bell, Quentin. *Virginia Woolf: A Biography*. London: Pimlico, 1996.

Lee, Hermione. *Virginia Woolf: A Biography*. London: Vintage, 1997; New York: Knopf, 1998.

Marder, Herbert. *The Measure of Life: Virginia Woolf's Last Years*. Ithaca, NY: Cornell University Press, 2000.

Stape, J. H., ed. *Virginia Woolf: Interviews and Recollections*. Basingstoke: Macmillan, 1995.

Works:

Two Stories, written and printed by Virginia Woolf and L. S. Woolf. London: Hogarth Press, 1917.

Kew Gardens. London: Hogarth Press, 1919.

Night and Day. London: Duckworth, 1920.

The Voyage Out. New York: Harcourt, Brace and Co., 1920.

Monday or Tuesday. New York: Harcourt, Brace and Co., 1921.

Jacob's Room. London: Hogarth Press, 1922.

Hogarth Essays. London: Hogarth Press, 1924.

Mr. Bennett and Mrs. Brown. London: Hogarth, 1924.

The Common Reader. London: Hogarth Press; New York: Harcourt, Brace and Co., 1925.

Mrs. Dalloway. New York: Harcourt, Brace and Co., 1925.

To the Lighthouse. London: Hogarth Press; New York, Harcourt, Brace and Co., 1927.

Orlando, a Biography. London: Hogarth Press; New York: Harcourt, Brace and Co., 1928.

Room of One's Own. London: Hogarth Press; New York: Harcourt, Brace and Co., 1929.

Beau Brummell. New York: Rimington & Hooper, 1930.

On Being Ill. London: Hogarth Press, 1930.

Street Haunting. San Francisco: Westgate Press, 1930.

The Waves. London: Hogarth Press, 1931.

Letter to a Young Poet. London: Hogarth Press, 1932.

The Second Common Reader. London. Penguin, 1944 (first published 1932).

Flush: A Biography. London: Hogarth Press; New York: Harcourt, Brace, 1933.

The Years. London: Hogarth Press New York: Harcourt, Brace and Co., 1937.

Three Guineas. London: Hogarth Press, 1938.

Reviewing. London: Hogarth Press, 1939.

Roger Fry, a Biography. London: Hogarth Press, 1940.

Posthumous Works:

Between the Acts. London: Hogarth Press; New York: Harcourt, Brace and Co., 1941.

Death of the Moth, and other Essays by Virginia Woolf. London: Hogarth Press, 1942.

Haunted House and Other Short Stories. London: Hogarth Press, 1943.

Moment and Other Essays. London: Hogarth Press, 1947.

Captain's Death Bed, and Other Essays. London: Hogarth Press; New York: Harcourt, Brace, 1950.

Writer's Diary: Being Extracts from the Diary of Virginia Woolf, ed. Leonard Woolf. London: Hogarth Press; New York: Harcourt, Brace and Co., 1953.

Letters: Virginia Woolf and Lytton Strachey, eds. Leonard Woolf and James Strachey. London: Chatto and Windus, 1956.

Hours in a Library. New York: Harcourt, Brace and Co., 1957.

Granite and Rainbow: Essays by Virginia Woolf. London: Hogarth; New York: Harcourt, Brace, 1958.

Collected Essays by Virginia Woolf. London: Hogarth Press; New York: Harcourt, Brace & World, 1966.

Moments of Being: Unpublished Autobiographical Writings, ed. Jeanne Schulkind. London: Chatto and Windus, 1976.

Books and Portraits: Some Further Selections from the Literary and Biographical Writings of Virginia Woolf, ed. Mary Lyon. London: Hogarth Press, 1977.

The Diary of Virginia Woolf, ed. Anne Olivier Bell. London: Hogarth Press, 1977–1984.

Letters of Vita Sackville-West to Virginia Woolf, eds. Louise DeSalvo and Mitchell A. Leaska. London: Hutchinson, 1984.

Hogarth Letters, intro. by Hermione Lee. London: Chatto and Windus, 1985.

Essays of Virginia Woolf, ed. Andrew McNeillie. London: Hogarth Press, 1986–1994.

Complete Shorter Fiction of Virginia Woolf, ed. Susan Dick. London: Hogarth Press, 1989.

Selected Essays, ed. Rachel Bowlby. London: Penguin, 1992–1993.

Criticism and Interpretation:

Abel, Elizabeth. *Virginia Woolf and the Fictions of Psychoanalysis.* Chicago: University of Chicago Press, 1989.

Batchelor, John. *Virginia Woolf: The Major Novels.* Cambridge; New York: Cambridge University Press, 1991.

Bazin, Nancy Topping. *Virginia Woolf and the Androgynous Vision.* New Brunswick, NJ: Rutgers University Press, 1973.

Beer, Gillian. *Virginia Woolf: The Common Ground.* Edinburgh: Edinburgh University Press, 1996.

Bowlby, Rachel. *Feminist Destinations and Further Essays on Virginia Woolf.* Edinburgh: Edinburgh University Press, 1997.

Bowlby, Rachel, ed. *Virginia Woolf.* London; New York: Longman, 1992.

Bloom, Harold, ed. *Virginia Woolf.* New York: Chelsea House, 1986.

Briggs, Julia, ed. *Virginia Woolf: Introductions to the Major Works.* London: Virago Press, 1994.

Brosnan, Leila. *Reading Virginia Woolf's Essays and Journalism: Breaking the Surface of Silence.* Edinburgh: Edinburgh University Press, 1997.

Caramagno, Thomas C. *Flight of the Mind: Virginia Woolf's Art and Manic-Depressive Illness.* Berkeley: University of California Press, 1992.

Dalgarno, Emily. *Virginia Woolf and the Visible World.* Cambridge: Cambridge University Press, 2001.

Dusinberre, Juliet. *Virginia Woolf's Renaissance: Woman Reader or Common Reader?* Basingstoke: Macmillan Press, 1997.

Ferrer, Daniel. *Virginia Woolf and the Madness of Language,* trans. Geoffrey Bennington and Rachel Bowlby. London; New York: Routledge, 1990.

Fleishman, Avrom. *Virginia Woolf: A Critical Reading.* Baltimore: Johns Hopkins University Press, 1975.

Fox, Alice. *Virginia Woolf and the Literature of the English Renaissance.* Oxford: Clarendon Press; New York: Oxford University Press, 1990.

Freedman, Ralph, ed. *Virginia Woolf: Revaluation and Continuity: A Collection of Essays.* Berkeley: University of California Press, 1980.

Goldman, Jane. *Feminist Aesthetics of Virginia Woolf: Modernism, Post-Impressionism, and the Politics of the Visual.* Cambridge, New York: Cambridge University Press, 1998.

Hawthorn, Jeremy. *Virginia Woolf's Mrs. Dalloway: A Study in Alienation*. London: Chatto & Windus, 1975.

Hussey, Mark. *Virginia Woolf and War: Fiction, Reality, and Myth*. Syracuse, NY: Syracuse University Press, 1991.

Lee, Hermione. *Novels of Virginia Woolf*. London: Methuen, 1977.

Majumdar, Robin and McLaurin, Allen, eds. *Virginia Woolf: The Critical Heritage*. London; Boston: Routledge & Kegan Paul, 1975.

Marcus, Jane. *Virginia Woolf and the Languages of Patriarchy*. Bloomington: Indiana University Press, 1987.

Marcus, Jane, ed. *New Feminist Essays on Virginia Woolf*. Lincoln: University of Nebraska Press, 1981.

Marcus, Jane, ed. *Virginia Woolf: A Feminist Slant*. Lincoln: University of Nebraska Press, 1983.

Marcus, Jane, ed. *Virginia Woolf and Bloomsbury: A Centenary Celebration*. Basingstoke, Hampshire: Macmillan, 1987.

McNichol, Stella. *Virginia Woolf and the Poetry of Fiction*. London; New York: Routledge, 1990.

Meisel, Perry. *Absent Father: Virginia Woolf and Walter Pater*. New Haven: Yale University Press, 1980.

Miller, Ruth C. *Virginia Woolf: The Frames of Art and Life*. Basingstoke: Macmillan, 1988.

Moore, Madeline. *Short Season Between Two Silences: The Mystical and the Political in the Novels of Virginia Woolf*. Boston: G. Allen & Unwin, 1984.

Newman, Herta. *Virginia Woolf and Mrs. Brown: Toward a Realism of Uncertainty*. New York: Garland, 1996.

Raitt, Suzanne. *Vita and Virginia: The Work and Friendship of V. Sackville-West and Virginia Woolf*. Oxford: Clarendon Press; Oxford; New York: Oxford University Press, 1993.

Richter, Harvena. *Virginia Woolf: The Inward Voyage*. Princeton: Princeton University Press, 1970.

Roe, Sue and Sellers, Susan, eds. *The Cambridge Companion to Virginia Woolf*. Cambridge; New York: Cambridge University Press, 2000.

Rosenthal, Michael. *Virginia Woolf*. New York: Columbia University Press; London: Routledge & Kegan Paul, 1979.

Silver, Brenda R. *Virginia Woolf, Icon*. Chicago: University of Chicago Press, 1999.

Spilka, Mark. *Virginia Woolf's Quarrel with Grieving*. Lincoln: University of Nebraska Press, 1980.

Squier, Susan Merrill. *Virginia Woolf and London: The Sexual Politics of the City*. Chapel Hill, NC: University of North Carolina Press, 1985.

Steele, Elizabeth. *Virginia Woolf's Literary Sources and Allusions: A Guide to the Essays*. New York: Garland, 1983.

Steele, Elizabeth. *Virginia Woolf's Rediscovered Essays: Sources and Allusions*. New York: Garland, 1987.

Wheare, Jane. *Virginia Woolf: Dramatic Novelist*. Basingstoke: Macmillan, 1989.

WILLIAM BUTLER YEATS (1865–1939)

Bibliographies:

Cross, K. G. W. and Dunlop, R. T. *Bibliography of Yeats Criticism, 1887–1965*. London and New York: Macmillan, 1971.

Jochum, K. P. S. *W. B. Yeats: A Classified Bibliography of Criticism*. Urbana: University of Illinois Press, 1978.

Stoll, John E. *Great Deluge: A Yeats Bibliography*. Troy, NY: Whitson, 1971.

Wade, Allan. *Bibliography of the Writings of W. B. Yeats*. London: Hart-Davis, 1968.

Biographies:

Aldritt, Keith. *W. B. Yeats: The Man and the Milieu*. London: John Murray, 1997.

Brown, Terence. *The Life of W. B. Yeats: A Critical Biography*. Malden, MA: Blackwell, 1999.

Coote, Stephen. *W.B. Yeats: A Life*. London: Sceptre, 1998.

Ellmann, Richard. *Yeats: The Man and the Masks*. London: Faber, 1961.

Foster, R. F. *W. B. Yeats: A Life*, 2 vols. Oxford: Oxford University Press, 1998–2003.

Jeffares, A. Norman. *W. B. Yeats: A New Biography*. London: Continuum, 2001.

Macrae, Alasdair D. F. *W. B. Yeats: A Literary Life*. Basingstoke: Macmillan, 1995.

Maddox, Brenda. *George's Ghost: A New Life of W. B. Yeats*. London: Picador, 1999.

Works:

The Wandering of Oisin and Other Poems. London: Kegan Paul, Trench & Co., 1889.

The Countess Kathleen and Various Legends and Lyrics. London: T. Fisher Unwin, 1892.

The Celtic Twilight: Men and Women, Dhouls and Faeries. London: Lawrence and Bullen, 1893.

The Land of Heart's Desire. London: T. Fischer Unwin, 1894.

The Secret Rose. London: Lawrence & Bullen; New York: Dodd, Mead & Co., 1897.

Wind Among the Reeds. London: E. Mathews; New York, London: Bodley Head, 1899.

The Shadowy Waters. London: Hodder and Stoughton, 1900.

Cathlee Ni Hoolihan: A Play in One Act and in Prose. London: A. H. Bullin, 1902.

Ideas of Good and Evil. London: A. H. Bullin; New York: Macmillan, 1903.

In the Seven Woods: Being Poems Chiefly of the Irish Heroic Age. London: Macmillan; New York: Macmillan, 1903.

The Hour Glass: A Morality. London: A. Bullen; New York, London: Macmillan, 1904.

The Tables of the Law and the Adoration of the Magi. London: Elkin Mathews, 1904.

On Baile's Strand. Dublin: Maunsel & Co., 1905.

Deirdre. London: A. H. Bullen, 1907.

The King's Threshold. Stratford upon Avon: Shakespeare Head, 1911.

Discoveries. Edmund Spencer. Poetry and Tradition & Other Essays. Stratford upon Avon: Shakespeare Head, 1911.

The Green Helmet and Other Poems. New York: R. Harold Paget, 1911.

The Cutting of an Agate. New York: Macmillan, 1912.

Responsibilities: Poems and a Play. Churchtown, Dundrum: Cuala Press, 1914; rpt. London: Macmillan, 1916.

Reveries over Childhood and Youth. London, New York: Macmillan, 1916.

The Wild Swan at Coole. Churchtown, Dundrum: Cuala Press, 1917; rpt. New York: Macmillan, 1919.

Per amica silentia lunae. London: Macmillan, 1918.

Four Plays for Dancers. London, New York: Macmillan, 1921.

Essays. London: Macmillan; New York: Macmillan, 1924.

The Bounty of Sweden: A Meditation and Lecture Delivered before the Royal Swedish Academy. Churchtown, Dundrum: Cuala Press, 1925.

A Vision: An Explanation of Life Founded upon the Writings of Giraldus and upon Certain Doctrines Attributed to Kusta ben Luka. London: Priv. print. for subscribers only by T. Werner Laurie, Ltd., 1925.

Autobiographies: Reveries over Childhood and Youth and The Trembling of the Veil. London: Macmillan, 1926.

The Tower. London: Macmillan; New York: Macmillan, 1928.

The Winding Stair. New York: Fountain Press, 1929; rpt. London: Macmillan; New York: Macmillan, 1933.

Words for Music Perhaps and Other Poems. Churchtown, Dundrum: Cuala Press, 1932.

Words upon the Window Pane: A Play in One Act, with Notes upon the Play and its Subject. Churchtown, Dundrum: Cuala Press, 1934.

Last Poems and Plays. Churchtown, Dundrum: Cuala Press, 1939.

Posthumous Works – Poetry:

Collected Poems of W. B. Yeats, ed. Augustine Martin. London: Vintage, 1992.

The Collected Poems of W. B. Yeats. London: Macmillan, 1950.

Under the Moon: The Unpublished Early Poetry of W. B. Yeats, ed. George Bornstein. New York: Scribner, 1995.

The Variorum Edition of the Poems of W. B. Yeats, eds. Peter Allt and Russell K. Aspach. New York: Macmillan, 1957, repr. 1973.

W. B. Yeats: Selected Poems, ed. Timothy Webb. Harmondsworth: Penguin, 1991.

W. B. Yeats: The Poems, ed. Daniel Albright. London: Dent, Everyman's Library, 1992; rev. edn. 1994.

Yeats's Poems, ed. Norman A. Jeffares. London: Macmillan, 1989.

Posthumous Works – Drama:

Collected Plays of W. B. Yeats. London: Macmillan, 1952.

The Variorum Edition of the Plays of W. B. Yeats, ed. Russell K. Alspach. London, New York: Macmillan, 1966; repr. 1979.

W. B. Yeats: Selected Plays, ed. Richard Cave. Harmondsworth: Penguin, 1997.

Posthumous Works – Selected Prose Writing:

A Critical Edition of Yeats's A Vision, eds. George Mills Harper and Walter Kelly Hood. London: Macmillan, 1978.

Essays and Introductions. London: Macmillan, 1961.

Explorations. London: Macmillan, 1962.

Memoirs, ed. Denis Donoghue. London and Basingstoke: Macmillan, 1972.

Mythologies. London and New York: Macmillan, 1959.

Uncollected Prose by W. B. Yeats, 2 vols., eds. John P. Frayne and Colton Johnson. London: Macmillan; New York: Columbia University Press, 1970–1975.

W. B. Yeats: Prefaces and Introductions, ed. William O'Donnell. London: Macmillan, 1988.

W. B. Yeats: Short Fiction, ed. G. J. Watson. Harmondsworth: Penguin, 1995.

W. B. Yeats: Writings on Irish Folklore, Legend and Myth, ed. Robert Welch. Harmondsworth: Penguin, 1993.

Posthumous Works – Occult Writing:

Yeats's Vision Papers, 3 vols., gen. ed. George Mills Harper. London and New York: Macmillan, 1992.

W. B. Yeats: A Vision and Related Writings, ed. A. Norman Jeffares. London: Arena, 1990.

Posthumous Works – Selected Editions of Letters:

The Collected Letters of W. B. Yeats, vol. 1, 1865–1895, ed. John Kelly, associate ed. Eric Domville. Oxford: Clarendon Press, 1986.

The Collected Letters of W. B. Yeats, vol. 2, 1896–1900, eds. Warwick Gould, John Kelly, and Deirdre Toomey. Oxford: Clarendon Press, 1997.

The Collected Letters of W. B. Yeats, vol. 3, 1900–1904, eds. John Kelly and Ronald Schuchard. Oxford: Clarendon Press, 1994.

The Gonne–Yeats Letters, 1893–1938, eds. Anna MacBride White and A. Norman Jeffares. London: Hutchinson, 1992; Pimlico, 1993.

The Letters of W. B. Yeats, ed. Allan Wade. London: Rupert Hart-Davis, 1954.

Criticism and Interpretation:

Adams, Joseph. *Yeats and the Mask of Syntax*. London and Basingstoke: Macmillan, 1984.

Albright, Daniel. *Myth Against Myth: A Study of Yeats's Imagination in Old Age*. London: Oxford University Press, 1972.

Bloom, Harold. *Yeats*. New York: Oxford University Press, 1972.

Bloom, Harold, ed. *William Butler Yeats*. New York: Chelsea House, 1986.

Castle, Gregory. *Modernism and the Celtic Revival*. Cambridge; New York: Cambridge University Press, 2001.

Chaudhry, Yug Mohit. *Yeats, the Irish Literary Revival and the Politics of Print*. Cork, Ireland: Cork University Press, 2001.

Clark, David R. *Yeats at Songs and Choruses*. Amherst, MA: University of Massachusetts Press, 2001.

Cullingford, Elizabeth. *Yeats, Ireland and Fascism*. London and Basingstoke: Macmillan, 1981.

Cullingford, Elizabeth. *Gender and History in Yeats's Love Poetry*. Cambridge; New York: Cambridge University Press, 1993.

Domville, Eric, ed. *Concordance to the Plays of W. B. Yeats*. Ithaca, NY: Cornell University Press, 1972.

Drake, Nicholas. *Poetry of W.B. Yeats*. London: Penguin Books, 1991.

Ellmann, Richard. *The Identity of Yeats*. London: Faber, 1964.

Flannery, James W. *W. B. Yeats and the Idea of a Theatre: The Early Abbey Theatre in Theory and Practice*. New Haven: Yale University Press, 1976.

Flannery, Mary Catherine. *Yeats and Magic: The Earlier Works*. Gerrards Cross: Smythe, 1977.

Fletcher, Ian. *W. B. Yeats and his Contemporaries*. Brighton, UK: Harvester Press, 1987.

Freyer, Grattan. *W. B. Yeats and the Anti-Democratic Tradition*. Dublin: Gill and Macmillan, 1981.

Friedman, Barton R. *Adventures in the Deeps of the Mind: The Cuchulain Cycle of W. B. Yeats*. Princeton: Princeton University Press, 1977.

Good, Maeve. *W. B. Yeats and the Creation of a Tragic Universe*. Basingstoke: Macmillan, 1987.

Greaves, Richard. *Transition, Reception, and Modernism in W. B. Yeats*. Basingstoke; New York: Palgrave, 2002.

Harper, George Mills. *Yeats's Golden Dawn*. London: Macmillan, 1974,

Harris, Daniel A. *Yeats: Coole Park & Ballylee*. Baltimore: Johns Hopkins University Press, 1974.

Holdridge, Jefferson. *Those Mingled Seas: The Poetry of W. B. Yeats, the Beautiful and the Sublime*. Dublin: University College Dublin Press, 2000.

Howes, Marjorie. *Yeats's Nations*. Cambridge: Cambridge University Press, 1996.

Jakobson, Roman. *Yeats' Sorrow of Love Through the Years*. Lisse: Peter de Ridder Press, 1977.

Jeffares, A. Norman and Knowland, A. S. *Commentary on the Collected Plays of W. B. Yeats*. Stanford: Stanford University Press, 1975.

Jeffares, A. Norman. *W. B. Yeats: the Critical Heritage*. London; Boston: Routledge and K. Paul, 1977.

Jeffares, A. Norman. *New Commentary on the Poems of W. B. Yeats*. Stanford: Stanford University Press, 1984.

Keane, Patrick J. *William Butler Yeats: A Collection of Criticism*. New York: McGraw-Hill, 1973.

Keane, Patrick J. *Yeats's Interactions with Tradition*. Columbia: University of Missouri Press, 1987.

Kline, Gloria C. *Last Courtly Lover: Yeats and the Idea of Woman*. Ann Arbor, MI: UMI Research Press, 1983.

Koch, Vivienne. *W. B. Yeats, the Tragic Phase: A Study of the Last Poems*. London: Routledge & K. Paul, 1951.

Larrissy, Edward. *Yeats the Poet: The Measures of Difference*. London; New York: Harvester Wheatsheaf, 1994

Levine, Herbert J. *Yeats's Daimonic Renewal*. Ann Arbor, MI: UMI Research Press, 1983.

Loizeaux, Elizabeth. *Yeats and the Visual Arts*. New Brunswick, NJ, and London: Rutgers University Press, 1986.

Malins, Edward Greenway. *Yeats and the Easter Rising*. Dublin: Dolmen Press, 1965.

Malins, Edward Greenway. *Preface to Yeats*. London; New York: Longman, 1974.

Marcus, Phillip L. *Yeats and the Beginning of the Irish Renaissance*. Ithaca, NY: Cornell University Press, 1970; Syracuse, NY: Syracuse University Press, 1987.

Meihuizen, Nicholas. *Yeats and the Drama of Sacred Space*. Amsterdam; Atlanta, GA: Rodopi, 1998.

Moore, John Rees. *Masks of Love and Death: Yeats as Dramatist*. Ithaca: Cornell University Press, 1971.

O'Hara, Daniel T. *Tragic Knowledge: Yeats's Autobiography and Hermeneutics*. New York: Columbia University Press, 1981.

Orr, Leonard ed. *Yeats and Postmodernism*. Syracuse, NY: Syracuse University Press, 1991.

Pierce, David. *Yeats's World: Ireland, England and the Poetic Imagination*. New Haven and London: Yale University Press, 1995.

Pritchard, William H., ed. *W. B. Yeats, a Critical Anthology*. Harmondsworth: Penguin, 1972.

Ramazani, Jahan. *Yeats and the Poetry of Death: Elegy, Self-Elegy, and the Sublime*. New Haven: Yale University Press, 1990.

Ronsley, Joseph. *Yeats's Autobiography: Life as Symbolic Pattern*. Cambridge, MA: Harvard University Press, 1968.

Rosenthal, M. L. *Running to Paradise: Yeats's Poetic Art*. New York: Oxford University Press, 1994.

Sena, Vinod. *W. B. Yeats, the Poet as Critic*. London: Macmillan, 1981.

Sidnell, Michael J. *Yeats's Poetry and Poetics*. Basingstoke: Macmillan; New York: St. Martin's Press, 1996

Skene, Reg. *Cuchulain Plays of W. B. Yeats: A Study*. New York: Columbia University Press, 1974.

Smith, Stan. *W. B. Yeats: A Critical Introduction*. Basingstoke: Macmillan Education, 1990.

Stanfield, Paul Scott. *Yeats and Politics in the 1930s*. London: Macmillan, 1998.

Steinman, Michael. *Yeats's Heroic Figures: Wilde, Parnell, Swift, Casement*. Albany: State University of New York Press, 1983.

Suess, Barbara Ann. *Progress and Identity in the Plays of W. B. Yeats, 1892–1907*. New York: Routledge, 2003.

Taylor, Richard. *Drama of W. B. Yeats: Irish Myth and the Japanese No*. New Haven: Yale University Press, 1976.

Taylor, Richard. *Reader's Guide to the Plays of W. B. Yeats*. London: Macmillan, 1984.

Thuente, Mary Helen. *Yeats and Irish Folklore*. Dublin: Gill and Macmillan; Totowa, NJ: Barnes and Noble, 1980.

Toomey, Deirdre. *Yeats and Women*. London: Macmillan Press, 1997.

Unterecker, John. *A Reader's Guide to W. B. Yeats*. London: Thames and Hudson, 1959.

Ure, Peter. *Yeats and Anglo-Irish Literature: Critical Essays*, ed. C. J. Rawson with a memoir by Frank Kermode. Liverpool: Liverpool University Press, 1974.

Vendler, Helen. *Yeats's "Vision" and the Last Plays*. Cambridge, MA: Harvard University Press, 1963.

Index of Authors and Titles